# Doyle, Keay and Curl: Annotate Legislation

## Tenth Edition

# Doyle, Keay and Curl: Annotated Insolvency Legislation

Tenth Edition

**General Editors**

**Louis Doyle QC, LLB, LLM, Barrister**

Kings Chambers, Manchester, Leeds and Birmingham, *and*
9 Stone Buildings, Lincoln's Inn

**Professor Andrew Keay, LLB, MDiv (Hons), LLM, PhD**

Professor of Corporate and Commercial Law, University of Leeds
Barrister, Kings Chambers, Manchester, Leeds and Birmingham, *and*
9 Stone Buildings, Lincoln's Inn

**Joseph Curl QC, BA, LLB, Barrister**

9 Stone Buildings, Lincoln's Inn
Deputy Insolvency and Companies Court Judge

**Consultant Editors**

**Chief Insolvency and Companies Court Judge Briggs**

**Insolvency and Companies Court Judge Burton**

and a team of specialist Contributing Editors

 LexisNexis®

## LexisNexis® UK & Worldwide

| | |
|---|---|
| United Kingdom | RELX (UK) Limited trading as LexisNexis®, 1–3 Strand, London WC2N 5JR |
| LNUK Global Partners | LexisNexis® encompasses authoritative legal publishing brands dating back to the 19th century including: Butterworths® in the United Kingdom, Canada and the Asia-Pacific region; Les Editions du Juris Classeur in France; and Matthew Bender® worldwide. Details of LexisNexis® locations worldwide can be found at www.lexisnexis.com |

ISBN 978-1-7847-3481-7

9 781784 734817

ISBN for this volume: 9781784734817

Printed and bound by Hobbs the Printers, Hampshire SO40 3WX

Visit LexisNexis at http://www.lexisnexis.co.uk

# Dedication

*To Edie Lambert*

# Foreword to Tenth Edition

I am delighted to have been asked to provide this Foreword to the tenth edition of *Doyle, Keay and Curl: Annotated Insolvency Legislation*; indeed I regard it as something of an honour, because the tenth edition of any book is a landmark, an indication that it has secured a foothold in a competitive market.

That *Doyle, Keay and Curl* is now an established work of reference is borne out by more than its simply having reached its tenth iteration: there are reasons why it has won its place. First, its one volume compactness is an advantage in itself: less volume and weight to carry are not, however, to be equated with superficiality or lack of weight in any broader sense. The ability of the authors to achieve so much in a concise form is an achievement, not just for practical reasons but for others alluded to in earlier introductions: for this text has not been allowed to expand under the weight of accretion; rather, the authors have exercised critical discipline in their selection of material for their commentary, including only the most essential and helpful authorities and references, discarding the superseded and often distracting wisdom of the past. They have done that, where appropriate, by producing what might be described as mini articles, each topic covered highlighted in bold print for ease of reference. In his Foreword to the ninth edition Mr Justice Snowden rightly praised the editorial skill of the contributors in identifying the real issues, a judgment which I gratefully adopt. If nothing else (and there is much else) *Doyle, Keay and Curl* is user friendly.

This will come as no surprise to those familiar with the general editors and the quality of their respective contributions to the law of insolvency, both corporate and personal. Louis Doyle QC and Joseph Curl QC bring to bear on their roles many years of practice in a wide range of insolvency cases; Professor Andrew Keay's work in the academic sphere (preceded, however, by 'coal face' work at the Bar and in the Australian courts) adds the dimension of academic objectivity.

If those are some of the reasons for *Doyle, Keay and Curl's* making it to its tenth edition, there is a more mundane one too: the pace of change in insolvency law. This edition comes off the press as we emerge (we hope) from a pandemic that has had a legislative as well as an economic and social impact from which insolvency law has not been spared; at the same time the insolvency professions are learning to cope with cross-border cases with which they must now grapple without the benefit of automatic recognition in the EU. The routine dissemination of judgments on Bailli has meant more case law 'out there' than ever before, making the task of sifting the wheat from the chaff harder than ever. We may be forgiven for feeling, like Macduff, that 'Confusion now hath made his master-piece'.

Users will judge in the coming years the value of the assistance the contributors have managed to provide in the face of potential confusion resulting from these difficult and developing areas, as well as others, but they can at least approach them in the confidence of sound guidance from Messrs Doyle, Keay and Curl. I commend this volume to all insolvency professionals, both to use on its own or for use in conjunction with other texts; and I do so in the sure and certain hope that *Doyle, Keay and Curl* will thrive in its tenth edition and for many editions to come.

**Stephen Baister**

**Deputy Insolvency and Companies Court Judge**

**Chief Registrar in Bankruptcy, 2004–2017**

*August 2021*

# Foreword to Ninth Edition by The Honourable Mr Justice Snowden

Doubtless with a view to enticing the reader to become a buyer, forewords often proclaim that a new edition arrives at a particularly propitious time. For once, that is no overstatement. The ninth edition of this book arrives at a time at which, regrettably, we may be facing the deepest recession and the largest wave of business failures and personal insolvency for decades as a result of the COVID-19 pandemic.

The response of the UK legislature was to enact the Corporate Insolvency and Governance Act 2020 with unprecedented speed. The new Act makes short term modifications to established insolvency procedures and introduces wholly new debtor-in-possession procedures by way of a moratorium and a restructuring scheme on a permanent basis. Time will tell whether those important new innovations are successful, but in the meantime, the existing framework of corporate and personal insolvency law will be under increased pressure and public scrutiny, both inside and outside the courts.

The international landscape is also changing at pace, but there is justifiable confidence that whatever post-Brexit agreements may or may not be reached, the insolvency profession and specialist judges in the UK will continue to advance their well-deserved reputations as leaders of the global restructuring community, combining expertise and innovation with constructive cross-border co-operation.

Against that background, this new edition provides practitioners and judges with an essential and up-to-date guide to the new insolvency landscape, at home and abroad. It incorporates all the key primary and secondary UK legislation, cross-border materials such as the UNCITRAL Model Law and EU Regulation, practice statements from the courts, and statements of insolvency practice.

If that were not enough, there are annotations and commentary from Louis Doyle QC and Professor Andrew Keay, whose well-established expertise and scholarship has been further strengthened by the addition of a leading junior in the insolvency field in the form of Joseph Curl, together with cross-border input from Professor Gerard McCormack. The fact that the authors have, as consultant editors, two distinguished and knowledgeable judges of the Insolvency and Companies Court in the form of Chief ICC Judge Briggs and ICC Judge Burton, is the icing on an already well-filled cake.

The judges who wrote the forewords to the last two editions both recognised that the strength of the authors' contribution lies in its concise accuracy, focussing on the key cases for the development of the principles of insolvency law, rather than simply providing ever more numerous examples of cases decided on their own facts. That remains a tried and tested feature of the new edition, which practitioners and judges alike will find particularly valuable as they strive to identify the real issues and find a clear path to a workable solution in the busy times ahead. The fact that such precision also enables the book to be confined to a single convenient and readily transportable volume is a very welcome bonus.

**Mr Justice Richard Snowden**

*Vice-Chancellor of the County Palatine of Lancaster and Supervising Judge of the Business and Property Courts for the Northern and North Eastern Circuits*
*August 2020*

# Contributors

## General Editors

**Louis Doyle QC, LLB, LLM, Barrister**

Kings Chambers, Manchester, Leeds and Birmingham *and*
9 Stone Buildings, Lincoln's Inn

**Professor Andrew Keay, LLB, MDiv (Hons), LLM, PhD**

Professor of Corporate and Commercial Law, University of Leeds
Barrister, Kings Chambers, Manchester, Leeds and Birmingham *and*
9 Stone Buildings, Lincoln's Inn

**Joseph Curl QC, BA, LLB, Barrister**

9 Stone Buildings, Lincoln's Inn
Deputy Insolvency and Companies Court Judge

## Consultant Editors

**Chief Insolvency and Companies Court Judge Briggs**

**Insolvency and Companies Court Judge Burton**

## Contributors

**Gerard McCormack**

*Professor of International Business Law, University of Leeds*

**Giselle McGowan**

**Faith Julian**

**Paul Wright**

**Andrew Mace**

*all Barristers at 9 Stone Buildings, Lincoln's Inn*

# Contents

Foreword to Tenth Edition vii

Foreword to Ninth Edition by The Honourable Mr Justice Snowden ix

Contributors xi

Table of Statutes xv

Table of Statutory Instruments xxxix

Table of International Legislation lv

Table of SIPs and Dear IPs lix

Table of Cases lxi

Introduction to Insolvency Legislation 1

Insolvency Act 1986 3

Insolvency (England and Wales) Rules 2016, SI 2016/1024 833

Insolvency Act 2000 1375

Enterprise Act 2002 1381

Corporate Insolvency and Governance Act 2020 1395

Regulation (EU) 2015/848 on Insolvency Proceedings 1471

Cross-Border Insolvency Regulations 2006 UNCITRAL Model Law 1569

Appendix 1 Statements of Insolvency Practice

SIP 1 An introduction to statements of insolvency practice 1631

SIP 2 Investigations by office holders in administrations and insolvent liquidations and the submission of conduct reports by office holders 1633

SIP 3.1 Individual voluntary arrangements 1636

SIP 3.2 Company voluntary arrangements 1640

SIP 6 Deemed consent and decision procedures in insolvency proceedings 1644

SIP 7 Presentation of financial information in insolvency proceedings 1646

SIP 9 Payments to insolvency office holders and their associates from an estate 1650

*Contents*

SIP 11 The handling of funds in formal insolvency appointments                 1655

SIP 13 Disposal of assets to connected parties in an insolvency
process                                                                         1657

SIP 14 A receiver's responsibility to preferential creditors                    1659

SIP 15 Reporting and providing information on their functions to
committees and commissioners                                                    1664

SIP 16 Pre-packaged sales in administrations                                    1666

SIP 17 An administrative receiver's responsibility for the com-
pany's records – England and Wales                                              1672

Appendix 2   Practice Direction Insolvency Proceedings (2018)
             (Amended July 2020)                                                1677

Appendix 3   Temporary Insolvency Practice Direction Supporting
             the Insolvency Practice Direction (2021)                           1701

Appendix 4   Insolvency Practice Direction Relating to the Corporate
             Insolvency and Governance Act 2020                                 1705

Appendix 5   Practice Statement (Companies: Schemes of Arrange-
             ment under Part 26 and Part 26A of the Companies Act
             2006)                                                              1709

Index                                                                           1713

# Table of Statutes

## A

Act of 1604 (1 Jac 1 c 15)
...................... 1.186, 1.404
Administration of Justice Act 1970
s 36 ............................ 1.386
Agricultural Marketing Act 1958
................................. 2.321
s 2 ............................. 1.176
Arbitration Act 1986
................................. 1.178
Arbitration Act 1996
............................. 1.628
s 9 ...................... 1.178, 1.383

## B

Banking Act 2009
s 113 ............................ 1.59
Bankruptcy Abuse Prevention and Consumer Protection Act 2005 (USA)
s 1507 .......................... 1.586
Bankruptcy Act 1869
s 16(3) ......................... 2.909
Bankruptcy Act 1883
s 53(2) ......................... 1.427
105(4) ......................... 1.503
Bankruptcy Act 1914
.. 1.396, 1.397, 1.398, 1.412, 2.530
s 9 ...................... 1.353, 1.660
15 ............................ 1.404
22(3) ......................... 1.452
25 ............................ 1.492
28(4) ......................... 1.393
29 ............................ 1.395
38(1) ......................... 1.427
42 .................... 1.302, 1.459
48(5) ......................... 1.429
51(2) ......................... 1.427
56(3) ......................... 1.433
74(2) ......................... 1.401
80 ................... 1.67, 1.414
93(3) ................. 1.410, 1.414
108(1) ......................... 2.814
147(1) ................. 1.504, 2.820
148 ............................ 1.505
154(1) ......................... 1.481
155 ............................ 1.488
167 ............................ 1.417
Bankruptcy Act 1966 (Australia)
s 369(1)(a), (b) .................. 1.488
Bankruptcy Code 1978 (USA)
s 101(23) ....................... 7.15
304 ....... 1.586, 7.2, 7.4, 7.34, 7.36
361 ............................ 7.34
Ch 7 (ss 701–784) ................ 7.36

Bankruptcy Code 1978 (USA) – *cont.*
Ch 11 (ss 1101–1174)
...................... 7.15, 7.28, 7.36
15 (ss 1501–1532)
.......... 6.5, 7.2, 7.4, 7.15, 7.30, 7.34
s 1523 .......................... 7.36
Bills of Sale Act 1878
............................. 1.470
Building Societies Act 1986
............................. 1.127
s 37(1)(a) ...................... 1.176
119 ............................ 1.627
Sch 15A ........................ 1.72
para 25 ........... 1.82, 1.83, 1.84
Building Societies Act 1997
s 39 ............................ 1.72

## C

Charging Orders Act 1979
s 3(5) .................... 1.431, 1.472
Charities Act 2006
s 113 ........................... 1.176
Child Support Act 1991
............................. 1.393
Children Act 1989 ..... 1.452, 1.489
Sch 1
para 5 ...................... 1.393
Civil Aviation Act 1982
s 88 ........................... 1.660
Civil Jurisdiction and Judgments Act 1982
................................. 1.433
Commonhold and Leasehold Reform Act 2002
s 43 ........................... 1.138
Companies Act 1862
............................. 1.128
Companies Act 1883
s 4 ............................. 1.84
Companies Act 1929
............................. 1.128
s 309 .......................... 1.80
Companies Act 1948
........................ 1.65, 1.128
s 352 .......................... 1.79
366 ........................... 1.74
367 ........................... 1.75
371(1) ......................... 1.80
Companies Act 1967
............................. 1.128
Companies Act 1976
............................. 1.128
Companies Act 1980
........................ 1.65, 1.128
Companies Act 1981
............................. 1.128

**Companies Act 1985**

|  |  |
|---|---|
| .................................... | 1.608 |
| Pt I (ss 1–42) .................... | 1.128 |
| s 14 ............................... | 1.129 |
| 30(1), (2) ..................... | 1.138 |
| (4) .......................... | 1.138 |
| 111A ........................... | 1.129 |
| 151 ............................ | 1.78 |
| 196 ............................ | 1.84 |
| 251 ............................ | 1.88 |
| Pt 13 (ss 281–361) |  |
| .................................... | 1.146 |
| s 283 ........................... | 1.138 |
| 288–295 ...................... | 1.138 |
| 307(1), (2) .................... | 1.138 |
| (4) .......................... | 1.138 |
| 447 ............................ | 1.177 |
| 458 ............................ | 1.271 |
| 459 .................... 1.65, 1.275 |  |
| 460 ............................ | 1.65 |
| 489 ............................ | 1.74 |
| 490 ............................ | 1.75 |
| 497 ............................ | 1.82 |
| 499 ............................ | 1.82 |
| 530 ............................ | 1.185 |
| 551 ............................ | 1.298 |
| 561 ............................ | 1.452 |
| 624 ............................ | 1.263 |
| 625 ............................ | 1.264 |
| 626 ............................ | 1.265 |
| 627 ............................ | 1.266 |
| 653 ............................ | 1.271 |
| 665 ............................ | 1.279 |
| 675(1) ......................... | 1.128 |
| 727 ............ 1.270, 1.272, 1.276 |  |
| 735(1) ................. 1.59, 1.728 |  |
| (a)–(c) .................. | 1.128 |
| 744 ............................ | 1.88 |
| 1040(1)(b) ..................... | 1.137 |

**Companies Act 1989**

|  |  |
|---|---|
| s 146(3) ........................ | 1.180 |
| Pt VII (ss 154–191) |  |
| s 155 .................. 1.302, 1.303 |  |
| (2) .................. 1.235, 1.243 |  |
| 159(4) ................. 1.442, 2.852 |  |
| 161(4) ......................... | 1.399 |
| 163(1), (2) ............. 1.442, 2.852 |  |
| 164(1) ................. 1.235, 1.243 |  |
| (3) .................. 1.180, 1.398 |  |
| 165(1)(a) ...................... | 1.302 |
| (b) ....................... | 1.303 |
| (3) .................. 1.302, 1.303 |  |
| 173 ............................ | 1.87 |
| (3)–(5) ............. 1.180, 1.398 |  |
| 175 ............................ | 1.87 |

**Companies Act 2006**

|  |  |
|---|---|
| .................... 1.59, 1.73, 1.279 |  |
| s 1 ............................. | 1.617 |
| (1) .................. 1.128, 1.728 |  |
| 33 ................... 1.129, 2.820 |  |
| 39 ................... 1.674, 1.686 |  |
| 44 ............ 1.631, 1.633, 1.728 |  |
| 47 ............................. | 1.77 |
| 102 ............................ | 1.132 |
| 122 ............................ | 1.325 |
| 168 ............................ | 1.674 |

**Companies Act 2006 – *cont.***

|  |  |
|---|---|
| s 171 ................... 1.618, 2.852 |  |
| (b) ......................... | 1.639 |
| 172 ...................... 1.244, 2.852 |  |
| (3) ......................... | 1.618 |
| 173–177 ........................ | 1.618 |
| 197 ............................ | 2.852 |
| 213 ............................ | 2.852 |
| 247(2) ......................... | 1.244 |
| 250 ............. 1.186, 1.300, 1.326 |  |
| 251 ............................ | 1.326 |
| (1) ......................... | 1.263 |
| 288, 289 ....................... | 1.639 |
| 754 ............................ | 1.228 |
| 761 ............................ | 1.174 |
| 859K ........................... | 1.83 |
| 869 ............................ | 1.90 |
| 871 ............................ | 1.90 |
| 877 ............................ | 1.207 |
| Pt 26 (ss 895–901) |  |
| .................... 1.620, 5.38 |  |
| s 895 .............. 1.163, 1.233, 1.666 |  |
| 896–901 ..................... | 1.666 |
| Pt 26A (ss 901A–901L) |  |
| ............ 1.58, 1.617, 1.666, 5.1, 6.2 |  |
| s 901A .......................... | 5.38 |
| 901C(4) ........................ | 5.38 |
| 901D–901F ...................... | 5.38 |
| 901G(3) ........................ | 5.38 |
| (5) ......................... | 5.38 |
| 993 .................... 1.265, 1.271 |  |
| 994 . 1.65, 1.174, 1.275, 1.429, 1.691 |  |
| 1024 ........................... | 1.257 |
| 1028(1) ........................ | 1.271 |
| 1029 ........................... | 1.257 |
| (1)(b) ..................... | 1.701 |
| (2)(j) ..................... | 1.701 |
| 1032 ........................... | 1.701 |
| (1) ......................... | 1.271 |
| 1043 ........................... | 1.280 |
| 1074 ........................... | 2.160 |
| 1077(1) ........................ | 1.183 |
| 1078(2) ........................ | 1.183 |
| 1080 ........................... | 2.175 |
| 1116 ........................... | 1.183 |
| 1121 ........................... | 1.664 |
| (1) ......................... | 1.593 |
| 1157 ............ 1.270, 1.272, 1.276 |  |
| 1171 .................... 1.128, 1.617 |  |
| 1173 ..... 1.184, 1.186, 1.263, 1.264, |  |
| | 1.300 |
| 1282 ........................... | 1.84 |

**Companies (Audit, Investigations and Community Enterprise) Act 2004**

|  |  |
|---|---|
| s 50 ............................ | 1.67 |

**Companies (Consolidation) Act 1908**

|  |  |
|---|---|
| .................................... | 1.128 |

**Companies (Winding Up) Act 1890**

|  |  |
|---|---|
| s 8 ............................. | 1.186 |

**Company Directors Disqualification Act 1986** ...................... 3.6, 4.1

|  |  |
|---|---|
| s 1(1) .......................... | 1.75 |
| 3(3) ........................... | 2.118 |
| 6 .............................. | 1.394 |
| 10 ............................. | 1.272 |
| 11 ............................. | 1.276 |

Company Directors Disqualification Act 1986
 – *cont.*
 s 17 ............................. 1.275
 Sch 1 ............................. 1.91
Consumer Credit Act 1974
 s 9 ............................... 1.308
 19 .............................. 1.469
 137, 138 ...................... 1.308
 139(1)(a) ..................... 1.469
  (2) ......................... 1.308
 140 ............................ 1.308
 140A–140C ................... 1.469
Contracts (Rights of Third Parties) Act
 1999 .......................... 1.64
Corporate Insolvency and Governance Act
 2020 ....... 1.617, 1.683, 5.38, 6.2
 12(1) ................. 1.272, 1.312
  (5)(a) ...................... 1.615
  (b) ...................... 1.615
 Sch 4
  para 5 ............... 1.5, 1.6, 1.7
   6(1)(a) .................... 1.5
    (b) ................... 1.8
    (c) ................. 1.615
   (2) ...................... 1.6
   7(a) ..................... 1.8
    (b) ................. 1.615
   8(2) ............... 1.12, 1.13
   (3) ................. 1.15
   9 ...................... 1.37
   10 ............. 1.40, 1.129
   13 ...................... 1.56
   24 ...................... 2.887
   25 ...................... 2.907
   26 ...................... 2.909
   27 ...................... 2.910
   28 ...................... 2.912
   47 . 2.754, 2.778, 2.787, 2.788,
                          2.801
   53 ...................... 1.55
 Sch 9 ......................... 5.1, 5.6
   10 ....................... 5.1, 5.8
  para 1(1) ........... 1.175, 1.176
   (2) ........... 1.176, 1.282
   2(1) ........... 1.175, 1.176
    (2) ................. 1.175
    (3) ........... 1.175, 1.176
    (4) ................. 1.175
   3(1) . 1.176, 1.282, 1.283,1.284
    (3) ........ 1.176, 1.284
   4(1) ................. 1.176
    (4) ................. 1.200
   5(1)(a) ................. 1.176
    (b) ................. 1.175
    (2) ................. 1.175
    (3) ................. 1.175
   6(1)(a) ................. 1.176
    (b) .... 1.282, 1.283, 1.284
    (2) ...... 1.281, 1.282, 1.283,
                          1.284
    (3) ...... 1.281, 1.282, 1.284
   7(1)(a) ........... 1.174, 1.281
    (5)(a) ........... 1.174, 1.281
    (6) ................. 1.200
   8 .............. 1.180, 1.182
    (1)(a) ................. 1.176

Corporate Insolvency and Governance Act
 2020 – *cont.*
  para 8(1)(b) .......... 1.174, 1.281
   9 ........... 1.180, 1.182
   10 ...................... 1.129
   11 ...................... 1.263
   12 ...................... 1.264
   13 ...................... 1.265
   14 ...................... 1.273
   15(2), (3) ............... 1.304
   16(2) ................... 1.306
    (3) ................... 1.306
   17 ...................... 1.307
   18(2), (3) ............... 1.309
   19(2) ................... 2.324
    (3) ................... 2.319
    (4) ................... 2.791
   21 .............. 1.180, 1.182
Corporations Act (Australia)
 s 596B ......................... 1.586
 1318 ......................... 1.272
County Courts Act 1984
 ............................... 1.592
Credit Unions Act 1979
 s 20(2) ......................... 1.176
Criminal Courts Act 1973
 ............................... 1.389
Criminal Justice Act 1988
 Pt V (ss 37–70) ................... 1.353
 s 71 ......................... 1.381
 101 ..................... 1.389, 1.392
 170(2) ................. 1.379, 1.381
 171(1) ..................... 1.382
 Sch 16 ................... 1.379, 1.381
Crown Proceedings Act 1947
 s 21 ............................. 1.65


D

Debtors Act 1969
 s 11 ............................. 1.481
Deeds of Arrangement Act 1914
 ............................... 1.506
Deregulation Act 2015
 ............................... 1.369
 s 17 ............................. 1.524
 Sch 6
  para 5 ....................... 1.641
  Pt 6 ......................... 1.524
Drug Trafficking Offences Act 1986
 s 8 ............................. 1.353


E

Electricity Act 1989
 ............................... 2.433
Employment Rights Act 1996
 ..................... 1.756, 2.852
 s 182 ........................... 1.474
 184 ........................... 1.474
 203 ............................. 1.59
Energy Act 2004
 s 159 ........................... 1.617
 Sch 20, 21 ..................... 1.617

Enterprise Act 2002
..... 1.1, 1.75, 1.159, 1.527, 1.620, 1.756
Pt 10 (ss 248–272)
.................................... 4.1
s 248 ............................. 4.2
249 ............................. 4.3
(1), (2) ..................... 1.627
251 ............. 1.84, 1.228, 1.520
254 ............................. 4.4
255 ............................. 4.5
256 ............................. 4.6
257 ..................... 1.394, 4.7
261 ............................. 4.8
264 ............................. 4.9
266 ............................. 4.10
267 ............................. 4.11
268 ..................... 1.394, 4.12
269 ............................. 4.13
270 ............................. 4.14
Sch 17 ........................... 4.15
para 18 .................... 1.692
47 ............. 1.687, 1.688
Sch 19 ........................... 4.16
20, 21 .................... 1.394
Environmental Protection Act 1990
..................... 1.353, 1.660
s 59 ............................. 2.183
European Communities Act 1972
.......................... 1.581
Sch 2
para 1(1) ...... 1.566, 1.567, 1.577, 1.578
European Union (Withdrawal) Act 2018
................................ 6.1
European Union (Withdrawal Agreement) Act 2020
s 33 ............................. 6.1
39 ............................. 6.1

**F**

Family Law Act 1996
s 33 ............... 1.456, 1.457, 1.458
Finance Act 2008
Sch 36
para 2 ...................... 1.414
Finance Act 2020
s 98 ............................. 1.228
(7) ......................... 1.522
99 ............................. 1.228
Financial Services Act 1986
.......................... 1.177
Financial Services and Markets Act 2000
.......................... 3.14
s 212(1) ......................... 1.138
215 ............................. 2.939
356, 357 ....................... 1.65
359 ..................... 1.629, 1.630
362 ............................. 2.939
(2)(a) ..................... 1.630
(3) ................ 1.669, 1.670
(4) ......................... 1.691
362A ........................... 1.646
363 ............................. 2.939

Financial Services and Markets Act 2000 – *cont.*
s 363(2) ......................... 1.79
(3) ......................... 1.85
(4) ......................... 1.92
(5) ......................... 1.93
364 ............................. 1.92
365 ............................. 2.939
367 ............. 1.176, 1.625, 1.630
371 ............................. 2.939
372 ............................. 1.379
373 ............................. 1.416
374 ............................. 2.939
(2) ......................... 1.379
(4) ......................... 1.412
375 ............................. 1.583
382(1)(a), (b) ................. 1.393
Financial Services (Banking Reform) Act 2013
Pt 6 (ss 111–128) ............... 1.617

**G**

Gas Act 1986 ............... 2.433

**H**

Higher Education Act 2004
s 42 ............................. 1.393
Housing Grants, Construction and Regeneration Act 1996
s 108 ............. 1.353, 1.660, 2.852
Human Rights Act 1998
. 1.186, 1.263, 1.265, 1.300, 1.302, 1.305, 1.394, 1.478, 1.482

**I**

Income and Corporation Taxes Act 1988
s 12(7ZA) ....................... 1.686
209 ......................... 1.162
Income Tax Act 2007
s 874 ........................... 2.850
Insolvency Act 1986
. 2.9, 2.76, 2.84, 2.99, 2.114, 2.121, 2.123, 2.126, 2.140, 2.148, 2.153, 2.155, 2.163, 2.173, 2.179, 2.181, 2.185, 2.195, 2.206, 2.208, 2.229, 2.233, 2.235, 2.251, 2.260, 2.269, 2.280, 2.298, 2.307, 2.317, 2.339, 2.365, 2.370, 2.395, 2.399, 2.407, 2.443, 2.448, 2.455, 2.467, 2.471, 2.475, 2.483, 2.490, 2.495, 2.503, 2.508, 2.516, 2.521, 2.525, 2.531, 2.561, 2.577, 2.584, 2.597, 2.625, 2.631, 2.641, 2.654, 2.658, 2.665, 2.671, 2.682, 2.689, 2.692, 2.697, 2.710, 2.719, 2.724, 2.729, 2.746, 2.750, 2.759, 2.775, 2.779, 2.790, 2.793, 2.804, 2.812, 2.828, 2.853, 2.876, 2.883, 2.893, 2.895, 2.906, 2.913, 2.914, 2.926, 2.939, 2.951, 2.960, 2.963, 2.969, 2.971, 2.973, 2.986, 2.1025, 2.1033, 3.1

Insolvency Act 1986 – *cont.*
 Pt A1 (ss A1–A55)  ...  1.617, 1.682, 5.1,
  5.3
 I (ss 1–7B)  ......  1.321, 1.322, 1.326,
  1.566, 2.48
 s 1  ........  1.1, 1.688, 1.690, 2.73, 2.75
  (1)  .....  1.58, 1.59, 1.60, 1.62, 1.64,
   1.67, 1.354, 1.359
  (2)  ....  1.59, 1.60, 1.62, 1.65, 1.291,
   1.354, 2.1.60, 2.482
  (3)  .......................  1.59, 1.60
  (4)  ......................  1.59, 1.728
 1A  ............  1.1, 1.60, 1.688, 1.690
 2  ...................  1.1, 1.688, 1.690
  (1)  ...........................  1.60
  (2)  ..  1.59, 1.67, 1.354, 1.356, 1.357,
   1.379, 1.388, 1.396, 2.81
   (a)  ....................  1.60, 1.61
   (b)  ....................  1.60, 1.61
  (3)  .............  1.60, 1.357, 1.358
   (b)  .........................  1.61
  (4)  ......................  1.59, 1.67
   (a), (b)  ..............  1.60, 1.358
 3  ....  1.1, 1.59, 1.62, 1.63, 1.64, 1.65,
   1.360, 1.688, 1.690
  (1)  ......................  1.61, 1.359
  (2)  ...........................  1.61
  (3), (4)  .................  1.61, 1.359
 4  ....................  1.1, 1.60, 1.688
  (1)  ...............  1.59, 1.62, 1.63
  (2)  ...............  1.59, 1.62, 1.67
  (3)  ........  1.62, 1.360, 1.666, 1.690
  (4)  ......................  1.58, 1.690
   (a), (b)  ..............  1.62, 1.360
  (5)  ...........................  1.62
  (6)  ......................  1.62, 1.65
  (6A)  ..........................  1.62
  (7)  ...........................  1.62
 4A  ...........  1.1, 1.67, 1.688, 1.690
  (1)  ......................  1.63, 1.64
  (2)  ...........................  1.62
   (a), (b)  ....................  1.63
  (3)  .........  1.62, 1.63, 1.64, 1.65
  (4)(b)  ........................  1.63
  (5)  ...........................  1.63
  (6)  ...................  1.63, 2.112
 5  ...................  1.1, 1.688, 1.690
  (1)  ......................  1.64, 1.362
  (2)  ........  1.354, 1.388, 2.75, 2.120
   (a)  ....................  1.64, 1.362
   (b)  ..  1.59, 1.61, 1.65, 1.67, 1.362,
    2.100
    (ii)  .......................  1.64
  (2A)  ..................  1.64, 1.362
  (3)  ...................  1.64, 2.115
  (4)  ...........................  1.64
   (a)  ...........................  1.65
 6  ......  1.1, 1.59, 1.688, 1.690, 2.550
  (1)  ......................  1.63, 1.233
   (a)  ..  1.58, 1.62, 1.65, 1.67, 1.364
   (b)  ...  1.58, 1.60, 1.61, 1.64, 1.65,
    1.67, 1.360, 1.364, 2.100
  (2)  ......................  1.65, 1.364
   (a)  ...........................  1.63
  (3)  ......................  1.63, 1.364
   (a)  ...........................  1.65

Insolvency Act 1986 – *cont.*
 s 6(4)(a), (b)  ...............  1.65, 1.364
  (5), (6)  .................  1.65, 1.364
  (7)  ....  1.61, 1.62, 1.64, 1.65, 1.360,
   1.364
 6A  ...........  1.1, 1.60, 1.688, 1.690
  (1), (2)  .................  1.66, 1.365
  (3)  ...........................  1.66
  (4)  ......................  1.66, 1.365
 7  ...................  1.1, 1.688, 1.690
  (1)  ......................  1.67, 1.368
  (2)  ...............  1.59, 1.67, 1.368
  (3)  ......................  1.67, 1.368
  (4)(a)  ..................  1.67, 1.368
   (b)  .....  1.67, 1.368, 1.629, 1.630
  (5)  ..........................  1.291
 7A  ...........  1.1, 1.68, 1.688, 1.690
 7B  ......  1.1, 1.64, 1.69, 1.688, 1.690
 Pt II (ss 8–27)  ......  1.71, 1.321, 1.322,
   1.326, 1.621, 1.622, 1.626,
   1.627, 1.629, 1.633, 1.683,
   1.700, 1.717, 2.127, 2.128,
   1.566, 2.48, 2.851
 s 8  ...................  1.1, 1.688, 1.690
  (1)(a)  .......................  1.628
   (b)  ...................  1.87, 1.628
  (2)  ..........................  1.618
  (3)  ...........................  1.59
   (a)  .........................  1.620
   (d)  .........................  1.620
 9  ............  1.1, 1.688, 1.690, 1.693
  (4)  ..........................  1.630
 10  ......  1.1, 1.353, 1.688, 1.690
  (1)(aa)  ........................  3.7
   (c)  .......................  1.660
 11  ...........  1.1, 1.353, 1.688, 1.690
  (3)(ba)  ........................  3.7
   (c)  ...................  1.62, 1.660
   (d)  ...................  1.67, 1.660
 12  ...........  1.1, 1.662, 1.688, 1.690
 13  ...............  1.1, 1.688, 1.690
 14  ...........  1.1, 1.685, 1.688, 1.690
  (1)(a), (b)  ...................  1.674
  (3)  ...................  1.660, 1.679
  (5)  ..........................  1.686
  (6)  ..........................  1.674
 15  ...............  1.1, 1.688, 1.690
  (2)  ...........................  1.87
 16  ...............  1.1, 1.688, 1.690
 17  ...........  1.1, 1.660, 1.688, 1.690
  (1)  ..........................  1.684
  (2)(a)  .......................  1.685
 18  ....  1.1, 1.682, 1.688, 1.690, 1.696
  (1)  ..........................  1.702
  (2)  ..........................  1.693
  (3)  ..........................  1.618
 19  ...............  1.1, 1.688, 1.690
  (1)  ..........................  1.698
  (4)  ............  1.81, 1.716, 2.115
  (5)  ..............  1.81, 1.716
 20  ...  1.1, 1.673, 1.688, 1.690, 1.692,
   1.697, 1.701
  (2), (3)  ....................  1.715
 21  ...............  1.1, 1.688, 1.690
 22  ...............  1.1, 1.688, 1.690
  (1)  ..........................  1.61

Insolvency Act 1986 – *cont.*
s 23 ........... 1.1, 1.685, 1.688, 1.690
　(1) ........................... 1.666
24–26 .............. 1.1, 1.688, 1.690
27 .... 1.1, 1.620, 1.688, 1.690, 1.691
Pt III (ss 28–72H) . 1.321, 1.322, 1.326,
　　　　　　　　　　1.566, 2.48
s 28 ...... 1.1, 1.72, 1.84, 1.117, 1.118,
　　1.119, 1.120, 1.121, 1.122, 1.123,
　　1.124, 1.125, 1.126, 1.688, 1.690,
　　　　　　　　　　　　　1.737
29 ................. 1.1, 1.688, 1.690
　(1) ....................... 1.71, 1.73
　(2) ... 1.71, 1.72, 1.79, 1.87, 1.629,
　　　　　　　　1.660, 2.209
　　(a) .... 1.73, 1.631, 1.656, 1.658
　　(b) ......................... 1.73
30 ...... 1.1, 1.72, 1.74, 1.688, 1.690
31 ............. 1.1, 1.72, 1.688, 1.690
　(3) ............................ 1.75
32 ...... 1.1, 1.72, 1.76, 1.688, 1.690
33 ..... 1.1, 1.72, 1.688, 1.690, 2.207
　(1)(a), (b) ...................... 1.77
　(2) ............................ 1.77
34 . 1.1, 1.72, 1.78, 1.79, 1.86, 1.638,
　　　　　1.651, 1.688, 1.690
35 ... 1.1, 1.72, 1.80, 1.81, 1.86, 1.87,
　　　　　1.88, 1.688, 1.690
　(1), (2) ....................... 1.79
36 . 1.1, 1.72, 1.79, 1.81, 1.688, 1.690
　(1) ............................ 1.80
　(2)(a), (c) ..................... 1.80
　(3) ............................ 1.80
37 ............. 1.1, 1.72, 1.688, 1.690
　(1)(a), (b) ............... 1.81, 1.88
　(2), (3) .................. 1.81, 1.88
　(4) ............................ 1.89
　　(a), (b) ..................... 1.81
38 ...... 1.1, 1.72, 1.85, 1.688, 1.690
　(2) ............................ 1.82
　(3)(b) ......................... 1.82
　(5) ............................ 1.82
39 ....... 1.1, 1.72, 1.77, 1.90, 1.662,
　　　　　　　1.688, 1.690
　(1) ............................ 1.83
40 ...... 1.1, 1.72, 1.89, 1.159, 1.228,
　　　　　　1.682, 1.688, 1.690
　(1)–(3) ........................ 1.84
41 ...... 1.1, 1.72, 1.82, 1.688, 1.690
　(1)(a), (b) ..................... 1.85
　(2) ............................ 1.85
42 ....... 1.1, 1.72, 1.73, 1.82, 1.680,
　　　　　　1.688, 1.690, 1.735
　(1) ....................... 1.71, 1.86
　(3) ............................ 1.86
43 ... 1.1, 1.71, 1.72, 1.73, 1.81, 1.86,
　　　　　　　1.688, 1.690
　(1), (2) ....................... 1.87
　(3)(a), (b) ..................... 1.87
　(4)–(7) ........................ 1.87
44 ....... 1.1, 1.71, 1.72, 1.73, 1.686,
　　　　　　1.688, 1.690, 1.716
　(1) ............................ 1.86
　　(a) ............. 1.81, 1.88, 1.92
　　(b), (c) ..................... 1.88
　(2) ............................ 1.88

Insolvency Act 1986 – *cont.*
s 44(2A)–(3D) ................... 1.88
　(3) ............................ 1.88
45 . 1.1, 1.71, 1.72, 1.73, 1.688, 1.690
　(1) ..................... 1.89, 1.634
　(2)–(5) ........................ 1.89
46 ...... 1.1, 1.72, 1.73, 1.688, 1.690,
　　　　　　　　　　　　　2.212
　(1) ............................ 1.83
　　(b) ......................... 1.90
　(4) ............................ 1.90
47 ...... 1.1, 1.72, 1.73, 1.267, 1.688,
　　　　1.690, 2.213, 2.214, 2.218
　(1), (2) ....................... 1.91
　(3)(c) ......................... 1.91
　(4) ............................ 1.91
　(5) ..................... 1.91, 2.217
　(6) ............................ 1.91
48 ...... 1.1, 1.72, 1.73, 1.688, 1.690,
　　　　　　　　2.220, 2.221
　(1), (2) ....................... 1.92
　(4) ............................ 1.92
　(6) .............. 1.92, 1.93, 2.219
　(7), (8) ....................... 1.92
49 ...... 1.1, 1.72, 1.73, 1.688, 1.690,
　　　　　　　　2.938, 2.940
　(1), (2) ....................... 1.93
50 ...... 1.1, 1.72, 1.94, 1.688, 1.690
51 . 1.1, 1.72, 1.73, 1.95, 1.688, 1.690
52 ...... 1.1, 1.72, 1.96, 1.688, 1.690
53 ...... 1.1, 1.72, 1.97, 1.688, 1.690
54 ...... 1.1, 1.72, 1.98, 1.688, 1.690
55 ...... 1.1, 1.72, 1.99, 1.688, 1.690
56 ..... 1.1, 1.72, 1.100, 1.688, 1.690
57 ..... 1.1, 1.72, 1.101, 1.688, 1.690
58 ..... 1.1, 1.72, 1.102, 1.688, 1.690
59 ..... 1.1, 1.72, 1.103, 1.688, 1.690
60 ..... 1.1, 1.72, 1.104, 1.688, 1.690
61 ..... 1.1, 1.72, 1.105, 1.688, 1.690
62 ..... 1.1, 1.72, 1.106, 1.688, 1.690
63 ..... 1.1, 1.72, 1.107, 1.688, 1.690
64 ..... 1.1, 1.72, 1.108, 1.688, 1.690
65 ..... 1.1, 1.72, 1.109, 1.688, 1.690
66 ..... 1.1, 1.72, 1.110, 1.688, 1.690
67 ..... 1.1, 1.72, 1.111, 1.688, 1.690
68 ..... 1.1, 1.72, 1.112, 1.688, 1.690
69 ..... 1.1, 1.72, 1.113, 1.688, 1.690
70 ..... 1.1, 1.72, 1.114, 1.688, 1.690
71 ..... 1.1, 1.72, 1.115, 1.688, 1.690
72 ........... 1.1, 1.116, 1.688, 1.690
72A ... 1.1, 1.71, 1.117, 1.118, 1.119,
　　1.120, 1.121, 1.122, 1.123, 1.124,
　　1.125, 1.126, 1.617, 1.629, 1.660,
　　　　　1.688, 1.690, 1.737, 4.1
　(4)(a) ......................... 1.631
72B–72F ..... 1.1, 1.71, 1.117, 1.118,
　　　　1.119, 1.120, 1.121, 1.122,
　　　　1.123, 1.124, 1.125, 1.126,
　　　　1.629, 1.631, 1.656, 1.660,
　　　　1.688, 1.690, 1.737, 4.1
72G, 72GA .. 1.1, 1.71, 1.117, 1.118,
　　　　1.119, 1.120, 1.121, 1.122,
　　　　1.123, 1.124, 1.125, 1.126,
　　　　1.629, 1.631, 1.656, 1.660,
　　　　　　1.688, 1.690, 1.737

Insolvency Act 1986 – *cont.*
  s 72H ... 1.1, 1.71, 1.117, 1.118, 1.119,
      1.120, 1.121, 1.122, 1.123, 1.124,
      1.125, 1.126, 1.688, 1.690, 1.737
  Pt IV (ss 73–219) .. 1.127, 1.322, 1.326,
      1.566, 1.604
  s 73 ........... 1.1, 1.128, 1.688, 1.690
  74 ... 1.1, 1.133, 1.176, 1.201, 1.266,
      1.325, 1.688, 1.690
    (1) ........... 1.129, 1.246, 1.682
    (2)(a) ............... 1.129, 1.131
      (b)–(c) ................... 1.129
      (f) .................. 1.129, 1.159
  75 .......... 1.1, 1.129, 1.688, 1.690
  76 .... 1.1, 1.130, 1.176, 1.688, 1.690
  77 ........... 1.1, 1.131, 1.688, 1.690
  78 ........... 1.1, 1.132, 1.688, 1.690
  79 ... 1.1, 1.129, 1.133, 1.286, 1.688,
      1.690
  80 .......... 1.1, 1.134, 1.688, 1.690
  81 .... 1.1, 1.129, 1.135, 1.688, 1.690
  82 ... 1.1, 1.129, 1.135, 1.136, 1.688,
      1.690
  83 .......... 1.1, 1.137, 1.688, 1.690
  84 ................ 1.1, 1.688, 1.690
    (1) ................... 1.128, 1.138
    (2A) ....................... 1.138
  85 .......... 1.1, 1.139, 1.688, 1.690
  86 .... 1.1, 1.140, 1.304, 1.688, 1.690
  87 .......... 1.1, 1.141, 1.688, 1.690
  88 .......... 1.1, 1.142, 1.688, 1.690
  89 ... 1.1, 1.143, 1.145, 1.688, 1.690,
      2.234
    (5) .......................... 1.143
  90 .... 1.1, 1.143, 1.144, 1.688, 1.690
  91 ... 1.1, 1.144, 1.145, 1.155, 1.688,
      1.690
  92 ... 1.1, 1.144, 1.146, 1.160, 1.688,
      1.690
  92A .. 1.1, 1.144, 1.147, 1.688, 1.690
  93 .......... 1.1, 1.144, 1.688, 1.690
  94 ... 1.1, 1.144, 1.148, 1.158, 1.199,
      1.688, 1.690, 2.243, 2.988
  95 ... 1.1, 1.144, 1.150, 1.688, 1.690,
      2.257, 2.261
    (1A)(a) ...................... 1.149
    (3) .......................... 1.267
  96 ... 1.1, 1.144, 1.149, 1.150, 1.688,
      1.690, 2.257, 2.271
  97 ... 1.1, 1.144, 1.151, 1.281, 1.688,
      1.690
  98 .... 1.1, 1.144, 1.151, 1.688, 1.690
    (1) .......................... 1.700
  99 ... 1.1, 1.144, 1.149, 1.267, 1.688,
      1.690, 2.262, 2.277
    (1) ..................... 1.61, 1.152
      (c) ...................... 1.218
    (2), (2A) ................... 1.152
  100 .. 1.1, 1.144, 1.192, 1.233, 1.688,
      1.690, 2.271, 2.274, 2.275, 2.281
    (3) ................... 1.153, 1.160
  101 .. 1.1, 1.144, 1.154, 1.194, 1.688,
      1.690, 2.279
  102 ... 1.1, 1.144, 1.154, 1.688, 1.690
  103 ... 1.1, 1.144, 1.155, 1.688, 1.690

Insolvency Act 1986 – *cont.*
  s 104 .. 1.1, 1.144, 1.153, 1.156, 1.160,
      1.688, 1.690, 2.282
  104A ............ 1.157, 1.688, 1.690
  105 ... 1.1, 1.144, 1.157, 1.688, 1.690
  106 .. 1.1, 1.144, 1.148, 1.158, 1.199,
      1.257, 1.688, 1.690, 2.289, 2.988
  107 .. 1.1, 1.144, 1.167, 1.183, 1.196,
      1.208, 1.520, 1.682, 1.688, 1.690
  108 ... 1.1, 1.89, 1.144, 1.160, 1.188,
      1.223, 1.224, 1.409, 1.688, 1.690,
      2.238, 2.241, 2.288
    (2) ......................... 1.705
  109 .. 1.1, 1.144, 1.161, 1.688, 1.690,
      2.18
    (1) .......................... 1.153
  110 ... 1.1, 1.144, 1.688, 1.690, 2.983
    (3)(b) ....................... 1.162
  111 ... 1.1, 1.144, 1.163, 1.688, 1.690
  112 ... 1.1, 1.81, 1.142, 1.144, 1.160,
      1.167, 1.169, 1.181, 1.186, 1.207,
      1.219, 1.223, 1.235, 1.298, 1.300,
      1.688, 1.690, 2.266, 2.274, 2.310,
      2.398, 2.756, 2.962, 2.990
    (1) ................... 1.138, 1.164
    (2) .......... 1.134, 1.164, 1.220
  113 ... 1.1, 1.144, 1.165, 1.688, 1.690
  114 .. 1.1, 1.144, 1.145, 1.166, 1.217,
      1.688, 1.690
  115 .. 1.1, 1.144, 1.159, 1.167, 1.688,
      1.690, 2.182, 2.266
  116 .. 1.1, 1.144, 1.168, 1.176, 1.178,
      1.688, 1.690
  Pt IV, Ch VI (ss 117–162)
      ............................ 1.128
  s 117 ........ 1.1, 1.164, 1.688, 1.690
    (2A) ....................... 1.169
    (5) .......................... 1.169
  118 ........ 1.1, 1.170, 1.688, 1.690
  119 ........ 1.1, 1.171, 1.688, 1.690
  120 ... 1.1, 1.169, 1.172, 1.688, 1.690
  121 ........ 1.1, 1.173, 1.688, 1.690
  122 ........ 1.1, 1.136, 1.688, 1.690
    (1)(a)–(d) .................. 1.174
      (e) ......... 1.174, 1.178, 2.315
      (f) . 1.174, 1.176, 1.178, 2.324,
      5.41
      (g) . 1.174, 1.175, 1.176, 1.178,
      1.196, 2.341, 2.344
  123 .. 1.1, 1.174, 1.272, 1.273, 1.284,
      1.302, 1.303, 1.304, 1.309, 1.321,
      1.383, 1.386, 1.628, 1.639, 1.688,
      1.690, 2.315
    (1)(a) . 1.175, 1.176, 1.282, 2.316,
      2.338
      (b)–(d) ........... 1.175, 1.176
      (e) ... 1.175, 1.176, 1.461, 5.41
    (2) ..... 1.175, 1.176, 1.461, 5.41
  124 .. 1.1, 1.129, 1.174, 1.175, 1.182,
      1.263, 1.264, 1.265, 1.282, 1.303,
      1.304, 1.309, 1.325, 1.515, 1.629,
      1.688, 1.690, 2.318, 2.321, 2.827,
      2.829
    (1) ......................... 1.67
    (2)(b) ...................... 1.176
    (3) ......................... 1.176

Insolvency Act 1986 – *cont.*

s 124(5) ......................... 1.168
124A ....... 1.1, 1.174, 1.176, 1.188,
    1.625, 1.688, 1.690, 2.354, 6.3
    (1), (2) ................... 1.177
124B .............. 1.1, 1.688, 1.690
124C .............. 1.1, 1.688, 1.690
125 .. 1.1, 1.251, 1.382, 1.629, 1.630,
    1.688, 1.690, 2.328, 2.333, 2.530,
                  2.550
    (1) ................. 1.175, 1.178
    (2) .......... 1.174, 1.176, 1.178
126 .. 1.1, 1.179, 1.181, 1.287, 1.688,
                  1.690
127 .. 1.1, 1.140, 1.174, 1.182, 1.183,
    1.188, 1.303, 1.398, 1.453, 1.617,
    1.630, 1.654, 1.657, 1.688, 1.690,
            2.324, 6.19, 7.33
    (2) ......................... 1.180
128 .. 1.1, 1.164, 1.181, 1.229, 1.240,
                1.688, 1.690
    (1) ......................... 1.140
129 .. 1.1, 1.263, 1.264, 1.265, 1.472,
                1.688, 1.690
    (1) .......... 1.177, 1.180, 1.304
    (1A) ............... 1.182, 1.630
    (2) .... 1.140, 1.177, 1.180, 1.182,
          1.304, 1.390, 1.657
130 ... 1.1, 1.399, 1.660, 1.688, 1.690
    (2) .... 1.164, 1.179, 1.182, 1.183,
           1.188, 1.288, 7.33
    (4) ......................... 1.183
131 .. 1.1, 1.164, 1.186, 1.267, 1.688,
                1.690
    (1) ..... 1.61, 1.184, 1.1.61, 2.356
    (3) .......... 1.184, 1.188, 2.356
132 .. 1.1, 1.174, 1.185, 1.554, 1.688,
                1.690
133 .. 1.1, 1.174, 1.184, 1.187, 1.267,
    1.404, 1.688, 1.690, 2.421, 2.429
    (1)(a) ..................... 1.186
    (c) ..................... 1.186
    (2) ................ 1.186, 2.824
    (3) ......................... 1.186
134 ......... 1.1, 1.187, 1.688, 1.690
135 .. 1.1, 1.177, 1.400, 1.688, 1.690,
          1.740, 2.348, 2.349
    (2) ......................... 1.188
136 .. 1.1, 1.189, 1.190, 1.193, 1.688,
              1.690, 2.371
    (2) ......................... 1.554
    (3) ......................... 1.258
    (4), (5) ................... 1.184
137 .. 1.1, 1.189, 1.190, 1.192, 1.193,
          1.688, 1.690, 2.376
138 ......... 1.1, 1.191, 1.688, 1.690
139 .. 1.1, 1.189, 1.192, 1.193, 1.688,
                1.690
140 ... 1.1, 1.193, 1.688, 1.690, 2.820
    (1), (2) ..................... 1.189
141 ... 1.1, 1.154, 1.688, 1.690, 2.820
    (2) ......................... 1.194
    (4), (5) ................... 2.968
142 ... 1.1, 1.195, 1.688, 1.690, 2.820
143 ... 1.1, 1.196, 1.688, 1.690, 2.820
144 ... 1.1, 1.197, 1.688, 1.690, 2.820

Insolvency Act 1986 – *cont.*

s 145 ......... 1.1, 1.688, 1.690, 2.820
    (2) ......................... 1.198
146 .. 1.1, 1.199, 1.261, 1.688, 1.690,
               2.820, 2.988
146A ....... 1.1, 1.688, 1.690, 2.820
147 .. 1.1, 1.164, 1.200, 1.688, 1.690,
                2.820
    (1) ................... 1.64, 1.655
148 .. 1.1, 1.129, 1.688, 1.690, 2.400,
              2.401, 2.820
    (2) ......................... 1.201
149 ......... 1.1, 1.688, 1.690, 2.820
    (2) ......................... 1.202
    (3) ................ 1.202, 2.852
150 ... 1.1, 1.203, 1.688, 1.690, 2.820
151 ......... 1.1, 1.203, 1.688, 1.690
152 .............. 1.1, 1.688, 1.690
    (1) ......................... 1.204
153 ... 1.1, 1.205, 1.212, 1.688, 1.690
154 ... 1.1, 1.206, 1.688, 1.690, 2.444
155 ... 1.1, 1.164, 1.207, 1.688, 1.690
156 .. 1.1, 1.167, 1.208, 1.688, 1.690,
           2.306, 2.433, 2.435
157 ......... 1.1, 1.209, 1.688, 1.690
158 ......... 1.1, 1.210, 1.688, 1.690
159 ......... 1.1, 1.211, 1.688, 1.690
160 ......... 1.1, 1.212, 1.688, 1.690
    (1) ......................... 1.205
    (b) ......................... 2.400
    (c) ......................... 2.398
    (d) ................ 1.203, 2.408
    (2) .......... 1.203, 2.397, 2.410
161 ......... 1.1, 1.213, 1.688, 1.690
162 ......... 1.1, 1.214, 1.688, 1.690
163 ......... 1.1, 1.215, 1.688, 1.690
164 .. 1.1, 1.216, 1.688, 1.690, 2.250,
           2.296, 2.394
165 .. 1.1, 1.217, 1.688, 1.690, 1.740,
              2.274
    (2) ......................... 1.741
    (4) ......................... 2.400
    (a) ......................... 1.201
    (b) ......................... 2.408
    (c) ......................... 1.201
    (5) ......................... 1.206
    (6) ......................... 1.217
166 .. 1.1, 1.166, 1.688, 1.690, 1.740,
              2.274
    (2) ......................... 1.218
    (5) ................ 1.152, 1.218
    (7) ......................... 1.218
167 ... 1.1, 1.194, 1.219, 1.688, 1.690
    (1) ......................... 1.741
    (3) ......................... 1.164
168 ......... 1.1, 1.688, 1.690, 1.740
    (3) ..... 1.81, 1.220, 1.235, 1.414
    (5) ..... 1.67, 1.220, 1.235, 1.414,
          2.440, 2.841, 2.962
169 ......... 1.1, 1.221, 1.688, 1.690
170 ... 1.1, 1.222, 1.249, 1.688, 1.690
171 .. 1.1, 1.270, 1.409, 1.688, 1.690,
        2.240, 2.241, 2.242, 2.286
    (2)(a) ..................... 1.160
    (b) ....... 1.160, 1.223, 1.224
    (3), (3A) ................... 1.160

Insolvency Act 1986 – *cont.*
s 171(5) .......................... 1.223
172 ... 1.1, 1.89, 1.223, 1.270, 1.688,
    1.690, 2.286, 2.288, 2.380, 2.384
(2) .......... 1.160, 1.224, 1.705
(6) .......................... 1.224
(8) .......................... 1.261
173 .. 1.1, 1.226, 1.270, 1.688, 1.690,
    2.248, 2.294
(2)(b) ...................... 1.225
174 .. 1.1, 1.225, 1.226, 1.270, 1.688,
    1.690
(3) .......................... 1.199
175 .. 1.1, 1.233, 1.270, 1.520, 1.688,
    1.690, 2.852
(1) .......... 1.159, 1.228, 1.682
(2)(a) ...................... 1.682
(b) ......... 1.84, 1.228, 1.682
176 ........ 1.1, 1.270, 1.688, 1.690
(2A) ........................ 1.229
(3) ................. 1.159, 1.229
176AZA ...................... 1.230
176ZA ..... 1.1, 1.159, 1.228, 1.270,
    1.688, 1.690, 2.308, 2.433,
    2.436, 2.437
(2) .............. 2.309, 2.439
(a) ................... 1.231
176ZB ...... 1.1, 1.270, 1.688, 1.690
(3) ..................... 1.232
176A .. 1.1, 1.84, 1.231, 1.270, 1.620,
    1.682, 1.688, 1.690, 2.75, 2.120,
    2.220, 2.273, 2.367, 4.1
(2) ..................... 1.233
(a) ............. 1.695, 1.725
(3)(a), (b) ............. 1.233
(4)(a), (b) ............. 1.233
(5)(a), (b) ............. 1.233
(9) ................. 1.71, 1.233
(6) ..................... 1.153
177 .. 1.1, 1.234, 1.270, 1.688, 1.690,
    2.414
178 .. 1.1, 1.238, 1.270, 1.434, 1.674,
    1.688, 1.690, 2.1013
(2) .......................... 1.235
(3)(b) ...................... 1.235
(4) .......................... 1.235
(6) .......................... 1.236
179 .. 1.1, 1.236, 1.270, 1.434, 1.436,
    1.674, 1.688, 1.690, 2.1013
180 .. 1.1, 1.237, 1.270, 1.434, 1.688,
    1.690, 2.1013
181 .. 1.1, 1.236, 1.239, 1.270, 1.434,
    1.688, 1.690, 2.1013
(2) .......................... 1.235
(b) ...................... 1.238
(4) .......................... 1.238
182 .. 1.1, 1.270, 1.434, 1.688, 1.690,
    2.1013
(1) .......................... 1.238
(4) .......................... 1.239
183 .. 1.1, 1.181, 1.241, 1.270, 1.472,
    1.688, 1.690
(1) .......................... 1.240
(2)(a) ...................... 1.240
(3)(a)–(c) ................. 1.240

Insolvency Act 1986 – *cont.*
s 184 .. 1.1, 1.196, 1.270, 1.472, 1.688,
    1.690
(4), (5) ..................... 1.241
185 ... 1.1, 1.242, 1.270, 1.688, 1.690
186 ... 1.1, 1.243, 1.270, 1.688, 1.690
187 ... 1.1, 1.244, 1.270, 1.688, 1.690
188 ... 1.1, 1.245, 1.662, 1.688, 1.690
189 ........ 1.1, 1.159, 1.688, 1.690
(2) ................. 1.129, 1.246
(4)(a), (b) ................. 1.246
190 ........ 1.1, 1.247, 1.688, 1.690
191 ........ 1.1, 1.248, 1.688, 1.690
192 ... 1.1, 1.222, 1.249, 1.688, 1.690
193 ........ 1.1, 1.250, 1.688, 1.690
194 ........ 1.1, 1.250, 1.688, 1.690
195 ........ 1.1, 1.251, 1.688, 1.690
(1) .......................... 1.178
196 ........ 1.1, 1.252, 1.688, 1.690
197 ........ 1.1, 1.253, 1.688, 1.690
198 ........ 1.1, 1.254, 1.688, 1.690
199 ........ 1.1, 1.255, 1.688, 1.690
200 ........ 1.1, 1.256, 1.688, 1.690
201 .. 1.1, 1.257, 1.258, 1.261, 1.688,
    1.690
(1), (2) ..................... 1.148
202 .. 1.1, 1.257, 1.259, 1.261, 1.688,
    1.690, 1.701
(5) .......................... 1.258
203 .. 1.1, 1.257, 1.259, 1.261, 1.688,
    1.690, 1.701
(1), (2) ..................... 1.258
204 ... 1.1, 1.257, 1.260, 1.688, 1.690
205 ........ 1.1, 1.257, 1.688, 1.690
(1) .......................... 1.261
Pt IV, Ch X (ss 206–219)
..................................... 1.477
s 206 .. 1.1, 1.263, 1.265, 1.267, 1.269,
    1.688, 1.690, 1.482
(1)(c) ......... 1.263, 1.266, 1.483
(2) .......................... 1.263
(3) ..... 1.66, 1.184, 1.186, 1.263,
    1.264, 1.300, 1.664
(4) .......................... 1.262
(5) .......................... 1.263
207 ................ 1.1, 1.688, 1.690
(1)(b) ...................... 1.264
(2)(a) ...................... 1.264
(b) ...................... 1.262
(3) .......................... 1.264
208 ........ 1.1, 1.267, 1.688, 1.690
(1)(a)–(e) ................. 1.265
(2) .......................... 1.265
(3) .......... 1.186, 1.264, 1.300
(4) .......................... 1.262
(a), (b) ................. 1.265
209 .. 1.1, 1.262, 1.266, 1.267, 1.688,
    1.690
210 ........ 1.1, 1.269, 1.688, 1.690
(1) ................. 1.184, 1.267
(2) .......................... 1.267
(3) ................. 1.186, 1.300
(4) ................. 1.262, 1.267
211 .. 1.1, 1.262, 1.267, 1.268, 1.688,
    1.690
(1)(a), (b) ................. 1.269

Insolvency Act 1986 – *cont.*
s 211(2) ................. 1.186, 1.300
  212 .. 1.1, 1.180, 1.271, 1.272, 1.688,
      1.690, 1.692, 1.715, 2.48, 2.433,
      2.751, 2.820, 2.834, 2.873, 6.8, 7.5
    (1), (2) ..................... 1.270
    (3) ......................... 1.415
    (4) ......................... 1.225
    (5) ......................... 1.270
  213 .. 1.1, 1.272, 1.274, 1.281, 1.311,
      1.617, 1.688, 1.690, 1.743
    (1), (2) ..................... 1.271
  214 .. 1.1, 1.270, 1.273, 1.274, 1.275,
      1.281, 1.312, 1.617, 1.688, 1.690,
      1.743, 2.433
    (1), (2) ..................... 1.272
    (4) ......................... 1.272
    (5) ......................... 1.272
    (8) ......................... 1.271
  214A(1) ....................... 1.273
    (2)(a) ...................... 1.273
      (b)(i) ................... 1.273
    (3) ......................... 1.273
    (5) ......................... 1.273
  215 ... 1.1, 1.271, 1.272, 1.688, 1.690
    (4) ......................... 1.274
  216 . 1.1, 1.276, 1.688, 1.690, 2.1041,
      2.1042, 2.1043
    (2)(b) ...................... 1.275
    (3) ......................... 2.1037
      (b), (c) ................. 1.275
    (6) ................. 1.275, 2.1044
  217 . 1.1, 1.263, 1.688, 1.690, 2.1037,
      2.1044
    (1)(b) ...................... 1.275
    (3) ......................... 1.276
    (4) ................. 1.275, 1.276
  218 ........... 1.1, 1.688, 1.690, 3.7
    (3) ......................... 1.277
    (5) ......................... 1.277
  219 ........... 1.1, 1.688, 1.690, 3.7
    (2A) ................... 1.278, 3.7
Pt V (ss 220–229) . 1.275, 1.321, 1.322,
      1.326, 1.566, 2.48
s 220 ... 1.1, 1.280, 1.688, 1.690, 1.728
  221 .. 1.1, 1.151, 1.279, 1.285, 1.688,
      1.690, 2.1048
    (1) ......................... 1.127
    (3)–(4) ..................... 1.281
    (5) ......................... 1.281
      (b) ...................... 1.282
  222 .. 1.1, 1.282, 1.283, 1.284, 1.688,
      1.690
  223 ... 1.1, 1.282, 1.283, 1.688, 1.690
  224 ................. 1.1, 1.688, 1.690
    (1) ......................... 1.284
      (a)–(d) .................. 1.282
    (2) ......................... 1.282
  225 ... 1.1, 1.183, 1.285, 1.688, 1.690
  226 ........ 1.1, 1.286, 1.688, 1.690
  227 ........ 1.1, 1.287, 1.688, 1.690
  228 ........ 1.1, 1.288, 1.688, 1.690
  229 ........ 1.1, 1.289, 1.688, 1.690
Pt VI (ss 230–246C)
    ................. 1.321, 1.322, 1.566
s 230 ........ 1.1, 1.291, 1.688, 1.690

Insolvency Act 1986 – *cont.*
s 231 ... 1.1, 1.77, 1.292, 1.688, 1.690,
      1.717
    (2) ................. 1.145, 1.153
  232 ...... 1.1, 1.77, 1.78, 1.86, 1.293,
      1.504, 1.688, 1.690, 1.721
  233 ... 1.1, 1.86, 1.294, 1.295, 1.498,
      1.688, 1.690
    (4) ......................... 1.63
  233A ........ 1.1, 1.295, 1.688, 1.690
  233B ........................... 5.1
  233C ........................... 5.1
  234 .... 1.1, 1.71, 1.86, 1.196, 1.415,
      1.688, 1.690, 2.398, 6.9
    (2) ................. 1.188, 1.298
    (3) ......................... 1.298
  235 ... 1.1, 1.71, 1.184, 1.277, 1.299,
      1.300, 1.405, 1.688, 1.690, 2.356
    (3) ......................... 2.267
  236 .... 1.1, 1.71, 1.80, 1.186, 1.267,
      1.299, 1.301, 1.586, 1.688, 1.690,
      1.740, 2.308, 2.426, 2.437, 2.765,
      2.767, 6.9, 7.34
    (2) ................. 1.300, 1.492
    (3) ........... 1.300, 1.492, 6.23
    (4)–(6) ..................... 1.300
  237 ......... 1.1, 1.493, 1.688, 1.690
    (1), (2) ..................... 1.301
    (4) ......................... 1.300
  238 .. 1.1, 1.178, 1.263, 1.290, 1.298,
      1.303, 1.304, 1.308, 1.309, 1.398,
      1.657, 1.688, 1.690, 1.700, 1.743,
      7.36
    (2) ......................... 1.302
    (3) .... 1.302, 1.305, 1.462, 1.582
    (4) ......................... 1.582
    (5) ......................... 1.459
  239 ... 1.1, 1.65, 1.178, 1.263, 1.271,
      1.290, 1.298, 1.302, 1.304, 1.308,
      1.309, 1.314, 1.324, 1.460, 1.604,
      1.657, 1.688, 1.690, 1.700, 1.743,
      2.48, 7.36
    (3) .......... 1.303, 1.305, 1.462
    (4)(a), (b) ................. 1.303
    (5) ................. 1.303, 1.582
    (6) ......................... 1.303
  240 .. 1.1, 1.178, 1.290, 1.309, 1.461,
      1.688, 1.690
    (1)(a), (b) ................. 1.304
    (2) ................. 1.302, 1.304
    (3) ........... 1.302, 1.303, 1.304
    (d) ...................... 1.700
    (e) ...................... 1.657
  241 .. 1.1, 1.178, 1.290, 1.462, 1.688,
      1.690
    (1) ......................... 1.584
    (a) ............... 1.302, 1.305
    (b), (c) ................. 1.305
    (d), (e) .......... 1.303, 1.305
    (f), (g) .................. 1.305
    (2) ................. 1.305, 1.584
    (2A) ............... 1.305, 1.584
    (3) ................. 1.305, 1.584
    (3A)–(3C) ................. 1.305
  242 .. 1.1, 1.178, 1.290, 1.306, 1.688,
      1.690, 1.743, 2.308, 2.437

Insolvency Act 1986 – *cont.*
s 243 .. 1.1, 1.178, 1.290, 1.307, 1.688,
 1.690, 1.743, 2.308, 2.437
 244 .. 1.1, 1.178, 1.290, 1.469, 1.688,
 1.690, 1.705, 1.743
 (3)–(5) ..................... 1.308
 245 ... 1.1, 1.65, 1.178, 1.290, 1.633,
 1.688, 1.690
 (2) ......................... 1.309
 (3)(a) ...................... 1.309
 (4)–(6) ..................... 1.309
 246 .. 1.1, 1.290, 1.310, 1.475, 1.688,
 1.690
 246ZA ...... 1.1, 1.271, 1.274, 1.311,
 1.617, 1.688, 1.690
 246ZB ...... 1.1, 1.272, 1.274, 1.312,
 1.617, 1.688, 1.690
 246ZC ...... 1.1, 1.274, 1.313, 1.688,
 1.690
 246ZD ..... 1.1, 1.617, 1.688, 1.690,
 1.743, 2.751, 2.820
 (2) .................... 1.314
 (b) ................... 1.272
 246ZE ...... 1.1, 1.507, 1.688, 1.690,
 2.271, 2.371, 2.874
 (7) ....................... 1.315
 (4) ....................... 1.153
 246ZF ...... 1.1, 1.316, 1.326, 1.508,
 1.688, 1.690, 2.271, 2.371, 2.874
 (5)(a) ............ 1.153, 2.274
 (6) .............. 1.153, 2.274
 246ZG ...... 1.1, 1.317, 1.688, 1.690
 246A ............... 1.1, 1.688, 1.690
 246B . 1.1, 1.319, 1.510, 1.688, 1.690
 246C ........ 1.1, 1.320, 1.688, 1.690
Pt VII (ss 247–251)
 .......................... 1.566, 2.48
s 247 ......... 1.1, 1.308, 1.688, 1.690
 (3)(a), (b) ................. 1.321
 248 .... 1.1, 1.62, 1.235, 1.322, 1.516
 (a) ......................... 1.690
 (b) ......................... 1.660
 (i) ....................... 1.688
 248A ........ 1.1, 1.323, 1.688, 1.690
 249 .. 1.1, 1.217, 1.302, 1.303, 1.309,
 1.324, 1.604, 1.688, 1.690
 250 .. 1.1, 1.134, 1.176, 1.325, 1.688,
 1.690
 251 ....... 1.1, 1.73, 1.77, 1.79, 1.84,
 1.164, 1.169, 1.184, 1.228, 1.309,
 1.324, 1.326, 1.656, 1.688, 1.690,
 1.728
Pt VIIA (ss 251A–251X)
 ................................. 2.48
s 251A ..................... 1.1, 1.328
 (2) ....................... 2.492
 (4) ....................... 2.492
 251B ..................... 1.1, 1.329
 251C ..................... 1.1, 1.330
 251D ..................... 1.1, 1.331
 251E ..................... 1.1, 1.332
 251F ..................... 1.1, 1.333
 251G ............. 1.1, 1.334, 1.399
 (2)(a) ................... 1.393
 251H ..................... 1.1, 1.335
 251I ...................... 1.1, 1.336

Insolvency Act 1986 – *cont.*
s 251J ..................... 1.1, 1.337
 251K ................... 1.1, 1.338
 251L ..................... 1.1, 1.339
 251M ................... 1.1, 1.340
 251N ................... 1.1, 1.341
 251O ................... 1.1, 1.342
 251P ................... 1.1, 1.343
 251Q ................... 1.1, 1.344
 251R ................... 1.1, 1.345
 251S .................... 1.1, 1.346
 251T ................... 1.1, 1.347
 251U ............. 1.1, 1.348, 2.492
 251V ................... 1.1, 1.349
 251W ................... 1.1, 1.350
 251X ................... 1.1, 1.351
 251A–251X ..................... 1.1
Pt VIII (ss 252–263G)
 ......................... 1.484, 2.48
s 252 .. 1.1, 1.354, 1.360, 1.503, 2.457,
 2.550
 (1) ......................... 1.353
 (2)(a) ....... 1.355, 1.356, 1.362
 (aa) ............. 1.353, 1.355
 (b) ........ 1.353, 1.355, 1.660
 253 ... 1.1, 1.355, 1.503, 2.451, 2.457
 (1) .................. 1.354, 1.360
 (2) ...... 1.60, 1.65, 1.354, 1.360,
 2.1.60
 (3) ......................... 1.358
 (b) ....................... 1.354
 (4) ....................... 1.354
 (5) .......... 1.353, 1.354, 1.358
 254 ........ 1.1, 1.503, 1.512, 2.457
 (1) ......................... 1.353
 (a), (b) .................. 1.355
 (2) .............. 1.353, 1.355
 255 ... 1.1, 1.503, 1.512, 2.119, 2.457
 (1) .................. 1.353, 1.358
 (a), (b) .................. 1.356
 (c) ......... 1.354, 1.356, 1.364
 (d) ....................... 1.356
 (2), (3) ................... 1.356
 (4) .................. 1.353, 1.356
 (5), (6) ..................... 1.356
 256 .. 1.1, 1.503, 1.512, 2.449, 2.450,
 2.451, 2.454, 2.463
 (1) .................. 1.67, 1.358
 (a) .............. 1.60, 1.357
 (aa) .......... 1.60, 1.61, 1.357
 (2) .................. 1.61, 1.357
 (3) ...... 1.59, 1.67, 1.354, 1.357,
 2.465
 (a) ....................... 1.60
 (5) .......... 1.353, 1.357, 1.358
 256A .. 1.1, 1.60, 1.353, 1.357, 1.503,
 1.512, 2.451, 2.454, 2.463
 (2) ........... 1.61, 1.358, 1.359
 (3) .................. 1.67, 1.358
 (b) .................... 1.61
 (4) ............... 1.67, 1.358
 (5) ....................... 1.358
 257 .. 1.1, 1.354, 1.357, 1.361, 1.362,
 1.363, 1.503, 1.512, 2.451
 (1) ........... 1.61, 1.358, 1.359
 (2) ................... 1.61, 1.359

Insolvency Act 1986 – *cont.*
s 257(3) .......................... 1.61
    (b) ...................... 1.359
258 .... 1.1, 1.60, 1.361, 1.503, 1.512
    (1) ............ 1.62, 1.354, 1.360
    (2) ............ 1.62, 1.67, 1.360
    (3) ........... 1.59, 1.354, 1.360
    (4) ........... 1.62, 1.353, 1.360
    (5)–(7) ..................... 1.360
259 ... 1.1, 1.362, 1.503, 1.512, 2.474
    (2) .......................... 1.361
260 ............... 1.1, 1.503, 1.512
    (1) .................. 1.64, 1.362
    (2)(a) ...................... 1.362
    (b) ............ 1.65, 1.362
        (ii) ................... 1.64
    (2A) .............. 1.362, 1.367
    (4) ................. 1.353, 1.362
    (5) ..................... 1.362
261 ............... 1.1, 1.503, 1.512
    (1) .......................... 1.393
    (2) ................. 1.363, 1.395
    (3) .......................... 1.363
262 ... 1.1, 1.59, 1.352, 1.357, 1.361,
        1.362, 1.363, 1.503, 1.512
    (1) ............ 1.64, 1.67, 1.360
    (a) .......... 1.62, 1.65, 1.364
    (b) ..... 1.60, 1.61, 1.65, 1.364
    (2) ................. 1.65, 1.364
    (3) ..... 1.65, 1.364, 1.366, 1.367
    (b) ..................... 1.359
    (4)(a) ......... 1.65, 1.364, 1.529
    (b) .............. 1.65, 1.364
    (5), (6) .............. 1.65, 1.364
    (7) ..................... 1.364
    (8) .................. 1.65, 1.364
262A ........ 1.1, 1.60, 1.503, 1.512
    (1), (2) ............ 1.66, 1.365
    (3) ..................... 1.365
262B .............. 1.1, 1.503, 1.512
    (2)(b) ...................... 1.366
262C .. 1.1, 1.64, 1.367, 1.503, 1.512
263 ............... 1.1, 1.503, 1.512
    (1) .......................... 1.368
    (2) ............ 1.67, 1.354, 1.368
    (3) ........ 1.65, 1.67, 1.368, 6.23
    (4) .......................... 1.368
    (a) ..................... 1.67
263A . 1.1, 1.368, 1.503, 1.512, 1.527
263B–263G .. 1.1, 1.368, 1.503, 1.512
Pt IX (ss 263H–371)
.................... 1.370, 1.511, 2.48
s 263H ....... 1.1, 1.358, 1.371, 1.379,
                1.503, 1.512
263I . 1.1, 1.358, 1.372, 1.377, 1.379,
                1.503, 1.512
263J . 1.1, 1.358, 1.373, 1.379, 1.402,
                1.503, 1.512
263K ....... 1.1, 1.358, 1.374, 1.379,
                1.503, 1.512, 1.553
263L . 1.1, 1.358, 1.375, 1.379, 1.503,
                1.512
263M ...... 1.1, 1.358, 1.376, 1.379,
                1.503, 1.512
263N . 1.1, 1.358, 1.379, 1.503, 1.512
    (5) ...................... 1.377

Insolvency Act 1986 – *cont.*
s 263O ...... 1.1, 1.358, 1.378, 1.379,
                1.503, 1.512
264 ........ 1.1, 1.381, 1.503, 1.512
    (1)(a) ....... 1.379, 1.382, 1.388
    (b)–(bb) ................. 1.379
    (c) ........ 1.368, 1.379, 1.388
    (d) ....... 1.379, 1.389, 1.392
    (2) ................. 1.379, 1.388
265 ............... 1.1, 1.503, 1.512
    (1)(a), (b) ................. 1.380
    (2) .......................... 1.379
    (a) ...................... 1.380
    (b)(i), (ii) .............. 1.380
    (3), (4) ................... 1.380
266 ... 1.1, 1.503, 1.512, 2.553, 2.555
    (1), (2) ..................... 1.381
    (3) .... 1.379, 1.381, 1.382, 2.550
    (4) .......................... 1.381
267 .. 1.1, 1.178, 1.381, 1.386, 1.503,
                1.512, 2.820
    (1)(a)–(c) ................. 2.530
    (2) .......................... 2.526
    (a) ...................... 2.530
    (b) .............. 1.382, 1.395
    (c) ......... 1.382, 1.383, 2.553
    (d) ......... 1.382, 1.385
    (3) .......................... 1.382
    (4) .......................... 1.379
268 .. 1.1, 1.175, 1.382, 1.503, 1.512,
                2.526, 2.527, 2.540
    (1) .......................... 2.553
    (a) ...................... 1.385
    (b) .............. 1.383, 2.820
    (2) ................. 1.383, 2.543
269 ........ 1.1, 1.503, 1.512, 2.526
    (1)(a) .............. 1.384, 1.516
    (b) ...................... 1.384
    (2) .......................... 1.382
270 .. 1.1, 1.382, 1.385, 1.386, 1.503,
                1.512, 2.548
271 .. 1.1, 1.175, 1.379, 1.382, 1.503,
                1.512, 2.550, 2.552
    (1)(a) ....... 1.384, 1.386, 2.530
    (b) ...................... 1.386
    (2) ................. 1.385, 1.386
    (3) .......................... 1.381
    (a) ...................... 1.386
    (c) ................. 1.386, 2.530
    (4) .......................... 1.386
    (5) ................. 1.386, 2.542
272 ........ 1.1, 1.387, 1.503, 1.512
    (1) .......................... 1.395
273 ... 1.1, 1.387, 1.400, 1.503, 1.512
274 ............ 1.1, 1.387, 1.503, 1.512
274A ........ 1.1, 1.387, 1.503, 1.512
275 ... 1.1, 1.387, 1.403, 1.503, 1.512
276 ............... 1.1, 1.503, 1.512
    (1) .......................... 1.379
    (a) ...................... 1.388
    (b)(i), (ii) .............. 1.388
    (c) ...................... 1.388
277 ... 1.1, 1.379, 1.389, 1.503, 1.512
278 ... 1.1, 1.390, 1.398, 1.503, 1.512
    (a) .......... 1.423, 1.448, 1.472

Insolvency Act 1986 – *cont.*
    s 279 .. 1.1, 1.390, 1.452, 1.497, 1.503,
                1.512
        (1) ........................ 1.403
        (2) .................. 1.391, 1.403
        (3) .................. 1.391, 1.394
    280 .. 1.1, 1.379, 1.390, 1.392, 1.503,
                1.512
    281 ... 1.1, 1.391, 1.394, 1.503, 1.512
        (1) .......... 1.354, 1.393, 1.515
        (3) ................. 1.381, 1.393
        (4), (4A) ........... 1.390, 1.393
        (5) ........................ 1.390
            (a) ...................... 1.393
        (6), (7) .............. 1.390, 1.393
        (8) ............. 1.390, 1.393, 2.829
    281A ....... 1.1, 1.394, 1.405, 1.488,
                1.503, 1.512, 1.751
    282 ... 1.1, 1.502, 1.503, 1.512, 2.672
        (1)(a), (b) ........... 1.363, 1.395
        (3) ........................ 1.391
    283 .. 1.1, 1.399, 1.417, 1.423, 1.490,
                1.503, 1.512
        (1) .................. 1.396, 1.479
            (a) ............... 1.382, 1.427
        (2) .................. 1.424, 1.427
            (a) ...................... 1.396
        (4)–(6) ................... 1.396
    283A ....... 1.1, 1.399, 1.423, 1.431,
                1.456, 1.503, 1.512
        (1), (2) .................. 1.397
        (3) ........................ 1.455
            (a) .................... 1.397
            (b)–(d) ......... 1.397, 1.432
            (e) ................... 1.397
        (4) ............... 1.397, 1.432
        (5)–(7) ................... 1.397
    284 ... 1.1, 1.396, 1.503, 1.512, 2.555
        (1) .... 1.180, 1.386, 1.398, 1.453
        (2) ........................ 1.398
        (4), (5) ................... 1.398
    285 ......... 1.1, 1.334, 1.503, 1.512
        (1), (2) .............. 1.399, 1.472
        (3) .......... 1.183, 1.393, 1.400
            (a), (b) .......... 1.399, 1.472
        (4) ........................ 1.399
        (5) ........................ 1.429
        (6) ........................ 1.399
    286 .. 1.1, 1.494, 1.503, 1.512, 2.348,
                2.578
        (1) ................. 1.400, 1.496
        (2) ........................ 1.496
        (3) ........................ 1.400
        (6)–(8) ................... 1.400
    287 ........ 1.1, 1.503, 1.512, 2.606
        (1) ................. 1.405, 1.496
        (2) ........................ 1.400
            (b) .................... 1.401
        (3) ........................ 1.400
            (a)–(c) .................. 1.401
        (4) ........................ 1.400
        (5) ........................ 1.401
    288 ........ 1.1, 1.503, 1.512, 2.588
        (1) ................. 1.402, 1.484
        (3) ........................ 1.402
    289 ... 1.1, 1.391, 1.503, 1.512, 1.554

Insolvency Act 1986 – *cont.*
    s 289(1) .................. 1.403, 1.405
        (4) ........................ 1.403
    290 ... 1.1, 1.186, 1.495, 1.503, 1.512
        (1), (2) ................... 1.404
        (4) ........................ 1.404
    291 ......... 1.1, 1.452, 1.503, 1.512
        (1) ........................ 1.430
            (b) ...................... 1.478
        (4)(b) ...................... 1.405
        (6) ........................ 1.490
    291A ....... 1.1, 1.369, 1.407, 1.417,
                1.489, 1.503, 1.512, 1.554
        (1) ........................ 1.406
    292 ... 1.1, 1.406, 1.417, 1.503, 1.512
        (1) ........................ 1.407
        (3) ........................ 1.407
    293 ......... 1.1, 1.407, 1.503, 1.512
    294 ......... 1.1, 1.407, 1.503, 1.512
    295 ......... 1.1, 1.407, 1.503, 1.512
    296 ......... 1.1, 1.417, 1.503, 1.512
        (1) ........................ 1.408
        (2) ........................ 1.408
        (3)–(5) ................... 1.408
    297 ......... 1.1, 1.408, 1.503, 1.512
        (3) ........................ 2.602
        (4), (5) ............. 1.401, 2.602
    298 ......... 1.1, 1.414, 1.503, 1.512
        (1) ........................ 1.409
        (4) ........................ 1.409
        (8) ........................ 1.450
    299 ................ 1.1, 1.503, 1.512
        (1) ........................ 1.410
        (2) .................. 1.410, 1.411
        (3) ........................ 1.410
            (d) ...................... 1.450
        (4) ........................ 1.410
        (5) .................. 1.410, 1.415
    300 ................ 1.1, 1.503, 1.512
        (1) ........................ 1.411
        (2) ........................ 1.417
            (b) ...................... 1.411
        (8) ........................ 1.411
    301 ... 1.1, 1.408, 1.413, 1.503, 1.512
        (2) ........................ 1.412
    302 ... 1.1, 1.412, 1.413, 1.503, 1.512
    303 ... 1.1, 1.391, 1.417, 1.503, 1.512
        (1) ..... 1.67, 1.401, 1.414, 1.416,
                1.427, 1.434, 1.489
        (2) .... 1.407, 1.414, 1.429, 1.489
        (2A)–(2C) ................... 1.414
    304 ... 1.1, 1.410, 1.414, 1.503, 1.512
        (1) .................. 1.417, 1.434
            (a) ...................... 1.415
        (2) .................. 1.415, 1.435
        (3) ........................ 1.415
    305 ......... 1.1, 1.393, 1.503, 1.512
        (2) .... 1.414, 1.415, 1.416, 1.417,
                1.434, 1.449, 1.452
    306 .. 1.1, 1.198, 1.398, 1.401, 1.408,
            1.417, 1.423, 1.456, 1.462, 1.473,
            1.490, 1.503, 1.512, 2.606
        (1) ...... 1.396, 1.427, 1.429
        (2) ........................ 1.429
    306A ....... 1.1, 1.419, 1.420, 1.421,
                1.422, 1.503, 1.512

Insolvency Act 1986 – *cont.*
s 306A(2), (3) ................... 1.418
  306AA ...... 1.1, 1.418, 1.419, 1.503,
                                       1.512
  306B . 1.1, 1.418, 1.420, 1.503, 1.512
  306BA ..... 1.1, 1.418, 1.421, 1.503,
                                       1.512
  306C ........ 1.1, 1.422, 1.503, 1.512
    (2), (3) ................... 1.418
  307 .. 1.1, 1.396, 1.426, 1.452, 1.473,
                     1.490, 1.503, 1.512
    (1) .......... 1.423, 1.427, 1.458
    (2)(c) .............. 1.393, 1.429
    (4)(b) ...................... 1.423
    (4A) ........................ 1.423
    (5) ................. 1.423, 1.427
    (7) ......................... 1.423
  308 .. 1.1, 1.423, 1.426, 1.454, 1.490,
              1.503, 1.512, 2.639, 2.640
    (1)(b) .............. 1.396, 1.424
    (3), (4) .................... 1.424
  308A ....... 1.1, 1.423, 1.425, 1.454,
                            1.503, 1.512
  309 ... 1.1, 1.396, 1.426, 1.503, 1.512
    (1)(a) ...................... 1.423
  310 .. 1.1, 1.424, 1.428, 1.473, 1.489,
              1.503, 1.512, 1.519
    (1) ......................... 1.427
    (1A)(b) ..................... 1.393
    (2) ......................... 1.427
    (6)(a) ...................... 1.393
    (6A) ........................ 1.427
    (7) ................. 1.396, 1.427
    (8), (9) .................... 1.427
  310A . 1.1, 1.423, 1.428, 1.503, 1.512
    (2) ......................... 1.427
  311 ......... 1.1, 1.430, 1.503, 1.512
    (1) .......... 1.396, 1.417, 1.429
    (2), (3) .................... 1.429
    (4) ................. 1.417, 1.429
    (5), (6) .................... 1.429
  312 .. 1.1, 1.429, 1.452, 1.503, 1.512
    (1) ................. 1.405, 1.430
  313 .. 1.1, 1.397, 1.451, 1.455, 1.503,
                                       1.512
    (2) ................. 1.411, 1.431
    (2A), (2B) .................. 1.431
    (3)–(5) ..................... 1.431
  313A ........ 1.1, 1.397, 1.503, 1.512
    (1)(a), (b) .............. 1.432
    (2) ......... 1.432, 1.455, 1.456
    (3) ......................... 1.432
  314 .. 1.1, 1.416, 1.503, 1.512, 1.752,
                                       1.755
    (1)(b) ...................... 1.433
    (5) ......................... 1.433
    (6)(b) ...................... 1.433
    (8) ......................... 1.433
    (2)(b) ...................... 1.433
  315 .. 1.1, 1.235, 1.396, 1.417, 1.438,
              1.439, 1.503, 1.512, 2.1013
    (1) ......................... 1.434
    (2) .... 1.434, 1.436, 1.437, 1.471
      (b) ...................... 1.401
    (3) ......................... 1.434
    (4) ................. 1.434, 1.435

Insolvency Act 1986 – *cont.*
s 315(5) ........................ 1.434
  316 . 1.1, 1.434, 1.503, 1.512, 2.1013
    (1)(b) ...................... 1.435
  317 .. 1.1, 1.435, 1.437, 1.503, 1.512,
                                       2.1013
    (1)(a) ...................... 1.436
  318 .. 1.1, 1.435, 1.437, 1.503, 1.512,
                                       2.1013
  319 . 1.1, 1.435, 1.503, 1.512, 2.1013
    (2) ......................... 1.438
  320 .. 1.1, 1.239, 1.435, 1.436, 1.440,
              1.503, 1.512, 2.1013
    (2)(a) ...................... 1.439
      (c) ...................... 1.439
    (3)(b) ...................... 1.439
    (4) ......................... 1.439
  321 .. 1.1, 1.435, 1.440, 1.503, 1.512,
                                       2.1013
  322 ............... 1.1, 1.503, 1.512
    (1) ......................... 1.441
      (a) ...................... 1.451
    (2) ................. 1.395, 1.441
    (3), (4) .................... 1.441
  323 .. 1.1, 1.442, 1.503, 1.512, 2.851,
                                       2.852
  324 ............... 1.1, 1.503, 1.512
    (1), (2) .................... 1.443
  325 ............... 1.1, 1.503, 1.512
    (1), (2) .................... 1.444
  326 ............... 1.1, 1.503, 1.512
    (2) ......................... 1.412
    (3) ................. 1.412, 1.445
  327 ......... 1.1, 1.446, 1.503, 1.512
  328 ......... 1.1, 1.503, 1.512, 2.691
    (4) ......................... 1.448
    (5) ................. 1.441, 1.447
    (6) ......................... 1.447
  329 ............... 1.1, 1.503, 1.512
    (2) ......................... 1.448
  330 ... 1.1, 1.415, 1.450, 1.503, 1.512
    (1)–(5) ..................... 1.449
  331 ... 1.1, 1.451, 1.503, 1.512, 2.988
    (1) ................. 1.449, 1.450
    (2)(b) ...................... 1.411
  332 ......... 1.1, 1.450, 1.503, 1.512
    (1), (2) .................... 1.451
  333 ... 1.1, 1.430, 1.455, 1.503, 1.512
    (1) .......... 1.405, 1.417, 1.452
    (2) ................. 1.423, 1.452
    (4) ................. 1.452, 1.490
  334 .. 1.1, 1.454, 1.503, 1.512, 2.693,
                                       2.694
    (2), (3) .................... 1.453
  335 .. 1.1, 1.453, 1.503, 1.512, 2.693,
                                       2.694
    (3) ......................... 1.454
    (5), (6) .................... 1.454
  335A ....... 1.1, 1.456, 1.457, 1.489,
              1.503, 1.512, 1.579
    (1) ......................... 1.455
    (2) ......................... 1.489
      (a) ...................... 1.455
      (b)(i) ................... 1.455
      (c) ...................... 1.455
    (3) ................. 1.431, 1.455

Insolvency Act 1986 – *cont.*

s 336 .. 1.1, 1.451, 1.457, 1.492, 1.503,
 1.512
 (1) ........................ 1.456
 (2)(a), (b) .................. 1.456
 (3) ......................... 1.455
 (4) ......................... 1.455
 (a) .................... 1.456
 (5) .................. 1.431, 1.456
337 ........ 1.1, 1.451, 1.503, 1.512
 (1) ......................... 1.457
 (2)(a), (b) .................. 1.457
 (3) ......................... 1.457
 (5) ......................... 1.457
 (6) .................. 1.455, 1.457
338 ........ 1.1, 1.458, 1.503, 1.512
339 .. 1.1, 1.302, 1.305, 1.469, 1.503,
 1.512
 (2) .................. 1.462, 1.582
 (3) ......................... 1.582
 (a)–(c) .................. 1.459
340 .. 1.1, 1.302, 1.459, 1.469, 1.503,
 1.512, 1.604
 (2) ......................... 1.462
 (5) ......................... 1.460
341 ........ 1.1, 1.459, 1.503, 1.512
 (2) .................. 1.461, 1.584
 (3) ......................... 1.584
342 .. 1.1, 1.397, 1.459, 1.462, 1.503,
 1.512
 (1) ......................... 1.584
342A ....... 1.1, 1.463, 1.465, 1.466,
 1.467, 1.468, 1.503, 1.512
342B . 1.1, 1.463, 1.464, 1.503, 1.512
342C ........ 1.1, 1.463, 1.503, 1.512
 (4)(a) .................. 1.465
 (7)–(9) .................. 1.465
342D . 1.1, 1.463, 1.466, 1.503, 1.512
342E . 1.1, 1.463, 1.467, 1.503, 1.512
342F . 1.1, 1.463, 1.468, 1.503, 1.512
343 .............. 1.1, 1.503, 1.512
 (2)–(4) .................. 1.469
 (6) ......................... 1.469
344 ........ 1.1, 1.453, 1.503, 1.512
 (3) ......................... 1.470
345 ............... 1.1, 1.503, 1.512
 (2), (3) .................. 1.471
346 ... 1.1, 1.393, 1.399, 1.503, 1.512
 (1)–(4) .................. 1.472
 (6) ......................... 1.472
347 .. 1.1, 1.229, 1.393, 1.399, 1.503,
 1.512
 (1)–(10) .................. 1.473
348 ... 1.1, 1.447, 1.474, 1.503, 1.512
349 ... 1.1, 1.310, 1.475, 1.503, 1.512
349A .. 1.1, 1.476, 1.503, 1.512, 7.33
350 .......... 1.1, 1.485, 1.503, 1.512
 (2), (3) .................. 1.478
351 ........ 1.1, 1.478, 1.503, 1.512
 (a) ......................... 1.479
352 .. 1.1, 1.480, 1.481, 1.482, 1.483,
 1.484, 1.485, 1.486, 1.487, 1.503,
 1.512
353 .. 1.1, 1.478, 1.479, 1.481, 1.482,
 1.503, 1.512
 (1)(b) .................. 1.480

Insolvency Act 1986 – *cont.*

s 354 .. 1.1, 1.478, 1.479, 1.481, 1.503,
 1.512
 (1) ......................... 1.482
 (b) .................. 1.480
 (2) ......................... 1.482
 (3) .................. 1.480, 1.482
355 .. 1.1, 1.478, 1.479, 1.480, 1.503,
 1.512
 (4), (5) .................. 1.483
356 .. 1.1, 1.405, 1.478, 1.479, 1.485,
 1.503, 1.512
 (1) .................. 1.480, 1.484
 (2) ......................... 1.480
 (b) .................. 1.484
357 .. 1.1, 1.405, 1.478, 1.479, 1.484,
 1.503, 1.512
 (1) .................. 1.480, 1.485
 (2), (3) .................. 1.485
358 .. 1.1, 1.478, 1.479, 1.480, 1.503,
 1.512
 (b) ......................... 1.486
359 ... 1.1, 1.478, 1.479, 1.503, 1.512
 (1) ......................... 1.487
 (2) ......................... 1.480
 (a), (b) .................. 1.487
 (3), (4) .................. 1.487
 (5) ......................... 1.487
360 ........ 1.1, 1.478, 1.503, 1.512
 (1) ......................... 1.480
 (a), (b) .................. 1.488
 (2) ......................... 1.488
 (4) ......................... 1.488
361, 362 .... 1.1, 1.488, 1.503, 1.512
363 ... 1.1, 1.407, 1.455, 1.503, 1.512
 (1) ......................... 1.489
 (2) .... 1.405, 1.414, 1.452, 1.489
 (4) .................. 1.405, 1.489
364 .......... 1.1, 1.503, 1.512, 7.33
 (1) ......................... 1.490
 (2)(b)–(d) .................. 1.490
365 .............. 1.1, 1.503, 1.512
 (1)–(3) .................. 1.491
366 .. 1.1, 1.404, 1.429, 1.452, 1.492,
 1.495, 1.503, 1.512, 2.765, 6.23,
 6.34, 7.34
 (3), (4) .................. 1.490
367 .. 1.1, 1.429, 1.493, 1.495, 1.503,
 1.512
368 ........ 1.1, 1.494, 1.503, 1.512
369 ............... 1.1, 1.503, 1.512
 (1), (2) .................. 1.495
370 .............. 1.1, 1.503, 1.512
 (1) ......................... 1.496
 (2) .................. 1.400, 1.496
 (3) ......................... 1.496
371 .............. 1.1, 1.503, 1.512
 (2) ......................... 1.497
Pt X (ss 372–379C)
 ............................. 2.48
s 372 .............. 1.1, 1.503, 1.512
 (1) ......................... 1.498
 (4) ......................... 1.499
 (d) ......................... 1.498
 (5)(c) ......................... 1.498
372A ........ 1.1, 1.499, 1.503, 1.512

Insolvency Act 1986 – *cont.*
s 373 .. 1.1, 1.455, 1.456, 1.457, 1.489,
1.501, 1.503, 1.512
(1) ......................... 1.500
(3) ......................... 1.500
374 .. 1.1, 1.455, 1.456, 1.457, 1.489,
1.501, 1.503, 1.512
(4)(a), (b) .................. 1.500
375 ......... 1.1, 1.381, 1.503, 1.512
(1) .... 1.356, 1.395, 1.502, 2.814
376 ... 1.1, 1.65, 1.364, 1.388, 1.503,
1.512, 1.693, 2.529
377 ......... 1.1, 1.503, 1.504, 1.512
378 ......... 1.1, 1.503, 1.505, 1.512
379 ......... 1.1, 1.503, 1.506, 1.512
379ZA ..... 1.1, 1.503, 1.507, 2.874
379ZB ...... 1.1, 1.503, 1.508, 2.874
379ZC ............ 1.1, 1.503, 1.509
379A ............... 1.1, 1.503, 1.509
379B ............... 1.1, 1.503, 1.510
379C ............... 1.1, 1.503, 1.511
Pt XI (ss 380–385)
.......................... 1.512, 2.48
s 380 ............ 1.1, 1.503, 1.513
381 ......... 1.1, 1.503, 1.513, 1.514
382 ... 1.1, 1.61, 1.359, 1.441, 1.503,
1.513, 2.827
(1) ......................... 1.393
(c) ...................... 1.515
(d) ...................... 1.395
(2) .................. 1.393, 1.395
(3) ........... 1.393, 1.515, 1.518
(4) .................. 1.393, 1.515
383 ......... 1.1, 1.359, 1.503, 1.513
(1) ......................... 1.516
(a) ............... 1.61, 1.379
(b) ...................... 1.379
(2) .... 1.175, 1.384, 1.386, 1.516,
2.530
(3) .................. 1.384, 1.516
383A ........ 1.1, 1.503, 1.513, 1.517
384 ......... 1.1, 1.503, 1.513, 1.518
385 ... 1.1, 1.61, 1.359, 1.437, 1.456,
1.457, 1.503, 1.513, 1.519
(1) .... 1.355, 1.397, 1.427, 1.432,
1.489
386 .. 1.1, 1.159, 1.228, 1.520, 1.521,
1.522
(1) ......................... 1.682
(1A), (1B) .................. 1.756
387 ......... 1.1, 1.159, 1.522, 1.756
(2) ........................... 1.62
(3)(b) ...................... 1.228
(ba) ...................... 1.700
(c) ...................... 1.228
(3A) ....................... 1.682
(4)(a) ...................... 1.228
(5), (6) ..................... 1.360
387A ........... 1.520, 1.523, 2.839
388 .... 1.1, 1.59, 1.145, 1.153, 1.291
(1) ..................... 1.71, 1.74
(a) ...................... 1.623
(2A)(c) .................... 1.525
(5)(a) ...................... 1.525
389 ... 1.1, 1.89, 1.145, 1.153, 1.291,
1.525, 1.526, 2.852

Insolvency Act 1986 – *cont.*
s 389(1) ......................... 1.71
389A ............... 1.1, 1.89, 1.526
389B ............... 1.1, 1.89, 1.527
390 ... 1.1, 1.89, 1.188, 1.291, 1.623,
2.387
(1) ..................... 1.71, 1.74
(3) .... 1.528, 2.211, 2.239, 2.377
390A ........ 1.1, 1.89, 1.528, 1.529
390B ............... 1.1, 1.89, 1.530
391 .... 1.1, 1.89, 1.524, 1.528, 1.531
391A ................... 1.1, 1.532
391B ................... 1.1, 1.533
391C ................... 1.1, 1.534
391D ................... 1.1, 1.535
391E ................... 1.1, 1.536
391F ................... 1.1, 1.537
391G ................... 1.1, 1.538
391H ................... 1.1, 1.539
391I ................... 1.1, 1.540
391J ................... 1.1, 1.541
391K ................... 1.1, 1.542
391L ................... 1.1, 1.543
391M ................... 1.1, 1.544
391N ................... 1.1, 1.545
391O ................... 1.1, 1.546
391P ................... 1.1, 1.547
391Q ................... 1.1, 1.548
391R ................... 1.1, 1.549
391S ................... 1.1, 1.550
391T ................... 1.1, 1.551
392 ................... 1.1, 1.551
393 ................ 1.1, 1.524, 1.551
394–398 ............... 1.1, 1.551
Pt XIV (ss 398A–410)
.......................... 1.552
s 398A ................... 1.1, 1.553
399 .......... 1.1, 1.76, 1.554, 2.822
400 .......... 1.1, 1.76, 1.555, 2.822
(2) ......................... 1.291
401 .......... 1.1, 1.76, 1.556, 2.822
402 ....................... 1.1, 1.557
403 ....................... 1.1, 1.558
404 ....................... 1.1, 1.559
405 ....................... 1.1, 1.559
406 ................... 1.1, 1.560, 3.7
407 ....................... 1.1, 1.561
408 ....................... 1.1, 1.562
409 ....................... 1.1, 1.563
410 ....................... 1.1, 1.564
Pt XV (ss 411–422)
.......................... 1.565
s 411 ............... 1.1, 1.567, 1.581
(2A), (2B) .................. 1.566
(3) ......................... 1.757
412 .............. 1.1, 1.400, 1.581
(2A), (2B) .................. 1.567
413 ................... 1.1, 1.568
414 ................... 1.1, 1.569
415 ............... 1.1, 1.570, 1.578
415A ................... 1.1, 1.571
416 ................... 1.1, 1.573
417 ................... 1.1, 1.574
417A ........................... 1.1
418 ................... 1.1, 1.575
419 ............... 1.1, 1.59, 1.576

Insolvency Act 1986 – *cont.*
s 420 ......... 1.1, 1.279, 1.353, 1.581
   (1A), (1B) .................. 1.577
  421 ............... 1.1, 1.398, 1.581
   (1) ........................... 3.7
   (1A), (1B) .................. 1.578
  421A ....................... 1.1, 3.7
   (9) ....................... 1.579
  422 ..................... 1.1, 1.580
   (1) ........................ 1.617
  422A ..... 1.566, 1.567, 1.577, 1.578,
          1.581
  423 .. 1.1, 1.302, 1.459, 1.485, 1.489,
        1.583, 2.48, 2.751, 6.8
   (1) ........................ 1.582
   (2) ................... 1.583, 1.584
    (a), (b) ................. 1.582
   (3)(a), (b) ................. 1.582
   (4) ........................ 1.582
   (5) ................... 1.582, 1.583
   (6) ........................ 1.582
  424 ............................. 1.1
   (1) ........................ 1.582
    (a)–(c) .................. 1.583
   (2) ........................ 1.583
  425 ............................. 1.1
   (1)(a)–(f) ................. 1.584
   (2) ................... 1.582, 1.584
   (3) ........................ 1.584
  Pt XVII (ss 426–434)
   ........................... 1.585
  s 426 .... 1.1, 1.59, 1.300, 6.1, 7.1, 7.4,
          7.20, 7.34
   (1)–(6) ..................... 1.586
   (9) ........................ 1.586
   (10)(d) ..................... 1.586
   (11), (12) .................. 1.586
  426A ................... 1.1, 1.587
  426B ................... 1.1, 1.588
  426C ................... 1.1, 1.589
  427 ............... 1.1, 1.393, 1.590
  428 ..................... 1.1, 1.591
  429 ..................... 1.1, 1.592
  430 . 1.1, 1.66, 1.74, 1.75, 1.82, 1.87,
    1.89, 1.90, 1.91, 1.92, 1.263, 1.264,
    1.275, 1.478, 1.485, 1.593, 1.635,
    1.637, 1.644, 1.646, 1.649, 1.664,
    1.666, 1.667, 1.669, 1.672, 1.688,
    1.694, 1.695, 1.697, 1.701, 1.703,
          1.706
  431 .......................... 1.1
   (4) ........................ 1.594
  432 ..................... 1.1, 1.595
  433 ............... 1.1, 1.402, 1.404
   (2) ........................ 1.596
   (3) .... 1.184, 1.186, 1.300, 1.596
   (4) ........................ 1.596
  434 ..................... 1.1, 1.597
  434A ................... 1.1, 1.598
  434B ................... 1.1, 1.599
   (a) ....................... 2.934
  434C ................... 1.1, 1.600
  434D ................... 1.1, 1.601
  434E ................... 1.1, 1.602
  Pt XVIII (ss 435–436B)
   ........................... 1.603

Insolvency Act 1986 – *cont.*
s 435 .. 1.1, 1.217, 1.461, 1.604, 2.249,
        2.295, 2.393, 2.912
   (7) ........................ 1.324
  436 .. 1.1, 1.181, 1.197, 1.235, 1.298,
    1.302, 1.310, 1.396, 1.423, 1.427,
    1.429, 1.434, 1.490, 1.582, 1.605,
          1.660, 1.728
  436A .......................... 1.1
  436B ....... 1.1, 1.483, 1.606, 1.725
  437 ..................... 1.1, 1.607
  438 ..................... 1.1, 1.608
  439 ..................... 1.1, 1.609
  440 ..................... 1.1, 1.610
   (2)(a) ..................... 1.87
  441 ..................... 1.1, 1.611
  442 ..................... 1.1, 1.612
  443 ..................... 1.1, 1.613
  444 ..................... 1.1, 1.614
  Sch ZA1 ........................ 5.1
   para 4 ..................... 1.272
  Sch ZA2 ........................ 5.1
   A1 ......... 1.58, 1.62, 1.639, 2.79
   para 3(2) ..................... 1.4
    6(1)(c) ................... 2.85
    (2) ..................... 2.87
    7(1)(a)–(d) ............... 2.88
    (e) ................... 2.88
    8(1) ..................... 2.88
    (2) ..................... 2.88
    (3) ..................... 2.88
    (4) ..................... 2.88
    (5) ..................... 2.88
    (6)–(8) ................. 2.88
    9 ....................... 2.88
    10 ...................... 2.88
    (11)(1) ................. 2.88
    12 ............... 2.88, 2.89
    13 ............... 2.88, 2.89
    14 ............... 2.88, 2.89
    15 ............... 2.88, 2.89
    16 ............... 2.88, 2.89
    17 ............... 2.88, 2.89
    18 ............... 2.88, 2.89
    19 ............... 2.88, 2.89
    20 ...................... 2.94
    25(1) ................... 2.95
    (4) ................... 2.95
    29 ...................... 2.88
    32 ...................... 2.88
    33 ...................... 2.88
    42 ...................... 1.66
    44(18) .................. 1.63
  Sch B1 ......................... 1.4
   para 1(2) .................. 1.660
      (a) ... 1.630, 1.659, 1.696,
       1.697, 1.698, 1.699, 1.700,
          1.701
      (b) ... 1.618, 1.650, 1.693,
          1.704, 2.136
      (c) .... 1.618, 1.696, 1.697,
          1.699, 1.700
      (d) .......... 1.618, 1.705
    2 .............. 1.618, 1.619
    3 ......... 1.617, 1.653, 2.164

Insolvency Act 1986 – *cont.*

para 3(1)(a) ... 1.620, 1.631, 1.654,
1.666, 1.680, 2.145
(b) ... 1.620, 1.631, 1.654,
1.666, 2.130, 2.145
(c) .... 1.620, 1.654, 1.668,
1.682
(2) ............. 1.620, 1.682
(3) ...... 1.403, 1.670, 1.683,
1.684, 1.685, 1.696, 1.697,
1.700, 1.701
(a), (b) ............. 1.620
(4)(a), (b) ............. 1.620
(5) ................... 1.620
4 ......... 1.617, 1.621, 1.693
5 .. 1.416, 1.618, 1.622, 1.636,
1.648, 1.679, 6.4
6 ......... 1.618, 1.619, 1.623
7 .. 1.619, 1.624, 1.630, 1.639,
1.720
8 ............... 1.619, 1.625
(1)(a) ................. 1.639
(b) .......... 1.639, 1.654
9 ............... 1.619, 1.626
10 . 1.617, 1.618, 1.626, 1.627,
2.136
11 ...................... 1.653
(a) ..... 1.620, 1.628, 1.630,
1.631, 1.652
(b) ..... 1.620, 1.627, 1.628,
1.630, 1.654
12 ............... 2.133, 2.164
(1) ....... 1.67, 1.630, 1.639
(a) .. 1.627, 1.629, 1.641,
2.127
(b) ... 1.627, 1.629, 1.641
(c) .. 1.627, 1.629, 1.634,
1.652
(d) ......... 1.627, 1.629
(2) ............. 1.624, 2.132
(a)–(c) ............. 1.629
(3) ................... 1.629
(4) ................... 1.629
(5) ....... 1.67, 1.629, 1.630
13 ........ 1.650, 2.164, 2.820
(1) ................... 1.634
(a) .. 1.618, 1.627, 1.628,
1.630, 1.685, 2.136,
2.814
(c) ......... 1.628, 1.630
(d) ......... 1.630, 1.661
(e) ............... 1.630
(f) ... 1.617, 1.630, 1.653,
1.661, 1.674, 1.679,
1.685, 1.693, 2.183
(2) ................... 2.136
(a), (b) ............. 1.630
(3) ................... 1.630
(4) ................... 1.630
14 . 1.304, 1.617, 1.618, 1.620,
1.627, 1.628, 1.629, 1.630,
1.634, 1.635, 1.636, 1.638,
1.641, 1.646, 1.650, 1.652,
1.653, 1.654, 1.657, 1.661,
1.693, 1.710, 1.713, 1.714,
1.715, 1.721, 1.728, 2.142

Insolvency Act 1986 – *cont.*

para 14(1) ................... 1.631
(2) ........... 1.632, 1.633
(a)–(d) ............. 1.631
(3) ................... 1.632
(a)–(c) ............. 1.631
15 . 1.633, 1.652, 1.713, 2.820
(1) ........... 1.643, 1.661
(a) ... 1.631, 1.632, 1.635
(b) ......... 1.632, 1.635
(2) ................... 1.632
16 . 1.631, 1.632, 1.633, 1.652,
1.713
17 ........ 1.641, 1.652, 1.713
(a) ................... 1.634
(b) ......... 1.634, 1.658
18 . 1.618, 1.631, 1.646, 2.142
(1) ..... 1.632, 1.636, 1.648
(b) ............... 1.635
(2) ........... 1.635, 1.636
(3) ................... 1.636
(5) ..... 1.632, 1.635, 1.636
(6) ................... 1.636
(7) ................... 1.635
19 . 1.618, 1.636, 1.650, 2.142
20(a) ........... 1.636, 1.637
(b) ................... 1.637
21 ............... 1.635, 1.651
(1) ................... 1.633
(a), (b) ............. 1.638
(2) ................... 1.638
22 . 1.304, 1.617, 1.618, 1.627,
1.634, 1.640, 1.641, 1.643,
1.644, 1.645, 1.646, 1.648,
1.649, 1.657, 1.661, 1.693,
1.711, 1.714, 1.715, 1.721,
1.722, 2.820
(1) ................... 2.127
(2) ................... 1.639
23 ............... 1.640, 1.641
(2) ................... 1.639
24(1) ................... 1.639
(3) ................... 1.639
25 ................... 1.634
(a) ........... 1.639, 1.641
(b) ................... 1.639
(c) ............. 1.639, 1.658
25A ............. 1.641, 1.642
(1) ................... 1.657
26 . 1.627, 1.644, 1.660, 2.149,
2.820
(1) ..... 1.643, 1.645, 1.647,
1.661
(2) ..... 1.632, 1.643, 1.645,
1.647
27 ............... 1.641, 1.645
(1) ........... 1.643, 1.644
(2) ........... 1.631, 1.644
(a) ............... 1.639
(3)(b) ............... 1.644
(4) ................... 1.644
28 ........ 1.644, 1.647, 2.820
(1) ................... 1.645
(2) ........... 1.645, 1.661
29 . 1.618, 1.631, 1.635, 1.639,
1.650, 2.59

Insolvency Act 1986 – *cont.*
para 29(2) ........... 1.643, 1.648
    (3) ................. 1.648
    (5) ........... 1.646, 1.648
    (6) ................. 1.648
    (7) ................. 1.646
30 ..................... 1.647
31 . 1.618, 1.636, 1.646, 1.648
32(a) ........... 1.648, 1.649
    (b) ................. 1.649
33 ..................... 1.650
    (a) ................. 1.646
34 ..................... 1.651
35 ....... 1.630, 1.631, 2.127
    (2)(a) ............... 1.628
    (b) ................. 1.652
36 . 1.356, 1.629, 1.656, 1.688
    (1)(b) ............... 1.653
    (2) ................. 1.653
37 ..................... 1.655
    (2) ................. 1.630
    (3)(a), (b) ............. 1.654
    (d) ................. 1.654
38 ....... 1.625, 1.654, 1.655
    (1) ................. 1.630
    (b) ................. 1.629
39 ..................... 1.629
    (1) ........... 1.630, 1.641
    (a) ........... 1.656, 1.661
    (b)–(d) ..... 1.653, 1.656,
                         1.661
    (2) ................. 1.656
40 . 1.353, 1.631, 1.659, 1.691
    (1)(a) ............... 1.657
    (b) .. 1.180, 1.634, 1.641,
                         1.657
    (2) ..... 1.625, 1.634, 1.641,
                         1.657
    (a) ................. 1.177
    (3) ..... 1.657, 1.679, 1.699
41 ........ 1.353, 1.656, 1.691
    (1) ..... 1.631, 1.634, 1.658,
                         1.660
    (2) ........... 1.631, 1.658
    (3)(a) ............... 1.658
    (4)(a) ............... 1.658
    (c) ................. 1.658
42 ........ 1.353, 1.631, 1.691
    (2) ..... 1.138, 1.659, 1.699
    (3) ..... 1.630, 1.657, 1.699
    (4) ..... 1.641, 1.659, 1.661,
                         1.699
    (5) ..... 1.659, 1.679, 1.699
43 . 1.353, 1.631, 1.643, 1.691,
                         7.33
    (1) ................. 1.660
    (2) ..... 1.658, 1.661, 1.688,
                         1.690
    (a) ................. 1.660
    (3) ................. 1.661
    (a) ................. 1.660
    (4) ..... 1.661, 1.688, 1.690
    (a) ................. 1.660
    (5) ................. 1.661
    (a) ................. 1.660
    (6) ....... 1.67, 1.183, 1.661

Insolvency Act 1986 – *cont.*
para 43(6)(a) ............... 1.660
    (b) ............... 1.686
    (6A) ................. 1.660
    (7), (8) ............... 1.660
44(1) ................. 1.661
    (2) ........... 1.631, 2.141
    (b) ............... 1.661
    (3) ................. 1.631
    (4) ..... 1.631, 1.643, 1.644
    (b) ............... 1.661
    (5) ..... 1.138, 1.631, 1.661
    (6) ................. 1.661
    (7)(d) ............... 1.661
45 ..................... 1.662
46(2) ............. 1.637, 1.649
    (9) ................. 1.663
47 ............. 1.267, 1.663
    (1) ............. 1.61, 1.664
    (2) ................. 1.664
    (3)(a) ............... 1.664
    (4) ................. 1.664
48 ..................... 1.663
    (2), (3) ............... 1.665
    (4) ................. 1.664
49 . 1.664, 1.667, 1.690, 1.696,
        1.715, 2.164, 2.175
    (1) ................. 1.620
    (2)(b) ......... 1.620, 1.666
    (3), (4) ............... 1.666
    (5)(a) ............... 1.685
    (b) ............... 1.666
    (7) ................. 1.666
    (8) ................. 1.724
50 ............. 1.666, 2.164
    (2) ................. 1.724
51 . 1.666, 1.670, 1.672, 2.164
    (1) ................. 1.668
    (2)(a), (b ............. 1.667
    (4) ................. 1.724
52 ............. 1.620, 2.164
    (1) ........... 1.667, 1.668
    (a) ............... 1.670
    (b) .. 1.670, 1.695, 1.700,
                         1.715
    (c) ......... 1.668, 1.670
    (2) ..... 1.666, 1.667, 1.670
    (d) ............... 1.668
53 ........ 1.670, 1.685, 2.164
    (1) ..... 1.667, 1.669, 1.700
    (2) ................. 1.667
    (a) ......... 1.671, 1.679
    (c) ................. 1.669
54 ........ 1.685, 1.697, 2.164
    (1)(a) ......... 1.670, 1.700
    (c) ................. 1.666
    (2)–(5) ............... 1.670
    (6) ................. 1.670
    (a) ......... 1.671, 1.679
55 . 1.630, 1.679, 1.685, 2.164
    (1) ................. 1.669
    (a) ......... 1.667, 1.671
    (b) ............... 1.671
    (2) ................. 1.671
    (a)–(c) ............. 1.667
    (d) ......... 1.657, 1.667

Insolvency Act 1986 – *cont.*

para 55(2)(e) .......... 1.667, 1.671
56 ..................... 1.672
(1)(b) .............. 1.667
57(2), (3) .............. 1.673
58 ..................... 1.673
59 ..................... 1.693
(1) ..... 1.674, 1.675, 1.678,
1.680
(2) ..... 1.674, 1.675, 1.680
(3) ........... 1.674, 1.686
60 . 1.630, 1.636, 1.648, 1.674,
1.675, 1.685, 1.693, 1.735
60A ..... 1.617, 1.675, 1.676,
1.693
61 .............. 1.675, 1.693
(a), (b) .............. 1.677
62 . 1.667, 1.670, 1.672, 1.675,
1.678, 1.693
63 . 1.622, 1.636, 1.648, 1.675,
1.679, 1.680, 1.682, 1.683,
1.685, 1.693, 1.699, 1.708
64 . 1.617, 1.677, 1.680, 1.693
(1) ................... 1.680
(2)(a) ............... 1.680
64A(2) ................. 1.682
65 ... 1.59, 1.617, 1.700, 1.701
(1) ........... 1.675, 1.682
(2) ..... 1.682, 1.683, 2.851
(3) ..... 1.679, 1.682, 1.683,
1.693
66 ........ 1.617, 1.675, 1.683
(3) ................... 1.682
67 ........ 1.660, 1.684, 1.693
68(1) ..... 1.620, 1.669, 1.670,
1.680, 1.685
(2) ..... 1.622, 1.630, 1.669,
1.670, 1.675, 1.679, 1.685,
1.686, 1.693
(3)(b) ............... 1.685
(c) ... 1.653, 1.670, 1.685
(d) ......... 1.653, 1.685
69 ........ 1.662, 1.675, 1.686
70 ........ 1.682, 1.688, 1.716
(1) ........... 1.86, 1.687
(2) ................... 1.687
71 . 1.679, 1.689, 1.696, 2.180
(1) ........... 1.687, 1.688
(2)(b) ............... 1.688
(3) ................... 1.687
(a), (b) ............. 1.688
72 . 1.679, 1.688, 1.689, 2.180
73(1) ................... 1.666
(a) ............... 1.690
(2) ................... 1.666
(a) ............... 1.690
(3) ................... 1.666
74 . 1.617, 1.679, 1.700, 2.837,
2.1008
(1) ................... 1.620
(a) ............... 1.691
(2) ........... 1.621, 1.691
(3) ................... 1.691
(4) ........... 1.621, 1.691
(5)(b) ............... 1.691
(6) ................... 1.691

Insolvency Act 1986 – *cont.*

para 75 .... 1.691, 1.693, 1.715, 7.5
(1), (2) .............. 1.692
(3) ................... 1.692
(c) ................ 1.621
(5), (6) .............. 1.692
76 . 1.617, 1.621, 1.694, 1.715
(1) ........... 1.618, 1.693
(2) ................... 1.618
(a) ......... 1.679, 1.693
(b) ......... 1.693, 1.695
77 ........ 1.621, 1.694, 1.695
(1)(a), (b) ............. 1.693
78(1) ................... 1.693
(a), (b) ............. 1.695
(2) ................... 1.693
(b)(ii) ............. 1.695
(3) ........... 1.693, 1.695
(4)(c) ................. 1.693
79 . 1.617, 1.671, 1.679, 1.700,
1.701, 1.715, 1.716
(1) ..... 1.618, 1.696, 1.697,
1.702, 1.703
(2) ........... 1.620, 1.697
(b) ............... 1.696
(3) ........... 1.696, 1.702
(4) ................... 1.702
(d) ............... 1.696
80 ........ 1.620, 1.715, 1.716
(2) ..... 1.667, 1.696, 1.697
(3) ........... 1.618, 1.697
81 . 1.691, 1.704, 1.705, 1.715,
1.716, 2.191, 2.814
(1) ..... 1.618, 1.698, 1.703
(2) ................... 1.698
(3)(d) ............... 1.698
82 ................... 1.659
(2) ................... 1.699
(3) ..... 1.657, 1.699, 1.703
(a) ............... 1.618
(b) ............... 1.625
(4) ........... 1.657, 1.699
83 . 1.620, 1.696, 1.715, 1.716
(1)(b) ......... 1.682, 1.700
(2) ................... 1.700
(b) ............... 1.682
(3) ........... 1.140, 1.700
(4), (5) .............. 1.700
(6) ................... 1.703
(a) ......... 1.618, 1.700
(b) ............... 1.321
(7) ................... 1.700
84 ........ 1.620, 1.715, 1.716
(1) ..... 1.667, 1.682, 1.700,
1.701
(2) ..... 1.682, 1.700, 1.701
(3) ................... 1.701
(4) ........... 1.618, 1.701
(5)–(7) .............. 1.701
(9) ................... 1.701
85 . 1.700, 1.701, 1.702, 1.715
(2) ........... 1.618, 1.696
86 ........ 1.696, 1.699, 1.700
(1) ................... 1.703
87 ........ 1.705, 1.715, 1.716
(2) ................... 1.704

Insolvency Act 1986 – *cont.*

para 88 . 1.679, 1.691, 1.704, 1.705, 1.715, 1.716, 2.196
(1) .................... 1.706
89 .............. 1.715, 1.716
(1) ............ 1.696, 1.706
90 . 1.673, 1.704, 1.705, 1.707, 1.709, 1.710, 1.712, 1.713, 1.714, 1.715
91 . 1.679, 1.704, 1.705, 1.707, 1.715, 1.716, 1.720
(1) .................. 1.712
(a) ................ 1.673
(b)–(e) ............. 1.708
(2)(b), (c) ............ 1.708
92 . 1.704, 1.705, 1.707, 1.708, 1.709, 1.712, 1.715, 1.716, 1.720
93 . 1.704, 1.705, 1.707, 1.708, 1.711, 1.712, 1.715, 1.716, 1.720
(2)(b) ................ 1.710
94 . 1.704, 1.705, 1.707, 1.708, 1.711, 1.712, 1.715, 1.716, 1.720
95 . 1.704, 1.705, 1.707, 1.708, 1.715, 1.716
(a) ........... 1.653, 1.712
(b) ........... 1.709, 1.712
96 . 1.707, 1.714, 1.715, 1.716, 1.720
(2), (3) ............... 1.713
97 . 1.707, 1.714, 1.715, 1.716, 1.720
98 .............. 1.692, 2.814
(1) .................. 1.715
(2) ..... 1.697, 1.701, 1.702
(a) ............... 1.715
(b) ......... 1.673, 1.715
(c) ............... 1.715
(3) .................. 1.715
(4)(a), (b) ............. 1.715
99 ..................... 2.183
(3) .... 1.687, 1.693, 2.115
(b) ......... 1.682, 1.716
(4) .... 1.682, 1.686, 1.687
(b) ............... 1.716
(5) .................. 1.686
(c) ............... 1.716
(6)(d) ............... 1.716
100 ................... 1.707
(1) ................. 1.717
(2) ........... 1.635, 1.717
101 ....... 1.707, 1.717, 1.718
102 ....... 1.707, 1.717, 1.719
103 ................... 1.707
(2)–(5) .............. 1.720
(6) .................. 1.717
104 ...... 1.504, 1.636, 1.638, 1.645, 1.648, 1.721
105 ...... 1.629, 1.639, 1.722, 2.127
106 ................... 1.723
(2)(a) .............. 1.637
(b) .............. 1.649
(d) .............. 1.664

Insolvency Act 1986 – *cont.*

para 106(2)(e) ............... 1.666
(f) ............... 1.667
(g) ............... 1.669
(j) ......... 1.672, 1.688
(l) ............... 1.694
(m) .............. 1.695
(n) .............. 1.697
(o) .............. 1.701
(p) .............. 1.703
(q) .............. 1.706
107 ...... 1.666, 1.667, 1.693, 1.724
108 ............. 1.666, 1.667
(1)–(3) .............. 1.725
(4)(a) ............... 1.725
(5)(d) ............... 1.725
109 ................... 1.726
110 ................... 1.727
111 ................... 1.729
(1) .... 1.628, 1.631, 1.632, 1.639, 1.656, 1.660, 1.687, 1.688, 1.716, 2.180
(1A) ............... 1.728
(c) .............. 1.618
(2) .......... 1.695, 1.725
(3) .......... 1.674, 1.715
111A ..... 1.618, 1.728, 1.729
112 ................... 1.730
113 ................... 1.731
114 ................... 1.732
115 ................... 1.733
116 ................... 1.734
Sch 1 .. 1.71, 1.86, 1.620, 1.675, 1.680, 1.685, 1.686, 1.735
para 2 ......................... 1.87
13 ........ 1.675, 1.682, 1.683
15, 16 ................... 1.87
Sch 2 ........................... 1.736
2A ........................... 1.737
para 6 ....................... 1.122
Sch 3
Pt I ......................... 1.738
II ......................... 1.739
Sch 4 ...... 1.198, 1.217, 1.219, 1.740, 1.752, 2.397, 2.440
Pt I ......................... 1.741
II ......................... 1.742
III ......................... 1.743
para 6 ....................... 1.197
Sch 4ZA ...................... 1.327
Pt 1 ......................... 1.748
2 ......................... 1.749
Sch 4ZB ................... 1.327, 1.750
4A ................... 1.403, 1.751
para 1 ............... 1.394, 1.488
2(1) .................... 1.394
(2) .................... 1.394
(a) ................... 1.488
(j) ................... 1.488
(3) .................... 1.394
3 ...................... 1.394
4, 5 .................... 1.394
7 ...................... 1.394
9–11 ................... 1.394
Sch 5 ............. 1.417, 1.496, 1.752

Insolvency Act 1986 – *cont.*
  Sch 5 – *cont.*
    Pt I ......................... 1.753
    para 1 ....................... 1.433
    Pt II ........................ 1.754
      III ........................ 1.755
    para 14 ...................... 1.433
  Sch 6 . 1.84, 1.159, 1.228, 1.233, 1.447,
      1.520, 1.521, 1.522, 1.682, 2.852
    para 1 ....................... 1.756
      3 .......................... 1.756
      8–15C ...................... 1.756
      15D ...... 1.228, 1.520, 1.756
  Sch 7 ......................... 1.756
    8
    para 7 ....................... 1.757
      28 ......................... 1.757
  Sch 9 ......................... 1.758
    para 9 ....................... 1.400
      20 ......................... 1.496
      21 .......................... 3.7
  Sch 10 ..... 1.66, 1.74, 1.75, 1.82, 1.87,
      1.89, 1.90, 1.91, 1.92, 1.263,
      1.264, 1.275, 1.478, 1.485, 1.526,
      1.592, 1.593, 1.635, 1.637, 1.644,
      1.646, 1.649, 1.664, 1.666, 1.667,
      1.669, 1.672, 1.688, 1.694, 1.695,
      1.697, 1.701, 1.703, 1.706, 1.723,
                                      1.759
    11
    Pt I ......................... 1.760
      II ......................... 1.761
      III ........................ 1.762
      IV ......................... 1.763
      V .......................... 1.764
  Sch 12 ........................ 1.608
Insolvency Act 1994
  s 2 ..................... 1.73, 1.81
Insolvency Act 2000
  .............................. 7.1
  s 1 ........................... 3.2
    2 ............................ 3.3
    3 ................. 1.353, 1.355, 3.4
    4 ............................ 3.5
    5–8 ....................... 3.1, 3.6
    9 ............................ 3.8
    10 ........................... 3.9
    11 ........................... 3.10
    12 ........................... 3.11
    13 ........................... 3.12
    14 ............. 3.1, 3.7, 3.13, 7.14
    15 ........................... 3.14
    16 ....................... 3.14, 3.15
    17 ....................... 3.14, 3.16
    18 ....................... 3.14, 3.17
  Sch 3 .................... 1.353, 1.355
    4 ............................ 3.6
Insolvency and the Enterprise Act 2002
  .............................. 1.233
Interpretation Act 1978
  s 6 ........................... 1.629

**J**

Joint Stock Companies Act 1840
  .............................. 1.128

Joint Stock Companies Winding Up Act
    1844
  s 15 .......................... 1.186
Judgments Act 1838
  .............................. 1.246
  s 17 .......................... 1.431
Judicature Act 1925
  .............................. 1.183

**L**

Land Charges Act 1972
  .............................. 1.417
Land Registration Act 1925
  s 61(5) ....................... 1.417
Land Registration Act 2002
  s 26 .......................... 1.88
    86 ........................... 1.417
Landlord and Tenant Act 1954
  Pt II (ss 23–46) .... 1.353, 1.396, 1.660
Landlord and Tenant (Covenants) Act 1995
  .............................. 1.235
  s 1(1) ........................ 1.238
    (3) .......................... 1.238
    5(1), (2) .................... 1.238
    31(1) ........................ 1.238
Law of Property Act 1925
  ........................ 1.71, 1.73
  s 30 .......................... 1.455
    101, 102 ..................... 1.87
    103 ...................... 1.77, 1.87
    104–107 ...................... 1.87
    109 .......................... 1.80
    146 .......................... 1.660
    172 .......................... 1.582
    205(1)(xxiii) ................ 1.438
Limitation Act 1980
  ........................ 1.183, 1.271
  s 8 .................... 1.302, 1.303
    (2) .......................... 1.459
    9 ............... 1.302, 1.303, 1.582
    (1) .......................... 1.459
    20(1) ........................ 1.431
    24 ...................... 1.176, 2.321
    (1) .......................... 1.382
    32(1), (2) ................... 1.582
Limitation Act 1989
  s 9(1) ........................ 1.272
Lotteries and Amusements Act 1976
  .............................. 1.177

**M**

Magistrates' Courts Act 1980
  s 32 ........ 1.263, 1.264, 1.275, 1.759
    150(1) ................... 1.393, 2.829
Matrimonial Causes Act 1973
  s 24 ...................... 1.180, 1.398
    37 ........................... 1.459

**N**

National Health Service Act 2006
  s 53 .......................... 1.59

## P

Partition Act 1868
s 4 .............................. 1.455
Partnership Act 1890
s 2, 3 ........................... 1.447
Pensions Act 2004 ........... 2.183
s 16 ............................ 1.393
43, 44 ................... 2.433, 2.827
100 ........................... 2.433
Perjury Act 1911
s 5 ... 1.91, 1.267, 1.484, 1.635, 1.644,
1.646
Postal Services Act 2011
s 35 ............................ 1.617
Proceeds of Crime Act 2002
....................... 1.276, 1.353
Pt 2 (ss 6–91) ................... 1.393
s 50 ............................ 1.418
52 ............................ 1.418
76(2) .......................... 1.275
Pt 3 (ss 92–155) ................. 1.393
s 128 ........................... 1.418
Pt 4 (ss 156–239) ............... 1.393
s 198 ........................... 1.418
200 ........................... 1.418
298 ........................... 1.417
317 ........................... 1.176
417 ..................... 1.396, 1.418
(4) ......................... 1.400
418 ........................... 1.418
(3) ......................... 1.423
419 ........................... 1.418
432(2) ......................... 1.401
Protection from Harassment Act 1997
.............................. 1.396
Policing and Crime Act 2009
.............................. 1.418

## R

Railways Act 1993
s 17 ...................... 1.353, 1.660
62(7) ........................... 1.83
Reserve Forces (Safeguard of Employment)
Act 1985 .................... 1.756

## S

Sea Fish (Conservation) Act 1992
.............................. 1.235
Senior Courts Act 1981
.............................. 1.300

Senior Courts Act 1981 – *cont.*
s 35A .......................... 1.303
39(1) .......................... 1.452
51 ............... 1.188, 2.136, 2.800
(1) ........................... 1.178
Small Business, Enterprise and Employment
Act 2015 ............. 1.433, 2.874
Pt 10 (ss 117–146)
................................. 1.524
s 120 .......................... 1.369
123 ........................... 1.369
125, 126 ...................... 1.369
127 ........................... 1.693
Sch 5
Pt 1, 2 ....................... 1.369
Social Security Administration Act 1992
.............................. 1.460
s 71 ............................ 1.334
78 ............................ 1.334
Solicitors Act 1974
.............................. 1.516

## T

Technical and Further Education Act 2017
Pt 2, Ch 4 (ss 15–35)
.............................. 1.617
s 20 ............................ 1.59
Third Parties (Rights Against Insurers) Act
1930 ................... 1.65, 1.399
Third Parties (Rights Against Insurers) Act
1999 ....................... 1.701
Trade Union and Labour Relations
(Consolidation) Act 1992
.............................. 2.827
s 188 ........................... 1.88
Trusts of Land and Appointment of Trustees
Act 1996 ................... 1.396
s 12, 13 ........................ 1.455
14 .................... 1.455, 1.489
15(4) .......................... 1.455
Tribunals, Courts and Enforcement Act
2007 ......................... 1.75
s 71 ..................... 1.181, 1.229
72 ............................ 1.181
115 ........................... 1.379
Sch 12 ................... 1.181, 1.229

## W

Welfare Reform and Pensions Act 1999
s 11 .... 1.396, 1.417, 1.427, 1.463, 6.9
12 ............. 1.396, 1.417, 1.463

# Table of Statutory Instruments

## A

Administration of Insolvent Estates of Deceased Persons Order 1986, SI 1986/1999 .................... 1.404
  art 3 ..................... 1.400, 1.401
    (1), (2) ..................... 1.578
    5(1) ......................... 1.578
  Sch 1
  Pt II
    para 13 ................... 1.400, 1.401
    15 ......................... 1.402
    16 ......................... 1.403
Administration (Restrictions on Disposal etc to Connected Persons) Regulations 2021, SI 2021/427 ....... 1.617, 1.676

## B

Banks (Former Authorised Institutions) (Insolvency) Order 2006, SI 2006/3107 ............................... 1.617

## C

Civil Jurisdiction and Judgments (Amendment) (EU Exit) Regulations 2019, SI 2019/479
  reg 92(1) ......................... 6.2
    (2)(d) ......................... 6.2
    (3) ........................... 6.2
Civil Procedure Rules 1998, SI 1998/3132 .................... 1.66, 1.630, 2.745
  Pt 1
  r 1.2 ........................... 2.781
  Pt 2
  r 2.3 ............................ 2.48
  Pt 3 ............................ 2.191
  r 3.1(2)(a) ....................... 1.503
    3.2(1) ......................... 1.63
    3.3(5) ......................... 2.530
    3.4 ........................... 2.744
    (2) ..................... 1.698, 2.48
    3.9 ............. 1.503, 2.814, 2.835
    3.10 .......................... 2.820
    (b) ......................... 1.646
  Pt 5
  r 5.4–5.4D ..................... 2.791
  Pt 6 ..................... 1.186, 1.582
  r 6.38 ......................... 1.300
  PD 6B
  para 3.1(20) ..................... 1.582
  Pt 7 ........ 1.489, 1.692, 2.751, 2.820
  r 7.5, 7.6 ...................... 2.754
    7.51A ......................... 1.414
  Pt 8 ........................... 2.751

Civil Procedure Rules 1998, SI 1998/3132 – cont.
  Pt 16
  r 16.6 .................... 1.660, 2.530
  Pt 17
  r 17.1 ......................... 2.542
  Pt 18 ......................... 2.776
  19
  r 19.2(2)(a) ..................... 1.583
  Pt 21
  r 21.3(3) ....................... 2.744
  Pt 22 ......................... 1.664
  24 ..................... 1.582, 1.660
  r 24.2 ........ 1.395, 1.698, 2.48, 2.530
  Pt 25 ......................... 1.400
  r 25.12 ......................... 7.19
  Pt 30
  r 30.2 ......................... 2.780
    (2) ......................... 2.781
    30.5 ......................... 2.780
  Pt 31 ......................... 2.776
  32
  r 32.5 .................... 2.744, 2.777
    32.14 ......................... 2.744
  Pt 39
  r 39.3(5) ....................... 2.814
  Pt 40
  r 40.7 ......................... 1.693
    40.9 ............. 1.79, 1.472, 2.814
    40.12 ......................... 2.814
  Pt 44 ......................... 2.744
  r 44.2 ......................... 2.913
    44.3 ......................... 1.414
    44.5 ......................... 1.414
  Pt 48
  r 48.2 ......................... 2.136
  Pt 51
  PD 51O
  para 2.1 ......................... 1.646
    5.3(2) ......................... 1.646
  Pt 52 ......................... 2.816
  55 ........................... 1.489
  72 ........................... 2.744
  81
  r 81.15 .................. 1.430, 1.489
  Other Practice Directions
  PD–Insolvency Proceedings
  ............................... 5.1
  para 5.5 ......................... 2.316
  8 ........................... 1.617
  9.1 .................... 1.175, 2.316
  9.2 ........................... 2.321
  9.3.1–9.3.4 ................. 2.321
  9.5 ........................... 2.319
  9.7 ........................... 2.319

Civil Procedure Rules 1998, SI 1998/3132 –
  *cont.*
  para 9.8.1 ........................ 2.324
    9.9.1 ........................ 2.334
    9.11 ........................ 1.180
  Sch 1–RSC
  Ord 3
  r 5 ............................ 1.63
  Ord 18
  r 19 ............................ 2.48
  Ord 20
  r 8 ............................ 2.542
  Ord 30
  r 3 ............................. 1.80

Civil Proceedings Fees Order 2008, SI
  2008/1053 ..................... 1.379

Companies Act 1980 (Commencement No
  2) Order 1980, SI 1980/1785
  ............................. 1.174

Companies Act 2006 (Consequential
  Amendments, Transitional Provisions
  and Savings) Order 2009, SI 2009/1941
  ............................... 1.59
  Sch 3 .......................... 1.174

Companies (Northern Ireland) Order 1986,
  SI 1986/1032 .................. 1.127

Companies (Tables A to F) Regulations
  1985, SI 1985/805
  Schedule
  Table A
  reg 30 ......................... 1.417
    70 .......................... 1.629

Co-operation of Insolvency Courts
  (Designation of Relevant Countries and
  Territories) Order 1986, SI 1986/2123
  ............................. 1.586

Co-operation of Insolvency Courts
  (Designation of Relevant Countries)
  Order 1996, SI 1996/253
  ............................. 1.586

Co-operation of Insolvency Courts
  (Designation of Relevant Country)
  Order 1998, SI 1998/2766
  ............................. 1.586

Co-operative and Community benefit
  Societies and Credit Unions
  (Arrangements, Reconstruction and
  Administration) (Amendment) Order
  2014, SI 2014/1822
  ............................. 1.617

Corporate Insolvency and Governance Act
  2020 (Coronavirus) (Amendment of
  Schedule 10) (No 2) Regulations 2021,
  SI 2021/1091 ................... 5.41

Corporate Insolvency and Governance Act
  2020 (Coronavirus) (Extension of the
  Relevant Period) Regulations 2021, SI
  2021/375
  reg 2 ..................... 1.272, 5.1

Corporate Insolvency and Governance Act
  2020 (Coronavirus) (Extension of the
  Relevant Period) (No 2) Regulations
  2021, 2021/718 ............. 5.1, 5.41

Corporate Insolvency and Governance Act
  2020 (Coronavirus) (Suspension of
  Liability for Wrongful Trading and
  Extension of the Relevant Period)
  Regulations 2020, SI 2020/1349
  reg 2 ..................... 1.272, 5.1

Credit Institutions (Reorganisation and
  Winding up) Regulations 2004, SI
  2004/1045 ................. 6.9, 6.20
  reg 36 ......................... 7.14

Cross-Border Insolvency Regulations 2006,
  SI 2006/1030 .... 1.281, 1.382, 1.398,
          1.660, 3.13, 6.1, 6.3, 7.3,
                                    7.4
  reg 2 ........................... 7.7
    (2)(c) ................... 7.1, 7.30
    3 ............................. 7.8
    4 ............................. 7.9
    5 ............................ 7.10
    6 ............................ 7.11
    7 ............................ 7.12
    8 ............................ 7.13
  Sch 1 ........................... 7.5
  art 1 ..................... 7.2, 7.14
    (2)(i) ....................... 7.14
    2 ............................ 7.30
    (i) .......................... 7.15
    3 ............................ 7.16
    4 ............................ 7.17
    5 ............................ 7.18
    6 ............................ 7.19
    7 ..................... 1.586, 7.20
    8 ............................ 7.21
    9 ............................ 7.22
    10 ........................... 7.23
    11 ........................... 7.24
    12 ........................... 7.25
    13(2), (3) ................... 7.26
    14 ........................... 7.27
    15 ........................... 7.28
    16(3) ........................ 7.29
    17(2) ........................ 7.30
    (3) ..................... 7.30, 7.32
    (4) .......................... 7.19
    18 ..................... 7.28, 7.31
    19 ........................... 7.32
    20 ........................... 7.37
    (1) .......................... 7.33
    (a) .......................... 7.34
    (2)–(4) ...................... 7.33
    (6) .......................... 7.33
    21 ........................... 7.40
    (1)(a) ....................... 7.34
    (d) .......................... 7.34
    (g) .......................... 7.34
    22 ........................... 7.35
    23(7) ........................ 7.36
    24 ........................... 7.37
    25 ..................... 7.39, 7.40
    (1), (2) ..................... 7.38
    26(1) ........................ 7.39
    27 ........................... 7.40

Cross-Border Insolvency Regulations 2006, SI
  2006/1030 – *cont.*
  Sch 1 – *cont.*
    art 28 ............................ 7.41
      29 ............................ 7.42
      30 ............................ 7.43
      31 ............................ 7.44
      32 ............................ 7.45
  Sch 2 ............................. 7.28
    Pt 1 ............................. 7.46
     2 ............................... 7.47
    para 4(1)(d) ..................... 7.28
    Pt 3 ............................. 7.48
     4 ............................... 7.49
     5 ............................... 7.50
     6 ............................... 7.51
     7 ............................... 7.52
     8 ......................... 7.5, 7.53
     9 ............................... 7.54
    10 .............................. 7.55
    11 .............................. 7.56
    12 .............................. 7.57
  Sch 3 ............................. 7.5
    4 ............................... 7.58

**E**

Education Administration Rules 2018, SI
  2018/1135 ..................... 1.617
Education (Student Loans) (Repayment)
  Regulations 2009, SI 2009/470
  reg 80(2)(a) ..................... 1.396
Education (Student Support) (No 2)
  Regulations 2002 (Amendment)
  Regulations 2004, SI 2004/2041
  reg 5 ........................... 1.393
Energy Supply Company Administration
  Rules 2013, SI 2013/1046
  ............................... 1.617
Enterprise Act 2002 (Commencement No 4
  and Transitional Provisions and
  Savings) Order 2003, SI 2003/2093
  art 7 ........................... 1.394

**F**

Financial Collateral Arrangements (No 2)
  Regulations 2003, SI 2003/3226
  ............................... 1.660
  reg 8(1)(b) ...................... 1.688
Financial Market Infrastructure
  Administration (England and Wales)
  Rules 2018, SI 2018/833
  ............................... 1.617
Financial Markets and Insolvency
  (Ecu Contracts) Regulations 1998, SI
  1998/27 ......................... 1.87
Financial Markets and Insolvency
  Regulations 1991, SI 1991/880
  ............................... 1.87
Financial Markets and Insolvency
  (Settlement Finality) Regulations 1999,
  SI 1999/2979 .... 1.180, 1.302, 1.303,
                        1.398

Financial Services and Markets Act 2000
  (Administration Orders Relating to
  Insurers) Order 2010, SI 2010/3023
  ............................... 1.617
Financial Services and Markets Act 2002
  (Administration Orders Relating to
  Insurers) Order 2002, SI 2002/1242
  ........................ 1.627, 1.668

**H**

Housing and Planning Act 2016
  (Commencement No 9 and Transitional
  and Saving Provisions) Regulations
  2018, SI 2018/805 .............. 1.617

**I**

Insolvency Act 1986 (Amendment) Order
  2015, SI 2015/922 .............. 1.382
Insolvency Act 1986 (Guernsey) Order
  1989, SI 1989/2409
  ............................... 1.586
Insolvency Act 1986 (HMRC Debts: Priority
  on Insolvency) Regulations 2020, SI
  2020/983 ...................... 1.756
  reg 2 ........................... 1.228
Insolvency Act 1986 (Prescribed Part) Order
  2003, SI 2003/2097
  art 2 ........................... 1.233
    3(1)(a), (b) ................... 1.233
    (2) ........................... 1.233
Insolvency (Amendment) (EU Exit)
  Regulations 2019, SI 2019/146
  ............................... 6.1
Insolvency (Amendment) (EU Exit)
  Regulations 2020, SI 2020/647
  ............................... 6.1
Insolvency (England and Wales) Rules 2016,
  SI 2016/1024 .................. 1.578
  Introductory Rules
  r 3 ............................. 2.205
  Pt 1 ...... 2.73, 2.76, 2.84, 2.99, 2.114,
       2.121, 2.123, 2.126, 2.140, 2.148,
       2.153, 2.155, 2.163, 2.173, 2.179,
       2.181, 2.185, 2.195, 2.206, 2.208,
       2.229, 2.233, 2.235, 2.251, 2.260,
       2.269, 2.280, 2.298, 2.307, 2.317,
       2.348, 2.356, 2.365, 2.370, 2.395,
       2.399, 2.407, 2.414, 2.421, 2.436,
       2.443, 2.448, 2.455, 2.467, 2.471,
       2.475, 2.483, 2.490, 2.495, 2.503,
       2.508, 2.516, 2.521, 2.525, 2.531,
       2.561, 2.577, 2.584, 2.597, 2.625,
       2.631, 2.641, 2.654, 2.658, 2.665,
       2.671, 2.682, 2.689, 2.692, 2.697,
       2.710, 2.719, 2.724, 2.729, 2.746,
       2.759, 2.775, 2.779, 2.790, 2.793,
       2.804, 2.812, 2.818, 2.828, 2.853,
       2.876, 2.883, 2.893, 2.895, 2.906,
       2.914, 2.926, 2.939, 2.951, 2.960,
       2.963, 2.969, 2.971, 2.973, 2.986,
    2.988, 2.1013, 2.1025, 2.1033, 2.1037

Insolvency (England and Wales) Rules 2016,
  SI 2016/1024 – *cont.*
  Pt 1, Ch 3 (rr 1.4–1.9)
  ................................. 1.180
  r 1.1 ............................... 2.8
  1.2 ............... 1.513, 2.9, 2.10
    (2) ...... 2.70, 2.874, 2.894, 2.912
    (3) .................... 1.62, 2.899
  1.3 ............. 1.503, 2.11, 2.1008
  1.4 ............................... 2.12
  1.5 ............................... 2.13
  1.6 . 2.14, 2.18, 2.24, 2.29, 2.39, 2.47
  1.7 ............................... 2.15
  1.8 ......................... 2.16, 2.48
  1.9 ............................... 2.17
  Pt 1, Ch 4 (rr 1.10–1.14)
  ................................. 2.18
  r 1.10 ...................... 2.19, 2.154
  1.11 ...................... 2.20, 2.154
  1.12 ...................... 2.21, 2.154
  1.13 ............................. 2.22
  1.14 ............................. 2.23
  Pt 1, Ch 5 (rr 1.15–1.18)
  ................................. 2.24
  r 1.15 ...................... 2.25, 2.166
  1.16 ...................... 2.26, 2.166
  1.17 ............................. 2.27
  1.18 ...................... 2.28, 2.166
  Pt 1, Ch 6 (rr 1.19–1.27)
  ................................. 2.29
  r 1.19 ............................ 2.30
  1.20 ............................. 2.31
  1.21 ............................. 2.32
  1.22 ............................. 2.33
  1.23 ............................. 2.34
  1.24 ............................. 2.35
  1.25 ............................. 2.36
  1.26 ............................. 2.37
  1.27 ............................. 2.38
  Pt 1, Ch 7 (rr 1.28–1.34)
  ................................. 2.39
  r 1.28 ............................ 2.40
  1.29 ............................. 2.41
  1.30 ............................. 2.42
  1.31 ............................. 2.43
  1.32 ............................. 2.44
  1.33 ............................. 2.45
  1.34 ............................. 2.46
  Pt 1, Ch 8 (r 1.35) ............... 2.47
  r 1.35 . 1.692, 2.48, 2.750, 2.751, 2.820
    (2) ......................... 1.362
  1.36 ............................. 2.49
  1.37 ................... 1.320, 2.50
  1.38 ............ 1.320, 1.323, 2.51
  1.39 ................... 1.320, 2.52
  1.40 ............................. 2.53
  1.41 ............................. 2.54
  1.42 ............................. 2.55
  1.43 ............................. 2.56
  1.44 ............................. 2.57
  1.45 ............................. 2.58
    (4) ......................... 1.663
  1.46 ...................... 1.663, 2.59
  1.47 ............. 1.510, 1.663, 2.60
  1.48 ...................... 1.663, 2.61
  1.49 ........ 1.319, 1.510, 1.663, 2.62

Insolvency (England and Wales) Rules 2016,
  SI 2016/1024 – *cont.*
  r 1.50 .............. 1.319, 1.663, 2.63
  1.51 ..................... 1.663, 2.64
  1.52 ..................... 1.663, 2.65
  1.53 ..................... 1.663, 2.66
  1.54 ............................. 2.67
  1.55 ............................. 2.68
  1.56 ..................... 1.478, 2.69
  1.57(3)(b) ....................... 2.70
  1.58 ..................... 1.412, 2.71
  Pt 2
  r 2.1 ............................. 2.72
  2.2(2) ........................... 2.74
    (3) .................... 1.60, 2.74
    (4) ......................... 2.74
  2.3 ............................. 1.60
    (1)(f)(iii) .................... 1.65
    (g) ............... 2.75, 2.119
    (j) ........................ 2.75
    (p) ........................ 2.75
    (u) ........................ 2.75
    (2), (3) ...................... 2.75
  2.4 ............................. 2.77
    (4) .......................... 1.60
  2.5 ...................... 1.60, 2.78
  2.6 ............... 1.267, 2.79, 2.85
    (1), (2) ..................... 1.60
  2.7 ...................... 1.60, 2.80
  2.8 ................. 1.60, 2.81, 2.85
  2.9 ............... 1.60, 1.61, 2.82
  2.10 .................. 1.60, 2.83
  2.11 .............. 1.60, 2.79, 2.85
  2.12 .................. 1.60, 2.86
  2.13 .................. 1.60, 2.87
  2.14 .... 1.60, 2.79, 2.88, 2.89, 2.91,
                             2.92, 2.93
  2.15 ............................ 1.60
    (2) .......................... 2.88
    (4) .......................... 2.88
    (6) ..................... 2.88, 2.89
  2.16 .................. 1.60, 2.90
  2.17 .................. 1.60, 2.91
  2.18 .................. 1.60, 2.92
  2.19 .............. 1.60, 2.88, 2.93
  2.20 .................. 1.60, 2.94
  2.21 .................. 1.60, 2.95
  2.22 .............. 1.60, 2.95, 2.96
  2.23 .................. 1.60, 2.97
  2.24 .................. 1.60, 2.98
  2.25 .............. 1.61, 1.62, 1.63
    (1), (2) ..................... 2.100
  2.26 .......... 1.62, 1.63, 2.101
    (3) .......................... 1.61
  2.27 ......... 1.61, 1.62, 1.63, 2.102
  2.28 .............. 1.61, 1.62, 2.103
    (2) ......................... 2.115
    (3) ................... 1.63, 2.115
  2.29 ......... 1.61, 1.62, 1.63, 2.104
  2.30 ......... 1.61, 1.62, 1.63, 2.105
  2.31 ........ 1.61, 1.62, 1.63, 2.1.61
  2.32 ........ 1.61, 1.62, 1.63, 2.1.62
  2.33 ......... 1.61, 1.62, 1.63, 2.1.63
  2.34 ........ 1.61, 1.62, 1.63, 2.109
  2.35 ........ 1.61, 1.62, 2.110, 2.111
  2.36 .............. 1.61, 1.62, 2.110

Insolvency (England and Wales) Rules 2016,
  SI 2016/1024 – *cont.*
  r 2.36(1) ....................... 2.111
    2.37 .................... 1.63, 2.112
    2.38(1) ......................... 2.113
      (2) ......................... 1.62
        (b) ..................... 2.113
      (3) .................... 1.62, 2.113
      (6) ......................... 1.62
    2.39 ........................... 1.67
      (1) ......................... 2.115
      (2) ......................... 1.64
        (b) ..................... 2.115
      (3) ......................... 1.64
        (a), (b) ................. 2.115
      (4)–(6) ............. 1.64, 2.115
    2.40 .............. 1.65, 1.67, 2.116
    2.41 ............. 1.67, 2.117, 2.118
    2.42 ................... 1.67, 2.118
    2.43 ........................... 1.67
      (a) ......................... 2.119
      (b)(ii) ..................... 2.119
    2.44 ........................... 1.67
      (1) ......................... 2.120
      (2)(d) ..................... 2.120
      (3), (4) ................... 2.120
    2.45 ................... 1.67, 2.122
  Pt 3
  r 3.1 ............. 2.124, 2.184, 2.977
    3.2(1) ......................... 2.130
      (f) ......................... 2.125
      (h) .............. 1.630, 2.125
  Pt 3, Ch 2 (rr 3.3–3.15)
    .................................. 2.750
  r 3.3(2)(i) ...................... 2.127
    3.4 ........................... 2.128
    3.5 ................... 1.67, 2.129
    3.6(1)(a) ..................... 1.629
      (3)(a)–(g) ................. 2.130
    3.7 ........................... 2.131
    3.8(4) ......................... 2.132
    3.9 .................... 1.416, 2.133
    3.10 .................. 2.132, 2.134
    3.11 ........................... 2.135
    3.12(1)(j) ..................... 2.136
      (2) ................. 2.136, 2.183
    3.13 .................. 1.693, 2.137
      (1)(j) ..................... 1.630
    3.14 ........................... 2.138
    3.15 ........................... 2.139
      (3) ......................... 1.630
    3.16 .................. 1.635, 1.644
      (1)–(4) ................... 2.141
    3.17 ...... 1.631, 1.635, 2.141, 2.142
    3.18 .................. 1.635, 2.143
    3.19 .................. 1.635, 2.144
    3.20 ........................... 1.635
      (1)(a) ..................... 2.145
      (9)(d) ..................... 2.145
    3.21 ........................... 2.146
    3.22 ........................... 2.147
      (2)(b) ..................... 2.145
    3.23 ........................... 2.149
      (2) ......................... 1.644
      (4)(d) ..................... 1.643
    3.24 .................. 1.636, 1.648

Insolvency (England and Wales) Rules 2016,
  SI 2016/1024 – *cont.*
  r 3.24(1)(j) .............. 1.646, 2.150
    3.25 .................... 2.149, 2.151
      (2) ......................... 1.646
    3.26 ........................... 2.152
    3.27 ........................... 2.154
    3.28 ........................... 2.156
    3.29 ........................... 2.157
    3.30 ........................... 2.158
      (6)(b) ..................... 2.160
    3.31 ........................... 2.159
    3.32 ........................... 2.160
      (1)(a) ..................... 2.160
    3.33 ........................... 2.161
    3.34 ........................... 2.162
    3.35(1)(j)(i) ............. 1.666, 2.164
      (10) ....................... 1.617
        (a) ..................... 2.164
    3.36 .................. 1.617, 2.165
    3.37 ........................... 2.166
    3.38 ........................... 1.668
      (4), (5) ................... 2.167
    3.39 ........................... 2.168
    3.40 ........................... 2.169
    3.41 .......... 1.669, 1.670, 2.170
    3.42 .................. 1.670, 2.171
    3.43 .................. 1.670, 2.172
    3.44 .................. 1.679, 2.174
    3.45 .................. 1.679, 2.175
    3.46 .................. 1.679, 2.176
    3.47 .................. 1.679, 2.177
    3.48 .................. 1.679, 2.178
    3.49 ........................... 2.180
    3.50 .................. 1.679, 2.182
    3.51 .................. 2.182, 2.691
      (2) ......................... 1.683
        (a) ..................... 2.183
        (c) .............. 1.630, 2.136
        (d) ..................... 1.630
        (e) ..................... 1.716
        (g) .............. 2.183, 2.964
        (i) .............. 2.184, 2.977
        (j) ..................... 1.686
      (3) ................. 2.136, 2.183
    3.52 ...... 1.617, 2.164, 2.165, 2.184
    3.53 ........................... 2.186
    3.54 ........................... 2.187
      (2) ......................... 1.693
      (5) ......................... 1.693
    3.55 ........................... 2.188
    3.56 ........................... 2.189
    3.57 .................. 1.671, 2.190
    3.58 ........................... 2.191
      (2) ......................... 2.191
    3.59 ........................... 2.192
    3.60 ........................... 2.193
    3.61 ........................... 2.194
    3.62 ............ 1.679, 1.704, 1.705
      (1), (2) ................... 2.196
    r 3.63 ........................... 2.197
    3.64 ........................... 2.198
    3.65(2) ......................... 2.199
    3.66 ........................... 2.200
    3.67 ........................... 2.201
    3.68 ........................... 2.202

Insolvency (England and Wales) Rules 2016,
 SI 2016/1024 – *cont.*
r 3.69 ........................... 2.203
 3.70 ........................... 2.204
Pt 4 ....... 2.205, 2.233, 2.258, 2.313
r 4.1 ........................ 1.90, 2.207
 (2) .......................... 1.77
 4.2 ........................... 2.209
 4.3 ...................... 1.91, 2.210
 4.4 ........................... 2.211
 4.5 .............. 1.77, 1.90, 2.212
 4.6 ...................... 1.91, 2.213
 4.7 ...................... 1.91, 2.214
 4.8 ...................... 1.91, 2.215
 4.9 ...................... 1.91, 2.216
 4.10 ..................... 1.91, 2.217
 4.11 ..................... 1.91, 2.218
 4.12 ..................... 1.92, 2.219
 4.13 ........................ 1.92
 (5)–(7) ................... 2.220
 4.14 ..................... 1.92, 2.221
 4.15 ........................... 2.222
 4.16 ..................... 1.87, 2.223
 4.17 ..................... 1.82, 2.224
 4.18 ..................... 1.89, 2.225
 4.19 ..................... 1.89, 2.226
 4.20 ............. 1.89, 1.658, 2.227
 4.21 ..................... 1.89, 2.228
Pt 4, Ch 3 (rr 4.22–4.24)
 .............................. 2.318
r 4.22 ........................... 2.230
 4.23 ................... 2.220, 2.231
 4.24 ................... 2.220, 2.232
Pt 5 ....... 1.144, 2.233, 2.258, 2.313
r 5.1 ..................... 1.143, 2.234
 5.2 ........................... 2.236
 (6) .......................... 1.145
 5.3 ........................... 2.237
 (1), (2) ..................... 1.138
 5.4 ........................... 2.238
 (2) .......................... 1.160
 5.5 ........................... 2.239
 5.6 ........................... 2.240
 (1), (2) ..................... 1.223
 5.7 ..................... 1.160, 2.241
 5.8 ........................... 2.242
 5.9 ..................... 1.148, 2.243
 5.10 ..................... 1.148, 2.244
 5.11 ..................... 1.146, 2.245
 5.12 ..................... 1.146, 2.246
 5.13 ........................... 2.247
 5.14 ..................... 1.225, 2.248
 5.15 ........................... 2.249
 5.16 ........................... 2.250
 5.17 ........................... 2.252
 (3) .................. 1.234, 2.909
 5.18 ........................... 2.253
 (1) .......................... 1.234
 5.19 ..................... 1.234, 2.254
 5.20 ..................... 1.234, 2.255
 5.21 ..................... 1.234, 2.256
 5.22 ..................... 1.149, 2.257
Pt 6 ....... 1.144, 2.233, 2.258, 2.313
r 6.1 ........................... 2.259
 6.2 ..................... 1.149, 2.261
 6.3 ..................... 1.152, 2.262

Insolvency (England and Wales) Rules 2016,
 SI 2016/1024 – *cont.*
r 6.4 ........................... 2.263
 6.5 ........................... 2.264
 6.6 ........................... 2.265
 6.7 ..................... 2.266, 2.362
 6.8 ........................... 2.267
 6.9 ........................... 2.268
 6.10 ........................... 2.270
 6.11(2) ........................ 2.271
 6.12 ........................... 2.272
 6.13 ........................... 2.273
 6.14 ........................... 2.274
 (2)–(5) ................... 1.153
 (7) .......................... 1.152
 (8) .......................... 1.153
 6.15 ........................... 2.275
 (1), (2) ............. 1.153, 1.233
 6.16 ........................... 2.276
 6.17 ........................... 2.277
 (1)–(3) ................... 1.152
 6.18 ........................... 2.278
 (1), (2) ................... 1.153
 6.19 ........................... 2.279
 6.20 ........................... 2.281
 (1)–(4) ................... 1.153
 (6), (7) ................... 1.153
 6.21 ..................... 1.156, 2.282
 6.22 ..................... 1.153, 2.283
 (2) .......................... 1.160
 6.23 ........................... 2.284
 6.24 ........................... 2.285
 6.25 ........................... 2.286
 (1), (2) ..................... 1.223
 (3) .......................... 1.386
 6.26 ........................... 2.287
 6.27 ........................... 1.160
 (5) .......................... 2.288
 6.28 ..................... 1.158, 2.289
 6.29 ..................... 2.290, 2.294
 6.30 ..................... 1.223, 2.291
 6.31 ........................... 2.292
 6.32 ........................... 2.293
 6.33 ..................... 1.225, 2.294
 6.34 ........................... 2.295
 6.35 ........................... 2.296
 6.36 ........................... 2.297
 6.37 ..................... 1.234, 2.299
 6.38 ........................... 2.300
 (1) .......................... 1.234
 (3) .......................... 1.234
 6.39 ..................... 1.234, 2.301
 6.40 ..................... 1.234, 2.302
 6.41 ..................... 1.234, 2.303
Pt 6, Ch 6 (r 6.42, 6.43)
 .............................. 2.304
r 6.42 ...... 1.167, 1.228, 1.231, 2.691
 (4) ......... 2.305, 2.433, 2.990
 (b) ................... 2.310
 (d) ................... 2.266
 (f) ................... 2.964
 6.43 ................... 1.231, 2.306
 (a) .......................... 1.167
 6.44 ........................... 1.159
 (1) .......................... 1.231
 (2) ................. 1.231, 2.308

Insolvency (England and Wales) Rules 2016,
  SI 2016/1024 – *cont.*
  r 6.45 ..................... 1.159, 1.231
    (1)(b)(c) ................... 2.309
    (2) ................. 2.308, 2.309
    (5) ......................... 2.309
  6.46 ...... 1.159, 1.231, 2.308, 2.310
    (1)(c) ...................... 2.311
    (3) ......................... 2.311
  6.47 ............ 1.159, 1.231, 2.308
    (2), (3) .................... 2.311
    (5) ......................... 2.311
  6.48 ...... 1.159, 1.231, 2.308, 2.310,
                                    2.312
  Pt 7 .............. 2.233, 2.258, 2.313
  r 7.1 ........................... 2.314
  7.2 .................... 1.175, 2.315
  7.3 ............................. 1.175
    (1)(k) ...................... 2.316
    (4) ......................... 2.316
  Pt 7, Ch 3 (rr 7.4–7.24)
  ..................................... 2.750
  r 7.4 . 1.67, 2.318, 2.322, 2.323, 2.325,
        2.328, 2.329, 2.333, 2.334, 2.335,
                   2.336, 2.340, 2.342
    (2) ......................... 2.339
  7.5 .................... 2.319, 2.321
    (1) ......................... 5.41
  7.6(6) .......................... 2.320
  7.7 .................... 1.176, 2.322
    (2)(b) ...................... 2.321
  7.8 .................... 1.176, 2.322
  7.9 .................... 1.176, 1.180
    (1) ......................... 2.323
    (4) ......................... 2.323
    (5) ................... 2.323, 2.324
  7.10 ............................ 1.176
    (1) ......................... 2.324
    (5) ......................... 2.324
  7.11 .................. 1.176, 2.325
  7.12 ........... 1.176, 2.326, 2.331
  7.13 ............................ 2.327
  7.14 ................... 1.180, 2.328
  7.15 .................. 2.328, 2.329
  7.16 ............................ 2.330
  7.17 .................. 1.180, 2.553
    (2) ......................... 2.331
  7.18 ............................ 2.332
  7.19 ............................ 2.333
  7.20 ............................ 2.334
  7.21 ............................ 2.335
  7.22 ............................ 2.336
  7.23 ............................ 2.337
  7.24 ........... 2.321, 2.324, 2.338
  Pt 7, Ch 4 (rr 7.25–7.32)
  .................... 2.317, 2.318, 2.750
  r 7.25 . 1.67, 2.331, 2.339, 2.339, 2.340
    (1) ... 2.322, 2.323, 2.325, 2.328,
        2.329, 2.333, 2.334, 2.335, 2.336
  7.26 .................... 1.67, 2.343
    (1)(o) ..................... 2.341
  7.27 .................... 1.67, 2.342
  7.28 .................... 1.67, 2.343
  7.29 ............................ 1.67
    (3) ......................... 2.344
  7.30 .................... 1.67, 2.345

Insolvency (England and Wales) Rules 2016,
  SI 2016/1024 – *cont.*
  r 7.31 ............. 1.67, 2.344, 2.346
  7.32 .................... 1.67, 2.347
  7.33 ............................ 2.349
    (1) ......................... 1.188
    (b) ......................... 1.634
    (5) ......................... 1.188
  7.34 ........... 1.188, 2.350, 2.354
  7.35(1)(h) ............. 1.188, 2.351
  7.36 .................. 1.188, 2.352
  7.37 ............................ 2.353
  7.38 ............................ 1.188
    (2), (3) .................... 2.354
  7.39 ............ 1.188, 1.634, 2.355
  7.40 .................. 1.184, 2.357
  7.41 .................. 1.184, 2.358
  7.42 .................. 1.184, 2.359
  7.43 .................. 1.184, 2.360
  7.44 .................. 1.184, 2.361
  7.45 .................. 1.184, 2.362
  7.46 ............................ 2.363
  7.47 ............................ 2.364
  Pt 7, Ch 7 (rr 7.48–7.51)
  ..................................... 2.365
  r 7.48 ................. 1.184, 2.366
  7.49 ............................ 2.367
  7.50 ............................ 2.368
  7.51 ............................ 2.369
  Pt 7, Ch 8 (rr 7.52–7.75)
  ..................................... 2.370
  r 7.52 .................. 1.189, 2.371
  7.53 ............................ 2.372
  7.54 ............................ 2.373
  7.55 ............................ 2.374
  7.56 ............................ 2.375
    (1), (2) ............. 1.192, 1.193
  7.57 ............... 1.190, 2.376
  7.58 ............................ 2.377
  7.59 ............................ 2.378
  7.60 ............................ 2.379
  7.61 ............................ 2.380
    (2) ......................... 1.224
  7.62 ............................ 2.381
  7.63 ............................ 2.382
  7.64 ............................ 2.383
  7.65 ............................ 2.384
    (2) ......................... 1.160
  7.66 ............................ 2.385
    (1)–(4) .................... 1.224
  7.67 ............................ 2.386
  7.68 ............................ 2.387
  7.69 ............ 1.199, 1.226, 2.388
  7.70 ............................ 2.389
  7.71 .................. 1.199, 2.390
  7.72 ............................ 2.391
  7.73 ............................ 2.392
    (1) ......................... 1.224
  7.74 ............................ 2.393
  7.75 ............................ 2.394
  7.76(1) ......................... 2.396
  7.77 ............................ 2.397
    (3) ......................... 1.194
  7.78 ........... 1.212, 1.298, 2.398
  7.79 ...... 1.129, 1.201, 1.212, 1.217,
                                    2.400

Insolvency (England and Wales) Rules 2016,
   SI 2016/1024 – *cont.*
r 7.80 ............. 1.201, 1.212, 2.401
   7.81 ............. 1.201, 1.212, 2.402
   7.82 ............. 1.201, 1.212, 2.403
   7.83 ............. 1.201, 1.212, 2.404
   7.84 ............. 1.201, 1.212, 2.405
   7.85 ............. 1.201, 1.212, 2.406
Pt 7, Ch 11 (rr 7.86–7.91)
   ................................. 2.401
r 7.86 ..................... 1.212, 2.408
   (2) ........................ 1.203
   7.87 ............. 1.203, 1.212, 2.409
   7.88 ..................... 1.212, 2.410
   7.89 ..................... 1.212, 2.411
   7.90 ..................... 1.212, 2.412
   7.91 ............. 1.203, 1.212, 2.413
Pt 7, Ch 12 (rr 7.92–7.97)
   ................................. 2.414
r 7.92 ..................... 1.234, 2.415
   7.93 ............................ 2.416
   (3) ........................ 1.234
   7.94 ............................ 2.417
   (1) ........................ 1.234
   7.95 ..................... 1.234, 2.418
   7.96 ..................... 1.234, 2.419
   7.97 ..................... 1.234, 2.420
Pt 7, Ch 13 (rr 7.98–7.107)
   ................................. 2.763
r 7.98 ..................... 1.186, 2.422
   7.99 ..................... 1.186, 2.423
   7.100 .................... 1.186, 2.424
   7.101 .......................... 2.425
   (3), (4) .................... 1.186
   7.102(2) ....................... 2.426
   (3) ........................ 1.186
   7.103 .......................... 1.186
   (5) ........................ 2.427
   7.104 .......................... 2.428
   (6) ........................ 1.186
   7.105 .......................... 2.429
   (1)(b) .................... 1.186
   7.106 .................... 1.186, 2.430
   7.107 .................... 1.186, 2.431
Pt 7, Ch 14 (rr 7.108–7.110)
   ................................. 2.432
r 7.108 ..... 1.188, 1.228, 2.434, 2.691
   (2)(b) .................... 2.433
   (e) .................... 2.433
   (3) ........................ 2.433
   (4) ........ 1.208, 2.305, 2.990
   (a) .................... 2.115
   (i) .................. 2.354
   (ii) .................. 2.433
   (f) .................... 2.354
   (h) .................... 2.433
   (i) .................... 2.417
   (m) .................... 2.433
   (n) .................... 2.964
   (r) .................... 2.115
   7.109 .................... 2.433, 2.434
   7.110 .................... 1.208, 2.435
   (2) ........................ 2.433
Pt 7, Ch 15 (rr 7.111–7.116)
   ................................. 2.436
r 7.111 ..... 2.308, 2.433, 2.437, 2.439

Insolvency (England and Wales) Rules 2016,
   SI 2016/1024 – *cont.*
r 7.111(1) ...................... 1.231
   7.112 .... 1.231, 2.308, 2.433, 2.437,
                                     2.438
   7.113 ..... 1.231, 2.308, 2.433, 2.437
   (1)(b)–(c) ................ 2.439
   (2)–(5) .................... 2.439
   7.114 .... 1.231, 2.308, 2.433, 2.437,
                                     2.440
   (1)(d) .................... 2.441
   (3) ........................ 2.441
   7.115 ..... 1.231, 2.308, 2.433, 2.437
   (2), (3) .................... 2.441
   (5) ........................ 2.441
   7.116 .... 1.231, 2.308, 2.433, 2.437,
                                     2.440
   (8) ........................ 2.442
   7.117 .......................... 2.444
   (2) ........................ 1.206
   (4) ........................ 1.206
   7.118 .......................... 2.445
   7.119 ........... 1.259, 1.261, 2.446
Pt 8
r 8.1 .......................... 2.447
   8.2 .................... 1.357, 2.449
   (2) ........................ 1.60
   8.3 .............. 1.60, 1.357, 2.450
   8.4 ............. 1.357, 2.451, 2.452
   8.5 ............. 1.357, 2.452
   (2) ........................ 1.60
   8.6 .................... 1.357, 2.453
   8.7 .................... 1.357, 2.454
   8.8 .................... 1.357, 2.456
   (4) ........................ 1.354
   8.9 .................... 1.357, 2.457
   8.10 .................... 1.357, 2.458
   8.11 .................... 1.357, 2.459
   8.12 .................... 1.357, 2.460
   8.13 .................... 1.357, 2.461
   8.14 .................... 1.357, 2.462
   8.15 .................... 1.357, 2.463
   8.16 .................... 1.357, 2.464
   8.17 .................... 1.357, 2.465
   8.18 .......................... 1.357
   (1) ........................ 2.466
   8.19 ........... 1.357, 1.358, 2.468
   8.20 ........... 1.357, 1.358, 2.469
   8.21 .................... 1.357, 2.470
   8.22 .............. 1.62, 1.360, 2.472
   (7) ........................ 1.359
   8.23 .......................... 2.473
   8.24 .......................... 2.474
   (2), (3) .................... 1.361
   8.25 ............. 1.67, 1.360, 2.476
   8.26 ............. 1.67, 1.360, 2.477
   8.27 ......... 1.65, 1.67, 1.360, 2.478
   8.28 ............. 1.67, 1.360, 2.479
   8.29 ............. 1.67, 1.360, 2.480
   8.30 ............. 1.67, 1.360, 2.481
   8.31 ..................... 1.67, 1.360
   (1) ........................ 2.482
   8.32 .......................... 2.484
   8.33 .......................... 2.485
   8.34 .......................... 2.486
   8.35 .......................... 2.487

Insolvency (England and Wales) Rules 2016,
  SI 2016/1024 – *cont.*
r 8.36 ........................... 2.488
  8.37 ........................... 2.489
  8.38 ........................... 2.491
Pt 9 ........................... 1.327
r 9.1 ........................... 2.493
  9.2 ................... 2.492, 2.494
  9.3 ........................... 2.496
  9.4 ........................... 2.497
  9.5 ........................... 2.498
  9.6 ........................... 2.499
  9.7 ........................... 2.500
  9.8 ........................... 2.501
  9.9 ........................... 2.502
  9.10 .......................... 2.504
  9.11 .......................... 2.505
  9.12 .......................... 2.506
  9.13 .......................... 2.507
  9.14 .......................... 2.509
  9.15 .......................... 2.510
  9.16 .......................... 2.511
  9.17 .......................... 2.512
  9.18 .......................... 2.513
  9.19 .......................... 2.514
  9.20 .......................... 2.515
  9.21 .......................... 2.517
  9.22 .......................... 2.518
  9.23 .......................... 2.519
  9.24 .......................... 2.520
  9.25 .......................... 2.522
  9.26 .......................... 2.523
  9.27 .......................... 2.524
Pt 10 ......................... 1.390
r 10.1 .................... 1.383, 2.530
  (1) ......................... 2.526
  10.2 ..... 1.175, 1.383, 2.527, 2.530,
                                    2.540
  10.3 ............ 1.383, 2.528, 2.530
  10.4 ............ 1.382, 1.383, 2.530
  (3) ......................... 2.529
  (6) ......................... 2.529
  10.5 ................. 2.550, 2.529
  (1) ......................... 2.530
  (4) ......................... 2.530
  (5) ................. 1.382, 1.383
  (a), (b) ................. 2.530
  (c) ........ 1.384, 1.516, 2.530
  (d) ..................... 2.530
  (8) ......................... 2.530
Pt 10, Ch 2 (rr 10.6–10.33)
............................... 2.750
r 10.6 .................... 1.379, 2.532
  10.7 ................... 1.379, 2.533
  10.8 ................... 1.379, 2.534
  10.9 ................... 1.379, 2.535
  10.10 .................. 1.379, 2.536
  10.11 .................. 1.379, 2.537
  10.12 .................. 1.379, 2.538
  10.13 .................. 1.379, 2.539
  10.14 ............ 1.379, 2.527, 2.540
  10.15 .................. 1.379, 2.541
  10.16 ............ 1.379, 1.386, 2.542
  10.17 .................. 1.379, 2.543
  10.18 .................. 1.379, 2.544
  10.19 .................. 1.379, 2.545

Insolvency (England and Wales) Rules 2016,
  SI 2016/1024 – *cont.*
r 10.20 ................... 1.379, 2.546
  10.21 ................... 1.379, 2.547
  (2) ......................... 1.385
  10.22 ................... 1.379, 2.548
  10.23 ................... 1.379, 2.549
  10.24 .... 1.379, 1.381, 1.382, 1.386,
          1.388, 2.549, 2.550, 2.556
  (1) ......................... 2.550
  (2) ................. 2.530, 2.550
  (5) ......................... 1.386
  10.25 ................... 1.379, 2.551
  10.26 ................... 1.379, 2.552
  10.27 ..... 1.379, 1.381, 2.553, 2.555
  10.28 ................... 1.379, 2.554
  10.29 ..... 1.379, 1.381, 2.553, 2.555
  (1) ......................... 1.386
  10.30 ......... 1.379, 1.381, 2.557
  10.31 ......... 1.379, 2.550, 2.558
  10.32 ........................ 1.379
  (5) ......................... 2.559
  10.33 ................. 1.379, 2.560
  10.34 ................. 1.402, 2.562
  10.35 ................. 1.402, 2.563
  10.36 ................. 1.402, 2.564
  10.37 ................. 1.402, 2.565
  10.38 ................. 1.402, 2.566
  10.39 ................. 1.402, 2.567
  10.40 ................. 1.402, 2.568
  10.41 ................. 1.402, 2.569
  10.42 ................. 1.402, 2.570
  10.43 ................. 1.402, 2.571
  10.44 ................. 1.402, 2.572
  10.45 ................. 1.402, 2.573
  10.46 ................. 1.402, 2.574
  10.47 ................. 1.402, 2.575
  10.48 ................. 1.402, 2.576
  10.49 ...................... 2.578
  (1) ......................... 1.400
  10.50 ................. 1.400, 2.579
  10.51 ................. 1.400, 2.580
  10.52 ................. 1.400, 2.581
  10.53 ................. 1.400, 2.582
  10.54 ...................... 2.583
  (2) ......................... 1.400
  10.55 ...................... 2.585
  10.56 ................. 1.402, 2.586
  10.57 ...................... 2.587
  10.58 ...................... 2.588
  (2) ......................... 1.402
  10.59 ...................... 2.589
  10.60 ...................... 2.590
  10.61 ...................... 2.591
  10.62 ...................... 2.592
  10.63 ...................... 2.593
  10.64 ...................... 2.594
  10.65 ...................... 2.595
  10.66 ...................... 2.596
  10.67 .......... 1.407, 1.417, 2.598
  10.68 .......... 1.407, 1.417, 2.599
  10.69 .......... 1.407, 1.417, 2.600
  10.70 .......... 1.407, 1.417, 2.601
  10.71 .......... 1.407, 1.417, 2.602
  10.72 .......... 1.407, 1.417, 2.603
  10.73 .......... 1.407, 1.417, 2.604

Insolvency (England and Wales) Rules 2016,
  SI 2016/1024 – *cont.*
r 10.74 ........... 1.407, 1.417, 2.605
  10.75 ..... 1.407, 1.417, 1.430, 2.606
  10.76 ................. 1.417, 2.607
  10.77 ........................ 1.409
     (3)(b) .................... 2.608
  10.78 ................. 1.409, 2.609
  10.79 ................. 1.409, 2.610
  10.80 ................. 1.409, 2.611
  10.81 ................. 1.409, 2.612
  10.82 ................. 1.409, 2.613
  10.83 ................. 1.409, 2.614
  10.84 ................. 1.409, 2.615
  10.85 ................. 1.409, 2.616
  10.86 ................. 1.410, 2.617
  10.87 ................. 1.410, 2.618
  10.88 ................. 1.410, 2.619
  10.89 ........................ 2.620
  10.90 ................. 1.430, 2.621
  10.91 ........................ 2.622
  10.92 ........................ 2.623
  10.93 ........................ 2.624
  10.94 ................. 1.496, 2.626
  10.95 ........................ 2.627
  10.96 ........................ 2.628
  10.97 ........................ 2.629
  10.98 ........................ 2.630
Pt 10, Ch 8 (rr 10.99–10.105)
  ............................. 2.763
r 10.99 ................. 1.404, 2.632
  10.100 ............... 1.404, 2.633
  10.101 ............... 1.404, 2.634
  10.102 ............... 1.404, 2.635
  10.103 ............... 1.404, 2.636
  10.104 ............... 1.404, 2.637
  10.105 ............... 1.404, 2.638
  10.106 ............... 1.424, 2.639
  10.107 ............... 1.424, 2.640
  10.108 ............... 1.427, 2.642
  10.109 ............... 1.427, 2.643
  10.110 ............... 1.427, 2.644
  10.111 ............... 1.427, 2.645
  10.112 ............... 1.427, 2.646
  10.113 ............... 1.427, 2.647
  10.114 ............... 1.427, 2.648
  10.114A ........ 1.427, 1.428, 2.650
  10.115 .......... 1.427, 1.428, 2.651
  10.116 .......... 1.427, 1.428, 2.652
  10.117 .......... 1.427, 1.428, 2.653
  10.118 ............... 1.495, 2.655
  10.119 ............... 1.495, 2.656
  10.120 ............... 1.495, 2.657
  10.121 ........................ 2.659
  10.122 ........................ 2.660
  10.123 ........................ 2.661
  10.124 ........................ 2.662
  10.125 ............... 1.423, 2.663
     (1) ...................... 1.452
  10.126 ............... 1.423, 2.664
  10.127 ........................ 2.666
  10.128 ........................ 2.667
  10.129 ........................ 2.668
  10.130 ........................ 2.669
  10.131 ........................ 2.670
  10.132 ............... 1.395, 2.672

Insolvency (England and Wales) Rules 2016,
  SI 2016/1024 – *cont.*
r 10.133 ................. 1.395, 2.673
  10.134 ................. 1.395, 2.674
  10.135 ................. 1.395, 2.675
  10.136 ................. 1.395, 2.676
  10.137 ................. 1.395, 2.677
  10.138 ........................ 2.678
     (2) ...................... 1.395
     (5)–(7) .................. 1.395
  10.139 ................. 1.395, 2.679
  10.140 ................. 1.395, 2.680
  10.141 ........................ 2.681
     (1) ...................... 1.395
  10.142 ........................ 2.683
     (5) ...................... 1.391
  10.143 ................. 1.391, 2.684
  10.144 ........................ 2.685
  10.145 ........................ 2.686
  10.146 ................. 1.393, 2.687
  10.147 ........................ 2.688
  10.148 ........ 1.449, 2.690, 2.1009
  10.149 ........ 1.447, 2.690, 2.1009
     (f) ...................... 1.496
     (i) ...................... 2.691
     (n) ...................... 2.964
  10.150 ................. 1.454, 2.693
     (1) ...................... 1.453
  10.151 ................. 1.453, 2.694
     (1) ...................... 1.454
  10.152 .......... 1.453, 1.454, 2.695
  10.153 .......... 1.453, 1.454, 2.696
  10.153A ...................... 2.698
  10.154 ........................ 2.699
  10.155 ........................ 2.700
  10.156 ........................ 2.701
  10.157 ........................ 2.702
  10.158 ........................ 2.703
  10.159 ........................ 2.704
  10.160 ........................ 2.705
  10.161 ........................ 2.706
  10.162 ........................ 2.707
  10.163 ........................ 2.708
  10.164 ........................ 2.709
  10.165 ........................ 2.711
  10.166 ........................ 2.712
  10.167 ........................ 2.713
  10.168 ................. 1.397, 2.714
  10.169 ................. 1.397, 2.715
  10.170 ................. 1.397, 2.716
  10.171 ................. 1.431, 2.717
Pt 11
r 11.1 .................... 1.750, 2.718
  11.2 ................. 1.750, 2.720
  11.3 ................. 1.750, 2.721
  11.4 ................. 1.750, 2.722
  11.5 ................. 1.750, 2.723
  11.6 ................. 1.750, 2.725
  11.7 ................. 1.750, 2.726
  11.8 ................. 1.750, 2.727
  11.9 ................. 1.750, 2.728
  11.10 ................ 1.751, 2.730
  11.11 ................ 1.751, 2.731
  11.12 ................ 1.751, 2.732
  11.13 ........................ 2.733
  11.14 ........................ 2.734

Insolvency (England and Wales) Rules 2016,
SI 2016/1024 – *cont.*

r 11.15 ......................... 2.735
11.16 ......................... 2.736
11.17 .................. 1.391, 2.737
11.18 ......................... 2.738
11.19 ......................... 2.739
11.20 ......................... 2.740
11.21 ......................... 2.741
11.22 ......................... 2.742
11.23 ......................... 2.743
Pt 12
r 12.1 ..... 2.777, 2.780, 2.781, 2.814
  (1) ......... 2.191, 2.744, 2.791
  (3) ......................... 2.744
12.2 ......................... 1.300
  (1) ......................... 2.745
  (3) ......................... 2.745
12.3 ......................... 2.747
12.4 ......................... 2.748
12.5 ......................... 2.749
12.6 ............. 2.750, 2.751, 2.820
12.7 ......................... 2.752
12.8 ......................... 2.753
12.9(3) ......................... 2.754
12.10 .................. 1.391, 2.755
12.11 .................. 2.756, 2.758
  (b) ......................... 2.776
12.12 ......................... 2.757
12.13(1), (2) .................. 2.758
12.14 .................. 2.759, 2.760
12.15 .................. 2.759, 2.761
12.16 ......................... 2.759
  (2) ......................... 2.762
  (4) ......................... 2.762
12.17 ..... 1.300, 2.421, 2.759, 2.764
12.18 ............. 2.421, 2.759
  (1)(b)(i)–(iii)
......................... 2.765
    (iv) .................. 1.300
  (2) ......................... 2.765
  (3) .................. 1.300, 2.765
12.19 ..... 1.300, 2.421, 2.759, 2.766
12.20 ............. 2.421, 2.759, 2.767
  (3) ......................... 1.300
12.21 ........... 1.300, 2.421, 2.759
  (4) ......................... 2.768
12.22 ........... 1.300, 2.421, 2.759
  (2) ............. 1.301, 2.769
Ch 4, Sub-div C .................. 2.770
r 12.23 .................. 2.759, 2.771
12.24 .................. 2.759, 2.772
12.25 .................. 2.759, 2.773
12.26 .................. 2.759, 2.774
12.27(1)(b) .................. 2.776
12.28(3) ......................... 2.777
12.29 ......................... 2.778
12.30 .................. 1.171, 1.500
  (2) ......................... 2.780
  (4)(a)–(c) .................. 2.780
12.31 ..... 1.170, 1.171, 1.500, 2.781
12.32 ........... 1.171, 1.500, 2.782
12.33 ........... 1.171, 1.500, 2.783
12.34 .................. 1.171, 1.500
  (4) ......................... 2.784
Ch 6, Sub-div B .................. 2.785

Insolvency (England and Wales) Rules 2016,
SI 2016/1024 – *cont.*

r 12.35 ............ 1.223, 1.500, 2.786
12.36 ..... 1.223, 1.500, 2.380, 2.787
12.37 ..... 1.223, 1.500, 2.380, 2.788
12.38 ............. 1.223, 1.500, 2.380
  (4) ......................... 2.789
12.39(1) ......................... 2.791
  (9) ......................... 2.791
12.40 ......................... 2.792
12.41 ......................... 2.794
  (3) ......................... 2.913
12.42 ......................... 2.795
12.43(4) ......................... 2.796
12.44 .................. 1.472, 2.797
12.45 ......................... 2.798
12.46 ......................... 2.799
12.47 ......................... 2.800
12.48(1) ......................... 2.801
12.49 ......................... 2.802
12.50 ......................... 2.803
12.51 .... 1.300, 1.301, 1.490, 1.491,
2.805
12.52 ..... 1.91, 1.184, 1.186, 1.300,
1.301, 1.490, 1.491, 2.806
  (1)(e) .................. 1.299
  (2)(a) .................. 1.664
  (3) .................. 1.299
12.53 .... 1.300, 1.301, 1.490, 1.491,
2.807
12.54 .... 1.187, 1.300, 1.301, 1.490,
1.491, 2.808
12.55 .... 1.300, 1.301, 1.490, 1.491,
2.809
12.56 ........... 1.490, 1.491, 2.810
12.57 ........... 1.490, 1.491, 2.811
12.58 ........... 1.502, 2.813, 2.816
12.59 ............. 1.79, 1.178, 2.328
  (1) .. 1.186, 1.200, 1.300, 2.814
  (2) ............. 1.200, 2.814
  (3) ......... 1.200, 1.502, 2.814
12.60 .................. 1.502, 2.815
12.61 ........... 1.502, 2.814, 2.816
12.62 .................. 1.502, 2.817
12.63 ......................... 2.819
12.64 ..... 1.175, 1.395, 1.504, 1.632,
1.633, 1.636, 1.639, 1.643, 1.645,
1.646, 1.648, 1.721, 2.150, 2.321,
2.324, 2.527, 2.540, 2.820, 2.967
12.65 .................. 1.629, 2.821
Pt 13
r 13.1 .................. 1.401, 2.822
13.2 .................. 1.401, 2.823
13.3 .................. 1.401, 2.824
13.4 .................. 1.401, 2.825
13.5 ......................... 2.826
Pt 14
r 14.1 ..... 1.303, 1.393, 1.515, 2.433,
2.829, 2.852
  (3) ... 1.129, 1.175, 2.830, 2.848,
2.849
  (a) ......................... 2.827
  (b) .................. 1.176, 2.827
  (c) ......................... 2.827
  (4) ......................... 2.827
  (5) .................. 1.175, 2.827

Insolvency (England and Wales) Rules 2016,
  SI 2016/1024 – *cont.*
  r 14.1(6) ................. 1.175, 1.176
  14.2 ...... 1.303, 1.515, 2.433, 2.827,
                              2.834, 2.839
    (1) ................ 1.441, 2.829
    (2) ....................... 1.441
      (c) ..................... 1.393
        (ii) ................. 2.829
    (3) ....................... 1.393
    (4) ......... 1.246, 1.393, 1.441
    (5) ....................... 2.829
  14.3 ........... 1.393, 1.441, 2.828
    (2) ....................... 2.830
    (3) ................ 2.827, 2.830
  14.4 ........... 1.393, 1.441, 2.828
    (1)(d) .................... 2.831
      (g) ..................... 1.441
  14.5 ........... 1.393, 2.828, 2.832
    (a) ....................... 1.441
  14.6 ........... 1.393, 2.828, 2.833
  14.7 ...... 1.393, 2.828, 2.834, 2.839
  14.8 ...... 1.393, 1.441, 2.828, 2.835,
                              2.860
  14.9 ........... 1.393, 2.828, 2.836
    (2) ....................... 2.913
  14.10 .......... 1.393, 2.828, 2.837
  14.11 ................. 1.393, 2.828
    (1)(a), (b) ............... 2.838
  14.12 ....................... 2.839
    (2) ....................... 1.682
  14.13 ....................... 2.840
  14.14 ................. 1.235, 2.841
  14.15 ....................... 2.842
    (1), (2) .................. 1.441
  14.16 ....................... 2.843
  14.17 ....................... 2.844
  14.18 ....................... 2.845
  14.19 ....................... 2.846
    (2) ....................... 1.233
  14.20 ................. 1.441, 2.847
  14.21 ................. 1.441, 2.848
  14.22 .... 1.441, 2.827, 2.829, 2.849
  14.23 ................. 1.441, 2.850
    (1) ....................... 1.246
  14.24 ................. 1.660, 2.852
    (1) ....................... 2.851
  14.25 ........... 1.442, 1.757, 2.851
    (2) ....................... 2.852
    (6) ....................... 2.852
    (7) ....................... 2.852
  14.26 ...... 1.67, 1.443, 1.682, 2.854
  14.27 ...... 1.67, 1.443, 1.682, 2.855
  14.28 ...... 1.67, 1.443, 1.682, 2.856
  14.29 ...... 1.67, 1.443, 1.682, 2.857
  14.30 ...... 1.67, 1.443, 1.682, 2.858
  14.31 ...... 1.67, 1.443, 1.682, 2.859
  14.32 ...... 1.67, 1.443, 1.682, 2.860
  14.33 ...... 1.67, 1.443, 1.682, 2.861
  14.34 ...... 1.67, 1.443, 1.682, 2.862
  14.35 ................. 1.67, 2.863
    (2) ....................... 1.443
  14.36 ...... 1.67, 1.443, 1.682, 2.864
  14.37 ........... 1.67, 1.682, 2.865
    (1) ....................... 1.443
  14.38 ...... 1.67, 1.443, 1.682, 2.866

Insolvency (England and Wales) Rules 2016,
  SI 2016/1024 – *cont.*
  r 14.39 ...... 1.67, 1.443, 1.682, 2.867
  14.40 ...... 1.67, 1.443, 1.682, 2.868
    (2) ....................... 1.205
  14.41 ...... 1.67, 1.443, 1.682, 2.869
  14.42 ...... 1.67, 1.443, 1.682, 2.870
  14.43 ...... 1.67, 1.443, 1.682, 2.871
  14.44 ...... 1.67, 1.443, 1.682, 2.851,
                              2.872
    (1) ....................... 1.441
    (2) ....................... 2.829
  14.45 ........... 1.67, 1.443, 2.861
    (2) ....................... 2.873
  Pt 15 ........................ 1.63
  Pt 15, Ch 1 (r 15.1)
  ............................. 2.271
  r 15.1 ....................... 2.875
    (1) ................. 2.272, 2.274
  Pt 15, Ch 2 (rr 15.2–15.7)
  ...................... 2.271, 2.371
  r 15.2 ................. 1.315, 2.874
    (1) ......... 1.153, 2.877, 2.887
    (2) ............... 2.877, 2.887
    (4) ....................... 2.877
  15.3 ...... 1.212, 1.223, 1.315, 2.272,
                              2.878
  15.4 ................. 1.315, 2.879
  15.5 ............. 1.315, 2.274, 2.880
  15.6 ............. 1.212, 1.315, 2.881
    (3) ....................... 1.153
  15.7 ...... 1.153, 1.316, 1.326, 2.274,
                         2.371, 2.874, 2.882
  Pt 15, Ch 3 (rr 15.8–15.16)
  ............................. 2.271
  r 15.8 ...... 1.149, 1.153, 1.223, 1.315,
                              2.884
  15.9 ................. 1.149, 1.315
    (3) ....................... 2.885
  15.10 ................. 1.315, 2.886
  15.11 ........... 1.315, 2.877, 2.887
    (2) ....................... 2.888
  15.12 ................. 1.315, 2.888
  15.13 ................. 1.315, 2.889
  15.14 ................. 1.315, 2.890
  15.15 ................. 1.315, 2.891
  15.16 ....................... 1.315
    (1), (2) .................. 2.892
  15.17 ....................... 2.894
  15.18 ........... 1.220, 2.877, 2.896
    (4) ............... 1.223, 1.224
  15.19(2)(a) .................. 2.897
  15.20 ....................... 2.898
  15.21 ....................... 2.899
  15.22 ....................... 2.900
  15.23 ................. 1.360, 2.901
  15.24 ....................... 2.902
  15.25 ....................... 2.903
  15.26 ....................... 2.904
  15.27 ....................... 2.905
  15.28 ........ 1.61, 1.62, 1.360, 2.907
    (5) ....................... 1.64
  15.29 . 1.61, 1.62, 1.360, 2.894, 2.908
  15.30 ........... 1.61, 1.62, 1.360
  15.31 ........... 1.62, 1.360, 2.913
    (1), (2) .................. 2.909

Insolvency (England and Wales) Rules 2016,
SI 2016/1024 – *cont.*
r 15.31(3) ...... 1.59, 1.61, 1.64, 2.909
15.32 . 1.61, 1.62, 1.360, 2.909, 2.910
15.33 .............. 1.61, 1.62, 1.360
(2) ...................... 2.911
(3) .............. 1.59, 2.911
15.34 .... 1.58, 1.59, 1.61, 1.62, 1.65,
1.360, 2.912
(6) ...................... 1.354
15.35 ......... 1.61, 1.62, 1.65, 1.360
(6) .......... 1.59, 2.744, 2.913
15.36 ............... 2.900, 2.915
15.37 ......................... 2.916
15.38 ......................... 2.917
15.39 ......................... 2.918
15.40 ......................... 2.919
15.41 ......................... 2.920
15.42 ......................... 2.921
15.43 ......................... 2.922
15.44 ......................... 2.923
15.45 ......................... 2.924
15.46 ................. 2.900, 2.925
Pt 16
r 16.1 ......................... 2.927
16.2(2)–(6) ................... 2.928
16.3(2)(b) ..................... 2.929
(4) ........................ 2.929
16.4 ......................... 2.930
16.5 ......................... 2.931
16.6 ......................... 2.932
16.7(1) ....................... 2.933
16.8 ......................... 2.935
16.9 ......................... 2.936
Pt 17 ......................... 2.168
r 17.1 ......................... 2.937
17.2 .................. 1.93, 2.938
17.3 ............. 1.93, 1.412, 2.940
(2) ................. 1.154, 2.279
(3) ........................ 1.194
17.4 ............. 1.93, 1.412, 2.941
17.5 ............. 1.93, 1.412, 2.942
17.6 ............. 1.93, 1.412, 2.943
(2), (3) .................... 1.194
(4) ........................ 1.194
17.7 ............. 1.93, 1.412, 2.944
17.8 ............. 1.93, 1.412, 2.945
17.9 ............. 1.93, 1.412, 2.946
17.10 ............ 1.93, 1.412, 2.947
17.11 ............ 1.93, 1.412, 2.948
17.12 ............ 1.93, 1.412, 2.949
17.13 ............ 1.93, 1.412, 2.950
17.14 ................. 1.93, 1.412
(2) ...................... 2.952
17.15 ............ 1.93, 1.412, 2.953
17.16 ............ 1.93, 1.412, 2.954
17.17 ............ 1.93, 1.412, 2.955
17.18 ............ 1.93, 1.412, 2.956
17.19 ............ 1.93, 1.412, 2.957
17.20 ............ 1.93, 1.412, 2.958
17.21 ............ 1.93, 1.412, 2.959
17.22 ............ 1.93, 1.412, 2.961
17.23 ................. 1.93, 1.412
(5) ...................... 2.962
17.24 ...... 1.93, 1.194, 1.412, 2.964
17.25 ...... 1.93, 1.194, 1.412, 2.965

Insolvency (England and Wales) Rules 2016,
SI 2016/1024 – *cont.*
r 17.26 ............. 1.93, 1.412, 2.966
17.27 ............. 1.93, 1.412, 2.967
17.28 .................... 1.412, 2.968
17.29 ......................... 2.970
(1) ...................... 1.193
(3) ...................... 1.193
Pt 18
r 18.1 ......................... 2.972
18.2 ......................... 2.974
18.3 ......................... 2.975
18.4 ......................... 2.976
18.5(2) ....................... 2.977
18.6 ......................... 2.978
18.7 ......................... 2.979
18.8 ......................... 2.980
18.9 ......................... 2.981
18.10 ......................... 2.982
18.11 ......................... 2.983
18.12 ......................... 2.984
18.13 ......................... 2.985
18.14 ........... 1.148, 1.158, 2.987
18.15 ......................... 2.989
18.16 .... 1.188, 2.990, 2.994, 2.997,
2.999
18.17 ......................... 2.991
18.18 ......................... 2.992
18.19 ......................... 2.993
18.20 ......................... 1.188
(4), (5) ................... 2.994
18.21 ......................... 2.995
18.22 ......................... 2.996
18.23 ......................... 2.997
18.24 ......................... 2.998
(b) ...................... 1.679
18.25 ......................... 2.999
18.26 ......................... 2.1000
18.27 ......................... 2.1001
18.28 ............... 1.679, 2.1002
18.29 .............. 2.1003, 2.1007
18.30 .............. 2.1004, 2.1007
18.31 ......................... 2.1005
18.32 .............. 2.1006, 2.1007
18.33 ......................... 2.1007
18.34 ......................... 2.1008
18.35 ......................... 2.690
(4) ...................... 2.1009
18.36 ......................... 2.1010
18.37 ......................... 2.1011
18.38 ......................... 2.1012
Pt 19 ......................... 2.1013
r 19.1 ......................... 2.1014
19.2 ...... 1.235, 1.434, 1.435, 1.436,
1.437, 1.438, 1.439, 2.1015
19.3 ...... 1.434, 1.435, 1.436, 1.437,
1.438, 1.439, 2.1016
19.4 ...... 1.236, 1.434, 1.435, 1.436,
1.437, 1.438, 1.439, 2.1017
19.5 ...... 1.434, 1.435, 1.436, 1.437,
1.438, 1.439, 2.1018
19.6 ...... 1.434, 1.435, 1.436, 1.437,
1.438, 1.439, 2.1019
19.7 ...... 1.434, 1.435, 1.436, 1.437,
1.438, 1.439, 2.1020

Insolvency (England and Wales) Rules 2016,
 SI 2016/1024 – *cont.*
  r 19.8 ...... 1.434, 1.435, 1.436, 1.437,
            1.438, 1.439, 2.1021
   19.9 ...... 1.235, 1.434, 1.436, 1.437,
            1.438, 1.439, 2.1022
    (1)–(3) .................... 1.435
   19.10 .... 1.434, 1.435, 1.436, 1.437,
            1.438, 1.439, 2.1023
   19.11 .... 1.238, 1.434, 1.435, 1.436,
            1.437, 1.438, 2.1024
    (2) ...................... 1.439
  Pt 20
  r 20.1 ........................ 2.1026
   20.2 ........................ 2.1027
   20.3 ........................ 2.1028
   20.4 ........................ 2.1029
   20.5 ........................ 2.1030
   20.6 ........................ 2.1031
   20.7 ........................ 2.1032
  Pt 21 ......................... 2.130
   21.4 ........................ 2.1035
   21.5 ........................ 2.1036
  Pt 22
  r 22.1 ................. 1.275, 2.1038
   22.2 ................. 1.275, 2.1039
   22.3 ................. 1.275, 2.1040
   22.4 .......... 1.275, 1.276, 2.1037
    (1) ...................... 2.1041
    (2) ............. 2.1041, 2.1042
    (3)(a) ................... 2.1041
    (4)(b) ................... 2.1041
   22.5 ........... 1.275, 1.276, 2.1042
   22.6 .... 1.275, 1.276, 2.1037, 2.1041
    (1) ...................... 2.1043
   22.7 .... 1.275, 1.276, 2.1037, 2.1041
    (b) ...................... 2.1044
  Sch 1 ........................ 2.1045
   2 ........................ 2.1046
  para 15 ........................ 2.16
  Sch 3 ............ 1.478, 2.69, 2.1047
   4 ........................ 2.1048
  para 1 .......................... 1.300
    (8) ...................... 1.582
   2 .......................... 1.176
   3 .......................... 2.132
   6 .......................... 1.176
  Sch 5 .......... 1.503, 2.1008, 2.1049
  para 3 .................... 2.120, 2.750
   4 ........................ 2.750
  Sch 6 ........................ 2.1050
   7
  Pt 1 ......................... 2.1051
   2 ......................... 2.1052
  Sch 8 ........................ 2.1053
   9 ........................ 2.1054
   10 ........................ 2.1055
   11 ................. 2.996, 2.1056

Insolvency (Northern Ireland) Order 1989,
 SI 1989/2405 (N.I. 19)
 art 277 ........................ 1.415

Insolvency Practitioners and Insolvency
 Services Account (Fees) Order 2003, SI
 2003/3363 .................... 1.571

Insolvency Practitioners (Recognised
 Professional Bodies) Order 1986, SI
 1986/1764 .................... 1.531
Insolvency Practitioners Regulations 1990,
 SI 1990/439 .................... 1.524
Insolvency Practitioners Regulations 2005,
 SI 2005/524 .................... 1.576
 reg 4(2), (3) .................... 1.524
 Sch 2
 para 2–8 ....................... 1.528
Insolvency Proceedings (Fees) Order 2004,
 SI 2004/593 .................... 1.379
Insolvency Proceedings (Fees) Order 2016,
 SI 2016/692 ...... 1.569, 1.570, 2.814
Insolvency Proceedings (Increase of
 Monetary Limits) Regulations 1984, SI
 1984/1199 .................... 1.382
Insolvency Proceedings (Monetary Limits)
 Order 1986, SI 1986/1996
  .... 1.327, 1.490, 1.573, 1.575, 1.756
Insolvency Proceedings (Monetary Limits)
 (Amendment) Order 2004, SI 2004/547
  ................. 1.482, 1.486, 1.488
 art 2 .......................... 1.432
Insolvency Regulations 1994, SI 1994/2507
 reg 23 .................... 1.443, 1.449
  31 .................... 1.443, 1.449
  35(1) ........................ 2.354
Insolvency Rules 1986, SI 1986/1925
  .... 2.271, 2.272, 2.279, 2.838, 2.874,
           2.912, 2.937, 2.977
 Pt 1
 r 1.17(3) ....................... 2.909
  1.17A(1), (2) ................. 2.911
   (4) ....................... 2.911
  1.30 .......................... 1.66
 Pt 2
 r 2.2 .................... 1.627, 2.130
  2.4(2)(e) .................... 2.130
  2.12(3) ....................... 2.136
  2.20(2)(d) .................... 1.643
  2.22 .......................... 1.639
  2.33(2) ....................... 1.666
   (m) ................... 1.700
   (6) ................... 1.685
  2.33A ......................... 2.175
  2.39 .......................... 2.913
  2.59–2.61 ..................... 2.607
  2.67(1)(c) .................... 1.617
   (f) ............. 1.716, 2.183
   (j) ....................... 1.686
  2.67A ......................... 1.620
  2.88 ................. 1.246, 2.850
  2.85 .......................... 2.851
  2.106 .................. 2.994, 2.997
  2.109 .............. 1.620, 2.1008
  2.114(1) ...................... 1.671
   (3) ....................... 1.671
  2.117(3) ...................... 1.700
  2.122(2) ...................... 2.199
 Pt 3
 r 3.23(4)(b) .................. 1.643
  3.56(6) ....................... 1.697
 Pt 4 .......................... 2.1037

Insolvency Rules 1986, SI 1986/1925 – *cont.*
r 4.8 .......................... 2.1048
4.38 .......................... 2.266
4.73 .......................... 1.67
   (1), (2) ..................... 2.830
4.74–4.82 ..................... 1.67
4.83 .......................... 1.67
   (4A) ..................... 2.835
4.84, 4.85 ..................... 1.67
4.86 .................. 1.67, 2.841
4.87 .......................... 1.67
4.88 .......................... 1.67
   (2) ......................... 1.233
4.89 .......................... 1.67
4.90 ............ 1.67, 1.757, 2.852
4.91–4.94 ..................... 1.67
4.114 ......................... 1.164
4.120(3) ...................... 2.288
4.125 ......................... 2.390
4.126 ......................... 2.289
4.127(5A) ..................... 2.994
4.153 ......................... 2.942
4.182(3) ...................... 2.873
4.184 ......................... 2.297
4.199 ......................... 2.404
4.204 ......................... 2.410
4.205 .................. 2.412, 2.413
4.206 ......................... 2.416
4.211 ......................... 2.426
4.213 .................. 2.423, 2.424
4.218 ......................... 2.434
   (1)(a) .................... 2.433
   (3) ......................... 2.433
4.218A ........................ 1.231
4.218B .......... 1.231, 2.308, 2.436
4.218C .......... 1.231, 2.308, 2.436
   (2)(b) ............ 2.310, 2.440
4.218D ... 1.231, 2.308, 2.311, 2.436, 2.441
4.218E ... 1.231, 2.308, 2.312, 2.436, 2.442
4.220(2) ...................... 2.433
4.229 ......................... 2.1043
4.230 ......................... 2.1044
Pt 6
r 6.5(1) ....................... 2.530
   (4)(a)–(d) .................. 2.530
   (6) ......................... 2.530
6.22 .................. 1.386, 2.542
6.25 .................. 1.382, 2.550
   (1) ......................... 1.388
6.26 .................. 2.552, 2.820
6.32 .......................... 1.379
6.119 ................. 2.846, 2.869
6.126(3) ...................... 1.704
6.135(3) ...................... 2.608
6.179(1), (2) .................. 1.436
   (4) ......................... 1.436
6.207 ......................... 1.395
6.209 ......................... 1.395
6.211(2), (3) .................. 1.395
   (6) ......................... 1.395
Pt 7
r 7.2 .......................... 2.48
7.4(6) ........................ 1.391
7.7(1) ........................ 2.777

Insolvency Rules 1986, SI 1986/1925 – *cont.*
r 7.10(2) ...................... 2.758
7.11 .......................... 2.780
7.15(3) ....................... 2.784
7.28(2), (3) ................... 2.791
7.31A(6) ...................... 2.791
7.34 .......................... 2.795
7.34A ......................... 2.795
7.39 .......................... 2.800
7.47(1) ....................... 2.814
   (4) ......................... 2.814
7.48 .......................... 2.815
7.51A(1) ...................... 2.744
   (2) ......................... 2.777
7.55 ...... 1.175, 1.395, 1.639, 1.645, 1.646, 1.721, 2.150, 2.527, 2.820
7.60 .......................... 2.777
Pt 8
r 8.1(6) ....................... 2.927
8.2(1) ........................ 2.929
8.3(6) ........................ 2.927
Pt 9
r 9.2 ..................... 2.763, 2.765
Pt 11
r 11.13 ....................... 1.235
Pt 12
r 12.3 ........................ 2.433
   (2)(a) .................... 2.829
   (3) ......................... 2.829
12.9(2) .............. 1.503, 1.693
12.18 ......................... 1.478
12A.4 ......................... 2.891
12A.10–12A.13 ................ 1.663
12A.55(2) ............ 1.503, 2.1008
Pt 13
r 13.12 ................. 2.183, 2.433
   (1)(b) .................... 1.176
Pt 14
r 14.26–14.44 ................. 1.682
Pt 15
r 15.23(2) ..................... 1.669
Sch 4 ......................... 2.16
Form 6.1–6.3 .................. 2.526
   6.4, 6.5 .................. 2.529
   6.11–6.13 ................. 2.528
   7.1A ...................... 2.48
Sch 5 ................. 1.478, 1.593

Insolvency (Amendment) Rules 1995, SI 1995/586 ...................... 1.87

Insolvency (Amendment) Rules 2003, SI 2003/1730
reg 5(2)–(4) ..................... 1.627

Insolvency (Amendment) Rules 2009, SI 2009/642 ..................... 2.324

Insolvency (Amendment) Rules 2010, SI 2010/686 ..................... 2.874

Insolvent Partnerships Order 1986, SI 1986/2142 ..................... 1.577
art 11 ......................... 1.353

Insolvent Partnerships Order 1994, SI 1994/2421 ............. 1.127, 1.627
art 4 .......................... 1.353
  5 .......................... 1.629

Insolvent Partnerships Order 1994, SI
  1994/2421 – *cont.*
    art 7 .......................... 1.279
        8 .......................... 1.520
        9 .......................... 1.279
        10, 11 ..................... 1.520
    Sch 1 ......................... 1.353
        2
    para 6 ........................ 1.629
    Sch 7
    para 1 ........................ 1.520
        23 ................. 1.520, 1.522
Insolvent Partnerships (Amendment) Order
  2005, SI 2005/1516
    .............................. 1.617
Insurers (Reorganisation and Winding-Up)
  Regulations 2004, SI 2004/353
  reg 21(2) ...................... 1.586
Investment Bank Special Administration
  (England and Wales) Rules 2011, SI
  2011/1301
  Pt 5, Ch 3 (rr 144–147)
    .............................. 1.617
Investment Bank Special Administration
  Regulations 2011, SI 2011/245
  reg 20, 21 ..................... 1.617

L

Limited Liability Partnerships Regulations
  2001, SI 2001/1090
    .............................. 1.627
  reg 5(1)(b) .................... 1.520

M

Model Articles of Association 2008, SI
  2008/3229
  art 3 .......................... 2.127

O

Occupational and Personal Pension Schemes
  (Bankruptcy) Regulations 2002, SI
  2002/427 ....................... 1.396
Occupational and Personal Pension Schemes
  (Bankruptcy) (No 2) Regulations 2002,
  SI 2002/836 .................... 1.465

P

Postal Administration Rules 2013, SI
  2013/3208 ...................... 1.617

T

Taking Control of Goods (Amendment)
  (Coronavirus) Regulations 2020, SI
  2020/1002 ...................... 1.229
Taking Control of Goods (Amendment)
  (Coronavirus) Regulations 2021, SI
  2021/300 ....................... 1.229
Taking Control of Goods and Certification
  of Enforcement Agents (Amendment)
  (Coronavirus) Regulations 2020, SI
  2020/451 ....................... 1.229
Taking Control of Goods and Certification
  of Enforcement Agents (Amendment)
  (No 2) (Coronavirus) Regulations 2020,
  SI 2020/614 .................... 1.229
Transfer of Undertakings (Protection of
  Employment) Regulations 2006, SI
  2006/246
  reg 8(7) ....................... 1.617

U

Unregistered Companies Regulations 2009,
  SI 2009/2436 ................... 1.280

# Table of International Legislation

## C

Convention on Jurisdiction and the
Enforcement of Judgments in Civil
and Commercial Matters 1968
(Brussels Convention)
.................................. 6.1
  art 16 .......................... 1.433
Convention on jurisdiction and the
recognition and enforcement of
judgments in civil and commercial
matters 1988 (Lugano Convention)
........................ 1.383, 6.1, 6.8
  art 23(1) .......................... 6.2

## D

Directive 98/26/EC on settlement finality in
payment and securities settlement
systems [1998] OJ L 166/45
.................................. 6.14
Directive 2001/17/EC on the reorganisation
and winding-up of insurance
undertakings [2001] OJ L 110/28
.............................. 1.586
Directive 2001/24/EC on the reorganisation
and winding-up of credit institutions
[2001] OJ L 125/15
.......................... 6.3
  art 10 .......................... 6.20
    (2)(c) ........................ 6.9
  30 ........................ 6.18
  32 ........................ 6.9, 6.20
Directive 2002/47/EC on financial collateral
arrangements [2002] OJ L 168/43
.............................. 1.660
Directive 2011/7/EU of the European
Parliament and of the Council on
combating late payment in commercial
transactions [2011] OJ L 48/1
  art 9 .......................... 6.12
Directive 2017/2399/EU of the European
Parliament and of the Council
amending Directive 2014/59/EU as
regards the ranking of unsecured debt
instruments in insolvency hierarchy
[2017] OJ L 345/96
.............................. 1.523

## E

European Convention on Human Rights
1950
  art 3 .......................... 1.427
  5 .......................... 1.490

European Convention on Human Rights 1950
  – *cont.*
  art 6 ....... 1.183, 1.186, 1.394, 1.399,
            1.455, 1.478, 1.482, 2.778
    (1) .................. 1.300, 1.596
    (2) .................. 1.262, 1.480
  8 ............. 1.186, 1.429, 1.455
    (2) ........................ 1.497
European Union Convention on Insolvency
Proceedings 1996 ................. 6.5

## R

Regulation (EC) No 1346/2000 of the
European Parliament and of
the Council on Insolvency Proceedings
[2000] OJ L 160/1 ...... 1.285, 1.566,
            1.567, 1.577, 1.578,
            1.586, 2.351, 6.36,
            6.45, 6.56, 6.64, 7.1
  Recital 11 ........................ 6.2
      33 ........................ 6.2
  art 1 .......................... 1.622
    (1) .................... 1.151, 6.3
    (2) .......................... 6.3
      (b) .......................... 6.2
    2(a) .......................... 1.59
      (b) ................. 1.188, 1.321
      (g) .......................... 6.5
    3 ........ 1.151, 1.169, 1.728, 2.130
    (1) ......... 1.59, 1.281, 6.8, 6.34
    (2) .................... 1.281, 6.34
    (3), (4) ...................... 1.281
    4 .......................... 6.8, 6.18
      (2)(b) .......................... 6.9
      (d) .......................... 6.9
      (f) ...................... 6.1, 6.9
    5 .......................... 6.1, 6.10
    6 .......................... 6.1, 6.11
    7 .......................... 6.1, 6.12
    8, 9 .......................... 6.1
    10 .......................... 6.1, 6.15
    11 .......................... 6.1, 6.16
    12 .......................... 6.1
    13 .......................... 6.1, 6.18
    14 .......................... 6.1, 6.19
    15 .................. 6.1, 6.9, 6.20
    16 .......................... 6.21
    17 .......................... 6.22
    18 .......................... 6.23
    19 .......................... 6.24
    20 .......................... 6.25
    21 .......................... 6.30
    24 .......................... 6.33
    25 .......................... 1.497
      (1), (2) .................... 6.34
    26 .......................... 6.35
    32 .......................... 6.48

Regulation (EC) No 1346/2000 of the European Parliament and of the Council on Insolvency Proceedings [2000] OJ L 160/1 – *cont.*
art 32(3) ........................ 1.691
   35 ..................... 6.1, 6.52
   36 ............................. 6.49
   37 ................... 1.304, 1.321
   38 ............................. 6.55
   40 ............................. 6.58
  Annex A ...... 1.59, 1.151, 1.622, 6.2

Regulation (EC) No 44/2001 of the European Parliament and of the Council on jurisdiction and the recognition and enforcement of judgments in civil and commercial matters [2001] OJ L 22/1
art 23 ........................... 6.9

Regulation (EC) No 593/2008 of the European Parliament and of the Council of 17 June 2008 on the law applicable to contractual obligations (Rome I) .............. 6.8, 6.9, 6.18

Regulation (EU) No 1215/2012 of the European Parliament and of the Council on jurisdiction and the recognition and enforcement of judgments in civil and commercial matters (Recast) [2012] OJ L 351/1
....................... 6.2, 6.8, 6.21
  Recital 21 ........................ 6.1
  art 1(1) .......................... 6.3
    (2)(b) ......................... 6.1
    4 ............................... 6.1
    31(2) ......................... 6.1

Regulation (EU) No 2015/848 of the European Parliament and of the Council on insolvency proceedings (Recast) [2015] OJ L 141/19
.... 1.380, 1.492, 1.566, 1.567, 1.577, 1.578, 1.586, 2.887, 7.1, 7.3, 7.40
  Recital 1 ......................... 6.1
    2–5 ...................... 6.1, 6.2
    6 ............................. 6.1
    7 ........................ 6.1, 6.2
    8 ............................. 6.1
    9 ................... 6.1, 6.2, 6.3
    10–12 ...................... 6.1
    13 ...................... 6.1, 7.29
    14, 15 ...................... 6.1
    16 ...................... 6.1, 6.2
    17–21 ...................... 6.1
    22–29 ................... 6.1, 6.2
    30 ...................... 6.1, 6.2
    31, 32 ................... 6.1, 6.2
    33–62 ...................... 6.1
    63 ..................... 6.1, 6.48
    64–70 ...................... 6.1
    71 ..................... 6.1, 6.14
    72–87 ...................... 6.1
    88 ...................... 6.1, 6.2
    89 ........................... 6.1
  art 1 ............................. 6.3
    (1) ...................... 6.2, 6.4
    (2)(b) ....................... 6.2

Regulation (EU) No 2015/848 of the European Parliament and of the Council on insolvency proceedings (Recast) [2015] OJ L 141/19 – *cont.*
art 2 .................. 6.4, 6.21, 6.34
    (3), (4) ....................... 6.5
    (5) ........................... 6.1
    (6) .......................... 1.59
    (9) ........................... 6.4
    (10) .......................... 6.5
    (11) ....................... 2.1034
   3 ........................ 6.2, 6.20
    (1) ........... 6.5, 6.8, 6.13, 7.15
    (2) ...................... 6.1, 6.21
    (4) ........................... 6.5
   4 ............................... 6.6
   5 ........................... 6.6, 6.7
   6(2) ........................... 6.8
   7 ..................... 6.2, 6.8, 6.18
    (2)(b) ....................... 6.12
    (d) .................... 6.9, 6.11
    (e) ......................... 6.13
    (f) .................... 6.9, 6.20
    (g) .......................... 6.9
    (h) .................... 6.9, 6.58
    (m) .. 6.9, 6.10, 6.11, 6.14, 6.18
   8 .... 6.1, 6.2, 6.9, 6.11, 6.22, 6.23, 6.25
    (1) .......................... 6.10
   9 ......... 6.1, 6.9, 6.11, 6.22, 6.23
    (1) .......................... 6.11
   10 .. 6.1, 6.9, 6.11, 6.12, 6.22, 6.23, 6.25
   11 .............. 6.1, 6.9, 6.22, 6.23
    (1), (2) ..................... 6.13
   12 ........ 6.1, 6.9, 6.14, 6.22, 6.23
   13 ........ 6.1, 6.9, 6.15, 6.22, 6.23
   14 ........ 6.1, 6.9, 6.16, 6.22, 6.23
   15 ........ 6.1, 6.9, 6.17, 6.22, 6.23
   16 ........ 6.1, 6.9, 6.18, 6.22, 6.23
   17 ........ 6.1, 6.9, 6.19, 6.22, 6.23
   18 ........ 6.1, 6.9, 6.20, 6.22, 6.23
   19 ............... 6.9, 6.21, 6.34
   20 .................... 6.9, 6.22
   21(1) ........................ 6.23
    (3) ......................... 6.23
   22 ........................... 6.24
   23(1), (2) .................... 6.25
   24 ...................... 6.26, 6.29
   25 ...................... 6.27, 6.29
   26 ...................... 6.28, 6.29
   27 ...................... 6.29, 6.29
   28 ........................... 6.30
   29 ........................... 6.31
   30 ........................... 6.32
   31 ...................... 6.33, 7.5
   32 ....... 6.8, 6.9, 6.13, 6.23, 6.34
   33 ...................... 6.35, 7.19
   34 ........................... 6.37
   35 ...................... 6.5, 6.38
   36 .................. 6.5, 6.36, 6.39
   37 ........................... 6.40
   38 ........................... 6.41
    (2), (3) ..................... 6.36
   39 ........................... 6.42
   40 ........................... 6.43

Regulation (EU) No 2015/848 of the European Parliament and of the Council on insolvency proceedings (Recast) [2015] OJ L 141/19 – *cont.*
art 41 ..................... 6.44, 6.46
 42 ..................... 6.45, 6.46
 43 ........................... 6.46
 44 ........................... 6.47
 45 ........................... 6.48
 46 ........................... 6.49
 47 ........................... 6.50
 48 ..................... 6.1, 6.51
 49 ..................... 6.1, 6.52
 50 ........................... 6.53
 51 ........................... 6.54
 52 ........................... 6.55
 53 ..................... 6.56, 6.57
 54 ..................... 6.56, 6.58
 55 ..................... 6.56, 6.59
 56 ..................... 6.60, 6.64
 57 ..................... 6.61, 6.64
 58 ..................... 6.62, 6.64
 59 ..................... 6.63, 6.64
 60 ........................... 6.64
 61 ........................... 6.66
  (1) ........................ 6.65
 62 ..................... 6.65, 6.67
 63 ..................... 6.65, 6.68
 64 ..................... 6.65, 6.69
 65 ..................... 6.65, 6.70
 66 ..................... 6.65, 6.71
 67 ..................... 6.65, 6.72
 68 ..................... 6.65, 6.73
 69 ..................... 6.65, 6.74
 70 ..................... 6.65, 6.75
 71 ..................... 6.65, 6.76
 72 ........................... 6.77
  (1)(b)(i) ................. 6.65
  (2)(b) .................... 6.65
  (e) ...................... 6.65
 73 ..................... 6.65, 6.78
 74 ..................... 6.65, 6.79
 75 ..................... 6.65, 6.80
 76 ..................... 6.65, 6.81
 77 ..................... 6.65, 6.82
 78 ........................... 6.83
 79 ........................... 6.84

Regulation (EU) No 2015/848 of the European Parliament and of the Council on insolvency proceedings (Recast) [2015] OJ L 141/19 – *cont.*
art 80 ........................... 6.85
 81 ........................... 6.86
 82 ........................... 6.87
 83 ........................... 6.88
 84 ........................... 6.89
 85 ........................... 6.90
 86 ........................... 6.91
 87 ..................... 6.29, 6.92
 88 ........................... 6.93
 89 ........................... 6.94
 90 ........................... 6.95
 91 ........................... 6.96
 92 ..................... 6.29, 6.97
Annex A ........... 6.2, 6.3, 6.4, 6.98
   B ...................... 6.99
   C ................ 1.188, 6.100

**S**

Singapore Model Law
art 16(3) ....................... 7.30

**T**

Treaty on European Union
art 1 ............................ 7.3
 4(3) ......................... 6.45
Treaty on the Functioning of the European Union (TFEU)
art 49 ........................... 6.9

**U**

UNCITRAL Model Law on Cross-Border Insolvency 1997 ... 3.13, 6.1, 6.3, 6.5, 7.1, 7.2, 7.3, 7.4, 7.5, 7.15, 7.20, 7.22, 7.29, 7.30, 7.37, 7.38, 7.40
art 15(1) ....................... 7.14
 16 ........................... 6.5
 20 .......................... 7.33
 21(1)(d) ................... 1.300
   (g) .................... 1.300
   (2) ............... 1.586, 7.34

# Table of SIPs and Dear IPs

### D

Dear IP Millenium Edition, December 2000
   Ch 20 ...... 1.263, 1.265, 1.275, 1.299
Dear IP No 26, March 2006
   .......................... 1.410, 2.791
Dear IP No 30, March 1994
   ................................ 2.791
Dear IP No 33, March 1995
   .......................... 1.59, 1.60
Dear IP No 43, January 1999
   ................................ 1.194
Dear IP, September 2014
   ................................ 1.617
Dear IP No 82, November 2018
   .............................. 2.789

### S

SIP 3.1 ......................... 1.60
   para 1 ........................... 1.59
      16 ......................... 1.67
SIP 3.2 .................... 1.59, 1.60
SIP 6 .................... 2.113, 2.874
SIP 9 ........ 1.59, 1.80, 2.119, 2.990
SIP 12 ........................ 2.113
SIP 13 ........................ 1.617
SIP 15
   para 9 ......................... 2.952
SIP 16 ................. 1.617, 2.130

# Table of Cases

## A

A v B [2021] EWHC 2289 (Ch), [2021] All ER (D) 37 (Aug) .......................... 5.41
A and BC Chewing Gum Ltd, Re, Topps Chewing Gum Inc v Coakley [1975] 1 All ER
   1017, [1975] 1 WLR 579, 119 Sol Jo 233 ............................................. 1.200
A & C Supplies Ltd, Re [1998] 1 BCLC 603, [1998] BCC 708, [1997] Lexis Citation
   4126, [1998] BPIR 303, [1997] All ER (D) 25 ................................. 1.89, 1.414
A & J Fabrications Ltd v Grant Thornton (a firm) [1998] 2 BCLC 227, [1998] Lexis
   Citation 1394 ...................................................................... 1.270, 1.415
A Bankrupt and in the matter of the Insolvency Act 1986 and the EC Regulation on
   Insolvency Proceedings, Re 2000 [2012] BPIR 469 .................................... 1.497
A Best Floor Sanding Pty Ltd v Skyer Australia Pty Ltd [1999] VSC 170, Vic S C ...... 1.176
A E Farr Ltd, Re [1992] BCLC 333, [1992] BCC 150 ............................... 1.300
A.R.G. (Mansfield) Ltd Gregory, Re v A.R.G. (Mansfield) Ltd [2020] EWHC 1133 (Ch),
   [2020] All ER (D) 79 (May) ............................................. 1.630, 1.646, 2.820
A Straume (UK) Ltd v Bradlor Developments Ltd [2000] BCC 333, (1999) Times,
   29 June .................................................................. 1.183, 1.353, 1.660
AA Mutual International Insurance Co Ltd, Re [2004] EWHC 2430 (Ch), [2005] 2 BCLC
   8, [2004] All ER (D) 34 (Dec) ........................................................ 1.628
ABC Coupler and Engineering Co Ltd, Re [1961] 1 All ER 354, [1961] 1 WLR 243, 105
   Sol Jo 109 .............................................................................. 1.178
ABC Coupler and Engineering Co Ltd (No 3), Re [1970] 1 All ER 650, [1970] 1 WLR
   702, 114 Sol Jo 242, 209 Estates Gazette 1197 ..................................... 2.433
ACN 003 671 387 and ACN 008 664 257, Re [2004] NSWSC 368 ............ 1.217, 1.270
AE Realisations (1985) Ltd, Re [1987] 3 All ER 83, [1988] 1 WLR 200, [1987] BCLC
   486, 3 BCC 136, 132 Sol Jo 51, [1988] 2 LS Gaz R 35 .............................. 1.236
AES Barry Ltd v TXU Europe Energy Trading (in administration) [2004] EWHC 1757
   (Ch), [2005] 2 BCLC 22, [2006] BPIR 1109, [2004] All ER (D) 160 (Sep) ......... 1.660
AIB Group (UK) plc v Mark Redler & Co Solicitors [2014] UKSC 58, [2015] AC 1503,
   [2015] 1 All ER 747, [2014] 3 WLR 1367, [2015] 2 All ER (Comm) 189, 18 ITELR
   216, [2015] EGLR 34, [2014] PLSCS 115, 164 NLJ 7632, [2015] WTLR 187,
   [2014] All ER (D) 49 (Nov), SC ...................................................... 1.644
AIB Group (UK) plc v St John Spencer Estates & Development Ltd [2012] EWHC 2317
   (Ch), [2013] 1 BCLC 718, [2012] All ER (D) 54 (Aug) ............................. 1.652
AMF International Ltd (No 2), Re [1996] 1 WLR 77, [1995] 2 BCLC 529, [1995] BCC
   439 ...................................................................................... 1.160
AMF International Ltd (No 2), Re [1996] 2 BCLC 9, [1996] BCC 335 ......... 2.834, 2.835
AMN Pty Ltd (in liqation), Re (1997) 15 ACLC 368 ............................... 1.220
AMP Enterprises Ltd (t/a Total Home Entertainment) v Hoffman [2002] EWHC 1899
   (Ch), [2003] 1 BCLC 319, [2002] BCC 996, (2002) Times, 13 August, [2003] BPIR 11,
   [2002] All ER (D) 393 (Jul) ........................................................... 1.160
ARMS (Multiple Sclerosis Research) Ltd, Re, Alleyne v A-G [1997] 2 All ER 679, [1997]
   1 WLR 877, [1997] 1 BCLC 157, (1996) Times, 29 November ...................... 1.220
ARV Aviation Ltd, Re [1989] BCLC 664, 4 BCC 708 ............................... 1.688
ASA Resource Group plc (in administration) (No. 02167843), Re Dearing v Skelton (joint
   administrators of ASA Resource Group plc) [2020] EWHC 1370 (Ch), [2020] All ER
   (D) 05 (Jun) .................................................................... 1.680, 1.691
ASIC v King [2020] HCA 4 ............................................................... 1.270
ASC v Solomon (1996) 19 ACSR 73 ................................................... 1.188
ASIC v Franklin [2014] FCAFC 85 ..................................................... 1.160
ASIC v Kingsley Brown Properties Pty Ltd [2005] VSC 506 ........................... 1.177
ASIC v Tax Returns Australia Dot Com Pty Ltd [2010] FCA 715 ..................... 1.188
ASIC v Westpoint Corpn Pty Ltd [2006] FCA 135, Aust Fed Ct ...................... 1.193
AY Bank Ltd (in administration), Re. See Rolph v AY Bank Ltd
Aardvark TMC Ltd [2013] EWHC 1774 (Ch), [2013] CRI 105 ...................... 1.218
Abbey Forwarding Ltd (in liq) v Hone [2010] EWHC 2029 (Ch), [2010] NLJR 1152,
   [2010] All ER (D) 24 (Aug) ........................................................... 1.271

Abbey Forwarding Ltd (In liqation) v Revenue and Customs Comrs [2015] EWHC 225
(Ch), [2015] Bus LR 882, [2015] All ER (D) 91 (Feb) ................................. 1.188
Abbey National plc v JSF Finance & Currency Exchange Co Ltd [2006] EWCA Civ 328,
[2006] All ER (D) 474 (Mar) ......................................................... 1.178
Abdulali v Finnegan [2018] EWHC 1806 (Ch), [2018] BPIR 1547 ............. 1.303, 1.460
Abdulla v Whelan [2017] EWHC 605 (Ch), [2018] 1 All ER 533, [2017] 1 WLR 3318,
[2017] BPIR 791, [2017] 2 P & CR D34, [2017] All ER (D) 102 (Apr) ............... 1.434
Abrahams v Trustee of the property of Abrahams (a bankrupt) (1999) Times, 26 July,
[1999] Lexis Citation 3432, [1999] BPIR 637, [1999] All ER (D) 780 ............... 1.396
Ad Valorem Factors Ltd v Ricketts [2003] EWCA Civ 1706, [2004] 1 All ER 894, [2003]
NLJR 1841, [2004] BPIR 825, [2003] All ER (D) 430 (Nov), sub nom Ricketts v Ad
Valorem Factors Ltd [2004] 1 BCLC 1, [2004] BCC 164 ..................... 1.275, 2.1044
Adams v Mason Bullock (a firm) [2004] EWHC 2910 (Ch), (2005) Times, 6 January,
[2005] BPIR 241, [2004] All ER (D) 292 (Dec) ...................................... 2.550
Adams (AJ) (Builders) Ltd, Re [1991] BCLC 359, [1991] BCC 62 ............. 1.160, 1.223
Addchance Ltd v Herojoy Trading Ltd [2019] HKCFI 1147 ......................... 2.338
Addlestone Linoleum Co, Re (1887) 37 ChD 191, 57 LJ Ch 249, 36 WR 227, 58 LT 428,
4 TLR 140, CA ....................................................................... 1.129
Addstone Pty Ltd (in liqation), Re (1997) 25 ACSR 357 ........................... 1.220
Adetula v Barking and Dagenham LBC (9 November 2017, unreported), ChD ........ 1.502
Adjei v Law For All [2011] EWHC 2672 (Ch), [2012] 2 BCLC 317, [2011] BCC 963,
[2011] 42 LS Gaz R 21, [2011] BPIR 1563, [2011] All ER (D) 154 (Oct) ...... 1.630, 1.643
Adlards Motor Group Holding Ltd, Re [1990] BCLC 68 ........................... 1.300
Adorian v Metropolitan Police Comr [2009] EWCA Civ 18, [2009] 4 All ER 227, [2009]
1 WLR 1859, (2009) Times, 23 February, [2009] All ER (D) 176 (Jan) ............... 1.183
Advance Housing Pty Ltd (in liqation) v Newcastle Classic Developments Pty Ltd
(1994) 14 ACSR 230 ................................................................. 1.160
Aetna Properties Ltd (in liqation) v GA Listing & Maintenance Pty Ltd (1994) 13 ACSR
422 ................................................................................... 1.200
Agilo Ltd v Henry [2010] EWHC 2717 (Ch), [2011] BPIR 297 ............... 1.383, 2.530
Agnew (as trustee in bankruptcy of the estate of Paul Dougan) v Moyola Estates Ltd
[2016] NICh 19 ...................................................................... 1.324
Agrenco Madeira - Comércio Internacional Lda, Re [2014] All ER (D) 118 (Apr) ..... 1.280
Agricultural Mortgage Corpn plc v Woodward [1995] 1 BCLC 1, 70 P & CR 53, [1996]
1 FLR 226, [1996] 2 FCR 796, [1996] Fam Law 149, [1994] BCC 688, [1995] 1 EGLR
1, [1995] 04 EG 143, (1994) Times, 30 May ................................... 1.302, 1.582
Agriculturist Cattle Insurance Co, Re, Baird's Case (1870) LR 5 Ch App 725, 18 WR
1094, 23 LT 424, [1861–73] All ER Rep Ext 1766, CACh ........................... 1.135
Agrimarche Ltd (in creditors' voluntary liq), Re [2010] EWHC 1655 (Ch),
[2011] 1 BCLC 1, [2010] BCC 775, [2010] All ER (D) 39 (Jul) ............... 1.164, 1.618
Agriplant Services Ltd (in liqation), Re [1997] 2 BCLC 598, [1997] BCC 842 .. 1.303, 1.305
Agrokor DD, Re [2018] EWHC 348 (Ch), [2018] All ER (D) 141 (Feb) ................ 7.34
Agrokor DD and in the matter of the Cross-Border Insolvency Regulations, Re 2006
[2017] EWHC 2791 (Ch), [2018] 2 BCLC 75, [2018] Bus LR 64, [2018] BPIR 1,
[2017] All ER (D) 83 (Nov) ................................................. 6.3, 7.15, 7.19
Ahajot (Count [2019] EWHC 1215 (Ch)Artsrunik) v Waller (Inspector of Taxes) [2004]
STC (SCD) 151, [2005] BPIR 82, SpecComm ....................................... 2.829
Ahmad v Bank of Scotland plc [2016] EWCA Civ 602, [2016] All ER (D) 184 (Jun)
.................................................................................... 1.88
Ahmad v IRC [2004] EWHC 2292 (Ch), [2005] BPIR 541, [2004] All ER (D) 435 (Jul)
.................................................................................... 1.382
Ahmed v Ingram (Joint trustees in bankruptcy of the estate of Ahmed the above-named
Debtor) [2018] EWCA Civ 519, [2018] BPIR 535, [2018] All ER (D) 144 (Mar) ..... 1.180,
                                                                                  1.398
Ahmed v Mogul Eastern Foods [2005] EWHC 3532 (Ch), [2007] BPIR 975,
[2005] All ER (D) 56 (Oct) .......................................................... 2.814
Aiglon Ltd and L'Aiglon SA v Gau Shan Co Ltd [1993] BCLC 1321, [1993] 1 Lloyd's Rep
164, (1992) Times, 8 July, [1992] Lexis Citation 1941 ............................. 1.582
Ailyan v Smith [2010] EWHC 24 (Ch), [2010] BPIR 289, [2010] All ER (D) 181 (Jun)
............................................................................. 1.302, 1.459
Air Ecosse Ltd v Civil Aviation Authority (1987) 3 BCC 492, [1987] Lexis Citation 89,
1987 SC 285, 1987 SLT 751, CtSess .................................................. 1.660
Airbase (UK) Ltd, Re [2008] EWHC 124 (Ch), [2008] 1 WLR 1516, [2008] 1 BCLC 437,
[2008] Bus LR 1076, [2008] BCC 213, [2008] All ER (D) 47 (Feb) ................... 1.233
Airfast Services Pty Ltd, Re (1976) 2 ACLR 1 ..................................... 1.178

Airlines Airspares Ltd v Handley Page Ltd [1970] Ch 193, [1970] 1 All ER 29n, [1970] 2 WLR 163 ........................................................................................ 1.81

Akers v Samba Financial Group [2017] UKSC 6, [2017] 2 All ER 799, [2017] 2 WLR 713, [2017] 2 All ER (Comm) 97, [2017] 1 BCLC 151, 20 ITELR 554, 167 NLJ 7733, (2017) Times, 06 February, [2017] AC 424, [2017] WTLR 373, [2017] BPIR 263, [2017] All ER (D) 06 (Feb), SC ........................................................... 1.180, 7.33

Akkurate Ltd (in liq), Re Wolloff (joint liquidators of Akkurate Ltd) v Calzaturificio Rodolfo Zengarini Srl company [2020] EWHC 1433 (Ch), [2020] All ER (D) 24 (Jun) ........................................................................... 1.300, 1.492, 6.23

Aktieselskabet Dansk Skibsfinansiering v Brothers [2001] 2 BCLC 324 ............... 1.271

Albany Building Ltd, Re [2007] BCC 591 ............................................. 1.654

Albert v Albert [1997] 2 FLR 791, [1998] 1 FCR 331, [1998] Fam Law 17, [1996] BPIR 232 ............................................................................... 1.399

Alberta Paper Co Ltd v Metropolitan Graphics Ltd (1983) 49 CBR (2d) 63 ............ 1.77

Alesi v Original Australian Art Co Pty Ltd (1989) 7 ACLC 595 ...................... 1.178

Alexander Sheridan Ltd, Re, Alexander Sheridan Ltd v Beaujersey Ltd [2004] EWHC 2072 (Ch), [2004] All ER (D) 21 (Aug) ............................................ 1.178

Alexanders Securities Ltd (No 2), Re [1983] 2 Qd R 597, 8 ACLR 434 ............... 1.176

Alitalia Linee Aeree Italiane SpA, Re [2011] EWHC 15 (Ch), [2011] 1 WLR 2049, [2011] 1 BCLC 606, [2011] Bus LR 926, [2011] BCC 579, [2011] NLJR 138, [2011] BPIR 308, [2011] All ER (D) 104 (Jan) .......................................... 6.38

All Leisure Holidays Ltd (In Administration), Re [2017] EWHC 870 (Ch), [2017] BPIR 1131, [2017] All ER (D) 142 (Jan) ......................................... 1.663, 2.175

Allan Ellis (Transport and Packing Services) Ltd, Re (1989) 5 BCC 835 ........ 1.222, 1.249

Allanfield Property Insurance Services Ltd (in administration) ("Apis") v Aviva Insurance Ltd [2015] EWHC 3721 (Ch), [2016] Lloyd's Rep IR 217, [2015] All ER (D) 198 (Dec) ........................................................................ 1.679

Allard Holdings Ltd, Re [2001] 1 BCLC 404, [2000] Lexis Citation 4440, [2002] BPIR 1, [2000] All ER (D) 1982 ....................................................... 2.838

Allders Department Stores Ltd, Re [2005] EWHC 172 (Ch), [2005] 2 All ER 122, [2006] 2 BCLC 1, [2005] ICR 867, [2005] BCC 289, (2005) Times, 2 March, [2005] All ER (D) 231 (Feb), CSRC vol 28 iss 25/3 .............................. 1.716

Allen, Re, Re a Debtor (No 367 of 1992) [1994] Lexis Citation 3883, [1998] BPIR 319 ................................................................................. 1.379

Allied Produce Co Ltd, Re [1967] 3 All ER 399n, [1967] 1 WLR 1469, 111 Sol Jo 848 ................................................................................. 1.177

Alman v Approach Housing Ltd [2001] 1 BCLC 530, [2002] BCC 723, [2001] BPIR 203, [2000] All ER (D) 2093 ............................................................ 1.64

Alpa Lighting, Re [1997] BPIR 341, CA ...................................... 1.59, 1.60, 1.67

Alpha Club (UK) Ltd, Re [2002] EWHC 884 (Ch), [2002] 2 BCLC 612, [2004] BCC 754, [2002] All ER (D) 202 (Apr) ....................................................... 1.177

Alt Landscapes Ltd, Re [1998] Lexis Citation 1936, [1999] BPIR 459 ................. 1.704

Altomart Ltd v Salford Estates (No 2) Ltd [2014] EWCA Civ 1575, [2015] Ch 589, [2015] 3 WLR 491, [2015] BPIR 399, [2014] All ER (D) 102 (Dec) ................. 1.178

Altomart Ltd v Salford Estates (No 2) Ltd [2014] EWCA Civ 1408, [2016] 2 All ER 328, [2015] 1 WLR 1825, (2014) Times, 09 December, [2014] 6 Costs LR 1013, [2014] All ER (D) 342 (Oct) ...................................................... 1.302

Amadeus Trading Ltd (No 1), Re (26 March 1997, unreported) ...................... 2.777

Amalgamated Investment and Property Co Ltd, Re [1985] Ch 349, [1984] 3 All ER 272, [1984] 3 WLR 1101, [1984] BCLC 341, 1985 FLR 11, 128 Sol Jo 798, [1985] LS Gaz R 276 .............................................................................. 1.441

Amalgamated Properties of Rhodesia (1913) Ltd, Re [1917] 2 Ch 115, 33 TLR 414, CA ................................................................................. 1.178

Amalgamated Syndicates Ltd, Re [1901] 2 Ch 181, 70 LJ Ch 726, 84 LT 864, 17 TLR 486 ................................................................................ 2.1008

American Energy Group Ltd v Hycarbex Asia Ltd [2014] EWHC 1091 (Ch) ........... 7.33

American Express International Banking Corpn v Hurley [1985] 3 All ER 564, [1986] BCLC 52, [1985] FLR 350, 2 BCC 98, 993, [1985] NLJ Rep 1034 ............. 1.88

Amihyia, Re [2004] EWHC 2617 (Ch), [2005] BPIR 264, [2004] All ER (D) 259 (Oct) ......................................................................... 1.381, 1.395

Anderson Owen Ltd (in liqation), Re [2009] EWHC 2837 (Ch), [2010] BPIR 37 ...... 2.820

Andrea Warwick (formerly Yarwood) v Trustee in Bankruptcy of Clive Graham Yarwood [2010] EWHC 2272 (Ch), [2010] 3 FCR 311, 154 Sol Jo (no 36) 33, [2010] BPIR 1443, [2010] All ER (D) 200 (Oct) .............................................. 1.398

Andrew, Re, ex p Official Receiver (Trustee) [1937] Ch 122, [1936] 3 All ER 450, 106 LJ Ch 195, [1936–7] B & CR 205, 80 Sol Jo 932, 155 LT 586, 53 TLR 90, CA .......... 1.240

Angel Group Ltd, Re [2015] EWHC 3624 (Ch), [2016] 2 BCLC 509, [2016] BPIR 260, [2016] All ER (D) 41 (Jan) ........................................................ 1.715

Angel Group Ltd Companies, Re [2015] EWHC 2372 (Ch), [2015] All ER (D) 33 (Sep) ................................................................................ 1.705, 2.776

Angel Group Ltd v British Gas Trading Ltd [2012] EWHC 2702 (Ch), [2012] All ER (D) 56 (Oct) ......................................................... 1.178, 2.338

Anglesea Colliery Co, Re (1866) LR 1 Ch App 555, 30 JP 692, 35 LJ Ch 809, 12 Jur NS 696, 14 WR 1004, 15 LT 127, CACh ............................................. 1.129

Anglesea Island Coal and Coke Co Ltd, Re, ex p Owen (1861) 4 LT 684 ............. 1.175

Anglican Insurance Ltd re [2008] NSWSC 41 ............................................ 1.164

Anglo American Insurance Co Ltd, Re [2002] BCC 715, [2000] Lexis Citation 1980, [2003] BPIR 793, [2000] All ER (D) 2558 ................................ 1.300, 2.765

Anglo-Austrian Printing and Publishing Union, Re, Brabourne v Anglo-Austrian Printing and Publishing Union [1895] 2 Ch 891, 65 LJ Ch 38, 2 Mans 614, 44 WR 186, 40 Sol Jo 68, 73 LT 442, 12 TLR 39, CA ...................................................... 1.270

Anglo-Austrian Printing and Publishing Union, Re, Isaacs' Case [1892] 2 Ch 158, 61 LJ Ch 481, 40 WR 518, 36 Sol Jo 427, 66 LT 593, 8 TLR 501, CA ...................... 1.201

Anglo-Baltic and Mediterranean Bank v Barber & Co [1924] 2 KB 410, 93 LJKB 1135, [1924] B & CR 224, [1924] All ER Rep 226, 132 LT 1, CA ........................... 1.164

Anglo-Bavarian Steel Ball Co, Re [1899] WN 80, CA ................................... 1.178

Anglo Irish Bank v Flannery [2012] EWHC 4090 (Ch), [2013] BPIR 165 ............. 1.380

Anglo Manx Bank Ltd v Aitkin [2001] Lexis Citation 2292, [2002] BPIR 215, [2001] All ER (D) 31 (Oct) ........................................................... 1.393

Annulment Funding Company Ltd v Cowey [2010] EWCA Civ 711, [2010] BPIR 1304, [2010] 2 P & CR D56, [2010] All ER (D) 205 (Jun) ................................. 1.395

Antal International Ltd, Re [2003] EWHC 1339 (Ch), [2003] 2 BCLC 406, [2003] BPIR 1067, [2003] All ER (D) 56 (May) ........................................... 1.88, 1.716

Apex Frozen Foods Ltd v Ali [2007] EWHC 469 (Ch), [2007] 6 Costs LR 818, [2007] BPIR 1437, [2007] All ER (D) 158 (Mar) .......................................... 1.188

Apex Global Management Ltd v Global Torch Ltd. See Re FI Call Ltd; Apex Global Management Ltd v FI Call Ltd

Apperley Investments Ltd v Monsoon Accessorize Ltd [2020] IEHC 523 ........ 6.13, 6.35

Appleyard v Reflex Recordings Ltd [2013] EWHC 4514 (Ch), [2014] All ER (D) 221 (Feb) .............................................................................. 2.183

Appleyard v Ritecrown Ltd [2007] EWHC 3515 (Ch), [2009] BPIR 235, [2007] All ER (D) 509 (Nov) ....................................................................... 1.67, 2.800

Appleyard v Wewelwala [2012] EWHC 3302 (Ch), [2013] 1 All ER 1383, [2013] 1 WLR 752, [2012] NLJR 1534, [2013] BPIR 15, [2012] All ER (D) 285 (Nov) ....... 1.386, 2.814

Application under Insolvency Rules 1986, an, Re [1994] 2 BCLC 104, [1994] BCC 369 ................................................................................ 2.791

Applied Data Base Ltd v Secretary of State for Trade and Industry [1995] 1 BCLC 272 ................................................................................ 2.324

Arauco Co, Re [1899] WN 134 ......................................................... 1.207

Arbuthnot Leasing International Ltd v Havelet Leasing Ltd (No 2) [1990] BCC 636, [1990] Lexis Citation 1212 ................................................ 1.582, 1.584

Archer Structures Ltd v Griffiths [2003] EWHC 957 (Ch), [2004] 1 BCLC 201, [2004] BCC 156, [2003] BPIR 1071, [2003] All ER (D) 172 (May), CSRC vol 27 iss 13/1 ........................................................................ 1.275, 1.276

Arctic Aviation Assets Designate Activity Company v Companies Act, 2014 [2021] IEHC 268 .................................................................................. 1.586, 7.4

Ardawa v Uppal [2019] EWHC 456 (Ch), [2019] Bus LR 1075, [2019] BPIR 475, [2019] All ER (D) 16 (Mar) ............................................... 1.395, 2.820

Ardawa v Uppal [2019] EWHC 1663 (Ch), 169 NLJ 7850, [2019] Bus LR 1943 [2019] BPIR 1086, [2019] All ER (D) 84 (Jul) ................. 1.489, 2.690, 2.795, 2.1009

Arena Corp Ltd v Customs and Excise Comrs [2004] EWCA Civ 371, [2004] BPIR 415, [2004] All ER (D) 494 (Mar) ........................................ 1.178, 6.1, 6.2

Argentum Lex Wealth Management Ltd v Giannotti [2011] EWCA Civ 1341 ......... 1.178

Argentum Reductions (UK) Ltd, Re [1975] 1 All ER 608, [1975] 1 WLR 186, 119 Sol Jo 97 .................................................................................. 1.180

Aria Inc v Credit Agricole Corporate and Investment Bank [2014] EWHC 872 (Comm), [2014] All ER (D) 244 (Mar) .............................................. 6.21, 6.23

Ariadne Capital Ltd, Re (unreported, Chief ICC Judge Briggs, 7 December 2018)

Arif v Zar [2012] EWCA Civ 986, [2012] BPIR 948, [2012] All ER (D) 243 (Jul) ..... 1.395, 2.784

Arlington Infrastructure Ltd (in administration) v Woolrych [2020] EWHC 3123 (Ch) ................................................................................ 1.633

Arm Asset Backed Securities S.A., Re [2013] EWHC 3351 (Ch), [2013] All ER (D) 107
(Nov) ................................................................... 6.3, 6.5
Arm Asset Backed Securities SA, Re [2014] EWHC 1097 (Ch), [2014] 2 BCLC 364,
[2014] All ER (D) 88 (Apr) ........................................... 6.9
Armitage v Gainsborough Properties Pty Ltd [2011] VSC 419 ..................... 1.183
Armstrong v Onyearu [2015] EWHC 1937 (Ch); affd sub nom Armstrong (as Trustee in
Bankruptcy of Onyearu) v Onyearu [2017] EWCA Civ 268, [2017] 3 WLR 1304,
(2017) Times, 09 June, [2017] WTLR 415, [2017] BPIR 869, [2017] 2 P & CR D36,
[2017] All ER (D) 141 (Apr) .......................................... 1.455
Armstrong Brands Ltd (In Administration), Re [2015] EWHC 3303 (Ch), [2015] All ER
(D) 172 (Nov) ................................................... 1.631, 1.728
Armvent Ltd, Re [1975] 3 All ER 441, [1975] 1 WLR 1679, 119 Sol Jo 845 .......... 1.176
Army and Navy Hotel, Re (1886) 31 ChD 644, 55 LJ Ch 511, 34 WR 389, 2 TLR 349
...................................................................... 2.321, 2.820
Aro Co Ltd, Re [1980] Ch 196, [1980] 1 All ER 1067, [1980] 2 WLR 453, 124 Sol Jo
15 ...................................................................... 1.179, 1.183
Arrowfield Services Ltd, Re [2015] EWHC 3046 (Ch) ......................... 2.768
Arrows Ltd (No 2), Re [1992] BCLC 1176, [1992] BCC 446, (1992) Times, 1 May; affd
[1994] 1 BCLC 355 ...................................................... 1.300
Arrows Ltd (No 3), Re [1992] BCLC 555, [1992] BCC 131 ..................... 1.630
Arrows Ltd (No 4) [1993] Ch 452, [1993] 3 All ER 861, [1993] 3 WLR 513,
[1993] BCLC 1222, [1993] BCC 473, [1993] 22 LS Gaz R 37, [1993] NLJR 690,
[1993] NLJR 688, [1993] NLJR 691, (1993) Times, 27 April, (1993) Times, 26 April;
affd sub nom Hamilton v Naviede [1995] 2 AC 75, [1994] 3 All ER 814, [1994] 3 WLR
656, [1994] 2 BCLC 738, [1994] BCC 641, [1994] NLJR 1203, HL .... 1.277, 1.299, 2.768
Artistic Colour Printing Co, Re (1880) 14 ChD 502, 49 LJ Ch 526, 28 WR 943, 42 LT
802 ...................................................................... 1.183
Artman v Artman, Debtor (No 622 of 1995), Re [1996] Lexis Citation 1242, [1996] BPIR
511 ...................................................................... 1.395
Ashapura Minechem Ltd, Re (2012) 480 BR 129 ..................... 7.15
Ashurst v Pollard [2001] Ch 595, [2001] 2 All ER 75, 150 NLJ 1787, (2000) Times,
29 November, [2000] Lexis Citation 2312, [2001] BPIR 131, [2000] All ER (D) 1900
...................................................................... 1.417, 1.433, 6.8
Ashworth v Newnote Ltd [2007] EWCA Civ 793, [2007] BPIR 1012, [2007] All ER (D)
436 (Jul) ............................................................. 1.178, 2.530
Askew v Peter Dominic Ltd [1995] Lexis Citation 1130, [1997] BPIR 163, CA ........ 1.395
Aslam v Finn [2013] EWHC 3405 (Ch), [2014] BPIR 1 ..................... 1.414
Aspinalls Club Ltd v Simone Halabi [1997] Lexis Citation 1195, [1998] BPIR 322 ... 1.386,
2.540
Association of Chartered Certified Accountants v Koumettou [2012] EWHC 1265 (Ch)
...................................................................... 2.785
Assured Logistics Solutions Ltd, Re [2011] EWHC 3029 (Ch), [2012] BCC 541 ....... 2.820
Astra Resources plc v Credit Veritas USA LLC [2015] EWHC 1830 (Ch), [2015] All ER
(D) 252 (Jun) ........................................................ 1.178
Atkinson v Varma [2020] EWHC 1868 (Ch), [2020] All ER (D) 106 (Jul); affd sub nom
Varma v Atkinson [2020] EWCA Civ 1602, [2021] Ch 180, [2021] 2 WLR 536,
[2020] All ER (D) 06 (Dec) .......................................... 2.744
Atlantic & General Investment Trust Ltd v Richbell Information Services Inc
[2000] 2 BCLC 778, [2000] BCC 111, (1999) Times, 21 January ....... 1.178, 1.180, 1.281
Atlantic Computer Systems plc, Re [1992] Ch 505, [1992] 1 All ER 476, [1992] 2 WLR
367, [1991] BCLC 606, [1990] BCC 859, (1990) Times, 18 September .. 1.81, 1.353, 1.622,
1.660, 1.683, 1.686
Atlantic Computers plc, Re [1998] BCC 200 ......................... 1.300
Atlantic Properties Ltd, Re [2006] EWHC 610 (Ch), [2006] All ER (D) 177 (Mar) .... 1.177
Atlas Shipping A/S 404 BR 726 , (April 27 2009, SDNY) ......................... 7.34
A-G v Jacobs-Smith [1895] 2 QB 341, 59 JP 468, 64 LJQB 605, 14 R 531, 43 WR 657, 39
Sol Jo 538, 72 LT 714, 11 TLR 411, CA ......................... 1.459
A-G v Parsons [1956] AC 421, [1956] 1 All ER 65, [1956] 2 WLR 153, 100 Sol Jo 51, 166
EG 748, HL ....................................................... 1.438
A-G's Reference (No 7 of 2000), Re (12 April 2001), The Times ..................... 1.478
A-G's Reference (No 1 of 2004), R v Edwards [2004] EWCA Crim 1025, [2005] 4 All ER
457, [2004] 1 WLR 2111, [2004] 2 Cr App Rep 424, [2004] Crim LR 832, [2004]
20 LS Gaz R 34, (2004) Times, 30 April, 148 Sol Jo LB 568, [2004] BPIR 1073,
[2004] All ER (D) 318 (Apr) ..................... 1.262, 1.263, 1.480, 1.485
Aurum Marketing Ltd (in liqation), Re [2000] 2 BCLC 645, [2002] BCC 31, (2000)
Times, 10 August, [2000] Lexis Citation 3333, [2000] All ER (D) 1009 ............... 1.177

Austin Australia Pty Ltd v De Martin & Gasparini Pty Ltd [2007] NSWSC 1238, NSW S Ct ................................................................................... 1.175
Austintel Ltd, Ex p. See Creditnet Ltd, Re
Australasian Alkaline Reduction and Smelting Syndicate Ltd, Re [1891] WN 209, 36 Sol Jo 139 .................................................................................. 2.328
Australasian Barrister Chambers Pty Ltd, Re [2020] NSWSC 304, (2020) 146 ACSR 1 ................................................................................... 1.225
Australian Beverage Distributors Pty Ltd v Evans & Tate Premium Wines Pty Ltd [2007] NSWCA 51 ............................................................................. 2.324
Australian Beverage Distributors Pty Ltd v The Redrock Co Pty Ltd [2007] NSWSC 966, [2007] 213 FLR 450 ....................................................... 1.176, 1.178
Australian Competition and Consumer Commission v Australian Institute of Professional Education Pty Ltd [2017] FCA 521 ......................................................... 1.183
Australian Consolidated Investments Ltd v Woodings (1996) 14 ACLC 1187 ......... 2.835
Australian Direct Steam Navigation Co, Re (1875) LR 20 Eq 325, 44 LJ Ch 676, Ct of Ch ................................................................................... 1.181
Australian Securities and Investments Commission v Planet Platinum Ltd [2015] VSC 273 .................................................................................. 1.188
Auto Management Services Ltd, Re [2007] EWHC 392 (Ch), [2008] BCC 761, [2007] All ER (D) 146 (Feb) ...................................................... 1.628
Autobrokers Ltd v Dymond [2015] EWHC 2691 (Admin) .......................... 1.164
Avery-Gee v Sibley [2021] EWHC 798 (Ch), [2021] All ER (D) 24 (Apr) .............. 1.679
Avonwick Holdings Ltd v Castle Investment Fund Ltd (15 December 2015, unreported) ................................................................................... 1.399
Avonwick Holdings Ltd v Azitio Holdings Ltd [2018] EWHC 2458 (Comm) ... 1.302, 1.582
Avatar Communications Ltd, Re (1988) 4 BCC 473 ............................... 1.187
Aveling Barford Ltd, Re [1988] 3 All ER 1019, [1989] 1 WLR 360, [1989] BCLC 122, 4 BCC 548, 133 Sol Jo 512, [1989] 18 LS Gaz R 36 ............................... 2.765
Avis v Turner. See Turner v Avis
Avonwick Holdings Ltd v Shlosberg [2016] EWCA Civ 1138, [2017] Ch 210, [2017] 2 WLR 1075, 166 NLJ 7725, [2017] BPIR 1, [2016] All ER (D) 141 (Nov) ..... 1.396, 1.416, 1.417, 1.429
Awan, Re [1999] Lexis Citation 4197, [2000] BPIR 241 ............................ 2.820
Awoyemi v Bowell [2005] EWHC 2138 (Ch), [2006] BPIR 1, [2005] All ER (D) 315 (Jul) .................................................................................. 1.455
Axnoller Events Ltd v Brake [2021] EWHC 828 (Ch), [2021] All ER (D) 52 (Apr) .... 2.758
Ayala Holdings Ltd, Re [1993] BCLC 256; revsd sub nom National Bank of Kuwait v Menzies [1994] 2 BCLC 306, sub nom Menzies v National Bank of Kuwait SAK [1994] BCC 119 ................................................... 1.582, 1.583
Ayala Holdings Ltd (No 2), Re [1996] 1 BCLC 467 ............................... 1.180
Ayerst (Inspector of Taxes) v C & K (Construction) Ltd [1976] AC 167, [1975] 2 All ER 537, [1975] 3 WLR 16, [1975] STC 345, 50 TC 651, 54 ATC 141, [1975] TR 117, 119 Sol Jo 424, HL ........................................................... 1.198
Azuonye v Kent (in her capacity as trustee of the bankrupt estate of Azuonye) [2018] EWHC 2766 (Ch), [2018] 4 WLR 157, 168 NLJ 7816, [2019] BPIR 23, [2018] All ER (D) 114 (Oct) ............................................................ 1.515
Azuonye v Kent (in her capacity as trustee of the bankrupt estate of the appellant) [2019] EWCA Civ 1289, [2019] 4 WLR 101, [2019] BPIR 1317, [2019] All ER (D) 123 (Jul) .......................................................... 1.427, 1.454, 1.515, 2.829

## B

B and M Quality Constructions Pty Ltd v WG Brady Pty Ltd (1994) 12 ACLC 970 ... 1.175
BAT Industries plc v Sequana SA [2016] EWHC 1686 (Ch), [2017] 1 BCLC 453, [2017] Bus LR 82, [2016] All ER (D) 96 (Jul) ................................... 1.582, 1.584
BAT Industries plc v Sequana SA [2017] EWHC 211 (Ch), 167 NLJ 7736, [2017] All ER (D) 176 (Feb) ................................................................ 1.582, 1.584
BCPMS (Europe) Ltd v GMAC Commercial Finance plc [2006] EWHC 3744 (Ch), [2006] All ER (D) 285 (Feb) ..................................................... 1.633
BHS Ltd (in administration), Re [2016] EWHC 1965 (Ch), [2016] All ER (D) 20 (Aug) ................................................................................... 1.720
BHT (UK) Ltd, Re [2004] EWHC 201 (Ch), [2004] 1 BCLC 568, [2004] All ER (D) 190 (Feb), sub nom BHT (UK) Ltd, Re; Duckworth v NatWest Finance Ltd [2004] BCC 301 ................................................................................... 1.84

BNY Corporate Trustee Services Ltd v Eurosail-UK 2007-3BL plc [2011] EWCA Civ 227,
[2011] 3 All ER 470, [2011] 1 WLR 2524, [2011] Bus LR 1359, [2011] BCC 399,
(2011) Times, 14 March, [2011] All ER (D) 74 (Mar); affd sub nom BNY Corporate
Trustee Services Ltd v Neuberger Berman Europe Ltd (on behalf of Sealink
Funding Ltd); BNY Corporate Trustee Services Ltd v Eurosail-UK 2007-3BL plc [2013]
UKSC 28, [2013] 3 All ER 271, [2013] 1 WLR 1408, [2013] 2 All ER (Comm) 531,
[2013] 1 BCLC 613, [2013] Bus LR 715, [2013] All ER (D) 107 (May), CSRC vol 37 iss
7/2, SC .................................................................... 1.175, 1.628, 2.127
BPE Solicitors v Gabriel [2015] UKSC 39, [2015] AC 1663, [2015] 4 All ER 672, [2015]
3 WLR 1, 165 NLJ 7658, [2015] 4 Costs LO 467, [2015] BPIR 779, [2015] All ER (D)
179 (Jun), SC ................................................................. 1.396
BPM Pty Ltd v HPM Pty Ltd (1996) 14 ACLC 857 ............................... 1.183
BPTC Ltd, Re (1992) 7 ACSR 291, on appeal (1993) 12 ACSR 181 ............... 1.207
BTI 2014 LLC v Sequana SA [2016] EWHC 1686 (Ch), [2017] 1 BCLC 453, [2017] Bus
LR 82, [2016] All ER (D) 96 (Jul); affd [2017] EWHC 211 (Ch), 167 NLJ 7736,
[2017] All ER (D) 176 (Feb); revsd in part sub nom BTI 2014 LLC v Sequana [2019]
EWCA Civ 112, [2019] 2 All ER 784, [2019] 2 All ER (Comm) 13, [2019] 1 BCLC
347, [2019] BPIR 562, [2019] All ER (D) 36 (Feb) ..................... 1.582, 1.584, 1.605
BW Estates Ltd, Re [2015] EWHC 517 (Ch), [2016] 1 BCLC 708, [2015] All ER (D) 27
(Mar) ............................................................... 1.618, 1.620, 2.1008
BXL Services, Re [2012] EWHC 1877 (Ch), [2012] BCC 657, [2012] All ER (D) 87
(Jul) ....................................................................... 1.643
Baars, Re [2002] EWHC 2159 (Ch), [2003] BPIR 523, [2002] All ER (D) 64 (Oct) ... 1.188,
1.400
Backman v Landsbanki Islands hf [2011] FCA 1430 ................................. 7.15
Bacon (MC) Ltd, Re [1990] BCLC 324, [1990] BCC 78, 11 LDAB 534, (1989) Times,
1 December ........................................................... 1.302, 1.303
Bacon (MC) Ltd, Re [1991] Ch 127, [1990] 3 WLR 646, [1990] BCLC 607, [1990] BCC
430, (1990) Times, 12 April .............................................. 1.582, 2.433
Badyal v Badyal [2018] EWHC 68 (Ch), [2018] All ER (D) 25 (Feb) ................. 1.174
Bae Systems Pension Funds Trustees Ltd v Bowmer and Kirkland Ltd [2018] EWHC 1222
(TCC) ...................................................................... 1.660
Bagnall v Official Receiver [2003] EWCA Civ 1925, [2004] 2 All ER 294, [2004] 1 WLR
2832, [2004] BPIR 445, [2003] All ER (D) 14 (Dec) ............................. 1.391
Bailey v Thurston & Co Ltd [1903] 1 KB 137, 72 LJKB 36, 10 Mans 1, 51 WR 162,
[1900–3] All ER Rep 818, 88 LT 43, CA ...................................... 1.396
Baillies Ltd (in liq), Re [2012] EWHC 285 (Ch), [2012] BCC 554, [2012] BPIR 665
............................................................. 1.582, 2.820, 6.8
Bairnsdale Food Products Ltd, Re [1948] VLR 624 ............................... 1.743
Bairstow v Queens Moat Houses plc, Marcus v Queens Moat Houses plc [2000] 1 BCLC
549, [2000] BCC 1025, [1999] Lexis Citation 4199, [1999] All ER (D) 1378; sub nom
Bairstow v Queens Moat Houses plc [2001] EWCA Civ 712, [2001] 2 BCLC 531,
[2002] BCC 91, [2001] All ER (D) 211 (May) ................................. 1.272
Baker v Biomethane (Castle Easton) Ltd [2019] EWHC 3298 (Ch) .................. 1.630
Baker v West Reading Social Club [2014] EWHC 3033 (Ch) ....................... 1.280
Bakhshiyeva (in her capacity as the foreign representative of the OJSC International Bank
of Azerbaijan) v Sberbank of Russia [2018] EWHC 59 (Ch), [2018] Bus LR 1270,
[2018] BPIR 287, [2018] All ER (D) 105 (Jan) ............................. 7.1, 7.34
Balfour v Wylie [1904] WN 72 ................................................. 1.207
Ball v Jones [2008] 2 FLR 1969, [2008] Fam Law 1184, [2008] BPIR 1051 .... 1.459, 1.460
Ballast plc (in admin), Re [2004] EWHC 2356 (Ch), [2005] 1 All ER 630, [2005] 1 WLR
1928, [2005] 1 BCLC 446, [2005] BCC 96, (2004) Times, 28 October, [2004] All ER
(D) 282 (Oct) ........................................................... 1.700, 1.701
Ballast plc, Re, St Paul Travellers Insurance Co Ltd v Dargan [2006] EWHC 3189 (Ch),
[2007] Lloyd's Rep IR 742, [2007] BCC 620, [2007] BPIR 117, [2006] All ER (D) 240
(Dec) ...................................................................... 1.238
Bamford Publishers Ltd, Re (2 June 1977, unreported) ........................... 1.177
Banco Nacional de Cuba v Cosmos Trading Corp [2000] 1 BCLC 813, [2000] BCC 910,
[1999] Lexis Citation 4202 ........................................ 1.169, 1.279, 1.281
Bangla Television Ltd, (in liqation), Re [2009] EWHC 1632 (Ch), [2010] BCC 143,
[2009] All ER (D) 170 (Jul) .................................................. 1.272
Bank Handlowy w Warszawie SA v Christanapol sp. zoo: C-116/11 (2012) C-116/11,
ECLI:EU:C:2012:7261, [2013] Bus LR 956, [2013] BPIR 174, [2012] All ER (D) 300
(Nov), EUCJ ........................................................ 6.2, 6.4, 6.34, 6.45
Bank Leumi (UK) plc, petitioner [2017] CSOH 129, [2018] 1 BCLC 204, 2017 SLT 1281,
[2018] BPIR 614, 2017 Scot (D) 6/10, CSOH ............................... 1.169, 6.2

Bank of Baroda v Maniar [2019] EWHC 2463 (Comm) .............................. 6.9
Bank of Baroda v Panessar [1987] Ch 335, [1986] 3 All ER 751, [1987] 2 WLR 208,
   [1986] BCLC 497, 2 BCC 99, 288, 131 Sol Jo 21, [1987] LS Gaz R 339, [1986] NLJ
   Rep 963 ...................................................................... 1.78, 1.638
Bank of Baroda v Patel [2008] EWHC 3390 (Ch), [2009] 2 FLR 753, [2009] 3 FCR 586,
   [2009] Fam Law 660, [2009] BPIR 255, [2009] All ER (D) 110 (Mar) ............... 1.414
Bank of Credit and Commerce International (Overseas) Ltd (in liq) v Habib Bank Ltd
   [1998] 4 All ER 753, [1999] 1 WLR 42, [1998] 2 BCLC 459, (1998) Times, 20 July,
   [1998] Lexis Citation 2771, [1999] BPIR 1, [1998] All ER (D) 295 ............ 2.835, 2.852
Bank of Credit and Commerce International SA, Re [1997] AC 213, [1997] Ch 213,
   [1996] 4 All ER 796, [1997] 2 WLR 172, [1997] 1 BCLC 80, [1996] BCC 980 ....... 1.586,
                                                                          2.852, 6.11
Bank of Credit and Commerce International SA (in liq), Re [2003] EWHC 1868 (Ch),
   [2004] 2 BCLC 236, [2003] BCC 735, [2003] All ER (D) 512 (Jul) ................. 1.271
Bank of Credit and Commerce International SA (in liq), Re [2004] EWHC 528 (Ch),
   [2005] 1 All ER (Comm) 209, [2004] 2 BCLC 279, [2004] BCC 404, [2004] All ER (D)
   378 (Mar); affd sub nom Morris v Bank of India [2005] EWCA Civ 693,
   [2005] 2 BCLC 328, (2005) Times, 19 July, [2005] BPIR 1067, [2005] All ER (D) 242
   (Jun), CSRC vol 29 iss 8/2, sub nom Bank of India v Morris [2005] BCC 739 ......... 1.271
Bank of Credit and Commerce International SA (No 2), Re [1992] BCLC 579,
   [1992] BCC 83 .................................................................. 1.188
Bank of Credit and Commerce International SA (No 2), Re, Banque Arabe et
   Internationale D'Investissement SA v Morris [2001] 1 BCLC 263, [2002] BCC 407,
   (2000) Times, 26 October, [2000] Lexis Citation 4053, [2000] All ER (D) 1437, CSRC
   vol 24 iss 8/2 ................................................................. 1.271
Bank of Credit and Commerce International SA (No 3), Re [1993] BCLC 1490,
   [1992] BCC 715 ...................................................... 1.219, 1.251, 1.741
Bank of Credit and Commerce International SA (No 6), Re [1994] 1 BCLC 450 ...... 2.777,
                                                                               2.835
Bank of Credit and Commerce International SA (No 7), Re [1994] 1 BCLC 458 ...... 1.300
Bank of Credit and Commerce International SA (No 8), Re [1996] Ch 245, [1996]
   2 All ER 121, [1996] 2 WLR 631, [1996] 2 BCLC 254, [1996] BCC 204, 140 Sol Jo LB
   36; affd [1998] AC 214, [1997] 4 All ER 568, [1997] 3 WLR 909, [1998] 2 LRC 292,
   [1998] 1 BCLC 68, [1997] BCC 965, 14 LDAB 10, [1997] NLJR 1653, 141 Sol Jo LB
   229, HL ...................................................................... 2.852
Bank of Credit and Commerce International SA (in liqation) (No 12), Re, Morris v Bank
   of America National Trust and Savings Association [1997] 1 BCLC 526, [1997] BCC
   561, (1997) Times, 10 February, [1997] Lexis Citation 3007 ...................... 1.300
Bank of Credit and Commerce International SA v Malik [1996] BCC 15, [1995] Lexis
   Citation 3553 ................................................................. 1.188
Bank of India v Morris. See Bank of Credit and Commerce International SA (in liq), Re
   [2004] EWHC 528 (Ch)
Bank of Melbourne Ltd v HPM Pty Ltd (1998) 16 ACLC 427 ...................... 1.220
Bank of Scotland plc (t/a Birmingham Midshires) v Breytenbach [2012] BPIR 1 . 1.183, 1.399
Bank of Scotland plc v Targetfollow Properties Holdings Ltd [2010] EWHC 3606 (Ch)
   ............................................................................. 1.629
Bank of South Australia (No 2), Re [1895] 1 Ch 578, 64 LJ Ch 397, 2 Mans 129, 12 R
   166, 43 WR 359, 39 Sol Jo 314, 72 LT 273, 11 TLR 265, CA .............. 1.168, 1.279
Bank of Tokyo-Mitsubishi UFJ Ltd v Owners of the MV Sanko Mineral [2014] EWHC
   3927 (Admlty), [2015] 2 All ER (Comm) 979, [2015] 1 Lloyd's Rep 247, [2014] All ER
   (D) 14 (Dec) .................................................................. 7.33
Banksia Securities Ltd, Re [2013] VSC 416 ..................................... 1.300
Bannai v Erez [2013] EWHC 4287 (Comm), [2014] BPIR 1369 ..................... 2.800
Bannai v Erez [2013] EWHC 3689 (Comm), [2014] BPIR 4, [2013] All ER (D) 288
   (Nov) ........................................................................ 7.33
Bannister v Islington London Borough Council (1971) LGR 239 .................... 1.88
Banque des Marchands de Moscou (Koupetschesky) v Kindersley [1951] Ch 112, [1950]
   2 All ER 549, 66 (pt 2) TLR 654, CA .......................................... 1.281
Barca v Mears [2004] EWHC 2170 (Ch), [2005] 2 FLR 1, [2005] BPIR 15, [2004] All ER
   (D) 153 (Sep) ................................................................. 1.455
Barcham, Re [2008] EWHC 1505 (Ch), [2009] 1 All ER 145, [2008] 2 P & CR D49,
   11 ITELR 507, [2008] 2 FCR 643, (2008) Times, 24 July, [2008] All ER (D) 64 (Jul),
   sub nom French v Barcham [2009] 1 WLR 1124, [2008] 3 EGLR 51, [2008] 39 EG
   126, [2008] BPIR 857 ......................................................... 1.455
Barclays Bank v Atay [2015] EWHC 3198 (Ch), [2016] BPIR 12 .................. 1.175
Barclays Bank plc v Choicezone Ltd [2011] EWHC 1303 (Ch), [2012] BCC 767 ...... 1.652

Barclays Bank plc v Eustice [1995] 4 All ER 511, [1995] 1 WLR 1238, [1995] 2 BCLC 630, [1995] BCC 978, [1995] NLJR 1503, (1995) Times, 3 August, [1996] BPIR 1 .... 1.582

Barclays Bank plc v Masters [2013] EWHC 2166 (Ch), [2013] BPIR 1058, [2013] All ER (D) 241 (Jul) .................................................................................... 1.380

Barclays Bank plc v Mogg [2003] EWHC 2645 (Ch), [2004] BPIR 259, [2003] All ER (D) 56 (Oct) ................................................................................................ 1.384

Barclays Bank plc (t/a Barclays Global Payment Acceptance) v Registrar of Companies [2015] EWHC 2806 (Ch), [2016] 2 BCLC 453, [2015] All ER (D) 279 (Oct) ......... 1.701

Barclays Mercantile Business Finance Ltd v Sibec Developments Ltd [1993] 2 All ER 195, [1992] 1 WLR 1253, [1993] BCLC 1077, [1993] BCC 148 ............. 1.353, 1.660, 1.679

Barker v Bajjon [2008] BPIR 771 ......................................................................... 1.489

Barker v Baxendale-Walker [2018] EWHC 1681 (Ch) ....................... 1.178, 2.550

Barker v Baxendale-Walker [2018] EWHC 2518 (Ch) .................. 1.406, 1.407, 1.489

Barleycorn Enterprises Ltd, Re, Mathias and Davies (a firm) v Down [1970] Ch 465, [1970] 2 All ER 155, [1970] 2 WLR 898, 114 Sol Jo 187 .........1.84, 1.159, 2.433

Barlow Clowes International Ltd v Henwood [2008] EWCA Civ 577, (2008) Times, 18 June, [2008] BPIR 778, [2008] All ER (D) 330 (May) ........................... 1.380

Barn Crown Ltd, Re [1994] 4 All ER 42, [1995] 1 WLR 147, [1994] 2 BCLC 186, [1994] BCC 381, 12 LDAB 579 ...................................................................... 1.180

Barnes (The Liquidator of Mistral Finance Ltd) v Premium Credit Ltd [2001] BCC 27, [2000] All ER (D) 39 ....................................................................... 1.302, 1.303

Barnes v Whitehead [2004] BPIR 693 ....................................... 1.386, 2.550

Barnett (Augustus) & Son Ltd, Re [1986] BCLC 170, 2 BCC 98, 904, [1986] PCC 167 .......................................................................................................... 1.271

Baron Cigarette Machine Co Ltd, Re (1912) 28 TLR 394 ...................... 1.160

Baron Investments (Holdings) Ltd (in liqation), Halstuk v Venvil [2000] 1 BCLC 272, [1999] Lexis Citation 3035, [1999] All ER (D) 391 ...................................... 1.433

Barrett v Barrett [2008] EWHC 1061 (Ch), [2008] 2 P & CR D18, [2008] 2 P & CR 345, [2008] 2 EGLR 81, [2008] 31 EG 90, [2008] BPIR 817, [2008] All ER (D) 233 (May) .................................................................................................. 1.452

Barrow Borough Transport Ltd, Re [1990] Ch 227, [1989] 3 WLR 858, [1989] BCLC 653, 5 BCC 646, 133 Sol Jo 1513 .......................................... 1.353, 1.660, 1.696

Barrows v Chief Land Registrar ( 20 October 1977, unreported) The Times ............ 1.88

Barton Manufacturing Co Ltd, Re [1999] 1 BCLC 740, [1998] BCC 827, [1997] Lexis Citation 5170 ................................................................................................. 1.302

Barton-upon-Humber and District Water Co, Re (1889) 42 ChD 585, 58 LJ Ch 613, 1 Meg 412, 38 WR 8, 61 LT 803 ....................................................................... 1.279

Basis Yield Alpha Fund, Re (2008) 381 BR 3 .......................................... 7.29

Bastable, Re, ex p Trustee [1901] 2 KB 518, 70 LJKB 784, 8 Mans 239, 49 WR 561, 45 Sol Jo 576, 84 LT 825, 17 TLR 560, CA .......................................................... 1.235

Bataillon v Shone [2016] EWHC 1174 (QB), [2016] BPIR 829, [2016] All ER (D) 199 (May) ............................................................................................................ 1.582

Bateson (John) & Co Ltd, Re [1985] BCLC 259 .......................................... 1.220

Batey, Re, ex p Emmanuel (1881) 17 Ch D 35, 50 LJ Ch 305, 29 WR 526, 44 LT 832, CA ............................................................................................................... 1.742

Batooneh v Asombang [2003] EWHC 2111 (QB), [2004] BPIR 1, [2003] All ER (D) 557 (Jul) .............................................................................................................. 1.308

Baxters Ltd, Re [1898] WN 60 ............................................................... 1.200

Bayliss v Saxton [2018] EWHC 3365 (QB) ............................................... 1.399

Baynton v Morgan (1888) 22 QBD 74, 53 JP 166, 58 LJQB 139, 37 WR 148, 5 TLR 99, CA ................................................................................................................. 1.64

Bayoil SA, Re, Seawind Tankers Corp v Bayoil SA [1999] 1 All ER 374, [1999] 1 WLR 147, [1999] 1 BCLC 62, [1999] 1 Lloyd's Rep 211, [1998] BCC 988, 14 LDAB 332, (1998) Times, 12 October, 142 Sol Jo LB 251 ............................. 1.178, 2.530

Beacon Leisure Ltd, Re [1992] BCLC 565, [1991] BCC 213 .......................... 1.303

Bear Stearns High-Grade Structured Credit Strategies Master Fund Ltd, Re (2007) 374 BR 122; (2008) 389 BR 325 .................................................................. 6.5, 7.29

Beattie v Smails [2011] EWHC 1563 (Ch), [2012] BPIR 135, [2011] All ER (D) 295 (May) ............................................................................................................. 1.160

Beaufort Asset Clearing Services Ltd (in special administration), Re [2018] EWHC 2287 ...................................................................................................... 1.617

Beaufort Asset Clearing Services Ltd, Re [2020] EWHC 2309 (Ch) ................... 1.679

Beaufort Asset Clearing Services Ltd, Re (in special administration) and other companies [2020] EWHC 3627 (Ch), [2021] All ER (D) 32 (Jan) ............................... 1.617

Beck Foods Ltd, Re. See Rees v Boston Borough Council

Beckham v Drake (1849) 2 HL Cas 579, 13 Jur 921, 9 ER 1213 ...................... 1.396

Beer v Higham (a bankrupt) [1997] BPIR 349 ........................................ 1.398

Bell (a bankrupt), Re [1998] BPIR 26, BCSC ...................................... 1.396

Bell v Birchall [2015] EWHC 1541 (Ch), [2016] 4 All ER 766, [2017] 1 WLR 667, [2015] BPIR 751, [2015] All ER (D) 57 (Jun) .............................................. 1.416

Bell v Brown [2007] EWHC 2788 (QB), [2008] BPIR 829, [2007] All ER (D) 456 (Nov) ................................................................................. 1.395

Bell v Long [2008] EWHC 1273 (Ch), [2008] 2 BCLC 706, [2008] BPIR 1211, [2008] All ER (D) 179 (Jun) ...................................................... 1.88

Bell Group Finance (Pty) Ltd (in liqation) v Bell Group (UK) Holdings Ltd [1996] 1 BCLC 304 ........................................................................ 1.174, 1.178

Bellaglade Ltd, Re [1977] 1 All ER 319 ......................................... 1.240

Bellmex International Ltd (in liq) v British American Tobacco Ltd [2001] 1 BCLC 91, [2001] BCC 253, [2000] 12 LS Gaz R 42, (2000) Times, 31 March, [2000] Lexis Citation 2921, 144 Sol Jo LB 133 ........................................... 1.300, 2.834

Belmont Park Investments PTY Ltd v BNY Corporate Trustee Services Ltd [2011] UKSC 38, [2012] 1 AC 383, [2012] 1 All ER 505, [2011] 3 WLR 521, [2012] 1 BCLC 163, [2011] Bus LR 1266, [2011] BCC 734, (2011) Times, 15 August, [2011] BPIR 1223, [2011] All ER (D) 259 (Jul), SC ...................................................... 1.159

Beloit Walmsley Ltd, Re [2008] EWHC 1888 (Ch), [2009] 1 BCLC 584, [2008] BPIR 1445 ...................................................................... 1.59, 1.63

Beni-Felkai Mining Co Ltd, Re [1934] Ch 406, 18 TC 632, 103 LJ Ch 187, [1934] B & CR 14, [1933] All ER Rep 693, 78 Sol Jo 29, 150 LT 370 .......................... 2.433

Benzon, Re, Bower v Chetwynd [1914] 2 Ch 68, 83 LJ Ch 658, 21 Mans 8, 58 Sol Jo 430, 110 LT 926, 30 TLR 435, CA ............................................. 1.393

Berkeley Applegate (Investment Consultants) Ltd (No 2), Re (1989) 4 BCC 279, [1987] Lexis Citation 1184 ................................................. 1.716, 2.433

Berkeley Applegate (Investment Consultants) Ltd, Re, Harris v Conway [1989] Ch 32, [1988] 3 All ER 71, [1988] 3 WLR 95, [1989] BCLC 28, 132 Sol Jo 896, [1988] 26 LS Gaz R 41 ............................................................ 1.618

Berkeley Applegate (Investment Consultants) Ltd, Re (No.2) [1988] 4 BCC 279 ....... 2.182

Berkshire Homes (Northern) Ltd v Newbury Venture Capital Ltd (in liq) [2018] EWHC 938 (Ch), [2018] All ER (D) 177 (Feb) ....................................... 1.629

Bernard Sport Surfaces Ltd v Astrosoccer4U Ltd [2017] EWHC 2425 (TCC), [2017] All ER (D) 34 (Oct) ................................................... 1.660

Bernasconi v Nicholas Bennett & Co (a firm) [2000] BCC 921, [1999] Lexis Citation 3624, [2000] BPIR 8, [1999] All ER (D) 1199 ................................. 1.271

Berntsen v Tait [2015] EWCA Civ 1001, [2015] All ER (D) 114 (Oct) ............... 1.691

Berry v Child Support Agency [2016] EWHC 1418 (Ch), [2016] WTLR 1327, [2016] BPIR 1256 ............................................................. 1.393

Berry (Herbert) Associates Ltd, Re [1977] 3 All ER 729, [1977] 1 WLR 617, 52 TC 113, [1977] TR 137, 121 Sol Jo 252, L(TC) 2627; affd sub nom Berry (Herbert) Associates Ltd v IRC [1978] 1 All ER 161, [1977] 1 WLR 1437, 52 TC 113, 121 Sol Jo 829, L(TC) 2666, HL ......................................... 1.183, 1.240

Best Beat Ltd v Rossall [2006] EWHC 1494 (Comm), [2006] BPIR 1357, [2006] All ER (D) 160 (Mar) ........................................................ 1.176

Betcorp Ltd, Re (2009) 400 BR 266 ............................................. 7.15

Betts, Re, ex p Betts [1897] 1 QB 50, 66 LJQB 14, 3 Mans 287, 45 WR 98, 41 Sol Jo 50, 75 LT 292, 13 TLR 23, CA .............................................. 1.381

Beverley Group plc v McClue [1995] 2 BCLC 407, [1995] BCC 751, [1996] BPIR 25 ................................................................. 1.59, 2.909

Bevis, Re [2001] All ER (D) 09 ................................................ 1.265

Bezier Acquisitions Ltd, Re [2011] EWHC 3299 (Ch), [2012] 2 BCLC 322, [2012] Bus LR 636, [2012] BCC 219, (2012) Times, 06 January, [2011] All ER (D) 119 (Dec), CSRC vol 35 iss 23/2 ....................................................... 2.132

Bhogal v Cheema [1998] 2 EGLR 50, [1998] 29 EG 117, [1999] BPIR 13 ...... 1.235, 1.236

Bhogal v Knight [2018] EWHC 2952 (Ch), [2019] BPIR 41 .......................... 2.836

Bill Hennessey Associates Ltd, Re. See Company, a (No 0013925 of 1991), Re, ex p Rousell

Bilta (UK) Ltd (in liq) v NatWest Markets plc company [2020] EWHC 546 (Ch), [2020] All ER (D) 82 (Mar) ............................................... 1.271

Bilta (UK) Ltd (in liq) v Nazir [2012] EWHC 2163 (Ch), [2014] Ch 52, [2013] 1 All ER
375, [2013] 2 WLR 825, [2012] STC 2424, [2012] 32 LS Gaz R 19, (2012) Times,
15 October, [2012] All ER (D) 49 (Aug); affd [2013] EWCA Civ 968, [2014] Ch 52,
[2014] 1 All ER 168, [2013] 3 WLR 1167, [2014] 1 All ER (Comm) 176, [2013] STC
2298, [2014] 1 BCLC 302, [2014] 1 Lloyd's Rep 113, [2013] All ER (D) 390 (Jul); affd
[2015] UKSC 23, [2016] AC 1, [2015] 2 All ER 1083, [2015] 2 WLR 1168, [2015]
2 All ER (Comm) 281, [2015] 1 BCLC 443, (2015) Times, 06 May, [2015] All ER (D)
149 (Apr), sub nom Jetivia SA v Bilta (UK) Ltd [2015] 2 Lloyd's Rep 61, SC .......... 1.271
Biposo Pty Ltd, Re (1995) 120 FLR 399 ............................................ 1.160
Bird, Re, ex p Debtor v IRC [1962] 2 All ER 406, [1962] 1 WLR 686, 41 ATC 137, [1962]
TR 173, 106 Sol Jo 507, CA ..................................................... 1.380
Bird v Hadkinson (1999) Times, 7 April, [1999] Lexis Citation 16, [1999] BPIR 653
......................................................................... 1.492
Birdi v Price [2018] EWHC 2943 (Ch), [2019] 3 All ER 250, [2019] BPIR 306,
[2018] All ER (D) 22 (Dec) ..................................................... 1.396
Birdi Miles v Price [2019] EWHC 291 (Ch), [2019] BPIR 498, [2019] All ER (D) 120
(Feb) ........................................ 1.409, 1.415, 2.896, 2.897, 2.1008
Birdi v Price [2019] EWHC 3943 (Ch), [2019] BPIR 306 ........................... 1.410
Bisgood v Henderson's Transvaal Estates Ltd [1908] 1 Ch 743, 77 LJ Ch 486, 15 Mans
163, [1908–10] All ER Rep 744, 52 Sol Jo 412, 98 LT 809, 24 TLR 510, CA ......... 1.163
Bishopsgate Investment Management Ltd (in liqation) v Maxwell [1993] BCLC 814,
[1993] BCC 120, (1993) Times, 12 January; affd sub nom Bishopsgate Investment
Management Ltd (in liqation) v Maxwell (No 2) [1994] 1 All ER 261, [1993] BCLC
1282, [1993] BCC 120, (1993) Times, 16 February ................................. 1.270
Bishopsgate Investment Management Ltd (in provisional liq) v Maxwell [1993] Ch 1,
[1992] 2 All ER 856, [1992] 2 WLR 991, [1992] BCLC 475, [1992] 18 LS Gaz R 35,
(1992) Times, 30 January, 136 Sol Jo LB 69 .............. 1.164, 1.186, 1.300, 1.404
Blackpool Motor Car Co Ltd, Re [1901] 1 Ch 77, 70 LJ Ch 61, 8 Mans 193, 49 WR 124,
45 Sol Jo 60 .................................................................. 1.303
Blackspur Group plc, Re [2007] EWCA Civ 425, [2008] 1 BCLC 153, [2007] All ER (D)
151 (May), CSRC vol 31 iss 4/1, sub nom Eastaway v Secretary of State for Trade and
Industry [2007] BCC 550 ....................................................... 2.814
Blair Carnegie Nimmo And Gerard Anthony Friar The Joint Administrators Of
Castlebridge Plant Ltd (In Admin) Noters For An Order Under Section 176A(5) Of The
Insolvency Act 1986 [2015] CSOH 165, CtSess ......................... 1.233, 2.762
Blake ex p Coker, Re (1875) 10 LR Ch App 652 .................................... 1.399
Blavo v Law Society (acting through the Solicitors Regulation Authority) [2017] EWHC
561 (Ch), [2017] 1 WLR 4514, 167 NLJ 7745, [2017] BPIR 909, [2017] All ER (D) 03
(May) ........................................................................ 1.382
Bletchley Boat Co Ltd, Re [1974] 1 All ER 1225, [1974] 1 WLR 630, 118 Sol Jo 182
......................................................................... 1.300
Blights Builders Ltd, Re [2006] EWHC 3549 (Ch), [2007] 3 All ER 776, [2008] 1 BCLC
245, [2007] Bus LR 629, [2007] BCC 712, [2007] All ER (D) 147 (Jan) ....... 1.641, 1.721,
2.321, 2.820
Block Transfer By Kaye And Morgan, Re [2010] EWHC 692 (Ch), [2010] BPIR 602
......................................................................... 2.785
Bloom v Harms Offshore AHT 'Taurus' GmbH & Co KG [2009] EWCA Civ 632, [2010]
Ch 187, [2010] 2 WLR 349, [2009] 2 BCLC 473, [2009] Bus LR 1663, [2010] BCC
822, (2009) Times, 10 July, [2009] All ER (D) 276 (Jun) ..................... 1.617, 1.660
Blue Co London LLP, Re (formerly known as Ince & Co LLP) (in administration) [2020]
EWHC 2385 (Ch), [2021] 2 BCLC 289 ........................................... 1.679
Blue Monkey Gaming Ltd v Hudson [2014] Lexis Citation 122, [2014] All ER (D) 222
(Jun) ........................................................................ 1.684
Blue Sennar Air Pty Ltd (in liq), Re [2016] NSWSC 772 ........................... 1.235
Bluebrook Ltd, Re [2009] EWHC 2114 (Ch), [2010] 1 BCLC 338, [2010] BCC 209,
[2009] All ER (D) 101 (Aug) .................................................... 5.35
Bolkiah v KPMG (a firm) [1999] 2 AC 222, [1999] 1 All ER 517, [1999] 2 WLR 215,
[1999] 3 LRC 568, [1999] 1 BCLC 1, [1999] NLJR 16, [1999] PNLR 220, (1999)
Times, 20 April, 143 Sol Jo LB 35, [1998] All ER (D) 767, HL ..................... 1.433
Bolsover District Council v Ashfield Nominees Ltd [2010] EWCA Civ 1129,
[2011] 2 BCLC 42, [2011] Bus LR 492, [2010] RA 523, [2012] BCC 803, [2010] NLJR
1490, [2010] 43 EG 98 (CS), [2011] BPIR 7, [2010] All ER (D) 177 (Oct) ........... 1.382
Bolsover District Council v Dennis Rye Ltd [2009] EWCA Civ 372, [2009] 4 All ER 1140,
[2009] RA 202, [2010] BCC 248, (2009) Times, 19 May, [2009] BPIR 778, [2009] Bus
LR D115, [2009] All ER (D) 41 (May) ............................................ 1.178

Bolton (HL) Engineering Co Ltd, Re [1956] Ch 577, [1956] 1 All ER 799, [1956] 2 WLR 844, 100 Sol Jo 263 ...................................................... 1.176, 1.429
Bombay Talkies (S) Pte Ltd v United Overseas Bank Ltd [2015] SGCA 66 ............. 1.175
Bonus Breaks Ltd, Re [1991] BCC 546 ................................................ 1.275
Booth v Mond [2010] EWHC 1576 (Ch), [2010] BPIR 1111, [2010] All ER (D) 285 (Jul) ............................................................................. 1.428, 2.829
Borneman v Wilson (1884) 28 ChD 53, 33 WLR 141, 54 LJ Ch 631, 51 LT 728, 1 TLR 64, CA .............................................................................. 1.396
Borodzicz v Horton, Re [2015] Lexis Citation 286, [2016] BPIR 24, [2015] All ER (D) 03 (Dec) ........................................................... 1.410, 1.414, 1.415
Bostels Ltd, Re [1968] Ch 346, [1967] 3 All ER 425, [1967] 3 WLR 1359, 111 Sol Jo 372 .................................................................. 1.180, 2.331
Boston Timber Fabrications Ltd, Re [1984] BCLC 328, 1 BCC 99 ..................... 1.178
Botleigh Grange Hotel Ltd v Revenue and Customs Comrs [2018] EWCA Civ 1032, 168 NLJ 7795, [2018] All ER (D) 56 (May) .............................................. 1.178
Bottomley v Brougham [1908] 1 KB 584, 77 LJKB 311, 52 Sol Jo 225, 99 LT 111, 24 TLR 262 .................................................................. 1.185, 1.403
Bourne, Re, Kaye v Bourne [2004] EWHC 3236 (Ch), [2005] BPIR 590, [2004] All ER (D) 384 (Nov) ......................................................................... 1.388
Bourne v Charit-Email Technology Partnership LLP (in liq) [2009] EWHC 1901 (Ch), [2010] 1 BCLC 210, [2009] All ER (D) 246 (Jul) ..................................... 1.183
Bournemouth and Boscombe Athletic Football Club Co Ltd, Re [1997] Lexis Citation 3402, [1998] BPIR 183 ................................................ 1.63, 1.65, 1.364
Bowen Travel Ltd, Re [2012] EWHC 3405 (Ch), [2013] Bus LR D21, [2012] All ER (D) 63 (Dec) ............................................................................. 1.630
Bowes v Directors of Hope Life and Insurance Guarantee Co (1865) 11 HL Cas 389, 35 LJ Ch 574, 11 Jur NS 643, 13 WR 790, 11 ER 1383, 12 LT 680, [1861–73] All ER Rep Ext 1443, HL ...................................................................... 1.178
Bowkett v Fuller's United Electric Works Ltd [1923] 1 KB 160, 92 LJKB 412, [1923] B & CR 75, [1922] All ER Rep 281, 128 LT 303, CA ..................................... 1.179
Bowman Power Systems re (UK) Ltd (27 October 2004, unreported), ChD ............. 1.275
Box Valley Pty Ltd v Kidd [2006] NSWCA 26, (2006) 24 ACLC 471 ................. 1.175
Boyden v Watson [2004] BPIR 1131, CC ............................................... 1.427
Brabon, Re, Treharne v Brabon [2001] 1 BCLC 11, [2000] BCC 1171, [2000] EGCS 38, [2000] Lexis Citation 2849, [2000] BPIR 537, [2000] All ER (D) 278 ............... 1.302
Brac Rent-A-Car International Inc, Re [2003] EWHC 128 (Ch), [2003] 2 All ER 201, [2003] 1 WLR 1421, [2003] 1 BCLC 470, [2003] BCC 248, [2003] 14 LS Gaz R 28, (2003) Times, 24 February, [2003] BPIR 531, [2003] All ER (D) 98 (Feb) .. 1.59, 1.281, 6.1, 6.5
Brackland Magazines Ltd, Re [1994] 1 BCLC 190, sub nom Gamlestaden plc v Brackland Magazines Ltd [1993] BCC 194 ............................................. 1.178, 1.188
Bradley-Hole (a bankrupt), Re [1995] 4 All ER 865, [1995] 1 WLR 1097, [1995] 2 BCLC 163, [1995] 2 FLR 838, [1996] 2 FCR 259, [1995] Fam Law 673, [1995] BCC 418 ................................................................... 1.64, 1.352
Brake (t/a Stay in Style), In re [2016] EWHC 1688 (Ch), [2017] 1 WLR 343, [2017] BPIR 1357 .............................................................. 1.617, 1.629
Brake v Guy [2021] EWHC 671 (Ch) .................................................. 1.492
Brake v Swift (as trustee of the estates of Nihal Brake and Andrew Brake) [2020] EWHC 1810 (Ch), [2020] 4 WLR 113, [2020] BPIR 1287, [2020] All ER (D) 99 (Jul) ........ 1.519
Bramston v Haut [2012] EWHC 1279 (Ch), [2012] BPIR 672, [2012] All ER (D) 263 (May); revsd [2012] EWCA Civ 1637, [2013] 1 WLR 1720, [2013] BPIR 25, [2012] All ER (D) 127 (Dec) ..................................... 1.353, 1.356, 1.391, 1.414
Bramston v Riaz [2014] BPIR 42 ...................................................... 1.459
Bransfield Engineering Ltd, Re (1985) 1 BCC 99, 409 ................................. 1.180
Brassford v Patel [2007] BPIR 1049, [2007] All ER (D) 256 (Feb) .................... 1.455
Brauch (a debtor), Re, ex p Britannic Securities and Investments Ltd [1978] Ch 316, [1978] 1 All ER 1004, [1977] 3 WLR 354, 121 Sol Jo 117 ........................... 1.380
Bremner (a bankrupt), Re [1999] 1 FLR 912, [1999] Fam Law 293, [1998] Lexis Citation 2968, [1998] Lexis Citation 3574, [1999] BPIR 185 ............................... 1.455
Brereton v Nicholls [1993] BCLC 593 ................................................. 1.310
LC 82, 182 ConLR 1, [2019] BPIR 377, [2019] All ER (D) 14 (Feb)
Bresco Electrical Services Ltd (in liq) v Michael J Lonsdale (Electrical) Ltd [2020] UKSC 25, [2020] 2 BCLC 147, 190 ConLR 1, [2020] PLSCS 117, [2020] All ER (D) 87 (Jun), SC reversing [2019] EWCA Civ 27, [2019] 3 All ER 337, [2019] 1 All ER (Comm) 1051 .......................................................... 2.834, 2.852, 2.831

Brewer (as joint liquidators of ARY Digital UK Ltd) v Iqbal [2019] EWHC 182 (Ch),
[2019] 1 BCLC 487, [2019] BPIR 529, [2019] All ER (D) 49 (Feb) .................. 1.692
Brickvest Ltd, Lumineau v Berlin Hyp AG [2019] EWHC 3084 (Ch) ........... 1.629, 2.820
Bridgend Goldsmiths Ltd, Re [1995] 2 BCLC 208, [1995] BCC 226 .................. 1.160
Bridgewater Engineering Co, Re (1879) 12 ChD 181, 48 LJ Ch 389 .................. 1.516
Bridport Old Brewery Co, Re (1867) LR 2 Ch App 191, 15 WR 291, 15 LT 643, CACh
........................................................................................................ 1.293
Brilliant Independent Media Specialists Ltd, Re [2014] Lexis Citation 201, [2014] BPIR
1395, [2014] All ER (D) 111 (Oct) ......................................... 1.194, 2.997
Brillouet v Hachette Magazines Ltd, Re a Debtor (No 27 of 1990) [1991] Lexis Citation
1907, [1996] BPIR 518, CA ...................................................... 2.550
Brinds Ltd v Offshore Oil NL [1987] LRC (Comm) 772, 2 BCC 98, 916, [1985] Lexis
Citation 327, PC ................................................................. 1.178
Brisbane Puntowners' Association, Re (1893) 5 QLJ 54 ............................... 1.202
Bristol Airport plc v Powdrill [1990] Ch 744, [1990] 2 All ER 493, [1990] 2 WLR 1362,
[1990] BCLC 585, [1990] 17 LS Gaz R 28, (1990) Times, 3 January, 1 S & B AvR
IV/121, sub nom Paramount Airways Ltd, Re, Bristol Airport plc v Powdrill
[1990] BCC 130 ....................................... 1.235, 1.310, 1.353, 1.605, 1.622, 1.660
Bristol & West Building Society v Back (bankrupt) (trustee) [1998] 1 BCLC 485, [1997]
BPIR 358 ..................................................................... 1.183, 1.399
Bristol Victoria Potteries Co, Re (1872) 20 WR 569 ............................... 1.200
Britannia Heat Transfer Ltd (in admin), Re [2007] BCC 470, [2007] BPIR 1038 ........ 1.59
British and Commonwealth Holdings plc (Nos 1 and 2), Re [1992] Ch 342, [1992]
2 All ER 801, [1992] 2 WLR 931, [1992] BCLC 641, [1992] BCC 172, [1992] BCC
165, (1991) Times, 31 December; affd sub nom British and Commonwealth
Holdings plc (joint administrators) v Spicer and Oppenheim (a firm) [1993] AC 426,
[1992] 4 All ER 876, [1992] 3 WLR 853, [1993] BCLC 168, [1992] BCC 977, HL ... 1.300,
2.765
British Eagle International Airlines Ltd v Compagnie Nationale Air France [1975]
2 All ER 390, [1975] 1 WLR 758, [1975] 2 Lloyd's Rep 43, 119 Sol Jo 368, HL ..... 1.159,
2.852
Briton Medical and General Life Assurance Association, Re (1886) 32 ChD 503, 55 LJ Ch
416, 34 WR 390, 54 LT 152, 2 TLR 344 ......................................... 1.183
Brittain (trustee of the estate in bankruptcy) v Haghighat. See Haghighat (a bankrupt), Re;
Brittain (trustee of the estate in bankruptcy) v Haghighat
Brittain v Whyte [2016] BPIR 1314 ................................................ 1.418
Broadside Colours & Chemicals Ltd, Re [2012] EWHC 195 (Ch) ..................... 2.814
Broadwick Financial Services Ltd v Spencer [2002] EWCA Civ 35, [2002] 1 All ER
(Comm) 446, [2002] GCCR 4601, [2002] All ER (D) 274 (Jan) ...................... 1.308
Brook v Reed (trustee in bankruptcy of estate of Helen Brook) [2011] EWCA Civ 331,
[2011] 3 All ER 743, [2012] 1 WLR 419, [2012] 1 BCLC 379, [2011] BCC 423, [2011]
14 LS Gaz R 21, [2011] NLJR 473, [2011] 4 Costs LR 622, [2011] BPIR 583,
[2011] All ER (D) 290 (Mar) ..................................................... 1.489
Brook Martin & Co (Nominees) Ltd, Re [1993] BCLC 328 ......................... 1.300
Brooker v Advanced Industrial Technology Corp Ltd [2019] EWHC 3160 (Ch) ....... 2.758
Brooks v Armstrong [2015] EWHC 2289 (Ch), [2016] BPIR 272, [2015] All ER (D) 45
(Aug) ........................................................................... 1.272
Brooks (Joint Liquidators of Robin Hood Centre plc in liqation) v Armstrong [2016]
EWHC 2893 (Ch), [2016] All ER (D) 117 (Nov) .................................. 1.272
Brown v Beat [2002] BPIR 421, [2001] All ER (D) 275 (Dec) ...................... 1.415
Brown v City of London Corpn [1996] 1 WLR 1070, [1996] 22 EG 118, sub nom
Sobam BV, Re [1996] 1 BCLC 446, [1996] BCC 351, sub nom Sobam BV and
Satelscoop BV, Re, Brown v City of London Corpn [1996] RA 93 ................... 1.88
Brown Bear Foods Ltd, Re [2014] EWHC 1132 (Ch), [2014] All ER (D) 101 (Apr) ... 1.630
Bryanston Finance Ltd v de Vries (No 2) [1976] Ch 63, [1976] 1 All ER 25, [1976] 2 WLR
41, 119 Sol Jo 709 ....................................................... 1.178, 2.338
Buccament Bay Resort Ltd, Re (SVG) Ltd, Re [2014] EWHC 4776 (Ch), [2015] 1 BCLC
646, [2014] All ER (D) 32 (Oct) .................................................. 1.281
Buchler v Al-Midani [2005] EWHC 3183 (Ch), [2006] BPIR 867, [2005] All ER (D) 273
(Nov) ........................................................................... 1.492
Buchler v Talbot. See Leyland Daf Ltd, Re, Buchler v Talbot
Buckingham International plc (No 2), Re [1998] 2 BCLC 369, [1998] BCC 943, [1998]
Lexis Citation 2248, [1998] All ER (D) 59 ....................................... 1.159
Budge v AF Budge (Contractors) Ltd (in receivership and liq) [1995] Lexis Citation 1741,
[1997] BPIR 366, CA ............................................................. 2.530

Budniok v The Adjudicator, Insolvency Service [2017] EWHC 368 (Ch), sub nom Re
  Budniok; Budniok v Adjudicator, Insolvency Service [2017] BPIR 521, [2017] All ER
  (D) 02 (Mar) ................................................ 1.372, 1.377, 1.502, 1.553
Buildlead Ltd, Re [2003] EWHC 1981 (Ch), [2003] 4 All ER 864, [2004] 1 BCLC 83,
  [2005] BCC 133, [2003] NLJR 1309, [2003] All ER (D) 59 (Aug) ................... 2.288
Buildlead Ltd, Re [2004] EWHC 2443 (Ch), [2006] 1 BCLC 9, [2005] BCC 138, [2004]
  BPIR 1139, [2004] All ER (D) 138 (Aug) ............................................. 1.160
Buildmat (Australia) Pty Ltd (1981) 5 ACLR 459, NSWSC ......................... 1.176
Bukhari (Trustee in Bankruptcy of) v Bukhari [1998] Lexis Citation 1441, [1999] BPIR
  157 ................................................................................ 1.416
Bulmer, Re, ex p Greaves [1937] Ch 499, [1937] 1 All ER 323, 106 LJ Ch 268,
  [1936–1937] B & CR 196, 81 Sol Jo 117, 156 LT 178, 53 TLR 303, CA ....... 1.194, 1.412
Bundeszentralamt Für Steuern (being the Federal Central Tax Office of the Federal
  Republic of Germany) v Heis (as the joint special administrators of MF Global UK Ltd
  [2019] EWHC 705 (Ch), [2020] 1 BCLC 649, [2019] All ER (D) 01 (Apr) ........... 1.617
Burford Midland Properties Ltd v Marley Extrusions Ltd [1995] 1 BCLC 102,
  [1994] BCC 604, [1995] 2 EGLR 15, [1995] 30 EG 89 ........................... 1.64
Burns v Stapleton (1959) 102 CLR 97, Aust HC .................................... 1.303
Burgo group SpA v Illochroma SA (in liq): C-327/13 (2014) C-327/13,
  ECLI:EU:C:2014:2158, [2015] 1 WLR 1046, [2014] All ER (D) 114 (Sep), EUCJ ........ 6.5
Burlington Loan Management Ltd v Lomas [2017] EWCA Civ 1462, [2018] Bus LR
  508 ................................................................................ 2.850
Burnden Holdings (UK) Ltd (in liq) v Fielding [2019] EWHC 1566 (Ch), [2019] Bus LR
  2878, [2020] BPIR 1, [2019] All ER (D) 136 (Jun) ........................... 1.414, 1.175
Burnden Group Holdings Ltd v Hunt (liquidator of Burnden Holdings (UK) Ltd) [2018]
  EWHC 463 (Ch), [2018] 2 BCLC 122, [2018] All ER (D) 106 (Mar) .......... 1.129, 2.833
Burness v Supaproducts Pty Ltd [2009] FCA 893, (2009) ALR 259 .................... 1.303
Burningnight Ltd and another company (in administration) MacKenzie (as joint
  administrators of Burningnight Ltd and another company (in administration)) v
  Crowdstacker Corporate Services Ltd [2020] EWHC 2663 (Ch), [2021] 1 BCLC 557,
  [2020] All ER (D) 59 (Oct) .................................................. 1.629, 1.693
Burr v Smith [1909] 2 KB 306, 78 LJKB 889, 16 Mans 210, [1908–10] All ER Rep 443,
  53 Sol Jo 502, 101 LT 194, 25 TLR 542, CA ..................................... 1.403
Burrows (J) (Leeds) Ltd (in liqation), Re [1982] 1 WLR 1177, [1982] 2 All ER 882,
  (1982) 126 SJ 227 ................................................................. 1.164
Burton v Burton [1986] 2 FLR 419, [1986] Fam Law 330 .......................... 1.398
Burton and Deakin Ltd, Re [1977] 1 All ER 631, [1977] 1 WLR 390, 121 Sol Jo 169
  ................................................................................... 1.180
Business City Express Ltd, Re [1997] 2 BCLC 510, [1997] BCC 826 ................. 1.586
Business Dream Ltd, Re [2011] EWHC 2860 (Ch), [2013] 1 BCLC 456, [2012] BCC 115,
  [2011] 46 LS Gaz R 20, [2012] BPIR 490, [2011] All ER (D) 113 (Nov) . 1.218, 1.644, 1.743
Business Mortgage Finance 6 plc v Roundstone Technologies Ltd [2019] EWHC 2917
  (Ch), [2019] All ER (D) 94 (Nov) .................................................. 1.78
Butler v Broadhead [1975] Ch 97, [1974] 2 All ER 401, [1974] 3 WLR 27, 118 Sol Jo
  115 ........................................................................ 1.205, 2.868
Butterworth v Soutter [2000] BPIR 582 ............................................ 1.395
Butterworth, Re, ex p Russell (1882) 19 ChD 588, 51 LJ Ch 521, 30 WR 584, 46 LT 113,
  CA ................................................................................ 1.582
Byblos Bank SAL v Al-Khudhairy [1987] BCLC 232, 2 BCC 99, 549, [1987] 1 FTLR
  35 .................................................................. 1.78, 1.175, 2.142
Byers v Yacht Bull Corp [2010] EWHC 133 (Ch), [2010] 2 BCLC 169, [2010] BCC 368,
  (2010) Times, 15 February, [2010] BPIR 535, [2010] All ER (D) 217 (Feb) .. 1.298, 6.1, 6.3,
  6.8
Byford v Butler [2003] EWHC 1267 (Ch), [2004] 1 P & CR 159, [2004] 1 FLR 56, [2004]
  2 FCR 454, [2004] Fam Law 14, [2003] 24 LS Gaz R 38, [2003] 31 LS Gaz R 32,
  (2003) Times, 13 June, [2003] BPIR 1089, [2003] All ER (D) 103 (Jun) ........ 1.397, 1.455

C

C A & T Developments Ltd, Re Koon v Bowes [2019] EWHC 3455 (Ch), [2020] All ER
  (D) 18 (Jan) .............................................................. 1.618, 1.698
C & M B Holdings Ltd, Re, Hamilton (Joint Trustees in Bankruptcy of Charles Newell
  Brown) v Brown company [2016] EWHC 191 (Ch), [2017] 1 BCLC 269, [2016] All ER
  (D) 103 (Feb) ....................................... 1.134, 1.174, 1.176, 1.325
C & W Berry Ltd v Armstrong-Moakes [2007] EWHC 2101 (QB), [2008] 1 P & CR D2,
  [2007] BPIR 1199, [2007] All ER (D) 82 (Sep) ..................................... 2.843

CFL Finance Ltd v Bass [2019] EWHC 1839 (Ch), [2019] BPIR 1327 ............... 1.178
CFL Finance Ltd v Laser Trust and another [2021] EWCA Civ 228, [2021] Costs LR 231,
[2021] BPIR 487, [2021] All ER (D) 115 (Feb) .................................. 1.65, 2.550
CNM Estates (Tolworth Tower) Ltd v VeCREF I SARL [2020] EWHC 1605 (Comm),
[2020] All ER (D) 11 (Jul) ..................................................... 1.88
CSSC (Qld) Pty Ltd, Re [2018] QSC 282 .......................................... 1.176
Cabletel Installations Ltd (in liq), Re [2005] BPIR 28 ........................... 1.489
Cabvision Ltd v Feetum. See Feetum v Levy
Cade (J E) & Son Ltd, Re [1992] BCLC 213, [1991] BCC 360, [1991] Lexis Citation
2492 ......................................................................... 1.174
Cadiz Waterworks Co v Barnett (1874) LR 19 Eq 182, 44 LJ Ch 529, 23 WR 208, 31 LT
640 .......................................................................... 1.178
Cadlock (The Trustee in Bankruptcy of Anthony Ivor Dunn) v Dunn [2015] EWHC 1318
(Ch), [2015] BPIR 739, [2015] All ER (D) 115 (May) ........................... 1.455
Cadmus Management Ltd, Re (in dissolution) [2016] EWHC 330 (Ch), [2017] BPIR
317 .......................................................................... 2.1024
Cadogan v Kennett (1776) 2 Cowp 432, 98 ER 1171 ............................. 1.582
Cadwell v Jackson [2000] Lexis Citation 4563, [2001] BPIR 966, [2000] All ER (D)
1975 ............................................................ 1.441, 2.829, 2.835
Cahillane v National Asset Loan Management Ltd [2014] EWHC 1992 (Ch), [2014]
BPIR 1093 ............................................................. 2.846, 2.869
Calder (in bankruptcy), Re [2011] EWHC 3192 (Ch), [2012] BPIR 63 ............... 1.461
Caldero Trading Ltd v Beppler & Jacobson Ltd [2012] EWHC 3648 (Ch), [2012] All ER
(D) 213 (Dec) ................................................................ 1.188
Calgary and Edmonton Land Co Ltd, Re [1975] 1 All ER 1046, [1975] 1 WLR 355, 119
Sol Jo 150 ............................................................ 1.164, 1.200
Calibre Solicitors Ltd (in administration), Re, Justice Capital Ltd v Murphy
(Administrators of Calibre Solicitors Ltd) [2014] Lexis Citation 259, [2015] BPIR 435,
[2014] All ER (D) 187 (Dec) .................................................. 2.1008
Calmex Ltd v C Lila Ltd [1989] 1 All ER 485, [1989] BCLC 299, 4 BCC 761 ........ 2.814
Cambrian Mining Co, Re (1882) 48 LT 114 ....................................... 1.743
Cambridge Gas Transport Corp v Official Committee of Unsecured Creditors of
Navigator Holdings plc [2006] UKPC 26, [2007] 1 AC 508, [2006] 3 All ER 829,
[2006] 3 WLR 689, [2006] 2 All ER (Comm) 695, [2006] 3 LRC 688, [2007] 2 BCLC
141, [2006] BCC 962, [2006] All ER (D) 225 (May), PC ......................... 1.198
Campbell (a bankrupt), Re [1997] Ch 14, [1996] 2 All ER 537, [1996] 3 WLR 626
............................................................................. 1.396
Campbell v Michael Mount PPB (1996) 14 ACLC 218 ............................. 1.180
Campbell Coverings Ltd, Re [1953] Ch 488, [1953] 2 All ER 74, [1953] 2 WLR 1135, 97
Sol Jo 372, CA .............................................................. 1.164
Campbell Coverings Ltd (No 2), Re [1954] Ch 225, [1954] 1 All ER 222, [1954] 2 WLR
204, 98 Sol Jo 93 ........................................................... 1.164
Cancol Ltd, Re [1996] 1 All ER 37, [1996] 1 BCLC 100, [1995] BCC 1133, [1995] NPC
156, [1995] EGCS 146, [1996] BPIR 252 ............... 1.59, 1.61, 1.62, 1.64, 1.65, 2.909
Candey Ltd v Crumpler and another (as joint liquidators of Peak Hotels and Resorts Ltd
(in liq)) [2020] EWCA Civ 26, [2020] Bus LR 1452, [2020] Costs LR 131 ............ 2.843
Canning v Irwin Mitchell LLP [2017] EWHC 718 (Ch), [2017] BPIR 934, [2017] All ER
(D) 74 (Apr) ............................................ 1.383, 2.527, 2.530, 2.540, 2.820
Cannon Screen Entertainment Ltd, Re [1989] BCLC 660, 5 BCC 207 ... 1.175, 1.178, 2.338
Canty v Boyden [2006] EWCA Civ 194, [2006] BPIR 624 .......................... 1.414
Canty (a bankrupt) (Trustee of the estate of) v Canty [2007] EWCA Civ 241, [2007] BPIR
299, [2007] All ER (D) 63 (Mar) .............................................. 1.455
Cape Breton Co v Fenn (1881) 17 ChD 198, 50 LJ Ch 321, 29 WR 386, 44 LT 445, CA
............................................................................. 1.220
Capital Annuities Ltd, Re [1978] 3 All ER 704, [1979] 1 WLR 170, 122 Sol Jo 315
............................................................................. 1.175
Capital Fire Insurance Association, Re (1882) 21 ChD 209, 52 LJ Ch 20, 30 WR 941, 47
LT 123 ...................................................................... 1.174
Capital For Enterprise Fund A LP and v Bibby Financial Services Ltd [2015] EWHC 2593
(Ch), [2015] All ER (D) 117 (Nov) ........................................... 1.617
Capital Prime Properties plc v Worthgate Ltd (in liq) [2000] 1 BCLC 647, [2000] BCC
525, [1999] Lexis Citation 3156 ....................................... 1.235, 1.434
Capital Project Homes Pty Ltd, Re (1992) 10 ACLC 75 ........................... 1.220
Capitol Films Ltd (in administration), Ress [2010] EWHC 3223 (Ch), [2011] BPIR 334,
[2010] All ER (D) 175 (Dec) ................................................. 1.688

Cardona, Re [1997] BCC 697, [1997] Lexis Citation 2549, [1997] BPIR 604 ... 1.65, 2.927, 2.930

Care Matters Partnership Ltd, Re [2011] EWHC 2543 (Ch), [2012] 2 BCLC 311, [2011] BCC 957 , [2011] All ER (D) 100 (Oct) ........................ 1.630, 1.721, 2.820

Care People Ltd, Re [2013] EWHC 1734 (Ch), [2013] BPIR 959, [2013] All ER (D) 254 (Oct) .......... 1.632, 1.633, 2.820

Caribbean Products (Yam Importers) Ltd, Re, Tickler v Swains Packaging Ltd [1966] Ch 331, [1966] 1 All ER 181, [1966] 2 WLR 153, 8 LDAB 435, 110 Sol Jo 32, CA ...... 1.240

Carl Stuart Jackson v Stephen Cohen (2017) [2017] EWHC 3677 (Ch) .............. 2.948

Carluccio's Ltd (in administration), Re [2020] EWHC 886 (Ch), [2020] 3 All ER 291, [2020] 2 All ER (Comm) 381, [2020] 1 BCLC 717, [2020] IRLR 510, [2020] All ER (D) 81 (Apr) .......... 1.716

Carman v Bucci [2013] EWHC 2371 (Ch), [2014] 2 BCLC 49, [2013] All ER (D) 03 (Aug); affd sub nom Carman (liquidator of Casa Estates (UK) Ltd) v Bucci [2014] EWCA Civ 383, [2014] 2 BCLC 49, [2014] BPIR 523, [2014] All ER (D) 33 (Apr) .... 1.175

Carman v Cronos Group SA [2005] EWHC 2403 (Ch), [2006] BCC 451, [2005] All ER (D) 90 (Nov) .......... 1.271

Carmarthenshire Anthracite Coal and Iron Co, Re (1875) 45 LJ Ch 200, 24 WR 109 .......... 2.328

Carr v British International Helicopters Ltd (in administration) [1994] 2 BCLC 474, [1994] IRLR 212, [1994] ICR 18, [1993] BCC 855, [1993] Lexis Citation 739, EAT .......... 1.353, 1.660

Carraway Guildford (Nominee A) Ltd [2021] EWHC 1294 (Ch), [2021] BPIR 1006 .......... 1.65

Carrier Air Conditioning Pty Ltd v Kurda (1993) 11 ACSR 247, SA S Ct ............. 1.175

Carringbush Corpn Pty Ltd v ASIC [2008] FCA 474 ............................... 1.180

Carter v Hewitt [2019] EWHC 3729 (Ch) ................................... 1.455, 1.489

Carter Moore Solicitors Ltd, Re [2020] EWHC 186 (Ch), [2020] All ER (D) 61 (Feb) .......... 1.646

Carter-Knight v Peat (2000) Times, 11 August, [2000] BPIR 968 ..................... 1.388

Carton Ltd, Re [1923] All ER Rep 622, 128 LT 629, 39 TLR 194 .................. 2.1008

Cartwright v Cartwright [2002] EWCA Civ 931, [2002] 2 FLR 610, [2002] 2 FCR 760, [2002] Fam Law 735, [2002] 35 LS Gaz R 37, (2002) Times, 31 July, 146 Sol Jo LB 177, [2002] BPIR 895, [2002] All ER (D) 34 (Jul) ................................ 2.829

Cartwright v Staffordshire and Moorlands District Council [1998] BPIR 328, CA ..... 2.526

Cases of Taffs Well Ltd, Re [1992] Ch 179, [1991] 3 WLR 731, [1992] BCLC 11, [1991] BCC 582 ..................... 1.183

Cash Generator Ltd v Fortune [2018] EWHC 674 (Ch), 168 NLJ 7792, [2018] All ER (D) 09 (May) ......................... 1.153, 1.160, 2.274

Cassegrain v CTK Engineering Pty Ltd [2005] NSWSC 495 (NSW Sup Ct) ............. 1.174

Casson v Law Society [2009] EWHC 1943 (Admin), 153 Sol Jo (no 41) 29, [2010] BPIR 49, [2009] All ER (D) 223 (Oct), DC .......... 1.393

Casterbridge Properties Ltd (in liq), Re, Jeeves v Official Receiver [2002] BCC 453, [2002] BPIR 428, [2001] All ER (D) 329 (Nov) sub nom Casterbridge Properties Ltd (in liqation), Re [2003] EWHC 1731 (Ch), [2003] BCC 724, [2003] All ER (D) 47 (Jul); affd sub nom Casterbridge Properties Ltd (in liq), Re, Jeeves v Official Receiver [2003] EWCA Civ 1246, [2003] 4 All ER 1041, [2004] 1 WLR 602, [2004] 1 BCLC 96, [2003] BCC 912, [2004] BPIR 46, [2003] All ER (D) 504 (Jul) ............... 1.186, 1.300

Castle New Homes Ltd, Re [1979] 2 All ER 775, [1979] 1 WLR 1075, 123 Sol Jo 568 .......... 1.300

Catholic Publishing and Bookselling Co Ltd, Re (1864) 33 LJ Ch 352, 12 WR 538, 10 LT 79 .......... 1.178

Ceart Risk Services Ltd, Re; Bootes v Ceart Risk Services Ltd [2012] EWHC 1178 (Ch), [2012] 2 BCLC 645, [2013] Bus LR 116, [2012] BCC 592, [2012] All ER (D) 43 (May) .......... 1.643, 1.646, 2.820

CeDe Group AB v KAN Sp. z o.o.C-198/18 (30 April 2019, unreported) ...... 6.8, 6.9, 6.11

Celtic Extraction Ltd (in liq), Re; Re Bluestone Chemicals Ltd (in liq) [2001] Ch 475, [1999] 4 All ER 684, [2000] 2 WLR 991, [1999] 2 BCLC 555, [1999] 3 EGLR 21, [1999] 46 EG 187, [1999] Lexis Citation 3024, [1999] BPIR 986, [1999] All ER (D) 783, sub nom Official Receiver v Environment Agency [2000] BCC 487, (1999) Times, 5 August .......... 1.235, 1.434, 1.605

Centaur Litigation SPC (in liq) v Terrill [2015] EWHC 3420 (Ch), [2015] All ER (D) 52 (Dec) .......... 1.586

Centenary Homes Ltd v Gershinson (19 September 2017, unreported) Queen's Bench Division .......... 1.88

Centenary Homes Ltd v Liddel [2020] EWHC 1080 (QB), [2020] All ER (D) 45 (May)
.................................................................................... 1.88
Central A1 Ltd, Re [2017] EWHC 220 (Ch) ........................ 1.167, 2.266, 2.268
Centralcrest Engineering Ltd, Re; IRC v Nelmes [2000] BCC 727 ............. 1.270, 1.742
Centre Reinsurance International Co v Freakley [2006] UKHL 45, [2006] 4 All ER 1153,
[2006] 1 WLR 2863, [2006] 2 All ER (Comm) 943, [2007] 1 BCLC 85, [2007] Bus LR
284, [2007] Lloyd's Rep IR 32, [2006] BCC 971, [2006] NLJR 1613, (2006) Times,
16 October, 150 Sol Jo LB 1395, [2006] BPIR 1405, [2006] All ER (D) 121 (Oct),
HL ...................................................................................... 1.716
Centrebind Ltd, Re [1966] 3 All ER 889, [1967] 1 WLR 377, 110 Sol Jo 905 .. 1.166, 1.218
Centrifugal Butter Co Ltd, Re [1913] 1 Ch 188, 82 LJ Ch 87, 20 Mans 34, 57 Sol Jo 211,
108 LT 24 ............................................................................. 1.270
Centrovincial Estates plc v Bulk Storage Ltd (1983) 46 P & CR 393, 127 Sol Jo 443,
[1983] 2 EGLR 45, 268 Estates Gazette 59 ............................................ 1.64
Chadwick (trustee in bankruptcy of Nash) v Nash [2012] BPIR 70 ...... 1.391, 1.427, 1.452
Chamberlin v Revenue and Customs Comrs [2011] EWCA Civ 271, [2011] STC 1237,
[2011] BPIR 691, [2011] All ER (D) 250 (Mar) ..................................... 1.382
Chan v First Strategic Development cssacoration Ltd [2015] QCA 28 affirming [2014]
QSC 60 ................................................................................ 1.175
Chan Sui Ko v Appasamy [2005] EWHC 3519 (Ch), [2008] 1 BCLC 314, [2008] BPIR
18, [2005] All ER (D) 165 (Mar) ...................................................... 2.530
Changtel Solutions UK Ltd (formerly Enta Technologies Ltd) v Revenue and
Customs Comrs. See Enta Technologies Ltd v Revenue And Customs Comrs
Chapel House Colliery Co, Re (1883) 24 ChD 259, 52 LJ Ch 934, 31 WR 933, 49 LT
575, [1881–5] All ER Rep Ext 1519, CA ...................................... 1.178, 1.251
Chapper v Jackson [2012] EWHC 3897 (Ch), [2012] BPIR 257 ...................... 1.415
Charalambous v B&C Associates [2009] EWHC 2601 (Ch), [2009] 43 EG 105 (CS)
...................................................................... 1.415, 1.692
Charit-Email Technology Partnership LLP v Vermillion International Investments Ltd
[2009] EWHC 388 (Ch), [2009] BPIR 762, [2009] All ER (D) 95 (Mar) .............. 1.176
Charlton v Funding Circle Trustee Ltd [2019] EWHC 2701 (Ch), [2020] BPIR 125 ... 1.380
Charlotte Emma Ward Caulfield v Sheikh Mohamad Al Jaber (2017) [2017] EWHC 3678
(Ch) .................................................................................. 1.300
Charnley Davies Business Services Ltd, Re (1987) 3 BCC 408, [1987] Lexis Citation
1182 .................................................................................. 1.193
Charnley Davies Ltd (No 2), Re [1990] BCLC 760, [1990] BCC 605, (1990) Times,
22 June ........................................................................ 1.685, 1.692
Charterlands Goldfields Ltd Re (1909) 26 TLR 182 ................................ 1.160
Chawda (in bankruptcy), Re; Lemon v Chawda [2013] Lexis Citation 88, [2014] BPIR
49 .................................................................................... 1.455
Chen v Delaney [2010] EWCA Civ 1455, [2012] 2 EGLR 15, [2012] 27 EG 95, [2011]
BPIR 39, [2010] All ER (D) 183 (Nov) ............................................... 1.582
Cherkasov v Nogotkov (Official Receiver of Dalnyaya Step LLC (in liqation)) [2017]
EWHC 756 (Ch), [2017] 1 WLR 4264, [2017] 2 BCLC 233, [2017] All ER (D) 11
(May) ........................................................................... 7.19, 7.28
Cheshire Banking Co, Re, Duff's Executors' Case (1886) 32 ChD 301, 54 LT 558, 2 TLR
440, CA .............................................................................. 1.135
Cheshire West And Chester Borough Council Petitioners In The Administration Of
Springfield Retail Ltd For An Order In Terms Of Paragraph 74(3)(E) Of Schedule B1 To
The Insolvency Act 1986 [2010] CSOH 115, CtSess ................................. 1.691
Chesterfield Catering Co Ltd, Re [1977] Ch 373, [1976] 3 All ER 294, [1976] 3 WLR
879, 120 Sol Jo 817 .................................................................. 1.176
Chesterfield United Inc, Re; Akers v Deutsche Bank AG [2012] EWHC 244 (Ch),
[2013] 1 BCLC 709, [2012] BCC 786 ......................................... 1.300, 7.34
Chesterton v Emson [2017] EWHC 3226 (Ch), [2018] BPIR 621 ............. 1.298, 1.300
Chesterton International Group plc v Deka Immobilien Inv Gmbh [2005] EWHC 656
(Ch), [2005] BPIR 1103 .............................................................. 1.656
Chevron Furnishers Pty Ltd (receiver and manager appointed) (in liqation), Re
(1992) 10 ACLC 1537 ................................................................ 1.220
Cheyne Finance plc, Re [2007] EWHC 2402 (Ch), [2008] 2 All ER 987, [2008] 1 BCLC
741, [2008] Bus LR 1562, [2008] BCC 182, [2007] All ER (D) 37 (Dec) ............. 1.175
Chief Constable of Greater Manchester Police v Wright [2015] EWHC 3824 (Ch), [2016]
BPIR 339, [2015] All ER (D) 270 (Nov), CC ................................. 1.396, 1.417
Chigwell, SS Ltd, Re (1888) 4 TLR 308 ........................................... 1.200

Child Maintenance and Enforcement Commission v Beesley [2010] EWCA Civ 1344,
[2011] 3 All ER 233, [2011] 1 WLR 1704, [2011] PTSR 893, [2011] 1 FLR 1547,
[2011] 1 FCR 380, [2011] Fam Law 134, (2011) Times, 13 January, [2011] BPIR 608,
[2010] All ER (D) 309 (Nov) ...................................................... 1.65
Chinn (Bankruptcy), Re [2016] BPIR 346 ............................................. 1.414
Chittenden v Pepper; Re Newlands (Seaford) Educational Trust [2006] EWHC 1511
(Ch), [2006] 2 EGLR 7, [2006] 33 EG 100, [2006] 27 EG 234 (CS), [2006] BPIR 1230,
[2006] All ER (D) 299 (Jun), sub nom Newlands (Seaford) Educational Trust, Re;
Chittenden v Pepper [2007] BCC 195 ...................................... 1.59, 2.909
Chohan v Saggar [1994] 1 BCLC 706, [1994] BCC 134 ........ 1.305, 1.582, 1.583, 1.584
Choudhri v Palta [1994] 1 BCLC 184, [1992] BCC 787, (1992) Times, 14 July ......... 1.81
Christofi v Barclays Bank plc [1999] 4 All ER 437, [2000] 1 WLR 937, [1999] 2 All ER
(Comm) 417, [2000] 1 FLR 163, [2000] Fam Law 161, [1999] 29 LS Gaz R 29, (1999)
Times, 1 July, [1999] Lexis Citation 2840, [1999] BPIR 855, [1999] All ER (D) 684
............................................................................... 1.452
Christonette International Ltd, Re [1982] 3 All ER 225, [1982] 1 WLR 1245, 126 Sol Jo
561, [1982] LS Gaz R 1025 ........................................................ 1.84
Christopher Moran Holdings Ltd v Bairstow. See Park Air Services, Re, Christopher
Moran Holdings Ltd v Bairstow
Christophorus 3 Ltd, Re [2014] EWHC 1162 (Ch), [2014] All ER (D) 195 (Apr) ...... 1.630
Chu v Lau (British Virgin Islands) [2020] UKPC 24, [2020] 1 WLR 4656, [2021] 1 BCLC
1, [2020] All ER (D) 116 (Oct), PC .............................................. 1.178
Churchill v First Independent Factors and Finance Ltd. See First Independent Factors and
Finance Ltd v Churchill
Ci4net.com Inc, Re [2004] EWHC 1941 (Ch), [2005] BCC 277 ....................... 1.628
Ciro Citterio Menswear plc (in administration), Re, Ciro Citterio Menswear plc v
Thakrar [2002] All ER (D) 399 (Mar) ............................................ 1.303
Citicorp Australia v Official Trustee in Bankruptcy [1996] FCA 1115 ......... 1.691, 2.754
Citro (a bankrupt), Re [1991] Ch 142, [1990] 3 All ER 952, [1990] 3 WLR 880, [1991] 1
FLR 71, [1990] Fam Law 428, 134 Sol Jo 806, [1990] 28 LS Gaz R 43, [1990] NLJR
1073, (1990) Times, 7 June ...................................................... 1.455
City and County Bank, Re (1875) LR 10 Ch App 470, 44 LJ Ch 716, 23 WR 936, 33 LT
344, CACh ...................................................................... 1.251
City and County Investment Co Ltd, Re (1877) 25 WR 342 ................... 1.160, 1.193
City Electrical Factors Ltd v Hardingham [1996] Lexis Citation 2794, [1996] BPIR 541
............................................................................... 2.530
City Life Assurance Co Ltd, Re, Grandfield's Case, Stephenson's Case [1926] Ch 191,
95 LJ Ch 65, [1925] B & CR 233, [1925] All ER Rep 453, 70 Sol Jo 108, 134 LT 207,
42 TLR 45, CA .................................................................. 2.852
City of Glasgow Bank, Re, Buchan's Case (1879) 4 App Cas 549, 583, HL ............ 1.135
Civil proceedings concerning MG Probud Gdynia sp z o o: C-444/07 (2010) C-444/07,
ECLI:EU:C:2010:24, [2010] ECR I-417, [2010] BCC 453, [2010] All ER (D) 17 (Feb),
EUCJ .......................................................................... 6.9, 6.21
Civil Service and General Stores, Re [1884] WN 158 ............................... 1.160
Clark (bankrupt), Re, ex p trustee of property of bankrupt v Texaco Ltd [1975] 1 All ER
453, [1975] 1 WLR 559, 118 Sol Jo 862 ........................................... 1.622
Clark v Clark Construction Initiatives (2008) UKEAT/0225/07, [2008] IRLR 364, [2008]
ICR 635, [2009] BCC 665, [2008] All ER (D) 440 (Feb), EAT; affd sub nom Clark v
Clark Construction Initiatives Ltd [2008] EWCA Civ 1446, [2009] ICR 718,
[2008] All ER (D) 191 (Dec) .................................................... 1.756
Clarke v Birkin [2006] EWHC 340 (Ch), [2006] BPIR 632, [2006] All ER (D) 56 (Jan)
............................................................................... 1.388
Clarke v Cognita Schools Ltd (t/a Hydesville Tower School) [2015] EWHC 932 (Ch),
[2016] 1 All ER 477, [2015] 1 WLR 3776, [2015] 2 All ER (Comm) 663, [2015] BPIR
444, [2015] All ER (D) 17 (Apr) ................................................. 2.530
Clarke v Harlowe [2005] EWHC 3062 (Ch), [2006] 1 P & CR D31, [2007] 1 FLR 1,
[2007] 3 FCR 726, [2006] Fam Law 846, [2006] BPIR 636, HC ..................... 1.455
Clarkson v Clarkson [1994] BCC 921, [1994] Lexis Citation 3545, [1996] BPIR 37, CA
............................................................................... 1.396
Claughton v Charalamabous [1999] 1 FLR 740, [1999] Fam Law 205, [1998] BPIR
558 ........................................................................... 1.455
Claybridge Shipping Co SA, Re [1997] 1 BCLC 572 ............................... 1.178
Clements v Udal [2002] 2 BCLC 606, [2001] BCC 658, (2000) Times, 7 July, [2001] BPIR
454 .............................................................. 1.160, 1.489, 1.720
Closegate Hotel Development (Durham) Ltd v McLean [2013] EWHC 3237 (Ch), [2014]
Bus LR 405, [2013] All ER (D) 308 (Oct) ....................................... 1.680

Cloverbay Ltd (joint administrators) v Bank of Credit and Commerce International SA [1991] Ch 90, [1991] 1 All ER 894, [1990] 3 WLR 574, [1991] BCLC 135, (1990) Times, 16 April ............................................................................ 1.300
Cloverbay Ltd, Re [1989] BCLC 724, 5 BCC 732 ........................... 1.300, 2.767
Club Superstores Ltd re (1993) 10 ACSR 730 ................................... 1.160
Clydesdale Financial Services Ltd v Smailes (No 1) [2009] EWHC 1745 (Ch), [2011] 2 BCLC 405, [2009] BCC 810, [2010] BPIR 62 ................ 1.160, 1.705, 2.199
Clydesdale Financial Services Ltd v Smailes (No 2) [2009] EWHC 3190 (Ch), [2011] 2 BCLC 405, [2010] BPIR 77 ............................................... 1.582
Coal Consumers' Association, Re (1876) 4 ChD 625, 46 LJ Ch 501, 25 WR 300, 35 LT 729 ....................................................................... 1.181, 1.516
Cockerton (Deborah Ann) (trustee in bankruptcy of saheeda begum) v Begum (Saheeda) [2015] EWHC 2042 (Ch) ...................................................... 1.455
Cohen (A Bankrupt), Re, ex p Bankrupt v IRC [1950] 2 All ER 36, 66 (pt 1) TLR 1207, CA .......................................................................... 2.814
Cohen (A Bankrupt), Re [1961] Ch 246, [1961] 1 All ER 646, [1961] 2 WLR 237, 105 Sol Jo 206, CA ................................................................... 1.427
Cohen v Selby [2001] 1 BCLC 176, [2000] Lexis Citation 2340, [2000] All ER (D) 1972 ..................................................................... 1.270, 1.272
Coilcolor Ltd v Camtrex Ltd [2015] EWHC 3202 (Ch), [2015] 6 Costs LO 753, [2016] BPIR 1129, [2015] All ER (D) 90 (Nov) ..................................... 1.178, 2.338
Collier v P & M J Wright (Holdings) Ltd [2007] EWCA Civ 1329, [2008] 1 WLR 643, [2007] BPIR 1452, [2007] All ER (D) 233 (Dec), CSRC vol 31 iss 25/1 .............. 2.530
Collins & Aikman Europe SA, Re [2006] EWHC 1343 (Ch), [2007] 1 BCLC 182, [2006] BCC 861, [2006] All ER (D) 80 (Jun) ................ 1.682, 1.683, 1.685, 6.5, 6.36
Colorado Products Pty Ltd [2013] NSWSC 1613 ................................. 1.188
Colt Telecom Group plc, Re [2002] EWHC 2815 (Ch), [2003] BPIR 324, [2002] All ER (D) 347 (Dec) ..................................................... 1.627, 1.628
Commercial and Industrial Insulations Ltd, Re [1986] BCLC 191, 2 BCC 98, 901 ..... 2.331
Commercial Bank of South Australia, Re (1886) 33 ChD 174, 55 LJ Ch 670, 55 LT 609, 2 TLR 714 .................................................................. 1.281
Comet Group Ltd (in liq), Re [2014] EWHC 3477 (Ch), [2015] BPIR 1, [2014] All ER (D) 336 (Oct) ..................................................... 1.300, 2.763
Comet Group Ltd, Re, Carton-Kelly (as additional liquidator of CGL Realisations Ltd) (formerly Comet Group Ltd) (in liq)) v Edwards (as liquidator of CGL Realisations Ltd) (formerly Comet Group Ltd) (in liq)) [2020] EWHC 131 (Ch), 170 NLJ 7875, [2020] All ER (D) 141 (Jan) ................................................... 2.791
Comite d'entreprise de Nortel networks SA v Rogeau: C-649/13 (2015) C-649/13, ECLI:EU:C:2015:384, [2016] QB 109, [2015] 3 WLR 1275, [2015] 2 BCLC 349, [2015] All ER (D) 143 (Jun), EUCJ ....................................... 6.5, 6.34
Comr of Corporate Affairs v Bracht (1989) 7 ACLC 40 ........................... 1.276
Comr of Taxation v Linter Australia Ltd (in liqation) [2005] HCA 20 ................ 1.198
Commonwealth v Hendon Industrial Park Pty Ltd (1995) 17 ACSR 358 ............. 1.188
Commonwealth Bank of Australia v Garuda Aviation Pty Ltd [2013] WASCA 61 ..... 1.175
Compania Merabello San Nicholas SA, Re [1973] Ch 75, [1972] 3 All ER 448, [1972] 3 WLR 471, [1972] 2 Lloyd's Rep 268, 116 Sol Jo 631 ............................ 1.281
Company, a, Re [1894] 2 Ch 349, 63 LJ Ch 565, 42 WR 585, 71 LT 15 ............. 1.176
Company (application to restrain advertisement), a, Re [2020] EWHC 1551 (Ch), [2020] 2 BCLC 307, [2020] BPIR 1100, [2020] All ER (D) 88 (Jun) ...... 1.175, 1.176, 5.41
Company, a (No 002567 of 1982), Re [1983] 2 All ER 854, [1983] 1 WLR 927, [1983] BCLC 151, 127 Sol Jo 508, [1983] LS Gaz R 2133 ......................... 1.178
Company, a (No 001573 of 1983), Re [1983] BCLC 492, 1 BCC 937 ................ 1.178
Company, a, Re [1984] 3 All ER 78, [1984] 1 WLR 1090, [1984] BCLC 322, 128 Sol Jo 580 ......................................................................... 1.175
Company, a, Re [1985] BCLC 37 ................................................. 1.175
Company, a, Re [1986] BCLC 362, sub nom Company , a (No 007623 of 1984), Re 2 BCC 99 ................................................. 1.175, 1.300, 2.324
Company, a (No 003843 of 1986), Re [1987] BCLC 562, 3 BCC 624 ................ 1.178
Company, a (No 007523 of 1986), Re [1987] BCLC 2001 .......................... 1.180
Company, a (No 00175 of 1987), Re [1987] BCLC 467, 3 BCC 124 ................. 1.630
Company, a (No 003318 of 1987), Re (1987) 3 BCC 564 ........................... 1.300
Company, a (No 00359 of 1987), Re [1988] Ch 210, [1987] 3 WLR 339, 3 BCC 160, 131 Sol Jo 938, [1987] LS Gaz R 1811, sub nom International Westminster Bank plc v Okeanos Maritime Corpn [1987] 3 All ER 137, [1988] LRC (Comm) 703, [1987] BCLC 450 .................................................... 1.281
Company, a (No 001992 of 1988), Re [1989] BCLC 9, 4 BCC 451 .................. 2.338

Company, a 001363 of 1988,Re (1989) 5 BCC 18 .................................... 1.174
Company, a (No 001448 of 1989), Re [1989] BCLC 715, 5 BCC 706 ................ 2.338
Company, a (No 008790 of 1990), Re [1991] BCLC 561, [1992] BCC 11 ............ 1.175
Company, a (No 0010656 of 1990), Re [1991] BCLC 464 .................... 1.178, 2.320
Company, a (No 004055 of 1991), Re [1991] 1 WLR 1003, [1991] BCLC 865 ....... 1.180
Company, a (No 0012209 of 1991), Re [1992] 2 All ER 797, [1992] 1 WLR 351,
    [1992] BCLC 865 ......................................................... 1.178, 2.338
Company, a (No 001127 of 1992), Re [1992] BCC 477, [1992] Lexis Citation 3071
    ................................................................................ 2.324
Company, a (No 006273 of 1992), Re [1993] BCLC 131, [1992] BCC 794 ........... 1.175
Company, a (No 004539 of 1993), Re [1995] 1 BCLC 459, [1995] BCC 116 .. 2.835, 2.911
Company, a (No 005374 of 1993), Re [1993] BCC 734, [1993] Lexis Citation 3375
    ................................................................................ 1.300
Company, a (No 007946 of 1993), Re [1994] Ch 198, [1994] 1 All ER 1007, [1994] 2
    WLR 438, [1994] 1 BCLC 565, [1994] 9 LS Gaz R 39, (1993) Times, 18 November
    ................................................. 1.127, 1.169, 1.177, 1.281, 2.324
Company, a (No 007816 of 1994), Re [1997] 2 BCLC 685 ......................... 1.177
Company, a (No 007923 of 1994), Re [1995] 1 WLR 953, [1995] 1 BCLC 440,
    [1995] BCC 634, [1995] 08 LS Gaz R 39, (1995) Times, 2 February .... 1.177, 2.324, 2.338
Company, a (No 007936 of 1994), Re [1995] BCC 705 ............................ 1.176
Company, a (No 006798 of 1995), Re [1996] 2 All ER 417, [1996] 1 WLR 491,
    [1996] 2 BCLC 48, 49 ConLR 39 .................................... 1.175, 1.178, 2.320
Company, a (No 004415 of 1996), Re [1997] 1 BCLC 479 ......................... 1.174
Company, a (No 006685 of 1996), Re [1997] 1 BCLC 639, [1997] BCC 830 ......... 1.178
Company, a (No 007020 of 1996), Re [1998] 2 BCLC 54 .................... 2.324, 2.346
Company, a (No 007070 of 1996), Re [1997] 2 BCLC 139 ................... 1.177, 1.188
Company, a (No 004601 of 1997), Re [1998] 2 BCLC 111 ......................... 1.178
Company, a (No 003689 of 1998), Re (1998) The Times, October 7, ChD .......... 1.175
Company, a (No 5669 of 1998), Re [2000] 1 BCLC 427, [1999] Lexis Citation 3632,
    [1999] All ER (D) 1065, sub nom Secretary of State for Trade and Industry v Travel
    Time (UK) Ltd [2000] BCC 792 .............................................. 1.177
Company, a (No 005174 of 1999), Re [2000] 1 WLR 502, [2000] 1 BCLC 593, [2000]
    ICR 263, [2000] BCC 698, (1999) Times, 2 November, [1999] Lexis Citation 3573,
    [1999] All ER (D) 982 .................................................... 1.88, 2.136
Company, a (No 003624 of 2002), Re [2002] All ER (D) 274 ..................... 1.178
Company, a (No 2507 of 2003), Re [2003] EWHC 1484 (Ch), [2003] 2 BCLC 346
    ................................................................................ 1.178
Company, a (No 160 of 2004), Re [2004] EWHC 380 (Ch), [2004] All ER (D) 352
    (Feb) ....................................................................... 1.178
Company, a (664 and 665 of 2014), Re [2014] EWHC 3925 (Ch), [2014] All ER (D) 270
    (Nov) ....................................................................... 1.177
Company, a, Re (13 November 2014, unreported), ChD .......................... 2.338
Company, a, Re (13 July 2016, unreported), ChD .............................. 2.338
Company, a (No 008654 of 2017), Re [2018] EWHC 1143 (Ch), [2018] All ER (D) 111
    (May) ....................................................................... 1.178
Company, a (No 005009 of 1987), Re, ex p Copp [1989] BCLC 13, 4 BCC 424 ...... 1.326
Company, a (No 00962 of 1991), Re, ex p Electrical Engineering Contracts (London) Ltd
    [1992] BCLC 248 ............................................................ 2.338
Company, a (No 001029 of 1990), Re, ex p F Ltd [1991] BCLC 567 ............... 2.321
Company, a (No 004502 of 1988), Re, ex p Johnson [1992] BCLC 701, [1991] BCC
    234 ......................................................................... 2.338
Company, a (No 003102 of 1991), Re, ex p Nyckeln Finance Co Ltd [1991] BCLC 539
    ......................................................................... 1.188, 1.281
Company, a (No 0013925 of 1991), Re, ex p Rousell [1992] BCLC 562, sub nom Re Bill
    Hennessey Associates Ltd [1992] BCC 386 .................................... 2.324
Condon, Re, ex p James (1874) LR 9 Ch App 609, 43 LJ Bcy 107, 22 WR 937,
    [1874–80] All ER Rep 388, 30 LT 773, CACh ................... 1.79, 1.491, 1.622
Condon v Rogers (1995) 120 FLR 399 ......................................... 1.160
Condor Insurance Co Ltd, Re (2010) 601 F 3d 319 ...................... 7.34, 7.36
Conegrade Ltd, Re [2002] EWHC 2411 (Ch), [2003] BPIR 358, [2002] All ER (D) 19
    (Nov) ....................................................................... 1.303
Coniston Hotel (Kent) LLP (in liq), Re [2013] EWHC 93 (Ch), [2013] 2 BCLC 405,
    [2013] All ER (D) 36 (Feb); affd [2013] All ER (D) 14 (Oct) ............ 1.691, 1.692
Connock v Fantozzi [2011] EWHC 15 (Ch), [2011] 1 WLR 2049, [2011] 1 BCLC 606,
    [2011] Bus LR 926, [2011] BCC 579, [2011] NLJR 138, [2011] BPIR 308,
    [2011] All ER (D) 104 (Jan) ................................................ 6.38

Consolidated Finance Ltd v Collins (Office of Fair Trading intervening) [2013] EWCA Civ 475, [2013] BPIR 543, [2013] GCCR 11720, [2013] All ER (D) 111 (May) ....... 1.395

Consolidated Finance Ltd v Cook [2010] EWCA Civ 369, [2010] BPIR 1331, [2010] All ER (D) 47 (Aug) ..................... 1.395

Consolidated Finance Ltd v Hunter [2010] BPIR 1322, CC ......................... 1.395

Constantinidis v JGL Trading Pty Ltd (1995) 17 ACSR 625 ....................... 1.188

Consumer and Industrial Press Ltd (No 2), Re (1987) 4 BCC 72, [1987] Lexis Citation 1192 ..................... 1.685

Consumer and Industrial Press Ltd, Re [1988] BCLC 177, 4 BCC 68, 11 LDAB 33 ... 1.628, 1.630

Continental Assurance Co of London (in liqation) (No 2), Re [1998] 1 BCLC 583 .... 2.820

Continental Assurance Co of London plc (in liq), Re [2007] 2 BCLC 287, [2001] Lexis Citation 2161, [2001] BPIR 733, [2001] All ER (D) 229 (Apr) ...................... 1.272

Contract Corpn, Re, Gooch's Case (1872) LR 7 Ch App 207, 41 LJ Ch 338, 20 WR 345, 26 LT 177, CACh ..................... 2.396

Cook, Re [1999] BPIR 881 ..................... 1.67, 1.414

Cook v Mortgage Debenture Ltd [2016] EWCA Civ 103, [2016] 3 All ER 975, [2016] 1 WLR 3048, [2016] 2 All ER (Comm) 296, [2016] 1 BCLC 479, 166 NLJ 7690, (2016) Times, 11 April, [2016] BPIR 565, [2016] All ER (D) 247 (Feb) ..................... 1.183

Cooke v Dunbar Assets plc [2016] EWHC 579 (Ch), [2016] BPIR 576, [2016] All ER (D) 49 (Apr) ..................... 1.381, 1.386, 1.455, 1.502

Cooke v Dunbar Assets plc [2016] EWHC 1888 (Ch), [2016] Bus LR 960, [2016] 4 Costs LR 781, [2016] BPIR 1339, [2016] All ER (D) 07 (Aug) ..................... 1.502, 2.690

Cooper, Re [2005] NICh 1, [2006] NI 103, [2007] BPIR 1206 ..................... 1.489

Cooper (Gerald) Chemicals Ltd, Re [1978] Ch 262, [1978] 2 All ER 49, [1978] 2 WLR 866, 121 Sol Jo 848 ..................... 1.271

Cooper v Official Receiver [2002] EWHC 1970 (Ch), [2003] BPIR 55 ..................... 1.379

Cooper v PRG Powerhouse Ltd (in creditors' voluntary liq) [2008] EWHC 498 (Ch), [2008] 2 All ER (Comm) 964, [2008] 2 P & CR D9, [2008] BCC 588, [2008] BPIR 492, [2008] All ER (D) 211 (Mar) ..................... 1.164, 1.219

Co-operative Bank plc v Phillips [2017] EWHC 1320 (Ch), 167 NLJ 7750, [2017] BPIR 1156, [2017] All ER (D) 50 (Jun) ..................... 1.64

Copeland & Craddock Ltd, Re [1997] BCC 294, CA ..................... 1.174

Corbenstoke Ltd, Re [1989] BCLC 496, 5 BCC 197 ..................... 2.324

Corbenstoke Ltd (No 2), Re [1990] BCLC 60, 5 BCC 767 ..................... 1.160

Corben v What Music Holdings Ltd (16 July 2003, unreported) (EWHC, Hart J) ..... 1.178

Cordova Union Gold Co, Re [1891] 2 Ch 580, 60 LJ Ch 701, 39 WR 536, 64 LT 772 ..................... 1.129

Core VCT plc (in liqation) Pagden (as liquidators of Core VCT plc, Core VCT IV plc and Core VCT V plc) v Fry [2019] EWHC 540 (Ch), [2019] BPIR 972, [2019] All ER (D) 102 (Mar) ..................... 1.160

Coregrange Ltd, Re [1984] BCLC 453 ..................... 1.183, 1.399

Corfe Joinery Ltd, Re. See Wills v Corfe Joinery Ltd (in liqation)

Cork v Rawlins [2001] EWCA Civ 202, [2001] Ch 792, [2001] 4 All ER 50, [2001] 3 WLR 300, (2001) Times, 15 March, [2001] BPIR 222, [2001] All ER (D) 39 (Feb) .... 1.396

Corke v Corke and Official Trustee in Bankruptcy (1994) 121 ALR 320 ............. 1.397

Cornelius v Casson [2008] Lexis Citation 1078, [2008] BPIR 504, [2008] All ER (D) 200 (Mar) ..................... 1.64, 1.65

Cornercare Ltd, Re [2010] EWHC 893 (Ch), [2010] BCC 592, [2010] All ER (D) 243 (May) ..................... 1.643, 1.645, 1.660, 2.130

Cornhill Insurance plc v Improvement Services Ltd [1986] 1 WLR 114, [1986] BCLC 26, 2 BCC 98, 942, 129 Sol Jo 828 ..................... 1.175, 5.41

Corporate Affairs Commission v ASC Timber Pty Ltd (1998) 16 ACLC 1642 ......... 1.741

Corporate Affairs Commission v Harvey (1979) 4 ACLR 259 ..................... 2.396

Corporate Jet Realisations Ltd, Re [2015] BCC 625 ..................... 2.806

Corporate Jet Realisations Ltd (In Liq), Re [2015] EWHC 221 (Ch), [2015] 2 BCLC 95, [2015] All ER (D) 203 (Feb) ..................... 1.299, 1.300

Corpn of West Kent and Ashford College (a further education corpn in education administration), Re [2020] EWHC 907 (Ch) ..................... 1.59

Cosco Bulk Carrier Co Ltd v Armada Shipping SA [2011] EWHC 216 (Ch), [2011] 2 All ER (Comm) 481, [2011] BPIR 626, [2011] All ER (D) 166 (Feb) ..................... 7.33

Coulon Sanderson and Ward Ltd v Ward (1985) 2 BCC 99, 207, [1986] PCC 57, [1985] Lexis Citation 1669, CA ..................... 2.338

Coulter v Chief of Dorset Police [2005] EWCA Civ 1113, [2006] BPIR 10, [2005] All ER (D) 155 (Jul) ..................... 2.550

County Bookshops Ltd v Grove [2002] EWHC 1160 (Ch), [2003] 1 BCLC 479, [2002] BPIR 772, [2002] BPIR 770, [2002] All ER (D) 65 (Jun) ............................ 1.59

Courts plc (in liq), Re [2008] EWHC 2339 (Ch), [2009] 2 All ER 402, [2009] 1 WLR 1499, [2009] 2 BCLC 363, [2009] Bus LR 741, [2008] BCC 917, [2008] All ER (D) 83 (Oct) ......................................................... 1.159, 1.233

Coutts & Co v Clarke [2002] EWCA Civ 943, [2002] BPIR 916, [2002] All ER (D) 98 (Jun) ......................................................................... 1.240

Coutts & Co v Passey [2007] BPIR 323 ...................................... 1.65, 1.515

Coutts & Co v Stock [2000] 2 All ER 56, [2000] 1 WLR 906, [2000] 1 BCLC 183, [2000] Lloyd's Rep Bank 14, [2000] BCC 247, (1999) Times, 30 November, [1999] Lexis Citation 3679, 144 Sol Jo LB 24, [2000] BPIR 400, [1999] All ER (D) 1312 .......... 1.180

Cover Europe Ltd, Re [2002] EWHC 861 (Ch), [2002] 2 BCLC 61, [2002] BPIR 931, [2002] All ER (D) 359 (Feb) ...................................................... 2.756

Cowey v Insol Funding Ltd [2012] EWHC 2421 (Ch), [2012] BPIR 958, [2012] All ER (D) 15 (Sep) ......................................................................... 1.396

Cowra Processors Pty Ltd, In re (1995) 15 ACLC 1582 ..................... 1.154, 2.940

Coyne v DRC Distribution Ltd [2008] EWCA Civ 488, [2008] BCC 612, [2008] BPIR 1247, [2008] All ER (D) 193 (May) .............................. 1.698, 1.704, 1.705

Craig v Humberclyde Industrial Finance Group Ltd [1999] 1 WLR 129, [1998] 2 BCLC 526, (1998) Times, 15 July, [1998] Lexis Citation 2037, [1999] BPIR 53 ....... 1.220, 1.414

Cranley Mansions Ltd, Re, Saigol v Goldstein [1994] 1 WLR 1610, [1995] 1 BCLC 290, [1994] BCC 576, [1995] 03 LS Gaz R 37, (1994) Times, 23 June ..................... 2.909

Creative Handbook Ltd, Re [1985] BCLC 1, 128 Sol Jo 645 ...................... 2.331

Credit Lucky Ltd v National Crime Agency [2014] EWHC 83 (Ch), [2014] All ER (D) 235 (Jan) ......................................................................... 2.814

Creditnet Ltd, Re [1996] 1 WLR 1291, [1996] 2 BCLC 133, [1996] NLJR 916, (1996) Times, 22 May; affd sub nom Austintel Ltd, Ex p [1997] 1 WLR 616, [1997] 1 BCLC 233, [1997] BCC 362, [1996] 43 LS Gaz R 26, (1996) Times, 11 November, 140 Sol Jo LB 254, [2000] BPIR 223 .................................................... 2.791

Crigglestone Coal Co Ltd, Re [1906] 2 Ch 327, 75 LJ Ch 662, 13 Mans 233, [1904–7] All ER Rep 894, 95 LT 510, 22 TLR 585, CA ...................... 1.178, 2.550

Croftbell Ltd, Re [1990] BCLC 844, [1990] BCC 781 ........................... 1.73, 1.631

Croshaw v Lyndhurst Ship Co [1897] 2 Ch 154, 66 LJ Ch 576, 45 WR 570, 41 Sol Jo 508, 76 LT 553 ......................................................................... 1.181

Crouch, Re [2007] NSWSC 1055, (2007) 214 FLR 244 ........................... 1.742

Crystal Reef Gold Mining Co, Re [1892] 1 Ch 408, 61 LJ Ch 208, 40 WR 235, 36 Sol Jo 217, 66 LT 111 ......................................................................... 1.176

Cuckmere Brick Co Ltd v Mutual Finance Ltd [1971] Ch 949, [1971] 2 All ER 633, [1971] 2 WLR 1207, 22 P & CR 624, 9 LDAB 212, 115 Sol Jo 288, [1971] RVR 126, 218 EG 1571 ......................................................................... 1.88

Cullen (R A) Ltd v Nottingham Health Authority (1986) 2 BCC 99, 368, [1986] Lexis Citation 1937, CA ...................................................................... 2.852

Cullinane V Comrs Of Inland Revenue [2000] Bpir 996 ..................... 1.382, 2.530

Cully v Parsons [1923] 2 Ch 512, 93 LJ Ch 42, 67 Sol Jo 750, 130 LT 178 ....... 1.71, 1.81

Cupit, Re [1996] BPIR 560n, CA ................................................ 1.61

Cursitan v Keenan [2011] NICh 23 ............................................. 1.698

Curistan v Keenan [2013] NICh 13 ............................................. 1.691

Currie v Consolidated Kent Collieries Corpn Ltd [1906] 1 KB 134, 75 LJKB 199, 13 Mans 61, 94 LT 148, CA ............................................... 1.164

Curtis (D H) (Builders) Ltd, Re [1978] Ch 162, [1978] 2 All ER 183, [1978] 2 WLR 28, 121 Sol Jo 707 ......................................................................... 2.852

Cushla Ltd, Re [1979] 3 All ER 415, [1979] STC 615 .......................... 2.852

Customs and Excise Comrs v Anglo Overseas Ltd [2004] EWHC 2198 (Ch), [2005] BPIR 137, [2004] All ER (D) 30 (Oct) ..................................................... 1.178

Cuthbertson & Richards Sawmills Pty Ltd v Thomas (1998) 28 ACSR 310 .......... 1.175


**D**

D & D Marketing (UK) Ltd, Re [2002] EWHC 660 (Ch), [2003] BPIR 539 .......... 1.382

DAP Holding NV, Re [2005] EWHC 2092 (Ch), [2006] BCC 48 ..................... 6.2

DFC Group AS (Societe) v Calli Invest (Societes) Cour de Cassation (France), 28 June 2016 ,[2017] IL Pr 3 ........................................................ 6.1

DHC Assets Ltd v Toon [2015] NZHC 140 ....................................... 1.183

DKG Contractors Ltd, Re [1990] BCC 903 ........................... 1.270, 1.272, 1.303

DKLL Solicitors, Re [2007] EWHC 2067 (Ch), [2008] 1 BCLC 112, [2007] BCC 908, [2007] All ER (D) 68 (Mar) ............................... 1.617, 1.630, 1.671

DPR Futures Ltd, Re [1989] 1 WLR 778, [1989] BCLC 634, 5 BCC 603, 133 Sol Jo 977, (1989) Times, 9 March ................................................................ 1.207
DSG Holdings Australia Pty Ltd v Helenic Pty Ltd [2014] NSWCA 96 ............... 1.183
DTX Australia Ltd, Re [1987] 5 ACLC 343 ........................................ 1.178
DW v CG [2016] EWHC 2965 (Fam), [2017] 4 WLR 80 ............................. 2.842
Daewoo Motor Co Ltd, Re [2005] EWHC 2799 (Ch), [2006] BPIR 415, [2005] All ER (D) 187 (Nov) ................................................................. 1.586
Dairy Farmers of Britain Ltd, Re [2009] EWHC 1389 (Ch), [2010] Ch 63, [2009] 4 All ER 241, [2010] 2 WLR 311, [2010] 1 BCLC 637, [2009] Bus LR 1627, [2010] BCC 637, [2009] All ER (D) 205 (Jun) ................................. 1.72, 1.728
Daisytek-ISA Ltd, Re [2003] BCC 562, [2004] BPIR 30, [2003] All ER (D) 312 (Jul) ................................................................. 1.59, 1.281, 6.5, 6.35
Dallhold Estates (UK) Pty Ltd, Re [1992] BCLC 621, [1992] BCC 394 ............... 1.586
Dallhold Investments Pty Ltd, Re (1994) 53 FCR 339 ........................... 1.300
Dalnyaya Step LLC (in liqation) [2017] EWHC 756 (Ch), [2017] 1 WLR 4264, [2017] 2 BCLC 233, [2017] All ER (D) 11 (May) ............................. 7.19, 7.28
Dalnyaya Step LLC (in liqation) [2017] EWHC 3153 (Ch), [2018] Bus LR 789, [2018] BPIR 378, [2017] All ER (D) 28 (Dec) ......................................... 7.19
Daltel Europe Ltd (in liq) v Makki [2004] EWHC 726 (Ch), [2005] 1 BCLC 594, [2004] All ER (D) 546 (Mar) ......................................................... 1.300
Dalton (a bankrupt), Re, ex p Herrington and Carmichael (a firm) v Trustee [1963] Ch 336, [1962] 2 All ER 499, [1962] 3 WLR 140, 8 LDAB 70, 106 Sol Jo 510, DC ...... 1.398
Damon v Widney plc [2002] BPIR 465 ............................................ 1.303
Dana (UK) Ltd, Re [1999] 2 BCLC 239 .......................................... 1.670
Danka Business Systems plc [2012] EWHC 579 (Ch), [2012] All ER (D) 146 (Mar); affd sub nom Danka Business Systems plc (in members' voluntary liq),[2013] EWCA Civ 92, [2013] Ch 506, [2013] 2 WLR 1398, [2013] 2 BCLC 313, [2013] BPIR 432, [2013] All ER (D) 217 (Feb) ......................................................... 2.841
Darjan Estate Co plc v Hurley [2012] EWHC 189 (Ch), [2012] 1 WLR 1782, [2012] BPIR 1021 ................................................................. 1.382
Darrell v Miller [2003] EWHC 2811 (Ch), [2004] BPIR 470, [2003] All ER (D) 123 (Nov) ................................................................. 1.630
Darty Holdings SAS (as successor to Kesa International Ltd) v Carton-Kelly (as liquidator of CGL Realisations Ltd (in liq) [2021] EWHC 1018 (Ch), [2021] BPIR 779, [2021] All ER (D) 85 (Apr) ......................................................... 1.604
Data Power Systems Ltd v Safehosts (London) Ltd [2013] EWHC 2479 (Ch), [2013] All ER (D) 15 (Sep) ................................................................. 1.630
Davey v Money [2018] EWHC 766 (Ch) .......... 1.617, 1.620, 1.666, 1.691, 1.692, 2.164
Davidson v Stanley [2004] EWHC 2595 (Ch), [2005] BPIR 279, [2004] All ER (D) 441 (Oct) ................................................................. 1.60
Davies v Directloans Ltd [1986] 2 All ER 783, [1986] 1 WLR 823, [1986] BTLC 277, 130 Sol Jo 392, [1986] LS Gaz R 1810, [1999] GCCR 795 ......................... 1.308, 1.469
Davis (S) & Co Ltd, Re [1945] Ch 402, 114 LJ Ch 253, 89 Sol Jo 269, 173 LT 40, 61 TLR 403 ................................................................. 2.433
Davis & Co Ltd v Brunswick (Australia) Ltd [1936] 1 All ER 299, PC ............... 1.174
Davey v Croxen [2015] EWHC 2372 (Ch), [2015] All ER (D) 33 (Sep) ............... 1.705
Davis (As trustee in bankruptcy of Jackson) v Jackson [2017] EWHC 698 (Ch), [2017] 1 WLR 4005, [2017] 2 FLR 1153, [2017] Fam Law 722, 167 NLJ 7745, [2017] WTLR 465, [2017] BPIR 950, [2017] All ER (D) 119 (Apr) ............................. 1.455
Davis v Trustee in Bankruptcy of the Estate of Davis [1995] Lexis Citation 1266, [1998] BPIR 572 ................................................................. 1.396
Davy v Pickering [2015] EWHC 380 (Ch), [2015] 2 BCLC 116, [2015] All ER (D) 238 (Feb); revsd [2017] EWCA Civ 30, [2017] 2 BCLC 260, (2017) Times, 08 March, [2017] All ER (D) 104 (Jan) ......................................................... 1.701
Dawodu (a bankrupt), Re [2001] BPIR 983, [2001] All ER (D) 251 (Jan) ...... 1.178, 1.381, 2.834
Day v Refulgent Ltd [2016] EWHC 7 (Ch), [2016] BPIR 594, [2016] All ER (D) 21 (Jan) ......................................................... 1.384, 1.386
Dean v Stout [2004] EWHC 3315 (Ch), [2006] 1 FLR 725, [2005] BPIR 1113, [2004] All ER (D) 72 (Dec) ......................................................... 1.455
Dean-Willcocks v Payee (Buildings) Pty Ltd (1 September 1994, unreported) NSW Sup Ct, Young J ................................................................. 1.138
Dean-Willcocks v Soluble Solution Hydroponics Pty Ltd (1997) 15 ACLC 833 ........ 1.220
Debenhams plc, Re [2020] EWHC 1755 (Ch) ..................................... 1.188

Debenhams Retail Ltd (in administration), Re [2020] EWHC 921 (Ch), [2020] 3 All ER 319, [2020] 2 All ER (Comm) 409, [2020] 1 BCLC 747, [2020] All ER (D) 111 (Apr) ................................................................................. 1.716

Debenhams Retail Ltd (in administration), Re Rowley (as joint administrators of Debenhams Retail Ltd) [2020] EWCA Civ 600, [2020] 3 All ER 319, [2020] 2 All ER (Comm) 409, [2020] 1 BCLC 747, [2020] Bus LR 788, [2020] IRLR 524, [2020] All ER (D) 42 (May) ........................................................ 1.716

Debtor (No 82 of 1926), Re [1927] 1 Ch 410, 136 LT 349, sub nom Mumford, Re, Debtor v Petitioning Creditor, ex p Official Receiver 96 LJ Ch 75, [1926] B & CR 165, DC

Debtor (No 17 of 1966), Re. See Debtor, Re ex p Debtor v Allen (infant by his father and next friend Allen)

Debtor, a (No 26A of 1975), Re [1984] 3 All ER 995, [1985] 1 WLR 6, 128 Sol Jo 685, [1984] LS Gaz R 3011 .................................................... 1.433

Debtor, a (No 1 of 1987, Lancaster), Re [1988] 1 All ER 959, [1988] 1 WLR 419, 132 Sol Jo 375, [1988] 10 LS Gaz R 44; affd sub nom Debtor, a (No 1 of 1987, Lancaster), Re, ex p Debtor v Royal Bank of Scotland plc [1989] 2 All ER 46, [1989] 1 WLR 271, 133 Sol Jo 290, [1989] 16 LS Gaz R 35, (1989) Times, 20 January ................. 1.175, 2.530

Debtor, a (No 2389 of 1989), Re [1991] Ch 326, [1991] 2 WLR 578, sub nom Re a Debtor (No 2389 of 1989), ex p Travel and General Insurance Co plc v Debtor [1990] 3 All ER 984 ......................................................... 2.815

Debtor, a (No 32/SD/1991), Re [1993] 2 All ER 991, [1993] 1 WLR 314 ............. 2.814

Debtor, a (Nos 49 and 50 of 1992), Re [1995] Ch 66, [1994] 3 WLR 847, CA ........ 2.530

Debtor, a (No 64 of 1992), Re [1994] 2 All ER 177, [1994] 1 WLR 264, [1994] BCC 55, (1993) Times, 12 November, [1993] Lexis Citation 2543 ........................... 1.64

Debtor, a (No 68 of 1992), Re (1993) Times, 12 February, [1993] Lexis Citation 1666, [1996] BPIR 478; on appeal sub nom Royal Bank of Scotland v Farley [1994] Lexis Citation 3153, [1996] BPIR 638, CA ......................................... 1.395

Debtor, a (No 222 of 1990), Re, ex p Bank of Ireland [1992] BCLC 137, (1991) Times, 27 June ................................................................... 1.59, 1.65

Debtor, a (No 222 of 1990), Re, ex p Bank of Ireland (No 2) [1993] BCLC 233, [1991] Lexis Citation 1451 ...................................................... 1.59, 1.60, 1.65

Debtor, a (No 22 of 1993), Re [1994] 2 All ER 105, [1994] 1 WLR 46 ........ 1.382, 1.385

Debtor, a (No 32 of 1993), Re [1995] 1 All ER 628, [1994] 1 WLR 899, [1994] BCC 438, [1994] 18 LS Gaz R 37, (1994) Times, 1 March ........................... 1.175, 1.386

Debtor, a (No 87 of 1993) (No 2), Re [1996] 1 BCLC 63, [1996] BCC 80, (1995) Times, 7 August, [1996] BPIR 64 ............................................... 1.65

Debtor, a (No 13A-IO-1995), Re; Debtor, a (No 14A-IO-1995), Re [1996] 1 All ER 691, [1995] 1 WLR 1127, [1995] 27 LS Gaz R 32 .................................. 1.353

Debtor (No 50A-SD-1995), Re [1997] Ch 310, [1997] 2 All ER 789, [1997] 2 WLR 57, [1997] 1 BCLC 280, sub nom Jelly v All Type Roofing Co [1996] Lexis Citation 2032, [1996] BPIR 565 ............................................... 1.176, 2.321

Debtor, a (No 574 of 1995), Re [1998] 2 BCLC 124 .............................. 1.388

Debtor, a (No 1401O of 1995), Re [1996] 2 BCLC 429 ........................... 1.357

Debtor, a (No 544/SD/98), Re [2000] 1 BCLC 103, CA ........................... 1.178

Debtor, a (No 101 of 1999), Re [2001] 1 BCLC 54, (2000) Times, 27 July, [2000] Lexis Citation 3650, [2000] BPIR 998, [2000] All ER (D) 949 ....................... 1.65

Debtor, a (No 78 of 2000), Re. See Skarzynski v Chalford Property Co Ltd

Debtor, Re, ex p Debtor v Allen (infant by his father and next friend Allen) [1967] Ch 590, [1967] 2 WLR 1528, 111 Sol Jo 130, sub nom Re Debtor (No 17 of 1966) [1967] 1 All ER 668, DC ................................................... 1.175

Debtor, a (No 310 of 1988), Re, ex p Debtor v Arab Bank Ltd [1989] 2 All ER 42, [1989] 1 WLR 452, [1989] 25 LS Gaz R 41 ................................... 1.516, 2.530

Debtor, Re, ex p Debtor v Dodwell (Trustee) [1949] Ch 236, [1949] 1 All ER 510, [1949] LJR 907, 93 Sol Jo 148, 65 TLR 150 .................................. 1.414

Debtor (No 757 of 1954), Re ex p Debtor v F A Dumont Ltd. See Majory, Re, ex p Debtor v F A Dumont Ltd

Debtor, a (No 784 of 1991), Re, ex p Debtor v IRC [1992] Ch 554, [1992] 3 All ER 376, [1992] 3 WLR 119, [1992] STC 549, 64 TC 612 .............................. 1.380

Debtor, a (No 415-SD-93), Re, ex p Debtor v IRC [1994] 2 All ER 168, [1994] 1 WLR 917, (1993) Times, 8 December ...................................... 1.386, 2.530

Debtor, a (No 490-SD-1991), Re, ex p Debtor v Printline (Offset) Ltd [1992] 2 All ER 664, [1992] 1 WLR 507, [1993] BCLC 164, (1992) Times, 9 April, [1992] Lexis Citation 3379 ........................................... 1.175, 2.316, 2.530

Debtor, a (No 51-SD-1991), Re, ex p Ritchie Bros Auctioneers v Debtor [1993] 2 All ER 40, [1992] 1 WLR 1294 .............................................. 1.175

Debtor (No 37 of 1976), Re, ex p Taylor v Debtor [1980] Ch 565, [1980] 1 All ER 129, [1980] 3 WLR 345, 124 Sol Jo 645 .................................................... 1.395

Debtor, a (No 2389 of 1989), Re, ex p Travel and General Insurance Co plc v Debtor. See Debtor, a (No 2389 of 1989), Re

Debtor, a (No 103 of 1994), Re, Cooper v Fearnley [1994] Lexis Citation 2827, [1997] BPIR 20 .......................................................................................... 1.60

Debtor, a (No 340 of 1992), Re, Debtor v First National Commercial Bank plc [1994] 3 All ER 269, [1994] 2 BCLC 171, (1993) Times, 19 July; affd [1996] 2 All ER 211, [1995] 15 LS Gaz R 40, (1995) Times, 6 March, 139 Sol Jo LB 82 ...... 1.175, 1.383, 2.820

Debtor, a (No 162 of 1993), Re, Doorbar v Alltime Securities Ltd. See Doorbar v Alltime Securities Ltd

Debtor, a (No 6349 of 1994), Re, IRC v Debtor [1996] BCC 971, [1995] Lexis Citation 2088, [1996] BPIR 271 ..................................................................... 1.386

Debtor (No 48810 of 1996), Re, JP v Debtor [1999] 2 BCLC 571, [1999] 1 FLR 926, [1999] 2 FCR 637, [1999] Fam Law 293, [1999] BPIR 206 .......................... 1.61

Debtor, a (No 10 of 1992), Re, Peck v Craighead. See Peck v Craighead

De Courcy v Clement [1971] Ch 693, [1971] 1 All ER 681, [1971] 2 WLR 210, 115 Sol Jo 93 ............................................................................................. 1.143

DeepOcean 1 UK Ltd, Re [2020] EWHC 3549 (Ch) ............................... 5.38

Dekala Pty Ltd (in liq) v Perth Land & Leisure Ltd (1989) 17 NSWLR 664, NSW S Ct ........................................................................................................ 1.235

Delaney v Staples (t/a De Montfort Recruitment) [1992] 1 AC 687, [1992] 1 All ER 944, [1992] 2 WLR 451, [1992] IRLR 191, [1992] ICR 483, [1992] 15 LS Gaz R 32, (1992) Times, 16 March, 136 Sol Jo LB 91, HL ................................................. 1.716

Delberry Ltd, Re [2008] EWHC 925 (Ch), [2008] BCC 653, [2008] BPIR 1277 . 1.80, 1.300

Delfin Marketing (UK) Ltd, Re [2000] 1 BCLC 71 ................................... 1.177

Deloitte & Touche AG v Johnson [1999] 1 WLR 1605, [1999] 4 LRC 281, [2000] 1 BCLC 485, 1 ITELR 771, (1999) Times, 16 June, PC ............... 1.160, 1.705

De Louville De Toucy v Bonhams 1793 Ltd [2011] EWHC 3809 (Ch), (2011) Times, 10 December, [2012] BPIR 793, [2011] All ER (D) 32 (Nov) ........................ 1.386

Demaglass Holdings Ltd, Re [2001] 2 BCLC 633, [2001] Lexis Citation 1736, [2001] All ER (D) 382 (Jul) ....................................................................... 1.178

Denney, Gasquet and Metcalfe v Conklin [1913] 3 KB 177, 82 LJKB 953, 109 LT 444, 29 TLR 598 ................................................................................................ 1.178

Dennis (a bankrupt), Re [1993] Ch 72, [1992] 3 All ER 436, [1992] 3 WLR 204, [1993] 1 FLR 313, [1993] 1 FCR 941, [1993] Fam Law 195, [1992] 27 LS Gaz R 33; revsd [1996] Ch 80, [1995] 3 All ER 171, [1995] 3 WLR 367, [1995] 2 FLR 387, [1995] 3 FCR 761, [1995] Fam Law 611, [1996] BPIR 106 ................................... 1.396

Denny v Yeldon [1995] 3 All ER 624, [1995] 1 BCLC 560, [1995] OPLR 115, [1995] PLR 37 ................................................................................................. 1.675

Denton v TH White Ltd [2014] EWCA Civ 906, [2015] 1 All ER 880, [2014] 1 WLR 3926, 154 ConLR 1, [2014] BLR 547, 164 NLJ 7614, [2014] 4 Costs LR 752, [2014] All ER (D) 53 (Jul) ....................................................................... 2.835

Denton Subdivisions Pty Ltd (in liq), Re (1968) 89 WN (NSW) (Pt 1) 231 ............ 2.433

Department for Environment Food and Rural Affairs v Feakins. See Secretary of State for the Environment, Food and Rural Affairs v Feakins

Department of Business, Innovation and Skills v Compton [2012] BPIR 1108, MagsCt ....................................................... 1.405, 1.480, 1.484, 1.485

Deputy Comr of Taxation v De Simeone Consulting Pty Ltd [2007] FCA 548, Aust Fed Ct .............................................................................................. 1.175

Derek Thomas Hood (a debtor, Re) [2020] EWHC 3232 (Ch), [2021] Ch 125, [2021] 2 WLR 313, [2021] BPIR 274 ........................... 1.180, 1.398, 1.605, 2.553, 2.555

Derfshaw Ltd, Re [2011] EWHC 1565 (Ch), [2012] 1 BCLC 814, [2011] BCC 631, [2011] NLJR 918, [2011] BPIR 1289, [2011] All ER (D) 144 (Jun) ................... 1.630

De Rothschild v Bell [2000] QB 33, [1999] 2 All ER 722, [1999] 2 WLR 1237, 78 P & CR D5, [1999] 1 FLR 1246, [1999] Fam Law 385, 32 HLR 274, [1999] NPC 23, [1999] 1 EGLR 35, [1999] 16 EG 155, [1999] EGCS 27, (1999) Times, 10 March, [1999] Lexis Citation 2262, [1999] BPIR 300, [1999] All ER (D) 160 ................ 1.396

Derry v Peek (1889) 14 App Cas 337, 54 JP 148, 58 LJ Ch 864, 1 Meg 292, 38 WR 33, [1886–90] All ER Rep 1, 61 LT 265, 5 TLR 625, HL ................................... 1.393

Designer Room Ltd, Re [2004] EWHC 720 (Ch), [2004] 3 All ER 679, [2005] 1 WLR 1581, [2004] BCC 904, [2004] All ER (D) 441 (Mar) ................................... 1.682

Deutsche Apotheker-Und Arztebank EG v Leitzbach [2018] EWHC 1544 (Ch), [2018] BPIR 1299, [2018] All ER (D) 166 (May) ............................................ 1.395

Devon and Somerset Farmers Ltd, Re [1994] Ch 57, [1994] 1 All ER 717, [1993] 3 WLR 866, [1994] 1 BCLC 99, [1993] BCC 410, [1993] 31 LS Gaz R 39, (1993) Times, 25 May ............................................................................................... 1.72
Dewrun Ltd, Re [2002] BCC 57 ............................................................... 1.180
Diamond Hangar Ltd Diamond Hangar Ltd v Abacus Lighting Ltd [2019] EWHC 224 (Ch), [2019] All ER (D) 69 (Feb) ...................................................... 2.814
Discovery (Northampton) Ltd and other companies v Debenhams Retail Ltd [2020] EWHC 260 (Ch), [2020] BPIR 1371, [2020] All ER (D) 171 (Feb) .................. 1.502
Direct Affinity Events Ltd companies, Re Revenue and Customs Comrs v Direct Affinity Events Ltd [2019] EWHC 3063 (Ch), [2020] BPIR 331, [2019] All ER (D) 67 (Dec) ........................................................................................ 2.321, 2.814
Dianoor Jewels Ltd, Re [2001] 1 BCLC 450, [2001] BPIR 234 ....................... 1.630
Dickinson v NAL Realisations (Staffordshire) Ltd [2017] EWHC 28 (Ch), [2018] 1 BCLC 623, [2017] BPIR 611, [2017] All ER (D) 155 (Feb) ............................... 1.582
Dicksmith (Manufacturing) Ltd (in liq), Re [1999] 2 BCLC 686, (1999) Times, 7 July, [1999] Lexis Citation 3015, [1999] All ER (D) 663 .................................. 1.164
Die Sparkasse v Armutcu [2012] EWHC 4026 (Ch), [2013] BPIR 210 ......... 1.372, 1.395
Digital Equipment Co Ltd v Bower. See MT Realisations Ltd, Re
Dikwa Holdings Pty Ltd v Oakbury Pty Ltd (1992) 10 ACLC 925 .................... 2.324
Discovery (Northampton) Ltd companies v Debenhams Retail Ltd [2019] EWHC 2441 (Ch), [2019] EGLR 47, [2019] All ER (D) 67 (Sep) .................... 1.59, 1.65, 2.827
Ditcham v Miller (1931) 100 LJPC 177, [1931] B & CR 86, PC ...................... 1.141
Divine Solutions UK Ltd, Re [2003] EWHC 1931 (Ch), [2004] 1 BCLC 373, [2004] BCC 325, [2003] All ER (D) 238 (Jul) ..................................................... 1.660
D'Jan of London Ltd, Re, Copp v D'Jan [1994] 1 BCLC 561, [1993] BCC 646, [1993] 31 LS Gaz R 38 ..................................................... 1.270, 1.272
Doherty v Fannigan Holdings Ltd [2018] EWCA Civ 1615, [2018] 2 BCLC 623, [2018] BPIR 1266 ................................................................................ 1.382
Doffmann v Wood [2011] EWHC 4008 (Ch), [2012] BPIR 972 ...................... 1.409
Dollar Land Holdings plc, Re [1993] BCC 823, [1994] 1 BCLC 404, ChD ............ 1.176
Dollar Land Holdings plc, Re [1994] 1 BCLC 404, [1993] BCC 823 .................. 1.174
Dollar Land (Feltham) Ltd, Re [1995] 2 BCLC 370, [1995] BCC 740 ......... 2.328, 2.814
Dolphin Quays Developments Ltd v Mills [2008] EWCA Civ 385, [2008] 4 All ER 58, [2008] 1 WLR 1829, [2008] 2 BCLC 774, [2008] Bus LR 1520, [2008] All ER (D) 257 (Apr), sub nom Mills v Birchall [2008] BCC 471, [2008] 4 Costs LR 599, [2008] BPIR 607 ......................................................................................... 1.86
Doltable Ltd v Lexi Holdings plc [2005] EWHC 1804 (Ch), [2006] 1 BCLC 384, [2006] BCC 918, [2005] All ER (D) 100 (Jun) ....................................... 1.620
Domestic & General Insulation Ltd, Re, Bevan v Walker [2018] EWHC 265 (Ch), [2018] Bus LR 923, [2018] All ER (D) 92 (Feb) ............................................ 1.138
Dominion of Canada Plumbago Co, Re (1884) 27 ChD 33, 53 LJ Ch 702, 33 WR 9, 50 LT 518, CA .............................................................. 2.306, 2.435
Donaldson v O'Sullivan [2008] EWHC 387 (Ch), [2008] BCC 328, [2008] BPIR 288; affd [2008] EWCA Civ 879, [2009] 1 All ER 1087, [2009] 1 WLR 924, [2009] BCC 99, [2008] NLJR 1226, (2008) Times, 6 October, [2008] BPIR 1288, [2008] All ER (D) 393 (Jul) ................................................................. 1.407
Donohoe v Ingram [2006] 2 FLR 1084, [2006] Fam Law 733, [2006] BPIR 417, [2006] All ER (D) 132 (Jan) ........................................................ 1.455
Doodes v Gotham [2005] EWHC 2576 (Ch), [2006] 1 WLR 729, [2006] 2 FLR 844, [2006] Fam Law 519, (2005) Times, 25 November, [2006] BPIR 36, [2005] All ER (D) 237 (Nov); revsd sub nom Gotham v Doodes [2006] EWCA Civ 1080, [2007] 1 All ER 527, [2007] 1 WLR 86, [2007] 1 FLR 373, [2007] 2 FCR 712, [2006] NLJR 1325, (2006) Times, 14 August, [2006] BPIR 1178, [2006] All ER (D) 348 (Jul) ............ 1.431
Doonin Plant Ltd, Noters [2018] CSOH 89, [2019] BCC 217 ................. 1.208, 2.183
Doorbar v Alltime Securities Ltd [1995] 1 BCLC 316, sub nom Re a Debtor (No 162 of 1993), Doorbar v Alltime Securities Ltd [1994] BCC 994; affd sub nom Doorbar v Alltime Securities Ltd [1996] 2 All ER 948, [1996] 1 WLR 456, [1996] 1 BCLC 487, [1995] BCC 1149, [1996] 2 EGLR 33, [1996] 06 LS Gaz R 28, [1996] 32 EG 70, (1995) Times, 7 December, 140 Sol Jo LB 8, [1996] BPIR 582 .. 1.59, 1.61, 1.64, 1.65, 2.909
Doorbar v Alltime Securities (No 2) [1995] 2 BCLC 513, [1995] BCC 728; affd sub nom Doorbar v Alltime Securities (No 2) [1996] 1 BCLC 487, [1996] BPIR 128, CA ........ 1.61
Doreen Boards Ltd, Re [1996] 1 BCLC 501 ........................... 1.178, 2.324, 2.346
Double S Printers Ltd, Re [1999] 1 BCLC 220, (1998) Times, 2 June, [1998] Lexis Citation 3571 ........................................................................... 1.164
Douglas Griggs Engineering Ltd, Re [1963] Ch 19, [1962] 1 All ER 498, [1962] 2 WLR 893, 106 Sol Jo 221 ....................................................... 1.175, 1.178

Downer Enterprises Ltd, Re [1974] 2 All ER 1074, [1974] 1 WLR 1460, 118 Sol Jo
   829 ........................................................................ 2.433
Downsview Nominees Ltd v First City Corpn Ltd [1993] AC 295, [1993] 3 All ER 626,
   [1993] 2 WLR 86, [1994] 1 BCLC 49, [1993] BCC 46, 12 LDAB 302, [1992]
   45 LS Gaz R 26, (1992) Times, 15 December, 136 Sol Jo LB 324, PC ................. 1.88
Drax Holdings Ltd, Re [2003] EWHC 2743 (Ch), [2004] 1 All ER 903, [2004] 1 WLR
   1049, [2004] 1 BCLC 10, [2004] BCC 324, [2003] All ER (D) 220 (Nov) .............. 6.5
Dry Docks Corpn of London, Re (1888) 39 ChD 306, 58 LJ Ch 33, 1 Meg 86, 37 WR 18,
   59 LT 763, 4 TLR 737, CA ....................................................... 1.188
Dubai Aluminium Co Ltd v Salaam [2007] BPIR 690 ............................... 1.382
Dummelow, Re, ex p Ruffle (1873) LR 8 Ch App 997, 42 LJ Bcy 82, 21 WR 932, 29 LT
   384, CACh .................................................................... 2.909
Dunbar Assets plc v Butler [2015] EWHC 2546 (Ch), 165 NLJ 7671, [2015] BPIR 1358,
   [2015] All ER (D) 138 (Sep) ................................................... 2.530
Dunbar Assets plc v Fowler [2012] Lexis Citation 108, [2013] BPIR 46, [2013] All ER (D)
   02 (Jan) ........................................... 1.381, 1.382, 1.386, 1.489
Dunraven Adare Coal and Iron Co, Re, Sheffield Wagon Co's Original Petition (1875) 1
   Char Pr Cas 2, 24 WR 37, 33 LT 371, CA ....................................... 1.169
Duomatic Ltd, Re [1969] 2 Ch 365, [1969] 1 All ER 161, [1969] 2 WLR 114, 112 Sol Jo
   922 .......................................................................... 1.639
Durkan v Patel [2018] EWHC 3231 (Ch) ........................................ 1.459

                                    E

E Squared Ltd, Re [2006] EWHC 532 (Ch), [2006] 3 All ER 779, [2006] 1 WLR 3414,
   [2006] 2 BCLC 277, [2006] BCC 379, [2006] All ER (D) 253 (Mar) ................. 1.700
ENEFI Energiahatékonysági Nyrt v Directia Generala Regionala a Finantelor Publice
   Brasov (DGRFP): C-212/15 (2016) C-212/15, ECLI:EU:C:2016:841, [2016] All ER (D)
   110 (Nov), EUCJ .............................................................. 6.9
ESS Production Ltd v Sully [2005] EWCA Civ 554, [2005] 2 BCLC 547, [2005] BCC 435,
   [2005] BPIR 691, [2005] All ER (D) 158 (May) ...... 1.275, 1.276, 2.1037, 2.1041, 2.1043,
                                                                                2.1044
Earp v Stevenson [2011] EWHC 1436 (Ch), [2012] 2 BCLC 65, [2011] All ER (D) 51
   (Jun), CSRC vol 35 iss 8/1 ................................................... 1.272
Eastaway v Secretary of State for Trade and Industry. See Blackspur Group plc, Re;
   Eastaway v Secretary of State for Trade and Industry
Ebbvale Ltd v Hosking (trustee in bankruptcy) [2013] UKPC 1, [2013] 2 BCLC 204,
   [2013] BPIR 219, [2013] All ER (D) 103 (Mar), PC .......................... 1.178, 1.382
Eberhardt & Co Ltd v Mair [1995] 3 All ER 963, [1995] 1 WLR 1180, [1995] BCC 845,
   (1995) Times, 9 May, [1996] BPIR 143 ..................................... 1.175, 1.178
Eberle's Hotels and Restaurant Co Ltd v Jonas (1887) 18 QBD 459, 56 LJQB 278, 35 WR
   467, 3 TLR 421, CA
Ebrahimi v Westbourne Galleries Ltd [1973] AC 360, [1972] 2 All ER 492, [1972] 2
   WLR 1289, 116 Sol Jo 412, HL ................................................. 1.174
Eco Link Resources Ltd, Re [2012] BCC 731 ............................... 1.632, 2.820
Eco Quest plc v GFI Consultants Ltd [2014] EWHC 4329 (QB), [2015] BPIR 244,
   [2015] All ER (D) 73 (Feb) ................................................... 1.399
Edennote Ltd, Re [1996] 2 BCLC 389, [1996] BCC 718, (1996) Times, 3 June, 140 Sol Jo
   LB 176 ............................................... 1.160, 1.220, 1.705
Edennote Ltd (No 2), Re [1997] 2 BCLC 89 .................................... 1.741
Edgeworth Capital Luxembourg SARL v Maud [2015] EWHC 3464 (Comm),
   [2015] All ER (D) 04 (Dec) ................................................... 6.9
Edwards, Re, ex p Chalmers (1873) LR 8 Ch App 289, 42 LJ Bcy 37, 21 WR 349, 28 LT
   325, CACh ................................................................... 1.471
Eichler (No 2) (a bankrupt), Re [2011] BPIR 1293 ........................... 1.372
El Ajou v Dollar Land Holdings plc [1994] 2 All ER 685, [1994] 1 BCLC 464,
   [1994] BCC 143, (1994) Times, 3 January ..................................... 1.303
El Ajou v Dollar Land (Manhattan) Ltd [2005] EWHC 2861 (Ch), [2007] BCC 953,
   [2005] All ER (D) 371 (Nov) ........................... 1.176, 1.178, 1.630
El Ajou v Stern [2006] EWHC 3067 (Ch), [2007] BPIR 693, [2006] All ER (D) 11
   (Dec) ........................................................................ 1.64
Elation Capital Ltd v Hoffgen [2021] 6 WLUK 480 ............................ 2.776
Electromagnetic (S) Ltd v Development Bank of Singapore [1994] SLR 734 .... 1.353, 1.660
Elgin Legal Ltd, Re (2016) [2016] EWHC 2523 (Ch), [2018] 1 BCLC 521, 166 NLJ 7720,
   [2017] BPIR 406, [2016] All ER (D) 124 (Oct) ............................... 1.629, 1.630

Ellis (Matthew) Ltd, Re [1933] Ch 458, 102 LJ Ch 65, [1933] B & CR 17, [1933] All ER Rep 583, 77 Sol Jo 82, 148 LT 434, CA .............................................. 1.309

Eloc Electro-Optieck and Communicatie BV, Re [1982] Ch 43, [1981] 2 All ER 1111, [1981] 3 WLR 176, [1981] ICR 732, 125 Sol Jo 412 ................................. 1.281

Elston v King [2020] EWHC 55 (Ch), [2020] BPIR 501, [2020] All ER (D) 110 (Jan) .................................................................................................. 1.428

Emap Active Ltd v Hill (t/a Bob Hill Motor Cycles) [2007] EWHC 1592 (Ch), [2007] BPIR 1228, [2007] All ER (D) 378 (May) ......................................... 1.386

Embassy Art Products Ltd, Re [1988] BCLC 1, 3 BCC 292 ......................... 1.300

Emerald Meats (London) Ltd, Re, McCarthy v Tann [2016] EWHC 542 (Ch), [2017] 2 BCLC 60 .......................................................................... 2.835

Emmadart Ltd, Re [1979] Ch 540, [1979] 1 All ER 599, [1979] 2 WLR 868, 123 Sol Jo 15 ................................................................................................ 1.176

Empire Builders Ltd, Re, Re Transvaal United Trust and Finance Co Ltd (1919) 88 LJ Ch 459, 63 Sol Jo 608, 121 LT 238 ................................................. 1.200

Employers' Liability Assurance Corpn v Sedgwick, Collins & Co. See Sedgwick, Collins & Co Ltd v Rossia Insurance Co of Petrograd

Energy Holdings (No 3) Ltd (in liq), Re [2010] EWHC 788 (Ch), [2011] 1 BCLC 84, [2010] BPIR 1339 ........................................................................... 1.67

Engel v Peri [2002] EWHC 799 (Ch), [2002] BPIR 961, [2002] All ER (D) 285 (Apr) ...................................................................................... 1.395, 1.489

England v Smith [2001] Ch 419, [2000] 2 WLR 1141, [1999] 47 LS Gaz R 29, (1999) Times, 3 December, [1999] Lexis Citation 3229, 144 Sol Jo LB 8, [1999] All ER (D) 1311, sub nom Southern Equities Corp Ltd (in liq), Re [2000] 2 BCLC 21, [2000] BCC 123, [2000] BPIR 28, CA ....................................................... 1.300, 1.586

English Bank of the River Plate, Re [1892] 1 Ch 391, 61 LJ Ch 205, 40 WR 325, 66 LT 177, 8 TLR 238 ............................................................................... 1.188

Enta Technologies Ltd v Revenue And Customs Comrs [2014] EWHC 548 (Ch), [2014] BPIR 543, [2014] All ER (D) 233 (Mar); revsd sub nom Changtel Solutions UK Ltd (formerly Enta Technologies Ltd) v Revenue and Customs Comrs [2015] EWCA Civ 29, [2015] 1 WLR 3911, [2015] 2 BCLC 586, 165 NLJ 7639, (2015) Times, 05 March, [2015] SWTI 248, [2015] BPIR 327, [2015] All ER (D) 211 (Jan) .................... 1.178

Enterprise Managed Services Ltd v Tony McFadden Utilities Ltd [2009] EWHC 3222 (TCC), [2011] 1 BCLC 414, [2010] BLR 89, [2010] All ER (D) 126 (Apr) ........... 2.852

Environment Agency v Clark (as administrator of Rhondda Waste Disposal Ltd) [2001] Ch 57, [2000] 3 WLR 1304, [2000] 1 EGLR 113, [2000] EGCS 25, (2000) Times, 2 March, [2000] Lexis Citation 2585, [2000] All ER (D) 162, sub nom Environment Agency v Clark (Administrator of Rhondda Waste Disposal Ltd) [2000] BCC 653, [2000] NLJR 227 ........................................................................ 1.353, 1.660

Environment Agency v Hillridge Ltd [2003] EWHC 3023 (Ch), [2004] 2 BCLC 358, [2003] All ER (D) 244 (Dec) ............................................................ 1.235

Equitas Ltd v Jacob [2005] EWHC 1440 (Ch), [2005] BPIR 1312 ............... 1.188, 2.70

Equiticorp International plc, Re [1989] 1 WLR 1010, [1989] BCLC 597, 5 BCC 599 .................................................................................. 1.176, 2.127

Equity and Provident Ltd, Re [2002] EWHC 186 (Ch), [2002] All ER (D) 239 (Feb), sub nom Re Equity & Provident Ltd [2002] 2 BCLC 78 ................................. 1.177

Erlam v Rahman (A Bankrupt) [2016] EWHC 111 (Ch), [2016] 2 P & CR D13, [2016] BPIR 856, [2016] All ER (D) 42 (Feb) ............................................ 1.455

Ernst & Young, Re (2008) 383 BR 773 ............................................. 7.29

Erste Bank Hungary Nyrt v Magyar Allam abd: C-527/10 (2012) C - 527/10, ECLI:EU:C:2012:417, [2012] NLJR 962, [2012] All ER (D) 62 (Jul), EUCJ ............ 6.10

Esal (Commodities) Ltd, Re [1989] BCLC 59, 4 BCC 475, (1988) Times, 30 May ..... 1.300

Esal (Commodities) Ltd (No 2), Re [1990] BCC 708, [1990] Lexis Citation 1470 ..... 1.300

Etic Ltd, Re [1928] Ch 861, 97 LJ Ch 460, [1928] B & CR 81, 140 LT 219 ........... 1.270

Euro Commercial Leasing Ltd v Cartwright & Lewis [1995] 2 BCLC 618, [1995] BCC 830 ................................................................................... 1.298

Eurocruit Europe Ltd (in liq) [2007] EWHC 1433 (Ch), [2007] 2 BCLC 598, [2008] Bus LR 146, [2007] BCC 916, (2007) Times, 16 July, [2007] All ER (D) 229 (Jun) ........ 1.270

Eurodis Electron Ltd plc, Re [2011] EWHC 1025 (Ch), [2012] 2 BCLC 257, [2012] BCC 57, [2011] 19 LS Gaz R 19, [2011] BPIR 1372, [2011] All ER (D) 48 (May) .. 1.281, 1.618, 6.21

Eurofood IFSC Ltd, Re [2004] IEHC 607, [2004] BCC 383; on appeal [2004] IESC 47, [2005] BCC 999, [2004] 4 IR 370, IrSC .............................................. 6.35

Eurofood IFSC Ltd, Re: C-341/04 (2006) C-341/04, ECLI:EU:C:2006:281, [2006] Ch 508, [2006] ECR I-3813, [2006] 3 WLR 309, [2006] All ER (EC) 1078, [2007] 2 BCLC 151, [2005] BCC 1021, [2006] BCC 397, [2006] BPIR 661, [2006] All ER (D) 20 (May), EUCJ ............................................................... 6.3, 6.4, 6.5, 6.64

Euromaster Ltd, Re [2012] EWHC 2356 (Ch), [2013] 1 BCLC 273, [2013] Bus LR 466, [2012] BCC 754, [2012] All ER (D) 84 (Aug), CSRC vol 36 iss 15/1 .......... 1.645, 2.820

Euromex Ventures Ltd v O'Connell [2013] EWHC 3007 (Ch), [2013] All ER (D) 106 (Oct) ................................................................... 1.298

European Assurance Society, Re [1872] WN 85 ..................................... 1.200

European Assurance Society Arbitration, Re, British Commercial Insurance Co v British Nation Life Assurance Association. See European Society Arbitration Acts, Re, ex p British Nation Life Assurance Association Liquidators

European Commission v AMI Semiconductor Belgium BVBA: C-294/02 (2005) C-294/02, ECLI:EU:C:2005:172, [2005] ECR I-2175, [2005] All ER (D) 315 (Mar), EUCJ ...................................................................... 6.9

European Directories DH6 BV, Re [2010] EWHC 3472 (Ch), [2012] BCC 46, [2011] BPIR 408 .................................................................... 6.5

European Society Arbitration Acts, Re, ex p British Nation Life Assurance Association Liquidators (1878) 8 ChD 679, 27 WR 88, 39 LT 136, sub nom Re European Assurance Society Arbitration, British Commercial Insurance Co v British Nation Life Assurance Association 48 LJ Ch 118, CA ...................................... 1.129

Evans v Finance-U-Ltd [2013] EWCA Civ 869, [2013] BPIR 1001, [2013] All ER (D) 233 (Jul) .............................................................. 1.393, 1.399

Evans v Rival Granite Quarries Ltd [1910] 2 KB 979, 79 LJKB 970, 18 Mans 64, 54 Sol Jo 580, 26 TLR 509, CA ...................................................... 1.77

Everitt v Budhram (a Bankrupt) [2009] EWHC 1219 (Ch), [2010] Ch 170, [2010] 2 WLR 637, (2009) Times, 14 July, [2010] BPIR 567 ...................................... 1.455

Everitt v Zeital [2018] EWHC 1316 (Ch) ........................................... 1.298

Everything Australian Pty Ltd, Re (1992) 11 ACLC 50, 9 ACSR 75 ................... 1.220

Exchange Securities and Commodities Ltd, Re [1983] BCLC 186 ..................... 1.183

Exchange Travel Agency Ltd v Triton Property Trust plc [1991] BCLC 396, [1991] BCC 341, [1991] 2 EGLR 50, [1991] 12 LS Gaz R 33, [1991] 35 EG 120 ................. 1.613

Exchange Travel (Holdings) Ltd, Re [1993] BCLC 887, [1992] BCC 954 ...... 1.193, 1.715

Exeter City Association Football Club Ltd v Football Conference Ltd [2004] EWHC 2304 (Ch), [2004] EWHC 831 (Ch), [2004] 4 All ER 1179, [2004] 1 WLR 2910, [2005] 1 BCLC 238, [2004] BCC 498, (2004) Times, 12 February, [2004] ArbLR 25, [2004] All ER (D) 09 (Nov) ..................................................... 1.176

Exeter City Council v Bairstow [2007] EWHC 400 (Ch), [2007] 4 All ER 437, [2007] 2 BCLC 455, [2007] Bus LR 813, [2007] 2 P & CR 129, [2007] RA 109, [2007] BCC 236, (2007) Times, 6 April, [2007] All ER (D) 45 (Mar) .......... 1.716, 2.183

Exhall Coal Mining Co Ltd, Re (1864) 4 De GJ & Sm 377, 33 LJ Ch 569n, 10 Jur NS 576, 4 New Rep 127, 46 ER 964 ......................................................... 1.183

Expo International Pty Ltd v Chant (1979) ACLC 34,043 (NSW), 4 ACLR 679, [1979] 2 NSWLR 820, NSWSC ...................................................... 1.89

Express Electrical Distributors Ltd v Beavis [2016] EWCA Civ 765, [2016] 1 WLR 4783, [2016] BPIR 1386, [2016] All ER (D) 118 (Jul) ................................... 1.180

Eyton (Adam) Ltd, Re, ex p Charlesworth (1887) 36 ChD 299, 57 LJ Ch 127, 36 WR 275, 57 LT 899, 3 TLR 738, CA .................................................... 1.160

Ezair v Conn (as joint administrators of Charlotte Street Properties Ltd) [2020] EWCA Civ 687, [2020] PLSCS 103, [2020] All ER (D) 09 (Jun) .................... 1.298, 1.300

### F

F-Tex SIA v Lietuvos-Anglijos UAB "Jadecloud-Vilma": C-213/10 (2012) C-213/10, ECLI:EU:C:2012:215, [2013] Bus LR 232, EUCJ .............................. 6.2, 6.8

F v F (divorce: insolvency) [1994] 1 FLR 359, [1994] 2 FCR 689, [1994] Fam Law 253, [1993] Lexis Citation 1572 ...................................................... 1.395

FI Call Ltd, Re, Apex Global Management Ltd v FI Call Ltd [2015] EWHC 3269 (Ch), [2015] All ER (D) 183 (Nov); affd sub nom Apex Global Management Ltd v Global Torch Ltd [2017] EWCA Civ 315, [2017] All ER (D) 157 (Apr) .............. 1.174, 1.176

FMS Financial Management Services Ltd, Re (1988) 5 BCC 191, [1988] Lexis Citation 1556 .................................................................... 1.59

FSA Business Software Ltd, Re [1990] BCLC 825, [1990] BCC 465 .................. 1.178

Fabric Sales Ltd v Eratex Ltd [1984] 1 WLR 863n, 128 Sol Jo 330, CA .............. 1.169

Fairfield Sentry Ltd, Re (2010) 440 BR 60 ........................................ 7.29

Fairway Graphics Ltd, Re [1991] BCLC 468 ....................................... 1.180

Fairway Magazines Ltd, Re [1993] BCLC 643, [1992] BCC 924 .............. 1.303, 1.309
Fakhry v Pagden [2020] EWCA Civ 1207, [2021] 2 BCLC 35, [2021] BPIR 526,
  [2020] All ER (D) 49 (Sep) ..................................................... 1.160, 1.270
Falcon RJ Development Ltd, Re [1987] BCLC 437, 3 BCC 146 ...................... 1.168
Fancy Dress Balls Co Ltd, Re [1899] WN 109, 43 Sol Jo 657 ...................... 1.178
Fargro Ltd v Godfroy [1986] 3 All ER 279, [1986] 1 WLR 1134, [1986] BCLC 370,
  2 BCC 99, 167, 130 Sol Jo 524, [1986] LS Gaz R 2326 ............................. 1.220
Farmizer (Products) Ltd, Re, Moore v Gadd [1997] 1 BCLC 589, [1997] BCC 655,
  [1997] 8 LS Gaz R 27, (1997) Times, 17 February, 141 Sol Jo LB 45 ........... 1.271, 1.272
Farnborough Airport Properties Co v Revenue and Customs Comrs [2019] EWCA Civ
  118, [2019] 2 All ER 435, [2019] 1 WLR 4077, [2019] STC 517 ...................... 1.88
Fashoff (UK) Ltd v Linton [2008] EWHC 537 (Ch), [2008] 2 BCLC 362, [2008] BCC
  542 ...................................................................................... 1.660
Feakins v Department for Environment Food and Rural Affairs. See Secretary of State for
  the Environment, Food and Rural Affairs v Feakins
Fearman (W F) Ltd, Re (1987) 4 BCC 139, [1987] Lexis Citation 1196 .............. 1.188
Fearman (W F) Ltd (No 2), Re (1987) 4 BCC 141, [1987] Lexis Citation 1197 . 1.167, 2.128
Federal Bank of Australia Ltd, Re [1893] WN 77, 62 LJ Ch 561, 2 R 416, 37 Sol Jo 441,
  68 LT 728, CA ......................................................................... 1.281
Federal-Mogul Aftermarket UK Ltd, Re. See Gleave v Board of the Pension Protection
  Fund
Feetum v Levy [2005] EWCA Civ 1601, [2006] Ch 585, [2006] 3 WLR 427,
  [2006] 2 BCLC 102, (2006) Times, 2 January, [2006] BPIR 379, [2005] All ER (D) 313
  (Dec), CSRC vol 29 iss 20/2, sub nom Cabvision Ltd v Feetum [2006] BCC 340 ...... 1.122
Fehily v Atkinson [2016] EWHC 3069 (Ch), [2017] Bus LR 695, [2017] BPIR 21,
  [2016] All ER (D) 20 (Dec) ............................................................. 1.64
Fenland District Council v Sheppard [2011] EWHC 2829 (Ch), [2012] 1 EGLR 49,
  [2012] 02 Estates Gazette 68, [2011] 45 EG 96 (CS), [2012] BPIR 289 .............. 1.439
Fenton, Re, ex p Fenton Textile Association Ltd [1931] 1 Ch 85, 99 LJ Ch 358, [1929] B
  & CR 189, [1930] All ER Rep 15, 74 Sol Jo 387, 143 LT 273, 46 TLR 478, CA ...... 2.852
Fern Advisers Ltd v Burford [2014] EWHC 762 (QB), [2014] BPIR 581 .............. 1.399
Ferrier & Knight v Civil Aviation Authority (1994) 48 FCR 163 ...................... 1.303
Field (a debtor), Re, ex p Debtor v H and J Quick Ltd [1978] Ch 371, [1978] 2 All ER
  981, [1977] 3 WLR 937, 121 Sol Jo 727 ............................................. 1.381
Fieldfisher LLP v Pennyfeathers Ltd [2016] EWHC 566 (Ch), [2016] BCC 697 . 1.178, 1.628,
                                                                              1.629
Fielding v Hunt (acting as Liquidator of the Burnden Group Ltd) [2017] EWHC 406 (Ch),
  167 NLJ 7737, [2017] 2 Costs LO 191, [2017] BPIR 585, [2017] All ER (D) 29
  (Mar) .................................................................................. 2.834, 2.836
Fielding v Seery [2004] BCC 315 ..................................................... 1.160
Fildes Bros Ltd, Re [1970] 1 All ER 923, [1970] 1 WLR 592, 114 Sol Jo 301 .. 1.175, 1.176
Financial Conduct Authority v Allied Wallet Ltd [2019] EWHC 2808 (Ch) ........... 1.630
Financial Services Compensation Scheme Ltd v Larnell (Insurances) Ltd [2005] EWCA
  Civ 1408, [2006] QB 808, [2006] 2 WLR 751, [2006] Lloyd's Rep IR 448, [2006] BCC
  690, 149 Sol Jo LB 1488, [2006] BPIR 1370, [2005] All ER (D) 388 (Nov) ........... 1.183
Finnerty v Clark [2010] EWHC 2538 (Ch), [2010] Bus LR 1747, [2011] BCC 64, [2010]
  NLJR 1613, [2011] BPIR 242, [2010] All ER (D) 84 (Nov); affd sub nom Finnerty v
  Clark [2011] EWCA Civ 858, [2012] 1 BCLC 286, [2012] Bus LR 594, [2011] BCC
  702, [2011] NLJR 1061, [2011] BPIR 1514, [2011] All ER (D) 201 (Jul) .............. 1.705
Firepower Operations Pty Ltd (No2), Re [2008] FCA 1228 ......................... 1.193
1st Credit Finance v Carr [2013] EWHC 2318 (Ch), [2013] BPIR 1012 .............. 1.395
1st Credit (Finance) Ltd v Bartram [2010] EWHC 2910 (Ch), [2011] BPIR 1 ......... 1.384
First Express Ltd, Re [1992] BCLC 824, [1991] BCC 782, (1991) Times, 10 October
  .......................................................................................... 1.298
First Independent Factors and Finance Ltd v Churchill [2006] EWCA Civ 1623,
  [2007] 1 BCLC 293, [2007] Bus LR 676, (2007) Times, 11 January, [2007] BPIR 14,
  [2006] All ER (D) 427 (Nov), CSRC vol 30 iss 21/1, sub nom Churchill v First
  Independent Factors and Finance Ltd [2007] BCC 45 ............................. 2.1041
First Independent Factors and Finance Ltd v Mountford [2008] EWHC 835 (Ch),
  [2008] 2 BCLC 297, [2008] BCC 598, [2008] BPIR 515, [2008] All ER (D) 330
  (Apr) ............................................................. 1.275, 1.276, 2.1044
First Line Distribution Pty Ltd v Whiley (1995) 13 ACLC 1216 ...................... 1.175
Fitch v Official Receiver [1996] 1 WLR 242, [1996] BCC 328, (1995) Times,
  21 November, 140 Sol Jo LB 22, [1996] BPIR 152, CA ............................... 2.814
Fitness Centre (South East) Ltd, Re [1986] BCLC 518, 2 BCC 99, 535, [1986] Lexis
  Citation 1117 ......................................................................... 1.168

Fivestar Properties Ltd, Re [2015] EWHC 2782 (Ch), [2016] 1 WLR 1104, 165 NLJ
7673, [2016] 1 P & CR D31, [2015] All ER (D) 76 (Oct) .......................... 1.701
Flagstaff Silver Mining Co of Utah, Re (1875) LR 20 Eq 268, 45 LJ Ch 136, 23 WR
611 ...................................................................................... 1.175
Flame Sa v Primera Maritime (Hellas) Ltd [2010] EWHC 2053 (Ch), [2010] All ER (D)
157 (Jul) ............................................................................. 2.1048
Fletcher v Vooght [2000] Lexis Citation 3099, [2000] BPIR 435, [2000] All ER (D) 257
............................................................................ 1.353, 1.358
Flett v Revenue and Customs Comrs [2010] EWHC 2662 (Ch), [2010] BPIR 1075 ... 1.382,
1.395
Flexi Containers Ltd, Re, Breese v (liquidator of Flexi Containers Ltd) v Hiley (by her
litigation friend Hiley) [2018] EWHC 12 (Ch), 168 NLJ 7778, [2018] BPIR 710,
[2018] All ER (D) 77 (Jan) ...................................................... 1.324
Flightline Ltd v Edwards [2003] EWCA Civ 63, [2003] 3 All ER 1200, [2003] 1 WLR
1200, [2003] 1 BCLC 427, [2003] BCC 361, [2003] 13 LS Gaz R 28, (2003) Times,
13 February, 147 Sol Jo LB 178, [2003] BPIR 549, [2003] All ER (D) 50 (Feb) . 1.183, 1.516
Flint (a bankrupt), Re [1993] Ch 319, [1993] 2 WLR 537, [1993] 1 FLR 763, [1993] 1
FCR 518, [1993] Fam Law 210, [1993] 5 LS Gaz R 40, (1992) Times, 16 July, 136 Sol
Jo LB 221 ............................................................... 1.180, 1.398
Fliptex Ltd v Hogg [2004] EWHC 1280 (Ch), [2004] BCC 870 .............. 1.636, 2.142
Floor Fourteen Ltd, Re; Lewis v IRC. See Lewis v IRC
Focus Insurance Co Ltd, Re [1997] 1 BCLC 219, [1996] BCC 659, (1996) Times,
6 May ............................................................................ 1.586
Foenander v Allan [2006] EWHC 2102 (Ch), [2006] BPIR 1392, [2006] All ER (D) 352
(Jul) ...................................................................... 1.455, 2.820
Fondazione Enasarco v Lehman Brothers Finance S.A. [2014] EWHC 34 (Ch),
[2014] 2 BCLC 662, [2014] All ER (D) 90 (Jan) ......................................... 6.8
Forcesun Ltd, Re [2002] EWHC 443 (Ch), [2002] 2 BCLC 302, [2002] All ER (D) 323
(Feb) .............................................................................. 1.177
Ford v Alexander (trustee of the estates of Daniel Ford and Liubov Ford) [2012] EWHC
266 (Ch), [2012] BPIR 528 ....................................................... 1.455
Ford v Wolverhampton City Council (Local Government Ombudsman's Report) [2008]
BPIR 1304 ....................................................................... 1.381
Ford & Carter Ltd v Midland Bank Ltd (1979) 10 LDAB 182, 129 NLJ 543, HL ...... 1.78
Forrester & Lamego Ltd, Re [1997] 2 BCLC 155 ................................... 1.188
Forstater, Re [2015] BPIR 21 .................................................... 2.905
Forster v Wilson (1843) 13 LJ Ex 209, 12 M & W 191, 152 ER 1165, ExCh ......... 1.159
Fortress Value Recovery Fund I LLC v Blue Skye Special Opportunities Fund L.P (A Firm)
[2013] EWHC 14 (Comm), [2013] 1 All ER (Comm) 973, [2013] 2 BCLC 351, [2013]
BPIR 276, [2013] All ER (D) 87 (Jan) ...................................... 1.582, 6.20
Fortune Copper Mining Co, Re (1870) LR 10 Eq 390, 40 LJ Ch 43, 22 LT 650 ...... 2.1048
4 Eng Ltd v Harper (No 2) [2009] EWHC 2633 (Ch), [2010] 1 BCLC 176, [2010] BCC
746, (2009) Times, 6 November, [2010] BPIR 1, [2010] Bus LR D58 .......... 1.582, 1.584
Four Private Investment Funds v Lomas [2008] EWHC 2869 (Ch), [2009] 1 BCLC 161,
[2009] BCC 632, [2009] Bus LR D28, [2008] All ER (D) 237 (Nov) ................... 1.691
Fourie v Le Roux [2005] EWHC 922 (Ch), [2005] BPIR 779, [2005] All ER (D) 263
(May) ............................................................................ 2.751
Fowlds (a bankrupt), Re, Fowlds v Bucknall (as joint trustees in bankruptcy of Peter
Herbert Fowlds) [2020] EWHC 329 (Ch), [2020] BPIR 541, [2020] All ER (D) 52
(Mar) ....................................................................... 1.427, 1.519
Fox Street Village Ltd, Re (in administration) [2020] EWHC 2541 (Ch), [2020] PLSCS
177, [2020] All ER (D) 05 (Oct) ............... 1.679, 1.688, 1.696, 1.704, 1.705, 2.196
Foxley v United Kingdom (Application 33274/96) (2000) 31 EHRR 637, (2000) Times,
4 July, 8 BHRC 571, [2000] BPIR 1009, EctHR ..................................... 1.497
Foyle v Turner [2007] BPIR 43 ................................................... 1.455
Francis v Solomon Taylor & Shaw (a firm) [2013] EWHC 9 (Ch), [2013] BPIR 314,
[2013] All ER (D) 39 (Jan) ...................................................... 1.382
Frank Saul (Fashions) Ltd v HMRC (18 May 2012, unreported), ChD ............... 1.178
Franses v Hay [2015] EWHC 3468 (Ch), [2016] BPIR 355 ......................... 2.482
Franses v Oomerjee [2005] BPIR 1320 ........................................... 1.423
Fraser Turner Ltd v PricewaterhouseCoopers LLP [2019] EWCA Civ 1290 .......... 1.691
Free Ties Leases Ltd, In the matter of [2015] EWHC 3974 (Ch) .............. 1.178, 2.324
Freeburn v Hunt [2010] BPIR 325 ............................................... 1.414
Freeman v General Publishing Co [1894] 2 QB 380, 63 LJQB 678, 1 Mans 366, 10 R 366,
42 WR 539, 38 Sol Jo 532, 70 LT 845, DC ....................................... 1.164
French v Barcham. See Barcham, Re

French v Cipolletta [2009] EWHC 223 (Ch), [2009] All ER (D) 155 (May) .......... 1.270
French's (Wine Bar) Ltd, Re [1987] BCLC 499, 3 BCC 173 ......................... 1.180
Frontsouth Ltd (in admin), Re [2011] EWHC 1668 (Ch), [2012] 1 BCLC 818, [2011] BCC 635, (2011) Times, 22 September, [2011] BPIR 1382, [2011] All ER (D) 41 (Jul) ................................................. 1.629, 1.630, 1.639, 2.127, 2.820
Frosdick v Fox [2017] EWHC 1737 (Ch), [2018] 1 WLR 38, 167 NLJ 7761, [2017] BPIR 1194, [2017] All ER (D) 35 (Aug) .................... 1.235, 1.396, 1.434, 1.435, 2.1022
Fryer v Brook [1984] LS Gaz R 2856, [1984] Lexis Citation 354, [1998] BPIR 687, CA ........................................................................................... 1.452
Fulham Football Club (1987) Ltd v Richards [2011] EWCA Civ 855, [2012] Ch 333 ........................................................................................... 1.174
Fuller v Cyracuse Ltd [2001] 1 BCLC 187, [2001] BCC 806, [2000] Lexis Citation 3754, sub nom Fuller v Cyracuse Ltd, Fuller v Realtime Partner UK Ltd [2000] All ER (D) 770 ............................................................................... 1.174, 1.178
Fulton v AIB Group (UK) plc [2014] NICh 8, [2014] BPIR 1169 .................... 1.660
Funding Corp Block Discounting Ltd v Lexi Holdings plc (in admin) [2008] EWHC 985 (Ch), [2008] 2 BCLC 596, [2008] All ER (D) 97 (May) ............................ 1.660
Fussell, Re, ex p Allen (1882) 20 ChD 341, 51 LJ Ch 724, 30 WR 601, 47 LT 65, CA ........................................................................................... 1.235

## G

G-Tech Construction Ltd, Re [2007] BPIR 1275 .................. 1.630, 1.721, 2.820
G & M Aldridge Pty Ltd v Walsh [2002] BPIR 482, AusHC ........................ 1.303
GBI Investments Ltd, Re [2010] EWHC 37 (Ch), [2010] 2 BCLC 624, [2010] BPIR 356, [2010] All ER (D) 171 (Jun) ........................................................ 1.178
GHE Realisations Ltd (formerly Gatehouse Estates Ltd), Re [2005] EWHC 2400 (Ch), [2006] 1 All ER 357, [2006] 1 WLR 287, [2006] BCC 139, (2005) Times, 11 November, [2005] All ER (D) 64 (Nov) .......................... 1.682, 1.700, 1.701
GP Aviation Group International (in liq), Re [2013] EWHC 1447 (Ch), [2014] 2 All ER 448, [2014] 1 WLR 166, [2014] 1 BCLC 474, [2013] NLJR 21, [2013] BPIR 576, [2013] All ER (D) 41 (Jun) ................................................ 1.396, 1.605
Gaardsoe v Optimal Wealth Management Ltd (in liq) [2012] EWHC 3266 (Ch), [2013] Ch 298, [2013] 2 WLR 550, [2013] BPIR 59 ................................... 1.660
Galileo Group Ltd, Re, Elles v Hambros Bank Ltd (Bank of England intervening) [1999] Ch 100, [1998] 1 All ER 545, [1998] 2 WLR 364, [1998] 1 BCLC 318, [1998] BCC 228, 14 LDAB 27, [1997] 46 LS Gaz R 30, (1997) Times, 10 December, 142 Sol Jo LB 21, [1997] All ER (D) 70 ................................................... 1.300
Gallagher (N T) & Son Ltd (in liq), Re, Shierson v Tomlinson [2002] EWCA Civ 404, [2002] 3 All ER 474, [2002] 1 WLR 2380, [2002] 2 BCLC 133, [2002] BCC 867, (2002) Times, 11 April, [2002] BPIR 565, [2002] All ER (D) 396 (Mar) . 1.59, 1.379, 1.388, 2.75, 2.482
Gallard, Re, ex p Gallard [1896] 1 QB 68, 65 LJQB 199, 2 Mans 515, 44 WR 121, [1895–9] All ER Rep 1002, 40 Sol Jo 99, 73 LT 457, 12 TLR 43, CA ................ 1.194
Gallidoro Trawlers Ltd, Re [1991] BCLC 411, [1991] BCC 691 ..................... 1.630
Galloppa v Galloppa [1999] BPIR 352 ............................................ 1.382
Galway and Salthill Tramways Co, Re [1918] 1 IR 62, 52 ILT 41 .................. 1.176
Gamlestaden plc v Brackland Magazines Ltd. See Brackland Magazines Ltd, Re; Gamelstaden plc v Brackland Magazines Ltd
Gardner v Lemma Europe Insurance Company Ltd (in liqation) [2016] EWCA Civ 484, [2016] All ER (D) 175 (May) ...................................................... 7.33
Garrow v Society of Lloyd's [2000] Lloyd's Rep IR 38, [1999] 42 LS Gaz R 40, (1999) Times, 28 October, [1999] Lexis Citation 3454, [1999] BPIR 885, [1999] All ER (D) 1096 ................................................................................ 2.530
Garton (Western) Ltd, Re [1989] BCLC 304, 5 BCC 198 ......................... 2.324
Garwood (Christopher) v Ambrose (Mark) [2012] EWHC 1494 (Ch), [2012] BPIR 996 ........................................................................................... 1.397
Garwood v Bolter [2015] EWHC 3619 (Ch), [2016] BPIR 367 ..................... 1.489
Gas and Electricity Markets Authority v GB Energy Supply Ltd [2016] EWHC 3341 (Ch), [2017] All ER (D) 49 (Jan) .......................................................... 1.617
Gate Gourmet Luxembourg IV Sarl v Morby [2015] EWHC 1203 (Ch), [2015] BPIR 787, [2015] All ER (D) 117 (May) .................................................... 1.380
Gategroup Guarantee Ltd, Re [2021] EWHC 304 (Ch) .......................... 6.2, 7.1
Gatnom Capital and Finance Ltd, Re [2010] EWHC 3353 (Ch), [2011] BPIR 1013, [2010] All ER (D) 233 (Dec) ...................................................... 1.65

Gatnom Capital and Finance Ltd, Re [2011] EWHC 3716 (Ch), [2012] BPIR 299, [2011] All ER (D) 218 (Nov) ...................................................... 1.65, 1.178
Geelong Building Society, Re (1996) 14 ACLC 334 ................................... 1.741
Geiger, Re [1915] 1 KB 439, 84 LJKB 589, [1915] HBR 44, [1914–15] All ER Rep 694, 59 Sol Jo 250, 112 LT 562, CA ........................................................ 1.194
Gendrot v Chadwick (joint trustees in bankruptcy of Edward Hagan) [2018] EWHC 48 (Ch), 168 NLJ 7778, [2018] BPIR 423, [2018] All ER (D) 91 (Jan) ................... 1.459
General Rolling Stock Co, Re, Joint Stock Discount Co's Claim (1872) LR 7 Ch App 646, 41 LJ Ch 732, 20 WR 762, [1861–73] All ER Rep 434, 27 LT 88, CACh ............. 1.183
General Works Co, Re, Gill's Case (1879) 12 ChD 755, 48 LJ Ch 774, 27 WR 934, 41 LT 21 ........................................................................ 1.202, 2.852
Gerah Imports Pty Ltd v The Duke Group Ltd (in liqation) (1994) 12 ACLC 116, (1994) 12 ACSR 513 ................................................................... 1.300
Gerard v Worth of Paris Ltd [1936] 2 All ER 905, 80 Sol Jo 633, CA ................. 1.164
German Graphics Graphische Maschinen GmbH v Schee: C-292/08 (2009) C-292/08, ECLI:EU:C:2009:544, [2009] ECR I-8421, [2009] All ER (D) 75 (Sep), EUCJ . 6.8, 6.9, 6.12
Gerrard (Thomas) & Son Ltd, Re [1968] Ch 455, [1967] 2 All ER 525, [1967] 3 WLR 84, 111 Sol Jo 329 ........................................................................ 1.270
Gertner v CFL Finance Ltd. See Re Gertner; CFL Finance Ltd v Rubin
Gertner v CFL Finance Ltd [2020] EWHC 1241 (Ch), [2020] BPIR 752, [2020] All ER (D) 147 (May) ..................................................................... 1.65, 2.550
Gertner, Re CFL Finance Ltd v Rubin [2017] EWHC 111 (Ch), [2017] BPIR 336, [2017] All ER (D) 102 (Feb); affd sub nom Gertner v CFL Finance Ltd [2018] EWCA Civ 1781, 168 NLJ 7806, [2018] All ER (D) 169 (Jul) .......................... 1.65, 2.907
Ghai and Maymask (228) Ltd [2020] UKUT 293 (LC), [2020] All ER (D) 112 (Oct) ........................................................................................... 1.88
Gibraltar Residential Properties Ltd v Gibralcon 2004 SA [2010] EWHC 2595 (TCC), [2011] BLR 126, [2010] All ER (D) 167 (Oct) ......................................... 6.9
Gibson Dunn & Crutcher (a firm) v Rio Properties Inc [2004] EWCA Civ 1043, [2004] 1 WLR 2702, 148 Sol Jo LB 946, [2004] BPIR 1203, [2004] All ER (D) 544 (Jul) ...... 1.188, 1.400
Giles v Rhind [2008] EWCA Civ 118, [2009] Ch 191, [2008] 3 All ER 697, [2008] 3 WLR 1233, [2008] 2 BCLC 1, [2008] Bus LR 1103, [2009] BCC 590, (2008) Times, 25 March, [2008] BPIR 342, [2008] All ER (D) 410 (Feb) ........................... 1.582
Gill v Quinn [2004] EWHC 883 (Ch), [2005] BPIR 129, [2004] All ER (D) 21 (Apr) ........................................................................................... 1.395
Gillan v HEC Enterprises Ltd applications [2016] EWHC 3179 (Ch), [2017] 1 BCLC 340, [2016] All ER (D) 103 (Dec) ............................................. 1.618, 1.716
Gilmartin (a bankrupt), Re, ex p bankrupt v International Agency and Supply Ltd [1989] 2 All ER 835, [1989] 1 WLR 513, 133 Sol Jo 877 ................................... 2.815
Glaser (W & A) Ltd, Re [1994] BCC 199, Ct of Ch ............. 1.194, 2.814, 2.942, 2.962
Glasgow City Council v Craig [2008] CSOH 171, [2009] 1 BCLC 742, [2009] RA 61, [2010] BCC 235, 2009 SC 185, 2009 SLT 212, 2008 Scot (D) 17/12, CSOH .......... 1.276
Glasgow (the bankruptcy trustee of Harlequin Property SVG Ltd) v ELS Law Ltd (Bar Council of England and Wales intervening) [2017] EWHC 3004 (Ch), [2018] 1 WLR 1564, [2018] 1 BCLC 339, [2018] 1 Costs LO 79, [2018] BPIR 431, [2017] All ER (D) 214 (Nov) ............................................................... 7.23
Gleave v Board of the Pension Protection Fund [2008] EWHC 1099 (Ch), [2008] All ER (D) 287 (May), sub nom Federal-Mogul Aftermarket UK Ltd, Re [2008] BPIR 846 .... 1.59, 1.67
Glenister v Rowe [2000] Ch 76, [1999] 3 All ER 452, [1999] 3 WLR 716, [1999] 20 LS Gaz R 39, [1999] NLJR 858, (1999) Times, 28 April, [1999] Lexis Citation 2161, 143 Sol Jo LB 156, [1999] BPIR 674, [1999] All ER (D) 401 ............ 1.460, 1.515
Glenn Maud Edgeworth Capital (Luxembourg) SARL, Re v Maud [2020] EWHC 974 (Ch), [2020] BPIR 903, [2020] All ER (D) 162 (Apr) ................... 1.178, 1.381, 2.550
Glenn Maud Edgeworth Capital (Luxembourg) SARL, Re v Maud [2020] EWHC 1469 (Ch), [2020] BPIR 903 ....................................... 1.178, 1.502, 2.553, 2.691
Glint Pay Ltd and other companies (in administration), Re [2020] EWHC 3078 (Ch), [2020] All ER (D) 142 (Nov) ..................... 1.633, 1.691 1.697, 1.715, 2.820
Global Acquirers Ltd v Laycatelcom LDA (2 July 2014, unreported), ChD ........... 2.338
Global Corporate Ltd v Hale [2017] EWHC 2277 (Ch), [2017] All ER (D) 50 (Sep) ........................................................................................... 1.303
Globe Legal Services Ltd, Re [2002] BCC 858 ...................................... 2.838

Globespan Airways Ltd (Formerly in Admin and now in Liq), In the matter of [2012] EWCA Civ 1159, [2012] 4 All ER 1124, [2013] 1 WLR 1122, [2013] 1 BCLC 339, [2012] 33 LS Gaz R 18, [2012] NLJR 1124, (2012) Times, 19 November, [2012] All ER (D) 144 (Aug) ...... 1.700

Glyncorrwg Colliery Co Ltd, Re, Railway Debenture and General Trust Co v Glyncorrwg Colliery Co Ltd [1926] Ch 951, 96 LJ Ch 43, [1926] All ER Rep 318, 70 Sol Jo 857, 136 LT 159 ...... 1.81

Godfrey v Torpy [2007] EWHC 919 (Ch), [2007] Bus LR 1203, (2007) Times, 16 May, [2007] BPIR 1538, [2007] All ER (D) 181 (Apr) ...... 1.583

Gold Co, Re (1879) 12 ChD 77, 48 LJ Ch 650, 27 WR 757, 40 LT 865, CA ...... 1.300

Goldacre (Offices) Ltd v Nortel Networks UK Ltd (in administration) [2010] Ch 455, [2010] 3 WLR 171, [2010] 2 BCLC 248, [2010] Bus LR 870, [2010] BCC 299, [2010] 1 EGLR 25, [2009] EWHC 3389 (Ch), [2010] 09 EG 168, [2010] All ER (D) 54 (Jan) ...... 2.183

Golden Chemical Products Ltd, Re [1976] Ch 300, [1976] 2 All ER 543, [1976] 3 WLR 1, 120 Sol Jo 401 ...... 1.177

Goldfarb v Alibhai (11 December 2017, unreported), Business and Property Courts ...... 1.271

Goldfarb v Higgins [2009] EWHC 601 (Ch), [2009] Bus LR 1141, [2010] BCC 787, (2009) Times, 2 April ...... 1.271

Goldfarb (liquidator of Overnight Ltd) v Higgins [2010] EWHC 613 (Ch), [2010] 2 BCLC 186, [2010] BCC 796, [2011] Bus LR D30, [2010] All ER (D) 268 (May) ...... 1.271

Goldman Sachs International v Novo Banco SA [2016] EWCA Civ 1092, [2017] 2 BCLC 277, [2016] All ER (D) 63 (Nov); affd sub nom Goldman Sachs International v Novo Banco SA [2018] UKSC 34, [2018] 1 WLR 3683, [2018] All ER (D) 18 (Jul), SC ...... 6.3

Goldspan Ltd, Re [2003] BPIR 93, [2001] All ER (D) 412 (Oct) ...... 1.61

Goldthorpe & Lacey Ltd, Re (1987) 3 BCC 595, [1987] Lexis Citation 441, CA ...... 2.331

Golstein v Bishop [2013] EWHC 1706 (Ch), [2013] BPIR 708 ...... 1.65

Golstein v Bishop [2016] EWHC 2187 (Ch), 166 NLJ 7714, [2016] All ER (D) 27 (Sep) ...... 1.65

Gomba Holdings UK Ltd v Homan [1986] 3 All ER 94, [1986] 1 WLR 1301, [1986] BCLC 331, 2 BCC 99, 102, 130 Sol Jo 821, [1987] LS Gaz R 36 ...... 1.82, 1.92

Gomba Holdings UK Ltd v Minories Finance Ltd (No 2) [1993] Ch 171, [1992] 4 All ER 588, [1992] 3 WLR 723, [1993] BCLC 7, [1992] BCC 877, 12 LDAB 217, (1992) Times, 14 February ...... 1.80, 1.88

Gonzalves, Re (a bankrupt) [2011] BPIR 419 ...... 1.489

Gordian Holdings Ltd v Sofroniou [2021] EWHC 235 (Comm), [2021] BPIR 808 ...... 1.582

Gordon & Breach Science Publishers Ltd, Re [1995] 2 BCLC 189, [1995] BCC 261, (1994) Times, 4 November ...... 1.168

Gosscott (Groundworks) Ltd, Re [1988] BCLC 363, 4 BCC 372, PCC 297, [1988] 2 FTLR 80, (1988) Times, 28 March ...... 1.630, 2.136

Gotham v Doodes. See Doodes v Gotham

Gould v Itmo Advent Computer Training Ltd [2010] EWHC 459 (Ch), [2011] BCC 44, [2010] All ER (D) 53 (Jun) ...... 1.663, 1.666, 1.724, 2.164

Gourdain v Nadler: C-133/78 [1979] ECR 733, [1979] 3 CMLR 180, EUCJ ...... 6.8

Government of India, Ministry of Finance (Revenue Division) v Taylor [1955] AC 491, [1955] 1 All ER 292, [1955] 2 WLR 303, 34 ATC 10, 48 R & IT 98, [1955] TR 9, 99 Sol Jo 94, HL ...... 7.26

Governor and Co of the Bank of Ireland v Colliers International UK plc (in admin) [2012] EWHC 2942 (Ch), [2013] Ch 422, [2013] 2 WLR 895, [2012] BPIR 1099, [2012] All ER (D) 255 (Oct) ...... 1.183, 1.399, 1.660

Grady v Prison Service [2003] EWCA Civ 527, [2003] 3 All ER 745, [2003] IRLR 474, [2003] ICR 753, [2003] 25 LS Gaz R 45, (2003) Times, 18 April, 147 Sol Jo LB 540, [2003] BPIR 823, [2003] All ER (D) 196 (Apr) ...... 1.396

Graham v Edge (1888) 20 QBD 683, 57 LJQB 406, 36 WR 529, 58 LT 913, 4 TLR 442, CA ...... 1.198

Graico Property Ltd, Re [2016] EWHC 2827 (Ch), [2017] BCC 15 ...... 1.176, 1.696

Grant v Baker [2016] EWHC 1782 (Ch), [2017] 2 FLR 646, [2016] Fam Law 1215, [2016] BPIR 1409, [2016] All ER (D) 108 (Jul) ...... 1.455

Grant v Hayes [2014] EWHC 2646 (Ch), [2014] BPIR 1455 ...... 1.396

Graveholt Ltd v Hughes [2005] EWCA Civ 897, [2005] 2 BCLC 421, [2005] BPIR 1345, [2005] All ER (D) 246 (Jul) ...... 1.235

Gray's Inn Construction Co Ltd, Re [1980] 1 All ER 814, [1980] 1 WLR 711, 10 LDAB 189, 124 Sol Jo 463 ...... 1.180

Great Britain Mutual Life Assurance Society, Re (1880) 16 ChD 246, 51 LJ Ch 10, 29 WR 202, 43 LT 684, CA ............. 1.178
Great Cwmsymtoy Silver Lead Co, Re (1868) 16 WR 270, 17 LT 463 ............. 2.1048
Great Eastern Electric Co Ltd, Re [1941] Ch 241, [1941] 1 All ER 409, 111 LJ Ch 1, [1940–1942] B & CR 45, 85 Sol Jo 190, 165 LT 366, 57 TLR 373 ............. 1.141, 1.742
Great Northern Copper Mining Co of South Australia Ltd, Re, ex p Great Northern Copper Mining Co of South Australia Ltd (1869) 17 WR 462, 20 LT 264; affd (1869) 20 LT 347 ............. 1.175
Great Western Forest of Dean Coal Consumers Co, Re, Carter's Case (1886) 31 ChD 496, 55 LJ Ch 494, 34 WR 516, 54 LT 531, 2 TLR 293 ............. 1.270
Green (trustee in bankruptcy of Austin) v Austina [2014] BPIR 1176, CC ............. 1.459
Green v BDO Stoy Hayward LLP [2005] EWHC 2413 (Ch), (2005) Times, 8 November, [2005] All ER (D) 16 (Nov), CSRC vol 29 iss 17/2 ............. 1.300
Green (liquidator of Al Fayhaa Mass Media Ltd) v Eltai [2014] Lexis Citation 310, [2015] BPIR 24 ............. 1.303, 1.304
Green v Gigi Brooks Ltd [2015] EWHC 961 (Ch) ............. 1.628
Green v Satsangi [1998] 1 BCLC 458, [1998] BPIR 55 ............. 1.415, 1.622
Green v Wright [2017] EWCA Civ 111, [2017] BPIR 430, [2017] All ER (D) 13 (Mar) ............. 1.59, 2.482
Greene King plc v Stanley [2001] EWCA Civ 1966, [2002] BPIR 491, [2002] All ER (D) 56 (Jan) ............. 1.59
Greenhaven Motors Ltd (in liqation), Re [1997] 1 BCLC 739, [1997] BCC 547; on appeal [1999] 1 BCLC 635, [1999] BCC 463 ............. 1.176, 1.219, 1.220, 1.741
Greenwood & Co, Re [1900] 2 QB 306, 69 LJQB 751, 7 Mans 456, 48 WR 607, 82 LT 843, DC ............. 1.168
Gregory v Portsmouth City Council [2000] 1 AC 419, [2000] 1 All ER 560, [2000] 2 WLR 306, [2000] 4 LRC 181, [2000] LGR 203, [2000] 06 LS Gaz R 36, [2000] NLJR 131, (2000) Times, 2 February, [2000] Lexis Citation 2538, 144 Sol Jo LB 82, [2000] All ER (D) 75, HL ............. 1.382
Greight Pty Ltd (in liqation), Re [2006] FCA 17, Aust Fed Ct ............. 1.160, 1.193
Gresham International Ltd v Moonie [2009] EWHC 1093 (Ch), [2010] Ch 285, [2010] 2 WLR 362, [2009] 2 BCLC 256, [2010] Bus LR 67, [2010] BPIR 122, [2009] All ER (D) 14 (Jun) ............. 2.297, 2.397
Grey Marlin Ltd, Re [1999] 4 All ER 429, [2000] 1 WLR 370, [1999] 2 BCLC 658, [2000] BCC 410, (1999) Times, 29 June, [1999] Lexis Citation 3027, [1999] All ER (D) 527 ............. 1.167, 1.188, 1.208, 2.354, 2.433
Greystoke v Hamilton-Smith, Re a Debtor (No 140 IO of 1995) [1997] BPIR 24 ............. 1.60
Griffin v Awoderu [2008] EWHC 349 (Ch), [2008] BPIR 877, [2008] All ER (D) 140 (Jan) ............. 1.582, 1.584
Griffith v Paget (1877) 5 ChD 894, 46 LJ Ch 493, 25 WR 523 ............. 1.162
Griffiths v Civil Aviation Authority [1997] BPIR 50, AusFC ............. 1.396
Griffiths v Yorkshire Bank plc [1994] 1 WLR 1427, [1994] 36 LS Gaz R 36 ............. 1.84
Grosvenor Hill (Qld) Pty Ltd v Barber (1994) 120 ALR 262 ............. 1.300
Grosvenor Metal Co Ltd, Re [1950] Ch 63, [1949] 2 All ER 948, 93 Sol Jo 774, 65 TLR 755 ............. 1.240
Grovewood Holdings plc v James Capel & Co Ltd [1995] Ch 80, [1994] 4 All ER 417, [1995] 2 WLR 70, [1994] 2 BCLC 782, [1995] BCC 760, [1994] NLJR 1405, (1994) Times, 15 August ............. 1.743
Guidezone Ltd, Re [2000] 2 BCLC 321, [2001] BCC 692, [2000] Lexis Citation 3146, [2000] All ER (D) 981 ............. 1.174
Guinan v Caldwell Associates Ltd [2003] EWHC 3348 (Ch), [2004] BPIR 531, [2004] All ER (D) 123 (Mar) ............. 1.395
Gunningham, Re [2002] BPIR 302 ............. 2.755, 2.758
Gursharan Randhawa v Andrew Turpin [2016] EWHC 2156 (Ch), [2017] 1 BCLC 240, [2016] All ER (D) 188 (Jul); revsd sub nom Randhawa v Turpin (as former Joint Administrators of BW Estates Ltd) [2017] EWCA Civ 1201, [2018] 2 WLR 1175, 167 NLJ 7760, (2017) Times, 05 October, [2017] All ER (D) 40 (Aug) ............. 1.639
Gwinnutt (as the First Defendant's Trustee in Bankruptcy) v George [2019] EWCA Civ 656, [2019] Ch 471, [2019] 3 WLR 229, [2019] BPIR 1195, [2019] All ER (D) 79 (Apr) ............. 1.396, 1.605
Gye v McIntyre (1991) 171 CLR 609, 98 ALR 393, 65 ALJR 221, AusHC ............. 2.852

# H

H v HK: C-295/13 (2014) C-295/13, ECLI:EU:C:2014:2410, [2014] All ER (D) 50 (Dec), EUCJ ............. 6.8

H & K (Medway) Ltd, Re, Mackay v IRC [1997] 2 All ER 321, sub nom H & K (Medway Ltd, Re [1997] 1 WLR 1422, sub nom H & K (Medway) Ltd (in administrative receivership), Re [1997] 1 BCLC 545 ................................. 1.83
H S Works Ltd, Re [2018] EWHC 1405 (Ch) ...................................... 2.754
HHO Licensing Ltd (In Liq), Re [2007] BPIR 1363 ............................ 1.302
HIH Casualty and General Insurance Ltd, Re [2005] EWHC 2125 (Ch), [2006] 2 All ER 671, [2007] BCC 335, [2005] All ER (D) 74 (Oct); affd [2006] EWCA Civ 732, [2007] 1 All ER 177, [2007] Bus LR 250, [2007] BCC 335, (2006) Times, 5 July, [2006] All ER (D) 65 (Jun); revsd [2008] UKHL 21, [2008] 3 All ER 869, [2008] 1 WLR 852, [2012] 2 BCLC 655, [2008] Bus LR 905, [2008] Lloyd's Rep IR 756, (2008) Times, 11 April, [2008] All ER (D) 116 (Apr), sub nom McGrath v Riddell [2008] BCC 349, [2008] BPIR 581, HL .......................................... 1.159, 1.246, 1.586, 7.34
HPJ UK Ltd (in admin), Re [2007] BCC 284 .................................... 1.682
HSBC Bank plc v Tambrook Jersey Ltd [2013] EWCA Civ 576, [2014] Ch 252, [2013] 3 All ER 850, [2014] 2 WLR 71, [2013] 2 BCLC 186, [2013] NLJR 17, (2013) Times, 02 July, [2013] BPIR 484, [2013] All ER (D) 247 (May) ........................ 1.586, 7.20
Hackney London Borough Council v Crown Estate Comrs (1995) 72 P & CR 233, [1996] 1 EGLR 151, [1996] 20 EG 118, [1996] BPIR 428 .......................... 1.439
Hagell v Currie, Re Breechloading Armoury Co [1867] WN 75 ..................... 1.183
Haghighat (a bankrupt), Re [2009] EWHC 90 (Ch), [2009] 1 P & CR D49, [2009] 1 FLR 1271, [2009] Fam Law 292, [2009] BPIR 268, [2009] All ER (D) 31 (Jan); affd sub nom Brittain (trustee of the estate in bankruptcy) v Haghighat [2010] EWCA Civ 1521, [2011] BPIR 328, [2011] All ER (D) 107 (Jan) ....................................... 1.455
Hague v Nam Tai Electronics [2008] UKPC 13, [2008] BPIR 363 .............. 1.415, 1.692
Haig v Aitken [2001] Ch 110, [2000] 3 All ER 80, [2000] 3 WLR 1117, [1999] Lexis Citation 4147, [2000] BPIR 462, [1999] All ER (D) 1001 .......................... 1.429
Haine v Day [2008] EWCA Civ 626, [2008] 2 BCLC 517, [2008] IRLR 642, [2008] ICR 1102, [2008] BCC 845, (2008) Times, 22 July, [2008] BPIR 1343, [2008] All ER (D) 121 (Jun) ..................................................................... 2.827
Haines v Hill [2007] EWCA Civ 1284, [2008] 2 All ER 901, [2007] 3 FCR 785, [2008] Fam Law 96, [2008] Fam Law 199, [2007] 50 EG 109 (CS), (2007) Times, 12 December, [2007] BPIR 1280, [2007] All ER (D) 56 (Dec), sub nom Hill v Haines [2008] Ch 412, [2008] 2 WLR 1250, [2008] 1 FLR 1192 ..................... 1.302, 1.459
Haines Watts, Re [2004] EWHC 1970 (Ch), [2005] BPIR 798 ..................... 2.791
Halabi v London Borough of Camden [2008] EWHC 322 (Ch), (2008) Times, 25 March, [2008] BPIR 370, [2008] All ER (D) 213 (Feb) ..................................... 1.395
Hall v Old Talargoch Lead Mining Co (1876) 3 ChD 749, 45 LJ Ch 775, 3 Char Pr Cas 40, 34 LT 901 ...................................................................... 1.183
Hall v Poolman [2007] NSWSC 1330, [2007] NSWSC 1494, [2008] BPIR 892, NSWSC ................................................................................... 1.175
Hall v Richards (1961) 108 CLR 84. ........................................... 1.181
Hall v Van der Heiden [2010] EWHC 537 (TCC), [2010] BPIR 585, [2010] All ER (D) 237 (Oct) .............................................................. 1.353, 1.519
Hamilton v Law Debenture Trustees Ltd, Re Barings plc [2001] 2 BCLC 159, [2001] Lexis Citation 1607, [2002] BPIR 85, [2001] All ER (D) 171 (Jun) ............ 1.164, 1.220
Hamilton v Naviede. See Arrows Ltd (No 4); Bishopsgate Investment Management Ltd, Re; Headington Investments Ltd, Re
Hamilton v Oades (1989) 166 CLR 486 ......................................... 1.300
Hamilton v The Official Receiver [1998] BPIR 602 ......................... 1.220, 1.414
Hamlet International plc (in admin), Re [1999] 2 BCLC 506, [1999] Lexis Citation 2242, [1999] All ER (D) 928, sub nom Trident International Ltd v Barlow [2000] BCC 602 ................................................................................... 1.728
Hammersmith Town Hall Co, Re (1877) 6 ChD 112 ............................... 1.188
Hammonds (a firm) v Pro-fit USA Ltd [2007] EWHC 1998 (Ch), [2008] 2 BCLC 159, [2007] All ER (D) 109 (Aug) ........................... 1.178, 1.628, 1.629, 2.164
Hampton Capital Ltd, Re [2015] EWHC 1905 (Ch), [2016] 1 BCLC 374, [2015] All ER (D) 118 (Jul) ......................................................................... 1.302
Handelsveem BV v Hill [2011] BPIR 1024, SC ........................... 1.492, 6.23, 6.34
Hans Brochier Holdings Ltd v Exner [2006] EWHC 2594 (Ch), [2007] BCC 127 . 2.134, 6.5
Hans Place Ltd, Re (in liq) [1993] BCLC 768, [1992] BCC 737, [1992] 2 EGLR 179, [1992] 44 EG 143 ...................................... 1.220, 1.235, 1.434
Hardy (a bankrupt) v Buchler [1997] BPIR 643 .................................. 1.489
Hardy v Focus Insurance Co Ltd (1996) Times, 19 July, [1996] Lexis Citation 1060, [1997] BPIR 77 ....................................................... 1.391, 1.414
Hargreaves (trustee in bankruptcy of Salt) v Salt [2010] EWHC 3549 (Fam), [2011] BPIR 656 .................................................................................. 1.459

Harlequin Management Services Ltd [2013] EWHC 1926 (Ch), [2013] All ER (D) 202
(May) ................................................................................. 2.820
Harmony Care Homes Ltd Between Hull v NP Securities No 3 Ltd [2009] EWHC 1961
(Ch) ......................................................................................... 1.79
Harmony Carpets v Chaffin-Laird [2000] BCC 893, [1999] Lexis Citation 3625, [2000]
BPIR 61, [1999] All ER (D) 1169 ............................................. 1.60, 1.65
Harper v Buchler [2004] BPIR 724 ................................................... 1.395
Harper v Buchler [2005] BPIR 577 ................................................... 1.395
Harper v London Borough of Camden Council [2020] EWHC 1001 (Ch) ...... 1.178, 2.338
Harriet Lock v Aylesbury Vale District Council [2018] EWHC 2015 (Ch), [2019] RVR
18, [2018] BPIR 1694, [2018] All ER (D) 136 (Aug) ................................ 1.381
Harris, Re, ex p Hasluck [1899] 2 QB 97, 68 LJQB 769, 6 Mans 259, 47 WR 544, 43 Sol
Jo 439, 80 LT 499 ...................................................................... 1.225
Harris v Gross [2001] BPIR 586 ........................... 1.67, 1.368, 1.379, 1.388
Harris Bus Co Ltd, Re [2000] BCC 1151 ............................................ 1.685
Harris Simons Construction Ltd, Re [1989] 1 WLR 368, [1989] BCLC 202, 5 BCC 11,
133 Sol Jo 122, [1989] 8 LS Gaz R 43 ..................................... 1.87, 1.628
Harvard Securities Ltd (in liq), Re, Holland v Newbury [1997] 2 BCLC 369, [1998] BCC
567, (1997) Times, 18 July, [1997] Lexis Citation 3856 ............................. 1.164
Harvest Finance Ltd (In liqation), Re [2014] EWHC 4237 (Ch), [2015] 2 BCLC 240,
[2015] BPIR 266, [2014] All ER (D) 216 (Dec) ............................. 1.300, 2.767
Harvey v Dunbar Assets plc (formerly Dunbar Bbank plc) [2017] EWCA Civ 60, [2017]
BPIR 450, [2017] All ER (D) 127 (Feb) ..................... 1.386, 1.395, 2.550
Hat & Mitre plc (in administration), Re [2020] EWHC 2649 (Ch), [2020] All ER (D) 42
(Oct) .................................................................................... 1.639
Hawk Insurance Co Ltd, Re [2001] BCC 57; revsd [2001] EWCA Civ 241,
[2001] 2 BCLC 480, [2002] BCC 300, [2001] All ER (D) 289 (Feb) ................. 1.188
Hawkes v Cuddy [2007] EWHC 1789 (Ch), [2008] 1 BCLC 527, [2007] BCC 671,
(2007) Times, 14 August, [2007] All ER (D) 27 (Aug); revsd in part sub nom Hawkes v
Cuddy [2007] EWCA Civ 1072, [2008] BCC 125, (2007) Times, 13 November, [2007]
BPIR 1217, [2007] All ER (D) 250 (Oct) ..................... 1.275, 1.276
Hawkes Hill Publishing Co Ltd (in liq), Re [2007] EWHC 3073 (Ch), 151 Sol Jo LB 743,
[2007] BPIR 1305, [2007] All ER (D) 422 (May) ......................... 1.272, 1.303
Hawkins (F T) & Co Ltd, Re [1952] Ch 881, [1952] 2 All ER 467, 96 Sol Jo 562, [1952]
2 TLR 281 ............................................................................ 1.194
Haworth v Cartmel [2011] EWHC 36 (Ch), [2011] BPIR 428, [2011] All ER (D) 23
(Mar) .......................................................................... 1.382, 1.395
Haycraft Gold Reduction and Mining Co, Re [1900] 2 Ch 230, 69 LJ Ch 497, 7 Mans
243, 83 LT 166, 16 TLR 350 ....................................................... 1.138
Hayes v Butters [2014] EWHC 4557 (Ch), [2015] Ch 495, [2015] 3 All ER 702, [2015] 2
WLR 1634, [2015] BPIR 287, [2014] All ER (D) 248 (Dec) ........................ 1.396
Hayes v Hayes [2012] EWHC 1240 (Ch), [2012] BPIR 739, [2012] All ER (D) 236
(Mar) .................................................................................... 1.393
Hayes v Hayes [2014] EWHC 2694 (Ch), [2014] Bus LR 1238, [2014] BPIR 1212 ... 1.178,
2.744, 2.777
Hayes v Willoughby (22 July 2015, unreported) ................................... 1.396
Hayward, Re [1997] Ch 45, [1997] 1 All ER 32, [1996] 3 WLR 674, [1997] BPIR 456
............................................................................... 1.433, 6.8
Heald v O'Connor [1971] 2 All ER 1105, [1971] 1 WLR 497, 115 Sol Jo 244 ......... 1.78
Heath v Tang [1993] 4 All ER 694, [1993] 1 WLR 1421, (1993) Times, 11 August ... 1.396,
1.414
Healthcare Management Services Ltd v Caremark Properties Ltd [2012] EWHC 1693
(Ch) ..................................................................................... 1.630
Heating Electrical Lighting and Piping Ltd (in liqation) v Ross [2012] EWHC 3764 (Ch),
[2012] BPIR 1122 ..................................................................... 1.399
Heis v Financial Services Compensation Scheme [2018] EWCA Civ 1327, [2018] BPIR
1142 ............................................................................ 1.64, 1.691
Helen Irene Borodzicz, Re [2015] Lexis Citation 286, [2016] BPIR 24, [2015] All ER (D)
03 (Dec) ........................................................ 1.410, 1.414, 1.415
Hellard (as Trustees in Bankruptcy for Mireskandari) v Chadwick (Trustee in Bankruptcy
for Tehrani) [2014] EWHC 2158 (Ch), [2014] BPIR 1234, [2014] All ER (D) 27 (Jul)
........................................................................... 1.399, 1.459
Hellard (as Trustees in Bankruptcy of Shahrokh Mireskandari) v Chadwick (as Trustee in
Bankruptcy of Mehrdad Jami Tehrani) and Shelley Jami Tehrani [2014] BPIR 163 ..... 1.399
Hellard v Graiseley Investments Ltd [2018] EWHC 2664 (Ch), [2018] All ER (D) 36
(Nov) .................................................................................... 1.742

Hellard v Kapoor [2013] EWHC 2204 (Ch), [2013] BPIR 745, [2013] All ER (D) 374 (Jul) .................................................................. 1.391, 1.452
Hellard and Goldfarb (The Joint Supervisors of Pinson Wholesale Ltd), Re [2007] BPIR 1322 ................................................................................ 1.64
Hellas Telecommunications II 535 BR 543 , 566-567 (Bkrtcy SDNY 2015) ............. 7.34
Hellas Telecommunications (Luxembourg) II SCA, Re [2009] EWHC 3199 (Ch), [2010] BCC 295 ...................................................... 1.617, 1.728, 2.134
Hellas Telecommunications (Luxembourg) II SCA (in admin), Re [2011] EWHC 3176 (Ch), [2013] 1 BCLC 426, [2011] All ER (D) 57 (Dec) ............................... 1.715
Hellas Telecommunications (Luxembourg) II SCA, Re [2013] BPIR 756 ................. 6.9
Hellenic Capital Investments Ltd v Trainfx Ltd [2015] EWHC 3713 (Ch) ...... 1.630, 1.652
Hemming (decd), Re [2008] EWHC 2731 (Ch), [2009] Ch 313, [2009] 2 WLR 1257, (2008) Times, 9 December, [2009] BPIR 50, [2008] All ER (D) 176 (Nov) ............ 1.605
Hemsley v Bance [2016] EWHC 1028 (Ch), [2016] BPIR 934 ................ 1.381, 1.393
Henderson v Merrett Syndicates [1995] 2 AC 145, [1994] 3 All ER 506, [1994] 3 WLR 761, [1994] 4 LRC 355, [1994] NLJR 1204, HL ........................................... 1.692
Henry (a bankrupt), Re Horton v Henry [2016] EWCA Civ 989, [2017] 3 All ER 735, [2017] 1 WLR 391, (2017) Times, 18 January, [2016] BPIR 1426, [2016] All ER (D) 50 (Oct) ....................................... 1.396, 1.427, 1.463, 1.489
Henry Butcher International Ltd v KG Engineering (a partnership) [2004] EWCA Civ 1597, 148 Sol Jo LB 1282, [2006] BPIR 60, [2004] All ER (D) 330 (Oct) ............. 1.178
Henwood v Customs and Excise [1994] Lexis Citation 3058, [1998] BPIR 339, CA ................................................................................. 1.395
HM Customs and Excise v Allen (2003) Times, 20 March, [2003] Lexis Citation 21, [2003] BPIR 830, [2003] All ER (D) 27 (Apr) ..................................... 1.160
HM Customs and Excise v Dougall [2001] BPIR 269 ..................... 1.175, 1.386
HM Revenue and Customs v Green Eye Events Ltd [2010] EWHC 1403 (Ch) ......... 2.324
Heritage Joinery (a firm) v Krasner [1999] BPIR 683 .................................. 1.60
Hertfordshire Investments Ltd v Bubb [2000] 1 WLR 2318, (2000) Times, 31 August, [2000] Lexis Citation 3234, [2000] All ER (D) 1052 ................................ 2.814
Hertz Corp v Friend (2010) 559 US 1, US Sup Ct ...................................... 7.29
Hester, Re, ex p Hester (1889) 22 QBD 632, 6 Morr 85, [1886–90] All ER Rep 865, 60 LT 943, 5 TLR 326, CA ............................................................... 1.200
Hewitt Brannan (Tools) Co Ltd, Re [1991] BCLC 80, [1990] BCC 354, [1990] Lexis Citation 1340 .......................................................................... 1.168
Hibernian Merchants Ltd, Re [1958] Ch 76, [1957] 3 All ER 97, [1957] 3 WLR 486, 101 Sol Jo 647 ........................................................................... 1.281
Hickling v Baker [2007] EWCA Civ 287, [2007] 4 All ER 390, [2007] 1 WLR 2386, (2007) Times, 19 April, [2007] BPIR 346, [2007] All ER (D) 51 (Apr) ............... 1.490
High Street Rooftop Holdings Ltd, Re [2020] EWHC 2572 (Ch) ............. 1.630, 1.652
High Street Services Ltd v Bank of Credit and Commerce International SA (in liq) (No 2) [1993] Ch 425, [1993] 3 All ER 769, [1993] 3 WLR 220, [1993] BCLC 1200, [1993] BCC 360, [1993] 21 LS Gaz R 40, [1993] NLJR 651, (1993) Times, 26 March, 137 Sol Jo LB 132, CA ...................................................................... 2.852
Highberry Ltd v Colt Telecom Group plc [2002] EWHC 2503 (Ch), [2003] 1 BCLC 290, [2003] 05 LS Gaz R 32, [2003] BPIR 311, [2002] All ER (D) 354 (Nov) ....... 2.776, 2.777
Highfield Commodities Ltd, Re [1984] 3 All ER 884, [1985] 1 WLR 149, [1984] BCLC 623, 128 Sol Jo 870 ...................................................................... 1.177
Highgrade Traders Ltd, Re [1984] BCLC 151 ........................................ 1.300
Hill (a trustee in bankruptcy) v Alex Lawrie Factors Ltd [2000] Lexis Citation 4614, [2000] BPIR 1038, [2000] All ER (D) 882 .......................................... 1.470
Hill v East and West India Dock Co (1884) 9 App Cas 448, 48 JP 788, 53 LJ Ch 842, 32 WR 925, 51 LT 163, HL ............................................................... 1.235
Hill v Haines. See Haines v Hill
Hill v Spread Trustee Co Ltd [2006] EWCA Civ 542, [2007] 1 All ER 1106, [2007] 1 WLR 2404, [2007] 1 BCLC 450, [2007] Bus LR 1213, [2006] BCC 646, (2006) Times, 10 July, [2006] BPIR 789, [2006] All ER (D) 202 (May) ...................... 1.302, 1.582
Hill v Stokes plc [2010] EWHC 3726 (Ch), [2011] BCC 473 .......... 1.643, 1.645, 2.820
Hill v Van Der Merwe [2007] EWHC 1613 (Ch), [2007] BPIR 1562 ................ 2.765
Hill Samuel & Co Ltd v Laing (1988) 4 BCC 9, 1988 SLT 452, CtSess; affd [1991] BCC 665, 1989 SC 301, 1989 SLT 760, 1989 SCLR 659, CtSess ........................... 1.81
Hill's Waterfall Estate and Gold Mining Co, Re [1896] 1 Ch 947, 65 LJ Ch 476, 3 Mans 158, 74 LT 341, 12 TLR 316 ...................................................... 1.220, 1.270
Hillig v Darkinjung Pty Ltd [2006] NSWSC 137, (2006) 205 FLR 450, S Ct (NSW) ................................................................................. 1.174

Hindcastle Ltd v Barbara Attenborough Associates Ltd [1997] AC 70, [1996] 1 All ER 737, [1996] 2 WLR 262, [1996] 2 BCLC 234, 13 LDAB 319, [1996] 1 EGLR 94, [1996] 12 LS Gaz R 29, [1996] NLJR 281, [1996] 15 EG 103, (1996) Times, 23 February, 140 Sol Jo LB 84, [1996] BPIR 595, HL .................. 1.235, 1.238, 1.434

Hinton (trustee in bankruptcy of Wotherspoon) v Wotherspoon [2016] EWHC 621 (Ch), [2016] BPIR 944, [2016] All ER (D) 43 (Jun) ......................................... 1.427

Hirani v Rendle [2003] EWHC 2538 (Ch), [2004] BPIR 274, [2003] All ER (D) 27 (Nov) ........................................................................................ 1.395

Hire Purchase Furnishing Co Ltd v Richens (1887) 20 QBD 387, CA ................. 1.141

Hoare (K G), Re [1997] Lexis Citation 2436, [1997] BPIR 683 ......................... 1.64

Hoare, Re, ex p Ashworth (1874) LR 18 Eq 705, 43 LJ Bcy 142, 22 WR 925, 30 LT 906 ............................................................................................ 1.395

Hobbs v Gibson [2010] EWHC 3676 (Ch) ................................................. 1.160

Hockin v Marsden [2014] EWHC 763 (Ch), [2014] 2 BCLC 531, [2014] Bus LR 441, [2014] BPIR 637, [2014] All ER (D) 206 (Mar) ........................................ 1.691

Hockley (William) Ltd, Re [1962] 2 All ER 111, [1962] 1 WLR 555, 106 Sol Jo 308 .................................................................................................. 1.176

Hofer v Strawson [1999] 2 BCLC 336, [1999] 13 LS Gaz R 31, (1999) Times, 17 April, [1999] Lexis Citation 2551, 143 Sol Jo LB 95, [1999] BPIR 501, [1999] All ER (D) 224 ......................................................................................... 2.530, 2.852

Holdenhurst Securities plc v Cohen [2001] 1 BCLC 460, [2000] Lexis Citation 2922, [2000] All ER (D) 447 ...................................................................... 1.67

Holland v Revenue and Customs Comrs. See Paycheck Services 3 Ltd, Re; Revenue and Customs Comrs v Holland

Hollicourt (Contracts) Ltd (in liq) v Bank of Ireland [2001] Ch 555, [2001] 1 All ER 289, [2001] 2 WLR 290, [2001] 1 All ER (Comm) 357, [2001] 1 BCLC 233, [2001] Lloyd's Rep Bank 6, [2000] BCC 1210, (2000) Times, 1 November, [2000] Lexis Citation 3781, [2001] BPIR 47, [2000] All ER (D) 1480, CSRC vol 24 iss 17/2 ....... 1.180

Hollinshead v Hazleton [1916] 1 AC 428, 85 LJPC 60, [1916] HBR 85, [1914–15] All ER Rep 1117, 60 Sol Jo 139, 114 LT 292, 32 TLR 177, HL ............................. 1.396

Holmes v Watt [1935] 2 KB 300, 104 LJKB 654, [1935] All ER Rep 496, 153 LT 58, CA ............................................................................................... 1.473

Holtham v Kelmanson [2006] EWHC 2588 (Ch), [2006] BPIR 1422, [2006] All ER (D) 271 (Oct) ................................................................................ 1.455, 1.489

Home and Colonial Insurance Co Ltd, Re [1930] 1 Ch 102, 34 Ll L Rep 463, 99 LJ Ch 113, [1929] B & CR 85, [1929] All ER Rep 231, 142 LT 207, 45 TLR 658 .... 1.196, 1.270

Home Assurance Association, Re (1871) LR 12 Eq 59, 41 LJ Ch 110, 19 WR 817, 24 LT 613 ............................................................................................. 2.327

Home Treat Ltd, Re [1991] BCLC 705, [1991] BCC 165 ............................... 1.686

Hong Kong Investments Group Ltd, Re [2018] HKCFI 984 ......................... 2.338

Hood v Revenue & Custom Comrs [2019] EWHC 2236 (Ch), [2019] BPIR 1425 .... 1.180, 1.398

Hook v Jewson Ltd [1997] 1 BCLC 664, [1997] BPIR 100 ............................. 1.60

Hooley Ltd, Petitioner [2016] CSOH 141, 2017 SLT 58, 2016 Scot (D) 12/10, CSOH ............................................................................................. 1.625, 1.633

Hooper (Trustee In Bankruptcy Of Surjit Singh Chowdhary) v Duncan Lewis (Solicitors) Ltd [2010] BPIR 591 ....................................................... 1.492

Hope v Premierpace (Europe) Ltd [1998] Lexis Citation 14, [1999] BPIR 695 .. 1.382, 1.395

Horler v Rubin [2012] EWCA Civ 4, [2013] 1 BCLC 1, [2012] BPIR 749, [2012] All ER (D) 142 (Jan) .............................................................................. 2.927

Hornet Aviation Pty Ltd v Ansett Australia Ltd (1995) 13 ACLC 613 ................ 1.175

Hosking v Apax Partners LLP [2018] EWHC 2732 (Ch), [2019] 1 WLR 3347, [2018] 5 Costs LR 1125 .............................................................................. 1.742

Hosking v Michaelides [2006] BPIR 1192, [2004] All ER (D) 147 (May) ............ 1.455

Hosking v Slaughter and May (a firm) [2014] EWHC 1390 (Ch); sub nom Hosking (as joint liquidators of Hellas Telecommunications (Luxembourg) II SCA) v Slaughter and May [2016] EWCA Civ 474, [2016] Bus LR 1219, 166 NLJ 7701, [2016] 3 Costs LR 617, [2016] BPIR 1190, [2016] All ER (D) 173 (May) ............................... 2.795

House Property and Investment Co Ltd, Re [1954] Ch 576, [1953] 2 All ER 1525, [1953] 3 WLR 1037, 97 Sol Jo 862, 162 EG 512 ........................................... 1.196

Housiaux (t/a Harpers of Weybridge) v HM Customs and Excise [2003] EWCA Civ 257, [2003] BPIR 858, [2003] All ER (D) 295 (Jan) ....................................... 1.395

Howard Holdings Inc, Re [1998] BCC 549 ..................................... 1.271, 1.272

Howell v Hughes [2019] EWHC 1559 (Ch), 169 NLJ 7846, [2019] BPIR 1211, [2019] All ER (D) 132 (Apr) ................................................................ 1.502, 2.559

Howell v Lerwick Commercial Mortgage Corpn Ltd [2015] EWHC 1177 (Ch), [2015] 1
WLR 3554, [2015] BPIR 821, [2015] All ER (D) 42 (May) .................... 1.383, 2.530
Huddersfield Fine Worsteds Ltd, Re [2005] EWCA Civ 1072, [2005] 4 All ER 886,
[2006] 2 BCLC 160, [2005] IRLR 995, [2006] ICR 205, [2005] BCC 915, [2005]
NLJR 1355, (2005) Times, 26 September, [2005] All ER (D) 65 (Aug), CSRC vol 29 iss
11/1 ......... 1.716
Hudson v Gambling Commission (Re Frankice (Golders Green) Ltd) [2010] EWHC 1229
(Ch), [2010] Bus LR 1608, [2010] NLJR 697, (2010) Times, 14 June, [2010] All ER (D)
59 (May) ......... 1.660
Hughes v Hannover Rückversicherungs AG [1997] 1 BCLC 497, (1997) Times, 6 March,
[1997] Lexis Citation 2964 ......... 1.586
Humber & Co v John Griffiths Cycle Co (1901) 85 LT 141, HL ......... 1.183
Hunt v Conwy County Borough Council [2013] EWHC 1154 (Ch), [2014] 1 WLR 254,
[2013] BPIR 790, [2013] All ER (D) 101 (May) ......... 1.239, 1.397, 1.439
Hunt v Fylde Borough Council [2008] BPIR 1368, CC ......... 1.381, 2.770
Hunt (as trustee in bankruptcy of Janan George Harb) v Harb [2011] EWCA Civ 1239,
[2012] 1 WLR 317, [2011] 44 LS Gaz R 20, [2011] NLJR 1556, [2012] 1 Costs LR 78,
[2012] BPIR 117, [2011] All ER (D) 244 (Oct) ......... 1.414
Hunt v Hosking [2013] EWCA Civ 1408, [2014] 1 BCLC 291, [2014] BPIR 285,
[2013] All ER (D) 188 (Nov) ......... 1.302
Hunt v Renzland [2008] BPIR 1380 ......... 2.768, 2.769
Hunt v Withinshaw (Former trustee in bankruptcy of Steven James Hunt) [2015] EWHC
3072 (Ch), [2016] BPIR 59, [2015] All ER (D) 253 (Oct) ......... 1.397, 1.439
Hunter v Lex Vehicle Finance Ltd [2005] EWHC 223 (Ch), [2005] BPIR 586,
[2005] All ER (D) 55 (Jan) ......... 1.395
Hussein v Haus of Vanity Ltd [2017] EWHC 2615 (Ch) ......... 1.174
Hurricane Energy plc, Re [2021] EWHC 1759 (Ch), [2021] All ER (D) 48 (Jul) ......... 5.38
Hurst v Bennett [2001] EWCA Civ 182, [2001] 2 BCLC 290, (2001) Times, 15 March,
[2001] BPIR 287, [2001] All ER (D) 189 (Feb) ......... 1.178, 2.530
Hurst v Bennett [2001] EWCA Civ 1398, [2002] BPIR 102, [2001] All ER (D) 423 (Jul)
......... 1.356
Hurst v Supperstone [2005] EWHC 1309 (Ch), [2006] 1 FLR 1245, [2006] 1 FCR 352,
[2006] Fam Law 101, [2005] BPIR 1231, [2005] All ER (D) 130 (Jun) ......... 1.60
Husky Group Ltd, Re [2014] EWHC 3003 (Ch), [2015] 3 Costs LO 337, [2014] All ER
(D) 319 (Oct), sub nom Watchorn v Jupiter Industries Ltd [2015] BPIR 184 ..... 1.304, 1.582
Hyde (joint administrators of BetIndex Ltd), Re [2021] EWHC 1542 (Ch), [2021] All ER
(D) 23 (Jun) ......... 1.679, 2.182
Hydrodam (Corby) Ltd, Re [1994] 2 BCLC 180, [1994] BCC 161, (1994) Times,
19 February ......... 1.270, 1.272, 1.326
Hydroserve Ltd, Re [2007] EWHC 3026 (Ch), [2008] BCC 175, [2007] All ER (D) 184
(Jun) ......... 1.233, 2.761

I

IACS Pty Ltd v Australian Flower Exports Pty Ltd (1993) 11 ACLC 618, (1993) 10 ACSR
769 ......... 1.207
ICI Chemicals and Polymers Ltd v TTE Training Ltd [2007] EWCA Civ 725,
[2007] All ER (D) 115 (Jun) ......... 2.530
ICS Incorporation Ltd v Michael Wilson & Partners Ltd [2005] EWHC 404 (Ch), [2005]
BPIR 804, [2005] All ER (D) 291 (Mar) ......... 1.178
ILG Travel Ltd (in administration), Re [1995] 2 BCLC 128, [1996] BCC 21 ......... 2.852
ING Bank N.V v Banco Santander S.A. [2020] EWHC 3561 (Comm), [2020] All ER (D)
120 (Dec) ......... 6.8
ITM Corpn Ltd, Re, Sterling Estates v Pickard UK Ltd (formerly Paxus Professional
Systems Ltd) [1997] 2 BCLC 389, [1997] BCC 554, [1997] 2 EGLR 33, [1997] 30 EG
122, [1998] BPIR 402 ......... 1.238
IV Fund Ltd SAC v Mountain [2021] EWHC 738 (Ch) ......... 1.500
Idessa Ltd, Re [2011] EWHC 804 (Ch), [2012] 1 BCLC 80, [2012] BCC 315, [2011]
BPIR 957, [2011] All ER (D) 129 (May) ......... 1.272
Imperial Bank of China, India and Japan, Re (1866) LR 1 Ch App 339, 35 LJ Ch 445, 12
Jur NS 422, 14 WR 594, 14 LT 211, CACh ......... 1.220
Imperial Hydropathic Hotel Co, Blackpool, Re (1882) 49 LT 147, CA ......... 1.178
Imperial Land Co of Marseilles, Re, Re National Bank (1870) LR 10 Eq 298, 39 LJ Ch
331, 18 WR 661, 22 LT 598 ......... 1.270
Imperial Motors (UK) Ltd, Re [1990] BCLC 29, 5 BCC 214 ......... 1.630
Imperial Silver Quarries Co Ltd, Re (1868) 16 WR 1220 ......... 1.178

Ince Gordon Dadds llp v Tunstall (2019) UKEAT/141/19, [2020] ICR 124, EAT ...... 1.660

Ince Hall Rolling Mills Co v Douglas Forge Co (1882) 8 QBD 179, 51 LJQB 238, 30 WR
442 ......... 2.852

Independent Insurance Co Ltd (in provisional liq), Re [2002] EWHC 1577 (Ch),
[2002] 2 BCLC 709, [2004] BCC 919, [2003] BPIR 562, [2002] All ER (D) 384 (Jul)
......... 1.188

Industria De Alimentos Nilza SA, Re and other companies Leite v Amicorp (UK) Ltd
[2020] EWHC 3560 (Ch), [2021] All ER (D) 54 (Jan) ......... 7.15

Industrial Diseases Compensation Ltd v Marrons [2001] BPIR 600 ........... 1.472, 2.814

IRC v Adam & Partners Ltd [2001] 1 BCLC 222, [2000] BPIR 986, [2000] All ER (D)
1315, sub nom IRC v Adam [2002] BCC 247 ......... 1.59

IRC v Bland [2003] EWHC 1068 (Ch), [2003] BPIR 1274 ......... 1.59

IRC v Conbeer [1996] BCC 189, [1996] BPIR 398 ......... 2.929

IRC v Duce (1998) Times, 29 December, [1998] Lexis Citation 3503, [1999] BPIR 189
......... 1.65

IRC v Goldblatt [1972] Ch 498, [1972] 2 All ER 202, [1972] 2 WLR 953, 47 TC 483,
116 Sol Jo 332 ......... 1.84

IRC v Hashmi [2002] EWCA Civ 981, [2002] 2 BCLC 489, [2002] BCC 943, [2002]
BPIR 271, [2002] BPIR 974, [2002] All ER (D) 71 (May) ......... 1.582

IRC v Khan [2005] BPIR 409 ......... 1.395

IRC v Lee-Phipps [2003] BPIR 803, [2003] All ER (D) 107 (Feb) ......... 2.550

IRC v Mills [2003] EWHC (Ch) 2022 ......... 1.164, 1.207

IRC v Nash [2003] EWHC 686 (Ch), [2004] BCC 150, [2003] BPIR 1138, [2003] All ER
(D) 373 (Mar) ......... 1.276

IRC v Wimbledon Football Club Ltd [2004] EWCA Civ 655, [2005] 1 BCLC 66,
[2004] BCC 638, 148 Sol Jo LB 697, [2004] BPIR 700, [2004] All ER (D) 437 (May)
......... 1.60, 1.62, 1.65

Inside Sport Ltd (in liqation), Re [2000] 1 BCLC 302, [2000] BCC 40, (1998) Times,
27 November, [1998] Lexis Citation 3626, [1998] All ER (D) 527 ......... 1.168

Inspired Asset Management Ltd, Re [2019] EWHC 3301 (Ch), [2019] All ER (D) 44
(Dec) ......... 1.674

Instrumentation Electrical Services Ltd, Re [1988] BCLC 550, 4 BCC 301, (1988) Times,
15 March ......... 1.176, 1.272

Integeral Ltd, Re [2013] EWHC 164 (Ch), [2013] All ER (D) 63 (Feb) ......... 1.630, 2.125

Integrated Medical Solutions Ltd, Re [2012] BCC 215 ......... 7.4

Interchase Corpn Ltd, Re (1996) 21 ACSR 375 ......... 1.300

Interedil Srl v Fallimento Interedil Srl: C-396/09 (2011) C-396/09, ECLI:EU:C:2011:671,
[2011] ECR I-9915, [2012] Bus LR 1582, [2012] BCC 851, [2011] BPIR 1639,
[2011] All ER (D) 195 (Oct), EUCJ ......... 6.2, 6.5

Intermain Properties Ltd, Re [1986] BCLC 265, 1 BCC 99, 555 ......... 1.200

International Air Transport Association v Ansett Australia Holdings Ltd [2008] HCA 3,
[2008] BPIR 57 ......... 1.159

International Bulk Commodities Ltd, Re [1993] Ch 77, [1993] 1 All ER 361, [1992] 3
WLR 238, [1992] BCLC 1074, [1992] BCC 463, [1992] 30 LS Gaz R 32 ......... 1.72

International Cat Manufacturing (in liq) v Rodrick [2013] QCA 372 ......... 1.175

International Championship Management Ltd, Re [2006] EWHC 768 (Ch),
[2007] 2 BCLC 274, [2007] BCC 95, [2006] All ER (D) 84 (Apr) ......... 1.272

International Pulp and Paper Co, Re (1876) 3 ChD 594, 45 LJ Ch 446, 24 WR 535, 35 LT
229 ......... 1.183

International Sections Ltd (in creditors' voluntary liq), Re [2009] EWHC 137 (Ch),
[2009] 1 BCLC 580, [2009] BCC 574, [2009] BPIR 297, [2009] All ER (D) 48 (Feb)
......... 1.233, 2.182, 2.761

International Tin Council, Re [1987] Ch 419, [1987] 1 All ER 890, [1987] 2 WLR 1229,
(1987) Times, 27 January, sub nom Re International Tin Council [1987] BCLC 272;
sub nom Maclaine Watson and Co Ltd v International Tin Council [1988] Ch 1, [1987]
3 All ER 787, [1987] 3 WLR 508, [1987] BCLC 653, 3 BCC 346, 131 Sol Jo 1062,
[1987] LS Gaz R 2764, (1987) Times, 19 May; [1989] Ch 253, [1988] 3 All ER 257,
[1988] 3 WLR 1033, [1988] 3 WLR 1169, [1988] BCLC 404, 4 BCC 559, 659, 132 Sol
Jo 1495, [1988] 39 LS Gaz R 42, (1988) Times, 4 May; affd sub nom JH Rayner
(Mincing Lane) Ltd v Department of Trade and Industry [1990] 2 AC 418, [1989] Ch
72, [1990] LRC (Const) 193, (1989) Times, 27 October, [1988] Lexis Citation 2500,
sub nom Maclaine Watson and Co Ltd v International Tin Council [1989] 3 All ER
523, [1989] 3 WLR 969, [1990] BCLC 102, 133 Sol Jo 1485, HL ......... 1.280

International Tin Council, In Re [1989] Ch 309, [1988] 3 WLR 1159, (1988) Times,
29 April, CA ......... 1.279, 1.280

International Westminster Bank plc v Okeanos Maritime Corpn. See Company, a (No 00359 of 1987), Re

Internet Investment Corpn Ltd, Re [2009] EWHC 2744 (Ch), [2010] 1 BCLC 458, [2009] All ER (D) 98 (Nov) ........................................................ 1.168

Investin Quay House Ltd, Re [2021] EWHC 2371 (Ch), [2021] All ER (D) 58 (Aug) ................................................................................ 5.41

Invicta Works Ltd, Re [1894] WN 39, 38 Sol Jo 290 ............................... 2.331

Irish Bank Resolution Corpn v Quinn [2012] NICh 1, [2012] BCC 608, [2012] BPIR 322 ..................................................................................... 6.2

Irish Reel Productions Ltd v Capitol Films Ltd [2010] EWHC 180 (Ch), [2010] Bus LR 854, [2010] BCC 588, [2010] All ER (D) 111 (Feb) .......................... 2.136, 2.183

Irwell Valley Housing Association Ltd v Docherty [2012] EWCA Civ 704 ............. 1.336

Isis Investments Ltd v Oscatello Investments Ltd [2013] EWCA Civ 1493, [2014] Bus LR 341, [2013] All ER (D) 327 (Nov) ............................................. 6.20

Islandsbanki HF v Stanford [2019] EWHC 307 (Ch), [2019] BPIR 641, [2019] All ER (D) 99 (Feb) .............................................................................. 1.176

Islandsbanki HF v Stanford [2019] EWHC 595 (Ch), [2019] BPIR 876, [2019] All ER (D) 166 (Mar) ....................................................................... 1.383, 2.553

Islandsbanki HF v Stanford [2020] EWCA Civ 480, [2020] BPIR 833, [2020] All ER (D) 20 (Apr) .............................................................................. 1.383

Isovel Contracts Ltd (in administration) v ABB Building Technologies Ltd [2002] 1 BCLC 390, [2001] Lexis Citation 2284, [2002] BPIR 525, [2001] All ER (D) 440 (Nov) ..... 2.851

Ivey v Genting Casinos (UK) Ltd (t/a Crockfords) [2017] UKSC 67, [2018] AC 391, [2018] 2 All ER 406, [2017] 3 WLR 1212, [2018] 1 Cr App Rep 180, [2018] Crim LR 395, (2017) Times, 13 November, [2017] All ER (D) 134 (Oct), SC .................. 1.393

Izod, Re, ex p Official Receiver [1898] 1 QB 241, 67 LJQB 111, 4 Mans 343, 46 WR 304, [1895–9] All ER Rep 1259, 42 Sol Jo 117, 77 LT 640, 14 TLR 115, CA .............. 1.200

# J

J Smiths Haulage Ltd, Re [2007] BCC 135 ................................... 1.180, 1.657

JCAM Commercial Real Estate Property XV Ltd v Davis Haulage Ltd [2017] EWCA Civ 267, [2018] 1 WLR 24, [2018] 1 BCLC 165, [2017] All ER (D) 62 (Apr) ............. 1.643

JGD Construction Ltd v Aaron Mills [2013] EWHC 572 (Ch), [2013] BPIR 811 ...... 1.240

JH Rayner (Mincing Lane) Ltd v Department of Trade and Industry. See International Tin Council, Re

JN2 Ltd, Re [1977] 3 All ER 1104, [1978] 1 WLR 183, 122 Sol Jo 46 ............... 1.201

JPF Clarke (Construction) Ltd, Re (in a company voluntary arrangement) Maze Inns Ltd (in liq) v Hunt [2019] Lexis Citation 379, [2020] BPIR 194, [2019] All ER (D) 181 (Oct) ..................................................................................... 2.834

JSC BTA Bank v Ablyazov [2018] EWCA Civ 1176, 168 NLJ 7797, [2018] All ER (D) 125 (May) ................................................................................. 1.582

JSF Finance and Currency Exchange Co Ltd v Akma Solutions Inc [2001] 2 BCLC 307, [2002] BPIR 535, [2001] All ER (D) 134 (Feb) .............................. 1.175, 1.176

JT Frith Ltd, Re [2012] EWHC 196 (Ch), [2012] BCC 634 ..................... 1.233, 2.843

Jackson v Casey [2019] EWHC 1657 (Ch) ....................................... 2.852

Jacob v UIC Insurance Co Ltd [2006] EWHC 2717 (Ch), [2007] 2 BCLC 46, [2007] Bus LR 568, [2007] BCC 167, [2007] BPIR 494, [2006] All ER (D) 30 (Nov), CSRC vol 30 iss 16/1 .............................................................................. 2.354, 2.814

Jacob v Vockrodt [2007] EWHC 2403 (QB), [2007] BPIR 1568, [2007] All ER (D) 166 (Oct) ..................................................................................... 1.178, 1.382

Jacob (Walter L) & Co Ltd, Re (1987) 3 BCC 532 ................................ 2.354

Jacob (Walter L) & Co Ltd, Re [1989] BCLC 345, 5 BCC 244, (1988) Times, 29 December ........................................................................ 1.177, 1.234

Jacqueline Anne Scott-Hake Scott-Hake v Frost [2020] EWHC 3677 (Ch), [2021] BPIR 414, [2020] All ER (D) 155 (Jan) ............................................. 1.133, 1.212

James, Re (1995) 15 ACLC 1582 ............................................ 1.154, 2.940

James Dolman & Co Ltd v Pedley [2003] EWCA Civ 1686, [2004] BCC 504, 147 Sol Jo LB 1121, [2004] BPIR 290, [2003] All ER (D) 171 (Sep), CSRC vol 27 iss 13/3 ....... 2.338

James Rose Projects Ltd (in administration), Re, Townsend v Biscoe [2010] WL 3166608 ................................................................................ 1.688

Janeash Ltd, Re [1990] BCC 250, [1990] Lexis Citation 1299 ..................... 1.178

Japan Leasing (Europe) plc, Re [1999] Lexis Citation 3061, [1999] BPIR 911, [1999] All ER (D) 940 ................................................................ 1.622

Japanese Koi Co Ltd, Re (13 July 2016, unreported) ....................... 1.630, 2.136

Jardio Holdings Pty Ltd v Dorcon Construction Pty Ltd (1984) 2 ACLC 574 ......... 1.180

Jarvis Conklin Mortgage Co, Re (1895) 11 TLR 373 .............................. 1.281
Jawett, Re [1929] 1 Ch 108, 98 LJ Ch 7, 140 LT 176 .............................. 1.404
Jelly v All Type Roofing Co. See Debtor (No 50A-SD-1995), Re
Jenkins v Official Receiver [2007] EWHC 1402 (Ch), [2007] BPIR 740, [2007] All ER (D)
   139 (Apr) ..................................................................... 1.394, 1.395
Jenkins v Supscaf Ltd [2006] 3 NZLR 264, NZHC ................................. 1.174
Jervis v Pillar Denton Ltd (Game Station) [2013] EWHC 2171 (Ch); revsd sub nom Pillar
   Denton Ltd v Jervis [2014] EWCA Civ 180, [2015] Ch 87, [2014] 3 All ER 519, [2014]
   3 WLR 901, [2014] 2 All ER (Comm) 826, [2014] 2 BCLC 204, [2014] 2 EGLR 9,
   (2014) Times, 16 April, [2014] All ER (D) 212 (Feb) ......................... 2.183, 2.433
Jetivia SA v Bilta (UK) Ltd. See Bilta (UK) Ltd (in liq) v Nazir
Joblin v Watkins and Roseveare (Motors) Ltd [1949] 1 All ER 47, 64 TLR 464 ....... 1.310
John Doyle Construction Ltd (in liq) v Erith Contractors Ltd [2020] EWHC 2451 .... 2.852
John Harlow (administrator of Blak Pearl Ltd) v Creative Staging Ltd [2014] EWHC
   2787 (Ch) ..................................................................... 1.657
John Holmes, Sadler v Holmes (unreported 20 February 2006), ChD ................. 2.48
John Lewis plc v Pearson-Burton [2004] BPIR 70, [2003] All ER (D) 140 (Oct) ....... 1.381
John Smith & Co (Edinburgh) Ltd v Hill [2010] EWHC 1016 (Ch), [2010] 2 BCLC 556,
   [2010] All ER (D) 73 (May) ..................................................... 1.686
John T Rhodes, Re (No.2) (1987) 3 BCC 588 ....................................... 2.765
Johnson, Re (12 April 2013, unreported) Bristol Crown Court ...................... 1.484
Johnson (B) & Co (Builders) Ltd, Re [1955] Ch 634, [1955] 2 All ER 775, [1955] 3 WLR
   269, 99 Sol Jo 490, CA ................................................ 1.78, 1.270, 1.638
Johnson (as Liquidator of Strobe 2) v Arden [2018] EWHC 1624 (Ch), [2019] 2 BCLC
   215, [2019] BPIR 901, [2018] All ER (D) 42 (Aug) .................... 1.305, 1.462, 1.584
Johnson v Davies [1999] Ch 117, [1998] 2 All ER 649, [1998] 3 WLR 1299,
   [1998] 2 BCLC 252, 79 P & CR 14, [1999] BCC 275, [1998] 3 EGLR 72, [1998]
   19 LS Gaz R 23, [1998] 49 EG 153, (1998) Times, 31 March, 142 Sol Jo LB 141,
   [1998] BPIR 607, [1998] All ER (D) 104 ............................... 1.59, 1.64, 1.65
Johnson v Tandridge District Council [2007] EWHC 3325 (Ch), [2008] BPIR 405,
   [2007] All ER (D) 350 (Oct) .......................................... 1.383, 1.386, 1.395
Johnson Machine and Tool Ltd, Re [2010] EWHC 582 (Ch), [2010] BCC 382, [2010]
   NLJR 805, [2010] All ER (D) 271 (May) ............................... 1.617, 2.164, 2.977
Joint administrators of Station Properties, petitioners [2013] CSOH 120, 2013 Scot (D)
   13/7, CtSess ................................................................... 1.697
Joint Liquidators of the Scottish Coal Co Ltd, Petitioners 2013 SLT 1055 ........... 1.235
Joint Stock Coal Co, Re (1869) LR 8 Eq 146, 38 LJ Ch 429, 17 WR 585, 20 LT 966
   ............................................................................... 1.251
Joint-Stock Discount Co, Re, Fyfe's Case (1869) LR 4 Ch App 768, 38 LJ Ch 725, 17 WR
   798, 21 LT 131, [1861–73] All ER Rep Ext 1869, CACh ........................... 1.142
Jonathan Digby-Rogers v Speechly Bircham LLP [2019] EWHC 1568 (Ch) ............. 2.550
Jones v Financial Conduct Authority [2013] EWHC 2731 (Ch), [2013] BPIR 1033 ..... 1.59
Jones v Kernott [2011] UKSC 53, [2012] 1 AC 776, [2012] 1 All ER 1265, [2011] 3 WLR
   1121, 14 ITELR 491, [2012] 1 FLR 45, [2011] 3 FCR 495, [2011] Fam Law 1338,
   [2012] HLR 188, (2011) Times, 10 November, [2011] BPIR 1653, [2012] 1 P & CR
   D22, [2011] All ER (D) 64 (Nov), SC ........................................... 1.455
Jones v Patel [2001] EWCA Civ 779, (2001) Times, 29 May, [2001] BPIR 919,
   [2001] All ER (D) 313 (May) ............................................ 1.417, 1.427
Jones (FC) & Sons (a firm) Trustee v Jones [1997] Ch 159, [1996] 4 All ER 721, [1996] 3
   WLR 703, [1996] 19 LS Gaz R 29, (1996) Times, 13 May, 140 Sol Jo LB 123, [1996]
   BPIR 644 ...................................................................... 1.396
Jyske Bank (Gibraltar) Ltd v Spjeldnaes [1999] 2 BCLC 101, [2000] BCC 16, [1998]
   46 LS Gaz R 35, (1998) Times, 6 November, [1998] Lexis Citation 3422, 142 Sol Jo LB
   287, [1999] BPIR 525, [1998] All ER (D) 515 ............................ 1.582, 2.751

## K

K/9 Meat Supplies (Guildford) Ltd, Re [1966] 3 All ER 320, [1966] 1 WLR 1112, 110 Sol
   Jo 348 ........................................................................ 1.429
KK v MA [2012] EWHC 788 (Fam), [2012] BPIR 1137 .................... 1.396, 1.447
Kam Leung Sui Kwan v Kam Kwan Lai [2015] HKCFA 79, [2015] 6 HKC 644 ....... 1.281
Kapoor v National Westminster Bank [2011] EWCA Civ 1083, [2012] 1 All ER 1201,
   [2011] NLJR 1417, [2011] BPIR 1680, [2012] Bus LR D25, [2011] All ER (D) 42
   (Oct) ................................................................ 1.64, 1.65, 2.907
Karnos Property Co Ltd, Re [1989] BCLC 340, 87 LGR 263, 5 BCC 14 .............. 1.176

Kasumu v Arrow Global (Guernsey) Ltd [2013] EWHC 789 (Ch), [2013] BPIR 1047 ............................................................................................ 2.820
Katoomba Coal & Slate Co, Re (North's Case) (1892) 18 LR (NSW) Eq 70 ........... 1.204
Katz v Bradney [2012] EWHC 1018 (Ch), [2012] 3 All ER 781, [2013] 1 BCLC 9, [2013] Bus LR 169, [2012] All ER (D) 163 (Apr) ........................................ 1.716
Katz v McNally [1999] BCC 291, [1998] Lexis Citation 2702, CA ................... 1.303
Katz v Oldham [2016] BPIR 83 ..................................................... 1.415
Kaupthing Capital Partners II Master LP Inc, Re [2010] EWHC 836 (Ch), [2011] BCC 338, sub nom Pillar Securitisation SARL v Spicer [2010] NLJR 655, [2010] All ER (D) 191 (Apr) ....................................... 1.646, 1.721, 6.5, 7.29
Kaupthing Singer and Friedlander Ltd (in administration), Re [2010] EWHC 316 (Ch), [2010] All ER (D) 35 (Jun) ..................................................... 2.851
Kavanagh v Crystal Palace FC (2000) Ltd [2013] EWCA Civ 1410, [2014] 1 All ER 1033, [2014] 2 BCLC 438, [2014] IRLR 139, [2014] ICR 251, [2013] All ER (D) 139 (Nov) ............................................................................ 1.617
Kayley Vending Ltd, Re [2009] EWHC 904 (Ch), [2011] 1 BCLC 114, [2009] BCC 578, [2009] All ER (D) 203 (Oct) ................................... 1.617, 2.130, 2.977
Kaytech International plc, Re, Secretary of State for Trade and Industry v Kaczer [1999] 2 BCLC 351, [1999] BCC 390, [1998] All ER (D) 655 ........................ 1.326
Kean v Lucas (as Liquidator of J&R Builders (Norwich) Ltd) [2016] EWHC 2684 (Ch), [2017] BPIR 128, [2016] All ER (D) 50 (Nov) ....................................... 1.223
Keely v Bell [2016] EWHC 308 (Ch), [2016] BPIR 653, [2016] All ER (D) 191 (Feb) ............................................................................ 1.452
Kean v Lucas (as liquidator of J&R Builders (Norwich) Ltd (in liq)) [2017] EWHC 250 (Ch), [2017] BPIR 702 .......................................................... 1.164
Keenan, Re [1998] BPIR 205 ....................................................... 1.388
Kelcrown Ltd (in liq), Re Hunt v Dolan [2017] EWHC 537 (Ch) ..................... 2.754
Kellar v BBR Graphic Engineers (Yorks) Ltd [2002] BPIR 544, [2001] All ER (D) 416 (Dec) ............................................................................. 2.530
Kelly and Sumpton v Inflexion Fund 2 2850 Ltd Partnership and Autocruise Co-Investment Ltd Partnership [2010] EWHC 2850 (Ch) ............................... 1.233
Kelvingrove (1993) Pty Ltd v Paratoo Pty Ltd (1998) 16 ACLC 964 ............... 2.331
Kema Plastics Pty Ltd v Mulford Plastics Pty Ltd [1981] ACLC 33 ................ 1.175
Kemsley v Barclays Bank plc [2013] EWHC 1274 (Ch), [2013] BPIR 839, [2013] All ER (D) 169 (May) ..................................................................... 1.399
Kenna & Brown Ltd v Kenna (1999) 32 ACSR 430 ................................. 1.272
Kent Coalfields Syndicate, Re [1898] 1 QB 754, 67 LJQB 500, 5 Mans 88, 46 WR 453, 42 Sol Jo 363, 78 LT 443, 14 TLR 305, CA ............................................. 1.207
Kentwood Constructions Ltd, Re [1960] 2 All ER 655n, [1960] 1 WLR 646, 104 Sol Jo 525 ............................................................................... 2.835
Keypak Homecare Ltd, Re [1987] BCLC 409, 3 BCC 558, [1987] Lexis Citation 1174 ............................................................................ 1.160
Keystone Knitting Mills Trade Mark, Re [1929] 1 Ch 92, 97 LJ Ch 316, 45 RPC 421, [1928] All ER Rep 276, 140 LT 9, CA ..................................... 1.183, 1.693
Keyworker Homes (North West) Ltd, Re Woodside (joint administrators of Keyworker Homes (North West) Ltd) v Keyworker Homes (North West) Ltd [2019] EWHC 3499 (Ch), 170 NLJ 7871, [2019] All ER (D) 194 (Nov) ................................ 1.645
Key2Law (Surrey) LLP v De'Antiquis (Secretary of State for Business, Innovation and Skills intervening). See Otg Ltd v Barke; Olds v Late Editions Ltd; Key2law (Surrey) Ltd v Antiquis; Secretary Of State For Business Innovations & Skills v Coyne; Head Entertainment Ltd v Walker
Khadzi-Murat Derev, Re [2021] EWHC 392 (Ch), [2021] Bus LR 685, [2021] BPIR 722 ................................................................................. 7.33
Khan, Re, Reynold Porter Chamberlain LLP v Khan [2016] Lexis Citation 9, [2016] BPIR 722, [2016] All ER (D) 92 (Feb) ................................................... 1.380
Khan v Permayer [2000] Lexis Citation 4739, [2001] BPIR 95, CA ................. 1.62
Khan v Whirlpool (UK) Ltd [2014] EWHC 3477 (Ch), [2015] BPIR 1, [2014] All ER (D) 336 (Oct) ....................................................... 1.300, 2.763
Khan-Ghauri v Dunbar Bank plc [2001] BPIR 618 ........................ 1.396, 1.434
Khawaja v FCA [2019] EWHC 2909 (Ch) ........................................... 1.630
Kilvert v Flackett (a bankrupt) [1998] OPLR 237, [1998] 2 FLR 806, [1998] Fam Law 582, (1998) Times, 3 August, [1998] BPIR 721 .................................. 1.427
King (C E) Ltd (in administration), Re [2000] 2 BCLC 297 ............... 1.673, 1.679
King v Anthony [1998] 2 BCLC 517, [1997] Lexis Citation 4174, [1999] BPIR 73, [1997] All ER (D) 58 ............................................................. 1.67
Kings Croft Insurance Co Ltd, Re [1994] 1 BCLC 80 ............................. 1.300

King's Cross Industrial Dwellings Co, Re (1870) LR 11 Eq 149, 19 WR 225, 23 LT 585 .................................................................................. 1.178
Kinnell (Charles P) & Co Ltd v Harding Wace & Co [1918] 1 KB 405, 87 LJKB 342, 62 Sol Jo 267, 118 LT 429, 34 TLR 217, sub nom Kinnell (Charles P) [1918–19] All ER Rep 594, CA ....................................................................... 2.321
Kiss Cards Ltd, Re, Smith v Lawson [2016] EWHC 2176 (Ch), [2016] BPIR 1450, [2016] All ER (D) 10 (Sep) ......................................................... 1.302
Klamer v Kyriakides and Braier (a firm) [2005] BPIR 1142 ................... 1.382, 2.530
Klempka (administrators of ISA Daisytek SAS) v ISA Daisytek SA [2003] BCC 984, FrCA ..................................................................................... 1.281
Knowles v Coutts & Co [1997] Lexis Citation 3443, [1998] BPIR 96 .................. 1.60
Knowles v Scott [1891] 1 Ch 717, 60 LJ Ch 284, 39 WR 523, 64 LT 135, 7 TLR 306 .................................................................................. 1.196
Kombinat Aluminjuma Podgorica A.D (In Bankruptcy), Re [2015] EWHC 750 (Ch), [2016] 1 BCLC 311, [2016] BPIR 1463, [2015] All ER (D) 287 (Mar) ............... 7.33
Kornhaas v Thomas Dithmar, acting as liquidator of the assets of Kornhaas Montage und Dienstleistung Ltd (2015) C-594/14, EUCJ ....................................... 6.8, 6.9
Koutrouzas v Lombard Natwest Factors Ltd [2002] EWHC 1084 (QB), [2003] BPIR 444, [2002] All ER (D) 273 (Apr) .................................................... 1.59
Krasner v Dennison, Lawrence v Lesser [2000] EWCA Civ 112, [2001] Ch 76, [2000] 3 All ER 234, [2000] 3 WLR 720, [2000] OPLR 299, [2000] NLJR 543, (2000) Times, 18 April, [2000] Lexis Citation 2801, 144 Sol Jo LB 205, [2000] BPIR 410, [2000] All ER (D) 485 ......................................................... 1.417, 1.427
Kumar (a bankrupt), Re, ex p Lewis v Kumar [1993] 2 All ER 700, [1993] 1 WLR 224, [1993] BCLC 548, [1993] 2 FLR 382, [1994] 2 FCR 373, [1993] Fam Law 470 ....... 1.302
Kumar v Hellard [2021] EWHC 181 (Ch), [2021] All ER (D) 68 (Feb) ............... 2.744
Kyrris v Oldham, Royle v Oldham [2003] EWCA Civ 1506, [2004] 1 BCLC 305, [2004] BCC 111, [2003] 48 LS Gaz R 17, (2003) Times, 7 November, [2004] BPIR 165, [2003] All ER (D) 45 (Nov), CSRC vol 27 iss 18/3, sub nom Oldham v Kyrris, Royle v Oldham 147 Sol Jo LB 1306 ...................................... 1.270, 1.415, 1.692

## L

L (a bankrupt), Re. See Landau (a bankrupt) Re, Pointer v Landau
L & N D Development and Design Ltd, Re) [2020] EWHC 2803 (Ch), [2021] 2 BCLC 110, [2021] BPIR 48, [2020] All ER (D) 119 (Oct) ................................... 1.691
LB Holdings Intermediate 2 Ltd (in administration) [2017] EWHC 2032 (Ch), 167 NLJ 7761, [2017] All ER (D) 45 (Aug) ................................................. 2.791
LB Holdings Intermediate 2 Ltd, Re (in administration) and another company [2020] EWHC 1681 (Ch) .......................................... 2.829, 2.834, 2.839
LBI hf (in winding up proceedings) v Stanford [2014] EWHC 3921 (Ch), [2014] All ER (D) 277 (Nov) ...................................................................... 6.9
LBI hf v Kepler Capital Markets SA: C-85/12 (2013) C-85/12, ECLI:EU:C:2013:697, [2013] All ER (D) 301 (Oct), EUCJ ............................................. 6.9, 6.20
LBI hf v Merrill Lynch International Ltd: E-28/13 (2014) E-28/13, [2015] All ER (D) 78 (Mar), EFTA Ct ......................................................................... 6.18
LCP Retail Ltd v Segal [2006] EWHC 2087 (Ch), [2007] BCC 584, [2007] 1 P & CR D22, [2006] All ER (D) 31 (Aug) ...................................................... 2.843
LF2 Ltd v Supperstone [2018] EWHC 1776 (Ch), [2019] 1 BCLC 38, 168 NLJ 7803, [2018] BPIR 1320, [2018] All ER (D) 86 (Jul) ................... 1.617, 1.691, 2.754, 2.801
LHF Wools Ltd, Re [1970] Ch 27, [1969] 3 All ER 882, [1969] 3 WLR 100, 113 Sol Jo 363 .................................................................................... 1.178
Lady Moon SPV SRL (a company incorporated under the Laws of Italy) v Petricca & Co Capital Ltd [2019] EWHC 439 (Ch), 169 NLJ 7832, [2019] All ER (D) 19 (Mar) ....... 6.3
Lady Moon SPV SRL v Petricca and Co [2019] EWHC 710 (Ch) .................... 2.852
Lafayette Electronics Europe Ltd, Re [2006] EWHC 1006 (Ch), [2007] BCC 890 ..... 1.176, 1.716
Lakehouse Contracts Ltd v UPR Services Ltd [2014] EWHC 1223 (Ch) ............... 1.178
Lam v IRC [2005] EWHC 592 (Ch), [2006] STC 893, [2009] BPIR 301, [2005] All ER (D) 234 (Mar) ........................................................................ 1.382
Lambeth London Borough Council v Kay [2006] UKHL 10, [2006] 2 AC 465, [2006] 4 All ER 128, [2006] 2 WLR 570, [2006] 5 LRC 158, [2006] LGR 323, [2006] 2 P & CR 511, [2006] 2 FCR 20, (2006) Times, 10 March, 150 Sol Jo LB 365, 20 BHRC 33, [2006] All ER (D) 120 (Mar), HL .................................................. 1.455
Lancashire Cotton Spinning Co, Re, ex p Carnelley (1887) 35 ChD 656, 56 LJ Ch 761, 36 WR 305, 57 LT 511, CA ........................................... 1.181, 1.183

Lancefield v Lancefield [2002] BPIR 1108 .......................................... 1.176
Land and Property Trust Co plc (No 2), Re [1991] BCLC 849, [1991] BCC 446; on appeal sub nom Land and Property Trust Co plc (No 4), Re [1994] 1 BCLC 232, (1993) Times, 16 February, sub nom Land and Property Trust Co plc (No 2), Re [1993] BCC 462, [1993] 11 LS Gaz R 43 ................................................ 1.671, 2.136
Land Development Association, Re [1892] WN 23 ................................. 1.251
Land Financiers' Association, Re (1878) 10 ChD 269, 27 WR 224 ................... 1.160
Landau (a bankrupt) Re, Pointer v Landau [1998] Ch 223, [1997] 3 All ER 322, [1997] 3 WLR 225, [1997] 2 BCLC 515, [1996] OPLR 371, (1997) Times, 1 January, 141 Sol Jo LB 28, [1997] BPIR 229, sub nom L (a bankrupt), Re [1997] 2 FLR 660, [1998] Fam Law 68 ........................................ 1.417, 1.427, 1.429
Langham Hotel Co, Re, ex p Liquidator (1869) 17 WR 463, 20 LT 163 .............. 2.991
Langham Skating Rink Co, Re (1877) 5 ChD 669, 46 LJ Ch 345, 36 LT 605, CA .... 1.176,
1.251
Langley Constructions (Brixham) Ltd v Wells [1969] 2 All ER 46, [1969] 1 WLR 503, 113 Sol Jo 203 ................................................................. 1.183
Langreen Ltd, Re (21 October 2011, unreported), ChD ........................... 1.272
Larsen v Navios International Inc [2011] EWHC 878 (Ch), [2012] 1 BCLC 151, [2012] Bus LR 1124, [2012] BCC 353, [2011] All ER (D) 246 (Apr), CSRC vol 35 iss 4/2 ..... 7.34
Lascomme Ltd v United Dominions Trust [1994] ILRM 224 ......................... 1.86
Lasytsya v Koumettou (trustees in bankruptcy of the estate of Lasytsya) [2020] EWHC 660 (Ch), [2020] BPIR 874, [2020] All ER (D) 196 (Mar) ........................... 1.491
Laverty v British Gas Trading Ltd [2014] EWHC 2721 (Ch), [2015] 2 All ER 430, [2015] 2 All ER (Comm) 166, [2015] 1 BCLC 295, [2015] Bus LR 17, [2014] All ER (D) 76 (Aug) ........................................................................ 2.433
Lavin v Swindell [2012] EWHC 2398 (Ch), [2012] BCC 864, [2012] All ER (D) 147 (Aug) ................................................................. 1.176, 1.671
Law Guarantee Trust and Accident Society Ltd, Re (1910) 26 TLR 565 .............. 2.410
Law Society v Beller [2014] EWHC 3923 (Ch), [2014] 5 Costs LO 683, [2014] BPIR 1480, [2014] All ER (D) 256 (Jul) ...................................................... 1.65
Law Society (acting through the Solicitors Regulation Authority) v Blavo [2018] EWCA Civ 2250, [2019] 1 WLR 1977, 168 NLJ 7814, [2018] BPIR 1704, [2018] All ER (D) 79 (Oct) ................................................................... 1.382
Law Society v Official Receiver [2007] EWHC 2841 (Ch), [2007] BPIR 1595, [2007] All ER (D) 488 (Nov), sub nom Law Society v Shah [2009] Ch 223, [2008] 3 WLR 1401, [2008] Bus LR 1742, [2008] Lloyd's Rep IR 442, (2007) Times, 20 December ................................................ 1.390, 1.393
Law Society v Southall [2001] EWCA Civ 2001, (2002) Times, 7 January, [2002] BPIR 336, [2001] All ER (D) 208 (Dec) ............................................... 1.582
Lawson (Inspector of Taxes) v Hosemaster Machine Co Ltd [1965] 3 All ER 401, [1965] 1 WLR 1399, 43 TC 337, 44 ATC 239, [1965] TR 253, 109 Sol Jo 902; revsd [1966] 2 All ER 944, [1966] 1 WLR 1300, 43 TC 337, 45 ATC 178, [1966] TR 157, 110 Sol Jo 407, CA ........................................................................ 1.81
Lazari GP Ltd v Jervis [2012] EWHC 1466 (Ch) .................................. 1.660
Lazari Properties 2 Ltd v New Look Retailers Ltd [2021] EWHC 1209 (Ch), [2021] Bus LR 915, [2021] BPIR 920 ................................................ 1.59, 1.65
Leading Guides International Ltd (in liqation), Re [1998] 1 BCLC 620 ............... 1.143
Leasing and Finance Services Ltd, Re [1991] BCC 29 ............................. 1.178
Ledingham-Smith (a bankrupt), Re, ex p trustee of the bankrupt v Pannell Kerr Forster (a firm) [1993] BCLC 635 ........................................ 1.303, 1.460
Lee v Lee [2000] 1 FLR 92, [1999] Fam Law 808, [2000] BCC 500, [1999] Lexis Citation 3298, [1999] BPIR 926, CA ..................................................... 1.238
Leeds United Association Football Club Ltd, Re [2007] EWHC 1761 (Ch), [2007] Bus LR 1560, [2007] ICR 1688, [2008] BCC 11, (2007) Times, 4 September, [2007] All ER (D) 385 (Jul) ...................................................................... 1.716
Legal Equitable Securities plc (in liq) [2010] EWHC 2046 (Ch), [2011] BCC 354, [2010] BPIR 1151 .................................................................. 2.835
Lehman Brothers Australia Ltd (in liq) (scheme administrators appointed) v Macnamara [2020] EWCA Civ 321, [2020] 3 WLR 147, [2020] BPIR 550, [2020] All ER (D) 32 (Mar) ........................................ 1.622, 1.691, 2.837
Lehman Brothers Europe Ltd (in administration), Re, [2017] EWHC 2031 (Ch), [2018] 2 All ER 367, [2018] 2 All ER (Comm) 75, [2018] Bus LR 439, 167 NLJ 7759, [2017] All ER (D) 44 (Aug) ........................................ 1.617, 1.685
Lehman Brothers Finance AG (in liqation) v Klaus Tschira Stiftung GmbH company [2014] EWHC 2782 (Ch), [2014] All ER (D) 42 (Aug) .............................. 7.33
Lehman Bros International (Europe), Re [2014] EWHC 1687, [2014] BPIR 1259 ..... 2.744

Lehman Brothers International (Europe) (in administration) [2018] EWHC 1980 (Ch), [2018] All ER (D) 04 (Aug) ............................................................. 6.3

Lehman Brothers International (Europe) (in administration), Re [2014] EWHC 704 (Ch), [2015] Ch 1, [2015] 2 All ER 111, [2014] 3 WLR 466, [2015] 1 All ER (Comm) 813, [2015] 1 BCLC 151, [2014] All ER (D) 153 (Mar); revsd in part sub nom Lehman Brothers International (Europe) (in administration), Re; subnom Joint Administrators of LB Holdings Intermediate 2 Ltd (in administration) v Lomas [2015] EWCA Civ 485, [2016] Ch 50 , [2016] 2 All ER 836, [2015] 3 WLR 1205, [2016] 1 All ER (Comm) 1079, [2015] 2 BCLC 433, 165 NLJ 7654, [2015] BPIR 1035, [2015] All ER (D) 139 (May); revsd in part sub nom Re Lehman Brothers International (Europe) (in administration) [2017] UKSC 38, [2018] AC 465, [2018] 1 All ER 205, [2017] 2 WLR 1497, [2018] 1 All ER (Comm) 629, [2017] 2 BCLC 149, (2017) Times, 29 May, [2017] All ER (D) 102 (May), SC ............ 1.129, 1.203, 1.246, 1.682, 2.834, 2.848, 2.852

Lehman Brothers International (Europe) (In Administration), Re, Lomas v Burlington Loan Management Ltd [2016] EWHC 2131 (Ch), [2016] All ER (D) 81 (Aug) ........ 1.246

Lehman Brothers Europe Ltd (in administration), Re [2020] EWHC 1369 (Ch), [2020] All ER (D) 11 (Jun) ......................................................... 1.715

Lehman Brothers Holdings plc (in administration) [2020] EWHC 3449 (Ch), [2020] All ER (D) 87 (Dec) .......................................................... 1.693

Lehman Brothers International (Europe) (in Administration) (No 8), Re, Lomas v Burlington Loan Management Ltd [2016] EWHC 2417 (Ch), [2017] 2 All ER (Comm) 275, [2017] Bus LR 1475, [2016] All ER (D) 40 (Oct) .............................. 2.850

Lehman Brothers International (Europe) Re (in administration) [2020] EWHC 1932 (Ch), [2020] Bus LR 1875, [2020] All ER (D) 132 (Jul) ..................................... 1.680

Lehman Brothers International (Europe) (in administration), Re. See Lehman Brothers International (Europe) (in administration), Re

Leibson Corpn v TOC Investments Corpn. See Re Beppler & Jacobson Ltd TOC Investments Corpn v Beppler & Jacobson Ltd

Leicester v Plumtree Farms Ltd [2003] EWHC 206 (Ch), [2004] BPIR 296 ............ 1.395

Leigh Estates (UK) Ltd, Re (in administrative receivership) [1994] RA 57, [1994] BCC 292 ....................................................................... 1.178, 2.550

Leighton Contracting (Qatar) WLL v Simms [2011] EWHC 1735 (Ch), [2011] BPIR 1395 ........................................................................... 2.909

Leisure (Norwich) II Ltd v Luminar Lava Ignite Ltd (in admin) [2012] EWHC 951 (Ch), [2014] Ch 165, [2012] 4 All ER 894, [2013] 3 WLR 1132, [2013] 2 BCLC 115, [2012] BCC 497, [2012] All ER (D) 165 (May) .............................. 2.183, 2.433

Leisure Study Group Ltd, Re [1994] 2 BCLC 65 ........................... 1.59, 2.115

Lemos v Church Bay Trust Company Ltd [2021] EWHC 1157 (Ch) ................. 1.583

Lemos, Re, Leeds v Lemos [2017] EWHC 1825 (Ch), [2018] Ch 81, [2018] 1 All ER 313, [2018] 2 WLR 73, 167 NLJ 7756, [2017] BPIR 1223, [2017] All ER (D) 157 (Jul) .... 1.396, 1.417, 1.429, 1.489, 1.492

Lennox Holdings plc, Re [2009] BCC 155 ........................................ 6.5

Leon v York-O-Matic Ltd [1966] 3 All ER 277, [1966] 1 WLR 1450, 110 Sol Jo 685 ................................................................. 1.220, 1.743, 1.617

Le Roux v Viana 2008 (2) SA 173 .............................................. 1.298

Leslie (J) Engineers Co Ltd, Re [1976] 2 All ER 85, [1976] 1 WLR 292, 120 Sol Jo 146 ............................................................................. 1.180

Leveraged Equities Ltd v Hilldale Australia Pty Ltd [2008] NSWSC 190 ............. 1.175

Levitt (Jeffrey S) Ltd, Re [1992] Ch 457, [1992] 2 All ER 509, [1992] 2 WLR 975, [1992] BCLC 250, [1992] BCC 137, (1991) Times, 6 November .............. 1.186, 1.300

Levy v Ellis-Carr [2012] EWHC 63 (Ch), [2012] BPIR 347, [2012] All ER (D) 196 (Jan) ............................................................................. 1.397

Levy v Legal Services Commission [2001] 1 All ER 895, [2001] 1 FLR 435, [2001] 1 FCR 178, [2001] Fam Law 92, (2000) Times, 1 December, [2000] Lexis Citation 3944, [2000] BPIR 1065, [2000] All ER (D) 1775 .......................... 1.379, 1.515, 2.829

Levy v Napier 1962 SC 468, 1962 SLT 264, CtSess ............................... 1.188

Levy McCallum Ltd v Mark Allen (liquidator of Fulford Hyman Ltd) [2007] NICh 3 ............................................................................. 1.302

Lewis v Doran [2004] NSWSC 608, [2005] NSWCA 243, (2005) 219 ALR 555 ....... 1.175

Lewis v IRC [2001] 3 All ER 499, (2000) Times, 14 November, (2000) Independent, 18 December, [2000] Lexis Citation 3874, [2000] All ER (D) 1641, sub nom Floor Fourteen Ltd, Re; Lewis v IRC [2001] 2 BCLC 392 ...................... 1.303, 2.433

Lewis v Metropolitan Property Realisation Ltd [2009] EWCA Civ 448, [2010] Ch 148, [2009] 4 All ER 141, [2010] 2 WLR 615, [2010] 1 FLR 86, [2009] 3 FCR 251, [2009] Fam Law 794, (2009) Times, 15 July, [2009] BPIR 820, [2009] All ER (D) 127 (Jun) ............................................................................. 1.397

Lewis Merthyr Consolidated Collieries Ltd, Re, Lloyds Bank v Lewis Merthyr Consolidated Collieries Ltd [1929] 1 Ch 498, 98 LJ Ch 353, 22 BWCC 20, 73 Sol Jo 27, 140 LT 321, CA ...................................................................... 1.84
Lewis's of Leicester Ltd, Re [1995] 1 BCLC 428, [1995] BCC 514 .................... 1.679
Leyland Daf Ltd, Re [1994] 2 BCLC 106, [1994] BCC 166, (1994) Times, 19 January ........................................................................................................................ 1.298
Leyland Daf Ltd, Re, Buchler v Talbot [2002] EWCA Civ 228, [2002] 1 BCLC 571, [2003] BCC 159, [2002] BPIR 690, [2002] All ER (D) 326 (Feb); revsd sub nom Buchler v Talbot [2004] UKHL 9, [2004] 2 AC 298, [2004] 1 All ER 1289, [2004] 2 WLR 582, [2004] 5 LRC 405, [2004] 1 BCLC 281, [2004] NLJR 381, (2004) Times, 5 March, 148 Sol Jo LB 299, [2004] All ER (D) 89 (Mar), sub nom Leyland Daf Ltd, Re [2004] BCC 214, HL .............. 1.84, 1.159, 1.196, 1.228, 1.231, 2.308, 2.433, 2.436
Licence-holder, Re a, Abbot [1997] BCC 666, [1998] BPIR 171 ....................... 1.160
Lictor Anstalt v MIR Steel UK Ltd [2014] EWHC 3316 (Ch), [2014] 6 Costs LO 918, [2014] All ER (D) 186 (Oct) ........................................................................... 1.686
Lightning Electrical Contractors Ltd, Re [1996] 2 BCLC 302, [1996] BCC 950 ....... 1.275
Lilley v American Express Europe Ltd [2000] BPIR 70 ................. 1.178, 1.382, 1.386
Linda Marie Ltd (in liqation), Re [1989] BCLC 46, 4 BCC 463 .. 1.208, 2.306, 2.435, 2.990
Lineas Navieras Bolivianas SAM, Re [1995] BCC 666, [1994] Lexis Citation 1396 .... 1.183
Linfoot (A Debtor), Re, Linfoot v (1) Adamson (2) Bank of Scotland plc (3) National Westminster Bank plc [2012] BPIR 1033, CC ............................................... 1.65
Linkrealm Ltd, Re [1998] BCC 478 ................................................................. 1.183
Liquidator of Glasgow and Weir Blacksmiths Ltd v Glasgow 2016 SLT 171, 2016 Scot (D) 10/3, SHCtemp ...................................................................................... 1.270
Liquidator of Marini Ltd v Dickenson [2003] EWHC 334 (Ch), [2004] BCC 172 ..... 1.272
Liquidator of Premier Housewares (Scotland) LLP v Rashid [2018] CSOH 23, 2018 SLT 386, 2018 Scot (D) 5/5, CSOH ...................................................... 1.175, 1.273
Lister v Hooson [1908] 1 KB 174, 77 LJKB 161, 15 Mans 17, 52 Sol Jo 93, 98 LT 75, [1904–7] All ER Rep Ext 1069, CA ........................................................ 2.852
Liverpool Civil Service Association, Re, ex p Greenwood (1874) LR 9 Ch App 511, 43 LJ Ch 609, 22 WR 636, 30 LT 451, CACh ......................................................... 1.180
Living Images Ltd, Re [1996] 1 BCLC 348, [1996] BCC 112, (1995) Times, 7 August ........................................................................................................................ 1.303
Lloyd (David) & Co, Re, Lloyd v David Lloyd & Co (1877) 6 ChD 339, 25 WR 872, 37 LT 83, CA ..................................................................................................... 1.183
Lloyds Bank plc v Byrne [1993] 1 FLR 369, [1993] 2 FCR 41, [1993] Fam Law 183, 23 HLR 472, CA ................................................................................................. 1.455
Lloyds Bank plc v Ellicott [2002] EWCA Civ 1333, [2003] BPIR 632, [2002] All ER (D) 121 (Feb) ..................................................................................................... 1.59
Lloyds Bank SF Nominees v Aladdin Ltd [1996] 1 BCLC 720, [1997] BPIR 111 ...... 1.238, 1.439
Llynvi and Tondu Co, Re (1889) 6 TLR 11 ...................................................... 1.160
Loch v John Blackwood Ltd [1924] AC 783, 93 LJPC 257, [1924] B & CR 209, [1924] All ER Rep 200, 68 Sol Jo 735, 131 LT 719, 40 TLR 732, PC .................. 1.174
Logitext UK Ltd, Re [2004] EWHC 2899 (Ch), [2005] 1 BCLC 326, [2004] All ER (D) 535 (Jul) ...................................................................................................... 1.620
Lomas v Burlington Loan Management Ltd; sub nom Re Lehman Brothers International (Europe) (in administration) [2015] EWHC 2269 (Ch), [2016] Bus LR 17, [2015] BPIR 1102, [2015] All ER (D) 11 (Aug) ................................................................. 2.850
Lomas v JFB Firth Rixson Inc [2012] EWCA Civ 419, [2012] 2 All ER (Comm) 1076, [2013] 1 BCLC 27, [2012] 2 Lloyd's Rep 548, [2012] All ER (D) 29 (Apr) ............ 1.159
Lomax Leisure Ltd, Re [2000] Ch 502, [1999] 3 All ER 22, [1999] 3 WLR 652, [1999] 2 BCLC 126, [2000] BCC 352, [1999] 2 EGLR 37, [1999] 21 LS Gaz R 38, [1999] 23 EG 143, [1999] EGCS 61, (1999) Times, 4 May, [1999] Lexis Citation 2566, [1999] All ER (D) 406 .......................................................................................... 1.628
Lomax Leisure Ltd (in liq) v Miller [2007] EWHC 2508 (Ch), [2008] 1 BCLC 262, [2008] BCC 686, [2007] BPIR 1615, [2007] All ER (D) 164 (Oct), CSRC vol 31 iss 16/1 ..................................................... 1.270, 1.415, 2.861, 2.862, 2.873
London and Caledonian Marine Insurance Co, Re (1879) 11 ChD 140, 27 WR 713, 40 LT 666, CA ................................................................................................. 1.158
London and General Bank, Re [1895] 2 Ch 166, 64 LJ Ch 866, 2 Mans 282, 12 R 263, 43 WR 481, [1895–9] All ER Rep 948, 39 Sol Jo 450, 72 LT 611, 11 TLR 374, CA ...... 1.270
London and Globe Finance Co Ltd, Re [1902] 2 Ch 416, 50 WR 253 ........... 1.186, 2.429
London and Manchester Industrial Association, Re (1875) 1 ChD 466, 45 LJ Ch 170, 24 WR 386, 33 LT 685 ............................................................................ 1.175, 1.188
London and Paris Banking Corpn, Re (1874) LR 19 Eq 444, 23 WR 643 ............. 1.175

London Borough of Redbridge v Mustafa [2010] EWHC 1105 (Ch), [2011] RVR 45, [2010] BPIR 893 ................................................................ 1.395

London Flats Ltd, Re [1969] 2 All ER 744, [1969] 1 WLR 711, 113 Sol Jo 304 ....... 1.160

London, Hamburg and Continental Exchange Bank, Re, Emmerson's Case (1866) LR 2 Eq 231, 35 LJ Ch 652, 14 WR 785, 14 LT 457; on appeal (1866) LR 1 Ch App 433, 36 LJ Ch 177, 12 Jur NS 592, 14 WR 905, 14 LT 746, CACh ...................... 1.188

London Iron and Steel Co Ltd, Re [1990] BCLC 372, [1990] BCC 159 ............... 1.298

London Metallurgical Co, Re [1895] 1 Ch 758, 64 LJ Ch 442, 2 Mans 276, 13 R 436, 43 WR 476, 39 Sol Jo 363, 72 LT 421, 11 TLR 308 .................................. 2.433

Lonergan v Gedling Borough Council [2009] EWCA Civ 745 [2009] EWCA Civ 696 [2009] EWCA Civ 1569, [2010] RVR 100, [2010] BPIR 911, [2009] EWCA Civ 1569 ...................................................................... 1.381

Longley v Chief Executive of Department of Environment and Heritage and Protection [2018] QCA 32 ....................................................... 1.235

Longmeade Ltd (In liq), Re [2016] EWHC 356 (Ch), [2017] 2 All ER 244, [2017] 2 All ER (Comm) 161, [2017] 1 BCLC 605, [2016] BPIR 666, [2016] All ER (D) 259 (Feb) ...................................................... 1.220, 1.741, 1.414

Lonnex Pty Ltd (in liq), Re (No 2) [2019] VSCA 62 ........................... 1.164

Loquitar Ltd, Re [2003] EWHC 999 (Ch), [2003] STC 1394, [2003] 2 BCLC 442, 75 TC 77, [2003] All ER (D) 123 (May) ....................................... 1.270

Lornamead Acquisitions Ltd v Kaupthing Bank HF [2011] EWHC 2611 (Comm), [2013] 1 BCLC 73, [2011] 43 LS Gaz R 22, [2011] All ER (D) 214 (Oct) ............... 6.9

Lovett v Carson Country Homes Ltd [2009] EWHC 1143 (Ch), [2009] 2 BCLC 196, [2011] BCC 789, [2009] All ER (D) 95 (Jun), CSRC vol 33 iss 3/1 .................. 1.633

Lowerstoft Traffic Services Ltd, Re [1986] BCLC 81, 2 BCC 98, 945 .......... 1.160, 1.168

Lowston Ltd, Re [1991] BCLC 570 ................................... 1.64, 1.1.64

Loy v O'Sullivan [2010] EWHC 3583 (Ch), [2011] BPIR 181 ........... 1.379, 1.380, 2.820

Lubell (Rolfe) & Co v Keith [1979] 1 All ER 860, [1979] 2 Lloyd's Rep 75, 123 Sol Jo 32 ....................................................................... 1.743

Lubin, Rosen and Associates Ltd, Re [1975] 1 All ER 577, [1975] 1 WLR 122, 119 Sol Jo 63 ....................................................................... 1.177

Ludsin Overseas Ltd v Maggs [2014] EWHC 3566 (Ch), [2015] BPIR 59, [2014] All ER (D) 09 (Nov) ....................................................... 2.530

Lummus Agricultural Services Ltd, Re [2001] 1 BCLC 137, [1998] Lexis Citation 1591 ................................................................... 1.178

Lundy Granite Co, Re, ex p Heavan (1871) LR 6 Ch App 462, 35 JP 692, 40 LJ Ch 588, 19 WR 609, 24 LT 922, CACh ............................................. 2.433

Lune Metal Products Ltd (in administration), Re [2006] EWCA Civ 1720, [2007] 2 BCLC 746, [2007] Bus LR 589, [2007] BCC 217, (2006) Times, 27 December, [2006] All ER (D) 225 (Dec) ..................................................... 1.618, 1.682

Lutz v Bauerle: C-557/13 (2015) C-557/13, ECLI:EU:C:2015:227, [2015] Bus LR 855, [2015] All ER (D) 139 (Apr), EUCJ ................................... 6.10, 6.18

Lyle (as joint trustees in bankruptcy of Jetson Ralph Bedborough) v Bedborough [2021] EWHC 220 (Ch), [2021] BPIR 581, [2021] All ER (D) 09 (Mar) ........ 1.302, 1.455, 1.459

Lympne Investments Ltd, Re [1972] 2 All ER 385, [1972] 1 WLR 523, 116 Sol Jo 332 ............................................................. 1.175, 1.178, 2.320

Lynch v Cadwallader (in his capacity as trustee in bankruptcy of the applicant) and another [2021] EWHC 328 (Ch), [2021] BPIR 854 ........................... 2.235

Lynch Hall & Hornby v Thakerar [2005] EWHC 2752 (Ch), [2006] 1 WLR 1513, (2006) Times, 9 January, [2005] All ER (D) 196 (Nov) ............................... 2.744

Lyric Club, Re (1892) 36 Sol Jo 801 ................................... 1.175

## M

M, Re [1992] QB 377, [1992] 1 All ER 537, [1992] 2 WLR 340, (1991) Times, 17 April ........................................................... 1.353

M (a minor) (contact order: committal), Re (31 December 1998, unreported) ......... 1.452

M (a minor) (contempt of court: committal of court's own motion), Re [1999] Fam 263, [1999] 2 All ER 56, [1999] 2 WLR 810, [1999] 1 FLR 810, [1999] 1 FCR 683, [1999] Fam Law 208, (1998) Times, 31 December, [1998] Lexis Citation 3143, 143 Sol Jo LB 36, [1998] All ER (D) 746 ................................................ 1.489

MBI Clifton Moor Ltd (in administration) [2020] EWHC 1835 (Ch) ............... 1.688

MBI Hawthorn Care Ltd, Re [2019] EWHC 2365 (Ch) ..................... 1.630, 1.674

MCH Services Ltd, Re [1987] BCLC 535, 3 BCC 179 ......................... 1.168

MCI WorldCom Ltd, Re, MCI WorldCom Ltd v Primus Telecommunications Ltd [2002] EWHC 2436 (Ch), [2003] 1 BCLC 330, [2003] BPIR 667, [2002] All ER (D) 237 (Nov) .................................................................. 1.178

MDA Investment Management Ltd, Re [2003] EWHC 2277 (Ch), [2004] 1 BCLC 217, [2005] BCC 783, [2004] BPIR 75, [2003] All ER (D) 128 (Oct) ..................... 1.302

MEPC plc v Scottish Amicable Life Assurance Society (1993) 67 P & CR 314, [1993] 2 EGLR 93, [1993] 36 EG 133, (1993) Times, 6 April, [1996] BPIR 447, CA .................................................................................. 1.434

MF Global UK Ltd, Re [2015] EWHC 2319 (Ch), [2016] Ch 325, [2016] 2 WLR 588, [2015] BPIR 1208, [2015] All ER (D) 22 (Aug) ................... 1.300, 1.301, 1.492

MG Rover Belux SA/NV (in admin), Re [2007] BCC 446, [2006] Lexis Citation 05 .................................................................................. 1.682

MG Rover Espana SA, Re [2006] EWHC 3426 (Ch), [2006] BCC 599, [2005] BPIR 1162 ............................................................................ 1.679, 1.683

MG Rover Group Ltd (in liq), Re, MG Rover Dealer Properties Ltd v Hunt [2012] BPIR 590 .................................................................................... 2.833

MHMH Ltd v Carwood Barker Holdings Ltd [2004] EWHC 3174 (Ch), [2006] 1 BCLC 279, [2005] BCC 536, [2005] BPIR 601, [2004] All ER (D) 327 (Dec) ............... 1.178

MK Airlines Property Ltd (in administration) v Katz (16 May 2012, unreported), ChD .................................................................................. 1.188

MK Airlines Ltd, Re [2012] EWHC 1018 (Ch), [2012] 3 All ER 781, [2013] 1 BCLC 9, [2013] Bus LR 169, [2012] All ER (D) 163 (Apr) ..................................... 1.716

MKG Convenience Ltd (in liq), Re Abdulali v NISA Retail Ltd [2019] EWHC 1383 (Ch), [2019] BPIR 1063, [2019] All ER (D) 55 (Jun) ..................................... 1.180

ML Design Group Ltd, Re [2006] EWHC 2224 (Ch), [2006] All ER (D) 75 (Jan) ..... 1.671

MMC Pty Ltd (in liqation), Re (1992) 10 ACLC 365 .............................. 1.207

MPOTEC Gmbh [2006] BCC 681 ................................................ 6.5

MS Fashions Ltd v Bank of Credit and Commerce International SA (in liq) (No 2) [1993] Ch 425, [1993] 3 All ER 769, [1993] 3 WLR 220, [1993] BCLC 1200, [1993] BCC 360, [1993] 21 LS Gaz R 40, [1993] NLJR 651, (1993) Times, 26 March, 137 Sol Jo LB 132, CA ................................................................................. 2.852

MT Realisations Ltd, Re [2003] EWHC 2895 (Ch), [2004] 1 All ER 577, [2004] 1 WLR 1678, [2004] 1 BCLC 119, [2003] All ER (D) 92 (Dec), sub nom Digital Equipment Co Ltd v Bower [2004] BCC 509, [2004] 04 LS Gaz R 31, (2003) Times, 29 December ................................................................. 1.208, 2.433

MTB Motors Ltd (in administration), Re [2010] EWHC 3751 (Ch), [2012] BCC 601 .................................................................... 1.646, 2.820

MTI Trading Systems Ltd (in administration), Re [1998] 2 BCLC 246 ............... 1.629

MTI Trading Systems Ltd v Winter [1998] BCC 591, [1997] Lexis Citation 1547 ..... 1.679

Mac Plant Services Ltd v Contract Lifting Services (Scotland) Ltd [2008] CSOH 158, 2009 SC 125, CSOH ................................................... 1.175, 1.178

McAllister v Society of Lloyd's [1999] Lloyd's Rep IR 487, [1999] BPIR 548 .......... 2.530

Macaria Investments Ltd v Gatnom Capital and Finance Ltd [2011] EWHC 3716 (Ch), [2012] BPIR 299, [2011] All ER (D) 218 (Nov) ............................. 1.65, 1.178

Macaria Investments Ltd v Sanders [2010] EWHC 3353 (Ch), [2011] BPIR 1013, [2010] All ER (D) 233 (Dec) .......................................................... 1.65

McAteer v Lismore [2012] NICh 7, [2012] BPIR 812 ............................... 1.415

McCarthy vTann [2015] EWHC 2049 (Ch), [2015] BPIR 1224 ...................... 2.835

McCurdy (E) Ltd, Re [1957] NZLR 752 .......................................... 2.320

McEwen v London, Bombay and Mediterranean Bank Ltd, Re London, Bombay and Mediterranean Bank Ltd [1866] WN 407, 15 WR 245, 15 LT 495 .................. 1.183

McGann v Bisping [2021] EWHC 704 (QB), [2021] BPIR 881 ....................... 1.396

McGrath v Riddell. See HIH Casualty and General Insurance Ltd, Re; McMahon v McGrath

McGruther v Seoble, Re [2004] SC 514 ............................................ 1.64

McGuinness Bros (UK) Ltd, Re (1987) 3 BCC 571, [1987] Lexis Citation 1198 ....... 1.180

McGuire v Rose (former trustee in bankruptcy of McGuire) [2013] EWCA Civ 429, [2014] BPIR 650 .................................................................. 1.415

McHale (James) Automobiles Ltd, Re [1997] 1 BCLC 273, [1997] BCC 202 ... 1.164, 1.300

McIsaac, Petitioner, Joint Liquidators of First Tokyo Index Trust Ltd, Re [1994] BCC 410, CtSess ...................................................................... 1.300

Mackay v Douglas (1872) LR 14 Eq 106, 41 LJ Ch 539, 20 WR 652, 26 LT 721 ...... 1.582

Mackay (as joint administrators) v Kaupthing Singer & Friedlander Ltd (in admin) [2013] EWHC 2553 (Ch), [2013] All ER (D) 127 (Aug) ................................. 1.660

Mackintosh (John) & Sons Ltd v Baker's Bargain Stores (Seaford) Ltd (1965) LR 5 RP 305, [1965] 3 All ER 412, [1965] 1 WLR 1182, 109 Sol Jo 678 ..................... 1.198

Maclaine Watson and Co Ltd v International Tin Council. See International Tin Council, Re

McLean & Co, Re [1881] WN 8 .................................................... 2.324

McIlroy-Rose and McIlroy-Rose as Personal Representative of the Estate of John McIlroy (Dec'd) v Mckeating [2021] NICh 17 ............................................ 1.582

McMullen & Sons Ltd v Cerrone [1994] 1 BCLC 152, 66 P & CR 351, [1994] BCC 25, [1994] 1 EGLR 99, [1993] NLJR 914, [1994] 19 EG 134, (1993) Times, 10 June ..... 1.353

McNulty v Revenue and Customs Comrs [2012] UKUT 174 (TCC), [2012] STC 2110, [2012] All ER (D) 92 (Aug) ........................................................ 1.396

Macpherson v Wise [2011] EWHC 141 (Ch), [2011] BPIR 472, [2011] All ER (D) 146 (Mar) .............................................................................. 2.530

McQuarrie v Jacques (1954) 92 CLR 262 ........................................... 1.181

Macquarie Bank Ltd v TM Investments Pty Ltd [2005] NSWSC 608 ................ 1.177

Macrae (P and J) Ltd, Re [1961] 1 All ER 302, [1961] 1 WLR 229, 105 Sol Jo 108, CA .......................................................................... 1.178, 2.550

McRoberts v McRoberts [2012] EWHC 2966 (Ch), [2013] 1 WLR 1601, [2013] BPIR 77, [2012] All ER (D) 12 (Nov) ...................................................... 1.393

McTear (liquidator of CJ & RA Eade LLP (in liq)) v Eade [2019] EWHC 1673 (Ch), [2019] BPIR 1380 ............................................................. 1.270, 1.273

McTear v Engelhard [2014] EWHC 1056 (Ch) ...................................... 1.680

Madoff Securities International Ltd, Re [2009] EWHC 442 (Ch), [2009] 2 BCLC 78, [2010] BCC 328, [2009] All ER (D) 31 (Mar) ................................... 1.299, 7.4

Madrid and Valencia Rly Co, Re, ex p James (1850) 19 LJ Ch 260, 2 Mac & G 169, 42 ER 65, Ct of Ch ............................................................. 1.174, 7.23

Magical Marking Ltd v Phillips [2008] EWHC 1640 (Pat), [2008] FSR 973 ......... 1.660

Magiera v Magiera [2016] EWCA Civ 1292, [2017] Fam 327, [2017] 3 WLR 41, 20 ITELR 47, [2018] 1 FLR 1131, [2017] Fam Law 286, [2017] WTLR 245, [2017] BPIR 472, [2016] All ER (D) 98 (Dec) ............................................ 1.433

Magnus Consultants Ltd, Re [1995] 1 BCLC 203 ........................... 1.160, 1.168

Mahomed v Morris [2000] 2 BCLC 536, [2001] BCC 233, [2000] 07 LS Gaz R 41, (2000) Times, 1 March, [2000] Lexis Citation 2584, [2000] All ER (D) 193 ................ 1.220

Maidstone Buildings Provisions Ltd, Re [1971] 3 All ER 363, [1971] 1 WLR 1085, 115 Sol Jo 464 ...................................................................... 1.271

Maira (No 3), The. See National Bank of Greece SA v Pinios Shipping Co

Majory, Re, ex p Debtor v F A Dumont Ltd [1955] Ch 600, [1955] 2 WLR 1035, 99 Sol Jo 316, sub nom Re Debtor (No 757 of 1954), ex p Debtor v F A Dumont Ltd [1955] 2 All ER 65, CA ................................................................. 1.381

Mal Bower's Macquarie Electrical Centre Pty Ltd (in liqation), Re [1974] 1 NSWLR 254 ................................................................................ 1.180

Malcolm v Benedict Mackenzie (a firm) [2004] EWCA Civ 1748, [2005] ICR 611, [2005] OPLR 301, [2005] 03 LS Gaz R 30, (2005) Times, 4 January, [2005] BPIR 176, [2004] All ER (D) 343 (Dec), sub nom Malcolm, Re [2005] 1 WLR 1238 ............ 1.417

Malcolm v Official Receiver [1998] Lexis Citation 13, [1999] BPIR 97 .............. 1.427

Mama Milla Ltd (in liq), Re [2014] EWCA Civ 761, [2015] BPIR 590 ............... 2.838

Manakau Timber Co, Re (1895) 13 NZLR 319 ...................................... 1.251

Managa Properties Ltd v Brittain [2009] EWHC 157 (Ch), [2009] 1 BCLC 689, [2010] Bus LR 599, [2009] BPIR 306, [2009] All ER (D) 60 (Feb) ................... 1.224, 2.834

Mander v Evans [2001] 3 All ER 811, [2001] 1 WLR 2378, [2001] 28 LS Gaz R 42, (2001) Times, 25 June, (2001) Independent, 9 July, [2001] Lexis Citation 1625, [2001] NLJR 818, 145 Sol Jo LB 158, [2001] BPIR 902, [2001] All ER (D) 185 (May) ....... 1.393

Manmac Farmers Ltd, Re [1968] 1 All ER 1150, [1968] 1 WLR 572, 112 Sol Jo 131 ................................................................................ 1.251

Mann v Goldstein [1968] 2 All ER 769, [1968] 1 WLR 1091, 112 Sol Jo 439 . 1.175, 1.178, 2.324, 2.331

Manolete Partners plc v Hayward and Barrett Holdings Ltd [2021] EWHC 1481 (Ch), [2021] All ER (D) 08 (Jun) .................... 1.270, 1.582, 1.692, 2.48, 2.751, 2.820

Manson v Smith (liquidator of Thomas Christy Ltd) [1997] 2 BCLC 161 ............ 2.852

Manual Work Services (Construction) Ltd, Re [1975] 1 All ER 426, [1975] 1 WLR 341, 118 Sol Jo 734 .................................................................... 2.820

Manuplastics Ltd v BPSW19 Ltd [2011] EWHC 3853 (Ch), [2012] BCC 368 ........ 1.162

Marann Brooks CSV Ltd, Re [2003] BCC 239, [2003] BPIR 1159, [2002] All ER (D) 42 (Dec) .......................................................................... 1.177, 6.3

March Estates plc v Gunmark Ltd [1996] 2 BCLC 1, [1996] 2 EGLR 38, [1996] 32 EG 75, (1996) Times, 1 April, [1996] BPIR 439 ..................................... 1.59, 1.62

Marches Credit Union Ltd 1986 [2013] EWHC 1731 (Ch) ........................... 1.176

Marcus v Institute of Chartered Accountants [2004] EWHC 3010 (Ch), [2005] BPIR 413, [2004] All ER (D) 27 (Dec) ........................................................ 2.829
Marine Investment Co Ltd, Re (1868) 17 LT 535 .................................. 1.183
Marine Mansions Co, Re (1867) LR 4 Eq 601, 37 LJ Ch 113, 17 LT 50 .............. 1.196
Mark One (Oxford St) plc, Re [1999] 1 All ER 608, [1999] 1 WLR 1445, [2000] 1 BCLC 462, [1998] BCC 984 ........................................................... 1.682
Market Wizard Systems (UK) Ltd, Re [1998] 2 BCLC 282, [1998] 33 LS Gaz R 34, (1998) Times, 31 July, 142 Sol Jo LB 229 ................................ 1.177, 1.276
Marks v Feldman (1870) LR 5 QB 275, 10 B & S 371, 39 LJQB 101, Exch .......... 1.303
Marlborough Club Co, Re (1868) LR 5 Eq 365, 37 LJ Ch 296, 16 WR 668, 18 LT 46 ...................................................................... 1.202
Marr (a bankrupt), Re [1990] Ch 773, [1990] 2 All ER 880, [1990] 2 WLR 1264, 11 LDAB 555, 134 Sol Jo 1009, [1990] 17 LS Gaz R 28, (1989) Times, 15 December ...................................................................... 1.386
Marseilles Extension Rly and Land Co, Re (1867) LR 4 Eq 692, 15 WR 1167, 17 LT 61 ...................................................................... 1.160
Marseilles Extension Rly and Land Co, Re [1867] WN 68 ........................ 1.188
Martin-Sklan v White [2006] EWHC 3313 (Ch), [2007] BPIR 76, [2006] All ER (D) 77 (Nov) ...................................................................... 1.455
Martin Wallis & Co, Re (1893) 37 Sol Jo 822 .................................. 1.178
Masri Apartments Pty Ltd v Perpetual Nominees Ltd (2004) 214 ALR 338, [2004] NSWCA 471, NSW CA ......................................................... 1.176
Masonic and General Life Assurance Co, Re (1885) 32 ChD 373, 55 LJ Ch 666, 34 WR 739 ...................................................................... 1.176
Massey, Re, Re Freehold Land and Brickmaking Co (1870) LR 9 Eq 367, 39 LJ Ch 492, 18 WR 444, 22 LT 195 .................................................. 2.306, 2.435
Masters v Leaver (1999) Times, 5 August, [1999] Lexis Citation 4690, [2000] BPIR 284, CA ...................................................................... 1.393
Matheson Bros Ltd, Re (1884) 27 ChD 225, 32 WR 846, 51 LT 111, [1881–5] All ER Rep Ext 1342 ................................................................. 1.281
Matthews (F P and C H) Ltd, Re [1982] Ch 257, [1982] 1 All ER 338, [1982] 2 WLR 495, 126 Sol Jo 63 ............................................................. 1.303
Maud, Re [2020] EWHC 674 (Ch) .............................................. 1.178
Maud, Re, Aabar Block S.A.R.L. v Maud [2018] EWHC 1414 (Ch), [2019] Ch 15, [2018] 3 WLR 1497, [2018] BPIR 1207, [2018] All ER (D) 75 (Jun) .......... 1.178, 1.381, 2.550
Maud, Re, Maud v Aabar Block S.a.r.l [2016] EWHC 2175 (Ch), [2016] Bus LR 1243, 166 NLJ 7715, [2016] BPIR 1486, [2016] All ER (D) 51 (Sep) ... 1.178, 1.381, 1.382, 2.550
Maud v Aabar Block SARL [2015] EWHC 1626 (Ch), [2015] BPIR 845, [2015] All ER (D) 97 (Jun) ........................................................ 1.178, 1.381, 2.530
Maville Hose Ltd, Re [1939] Ch 32, [1938] 3 All ER 621, 108 LJ Ch 78, 88 Sol Jo 625, 159 LT 410, 54 TLR 1056 ............................................... 1.300
Mawcon Ltd, Re [1969] 1 All ER 188, [1969] 1 WLR 78, 112 Sol Jo 1004 .......... 2.433
Mawer v Bland [2013] EWHC 3122 (Ch), [2015] BPIR 66 ......................... 1.391
Maxwell v Brookes [2014] Lexis Citation 201, [2014] BPIR 1395, [2014] All ER (D) 111 (Oct) ................................................................ 1.194, 2.997
Maxwell Communication Corpn plc, Re [1992] BCLC 465, [1992] BCC 372 .. 1.407, 1.433, 1.671
Maxwell Communications Corpn plc (No 2), Re [1994] 1 All ER 737, [1993] 1 WLR 1402, [1994] 1 BCLC 1, [1993] BCC 369, (1993) Times, 1 April .................... 1.159
Maxwell Communications Corpn plc (No 3), Re [1995] 1 BCLC 521, [1994] BCC 741 ...................................................................... 1.300, 2.765
Mazur Media Ltd v Mazur Media GmbH [2004] EWHC 1566 (Ch), [2004] 1 WLR 2966, [2005] 1 BCLC 305, [2005] 1 Lloyd's Rep 41, (2004) Times, 29 July, [2004] BPIR 1253, [2004] All ER (D) 110 (Jul) ........................................ 1.183
Meadrealm Ltd v Transcontinental Golf Construction (29 November 1991, unreported), ChD ........................................................... 1.73, 1.631
Meaford Manufacturing Co, Re (1919) 46 OLR 252 .............................. 1.178
Medforth v Blake [2000] Ch 86, [1999] 3 All ER 97, [1999] 3 WLR 922, [1999] 2 BCLC 221, [1999] 2 EGLR 75, [1999] 24 LS Gaz R 39, [1999] NLJR 929, [1999] 29 EG 119, [1999] EGCS 81, (1999) Times, 22 June, [1999] Lexis Citation 2390, 143 Sol Jo LB 158, [1999] BPIR 712, [1999] All ER (D) 546 ......................... 1.88, 1.620
Medisco Equipment Ltd, Re [1983] BCLC 305, [1983] Com LR 232, 1 BCC 98, 944 ...................................................................... 1.168, 1.178
Meek (David) Plant Ltd, Re [1994] 1 BCLC 680, [1993] BCC 175 .................. 1.660

Meem SL Ltd (an administration), Re, Goel v Grant (as joint administrators of Meem SL Ltd) [2017] EWHC 2688 (Ch), [2018] Bus LR 393, [2017] All ER (D) 114 (Dec) ............................................................................................ 1.691

Meesan Investments Ltd, Re. See Royal Trust Bank v Buchler

Meisels v Martin [2005] EWHC 845 (Ch), [2005] BPIR 1151, [2005] All ER (D) 88 (May) .................................................................................. 2.837

Mekarska v Ruiz [2011] EWHC 913 (Fam), [2011] 2 FLR 1351, [2011] 2 FCR 608, [2011] Fam Law 802, [2011] NLJR 849, [2011] BPIR 1139, [2011] All ER (D) 14 (Jun) ............................................................................... 1.395, 1.456

Melars Group Ltd Melars Group Ltd, Re (in liq) v East-West Logistics LLP [2021] EWHC 1523 (Ch), [2021] All ER (D) 26 (Jun) ............................................... 6.5

Melcann Ltd v Marmlon Holdings (1991) 9 ACLC 678 ............................ 2.324

Melson Velcrete Pty Ltd re (1996) 14 ACLC 778 ................................... 1.77

Memon v Cork [2018] EWHC 594 (Ch) ............................................... 1.160

Menastar Finance Ltd (in liq), Re, Menastar Ltd v Simon [2002] EWHC 2610 (Ch), [2003] 1 BCLC 338, (2002) Times, 11 November, [2002] All ER (D) 26 (Nov), CSRC vol 26 iss 17/1 ................................................... 1.178, 2.834, 2.835

Menzies v National Bank of Kuwait SAK. See Ayala Holdings Ltd, Re

Mercantile Bank of Australia Ltd v Dinwoodie (1902) 28 VLR 491 ............... 1.293

Mercantile Finance & Agency Co Re (1894) 13 NZLR 472 ....................... 1.160

Mercer and Moore, Re (1880) 14 ChD 287, 49 LJ Ch 201, 28 WR 485, 42 LT 311 ............................................................................................ 1.235

Mercy & Sons Pty Ltd v Wanari Pty Ltd [2000] NSWSC 75 ..................... 1.200

Mederco (Cardiff) Ltd, Re (09477164) [2021] EWHC 386 (Ch), [2021] 2 BCLC 60 ................................................................... 1.693, 2.137, 6.1

Mersey Steel and Iron Co v Naylor, Benzon & Co (1884) 9 App Cas 434, 53 LJQB 497, 32 WR 989, [1881–5] All ER Rep 365, 51 LT 637, HL .......................... 1.180

Merton v Hammond Suddards [1996] 2 BCLC 470 ................................. 1.180

Metalloy Supplies Ltd (in liqation) v MA (UK) Ltd [1997] 1 All ER 418, [1997] 1 WLR 1613, [1997] 1 BCLC 165, (1996) Times, 12 December, [1998] 1 Costs LR 85 ........ 1.178

Metro Nominees (Wandsworth) (No 1) Ltd v Rayment [2008] BCC 40, CC ........... 1.660

Metrocab Ltd, Re [2010] EWHC 1317 (Ch), [2010] 2 BCLC 603, [2010] BPIR 1368, [2010] Bus LR D149, [2010] All ER (D) 89 (Jun) .................................. 2.814

Metropolitan Bank, Re, Heiron's Case (1880) 15 ChD 139, 49 LJ Ch 651, 43 LT 299, CA ............................................................................................ 1.300

Metropolitan Rly Warehousing Co Ltd, Re (1867) 36 LJ Ch 827, 15 WR 1121, 17 LT 108 ............................................................................................ 1.174

Metzeler, Re (1987) 78 BR 674 ............................................... 7.34, 7.36

Michael v The Official Receiver [2010] EWHC 2246 (Ch) ......................... 1.394

Michael Bernard McNamara Wilson (joint trustees in bankruptcy of Michael Bernard McNamara), Re v McNamara [2020] EWHC 98 (Ch), [2020] BPIR 661, [2020] All ER (D) 107 (Jan) ................................................................... 6.8

Micklethwait, Re [2002] EWHC 1123 (Ch), [2003] BPIR 101, [2002] All ER (D) 351 (May) .................................................................................. 1.381

Mid East Trading Ltd, Re [1998] 1 All ER 577, [1998] 1 BCLC 240, [1998] BCC 726, [1998] 03 LS Gaz R 24, [1997] Lexis Citation 4754, 142 Sol Jo LB 45, [1997] All ER (D) 106 ............................................................. 1.186, 1.300, 2.814

Middlesborough Assembly Rooms Co, Re (1880) 14 ChD 104, 49 LJ Ch 413, 28 WR 868, 42 LT 609, CA ..................................................................... 1.174

Midland Bank plc v Wyatt [1997] 1 BCLC 242, [1995] 1 FLR 696, [1995] 3 FCR 11, [1995] Fam Law 299, [1996] BPIR 288 ............................................. 1.582

Midland Counties District Bank Ltd v Attwood [1905] 1 Ch 357, 74 LJ Ch 286, 12 Mans 20, 2 LDAB 70, [1904–7] All ER Rep 648, 92 LT 360, 21 TLR 175 ................. 1.145

Migration Services International, Re [2000] 1 BCLC 666, [2000] BCC 1095, [1999] 47 LS Gaz R 29, (1999) Times, 2 December, [1999] Lexis Citation 4082, [1999] All ER (D) 1259 .................................................................... 1.275

Mikki v Duncan [2017] EWCA Civ 57, [2017] 1 WLR 2907, (2017) Times, 23 February, [2017] BPIR 490, [2017] All ER (D) 157 (Feb) ............................. 1.396, 1.424

Milford Docks Co, Re (1883) 23 ChD 292, 52 LJ Ch 744, 48 LT 560 ............. 1.176

Millennium Advanced Technology Ltd, Re [2004] EWHC 711 (Ch), [2004] 4 All ER 465, [2004] 1 WLR 2177, [2004] 2 BCLC 77, (2004) Times, 29 April, [2004] All ER (D) 45 (Apr) .......................................................................... 1.174, 1.177

Millennium Global Emerging Credit, Re (2011) 458 BR 63 (Bankr SDNY 2011) ....... 7.30

Miller v Bain [2002] BCC 899, [2000] Lexis Citation 4630, [2003] BPIR 959, [2000] All ER (D) 2019 ............................................................. 2.768

Miller v Bayliss [2009] EWHC 2063 (Ch), [2009] BPIR 1438 ..................... 1.414

Mills v Birchall. See Dolphin Quays Developments Ltd v Mills

Mills v Edict Ltd [1999] BPIR 391 ................................. 1.303, 1.305, 1.324

Minmar Ltd v Khalatschi [2011] EWHC 1159 (Ch), [2012] 1 BCLC 798, [2011] BCC 485, [2011] NLJR 1449, [2011] All ER (D) 99 (Oct) ..... 1.629, 1.639, 1.643, 1.722, 2.127, 2.820

Minotaur Data Systems Ltd, Re, Official Receiver v Brunt [1999] 3 All ER 122, [1999] 1 WLR 1129, [1999] 2 BCLC 766, [1999] NPC 27, [1999] NLJR 415, (1999) Times, 18 March, [1999] Lexis Citation 2024, 143 Sol Jo LB 97, [1999] 2 Costs LR 97, [1999] BPIR 560, [1999] All ER (D) 215 .................................................... 1.554

Minrealm Ltd, Re [2007] EWHC 3078 (Ch), [2008] 2 BCLC 141, [2007] All ER (D) 320 (Dec), CSRC vol 31 iss 22/1 ........................................................ 1.176

Mirror Group (Holdings) Ltd, Re [1993] BCLC 538, [1992] BCC 972, [1992] NPC 139, [1992] EGCS 126, (1992) Times, 12 November ...................................... 1.679

Mirror Group Newspapers plc (inquiry), Re [1999] 2 All ER 641, [1999] 3 WLR 583, [1999] 1 BCLC 690, [2000] BCC 217 ................................................... 1.277

Mirror Group Newspapers plc v Maxwell [1998] 1 BCLC 638, [1998] BCC 324, (1997) Times, 15 July .................................................................... 1.80

Mitchell (joint liquidators of MBI International & Partners Inc (in liq)) v Al Jaber [2021] EWHC 912 (Ch), [2021] 3 WLR 15, [2021] All ER (D) 36 (May); revsd sub nom Al Jaber v Mitchell [2021] EWCA Civ 1190, [2021] All ER (D) 21 (Aug) ............... 1.300

Mitchell v Buckingham International plc (in liq) [1998] 2 BCLC 369, [1998] BCC 943, [1998] Lexis Citation 2248, [1998] All ER (D) 59 ................................... 1.220

Mitchell v Carter [1997] 1 BCLC 673, CA ........................................... 1.240

Mitchell McFarlane & Partners Ltd, Re, Mitchell McFarlane & Partners Ltd v Foremans Ltd [2002] EWHC 3203 (Ch) ............................................... 1.178

Mittal v RP Capital Explorer Master Fund [2014] BPIR 1537 ....................... 1.382

Modern Jet Support Centre Ltd, Re [2005] EWHC 1611 (Ch), [2005] 1 WLR 3880, [2006] STC 808, [2006] 1 BCLC 703, [2006] BCC 174, [2005] RVR 379, (2005) Times, 19 September, [2005] BPIR 1382, [2005] All ER (D) 314 (Jul) ................ 1.240

Mond v Hyde [1999] QB 1097, [1998] 3 All ER 833, [1999] 2 WLR 499, [1998] 2 BCLC 340, [1998] 31 LS Gaz R 35, (1998) Times, 29 July, [1998] Lexis Citation 2816, 142 Sol Jo LB 242, [1999] BPIR 728, [1998] All ER (D) 346 ......... 1.185, 1.554, 1.555, 2.800

Mond v Synergi Partners Ltd [2015] EWHC 964 (Ch), [2015] 2 BCLC 229, [2015] BPIR 1300, [2015] All ER (D) 81 (Apr) ...................................................... 1.630

Mondelphous Engineering Associates (No 2) Ltd (in liqation), Re (1989) 7 ACLC 220 ............................................................................. 1.186

Montgomery v Wanda Modes Ltd [2002] 1 BCLC 289, [2003] BPIR 457, [2001] All ER (D) 374 (Dec) ......................................................................... 1.178

Montin Ltd, Re [1999] 1 BCLC 663 ................................................. 1.685

Montratier Asphalte Co, Re (1874) 22 WR 527 ..................................... 1.160

Moodliar v Hendricks 2011 (2) SA 199 ............................................. 1.188

Moon v Franklin [1996] BPIR 196 .................................................. 1.582

Morby v Gate Gourmet Luxembourg IV Sarl [2016] EWHC 74 (Ch), [2016] Bus LR 218, [2016] BPIR 414, [2016] All ER (D) 157 (Jan) ................................. 1.380, 2.540

Mordant, Re, Mordant v Halls [1995] Lexis Citation 4250, [1996] BPIR 302, CA .... 2.800

Morecambe Bowling Ltd, Re [1969] 1 All ER 753, [1969] 1 WLR 133, 113 Sol Jo 104 ............................................................................. 1.270

Morgan v Gray [1953] Ch 83, [1953] 1 All ER 213, [1953] 2 WLR 140, 97 Sol Jo 48 ......................................................................... 1.417, 1.429

Morning Mist v Krys (In re Fairfield Sentry Ltd), 714 F 3d 127 (2d Cir 2013) .......... 7.30

Morphitis v Bernasconi [2003] EWCA Civ 289, [2003] Ch 552, [2003] 2 WLR 1521, [2003] 2 BCLC 53, [2003] BCC 540, [2003] 19 LS Gaz R 30, (2003) Times, 12 March, 147 Sol Jo LB 300, [2003] BPIR 973, sub nom Morphites v Bernasconi [2003] All ER (D) 33 (Mar) ............................................................... 1.271, 1.272

Morris v Bank of America National Trust & Saving Association [1997] BCC 651 ..... 2.767

Morris v Bank of America National Trust and Savings Association [2000] 1 All ER 954, [2001] 1 BCLC 771, [2000] BCC 1076, [2000] 03 LS Gaz R 37, (2000) Times, 25 January, [1999] Lexis Citation 4067, 144 Sol Jo LB 48, [2000] BPIR 83, [1999] All ER (D) 1507 ................................................................... 1.271

Morris v Bank of India. See Bank of Credit and Commerce International SA (in liq), Re [2004] EWHC 528 (Ch)

Morris v European Islamic Ltd (002828 of 1999) [1999] CLY 3283, ChD ........... 1.300

Morris v Kanssen [1946] AC 459, [1946] 1 All ER 586, 115 LJ Ch 177, 174 LT 353, 62 TLR 306, HL ................................................................. 1.78, 1.638

Morris v Morgan [1998] Lexis Citation 2429, [1998] BPIR 764, CA ................. 1.396

Morris v Murjani [1996] 2 All ER 384, [1996] 1 WLR 848, (1995) Times, 27 December, [1996] BPIR 458 ............................................................................... 1.452

Morris v State Bank of India [2003] EWHC 1868 (Ch), [2004] 2 BCLC 236, [2003] BCC 735, [2003] All ER (D) 512 (Jul) ...................................................... 1.271

Morrside Investments Ltd v DAG Construction Ltd (1 November 2007, unreported), ChD ..................................................................................................... 1.178

Mortgage Corp Ltd v Shaire, Mortgage Corp Ltd v Lewis Silkin (a firm) [2001] Ch 743, [2001] 4 All ER 364, [2001] 3 WLR 639, 80 P & CR 280, [2000] 1 FLR 973, [2000] 2 FCR 222, [2000] Fam Law 402, [2000] 3 EGLR 131, [2000] 11 LS Gaz R 37, [2000] EGCS 35, (2000) Times, 21 March, [2000] Lexis Citation 2740, [2000] BPIR 483, [2000] All ER (D) 254 ........................................................................ 1.455

Morton v Confer [1963] 2 All ER 765, [1963] 1 WLR 763, 61 LGR 461, 127 JP 433, 107 Sol Jo 417, DC ......................................................................... 1.262

Moscow Savings Bank and the Russian Federation v Amadeus Trading Ltd (26 March 1997, unreported) ............................................................................ 2.777

Moseley V Else Solicitors LLP [2010] Lexis Citation 67, [2010] BPIR 1192, CC ....... 1.382

Moss, Re, ex p Hallet [1905] 2 KB 307, 74 LJKB 764, 12 Mans 227, 53 WR 558, [1904–7] All ER Rep 713, 49 Sol Jo 538, 92 LT 777, DC ................................ 1.393

Moss Groundworks Ltd, Re [2019] EWHC 3079 (Ch), [2019] All ER (D) 91 (Sep) .... 1.617

Motor Auction Pty Ltd v John Joyce Wholesale Cars Pty Ltd (1997) 15 ACLC 987, NSW Sup Ct ............................................................................................ 1.263

Motor Terms Co Pty Ltd v Liberty Insurance Ltd (1967) 116 CLR 177, HCA ......... 1.176

Mountney v Treharne [2002] EWCA Civ 1174, [2003] Ch 135, [2002] 3 WLR 1760, [2002] 2 FLR 930, [2002] 3 FCR 97, [2002] Fam Law 809, [2002] 39 LS Gaz R 38, (2002) Times, 9 September, [2002] BPIR 1126, [2002] All ER (D) 35 (Aug) .... 1.396, 1.398

Mourant & Co Trustees Ltd v Sixty UK Ltd (in liq) [2010] EWHC 1890 (Ch), [2011] 1 BCLC 383, [2010] BCC 882, [2010] 2 EGLR 125, (2010) Times, 2 November, [2010] BPIR 1264, [2010] All ER (D) 250 (Jul) ................................. 1.59, 1.65

Mowbary v Saunders [2015] EWHC 2317 (Ch) .............................................. 1.395

Mowbray v Sanders [2015] EWHC 296 (Ch), [2015] BPIR 665, [2015] All ER (D) 161 (Feb) ............................................................................................... 1.395

Mulalley and Company Ltd v Regent Building Services Ltd [2017] EWHC 2962 (Ch), 167 NLJ 7772, [2017] All ER (D) 200 (Nov) ................................................ 2.338

Mulkerrins v PricewaterhouseCoopers (a firm) [2003] UKHL 41, [2003] 4 All ER 1, [2003] 1 WLR 1937, [2003] 37 LS Gaz R 32, (2003) Times, 1 August, 147 Sol Jo LB 935, [2003] BPIR 1357, [2003] All ER (D) 549 (Jul), HL ............................ 1.396

Multi Guarantee Co Ltd, Re [1987] BCLC 257 ............................................... 1.622

Mulvey v Secretary of State for Social Security (1997) Times, 20 March, 1997 SC (HL) 105, 1997 SLT 753, 1997 SCLR 348, [1997] BPIR 696, HL ......................... 1.396

Mulville v Sandelson [2019] EWHC 3287 (Ch), [2020] BPIR 392 ....................... 1.382

Mumford, Re, Debtor v Petitioning Creditor, ex p Official Receiver. See Debtor (No 82 of 1926), Re

Mumtaz Properties Ltd, Re [2011] EWCA Civ 610, [2012] 2 BCLC 109, [2011] NLJR 779, [2011] All ER (D) 237 (May) ......................................................... 1.270

Munns v Perkins [2002] BPIR 120 .................................................... 1.79, 1.80

Munro and Rowe, Singer v Trustee in Bankruptcy, Re. See Singer v Trustee of the Property of Munro (bankrupts)

Murjani (a bankrupt), Re [1996] 1 All ER 65, [1996] 1 WLR 1498, [1996] 1 BCLC 272, [1996] BCC 278, [1996] BPIR 325 .................... 1.300, 1.429, 1.492, 2.765

Murray Engineering Co, Re [1925] SASR 330 .............................................. 1.201

Murphy v Gooch [2007] EWCA Civ 603, 10 ITELR 300, [2007] 2 FLR 934, [2007] 3 FCR 96, [2007] Fam Law 905, 151 Sol Jo LB 896, [2007] BPIR 1123, [2007] 2 P & CR D46, [2007] All ER (D) 350 (Jun) ....................................................... 1.455

Myers v Kestrel Acquistions Ltd [2015] EWHC 916 (Ch), [2016] 1 BCLC 719, [2015] All ER (D) 11 (Apr) .................................................................. 1.175

Mytre Investments Ltd v Reynolds (No 2) [1996] BPIR 464 .................... 1.61, 1.359

## N

N (a debtor), Re [2002] BPIR 1024 ........................................................... 1.61

NFU (or National Farmers' Union) Development Trust Ltd, Re [1973] 1 All ER 135, [1972] 1 WLR 1548, 116 Sol Jo 679 ...................................................... 1.58

NJM Clothing Ltd, Ross v Fashion Design Solutions [2018] EWHC 2388 (Ch), [2018] BCC 875 ................................................... 1.646, 2.150, 2.820

NK v BNP Paribas Fortis NV (2019) C-535/17, ECLI:EU:C:2019:96, [2019] All ER (D) 25 (Feb), EUCJ ............................................................................... 6.8

NMC Healthcare Ltd (in administration) and the companies listed in the application schedule [2021] EWHC 1806 (Ch) .................................................... 1.660, 7.30
NMUL Realisations Ltd, Re [2021] EWHC 94 (Ch), [2021] All ER (D) 76 (Jan) ...... 1.632, 1.643, 2.820
NS Distribution Ltd, Re [1990] BCLC 169 ................................ 1.679, 1.685
Naeem (a bankrupt) (No 18 of 1988), Re [1990] 1 WLR 48 .................... 1.62, 1.65
Namco UK Ltd, Re [2003] EWHC 989 (Ch), [2003] 2 BCLC 78, [2003] BPIR 1170, [2003] All ER (D) 118 (Apr) ........................................................ 1.188
Namulas Pension Trustees Ltd v Mouzakis [2011] BPIR 1724, CC ..................... 1.61
Narandas-Girdhar v Bradstock [2016] EWCA Civ 88, [2016] 1 WLR 2366, 166 ConLR 1, (2016) Times, 06 April, [2016] BPIR 428, [2016] All ER (D) 151 (Feb) . 1.61, 1.65, 1.360
Narinen v Finland (Application no 45027/98) [2004] BPIR 914, [2004] ECHR 45027/98, EctHR ................................................................................ 1.497
Nathan, Newman & Co, Re (1887) 35 ChD 1, 56 LJ Ch 752, 35 WR 293, 56 LT 95, 3 TLR 363, CA .......................................................................... 1.201, 2.404
National Acceptance Corpn Pty Ltd v Benson (1988) 12 NSWLR 213, (1988) 6 ACLC 685, NSWCA ........................................................................... 1.180
National Arms and Ammunition Co, Re (1885) 28 ChD 474, 54 LJ Ch 673, 33 WR 585, 52 LT 237, 1 TLR 240, CA ......................................................... 2.433
National Australia Bank Ltd v KDS Construction Services Pty Ltd (1987) 163 CLR 668, 76 ALR 27, 6 ACLC 28, 12 ACLR 663, 62 ALJR 63, AusHC ....................... 1.303
National Bank of Greece SA v Pinios Shipping Co [1990] 1 AC 637, [1990] 1 All ER 78, [1989] 3 WLR 1330, [1990] LRC (Comm) 20, 11 LDAB 518, 134 Sol Jo 261, [1990] 3 LS Gaz R 33, (1989) Times, 1 December, [1999] GCCR 1385, sub nom National Bank of Greece SA v Pinios Shipping Co and George Dionysios Tsitsilianis, The Maira (No 3) [1990] 1 Lloyd's Rep 225, HL .................................... 1.78, 1.638
National Bank of Kuwait v Menzies. See Ayala Holdings Ltd, Re
National Bank of Wales, In Re, Taylor, Phillips and Rickards' Case [1896] 2 Ch 851 ................................................................................................ 1.142
National Bank of Wales, Re, Taylor, Phillips and Rickards' Cases [1897] 1 Ch 298, 66 LJ Ch 222, 4 Mans 59, 45 WR 401, 76 LT 1, 13 TLR 179, CA ......................... 1.129
National Bank Trust (a company incorporated in Russia) v Yurov [2020] EWHC 100 (Comm) .......................................................................... 1.462
National Crime Agency v GTG Management Ltd company [2020] EWHC 963 (Ch), [2020] All ER (D) 203 (Mar) ............................................... 1.176, 1.271
National Mutual Life Association of Australia Ltd v Oasis Developments Pty Ltd (1983) 1 ACLC 1263 ......................................................... 1.178
National Permanent Building Society, Re, ex p Williamson (1869) 5 Ch App 309, 34 JP 341, 18 WR 388 ......................................................... 1.176
National Union of Flint Glassworkers, Re [2006] BCC 828 ......................... 1.280
National United Investment Corpn, Re [1901] 1 Ch 950, 70 LJ Ch 461, 8 Mans 399, 84 LT 766, 17 TLR 396 ......................................................... 1.181
National Westminster Bank Ltd v Halesowen Presswork and Assemblies Ltd [1972] AC 785, [1972] 1 All ER 641, [1972] 2 WLR 455, [1972] 1 Lloyd's Rep 101, 9 LDAB 253, 116 Sol Jo 138, HL ......................................................... 2.852
National Westminster Bank plc v Jones [2001] 1 BCLC 98, [2000] NPC 73, [2000] EGCS 82, (2000) Times, 7 July, [2000] BPIR 1092, [2000] All ER (D) 857; affd [2001] EWCA Civ 1541, [2002] 1 BCLC 55, [2002] 1 P & CR D20, [2001] 44 LS Gaz R 35, (2001) Times, 19 November, 145 Sol Jo LB 246, [2002] BPIR 361, [2001] All ER (D) 333 (Oct) ......................................................... 1.302
National Westminster Bank plc v Msaada Group [2011] EWHC 3423 (Ch), [2012] 2 BCLC 342, [2012] BCC 226 ..................................... 1.643, 2.820
National Westminster Bank plc v Scher [1998] BCLC 124, [1997] Lexis Citation 2901, [1998] BPIR 224 ......................................................... 1.60, 1.65
National Westminster Bank plc v Spectrum Plus Ltd [2005] UKHL 41, [2005] 2 AC 680, [2005] 4 All ER 209, [2005] 3 WLR 58, [2006] 2 LRC 243, [2005] 2 BCLC 269, [2005] 2 Lloyd's Rep 275, [2005] NLJR 1045, (2005) Times, 1 July, [2005] All ER (D) 368 (Jun) ......................................................... 1.632
National Wholemeal Bread and Biscuit Co, Re [1892] 2 Ch 457, 61 LJ Ch 712, 40 WR 591, 36 Sol Jo 523, 540, 67 LT 293 ....................................... 2.834, 2.836
Nationwide Accident Repair Services Ltd and other companies, Re [2020] EWHC 2420 (Ch) ......................................................... 1.629
Natwest Bank plc v Yadgaroff [2011] EWHC 3711 (Ch), [2012] BPIR 371 ............. 1.59
Neath Harbour Smelting and Rolling Works, Re [1887] WN 87, 35 WR 827, 56 LT 727, 3 TLR 568 ......................................................... 1.180

Neath Rugby Ltd, Re [2007] EWHC 1789 (Ch), [2008] 1 BCLC 527, [2007] BCC 671, (2007) Times, 14 August, [2007] All ER (D) 27 (Aug); revsd in part sub nom Hawkes v Cuddy [2007] EWCA Civ 1072, [2008] BCC 125, (2007) Times, 13 November, [2007] BPIR 1217, [2007] All ER (D) 250 (Oct) .................................... 1.275, 1.276
Neesam Investments Ltd, Re (1988) 4 BCC 788 ...................... 1.660
Nektan (Gibraltar) Ltd, Re [2020] EWHC 65 (Ch), 170 NLJ 7872, [2020] All ER (D) 53 (Jan) ................................................................. 1.618
Neon Signs (Australasia) Ltd, Re [1965] VR 125 .................... 1.89
Neufeld v Secretary of State for Business, Enterprise and Regulatory Reform [2009] EWCA Civ 280, [2009] 3 All ER 790, [2009] 2 BCLC 273, [2009] IRLR 475, [2009] ICR 1183, [2009] BCC 687, (2009) Times, 10 April, [2009] BPIR 909, [2009] All ER (D) 40 (Apr) ................................................................. 1.756
Neumans LLP v Andronikou [2013] EWCA Civ 916, [2014] 1 All ER 12, [2014] 1 BCLC 1, [2013] Bus LR 1152, [2013] 6 Costs LO 934, [2013] All ER (D) 284 (Jul) ......... 2.183
New Cap Reinsurance Corp Ltd (in liq), Re. See Rubin v Eurofinance SA
New Cap Reinsurance Corp Ltd (in liq) v A E Grant [2008] NSWSC 1015 ............ 1.175
New Cap Reinsurance Corp Ltd v HIH Casualty and General Insurance Ltd [2002] EWCA Civ 300, [2002] 2 BCLC 228, [2002] BPIR 809, [2002] All ER (D) 413 (Feb) ........................................................................... 1.183
New Hampshire Insurance Co v Rush & Tompkins Group plc [1998] 2 BCLC 471 ... 1.281
New Millennium Experience Co Ltd, Re [2003] EWHC 1823 (Ch), [2004] 1 All ER 687, [2004] 1 BCLC 19, [2003] All ER (D) 399 (Jul), CSRC vol 27 iss 11/1 ........... 1.143
Newark Pty Ltd, Re [1993] 1 Qd R 409, (1991) 6 ACSR 255, Qld S Ct (Full Ct) ...... 1.175
Newdigate Colliery Ltd, Re, Newdigate v Newdigate Colliery Ltd [1912] 1 Ch 468, 81 LJ Ch 235, 19 Mans 155, 106 LT 133, 28 TLR 207, CA ................................. 1.81
Newhart Developments Ltd v Co-operative Commercial Bank Ltd [1978] QB 814, [1978] 2 All ER 896, [1978] 2 WLR 636, 121 Sol Jo 847 ................................. 1.86
Newheadspace Pty Ltd (in liq), Re [2020] NSWSC 173 ............................ 1.300
Newlands (Seaford) Educational Trust, Re; Chittenden v Pepper. See Chittenden v Pepper; Re Newlands (Seaford) Educational Trust
Newman Shopfitters (Cleveland) Ltd, Re [1991] BCLC 407 ........................ 1.87
Newtons Coaches Ltd, Re [2016] EWHC 3068 (Ch), [2018] 1 BCLC 285, [2016] All ER (D) 109 (Dec) .................................................. 1.275, 2.1044
Ng (a bankrupt), Re, Ng v Ng (trustee) [1998] 2 FLR 386, [1998] Fam Law 515, [1997] BCC 507, [1997] BPIR 267 .................................................. 1.416
Nicholls v Lan [2006] EWHC 1255 (Ch), [2007] 1 FLR 744, (2006) Times, 4 August, [2006] BPIR 1243, [2006] All ER (D) 16 (Jun) .................................... 1.455
Nicholson v Fayinka [2014] BPIR 692 ........................................... 1.491
Nicholson v Fielding [2017] Lexis Citation 313, [2017] All ER (D) 156 (Oct) ......... 1.272
Nickel & Goeldner Spedition GmbH v Kintra UAB: C-157/13 (2014) C-157/13, ECLI:EU:C:2014:2145, [2015] QB 96, [2014] 3 WLR 1299, [2015] RTR 75, [2014] All ER (D) 129 (Sep), EUCJ .................................................. 6.2, 6.8
Nicola Jane Ide (in bankruptcy), Re [2020] EWCA Civ 1469, [2021] 1 WLR 1076, [2021] 2 All ER (Comm) 649, [2021] BPIR 113, [2020] All ER (D) 65 (Nov) ......... 2.754, 2.780
Nicoll v Cutts [1985] BCLC 322, 1 BCC 99,427, [1985] PCC 311 .................... 1.88
Nicou v Ngan [2005] NSWSC 446, (2005) 53 ACSR 529, NSW Sup Ct ............. 1.224
Nike European Operations Netherlands BV v Sportland Oy: C-310/14 (2015) C-310/14, ECLI:EU:C:2015:690, [2016] 1 BCLC 297, [2015] All ER (D) 151 (Oct), EUCJ ...... 6.18
Nimat Halal Food Ltd company v Patel (in his capacity as administrator of Tariq Halal Meat (Ilford) Ltd) [2020] EWHC 734 (Ch), [2020] BPIR 976, [2020] All ER (D) 38 (Apr) ................................................... 2.834, 2.835, 2.836, 2.913
19 Entertainment Ltd, Re [2016] EWHC 1545 (Ch) ............................... 7.28
90 Nine Ltd v Luxury Rentals NZ Ltd [2019] NZCA 424 .......................... 1.178
Noble Group Ltd, Re [2018] EWHC 3092 (Ch), [2019] 2 BCLC 548, [2018] All ER (D) 100 (Nov) ................................................................. 1.586
Nolton Business Centres Ltd, Re, Eliades v City of London Common Council [1996] 1 BCLC 400, [1996] RA 116 ............................................ 2.433
Normandy Marketing Ltd, Re [1993] BCC 879, [1993] Lexis Citation 3974 ......... 2.338
Nortel GmbH, Re (in administration) [2011] EWCA Civ 1124, [2012] 1 All ER 1455, [2012] 1 BCLC 248, [2012] Bus LR 818, [2012] BCC 83, [2011] 42 LS Gaz R 21, [2011] All ER (D) 124 (Oct); revsd [2013] UKSC 52, [2014] AC 209, [2013] 4 All ER 887, [2013] 2 BCLC 135, (2013) Times, 19 August, [2013] BPIR 866, [2013] All ER (D) 283 (Jul), SC . 1.64, 1.65, 1.159, 1.176, 1.382, 1.393, 1.460, 1.515, 1.618, 1.682, 1.716, 2.183, 2.433, 2.827, 2.829, 2.852
Nortel Networks France SAS, Re [2019] EWHC 2447 (Ch), [2019] All ER (D) 134 (Oct) ............................................................. 1.696, 1.715

Nortel Networks SA, Re [2009] EWHC 206 (Ch), [2009] BCC 343, [2009] BPIR 316,
[2009] All ER (D) 128 (Feb) ......................................................... 6.36
Nortel Networks UK Ltd ("NNUK"), Re [2014] EWHC 2614 (Ch) .................. 1.679
Nortel Networks UK Ltd, Re [2015] EWHC 2506 (Ch), [2017] 2 BCLC 555,
[2015] All ER (D) 05 (Sep) .......................................................... 1.682
Nortel Networks UK Ltd, Re [2016] EWHC 2769 (Ch), [2017] 2 BCLC 572, [2017] Bus
LR 590, 166 NLJ 7722, [2016] All ER (D) 205 (Jun) ............................. 1.679
Nortel Networks UK Ltd, Re [2017] EWHC 1429 (Ch), [2017] 2 BCLC 592, [2018] Bus
LR 206, [2017] All ER (D) 94 (Jun) ........................................ 1.682, 2.182
Nortel Networks UK Ltd, Re [2017] EWHC 3299 (Ch), [2018] 1 BCLC 513,
[2018] All ER (D) 06 (Feb) .......................................................... 1.693
North Australian Territory Co, Re (1890) 45 ChD 87, 59 LJ Ch 654, 2 Meg 239, 38 WR
561, 63 LT 77, 6 TLR 348, CA ....................................................... 1.300
North Brazilian Sugar Factories Ltd, Re (1887) 37 ChD 83, 57 LJ Ch 110,
[1886–90] All ER Rep 686, 58 LT 4, 4 TLR 61, CA ............................... 1.207
North Eastern Insurance Co Ltd, Re (1915) 85 LJ Ch 751, [1916] HBR 154, 59 Sol Jo
510, 113 LT 989, 31 TLR 428 ....................................................... 1.194
North Point Global Ltd, Re Brittain (joint liquidators of Baltic House Developments Ltd)
v Chamberlain (supervisor of a voluntary arrangement relating to North Point
Global Ltd) [2020] EWHC 1648 (Ch), [2020] All ER (D) 06 (Jul) .. 1.59, 1.64, 2.827, 2.829
North West Holdings plc, Re [2000] BCC 731 ..................................... 1.177
North West Holdings plc, Re [2001] EWCA Civ 67, [2001] 1 BCLC 468, [2002] BCC
441, (2001) Times, 23 February, (2001) Independent, 9 February, 145 Sol Jo LB 53,
[2001] All ER (D) 184 (Jan), CSRC vol 24 iss 23/2 ............................. 1.177
Northbuild Constructions Pty Ltd v ACN 103 753 484 Pty Ltd [2008] QSC 182 ...... 1.160
Northsea Base Investment Ltd, Re [2015] EWHC 121 (Ch), [2015] 1 BCLC 539,
[2015] All ER (D) 202 (Jan) ......................................................... 6.5
Norwich and Peterborough Building Society v McGuinness [2011] EWCA Civ 1286,
[2012] 2 All ER (Comm) 265, [2012] 2 BCLC 233, (2011) Times, 21 December, [2012]
BPIR 145, [2011] All ER (D) 63 (Nov) .............................................. 1.382
Nottingham City Council v Pennant [2009] EWHC 2437 (Ch), [2009] RVR 348, [2010]
BPIR 430 ............................................................................. 1.386
Nottingham General Cemetery Co, Re [1955] Ch 683, [1955] 2 All ER 504, [1955] 3
WLR 61, 53 LGR 519, 119 JP 443, 99 Sol Jo 400 ................................ 1.235
Nowmost Co Ltd. Re, [1996] 2 BCLC 492 .......................................... 1.178
Nunn (bankruptcy: divorce: pension rights), Re [2004] 1 FLR 1123, [2004] Fam Law
324, sub nom Roberts v Nunn [2004] BPIR 623, [2004] All ER (D) 233 (Jan) ......... 1.396

O

OBG Ltd v Allan [2007] UKHL 21, [2008] 1 AC 1, [2007] 4 All ER 545, [2007] 2 WLR
920, [2008] 1 All ER (Comm) 1, [2008] 1 LRC 279, [2007] Bus LR 1600, [2007] IRLR
608, [2007] 19 EG 165 (CS), (2007) Times, 4 May, 151 Sol Jo LB 674, [2007] EMLR
325, [2007] BPIR 746, [2007] All ER (D) 44 (May), HL ......................... 1.78, 1.293
OGX Petróleo e Gás SA Nordic Trustee A.S.A. v Ogx Petroleo E Gas S.A. (Em
Recuperação Judicial) [2016] EWHC 25 (Ch), [2017] 2 All ER 217, [2017] 1 All ER
(Comm) 910, [2016] Bus LR 121, [2016] All ER (D) 62 (Jan) ......... 7.19, 7.28, 7.31, 7.33
OJSC ANK Yugraneft, Re, Millhouse Capital UK Ltd v Sibir Energy plc [2008] EWHC
2614 (Ch), [2009] 1 BCLC 298, [2010] BCC 475, [2009] Bus LR D33, [2008] All ER
(D) 311 (Oct) ........................................................................ 1.281
OJSC International Bank of Azerbaijan, Re [2017] EWHC 2075 (Ch) .................. 7.14
OJSC International Bank of Azerbaijan, Bakhshiyeva v Sberbank of Russia [2018] EWCA
Civ 2802, [2019] 2 All ER 713, [2019] 1 All ER (Comm) 597, [2019] 1 BCLC 1, [2019]
BPIR 269, [2018] All ER (D) 83 (Dec) ................................. 1.586, 7.1, 7.34
OMP Leisure Ltd, Re [2008] BCC 67 ............................................... 1.632
OPC Managed Rehab Ltd v Accident Compensation Corpn [2006] 1 NZLR 778,
NZCA ................................................................................ 1.175
Oakes v Simms [1996] Lexis Citation 3158, [1997] BPIR 499, CA ............. 1.490, 1.492
Oakland v Wellswood (Yorkshire) Ltd [2009] EWCA Civ 1094, [2010] IRLR 82, [2010]
ICR 902, [2010] BCC 263, [2009] All ER (D) 11 (Nov) ............................ 1.617
Oakley v Ultra Vehicle Design Ltd (in liq) [2005] EWHC 872 (Ch), [2006] BCC 57,
[2006] BPIR 115, [2005] All ER (D) 380 (May) .................................... 6.8
Oakley Smith v Greenberg [2002] EWCA Civ 1217, [2005] 2 BCLC 74, [2003] BPIR 709,
[2002] All ER (D) 36 (Aug) .............................................. 1.696, 1.697
Oakrock Ltd v Travelodge Hotels Ltd [2015] EWHC 30 (TCC), [2015] BPIR 360,
[2015] All ER (D) 119 (Jan) ......................................................... 1.64

Oakwell Collieries Co, Re [1879] WN 65 ........................................... 1.298
Oakwood Storage Services Ltd, Re [2003] EWHC 2807 (Ch), [2004] 2 BCLC 404,
  [2003] All ER (D) 117 (Nov) ..................................................... 2.814
Oasis Merchandising Services, Re [1995] 2 BCLC 493, [1995] BCC 911, (1995) Times,
  19 June; affd sub nom Re Oasis Merchandising Services, Ward v Aitkin [1998] Ch 170,
  [1997] 1 All ER 1009, [1997] 2 WLR 764, [1997] 1 BCLC 689, [1996] NLJR 1513,
  (1996) Times, 14 October ..................................... 1.271, 1.272, 1.303, 1.692
Oben v Blackman [2000] BPIR 302 ................................................ 2.820
Oceanic Life Ltd v Insurance and Retirement Services Pty Ltd (in liqation)
  (1993) 11 ACLC 1157 ............................................................ 1.183
O'Connor v Atlantis Fisheries Ltd 1998 SCLR 401, 1998 SLT (Sh Ct) 61, 1998 GWD
  8–359, Sh Ct ..................................................................... 1.176
Odessa Promotions Pty Ltd (in liqation)Re (1979) ACLC 49 ........................ 1.80
Officeserve Technologies Ltd (in compulsory liq) v Anthony-Mike [2017] EWHC 1920
  (Ch), 167 NLJ 7759, [2017] BPIR 1291, [2017] All ER (D) 37 (Aug) ............... 1.180
Officeserve Technologies Ltd (in Compulsory Liq) v Annabel's (Berkeley Square) Ltd
  [2018] EWHC 2168 (Ch), [2019] Ch 103, [2018] 3 WLR 1568, [2018] BPIR 1743,
  [2018] All ER (D) 96 (Aug) ...................................................... 1.180
Official Receiver v Baars [2009] BPIR 524 ....................................... 1.394
Official Receiver v Baker [2013] EWHC 4594 (Ch), [2014] BPIR 724 ................ 1.427
Official Receiver v Bathurst [2008] EWHC 1724 (Ch), [2008] BPIR 1548, [2008] All ER
  (D) 286 (May); affd [2008] EWHC 2572 (Ch), [2008] All ER (D) 18 (Jun) ........... 1.394
Official Receiver v Brown [2017] EWHC 2762 (Ch), [2018] BPIR 98, [2017] All ER (D)
  97 (Nov) ......................................................................... 1.430
Official Receiver v Cummings-John [2000] BPIR 320 ............................... 1.489
Official Receiver v Deuss [2020] EWHC 3441 (Ch), [2021] BPIR 466, [2020] All ER (D)
  95 (Dec) ......................................................................... 1.186
Official Receiver v Doganci [2007] BPIR 87 ...................................... 1.394
Official Receiver v Doshi [2001] 2 BCLC 235, [2001] Lexis Citation 1193, [2001] All ER
  (D) 09 (Mar) ..................................................................... 1.272
Official Receiver v Environment Agency. See Celtic Extraction Ltd (in liq), Re; Re
  Bluestone Chemicals Ltd (in liq)
Official Receiver v Going [2011] EWHC 786 (Ch), [2011] BPIR 1069 ................ 1.394
Official Receiver v Hollens [2007] EWHC 754 (Ch), [2007] 3 All ER 767, [2007] Bus LR
  1402, [2007] BPIR 830, [2007] All ER (D) 94 (Apr) .............................. 1.414
Official Receiver v Lloyd [2015] BPIR 374, CC ................................... 1.396
Official Receiver v McKay [2009] EWCA Civ 467, [2010] Ch 303, [2010] 2 WLR 891,
  [2009] BPIR 1061, [2009] All ER (D) 144 (Jun) .................................. 2.837
Official Receiver v May [2008] EWHC 1778 (Ch), [2008] BPIR 1562 ................ 1.394
Official Receiver v Meade-King (a firm) [2003] UKHL 49, [2004] 1 AC 158, [2003]
  4 All ER 18, [2003] 3 WLR 767, [2003] 2 BCLC 257, [2003] BCC 659, [2003] NLJR
  1346, (2003) Times, 7 August, 147 Sol Jo LB 936, [2004] BPIR 139, [2003] All ER (D)
  553 (Jul), HL .................................................................... 1.300
Official Receiver v Negus [2011] EWHC 3719 (Ch), [2012] 1 WLR 1598, (2012) Times,
  21 February, [2012] BPIR 382, [2012] All ER (D) 124 (Jan) ...................... 1.427
Official Receiver v Norriss [2015] EWHC 2697 (Ch), [2016] BPIR 188, [2015] All ER (D)
  69 (Nov) ................................................................... 1.300, 1.492
Official Receiver v Pyman [2007] EWHC 2002 (Ch), [2007] BPIR 1150, [2007] All ER
  (D) 25 (Mar) ..................................................................... 1.394
Official Receiver v Southey [2009] BPIR 89 ...................................... 1.394
Official Receiver v Wilson [2013] BPIR 907 ...................................... 1.427
Official Receiver for Northern Ireland v O'Brien [2012] NICh 12, [2012] BPIR 826
  ................................................................................. 1.455
Official Receiver for Northern Ireland v Rooney [2008] NICh 22, [2009] 2 FLR 1437,
  [2009] Fam Law 923, [2009] BPIR 536 .......................................... 1.455
Official Receiver For Northern Ireland v Stranaghan [2010] NICh 8, [2010] BPIR 928
  ................................................................................. 1.459
Oi Brasil Holdings, Re (4 December 2017, unreported) ............................. 7.3
Oldham v Kyrris, Royle v Oldham. See Kyrris v Oldham, Royle v Oldham
Olympia & York Canary Wharf Ltd, Re, American Express Europe Ltd v Adamson
  [1993] BCLC 453, [1993] BCC 154 ...................................... 1.353, 1.660
Olympic Airlines SA, Re [2015] UKSC 27, [2015] 3 All ER 694, [2015] 1 WLR 2399,
  [2015] 2 All ER (Comm) 393, [2015] 1 BCLC 589, 165 NLJ 7651, (2015) Times,
  14 May, [2016] BPIR 1532, [2015] All ER (D) 224 (Apr), SC ..................... 6.1, 6.4
Omar (a bankrupt), Re [2000] BCC 434, [1999] BPIR 1001, [1999] All ER (D) 560
  ................................................................................. 1.429

Omgate Ltd v Gordon [2001] Lexis Citation 1351, [2001] BPIR 909, [2001] All ER (D)
  83 (Apr) .................................................................................. 2.552
Omni Trustees Ltd, Re [2015] EWHC 2122 (Ch), [2015] All ER (D) 268 (Jul) ........ 1.300
Omokwe v HFC Bank Ltd [2007] BPIR 1157, HC ............................. 1.395, 2.527
One Blackfriars Ltd, Re (in liq) [2021] EWHC 684 (Ch), [2021] All ER (D) 110 (Mar)
  .................................................................................................. 1.692
115 Constitution Road Pty Ltd v Downey [2008] NSWSC 997 ...................... 2.316
One World Logistics Freight Ltd, Re [2018] EWHC 264 (Ch) (Alison Foster QC) ..... 1.630
Onslow, Re, ex p Kibble (1875) LR 10 Ch App 373, 44 LJ Bcy 63, 23 WR 433, 32 LT 138,
  CACh ........................................................................................ 1.178
Onward Building Society, Re [1891] 2 QB 463, 56 JP 260, 60 LJQB 752, 40 WR 26, 65
  LT 516, 7 TLR 601, [1891–4] All ER Rep Ext 1953, CA ...................... 1.142, 1.180
Opera Ltd, Re [1891] 3 Ch 260, 60 LJ Ch 839, 39 WR 705, 65 LT 371, 7 TLR 655,
  CA .......................................................................................... 1.77
Oracle (North West) Ltd v Pinnacle Services (UK) Ltd [2008] EWHC 1920 (Ch),
  [2009] BCC 159, [2008] All ER (D) 77 (Sep) ......................................... 1.630
Oraki, Re, Oraki v Dean & Dean (a firm taken over by the Law Society) [2017] EWHC 11
  (Ch), [2017] Bus LR 545, [2017] BPIR 750, [2017] All ER (D) 26 (Jan) .............. 1.502
Oraki v Bramston [2014] EWHC 2982 (Ch), [2014] BPIR 1374, [2014] All ER (D) 109
  (Sep) ........................................................................................ 1.414
Oraki v Bramston [2017] EWCA Civ 403, [2018] 3 WLR 569, 167 NLJ 7749, [2017]
  BPIR 1021, [2017] All ER (D) 174 (May) ....................... 1.410, 1.415, 1.416, 1.449
Oraki v Dean & Dean (a firm) [2012] EWHC 2885 (Ch), [2013] BPIR 88, [2012] All ER
  (D) 322 (Oct); affd [2013] EWCA Civ 1629, [2014] BPIR 266, [2013] All ER (D) 170
  (Dec) ........................................................................................ 1.395
Oraki v Hall (trustee in bankruptcy of Sheida Oraki) [2019] EWHC 1515 (Ch),
  [2019] All ER (D) 169 (Jul) ............................................................. 2.604
Ord v Upton (as trustee to the property of Ord) [2000] Ch 352, [2000] 1 All ER 193,
  [2000] 2 WLR 755, (2000) Times, 11 January, [2000] 01 LS Gaz R 22, [1999] NLJR
  1904, [1999] Lexis Citation 3683, 144 Sol Jo LB 35, [2000] BPIR 104, [1999] All ER
  (D) 1384 .................................................................................... 1.396
Orexim Trading Ltd v Mahavir Port and Terminal Private Ltd [2017] EWHC 2663
  (Comm), [2018] 2 All ER (Comm) 365, [2018] Bus LR 470, [2018] BPIR 124,
  [2017] All ER (D) 03 (Nov); affd on other grounds sub nom Orexim Trading Ltd v
  Mahavir Port And Terminal Private Ltd (formerly known as Fourcee Port and Terminal
  Private Ltd) [2018] EWCA Civ 1660, [2018] All ER (D) 101 (Jul) ................... 1.582
Oriental Bank Corpn, Re, ex p Guillemin (1884) 28 ChD 634, 54 LJ Ch 322, 52 LT 167,
  1 TLR 9 ..................................................................................... 1.279
Oriental Credit Ltd, Re [1988] Ch 204, [1988] 1 All ER 892, [1988] 2 WLR 172, 132 Sol
  Jo 127, [1988] 7 LS Gaz R 39 ........................................................... 1.300
Orleans Motor Co Ltd, Re [1911] 2 Ch 41, 80 LJ Ch 477, 18 Mans 287, 104 LT 627
  .................................................................................................. 1.309
Orrick, Herrington & Sutcliffe (Europe) LLP v Frohlich [2012] BPIR 169 ............ 1.382
Orton v Towcester Racecourse Company Ltd (in administration) [2018] EWHC 2902
  (Ch), 168 NLJ 7817, [2019] BPIR 411, [2018] All ER (D) 10 (Nov) .................. 1.646
Osborn v Cole [1999] BPIR 251 ............................................................ 1.414
Osmosis Group Ltd, Re [1999] 2 BCLC 329, [2000] BCC 428, [1999] Lexis Citation
  2738, [1999] All ER (D) 534 .............................................................. 1.685
O'Sullivan, Re [2001] BPIR 534 ................................................... 2.75, 2.119
Otg Ltd v Barke [2011] IRLR 272, [2011] ICR 781, [2011] All ER (D) 241 (Mar), sub
  nom Otg Ltd v Barke; Olds v Late Editions Ltd; Key2law (Surrey) Ltd v Antiquis;
  Secretary Of State For Business Innovations [2011] BCC 608, EAT; affd sub nom
  Key2Law (Surrey) LLP v De'Antiquis (Secretary of State for Business, Innovation and
  Skills intervening) [2011] EWCA Civ 1567, [2012] 2 BCLC 195, [2012] IRLR 212,
  [2012] ICR 881, [2012] BCC 375, [2011] All ER (D) 194 (Dec) ........ 1.617, 1.620, 1.628
Ouvaroff (a Bankrupt), Re [1997] BPIR 712 ............................................. 1.429
Ovenden Colbert Printers Ltd, Re [2013] EWCA Civ 1408, [2014] 1 BCLC 291, [2014]
  BPIR 285, [2013] All ER (D) 188 (Nov) ................................................ 1.302
Overend, Gurney & Co, Re, Grissell's Case (1866) LR 1 Ch App 528, 30 JP 548, 35 LJ Ch
  752, 12 Jur NS 718, 14 WR 1015, 14 LT 843, CACh ...................... 1.202, 2.852
Overnight Ltd, Re [2009] EWHC 601 (Ch), [2009] Bus LR 1141, [2010] BCC 787,
  (2009) Times, 2 April ....................................................................... 1.271
Overnight Ltd (in liq), Re [2010] EWHC 613 (Ch), [2010] 2 BCLC 186, [2010] BCC 796,
  [2011] Bus LR D30, [2010] All ER (D) 268 (May) ..................................... 1.271
Overseas Aviation Engineering (GB) Ltd, Re [1963] Ch 24, [1962] 3 All ER 12, [1962] 3
  WLR 594, CA ............................................................................... 1.181

Owen v Revenue and Customs Comrs [2007] EWHC 395 (Ch), [2008] BPIR 164, [2007] All ER (D) 266 (Jan) ......................................................... 2.530
Owners of Strata Plan 5290 v CGS & Co Pty Ltd [2011] NSWCA 168 .............. 1.743
Owo-Samson v Barclays Bank plc [2003] EWCA Civ 714, [2003] 28 LS Gaz R 30, (2003) Times, 27 May, 147 Sol Jo LB 658, [2003] BPIR 1373, [2003] All ER (D) 285 (May) ................................................................................ 1.395, 2.530

## P

PAG Asset Preservation Ltd, Re [2019] EWHC (Ch), [2020] BCC 167 ............... 1.177
PD Fuels Ltd, Re [1999] BCC 450 ................................................... 1.685
PFTZM Ltd, Re, Jourdain v Paul [1995] 2 BCLC 354, [1995] BCC 280 ....... 1.300, 1.326
PGH Investments Ltd PGH, Re [2021] EWHC 533 (Ch) ............................ 5.41
PJSC Bank Finance and Credit (in liquidation), Re [2021] EWHC 1100 (Ch), [2021] All ER (D) 35 (May) ...................................................... 7.14
PJSC VTB Bank v Laptev [2020] EWHC 321 (Ch), [2020] BPIR 624, [2020] All ER (D) 71 (Mar) ........................................................................ 1.382
PNC Telecom plc (in administration), Re [2003] EWHC 2220 (Ch), [2004] BPIR 314, [2003] All ER (D) 56 (Aug) .................................................... 1.300
PT Garuda Indonesia v Grellman (1992) 107 ALR 199 ........................... 1.398
Pacific and General Insurance Co Ltd v Hazell [1997] BCC 400, [1996] Lexis Citation 5062, [1997] LRLR 65 ........................................................... 1.188
Pacific Coast Fisheries Pty, Re (1980) 5 ACLR 354 .............................. 1.180
Pacific Communications Rentals Pty Ltd v Walker (1994) 12 ACSR 287, 12 ACLC 5 ...................................................................................... 1.178
Paget, Re, ex p Official Receiver [1927] 2 Ch 85, 96 LJ Ch 377, [1927] B & CR 118, [1927] All ER Rep 465, 71 Sol Jo 489, 137 LT 369, 43 TLR 455, CA ................ 1.404
Palmer Marine Surveys Ltd, Re [1986] 1 WLR 573, [1986] BCLC 106, 1 BCC 99, 557, 130 Sol Jo 372, [1986] LS Gaz R 1895 ..................................... 1.153, 1.168
Pan Ocean Co. Ltd, Re [2014] EWHC 2124 (Ch), [2014] Bus LR 1041, [2014] All ER (D) 03 (Jul) ................................................................ 7.33, 7.34, 7.36
Pannell v The Official Receiver [2008] EWHC 736 (Ch), [2008] BPIR 629 ............ 1.397
Pantmaenog Timber Co Ltd (in liq), Re [2003] UKHL 49, [2004] 1 AC 158, [2003] 4 All ER 18, [2003] 3 WLR 767, [2003] 2 BCLC 257, [2003] BCC 659, [2003] NLJR 1346, (2003) Times, 7 August, 147 Sol Jo LB 936, [2004] BPIR 139, [2003] All ER (D) 553 (Jul), HL ...................................................................... 1.300
Papanicola v Fagan [2008] EWHC 3348 (Ch), [2009] BPIR 320 ..................... 1.582
Papanicola (as trustee in bankruptcy for Mak) v Humphreys [2005] EWHC 335 (Ch), [2005] 2 All ER 418, (2005) Times, 28 April, [2006] BPIR 135, [2005] All ER (D) 220 (Mar) ........................................................................... 2.814
Paperback Collection and Recycling Ltd, Re Ratten v Natural Resource Body for Wales [2019] EWHC 2904 (Ch) ................................................... 1.164, 1.179
Paperback Collection and Recycling Ltd, Re (in liquidation) [2020] EWHC 1601 (Ch), [2021] 1 All ER (Comm) 1132, [2020] BPIR 1200, [2020] All ER (D) 142 (Jun) ...... 2.827, 2.829
Paragon Finance plc v Staunton, Paragon Finance plc v Nash [2001] EWCA Civ 1466, [2002] 2 All ER 248, [2002] 1 WLR 685, [2001] 2 All ER (Comm) 1025, [2002] 1 P & CR D22, [2002] 2 P & CR 279, [2001] 44 LS Gaz R 36, (2001) Times, 24 October, 145 Sol Jo LB 244, [2002] GCCR 3073, [2001] All ER (D) 202 (Oct) .................... 1.308
Paragon Offshore plc (in liq), Re [2020] EWHC 2740 (Ch), [2020] All ER (D) 102 (Oct) ........................................................................... 2.814
Paragon Offshore plc (in liq), Re [2020] EWHC 1925 (Ch), [2020] All ER (D) 114 (Jul) ...................................................................................... 1.715
Paramount Airways Ltd (in admin), Re [1993] Ch 223, [1992] 3 All ER 1, [1992] 3 WLR 690, [1992] BCLC 710, [1992] BCC 416, (1992) Times, 5 March, 136 Sol Jo LB 97 .................................................... 1.281, 1.302, 1.305, 1.582
Paramount Airways Ltd, Re, Bristol Airport plc v Powdrill. See Bristol Airport plc v Powdrill
Paramount Powders (UK) Ltd, Re [2019] EWCA Civ 1644; [2020] BCC 152 ......... 1.174
Park Air Services, Re, Christopher Moran Holdings Ltd v Bairstow [2000] 2 AC 172, [1999] 1 All ER 673, [1999] 1 BCLC 155, [1999] NLJR 195, [1999] BPIR 786, [1999] All ER (D) 106, sub nom Christopher Moran Holdings Ltd v Bairstow [1999] 2 WLR 396, [1999] 14 EG 149, [1999] EGCS 17, HL .............. 1.62, 1.235, 1.236, 1.322
Parkdawn Ltd, Re (15 June 1993, unreported) ..................................... 1.160
Parke v Daily News Ltd [1962] Ch 927, [1962] 2 All ER 929, [1962] 3 WLR 566, 106 Sol Jo 704 ................................................................. 1.244

Parker-Tweedale v Dunbar Bank plc (No 2) [1991] Ch 26, [1990] 2 All ER 588, [1990] 3
    WLR 780, 134 Sol Jo 1040, [1990] 29 LS Gaz R 33, (1990) Times, 23 February ....... 1.80
Parkins, Re [2014] Lexis Citation 47, [2014] BPIR 1054, [2014] All ER (D) 68 (Apr)
    ...................................................................................... 1.431
Parkinson Engineering Services plc (in liq) v Swan [2009] EWCA Civ 1366,
    [2010] 1 BCLC 163, [2010] Bus LR 857, (2010) Times, 13 January, [2010] BPIR 437,
    [2009] All ER (D) 232 (Dec) ......................................................... 1.415
Parkwell Investments Ltd, Re [2014] EWHC 3381 (Ch), [2015] Bus LR 40, 164 NLJ
    7634, [2015] BPIR 74, [2014] All ER (D) 214 (Oct) .................................. 1.188
Parmalat Capital Finance Ltd v Food Holdings Ltd (in liq) [2008] UKPC 23,
    [2009] 1 BCLC 274, [2008] BCC 371, [2008] BPIR 641, [2008] All ER (D) 124 (Apr),
    PC .......................................................................... 1.178, 1.407
Parmeko Holdings Ltd (in liq), Re (2013) 164 NLJ 7591, [2013] Lexis Citation 120,
    [2014] All ER (D) 39 (Jan) ........................................................... 1.671
Paramount Airways Ltd (No 3) re, Powdrill v Watson [1993] BCC 662  ............... 1.88
Partizan Ltd v OJ Kilkenny & Co Ltd [1998] 1 BCLC 157, [1998] BCC 912, [1997] Lexis
    Citation 4781 ....................................................................... 1.178
Parveen v Manchester City Council [2010] BPIR 152, CC  .......................... 1.395
Patley Wood Farm LLP v Brake [2016] EWHC 1688 (Ch), [2017] 1 WLR 343, [2017]
    BPIR 1357 ..................................................................... 1.617, 1.629
Paton, as liquidator of Ricky Martin (Racing) Ltd v Kelly Martin, Elizabeth Martin,
    Richard John Martin [2016] SC AIR 57 .............................................. 1.272
Paul Flatman Ltd (in Creditors' Voluntary Liq); Flatman v Wiles [2019] EWHC 3338
    (Ch), [2020] BPIR 522 ............................................................... 1.303
Paulin v Paulin [2009] EWCA Civ 221, [2009] 3 All ER 88n, [2010] 1 WLR 1057, [2009]
    2 FLR 354, [2009] 2 FCR 477, [2009] Fam Law 567, [2009] NLJR 475, [2009] BPIR
    572, [2009] All ER (D) 187 (Mar) .................................................... 1.395
Pavlou (a bankrupt), Re [1993] 3 All ER 955, [1993] 1 WLR 1046, [1993] 2 FLR 751,
    [1993] Fam Law 629, [1993] 11 LS Gaz R 43 ....................................... 1.455
Paycheck Services 3 Ltd, Re [2008] EWHC 2200 (Ch), [2008] STC 3142, [2008] 2 BCLC
    613, [2009] Bus LR 1, [2009] BCC 37, [2008] All ER (D) 319 (Jun), CSRC vol 32 iss
    7/1 .................................................................................. 1.270
Payne v Secretary of State for Work and Pensions [2011] UKSC 60, [2012] 2 AC 1, [2012]
    2 All ER 46, [2012] 2 WLR 1, [2012] PTSR 310, [2011] NLJR 31, (2011) Times,
    28 December, [2012] BPIR 224, [2011] All ER (D) 94 (Dec), SC  . 1.327, 1.334, 1.393, 1.396,
    1.515
Payroller Ltd (in liqation) v Little Panda Consultants Ltd [2018] EWHC 3161 (QB),
    [2019] BPIR 205, [2018] All ER (D) 97 (Nov) ...................................... 1.584
Peace (Joseph) & Co, Re [1873] WN 127  ......................................... 1.183
Peak Hotels and Resorts Ltd (in liq), Re, Candey Ltd v Crumpler (as joint liquidators of
    Peak Hotels and Resorts Ltd (in liq)) [2019] EWHC 282 (Ch), [2019] Bus LR 1901,
    [2019] All ER (D) 116 (Feb) ......................................................... 2.843
Peak Hotels and Resorts Ltd Crumpler (joint liquidators of Peak Hotels and Resorts Ltd)
    v Candey Ltd [2019] EWCA Civ 345, 169 NLJ 7833, [2019] BPIR 623, [2019] All ER
    (D) 48 (Mar) ......................................................................... 1.309
Pearl Maintenance Services Ltd, Re [1995] 1 BCLC 449, [1995] BCC 657  ............ 1.84
Pearson (in his capacity as additional liquidator of Herald Fund SPC (in official liq)) v
    Primeo Fund (in official liq) (Cayman Islands) [2020] UKPC 3, [2020] All ER (D) 128
    (Jan), PC ............................................................................ 2.852
Peck v Craighead [1995] 1 BCLC 337, sub nom Debtor, a (No 10 of 1992), Re, Peck v
    Craighead [1995] BCC 525, (1995) Times, 1 February .......................... 1.62, 1.65
Pen-y-Van Colliery Co, Re (1877) 6 ChD 477  ................................... 1.176
Pendigo Ltd, Re [1996] 2 BCLC 64, [1996] BCC 608  ............................. 1.178
Pennington, Re, ex p Pennington (1888) 5 Morr 268, 5 TLR 29, CA  ........... 1.300, 2.429
Pennington and Owen Ltd, Re [1925] Ch 825, 95 LJ Ch 93, [1926] B & CR 39,
    [1925] All ER Rep 354, 69 Sol Jo 759, 134 LT 66, 41 TLR 657, CA ................. 2.852
Penrose v Official Receiver [1996] 2 All ER 96, [1996] 1 BCLC 389, [1996] BCC 311,
    (1995) Times, 19 December, sub nom Penrose v Secretary of State for Trade and
    Industry [1996] 1 WLR 482 ...................................... 1.275, 2.1041
Pensions Regulator v Payae Ltd [2018] EWHC 36 (Ch), [2018] ICR D3, [2018] All ER
    (D) 118 (Jan) ....................................................................... 1.393
Peppard, Re [2009] BPIR 331 ............................................... 1.302, 1.459
Perak Pioneer Ltd v Petroliam Nasional Bhd [1986] AC 849, [1986] 3 WLR 105, 2 BCC
    99, 128, 130 Sol Jo 467, [1986] LS Gaz R 1719, PC .................................. 2.331
Performing Right Society Ltd v Rowland [1997] 3 All ER 336, [1998] BPIR 128,
    Halsburys Laws 1997 Abr para 2439 ................................................. 1.396

Permacell Finesse Ltd (in liq), Re [2007] EWHC 3233 (Ch), [2008] BCC 208 ......... 1.233
Permanent Trustee Co v Palmer (1929) 42 CLR 277 ................................. 1.135
Peruvian Railway Construction Co Ltd, Re [1915] 2 Ch 144, 59 Sol Jo 579, 31 TLR 464;
    affd [1915] 2 Ch 442, 85 LJ Ch 129, 60 Sol Jo 25, 113 LT 1176, 32 TLR 46,
    [1914–15] All ER Rep Ext 1397, CA ............................................... 2.852
Peskin v Anderson [2001] 1 BCLC 372, [2001] BCC 874, [2000] All ER (D) 2278 .... 1.415
Peter Herbert Fowlds (a bankrupt), Re Bucknall (as joint trustees in bankruptcy of Peter
    Herbert Fowlds) v Wilson [2020] EWHC 1200 (Ch), [2020] All ER (D) 153 (May) ... 1.459,
                                                                    1.303, 1.305, 1.584
Peter Jones (China) Ltd, Re Smith (joint administrators of Peter Jones (China) Ltd) v
    Registrar of Companies [2021] EWHC 215 (Ch), [2021] All ER (D) 48 (Feb) ......... 2.160
Peterkin v London Borough of Merton [2011] EWHC 376 (Ch), [2012] BPIR 388 ...... 1.64
Petersburgh & Viborg Gas Co, Re (1874) WN 1996 ................................. 1.174
Pettit v Bradford Bulls (Northern) Ltd (in administration) [2016] EWHC 3557 (Ch),
    [2017] 2 BCLC 519, [2016] Lexis Citation 1667, [2016] All ER (D) 191 (Nov) ....... 1.630,
                                                                    1.646, 1.696
Pettit (trustee in bankruptcy of Steven Anthony Thrussell) v Novakovic [2007] BCC 462,
    [2007] Lexis Citation 2, [2007] BPIR 1643, [2007] All ER (D) 310 (Jan) ....... 1.180, 1.398
Peveril Gold Mines Ltd, Re [1898] 1 Ch 122, 67 LJ Ch 77, 4 Mans 398, 46 WR 198, 42
    Sol Jo 96, 77 LT 505, 14 TLR 86, CA ............................................. 1.176
Pham Thai Duc v PTS Australian Distributor Pty Ltd [2005] NSWSC 98, NSW Sup Ct
    ...................................................................................... 1.174
Phillips v Brewin Dolphin Bell Lawrie Ltd [1999] 2 All ER 844, [1999] 1 WLR 2052,
    [1999] 1 BCLC 714, (1999) Times, 30 March, [1999] Lexis Citation 2368, [1999]
    BPIR 797, [1999] All ER (D) 279; affd sub nom Phillips v Brewin Dolphin Bell
    Lawrie Ltd [2001] UKHL 2, [2001] 1 All ER 673, [2001] 1 WLR 143, [2001] 1 BCLC
    145, [2001] BCC 864, [2001] 12 LS Gaz R 43, (2001) Times, 23 January, [2001] Lexis
    Citation 1136, 145 Sol Jo LB 23, [2001] BPIR 119, [2001] All ER (D) 84 (Jan), HL
    ........................................................... 1.302, 1.303, 1.305, 1.605
Phillips v McGregor-Paterson [2009] EWHC 2385 (Ch), [2010] 1 BCLC 72, [2010] BPIR
    239, [2009] All ER (D) 58 (Oct) ...................................... 1.180, 1.270, 2.820
Phillips (Joseph) Ltd, Re [1964] 1 All ER 441, [1964] 1 WLR 369, 108 Sol Jo 278 .... 2.354
Philpott (as joint liquidators of WGL Realisations 2010 Ltd) v Lycee Francais Charles de
    Gaulle School [2015] EWHC 1065 (Ch), [2016] 1 All ER (Comm) 1, [2015] BLR 495,
    [2016] BPIR 448, [2015] All ER (D) 175 (Apr)
Phoenix Oil and Transport Co Ltd, Re [1958] Ch 560, [1957] 3 All ER 218, [1957] 3
    WLR 633, 101 Sol Jo 779 ...................................................... 1.129, 1.201
Phoenix Oil and Transport Co Ltd (No 2), Re [1958] Ch 565, [1958] 1 All ER 158,
    [1958] 2 WLR 126, 102 Sol Jo 87 ................................................. 1.743
Picard v FIM Advisers LLP [2010] EWHC 1299 (Ch), [2011] 1 BCLC 129, [2010] NLJR
    1077, [2010] All ER (D) 216 (Jul) .................................................. 7.34
Picard v Primeo Fund (16 April 2014, unreported) Cayman Court of Appeal .......... 7.36
Piccadilly Property Management Ltd, Re [1999] 2 BCLC 145, [2000] BCC 44, [1999]
    BPIR 260, [1998] All ER (D) 619 ........................... 1.178, 2.328, 2.330, 2.814
Pick v Chief Land Registrar [2011] EWHC 206 (Ch), [2012] Ch 564, [2012] 3 WLR 3,
    [2012] 3 EGLR 17, [2012] 39 Estates Gazette 125, [2011] BPIR 1090 ................ 1.417
Pick v Sumpter [2010] EWHC 685 (Ch), [2010] BPIR 638, [2010] All ER (D) 103 (Jun)
    ...................................................................................... 1.455
Pickard (Joint Trustees in Bankruptcy of Constable) v Constable [2017] EWHC 2475
    (Ch), [2018] BPIR 140, [2017] All ER (D) 99 (Oct) .................................. 1.455
Pierson (Brian D) (Contractors) Ltd, Re [2001] 1 BCLC 275, [1999] BCC 26, [1998]
    Lexis Citation 3707, [1999] BPIR 18, CSRC vol 25 iss 1/1 ............. 1.270, 1.272, 1.303
Pike (a bankrupt) v Cork Gully [1997] BPIR 723 ................................... 1.423
Pillar Denton Ltd v Jervis. See Jervis v Pillar Denton Ltd (Game Station)
Pillar Securitisation SARL v Spicer. See Kaupthing Capital Partners II Master LP Inc, Re
Pilmer v HIH Casualty Insurance Ltd (2004) 90 SASR 465 .......................... 1.180
Pinecord Ltd (in liqation), Re [1995] 2 BCLC 57, [1995] BCC 483 ................... 2.404
Pinstripe Farming Co Ltd, Re [1996] 2 BCLC 295 ..................... 1.160, 1.168, 1.188
Pitt v Mond [2001] BPIR 624 ...................................................... 1.60
Pittortou (a bankrupt), Re, ex p Trustee of the Property of the Bankrupt v Bankrupt
    [1985] 1 All ER 285, [1985] 1 WLR 58, 129 Sol Jo 47, [1985] LS Gaz R 680 ......... 1.455
Plant v Plant [1998] 1 BCLC 38, [1998] BPIR 243 ............................. 1.65, 1.364
Platts v Western Trust & Savings Ltd [1993] 22 LS Gaz R 38, (1993) Times, 7 April,
    [1993] Lexis Citation 3929, [1996] BPIR 339, CA ................................. 2.530
Pleatfine Ltd, Re [1983] BCLC 102, 1 BCC 98, 942 ................................ 1.178

Plummer v IRC [1988] 1 All ER 97, [1988] 1 WLR 292, [1987] STC 698, 60 TC 452, 132
  Sol Jo 54, [1987] LS Gaz R 3415, (1987) Times, 24 October ........................ 1.380
Plummer, Re [2004] BPIR 767, HC .......................................... 1.65, 1.360
Polly Peck International plc, Re, ex p Joint Administrators [1994] BCC 15 ............ 1.299
Polly Peck International plc (in admin), Re [1996] 2 All ER 433, [1996] 1 BCLC 428
  ................................................................................ 1.220
Polly Peck International plc v Nadir [1992] BCLC 746 ............................. 1.399
Polymer Vision R & D Ltd v Van Dooren [2011] EWHC 2951 (Comm), [2011] 47 LS Gaz
  R 21, [2011] All ER (D) 170 (Nov) ..................................................... 6.8
Poole Firebrick and Blue Clay Co, Re (1873) 17 Eq 268, 43 LJ Ch 447, 22 WR 247
  ................................................................................ 1.164
Popely v Popely [2004] EWCA Civ 463, [2004] 19 LS Gaz R 29, (2004) Times, 14 May,
  148 Sol Jo LB 569, [2004] BPIR 778, [2004] All ER (D) 346 (Apr) ................... 1.178
Popham v Information Governance Holdings Ltd [2013] EWHC 2611 (Ch),
  [2013] All ER (D) 262 (Oct) .................................................. 1.628, 1.630
Port v Auger [1994] 3 All ER 200, [1994] 1 WLR 862, (1993) Times, 16 December
  ................................................................... 1.67, 1.414, 2.48
Portbase Clothing Ltd, Re [1993] Ch 388, [1993] 3 All ER 829, [1993] 3 WLR 14,
  [1993] BCLC 796, [1993] BCC 96, 12 LDAB 332, [1992] Lexis Citation 2968 .. 1.84, 1.159
Portedge Ltd, Re [1997] BCC 23 ............................................... 2.338
Portman Building Society v Gallwey [1955] 1 All ER 227, [1955] 1 WLR 96, 99 Sol Jo
  95 ...................................................................... 1.74, 1.75
Portsmouth Borough (Kingston Fratton and Southsea) Tramways, Re [1892] Ch 362
  ................................................................................ 1.176
Portsmouth City Football Club Ltd (in liq), Re [2012] EWHC 3088 (Ch), [2013] 1 All ER
  975; affd [2013] EWCA Civ 916, [2014] 1 All ER 12, [2014] 1 BCLC 1, [2013] Bus LR
  1152, [2013] 6 Costs LO 934, [2013] All ER (D) 284 (Jul) .................... 2.183, 1.429
Post Office v Norwich Union Fire Insurance Society Ltd [1967] 2 QB 363, [1967] 1 All ER
  577, [1967] 2 WLR 709, [1967] 1 Lloyd's Rep 216, 111 Sol Jo 71 .................... 1.399
Pott v Clegg (1847) 16 LJ Ex 210, 11 Jur 289, 16 M & W 321, 153 ER 1212, 8 LTOS
  493, ExCh ................................................................... 2.852
Potters Oil Ltd (No 2), Re [1986] 1 All ER 890, [1986] BCLC 98, 1 BCC 99, 593, 130 Sol
  Jo 166, sub nom Re Potters Oils Ltd [1986] 1 WLR 201 ............................. 1.80
Powdrill v Watson [1994] 2 All ER 513, [1994] 2 BCLC 118, [1994] IRLR 295, [1994]
  ICR 395, [1994] BCC 172, [1994] 15 LS Gaz R 35, (1994) Times, 1 March, 138 Sol Jo
  LB 76; varied sub nom Powdrill v Watson [1995] 2 AC 394, (1995) Times, 23 March,
  sub nom Powdrill v Watson [1995] 2 All ER 65, [1995] 2 WLR 312, [1995] 1 BCLC
  386, [1995] IRLR 269, [1995] ICR 1100, [1995] BCC 319, [1995] 17 LS Gaz R 47,
  [1995] NLJR 449, HL ................................................. 1.81, 1.88, 1.716
Power v Brown [2009] EWHC 9 (Ch), [2009] BPIR 340, [2009] All ER (D) 77 (Jan)
  ................................................................................ 1.180
Power v Sharp Investments Ltd. See Shoe Lace Ltd, Re
Practice Direction (Companies Court: Contributory's Petition) [1990] 1 WLR 490
Practice Direction: Insolvency Proceedings [2012] BPIR 409 ................... 1.489, 1.503
Practice Direction: Insolvency Proceedings (July 2020) [2020] BPIR 1211 ..... 1.169, 1.174,
  1.175, 1.176, 1.178, 1.180, 1.187, 1.281–1.284, 1.386, 1.398, 1.489, 1.503, 2.48, 2.316, 2.319,
      2.321, 2.323, 2.527, 2.530, 2.540, 2.550, 2.553, 2.812, 2.813, 2.814, 2.990, 2.997, 5.1
Practice Direction (Insolvency) relating to the Corporate Insolvency and Governance Act
  2020 [2020] BPIR 1207 . 1.174, 1.175, 1.281, 1.282, 1.283, 1.284, 1.617, 2.319, 2.323, 5.1,
                                                                                        5.41
Practice Note [2020] BCC 211 ......................................... 1.617, 1.646, 2.59
Premier Motor Auctions Leeds Ltd (In liqation), Re [2015] EWHC 3568 (Ch),
  [2015] All ER (D) 126 (Dec) .................................................. 2.312, 2.442
Premier Permanent Building Society, Re (1890) 16 VLR 643 ......................... 1.743
Prest v Prest [2012] EWCA Civ 1395, [2013] 2 AC 415, [2013] 1 All ER 795, [2013] 2
  WLR 557, [2013] 2 FLR 576, [2012] 3 FCR 588, (2013) Times, 02 January, [2013]
  2 Costs LO 249, [2012] All ER (D) 293 (Oct); revsd sub nom Prest v Petrodel
  Resources Ltd [2013] UKSC 34, [2013] 2 AC 415, [2013] 4 All ER 673, [2013] 3 WLR
  1, [2014] 1 BCLC 30, [2013] 2 FLR 732, [2013] 3 FCR 210, [2013] Fam Law 953,
  [2013] NLJR 27, (2013) Times, 24 July, 157 Sol Jo (no 24) 37, [2013] All ER (D) 90
  (Jun), SC ...................................................................... 6.64
Preston & Duckworth Ltd, Re [2006] BCC 133, HC ............................... 1.701
Price v Davis [2014] EWCA Civ 26, [2014] 1 WLR 2129, [2015] Fam Law 252, [2014]
  BPIR 494, [2014] All ER (D) 244 (Jan) ............. 1.61, 1.64, 1.65, 1.362, 2.907, 2.909
Priestman (Alfred) & Co (1929) Ltd, Re [1936] 2 All ER 1340, 80 Sol Jo 720 ........ 1.164
Priory Garage (Walthamstow) Ltd, Re [2001] BPIR 144 ............... 1.302, 1.303, 1.459

Pritchard, Re, Pritchard v Deacon [1963] Ch 502, [1963] 1 All ER 873, [1963] 2 WLR 685, 107 Sol Jo 154, CA ..................................................................... 1.178
Pritchard (a Bankrupt), Re, Williams v Pritchard [2007] BPIR 1385 .................. 1.396
Pro Image Productions (Vic) Pty Ltd v Catalyst Television Productions Pty Ltd (1988) 6 ACLC 888 .................................................................................. 1.175
Procureur-General Bij Het Hof Van Beroep Te Antwerpen v Zaza Retail BV: C-112/10 (2011) C-112/10, ECLI:EU:C:2011:743, [2011] ECR I-11525, [2012] BPIR 438, EUCJ ................................................................................................ 6.5
Produce Marketing Consortium Ltd, Re [1989] 3 All ER 1, [1989] 1 WLR 745, [1989] BCLC 513, 5 BCC 569, 133 Sol Jo 945 ...................................... 1.272
Produce Marketing Consortium Ltd, (No 2), Re [1989] BCLC 520, 5 BCC 569, 11 LDAB 373, (1989) Times, 7 April ............................................................... 1.272
Professional Computer Group Ltd, Re [2008] EWHC 1541 (Ch), [2009] 1 BCLC 88, [2009] BCC 323, [2008] All ER (D) 62 (Jul) ......................................... 2.136
Promontoria (Chestnut) Ltd v Craig [2017] EWHC 2405 (Ch) ............... 1.660, 2.167
Promontoria (Chestnut) Ltd v Bell [2019] EWHC 1581 (Ch), 169 NLJ 7847, [2019] BPIR 1241 ........................................................................... 1.516, 2.530
Property Professionals Ltd, Re [2013] EWHC 1903 (Ch), [2014] 1 BCLC 466, [2013] All ER (D) 110 (Jul) ............................................................ 1.693, 1.700
Prosser v Castle Sanderson Solicitors (a firm) [2002] EWCA Civ 1140, [2002] Lloyd's Rep PN 584, [2003] BCC 440, [2002] BPIR 1163, [2002] All ER (D) 507 (Jul) ............. 1.60
Prudential Assurance Co Ltd v PRG Powerhouse Ltd [2007] EWHC 1002 (Ch), [2008] 1 BCLC 289, [2007] Bus LR 1771, [2007] BCC 500, [2007] 3 EGLR 131, [2007] 19 EG 164 (CS), [2007] BPIR 839, [2007] All ER (D) 21 (May) .......... 1.59, 1.65
Public Joint Stock Co Aeroflot Russian Airlines v Berezovsky (16 December 2015, unreported) ..................................................................................... 1.399
Pudsey Steel Services ltd, Re [2015] BPIR 1459 ...................................... 1.671
Pui-Kwan v Kam-Ho [2015] EWHC 621 (Ch), [2015] 2 All ER (Comm) 1139, [2015] 1 BCLC 518, [2016] Bus LR 101, [2015] All ER (D) 133 (Mar) .............. 1.639
Purewal v Countrywide Residential Lettings Ltd [2015] EWCA Civ 1122, [2016] 4 WLR 31, [2016] 1 P & CR 196, [2016] HLR 41, [2016] EGLR 11, [2016] BPIR 177, [2015] All ER (D) 60 (Nov) ....................................................................... 1.417
Purpoint Ltd, Re [1991] BCLC 491, [1991] BCC 121 ........................ 1.270, 1.272

**Q**

Quartz Hill Consolidated Gold Mining Co v Eyre (1883) 11 QBD 674, 52 LJQB 488, 31 WR 668, 49 LT 249, [1881–5] All ER Rep Ext 1474, CA ............................ 1.178
Queensland Mercantile Agency Co Ltd, Re (1888) 58 LT 878, 4 TLR 387 ............ 1.183
Queensland Mining Corpn Ltd v Butmall Pty Ltd, in the matter of Butmall Pty Ltd (in liq) [2016] FCA 16 ..................................................................................... 1.160
Queensland Stations Re Pty Ltd (in liqation) (1991) 9 ACLC 1341 .................. 1.160
Qureshi (in her capacity as liquidator of Edgware Constitutional Club Ltd) v Association of Conservative Clubs Ltd [2019] EWHC 1165 (Ch), [2019] All ER (D) 68 (May) .... 1.159

**R**

R (on the application of Monarch Airlines Ltd (in admin) v Airport Coordination Ltd [2017] EWCA Civ 1892, [2017] All ER (D) 179 (Nov) .............................. 1.628
R v Austen (1985) 7 Cr App Rep (S) 214, 1 BCC 99, 528, [1985] LS Gaz R 2499, CA .................................................................................................. 1.276
R v Barnet Justices, ex p Phillippou [1997] BPIR 134 ...................... 1.353, 2.829
R (on the application of Steele) v Birmingham City Council [2005] EWCA Civ 1824, [2007] 1 All ER 73, [2006] 1 WLR 2380, [2006] ICR 869, [2006] RVR 120, (2006) Times, 26 April, [2006] BPIR 856, [2005] All ER (D) 243 (Dec) ........ 1.176, 1.460, 1.515
R v Bolus (1870) 11 Cox CC 610, 23 LT 339 ........................................... 1.481
R v Brady [2004] EWCA Crim 1763, [2004] 3 All ER 520, [2004] 1 WLR 3240, [2005] 1 Cr App Rep 78, [2005] BCC 357, [2004] 29 LS Gaz R 29, (2004) Times, 9 July, 148 Sol Jo LB 1149, [2004] BPIR 962, [2004] All ER (D) 234 (Jun) .................... 1.277, 1.299
R v Campbell (1984) 80 Cr App Rep 47, CA ............................................. 1.276
R v Carass [2001] EWCA Crim 2845, [2002] 1 WLR 1714, [2002] 2 Cr App Rep 77, (2002) Times, January 21, 146 Sol Jo LB 28, [2002] BPIR 821, [2001] All ER (D) 300 (Dec), CSRC vol 25 iss 21/3 ...................................................................... 1.480
R v Chelmsford Justices ex p Lloyd (5 December 2000, unreported) .................. 1.275
R v Cole [1998] 2 BCLC 234, [1997] 1 Cr App Rep (S) 228, [1997] 28 LS Gaz R 25, (1997) Times, 16 July, 141 Sol Jo LB 160, sub nom R v Cole [1998] BCC 87, CA ..... 1.275

R v Daniel [2002] EWCA Crim 959, [2003] 1 Cr App Rep 99, (2002) Times, 8 April, 146 Sol Jo LB 93, [2002] BPIR 1193, [2002] All ER (D) 354 (Mar) .............. 1.480, 1.482

R v Dawson (29 June 2001, unreported) ............................................. 1.66

R v Derby Magistrates' Court, ex p B [1996] AC 487, [1995] 4 All ER 526, [1995] 3 WLR 681, [1996] 1 Cr App Rep 385, [1996] 1 FLR 513, [1996] Fam Law 210, 159 JP 785, [1996] Crim LR 190, [1995] NLJR 1575, (1995) Times, 25 October, 139 Sol Jo LB 219, HL ............................................................................ 1.429

R v Dickson (1991) 94 Cr App Rep 7, [1991] Crim LR 854, [1991] BCC 719, [1991] Lexis Citation 3539 ...................................................... 1.183

R v Doring [2002] EWCA Crim 1695, [2003] 1 Cr App Rep 143, [2002] Crim LR 817, [2002] BCC 838, [2002] 33 LS Gaz R 21, (2002) Times, 27 June, 146 Sol Jo LB 184, [2002] BPIR 1204, [2002] All ER (D) 182 (Jun), CSRC vol 26 iss 7/3 ................ 1.275

R v Duke of Leinster [1924] 1 KB 311, 17 Cr App Rep 176, 87 JP 191, 93 LJKB 144, 27 Cox CC 574, [1924] B & CR 78, [1923] All ER Rep 187, 68 Sol Jo 211, 130 LT 318, 40 TLR 33, NICrCA ................................................................ 1.488

R v Edwards (Jeremy Nicholas) [2010] EWCA Crim 1682 .......................... 1.481

R v Enver (20 January 2000, unreported) .................................... 1.264, 1.275

R v Faryab [2000] Crim LR 180, [1999] Lexis Citation 3464, [1999] BPIR 569 ....... 1.300

R v French [2000] 2 BCLC 438, [2000] BCC 617, (1999) Times, 5 October, [1999] Lexis Citation 4024, [2000] BPIR 1129, [1999] All ER (D) 936, CSRC vol 24 iss 15/2 ..... 1.265, 1.275

R v Grantham [1984] QB 675, [1984] 3 All ER 166, [1984] 2 WLR 815, [1984] BCLC 270, 79 Cr App Rep 86, [1984] Crim LR 492, 10 LDAB 473, 128 Sol Jo 331, [1984] LS Gaz R 1437 ...................................................... 1.271

R v Hilsdon [2021] EWCA Crim 52 .............................................. 1.478

R v Hussain [2013] EWCA Crim 2243, [2014] 2 Cr App Rep (S) 114 .......... 1.484, 1.485

R v Johnstone [2003] UKHL 28, [2003] 3 All ER 884, [2003] 1 WLR 1736, [2003] 2 Cr App Rep 493, [2003] FSR 748, 167 JP 281, [2004] Crim LR 244, [2003] IP & T 901, [2003] 26 LS Gaz R 36, (2003) Times, 29 May, 147 Sol Jo LB 625, [2003] All ER (D) 323 (May), HL ................................................................ 1.262

R v Kansal (No 2) [2001] UKHL 62, [2002] 2 AC 69, [2002] 1 All ER 257, [2001] 3 WLR 1562, [2002] 4 LRC 245, [2002] 1 Cr App Rep 478, [2002] 03 LS Gaz R 25, (2001) Times, 4 December, 145 Sol Jo LB 275, [2002] BPIR 370, [2001] All ER (D) 418 (Nov), HL ........................................................................ 1.478

R v Kearns [2002] EWCA Crim 748, [2002] 1 WLR 2815, [2003] 1 Cr App Rep 111, (2002) Times, 4 April, 146 Sol Jo LB 101, [2002] BPIR 1213, [2002] All ER (D) 363 (Mar) .................................................................. 1.403, 1.482

R v Kelly, A-G's Reference (No 53 of 1998) [2000] QB 198, [1999] 2 All ER 13, [1999] 2 WLR 1100, [1999] 2 Cr App Rep 36, [1999] 2 Cr App Rep (S) 176, [1999] Crim LR 240, (1998) Times, 29 December, [1998] Lexis Citation 2908, [1998] All ER (D) 734 ...................................................................... 1.455

R v Kemp [1988] QB 645, [1988] 2 WLR 975, [1988] BCLC 217, 87 Cr App Rep 95, 152 JP 461, [1988] Crim LR 376, 4 BCC 203, 132 Sol Jo 461, [1988] 10 LS Gaz R 44, (1988) Times, 9 February .................................................. 1.271

R v McCredie [2000] 2 BCLC 438, [2000] BCC 617, (1999) Times, 5 October, [1999] Lexis Citation 4024, [2000] BPIR 1129, [1999] All ER (D) 936, CSRC vol 24 iss 15/2 ................................................................ 1.265, 1.275

R v Mohammed Ramzan [1998] 2 Cr App R 328 ................................ 1.488

R v Mungroo [1997] 25 LS Gaz R 33, (1997) Times, 3 July, [1997] Lexis Citation 1216, 141 Sol Jo LB 129, [1998] BPIR 784 ........................................ 1.485

R (on the application of Howard) v Official Receiver [2013] EWHC 1839 (Admin), [2014] QB 930, [2014] 2 WLR 1518, [2013] NLJR 20, [2014] BPIR 204, [2013] All ER (D) 73 (Jul) ........................................................................ 1.339

R (on the application of Singh) v Revenue and Customs Comrs [2010] UKUT 174 (TCC), [2010] STC 2020, [2010] BPIR 933, [2010] All ER (D) 39 (Jun) ...................... 1.396

R (on the application of Griffin) v Richmond Magistrates' Court [2008] EWHC 84 (Admin), [2008] 3 All ER 274, [2008] 1 WLR 1525, [2008] 1 BCLC 681, [2008] Bus LR 1014, [2008] 1 Cr App Rep 453, [2008] BCC 575, (2008) Times, 31 March, [2008] BPIR 468, [2008] All ER (D) 181 (Jan), DC ......................... 1.263, 1.265, 1.275

R v Salter [1968] 2 QB 793, [1968] 2 All ER 951, [1968] 3 WLR 39, 52 Cr App Rep 549, 112 Sol Jo 480 ................................................................ 1.482

R v Scott [1998] BPIR 471 .................................................. 1.488

R (on the application of Balding) v Secretary of State for Work and Pensions [2007] EWCA Civ 1327, [2008] 3 All ER 217, [2008] 1 WLR 564, [2007] BPIR 1669, [2007] All ER (D) 200 (Dec) ................................................ 1.393, 1.515

R v Soneji [2005] UKHL 49, [2006] 1 AC 340, [2005] 4 All ER 321, [2005] 3 WLR 303, [2006] 2 Cr App Rep 298, [2006] 1 Cr App Rep (S) 430, [2006] Crim LR 167, [2005] 31 LS Gaz R 26, [2005] NLJR 1315, (2005) Times, 22 July, [2005] All ER (D) 294 (Jul), HL .................................................................... 1.646, 2.820

R (on the application of Prudential plc) v Special Comr of Income Tax [2013] UKSC 1, [2013] 2 AC 185, [2013] 2 All ER 247, [2013] 2 WLR 325, [2013] STC 376, [2013] 4 LRC 546, [2013] 1 FCR 545, [2013] NLJR 109, (2013) Times, 05 February, [2013] 2 Costs LR 275, [2013] All ER (D) 146 (Jan), CSRC vol 36 iss 25/1, SC .............. 1.429

R v Taylor [2011] EWCA Crim 728, [2011] 1 WLR 1809, [2011] Bus LR 1011, [2011] 2 Cr App Rep 47, [2011] Crim LR 798, [2012] BCC 663, (2011) Times, 24 June, [2011] All ER (D) 283 (Mar) ........................................................ 1.483

R (on the application of Eliades) v The Institute of Chartered Accountants of England and Wales [2000] Lexis Citation 3489, [2001] BPIR 363, [2000] All ER (D) 2059 ......... 1.531

R v Theivendran (Sundranpillai) (1992) 13 Cr App R(S) 601 ......................... 1.478

R v S [2019] EWCA Crim 1728, [2020] 1 WLR 109, [2020] 1 Cr App R 13, [2020] BPIR 278 ..................................................................................... 1.418

R v Weintroub [2011] EWCA Crim 2167, [2011] All ER (D) 126 (Jul) ......... 1.275, 1.276

R & R Consultants Pty Ltd v Comr of Taxation [2006] NSWSC 1152, (2006) 204 FLR 149, NSW S Ct ......................................................................... 1.175

RA Noble & Sons Ltd, re [1997] BCC 294 ............................................ 1.174

RA Price Securities Ltd v Henderson [1989] 2 NZLR 257, NZCA ...................... 1.81

RA Securities Ltd v Mercantile Credit Co Ltd [1995] 3 All ER 581, [1994] 2 BCLC 721, [1994] BCC 598, [1994] NPC 76, [1994] 2 EGLR 70, [1994] 44 EG 242 .............. 1.64

RBG Resources Ltd, Re, Shierson v Rastogi [2002] EWCA Civ 1624, [2003] 1 WLR 586, [2002] BCC 1005, [2003] 02 LS Gaz R 31, (2002) Times, 20 November, [2003] BPIR 148, [2002] All ER (D) 124 (Nov), CSRC vol 27 iss 3/2 .............................. 1.300

RC Brewery Ltd v Revenue and Customs Comrs [2013] EWHC 1184 (Ch), [2013] NLJR 21, [2013] All ER (D) 130 (May) ...................................................... 1.180

RH Trevan Pty Ltd, Re [2013] NSWSC 1445 ......................................... 1.206

RJH Stanhope Ltd Poxon, Re (as joint liquidators of RJH Stanhope Ltd) v Harriss [2020] EWHC 2808 (Ch), [2020] All ER (D) 25 (Nov) ...................................... 2.834

RWH Enterprises Ltd v Portedge Ltd [1998] BCC 556, [1996] Lexis Citation 5464, CA
.............................................................................................. 2.338

Radford and Bright Ltd, Re [1901] 1 Ch 272, 70 LJ Ch 78, 9 Mans 98, 49 WR 270, 17 TLR 81 .............................................................................. 1.194, 2.940

Rae, Re [1995] BCC 102, (1994) Times, 27 October, [1994] Lexis Citation 4303 ..... 1.235, 1.396, 1.605

Rafidain Bank, Re [1992] BCLC 301, [1992] BCC 376, (1991) Times, 22 July ........ 1.180

Railtrack plc (in railway admin), Re, Winsor v Bloom [2002] EWHC 1027 (Ch), [2002] 3 All ER 140, [2002] 2 BCLC 308, [2002] All ER (D) 316 (May); revsd [2002] EWCA Civ 955, [2002] 4 All ER 435, [2002] 1 WLR 3002, [2002] 2 BCLC 755, (2002) Times, 15 July, [2003] BPIR 507, [2002] All ER (D) 152 (Jul) ....................... 1.353, 1.660

Railway Finance Co Ltd, Re (1866) 14 WR 956 ....................................... 1.175

Raithatha (as Trustee in Bankruptcy of Michael Roy Williamson) v Williamson [2012] EWHC 909 (Ch), [2012] 3 All ER 1028, [2012] 1 WLR 3559, [2012] NLJR 543, (2012) Times, 17 July, [2012] BPIR 621, [2012] All ER (D) 57 (Apr) ................. 1.427

Raja v Rubin [2000] Ch 274, [1999] 3 All ER 73, [1999] 3 WLR 606, [1999] 1 BCLC 621, [1999] BCC 579, (1999) Times, 14 April, [1999] Lexis Citation 2288, [1999] BPIR 575, [1999] All ER (D) 299 .................................................. 1.60

Rajapakse (note), Re [2007] BPIR 99 ................................................. 7.28

Ralls Builders Ltd (in liqation), Re, Grant (Joint Liquidators of Ralls Builders Ltd) v Ralls [2016] EWHC 243 (Ch), [2016] Bus LR 555, [2016] All ER (D) 142 (Feb) ........... 1.272

Ram v Ram [2004] EWCA Civ 1452, [2005] 2 BCLC 476, [2005] 2 FLR 63, [2004] 3 FCR 425, [2005] Fam Law 274, 148 Sol Jo LB 1317, [2005] BPIR 616, [2004] All ER (D) 89 (Nov) .............................................................................. 2.829

Rambaldi (Trustee) v Comr of Taxation [2017] FCAFC 217 ........................... 1.303

Ramora UK Ltd, Re [2011] EWHC 3959 (Ch), [2012] BCC 672 ...................... 1.641

Ramsay Health Care Australia Pty Ltd v Compton [2017] HCA 28, [2017] BPIR 1638, AusHC ................................................................................. 1.178

Randall (Derek) Enterprises Ltd (in liqation) v Randall [1991] BCLC 379, [1990] BCC 749, (1990) Times, 28 August, CA ................................................... 1.270

Randhawa v Official Receiver [2006] EWHC 2946 (Ch), [2007] 1 All ER 755, [2007] 1 WLR 1700, [2006] BPIR 1435, [2006] All ER (D) 02 (Jul) ........................... 1.394

Randhawa v Turpin [2015] EWHC 517 (Ch), [2016] 1 BCLC 708, [2015] All ER (D) 27 (Mar) ...................................................................... 1.618, 1.620, 2.1008

Randhawa v Turpin (as former Joint Administrators of BW Estates Ltd). See Gursharan
    Randhawa v Andrew Turpin
Rankin v Dissington Lending Company Ltd [2021] EWHC 172 (Ch) .......... 1.503, 2.529
Rastelli Davide e C Snc v Hidoux (in his capacity as liquidator appointed by the court for
    the company Médiasucre International): C-191/10 (2011) C-191/10,
    ECLI:EU:C:2011:838, [2012] All ER (EC) 239, [2013] 1 BCLC 329, EUCJ ........... 6.64
Ratford v Northavon District Council [1987] QB 357, [1986] 3 All ER 193, [1986] 3
    WLR 770, [1986] BCLC 397, 85 LGR 443, [1986] RA 137, 150 JP 605, 2 BCC 99,
    242, 130 Sol Jo 786 ................................................................ 1.88
Rathbone (Arthur) Kitchens Ltd, Re [1997] 2 BCLC 280, [1998] BCC 450, [1998] BPIR
    1 .................................................................. 1.67, 1.168, 1.368
Ravichandran, Re [2004] BPIR 814, Hc ........................................... 1.354
Rayatt, Re [1998] 2 FLR 264, [1998] Fam Law 458, (1998) Times, 4 May, [1998] Lexis
    Citation 2708, [1998] BPIR 495 .................................................. 1.427
Razzaq v Pala [1997] 1 WLR 1336, [1998] BCC 66, [1997] 24 LS Gaz R 32, [1997] 38
    EG 157, [1997] EGCS 75, (1997) Times, 6 June, 141 Sol Jo LB 120, [1997] BPIR 726
    .................................................... 1.62, 1.516, 1.688, 1.690
Real Estate Development Co, Re [1991] BCLC 210 ................ 1.177, 1.279, 1.281
Realstar Ltd, Re [2007] EWHC 2921 (Ch), [2008] BPIR 1391, [2007] All ER (D) 171
    (Aug) ........................................................................... 1.178
Rees v Boston Borough Council [2001] EWCA Civ 1934, [2002] 1 WLR 1304, (2002)
    Times, 15 January, sub nom Beck Foods Ltd, Re [2002] BCC 495, [2002] BPIR 665,
    [2001] All ER (D) 337 (Dec) ..................................................... 1.88
Regent United Service Stores, Re (1878) 8 ChD 75, 26 WR 425, 38 LT 84, CA ...... 2.1048
Regent's Canal Ironworks Co, Re, ex p Grissell (1875) 3 ChD 411, CA .............. 1.743
Regis Direct Ltd v Hakeem [2012] EWHC 4328 (Ch) ............................. 1.382
Regis UK Ltd (in administration) [2019] EWHC 3073 (Ch) ....................... 1.65
Registrar of Companies v Swarbrick (Joint Administrators of Gardenprime Ltd in Admin)
    [2014] EWHC 1466 (Ch), [2014] 2 BCLC 695, [2014] All ER (D) 144 (May) .. 2.175, 2.177
Reigate v Union Manufacturing Co (Ramsbottom) Ltd and Elton Cop Dyeing Co Ltd
    [1918] 1 KB 592, 87 LJKB 724, [1918–19] All ER Rep 143, 118 LT 479, CA ......... 1.141
Reiter Bros Exploratory Drilling Pty Ltd, Re (1994) 12 ACLC 430 ................... 2.990
Reliance Wholesale Ltd v AM2PM Feltham Ltd [2019] EWHC 1079 (Ch), [2019] All ER
    (D) 52 (May) .................................................................... 1.178
Rendle v Panelform Ltd [2020] EWHC 2810 (Ch) ............................... 1.176
Report of an Investigation into Complaint No 08 002 300 against Exeter City Council
    [2009] BPIR 598 ................................................................ 1.381
Report of an Investigation into Complaint No 07/A/12661 against The London Borough
    of Camden [2008] BPIR 1572 .................................................... 1.381
Report on an Investigation into Complaint (No 10 002 564) Against Torbay Council
    [2011] BPIR 1098 ............................................................... 1.381
Rescupine Ltd, Re [2003] EWHC 216 (Ch), [2003] 1 BCLC 661, [2003] All ER (D) 161
    (Jan) ........................................................................... 1.180
Revenue and Customs Comrs v Ariel (as Trustee of the Estate in Bankruptcy of Halabi)
    [2016] EWHC 1674 (Ch), [2017] 1 WLR 319, [2016] BPIR 1144, [2016] All ER (D)
    151 (Jul) ....................................................................... 1.414
Revenue and Customs Comrs v Cassells [2008] EWHC 3180 (Ch), [2009] STC 1047,
    [2009] BPIR 284, [2008] All ER (D) 52 (Dec) ................................... 2.814
Revenue and Customs Comrs v Crossman [2007] EWHC 1585 (Ch), [2008] 1 All ER
    483, [2007] BPIR 1068, [2007] All ER (D) 112 (Jul) ............................. 1.381
Revenue and Customs Comrs v Dempster (t/a Boulevard) [2008] EWHC 63 (Ch), [2008]
    STC 2079, [2008] All ER (D) 175 (Jan) .......................................... 1.271
Revenue and Customs Comrs v Earley [2011] EWHC 1783 (Ch), [2011] BPIR 1590
    ...................................................... 1.65, 1.175, 1.500
Revenue and Customs Comrs v Football League Ltd [2012] EWHC 1372 (Ch),
    [2013] 1 BCLC 285, [2012] Bus LR 1539, [2012] 24 LS Gaz R 20, [2012] NLJR 781,
    (2012) Times, 28 June, [2012] BPIR 686, [2012] All ER (D) 214 (May) ............. 1.159
Revenue and Customs Comrs v Garwood [2012] BPIR 575 .................... 1.175, 1.386
Revenue and Customs Comrs v Joint Administrators of Lehman Brothers International
    [2019] UKSC 12, [2019] 2 All ER 559, [2019] 1 WLR 2173, [2019] STC 661,
    [2019] 1 BCLC 609, 169 NLJ 7833, [2019] SWTI 705, [2019] All ER (D) 61 (Mar),
    SC ..................................................................... 1.246, 2.850
Revenue and Customs Comrs v Maxwell [2010] EWCA Civ 1379, [2011] 2 BCLC 301,
    [2011] Bus LR 707, [2012] BCC 30, (2011) Times, 19 January, [2010] SWTI 3242,
    [2011] BPIR 480, [2010] All ER (D) 100 (Dec) ................................... 2.913

Revenue and Customs Comrs v Munir [2015] EWHC 1366 (Ch), [2015] All ER (D) 133
(May) .......................................................................................... 1.188
Revenue and Customs Comrs v Portsmouth City Football Club Ltd (in administration)
[2010] EWHC 2013 (Ch), [2011] BCC 149, [2010] BPIR 1123, [2010] All ER (D) 58
(Aug) .......................................................................................... 1.65
Revenue and Customs Comrs v Rochdale Drinks Distributors Ltd [2011] EWCA Civ
1116, [2012] STC 186, [2012] 1 BCLC 748, [2011] BPIR 1604, [2011] All ER (D) 122
(Oct) ............................................................................ 1.177, 1.188
Revenue and Customs Comrs v Royal Bank of Scotland plc [2007] EWCA Civ 1262,
[2008] 1 BCLC 204, [2008] Bus LR 1213, [2008] BCC 135, [2007] All ER (D) 470
(Nov) ........................................................................................ 1.228
Revenue and Customs Comrs v Smart [2016] Lexis Citation 78, [2016] BPIR 1329,
[2016] All ER (D) 158 (Jun) ....................................................... 1.175
Revenue and Customs Comrs v Walsh [2005] EWHC 1304 (Ch), [2005] 2 BCLC 455,
[2006] BCC 431, [2005] BPIR 1105, [2005] All ER (D) 46 (Jun) ................... 1.275
Revenue and Customs Comrs v Winnington Networks Ltd [2014] EWHC 1259 (Ch), 164
NLJ 7609, [2014] All ER (D) 207 (May) ............................... 1.400, 1.188
Revere Trust Ltd v Wellington Handkerchief Works Ltd [1931] NI 55, CA ............ 1.309
Reynard v Fox [2018] EWHC 2141 (Ch), 168 NLJ 7810, [2018] BPIR 1780,
[2018] All ER (D) 51 (Sep) ......................................................... 1.415
Rhine Film Corp (UK) Ltd, Re (1986) 2 BCC 98, 949 ............................... 1.168
Rhino Enterprises Holdings Ltd, Re [2020] EWHC 2370 (Ch), [2021] BPIR 144 ....... 1.64
Rica Gold Washing Co, Re (1879) 11 ChD 36, 27 WR 715, 40 LT 531, [1874–80] All ER
Rep Ext 1570, CA ...................................................................... 1.176
Richbell Strategic Holdings Ltd, Re [1997] 2 BCLC 429 ................... 1.176, 1.178
Richbell Strategic Holdings Ltd (in liq) (No 2), Re [2000] 2 BCLC 794, [2001] BCC 409,
(2000) Times, 14 June, [2000] Lexis Citation 2481 .................... 1.186, 1.300, 2.429
Ricketts v Ad Valorem Factors Ltd. See Ad Valorem Factors Ltd v Ricketts
Ridgeway Motors (Isleworth) Ltd v Altis Ltd [2004] EWHC 1535 (Ch), [2004] BPIR
1323, [2004] All ER (D) 320 (May); affd sub nom Ridgeway Motors (Isleworth) Ltd v
ALTS Ltd [2005] EWCA Civ 92, [2005] 2 All ER 304, [2005] 1 WLR 2871,
[2005] 2 BCLC 61, [2005] BCC 496, [2005] RVR 173, (2005) Times, 24 February,
[2005] BPIR 423, [2005] All ER (D) 147 (Feb) ...................... 1.176, 1.382, 2.321
Rightmatch Ltd (acting by its LPA Receiver) v Meisels [2014] BPIR 733 ............. 1.178
Rio Grande Do Sul Steamship Co, Re (1877) 5 ChD 282, 46 LJ Ch 277, 3 Asp MLC 424,
25 WR 328, 36 LT 603, CA ........................................................... 1.183
Rio Properties Inc v Al-Midani [2003] BPIR 128, [2002] All ER (D) 135 (Oct) . 1.180, 1.398
Riviera Pearls Ltd, Re [1962] 2 All ER 194n, [1962] 1 WLR 722, 106 Sol Jo 328 ..... 1.168
Rloans LLP v The Registrar of Companies [2012] Lexis Citation 123, [2013] All ER (D)
180 (May) .................................................................................. 1.701
Roberts, Re [1900] 1 QB 122, 69 LJQB 19, 7 Mans 5, 48 WR 132, 44 Sol Jo 44, 81 LT
467, 16 TLR 29, [1895–91] All ER Rep Ext 1320, CA ............................... 1.427
Roberts v Frohlich [2011] EWHC 257 (Ch), [2011] 2 BCLC 625, [2012] BCC 407,
[2011] All ER (D) 211 (Feb) ........................................................ 1.272
Roberts v Nunn. See Nunn (bankruptcy: divorce: pension rights), Re
Roberts v Procurator Fiscal, Kilmarnock [2019] SAC (Crim) 10 ...................... 1.594
Roberts Petroleum Ltd v Bernard Kenny Ltd [1983] 2 AC 192, [1982] 1 All ER 685,
[1982] 1 WLR 301, 126 Sol Jo 81; revsd [1983] 2 AC 192, [1983] 1 All ER 564, [1983]
2 WLR 305, [1983] BCLC 28, [1983] Com LR 564, 10 LDAB 393, 127 Sol Jo 138,
HL ................................................................................ 1.240, 1.399
Robertson (a bankrupt), Re [1989] 1 WLR 1139 ................................... 1.395
Robertson v Wojakovski [2020] EWHC 2737 (Ch), [2021] BPIR 178, [2020] All ER (D)
80 (Oct) .................................................................................. 2.550
Robinson v Burnell's Vienna Bakery Co [1904] 2 KB 624, 73 LJKB 911, 52 WR 526, 48
Sol Jo 299, 91 LT 375, 20 TLR 284 ................................................. 1.77
Robinson v H. G. Robinson & Sons Ltd [2020] EWHC 1 (Ch), [2020] All ER (D) 40
(May) ............................................................................ 1.174, 1.178
Rochay Productions Ltd (in liquidation), Re [2020] EWHC 1737 (Ch), [2020] BPIR
1423 ....................................................................................... 2.913
Rocks v Brae Hotel (Shetland) Ltd 1997 SLT 474, CtSess ........................... 1.174
Rococo Developments Ltd (in liq), Re, Evans v Jones [2016] EWCA Civ 660, [2017] Ch 1,
[2016] 3 WLR 1480, [2017] 1 BCLC 184, 166 NLJ 7707, [2016] BPIR 1207,
[2016] All ER (D) 36 (Jul) .......................................................... 1.175
Rodencroft Ltd, Re [2004] EWHC 862 (Ch), [2004] 3 All ER 56, [2004] 1 WLR 1566,
[2004] BCC 631, (2004) Times, 13 May, [2004] All ER (D) 219 (Apr) .............. 1.177

Rodenstock GmbH, Re [2011] EWHC 1104 (Ch), [2011] Bus LR 1245, [2012] BCC 459, [2011] All ER (D) 62 (May) .................................................. 6.2, 6.3, 6.4

Roderick John Lynch Inspiration Finance Ltd, Re v Cadwallader (in his capacity as trustee in bankruptcy of Roderick John Lynch) [2020] EWHC 15 (Ch), [2020] BPIR 573, [2020] All ER (D) 78 (Jan) ............................................. 1.414, 1.489

Rogers v Spence (1846) 12 Cl & Fin 700 ........................................... 1.396

Rohl v Bickland Ltd (in admin) [2012] EWHC 706 (Ch), [2012] 2 BCLC 751, [2013] Bus LR 361, [2012] BCC 884 ........................................................ 2.183

Rollings (as Joint Administrators of Musion Systems Ltd) v O'Connell [2014] EWCA Civ 639, [2014] All ER (D) 210 (May) ................................................ 1.688

Rolls Razor Ltd, Re [1968] 3 All ER 698 .......................................... 1.300

Rolls Razor Ltd (No 2), Re [1970] Ch 576, [1969] 3 All ER 1386, [1970] 2 WLR 100, 113 Sol Jo 938 ................................................................. 1.300

Rolph v AY Bank Ltd [2002] BPIR 1231, sub nom AY Bank Ltd (in administration), Re [2001] All ER (D) 431 (Dec) ........................................................ 1.682

Ronelp Marine Ltd v STX Offshore & Shipbuilding Co Ltd [2016] EWHC 2228 (Ch), [2017] BPIR 203, [2016] All ER (D) 77 (Oct) ................................. 1.660, 7.33

Rooney v Cardona [1999] 1 WLR 1388, [1999] 1 FLR 1236, [1999] Fam Law 542, (1999) Times, 4 March, [1999] Lexis Citation 2268, [1999] BPIR 291, [1999] All ER (D) 124 ................................................................. 1.417, 1.429

Rooney v Das [1999] BPIR 404 ............................................... 1.303, 1.460

Roselmar Properties Ltd (No 2), Re (1986) 2 BCC 99, 157, [1986] Lexis Citation 1118 .................................................................................... 1.168

Ross (a Bankrupt) (No 2), Re (2000) Times, 10 May, [2000] Lexis Citation 2814, [2000] BPIR 636, [2000] All ER (D) 583 .................................................. 1.381

Ross v P J Heeringa Ltd [1970] NZLR 170 .......................................... 1.138

Ross v Revenue and Customs Comrs [2010] EWHC 13 (Ch), [2010] 2 All ER 126, [2010] STC 657, [2010] NLJR 103, [2010] BPIR 652, [2010] All ER (D) 49 (Jan) ..... 1.386, 2.550

Rossair Ltd v Primus Build Ltd [2017] EWHC 2430 (TCC) ........................... 1.183

Rottenberg v Monjack [1993] BCLC 374, [1992] BCC 688, [1992] NPC 89 ........... 1.89

Rottmann v Brittain [2009] EWCA Civ 473, [2010] 1 WLR 67, [2009] Bus LR 1604, [2009] BPIR 1148, [2009] All ER (D) 213 (Jul) ..................................... 1.300

Rottmann v Official Receiver [2008] EWHC 1794 (Ch), [2009] Bus LR 284, [2009] BPIR 617 .................................................................................... 1.404

Roundwood Colliery Co, Re, Lee v Roundwood Colliery Co [1897] 1 Ch 373, 66 LJ Ch 186, 45 WR 324, [1895–9] All ER Rep 530, 41 Sol Jo 240, 75 LT 641, 13 TLR 175, CA ...................................................................................... 1.164

Rowbotham Baxter Ltd, Re [1990] BCLC 397, [1990] BCC 113 .............. 1.620, 1.627

Rowbury v Official Receiver [2015] EWHC 2276 (Ch), [2016] BPIR 477, [2015] All ER (D) 129 (Sep) ..................................................................... 1.65, 2.905

Rowe v Sanders [2002] EWCA Civ 242, [2002] 2 All ER 800, [2002] BPIR 847, [2002] All ER (D) 103 (Feb) ........................................................ 1.417

Rowellian Football Social Club, Re [2011] EWHC 1301 (Ch), [2012] Ch 125, [2011] 3 WLR 1147, [2011] 2 BCLC 610, [2011] All ER (D) 230 (May) ...................... 1.728

Rowntree Ventures Ltd v Oak Property Partners Ltd [2017] EWCA Civ 1944 ......... 1.630

Rowse (Tony) NMC Ltd, Re [1996] 2 BCLC 225, [1996] BCC 196 .......... 2.434, 2.1002

Royal Bank of Canada v Chetty [1997] BPIR 137, SKCA ........................... 1.396

Royal Bank of Scotland plc v Munikwa [2020] EWHC 786 (Ch) ..................... 1.65

Royal Bank of Scotland v Farley. See Debtor, a (No 68 of 1992), Re

Royal Trust Bank v Buchler [1989] BCLC 130, sub nom Meesan Investments Ltd, Re 4 BCC 788 ......................................................................... 1.660

Royscott Spa Leasing Ltd v Lovett [1995] BCC 502, [1994] NPC 146, [1994] Lexis Citation 2180, CA ...................................................................... 1.582

Rubber and Produce Investment Trust, Re [1915] 1 Ch 382, 84 LJ Ch 534, [1915] HBR 120, 112 LT 1129, 31 TLR 253 ................................................. 1.160, 2.949

Rubin v Cobalt Pictures Ltd [2010] EWHC 3223 (Ch), [2011] BPIR 334, [2010] All ER (D) 175 (Dec) ......................................................................... 1.688

Rubin v Coote [2009] EWHC 2266 (Ch), [2010] BPIR 262; affd [2011] EWCA Civ 106, [2011] BCC 596, [2011] BPIR 558, [2011] All ER (D) 102 (Feb) ..................... 1.741

Rubin (Trustee of Dweck) v Dweck [2012] BPIR 854 ............................... 1.582

Rubin v Eurofinance SA [2010] EWCA Civ 895, [2011] Ch 133, [2011] 2 WLR 121, [2011] 1 All ER (Comm) 287, [2011] 2 BCLC 473, [2011] Bus LR 84, [2011] BCC 649, [2010] NLJR 1192, (2010) Times, 5 October, [2011] BPIR 1110, [2010] All ER (D) 358 (Jul); sub nom New Cap Reinsurance Corpn Ltd (in liq), Re [2011] EWHC 677 (Ch), [2011] All ER (D) 54 (Aug); [2011] EWCA Civ 971, [2012] Ch 538, [2012] 1 All ER 755, [2012] 2 WLR 1095, [2012] 1 All ER (Comm) 1207, [2012] Bus LR 772, [2011] BCC 937, [2011] BPIR 1428, [2011] All ER (D) 55 (Aug); sub nom Rubin v Eurofinance SA; New Cap Reinsurance Corp (in liq) v Grant [2012] UKSC 46, [2013] 1 AC 236, [2013] 1 All ER 521, [2012] 3 WLR 1019, [2013] 1 All ER (Comm) 513, [2013] 4 LRC 132, [2012] 2 BCLC 682, [2013] Bus LR 1, [2012] 2 Lloyd's Rep 615, (2012) Times, 09 November, [2012] BPIR 1204, [2012] All ER (D) 258 (Oct), SC ..... 7.15, 7.34, 7.40
Rudd & Son Ltd, Re [1991] BCLC 378, [1986] 2 BCC 98 ............................ 1.89
Ruiz (a bankrupt), Re, Mekaraska v Ruiz [2011] EWCA Civ 1646, [2012] BPIR 446 .......................................................................................... 1.395, 1.456
Rushcutters Court Pty Ltd (No 2), Re (1978) ACLC 29, 965 ....................... 1.180
Rushleigh Services Pty Ltd v Forge Group Ltd [2016] FCA 1471 ................... 1.183
Russell (J) Electronics Ltd, Re [1968] 2 All ER 559, [1968] 1 WLR 1252, 112 Sol Jo 621 ................................................................................................ 1.168
Ryan Developers Ltd, Re [2002] EWHC 1121 (Ch), [2002] 2 BCLC 792, [2003] BPIR 482, [2002] All ER (D) 121 (May) ...................................................... 1.178
Ryder Installations Ltd, Re [1966] 1 All ER 453n, [1966] 1 WLR 524, 110 Sol Jo 246 .................................................................................................. 1.160
Ryohin Keikaku Europe Ltd V Hollis and O'reilly (Joint Administrators and Supervisors of Sixty Uk Ltd) [2009] EWHC 3866 (Ch), [2010] BPIR 1234 ......................... 1.59

## S

S & A Conversions Ltd, Re (1988) 4 BCC 384, [1988] NLJR 169, [1988] Lexis Citation 2151, CA ...................................................................... 1.222, 1.249
S & D International Pty Ltd (in liqation) (No 7), Re [2012] VSC 551 ................. 1.741
S & D International (in liq) v MIG Property Services Pty Ltd [2010] VSC 336 ......... 1.164
S.J. Henderson & Co Ltd, Re; Re Triumph Furniture Ltd [2019] EWHC 2742 (Ch), [2019] All ER (D) 126 (Oct) ................................................ 1.646, 2.820
SA & D Wright Ltd, Re, Denney v John Hudson & Co Ltd [1992] BCLC 901, [1992] BCC 503 ............................................................................. 1.180
SCI Senior Home, in administration, v Gemeinde Wedemark: C-195/15 (2016) C-195/15, ECLI:EU:C:2016:804, [2018] BPIR 173, [2016] All ER (D) 23 (Nov), EUCJ ........... 6.10
SCL Building Services Ltd, Re [1990] BCLC 98, 5 BCC 746 ......................... 1.671
SCT Industri AB i Likvidation v Alpenblume AB: C-111/08 (2009) C-111/08, ECLI:EU:C:2009:419, [2009] ECR I-5655, [2010] Bus LR 559, [2009] All ER (D) 47 (Jul), EUCJ ......................................................................... 6.1, 6.8
SED Essex Ltd, Re [2013] EWHC 1583 (Ch), [2013] All ER (D) 151 (Jun) ............ 1.188
SEIL Trade Finance Ltd, Re [1992] BCC 538 ....................................... 1.310
SHB Realisations Ltd (formerly BHS Ltd) (in liqation), Re, Wright (as joint liquidators of SHB Realisations Ltd (formerly BHS Ltd) (in liqation)) v Prudential Assurance Company Ltd [2018] EWHC 402 (Ch), [2018] Bus LR 1173, 168 NLJ 7785, [2018] BPIR 818, [2018] All ER (D) 58 (Mar) ................................. 1.64, 1.65
SK Shipping Co Ltd v STX Pan Ocean Co Ltd (29 July 2014, unreported) Chancery Division ...................................................................................... 7.33
SMU Investments Ltd Kirker, Re (liquidator of SMU Investments Ltd) v Holyoak Investments Inc [2020] EWHC 875 (Ch), [2020] All ER (D) 91 (Apr) ................. 1.324
SN Group plc, Re [1994] 1 BCLC 319, [1993] BCC 808 ............................ 2.814
SNR Denton UK LLP v Kirwan (2012) UKEAT/0158/12/ZT, [2012] IRLR 966, [2013] ICR 101, [2012] All ER (D) 215 (Oct), EAT ....................................... 1.686
SSRL Realisations Ltd (In Administration), Re, Lazari Investments Ltd v Saville [2015] EWHC 2590 (Ch), [2016] 1 P & CR 13, [2015] All ER (D) 74 (Sep) ................ 1.660
SSSL Realisations (2002) Ltd (in liq), Re [2006] EWCA Civ 7, [2006] Ch 610, [2006] 2 WLR 1369, [2007] 1 BCLC 29, (2006) Times, 20 January, [2006] BPIR 457, [2006] All ER (D) 98 (Jan), sub nom Squires (liquidators of SSSL Realisations (2002) Ltd) v AIG Europe (UK) Ltd [2006] BCC 233 ............................. 1.235
Saad Investments Company Ltd (in liqation), Re, Akers v Hayley [2016] Lexis Citation 69, [2017] BPIR 1700, [2016] All ER (D) 103 (Jun) ................................ 2.769
Sabre International Products Ltd, Re [1991] BCLC 470, [1991] BCC 694 ............. 1.622
Safe Business Solutions Ltd (in liqation) v Cohen [2017] EWHC 145 (Ch), [2017] All ER (D) 82 (Feb) ...................................................................... 1.660

Sahaviriya Steel Industries UK Ltd, Re; Subnom Official Receiver v Sahaviriya Steel
    Industries Public Company Ltd [2015] EWHC 2877 (Ch), [2016] 1 BCLC 758,
    [2015] All ER (D) 269 (Oct) .......................................... 1.294, 1.300, 1.404
Sahaviriya Steel Industries UK Ltd v Hewden Stuart Ltd [2015] EWHC 2726 (Ch),
    [2015] All ER (D) 148 (Oct) ..................................................... 1.180
Saini v Petroform Ltd [1995] Lexis Citation 2391, [1997] BPIR 515, CA ............ 1.396
St James's Club, Re (1852) 2 De GM & G 383, 16 Jur 1075, 42 ER 920, 19 LTOS 307
    ................................................................................. 1.280
St Nazaire Co, Re (1879) 12 ChD 88, 27 WR 854, 41 LT 110, CA .................. 1.200
Salcombe Hotel Development Co Ltd, Re [1991] BCLC 44, 5 BCC 807, (1988) Times,
    25 November, [1988] Lexis Citation 1749 ........................................ 1.218
Salliss v Hunt (trustee in bankruptcy of Salliss) [2014] EWHC 229 (Ch), [2014] 2 All ER
    1002, [2014] 1 WLR 2402, [2014] BPIR 754, [2014] All ER (D) 99 (Feb) ...... 1.395, 1.489
Salmet International Ltd (in administration), Re [2001] BCC 796, sub nom Spring Valley
    Properties Ltd v Harris [2001] BPIR 709 ............................... 1.81, 1.622, 1.716
Salter v Wetton [2011] EWHC 3192 (Ch), [2012] BPIR 63 ......................... 1.461
Salters Hall School Ltd (in liqation), Re, Merrygold v Horton [1998] 1 BCLC 401,
    [1998] BCC 503, (1997) Times, 11 July, [1997] Lexis Citation 1165 .................. 2.990
Salvage Association, Re [2003] EWHC 1028 (Ch), [2003] 3 All ER 246, [2004] 1 WLR
    174, [2003] 2 BCLC 333, [2003] BCC 504, [2003] 24 LS Gaz R 36, (2003) Times,
    21 May, [2003] BPIR 1181, [2003] All ER (D) 108 (May), CSRC vol 27 iss 6/2 . 1.59, 1.728
Sandell v Porter (1966) 115 CLR 666, AusHC ...................................... 1.175
Sandelson v Mulville [2019] EWHC 1620 (Ch), [2019] BPIR 1253 .................... 2.744
Sanders v Donovan [2012] BPIR 219 .............................................. 1.398
Sandford Farm Properties Ltd, Re (26 June 2015, unreported), ChD .................. 1.300
Sands v Clitheroe [2006] BPIR 1000 .............................................. 1.582
Sands (as trustee in bankruptcy of the estate of Layne (a bankrupt)) v Layne [2016]
    EWCA Civ 1159, [2017] 1 WLR 1782, [2017] BPIR 215, [2016] All ER (D) 160
    (Nov) ......................................................................... 1.502
Sands v Singh [2015] EWHC 2219 (Ch), [2015] BPIR 1293, [2015] All ER (D) 304
    (Jun) ......................................................................... 1.397
Sands and Treharne [2010] BPIR 1437 ............................................ 1.398
Sandwell Copiers Ltd, Re [1988] BCLC 209, 4 BCC 227 ........................... 1.167
Sankey Furniture Ltd, Re, ex p Harding [1995] 2 BCLC 594 .................. 1.160, 2.781
Sarjanda Ltd, Re [2021] EWHC 210 (Ch), [2021] All ER (D) 76 (Feb) .............. 2.814
Sarflax Ltd, Re [1979] Ch 592, [1979] 1 All ER 529, [1979] 2 WLR 202, 143 JP 225, 123
    Sol Jo 97 ..................................................................... 1.271
Sasea Finance Ltd (in liqation) v KPMG [1998] BCC 216, [1997] Lexis Citation 3701
    ................................................................................. 1.300
Sat-Elite Ltd, Re [2003] EWHC 2990 (Ch), [2003] All ER (D) 222 (Nov) ............ 1.178
Saunders (G L) Ltd, Re [1986] 1 WLR 215, [1986] BCLC 40, 130 Sol Jo 166,
    [1986] LS Gaz R 779 ........................................................... 1.84
Saunders (a bankrupt), Re [1997] Ch 60, [1997] 3 All ER 992, [1996] 3 WLR 473, [1996]
    BPIR 355 ..................................................................... 1.399
Saunders v United Kingdom (Application 19187/91) [1998] 1 BCLC 362, 23 EHRR 313,
    [1997] BCC 872, (1996) Times, 18 December, 2 BHRC 358, [1996] ECHR 19187/91,
    EctHR ................................................................. 1.300, 1.596
Savage v Howard [2006] EWHC 3693 (Ch), [2007] BPIR 1097, [2006] All ER (D) 13
    (Feb) ......................................................................... 1.395
Savage v Norton [1908] 1 Ch 290, 77 LJ Ch 198, 98 LT 382 ....................... 1.452
Saw (SW) 2010 Ltd v Wilson (as joint administrators of Property Edge Lettings Ltd)
    [2017] EWCA Civ 1001, [2018] Ch 213, [2018] 2 WLR 636, [2018] 1 BCLC 291, 167
    NLJ 7761, [2017] All ER (D) 48 (Aug) .................... 1.73, 1.326, 1.631, 1.632, 1.633
Sayers v Clarke Walker (a firm) [2002] EWCA Civ 645, [2002] 3 All ER 490, [2002] 1
    WLR 3095, (2002) Times, 3 June, [2002] All ER (D) 189 (May) .................... 2.814
Scandon Pty Ltd, Re (1996) 14 ACLC 124 ......................................... 1.175
Schmid v Hertel: C-328/12 (2014) C-328/12, ECLI:EU:C:2014:6, [2014] 1 WLR 633,
    164 NLJ 7593, [2014] BPIR 504, [2014] All ER (D) 221 (Jan), EUCJ .............. 6.1, 6.8
Schmitt v Deichmann [2012] EWHC 62 (Ch), [2013] Ch 61, [2012] 2 All ER 1217,
    [2012] 3 WLR 681, [2014] 1 BCLC 663, [2012] BCC 561, [2012] NLJR 214, (2012)
    Times, 31 January, [2012] BPIR 392, [2012] All ER (D) 177 (Jan) .................... 1.583
Schooler v Customs and Excise Comrs [1995] 2 BCLC 610, (1995) Times, 9 August,
    [1996] BPIR 207 ............................................................... 1.382
Schroder Exempt Property Unit Trust v Birmingham City Council [2014] EWHC 2207
    (Admin), [2014] 2 P & CR 251, [2015] RA 24, [2014] 3 EGLR 91, [2014] BPIR 1338,
    [2014] All ER (D) 143 (Jul) ..................................................... 1.235

Schuppan (a bankrupt), Re [1996] 2 All ER 664, [1997] 1 BCLC 211, [1996] BPIR 486
............................................................. 1.416, 1.433
Schuppan (a bankrupt) (No 2), Re [1997] 1 BCLC 256, [1997] BPIR 271 ............. 1.302
Science & Media LLP, Re [2014] BPIR 774 ........................................ 1.240
Science Research Council v Nasse [1980] AC 1028, [1979] 3 All ER 673, [1979] 3 WLR
762, [1979] IRLR 465, [1979] ICR 921, 123 Sol Jo 768, HL ........................ 1.660
Scientific Investment Pension Plan (Trusts), Re [1999] Ch 53, [1998] 3 All ER 154, [1998]
3 WLR 1191, [1998] 2 BCLC 360, [1998] OPLR 41, [1998] 2 FLR 761, [1998] Fam
Law 582, (1998) Times, 5 March, [1998] Lexis Citation 2681, [1998] BPIR 410,
[1998] All ER (D) 72 ........................................................... 1.417
Scmlla Properties Ltd v Gesso Properties (BVI) Ltd [1995] BCC 793, [1995] NPC 48,
[1995] Lexis Citation 3080 ...................................................... 1.235
Scotch Granite Co, Re (1867) 17 LT 533 ......................................... 1.160
Scott (a bankrupt), Re [2003] BPIR 1009, [2003] All ER (D) 214 (Feb) .............. 1.427
Scottish & Newcastle Ltd v Raguz [2010] EWHC 1384 (Ch), [2010] NLJR 878, [2010]
BPIR 945, [2010] All ER (D) 63 (Jun) ........................................... 2.814
Scottish Environment Protection Agency v Joint Liquidators of The Scottish Coal Co Ltd
[2013] CSIH 108, 2014 SC 372, 2014 SLT 259, 2013 Scot (D) 14/12, CtSess ......... 1.434
Scottish Widows plc v Tripipatkul [2003] EWHC 1874 (Ch), [2004] 1 P & CR 461,
[2004] BCC 200, [2003] BPIR 1413, [2003] All ER (D) 24 (Aug) ..................... 1.235
Scranton's Trustee v Pearse [1922] 2 Ch 87, 91 LJ Ch 579, [1922] B & CR 52,
[1922] All ER Rep 764, 66 Sol Jo 503, 127 LT 698, 38 TLR 629, CA ................ 1.622
Scriven, Re [2004] EWCA Civ 683, 148 Sol Jo LB 757, [2004] BPIR 972, [2004] All ER
(D) 185 (Jun) ................................................................. 1.404
Sea Management Singapore Pte Ltd v Professional Service Brokers Ltd [2012]
CIV-2011-404-5315 ............................................................ 1.174
Sea Voyager Maritime Inc v Bielecki (t/a Hughes Hooker & Co) [1999] 1 All ER 628,
[1999] 1 BCLC 133, [1998] Lexis Citation 3577, [1998] BPIR 655, sub nom Sea
Voyager Maritime Inc v Bielecki (t/a Hughes Hooker (1998) Times, 23 October .. 1.64, 1.65
Seabrooke Road Ltd, Re [2021] EWHC 436 (Ch), [2021] All ER (D) 105 (Jan) ... 1.643
Seagon v Deko Marty Belgium NV: C-339/07 (2009) C-339/07, ECLI:EU:C:2009:83,
[2009] ECR I-767, [2009] 1 WLR 2168, [2009] Bus LR 1151, [2009] BCC 347,
[2009] All ER (D) 112 (Feb), EUCJ ............................................. 6.8
Seagull Manufacturing Co Ltd (in liqation), Re [1993] Ch 345, [1993] 2 All ER 980,
[1993] 2 WLR 872, [1993] BCLC 1139, [1993] BCC 241, (1993) Times, 8 February
.................................................... 1.186, 1.300, 1.404, 2.426
Seah Teong Kang v Seah Yong Chwan [2015] SGCA 48 ........................... 1.180
Seal v Chief Constable of South Wales Police [2007] UKHL 31, [2007] 4 All ER 177,
[2007] 1 WLR 1910, 97 BMLR 172, (2007) Times, 5 July, 22 BHRC 769, [2007] BPIR
1396, [2007] All ER (D) 49 (Jul), HL ...................................... 1.183, 1.399
Secondus v Atkinson (As Trustee in Bankruptcy of Ene Baleme Secondus) [2013] BPIR
632 ......................................................................... 1.395
Secretary of State for Business Energy and Industrial Strategy v Celtic Consultancy and
Enterprises Ltd [2021] EWHC 1240 (Ch), [2021] Bus LR 1071 ...................... 1.177
Secretary of State for Business, Energy and Industrial Strategy v Rigel Kent
Acquisitions Ltd [2017] EWHC 3636 (Ch) ....................................... 1.188
Secretary of State for Business, Enterprise and Regulatory Reform v Amway (UK) Ltd
[2009] EWCA Civ 32, [2009] BCC 781, (2009) Times, 18 March, [2009] Bus LR
D121, [2009] All ER (D) 239 (Jan) ............................................. 1.177
Secretary of State for Business, Enterprise and Regulatory Reform v Art IT plc [2008]
EWHC 258 (Ch), [2009] 1 BCLC 262, [2008] All ER (D) 237 (Jan) ................. 1.177
Secretary of State for Business, Innovation and Skills v APW Asset Management Ltd
[2015] Lexis Citation 57, [2015] All ER (D) 160 (Apr) ........................... 2.324
Secretary of State for Business Innovation and Skills v PAG Management Services Ltd
[2015] EWHC 2404 (Ch), [2015] RA 519, [2015] All ER (D) 74 (Aug) ........ 1.177, 1.178
Secretary of State for Business, Innovation and Skills v PGMRS Ltd [2010] EWHC 2864
(Ch), [2011] 1 BCLC 443, [2011] BCC 368, [2010] All ER (D) 132 (Nov) ............ 1.177
Secretary of State for Education v Corpn of Hadlow College [2019] EWHC 2035 (Ch),
[2019] All ER (D) 164 (May) ................................................... 1.617
Secretary of State for the Environment, Food and Rural Affairs v Feakins [2004] EWHC
2735 (Ch), [2005] 05 LS Gaz R 28, [2004] 49 EG 135 (CS), (2004) Times,
29 December, [2005] BPIR 292, [2004] All ER (D) 417 (Nov); revsd in part sub nom
Department for Environment Food and Rural Affairs v Feakins [2005] EWCA Civ
1513, (2005) Times, 22 December, [2006] BPIR 895, [2005] All ER (D) 153 (Dec), sub
nom Feakins v Department for Environment Food and Rural Affairs [2007] BCC 54
............................................................................. 1.582

Secretary of State for Trade and Industry v Arnold [2007] EWHC 1933 (Ch),
  [2008] 1 BCLC 581, [2008] BCC 119, [2007] All ER (D) 65 (Aug), CSRC vol 31 iss
  10/2 .................................................................................................... 1.701
Secretary of State for Trade and Industry v Becker [2002] EWHC 2200 (Ch),
  [2003] 1 BCLC 555, [2002] All ER (D) 280 (Oct) .............................................. 1.326
Secretary of State for Trade and Industry v Bell Davies Trading Ltd [2004] EWCA Civ
  1066, [2005] 1 All ER 324, [2005] 1 BCLC 516, [2005] BCC 564, [2004] 36 LS Gaz R
  33, (2004) Times, 21 September, [2004] All ER (D) 598 (Jul) ............................... 1.177
Secretary of State for Trade and Industry v Bottrill [2000] 1 All ER 915, [2000] 2 BCLC
  448, [1999] IRLR 326, [1999] ICR 592, [1999] BCC 177, (1999) Times, 24 February,
  [1999] Lexis Citation 2021, 143 Sol Jo LB 73, 615 IRLB 12, [1999] All ER (D) 138,
  CSRC vol 24 iss 15/3 ............................................................................. 1.756
Secretary of State for Trade and Industry v Deverell [2001] Ch 340, [2000] 2 All ER 365,
  [2000] 2 WLR 907, [2000] 2 BCLC 133, [2000] BCC 1057, [2000] 03 LS Gaz R 35,
  (2000) Times, 21 January, [1999] Lexis Citation 4075, 144 Sol Jo LB 49, [1999] All ER
  (D) 1497 ............................................................................................. 1.326
Secretary of State for Trade and Industry v Leyton Housing Trustees Ltd [2000] 2 BCLC
  808 .................................................................................................... 1.177
Secretary of State for Trade and Industry v Liquid Acquisitions Ltd [2002] EWHC 180
  (Ch), [2003] 1 BCLC 375, [2002] All ER (D) 287 (Jan) ...................................... 1.177
Secretary of State for Trade and Industry v North West Holdings plc [1999] 1 BCLC
  425 .................................................................................................... 2.324
Secretary of State for Trade and Industry v Tjolle [1998] 1 BCLC 333, [1998] BCC 282,
  [1997] 24 LS Gaz R 31, (1997) Times, 9 May, 141 Sol Jo LB 119 ......................... 1.326
Secretary of State for Trade and Industry v Travel Time (UK) Ltd. See Company, a (No
  5669 of 1998), Re
Secure and Provide plc, Re [1992] BCC 405 .................................... 1.177, 2.354
Securities and Investments Board v Lancashire and Yorkshire Portfolio Management Ltd
  [1992] BCLC 281, [1992] BCC 381 ................................................................ 1.68
Security Directors Pty Ltd (in liq), Re (1997) 24 ACSR 558, Vic S Ct ................. 1.194
Sedgwick, Collins & Co Ltd v Rossia Insurance Co of Petrograd [1926] 1 KB 1, 95 LJKB
  7, 133 LT 808, 41 TLR 663, CA; affd sub nom Employers' Liability Assurance Corpn v
  Sedgwick, Collins & Co [1927] AC 95, 95 LJKB 1015, [1926] All ER Rep 388, 42 TLR
  749, sub nom Sedgwick, Collins & Co Ltd v Rossia Insurance Co of Petrograd 136 LT
  72, 42 TLR 749, HL ................................................................................ 1.181
Seear v Lawson (1880) 15 ChD 426, 49 LJ Bcy 69, 28 WR 929, 42 LT 893, CA ...... 1.743
Segal v Pasram [2008] 1 FLR 271, [2007] Fam Law 892, [2007] BPIR 881, [2007] All ER
  (D) 35 (Jun) ........................................................................................ 1.459
Sekhon v Edginton [2015] EWCA Civ 816, [2015] 1 WLR 4435, [2015] BPIR 1397
  ............................................................................ 1.178, 1.386, 2.550
Sell Your Car With Us Ltd v Sareen [2019] EWHC 2332 (Ch), [2019] All ER (D) 76
  (Sep) .................................................................................................. 2.338
Selectmove Ltd, Re [1995] 2 All ER 531, [1995] 1 WLR 474, [1995] STC 406, 66 TC
  552, (1994) Times, 13 January ..................................................................... 1.178
Senator Hanseatische Verwaltungsgesellschaft mbH, Re [1996] 4 All ER 933, [1997] 1
  WLR 515, [1996] 2 BCLC 562, (1996) Times, 30 July ............................... 1.177, 6.3
Serene Shoes Ltd, Re [1958] 3 All ER 316, [1958] 1 WLR 1087, 102 Sol Jo 777 ...... 1.164
Sevenoaks Stationers (Retail) Ltd, Re [1991] Ch 164, [1991] 3 All ER 578, [1990] 3 WLR
  1165, [1991] BCLC 325, [1990] BCC 765, 134 Sol Jo 1367, (1990) Times,
  21 August ........................................................................................... 1.394
Shah v Cooper [2003] BPIR 1018 .............................................................. 1.60
Shalson v DF Keane Ltd [2003] EWHC 599 (Ch), [2003] BPIR 1045, [2003] ArbLR 38
  ......................................................................................................... 1.383
Sharples v Places for People Homes Ltd; Godfery v A2 Dominion Homes Ltd [2011]
  EWCA Civ 813, [2012] Ch 382, [2012] 1 All ER 582, [2012] 2 WLR 584, [2012] PTSR
  401, [2011] HLR 704, [2011] NLJR 1062, [2011] BPIR 1488, [2011] All ER (D) 170
  (Jul) ......................................................................................... 1.334, 1.399
Sharps of Truro Ltd, Re [1990] BCC 94 ..................................................... 2.814
Sharyn Development Co Pty Ltd (in liq) v Official Receiver in Bankruptcy as Trustee of the
  Estate of Bridgland (1980) 5 ACLR 1 .......................................................... 1.303
Shaw (Joshua) & Sons Ltd, Re [1989] BCLC 362, 5 BCC 188 ......................... 1.176
Shaw v Doleman [2009] EWCA Civ 279, [2009] 2 BCLC 123, [2009] Bus LR 1175,
  [2009] 2 P & CR 205, [2009] BCC 730, [2009] 2 EGLR 35, [2009] 27 EG 92, [2009]
  14 EG 86 (CS), (2009) Times, 22 April, [2009] BPIR 945, [2009] 2 P & CR D23,
  [2009] All ER (D) 34 (Apr) ...................................................................... 1.235

Sheldrake v DPP, A-G's Reference (No 4 of 2002) [2004] UKHL 43, [2005] 1 AC 264,
    [2005] 1 All ER 237, [2004] 3 WLR 976, [2005] 3 LRC 463, [2005] RTR 13, [2005] 1
    Cr App Rep 450, 168 JP 669, [2004] 43 LS Gaz R 33, (2004) Times, 15 October, 148
    Sol Jo LB 1216, 17 BHRC 339, [2004] All ER (D) 169 (Oct), HL ............. 1.263, 1.480
Shepheard v Lamey [2001] BPIR 939 ............................... 1.160, 1.224, 1.705
Shepherd v Legal Services Commission [2003] BCC 728, [2003] BPIR 140 ............ 1.381
Shepherd v Official Receiver [2006] EWHC 2902 (Ch), [2007] BPIR 101, [2006] All ER
    (D) 72 (Nov) ...................................................................... 1.414
Sherborne Associates Ltd, Re [1995] BCC 40 ............................... 1.271, 1.272
Sheridan (Brian) Cars Ltd, Re, Official Receiver v Sheridan [1996] 1 BCLC 327,
    [1995] BCC 1035 ................................................................. 2.814
Sheridan Securities Ltd, Re (1988) 4 BCC 200, [1988] Lexis Citation 1773 ........... 1.716
Shettar, Re [2003] EWHC 220 (Ch), [2003] BPIR 1055, [2003] All ER (D) 329 (Jan)
    ...................................................................................... 1.414
Shierson v Rastogi [2007] EWHC 1266 (Ch), [2007] BPIR 891, [2007] All ER (D) 446
    (May) .............................................................................. 1.391
Shierson v Vlieland-Boddy [2005] EWCA Civ 974, [2005] 1 WLR 3966, [2006] 2 BCLC
    9, [2005] BCC 949, (2005) Times, 26 September, [2005] BPIR 1170, [2005] All ER (D)
    391 (Jul) ............................................................ 1.380, 6.1, 6.2
Shilabeer v Lanceley [2019] EWHC 3380 (QB) ................................... 1.455
Shindler v Northern Raincoat Co Ltd [1960] 2 All ER 239, [1960] 1 WLR 1038, 104 Sol
    Jo 806 .............................................................................. 1.677
Shiraz Nominees (in liqation) v Collinson (1985) 3 ACLC 706 ...................... 1.220
Shlosberg, Re [2018] EWHC 603 (Ch) ............................................. 1.492
Shoe Lace Ltd, Re [1992] BCLC 636, [1992] BCC 367; affd sub nom Power v Sharp
    Investments Ltd [1994] 1 BCLC 111, [1993] BCC 609, (1993) Times, 3 June ......... 1.309
Shrimpton v Darbys Solicitors LLP [2011] EWHC 3796 (Ch), [2012] BPIR 631 ....... 1.386
Shruth Ltd, Re [2005] EWHC 1293 (Ch), [2006] 1 BCLC 294, [2007] BCC 960, [2005]
    BPIR 1455, [2005] All ER (D) 275 (Jun) ....................... 1.160, 2.834, 2.835, 2.931
Siddiqi v Taparis Ltd [2019] EWHC 417 (Ch), [2019] BPIR 1025 ....... 1.500, 2.544, 2.550
Sidebotham, Re, ex p Sidebotham (1880) 14 ChD 458, 49 LJ Bcy 41, 28 WR 715,
    [1874–80] All ER Rep 588, 42 LT 783, CA ....................................... 1.220
Signland Ltd, Re [1982] 2 All ER 609n ........................................... 2.324
Silven Properties Ltd v Royal Bank of Scotland plc [2003] EWCA Civ 1409, [2004]
    4 All ER 484, [2004] 1 WLR 997, [2004] 1 BCLC 359, [2004] 1 P & CR D13,
    [2003] BCC 1002, [2003] 3 EGLR 49, [2003] 44 LS Gaz R 33, [2003] 50 EG 96,
    (2003) Times, 27 October, 147 Sol Jo LB 1239, [2003] BPIR 1429, [2003] All ER (D)
    335 (Oct) ..................................................... 1.71, 1.81, 1.88
Silver Valley Mines, Re (1882) 21 ChD 381, 31 WR 96, 47 LT 597, CA .............. 2.990
Simmon Box (Diamonds) Ltd, Re [2000] BCC 275, [1999] Lexis Citation 1955; revsd
    [2002] BCC 82, CSRC vol 24 iss 21/2, CA ...................................... 1.272
Simmonds (as trustee in bankruptcy of Mr Albert James Pearce) v Pearce (a bankrupt)
    [2017] EWHC 3126 (Admin), [2018] 1 WLR 1849, [2018] BPIR 206, [2017] All ER
    (D) 10 (Dec) ................................................. 1.430, 1.489, 1.596
Simms v Oakes [2002] EWCA Civ 08, [2002] BPIR 1244, [2002] All ER (D) 37 (Jan)
    ...................................................................................... 1.302
Simon Carves Ltd, Re [2013] EWHC 685 (Ch), [2013] 2 BCLC 100, [2013] All ER (D)
    304 (Mar) .......................................................................... 1.583
Sinclair, Re, ex p Payne (1885) 15 QBD 616, 2 Morr 255, [1881–5] All ER Rep 173, 53
    LT 767 ............................................................................. 1.398
Singh v Hicken (trustee in bankruptcy of Singh) [2018] EWHC 3277 (Ch), [2019] BPIR
    216, [2018] All ER (D) 28 (Dec) ............................................... 2.1009
Sino Strategic International Ltd, Re [2015] FCA 709 .............................. 1.174
Singer v Trustee of the Property of Munro (bankrupts) [1981] 3 All ER 215, sub nom
    Munro and Rowe, Singer v Trustee in Bankruptcy, Re [1981] 1 WLR 1358, 125 Sol Jo
    512 ...................................................................... 1.410, 1.414
Singer (A) & Co (Hat Manufacturers) Ltd, Re [1943] Ch 121, [1943] 1 All ER 225,
    112 LJ Ch 113, 5 LDAB 339, 87 Sol Jo 102, 168 LT 132, 59 TLR 176, CA .......... 1.270
Singh v Singh [2013] EWHC 4783 (Ch), [2014] BPIR 1555 ......................... 1.356
Singh v The Official Receiver [1996] Lexis Citation 3149, [1997] BPIR 530 ........... 1.497
Singh Sandhu (t/a Isher Fashions UK) v Jet Star Retail Ltd [2011] EWCA Civ 459,
    [2011] All ER (D) 192 (Apr) ..................................................... 1.684
Singh Sands (as trustee in bankruptcy of Singh) v Singh [2016] EWHC 636 (Ch), [2016]
    BPIR 737, [2016] All ER (D) 209 (Mar) ........................................... 1.459
Singla v Brown [2007] EWHC 405 (Ch), [2008] Ch 357, [2008] 2 WLR 283, [2008] 2
    FLR 125, [2008] Fam Law 413, [2007] BPIR 424, [2007] All ER (D) 05 (Mar) . 1.459, 1.305

Sisu Capital Fund Ltd v Tucker [2005] EWHC 2321 (Ch), [2006] 1 All ER 167, [2006] FSR 409, [2006] BCC 463, [2005] NLJR 1686, (2005) Times, 4 November, [2006] 2 Costs LR 262, [2006] BPIR 154, [2005] All ER (D) 351 (Oct) ......... 1.65, 1.691, 1.705
Sisu Capital Fund Ltd v Tucker [2005] EWHC 2170 (Ch), [2006] BCC 463, [2006] BPIR 154, [2005] All ER (D) 200 (Oct) ............................................................... 1.160
Sir John Moore Gold Mining Co Re(1879) 12 ChD 326 ............................ 1.160
Sixty Uk Ltd (in Admin and Co Voluntary Arrangement), Re [2009] EWHC 3866 (Ch), [2010] BPIR 1234 ........................................................................... 1.59
Skandinaviska Enskilda Banken AB (Publ) v Conway (as joint official liquidators of Weavering Macro Fixed Income Fund Ltd) (Cayman Islands) [2019] UKPC 36, [2019] 3 WLR 493, [2019] 2 BCLC 431, [2019] BPIR 1562, [2019] All ER (D) 170 (Jul), PC ............................................................................................................. 1.303
Skarb v Stephan Riel Case C-47/18 (ECLI:EU:C:2019:754, (18 September 2019, unreported) ............................................................................................... 6.8
Skarzynski v Chalford Property Co Ltd [2000] Lexis Citation 4284, [2001] BPIR 673, sub nom Debtor (No 78 of 2000), a, Re [2000] All ER (D) 2117 ..................... 1.383
Skay Fashions Pty Ltd (in liqation), Re (1986) 10 ACLR 743 ....................... 1.742
Skeggs Beef Ltd Eason, Re (as joint administrators of Skeggs Beef Ltd (in administration)) v Skeggs Beef Ltd (in administration) [2019] EWHC 2607 (Ch), [2019] All ER (D) 129 (Oct) .................................................... 1.632, 1.643, 1.646, 2.820
Skipton Building Society v Collins [1997] Lexis Citation 3618, [1998] BPIR 267 ....... 1.64
Skjevesland v Geveren Trading [2002] EWHC 2898 (Ch), [2003] BCC 391, [2003] BPIR 924, [2003] All ER (D) 61 (May) ..................................................... 1.380
Sky Building Ltd v Revenue and Customs Commissioners and another [2020] EWHC 3139 (Ch), [2020] PLSCS 212, [2020] All ER (D) 121 (Nov) ....................... 1.688
Skypac Aviation Pty Ltd, Re [2019] NSWSC 291 ................................... 1.180
Sleight (as trustee of the estate of Jillian Paula Mascall dec'd) v Crown Estate Comrs [2018] EWHC 3489 (Ch), [2019] PLSCS 4, [2019] BPIR 430, [2019] 1 P & CR D40, [2018] All ER (D) 111 (Dec) ........................................................... 1.439
Smallman Construction Ltd, Re [1989] BCLC 420, 4 BCC 784 ..................... 1.685
Smeaton v Equifax plc [2013] EWCA Civ 108, [2013] 2 All ER 959, [2013] BPIR 231, [2013] All ER (D) 238 (Feb) ........................................................... 1.395
Smedley v Brittain [2008] BPIR 219 ............................ 1.409, 1.430, 1.497
Smile Stylist Ltd v Harte Solutions Ltd [2017] EWHC 2971 (Ch) ................... 1.178
Smith (a bankrupt), Re, ex p Braintree District Council, Braintree District Council v Bankrupt [1988] Ch 457, [1988] 3 All ER 203, [1988] 3 WLR 327, 132 Sol Jo 995, [1988] 27 LS Gaz R 41; revsd sub nom Smith (a bankrupt) v Braintree District Council [1990] 2 AC 215, [1989] 3 All ER 897, [1989] 3 WLR 1317, 88 LGR 393, [1990] RA 1, 154 JP 304, 134 Sol Jo 285, [1990] 2 LS Gaz R 39, (1989) Times, 4 December, HL ............................................................................................................. 1.399
Smith (Wallace) & Co Ltd, Re [1992] BCLC 970 ................................... 1.281
Smith (Wallace) Trust Co Ltd, Re [1992] BCC 707 ............ 1.184, 1.186, 2.806
Smith (Administrator of Cosslett (Contractors) Ltd) v Bridgend County Borough Council [2001] UKHL 58, [2002] 1 AC 336, [2002] 1 All ER 292, [2001] 3 WLR 1347, [2002] 1 BCLC 77, 80 ConLR 172, [2001] BCC 740, [2002] BLR 160, [2002] GCCR 3095, [2001] All ER (D) 118 (Nov), HL ....................................... 1.298, 2.852
Smith v Duke of Manchester (1883) 24 ChD 611, 53 LJ Ch 96, 32 WR 83, 49 LT 96 ............................................................................................................. 1.176
Smith v Ian Simpson & Co (a firm) [2001] Ch 239, [2000] 3 All ER 434, [2000] 3 WLR 495, [2000] NLJR 582, (2000) Times, 24 April, [2000] Lexis Citation 2778, [2000] BPIR 667, [2000] All ER (D) 527 ..................................................... 1.386
Smith v UIC Insurance Co Ltd [2001] BCC 11, [2000] All ER (D) 33 ................. 1.188
Smith-Evans v Smailes [2013] EWHC 3199 (Ch), [2014] 1 WLR 1548, [2014] BPIR 306 ........................................................ 1.61, 1.62, 1.64, 1.65, 1.361
Smith (W H) Ltd v Wyndham (or Wyndram) Investments Ltd [1994] 2 BCLC 571, 70 P & CR 21, [1994] BCC 699, (1994) Times, 26 May ..................... 1.235, 2.1024
Smiths Ltd v Middleton [1979] 3 All ER 842 ............................. 1.82, 1.92
Smolen v Tower Hamlets London Borough Council [2006] EWHC 3628 (Ch), [2007] BPIR 448, [2006] All ER (D) 48 (Apr) ........................................... 1.382
Smurthwaite v Simpson-Smith [2006] EWCA Civ 1183, [2006] BPIR 1504, [2006] All ER (D) 368 (Jul) ......................................................................... 2.913
Snook v London and West Riding Investments Ltd [1967] 2 QB 786, [1967] 1 All ER 518, [1967] 2 WLR 1020, 111 Sol Jo 71, [1999] GCCR 333 ........................... 1.582
Sobam BV, Re. See Brown v City of London Corpn
Sobam BV and Satelscoop BV, Re, Brown v City of London Corpn. See Brown v City of London Corpn

Sobey (A Bankrupt), Re [1999] BPIR 1009 .......................................... 1.396
Society of Lloyds v Waters [2001] BPIR 698 ....................................... 1.395
Soden v British and Commonwealth Holdings plc [1998] AC 298, [1997] 4 All ER 353,
  [1997] 3 WLR 840, [1998] 2 LRC 225, [1997] 2 BCLC 501, [1997] BCC 952, [1997]
  41 LS Gaz R 28, [1997] NLJR 1546, (1997) Times, 22 October, [1997] Lexis Citation
  4216, [1997] All ER (D) 24, HL ............................................ 1.129, 1.582
Soden v Burns [1996] 3 All ER 967, [1996] 1 WLR 1512, [1996] 2 BCLC 636,
  [1997] BCC 308, (1996) Times, 5 July .......................................... 1.300
Sofaer v Anglo Irish Asset Finance plc [2011] EWHC 1480 (Ch), [2011] BPIR 1736
  .......................................................................... 1.59, 1.382
Solomons v Williams [2001] Lexis Citation 1606, [2001] BPIR 1123, [2001] All ER (D)
  299 (May) ................................................................... 1.423
Somerfield Stores Ltd v Spring (Sutton Coldfield) Ltd [2009] EWHC 2384 (Ch),
  [2010] 2 BCLC 452, [2009] 3 EGLR 57, [2009] 48 EG 104, [2009] All ER (D) 68
  (Oct) ....................................................................... 1.660
Somji v Cadbury Schweppes plc [2001] 1 WLR 615, [2001] 1 BCLC 498, (2001) Times,
  16 January, [2000] Lexis Citation 3500, [2001] BPIR 172, [2000] All ER (D) 2397,
  CSRC vol 24 iss 20/1 ..................................................... 1.65, 1.388
Sonatacus Ltd, Re [2007] EWCA Civ 31, [2007] 2 BCLC 627, [2007] BCC 186, [2007]
  BPIR 106, [2007] All ER (D) 203 (Jan) ......................................... 1.305
Souster v Carman Construction Co Ltd [1999] Lexis Citation 1864, [2000] BPIR 371
  .......................................................................... 1.168
South Barrule Slate Quarry Co, Re (1869) LR 8 Eq 688 ..................... 1.164, 1.200
South Coast Construction Ltd v Iverson Road Ltd [2017] EWHC 61 (TCC), [2017]
  1 All ER (Comm) 653, [2017] BLR 169, [2017] All ER (D) 114 (Jan) .......... 1.183, 1.660
South East Water v Kitoria Pty Ltd (1996) 14 ACLC 1328 ....................... 1.178
South India Shipping Corpn Ltd v Export-Import Bank of Korea [1985] 2 All ER 219,
  [1985] 1 WLR 585, [1985] BCLC 163, [1985] 1 Lloyd's Rep 413, [1985] FLR 106,
  [1985] PCC 125, 129 Sol Jo 268, [1985] LS Gaz R 1005 ........................ 1.281
South Kensington Co-operative Stores, Re (1881) 17 ChD 161, 50 LJ Ch 446, 29 WR
  662, 44 LT 471 ............................................................. 2.433
South London Fish Market Co, Re (1888) 39 ChD 324, 1 Meg 92, 37 WR 3, 60 LT 68, 4
  TLR 764, CA ................................................................ 1.279
South Luipaards Vlei Gold Mines Ltd, Re (1897) 13 TLR 504, CA ................. 1.174
South Wales Atlantic Steamship Co, Re (1876) 2 ChD 763, 46 LJ Ch 177, 35 LT 294,
  CA ......................................................................... 1.176
South West Car Sales Ltd (in liqation), Re [1998] BCC 163, [1997] Lexis Citation 2565
  .......................................................................... 1.622
Southern Cross Airlines Holdings Ltd v Arthur Anderson & Co (1998) 16 ACLC 485
  .......................................................................... 1.194
Southern Cross Group plc v Deka Immobilien Investment [2005] EWHC 3459 (Ch),
  [2005] BPIR 1010, [2005] All ER (D) 374 (Feb) ................................ 1.178
Southern Equities Corp Ltd (in liq), Re; England v Smith. See England v Smith
Southern Foundries (1926) Ltd v Shirlaw [1940] AC 701, [1940] 2 All ER 445, 109 LJKB
  461, 84 Sol Jo 464, 164 LT 251, 56 TLR 637, HL ............................. 1.677
Soutzos v Asombang [2010] EWHC 842 (Ch), [2010] BPIR 960, [2010] All ER (D) 213
  (Apr) ...................................................................... 1.393
Sowman v David Samuel Trust Ltd [1978] 1 All ER 616, [1978] 1 WLR 22, 36 P & CR
  123, 121 Sol Jo 757 ..................................................... 1.88, 1.180
Spaceright Europe Ltd v Baillavoine [2011] EWCA Civ 1565, [2012] 2 All ER 812,
  [2012] IRLR 111, [2012] ICR 520, [2012] NLJR 68, [2011] All ER (D) 106 (Dec),
  Spaceright Europe Ltd v Baillavoine ......................................... 1.617
Spaces London Bridge Ltd, Re [2018] EWHC 3099 (Ch), [2019] BPIR 660, [2018] All ER
  (D) 99 (Nov) ......................................................... 1.646, 2.150, 2.820
Spackman, Re ex p Foley (No 1) [1886–90] All ER Rep 1128 ..................... 1.398
Sparkasse Hilden Ratingen Verlbert v Benk [2012] EWHC 2432 (Ch), [2012] BPIR 1258,
  [2012] All ER (D) 88 (Sep) .................................................... 6.2
Specialised Mouldings Ltd (Chancery Division), Re (13 February 1987, unreported)
  .......................................................................... 1.88
Spicer, noters [2011] CSOH 87, 2011 SCLR 678, 2011 Scot (D) 3/6, CSOH .......... 1.160
Spiraflite Ltd, Re [1979] 2 All ER 766, [1979] 1 WLR 1096n ................... 1.300
Spirit Motorsport Ltd, Re [1996] 1 BCLC 684, [1997] BPIR 288 ................. 1.238
Sporting Options plc, Re [2004] EWHC 3128 (Ch), [2005] BCC 88, [2005] BPIR 435,
  [2004] All ER (D) 30 (Dec) ......................................... 1.663, 1.666, 2.164
Sports Betting Media Ltd, Re [2007] EWHC 2085 (Ch), [2008] 2 BCLC 89, [2008] BCC
  177, [2007] All ER (D) 123 (Jul) ............................................. 1.716

Spring Valley Properties Ltd v Harris. See Salmet International Ltd (in administration), Re
Squires (liquidators of SSSL Realisations (2002) Ltd) v AIG Europe (UK) Ltd. See SSSL
   Realisations (2002) Ltd (in liq), Re.
Stack v Dowden [2007] UKHL 17, [2007] 2 AC 432, [2007] 2 All ER 929, [2007] 2 WLR
   831, [2008] 2 P & CR 56, 9 ITELR 815, [2007] 1 FLR 1858, [2007] 2 FCR 280, [2007]
   Fam Law 593, [2007] NLJR 634, (2007) Times, 26 April, 151 Sol Jo LB 575, [2007]
   BPIR 913, [2007] 2 P & CR D28, [2007] All ER (D) 208 (Apr), HL .................. 1.455
Stallton Distribution Ltd, Re [2002] BCC 486 ....................................... 1.630
Standard Chartered Bank Ltd v Walker [1982] 3 All ER 938, [1982] 1 WLR 1410,
   [1982] Com LR 233, 10 LDAB 365, 126 Sol Jo 479, [1982] 2 EGLR 152,
   [1982] LS Gaz R 1137, 264 Estates Gazette 345 ............................. 1.78, 1.638
Standard Contract and Debenture Corpn, Re (1892) 8 TLR 485, CA ................. 1.281
Standard Manufacturing Co, Re [1891] 1 Ch 627, 60 LJ Ch 292, 2 Meg 418, 39 WR 369,
   [1891–4] All ER Rep 1242, 64 LT 487, 7 TLR 282, CA ...................... 1.77, 1.240
Stanford v Akers and McDonald (as Joint liquidators of Chesterfield United Inc,
   Appeal BVIHCMAP 2017/0019, 12 July 2018 ...................................... 1.220
Stanford International Bank Ltd, Re [2009] EWHC 1661 (Ch), [2009] BPIR 1157  .. 6.5, 7.2,
                                                                                7.3, 7.29
Stanford International Bank Ltd, Re [2009] EWHC 1441 (Ch), [2009] BPIR 1157 ...... 7.15
Stanford International Bank Ltd, Re [2010] EWCA Civ 137, [2011] Ch 33, [2010] 3 WLR
   941, [2010] Bus LR 1270, [2011] BCC 211, [2010] BPIR 679, [2010] All ER (D) 219
   (Apr) ................................................................. 2.134, 6.3, 7.15, 7.29
Stanhope Silkstone Collieries Co, Re (1879) 11 ChD 160, 48 LJ Ch 409, 27 WR 561, 40
   LT 204, CA ........................................................................ 1.181
Stanley v TMK Finance Ltd [2010] EWHC 3349 (Ch), [2011] BPIR 876, [2011] Bus LR
   D93, [2010] All ER (D) 295 (Dec) ................................................. 1.302
Stanley v Wilson [2017] BPIR 227 ................................................... 1.463
Stanley J Holmes & Sons Ltd v Davenham Trust plc [2006] EWCA Civ 1568, [2007] BCC
   485, [2006] All ER (D) 110 (Oct) ................................................. 1.688
Stanley & Watson v A Debtor (unreported, Ch D, 2019, Deputy ICC  ................. 1.180
Stanleybet UK Investments Ltd, Re [2011] EWHC 2820 (Ch), [2012] BCC 550 ....... 1.671
Stanton (F and E) Ltd, Re [1928] 1 KB 464, 97 LJKB 131, [1927] B & CR 187, 138 LT
   175, 44 TLR 118 ................................................................... 1.169
Star v O'Brien (1997) 15 ACLC 144 ................................................. 1.303
State Bank of India v Mallya [2019] EWHC 995 (QB), [2019] All ER (D) 96 (Apr)  .... 1.472
State Bank of India v Mallya [2020] EWHC 96 (Ch) ................................. 1.384
State Bank of New South Wales v Turner Corpn Ltd (1994) 14 ACSR 480 ............. 1.741
Statebourne, Re (Cryogenic) Ltd [2020] EWHC 231 (Ch) ..................... 1.645, 2.820
State of Wyoming Syndicate, Re [1901] 2 Ch 431, 70 LJ Ch 727, 8 Mans 311, 49 WR
   650, 45 Sol Jo 656, 84 LT 868, 17 TLR 631 ....................................... 1.138
Staubitz-Schreiber (Proceedings concerning): C-1/04 (2006) C-1/04, ECLI:EU:C:2006:39,
   [2006] ECR I-701, [2006] BCC 639, [2006] BPIR 510, [2006] All ER (D) 65 (Jan),
   EUCJ ..................................................................... 6.2, 6.21, 6.35
Stonham v Ramrattan [2010] EWHC 1033 (Ch), [2010] BPIR 1210 ........... 1.305, 1.459
Stooke v Taylor (1880) 5 QBD 565 ................................................. 1.175
Stead, Hazel & Co v Cooper [1933] 1 KB 840, 102 LJKB 533, [1933] B & CR 72,
   [1933] All ER Rep 770, 77 Sol Jo 117, 148 LT 384, 49 TLR 200 ....... 1.235, 1.743, 2.433
Stealth Construction Ltd, Re [2011] EWHC 1305 (Ch), [2012] 1 BCLC 297, [2011] BPIR
   1173, [2011] All ER (D) 239 (May) ................................................. 1.303
Steel Wing Co Ltd, Re [1921] 1 Ch 349, 90 LJ Ch 116, [1920] B & CR 160, [1920] All ER
   Rep 292, 65 Sol Jo 240, 124 LT 664 ....................................... 1.175, 1.176
Stein v Blake [1996] AC 243, [1995] 2 All ER 961, [1995] 2 WLR 710, [1995] 2 BCLC
   94, [1995] BCC 543, 13 LDAB 83, [1995] NLJR 760, (1995) Times, 19 May, HL ..... 1.59,
                                                                       1.159, 1.442, 2.852
Stein v Blake [1994] Ch 16, [1993] 4 All ER 225, [1993] 3 WLR 718, [1993] BCLC 1478,
   [1993] BCC 587, (1993) Times, 13 May; affd [1996] AC 243, [1995] 2 All ER 961,
   [1995] 2 WLR 710, [1995] 2 BCLC 94, [1995] BCC 543, 13 LDAB 83, [1995] NLJR
   760, (1995) Times, 19 May, HL ................................................... 2.852
Stella v Harris [2014] EWHC 4492 (Ch), [2015] BPIR 926 ......................... 1.353
Stella Metals (in liqation), Re [1997] BCC 626, [1996] Lexis Citation 5512, [1997] BPIR
   293 ........................................................................ 1.160, 1.706
Stephen and Hill, joint administrators of QMD Hotels Ltd, Noters [2010] CSOH 168,
   [2012] BCC 794, CtSess ........................................................... 1.233
Stephen Jones (Tc06009) [2017] Ukftt 567 (Tc) ................................... 1.515
Stericker v Horner [2012] BPIR 645 ............................................... 1.67
Stetzel Thomson & Co Ltd, Re (1988) 4 BCC 74, [1987] Lexis Citation 1191  .. 1.164, 1.220

Stevensdrake Ltd v Hunt [2015] EWHC 1527 (Ch), [2015] 4 Costs LR 639, [2015] BPIR
1462, [2015] All ER (D) 229 (May) ..................................................... 1.686
Stevenson v Newnham (1853) 13 CB 285, 22 LJCP 110, 17 Jur 600, 138 ER 1208,
20 LTOS 279, Exch .......................................................... 1.305
Stichting Shell Pensioenfonds v Krys [2014] UKPC 41, [2015] AC 616, [2015] 2 WLR
289, [2015] 2 All ER (Comm) 97, [2015] 4 LRC 117, [2015] 1 BCLC 597, (2015)
Times, 01 January, [2014] All ER (D) 280 (Nov), PC .................................. 6.35
Stockley Construction Company Ltd, Re (26 June 2000, ) .......................... 1.218
Stocznia Gdanska SA v Latreefers Inc (No 2) [2001] 2 BCLC 116, [2001] BCC 174,
(2000) Times, 15 March, [2000] Lexis Citation 2603, [2000] All ER (D) 148 .. 1.272, 1.281
Stocznia Gdynia SA v Bud-Bank Leasing Sp zoo [2010] BCC 255 ...................... 7.15
Stone v Vallance [2008] BPIR 236 ................................................. 2.530
Stone and Rolls Ltd v Micro Communications Inc [2005] EWHC 1052 (Ch),
[2005] All ER (D) 390 (May) ...................................................... 1.302
Stonegate Securities Ltd v Gregory [1980] Ch 576, [1980] 1 All ER 241, [1980] 3 WLR
168, 124 Sol Jo 495 .......................................................... 1.176, 1.178
Stonham (trustee in bankruptcy of Sebastian Satyanard Ramrattan) v Ramrattan [2011]
EWCA Civ 119, [2011] 4 All ER 392, [2011] 1 WLR 1617, [2011] BPIR 518,
[2011] All ER (D) 175 (Feb) .............................. 1.302, 1.397, 1.459, 1.462
Strand Capital Ltd, Re [2019] EWHC 1449 (Ch) ..................................... 1.617
Strategic Advantage SPC (for and on behalf of Arlington 1 SP and Arlington 3 SP) v ARL
O09 Ltd and other companies [2020] EWHC 3350 (Ch), [2020] All ER (D) 71 (Dec)
.................................................................... 1.630, 2.136
Street v Mountford [1985] AC 809, [1985] 2 All ER 289, [1985] 2 WLR 877, 50 P & CR
258, 17 HLR 402, 129 Sol Jo 348, [1985] 1 EGLR 128, [1985] LS Gaz R 2087, [1985]
NLJ Rep 460, 274 Estates Gazette 821, HL ..................................... 1.353, 1.85
Structures and Computers Ltd, Re [1998] 1 BCLC 292, [1998] BCC 348, (1997) Times,
3 October ..................................................... 1.671, 2.136
Sturgeon Central Asia Balanced Fund Ltd (in liq), Re [2019] EWHC 1215 (Ch), 169 NLJ
7842, [2019] 2 BCLC 412, [2019] BPIR 1035, [2019] All ER (D) 96 (May) .. 7.1, 7.15, 7.30
Sturgeon Central Asia Balanced Fund Ltd (in liq), Re Carter v Bailey (as foreign
representatives of Sturgeon Central Asia Balanced Fund Ltd) [2020] EWHC 123 (Ch),
[2020] 1 BCLC 600, [2020] All ER (D) 123 (Jan) ............................... 7.15, 7.30
Sugar Properties (Derisley Wood) Ltd, Re [1988] BCLC 146, 3 BCC 88 .............. 1.180
Suidair International Airways Ltd (in liqation), Re [1951] Ch 165, [1950] 2 All ER 920,
94 Sol Jo 742, 66 (pt 2) TLR 909 ................................................ 1.240
Sunberry Properties Ltd v Innovate Logistics Ltd (in administration) [2008] EWCA Civ
1321, [2009] 1 BCLC 145, [2009] BCC 164, [2008] All ER (D) 163 (Nov) .......... 1.660
Sunlight Incandescent Gas Lamp Co Ltd, Re (1900) 16 TLR 535 ..................... 1.270
Sunshine Porcelain Potteries Proprietary Ltd v Nash [1961] AC 927, [1961] 3 All ER 203,
[1961] 3 WLR 727, PC .......................................................... 1.630
Sunwing Vacation Inc, Re [2011] EWHC 1544 (Ch), [2012] 2 BCLC 104, [2011] BCC
889, [2011] BPIR 1524, [2011] All ER (D) 01 (Sep) ........................... 1.164, 1.207
Supercapital Ltd, Re [2020] EWHC 1685 (Ch), [2021] 1 BCLC 355 .................. 1.679
Supperstone v Auger [1999] BPIR 152 ............................................. 1.414
Supperstone v Hurst [2006] EWHC 2147 (Ch), [2006] BPIR 1263, [2006] All ER (D) 59
(Jun) ........................................................................ 1.414
Supperstone v Lloyd's Names Working Party [1999] Lexis Citation 2803, [1999] BPIR
832, [1999] All ER (D) 685 ................................................ 1.423, 1.427
Suppipat v Narongdej [2020] EWHC 3191 (Comm), [2020] Costs LR 1649, [2021] BPIR
756 ........................................................................ 1.302, 1.582
Supporting Link Ltd, Re [2004] EWHC 523 (Ch), [2005] 1 All ER 303, [2004] 1 WLR
1549, [2004] 2 BCLC 486, [2004] BCC 764, (2004) Times, 28 April, [2004] All ER (D)
396 (Mar) ..................................................................... 1.177
Surplus Properties (Huddersfield) Ltd, Re [1984] BCLC 89 ................... 1.143, 1.168
Sushinho Ltd [2011] All ER (D) 32 (Mar) ......................................... 1.176
Sussman (J and P) Ltd, Re [1958] 1 All ER 857, [1958] 1 WLR 519, 102 Sol Jo 347
.................................................... 2.321, 2.324, 2.820
Swain (JD) Ltd, Re [1965] 2 All ER 761, [1965] 1 WLR 909, 109 Sol Jo 329, CA .... 1.168,
1.178
Swaby v Lift Capital Partners Pty Ltd [2009] FCA 749 ............................. 1.183
Sweatfield Ltd, Re [1997] BCC 744, [1998] BPIR 276 ......................... 1.59, 1.65
Swift Advances plc v Ahmed [2015] EWHC 3265 (Ch), 165 NLJ 7678, [2016] WTLR
1059, [2016] BPIR 197, [2016] 1 P & CR D 41, [2015] All ER (D) 177 (Nov) ........ 1.582
Swindon Town Properties Ltd v Swindon Football Company Ltd [2003] BPIR 253,
[2002] All ER (D) 85 (Jul) ....................................................... 1.65

Swissair Schweizerische Luftverkehr-Aktiengesellschaft, Re [2009] EWHC 2099 (Ch), [2010] BCC 667, [2009] BPIR 1505, [2009] All ER (D) 153 (Aug) ..................... 7.34
Swissport (UK) Ltd v Aer Lingus Ltd [2007] EWHC 1089 (Ch), [2009] BCC 113, [2007] All ER (D) 197 (May) ...................................................... 2.852
Switch Services Ltd (in administration), Re, SB Corporate Solutions Ltd v Prescott [2012] Bus LR D91 ............................................................................ 1.630
Sykes & Son Ltd v Teamforce Labour Ltd [2012] EWHC 1005 (Ch), [2013] Bus LR 106, [2012] BPIR 1273, [2012] All ER (D) 173 (Apr) ..................................... 1.178
Symes (a debtor), Re, Kent Carpets Ltd v Symes [1995] 2 BCLC 651, [1996] BCC 137, [1996] BPIR 169 ..................................................................... 1.361
Symm & Company Ltd, Re [2020] EWHC 317 (Ch), [2020] All ER (D) 107 (Feb) ... 1.646, 2.820
Synthetic Technology Ltd, Re [1990] BCLC 378 ..................................... 1.679
Syska (acting as the administrator of Elektrim SA (in bankruptcy)) v Vivendi Universal SA [2009] EWCA Civ 677, [2009] 2 All ER (Comm) 891, [2010] 1 BCLC 467, [2010] BCC 348, [2009] NLJR 1033, [2009] Bus LR 1494, [2009] BPIR 1304, [2009] All ER (D) 91 (Jul) ......................................................... 6.1, 6.20
System Building Services Group Ltd (in liq), Re; Hunt (as liquidator of System Building Services Group Ltd) v Michie [2020] EWHC 54 (Ch), [2020] 1 BCLC 205, [2020] All ER (D) 91 (Jan) ......................................................... 1.618

# T

T & D Industries plc (in administration), Re; T & D Automotive Ltd (in administration), Re [2000] 1 All ER 333, [2000] 1 WLR 646, [2000] 1 BCLC 471, [2000] BCC 956, [1999] 46 LS Gaz R 37, (1999) Times, 23 November, [1999] Lexis Citation 3655, [1999] All ER (D) 1239 ..................................... 1.79, 1.414, 1.679, 1.685
T & N Ltd, Re [2005] EWHC 2870 (Ch), [2006] 3 All ER 697, [2006] 1 WLR 1728, [2006] 2 BCLC 374, [2006] BPIR 532, [2005] All ER (D) 211 (Dec) ........... 2.827, 2.829
TAG World Services Ltd, Re [2008] EWHC 1866 (Ch), [2008] All ER (D) 395 (Jul) ............................................................................... 1.177
TH Knitwear (Wholesale) Ltd, Re [1988] Ch 275, [1988] 1 All ER 860, [1988] 2 WLR 276, [1988] STC 79, [1988] BCLC 195, 4 BCC 102, 131 Sol Jo 1696, [1988] 4 LS Gaz R 35 ............................................................ 1.220, 1.618, 1.622
TJ Ross (Joiners) Ltd v High Range Developments Ltd 2000 SCLR 161 .............. 1.178
TM Kingdom Ltd (in admin), Re [2007] BCC 480 ................................... 1.696
TOC Investments Corpn v Beppler & Jacobson Ltd [2016] EWHC 20 (Ch), [2016] All ER (D) 37 (Jan); revsd sub nom Leibson Corpn v TOC Investments Corpn [2018] EWCA Civ 763, [2018] 2 Costs LR 293, [2018] All ER (D) 72 (Apr) ....................... 2.354
TPS Investments (UK) Ltd (in administration) Mark Grahame Tailby (administrator), , Re [2020] EWHC 1135 (Ch) ............................................................ 1.629
TSB Bank plc v Katz (1994) Times, 2 May, [1997] BPIR 147 ........................ 2.751
TSB Bank plc v Platts [1997] BPIR 151 ............................................. 1.381
TSB Bank plc v Platts [1998] 2 BCLC 1, [1998] 12 LS Gaz R 28, (1998) Times, 4 March, [1998] Lexis Citation 2565, [1998] Lexis Citation 3733, 142 Sol Jo LB 93, [1998] BPIR 284 ........................................................... 1.382, 2.530
TT Industries Ltd, Re [2006] BCC 372, [2006] BPIR 597 ........................... 1.693
TXU Europe German Finance BV, Re [2005] BCC 90, [2005] BPIR 209 ....... 1.151, 1.281
TXU Group plc, Re [2011] EWHC 2072 (Ch), [2012] BCC 363, [2012] BPIR 463, [2011] All ER (D) 104 (Jul) ......................................................... 1.67
TXU UK Ltd (in administration), Re [2002] EWHC 2784 (Ch), [2003] 2 BCLC 341, [2003] BPIR 1062, [2003] All ER (D) 437 (Mar) ................................... 1.683
Tack, Re [1998] Lexis Citation 2089, [2000] BPIR 164 ............................ 1.388
Tager v Westpac Banking Corpn [1997] 1 BCLC 313, [1998] BCC 73, (1996) Times, 24 December, [1997] BPIR 543 ................................... 1.65, 1.364, 2.909
Tagore Investments SA v Official Receiver [2008] EWHC 3495 (Ch), [2009] BPIR 392, [2009] All ER (D) 63 (Jan) ........................................................ 1.472
Tailby v HSBC Bank plc [2015] BPIR 143 ........................................... 1.459
Tailby (as joint administrators of TPS Investments (UK) Ltd ) v Hutchinson Telecom FZCO [2018] EWHC 360 (Ch), [2019] 1 BCLC 61, [2018] All ER (D) 15 (Mar) ...... 1.160
Tain Construction Ltd, Re [2003] EWHC 1737 (Ch), [2003] 1 WLR 2791, [2003] 2 BCLC 374, [2004] BCC 11, [2003] 30 LS Gaz R 31, (2003) Times, 8 July, [2003] BPIR 1188, [2003] All ER (D) 91 (Jun) ...................................... 1.180
Takavarasha v Newham London Borough Council [2004] EWHC 3232 (Ch), [2006] BPIR 311, [2004] All ER (D) 222 (Dec) ............................................ 2.527
Tallington Lakes Ltd v South Kesteven District Council [2012] EWCA Civ 443 ....... 2.338

Tamlin v Edgar [2011] EWHC 3949 (Ch), (2012) Times, 23 February, [2015] WTLR
485 .................................................................................................. 1.679
Tanner v Everitt [2004] EWHC 1130 (Ch), [2004] BPIR 1026, [2004] All ER (D) 192
(May) ............................................................................................... 1.64
Tanning Research Laboratories Inc v O'Brien [1990] LRC (Comm) 664, 169 CLR 332, 91
ALR 180, AusHC ................................................................................. 2.835
Tarragó da Silveira v Massa Insolvente da Espírito Santo Financial GroupSA (2018)
C-250/17, ECLI:EU:C:2018:398, [2018] 1 WLR 4148, [2018] BPIR 1516,
[2018] All ER (D) 29 (Jun), EUCJ ............................................... 6.1, 6.20
Tasarruf Mevduati Sigorta Fonu v Merrill Lynch Bank and Trust Co (Cayman) Ltd [2011]
UKPC 17, [2011] 4 All ER 704, [2012] 1 WLR 1721, 80 WIR 222, [2011] 5 LRC 190,
14 ITELR 102, [2011] BPIR 1743, [2011] All ER (D) 163 (Jun), PC .................. 1.396
Tate Building Services Ltd v B and M McHugh Ltd [2014] EWHC 2971 (TCC), [2014]
BPIR 1560 .......................................................................................... 1.59
Taunton Logs Ltd (in administration), Re [2020] EWHC 3480 (Ch), [2021] BPIR 427,
[2021] All ER (D) 18 (Jan) ..................................................................... 2.820
Tavistock Ironworks Co, Re (1871) 19 WR 672, 24 LT 605 ........................... 1.160
Taylor, Re [1934] NZLR 117 .................................................................. 1.220
Taylor (a bankrupt), Re [2006] EWHC 3029 (Ch), [2007] Ch 150, [2007] 3 All ER 638,
[2007] 2 WLR 148, [2007] BPIR 175, [2006] All ER (D) 288 (Nov) .................. 1.399
Taylor (J N) Finance Pty Ltd, Re, England v Purves [1999] 2 BCLC 256, (1998) Times,
29 January, [1998] BPIR 347 ....................................................... 1.300, 1.586
Taylor v Glenrinnes Farms Ltd [1994] 2 BCLC 522, 1993 SCLR 199, CtSess ......... 1.176
Taylor v Pace Developments Ltd [1991] BCC 406, (1991) Times, 7 May, [1991] Lexis
Citation 2813, CA ............................................................................... 1.178
Taylor v The MacDonald Partnership [2015] EWCA Civ 921 ......................... 1.395
Taylor Made Foods plc, Re (28 February 2010, unreported) ......................... 1.693
Taylor Pearson (Construction) Ltd (in administration), Re [2020] EWHC 2933 (Ch),
[2021] 1 BCLC 725, [2020] All ER (D) 88 (Nov) ............... 1.620, 1.668, 1.682, 2.167
Taylor Sinclair (Capital) Ltd, Re [2001] 2 BCLC 176, [2001] Lexis Citation 1485, [2002]
BPIR 203, [2001] All ER (D) 113 (Jun) ....................................................... 1.302
Taylors Industrial Flooring Ltd v M & H Plant Hire (Manchester) Ltd [1990] BCLC 216,
[1990] BCC 44, (1989) Times, 31 October ................................... 1.175, 1.178
Tchenguiz v Grant Thornton UK LLP [2015] EWHC 1864 (Comm), [2015] 2 BCLC 307,
[2015] All ER (D) 36 (Jul); affd sub nom Tchenguiz v Kaupthing Bank HF [2017]
EWCA Civ 83, [2018] QB 695, [2018] 2 WLR 834, [2017] 2 BCLC 299, [2017] All ER
(D) 40 (Mar) ............................................................................... 6.8, 6.9
Tea Corpn Ltd, Re, Sorsbie v Tea Corpn Ltd [1904] 1 Ch 12, 73 LJ Ch 57, 11 Mans 34,
52 WR 177, 48 Sol Jo 99, 89 LT 516, 20 TLR 57, CA .................................. 5.38
Telescriptor Syndicate Ltd, Re [1903] 2 Ch 174, 72 LJ Ch 480, 10 Mans 213, 51 WR 409,
88 LT 389, 19 TLR 271 ......................................................................... 1.200
Television Trade Rentals Ltd, Re [2002] EWHC 211 (Ch), [2002] BCC 807, [2002] BPIR
859, [2002] All ER (D) 259 (Feb) ................................................. 1.59, 1.586
Telia AB v Hillcourt (Docklands) Ltd (14 Feb 2006, unreported), ChD .............. 1.169
Tennant's Application, Re [1956] 2 All ER 753, [1956] 1 WLR 874, 100 Sol Jo 509,
CA ................................................................................................... 1.427
Tertiary Enterprises Ltd re (3 August 2006, unreported), ChD ....................... 1.270
Tesco Supermarkets Ltd v Nattrass [1972] AC 153, [1971] 2 All ER 127, [1971] 2 WLR
1166, 69 LGR 403, 135 JP 289, 115 Sol Jo 285, HL .................................... 1.303
Testro Bros Consolidated, Re [1965] VR 18, Vic S Ct .................................. 1.176
Tetteh v London Borough of Lambeth [2008] BPIR 241 ............................... 1.395
Thames Chambers Solicitors v Miah [2013] EWHC 1245 (QB), [2013] 4 Costs LR 582,
[2013] BPIR 650, [2013] All ER (D) 249 (May) ........................................... 1.396
Thames Plate Glass Co v Land and Sea Construction Telegraph Co (1871) 6 Ch App
643 .................................................................................................. 1.183
Thellusson, Re, ex p Abdy [1919] 2 KB 735, 88 LJKB 1210, [1918–1919] B & CR 249,
3 LDAB 211, [1918–19] All ER Rep 729, 63 Sol Jo 788, 122 LT 35, 35 TLR 732, CA
........................................................................................................ 1.622
Theophile v Solicitor-General [1950] AC 186, [1950] 1 All ER 405, 43 R & IT 180, 94
Sol Jo 208, 66 (pt 1) TLR 441, HL .......................................................... 1.380
Therm-a-Stor Ltd, Re [1996] 3 All ER 228, [1996] 1 WLR 1338, [1996] 2 BCLC 400,
(1996) Times, 29 March ........................................................................ 1.79
Thirty-Eight Building Ltd, Re [1999] 1 BCLC 416, [1999] OPLR 319, (1999) Times,
14 January, [1999] BPIR 620, [1998] All ER (D) 677 ................................... 1.303
Thirty-Eight Building Ltd (in liq), Re [2000] 1 BCLC 201, [2000] BCC 422, [1999] Lexis
Citation 2795, [2000] BPIR 158, [1999] All ER (D) 533 ............................... 2.814

Thoars (decd), Re, Reid v Ramlort Ltd [2002] EWHC 2416 (Ch), [2003] 1 BCLC 499, (2002) Times, 22 November, [2003] BPIR 489, [2002] All ER (D) 235 (Nov) ......... 1.302
Thoars (decd), Re, Reid v Ramlort Ltd [2004] EWCA Civ 800, [2005] 1 BCLC 331, 148 Sol Jo LB 877, [2004] BPIR 985, [2004] All ER (D) 85 (Jul) ............ 1.302, 1.305, 1.459
Thomas v D'Eye [2016] Lexis Citation 50, [2016] BPIR 883, [2016] All ER (D) 66 (May) ................................................................................................ 1.180
Thomas (trustees in bankruptcy of Edmondson) v Edmondson [2014] EWHC 1494 (Ch), [2014] 3 All ER 976, [2015] 1 WLR 1395, [2014] BPIR 1070, [2014] All ER (D) 96 (May) ...................................................................................... 1.427, 1.428
Thomas v Frogmore Real Estate Partners GP1 Ltd, Frogmore Real Estate Partners GP1 Ltd v Thomas [2017] EWHC 25 (Ch), [2017] 2 BCLC 101, [2017] BPIR 771, [2017] All ER (D) 73 (Jan) ................................................................ 1.698, 6.5
Thorne v Heard and Marsh [1895] AC 495, 64 LJ Ch 652, 11 R 254, 44 WR 155, 73 LT 291, 11 TLR 464, HL ............................................................................ 1.87
Thorne v Silverleaf [1994] 1 BCLC 637, [1994] BCC 109 ........................ 1.275, 1.276
Thornhill v Atherton [2004] EWCA Civ 1858, [2005] BPIR 437, [2004] All ER (D) 316 (Dec) ................................................................................................ 1.395
Thorniley v Revenue and Customs Comrs [2008] EWHC 124 (Ch), [2008] 1 WLR 1516, [2008] 1 BCLC 437, [2008] Bus LR 1076, [2008] BCC 213, [2008] All ER (D) 47 (Feb) ................................................................................................. 1.233
Thorpe (William) & Son, Re (1988) 5 BCC 156, [1988] Lexis Citation 1780 ... 1.168, 1.178
Three Rivers District Council v Bank of England [2002] EWCA Civ 1182, [2002] 4 All ER 881, [2003] 1 WLR 210, [2002] 39 LS Gaz R 40, (2002) Times, 4 October, [2002] All ER (D) 27 (Aug) ................................................................... 5.41
Thulin (a debtor), Re [1995] 1 WLR 165, [1995] 02 LS Gaz R 35 .................... 1.381
Thurso New Gas Co, Re (1889) 42 ChD 486, 1 Meg 330, 38 WR 156, 61 LT 351, 5 TLR 562 ..................................................................................................... 1.164
Thynne (Marchioness of Bath) v Thynne (Marquess of Bath) [1955] P 272, [1955] 3 All ER 129, [1955] 3 WLR 465, 99 Sol Jo 580, CA ............................... 2.814
Timbatec Pty Ltd, Re (1974) 24 FLR 30, Fed CA ........................... 1.175, 1.303
Timberland Ltd, Re (1979) 4 ACLR 259 ........................................... 2.396
Times Newspapers Ltd v McNamara [2013] Lexis Citation 66, [2013] BPIR 1092, [2013] All ER (D) 121 (Aug) ............................................................... 2.791
Timothy, Re [2005] EWHC 1885 (Ch), [2006] BPIR 329, [2005] All ER (D) 296 (Jul) ..................................................................................................... 1.67
Titan International Inc, Re [1998] 1 BCLC 102 ............................... 1.177, 1.281
Titterton v Cooper (1882) 9 QBD 473, 51 LJQB 472, 30 WR 866, [1881–5] All ER Rep 757, 46 LT 870, CA .................................................................... 1.235
Tokenhouse VB Ltd (formerly VAT Bridge 7 Ltd), Re [2020] EWHC 3171 (Ch), [2021] 2 All ER (Comm) 532, [2020] All ER (D) 86 (Oct) .............. 1.632, 1.633, 1.643, 2.820
Tombs v Moulinex SA [2004] EWHC 454 (Ch), [2004] 2 BCLC 397, [2004] All ER (D) 208 (Mar) .......................................................................................... 1.164
Tomkins (H J) & Son Ltd, Re [1990] BCLC 76 ...................................... 1.168
Tomlin Patent Horse Shoe Co Ltd, Re (1886) 55 LT 314 ........................... 1.174
Tomlinson (Trustee in Bankruptcy of Smalley) v Bridging Finance Ltd [2010] BPIR 759, CC ................................................................................... 1.398, 1.417
Top Brands Ltd v Sharma [2014] EWHC 2753 (Ch), [2015] 2 All ER 581, [2015] 1 All ER (Comm) 1142, [2015] 1 BCLC 546, [2015] BPIR 621, [2014] All ER (D) 32 (Aug); affd sub nom Top Brands Ltd v Sharma (as former Liquidator of Mama Milla Ltd) [2015] EWCA Civ 1140, [2017] 1 All ER 854, [2017] 1 All ER (Comm) 158, [2016] BPIR 111, [2015] All ER (D) 77 (Nov) ...................................................... 1.270
Toshoku Finance UK plc, Re, Kahn v IRC [2002] UKHL 6, [2002] 3 All ER 961, [2002] 1 WLR 671, [2002] STC 368, [2002] 1 BCLC 598, [2002] BCC 110, (2002) Times, 25 February, [2002] BPIR 790, [2002] All ER (D) 276 (Feb), HL .............. 1.757, 2.433
Totalbrand Ltd, Re [2020] EWHC 2917 (Ch), [2021] 2 All ER (Comm) 217, [2020] All ER (D) 14 (Nov) ................................................................. 1.314
Tottenham Hotspur plc v Edennote plc [1995] 1 BCLC 65, [1994] BCC 681 ... 1.178, 2.827
Tournier v National Provincial and Union Bank of England [1924] 1 KB 461, 93 LJKB 449, 29 Com Cas 129, 3 LDAB 305, [1923] All ER Rep 550, 68 Sol Jo 441, 130 LT 682, 40 TLR 214, CA .................................................................... 1.452
Town Investments Ltd Underlease, Re, McLaughlin v Town Investments Ltd [1954] Ch 301, [1954] 1 All ER 585, [1954] 2 WLR 355, 98 Sol Jo 162, 163 EG 191 ........... 1.440
Trading Partners Ltd, Re [2002] 1 BCLC 655, [2001] Lexis Citation 2168, [2002] BPIR 606, [2001] All ER (D) 68 (Sep) ............................................................ 1.300
Tradition (UK) Ltd v Ahmed [2008] EWHC 2946 (Ch), [2009] BPIR 626, [2008] All ER (D) 72 (Dec) ........................................................................ 1.59, 1.60, 1.65

Tramway Building and Construction Co Ltd, Re [1988] Ch 293, [1988] 2 WLR 640, [1987] BCLC 632, 3 BCC 443, 132 Sol Jo 460, [1988] 16 LS Gaz R 41, (1987) Times, 21 August .................. 1.180

Transbus International Ltd, Re [2004] EWHC 932 (Ch), [2004] 2 All ER 911, [2004] 1 WLR 2654, [2004] 2 BCLC 550, [2004] BCC 401, [2004] All ER (D) 293 (Apr) ..... 1.679, 1.685

Transfield ER Cape Ltd, Re [2010] EWHC 2851 (Ch) ........................... 7.33

Transfloors Pty Ltd v SWF Hoists & Industrial Equipment Pty Ltd (1985) 3 ACLC 66 .................................................. 1.175

Transworld Payments UK Ltd, Re [2020] EWHC 115 ............... 1.186, 2.433

Transworld Trading Ltd, Re [1998] Lexis Citation 3362, [1999] BPIR 628 ............ 1.303

Treasure Traders Corpn Ltd, Re [2005] EWHC 2774 (Ch), [2005] All ER (D) 25 (Dec) .................................................. 1.177

Treharne v Forrester [2003] EWHC 2784 (Ch), [2004] 1 FLR 1173, [2004] Fam Law 486, [2004] BPIR 338, [2003] All ER (D) 36 (Nov) ....................... 1.398

Trench Tubeless Tyre Co, Re, Bethell v Trench Tubeless Tyre Co [1900] 1 Ch 408, 69 LJ Ch 213, 8 Mans 85, 48 WR 310, 44 Sol Jo 260, 82 LT 247, 16 TLR 207, CA .. 1.138, 1.145

Trepca Mines Ltd, Re [1960] 3 All ER 304n, [1960] 1 WLR 1273, 104 Sol Jo 979, CA .................................................. 1.178, 2.835

Tri-Continental Exchange Ltd, Re (2006) 349 BR 627 .................... 7.29

Trident Fashions plc (in administration), Re, Anderson v Kroll Ltd [2004] EWHC 351 (Ch), [2004] 2 BCLC 28, [2004] All ER (D) 274 (Jan) ................. 1.693

Trident International Ltd v Barlow. See Hamlet International plc (in admin), Re; Trident International Ltd v Barlow

Trillium (Nelson) Properties Ltd v Office Metro Ltd [2012] EWHC 1191 (Ch), [2012] BCC 829, [2012] NLJR 714, [2012] BPIR 1049, [2012] All ER (D) 98 (May) .................................................. 6.1

Tru Floor Service Pty Ltd v Jenkins (No 2) [2006] FCA 632, Aust Fed Ct ............ 1.175

Truex v Toll [2009] EWHC 396 (Ch), [2009] 4 All ER 419, [2009] 1 WLR 2121, [2009] 2 FLR 250, [2009] Fam Law 474, [2009] NLJR 429, [2009] 5 Costs LR 758, [2009] BPIR 692, [2009] All ER (D) 98 (Mar) ....................... 1.382

Trustee in Bankruptcy of Gordon Robin Claridge v Gordon Robin Claridge [2011] EWHC 2047 (Ch), [2012] 1 FCR 388, [2011] BPIR 1529, [2011] All ER (D) 27 (Aug) .................................................. 1.459, 1.305

Tucker (a bankrupt), Re, ex p Tucker [1990] Ch 148, [1988] 1 All ER 603, [1988] 2 WLR 748, 132 Sol Jo 497, [1988] 15 LS Gaz R 33 ..................... 1.300, 1.492

Tucker v Atkins (trustee in bankruptcy of Tucker) [2013] EWHC 4469 (Ch), [2014] BPIR 1359 .................................................. 1.353

Tucker v Atkins [2014] EWHC 2260 (Ch), [2014] BPIR 1569 ............... 1.356

Tucker (joint supervisors of Energy Holdings (No 3) (in liq) v Gold Fields Mining LLC [2009] EWCA Civ 173, [2009] 1 BCLC 567, [2010] BCC 544, [2009] BPIR 704, [2009] All ER (D) 123 (Mar) .................................... 1.64, 1.65

Tudor Grange Holdings Ltd v Citibank NA [1992] Ch 53, [1991] 4 All ER 1, [1991] 3 WLR 750, [1991] BCLC 1009, 12 LDAB 28, (1991) Times, 30 April .............. 1.86

Tully, Re [2017] NICh 18 .................................................. 1.414

Tünkers France v Expert France (2017) C-641/16, ECLI:EU:C:2017:847, [2017] All ER (D) 80 (Nov), EUCJ .................................................. 6.8

Turner v Avis [2007] EWCA Civ 748, [2007] 4 All ER 1103, [2007] 2 FCR 695, [2007] Fam Law 979, [2007] 30 EG 132 (CS), (2007) Times, 22 August, 151 Sol Jo LB 986, [2007] BPIR 663, [2007] All ER (D) 309 (Jul), sub nom Avis v Turner [2008] Ch 218, [2008] 2 WLR 1, [2008] 1 FLR 1127, [2007] 3 EGLR 51, [2007] 48 EG 146 ........ 1.396

Turner v Avis [2009] 1 FLR 74, [2008] Fam Law 1185, [2008] BPIR 1143 ............ 1.455

Turner v Royal Bank of Scotland [2000] Lexis Citation 3293, [2000] BPIR 683, CA .................................................. 1.386, 2.550

Tweeds Garages Ltd, Re [1962] Ch 406, [1962] 1 All ER 121, [1962] 2 WLR 38, 105 Sol Jo 1085 .................................................. 1.175, 1.178

Tyler, Re, ex p Official Receiver [1907] 1 KB 865, 76 LJKB 541, 14 Mans 73, [1904–7] All ER Rep 181, 51 Sol Jo 291, 97 LT 30, 23 TLR 328, CA ............... 1.622

Tyne Chemical Co Ltd, Re (1874) 43 LJ Ch 354 .......................... 1.300

Tyneside Permanent Benefit Building Society, Re [1885] WN 148, 20 LJNC 130 ....... 2.327

## U

UB v VA (2019) C-493/18, ECLI:EU:C:2019:1046, [2020] 1 WLR 2955, [2020] 2 All ER (Comm) 444, [2020] All ER (D) 51 (Jan), EUCJ ..................... 6.13

UBS AG (as successor to Swiss Bank Corpn) v Omni Holding AG (in liqation) [2000] 1
WLR 916, [2000] 1 All ER (Comm) 42, [2000] 2 BCLC 310, [2000] BCC 593, [1999]
Lexis Citation 3036, [1999] All ER (D) 910 .......................................... 6.8
UBS AG New York v Fairfield Sentry Ltd (in liqation) (British Virgin Islands) [2019]
UKPC 20, [2019] 2 BCLC 1, [2019] BPIR 1054, [2019] All ER (D) 122 (May), PC ..... 7.34
UK Coal Operations Ltd, In the matter of [2013] EWHC 2581 (Ch), [2014] 1 BCLC 471,
[2013] All ER (D) 71 (Sep) ........................................................ 1.666
UK-Euro Group plc, Re [2006] EWHC 2102 (Ch), [2007] 1 BCLC 812, [2006] All ER
(D) 394 (Jul) ..................................................................... 1.177
UK Housing Alliance (North West) Ltd (in administration), Re [2013] EWHC 2553 (Ch),
[2013] All ER (D) 127 (Aug) ...................................................... 1.660
UK Steelfixers Ltd, Re [2012] EWHC 2409 (Ch), [2012] BCC 751 .............. 1.617, 1.630
UOC Corpn, Re [1997] 2 BCLC 569 ........................................... 2.354, 2.355
UOC Corpn, Re, Alipour v Ary [1997] 1 WLR 534, [1997] 1 BCLC 557, [1997] BCC
377, (1996) Times, 18 December ................................................... 1.178
US Ltd, Re (1983) 1 BCC 98, 985 ............................................ 1.234, 2.320
Ulf Kazimierz Radziejewski v Kronofogdemyndigheten i Stockholm: C-461/11 (2012)
C-461/11, ECLI:EU:C:2012:9626, EUCJ ......................................... 6.2, 6.4
Ulster Bank Ltd v Taggart [2018] NIMaster 7 ............................... 2.907, 2.913
Ultra Motorhomes International Ltd, Re [2005] EWHC 872 (Ch), [2006] BCC 57, [2006]
BPIR 115, [2005] All ER (D) 380 (May) ............................................ 6.8
Ultraframe (UK) Ltd v Rigby [2005] EWCA Civ 276, [2005] All ER (D) 139 (Jan) .... 1.743
Unadkat & Co (Accounts) Ltd v Bhardwaj (former liquidator of Isher Fashions Ltd)
[2007] BCC 452 ............................................................. 2.306, 2.435
Unidare plc v Cohen [2005] EWHC 1410 (Ch), [2006] Ch 489, [2005] 3 All ER 730,
[2006] 2 WLR 974, [2006] 2 BCLC 140, [2005] BPIR 1472, [2005] All ER (D) 12
(Jul) ...................................................................... 1.620, 1.700
Union Accident Insurance Co Ltd, Re [1972] 1 All ER 1105, [1972] 1 WLR 640, [1972]
1 Lloyd's Rep 297, 340, 116 Sol Jo 274 ........................................... 1.188
Unit 2 Windows Ltd, Re [1985] 3 All ER 647, [1985] 1 WLR 1383, [1986] BCLC 31,
1 BCC 99, 129 Sol Jo 829 ......................................................... 2.852
Unite the Union v Nortel Networks UK Ltd (in administration) [2010] EWHC 826 (Ch),
[2010] 2 BCLC 674, [2010] IRLR 1042, [2010] BCC 21, (2010) Times, 18 May, [2010]
BPIR 1003, [2010] All ER (D) 164 (Apr) ...................................... 1.660, 2.829
United Drug (UK) Holdings Ltd v Bilcare Singapore Pte Ltd [2013] EWHC 4335 (Ch),
[2014] All ER (D) 190 (Jan) ....................................................... 7.33
United Stock Exchange Co Ltd, Re [1884] WN 251, 51 LT 687 ..................... 1.178
Up Energy Development Group Ltd, re [2017] SC (Bda) 85 Com ................... 1.178
Uralkali v Rowley [2020] EWHC 3442 (Ch) ................................. 1.691, 1.692
Urmston Grange Steamship Co Ltd, Re (1901) 45 Sol Jo 555, 17 TLR 553, CA ....... 1.160

## V

VST Enterprises Ltd Interactive, Re [2021] EWHC 887 (Ch), [2021] All ER (D) 67
(Apr) ............................................................................. 1.630
VTB Capital plc v Nutritek International Corp [2013] UKSC 5, [2013] 2 AC 337, [2013]
1 All ER 1296, [2013] 2 WLR 398, [2013] 1 All ER (Comm) 1009, [2013] 1 BCLC
179, [2013] 1 Lloyd's Rep 466, [2013] All ER (D) 47 (Feb), SC ..................... 6.64
Vadher v Weisgard [1996] Lexis Citation 3050, [1998] BPIR 295 ................... 1.388
Van Buggenhout v Banque Internationale a Luxembourg SA: C-251/12 (2013) C-251/12,
ECLI:EU:C:2013:566, [2013] All ER (D) 158 (Nov), EUCJ .......................... 6.33
Van Gansewinkel Groep B.V, Re [2015] EWHC 2151 (Ch), [2016] 2 BCLC 138, [2015]
Bus LR 1046, [2015] All ER (D) 241 (Jul) .......................................... 6.2
Varden Nuttall Ltd v Nuttall [2018] EWHC 3868 (Ch), [2019] BPIR 738, [2018] All ER
(D) 172 (May) ..................................................................... 1.59
Ve Interactive Ltd (in administration), Re, Ve Vegas Investors IV LLC v Shinners [2018]
EWHC 186 (Ch), [2018] All ER (D) 34 (Mar) ................. 1.160, 1.617, 1.705, 2.196
Vedmay Ltd, Re [1994] 1 BCLC 676, 69 P & CR 247, 26 HLR 70, [1994] 1 EGLR 74,
[1994] 10 EG 108, (1993) Times, 21 October ...................................... 1.239
Vickers v Mitchell [2004] All ER (D) 414 (May) ................................. 1.423
Videology Ltd, Re [2018] EWHC 2186 (Ch), [2019] BCC 195, [2018] BPIR 1795,
[2018] All ER (D) 149 (Aug) ......................... 6.5, 7.3, 7.15, 7.29, 7.30, 7.34
Vidiofusion Ltd, Re [1975] 1 All ER 76n, [1974] 1 WLR 1548, 118 Sol Jo 848 ....... 2.321,
                                                                          2.324, 2.820
Vieira v Revenue and Customs Comrs [2017] EWHC 936 (Ch), [2017] 4 WLR 86, [2017]
STC 1328, [2017] BPIR 1062, [2017] All ER (D) 32 (May) ...... 1.178, 1.382, 2.530, 2.550

Vink v Tuckwell [2008] VSC 100, [2008] 216 FLR 309 ............................ 1.270
Vinyls Italia Spa v Mediterranea di Navigazione Spa (2017) C-54/16,
 ECLI:EU:C:2017:433, [2018] 1 WLR 543, [2017] All ER (D) 60 (Jun), EUCJ .......... 6.18
Virgin Active Holdings Ltd and other companies, Re [2021] EWHC 814 (Ch),
 [2021] All ER (D) 44 (Apr) ......................................................... 5.38
Virgin Active Holdings Ltd and other companies, Re [2021] EWHC 1246 (Ch),
 [2021] All ER (D) 100 (May) .................................................. 1.58, 5.38
Virgin Atlantic Airways Ltd, Re [2020] EWHC 2191 (Ch), [2021] 1 BCLC 87 ......... 5.38
Virgin Atlantic Airways Ltd, Re [2020] EWHC 2376 (Ch), [2021] 1 BCLC 105,
 [2020] All ER (D) 08 (Sep) .................................................. 2.35, 5.38
Virgo Systems Ltd, Re [1990] BCLC 34, 5 BCC 833 ............................... 2.814
Virtualpurple Professional Services Ltd, Re [2011] EWHC 3487 (Ch), [2012] 2 BCLC
 330, [2012] BCC 254, [2012] NLJR 179, [2012] All ER (D) 149 (Jan), CSRC vol 35 iss
 23/1 .................................................................... 1.643, 2.820
Viscount St Davids v Lewis [2015] EWHC 2826 (Ch), [2015] BPIR 1471, [2015] All ER
 (D) 73 (Oct) ....................................................................... 1.423
Vlieland-Boddy v Dexter Ltd [2003] EWHC 2592 (Ch), [2004] BPIR 235, [2003] All ER
 (D) 423 (Oct) ............................................................... 1.61, 1.357

# W

WBSL Realisations 1992 Ltd, Re; Re Ward Group plc [1995] 2 BCLC 576, [1995] BCC
 1118 ............................................................................. 1.682
WF Fearman Ltd (No 2), Re (1988) 4 BCC 141 ................................... 2.136
Wadling v Oliphant (1875) 1 QBD 145, 45 LJQB 173, 24 WR 246, 33 LT 837 ....... 1.396
Walden v Atkins [2013] EWHC 1387 (Ch), [2013] BPIR 943, [2013] All ER (D) 353
 (May) ........................................................................... 1.396
Walkden Sheet Metal Co Ltd, Re [1960] Ch 170, [1959] 3 All ER 333, [1959] 3 WLR
 616, 103 Sol Jo 833 ...................................................... 1.240, 1.241
Walker v National Westminster Bank plc [2015] EWHC 315 (Ch), [2016] BCC 355
 ................................................................................. 1.716
Walker v WA Personnel Ltd [2002] BPIR 621 .............................. 1.302, 1.305
Walker Morris (a firm) v Khalastchi [2001] 1 BCLC 1, [2000] Lexis Citation 3649,
 [2000] All ER (D) 994 ..................................................... 1.89. 1.360
Wallace (as liquidator of Carna Meats (UK) Ltd) v Wallace [2019] EWHC 2503 (Ch),
 [2020] 1 WLR 1176, [2020] 1 All ER (Comm) 429, [2020] 1 BCLC 380, [2020] BPIR
 299, [2019] All ER (D) 07 (Oct) ..................................... 1.300, 1.492, 6.23
Wallace v Universal Automatic Machines Co [1894] 2 Ch 547, 63 LJ Ch 598, 1 Mans
 315, 7 R 316, [1891–4] All ER Rep 1156, 70 LT 852, 10 TLR 501, CA .............. 2.872
Wallace LLP v Yates [2010] EWHC 1098 (Ch), [2010] BPIR 1041, [2010] All ER (D) 81
 (Jun) ........................................................................... 1.382
Ward v Official Receiver [2012] BPIR 1073, CC ................................. 1.396
Ward v Perks [2007] EWHC 3073 (Ch), 151 Sol Jo LB 743, [2007] BPIR 1305,
 [2007] All ER (D) 422 (May) ..................................................... 1.303
Warley Continental Services Ltd v Johal (2002) Times, 28 October, [2004] BPIR 353,
 [2002] All ER (D) 224 (Oct) ...................................... 1.65, 1.364, 1.423
Warne v GDK Financial Solutions Pty Ltd [2006] NSWSC 464, (2006) 233 ALR 181
 ................................................................................. 1.742
Warnford Investments Ltd v Duckworth [1979] Ch 127, [1978] 2 All ER 517, [1978] 2
 WLR 741, 76 P & CR 295, 122 Sol Jo 63 ....................................... 1.235
Wasu Edwards (trustee in bankruptcy of Wasu) v Aurora Leasing Ltd [2021] EWHC 96
 (Ch), [2021] BPIR 259 .................................................. 1.180, 1.398
Watchorn v Jupiter Industries Ltd. See Husky Group Ltd, Re
Watford Printers Ltd (in liq), Re [2018] EWHC 329 (Ch) ......................... 1.159
Watts v Midland Bank plc [1986] BCLC 15, 2 BCC 98, 961 ......................... 1.86
Wave Lending Ltd v Parmar [2017] EWHC 681 (Ch), [2019] BPIR 451 .............. 1.384
Wavern Engineering Co Ltd, Re (1987) 3 BCC 3, [1986] Lexis Citation 1112 ......... 2.327
Wear Engine Works Co, Re (1875) LR 10 Ch App 188, 44 LJ Ch 256, 23 WR 735, 32 LT
 314, [1874–80] All ER Rep Ext 1889, DC .................................. 1.138, 1.176
Wearmouth Crown Glass Co, Re (1882) 19 ChD 640, 30 WR 316, 45 LT 757 ........ 2.433
Webb v Webb: C-294/92 (1994) C-294/92, ECLI:EU:C:1994:193, [1994] QB 696, [1994]
 3 All ER 911, [1994] ECR I-1717, [1994] 3 WLR 801, (1994) Times, 27 June, EUCJ
 ................................................................................. 1.433
Webb v Whiffin (1872) LR 5 HL 711, 42 LJ Ch 161, HL ........................... 1.129
Weddell v JA Pearce & Major [1988] Ch 26, [1987] 3 All ER 624, [1987] 3 WLR 592,
 131 Sol Jo 1120 ................................................................. 1.429

Wehmeyer v Wehmeyer [2001] 2 FLR 84, [2001] BPIR 548 .................... 1.385, 2.829

Weir (as trustee in bankruptcy of Claire Elizabeth Hilsdon) v Hilsdon [2017] EWHC 983 (Ch), [2017] BPIR 1088, [2017] All ER (D) 33 (May) ........................ 1.391, 1.427

Weisgard v Pilkington [1995] BCC 1108, [1995] Lexis Citation 2150 ................. 1.303

Welsby v Brelec Installations Ltd (in liq) [2000] 2 BCLC 576, [2001] BCC 421, (2000) Times, 18 April, [2000] Lexis Citation 3163, [2001] BPIR 210, [2000] All ER (D) 515 .................................................................................... 1.64, 1.388

Welsh Brick Industries Ltd, Re [1946] 2 All ER 197, 90 Sol Jo 430, CA ............. 1.178

Welsh Development Agency v Export Finance Co Ltd [1992] BCLC 148, [1992] BCC 270, (1991) Times, 28 November ........................................... 1.298, 1.415

Wentworth Sons Sub-Debt SARL v Lomas [2017] EWHC 3158 (Ch), [2018] 2 BCLC 696, [2017] All ER (D) 39 (Dec) ..................................................... 2.835

West End Networks Ltd (in liq), Re; Secretary of State for Trade and Industry v Frid [2004] UKHL 24, [2004] 2 AC 506, [2004] 2 All ER 1042, [2004] 2 WLR 1279, [2004] 2 BCLC 1, [2004] BCC 525, [2004] NLJR 770, (2004) Times, 14 May, 148 Sol Jo LB 631, [2004] BPIR 841, [2004] All ER (D) 180 (May), HL ..................... 2.852

West End Quay Estate Management, Re (6 February 2017, unreported) ............. 1.696

West Park Golf & Country Club, Re [1997] 1 BCLC 20 ........................... 1.630

Westaway v Durkan [2016] EWHC 3101 (Ch) ....................................... 1.175

Westbury v Twigg & Co [1892] 1 QB 77, 61 LJQB 32, 40 WR 208, 66 LT 225 ....... 1.164

Westdock Realisations Ltd, Re [1988] BCLC 354, 4 BCC 192, (1988) Times, 25 January .................................................................................... 1.79

Western Benefit Building Society (1864) 33 Beav 368, 33 LJ Ch 179, 55 ER 409 ...... 2.320

Western Intelligence Ltd v KDO Label Printing Machines Ltd [1998] BCC 472, (1998) Times, 15 July, [1998] Lexis Citation 1800 .................................. 1.275

Western of Canada Oil, Lands and Works Co, Re (1873) LR 17 Eq 1, 43 LJ Ch 184, 22 WR 44 .................................................................... 1.178, 1.251

Western Welsh International System Buildings Ltd, Re (1985) 1 BCC 99 . 1.159, 1.180, 1.304

Westlowe Storage and Distribution Ltd (in liqation), Re [2000] 2 BCLC 590, [2000] BCC 851, [1999] Lexis Citation 3647, [1999] All ER (D) 1108 ........................ 1.270

Westmead Consultants Ltd, Re, Ward v Evans [2002] 1 BCLC 384, [2001] Lexis Citation 1831, [2001] All ER (D) 37 (Dec) ................................................... 1.300

Westminster City Council v Treby [1936] 2 All ER 21, 80 Sol Jo 465 ................ 1.84

Westminster Corpn v Haste [1950] Ch 442, [1950] 2 All ER 65, 49 LGR 67, 114 JP 340, 66 (pt 1) TLR 1083 ............................................................. 1.84

Westmoreland Green and Blue Slate Co v Feilden [1891] 3 Ch 15, 60 LJ Ch 680, 40 WR 23, 65 LT 428, 7 TLR 585, CA ..................................................... 1.203

Westshield Ltd v Whitehouse [2013] EWHC 3576 (TCC), [2014] Bus LR 268, [2014] 1 EGLR 1, [2014] BPIR 317, [2013] All ER (D) 292 (Nov) ..................... 1.59

Westways Garage Ltd, Re [1942] Ch 356, [1942] 2 All ER 147, 111 LJ Ch 294, 86 Sol Jo 217, 58 TLR 292 .................................................................. 1.201

Whig v Whig [2007] EWHC 1856 (Fam), [2008] 1 FLR 453, [2007] Fam Law 1127, [2008] Fam Law 201, [2007] BPIR 1418 ........................................... 1.395

White v Davenham Trust Ltd [2010] EWHC 2748 (Ch), [2011] Bus LR 615, [2011] BCC 77, [2011] BPIR 280, [2010] All ER (D) 31 (Nov); affd [2011] EWCA Civ 747, [2012] 1 BCLC 123, [2011] Bus LR 1443, [2011] 27 EG 76 (CS), [2011] BPIR 1187, [2011] All ER (D) 230 (Jun), CSRC vol 35 iss 11/2 ........................... 1.308, 1.386

Whitehead v Household Mortgage Corp plc [2002] EWCA Civ 1657, [2003] 1 All ER 319, [2003] 1 WLR 1173, [2003] 1 All ER (Comm) 263, [2003] 2 FCR 369, [2003] 04 LS Gaz R 32, (2002) Times, 29 November, 146 Sol Jo LB 262, 147 Sol Jo LB 26, [2003] BPIR 1482, [2002] All ER (D) 203 (Nov) ................................ 1.62, 1.399

Whitehouse v Wilson (liquidator of Vol-Mec Ltd). See Wilson v Whitehouse

Whitfield v Bin Issa Al Jaber [2013] EWHC 3925 (Ch) ............................. 1.716

Wiemer & Trachte GmbH (in liq) v Tadzher (2018), ECLI:EU:C:2018:902, C-296/17 [2019] BPIR 252, [2018] All ER (D) 76 (Nov), EUCJ ................................. 6.8

Wightman v Bennett [2005] BPIR 470 ............................................ 1.270

Wilcock v Duckworth [2005] BPIR 682 ............................................ 1.395

Wilcox v Tait [2006] EWCA Civ 1867, [2007] 2 FLR 871, [2007] 3 FCR 611, [2007] Fam Law 988, [2007] Fam Law 667, [2007] BPIR 262, [2007] All ER (D) 167 (Mar) ...... 1.455

Wilkinson v IRC [1998] BPIR 418 ........................................... 1.380, 2.777

Willgress v Scaife [2011] EWCA Civ 728 .......................................... 1.263

Williams, Re [2002] EWHC 1393 (Ch), [2003] BPIR 545, sub nom Williams v Dreamings Ltd (in liqation) [2002] All ER (D) 153 (Jun) .......................... 1.414

Williams v Bateman [2009] EWHC 1760 (Ch), [2009] BPIR 973, [2009] All ER (D) 317 (Jul) ........................................................................ 1.442

Williams (trustee of the insolvent estate of John Owen Napier Lawrence decd) v Lawrence [2011] EWHC 2001 (Ch), [2011] BPIR 1761 ........................................ 1.398

Williams (trustee of the property of Nassim Mohammed) v Mohammed [2011] EWHC 3293 (Ch), [2011] BPIR 1787 ...................................... 1.481

Williams (trustee of the property of Nassim Mohmmed) v Mohammed (No 2) [2012] BPIR 238 .................................................................. 1.491

Williams v Taylor [2012] EWCA Civ 1443, [2013] BPIR 133, [2012] All ER (D) 262 (Oct) ................................................................... 1.582

Williams Pickles plc, Re [1996] 1 BCLC 681, [1996] BCC 408, (1996) Times, 13 February, 140 Sol Jo LB 65 ......................................... 1.164

Willmont (as joint liquidators of Webinvest Ltd) v Willmont (as joint trustees in bankruptcy of Shlosberg) [2017] EWHC 2446 (Ch), [2018] BPIR 182, [2017] All ER (D) 64 (Oct) ................................................. 1.407, 1.492

Wills v Corfe Joinery Ltd (in liqation) [1998] 2 BCLC 75, [1997] BCC 511, (1997) Times, 21 January, sub nom Corfe Joinery Ltd, Re [1997] 7 LS Gaz R 29, [1997] BPIR 611 ........................................................................ 1.303, 1.304

Wilmott Forests Ltd (in liqation), Re [2013] HCA 51 ............................... 1.235

Wilmott Trading Ltd (in liqation) (No 2), Re [1999] 2 BCLC 541, [1999] 25 LS Gaz R 29, (1999) Times, 17 June, [1999] Lexis Citation 2793, [1999] All ER (D) 583, sub nom Wilmott Trading Ltd, Re; Henry v Environment Agency [2000] BCC 321 ...... 1.158, 1.257

Wilson, Re, ex p Vine (1878) 8 ChD 364, 47 LJ Bcy 116, 26 WR 582, 38 LT 730, CA ........................................................................... 1.396

Wilson v PLT Pipetech Pty Ltd (1989) 7 ACLC 191 ............................. 1.251

Wilson v SMC Properties Ltd [2015] EWHC 870 (Ch), [2015] 2 BCLC 173, [2015] All ER (D) 115 (Apr) ....................................... 1.180, 1.398

Wilson v SMC Properties Ltd [2016] EWHC 444 (Ch), [2016] BPIR 1074, [2016] All ER (D) 246 (Jan) ...................................................... 1.180

Wilson v Specter Partnership [2007] EWHC 133 (Ch), [2007] 6 Costs LR 802, [2007] BPIR 649, [2007] All ER (D) 05 (Feb) ......................................... 2.814

Wilson v United Counties Bank Ltd [1920] AC 102, 88 LJKB 1033, [1918–19] All ER Rep 1035, 122 LT 76, HL ..................................................... 1.396

Wilson v Whitehouse [2006] EWCA Civ 1688, [2007] BPIR 230, [2006] All ER (D) 93 (Dec), sub nom Whitehouse v Wilson (liquidator of Vol-Mec Ltd) [2007] BCC 595 .... 1.164

Wilson v Williams (Trustee in Bankruptcy for John Wilson) [2015] EWHC 1841 (Ch), [2015] BPIR 1319, [2015] All ER (D) 275 (Jun) ......................................... 1.391

Wilson and Sharp Investments Ltd v Harbourview Developments Ltd [2015] EWCA Civ 1030, 162 ConLR 154, [2015] BPIR 1496, [2015] All ER (D) 08 (Nov) .............. 1.178

Wilton UK Ltd (suing on behalf of itself as shareholder in Banks Mount Oswald Ltd, fifth defendant) v Shuttleworth [2017] EWHC 2195 (Ch), [2018] Bus LR 258, [2017] All ER (D) 21 (Sep) ................................................ 1.399

Wiltshire Iron Co, Re, ex p Pearson (1868) LR 3 Ch App 443, 37 LJ Ch 554, 16 WR 682, 18 LT 423, CACh .............................................................. 1.180

Winding-up board of Landsbanki Islands HF v Mills [2010] CSOH 100, [2011] 2 BCLC 437, 2010 Scot (D) 21/7, CSOH ........................................... 6.9

Windsor Refrigerator Co Ltd v Branch Nominees Ltd [1961] Ch 375, [1961] 1 All ER 277, [1961] 2 WLR 196, 7 LDAB 259, 105 Sol Jo 205, CA ......................... 1.77

Windsor Steam Coal Co (1901) Ltd, Re [1929] 1 Ch 151, 98 LJ Ch 147, 140 LT 80, CA ......................................................................... 1.220

Wine National Pty Ltd, Re [2014] NSWSC 507 .......................... 1.183, 1.200

Winis Trading Pty Ltd, Re (1984) 3 ACLC 39 ......................... 1.176

Winter v IRC [1963] AC 235, [1961] 3 All ER 855, [1961] 3 WLR 1062, 40 ATC 361, [1961] TR 349, 105 Sol Jo 929, HL ..................................... 1.515

Winterbottom (G) (Leeds) Ltd, Re [1937] 2 All ER 232, 81 Sol Jo 377 ............... 1.240

Wise v Lansdell [1921] 1 Ch 420, 90 LJ Ch 178, [1920] B & CR 145, [1920] All ER Rep 648, 124 LT 502, 37 TLR 167 .......................................... 1.417

Wisepark Ltd, Re [1994] BCC 221 ......................................... 1.59

Witney Town Football and Social Club, Re [1994] 2 BCLC 487, [1993] BCC 874, (1993) Times, 19 November .......................................... 1.280

Woking UDC (Basingstoke Canal) Act 1911, Re [1914] 1 Ch 300, 12 LGR 214, 78 JP 81, 83 LJ Ch 201, 110 LT 49, 30 TLR 135, CA ................................... 1.141

Wolf International Ltd [2021] 1 WLUK 104 ............................ 1.630

Wolf Rock (Cornwall) Ltd v Langhelle [2020] EWHC 2500 (Ch), [2021] 2 All ER (Comm) 625, [2020] Bus LR 2348, [2020] All ER (D) 08 (Oct) .................. 1.176

Wood v Baker [2015] EWHC 2536 (Ch), [2015] BPIR 1524 .................. 1.423, 1.452

Wood v Capita Insurance Services Ltd [2017] UKSC 24, [2017] 4 All ER 615, [2017] 2 WLR 1095, [2018] 1 All ER (Comm) 51, 171 ConLR 1, 167 NLJ 7741, [2017] All ER (D) 182 (Mar), SC ............................................................ 1.64

Wood v Targett (1997) 23 ACSR 291 ............................................ 1.160

Wood (supervisor of a company voluntary arrangement in respect of the Heart Hospital Ltd) v The Heart Hospital Ltd [2009] BPIR 1538 ................ 1.64, 1.65

Wood and Martin (Bricklaying Contractors) Ltd, Re [1971] 1 All ER 732, [1971] 1 WLR 293, 115 Sol Jo 57 ................................................................ 1.79

Woodbridge v Smith [2004] BPIR 247 ........................................... 1.414

Woodland-Ferrari v UCL Group Retirement Benefits Scheme [2002] EWHC 1354 (Ch), [2003] Ch 115, [2002] 3 All ER 670, [2002] 3 WLR 1154, (2002) Times, 17 July, [2002] BPIR 1270, [2002] All ER (D) 88 (Jul) ........................................ 1.393

Woodley v Woodley (No 2) [1993] 4 All ER 1010, [1994] 1 WLR 1167, [1993] 2 FLR 477, [1993] 2 FCR 661, [1993] 2 FCR 660, [1993] Fam Law 471, [1993] NLJR 475n, (1993) Times, 15 March ....................................................... 1.482

Woods (Bristol) Ltd, Re [1931] 2 Ch 320, 100 LJ Ch 335, [1931] B & CR 17, [1931] All ER Rep 777, 75 Sol Jo 458, 145 LT 444, 47 TLR 464 ............... 1.241

Woolsey v Payne [2015] EWHC 968 (Ch), [2015] BPIR 933, [2015] GCCR 13049, [2015] All ER (D) 24 (May) ...................................................... 1.395

Wordsworth v Dixon [1994] Lexis Citation 2624, [1997] BPIR 337, CA ........ 1.396

Working Project Ltd, Re, Fosterdown Ltd, Re, Davies Flooring (Southern) Ltd, Re [1995] 1 BCLC 226, [1995] BCC 197, (1994) Times, 27 October ............... 1.257

World Class Homes Ltd, Re [2004] EWHC 2906 (Ch), [2005] 2 BCLC 1, [2004] All ER (D) 79 (Nov) ................................................................. 1.630

Worldspreads Ltd, Re [2012] EWHC 1263 (Ch) ................................ 6.3

Wormleighton and another (joint administrators of Fortuna Fix Ltd (in administration)) v Salamander Invest A/S [2020] EWHC 2369 (Ch), [2020] All ER (D) 66 (Sep) ......... 1.671

Worthing Royal Sea House Hotel Co, Re [1872] WN 74 ......................... 2.324

Worthley v England (1994) 14 ACSR 407 ........................................ 1.207

Wreck Recovery and Salvage Co, Re (1880) 15 ChD 353, 29 WR 266, [1874–80] All ER Rep 755, 43 LT 190, CA ............................................................ 1.742

Wright, Re, ex p Willey (1883) 23 ChD 118, 52 LJ Ch 546, 31 WR 553, 48 LT 380, CA ........................................................................... 1.300

Wright v HMV Ecommerce Ltd and another company [2019] EWHC 903 (Ch), [2019] 2 BCLC 288, [2019] BPIR 1310, [2019] All ER (D) 172 (Jan) ............... 2.820

Wright v Nationwide Building Society [2009] EWCA Civ 811, [2010] Ch 318, [2010] 2 WLR 1097, [2009] 2 BCLC 695, [2009] 3 EGLR 39, [2009] 40 EG 132, [2009] 31 EG 73 (CS), [2009] BPIR 1047, [2009] All ER (D) 305 (Jul) ........................... 1.472

Wright v Official Receiver [2001] BPIR 196, CC ......................... 1.354, 1.358

Wright Hassall LLP v Morris (administrator of Marketbalance Ltd) [2012] EWCA Civ 1472, [2012] BPIR 1310, [2012] All ER (D) 198 (Nov) ........................... 1.686

Wyley v Exhall Coal Mining Co Ltd (1864) 33 Beav 538, 55 ER 478 ............ 1.183

Wyvern Developments Ltd, Re [1974] 2 All ER 535, [1974] 1 WLR 1097, 118 Sol Jo 531 ........................................................................ 1.220, 1.622

## X

X (a bankrupt), Re [1996] BPIR 494 ............................................. 1.393

X (Application to open Insolvency Proceedings), Re [2014] ILPr 35 ............... 6.21

X v Service Navigation de Plaisance Boat Service [2014] ILPr 24 .................. 6.58

X-Fab Semiconductor Foundries AG v Plessey Semiconductors Ltd [2014] EWHC 3190 ........................................................................... 1.660

Xyllyx plc (No 2), Re [1992] BCLC 378 ......................................... 1.177

XYZ (acting as liq of ABC Ltd) v HM Revenue and Customs [2010] EWHC 1645 (Ch), [2010] NLJR 905, [2011] SWTI 1939, [2010] BPIR 1297, [2010] All ER (D) 139 (Jun) ........................................................................... 1.300

## Y

Yagerphone Ltd, Re [1935] Ch 392, 104 LJ Ch 156, [1934–1935] B & CR 240, [1935] All ER Rep 803, 79 Sol Jo 162, 152 LT 555, 51 TLR 226 ................... 1.303

Yang v Official Receiver [2017] EWCA Civ 1465, [2018] Ch 178, [2018] 2 WLR 307, [2018] RVR 152, 167 NLJ 7767, (2017) Times, 06 December, (2017) Times, 13 December, [2018] BPIR 255, [2017] All ER (D) 65 (Oct) ........... 1.178, 1.395, 1.502

Yate Collieries and Limeworks Co, Re [1883] WN 171 ........................... 1.175

Yates (a bankrupt), Re; Carman (trustee of the estate in bankruptcy) v Yates [2004] EWHC 3448 (Ch), [2005] BPIR 476, [2004] All ER (D) 373 (Nov) .................. 1.302

Yehuda Gershon Crammer V West Bromwich Building Society [2012] Ewca Civ 517, [2012] Bpir 963 ........................................................... 1.395, 1.502

Yeovil Glove Co Ltd, Re [1965] Ch 148, [1964] 2 All ER 849, [1964] 3 WLR 406, 8 LDAB 267, 108 Sol Jo 499, CA .................................................... 1.309

Yew Bon Tew v Kenderaan Bas Mara [1983] 1 AC 553, [1982] 3 All ER 833, [1982] 3 WLR 1026, 126 Sol Jo 729, PC ...................................... 1.630

York Gas Ltd (In Creditors' Voluntary Liq), Re [2010] EWHC 2275 (Ch), [2011] BCC 447 .................................................................................. 1.160

Young, Re [2014] EWHC 4315 (Ch) ....................................................... 1.489

Young, Re, Allen (trustee in bankruptcy of Young) v Young [2017] Lexis Citation 50, [2017] BPIR 1116, [2017] All ER (D) 65 (Apr) ...................................... 1.622

Young v Hamilton [2010] NICh 11, [2010] BPIR 1468 ...................... 1.396, 1.434

Young v Official Receiver [2010] EWHC 1591 (Ch), [2010] BPIR 1477 . 1.235, 1.396, 1.434

## Z

ZM v E.A. Frerichs (2021) C-73/20, EUCJ ......................................... 6.18

Zandfarid v Bank of Credit and Commerce International SA (in liqation) [1996] 1 WLR 1420, [1997] 1 FLR 274, [1997] 1 FCR 78, [1996] BPIR 501 ...................... 1.384

Zebra Industrial Projects Ltd (in liqation), Re [2004] EWHC 549 (Ch), [2005] BCC 104, [2005] BPIR 1022 ........................................................... 1.64

Zegna III Holdings Inc (in administration), Re; BLV Realty [2009] EWHC 2994 (Ch), [2010] BPIR 277 ............................................................... 1.691

Zetta Jet Pte Ltd (Asia Aviation Holdings Pte Ltd, intervener) [2019] SGHC 53 ........ 7.30

Zinc Hotels (Investment) Ltd v Beveridge [2018] EWHC 1936 (Ch) .... 1.620, 1.630, 1.705, 1.709, 1.720

Zirceram Ltd (in liqation), Re; J Paterson Brodie & Son (a firm) v Zirceram Ltd (in liqation) [2000] 1 BCLC 751, [2000] BCC 1048, [1999] Lexis Citation 4109, [1999] All ER (D) 1399 ......................................................... 1.160, 1.168

Zoom UK Distribution Ltd (in administration), Re [2021] EWHC 800 (Ch), [2021] All ER (D) 31 (Apr) ................................................... 1.643, 2.820

Decisions of the European Court of Justice are listed below numerically. These decisions are also included in the preceding alphabetical list.

C-133/78: Gourdain v Nadler [1979] ECR 733, [1979] 3 CMLR 180, EUCJ ........... 6.8

C-294/92: Webb v Webb C-294/92, ECLI:EU:C:1994:193, [1994] QB 696, [1994] 3 All ER 911, [1994] ECR I-1717, [1994] 3 WLR 801, (1994) Times, 27 June, EUCJ ....................................................................................... 1.433

C-294/02: European Commission v AMI Semiconductor Belgium BVBA C-294/02, ECLI:EU:C:2005:172, [2005] ECR I-2175, [2005] All ER (D) 315 (Mar), EUCJ ......... 6.9

C-1/04: Staubitz-Schreiber (Proceedings concerning) C-1/04, ECLI:EU:C:2006:39, [2006] ECR I-701, [2006] BCC 639, [2006] BPIR 510, [2006] All ER (D) 65 (Jan), EUCJ ............................................................... 6.2, 6.21, 6.35

C-341/04: Eurofood IFSC Ltd, Re C-341/04, ECLI:EU:C:2006:281, [2006] Ch 508, [2006] ECR I-3813, [2006] 3 WLR 309, [2006] All ER (EC) 1078, [2007] 2 BCLC 151, [2005] BCC 1021, [2006] BCC 397, [2006] BPIR 661, [2006] All ER (D) 20 (May), EUCJ ...................................................... 6.3, 6.4, 6.5, 6.64

C-339/07: Seagon v Deko Marty Belgium NV C-339/07, ECLI:EU:C:2009:83, [2009] ECR I-767, [2009] 1 WLR 2168, [2009] Bus LR 1151, [2009] BCC 347, [2009] All ER (D) 112 (Feb), EUCJ ............................................... 6.8

C-444/07: Civil proceedings concerning MG Probud Gdynia sp z o o C-444/07, ECLI:EU:C:2010:24, [2010] ECR I-417, [2010] BCC 453, [2010] All ER (D) 17 (Feb), EUCJ .................................................................... 6.9, 6.21

C-111/08: SCT Industri AB i Likvidation v Alpenblume AB C-111/08, ECLI:EU:C:2009:419, [2009] ECR I-5655, [2010] Bus LR 559, [2009] All ER (D) 47 (Jul), EUCJ .................................................................. 6.1, 6.8
C-292/08: German Graphics Graphische Maschinen GmbH v Schee C-292/08, ECLI:EU:C:2009:544, [2009] ECR I-8421, [2009] All ER (D) 75 (Sep), EUCJ . 6.8, 6.9, 6.12
C-396/09: Interedil Srl v Fallimento Interedil Srl C-396/09, ECLI:EU:C:2011:671, [2011] ECR I-9915, [2012] Bus LR 1582, [2012] BCC 851, [2011] BPIR 1639, [2011] All ER (D) 195 (Oct), EUCJ .................................. 6.2, 6.5
C-112/10: Procureur-General Bij Het Hof Van Beroep Te Antwerpen v Zaza Retail BV C-112/10, ECLI:EU:C:2011:743, [2011] ECR I-11525, [2012] BPIR 438, EUCJ ......... 6.5
C-191/10: Rastelli Davide e C Snc v Hidoux (in his capacity as liquidator appointed by the court for the company Médiasucre International) C-191/10, ECLI:EU:C:2011:838, [2012] All ER (EC) 239, [2013] 1 BCLC 329, EUCJ ................................. 6.64
C-213/10: F-Tex SIA v Lietuvos-Anglijos UAB "Jadecloud-Vilma" C-213/10, ECLI:EU:C:2012:215, [2013] Bus LR 232, EUCJ ................................. 6.2, 6.8
C-527/10: Erste Bank Hungary Nyrt v Magyar Allam abd C - 527/10, ECLI:EU:C:2012:417, [2012] NLJR 962, [2012] All ER (D) 62 (Jul), EUCJ ............. 6.10
C-116/11: Bank Handlowy w Warszawie SA v Christanapol sp. zoo C-116/11, ECLI:EU:C:2012:7261, [2013] Bus LR 956, [2013] BPIR 174, [2012] All ER (D) 300 (Nov), EUCJ ............................... 6.2, 6.4, 6.34, 6.45
C-461/11: Ulf Kazimierz Radziejewski v Kronofogdemyndigheten i Stockholm C-461/11, ECLI:EU:C:2012:9626, EUCJ ...................................... 6.2, 6.4
C-85/12: LBI hf v Kepler Capital Markets SA C-85/12, ECLI:EU:C:2013:697, [2013] All ER (D) 301 (Oct), EUCJ ................................. 6.9, 6.20
C-251/12: Van Buggenhout v Banque Internationale a Luxembourg SA C-251/12, ECLI:EU:C:2013:566, [2013] All ER (D) 158 (Nov), EUCJ .......................... 6.33
C-328/12: Schmid v Hertel C-328/12, ECLI:EU:C:2014:6, [2014] 1 WLR 633, 164 NLJ 7593, [2014] BPIR 504, [2014] All ER (D) 221 (Jan), EUCJ ...................... 6.1, 6.8
C-157/13: Nickel & Goeldner Spedition GmbH v Kintra UAB C-157/13, ECLI:EU:C:2014:2145, [2015] QB 96, [2014] 3 WLR 1299, [2015] RTR 75, [2014] All ER (D) 129 (Sep), EUCJ ............................. 6.2, 6.8
C-295/13: H v HK C-295/13, ECLI:EU:C:2014:2410, [2014] All ER (D) 50 (Dec), EUCJ ................................................................ 6.8
C-327/13: Burgo group SpA v Illochroma SA (in liq) C-327/13, ECLI:EU:C:2014:2158, [2015] 1 WLR 1046, [2014] All ER (D) 114 (Sep), EUCJ .............................. 6.5
C-557/13: Lutz v Bauerle C-557/13, ECLI:EU:C:2015:227, [2015] Bus LR 855, [2015] All ER (D) 139 (Apr), EUCJ ............................... 6.10, 6.18
C-649/13: Comite d'entreprise de Nortel networks SA v Rogeau C-649/13, ECLI:EU:C:2015:384, [2016] QB 109, [2015] 3 WLR 1275, [2015] 2 BCLC 349, [2015] All ER (D) 143 (Jun), EUCJ ............................... 6.5, 6.34
C-310/14: Nike European Operations Netherlands BV v Sportland Oy C-310/14, ECLI:EU:C:2015:690, [2016] 1 BCLC 297, [2015] All ER (D) 151 (Oct), EUCJ ........ 6.18
C-594/14: Kornhaas v Thomas Dithmar, acting as liquidator of the assets of Kornhaas Montage und Dienstleistung Ltd, EUCJ .......................................... 6.8, 6.9
C-195/15: SCI Senior Home, in administration, v Gemeinde Wedemark C-195/15, ECLI:EU:C:2016:804, [2018] BPIR 173, [2016] All ER (D) 23 (Nov), EUCJ ........... 6.10
C-212/15: ENEFI Energiahatékonysági Nyrt v Directia Generala Regionala a Finantelor Publice Brasov (DGRFP) C-212/15, ECLI:EU:C:2016:841, [2016] All ER (D) 110 (Nov), EUCJ ................................................................ 6.9
C-54/16: Vinyls Italia Spa v Mediterranea di Navigazione Spa, ECLI:EU:C:2017:433, [2018] 1 WLR 543, [2017] All ER (D) 60 (Jun), EUCJ .......................... 6.18
C-641/16: Tünkers France v Expert France (2017), ECLI:EU:C:2017:847, [2017] All ER (D) 80 (Nov), EUCJ ....................................................... 6.8
C-250/17: Tarragó da Silveira v Massa Insolvente da Espírito Santo Financial GroupSA (2018), ECLI:EU:C:2018:398, [2018] 1 WLR 4148, [2018] BPIR 1516, [2018] All ER (D) 29 (Jun), EUCJ .................................... 6.1, 6.20
C-296/17: Wiemer & Trachte GmbH (in liq) v Tadzher (2018), ECLI:EU:C:2018:902, [2019] BPIR 252, [2018] All ER (D) 76 (Nov), EUCJ .......................... 6.8
C-535/17: NK v BNP Paribas Fortis NV (2019), ECLI:EU:C:2019:96, [2019] All ER (D) 25 (Feb), EUCJ .......................................................... 6.8
C-47/18: Skarb v Stephan Riel Case (ECLI:EU:C:2019:754, (18 September 2019, unreported) ........................................................... 6.8
C-198/18: CeDe Group AB v KAN Sp. z o.o. (30 April 2019, unreported) ..... 6.8, 6.9, 6.11
C-493/18: UB v VA (2019), ECLI:EU:C:2019:1046, [2020] 1 WLR 2955, [2020] 2 All ER (Comm) 444, [2020] All ER (D) 51 (Jan), EUCJ ................................. 6.13
ZM v E.A. Frerichs (2021) C-73/20, EUCJ .......................................... 6.18

# INTRODUCTION TO THE INSOLVENCY LEGISLATION

[0.1]

Our starting point in this book is the Insolvency Act 1986 ('the Act'). The need for this legislation resulted from the work done by the Insolvency Law Review Committee and contained in its Report, titled *Insolvency Law and Practice* (Cmnd 8558) – known as 'the Cork Report' – handed down in 1982. The Cork Report made many recommendations and a good number of them were taken up by the Government. From the earliest times, and at the time of the Cork Committee's work, UK insolvency law was provided for mainly in two pieces of legislation: the Bankruptcy Act for personal insolvency and the Companies Act for corporate insolvency. The Committee advocated unified legislation, something that already existed in the United States.

The Insolvency Act 1986 represented a major reform of insolvency law in the UK. The process that led to the advent of this legislation began with the enactment of the Insolvency Act 1985. It provided for the bankruptcy of individuals and partly for the insolvency of companies, but the Companies Act 1985 still governed aspects of corporate insolvency[1]. The Insolvency Act became law on 30 October 1985, but few of its provisions became operative. The Government had decided to put forward a fresh Insolvency Bill. This latter Bill, to become the Insolvency Act 1986, was to act as a consolidating statute in relation to most of the Insolvency Act 1985[2] and to the parts of the Companies Act 1985 which covered corporate insolvency, so giving us unified legislation[3]. At the same time the Government decided to consolidate the law as it related to company director disqualification, and so the Company Directors' Disqualification Act 1986 was enacted. This legislation and the Insolvency Act began to operate from 29 December 1986. Contemporaneously, the Insolvency Rules 1986 came into force. While personal and corporate insolvency are now contained within the four corners of the same statute, the statute does not provide for a unified system per se. This is because, in the main, separate procedures and rules are maintained for the two forms of insolvency.

There have been a number of pieces of insolvency legislation enacted subsequent to the advent of the Insolvency Act 1986, both primary and secondary. The Insolvency Act 2000 is of particular note, although the biggest change came with the enactment of the Enterprise Act 2002. Part 10 of that legislation introduced a number of critical changes to both corporate and personal insolvency. Other legislation has been enacted, like the Enterprise Act 2002, that is not dedicated to insolvency law, but amends the Insolvency Act 1986 in

1

some way. In recent times there has been the Deregulation Act 2015 and the Small Business Enterprise and Employment Act 2015. The former included one Schedule, Schedule 6, which addresses some issues relating to insolvency. The Small Business Enterprise and Employment Act 2015 made even more important amendments to insolvency law and practice. Like the Deregulation Act, this legislation also addressed several areas of law. The amendments made by these two pieces of legislation to insolvency law have been included in the Insolvency Act.

Another piece of relatively recent legislation is the Insolvency (England and Wales) Rules 2016. These Rules came into force on 6 April 2017 and have been long awaited. The Insolvency Service indicated some years ago that it wished to provide a consolidated version of the Insolvency Rules (the 1986 Rules were amended by 28 different statutory instruments over the years) and to take into account in such a consolidation changes in practice and technology that have occurred since 1986. The Insolvency Rules Committee worked hard for a long time on producing the Rules, seeking to take into account stakeholder input. Besides consolidating the Rules and reducing repetition, the 2016 Rules restructured the Rules and updated the language. Also they modernise the Rules to take account of the changes made to the Insolvency Act by the Deregulation Act 2015 and the Small Business, Enterprise and Employment Act 2015 and in particular amendments enabling modern methods of communication and decision making to be used in place of paper communications and physical meetings[4], although both are still possible. The Rules also see the discontinuation of the use of statutory forms.

Very recently, the Parliament enacted a new statute, the Corporate Insolvency and Governance Act 2020, that encompassed plans that the Government has had for some while to introduce a moratorium procedure that was not attached to any particular insolvency regime and that was designed to facilitate corporate rescue. The Act also included provisions which were introduced to response to the COVID-19 pandemic that hit the country and many parts of the world hard. Many of these latter provisions were temporary in nature. The Act is discussed elsewhere in this volume.

[1]   For example, winding up in ss 501–650 and 659–674.
[2]   For example, ss 12–14, 16, 17 and Sch 2 were consolidated into the Company Directors' Disqualification Act 1986.
[3]   Sections 467–650 and 659–674.
[4]   See the Explanatory Memorandum to the Insolvency (England and Wales) Rules which are accessible at: http://www.legislation.gov.uk/uksi/2016/1024/pdfs/uksiem_20161024_en.pdf.

# INSOLVENCY ACT 1986

**[1.1]**

As explained in the Introduction, this legislation was a result of a comprehensive review of UK insolvency law and practice undertaken by the Cork Committee from 1977 until 1982. The Act is the first time that the UK has had unified insolvency legislation. Until this legislation was enacted, personal insolvency was covered by the various Bankruptcy Acts and corporate insolvency was covered by the various Companies Acts. But besides covering insolvent companies the legislation also deals with the liquidation and receivership of solvent companies. While the legislation is unified to a certain extent, there are significant parts that are devoted to either companies or individuals. The same level of unification as the Americans have was not achieved.

The legislation is divided broadly into three Groups of Parts. The first Group addresses corporate insolvency (ss 1–251, inclusive of a definition Part). The second group deals with personal insolvency, including bankruptcy. It covers ss 252–385, again including a Part addressing interpretation issues. The third Group (ss 386–444) deals with miscellaneous matters, including important aspects relevant to the administration of insolvency practice, and many of the provisions cover both personal and corporate insolvency regimes. The major elements of the legislation are Parts. The larger Parts are then divided into Chapters. The two largest Parts are Part IV dealing with liquidation, and Part IX dealing with bankruptcy. The Schedules to the Act are more important than schedules attached to many statutes. Of particular importance is Sch B1, which houses most of the provisions that deal with administrations following changes brought about by the enactment of the Enterprise Act 2002.

As one might expect, the statute is long and quite complex in places. The legislation covers the following corporate insolvency regimes: company voluntary arrangements, administrations, administrative receiverships, provisional liquidations, and liquidations. The following personal insolvency regimes are covered: individual insolvency arrangements, interim receiverships, debt relief orders and bankruptcies.

Until the advent of the Enterprise Act 2002 the Act was only amended in relatively minor ways. But the Enterprise Act led to some extensive changes. These are addressed in the *Introduction to the Enterprise Act*, found later in the book. Provisions in the Enterprise Act that addressed corporate insolvency became operative from 15 September 2003, and the personal insolvency provisions from 1 April 2004. Amendments to the Act brought about by the Deregulation Act 2015 and the Small Business, Enterprise and Employment Act 2015 have also made changes to most insolvency regimes.

# INSOLVENCY ACT 1986

## ARRANGEMENT OF SECTIONS

### THE FIRST GROUP OF PARTS
### COMPANY INSOLVENCY; COMPANIES WINDING UP

### PART A1
### MORATORIUM

*Chapter 1 Introductory*

| | | |
|---|---|---|
| A1 | Overview | 1.3 |
| A2 | Eligible companies | 1.4 |

*Chapter 2 Obtaining a Moratorium*

| | | |
|---|---|---|
| A3 | Obtaining a moratorium by filing or lodging documents at court | 1.5 |
| A4 | Obtaining a moratorium for company subject to winding-up petition | 1.6 |
| A5 | Obtaining a moratorium for other overseas companies | 1.7 |
| A6 | The relevant documents | 1.8 |
| A7 | Beginning of moratorium and appointment of monitor | 1.9 |
| A8 | Obligations to notify where moratorium comes into force | 1.10 |

*Chapter 3 Length of Moratorium*

*Initial period*

| | | |
|---|---|---|
| A9 | End of the moratorium | 1.11 |

*Extension of moratorium*

| | | |
|---|---|---|
| A10 | Extension by directors without creditor consent | 1.12 |
| A11 | Extension by directors with creditor consent | 1.13 |
| A12 | Creditor consent for the purposes of section A11 | 1.14 |
| A13 | Extension by court on application of directors | 1.15 |
| A14 | Extension while proposal for CVA pending | 1.16 |
| A15 | Extension by court in the course of other proceedings | 1.17 |

*Early termination on certain grounds*

| | | |
|---|---|---|
| A16 | Company enters into insolvency procedure etc | 1.18 |

*Obligations to notify change in end of moratorium*

| | | |
|---|---|---|
| A17 | Obligations to notify change in end of moratorium | 1.19 |

*Chapter 4 Effects of Moratorium*

*Introductory*

| | | |
|---|---|---|
| A18 | Overview and construction of references to payment holidays | 1.20 |

*Publicity about moratorium*

| | | |
|---|---|---|
| A19 | Publicity about moratorium | 1.21 |

*Effect on creditors etc*

| | | |
|---|---|---|
| A20 | Restrictions on insolvency proceedings etc | 1.22 |
| A21 | Restrictions on enforcement and legal proceedings | 1.23 |
| A22 | Floating charges | 1.24 |
| A23 | Enforcement of security granted during moratorium | 1.25 |

*Notification of insolvency proceedings*

| | | |
|---|---|---|
| A24 | Duty of directors to notify monitor of insolvency proceedings etc | 1.26 |

*Restrictions on transactions*

| | | |
|---|---|---|
| A25 | Restrictions on obtaining credit | 1.27 |
| A26 | Restrictions on grant of security etc | 1.28 |
| A27 | Prohibition on entering into market contracts etc | 1.29 |

*Restrictions on payments and disposal of property*

| | | |
|---|---|---|
| A28 | Restrictions on payment of certain pre-moratorium debts | 1.30 |
| A29 | Restrictions on disposal of property | 1.31 |
| A30 | Restrictions on disposal of hire-purchase property | 1.32 |

*Disposals of property free from charges etc*

| | | |
|---|---|---|
| A31 | Disposal of charged property free from charge | 1.33 |
| A32 | Disposal of hire-purchase property | 1.34 |

*Effect of contravention of certain provisions of Chapter*

| | | |
|---|---|---|
| A33 | Contravention of certain requirements imposed under this Chapter | 1.35 |

*Chapter 5 The Monitor*

| | | |
|---|---|---|
| A34 | Status of monitor | 1.36 |
| A35 | Monitoring | 1.37 |
| A36 | Provision of information to monitor | 1.38 |
| A37 | Application by monitor for directions | 1.39 |
| A38 | Termination of moratorium by monitor | 1.40 |
| A39 | Replacement of monitor or appointment of additional monitor | 1.41 |
| A40 | Application of Part where two or more persons act as monitor | 1.42 |
| A41 | Presumption of validity | 1.43 |

*Chapter 6 Challenges*

| | | |
|---|---|---|
| A42 | Challenge to monitor's actions | 1.44 |
| A43 | Challenges to monitor remuneration in insolvency proceedings | 1.45 |
| A44 | Challenge to directors' actions | 1.46 |
| A45 | Challenge brought by Board of the Pension Protection Fund | 1.47 |

*Chapter 7 Offences: General*

| | | |
|---|---|---|
| A46 | Offence of fraud etc during or in anticipation of moratorium | 1.48 |
| A47 | Offence of false representation etc to obtain a moratorium | 1.49 |
| A48 | Prosecution of delinquent officers of company | 1.50 |

*Chapter 8 Miscellaneous and General*

*Special rules for certain kinds of company etc*

| | | |
|---|---|---|
| A49 | Regulated companies: modifications to this Part | 1.51 |
| A50 | Power to modify this Part etc in relation to certain companies | 1.52 |
| A51 | Power to make provision in connection with pension schemes | 1.53 |

*Floating charges*

| | | |
|---|---|---|
| A52 | Void provisions in floating charge documents | 1.54 |

*Interpretation of this Part*

| | | |
|---|---|---|
| A53 | Meaning of "pre-moratorium debt" and "moratorium debt" | 1.55 |
| A54 | Interpretation of this Part: general | 1.56 |

*Regulations*

| | | |
|---|---|---|
| A55 | Regulations | 1.57 |

PART I
COMPANY VOLUNTARY ARRANGEMENTS

*The proposal*

| | | |
|---|---|---|
| 1 | Those who may propose an arrangement | 1.59 |
| 1A | (*Repealed*) | |
| 2 | Procedure where nominee is not the liquidator or administrator | 1.60 |
| 3 | Consideration of proposal | 1.61 |

*Consideration and implementation of proposal*

| | | |
|---|---|---|
| 4 | Decisions of meetings the company and its creditors | 1.62 |
| 4A | Approval of arrangement | 1.63 |
| 5 | Effect of approval | 1.64 |
| 6 | Challenge of decisions | 1.65 |
| 6A | False representations, etc | 1.66 |
| 7 | Implementation of proposal | 1.67 |
| 7A | Prosecution of delinquent officers of company | 1.68 |
| 7B | Arrangements coming to an end prematurely | 1.69 |

PART II
ADMINISTRATION

| | | |
|---|---|---|
| 8 | Administration | 1.70 |

PART III
RECEIVERSHIP

CHAPTER I
RECEIVERS AND MANAGERS (ENGLAND AND WALES)

*Preliminary and general provisions*

| | | |
|---|---|---|
| 28 | Extent of this Chapter | 1.72 |
| 29 | Definitions | 1.73 |
| 30 | Disqualification of body corporate from acting as receiver | 1.74 |
| 31 | Disqualification of bankrupt or person in respect of whom a debt relief order is made | 1.75 |
| 32 | Power for court to appoint official receiver | 1.76 |

*Receivers and managers appointed out of court*

| | | |
|---|---|---|
| 33 | Time from which appointment is effective | 1.77 |
| 34 | Liability for invalid appointment | 1.78 |
| 35 | Application to court for directions | 1.79 |
| 36 | Court's power to fix remuneration | 1.80 |
| 37 | Liability for contracts, etc | 1.81 |
| 38 | Receivership accounts to be delivered to registrar | 1.82 |

*Provisions applicable to every receivership*

| | | |
|---|---|---|
| 39 | Notification that receiver or manager appointed | 1.83 |
| 40 | Payment of debts out of assets subject to floating charge | 1.84 |
| 41 | Enforcement of duty to make returns | 1.85 |

*Administrative receivers: general*

| | | |
|---|---|---|
| 42 | General powers | 1.86 |
| 43 | Power to dispose of charged property, etc | 1.87 |
| 44 | Agency and liability for contracts | 1.88 |
| 45 | Vacation of office | 1.89 |

*Administrative receivers: ascertainment and investigation of company's affairs*

| | | |
|---|---|---|
| 46 | Information to be given by administrative receiver | 1.90 |
| 47 | Statement of affairs to be submitted | 1.91 |
| 48 | Report by administrative receiver | 1.92 |
| 49 | Committee of creditors | 1.93 |

CHAPTER II
RECEIVERS (SCOTLAND)

| | | |
|---|---|---|
| 50 | Extent of this Chapter | 1.94 |
| 51 | Power to appoint receiver | 1.95 |
| 52 | Circumstances justifying appointment | 1.96 |
| 53 | Mode of appointment by holder of charge | 1.97 |
| 54 | Appointment by court | 1.98 |
| 55 | Powers of receiver | 1.99 |
| 56 | Precedence among receivers | 1.100 |
| 57 | Agency and liability of receiver for contracts | 1.101 |
| 58 | Remuneration of receiver | 1.102 |
| 59 | Priority of debts | 1.103 |
| 60 | Distribution of moneys | 1.104 |
| 61 | Disposal of interest in property | 1.105 |
| 62 | Cessation of appointment of receiver | 1.106 |
| 63 | Powers of court | 1.107 |
| 64 | Notification that receiver appointed | 1.108 |
| 65 | Information to be given by receiver | 1.109 |
| 66 | Company's statement of affairs | 1.110 |
| 67 | Report by receiver | 1.111 |
| 68 | Committee of creditors | 1.112 |
| 69 | Enforcement of receiver's duty to make returns, etc | 1.113 |
| 70 | Interpretation for Chapter II | 1.114 |
| 71 | Prescription of forms etc; regulations | 1.115 |

CHAPTER III
RECEIVERS' POWERS IN GREAT BRITAIN AS A WHOLE

| | | |
|---|---|---|
| 72 | Cross-border operation of receivership provisions | 1.116 |

CHAPTER IV

PROHIBITION OF APPOINTMENT OF ADMINISTRATIVE RECEIVER

| | | |
|---|---|---|
| 72A | Floating charge holder not to appoint administrative receiver | 1.117 |
| 72B | First exception: capital market | 1.118 |
| 72C | Second exception: public-private partnership | 1.119 |
| 72D | Third exception: utilities | 1.120 |
| 72DA | Exception in respect of urban regeneration projects | 1.121 |
| 72E | Fourth exception: project finance | 1.122 |
| 72F | Fifth exception: financial market | 1.123 |
| 72G | Sixth exception: social landlords | 1.124 |
| 72GA | Exception in relation to protected railway companies etc | 1.125 |
| 72H | Sections 72A to 72G: supplementary | 1.126 |

PART IV

WINDING UP OF COMPANIES REGISTERED UNDER THE COMPANIES ACTS

CHAPTER I

PRELIMINARY

*Introductory*

| | | |
|---|---|---|
| 73 | Scheme of this Part | 1.128 |

*Contributories*

| | | |
|---|---|---|
| 74 | Liability as contributories of present and past members | 1.129 |
| 75 | (*Repealed*) | |
| 76 | Liability of past directors and shareholders | 1.130 |
| 77 | Limited company formerly unlimited | 1.131 |
| 78 | Unlimited company formerly limited | 1.132 |
| 79 | Meaning of "contributory" | 1.133 |
| 80 | Nature of contributory's liability | 1.134 |
| 81 | Contributories in case of death of a member | 1.135 |
| 82 | Effect of contributory's bankruptcy | 1.136 |
| 83 | Companies registered but not formed under the Companies Act 2006 | 1.137 |

CHAPTER II

VOLUNTARY WINDING UP (INTRODUCTORY AND GENERAL)

*Resolutions for, and commencement of, voluntary winding up*

| | | |
|---|---|---|
| 84 | Circumstances in which company may be wound up voluntarily | 1.138 |
| 85 | Notice of resolution to wind up | 1.139 |
| 86 | Commencement of winding up | 1.140 |

*Consequences of resolution to wind up*

| | | |
|---|---|---|
| 87 | Effect on business and status of company | 1.141 |
| 88 | Avoidance of share transfers, etc after winding-up resolution | 1.142 |

*Declaration of solvency*

| | | |
|---|---|---|
| 89 | Statutory declaration of solvency | 1.143 |
| 90 | Distinction between "members'" and "creditors'" voluntary winding up | 1.144 |

CHAPTER III

MEMBERS' VOLUNTARY WINDING UP

| | | |
|---|---|---|
| 91 | Appointment of liquidator | 1.145 |
| 92 | Power to fill vacancy in office of liquidator | 1.146 |
| 92A | Progress report to company | 1.147 |
| 93 | (*Repealed*) | |
| 94 | Final account prior to dissolution | 1.148 |
| 95 | Effect of company's insolvency | 1.149 |
| 96 | Conversion to creditors' voluntary winding up | 1.150 |

CHAPTER IV

CREDITORS' VOLUNTARY WINDING UP

| | | |
|---|---|---|
| 97 | Application of this Chapter | 1.151 |
| 98 | (*Repealed*) | |
| 99 | Directors to lay statement of affairs before creditors | 1.152 |
| 100 | Appointment of liquidator | 1.153 |
| 101 | Appointment of liquidation committee | 1.154 |
| 102 | (*Repealed*) | |

| | | |
|---|---|---|
| 103 | Cesser of directors' powers | **1.155** |
| 104 | Vacancy in office of liquidator | **1.156** |
| 104A | Progress report to company and creditors | **1.157** |
| 105 | (*Repealed*) | |
| 106 | Final account prior to dissolution | **1.158** |

### CHAPTER V
### PROVISIONS APPLYING TO BOTH KINDS OF VOLUNTARY WINDING UP

| | | |
|---|---|---|
| 107 | Distribution of company's property | **1.159** |
| 108 | Appointment or removal of liquidator by the court | **1.160** |
| 109 | Notice by liquidator of his appointment | **1.161** |
| 110 | Acceptance of shares, etc, as consideration for sale of company property | **1.162** |
| 111 | Dissent from arrangement under s 110 | **1.163** |
| 112 | Reference of questions to court | **1.164** |
| 113 | Court's power to control proceedings (Scotland) | **1.165** |
| 114 | No liquidator appointed or nominated by company | **1.166** |
| 115 | Expenses of voluntary winding up | **1.167** |
| 116 | Saving for certain rights | **1.168** |

### CHAPTER VI
### WINDING UP BY THE COURT

#### *Jurisdiction (England and Wales)*

| | | |
|---|---|---|
| 117 | High Court and county court jurisdiction | **1.169** |
| 118 | Proceedings taken in wrong court | **1.170** |
| 119 | Proceedings in county court; case stated for High Court | **1.171** |

#### *Jurisdiction (Scotland)*

| | | |
|---|---|---|
| 120 | Court of Session and sheriff court jurisdiction | **1.172** |
| 121 | Power to remit winding up to Lord Ordinary | **1.173** |

#### *Grounds and effect of winding-up petition*

| | | |
|---|---|---|
| 122 | Circumstances in which company may be wound up by the court | **1.174** |
| 123 | Definition of inability to pay debts | **1.175** |
| 124 | Application for winding up | **1.176** |
| 124A | Petition for winding up on grounds of public interest | **1.177** |
| 124B | (*Repealed*) | |
| 124C | (*Repealed*) | |
| 125 | Powers of court on hearing of petition | **1.178** |
| 126 | Power to stay or restrain proceedings against company | **1.179** |
| 127 | Avoidance of property dispositions, etc | **1.180** |
| 128 | Avoidance of attachments, etc | **1.181** |

#### *Commencement of winding up*

| | | |
|---|---|---|
| 129 | Commencement of winding up by the court | **1.182** |
| 130 | Consequences of winding-up order | **1.183** |

#### *Investigation procedures*

| | | |
|---|---|---|
| 131 | Company's statement of affairs | **1.184** |
| 132 | Investigation by official receiver | **1.185** |
| 133 | Public examination of officers | **1.186** |
| 134 | Enforcement of s 133 | **1.187** |

#### *Appointment of liquidator*

| | | |
|---|---|---|
| 135 | Appointment and powers of provisional liquidator | **1.188** |
| 136 | Functions of official receiver in relation to office of liquidator | **1.189** |
| 137 | Appointment by Secretary of State | **1.190** |
| 138 | Appointment of liquidator in Scotland | **1.191** |
| 139 | Choice of liquidator by creditors and contributories | **1.192** |
| 140 | Appointment by the court following administration or voluntary arrangement | **1.193** |

#### *Liquidation committees*

| | | |
|---|---|---|
| 141 | Liquidation committee (England and Wales) | **1.194** |
| 142 | Liquidation committee (Scotland) | **1.195** |

#### *The liquidator's functions*

| | | |
|---|---|---|
| 143 | General functions in winding up by the court | **1.196** |
| 144 | Custody of company's property | **1.197** |

| | | |
|---|---|---|
| 145 | Vesting of company property in liquidator | 1.198 |
| 146 | Final account | 1.199 |
| 146A | (*Repealed*) | |

*General powers of court*

| | | |
|---|---|---|
| 147 | Power to stay or sist winding up | 1.200 |
| 148 | Settlement of list of contributories and application of assets | 1.201 |
| 149 | Debts due from contributory to company | 1.202 |
| 150 | Power to make calls | 1.203 |
| 151 | (*Repealed*) | |
| 152 | Order on contributory to be conclusive evidence | 1.204 |
| 153 | Power to exclude creditors not proving in time | 1.205 |
| 154 | Adjustment of rights of contributories | 1.206 |
| 155 | Inspection of books by creditors, etc | 1.207 |
| 156 | Payment of expenses of winding up | 1.208 |
| 157 | Attendance at company meetings (Scotland) | 1.209 |
| 158 | Power to arrest absconding contributory | 1.210 |
| 159 | Powers of court to be cumulative | 1.211 |
| 160 | Delegation of powers to liquidator (England and Wales) | 1.212 |

*Enforcement of, and appeal from, orders*

| | | |
|---|---|---|
| 161 | Orders for calls on contributories (Scotland) | 1.213 |
| 162 | Appeals from orders in Scotland | 1.214 |

## CHAPTER VII

## LIQUIDATORS

*Preliminary*

| | | |
|---|---|---|
| 163 | Style and title of liquidators | 1.215 |
| 164 | Corrupt inducement affecting appointment | 1.216 |

*Liquidator's powers and duties*

| | | |
|---|---|---|
| 165 | Voluntary winding up | 1.217 |
| 166 | Creditors' voluntary winding up | 1.218 |
| 167 | Winding up by the court | 1.219 |
| 168 | Supplementary powers (England and Wales) | 1.220 |
| 169 | Supplementary powers (Scotland) | 1.221 |
| 170 | Enforcement of liquidator's duty to make returns, etc | 1.222 |

*Removal; vacation of office*

| | | |
|---|---|---|
| 171 | Removal, etc (voluntary winding up) | 1.223 |
| 172 | Removal, etc (winding up by the court) | 1.224 |

*Release of liquidator*

| | | |
|---|---|---|
| 173 | Release (voluntary winding up) | 1.225 |
| 174 | Release (winding up by the court) | 1.226 |
| 174A | Moratorium debts etc: priority | 1.227 |

## CHAPTER VIII

## PROVISIONS OF GENERAL APPLICATION IN WINDING UP

*Preferential debts*

| | | |
|---|---|---|
| 175 | Preferential debts (general provision) | 1.228 |
| 176 | Preferential charge on goods distrained, etc | 1.229 |

*Non-preferential debts*

| | | |
|---|---|---|
| 176AZA | Non-preferential debts of financial institutions | 1.230 |

*Property subject to floating charge*

| | | |
|---|---|---|
| 176ZA | Payment of expenses of winding up (England and Wales) | 1.231 |
| 176ZB | Application of proceeds of office-holder claims | 1.232 |
| 176A | Share of assets for unsecured creditors | 1.233 |

*Special managers*

| | | |
|---|---|---|
| 177 | Power to appoint special manager | 1.234 |

*Disclaimer (England and Wales only)*

| | | |
|---|---|---|
| 178 | Power to disclaim onerous property | 1.235 |
| 179 | Disclaimer of leaseholds | 1.236 |
| 180 | Land subject to rentcharge | 1.237 |

| | | |
|---|---|---|
| 181 | Powers of court (general) | 1.238 |
| 182 | Powers of court (leaseholds) | 1.239 |

*Execution, attachment and the Scottish equivalents*

| | | |
|---|---|---|
| 183 | Effect of execution or attachment (England and Wales) | 1.240 |
| 184 | Duties of officers charged with execution of writs and other processes (England and Wales) | 1.241 |
| 185 | Effect of diligence (Scotland) | 1.242 |

*Miscellaneous matters*

| | | |
|---|---|---|
| 186 | Rescission of contracts by the court | 1.243 |
| 187 | Power to make over assets to employees | 1.244 |
| 188 | Notification that company is in liquidation | 1.245 |
| 189 | Interest on debts | 1.246 |
| 190 | Documents exempt from stamp duty | 1.247 |
| 191 | Company's books to be evidence | 1.248 |
| 192 | Information as to pending liquidations | 1.249 |
| 193 | Unclaimed dividends (Scotland) | 1.250 |
| 194 | (*Repealed*) | |
| 195 | Court's powers to ascertain wishes of creditors or contributories | 1.251 |
| 196 | Judicial notice of court documents | 1.252 |
| 197 | Commission for receiving evidence | 1.253 |
| 198 | Court order for examination of persons in Scotland | 1.254 |
| 199 | Costs of application for leave to proceed (Scottish companies) | 1.255 |
| 200 | Affidavits etc in United Kingdom and overseas | 1.256 |

CHAPTER IX

DISSOLUTION OF COMPANIES AFTER WINDING UP

| | | |
|---|---|---|
| 201 | Dissolution (voluntary winding up) | 1.257 |
| 202 | Early dissolution (England and Wales) | 1.258 |
| 203 | Consequence of notice under s 202 | 1.259 |
| 204 | Early dissolution (Scotland) | 1.260 |
| 205 | Dissolution otherwise than under ss 202–204 | 1.261 |

CHAPTER X

MALPRACTICE BEFORE AND DURING LIQUIDATION; PENALISATION OF COMPANIES AND COMPANY OFFICERS; INVESTIGATIONS AND PROSECUTIONS

*Offences of fraud, deception, etc*

| | | |
|---|---|---|
| 206 | Fraud, etc in anticipation of winding up | 1.263 |
| 207 | Transactions in fraud of creditors | 1.264 |
| 208 | Misconduct in course of winding up | 1.265 |
| 209 | Falsification of company's books | 1.266 |
| 210 | Material omissions from statement relating to company's affairs | 1.267 |
| 211 | False representations to creditors | 1.268 |

*Penalisation of directors and officers*

| | | |
|---|---|---|
| 212 | Summary remedy against delinquent directors, liquidators, etc | 1.270 |
| 213 | Fraudulent trading | 1.271 |
| 214 | Wrongful trading | 1.272 |
| 214A | Adjustment of withdrawals | 1.273 |
| 215 | Proceedings under ss 213, 214 | 1.274 |
| 216 | Restriction on re-use of company names | 1.275 |
| 217 | Personal liability for debts, following contravention of s 216 | 1.276 |

*Investigation and prosecution of malpractice*

| | | |
|---|---|---|
| 218 | Prosecution of delinquent officers and members of company | 1.277 |
| 219 | Obligations arising under s 218 | 1.278 |

PART V

WINDING UP OF UNREGISTERED COMPANIES

| | | |
|---|---|---|
| 220 | Meaning of "unregistered company" | 1.280 |
| 221 | Winding up of unregistered companies | 1.281 |
| 222 | Inability to pay debts: unpaid creditor for £750 or more | 1.282 |
| 223 | Inability to pay debts: debt remaining unsatisfied after action brought | 1.283 |
| 224 | Inability to pay debts: other cases | 1.284 |
| 225 | Company incorporated outside Great Britain may be wound up though dissolved | 1.285 |

| | | |
|---|---|---|
| 226 | Contributories in winding up of unregistered company | 1.286 |
| 227 | Power of court to stay, sist or restrain proceedings | 1.287 |
| 228 | Actions stayed on winding-up order | 1.288 |
| 229 | Provisions of this Part to be cumulative | 1.289 |

## PART VI
### MISCELLANEOUS PROVISIONS APPLYING TO COMPANIES WHICH ARE INSOLVENT OR IN LIQUIDATION

*Office-holders*

| | | |
|---|---|---|
| 230 | Holders of office to be qualified insolvency practitioners | 1.291 |
| 231 | Appointment to office of two or more persons | 1.292 |
| 232 | Validity of office-holder's acts | 1.293 |

*Management by administrators, liquidators, etc*

| | | |
|---|---|---|
| 233 | Supplies of gas, water, electricity, etc | 1.294 |
| 233A | Further protection of essential supplies | 1.295 |
| 233B | Protection of supplies of goods and services | 1.296 |
| 233C | Powers to amend section 233B and Schedule 4ZZA | 1.297 |
| 234 | Getting in the company's property | 1.298 |
| 235 | Duty to co-operate with office-holder | 1.299 |
| 236 | Inquiry into company's dealings, etc | 1.300 |
| 237 | Court's enforcement powers under s 236 | 1.301 |

*Adjustment of prior transactions (administration and liquidation)*

| | | |
|---|---|---|
| 238 | Transactions at an undervalue (England and Wales) | 1.302 |
| 239 | Preferences (England and Wales) | 1.303 |
| 240 | "Relevant time" under ss 238, 239 | 1.304 |
| 241 | Orders under ss 238, 239 | 1.305 |
| 242 | Gratuitous alienations (Scotland) | 1.306 |
| 243 | Unfair preferences (Scotland) | 1.307 |
| 244 | Extortionate credit transactions | 1.308 |
| 245 | Avoidance of certain floating charges | 1.309 |
| 246 | Unenforceability of liens on books, etc | 1.310 |

*Administration: penalisation of directors etc*

| | | |
|---|---|---|
| 246ZA | Fraudulent trading: administration | 1.311 |
| 246ZB | Wrongful trading: administration | 1.312 |
| 246ZC | Proceedings under section 246ZA or 246ZB | 1.313 |

*Power to assign certain causes of action*

| | | |
|---|---|---|
| 246ZD | Power to assign | 1.314 |

*Decisions by creditors and contributories*

| | | |
|---|---|---|
| 246ZE | Decisions by creditors and contributories: general | 1.315 |
| 246ZF | Deemed consent procedure | 1.316 |
| 246ZG | Power to amend sections 246ZE and 246ZF | 1.317 |

*Remote attendance at meetings*

| | | |
|---|---|---|
| 246A | Remote attendance at meetings | 1.318 |

*Giving of notices etc by office-holders*

| | | |
|---|---|---|
| 246B | Use of websites | 1.319 |
| 246C | Creditors' ability to opt out of receiving certain notices | 1.320 |

## PART VII
### INTERPRETATION FOR FIRST GROUP OF PARTS

| | | |
|---|---|---|
| 247 | "Insolvency" and "go into liquidation" | 1.321 |
| 248 | "Secured creditor", etc | 1.322 |
| 248A | "Opted-out creditor" | 1.323 |
| 249 | "Connected" with a company | 1.324 |
| 250 | "Member" of a company | 1.325 |
| 251 | Expressions used generally | 1.326 |

THE SECOND GROUP OF PARTS
INSOLVENCY OF INDIVIDUALS; BANKRUPTCY

PART VIIA
DEBT RELIEF ORDERS

*Preliminary*

| | | |
|---|---|---|
| 251A | Debt relief orders | 1.328 |

*Applications for a debt relief order*

| | | |
|---|---|---|
| 251B | Making of application | 1.329 |
| 251C | Duty of official receiver to consider and determine application | 1.330 |
| 251D | Presumptions applicable to the determination of an application | 1.331 |

*Making and effect of debt relief order*

| | | |
|---|---|---|
| 251E | Making of debt relief orders | 1.332 |
| 251F | Effect of debt relief order on other debt management arrangements | 1.333 |
| 251G | Moratorium from qualifying debts | 1.334 |
| 251H | The moratorium period | 1.335 |
| 251I | Discharge from qualifying debts | 1.336 |

*Duties of debtor*

| | | |
|---|---|---|
| 251J | Providing assistance to official receiver etc | 1.337 |

*Objections, investigations and revocation*

| | | |
|---|---|---|
| 251K | Objections and investigations | 1.338 |
| 251L | Power of official receiver to revoke or amend a debt relief order | 1.339 |

*Role of the court*

| | | |
|---|---|---|
| 251M | Powers of court in relation to debt relief orders | 1.340 |
| 251N | Inquiry into debtor's dealings and property | 1.341 |

*Offences*

| | | |
|---|---|---|
| 251O | False representations and omissions | 1.342 |
| 251P | Concealment or falsification of documents | 1.343 |
| 251Q | Fraudulent disposal of property | 1.344 |
| 251R | Fraudulent dealing with property obtained on credit | 1.345 |
| 251S | Obtaining credit or engaging in business | 1.346 |
| 251T | Offences: supplementary | 1.347 |

*Supplementary*

| | | |
|---|---|---|
| 251U | Approved intermediaries | 1.348 |
| 251V | Debt relief restrictions orders and undertakings | 1.349 |
| 251W | Register of debt relief orders etc | 1.350 |
| 251X | Interpretation | 1.351 |

PART VIII
INDIVIDUAL VOLUNTARY ARRANGEMENTS

*Moratorium for insolvent debtor*

| | | |
|---|---|---|
| 252 | Interim order of court | 1.353 |
| 253 | Application for interim order | 1.354 |
| 254 | Effect of application | 1.355 |
| 255 | Cases in which interim order can be made | 1.356 |
| 256 | Nominee's report on debtor's proposal | 1.357 |

*Procedure where no interim order made*

| | | |
|---|---|---|
| 256A | Debtor's proposal and nominee's report | 1.358 |

*Creditors' decisions*

| | | |
|---|---|---|
| 257 | Consideration of debtor's proposal by creditors | 1.359 |

*Consideration and implementation of debtor's proposal*

| | | |
|---|---|---|
| 258 | Approval of debtor's proposal | 1.360 |
| 259 | Report of decisions to court | 1.361 |
| 260 | Effect of approval | 1.362 |
| 261 | Additional effect on undischarged bankrupt | 1.363 |
| 262 | Challenge of creditors' decision | 1.364 |
| 262A | False representations etc | 1.365 |
| 262B | Prosecution of delinquent debtors | 1.366 |
| 262C | Arrangements coming to an end prematurely | 1.367 |

263        Implementation and supervision of approved voluntary arrangement        **1.368**
263A–263G    (*Repealed*)

## PART IX
## BANKRUPTCY

### CHAPTER A1
#### ADJUDICATORS: BANKRUPTCY APPLICATIONS BY DEBTORS AND BANKRUPTCY OR-DERS

263H       Bankruptcy applications to an adjudicator        **1.371**
263I       Debtors against whom an adjudicator may make a bankruptcy order        **1.372**
263J       Conditions applying to bankruptcy application        **1.373**
263K       Determination of bankruptcy application        **1.374**
263L       Adjudicator's requests for further information        **1.375**
263M       Making of bankruptcy order        **1.376**
263N       Refusal to make a bankruptcy order: review and appeal etc        **1.377**
263O       False representations and omissions        **1.378**

### CHAPTER I
#### THE COURT: BANKRUPTCY PETITIONS AND BANKRUPTCY ORDERS

*Preliminary*

264        Who may present a bankruptcy petition        **1.379**
265        Creditor's petition: debtors against whom the court may make a bank-
           ruptcy order        **1.380**
266        Other preliminary conditions        **1.381**

*Creditor's petition*

267        Grounds of creditor's petition        **1.382**
268        Definition of "inability to pay", etc; the statutory demand        **1.383**
269        Creditor with security        **1.384**
270        Expedited petition        **1.385**
271        Proceedings on creditor's petition        **1.386**
272–275A    (*Repealed*)

*Other cases for special consideration*

276        Default in connection with voluntary arrangement        **1.388**
277        Petition based on criminal bankruptcy order        **1.389**

### CHAPTER 1A
#### COMMENCEMENT AND DURATION OF BANKRUPTCY

278        Commencement and continuance        **1.390**
279        Duration        **1.391**
280        Discharge by order of the court        **1.392**
281        Effect of discharge        **1.393**
281A       Post-discharge restrictions        **1.394**
282        Court's power to annul bankruptcy order        **1.395**

### CHAPTER II
#### PROTECTION OF BANKRUPT'S ESTATE AND INVESTIGATION OF HIS AFFAIRS

283        Definition of bankrupt's estate        **1.396**
283A       Bankrupt's home ceasing to form part of estate        **1.397**
284        Restrictions on dispositions of property        **1.398**
285        Restriction on proceedings and remedies        **1.399**
286        Power to appoint interim receiver        **1.400**
287        Powers of interim receiver        **1.401**
288        Statement of affairs        **1.402**
289        Investigatory duties of official receiver        **1.403**
290        Public examination of bankrupt        **1.404**
291        Duties of bankrupt in relation to official receiver        **1.405**

### CHAPTER III
#### TRUSTEES IN BANKRUPTCY

*Tenure of office as trustee*

291A       First trustee in bankruptcy        **1.406**
292        Appointment of trustees: general provision        **1.407**
293–295     (*Repealed*)

| | | |
|---|---|---|
| 296 | Appointment of trustee by Secretary of State | 1.408 |
| 297 | (*Repealed*) | |
| 298 | Removal of trustee; vacation of office | 1.409 |
| 299 | Release of trustee | 1.410 |
| 300 | Vacancy in office of trustee | 1.411 |

*Control of trustee*

| | | |
|---|---|---|
| 301 | Creditors' committee | 1.412 |
| 302 | Exercise by Secretary of State of functions of creditors' committee | 1.413 |
| 303 | General control of trustee by the court | 1.414 |
| 304 | Liability of trustee | 1.415 |

CHAPTER IV

ADMINISTRATION BY TRUSTEE

*Preliminary*

| | | |
|---|---|---|
| 305 | General functions of trustee | 1.416 |

*Acquisition, control and realisation of bankrupt's estate*

| | | |
|---|---|---|
| 306 | Vesting of bankrupt's estate in trustee | 1.417 |
| 306A | Property subject to restraint order | 1.418 |
| 306AA | Property released from detention | 1.419 |
| 306B | Property in respect of which receivership or administration order made | 1.420 |
| 306BA | Property in respect of which realisation order made | 1.421 |
| 306C | Property subject to certain orders where confiscation order discharged or quashed | 1.422 |
| 307 | After-acquired property | 1.423 |
| 308 | Vesting in trustee of certain items of excess value | 1.424 |
| 308A | Vesting in trustee of certain tenancies | 1.425 |
| 309 | Time-limit for notice under s 307 or 308 | 1.426 |
| 310 | Income payments orders | 1.427 |
| 310A | Income payments agreement | 1.428 |
| 311 | Acquisition by trustee of control | 1.429 |
| 312 | Obligation to surrender control to trustee | 1.430 |
| 313 | Charge on bankrupt's home | 1.431 |
| 313A | Low value home: application for sale, possession or charge | 1.432 |
| 314 | Powers of trustee | 1.433 |

*Disclaimer of onerous property*

| | | |
|---|---|---|
| 315 | Disclaimer (general power) | 1.434 |
| 316 | Notice requiring trustee's decision | 1.435 |
| 317 | Disclaimer of leaseholds | 1.436 |
| 318 | Disclaimer of dwelling house | 1.437 |
| 319 | Disclaimer of land subject to rentcharge | 1.438 |
| 320 | Court order vesting disclaimed property | 1.439 |
| 321 | Order under s 320 in respect of leaseholds | 1.440 |

*Distribution of bankrupt's estate*

| | | |
|---|---|---|
| 322 | Proof of debts | 1.441 |
| 323 | Mutual credit and set-off | 1.442 |
| 324 | Distribution by means of dividend | 1.443 |
| 325 | Claims by unsatisfied creditors | 1.444 |
| 326 | Distribution of property in specie | 1.445 |
| 327 | Distribution in criminal bankruptcy | 1.446 |
| 328 | Priority of debts | 1.447 |
| 329 | Debts to spouse or civil partner | 1.448 |
| 330 | Final distribution | 1.449 |
| 331 | Final report | 1.450 |
| 332 | Saving for bankrupt's home | 1.451 |

*Supplemental*

| | | |
|---|---|---|
| 333 | Duties of bankrupt in relation to trustee | 1.452 |
| 334 | Stay of distribution in case of second bankruptcy | 1.453 |
| 335 | Adjustment between earlier and later bankruptcy estates | 1.454 |

## CHAPTER V
## EFFECT OF BANKRUPTCY ON CERTAIN RIGHTS, TRANSACTIONS, ETC

### *Rights under trusts of land*

335A    Rights under trusts of land    1.455

### *Rights of occupation*

336    Rights of occupation etc of bankrupt's spouse or civil partner    1.456
337    Rights of occupation of bankrupt    1.457
338    Payments in respect of premises occupied by bankrupt    1.458

### *Adjustment of prior transactions, etc*

339    Transactions at an undervalue    1.459
340    Preferences    1.460
341    "Relevant time" under ss 339, 340    1.461
342    Orders under ss 339, 340    1.462
342A    Recovery of excessive pension contributions    1.463
342B    Orders under section 342A    1.464
342C    Orders under section 342A: supplementary    1.465
342D    Recovery of excessive contributions in pension-sharing cases    1.466
342E    Orders under section 339 or 340 in respect of pension-sharing transactions    1.467
342F    Orders under section 339 or 340 in pension-sharing cases: supplementary    1.468
343    Extortionate credit transactions    1.469
344    Avoidance of general assignment of book debts    1.470
345    Contracts to which bankrupt is a party    1.471
346    Enforcement procedures    1.472
347    Distress, etc    1.473
348    Apprenticeships, etc    1.474
349    Unenforceability of liens on books, etc    1.475
349A    Arbitration agreements to which bankrupt is party    1.476

## CHAPTER VI
## BANKRUPTCY OFFENCES

### *Preliminary*

350    Scheme of this Chapter    1.478
351    Definitions    1.479
352    Defence of innocent intention    1.480

### *Wrongdoing by the bankrupt before and after bankruptcy*

353    Non-disclosure    1.481
354    Concealment of property    1.482
355    Concealment of books and papers; falsification    1.483
356    False statements    1.484
357    Fraudulent disposal of property    1.485
358    Absconding    1.486
359    Fraudulent dealing with property obtained on credit    1.487
360    Obtaining credit; engaging in business    1.488
361    (*Repealed*)
362    (*Repealed*)

## CHAPTER VII
## POWERS OF COURT IN BANKRUPTCY

363    General control of court    1.489
364    Power of arrest    1.490
365    Seizure of bankrupt's property    1.491
366    Inquiry into bankrupt's dealings and property    1.492
367    Court's enforcement powers under s 366    1.493
368    Provision corresponding to s 366, where interim receiver appointed    1.494
369    Order for production of documents by inland revenue    1.495
370    Power to appoint special manager    1.496
371    Re-direction of bankrupt's letters, etc    1.497

## PART X
## INDIVIDUAL INSOLVENCY: GENERAL PROVISIONS

372    Supplies of gas, water, electricity, etc    1.498

| | | |
|---|---|---|
| 372A | Further protection of essential supplies | 1.499 |
| 373 | Jurisdiction in relation to insolvent individuals | 1.500 |
| 374 | Insolvency districts | 1.501 |
| 375 | Appeals etc from courts exercising insolvency jurisdiction | 1.502 |
| 376 | Time-limits | 1.503 |
| 377 | Formal defects | 1.504 |
| 378 | Exemption from stamp duty | 1.505 |
| 379 | Annual report | 1.506 |

*Creditors' decisions*

| | | |
|---|---|---|
| 379ZA | Creditors' decisions: general | 1.507 |
| 379ZB | Deemed consent procedure | 1.508 |
| 379ZC | Power to amend sections 379ZA and 379ZB | 1.509 |

*Remote attendance at meetings*

| | | |
|---|---|---|
| 379A | (*Repealed*) | |

*Giving of notices etc by office-holders*

| | | |
|---|---|---|
| 379B | Use of websites | 1.510 |
| 379C | Creditors' ability to opt out of receiving certain notices | 1.511 |

## PART XI
### INTERPRETATION FOR SECOND GROUP OF PARTS

| | | |
|---|---|---|
| 380 | Introductory | 1.513 |
| 381 | "Bankrupt" and associated terminology | 1.514 |
| 382 | "Bankruptcy debt", "liability" | 1.515 |
| 383 | "Creditor", "security", etc | 1.516 |
| 383A | "Opted-out creditor" | 1.517 |
| 384 | "Prescribed" and "the rules" | 1.518 |
| 385 | Miscellaneous definitions | 1.519 |

## THE THIRD GROUP OF PARTS
### MISCELLANEOUS MATTERS BEARING ON BOTH COMPANY AND INDIVIDUAL INSOLVENCY; GENERAL INTERPRETATION; FINAL PROVISIONS

## PART XII
### PREFERENTIAL DEBTS IN COMPANY AND INDIVIDUAL INSOLVENCY

| | | |
|---|---|---|
| 386 | Categories of preferential debts | 1.521 |
| 387 | "The relevant date" | 1.522 |
| 387A | Financial institutions and their non-preferential debts | 1.523 |

## PART XIII
### INSOLVENCY PRACTITIONERS AND THEIR QUALIFICATION

*Restrictions on unqualified persons acting as liquidator, trustee in bankruptcy, etc*

| | | |
|---|---|---|
| 388 | Meaning of "act as insolvency practitioner" | 1.525 |
| 389 | Acting without qualification an offence | 1.526 |
| 389A | (*Repealed*) | |
| 389B | Official receiver as nominee or supervisor | 1.527 |

*The requisite qualification, and the means of obtaining it*

| | | |
|---|---|---|
| 390 | Persons not qualified to act as insolvency practitioners | 1.528 |
| 390A | Authorisation | 1.529 |
| 390B | Partial authorisation: acting in relation to partnerships | 1.530 |
| 391 | Recognised professional bodies | 1.531 |
| 391A | Application for recognition as recognised professional body | 1.532 |

*Regulatory objectives*

| | | |
|---|---|---|
| 391B | Application of regulatory objectives | 1.533 |
| 391C | Meaning of "regulatory functions" and "regulatory objectives" | 1.534 |

*Oversight of recognised professional bodies*

| | | |
|---|---|---|
| 391D | Directions | 1.535 |
| 391E | Directions: procedure | 1.536 |
| 391F | Financial penalty | 1.537 |
| 391G | Financial penalty: procedure | 1.538 |
| 391H | Appeal against financial penalty | 1.539 |
| 391I | Recovery of financial penalties | 1.540 |
| 391J | Reprimand | 1.541 |
| 391K | Reprimand: procedure | 1.542 |

*Revocation etc of recognition*

| | | |
|---|---|---|
| 391L | Revocation of recognition at instigation of Secretary of State | 1.543 |
| 391M | Orders under section 391L: procedure | 1.544 |
| 391N | Revocation of recognition at request of body | 1.545 |

*Court sanction of insolvency practitioners in public interest cases*

| | | |
|---|---|---|
| 391O | Direct sanctions orders | 1.546 |
| 391P | Application for, and power to make, direct sanctions order | 1.547 |
| 391Q | Direct sanctions order: conditions | 1.548 |
| 391R | Direct sanctions direction instead of order | 1.549 |

*General*

| | | |
|---|---|---|
| 391S | Power for Secretary of State to obtain information | 1.550 |
| 391T | Compliance orders | 1.551 |
| 392–398 | (*Repealed*) | |

### PART XIV
### PUBLIC ADMINISTRATION (ENGLAND AND WALES)

*Adjudicators*

| | | |
|---|---|---|
| 398A | Appointment etc of adjudicators and assistants | 1.553 |

*Official receivers*

| | | |
|---|---|---|
| 399 | Appointment, etc of official receivers | 1.554 |
| 400 | Functions and status of official receivers | 1.555 |
| 401 | Deputy official receivers and staff | 1.556 |

*The Official Petitioner*

| | | |
|---|---|---|
| 402 | Official Petitioner | 1.557 |

*Insolvency Service finance, accounting and investment*

| | | |
|---|---|---|
| 403 | Insolvency Services Account | 1.558 |
| 404 | Investment Account | 1.559 |
| 405 | (*Repealed*) | |
| 406 | Interest on money received by liquidators or trustees in bankruptcy and invested | 1.560 |
| 407 | Unclaimed dividends and undistributed balances | 1.561 |
| 408 | Adjustment of balances | 1.562 |
| 409 | Annual financial statement and audit | 1.563 |

*Supplementary*

| | | |
|---|---|---|
| 410 | Extent of this Part | 1.564 |

### PART XV
### SUBORDINATE LEGISLATION

*General insolvency rules*

| | | |
|---|---|---|
| 411 | Company insolvency rules | 1.566 |
| 412 | Individual insolvency rules (England and Wales) | 1.567 |
| 413 | Insolvency Rules Committee | 1.568 |

*Fees orders*

| | | |
|---|---|---|
| 414 | Fees orders (company insolvency proceedings) | 1.569 |
| 415 | Fees orders (individual insolvency proceedings in England and Wales) | 1.570 |
| 415A | Fees orders (general) | 1.571 |
| 415B | Monetary limits (companies moratorium) | 1.572 |

*Specification, increase and reduction of money sums relevant in the operation of this Act*

| | | |
|---|---|---|
| 416 | Monetary limits (companies winding up) | 1.573 |
| 417 | Money sum in 222 | 1.574 |
| 417A | (*Repealed*) | |
| 418 | Monetary limits (bankruptcy) | 1.575 |

*Insolvency practice*

| | | |
|---|---|---|
| 419 | Regulations for purposes of Part XIII | 1.576 |

*Other order-making powers*

| | | |
|---|---|---|
| 420 | Insolvent partnerships | 1.577 |
| 421 | Insolvent estates of deceased persons | 1.578 |
| 421A | Insolvent estates: joint tenancies | 1.579 |
| 422 | Formerly authorised banks | 1.580 |

422A     Meaning of "relevant offence"     1.581

## PART XVI
### PROVISIONS AGAINST DEBT AVOIDANCE (ENGLAND AND WALES ONLY)

423     Transactions defrauding creditors     1.582
424     Those who may apply for an order under s 423     1.583
425     Provision which may be made by order under s 423     1.584

## PART XVII
### MISCELLANEOUS AND GENERAL

426     Co-operation between courts exercising jurisdiction in relation to insolvency     1.586
426A     Disqualification from Parliament (England and Wales and Northern Ireland)     1.587
426B     Devolution     1.588
426C     Irrelevance of privilege     1.589
427     Disqualification from Parliament (Scotland)     1.590
428     Exemptions from Restrictive Trade Practices Act     1.591
429     Disabilities on revocation of administration order against an individual     1.592
430     Provision introducing Schedule of punishments     1.593
431     Summary proceedings     1.594
432     Offences by bodies corporate     1.595
433     Admissibility in evidence of statements of affairs, etc     1.596
434     Crown application     1.597

## PART XVIIA
### SUPPLEMENTARY PROVISIONS

434A     Introductory     1.598
434B     Representation of corporations in decision procedures and at meetings     1.599
434C     Legal professional privilege     1.600
434D     Enforcement of company's filing obligations     1.601
434E     Application of filing obligations to overseas companies     1.602

## PART XVIII
### INTERPRETATION

435     Meaning of "associate"     1.604
436     Expressions used generally     1.605
436A     (*Repealed*)
436B     References to things in writing     1.606

## PART XIX
### FINAL PROVISIONS

437     Transitional provisions, and savings     1.607
438     Repeals     1.608
439     Amendment of enactments     1.609
440     Extent (Scotland)     1.610
441     Extent (Northern Ireland)     1.611
442     Extent (other territories)     1.612
443     Commencement     1.613
444     Citation     1.614
    Schedules
    Schedule ZA1 Moratorium: Eligible Companies     1.615
    Schedule ZA2 Moratorium: Contract or other Instrument Involving Financial Services     1.616
    Schedule A1 (*Repealed*)
    Schedule B1 Administration     1.617
    Schedule 1 Powers of Administrator or Administrative Receiver     1.735
    Schedule 2 Powers of a Scottish Receiver (Additional to Those Conferred on him by the Instrument of Charge)     1.736
    Schedule 2A Exceptions to Prohibition on Appointment of Administrative Receiver: Supplementary Provisions     1.737
    Schedule 3 Orders in Course of Winding Up Pronounced in Vacation (Scotland)
    Part I Orders Which are to be Final     1.738
    Part II Orders Which are to take Effect Until Matter Disposed of by Inner House     1.739
    Schedule 4 Powers of Liquidator in a Winding Up     1.740
    Schedule 4ZZA Protection of Supplies under Section 233B: Exclusions
    Part 1 Essential Supplies     1.744

Part 2  Part 2 Persons Involved in Financial Services                                    1.745
Part 3  Contracts Involving Financial Services                                           1.746
Part 4  Other Exclusions                                                                 1.747
Schedule 4ZA  Conditions for Making a Debt Relief Order
Part 1  Conditions which Must be Met                                                     1.748
Part 2  Other Conditions                                                                 1.749
Schedule 4ZB  Debt Relief Restrictions Orders and Undertakings                           1.750
Schedule 4A  Bankruptcy Restrictions Order and Undertaking                               1.751
Schedule 5  Powers of Trustee in Bankruptcy                                              1.752
Schedule 6  The Categories of Preferential Debts                                         1.756
Schedule 7  (*Repealed*)
Schedule 8  Provisions Capable of Inclusion in Company Insolvency Rules                  1.757
Schedule 9  Provisions Capable of Inclusion in Individual Insolvency Rules               1.758
Schedule 10  Punishment of Offences under this Act                                       1.759
Schedule 11  Transitional Provisions and Savings
Part I  Company Insolvency and Winding Up                                                1.760
Part II  Individual Insolvency                                                           1.761
Part III  Transitional Effect of Part XVI                                                1.762
Part IV  Insolvency Practitioners                                                        1.763
Part V  General Transitional Provisions and Savings                                      1.764

## FIRST GROUP OF PARTS
## COMPANY INSOLVENCY; COMPANIES WINDING UP

### PART A1  MORATORIUM

**[1.2]**

**Introduction to the 2020 legislation and its aims**—The Corporate Insolvency and Governance Bill was introduced to the House of Commons on 20 May 2020. According to paras 78–86 of the Explanatory Notes produced upon the Bill being brought from the House of Commons on 3 June 2020 (HL Bill 58-EN (2019–21)), the entire Bill was fast-tracked through Parliament because its provisions were aimed at creating an environment where companies were supported in surviving the Covid-19 pandemic emergency with a view to continuing as going concerns. The Corporate Insolvency and Governance Act ('CIGA 2020') received the Royal Assent on 25 July 2020. It came into force the next day.

The three permanent measures introduced by the CIGA 2020, including the new moratorium procedure provided for in the new Part A1 introduced into the Insolvency Act 1986 ('IA 1986') (together with a rescue plan procedure under a new Part 26A of the Companies Act 2006 and restrictions on contractual supplier termination clauses), are innovative and far-reaching and are likely to have a significant impact on the practice of corporate insolvency in the UK, but these innovations are not newly devised. Rather, their implementation was brought forward in response to the Covid-19 pandemic and its serious economic impact. The Government consulted on the permanent measures now contained in the CIGA 2020 in 2016 and 2018 and published a response to those consultations on 26 August 2018, indicating a plan to take the proposals into legislation. That response, *Department for Business, Energy and Industrial Strategy, Insolvency and Corporate Governance: Government Response*, 26 August 2018, focused on reducing the risk of major company failures occurring through poor governance and improving the existing insolvency framework in such situations. In reality, the new permanent measures have been appropriated and modified in response to the pandemic and hurried through Parliament; experience may demonstrate that the provisions require further modification, and the Insolvency Service has said as much.

**The key statutory provisions**—Section 1 of the CIGA 2020 inserts a new Part A1 immediately before the existing CVA provisions in Part 1 of the IA 1986. The key CIGA 2020 provisions are: Schedule 1, which includes Schedules ZA1 and ZA2 (eligible companies); Schedule 2 (contracts involving financial services); Section A2 and Schedule 3 (further amendments and transition); and Section A3 and Schedule 4 (temporary modifications).

**The nature of the moratorium procedure**—Part A1 is innovative in two ways. First, it provides for the first free-standing moratorium in UK insolvency law. Secondly, it introduces for the first time in UK law a debtor-in-possession procedure, which bears some similarities to the US Chapter 11 model, by which the company (as debtor) remains under control of and management by the company's directors, subject to oversight by a monitor who must be a licensed insolvency practitioner. The single purpose of the new procedure is facilitating the rescue of the entity of the company debtor, rather than the company's business or the realisation of its assets; such an outcome is often the purpose underpinning a CVA but far less commonly the purpose of an administration. The scheme of Part A1 is to achieve that purpose by affording a company, which must be insolvent or likely to become insolvent, a temporary breathing space – initially by way of an extendable 20-day period – during which the company is protected from creditor claims by way of what is termed a payment holiday (although other non-monetary and proprietary claims are also barred), subject to certain exceptions stipulated in s A18(3), and can seek to reorganise itself at what is envisaged as relatively low cost subject to what has been termed 'light touch' oversight by a monitor. (It remains to be seen how the obvious tension between such anticipated low cost and the inherent rigour necessary in even light-touch oversight by a responsible professional is to be resolved, if it can be.)

There is no stipulated outcome or exit route from the moratorium procedure; at one extreme a company may need no more than breathing space for a limited period to stabilise itself financially whereas, at the other, it may be that the process culminates in an insolvency procedure, most likely, but not necessarily, a CVA.

Finally, the moratorium procedure is an addition to the corporate rescue toolbox and does nothing to detract from the existing procedures under the 1986 Act or other legislation, most obviously schemes of arrangement and the rescue plan procedure now available under the new Part 26A of the Companies Act 2006.

**Eligibility**—Section A2 provides that Sch ZA1, which appears within Sch 1, contains provisions for determining whether a company is eligible. The scheme of the legislation is that all companies are eligible for the moratorium procedure unless characterised as ineligible.

Ineligible companies include: a company operating in a specific sector which is subject to a specific statutory insolvency process (such as banks, insurers, payment institutions, designated exchanges etc); a company with over £10m of capital market debt (including bonds); a company which, on filing date or in the preceding 12 months, is or has been subject to a moratorium or 'insolvency procedure' (defined as a CVA, administration, interim moratorium under para 44 of Sch B1 to the IA 1986 ('Sch B1'), administrative receivership, winding-up or extant public interest winding-up petition, but not including a company that has been subject to a winding-up petition that has been dismissed); an overseas company unless capable of being wound up in the UK on which see ss 221 and 222 of the IA 1986 (Sch ZA1, para 18).

An LLP is eligible for the moratorium procedure.

**Procedure: Part A1, Chapter 3, ss A3 to A8**—An application may be made by way of filing requisite documents at court or by court application.

Obtaining a moratorium by the filing route involves the directors of the company filing 'relevant documents' (s A6) which include the proposed monitor confirming consent to act, that the company is eligible and that, in the monitor's view, 'it is likely that a moratorium for the company would result in the rescue of the company as a going concern' (s A4). This last requirement is fundamental and will almost certainly require judicial clarification in time. The view taken here is that there are good, practical reasons why 'likely' should be attributed a meaning the same as or more or less equivalent to the now well-established real prospect test applicable to court applications in Sch B1 administration – see the notes to Sch B1, para 13 – as opposed to more likely than not (as was the test applicable for a limited time in the early days of the former Part II administration regime).

The *Guide to Monitors* produced by the Insolvency Service (see below) spells out that the moratorium procedure is inappropriate where there is no such likelihood of the rescue of the company such that the moratorium constitutes no more than a method of the company buying time from its creditors.

It also remains to be seen how willing a suitably qualified practitioner is to make such a declaration as to likelihood on what is necessarily limited information and the extent to which the proposed monitor is expected to seek out and verify information provided. Although the monitor's principal source of information will be the directors, there will be cases in which it is clearly appropriate for the monitor to consider looking to, say, the company's bank or major creditors or other plainly interested parties capable of assisting the monitor to make an informed assessment of the position. Such additional work, of course, necessarily brings additional time and cost. There are, it is submitted, obvious parallels with the position of a nominee acting in relation to a CVA in terms of the extent to which the responsible practitioner has to be active or reactive to relevant information.

A court application is necessary to obtain a moratorium where the company is subject to an extant winding-up petition (s A5) or is an overseas company (s A6). Section A8 imposes notification requirements on a monitor in giving notice to the Registrar of Companies and every creditor upon becoming aware of a moratorium being effective. There are also publicity requirements (name of monitor and that moratorium in force) at place of business and on website and business documents in s A19.

Because the court can make a moratorium on a time unlimited basis, there may be cases in which the filing route is used to initiate the procedure following which an application is made to court to extend the period.

**Terminology: pre-moratorium debts with and without a payment holiday, moratorium debts and priority pre-moratorium debts**—An understanding of the impact of a moratorium under

Part A1 requires an understanding of the statutory terminology. Pre-moratorium debts are debts which have fallen due before the moratorium or which fall due during the moratorium and are sub-divided into those debts which are subject to a payment holiday in a moratorium, and those expressly excluded by s A18(3) from the payment holiday.

A moratorium debt, on the other hand, is a debt which either arises during the moratorium or which arises after the moratorium but due to an obligation incurred during the moratorium. By way of example, a tax liability to HMRC arising during a moratorium will constitute a moratorium debt whereas tax arrears (or, arguably, a deferred tax liability) in existence at the time the moratorium comes into effect will constitute a pre-moratorium debt which is not expressly carved out from the payment holiday by s A18(3).

Finally, priority pre-moratorium debts are a narrower category of pre-moratorium debts without a payment holiday which are afforded super-priority in any liquidation or administration which occurs within 12 weeks of the moratorium ending (see below).

**Effect of the moratorium on creditors: Part A1, Chapter 4, ss A18 to A33**—A moratorium provides a payment holiday – such debts remain ultimately payable – during the moratorium in respect of pre-moratorium debts subject to the specific exclusions prescribed by s A18(3) (see below).

A moratorium also has the following effects: a restriction on insolvency proceedings, as defined (s A20); a restriction on enforcement and legal proceedings (s A21); a restriction on the crystallisation of floating charge (through the technique of the legislation overriding the relevant contractual provisions) (s A22); and a restriction on the enforcement of security granted by the company during the moratorium save with the consent of the monitor (s A23).

The moratorium provisions applicable in administration by paras 42 and 43 of Sch B1 will be of assistance by way of analogy here in relation to ss A20 and A21. The moratorium will not prevent all action by a creditor (eg service of a notice of default) or self-help remedies such as the exercise of a right of set-off.

**Effect of the moratorium, restriction on transactions: Part A1, Chapter 4, ss A18 to A33**—A moratorium imposes a restriction on the obtaining of credit of more than £500 unless the creditor is informed that the moratorium in force (s A25); a restriction on the creation of security save with the consent of the monitor (s A26); a restriction on entering into market contracts etc (s A27); a restriction on payment of pre-moratorium debts exceeding the greater of £5,000 (in total) or 1% of the value of all unsecured creditors as at date of moratorium save with the consent of the monitor (s A28); and a restriction on the disposal of property save in the ordinary course of business or with the consent of the monitor or pursuant to court order (s A29).

Section 127 of the IA 1986 is disapplied during the course of the moratorium.

**Debts not protected against by the moratorium: s A18(3)**—The following amounts payable are not subject to a payment holiday: the monitor's remuneration or expenses (but not pre-moratorium remuneration for which separate provision needs to be made) (s A18(3)(a) and (7)); goods or services supplied during the moratorium (subject to definition in the Rules) (s A18(3)(b)); 'rent in respect of a period during the moratorium' (s A18(3)(c)); wages or salary (which are uncapped) arising under a contract of employment (s A18(3)(d)) (including holiday pay accruing in the moratorium period) (s A18(7)); redundancy payments (also uncapped, and including sums payable on agreed termination where the employee would have been entitled to redundancy) (s 18A(3)(e) and (7)); and 'debts or other liabilities arising under a contract or other instrument involving financial services', as defined (s A18(3)(e)).

There is clearly significant scope for litigation over the meaning of these new provisions. The scope for accelerated payments under s A18(3)(e) effectively stifling a moratorium because a monitor is obliged to terminate if a company cannot pay such liabilities as they fall due is not difficult to see. Rent is another prime example. The wording in s A18(3)(b) cited above addresses the period for which rent is payable but appears to draw no distinction between rent payable in respect of empty or unused premises and premises used in the course of the moratorium. This contrasts sharply with the position in administration where rent is only payable in respect of property used for the purpose of the administration following *Re Game Station, Jervis v Pillar Denton* [2014] EWCA Civ 180. Where rent is payable in advance, it would appear that only that apportioned part of the rent relating to the period of the moratorium would lose payment holiday protection. Equally, where rent is payable in arrears, it would appear that rent due for a period ending prior to the start of the moratorium would fall outside of s A18(3)(c) so as to be subject to a payment holiday, as might prompt the tactical use of the procedure where such rent constitutes a significant liability.

**Super-priority of certain debts in subsequent liquidation or administration: Paras 13 and 31 of Schedule 3 inserting s 174A into the IA 1986 (liquidation) and para 64A into Sch B1 (administration)**—If within 12 weeks of the end of the moratorium a company enters into administration or liquidation, unpaid moratorium debts and priority pre-moratorium debts are afforded super-priority status in that insolvency process. Those two classes of debt rank subject to any fixed charges but in priority to: the expenses and remuneration of the liquidator/administrator; preferential creditors; the prescribed part; floating charge holders; and ordinary unsecured creditors.

**Roles and functions of the monitor: Chapter 5, ss A34 to A41**—On 16 June 2020 the Insolvency Service published in draft *The Insolvency Service's Guide for Monitors* which was published in virtually the same final form on 26 June 2020. The *Guide* does little more in substance than make reference to the statutory requirements (although, to be fair, it also goes much further than simply providing guidance to monitors).

The following are of particular note. Section 388(1) of IA 1986 has been amended so that 'office-holder' now includes monitors. (Although never in possession of the company's assets, a monitor must also be bonded to the value of those assets.) As an officer of the court (s A34), a monitor is subject to consequences of such status, court control and has a duty to act with integrity and good faith in line with the rule in *Ex parte James*. A monitor will be subject to the ethical and regulatory guidelines of the relevant Regulatory Professional Bodies and the new *Insolvency Code of Ethics*, effective from 1 May 2020. After consenting to act, the monitor's role is to supervise the company's continued eligibility at and following the commencement of the procedure, in particular that it is likely that the company can be rescued as a going concern (on which note, in particular, s A38(1) in the event of the monitor not being of that view). The monitor may require directors to provide information required for carrying out his or her functions (s A36). In default of compliance as soon as practicable, the monitor may file notice at court ending the moratorium (s A38(1)(c)). There is no obligation on a monitor to provide creditors with information other than start and changes to end date and replacement of monitor, but s A42 enables a creditor to challenge a monitor's actions by court application. A monitor has standing to apply to court for directions under s A37.

No guidance is given as to the taking of a subsequent appointment in respect of a company by a former monitor. Presumably, the same considerations will apply as on any other subsequent appointment, such as where an office-holder takes appointment as a liquidator following an administration; of particular note will be whether or not the view expressed by the monitor as to the survival of the company was borne out, the level of fees charged by the monitor, whether it is more efficient to retain the monitor as office-holder and any objections or complaints raised in relation to the monitor during the course of or following the moratorium.

**Extending the term of the moratorium: Part A1, Chapter 3**—The initial period of the moratorium is 20 business days beginning with the day following the moratorium coming into force (s A9(2)). That period is extendable by a further 20 days without creditor consent by way of the directors filing the documents prescribed by s A10(1) documents, but only after the first 15 business days of the initial 20-day period. The extension of the moratorium period requires the continued certification by the monitor as to the likelihood of the rescue of the company as a going concern.

With creditor consent, the moratorium period can be extended up to one-year (s A12(3)) by directors filing prescribed s A11(1) documents, but only after 15 business days of initial 20-day period. Absent creditor consent, the court can extend the moratorium period without limit on and application by the directors under s A13. Section A13(5) is bound to give rise to case law where the courts are faced with the views of opposing creditors notwithstanding what may be the merits of extending the term of the moratorium for the purpose of achieving its purpose.

The CIGA 2020 makes no provision for the curing retrospectively of a defective appointment. Presumably, this very obvious omission is a potential problem Parliament has left for resolution by the courts, perhaps by the development of a jurisdiction similar to the *Re G-Tech Construction Ltd* [2007] BPIR 1275 line of authorities on retrospective administration appointments, a jurisdiction well established and well used at first instance as a judicially established tool of great pragmatic utility which is nonetheless widely recognised as being almost indefensible in terms of its technical integrity: see the notes to Sch B1 para 13.

**Exit routes: Part A1, Chapter 3**—The monitor 'must' – the provision imposes a mandatory and unqualified obligation once triggered – bring a moratorium to an end by filing a notice (of which 3 business days' notice must be given to the company) if (s A38(1)) the monitor 'thinks' (on which term see the notes to Sch B1 administration): (a) the moratorium is no longer likely to result in rescue of the company as a going concern; (b) the objective of rescuing the company as going concern has been achieved; (c) by reason of a s A36 (provision of information) default, the monitor is unable properly to carry out his or her functions; or (d) the company is unable to pay due (i) moratorium debts, or (ii) pre-moratorium debts for which the company does not have a payment holiday.

A moratorium will also come to an end if: the company enters into another insolvency process (liquidation, CVA, administration (including the filing of a notice of intention to appoint)); a restructuring plan or scheme of arrangement is sanctioned; the court so orders; or automatically upon the expiration of the term of the moratorium.

**Challenges to the monitor and the directors: Part A1, Chapter 6**—There are various grounds upon which the conduct of the monitor or the directors may be challenged. Notably, there is no provision which expressly envisages a claim for damages or compensation against a monitor (equivalent to s 212 of the 1986 Act or para 75 of Sch B1), as appears to reflect the status of the monitor as having oversight but not control of the company and its assets (subject, of course, to a monitor attracting such liability for conduct, say, capable of characterising the monitor as a shadow director).

Any act, omission or decision of the monitor during moratorium is open to challenge by a creditor, director, member or other person affected by the moratorium on the ground that the monitor 'has unfairly harmed the interests of the applicant' (s A42). The court has a wide discretion in terms of remedy but 'must have regard to the need to safeguard the interests' of bona fide third parties who have dealt with the company for value.

Rules may provide for a challenge to a monitor's remuneration on the ground of the remuneration being excessive, but only by a liquidator or administrator (s A43). Such an application might be forthcoming where the monitor's assessment of the likelihood of the rescue of the company as a going concern is clearly open to question in circumstances where the remuneration charged is on its face disproportionate relative to the task apparently undertaken by the monitor.

Finally, a creditor or member is afforded a specific application against the company's directors on the ground that actual or future management by the directors has unfairly harmed the interests of the applicant (s A44).

**Remuneration**—SIP 9 has not been amended to extend to the remuneration of monitors although that step may be considered necessary depending on the experience of the level of fees found to be charged for the services of a monitor.

**Temporary Covid–19 measures applicable until 30 September 2020 (subject to extension)**—Under these temporary measures, the directors may file the requisite documents to invoke a moratorium notwithstanding any extant winding-up petition. The proposed monitor may disregard any worsening of the company's position related to Covid-19 with a modified statement to that effect in expressing the likelihood of the company being rescued as a going concern. Further, there is no bar on a moratorium being obtained by reason of any previous moratorium, CVA or administration. Although the monitor remains obligated to form a view that the company is likely to be rescued as a going concern, or would be were it not for Coronavirus, the monitor must terminate the moratorium if he or she forms the view that the company is not likely to be rescued and would not have been likely to be rescued even absent Coronavirus.

## CHAPTER 1

### INTRODUCTORY

## [1.3]

**A1 Overview**

(1) This Part contains provision that enables an eligible company, in certain circumstances, to obtain a moratorium, giving it various protections from creditors set out in this Part.

(2) In this Chapter section A2 introduces Schedule ZA1 (which defines what is meant by an "eligible" company).

(3) Chapter 2 sets out how an eligible company may obtain a moratorium.

(4) Chapter 3 sets out for how long a moratorium has effect.

(5) Chapter 4 sets out the effects of a moratorium on the company and its creditors.

(6) Chapter 5 contains provision about the monitor.

(7) Chapter 6 contains provision about challenges.

(8) Chapter 7 contains provision about certain offences.

(9) Chapter 8 contains miscellaneous and general provision, including—

    (a) special provision for certain kinds of company;

    (b) definitions for the purposes of this Part;

    (c) provision about regulations under this Part.

**Amendments**—Inserted by Corporate Insolvency and Governance Act 2020, s 1(1).

**[1.4]**

**A2 Eligible companies**

Schedule ZA1 contains provision for determining whether a company is an eligible company for the purposes of this Part.

Amendments—Inserted by Corporate Insolvency and Governance Act 2020, s 1(1).

CHAPTER 2

OBTAINING A MORATORIUM

**[1.5]**

**A3 Obtaining a moratorium by filing or lodging documents at court**

(1)   This section applies to an eligible company that—
>   (a)   is not subject to an outstanding winding-up petition, and
>   (b)   is not an overseas company.

(2)   The directors of the company may obtain a moratorium for the company by filing the relevant documents with the court (for the relevant documents, see section A6).

(3)   For the purposes of this Chapter a company is "subject to an outstanding winding-up petition" if—
>   (a)   a petition for the winding up of the company has been presented, and
>   (b)   the petition has not been withdrawn or determined.

Amendments—Inserted by Corporate Insolvency and Governance Act 2020, s 1(1).

CIGA 2020—This provision is affected by temporary measures at Sch 4, paras 5 and 6(1)(a) of CIGA 2020 and by the *Insolvency Practice Direction relating to the Corporate Insolvency and Governance Act* 2020 (at APPENDIX 4 of this book).

**[1.6]**

**A4 Obtaining a moratorium for company subject to winding-up petition**

(1)   This section applies to an eligible company that is subject to an outstanding winding-up petition.

(2)   The directors of the company may apply to the court for a moratorium for the company.

(3)   The application must be accompanied by the relevant documents (for the relevant documents, see section A6).

(4)   On hearing the application the court may—
>   (a)   make an order that the company should be subject to a moratorium, or
>   (b)   make any other order which the court thinks appropriate.

(5)   The court may make an order under subsection (4)(a) only if it is satisfied that a moratorium for the company would achieve a better result for the company's creditors as a whole than would be likely if the company were wound up (without first being subject to a moratorium).

Amendments—Inserted by Corporate Insolvency and Governance Act 2020, s 1(1).

CIGA 2020—This provision is affected by temporary measures at Sch 4, paras 5 and 6(2) of CIGA 2020.

**[1.7]**

**A5 Obtaining a moratorium for other overseas companies**

(1)   This section applies to an eligible company that—
>   (a)   is not subject to an outstanding winding-up petition, and
>   (b)   is an overseas company.

(2)   The directors of the company may apply to the court for a moratorium for the company.

(3)   The application must be accompanied by the relevant documents (for the relevant documents, see section A6).

(4)   On hearing the application the court may—
- (a)   make an order that the company should be subject to a moratorium, or
- (b)   make any other order which the court thinks appropriate.

**Amendments**—Inserted by Corporate Insolvency and Governance Act 2020, s 1(1).

**CIGA 2020**—This provision is affected by temporary measures at Sch 4, para 5 of CIGA 2020.

## [1.8]

### A6   The relevant documents

(1)   For the purposes of this Chapter, "the relevant documents" are—
- (a)   a notice that the directors wish to obtain a moratorium,
- (b)   a statement from a qualified person ("the proposed monitor") that the person—
    - (i)   is a qualified person, and
    - (ii)   consents to act as the monitor in relation to the proposed moratorium,
- (c)   a statement from the proposed monitor that the company is an eligible company,
- (d)   a statement from the directors that, in their view, the company is, or is likely to become, unable to pay its debts, and
- (e)   a statement from the proposed monitor that, in the proposed monitor's view, it is likely that a moratorium for the company would result in the rescue of the company as a going concern.

(2)   Where it is proposed that more than one person should act as the monitor in relation to the proposed moratorium—
- (a)   each of them must make a statement under subsection (1)(b), (c) and (e), and
- (b)   the statement under subsection (1)(b) must specify—
    - (i)   which functions (if any) are to be exercised by the persons acting jointly, and
    - (ii)   which functions (if any) are to be exercised by any or all of the persons.

(3)   The rules may make provision about the date on which a statement comprised in the relevant documents must be made.

(4)   The Secretary of State may by regulations amend this section for the purposes of adding to the list of documents in subsection (1).

(5)   Regulations under subsection (4) are subject to the affirmative resolution procedure.

**Amendments**—Inserted by Corporate Insolvency and Governance Act 2020, s 1(1).

**CIGA 2020**—This provision is affected by temporary measures at Sch 4, paras 6(1)(b) and 7(a) of CIGA 2020.

## [1.9]

### A7   Beginning of moratorium and appointment of monitor

(1)   A moratorium for a company comes into force at the time at which—
- (a)   in the case of a company to which section A3 applies, the relevant documents are filed with the court under subsection (2) of that section;
- (b)   in the case of a company to which section A4 applies, an order is made under section A4(4)(a);
- (c)   in the case of a company to which section A5 applies, an order is made under section A5(4)(a).

(2)   On the coming into force of a moratorium, the person or persons who made the statement mentioned in section A6(1)(b) become the monitor in relation to the moratorium.

**Amendments**—Inserted by Corporate Insolvency and Governance Act 2020, s 1(1).

**[1.10]**

**A8 Obligations to notify where moratorium comes into force**

(1)   As soon as reasonably practicable after a moratorium for a company comes into force, the directors must notify the monitor of that fact.

(2)   As soon as reasonably practicable after receiving a notice under subsection (1), the monitor must notify the following that a moratorium for the company has come into force—

    (a)    the registrar of companies,

    (b)    every creditor of the company of whose claim the monitor is aware,

    (c)    in a case where the company is or has been an employer in respect of an occupational pension scheme that is not a money purchase scheme, the Pensions Regulator, and

    (d)    in a case where the company is an employer in respect of such a pension scheme that is an eligible scheme within the meaning given by section 126 of the Pensions Act 2004, the Board of the Pension Protection Fund.

(3)   A notice under subsection (2) must specify—

    (a)    when the moratorium came into force, and

    (b)    when, subject to any alteration under or by virtue of any of the provisions mentioned in section A9(3) or (4), the moratorium will come to an end.

(4)   If the directors fail to comply with subsection (1), any director who did not have a reasonable excuse for the failure commits an offence.

(5)   If the monitor without reasonable excuse fails to comply with subsection (2), the monitor commits an offence.

**Amendments**—Inserted by Corporate Insolvency and Governance Act 2020, s 1(1).

CHAPTER 3

LENGTH OF MORATORIUM
*Initial period*

**[1.11]**

**A9 End of the moratorium**

(1)   A moratorium ends at the end of the initial period unless it is extended, or comes to an end sooner, under or by virtue of a provision mentioned in subsection (3) or (4).

(2)   In this Chapter "the initial period", in relation to a moratorium, means the period of 20 business days beginning with the business day after the day on which the moratorium comes into force.

(3)   For provision under or by virtue of which a moratorium is or may be extended, see—

    section A10 (extension by directors without creditor consent);

    section A11 (extension by directors with creditor consent);

    section A13 (extension by court on application of directors);

    section A14 (extension while proposal for CVA pending);

    section A15 (extension by court in course of other proceedings).

(4)   For provision under or by virtue of which the moratorium is or may be terminated, see—

    section A16 (termination on entry into insolvency procedure etc);

    section A38 (termination by monitor);

    section A42 or A44 (termination by court).

(5)   A moratorium may not be extended under a provision mentioned in subsection (3) once it has come to an end.

(6)   Where the application of two or more of the provisions mentioned in subsections (3) and (4) would produce a different length of moratorium, the provision that applies last is to prevail (irrespective of whether that results in a shorter or longer moratorium).

**Amendments**—Inserted by Corporate Insolvency and Governance Act 2020, s 1(1).

*Extension of moratorium*

**[1.12]**

**A10 Extension by directors without creditor consent**

(1) During the initial period, but after the first 15 business days of that period, the directors may extend the moratorium by filing with the court—

    (a)    a notice that the directors wish to extend the moratorium,

    (b)    a statement from the directors that all of the following that have fallen due have been paid or otherwise discharged—

        (i)    moratorium debts, and

        (ii)    pre-moratorium debts for which the company does not have a payment holiday during the moratorium (see section A18),

    (c)    a statement from the directors that, in their view, the company is, or is likely to become, unable to pay its pre-moratorium debts, and

    (d)    a statement from the monitor that, in the monitor's view, it is likely that the moratorium will result in the rescue of the company as a going concern.

(2) The rules may make provision about the date on which a statement mentioned in subsection (1) must be made.

(3) On the filing with the court of the documents mentioned in subsection (1), the moratorium is extended so that it ends at the end of the period—

    (a)    beginning immediately after the initial period ends, and

    (b)    ending with the 20th business day after the initial period ends.

**Amendments**—Inserted by Corporate Insolvency and Governance Act 2020, s 1(1).

**CIGA 2020**—This provision is affected by temporary measures at Sch 4, para 8(2) of CIGA 2020.

**[1.13]**

**A11 Extension by directors with creditor consent**

(1) At any time after the first 15 business days of the initial period the directors may, if they have obtained creditor consent, extend the moratorium by filing with the court—

    (a)    a notice that the directors wish to extend the moratorium,

    (b)    a statement from the directors that all of the following that have fallen due have been paid or otherwise discharged—

        (i)    moratorium debts, and

        (ii)    pre-moratorium debts for which the company does not have a payment holiday during the moratorium (see section A18),

    (c)    a statement from the directors that, in their view, the company is, or is likely to become, unable to pay its pre-moratorium debts,

    (d)    a statement from the monitor that, in the monitor's view, it is likely that the moratorium will result in the rescue of the company as a going concern, and

    (e)    a statement from the directors that creditor consent has been obtained, and of the revised end date for which that consent was obtained.

(2) The rules may make provision about the date on which a statement mentioned in subsection (1) must be made.

(3) On the filing with the court of the documents mentioned in subsection (1), the moratorium is extended so that it ends with the revised end date mentioned in the statement under subsection (1)(e).

(4) A moratorium may be extended under this section more than once.

**Amendments**—Inserted by Corporate Insolvency and Governance Act 2020, s 1(1).

**CIGA 2020**—This provision is affected by temporary measures at Sch 4, para 8(2) of CIGA 2020.

**[1.14]**

### A12 Creditor consent for the purposes of section A11

(1)   References in section A11 to creditor consent are to the consent of pre-moratorium creditors to a revised end date for the moratorium.

(2)   The decision as to consent is to be made using a qualifying decision procedure.

(3)   The revised end date must be a date before the end of the period of one year beginning with the first day of the initial period.

(4)   In this section "pre-moratorium creditor" means a creditor in respect of a pre-moratorium debt—

  (a)   for which the company has a payment holiday during the moratorium (see section A18), and

  (b)   which has not been paid or otherwise discharged.

(5)   In determining for the purposes of subsection (4) what counts as a pre-moratorium debt for which the company has a payment holiday during the moratorium, sections A18(3) and A53(1)(b) apply as if the references to the moratorium were to the moratorium as proposed to be extended.

(6)   The Secretary of State may by regulations amend this section for the purposes of changing the definition of "pre-moratorium creditor".

(7)   Regulations under subsection (6) are subject to the affirmative resolution procedure.

**Amendments**—Inserted by Corporate Insolvency and Governance Act 2020, s 1(1).

**[1.15]**

### A13 Extension by court on application of directors

(1)   At any time after the first 15 business days of the initial period, the directors may apply to the court for an order that the moratorium be extended.

(2)   The application must be accompanied by—

  (a)   a statement from the directors that all of the following that have fallen due have been paid or otherwise discharged—

    (i)   moratorium debts, and

    (ii)   pre-moratorium debts for which the company does not have a payment holiday during the moratorium (see section A18),

  (b)   a statement from the directors that, in their view, the company is, or is likely to become, unable to pay its pre-moratorium debts,

  (c)   a statement from the directors as to whether pre-moratorium creditors (as defined by section A12(4) and (5)) have been consulted about the application and if not why not, and

  (d)   a statement from the monitor that, in the monitor's view, it is likely that the moratorium will result in the rescue of the company as a going concern.

(3)   The rules may make provision about the date on which a statement mentioned in subsection (2) must be made.

(4)   On hearing the application the court may—

  (a)   make an order that the moratorium be extended to such date as is specified in the order, or

  (b)   make any other order which the court thinks appropriate.

(5)   In deciding whether to make an order under subsection (4)(a) the court must, in particular, consider the following—

  (a)   the interests of pre-moratorium creditors, as defined by section A12(4) and (5), and

  (b)   the likelihood that the extension of the moratorium will result in the rescue of the company as a going concern.

(6)   Subsection (7) applies where—

  (a)   an application under this section is made, and

    (b)    apart from that subsection, the moratorium would end at a time before the application has been disposed of.

(7)   The moratorium—

    (a)    does not end at the time mentioned in subsection (6)(b), and

    (b)    instead, ends—

        (i)    in a case in which the court makes an order under subsection (4)(a), in accordance with the order;

        (ii)    otherwise, when the application is withdrawn or disposed of.

(8)   A moratorium may be extended under this section more than once.

**Amendments**—Inserted by Corporate Insolvency and Governance Act 2020, s 1(1).

**CIGA 2020**—This provision is affected by temporary measures at Sch 4, para 8(3) of CIGA 2020.

## [1.16]

### A14 Extension while proposal for CVA pending

(1)   Subsection (2) applies where—

    (a)    at any time, the directors make a proposal under Part 1 (company voluntary arrangements), and

    (b)    apart from that subsection, the moratorium would end at a time before the proposal is disposed of.

(2)   The moratorium—

    (a)    does not end at the time mentioned in subsection (1)(b), and

    (b)    instead, ends when the proposal is disposed of.

(3)   For the purposes of this section a proposal under Part 1 is "disposed of" when any of the following takes place—

    (a)    the company and its creditors both decide under section 4 not to approve the voluntary arrangement contained in the proposal;

    (b)    the decisions taken by the company and its creditors under section 4 differ, and—

        (i)    the period for making an application under section 4A(3) expires and either no application has been made within that period or any application made within that period has been withdrawn, or

        (ii)    an application is made under section 4A(3) and that application is disposed of, or it is withdrawn after the expiry of the period for making an application under section 4A(3);

    (c)    the voluntary arrangement contained in the proposal takes effect under section 5;

    (d)    the proposal is withdrawn.

**Amendments**—Inserted by Corporate Insolvency and Governance Act 2020, s 1(1).

## [1.17]

### A15 Extension by court in the course of other proceedings

(1)   Subsection (2) applies where—

    (a)    an application is made under section 896 or 901C(1) of the Companies Act 2006 (arrangements and reconstructions: court order for holding of meeting) in respect of a company, and

    (b)    during proceedings before a court in connection with the application, a moratorium for the company is in force.

(2)   The court may make an order that the moratorium be extended to such date as is specified in the order.

**Amendments**—Inserted by Corporate Insolvency and Governance Act 2020, s 1(1).

*Early termination on certain grounds*

**[1.18]**

**A16 Company enters into insolvency procedure etc**

(1)   A moratorium comes to an end at any time at which the company—

(a)   enters into a compromise or arrangement (see subsection (2)), or

(b)   enters into a relevant insolvency procedure (see subsection (3)).

(2)   For the purposes of this section a company enters into a compromise or arrangement if an order under section 899 or 901F of the Companies Act 2006 (court sanction for compromise or arrangement) comes into effect in relation to the company.

(3)   For the purposes of this section a company enters into a relevant insolvency procedure if—

(a)   a voluntary arrangement takes effect under section 5 in relation to the company,

(b)   the company enters administration (within the meaning of Schedule B1 (see paragraph 1(2)(b) of that Schedule)),

(c)   paragraph 44 of Schedule B1 (administration: interim moratorium) begins to apply in relation to the company, or

(d)   the company goes into liquidation (see section 247).

**Amendments**—Inserted by Corporate Insolvency and Governance Act 2020, s 1(1).

*Obligations to notify change in end of moratorium*

**[1.19]**

**A17   Obligations to notify change in end of moratorium**

(1)   The table imposes obligations on the directors of a company to notify the monitor where a moratorium for the company is extended or comes to an end.

| | Where a moratorium is extended or comes to an end under or by virtue of the following provision | the directors must |
|---|---|---|
| 1 | Section A10 | Notify the monitor of the extension. |
| 2 | Section A11 | Notify the monitor of the extension and of the revised end date. |
| 3 | Section A13(4) | Notify the monitor of the extension and provide the monitor with the court order under section A13(4). |
| 4 | Section A13(7)(a) | Notify the monitor of the extension. |
| 5 | Section A13(7)(b)(ii) | Notify the monitor that the moratorium has come to an end and of the date that it ended. |
| 6 | Section A14(2)(a) | Notify the monitor of the extension. |
| 7 | Section A14(2)(b) | Notify the monitor that the moratorium has come to an end and of the date that it ended. |

| 8 | Section A15 | Notify the monitor of the extension and provide the monitor with any court order under section A15. |
|---|---|---|
| 9 | Section A16 | Notify the monitor that the moratorium has come to an end. |
| 10 | Section A42 | Notify the monitor that the moratorium has come to an end and provide the monitor with the court order under section A42. |
| 11 | Section A44 | Notify the monitor that the moratorium has come to an end and provide the monitor with the court order under section A44. |

(2) After receiving a notice under subsection (1), other than a notice under entry 4 or 6 of the table, the monitor must notify the relevant persons of when the moratorium ended or, subject to any alteration under or by virtue of any of the provisions mentioned in section A9(3) or (4), the moratorium will come to an end.

(3) After receiving a notice under entry 4 or 6 of the table, the monitor must notify the relevant persons.

(4) If a moratorium comes to an end under section A38 (termination by monitor), the monitor must notify the company and the relevant persons of when the moratorium ended.

(5) The rules may—

    (a) make further provision about the timing of a notice required to be given under this section;

    (b) require a notice to be accompanied by other documents.

(6) If the directors fail to comply with subsection (1), any director who did not have a reasonable excuse for the failure commits an offence.

(7) If the monitor without reasonable excuse fails to comply with any of subsections (2) to (4), the monitor commits an offence.

(8) In this section "the relevant persons" means—

    (a) the registrar of companies,

    (b) every creditor of the company of whose claim the monitor is aware,

    (c) in a case where the company is or has been an employer in respect of an occupational pension scheme that is not a money purchase scheme, the Pensions Regulator, and

    (d) in a case where the company is an employer in respect of such a pension scheme that is an eligible scheme within the meaning given by section 126 of the Pensions Act 2004, the Board of the Pension Protection Fund.

**Amendments**—Inserted by Corporate Insolvency and Governance Act 2020, s 1(1).

## CHAPTER 4

### Effects of Moratorium
*Introductory*

**[1.20]**

**A18 Overview and construction of references to payment holidays**

(1) This Chapter makes provision about the main effects of a moratorium for a company.

(2) The provision made by this Chapter includes restrictions on the enforcement or payment of the debts that are defined by subsection (3) as pre-moratorium debts for which a company has a payment holiday during a moratorium.

(3)   In this Part a reference to pre-moratorium debts for which a company has a payment holiday during a moratorium is to its pre-moratorium debts that have fallen due before the moratorium, or that fall due during the moratorium, except in so far as they consist of amounts payable in respect of—

    (a)    the monitor's remuneration or expenses,

    (b)    goods or services supplied during the moratorium,

    (c)    rent in respect of a period during the moratorium,

    (d)    wages or salary arising under a contract of employment,

    (e)    redundancy payments, or

    (f)    debts or other liabilities arising under a contract or other instrument involving financial services.

(4)   The rules may make provision as to what is, or is not, to count as the supply of goods or services for the purposes of subsection (3)(b).

(5)   The Secretary of State may by regulations amend this section for the purposes of changing the list in subsection (3).

(6)   Regulations under subsection (5) are subject to the affirmative resolution procedure.

(7)   In this section—

"contract or other instrument involving financial services" has the meaning given by Schedule ZA2;

"monitor's remuneration or expenses" does not include remuneration in respect of anything done by a proposed monitor before the moratorium begins;

"redundancy payment" means—

    (a)    a redundancy payment under Part 11 of the Employment Rights Act 1996 or Part 12 of the Employment Rights (Northern Ireland) Order 1996, or

    (b)    a payment made to a person who agrees to the termination of their employment in circumstances where they would have been entitled to a redundancy payment under that Part if dismissed;

"wages or salary" includes—

    (a)    a sum payable in respect of a period of holiday (for which purpose the sum is to be treated as relating to the period by reference to which the entitlement to holiday accrued),

    (b)    a sum payable in respect of a period of absence through illness or other good cause,

    (c)    a sum payable in lieu of holiday, and

    (d)    a contribution to an occupational pension scheme.

**Amendments**—Inserted by Corporate Insolvency and Governance Act 2020, s 1(1).

*Publicity about moratorium*

**[1.21]**

### A19   Publicity about moratorium

(1)   During a moratorium, the company must, in any premises—

    (a)    where business of the company is carried on, and

    (b)    to which customers of the company or suppliers of goods or services to the company have access,

display, in a prominent position so that it may easily be read by such customers or suppliers, a notice containing the required information.

(2)   During a moratorium, any websites of the company must state the required information.

(3)   During a moratorium, every business document issued by or on behalf of the company must state the required information.

(4)   For the purposes of subsections (1), (2) and (3), "the required information" is—

    (a)    that a moratorium is in force in relation to the company, and

(b)    the name of the monitor.
(5)  If subsection (1), (2) or (3) is contravened—
(a)    the company commits an offence, and
(b)    any officer of the company who without reasonable excuse authorised or permitted the contravention commits an offence.
(6)  In this section "business document" means—
(a)    an invoice,
(b)    an order for goods or services,
(c)    a business letter, and
(d)    an order form,
whether in hard copy, electronic or any other form.

**Amendments**—Inserted by Corporate Insolvency and Governance Act 2020, s 1(1).

*Effect on creditors etc*

**[1.22]**

**A20  Restrictions on insolvency proceedings etc**
(1)  During a moratorium—
(a)    no petition may be presented for the winding up of the company, except by the directors,
(b)    no resolution may be passed for the voluntary winding up of the company under section 84(1)(a),
(c)    a resolution for the voluntary winding up of the company under section 84(1)(b) may be passed only if the resolution is recommended by the directors,
(d)    no order may be made for the winding up of the company, except on a petition by the directors,
(e)    no administration application may be made in respect of the company, except by the directors,
(f)    no notice of intention to appoint an administrator of the company under paragraph 14 or 22(1) of Schedule B1 may be filed with the court,
(g)    no administrator of the company may be appointed under paragraph 14 or 22(1) of Schedule B1, and
(h)    no administrative receiver of the company may be appointed.
(2)  Subsection (1)(a) does not apply to an excepted petition; and subsection (1)(d) does not apply to an order on an excepted petition.
(3)  For these purposes, "excepted petition" means a petition under—
(a)    section 124A, 124B or 124C, or
(b)    section 367 of the Financial Services and Markets Act 2000 on the ground mentioned in subsection (3)(b) of that section.

**Amendments**—Inserted by Corporate Insolvency and Governance Act 2020, s 1(1).

**[1.23]**

**A21  Restrictions on enforcement and legal proceedings**
(1)  During a moratorium—
(a)    a landlord or other person to whom rent is payable may not exercise a right of forfeiture by peaceable re-entry in relation to premises let to the company, except with the permission of the court,
(b)    in Scotland, a landlord or other person to whom rent is payable may not exercise a right of irritancy in relation to premises let to the company, except with the permission of the court,
(c)    no steps may be taken to enforce any security over the company's property except—

      (i)     steps to enforce a collateral security charge (within the meaning of the Financial Markets and Insolvency (Settlement Finality) Regulations 1999 (SI 1999/2979)),

      (ii)    steps to enforce security created or otherwise arising under a financial collateral arrangement (within the meaning of regulation 3 of the Financial Collateral Arrangements (No 2) Regulations 2003 (SI 2003/3226)), or

      (iii)   steps taken with the permission of the court,

  (d)    no steps may be taken to repossess goods in the company's possession under any hire-purchase agreement, except with the permission of the court, and

  (e)    no legal process (including legal proceedings, execution, distress or diligence) may be instituted, carried out or continued against the company or its property except—

      (i)     employment tribunal proceedings or any legal process arising out of such proceedings,

      (ii)    proceedings, not within sub-paragraph (i), involving a claim between an employer and a worker, or

      (iii)   a legal process instituted, carried out or continued with the permission of the court.

(2) An application may not be made for permission under subsection (1) for the purposes of enforcing a pre-moratorium debt for which the company has a payment holiday during the moratorium.

(3) An application may not be made for permission under subsection (1)(c), (d) or (e) with a view to obtaining—

  (a)    the crystallisation of a floating charge, or

  (b)    the imposition, by virtue of provision in an instrument creating a floating charge, of any restriction on the disposal of any property of the company.

(4) Permission of the court under subsection (1) may be given subject to conditions.

(5) Subsection (1)(c)(iii) is subject to section A23(1).

(6) In this section—

"agency worker" has the meaning given by section 13(2) of the Employment Relations Act 1999;

"employer"—

  (a)    in relation to an agency worker, has the meaning given by section 13(2) of the Employment Relations Act 1999;

  (b)    otherwise, has the meaning given by section 230(4) of the Employment Rights Act 1996;

"worker" means an individual who is—

  (a)    a worker within the meaning of section 230(3) of the Employment Rights Act 1996, or

  (b)    an agency worker.

**Amendments**—Inserted by Corporate Insolvency and Governance Act 2020, s 1(1).

## [1.24]

### A22 Floating charges

(1) This section applies where there is an uncrystallised floating charge on the property of a company for which a moratorium is in force.

(2) During the moratorium, the holder of the floating charge may not give any notice which would have the effect of—

  (a)    causing the floating charge to crystallise, or

  (b)    causing the imposition, by virtue of provision in the instrument creating the charge, of any restriction on the disposal of property of the company.

(3) No other event occurring during the moratorium is to have the effect mentioned in subsection (2)(a) or (b).

(4) Subsection (5) applies where—

(a)     the holder of a floating charge ("the chargee") is prevented by subsection (2) from giving a notice mentioned there during the moratorium, and

(b)     under the terms of the floating charge, the time for giving such a notice ends during the moratorium or before the chargee is given notice of the end of the moratorium under section A17.

(5)   The chargee may give notice later than is required under the terms of the floating charge, but only if the chargee does so as soon as is practicable after—

(a)     the end of the moratorium, or

(b)     if later, the day on which the chargee is notified of the end of the moratorium.

(6)   Where—

(a)     subsection (3) prevents an event which occurs during the moratorium from having the effect mentioned there, and

(b)     the holder of the floating charge gives notice of the event to the company as soon as is practicable after—

(i)     the end of the moratorium, or

(ii)     if later, the day on which the chargee is notified of the end of the moratorium,

the event is to be treated as if it had occurred when the notice was given.

(7)   This section does not apply in relation to a floating charge that is—

(a)     a collateral security (as defined by section A27);

(b)     a market charge (as defined by section A27);

(c)     a security financial collateral arrangement (within the meaning of regulation 3 of the Financial Collateral Arrangements (No 2) Regulations 2003 (SI 2003/3226));

(d)     a system-charge (as defined by section A27).

**Amendments**—Inserted by Corporate Insolvency and Governance Act 2020, s 1(1).

## [1.25]

### A23 Enforcement of security granted during moratorium

(1)   Security granted by a company during a moratorium in relation to the company may be enforced only if the monitor consented to the grant of security under section A26.

(2)   See also section A21(1)(c), which restricts enforcement during a moratorium.

**Amendments**—Inserted by Corporate Insolvency and Governance Act 2020, s 1(1).

*Notification of insolvency proceedings*

## [1.26]

### A24 Duty of directors to notify monitor of insolvency proceedings etc

(1)   The directors of a company must notify the monitor before taking any of the following steps during a moratorium—

(a)     presenting a petition for the winding up of the company;

(b)     making an administration application in respect of the company;

(c)     appointing an administrator under paragraph 22(2) of Schedule B1.

(2)   The directors of a company must notify the monitor if, during a moratorium for the company, they recommend that the company passes a resolution for voluntary winding up under section 84(1)(b).

(3)   The rules may make provision about the timing of a notice required to be given under subsection (1) or (2).

(4)   If the directors fail to comply with subsection (1) or (2), any director who did not have a reasonable excuse for the failure commits an offence.

**Amendments**—Inserted by Corporate Insolvency and Governance Act 2020, s 1(1).

*Restrictions on transactions*

**[1.27]**

### A25 Restrictions on obtaining credit

(1)   During a moratorium, the company may not obtain credit to the extent of £500 or more from a person unless the person has been informed that a moratorium is in force in relation to the company.

(2)   The reference to the company obtaining credit includes—

    (a)   the company entering into a conditional sale agreement in accordance with which goods are to be sold to the company,

    (b)   the company entering into any other form of hire-purchase agreement under which goods are to be bailed (in Scotland, hired) to the company, and

    (c)   the company being paid in advance (whether in money or otherwise) for the supply of goods or services.

(3)   If a company contravenes subsection (1)—

    (a)   the company commits an offence, and

    (b)   any officer of the company who without reasonable excuse authorised or permitted the obtaining of the credit commits an offence.

**Amendments**—Inserted by Corporate Insolvency and Governance Act 2020, s 1(1).

**[1.28]**

### A26 Restrictions on grant of security etc

(1)   During a moratorium, the company may grant security over its property only if the monitor consents.

(2)   The monitor may give consent under subsection (1) only if the monitor thinks that the grant of security will support the rescue of the company as a going concern.

(3)   In deciding whether to give consent under subsection (1), the monitor is entitled to rely on information provided by the company unless the monitor has reason to doubt its accuracy.

(4)   If the company grants security over its property during the moratorium otherwise than as authorised by subsection (1)—

    (a)   the company commits an offence, and

    (b)   any officer of the company who without reasonable excuse authorised or permitted the grant of the security commits an offence.

(5)   For the consequences of a company granting security over its property in contravention of subsection (1), see also section A23.

(6)   The monitor may not give consent under this section if the granting of security is an offence under section A27.

**Amendments**—Inserted by Corporate Insolvency and Governance Act 2020, s 1(1).

**[1.29]**

### A27 Prohibition on entering into market contracts etc

(1)   If a company enters into a transaction to which this section applies during a moratorium for the company—

    (a)   the company commits an offence, and

    (b)   any officer of the company who without reasonable excuse authorised or permitted the company to enter into the transaction commits an offence.

(2)   A company enters into a transaction to which this section applies if it—

    (a)   enters into a market contract,

    (b)   enters into a financial collateral arrangement,

    (c)   gives a transfer order,

    (d)   grants a market charge or a system-charge, or

    (e)   provides any collateral security.

(3)   Where during the moratorium a company enters into a transaction to which this section applies, nothing done by or in pursuance of the transaction is to be treated as done in contravention of any of sections A19, A21, A25, A26 and A28 to A32.

(4)   In this section—

"collateral security" has the same meaning as in the Financial Markets and Insolvency (Settlement Finality) Regulations 1999 (SI 1999/2979);

"financial collateral arrangement" has the same meaning as in the Financial Collateral Arrangements (No 2) Regulations 2003 (SI 2003/3226);

"market charge" has the same meaning as in Part 7 of the Companies Act 1989;

"market contract" has the same meaning as in Part 7 of the Companies Act 1989;

"system-charge" has the meaning given by the Financial Markets and Insolvency Regulations 1996 (SI 1996/1469);

"transfer order" has the same meaning as in the Financial Markets and Insolvency (Settlement Finality) Regulations 1999.

**Amendments**—Inserted by Corporate Insolvency and Governance Act 2020, s 1(1).

*Restrictions on payments and disposal of property*

## [1.30]

### A28   Restrictions on payment of certain pre-moratorium debts

(1)   During a moratorium, the company may make one or more relevant payments to a person that (in total) exceed the specified maximum amount only if—

(a)   the monitor consents,

(b)   the payment is in pursuance of a court order, or

(c)   the payment is required by section A31(3) or A32(3).

(2)   In subsection (1)—

"relevant payments" means payments in respect of pre-moratorium debts for which the company has a payment holiday during the moratorium (see section A18);

"specified maximum amount" means an amount equal to the greater of—

(a)   £5000, and

(b)   1% of the value of the debts and other liabilities owed by the company to its unsecured creditors when the moratorium began, to the extent that the amount of such debts and liabilities can be ascertained at that time.

(3)   The monitor may give consent under subsection (1)(a) only if the monitor thinks that it will support the rescue of the company as a going concern.

(4)   In deciding whether to give consent under subsection (1)(a), the monitor is entitled to rely on information provided by the company unless the monitor has reason to doubt its accuracy.

(5)   If the company makes a payment to which subsection (1) applies otherwise than as authorised by that subsection—

(a)   the company commits an offence, and

(b)   any officer of the company who without reasonable excuse authorised or permitted the payment commits an offence.

**Amendments**—Inserted by Corporate Insolvency and Governance Act 2020, s 1(1).

## [1.31]

### A29   Restrictions on disposal of property

(1)   During a moratorium, the company may dispose of its property only if authorised by subsection (2) or (5).

(2)   In the case of property that is not subject to a security interest, the company may dispose of the property if—

(a)   the disposal is made in the ordinary way of the company's business,

(b)     the monitor consents, or

(c)     the disposal is in pursuance of a court order.

(3)   The monitor may give consent under subsection (2)(b) only if the monitor thinks that it will support the rescue of the company as a going concern.

(4)   In deciding whether to give consent under subsection (2)(b), the monitor is entitled to rely on information provided by the company unless the monitor has reason to doubt its accuracy.

(5)   In the case of property that is subject to a security interest, the company may dispose of the property if the disposal is in accordance with—

(a)     section A31(1), or

(b)     the terms of the security.

(6)   If the company disposes of its property during the moratorium otherwise than as authorised by this section—

(a)     the company commits an offence, and

(b)     any officer of the company who without reasonable excuse authorised or permitted the disposal commits an offence.

**Amendments**—Inserted by Corporate Insolvency and Governance Act 2020, s 1(1).

## [1.32]

### A30   Restrictions on disposal of hire-purchase property

(1)   During a moratorium, the company may dispose of any goods in the possession of the company under a hire-purchase agreement only if the disposal is in accordance with—

(a)     section A32(1), or

(b)     the terms of the agreement.

(2)   If the company disposes of goods in the possession of the company under a hire-purchase agreement otherwise than as authorised by subsection (1)—

(a)     the company commits an offence, and

(b)     any officer of the company who without reasonable excuse authorised or permitted the disposal commits an offence.

**Amendments**—Inserted by Corporate Insolvency and Governance Act 2020, s 1(1).

*Disposals of property free from charges etc*

## [1.33]

### A31   Disposal of charged property free from charge

(1)   During a moratorium, the company may, with the permission of the court, dispose of property which is subject to a security interest as if it were not subject to the security interest.

(2)   The court may give permission under subsection (1) only if the court thinks that it will support the rescue of the company as a going concern.

(3)   Where the court gives permission under subsection (1) other than in relation to a floating charge, the company must apply the following towards discharging the sums secured—

(a)     the net proceeds of disposal of the property, and

(b)     any money required to be added to the net proceeds so as to produce the amount determined by the court as the net amount which would be realised on a sale of the property in the open market by a willing vendor.

(4)   Where the permission relates to two or more security interests, the condition in subsection (3) requires the application of money in the order of the priorities of the security interests.

(5)   Where property subject to a floating charge is disposed of under subsection (1), the holder of the floating charge has the same priority in respect of acquired property as they had in respect of the property disposed of.

(6)   In subsection (5) "acquired property" means property of the company which directly or indirectly represents the property disposed of.

(7)   Where the court makes an order giving permission under subsection (1), the directors must, within the period of 14 days beginning with the date of the order, send a copy of it to the registrar of companies.

(8)   If the directors fail to comply with subsection (7), any director who did not have a reasonable excuse for the failure commits an offence.

(9)   Where property in Scotland is disposed of under subsection (1), the company must grant to the disponee an appropriate document of transfer or conveyance of the property, and—

    (a)   that document, or

    (b)   recording, intimation or registration of that document (where recording, intimation or registration of the document is a legal requirement for completion of title to the property),

has the effect of disencumbering the property of or, as the case may be, freeing the property from, the security interest.

(10)   If a company fails to comply with subsection (3) or (9)—

    (a)   the company commits an offence, and

    (b)   any officer of the company who without reasonable excuse authorised or permitted the failure commits an offence.

(11)   Subsection (1) does not apply in relation to any property which is subject to a financial collateral arrangement, a market charge, a system-charge or a collateral security (as defined by section A27).

**Amendments**—Inserted by Corporate Insolvency and Governance Act 2020, s 1(1).

## [1.34]

### A32   Disposal of hire-purchase property

(1)   During a moratorium, the company may, with the permission of the court, dispose of goods which are in the possession of the company under a hire-purchase agreement as if all of the rights of the owner under the agreement were vested in the company.

(2)   The court may give permission under subsection (1) only if the court thinks that it will support the rescue of the company as a going concern.

(3)   Where the court gives permission under subsection (1), the company must apply the following towards discharging the sums payable under the hire-purchase agreement—

    (a)   the net proceeds of disposal of the goods, and

    (b)   any additional money required to be added to the net proceeds so as to produce the amount determined by the court as the net amount which would be realised on a sale of the goods in the open market by a willing vendor.

(4)   If a company fails to comply with subsection (3)—

    (a)   the company commits an offence, and

    (b)   any officer of the company who without reasonable excuse authorised or permitted the failure commits an offence.

(5)   Where the court makes an order giving permission under subsection (1), the directors must, within the period of 14 days beginning with the date of the order, send a copy of it to the registrar of companies.

(6)   If the directors fail to comply with subsection (5), any director who did not have a reasonable excuse for the failure commits an offence.

(7)   In Scotland, where goods in the possession of the company under a hire-purchase agreement are disposed of under subsection (1), the disposal has the effect of extinguishing, as against the disponee, all rights of the owner of the goods under the agreement.

**Amendments**—Inserted by Corporate Insolvency and Governance Act 2020, s 1(1).

*Effect of contravention of certain provisions of Chapter*

**[1.35]**

**A33 Contravention of certain requirements imposed under this Chapter**
The fact that a company contravenes section A19 or any of sections A25 to A32 does not—

(a) make any transaction void or unenforceable, or

(b) affect the validity of any other thing.

Amendments—Inserted by Corporate Insolvency and Governance Act 2020, s 1(1).

CHAPTER 5

THE MONITOR

**[1.36]**

**A34 Status of monitor**
The monitor in relation to a moratorium is an officer of the court.

Amendments—Inserted by Corporate Insolvency and Governance Act 2020, s 1(1).

**[1.37]**

**A35 Monitoring**
(1) During a moratorium, the monitor must monitor the company's affairs for the purpose of forming a view as to whether it remains likely that the moratorium will result in the rescue of the company as a going concern.
(2) In forming the view mentioned in subsection (1), the monitor is entitled to rely on information provided by the company, unless the monitor has reason to doubt its accuracy.

Amendments—Inserted by Corporate Insolvency and Governance Act 2020, s 1(1).
CIGA 2020—This provision is affected by temporary measures at Sch 4, para 9 of CIGA 2020.

**[1.38]**

**A36 Provision of information to monitor**
(1) The monitor may require the directors of the company to provide any information required by the monitor for the purpose of carrying out the monitor's functions.
(2) The directors must comply with a requirement to provide information as soon as practicable.
(3) For the potential consequences of failing to comply with a requirement to provide information, see section A38.

Amendments—Inserted by Corporate Insolvency and Governance Act 2020, s 1(1).

**[1.39]**

**A37 Application by monitor for directions**
The monitor in relation to a moratorium may apply to the court for directions about the carrying out of the monitor's functions.

Amendments—Inserted by Corporate Insolvency and Governance Act 2020, s 1(1).

**[1.40]**

**A38 Termination of moratorium by monitor**
(1) The monitor must bring a moratorium to an end by filing a notice with the court if—

(a) the monitor thinks that the moratorium is no longer likely to result in the rescue of the company as a going concern,

(b)   the monitor thinks that the objective of rescuing the company as a going concern has been achieved,

(c)   the monitor thinks that, by reason of a failure by the directors to comply with a requirement under section A36, the monitor is unable properly to carry out the monitor's functions, or

(d)   the monitor thinks that the company is unable to pay any of the following that have fallen due—

(i)   moratorium debts;

(ii)   pre-moratorium debts for which the company does not have a payment holiday during the moratorium (see section A18).

(2)   The rules may provide for debts that are to be disregarded for the purposes of subsection (1)(d).

(3)   On the filing with the court of a notice under subsection (1), the moratorium comes to an end.

(4)   The rules may make provision about the timing of a notice required to be given under subsection (1).

(5)   The Secretary of State may by regulations amend this section for the purposes of changing the circumstances in which the monitor must bring a moratorium to an end under subsection (1).

(6)   Regulations under subsection (5) are subject to the affirmative resolution procedure.

(7)   See also section A17 (obligations to notify change in end of moratorium).

**Amendments**—Inserted by Corporate Insolvency and Governance Act 2020, s 1(1).

**CIGA 2020**—This provision is affected by temporary measures at Sch 4, para 10 of CIGA 2020.

## [1.41]

### A39   Replacement of monitor or appointment of additional monitor

(1)   The court may make an order authorising the appointment of a qualified person to act as the monitor in relation to a moratorium instead of, or in addition to, a person who already acts as the monitor.

(2)   The court may make an order providing that a person ceases to act as the monitor in relation to a moratorium.

(3)   An order under subsection (1) or (2) may be made only on an application by the directors or the monitor.

(4)   The court may make an order authorising the appointment of a monitor under subsection (1) only if the person has provided the court with a statement that the person—

(a)   is a qualified person, and

(b)   consents to act as the monitor in relation to the moratorium.

(5)   Where it is proposed that more than one person should act as the monitor in relation to the moratorium, the statement under subsection (4) must specify—

(a)   which functions (if any) are to be exercised by the persons acting jointly, and

(b)   which functions (if any) are to be exercised by any or all of the persons.

(6)   The rules may make provision about the date on which the statement under subsection (4) must be made.

(7)   Where the court makes an order under subsection (1) or (2) the person begins to act as the monitor, or ceases to act as the monitor, in relation to the moratorium at the time specified in, or determined in accordance with, the order ("the relevant time").

(8)   As soon as reasonably practicable after the relevant time, the monitor must notify the following of the effect of the order—

(a)   the registrar of companies,

(b)   every creditor of the company of whose claim the monitor is aware,

(c)   in a case where the company is or has been an employer in respect of an occupational pension scheme that is not a money purchase scheme, the Pensions Regulator, and

    (d)    in a case where the company is an employer in respect of such a pension scheme that is an eligible scheme within the meaning given by section 126 of the Pensions Act 2004, the Board of the Pension Protection Fund.

(9) If the monitor without reasonable excuse fails to comply with subsection (8), the monitor commits an offence.

*Amendments*—Inserted by Corporate Insolvency and Governance Act 2020, s 1(1).

## [1.42]

### A40 Application of Part where two or more persons act as monitor

(1) Where two or more persons act jointly as the monitor—
    (a)    a reference in this Act to the monitor is a reference to those persons acting jointly;
    (b)    where an offence of omission is committed by the monitor, each of the persons appointed to act jointly—
        (i)    commits the offence, and
        (ii)    may be proceeded against and punished individually.

(2) Where persons act jointly in respect of only some of the functions of the monitor, subsection (1) applies only in relation to those functions.

(3) Where two or more persons act concurrently as the monitor a reference in this Act to the monitor is a reference to any of the persons appointed (or any combination of them).

*Amendments*—Inserted by Corporate Insolvency and Governance Act 2020, s 1(1).

## [1.43]

### A41 Presumption of validity

An act of the monitor is valid in spite of a defect in the monitor's appointment or qualification.

*Amendments*—Inserted by Corporate Insolvency and Governance Act 2020, s 1(1).

CHAPTER 6

CHALLENGES

## [1.44]

### A42 Challenge to monitor's actions

(1) Any of the persons specified below may apply to the court on the ground that an act, omission or decision of the monitor during a moratorium has unfairly harmed the interests of the applicant.

(2) The persons who may apply are—
    (a)    a creditor, director or member of the company, or
    (b)    any other person affected by the moratorium.

(3) An application under subsection (1) may be made during the moratorium or after it has ended.

(4) On an application under subsection (1) the court may—
    (a)    confirm, reverse or modify any act or decision of the monitor,
    (b)    give the monitor directions, or
    (c)    make such other order as it thinks fit (but may not, under this paragraph, order the monitor to pay any compensation).

(5) Where an application under subsection (1) relates to a failure by the monitor to bring the moratorium to an end under section A38(1), an order under subsection (4) may, in particular, bring the moratorium to an end and make such consequential provision as the court thinks fit.

(6) Where an application under subsection (1) relates to the monitor bringing a moratorium to an end under section A38(1), an order under subsection (4) may, in particular, provide that the moratorium is not to be taken into account for the purposes

of paragraph 2(1)(b) of Schedule ZA1 (company not eligible for moratorium if moratorium in force within previous 12 months).

(7)   In making an order under subsection (4) the court must have regard to the need to safeguard the interests of persons who have dealt with the company in good faith and for value.

(8)   See also section A17 (obligations to notify change in end of moratorium).

**Amendments**—Inserted by Corporate Insolvency and Governance Act 2020, s 1(1).

## [1.45]

### A43  Challenges to monitor remuneration in insolvency proceedings

(1)   The rules may confer on an administrator or liquidator of a company the right to apply to the court on the ground that remuneration charged by the monitor in relation to a prior moratorium for the company was excessive.

(2)   Rules under subsection (1) may (among other things) make provision as to—

    (a)   time limits;

    (b)   disposals available to the court;

    (c)   the treatment of costs (or, in Scotland, the expenses) of the application in the administration or winding up.

**Amendments**—Inserted by Corporate Insolvency and Governance Act 2020, s 1(1).

## [1.46]

### A44  Challenge to directors' actions

(1)   A creditor or member of a company may apply to the court for an order under this section on the ground that—

    (a)   during a moratorium, the company's affairs, business and property are being or have been managed by the directors in a manner which has unfairly harmed the interests of its creditors or members generally or of some part of its creditors or members (including at least the applicant), or

    (b)   any actual or proposed act or omission of the directors during a moratorium causes or would cause such harm.

(2)   An application under subsection (1) may be made during the moratorium or after it has ended.

(3)   On an application under subsection (1) the court may make such order as it thinks fit.

(4)   An order under subsection (3) may in particular—

    (a)   regulate the management by the directors of the company's affairs, business and property during the remainder of the moratorium,

    (b)   require the directors to refrain from doing or continuing an act complained of by the applicant or to do an act which the applicant has complained they have omitted to do,

    (c)   require a decision of the company's creditors to be sought (using a qualifying decision procedure) on such matters as the court may direct, or

    (d)   bring the moratorium to an end and make such consequential provision as the court thinks fit.

(5)   In making an order under subsection (3) the court must have regard to the need to safeguard the interests of persons who have dealt with the company in good faith and for value.

(6)   See also section A17 (obligations to notify change in end of moratorium).

**Amendments**—Inserted by Corporate Insolvency and Governance Act 2020, s 1(1).

## [1.47]

### A45  Challenge brought by Board of the Pension Protection Fund

(1)   This section applies where—

    (a)   a moratorium—

        (i)     is in force in relation to a company that is an employer in respect of an eligible scheme, or

        (ii)    is or has been in force in relation to a company that has been an employer in respect of an eligible scheme at any time during the moratorium, and

    (b)    the trustees or managers of the scheme are a creditor of the company.

(2)   The Board of the Pension Protection Fund may make any application under section A42(1) or A44(1) that could be made by the trustees or managers as a creditor.

(3)   For the purposes of such an application, any reference in section A42(1) or A44(1) to the interests of the applicant is to be read as a reference to the interests of the trustees or managers as a creditor.

(4)   In this section "eligible scheme" has the meaning given by section 126 of the Pensions Act 2004.

**Amendments**—Inserted by Corporate Insolvency and Governance Act 2020, s 1(1).

## CHAPTER 7

### OFFENCES: GENERAL

[1.48]

#### A46  Offence of fraud etc during or in anticipation of moratorium

(1)   An officer of a company commits an offence if, during a moratorium for the company or at any time within the period of 12 months ending with the day on which a moratorium for the company comes into force, the officer—

    (a)    does any of the things mentioned in subsection (2), or

    (b)    was privy to the doing by others of any of the things mentioned in subsection (2)(c), (d) and (e).

(2)   Those things are—

    (a)    concealing any part of the company's property to the value of £500 or more, or concealing any debt due to or from the company,

    (b)    fraudulently removing any part of the company's property to the value of £500 or more,

    (c)    concealing, destroying, mutilating or falsifying any document affecting or relating to the company's property or affairs,

    (d)    making any false entry in any document affecting or relating to the company's property or affairs,

    (e)    fraudulently parting with, altering or making any omission in any document affecting or relating to the company's property or affairs, or

    (f)    pawning, pledging or disposing of any property of the company which has been obtained on credit and has not been paid for (unless the pawning, pledging or disposal was in the ordinary way of the company's business).

(3)   It is a defence—

    (a)    for a person charged with an offence under subsection (1) in respect of any of the things mentioned in subsection (2)(a) or (f) to prove that the person had no intent to defraud, and

    (b)    for a person charged with an offence under subsection (1) in respect of any of the things mentioned in subsection (2)(c) or (d) to prove that the person had no intent to conceal the state of affairs of the company or to defeat the law.

(4)   Where a person pawns, pledges or disposes of any property of a company in circumstances which amount to an offence under subsection (1), every person who takes in pawn or pledge, or otherwise receives, the property commits an offence if the person knows it to be pawned, pledged or disposed of in circumstances which—

    (a)    amount to an offence under subsection (1), or

    (b)    would, if a moratorium were obtained for the company within the period of 12 months beginning with the day on which the pawning, pledging or disposal took place, amount to an offence under subsection (1).

(5)   In this section, "officer" includes a shadow director.

**Amendments**—Inserted by Corporate Insolvency and Governance Act 2020, s 1(1).

## [1.49]

### A47  Offence of false representation etc to obtain a moratorium

(1)   An officer of a company commits an offence if, for the purpose of obtaining a moratorium for the company or an extension of a moratorium for the company, the officer—

- (a)      makes any false representation, or
- (b)      fraudulently does, or omits to do, anything.

(2)   Subsection (1) applies even if no moratorium or extension is obtained.

(3)   In this section, "officer" includes a shadow director.

**Amendments**—Inserted by Corporate Insolvency and Governance Act 2020, s 1(1).

## [1.50]

### A48  Prosecution of delinquent officers of company

(1)   This section applies where a moratorium has been obtained for a company.

(2)   If it appears to the monitor that any past or present officer of the company has committed an offence in connection with the moratorium, the monitor must forthwith—

- (a)      report the matter to the appropriate authority, and
- (b)      provide the appropriate authority with such information and give the authority such access to and facilities for inspecting and taking copies of documents (being information or documents in the possession or under the control of the monitor and relating to the matter in question) as the authority requires.

(3)   In subsection (2), "the appropriate authority"—

- (a)      in the case of a company registered in England and Wales, means the Secretary of State,
- (b)      in the case of a company registered in Scotland, means the Lord Advocate, and
- (c)      in the case of an unregistered company means—
    - (i)      if it has a principal place of business in England and Wales but not Scotland, the Secretary of State,
    - (ii)     if it has a principal place of business in Scotland but not England and Wales, the Lord Advocate,
    - (iii)    if it has a principal place of business in both England and Wales and Scotland, the Secretary of State and the Lord Advocate, and
    - (iv)    if it does not have a principal place of business in England and Wales or Scotland, the Secretary of State.

(4)   Where a matter is reported to the Secretary of State under subsection (2), the Secretary of State may, for the purpose of investigating the matter and such other matters relating to the affairs of the company as appear to the Secretary of State to require investigation, exercise any of the powers which are exercisable by inspectors appointed under section 431 or 432 of the Companies Act 1985.

(5)   For the purpose of such an investigation any obligation imposed on a person by any provision of the Companies Acts to produce documents or give information to, or otherwise to assist, inspectors so appointed is to be regarded as an obligation similarly to assist the Secretary of State in the Secretary of State's investigation.

(6)   Where a question is put to a person in exercise of the powers conferred by subsection (4), the person's answer may be used in evidence against them.

(7)   However, in criminal proceedings in which the person is charged with an offence other than a false statement offence—

- (a)      no evidence relating to the answer may be adduced, and
- (b)      no question relating to it may be asked,

by or on behalf of the prosecution, unless evidence relating to it is adduced, or a question relating to it is asked, in the proceedings by or on behalf of the person.

(8)   In subsection (7) "false statement offence" means—

(a)   an offence under section 2 or 5 of the Perjury Act 1911 (false statements made on oath otherwise than in judicial proceedings or made otherwise than on oath), or

(b)   an offence under section 44(1) or (2) of the Criminal Law (Consolidation) (Scotland) Act 1995 (false statements made on oath or otherwise than on oath).

(9)   Where a prosecuting authority institutes criminal proceedings following any report under subsection (2), the monitor, and every officer and agent of the company past and present (other than the defendant or defender), must give the authority all assistance in connection with the prosecution which they are reasonably able to give.

(10)   For this purpose—

"agent" includes any banker or solicitor of the company and any person employed by the company as auditor, whether that person is or is not an officer of the company;

"prosecuting authority" means the Director of Public Prosecutions, the Lord Advocate or the Secretary of State.

(11)   The court may, on the application of the prosecuting authority, direct a person who has failed to comply with subsection (9) to comply with it.

**Amendments**—Inserted by Corporate Insolvency and Governance Act 2020, s 1(1).

## CHAPTER 8

### MISCELLANEOUS AND GENERAL
*Special rules for certain kinds of company etc*

## [1.51]

### A49   Regulated companies: modifications to this Part

(1)   For the purposes of sections A3 and A4 as they apply in relation to a regulated company, section A6(1) has effect as if the documents listed there included a reference to the written consent of the appropriate regulator to the appointment of the proposed monitor.

(2)   The remaining provisions of this section apply in relation to a moratorium for a regulated company.

(3)   Any notice under section A8(2), A17(2) to (4) or A39(8) must also be sent by the monitor to the appropriate regulator.

(4)   The directors must give the appropriate regulator notice of any qualifying decision procedure by which a decision of the company's creditors is sought for the purposes of section A12(2) or A44(4)(c).

(5)   If the directors fail to comply with subsection (4), any director who did not have a reasonable excuse for the failure commits an offence.

(6)   The appropriate regulator, or a person appointed by the appropriate regulator, may in the way provided for by the rules, participate (but not vote) in any qualifying decision procedure by which a decision of the company's creditors is sought for the purposes of this Part.

(7)   The appropriate regulator is entitled to be heard on any application to the court for permission under section A31(1) or A32(1) (disposal of charged property, etc).

(8)   The court may make an order under section A39(1) only if the appropriate regulator has given its written consent to the appointment of the proposed monitor.

(9)   The persons who may apply to the court under section A39(3), A42(1) or A44(1) include the appropriate regulator.

(10)   If a person other than a regulator applies to the court under section A39(3), A42(1) or A44(1) the appropriate regulator is entitled to be heard on the application.

(11) If either regulator makes an application to the court under section A39(3), A42(1) or A44(1) in relation to a PRA-regulated company, the other regulator is entitled to be heard on the application.

(12) This section does not affect any right that the appropriate regulator has (apart from this section) as a creditor of a regulated company.

(13) In this section—

"the appropriate regulator" means—

    (a)    where the regulated company is a PRA-regulated company, each of the Financial Conduct Authority and the Prudential Regulation Authority, and

    (b)    where the regulated company is not a PRA-regulated company, the Financial Conduct Authority;

"PRA-authorised person" has the meaning given by section 2B(5) of the Financial Services and Markets Act 2000;

"PRA-regulated company" means a regulated company which—

    (a)    is, or has been, a PRA-authorised person,

    (b)    is, or has been, an appointed representative within the meaning given by section 39 of the Financial Services and Markets Act 2000, whose principal (or one of whose principals) is, or was, a PRA-authorised person, or

    (c)    is carrying on, or has carried on, a PRA-regulated activity (within the meaning of section 22A of that Act) in contravention of the general prohibition;

"regulated activity" has the meaning given by section 22 of the Financial Services and Markets Act 2000, taken with Schedule 2 to that Act and any order under that section;

"regulated company" means a company which—

    (a)    is, or has been, an authorised person within the meaning given by section 31 of the Financial Services and Markets Act 2000,

    (b)    is, or has been, an appointed representative within the meaning given by section 39 of that Act, or

    (c)    is carrying on, or has carried on, a regulated activity in contravention of the general prohibition within the meaning given by section 19 of that Act;

"regulator" means the Financial Conduct Authority or the Prudential Regulation Authority.

(14) The Secretary of State may by regulations amend this section for the purposes of changing the definition of "regulated company" in subsection (13).

(15) Regulations under subsection (14) are subject to the affirmative resolution procedure.

**Amendments**—Inserted by Corporate Insolvency and Governance Act 2020, s 1(1).

## [1.52]

### A50 Power to modify this Part etc in relation to certain companies

(1) The Secretary of State may by regulations make provision under the law of England and Wales or Scotland—

    (a)    to modify this Part as it applies in relation to a company for which there is a special administration regime, or

    (b)    in connection with the interaction between this Part and any other insolvency procedure in relation to such a company.

(2) The Welsh Ministers may by regulations make provision under the law of England and Wales—

    (a)    to modify this Part as it applies in relation to a company that is a social landlord registered under Part 1 of the Housing Act 1996, or

    (b)    make provision in connection with the interaction between this Part and any other insolvency procedure in relation to such a company.

(3) The Scottish Ministers may by regulations make provision under the law of Scotland—

    (a)    to modify this Part as it applies in relation to a company that is a social landlord registered under Part 2 of the Housing (Scotland) Act 2010 (asp 17), or

    (b)    make provision in connection with the interaction between this Part and any other insolvency procedure in relation to such a company.

(4) The Secretary of State may, by regulations, make any provision under the law of England and Wales, Scotland or Northern Ireland that appears to the Secretary of State to be appropriate in view of provision made under subsection (1), (2) or (3).

(5) The power in subsection (1), (2), (3) or (4) may, in particular, be used to amend, repeal, revoke or otherwise modify any provision made by an enactment.

(6) Regulations under subsection (1) or (4) are subject to the affirmative resolution procedure.

(7) A statutory instrument containing regulations under subsection (2) may not be made unless a draft of the statutory instrument containing them has been laid before and approved by a resolution of Senedd Cymru.

(8) Regulations made by the Scottish Ministers under subsection (3) are subject to the affirmative procedure (see section 29 of the Interpretation and Legislative Reform (Scotland) Act 2010 (asp 10)).

(9) In this section—

    "insolvency procedure" includes—

        (a)    in relation to subsection (1)(b), the provision made by sections 143A to 159 of the Housing and Regeneration Act 2008;

        (b)    in relation to subsection (2)(b), the provision made by sections 39 to 50 of the Housing Act 1996;

        (c)    in relation to subsection (3)(b), the provision made by Part 7 of the Housing (Scotland) Act 2010;

    "ordinary administration" means the insolvency procedure provided for by Schedule B1;

    "special administration regime" means provision made by an enactment for an insolvency procedure that—

        (a)    is similar or corresponds to ordinary administration, and

        (b)    provides for the administrator to have one or more special objectives instead of or in addition to the objectives of ordinary administration.

**Amendments**—Inserted by Corporate Insolvency and Governance Act 2020, s 1(1).

**[1.53]**

**A51  Power to make provision in connection with pension schemes**

(1) The Secretary of State may by regulations provide that, in a case where—

    (a)    a moratorium—

        (i)    is in force in relation to a company that is an employer in respect of an eligible scheme, or

        (ii)    is or has been in force in relation to a company that has been an employer in respect of an eligible scheme at any time during the moratorium, and

    (b)    the trustees or managers of the scheme are a creditor of the company,

the Board of the Pension Protection Fund may exercise any of the following rights.

(2) The rights are those which are exercisable by the trustees or managers as a creditor of the company under or by virtue of—

    (a)    section A12, or

    (b)    a court order under section A44(4)(c).

(3) Regulations under subsection (1) may provide that the Board may exercise any such rights—

    (a)    to the exclusion of the trustees or managers of the scheme, or

    (b)    in addition to the exercise of those rights by the trustees or managers of the scheme.

(4)    Regulations under subsection (1)—

    (a)    may specify conditions that must be met before the Board may exercise any such rights;

    (b)    may provide for any such rights to be exercisable by the Board for a specified period;

    (c)    may make provision in connection with any such rights ceasing to be so exercisable at the end of such a period.

(5)    Regulations under subsection (1) are subject to the affirmative resolution procedure.

(6)    In this section "eligible scheme" has the meaning given by section 126 of the Pensions Act 2004.

    **Amendments**—Inserted by Corporate Insolvency and Governance Act 2020, s 1(1).

*Floating charges*

## [1.54]

### A52 Void provisions in floating charge documents

(1)    A provision in an instrument creating a floating charge is void if it provides for the obtaining of a moratorium, or anything done with a view to obtaining a moratorium, to be—

    (a)    an event causing the floating charge to crystallise,

    (b)    an event causing restrictions which would not otherwise apply to be imposed on the disposal of property by the company, or

    (c)    a ground for the appointment of a receiver.

(2)    The reference in subsection (1) to anything done with a view to obtaining a moratorium includes any preliminary decision or investigation.

(3)    In subsection (1) "receiver" includes a manager and a person who is appointed both receiver and manager.

(4)    Subsection (1) does not apply to a provision in an instrument creating a floating charge that is—

    (a)    a collateral security (as defined by section A27);

    (b)    a market charge (as defined by section A27);

    (c)    a security financial collateral arrangement (within the meaning of regulation 3 of the Financial Collateral Arrangements (No 2) Regulations 2003 (SI 2003/3226));

    (d)    a system-charge (as defined by section A27).

    **Amendments**—Inserted by Corporate Insolvency and Governance Act 2020, s 1(1).

*Interpretation of this Part*

## [1.55]

### A53 Meaning of "pre-moratorium debt" and "moratorium debt"

(1)    In this Part "pre-moratorium debt", in relation to a company for which a moratorium is or has been in force, means—

    (a)    any debt or other liability to which the company becomes subject before the moratorium comes into force, or

    (b)    any debt or other liability to which the company has become or may become subject during the moratorium by reason of any obligation incurred before the moratorium comes into force,

but this is subject to subsection (3).

(2)    In this Part "moratorium debt", in relation to a company for which a moratorium is or has been in force, means—

    (a)    any debt or other liability to which the company becomes subject during the moratorium, other than by reason of an obligation incurred before the moratorium came into force, or

    (b)    any debt or other liability to which the company has become or may become subject after the end of the moratorium by reason of an obligation incurred during the moratorium,

but this is subject to subsection (3).

(3)    For the purposes of this Part—

    (a)    a liability in tort or delict is a "pre-moratorium debt" if either—

        (i)    the cause of action has accrued before the moratorium comes into force, or

        (ii)    all the elements necessary to establish the cause of action exist before the moratorium comes into force except for actionable damage;

    (b)    a liability in tort or delict is a "moratorium debt" if it does not fall within paragraph (a) and either—

        (i)    the cause of action has accrued during the moratorium, or

        (ii)    all the elements necessary to establish the cause of action exist before the moratorium comes to an end except for actionable damage.

(4)    The Secretary of State may by regulations amend this section for the purposes of changing the definition of "pre-moratorium debt" or "moratorium debt" in this Part.

(5)    Regulations under subsection (4) are subject to the affirmative resolution procedure.

**Amendments**—Inserted by Corporate Insolvency and Governance Act 2020, s 1(1).

## [1.56]

### A54  Interpretation of this Part: general

(1)    In this Part—

"company" means—

    (a)    a company registered under the Companies Act 2006 in England and Wales or Scotland, or

    (b)    an unregistered company that may be wound up under Part 5 of this Act;

"the court", in relation to a company, means a court having jurisdiction to wind up the company;

"eligible", in relation to a company, has the meaning given by Schedule ZA1;

"employer", in relation to a pension scheme—

    (a)    in sections A8(2)(c), A17(8)(c) and A39(8)(c), means an employer within the meaning of section 318(1) of the Pensions Act 2004;

    (b)    elsewhere in this Part, has the same meaning that it has for the purposes of Part 2 of the Pensions Act 2004 (see section 318(1) and (4) of that Act);

"enactment" includes an Act of the Scottish Parliament and an instrument made under such an Act;

"hire-purchase agreement" includes a conditional sale agreement, a chattel leasing agreement and a retention of title agreement;

"liability" means (subject to subsection (2)) a liability to pay money or money's worth, including any liability under an enactment, a liability for breach of trust, any liability in contract, tort, delict or bailment, and any liability arising out of an obligation to make restitution;

"money purchase scheme" has the meaning given by section 181(1) of the Pension Schemes Act 1993;

"the monitor", in relation to a moratorium, means the person who has the functions of the monitor in relation to the moratorium (see also section A40 for cases where two or more persons act as the monitor);

"moratorium" means a moratorium under this Part;

"moratorium debt" has the meaning given by section A53;

"occupational pension scheme" has the meaning given by section 1 of the Pension Schemes Act 1993;

"pension scheme" has the meaning given by section 1 of the Pension Schemes Act 1993;

"pre-moratorium debt" has the meaning given by section A53;

"qualified person" means a person qualified to act as an insolvency practitioner;

"unable to pay its debts"—

(a)   in relation to a registered company, has the same meaning as in Part 4 (see section 123);

(b)   in relation to an unregistered company, has the same meaning as in Part 5 (see sections 222 to 224).

(2)   For the purposes of references in any provision of this Part to a debt or liability it is immaterial whether the debt or liability is present or future, whether it is certain or contingent, or whether its amount is fixed or liquidated, or is capable of being ascertained by fixed rules or as a matter of opinion.

(3)   In this Part references to filing a document with the court are, in relation to a court in Scotland, references to lodging it in court.

(4)   The Secretary of State may by regulations amend this section for the purposes of changing the definition of "qualified person" in subsection (1).

(5)   Regulations under subsection (4) are subject to the affirmative resolution procedure.

**Amendments**—Inserted by Corporate Insolvency and Governance Act 2020, s 1(1).

**CIGA 2020**—This provision is affected by temporary measures at Sch 4, paras 13 and 53 of CIGA 2020.

*Regulations*

## [1.57]

### A55  Regulations

(1)   Regulations under this Part may make—

(a)   different provision for different purposes;

(b)   consequential, supplementary, incidental or transitional provision or savings.

(2)   Regulations under this Part are to be made by statutory instrument, unless they are made by the Scottish Ministers.

(3)   Where regulations of the Secretary of State under this Part are subject to "the affirmative resolution procedure", they may not be made unless a draft of the statutory instrument containing them has been laid before Parliament and approved by a resolution of each House of Parliament.

**Amendments**—Inserted by Corporate Insolvency and Governance Act 2020, s 1(1).

## PART I   COMPANY VOLUNTARY ARRANGEMENTS

## [1.58]

**Introductory note to company voluntary arrangements**—The company voluntary arrangement (CVA) was a creation of the 1986 Act. This new mechanism followed observations made in paras 400–403 of the Cork Committee Report to the effect that company law was deficient in failing to provide a straightforward mechanism by which a company might reach a binding arrangement with its unsecured creditors.

Section 1(1) defines a voluntary arrangement as either a composition by a company in satisfaction of its debts or a scheme of arrangement of its affairs. The difference between a composition and a scheme is discussed in the notes to s 1. It should be understood that, strictly, there is no requirement for a company to be insolvent under any provision in Part I as a pre-requisite of a company proposing a CVA. In practice, however, a CVA might only conceivably have any practical use to a solvent company where that company has real grounds for anticipating its impending and unavoidable liquidation or, possibly, pursuant to a restructuring. CVAs are commonly used as an exit route from administration.

The key feature of a CVA lies in the ability of a company and a requisite majority of its creditors – on which see r 15.34 – to bind a dissentient minority in the way of what amounts to a form of statutory binding. In this sense a CVA has more than a passing resemblance to a scheme of arrangement: see *Re NFU Development Trust* [1972] 1 WLR 1548. Section 6(1)(a) and (b) allows for a creditor to challenge either the approval of a CVA as a material irregularity or the 'effect' of the arrangement as being unfairly prejudicial. Those matters are discussed in the notes to those provisions.

Many (although by no means all) of the statutory provisions concerning CVAs are in mirror form to those concerning the analogous individual voluntary arrangement ('IVA') procedure, found in Part XIII of the IA 1986. In such instances, cases decided under one species of voluntary arrangement are generally relevant to and are appropriately cited in respect of cases arising under the other.

**Coronavirus and the future**—Even before the onset of the coronavirus pandemic, changing retail habits had seen a flurry of famous high-street names engaging in CVAs, including Mothercare, House of Fraser, Arcadia and Debenhams in the recent past. Concern had been expressed (notably by industry bodies such as the British Property Federation) over the perceived unfairness of the rent reductions achieved by companies in CVA, with landlords (often investing on behalf of pension funds) asked to shoulder disproportionate pain compared with shareholders and banks. The existing bleak outlook for retail was compounded by the consequences of coronavirus and further famous names on the British high-street to have entered into CVAs during the pandemic include Clarks, Café Nero and New Look, with the latter two attracting court challenges. It is possible that this trend will continue when the moratorium on landlord and other creditor action that has been in place since March 2020 is eventually lifted: in some cases, rent will not have been paid for the entire period, which will present a significant debt burden.

The future popularity of CVAs as a restructuring tool may, however, be uncertain for two reasons. Firstly, it is too early to tell what effect the restoration of Crown preference could be. Since the coming into force of the Finance Act 2020 on 1 December 2020, HMRC has enjoyed the status of a secondary preferential creditor, which means its 'concurrence' is required for its priority status to be modified: see note to s 4(4) below. Secondly, the new form of restructuring plan under Pt 26A of the Companies Act 2006 introduced by the Corporate Governance and Insolvency Act 2020 ('CIGA 2020') remains in its infancy and it remains to be seen whether it will become widely popular. The ability of a distressed company to obtain, under certain conditions, a cross-class cram down in the face of creditor opposition, and to discount altogether those classes without a 'genuine economic interest', may mean that the Pt 26A plan becomes more attractive as a restructuring tool than the CVA, for which the approval of 75% of all creditors is required. In granting sanction to a Pt 26A plan in *Re Virgin Active Holdings Ltd* [2021] EWHC 1246 (Ch), Snowden J remarked that there was nothing inappropriate in the plan companies choosing to utilise Pt 26A rather than a CVA in circumstances where the evidence suggested the dissentient landlords would have been in a stronger position had a CVA been proposed ([275]–[276]).

*The proposal*

## [1.59]

### 1 Those who may propose an arrangement

(1)   The directors of a company (other than one which is in administration or being wound up) may make a proposal under this Part to the company and to its creditors for a composition in satisfaction of its debts or a scheme of arrangement of its affairs (from here on referred to, in either case, as a "voluntary arrangement").

(2)   A proposal under this Part is one which provides for some person ("the nominee") to act in relation to the voluntary arrangement either as trustee or otherwise for the purpose of supervising its implementation; and the nominee must be a person who is qualified to act as an insolvency practitioner . . . in relation to the voluntary arrangement.

(3)   Such a proposal may also be made—

   (a)   where the company is in administration, by the administrator, and

   (b)   where the company is being wound up, by the liquidator.

(4)   In this Part "company" means—

    (a)    a company registered under the Companies Act 2006 in England and Wales or Scotland;

    (b)    a company incorporated in an EEA State *other than the United Kingdom*; or

    (c)    a company not incorporated in an EEA State but having its centre of main interests in a member State *other than Denmark* (other than Denmark) or in the United Kingdom.

(5)   In subsection (4), in relation to a company, "centre of main interests" has the same meaning as in Article 3 of the EU Regulation.

(6)   If a company incorporated outside the United Kingdom has a principal place of business in Northern Ireland, no proposal under this Part shall be made in relation to it unless it also has a principal place of business in England and Wales or Scotland (or both in England and Wales or Scotland).

**Amendments**—Insolvency Act 2000, s 2, Sch 2, paras 1, 2; Enterprise Act 2002, s 248(3), Sch 17, paras 9, 10(a); SI 2002/1240; SI 2005/879; SI 2009/1941; Deregulation Act 2015, s 19, Sch 6, Pt 6, para 20(1), (2)(a); SI 2017/702; SI 2019/146, as from IP completion day (as defined in the European Union (Withdrawal Agreement) Act 2020, s 39(1)–(5)).

**General note**—Despite its heading, this provision touches on a wide range of issues which, for convenience, are considered here.

### SECTION 1(1)

**Eligible applicants**—Other than where a company is in administration (ie under the former Part II or under the new Sch B1) or a company is being wound up compulsorily or voluntarily – in which case the office-holder may put a proposal under s 1(3) – s 1(1) envisages only the directors of a company making a proposal to the company and its creditors for what is commonly termed a CVA. There is no provision for a proposal to be put by either the members or creditors of a company, or any other person.

The Independent Regulator may direct an NHS foundation trust to have recourse to a CVA by virtue of s 53 of the National Health Service Act 2006. Pursuant to s 113 of the Banking Act 2009, a bank liquidator may also propose a CVA.

The administrators of an education corporation subject to an education administration order under s 20 of the Technical and Further Education Act 2017 have the power under s 1 to propose a CVA to creditors: *Re Corporation of West Kent and Ashford College (a further education corporation in education administration)* [2020] EWHC 907 (Ch).

**The scope of the term 'creditor'**—Whilst the legislation provides no definition of the word 'creditor' for the purposes of CVA, the term extends not only to unliquidated debts (given specific language to that effect in r 15.31(3)) but also to future or contingently payable debts: *Re Cancol Ltd* [1996] 1 All ER 37 (Knox J, future payments of rents to fall due under an existing lease) applying to CVAs the reasoning applied by the Court of Appeal in *Doorbar v Alltime Securities Ltd (No 2)* [1995] BCC 1, 149, affirming Knox J at first instance [1994] BCC 728, in relation to individual voluntary arrangements. *Re Cancol* and *Doorbar* were applied by Norris J in *Discovery (Northampton) Ltd v Debenhams Retail Ltd* [2019] EWHC 2441 (Ch), [2020] BCC 9, who regarded both cases as rightly decided and held that future rent may be included in a CVA ([57]–[61]). Norris J held in the same case, however, that the CVA could not validly restrain a landlord's right of re-entry, which was a proprietary (not a security) right. Norris J held that a CVA can modify any pecuniary obligation upon breach of which the right of re-entry may be exercised, but it cannot modify the right of re-entry itself ([99]). The offending provision was simply deleted from the CVA, which otherwise continued in operation ([139]).

In *Re North Point Global Limited; Brittain v Chamberlain* [2020] EWHC 1648 (Ch), [2020] 2 BCLC 676, a liquidator with a statutory preference claim against the company in CVA was a creditor for the purposes of the CVA, even where the winding up post-dated the approval of the CVA. HHJ Davies-White QC (sitting as a High Court judge) rejected the Supervisor's contention that the claim post-dated the CVA and, as such, fell outside the arrangement.

For analysis as to how CVAs and arbitral awards interact, reference can be made to the two High Court decisions *Westshield Ltd v Whitehouse* [2013] EWHC 3576 (TCC), [2014] BPIR 317 and *Tate Building Services Ltd v B&M McHugh Ltd* [2014] EWHC 2971 (TCC), [2014] BPIR 1560.

**Unliquidated debts**—Rule 15.31(3) provides that a creditor voting in respect of an unliquidated amount or any debt whose value is not ascertained shall, for voting purposes only, have the debt valued at £1 unless the convener or chair agrees to put a higher value on it. However, the chairman may not be passive: Norris J observed in *National Westminster Bank plc v Yadgaroff* [2011] EWHC 3711 (Ch), [2012] BPIR 371 at [15] that where the chairman decides that a debt is unliquidated or unascertained, he must examine the evidence and, if the evidence leads to the conclusion that he can safely place a minimum value higher than £1 on the debt, he should do so. For further illustrations on the treatment of such creditor claims see *Beverley Group plc v McClue* [1995] BCC 751 (Knox J); *Re Sweatfield Ltd* [1997] BCC 744 (HHJ Weeks QC); *Re Wisepark Ltd* [1994] BCC 221 (untaxed (ie unassessed) litigation costs not a debt for CVA purposes) and *County Bookshops Ltd v Grove* [2002] BPIR 772 (Neuberger J, contractual instalment payments which had not fallen due as at date of CVA admitted to arrangement as contingent debts). In *Sofaer v Anglo Irish Asset Finance plc* [2011] EWHC 1480 (Ch), [2011] BPIR 1736 (Lewison J), one of the debtor's arguments was that his liability to the relevant creditor was under a guarantee and so was unliquidated. That argument was rejected by Lewison J, who held in any event, following *Re Newlands (Seaford) Educational Trust (In Administration); Chittenden and Others v Pepper and Others* [2006] EWHC 1511 (Ch), [2006] BPIR 1230 that r 5.21(3) of the 1986 Rules (replaced by r 15.31(3)) was not engaged where the chairman agreed to put a higher value on the debt.

**Disputed debts**—In the case of disputed debts the proper course under r 15.33(3) is for the convener or chair to mark the claims as objected to and allow the creditor to vote for the full amount, on which see *Re A Debtor (No 222 of 1990) ex parte Bank of Ireland* [1992] BCLC 137 at 144F–144H (Harman J).

**Contingent debts**—The decision of David Richards J in *Re Federal-Mogul Aftermarket UK Ltd* [2008] EWHC 1099 (Ch), [2008] BPIR 846 includes valuable guidance on the application of the so-called 'hindsight principle' – that is, in valuing a contingent debt it is necessary to take into account everything which has actually happened between the date of valuation and the date on which the contingent liability is actually calculated – as explained by Lord Hoffmann in *Stein v Blake* [1996] 1 AC 243 at 252E–252F.

**Court control over the admission of creditor's proof**—The court has jurisdiction to direct that a creditor be admitted to proof in an arrangement: *Re FMS Financial Management Services Ltd* (1988) 5 BCC 191 (Hoffmann J, joint administrators proposing CVA directed to admit to proof shareholders with prima facie good claim against the company for misrepresentation). But it should be noted that the standing of FMS, an ex tempore judgment upon an appearance by administrators only without reference to authority, is, to use the words of HHJ Pelling QC (sitting as a High Court judge) in *Re Beloit Walmsley Ltd* [2008] BPIR 1445 at [20], 'seriously circumscribed'. Certainly in *Re Alpa Lighting Ltd* [1997] BPIR 341 at 347A–347B Nourse LJ had distinguished FMS on the basis that in FMS no amendment of the CVA had been sought and that it was unnecessary to go into the question of whether the admission of a new class of creditors to an arrangement amounted to such an amendment.

**The effect of an arrangement on third parties**—Although a CVA is capable either expressly or by necessary implication of varying the relationship between a creditor of the company and a third party (eg so as to release a co-debtor or security which is not itself a party to the arrangement), an arrangement will ordinarily be construed as reserving the rights of creditors against third parties: see *March Estates plc v Gunmark* [1996] 2 BCLC 1 at 5H–6G (Lightman J) and the cases cited therein: see also *Lombard NatWest Factors Ltd v Koutrouzas* [2002] EWHC 1084 (QB), [2003] BPIR 444 (surety not released by IVA of co-surety where guarantee expressly provided that guarantee would not be affected by indulgence granted to co-surety). On the release of a surety on the IVA of a principal debtor see *Greene King plc v Stanley* [2002] BPIR 491 at [58]–[86] (Jonathan Parker LJ). On a proper construction of the agreement, liability was reserved against a co-debtor in *Jones v Financial Conduct Authority* [2013] EWHC 2731 (Ch), [2013] BPIR 1033 (HHJ Kaye QC, sitting as a High Court judge). For the appropriate procedure where one of two co-debtors has entered into an IVA where the creditor wishes to pursue the debt and the non-IVA co-debtor wishes to pursue an indemnity and contribution claim against the IVA co-debtor see [2003] BPIR 632 at [54] (Chadwick LJ). For an unsuccessful attempt at materially affecting the rights of third parties, see *Re Sixty UK Ltd (in Administration and Company Voluntary Arrangement); Mourant & Co Trustees Ltd and Mourant Property Trustees Ltd v Sixty UK Ltd (in Administration), Hollis and O'Reilly* [2009] EWHC 3866 (Ch), [2010] BPIR 1234 which was a CVA which failed on the grounds of unfair prejudice (cf *Prudential Assurance Co Ltd v PRG Powerhouse Ltd* [2007] EWHC 1002 (Ch), [2007] BPIR 839). Construction of an arrangement term purporting to modify third party rights is not a matter of general principle and depends on the surrounding circumstances and account being taken not only of the express words employed in the arrangement but also any terms which may be properly implied: *Johnson v Davies* [1998] 2 BCLC 252 at 259B–259D (Chadwick LJ). A CVA does not constitute an 'agreement' for the purposes of s 203 of the Employment Rights Act 1996: *Re Britannia Heat Transfer Ltd* [2007] BCC 470, [2007] BPIR 1038 (HHJ Norris QC sitting as a High Court judge).

For further general guidance on the construction of voluntary arrangements see the notes under that heading to s 5(2)(b) below.

**The scope of the terms 'voluntary arrangement', 'composition' and 'scheme of arrangement'**—The distinction between the terms 'composition' and 'scheme of arrangement' was considered by the Court of Appeal in *Commissioners of Inland Revenue v Adams* [2001] 1 BCLC 222 at 230G–231F (Mummery LJ), affirming the decision of Nicholas Warren QC (sitting as a deputy High Court judge) at [1999] 2 BCLC 730. A composition is an arrangement to pay a sum in lieu of a larger debt or other obligation, or forbearance to sue for the full amount being exchanged for a money payment or other consideration. A scheme of arrangement, on the other hand, involves something less than the release or discharge of creditor debts (as on a composition) and might include nothing more than a moratorium on the enforcement of creditor claims so as to suspend the date for repayment of such debts, with or without the payment of a dividend in the interim: see *March Estates plc v Gunmark* [1996] 2 BCLC 1 at 5A–5G (Lightman J). Accordingly, the approved proposal in *Adams*, which imposed a moratorium on the prosecution of creditor claims for a 3-year period with no prospect of a dividend to preferential or unsecured creditors, constituted a scheme of arrangement so as to amount to a voluntary arrangement within s 1(1). A scheme of arrangement which amounts to nothing more than a moratorium on creditor claims, even if capable of being brought within the definition of a voluntary arrangement, will not usually be of great attraction to a debtor for the simple reason that arrangement creditors will be free to pursue their claims against the debtor on the cessation of the moratorium. In practice, therefore, a debtor might seek to obtain the fuller advantage of a composition by offering a dividend, even a very small dividend, to creditors in consideration for the discharge in full of creditor claims.

The applicant landlords in *Lazari Properties 2 Ltd v New Look Retailers Ltd* [2021] EWHC 1209 (Ch) submitted that a proposal for a CVA can only constitute a 'composition' or an 'arrangement' within s 1(1) if, having regard to the existing rights of creditors and the rights conferred by the proposal, all the creditors would fall into a single class if the terms of proposal had been included within a scheme of arrangement. This submission was derived from the case law on class composition in schemes of arrangement. Zacaroli J described it as a 'root and branch attack on the use of CVAs' ([67]) and rejected it on the basis that it was not supported by s 1(1): [65]–[67], [157]–[166].

**Proposals which do not amount to a composition or a scheme of arrangement**—If a proposal is put to creditors which amounts to neither a composition nor a moratorium, then the original proposal remains a nullity such that the proposal is not capable of being saved by modifications introduced at the first statutory meeting of creditors, even where the creditors support such modifications: *Commissioners of Inland Revenue v Bland* [2003] BPIR 1274 (Lloyd J, original IVA proposal which offered nothing to creditors successfully challenged by Revenue under s 262 notwithstanding modifications introduced to provide for dividend). The same considerations as apply to IVAs apply to CVAs: *Bland* at [39].

### SECTION 1(2)

**Implementation**—A valid proposal is implemented on being approved under s 4(1) by a creditors' decision procedure under s 3 by the requisite majority of creditors as provided for in r 15.34. Thereafter, the nominee – or any person appointed in his or her stead under s 2(4) or s 4(2) – is known as the supervisor of the voluntary arrangement: see s 7(2) and the notes thereto.

**Qualifications of the nominee**—In addition to the observations as to the nature of a voluntary arrangement in the notes to s 1(1) above, s 1(2) imposes a requirement that, so as to constitute a proposal, a proposed CVA must provide for a person who is qualified to act as an insolvency practitioner 'in relation to the voluntary arrangement.

The phrase 'act as an insolvency practitioner' is defined in s 388: see also s 419.

**Identity of the nominee**—In practice the nominee is invariably the same individual who takes office subsequently as supervisor, although s 4(2) (s 258(3) in the case of an IVA) provides that a modification to the proposal replacing the nominee with another individual (who will then take office as supervisor) may be approved by creditors at the meeting summoned to consider the proposal. The nominee may also be replaced by the court under s 2(4) (s 256(3) in the case of IVAs) on prescribed grounds.

**Proposal by administrator or liquidator**—Under the former Part II of the Act relating to administration orders, a CVA – in contrast with the other purposes identified in s 8(3) – constituted a common 'exit route' by which assets could be distributed to creditors in the administration. Although a CVA will continue to be used as an exit route by administrators appointed under Sch B1 of the Act, it should be noted that an administrator is now empowered by para 65 of Sch B1 to make distributions to creditors, subject to court permission where the distribution is to an unsecured creditor.

CVA proposals by liquidators are rare in practice.

**Role of the nominee**—The legislation confers no powers on a nominee in relation to the company or the assets of the company subject to the proposed CVA. In practice, the nominee will usually play a significant role in assisting the directors of the company in the drafting of the proposal, although the proposal itself remains that of the directors (or an office-holder under s 1(3)). The nominee is not, however, the agent of the debtor: *Re A Debtor (No 222 of 1990) ex parte Bank of Ireland (No 2)* [1993] BCLC 233 at 235D (Harman J).

The involvement of the nominee in the proposal process must be tempered with the fundamental requirement for the nominee to retain objectivity in the discharge of his or her function and in the preparation of the nominee's report to the court under s 2(2).

SIP 3.1 (relating to IVAs) and SIP 3.2 (relating to CVAs) were first introduced in July 2014 and identify best practice in relation to voluntary arrangements. SIP 3.2 was updated from 1 April 2021. Paragraph 1 of SIP 3.1 provides that 'The particular nature of an insolvency practitioner's position renders transparency and fairness in all dealings of primary importance. The debtor and creditors should be confident that an insolvency practitioner will act professionally and with objectivity in each role associated with the arrangement. Failure to do so may prejudice the interests of both the debtor and creditors, and is likely to bring the practitioner and the profession into disrepute.' The Insolvency Service's Dear IP Letter No 33 of March 1995 titled 'The Role of the Nominee and Application of Professional Judgment' suggests that practitioners pose the following questions in relation to a proposed arrangement: (1) Is it feasible? (2) Is it fair to the creditors? (3) Is it an acceptable alternative to formal insolvency? (4) Is it fit to be considered by the creditors? (5) Is it fair to the debtor? The loss of professional objectivity in theory carries with it the risk of professional criticism and sanction. In addition, where a nominee falls significantly below the standards required of a licensed insolvency practitioner the court may, on an application under s 6 (s 262 in the case of an IVA), require the nominee to pay all or part of the costs of any proceedings arising out of the inadequate discharge of his duties, including his conduct as chairman of the creditors' meeting: *Re A Debtor (No 222 of 1990) ex parte Bank of Ireland (No 2)* [1993] BCLC 233 (Harman J) and see also the decision of Andrew Simmonds QC in *Tradition (UK) Ltd v Ahmed and Other* [2008] EWHC 3448 (Ch), [2009] BPIR 626 for an unsuccessful attempt at making the nominee liable for all of the costs of an application to challenge a voluntary arrangement – the decision contains a useful analysis of the principles to be applied when determining whether a proposed nominee should be liable for costs. This is the case even where the application could have been pursued by way of an appeal under r 15.35, in relation to which r 15.35(6) provides that the person who makes a decision in connection with the meeting will not be personally liable for the costs of such an appeal unless the court makes an order to that effect. It is vitally important, therefore, that a nominee (or supervisor) maintains objectivity throughout, remaining, in effect, between the debtor and the creditors, and is not seen to take up the debtor's cause where a creditor raises a legitimate complaint.

**Role of the supervisor**—In *Varden Nuttall Ltd v Nuttall* [2018] EWHC 3868 (Ch), [2019] BPIR 738, the court emphasised that estate monies in individual voluntary arrangements are held on trust for the purposes of those IVAs. At [63], HHJ Pelling QC (sitting as a High Court judge) held that SIP 9 governs the way in which the supervisor of a voluntary arrangement should conduct themselves. Where sums paid to third party service providers had included a referral fee element amounting to a secret commission that had ultimately benefited the supervisor, this amounted to a dishonest breach of duty as supervisor: [69]–[75], [102]. SIP 9 was updated from 1 April 2021 in a form that appears to have been designed to address the abuse present in *Varden Nuttall*.

**The status of arrangement assets in a winding up or bankruptcy**—In *Re NT Gallagher & Son Ltd, Shierson v Tomlinson* [2002] 2 BCLC 133, [2002] EWCA Civ 404 Peter Gibson LJ, giving the judgment of the court (also comprising Ward and Dyson LJJ) considered the issue of whether arrangement assets held on a trust for CVA creditors survived liquidation and whether the arrangement creditors were entitled to prove in an ensuing liquidation. The guidance provided in the *Gallagher* judgment was much needed given the eleven hardly reconcilable first instance decisions considered in the judgment. The following conclusions were identified (at [54]):

'(1) Where a CVA or IVA provide for money or other assets to be paid to or transferred or held for the benefit of CVA or IVA creditors, this will create a trust of those moneys or assets for those creditors. (2) The effect of the liquidation of the company or the bankruptcy of the debtor on a trust created by the CVA or IVA will depend on the provision of the CVA or IVA relating thereto. (3) If the CVA or IVA provides what is to happen on liquidation or bankruptcy (or a failure of the CVA or IVA), effect must be given thereto. (4) If the CVA or IVA does not so provide, the trust will continue notwithstanding the liquidation, bankruptcy or failure and must take effect according to its terms. (5) The CVA or IVA creditors can prove in the liquidation or bankruptcy for so much of their debt as remains after payment of what has been or will be recovered under the trust.'

The *Gallagher* judgment was applied to an IVA by the Court of Appeal in *Green v Wright* [2017] EWCA Civ 111, [2017] BPIR 430. The Court of Appeal (reversing the County Court and the Chancery Division) held that the trusts of the debtor's assets constituted by the IVA did not come to an end on successful completion of the IVA. This meant that the proceeds of claims that had been assets of the arrangement, but which only paid out after the notice of completion had been given, were to be distributed to creditors in accordance with the terms of the IVA.

For the purposes of conclusion (1) in the *Gallagher* case it should be noted that the Court of Appeal approved of the concession by counsel for the CVA supervisors, by reference to the decision of Harman J in *Re Leisure Study Group Ltd* [1994] 2 BCLC 65, to the effect that the supervisors were trustees of the assets in their hands notwithstanding the absence of an express trust having been created by the CVA. The combined effects of conclusions (3) and (4) is that arrangement assets will remain ring-fenced for arrangement creditors on a liquidation or bankruptcy or failure of the arrangement unless the arrangement itself specifically provides that the arrangement assets are to be treated differently, most obviously by way of falling into the liquidation or bankruptcy for the benefit of liquidation or bankruptcy creditors. The justification for what might be termed the default rule on ring-fencing in conclusions (3) and (4) appears in the judgment (at [50]) and provided, following an observation that the general law leaves trusts of assets not held for a company unaffected by the debtor's liquidation or bankruptcy:

'Further, as a matter of policy, in the absence of any provision in the CVA as to what should happen to trust assets on liquidation of the company, the court should prefer a default rule which furthers rather than hinders what might be taken to be the statutory purpose of Part I of the Act. Parliament plainly intended to encourage companies and creditors to enter into CVAs so as to provide creditors with a means of recovering what they are owed without recourse to the more expensive means provided by winding-up or administration, thereby giving many companies the opportunity to continue to trade.'

Precisely the same rationale justifies the operation of the default rule on ring-fencing in IVAs under Part VIII, which were introduced as a means of avoiding the consequences of bankruptcy, subject to approval by the statutory requisite majority of creditors.

The court has no jurisdiction to authorise the supervisor of a CVA to breach the trust of the CVA assets for the benefit of the CVA creditors: Re *Beloit Walmsley Ltd* [2008] EWHC 1888 (Ch), [2008] BPIR 1445 (HHJ Pelling QC, sitting as a High Court judge), a decision which includes a useful review of the authorities dealing with the court's jurisdiction to interfere with the terms of a voluntary arrangement, Re *FMS Financial Management Services Ltd* (1989) 5 BCC 191, in particular, being identified as doubtful, or at least 'seriously circumscribed'.

SECTION 1(4)

**The meaning of the term 'company'**—Since 1 October 2009, the term 'company' is defined by reference to the Companies Act 2006 (see the Companies Act 2006 (Consequential Amendments, Transitional Provisions and Savings) Order 2009 (SI 2009/1942).

Section 1(4) was originally introduced with effect from 31 May 2002 by reg 4 of the Insolvency Act 1986 (Amendment) (No 2) Regulations 2002 (SI 2002/1240) and had the effect of extending the scope of the statutory definition. However, following the confusion caused by the decision in Re *The Salvage Association* [2003] BCC 504 (Blackburne J) as to whether the EC Regulation (since replaced by the EU Regulation) permitted an unincorporated entity to avail itself of a CVA, s 1(4) was amended with effect from 13 April 2005 by the Insolvency Act 1986 (Amendment) Regulations 2005 (SI 2005/879) so as to limit the scope of Part I to companies as defined in s 735(1) of the Companies Act 1985 and certain overseas companies. The provision was amended again with effect from 1 October 2009, as described above.

**Article 3(1) of the EU Regulation**—Voluntary arrangements under insolvency legislation are expressly included in Annex A of the EU Regulation on Insolvency Proceedings 2000 as 'insolvency proceedings' within the meaning of Art 2(a) for the purposes of the Regulation. Although Art 3(1) refers to the 'courts' of a Member State having jurisdiction to open main insolvency proceedings, the term, in line with Art 2(6) of the Regulation and para 66 of the Virgos-Schmit Report's commentary on the earlier draft EC Bankruptcy Convention, includes not only the judiciary but also any other competent body empowered by national law to open or make decisions in the course of those proceedings, such as meetings of members and creditors in a CVA.

A CVA may be proposed in relation to a company incorporated outside a member state if the company's centre of main interests can be shown to be within the United Kingdom: Re *BRAC Rent-a-Car International Inc* [2003] 1 WLR 1421 (Lloyd J, administration order made in respect of Delaware incorporated company) and to similar effect see *Daisytek-ISA Ltd* [2003] BCC 562 (HHJ McGonigal sitting as a judge of the High Court).

The decisions in *Salvage Association* and *Rent-a-Car* were preceded by that of Lawrence Collins J in Re *Television Trade Rentals Ltd* [2002] BCC 807 where orders (which were not retrospective) were granted in favour of the provisional liquidators of two Isle of Man registered companies with strong English trading connections in response to a letter of request by the Isle of Man court asking the English court to direct and declare that Part I of the IA 1986, which had no equivalent in the Isle of Man, should apply to the companies pursuant to s 426. It would now appear that, subject to the revised scope of s 1(4) and a debtor company establishing eligibility to make a proposal under s 1 and centre of main interests within the United Kingdom, a non-member state corporation need not have recourse to s 426 in pursuing a CVA.

**1A**

*(Repealed)*

**Amendments**—Repealed by the Corporate Insolvency and Governance Act 2020, s 2(1), Sch 3, paras 1, 2.

**[1.60]**

## 2 Procedure where nominee is not the liquidator or administrator

(1)   This section applies where the nominee under section 1 is not the liquidator or administrator of the company . . ..

(2)   The nominee shall, within 28 days (or such longer period as the court may allow) after he is given notice of the proposal for a voluntary arrangement, submit a report to the court stating—

(a)   whether, in his opinion, the proposed voluntary arrangement has a reasonable prospect of being approved and implemented,

(b)   whether, in his opinion, the proposal should be considered by a meeting of the company and by the company's creditors, and

(c)   if in his opinion it should, the date on which, and time and place at which, he proposes a meeting of the company should be held.

(3)   For the purposes of enabling the nominee to prepare his report, the person intending to make the proposal shall submit to the nominee—

(a)   a document setting out the terms of the proposed voluntary arrangement, and

(b)   a statement of the company's affairs containing—

(i)   such particulars of its creditors and of its debts and other liabilities and of its assets as may be prescribed, and

(ii)   such other information as may be prescribed.

(4)   The court may—

(a)   on an application made by the person intending to make the proposal, in a case where the nominee has failed to submit the report required by this section or has died, or

(b)   on an application made by that person or the nominee, in a case where it is impracticable or inappropriate for the nominee to continue to act as such,

direct that the nominee be replaced as such by another person qualified to act as an insolvency practitioner . . . in relation to the voluntary arrangement.

**Amendments**—Insolvency Act 2000, s 2, Sch 2, paras 1, 3; Deregulation Act 2015, s 19, Sch 6, Pt 6, para 20(1), (2)(b); Small Business, Enterprise and Employment Act 2015, s 126, Sch 9, Pt 1, paras 1, 2; SI 2002/2711; Corporate Insolvency and Governance Act 2020, s 2(1), Sch 3, paras 1, 3.

**General note**—The detailed procedural rules governing the preparation and contents of CVA proposals together with the preparation of the proposal and the nominee's report to the court are set out in rr 2.2–2.24.

### SECTION 2(1)

**Scope of provision**—Section 2 applies either where the CVA proposal is made by the directors under s 1(1) (but not where it is proposed to take steps to obtain a moratorium under s 1A) or where (far less commonly) an administrator or liquidator proposing an arrangement under s 1(3) nominates an individual other than himself or herself as nominee.

### SECTION 2(2)

**The viability of the proposal and the duties of the nominee in reporting to the court**—In *Re A Debtor (No 222 of 1990) ex parte Bank of Ireland and Others (No 2)* [1993] BCLC 233 at 234E–234G Harman J, in the course of a judgment heavily critical of a nominee, expressed the following view:

'In my judgment, the nominee both in making his report and in acting as chairman of the meeting is to be taken as having a duty (arising from the requirement in the statute that he shall report his own opinion to the court) to exercise a professional independent judgment. The fact that judgment is required to be that of a licensed insolvency practitioner emphasises the fact that the court is to receive a report from a qualified person skilled and experienced in these matters, who is exercising his own professional functions in judging whether the matter is, in his opinion, fit to go forward.'

The substance of the judgment in *Bank of Ireland* is reflected in the guidance in SIP 3.1 and SIP 3.2 and was referred to in the Dear IP Letter of March 1995 noted under the heading 'Role of the nominee' to s 1(2) above.

In *Greystoke v Hamilton-Smith* [1997] BPIR 24 at 28B–28F Lindsay J made reference to the Dear IP Letter of March 1995 as representing 'a fair view in general terms of responsibilities which the legislation casts upon a nominee.' The judge, however, went on to express the view that a nominee cannot be expected in every case to have verified personally every figure and to have tested every part of the proposal where, for example, financial resources preclude such enquiries. Lindsay J did, nonetheless, consider that a nominee has an obligation to satisfy himself of three specific matters, 'at least in those cases where the fullness or candour of the debtor's information has properly come into question', namely (1) that the debtor's true position as to assets and liabilities does not appear to him in any material respect to differ substantially from that as it is to be represented to creditors, (2) that the debtor's proposal to creditors has a real prospect of being implemented in the way it is to be represented that it will be (bearing in mind that a measure of modification to proposals is possible under s 4 (s 258 in the case of an IVA), and (3) that the information provides a basis for the view that no already manifest yet unavoidable prospective unfairness in relation to the nominee's functions of admitting or rejecting claims to vote and agreeing values for voting purposes is present. In each particular case, therefore, it is submitted that the question of further enquiry or investigation by the nominee remains a judgment call for the nominee, whose decision must be capable of being justified, objectively speaking, in those circumstances which are known or ought to be known to him or her. His Lordship also considered but rejected the proposition that the arrangement must appear to offer a reasonable prospect of a better recovery than bankruptcy (or liquidation).

Having identified the above three minimum steps, Lindsay J went on in *Greystoke* (at 28H–29A) to qualify his view with the proviso that the steps which it is reasonable for a nominee to take in satisfying himself of the matters identified will, amongst a host of variables particular to any case, include the availability of funds to meet the expense entailed in such further enquiries. That view is consistent with the approach adopted subsequently by HHJ Cooke (sitting as a High Court judge) in *Pitt v Mond* [2001] BPIR 624 at 640F–641B, to the effect that, whilst a nominee is entitled to rely on information provided by a debtor, he or she is under a duty to investigate further any fact or matter which appears to him or her to be doubtful, but only by the taking of such steps as are reasonable on the facts of the case.

For further cases involving claims against nominees see *Heritage Joinery (a firm) v Krasner* [1999] BPIR 683; *Harmony Carpets v Chaffin-Laird* [2000] BPIR 61 (Rattee J); and *Prosser v Castle Sanderson (a firm)* [2002] BPIR 1163 (Mummery, Clarke and Hale LJJ, insolvency practitioner did not owe duty of care to debtor as nominee or chairman of creditors' meeting, but did owe such a duty in his capacity as the debtor's adviser during the short adjournment of the creditors' meeting) and *Tradition (UK) Ltd v Ahmed and Other* [2008] EWHC 3448 (Ch), [2009] BPIR 626.

'Whether . . . the proposed voluntary arrangement has a reasonable prospect of being approved and implemented'—This requirement in s 2(2)(a) (s 256(1)(a) in the case of an IVA) differs from that in s 2(2)(b) (s 256(1)(aa) in the case of an IVA) in that the latter requires consideration of whether meetings of the company and its creditors should be summoned (which brings into play the 'serious and viable' test considered under the next heading), whereas the former provision requires the nominee to express a view not only as to whether the proposal has a reasonable prospect of being approved by creditors but also, it is submitted, whether the approved arrangement is capable of being implemented as envisaged by the proposal.

The formation of an opinion on the prospects of approval must, it is submitted, involve a consideration of the likely attitude of the debtor's unsecured creditors to the proposal. This was in fact the view adopted by the court in *Tradition (UK) Ltd v Ahmed and Other* [2008] EWHC 3448 (Ch), [2009] BPIR 626 in the context of an IVA (at [226]), although in that case, the court questioned to some extent whether spending time and effort trying to predict the outcome of the creditors' meeting would be a productive exercise given that known creditors may not vote, unknown creditors may emerge and in either case a creditor may change their mind. It is suggested that it may be sufficient for a nominee to be satisfied that the proposal has the support of at least one creditor or a group of creditors of a substantial size (see [229]). SIP 3.1 indicates that, as a matter of best practice, the nominee needs to be satisfied at each stage of the process that there are procedures in place to ensure that an assessment is made of viability, the debtor's understanding of the process and commitment to it, and the likely attitude of any key creditors and the general body of creditors. It is submitted that s 2(2)(a) (s 256(1)(a) in the case of an IVA) does not of itself impose an obligation on the nominee to make contact with creditors for the purpose of taking soundings, although a nominee may well regard such a step as prudent in a particular case. Equally, the nominee may, in the absence of suspicion, rely upon representations made to him by the directors as to the likely attitude of any particular creditor. In many cases, however, neither the directors nor the nominee will be in a position to express an opinion as to the likely position of creditors, other than where the proposal is plainly derisory in terms of any proposed dividend.

The question of implementation involves the nominee making an informed assessment as to the viability of the proposal on its terms. It is submitted that any mechanism within the proposal for the post-approval modification of the arrangement will usually constitute a factor affecting implementation.

There is no authority on the meaning of the term 'reasonable prospect' in the present context. It is suggested that this threshold test is relatively low and, by definition, will not be met only where there is no reasonable prospect of the proposal being both approved and – just as importantly and perhaps rather more stringently – implemented.

**Whether the proposal should be considered by the creditors: the 'serious and viable' test**—In *Cooper v Fearnley* [1997] BPIR 20 at 21B–21C Aldous J considered, in the context of an appeal against the decision of a deputy district judge to refuse the making of an interim order in relation to a proposed individual voluntary arrangement, that a proposal must be 'serious and viable'. That yardstick was adopted by Sir Richard Scott V-C in *Hook v Jewson Ltd* [1997] BPIR 100 at 105D and is now well established.

The serious and viable threshold requires not merely that a proposal is seriously made or is made bona fide; rather, the proposal must have both substance and be one which should seriously be considered by the creditors or, alternatively, be capable of serious consideration by creditors, even if there were serious and well-founded doubts and questions over the proposal itself: *Shah v Cooper* [2003] BPIR 1018 (Deputy Registrar Shekerdemian). The fact that a proposal offers only a modest projected dividend to creditors is a relevant factor, but need not of itself mean that the proposal is not serious and viable, since the matter can be left for approval or rejection by creditors: *Knowles v Coutts* [1998] BPIR 96 at 99E–100F (proposal of 1.4 pence in the pound) and *National Westminster Bank plc v Scher* [1998] BPIR 224 (proposed dividend of 0.06 pence in the pound). For a case in which Blackburne J regarded the proposal as 'an essay in make-believe' see *Davidson v Stanley* [2004] EWHC 2595 (Ch), [2005] BPIR 279, an IVA case.

For best practice guidance see SIP 3.1 (IVAs) and SIP 3.2 (CVAs).

### SECTION 2(3)

'a document setting out the terms of the proposed voluntary arrangement'—The proposal, as distinct from the statement of the company's affairs, provides the basis for the conduct of the voluntary arrangement. The detailed information which must appear in the proposal is prescribed in r 2.3 (rr 8.2–8.3 in the case of an IVA).

A proposal does not extend to an agreement or other understanding between a third party and creditors where the distribution to those creditors is to be made from funds advanced by the third party: *IRC v Wimbledon Football Club Ltd* [2004] EWCA Civ 655, [2005] 1 BCLC 66 at [59] (Neuberger LJ).

In practice, it will frequently be necessary to supplement that information prescribed by r 2.3 (rr 8.2–8.3 in the case of an IVA) with further details so as to enable the nominee to report to the court and for the purpose of enabling creditors to make an informed assessment of what is proposed. For example, in the case of a 'trading' arrangement (more common in CVAs than IVAs) the debtor will usually wish to provide something akin to a business plan which extends beyond the very general and which identifies the company's strategy and objectives through ongoing trading. A proposal will also usually identify clearly those assets of the debtor which are included within an arrangement and those which are not. In *Supperstone v Hurst* [2005] BPIR 1231 it was held that statements in an IVA proposal as to the nature and extent of a debtor's interest in a property could not constitute declarations of trust and could not form the basis of inferring a shared common intention of beneficial ownership.

A proposal will also commonly include certain procedural and administrative provisions which allow for the operation of the arrangement itself. Such provisions commonly include an express statement of the supervisor's powers, together with an indication of whether the supervisor is deemed to act as agent for the debtor in the exercise of those powers, given the absence of any statutory provision providing for such agency.

It is also common for arrangements to provide for the treatment of disputed, contingent and/or prospective debts, the status of claims asserted against the debtor which are not known to exist at the time of the proposal together with a facility for the subsequent modification of the arrangement by, typically, 75% of creditors voting on any modification, given that an arrangement may only be modified with the unanimous approval of all creditors in the absence of such a provision: *Raja v Rubin* [1999] 3 WLR 606, CA; and see *Re Alpa Lighting Ltd, Mills v Samuels* [1997] BPIR 341, CA (court has no jurisdiction to direct modifications to approved proposal).

The 28-day period in s 2(2) runs from the date from which the directors' proposal is received: r 2.4(4).

The directors' proposal may be amended at any time prior to the delivery of the nominee's report to the court under s 2(2): r 2.2(3) (s 256 or s 256A and r 8.2(2) in the case of an IVA).

'a statement of . . . affairs'—In practice, both the proposal and the statement of affairs are almost always delivered together. The statement of affairs must be made up to a date which is not earlier than 2 weeks before the date of the proposal: r 2.6(2) (r 8.5(2) in the case of an IVA).

The statement of affairs must include those particulars prescribed by r 2.6(1) (r 8.5 in the case of an IVA) and must supplement or amplify those particulars already given in the directors' proposal 'so far as is necessary for clarifying the state of the company's [or debtor's] affairs'.

A mis-statement of the amount of the assets and liabilities of the debtor may be actionable by an aggrieved creditor as a material irregularity within the meaning of s 6(1)(b) (s 262(1)(b) in the case of an IVA) with the potential for revocation of approval of the arrangement.

**False representations etc**—For the criminal consequences of an offer of a company falsely or fraudulently obtaining the approval of the members of creditors to a voluntary arrangement proposal see s 6A (s 262A in the case of an IVA).

### SECTION 2(4)(a), (b)

**Scope of provision**—This provision (s 256(3)(a) in the case of an IVA) allows for the replacement (and not merely the removal) of the nominee by the court where the nominee has died or failed to submit his or her report to the court within the extendable 28-day period stipulated in s 2(2). Applications to replace a nominee in default of the reporting obligations will be rare since, in cases where the nominee is unwilling to vacate office voluntarily, the debtor is properly entitled to abort the process and to proceed with an alternative nominee. In those circumstances it is submitted that the original nominee would not, on being given notice of the company's (or debtor's in the case of IVAs) position, fall within the definition of 'nominee' in s 1(2) (s 253(2) in the case of an IVA) and would therefore have no obligation to report to the court under s 2(2) (s 256(1) in the case of an IVA).

**'in a case where it is impracticable or inappropriate for the nominee to continue to act as such'**—The observations in the preceding note apply equally here. Alternatively, the person intending to make the proposal or the nominee may make application if, say, the nominee is subject to geographical relocation or is professionally embarrassed.

If an application is made to replace a nominee on professional grounds, then the proposed replacement nominee should, as a matter of good practice, confirm to the court that his appointment does not conflict with any statement of professional ethics or professional guidelines which apply to him.

## [1.61]

### 3 Consideration of proposal

(1)   Where the nominee under section 1 is not the liquidator or administrator, and it has been reported to the court under section 2(2) that the proposal should be considered by a meeting of the company and by the company's creditors, the person making the report shall (unless the court otherwise directs)—

  (a)    summon a meeting of the company to consider the proposal for the time, date and place proposed in the report, and

  (b)    seek a decision from the company's creditors as to whether they approve the proposal.

(2)   Where the nominee is the liquidator or administrator, he shall—

  (a)    summon a meeting of the company to consider the proposal for such time, date and place as he thinks fit, and

  (b)    seek a decision from the company's creditors as to whether they approve the proposal.

(3)   A decision of the company's creditors as to whether they approve the proposal is to be made by a qualifying decision procedure.

(4)   Notice of the qualifying decision procedure must be given to every creditor of the company of whose claim and address the person seeking the decision is aware.

**Amendments**—Small Business, Enterprise and Employment Act 2015, s 126, Sch 9, Pt 1, paras 1, 3(1)–(5).

**General note**—For the detailed procedural rules governing decision procedures see rr 15.28–15.35. Most of the case law in this area concerns IVAs rather than CVAs.

It had been held that a meeting is not valid if not summoned in accordance with the provisions of IA 1986: *Vlieland-Boddy v Dexter* [2004] BPIR 235. However, subsequent decisions indicated that where a properly summoned creditors' meeting considered a proposal that was properly made, a breach of the Act or the Rules or some other default in obtaining approval was unlikely to render the purported approval a nullity. It is submitted that a similar approach will be taken under the qualifying decision procedure regime. HHJ Purle QC, sitting as a High Court judge, held in *Smith-Evans v Smailes* [2013] EWHC 3199 (Ch), [2014] BPIR 306, at [25], that unless challenged in a timely manner using the machinery in s 262 (s 6 in the case of a CVA), the result of a meeting reported to the court should be taken at face value and accepted. An unauthorised exercise of a proxy was a material irregularity, not a nullity, and could be retrospectively ratified. HHJ Purle QC accepted that his approach did some violence to the literal statutory language, but considered a purposive construction was necessary to avoid potential chaos years down the line (at [31]–[32]).

The Court of Appeal approved HHJ Purle QC's approach in *Narandas-Girdhar v Bradstock* [2016] 1 WLR 2366, at [49]. These decisions are consistent with the modern purposive approach to the voluntary arrangement regime, exemplified by the Court of Appeal's decision in *Price v Davis* [2014] EWCA Civ 26, [2014] BPIR 494, see notes to ss 6(1)(b) and 6(7). Failure to give notice of a creditors' decision procedure to a person so entitled is capable of having serious practical consequences, since a person not properly summoned may challenge the arrangement on the 'material irregularity' grounds in s 6(1)(b) (s 262(1)(b) in the case of an IVA).

### SECTION 3(1)

**Scope of provision**—If the nominee files a positive report for the purposes of s 2(2)(a) (s 256(1)(aa) or s 256A(3)(b) for IVAs), then he is under an obligation to summon meetings of the company (or debtor in the case of an IVA) and of its creditors, subject to contrary order of the court, in accordance with his proposals under s 2(2)(b). In practice, a positive report will not usually elicit any response from the court such that the nominee will normally proceed to summon the meetings as a matter of course in accordance with his or her proposals. The subsection appears to anticipate that a contrary order of the court may be made of the court's own volition or following an application by any party with a genuine interest in the business of the proposed meetings of the creditors.

In *Re N (a Debtor)* [2002] BPIR 1024 at [6] Registrar Baister emphasised that s 257(1) (s 3(1) in the case of a CVA) is mandatory and that a meeting should be convened in strict compliance with it. If, as in that case, the nominee fails to hold the meeting at the time and date stipulated then the meeting, and any arrangement there approved, is a nullity and the nominee is at risk of costs personally on any subsequent proceedings in relation thereto. See general notes to ss 3 and 6(7).

**Timing of the meetings of the company and creditors**—Rules 2.26(3) and 2.27 provide that the meetings of the company and the relevant decision procedure in the case of the creditors must be (in the case of creditors) not less than 14, nor more than 28 days from the date on which the nominee's report is filed in court under r 2.9. Under the old IR 1986, the reference to 14 days' notice is to 14 days' clear notice being given to a creditor; there is no scope for arguing for 'substantial compliance' with the provision where less than 14 days' clear notice has been given: *Mytre Investments Ltd v Reynolds (No 2)* [1996] BPIR 464 at 468H–470H. This point is relevant to the question of whether a creditor can be said to have had notice of a creditors' decision procedure 'in accordance with the rules' under s 5(2)(b).

### SECTION 3(2)

**Scope of provision**—The procedure under s 2 has no application where the nominee is the liquidator or administrator, in which case the office-holder proceeds directly to the summoning of meetings of the company and seeking a decision from the creditors without notification to the court. The absence of court involvement would explain the absence of any provision in the section allowing for a contrary order of the court in the summoning of meetings.

For the summoning of meetings where the nominee is liquidator or administrator of the company see rr 2.25–2.36.

### SECTION 3(3), (4)

**Scope of provision**—Section 3(3) (s 257(2), s 257(2A) and s 257(2B) in the case of an IVA) specifies the manner in which a decision of the company's creditors must be reached. Part 15 of the Rules contains rules about decision making and decision making procedures.

In a case concerning an IVA, the importance of complying with s 257(2) was emphasised: *(1) Namulas Pension Trustees Ltd (2) Boyd v (1) Mouzakis (2) Mouzakis (3) Hogg (4) Grant* [2011] BPIR 1724.

The most obvious source of information regarding the identity of the creditors of the company is the statement of affairs submitted to the nominee under s 2(3)(b) (where that section applies) or produced for or provided to a liquidator under s 99(1) or 131(1) or an administrator under s 22(1) (Part II) or para 47(1) of Sch B1 (s 256(2) or s 256A(2) in IVAs). Plainly the nominee should not rely blindly on the list of creditors particularised in the statement of affairs if the nominee has reason to believe that other creditors may exist, given that the subsection is based on the nominee's state of knowledge.

For the binding effect of a voluntary arrangement on persons entitled to notice of the decision procedure in accordance with the rules see s 5(2)(b) and the notes thereto.

**The scope of the term 'creditor'**—The scope of the term 'creditor' and related terms is provided for in ss 382, 383 and 385, a point relevant to a proposal by an undischarged bankrupt, on which see s 257(3) and the notes thereto. In *Re A Debtor, JP v A Debtor* [1999] BPIR 206 Sir John Vinelott held that a petitioning former wife was a creditor within the scope of s 383(1)(a) and was therefore bound by the arrangement proposed by her former husband.

The term extends not only to unliquidated debts (given the above provisions and the specific language to that effect in r 15.31(3)) but also to future or contingent payable debts: *Re Cancol Ltd* [1996] 1 All ER 37 (Knox J, future payments of rents to fall due under an existing lease) applying to CVAs the reasoning applied by the Court of Appeal in *Doorbar v Alltime Securities Ltd (No 2)* [1995] BCC 1149, which affirmed Knox J at first instance [1994] BCC 728, in relation to IVAs.

The Court of Appeal has expressed the view informally that an IVA may extend to joint debts: *Re Cupit (Note)* [1996] BPIR 560 at 563E–564E (Sir Thomas Bingham MR).

There is no conceptual difficulty in the terms of an arrangement being construed so as to extend to post-arrangement debts, subject to the particular terms and circumstances of each case: *Re Goldspan Ltd* [2003] BPIR 93 (Leslie Kosmin QC sitting as a deputy High Court judge).

*Consideration and implementation of proposal*

## [1.62]

### 4 Decisions of the company and its creditors

(1)　This section applies where, under section 3—

(a)　a meeting of the company is summoned to consider the proposed voluntary arrangement, and

(b)　the company's creditors are asked to decide whether to approve the proposed voluntary arrangement.

(1A)　The company and its creditors may approve the proposed voluntary arrangement with or without modifications.

(2)　The modifications may include one conferring the functions proposed to be conferred on the nominee on another person qualified to act as an insolvency practitioner . . . in relation to the voluntary arrangement.

But they shall not include any modification by virtue of which the proposal ceases to be a proposal such as is mentioned in section 1.

(3)　Neither the company nor its creditors may approve any proposal or modification which affects the right of a secured creditor of the company to enforce his security, except with the concurrence of the creditor concerned.

(4)　Subject as follows, neither the company nor its creditors may approve any proposal or modification under which—

(a)　any preferential debt of the company is to be paid otherwise than in priority to such of its debts as are not preferential debts, . . .

(aa)　any ordinary preferential debt of the company is to be paid otherwise than in priority to any secondary preferential debts that it may have,

(b)　a preferential creditor of the company is to be paid an amount in respect of an ordinary preferential debt that bears to that debt a smaller proportion than is borne to another ordinary preferential debt by the amount that is to be paid in respect of that other debt, . . .

(c)　a preferential creditor of the company is to be paid an amount in respect of a secondary preferential debt that bears to that debt a smaller proportion than is borne to another secondary preferential debt by the amount that is to be paid in respect of that other debt, or

(d)　in the case of a company which is a relevant financial institution (see section 387A), any non-preferential debt is to be paid otherwise than in accordance with the rules in section 176AZA(2) or (3).

However, . . . such a proposal or modification may be approved with the concurrence of the . . . creditor concerned.

(4A)　Subject to subsection (4B), where the nominee's report under section 2(2) is submitted to the court before the end of the period of 12 weeks beginning with the day after the end of any moratorium for the company under Part A1, neither the company nor its creditors may approve any proposal or modification under which the following are to be paid otherwise than in full—

(a)　moratorium debts (within the meaning given by section 174A);

(b)　priority pre-moratorium debts (within the meaning given by section 174A).

(4B)　Subsection (4A) does not prevent the approval of such a proposal or modification with the concurrence of the creditor concerned.

(5) Subject as above, the meeting of the company and the qualifying decision procedure shall be conducted in accordance with the rules.

(6) After the conclusion of the company meeting in accordance with the rules, the chairman of the meeting shall report the result of the meeting to the court, and, immediately after reporting to the court, shall give notice of the result of the meeting to such persons as may be prescribed.

(6A) After the company's creditors have decided whether to approve the proposed voluntary arrangement the person who sought the decision must—

(a)    report the creditors' decision to the court, and

(b)    immediately after reporting to the court, give notice of the creditors' decision to such persons as may be prescribed.

(7) References in this section to preferential debts, ordinary preferential debts, secondary preferential debts and preferential creditors are to be read in accordance with section 386 in Part XII of this Act.

**Amendments**—Insolvency Act 2000, s 2, Sch 2, paras 1, 4; SI 2014/3486; Deregulation Act 2015, s 19, Sch 6, Pt 6, para 20(1), (2)(c); Small Business, Enterprise and Employment Act 2015, s 126, Sch 9, Pt 1, paras 1, 4(1)-(8); SI 2018/1244; Corporate Insolvency and Governance Act 2020, s 2(1) Sch 3, paras 1, 4.

**General note**—For the procedural rules governing decisions see rr 2.25–2.36 (r 8.22 in the case of an IVA) and rr 15.28–15.35.

A proposal does not extend to an agreement or other understanding between a third party and creditors where the money from which a distribution is to be made will be from the third party's 'free money', being money which is not advanced at the cost of the debtor: *IRC v Wimbledon Football Club Ltd* [2004] EWCA Civ 655, [2005] 1 BCLC 66 at [59] (Neuberger LJ).

## SECTION 4(1)

**Scope of provision**—The decision of the meetings of the company and the decision of the creditors are, notwithstanding the heading to s 4, referred to in the sub-heading as a single decision. This accords with s 4A(2) by which a decision of the creditors' decision procedure overrides a contrary decision of the members' meeting subject to the standing of a member to apply to court under s 4A(3).

**'with or without modifications'**—Whilst it appears implicit that the meetings of the company and its creditors must each consider identical forms of the proposed voluntary arrangement, whether or not in modified form, note that s 4A(2) provides that approval under s 4(1) requires only the approval of the creditors.

Where modifications are introduced, it is prudent to include a provision of a kind frequently required as a condition of support for a proposal by Crown creditors to the effect that any modification is deemed to override any term in the original proposal where an inconsistency arises between the two.

## SECTION 4(2)

**Scope of provision**—Any modification altering the identity of the nominee squares with s 1(2) in that the amendment will not deprive the CVA proposal of its status as such.

'  . . .  **any modification by virtue of which the proposal ceases to be a proposal** . . . '—Section 4(2) imposes no limitation on the extent of the modifications which may be proposed. In practice, such modifications are common enough and may be insisted upon by a significant creditor or creditors as the price for their support of the proposal, subject to the standing of an eligible applicant making application to the court complaining of unfair prejudice or material irregularity under s 6(1). In theory, therefore, there is no good reason why the proposal should not be modified extensively at the meetings stage, provided that the modifications do not fall within the scope of challenge under s 6(1).

The specific limitation imposed prevents the proposal being modified so as to deprive it of its status as a composition or a scheme of arrangement such that, if approved, the proposal would not constitute a voluntary arrangement as defined in s 1(1).

**No requirement for consent to modifications**—There is no requirement for a company or its directors to agree to modifications to a proposal as submitted by creditors, or even the members of the company or the chairman of the meeting. This is one of the key distinctions between CVAs and IVAs; in an IVA, the debtor's consent is required under s 258(2).

## SECTION 4(3)

**Scope of provision**—A proposal or modified proposal is incapable of affecting the rights of a secured creditor 'to enforce his security' other than with the 'concurrence' of the secured creditor. For the definition of 'secured creditor' and of 'security' see s 248. Schedule A1 provides no definition of the term 'security' where a CVA is coupled with a moratorium; it is submitted, however, that there is no good reason why the term should have any meaning other than that attributed by s 248.

' . . . to enforce his security . . . '—The prohibition in s 4(3) (s 258(4) in IVAs) does not safeguard the rights of a non-concurring secured creditor generally, but only the rights of such a creditor 'to enforce his security'. In *Razzaq v Pala* [1998] BCC 66 Lightman J confirmed (in the context of the former s 11(3)(c)) that the term 'security' does not include a landlord's right of re-entry as Lightman J had previously held to be the case, albeit without full argument on the point, in *March Estates plc v Gunmark Ltd* [1996] BPIR 439. The adoption of Lightman J's approach in *Razzaq* by the House of Lords in *Re Park Air Services plc* [1999] 2 WLR 396 confirms that a landlord's right of re-entry does not constitute security for the performance of lease covenants including, most obviously, a covenant for the payment of rent reserved. It follows that a voluntary arrangement may affect the right of a landlord to exercise the right of re-entry under a lease without the concurrence of the landlord, subject to the standing of the landlord to challenge such a decision as unfairly prejudicial under s 6(1)(a) (s 262(1)(a) in the case of an IVA). A voluntary arrangement is capable of modifying a landlord's right as a creditor in relation to reserved rent, including arrears and/or future rent: *Re Cancol Ltd* [1996] 1 All ER 37. In *Re Naeem (a Bankrupt)* [1990] 1 WLR 48 at 50 Hoffmann J rejected a landlord's complaint of unfair prejudice and held that, in keeping with the modification of the claims of other creditors, the right of the landlord to forfeit under a lease should operate for the recovery of rent as modified by the arrangement and not the landlord's original claim. The decision in *Re Naeem*, it is submitted, is consistent with that in *Razzaq*.

It is suggested that there are at least two obvious reasons why the reasoning of Hoffmann J in *Re Naeem*, as it applies to the modification of a landlord's claim for rent, would not apply to a debt due to a creditor secured by a mortgage or charge. First, a mortgagee or chargee obtains an immediate proprietary interest by way of security in the debtor's property, which encumbrance the debtor is only able to discharge through payment in full of the underlying indebtedness. A landlord, on the other hand, obtains no such proprietary interest in the debtor's property, but enjoys instead proprietary *remedies* (forfeiture, re-entry etc) which are exercisable in relation to the leased property. Secondly, it is extremely unlikely that Parliament could have intended to allow for the modification of the security rights of a non-concurring mortgage or charge-holder under the terms of a voluntary arrangement where the same rights would be unaffected by the process of liquidation or administration.

' . . . except with the concurrence of the creditor concerned . . . '— The word 'concurrence' in this context means positive consent or agreement, not merely passive acquiescence. In *Peck v Craighead* [1995] 1 BCLC 337 Martin Mann QC, sitting as a deputy High Court judge, found a material irregularity where security rights were modified without consent.

A secured creditor is not automatically deemed to have waived its security rights through the acceptance of a dividend under a voluntary arrangement: *Whitehead v Household Mortgage Corporation* [2002] EWCA Civ 1657; compare *Khan v Permayer* [2001] BPIR 95.

## SECTION 4(4)

Scope of provision—This subsection prohibits the variation of the priority status afforded to preferential debts and the treatment of any preferential debt vis-à-vis other preferential debts other than with the concurrence of the preferential creditor concerned.

For the meaning of 'preferential debts' and 'preferential creditors' see s 4(7). On the term 'concurrence' see the note to s 4(3) above.

## SECTION 4(4)(a), (b)

Scope of provision—A decision under s 4(1) (s 258(1) in the case of an IVA) cannot take away the priority afforded to preferential debts by statute. Neither is a voluntary arrangement capable of modifying the claim of a single preferential creditor such that the reduction in that preferential creditor's claim would be greater than the reduction suffered by any other preferential creditor.

## SECTION 4(5)

Scope of provision—See rr 2.25–2.34 (r 8.22 in IVAs) and rr 15.28–15.35.

## SECTIONS 4(6), (6A)

Scope of provision—Rule 2.28 provides that the creditors' decision must be made in advance of the company meeting and the members' decision must be made not later than 5 business days later than the creditors' decision. Those rules envisage that there is no purpose in a meeting of members if the creditors have rejected the proposal. Rule 2.34 provides that the chair of any meeting is to be the nominee or an 'appointed person', an expression defined in r 1.2(3) and includes either a person qualified to act as an insolvency practitioner or a person experienced in insolvency matters who is a member or employee of the office-holder's (presumably, office-holder in this context refers to nominee's) firm or an employee of the office-holder (again, presumably office-holder refers in this context to the nominee). Rule 2.38 provides that a report of the consideration of the proposal is to be prepared by the chairman. Rule 2.38(2) prescribes the contents of the report, which must be filed with the court under r 2.38(3) within 4 business days of the company meeting being held. If the arrangement is approved, then the supervisor must also send a copy of the chairman's report to the Registrar of Companies: r 2.38(6). The chairman must also send a notice of the result – but not necessarily a copy of the chairman's report – to all those persons who were sent notice of the qualifying decision procedure under s 3, and he must do so as soon as reasonably practicable.

The filing of the chairman's report with the court amounts to a reporting obligation only and has no substantive consequence. The CVA comes into being as a consequence of approval under s 4A alone; the court is not involved in the ongoing conduct of the arrangement in the absence of an application to it. In the case of an IVA, it was held that the result of a meeting reported to the court must be taken at face value and accepted in the absence of a timely application to the court pursuant to s 262 (s 6 in the case of a CVA): *Smith-Evans v Smailes* [2013] EWHC 3199 (Ch), [2014] BPIR 306 (HHJ Purle QC, sitting as a High Court judge, at [25]). See note to s 6(7).

**SECTION 4(7)**

**Scope of provision**—The 'relevant date' for the assessment of preferential debts is the date on which the voluntary arrangement takes effect or, if the company is in administration, the date on which it entered administration: s 387(2). The fact that the company is in receivership will not affect the relevant date for the assessment of preferential debts in a company voluntary arrangement.

## [1.63]

### 4A Approval of arrangement

(1)   This section applies to a decision, under section 4, with respect to the approval of a proposed voluntary arrangement.

(2)   The decision has effect if, in accordance with the rules—

   (a)   it has been taken by the meeting of the company summoned under section 3 and by the company's creditors pursuant to that section, or

   (b)   (subject to any order made under subsection (6)) it has been taken by the company's creditors pursuant to that section.

(3)   If the decision taken by the company's creditors differs from that taken by the company meeting, a member of the company may apply to the court.

(4)   An application under subsection (3) shall not be made after the end of the period of 28 days beginning with—

   (a)   the day on which the decision was taken by the company's creditors, or

   (b)   where the decision of the company meeting was taken on a later day, that day.

(5)   Where a member of a regulated company, as defined by section A49(13), applies to the court under subsection (3), the appropriate regulator is entitled to be heard on the application.

(5A)   The "appropriate regulator" means—

   (a)   where the regulated company is a PRA-regulated company as defined by section A49(13), the Financial Conduct Authority and the Prudential Regulation Authority, and

   (b)   in any other case, the Financial Conduct Authority.

(6)   On an application under subsection (3), the court may—

   (a)   order the decision of the company meeting to have effect instead of the decision of the company's creditors, or

   (b)   make such other order as it thinks fit.

**Amendments**—Inserted by Insolvency Act 2000, s 2, Sch 2, paras 1, 5. Amended by Financial Services Act 2012, s 114(1), Sch 18, Pt 2, paras 51, 52(1)-(3); Small Business, Enterprise and Employment Act 2015, s 126, Sch 9, Pt 1, paras 1, 5(1)-(3); Corporate Insolvency and Governance Act 2020, s 2(1), Sch 3, paras 1, 5(1).

**General note**—These provisions were introduced, with effect from 1 January 2003, by Insolvency Act 2000, s 2 and Sch 2 thereto. Save for s 4A(5) the provisions confirm that, in effect, only the requisite support of the creditors is required to approved a proposed CVA, subject to the standing of a member of the company to apply to the court under s 4A(3) for relief under s 4A(6) where the meeting of the company does not approve the proposal.

**SECTION 4A(1)**

**Scope of provision**—The scope of s 4A is limited to the decision under s 4(1) to approve the proposed CVA, with or without modifications. The provisions have no wider scope.

The date on which a voluntary arrangement takes effect, or any associated moratorium comes into force, amounts to the 'effective date' for the purposes of s 233(4) (supplies of gas, water, electricity, etc to company).

**SECTION 4A(2)(a), (b)**

**Scope of provision**—Subject to any contrary order under s 4A(4) the decision under s 4(1) requires only the approval of the creditors.

' . . . **in accordance with the rules** . . . '—A decision under s 4(1) can only have effect if the meeting of the company has been summoned and the creditors' decision has been conducted under s 3 in accordance with rr 2.25–2.34 and Part 15, although it is arguable from the wording of s 4A(2)(b) that only the creditors' decision needs to have been arrived at in accordance with s 3 and the applicable rules.

**SECTION 4A(3)**

**Scope of provision**—To make an application to court under this subsection a member of a company need establish no other grounds than the fact of the creditors having made a decision for s 4(1) purposes which differs from that of the company meeting. Whilst the court has the broadest powers under s 4A(6) on such an application, it is difficult to envisage circumstances in which those powers might properly be exercised. If the creditors have approved a proposed CVA without the support of the company meeting, then it is far from clear on what basis the court might interfere, at least where the company is insolvent, by allowing the decision of the company meeting to override that of the creditors so as, in effect, to withdraw the approval provided for in s 4A(2)(b). Equally, the court's interference by order under s 4A(6) is unlikely to be justified in a case where the creditors have not given their approval to the proposal, at least, again, where the company is insolvent.

An application under s 4A(3) does not apparently require proof that the CVA prejudices the interests of a creditor, member or contributory or that there has been some material irregularity at, or in relation to, the meeting of the company or the creditors' decision procedure. Proof of either such matter, however, is required on an application under s 6(1) by a member eligible under s 6(2)(a). The absence of either such ground in an application under s 4A(3), it is submitted, can only militate against the making of an order under s 4A(6) where the decision of the creditors has been validly made in accordance with s 3 and the rules thereto.

**SECTION 4A(4)**

**Scope of provision**—For the purposes of s 4A(4)(b) a company meeting must be held within 5 business days of the creditors' decision: r 2.28(3).

**Extension by the court of the 7-day period?**—Based on the reasoning of Lloyd J in *Re Bournemouth & Boscombe AFC Co Ltd* [1998] BPIR 183 at 186A–186D in relation to very similar wording in s 6(3), the 28-day time limit prescribed in this subsection will not be capable of extension by the court. In *Re Beloit Walmsley Ltd* [2008] EWHC 1888 (Ch), [2008] BPIR 1445 at [29] HHJ Pelling QC (sitting as a High Court judge), confirmed that the reasoning in the *Bournemouth* case, which had been decided by reference to the formerly operative RSC Ord 3, r 5, continued to apply following the implementation of CPR 3.2(1). See note to s 6(3).

**SECTION 4A(5)**

**Scope of provision**—The term 'regulated company' is defined in para 44(18) of Sch A1.

**SECTION 4A(6)**

**Scope of provision**—The court has an unfettered discretion in terms of the scope of any order it may make. See, however, the notes to s 4A(3) above.

For the procedure following the making of an order under s 4A(6) see r 2.37.

## [1.64]

### 5 Effect of approval

(1) This section applies where a decision approving a voluntary arrangement has effect under section 4A.

(2) The . . . voluntary arrangement—

    (a)    takes effect as if made by the company at the time the creditors decided to approve the voluntary arrangement, and

    (b)    binds every person who in accordance with the rules—

(i)     was entitled to vote in the qualifying decision procedure by which the creditors' decision to approve the voluntary arrangement was made, or

(ii)    would have been so entitled if he had had notice of it,

as if he were a party to the voluntary arrangement.

(2A)  If—

(a)     when the arrangement ceases to have effect any amount payable under the arrangement to a person bound by virtue of subsection (2)(b)(ii) has not been paid, and

(b)     the arrangement did not come to an end prematurely,

the company shall at that time become liable to pay to that person the amount payable under the arrangement.

(3)  Subject as follows, if the company is being wound up or is in administration, the court may do one or both of the following, namely—

(a)     by order stay or sist all proceedings in the winding up or provide for the appointment of the administrator to cease to have effect;

(b)     give such directions with respect to the conduct of the winding up or the administration as it thinks appropriate for facilitating the implementation of the . . . voluntary arrangement.

(3A)  Where immediately before the voluntary arrangement took effect a moratorium for the company was in force under Part A1 and a petition for the winding up of the company, other than an excepted petition within the meaning of section A20, was presented before the beginning of the moratorium, the court must dismiss the petition.

(4)  The court shall not make an order under subsection (3)(a) or dismiss a petition under subsection (3A)—

(a)     at any time before the end of the period of 28 days beginning with the first day on which each of the reports required by section 4(6) and (6A) has been made to the court, or

(b)     at any time when an application under the next section or an appeal in respect of such an application is pending, or at any time in the period within which such an appeal may be brought.

(5)  Where the company is in energy administration, the court shall not make an order or give a direction under subsection (3) unless—

(a)     the court has given the Secretary of State or the Gas and Electricity Markets Authority a reasonable opportunity of making representations to it about the proposed order or direction; and

(b)     the order or direction is consistent with the objective of the energy administration.

(6)  In subsection (5) "in energy administration" and "objective of the energy administration" are to be construed in accordance with Schedule B1 to this Act, as applied by Part 1 of Schedule 20 to the Energy Act 2004.

**Amendments**—Insolvency Act 2000, ss 2, 15(1), Sch 2, paras 1, 6, Sch 5; Enterprise Act 2002, s 248(3), Sch 17, paras 9, 11; Energy Act 2004, s 159(1), Sch 20, Pt 4, para 43; Small Business, Enterprise and Employment Act 2015, s 126, Sch 9, Pt 1, paras 1, 6(1)-(3); Corporate Insolvency and Governance Act 2020, s 2(1), Sch 3, paras 1, 6(1).

**General note**—Taken together, these provisions, together with s 4A, identify the decision of the creditors as the key event for the bringing of the arrangement into effect. An approved arrangement remains in force until either revoked by way of a modification validly approved by creditors or until the making of any order setting aside the arrangement under s 6 (s 262 in IVAs).

### SECTION 5(1)

**Scope of provision**—Section 5 applies only where s 4A(1) has effect. The application of the section is not affected by the fact of an application to court under s 4A(3) or s 6(1), subject to any order of the court.

It appears that the reference to creditors having decided to approve a proposal in s 5(1) should now be taken to include a *purported* approval where the approval is capable of being impugned by some breach of the Act or Rules or some other default in obtaining the approval. In *Smith-Evans v Smailes* [2013] EWHC 3199 (Ch), [2014] BPIR 306, [25]-[27] (a case concerning the similar provision applicable to IVAs in s 260(1)), it was held that such a purported approval must be taken at face value and accepted unless challenged by a timely application under s 262 (s 6 in the case of a CVA). See notes to ss 3, 6(1)(b) and 6(7).

## SECTION 5(2)

**Scope of provision**—This is a deeming provision, which provides for the binding nature of the CVA (s 260(2) in the case of an IVA). The effect of the arrangement taking effect as if made by the company (or debtor in the case of an IVA) operates so as to bind it to the arrangement. This provision also binds to the arrangement all creditors entitled to vote at the meeting that approved it, whether they voted for it or not. It has been held (in a case concerning an IVA) that where a voluntary arrangement is approved at a further meeting held under s 262 (s 6 in the case of a CVA), the statutory binding in s 260(2) (s 5(2) in CVAs) applies to the creditors as at the date of the summoning of that further meeting, not merely those who were entitled to vote at the time of the original meeting: *Price v Davis* [2014] EWCA Civ 26, [2014] BPIR 494, [25]. In another case concerning an IVA, *Fehily v (1) Atkinson (2) Mummery* [2016] EWHC 3069 (Ch), [2017] BPIR 21 Stephen Jourdan QC (sitting as a deputy High Court judge) held that the statutory binding in s 260(2) (s 5(2) in the case of a CVA) is not rendered void on the ground that the debtor lacks mental capacity ([117]–[127]).

The effect of this 'statutory hypothesis' or deeming is that the court is compelled to apply a contractual analysis to the construction of a CVA: *In re SHB Realisations Ltd (formerly BHS Ltd) (in liquidation)* [2018] EWHC 402 (Ch), [2018] Bus LR 1173, at [28], per Christopher Pymont QC (sitting as a deputy High Court judge). The deputy judge held, however, that it is unnecessary and inappropriate to consider any of the usual principles of contract formation (offer, acceptance, consideration, intention to create legal relations), all of which are irrelevant. The law on penalties is also impossible to apply, because a CVA put forward by or on behalf of a company in the interests of itself, its members and creditors, cannot be said to have oppressed the company, at [29]. Building on the analysis in *In re SHB Realisations Ltd*, HHJ Simon Barker QC (sitting as a High Court judge) suggested in *Re Rhino Enterprises Holdings Ltd* [2020] EWHC 2370 (Ch), [2021] BPIR 144 that the 'statutory hypothesis' characterisation made clear that a CVA is different from, and is not in fact, a contract. The judge declined to make an outright finding but held that it was at least as likely as not that a CVA is not a contract and that the Contract (Rights of Third Parties) Act 1999 had no application ([83]–[86]).

**The court's approach to the construction of voluntary arrangements**—The judgment of Blackburne J in *Welsby v Brelec Installations Ltd* [2000] 2 BCLC 576 concerned in part the construction of certain express terms employed in a CVA for the purpose of determining if and when there had been 'failure' for the purposes of that arrangement:

> 'An arrangement is usually put together with some haste. Modifications to it are frequently made at the statutory meeting of creditors with little time to reflect on how they relate to the other terms of the debtor's proposal. Quite often, as this case demonstrates, the resulting terms are clumsily worded. The arrangement ought therefore to be construed in a practical fashion. Otherwise there is a risk that careless drafting coupled with a too-literal approach to its construction will serve to frustrate rather than achieve the purpose of the arrangement. The underlying purpose in most arrangements – and certainly this one – is to provide the arrangement creditors with a means of debt recovery which avoids the need to have recourse to the formal and more expensive mechanisms of winding up or administration (or bankruptcy in the case of an individual) and, if the arrangement is successful, to give the debtor the chance to continue trading in the longer term.'

For a case adopting the *Welsby* approach to construction of a CVA, which involved reconciliation of terms as to a CVA providing for failure and termination through the issue of a certificate of non-compliance or an abort certificate so as to determine the destination of CVA trust assets see *Re Zebra Industrial Projects Ltd* [2005] BPIR 1022 (John Martin QC, sitting as a deputy High Court judge).

It is necessary, in construing specific terms of a CVA, to analyse such terms carefully. However, in undertaking that analysis, it must be borne in mind that the CVA must be read as a whole, and further that specific terms must not be analysed so closely as to overlook the overall commercial context or the practical consequences: see *Tucker and Spratt (Joint Supervisors of Energy Holdings (No 3) (In Liquidation) v Gold Fields Mining LLC* [2009] EWCA Civ 173, [2009] BPIR 704.

Any suggestion, however, that the decision in *Welsby* should be taken to mean that the court is not constrained by the ordinary rules on contractual interpretation in the case of a CVA is unlikely to survive the Court of Appeal's decision in *Re MF Global UK Ltd (in special administration)*; *Heis v Financial Services Compensation Scheme Ltd* [2018] EWCA Civ 1327, [2018] BPIR 1142. Sir Colin Rimer (McFarlane and Asplin LJJ concurring) agreed with the parties (at [22]) that the ordinary principles of interpretation, as summarised by the *Supreme Court in Wood v Capita Insurance Services Ltd* [2017] UKSC 24, apply to CVAs. Accordingly, meaning must be assessed in the light of: (i) the natural and ordinary meaning of the clause; (ii) any other relevant provisions of the instrument; (iii) the overall purpose of the clause and the instrument; (iv) the facts and circumstances known or assumed by the parties at the time of execution; and (v) commercial common sense; but (vi) disregarding subjective evidence of any party's intentions.

**The implication of terms into an arrangement**—As regards terms implied into a voluntary arrangement, given that an arrangement is ordinarily a lengthy and complex document and has the effect by statutory force under s 5(2) (s 260(2) in the case of an IVA) of binding all creditors entitled to notice of it, it is perhaps not surprising that the court will be slow to imply a term unless it is necessary to give efficacy to an arrangement. In the words of Chadwick LJ in *Johnson v Davies* [1999] Ch 117 at 138A–138B, in the context of a case which considered whether an IVA was capable of releasing a co-debtor from liability:

'Under Part VIII of the 1986 Act, the discharge of the debtor depends entirely on the terms of the arrangement. One must look at the arrangement, and nothing else, in order to find the terms (if any) under which the debtor is discharged. This is emphasised by the words in s 260(2) (s 5(2) in the case of a CVA) of the 1986 Act . . . '

In *El Ajou v Stern* [2006] EWHC 3067 (Ch), [2007] BPIR 693 at [31]–[34] Kitchin J accepted that an IVA was subject to an implied term that creditors subject to the IVA would take no steps to enforce their claim against the debtor since such a term was necessary to give business efficacy to the arrangement, mindful of the comments of Chadwick LJ in *Johnson* at 128F–128G to the effect that such a term must be implied if an arrangement is to work as intended. Kitchin J could not, however, find any basis for implying a term prohibiting a creditor from pursuit of a claim to judgment following discharge of the interim order imposing a stay. A similar conclusion was reached by Rimer J in *Alman v Approach Housing Ltd* [2001] BCLC 530 (a CVA case) where the arrangement contained no machinery for the determination of disputed claims.

In *Re Hellard and Goldfarb* [2007] BPIR 1322 HHJ Norris QC (sitting as a High Court judge) was prepared to imply a term (by way of a direction to that effect) that supervisors of a CVA were entitled to draw remuneration from arrangement assets on a time cost basis where a cap on fees had been reached and where a further meeting to seek sanction for the drawing of further fees in accordance with the terms of the CVA had been inquorate upon nobody attending.

In *Oakrock Ltd v Travelodge Hotels Ltd and others* [2015] EWHC 30 (TCC), [2015] BPIR 360, the court (Edwards-Stuart J) accepted, on the basis of a concession by counsel in that case, that a CVA can include an implied term that the company will not rely on a limitation period whilst it is in a CVA. The concession was made on the basis of the decision of Mann J in *Tanner v Everitt* [2004] EWHC 1130 (Ch), [2004] BPIR 1026. On a contested appeal, HHJ Paul Matthews (sitting as a High Court judge) applied *Tanner v Everitt* to imply a similar term into an IVA in *The Co-operative Bank plc v Phillips* [2017] EWHC 1320 (Ch), [2017] BPIR 1156.

**SECTION 5(2)(a)**

**Scope of provision**—The word 'made' replaced the word 'approved' by amendment under Sch 5 of the Insolvency Act 2000. The earlier version of s 5(2) was considered by the court in *Wood v Heart Hospital* [2009] BPIR 1538.

**SECTION 5(2)(b)**

**The meaning of 'notice'**—This new provision was inserted by Insolvency Act 2000, s 2 (s 3 in the case of an IVA) and Sch 2 (Sch 3 in the case of an IVA) thereto and represents a significant change from the previous position. Formerly, it had been held that a creditor must have actual notice of the creditors' decision procedure so as to be bound by the arrangement; in particular, the court had rejected the operation of a doctrine of deemed notice: see *Re a Debtor (No 64 of 1992)* [1994] BCC 55, and *Skipton Building Society v Collins* [1998] BPIR 267 (Jonathan Parker J). The new provision does away with the requirement for actual notice. Instead, s 5(2)(b) (s 260(2)(b) in the case of an IVA) binds two classes of person (see below) as party to the voluntary arrangement on the assumption that any such person would have been entitled to participate in the creditors' decision making process. In this regard, r 15.28(5) (entitlement to vote) must be read in light of s 5(2)(b) (s 260(2)(b) in the case of an IVA) to the extent that the former provision refers to 'every creditor who has notice of the decision procedure'; s 5(2)(b) (s 260(2)(b) in the case of an IVA) suggests that those words must be interpreted as meaning every creditor who has notice or would have been entitled to have had notice of the creditors' decision procedure.

**The two classes of person within s 5(2)(b) (s 260(2)(b) in IVAs)**—The two classes of person bound by s 5(2)(b) (s 260(2)(b) in the case of an IVA) are (i) every person entitled to vote in a creditors' decision process (ie who had notice of the decision process, irrespective of whether or not he participated), or (ii) any person who would have been entitled to have had such notice (ie irrespective of whether such notice was received or otherwise communicated). Class (i) will not extend to a person who is not entitled to vote: *RA Securities Ltd v Mercantile Credit Co Ltd* [1994] BCC 598 at 600H (Jacob J); and see also *Burford Midland Properties Ltd v Marley Extrusions Ltd* [1994] BCC 604 (HHJ Roger Cooke sitting as a High Court judge). Class (ii) will catch both creditors who are not known to the nominee initiating the creditors' decision process and also creditors who are known but to whom notice is not given through, say, an administrative oversight or even a deliberate omission. In *Re North Point Global Limited; Brittain v Chamberlain* [2020] EWHC 1648 (Ch), HHJ Davies-White QC (sitting as a High Court judge) held that a liquidator with a preference claim against a company in CVA was within the scope of s 5(2)(b)(ii), even where the winding up post-dated the approval of the CVA and the liquidator had neither been in office nor had a claim at the time of the decision to approve the CVA (at [112]–[125]).

**Failure to give notice as ground for alleging unfair prejudice/material irregularity under s 6 (s 262 in IVAs)**—The fact of a creditor being bound by an arrangement under s 5(2)(b) (s 262(2)(b) in the case of an IVA) in circumstances where that creditor can establish, as a matter of fact, that it had not been given notice is capable of founding an application alleging material irregularity and/or, possibly, unfair prejudice under s 6(1) (s 262(1) in the case of an IVA), but only where that creditor would have been capable of affecting or influencing the outcome of the decision procedure.

**Unliquidated, future or contingent debts, co-debtors and third parties**—For the treatment of unliquidated, future or contingent debts in a voluntary arrangement and the position of co-debtors and third parties, see the notes to s 1(1) above.

**The effect of an arrangement on assignees**—Subject to an effective contrary term within an arrangement, the assignee of a contractual right which is modified by an arrangement prior to assignment acquires only the benefit of that right as modified by the arrangement. In the context of leases it is well established that an assignee may reach agreement with his or her landlord to alter the terms on which the assignee holds the estate so as to bind an original tenant: *Baynton v Morgan* (1888) 22 QBD 74l, and see *Centrovincial Estates plc v Bulk Storage Ltd* (1983) 46 PCR 393. Whether or not future rent under a lease falls within the scope of the arrangement as a prospective debt will depend on the particular terms and construction of the arrangement. Note that, pursuant to the decision of the Court of Appeal in *Kapoor v (1) National Westminster Bank plc (2) Tan* [2011] EWCA Civ 1083, [2011] BPIR 1680 an assignee of a creditor is able to vote at a meeting of creditors called to consider an IVA proposal (although on the facts of that case, there was a material irregularity arising from the circumstances and the lack of good faith in respect of the assignment).

**Single creditor with a claim within and a claim outside the arrangement**—One problem which may arise in relation to s 5(2)(b) (s 260(2)(b) in the case of an IVA) concerns the position where a creditor maintains two separate claims against the debtor where one of the claims does not fall plainly within the scope of the arrangement. The decision on Knox J in *Doorbar v Alltime Securities Ltd* [1994] BCC 994 involved claims by a landlord in respect of arrears and interest for a liquidated sum together with a further claim for the aggregate of rent prospectively payable until the end of the contractual term of the lease disregarding possible upward rent reviews. At 1000E of his judgment Knox J opined that a creditor entitled to vote in respect of one debt was not bound by an approved arrangement in respect of a different debt if (as was the case on the facts of *Doorbar*) the creditor was not entitled to vote in respect of that different debt. That position appears to have been assumed in the judgment of the Court of Appeal given by Peter Gibson LJ: see [1995] BCC 1149 at 1155C. That view, as expressed, however, runs contrary to the decision of Rimer J in *Re Bradley-Hole (a Bankrupt)* [1995] BCC 418 at 434B–434C which held that a creditor is bound by an arrangement in respect of both debts where one carried an entitlement to vote and the other did not. This problem is probably now more apparent than real following the Court of Appeal's decision in *Doorbar* and the finding (at 1157E) that a chairman is entitled to place an estimated minimum value on an unliquidated debt for voting purposes, on which see now the express wording in r 15.31(3) and the notes to that provision. Where a creditor disagrees with that minimum value it can hardly be said that the creditor has no entitlement to vote for the purposes of s 5(2)(b) (s 260(2)(b) in the case of an IVA). In *Peterkin v London Borough of Merton and Another* [2011] EWHC 376 (Ch), [2012] BPIR 388, Vos J held that a moratorium imposed by an IVA could not preclude a participating creditor from seeking to enforce a debt which arose after the IVA and which was outside the scope of the IVA. *Cornelius v Casson* [2008] BPIR 504 is another example of a case in which the court (Thomas Ivory QC, sitting as a deputy High Court judge) considered which debts of a participating creditor fell within an IVA. Following the Supreme Court's decision in *In re Nortel GmbH (in administration)* [2013] UKSC 52, [2014] AC 209, earlier authorities on this area should be approached with caution.

Where the chairman declines to admit a claim for unliquidated damages and attributes to it only a nominal value, in circumstances where the same creditor is admitted to the arrangement for a liquidated sum relating to a separate debt so as to be bound by it in respect of the liquidated debt, any entitlement to pursue the unliquidated claim outside the terms of the arrangement will depend on a construction of those terms. In *Sea Voyager Maritime Inc v Bielecki (t/a Hughes Hooker & Co)* [1999] 1 BCLC 133 at 150–151, Richard McCombe QC (sitting as a deputy High Court judge), held that it was implicit in the terms of that particular arrangement that those bound by it were prevented from commencing or pursuing proceedings outside the arrangement. No such bar was held to have been implied in the less elaborately drawn CVA considered by Rimer J in *Alman v Approach Housing Ltd* [2001] BPIR 203. Ultimately, the implication of a term into a voluntary arrangement turns on whether the term is necessary to give efficacy to the arrangement; although such terms will not be implied lightly: see *Johnson v Davies* [1999] Ch 117 at 128G–128H (Chadwick LJ).

**Single creditor pursuing only part of single debt in arrangement**—What of the position where a single creditor seeks to be bound only in respect of part of that debt? It is submitted that that possibility now seems doubtful, given the revised wording in s 5(2)(b).

In *Re C J Hoare* [1997] BPIR 683 Edward Nugee QC (sitting as a deputy High Court judge) held (at 695D), following the decision of the Court of Appeal in *Doorbar v Alltime Securities Ltd* and adopting the approach of Knox J in *Re Cancol Ltd* [1996] 1 All ER 37, that it is not open to a creditor to put an estimated figure on his debts which is stated as being subject to verification and possible amendment, only to claim later that he or she is owed some other debt which was not included in the original figure and in respect of which the debtor is not bound by the arrangement. Whilst the deputy judge accepted the possibility of a distinction being drawn between two separate debts arising out of the same claim (at 694G), it now seems unlikely, given the amended form of s 5(2) (s 260(2) in the case of an IVA), that a single debt might be divided so as to allow part of it to be pursued outside of the arrangement other than where the terms of the arrangement expressly provide for such an outcome.

### SECTION 5(2A)

**Scope of provision**—This provision was inserted by Insolvency Act 2000, s 2 (s 3 in the case of an IVA) and Sch 2 (Sch 3 in the case of an IVA) thereto. Its effect is such that, where an arrangement does not end prematurely, a creditor who is bound by an arrangement, but has not had notice of it by virtue of s 5(2)(b)(ii) (s 260(2)(b)(ii) in the case of an IVA), is entitled to any sum due to him under the arrangement to the extent that that creditor has not already been paid. The provision does not, however, confer any entitlement to vote on such a creditor.

For the meaning of the term 'comes to an end prematurely' see s 7B (s 262C in the case of an IVA).

### SECTION 5(3), (4)

**Scope of provision**—These provisions are largely self-explanatory and are designed, subject to the constraints imposed by s 5(4), to enable the court to stay winding-up proceedings or, apparently, to discharge the appointment of an administrator for the purpose of 'facilitating the implementation of the voluntary arrangement'. For cases under the equivalent s 147(1) see *Re Lowston* [1991] BCLC 570, ChD (Harman J) and the authorities therein.

The provisions do not identify the parties eligible to make an application for an order under s 5(3). Procedurally, an application should be made in any winding-up or administration proceedings. It is submitted that such an application may be made by any party with an interest in the CVA, which would include the company itself, the nominee or supervisor, a liquidator or administrator, a member of the company or a creditor, whether or not an arrangement creditor. In Scotland it has been held that the burden rests on the applicant in satisfying the court that an order should be made and that the court must consider the rights and interests of all who may be affected by the decision: *Re McGruther v Seoble* [2004] SC 514 at [16]–[18].

For the discharge of the remuneration etc of a liquidator or administrator where a voluntary arrangement is approved, see r 2.39(2)–(6).

## [1.65]

### 6 Challenge of decisions

(1) Subject to this section, an application to the court may be made, by any of the persons specified below, on one or both of the following grounds, namely—

    (a)    that a voluntary arrangement which has effect under section 4A unfairly prejudices the interests of a creditor, member or contributory of the company;

    (b)    that there has been some material irregularity at or in relation to the meeting of the company, or in relation to the relevant qualifying decision procedure.

(1A) In this section—

    (a)    the "relevant qualifying decision procedure" means the qualifying decision procedure in which the company's creditors decide whether to approve a voluntary arrangement;

    (b)    references to a decision made in the relevant qualifying decision procedure include any other decision made in that qualifying decision procedure.

(2) The persons who may apply under subsection (1) are—

- (a) a person entitled, in accordance with the rules, to vote at the meeting of the company or in the relevant qualifying decision procedure;
- (aa) a person who would have been entitled, in accordance with the rules, to vote in the relevant qualifying decision procedure if he had had notice of it;
- (b) the nominee or any person who has replaced him under section 2(4) or 4(2); and
- (c) if the company is being wound up or is in administration, the liquidator or administrator.

(2A)   Subject to this section, where a voluntary arrangement in relation to a company in energy administration is approved at the meetings summoned under section 3, an application to the court may be made—

- (a) by the Secretary of State, or
- (b) with the consent of the Secretary of State, by the Gas and Electricity Markets Authority,

on the ground that the voluntary arrangement is not consistent with the achievement of the objective of the energy administration.

(3)   An application under this section shall not be made—

- (a) after the end of the period of 28 days beginning with the first day on which each of the reports required by section 4(6) and (6A) has been made to the court, or
- (b) in the case of a person who was not given notice of the relevant qualifying decision procedure, after the end of the period of 28 days beginning with the day on which he became aware that the relevant qualifying decision procedure had taken place,

but (subject to that) an application made by a person within subsection (2)(aa) on the ground that the voluntary arrangement prejudices his interests may be made after the arrangement has ceased to have effect, unless it came to an end prematurely.

(4)   Where on such an application the court is satisfied as to either of the grounds mentioned in subsection (1) or, in the case of an application under subsection (2A), as to the ground mentioned in that subsection, it may do any of the following, namely—

- (a) revoke or suspend any decision approving the voluntary arrangement which has effect under section 4A or, in a case falling within subsection (1)(b), any decision taken by the meeting of the company, or in the relevant qualifying decision procedure, which has effect under that section;
- (b) give a direction to any person for the summoning of a further company meeting to consider any revised proposal the person who made the original proposal may make or, in a case falling within subsection (1)(b) and relating to the company meeting, a further company meeting to reconsider the original proposal;
- (c) direct any person—
  - (i) to seek a decision from the company's creditors (using a qualifying decision procedure) as to whether they approve any revised proposal the person who made the original proposal may make, or
  - (ii) in a case falling within subsection (1)(b) and relating to the relevant qualifying decision procedure, to seek a decision from the company's creditors (using a qualifying decision procedure) as to whether they approve the original proposal.

(5)   Where at any time after giving a direction under subsection (4)(b) or (c) in relation to a revised proposal the court is satisfied that the person who made the original proposal does not intend to submit a revised proposal, the court shall revoke the direction and revoke or suspend any decision approving the voluntary arrangement which has effect under section 4A.

(6)   In a case where the court, on an application under this section with respect to any meeting or relevant qualifying decision procedure—

- (a) gives a direction under subsection (4)(b) or (c), or
- (b) revokes or suspends an approval under subsection (4)(a) or (5),

the court may give such supplemental directions as it thinks fit and, in particular, directions with respect to things done under the voluntary arrangement since it took effect.

(7)  Except in pursuance of the preceding provisions of this section,

  (a)  a decision taken at a company meeting summoned under section 3 is not invalidated by any irregularity at or in relation to the meeting, and

  (b)  a decision of the company's creditors made in the relevant qualifying decision procedure is not invalidated by any irregularity in relation to the relevant qualifying decision procedure.

(8)  In this section "in energy administration" and "objective of the energy administration" are to be construed in accordance with Schedule B1 to this Act, as applied by Part 1 of Schedule 20 to the Energy Act 2004.

**Amendments**—Insolvency Act 2000, s 2, Sch 2, paras 1, 7; Enterprise Act 2002, s 248(3), Sch 17, paras 9, 12; Energy Act 2004, s 159(1), Sch 20, Pt 4, para 44; Small Business, Enterprise and Employment Act 2015, s 126, Sch 9, Pt 1, paras 1, 7(1)–(13).

**General note**—This section allows for an application to court by any of the applicants within s 6(2) (s 262(2) in the case of an IVA) on either or both of the grounds identified in s 6(1) (s 262(1) for IVAs), either of which may extend to breach of a substantive statutory prohibition: *IRC v Wimbledon Football Club Ltd* [2004] EWCA Civ 655, [2005] 1 BCLC 66 at [37] (Neuberger LJ). The use of the words 'an application to the court may be made' in s 6(1) (s 262(1) in the case of an IVA) together with the reference to 'a voluntary arrangement which has effect' in s 6(1)(a) (s 262(1)(a) in the case of an IVA) strongly suggests that an application may only be made once an arrangement has actually been approved by creditors, such that no grounds are available for an application in respect of prospective or anticipated unfair prejudice or material irregularity prior to approval of the arrangement.

The court has wide powers under s 6(4)–(6) (s 262(4)–(6) in the case of an IVA) to tailor its order to the circumstances of the case, including the revocation of the approval of the voluntary arrangement or directions for the summoning of further meetings to consider either the original proposal or any revised proposal with which the debtor seeks to proceed. Many of the reported first instance decisions on applications under s 6 (s 262 in the case of an IVA) are of very limited assistance in terms of general application, given that the grounds in s 6(1) (s 262 for IVAs), and any order or direction made by the court, necessarily depend on the particular facts of each case.

Save for s 6 (s 262 for IVAs), an application to court may also be available under s 4A(3) (s 263(3) for IVAs): see the notes to that subsection. A creditor or member of the company may also appeal the chairman's decision on the admission of any creditor claim for voting purposes under r 15.35.

One of the key distinctions between CVAs and IVAs is that the 28-day time limit imposed by s 6(3) is not extendable by the court in the case of CVAs. See notes to s 6(3).

### SECTION 6(1)(a)

**Scope of provision**—The language of the subsection requires that the unfair prejudice complained of must be caused by the voluntary arrangement giving rise to some unfairness, and not merely prejudice caused by the existence of a voluntary arrangement taking effect through statutory force under s 4A.

In *Re A Debtor (No 222 of 1990) ex parte Bank of Ireland* [1992] BCLC 137 at 145C–145G Harman J (in considering the virtually identical provisions in s 262(1)(a), applicable to IVAs) considered that subsection (a) 'plainly looks at the arrangement itself and requires consideration of whether it prejudices the creditor, presumably because of some differential treatment, some restriction upon the creditors or some advantage to another creditor so that there is an unfair prejudice by reason of the voluntary arrangement itself': see also *Re A Debtor (No 87 of 1993) (No 2)* [1996] 1 BCLC 63 at 86 (Rimer J) in which, having cited and relied upon the above passage, counsel for the claimant was forced to abandon an argument to the effect that the court may embark upon consideration of the overall merits of the arrangement on an unfair prejudice complaint and to accept that there is no relevant prejudice to any creditor if each creditor under the scheme is put in the same position as the other creditors and suffers no discriminatory treatment as a consequence. Subsection (b), on the other hand, 'seems plainly to divide the matter into events occurring at the meeting which are wrong, which are irregularities, and matters in relation to the voluntary arrangement which could be unfairly prejudicial.' Accordingly, a wrong decision at a meeting to exclude or prohibit a vote gives rise to a complaint of material irregularity and not unfair prejudice.

To similar effect, in *Peck v Craighead* [1995] 1 BCLC 337 Martin Mann QC (sitting as a deputy High Court judge) observed at 343E that 'Irregularity involving unlawfulness at a meeting of creditors is conceptually different from unfair prejudice which predicates unfairness inherent in a proposal or modification which otherwise lawfully affects a creditor's interest.'

' . . . unfairly prejudices the interests of the creditor, member or contributory of the company'—The term 'unfairly prejudicial' is also employed in s 994 of the Companies Act 2006, which together with its predecessors ss 459, 460 of the Companies Act 1985 and the Companies Acts of 1948 and 1980, have given rise to a plethora of reported case law. The term 'unfairly prejudicial' is, however, employed in a very different context in s 994 of the 2006 Act, in that it relates to the conduct of the management of a company. As a consequence, authorities on s 994 and its predecessors are unlikely to be of any assistance in the present context, on which see the comments in *Doorbar v Alltime Securities Ltd* [1995] BCC 1149 at 1159A (Peter Gibson LJ).

The meaning and scope of unfair prejudice—In the context of voluntary arrangements, the Court of Appeal addressed the test applicable to unfair prejudice in *Cadbury Schweppes plc v Somji* [2001] 1 WLR 615 to the extent that Robert Walker LJ referred to the 'fairly strong line of first instance authority' which is 'uniformly in favour of limiting the effect of the provisions to unfairness brought about by the terms of the [arrangement] itself'. At least two key principles are clear enough from decisions at first instance. First, the unfair prejudice must result from the arrangement itself: *Re A Debtor (No 222 of 1990) ex parte Bank of Ireland*. Secondly, whether the interests of an applicant are unfairly prejudiced requires the court to consider all the circumstances of the case: *Re A Debtor (No 101 of 1999)* [2001] 1 BCLC 54 at 63D (Ferris J). It is not sufficient that an applicant establishes mere prejudice resulting from the arrangement; rather, the prejudice must be unfair. The judgment of Lightman J at first instance in *IRC v Wimbledon Football Club Ltd* [2004] EWCA Civ 655, [2005] 1 BCLC 66 also contains useful guidance on the issue of unfair prejudice. In particular (at [18]) 'the unfair prejudice must have been caused by the terms of the arrangement' and (at [23]) 'the question of fairness of the arrangement requires consideration of all of the circumstances and in particular the alternatives available and the practical consequences of a decision to confirm or reject the arrangement'.

The 'vertical' and 'horizontal' comparators—In considering whether an arrangement is unfairly prejudicial, the courts have developed two tests, labelled the 'vertical' and 'horizontal' comparators: see *Prudential Assurance Co Ltd v PRG Powerhouse Ltd* [2007] EWHC 1002 (Ch), [2008] 1 BCLC 289, [75], per Etherton J. The relevant case law on these comparators was succinctly reviewed by Zacaroli J in *Lazari Properties 2 Ltd v New Look Retailers Ltd* [2021] EWHC 1209 (Ch). The 'vertical' comparator is a comparison with what the creditors' position would have been in the event that the CVA was not approved, typically their position in winding up or bankruptcy. This was described by Henderson J as the 'irreducible minimum' below which the return in a CVA cannot go: *Mourant & Co Trustees Ltd v Sixty UK Ltd (in administration)* [2010] EWHC 1890 (Ch), [2011] 1 BCLC 384, [67]. It is emphatically not enough to preclude a finding of unfair prejudice that the vertical comparator test is satisfied in respect of objecting creditors: it is also necessary to consider the 'horizontal' comparator, which compares the treatment of creditors between themselves, and requires particularly careful scrutiny of any differential treatment.

Differential treatment of creditors which is not assented to by a creditor may give cause for an inquiry, but does not of itself necessarily establish unfair prejudice, in that there may well be an explanation justifying such differential treatment: *Re a Debtor (No 101 of 1999)* [2001] 1 BCLC 54, 63c, per Ferris J. In that case, an arrangement that achieved the differential treatment of the Crown by means of the votes of various friends of the debtor, while preserving their own rights and remedies in full, was held to be unfairly prejudicial. But it is necessary to consider all the circumstances and differential treatment may be justified where it is necessary to ensure the continuation of the business that underlies the arrangement: *Prudential Assurance Co Ltd v PRG Powerhouse Ltd*, [90]; *Mourant & Co Trustees Ltd v Sixty UK Ltd (in administration)*, [67]; *Discovery (Northampton) Ltd v Debenhams Retail Ltd* [2019] EWHC 2441 (Ch), [2020] BCC 9, [110], per Norris J. It is not necessarily unfairly prejudicial to a sub-group of compromised creditors that the statutory majority is achieved by the votes of unimpaired creditors, or those who receive substantially different treatment, but that will be a highly relevant factor in determining whether there is unfair prejudice: *Lazari Properties 2 Ltd v New Look Retailers Ltd* [156], per Zacaroli J.

The differential treatment of landlords has been to the fore in challenges to a number of high-street CVAs. In *Discovery (Northampton) Ltd v Debenhams Retail Ltd* [2019] EWHC 2441 (Ch), [2020] BCC 9, Norris J held that a CVA that reduces rent under an existing lease is not automatically 'unfair', and the landlords' ability to terminate the varied relationship rendered it fair in that case ([76]). In *Lazari Properties 2 Ltd v New Look Retailers Ltd* [2021] EWHC 1209 (Ch) and *Carraway Guildford (Nominee A) Ltd v Regis UK Ltd* [2021] EWHC 1294 (Ch), Zacaroli J declined an invitation not to follow Norris J on this point. It appears from these cases that where a landlord is given the option to terminate the lease as an alternative to accepting a compromise of ongoing rights under a CVA, this will be a key factor weighing against a finding of unfair prejudice, provided that the terms of the termination are at least as beneficial as the vertical comparator: *New Look Retailers Ltd* [202]–[218] and *Regis UK Ltd*, [168]–[177]. In *Regis UK Ltd*, however, the CVA was revoked on an alternative basis that the preferential treatment of a particular creditor was without justification and unfairly prejudicial to those creditors whose debts were impaired, [153]–[160].

In considering unfair prejudice it is not for the court to speculate as to whether the terms proposed were the best that could have been achieved. Unless the court can be satisfied that such alternatives would certainly have been on offer the comparison must be between the proposed compromise and no compromise at all as at the date of the vote on the arrangement: *SISU Capital Fund Ltd v Tucker* [2006] BPIR 154 at [73].

**Cases on unfair prejudice**—For further cases on unfair prejudice see *Cadbury Schweppes plc v Somji* [2001] 1 WLR 615, CA (secret deal with two creditors inducing their support of a voluntary arrangement not unfairly prejudicial but a fraud on creditors); *National Westminster Bank plc v Scher* [1998] BPIR 224 (John Martin QC, sitting as a deputy High Court judge, no unfair prejudice to two bank creditors prevented from enforcing rights against debtor's wife under terms of arrangement where wife had no separate assets or income); *Sea Voyager Maritime Inc v Bielecki (t/a Hughes Hooker & Co)* [1999] 1 BCLC 133 (Richard McCombe QC, sitting as a deputy High Court judge), creditor unfairly prejudiced by arrangement which prevented creditor from proceeding to judgment against debtor with consequence that creditor unable to make recovery from debtor's insurers under the Third Parties (Rights Against Insurers) Act 1930); *Re Naeem (a Bankrupt) (No 18 of 1988)* [1990] 1 WLR 48 (Hoffmann J), arrangement reducing debtor's liability for rent for which landlord retained usual enforcement remedies prejudicial but not unfairly prejudicial to landlord); and *Re Cancol Ltd* [1995] BCC 1133 (Knox J, no unfair prejudice to landlord under terms of arrangement providing for landlord to be paid either rent in full whilst debtor occupied premises or a dividend on premises being vacated where landlord not deprived of right of forfeiture on rent ceasing to be paid in full).

A creditor may also apply to court alleging unfair prejudice where an arrangement has the effect of releasing a co-debtor against whom that creditor would otherwise have a right of action: *Johnson v Davies* [1998] 3 WLR 1299 at 1317B (Chadwick LJ). In *Prudential Assurance Co Ltd v PRG Powerhouse Ltd* [2007] EWHC 1002 (Ch), [2008] 1 BCLC 289 Etherton J held that, whilst each case must turn on its own facts, the landlords of properties occupied by the company had been unfairly prejudiced by the terms of a CVA which operated to release the company's parent from guarantees given to the landlords. *Mourant & Co Trustees Limited & Anor v Sixty UK Limited (in administration) & Ors* [2010] EWHC 1890 (Ch), [2010] BPIR 1264 was another attempt at guarantee stripping which also failed. The judge (Henderson J), after undertaking both a vertical and a horizontal comparison, concluded that the voluntary arrangement did unfairly prejudice the interests of the applicant landlords whose guarantees had been stripped. The judge, somewhat emphatically, stated: 'This is, in my view, a CVA that should never have seen the light of day . . . ' although he also went on to observe 'I do not say that it is necessarily impossible to propose a fair CVA of this type but the greatest care is needed to ensure fairness to the [minority creditors who are to be deprived of valuable contractual rights], both in the substance of what is proposed and in the procedure that is adopted'.

In *HM Revenue and Customs v Portsmouth City Football Club Limited (in administration) & Ors* [2010] EWHC 2013 (Ch) [2010] BPIR 1123, HMRC sought to challenge a voluntary arrangement on the grounds that it (in particular in upholding the so-called football creditors rule) was unfairly prejudicial. Mann J, who had an eye on the commercial realities, rejected the challenge. *Child Maintenance and Enforcement Commission v Beesley and Whyman* [2010] EWCA Civ 1344 (Ch), [2011] BPIR 608 was a case in which CMEC brought a challenge in the context of an individual voluntary arrangement and in which the Court of Appeal considered CMEC's alternative contention that the voluntary arrangement was unfairly prejudicial. Both at first instance in that case, and on appeal, the Court concluded that the voluntary arrangement was unfairly prejudicial to CMEC.

## SECTION 6(1)(b)

**The meaning and scope of material irregularity**—Section 6(7) (s 262(8) for in the case of an IVA) expressly provides that, in the absence of an application under s 6 (s 262 in the case of an IVA), the mere fact of an irregularity at, or in relation to, either the company meeting or in relation to the creditors' decision procedure, does not of itself invalidate any decision in relation to the arrangement. To obtain a remedy under s 6 (s 262 in the case of an IVA) an applicant must establish not only an irregularity, but also the fact of its materiality: *Re Sweatfield Ltd* [1997] BCC 744 at 750E (HHJ Weeks QC, sitting as a High Court judge). In *Discovery (Northampton) Ltd v Debenhams Retail Ltd* [2019] EWHC 2441 (Ch), [2020] BCC 9, Norris J explained that an irregularity will be 'material' for the purposes of s 6(1)(b) if (and only if) objective assessed, there is a substantial chance that if the irregularity had not occurred, it would have made a material difference to the way in which the creditors would have considered and assessed the terms of the CVA. In that case, a failure to identify in a CVA proposal information about possible claims that might exist under ss 239 and 245 in the event that the company entered administration or liquidation (as is required by r 2.3(1)(f)(iii)) was not 'material' for these purposes ([128]–[130]).

It appears that breaches of the Act or the Rules or other shortcomings in obtaining the purported approval of a voluntary arrangement are more likely than previously to be treated as material irregularities, rather than nullities. See general note to s 3 and note to 6(7). See *Smith-Evans v Smailes* [2014] BPIR 306 at [29]–[31], approved by the Court of Appeal in *Narandas-Girdhar v Bradstock* [2016] 1 WLR 2366 at [49].

In *Cadbury Schweppes plc v Somji* [2001] 1 WLR 615 at 626 Robert Walker LJ identified that the test for materiality is whether objectively assessed an error or omission 'would be likely to have made a material difference to the way in which creditors would have considered and assessed the terms of the proposed IVA'. But that objectivity does not mean that the anticipated behaviour of the actual creditors is to be ignored: if the court finds a material irregularity, but is satisfied the proposal would nonetheless have been approved, it might decline to provide a remedy applying its discretion in s 262(4): *Golstein v (1) Bishop; (2) Barnett* [2016] EWHC 2187 (Ch), [2017] BPIR 51, [66]–[68], per Warren J.

Perhaps the most obvious form of material irregularity in relation to meetings concerns the assertion and treatment of voting rights. In *Doorbar v Alltime Securities Ltd* [1995] BCC 1149 at 1158D–1158H the Court of Appeal rejected an allegation of material irregularity by a landlord in circumstances where the chairman of the creditors' meeting had placed a minimum value of one year's rent on the landlord's claim in making allowance for the possibility that the landlord would exercise its power of re-entry and, in so doing, had rejected the landlord's claim for the aggregate of the whole of the future rent under the lease. Given that the chairman's approach was entirely reasonable, and that the landlord would only have had 25% or more of the voting power of the meeting if the estimated value of its claim was increased threefold, there could be no material irregularity.

In *Commissioners of Inland Revenue v Duce* [1999] BPIR 189 Hazel Williamson QC, sitting as a deputy High Court judge, considered an allegation of material irregularity by the Inland Revenue where a debtor had failed to disclose the fact that a significant creditor supporting approval of the arrangement had taken assignment of the debt from a company in which the debtor had a substantial interest and where the debtor had failed to identify accurately the creditor which was to purchase the debtor's property for full market value less £90,000 so as to produce funds in full and final settlement of all creditor claims. The deputy judge took the view that the judge below had erred in principle in failing to undertake a balancing exercise which took full account of the circumstances of the case, namely the seriousness and heinousness of the irregularity on the one hand, and the likely attitude of the other creditors on the other. On the basis that creditors ought to be given the opportunity to reconsider an arrangement with knowledge of the proper facts, the deputy judge directed the re-convening of the creditors' meeting.

Material irregularity may also arise by virtue of a decision procedure failing to acknowledge the security rights of a creditor whose consent would otherwise be required for the modification of such rights. For example, in *Peck v Craighead* [1995] 1 BCLC 337 Martin Mann QC, sitting as a deputy High Court judge, found material irregularity (under the equivalent provision, namely s 262(1)(b) in the context of an individual voluntary arrangement) where the meeting of creditors had approved an arrangement which envisaged the sale of chattels which had been used by the debtors, but over which the complainant creditor had obtained a writ of fi fa and walking possession pursuant to a consent judgment. Given that the complainant creditor had not consented to the modification of what amounted to its rights as a secured creditor, the deputy judge held that the approval constituted a material irregularity, as a consequence of which the complainant creditor's execution could proceed notwithstanding the approval of the arrangement.

An application may be made under s 6(1)(b) (s 262(1)(b) in the case of an IVA) by a creditor who is bound by an arrangement through the operation of s 5(2)(b) (s 260(2)(b) in the case of an IVA) where the creditor would have been entitled to vote in the decision procedure but did not have notice of it in circumstances where that creditor could have affected or influenced the outcome: see, for example, *Tager v Westpac Banking Corp* [1997] 1 BCLC 313 at 325F–325G (HHJ Weeks QC, sitting as a High Court judge).

The treatment of proxies has caused material irregularities to arise leading to revocation. In *Re Cardona* [1997] BCC 697, the chairman of the creditors' meeting wrongly refused to allow the Inland Revenue, being the debtor's largest creditor, to withdraw a proxy form lodged for the purposes of a creditors' meeting, which was adjourned, and to lodge a second proxy for the purposes of the re-convened meeting. In *Rowbury v Official Receiver* [2015] EWHC 2276 (Ch), [2016] BPIR 477, a chairman's refusal to suspend a meeting to enable an obviously incorrectly completed proxy to be corrected gave rise to a material irregularity and (amongst other defects) led to revocation [43]–[48]). *Royal Bank of Scotland plc v Munikwa* [2020] EWHC 786 (Ch) was an extreme case of material irregularity on a significant scale in relation to treatment of proxies. A creditor brought 8 test cases under s 262(1)(b) against a volume IVA provider whose practice when acting as proxy-holder was to vote such proxies in favour of proposals without modification, despite those proxies being expressly conditional on the acceptance of modifications proposed by the creditor. ICC Judge Prentis held that the supervisor's reports to creditors were 'indefensible in their terms' ([44]) and indicated that the judgment would be sent to the supervisor's regulator ([64]).

*Commissioners for Her Majesty's Revenue and Customs v (1) Earley (2) Heron (3) Fisher* [2011] EWHC 1783 (Ch), [2011] BPIR 1590 is a decision of Sir Andrew Morritt, the then Chancellor of the High Court, in which he found that there was a material irregularity in relation to an IVA (a without notice injunction had been obtained against HMRC preventing HMRC from voting at the meeting in the full amount of its debt in circumstances where, pursuant to s 21 of the Crown Proceedings Act 1947, the court could not make an injunction against the Crown).

*Re Linfoot (A Debtor); Linfoot v (1) Adamson (2) Bank of Scotland plc (3) National Westminster Bank plc* [2012] BPIR 1033 was a case in which an individual had made an application challenging a decision taken at a creditors' meeting called by the supervisor of the IVA sometime after the IVA had been approved. HHJ Behrens (sitting as a High Court judge) held that s 262 was not engaged on such an application, whereas s 263 was.

For an unsuccessful allegation of material irregularity which was based on fundamental misunderstandings on the part of the secured creditor as to the effect of the CVA and unsubstantiated allegations of irregularities at the creditors' meeting and the counting of votes see *Swindon Town Properties Ltd v Swindon Town Football Co Ltd* [2003] BPIR 253 (Hart J). A challenge based on an alleged material irregularity succeeded in *Re Gatnom Capital & Finance Ltd; Macaria Investments Ltd v (1) Sanders (2) Gatnom Capital & Finance Ltd* [2010] EWHC 3353 (Ch) [2011] BPIR 1013. In that case, Roth J accepted the applicant's contention that two land contracts were shams, and accordingly, creditors under those contracts who had been allowed to vote at the creditor's meeting should not have been allowed to vote. The same amounted to a material irregularity.

Section 6(1)(b) (s 262(1)(b) in the case of an IVA) is sufficiently broad to extend to a material irregularity in a debtor's proposal or statement of affairs: *Re A Debtor (No 87 of 1993) (No 2)* [1996] BCL 80 at 107C–108E (Rimer J), an IVA case. That case, which resulted in the court revoking the arrangement, involved an application by four creditors of the debtor alleging that the debtor's proposal was dishonest and misleading in that it falsely disclosed a non-existent asset, it failed to disclose all of the debtor's assets, and made false representation with regard to those assets and liabilities which had been disclosed by the debtor.

It is submitted that a finding of material irregularity involves a finding of fact alone and is in no way dependent on any finding of fault.

**The 'good faith' principle**—A debtor is subject to an obligation of transparency and good faith in putting forward a proposal for a voluntary arrangement: *Cadbury Schweppes plc v Somji* [2001] 1 WLR 615, [40], per Judge LJ. In certain circumstances, creditors may be exposed to the effects of the good faith rule. The Court of Appeal in *Kapoor v (1) National Westminster Bank plc (2) Tan* [2011] EWCA Civ 1083, [2011] BPIR 1680 considered that it was a material irregularity for a connected creditor to have assigned his or her debt to an unconnected creditor (notwithstanding that the assignment was effective) for the purposes of circumventing IR 1986, r 5.23 (replaced by IR 2016, r 15.34). This was a breach of the requirement of complete good faith between a debtor and his creditors and between competing unsecured creditors, which meant there was a material irregularity. *Kapoor* was applied by the Court of Appeal in the first round of litigation in *Gertner v CFL Finance Ltd and Rubin* [2018] EWCA Civ 1781, [2018] BPIR 1605. An IVA was revoked in that case for material irregularity where a debtor had entered into a settlement agreement (undisclosed at the time of the creditors' meeting) with the biggest creditor that had the dual purpose of simultaneously preserving (for the purposes of voting through the IVA) and compromising (by way of benefits from a third party) the creditor's claim. Patten LJ held at [79]–[80] that the arrangement provided the creditor with a collateral advantage not available to other creditors, which placed it in a position of conflict with the interests of other creditors. That was a breach of the good faith principle, which fell to be strictly applied. The good faith principle was significantly qualified, however, in proceedings on a subsequent petition against the same debtor. In *Gertner and Laser Trust v CFL Finance Ltd* [2020] EWHC 1241 (Ch), [2020] BPIR 752, Marcus Smith J allowed an appeal against a bankruptcy order made by Chief ICC Judge Briggs. An assignee of the rights of the creditor with the benefit of the tainted settlement agreement had sought a stay of the bankruptcy petition to enable a further proposal for an IVA to be voted on. Judge Briggs had refused the stay and made a bankruptcy order, on the ground that the assignment to the new entity did not prevent the strict application of the good faith principle and did not mean that the assignee had not received a collateral advantage not available to other creditors, inferring that the new entity was not wholly independent of the debtor. Marcus Smith J held that Judge Briggs had erred in the scope of the good faith rule, which was not a general rule of good faith but was an obligation that fell on the debtor. In order to affect a creditor, it was necessary to show that an illicit collateral advantage had been conferred on that creditor, and this had not been shown in the case of the assignee. The judge held that the case could be distinguished from *Kapoor*, because, unlike *Kapoor*, neither the original creditor nor the assignee were associates of the debtor ([94]–[95]). The debtor's appeal from Judge Briggs was allowed by the Court of Appeal on an additional ground in relation to the Consumer Credit Act 1974 in *CFL Finance Ltd v (1) Laser Trust (2) Gertner* [2021] EWCA Civ 228, [2021] BPIR 487, [54]–[55] (Newey LJ), with the balance of Marcus Smith J's order undisturbed.

**Material irregularity and creditors for costs**—In *Coutts & Co v Passey* [2007] BPIR 323 Registrar Nicholls allowed an appeal against the decision of the chairman of a creditors' meeting on the basis that the chairman should have allowed the creditor to vote in full for legal costs incurred by it, but not assessed by the court, where the creditor had a contractual entitlement to such costs incurred from the debtor. The chairman's decision constituted a material irregularity justifying the setting aside of the IVA and discharge of the interim order given that the appellant was thus capable of voting down the debtor's proposal. There is authority that where a liability to pay costs arises out of a pre-IVA agreement, but is not imposed until after approval of the IVA, the costs claim, subject to the terms of the IVA, will not be caught by the IVA: *Cornelius v Casson* [2008] BPIR 504 (Thomas Ivory QC, sitting as a deputy High Court judge).

However, the effect of the R3 standard terms used in the IVA at issue in *Golstein v Bishop* [2013] EWHC 1706 (Ch), [2013] BPIR 708 was that costs that crystalised post-IVA were a debt within the scope of the IVA (Christopher Nugee QC, sitting as a deputy High Court judge). It is submitted that following the Supreme Court's decision in *In re Nortel GmbH (in administration)* [2013] UKSC 52, [2014] AC 209, an adverse costs order made after the approval of a voluntary arrangement in proceedings that were extant at the date of the approval will be a debt within the arrangement, even where the possibility of such a future costs order being made is entirely contingent at the date of the approval. Pre-*Nortel* cases to contrary effect such as *Cornelius v Casson* are now to be doubted. See also *The Law Society v Beller* [2014] EWHC 3923 (Ch), [2014] BPIR 1480: where the Law Society intervened in a solicitor's practice prior to the solicitor's entry into an IVA, the costs of the intervention (incurred both before and after the IVA was approved) constituted a debt within the IVA and could not (contrary to the Law Society's contention) be paid from recoveries from the solicitor's clients (George Bompas QC, sitting as a deputy High Court judge).

### SECTION 6(2)

**Scope of provision**—For the standing of the FCA to apply and be heard on applications under s 6 (s 262 in the case of an IVA) see ss 356 and 357 of the Financial Services and Markets Act 2000.

**Eligible applicants**—Categories (a) and (aa) are clear enough by reference to the two grounds in s 6(1).

It appears that either the nominee (or his replacement) or a liquidator or administrator has standing to make application under s 6(1)(a), although such an application may only proceed on the basis of alleged unfair prejudice to the interests of a creditor, member or contributory and, as such, and in the absence of an application by either such party, such applications are unlikely. More obviously plausible are applications under s 6(1)(b), since these are not restricted to prejudice to the interests of a creditor's member or contributory. A nominee, for example, may consider an application if the effect of the decision is to inhibit the discharge of his or her function under s 1(2) or, given that no standing to apply is conferred on the company itself or its directors, to challenge a decision which approves a modified proposal where the consent of the directors has not been forthcoming to such modifications.

The company itself may not apply and has no voice in this process, save in so far as matters that could be said to affect its interests are taken up by the persons who are entitled to apply: *In re SHB Realisations Ltd (formerly BHS Ltd) (in liquidation)* [2018] EWHC 402 (Ch), [2018] Bus LR 1173, at [30], per Christopher Pymont QC (sitting as a deputy High Court judge).

**Procedure on a s 6(2) application**—Care must be taken in naming the respondents to an application under s 6(1) (s 262(1) in the case of an IVA). In *Re Naeem (a Bankrupt) (No 18 of 1988)* [1990] 1 WLR 48, a case involving an unsuccessful allegation of unfairly prejudicial conduct in the context of an individual voluntary arrangement, Hoffmann J indicated that the applicant had been wrong to join the nominee and two creditors as respondents to the application. His Lordship also held that a nominee should not be ordered to pay the costs of a successful application in the absence of actual misconduct on the nominee's part. Hoffmann J did comment, however, that convenience may dictate giving the nominee notice of the application in such a case. In the words of Hoffmann J in *Naeem* (at [51]), 'If there had been some personal conduct on the part of the nominee which would justify an order for costs against him, that could be done.'

It is suggested that it will usually be appropriate to join the nominee, and possibly one or more creditors, to an application alleging material irregularity at or in relation to a meeting at which the nominee and/or such creditors have played a part.

For further discussion on costs in this context, see *Re A Debtor (No 222 of 1990) ex parte Bank of Ireland* [1992] BCLC 137 and *(No 2)* [1993] BCLC 233 (Harman J); and *Harmony Carpets v Chaffin-Laird* [2000] BPIR 61 (Rattee J, no order for costs against nominee of individual voluntary arrangement notwithstanding criticisms of nominee in reporting to court on the basis that it was not clear, had proper reports been made, that the court would have declined to allow meetings of creditors to take place such that the complainant would still have incurred the costs of challenging the decision of the meeting). The decision of Andrew Simmonds QC (sitting as a deputy High Court judge) in *Tradition (UK) Ltd v Ahmed and Others* [2008] EWHC 3448 (Ch), [2009] BPIR 626 concerned an unsuccessful attempt to make a nominee liable for all of the costs of an application to challenge a voluntary arrangement and contains a useful analysis of the principles to be applied when determining whether a proposed nominee should be liable for costs.

For the possibility of obtaining costs against non-parties, see *Re Gatnom Capital & Finance Ltd; Macaria Investments Ltd v (1) Sanders (2) Gatnom Capital & Finance Ltd (3) Omatov (No 2)* [2011] EWHC 3716 (Ch), [2012] BPIR 299.

### SECTION 6(3)

' . . . **shall not be made** . . . **after the end of the period of 28 days** . . . '—These words are not a common formulation for the computation of time under statute although they do correspond with the formulation employed in s 5(4)(a). The 28-day period begins with and includes the dates specified in s 6(3)(a) and (b). In the case of s 6(3)(a) the reference to 'the reports' envisages separate reports being filed for the purposes of s 4(6), although in practice the chairman of the company meeting and the convener of the creditors' decision procedure will usually file a single report at the same time. If separate reports were filed at different times, then it would follow that two differing 28-day periods would come into effect, one affecting the standing of creditors and the other applying to applications by members of contributories of the company.

In sharp distinction from the position in IVAs, in the case of CVAs the 28-day period cannot be extended by the court: *Re Bournemouth & Boscombe Athletic Football Club Co Ltd* [1998] BPIR 183 (Lloyd J) (this proposition was also accepted without comment in the Court of Appeal in *Tucker and Spratt (Joint Supervisors of Energy Holdings (No 3) (In Liquidation) v Gold Fields Mining LLC* [2009] EWCA Civ 173, [2009] BPIR 704 and was applied by Registrar Jaques in *Wood v Heart Hospital* [2009] BPIR 1538). Neither is it appropriate to allow an application out of time to be joined with a live s 6 application made within the 28-day period since such a course would serve to defeat the purpose of the stipulated limitation period. If a proposal has been approved, but can nonetheless be shown to have been invalid then, at least where the proposal is advanced bona fide and approved and implemented accordingly, and in particular where the invalidity is overlooked by all concerned up to the time of approval and expiration of the 28-day period, the arrangement should be treated as valid notwithstanding the infringement giving rise to the apparent invalidity: *IRC v Wimbledon Football Club Ltd* [2004] EWCA Civ 655, [2005] 1 BCLC 66 at [38] (Neuberger LJ). Technically, but without any real substantive justification, the position in CVAs differs from that in IVAs, in relation to which the 28-day period in s 262(3) is capable of extension under s 376 (time limits): *Tager v Westpac Banking Corp* [1997] 1 BCLC 313. There is no equivalent to s 376 applicable to Part I. In the context of IVAs HHJ Weeks QC (sitting as a High Court judge) held in *Tager* (at 325D) that the factors relevant to the exercise of discretion and extending time are the length of delay, the reasons for the delay, the apparent merits of the underlying application and the prejudice to each side other than the inevitable prejudice inherent in re-opening the question of approval of the arrangement. The conclusion of HHJ Weeks QC in extending was approved of by Carnwath J in *Plant v Plant* [1998] 1 BCLC 38. In *Warley Continental Services Ltd (in liquidation) v Johal* (2002) *The Times*, October 28 HHJ Norris QC (sitting as a High Court judge) also identified the conduct of the parties as being of potential significance in a wide range of cases; an extension of time in that case was refused, given the unjustifiable and significant delay in making the application, notwithstanding the obvious merits of the case.

### SECTION 6(4)

**Remedies and relief on a s 6(2) (s 262(2) for IVAs) application**—Whilst the discretion of the court in making an order under this subsection appears unfettered through the use of the word 'may', the court has a positive duty to act in setting aside an arrangement where the arrangement is in clear conflict with a statutory provision (see below). In other cases the court would be perfectly entitled in the exercise of its discretion to refuse to make any order if the practical effect of, most obviously, setting aside an arrangement would be to harm the interests of the creditors of the debtor generally, say where the purpose of the arrangement was all but complete, even where the court was satisfied as to the fact of unfair prejudice and/or material irregularity.

The scope of any such order made is defined in fairly restrictive terms by s 6(4)(a) and (b) (s 262(4)(a) and (b) in the case of an IVA) which do not read as being mutually exclusive in that the court may make an order suspending the decision under (a) whilst at the same time providing directions under (b). In particular, the court has no power to direct the modification of a proposal or that any particular modification should be considered by any further meeting, since the formulation of the proposal remains at all times entirely a matter for the party making the proposal.

### SECTION 6(4)(a)

**Scope of provision**— Revocation means the voluntary arrangement is gone forever. Suspension defers the decision, but if never lifted has the same effect as revocation. While an arrangement is suspended, no arrangement is in force: *Price v Davis* [2014] EWCA Civ 26, [2014] BPIR 494, at [30]–[31]. If an arrangement is revoked or suspended then there is nothing to prevent a fresh proposal being formulated and advanced, even by way of a proposal in identical terms to that revoked or suspended.

The court's discretion to revoke survives the termination of the arrangement. In *Regis UK Limited (in administration)* [2019] EWHC 3073 (Ch), Mr James Morgan QC (sitting as a deputy High Court judge) refused on that basis an application to strike-out or grant summary judgment on an application for revocation, observing that the wording of s 6(4) was not expressly limited by reference to whether or not the arrangement had terminated and that there were likely to be cases where revocation would have a practical effect notwithstanding termination ([26]). The CVA in that case was subsequently revoked by Zacaroli J in *Carraway Guildford (Nominee A) Ltd v Regis UK Ltd* [2021] EWHC 1294 (Ch), [220]–[224].

### SECTION 6(4)(b)

**Scope of provision**—The provision for the giving of a direction 'to any person' for the summoning of further meetings is probably designed to allow for summoning by a person other than the incumbent nominee where the court forms the view that future conduct by that individual is inappropriate although in those circumstances further steps would be required to replace the nominee for the purposes of s 1(2) (s 253(2) in the case of an IVA). In the absence of grounds for concern, the court's direction will be to the incumbent nominee.

The court will not ordinarily be inclined to direct the summoning of further meetings to consider any revised proposal if it is satisfied on evidence before it that a sufficient number of creditors in value will vote against, so as to defeat, approval of the proposal. Even where such a direction is given, the court must revoke the direction under s 6(5) if satisfied that the party making the original proposal does not intend to proceed with a revised proposal. Creditors for the purpose of further meetings are those known to the nominee at the date of the summoning of the further meeting, not merely those entitled to vote at the original meeting: *Price v Davis* [2014] EWCA Civ 26, [2014] BPIR 494, [25], decided under s 262 (the equivalent provision for IVAs).

### SECTION 6(5)

The court may revoke an arrangement under s 6(5) (s 262(5) for IVAs) if satisfied that the party making the original proposal does not intend to proceed with a revised proposal and squarely accepts the merit of the application under s 6(1) (s 262(1) in the case of an IVA).

For action following the revocation or suspension of an arrangement see r 2.40 (r 8.27 in the case of an IVA).

### SECTION 6(6)

**Scope of provision**—Although the court may tailor any supplemental directions to complement any order under s 6(4) or (5) (s 262(4) or (5) in the case of an IVA), this provision addresses in particular the interim period between the approval of an arrangement and the making of any such order, given that an arrangement remains valid pending the making of such an order.

### SECTION 6(7)

**Scope of provision**—See the note to s 6(1)(b). See the general note to ss 3 and 6(1)(b). Unless challenged using the machinery in s 6 (s 262(8) in the case of an IVA), an approval is not invalidated by any irregularity at or in relation to a company meeting or qualifying decision procedure. It appears that a wide approach will now be taken to the scope of such non-invalidating irregularities, which must either be subject to a timely challenge or left alone. The distinction between 'material irregularities' within the ambit of this provision that are incapable of invalidating an approval, and defects capable of rendering a voluntary arrangement invalid, appears to depend upon whether or not the defect occurred 'at or in relation to' a properly summoned meeting or decision procedure: *Narandas-Girdhar v Bradstock* [2016] 1 WLR 2366, [53], per Briggs LJ. The narrower approach, exemplified by *Re Plummer* [2004] BPIR 767, was disapproved by Briggs LJ ([53]).

## [1.66]

### 6A False representations, etc

(1) If, for the purpose of obtaining the approval of the members or creditors of a company to a proposal for a voluntary arrangement, a person who is an officer of the company—

    (a)    makes any false representation, or

    (b)    fraudulently does, or omits to do, anything,

he commits an offence.

(2) Subsection (1) applies even if the proposal is not approved.

(3) For purposes of this section "officer" includes a shadow director.

(4)   A person guilty of an offence under this section is liable to imprisonment or a fine, or both.

**Amendments**—Inserted by Insolvency Act 2000, s 2, Sch 2, paras 1, 8.

**General note**—These provisions were effective from 1 January 2003 on implementation under s 2 (s 3 for IVAs) of the Insolvency Act 2000 and para 8 of Sch 2 (Sch 3 for IVAs) thereto; the formerly operative r 1.30 was revoked by the Insolvency (Amendment) (No 2) Rules 2002 (SI 2002/2712). In practice, a proposal will typically include a declaration that the directors had been made aware of s 6A (s 262A for IVAs). Some proposals also include a statement of truth of a kind employed in witness statements and statements of case under the Civil Procedure Rules 1998 which verifies the deponent's belief as to the matters of fact represented in the proposal.

### SECTION 6A(1)

**Scope of provision**—The actus reus of the offence includes the making of a false representation or, alternatively, the fraudulent commission, or omission, of anything for the purpose of obtaining the approval of the members or creditors of a company to a proposal.

For a criminal prosecution for fraudulent representation in the context of an IVA proposal see *R v Dawson* (unreported, 29 June 2001). The scope of s 6A (s 262A(1) in the case of an IVA) has been extended to the obtaining of a moratorium in connection with a CVA by para 42 of Sch A1. The wording of the subsection, it is suggested, does not extend to obtaining approval for the modification to the terms of a subsisting arrangement.

### SECTION 6A(2)

**Scope of provision**—The fact that a proposal is not approved has no bearing on the committing of an offence under s 6A(1) (262A(2) in the case of an IVA), which requires only proof of the acts or omissions within its scope 'for the purpose' of obtaining approval of the arrangement.

### SECTION 6A(3)

**Scope of provision**—For the terms 'officer' and 'shadow director' see the note to s 206(3).

### SECTION 6A(4)

**Scope of provision**—On penalties see s 430 and Sch 10.

## [1.67]

### 7  Implementation of proposal

(1)   This section applies where a voluntary arrangement has effect under section 4A.

(2)   The person who is for the time being carrying out in relation to the voluntary arrangement the functions conferred—

(a)   on the nominee by virtue of the approval of the voluntary arrangement by the company or its creditors (or both) pursuant to section 3,

(b)   by virtue of section 2(4) or 4(2) on a person other than the nominee,

shall be known as the supervisor of the voluntary arrangement.

(3)   If any of the company's creditors or any other person is dissatisfied by any act, omission or decision of the supervisor, he may apply to the court; and on the application the court may—

(a)   confirm, reverse or modify any act or decision of the supervisor,

(b)   give him directions, or

(c)   make such other order as it thinks fit.

(4)   The supervisor—

(a)   may apply to the court for directions in relation to any particular matter arising under the voluntary arrangement, and

(b)   is included among the persons who may apply to the court for the winding up of the company or for an administration order to be made in relation to it.

(5)   The court may, whenever—

(a)   it is expedient to appoint a person to carry out the functions of the supervisor, and

(b)   it is inexpedient, difficult or impracticable for an appointment to be made without the assistance of the court,

make an order appointing a person who is qualified to act as an insolvency practitioner in relation to the voluntary arrangement, either in substitution for the existing supervisor or to fill a vacancy.

(6)   The power conferred by subsection (5) is exercisable so as to increase the number of persons exercising the functions of supervisor or, where there is more than one person exercising those functions, so as to replace one or more of those persons.

**Amendments**—Insolvency Act 2000, s 2, Sch 2, paras 1, 9; Deregulation Act 2015, s 19, Sch 8, Pt 6, para 20(1), (2)(d); Small Business, Enterprise and Employment Act 2015, s 126, Sch 9, Pt 1, paras 1, 8.

**General note**—These provisions provide for the automatic appointment of the supervisor following approval of the voluntary arrangement (under s 7(2) (s 263(2) in the case of an IVA)) and for the making of applications to court in the event of dissatisfaction with the conduct of the supervisor (under s 7(3) (s 263(3) in the case of an IVA)) or where the supervisor requires the assistance of the court in relation to the voluntary arrangement or seeks a winding-up order against the company (under s 7(4)).

Best practice guidance on the implementation of a voluntary arrangement appears at para 16 of SIP 3.1. In particular, para 16(d) provides that 'Any departures from the terms of the IVA are identified at an early stage and appropriate action is then taken promptly by the supervisor'.

Despite the heading to s 7 (s 263 in the case of an IVA), its provisions provide no specific guidance on the implementation of the proposal itself. Detailed procedural rules do, however, appear in rr 2.39–2.44 (rr 8.25–8.31 in the case of an IVA). In addition, the terms of the arrangement itself will dictate the method of implementation on a case-by-case basis. Rule 2.45 also contains rules on time recording which a supervisor must comply with.

On the declaration of payment of dividends generally see rr 14.26–14.45.

In practice, it used to be common to find that the terms of a CVA imported the provisions in rr 4.73–4.94 of the IR 1986, which provide a procedure for proof and quantification of claims for dividend purposes in liquidation. The new rules on dividends and proving are contained in rr 14.26–14.45.

*Appleyard Ltd v Ritecrown Ltd* [2007] EWHC 3515 (Ch), [2009] BPIR 235 is a case in which Lewison J considered the scope of the supervisor's duty. He stated (at para 38): 'The primary duty of the supervisor is to implement the CVA in accordance with the Insolvency Act, the Insolvency Rules, and the terms of the proposals as modified. Any power or discretion given to him under those proposals is in my judgment to be exercised for that purpose, and that purpose only, and not for a collateral purpose. It is common ground that as an officer of the court the supervisor must also act reasonably'.

## SECTION 7(1)

**Scope of provision**—For guidance see the notes to s 4A.

## SECTION 7(2)

**Scope of provision**—The nominee, or his replacement, becomes known as the supervisor of the voluntary arrangement automatically by force of this provision on the arrangement coming into effect under s 4A.

The circumstances in which the nominee does not become supervisor are specified in ss 2(4) and 4(2) (ss 256(3), 256A(4) and 258(2) in the case of an IVA). The first arises where the court has appointed a replacement nominee because the original nominee failed to submit a report to the court in accordance with s 2(2) (ss 256(1) and 256A(3) in the case of an IVA). The second situation arises where the proposal has been modified so as to confer the functions of the nominee on another appropriately qualified person.

The consequence of the supervisor's appointment is that the person so appointed becomes entitled, indeed obliged, to discharge his functions and exercise his powers under and in accordance with the arrangement.

## SECTION 7(3)

**Scope of provision**—This subsection is concerned only with complaints directed against a supervisor; it has no bearing on whether a creditor is able to sustain a claim against a company, notwithstanding the approval of the voluntary arrangement, on which see the notes to s 5(2)(b).

Provided that the court is not minded to strike out an underlying claim on the basis that it is bound to fail, s 7(3) will permit an application seeking declaratory relief against a company in CVA as to the existence and quantum of a debt, and as against the supervisors of the CVA as regards admission of the debt to the CVA, without contravention of s 11(3)(d) (now para 43(6) of Sch B1) where the company in CVA is also in administration since ss 7 and 11 have different purposes and do not conflict: *Holdenhurst Securities plc v Cohen* [2001] 1 BCLC 460 at [11]–[17] (Laddie J).

'  . . .  **any other person**  . . . '—This term will, it is submitted, extend to any person capable of establishing to the court that he has a sufficient interest in the voluntary arrangement. This might include the directors of the company or, alternatively, a person with a beneficial interest in the arrangement assets: see *Port v Auger* [1994] 1 WLR 862 at 873–874 (Harman J, considering similar wording in s 303). The provision might also catch a third party who claims not to be bound by an arrangement but is treated as such by the supervisor in circumstances where the supervisor refuses to seek clarification of the issue by way of an application under s 262 at the behest of the third party: *Re Timothy* [2006] BPIR 329 at [49] (Warren J). HHJ Langan QC (sitting as a High Court judge) in *Stericker v Horner* [2012] BPIR 645 gave some limited consideration to the scope of the phrase 'any other person' ([37]–[38]).

' . . . is dissatisfied . . . '—This phrase also appears in s 263(3) in relation to IVAs, as it does in s 303(1) in relation to complaints made against a trustee in bankruptcy. The term is to be contrasted with 'is aggrieved by', which applies to complaints made against a liquidator under s 168(5) in a compulsory liquidation and which also appeared in the former s 80 of the Bankruptcy Act 1914 in relation to trustees-in-bankruptcy. In *Re Dennis Michael Cooke* [1999] BPIR 881 Stanley Burnton QC, sitting as a deputy High Court judge, considered (at 883F–883G), in the context of an application under s 303, that the term 'dissatisfied' is certainly no narrower than 'aggrieved', and is arguably wider and should not be given a restricted interpretation so as to include a person who has a genuine grievance against the actions of the office-holder, but not merely busybody interfering in things which do not concern him. That interpretation, it is submitted, would apply equally in the context of the present provision.

' . . . by any act, omission or decision of the supervisor . . . '— The subsection distinguishes a 'decision' from an 'act' or 'omission'. If those three terms are mutually exclusive, then it would follow that an omission extends to a failure to do something, say through an oversight or through ignorance, but not a failure to do something as a consequence of a decision to that effect. The scope of the conduct capable of falling within the cumulative scope of the three terms is plainly broad, but will only include relevant conduct on the part of the supervisor acting as such, including such conduct undertaken on his behalf, say by a member of the supervisor's staff.

**Does s 7(3) preclude the existence of a private right of action outside of the provision in favour of a creditor?**—In *King v Anthony* [1999] BPIR 73 the Court of Appeal (Nourse, Schiemann and Brooke LJJ) held (in the judgment of Brooke LJ at 78H–79B), in relation to the identical provision in s 263(3) applicable to IVAs, that a creditor had no private right of action allowing for complaint to be made against a supervisor, since s 263(3) provided an effective means of enforcing the duties of a supervisor. Furthermore, Part VIII of the IA 1986 constitutes a self-contained statutory scheme which in s 263(3) provides expressly for the court to give appropriate directions to a supervisor, thereby allowing the court to maintain control over the performance of its officer. This issue had arisen in that case in the context of a claim by a supervisor against two debtors who had served a defence and counterclaim which alleged a private law remedy against the supervisor which sounded in damages and which constituted a set-off against the supervisor's claim. Based on its construction of s 263 the Court of Appeal upheld the decision of the judge below in striking out the defence and counterclaim.

**Is a private law remedy available against a nominee?**—Section 7(3) applies only to a supervisor. *King v Anthony*, therefore, cannot operate so as to limit any private law remedy available against a nominee, as opposed to a supervisor. It would appear to follow from the reasoning in *King v Anthony* that misconduct by a nominee which constitutes unfair prejudice and/or material irregularity within the meaning of s 6(1)(a) and/or (b) (s 262(1) and/or (b) in the case of an IVA) is actionable only under these provisions and will not be open to a private law remedy. However, to the extent that any breach of the nominee's duties – on which see the notes to s 2(2) – falls outside s 6(1) (s 262(1) in the case of an IVA), that conduct would appear actionable by way of a private law remedy, say in a claim for breach of duty and/or negligence.

SECTION 7(4)(a)

' . . . directions in relation to any particular matter arising under the voluntary arrangement . . . '—There is no authority which deals with the scope of s 7(4)(a) (s 263(4)(a) in the case of an IVA), most likely because the court will usually be willing to respond to a genuine request for assistance by a supervisor in connection with any specific (or 'particular') matter which arises under – seemingly, in connection with or caused by – the voluntary arrangement. The objective of the provision, it is submitted, is to afford a supervisor easy access to court for the resolution of such genuine difficulties. Whilst plainly drafted more broadly in scope than s 7(3) (s 263(3) in the case of an IVA), the s 7(4)(a) (s 263(4)(a) in the case of an IVA) facility should not be employed for the purpose of seeking the court's approval or 'rubber stamp' – which will most likely be refused in any case – where the substance of the particular matter raised amounts to a commercial decision for the office-holder personally. Neither, it is submitted, is an application for directions appropriate where the application constitutes an obvious attempt on the part of the supervisor to avoid alternative and plainly more appropriate proceedings.

The Court of Appeal has held that the court has no jurisdiction to give directions modifying the terms of an approved arrangement since the power to give directions in relation to an arrangement is something very different from a power to amend an arrangement: *Re Alpa Lighting Ltd* [1997] BPIR 341 and see the note 'Control over the admission of creditor's proof' to s 1(1). There have been a number of recent cases in which supervisors have made applications for directions under s 7(4) (s 263(4) in the case of an IVA). For instance *Re Federal-Mogul Aftermarket Ltd* [2008] BPIR 846, *Re Energy Holdings (No 3) Ltd* [2010] BPIR 1339 and *TXU Europe Group Plc* [2011] EWHC 2072 (Ch), [2012] BPIR 463.

## SECTION 7(4)(b)

**Petition by supervisor for winding up**—In the absence of the supervisor of a CVA appearing within the classes of person eligible to petition for the winding up of a company within s 124(1), this provision expressly provides such standing.

In practice, the provisions of a CVA will commonly require a supervisor either to petition or to consider petitioning for winding up in the event of one or more specified defaults. The supervisor of a CVA does not necessarily lose standing to petition under this provision by virtue of the fact that an arrangement is no longer functioning (as in a trading arrangement) as originally envisaged. In *Re Arthur Rathbone Kitchens Ltd* [1997] 2 BCLC 280 Roger Kaye QC, sitting as deputy High Court judge, rejected submissions to the effect that a supervisor could not petition for winding up under s 7(4)(b) if the CVA was not still on foot so as to deprive the supervisor of locus standi as 'supervisor' within the meaning of s 7(2). The deputy judge identified that, on the particular terms of the CVA, the arrangement had not terminated, although the company was in default, at the time of the presentation of the supervisor's petition. Neither does a supervisor lose standing to petition on the expiration of a fixed-term arrangement, provided that, at the time of presentation of the petition, the supervisor was still 'carrying out in relation to the voluntary arrangement the functions conferred on the supervisor by virtue of s 7(2) (or s 263(2) in the case of an IVA): *Harris v Gross* [2001] BPIR 586 (HHJ Maddocks sitting as a High Court judge, bankruptcy orders made on petitions presented by IVA supervisor one month after expiration of 4-year fixed term interlocking IVAs in respect of ongoing defaults committed during the term of the fixed period of the arrangements).

A CVA supervisor's winding-up petition is treated as if it were a contributories' petition: see rr 7.4 and 7.25–7.32.

**Application by supervisor for administration order**—The supervisor of a CVA is not identified in para 12(1) of Sch B1 as a person having standing to apply to the court for the making of an administration order. It is plain, however, that a supervisor has such standing from s 7(4)(b) and from para 12(5) of Sch B1, which provides that para 12(1) is without prejudice to s 7(4)(b). Rule 3.5 provides that an application for an administration order by the supervisor of a CVA is to be treated as if it were an application by the company.

## [1.68]

### 7A Prosecution of delinquent officers of company

(1)   This section applies where the approval of a voluntary arrangement in relation to a company has taken effect under section 4A.

(2)   If it appears to the supervisor that any past or present officer of the company has committed an offence in connection with the voluntary arrangement, the supervisor must forthwith—

(a)   report the matter to the appropriate authority, and

(b)   provide the appropriate authority with such information and give the authority such access to and facilities for inspecting and taking copies of documents (being information or documents in the possession or under the control of the . . . supervisor and relating to the matter in question) as the authority requires.

In this subsection, "the appropriate authority" means—

(i)   in the case of a company registered in England and Wales, the Secretary of State, and

(ii)   in the case of a company registered in Scotland, the Lord Advocate.

(3)   Where a report is made to the Secretary of State under subsection (2), he may, for the purpose of investigating the matter reported to him and such other matters relating to the affairs of the company as appear to him to require investigation, exercise any of the powers which are exercisable by inspectors appointed under section 431 or 432 of the Companies Act 1985 to investigate a company's affairs.

(4)   For the purpose of such an investigation any obligation imposed on a person by any provision of the Companies Acts to produce documents or give information to, or otherwise to assist, inspectors so appointed is to be regarded as an obligation similarly to assist the Secretary of State in his investigation.

(5)  An answer given by a person to a question put to him in exercise of the powers conferred by subsection (3) may be used in evidence against him.

(6)  However, in criminal proceedings in which that person is charged with an offence to which this subsection applies—

  (a)  no evidence relating to the answer may be adduced, and

  (b)  no question relating to it may be asked,

by or on behalf of the prosecution, unless evidence relating to it is adduced, or a question relating to it is asked, in the proceedings by or on behalf of that person.

(7)  Subsection (6) applies to any offence other than—

  (a)  an offence under section 2 or 5 of the Perjury Act 1911 (false statements made on oath otherwise than in judicial proceedings or made otherwise than on oath), or

  (b)  an offence under section 44(1) or (2) of the Criminal Law (Consolidation) (Scotland) Act 1995 (false statements made on oath or otherwise than on oath).

(8)  Where a prosecuting authority institutes criminal proceedings following any report under subsection (2), the . . . supervisor, and every officer and agent of the company past and present (other than the defendant or defender), shall give the authority all assistance in connection with the prosecution which he is reasonably able to give.

  For this purpose—

    "agent" includes any banker or solicitor of the company and any person employed by the company as auditor, whether that person is or is not an officer of the company,

    "prosecuting authority" means the Director of Public Prosecutions, the Lord Advocate or the Secretary of State.

(9)  The court may, on the application of the prosecuting authority, direct any person referred to in subsection (8) to comply with that subsection if he has failed to do so.

**Amendments**—Inserted by Insolvency Act 2000, s 2, Sch 2, paras 1, 10. Amended by SI 2009/1941; Corporate Insolvency and Governance Act 2020, s 2(1), Sch 3, paras 1, 7(1).

## [1.69]

### 7B Arrangements coming to an end prematurely

For the purposes of this Part, a voluntary arrangement the approval of which has taken effect under section 4A . . . comes to an end prematurely if, when it ceases to have effect, it has not been fully implemented in respect of all persons bound by the arrangement by virtue of section 5(2)(b)(i) . . ..

**Amendments**—Inserted by Insolvency Act 2000, s 2, Sch 2, paras 1, 10. Amended by Corporate Insolvency and Governance Act 2020, s 2(1), Sch 3, paras 1, 8(a), (b).

## PART II  ADMINISTRATION

## [1.70]

**General comment on Part II**—With effect from 15 September 2003 a new statutory regime in Sch B1 of the 1986 Act governing administration of companies came into effect and replaced the provisions in Part II (being ss 8–27). That new regime amounts to a re-modelled, streamlined mechanism, which is outlined in the introductory note to Sch B1. For those undertakings to which the former Part II continues to apply, see the notes under that heading to para 10 of Sch B1.

### 8 Administration

Schedule B1 to this Act (which makes provision about the administration of companies) shall have effect.

### 9–27

*(Repealed)*

## PART III   RECEIVERSHIP

**[1.71]**

**References**—For clarity, in the commentary to Part III of the IA 1986 reference to 'non-administrative receivers' means receivers and managers described by s 29(1) and reference to 'administrative receivers' means receivers and managers described by s 29(2).

**General introduction to receivership**—Receivership is a formal method of debt enforcement which can be traced back to Elizabethan times and which allows a secured creditor to enforce his security through the appointment of a receiver, or more commonly a receiver and manager, over the assets of the debtor with a view to recouping monies due to him or her. The administrative receiver (being an individual appointed, most commonly, by a financial institution over the whole or substantially the whole of the company's assets and undertakings pursuant to a 'global' floating charge which in practice is invariably supplemented by one or more fixed charges over specific assets) was a creation of the 1986 Act. Administrative receivership was, by its nature, mutually exclusive with the procedure of administration introduced under Part II of the 1986 Act.

**Administrative receivers and non-administrative receivers distinguished: powers**—An administrative receiver has conferred on him or her the investigatory and related powers in ss 234–236. Further, the powers derive from Sch 1, which is implied into the debenture pursuant to which the administrative receiver is appointed, subject to contrary provision therein: see s 42(1). In addition, an administrative receiver may apply for an order for sale under s 43 where charged property is subject to security ranking in priority to that pursuant to which he or she is appointed. A non-administrative receiver's powers derive from the debenture pursuant to which he or she was appointed (as supplemented by the Law of Property Act 1925 in the case of a LPA receiver) without the implication of powers from Sch 1. In practice, equivalent powers should be expressly bestowed on the non-administrative receiver by the terms of the debenture. For both types of receiver, reference should be made to the commentary to s 42.

**Administrative receivers and other non-administrative receivers and managers distinguished: agency**—An administrative receiver is deemed to be the agent of the company pursuant to s 44. There is no corresponding provision that applies to a non-administrative receiver but, in practice, this is usually expressly provided for in the debenture pursuant to which he or she is appointed. In the absence of any such provision, it is for the court to consider the nature of the receiver's agency as a matter of construction of the debenture: *Cully v Parsons* [1923] 2 Ch 512. In either case, the special nature of this agency to the company has some 'peculiar incidents': *Silven Properties Ltd v Royal Bank of Scotland plc* [2003] EWCA Civ 1409, [2004] 1 WLR 997, [2004] 1 BCLC 359, [2003] BPIR 1429 at [26] to [27]. For both types of receiver, reference should be made to the commentary to s 44.

**Administrative receivers and non-administrative receivers distinguished: removal**—Unlike a non-administrative receiver (who may be removed by the appointor at any time) an administrative receiver may only be removed by order of the court under s 45.

**Administrative receivers and non-administrative receivers distinguished: qualification to act**—A person who acts as an administrative receiver of a company acts in relation to it as an insolvency practitioner and must be qualified to act as such on pain of criminal sanction: see ss 388(1), 389(1) and 390(1). A non-administrative receiver need not be qualified to act as an insolvency practitioner in relation to a company. Indeed, in practice, this is often the case with, for example, real estate specialists being appointed to realise a company's property.

**Role of receivership today**—With the passage of time it became increasingly difficult to characterise administrative receivership as a rescue mechanism in common with the other procedures under the 1986 Act (which were, unlike receivership, collective insolvency proceedings) and which were increasingly referred to as constituent parts of the so-called 'rescue culture'. In perhaps the most far-reaching amendment to the insolvency legislation since the implementation of the 1986 Act, a new s 72A, introduced by s 250 of the Enterprise Act 2002 and effective from 15 September 2003, effectively abolished administrative receivership from that date. The abolition, however, was not without its provisos. First, s 72A has no effect on floating charge security created prior to 15 September 2003 and compliant with s 29(2). Secondly, by virtue of s 176A(9), the charge-holder enforcing floating charge security created prior to 15 September 2003 enjoys not only freedom from the prescribed-part provisions in s 176A but also benefits from the abolition of Crown preference. Thirdly, those excepted cases provided for in ss 72B–72H allow for the appointment of an administrative receiver in relation to such undertakings, irrespective of the date of the creation of the requisite floating charge under s 29(2).

These changes dramatically reduced the role that the administrative receiver now plays in the insolvency process. In the three years before these changes came into force, 11% of all new insolvencies were administrative receiverships. In the three years following these changes, that figure dropped to just 5%. This trend has continued until administrative receivership made up just 0.02% of the total number of new insolvencies in 2020. The latest statistics can be accessed at: https://www.gov.uk/government/collections/insolvency-service-official-statistics.

Section 72A has no effect on the appointment of non-administrative receivers pursuant to security which is either fixed in nature or which is a crystallised floating charge but less extensive than the s 29(2) threshold. It is the non-administrative receiver that still plays a crucial role in the insolvency process today.

CHAPTER I

RECEIVERS AND MANAGERS (ENGLAND AND WALES)
*Preliminary and general provisions*

## [1.72]

### 28 Extent of this Chapter

(1)   In this Chapter "company" means a company registered under the Companies Act 2006 in England and Wales or Scotland.

(2)   This Chapter does not apply to receivers appointed under Chapter 2 of this Part (Scotland).

Amendments—SI 2009/1941.

General note—Chapter I, comprising ss 28–49, applies only to receivers and managers appointed under the law of England and Wales. Chapter II, comprising ss 50–71, governs receivers appointed under Scottish law.

Jurisdiction—In practice it is usual for standard form debentures to provide that the debenture itself and any receiver appointed pursuant to its terms is to be construed in accordance with and governed by the law of a specified jurisdiction.

'. . . a company . . .'—This definition of the term 'company' was inserted by the Companies Act 2006 (Consequential Amendments, Transitional Provisions and Savings) Order 2009. The original drafting of the IA 1986 contained no such definition. Previous cases considered it possible to appoint a receiver and manager in relation to a foreign company (*Re International Bulk Commodities Ltd* [1993] Ch 77, [1992] BCLC 1074). This is clearly no longer the case.

Under the previous drafting of this provision, HHJ Hague QC (sitting as a High Court judge) held that a receiver and manager appointed to an industrial and provident society is incapable of constituting an administrative receiver because such an unregistered company falls outside the definition of the term 'company' for s 29(2) purposes: *Re Devon and Somerset Farmers Ltd* [1994] Ch 57, [1994] 2 BCLC 99. Henderson J agreed that an industrial and provident society is outside the administrative receivership regime in *Re Dairy Farmers of Britain Ltd* [2009] EWHC 1389 (Ch), [2010] Ch 63, [2010] 1 BCLC 637.

Building societies—Chapter I also applies to building societies subject to certain modifications provided for in Sch 15A and the Building Societies Act 1997, s 39.

## [1.73]

### 29 Definitions

(1)   It is hereby declared that, except where the context otherwise requires—

    (a)    any reference in this Act to a receiver or manager of the property of a company, or to a receiver of it, includes a receiver or manager, or (as the case may be) a receiver of part only of that property and a receiver only of the income arising from the property or from part of it; and

    (b)    any reference in this Act to the appointment of a receiver or manager under powers contained in an instrument includes an appointment made under powers which, by virtue of any enactment, are implied in and have effect as if contained in an instrument.

(2)   In this Chapter "administrative receiver" means—

    (a)    a receiver or manager of the whole (or substantially the whole) of a company's property appointed by or on behalf of the holders of any debentures of the company secured by a charge which, as created, was a floating charge, or by such a charge and one or more other securities; or

    (b)    a person who would be such a receiver or manager but for the appointment of some other person as the receiver of part of the company's property.

**Amendments**—SI 2009/1941.

**General note**—This provision defines the scope of a receiver and manager (in s 29(1)) as distinct from the statutorily created receiver and manager known as the administrative receiver (as defined in s 29(2)). Sections 42–49 apply only to administrative receivers (though some of the concepts discussed in the commentary to those sections below apply equally to non-administrative receivers), as does s 2 of the Insolvency Act 1994.

A receiver and manager appointed under s 51 (Scotland) may also be an administrative receiver, on which see the definitions in s 251.

## SECTION 29(1)

**Scope of provision**—There are two types of non-administrative receiver commonly referred to in practice: the fixed charge receiver (a receiver appointed pursuant to a fixed charge or a floating charge (other than a qualifying floating charge) that has crystallised into a fixed charge) and a LPA receiver (a receiver appointed pursuant to the powers in the Law of Property Act 1925 on which consider the effect of *Meadrealm Ltd v Transcontinental Golf Construction* (unreported) 29 November 1991, ChD (Vinelott J), noted under s 29(2)(a) below). Save where the context otherwise requires, the term receiver and manager in the legislation will catch both a fixed charge receiver and a LPA receiver.

' . . . **receiver or manager** . . . '—Although the wording envisages the appointment of a receiver 'or' manager, in practice appointees invariably take office as both.

## SECTION 29(2)(a)

**Scope of provision**—Despite a number of anomalies, there is no reported judgment which includes a detailed analysis of the ambiguous terminology employed in this provision.

' . . . **the whole or substantially the whole of the company's property** . . . '—This phrase is open to a number of possible interpretations. Reference to 'substantially the whole' necessitates some objective criteria by which that element of the company's property may be adjudged to amount to such in comparison with that element of the company's property to which the appointment does not extend (ie that part other than substantially the whole). The most obvious objective criterion which, it is suggested, is also entirely appropriate and workable for these purposes is the financial value of the relevant property subject to the floating charge security as at the date of the appointment, as valued, not by the appointing debenture-holder, but by the company itself, say by reference to the company's most recent financial statements or audited accounts, provided those sources include objective and credible values.

' . . . **a company** . . . '—The term 'company' in the context of s 29(2) means 'a company registered under the Companies Act 2006 in England and Wales or Scotland' (pursuant to s 28 above and the commentary thereto).

' . . . **appointed by or on behalf of the holders of any debentures of the company** . . . '—This reference excludes court appointed receivers from the definition of the term 'administrative receiver'; a court appointment on the application of the holder of a debenture cannot, it is suggested, at least not realistically be argued to be made 'on behalf of' the applicant.

' . . . **secured by a charge which, as created, was a floating charge** . . . '—The key element of the phrase 'secured by a charge which, as created, was a floating charge, or by such a charge in one or more other securities' is the reference to a prerequisite floating charge as defined in s 251. The reference to 'one or more other securities' covers the common scenario where an appointing debenture-holder holds one or more fixed charges over specific property in addition to a 'global' floating charge which will convert to a fixed equitable charge on crystallisation. More importantly, however, the reference to a floating charge on either side of the word 'or' in the above phrase denotes that the floating charge must be a global security which extends at least to substantially the whole of the company's property. Consistent with this approach, a receiver appointed under a fixed charge or charges has been held not to amount to an administrative receiver, even where the appointing debenture-holder held, but made no appointment pursuant to, a global floating charge: *Meadrealm Ltd v Transcontinental Golf Construction Ltd* (unreported) 29 November 1991 (ChD, Vinelott J).

**'Lightweight' floating charges**—The validity of an instrument as a floating charge at the time of creation does not depend upon the existence of uncharged assets to which the floating charge can attach or upon a power in the chargor company to acquire assets in the future free from any fixed charge but rather as a matter of construction of the relevant instrument creating the charge: *SAW (SW) 2010 Ltd v Wilson* [2017] EWCA Civ 1001, [2018] 2 WLR 636, [2018] 1 BCLC 291 at [24] (though this case actually considered para 14 to Sch B1, Briggs LJ held (at [26]) that the definition of 'floating charge' was identical in these provisions and expressly relied upon the earlier receivership case of *Re Croftbell Ltd* [1990] BCLC 844). Reference should be made to commentary to para 14.

SECTION 29(2)(b)

**Scope of provision**—This provision preserves the status of an administrative receiver where a receiver and manager (within s 29(1)) is previously appointed over part only of a company's property where the residual part over which that appointment is not made amounts to less than substantially the whole of the company's property.

Section 29(2)(b), it is suggested, precludes the contemporaneous appointment of two or more administrative receivers (ie other than as joint appointees).

## [1.74]

### 30 Disqualification of body corporate from acting as receiver

A body corporate is not qualified for appointment as receiver of the property of a company, and any body corporate which acts as such a receiver is liable to a fine.

**General note**—This provision continues the bar on corporate receivers (ie appointed in or out of court) as was previously provided for in the now repealed s 366 of the Companies Act 1948 and s 489 of the Companies Act 1985. The appointment of a corporate receiver is a nullity: *Portman Building Society v Gallwey* [1955] 1 WLR 96 at 100 (Wynn Parry J).

Any body corporate acting as receiver of the property of a company is liable to a fine as prescribed in s 430 and in Sch 10.

For the more general bar on bodies corporate being qualified to act as insolvency practitioners and related criminal sanctions, see ss 389(1) and 390(1).

## [1.75]

### 31 Disqualification of bankrupt or person in respect of whom a debt relief order is made

(1)   A person commits an offence if he acts as receiver or manager of the property of a company on behalf of debenture holders while—

(a)   he is an undischarged bankrupt,

(aa)   a moratorium period under a debt relief order applies in relation to him, or

(b)   a bankruptcy restrictions order or a debt relief restrictions order is in force in respect of him.

(2)   A person guilty of an offence under subsection (1) shall be liable to imprisonment, a fine or both.

(3)   This section does not apply to a receiver or manager acting under an appointment made by the court.

**Amendments**—Enterprise Act 2002, s 257(3), Sch 21, para 1; Tribunals, Courts and Enforcement Act 2007, s 108(3), Sch 20, Pt 1, paras 1, 2.

**General note**—This provision, amended by Sch 21 of the Enterprise Act 2002 and effective from 1 April 2004, continues the bar on an undischarged bankrupt, but not a discharged bankrupt, acting as a receiver or manager of the property of a company. The bar was extended even further to persons subject to a bankruptcy restriction order (by the Enterprise Act 2002) or subject to a debt relief order and debt relief restrictions order (by the Tribunals, Courts and Enforcement Act 2007). Although s 31(3) envisages the possibility of such a barred person from being appointed as a court appointed receiver or manager, in practice the court will be very unlikely to accede to such an application.

A substantively similar prohibition appeared previously in the now repealed s 367 of the Companies Act 1948 and s 490 of the Companies Act 1985. Such appointment would appear to be a nullity, based on the reasoning of Wynn Parry J in *Portman Building Society v Gallwey* [1955] 1 WLR 96 at 100.

Any person acting in contravention of s 31 is liable to imprisonment or a fine as prescribed in s 430 and Sch 10.

A person disqualified from acting as a company director is also disqualified from acting as a receiver of a company's property (unless there is leave of the court) and an insolvency practitioner: see s 1(1) of the Company Directors Disqualification Act 1986.

**[1.76]**

## 32 Power for court to appoint official receiver

Where application is made to the court to appoint a receiver on behalf of the debenture holders or other creditors of a company which is being wound up by the court, the official receiver may be appointed.

**General note**—Applications under this provision are very rare in practice but might conceivably arise where a defect within a debenture precludes the appointment of a receiver and manager in circumstances where an incumbent liquidator disputes the validity of the security comprised in the debenture where the secured assets are in need of immediate protection or management; in these circumstances, however, any prospective applicant might well prefer an appointee of his own choice other than the official receiver.

Sections 399–401 deal with the appointment, functions and status of official receivers as office-holders under the legislation.

*Receivers and managers appointed out of court*

**[1.77]**

## 33 Time from which appointment is effective

(1) The appointment of a person as a receiver or manager of a company's property under powers contained in an instrument—

   (a)   is of no effect unless it is accepted by that person before the end of the business day next following that on which the instrument of appointment is received by him or on his behalf, and

   (b)   subject to this, is deemed to be made at the time at which the instrument of appointment is so received.

(2) This section applies to the appointment of two or more persons as joint receivers or managers of a company's property under powers contained in an instrument, subject to such modifications as may be prescribed by the rules.

**General note**—This provision requires acceptance by an appointee or appointees within a relatively stringent timescale as a pre-condition of the effective appointment of a receiver and manager out of court. In practice, an appointor will invariably confirm willingness to act with an appointee prior to offering appointment.

The timing of an effective appointment is relevant because the most common event of external intervention giving rise to the crystallisation of a floating charge is the out of court appointment of a receiver and manager, on which see *Evans v Rival Granite Quarries Ltd* [1910] 2 KB 979 at 1000–1001 (Buckley LJ). In the absence of specific provision in a debenture, there is no requirement for notification of appointment of a receiver and manager to the chargor or any other third party for the purpose of effecting crystallisation of a floating charge. Crystallisation of a floating charge confers priority in favour of the charge-holder over secured assets over which execution has been levied but not completed by way of payment of monies over to the execution creditor: *Re Standard Manufacturing Co Ltd* [1891] 1 Ch 627, CA; *Re Opera Ltd* [1891] 3 Ch 260; and see, though on unusual facts, *Robinson v Burnell's Bakery* [1904] 2 KB 624.

Section 33 and its associated formalities, noted below, are not dependent on the taking of possession of charged assets by a receiver, which would in any case be unnecessary, given that the execution of a debenture allowing for the appointment of a receiver can be taken as a surrender by the chargor company of those powers assumed by a receiver on appointment: *Alberta Paper Co Ltd v Metropolitan Graphics Ltd* (1983) 49 CBR (2d) 63.

Effective appointment of a receiver and manager is not in itself confirmatory of the substantive validity of the appointment.

**Procedure on appointment**—For the formalities on acceptance and confirmation of appointment see rr 4.1 and 4.5 and the notes thereto. For the notification of the appointment of a receiver and manager see also s 39.

The legislation does not prescribe any statutory form for confirmation or evidencing of the appointment of a receiver or manager. A debenture may, however, and commonly will, prescribe formalities necessary on the effecting of an appointment. It is useful for the instrument of appointment to confirm compliance with such formalities such as the obtaining of any prescribed consent or the service of a demand on the chargor company prior to appointment. Such instrument should usually be executed as a deed so that the receiver can execute deeds on behalf of his or her appointor (s 47 of the Companies Act 2006).

On the validity of an office-holder's acts notwithstanding defects in appointment, nomination or qualifications, see s 232 and the notes thereto. Section 33(1)(a) and (b)

**Scope of provision**—Provided that acceptance of appointment is effected within the period prescribed by s 33(1)(a), s 33(1)(b) deems appointment to have been effected at the time of receipt of the instrument or offer of appointment.

'. . . **powers contained in an instrument** . . . '—The debenture itself usually provides the terms upon which the power to appoint a receiver is exercisable by the debenture-holder. In the case of a LPA receiver, s 103 of the Law of Property Act 1925 provides that a mortgagee's power of sale under that Act cannot be exercised unless and until certain conditions are complied with. To avoid the need to satisfy these conditions, the debenture can and most commonly will expressly exclude s 103.

'**Business day**'—For the meaning of 'business day' in s 33(1)(a), see s 251.

**Instrument of appointment executed in anticipation of appointment**—There is nothing objectionable in an instrument of appointment being executed, signed and dated in readiness for the possible future appointment of a receiver: *Windsor Refrigerator Co Ltd v Branch Nominees Ltd* [1961] Ch 375 at 397 (Harman LJ).

## SECTION 33(2)

**Scope of provision**—In the case of a joint appointment – usually, in practice, partners in the same firm – r 4.1(2) provides that each joint appointee must accept appointment as if each were a sole appointee, consequent upon which any such appointment will be effective from the time at which the instrument of appointment was received by or on behalf of all the appointees.

On joint appointments see also s 231 (appointment to office of two or more persons) and the discussion in *Re Melson Velcrete Pty Ltd* (1996) 14 ACLC 778 on the joint, several and joint, and several roles of multiple receivers.

## [1.78]

### 34 Liability for invalid appointment

Where the appointment of a person as the receiver or manager of a company's property under powers contained in an instrument is discovered to be invalid (whether by virtue of the invalidity of the instrument or otherwise), the court may order the person by whom or on whose behalf the appointment was made to indemnify the person appointed against any liability which arises solely by reason of the invalidity of the appointment.

**General note**—This provision confers a discretion on the court to order that the appointor of a person appointed as receiver or manager of a company's property indemnifies the appointee in respect of any liability arising 'solely' by reason of the invalidity of the appointment.

The tort of unlawful interference with contractual relations does not arise where an invalidly appointed receiver takes charge of a company's contractual relations without the intention to induce the company to breach any of its contracts; neither does English law recognise a tort of conversion of a chose in action: *OBG v Allan & Others* [2007] UKHL 21, [2008] 1 AC 1, [2007] BPIR 746. Procedurally, the proper course in assessing liability consequent on the defective appointment of a receiver is the provision of directions for the taking of an inquiry.

Quite apart from s 34 it is a well-established principle that a debenture holder may rely on any circumstance, existing at the time of the appointment of the receivers, which would justify their appointment notwithstanding that that circumstance was not being expressly relied on by the debenture holder at the time the appointment was made: *Byblos Bank SAL v Al-Khudairy* (1986) 2 BCC 99, 549 at 99, 564 (Nicholls LJ).

**Invalid and defective appointments distinguished**—A distinction is drawn between invalidity in appointment under this provision, say where there is no power to appoint or no substantive appointment (on which see *Morris v Kanssen* [1946] AC 459), and mere defects in the formalities or procedure by which appointment is effected, which defects may be cured by s 232, by which the actions of an improperly appointed receiver may also remain valid: *OBG v Allan & Others*.

'. . . **any liability** . . . '—The reference to 'any liability' appears wide enough to cover liabilities flowing solely from the invalidity of the appointment and which are incurred by the appointee either to the company itself, save for wrongful interference with goods or conversion, or to a third party with whom the appointee has had dealings as receiver. However, it is doubtful that any such liability will arise 'solely' from any invalidity in appointment where the liability is incurred by the appointee contracting with personal liability as receiver on the basis of an indemnity from the company's assets (which indemnity would be lost by virtue of the invalidity of the appointment).

The exercise of the court's discretion under this provision will depend on the extent to which the appointor and appointee can each be shown to have been aware of the invalidity of the appointment or capable of establishing such invalidity on reasonable investigation.

**Invalidly appointed receiver: agent of appointor?**—In the case of an invalidly appointed receiver, quite apart from s 34, the appointor will be vicariously liable for the acts of his or her agent, the purported receiver, where the purported receiver acts on the instructions or directions of the appointor: *Standard Chartered Bank v Walker* [1982] 1 WLR 1410 at 1416A, CA. Section 34 itself, it is suggested, does not preclude the existence of such an agency relationship; compare the reasoning of Walton J in *Bank of Baroda v Panessar* [1987] Ch 335 to opposite effect. However, neither does the mere fact of appointment automatically trigger an agency relationship between appointor and appointee in the usual absence of a provision to such effect in the debenture: *National Bank of Greece v Pinios* [1990] 1 AC 637 at 648–649 (Lloyd LJ).

A third party cannot rely on the ostensible authority of an invalidly appointed receiver unless they could satisfy the court that there was some holding out or representation emanating from the putative principal: *Business Mortgage Finance 6 plc v Roundstone Technologies Ltd* [2019] EWHC 2917 (Ch) (Mann J) at [56].

**Invalidly appointed receiver: estoppel**—Where the directors of a company treat the receiver as validly appointed, the court may find it unconscionable to permit the company to later deny that which they have encouraged the appointor and the receiver to assume to their detriment (ie that the appointment was valid): *Bank of Baroda v Panessar* [1987] Ch 335 at 339.

**Indemnities beyond s 34**—The statutory indemnity provided for in s 34 is also discrete from any indemnity which may be claimed by a receiver who incurs liability to the chargor company or any third party in the course of acting on the instructions of the appointor: *Re B Johnson & Co (Builders) Ltd* [1955] Ch 634 at 647–648 (Evershed MR).

Where there are concerns over the validity of an appointment, a prospective appointee may seek a contractual indemnity, usually in the form of a deed, from the appointor to cover consequential liabilities as a condition of his or her appointment. The provision of indemnities very much varies in practice. An indemnity will ordinarily only protect a receiver from liability arising from invalidity in the debenture or in the form of appointment. The provision of an indemnity in respect of a receiver's acts or omissions, certainly by an institutional lender, is usually commercially inconceivable. For examples of invalid appointment see *Heald v O'Connor* [1971] 1 WLR 497 (mortgagor guaranteed loan in contravention of the predecessor to s 151 of the Companies Act 1985 rendering unlawful the giving of financial assistance by a company for the acquisition of its shares) and *Ford & Carter v Midland Bank plc* (1979) 129 NLJ 543, HL (no subsisting debt for which debenture holder bank could make demand).

## [1.79]

### 35 Application to court for directions

(1)   A receiver or manager of the property of a company appointed under powers contained in an instrument, or the persons by whom or on whose behalf a receiver or manager has been so appointed, may apply to the court for directions in relation to any particular matter arising in connection with the performance of the functions of the receiver or manager.

(2)   On such an application, the court may give such directions, or may make such order declaring the rights of persons before the court or otherwise, as it thinks just.

**General note**—This provision provides a useful facility for the resolution of disputes within the scope of s 35(1) on the application of a receiver or manager or the appointor. Appointors were not afforded such a facility in the earlier legislation. It is very doubtful that the court retains some inherent jurisdiction to entertain applications by persons outside the scope of s 35(1), not only because of the specific and express scope of s 35(1), but also because appointments covered by s 35 are effected out of court and remain a matter of contract between the chargor company and chargee creditor. Such a wide-ranging jurisdiction would also be inconsistent with the fact that a receiver appointed out of court is not subject to the control of the court under the rule in *Ex parte James* (1874) 9 Ch App 609.

The court should not be troubled with matters of commercial judgment, which remain the sole professional responsibility of the office-holder: *Re T & D Industries* [2000] 1 WLR 646, [2000] 1 BCLC 471 (Neuberger J, in the context of a directions application in an old-style administration: the court should not be seen as a 'bomb shelter' in the face of what amounts essentially to a commercial decision on the part of the office-holder).

#### SECTION 35(1)

**Destination of the application**—Any application pursuant to s 35(1) should be made to the court having jurisdiction to wind up the company (s 251).

**Eligible applicants**—The scope of applicants under this provision is limited to a receiver 'or' manager of the property of the company, including an administrative receiver. Alternatively, the application may be made by the person or persons by whom or on whose behalf the appointment 'has' been made, being, most commonly, the appointor under a debenture or, less commonly, trustees under a debenture trust stock deed or those for whom such trustees act. The provision therefore does not extend to ordinary creditors, or a creditor who may be entitled to effect appointment of a receiver or manager outside the scope of s 29(2). The FCA and PRA has standing to be heard on an application in an appropriate case: FMSA 2000, s 363(2).

**The scope of a s 35 application**—The scope of the directions which may be sought extends to any 'matter arising in connection with the performance of [the receiver's] functions'. This confers on the court a very broad jurisdiction and will include, for example, issues concerning the nature or priority of security under which a receiver is accountable or whether funds available for payment of preferential claims may be employed in ongoing trading. The provision also extends to disputes concerning a receiver's or manager's remuneration: *Re Therm-a-Stor Ltd* [1996] 1 WLR 1338, [1996] 2 BCLC 400 (Laddie J); and see *Mumms v Perkins* [2002] BPIR 120 (Evans-Lombe J) and the notes to s 36 below.

A strict construction of the wording in s 35(1) would appear to preclude an application by a receiver or his or her appointor to consider the validity of the receiver's appointment (for example where validity is disputed by others). However, such a conclusion is doubtful and at odds with both the apparent purpose of the provision and the practical requirement for the speedy resolution of any such issue, given the receiver's recourse to company assets in respect of his or her remuneration and the statutory indemnity in his or her favour under s 34. This purposive approach to s 35(1) would also bring the provision in line with the substance of the court's approach in *Re Wood and Martin Ltd* [1971] 1 WLR 293 (Megarry J) to s 352 of the Companies Act 1948 which, whilst being drafted very differently to s 35, was held to allow an invalidly appointed liquidator to seek a declaration that the dissolution of the company was void as a 'person interested', albeit not as 'liquidator'.

## SECTION 35(2)

**Remedies and relief on a s 35 application**—The court enjoys an unfettered discretion in resolving the dispute or issue before it. This includes the making of orders, which affect not only those before the court, on which see r 12.59 (review of the court's decisions) and CPR 40.9 (applications to vary or set aside by non-parties). The court may also give such directions or other form of relief as it thinks just. In the context of the application the court may consider making costs orders which regulate the extent to which the costs of any particular party may or may not be claimed as an expense of the receivership.

**Costs on a s 35 application**—There is no fixed practice in the Business and Property Courts as to the proper order on costs in cases where a receiver issues an application to determine questions arising in the course of the receivership. In hostile cases involving, say, ownership of property, costs will normally follow the event. On the other hand, the court will usually consider meeting the costs of a representative respondent, who is joined into the proceedings to argue a point on behalf of a class, out of the assets of the company: *Re Westdock Realisations Ltd* [1988] BCLC 354 (Browne-Wilkinson V-C). An office-holder will usually be awarded costs from the assets of the company as an expense of office: *Re Harmony Care Homes Ltd* [2009] EWHC 1961 (Ch). The court may order that such costs should constitute a personal liability of the office-holder where some exceptional circumstances justify such a draconian consequence.

## [1.80]

### 36 Court's power to fix remuneration

(1) The court may, on an application made by the liquidator of a company, by order fix the amount to be paid by way of remuneration to a person who, under powers contained in an instrument, has been appointed receiver or manager of the company's property.

(2) The court's power under subsection (1), where no previous order has been made with respect thereto under the subsection—

    (a)    extends to fixing the remuneration for any period before the making of the order or the application for it,

    (b)    is exercisable notwithstanding that the receiver or manager has died or ceased to act before the making of the order or the application, and

    (c)    where the receiver or manager has been paid or has retained for his remuneration for any period before the making of the order any amount in excess of that so fixed for that period, extends to requiring him or his personal representatives to account for the excess or such part of it as may be specified in the order.

But the power conferred by paragraph (c) shall not be exercised as respects any period before the making of the application for the order under this section, unless in the court's opinion there are special circumstances making it proper for the power to be exercised.

(3) The court may from time to time on an application made either by the liquidator or by the receiver or manager, vary or amend an order made under subsection (1).

**General note**—A receiver's right to remuneration, costs, disbursements etc will usually be provided for expressly in a well-drawn debenture. Such contractual provisions may also provide for remuneration on a time-cost basis, with or without stipulations being made as to specific rates, or as a percentage of recoveries. Section 109 of the Law of Property Act 1925 (which provides a cap on the rate of commission at 5% of the gross amount of money received) is either varied or, more commonly, excluded.

Section 36(1) repeats s 371(1) of the Companies Act 1948 and confers a limited right on a liquidator – and only a liquidator – to apply to the court to fix the amount to be paid by way of remuneration to a person appointed out of court as receiver or manager of a company's property. Where, however, such an order has been made, an application to vary or amend the order may be made under s 36(3) by either the liquidator 'or' by the receiver or manager.

A liquidator who has credible evidence of the drawing of excessive remuneration by a receiver will need very good reasons for justifying inaction to creditors. The absence of a large number of reported cases on s 36(1) applications may be explicable by reference to the fact that, in practice, any such claim, for very obvious reasons, may well be capable of compromise between liquidator and receiver without the need for resolution by the court.

## SECTION 36(1)

**Scope of provision**—Section 36(1) is limited to the fixing of remuneration only and makes no mention of costs, disbursements etc.

The reference to appointment under powers in an instrument in s 36(1) precludes an application relating to a receiver appointed either under statutory powers or by the court (on which see RSC Ord 30, r 3 within CPR, Sch 1).

The provisions in s 36 are distinct from the standing of a mortgagor to apply to the court for the fixing of an account between mortgagor and mortgagee, the scope of which extends beyond remuneration, and on which see *Parker-Tweedale v Dunbar Bank plc (No 2)* [1991] Ch 26 (Nourse LJ) and generally *Gomba Holdings Ltd v Minories Finance Ltd (No 2)* [1993] Ch 171 (Scott LJ).

Irrespective of s 36, there appears to be no English authority for the proposition that a receiver may apply to the court for an increase in the remuneration to which the receiver is entitled under the debenture pursuant to which he or she is appointed. However, in *Odessa Promotions Pty Ltd (in liquidation)* (1979) ACLC 49–253 the Supreme Court of Victoria refused to allow receivers to claim scale rates agreed with their appointing debenture-holder following appointment, where those scale rates were in excess of the 5% of all gross monies recovered rate as expressly provided for in the debenture, on the basis that no statutory power existed for such provision to be made.

In *Re Delberry Ltd* [2008] EWHC 925 (Ch), [2008] BPIR 1277, Terence Mowschenson QC (sitting as a deputy High Court judge) held that it was not improper for a liquidator to use s 236 to gather information to determine whether to make an application under s 36.

**The court's approach to an application under s 36(1)**—Section 36(1) allows the court to interfere with the contractual rights of the receiver and mortgagee and involves the court in the exercise of two separate and unfettered discretions. First, the court has a discretion as to whether to interfere at all. Interference, however, should be confined to cases in which the remuneration claimed can be seen on its face, or after only preliminary inquiry, to be excessive rather than the application taking the form of a routine assessment by the court of a receiver's remuneration: *Re Potters Oils Ltd (No 2)* [1986] 1 WLR 201 (Hoffmann J, application by liquidator under s 371 of the Companies Act 1948 dismissed where sum claimed not unreasonable by comparison with official receiver's statutory fees and in any case less than maximum stipulated in debenture). The second discretion, once a decision has been made to fix remuneration, is as to the quantum of such remuneration.

In *Mumms v Perkins* [2002] BPIR 120, applying *Potters Oils*, Evans-Lombe J allowed on appeal a receiver's claim for remuneration equating to 4.2% of the value of assets realised following an application by the debenture-holder under s 35, complaining that the fee in the region of £11,000 claimed by the receiver exceeded an estimate of £3,000 to £4,000 given by telephone prior to appointment. Evans-Lombe J noted in particular that the debenture itself allowed for a remuneration on a time-cost basis, that the conduct of the receivership had largely involved unusual work by way of transferring assets in specie, and that much of the work was conducted by a senior manager.

For some guidance on office-holders' remuneration generally see *Mirror Group Newspapers plc v Maxwell (No 2)* [1998] 1 BCLC 638 (Ferris J) and the report on taxation (now assessment) of Chief Taxing Master Hurst at [1999] BCC 694. The Chief Taxing Master allowed £659,260 of £744,289 remuneration claimed and indicated (at 681E) that 'The correct viewpoint to be taken by a taxing officer in considering whether any step was reasonable was that of a sensible solicitor considering what, in the light of his then knowledge, was reasonable in the interests of his client . . . in assessments on either the standard or indemnity basis'. For further guidance see SIP 9.

SECTION 36(2)

**Scope of provision**—These powers appear exercisable only in the course of an application under s 36(1). Once an order is made under that provision, the court's power is restricted to variation or amendment under s 36(3).

The original form of s 36(2)(a) appeared in s 309 of the Companies Act 1929, which applied only to remuneration claimed after the date of the order.

The meaning of 'special circumstances' in s 36(2)(c) remains unclear; the provision appears to anticipate that a receiver or manager or his personal representatives will only be required to account for pre-order remuneration paid or retained where some exceptional factor, such as remuneration having been drawn on a plainly excessive or exorbitant basis, is at play.

SECTION 36(3)

**Scope of provision**—In practice only a material change in circumstances will warrant an application for variation or amendment under this provision which, it is suggested, is not intended as an appeal mechanism from any order made under s 36(1).

## [1.81]

### 37 Liability for contracts etc

(1)   A receiver or manager appointed under powers contained in an instrument (other than an administrative receiver) is, to the same extent as if he had been appointed by order of the court—

   (a)   personally liable on any contract entered into by him in the performance of his functions (except in so far as the contract otherwise provides) and on any contract of employment adopted by him in the performance of those functions, and

   (b)   entitled in respect of that liability to indemnity out of the assets.

(2)   For the purposes of subsection (1)(a), the receiver or manager is not to be taken to have adopted a contract of employment by reason of anything done or omitted to be done within 14 days after his appointment.

(3)   Subsection (1) does not limit any right to indemnity which the receiver or manager would have apart from it, nor limit his liability on contracts entered into without authority, nor confer any right to indemnity in respect of that liability.

(4)   Where at any time the receiver or manager so appointed vacates office—

   (a)   his remuneration and any expenses properly incurred by him, and

   (b)   any indemnity to which he is entitled out of the assets of the company,

shall be charged on and paid out of any property of the company which is in his custody or under his control at that time in priority to any charge or other security held by the person by or on whose behalf he was appointed.

General note—These provisions apply to non-administrative receivers. Very similar provisions relating to administrative receivers appear in certain parts of s 44, although those provisions, in contrast to s 37, provide expressly – in s 44(1)(a) – that an administrative receiver is the deemed agent of a company until the company's liquidation. The debenture pursuant to which a non-administrative receiver is appointed will usually expressly provide that the receiver is an agent of the company. In the absence of any such provision, it is for the court to consider the nature of the receiver's agency as a matter of construction of the debenture: *Cully v Parsons* [1923] 2 Ch 512. The special nature of the receiver's agency has some 'peculiar incidents': *Silven Properties Ltd v Royal Bank of Scotland plc* [2003] EWCA Civ 1409, [2004] 1 WLR 997, [2004] 1 BCLC 359, [2003] BPIR 1429 at [26]–[27]. Those incidents are explained in the commentary to s 44 to which reference should be made.

The personal liability imposed and the corresponding indemnity provided by these provisions arises 'to the same extent as if [the receiver or manager] had been appointed by order of the court' and applies only to contractual liability. Section 37(3) makes clear, however, that this statutory liability and indemnity will not limit or vary the personal liability of a receiver who enters into a contract without authority, in which circumstances no corresponding indemnity will arise in the receiver's favour. Conversely, and notwithstanding these provisions, a receiver will remain entitled to an indemnity from the company's assets under the terms of any contractual indemnity obtained from the appointing debenture-holder, although in practice the provision of such indemnities by institutional lenders remains a matter for individual cases and is uncommon. Private lenders may be more open to providing a suitable indemnity as a pre-condition of an appointee taking office. In New Zealand it has been held that failure to advise a receiver to obtain such an indemnity may form a basis for a negligence claim by a receiver against an advising solicitor: *RA Price Securities Ltd v Henderson* [1989] 2 NZLR 257, NZCA.

A prospective receiver should always ensure that he or she has in place professional indemnity insurance of an appropriate level to cover the risk of his or her own negligence and that of subordinates.

Section 37 is not concerned with the effects of a receiver causing a company to terminate a subsisting contract with the company in receivership, on which see *Re Newdigate Colliery Ltd* [1912] 1 Ch 468 and *Airline Airspares Ltd v Handley Page Ltd* [1970] Ch 193.

### SECTION 37(1)(a)

**Scope of provision**—The wording of this subparagraph plainly envisages a receiver contracting out of personal liability on contracts – including employment contracts – entered into by him or her 'in the performance of his or her functions'. Such contracting out is usual practice.

**Implying an exclusion of personal liability**—The exclusion of personal liability in practice is frequently not a matter of express agreement but one which is communicated by words endorsed to that effect on the company's notepaper and documents. In *Hill Samuel & Co Ltd v Laing* (1988) 4 BCC 9 the Court of Session in Scotland considered a receiver's claim that express wording in a bank debenture excluded the receiver from personal liability on a loan contract to the bank. In rejecting the view of Cross J, expressed obiter at first instance in *Lawson v Hosemaster Co Ltd* [1965] 1 WLR 1399 at 1410–1411, to the effect that the exclusion of personal liability requires express provision, Lord Cullen indicated that such exclusion is capable of being implied. This approach accords with the common practice in receiverships.

**The adoption by a non-administrative receiver of contracts and contracts of employment**—A receiver does not incur personal liability on an existing contract between the company and a third party, other than a contract of employment, as considered below: *Re Atlantic Computer Systems plc* [1992] Ch 505, [1991] BCLC 606 at 524 (Nicholls LJ).

The question of whether a contract of employment has been 'adopted' by a receiver is one of fact and is considered further in the note to s 37(2) below. Following the House of Lords' decision in *Re Paramount Airways Ltd (No 3), Powdrill v Watson* [1994] 2 BCLC 118 (also considered below) the amending legislation in s 2 of the Insolvency Act 1994 was not extended to non-administrative receivers. There is no good reason why it should not have been.

It follows that a non-administrative receiver may have no option but to terminate subsisting contracts of employment within the 14-day period provided for in s 37(1)(b), with the possible hope of re-negotiating fresh contracts of employment, in the absence of sufficient assets or a contractual indemnity to meet such liabilities as would otherwise be incurred by the non-administrative receiver personally. One practical alternative, albeit one requiring some speed within the 14-day period in s 37(2), is to seek to contract out of such liabilities by express agreement with employees, a possibility which is not excluded by the present provisions and which is hardly in conflict with public policy. In *Powdrill* Dillon LJ resiled from expressing a view on the possibility of contracting out, despite arguments before the Court of Appeal on the point: see [1994] BCC 172 at 180C–180D. The point was neither an issue in, nor discussed on, the subsequent appeal to the House of Lords.

### SECTION 37(1)(b)

**Scope of provision**—The statutory indemnity provided by s 37(1)(b) is only as good as the extent to which a company's assets are capable of meeting those liabilities under s 37(1)(a) to which the indemnity relates.

**The priority of the receiver's claim for remuneration and expenses**—In practice, a well-drawn standard form debenture will ordinarily include an express contractual provision to the effect that a receiver's remuneration and expenses are to be met out of receipts and realisations in priority to the sums secured by the debenture. Even in the absence of such an express provision, a receiver enjoys such priority over the claims of the appointing debenture-holder and preferential creditors, but only from company assets which are not subject to the security of a prior-ranking debenture-holder: *Re Glyncorrwg Colliery Co Ltd* [1926] Ch 951.

### SECTION 37(2)

The 'adoption' of a contract of employment by a receiver—In *Re Paramount Airways Ltd (No 3), Powdrill v Watson* [1994] 2 BCLC 118 Lord Browne-Wilkinson considered that adoption in the context of this subsection arises as a matter of fact if a receiver causes or allows a company to continue a contract of employment for more than 14 days after his appointment by virtue of not taking steps to terminate or repudiate such a contract. Accordingly, correspondence of the so-called *Specialised Mouldings*-type, as commonly employed previously by receivers and administrators as a means of excluding personal liability on employment contracts by unilateral notice, is of no effect in law. The judgment in *Powdrill* lends weight to the view that a contract of employment is capable of termination through a repudiatory act notwithstanding the absence of acceptance of the repudiatory act by the other party, an exception to the general rule to the contrary in contract law.

### SECTION 37(3)

Scope of provision—See the general note above and the note to s 37(1)(b) above for the limits on the scope of this indemnity.

### SECTION 37(4)

Scope of provision—The statutory charge created by this provision in respect of remuneration, expenses and the receiver's indemnity is triggered only on the receiver's vacation from office. Despite its wording, however, this provision will not prevent the receiver drawing remuneration and expenses and claiming on any indemnity during the course of the receivership, such that the charge may only catch outstanding claims on vacation: see *Re Paramount Airways Ltd (No 3), Powdrill v Watson* [1994] 2 BCLC 118 (Dillon LJ); and see *Re Salmet International Ltd* [2001] BPIR 709 (Blackburne J) on very similar wording to the same effect in administrations under the former s 19(4) and (5).

The priority of the s 37(4) statutory charge—The statutory charge secures priority for the receiver only over the security of the appointor. In *Choudhri v Palta* [1992] BCC 787 the Court of Appeal held, in a case involving a court appointed receiver and without addressing s 37 or s 44 specifically, but in making note of s 43, that the court has no jurisdiction to order that a charge, created in that case by order of the court, securing a receiver's remuneration and costs should stand in priority to any prior ranking security. It is submitted that there is no good reason why the position should be different in the case of a non-administrative receiver. For the position of an administrative receiver see s 43 and the notes thereto.

' . . . remuneration . . . '—On the term 'remuneration' in s 37(4)(a), see the notes to s 36. Whether expenses are 'properly incurred' is an issue capable of confirmation by a receiver or the appointor under s 35 or challenged by a liquidator under s 112 or s 168(3) on an application to the court for directions.

' . . . any indemnity . . . '—The reference to 'any indemnity' in s 37(4)(b) extends the charge to both the statutory indemnity in s 37(1)(b) and any contractual indemnity existing in favour of the receiver.

## [1.82]

### 38 Receivership accounts to be delivered to registrar

(1) Except in the case of an administrative receiver, every receiver or manager of a company's property who has been appointed under powers contained in an instrument shall deliver to the registrar of companies for registration the requisite accounts of his receipts and payments.

(2) The accounts shall be delivered within one month (or such longer period as the registrar may allow) after the expiration of 12 months from the date of his appointment and of every subsequent period of 6 months, and also within one month after he ceases to act as receiver or manager.

(3) The requisite accounts shall be an abstract in the prescribed form showing—

  (a) receipts and payments during the relevant period of 12 or 6 months, or

  (b) where the receiver or manager ceases to act, receipts and payments during the period from the end of the period of 12 or 6 months to which the last preceding abstract related (or, if no preceding abstract has been delivered under this section, from the date of his appointment) up to the date of his so ceasing, and the aggregate amount of receipts and payments during all preceding periods since his appointment.

(4) In this section "prescribed" means prescribed by regulations made by statutory instrument by the Secretary of State.

(5) A receiver or manager who makes default in complying with this section is liable to a fine and, for continued contravention, to a daily default fine.

**Amendments**—SI 2013/1947.

**General note**—This provision imposes an obligation on non-administrative receivers to file abstracts of receipts and payments with the Registrar of Companies on a periodical basis. The obligation is enforceable under s 41. The analogous obligations imposed on an administrative receiver are provided for in IR 2016, r 4.17.

**The nature and scope of the receiver's duty to provide information**—In *Gomba Holdings UK Ltd v Homan* [1986] 1 WLR 1301 at 1308 Hoffmann J held that a receiver's duty to provide accounts or other information to a debtor company extended beyond the statutory obligations to account (then contained in ss 497 and 499 of the Companies Act 1985) and included an equitable duty to the company to provide information subject to the company 'demonstrating a "need to know" for the purpose of enabling the board to exercise its residual rights [on which see the note to s 42 below] or perform its duties'. Thus, 'A board which demonstrates a *bona fide* intention and ability to redeem is entitled not merely to a redemption statement showing how much is still owing but also to reasonable information about the nature of the assets remaining in the hands of the receivers. On the other hand, comfortably with the principles I have discussed, I think that the receiver's duty to provide such information must be subordinated to his primary duty not to do anything which may prejudice the interests of the debenture-holder.' Notwithstanding Hoffmann J's reference here to the board of a company, there is no good reason, it is submitted, why this equitable duty should not also be enforceable by a liquidator.

Notwithstanding s 38(2), a receiver is under a general duty to account to the company at the end of the receivership: *Smiths Ltd v Middleton* [1979] 3 All ER 842 (Blackett-Ord V-C).

**SECTION 38(2), (3)(b)**

**Scope of provision**—This obligation triggers where an incumbent receiver or manager 'ceases to act', which will extend to his removal or vacation from office as well as the closure of the receivership.

**SECTION 38(3)**

**Scope of provision**—For building societies see para 25, Sch 15A as inserted by s 6 and Sch 6 of the Building Societies Act 1997.

**SECTION 38(5)**

**Scope of provision**—On penalties see s 430 and Sch 10.

*Provisions applicable to every receivership*

**[1.83]**

### 39 Notification that receiver or manager appointed

(1) Where a receiver or manager of the property of a company has been appointed—

    (a)    every invoice, order for goods or services, business letter or order form (whether in hard copy, electronic or any other form) issued by or on behalf of the company or the receiver or manager or the liquidator of the company; and

    (b)    all the company's websites,

must contain a statement that a receiver or manager has been appointed.

(2) If default is made in complying with this section, the company and any of the following persons, who knowingly and wilfully authorises or permits the default, namely, any officer of the company, any liquidator of the company and any receiver or manager, is liable to a fine.

**Amendments**—SI 2008/1897.

**General note**—In addition to the obligations in s 39(1), an administrative receiver must also comply with the notice and advertisement obligations in s 46(1).

The appointor of a receiver or manager (including an administrative receiver) must, within 7 days of the appointment, give notice to the Registrar of Companies along with any other information as necessary pursuant to s 859K of the Companies Act 2006. The appointment is then entered on the company's register of charges.

**Railway companies and building societies**—The enforcement of security against the assets of a railway company is subject to advance notice requirements imposed by the Railways Act 1993, s 62(7). For building societies see para 25, Sch 15A as inserted by the Building Societies Act 1997, s 6 and Sch 6.

## [1.84]

### 40 Payment of debts out of assets subject to floating charge

(1) The following applies, in the case of a company, where a receiver is appointed on behalf of the holders of any debentures of the company secured by a charge which, as created, was a floating charge.

(2) If the company is not at the time in course of being wound up, its preferential debts (within the meaning given to that expression by section 386 in Part XII) shall be paid out of the assets coming to the hands of the receiver in priority to any claims for principal or interest in respect of the debentures.

(3) Payments made under this section shall be recouped, as far as may be, out of the assets of the company available for payment of general creditors.

General note—Section 40 is of considerable practical importance, in that practitioners must be alive to the risk of trading on floating charge realisations, given the obligations imposed by these provisions. The relevance of preferential claims is now very much reduced, on which see the note to s 40(2). Preferential claims are considered in some detail in Sch 6 and the notes thereto.

The application of s 40 to receivership has the same effect as the Companies Act 1985, s 196 (as amended by the Insolvency Act 1986, s 439(1) and Sch 13) had on a debenture-holder taking possession: *Re H & K (Medway) Ltd* [1997] 1 WLR 1422 at 1426 (Neuberger J). Under the Companies Act 2006, the priorities where debentures are secured by floating charge are now set out at s 754.

The operation of this provision depends very much on the categorisation of security as fixed or floating by the office-holder and, in case of any dispute, the court, on which see the note on floating charges in s 251. The allocation of receivership expenses between fixed and floating charge accounts is also of great practical relevance, since receivership expenses take in priority to preferential claims and floating charge claims.

### SECTION 40(1)

Scope of provision—The combined effect of this provision and s 40(2) is to afford preferential creditors priority over the claims of holders of any charge which, as created, was a floating charge in contrast to the position under the previous legislation. The priority point, therefore, is not concerned with the timing or the fact of the crystallisation of the floating charge.

'... which, as created, was a floating charge'—Under the earlier legislation, in which a floating charge was not defined as in this provision, a floating charge holder could avoid the priority afforded to preferential claims by crystallising the floating charge so that the charge was fixed at the relevant date for the assessment of preferential liabilities. The technique employed in the drafting of this subsection is also employed in s 175(2)(b) and s 251, to which reference should also be made.

### SECTION 40(2)

Scope of provision—The scope of preferential debts was much reduced by the abolition of Crown debts by operation of s 251 of the Enterprise Act 2002, effective from 15 September 2003. Contributions to occupational pension schemes and state pension schemes and certain employee entitlements as identified in Categories 4 and 5 respectively to Sch 6 of the 1986 Act remain preferential. Despite the effective date of the provisions of the 2002 Act, the virtual abolition of preferential debts will also apply to the appointment of administrative receivers pursuant to security created prior to 15 September 2002. In February 2019, HMRC consulted on a proposal announced by the government in its Budget in Autumn 2018 to make HMRC a secondary preferential creditor for taxes paid by employees and customers. The consultation came to an end in May 2019 but, at the time of writing, there had been no update as to how this change would be implemented or when this change will come into effect.

An administrative receiver appointed pursuant to security on or after 15 September 2003 will also fall subject to the obligation to make available a prescribed part of the company's net property under s 176A, although a receiver appointed pursuant to security created prior to that date will not.

'... a company ...'—See here the note under this heading to s 28.

'... in the course of being wound up ...'—A company is 'in the course of being wound up' once a winding-up order has been made against it or a resolution for winding up has been passed: *Re Christonette International Ltd* [1982] 1 WLR 1245 at 1252 (Vinelott J). Also, see, s 247(2). Once a company goes into liquidation, the operation of s 40 is not entirely superseded by s 175(2) whilst the receiver remains in office: see *Re Pearl Maintenance Services Ltd* [1995] 1 BCLC 449 as noted under the heading 'in priority to any claims for principal or interest' below.

**Priority of preferential and secured claims and the receiver's claims for remuneration, costs and expenses where company being wound up**—In *Re Leyland DAF Ltd, Buchler v Talbot* [2004] UKHL 9, [2004] 2 AC 298, [2004] 1 BCLC 281 the House of Lords provided much-needed clarification on the interplay between s 40 and s 175(2)(b), being the current re-enactment of a provision which could be traced back to s 4 of the Companies Act 1883 (and further in bankruptcy), which confers priority on preferential claims over what s 175(2)(b) now terms ' . . . the assets of the company available for payment of general creditors', which are now perhaps more conveniently labelled 'the company's free assets'. In overruling the decision of the Court of Appeal in *Re Barleycorn Enterprises Ltd* [1970] Ch 465 their Lordships were of the opinion in *Buchler* that, whilst s 175(2)(b) amounted to an incursion on the proprietary rights of debenture-holders by way of making provision for the payment of preferential debts out of property subject to a floating charge and in priority to the claims of the charge holder, neither s 175(2)(b) nor any of its statutory predecessors had the effect of authorising the liquidator's costs and expenses of a winding up to be paid out of the assets subject to a floating charge in priority to the claims of the charge holder. The decision in *Buchler* had potentially far-reaching (and unhelpful) implications and has been reversed by way of s 1282 of the Companies Act 2006.

' . . . **assets coming to the hands of the receiver** . . . '—This is a term which does not extend to property subject to a fixed charge, which takes free of this provision, subject to any deed of priority providing otherwise: *Re Lewis Merthyr Consolidated Collieries* [1929] 1 Ch 498 at 511 (Lord Hanworth MR) and 512 (Lawrence LJ) and see also on this point the explanation by Chadwick J in *Re Portbase (Clothing) Ltd* [1993] Ch 388, [1993] BCLC 796.

**Application of fixed charge surplus where debenture-holder discharged in full**—Where a debenture-holder is discharged in full, any fixed charge surplus is payable to the company (or its liquidator) and does not fall subject to any floating charge and is not therefore subject to any preferential claims which would otherwise bite on floating charge assets: *Re GL Saunders* [1986] 1 WLR 215.

**Consequences of a receiver's breach of the positive duty imposed by s 40(2)**—Section 40(2) imposes a positive duty on a receiver to account to preferential creditors from available assets coming into a receiver's hands. Breach of this statutory duty renders the receiver personally liable in damages for resultant loss or, arguably, in tort: *Westminster City Council v Traby* [1936] 2 All ER 21 (Farwell J); *Westminster Corpn v Haste* [1950] Ch 442 at 447 (Danckwerts J).

In *IRC v Goldblatt* [1972] Ch 498, when monies were paid over by a receiver to the company in the knowledge that the company would pay over the monies to the debenture-holder with notice of the receiver's statutory duty in satisfaction of the debenture-holder's claim, Goff J held that the debenture-holder held the monies on constructive trust for the preferential creditor, although it must be doubtful, it is submitted, that notice is relevant to such a claim where damages are sought on a restitutionary basis. Where a claim is brought against a receiver by a creditor in such circumstances, the receiver will be entitled to an indemnity from the debenture-holder: see *Westminster City Council v Traby*.

For an unsuccessful restitutionary claim against a charge holder following a payment by administrative receivers in contravention of s 40, see *Re BHT (UK) Ltd, Duckworth v Nat West Finance Ltd* [2004] EWHC 201 (Ch), [2004] 1 BCLC 569.

' . . . **in priority to any claims for principal or interest** . . . '—Whilst it might be argued that the term 'in priority to any claims for principal or interest' points to the positive duty imposed by s 40(2) ceasing once claims of floating charge holders have been met in full, a contrary view was reached by Carnwarth J in *Re Pearl Maintenance Services Ltd* [1995] 1 BCLC 449. Notwithstanding appointment by a debenture-holder, the duty imposed by s 40(2) is capable of a separate life of its own which is not brought to an end on discharge of a debt secured by a floating charge. Until vacation of office, the receiver remains under a duty to meet preferential claims so far as possible out of floating charge assets.

' . . . **the debentures** . . . '—The reference to 'the debentures' at the end of this subsection is a reference back to 'any debentures of the company secured by a charge which, as created, was a floating charge' in s 40(1) and, as such, is not merely a reference to any debenture or debentures pursuant to which a receiver has been appointed: *Re H & K (Medway) Ltd* [1997] 1 WLR 1422, [1997] 1 BCLC 545 at 1427. The statutory duty imposed on the receiver and manager extends to all such debentures. In *Medway* Neuberger J departed from the decision in *Griffiths v Yorkshire Bank plc* [1994] 1 WLR 1427, in which Morritt J in considering s 196 of the Companies Act 1985 in its earlier form, had construed the term 'the debentures' in the narrower sense. Neuberger J noted, however, that Morritt J had not heard submissions on behalf of preferential creditors and that the report of the decision in *Griffiths* was doubtful.

**Building societies**—These provisions are inapplicable to building societies: see para 27, Sch 15A as inserted by the Building Societies Act 1997, s 39 and Sch 6.

SECTION 40(3)

Scope of provision—The receiver's right of recoupment from assets which would otherwise become available to unsecured creditors under this subsection is only triggered once payment to preferential creditors is made from floating charge assets pursuant to s 40(2).

## [1.85]

### 41 Enforcement of duty to make returns

(1)  If a receiver or manager of a company's property—

    (a)    having made default in filing, delivering or making any return, account or other document, or in giving any notice, which a receiver or manager is by law required to file, deliver, make or give, fails to make good the default within 14 days after the service on him of a notice requiring him to do so, or

    (b)    having been appointed under powers contained in an instrument, has, after being required at any time by the liquidator of the company to do so, failed to render proper accounts of his receipts and payments and to vouch them and pay over to the liquidator the amount properly payable to him,

the court may, on an application made for the purpose, make an order directing the receiver or manager (as the case may be) to make good the default within such time as may be specified in the order.

(2)  In the case of the default mentioned in subsection (1)(a), application to the court may be made by any member or creditor of the company or by the registrar of companies; and in the case of the default mentioned in subsection (1)(b), the application shall be made by the liquidator.

In either case the court's order may provide that all costs of and incidental to the application shall be borne by the receiver or manager, as the case may be.

(3)  Nothing in this section prejudices the operation of any enactment imposing penalties on receivers in respect of any such default as is mentioned in subsection (1).

General note—These enforcement provisions are not restricted to the obligations prescribed by s 38.

SECTION 41(1)(a)

Scope of provision—No form is prescribed for a notice under s 41(1)(a).

SECTION 41(1)(b)

Scope of provision—This provision extends beyond the accounts etc identified in s 41(1)(a) and permits a liquidator specifically, following a request for such information by or on his or her behalf, to seek an order requiring not only the rendering and vouching of proper receipts and payments accounts but also payment of the account properly due to the liquidator. For a receiver's duty to account see s 38 and the notes thereto.

SECTION 41(2)

Scope of provision—Although the court would in any case have jurisdiction to make an order against the receiver or manager personally, this subsection confirms that the court should positively consider the making of such an order. A direction within an order precluding the receiver from recouping such costs from the assets of the company will prevent those costs being borne ultimately by the company's unsecured creditors.

For the standing of the FCA and PRA to apply for an enforcement order see FMSA 2000, s 363(3).

*Administrative receivers: general*

## [1.86]

### 42 General powers

(1)  The powers conferred on the administrative receiver of a company by the debentures by virtue of which he was appointed are deemed to include (except in so far as they are inconsistent with any of the provisions of those debentures) the powers specified in Schedule 1 to this Act.

(2)  In the application of Schedule 1 to the administrative receiver of a company—

(a)    the words "he" and "him" refer to the administrative receiver, and

(b)    references to the property of the company are to the property of which he is or, but for the appointment of some other person as the receiver of part of the company's property, would be the receiver or manager.

(3)    A person dealing with the administrative receiver in good faith and for value is not concerned to inquire whether the receiver is acting within his powers.

**General note**—In addition to the powers identified in the note to s 42(1) below, an administrative receiver, like a non-administrative receiver, will, in this capacity as an agent, and subject to contrary provision in the debenture pursuant to which he or she is appointed, enjoy implied authority to do all those things necessary for or incidental to the effective exercise of the receiver's express authority in the ordinary course. For the nature of the agency of an administrative receiver see the note to s 44(1) below.

Notably, s 43 confers an additional power to dispose of property subject to prior or equal ranking security, which is unique to an administrative receiver, but similar to a less extensive power available to an administrator under para 70(1) of Sch B1. An administrative receiver is also empowered to require continued supply of utilities (s 233) and delivery up of property (s 234).

### SECTION 42(1)

**Scope of provision**—The technique adopted by the legislation here is to imply into the contractual debenture pursuant to which an administrative receiver is appointed those express powers in Sch 1, save to the extent that the debenture provides to the contrary. In practice, standard form debentures commonly provide such express powers, in any case, which will be effective on the appointment of a non-administrative receiver whose powers do not derive from Sch 1 but are dictated by the debenture itself. For further commentary on the nature of the Sch 1 powers and for the effect of liquidation on the exercise of a receiver's powers, see the notes to s 44(1) below.

**The liability of receivers for costs in proceedings brought by a company in receivership**—Where receivers cause a company to bring proceedings there is no general rule that the receivers should be personally liable for the costs of the successful party; the normal expectation is that the successful party would and should seek an order for security for costs against the company in receivership: *Dolphin Quays Developments Ltd v Mills* [2008] EWCA Civ 385, [2008] 1 WLR 1829, [2008] 2 BCLC 774 (Mummery, Lawrence Collins LJJ and Munby J upholding the decision of Morritt C to the effect that neither the appointing bank nor the receivers was a real party to the proceedings, which involved the enforcement of a contractual claim, and that there were no exceptional circumstances taking the case out of the ordinary run of cases to justify the imposition of a personal costs order).

**The residual status and powers of directors in receivership**—The appointment of an administrative receiver or, indeed, any receiver, does not displace the directors from office. Rather, the directors remain in office, although their powers as such are effective only to the extent that the same powers are not assumed by the administrative receiver either by virtue of the Sch 1 powers or by virtue of the appointing debenture-holder's security encompassing property, such as a cause of action, which would otherwise be available to the company: *Newhart v Co-operative Commercial Bank* [1978] QB 814 at 819 (Shaw LJ). It is suggested that, in order to avoid an unhelpful and unintended confusion of interests between the company and receiver/debenture-holder, the directors may assume a right to exercise a power or control of an asset available to an administrative receiver only on the receiver, as agent of the debenture-holder, giving a clear and unambiguous indication of his or her consent to such a course. In some cases, most obviously involving a cause of action caught by a debenture-holder's security, it may be necessary for the debenture-holder to re-assign the asset to the company so as to allow for its pursuit or realisation by the company acting by its directors.

In *Newhart* Shaw LJ was mindful of the potential embarrassment to receivers seeking to enforce causes of action against their appointing debenture-holders and perceived no difficulty in such claims being pursued by the company itself: see, for example, *Watts v Midland Bank* [1986] 2 BCC 98, 961 (Peter Gibson J) (no reason why a company should not sue a receiver in respect of an improper exercise of powers). In *Tudor Grange Holdings Ltd v Citibank* [1992] Ch 53, [1991] BCLC 1009 Browne-Wilkinson V-C doubted the reasoning in *Newhart* and identified s 35 as a mechanism by which a receiver might avoid embarrassment by seeking directions as to the proper course to be taken by him or her in a case involving the appointor. Whilst bound by *Newhart*, the Vice-Chancellor took the view that any claim by the company acting by its directors would be liable to be struck out in the absence of a complete indemnity from the directors for the costs of the proposed action. It should be noted that it is only the provision of such an indemnity which guards against the risk of the dissipation of company assets to the cost of the debenture-holder and/or the company's unsecured creditors, a point underpinning the reasoning of Keane J in the Irish High Court in *Lascomme Ltd v United Dominions Trust* [1994] ILRM 224 in reconciling the decision in *Newhart* with that in *Tudor Grange*.

SECTION 42(3)

Scope of provision—Whilst the third party is not required to inquire as to whether a receiver is acting within powers, this provision is predicated on the assumption that the receiver is validly appointed. No protection is afforded to a third party dealing with a receiver who is never validly appointed. For the distinction between an invalid appointment and one subject to procedural defects, see ss 34 and 232 and the notes thereto.

## [1.87]

### 43 Power to dispose of charged property etc

(1)   Where, on an application by the administrative receiver, the court is satisfied that the disposal (with or without other assets) of any relevant property which is subject to a security would be likely to promote a more advantageous realisation of the company's assets than would otherwise be effected, the court may by order authorise the administrative receiver to dispose of the property as if it were not subject to the security.

(2)   Subsection (1) does not apply in the case of any security held by the person by or on whose behalf the administrative receiver was appointed, or of any security to which a security so held has priority.

(3)   It shall be a condition of an order under this section that—

    (a)    the net proceeds of the disposal, and

    (b)    where those proceeds are less than such amount as may be determined by the court to be the net amount which would be realised on a sale of the property in the open market by a willing vendor, such sums as may be required to make good the deficiency,

shall be applied towards discharging the sums secured by the security.

(4)   Where a condition imposed in pursuance of subsection (3) relates to two or more securities, that condition shall require the net proceeds of the disposal and, where paragraph (b) of that subsection applies, the sums mentioned in that paragraph to be applied towards discharging the sums secured by those securities in the order of their priorities.

(5)   A copy of an order under this section shall, within 14 days of the making of the order, be sent by the administrative receiver to the registrar of companies.

(6)   If the administrative receiver without reasonable excuse fails to comply with subsection (5), he is liable to a fine and, for continued contravention, to a daily default fine.

(7)   In this section "relevant property", in relation to the administrative receiver, means the property of which he is or, but for the appointment of some other person as the receiver of part of the company's property, would be the receiver or manager.

Amendments—SI 2009/1941.

General note—It is, of course, open to a debenture-holder to sell property subject to its security, without the requirement for a court order, either as mortgagee-in-possession or by way of its receiver, so as to override the interests of subsequent mortgagees. The detailed provisions dealing with a mortgagee's power of sale appear in ss 101–107 of the Law of Property Act 1925. Where there are several mortgagees interested in the same land, a prior mortgagee holds any surplus proceeds on trust for later mortgagees of whose incumbrances the prior mortgagee has notice, subject to the payment of the expenses of sale: *Thorne v Heard and Marsh* [1895] AC 495, and see s 105 of the Law of Property Act 1925. However, no such power exists in relation to a security interest ranking in priority or equal to that of a mortgagee wishing to realise its security. So as to facilitate rescue schemes and to avoid the potentially obstructive fetter of such security, s 43, in accordance with a recommendation of the Cork Committee in its review (at paras 1510–1513), provides an additional power to an administrative receiver to seek the authority of the court for a sale of such property charged in favour of a prior ranking mortgagee as if the property were not subject to such security. Although the above commentary refers to interests in land, s 43 has general application to security interests held over property in any form.

Section 43 has no application in Scotland: s 440(2)(a).

For the non-application of this provision to so-called market charges within the meaning of s 173 of the Companies Act 1989, see s 175 of the Companies Act 1989 and the Financial Markets and Insolvency Regulations 1991 (SI 1991/880, 1995/586 and 1998/27).

Procedure—For procedure see r 4.16.

**SECTION 43(1)**

Scope of provision—The phrase 'with or without other assets' envisages the possibility of certain parts of the charged property being subject to prior or equal security where a composite sale, typically of a business as a going concern (on which see paras 2, 15 and 16 of Sch 1), is envisaged.

The term 'likely' should, it is suggested, be construed in accordance with the relatively low threshold of the 'real prospect' test laid down by Hoffmann J in *Re Harris Simons Construction Ltd* [1989] 1 WLR 368, [1989] BCLC 202 in relation to the former administration order regime under s 8(1)(b).

**SECTION 43(2)**

Scope of provision—No application is necessary where, for example, an administrative receiver is appointed under a floating charge (and, usually, accompanying fixed charges in the same debenture) where the appointing debenture-holder itself also holds prior ranking security pursuant to which the appointment is not made.

**SECTION 43(3)**

Scope of provision—These conditions (and those in s 43(4) below) must be taken as binding by statutory force on a debenture-holder, even if not incorporated – as they should be – in the court's order following a s 43 application.

' . . . net proceeds . . . '—The reference to 'net proceeds' in s 43(3)(a) allows for the costs of realisation in favour of the appointing debenture-holder.

' . . . where those proceeds are less than such amount as may be determined by the court . . . '—The practical effect of s 43(3)(b) is that, where the proceeds are less than the amount specified by the court on the hearing of the application, the shortfall must be paid to the prior or equal ranking security holder by, and from the assets available to, the appointing debenture-holder – and seemingly from it in any case if those funds are insufficient – in priority to any preferential claims and those of any other creditors.

Where the net realisation figure assessed by the court is higher than the actual open-market value, s 43(3)(b) dictates that the prior or equal ranking security holder stands to benefit from any windfall in terms of the potential consequent shortfall to be made good by the appointing debenture-holder. In these circumstances an application may be made for a revision by the court of its assessment of the net realisation figure prior to sale. The provisions in s 43(3) do not envisage any such application being made following sale.

Section 43 application coinciding with dispute as to validity of security—Where an application coincides with a dispute as to the validity of a prior ranking security or the competing priority of securities there is, it is submitted, every good reason why the court should not entertain a s 43 application and should instead make an order pursuant to s 43(1) or s 35 or the court's inherent jurisdiction to the effect that the proceeds of sale are to be held as directed by the court, or as agreed between the parties, pending resolution of the dispute: compare the contrary and, with respect, doubtful view of HHJ O'Donoghue in *Re Newman Shopfitters (Cleveland) Ltd* [1991] BCLC 407 in relation to an administration case under the former s 15(2).

**SECTION 43(4)**

Scope of provision—This provision is a logical extension of s 43(3) where there are two or more prior or equal ranking securities.

**SECTION 43(5), (6)**

Scope of provision—For the penalties in relation to these administrative provisions see s 430 and Sch 10.

**SECTION 43(7)**

Scope of provision—This provision defines the term 'relevant property' as employed in s 43(1). For further explanation see the notes to s 29(2).

**[1.88]**

**44 Agency and liability for contracts**

(1) The administrative receiver of a company—

    (a)    is deemed to be the company's agent, unless and until the company goes into liquidation;

    (b)    is personally liable on any contract entered into by him in the carrying out of his functions (except in so far as the contract otherwise provides) and, to the extent of any qualifying liability, on any contract of employment adopted by him in the carrying out of those functions; and

(c)     is entitled in respect of that liability to an indemnity out of the assets of the company.

(2)   For the purposes of subsection (1)(b) the administrative receiver is not to be taken to have adopted a contract of employment by reason of anything done or omitted to be done within 14 days after his appointment.

(2A)   For the purposes of subsection (1)(b), a liability under a contract of employment is a qualifying liability if—

(a)     it is a liability to pay a sum by way of wages or salary or contribution to an occupational pension scheme,

(b)     it is incurred while the administrative receiver is in office, and

(c)     it is in respect of services rendered wholly or partly after the adoption of the contract.

(2B)   Where a sum payable in respect of a liability which is a qualifying liability for the purposes of subsection (1)(b) is payable in respect of services rendered partly before and partly after the adoption of the contract, liability under subsection (1)(b) shall only extend to so much of the sum as is payable in respect of services rendered after the adoption of the contract.

(2C)   For the purposes of subsections (2A) and (2B)—

(a)     wages or salary payable in respect of a period of holiday or absence from work through sickness or other good cause are deemed to be wages or (as the case may be) salary in respect of services rendered in that period, and

(b)     a sum payable in lieu of holiday is deemed to be wages or (as the case may be) salary in respect of services rendered in the period by reference to which the holiday entitlement arose.

(2D)   . . .

(3)   This section does not limit any right to indemnity which the administrative receiver would have apart from it, nor limit his liability on contracts entered into or adopted without authority, nor confer any right to indemnity in respect of that liability.

**Amendments**—Insolvency Act 1994, s 2; Deregulation Act 2015, s 19, Sch 6, Pt 7, paras 24, 26.

**General note**—Section 44 applies to administrative receivers only. Sections 44(1)(b) and (c) and 44(2) mirror those provisions in ss 37(1)(a) and (b) and 37(2) in relation to non-administrative receivers. Administrative receivers alone, however, are afforded the protection of the 'qualifying liability' regime provided for in ss 44(1)(b) and 44(2A)–(2D) as modified and inserted by s 2(1), (3) and (4) of the Insolvency Act 1994. Those new provisions limit the personal liability of an administrative receiver for services rendered wholly or in part after adoption of a contract for such services on or after 15 March 1994 and were introduced by Parliament in response to the decision of the Court of Appeal in *Re Paramount Airways Ltd (No 3), Powdrill v Watson* [1993] BCC 662.

### SECTION 44(1)(a)

**Scope of provision**—The deeming of an administrative receiver as agent of a company until liquidation is consistent with an express term to such effect commonly found in practice in debenture documents. This deemed agency, however, is unusual in nature since it does not operate for the benefit of the company – which itself has no power to determine the agency relationship or to control the function of the administrative receiver – but, rather, serves to protect the appointing debenture-holder's security: *Gomba Holdings UK Ltd v Minories Finance Ltd* [1993] Ch 171 (Fox LJ). The deeming of the administrative receiver as agent of the company also serves to insulate the appointing debenture-holder from liability for the acts or omissions of the receiver. The debenture-holder is, however, at risk of incurring such liability if the acts or omissions of the receiver can be shown to have been undertaken on the instructions of the debenture-holder, in which case the receiver will amount to the de facto agent of the debenture-holder notwithstanding s 44(1)(a): *American Express International Banking Corp v Hurley* [1986] BCLC 52 (Mann J).

**The receiver's duties to the company in receivership are subordinate to the duties owed to the appointing debenture-holder**—The receiver's position is dual-faceted in terms of the duties owed contemporaneously to the company and to the appointing debenture-holder. It is well established that the receiver's duties to the company over the assets of which he or she is appointed are subordinate to the receiver's primary duties owed to his or her appointing debenture-holder: *Downsview Nominees Ltd v First City Corp Ltd* [1993] AC 295, [1994] 2 BCLC 49 (Lord Templeman). The receiver owes an equitable duty to the company (together with all those interested in the equity of redemption) but owes a further primary duty to the appointor to exercise powers to bring about a situation in which the secured debt of the appointor is repaid: *Silven Properties Ltd v Royal Bank of Scotland plc* [2003] EWCA Civ 1409, [2004] 1 WLR 997,

[2004] 1 BCLC 359, [2003] BPIR 1429 at [26]–[27]. It is possible to exclude liability for a non-administrative receiver's equitable duty to the company, but clear language will be required to do so: *CNM Estates (Tolworth Tower) Ltd v Vecref I Sarl* [2020] EWHC 1605 (Comm), [2020] PNLR 27, per Foxton J at [34]–[40].

**Termination of the receiver's agency consequent upon liquidation**—An administrative receiver may cause a company to enter into contractual and other liabilities or, alternatively, the receiver may enter into such liabilities personally as agent of the company. Liquidation has the effect of terminating the power of the receiver to act as agent and to cause the company to commit to such liabilities, in addition to bringing to an end the indemnity out of the company's assets in favour of the receiver under s 44(1)(c). The fact of liquidation, however, does nothing to terminate the receivership itself or the standing of the receiver to exercise in rem security rights, in the name of the appointing debenture-holder as mortgagee or chargee or in the name of the company, for the benefit of the debenture-holder: *Sowman v David Samuel Trust Ltd* [1978] 1 WLR 22 (Goulding J) and the later decision in *Barrows v Chief Land Registrar* (1977) *The Times*, October 20 (receiver entitled to exercise power of sale in debenture in conveying legal estate in the name of company in receivership following winding up).

**The duties of a receiver in carrying on the business of a company**—A receiver will incur no liability to the company, or, indeed, to a junior ranking secured creditor, a guarantor or any other party with an interest in the equity of redemption if he or she acts in good faith and (a) in exercising powers of management he or she tries to bring about a situation in which interests on the secured debt can be paid and the debt itself repaid, and (b) in carrying on the business constituted by the charged assets (there being no such obligation imposed on the receiver) all reasonable steps are taken to carry on the business profitably: *Medforth v Blake* [2000] Ch 86, [1999] 2 BCLC 221, [1999] BPIR 712 (Sir Richard Scott V-C). Yet the receiver is not managing the mortgagor's property for the mortgagor's benefit but, rather, the mortgagee's security for the mortgagee's benefit: *Silven Properties Ltd v Royal Bank of Scotland plc* [2003] EWCA Civ 1409, [2004] 1 WLR 997, [2004] 1 BCLC 359, [2003] BPIR 1429 (Lightman J delivering judgment, Aldous and Tuckey LJJ agreeing).

**The duties of a receiver as regards sale of property under his control: timing**—In *Bell v Long* [2008] EWHC 1273 (Ch), [2008] 2 BCLC 706, [2008] BPIR 1211 Patten J held that though a receiver is effectively in the same position as a mortgagee and owes duties to those with an interest in the equity of redemption, the receiver is not trustee of the power to sell for the mortgagor and is therefore entitled to choose the time for sale, even if that course later turns out to have been disadvantageous to the mortgagor. However, unlike the mortgagee, the receiver is not able to remain passive and must act if failure to do so would damage the interests of the mortgagor or mortgagee: *Silven Properties Ltd v Royal Bank of Scotland plc* [2003] EWCA Civ 1409, [2004] 1 WLR 997, [2004] 1 BCLC 359, [2003] BPIR 1429 at [23]. Generally, the position is that a receiver is under no duty to exercise a power of sale but, if goods under his or her control are perishable, such a duty may arise: *Silven Properties Ltd* at [23].

**The duties of a receiver as regards the sale of property under his control: price**—In *Cuckmere Brick Co Ltd v Mutual Finance Ltd* [1971] Ch 949 the Court of Appeal held that a mortgagee exercising power of sale was under an equitable duty to take reasonable care to obtain a 'proper price' (or 'true market value' as preferred by Salmon LJ). Where a property has been exposed to the market before sale, the court should assess whether it achieved a proper price by considering first the steps taken to market the property and then to consider whether, in all the circumstances, it was reasonable to sell at that price: *Centenary Homes Ltd v Liddell* [2020] EWHC 1080 (QB), John Kimbell QC (sitting as a deputy High Court judge) at [118]. A receiver exercising power of sale also owes the same specific duties as the mortgagee: *Medforth v Blake* [2000] Ch 86, [1999] 2 BCLC 221, [1999] BPIR 712 at 98. Patten J has more recently remarked that the characterisation of the receiver's duty as a duty to obtain the 'best price reasonably obtainable at the time of sale' is not an accurate or adequate description of the duty as an absolute test of liability regardless of the circumstances prevailing at the time of the decision to market and sell: *Bell v Long* [2008] EWHC 1273 (Ch), [2008] 2 BCLC 706, [2008] BPIR 1211. This duty does not, however, require the receiver to undertake any improvement to the property so as to increase its value: *Ahmad v Bank of Scotland* [2016] EWCA Civ 602, per Lewison LJ at [38]. As such, if a receiver decides to sell a property with a known defect, that will not automatically give rise to an argument that the sale was at an undervalue where, if that defect had been remedied, it could have achieved a higher sale price: *Centenary Homes Ltd v Liddell* [2020] EWHC 1080 (QB), John Kimbell QC (sitting as a deputy High Court judge) at [116].

**The duties of a receiver as regards the sale of property under his control: method**—In *Bell v Long* Patten J held that administrative receivers were entitled to sell four properties as a portfolio at a discount on their individual valuations since such a sale guaranteed realisation as opposed to the uncertainties of a longer marketing period in uncertain market conditions. To challenge a receiver's decision to sell property under his or her control by a particular method it is necessary to identify from the outset (i) what specific duties are relied upon, as can run collaterally and without conflict to the duties owed to the mortgagee and (ii) the facts relied upon as establish a breach of those duties. Merely identifying alternative strategies or decisions the receivers might have made in general terms is insufficient: *Centenary Homes Limited v Gershinson* (unreported) Queen's Bench Division, 19 September 2017, Master Thornett at [35]–[36].

**Liability of the receiver for rates**—In *Re Beck Foods Ltd, Boston BC v Rees* [2001] EWCA Civ 1934, [2002] 1 WLR 1304, [2002] BPIR 665 the Court of Appeal (Pill and Jonathan Parker LJJ) confirmed that the management and carrying on of a business by a receiver does not bring to an end the rateable occupation of a property by the company so as to make the receiver personally liable as the rateable occupier. That decision is consistent with the earlier judgment of the Court of Appeal in *Ratford v Northavon District Council* [1987] QB 357, and in particular the judgment of Slade LJ at 374E and 376E, which had held that the fact of a receiver entering into a company's premises for the purpose of managing and carrying on its business did not of itself bring about the cessation of the company's rateable occupation. The position is not affected by the fact of the company going into liquidation during the course of the receivership. In *Beck* the company had been placed into creditors' voluntary liquidation less than 3 months after the appointment of the receivers, following which part of the company's business was continued by the receivers at the company's premises until the eventual sale of all of the assets some 7 months later; the liquidation, which had been brought about by the receivers themselves for the purpose of protecting the interests of unsecured creditors, involved no change in the day-to-day conduct of the business which was monitored by the receivers by way of a weekly site visit. It is submitted that a receiver may incur liability for rateable occupation if, as a matter of fact, the receiver can be said to have taken possession and gone into occupation of the premises; in those circumstances a receiver will be personally liable for rates if he or she has lost his or her position as agent of the company through liquidation, subject to any indemnity in the receiver's favour from the appointor. It is further submitted that, based on the reasoning in both *Beck* and *Ratford*, a receiver will not incur a liability for rates if premises are actually unoccupied, on which see *Bannister v Islington London Borough Council* (1971) LGR 239 and *Re Sobam BV* [1996] 1 WLR 1070, [1996] 1 BCLC 446. An administrative receiver cannot be required by a rating authority to exercise any power or discretion to pay rates; neither are such rates payable as an expense of the receivership: *Brown v City of London Corporation* [1996] 1 WLR 1070, [1996] 1 BCLC 446.

**Administrative receiver as shadow director?**—It is inconceivable that an administrative receiver would fall within the definition of 'shadow director' in s 251 and s 744 of the Companies Act 1985 by virtue of deemed agency for the company alone, though the point might be arguable where the administrative receiver acts beyond the scope of his or her office.

**Change of control**—In the context of obtaining group relief from UK corporation tax, the appointment of an administrative receivership constituted a change of control (Henderson LJ in *Farnborough Airport Properties Co v HMRC* [2019] EWCA Civ 118, [2019] 1 WLR 4077, at [64]–[70]). This decision was predicated on the particular interpretation of 'control' for the purposes of s 154 of the Corporation Tax Act 2010.

Outside the context of group relief from UK corporation tax, the Lands Chamber of the Upper Tribunal considered the validity of a company's sale of a property that had been effected by the company's director after a receiver had been appointed. It was found that the sale was valid as s 26 of the Land Registration Act 2002 provided that a purchaser was entitled to assume that the seller had the power to make the disposition unless a suitable restriction was recorded by an entry in the register of title. In such circumstances, receivers appointed in respect of property may be well advised to make such an entry on the register to reflect their appointment and the limitation on the power of the company to make dispositions of the property. *Ghai v Maymask (228) Ltd* [2020] UKUT 293 (LC).

## SECTION 44(1)(b)

**Scope of provision**—This provision provides that administrative receivers are personally liable on a contract entered into by them in two distinct scenarios. First, personal liability arises where the administrative receiver enters into a contract, save to the extent that the contract provides to the contrary, most obviously by identifying the principal company – and not the administrative receiver – as the contracting party. The administrative receiver's powers to cause the company to enter into such a contract terminate on liquidation: see s 44(1)(a) above. The commentary on the contracting out of personal liability by a receiver in the notes to s 37(1)(a) above applies equally to an administrative receiver. The second scenario in which an administrative receiver incurs personal liability on a contract arises where a contract of employment is 'adopted by him', in which case liability is capped to the extent that the liability amounts to a 'qualifying liability' as defined and provided for in s 44(2A)–(2D).

**The concept of 'qualifying liability'**—The introduction of the concept of capping the administrative receiver's liabilities to the extent of one or more qualifying liabilities in the modifications and amendments introduced by the Insolvency Act 1994 followed from the decision of the Court of Appeal in *Re Paramount Airways Ltd (No 3), Powdrill v Watson* [1993] BCC 662, which severely hampered the objective of corporate rescue in rejecting any legal basis for the common (former) practice by which administrative receivers (and administrators) had written to employees within the 14-day period provided for in s 44(2) giving unilateral notice in standard form that an employee's contract of employment would be continued as previously but that the administrative receiver (or administrator) was not to be taken as adopting a contract and, as such, assumed no personal liability on the contract of employment. That practice had been followed by office-holders based on an unreported decision of Harman J (which had never been reduced to writing) in *Re Specialised Mouldings Ltd* (Chancery Division, 13 February 1987) which, on an application by an administrative receiver for directions under s 35, had held that such letters were effective in avoiding adoption notwithstanding the continuation of any affected contract of employment in fact beyond the s 44(2) 14-day period. As such, *Specialised Mouldings* letters had had the effect of protecting office-holders from the effects of the decision in *Nicoll v Cutts* [1985] BCLC 322.

The true meaning of adoption—In *Paramount* the Court of Appeal had upheld the decision of Evans-Lombe J at first instance to the effect that adoption by an office-holder was a question of fact which was determined by any act or acquiescence after the 14-day statutory period and which was indicative of the office-holder's intention to treat the contract as being on foot. In addition, the Court of Appeal held that a continuing contract which had been adopted by an office-holder was only capable of being adopted in its entirety.

The appeal from the decision of the Court of Appeal in *Paramount* was consolidated with appeals from the decisions of Lightman J in *Re Leyland DAF Ltd (No 2)* and *Re Ferranti International plc* [1994] BCC 654. On appeal, the House of Lords held that adoption may only apply to a contract as a whole and requires conduct amounting to an election as a matter of fact on the part of the office-holder to treat the continued employment as a separate liability in the receivership (or administration), although that conduct may apparently involve nothing more than a failure on the part of the office-holder to terminate or repudiate a contract of employment within the statutory 14-day period: see [1995] 2 AC 394, [1994] 1 BCLC 386 at 448, 449, 450 and 452 (Lord Brown-Wilkinson).

In *Re Antal International Ltd (in administration)* [2003] EWHC 1339 (Ch), [2003] 2 BCLC 406, [2003] BPIR 1067 the court was asked to determine whether administrators had adopted contracts of employment where the administrators had genuinely but erroneously believed that employees were employed by a French subsidiary where, on discovering that the French subsidiary did not exist, the administrators had taken all necessary steps to terminate the employment contracts in accordance with French law. Neuberger J held that the contracts of employment had not been adopted on the basis that there was no evidence of conduct on the part of the administrators capable of constituting an election to carry on the contracts.

Can an office-holder contract out of adoption?—It is suggested that there is no good reason why, in principle, an administrative receiver should not seek to contract out of the consequences of adoption of a contract of employment. Such express contracting-out would, however, it is further submitted, require the express agreement of employees and might be seen as less likely in any case, given the reduction of the receiver's liabilities by way of the introduction of the scheme of qualifying liabilities.

For the notification of proposed redundancies to a trade union or employee representative see s 188 of the Trade Union and Labour Relations (Consolidation) Act 1992.

' . . . in the carrying out of his functions . . . '—Both scenarios in which an administrative receiver may incur personal liability on a contract, as discussed above in the note to s 44(1)(b), assume the contract had been entered into by an administrative receiver 'in the carrying out of his functions'. It is very difficult to see how an administrative receiver might incur personal liability other than in the carrying out of his or her functions other than where an office-holder intentionally incurs a liability which is not in any way incidental to the preservation and/or realisation of secured assets; in such circumstances the administrative receiver will not have the benefit of the indemnity in s 44(1)(c).

## SECTION 44(2)

Scope of provision—On adoption of a contract of employment see the notes to s 44(1)(b) above.

## SECTION 44(2A)–(2D)

Scope of provision—These provisions elaborate on the term 'qualifying liability' in s 44(1)(b). Essentially, qualifying liabilities are limited to those restricted classes incurred under the adopted contract of employment whilst the administrative receiver is in office.

Statutory compensation for unfair dismissal will not amount to a qualifying liability, since such liability does not accrue under a contract of employment: *Re Paramount (No 3)* [1994] 2 BCLC 118 at 132E.

Whether or not a particular liability amounts to a qualifying liability is a question determined on the particular facts of the case based on all surrounding circumstances which are known or ought to have been known to the parties: *Re A Company (No 005174 of 1999)* [2000] 1 WLR 502, [2000] 1 BCLC 593 at 508 (Neuberger J).

## SECTION 44(3)

**Scope of provision**—The commentary and the notes to s 37(1)(b), s 37(3) and the general note to s 37 apply equally to this provision.

## [1.89]

### 45 Vacation of office

(1) An administrative receiver of a company may at any time be removed from office by order of the court (but not otherwise) and may resign his office by giving notice of his resignation in the prescribed manner to such persons as may be prescribed.

(2) An administrative receiver shall vacate office if he ceases to be qualified to act as an insolvency practitioner in relation to the company.

(3) Where at any time an administrative receiver vacates office—

    (a)    his remuneration and any expenses properly incurred by him, and

    (b)    any indemnity to which he is entitled out of the assets of the company,

shall be charged on and paid out of any property of the company which is in his custody or under his control at that time in priority to any security held by the person by or on whose behalf he was appointed.

(4) Where an administrative receiver vacates office otherwise than by death, he shall, within 14 days after his vacation of office, send a notice to that effect to the registrar of companies.

(5) If an administrative receiver without reasonable excuse fails to comply with subsection (4), he is liable to a fine *and, for continued contravention, to a daily default fine.*

**Amendments**—Words in italics prospectively repealed by Companies Act 1989, ss 107, 212, Sch 16, para 3(3), Sch 24, from a date to be appointed.

**General note**—An administrative receiver will hold office until his resignation or removal by the court under s 45(1) or, alternatively, in the event of ceasing to be qualified to act as an insolvency practitioner in relation to a company under s 45(2), on death (on which see r 4.19) or on vacating office on completion of the receivership (on which see rr 4.20–4.21). Unlike a non-administrative receiver, an administrative receiver may not be removed by the appointing debenture-holder. The logic in this apparently harsh rule lies in preventing interference by the debenture-holder with the statutory obligations imposed on the appointee, perhaps most obviously the discharge of senior-ranking secured debt and the payment of preferential debts under s 40.

**The receiver's duty to cease acting**—As regards vacating office on completion of the receivership, the decision of HHJ Roger Cooke (sitting as a High Court judge) in *Rottenberg v Monjack* [1993] BCLC 374, is authority for the proposition that a cause of action arises in favour of a company in respect of any breach on the part of a receiver of his or her duty to cease acting where the receiver has in his or her hands sufficient funds to discharge the total debt under the security pursuant to which the receiver was appointed in addition to remuneration and all possible claims which could be made against him or her. For an Australian authority to similar effect see *Expo International Pty Ltd v Chant* [1979] 2 NSWLR 820. The duty to cease acting is not, however, triggered where there remains outstanding a contingent liability due to the debenture-holder: *Re Rudd & Son Ltd* (1986) BCC 98, 955, CA.

The duty to vacate is not affected by the views of the receivers or the appointing debenture-holder as to the merits of handing control of the company back to its directors and, furthermore, operates irrespective of the liquidation of the company. Insolvency practitioners will act in breach of the duty to vacate if they fail to vacate office on the sole basis of an objectively unsustainable outstanding claim under the security of the debenture pursuant to which they were appointed.

**Procedure**— 4.18–4.21.

On an application to remove an administrative receiver under s 45(1) notice should ordinarily be given to the appointee.

## SECTION 45(1)

**Scope of provision**—Where an incumbent office-holder will not resign voluntarily, any application under this provision to remove him or her will usually be combative.

**Eligible applicants under s 45(1)**—The provisions give no guidance as to the eligible applicants or the appropriate test applicable to a removal application. It is suggested that, as a first step, the court will only entertain an application by an individual with a sufficient interest in the receivership. Such persons might include the appointee's professional body, a co-appointee, the appointing debenture-holder, the holder of other security affected by the receivership or a liquidator. However, it is doubtful that a minority shareholder or an unsecured creditor for a relatively small sum will be able to establish sufficient interest in the absence of some exceptional circumstances: see *Walker Morris (a firm) v Khalastchi* [2001] 1 BCLC 1. As a second step, it is suggested, the court must be satisfied that cause can be shown justifying removal. It is suggested that there is good reason that that test should require proof to the standard applicable to removal of liquidators, on which see the notes to ss 108 and 172. Commonwealth authority suggests that the court will usually intervene by removing an office-holder where guilty of a flagrant breach of duty jeopardising the debenture-holder's security: see *Re Neon Signs (Australasia) Ltd* [1965] VR 125.

**Replacement following removal of a receiver**—On removal, a debenture-holder will usually wish to appoint a replacement office-holder of its choice although the court might appoint a receiver, if only to hold the proverbial ring, where a replacement cannot be appointed for any reason. In *Re A & C Supplies Ltd* [1998] 1 BCLC 603, [1998] BPIR 303 at 609F Blackburne J, in the context of a contested block appointment transfer application, held that the court has no jurisdiction to appoint an administrative receiver.

### SECTION 45(2)

**Scope of provision**—For the meaning of being qualified to act as an insolvency practitioner in relation to a company see ss 389–391.

### SECTION 45(3)

**Scope of provision**—This provision is in identical form to s 37(4), on which see the notes to that section.

### SECTION 45(4), (5)

**Scope of provision**—The ongoing daily default fine previously imposed by s 45(5) was abolished by Schs 16 and 24 of the Companies Act 1989.

For penalties see s 430 and Sch 10.

*Administrative receivers: ascertainment and investigation of company's affairs*

## [1.90]

### 46 Information to be given by administrative receiver

(1)   Where an administrative receiver is appointed, he shall—

(a)   forthwith send to the company and publish in the prescribed manner a notice of his appointment, and

(b)   within 28 days after his appointment, unless the court otherwise directs, send such a notice to all the creditors of the company (so far as he is aware of their addresses).

(2)   This section and the next do not apply in relation to the appointment of an administrative receiver to act—

(a)   with an existing administrative receiver, or

(b)   in place of an administrative receiver dying or ceasing to act,

except that, where they apply to an administrative receiver who dies or ceases to act before they have been fully complied with, the references in this section and the next to the administrative receiver include (subject to the next subsection) his successor and any continuing administrative receiver.

(3)   If the company is being wound up, this section and the next apply notwithstanding that the administrative receiver and the liquidator are the same person, but with any necessary modifications arising from that fact.

(4)   If the administrative receiver without reasonable excuse fails to comply with this section, he is liable to a fine and, for continued contravention, to a daily default fine.

**General note**—These administrative provisions provide for the publicising of the appointment of an administrative receiver and should be read with rr 4.1 and 4.5. Whilst criminal sanctions are imposed in default, non-compliance with these formalities, however significant the consequence, will not affect the validity of an appointment.

### SECTION 46(1)

**The extent of the duty to give notice**—Save for the general duty to give notice within 28 days in the manner described in s 46(1)(b) an administrative receiver is under no obligation to bring the fact of the appointment to the attention of any particular creditor or any other party.

' . . . **unless the court otherwise directs** . . . '—These words in s 46(1)(b) suggest that an appointee sending notice to creditors outside the 28-day period without court permission will, whatever the reasons for default, incur liability for the criminal sanctions in s 46(4). An application to the court will be by way of originating application with witness statement in support and should name the appointing debenture-holder as respondent.

**Procedure**—For the contents of the notice and advertisement see r 4.5.

Quite apart from the provisions in s 46, a person appointing a receiver and manager of the property of a company under any powers contained in an instrument (including statutorily implied powers in an instrument) must, within 7 days from the date of the appointment, give notice of the fact of the appointment to the Registrar of Companies, who is then obliged to register the fact on the company's register of charges: Companies Act 2006, s 871, and see s 869 for the register.

**Section 39 obligations**—An administrative receiver is also bound to comply with the obligations in s 39 relating to statements and invoices and the like.

SECTION 46(4)
**Penalties**—See s 430 and Sch 10.

## [1.91]

### 47 Statement of affairs to be submitted

(1)   Where an administrative receiver is appointed, he shall forthwith require some or all of the persons mentioned below to make out and submit to him a statement in the prescribed form as to the affairs of the company.

(2)   A statement submitted under this section shall be verified by a statement of truth by the persons required to submit it and shall show—

- (a)   particulars of the company's assets, debts and liabilities;
- (b)   the names and addresses of its creditors;
- (c)   the securities held by them respectively;
- (d)   the dates when the securities were respectively given; and
- (e)   such further or other information as may be prescribed.

(3)   The persons referred to in subsection (1) are—

- (a)   those who are or have been officers of the company;
- (b)   those who have taken part in the company's formation at any time within one year before the date of the appointment of the administrative receiver;
- (c)   those who are in the company's employment, or have been in its employment within that year, and are in the administrative receiver's opinion capable of giving the information required;
- (d)   those who are or have been within that year officers of or in the employment of a company which is, or within that year was, an officer of the company.

In this subsection "employment" includes employment under a contract for services.

(4)   Where any persons are required under this section to submit a statement of affairs to the administrative receiver, they shall do so (subject to the next subsection) before the end of the period of 21 days beginning with the day after that on which the prescribed notice of the requirement is given to them by the administrative receiver.

(5)   The administrative receiver, if he thinks fit, may—

- (a)   at any time release a person from an obligation imposed on him under subsection (1) or (2), or
- (b)   either when giving notice under subsection (4) or subsequently, extend the period so mentioned;

and where the administrative receiver has refused to exercise a power conferred by this subsection, the court, if it thinks fit, may exercise it.

(6)   If a person without reasonable excuse fails to comply with any obligation imposed under this section, he is liable to a fine and, for continued contravention, to a daily default fine.

**Amendments**—SI 2010/18.

**General note**—These provisions stipulate the requirements for the preparation and submission of a statement of affairs to the administrative receiver. The failure to comply with the obligation to deliver up a statement of affairs is a matter within Sch 1 of the Company Directors Disqualification Act 1986 in determining the unfitness of a company director on an application for a disqualification order.

**Procedure**—Detailed procedural provisions appear in rr 4.6–4.11.

## SECTION 47(1), (4)

**Scope of provision**—The administrative receiver is under an obligation – through use of the word 'shall' – to require submission to him or her of the statement of affairs 'forthwith' – and not within, say, a reasonable time – following his appointment. By s 47(2) the recipients of the prescribed form are afforded 21 days from receipt to submit the completed document; the word 'given' connotes actual receipt.

Subject to s 47(5), provided that the administrative receiver discharges his or her obligation to require submission of the statement of affairs, by way of the imposition of that requirement on one or more of the individuals in s 47(3), the receiver has a discretion as to which specific individuals are made subject to the s 47(2) obligation.

Under r 4.8 an administrative receiver may also require any one of those persons mentioned in s 47(3) to submit an affidavit of concurrence stating that the deponent concurs in the statement of affairs submitted.

**Enforcement of the obligation by the receiver**—The obligation to submit a statement of affairs is enforceable by the administrative receiver under r 12.52.

## SECTION 47(2)

**Scope of provision**—The swearing of the statement of affairs renders a deponent liable to prosecution under s 5 of the Perjury Act 1911 for false or misleading statements.

## SECTION 47(3)

**Scope of provision**—Section 47(3)(c) will extend to employment under a contract for services.

## SECTION 47(4)

**Scope of provision**—See the note to s 47(1) above.

For the recovery by a 'nominated person' under r 4.3 of his or her expenses in making the statement of affairs and supporting statement of truth see r 4.11.

## SECTION 47(5)

**Scope of provision**—An administrative receiver may either release an individual from the obligation under s 47(1) or (2) (ie irrespective of whether a s 47(4) notice has been served) or, alternatively, extend the 21-day period in s 47(4). This provision anticipates that an application to the court for the same relief, which would be in the form of an originating application with witness statement or affidavit in support, may only be made following a refusal by the administrative receiver of such release or extension of time.

**Procedure**—For procedure on the release from duty to submit the statement of affairs or for the extension of time see r 4.10.

## SECTION 47(6)

**Penalties**—See s 430 and Sch 10.

## [1.92]

### 48 Report by administrative receiver

(1) Where an administrative receiver is appointed, he shall, within 3 months (or such longer period as the court may allow) after his appointment, send to the registrar of companies, to any trustees for secured creditors of the company and (so far as he is aware of their addresses) to all such creditors, other than opted-out creditors, a report as to the following matters, namely—

    (a)    the events leading up to his appointment, so far as he is aware of them;

    (b)    the disposal or proposed disposal by him of any property of the company and the carrying on or proposed carrying on by him of any business of the company;

    (c)    the amounts of principal and interest payable to the debenture holders by whom or on whose behalf he was appointed and the amounts payable to preferential creditors; and

    (d)    the amount (if any) likely to be available for the payment of other creditors.

(2) The administrative receiver shall also, within 3 months (or such longer period as the court may allow) after his appointment, either—

(a)    send a copy of the report (so far as he is aware of their addresses) to all unsecured creditors of the company, other than opted-out creditors; or

(b)    publish in the prescribed manner a notice stating an address to which unsecured creditors of the company should write for copies of the report to be sent to them free of charge,

(3)  . . .

(4)  Where the company has gone or goes into liquidation, the administrative receiver—

(a)    shall, within 7 days after his compliance with subsection (1) or, if later, the nomination or appointment of the liquidator, send a copy of the report to the liquidator, and

(b)    where he does so within the time limited for compliance with subsection (2), is not required to comply with that subsection.

(5)  A report under this section shall include a summary of the statement of affairs made out and submitted to the administrative receiver under section 47 and of his comments (if any) upon it.

(6)  Nothing in this section is to be taken as requiring any such report to include any information the disclosure of which would seriously prejudice the carrying out by the administrative receiver of his functions.

(7)  Section 46(2) applies for the purposes of this section also.

(8)  If the administrative receiver without reasonable excuse fails to comply with this section, he is liable to a fine and, for continued contravention, to a daily default fine.

**Amendments**—Small Business, Enterprise and Employment Act 2015, s 126, Sch 9, Pt 1, paras 1, 12.

**General note**—The detailed requirements of this section are largely prescriptive and provide for the provision of specific information by an administrative receiver within the extendable 3-month period following the receiver's appointment, as provided for in s 48(1), subject to the facility for the limiting of disclosure under s 48(6). In practice, the provision of information by an administrative receiver commonly amounts to little more than a formalistic disclosure exercise with little practical consequence.

**The equitable duty to account as an agent and the receiver's duty as a fiduciary**—Quite apart from the requirements under s 48 a receiver, including an administrative receiver, is under an equitable duty to the company, as its agent and as a fiduciary, to account for his or her conduct of the receivership. As a basic principle, this duty will ordinarily require the receiver to keep full accounts and to produce those accounts to the company on being required to do so: *Smith v Middleton* [1979] 3 All ER 842 (Blackett-Ord V-C). However, the scope of the duty is variable, depending upon the nature of the receivership and, in particular, two specific factors. First, the right of the company to require information is dependent on the company being able to establish that the information sought is necessary for the purpose of enabling the directors to discharge any of the residual obligations remaining on them, most obviously the filing of accounts or the redemption of the debenture-holder's security: *Gomba Holdings (UK) Ltd v Homan, Same v Johnson Matthey Bankers* [1986] 1 WLR 1301 (Hoffmann J). Secondly, given his primary duty to the appointing debenture-holder (on which see the notes to s 44(1)(a)) the receiver may refuse to disclose information if he or she is of the objectively reasonable subjective view that such disclosure would be prejudicial to the interests of the debenture-holder in realising the security: *Gomba Holdings*.

**Whistle-blowing obligation**—An administrative receiver is subject to a so-called whistle-blowing duty to the FCA and PRA by virtue of s 364 of the FSMA 2000.

**Procedure**— 4.13–4.14.

## SECTION 48(1), (4)

**Scope of provision**—The parties to whom the administrative receiver must submit a report include not only those listed in s 48(1) but also, by virtue of s 48(4), any liquidator of the company and, if appropriate, the FCA and PRA by virtue of FSMA 2000, s 363(4).

## SECTION 48(2)

**Scope of provision**—Section 48(2) previously placed an obligation on the administrative receiver to summon a meeting of unsecured creditors on not less than 14 days' notice within 3 months of his appointment. That obligation has now been removed.

## SECTION 48(6)

'. . . **any information the disclosure of which would seriously prejudice the carrying out** . . . **of his functions**'—The most obvious examples of such information are price-sensitive information where the viability of the company's business might be damaged by the disclosure of such information to creditors and/or business competitors or details of offers received by the administrative receiver to date for the whole or part of the company's undertaking where such disclosure might prejudice the making of what would otherwise be a significantly more competitive bid.

For procedure on the application to court, see r 4.12.

### SECTION 48(7)

**Scope of provision**—The obligations imposed by this section do not apply to an administrative receiver who is appointed to act with an administrative receiver or, save to the extent that an outgoing administrative receiver has failed to comply with his obligations under the section, an administrative receiver appointed to replace one who has died or ceased to act as such.

### SECTION 48(8)

**Scope of provision**—For penalties see s 430 and Sch 10.

## [1.93]

### 49 Committee of creditors

(1) Where an administrative receiver has sent or published a report as mentioned in section 48(2) the company's unsecured creditors may, in accordance with the rules, establish a committee ("the creditors' committee") to exercise the functions conferred on it by or under this Act.

(2) If such a committee is established, the committee may, on giving not less than 7 days' notice, require the administrative receiver to attend before it at any reasonable time and furnish it with such information relating to the carrying out by him of his functions as it may reasonably require.

**Amendments**—Small Business, Enterprise and Employment Act 2015, s 126, Sch 9, Pt 1, paras 1, 13.

**General note**—The practical significance of the creditors' committee very much depends upon the level of interest on the part of creditors in the conduct and outcome of the administrative receivership. In some cases, as s 49(1) envisages, the creditors receiving a report under s 48 may not see fit even to establish a creditors' committee.

With the abolition of the creditors' meeting convened under s 48, there is a real power in the creditors' committee in the terms of s 49(2), on which see the notes below. Conversely, however, the creditors' committee is to 'assist the office-holder in discharging the office-holder's functions' and 'act in relation to the office-holder in such manner as may from time to time be agreed: r 17.2.

**Procedure**—For procedure and formalities in relation to the creditors' committee see rr 17.3–17.27. Rule 17.27 provides that the acts of the creditors' committee are valid notwithstanding any defect in the appointment, election or qualifications of a member of the committee or any committee-member's representative or in the formalities of its establishment.

### SECTION 49(1)

**Scope of provision**—Despite the apparent suggestion that there may be functions conferred on the creditors' committee by the 1986 Act, in fact the only functions provided for are in the very general terms of r 17.2 which appears in substance in the general note above. That provision does, however, envisage that specific functions on the part of the creditors' committee may be agreed between the committee and the administrative receiver from time to time.

The administrative receiver shall call a first meeting of the creditors' committee not later than 6 weeks after its establishment and thereafter in accordance with the request or direction of the committee itself in accordance with r 17.14.

For the position of the FCA and PRA in relation to the creditors' committee see FSMA 2000, s 363(5).

**Chairman of the creditors' committee**—See r 17.15.

**Quorum**—See r 17.16.

### SECTION 49(2)

'. . . as it may reasonably require'—The limit on information to be furnished by the administrative receiver by reference to the words 'reasonably require' guards, it is submitted, against two scenarios. First, it cannot be envisaged that the committee might require the administrative receiver to disclose something to it, which the administrative receiver would not be required to disclose in the report to creditors under s 48(6) on the grounds that such disclosure would seriously prejudice the carrying out by the administrative receiver of his or her functions.

Secondly, the sub-provision protects the administrative receiver from vexatious, irrelevant or disproportionate (in terms of time and expense as against perceived benefit) requests for information.

## CHAPTER II

### Receivers (Scotland)

**[1.94]**

#### 50 Extent of this Chapter
This Chapter extends to Scotland only.

**[1.95]**

#### 51 Power to appoint receiver
(1) It is competent under the law of Scotland for the holder of a floating charge over all or any part of the property (including uncalled capital), which may from time to time be comprised in the property and undertaking of an incorporated company (whether a company registered under the Companies Act 2006 or not)—

    (a)    which the Court of Session has jurisdiction to wind up; or

    (b)    where paragraph (a) does not apply, in respect of which a court of a member state . . . has under the EU Regulation jurisdiction to open insolvency proceedings,

to appoint a receiver of such part of the property of the company as is subject to the charge.

(2) It is competent under the law of Scotland for the court, on the application of the holder of such a floating charge, to appoint a receiver of such part of the property of the company as is subject to the charge.

(2ZA) . . .

(2A) Subsections (1) and (2) are subject to section 72A.

(3) The following are disqualified from being appointed as receiver—

    (a)    a body corporate;

    (b)    an undischarged bankrupt;

    (ba)    a person subject to a bankruptcy restrictions order; and

    (c)    a firm according to the law of Scotland.

(4) A body corporate or a firm according to the law of Scotland which acts as a receiver is liable to a fine.

(5) An undischarged bankrupt or a person subject to a bankruptcy restrictions order who so acts is liable to imprisonment or a fine, or both.

(6) In this section, "receiver" includes joint receivers; and

    "bankruptcy restrictions order" means—

        (a)    a bankruptcy restrictions order made under section 155 of the Bankruptcy (Scotland) Act 2016;

        (b)    . . .

        (c)    a bankruptcy restrictions order made under paragraph 1 of Schedule 4A to this Act; or

        (d)    a bankruptcy restrictions undertaking entered into under paragraph 7 of that Schedule

    "the EU Regulation" is Regulation (EU) 2015/848 of the European Parliament and of the Council on insolvency proceedings as that Regulation has effect in the law of the European Union;

    "court" is to be construed in accordance with Article 2(6) of the EU Regulation;

    "insolvency proceedings" is to be construed in accordance with Article 2(4) of the EU Regulation.

**Amendments**—Enterprise Act 2002, s 248(3), Sch 17, paras 9, 13; Bankruptcy and Diligence etc (Scotland) Act 2007, s 3; SI 2009/1941; SSI 2011/140; Bankruptcy and Debt Advice (Scotland) Act

2014, s 56(2), Sch 4; SSI 2016/141; SSI 2016/1034; SSI 2017/210; SSI 2019/94 having effect from IP completion day (as defined in the European Union (Withdrawal Agreement) Act 2020, s 39(1)–(5)).

**[1.96]**

### 52 Circumstances justifying appointment

(1)   A receiver may be appointed under section 51(1) by the holder of the floating charge on the occurrence of any event which, by the provisions of the instrument creating the charge, entitles the holder of the charge to make that appointment and, in so far as not otherwise provided for by the instrument, on the occurrence of any of the following events, namely—

> (a)   the expiry of a period of 21 days after the making of a demand for payment of the whole or any part of the principal sum secured by the charge, without payment having been made;
>
> (b)   the expiry of a period of 2 months during the whole of which interest due and payable under the charge has been in arrears;
>
> (c)   the making of an order or the passing of a resolution to wind up the company;
>
> (d)   the appointment of a receiver by virtue of any other floating charge created by the company.

(2)   A receiver may be appointed by the court under section 51(2) on the occurrence of any event which, by the provisions of the instrument creating the floating charge, entitles the holder of the charge to make that appointment and, in so far as not otherwise provided for by the instrument, on the occurrence of any of the following events, namely—

> (a)   where the court, on the application of the holder of the charge, pronounces itself satisfied that the position of the holder of the charge is likely to be prejudiced if no such appointment is made;
>
> (b)   any of the events referred to in paragraphs (a) to (c) of subsection (1).

**[1.97]**

### 53 Mode of appointment by holder of charge

(1)   The appointment of a receiver by the holder of the floating charge under section 51(1) shall be by means of an instrument subscribed in accordance with the Requirements of Writing (Scotland) Act 1995 ("the instrument of appointment"), a copy (certified in the prescribed manner to be a correct copy) whereof shall be delivered by or on behalf of the person making the appointment to the registrar of companies for registration within 7 days of its execution and shall be accompanied by a notice in the prescribed form.

(2)   If any person without reasonable excuse makes default in complying with the requirements of subsection (1), he is liable to a fine *and, for continued contravention, to a daily default fine.*

(3)   . . .

(4)   If the receiver is to be appointed by the holders of a series of secured debentures, the instrument of appointment may be executed on behalf of the holders of the floating charge by any person authorised by resolution of the debenture-holders to execute the instrument.

(5)   On receipt of the certified copy of the instrument of appointment in accordance with subsection (1), the registrar shall, on payment of the prescribed fee, enter the particulars of the appointment in the register.

(6)   The appointment of a person as a receiver by an instrument of appointment in accordance with subsection (1)—

> (a)   is of no effect unless it is accepted by that person before the end of the business day next following that on which the instrument of appointment is received by him or on his behalf, and

(b)      subject to paragraph (a), is deemed to be made on the day on and at the time at which the instrument of appointment is so received, as evidenced by a written docquet by that person or on his behalf;

and this subsection applies to the appointment of joint receivers subject to such modifications as may be prescribed.

(7)    On the appointment of a receiver under this section, the floating charge by virtue of which he was appointed attaches to the property then subject to the charge; and such attachment has effect as if the charge was a fixed security over the property to which it has attached.

**Amendments**—Words in italics prospectively repealed by Companies Act 1989, ss 107, 212, Sch 16, para 3(3), Sch 24, as from a date to be appointed; Law Reform (Miscellaneous Provisions) (Scotland) Act 1990, s 74, Sch 8, para 35, Sch 9; Requirements of Writing (Scotland) Act 1995, s 14(1), Sch 4, para 58; SI 2013/600.

## [1.98]

### 54  Appointment by court

(1)    Application for the appointment of a receiver by the court under section 51(2) shall be by petition to the court, which shall be served on the company.

(2)    On such an application, the court shall, if it thinks fit, issue an interlocutor making the appointment of the receiver.

(3)    A copy (certified by the clerk of the court to be a correct copy) of the court's interlocutor making the appointment shall be delivered by or on behalf of the petitioner to the registrar of companies for registration, accompanied by a notice in the prescribed form, within 7 days of the date of the interlocutor or such longer period as the court may allow.

If any person without reasonable excuse makes default in complying with the requirements of this subsection, he is liable to a fine *and, for continued contravention, to a daily default fine.*

(4)    On receipt of the certified copy interlocutor in accordance with subsection (3), the registrar shall, on payment of the prescribed fee, enter the particulars of the appointment in the register.

(5)    The receiver is to be regarded as having been appointed on the date of his being appointed by the court.

(6)    On the appointment of a receiver under this section, the floating charge by virtue of which he was appointed attaches to the property then subject to the charge; and such attachment has effect as if the charge were a fixed security over the property to which it has attached.

(7)    In making rules of court for the purposes of this section, the Court of Session shall have regard to the need for special provision for cases which appear to the court to require to be dealt with as a matter of urgency.

**Amendments**—Words in italics prospectively repealed by Companies Act 1989, ss 107, 212, Sch 16, para 3(2), Sch 24, as from a date to be appointed; SI 2013/600.

## [1.99]

### 55  Powers of receiver

(1)    Subject to the next subsection, a receiver has in relation to such part of the property of the company as is attached by the floating charge by virtue of which he was appointed, the powers, if any, given to him by the instrument creating that charge.

(2)    In addition, the receiver has under this Chapter the powers as respects that property (in so far as these are not inconsistent with any provision contained in that instrument) which are specified in Schedule 2 to this Act.

(3)    Subsections (1) and (2) apply—

(a)      subject to the rights of any person who has effectually executed diligence on all or any part of the property of the company prior to the appointment of the receiver, and

(b)    subject to the rights of any person who holds over all or any part of the property of the company a fixed security or floating charge having priority over, or ranking pari passu with, the floating charge by virtue of which the receiver was appointed.

(4)   A person dealing with a receiver in good faith and for value is not concerned to enquire whether the receiver is acting within his powers.

## [1.100]

### 56 Precedence among receivers

(1)   Where there are two or more floating charges subsisting over all or any part of the property of the company, a receiver may be appointed under this Chapter by virtue of each such charge; but a receiver appointed by, or on the application of, the holder of a floating charge having priority of ranking over any other floating charge by virtue of which a receiver has been appointed has the powers given to a receiver by section 55 and Schedule 2 to the exclusion of any other receiver.

(2)   Where two or more floating charges rank with one another equally, and two or more receivers have been appointed by virtue of such charges, the receivers so appointed are deemed to have been appointed as joint receivers.

(3)   Receivers appointed, or deemed to have been appointed, as joint receivers shall act jointly unless the instrument of appointment or respective instruments of appointment otherwise provide.

(4)   Subject to subsection (5) below, the powers of a receiver appointed by, or on the application of, the holder of a floating charge are suspended by, and as from the date of, the appointment of a receiver by, or on the application of, the holder of a floating charge having priority of ranking over that charge to such extent as may be necessary to enable the receiver second mentioned to exercise his powers under section 55 and Schedule 2; and any powers so suspended take effect again when the floating charge having priority of ranking ceases to attach to the property then subject to the charge, whether such cessation is by virtue of section 62(6) or otherwise.

(5)   The suspension of the powers of a receiver under subsection (4) does not have the effect of requiring him to release any part of the property (including any letters or documents) of the company from his control until he receives from the receiver superseding him a valid indemnity (subject to the limit of the value of such part of the property of the company as is subject to the charge by virtue of which he was appointed) in respect of any expenses, charges and liabilities he may have incurred in the performance of his functions as receiver.

(6)   The suspension of the powers of a receiver under subsection (4) does not cause the floating charge by virtue of which he was appointed to cease to attach to the property to which it attached by virtue of section 53(7) or 54(6).

(7)   Nothing in this section prevents the same receiver being appointed by virtue of two or more floating charges.

## [1.101]

### 57 Agency and liability of receiver for contracts

(1)   A receiver is deemed to be the agent of the company in relation to such property of the company as is attached by the floating charge by virtue of which he was appointed.

(1A)   Without prejudice to subsection (1), a receiver is deemed to be the agent of the company in relation to any contract of employment adopted by him in the carrying out of his functions.

(2)   A receiver (including a receiver whose powers are subsequently suspended under section 56) is personally liable on any contract entered into by him in the performance of his functions, except in so far as the contract otherwise provides, and, to the extent of any qualifying liability, on any contract of employment adopted by him in the carrying out of those functions.

(2A)   For the purposes of subsection (2), a liability under a contract of employment is a qualifying liability if—

    (a)    it is a liability to pay a sum by way of wages or salary or contribution to an occupational pension scheme,

    (b)    it is incurred while the receiver is in office, and

    (c)    it is in respect of services rendered wholly or partly after the adoption of the contract.

(2B)   Where a sum payable in respect of a liability which is a qualifying liability for the purposes of subsection (2) is payable in respect of services rendered partly before and partly after the adoption of the contract, liability under that subsection shall only extend to so much of the sum as is payable in respect of services rendered after the adoption of the contract.

(2C)   For the purposes of subsections (2A) and (2B)—

    (a)    wages or salary payable in respect of a period of holiday or absence from work through sickness or other good cause are deemed to be wages or (as the case may be) salary in respect of services rendered in that period, and

    (b)    a sum payable in lieu of holiday is deemed to be wages or (as the case may be) salary in respect of services rendered in the period by reference to which the holiday entitlement arose.

(3)   A receiver who is personally liable by virtue of subsection (2) is entitled to be indemnified out of the property in respect of which he was appointed.

(4)   Any contract entered into by or on behalf of the company prior to the appointment of a receiver continues in force (subject to its terms) notwithstanding that appointment, but the receiver does not by virtue only of his appointment incur any personal liability on any such contract.

(5)   For the purposes of subsection (2), a receiver is not to be taken to have adopted a contract of employment by reason of anything done or omitted to be done within 14 days after his appointment.

(6)   This section does not limit any right to indemnity which the receiver would have apart from it, nor limit his liability on contracts entered into or adopted without authority, nor confer any right to indemnity in respect of that liability.

(7)   Any contract entered into by a receiver in the performance of his functions continues in force (subject to its terms) although the powers of the receiver are subsequently suspended under section 56.

Amendments—Insolvency Act 1994, s 3; SSI 2016/141.

## [1.102]

### 58 Remuneration of receiver

(1)   The remuneration to be paid to a receiver is to be determined by agreement between the receiver and the holder of the floating charge by virtue of which he was appointed.

(2)   Where the remuneration to be paid to the receiver has not been determined under subsection (1), or where it has been so determined but is disputed by any of the persons mentioned in paragraphs (a) to (d) below, it may be fixed instead by the Auditor of the Court of Session on application made to him by—

    (a)    the receiver;

    (b)    the holder of any floating charge or fixed security over all or any part of the property of the company;

    (c)    the company; or

    (d)    the liquidator of the company.

(3)   Where the receiver has been paid or has retained for his remuneration for any period before the remuneration has been fixed by the Auditor of the Court of Session under subsection (2) any amount in excess of the remuneration so fixed for that period, the receiver or his personal representatives shall account for the excess.

**[1.103]**

### 59 Priority of debts

(1) Where a receiver is appointed and the company is not at the time of the appointment in course of being wound up, the debts which fall under subsection (2) of this section shall be paid out of any assets coming to the hands of the receiver in priority to any claim for principal or interest by the holder of the floating charge by virtue of which the receiver was appointed.

(2) Debts falling under this subsection are preferential debts (within the meaning given by section 386 in Part XII) which, by the end of a period of 6 months after advertisement by the receiver for claims in the Edinburgh Gazette and in a newspaper circulating in the district where the company carries on business either—

  (i)   have been intimated to him, or

  (ii)  have become known to him.

(3) Any payments made under this section shall be recouped as far as may be out of the assets of the company available for payment of ordinary creditors.

**[1.104]**

### 60 Distribution of moneys

(1) Subject to the next section, and to the rights of any of the following categories of persons (which rights shall, except to the extent otherwise provided in any instrument, have the following order of priority), namely—

  (a)   the holder of any fixed security which is over property subject to the floating charge and which ranks prior to, or pari passu with, the floating charge;

  (b)   all persons who have effectually executed diligence on any part of the property of the company which is subject to the charge by virtue of which the receiver was appointed;

  (c)   creditors in respect of all liabilities, charges and expenses incurred by or on behalf of the receiver;

  (d)   the receiver in respect of his liabilities, expenses and remuneration, and any indemnity to which he is entitled out of the property of the company; and

  (e)   the preferential creditors entitled to payment under section 59,

the receiver shall pay moneys received by him to the holder of the floating charge by virtue of which the receiver was appointed in or towards satisfaction of the debt secured by the floating charge.

(2) Any balance of moneys remaining after the provisions of subsection (1) and section 61 below have been satisfied shall be paid in accordance with their respective rights and interests to the following persons, as the case may require—

  (a)   any other receiver;

  (b)   the holder of a fixed security which is over property subject to the floating charge;

  (c)   the company or its liquidator, as the case may be.

(3) Where any question arises as to the person entitled to a payment under this section, or where a receipt or a discharge of a security cannot be obtained in respect of any such payment, the receiver shall consign the amount of such payment in any joint stock bank of issue in Scotland in name of the Accountant of Court for behoof of the person or persons entitled thereto.

**[1.105]**

### 61 Disposal of interest in property

(1) Where the receiver sells or disposes, or is desirous of selling or disposing, of any property or interest in property of the company which is subject to the floating charge by virtue of which the receiver was appointed and which is—

(a)   subject to any security or interest of, or burden or encumbrance in favour of, a creditor the ranking of which is prior to, or pari passu with, or postponed to the floating charge, or

(b)   property or an interest in property affected or attached by effectual diligence executed by any person,

and the receiver is unable to obtain the consent of such creditor or, as the case may be, such person to such a sale or disposal, the receiver may apply to the court for authority to sell or dispose of the property or interest in property free of such security, interest, burden, encumbrance or diligence.

(1A)   For the purposes of subsection (1) above, an inhibition which takes effect after the creation of the floating charge by virtue of which the receiver was appointed is not an effectual diligence.

(1B)   For the purposes of subsection (1) above, an arrestment is an effectual diligence only where it is executed before the floating charge, by virtue of which the receiver was appointed, attaches to the property comprised in the company's property and undertaking.

(2)   Subject to the next subsection, on such an application the court may, if it thinks fit, authorise the sale or disposal of the property or interest in question free of such security, interest, burden, encumbrance or diligence, and such authorisation may be on such terms or conditions as the court thinks fit.

(3)   In the case of an application where a fixed security over the property or interest in question which ranks prior to the floating charge has not been met or provided for in full, the court shall not authorise the sale or disposal of the property or interest in question unless it is satisfied that the sale or disposal would be likely to provide a more advantageous realisation of the company's assets than would otherwise be effected.

(4)   It shall be a condition of an authorisation to which subsection (3) applies that—

(a)   the net proceeds of the disposal, and

(b)   where those proceeds are less than such amount as may be determined by the court to be the net amount which would be realised on a sale of the property or interest in the open market by a willing seller, such sums as may be required to make good the deficiency,

shall be applied towards discharging the sums secured by the fixed security.

(5)   Where a condition imposed in pursuance of subsection (4) relates to two or more such fixed securities, that condition shall require the net proceeds of the disposal and, where paragraph (b) of that subsection applies, the sums mentioned in that paragraph to be applied towards discharging the sums secured by those fixed securities in the order of their priorities.

(6)   A copy of an authorisation under subsection (2) shall, within 14 days of the granting of the authorisation, be sent by the receiver to the registrar of companies.

(7)   If the receiver without reasonable excuse fails to comply with subsection (6), he is liable to a fine and, for continued contravention, to a daily default fine.

(8)   Where any sale or disposal is effected in accordance with the authorisation of the court under subsection (2), the receiver shall grant to the purchaser or disponee an appropriate document of transfer or conveyance of the property or interest in question, and that document has the effect, or, where recording, intimation or registration of that document is a legal requirement for completion of title to the property or interest, then that recording, intimation or registration (as the case may be) has the effect, of—

(a)   disencumbering the property or interest of the security, interest, burden or encumbrance affecting it, and

(b)   freeing the property or interest from the diligence executed upon it.

(9)   Nothing in this section prejudices the right of any creditor of the company to rank for his debt in the winding up of the company.

**Amendments**—Bankruptcy and Diligence etc (Scotland) Act 2007, s 155(1), (2) and s 226(1), Sch 5, para 14(1), (2), partly as from a date to be appointed; SI 2009/1941.

**[1.106]**

**62 Cessation of appointment of receiver**

(1)   A receiver may be removed from office by the court under subsection (3) below and may resign his office by giving notice of his resignation in the prescribed manner to such persons as may be prescribed.

(2)   A receiver shall vacate office if he ceases to be qualified to act as an insolvency practitioner in relation to the company.

(3)   Subject to the next subsection, a receiver may, on application to the court by the holder of the floating charge by virtue of which he was appointed, be removed by the court on cause shown.

(4)   Where at any time a receiver vacates office—

(a)     his remuneration and any expenses properly incurred by him, and

(b)     any indemnity to which he is entitled out of the property of the company,

shall be paid out of the property of the company which is subject to the floating charge and shall have priority as provided for in section 60(1).

(5)   When a receiver ceases to act as such otherwise than by death he shall, and, when a receiver is removed by the court, the holder of the floating charge by virtue of which he was appointed shall, within 14 days of the cessation or removal (as the case may be) give the registrar of companies notice to that effect, and the registrar shall enter the notice in the register.

If the receiver or the holder of the floating charge (as the case may require) makes default in complying with the requirements of this subsection, he is liable to a fine *and, for continued contravention, to a daily default fine.*

(6)   If by the expiry of a period of one month following upon the removal of the receiver or his ceasing to act as such no other receiver has been appointed, the floating charge by virtue of which the receiver was appointed—

(a)     thereupon ceases to attach to the property then subject to the charge, and

(b)     again subsists as a floating charge;

and for the purposes of calculating the period of one month under this subsection no account shall be taken of any period during which the company is in administration under Part II of this Act.

   **Amendments**—Words in italics prospectively repealed by Companies Act 1989, ss 107, 212, Sch 16, para 3(3), Sch 24, as from a date to be appointed; SI 2003/2096; SI 2013/600.

**[1.107]**

**63  Powers of court**

(1)   The court on the application of—

(a)     the holder of a floating charge by virtue of which a receiver was appointed, or

(b)     a receiver appointed under section 51,

may give directions to the receiver in respect of any matter arising in connection with the performance by him of his functions.

(2)   Where the appointment of a person as a receiver by the holder of a floating charge is discovered to be invalid (whether by virtue of the invalidity of the instrument or otherwise), the court may order the holder of the floating charge to indemnify the person appointed against any liability which arises solely by reason of the invalidity of the appointment.

**[1.108]**

**64  Notification that receiver appointed**

(1)   Where a receiver has been appointed—

(a)     every invoice, order for goods or services, business letter or order form (whether in hard copy, electronic or any other form) issued by or on behalf of the company or the receiver or the liquidator of the company; and

(b)     all the company's websites,

must contain a statement that a receiver has been appointed.

(2) If default is made in complying with the requirements of this section, the company and any of the following persons who knowingly and wilfully authorises or permits the default, namely any officer of the company, any liquidator of the company and any receiver, is liable to a fine.

Amendments—SI 2008/1897.

## [1.109]

### 65 Information to be given by receiver

(1) Where a receiver is appointed, he shall—
- (a) forthwith send to the company and publish notice of his appointment, and
- (b) within 28 days after his appointment, unless the court otherwise directs, send such notice to all the creditors of the company (so far as he is aware of their addresses).

(2) This section and the next do not apply in relation to the appointment of a receiver to act—
- (a) with an existing receiver, or
- (b) in place of a receiver who has died or ceased to act,

except that, where they apply to a receiver who dies or ceases to act before they have been fully complied with, the references in this section and the next to the receiver include (subject to subsection (3) of this section) his successor and any continuing receiver.

(3) If the company is being wound up, this section and the next apply notwithstanding that the receiver and the liquidator are the same person, but with any necessary modifications arising from that fact.

(4) If a person without reasonable excuse fails to comply with this section, he is liable to a fine and, for continued contravention, to a daily default fine.

## [1.110]

### 66 Company's statement of affairs

(1) Where a receiver of a company is appointed, the receiver shall forthwith require some or all of the persons mentioned in subsection (3) below to make out and submit to him a statement in the prescribed form as to the affairs of the company.

(2) A statement submitted under this section shall contain a statutory declaration by the persons required to submit it and shall show—
- (a) particulars of the company's assets, debts and liabilities;
- (b) the names and addresses of its creditors;
- (c) the securities held by them respectively;
- (d) the dates when the securities were respectively given; and
- (e) such further or other information as may be prescribed.

(3) The persons referred to in subsection (1) are—
- (a) those who are or have been officers of the company;
- (b) those who have taken part in the company's formation at any time within one year before the date of the appointment of the receiver;
- (c) those who are in the company's employment or have been in its employment within that year, and are in the receiver's opinion capable of giving the information required;
- (d) those who are or have been within that year officers of or in the employment of a company which is, or within that year was, an officer of the company.

In this subsection "employment" includes employment under a contract for services.

(4) Where any persons are required under this section to submit a statement of affairs to the receiver they shall do so (subject to the next subsection) before the end of the period of 21 days beginning with the day after that on which the prescribed notice of the requirement is given to them by the receiver.

(5) The receiver, if he thinks fit, may—

    (a)    at any time release a person from an obligation imposed on him under subsection (1) or (2), or

    (b)    either when giving the notice mentioned in subsection (4) or subsequently extend the period so mentioned,

and where the receiver has refused to exercise a power conferred by this subsection, the court, if it thinks fit, may exercise it.

(6) If a person without reasonable excuse fails to comply with any obligation imposed under this section, he is liable to a fine and, for continued contravention, to a daily default fine.

    **Amendments**—SSI 2016/141.

## [1.111]

### 67 Report by receiver

(1) Where a receiver is appointed under section 51, he shall within 3 months (or such longer period as the court may allow) after his appointment, send to the registrar of companies, to the holder of the floating charge by virtue of which he was appointed and to any trustees for secured creditors of the company and (so far as he is aware of their addresses) to all such creditors, other than opted-out creditors, a report as to the following matters, namely—

    (a)    the events leading up to his appointment, so far as he is aware of them;

    (b)    the disposal or proposed disposal by him of any property of the company and the carrying on or proposed carrying on by him of any business of the company;

    (c)    the amounts of principal and interest payable to the holder of the floating charge by virtue of which he was appointed and the amounts payable to preferential creditors; and

    (d)    the amount (if any) likely to be available for the payment of other creditors.

(2) The receiver shall also, within 3 months (or such longer period as the court may allow) after his appointment, either—

    (a)    send a copy of the report (so far as he is aware of their addresses) to all unsecured creditors of the company, other than opted-out creditors, or

    (b)    publish in the prescribed manner a notice stating an address to which unsecured creditors of the company should write for copies of the report to be sent to them free of charge,

. . .

(3)  . . .

(4) Where the company has gone or goes into liquidation, the receiver—

    (a)    shall, within 7 days after his compliance with subsection (1) or, if later, the nomination or appointment of the liquidator, send a copy of the report to the liquidator, and

    (b)    where he does so within the time limited for compliance with subsection (2), is not required to comply with that subsection.

(5) A report under this section shall include a summary of the statement of affairs made out and submitted under section 66 and of his comments (if any) on it.

(6) Nothing in this section shall be taken as requiring any such report to include any information the disclosure of which would seriously prejudice the carrying out by the receiver of his functions.

(7) Section 65(2) applies for the purposes of this section also.

(8) If a person without reasonable excuse fails to comply with this section, he is liable to a fine and, for continued contravention, to a daily default fine.

(9) In this section "secured creditor", in relation to a company, means a creditor of the company who holds in respect of his debt a security over property of the company, and "unsecured creditor" shall be construed accordingly.

Amendments—Small Business, Enterprise and Employment Act 2015, s 126, Sch 9, Pt 1, paras 1, 14(1)–(4).

## [1.112]

### 68 Committee of creditors

(1)   Where a receiver has sent or published a report as mentioned in section 67(2) the company's unsecured creditors may, in accordance with the rules, establish a committee ("the creditors' committee") to exercise the functions conferred on it by or under this Act.

(2)   If such a committee is established, the committee may on giving not less than 7 days' notice require the receiver to attend before it at any reasonable time and furnish it with such information relating to the carrying out by him of his functions as it may reasonably require.

Amendments—Small Business, Enterprise and Employment Act 2015, s 126, Sch 9, Pt 1, paras 1, 15.

## [1.113]

### 69 Enforcement of receiver's duty to make returns etc

(1)   If any receiver—

   (a)   having made default in filing, delivering or making any return, account or other document, or in giving any notice, which a receiver is by law required to file, deliver, make or give, fails to make good the default within 14 days after the service on him of a notice requiring him to do so; or

   (b)   has, after being required at any time by the liquidator of the company so to do, failed to render proper accounts of his receipts and payments and to vouch the same and to pay over to the liquidator the amount properly payable to him,

the court may, on an application made for the purpose, make an order directing the receiver to make good the default within such time as may be specified in the order.

(2)   In the case of any such default as is mentioned in subsection (1)(a), an application for the purposes of this section may be made by any member or creditor of the company or by the registrar of companies; and, in the case of any such default as is mentioned in subsection (1)(b), the application shall be made by the liquidator; and, in either case, the order may provide that all expenses of and incidental to the application shall be borne by the receiver.

(3)   Nothing in this section prejudices the operation of any enactments imposing penalties on receivers in respect of any such default as is mentioned in subsection (1).

## [1.114]

### 70 Interpretation for Chapter II

(1)   In this Chapter, unless the contrary intention appears, the following expressions have the following meanings respectively assigned to them—

   "company"' means an incorporated company (whether or not a company registered under the Companies Act 2006) which the Court of Session has jurisdiction to wind up;

   "fixed security", in relation to any property of a company, means any security, other than a floating charge or a charge having the nature of a floating charge, which on the winding up of the company in Scotland would be treated as an effective security over that property, and (without prejudice to that generality) includes a security over that property, being a heritable security within the meaning of the Conveyancing and Feudal Reform (Scotland) Act 1970;

   "instrument of appointment" has the meaning given by section 53(1);

   "prescribed fee" means the fee prescribed by regulations made under this Chapter by the Secretary of State;

"receiver" means a receiver of such part of the property of the company as is subject to the floating charge by virtue of which he has been appointed under section 51;

"the register" has the meaning given by section 1080 of the Companies Act 2006;

"secured debenture" means a bond, debenture, debenture stock or other security which, either itself or by reference to any other instrument, creates a floating charge over all or any part of the property of the company, but does not include a security which creates no charge other than a fixed security; and

"series of secured debentures" means two or more secured debentures created as a series by the company in such a manner that the holders thereof are entitled pari passu to the benefit of the floating charge.

(2)   Where a floating charge, secured debenture or series of secured debentures has been created by the company, then, except where the context otherwise requires, any reference in this Chapter to the holder of the floating charge shall—

(a)    where the floating charge, secured debenture or series of secured debentures provides for a receiver to be appointed by any person or body, be construed as a reference to that person or body;

(b)    where, in the case of a series of secured debentures, no such provision has been made therein but—

(i)     there are trustees acting for the debenture-holders under and in accordance with a trust deed, be construed as a reference to those trustees, and

(ii)    where no such trustees are acting, be construed as a reference to—

(aa)    a majority in nominal value of those present or represented by proxy and voting at a meeting of debenture-holders at which the holders of at least one-third in nominal value of the outstanding debentures of the series are present or so represented, or

(bb)    where no such meeting is held, the holders of at least one-half in nominal value of the outstanding debentures of the series.

(3)   Any reference in this Chapter to a floating charge, secured debenture, series of secured debentures or instrument creating a charge includes, except where the context otherwise requires, a reference to that floating charge, debenture, series of debentures or instrument as varied by any instrument.

(4)   References in this Chapter to the instrument by which a floating charge was created are, in the case of a floating charge created by words in a bond or other written acknowledgement, references to the bond or, as the case may be, the other written acknowledgement.

**Amendments**—SI 2009/1941; SI 2013/600; SSI 2017/209.

## [1.115]

### 71 Prescription of forms etc; regulations

(1)   The notice referred to in section 62(5), and the notice referred to in section 65(1)(a) shall be in such form as may be prescribed.

(2)   Any power conferred by this Chapter on the Secretary of State to make regulations is exercisable by statutory instrument; and a statutory instrument made in the exercise of the power so conferred to prescribe a fee is subject to annulment in pursuance of a resolution of either House of Parliament.

## CHAPTER III

### RECEIVERS' POWERS IN GREAT BRITAIN AS A WHOLE

**[1.116]**

**72 Cross-border operation of receivership provisions**

(1)   A receiver appointed under the law of either part of Great Britain in respect of the whole or any part of any property or undertaking of a company and in consequence of the company having created a charge which, as created, was a floating charge may exercise his powers in the other part of Great Britain so far as their exercise is not inconsistent with the law applicable there.

(2)   In subsection (1) "receiver" includes a manager and a person who is appointed both receiver and manager.

## CHAPTER IV

### PROHIBITION OF APPOINTMENT OF ADMINISTRATIVE RECEIVER

**[1.117]**

**72A Floating charge holder not to appoint administrative receiver**

(1)   The holder of a qualifying floating charge in respect of a company's property may not appoint an administrative receiver of the company.

(2)   In Scotland, the holder of a qualifying floating charge in respect of a company's property may not appoint or apply to the court for the appointment of a receiver who on appointment would be an administrative receiver of property of the company.

(3)   In subsections (1) and (2)—

"holder of a qualifying floating charge in respect of a company's property" has the same meaning as in paragraph 14 of Schedule B1 to this Act, and

"administrative receiver" has the meaning given by section 251.

(4)   This section applies—

(a)   to a floating charge created on or after a date appointed by the Secretary of State by order made by statutory instrument, and

(b)   in spite of any provision of an agreement or instrument which purports to empower a person to appoint an administrative receiver (by whatever name).

(5)   An order under subsection (4)(a) may—

(a)   make provision which applies generally or only for a specified purpose;

(b)   make different provision for different purposes;

(c)   make transitional provision.

(6)   This section is subject to the exceptions specified in sections 72B to 72GA.

**Amendments**—Inserted by Enterprise Act 2002, s 250(1). Amended by SI 2003/1832.

**General note**—On ss 72A–72H see the commentary in the general introduction to receivership preceding s 28.

**[1.118]**

**72B First exception: capital market**

(1)   Section 72A does not prevent the appointment of an administrative receiver in pursuance of an agreement which is or forms part of a capital market arrangement if—

(a)   a party incurs or, when the agreement was entered into was expected to incur, a debt of at least £50 million under the arrangement, and

(b)   the arrangement involves the issue of a capital market investment.

(2)   In subsection (1)—

"capital market arrangement" means an arrangement of a kind described in paragraph 1 of Schedule 2A, and "capital market investment" means an investment of a kind described in paragraph 2 or 3 of that Schedule.

**Amendments**—Inserted by Enterprise Act 2002, s 250(1).

**General note**—On ss 72A–72H see the commentary in the general introduction to receivership preceding s 28.

## [1.119]

### 72C  Second exception: public-private partnership

(1)  Section 72A does not prevent the appointment of an administrative receiver of a project company of a project which—

  (a)  is a public-private partnership project, and

  (b)  includes step-in rights.

(2)  In this section "public-private partnership project" means a project—

  (a)  the resources for which are provided partly by one or more public bodies and partly by one or more private persons, or

  (b)  which is designed wholly or mainly for the purpose of assisting a public body to discharge a function.

(3)  In this section—

  "step-in rights" has the meaning given by paragraph 6 of Schedule 2A, and

  "project company"' has the meaning given by paragraph 7 of that Schedule.

**Amendments**—Inserted by Enterprise Act 2002, s 250(1).

**General note**—On ss 72A–72H see the commentary in the general introduction to receivership preceding s 28.

## [1.120]

### 72D  Third exception: utilities

(1)  Section 72A does not prevent the appointment of an administrative receiver of a project company of a project which—

  (a)  is a utility project, and

  (b)  includes step-in rights.

(2)  In this section—

  (a)  "utility project" means a project designed wholly or mainly for the purpose of a regulated business,

  (b)  "regulated business" means a business of a kind listed in paragraph 10 of Schedule 2A,

  (c)  "step-in rights" has the meaning given by paragraph 6 of that Schedule, and

  (d)  "project company" has the meaning given by paragraph 7 of that Schedule.

**Amendments**—Inserted by Enterprise Act 2002, s 250(1).

**General note**—On ss 72A–72H see the commentary in the general introduction to receivership preceding s 28.

## [1.121]

### 72DA  Exception in respect of urban regeneration projects

(1)  Section 72A does not prevent the appointment of an administrative receiver of a project company of a project which—

  (a)  is designed wholly or mainly to develop land which at the commencement of the project is wholly or partly in a designated disadvantaged area outside Northern Ireland, and

  (b)  includes step-in rights.

(2)  In subsection (1) "develop" means to carry out—

  (a)  building operations,

    (b)    any operation for the removal of substances or waste from land and the levelling of the surface of the land, or

    (c)    engineering operations in connection with the activities mentioned in paragraph (a) or (b).

(3)   In this section—

    "building" includes any structure or erection, and any part of a building as so defined, but does not include plant and machinery comprised in a building,

    "building operations" includes—

        (a)    demolition of buildings,

        (b)    filling in of trenches,

        (c)    rebuilding,

        (d)    structural alterations of, or additions to, buildings and

        (e)    other operations normally undertaken by a person carrying on business as a builder,

    "designated disadvantaged area" means an area designated as a disadvantaged area under section 92 of the Finance Act 2001,

    "engineering operations" includes the formation and laying out of means of access to highways,

    "project company" has the meaning given by paragraph 7 of Schedule 2A,

    "step-in rights" has the meaning given by paragraph 6 of that Schedule,

    "substance" means any natural or artificial substance whether in solid or liquid form or in the form of a gas or vapour, and

    "waste" includes any waste materials, spoil, refuse or other matter deposited on land.

**Amendments**—Inserted by SI 2003/1832.

**General note**—On ss 72A–72H see the commentary in the general introduction to receivership preceding s 28.

## [1.122]

### 72E Fourth exception: project finance

(1)   Section 72A does not prevent the appointment of an administrative receiver of a project company of a project which—

    (a)    is a financed project, and

    (b)    includes step-in rights.

(2)   In this section—

    (a)    a project is "financed" if under an agreement relating to the project a project company incurs, or when the agreement is entered into is expected to incur, a debt of at least £50 million for the purposes of carrying out the project,

    (b)    "project company" has the meaning given by paragraph 7 of Schedule 2A, and

    (c)    "step-in rights" has the meaning given by paragraph 6 of that Schedule.

**Amendments**—Inserted by Enterprise Act 2002, s 250(1).

**General note**—On ss 72A–72H see the commentary in the general introduction to receivership preceding s 28.

'**Step-in rights**'—In *Feetum v Levy* [2005] EWCA Civ 1601, [2006] Ch 585, [2006] 2 BCLC 102, [2006] BPIR 379 at [93] the Court of Appeal (Jonathan Parker LJ, Sir Peter Gibson and Ward LJ agreeing) identified a number of propositions regarding the meaning and scope of para 6 of Sch 2A which could be stated with 'some degree of confidence' despite the concerns expressed over the state of the drafting of the provisions.

## [1.123]

### 72F Fifth exception: financial market

Section 72A does not prevent the appointment of an administrative receiver of a company by virtue of—

(a)   a market charge within the meaning of section 173 of the Companies Act 1989 (c 40),

(b)   a system-charge within the meaning of the Financial Markets and Insolvency Regulations 1996 (SI 1996/1469),

(c)   a collateral security charge within the meaning of the Financial Markets and Insolvency (Settlement Finality) Regulations 1999 (SI 1999/2979).

**Amendments**—Inserted by Enterprise Act 2002, s 250(1).

**General note**—On ss 72A–72H see the commentary in the general introduction to receivership preceding s 28.

## [1.124]

### 72G  Sixth exception: social landlords

Section 72A does not prevent the appointment of an administrative receiver of a company which is—

(a)   a private registered provider of social housing, or

(b)   registered as a social landlord under Part I of the Housing Act 1996 (c 52) or under Part 2 of the Housing (Scotland) Act 2010 (asp 17).

**Amendments**—Inserted by Enterprise Act 2002, s 250(1); SI 2010/866; SI 2012/700.

**General note**—On ss 72A–72H see the commentary in the general introduction to receivership preceding s 28.

## [1.125]

### 72GA  Exception in relation to protected railway companies etc

Section 72A does not prevent the appointment of an administrative receiver of—

(a)   a company holding an appointment under Chapter I of Part II of the Water Industry Act 1991,

(b)   a protected railway company within the meaning of section 59 of the Railways Act 1993 (including that section as it has effect by virtue of section 19 of the Channel Tunnel Rail Link Act 1996, or

(c)   a licence company within the meaning of section 26 of the Transport Act 2000.

**Amendments**—Inserted by SI 2003/1832.

**General note**—On ss 72A–72H see the commentary in the general introduction to receivership preceding s 28.

## [1.126]

### 72H  Sections 72A to 72G: supplementary

(1)   Schedule 2A (which supplements sections 72B to 72G) shall have effect.

(2)   The Secretary of State may by order—

(a)   insert into this Act provision creating an additional exception to section 72A(1) or (2);

(b)   provide for a provision of this Act which creates an exception to section 72A(1) or (2) to cease to have effect;

(c)   amend section 72A in consequence of provision made under paragraph (a) or (b);

(d)   amend any of sections 72B to 72G;

(e)   amend Schedule 2A.

(3)   An order under subsection (2) must be made by statutory instrument.

(4)   An order under subsection (2) may make—

(a)   provision which applies generally or only for a specified purpose;

(b)   different provision for different purposes;

(c)   consequential or supplementary provision;

(d)   transitional provision.

(5)   An order under subsection (2)—

(a)   in the case of an order under subsection (2)(e), shall be subject to annulment in pursuance of a resolution of either House of Parliament,

(b)   in the case of an order under subsection (2)(d) varying the sum specified in section 72B(1)(a) or 72E(2)(a) (whether or not the order also makes consequential or transitional provision), shall be subject to annulment in pursuance of a resolution of either House of Parliament, and

(c)   in the case of any other order under subsection (2)(a) to (d), may not be made unless a draft has been laid before and approved by resolution of each House of Parliament.

**Amendments**—Inserted by Enterprise Act 2002, s 250(1).

**General note**—On ss 72A–72H see the commentary in the general introduction to receivership preceding s 28.


## PART IV   WINDING UP OF COMPANIES REGISTERED UNDER THE COMPANIES ACTS

**[1.127]**

**General comment on Part IV**—This Part deals with the winding up of the vast majority of companies in England and Wales, and Scotland, namely those that are registered pursuant to the Companies Acts. The next Part (Part V) of the Act deals with the winding up of unregistered companies. This latter category covers oversea companies and other companies the liquidation of which is not dealt with in separate legislation. Some specialist companies are wound up under specific legislation, eg building societies (Building Societies Act 1986). Companies in Northern Ireland are wound up pursuant to the Companies (Northern Ireland) Order 1986, although such companies may be wound up as unregistered companies under s 221(1) if they have a principal place of business in Great Britain: *Re a Company (No 007946 of 1993)* [1994] Ch 198. Insolvent partnerships are able to be wound up as unregistered companies due to the operation of the Insolvent Partnerships Order 1994 (SI 1994/2421).

Winding up involves the administration of the affairs of a company so as to prepare it for corporate death, ie dissolution.


### CHAPTER I

#### PRELIMINARY
*Introductory*


**[1.128]**

### 73  Scheme of this Part

(1)   This Part applies to the winding up of a company registered under the Companies Act 2006 in England and Wales or Scotland.

(2)   The winding up may be either—

(a)   voluntary (see Chapters 2 to 5), or

(b)   by the court (see Chapter 6).

(3)   This Chapter and Chapters 7 to 10 relate to winding up generally, except where otherwise stated.

**Amendments**—SI 2009/1941.

**General note**—The provision identifies two forms of liquidation – voluntary winding up and winding up by the court, with the latter being more usually referred to as compulsory winding up. The former is initiated by the company, and is brought about by a resolution for winding up passed by the company in general meeting (s 84(1)). If the company is solvent, the liquidator is appointed by the members and such liquidations are known as 'members' voluntary liquidations'. It might seem strange that companies that are solvent at the point of winding up are dealt with pursuant to the Insolvency Act, but it is probably efficient and convenient to have all companies that are wound up regulated by the same statute. Notwithstanding that some companies are solvent when they are wound up either voluntarily or by the court, the vast majority of companies that are liquidated each year are insolvent to varying degrees.

Compulsory liquidations are commenced only by a court order. See Chapter VI of this Part.

**A company**—This term is not defined in the Act, but s 251 provides that 'any expression for whose interpretation provision is made by Part XXVI of the Companies Act 1985, other than an expression defined above in this section, is to be construed in accordance with that provision.' 'Company' is defined in ss 1(1) and 1171 of the Companies Act 2006 as a company formed and registered under that statute, or an existing company (s 735(1)(a)). Section 735(1)(b) provides that an existing company is a company formed and registered pursuant to the former Companies Acts, but does not include a company registered under the Joint Stock Companies Acts, the Companies Act 1862 or the Companies (Consolidation) Act 1908 in what was, when the legislation was passed, Ireland. 'The former Companies Acts' are defined to mean the Joint Stock Companies Acts, the Companies Act 1862 or the Companies (Consolidation) Act 1908, the Companies Act 1929 and the Companies Acts 1948 to 1983 (s 735(1)(c)). In relation to existing companies, s 675(1) of the Companies Act 1985 provides that in its application to existing companies the Companies Act applies just as if they had been formed and registered pursuant to Part I of the legislation. The upshot from all of this is that no matter under which legislation a company was registered, it is to be viewed in the same manner for the purposes of the Companies Act 1985, and can be wound up under the Insolvency Act as a company registered in England and Wales or Scotland.

## Contributories

**[1.129]**

### 74 Liability as contributories of present and past members

(1)   When a company is wound up, every present and past member is liable to contribute to its assets to any amount sufficient for payment of its debts and liabilities, and the expenses of the winding up, and for the adjustment of the rights of the contributories among themselves.

(2)   This is subject as follows—

(a)   a past member is not liable to contribute if he has ceased to be a member for one year or more before the commencement of the winding up;

(b)   a past member is not liable to contribute in respect of any debt or liability of the company contracted after he ceased to be a member;

(c)   a past member is not liable to contribute, unless it appears to the court that the existing members are unable to satisfy the contributions required to be made by them;

(d)   in the case of a company limited by shares, no contribution is required from any member exceeding the amount (if any) unpaid on the shares in respect of which he is liable as a present or past member;

(e)   nothing in the Companies Acts or this Act invalidates any provision contained in a policy of insurance or other contract whereby the liability of individual members on the policy or contract is restricted, or whereby the funds of the company are alone made liable in respect of the policy or contract;

(f)   a sum due to any member of the company (in his character of a member) by way of dividends, profits or otherwise is not deemed to be a debt of the company, payable to that member in a case of competition between himself and any other creditor not a member of the company, but any such sum may be taken into account for the purpose of the final adjustment of the rights of the contributories among themselves.

(3)   In the case of a company limited by guarantee, no contribution is required from any member exceeding the amount undertaken to be contributed by him to the company's assets in the event of its being wound up; but if it is a company with a share capital, every member of it is liable (in addition to the amount so undertaken to be contributed to the assets), to contribute to the extent of any sums unpaid on shares held by him.

**Amendments**—SI 2009/1941.

**CIGA 2020**—This provision is affected by temporary measures at Sch 10, para 10 of CIGA 2020.

**General**—Section 74(1) involves liquidators undertaking an assessment of what the liabilities of the company might be, which consequently leads, at least in part, to an assessment of what its assets are. Liquidators will have to make a judgment as to the liabilities, the assets available to pay them, and the costs of getting in the assets. The result of that consideration will determine the liability to contribute as defined in s 74(1): *Scott-Hake v Frost* [2020] EWHC 3677 (Ch) at [38].

**Past member**—The reference to one year is varied where a winding-up order was made as a result of a petition presented under s 124 during the period of 27 April 2020 to 30 September 2021 on the basis that the company was unable to pay its debts. In such a case s 74(2)(a) has effect as if the reference to one year or more before the commencement of the winding up were to one year or more before the day on which the petition was presented, or if the winding-up order was made more than 6 months after the day on which the petition was presented, 18 months or more before the day on which the winding-up order was made (para 10 of Sch 10 of the Corporate Insolvency and Governance Act 2020) (as amended by The Corporate Insolvency and Governance Act 2020 (Coronavirus) (Extension of the Relevant Period) Regulations 2020 (SI 2020/1031), reg 2, The Corporate Insolvency and Governance Act 2020 (Coronavirus) (Extension of the Relevant Period) (No 2) Regulations 2020 (SI 2020/1483), reg 2, The Corporate Insolvency and Governance Act 2020 (Coronavirus) (Extension of the Relevant Period) Regulations 2021 (SI 2021/375), reg 3(4) and The Corporate Insolvency and Governance Act 2020 (Coronavirus) (Extension of the Relevant Period) (No 2) Regulations 2021 (SI 2021/718), reg 2).

**Contributory**—'Contributory' is a term that is defined in s 79. It involves any member or past member who is liable to contribute to the assets of a company on winding up. This seems to indicate that one is only a contributory if at the point of winding up, one is liable to make payment to the company. However, this would mean that a fully paid up shareholder was not a contributory, and yet it has been settled for many years that such a shareholder is a contributory: *Re Anglesea Colliery Co* (1866) 1 Ch App 555; *Re Phoenix Oil & Transport Co* [1958] Ch 560, and affirmed recently: *Burnden Group Holdings Ltd v Hunt* [2018] EWHC 463 (Ch) at [52]. A person or company who owes a debt to the company is not a contributory (*Re European Society Arbitration Acts* (1878) 8 ChD 679 at 708), but treated as owing a debt to the company. The law acknowledges that there is a distinction to be made between the status of being a contributory, and a liability to contribute to the assets. Being a contributory means essentially that one is part of the membership of the company, and this status can exist before winding up, while having a liability to contribute only occurs when the winding up commences. There are two kinds of persons who, though not registered as members of the company, are, according to ss 81 and 82, to be regarded as contributories, namely the personal representatives of a deceased contributory and the trustee of a bankrupt contributory. See the comments accompanying ss 81 and 82, which specifically deal with these kinds of contributories.

The sums that are recovered from contributories are deposited in a fund that will be used to repay creditors (*Webb v Whiffin* (1872) LR 5 HL 711), provided that there are sufficient funds following the payment of the costs and expenses of the liquidation.

Section 74 first provides that all present and past members are liable to contribute to its assets to the extent of paying off debts and liabilities and meeting the expenses of winding up, as well as providing for the adjustment of rights amongst the contributories. Then it states that certain persons are effectively exempt from payment or their contribution is limited. This restriction on liability recognises the concept of limited liability.

The liquidator is charged with the job of recovering contributions from the members in winding up. First, the liquidator will ascertain or identify those who are liable to contribute, and this is achieved by what is known as 'settling the list of contributories'. The obligation is, according to s 148, something that falls to the court, but r 7.79 provides that the liquidator is to discharge this court duty as a delegate of the court. After the completion of the settling, the liquidator makes and enforces calls on as many of those persons listed (to the full extent of their liability) as is necessary in order to discharge the debts of the company or to adjust the rights of contributories. Adjustment occurs in order to have losses evenly distributed amongst all the members. See the comments attaching to s 148.

If the articles permit shares to be paid for in instalments, this arrangement will cease if liquidation intervenes before the date on which the instalments become due and payable: *Re Cordova Union Gold Co* [1891] 2 Ch 580.

**Liable to contribute**—Contributories' liability in unlimited companies extends to the payment of statutory interest on proved debts and unprovable liabilities: *Re Lehman Brothers International (Europe) (No 7)* [2014] EWHC 704 (Ch), [2015] 1 BCLC 151 and affirmed on appeal: [2015] EWCA Civ 485, [2016] Ch 50, [2015] 2 BCLC 433. The Court of Appeal stated that a statutory requirement for payment of a sum out of the assets of a company should be regarded as a liability of the company to the person entitled to the payment, certainly for the purposes of this section. The Court also stated that the liability of members under s 74(1) to contribute to the assets of a company in liquidation 'to any amount sufficient for payment of its debts and liabilities' was not restricted to the funds required to pay the debts and liabilities proved in the liquidation but also, by s 189(2), included funds required for the payment of statutory interest on those debts and any non-provable liabilities. Furthermore, the future or contingent liability of a member to meet a call in respect of its liability under s 74(1) is a provable debt in the insolvency of the member within the meaning of r 14.1(3)

**Past members**—Their liability is limited in various ways by s 74(2)(a)–(c). The obligation of past members to contribute is further restricted to the amount left unpaid by the present members on the shares that they once held.

Past members are those who have ceased for any reason, perhaps because of death, transfer, or forfeiture, to be members: *Re National Bank of Wales; Taylor, Phillips and Rickards' Case* [1897] 1 Ch 298 at 307.

**In the character of a member**—According to s 74(2)(f), in circumstances where a member is liable to pay a sum to the liquidator, then that member is unable to prove in the liquidation, in competition with other creditors who are not members of the company, for any amount owed to the member 'in his character of a member'. This phrase has caused problems for the courts. Sums due 'in his character of a member' will include sums owed as dividends, profits or otherwise, but they will not include claims that might have depended on membership of the company, and where membership was not the foundation of the cause of action: *Soden v British and Commonwealth Holdings plc* [1998] AC 298, [1997] 2 WLR 206, [1997] 2 BCLC 501 HL. So damages that emanate from a claim against the company for misrepresentation after the purchase of shares from a third party is not a claim in the character of a member (*Soden*). In delivering the leading speech in *Soden*, Lord Browne-Wilkinson said ([1998] AC at 298 at 323) that:

> '[I]n the absence of any contrary indication sums due to a member "in his character of a member" are only those sums the right to which is based by way of cause of action on the statutory contract [between the members and the company and provided by s 14 of the Companies Act 1985 (now s 33 of the Companies Act 2006)].'

However, where members purchased the shares by subscription from the company and had a claim for misrepresentation, the claim would be one in the character of a member: *Re Addlestone Linoleum Co* (1887) 37 ChD 191; *Webb Distributors (Aust) Pty Ltd v The State of Victoria* (1993) 11 ACLC 1178, (1993) 11 ACSR 731, Aust HC. The advent of s 111A of the Companies Act 1985 (now Companies Act 2006, might well mean that these cases would now be decided differently on the relevant point.

According to *Soden*, loans made by a member to the company, sums due to a member under a contract for the sale of goods by the member to the company, and arrears of remuneration due to a member in his or her capacity as a director would not be affected by s 74(2)(f), so members with these sorts of claims could line up for payment with the creditors of the company: [1998] AC 298 at 306. *Soden* provides that there was not a 'members come last' principle in a winding up, for a member with an independent claim is in no worse position than a creditor; it is only in considering the rights of a member *qua* member that his or her rights are placed last.

Any amount owed in the character of a member may be taken into account for the purpose of the final adjustment of the rights of contributories amongst each other.

For a detailed discussion of contributories, see A Keay *McPherson and Keay's Law of Company Liquidation* (Sweet and Maxwell, 4th edn, 2018), Ch 10.

## 75
*(Repealed)*

## [1.130]

### 76 Liability of past directors and shareholders

(1)  This section applies where a company is being wound up and—

   (a)  it has under Chapter 5 of Part 18 of the Companies Act 2006 (acquisition by limited company of its own shares: redemption or purchase by private company out of capital) made a payment out of capital in respect of the redemption or purchase of any of its own shares (the payment being referred to below as "the relevant payment"), and

   (b)  the aggregate amount of the company's assets and the amounts paid by way of contribution to its assets (apart from this section) is not sufficient for payment of its debts and liabilities, and the expenses of the winding up.

(2)  If the winding up commenced within one year of the date on which the relevant payment was made, then—

   (a)  the person from whom the shares were redeemed or purchased, and

   (b)  the directors who signed the statement made in accordance with section 714(1) to (3) of the Companies Act 2006 for purposes of the redemption or purchase (except a director who shows that he had reasonable grounds for forming the opinion set out in the statement), are, so as to enable that insufficiency to be met, liable to contribute to the following extent to the company's assets.

(3)   A person from whom any of the shares were redeemed or purchased is liable to contribute an amount not exceeding so much of the relevant payment as was made by the company in respect of his shares; and the directors are jointly and severally liable with that person to contribute that amount.

(4)   A person who has contributed any amount to the assets in pursuance of this section may apply to the court for an order directing any other person jointly and severally liable in respect of that amount to pay him such amount as the court thinks just and equitable.

(5)   Section 74 does not apply in relation to liability accruing by virtue of this section.

(6)   . . .

**Amendments**—SI 2009/1941; SI 2011/1265.

**General note**—Here the legislature is concerned that the company will have been divested of capital, which could have been used to pay creditors, in order to pay the seller of the shares. Hence, it is a measure that is designed to protect the unsecured creditors, who will have recourse to the company's capital on liquidation.

## [1.131]

### 77  Limited company formerly unlimited

(1)   This section applies in the case of a company being wound up which was at some former time registered as unlimited but has re-registered as a limited company.

(2)   Notwithstanding section 74(2)(a) above, a past member of the company who was a member of it at the time of re-registration, if the winding up commences within the period of 3 years beginning with the day on which the company was re-registered, is liable to contribute to the assets of the company in respect of debts and liabilities contracted before that time.

(3)   If no persons who were members of the company at that time are existing members of it, a person who at that time was a present or past member is liable to contribute as above notwithstanding that the existing members have satisfied the contributions required to be made by them.

This applies subject to section 74(2)(a) above and to subsection (2) of this section, but notwithstanding section 74(2)(c).

(4)   Notwithstanding section 74(2)(d) and (3), there is no limit on the amount which a person who, at that time, was a past or present member of the company is liable to contribute as above.

**Amendments**—SI 2009/1941.

**General note**—This constitutes a qualification to the restriction on the liability of a past member in s 74(2)(a). In the circumstance set out in the section a past member can be liable for up to 3 years since he or she ceased to be a member.

## [1.132]

### 78  Unlimited company formerly limited

(1)   This section applies in the case of a company being wound up which was at some former time registered as limited but has been re-registered as unlimited.

(2)   A person who, at the time when the application for the company to be re-registered was lodged, was a past member of the company and did not after that again become a member of it is not liable to contribute to the assets of the company more than he would have been liable to contribute had the company not been re-registered.

**Amendments**—SI 2009/1941.

**General note**—Where the change of a company's status is from public company to unlimited company, pursuant to s 102 of the Companies Act 2006, then past members at the time of the change (who did not again become members of the company) are protected in that they are not liable to contribute more than what they would have been liable to contribute had the company not changed status.

**[1.133]**

**79 Meaning of "contributory"**

(1)   In this Act the expression "contributory" means every person liable to contribute to the assets of a company in the event of its being wound up, and for the purposes of all proceedings for determining, and all proceedings prior to the final determination of, the persons who are to be deemed contributories, includes any person alleged to be a contributory.

(2)   The reference in subsection (1) to persons liable to contribute to the assets does not include a person so liable by virtue of a declaration by the court under section 213 (imputed responsibility for company's fraudulent trading) or section 214 (wrongful trading) in Chapter X of this Part.

(3)   A reference in a company's articles to a contributory does not (unless the context requires) include a person who is a contributory only by virtue of section 76.

Amendments—SI 2009/1941.

General note—See the notes accompanying s 74.

Contributory—This term includes reference to an alleged contributory: *Scott-Hake v Frost* [2020] EWHC 3677 (Ch) at [65].

**[1.134]**

**80 Nature of contributory's liability**

The liability of a contributory creates a debt (in England and Wales in the nature of an ordinary contract debt) accruing due from him at the time when his liability commenced, but payable at the times when calls are made for enforcing the liability.

Amendments—SI 2009/1941.

General note—If a person is liable as a contributory, then this creates a debt, a specialty debt (in England and Wales) owed to the company, and payable at the time when calls are made for the enforcing of the liability. The limitation period for specialty debts is 12 years.

The meaning of 'contributory' includes those who are regarded as members within s 250, and this is so 'notwithstanding that the name of the qualifying transferee or of the person to whom shares are transmitted by law is not entered into a company's register of members. It is also notwithstanding that a member has to have their name registered in the register of members.' (s 112(2) CA): *Hamilton v Brown*, sub nom, *Re C and MB Holdings Ltd* [2016] EWHC 191 (Ch), [2017] 1 BCLC 269, [2016] BPIR 531 at [46].

**[1.135]**

**81 Contributories in case of death of a member**

(1)   If a contributory dies either before or after he has been placed on the list of contributories, his personal representatives, and the heirs and legatees of heritage of his heritable estate in Scotland, are liable in a due course of administration to contribute to the assets of the company in discharge of his liability and are contributories accordingly.

(2)   Where the personal representatives are placed on the list of contributories, the heirs or legatees of heritage need not be added, but they may be added as and when the court thinks fit.

(3)   If in England and Wales the personal representatives make default in paying any money ordered to be paid by them, proceedings may be taken for administering the estate of the deceased contributory and for compelling payment out of it of the money due.

General note—This provision (and s 82) constitutes an exception to the rule that the group of contributories consists of members present or past.

The executors of the estate of a deceased member do not become personally liable unless they agree to be registered as members: *Re City of Glasgow Bank; Buchan's Case* (1879) 4 App Cas 583; *Re Cheshire Banking Co; Duff's Executors Case* (1885) 32 ChD 301.

It might be thought that, as the death of a member terminates his or her membership of the company (*Permanent Trustee Co v Palmer* (1929) 42 CLR 277 at 283), the estate of a member dying before winding up would be liable only as a past member. But it is settled that, while the name of the deceased member remains on the register of members, the deceased's estate is a member of the company and so the liability is that of a present member: *Re Agriculturist Cattle Insurance Co; Baird's Case* (1870) 5 Ch App 725 at 735.

## [1.136]

### 82 Effect of contributory's bankruptcy

(1)   The following applies if a contributory becomes bankrupt, either before or after he has been placed on the list of contributories.

(2)   His trustee in bankruptcy represents him for all purposes of the winding up, and is a contributory accordingly.

(3)   The trustee may be called on to admit to proof against the bankrupt's estate, or otherwise allow to be paid out of the bankrupt's assets in due course of law, any money due from the bankrupt in respect of his liability to contribute to the company's assets.

(4)   There may be proved against the bankrupt's estate the estimated value of his liability to future calls as well as calls already made.

General note—If the trustee in bankruptcy of a member is registered in place of the bankrupt member, the trustee becomes personally liable unless he or she disclaims the shares. It is unusual for the trustee to be registered if the shares are of no value. In a liquidation it is the trustee and not the bankrupt who is the contributory. Hence, the trustee represents the bankrupt for all the purposes of winding up and the liquidator is entitled to prove against the bankrupt estate.

See the comments relating to 'contributory' in s 122.

## [1.137]

### 83 Companies registered but not formed under the Companies Act 2006

(1)   The following applies in the event of a company being wound up which is registered but not formed under the Companies Act 2006.

(2)   Every person is a contributory, in respect of the company's debts and liabilities contracted before registration, who is liable—

  (a)   to pay, or contribute to the payment of, any debt or liability so contracted, or

  (b)   to pay, or contribute to the payment of, any sum for the adjustment of the rights of the members among themselves in respect of any such debt or liability, or

  (c)   to pay, or contribute to the amount of, the expenses of winding up the company, so far as relates to the debts or liabilities above-mentioned.

(3)   Every contributory is liable to contribute to the assets of the company, in the course of the winding up, all sums due from him in respect of any such liability.

(4)   In the event of the death, bankruptcy or insolvency of any contributory, provisions of this Act, with respect to the personal representatives, to the heirs and legatees of heritage of the heritable estate in Scotland of deceased contributories and to the trustees of bankrupt or insolvent contributories respectively, apply.

Amendments—SI 2009/1941.

General note—This relates to companies covered by s 1040 of the Companies Act 2006, namely those that have not been registered under the Companies Act, but which are entitled to become so registered. An example is a company formed pursuant to an Act of Parliament (s 1040(1)(b)).

CHAPTER II

VOLUNTARY WINDING UP (INTRODUCTORY AND GENERAL)
*Resolutions for, and commencement of, voluntary winding up*

## [1.138]

### 84 Circumstances in which company may be wound up voluntarily

(1)   A company may be wound up voluntarily—

  (a)   when the period (if any) fixed for the duration of the company by the articles expires, or the event (if any) occurs, on the occurrence of which the

> articles provide that the company is to be dissolved, and the company in general meeting has passed a resolution requiring it to be wound up voluntarily;
>
> (b)    if the company resolves by special resolution that it be wound up voluntarily;
>
> (c)    . . .

(2)   In this Act the expression "a resolution for voluntary winding up" means a resolution passed under either of the paragraphs of subsection (1).

(2A)   Before a company passes a resolution for voluntary winding up it must give written notice of the resolution to the holder of any qualifying floating charge to which section 72A applies.

(2B)   Where notice is given under subsection (2A) a resolution for voluntary winding up may be passed only—

> (a)    after the end of the period of five business days beginning with the day on which the notice was given, or
>
> (b)    if the person to whom the notice was given has consented in writing to the passing of the resolution.

(3)   Chapter 3 of Part 3 of the Companies Act 2006 (resolutions affecting a company's constitution) applies to a resolution under paragraph (a) of subsection (1) as well as a special resolution under paragraph (b).

(4)   This section has effect subject to section 43 of the Commonhold and Leasehold Reform Act 2002.

**Amendments**—Commonhold and Leasehold Reform Act 2002, s 68, Sch 5, para 6; SI 2003/2096; SI 2007/2194.

**General note**—Voluntary liquidation manifests the policy of allowing the creditors and contributories in winding up to manage what essentially are their own affairs: *Re Wear Engine Works Co* (1875) 10 Ch App 188 at 191. As the section provides, no application to court is necessary in order to initiate this form of winding up, and the liquidator is appointed by, and answerable to, the creditors or contributories who exercise some degree of control over what he or she does in administering the winding up. There is no court involvement in the liquidation process except on certain occasions when court involvement is necessary, such as when: there is a need for the determination of questions arising in winding up and an application is made under s 112(1); some disagreement occurs amongst those persons who are interested in the winding up; or the liquidator has commenced proceedings in order to recover property disposed of, or obtained improperly, before the commencement of the winding up.

A voluntary winding up commences with the passing by the members of one of the two kinds of resolutions set out in s 84(1). The usual company law rules regulating the calling and conduct of company meetings apply in relation to matters such as notice, quorum, voting and procedure.

Members may call the meeting, but usually it is convened by the board of directors, and is valid only if issued with the authority of the directors: *Re Haycraft Gold Reduction Co* [1900] 2 Ch 230; *Re State of Wyoming Syndicate* [1901] 2 Ch 431.

With private companies, a resolution may be passed without the need for a general meeting being held. To do this all the members who are entitled to vote on the resolution must sign a document containing a statement that they support the resolution that is stated in the document (Companies Act 2006, ss 288, 289 (and note the procedure for circulation of the document under ss 290–295)).

The resolution sometimes includes a further resolution to appoint a liquidator. If not, then a separate resolution can be passed after the resolution to wind up has been passed, and this second resolution can be passed without notice: *Bethell v Trench Tubeless Tyres Co* [1900] 1 Ch 408.

A resolution to wind up cannot be passed during the time in which a company is in administration (Sch B1, para 42(2)). Also, a resolution to wind up cannot be passed during the period between the presentation of an application for an administration order and either the making of an administration order or dismissal of the application (Sch B1, para 44(5)). The same paragraph covers the situation where an administration order has been made, but has not taken effect.

Australasian authority provides that the members are not able to revoke a resolution to wind up (*Ross v PJ Heringa Pty Ltd* [1970] NZLR 170; *Dean-Willcocks v Payee (Buildings) Pty Ltd* (unreported, NSW Sup Ct, Young J, 1 September 1994)); application for a court order terminating the winding up would have to be made by the company: *Dean-Willcocks*.

The failure to give notice to the qualifying floating chargeholder under s 84(2A) will not necessarily impugn the appointment of the liquidator by the members' meeting provided that a special resolution to wind up has been passed according to the company's articles: *Re Domestic and General Insulation Ltd* [2018] EWHC 265 (Ch) at [9]. In such a case a qualifying charge holder may have a remedy, if unhappy with this state of affairs, such as petitioning for the compulsory winding up of the company or applying for a stay of the winding up so as to enable an administrator to be appointed (*Re Domestic and General Insulation Ltd* at [9]).

See A Keay *McPherson and Keay's Law of Company Liquidation* (Sweet and Maxwell, 4th edn, 2018) at 42–45 for further explanation of the practice and procedure prior to, and, at the meeting.

The section is subject to the Commonhold and Leasehold Reform Act 2002 and this provides in s 43 for the winding up of commonhold associations (private companies limited by guarantee).

**Resolution**—An ordinary resolution merely requires a simple majority of the members attending the meeting for it to be passed. Special resolutions require a majority of not less than three-fourths (Companies Act 2006, s 283). 14 days' notice of the meeting is required (Companies Act 2006, s 307(1), (2)) (21 days for an annual general meeting of public companies) for whatever resolution is required at the meeting. The members can agree to a shorter notice period (Companies Act 2006, s 307(4)).

**Copy of resolution filed**—The liquidator is obliged to file with the registrar of companies a copy of the resolution within 15 days, or else the liquidator is liable for a fine (Companies Act 2006, s 30(1), (2), (4)).

For a detailed and integrated discussion of voluntary liquidation, see A Keay *McPherson and Keay's Law of Company Liquidation* (Sweet and Maxwell, 4th edn, 2018) at 42–45.

**Authorised deposit-taker**—Where the company falls within this description, notice of the meeting must be delivered by the directors to the Financial Conduct Authority and to the scheme manager established under s 212(1) of the Financial Services and Markets Act 2000: IR 2016, r 5.3(1), (2).

## [1.139]

### 85 Notice of resolution to wind up

(1) When a company has passed a resolution for voluntary winding up, it shall, within 14 days after the passing of the resolution, give notice of the resolution by advertisement in the Gazette.

(2) If default is made in complying with this section, the company and every officer of it who is in default is liable to a fine and, for continued contravention, to a daily default fine.

For purposes of this subsection the liquidator is deemed an officer of the company.

## [1.140]

### 86 Commencement of winding up

A voluntary winding up is deemed to commence at the time of the passing of the resolution for voluntary winding up.

**General note**—The date of the commencement of a winding up is a critical point, as a number of provisions of the Act refer to this time. For instance, the date of commencement terminates the power of the company to dispose of its property (s 127), it fixes the status and liability of contributories, and it deprives creditors of their ordinary remedies against the company (s 128(1)). The time of the commencement in voluntary winding up is to be contrasted with the commencement of a compulsory winding up. In the latter case, while a company is not actually in winding up until a court order is made to that effect, a winding up is nevertheless deemed to have commenced at the time of the presentation of the petition, if an order is made subsequently (s 129(2)).

If a company should move from administration to creditors' winding up under para 83 of Sch B1, then the commencement date under s 86 will be, according to para 83, as if the reference to the time of the passing of the resolution for voluntary winding up were a reference to the beginning of the date of registration of the notice under para 83(3), that is when the administrator sends a notice to the registrar of companies that para 83 is to apply.

*Consequences of resolution to wind up*

**[1.141]**

### 87 Effect on business and status of company

(1)   In case of a voluntary winding up, the company shall from the commencement of the winding up cease to carry on its business, except so far as may be required for its beneficial winding up.

(2)   However, the corporate state and corporate powers of the company, notwithstanding anything to the contrary in its articles, continue until the company is dissolved.

**General note**—This provision details an important effect that the advent of liquidation has on the company and clarifies the fact that the company continues to exist as a corporate entity.

**Ceasing business**—A liquidator in a voluntary liquidation is empowered to carry on the company's business so far as is necessary for its beneficial disposal: *Re Great Eastern Electric Co Ltd* [1941] 1 Ch 241. A person wishing to impugn the decision to carry on the business on the basis that it is not beneficial for the company has the onus of proving it: *The Hire Purchase Furnishing Co Ltd v Richens* (1887) 20 QBD 387, CA.

**Corporate state and powers**—A voluntary liquidation does not affect the corporate personality of the company (*Reigate v Union Manufacturing Co* [1918] 1 KB 592 at 606), which remains a separate entity from the members who comprise it (*Ditcham v Miller* (1931) 100 LJPC 177), and the company's powers are not limited by the fact that it has gone into liquidation: *Re Woking Urban District Council Act* [1914] 1 Ch 300.

**[1.142]**

### 88 Avoidance of share transfers etc after winding-up resolution

Any transfer of shares, not being a transfer made to or with the sanction of the liquidator, and any alteration in the status of the company's members, made after the commencement of a voluntary winding up, is void.

**General note**—This provision is aimed at preventing shareholders from evading liability as contributories by transferring, after winding up has commenced, shares to someone who is impecunious (*Rudge v Bowman* (1865) LR 3 QB 659 at 695; *Re National Bank of Wales* [1896] 2 Ch 851 at 857, 858), but courts have, on occasions, even refused to approve transfers in the case of solvent companies, for instance where it was done for speculative purposes: *Re Onward Building Society* [1891] 2 QB 463.

The transferring of shares is not the only way that a shareholder might seek to evade liability to contribute, and so Parliament probably had this in mind when it provided in this section that no alteration in the status of a member of the company should be valid if it occurs after winding up has commenced.

If agreement was reached in relation to a transfer of shares before winding up, and the transfer has not been registered by the time of winding up because of the failure of the directors of the company to act, the court will order the liquidator to register it: *Re Joint Stock Discount Co* (1869) 4 Ch App 768.

**Sanction of the liquidator**—If the liquidator refuses to sanction the transfer, an application could be made to the court under s 112.

*Declaration of solvency*

**[1.143]**

### 89 Statutory declaration of solvency

(1)   Where it is proposed to wind up a company voluntarily, the directors (or, in the case of a company having more than two directors, the majority of them) may at a directors' meeting make a statutory declaration to the effect that they have made a full inquiry into the company's affairs and that, having done so, they have formed the opinion that the company will be able to pay its debts in full, together with interest at the official rate (as defined in section 251), within such period, not exceeding 12 months from the commencement of the winding up, as may be specified in the declaration.

(2)   Such a declaration by the directors has no effect for purposes of this Act unless—

(a) it is made within the 5 weeks immediately preceding the date of the passing of the resolution for winding up, or on that date but before the passing of the resolution, and

(b) it embodies a statement of the company's assets and liabilities as at the latest practicable date before the making of the declaration.

(3) The declaration shall be delivered to the registrar of companies before the expiration of 15 days immediately following the date on which the resolution for winding up is passed.

(4) A director making a declaration under this section without having reasonable grounds for the opinion that the company will be able to pay its debts in full, together with interest at the official rate, within the period specified is liable to imprisonment or a fine, or both.

(5) If the company is wound up in pursuance of a resolution passed within 5 weeks after the making of the declaration, and its debts (together with interest at the official rate) are not paid or provided for in full within the period specified, it is to be presumed (unless the contrary is shown) that the director did not have reasonable grounds for his opinion.

(6) If a declaration required by subsection (3) to be delivered to the registrar is not so delivered within the time prescribed by that subsection, the company and every officer in default is liable to a fine and, for continued contravention, to a daily default fine.

**General note**—This is a critical section in the voluntary winding-up process. Unless a declaration of solvency can be made by the directors, the liquidation of a company must proceed as a creditors' voluntary liquidation; for a members' voluntary liquidation of a company, there must be this declaration of solvency. The two forms of voluntary liquidation are referred to in s 90.

The section deters directors from acting imprudently in making a declaration. First, s 89(5) provides that they have the burden of overcoming a presumption that they did not have reasonable grounds for the opinion that is expressed in the statement. Second, civil and criminal consequences might flow from a breach of the section.

**A statutory declaration**—While the declaration is often referred to as a declaration of solvency, the directors do not have to state that the company is, or will be, solvent. The directors must, in the declaration, state when, in their view, the company's debts, in a period not exceeding 12 months, will be paid in full. The declaration is only effective if made either within 5 weeks immediately preceding the date of the passing of the resolution for voluntary winding up, or on that date, but before the passing of the resolution, and it includes a statement of the company's assets and liabilities as at the latest practicable date before the declaration is made. The time period set for the compilation of the statement is designed, obviously, to ensure that the statement shows, as much as possible, the current state of the company's affairs.

Rule 5.1 sets out the details that are to be included in the declaration of solvency.

If, after a statement has been made, errors and omissions are found, it will not prevent the statement from being a statement within the terms of the section: *De Courcy v Clement* [1971] Ch 693, [1971] 1 All ER 681; *Re New Millennium Experience Co Ltd* [2003] EWHC 1823, [2004] 1 BCLC 19 at [107], [111].

If the company is the subject of a petition for winding up, following a voluntary winding up it is then the statement is likely to be scrutinised, as in *Re Leading Guides International Ltd (in liquidation)* [1998] 1 BCLC 620.

**Penalty**—Directors who breach the section may be subject to a civil penalty (having to pay the company's debts) and a criminal penalty (a fine or imprisonment or both). The fine is unlimited and the term of imprisonment could be anything up to 2 years if the prosecution is tried on indictment (Sch 10): see the comments of Harman J in *Re Surplus Properties (Huddersfield) Ltd* [1984] 1 BCLC 89 at 91.

## [1.144]

### 90 Distinction between "members'" and "creditors'" voluntary winding up

A winding up in the case of which a directors' statutory declaration under section 89 has been made is a "members' voluntary winding up"; and a winding up in the case of which such a declaration has not been made is a "creditors' voluntary winding up".

**General note**—This sets out the distinction between the two forms of voluntary liquidation. Sections 91–96 cover members' voluntary liquidation and ss 97–106 address creditors' voluntary liquidation. Then ss 107–116 are provisions that apply to both forms.

Part 5 of the Rules applies to members' voluntary liquidations and Part 6 to creditors' voluntary liquidations.

## CHAPTER III

### MEMBERS' VOLUNTARY WINDING UP

## [1.145]

### 91 Appointment of liquidator

(1) In a members' voluntary winding up, the company in general meeting shall appoint one or more liquidators for the purpose of winding up the company's affairs and distributing its assets.

(2) On the appointment of a liquidator all the powers of the directors cease, except so far as the company in general meeting or the liquidator sanctions their continuance.

**General note**—This provision deals exclusively with members' voluntary winding up. Creditors do not become involved in this form of winding up because they have no financial interest in the outcome of the liquidation, as the company will be able to pay all its debts in full (provided that the statutory declaration in s 89 is correct).

Rule 5.2 sets out the requirements that have to be completed for the liquidator's appointment.

See A Keay *McPherson and Keay's Law of Company Liquidation* (Sweet and Maxwell, 4th edn, 2018) at 40–45 for further discussion concerning the members' voluntary winding up process.

**Appointing a liquidator**—The members' meeting appoints the liquidator (who consents) by resolution. This appointment can be part of the resolution to wind up. If this does not occur, then the liquidator can be appointed by ordinary resolution, and such a resolution can be put and passed without notice after the resolution to wind up has been passed: *Bethell v Trench Tubeless Tyres Co* [1900] 1 Ch 408. The members may appoint more than one liquidator (*Bethell*), although this would be unusual. Where more than one liquidator is appointed, the resolution should state whether the liquidators are to exercise their powers and duties jointly or separately (see s 231(2)). Anyone who is nominated as a liquidator must be qualified to act as an insolvency practitioner pursuant to ss 388 and 389.

The liquidator has 28 days from appointment to deliver notice of the appointment to the creditors of the company: r 5.2(6).

**Directors' powers**—While the powers of directors terminate on winding up, the office of a director does not come to an end, because the Act permits directors to exercise certain powers in some circumstances after the commencement of winding up. There is judicial authority that supports such a view (*Midland Counties District Bank Ltd v Attwood* [1905] 1 Ch 357), as does s 114.

## [1.146]

### 92 Power to fill vacancy in office of liquidator

(1) If a vacancy occurs by death, resignation or otherwise in the office of liquidator appointed by the company, the company in general meeting may, subject to any arrangement with its creditors, fill the vacancy.

(2) For that purpose a general meeting may be convened by any contributory or, if there were more liquidators than one, by the continuing liquidators.

(3) The meeting shall be held in manner provided by this Act or by the articles, or in such manner as may, on application by any contributory or by the continuing liquidators, be determined by the court.

**Arrangement with the creditors**—Given the fact that this is a members' voluntary liquidation, it is hard to see why the reference to the creditors has any relevance.

**This Act**—The reference to 'this Act' is undoubtedly meant to be a reference to the companies legislation, and not to the Insolvency Act, as the latter makes no provision for the convening of members' meetings. Part 13 of the Companies Act 2006 now covers the convening of meetings for companies.

Rule 5.11 covers the situation where the appointed liquidator dies, and r 5.12 addresses the situation where the liquidator is no longer qualified to act as an insolvency practitioner.

**[1.147]**

**92A Progress report to company . . . . . .**

(1)  Subject to section 96, . . . the liquidator must—

  (a)  for each prescribed period produce a progress report relating to the prescribed matters; and

  (b)  within such period commencing with the end of the period referred to in paragraph (a) as may be prescribed send a copy of the progress report to—

   (i)  the members of the company; and

   (ii)  such other persons as may be prescribed.

(2)  A liquidator who fails to comply with this section is liable to a fine.

**Amendments**—Inserted by SI 2010/18. Amended by Small Business, Enterprise and Employment Act 2015, ss 126, 136(1), (2), Sch 9, Pt 1, paras 1, 16; SSI 2016/141.

**93**

*(Repealed)*

**Amendments**—Repealed by SSI 2016/141.

**[1.148]**

**94 Final account prior to dissolution**

(1)  As soon as the company's affairs are fully wound up the liquidator must make up an account of the winding up, showing how it has been conducted and the company's property has been disposed of.

(2)  The liquidator must send a copy of the account to the members of the company before the end of the period of 14 days beginning with the day on which the account is made up.

(3)  The liquidator must send a copy of the account to the registrar of companies before the end of that period (but not before sending it to the members of the company).

(4)  If the liquidator does not comply with subsection (2) the liquidator is liable to a fine.

(5)  If the liquidator does not comply with subsection (3) the liquidator is liable to a fine and, for continued contravention, a daily default fine.

**Amendments**—Substituted by Small Business, Enterprise and Employment Act 2015, s 126, Sch 9, Pt 1, paras 1, 18.

**General note**—At the end of 3 months from the delivery of the liquidator's final account and statement to the registrar of companies, the company is automatically dissolved (s 201(1), (2)). See the comments accompanying s 201, which deals with dissolution.

See r 5.9 for the process and the fact that a notice must be sent to the members with the proposed final account and giving the members a minimum of 8 weeks' notice of a specified date on which the liquidator intends to deliver the final account.

Rule 5.10 provides that the contents of the final account which the liquidator is required to make up must comply with the requirements of r 18.14. The former rule also states that a notice must accompany the final account and it describes what the notice must do.

Section 94 is essentially the same as s 106, which covers creditors' voluntary liquidations. See the notes accompanying that latter section.

**[1.149]**

**95 Effect of company's insolvency**

(1)  This section applies where the liquidator is of the opinion that the company will be unable to pay its debts in full (together with interest at the official rate) within the period stated in the directors' declaration under section 89.

(1A)  The liquidator must before the end of the period of 7 days beginning with the day after the day on which the liquidator formed that opinion—

  (a)  make out a statement in the prescribed form as to the affairs of the company, and

  (b)  send it to the company's creditors.

(2)  . . .

(2A)   ...

(3)   ...

(4)   The statement as to the affairs of the company ... shall show—

    (a)    particulars of the company's assets, debts and liabilities;

    (b)    the names and addresses of the company's creditors;

    (c)    the securities held by them respectively;

    (d)    the dates when the securities were respectively given; and

    (e)    such further or other information as may be prescribed.

(4A)   The statement as to the affairs of the company shall ...—

    (a)    in the case of a winding up of a company registered in England and Wales be verified by the liquidator, by a statement of truth; and

    (b)    in the case of a winding up of a company registered in Scotland, contain a statutory declaration by the liquidator.

(4B)   The company's creditors may in accordance with the rules nominate a person to be liquidator.

(4C)   The liquidator must in accordance with the rules seek such a nomination from the company's creditors.

(5)   ...

(6)   ...

(7)   ...

(8)   If the liquidator without reasonable excuse fails to comply with subsections (1) to (4A), he is liable to a fine.

**Amendments**—SI 2009/864; SI 2010/18; Small Business, Enterprise and Employment Act 2015, s 126, Sch 9, Pt 1, paras 1, 19(1)–(5); SSI 2016/141.

**General note**—If the situation provided for in this section occurs, then the liquidation proceeds as a creditors' voluntary winding up (s 96).

The rules in Chapter 2 of Part 6 apply to the statement of affairs made out by the liquidator under s 95(1A)(a): r 5.22.

The details that the liquidator has to supply to creditors are equivalent to what the directors have to provide under s 99 where there is a creditors' voluntary liquidation right from the beginning of the winding-up process.

In general see rr 15.8, 15.9.

**Statement of affairs**—See r 6.2.

## [1.150]

### 96 Conversion to creditors' voluntary winding up

(1)   The winding up becomes a creditors' voluntary winding up as from the day on which—

    (a)    the company's creditors under section 95 nominate a person to be liquidator, or

    (b)    the procedure by which the company's creditors were to have made such a nomination concludes without a nomination having been made.

(2)   As from that day this Act has effect as if the directors' declaration under section 89 had not been made.

(3)   The liquidator in the creditors' voluntary winding up is to be the person nominated by the company's creditors under section 95 or, where no person has been so nominated, the existing liquidator.

(4)   In the case of the creditors nominating a person other than the existing liquidator any director, member or creditor of the company may, within 7 days after the date on which the nomination was made by the creditors, apply to the court for an order either—

    (a)    directing that the existing liquidator is to be liquidator instead of or jointly with the person nominated by the creditors, or

    (b)    appointing some other person to be liquidator instead of the person nominated by the creditors.

(4A)   The court shall grant an application under subsection (4) made by the holder of a qualifying floating charge in respect of the company's property (within the meaning of paragraph 14 of Schedule B1) unless the court thinks it right to refuse the application because of the particular circumstances of the case.

(5) The "existing liquidator" is the person who is liquidator immediately before the winding up becomes a creditors' voluntary winding up.

**Amendments**—Small Business, Enterprise and Employment Act 2015, s 126, Sch 9, Pt 1, paras 1, 20(1)–(2).

**General note**—This section makes it clear that the liquidation that began as a members' voluntary is converted into a creditors' voluntary liquidation. All that has been done up until and including the point where the creditors make a decision concerning the liquidator (referred to in s 95) are deemed equivalent to initiating a creditors' voluntary liquidation.

The creditors are by their decision entitled to change liquidators if they so wish, the first liquidator being appointed by the members.

## CHAPTER IV

### CREDITORS' VOLUNTARY WINDING UP

## [1.151]

**97 Application of this Chapter**
(1) Subject as follows, this Chapter applies in relation to a creditors' voluntary winding up.
(2) Sections 99 and 100 do not apply where, under section 96 in Chapter III, a members' voluntary winding up has become a creditors' voluntary winding up.

**Amendments**—Small Business, Enterprise and Employment Act 2015, s 126, Sch 9, Pt 1, paras 1, 21.

**General note**—A creditors' voluntary liquidation is regarded as a collective proceeding that is covered by the EU Regulation on Insolvency Proceedings (Art 1(1)). Annex A to the EU Regulation refers to creditors' voluntary winding up in relation to the UK.

Pursuant to Art 3 of the EU Regulation on Insolvency Proceedings, a foreign company that has its centre of main interests in the UK may be wound up by way of a creditors' voluntary winding up: *Re TXU Europe German Finance BV* [2005] BCC 90.

See the comments under the heading of 'Voluntary Liquidation' in relation to s 221.

## 98

*(Repealed)*

**Amendments**—Repealed by Small Business, Enterprise and Employment Act 2015, s 126, Sch 9, Pt 1, paras 1, 22.

## [1.152]

**99 Directors to lay statement of affairs before creditors**
(1) The directors of the company must, before the end of the period of 7 days beginning with the day after the day on which the company passes a resolution for voluntary winding up—
    (a)    make out a statement in the prescribed form as to the affairs of the company, and
    (b)    send the statement to the company's creditors.
(2) The statement as to the affairs of the company . . . shall show—
    (a)    particulars of the company's assets, debts and liabilities;
    (b)    the names and addresses of the company's creditors;
    (c)    the securities held by them respectively;
    (d)    the dates when the securities were respectively given; and
    (e)    such further or other information as may be prescribed.
(2A) The statement as to the affairs of the company shall . . .—
    (a)    in the case of a winding up of a company registered in England and Wales, be verified by some or all of the directors by a statement of truth; and
    (b)    in the case of a winding up of a company registered in Scotland, contain a statutory declaration by some or all of the directors.

(3)   If the directors without reasonable excuse fail to comply with subsection (1), (2) or (2A), they are guilty of an offence and liable to a fine.

**Amendments**—SI 2010/18; Small Business, Enterprise and Employment Act 2015, s 126, Sch 9, Pt 1, paras 1, 23; SSI 2016/141.

**General note**—If the directors fail to comply with s 99(1), (2) or (2A), the liquidator shall, within 7 days of the relevant day, apply to the court for directions as to the manner in which that default is to be remedied: s 166(5).

**Statement of affairs**—The details to be included in the statement are set out in r 6.3.

The directors must deliver to the creditors a copy of the statement of affairs required under s 99 not later than on the business day before the decision date (r 6.14(7)) (the decision relates to the appointment of a liquidator).

Where the statement of affairs sent to creditors under s 99(1) does not, or will not, state the company's affairs at the decision date for the creditors' nomination of a liquidator, the directors of the company must cause a report (written or oral) to be made to the creditors in accordance with this rule on any material transactions relating to the company occurring between the date of the making of the statement and the decision date (r 6.17(1)). Where a decision being taken is at a meeting, the report must be made at the meeting by the director chairing the meeting or by another person with knowledge of the relevant matters (r 6.17(2)). Alternatively, where the deemed consent procedure is used, the report must be delivered to creditors as soon as reasonably practicable after the material transaction takes place in the same manner as the deemed consent procedure (r 6.17(3)).

## [1.153]

### 100 Appointment of liquidator

(1)   The company may nominate a person to be liquidator at the company meeting at which the resolution for voluntary winding up is passed.

(1A)   The company's creditors may in accordance with the rules nominate a person to be liquidator.

(1B)   The directors of the company must in accordance with the rules seek such a nomination from the company's creditors.

(2)   The liquidator shall be the person nominated by the creditors or, where no person has been so nominated, the person (if any) nominated by the company.

(3)   In the case of different persons being nominated, any director, member or creditor of the company may, within 7 days after the date on which the nomination was made by the creditors, apply to the court for an order either—

(a)   directing that the person nominated as liquidator by the company shall be liquidator instead of or jointly with the person nominated by the creditors, or

(b)   appointing some other person to be liquidator instead of the person nominated by the creditors.

(4)   The court shall grant an application under subsection (3) made by the holder of a qualifying floating charge in respect of the company's property (within the meaning of paragraph 14 of Schedule B1) unless the court thinks it right to refuse the application because of the particular circumstances of the case.

**Amendments**—Subsection (4) inserted by Enterprise Act 2002, s 248(3), Sch 17, paras 9, 14, from a date to be appointed; Small Business, Enterprise and Employment Act 2015, s 126, Sch 9, Pt 1, paras 1, 24.

**General note**—The creditors may nominate a person(s) to act as liquidator. It is likely that in some cases, particularly where the person nominated by the directors of the insolvent company to act as liquidator is not to the liking of the creditors, that the creditors will appoint. This is especially the case if it is likely that the liquidator will need to investigate the conduct of the directors and there is concern that the liquidator is too close to the directors: see *Re Palmer Marine Surveys Ltd* [1986] BCLC 106. This, however, is not as likely now since the introduction in the Act of a strict regime for the appointment of insolvency practitioners.

The directors are obliged to deliver to the creditors a notice seeking their decision on the nomination of a liquidator by the deemed consent procedure or a virtual meeting: r 6.14(2). The contents of the notice are provided for in r 6.14(8). Also the directors must deliver the information required by rr 15.7 (deemed consent) and 15.8 (notices to creditors of decision procedure) (r 6.14(8)).

The decision date for the decision of the creditors on the nomination of a liquidator must be not earlier than 3 business days after the notice under r 6.14(2) is delivered but not later than 14 days after the resolution is passed to wind up the company (r 6.14(3)). This can be a tight time frame as acknowledged by ICC Judge Jones in *Cash Generator Ltd v Fortune* [2018] EWHC 674 (Ch), [2019] 1 BCLC 475. A decision date in this case is either the date that the decision is to be made (using the decision procedure) or deemed to have been made (if using the deemed consent process) (r 15.2(1)). Where the directors have sought a decision from the creditors through the deemed consent procedure but, pursuant to s 246ZF(5)(a), more than the specified number of creditors object so that the decision cannot be treated as having been made, the directors must then seek a decision from the creditors on the nomination of a liquidator by holding a physical meeting under r 15.6 as if a physical meeting had been required under s 246ZE(4) (r 6.14(4)). Where this situation applies, the meeting must not be held earlier than 3 business days after the notice under r 15.6(3) is delivered or later than 14 days after the level of objections needed reach that which is described in the Rules (r 6.14(5)) and this will be 10% in value of the creditors (s 246ZF(6)).

Where the chosen route to obtain a creditors' nomination for liquidator under s 100(3) is the deemed consent procedure and one or more of the creditors have not been sent notices the appointment of the liquidator appointed is not, according to ICC Judge Jones in *Cash Generator Ltd v Fortune* [2018] EWHC 674 (Ch), [2019] 1 BCLC 475, invalid as this is not said by the legislation to be a consequence of non-compliance; the effect of failing to send is that the directors commit a criminal offence (under r 6.14(13) (at [13])).

Where there is a decision on the nomination of a liquidator by the creditors, and on any vote there are two nominees, the person who obtains the most support is appointed. If there are three or more nominees, and one of them has a clear majority over both or all the others together, that one is appointed, and in any other case the convener (for a deemed consent procedure) or chair (for a meeting) must continue to take votes (disregarding at each vote any nominee who has withdrawn and, if no nominee has withdrawn, the nominee who obtained the least support last time) until a clear majority is obtained for any one nominee (r 6.18(1)). Where there is a creditors' meeting the chair may at any time put to the meeting a resolution for the joint nomination of any two or more nominees (r 6.18(2)).

The liquidator must deliver to the creditors and contributories within 28 days of his or her appointment under s 100 a notice which must—(a) be accompanied by a statement of affairs or a summary where the notice is delivered to any contributory or creditor to whom the notice under r 6.14 was not delivered; (b) be accompanied by a report on the decision procedure or deemed consent procedure under r 6.14; and (c) be accompanied by certain information (r 6.15(1)). This information is an estimate to the best of the liquidator's knowledge and belief of—(a) the value of the prescribed part under s 176A; and (b) the value of the company's net property (as defined by s 176A(6)) (r 6.15(2)).

Where a liquidator is appointed by creditors or the company, the appointment must be certified by the convener or chair of the decision procedure or deemed consent procedure, or where there was an appointment by the company, the chair of the company meeting or a director or the secretary of the company (in the case of a written resolution) (r 6.20(1)–(3)). The person certifying the appointment must not do so unless and until the proposed liquidator has provided a statement of being an insolvency practitioner qualified under the Act to be the liquidator and of consenting to act (r 6.20(4)). The person who certifies the appointment must deliver the certificate as soon as reasonably practicable to the liquidator, who must keep it as part of the records of the winding up (r 6.20(7)). If two or more liquidators are appointed then the certificate of appointment should indicate whether the liquidators are to exercise their powers and duties jointly or separately (s 231(2), r 6.20(6)). The liquidator once appointed must publish, within 14 days after, in the Gazette and deliver to the registrar of companies for registration a notice of appointment (s 109(1)).

Once the position of liquidator is determined, any subsequent vacancies in the office of liquidator may be filled by the creditors (s 104).

As far as any appointment made by the court as a result of s 100(3), see r 6.22.

Anyone who is nominated as a liquidator must be qualified to act as an insolvency practitioner pursuant to ss 388 and 389.

## [1.154]

### 101 Appointment of liquidation committee

(1) The creditors may in accordance with the rules appoint a committee ("the liquidation committee") of not more than 5 persons to exercise the functions conferred on it by or under this Act.

(2) If such a committee is appointed, the company may, either at the meeting at which the resolution for voluntary winding up is passed or at any time subsequently in general

meeting, appoint such number of persons as they think fit to act as members of the committee, not exceeding 5.

(3) However, the creditors may, if they think fit, decide that all or any of the persons so appointed by the company ought not to be members of the liquidation committee; and if the creditors so decide—

    (a)    those persons are not then, unless the court otherwise directs, qualified to act as members of the committee; and

    (b)    on any application to the court under this provision the court may, if it thinks fit, appoint other persons to act as such members in place of those persons.

(4) In Scotland, the liquidation committee has, in addition to the powers and duties conferred and imposed on it by this Act, such of the powers and duties of commissioners on a bankrupt estate as may be conferred and imposed on liquidation committees by the rules.

**Amendments**—Small Business, Enterprise and Employment Act 2015, s 126, Sch 9, Pt 1, paras 1, 25.

**General note**—The liquidation committee is designed to enable the creditors to have some control over the administration of the liquidation. It also can be a body from which the liquidator can seek advice and gauge the opinions of some of the major creditors. The equivalent provision for compulsory liquidations is s 141.

It has been held in Australia that if it is clear that creditors will not receive full payment from the winding up, then providing that all other matters are equal all members of the committee should represent creditors, but if all creditors will be paid in full, then contributories should have fair representation on the committee: *Re James; In re Cowra Processors Pty Ltd* (1995) 15 ACLC 1582.

In a creditors' voluntary winding up the committee must have three members before it can be established (r 17.3(2)).

See Part 17 of the IR 2016 which deal with the liquidation committee.

See the notes accompanying s 141 which addresses liquidation committees in court windings up and Part 17 of the IR 2016.

See A Keay *McPherson and Keay's Law of Company Liquidation* (Sweet and Maxwell, 4th edn, 2018) at 510–520 for a detailed discussion of the liquidation committee.

## 102

*(Repealed)*

**Amendments**—Repealed by Small Business, Enterprise and Employment Act 2015, s 126, Sch 9, Pt 1, paras 1, 26.

## [1.155]

### 103 Cesser of directors' powers

On the appointment of a liquidator, all the powers of the directors cease, except so far as the liquidation committee (or, if there is no such committee, the creditors) sanction their continuance.

**General note**—See the note under 'Directors' powers' in relation to s 91.

## [1.156]

### 104 Vacancy in office of liquidator

If a vacancy occurs, by death, resignation or otherwise, in the office of a liquidator (other than a liquidator appointed by, or by the direction of, the court), the creditors may fill the vacancy.

**General note**—Where there is a need to fill a vacancy, a decision procedure may be instituted by any creditor, or where there was more than one liquidator the decision procedure may be instituted by the liquidator(s) who intend(s) to continue in office (r 6.21).

## [1.157]

### 104A Progress report to company and creditors . . . . . .

(1) The liquidator must—

(a) for each prescribed period produce a progress report relating to the prescribed matters; and

(b) within such period commencing with the end of the period referred to in paragraph (a) as may be prescribed send a copy of the progress report to—

  (i) the members and creditors, other than opted-out creditors of the company; and

  (ii) such other persons as may be prescribed.

(2) A liquidator who fails to comply with this section is liable to a fine.

**Amendments**—Inserted by SI 2010/18. Amended by Small Business, Enterprise and Employment Act 2015, ss 126, 136(1), (3), Sch 9, Pt 1, paras 1, 27; SSI 2016/141.

## 105
*(Repealed)*

## [1.158]

### 106 Final account prior to dissolution

(1) As soon as the company's affairs are fully wound up the liquidator must make up an account of the winding up, showing how it has been conducted and the company's property has been disposed of.

(2) The liquidator must, before the end of the period of 14 days beginning with the day on which the account is made up—

(a) send a copy of the account to the company's members,

(b) send a copy of the account to the company's creditors (other than opted-out creditors), and

(c) give the company's creditors (other than opted-out creditors) a notice explaining the effect of section 173(2)(e) and how they may object to the liquidator's release.

(3) The liquidator must during the relevant period send to the registrar of companies—

(a) a copy of the account, and

(b) a statement of whether any of the company's creditors objected to the liquidator's release.

(4) The relevant period is the period of 7 days beginning with the day after the last day of the period prescribed by the rules as the period within which the creditors may object to the liquidator's release.

(4A) . . .

(4B) . . .

(5) If the liquidator does not comply with subsection (2) the liquidator is liable to a fine.

(6) If the liquidator does not comply with subsection (3) the liquidator is liable to a fine and, for continued contravention, a daily default fine.

(7) . . .

(8) . . .

**Amendments**—Substituted by Small Business, Enterprise and Employment Act 2015, s 126, Sch 9, Pt 1, paras 1, 29. Amended by SI 2017/702; SI 2019/146, as from IP completion day (as defined in the European Union (Withdrawal Agreement) Act 2020, s 39(1)–(5)).

**General note**—The provision is the same as s 94. See rr 6.28 and 18.14 and the accompanying notes, and the notes relating to s 94.

**The affairs are fully wound up**—It has been held that a company's affairs are able to be regarded as fully wound up in situations where there is property still retained by the liquidator, but all that can be done has been done: *Re London & Caledonian Marine Insurance* Co (1879) 11 ChD 140 at 143; *Re Wilmott Trading Ltd (in liquidation) (No 1 and 2)*; sub nom *Henry v Environmental Agency (No 2)* [1999] 2 BCLC 541 (the continued holding of a waste management licence).

CHAPTER V

PROVISIONS APPLYING TO BOTH KINDS OF VOLUNTARY WINDING UP

**[1.159]**

### 107 Distribution of company's property

Subject to the provisions of this Act as to preferential payments, the company's property in a voluntary winding up shall on the winding up be applied in satisfaction of the company's liabilities pari passu and, subject to that application, shall (unless the articles otherwise provide) be distributed among the members according to their rights and interests in the company.

**General note**—This provision embraces what is often regarded as the most fundamental principle of insolvency law, namely the pari passu principle (*Re Western Welsh International System Buildings Ltd* (1985) 1 BCC 99, 296 at 99, 297). The principle can be traced back to the bankruptcy statute of 1570 (13 Eliz c 7).

The implementation of the pari passu principle is made subject to the payment of preferential payments, which includes the costs and expenses of winding up (s 115) and preferential debts covered in s 386 and Sch 6. Besides such payments, the pari passu principle is pushed aside and made subject to other arrangements, such as set-off. The reason for permitting set-off in liquidations and bankruptcy is 'to do substantial justice between the parties, where a debt is really due from the debtor to his estate' (*Forster v Wilson* (1843) 12 M & W 191 at 204, 152 ER 1165 at 1171). See *Stein v Blake* [1993] BCLC 1478. See also r 14.25 and the note accompanying it.

In distributing company funds a liquidator will normally apply the funds generally in the following way (see *Re Nortel GmbH* [2013] UKPC 52, [2014] AC 209 at [117]):

- costs and expenses of winding up (s 115);
- preferential debts (s 175(1), ss 386, 387 and Sch 6);
- any preferential charge on goods distrained that arises pursuant to s 176(3);
- general body of ordinary unsecured creditors;
- post-liquidation interest on debts (s 189);
- deferred creditors – mentioned in s 74(2)(f);
- any balance is divided amongst the contributories pursuant to the memorandum and articles.

For a recent decision considering distribution to the members, see *Re Finch (Watford Printers Ltd)* [2018] EWHC 329 (Ch) where Chief ICC Judge Briggs applied s 107 in the absence of any provisions in the articles dealing with solvent winding up.

Because of the many exceptions to the pari passu rule, demonstrated, in part, by the above hierarchy, it is highly questionable whether the rule is as important as many assert. However, when it comes to case authority, the courts do focus on the rule and many have maintained the fundamental importance of it to insolvency law (eg *Re HIH Casualty and General Insurance Ltd* [2005] EWHC 2125 (Ch)); *Re Courts plc* [2008] EWHC 2339 (Ch); *Re Nortel GmbH* [2011] EWCA Civ 1124; *Revenue and Customs Commissioners v Football League Ltd* [2012] EWHC 1372 (Ch)). The rule effectively only applies to the general body of unsecured creditors who have no right to preferential treatment. But having said, that there might be other exceptions, such as set-off, which will also affect the application of the rule as far as the general unsecured creditors are concerned.

Of course, a company that is in liquidation might be subject to a floating charge. The question that has arisen in this context is whether a liquidator is entitled to pay liquidation expenses from the property subject to the charge before paying the preferential debts. Except where a receiver has been appointed over the assets covered by a floating charge and had made distributions to the chargeholder before the advent of winding up, the law was that a liquidator was able to have recourse to the assets subject to floating charges, whether the charge crystallised by reason of, and immediately after the commencement of winding up, or before the commencement of winding up: *Re Barleycorn Enterprises Ltd* [1970] Ch 465 at 474, CA; *Re Portbase (Clothing) Ltd* [1993] Ch 388; *Re Leyland DAF Ltd* [2002] 1 BCLC 571, CA. But in *Buchler v Talbot* [2004] UKHL 9, [2004] 2 AC 298, [2004] 1 BCLC 281, a decision of the House of Lords when hearing an appeal in the *Leyland DAF* litigation, it was held that this previous position was, in fact, incorrect. Their Lordships stated that liquidation expenses are not to be paid out of assets subject to the charge. It was wrong to permit a liquidator to make such an incursion into the chargeholder's rights. Their Lordships noted that where a company is in both administrative receivership and liquidation, its assets are comprised in two different funds. One fund involved some assets that were subject to a floating charge and the other fund involved assets that were just subject to the liquidation. Generally each fund bears its own costs and, as the chargeholder has no interest in the liquidation, he or she should not have to contribute towards the liquidation expenses ([2004] UKHL 9, [2004]

2 AC 298, [2004] 1 BCLC 281 at [30] and [31]). See R Mokal 'Liquidation Expenses and Floating Charges – The Separate Funds Fallacy' [2004] LMCLQ 387; H Rajak 'Liquidation Expenses Versus a Claim Secured by a Floating Charge' (2005) 18 *Insolvency Intelligence* 97.

This position was overturned by the enactment of s 176ZA (introduced through the Companies Act 2006 (s 1282) and came into force on 6 April 2008). The amendment does not have retrospective effect. See s 176ZA and rr 6.44–6.48, as well as the notes accompanying the section and the rules.

If the liquidator does not pay the preferential debts, a receiver acting for the chargeholder will be required to pay out those debts before making distributions to the chargeholder (s 40).

Preferential debts are now not as important a concern as they once were. Since the corporate insolvency provisions of the Enterprise Act 2002 became operational from 15 September 2003, the main preferential debts are likely to be the wages and leave entitlements of the employees of the company. Previously, the Crown was entitled to claim certain debts owed to it as preferential (eg VAT payments) and these often constituted large sums that had to be paid before the floating chargeholder and the unsecured creditors were paid.

Attempts have been made from time to time to circumvent the statutory order set out above. But English courts have generally been set against such action: *Re Buckingham International plc (No 2)* [1998] 2 BCLC 369. They have, for the most part, frowned on debt subordination schemes, where one debtor seeks, other than through security-taking, to push himself or herself into a priority position on the basis that it is against public policy to contract out of the pari passu rule: see *British Eagle International Air Lines Ltd v Compagnie Nationale Air France* [1975] 1 WLR 758. Yet in *Re Maxwell Communications Corporation plc (No 3)* [1993] BCC 369, Vinelott J favoured permitting a liquidator to distribute according to an agreement entered into before liquidation whereby it is agreed for some reason that an unsecured creditor's debt ranks ahead of other unsecured creditors, providing that to do so would not adversely affect any creditor not a party to the agreement, ie creditors not involved in the subordination agreement would receive less under that agreement than would have been received if distributions had been made according to the statutory scheme. In *International Air Transport Association v Ansett Australia Holdings Ltd* [2008] HCA 3, [2008] BPIR 57 the Australian High Court considered the clearing house rules that were the subject of the *British Eagle* decision. For further discussion, see E Ferran 'Recent Developments in Unsecured Debt Subordination' in B A K Rider (ed) *The Realm of Company Law* (Kluwer Law International, 1998).

**Anti-deprivation**—The notion that it is contrary to public policy to contract out of the pari passu principle overlaps with the anti-deprivation rule, both of which are sub-rules of the general rule that parties are not permitted to contract out of the insolvency legislation: *Belmont Park Investments Pty Ltd v BNY Corporate Trustee Services Pty Ltd* [2011] UKSC 38, [2011] BPIR 1223. The anti-deprivation rule is aimed at preventing attempts to withdraw assets from the creditors in an insolvency regime such as liquidation so as to reduce the size of the insolvent estate. Such action would, of course, reduce the dividends received by creditors. The rule only applies where there is a deliberate intention to evade the insolvency laws: *Belmont Park* at [78]–[79]. There is some overlap with the pari passu principle, but it is separate from it and aimed at a different mischief (*Belmont Park* at [1]). It applies only if the deprivation is triggered by an insolvency proceeding, and the deprivation must be of an asset of the debtor which would otherwise be available to creditors (*Revenue and Customs Commissioners v Football League Ltd* [2012] EWHC 1372 (Ch) at [67]). The Court of Appeal in *Lomas v JFB Firth Rixson Inc* [2012] EWCA Civ 419 stated that: 'The anti-deprivation principle therefore protects the value of the estate from attempts to evade the insolvency laws and, as a consequence, facilitates the application of the pari passu rule. But their areas of operation are distinct and it is clear that the pari passu rule is only engaged in respect of assets of the estate as at the commencement of the bankruptcy or liquidation' (at [97]). Pari passu deals with the situation where the assets which form the insolvent estate have been identified, and it ensures that the assets identified are distributed according to the statutory scheme. To be void a provision in a contract had to be interpreted as a deliberate attempt to evade the insolvency laws, although the intention did not have to be subjective. See R Calnan, 'Anti-deprivation: a missed opportunity' (2011) 9 JIBFL 531; R Cole, 'Anti-deprivation: a rule of 'purgatorial complexity' (2011) CRI 149 (Oct); T Cleary, 'Perpetuating Uncertainty: The Anti-Deprivation Principle and Contractual Rights in the Post-Lehman World' (2011) 20 IRR 185.

**Distributed among the members**—After all the property of the company has been got in and realised, and there has been a distribution to creditors so that all the debts and liabilities, including the costs of winding up, have been paid or provided for, the liquidator may proceed to distribute any surplus among the members. The rights of sharing in the surplus may be prescribed in the company's constitution, but if not then the distribution will be on the basis of equality. To do all of this the liquidator may have to adjust the rights of the contributories inter se, and this will be done by making calls on those who have paid less on their shares than other members in order to ensure that losses are evenly distributed among all the members of the company.

For two recent cases where the provision was employed in ruling on the distribution of surplus assets in a voluntary liquidation of a solvent company, see *Re Watford Printers Ltd* [2018] EWHC 329 (Ch); *Qureshi v Association of Conservative Clubs Ltd* [2019] EWHC 1165 (Ch). In both cases distributions were ordered to be in favour of the members.

See A Keay *McPherson and Keay's Law of Company Liquidation* (Sweet and Maxwell, 4th edn, 2018), Chs 13 and 14.

## [1.160]

### 108 Appointment or removal of liquidator by the court

(1) If from any cause whatever there is no liquidator acting, the court may appoint a liquidator.

(2) The court may, on cause shown, remove a liquidator and appoint another.

**General note**—The provision entitles a court to do two things: appoint a liquidator where none is acting; and remove a liquidator. The former can also be done by the members in a members' voluntary liquidation (s 92) or the creditors in a creditors' voluntary liquidation (s 104). Removal in a creditors' voluntary liquidation is to by a decision of the creditors made by a qualifying decision procedure instituted specifically to consider removal (s 171(2)(b)) and, in a members' voluntary winding up, by the general meeting of the company (ie the members) (s 171(2)(a)).

It seems a little strange that the court is given the power to remove liquidators in voluntary liquidations by both s 108 and s 171. The difference between the two provisions is that only the former sets out any reason, namely there has to be 'cause shown'. It is, however, unlikely that a court would remove under s 171 unless a cause was shown. Therefore, one wonders why two provisions should continue to exist.

**No liquidator acting**—It can be said that there is no liquidator acting in the situation where the liquidator is not performing his or her function: *Clements v Udal* [2002] 2 BCLC 606, [2001] BPIR 454.

If a liquidator has been appointed under this section, in relation to a members' voluntary winding up, a meeting to consider removal shall be summoned only if:

(a)     the liquidator thinks fit,

(b)     the court so directs, or

(c)     the meeting is requested in accordance with the rules by members representing not less than one-half of the total voting rights of all the members having at the date of the request a right to vote at the meeting (s 171(3))

If a liquidator has been appointed under this section, in relation to a creditors' voluntary winding up, a qualifying decision procedure is to be instigated only if:

(a)     the liquidator thinks fit,

(b)     the court so directs, or

(c)     it is requested in accordance with the rules by not less than one-half in value of the company's creditors (s 171(3A)).

In cases involving the withdrawal of a liquidator's authority to act, which terminates the liquidator's office automatically, the Secretary of State for Business Energy and Industrial Strategy has been permitted to apply for the appointment of a new liquidator: *Re Bridgend Goldsmiths Ltd* [1995] 2 BCLC 208.

Where appropriate, courts are able to appoint additional liquidators on a temporary basis: *Clements v Udal* [2002] 2 BCLC 606, [2001] BPIR 454.

**Removal**—With an application to the court for removal or for an order directing the liquidator to initiate a decision procedure for creditors for the purpose of removing the liquidator, r 6.27 sets out what is to occur and the contents of the order. Where a person is aggrieved by a decision which the liquidator has taken, he or she should apply pursuant to s 112 for a review of the decision, rather than seeking removal of the liquidator.

Applications should not be made ex parte, except in circumstances where either the need for relief was so urgent that it was not possible to notify the defendant of the proposed application or the kind of relief sought meant that it was inappropriate to notify because that would risk making any relief granted nugatory (*Clements v Udal* [2002] 2 BCLC 606, [2001] BPIR 454).

A court will not remove a liquidator simply because it disagrees with a decision which he or she has taken: *Re Shruth Ltd* [2005] EWHC 1293 (Ch), [2005] BPIR 1455, [2006] 1 BCLC 294 at [40].

**On cause shown**—The equivalent provision for a compulsory liquidation is said to be s 172(2) (*Re Sankey Furniture Ltd* [1995] 2 BCLC 594 at 597), although this latter provision is worded differently and includes no reference to 'on cause shown'. Notwithstanding this, r 7.65(2), together with past case law, indicates that the same criterion applies, ie that a cause must be shown for removal to be ordered.

It only takes the establishing of one good ground or cause by an applicant as to why a person should be removed if the applicant is to succeed. The applicant does not have 'prove everything in sight': *Shepheard v Lamey* [2001] BPIR 939. The words of the section are very wide and it is not appropriate either to limit the cause for which removal is the correct remedy (*Re Keypak Homecare Ltd* [1987] BCLC 409 or to lay down the circumstances that would establish the grounds for removal (*AMP Enterprises Ltd v Hoffman*; sub nom *AMP Music Box Enterprises Ltd v Hoffman* [2002] EWHC 1899 (Ch), [2003] 1 BCLC 319, [2003] BPIR 11; *Re Buildlead Ltd (No 2)* [2004] EWHC 2443 (Ch), [2004] BPIR 1139). Simply, the applicant must establish good grounds for the removal: *AMP Enterprises Ltd v Hoffman*. The difficult task for a court is to effect a balance between the requirement for liquidators to be efficient, vigorous and unbiased in their conduct of liquidations, as against the fact that courts must be careful before they remove liquidators who have generally been effective and honest: *AMP Enterprises Ltd v Hoffman*; *Re Buildlead Ltd (No 2)* [2004] EWHC 2443 (Ch), [2004] BPIR 1139.

It is not necessary for an applicant for a removal to establish misconduct or personal unfitness on the part of the liquidator, or that he or she has a personal grievance against the liquidator. Cause can be that there is an unavoidable interruption in the ability of the liquidator to do his or her job (*Re Parkdawn Ltd* (unreported) 15 June 1993, per Harman J; *Re Sankey Furniture Ltd* [1995] 2 BCLC 594 at 602), such as where the liquidator is experiencing ill health: *Re Sankey Furniture Ltd*. Courts have to take into account all the circumstances: *Re Marseilles Extension Railway and Land Co* (1867) LR 4 Eq 692. In an Australian decision, the Queensland Supreme Court ordered removal because the liquidator had given personal advice to the directors at a conference that occurred before liquidation: *Re Club Superstores Ltd* (1993) 10 ACSR 730. The advice included advising on the effect of a winding up on the interests of the directors, and this raised the possibility of a conflict, even though the advice was given without charge and was delivered with no ulterior or improper motives.

It appears that if a court is satisfied on the evidence before it that it is against the interest of the liquidation, and this includes all those who have some interest in the company being liquidated, that a liquidator should remain in post, then the court has the power to remove the liquidator: *Re Adam Eyton Ltd* (1887) 36 ChD 299; *Re Edennote Ltd* [1996] 2 BCLC 389; *Re Pinstripe Farming Co Ltd* [1996] 2 BCLC 295. Clearly, the courts are not limited in what they consider, and it is wrong for a court to seek to limit or define the kind of cause which is required for removal: *Re Keypak Homecare Ltd* [1996] 2 BCLC 295. In some cases it may well be appropriate to remove a liquidator even though there is nothing that can be said against him or her as an individual (*Re Adam Eyton Ltd*), or where no particular breaches are identified: *Re Buildlead Ltd (No 2)* [2004] EWHC 2443 (Ch), [2004] BPIR 1139. For instance, a liquidator might be removed, and replaced, if he or she resides and practices a considerable distance from where the company operated and where its offices and facilities are to be found, because of the additional expense and inconvenience that this might precipitate for the winding up: *Northbuild Constructions Pty Ltd v ACN 103 753 484 Pty Ltd* [2008] QSC 182. Liquidators may be removed for unfitness on the basis of their personal standing (although private immorality is not sufficient for removal: *Re Urmston Grange Steam Ship Co* (1901) 17 TLR 553); their personal conduct (such as relations with the directors); or in the conduct of the particular liquidation (*Re Keypak Homecare Ltd*). Liquidators have, in removing a liquidator, taken into account the fact that a considerable number of creditors are opposed to the liquidator remaining in office (*Re Adam Eyton Ltd*), or the fact that the creditors have lost faith in the liquidator, and this loss of faith is reasonable in the circumstances: *Re Edennote Ltd* [1996] 2 BCLC 389, CA; *Re Buildlead Ltd (No 2)*. The wishes of a majority of creditors (*Re Edennote Ltd* [1996] 2 BCLC 389 at 398; *Re Ve Interactive Ltd* [2018] EWHC 186 (Ch) at [37] (an administration case but applying equally to liquidation)) in a creditors' voluntary or a majority of the members in a members' voluntary (*Re Core VCT plc* [2019] EWHC 540 (Ch) at [82])) are certainly not decisive, as removal is a very serious matter for the liquidator and that fact requires to be taken into consideration so as to be fair to the liquidator: *Re Adam Eyton & Co* (1887) 36 ChD 299 at 306. Thus, the courts will have regard to the impact of removal of a liquidator on his or her professional standing and reputation (*Re Edennote Ltd* at 398), but will not refrain from ordering removal just because such an action would redound to the point of discrediting the liquidator: *AMP Enterprises Ltd v Hoffman*; sub nom *AMP Music Box Enterprises Ltd v Hoffman* [2002] EWHC 1899 (Ch), [2003] 1 BCLC 319, [2003] BPIR 11. But even if removal may lead to the discredit of a liquidator, courts should not fail to remove in appropriate cases (*AMP Enterprises Ltd v Hoffman*). Notwithstanding this, removal of a professional is not to be undertaken lightly (*Hobbs v Gibson* [2010] EWHC 3676 (Ch) at [47]), even if conduct has fallen below what is ideal (*Re Ve Interactive Ltd* [2018] EWHC 186 (Ch) at [36]; *Cash Generator Ltd v Fortune* [2018] EWHC 674 (Ch), [2019] 1 BCLC 475 at [29]) and those who submit that a liquidator should be removed are under a duty to establish at least a prima facie case that this is for the general advantage of the persons interested in the winding up (*Re Mercantile Finance & Agency Co* (1894) 13 NZLR 472). The courts will be careful that they do not encourage applications by disgruntled creditors: *AMP Enterprises Ltd v Hoffman*.

In *Re Keypak Homecare Ltd* [1996] 2 BCLC 295 the liquidator was removed because he had been too relaxed in his conduct of the liquidation, and the creditors were justified in thinking that the liquidator would fail to pursue proceedings against the directors with the necessary vigour. If a liquidator fails to carry out his or her duties, that constitutes a cause for removal: *Re Ryder Installations Ltd* [1966] 1 WLR 524. The courts are likely to consider whether there is a possibility that the liquidator will not act impartially or objectively in relation to the company's affairs: *Re Lowestoft Traffic Services Ltd* [1986] BCLC 81; *Re Magnus Consultants Ltd* [1995] 1 BCLC 203. Courts will remove liquidators where their independence (*Re Zirceram Ltd* [2000] 1 BCLC 751 at 760; *HM Customs and Excise v Allen* [2003] BPIR 830) or fiduciary position (*Re Queensland Stations Pty Ltd (in liquidation)* (1991) 9 ACLC 1341) is compromised, such as where there is a conflict of interest (*Re Charterlands Goldfields Ltd* (1909) 26 TLR 182; *Re Corbenstoke Ltd (No 2)* [1990] BCLC 60) or where the liquidator fails to act in an efficient manner within a reasonable period of time: *Re Buildlead Ltd (No 2)* [2004] EWHC 2443 (Ch), [2004] BPIR 1139. According to the Federal Court of Australia, a conflict of interest allegation against a liquidator must demonstrate that there was a real conflict and not a theoretical possibility of a conflict: *Queensland Mining Corporation Ltd v Butmall Pty Ltd, in the matter of Butmall Pty Ltd (in liq)* [2016] FCA 16. In *SISU Capital Fund Ltd v Tucker* [2005] EWHC 2170 (Ch), [2006] BPIR 154 at [96], it was acknowledged that there are likely to be more conflicts in large insolvencies as there are so few accounting firms competent to deal with them. Conflicts will not necessarily lead to removal (*Cash Generator Ltd v Fortune* [2018] EWHC 674 (Ch), [2019] 1 BCLC 475 at [29]). Applications to remove on the basis of conflict should never be made without careful consideration of the position and an attempt, by both sides acting co-operatively, to proceed in a constructive and time – and cost-efficient manner (*Re TPS Investments (U) Ltd* [2018] EWHC 360 (Ch)). HHJ Davies in *Tailby v Hutchinson Telecom FZCO* [2018] EWHC 360 (Ch), [2019] 1 BCLC 61 said that whether the post of administrator should be relinquished because of conflict depended on: the nature of the conflict; the point in the administration when the issue is being considered; whether the conflict could be managed; the consequences for and against removal in terms of cost and time. These points could be applied equally to liquidators. In relation to the third of those points, in *SISU Capital Fund Ltd v Tucker* Warren J pointed to a number of cases where the courts suggested that conflicts can often be managed (eg at [112]). Subsequently, Norris J stated in *Re Kimberly Scott Services Ltd* [2011] EWHC 1563 (Ch), [2012] BPIR 135, that removal would not occur where any conflicts of interest could be managed by way of applications to court for directions. One way to manage a conflict situation was to appoint an additional liquidator from a firm that is different from the firm to which the existing liquidator belongs: *Re York Gas Ltd* [2010] EWHC 2275 (Ch); *Re Ve Interactive Limited (In Administration)* [2018] EWHC 186 (Ch).

If an office-holder acted for companies related to the one(s) over whose affairs he or she has been appointed and this led to an actual conflict of interest, that of itself was not sufficient to demand that an office-holder cease to act as a court would moderate the fiduciary principle if it was in the creditors' interests, in relation to costs and time, for the office-holder to remain in post: *Tailby v Hutchinson Telecom FZCO* [2018] EWHC 360 (Ch), [2019] 1 BCLC 61.

Instances of removal include the following circumstances: the liquidator trying to prevent misfeasance proceedings from being commenced against him or her (*Re Sir John Moore Gold Mining Co* (1879) 12 ChD 326); the liquidator has been closely associated with promoters or directors whose conduct required investigation (*Re Charterlands Goldfields Ltd*); the liquidator has demonstrated a propensity to prefer one person's interests over those of another (*Re City & County Investment Co* (1877) 25 WR 342; *Re Rubber & Produce Investment Trust* [1915] 1 Ch 382); the liquidator has taken action or failed to act because of personal animosity toward some of those interested in the winding up (*Re London Flats Ltd* [1969] 1 WLR 711); the liquidator is guilty of being dilatory in dealing with creditors' claims: *Re AMF International Ltd* [1995] 2 BCLC 529; *the liquidator was previously the administrator of the company and this was undesirable: Hobbs v Gibson* [2011] EWHC 3676 (Ch). Liquidators were removed where they were connected professionally with a former liquidator (removed by the court on the liquidator's own application). The court did this because it had removed the former liquidator on the basis of his alleged ill health, yet the real reason why he wished to be removed was that he was insolvent: *HM Customs and Excise v Allen* [2003] BPIR 830.

A primary reason for removal is that there is a real or apprehended conflict of interest involving the liquidator or he or she is biased. In this context bias is where circumstances exist that might lead a liquidator to make a decision other than based on merit. The test for bias is whether a reasonably fair-minded observer might think that the liquidator was biased or had a conflict of interest: *ASIC v Franklin* [2014] FCAFC 85. A court might decide to remove liquidators where there is no imputation against them personally but where there needs to be an investigation that would entail a consideration of their actions, and the liquidators cannot be expected to investigate themselves: *Clydesdale Financial Services v Smailes* [2009] EWHC 1745 (Ch), (2009) BCC 810; *Fakhry v Pagden* [2020] EWCA Civ 1207, [2021] BPIR 526 at [16]).

A liquidator should not be removed simply because he or she is the choice of a creditor(s) who is concerned to see the claims of the company pursued by the liquidator: *Fielding v Seery* [2004] BCC 315 at 322. An applicant will, in order to succeed, have to establish more that the fact that a new liquidator 'might spot something that the current [liquidator] . . . may have missed . . .': *Memon v Cork* [2018] EWHC 594 (Ch) per ICC Judge Barber.

Misconduct or unfitness may be constituted by some breach of duty (*Re Scotch Granite Co* (1867) 17 LT 533; *Re Baron Cigarette Machine Co* (1912) 28 TLR 394) or appearance of partiality on the part of the liquidator (*Re London Flats Ltd* [1969] 1 WLR 711), but it also seems to be enough for removal if one can show that winding up can be conducted more cheaply (*Re Tavistock Ironworks & Co* (1871) 24 LT 605; *Re Association of Land Financiers* (1878) 10 ChD 269) or more effectively (*Re Montratier Asphalte Co* (1874) 22 WR 527) by a different liquidator who can be appointed following removal.

It will be hard for an applicant for removal to discharge the burden of proof if the liquidator has become conversant with the business and affairs of the company (*Re Civil Service & General Stores Ltd* [1884] WN 158; *Re Urmston Grange Steam Ship Co* (1909) 17 TLR 553), or the process of winding up has almost reached completion: *Re Llynvi & Tondu Co* (1889) 6 TLR 11. In some Australian cases courts have been of the opinion they should be less ready to discharge a liquidator towards the end of a winding up: *Advance Housing Pty Ltd (in liquidation) v Newcastle Classic Developments Pty Ltd* (1994) 14 ACSR 230 at 237; *Wood v Targett* (1997) 23 ACSR 291. The fact that removal of a liquidator could lead to disruption and extra cost should be considered: *AMP Enterprises Ltd v Hoffman*; sub nom *AMP Music Box Enterprises Ltd v Hoffman* [2002] EWHC 1899 (Ch), [2003] 1 BCLC 319, [2003] BPIR 11. One Australian appellate court has indicated that courts should be cautious in removing a liquidator where it seems possible that the applicant is trying to avoid the consequences of some wrongdoing by attacking the liquidator and seeking his or her removal: *Re Biposo Pty Ltd; Condon v Rogers* (1995) 120 FLR 399 at 403.

If there is the possibility that misfeasance proceedings will be taken against a liquidator then he or she should step aside: *Shepheard v Lamey* [2001] BPIR 939.

**Applicants**—The section gives no indication as to who may apply for removal. It is a matter that is left to the court to determine whether the applicant has a sufficient interest to make the application: *Fakhry v Pagden* [2020] EWCA Civ 1207, [2021] BPIR 526 at [48]. As to who may be permitted to apply, it is likely that it will depend very much on the circumstances of each case. A person who applies for removal must demonstrate both that he or she is entitled to make the application and that he or she is a proper person to make the application: *Deloitte Touche AG v Johnson* [1999] 1 WLR 1605, [2000] 1 BCLC 485, PC. A creditor is entitled to apply (*HM Customs and Excise v Allen* [2003] BPIR 830). It has been held in Australia, in *Re Greight Pty Ltd (in liquidation)* [2006] FCA 17, that a person who is a possible creditor of the company may also apply.

It is probably correct to say that a contributory who is fully paid up is not entitled to apply for removal, because in *Re Corbenstoke Ltd (No 2)* [1990] BCLC 60 it was said (at 61–62) that only someone who has an interest in the outcome of a liquidation can apply for removal, and if a company is insolvent then a contributory has no such interest: see also *Deloitte and Touche AG v Johnson* [1999] 1 WLR 1605, [2000] 1 BCLC 485. Defendants to a legal action commenced by the liquidator, such as the former auditors of the company in liquidation, were not able to bring proceedings for the removal of the liquidator for they were deemed to be strangers to the liquidation: *Deloitte and Touche AG v Johnson*. In *Re Core VCT plc* [2019] EWHC 540 (Ch) a former liquidator and a shareholder were refused an order of removal of the current liquidators as the application could be seen to be an attempt to prevent an investigation of the company's affairs.

A liquidator whose authorisation to act as a liquidator has been suspended may apply for an order of removal: *Re AJ Adams (Builders) Ltd* [1991] BCLC 359. In similar circumstances, an application by the Insolvency Practitioners' Association, a recognised professional body for the accrediting of practitioners under the IA 1986, was allowed (*Re Stella Metals Ltd (in liquidation)* [1997] BPIR 293), because it was held to be appropriate for the Insolvency Practitioners' Association to bring such an application. The courts have even permitted an insolvency practitioner (with the support of the Secretary of State)) to apply under this provision for the liquidator to be removed and replaced where the liquidator is no longer authorised to act: *Re a Licence-holder* [1998] BPIR 171.

If a liquidator is removed then in Scotland he or she cannot retain from the company's assets any assets as security for costs, but in England and Wales the courts have a discretion to permit him or her to do so: *Re Echelon Wealth Management Ltd* [2011] CSOH 87; 2011 SCLR 678.

See rr 6.27 and 5.7 concerning the removal of a liquidator in creditors' voluntary liquidations and members' voluntary liquidations respectively. Also, see rr 6.22 and 5.4 concerning the appointment of a liquidator under s 108. Rule 6.22(2) states what must be included in the order of the court where an order is made for appointment under either s 100(3) or s 108. Rule 5.4(2) does the same in relation to a members' voluntary liquidation and where an order is made under s 108.

See, M Shekerdemian and J Curl, 'Administrators: Conflict of Interest and Removal' (2019) 16 ICR 4.

## [1.161]

### 109 Notice by liquidator of his appointment

(1)   The liquidator shall, within 14 days after his appointment, publish in the Gazette and deliver to the registrar of companies for registration a notice of his appointment in the form prescribed by statutory instrument made by the Secretary of State.

(2)   If the liquidator fails to comply with this section, he is liable to a fine and, for continued contravention, to a daily default fine.

*Refer to r 6.23
23A*

## [1.162]

### 110 Acceptance of shares etc as consideration for sale of company property

(1)   This section applies, in the case of a company proposed to be, or being, wound up voluntarily, where the whole or part of the company's business or property is proposed to be transferred or sold—

   (a)   to another company ("the transferee company"), whether or not the latter is a company registered under the Companies Act 2006, or

   (b)   to a limited liability partnership (the "transferee limited liability partnership").

(2)   With the requisite sanction, the liquidator of the company being, or proposed to be, wound up ("the transferor company") may receive, in compensation or part compensation for the transfer or sale—

   (a)   in the case of the transferee company, shares, policies or other like interests in the transferee company for distribution among the members of the transferor company, or

   (b)   in the case of the transferee limited liability partnership, membership in the transferee limited liability partnership for distribution among the members of the transferor company.

(3)   The san     ion (2) is—

   (a)         ' voluntary winding up, that of a special
               conferring either a general authority on the
               ı respect of any particular arrangement, and

   (b)         luntary winding up, that of either the court or

(4)   Alternat     iquidator may (with that sanction) enter into
any other arr     ıbers of the transferor company may—

   (a)         e company, in lieu of receiving cash, shares,
               sts (or in addition thereto) participate in the
               ıer benefit from, the transferee company, or

   (b)   iı.   imited liability partnership, in lieu of receiving
         cası.  ddition thereto), participate in some other way
         in the     any other benefit from, the transferee limited
         liability partnership.

(5)   A sale or arrangement in pursuance of this section is binding on members of the transferor company.

(6)   A special resolution is not invalid for purposes of this section by reason that it is passed before or concurrently with a resolution for voluntary winding up or for appointing liquidators; but, if an order is made within a year for winding up the company by the court, the special resolution is not valid unless sanctioned by the court.

   **Amendments**—SI 2001/1090; SI 2009/1941.

   **General note**—This provision deals with a relatively infrequent occurrence, namely where a company in liquidation is subject to a scheme of reorganisation. The company's business is sold by the liquidator to another company and in return either the liquidator will distribute to the members, in a members' voluntary liquidation, shares or other securities in the company buying the business of the former company, or the members will be able to participate in the profits of the company buying the business. Certain tax advantages can be obtained from a reorganisation under this provision, such as a reorganisation would not be a distribution within s 209 of the Income and Corporation Taxes Act 1988 (R Richards and J Tribe 'Members' Liquidations' (2005) 26 Co Law 132 at 133).

The provision may also apply to a creditors' voluntary liquidation (see s 110(3)(b)), but it is hard to envisage the circumstances where this will occur, as the company will be insolvent and the creditors will not receive full payment of their debts. Perhaps the only situation where this might occur is where the company in creditors' voluntary liquidation is eventually found to be solvent.

If a company has more than one class of shares, the company can only decide on the nature of consideration to be accepted, and it is not able to decide, given a statutory majority, the mode of distribution of the consideration accepted as between the various classes of shareholders: *Griffith v Padget* (1877) 5 ChD 894.

The courts are willing to assist by exercising their equitable jurisdiction where the correct order required by a scheme entered into to take advantage of s 110 has not been adhered to because of a mistake: *Manuplastics Ltd v BPSW19 Ltd* [2011] EWHC 3853 (Ch).

## [1.163]

### 111 Dissent from arrangement under s 110

(1) This section applies in the case of a voluntary winding up where, for the purposes of section 110(2) or (4), there has been passed a special resolution of the transferor company providing the sanction requisite for the liquidator under that section.

(2) If a member of the transferor company who did not vote in favour of the special resolution expresses his dissent from it in writing, addressed to the liquidator and left at the company's registered office within 7 days after the passing of the resolution, he may require the liquidator either to abstain from carrying the resolution into effect or to purchase his interest at a price to be determined by agreement or by arbitration under this section.

(3) If the liquidator elects to purchase the member's interest, the purchase money must be paid before the company is dissolved and be raised by the liquidator in such manner as may be determined by special resolution.

(4) For purposes of an arbitration under this section, the provisions of the Companies Clauses Consolidation Act 1845 or, in the case of a winding up in Scotland, the Companies Clauses Consolidation (Scotland) Act 1845 with respect to the settlement of disputes by arbitration are incorporated with this Act, and—

    (a)    in the construction of those provisions this Act is deemed the special Act and "the company" means the transferor company, and

    (b)    any appointment by the incorporated provisions directed to be made under the hand of the secretary or any two of the directors may be made in writing by the liquidator (or, if there is more than one liquidator, then any two or more of them).

General note—Any attempt to circumvent the thrust of the provision, such as requiring in the company's constitution that dissenting members must accept a scheme, set out in the constitution, for providing compensation to members, will not be enforced: *Bisgood v Henderson's Transvaal Estates* [1908] 1 Ch 743, CA. Due to the need for the shares of dissenters to be bought, a scheme under the s 895 of the Companies Act 2006 procedure might be easier and less expensive, although the process under this provision is not quick and inexpensive.

## [1.164]

### 112 Reference of questions to court

(1) The liquidator or any contributory or creditor may apply to the court to determine any question arising in the winding up of a company, or to exercise, as respects the enforcing of calls or any other matter, all or any of the powers which the court might exercise if the company were being wound up by the court.

(2) The court, if satisfied that the determination of the question or the required exercise of power will be just and beneficial, may accede wholly or partially to the application on such terms and conditions as it thinks fit, or may make such other order on the application as it thinks just.

(3) A copy of an order made by virtue of this section staying the proceedings in the winding up shall forthwith be forwarded by the company, or otherwise as may be

prescribed, to the registrar of companies, who shall enter it in his records relating to the company.

**General note**—While it is not mandatory to have any court involvement in a voluntary liquidation, it might be necessary at some point during the course of a voluntary liquidation for the liquidator to obtain a court order or direction on a given matter. As this provision enables the court in voluntary winding up to exercise all or any of the powers which it might exercise if the company were being wound up by the court, and because of the liberal interpretation of the section (*Re Campbell Coverings Ltd* [1953] Ch 488), there is not a lot of difference between compulsory and creditors' voluntary liquidations. For instance, public examinations can be initiated in relation to voluntary liquidations through the agency of s 112 (*Re Campbell Coverings Ltd (No 2)* [1954] Ch 225; *Re Serene Shoes Ltd* [1958] 1 WLR 1087; *Bishopsgate Investment Management Ltd (in prov liq) v Maxwell* [1993] Ch 1 at 24 and 46, CA), even though public examinations are only allowed under s 131 in compulsory liquidations. But the section cannot be used as an alternative basis for a creditor instigating the private examination process, where this process might not be available and it would give a liquidator of a voluntary liquidation more powers than a liquidator in a compulsory liquidation: *Re James McHale Automobiles Ltd* [1997] 1 BCLC 273. An application can be made under 112 in a voluntary liquidation whereby a court can exercise the power set out in s 167(3) allowing the court to control the exercise of powers by a liquidator: *Cooper v PRG Powerhouse Ltd* [2008] EWHC 498 (Ch). In fact s 112(1) and s 112(2) when considered together give the courts the same powers in addressing the position of a company in voluntary liquidation that they would have in relation to a company that was in compulsory liquidation: *Re Paperback Collection and Recycling Ltd* [2019] EWHC 2904 (Ch).

While the section is wide in application it does include a threshold requirement, namely before the court will entertain making an order, it must be satisfied that the determination of the question posed will be just and beneficial: *Kean v Lucas* [2017] EWHC 250 (Ch), [2017] BCC 311, [2017] BPIR 689 at [16].

Often an application under s 112 will be made by a liquidator seeking directions concerning an issue of importance in the winding-up process. For instance, in *Re Harvard Securities Ltd (in liquidation)* [1997] 2 BCLC 369 the liquidator needed guidance as to who were the beneficial owners of shares, and the liquidator in *Re Agrimarche Ltd* [2010] EWHC 1655 (Ch), had the need of directions concerning the valuation of call options held by the company. In *Whitehouse v Wilson* [2006] EWCA Civ 1688, [2007] BPIR 230, a liquidator in a creditors' voluntary liquidation applied for the sanction of the court in relation to his decision to compromise his misfeasance claim against a director. An application can be made by a liquidator of more than one company in a group where the subject matter is common to all of the companies: *Re William Pickles plc (in liquidation)* [1996] 1 BCLC 681. Liquidators can apply under s 112 for directions whether and to what extent a debenture grants a valid and enforceable fixed charge of the assets of the company: *Re Double S Printers Ltd (in liquidation)* [1999] 1 BCLC 220.

Where a company has sufficient funds and the matter can be best dealt with pursuant to ordinary litigation, a court might well decline to hear any application for directions: *Re Stetzel Thompson & Co Ltd* (1988) 4 BCC 74.

The court has a discretion as to whether it will make an order under s 112, with the conditions governing its exercise being set out in s 112(2). But it has been said that an application under s 112 will only be entertained where its purpose is a legitimate purpose of winding up: *IRC v Mills* [2003] EWHC 2022 (Ch). Directions should only be provided for where it is just and beneficial and it will be of advantage in the liquidation: *S & D International (in liq) v MIG Property Services Pty Ltd* [2010] VSC 336. Along these lines, HHJ Cooke (sitting as a High Court judge) said in *Autobrokers Ltd v Dymond* [2015] EWHC 2691 (Admin), quoting from *Re Barings Plc; Hamilton v Law Debenture Trustees Ltd* [2001] 2 BCLC 159 at [8], that the test to be applied on an application is ' . . . whether . . . it [the direction sought] will be conducive to both the proper operation of the process of liquidation and to justice between all those interested in the liquidation'.

The court is able to direct a liquidator not to comply with a requirement, or be relieved from complying with an obligation, contained in the IR 2016 but a strong reason must be given for this to be ordered: *Autobrokers Ltd v Dymond* [2015] EWHC 2691 (Admin).

In *Tombs v Moulinex SA* [2004] EWHC 454 (Ch), [2004] 2 BCLC 397, involving a members' voluntary liquidation, the liquidators were seeking directions on the possible distribution of funds remaining under their control. In this case there was some possibility of future consumer actions against the company as a result of products that it had sold. The court does have jurisdiction to order distribution in a members' voluntary liquidation notwithstanding the existence of future creditors emerging: *Re R-R Realisations Ltd* [1980] 1 WLR 805. In *Re Sunwing Vacations Inc* [2011] EWHC 1544 (Ch), [2011] BPIR 1524 there was an application by a creditor that the liquidator disclose company documents to the applicant (the provision in compulsory liquidation is s 155). In *Autobrokers Ltd v Dymond* [2015] EWHC 2691 (Admin) the court made an order under s 112 that the liquidators convene a meeting of creditors after the creditors issued a valid requisition for the meeting under the process that was found in the now repealed IR 1986, r 4.114. The case remains indicative of the kind of order that the courts might make under s 112.

In *Re Anglican Insurance Ltd* [2008] NSWSC 41, the New South Wales Supreme Court, in dealing with the Australian equivalent of s 112 of the Insolvency Act, said that it could not make orders affecting the rights of outsiders, and it was not the task of the court to determine the rights and liabilities arising from the company's transactions entered into before the commencement of liquidation.

Any application that is made under the section should be made to the court which has jurisdiction to wind up the company ('the court' – s 251 of the Insolvency Act).

See the notes related to s 117.

'**Creditor**'—This includes a secured creditor: *Re Alfred Priestman & Co* (1929) [1936] 2 All ER 1340.

**Stay on proceedings against the company**—In compulsory liquidations there is a specific statutory provision, namely s 130(2), that prohibits, automatically, the initiation or prosecution of proceedings against the company unless leave is obtained from the courts. There is no corresponding provision in voluntary liquidations, but it has always been the practice for the court, upon application by the liquidator under s 112(1), to exercise its power in s 130(2) of staying actions and proceedings after commencement of voluntary winding up: *Freeman v General Publishing Co* [1894] 2 QB 380; *Anglo-Baltic & Mediterranean Bank v Barber* [1924] 2 KB 410; *Re Dicksmith (Manufacturing) Ltd (in liquidation)* [1999] 2 BCLC 686. The liquidator has the onus of establishing that there are special reasons for making the stay: *Re Roundwood Colliery Co* [1897] 1 Ch 373 at 381; *Currie v Consolidated Kent Collieries Corp* [1906] 1 KB 134.

To ensure the implementation of the principle of rateable division of assets, there has been a trend for stays to be ordered in relation to execution proceedings, on the application of the liquidator under s 112, where voluntary liquidation has commenced (*Re Poole Firebrick & Blue Clay Co* (1873) 17 Eq 268; *Re Thurso New Gas Co* (1889) 42 ChD 486; *Westbury v Twigg* [1892] 1 QB 77), so that through s 112 the court's powers under s 128 are applied in a creditors' voluntary winding up. However, this is not the case with members' voluntary windings up. It has been held that this practice would not be followed in a members' voluntary winding up, as it could be assumed that the company was able to pay its debts in full: *Gerard v Worth of Paris, Ltd* [1936] 2 All ER 905, CA.

See the notes related to s 130 for a discussion of the principles that apply when a court is faced with an application for leave to commence, or continue with, an action.

**Stay on winding-up proceedings**—The section can be used in a voluntary liquidation to obtain a stay of the liquidation proceedings (*Re Serene Shoes Ltd* [1958] 1 WLR 1087, [1958] 3 All ER 316; *Re Calgary and Edmonton Land Co Ltd* [1975] 1 WLR 355, [1975] 1 All ER 1046), just as one can with compulsory liquidations under s 147: *Re South Barrule Slate Quarry Co* (1869) 8 Eq 688; *Re J Burrows (Leeds) Ltd (in liquidation)* (1982) 126 SJ 227.

**Costs**—It has been held by the Victorian Court of Appeal in *Re Lonnex Pty Ltd (in liq) (No 2)* [2019] VSCA 62 that a liquidator should have his or her costs in seeking directions from the court paid out of the estate, provided that they were honestly and reasonably incurred. However, if liquidators appeal from a determination of the court they do so at their own risk and must take the usual consequences, so that if the liquidators are unsuccessful in their appeal they must be responsible personally for their own costs and that of any successful party; they cannot have recourse to the company's funds and assets. The only exception might be, it would seem from what the court said, where there was controversy as to legal principle.

See s 147 and the notes accompanying that section.

**[1.165]**

### 113 Court's power to control proceedings (Scotland)

If the court, on the application of the liquidator in the winding up of a company registered in Scotland, so directs, no action or proceeding shall be proceeded with or commenced against the company except by leave of the court and subject to such terms as the court may impose.

**[1.166]**

### 114 No liquidator appointed or nominated by company

(1) This section applies where, in the case of a voluntary winding up, no liquidator has been appointed or nominated by the company.

(2) The powers of the directors shall not be exercised, except with the sanction of the court or (in the case of a creditors' voluntary winding up) so far as may be necessary to

secure compliance with sections 99 (statement of affairs) and 100(1B) (nomination of liquidator by creditors), during the period before the appointment or nomination of a liquidator of the company.

(3)   Subsection (2) does not apply in relation to the powers of the directors—

    (a)      to dispose of perishable goods and other goods the value of which is likely to diminish if they are not immediately disposed of, and

    (b)      to do all such other things as may be necessary for the protection of the company's assets.

(4)   If the directors of the company without reasonable excuse fail to comply with this section, they are liable to a fine.

**Amendments**—Small Business, Enterprise and Employment Act 2015, s 126, Sch 9, Pt 1, paras 1, 30.

**General note**—This provision covers the period from the time of the resolution to wind up to the appointment of the liquidator. It is aimed at ensuring, inter alia, that the assets of the company are protected from dissipation during the interim period between the resolution to wind up and the appointment of a liquidator. The provision is designed to encourage the early appointment of a liquidator. It was introduced in the 1986 Act, together with s 166, to proscribe what was known as 'centrebinding'. This process derived its name from the case of *Re Centrebind Ltd* [1967] 1 WLR 377, [1966] 3 All ER 889. See the notes accompanying s 166 for more discussion.

This provision restricts the powers that the directors can exercise.

## [1.167]

### 115   Expenses of voluntary winding up

After the payment of any liabilities to which section 174A applies, all expenses properly incurred in the winding up, including the remuneration of the liquidator, are payable out of the company's assets in priority to all other claims.

**Amendments**—Corporate Insolvency and Governance Act 2020, s 2(1), Sch 3, paras 1, 9.

**General note**—In general terms the expenses of the winding up are paid out of the company's assets before any other unsecured creditors (see notes accompanying s 107). The section does not identify the expenses to which it refers. It is supplemented by r 6.42: *Re Central A1 Ltd* [2017] EWHC 220 (Ch) at [23]. The kinds of expenses that can be claimed are detailed in r 6.42 for creditors' voluntary liquidations, which also sets out the order of priority as far as payment occurs if there are insufficient assets to pay all expenses. This order may be varied by the courts under a combination of ss 112 and 156. However, the courts will not be quick to vary the priority order, as they are generally content to adopt the order of priorities in r 6.42: *Re Grey Marlin Ltd* [2000] 1 WLR 370, [2000] 2 BCLC 658. Rule 6.43(a) expressly permits courts to, in effect, re-order the priorities set out in r 6.42.

**'Incurred in the winding up'**—This does not encompass any expenses incurred prior to the making of the resolution to wind up unless they directly related to the obtaining of the resolution or were required by legislation (*Re WF Fearman Ltd (No 2)* (1988) 4 BCC 141 (costs of the preparation of a petition for an administration order – presented after the winding-up petition – were permitted, but no other costs); *Re Sandwell Copiers Ltd* [1988] BCLC 209 (an accountant could not claim his fees out of the funds held in the liquidation for collecting company debts prior to a commencement of the winding up)).

See the note relating to s 156.

## [1.168]

### 116   Saving for certain rights

The voluntary winding up of a company does not bar the right of any creditor or contributory to have it wound up by the court; but in the case of an application by a contributory the court must be satisfied that the rights of the contributories will be prejudiced by a voluntary winding up.

**General note**—When confronted with a petition by a creditor, in relation to a company that is in a creditors' voluntary liquidation, the general issue that a court must consider is whether it is preferable for the creditors that a winding-up order is made or the voluntary winding up continues: *Re Fitness Centre (South East) Ltd* [1986] BCLC 518; *Re Rhine Film Corp (UK) Ltd* (1986) 2 BCC 98, 949.

An order will not be made unless the court is satisfied that the voluntary winding up cannot be continued having regard to the interests of the members and creditors. It has been held that where a declaration of solvency had been completed then it was proper to hear the views of contributories on a petition for a winding up by the court: *Re Surplus Properties (Huddersfield) Ltd* [1984] BCLC 89 at 91.

If a creditor has a concern over the identity of the liquidator of a creditors' voluntary winding up, the creditor should not petition for a compulsory winding up, but rather apply for removal of the liquidator: *Re Inside Sports Ltd* [2000] 1 BCLC 302.

It appears that a creditor petitioning for an order must demonstrate that it would be detrimental to the interests of creditors if voluntary liquidation were to continue: *Re Riviera Pearls Ltd* [1962] 1 WLR 722; *Re Medisco Equipment Ltd* [1983] BCLC 305; *Re Magnus Consultants Ltd* [1995] BCLC 203. To secure an order, it is unnecessary for the liquidator's probity or competence to be challenged: *Re Lowestoft Traffic Services Ltd* [1986] BCLC 81; *Re Palmer Marine Surveys Ltd* [1986] 1 WLR 573, [1986] BCLC 106; *Re Falcon RJ Development Ltd* [1987] BCLC 437.

An order would not be made against the wishes of the majority as they have the largest stake in the company (*Re JD Swain Ltd* [1965] 1 WLR 909 at 913, 915, 916, [1965] 1 All ER 761 at 764, 765, 766, CA; *Re Zirceram Ltd* [2000] 1 BCLC 751 at 758) unless good reason was given for the court deciding to refrain from accepting the wishes of the majority. But in taking into account the wishes of the majority, the views of outside creditors will be given greater weight than those who are also members: *Re Medisco Equipment Ltd* [1983] BCLC 305; *Re H J Tomkins Ltd* [1990] BCLC 76. It has been said that it would not be right to refuse a winding-up order if the refusal would lead to the majority of creditors who are substantial and independent having a justified strong feeling of grievance that they had been unfairly denied the chance of having an independent liquidator being given the conduct of the winding up: *Re Falcon RJ Development Ltd* [1987] BCLC 437; *Re Palmer Marine Surveys Ltd* [1986] 1 WLR 573, [1986] BCLC 106; *Re MCH Services Ltd* [1987] BCLC 535. Furthermore, in arriving at a decision, the courts must consider: the quantity and the quality of debts owed by the company; and connections between any particular creditor with the company which may indicate any motivation for the creditor voting one way or the other: *Re Inside Sports Ltd* [2000] 1 BCLC 302.

Courts will exercise their discretion and order a winding up, on the basis of fairness and commercial morality, when they feel that the circumstances of the company warrant special scrutiny and to ensure that the creditors' interests are not prejudiced: *Re Zirceram Ltd* [2000] 1 BCLC 751 at 758. Courts have made orders where: the creditors lack confidence in the liquidator, and the latter is perceived as not being impartial (*Re Palmer Marine Surveys Ltd* [1986] 1 WLR 573, [1986] BCLC 106; *Re Roselmar Properties Ltd (No 2)* (1986) 2 BCC 99, 157; *Re Pinstripe Farming Co Ltd* [1996] 2 BCLC 295; *Re Zirceram Ltd* [2000] 1 BCLC 751 at 760); the liquidator has admitted into proof inflated or non-substantiated claims against the company (*Re Magnus Consultants Ltd* [1995] 1 BCLC 203; *Re Gordon & Breach Science Publishers Ltd* [1995] 2 BCLC 189; the liquidator had transferred company assets to associated companies for inadequate consideration (*Re Palmer Marine Surveys Ltd*); there have been inordinate delays in the winding up (*Re Hewitt Brannon (Tools) Co Ltd* [1991] BCLC 80); and there is a need for an urgent and quick investigation of the company's affairs (*Re William Thorpe & Son Ltd* (1988) 5 BCC 156).

It has been said that a factor in a decision to order a compulsory winding up could be the fact that the liquidator in a voluntary liquidation had not progressed far: *Souster v Carman Construction Co Ltd* [2000] BPIR 371 at 380. It is less likely that a court will make an order where the voluntary liquidation is nearly finalised and the liquidator undertakes to complete the winding up promptly: *Re J Russell Electronics Ltd* [1968] 1 WLR 1252, [1968] 2 All ER 559.

At the hearing of the petition: the incumbent liquidator is entitled (*Re Medisco Equipment* [1983] BCLC 305, (1983) 1 BCC 98, 944), and is probably advised, to appear by counsel; the liquidator may merely give evidence of the current state of the liquidation; and the liquidator should remain independent and refrain from expressing a view as to the desirability of a compulsory winding-up order: *Re Medisco Equipment Ltd* [1983] BCLC 305, (1983) 1 BCC 98, 944; *Re Arthur Rathbone Kitchens Ltd* [1997] 2 BCLC 280; *Souster v Carman Construction Co Ltd* [2000] BPIR 371. If he or she appears, the liquidator would be allowed the costs of doing so (*Re Roselmar Properties Ltd (No 2)* (1986) 2 BCC 99, 157), unless he or she adopts a less than independent approach, where the court may decide not to allow his or her costs out of the company's property: *Re Roselmar Properties Ltd (No 2)*; *Re Pinstripe Farming Co Ltd* [1996] 2 BCLC 295.

The official receiver is given specific power by s 124(5) to petition for a winding-up order in relation to a company that is in voluntary liquidation.

'Creditor'—Any creditor of the company, whether a pre- or post-voluntary liquidation creditor, may petition: *Re Bank of South Australia (No 2)* [1895] 1 Ch 578; *Re Greenwood and Co* [1900] 2 QB 306.

'**Petition by contributory**'—The same issues that apply when a creditor petitions apply when a contributory petitions: *Re Internet Investment Corporation Ltd* [2009] EWHC 2744 (Ch), [2010] 1 BCLC 458

For further discussion, see A Keay *McPherson and Keay's Law of Company Liquidation* (Sweet and Maxwell, 4th edn, 2013) at 181–188.

## CHAPTER VI

### WINDING UP BY THE COURT JURISDICTION (ENGLAND AND WALES)

[1.169]

### 117 High Court and county court jurisdiction

(1) The High Court has jurisdiction to wind up any company registered in England and Wales.

(2) Where in the case of a company registered in England and Wales the amount of its share capital paid up or credited as paid up does not exceed £120,000, then (subject to this section) the county court . . . has concurrent jurisdiction with the High Court to wind up the company.

(2A) Despite subsection (2), proceedings for the exercise of the jurisdiction to wind up a company registered in England and Wales may be commenced only in the High Court if the place which has longest been the company's registered office during the 6 months immediately preceding the presentation of the petition for winding up is in the district that is the London insolvency district for the purposes of the second Group of Parts of the Act.

(3) The money sum for the time being specified in subsection (2) is subject to increase or reduction by order under section 416 in Part XV.

(4) . . .

(5) Every court in England and Wales having winding-up jurisdiction has for the purposes of that jurisdiction all the powers of the High Court; and every prescribed officer of the court shall perform any duties which an officer of the High Court may discharge by order of a judge of that court or otherwise in relation to winding up.

(6) . . .

(7) . . .

(8) The Lord Chief Justice may nominate a judicial office holder (as defined in section 109(4) of the Constitutional Reform Act 2005) to exercise his functions under this section.

**Amendments**—SI 2002/1240; Constitutional Reform Act 2005, s 15(1), Sch 4, Pt 1, paras 185, 186(1); Crime and Courts Act 2013, s 17(5), Sch 9, Pt 3, para 93; SI 2014/821; SI 2017/702; SI 2019/146, as from IP completion day (as defined in the European Union (Withdrawal Agreement) Act 2020, s 39(1)–(5)).

**General note**—For a winding-up order to be made, the European Union Regulation on Insolvency Proceedings requires that the company's centre of main interests is the jurisdiction where insolvency proceedings are to be opened. But for the purposes of this Regulation the UK is treated as one jurisdiction. Thus, a company registered in England and Wales could not be wound up in Scotland merely because its centre of main interests was in Scotland; it has to be wound up in England and Wales: *Bank Leumi (UK) plc v Screw Conveyor Ltd* [2017] CSOH 129.

Where a company has been registered in Scotland, it must be wound up in Scotland (see s 120), while a company that is registered in Northern Ireland may be wound up by the High Court of England and Wales as an unregistered company if it has a principal place of business in England or Wales: *Re Normandy Marketing Ltd* [1994] Ch 198, [1994] 2 WLR 438, [1994] 1 All ER 1007, [1994] 1 BCLC 565.

It is stated in s 117(5) that every court which has a winding-up jurisdiction has all of the powers of the High Court, and as a result the county court is able, while hearing proceedings in relation to the winding up, to resolve issues where the value of the assets or the claim is in excess of its normal jurisdictional limit: *Re F & E Stanton Ltd* [1928] 1 KB 464. In the case of voluntary liquidation, where an application needs to be made to a court (such as pursuant to s 112), then the court to which the application is made is to the court which has jurisdiction to wind up the company (s 251 of the Insolvency Act).

All of the High Court judges are able to exercise jurisdiction in relation to an application that is in some way incidental to a liquidation: *Fabric Sales Ltd v Eratex Ltd* [1984] 1 WLR 863 at 865.

While taking proceedings in the county court may be more convenient, at times the practice has tended to be to use the High Court more than the county court, but now s 117(2A) limits that, probably in an attempt to reduce the number of petitions being dealt with by the High Court.

The Court of Appeal is only able to hear appeals relating to petitions for winding-up orders, and it does not have the power to hear petitions at first instance: *Re Dunraven Adare Coal & Iron Co* (1875) 33 LT 371.

Where appropriate, hearings may be held in private: *Banco Nacional de Cuba v Cosmos Trading Corp* [2000] 1 BCLC 813 at 816, CA.

The provision is subject to Art 3 of the EU Regulation on Insolvency Proceedings. The article provides that ⟨...⟩ sts is in a Member State of the EU, that State will have ju⟨...⟩ and the place where a company has its registered office i⟨...⟩ pany's main interests. Proceedings cannot be commenc⟨...⟩ company has an establishment in that State's territory⟨...⟩ ..td) the court took the view that winding-up proceedi⟨...⟩ Vales against a Swedish company as the company had no⟨...⟩ held that the existence of business premises was not suf⟨...⟩ blishment here, for the purposes of Art 3. In a case whe⟨...⟩ Member State then any proceedings commenced elsewher⟨...⟩ proceedings. See the notes relating to Art 3 of the EU R⟨...⟩

Importantly para 3.1 of the *Practice Direction – Insolvency Proceedings* (July 2020) [2020] BPIR 1211 states that in the High Court, all petitions and applications, are to be listed for an initial hearing before an ICC judge in the Royal Courts of Justice, or a district judge sitting in a District Registry except for those matters set out in para 3.3.

[1.170]

**118 Proceedings taken in wrong court**

(1) Nothing in section 117 invalidates a proceeding by reason of its being taken in the wrong court.

(2) The winding up of a company by the court in England and Wales, or any proceedings in the winding up, may be retained in the court in which the proceedings were commenced, although it may not be the court in which they ought to have been commenced.

**General note**—In such circumstances the court may make one of three orders: that the proceedings be transferred to the correct court; that the proceedings continue in the court; or that the proceedings be struck out (r 12.31).

[1.171]

**119 Proceedings in county court; case stated for High Court**

(1) If any question arises in any winding-up proceedings in a county court which all the parties to the proceedings, or which one of them and the judge of the court, desire to have determined in the first instance in the High Court, the judge shall state the facts in the form of a special case for the opinion of the High Court.

(2) Thereupon the special case and the proceedings (or such of them as may be required) shall be transmitted to the High Court for the purposes of the determination.

**General note**—See rr 12.30–12.34 and the notes attaching thereto.

*Jurisdiction (Scotland)*

[1.172]

**120 Court of Session and sheriff court jurisdiction**

(1) The Court of Session has jurisdiction to wind up any company registered in Scotland.

(2) When the Court of Session is in vacation, the jurisdiction conferred on that court by this section may (subject to the provisions of this Part) be exercised by the judge acting as vacation judge . . .

(3)   Where the amount of a company's share capital paid up or credited as paid up does not exceed £120,000, the sheriff court of the sheriffdom in which the company's registered office is situated has concurrent jurisdiction with the Court of Session to wind up the company; but—

- (a)   the Court of Session may, if it thinks expedient having regard to the amount of the company's assets to do so—
  - (i)   remit to sheriff court any petition presented to the Court of Session for winding up such a company, or
  - (ii)   require such a petition presented to a sheriff court to be remitted to the Court of Session; and
- (b)   the Court of Session may require any such petition as above-mentioned presented to one sheriff court to be remitted to another sheriff court; and
- (c)   in a winding up in the sheriff court the sheriff may submit a stated case for the opinion of the Court of Session on any question of law arising in that winding up.

(4)   For purposes of this section, the expression "registered office" means the place which has longest been the company's registered office during the 6 months immediately preceding the presentation of the petition for winding up.

(5)   The money sum for the time being specified in subsection (3) is subject to increase or reduction by order under section 416 in Part XV.

(6)   . . .

**Amendments**—Court of Session Act 1988, s 52(2), Sch 2, Pt I; SI 2002/1240; SI 2017/702; SI 2019/146, as from IP completion day (as defined in the European Union (Withdrawal Agreement) Act 2020, s 39(1)–(5)).

## [1.173]

### 121   Power to remit winding up to Lord Ordinary

(1)   The Court of Session may, by Act of Sederunt, make provision for the taking of proceedings in a winding up before one of the Lords Ordinary; and, where provision is so made, the Lord Ordinary has, for the purposes of the winding up, all the powers and jurisdiction of the court.

(2)   However, the Lord Ordinary may report to the Inner House any matter which may arise in the course of a winding up.

*Grounds and effect of winding-up petition*

## [1.174]

### 122   Circumstances in which company may be wound up by the court

(1)   A company may be wound up by the court if—

- (a)   the company has by special resolution resolved that the company be wound up by the court,
- (b)   being a public company which was registered as such on its original incorporation, the company has not been issued with a trading certificate under section 761 of the Companies Act 2006 (requirement as to minimum share capital) and more than a year has expired since it was so registered,
- (c)   it is an old public company, within the meaning of Schedule 3 to the Companies Act 2006 (Consequential Amendments, Transitional Provisions and Savings) Order 2009,
- (d)   the company does not commence its business within a year from its incorporation or suspends its business for a whole year,
- (e)   . . .
- (f)   the company is unable to pay its debts,
- (fa)   . . .
- (g)   the court is of the opinion that it is just and equitable that the company should be wound up.

(2)   In Scotland, a company which the Court of Session has jurisdiction to wind up may be wound up by the Court if there is subsisting a floating charge over property comprised in the company's property and undertaking, and the court is satisfied that the security of the creditor entitled to the benefit of the floating charge is in jeopardy.

For this purpose a creditor's security is deemed to be in jeopardy if the Court is satisfied that events have occurred or are about to occur which render it unreasonable in the creditor's interests that the company should retain power to dispose of the property which is subject to the floating charge.

**Amendments**—Insolvency Act 2000, s 1, Sch 1, paras 1, 6; SI 2008/948; SI 2009/1941; SI 2011/1265; Corporate Insolvency and Governance Act 2020, s 2(1), Sch 3, paras 1, 10.

**CIGA 2020**—This provision is affected by temporary measures at Sch 10, paras 7(1)(a), 7(5)(a) and 8(1)(b) of CIGA 2020 and by the *Insolvency Practice Direction relating to the Corporate Insolvency and Governance Act 2020* [2020] BPIR 1207 (at APPENDIX 4 of this book).

**General note**—This provision, together with s 125, makes it clear that the court has a discretion as to whether it orders the winding up of a company. The section sets out the circumstances when an order may be made.

Only one of the grounds set out in this section makes insolvency the basis for a winding-up order (s 122(1)(f)), but this ground is by far the most frequent ground relied on by a winding-up petition. It must always be remembered that the Act does not deal exclusively with issues of insolvency, as can be seen from the fact that it encompasses members' voluntary windings up. Solvent companies are wound up under the Act.

## SECTION 122(1)(a)

**Where there is a special resolution**—As a company can be wound up pursuant to the voluntary liquidation process if a special resolution to wind up is passed, it is difficult to envisage circumstances where the members are going to prefer the more complicated and expensive compulsory form of winding up. A possible reason is where it is felt that it is desirable that the official receiver's investigative powers are exercised under ss 132–133.

The courts have a discretion whether or not to make a winding-up order or not under this ground. Generally speaking the court's discretion should be exercised in favour of making an order: *Hillig v Darkinjung Pty Ltd* [2006] NSWSC 137, (2006) 205 FLR 450.

## SECTION 122(1)(b)

**Public company not meeting share capital requirements**—Here the company is a public company which was registered on or after 22 December 1980, being the date on which a new definition of 'public company' came into operation (Companies Act 1980 (Commencement No 2) Order 1980 (SI 1980/1785)), and which has not, for more than a year since its registration, been issued with a certificate of compliance under s 761 of the Companies act 2006 with the share capital requirements.

## SECTION 122(1)(c)

**An old public company**—This refers to an old public company, within the meaning of Sch 3 to the Companies Act 2006 (Consequential Amendments, Transitional Provisions and Savings) Order 2009. For the purposes of Sch 3 an 'old public company' is a company limited by shares, or a company limited by guarantee and having a share capital, in respect of which certain conditions are fulfilled.

## SECTION 122(1)(d)

**Company does not commence business**—Originally, this ground was designed essentially to enable shareholders to have a way of recovering their investment from a company which fails to carry on its intended business. To succeed, the petitioner must establish that the company had no intention of carrying on business: *Re Middlesborough Assembly Rooms* (1879) 14 ChD 104. Even if the petitioner is able to do this, the court retains a discretion whether or not to make an order (*Re Metropolitan Rly Warehousing Co* (1867) 36 LJ Ch 287, (1867) 17 LT 108), and in exercising this discretion the courts will take into account the wishes of the majority of the shareholders: *Re Tomlin Patent Horse Shoe Co* (1886) 55 LT 314.

'Business'—At one stage this was taken to refer to the business specified in the objects' clause of the company's memorandum. Now, with the abolition (virtually) of the ultra vires rule and courts taking a liberal view on objects' clauses, it is probable that courts will interpret the term 'business' far more broadly.

'Commencement'—For the commencement of a business the company must 'actually set to work' (*Re South Luipaard's Vlei Gold Mines Co* (1897) 13 TLR 504), and this does not include merely allotting shares (*Re South Luipaard's*), making calls, or holding board meetings: *Re Capital Fire Insurance Association* (1882) 21 ChD 209. Action which involves making arrangements which are necessary before starting business may be sufficient for a commencement: *Re Petersburgh & Viborg Gas Co* (1874) WN 1996.

'Suspension'—Suspension occurs where the business is abandoned either with the deliberate intention of abandoning it (*Re Madrid & Valencia Ry Co* (1850) 19 LJ Ch 260), or because of inability to proceed: *Re Middlesborough Assembly Rooms Co* (1879) 14 ChD 104; *Re Tomlin Patent Horse Shoe Co* (1886) 55 LT 314.

## SECTION 122(1)(f)

The company is unable to pay its debts—This is the main ground upon which companies are liquidated. Companies falling into this category are insolvent.

The meaning of 'unable to pay its debts' is explained in s 123. See the notes relating to that section.

## SECTION 122(1)(g)

Just and equitable—Following the previous ground, this is the next most popular ground under section 122 for founding a winding-up petition. Ordinarily this ground will be relied on by a contributory of the company. Most frequently it is invoked in relation to quasi-partnerships where there has been a breakdown in the relations between the controllers. It is, together with s 994 of the Companies Act 2006, the ground on which the majority of contributories' petitions rely where contributories are dissatisfied with the way in which the company is being run or they feel that the controllers of companies have acted improperly and unfairly towards them. But creditors do have the right to rely on the just and equitable ground (*Re Dollar Land Holdings plc* [1994] 1 BCLC 404; *Bell Group Finance Pty Ltd (in liquidation) v Bell Group (UK) Holdings Ltd* [1996] 1 BCLC 304; *Morrice v Brae Hotel (Shetland) Ltd* 1997 SLT 474, [1997] BCC 670), provided that the creditor is able to establish that he or she has the necessary standing to bring the proceedings: *Morrice v Brae Hotel (Shetland) Ltd*. A creditor is not entitled to rely on the ground where the bases for the petition are public interest reasons, as Parliament has determined that where such reasons exist the Secretary of State for Business Energy and Industrial Strategy should present a petition under s 124A: *Re Millennium Advanced Technology Ltd* [2004] EWHC 711(Ch) at [33], [2004] 1 BCLC 77 at 85.

With quasi-partnerships mutual trust and confidence is very important. However, the Court of Appeal in *Re Paramount Powders (UK) Ltd* [2019] EWCA Civ 1644, [2020] BCC 152, affirming the decision at first instance (*Badyal v Badyal* [2018] EWHC 68 (Ch)) has indicated that the loss of mutual trust and confidence will not, alone, suffice for an order to wind up. It was indeed a relevant factor, but only one to be taken into account (at [34]). Probity and good faith were also relevant factors (at [36]). If the breakdown in trust and confidence was due to the petitioner's own misconduct the petitioner might not be able to secure a winding-up order (at [39]).

In deciding petitions courts will assess the factual matrix of the case: *Re Sino Strategic International Ltd* [2015] FCA 709.

Section 125(2) provides that where a contributory presents a petition on the just and equitable ground the company should be wound up, if the court is of the opinion that (a) the petitioners are entitled to relief either by winding up the company or by some other means, and (b) in the absence of any other remedy it would be just and equitable that the company should be wound up. However, this does not apply if the court is also of the opinion both that some other remedy is available to the petitioners and that they are acting unreasonably in seeking to have the company wound up instead of pursuing that other remedy. Notwithstanding this and the fact that an alternative remedy exists and the petitioner is acting unreasonably, courts have a wide discretion in deciding whether to make an order or not: *Re a Company 001363 of 1988* (1989) 5 BCC 18; *Re Cyracuse Ltd* [2001] 1 BCLC 187; *Robinson v H G Robinson and Sons Ltd* [2020] EWHC 1 (Ch) at [29]. However, winding up is seen as a last resort and an exceptional way of resolving shareholder conflicts: *Fulham Football Club (1987) Ltd v Richards* [2011] EWCA Civ 855, [2012] Ch 333. One alternative is to bring an action under s 994 of the Companies Act 2006 (unfair prejudice ground). Another alternative is where there is an offer to purchase shares at a reasonable value: *Re Cyracuse Ltd* [2001] 1 BCLC 187; *Robinson v H G Robinson and Sons Ltd* [2020] EWHC 1 (Ch) at [45]. It is possible that where there is an alternative remedy, a petition will be struck out: *Re a Company* [1997] 1 BCLC 479; *Robinson* [2020] EWHC 1 (Ch).

As mentioned above, parties may seek a winding-up order or a remedy under s 994 of the Companies Act 2006 in the alternative. It might be thought to be a bit of a gamble to do this now, as the courts have, on occasions, struck out such petitions and, in fact, *Practice Direction – Insolvency Proceedings* (July 2020) [2020] BPIR 1211 in para 22(1) makes it plain that it is undesirable to seek, as a matter of course, a winding up order as an alternative to an order under s 994 of the Companies Act 2006. The Practice Direction states that: 'The petition should not ask for a winding up order unless that is the remedy which the petitioner prefers, or it is thought that it may be the only remedy to which the petitioner is entitled.' Notwithstanding this, it has been said in the past that courts will accept, on occasions, that the pleading of an alternative remedy is allowed (*Re Copeland and Craddock Ltd* [1997] BCC 294), and this is likely to be where it is

167

unclear on the facts whether unfairly prejudicial conduct under s 994 can be made out: *Re RA Noble & Sons Ltd* [1997] BCC 294. In *Re FI Call Ltd* [2015] EWHC 3269 (Ch) the court permitted petitions for relief under s 994 of the Companies Act 2006 and one for winding up under s 122(1)(g) to run concurrently. Of importance in making any decisions on this score is the judicial comment that the just and equitable ground does not provide a wider basis for granting relief, with the result that if conduct was not sufficient to obtain an order under s 994, then a court would not grant a winding-up order on the basis of s 122(1)(g), for the jurisdiction to wind up is not more extensive than that under s 994: *Re Guidezone Ltd* [2000] 2 BCLC 321. But winding up is only permitted pursuant to a claim under the just and equitable ground, and not pursuant to a claim under s 994.

It has been made clear in the leading case that there should be flexibility with this ground and courts should refrain from setting down categories into which petitioners have to bring themselves: *Ebrahimi v Westbourne Galleries Ltd* [1973] AC 360, HL. Most cases have involved small private companies (closely-held companies) that are, substantially, in the nature of a partnership, whose members are unable to co-operate in the conduct of its affairs: *Ebrahimi v Westbourne Galleries Ltd*. For a case where Chief Registrar Briggs (as he then was) set out the factors that could be taken into account when deciding whether to grant a winding-up petition under this ground, see *Hussein v Haus of Vanity Ltd* [2017] EWHC 2615 (Ch) at [48]. One of those factors was that there is a public interest in investigating management.

It has been held that a petitioner must come with clean hands, and if he or she does not do so then his or her relevant misconduct could mean that relief will be denied: *Ebrahimi v Westbourne Galleries Ltd*. However, in a recent Australian case it was said that while the actions of the applicant for a winding-up order on this ground should be an important consideration for the court when deciding whether or not to grant the order, unclean hands would not constitute an absolute bar to an applicant in a winding-up application, as in many instances both parties will come with unclean hands: *Pham Thai Duc v PTS Australian Distributor Pty Ltd* [2005] NSWSC 98.

Courts will only order winding up on the petition of a contributory if he or she is endeavouring to protect his or her position as a member, for a member is not permitted to obtain a winding-up order under s 122(1)(f) to protect a wider range of interests than could be protected under s 994 of the Companies Act 2006: *Re JE Cade & Son Ltd* [1992] BCLC 213.

In *Sea Management Singapore Pte Ltd v Professional Service Brokers Ltd* [2012] CIV-2011–404–5315, the New Zealand High Court stated that the petitioner has the onus of establishing that it is either impracticable or inequitable for him or her to be limited to remedies in any shareholders' agreement. Also in New Zealand it has been held that the court would not regard the possible impact on a shareholder who was not involved directly in the circumstances that led to the breakdown of confidence as a sufficient reason to deny a winding-up order (*Jenkins v Supscaf Ltd* [2006] 3 NZLR 264, NZHC).

A trustee in bankruptcy of a member of a company is entitled to petition for winding up under this ground: *Hamilton v Brown*, sub nom, *Re C and MB Holdings Ltd* [2016] EWHC 191 (Ch), [2017] 1 BCLC 269, [2016] BPIR 531. See notes under s 124.

The *Practice Direction – Insolvency Proceedings* (July 2020) [2020] BPIR 1211 makes it incumbent in para 22.2 on the petitioner to state whether he or she is willing to consent to a validating order under s 127 in the standard form. The problem for the company is that once a petition has been presented it can be restricted in its dealings. See the notes attached to s 127.

At one time it was thought that this ground was to be construed in the light of other grounds, namely those now contained in s 122(1)(a)–(f), but clearly this ground is now regarded as being independent of the other grounds in s 122(1): *Loch v John Blackwood Ltd* [1924] AC 783 at 788–790; *Davis & Co v Brunswick (Australia) Ltd* [1936] 1 All ER 299; *Ebrahimi v Westbourne Galleries Ltd* [1973] AC 360.

If a controlling shareholder causes a company to oppose unreasonably a petition for a winding-up order on this ground, he or she might be held liable personally for the costs: *Cassegrain v CTK Engineering Pty Ltd* [2005] NSWSC.

A petition on this ground will not be valid if it is designed to vindicate personal or business reputation save where it is incidental to a decision as to whether the relief sought is justified or not: *Re FI Call Ltd* [2015] EWHC 3269 (Ch) at [64].

See A Keay *McPherson and Keay's Law of Company Liquidation* (Sweet and Maxwell, 4th edn, 2018) at 239–257.

**[1.175]**

### 123 Definition of inability to pay debts

(1)   A company is deemed unable to pay its debts—

    (a)   if a creditor (by assignment or otherwise) to whom the company is indebted in a sum exceeding £750 then due has served on the company, by

> leaving it at the company's registered office, a written demand (in the prescribed form) requiring the company to pay the sum so due and the company has for 3 weeks thereafter neglected to pay the sum or to secure or compound for it to the reasonable satisfaction of the creditor, or

(b)    if, in England and Wales, execution or other process issued on a judgment, decree or order of any court in favour of a creditor of the company is returned unsatisfied in whole or in part, or

(c)    if, in Scotland, the induciae of a charge for payment on an extract decree, or an extract registered bond, or an extract registered protest, have expired without payment being made, or

(d)    if, in Northern Ireland, a certificate of unenforceability has been granted in respect of a judgment against the company, or

(e)    if it is proved to the satisfaction of the court that the company is unable to pay its debts as they fall due.

(2)    A company is also deemed unable to pay its debts if it is proved to the satisfaction of the court that the value of the company's assets is less than the amount of its liabilities, taking into account its contingent and prospective liabilities.

(3)    The money sum for the time being specified in subsection (1)(a) is subject to increase or reduction by order under section 416 in Part XV.

**CIGA 2020**—This provision is affected by temporary measures as at Sch 10, paras 1(1), 2(1), 2(3), 5(1)(b), 5(2) and 5(3) of CIGA 2020 and by the *Insolvency Practice Direction relating to the Corporate Insolvency and Governance Act 2020* [2020] BPIR 1207 (at Appendix 4 of this book).

**General note**—The provision details six instances where a company will be deemed to be unable to pay its debts. Where any of these can be established, a court will presume the company to be insolvent, and the onus is then on the company to prove that it is able to pay its debts.

The fact that a creditor is able to establish that the company is unable to pay its debts does not mean that a winding-up order will be made automatically: the court has an unfettered discretion (s 125(1)). The company might be able to establish positively that it is solvent. After saying that, a court may still make a winding-up order if the assets of the company are greater than liabilities, and if the company does not dispute the fact that it owes money to the creditor who has requested payment, because non-payment gives rise to a legitimate suspicion of inability to pay: *Cornhill Insurance plc v Improvement Services Ltd* [1986] 1 WLR 114. But it might be necessary to be able to prove first that any sum owed has been demanded from the company: *Re a Company (No 006798 of 1995)* [1996] 2 BCLC 48.

According to *Re Fildes Bros Ltd* [1970] 1 WLR 592 at 597 petitioners must be able to establish that the ground on which they rely exists at the time of the hearing as well as when the petition was presented, but this case was based on the just and equitable ground (s 122(1)(g)) and not on an inability to pay debts.

As a temporary restriction, and as part of the Government's response to the COVID-19 (coronavirus) pandemic in 2020–2021, paras 2(1), (2), (3), (4) of Sch 10 of the Corporate Insolvency and Governance Act 2020 provided (and as amended by The Corporate Insolvency and Governance Act 2020 (Coronavirus) (Extension of the Relevant Period) Regulations 2020 (SI 2020/1031), reg 2, The Corporate Insolvency and Governance Act 2020 (Coronavirus) (Extension of the Relevant Period) (No 2) Regulations 2020 (SI 2020/1483), reg 2, The Corporate Insolvency and Governance Act 2020 (Coronavirus) (Extension of the Relevant Period) Regulations 2021 (SI 2021/375), reg 3(4) and The Corporate Insolvency and Governance Act 2020 (Coronavirus) (Extension of the Relevant Period) (No 2) Regulations 2021 (SI 2021/718), reg 2) that during the period between 27 April 2020 and 30 September 2021 a petition could not be presented on the basis of non-compliance with s 123(1)(a)–(d) (where s 123(1)(a) is relied on the demand could not have been served between 1 March 2020 and 30 September 2021) unless the petitioner/creditor had reasonable grounds for believing that coronavirus did not have a financial effect on the company or the facts to which the ground on which the petition is based would have occurred even if coronavirus had no financial effect on the company or non-compliance with s 123(1)(e) or s 123(2) unless coronavirus did not have a financial effect on the company, or the relevant ground would apply even if coronavirus had not had a financial effect on the company. The burden of establishing that the virus had a financial effect is on the company, but it merely requires the company to make out a prima facie case, and it is, therefore, not a heavy burden: *Re A Company* [2020] EWHC 1551 (Ch), [2020] 2 BCLC 307, [2020] BPIR 1100.

**Written demand**—This demand is referred to as a 'statutory demand' in winding-up proceedings (r 7.2), and is a procedure that dates back to the Companies Act 1862. There is no limit to the life of a demand nor any time specified in which a petition, when it is founded on the non-compliance with a demand, is to be presented. But one would think that the court may take the view that reliance on the failure to comply with a demand served many months or even weeks before the presentation of the petition would not be appropriate, as the company's situation might have changed in that time.

There seems nothing to prohibit a creditor using the non-compliance with a statutory demand to found a petition even where the demand was served by another creditor, as the only effect of a failure to comply is to lead to the presumption of insolvency: *Re Island of Anglesea Coal Co* (1861) 4 LT 684. Yet to do so the creditor would surely have to establish that in excess of £750 was owed and that the creditor had demanded payment in some way.

The company must be given a complete 3-week period in which to comply, and a petition should not be presented until a full 21 days have elapsed.

Now there is no prescribed form for a demand. Nevertheless, the *Practice Direction – Insolvency Proceedings* (July 2020) [2020] BPIR 1211 provides at para 9.1 that where a winding up petition is presented following service of a statutory demand, the statutory demand must contain the information set out in r 7.3 and should, as far as possible, follow the form provided on the Government website (Form SD1. See https://www.gov.uk/government/publications/demand-imme diate-payment-of-a-debt-from-a-limited-company-form-sd1). See r 7.3 and the notes under that rule.

The non-compliance with a statutory demand only provides a presumption that the company is unable to pay its debts. So, the company might be able to present evidence, besides arguing that the debt on which the petition is founded is disputed, that rebuts the presumption of insolvency. To rebut the presumption a company that wishes to establish the fact of solvency must adduce evidence for that purpose. Once that is done then the judge will decide whether the evidence is relevant, followed by a determination as to whether the evidence is admissible. Then the judge will assess the probative value of the evidence. That assessment is inductive. Finally the judge will decide whether the claimed solvency is probable or more probable than not: *Deputy Commissioner of Taxation v De Simeone Consulting Pty Ltd* [2007] FCA 548 at [12].

See r 7.3 and the notes attached to that rule for the required contents of demands.

**Creditor**—To be able to invoke s 123(1)(a), the person who serves a statutory demand must be a creditor owed in excess of £750. The meaning of creditor is discussed under 'Creditor' in the notes attached to s 124.

A person who is the creditor by assignment may serve a demand, but an equitable assignee is not able to, as it must be served by the person who holds the legal title to the debt: *Re Steel Wing Co* [1921] 1 Ch 349 at 356.

Creditors who serve a demand on a company may be held liable for the costs of the company if it applies successfully for an order restraining the presentation of a petition on the basis of a dispute over the debt relied on in the demand: *Cannon Screen Entertainment Ltd v Handmade Films (Distributors) Ltd* [1989] BCLC 660.

Where a company has been served with a demand and the company wishes to resist the demand, the appropriate course of action is to apply for an injunction to prevent the creditor from either presenting a petition or advertising a petition that is presented.

**The debt**—A debt must be due, and must be payable to the one serving the demand at that time, so this rules out contingent claims (it has been held that while a contingent debt is a debt for the purposes of winding up, such a debt could not be used as the basis for a statutory demand until the relevant contingency has happened (*JSF Finance and Current Exchange Co Ltd v Akma Solutions Inc* [2001] 2 BCLC 307, [2002] BPIR 621) and prospective debts, as well as unliquidated sums.

It has been held that a claim for money had and received, whilst restitutionary, is able to be treated as a debt due for the purposes of a provision like s 123: *OPC Managed Rehab Ltd v Accident Compensation Corporation* [2006] 1 NZLR 778, NZCA.

In circumstances where the debt is owed in a foreign currency then, as there is no express provision requiring conversion, the creditor may make the demand in the foreign currency, or the creditor may convert the amount into pounds sterling: *Re a Debtor (No 51/SD/91)* [1992] 1 WLR 1294, [1993] 2 All ER 40. If the debt is converted into pounds sterling it would appear that the creditor is not obliged to state the rate of exchange or the date of conversion (*Re a Debtor (No 51/ SD/91)*), which might appear to be unfair to the company.

In *HMRC v Earley* [2011] EWHC1783 (Ch), [2011] BPIR 1590, it was held that the amount of an assessment of tax was a debt and it was liquidated and ascertained.

**The demand**—At one time demands were construed very strictly by the courts and minor mistakes would invalidate them for the purposes of s 123. But now, as with demands relied on before the presentation of bankruptcy petitions, the courts have exhibited a more liberal approach. For instance, in *Re a Debtor (No 1 of 1987)* [1988] 1 All ER 959, the court refused to set aside a defective demand served on an individual debtor even though it was perplexing. On appeal the decision was affirmed ([1989] 1 WLR 271, [1989] 2 All ER 46, CA) and Nicholls LJ said that while the demand may have been confusing for the debtor, it was not confusing enough to set aside the demand. Where there is a defective demand, but no prejudice to the debtor and no indication that the debtor would have complied with a demand, which was not defective, the demand should not be regarded as fatally flawed: *Re a Debtor (No 1 of 1987)* [1987] 1 WLR 271 at 279. If a demand overstates the amount owed by a debtor to a creditor, it has been held that the demand is not necessarily invalid, as the debtor could have avoided the presumption of insolvency by paying what he or she admitted was owing and taking issue with the demand as far as the balance was concerned: *Re A Debtor (No 490/SD/91)* [1992] 1 WLR 507, [1992] 2 All ER 664, [1993] BCLC 164 – following *Re a Debtor (No 1 of 1987)* [1989] 1 WLR 271, [1989] 2 All ER 46, CA. But all of this should not be seen as a signal to creditors and their advisers that they can be slipshod in their preparation of demands: *Re a Debtor (No 1 of 1987)* [1989] 2 All ER 46 at 51.

See Milman 'Statutory Demands in the Courts: A Retreat from Formalism in Bankruptcy Law' [1994] Conv 289.

There is no English authority that determines whether the insertion in the demand of a wrong name for the company is defective. There is divergence of opinion in Australia, but the stronger view is that the court will make an allowance for minor errors (*Transfloors Pty Ltd v SWF Hoists & Industrial Equipment Pty Ltd* (1985) 3 ACLC 66) or for errors which do not frustrate the purpose of the provisions or do not deprive a party of a right (*Pro Image Production (Vic) Pty Ltd v Catalyst Television Productions Pty Ltd* (1988) 6 ACLC 888; *Hornet Aviation Pty Ltd v Ansett Australia Ltd* (1995) 13 ACLC 613). But there is an opposite view, namely that the use of the wrong company name is a defect which makes the demand invalid: *B&M Quality Constructions Pty Ltd v WG Brady Pty Ltd* (1994) 12 ACLC 970; *Re Scandon Pty Ltd* (1996) 14 ACLC 124.

There is Australian authority to the effect that a multiple number of creditors are unable to serve a single demand on one company – it is a defect which would cause a substantial injustice: *First Line Distribution Pty Ltd v Whiley* (1995) 13 ACLC 1216 at 1220. Australian authority also provides that a valid demand can claim a portion of the debt owed to the creditor: *Commonwealth Bank of Australia v Garuda Aviation Pty Ltd* [2013] WASCA 61.

If a creditor serves a demand and the company applies to restrain the presentation of a winding-up petition leading to the creditor agreeing not to present a petition because of the evidence put before it, the creditor will not be entitled to its costs: *Re Cannon Screen Entertainment Ltd* [1989] BCLC 660.

**Service**—The creditor has the obligation to do all that he or she can reasonably do to bring the demand to the notice of the company. Unlike bankruptcy, where the creditor is required, if practicable, to serve the demand personally (r 10.2; para 11.2 of the *Practice Direction – Insolvency Proceedings* (July 2020) [2020] BPIR 1211), there is no indication in the 1986 Act or 2016 Rules as to what constitutes effective service on companies.

While it has been said that service by post does not constitute leaving the demand at the company's registered office (something required by the provision) (*Re a Company* [1985] BCLC 37), judges are willing to accept service by post provided that it can be proved that the demand had arrived at the office. If that can be established, then the view is that the demand has been left at the office by the postal worker who delivered it: *Re a Company No 008790 of 1990* [1991] BCLC 561. So the consequence of this is that where a company denies receipt of a demand by post, a creditor is not going to be able to rely on the demand, even if proof of posting could be adduced.

It has been held that 'leaving it at the registered office' does not mean serving the company at its registered office by telex (*Re a Company* [1985] BCLC 37) and it is assumed that the same view would apply to attaching the demand to an email message; however, it is thought that if the company admitted receiving the telex or fax, then, on the basis of the approach in *Re a Company No 008790 of 1990*, the demand would be effective.

It was held in the Australian case of *R & R Consultants Pty Ltd v Commissioner of Taxation* [2006] NSWSC 1152, (2006) 204 FLR 149 that the service of a photocopy of a signed statutory demand that is in the prescribed form is valid, but it is highly debatable whether a court in England or Wales would take the same view.

For further discussion, see Keay 'The Service of Statutory Demands on Companies' [2003] *Insolvency Lawyer* 148.

**Neglected to pay**—This phrase does not mean fail to pay, but a failure to pay without a reasonable excuse: *Re London and Paris Banking Corp* (1875) 19 Eq 444; *Mann v Goldstein* [1968] 1 WLR 1091; *Re Lympne Investments Ltd* [1972] 1 WLR 523, [1972] 2 All ER 385; *Re a Company (No 033729 of 1982)* [1984] 1 WLR 1090, [1984] 3 All ER 78; *Re a Company (No 006273 of 1992)* [1993] BCLC 131. As a consequence, where a company refuses to pay on the basis that it believes that the debt claimed is not actually owing, ie there is a genuine dispute, then the company cannot be said to be presumed insolvent: *Re Lympne Investments Ltd* [1972] 1 WLR 523 at 527, [1972] 2 All ER 385 at 389. For a discussion as to a genuine dispute concerning a debt, see the notes accompanying s 125.

**Secure or compound to the reasonable satisfaction of the creditor**—A bankruptcy provision, s 383(2), states that the securing of a debt involves the giving of a mortgage, charge, lien or other security over the property of the debtor: see *Re a Debtor (No 310 of 1988)* [1989] 1 WLR 271, [1989] 2 All ER 42.

The court is to consider whether a reasonable hypothetical creditor in the position of the petitioner would accept or refuse the offer: *HMRC v Garwood* [2012] BPIR 575.

A compounding of the debt occurs when the creditor and the debtor company come to some arrangement which reasonably satisfies the creditor. In Singapore the Court of Appeal has held that for a debt to be compounded the original obligation must have been discharged by the agreement and the new arrangement overtakes the original one to the point where the creditor is unable to enforce the original debt: *Bombay Talkies (S) Pte Ltd v United Overseas Bank Ltd* [2015] SGCA 66. The test of whether an offer to compound is reasonable and should be accepted by a creditor is objective and depends on whether a reasonable hypothetical creditor in the position of the petitioning creditor, and in the light of the actual history of the dealings between the creditor and the debtor, could have reached the conclusion that the petitioning creditor reached: *Re a Debtor (No 32 of 1993)* [1995] 1 All ER 628; *HM Customs and Excise v Dougall* [2001] BPIR 269; *Revenue and Customs Commissioners v Smart* [2016] BPIR 1329, [2016] All ER (D) 158 (Jun). The history of dealings between the parties may be taken into account (*HMRC v Garwood* [2012] BPIR 575) and a creditor would usually be entitled to reject an offer from a debtor if the debtor had previously defaulted on a similar repayment agreement: *Barclays Bank Plc v Atay* [2015] EWHC 3198 (Ch). There may be a range of reasonable positions that the hypothetical reasonable creditor could take and a rejection of an offer by the petitioner is only to be regarded as unreasonable if the refusal is beyond the range of reasonable responses to it: *HM Customs and Excise v Dougall* [2001] BPIR 269 at 272. The court has to look at the position as at the date of the hearing: *HMRC v Garwood* [2012] BPIR 575. The court went on to say that it is necessary to consider the extent to which the reasonably hypothetical creditor may be taken to have the characteristics of the petitioner and the court must not be limited to considering the matters taken into account by the petitioner when the offer to secure was made; all relevant factors and their impact on the reasonable hypothetical creditors must be taken into account. The debtor must be full, frank and open with the creditor and provide all the information that a creditor needs in order to make an informed decision: *HM Customs and Excise v Dougall*; *Barclays Bank Plc v Atay* [2015] EWHC 3198 (Ch). Where a creditor has a very rigid policy of rejecting offers that could tell against it, but coherent in-house policies adopted by a creditor were not necessarily wrong. A creditor is not obliged to be patient or generous and could be concerned about its own interests. In this regard the costs implications for a creditor were a highly material consideration: *HMRC v Garwood* [2012] BPIR 575 and if the claim which is the subject of the petition has a long history, that might be something that is to be considered by a court: *Westaway v Durkan* [2016] EWHC 3101 (Ch). If a reasonable offer to compound is accepted, the creditor cannot renege on the arrangement: *Kema Plastics Pty Ltd v Mulford Plastics Pty Ltd* [1981] ACLC 33, 225.

In *Re a Debtor (No 32 of 1993)* [1995] 1 All ER 628 an offer by a debtor of £15,000 in full settlement of a debt over £33,000 was held to be an offer to compound for a debt.

**Unsatisfied execution**—It is not possible to petition for winding up on the basis of unsatisfied execution if the sheriff is unable to gain access to the company's premises, as that would merely be a failure to levy execution and not a case of execution not being satisfied: *Re A Debtor (No 340 of 1992)*; *The Debtor v First National Commercial Bank plc* [1994] 3 All ER 269, [1994] 2 BCLC 171 (affirmed on appeal in [1996] 2 All ER 211). If a petitioner did seek to do so then this would be a serious defect within the meaning of IR 1986, r 7.55 (replaced by IR 2016, r 12.64): *Re A Debtor (No 340 of 1992)*. Petitioning creditors have to satisfy the words of s 123(1)(b) strictly (*Re A Debtor (No 340 of 1992)*) and the court is not able to waive parts of the paragraph: *Re A Debtor (No 340 of 1992)*.

Courts may go behind any return in order to determine whether the execution was in fact unsatisfied. Also, they may even investigate the judgment on which proceedings were based: *Re Railway Finance Co* (1866) 14 WR 956; *Eberhardt v Mair* [1995] 1 WLR 1180. See the notes under the heading 'Judgment obtained in relation to petition debt' found under s 125.

See the comments accompanying s 268.

**Unable to pay debts as they fall due**—This provides for a cash flow test of insolvency, and tends to be the ground relied on most frequently now by petitioning creditors in practice. Companies that are covered by this phrase are those that are unable to meet current demands (*Re Capital Annuities Ltd* [1979] 1 WLR 170), irrespective of whether the company is possessed of assets which, if realised, would enable it to discharge its liabilities in full. It has been held that where a debt is due, an invoice has been sent and the debt is not disputed, if the company fails to pay then that is evidence of inability to pay: *Taylor's Industrial Flooring Ltd v M & H Plant Hire (Manchester) Ltd* [1990] BCLC 216, CA. But it has been said that if the creditor has not made a demand for payment prior to petitioning, courts should be less ready to infer inability of a company to pay its debts: *Mac Plant Services Ltd v Contract Lifting Services (Scotland) Ltd* [2008] CSOH 158, 2009 SC 125 at [68].

Debts in this context are usually regarded as liquidated claims, namely claims for amounts that are able to be ascertained or readily ascertained: *Stooke v Taylor* (1880) 5 QBD 565 at 575. An important issue is whether future debts are to be taken into account in determining ability to pay, or are we limited to a consideration of debts presently due? Whilst old authority has held that contingent and prospective debts cannot be taken into consideration: *Re London & Manchester Industrial Association* (1875) 1 ChD 466 at 472, they dealt with differently worded legislation, and the answer to the question now appears to be 'yes,' according to Briggs J in *Re Cheyne Finance plc* [2007] EWHC 2402 (Ch), [2008] 1 BCLC 741, because the words 'as they fall due' invite considerations of futurity (the words were regarded as synonymous with 'become due' which in Australia has led courts to look to future debts in assessing ability to pay within the equivalent of s 123(1)(e) (at [53])). His Lordship said that the fact that s 123(2) required one to consider contingent and prospective liabilities in determining solvency under that provision, did not mean that prospective liabilities could not be taken into account under s 123(1)(e). *Re Cheyne Finance* does not resolve the issue of how far in the future must the debt be due. Briggs J specifically indicated that a debt coming due in 6 months would be able to be taken into account. In *New Cap Reinsurance Corporation Ltd (in liq) v A E Grant* [2008] NSWSC 1015 at [44] the court said that one looks to the reasonably immediate future, which is what Briggs J probably did. Briggs J approved of the view of the New South Wales Court of Appeal in *Lewis v Doran* [2005] NSWCA 243, (2005) 219 ALR 555 at [103] that how far one goes into the future depends on the kind of business conducted by the company and, if known, the company's future liabilities. As pointed out by Lewison LJ in his leading judgment in *Evans v Davies* [2016] EWCA Civ 660, [2016] 3 WLR 1480 at [24], Briggs J was indicating that even though a company may continue to pay its debts it may yet be 'on any commercial view insolvent'.

The approach adopted in *Re Cheyne Finance* permits flexibility but does introduce a fair amount of uncertainty. In *BNY Corporate Trustee Services Limited v Eurosail-UK 2007-3BL Plc* [2013] UKSC 28, [2013] 1 WLR 1408, [2013] 1 BCLC 613 at [37] the Supreme Court confirmed the approach taken by Briggs J in *Cheyne* accepting the fact that the cash flow test is concerned both with due debts and with debts falling due from time to time in the 'reasonably near' future (which will depend on all the circumstances, but especially on the nature of the company's business). The court said that beyond the reasonably near future any attempt to apply a cash flow test is completely speculative, and a comparison of present assets with present and future liabilities (discounted for contingencies and deferment) is the only sensible way to proceed, even though it is far from an exact science. In *Re Casa Estates (UK) Ltd* [2013] EWHC 2371 (Ch) at [34] Warren J said that balance sheet insolvency is not irrelevant to a company's ability to pay debts as they fall due. His Lordship did not think that the judgments in *BNY Corporate Trustee Services Limited v Eurosail-UK 2007-3BL PLC* suggested a rigid demarcation between cash flow and balance sheet insolvency. His Lordship had earlier said that anticipated income and outgoings over the reasonably near future cannot be taken into account (at [29]), but that might not rule out what was said in the much-cited Australian case of *Sandell Porter* (1966) 115 CLR 666, (1966) 40 ALJR 71 that a company can rely upon money which might be obtained from the sale of assets or upon loan money where the loan was granted because security could be taken against the company's assets. The Court of Appeal in the appeal from the decision of Warren J, *Bucci v Carman* [2014] EWCA Civ 383, [2014] 2 BCLC 49, [2014] BPIR 523 agreed that the two tests, cash flow and balance sheet stand side by side and are relevant to one another (at [27]). Warren J said: 'Consider a company which is balance sheet insolvent on the basis of its current debts that is to say debts which have fallen due for payment or will in the reasonably near future fall due for payment. Those are precisely the debts which need to be taken into account in making an assessment under the cash flow test in accordance with section 123(1)(e). It is difficult to see how the company could then be said, with nothing more, to be cash flow solvent. However, immediate cash flow problems might be subject to amelioration; for instance, immediate debts could be covered by a short term loan or by an overdraft facility, although that assumes the creation of new liabilities on the part of the Company which will either be themselves liabilities which will fall due for payment within the reasonably near future, in which case the cash flow problem still arises, or one posits a series of loans running past the reasonably near future, in which case the commercial reality is no different from that of a prospective liability to which it would be appropriate to apply section 123(2), with liabilities exceeding assets. The same would apply if a particular creditor (eg a shareholder or director) agreed to postpone the calling-in of his debt. In contrast, if immediate liabilities were to be financed by further long-term funding, then that funding would give rise to a prospective or contingent liability which would not fall to be taken account of when applying the section 123(1)(e) test; but that is just the sort of case where the test in s 123(2) would apply with the result in this example, that liabilities exceed assets.' (*Re Casa Estates (UK) Ltd* [2013] EWHC 2371 (Ch) at [35]).

The Supreme Court in *BNY Corporate Trustee Services Ltd v Eurosail–UK 2007-3BL plc* said in obiter that s 123(1)(e) 'does not treat proof of a single specific default by a company as conclusive of the general issue of its inability to pay its debts.' The court said that the scope of s 123(1)(e) is wider than a single debt (at [25]). Thus this might call into question the decision of *Taylor's Industrial Flooring Ltd v M & H Plant Hire (Manchester) Ltd* [1990] BCLC 216, CA.

An issue that does not appear to have been decided in England is whether a claim for unliquidated damages is to be taken into account in deciding the quantum of the debts of the company. This is probably because the answer is relatively straightforward. At the time one is determining whether the company is unable to pay, for the purposes of s 123, the claim has yet to be decided on and, therefore, the amount of the claim could not be taken into account. This is despite the fact that r 14.1(3) provides that 'debt' means, inter alia, 'any debt or liability to which the company may become subject after that date by reason of any obligation incurred before that date.' This latter provision is referring to someone proving in a winding up and cannot be applied to a decision concerning the solvency of a company under s 123. The New South Wales Court of Appeal in *Box Valley Pty Ltd v Kidd* [2006] NSWCA 26, (2006) 24 ACLC 471, stated that even if it was highly probable that a claim would lead to a liability to pay damages it could not be considered as a debt in determining inability to pay. The type of claim envisaged in this paragraph cannot, of course, be classified as a prospective debt as there is no certainty that it will be due in the future.

There has been significant uncertainty as to whether the fact that a creditor grants the debtor company some forbearance in requiring payment of a debt (such as an extension of time to pay) that is due can be regarded as meaning that that debt has not fallen due for the purposes of determining the debtor's solvency. In Australia there is a divergence of opinion, with cases such as *Carrier Air Conditioning Pty Ltd v Kurda* (1993) 11 ACSR 247 taking the view that forbearance should not be taken into account in determining whether a debt has fallen due, while other cases, such as *Re Newark Pty Ltd* [1993] 1 Qd R 409, (1991) 6 ACSR 255 and, more recently, *Tru Floor Service Pty Ltd v Jenkins (No 2)* [2006] FCA 632 have adopted a more liberal line and held that forbearance might be considered. An obiter comment of Warren J in *Re Casa Estates (UK) Ltd* [2013] EWHC 2371 (Ch) at [75] suggests that his Lordship would agree with the approach taken in *Carrier Air Conditioning Pty Ltd v Kurda*.

In determining whether a company is able to pay its debts, the courts must take into account what current revenue the company has as well as what the company can procure by realising assets within a relatively short time: *Re Capital Annuities Ltd* [1979] 1 WLR 170 at 182, 188. As mentioned above, it has been said that a company is not limited to its own cash on hand in determining whether it has the ability to pay its debts. A company can rely upon money which might be obtained from the sale of assets or upon loan money where the loan was granted because security could be taken against the company's assets: *Sandell v Porter* (1966) 115 CLR 666, (1966) 40 ALJR 71; *Lewis v Doran* [2005] NSWCA 243, (2005) 219 ALR 555. Where the sale of a major asset is near enough to certain, the funds that will be realised may be taken into account: *Cuthbertson & Richards Sawmills Pty Ltd v Thomas* (1998) 28 ACSR 310 at 319. But a hope or expectation that the company will obtain future assets would not be able to be taken into account unless there was a right to hold that hope or expectation: *Byblos Bank SAL v Al Khudhairy* [1987] BCLC 232; *BNY Corporate Trustee Services Ltd v Eurosail–UK 2007–3BL plc* [2010] EWHC 2005 (Ch) at [35]. It has been held in Australia that property could not be taken into account when it would take 6 months to realise it and debts were falling due within a month: *Hall v Poolman* [2007] NSWSC 1330, (2007) 215 FLR 243, [2008] BPIR 892 at [187].

Other Australian authority has held that a debtor could not rely on realising assets which would involve a cessation or breaking up of its business: *Re Timbatec Pty Ltd* (1974) 24 FLR 30 at 36–37. While still other Australian authority has stated that a court might take into account the fact that the company is able to obtain funds under an unsecured loan provided that the court was convinced that the third party lender was clearly willing to extend funds to the company: *Lewis v Doran* [2004] NSWSC 608, (2005) 50 ACSR 175 at [113] (NSW S Ct) and accepted on appeal in *Lewis v Doran* [2005] NSWCA 243, (2005) 219 ALR 555. In *Leveraged Equities Ltd v Hilldale Australia Pty Ltd* [2008] NSWSC 190 it was said that the promised provision of a loan which would enable the company to pay its debts could be taken into account in determining whether the company was insolvent or not. There are indications that the judgment of Warren J in *Re Casa Estates (UK) Ltd* [2013] EWHC 2371 (Ch) at [35] supports that approach, with qualifications. Yet the English Court of Appeal in *Bucci v Carman* [2014] EWCA Civ 383, [2014] 2 BCLC 49, [2014] BPIR 523 indicated that the obtaining of loans is not likely to be seen as supporting solvency if the result of the lending means that the company goes further and further into long-term debt (at [31]). In *Burnden Holdings (UK) Ltd v Fielding* ([2019] EWHC 1566 (Ch)) at [289] Zacaroli J said that a company would clearly not be avoiding balance sheet insolvency if it borrowed funds but doing that might enable it to avoid cash flow insolvency. Something similar was said in the Scottish case of *Milne v Rashid* ([2018] CSOH 23, [2018] 2 BCLC 673 at [49]). It has been said that when assessing whether a company is able to pay its debts as and when they are owed, the company's position must be considered by reference to the company's legal rights and obligations as well as the relative likelihood that it will have funds available to it: *Chan v First Strategic Development Corporation Ltd* [2015] QCA 28. Australian authority suggests that a court can take into account funds from sources with whom there is no formalised agreement and in principle there is no objection to a court considering loans from parties related to the company or its directors: *First Strategic Development Corporation Ltd v Chan* [2014] QSC 60 (affirmed on appeal at [2015] QCA 28), *International Cat Manufacturing (in liq) v Rodrick* [2013] QCA 372, but there must be cogent evidence which enables a court to conclude that there is a degree of commitment from the provider of support to continue it, such that it can be said that any point of time it was likely to be continued so that the company would be able to pay its debts as they fell due: *Chan v First Strategic Development Corporation Ltd* [2015] QCA 28.

In a situation where one company in a corporate group had recourse to the assets of another company in the group and such a recourse did not cause the second company to become insolvent or involves merely delaying the inevitable insolvency of the first, this would be taken into account in determining whether the first company was able to pay its debts as they fall due: *Hall v Poolman* [2007] NSWSC 1330, (2007) 215 FLR 243, [2008] BPIR 892, NSW S Ct.

Generally, determining whether a company is cash flow insolvent is a question of fact, that may be established by a receiver for debenture-holders taking possession of all of the company's assets: *Re Lyric Club* (1892) 36 Sol Jo 801. Indicators of cash flow insolvency are that: the company has a large number of outstanding debts and unsatisfied judgments (*Re Tweeds Garages Ltd* [1962] Ch 406); the company or its solicitors have admitted that the company is unable to pay (*Re Great Northern Copper Co* (1869) 20 LT 264); or the absence of assets on which execution can be levied: *Re Flagstaff Silver Mining Co of Utah* (1875) 20 Eq 268; *Re Yate Collieries Co* [1883] WN 171; *Re Douglas Griggs Engineering Ltd* [1963] Ch 19. An Australian decision has indicated that the question of inability to pay debts is a question of commercial reality having regard to the facts of the particular case: *Lewis v Doran* (2004) NSWSC 608, (2005) 50 ACSR 175. In the Australian case of *Austin Australia Pty Ltd v De Martin & Gasparini Pty Ltd* [2007] NSWSC 1238 it was said that the following might be taken into account in order to determine whether a company is unable to pay its debts: a history of dishonoured cheques; suppliers insisting on cash on delivery; the issuing of post-dated cheques; the issuing of rounded cheques (suggesting part payment of debts); special arrangements with creditors; inability to produce timely audited accounts; non-payment of workers' compensation premiums, VAT, pension payments and group tax; demands from bankers to reduce amount owing on overdraft; receipt of letters of demand and court processes.

For further discussion, see RM Goode *Principles of Corporate Insolvency Law* (Sweet and Maxwell, 4th edn, 2011) at 121–129; K Baird and P Sidle 'Cash Flow Insolvency' (2008) 21 *Insolvency Intelligence* 40.

**Value of assets less than liabilities**—Section 123(2) provides for a balance sheet test of insolvency.

This test is not excluded from consideration merely because the company is able to pay its debts as they fall due: *Bucci v Carman* [2014] EWCA Civ 383, [2014] 2 BCLC 49, [2014] BPIR 523 at [29]).

In determining insolvency on this basis a court is able to take into account contingent and prospective liabilities, but not contingent and prospective assets: *Byblos Bank SAL v Al-Khudhairy* (1986) 2 BCC 99,549, CA; *BNY Corporate Trustee Services Ltd v Eurosail-UK 2007-3BL plc* [2010] EWHC 2005 (Ch) at [35] (affirmed on appeal – [2011] EWCA Civ 227, and [2013] UKSC 28, [2013] 1 WLR 1408; *Evans v Jones* [2016] EWCA Civ 660 at [20]). 'Liabilities' is a broader term than 'debts' (*Re A Debtor (No 17 of 1966)* [1967] Ch 590, [1967] 1 All ER 668) and is defined for the purposes of winding up in r 14.1(6). Rule 14.1(5) states that it is immaterial whether the liability is present or future, whether it is certain or contingent, or whether its amount is fixed or liquidated, or is capable of being ascertained by fixed rules or as a matter of opinion. See the comments relating to 'Contingent or prospective creditors' in relation to s 124.

The starting point in relation to a company is that if its immediate liabilities are in excess of the assets the company is insolvent: *Re Casa Estates (UK) Ltd* [2013] EWHC 2371 (Ch) at [81] (the evidential burden would fall on the company to demonstrate why it can, notwithstanding its balance sheet, reasonably be expected to meet its liabilities). But, while this test seems to be quite simple to apply, it has been made clear in the *BNY Corporate Trustee Services Ltd v Eurosail–UK 2007–3BL plc* litigation [2010] EWHC 2005 (Ch) by Sir Andrew Morritt C and by the Court of Appeal on appeal (affirming the judgment at first instance ([2011] EWCA Civ 227) and the Supreme Court on appeal from the Court of Appeal ([2013] UKSC 28)) that this is not always the case. In the Supreme Court it was indicated that employing the balance sheet test did not simply involve computing the asset value and that of the liabilities and comparing them, without allowing some discount to take account of deferment and contingencies. The Court of Appeal said that it would be impractical as well as undesirable for a company to be deemed balance sheet insolvent every time its liabilities exceeded its assets. The provision does not call for an annual balance sheet in order to provide a snapshot of the affairs of the company at any specific time (as is the usual reason for accounting reasons). So, a company's audited accounts that show a net liability will not be conclusive evidence of insolvency for s 123(2) purposes. The court must look at the company's finances from a commercial and overall perspective and consider the facts of each case; the fact that there are temporary imbalances will not mean that insolvency is to be concluded. The courts will look at whether it is clear in practical terms that because of incurable deficiencies in assets it will not be able to meet future or prospective liabilities (*BNY Corporate Trustee Services Ltd v Eurosail–UK 2007–3BL plc* [2011] EWCA Civ 227 at [48]). The Supreme Court did not appear to demur to these views and in fact expressly endorsed aspects of it (at [38]). It did reject

Lord Neuberger's 'end of the road' test, namely a company is to be seen as insolvent if it has reached the end of the road and put up the shutters. The Supreme Court did say that whether or not the balance sheet test was satisfied relied on the evidence of the company's circumstances in any given case (at [38]). The court accepted the fact that the more distant a liability is the more difficult it is to establish it (at [42]). The court also said that for the purposes of the 'balance-sheet' test the ability of a company to meet liabilities, both prospective and contingent, is to be determined on the balance of probabilities with the burden of proof on the party asserting balance-sheet insolvency (at [48]).

What 'taking account' means must be considered in the context of the overall question of whether the company is to be deemed to be insolvent because the amount of its liabilities exceeds the value of its assets. 'This will involve consideration of the relevant facts of the case, including when the prospective liability falls due, whether it is payable in sterling or some other currency, what assets will be available to meet it and what if any provision is made for the allocation of losses in relation to those assets': *BNY Corporate Trustee Services Ltd v Eurosail–UK 2007–3BL plc* [2010] EWHC 2005 (Ch) at [35] per Sir Andrew Morritt C. The Court of Appeal affirmed the judgment of Morritt C and these decisions appear to provide courts with greater discretion than was once thought when dealing with this test. While the Supreme Court disapproved of some of the things that the Court of Appeal said this seems correct.

A court may only take into account the assets of the company held at that time; so assets which are expected to be received in the future by the company or funds that it has on loan are both excluded from being taken into account: *Byblos Bank SAL v Al-Khudairy* (1986) 2 BCC 99, 549 at 99, 562 and 99, 563.

But while a court will not permit a mere hope of restructuring for the company to act as a rebuttal to the presumption of insolvency, it would seem that if credible evidence can be adduced that a restructuring plan is able to be set in train and it has support then the court might hold that the company is not insolvent: *Myers v Kestrel Acquisitions Ltd* [2015] EWHC 916 (Ch), [85], [91], [92].

For further discussion, see RM Goode *Principles of Corporate Insolvency Law* (Sweet and Maxwell, 4th edn, 2011) at 129–147; P Walton '"Inability to pay debts": Beyond the Point of No Return' [2013] JBL 160; P Walton '*BNY Corporate Trustee Services Ltd v Eurosail–UK 2007–3BL plc* – from the point of no return to crystal ball gazing' (2013) 26 Insol Intel 124; A Keay *McPherson and Keay's Law of Company Liquidation* (4th edn, Sweet and Maxwell, 2018) at 93–116.

See the notes accompanying s 271.

## [1.176]

### 124 Application for winding up

(1)   Subject to the provisions of this section, an application to the court for the winding up of a company shall be by petition presented either by the company, or the directors, or by any creditor or creditors (including any contingent or prospective creditor or creditors), contributory or contributories, . . . appointed in proceedings by virtue of Article 3(1) of the EU Regulation or a temporary administrator (within the meaning of Article 52 of the EU Regulation) or by the designated officer for a magistrates' court in the exercise of the power conferred by section 87A of the Magistrates' Courts Act 1980 (enforcement of fines imposed on companies), or by all or any of those parties, together or separately.

(2)   Except as mentioned below, a contributory is not entitled to present a winding-up petition unless either—

(a)   the number of members is reduced below 2, or

(b)   the shares in respect of which he is a contributory, or some of them, either were originally allotted to him, or have been held by him, and registered in his name, for at least 6 months during the 18 months before the commencement of the winding up, or have devolved on him through the death of a former holder.

(3)   A person who is liable under section 76 to contribute to a company's assets in the event of its being wound up may petition on either of the grounds set out in section 122(1)(f) and (g), and subsection (2) above does not then apply; but unless the person is a contributory otherwise than under section 76, he may not in his character as contributory petition on any other ground.

. . .

(3A)   . . .

(4) A winding-up petition may be presented by the Secretary of State—

    (a)    if the ground of the petition is that in section 122(1)(b) or (c), or

    (b)    in a case falling within section 124A or 124B below.

(4AA) A winding up petition may be presented by the Financial Conduct Authority in a case falling within section 124C(1) or (2).

(4A) A winding-up petition may be presented by the Regulator of Community Interest Companies in a case falling within section 50 of the Companies (Audit, Investigations and Community Enterprise) Act 2004.

(5) Where a company is being wound up voluntarily in England and Wales, a winding-up petition may be presented by the official receiver attached to the court as well as by any other person authorised in that behalf under the other provisions of this section; but the court shall not make a winding-up order on the petition unless it is satisfied that the voluntary winding up cannot be continued with due regard to the interests of the creditors or contributories.

**Amendments**—Criminal Justice Act 1988, s 62(2)(b); Companies Act 1989, s 60(2); Access to Justice Act 1999, s 90, Sch 13, para 133; Insolvency Act 2000, s 1, Sch 1, paras 1, 7; SI 2002/1240; Courts Act 2003, s 109(1), Sch 8, para 294; SI 2004/2326; Companies (Audit, Investigations and Community Enterprise) Act 2004, s 50(3); SI 2006/2078; SI 2009/1941; SI 2013/496; SI 2017/702; SI 2019/146, as from IP completion day (as defined in the European Union (Withdrawal Agreement) Act 2020, s 39(1)–(5)); Corporate Insolvency and Governance Act 2020, s 2(1), Sch 3, paras 1, 11.

**CIGA 2020**—This provision is affected by temporary measures at Sch 10, paras 1(1), 1(2), 2(1), 2(3), 3(1), 3(3), 4(1), 5(1)(a), 6(1)(a) and 8(1)(a) of CIGA 2020.

**General note**—This provision sets out who is entitled to present a petition for winding up. But it must be noted that there are pieces of legislation that give other parties the right to present petitions. These are, for example, Charities Act 2006, s 113 (Attorney-General); Building Societies Act 1986, s 37(1)(a) (Prudential Regulation Authority) Financial Services and Markets Act 2000, s 367 (Financial Conduct Authority); Credit Unions Act 1979, s 20(2) (Financial Conduct Authority); Agricultural Marketing Act 1958, s 2 (Minister for Agriculture); Companies (Audit, Investigations and Community Enterprise) Act 2004, s 50 (Regulator of Community Interest Companies). The National Crime Agency may have the right to petition for a winding-up order pursuant to s 317 of the Proceeds of Crime Act 2002: *National Crime Agency v GTG Management Ltd* [2020] EWHC 963 (Ch).

As a temporary restriction, and as part of the Government's response to the COVID-19 (coronavirus) pandemic in 2020–2021, if a creditor presents a petition for winding up under s 124 between 27 April 2020 and 30 September 2021 and the company is deemed unable to pay its debts on a ground specified in s 123(1) or (2), certain conditions must be fulfilled before a petition succeeds. The court may wind the company up under s 122(1)(f) on a ground specified in s 123(1)(a) to (d) only if the court is satisfied that the creditor has reasonable grounds for believing that coronavirus has not had a financial effect on the company and the facts by reference to which that ground applies would have arisen even if coronavirus had not had a financial effect on the company. The court may wind the company up under s 122(1)(f) on the ground specified in s 123(1)(e) or (2) if the court is satisfied that the creditor has reasonable grounds for believing that coronavirus has not had a financial effect on the company and the ground would apply even if coronavirus had not had a financial effect on the company: para 5 of Sch 10 of the Corporate Insolvency and Governance Act 2020 (as amended by The Corporate Insolvency and Governance Act 2020 (Coronavirus) (Extension of the Relevant Period) Regulations 2020 (SI 2020/1031), regs 1, 2(3), The Corporate Insolvency and Governance Act 2020 (Coronavirus) (Extension of the Relevant Period) (No 2) Regulations 2020 (SI 2020/1483), reg 2, The Corporate Insolvency and Governance Act 2020 (Coronavirus) (Extension of the Relevant Period) Regulations 2021 (SI 2021/375), reg 3(4) and The Corporate Insolvency and Governance Act 2020 (Coronavirus) (Extension of the Relevant Period) (No 2) Regulations 2021 (SI 2021/718), reg 2) . The burden of establishing that the virus had a financial effect is on the company, but it merely requires the company to make out a prima facie case, and it is, therefore, not a heavy burden: *Re A Company* [2020] EWHC 1551 (Ch), [2020] 2 BCLC 307, [2020] BPIR 1100.

In very exceptional circumstances a court may order winding up on its own motion provided that one of the circumstances in s 122 existed: *Lancefield v Lancefield* [2002] BPIR 1108 (a case actually dealing with an insolvent partnership); *Re Marches Credit Union Ltd* [2013] EWHC 1731 (Ch) (this involved an entity that was an Industrial and Provident Society and winding up was ordered on a public interest basis); *Re Graico Property Co Ltd* (in admin) [2016] EWHC 2827 (Ch) (a case involving a company that was in administration and the petition was made by the administrators; *Rendle v Panelform Ltd* [2020] EWHC 2810 (a trustee in bankruptcy sought the compulsory winding-up of a company associated with the bankrupt but failed as he was seeking to bypass the statutorily prescribed mechanism for obtaining a winding-up order). The court will use the power cautiously (*Lancefield v Lancefield* [2002] BPIR 1108; *Rendle v Panelform Ltd* [2020] EWHC 2810). A court must be convinced that one of the grounds for winding up has been fulfilled before considering whether to make a winding-up order on its own (*Lancefield v Lancefield*; *Re BTR (UK) Ltd* [2012] EWHC 2398 (Ch), [2012] BCC 864, *Re Graico Property Ltd*). Furthermore, the court will only act if the company was already before the court, where there is no petition (*Lancefield v Lancefield, Rendle v Panelform Ltd*). Winding up will not be ordered where the applicant is endeavouring to circumvent the statutory mechanism for winding up, unless the applicant for winding up is incidental to, or arising as a means of, resolving difficulties shown by other issues already before the court (*Rendle v Panelform Ltd* at [17]).

**The petition**—The petition is not to contain matters of evidence: *Re Rica Gold Washing Co* (1879) 11 ChD 36 at 43. It does not have to be signed by the petitioner: *Re Testro Bros Consolidated Ltd* [1965] VR 18. A petitioner can only rely, at the hearing, on the grounds set out in the petition (*Re Fildes Bros Ltd* [1970] 1 WLR 592; *Re Armvent Ltd* [1975] 1 WLR 1679), and if a petition fails to provide a ground for winding up, or states one that is not covered by the Act, then, unless the court allows amendment of the petition, it will be dismissed: *Re Wear Engine Works Co* (1875) 10 Ch App 188. Leave can be granted to amend a petition to enable reliance to be placed on a post-petition debt, and this is despite the fact that otherwise the petition would have been liable to be struck out: *Re Richbell Strategic Holdings Ltd* [1997] 2 BCLC 429.

As a petition is not an action on a judgment for the purposes of s 24 of the Limitation Act 1980, a petitioner is not required to present a petition within 6 years of the judgment on which the petition relies: *Ridgeway Motors (Isleworth) Ltd v Altis Ltd* [2004] EWHC 1535 (Ch), [2004] BPIR 1323 (disagreeing with *Re A Debtor* (No 50A-SD-1995) [1997] Ch 310, [1997] 2 WLR 57, [1997] 1 BCLC 280, [1996] BPIR 565 which involved a bankruptcy petition).

A petition is not to be classified as a claim or counterclaim in law, although it is a species of legal proceedings: *Best Beat Ltd v Rossall* [2006] EWHC 1494 (Comm), [2006] BPIR 1357. See rr 7.7–7.12 of and Sch 4, paras 2 and 6 to the IR 2016, and the comments accompanying those rules.

The *Practice Direction – Insolvency Proceedings* (July 2020) [2020] BPIR 1211 makes the point that before presenting a winding up petition, the creditor must conduct a search to ensure that no petition is pending. Save in exceptional circumstances a second winding up petition should not be presented whilst a prior petition is pending. A petitioner who presents a petition while another petition is pending does so at risk as to costs (para 9.2).

For a case where there were multiple petitions, see *Islandsbanki HF v Kevin Gerald Stanford* [2019] EWHC 307 (Ch). In this case and on the facts it was held that the first in time warranted being decided.

**Company**—Applications by companies to have themselves wound up by the court are rather rare (eg *Re Winis Trading Pty Ltd* (1984) 3 ACLC 39), probably because where it is thought proper for the company to wind up, a resolution to wind up will be obtained, and voluntary liquidation will ensue. However, this requires an extraordinary or special resolution, and for some reason or other this might not be possible, as a three-fourths majority of shareholders able to vote and voting must support a resolution. It might be possible, however, to secure an ordinary resolution, sufficient for the company to apply for a winding-up order.

If the directors were to present a petition in the name of the company, but without securing the necessary vote in support, the court might adjourn the petition and permit the company meeting to ratify what the directors had done: *Re Galway and Salthill Tramways Co* [1918] IR 62.

Where a company presents a petition, it may rely on any ground contained in s 122(1): *Re Langham Skating Rink Co* (1877) 5 ChD 669; *Smith v Duke of Manchester* (1883) 24 ChD 611; *Re Emmadart Ltd* [1979] Ch 540, [1979] 1 All ER 599.

**Directors**—The reference to 'directors' means all of the directors and not one or a majority of them can petition; consequently, absent a proper board resolution, all of the directors must agree to the presentation of the petition: *Re Instrumentation Electrical Services Ltd* [1988] BCLC 550. All directors are bound by a proper resolution for the winding up of the company passed by the board, and one director may present a petition on behalf of all: *Re Equiticorp International plc* [1989] 1 WLR 1010. For an example, see *Re Minrealm Ltd* [2007] EWHC 3078 (Ch) (petition brought by directors – majority supported it and passed a board resolution to wind up).

If a sole director were to petition, such action could be regarded as an abuse of process and liability for costs may be imposed on him or her: *Re a Company (No 003689 of 1998)* (1998) *The Times*, October 7.

**Creditor**—The petitioner must be a person to whom the company owes a debt, which has not been paid at the date of the presentation of the petition (*Re William Hockley Ltd* [1962] 1 WLR 555), and so there must be a debtor-creditor relationship.

A person who is owed an obligation to pay damages or like compensation for breach of some legal duty is not, without more, a 'creditor,' because such a person is not owed a 'debt': *Wolf Rock (Cornwall) Ltd v Langhelle* [2020] EWHC 2500 (Ch).

Where a court had delivered a judgment in favour of the petitioner then the petitioner is a creditor for the purposes of winding up even if the judgment is subject to an appeal: *El Ajou v Dollar Land (Manhattan) Ltd* [2005] EWHC 2861 (Ch).

A debt may be defined as a sum payable by one person to another in respect of a liquidated sum in money. See r 14.1 and its definition of 'debt' for winding up purposes, as well as the notes accompanying that rule. While r 14.1(6) provides that liability means liability to pay money or money's worth, including any liability under an enactment, any liability for breach of trust, any liability in contract, tort or bailment, and any liability arising out of any obligation to make restitution, a person with an unliquidated claim in tort or contract is not able to present a petition: *Re Pen-y-van Colliery Co* (1877) ChD 477; *Re Milford Docks Co* (1883) 23 ChD 292.

There is Australian authority to the effect that a creditor, to whom the company is jointly and severally liable with another person, can apply for a winding-up order: *Re Buildmat (Aust) Pty Ltd* (1981) 5 ACLR 459. A creditor by subrogation is entitled to petition: *Re National Permanent Building Society* (1869) 5 Ch App 309. Any debt owed must be a valid debt and a person who claims a debt resulting from an illegal transaction is not able to petition: *Re South Wales Atlantic Steamship Co* (1875) 2 ChD 763. The executor of a creditor of the company is able to petition as a creditor provided that probate was granted prior to when the petition is heard: *Re Masonic and General Life Assurance Co* (1885) 32 ChD 373. A person who has obtained an order for costs against a company can petition for a winding-up order on the basis of being a creditor.

While an equitable assignee of a debt is not able to serve a demand under s 123(1)(a), he or she is entitled to petition for winding up on the basis of the debt: *Re Steel Wing Co* [1921] 1 Ch 349 at 356.

If a creditor's claim, at the time of presentation of a petition, is statute-barred, he or she is not able to be classified as a 'creditor' for winding up purposes: *Re Karnose Property Trust Ltd* [1989] BCLC 340; *Re Joshua Shaw & Sons Ltd* [1989] BCLC 362. But if a creditor's claim became statute-barred after the presentation of the petition and before the hearing of the petition, the creditor still has standing to obtain a winding up order: *Motor Terms Co Pty Ltd v Liberty Insurance Ltd* (1967) 116 CLR 177.

Where a petitioner has standing as a creditor at the time of the presentation of the petition, but is not a creditor at the time of the hearing of the petition, the court has a discretion whether or not to make a winding-up order: *Australian Beverage Distributors Pty Ltd v The Redrock Co Pty Ltd* [2007] NSWSC 966, [2007] 213 FLR 450 at [33], [34].

Australian authority would seem to permit a director to petition for the winding up of his or her company, based on the fact that he or she is a creditor, without it constituting a breach of duty on the director's part and an abuse of process: *Re CSSC (Qld) Pty Ltd* [2018] QSC 282.

**Secured creditor**—It has been said that a secured creditor is a creditor, even following the appointment of a receiver (*Re Portsmouth Borough (Kingston Fratton and Southsea) Tramways Co* [1892] Ch 362), and so it is assumed that such a creditor, whether the debt is fully or partly secured, may petition: (*Masri Apartments Pty Ltd v Perpetual Nominees Ltd* (2004) 214 ALR 338, [2004] NSWCA 471). This seems to be supported by the fact that in *Re Lafayette Electronics Europe Ltd* [2006] EWHC 1006 (Ch) at [7], HHJ Norris QC indicated that he was not convinced that a secured creditor was unable to present a petition. Subsequently Mann J in *Re Sushinho Ltd* [2011] All ER (D) 32 (Mar) had unreservedly accepted that a secured creditor may petition. It has been held in Australia that it is not incumbent on the creditor to realise its security prior to, or instead of, petitioning: *Re Alexander's Securities (No 2)* [1983] 2 Qd R 597.

**Contingent or prospective creditors**—A contingent creditor is 'a person towards whom, under an existing obligation, the company may or will become subject to a present liability on the happening of some future event or at some future date': *Re William Hockley Ltd* [1962] 1 WLR 555 at 558, although Arden LJ (in obiter) felt that this would be a future or prospective liability: *R v Birmingham City Council* [2005] EWCA Civ 1824, [2006] 1 WLR 2380 at [24]. It must be noted that in this last case Arden LJ did say that what is a contingent liability will depend on the circumstances and context: *R v Bimingham City Council* [2005] EWCA Civ 1824, [2006] 1 WLR 2380 at [21].

It has been explained that a prospective creditor is one who is owed a debt which will certainly become due in the future, either on some determined date or some date which will be determined by reference to future events (*Stonegate Securities Ltd v Gregory* [1980] 1 Ch 576 at 579), and will include a claim that is unable to be disputed and involves unliquidated damages which remain to be quantified: *Re Dollar Land Holdings Ltd* [1994] BCLC 404.

While a contingent debt is a debt for the purposes of winding up, such a debt could not be used as the basis for a statutory demand and a subsequent petition, until the relevant contingency has happened: *JSF Finance and Current Exchange Co Ltd v Akma Solutions Inc* [2001] 2 BCLC 307, [2002] BPIR 621.

The judgment of Lord Neuberger in *Re Nortel GmbH* [2013] UKSC 52, [2013] 3 WLR 504, [2013] 2 BCLC 135, [2013] BPIR 866 appears to be of some assistance in understanding contingent liabilities. His Lordship was focusing on what is now r 14.1(3)(b) of the 2016 Rules and which was, at the time of the judgment, r 13.12(1)(b) of the 1986 Rules. He said that in determining whether it can be said that an obligation involved a liability which arose 'by reason of any obligation incurred before' the insolvency event, such as liquidation, ordinarily for a company to have incurred a liability it must have taken, or been subjected to, 'some step or combination of steps which (a) had some legal effect (such as putting it under some legal duty or into some legal relationship), and which (b) resulted in it being vulnerable to the specific liability in question, such that there would be a real prospect of that liability being incurred. If these two requirements are satisfied, it is also, I think, relevant to consider (c) whether it would be consistent with the regime under which the liability is imposed to conclude that the step or combination of steps gave rise to an obligation under rule 13.12(1)(b)' (at [77]).

Contributory—See the notes accompanying s 74 for a discussion of who is a contributory.

No provision in the memorandum or the articles can prohibit a contributory from presenting a petition, because the legislation specifically permits contributories to be able to do so: *Re Peveril Gold Mines Ltd* [1898] 1 Ch 122. Nor can the right of a contributory to petition be removed by contract: *A Best Floor Sanding Pty Ltd v Skyer Australia Pty Ltd* [1999] VSC 170, Vic S C (approved in *Exeter City AFC Ltd v Football Conference Ltd* [2004] EWHC 831 (Ch), [2004] 1 WLR 2910, [2004] 4 All ER 1179, [2005] 1 BCLC 238).

It was held in *Hamilton v Brown* [2016] EWHC 191 (Ch), [2017] 1 BCLC 269, [2016] BPIR 531 that the trustees in bankruptcy of a shareholder had standing as a contributory to present a petition for the winding up of the company. Registrar Jones' holding was made despite the fact that the company shares, which had vested in them upon their appointment, had not been registered in their name for the 6-month period before liquidation as required by s 124(2)(b) (see below). The consequence of s 250 was that persons in the trustee's position should be regarded as a 'member' (with standing to present a petition) from the date when he or she acquired the shares, as opposed to the date when the shares were registered in the trustee's name (at [48], [51]).

Restrictions—The right of a contributory to petition is restricted by s 124(2), although s 124(3) exempts some contributories that would ordinarily fall within s 124(2). Section 124(2) applies where the company is a public or unlimited company. The condition in that subsection that one must have held the shares for at least 6 months is designed to prevent a person from obtaining a share in a company with the aim only of presenting a petition: *Re a Company* [1894] 2 Ch 349. The restriction in s 124(2) applies to a trustee in bankruptcy of a member: *Re HL Bolton Engineering Co Ltd* [1956] Ch 577, [1956] 1 All ER 799; *Taylor v Glenrinnes Farms Ltd* [1994] 2 BCLC 522.

Section 124(3) provides an exemption and a limitation. A contributory, because of s 76, is entitled to petition, but he or she must do so under either s 122(1)(f) or s 122(1)(g).

A further restriction is contained in s 125(2). See the notes relating to s 125, and particularly under the heading 'Restrictions on making an order on the petition of a contributory' for details.

A general rule, formulated at common law, also restricts which contributories are entitled to petition. The rule is that a contributory must demonstrate a tangible interest in the company if he or she is to petition: *Re Rica Gold Washing Co* (1879) 11 Ch D 36; *Re Chesterfield Catering Co Ltd* [1977] Ch 373; *Re Greenhaven Motors Ltd* [1997] 1 BCLC 739; *O'Connor v Atlantis Fisheries Ltd* 1998 SCLR 401. With insolvent companies, fully paid-up shareholders are normally unable to show a tangible interest, as they are only entitled to share in the assets of such companies after both the creditors have been paid in full and the costs of winding up have been paid. It has been made clear that a shareholder who seeks to petition is not able to establish the necessary interest by asserting the possibility that a surplus might be produced by means of recoveries from future litigation to be brought within the liquidation itself: *Re Rica Gold Washing Co* (1879) 11 Ch D 36 at 43. A tangible interest appears not to be limited to an interest in a monetary surplus, but might include achievement of some substantial advantage or the minimization of some disadvantage: *Re Chesterfield Catering Co Ltd*; *Re FI Call Ltd* [2015] EWHC 3269 (Ch) at [56]. It has been recognised that there can be exceptions to the general rule: *Re Rica Gold Washing Co* at 43; *Re Chesterfield Catering Co Ltd* at 380; *The Charit-Email Technology Partnership LLP v Vermillion International Investments Limited* [2009] EWHC 388 (Ch), [2009] BPIR 762. An example is *Re a Company (No 007936 of 1994)* [1995] BCC 705 where a contributory was allowed to petition in circumstances where he could not ascertain whether he had a tangible interest in the company because the company failed to provide proper access to financial details.

A contributory who is in arrears with calls on his or her shares is not able to petition unless he or she agrees to pay the arrears to the company or into court, or consents to adhere to any order which the court determines should be made in relation to the calls: *Re Crystal Reef Gold Mining Co* [1892] 1 Ch 408.

Secretary of State—The Secretary of State for Business, Energy and Industrial Strategy is the political head of the Department of Business, Innovation and Skills, which has the function of regulating the formation, management and insolvency of companies. In this capacity he or she is given the power to petition for winding up. The provision under which the Secretary of State most often petitions is s 124A.

**Official receiver**—The official receiver is entitled to petition for a winding-up order where a company is in voluntary liquidation. See notes relating to s 116 for discussion of when a court is likely to order a court winding up of a company that is in voluntary liquidation. There is more likely to be a petition filed by the official receiver where there is a need for careful investigation of the affairs of the company.

## [1.177]

### 124A Petition for winding up on grounds of public interest

(1) Where it appears to the Secretary of State from—

    (a)    any report made or information obtained under Part XIV (except section 448A) of the Companies Act 1985 (company investigations, &c.),

    (b)    any report made by inspectors under—

        (i)    section 167, 168, 169 or 284 of the Financial Services and Markets Act 2000, or

        (ii)    where the company is an open-ended investment company (within the meaning of that Act), regulations made as a result of section 262(2)(k) of that Act;

    (bb)    any information or documents obtained under section 165, 171, 172, 173 or 175 of that Act,

    (c)    any information obtained under section 2 of the Criminal Justice Act 1987 or section 52 of the Criminal Justice (Scotland) Act 1987 (fraud investigations), or

    (d)    any information obtained under section 83 of the Companies Act 1989 (powers exercisable for purpose of assisting overseas regulatory authorities),

that it is expedient in the public interest that a company should be wound up, he may present a petition for it to be wound up if the court thinks it just and equitable for it to be so.

(2) This section does not apply if the company is already being wound up by the court.

**Amendments**—Inserted by Companies Act 1989, s 60(3). Amended by SI 2001/3649; Companies (Audit, Investigations and Community Enterprise Act 2004, s 25(1), Sch 2, Pt 3, para 27.

**General note**—The Secretary of State for Business, Energy and Industrial Strategy intervenes by petitioning for a winding-up order under this provision in order to safeguard the public from the activities of the company. Hence, petitions presented under this provision are known commonly as 'public interest petitions': *Re a Company (No 007816 of 1994)* [1997] 2 BCLC 685 at 687, CA; *Re Titan International Inc* [1998] 1 BCLC 102 at 107, CA; *Re Delfin International (SA) Ltd* [2000] 1 BCLC 71.

It has been held that only the Secretary of State is entitled to present a petition under this section as he or she has been identified by Parliament as the guardian of the public interest: *Re Millennium Advanced Technology Ltd* [2004] EWHC 711 (Ch), [2004] 1 WLR 2177, [2004] 4 All ER 465, [2004] 2 BCLC 77 at [33]. It was further stated that Parliament's intention was that the Secretary of State should act as a filter as to what is in the public interest. Anyone concerned about the activities of a company being against the public interest should bring these concerns to the attention of the Secretary of State: *Millennium Advanced Technology* at [38].

Often the Secretary of State will, following presentation of the petition, file an application for the appointment of a provisional liquidator (eg *Re a Company (No 007070 of 1996)* [1997] 2 BCLC 139), and this is frequently done because of the need for an early and rigorous examination of the affairs of a company. For comments on provisional liquidation, see the notes relating to s 135. But courts are slow to appoint a provisional liquidator unless there is a good prima facie case for saying that a winding-up order would be made: *Re Treasure Traders Corporation Ltd* [2005] EWHC 2774 (Ch).

A company that is associated with another company, against which a winding-up order is made under this ground, will not suffer the same fate, merely because of the association, where it is carrying on its own discrete business: *Re Tag World Services Ltd* [2008] EWHC 1866 (Ch).

It has been held in obiter comments that s 124A petitions are neither within the EU Regulation on Insolvency Proceedings nor the Brussels Convention on Jurisdiction and Enforcement of Judgments in Civil and Commercial Matters: *Re Marann Brooks CSV Ltd* [2003] BPIR 1159.

Orders might be made under this section against companies that are in voluntary liquidation (*Re ForceSun Ltd* [2002] 2 BCLC 302; *Re Alpha Club (UK) Ltd* [2002] 2 BCLC 612) or in administration (para 40(2)(a) of Sch B1).

While the Secretary of State is empowered to petition for the winding up of a company pursuant to s 124A of a company that is registered outside of Great Britain, provided that the company has a principal place of business in England or Wales (*Re Normandy Marketing Ltd* [1994] Ch 198 at 204, [1994] 2 WLR 438, [1994] 1 All ER 1007, [1994] 1 BCLC 565), he or she must satisfy the court that a real or sufficient connection between the company and the jurisdiction of the English and Welsh courts exists: *Re Real Estate Development Co Ltd* [1991] BCLC 210; *Re Titan International plc* [1998] 1 BCLC 102 at 107.

If a company has gone some way to rectifying concerns that the Secretary of State had with its business and affairs and at the time of the hearing there were no grounds for winding up then an order would not be given. Matters had to be looked at as at the time of the hearing of the petition and as a whole. By that time in *Secretary of State for Business Enterprise and Regulatory Reform v Amway (UK) Ltd* [2009] EWCA Civ 32, [2011] 2 BCLC 716, the company had responded to the concerns identified by the Secretary of State. The court said that there is no rule of law or binding principle of discretion that past misconduct or past misconduct which was sufficiently serious led inevitably to winding up.

An application to appoint a provisional liquidator should not be used instead of a winding-up petition under s 124A where the latter was appropriate: *The Commisioners for HMRC v Rochdale Drinks Distributors Ltd* [2011] EWCA Civ 1116, [2012] 1 BCLC 748, [2011] BPIR 1604.

**Grounds**—The expression 'in the public interest' is of the widest import, and the Secretary of State is not limited, in presenting petitions, to cases where illegal activity is alleged: *Re SHV Senator Hanseatische Verwaltungs Gesellschaft mbH* [1997] 1 WLR 515, [1996] 4 All ER 933, [1996] 2 BCLC 597, CA; a company might be wound up if its business was 'inherently objectionable' because its activities were contrary to a clearly identified public interest: *Secretary of State for Business Innovation and Skills Ltd v PAG Management Services Ltd* [2015] EWHC 2404 (Ch) at [5]; *Re PAG Asset Preservation Ltd* [2019] EWHC (Ch), [2020] BCC 167 (and affirmed on appeal: [2020] EWCA Civ 1017, [2020] BCC 979). It is desirable, although not essential, that a petition alleges intentional and dishonest deceit of the public: *Re a Company (No 5669 of 1998)* [2000] 1 BCLC 427. It has been held in Australia that it could be in the public interest to wind up a company even where it had no current trading activity: *ASIC v Kingsley Brown Properties Pty Ltd* [2005] VSC 506. It has been said that subverting the purpose of the liquidation process was against the public interest: *Secretary of State for Business Innovation and Skills Ltd v PAG Management Services Ltd* [2015] EWHC 2404 (Ch).

While companies against which petitions are presented are often insolvent, it is not a prerequisite to such proceedings (*Re Marann Brooks CSV Ltd* [2003] BPIR 1159), as insolvency itself is not a ground for granting a winding-up order under this section (*Re SHV Senator Hanseatische Verwaltungs Gesellschaft mbH* [1997] 1 WLR 515, [1996] 4 All ER 933, [1996] 2 BCLC 597, CA); more must be demonstrated than insolvency in obtaining an order, namely that the order sought is in the public interest. Nevertheless, the reasons why, and the circumstances in which, a company has become insolvent might be highly pertinent to the granting of an order: *Re UK-Euro Group plc* [2006] EWHC 2102 (Ch), [2007] 1 BCLC 812. In Australia the fact that a company is insolvent has been held to be a factor in making a winding-up order under that jurisdiction's equivalent provision: *Macquarie Bank Ltd v TM Investments Pty Ltd* [2005] NSWSC 608. One would think that in some cases permitting an insolvent company to continue in business would be against the public interest. Clearly there are situations where it is in the public interest that a solvent company be wound up: *Re a Company (No 007923 of 1994)* [1995] 1 WLR 953, [1995] 1 BCLC 440. Companies may be wound up on the basis of the section where they have been guilty of conduct that is below the generally accepted standards of commercial behaviour: *Re Marann Brooks CSV Ltd*.

The sort of conduct that may well see a petition succeed is where there is a lack of commercial probity *Secretary of State for Business for Business Energy and Skills v PGMRS Ltd* [2010] EWHC 2983 (Ch), [2011] 1 BCLC 443 and while this may well involve a company inducing members of the public to become involved in transactions that will cause them loss, it might also constitute activity that is detrimental to the public in general: *Secretary of State for Business Energy and Industrial Strategy v Celtic Consultancy and Enterprises Ltd* [2021] EWHC 1240 (Ch) at [122].

Petitions have been presented for a variety of reasons, such as: the company never had, during its existence, a sufficient paid up capital to finance its activities (*In re Rubin, Rosen and Associated Ltd* [1975] 1 WLR 122); the company has committed serious breaches of the Companies Act (*Re Allied Produce Co Ltd* [1967] 1 WLR 1469); the affairs of the company were being conducted fraudulently (*In re Golden Chemical Products Ltd* [1976] 1 Ch 300); the company has engaged in making fraudulent misrepresentations (*Re Secure & Provide plc* [1992] BCC 405; *Re a Company (No 5669 of 1998)* [2000] 1 BCLC 427); the company has been party to a conspiracy to defraud customers (*Re Highfield Commodities Ltd* [1985] 1 WLR 149, [1984] BCLC 623,); the company's records were inadequately maintained and members of the public had been misled (*Re Walter L Jacob Ltd* [1989] BCLC 345); the company had no authorisation to conduct investment business pursuant to the Financial Services Act 1986 (legislation now repealed) and had made statements in promotional literature that were misleading and contrary to that legislation (*Re Market Wizard Systems (UK) Ltd* [1998] 2 BCLC 282); the company had been carrying on an insurance business without authorisation (*Re a Company (No 007816 of 1994)* [1997] 2 BCLC 685); the company was delivering unordered goods to consumers and impersonating bona fide suppliers (*Re Forcesun Ltd* [2002] 2 BCLC 302); the company was conducting a pyramid selling scheme and a breach of the Lotteries and Amusements Act 1976 (*Re Alpha Club (UK) Ltd* [2002] 2 BCLC 612); and the company was taking advance fees and not doing the work agreed to be done: *Re Marann Brooks CSV Ltd* [2003] BPIR 1159. Petitions in some of these cases were not successful. Often petitions are based on several grounds. An instance is *Re Atlantic Properties Ltd* [2006] EWHC 610 (Ch), where an order was made because the company had failed to comply with an order for disclosure of documents under s 447 of the Companies Act 1985, it had failed to keep proper financial records and it was insolvent.

As a prerequisite to the presenting of a petition, the Secretary of State must be, according to the section, of the opinion that it is expedient in the public interest that the company should be wound up: *Re Walter L Jacob Ltd* [1989] BCLC 345, CA. It is permissible to petition where the Secretary of State has not formed the necessary opinion, but a senior officer in the Department, has done so: In *Re Golden Chemical Products Ltd* [1976] 1 Ch 300.

**The decision-making process**—When hearing a petition, a court will examine the evidence presented and submissions made to it and undertake a balancing exercise, weighing the factors which constitute reasons for the making of a winding-up order as against those factors which are reasons for not winding up the company: *Re Walter L Jacob Ltd* [1989] BCLC 345, CA *Re Market Wizard Systems (UK) Ltd* [1998] 2 BCLC 282 at 285; *Secretary of State for Trade and Industry v Leyton Housing Trustees Ltd* [2000] 2 BCLC 808 at 810; *Secretary of State for Business Enterprise and Regulatory Reform v Art IT plc* [2008] All ER (D) 237 (Jan). Once having done the balancing, the court had to then be able to identify for itself the aspects of the public interest which would be promoted by making a winding-up order: *Re PAG Asset Preservation Ltd* [2019] EWHC (Ch), [2020] BCC 167. In their deliberations, courts will consider the views of creditors opposing the petition: In *Re Rubin, Rosen and Associated Ltd* [1975] 1 WLR 122 at 128–129. An order will not be made unless a court is convinced that there is a reasonable prospect that the public interest will be fostered by a winding up: *Re Titan International plc* [1998] 1 BCLC 102 at 107, CA. A judge has complete discretion whether or not to make a winding–up order: *Secretary of State for Trade and Industry v Bell Davies Trading Ltd* [2004] EWCA Civ 1066; *Secretary of State for Business Enterprise and Regulatory Reform v Amway (UK) Ltd* [2009] EWCA Civ 32. At first instance in *Secretary of State for Business Enterprise and Regulatory Reform v Amway (UK) Ltd* [2008] EWHC 1054 (Ch), Norris J said that a court was entitled to make an order simply because the company was managing its business in a way that was not consistent with the generally accepted minimum standards of commercial behaviour. In *Secretary of State for Business Enterprise and Regulatory Reform v Art IT* [2008] All ER (D) 237 (Jan) the court balanced the various factors involved and ordered winding up as the company had: failed to file accounts; issued a misleading advertisement claiming the company was being floated on the AIM when it was not; and failed to comply with company investigators. In making a decision the judge is permitted to consider past misconduct, but it should not be seen as conclusive and a judge could take into account changed circumstances and accept undertakings of a company that indicated its intention to improve the situation, even where the Secretary of State had declined to accept such undertakings, although a court would only do so in rare cases: *Secretary of State for Business Enterprise and Regulatory Reform v Amway (UK) Ltd* [2009] EWCA Civ 32.

The wrongdoing that is alleged to found a petition does not have to have been carried out by the directing mind of the company: *Secretary of State for Business Enterprise and Regulatory Reform v Amway (UK) Ltd* [2008] EWHC 1054 (Ch).

**Opposing a petition**—The company is naturally entitled to oppose a petition. But can a contributory of the company do so? The answer appears to be in the affirmative if the contributory can establish that the company is solvent: *Re Rodencroft Ltd*, sub nom *Allso v Secretary of State for Trade and Industry* [2004] EWHC 862 (Ch).

The company might always seek to obtain an injunction to prevent the advertisement of a petition. The company would have the burden of establishing the fact that the normal advertising process should not take effect. The court would balance the need for the advertising of the petition to proceed and the interests of those who had a need to be informed of the petition, as against the damage that might be done to the company: *Secretary of State for Business Innovation and Skills v Broomfield Developments Ltd* [2014] EWHC 3925 (Ch).

**The inter-relationship and consequences of s 124A(2) and s 129(2) (commencement of winding up)**—Other than in the circumstances prescribed in s 129(1) and (2), the winding up of a company is deemed to commence at the time of the presentation of a winding-up petition. Read literally, and, it is submitted, reasonably and objectively, s 124A cannot be invoked where a winding-up petition is extant. The point is significant since it goes to jurisdiction and is not a matter for the court's discretion. If that analysis is correct then it would appear to follow that s 124A cannot engage in the face of a winding-up petition though the provision would be capable of being engaged upon such a petition being dismissed subject to s 129(1) and (2). To the extent that any order has been made under s 124A(1) in the face of an extant winding-up petition then that order, and, apparently, any consequences following from it, would appear capable of being challenged on the footing that the order amounts to a nullity in the absence of the court having any jurisdiction to make it.

**Undertakings**—Companies that are the subject of public interest petitions might be willing to offer undertakings, usually to cease to continue the activity that is the subject of the Secretary of State's concerns, and courts have the discretion whether or not to accept an undertaking as to future conduct: *Secretary of State for Business Enterprise and Regulatory Reform v Amway (UK) Ltd* [2008] EWHC 1054 (Ch). But undertakings offered have been refused by judges: *Re Equity & Provident Ltd* [2002] 2 BCLC 78. In *Re Bamford Publishers Ltd* ((unreported) 2 June 1977, but considered by the Vice-Chancellor in *Re The Supporting Link Ltd* [2004] EWHC 523 (Ch)), Brightman J adverted to the problem with undertakings, namely that it is not the function of either the court or the Department of Business, Energy and Industrial Strategy to police undertakings. A judge hearing a public interest petition is entitled to: dismiss the petition where undertakings have been given by the company (the judge being satisfied that the offending activity had ceased or the Secretary of State had accepted the undertakings); dismiss, in unusual circumstances, the petition on the giving of undertakings, even if the Secretary of State was opposed to this; or refuse to accept undertakings and make a winding-up order if, for instance, the judge was not satisfied that the ones giving the undertakings were trustworthy: *Secretary of State for Trade and Industry v Bell Davies Trading Ltd* [2004] EWCA Civ 1066. If an undertaking is given by a company, it is not entitled to appeal against it: *Bell Davies Trading Ltd*.

**Costs**—If the Secretary of State obtains a winding-up order, the Department of Business, Energy and Industrial Strategy will, usually, be awarded costs against the company (*Re Xyllyx plc (No 2)* [1992] BCLC 378 at 385), although the courts have awarded the costs against a director of the company personally where he or she is in control of the company's affairs and had acted in his or her interests rather than the interests of the company: *Re Aurum Marketing Ltd* [2000] 2 BCLC 645 at 650, CA; *Re Northwest Holdings plc* [2000] BCC 731 (upheld on appeal to the Court of Appeal – [2001] 1 BCLC 468); *Secretary of State for Trade and Industry v Liquid Acquisitions Ltd* [2003] 1 BCLC 375. It was clear that it was not the normal rule that directors should be made to pay the costs of the company, even if they knew that the company would not be able to pay any costs if the defence failed: *Re Northwest Holdings plc* [2001] EWCA Civ 67, [2001] 1 BCLC 468 at [33], CA (dismissing an appeal from Hart J). A director should not be liable for costs where he or she had a bona fide belief that the company had an arguable defence and it was in the company's interests that the defence be advanced: *Re Northwest Holdings plc* at [33]–[34].

If the petition fails, costs may be awarded against the Department for Business Enterprise and Regulatory Reform (*Re Secure & Provide plc* [1992] BCC 405 at 415), but this is not an automatic result, because the court needs to undertake a balancing exercise: *Re Xyllyx plc (No 2)* [1992] BCLC 378.

See Keay 'Public Interest Petitions' (1999) 20 *Company Lawyer* 296; Finch 'Public interest liquidation: PIL or Placebo?' [2002] *Insolvency Lawyer* 157; A Keay *McPherson and Keay's Law of Company Liquidation* (Sweet and Maxwell, 4th edn, 2018) at 277–292.

## 124B

*(Repealed)*

**Amendments**—Inserted by SI 2004/2326. Repealed by SI 2019/710 having effect from IP completion day (as defined in the European Union (Withdrawal Agreement) Act 2020, s 39(1)–(5)).

**General note**—This section mirrors s 124A as far as the new European company (Societas Europea) is concerned.

## 124C

*(Repealed)*

**Amendments**—Inserted by SI 2006/2078. Amended by SI 2013/496. Repealed by SI 2019/710 having effect from IP completion day (as defined in the European Union (Withdrawal Agreement) Act 2020, s 39(1)–(5)).

General note—This section mirrors s 124A as far as a European Cooperative Society is concerned.

**[1.178]**

### 125 Powers of court on hearing of petition

(1)   On hearing a winding-up petition the court may dismiss it, or adjourn the hearing conditionally or unconditionally, or make an interim order, or any other order that it thinks fit; but the court shall not refuse to make a winding-up order on the ground only that the company's assets have been mortgaged to an amount equal to or in excess of those assets, or that the company has no assets.

(2)   If the petition is presented by members of the company as contributories on the ground that it is just and equitable that the company should be wound up, the court, if it is of opinion—

(a)   that the petitioners are entitled to relief either by winding up the company or by some other means, and

(b)   that in the absence of any other remedy it would be just and equitable that the company should be wound up,

shall make a winding-up order; but this does not apply if the court is also of the opinion both that some other remedy is available to the petitioners and that they are acting unreasonably in seeking to have the company wound up instead of pursuing that other remedy.

General note—The courts are granted an unfettered discretion and they can make any of the orders contemplated by s 125(1). This is subject to the proviso that the court shall not refuse to make a winding-up order only because the company's assets have been mortgaged to the value of the assets, or in excess of the assets, or where the company has no assets.

As far as the hearing of petitions presented in relation to companies in voluntary liquidation is concerned, see s 116 and the notes relating to it.

Discretion—While the court has a discretion as to whether or not to make a winding-up order, the general approach is that a petitioner who can prove that a debt is unpaid and that the company is insolvent is entitled to a winding-up order ex debito justitiae: *Re Western of Canada Oil* (1873) 17 Eq 1; *Re Demaglass Holdings Ltd* [2001] 2 BCLC 633; *Re Maud* [2020] EWHC 674 (Ch). In this context this is taken to mean that, pursuant to settled practice, the court can exercise its discretion in only one way, namely by granting the order sought: *Re Pritchard* [1963] Ch 502 at 521. The New Zealand Court of Appeal has cautioned that courts should use the power to refuse to make an order sparingly where it is faced with a creditor's petition, and this should still be the case where there are few assets available to creditors: *90 Nine Ltd v Luxury Rentals NZ Ltd* [2019] NZCA 424 at [15], [16]. But, as indicated above, it is now settled that the rights of a creditor are always subject to the overriding discretion which the court has, and found in s 125(1): *Re P & J MacRae Ltd* [1961] 1 WLR 229 at 238, so that the court is never bound to make an order, even where there is proof that a ground for winding up exists, but has a discretion to decide whether or not it will do so. Notwithstanding this, the power of the court to deny an order is exercised in accordance with principles which are relatively well defined. Courts tend only to refuse orders in the following cases: (1) the debt is bona fide disputed by the company, (2) the petition constitutes an abuse of process, (3) the company has paid or tendered payment of the petitioner's debt, (4) winding up is opposed by other creditors, (5) the company is in the process of being wound up voluntarily; and (6) the English and Welsh courts are not the most appropriate jurisdiction for the issues to be resolved (see A Keay, *McPherson and Keay's Law of Company Liquidation* (Sweet and Maxwell, 4th edn, 2018) at 137–188).

Courts will not usually exercise their discretion against petitioners who have ulterior motives in initiating the proceedings, such as ill-will towards the company unless it is otherwise an abuse of process: *Bryanston Finance Ltd v De Vries (No 2)* [1976] 1 Ch 63, *Maud v Aabar Block Sarl* [2016] EWHC 2175 (Ch), [2016] BPIR 1486. But, in *HM Commissioners of Customs and Excise v Anglo Overseas Ltd* [2004] EWHC 2198 (Ch), [2005] BPIR 137, Lewison J did say that the circumstances under which the petition was presented were a relevant consideration in deciding whether to make a winding-up order, although this case, it must be noted, did involve somewhat unusual facts. Even if a petition is not held to be an abuse of process, the motives or objectives of a petitioner in seeking a liquidation do not become irrelevant; they can be relevant in relation to the situation where other creditors oppose the making of a petition: *Maud v Aabar Block Sarl* [2016] EWHC 2175 (Ch), [2016] BPIR 1486 (a bankruptcy case but the same principles apply).

Where a petitioner has standing as a creditor at the time of the presentation of the petition, but is not a creditor at the time of the hearing of the petition, Australian authority has stated that the court has a discretion whether or not to make a winding-up order: *Australian Beverage Distributors Pty Ltd v The Redrock Co Pty Ltd* [2007] NSWSC 966, [2007] 213 FLR 450 at [33], [34].

**Amount of the debt relied on in the petition**—While there is no minimum amount that must be owed before a court will order winding up, courts have, traditionally, been wary about making an order where the amount owed is less than £750. The reason for this is that the courts do not wish to see winding up used as an avenue for the collection of small debts (*Re Fancy Dress Balls* Co [1899] WN 109) and this accords with the approach taken in Australia, for instance: *South East Water v Kitoria Pty Ltd* (1996) 14 ACLC 1328. In *Lilley v American Express Europe Ltd* [2000] BPIR 70, a bankruptcy case, it was held that the court retained jurisdiction to make a bankruptcy order even where the debtor had reduced the outstanding petition debt to beneath the bankruptcy level by the time of the hearing of the petition, and a bankruptcy order might well be made where it was clear that the debtor was 'playing cat and mouse with the petitioner' (at 74–75). See the comments accompanying s 267, where the latter case is discussed in more detail.

**Debt relied on in the petition is disputed**—There is no rule of law (*Re Claybridge Shipping Co SA* [1997] 1 BCLC 572, CA; *Re UOC Corp*; *Alipour v Ary* [1997] 1 WLR 534), that a winding-up order will not be made on a petition founded on a disputed debt, but there tends to be a rule of practice that a petition will be struck out or dismissed in such a case (*Botleigh Grange Hotels Ltd v Revenue and Customs Commissioners* [2018] EWCA Civ 1032 at [8]). The courts retain a discretion to make a winding-up order (*Re Claybridge Shipping Co SA, Parmalat Capital Finance Ltd v Food Holdings Ltd (in liq)* [2008] UKPC 23, [2008] BPIR 641 at [9]; *Botleigh Grange Hotels Ltd v Revenue and Customs Commissioners* at [8]). In *Botleigh Grange Hotels Ltd* the Court of Appeal said that a court might determine the merits of a disputed debt because: all of the relevant evidence is before the court; the issue is able to be decided on the documents that have been filed alone and this accepted by the parties; counsel is prepared to argue the merits of the dispute; the court has sufficient to do so (at [8]).

The rule of practice applies to petitions brought by creditors no matter on what ground in s 122 they are relying. The rule provides that for dismissal of a petition the company must be able to establish that the debt is bona fide disputed, and the dispute is based on some substantial ground: *Mann v Goldstein* [1968] 1 WLR 1091 at 1098–1099; *Re Richbell Strategic Holdings Ltd* [1997] 2 BCLC 429; *Re UOC Corp*; *Alipour v Ary* [1997] 1 WLR 534, CA; *Re A Company (No.006685)* [1997] 1 BCLC 639 at 642; *Abbey National v JSF Finance* [2006] EWCA Civ 328 at [46]). In *ICS Incorporation Ltd v Michael Wilson Partners Ltd* [2005] EWHC 404 (Ch), [2005] BPIR 804 the judge preferred 'substantial dispute' to 'bona fide dispute', since the latter might turn on issues of credibility of witnesses. In *Argentum Lex Wealth Management Ltd v Giannotti* [2011] EWCA Civ 1341 it was said that the test of substantial grounds was not very different from the test for granting judicial review applications in the administrative courts or granting permission to appeal to the Court of Appeal, and what must exist is a realistic prospect of success (at [17]). The rationale for dismissing a petition where the debt on which it is based is disputed genuinely on substantial grounds is that a winding-up petition is not to be used for the improper purpose of compelling a solvent company to pay a disputed debt which would certainly be discharged as soon as the company's liability was clearly shown to exist (*Re Imperial Silver Quarries* (1868) 14 WR 1220; *Re Imperial Hydropathic Hotel Co* (1882) 49 LT 147 at 150) and where irreparable damage could be caused to the company: *Cadiz Waterworks Company v Barnett* (1874) LR 19 Eq 182. The legal reason for the striking out of the petition is that a creditor whose debt is disputed lacks the qualification necessary to be a petitioner: *Mann v Goldstein* [1968] 1 WLR 1091; *Re Selectmove Ltd* [1995] 2 All ER 531, [1995] 1 WLR 474.

The courts will not permit the rule of practice that means a court will ordinarily dismiss a petition when the underlying debt is disputed to allow a company to throw up a cloud of objections to the claim in the petition so as to be able to argue that there is a substantial dispute. A court is entitled to determine whether on the evidence before it there is indeed a dispute on substantial grounds; this is even if, in performing that task, the court may be engaged in much the same exercise as that which would be required of a court faced with an application for summary judgment: *Re A Company (No 006685)* [1997] 1 BCLC 639 at 645; *Angel Group v British Gas* [2012] EWHC 2702 (Ch) at [22]. The courts must apply critical analysis to assertions of dispute made by debtors, and assertions must be considered in light of all of the admissible evidence and material and to determine if the assertion of dispute has substance (*CFL Finance Ltd v Bass* [2019] EWHC 1839 (Ch), [2019] BPIR 1327 at [91]).

To resist a petition on the basis that the petition debt is disputed, a company must establish that the dispute is real and substantial; the fact that the company is clearly solvent is not sufficient as solvency is not a defence to a petition based on an undisputed claim. Nevertheless, the court would want to be satisfied that the remedy was not being sought as a way of putting pressure on a company the solvency of which is not in real doubt, and where there is a dispute as to indebtedness (*Coilcolor Limited v Camtrex Limited* [2015] EWHC 3202 (Ch), [2016] BPIR 1129 at [42]).

The courts have indicated that the winding-up process should not be used as a method of debt collection where there was a dispute: *Hammonds (A Firm) v Pro-Fit USA Ltd* [2007] EWHC 1998 (Ch) at [27]; *Re GBI Investments Ltd* [2010] EWHC 37 (Ch), [2010] BPIR 356 at [80].

A company which claims to dispute a debt has a duty 'to bring forward a prima facie case which satisfies the court that there is something to be tried' (*Re Great Britain Mutual Life Assurance Society* (1880) 26 ChD 246 at 253 per Jessel MR), and it is not sufficient if the company has a mere honest belief that payment to the petitioner is not due: *Taylor's Industrial Flooring Ltd v M & H Plant Hire (Manchester) Ltd* [1990] BCLC 216 CA. But where there is a substantial dispute, courts are likely to refuse to make a winding-up order even where the defence of the company to the claim in the petition is 'shadowy': *ICS Incorporation Ltd v Michael Wilson Partners Ltd* [2005] EWHC 404 (Ch), [2005] BPIR 804 at [12].

In seeking to determine whether there is a dispute on substantial grounds, a court should consider the witness statements and other documentary evidence: *Mac Plant Services Ltd v Contract Lifting Services (Scotland) Ltd* [2008] CSOH 158, 2009 SC 125 at [9]. If a not insignificant period has elapsed between presentation of the petition and the hearing of it a court should not be required to look just at the circumstances that exist at the time of the hearing, but also the circumstances as they existed at the time of presentation: *Mac Plant Services Ltd v Contract Lifting Services (Scotland) Ltd* [2008] CSOH 158, 2009 SC 125 at [64].

Courts may, although they do so infrequently, ascertain, where they feel that it is appropriate, what is the true position between the company and the petitioner where a dispute is alleged, namely determining whether the company does in fact owe the debt relied on in the petition: *Brinds Ltd v Offshore Oil NL* [1985] 2 BCC 98, 916 (PC); *Re Janeash Ltd* [1990] BCC 250; (*Re A Company (No 006685)* [1997] 1 BCLC 639 at 642). *Corben v What Music Holdings Ltd* (unreported) 16 July 2003 (EWHC, Hart J). It has been said that the court may determine what the position is between the petitioner and the company and make a winding-up order where there was an unusual and extreme set of facts justifying an exception to the normal rule: *Re The Arena Corporation Ltd* [2004] BPIR 415 at 432. Factors that are relevant in determining that there ~~[2003]~~ are exceptional circumstances are: the company is insolvent absent the petition debt; the company ~~EWCA~~ is not going to suffer any prejudice; the petitioner has no adequate alternative remedy to ~~Civ~~ liquidation: *Re GBI Investments Ltd* [2010] EWHC 37 (Ch), [2010] BPIR 356 at [160]–[163]. But ~~87~~ the courts will not ordinarily undertake an inquiry into whether the debt is actually owed as that ~~[?]~~ should be determined by the normal court process.

Where only part of the debt is disputed and the amount that is not in dispute exceeds £750, then a court should order a winding up: *Re Tweeds Garages Ltd* [1962] Ch 406; *Taylor's Industrial Flooring Ltd v M & H Plant Hire (Manchester) Ltd* [1990] BCLC 216, CA; *Mac Plant services Ltd v Contract Lifting Services (Scotland) Ltd* [2008] CSOH 158, 2009 SC 125 at [10]; *Astra Resources Plc v Credit Veritas USA LLC* [2015] EWHC 1830 (Ch).

Where a court had delivered a judgment in favour of the petitioner then the petitioner is a creditor for the purposes of winding up even if the judgment is subject to an appeal: *El Ajou v Dollar Land (Manhattan) Ltd* [2005] EWHC 2861 (Ch).

Where a debt is disputed and the parties are subject to an agreement that requires disputes to go to arbitration a court has the discretion to order the winding up of the debtor on the petition of the creditor. The court is not stopped from doing so because of the arbitration provision, as a winding-up petition is not a claim for the payment of a debt within the terms of s 9 of the Arbitration Act: *Salford Estates (No 2) Ltd v Altomart Ltd* [2014] EWCA 1575, [2015] BPIR 399). Nevertheless, the Court of Appeal in this case seemed to suggest that, in practice and save in very exceptional circumstances, where the debt constituting the foundation of a winding-up petition is disputed and falls within the scope of matters which the parties agreed to refer to arbitration, then the courts will exercise their discretion in such a way as to stay or dismiss the petition. It was said in this case (at [39]) that it was difficult to envisage exceptional circumstances that would lead to a court declining to dismiss the petition. Later, in the Court of Appeal in *Re Enta Technologies Ltd* ([2015] EWCA Civ 29, [2015] BPIR 327, [2015] 2 BCLC 586 at [29]) and then in *Re Telnic* ([2020] EWHC 1615 (Ch) at [12]) Vos C opined that a court is not prevented, because of an arbitration provision, from determining whether the debt on which a petition is based is disputed on substantial grounds and he did not think that the Court of Appeal in *Salford Estates (No 2) Ltd v Alomart Ltd* had set down a view that was against such a conclusion (at [12]). The judge did add that the occasions where a court would not stay or dismiss would be rare (at [13]). He said that it would be exacting for petitioners to bring themselves within the term 'exceptional circumstances.' (at [30]). Exceptional or rare circumstances would not be constituted by the situation where the company had made past admissions concerning the fact that it owed the debt (at [27]). According to Vos C and an earlier decision (*Fieldfisher LLP v Pennyfeathers Ltd* [2016] EWHC 566 (Ch) at [28]–[29]), the reasons for the courts taking this approach were that it was designed to: '(a) uphold the policy of the Arbitration Act 1986, (b) discourage parties to an arbitration agreement from bypassing it as a tactic by presenting a winding up petition, (c) prevent one party applying pressure on an alleged debtor to pay up immediately or face the burden of satisfying the court that the debt was bona fide disputed on substantial grounds, and (d) require the parties to adhere to their agreement as to the proper forum for the resolution of such an issue.' (at [27]).

The kind of dispute—While, generally, courts in England and Wales will strike out a petition based on a disputed debt, there is case law to the effect that the court still has a discretion as to whether a winding-up order is to be made: *Brinds Ltd v Offshore Oil NL* [1985] 2 BCC 98, 916t 98, 921; *Parmalat Capital Finance Ltd v Food Holdings Ltd (in liq)* [2008] UKPC 23, [2008] BPIR 641 at [9]. But in *Re Bayoil SA* [1999] 1 BCLC 62 the Court of Appeal said that where a company disputes a petition on substantial grounds then whether or not there should be a dismissal of the petition is not, at any rate initially, a matter for the discretion of the court (at 66). The upshot is that the principle that a dispute over a debt founding the petition will lead to dismissal tends to be applied generally, except in special circumstances. Whether or not there is a dispute on substantial grounds is a matter to be decided in each case. The kind of dispute that is contemplated is one which involves substantially disputed questions of fact which demand the taking of viva voce evidence: *Re Lympne Investments Ltd* [1972] 2 All ER 385 at 389. A company must demonstrate that the dispute is genuine and bona fide, both in the sense that it must be honestly believed to exist by those who allege it (*Stonegate Securities Ltd v Gregory* [1980] Ch 576 at 580, [1980] 1 All ER 241 at 243–244, CA), and in the sense that the belief must be based on reasonable (*Stonegate Securities Ltd v Gregory*) or substantial grounds (*Re Welsh Brick Industries Ltd* [1946] 2 All ER 197 at 198; *Taylor's Industrial Flooring Ltd v M & H Plant Hire (Manchester) Ltd* [1990] BCLC 216, CA; *Re a Company (No 0010656 of 1990)* [1991] BCLC 464 at 466). But it has been said that the courts will be wary of a company which seeks to raise objections to a petition in order to allow them to submit that a disputed debt exists where the objections are not able to be determined on affidavit (now witness statements) evidence and without cross-examination (*Re a Company (No 006685 of 1996)* [1997] 1 BCLC 639). Courts might be willing to accept, although thus far they have not considered it, that they are not required to find that a company had no triable defence before they can order winding up, as this kind of approach has been adopted in relation to cases involving applications to restrain the advertising of a petition: *Re a Company (No 0160 of 2004)* [2004] All ER (D) 352 (Feb) at [28].

A dispute will not be viewed as substantial if it has no rational prospect of success: *Re a Company (No 0012209 of 1991)* [1992] 1 WLR 351, [1992] BCLC 865; *Angel Group Ltd v British Gas Trading Ltd* [2012] EWHC 2702 (Ch). A dispute will not be put in good faith if the company is merely seeking to take for itself credit which it is not allowed under the contract with the alleged creditor: *Re a Company (No 0012209 of 1991)* [1992] 1 WLR 351 at 354, [1992] BCLC 865. In the course of determining whether a dispute is genuine or not the court is able to reject evidence going towards establishing this if it is inherently implausible or is contradicted by other evidence: *Smile Stylist Ltd v Harte Solutions Ltd* [2017] EWHC 2971 (Ch) at [19].

A company might succeed on the basis of a dispute where the petitioner is an assignee of a debt and no notice of the assignment had been given to the company by the date of the presentation of the petition: *Re a Company (No 003624 of 2002)* [2002] All ER (D) 274. The relevant test is whether any notice relied upon is brought to the company's notice with reasonable certainty: *Denny, Gasquet and Metcalfe v Conklin* [1913] 3 KB 177 at 180; *Mitchell McFarlane & Partners Ltd v Foremans Ltd* [2002] EWHC 3203 (Ch) (ChD, Mr N Strauss, 18 December 2002).

While there has been a long line of cases in which insolvency courts have declined to go behind a tax assessment and have treated them as correct (*Vieira v The Commissioners for HMRC* [2017] EWHC 936 (Ch), [2017] BPIR 1062), there has been uncertainty over whether tax assessments can form the basis of a petition or are a disputed debt, where the First-tier Tribunal Tax Chamber has granted an extension to a company to appeal an assessment. The matter now seems to have been resolved by the decision of the Court of Appeal in *Re Enta Technologies Ltd sub nom Revenue and Customs Commissioners v Changtel Solutions UK Ltd* [2015] EWCA Civ 29, [2015] BPIR 327, [2015] 2 BCLC 586. The court held that the decision of the First-tier Tribunal Tax Chamber that a company should be granted an extension to permit it to appeal as the company's case was not hopeless was to be taken into account and was an important factor for the court hearing the winding-up petition to consider. But the court retained a discretion on the petition and the view of the Chamber was not determinative concerning whether there was a substantial dispute. The court should not defer to the Chamber. The issue that had to be decided by the court on hearing a petition that was based on an unpaid tax assessment was not the same as that which the tax tribunal had to address, and so in presenting a petition it could not be said necessarily to be an indirect means by which HMRC could succeed on the appeal. In this case the court said that the evidence before the winding-up court was not sufficient for the court to decide that the petition debt was disputed on substantial grounds. The court ordered a winding up.

Sometimes where the dispute can be resolved without a great deal of time and the taking of evidence, the court has indicated that it might determine the dispute on the hearing of the petition: *Re King's Cross Industrial Dwellings Co* (1870) 11 Eq 149; *Re Welsh Brick Industries Ltd* [1946] 2 All ER 197; *Brinds Ltd v Offshore Oil NL* (1986) 2 BCC 98, 916, PC.

Set-off or cross-claim—The company might argue that the debt relied on in the petition is not owed because it has a set-off or cross-claim which equals or exceeds the amount of the petitioner's debt, and which could be pleaded in response to a claim for that debt if the petitioner were to bring proceedings to recover it. If, when a cross-claim is taken into account, there is a significant amount owed to the petitioner, the petition will be allowed to proceed: *Alexander Sheridan Ltd v Beaujersey Ltd* [2004] EWHC 2072 (Ch) at [59]. While neither a set-off nor a cross-claim is a complete answer to a petition (*Re Douglas Griggs Engineering Ltd* [1963] 1 Ch 19; *Re FSA Business Software Ltd* [1990] BCLC 825; *Re Leasing and Finance Services Ltd* [1991] BCC 29), where it can be shown that the alleged set-off or cross-claim is genuine and based on a substantial ground, the court can refuse to make a winding-up order in the exercise of its discretion: *Re LHF Wools Ltd* [1970] Ch 27, [1969] 3 All ER 882, CA; *Re Bayoil SA* [1999] 1 BCLC 62, CA; *MCI WorldCom Ltd v Primus Telecommunications Ltd* [2002] EWHC 2436 (Ch), [2003] 1 BCLC 330; *Re a Company (No 008654 of 2017)* [2018] EWHC 1143 (Ch). It is necessary for a company, in addition to establishing the fact that the cross-claim is genuine and serious, to show that the cross-claim was one which the company had been unable to litigate and it is greater than the claim of the petitioning creditor: *Re Bayoil SA* [1999] 1 BCLC 62, CA; *Ashworth v Newnote Ltd* [2007] EWCA Civ 793, [2007] BPIR 1012 at [35]. In the latter case the Court of Appeal added that the cross-claim, in order to resist the petition, might raise a genuine triable issue and this means the same as a real prospect of success on the claim (at [33]–[35]). Where the company delays in taking action in relation to an alleged cross-claim, it must demonstrate a good reason for the delay (*Re Bayoil SA*), although more recently it has been held that a company is not precluded from relying on a cross-claim because it could reasonably have litigated the cross-claim before the petition was presented: *Montgomery v Wanda Modes Ltd* [2002] 1 BCLC 289; *Denis Rye Ltd v Bolsover District Council* [2009] EWCA Civ 372, [2009] BPIR 778; *Wilson and Sharp Investments Ltd v Harbourview Developments Ltd* [2015] EWCA Civ 1030. It has been said that there was no absolute requirement that a debtor had to demonstrate that he or she had been unable to litigate the cross-claim, and where there had been delay in the prosecution of a cross-claim, that delay could not be such as to throw real doubt on the genuineness of the cross-claim: *Popely v Popely* [2004] EWCA Civ 463, [2004] BPIR 778, *Hayes v Hayes* [2014] EWHC 2694 (Ch), [2014] BPIR 1212. But in deciding whether a cross-claim is genuine and serious the fact that the company had not sought to litigate the cross-claim or that there were reasons it had not done so might persuade a court that the cross-claim was not sufficiently serious or genuine (*Denis Rye Ltd v Bolsover District Council* [2009] EWCA (Civ) 372, [2009] BPIR 778; *Barker v Baxendale-Walker* [2018] EWHC 1681 (Ch), [2018] BPIR 1243 at [35]). In bankruptcy it has been said that any delay in alleging a cross-claim might lead to the inference that the allegation is not made in good faith, but to stave off bankruptcy: *Re a Debtor (No 554/SD/98)* [2000] 1 BCLC 103, CA. Certainly courts might be averse to restraining a petition where a cross-claim is asserted late in the day and where it might be seen as a ploy to stave off liquidation: *Southern Cross Group plc v Deka Immobilien Investment* [2005] BPIR 1010.

A court has to take account of the fact that a cross-claim was not raised prior to the commencement of the winding-up proceedings, with the consequence that the company's evidence has to be approached with considerable caution: *Rightmatch Ltd v Meisels* [2014] BPIR 733.

While a court has a discretion as to whether to order winding up where there is a genuine and serious cross-claim, if a court has determined that a genuine and serious cross-claim exists, then it has been held that ordinarily the court should strike out the petition. It is only if special circumstances exist that a court has a real discretion and may wind up the company: *Re Bayoil SA* [1999] 1 BCLC 62 at 70. In *Morrside Investments Ltd v DAG Construction Ltd* (unreported, 1 November 2007, ChD, Warren J) Dismissal of a petition where there is a genuine and substantial dispute is not a rule of law, but a practice that applies save where exceptional circumstances exist. For an example of a case where there were special circumstances, and a court refused to dismiss a petition, see *Atlantic & General Information Investment Trust Ltd v Richbell Information Services Inc* [2000] 2 BCLC 778.

Where the claim in the petition is substantiated, but the company has a cross-claim pending in another court, the court hearing the petition has a discretion whether or not to order winding up: *Re FSA Business Software Ltd* [1990] BCLC 825. It has been held that where a disputed cross-claim exists, yet the company is unable to dispute that some money is owed by it to the petitioner, a court may make a winding-up order. In such a case the company's claim must be equal to or exceed the creditor's claim for it to escape a winding-up order: *Re Pendigo Ltd* [1996] 2 BCLC 64; *Re Bayoil SA* [1999] 1 BCLC 62, CA.

It should be noted that in Scotland it has been indicated that where a company that is the subject of a petition presented by a creditor has claims against the petitioner, an order might still be made if there are other major creditors that have not been paid: *Innes, petitioner* (P158/04 (OH), Lady Paton, 16 March 2004). The court said that while a creditor must demonstrate some debt owed to him or her, the terms of s 122(1)(f) and s 123(1)(e) permit a court to take a general and overall view of the company's financial position, 'rather than a view restricted to the company's standing and relationship with one creditor' (at [18]). This appears to accord with the view expressed in Australia in several cases: eg *National Mutual Life Association of Australasia Ltd v Oasis Developments Pty Ltd* (1983) 1 ACLC 1263.

While a set-off must exist between the creditor and the debtor in the same right, this is not the case with a cross-claim: *Hurst v Bennett* [2001] 2 BCLC 290, CA at [52] per Peter Gibson LJ. A cross-claim, unlike a set-off, would not need to have any procedural or juridical relationship to the debt claimed in the petition, but is a claim by the company against the creditor: *Popely v Popely* [2004] EWCA Civ 463 at [113].

Any cross-claim relied upon by the company must be against the petitioner, and not against a subsidiary company of the petitioner: *Tottenham Hotspur plc v Edennote plc* [1995] 1 BCLC 65.

**Judgment obtained in relation to petition debt**—Where the petition is based on an unpaid judgment debt or costs, a petition may succeed even if the company has lodged an appeal (*Re Amalgamated Properties of Rhodesia Ltd* [1917] 2 Ch 115; also, see *El Ajou v Dollar Land (Manhattan) Ltd* [2005] EWHC 2861 (Ch)) against the judgment or award. The company should seek both a stay of execution of the judgment pending determination of the appeal and an adjournment of the winding-up petition. In the opposite situation, where the petition is based on a judgment debt, and the judgment has since been overturned, the petition will be struck out notwithstanding the fact that the petitioner has appealed: *Re Anglo-Bavarian Steel Ball Co* [1899] WN 80.

If the company submits that a judgment which has produced the debt upon which the petition is based was obtained by fraud or collusion, the petition will be ordered to stand over (*Bowes v Hope Life Insurance Society* (1865) 11 HLC 389; 11 ER 1383) until the company establishes, by means of evidence (*Re Universal Stock Exchange Co* [1884] WN 251), or in proceedings taken to challenge the judgment (*Bowes v Hope Life Insurance Society*), that the judgment was obtained improperly.

In only exceptional circumstances will a court go behind a judgment: *Dawodu v American Express Bank* [2001] BPIR 983 at 990. The courts have a discretion to go behind the judgment relied on by the creditor where there is a possibility of fraud, collusion or miscarriage of justice so as to ensure that injustice is not done (*Ex parte Kibble* (1875) LR 10 Ch App 373 at 378, CA; *Eberhardt v Mair* [1995] 1 WLR 1180 at 1186; *Re Menastar Finance Ltd* [2003] 1 BCLC 338; *Denis Rye Ltd v Bolsover District Council* [2009] EWCA (Civ) 372, [2009] BPIR 778, *Dawodu v American Express Bank*; *Yang v Official Receiver* [2017] EWCA Civ 1465, [2018] Ch 178 at [55]), and the court is not limited to the evidence that was presented at the original hearing of the petitioner's claim: *Re Treka Mines Ltd* [1960] 1 WLR 1273; *Re Menastar Finance Ltd*. In the High Court of Australia, after a lengthy consideration of the case law, it was said that while it would be rare, a court could go behind a judgment absent fraud, collusion or miscarriage of justice: *Ramsay Health Care Australia Pty Ltd v Compton* [2017] HCA 28, [2017] BPIR 1638. The same principles apply to liability orders made by a court in relation to unpaid council rates (*Harper v London Borough of Camden Council* [2020] EWHC 1001).

**Costs**—If a petition succeeds then costs will usually be awarded to the petitioner and to be paid out of the funds of the company. Occasionally a court might actually award costs against a non-party. This will usually be the directors of the company where the petitioner succeeds. To be liable a non-party must have been guilty of some bad faith or impropriety: *Metalloy Supplies Ltd v MA (UK) Ltd* [1997] 1 WLR 1613. A director of a company that was wound up was held liable for costs in *Gatnom Capital v Sanders and Others* [2011] EWHC 3716 (Ch) at [9]–[15], because he was the only director, he was the guiding force behind the company's conduct in the proceedings, which was improper, he funded the defence to the winding-up proceedings, he acted improperly, and at all relevant times the company was insolvent.

If a petition is dismissed on the basis that there is a substantial dispute on genuine grounds, a court is likely to award indemnity costs against the petitioner: *Re a Company (No 0012209 of 1991)* [1992] 1 WLR 351, [1992] BCLC 865; *Re a Company (No 2507 of 2003)* [2003] 2 BCLC 346; see also *TJ Ross (Joiners) Ltd v High Range Developments Ltd* 2000 SCLR 161, save in exceptional circumstances: *Re Sykes & Sons Ltd* [2012] EWHC 1005 (Ch). In ascertaining whether there are exceptional circumstances to disregard the general rule, courts are entitled to take into account the parties' communications prior to the presentation of the petition: *Re Sykes & Sons Ltd* [2012] EWHC 1005 (Ch). In this case the petition was dismissed but the petitioner was only held liable for costs on a standard basis as it had given the company every reasonable opportunity to explain the basis of its dispute and the company had not done so in any meaningful way and so this warranted departing from the general rule on costs. Where the petitioner has given the debtor company significant notice of the petitioner's intention to advertise the petition, giving the company time in which to give notice of its intention to apply for an injunction to prevent advertising, the petitioner might be ordered only to pay the company's costs on the standard basis: *Re Realstar Ltd* [2007] EWHC 2921 (Ch), [2008] BPIR 1391.

If a petition is dismissed by consent after the company has satisfied the debt owed to the petitioner after the presentation of a petition, it is normal for the court to order that the company pay the costs provided that notice of the petition has been given (*Re Ryan Developments Ltd* [2002] EWHC 1121 (Ch), [2002] 2 BCLC 792; *Reliance Wholesale Ltd v AM2PM Feltham Ltd* [2019] EWHC 1079 (Ch)). If the company wishes to oppose such an order it must place before the court material that will convince a court that it should displace the normal order for costs (*Reliance Wholesale Ltd v AM2PM Feltham Ltd* [2019] EWHC 1079 (Ch) at [22]). The material does not have to be formal evidence and the court may adopt a pragmatic approach to the acceptability of the material put before the court, but it is not sufficient for the company to rely on disputed averments or submissions, unsupported evidence, formal or otherwise (*Reliance Wholesale Ltd v AM2PM Feltham Ltd* [2019] EWHC 1079 (Ch) at [22]).

If a winding-up order is made and defects are found in the petition an application for permission to amend the errors is to be made to the member of court staff in charge of the winding up list in the Royal Courts of Justice or to a District Judge sitting in a District Registry or District Judge (*Practice Direction – Insolvency Proceedings* (July 2020) [2020] BPIR 1211, para 9.9.1).

The company may take proceedings against the petitioner for damages for malicious prosecution: *Quartz Hill Gold Mining v Eyre* (1883) 11 QBD 674; *Partizan Ltd v OJ Kenny & Co Ltd* [1998] 1 BCLC 157. Malice could involve improper motive in the presenting of a petition as well as ill-will or spite. Reliance on legal advice by a petitioner makes it almost impossible to establish malice: *Jacob v Vockrodt* [2007] EWHC 2403 (QB), [2007] BPIR 1568.

See Keay 'Claims for Malicious Presentation: The Peril Lurking on the Sidelines for Petitioning Creditors' [2001] *Insolvency Lawyer* 136.

See Galatopoulos 'Cross-Claims, Winding up and Judicial Discretion: An Overview' [1999] *Insolvency Lawyer* 240; Keay 'Disputing Debts Relied On By Petitioning Creditors Seeking Winding-up orders' (2001) 22 *Company Lawyer* 40; Lee 'The Court's Jurisdiction to Restrain a Creditor from Presenting a Winding Up Petition Where a Cross-Claim Exists' (2010) 69 CLJ 113 for more detailed discussions of the whole issue of disputing a petition debt.

**Abuse of process**—The court has an inherent power to prevent abuse of its process, and may, in its discretion, grant an injunction to restrain the presentation, and advertisement, of a petition (*Stonegate Securities Ltd v Gregory* [1980] 1 All ER 241) or dismiss it with costs (*Re Doreen Boards Ltd* [1996] 1 BCLC 501) in circumstances other than where the debt founding the petition is disputed. These are: if the proceedings are bound to fail because the petitioner will not be able to establish that he or she is a creditor and, therefore, obtain the necessary standing to petition, or an inability to prove that the company is unable to pay its debts (*Pacific Communications Rentals Pty Ltd v Walker* (1994) 12 ACSR 287 at 288–289; (1994) 12 ACLC 5 at 6); the petition is presented to achieve some improper purpose: *Re a Company (No 004601 of 1997)* [1998] 2 BCLC 111. It is an improper use of the winding-up process if the aim is to put improper pressure on the company to settle liabilities that were not those on which the petition was based: *Re a Company (No 004601 of 1997)* [1998] 2 BCLC 111.

In *Re Maud* ([2015] EWHC 1626 (Ch)), a bankruptcy case, Rose J said that an abuse of process could exist in two cases where the petition debt was undisputed. First, where the petitioner does not really want to obtain the liquidation of the company at all, but issues or threatens to issue the proceedings to put pressure on the target to take some other action. Secondly 'where the petitioner does want to achieve the relief sought but he is not acting in the interests of the class of creditors of which he is one or where the success of his petition will operate to the disadvantage of the body of creditors' (at [29]). Subsequently, in *Aabar Block Sarl v Maud* ([2018] EWHC 1414 (Ch), [2019] Ch 15, [2018] BPIR 1207) Snowden J accepted that a bankruptcy petition will not be an abuse of process if, in addition to wishing to receive a dividend on his or her debt in the bankruptcy together with other creditors, the petitioner has a collateral purpose which is not shared with the other creditors, but which will not cause them any detriment if achieved (at [82]). In an earlier judgment, Snowden J said that if a creditor has a collateral purpose which would operate to the detriment of the class of creditors, the creditor/petitioner cannot save the petition by asserting that he would still wish to receive a dividend upon his debt in the bankruptcy, because the effect of the petitioner achieving his collateral purpose would be to reduce that dividend for all creditors (*Maud v Aabar Block Sarl* [2016] EWHC 2175 (Ch), [2016] BPIR 1486 at [94]). The judge said in the 2018 judgment that it might be an abuse if the petitioner was pursuing the petition not to recover the petition debt at all, but solely for an extraneous purpose, even though that did not harm the interests of creditors (*Aabar Block Sarl v Maud* [2018] EWHC 1414 (Ch), [2019] Ch 15, [2018] BPIR 1207 at [84]).

For a discussion of this matter, see the Privy Council's decision in *Ebbvale Ltd v Hosking* [2013] UKPC 1, [2013] 2 BCLC 204, [2013] BPIR 219. In that case The Judicial Committee said that a court will not refuse a winding-up order if the petitioner might have, as one purpose in presenting a petition, an ulterior purpose if one of the purposes of presentation was legitimate; in fact the bringing of winding-up proceedings does not have to be the principal object of the petitioner provided that an order would be of substantial advantage to him in his capacity as the petitioning creditor (at [33]).

The courts will ordinarily dismiss a petition as an abuse of process where the petitioner has intentionally flouted the procedural rules relating to the winding-up proceedings: *Re Free of Ties Leases Ltd* [2015] EWHC 3974 (Ch).

**Creditor opposition to the petition**—The other creditors of the company that is the subject of a petition may, on occasions, oppose the making of a winding-up order sought by the petitioning creditor. The right to have an order belongs to the creditors as a class, rather than being a right just belonging to the petitioner, so all creditors are entitled to be consulted on the desirability of such a course: *Re Crigglestone Coal Co* [1906] 2 Ch 327 at 332.

Creditors would be entitled to raise the fact that the petitioner had a collateral purpose in presenting the petition and they could have the matter revisited in light of recent evidence (*Aabar Block Sarl v Maud* [2018] EWHC 1414 (Ch), [2019] Ch 15, [2018] BPIR 1207). In determining whether or not to give effect to the class remedy it is not a matter that is limited to a question of simple mathematics (how much debt is represented by creditors for and against winding up) as the court will consider the reasons put forward by the creditors whether for or against liquidation in order to assess whether the reasons are commercially rational. The court will also take into account other evidence 'to assess whether the weight and rationality of a particular creditor's approach is diminished by any extraneous factors such as personal antipathy or affection on the part of the creditor for the debtor (or those connected with it in the case of a company)'. (*Re Maud* [2020] EWHC 674 (Ch) at [78]). Snowden J rejected an argument that the authorities support a proposition that it is for a judge to formulate some view of a hypothetical rational creditor who is a member of the class, or to impose his or her own view of the commercial merits or the best interests of the class (at [79]). See the discussion under 'Abuse of process' above.

The courts will be more concerned with the opposition of unsecured as opposed to secured creditor opposition: *Re Crigglestone Coal Co; Re Demaglass Holdings Ltd* [2001] 2 BCLC 633. The court is empowered by s 195(1) to have regard to the wishes of the creditors, as proved to it by any sufficient evidence.

It is incumbent on the court to balance the right of an unpaid creditor to a winding-up order in relation to an insolvent company, as against the fact that the majority in value of creditors may wish the company to continue: *Re Demaglass Holdings Ltd* [2001] 2 BCLC 633. The court may, in exercising its discretion, decide to refrain from making an order because of the attitude of the majority of creditors in number and value, and the fact that the creditors can demonstrate good reasons for their opposition to the order: *Re P & J Macrae Ltd* [1961] 1 WLR 229; *Re JD Swain Ltd* [1965] 1 WLR 909 at 914–915, CA; *Re Demaglass Holdings Ltd* [2001] 2 BCLC 633. But even then, the court might overlook the opposition if the petitioner can demonstrate the fact that special circumstances exist warranting the making of an order: *Re P & J Macrae Ltd; Re ABC Coupler & Engineering Co* [1961] 1 WLR 243, CA. The court will also take into account whether the petitioning creditor is seeking to gain an unfair advantage vis à vis the other creditors: *Re Leigh Estates (UK) Ltd* [1994] BCC 292.

It must be noted that the court will take cognisance of the nature of the creditors who oppose the order, as well as the quality of their debts: *Re P & J Macrae Ltd*. The court will not disregard totally the views of creditors with vested interests in the company, such as the directors of the company and creditors who are associated with the company (*Re Medisco Equipment Ltd* [1983] BCLC 305), but they will carry far less weight at the point where a court looks at which view has the majority support (*Re HJ Tompkins Ltd* [1990] BCLC 76; *Re Demaglass Holdings Ltd* [2001] 2 BCLC 633), and they may well be discounted: *Re Lummus Agricultural Services Ltd* [2001] 1 BCLC 137.

Where creditors oppose the winding up, but a court decides to make a winding-up order, the creditors may be granted their costs out of the company's assets if their views were entitled to be put forward in the circumstances: *Re William Thorpe & Son Ltd* (1988) 5 BCC 156.

If there are creditors as joint petitioners and they disagree as to what should be the outcome of the petition then the court is unable to make an order sought by one or the other unless it can be shown that one is acting in breach of trust (*Aabar Block Sarl v Maud* [2018] EWHC 1414 (Ch), [2019] Ch 15, [2018] BPIR 1207 at [114]–[115]). In *Re Maud* ([2020] EWHC 1469 (Ch) at [66]) Snowden J said that where there is opposition to a winding-up order from other creditors, it would be illogical for the court to take heed of the voice of the debtor who is not involved in that contest.

For a discussion both of what might constitute good reasons for opposing the petition and what might constitute special circumstances in favour of the petitioner where a majority is against an order, see A Keay *McPherson and Keay's Law of Company Liquidation* (Sweet and Maxwell, 4th edn, 2018) at 178–181.

**Adjourn**—The general practice, in the past, has been, where the debt relied on in the petition is disputed at the winding-up hearing, to dismiss the petition (*Re Martin Wallis & Co* (1893) 37 Sol Jo 822; *Re Meaford Manufacturing Co* (1919) 46 OLR 252), but the court has on a few occasions exercised the power to adjourn in order to allow the petitioner to bring an action to establish the debt relied on (*Re Catholic Publishing Co* (1864) 33 LJ Ch 325; *Brinds Ltd v Offshore Oil NL* (1986) 2 BCC 98, 916, PC), or to enable the company to take proceedings to have a judgment set aside for fraud: *Bowes v Hope Life Insurance Society Ltd* (1865) 11 HLC 389, (1865) 11 ER 1383.

Where the majority of creditors oppose the making of a winding-up order, the court will grant an adjournment ordinarily if there is a good reason to do so, such as being able to sell company stock in trade for a higher price while the company was trading compared with if it was in liquidation: *Re Demaglass Holdings Ltd* [2001] 2 BCLC 633. The Supreme Court of Bermuda has granted an adjournment to permit a possible restructuring of the company where there is some evidence that a majority of unsecured creditors favoured such a course of action: *Re Up Energy Development Group Ltd* [2017] SC (Bda) 85 Com.

The court may well grant an adjournment if the application is not in order, for instance giving notice of the petition has not occurred. It is the practice of the High Court to grant only one adjournment to permit the application to be put in order. More than one adjournment will not usually be able to be secured merely because the petitioner is negotiating with the company. Nevertheless, if the application is in order the court will listen to an application for an adjournment to permit negotiating to take place (or for payment to be arranged) (Chief Registrar Baister 'The hearing of the petition' (2008) CRI 115 at 115).

Courts have tended to be against the granting of adjournments, either for long or indefinite periods, or on a repeated basis (*Re Boston Timber Fabrications Ltd* [1984] BCLC 328 at 333, CA), whether the application for adjournment has or has not been opposed. The courts will not be willing to order adjournments one after another even if the parties all agree: *Re a Company (No 001573 of 1983)* [1983] BCLC 492; *Re Pleatfine Ltd* [1983] BCLC 102. But short adjournments are often granted so as to permit the petition to be re-advertised, to enable further witness statements to be filed, to enable the ascertainment of the creditors' wishes concerning the petition (under s 195), to provide a chance for creditors to obtain advice, or to give an opportunity for a compromise to be reached, settling a scheme of arrangement or proposing a company voluntary arrangement: *Re Piccadilly Property Management Ltd* [1999] 2 BCLC 145. Having said all of that, courts will also stand over petitions where there are sufficiently exceptional circumstances (*MHMH Ltd v Carwood Barker Holdings Ltd* [2004] EWHC 3174 (Ch); *CFL Finance Ltd v Bass* [2019] EWHC 1839 (Ch), [2019] BPIR 1327). There is Australian authority to the effect that the principles that are to guide a court when hearing an application for an adjournment, are the same as those when exercising its discretion on whether to make a winding-up order: *Re Airfast Services Pty Ltd* (1976) 2 ACLR 1; *Re DTX Australia Ltd* (1987) 5 ACLC 343 at 350. This is evident to a degree in the judgment of Chief ICC Judge Briggs in *CFL Finance Ltd v Bass* ([2019] EWHC 1839 (Ch), [2019] BPIR 1327) which, although involving a bankruptcy petition, could be applied to winding-up petitions. In this case the judge said that in exercising discretion to adjourn a hearing the court ought to consider: '(i) the class remedy nature of insolvency (ii) if a meeting of creditors is held, whether it is likely that a majority by reference to the value of votes will pass the proposals (iii) the proposal in the context of the claims to identify if a commercial return would be provided to creditors and (iv) all the circumstances of the case'. (at [119]). The judge noted that the aforementioned list should not be regarded as exhaustive. The Court of Appeal in *Sekhon v Edginton* ([2015] EWCA Civ 816, [2015] 1 WLR 4435, [2015] BPIR 1397 at [19]) said that an adjournment will only be granted if there is credible evidence that there is a reasonable prospect that the petition debt will be paid within a reasonable time. If the company does not produce any evidence of its ability to pay it takes the risk that the court will not accept a bare assertion as to the means and ability to pay.

Courts might allow an adjournment of a petition where the company is not legally represented and the matters that surround it are complex: *Henry Butcher International Ltd v K G Engineering* [2004] EWCA Civ 1597.

**'The ground only that . . . the company has no assets'**—At one stage the courts would not make a winding-up order against a company that held no assets which could be made available for the payment of debts: *Re Chapel House Colliery Co* (1883) 24 Ch D 259. But this led to abuse and to the introduction of the relevant words in s 125(1). It must be noted that the use of the word 'only' in s 125(1) indicates that the intention of Parliament was not to prevent the court from taking into account the total absence of property as one of the factors that might lead it to refuse the order. See *Bell Group Finance Pty Ltd v Bell Group (UK) Holdings Ltd* [1996] BCLC 304 for a case where Chadwick J acknowledged that the company had no assets, but said that that was not a sufficient reason for not making a winding-up order. A liquidator might always be able to recover money and assets by invoking some provisions, such as those known as the adjustment provisions (ss 238–245), or taking legal action against directors for breach of their duties, fraudulent trading or wrongful trading.

The cases now seem to provide that the court may, but only in exceptional cases, exercise its general discretion to decline to make a winding-up order if it is satisfied that the order will serve no useful purpose because there will be no assets available in the insolvent estate for creditors (*Re Maud* [2016] EWHC 2175, [2016] BPIR 1486 at [103]; *Aabor Block Sarl v Maud* [2020] EWHC 674 (Ch) at [115]). In the former case, one dealing with bankruptcy, Snowden J said, and he affirmed this in the latter decision of *Re Maud* ([2020] EWHC 974 (Ch) at [115]), that a debtor faced a heavy burden in persuading the court not to make an order on the basis that there was an absence of assets (at [103]), and now that might well be said to be the case in liquidation as well. In *Maud* Snowden J said that it would only be in exceptional circumstances that a court would not make a bankruptcy order on the basis that the debtor has an absence of assets (at [115]).

**Restrictions on making an order on the petition of a contributory**—Section 125(2) provides that where a contributory presents a petition on the basis of s 122(1)(g) (the just and equitable ground) the court should not make an order, even if the petitioner is entitled to the relief, if it is of the opinion that some remedy other than winding up is available to contributories and they are acting unreasonably in seeking a winding-up order rather than pursuing their other remedy. This is so even if, in the absence of any other remedy, the court is of the opinion that the company should be wound up. 'Other remedy' here means other causes of action available under the general law or statute, or even an offer to purchase the members' shares: *Re a Company* [1983] 1 WLR 927, [1983] 2 All ER 854; *Re a Company* [1987] BCLC 562 at 571; *Re Cyracuse Ltd* [2001] 1 BCLC 187; *Chu v Lau* [2020] UKPC 24, [2021] 1 BCLC 1. The corollary of the foregoing is that if the other remedy is not viable then a contributory would not be acting unreasonably in seeking a winding-up order: *Alesi v Original Australian Art Co Pty Ltd* (1989) 7 ACLC 595 at 597. Judges, in taking into account whether a member has some other remedy available to him or her, will not restrict themselves only to considering remedies that result either from a member's legal rights or from the company's constitution: *Re a Company* [1983] 1 WLR 927, [1983] 2 All ER 854. Critically, anyone resisting the petition must establish two distinct elements, namely that some other remedy was available to the petitioner, *and* that the petitioner is unreasonable in seeking winding up rather than pursuing the other remedy: *Re Cyracuse Ltd* [2001] 1 BCLC 187; *Robinson v H G Robinson and Sons Ltd* [2020] EWHC 1 (Ch) at [29].

See the notes under 'Just and equitable' in relation to s 122.

**Costs**—The court has a wide jurisdiction, under s 51(1) of the Senior Courts Act 1981, in awarding costs: *Cannon Screen Entertainment Ltd v Handmade Films (Distributors) Ltd* [1989] BCLC 660; *Re Ryan Developments Ltd* [2002] EWHC 1121 (Ch), [2002] 2 BCLC 792. If a petitioner succeeds in obtaining a winding-up order, then usually the petitioner is entitled to his or her reasonable costs of and in connection with the petition: *Re Ryan Developments Ltd*. If a debt is paid after winding-up proceedings have been instituted, normally the petitioner will be seen as having succeeded and will be entitled to costs of, and in connection with, the petition (*Re Donald Fisher (Ealing) Ltd* [2001] All ER (D) 278; *Re Ryan Developments Ltd*), including the costs associated with being heard on any application by the company to stay the winding-up petition: *Re Ryan Developments Ltd*. A court is entitled to take account of the conduct of the parties both before and after proceedings have been instituted as well as during the course of proceedings: *Frank Saul (Fashions) Ltd v HMRC* (unreported, 18 May 2012, ChD, Vos J). If a court determines that a petition had been wrongly presented as the debt on which it relied was genuinely disputed on substantial grounds, the company is likely to be entitled to its costs of resisting the petition on the indemnity basis (*Sat-Elite Ltd v Strong* [2003] EWHC 2990 (Ch) at [24]), but if its conduct in the litigation became unreasonable at some point, then costs would only be awarded up to that point: *Lakehouse Contracts Ltd v UPR Services Ltd* [2014] EWHC 1223 (Ch).

Where a winding-up petition is dismissed by consent as the company has paid the alleged debt due in the petition but after the presentation of the petition, the usual practice is for the court in its discretion to order the company to pay the petitioner's costs. The petitioner is regarded as having been successful and the normal rule applies that costs follow the event. The company has the burden of providing the court with material as to why such order should not be made, although this material does not have to be formal evidence properly so described: *Re Nowmost Co Ltd* [1996] 2 BCLC 492, 496.

A court may, if it deems it appropriate, order that some person other than the company or the petitioner pay the costs personally (*Re a Company (No 006798 of 1995)* [1996] 2 BCLC 48), eg the directors of the company: *Re Brackland Magazines Ltd* [1994] 1 BCLC 190 (directors had improperly caused the company and the petitioner to incur costs in relation to a petition). But the courts will not make orders for costs as a matter of course against directors of one person companies unless they have acted improperly: *Taylor v Pace Developments Ltd* [1991] BCC 406, CA.

**Winding-up order**—If the court decides to make the order it will, after doing so, make a declaration concerning the applicability of the EU Regulation on Insolvency Proceedings and whether the proceedings were main, territorial or secondary. The decision it makes in this regard could have effects on other litigation commenced subsequently in the EU (except for Denmark).

**Review or rescission of winding-up order**—See r 12.59 and the notes accompanying it.

[1.179]

### 126 Power to stay or restrain proceedings against company

(1)  At any time after the presentation of a winding-up petition, and before a winding-up order has been made, the company, or any creditor or contributory, may—

(a)  where any action or proceeding against the company is pending in the High Court or Court of Appeal in England and Wales or Northern Ireland, apply to the court in which the action or proceeding is pending for a stay of proceedings therein, and

(b)  where any other action or proceeding is pending against the company, apply to the court having jurisdiction to wind up the company to restrain further proceedings in the action or proceeding;

and the court to which application is so made may (as the case may be) stay, sist or restrain the proceedings accordingly on such terms as it thinks fit.

(2)  In the case of a company registered but not formed under the Companies Act 2006, where the application to stay, sist or restrain is by a creditor, this section extends to actions and proceedings against any contributory of the company.

(3)  Subsection (1) applies in relation to any action being taken in respect of the company under Part 1 of Schedule 8 to the Finance (No 2) Act 2015 (enforcement by deduction from accounts) as it applies in relation to any action or proceeding mentioned in paragraph (b) of that subsection.

**Amendments**—SI 2009/1941; Finance (No 2) Act 2015, s 51, Sch 8, Pt 2, paras 26, 27.

**General note**—Probably, the aims of this provision are, as with the analogous provision in s 130(2), to prevent a company (which is possibly going to enter liquidation) from having its assets wasted in litigation, and to make sure that there is a distribution of company assets according to the statutory scheme, should liquidation eventuate: *Bowkett v Fuller United Electic Works Ltd* [1923] 1 KB 160.

The applicable principles identified by courts under s 130 are closely analogous to those applying under s 126: *Re Aro Ltd* [1980] Ch 196.

It has been decided that the power in s 126 did not confer jurisdiction on an insolvency court to stay proceedings before another court: *Re Paperback Collection and Recycling Ltd* [2019] EWHC 2904 (Ch) at [22]. In any event staying proceedings might not always be appropriate because of public interest grounds favouring the continuation of the proceedings: *Re Paperback Collection and Recycling Ltd* (at [34]).

## [1.180]

### 127 Avoidance of property dispositions, etc

(1)  In a winding up by the court, any disposition of the company's property, and any transfer of shares, or alteration in the status of the company's members, made after the commencement of the winding up is, unless the court otherwise orders, void.

(2)  This section has no effect in respect of anything done by an administrator of a company while a winding-up petition is suspended under paragraph 40 of Schedule B1.

(3)  This section has no effect in respect of anything done during a moratorium under Part A1, or during a period mentioned in section 5(4)(a) following the end of a moratorium, where the winding-up order was made on a petition presented before the moratorium begins, unless the petition was presented under section 367 of the Financial Services and Markets Act 2000 on the ground mentioned in section 367(3)(b) of that Act.

**Amendments**—Enterprise Act 2002, s 248(3), Sch 17, paras 9, 15; Corporate Insolvency and Governance Act 2020, s 2(1), Sch 3, paras 1, 12.

**General note**—Following presentation of a winding-up petition, the rendering void of any disposition of a company's property (and those other matters relating to share transfers and the alteration of the company' membership) is triggered on the making of a winding-up order against the company. This effect may be stopped by a court order validating dispositions. The scope of the provision in rendering dispositions void involves a 'relation back' to the commencement of the winding up (being the presentation of the petition or any earlier resolution to wind up the company) as defined in s 129. It has been said that the purpose of the 'relation back' is in seeking to preserve the pari passu principle of distribution in the period in which a winding-up petition is pending: *Re Wiltshire Iron Co* (1868) 3 Ch App 443 at 447. A similar statement by Lightman J in *Coutts & Co v Stock* [2000] 1 WLR 906, [2000] 2 All ER 56, [2000] 1 BCLC 183 at 186 ('part of the statutory scheme') was approved by the Court of Appeal in *Hollicourt (Contracts) Ltd v Bank of Ireland Ltd* [2001] 2 WLR 290 at 296. The provision as cast, however, is far broader in scope than is necessary for achieving this purpose alone and will render void all post-petition dispositions, including not only dispositions which are harmful to the company but also those involved in bona fide transactions, transactions entered into in the ordinary course of the company's business, payments into and out of the company's bank account and transactions which operate significantly to the benefit of the company through an increase in its net assets. So as to avoid the prejudicial consequences of s 127, it is imperative that a contrary order of the type mentioned in the provision, commonly termed a validating order, is obtained. Dispositions of property to a company against which a winding-up petition has been presented are not caught by s 127. In the Court of Appeal decision in *Electrical Distributors Ltd v Beavis* [2016] EWCA Civ 765, [2016] 1 WLR 4783, [2016] BPIR 1386, Sales LJ (with whom the other judges agreed) said that the policy of pari passu was central to s 127. In *Officeserve Technologies Ltd v Anthony-Mike* [2017] EWHC 1920 (Ch), [2017] BPIR 1291 at [62], [90] HHJ Matthews said that the mischief against which the provision was aimed was the destruction or reduction in value of the property right belonging to the company leading to an immediate and equivalent accrual in value to another person. The judge later said that the section 'is not, and is not intended to be, a prescription for the behaviour of company directors in future. Instead it is intended to, and does, help resolve problems of the past, each on the particular facts of their case' (at [110]).

The provision does not in itself provide the liquidator with any cause of action against the directors of the company which has made the disposition: *Phillips v McGregor-Paterson* [2009] EWHC 2385 (Ch), [2010] BPIR 239 at [35]. The provision simply determines whether a disposition is void or not, and it does not lay down what remedy is available to the liquidator where a disposition is avoided; the appropriate remedy is determined by the general law: *Hollicourt (Contracts) Ltd v Bank of Ireland* [2001] 2 WLR 290; *Ahmed v Ingram* [2018] EWCA Civ 519.

The right to recover under the provision is restitutionary: *Hollicourt (Contracts) Ltd v Bank of Ireland* [2001] 2 WLR 290; *Ahmed v Ingram* [2018] EWCA Civ 519, [2018] BPIR 535 at [33]. Anyone in receipt of payments from the funds of an insolvent holds them for the insolvent's estate: *Re D'Eye* [2016] BPIR 883 (a case dealing with the bankruptcy equivalent, s 284). Any claim will be for money had and received: *Officeserve Technologies Ltd v Annabel's (Berkeley Square) Ltd* [2018] EWHC 2168 (Ch), [2019] Ch 103, [2018] 3 WLR 1568, [2018] BPIR 1743.

It has been held in the Australian case of *Re Skypac Aviation Pty Ltd* [2019] NSWSC 291 that a disposition that is made on the date of the commencement of winding up will not be void.

Section 127 is expressly disapplied in the case of certain financial market transactions prescribed in Companies Act 1989, ss 164(3), 173(3)–(5). Similar exemptions applicable to financial and security settlements and associated security arrangements are provided for in the Financial Markets and Insolvency (Settlement Finality) Regulations 1999 (SI 1999/2979).

As a consequence of the enactment of the Corporate Insolvency and Governance Act 2020 (Sch 10, paras 8, 9 and 21) and its subsequent amendment by the Corporate Insolvency and Governance Act 2020 (Coronavirus) (Extension of the Relevant Period) Regulations 2020 (SI 2020/1031), reg 2(3), the Corporate Insolvency and Governance Act 2020 (Coronavirus) (Extension of the Relevant Period) (No 2) Regulations 2020 (SI 2020/1483), reg 2, The Corporate Insolvency and Governance Act 2020 (Coronavirus) (Extension of the Relevant Period) Regulations 2021 (SI 2021/375), reg 3(4) and The Corporate Insolvency and Governance Act 2020 (Coronavirus) (Extension of the Relevant Period) (No 2) Regulations 2021 (SI 2021/718), reg 2, if a winding-up order was made as a result of a petition presented under s 124 during the period of 27 April 2020 to 30 September 2021 on the basis that the company was unable to pay its debts, then the commencement of winding up is not, as provided for in s 129(2), the date of the presentation of the petition but the date of the winding-up order.

See, for a detailed discussion of s 127, A Keay, *McPherson and Keay's Law of Company Liquidation* (Sweet and Maxwell, 4th edn, 2018) at 332–364.

'**Commencement of the winding up**'—For the most part, the commencement of winding up will be the date of the presentation of the petition to wind up, but in some cases it can be earlier than that. For example, if the company passed a resolution to wind up before the presentation of the petition, then commencement will be, if a winding-up order is eventually made, the date of the resolution (s 129(1)) and, of course, this makes the period during which dispositions may be set aside longer.

'**Void**'—'Void' means void for all purposes related to or incidental to the administration of the winding up: *National Acceptance Corp Pty Ltd v Benson* (1988) 12 NSWLR 213 at 229, (1988) 6 ACLC 685 at 689, NSWCA; *Monds v Hammond and Suddards* [1996] 2 BCLC 470 at 474.

**Disposition**—The term 'disposition' is not defined in the legislation but must be attributed the widest possible meaning, given the unlimited wording employed in the provision and its underlying purpose. What is needed for s 127 to operate is a disposition amounting to an alienation of the company's property: *Mersey Steel & Iron Co Ltd v Naylor* (1884) 9 App Cas 434 at 440. The term will, therefore, include not only all forms of dealing by the company in its tangible and intangible property but also, for example, a surrender of a company's contractual rights or the taking of any other step by the company conferring value on a third party, such as the conferring of the benefit of a lien. While the term is wide (*Officeserve Technologies Ltd v Anthony-Mike* [2017] EWHC 1920

(Ch), [2017] BPIR 1291), in Australia 'disposition' has been held not to catch the abandonment by a company of an alleged claim for damages: *Re Mal Bower's Macquarie Electrical Centre Pty Ltd (in liquidation)* [1974] 1 NSWLR 254. The disposition of property in the section covers the release of contractual rights, the cancellation of a charge on property, the 'destruction, or at least the *reduction* in value, of a property right belonging to the company, causing an immediate and equivalent *accrual* in value to another person . . . ' and payments by a company to a person as part of a settlement of all obligations owed by the person to the company or owed to the person by the company: *Officeserve Technologies Ltd v Anthony-Mike* [2017] EWHC 1920 (Ch), [2017] BPIR 1291 at [90]. But it does not cover the 'mere effluxion of time of a wasting asset, such as a lease. Nor is it apt to cover deliberate consumption or waste by the company of its assets': *Officeserve Technologies Ltd v Anthony-Mike* at [98]. Also, disposition does not extend to the process by which a person with a beneficial interest in the property of a company, such as a bank with a fixed and floating charge over its assets, obtains that property, or the proceeds of the sale of that property: *Re French's Wine Bar Ltd* [1987] BCLC 499. Furthermore, the assumption of liabilities by a company is not within s 127, as it does not involve a disposition of the company's property: *Coutts & Co v Stock* [2000] 1 WLR 906, [2000] 2 All ER 56, [2000] 1 BCLC 183. A disposition which is effected by a company pursuant to a court order will nevertheless apparently fall within s 127: *Re Flint* [1993] Ch 319 (transfer of a husband's interest in matrimonial home to wife pursuant to an order under Matrimonial Causes Act 1973, s 24 and analogous to s 284(1) of the Insolvency Act, applicable in bankruptcy); reference should be made here to the observations on the judgment in *Flint* in the note with the same heading as here and under s 284 (but it must be noted that s 284 is in different terms to s 127 and so one cannot approach this section with the assumption that it is designed to achieve the same outcome as s 127, and one cannot necessarily apply a case decided under one section to the other section: *Pettit v Novakovic* [2007] BPIR 1643), *Edwards v Aurora Leasing Ltd* [2021] EWHC 96 (Ch), [2021] BPIR 259.

Post-petition payments made under what is now termed a third party debt order (formerly a garnishee order) would fall within s 127, as would the assignment of a company owned debt to another person: *Officeserve Technologies Ltd v Anthony-Mike* [2017] EWHC 906 (Ch), [2017] BPIR 1291.

Lord Neuberger in *Akers v Samba Financial Group* [2017] UKSC 6, [2017] AC 424, [2017] 1 BCLC 151, [2017] BPIR 263 said (at [65]) that 'it is fair to say that the word 'disposition' is linguistically capable of applying to a transaction which involves the destruction or termination of an interest.'. In the same case, Lord Mance (with whom the other justices agreed) said that he did not see any basis for extending, or any need to extend, s 127 to cover three-party situations where legal title is held and disposed of to a third party by a trustee, and the beneficiary's beneficial interest either survives or is overridden by virtue of the disposition of the legal title to the third party (at [56]). His Lordship went on to say that the law regulates, protects and circumscribes beneficial interests under a trust in a manner which is separate from and outside the scope of s 127 (at [56]). According to the court, if there is a transfer of the legal interest in property that was improper the beneficiary has the right to take proceedings against the trustee if he or she acted in breach of trust. If legal title to property is transferred to a bona fide purchaser for value and without notice (of the existence of the holder of the equitable interest) and not by or for the company, then s 127 cannot apply to void the transfer as there is not a disposition within the provision: *Akers v Samba Financial Group*. The court said that the section covered the case where the company's property was held by a director or an agent and the director or agent disposes of the property to some third party: *Akers v Samba Financial Group* at [53].

*Hollicourt (Contracts) Ltd v Bank of Ireland* [2001] 2 WLR 290 the Court of Appeal (Mummery LJ delivering the judgment of the court) departed from its earlier decision in *Re Gray's Inn Construction Ltd* [1980] 1 WLR 711 (Buckley LJ with whom Goff LJ and Sir David Cairns agreed) so as to hold that, whilst a payment out of a company's bank account constitutes a disposition of the company's property in favour of the creditor, such a payment does not involve a disposition in favour of the bank. On a payment out of a bank account a bank acts merely as the company's agent such that the avoidance of the disposition in favour of the creditor does not affect the validity of any intermediate, related transaction, most commonly the bank honouring the cheque tendered by the company to its customer, irrespective of whether the company's account is in credit or overdrawn: *Hollicourt* at 299–300. Approving the decision in *Coutts & Co v Stock* [2000] 1 WLR 906, [2000] 2 All ER 56, [2000] 1 BCLC 183 to similar effect, the Court of Appeal in *Hollicourt* identified not only (a) that *Re Gray's Inn* concerned payments into an overdrawn bank account but also (b) that certain observations in the judgment of Buckley LJ relied on a questionable concession by counsel for the bank to the effect that payments from the account in discharge of pre-liquidation debts amounted to dispositions of property unless, properly analysed, the payments did not amount to dispositions of property but operated to do no more than increase the company's liability on its overdraft to the bank. Despite *Hollicourt*, it might be argued, though it is thought to be doubtful, that a claim for breach of duty remains against a bank which honours payments from a company's bank account following the giving notice of a winding-up petition, in light of the statement in *Hollicourt* to the effect that the case is restricted to s 127 without discounting the possibility of alternative lines of argument.

A payment made into a bank account which is in credit has been held not to amount to a disposition within s 127: *Re Barn Crown Ltd* [1994] 4 All ER 42. The analysis in that case (at 45) to the effect that payment on the collected cheque involves nothing more than an adjustment in favour of the company on the statement of account between the company and its bank misses the fact of the transfer of funds from the company to its bank (ie the funds collected by the bank on the cheque) in consideration for the bank's promise of repayment in accordance with the terms of the account: see also *Gray's Inn* at 818. A payment made into a bank account which is in overdraft amounts to a disposition of the company's property by way of the transfer of funds collected by the bank on the cheque in reduction of the company's indebtedness to the bank.

A disposition by X of Y Ltd's property, held by X on behalf of Y Ltd, may be set aside under s 127 even though the disposition of the property is not directly made by Y Ltd: *Re J Leslie Engineers Co Ltd (in liquidation)* [1976] 2 All ER 85 at 89, *Akers v Samba Financial Group* [2017] UKSC 6, [2017] AC 424, [2017] 1 BCLC 151, [2017] BPIR 263 at [53]. If the petitioner is paid out by the company, and another creditor successfully applies to be substituted as the petitioner, and that new petitioner obtains a winding-up order, the original petitioner will have to repay the sum received less his or her reasonable costs in bringing the petition: *Re Bostels Ltd* [1968] Ch 346; *Re Western Welsh International System Buildings Ltd* (1985) 1 BCC 99, 296.

The South Australian Supreme Court has held that a payment into court is not a disposition, despite the fact that the company does not retain any legal interest in the money. A disposition will only exist where the company has a beneficial interest in the money at the time of payment out: *Pilmer v HIH Casualty Insurance Ltd* (2004) 90 SASR 465.

'The company's property'—The term means property that is legally or beneficially owned by the company. The term will not catch property which is taken out of the ownership of the company under the security of a third party; accordingly the court's validation will not be required for the enforcement of fixed or floating security or the realisation of assets by a mortgagee, whether as mortgagee-in-possession or through the appointment of a receiver (*Sowman v David Samuel Trust Ltd* [1978] 1 WLR 22; also see, *Stanley & Watson v A Debtor* (unreported, Ch D, 2019, Deputy ICC Judge Middleton) which dealt with s 284); neither will s 127 catch the vesting of property under an after-acquired property provision within contractual security. To similar effect, in *Re French's Wine Bar Ltd* [1987] BCLC 499 it was held that s 127 did not prevent completion of an unconditional contract for the sale of leasehold property, since the property had passed in equity on exchange of contracts prior to the presentation of the winding-up petition.

Where a petitioning creditor's debt is to be discharged from company funds, it will be necessary to obtain a validating order in respect of the disposition to avoid subsequent recovery by a liquidator if a supporting creditor is to be substituted on discharge of the debt: *Re Liverpool Civil Service Association* (1874) 9 Ch App 511.

Transfer of shares—The section does not affect the parties to the transfer as far as their liability to each other; the transfer is void 'so far as regards any effect to be given to it by or against the company': *In Re Onward v Building Society* (1891) 2 QB 463 at 475 per Lord Esher (our emphasis). Whether or not a transfer will be approved is dependent on whether it would be 'beneficial to the company' (*Onward Building Society* per Bowen LJ at 480) and would it benefit the creditors (*Onward Building Society* per Kay LJ at 481–482). The considerations that are relevant to whether a disposition of property ought to be approved are quite different from those that apply to a transfer of shares, and this is especially the case where the shares are fully paid up and so no calls can be made on them: *Carringbush Corporation Pty Ltd v ASIC* [2008] FCA 474 at [29].

It has been held by the Singaporean Court of Appeal in *Seah Teong Kang v Seah Yong Chwan* [2015] SGCA 48 that the equivalent of s 127 does not make void a transfer of the beneficial title to shares; this is not something that requires court validation.

In relation to the bankruptcy equivalent of s 127, s 284, *Re Hood* ([2020] EWHC 3232 (Ch)) held that a payment by a third party to the petitioning creditor of a debtor that purported to discharge the petition debt of the indebted company so as to lead to the dismissal of the petition was not a disposition of property and thus there was not a void disposition. This is even if the debtor has agreed to repay or reimburse the third party. The reason for this decision was that the money paid to the petitioner was not the debtor's.

Validating orders—The section makes no mention of the parties eligible to apply for a validating order. Details relating to an application are provided for in *Practice Direction – Insolvency Proceedings* (July 2020) [2020] BPIR 1211 at para 9.11. The procedure is set out in para 9.11.1–9.11.3 of the Practice Direction. The contents of an application are set out in paras 9.11.4, 9.11.6 and 9.11.7 of the Practice Direction. Where an application is made urgently to enable payments to be made which are essential to continued trading and all the evidence mentioned in para 9.11.4 cannot be obtained, the court may consider granting limited relief for a short period. However, there should be sufficient evidence to satisfy the court that the interests of creditors are unlikely to be prejudiced by the grant of limited relief (para 9.11.5).

The company that is the respondent to a winding-up petition is in practice the most common applicant. An application by a shareholder, whose legitimate concern could be shown to be that there would be a share devaluation if there was a failure to validate a particular transaction, has been permitted: *Re Argentum Reductions (UK) Ltd* [1975] 1 WLR 186 at 190–191. There is no good reason why the court should not entertain an application by any party able to establish a legitimate interest in the validation. In practice, other than the company and a shareholder (see above) this might conceivably include any of the company's directors (if the company itself will not apply), or the other party to any potentially void disposition. In practice, the obvious difficulty facing parties other than the company is provision of the financial information necessary to support such an application. Certainly, in Australia, reluctance to grant an order has been expressed in the absence of evidence from the company itself as to the benefit of the proposed disposition: *Re Pacific Coast Fisheries Pty* (1980) 5 ACLR 354.

The applicant for a validating order has the onus of showing why a validating order should be made: *Re Rushcutters Court Pty Ltd (No 2)* (1978) ACLC 29, 965. The Court of Appeal has said that an order should only be made in relation to an insolvent company if there is some special circumstance which demonstrates that the disposition will benefit or has benefitted the general body of unsecured creditors and so it is appropriate to disapply the pari passu principle: *Express Electrical Distributors Ltd v Beavis* [2016] EWCA Civ 765, [2016] BPIR 1386 at [56] and affirmed by the Supreme Court in *Akers v Samba Financial Group* [2017] UKSC 6, [2017] AC 424, [2017] 1 BCLC 151, [2017] BPIR 263 at [47]. This view stands even if there was a disposition carried out in good faith in the ordinary course of business at a time when the parties to the transaction were unaware of the presentation of a petition (*Express Electrical Distributors Ltd v Beavis* at [52]). In *Officeserve Technologies Ltd v Annabel's (Berkeley Square) Ltd* [2018] EWHC 2168 (Ch), [2019] Ch 103, [2018] 3 WLR 1568, [2018] BPIR 1743 (at [17], [36], HHJ Mathews said that just because goods or services were supplied in good faith did not affect the operation of s 127 in making the disposition of property void. He emphasised that there is no exception in the section for receipt in good faith (there was no argument from the company and thus it is limited in being cited as authority). Back to *Express Electrical*, Sales LJ (with whom the other judges agreed) emphasised the fact that the pari passu principle was central in the application of s 127 and in considering whether a validating order could be made. In obiter comments his Lordship did say that there may be exceptional circumstances which might possibly justify the making of a validation order in a retrospective application case and he gave (at [40]) the following example: 'if a director of the company who knows about the winding-up petition suppresses that information and deceives someone into dealing with the company: the merits in such a case would need to be argued out between the person dealing with the company and its liquidator and I express no view on what the result should be'. Nevertheless the thrust of his Lordship's judgment was that orders should only be made where the creditors of the debtor are not prejudiced.

The granting of validating orders has developed upon what are now well settled principles, although the court has a broad, unfettered discretion: In *Re Tramways Building & Construction Co Ltd* [1988] 1 Ch 293; *Denney v John Hudson & Co Ltd* [1992] BCLC 901, CA. Because of the discretion, an exhaustive consideration of authority at first instance is of very little practical assistance, since the cases involve the application of these principles to the particular facts of each case, though for examples of cases where orders have been refused, see *Re J Leslie Engineers Co Ltd* [1976] 1 WLR 292 (the proposed transaction promised no benefit to creditors), *Re Rafidain Bank* [1992] BCLC 301 (there was an absence of benefit to creditors generally). As circumstances will differ and the fact that the discretion of a judge is at large one judge might exercise discretion in one way and another judge might exercise it in another way: *Wilson v SMC Properties Ltd* [2016] EWHC 444 (Ch), [2016] BPIR 1074.

In *Richbell Information Services Inc v Atlantic General Investments Ltd* [1999] BCC 871 an order facilitating litigation funding for a company to recover was granted. For a highly pragmatic approach, see *Re Dewrum Ltd* [2002] BCC 57, in which Neuberger J granted a bank's application for validation only of a charge granted to it by A on the same day that the said property had been transferred to A by Dewrum Ltd against which a winding-up petition had been presented on the basis that the bank sought a limited validation in respect of the charge to which Dewrum Ltd was not party, and the need to do justice between the parties.

In deciding whether to order the validation of a transaction a court may rely on the evidence of expert valuers as far as the value of property that is part of the transaction is concerned rather than prices agreed to be paid under uncompleted purchases: *Wilson v SMC Properties Ltd* [2016] EWHC 444 (Ch), [2016] BPIR 1074. The court is entitled to look at what occurred subsequent to any agreement to which an application to validate relates: *Officeserve Technologies Ltd v Anthony-Mike* [2017] EWHC 1920 (Ch), [2017] BPIR 1291 at [110].

Wherever practicable, an application should be made to seek prospective validation of a transaction; the court's discretion is less likely to be exercised favourably where validation is sought retrospectively, particularly where there is any period of unexplained delay. But the court should be cautious on prospective applications of pre-empting the work of a liquidator and should not ordinarily grant a validating order where the subsequent making of a winding-up order is inevitable: *Re Bransfield Engineering Ltd* (1985) 1 BCC 99, 409 at 99, 411. It is not helpful for the court, when hearing an application for a validation of a transaction ex post, on every occasion to consider what the position would have been had a prospective application been made: *Wilson v SMC Properties Ltd* [2016] EWHC 444 (Ch), [2016] BPIR 1074.

There is no reason in principle why a validating order should not be sought in respect of only a part of a transaction, although in Australia, some reluctance has been expressed at acceding to applications to validate parts only of a transaction: see *Jardio Holdings Pty Ltd v Dorcon Construction Pty Ltd* (1984) 2 ACLC 574.

The Court of Appeal in *Denney v John Hudson & Co Ltd* [1992] BCLC 901 Fox LJ (with whom Russell and Staughton LJJ agreed) identified the following principles as having been approved in *Re Gray's Inn Construction Ltd* [1980] 1 WLR 711(references are to pages in the report of the latter case):

(1)     The discretion vested in the court by s 127 is entirely at large, subject to the general principles which apply to any kind of discretion, and subject also to limitation that the discretion must be exercised in the context of the liquidation provisions of the statute (at 717).

(2)     The basic principle of law governing the liquidation of insolvent estates is that the assets of the insolvent at the time of the commencement of the liquidation will be distributed pari passu among the insolvent's unsecured creditors as at the date of the liquidation. In a company's compulsory liquidation this is achieved by s 127 (at 717).

(3)     There are occasions, however, when it may be beneficial not only for the company but also for the unsecured creditors, that the company should be able to dispose of some of its property during the period after the petition has been presented, but before the winding-up order has been made. Thus, it may sometimes be beneficial to the company and its creditors that the company should be able to continue the business in its ordinary course (at 717).

(4)     In considering whether to make a validating order, the court must always do its best to ensure that the interests of the unsecured creditors will not be prejudiced (at 717).

(5)     The desirability of the company being able to carry on its business is likely to be more speculative and will be likely to depend on whether a sale of a company's business is more beneficial than a realisation of individual assets (at 717).

(6)     The court should not validate any transaction or series of transactions which might result in one or more pre-liquidation creditors being paid in full at the expense of other creditors, who will only receive a dividend, in the absence of special circumstances making such a course desirable in the interests of the creditors generally. If, for example, it were in the interests of the creditors generally that the company's business should be carried on, and this could only be achieved by paying for goods already supplied to the company when the petition is presented but not yet paid for, the court might exercise its discretion to validate payments for those goods (at 718).

(7)     A disposition carried out in good faith in the ordinary course of business at a time when the parties were unaware that a petition had been presented would usually be validated by the court unless there is ground for thinking that the transaction may involve an attempt to prefer the disponee – in which case the transaction would not be validated (at 718). This proposition must be taken with caution as indicated by what Sales LJ said in *Express Electrical Distributors Ltd v Beavis* [2016] EWCA Civ 765, [2016] BPIR 1386 at [56]. His Lordship said (at [55]) that the proposition is misleading not least because Fox LJ did not apply it. Fox LJ had taken the view (indicated in proposition 4 above) that the ultimate issue was whether the general body of creditors would be or had been prejudiced by the disposition. Sales LJ agreed with this approach, as noted earlier in these notes.

(8)     Despite the strength of the principle of securing pari passu distribution, the principle has no application to post-liquidation creditors; for example, the sale of an asset at full market value after the presentation of the petition. That is because such a transaction involves no dissipation of the company's assets for it does not reduce the value of its assets (at 719).

For a validation order, the applicant needs to establish that either the company is solvent or that the order will be for the benefit of company creditors: *Re McGuinness Bros (UK) Ltd* (1987) 3 BCC 571 at 574; *Re Fairway Graphics Ltd* [1991] BCLC 468 at 468; *Practice Direction – Insolvency Proceedings* (July 2020) [2020] BPIR 1211 at para 9.11. Despite the need for creditor benefit, there may be exceptional cases where a validation order is granted on other grounds such as in allowing a company to make payment to enable its solicitors to raise bona fide grounds of opposition to a winding-up petition presented against it; see, by analogy, *Rio Properties v Al-Midani* [2003] BPIR 128 at 135–139.An order might be made where to do so would further the interests of the unsecured creditors by increasing the prospect of the company finalizing a financial restructuring or sale of the business of the company as a going concern: *Sahaviriya Steel UK Ltd v Hewden Stuart Ltd* [2015] EWHC 2726 (Ch). In determining solvency in the context of a validation application debts disputed on genuine and substantial grounds should not be taken into account: *Hood v JD Classics Ltd* [2019] EWHC 2236 (Ch), [2019] BPIR 1423.

The solvency of a company does not preclude the making of a validating order. Such an order will be more easily obtained where solvency can be demonstrated, although the court will entertain objections by parties with a legitimate interest: *Re Burton & Deakin Ltd* [1977] 1 WLR 390. A validation order might be made where a creditor who has benefited from a disposition and has changed its position as a result of the disposition, in circumstances where the creditor did not know and could not have known of the existence of the petition (because the petition had not been advertised): *Re Tain Construction Ltd* [2003] 2 BCLC 374 at [41] (where the change of position argument failed). But the change of position defence could not be relied on if the respondent knows at the time of the change of position that the disposition was invalid, as the respondent would not be acting in good faith (*Tain* at [43]). In *Officeserve Technologies Ltd v Annabel's (Berkeley Square) Ltd* [2018] EWHC 2168 (Ch), [2019] Ch 103, [2018] 3 WLR 1568, [2018] BPIR 1743, HHJ Mathews confirmed that the change of position defence was available in the appropriate case. Subsequently, in *Abdulali v Nisa Retail Ltd* ([2019] EWHC 1383 (Ch), [2019] BPIR 1063) ICC Judge Jones said that the circumstances in which a change of position defence is able to succeed are constrained in the same way and for the same reasons as the exercise of the court's discretion to validate. He went on to say that it was not 'easy to think of circumstances in which the court would decline to make a validation order, but nevertheless find it inequitable to order repayment of a benefit received, particularly when one takes account of the availability of "exceptional circumstances" as justification for a validation order.' (at [69]).

It has been held that as the making of a validation order is squarely in the discretion of the court, the court would consider all evidence placed before it, from whatever source (including from people who did not have locus standi), if it was relevant to the exercise of the discretion: *Re Rescupine Ltd* [2003] 1 BCLC 661. While there is a broad discretion it has been said that an order will only be made where there was no serious risk to the creditors or where the court was satisfied that the company's position and hence the position of the creditors would be improved by the transaction being validated: *RC Brewery Ltd v Revenue and Customs Commissioners* [2013] EWHC 1184 (Ch). The courts may make an order where full value was not obtained pursuant to the transaction, although they will not do so if the transaction contravenes the policy behind the provision: *Wilson v SMC Properties Ltd* [2015] EWHC 870 (Ch), [2015] 2 BCLC 173.

A court might order the hearing of an application for a validation order in private if a public hearing could be deleterious to confidential negotiations concerning the restructuring of the company or sale of the company or its business as a going concern: *Sahaviriya Steel UK Ltd v Hewden Stuart Ltd* [2015] EWHC 2726 (Ch).

In *RC Brewery Ltd v Revenue and Customs Commissioners* ([2013] EWHC 1184 (Ch) at [8]) Warren J that where a company is defending a petition on the basis that the debt founding it is subject to a genuine and substantial dispute it might be correct to grant validation to the payment of the company's lawyers.

**The consequence of failing to obtain a validating order**—A claim for recovery of property disposed of without the protection of a validating order constitutes a statutory cause of action which is created automatically on the making of a winding-up order, and not the election of a liquidator. The method of recovery is not prescribed in the legislation and remains a matter of general law, which would allow for trading on equitable principles: *Re J Leslie Engineers Co Ltd* [1976] 2 All ER 85 at 89. A claim to recover property will ordinarily be pursued by way of relief consequent upon an application for a declaration that the disposition pursued is void under s 127. The claim is available to the liquidator only (*Campbell v Michael Mount PPB* (1996) 14 ACLC 218), although in *Mond v Hammond Suddards* [1996] 2 BCLC 470 at 473 it was said that s 127 imposes no limit on who is able to bring a claim; with respect, this appears to be misconceived in that it ignores the class nature of liquidation. No other English authority seems to adopt such a wide view as that in *Mond*, although in *Power v Brown* [2009] EWHC 9 (Ch) Gabriel Moss QC (sitting as a deputy judge of the High Court) appeared to accept what Judge Kolbert had said, and the learned deputy judge in *Power* said in that in an appropriate case s 284 (the bankruptcy equivalent of s 127) could be relied on by parties other than the bankruptcy trustee (at [20], [21]). One must always bear in mind that s 284 is different from s 127.

A recovery made in respect of a void disposition under s 127 enures for the benefit of the company in liquidation since the property recovered remained at all times, notwithstanding any purported disposition, the property of the company. As such, the property will remain subject to any security existing at the date of the winding-up order.

Where a liquidator is unable to recover a void disposition, then a prima facie claim for damages equating to the loss suffered by the company as a consequence of the disposition, less any partial recovery made, will be available to the liquidator against the company's directors in misfeasance proceedings under s 212: *Re Neath Harbour Smelting and Rolling Works Co* [1887] WN 87.

A liquidator may not assign a claim under s 127: *Re Ayala Holdings Ltd (No 2)* [1996] 1 BCLC 467.

For the procedure to be followed for applying for a validation order, see para 9.11 of the *Practice Direction – Insolvency Proceedings* (July 2020) [2020] BPIR 1211.

**Practice and procedure**—The liquidator will seek a declaration that a disposition is void and in the same proceedings the company or a third party will usually seek an order validating the disposition.

Notwithstanding the decision in *Hollicourt (Contracts) Ltd v Bank of Ireland* [2001] 2 WLR 290, which suggests that a bank will not face a potential recovery claim under s 127 by a liquidator, it is usual practice for a clearing bank to freeze a customer company's accounts on the giving of notice of a winding-up petition. On a validation order being granted to the bank's satisfaction, the bank will usually operate a new account having 'ruled off' liability on the old account.

An application for a validating order must be supported by the evidence specified in para 9.11.4 of the *Practice Direction – Insolvency Proceedings* (July 2020) [2020] BPIR 1211. The scrutiny to which such information is subjected by the court is likely to be more exacting where the company proposes ongoing trading and seeks multiple or repeat validations. For examples of the exercise of the jurisdiction see (on the particular facts in each) *Re a Company (No 007523 of 1986)* [1987] BCLC 2001 (validation refused where the company was involved in loss-making and the trend was apparently irreversible, though note the possibility of reduced loss through the proposed transaction) and *Richbell Information Service Inc v Atlantic General Investments Trust Ltd* [1999] BCC 871 (inappropriate to validate disposition in absence of petitioning creditor's consent where disposition contrary to petitioner's contractual rights).

**Procedure and forms**—An application for a validating order must be involve the giving of notice to: (a) the petitioning creditor; (b) any person entitled to receive a copy of the petition pursuant to rule 7.9; (c) any creditor who has given notice to the petitioner of their intention to appear on the hearing of the petition pursuant to rule 7.14; and (d) any creditor who has been substituted as petitioner pursuant to rule 7.17, except in exceptional circumstances (para 9.11.2 of the *Practice Direction – Insolvency Proceedings* (July 2020) [2020] BPIR 1211). Section 127 is applicable in the winding up of a foreign company in England and Wales: *Re Sugar Properties (Deriseley Wood) Ltd* [1988] BCLC 146. See Chapter 3 of Part 1 of the 2016 Rules and para 9.11.4 of the *Practice Direction – Insolvency Proceedings* (July 2020) [2020] BPIR 1211 as to the required contents of an application to the court for an order.

An application for a validation order should be initially listed before an ICC judge or a district judge in a District Registry (para 3.1 of the *Practice Direction – Insolvency Proceedings* (July 2020) [2020] BPIR 1211). An application under s 127 should only be made in the winding-up proceedings established on presentation of the winding-up petition.

**'anything done by an administrator of a company while a winding-up petition is suspended'**—This was introduced by the Enterprise Act 2002. For a discussion, see the comments accompanying para 40 of Sch B1. Also, see *Re J Smiths Haulage Ltd* [2007] BCC 135, where an administrator was appointed subsequent to the presentation of a petition to wind up and disposed of company property without knowledge of the petition. It was said that such a disposition was not be void under s 127 as the effect of the administrator's appointment was to suspend the petition (para 40(1)(b)), and s 127(2) confirms this.

## [1.181]

### 128 Avoidance of attachments etc

(1)  Where a company registered in England and Wales is being wound up by the court, any attachment, sequestration, distress or execution put in force against the estate or effects of the company after the commencement of the winding up is void.

(2)  This section, so far as relates to any estate or effects of the company situated in England and Wales, applies in the case of a company registered in Scotland as it applies in the case of a company registered in England and Wales.

(3)  In subsection (1) "attachment" includes a hold notice or a deduction notice under Part 1 of Schedule 8 to the Finance (No 2) Act 2015 (enforcement by deduction from accounts) and, if subsection (1) has effect in relation to a deduction notice, it also has effect in relation to the hold notice to which the deduction notice relates (whenever the hold notice was given).

**Amendments**—Finance (No 2) Act 2015, s 51, Sch 8, Pt 2, paras 26, 28.

**General note**—This provision denies creditors their ordinary remedies against the company, to ensure that an insolvent company's property shall, once in liquidation, be applied in satisfaction of creditors according to the statutory scheme. This denial commences when the company enters liquidation, although it could be effected after the presentation of the winding-up petition, if a stay on proceedings under s 126 is obtained.

See s 183 and the notes relating to that section for further consideration of execution and attachment. See s 112 and the general note under that section for the position with respect to voluntary liquidations.

'**Attachment**'—Attachment encompasses the process by which a judgment creditor obtains a garnishee order attaching a debt that is owed by a third party to the debtor company. An attachment does not occur when the garnishee order is obtained (*Re Stanhope Silkstone Collieries Co* (1879) 11 ChD 160), but only when it is served on the garnishee: *Re National United Investments Corp* [1901] 1 Ch 950; *Sedgwick Collins & Co v Rossia Insurance Co* [1926] 1 KB 1.

'**Sequestration**'—This term has no particular technical meaning, and it means 'the detention of property by a court so as to permit the answering of a demand which is made': *Re Australian Direct Steam Navigation Co* (1875) 20 Eq 325 at 326.

'**Distress**'—This is an extra-judicial process used mainly in order to enforce the payment of arrears of rent that is owed pursuant to a lease, or payment of outstanding instalments of principal and interest owing under a mortgage or mortgage debenture which either expressly grants the right to distrain or includes a provision in terms of which the mortgagor attorns the tenant to the mortgagee. 'Distrain' in the context of the renting of land is a right to resort to the chattels on the land occupied by the tenant: *Re Coal Consumers' Association* [1876] 4 ChD 625 at 629–630. 'Distress' as a remedy has been abolished, by s 71 of the Tribunals, Courts and Enforcement Act 2007 and effectively replaced, according to s 72 of the same Act, by a new remedy, known as Commercial Rent Arrears Recovery ('CRAR'). In s 436 of the IA 1986, 'distress' is defined and refers specifically to the use of the CRAR procedure contained in Sch 12 to the Tribunals, Courts and Enforcement Act 2007 which provides for the process to be followed by enforcement officers.

'**Execution**'—This has been referred to as 'the process for enforcing or giving effect to the judgment of the court': *Re Overseas Aviation Engineering Ltd* [1963] Ch 24 at 39.

'**Put in force**'—What this constitutes depends on the remedy involved. It may take the form of legal, equitable or statutory execution. The form of execution can determine when it is actually put in force. With attachment, service on the garnishee is the critical issue: *Re Stanhope Silkstone Collieries Co* (1879) 11 ChD 160; *Croshaw v Lyndhurst Ship Co* [1897] 2 Ch 154. All forms of execution have been put in force when proceedings have led to the creditor obtaining a charge over the property with the result that the creditor is made secured: *Croshaw v Lyndhurst Ship Co* [1897] 2 Ch 154. In relation to execution against goods a charge is not created until the relevant goods have been taken control of by a High Court Enforcement Officer: *McQuarrie v Jacques* (1954) 92 CLR 262, *Hall v Richards* (1961) 108 CLR 84.

**Leave to proceed**—While s 128 makes no mention of any right of a creditor to seek and obtain leave to proceed, it has been held that the courts may give leave to a creditor to proceed with execution where it has been instigated, but not put in force, when winding up commenced: *Re Lancashire Cotton Spinning Co* (1887) 35 ChD 656.

*Commencement of winding up*

**[1.182]**

### 129 Commencement of winding up by the court

(1) If, before the presentation of a petition for the winding up of a company by the court, a resolution has been passed by the company for voluntary winding up, the winding up of the company is deemed to have commenced at the time of the passing of the resolution; and unless the court, on proof of fraud or mistake, directs otherwise, all proceedings taken in the voluntary winding up are deemed to have been validly taken.

(1A) Where the court makes a winding-up order by virtue of paragraph 13(1)(e) of Schedule B1, the winding up is deemed to commence on the making of the order.

(2) In any other case, the winding up of a company by the court is deemed to commence at the time of the presentation of the petition for winding up.

**Amendments**—Enterprise Act 2002, s 248(3), Sch 17, paras 9, 16.

**CIGA 2020**—This provision is affected by temporary measures at Sch 10, para 9 of CIGA 2020.

**General note**—This provision states that voluntary liquidations commence at the time when the company resolves to wind up, whereas a compulsory liquidation commences not with the making of the winding-up order, but with the presentation of the petition on which the winding-up order is subsequently made. However, where a winding-up order is made in relation to a company that was in voluntary liquidation at the time of the making of the order, then the winding up is said to commence at the time of the resolution to wind up. So, while the commencement of winding up in voluntary liquidation is the time when winding up actually begins, in compulsory liquidation there is an artificial date for the commencement. Commencement in this latter form of winding up relates back to the point when the winding up proceedings were initiated.

Subsection (1A) was introduced by the Enterprise Act 2002 and effectively means that if a court decides to make a winding-up order when hearing an application for an administration order, the date of the winding-up order is the commencement of winding up, and, therefore, there is no back-dating.

The commencement of winding up is of significant importance: for example, it brings to an end the power of the company to dispose of its property (s 127) and it is the time from which the status and liability of contributories is determined. But while it is the point of time that is crucial for determining many things in a liquidation, the actual date when the liquidation commences is used for a few matters: for instance, an automatic stay applies from the time of the actual winding up (s 130(2)).

As a consequence of the enactment of the Corporate Insolvency and Governance Act 2020 (Sch 10, paras 8, 9 and 21) and its subsequent amendment by the Corporate Insolvency and Governance Act 2020 (Coronavirus) (Extension of the Relevant Period) Regulations 2020 (SI 2020/1031), reg 2(3), the Corporate Insolvency and Governance Act 2020 (Coronavirus) (Extension of the Relevant Period) (No 2) Regulations 2020 (SI 2020/1483), reg 2, The Corporate Insolvency and Governance Act 2020 (Coronavirus) (Extension of the Relevant Period) Regulations 2021 (SI 2021/375), reg 3(4) and The Corporate Insolvency and Governance Act 2020 (Coronavirus) (Extension of the Relevant Period) (No 2) Regulations 2021 (SI 2021/718), reg 2, if a winding-up order was made as a result of a petition presented under s 124 during the period of 27 April 2020 to 30 September 2021 on the basis that the company was unable to pay its debts, then the commencement of winding up is not, as provided for in s 129(2), the date of the presentation of the petition but the date of the winding-up order.

## [1.183]

### 130 Consequences of winding-up order

(1)  On the making of a winding-up order, a copy of the order must forthwith be forwarded by the company (or otherwise as may be prescribed) to the registrar of companies, who shall enter it in his records relating to the company.

(2)  When a winding-up order has been made or a provisional liquidator has been appointed, no action or proceeding shall be proceeded with or commenced against the company or its property, except by leave of the court and subject to such terms as the court may impose.

(3)  When an order has been made for winding up a company registered but not formed under the Companies Act 2006, no action or proceeding shall be commenced or proceeded with against the company or its property or any contributory of the company, in respect of any debt of the company, except by leave of the court, and subject to such terms as the court may impose.

(3A)  In subsections (2) and (3), the reference to an action or proceeding includes action in respect of the company under Part 1 of Schedule 8 to the Finance (No 2) Act 2015 (enforcement by deduction from accounts).

(4)  An order for winding up a company operates in favour of all the creditors and of all contributories of the company as if made on the joint petition of a creditor and of a contributory.

**Amendments**—SI 2009/1941; Finance (No 2) Act 2015, s 51, Sch 8, Pt 2, paras 26, 29.

**General note**—This provision states some of the major effects of compulsory winding up. The fact that a company is subject to winding up is something that the public is not expected to be aware of until official notification has occurred. This occurs when the registrar of companies places a notice in the *London Gazette* informing the world that he or she has received a copy of a winding-up order made against the company concerned (Companies Act 2006, ss 1077(1) and 1078(2); also, see s 1116. The difficulty is that the making of the winding-up order is made retrospective and can affect parties who have no notice of the fact that winding-up proceedings are on foot against the company, but deal with the company before a winding-up order is made. See, for instance, s 127.

Section 130(2) enforces an automatic stay on all legal proceedings, and it has effect all over the United Kingdom (In Re *International Pulp and Paper Co* (1876) 3 ChD 594), but while the provision can apply to a winding up of a foreign company in England and Wales, it does not apply to a foreign insolvency proceeding: *Mazur Media Ltd v Mazur Media GmbH* [2004] BPIR 1253. The aim behind the stay is to assist the liquidator to achieve the purposes of liquidation (*South Coast Construction Ltd v Iverson Road Ltd* [2017] EWHC 61 (TCC) at [15]), and specifically it is designed to ensure that liquidators are not required to defend a significant body of litigation instituted by disaffected creditors, thereby dissipating the company's funds: In *Re David Lloyd & Co* (1877) 6 ChD 339. Such a result would impact on all creditors. The right of the creditors to claim a remedy through the courts is effectively replaced with a right to lodge a proof of debt in the company's liquidation and to obtain, it is hoped, a share of the company's funds. This process should, generally, be far less expensive than litigation. It must not be forgotten that the prohibition in s 130(2) is also directed equally at actions that are being taken, or might be taken, by shareholders and others.

The imposition of the stay supports the notion that winding up ought to be seen as an orderly, effective process that prima facie treats creditors equally (but see the notes to s 107).

As s 130(4) indicates, the winding-up order operates in relation to all creditors and all contributories. This demonstrates the collective nature of the winding-up process and so where the petitioner is a creditor, he or she obtains the order as a representative of all of the creditors. In some ways this provision is the benefit given to creditors for having their right to initiate or continue legal proceedings stayed by s 130(2).

'**Action or proceeding**'—There is not a critical difference between these two terms. 'Action' is a generic term and the Judicature Act 1925 provides that it means 'a civil proceeding' (s 225).

The latter term has been held to include any kind of action (*Re Keystone Knitting Mills' Trade Mark* [1929] 1 Ch 92 at 102), and should be interpreted widely: *Langley Constructions (Brixham) Ltd v Wells* [1969] 1 WLR 503 at 509. See the commentary attaching to para 43 of Sch B1.

As far as specific kinds of proceedings are concerned, it has been held that the following fall within s 130(2) (this is not exhaustive): counterclaims (*Langley Constructions*); proceedings for recovery of a statutory penalty (*Re Briton Medical & General Life Assurance Association* (1886) 32 ChD 503); the process directed against the property of a company such as levying execution (*Re Artistic Colour Printing Co* (1880) 14 ChD 502 at 505); distress (*Re Exhall Coal Mining Co* (1864) 4 De GJ & S 377; *Re Lancashire Cotton Spinning Co* (1887) 35 ChD 656 at 661); enforcing a garnishee order (*Re Herbert Berry Associates Ltd* [1977] 1 WLR 617); criminal prosecutions (*R v Dickson* (1992) 94 Cr. App. R. 7); and arbitration proceedings (*A Straume (UK) Ltd v Bradlor Developments Ltd* (1999) *The Times*, August 13). But applying for security for costs against the company (*BPM Pty Ltd v HPM Pty Ltd* (1996) 14 ACLC 857) is not a proceeding within s 130(2), nor is the lodging of an appeal if it was the company that initiated proceedings either before or after entry into liquidation, and the defendant wishes to appeal against the judgment given in favour of the company (*Humber & Co v John Griffiths Cycle Co* (1901) 85 LT 141, HL).

It has been held in a case dealing with the stay in administrations that an application by a party to be joined as an additional defendant in an appeal where the initial action had been instigated by a company in administration did not constitute legal proceedings within para 43(6) of Sch B1 and so no leave was required by the party wishing to be joined: *Cook v Mortgage Debenture Ltd* [2016] EWCA Civ 103, [2016] BPIR 565. The court did say that a critical element of legal proceedings within the provision was that they had to be proceedings brought against the company and what was essentially a defensive initiative in wanting to be joined was not within the provision. The court also made it clear that the law relating to the administration provision could be applied to s 130(2).

**Leave**—Where an action or proceeding falls within s 130(2), leave of the court to initiate or continue proceedings is necessary. The provision does not state when leave will be given; rather the courts have an unfettered discretion as to when they will grant leave: *Re Aro Co Ltd* [1980] Ch 196; *New Cap Reinsurance Corp Ltd v HIH Casualty and General Insurance Ltd* [2002] 2 BCLC 228, [2002] BPIR 809, CA.

There has not been significant examination in the UK as to when leave will be granted. It has been said that courts are to do what is right and fair in all of the circumstances (*Re Aro Co Ltd* [1980] Ch 196; *Re Exchange Securities & Commodities Ltd* [1983] BCLC 186 at 195; *New Cap Reinsurance Corp Ltd v HIH Casualty and General Insurance Ltd* [2002] 2 BCLC 228, [2002] BPIR 809, CA).

A court is not required to, nor should it, investigate the merits of proposed or existing proceedings, except to satisfy itself that there was a genuine claim: *Bourne v Charit-Email Technology Partnership LLP* [2010] EWHC 1901 (Ch), [2010] 1 BCLC 210. The court in this case said that the resources available to the liquidator should be taken into account in making a decision. The court is to be cautious in placing a liquidator under the burden of having to deal with difficult and time-consuming litigation.

Some types of claims will find favour with the court as far as leave is concerned. Where a person is seeking to claim from the company what is in effect his or her own property, leave to proceed will be granted as a formality (*Re David Lloyd & Co* (1877) 6 ChD 339; *Re Lineas Navieras*

*Boliviarnas SAM* [1995] BCC 666), because of the fact that a liquidation should not deprive a person from having his or her property (*Re David Lloyd & Co* at 344); such property is not, of course, available for distribution among the general body of creditors. For instance, proceedings will be allowed by a mortgagee for the enforcement of security: *Re David Lloyd & Co*. In *Edwards and Smith v Flightline Ltd* [2003] EWCA Civ 63 the court at first instance had granted leave to the applicant (F) to continue an action on the basis that it had a secured interest in funds in a joint bank account which would make it a secured creditor in relation to any judgment obtained. But the Court of Appeal allowed an appeal against this ruling because it held that there were no security rights in favour of F. It has been held in New Zealand that leave should be granted to permit a party to seek adjudication proceedings against a company in liquidation under construction legislation where there was a dispute over the final payment in a construction agreement: *DHC Assets Ltd v Toon* [2015] NZHC 140.

The question of expedience and convenience might be a major factor (*Re Queensland Mercantile Agency Co* (1888) 58 LT 878), and leave will be withheld where the action raises issues which could be dealt with in the liquidation as conveniently as in other proceedings and with both less delay and expense: *Re Exchange Securities & Commodities Ltd* [1983] BCLC 186 at 196. So, where there are proceedings which are aimed primarily against persons other than the company, and the company is a party only as a formality, the courts normally give leave: *McEwan v London, Bombay & Mediterranean Bank* (1886) 15 LT 495; *Hall v Old Talargoch Lead Mining Co* (1876) 3 ChD 749; *Re Rio Grande du Sol Steamship Co* (1877) 5 ChD 282. Courts will tend to grant leave where there are claims likely to be more difficult or more expensive if handled by way of the proving of claims process in a liquidation, rather than by the normal litigious process: *Thames Plate Glass Co v Land & Sea Telegraph Co* (1871) 6 Ch App 643; *Re Joseph Pease & Co* [1873] WN 127. Also, leave is far more likely in situations where the claim is for declaratory and injunctive relief (*Wyley v Exhall Gold Mining Co* (1864) 33 Beav 538; 55 ER 478), or other equitable relief, such as for specific performance or rescission of a contract (*Re Coregrange Ltd* [1984] BCLC 453), which cannot be adjudicated on in the winding-up process very easily.

A court might refrain from granting leave if the liquidator indicates that he or she would admit a proof of debt lodged by the applicant for leave as a contingent debt: *Swaby v Lift Capital Partners Pty Ltd* [2009] FCA 749.

While an applicant for leave is not required to demonstrate that granting of leave would not prejudice the creditors or the orderly winding up of the company, if the applicant cannot do so it might well tell against the granting of leave: *DSG Holdings Australia Pty Ltd v Helenic Pty Ltd* [2014] NSWCA 96.

When considering whether to grant a stay a court is not to determine the matter by reference to the principles applicable to interlocutory relief, as the application involves a request for final relief. In making a determination a court must consider matters of commercial morality and this might mean refusing to stay the winding up if there is serious impropriety: *Re Wine National Pty Ltd* [2014] NSWSC 507. Another Australian authority has held that the court will have regard to the likely sources of any recoveries obtained from an action or from one permitted to proceed and the impact on creditors' returns: *Rushleigh Services Pty Ltd v Forge Group Ltd* [2016] FCA 1471.

Leave may be granted retrospectively, ie after proceedings have been issued against a company in liquidation (*Re Saunders* [1997] Ch 60; *Bristol & West Building Society v Alexander* [1997] BPIR 358, [1998] 1 BCLC 485, *Re Linkrealm Ltd* [1998] BCC 478, *Adorian v Commissioner of Police of the Metropolis* [2009] EWCA Civ 18, [2009] 1 WLR 1859, *Bank of Scotland v Breytenbach* [2012] BPIR 1; *Re Colliers International UK plc* [2012] EWHC 2942 (Ch)), and there is Australian authority to the effect that simply delaying in applying for leave will not, in itself, prevent leave being granted: *Ex parte Walker* (1982) 6 ACLR 423, but it might tell against the granting of leave if the delay is unexplained: *DSG Holdings Australia Pty Ltd v Helenic Pty Ltd* [2014] NSWCA 96.

The granting of leave by a court might be subject to certain conditions, which may be seen as limiting the interference with the winding-up process: *Oceanic Life Ltd v Insurance and Retirement Services Pty Ltd (in liquidation)* (1993) 11 ACLC 1157 at 1159. One condition that might be specified is the requirement on the part of the applicant for leave to give an undertaking that judgment will not be enforced without obtaining further leave of the court: *Hazell v Currie* (1867) WN 68; *Re Marine Investment Co* (1868) 17 LT 535.

Australian authority has held that leave to proceed may be granted where it can be demonstrated that serious and substantial questions of public interest demand that litigation is able to be initiated or continued: *Australian Competition and Consumer Commission v Australian Institute of Professional Education Pty Ltd* [2017] FCA 521.

Courts have lifted the stay to enable the enforcement of an adjudicator's decision in a construction dispute: *South Coast Construction Ltd v Iverson Road Ltd* [2017] EWHC 61 (TCC); *Rossair Ltd v Primus Build Ltd* [2017] EWHC 2430 (TCC). These cases were in relation to companies in administration and there was some suggestion that the insolvency procedure was being used by the companies to avoid payment.

If a claim is to be brought against a liquidator, in a compulsory liquidation, in his or her personal capacity and when he or she was carrying out his or her duties as a liquidator, then according to several Australian authorities leave of the court is needed to bring proceedings during the period of the company's liquidation: eg *Armitage v Gainsborough Properties Pty Ltd* [2011] VSC 419 at [34] and [42].

Making leave a requirement has been held, in relation to other legislation, not to infringe Art 6 of the European Convention for the Protection of Human Rights for if an applicant for leave had an arguable case leave would be granted: *Seal v Chief Constable of South Wales Police* [2007] UKHL 31, [2007] BPIR 1396.

**Limitation of actions**—The time from which the Limitation Act 1980 runs as far as determining when proceedings have to be brought by or against the company, is the date of any winding-up order: *Re General Rolling Stock Co* (1872) 7 Ch App 646; *Re Cases of Taff Wells Ltd* [1992] Ch 179, [1992] BCLC 11. The limitation period ceases to run during the period in which a company is in liquidation: *Re General Rolling Stock Co* (1872) 7 Ch App 646; *Financial Services Compensation Scheme Ltd v Larnell (Insurances) Ltd* [2005] EWCA Civ 1408, [2006] BPIR 1370 at [18]. However, there are exceptions to the principle enunciated in *Re General Rolling Stock Co*. These exceptions are discussed in *Financial Services Compensation Scheme Ltd v Larnell (Insurances) Ltd* (at [20]–[28]).

See the notes under the heading, 'The scope of s 285(3) and the principles governing permission to proceed' in relation to s 285.

*Investigation procedures*

**[1.184]**

**131 Company's statement of affairs**

(1) Where the court has made a winding-up order or appointed a provisional liquidator, the official receiver may require some or all of the persons mentioned in subsection (3) below to make out and submit to him a statement in the prescribed form as to the affairs of the company.

(2) The statement shall show—

  (a) particulars of the company's assets, debts and liabilities;
  (b) the names and addresses of the company's creditors;
  (c) the securities held by them respectively;
  (d) the dates when the securities were respectively given; and
  (e) such further or other information as may be prescribed or as the official receiver may require.

(2A) The statement shall—

  (a) in the case of an appointment of a provisional liquidator or a winding up by the court in England and Wales, be verified by the persons required to submit it by a statement of truth; and
  (b) in the case of an appointment of a provisional liquidator or a winding up by the court in Scotland, contain a statutory declaration by the persons required to submit it.

(3) The persons referred to in subsection (1) are—

  (a) those who are or have been officers of the company;
  (b) those who have taken part in the formation of the company at any time within one year before the relevant date;
  (c) those who are in the company's employment, or have been in its employment within that year, and are in the official receiver's opinion capable of giving the information required;
  (d) those who are or have been within that year officers of, or in the employment of, a company which is, or within that year was, an officer of the company.

(4) Where any persons are required under this section to submit a statement of affairs to the official receiver, they shall do so (subject to the next subsection) before the end of the period of 21 days beginning with the day after that on which the prescribed notice of the requirement is given to them by the official receiver.

(5) The official receiver, if he thinks fit, may—

(a)   at any time release a person from an obligation imposed on him under subsection (1) or (2) above; or

(b)   either when giving the notice mentioned in subsection (4) or subsequently, extend the period so mentioned;

and where the official receiver has refused to exercise a power conferred by this subsection, the court, if it thinks fit, may exercise it.

(6)   In this section—

"employment" includes employment under a contract for services; and

"the relevant date" means—

(a)   in a case where a provisional liquidator is appointed, the date of his appointment; and

(b)   in a case where no such appointment is made, the date of the winding-up order.

(7)   If a person without reasonable excuse fails to comply with any obligation imposed under this section, he is liable to a fine and, for continued contravention, to a daily default fine.

(8)   In the application of this section to Scotland references to the official receiver are to the liquidator or, in a case where a provisional liquidator is appointed, the provisional liquidator.

**Amendments**—SI 2010/18; SSI 2016/141.

**General note**—In the course of investigating a compulsory winding up, the official receiver may, on the making of a winding-up order, require, by notice, some or all of the persons referred to in s 131(3) to make out and submit to him or her a statement of affairs of the company (s 131(1)).

**Statement of affairs**—The official receiver may, if he or she chooses, call for a statement of affairs. The statement of affairs will be of assistance usually to the official receiver in discovering the assets of the company, in deciding whether to apply for an examination of officers and others in relation to the company's affairs, and to ascertain who are the creditors if the official receiver decides to seek nominations from the creditors and contributories for the purpose of choosing a person to be the liquidator of the company: see s 136(4), (5). The statement can be used in subsequent civil proceedings, but it cannot be used in any criminal proceedings, save those mentioned in s 433(3). For further details, see the notes accompanying s 433. If, in preparing a statement of affairs, a former or present officer of the company were to make a material omission, he or she commits an offence (s 210(1)). The contents of the statement of affairs are set out in r 7.41

**'Officer'**—This term is not specifically defined by the Act. It will include those persons mentioned in s 1173 of the Companies Act 2006 (incorporated by s 251), namely directors, managers and secretaries. In s 206, the term includes shadow directors (s 206(3)), which is itself defined in s 251, but it might well be argued that as no specific reference is made to a shadow director being an officer, the section did not intend to include such persons as officers. It is highly unlikely that a person who acted as liquidator of a company, the liquidation of which was converted from voluntary to compulsory, would be classified as an officer, because there are cases in the Act where the legislature refers to officers and liquidators separately (eg s 235).

**Failure to submit**—If there is non-compliance with the official receiver's requirement, then the official receiver may apply to the court, pursuant to r 12.52, asking it to make such orders as are necessary to require persons to fulfil their obligations: *Re Wallace Smith Trust Co Ltd* [1992] BCC 707. It is more appropriate that such action is taken, rather than seeking a public examination under s 133: *Re Wallace Smith Trust Co Ltd.*

**Report**—Where the official receiver has required a statement of affairs and a statement has been filed, the official receiver must send out to creditors and contributories a report, unless he or she has previously reported. See r 7.48.

See rr 7.40–7.45 and the comments thereto.

## [1.185]

### 132 Investigation by official receiver

(1)   Where a winding-up order is made by the court in England and Wales, it is the duty of the official receiver to investigate—

(a)   if the company has failed, the causes of the failure; and

(b)   generally, the promotion, formation, business, dealings and affairs of the company,

and to make such report (if any) to the court as he thinks fit.

(2)   The report is, in any proceedings, prima facie evidence of the facts stated in it.

**General note**—While the official receiver is obliged to investigate the causes of the failure of a company and generally the promotion, formation, business, dealings and affairs of a company in liquidation, he or she is given a discretion as to whether to make a report. It is likely that the report of the official receiver made pursuant to s 132 will be absolutely privileged, such that a libel action could not be sustained against the official receiver for any comments made in the report. The reason for saying this is that it was held that a report made under s 530 of the Companies Act 1985, a predecessor of s 132, could not lead to liability for defamation: *Bottomley v Brougham* [1908] KB 584. In addition, it is likely that the official receiver could not be sued in relation to any negligent misstatements contained in the report, as he or she is immune from legal suit in respect of statements that are made in the capacity of official receiver and made in relation to the liquidation proceedings: *Mond v Hyde* [1999] QB 1097, CA.

## [1.186]

### 133  Public examination of officers

(1)   Where a company is being wound up by the court, the official receiver or, in Scotland, the liquidator may at any time before the dissolution of the company apply to the court for the public examination of any person who—

(a)   is or has been an officer of the company; or

(b)   has acted as liquidator or administrator of the company or as receiver or manager or, in Scotland, receiver of its property; or

(c)   not being a person falling within paragraph (a) or (b), is or has been concerned, or has taken part, in the promotion, formation or management of the company.

(2)   Unless the court otherwise orders, the official receiver or, in Scotland, the liquidator shall make an application under subsection (1) if he is requested in accordance with the rules to do so by—

(a)   one-half, in value, of the company's creditors; or

(b)   three-quarters, in value, of the company's contributories.

(3)   On an application under subsection (1), the court shall direct that a public examination of the person to whom the application relates shall be held on a day appointed by the court; and that person shall attend on that day and be publicly examined as to the promotion, formation or management of the company or as to the conduct of its business and affairs, or his conduct or dealings in relation to the company.

(4)   The following may take part in the public examination of a person under this section and may question that person concerning the matters mentioned in subsection (3), namely—

(a)   the official receiver;

(b)   the liquidator of the company;

(c)   any person who has been appointed as special manager of the company's property or business;

(d)   any creditor of the company who has tendered a proof or, in Scotland, submitted a claim in the winding up;

(e)   any contributory of the company.

**General note**—The examination of insolvents has a long lineage, going back to the Act of 1604 (1 Jac 1 c 15). The first examination provision in liquidation law was introduced in s 15 of the Joint Stock Companies Winding Up Act 1844. The first public examination procedure was provided for in s 8 of the Companies (Winding Up) Act 1890. But until s 133 was introduced, public examinations had fallen into relative disuse. Reference can be had to the notes accompanying s 236 (private examinations) for further details.

Public examinations can be employed in any compulsory liquidation, but they are generally only utilised in insolvent liquidations.

Public examinations are not to be used if the only purpose is to force the examinee to co-operate with the official receiver. Where non-compliance of officers of the company occurs it is appropriate for the official receiver to apply to the court pursuant to r 12.52 seeking such orders as are necessary to enforce compliance with the obligations involved: *Re Wallace Smith Trust Co Ltd* [1992] BCC 707. Nevertheless, a public examination might be a legitimate way of obtaining the information that an officer should provide in the statement of affairs under s 131: *Re Wallace Smith Trust Co Ltd* [1992] BCC 707.

See rr 7.98–7.107 and the notes relating to them.

Reference should also be made to the notes accompanying s 236 (private examinations) and s 290 (bankruptcy). For a more detailed discussion of public examinations, see A Keay *McPherson and Keay's Law of Company Liquidation* (Sweet and Maxwell, 4th edn, 2018) at 969–980.

**Purpose**—The section was designed to fulfil the purposes enumerated in the Cork Report, namely:

> '(a) to form the basis of reports, which the official receiver may have to submit to the Department concerning the affairs of the company; for example concerning possible offences by officers of the company and others, (b) to obtain material information for the administration of the estate which cannot as well be obtained privately; and (c) to give publicity, for the information of creditors and the community at large, to the salient facts and unusual features connected with the company's failure' (*Re Seagull Manufacturing Co Ltd (in liquidation)* [1993] BCLC 1139 at 1145, CA per Peter Gibson LJ).

**Voluntary liquidation**—While s 133 falls within that part of the Act that is devoted to compulsory liquidation, applications for examinations are able to be made in voluntary liquidations by way of s 112: *Bishopsgate Investment Management Ltd (in provisional liquidation) v Maxwell* [1992] Ch 1 at 24 and 46, CA. Having said that, it is likely to be uncommon for applications to be made in voluntary liquidations.

**The examinees**—Subsection (1) provides that the range of persons who might be subjected to an examination is broad, and includes a liquidator of the company. This enables, for instance, the official receiver, where a voluntary liquidation has been converted to a compulsory liquidation, to examine the liquidator who administered the company previously in voluntary liquidation.

As far as costs and expenses of examinees go, see r 7.107 and the notes accompanying them.

## SECTION 133(1)(a)

**'Officer'**—There are a number of definitions of 'officer' in the Act (eg ss 206(3), 208(3), 210(3) and 211(2)), as well as a definition in the Companies Act 2006, s 1173. The latter section includes directors, managers and secretaries. 'Director' is explained in CA 2006, s 250 as including any person occupying the position of director by whatever name called.

**Applications for an examination**—The official receiver has a discretion as to whether to apply for an examination, save where he or she is requested to do so by those acting in accordance with the rules (see rr 7.99 and 7.100) and mentioned in s 133(2). The official receiver has a supervisory or filtering role to play (*Re Transworld Payments UK Ltd* [2020] EWHC 115, [2021] BPIR 469 at [10]). The official receiver may, if of the opinion that the request of the creditors or the contributories is an unreasonable one in the circumstances, apply to the court for an order relieving the official receiver from the obligation to make the application (r 7.101(4)). If no such application is made by the official receiver, he or she is obliged, within 28 days of receiving the request from the creditors or contributories, to make the application as required by s 133(2) (r 7.101(3)). For details concerning the procedure relating to requests by creditors and contributories, see r 7.101.

An application may be made ex parte if supported simply by evidence in the form of a report by the official receiver to the court (r 7.104(6)). Quaere whether it may be argued that an ex parte hearing is not consistent with Art 6 of the European Convention on Human Rights (applied by the Human Rights Act 1998), which gives persons the right to a fair hearing.

The court has no discretion as to whether it will order an examination, for it must direct that an examination of the person mentioned in the application be held on an appointed date (s 133(3)). However, it must not be thought that the function of the court is to act as 'a rubber stamp' to the application of the official receiver, for the court must be satisfied that the company is being wound up by the court and that the proposed examinee falls within one of the categories contained in s 133(1): *Jeeves v Official Receiver* [2003] EWCA Civ 1246, [2004] 1 WLR 602, [2004] 1 BCLC 96, CA. But, it has been said that it would only be in an exceptional case where the court could gauge, at the time of the application, that there were no questions that could be put to the prospective examinee at the examination hearing or that the examination would not serve a useful purpose: *Jeeves v Official Receiver*. Simon Brown LJ in a form of postscript in *Jeeves* (at [59]) was of the view that it would be very rare for a court to be in a position to say that an examination would serve no useful purpose, as the court could not be alive to the detailed circumstances of the case. Subsequently in *Official Receiver v Deuss*, Chief ICC Judge Briggs ([2020] EWHC 3441 (Ch), [2021] BPIR 448) said that the words 'useful purpose' was to be considered in the context of the functions of the official receiver such as the function to provide a 'D' report, obtain information regarding the administration of the estate and to give publicity concerning the reasons for the company's failure (at [26]).

**Application to set aside an order**—Once an order has been made and served, the person named as the examinee may apply for the rescission of the order (r 12.59(1)): *Jeeves v Official Receiver* [2003] EWCA Civ 1246, [2004] 1 WLR 602, [2003] BCC 912, [2004] 1 BCLC 96, CA. The applicant for rescission has the onus of establishing that the order should not have been made: *Re Casterbridge Properties Ltd (in liquidation) (No 2)* [2002] BPIR 428. A court may rescind any order of examination where it is satisfied that the person to whom the order is directed is not a person within s 133(1)(c) (see 7.102(3)), or the examination would serve no useful purpose: *Re Casterbridge Properties Ltd*. If there was a real risk that the examinee would be liable to some sanction in a foreign jurisdiction, if he or she answered questions at a public examination, then the order might be set aside as being unduly oppressive, especially where some other way was available by which the information sought by the official receiver could be obtained: *Re Mid-East Trading Ltd* [1998] 1 All ER 577, [1998] 1 BCLC 240; *Re Casterbridge Properties Ltd (in liquidation)* [2003] EWHC 1731 (Ch).

**Examinations**—The procedure and issues relating to the conducting of an examination are discussed in notes relating to r 7.98 et seq. Importantly, an examinee is not able to rely on the privilege against self-incrimination in relation to any question put to him or her (*Re Jeffery S Levitt Ltd* [1992] Ch 457, [1992] 2 WLR 975, [1992] 2 All ER 509, [1992] BCLC 250 (affirmed by the Court of Appeal [1992] Ch 578, [1992] 2 WLR 850, [1992] 2 All ER 842, [1992] BCLC 285), *Bishopsgate Investment Management Ltd (in provisional liquidation) v Maxwell* [1992] Ch 1, [1992] 2 All ER 856, [1992] BCLC 475, CA), no matter whether the examination relates to a compulsory or a voluntary liquidation. Any refusal to answer a question, on the basis of self-incrimination, is a contempt of court: *Bishopsgate Investment Management Ltd*. The self-incriminating answers of an examinee cannot be used in evidence in criminal proceedings, save those mentioned in s 433(3).

An examinee should be entitled at the examination to raise particular questions or areas of inquiry to which he or she could take objection: *Jeeves v Official Receiver* [2003] EWCA Civ 1246, [2004] 1 BCLC 96.

The court's function is to ensure that there is fair play between the person being examined and those questioning the examinee: *Re Mondelphous Engineering Associates (No 2) Ltd (in liquidation)* (1989) 7 ACLC 220. While the court that orders an examination may give a direction as to the hearing, a judge presiding at the examination has a broad discretion to allow or disallow questions (r 7.105(1)(b)): *Re Richbell Strategic Holdings Ltd (in liquidation) (No 2)* [2000] 2 BCLC 794. Questions asked only for reasons of malevolence, and not bona fide for the benefit of the creditors, contributories or the public, may be disallowed by a court: *Re London & Globe Finance Co* [1902] 2 Ch 416, 50 WR 253. Examinees are required to provide the best answers that they can to questions: *Re Richbell Strategic Holdings Ltd*. Where the company whose affairs are being examined is involved in multiple intra-group transactions, relevant questions concerning other companies in the same group may be allowed: *Re Richbell Strategic Holdings Ltd*.

It is likely that statements are able to be used in relation to civil proceedings because while the examinee is compelled to answer questions, and this might be seen as an interference with the examinee's right to privacy under Art 8 of the European Convention on Human Rights, this interference may well be seen as justified in achieving a legitimate aim (see Simmons and Smith 'The Human Rights Act 1998: the practical impact on insolvency' (2000) IL & P 167 at 171).

The procedure to be followed at a hearing is detailed in r 7.105.

The effect of non-compliance with an order to attend an examination is considered in the next section.

**Examinees out of the jurisdiction**—Courts are empowered to order the service of an order of examination on a person who is outside the jurisdiction and resident abroad, whether or not that person is a British subject: *Re Seagull Manufacturing Co Ltd (in liquidation)* [1993] Ch 345, CA (affirming [1992] Ch 128). This represents an exception to the customary approach of not applying statutes outside the jurisdiction unless they contain express wording to that effect. But, on application to set aside the order for examination, the court may consider and find that it is not appropriate to permit the examination of the respondent who is resident in a foreign jurisdiction if he or she would be liable to some sanction in that jurisdiction as a result of answering questions at an examination: *Jeeves v Official Receiver* [2003] EWCA Civ 1246 [2004] 1 BCLC 96, CA. It should be noted that the decision in *Re Seagull Manufacturing Co Ltd (in liquidation)* was delivered under previous insolvency rules where there was a rule that allowed for service. Now there would be reliance on Part 6 of the CPR: see Sch 4, para 8 of the Rules.

An examination would be rescinded where it was clear that the order would not be enforceable out of the jurisdiction: *Re Casterbridge Properties Ltd (in liquidation) (No 2)* [2002] BPIR 428.

## SECTION 133(2)

The question of whether requests had been made by 50% in value of the company's creditors was not a matter with which the court should normally become involved: *Re Transworld Payments UK Ltd* [2020] EWHC 115, [2021] BPIR 469 at [25], [59].

**[1.187]**

**134 Enforcement of s 133**

(1) If a person without reasonable excuse fails at any time to attend his public examination under section 133, he is guilty of a contempt of court and liable to be punished accordingly.

(2) In a case where a person without reasonable excuse fails at any time to attend his examination under section 133 or there are reasonable grounds for believing that a person has absconded, or is about to abscond, with a view to avoiding or delaying his examination under that section, the court may cause a warrant to be issued to a constable or prescribed officer of the court—

    (a)    for the arrest of that person; and

    (b)    for the seizure of any books, papers, records, money or goods in that person's possession.

(3) In such a case the court may authorise the person arrested under the warrant to be kept in custody, and anything seized under such a warrant to be held, in accordance with the rules, until such time as the court may order.

**General note**—This section is to be considered with s 133 in that it provides enforcement of s 133 if an examinee fails to attend an examination. Rule 12.54 should be read with s 134.

*Practice Direction – Insolvency Proceedings* (July 2020) [2020] BPIR 1211 provides in para 3.2 that an application for committal for contempt must be listed before a High Court judge.

**Warrant for arrest**—If the examinee appeals against the making of an arrest warrant, and fails, then he or she is close to contempt and may be ordered to pay, on an indemnity basis, the costs of the official receiver: *Re Avatar Communications Ltd* (1988) 4 BCC 473.

*Appointment of liquidator*

**[1.188]**

**135 Appointment and powers of provisional liquidator**

(1) Subject to the provisions of this section, the court may, at any time after the presentation of a winding-up petition, appoint a liquidator provisionally.

(2) In England and Wales, the appointment of a provisional liquidator may be made at any time before the making of a winding-up order; and either the official receiver or any other fit person may be appointed.

(3) In Scotland, such an appointment may be made at any time before the first appointment of liquidators.

(4) The provisional liquidator shall carry out such functions as the court may confer on him.

(5) When a liquidator is provisionally appointed by the court, his powers may be limited by the order appointing him.

**General note**—A court can, by the appointment of a provisional liquidator, give interim control of the company to a liquidator, from the time of the appointment until the final determination of the winding-up petition: *Re Forrester & Lamego Ltd* [1997] 2 BCLC 155 at 158. The court has a wide and unfettered discretion whether or not to appoint a provisional liquidator: *Re Union Accident Insurance Co Ltd* [1972] 1 All ER 1105 at 1109. The courts have, in recent years, been more flexible in appointing provisional liquidators: *Smith v UIC Insurance Co Ltd* [2001] BCC 11 at 20–21; *Re Namco Ltd* [2003] BPIR 1170.

The main reason for the filing of an application for the appointment of a provisional liquidator is that there is a concern that the assets and affairs of the company are in jeopardy, pending the hearing of the winding-up petition: *Re Namco Ltd* [2003] BPIR 1170 at 1174. Specifically, there can be concern that the directors and/or shareholders might dissipate the assets, disadvantaging the creditors should the company eventually be wound up. 'Dissipation' in this regard does not just mean the directors and/or others making away with the assets, it can also refer to the fact that there is a serious risk that the assets may not continue to be available to the company: *The Commisioners for HMRC v Rochdale Drinks Distributors Ltd* [2011] EWCA Civ 1116, [2012] 1 BCLC 748, [2011] BPIR 1604 at [99]. This could be where, notwithstanding the presentation of a petition, the directors continue to trade a loss-making company without securing an order under s 127: ibid. In the context of the company's assets, 'assets' is to be given a broad meaning: *HMRC v Winnington Networks Ltd* [2014] EWHC 1259 (Ch) at [9].

A provisional liquidator is appointed to preserve the status quo (*Re Dry Docks Corporation of London* (1888) 39 ChD 306; *Re Namco Ltd* [2003] BPIR 1170 at 1173), but on occasions it might be appropriate for the provisional liquidator to wind down the company's business so as to reduce costs: *Re Union Accident Insurance Co Ltd* [1972] 1 All ER 1105.

The power provided for in this section has been referred to as a draconian power (*Re Forrester & Lamego Ltd* [1997] 2 BCLC 155 at 158) as it involves a serious intrusion into the affairs of the company, and it can often paralyse the company: *Re London, Hamburg & Continental Exchange Bank, Emmerson's Case* [1866] LR 2 Eq 231 at 237. So, if there are other adequate ways of preserving the status quo, they should be considered first: *Constantinidis v JGL Trading Pty Ltd* (1995) 17 ACSR 625 at 635, 647. The courts are particularly cautious about making an order where its consequence is almost inevitably to end the trading of the company: *Re Parkwell Investments Ltd* [2014] EWHC 3381 (Ch).

In hearing an application for the appointment of a provisional liquidator the court should first determine whether the applicant is likely to obtain a winding-up order on the hearing of the petition: *The Commissioners for HMRC v Rochdale Drinks Distributors Ltd* [2011] EWCA Civ 1116, [2012] 1 BCLC 748, [2011] BPIR 1604 at [77], [78]. In this respect John Randall QC (sitting as a deputy judge of the High Court) in *Re SED Essex Ltd* ([2013] EWHC 1583 (Ch) at [8]) said that a company has a burden to show a good arguable case where the evidential burden has switched to it (after the applicant has laid down a basis for an appointment), the company then has to make out a sufficiently strong case to negate such likelihood. If the company cannot provide sufficient evidence then the court must consider whether in the circumstances of the case it is right for a provisional liquidator to be appointed: *Re Union Accident Insurance Co Ltd* [1972] 1 All ER 1105 at 1110 and approved by the Court of Appeal in *The Commissioners for HMRC v Rochdale Drinks Distributors Ltd* at [77]. In arriving at its decision the court should take into account the prejudice which the applicant may suffer if there is no appointment or the company may suffer if it is: ibid at [109]. Although not generally required the court might require the applicant for an order to provide an undertaking to pay damages on the appointment of a provisional liquidator: (*HMRC v Winnington Networks Ltd* [2014] EWHC 1259 (Ch)). If an undertaking is required and given then the undertaking is not automatically at an end once a winding-up order is made by the court so as to deprive the courts of jurisdiction to enforce the undertaking. The courts can still order an inquiry as to damages: *Abbey Forwarding Ltd v HRMC* [2015] EWHC 225 (Ch). In *Re Parkwell Investments Ltd* [2014] EWHC 3381 (Ch) it has been said that it was not appropriate to require HMRC to give an undertaking as to damages as they could be distinguished from a private litigant on the basis they have a public interest function to discharge. In *Re Rigil Kent Acquisitions Ltd* [2017] EWHC 3636 (Ch), [2018] BCC 591, Smith J said that when the Crown is taking proceedings to enforce the law there was no requirement as to an undertaking in damages unless the respondent demonstrated special circumstances. This is in contrast to where the Crown is taking proceedings to enforce some proprietary right.

While it has been held that applications may be made ex parte (eg *Re a Company (No 007070 of 1996)* [1997] 2 BCLC 139 at 142), normally an order will not be made on an ex parte application as the company should be served with notice of the application, except where this is not practicable: *Re London and Manchester Industrial Association* (1875) 1 ChD 466, such as in the circumstances where there is no time to give notice before the appointment is required to prevent the threatened wrongful act: *Commissioners for HMRC v Rochdale Drinks Distributors Ltd* [2011] EWCA Civ 1116, [2012] 1 BCLC 748, [2011] BPIR 1604 at [111], or either the effect of giving notice would enable the directors or others to take steps to defeat the purpose behind the appointment: *The Commissioners for HMRC v Rochdale Drinks Distributors Ltd* at [111]. In this case the court said that any notice is better than nothing: at [111]. More recently Norris J has said that before making an order on an ex parte application, exceptional circumstances need to exist (*HMRC v Winnington Networks Ltd* [2014] EWHC 1259 (Ch) at [4]) and a court had to have a fair picture of the prevailing circumstances and that the petitioner has provided full and frank disclosure. The court is entitled to consider the company's engagement with and response to any earlier investigative steps undertaken by the petitioner: *HMRC v Winnington Networks Ltd* [2014] EWHC 1259 (Ch) at [7]). In *Re Debenhams plc* ([2020] EWHC 1755 (Ch) at [12]) ICC Judge Mullen indicated that he would be very cautious about making an order where the application was without notice.

In exceptional circumstances an appointment will be made where a petition for winding up has been presented against a company that is in voluntary liquidation: *Securities and Investments Board v Lancashire and Yorkshire Portfolio Management Ltd* [1992] BCLC 281; *Re a Company (No 007070 of 1996)* [1997] 2 BCLC 139; *Re Pinstripe Farming Co Ltd* [1996] 2 BCLC 295.

The appointment of a provisional liquidator does not affect the company's legal position. It does not mean that any contracts of the company are terminated, unless there is some provision in the contract itself to this effect: *BCCI v Malik* [1996] BCC 15 at 17. The appointment does mean that there is an automatic stay on the commencement and prosecution of legal proceedings, unless the leave of the court is obtained (s 130(2)). Also, in order to ensure that the provisional liquidator is placed in control of the company's affairs, the authority of any agent of the company appointed by or on the behalf of the directors is revoked: *Pacific & General Insurance Ltd (in liquidation) v Home & Overseas Insurance Co Ltd* [1997] BCC 400.

The provisional liquidator may require some or all of the persons referred to in s 131(3) to make out and submit a statement of affairs of the company (s 131(1)), as well as require any persons who have in their possession or control company property etc to pay, deliver, convey, surrender or transfer the property etc of the company to the provisional liquidator (s 234(2)).

The notion of appointing a provisional liquidator is analogous to the appointment of an interim receiver when a bankruptcy petition has been presented: eg *Re Baars* [2003] BPIR 523.

In regard to a provisional liquidator being liable to pay non-party costs in relation to legal proceedings under s 51 of the Supreme Court Act 1981, a provisional liquidator is seen as being closer to a liquidator than a director and so a court would be less inclined to make an order under s 51: *Apex Frozen Foods Ltd v Ali* [2007] EWHC 469 (Ch), [2007] BPIR 1437.

The principle which enables rent falling due during liquidation to be treated as if it were a liquidation expense if the property is retained for the benefit of the liquidation, applies to provisional liquidation (see the notes to r 7.108): *MK Airlines Property Ltd (in administration) v Katz* (unreported) (Mr N Strauss QC, 16 May 2012, ChD).

It is notable that a provisional liquidator is now a liquidator for the purposes of art 2(b) of the EU Regulation on Insolvency Proceedings (see Annex C to the Regulation).

The procedure and practice is detailed in rr 7.33–7.39. See those rules and the notes relating to them.

**Hearing**—Ordinarily, the hearing should be in public. But, given the fact that appointments may have significant ramifications for a company, a judge could order that the hearing be heard in camera.

**Grounds**—As no grounds are specified in the section (and the relevant rule, r 7.33(5) merely refers to sufficient grounds) and the courts have a wide discretion, it is not possible to identify with any certainty what grounds will suffice for an order: *ASC v Solomon* (1996) 19 ACSR 73. Often an order will be made because of a number of factors: *Commonwealth v Hendon Industrial Park Pty Ltd* (1995) 17 ACSR 358.

**Urgency**—Appointments often are required to be made on the basis of urgency: eg *Re Hammersmith Town Hall Company* (1877) 6 ChD 112. Because of this, courts might not require strict adherence to the relevant procedure. In *Re WF Fearman Ltd* (1987) 4 BCC 139 an application for an appointment was heard in circumstances where there was no application in writing and the usual procedural requirements had not been followed, and yet the appointment was made.

**Other grounds**—These include: danger to assets (*Re Marseilles Extension Railway and Land Co* [1867] WN 68; *Re a Company (No 003102 of 1991)* [1991] BCLC 539); deadlock in company affairs because of disputes between shareholders or directors; the affairs of the company are in jeopardy because of the directors (*Re Brackland Magazines Ltd*, sub nom *Gamlestaden plc v Brackland Magazines Ltd* [1994] 1 BCLC 190; a need for a speedy and careful investigation of the company's affairs: *Re a Company (No 007070 of 1996)* [1997] 2 BCLC 139; where there is real concern over the integrity of the management of the company and as to the quality of the accounting and record-keeping function of management: *Commissioners for HMRC v Rochdale Drinks Distributors Ltd* [2011] EWCA Civ 1116, [2012] 1 BCLC 748, [2011] BPIR 1604 at [100]. In *Re SED Essex Ltd* [2013] EWHC 1583 (Ch) at [16] John Randall QC (sitting as a deputy judge of the High Court) said that in determining whether there should be an appointment or retention of provisional liquidators in office, the factors a court should consider include whether there are real questions as to the integrity of the management of the company and/or as to the quality of the company's accounting and record keeping function, whether there is any real risk of dissipation of the company's assets and/or any real need to take steps to preserve them, whether there is any real risk that the company's books and records will be destroyed and/ or any real need for steps to be taken to ensure that they are properly preserved and maintained, whether there is any real need for steps to be taken to facilitate immediate inquiries into the conduct of the company's management and affairs and/or to investigate and consider possible claims against directors (eg for fraudulent or wrongful trading), whether or not the company has a realistic prospect of obtaining a validation order under s 127 of the Act.

A provisional liquidator has been appointed when the court is of the view that the company's affairs are in a chaotic state and a danger to the public interest: *ASIC v Tax Returns Australia Dot Com Pty Ltd* [2010] FCA 715. In another Australian case it has been said that in deciding whether to appoint a provisional liquidator the public interest in general is a relevant consideration: *Australian Securities and Investments Commission v Planet Platinum Ltd* [2015] VSC 273.

**Applicants**— These are enumerated in r 7.33(1). The most frequent applicants are creditors and the Secretary of State for Business, Energy and Industrial Strategy, the latter where he or she is seeking to wind up the company under s 124A. But contributories have been successful. For a recent example, see *Re Beppler and Jacobson* [2012] EWHC 3648 (Ch).

'**Any other fit person**'—While the official receiver will often be appointed as the provisional liquidator, s 135(2) provides that it could also be any other fit person. This designation is a reference to a licensed insolvency practitioner who is qualified to act in relation to the company (s 390): for an example, see In *Re Grey Marlin Ltd* [1999] 2 BCLC 658. This accords with the decision of the Court of Appeal in *Gibson Dunn & Crutcher v Rio Properties Inc* [2004] EWCA Civ 1043 where it held, in relation to the appointment of an interim receiver in bankruptcy, that someone other than the official receiver could be appointed. Where an insolvency practitioner is appointed, he or she must fulfil the same qualities that generally apply to the appointment of liquidators. This will involve avoiding the appointment of persons who have associations with the applicant and the company. The court will want someone who is independent: *Levy v Napier* 1962 SC 468 at 475, 478. See the notes relating to s 108.

**Order**—The contents of an order are enumerated in r 7.35. The court has a discretion as to what orders are made besides the actual appointment, and wide powers can be conferred in the order (eg *Re BCCI* [1992] BCLC 579; *Smith v UIC Insurance Co Ltd* [2001] BCC 11), such as those powers mentioned in Sch 4 relating to liquidators: *Re Hawk Insurance Co Ltd* [2001] BCC 57. In determining the powers that the court will bestow on the liquidator the court has to decide whether, based on the evidence, the powers were ultimately necessary to the liquidator to perform his or her mandate: *Moodliar v Hendricks* 2011 (2) SA 199.

It has often been the case that the order indicates the property over which the appointee will have power. On limited occasions, the order may specify that the provisional liquidator shall have some of the powers of a permanent liquidator, including the power of settling a list of contributories, making calls and admitting and rejecting creditors' proofs of debt: *Re English Bank of the River Plate* [1892] 1 Ch 391. The order is to state what functions the provisional liquidator is to carry out (r 7.35(1)(h)). Courts may grant liquidators the power, in unusual circumstances, to circulate material about creditors of the company to other creditors: *Equitas Ltd v Jacob* [2005] EWHC 1440 (Ch), [2005] BPIR 1312.

There is Australian authority to the effect that courts are able to make an order retrospectively granting a provisional liquidator power to do something: *Re Colorado Products Pty Ltd* [2013] NSWSC 1613.

**Remuneration**—The general principles are discussed in *Re Independent Insurance Company Ltd (No 1)* [2003] BPIR 562. Also, see rr 7.38, 18.16 and 18.20 and the notes accompanying r 7.38.

If provisional liquidators are impeded in the execution of their duties and their tasks by the officers of the company then the court can hold the latter in contempt: *HMRC v Munir* [2015] EWHC 1366 (Ch).

For further details, see Husband 'Application by a petitioning company for the appointment of a provisional liquidator' (2000) 16 IL & P 3; A Keay *McPherson and Keay's Law of Company Liquidation* (Sweet and Maxwell, 4th edn, 2018), Ch 6.

For discussion of the powers of provisional liquidators, see notes accompanying r 7.35.

Generally, see rr 7.33–7.39 and the accompanying notes.

**[1.189]**

### 136 Functions of official receiver in relation to office of liquidator

(1)   The following provisions of this section have effect, subject to section 140 below, on a winding-up order being made by the court in England and Wales.

(2)   The official receiver, by virtue of his office, becomes the liquidator of the company and continues in office until another person becomes liquidator under the provisions of this Part.

(3)   The official receiver is, by virtue of his office, the liquidator during any vacancy.

(4)   At any time when he is the liquidator of the company, the official receiver may in accordance with the rules seek nominations from the company's creditors and contributories for the purpose of choosing a person to be liquidator of the company in place of the official receiver.

(5)   It is the duty of the official receiver—

    (a)   as soon as practicable in the period of 12 weeks beginning with the day on which the winding-up order was made, to decide whether to exercise his power under subsection (4), and

    (b)   if in pursuance of paragraph (a) he decides not to exercise that power, to give notice of his decision, before the end of that period, to the court and to the company's creditors and contributories, and

(c)     (whether or not he has decided to exercise that power) to exercise his power under subsection (4) if he is at any time requested, in accordance with the rules, to do so by one-quarter, in value, of the company's creditors;

and accordingly, where the duty imposed by paragraph (c) arises before the official receiver has performed a duty imposed by paragraph (a) or (b), he is not required to perform the latter duty.

(6)   A notice given under subsection (5)(b) to the company's creditors shall contain an explanation of the creditors' power under subsection (5)(c) to require the official receiver to seek nominations from the company's creditors and contributories.

**Amendments**—Small Business, Enterprise and Employment Act 2015, s 126, Sch 9, Pt 1, paras 1, 31.

**General note**—It is necessary to read the section in light of s 137.

While in most cases the official receiver becomes the liquidator on the making of a winding-up order, there are two exceptions to this. First, in the case where a winding-up order immediately follows the discharge of an administration order. Here the court may appoint the person who occupied the position of administrator as liquidator (s 140(1)). Second, where a winding-up order is made when there is a supervisor of a company voluntary arrangement in post. In such a case a court may appoint the supervisor as liquidator at the time of the making of the winding-up order (s 140(2)). In each of these situations the insolvency practitioner who was acting as either the administrator or the supervisor would be aware of the affairs of the company, and it would be sensible for him or her to continue to administer the affairs of the company.

**Nominations**—This is covered by r 7.52 and s 139.

## [1.190]

### 137 Appointment by Secretary of State

(1)   In a winding up by the court in England and Wales the official receiver may, at any time when he is the liquidator of the company, apply to the Secretary of State for the appointment of a person as liquidator in his place.

(2)   If nominations are sought from the company's creditors and contributories in pursuance of a decision under section 136(5)(a), but no person is chosen to be liquidator as a result, it is the duty of the official receiver to decide whether to refer the need for an appointment to the Secretary of State.

(3)   On an application under subsection (1), or a reference made in pursuance of a decision under subsection (2), the Secretary of State shall either make an appointment or decline to make one.

(4)   Where a liquidator has been appointed by the Secretary of State under subsection (3), the liquidator shall give notice of his appointment to the company's creditors or, if the court so allows, shall advertise his appointment in accordance with the directions of the court.

(5)   In that notice or advertisement the liquidator must explain the procedure for establishing a liquidation committee under section 141.

**Amendments**—Small Business, Enterprise and Employment Act 2015, s 126, Sch 9, Pt 1, paras 1, 32.

'**Apply for the appointment of a person as liquidator**'—This is a right that is able to be exercised instead of seeking the views of the creditors and the contributories under s 136.

See r 7.57.

## [1.191]

### 138 Appointment of liquidator in Scotland

(1)   Where a winding-up order is made by the court in Scotland, a liquidator shall be appointed by the court at the time when the order is made.

(2)   The liquidator so appointed (here referred to as "the interim liquidator") continues in office until another person becomes liquidator in his place under this section or the next.

(3)   The interim liquidator shall (subject to the next subsection) as soon as practicable in the period of 28 days beginning with the day on which the winding-up order was made or such longer period as the court may allow, in accordance with the rules seek

nominations from the company's creditors and contributories for the purpose of choosing a person (who may be the person who is the interim liquidator) to be liquidator of the company in place of the interim liquidator.

(4)   If it appears to the interim liquidator, in any case where a company is being wound up on grounds including its inability to pay its debts, that it would be inappropriate to seek a nomination from the company's contributories under subsection (3), he may seek a nomination only from the company's creditors for the purpose mentioned in that subsection.

(5)   If a nomination is sought from the company's creditors, or nominations are sought from the company's creditors and contributories, in pursuance of this section but no person is appointed or nominated as a result, the interim liquidator shall make a report to the court which shall appoint either the interim liquidator or some other person to be liquidator of the company.

(6)   A person who becomes liquidator of the company in place of the interim liquidator shall, unless he is appointed by the court, forthwith notify the court of that fact.

**Amendments**—Small Business, Enterprise and Employment Act 2015, s 126, Sch 9, Pt 1, paras 1, 33.

## [1.192]

### 139 Choice of liquidator by creditors and contributories

(1)   This section applies where a company is being wound up by the court and nominations are sought from the company's creditors and contributories for the purpose of choosing a person to be liquidator of the company.

(2)   The creditors and the contributories may in accordance with the rules nominate a person to be liquidator.

(3)   The liquidator shall be the person nominated by the creditors or, where no person has been so nominated, the person (if any) nominated by the contributories.

(4)   In the case of different persons being nominated, any contributory or creditor may, within 7 days after the date on which the nomination was made by the creditors, apply to the court for an order either—

  (a)    appointing the person nominated as liquidator by the contributories to be a liquidator instead of, or jointly with, the person nominated by the creditors; or

  (b)    appointing some other person to be liquidator instead of the person nominated by the creditors.

**Amendments**—Small Business, Enterprise and Employment Act 2015, s 126, Sch 9, Pt 1, paras 1, 34.

**General note**—This is analogous to s 100, which deals with the appointment of a liquidator in a creditors' voluntary liquidation.

The creditors will usually nominate a liquidator and that nomination will normally prevail.

See the notes under 'Secretary of State shall make an appointment or decline to make one' in s 137 relating to the fact that creditors do not seem to have the right to convene a meeting to consider the appointee.

The court must not issue the order of appointment unless and until the appointee files in court a statement to the effect that he or she is a licensed insolvency practitioner, duly qualified to act as the liquidator and that he or she consents to acting as the liquidator (r 7.56(1), (2)).

See r 7.53.

## [1.193]

### 140 Appointment by the court following administration or voluntary arrangement

(1)   Where a winding-up order is made immediately upon the appointment of an administrator ceasing to have effect, the court may appoint as liquidator of the company the person whose appointment as administrator has ceased to have effect.

(2)   Where a winding-up order is made at a time when there is a supervisor of a voluntary arrangement approved in relation to the company under Part I, the court may appoint as liquidator of the company the person who is the supervisor at the time when the winding-up order is made.

(3)   Where the court makes an appointment under this section, the official receiver does not become the liquidator as otherwise provided by section 136(2), and section 136(5)(a) and (b) does not apply.

**Amendments**—Enterprise Act 2002, s 248(3), Sch 17, paras 9, 17; Small Business, Enterprise and Employment Act 2015, s 126, Sch 9, Pt 1, paras 1, 30.

**General note**—The section grants to the court a discretionary power to by-pass the normal procedure for the appointment of liquidators prescribed by ss 136 and 139: *Re Exchange Travel (Holdings) Ltd* [1993] BCLC 887. Section 140 provides two instances where the official receiver might not become the liquidator of a company following the making of a winding-up order. These exceptions exist probably because it is sensible and cost-effective to allow the insolvency practitioner who has acted either as the administrator of the company or the supervisor of a company voluntary arrangement to continue to administer the company's affairs, as he or she will be aware of the issues that need addressing, know the company's background and will not have to do some of the things that a liquidator, coming fresh to the company, would have to do. However, it is necessary also to consider the fact that the creditors should have a say in who acts as liquidator; they will have had contact with the administrator and they may have some concerns over him or her being appointed as liquidator.

The court might decide to invoke s 140(1) even where there is a question mark against the administrator or supervisor. In *Re Charnley Davies Business Services Ltd* (1987) 3 BCC 408 the court appointed the person who was the former administrator despite pending proceedings against the administrator alleging irregularities on his part while acting as administrator. The reasons for this decision were somewhat pragmatic, namely, taking into account the time lapse in appointing the official receiver, and the fact that there was no other nominee: *Re Charnley Davies* at 412.

If there is a dispute between a creditor and the administrator who wishes to become liquidator, and the creditor is against the administrator becoming liquidator, the administrator should remain neutral as to his or her appointment as liquidator: *Re Ariadne Capital Ltd* (unreported, Chief ICC Judge Briggs, 7 December 2018, [7]).

The court must not issue the order of appointment unless and until the appointee files in court a statement to the effect that he or she is an insolvency practitioner, duly qualified to act as the liquidator and that he or she consents to acting as the liquidator (r 7.56(1), (2)).

If an administration order is discharged and followed by a compulsory winding up, with the administrator being appointed liquidator under this section, then any creditors' committee established for the administration becomes the liquidation committee and is deemed to have been established pursuant to s 140 (r 17.29(1)), unless fewer than three members of that committee have agreed to act (r 17.29(3)).

It has been held in *Re Firepower Operations Pty Ltd (No 2)* [2008] FCA 1228 by the Australian Federal Court that in considering whether to appoint to the position of liquidator the incumbent administrator or another practitioner, the court may take into account the relative funding capabilities of each. There is other Australian authority to the effect that a court is able to appoint a single liquidator to deal with the liquidation of more than one company in a corporate group in the situation where a number of companies in the group occupied debtor/creditor relationships in respect of one another: *ASIC v Westpoint Corporation Pty Ltd* [2006] FCA 135. One assumes that this would be subject to the rider that the liquidator would not be placed potentially in a conflict of interest situation (*Re City & County Investment Co* (1877) 25 WR 342; *Re Greight Pty Ltd (in liquidation)* [2006] FCA 17).

See the notes under 'Secretary of State shall make an appointment or decline to make one' in s 137 relating to the fact that creditors do not seem to be able to requisition a decision on the appointee.

*Liquidation committees*

## [1.194]

### 141  Liquidation committee (England and Wales)
(1)   This section applies where a winding up order has been made by the court in England and Wales.

(2)   If both the company's creditors and the company's contributories decide that a liquidation committee should be established, a liquidation committee is to be established in accordance with the rules.

(3)   If only the company's creditors, or only the company's contributories, decide that a liquidation committee should be established, a liquidation committee is to be established in accordance with the rules unless the court orders otherwise.

(3A)  A "liquidation committee" is a committee having such functions as are conferred on it by or under this Act.

(3B)  The liquidator must seek a decision from the company's creditors and contributories as to whether a liquidation committee should be established if requested, in accordance with the rules, to do so by one-tenth in value of the company's creditors.

(3C)  Subsection (3B) does not apply where the liquidator is the official receiver.

(4)  The liquidation committee is not to be able or required to carry out its functions at any time when the official receiver is liquidator; but at any such time its functions are vested in the Secretary of State except to the extent that the rules otherwise provide.

(5)  Where there is for the time being no liquidation committee, and the liquidator is a person other than the official receiver, the functions of such a committee are vested in the Secretary of State except to the extent that the rules otherwise provide.

**Amendments**—Small Business, Enterprise and Employment Act 2015, s 126, Sch 9, Pt 1, paras 1, 36.

**General note**—This is the compulsory winding up equivalent to s 101 that applies to creditors' voluntary liquidations. Liquidation committees are consultative rather than administrative or supervisory bodies. Australian authority indicates that they have an oversight role on behalf of the creditors: *Southern Cross Airlines Holdings Ltd v Arthur Anderson & Co* (1998) 16 ACLC 485 at 462.

The members of the committee are in a fiduciary position in relation to the creditors and contributories (*Re Geiger* [1915] 1 KB 439 at 447; *Re Bulmer* [1937] Ch 499 at 502), and as a consequence they are not permitted either to obtain a profit from their office, or to allow their private interests to conflict with their duties as committee members. Members must seek the approval of the court to benefit from their positions, and this must be obtained before any transaction is entered into that leads to a profit for a committee member: *Re Gallard* [1896] 1 QB 68 at 72–73; *Re FT Hawkins & Co* [1952] Ch 881 at 884.

If the creditors do not decide that a liquidation committee should be established, or decide that a committee should not be established, the contributories may decide to appoint one of their number to make application to the court for an order requiring the liquidator to seek a further decision from the creditors on whether to establish a liquidation committee; and the court may, if it thinks that there are special circumstances to justify it, make such an order; and the creditors' decision sought by the liquidator in compliance with the order is deemed to have been a decision under s 141 (r 17.6(2)). If the creditors decide not to establish a liquidation committee, the contributories may establish a committee (r 17.6(3)). In such a situation the committee must then consist of at least three, and not more than five, contributories elected by the contributories (r 17.6(4)).

The court is not empowered to remove a member of the committee, but it may direct the liquidator to convene a decision procedure of the creditors and contributories for them to consider removal (*Re Radford & Bright Ltd* [1901] 1 ChD 272).

For the powers and functions of the committee, see s 167 and the notes relating to that section. Although the duties in s 167 focus on the supervisory nature of the committee, in practice the committee tends to function more in a consultative capacity. Notwithstanding the wide powers and functions of the committee, members do not have the right to inspect, or ask the liquidator questions about documents that might be conveyed between the liquidator and the Department of Business, Energy and Industrial Strategy relating to the possible disqualification of directors of the company: *Re W&A Glaser Ltd* [1994] BCC 199 at 205. By analogy with creditors' committees in administration, the views of a liquidation committee should be considered by a liquidator as representing the views of the creditors, but it is not for the committee to decide how a liquidation should be conducted. That was for the liquidator: *Re Brilliant Independent Media Specialists Ltd* [2014] BPIR 1395.

Where a committee will not sanction a course of action for which the liquidator needs sanction, the liquidator is entitled to apply to the court for approval, and while the court will consider the opinion of the committee, it is able to overrule the committee's decision: *Re Northern Assurance Co Ltd* (1915) 113 LT 989.

**SECTION 141(2)**

**Composition of committee**—Rule 17.3 provides that in a compulsory winding up, where a committee is established under s 141 the committee is to consist of at least three, and not more than five members, elected by the creditors and where the grounds on which the company was wound up do not include an inability to pay its debts, and where the contributories so decide, up to three contributory members elected by the contributories: r 17.3(3).

While a court is not granted any express power to interfere with the composition of a committee that has been established in line with the requirements in the Act and Rules, the court is to ensure that no creditor or class of creditors with a substantial interest is excluded from the representation which it wishes to have: *Re Radford & Bright Ltd* [1901] 1 ChD 272 at 277.

**Remuneration**—No provision in the Act or Rules provides for remuneration of the committee members. Court approval has to be obtained before a member receives any remuneration (r 17.25). Such approval is likely to be rare, and might only be granted where the member(s) has rendered special services in the course of liquidation: *Re Security Directors Pty Ltd (in liquidation)* (1997) 24 ACSR 558, Vic S Ct).

**Expenses**—The liquidator must pay, as an expense of the insolvency proceedings, the reasonable travelling expenses directly incurred by members of the committee or their representatives in attending the committee's meetings or otherwise on the committee's business (r 17.24).

**No committee**—In such a case the Secretary of State has the functions of a committee vested in him or her. Dear IP No 43, January 1999 sets out the guidelines for requests for sanction.

Where the liquidator has done anything without permission, when he or she needed permission, the liquidation committee may, for the purpose of enabling the liquidator to meet the liquidator's expenses out of the assets, ratify what the liquidator has done; but it must not do so unless satisfied that the liquidator has acted in a case of urgency and has sought ratification without undue delay (r 7.77(3)).

Generally, see Pt 17 of the IR 2016 and the notes accompanying those rules.

## [1.195]

### 142 Liquidation committee (Scotland)

(1) This section applies where a winding up order has been made by the court in Scotland.

(2) If both the company's creditors and the company's contributories decide that a liquidation committee should be established, a liquidation committee is to be established in accordance with the rules.

(3) If only the company's creditors, or only the company's contributories, decide that a liquidation committee should be established, a liquidation committee is to be established in accordance with the rules unless the court orders otherwise.

(3A) A "liquidation committee" is a committee having such functions as are conferred on it by or under this Act.

(4) A liquidator appointed by the court other than under section 139(4)(a) must seek a decision from the company's creditors and contributories as to whether a liquidation committee should be established if requested, in accordance with the rules, to do so by one-tenth in value of the company's creditors.

(5) Where in the case of any winding up there is for the time being no liquidation committee, the functions of such a committee are vested in the court except to the extent that the rules otherwise provide.

(6) A "liquidation committee" is a committee having the powers and duties conferred and imposed on it by this Act, and such of the powers and duties of commissioners in a sequestration as may be conferred and imposed on such committees by the rules.

**Amendments**—Small Business, Enterprise and Employment Act 2015, s 126, Sch 9, Pt 1, paras 1, 37.

*The liquidator's functions*

## [1.196]

### 143 General functions in winding up by the court

(1) The functions of the liquidator of a company which is being wound up by the court are to secure that the assets of the company are got in, realised and distributed to the company's creditors and, if there is a surplus, to the persons entitled to it.

(2) It is the duty of the liquidator of a company which is being wound up by the court in England and Wales, if he is not the official receiver—

    (a)    to furnish the official receiver with such information,

    (b)    to produce to the official receiver, and permit inspection by the official receiver of, such books, papers and other records, and

    (c)    to give the official receiver such other assistance,

as the official receiver may reasonably require for the purposes of carrying out his functions in relation to the winding up.

**General note**—This provision sets out in general terms the functions that must be completed by a liquidator. How the liquidator actually carries out the functions contained in the section is, generally, left to his or her judgment and discretion. However, some matters (eg the making of calls on contributories and dealing with claims by creditors) are specifically addressed by the Act and the Rules. In discharging his or her functions the liquidator is acting as a fiduciary whose obligations are owed to the company and the body of creditors (*Knowles v Scott* [1891] 1 Ch 717 at 723; *Re Home & Colonial Insurance Co* [1930] 1 Ch 102 at 125, 133), and as a consequence the liquidator is required to act honestly, with due care, and with such a degree of diligence that will ensure that the winding up will be completed within a reasonable time frame, though what is reasonable will depend very much on the circumstances of the company in question: *Re House Property & Investment Co* [1954] Ch 576 at 612.

**'Assets are got in'**—The liquidator might make use of s 234 to assist in the collection of assets. See the notes accompanying that section.

Where any property of the company has been seized in execution, the liquidator should serve notice on the High Court enforcement officers requiring delivery of the property to the liquidator together with any money seized or received in part satisfaction of the execution (s 184).

**'Realised'**—In order to do this the liquidator is authorised by para 6 of Sch 4 to sell or otherwise dispose of all or any part of the property of the company. If the liquidator realises property that is subject to mortgages or charges, or other securities, he or she may deduct a reasonable sum from the proceeds in order to meet the cost of realisation before paying the proceeds to the extent of the principal debt and any outstanding interest due to the secured creditor: *Re Marine Mansions Co* (1867) 4 Eq 601; *Buchler v Talbot* [2004] UKHL 9, [2004] 2 AC 298, [2004] 2 WLR 582, [2004] 1 BCLC 281.

The realisation of the assets of the company should be carried out in the most efficient way, so as to obtain the highest possible price for the assets, and the winding up should not be unnecessarily protracted.

**'Distributed to the company's creditors'**—Reference should be had to the notes accompanying s 107. Also, see A Keay *McPherson and Keay's Law of Company Liquidation* (Sweet and Maxwell, 4th edn, 2018), Ch 13.

**Distributed a surplus to the persons entitled**—In a compulsory liquidation, this is a very unlikely occurrence, save where the winding up is made pursuant to s 122(1)(g)).

See the notes accompanying s 107 and A Keay *McPherson and Keay's Law of Company Liquidation* (Sweet and Maxwell, 4th edn, 2018), Ch 14.

See s 212 and r 12.52(1)(d) and the notes relating to that section and rule.

For a detailed discussion of the functions, duties and powers of liquidators, see A Keay *McPherson and Keay's Law of Company Liquidation* (Sweet and Maxwell, 4th edn, 2018) at 468–477 and Ch 9.

## [1.197]

### 144 Custody of company's property

(1) When a winding-up order has been made, or where a provisional liquidator has been appointed, the liquidator or the provisional liquidator (as the case may be) shall take into his custody or under his control all the property and things in action to which the company is or appears to be entitled.

(2) In a winding up by the court in Scotland, if and so long as there is no liquidator, all the property of the company is deemed to be in the custody of the court.

**General note**—This is a wide duty placed on the liquidator, for he or she must collect or control all of the company's property, including property to which the company appears to be entitled. It is likely that a liquidator will take charge of any property over which ownership rights are in doubt and then negotiate with anyone who appears to have a claim to the property.

**'Property'**—This is defined very broadly in s 436.

## [1.198]

### 145 Vesting of company property in liquidator

(1) When a company is being wound up by the court, the court may on the application of the liquidator by order direct that all or any part of the property of whatsoever

description belonging to the company or held by trustees on its behalf shall vest in the liquidator by his official name; and thereupon the property to which the order relates vests accordingly.

(2)   The liquidator may, after giving such indemnity (if any) as the court may direct, bring or defend in his official name any action or other legal proceeding which relates to that property or which it is necessary to bring or defend for the purpose of effectually winding up the company and recovering its property.

General note—On winding up, while the company is divested of the beneficial interest in its property, the legal title remains in the company: *Ayerst v C & K (Constructions) Ltd* [1976] AC 167, HL. While the Privy Council has endorsed this view (*Cambridge Gas Transport Corporation v Official Committee of Unsecured Creditors of Navigator Holdings plc* [2006] UKPC 26), a majority of the Australian High Court (Kirby J dissenting) has declined to follow *Ayerst* and has held that on winding up there is not a change in beneficial ownership of company assets: *Commissioner of Taxation v Linter Australia Ltd (in liquidation)* [2005] HCA 20. See Mokal, 'What Liquidation Does For Secured Creditors, And What It Does For You' (2008) 71 MLR 699 for an interesting discussion of some aspects of the case law and the relevant concepts involved.

Unlike with bankruptcy, where a bankruptcy order vests the bankrupt's property in the trustee in bankruptcy (s 306), a winding-up order does not have that effect, and company property continues to belong to the company: *John Mackintosh & Sons Ltd v Baker's Bargain Stores (Seaford) Ltd* [1965] 1 WLR 1182. Notwithstanding that, liquidators may apply for and obtain an order vesting in them all of any portion of the property of the company, in which case it vests in liquidators in their official capacity: *Graham v Edge* (1888) 20 QBD 683. Section 145(2) permits liquidators to bring and defend legal proceedings in respect of vested property in their own official name, namely 'X as the liquidator of ABC Ltd'.

Applications for vesting orders are extremely uncommon, probably because the liquidator is given wide powers by the Act in Sch 4.

## [1.199]

### 146 Final account

(1)   This section applies where a company is being wound up by the court and the liquidator is not the official receiver.

(2)   If it appears to the liquidator that the winding up of the company is for practical purposes complete the liquidator must make up an account of the winding up, showing how it has been conducted and the company's property has been disposed of.

(3)   The liquidator must—

(a)     send a copy of the account to the company's creditors (other than opted-out creditors), and

(b)     give the company's creditors (other than opted-out creditors) a notice explaining the effect of section 174(4)(d) and how they may object to the liquidator's release.

(4)   The liquidator must during the relevant period send to the court and the registrar of companies—

(a)     a copy of the account, and

(b)     a statement of whether any of the company's creditors objected to the liquidator's release.

(5)   The relevant period is the period of 7 days beginning with the day after the last day of the period prescribed by the rules as the period within which the creditors may object to the liquidator's release.

(6)   . . .

(7)   . . .

Amendments—Substituted by Small Business, Enterprise and Employment Act 2015, s 126, Sch 9, Pt 1, paras 1, 38. Amended by SI 2017/702; SI 2019/146, as from IP completion day (as defined in the European Union (Withdrawal Agreement) Act 2020, s 39(1)–(5)).

General note—This is the compulsory winding-up equivalent of the provision covering creditors' voluntary winding up (s 106) and the provision covering members' voluntary winding up (s 94). See the notes accompanying these sections. Also, see rr 7.69 and 7.71.

The official receiver, where he or she is the liquidator, will apply to the Secretary of State for release (s 174(3)).

**146A**

*(Repealed)*

**Amendment**—Inserted by SI 2017/702. Repealed by SI 2019/146, as from IP completion day (as defined in the European Union (Withdrawal Agreement) Act 2020, s 39(1)–(5)).

*General powers of court*

**[1.200]**

**147 Power to stay or sist winding up**

(1) The court may at any time after an order for winding up, on the application either of the liquidator or the official receiver or any creditor or contributory, and on proof to the satisfaction of the court that all proceedings in the winding up ought to be stayed or sisted, make an order staying or sisting the proceedings, either altogether or for a limited time, on such terms and conditions as the court thinks fit.

(2) The court may, before making an order, require the official receiver to furnish to it a report with respect to any facts or matters which are in his opinion relevant to the application.

(3) A copy of every order made under this section shall forthwith be forwarded by the company, or otherwise as may be prescribed, to the registrar of companies, who shall enter it in his records relating to the company.

**CIGA 2020**—This provision is affected by temporary measures at Sch 10, paras 4(4) and 7(6) of CIGA 2020.

**General note**—An application for an order staying proceedings in relation to the winding up may be made by the court at any time after a winding-up order has been made.

A stay has been granted where the winding-up order was fundamentally defective: *Re Intermain Properties Ltd* [1986] BCLC 265. But the correct procedure now would be to seek rescission of the order under r 12.59(1), provided that action can be taken within 5 business days of the making of the winding-up order (r 12.59(3)).

If the company or some other party seeks to challenge a winding-up order, the proper procedure in general is to appeal, pursuant to r 12.59(2): *Re St Nazaire Co* (1879) 12 ChD 88. Normally an application under this section to obtain an order staying proceedings is not sought (*Re A & BC Chewing Gum Ltd* [1975] 1 All ER 1017), except where the appeal cannot be heard swiftly.

It is not possible to challenge the making of the winding-up order at the hearing of the application for a stay: *Re Empire Builders Ltd* (1919) 88 LJ Ch 459.

As the language of the section indicates, the court has a discretion (*Re Telescriptor Syndicate Ltd* [1903] 2 Ch 174 at 180) whether or not to stay proceedings, and while there are no rigid rules (*Re Calgary and Edmonton Land Co Ltd* [1975] 1 All ER 1046 at 1051), the courts operate within certain principles, many of which derive from those used when considering applications for annulments in bankruptcy: *Re Telescriptor Syndicate Ltd.* The applicant for a stay does not have to show special circumstances, but the court must base its decision to order a stay on some valid reason: *Aetna Properties Ltd (in liquidation) v GA Listing & Maintenance Pty Ltd* (1994) 13 ACSR 422. If a court is in doubt, a stay will not be ordered: *Re Calgary and Edmonton Land Co Ltd*, [1975] 1 WLR 355, [1975] 1 All ER 1046; *Re Lowston Ltd* [1991] BCLC 570. Australian authority has suggested that in determining whether to order a stay a court must consider the following (in order): the creditors' interests, the interests of the liquidator, the interests of the contributories, the public interest: *Mercy & Sons Pty Ltd v Wanari Pty Ltd* [2000] NSWSC 756, *Re Wine National Pty Ltd* [2014] NSWSC 507.

At a hearing for a stay, the applicant has to make out a clear case why a stay should be granted (*Re Telescriptor Syndicate Ltd* [1903] 2 Ch 174; *Re Calgary & Edmonton Land Co Ltd* [1975] 1 WLR 355, [1975] 1 All ER 1046) and the interests of the liquidator, the creditors and the members are taken into account by the court: *Re Calgary & Edmonton Land Co Ltd.* Also, the court will decide whether a stay would prejudice commercial morality and the public interest. In *Re Hester* (1889) 22 QBD 632 at 634, 636 and in the appeal at 640, 641; *Re Izod* [1897] 1 QB 241 at 255; *Re Telescriptor Syndicate Ltd* [1903] 2 Ch 174 at 180. In making a decision, the following may be considered: directors have failed to assist the official receiver; an investigation is warranted as far as aspects of the promotion, formation or demise of the company are concerned; and the business affairs of the company require investigation: *Re Telescriptor Syndicate Ltd.*

If the court finds that there has been misfeasance or improper activities in the life of the company, it will reject an application for a stay: *Re Calgary and Edmonton Land Co Ltd* [1975] 1 WLR 355,

[1975] 1 All ER 1046. Before ordering a stay the court will want to be assured that the liquidator's position is protected as far as his or her remuneration and expenses are concerned: *Re Calgary and Edmonton Land Co Ltd*.

It has been said that a stay is in the nature of final relief and as such the issue of whether there should be a stay or not is not be decided by referring to principles governing applications for interlocutory relief: *Re Wine National Pty Ltd* [2014] NSWSC 507.

'**All proceedings**'—The court has no power to stay only part of the proceedings (*Re European Assurance Society* [1872] WN 85), although it may attach terms and conditions to the order.

**The effect of the stay**—Where a perpetual stay is ordered, the winding–up process terminates, and the company can thereupon resume the conduct of its business and affairs as if no winding up ever existed. In such a case, the liquidator is entitled to a discharge.

If the stay is in respect of a compulsory winding up that was initiated subsequent to a voluntary one, the voluntary liquidation will proceed unless it is stayed: *Re Bristol Victoria Potteries Co Ltd* (1872) 20 WR 569.

'**Such terms and conditions as the court thinks fit**'—The court has, pursuant to this part of the provision, ordered that: dissenting shareholders should be allowed to retire from the company and be paid the value of their shares (*Re South Barrule Slate Quarry Co* (1869) 8 Eq 688; *Re Steamship 'Chigwell' Ltd* (1888) 4 TLR 308); any creditor has liberty to apply within a certain period to have the stay set aside: *Re Baxters' Ltd* [1898] WN 60.

## [1.201]

### 148 Settlement of list of contributories and application of assets

(1)   As soon as may be after making a winding-up order, the court shall settle a list of contributories, with power to rectify the register of members in all cases where rectification is required, and shall cause the company's assets to be collected, and applied in discharge of its liabilities.

(2)   If it appears to the court that it will not be necessary to make calls on or adjust the rights of contributories, the court may dispense with the settlement of a list of contributories.

(3)   In settling the list, the court shall distinguish between persons who are contributories in their own right and persons who are contributories as being representatives of or liable for the debts of others.

**Amendments**—SI 2009/1941.

**General note**—The provision enables duties given to the court under this section to be delegated to the liquidator, who exercises them in a quasi-judicial capacity (*Re Westaway's Garages Ltd* [1942] Ch 356 at 364), pursuant to the rules. See rr 7.79–7.85. Section 165(4)(a) gives the liquidator in a voluntary liquidation the power of the court to settle a list of contributories.

The liquidator must follow the settling process and has no right to apply to the court for a declaration that a contributory ought to be placed on the list: *Re Nathan Newman & Co* (1887) 35 ChD 1.

For the procedure of settling a list, see r 7.82 and the related notes.

'**Settle**'—The liquidator is permitted to regard the register of members as prima facie evidence concerning membership, and of the existence of an unpaid liability, but it is not conclusive. The list may well reflect the register completely, but the liquidator is certainly not bound by the register: *Isaacs' Case* [1892] 2 Ch 158; *Re J N 2 Ltd* [1978] 1 WLR 183.

The word 'settle' here involves the considering of who is a member and who is to contribute: *Re Murray Engineering Co* [1925] SASR 330 at 333.

Notwithstanding the fact that the 2016 Rules (or its precursors) do not so require, two lists of contributories are often compiled, namely the A list and the B list. The A list includes all those who were members of the company at the time winding up commenced and who have not since died, become bankrupt or transferred their shares, and the personal representatives and trustees in bankruptcy respectively of members who have died or become bankrupt subsequent to the commencement of the winding up. The B list, which does not have to be compiled until the liquidator ascertains that the A list contributories will not be able to satisfy the contribution payments that they are liable to pay, includes all remaining contributories.

'**Contributories**'—See the comments accompanying s 74 concerning the meaning of the term and the extent of their liability.

**Dispensing with the list**—This would occur where all shares are fully paid up. As to whether it would occur in other situations, it will depend on the facts, but it should only be done following careful consideration: *Re Phoenix Oil and Transport Co Ltd* [1958] Ch 560.

While there is no corresponding provision to s 148(2) for voluntary winding up, it can be assumed that as the liquidator in a voluntary liquidation is given the power of the court to settle a list (s 165(4)(c)), he or she would also have the power, in the appropriate case, to dispense with settling a list.

## [1.202]

### 149 Debts due from contributory to company

(1)   The court may, at any time after making a winding-up order, make an order on any contributory for the time being on the list of contributories to pay, in manner directed by the order, any money due from him (or from the estate of the person who he represents) to the company, exclusive of any money payable by him or the estate by virtue of any call.

(2)   The court in making such an order may—

    (a)    in the case of an unlimited company, allow to the contributory by way of set-off any money due to him or the estate which he represents from the company on any independent dealing or contract with the company, but not any money due to him as a member of the company in respect of any dividend or profit, and

    (b)    in the case of a limited company, make to any director or manager whose liability is unlimited or to his estate the like allowance.

(3)   In the case of any company, whether limited or unlimited, when all the creditors are paid in full (together with interest at the official rate), any money due on any account whatever to a contributory from the company may be allowed to him by way of set-off against any subsequent call.

**Amendments**—SI 2009/1941.

**General note**—While the provision does not state it expressly, it has been held that the money owed by a contributory and covered by this section only includes sums owed by a member in his or her capacity as a member: *Re Marlborough Club Co* (1868) LR 5 Eq 365; *Re Brisbane Puntowners' Association* (1893) 5 QLJ 54.

**Set-off**—Where a liquidator is seeking to enforce a liability to contribute to the assets of a company in winding up, the contributory is not entitled to set-off against that liability amounts which are due from the company to that contributory: *Re Overend, Gurney & Co; Grissell's Case* (1866) 1 Ch App 528; *Re General Works Co; Gill's Case* (1879) 12 ChD 755. But set-off may be permitted by a court either in the circumstances set out in s 149(2) or s 149(3), ie when all the company's creditors have been paid in full or the company is an unlimited one, although s 149(2) does not allow set-off in relation to dividends or profits due to a member in his or her position as a member of an unlimited company.

## [1.203]

### 150 Power to make calls

(1)   The court may, at any time after making a winding-up order, and either before or after it has ascertained the sufficiency of the company's assets, make calls on all or any of the contributories for the time being settled on the list of the contributories to the extent of their liability, for payment of any money which the court considers necessary to satisfy the company's debts and liabilities, and the expenses of winding up, and for the adjustment of the rights of the contributories among themselves, and make an order for payment of any calls so made.

(2)   In making a call the court may take into consideration the probability that some of the contributories may partly or wholly fail to pay it.

**General note**—The provision vests the power to make calls on contributories in the court, but this power can be delegated to the liquidator pursuant to a combination of s 160(1)(d) and rr 7.86 and 7.91. The liquidator must seek the approval of the court, save where a liquidation committee exists (rr 7.86(2) and 7.87) or special leave has been granted by the court (s 160(2)).

Any money paid on a call under s 150 is paid to the liquidator and not the company. It is held by the liquidator on statutory trust for distribution by the liquidator: *The Joint Administrators of LB Holdings Intermediate 2 Ltd v the Joint Administrators of Lehman Brothers International (Europe)* [2017] UKSC 38, [2017] 2 WLR 1497, [2017] 2 BCLC 149 at [156].

A liquidator will always have to make calls on contributories where the contributories' liability has not become due and payable prior to winding up. If a contributory fails to pay, the liquidator may need to obtain an order of the court ('a balance order') under r 7.91(2) enforcing the payment of the call.

When winding up commences, if sums are already due from a contributory to the company, such as calls previously made by the company, the liquidator may either make and, with court approval, enforce a call in respect of the sum already payable, or the existing right to payment may be enforced instead as a debt due to the company: *Westmoreland Green & Blue Slate Co v Feilden* [1891] 3 Ch 15.

## 151
*(Repealed)*

## [1.204]

### 152 Order on contributory to be conclusive evidence

(1)    An order made by the court on a contributory is conclusive evidence that the money (if any) thereby appearing to be due or ordered to be paid is due, but subject to any right of appeal.

(2)    All other pertinent matters stated in the order are to be taken as truly stated as against all persons and in all proceedings except proceedings in Scotland against the heritable estate of a deceased contributory; and in that case the order is only prima facie evidence for the purpose of charging his heritable estate, unless his heirs or legatees of heritage were on the list of contributories at the time of the order being made.

General note—As s 152(1) provides that an order is conclusive evidence of money being due on an order of the court for payment of calls in winding up, contributories will struggle to challenge successfully the validity of proceedings taken prior to the making of the call, particularly if the contributory has been cognisant of the existence of a defect from the very beginning, but has only raised it for the first time when proceedings are initiated: *Re Katoomba Coal & Slate Co; North's Case* (1892) 18 LR (NSW) Eq 70.

## [1.205]

### 153 Power to exclude creditors not proving in time

The court may fix a time or times within which creditors are to prove their debts or claims or to be excluded from the benefit of any distribution made before those debts are proved.

General note—So as to ensure that all the liabilities of the company are proved in winding up within a reasonable time, the liquidator will fix a date for the proving of debts. The power to fix the date is delegated to the liquidator by the court under s 160(1).

Where a creditor does not prove within the time fixed by a liquidator, he or she is unable to participate in a distribution that has been made before proving (*Butler v Broadhead* [1975] Ch 97), but the creditor may be paid from any assets that remain or come into the liquidator's hands after the distribution (r 14.40(2)).

## [1.206]

### 154 Adjustment of rights of contributories

The court shall adjust the rights of the contributories among themselves and distribute any surplus among the persons entitled to it.

General note—The amount to be paid by a contributory may be varied because, after the making of calls, the court may need to adjust, under this section, the rights of contributories among themselves. The equivalent for voluntary liquidation is s 165(5). Adjustment occurs in order to provide a result whereby contributories bear the loss of capital equally. Whether equal loss is to be implemented will depend on the articles.

The liquidator is not permitted to make a distribution. He or she may only distribute it after obtaining special leave from the court. The liquidator must apply to the court for an order under r 7.117. A list of persons to whom it is intended to return capital must accompany the application (r 7.117(2)). If an order is made then the liquidator is sent a sealed copy of the order and he or she is to follow the procedures set out in r 7.118 (r 7.117(4)). In the Australian case of *Re RH Trevan*

*Pty Ltd* [2013] NSWSC 1445 it was held that the purpose of the equivalent provision was to ensure that the liquidator took all necessary steps to verify the fact that there was a surplus and that members' entitlements had been ascertained.

## [1.207]

### 155 Inspection of books by creditors etc

(1)   The court may, at any time after making a winding-up order, make such order for inspection of the company's books and papers by creditors and contributories as the court thinks just; and any books and papers in the company's possession may be inspected by creditors and contributories accordingly, but not further or otherwise.

(2)   Nothing in this section excludes or restricts any statutory rights of a government department or person acting under the authority of a government department.

(3)   For the purposes of subsection (2) above, references to a government department shall be construed as including references to any part of the Scottish Administration.

**Amendments**—SI 1999/1820.

**General note**—Before liquidation, some of a company's books, such as the register of charges (Companies Act 2006, s 877 are open to inspection by the members and creditors without a fee. On liquidation this right of inspection ends, with outsiders having no right to inspect (*Re Kent Coalfields Syndicate* [1898] 1 QB 754), and there is Australian authority (*IACS Pty Ltd v Australian Flower Exports Pty Ltd* (1993) 10 ACSR 769) to the effect that the liquidator cannot permit inspection. The right to inspect for creditors and contributories depends on this section. The court has power to make an order for inspection of any books and papers in the possession of the company, but does not cover the case where the papers are in the possession of some third party (*Re North Brazilian Sugar Factories* (1887) 37 ChD 83 (no order where books relating to formerly held property of the company in liquidation were in the possession of a company to whom the company in liquidation had transferred its property)). It is permissible for copies to be taken of documents inspected: *Re Arauco Co* [1899] WN 134; *Re Gold Coast Syndicate Ltd* [1904] WN 72.

The predominance of authority seems to indicate that inspection exists for the purpose of the winding up and not, for example, for the benefit of individual shareholders or creditors (to enable them, for instance, to obtain information that might assist in bringing actions against directors of the company): *Re North Brazilian Sugar Factories* (1887) 35 ChD 83; *Re DPR Futures Ltd* [1989] 1 WLR 778; *IRC v Mills* [2003] EWHC 2022 (Ch). But, in *Re Sunwing Vacations Inc* [2011] EWHC 1544 (Ch), [2011] BPIR 1524, Morgan J was willing to make an order of disclosure (under s 112 as the company was in voluntary liquidation) because he was persuaded that if the applicants (who were creditors of the company in liquidation) obtained the information from the liquidator then they would be able to succeed against a third party, and if this occurred then the applicants' claim against the company in liquidation would be reduced (at [17]). His Lordship saw this as an order that was being made for the purpose of the winding up (at [18]). The fact was that the benefit for the company would be indirect, but that sufficed as far as Morgan J was concerned (at [19]).

In several Australian cases creditors have been able to obtain orders for inspection for the purpose of furthering their own interests rather than benefiting the winding up: *Re MMC Pty Ltd (in liquidation)* (1992) 10 ACLC 365 (creditors were able to inspect in circumstances where their purpose was to assist in the preparation of their own action against the directors); *Re BPTC Ltd* (1992) 7 ACSR 291, on appeal (1993) 12 ACSR 181 (inspection was sought to enable the furtherance of proceedings against the company's insurers); *IACS Pty Ltd v Australian Flower Exports Pty Ltd* (1993) 11 ACLC 618, although an appellate court in Australia has counselled against the use of the power to inspect being overly extended: *Worthley v England* (1994) 14 ACSR 407 at 427–428.

As the section suggests, only books and papers in the possession of the company can be inspected, therefore ruling out any books or papers of the company which are held by others.

## [1.208]

### 156 Payment of expenses of winding up

The court may, in the event of the assets being insufficient to satisfy the liabilities, make an order as to the payment out of the assets of the expenses incurred in the winding up in such order of priority as the court thinks just.

**General note**—This section provides for the re-ordering of priorities established in r 7.108: *Digital Equipment Co Ltd v Bower* [2004] BCC 509. Also, see r 7.110.

The court has an unfettered discretion, although the courts are not quick to vary the priority order, as they are generally content to adopt the order of priorities in r 7.108(4): *Re Grey*

*Marlin Ltd* [2000] 1 WLR 370, [1999] 4 All ER 429. Courts are able to include the costs of successful litigation against the liquidator in any decision alter the order of priority.

Courts will only give a liquidator priority for his or her remuneration over liquidation expenses that would normally rank ahead of it, where there are exceptional circumstances: *Re Linda Marie Ltd (in liquidation)* (1988) 4 BCC 463 at 472.

For a recent example of a case where a court made an order under s 156, see *Re Doonin Plant Ltd* [2018] CSOH 89, [2018] BPIR 1580.

Reference should be had to the notes to s 107 as far as assets covered by floating charges are concerned.

## [1.209]

### 157 Attendance at company meetings (Scotland)

In the winding up by the court of a company registered in Scotland, the court has power to require the attendance of any officer of the company at any meeting of creditors or of contributories, or of a liquidation committee, for the purpose of giving information as to the trade, dealings, affairs or property of the company.

## [1.210]

### 158 Power to arrest absconding contributory

The court, at any time either before or after making a winding-up order, on proof of probable cause for believing that a contributory is about to quit the United Kingdom or otherwise to abscond or to remove or conceal any of his property for the purpose of evading payment of calls, may cause the contributory to be arrested and his books and papers and moveable personal property to be seized and him and them to be kept safely until such time as the court may order.

## [1.211]

### 159 Powers of court to be cumulative

Powers conferred on the court by this Act are in addition to, and not in restriction of, any existing powers of instituting proceedings against a contributory or debtor of the company, or the estate of any contributory or debtor, for the recovery of any call or other sums.

**Amendments**—SI 2009/1941.

## [1.212]

### 160 Delegation of powers to liquidator (England and Wales)

(1) Provision may be made by rules for enabling or requiring all or any of the powers and duties conferred and imposed on the court in England and Wales in respect of the following matters—

(a) the seeking of decisions on any matter from creditors and contributories,

(b) the settling of lists of contributories and the rectifying of the register of members where required, and the collection and application of the assets,

(c) the payment, delivery, conveyance, surrender or transfer of money, property, books or papers to the liquidator,

(d) the making of calls,

(e) the fixing of a time within which debts and claims must be proved,

to be exercised or performed by the liquidator as an officer of the court, and subject to the court's control.

(2) But the liquidator shall not, without the special leave of the court, rectify the register of members, and shall not make any call without either that special leave or the sanction of the liquidation committee.

**Amendments**—SI 2009/1941; Small Business, Enterprise and Employment Act 2015, s 126, Sch 9, Pt 1, paras 1, 39.

**General note**—In relation to the exercise of powers by the liquidator, see rr 15.3 and 15.6 in respect of the calling of meetings, rr 7.79–7.85 in respect of the settling of the list of contributories, r 7.79 in respect of rectifying the register of members, r 7.78 in respect of enforcing delivery of company property, rr 7.86–7.91 in respect of the making of calls, and s 153 in respect of fixing the time in which to prove debts.

This provision delegates to rule-makers the ability to make rules covering certain subject-matter areas and this includes the making of calls: *Scott-Hake v Frost* [2020] EWHC 3677 (Ch) at [53]. The answer as to what a liquidator may do when making the call is not in the IA 1986, but in the IR 2016: *Scott-Hake v Frost* at [54]. The IR 2016 then delegate the duty to the liquidator.

*Enforcement of, and appeal from, orders*

**[1.213]**

**161 Orders for calls on contributories (Scotland)**

(1)   In Scotland, where an order, interlocutor or decree has been made for winding up a company by the court, it is competent to the court, on production by the liquidators of a list certified by them of the names of the contributories liable in payment of any calls, and of the amount due by each contributory, and of the date when that amount became due, to pronounce forthwith a decree against those contributories for payment of the sums so certified to be due, with interest from that date until payment (at 5 per cent per annum) in the same way and to the same effect as if they had severally consented to registration for execution, on a charge of 6 days, of a legal obligation to pay those calls and interest.

(2)   The decree may be extracted immediately, and no suspension of it is competent, except on caution or consignation, unless with special leave of the court.

**[1.214]**

**162 Appeals from orders in Scotland**

(1)   Subject to the provisions of this section and to rules of court, an appeal from any order or decision made or given in the winding up of a company by the court in Scotland under this Act lies in the same manner and subject to the same conditions as an appeal from an order or decision of the court in cases within its ordinary jurisdiction.

(2)   In regard to orders or judgments pronounced by the judge acting as vacation judge—

    (a)    none of the orders specified in Part I of Schedule 3 to this Act are subject to review, reduction, suspension or stay of execution, and

    (b)    every other order or judgment (except as mentioned below) may be submitted to review by the Inner House by reclaiming motion enrolled within 14 days from the date of the order or judgment.

(3)   However, an order being one of those specified in Part II of that Schedule shall, from the date of the order and notwithstanding that it has been submitted to review as above, be carried out and receive effect until the Inner House have disposed of the matter.

(4)   In regard to orders or judgments pronounced in Scotland by a Lord Ordinary before whom proceedings in a winding up are being taken, any such order or judgment may be submitted to review by the Inner House by reclaiming motion enrolled within 14 days from its date; but should it not be so submitted to review during session, the provisions of this section in regard to orders or judgments pronounced by the judge acting as vacation judge apply.

(5)   Nothing in this section affects provisions of the Companies Acts or this Act in reference to decrees in Scotland for payment of calls in the winding up of companies, whether voluntary or by the court.

**Amendments**—Court of Session Act 1988, s 52(2), Sch 2, Pt I; SI 2009/1941.

CHAPTER VII

LIQUIDATORS
*Preliminary*

**[1.215]**

**163 Style and title of liquidators**
The liquidator of a company shall be described—
  (a)   where a person other than the official receiver is liquidator, by the style of "the liquidator" of the particular company, or
  (b)   where the official receiver is liquidator, by the style of "the official receiver and liquidator" of the particular company;
and in neither case shall he be described by an individual name.

**[1.216]**

**164 Corrupt inducement affecting appointment**
A person who gives, or agrees or offers to give, to any member or creditor of a company any valuable consideration with a view to securing his own appointment or nomination, or to securing or preventing the appointment or nomination of some person other than himself, as the company's liquidator is liable to a fine.

*Liquidator's powers and duties*

**[1.217]**

**165 Voluntary winding up**
(1)   This section has effect where a company is being wound up voluntarily, but subject to section 166 below in the case of a creditors' voluntary winding up.
(2)   The liquidator may exercise any of the powers specified in Parts 1 to 3 of Schedule 4.
(4)   The liquidator may—
  (a)   exercise the court's power of settling a list of contributories (which list is prima facie evidence of the liability of the persons named in it to be contributories),
  (b)   exercise the court's power of making calls,
  (c)   summon general meetings of the company for the purpose of obtaining its sanction by special resolution or for any other purpose he may think fit.
(5)   The liquidator shall pay the company's debts and adjust the rights of the contributories among themselves.
(6)   Where the liquidator in exercise of the powers conferred on him by this Act disposes of any property of the company to a person who is connected with the company (within the meaning of section 249 in Part VII), he shall, if there is for the time being a liquidation committee, give notice to the committee of that exercise of his powers.

  **Amendments**—Amended by SI 2007/2194; Small Business, Enterprise and Employment Act 2015, s 120(1), (2).
  **General note**—This section must be considered in conjunction with Sch 4 to the Act where the detailed powers of a liquidator are enumerated.
  **Settle a list of contributories**—The court's power to do this is delegated to the liquidator. Interestingly, provision of a delegation of the power to liquidators in compulsory liquidations is by way of the IR 2016(see r 7.79).

SECTION 165(6)
  '**A person who is connected with the company**'—Where any property is disposed of to such a person, notice must be given to any liquidation committee, if one exists. The expression 'connected with the company' is defined in s 249 to include a director of the company, an associate of a director or an associate of the company. 'Associate' is then defined broadly in s 435. See the notes

relating to these sections for further details. Parliament obviously is concerned that if property is to go to connected persons, then the liquidation committee should be given forewarning so as to thwart possible improper dealings. See the unusual facts in the Australian case of *Re ACN 003 671 387* [2004] NSWSC 368, where the judge permitted the sale of shares in companies being wound up by a liquidator to the trustee of a service trust. The liquidator was a partner in an accounting firm and the service trust involved was the firm's service trust.

## [1.218]

### 166 Creditors' voluntary winding up

(1) This section applies where, in the case of a creditors' voluntary winding up, a liquidator has been nominated by the company.

(1A) The exercise by the liquidator of the power specified in paragraph 6 of Schedule 4 to this Act (power to sell any of the company's property) shall not be challengeable on the ground of any prior inhibition.

(2) The powers conferred on the liquidator by section 165 shall not be exercised, except with the sanction of the court, before—

    (a)    the company's creditors under section 100 nominate a person to be liquidator, or

    (b)    the procedure by which the company's creditors were to have made such a nomination concludes without a nomination having been made.

(3) Subsection (2) does not apply in relation to the power of the liquidator—

    (a)    to take into his custody or under his control all the property to which the company is or appears to be entitled;

    (b)    to dispose of perishable goods and other goods the value of which is likely to diminish if they are not immediately disposed of; and

    (c)    to do all such other things as may be necessary for the protection of the company's assets.

(4) . . .

(5) If the directors fail to comply with—

    (a)    section 99(1), (2) or (2A), or

    (b)    section 100(1B),

the liquidator shall, within 7 days of the relevant day, apply to the court for directions as to the manner in which that default is to be remedied.

(6) "The relevant day" means the day on which the liquidator was nominated by the company or the day on which he first became aware of the default, whichever is the later.

(7) If the liquidator without reasonable excuse fails to comply with this section, he is liable to a fine.

**Amendments**—Bankruptcy and Diligence etc (Scotland) Act 2007, s 155(1), (3); SI 2009/864, SI 2010/18; Small Business, Enterprise and Employment Act 2015, s 126, Sch 9, Pt 1, paras 1, 40.

**General note**—This provision has limited operation. It applies only to companies in creditors' voluntary liquidation where the liquidator was appointed by the members, and only in relation to the period between the liquidator's appointment and the decision of the creditors concerning the nomination of a liquidator or after the expiration of the period in which the creditors could decide to nominate.

In the period covered by the section, the liquidator is not to exercise the powers referred to in s 165 without the sanction of the court. This provision, together with s 114, was introduced to prevent the practice of 'centrebinding'. This process derived its name from the case of *Re Centrebind Ltd* [1967] 1 WLR 377, [1966] 3 All ER 889. Subsequent to this case, some companies appointed unscrupulous liquidators who delayed the holding of the creditors' meeting (which could nominate the liquidator) until after the assets of the company were disposed of at a very low price to a company which was connected with the members of the company, and the creditors could take no action whatsoever.

For a discussion of the application of this rule in relation to actions of liquidators in CVLs before the decision of the creditors to nominate a liquidator, see *Re Aardvark TMC Ltd* [2013] EWHC 1774 (Ch) (and discussed in [2013] CRI 105). In this case Arnold J said that s 166(2) does not apply to the power to disclaim (at [13]), but this appears to be at odds with *Re Business Dream Ltd* [2011] EWHC 2860 (Ch), although in the latter the comments were obiter.

'Apply to the court for directions'— If the company fails to adopt the correct procedure for the calling of a decision by the creditors, then the liquidator is required by s 166(5) to apply to the court for directions as to how the default can be remedied. In *Re Salcombe Hotel Development Co Ltd* [1991] BCLC 44 it was said that this subsection is directory and not mandatory and, consequently, it is not incumbent on liquidators to seek directions in cases where there is no need for directions. Yet the language of the provision, and especially the inclusion of the word 'shall' seems to suggest that liquidators must apply for directions. The fact that a liquidator is subject to a penalty for non-compliance under s 166(7) might cause liquidators to err on the side of caution and to apply for directions. More recently, in *Re Stockley Construction Company Ltd* (unreported) 26 June 2000 (but noted at (2000) 16 IL & P 218) Laddie J emphasised the fact that the liquidators had acted quite properly in seeking directions under s 166(5) where the liquidators were unable to obtain a commitment from a director to attend the adjourned meeting of the creditors, as was required by s 99(1)(c), as it was then drafted.

## [1.219]

### 167 Winding up by the court

(1)   Where a company is being wound up by the court, the liquidator may exercise any of the powers specified in Parts 1 to 3 of Schedule 4.

(2)   Where the liquidator (not being the official receiver), in exercise of the powers conferred on him by this Act—

(a)      disposes of any property of the company to a person who is connected with the company (within the meaning of section 249 in Part VII), or

(b)      employs a solicitor to assist him in the carrying out of his functions,

he shall, if there is for the time being a liquidation committee, give notice to the committee of that exercise of his powers.

(3)   The exercise by the liquidator in a winding up by the court of the powers conferred by this section is subject to the control of the court, and any creditor or contributory may apply to the court with respect to any exercise or proposed exercise of any of those powers.

Amendments—Small Business, Enterprise and Employment Act 2015, s 120(1), (3).

General note—At one time a liquidator of a company in compulsory liquidation was required to obtain sanction before he or she exercised certain powers. That has changed. But the exercise of powers is still subject to the control of the court. Any creditor or contributory may still apply to the court with respect to any exercise or proposed exercise of any of the powers. In making a decision, the court is not bound by the views of creditors or contributories (*Re Bank of Credit and Commerce International SA (No 2)* [1993] BCLC 1490; *Re Greenhaven Motors Ltd* [1999] 1 BCLC 635, CA), but they will normally be accepted, save in exceptional circumstances: *Re Bank of Credit and Commerce International SA (No 2)*.

The provision only applies to court winding up, but in voluntary liquidations an application may be brought under s 112 as the court is entitled to control the exercise of a liquidator's powers: *Cooper v PRG Powerhouse Ltd* [2008] EWHC 498 (Ch).

See Sch 4 to the Act and the notes relating to it.

## [1.220]

### 168 Supplementary powers (England and Wales)

(1)   This section applies in the case of a company which is being wound up by the court in England and Wales.

(2)   The liquidator may seek a decision on any matter from the company's creditors or contributories; and must seek a decision on a matter—

(a)      from the company's creditors, if requested to do so by one-tenth in value of the creditors;

(b)      from the company's contributories, if requested to do so by one-tenth in value of the contributories.

(3)   The liquidator may apply to the court (in the prescribed manner) for directions in relation to any particular matter arising in the winding up.

(4)   Subject to the provisions of this Act, the liquidator shall use his own discretion in the management of the assets and their distribution among the creditors.

(5)   If any person is aggrieved by an act or decision of the liquidator, that person may apply to the court; and the court may confirm, reverse or modify the act or decision complained of, and make such order in the case as it thinks just.

(5A)   Where at any time after a winding-up petition has been presented to the court against any person (including an insolvent partnership or other body which may be wound up under Part V of the Act as an unregistered company), whether by virtue of the provisions of the Insolvent Partnerships Order 1994 or not, the attention of the court is drawn to the fact that the person in question is a member of an insolvent partnership, the court may make an order as to the future conduct of the insolvency proceedings and any such order may apply any provisions of that Order with any necessary modifications.

(5B)   Any order or directions under subsection (5A) may be made or given on the application of the official receiver, any responsible insolvency practitioner, the trustee of the partnership or any other interested person and may include provisions as to the administration of the joint estate of the partnership, and in particular how it and the separate estate of any member are to be administered.

(5C)   Where the court makes an order for the winding up of an insolvent partnership under—

   (a)   section 72(1)(a) of the Financial Services Act 1986;
   (b)   section 92(1)(a) of the Banking Act 1987; or
   (c)   section 367(3)(a) of the Financial Services and Markets Act 2000,

the court may make an order as to the future conduct of the winding up proceedings, and any such order may apply any provisions of the Insolvent Partnerships Order 1994 with any necessary modifications.

**Amendments**—SI 1994/2421; SI 2002/1555; Small Business, Enterprise and Employment Act 2015, s 126, Sch 9, Pt 1, paras 1, 41.

**General note**—The Act protects creditors and contributories. This section is one of the group of provisions that seek to achieve that objective. The section does so by providing creditors and contributories with the right to request the liquidator to call meetings, or they can apply to the court to have decisions of liquidators reviewed. The section also protects, or at least aids, liquidators in that they are permitted to seek directions from the courts.

**Decisions of creditors or contributories**—While a liquidator must seek decisions when they are requisitioned properly, a court can override the duty of a liquidator to seek a decision by directing him or her not to seek the decision: *Re Barings plc* [2001] 2 BCLC 159 at 171 (which dealt with the 1986 Rules and related to the calling of meetings).

See r 15.18.

**Directions**—The role of s 168(3) is to provide a procedure for a liquidator to obtain some guidance from the court in conducting a liquidation and so as to give protection against a claim for breach of duty. Applications are so common that it is of little help to catalogue all the situations in which such an application may be made. Instances have been where the liquidator wishes: to know whether testamentary gifts to a charitable company that had gone into liquidation were ineffective (*Alleyne v Attorney-General* [1997] 1 WLR 877, [1997] 2 All ER 679, [1997] 1 BCLC 157); to know how to deal with a claim of a creditor (*Re Polly Peck International plc* [1996] 2 All ER 433, [1996] 1 BCLC 428); to know whether to admit a particular debt or claim to proof in the winding up; to seek guidance on the sale of a cause of an action (*Craig v Humberclyde Industrial Finance Ltd* [1999] 1 WLR 129, [1998] 2 BCLC 526, CA). The courts have said that in cases of real doubt the correct procedure for a liquidator is to seek directions.

Courts will not entertain applications for directions where the liquidator is seeking, in effect, to have the court make a commercial decision for him or her: *Re Stetzel Thomson & Co Ltd* (1988) 4 BCC 74; *Shiraz Nominees (in liquidation) v Collinson* (1985) 3 ACLC 706. Also, there is Australian authority to the effect that the section is not to be employed where there is a dispute between two parties over a right to claim company funds. In such a case the liquidator should commence substantive proceedings against the two parties and seek a declaratory order: *Re Everything Australian Pty Ltd* (1993) 11 ACLC 50 at 51; *Re AMN Pty Ltd (in liquidation)* (1997) 15 ACLC 368. While liquidators should not 'run' to the courts at any time that a problem is raised, an application for directions should be initiated if there is any doubt in the liquidator's mind as to what action he or she should take: *Re Windsor Steam Coal Co* [1929] 1 Ch 151 at 159.

Directions will be given if a proposed decision of the liquidator is subject to criticism by a creditor or creditors on the basis that it is unreasonable or there is evidence of bad faith: *Re Addstone Pty Ltd (in liquidation)* (1997) 25 ACSR 357 at 363. It seems that ex parte hearings of the application for directions are allowed, but every case must be considered on its facts, and where there are conflicting interests to be considered such a procedure may be inappropriate: *Bank of Melbourne Ltd v HPM Pty Ltd* (1998) 16 ACLC 427 at 429.

In taking any decision a liquidator, even after the change in the law that permitted liquidators to commence or defend legal proceedings without the need for this to be sanctioned, must have regard for the best interests of the company and all who have an interest in it. Liquidators did not have to, but could consult the creditors. Liquidators should ordinarily give weight to the reasoned views of the majority of creditors: *Re Longmeade Ltd* [2016] EWHC 356 (Ch), [2016] BPIR 666.

It has been known for judges to direct liquidators to apply to the court for directions: *Craig v Humberclyde Industrial Finance Ltd* [1999] 1 WLR 129, [1998] 2 BCLC 526, CA.

The equivalent of s 168(3) for voluntary liquidation is s 112. Even though a liquidator in a voluntary winding up is not an officer of the court (*Re Hill's Waterfall Estate & Gold Mining Co* [1896] 1 Ch 947; *Re John Bateson & Co* [1985] BCLC 259; In *Re Knitwear (Wholesale) Ltd* [1988] 1 Ch 275), much of what has been decided in relation to s 168(5) can be applied to liquidators in voluntary liquidations because s 168(5), which provides, in effect, that courts may supervise liquidators, applies to all liquidators.

In general s 168(3) and s 112 have been seen as broadly the same. However, the Australian case of *Dean-Willcocks v Soluble Solution Hydroponics Pty Ltd* (1997) 15 ACLC 833 doubted this, as it was noted that the court may, under the equivalent of s 168(3), direct the liquidator, its officer, to commit a breach of trust or to do something which it is arguable that the liquidator has no power to do, while under s 112(2) the court is only given power to avoid expensive procedures. Also, under s 112 a creditor or contributory, as well as a liquidator, is entitled to apply for directions.

'**Person aggrieved**'—For the section to operate there must be an application by a person who is 'aggrieved' by an act, omission or decision of the liquidator. The meaning of 'aggrieved' has not yet been settled. It has been said that the person must be someone who has suffered a legal grievance or has been wrongly deprived of something or affected his or her right to something: *Re S ex parte Sidebotham* (1880) 14 ChD 458 at 465. Yet this might well be regarded as being too narrow, as the expression should not be limited to those with a definite legal grievance. Any attempt at classifying those who may be persons aggrieved has been said to be undesirable: *Re Edennote Ltd* [1996] 2 BCLC 389 at 393. Clearly the expression includes creditors, unless the company's liquidation will yield a surplus. So, those who can apply include creditors whose proofs of debt have been rejected by the liquidator (*Re Taylor* [1934] NZLR 117 at 127), creditors wishing to complain about the fact that the liquidator admitted another creditor's claim (*Re Capital Project Homes Pty Ltd* (1992) 10 ACLC 75), creditors where a liquidator has disposed of an asset at a undervalue (*Re Edennote Ltd* [1996] 2 BCLC 389 at 393), and those creditors who have been prevented from attending creditors' meetings (*Re Chevron Furnishers Pty Ltd (receiver and manager appointed) (in liquidation)* (1992) 10 ACLC 1537). It also includes contributories in situations where there will be a surplus of assets: *Re Edennote Ltd* [1996] 2 BCLC 389 at 393, CA. Additionally, it includes those who are directly affected by the exercise of a liquidator's power and, absent this provision, would be unable to challenge the exercise of power: *Mahomed v Morris* [2000] 2 BCLC 536 at 555, CA. An example is someone prejudiced by a disclaimer of company property: *Re Hans Place Ltd* [1993] BCLC 768; *Mahomed v Morris* at 555. But outsiders to the liquidation, dissatisfied with some act or decision of the liquidator, will not be able to bring proceedings: *Mahomed v Morris* at 555. Furthermore, courts will not, normally, accede to applications which will lead to interference with matters of day-to-day administration or where the liquidator has exercised discretionary powers in good faith, as this would make it very difficult, if not impossible, to accomplish the winding-up process: *Leon v York-o-Matic Ltd* [1966] 1 WLR 1450; *Re Wyvern Developments Ltd* [1974] 1 WLR 1097; *Mitchell v Buckingham International plc* [1998] 2 BCLC 369 at 390–391, CA.

According to the BVI Court of Appeal whether a person has standing as an aggrieved person within the equivalent of s 168(5) is not founded on whether he or she has a relationship to the liquidation but rather it must be demonstrated that the person has a legitimate interest in the relief sought, and the more remote the relationship of the person to the liquidation the less likely he or she will have a legitimate interest: *Stanford v Akers and McDonald (as Joint liquidators of Chesterfield United Inc*, Appeal BVIHCMAP 2017/0019, 12 July 2018.

**Review of a decision**—The courts are concerned about ensuring that the fiduciary and other duties and powers of liquidators are exercised properly: *Craig v Humberclyde Industrial Finance Ltd* [1999] 1 WLR 129, [1998] 2 BCLC 526, CA. It has been said that the exercise of a liquidator's discretion may be questioned where it can be established that the liquidator, notwithstanding he or she was acting in good faith, considered issues which ought not to have been considered: *Re Edennote Ltd* [1995] 2 BCLC 248 at 257–258. Also, the liquidator's discretion might be queried where it can be demonstrated that the liquidator failed to take into account issues which should have been taken into account: *Re Edennote Ltd* at 257–258.

When assessing an application and deciding what to do about a decision of a liquidator, a court will give significant weight to the commercial decisions of liquidators: *Re Edennote Ltd*

[1996] 2 BCLC 389 at 394; *Mitchell v Buckingham International plc* [1998] 2 BCLC 369 at 390–391, CA.

Frequently, an application is made to have a liquidator removed because of a decision which he or she has taken. In such cases an application for removal of the liquidator would be more appropriate than to apply pursuant to s 168(5) for a review of the decision.

The court may, after reviewing a liquidator's decision and if the circumstances so demand, reverse a transaction into which a liquidator entered: *Re Edennote Ltd* [1996] 2 BCLC 389 at 393.

Proceedings may be taken under s 168(5) by creditors or contributories and they may seek to have the liquidator's decision not to initiate or defend legal proceedings reviewed. The court might see fit to give leave to persons other than the liquidator to take proceedings in the name of the company or that of the liquidator: *Re Imperial Bank of China, Hindustan & Japan* (1866) 1 Ch App 339; *Cape Breton Co v Fenn* (1881) 17 ChD 198 at 208; *Fargro Ltd v Godfroy* [1986] 1 WLR 1134 at 1136–1138.

'**Make such order as it thinks fit**'—When hearing applications pursuant to s 168(5) the court will not readily interfere with a decision of the liquidator: *Mitchell v Buckingham International plc* [1998] 2 BCLC 369 at 391, CA. In fact, it will not do so except where the decision of the liquidator is such that no reasonable liquidator could, properly instructed and advised in the circumstances, come to it: *Re Hans Place Ltd* [1993] BCLC 768; *Re Greenhaven Motors Ltd* [1997] 1 BCLC 739; *Re Edennote Ltd* [1996] 2 BCLC 389, CA; *Hamilton v Official Receiver* [1998] BPIR 602. A later decision has said that a court would not interfere with a liquidator's decision unless it did not withstand logical analysis (*Re Meem SL Ltd* [2017] EWHC 2688 (Ch), [2018] BCC 652, dealing with an administrator). Other case law has employed the test of perversity, that is, absent bad faith or fraud, did the liquidator act in a manner that is so utterly unreasonable or absurd that it is properly to be regarded as perverse? (*Leon v York-O-Matic Ltd* [1966] 1 WLR 1450; *Re Edennote Ltd* [1996] 2 BCLC 389 at 394). This is particularly the case with commercial decision-making: *Mahomed v Morris* [2000] 2 BCLC 536 at 557, CA. An example of a liquidator acting unreasonably is where the liquidator refused to assign to a former controller of the company in liquidation a claim which the company had against a firm of solicitors: *Hamilton v Official Receiver* [1998] BPIR 602.

See Keay 'The Supervision and Control of Liquidators' [2000] *The Conveyancer and Property Lawyer* 295.

## [1.221]

### 169 Supplementary powers (Scotland)

(1)   . . .

(2)   In a winding up by the court in Scotland, the liquidator has (subject to the rules) the same powers as a trustee on a bankrupt estate.

**Amendments**—Small Business, Enterprise and Employment Act 2015, s 120(1), (4).

## [1.222]

### 170 Enforcement of liquidator's duty to make returns etc

(1)   If a liquidator who has made any default—

    (a)    in filing, delivering or making any return, account or other document, or

    (b)    in giving any notice which he is by law required to file, deliver, make or give,

fails to make good the default within 14 days after the service on him of a notice requiring him to do so, the court has the following powers.

(2)   On an application made by any creditor or contributory of the company, or by the registrar of companies, the court may make an order directing the liquidator to make good the default within such time as may be specified in the order.

(3)   The court's order may provide that all costs of and incidental to the application shall be borne by the liquidator.

(4)   Nothing in this section prejudices the operation of any enactment imposing penalties on a liquidator in respect of any such default as is mentioned above.

**General note**—If a court makes an order under this section and the liquidator fails to comply with it, then he or she is in contempt of court and it can lead to serious consequences for the liquidator: see *Re S & A Conversion Ltd* (1988) 4 BCC 384, CA. A liquidator was ordered to be imprisoned for failing to provide the registrar of companies with the particulars required in what is now s 192, after being ordered to do so by the court; in *Re Allan Ellis (Transport and Packing Services) Ltd* (1989) 5 BCC 835. The courts in these two cases emphasised the seriousness of not complying with court orders.

*Removal; vacation of office*

[1.223]

### 171 Removal, etc (voluntary winding up)

(1)   This section applies with respect to the removal from office and vacation of office of the liquidator of a company which is being wound up voluntarily.

(2)   Subject to the next subsection, the liquidator may be removed from office only by an order of the court or—

    (a)   in the case of a members' voluntary winding up, by a general meeting of the company summoned specially for that purpose, or

    (b)   in the case of a creditors' voluntary winding up, by a decision of the company's creditors made by a qualifying decision procedure instigated specially for that purpose in accordance with the rules.

(3)   Where the liquidator in a members' voluntary winding up was appointed by the court under section 108, a meeting such as is mentioned in subsection (2)(a) shall be summoned only if—

    (a)   the liquidator thinks fit,

    (b)   the court so directs, or

    (c)   the meeting is requested in accordance with the rules by members representing not less than one-half of the total voting rights of all the members having at the date of the request a right to vote at the meeting.

(3A)   Where the liquidator in a creditors' voluntary winding up was appointed by the court under section 108, a qualifying decision procedure such as is mentioned in subsection (2)(b) is to be instigated only if—

    (a)   the liquidator thinks fit,

    (b)   the court so directs, or

    (c)   it is requested in accordance with the rules by not less than one-half in value of the company's creditors.

(4)   A liquidator shall vacate office if he ceases to be a person who is qualified to act as an insolvency practitioner in relation to the company.

(5)   A liquidator may, in the prescribed circumstances, resign his office by giving notice of his resignation to the registrar of companies.

(6)   In the case of a members' voluntary winding up where the liquidator has produced an account of the winding up under section 94 (final account), the liquidator vacates office as soon as the liquidator has complied with section 94(3) (requirement to send final account to registrar).

(7)   In the case of a creditors' voluntary winding up where the liquidator has produced an account of the winding up under section 106 (final account), the liquidator vacates office as soon as the liquidator has complied with section 106(3) (requirement to send final account etc to registrar).

**Amendments**—Small Business, Enterprise and Employment Act 2015, s 126, Sch 9, Pt 1, paras 1, 42.

**General note**—The provision deals with the removal or resignation of a liquidator in a voluntary liquidation. Compulsory liquidation is covered by s 172.

**Qualifying decision procedure**—A person who is the convener must instigate a decision procedure and this can follow any of those procedures set out in r 15.3. The convener is required to send a notice to the creditors in conformity with r 15.8.

A decision procedure must be instigated under s 171(2)(b) for the removal of the liquidator in a creditors' voluntary liquidation, other than a liquidator appointed by the court under s 108, if 25% in value of the company's creditors, excluding those who are connected with the company, request it (r 15.18(4)).

**Vacation of office**—A liquidator whose authorisation to act as a liquidator has been suspended may apply for an order of removal and to have another liquidator to replace him or her: *Re AJ Adams (Builders) Ltd* [1991] BCLC 359.

See r 6.30.

**Resign**—The prescribed circumstances referred to in s 171(5) are set out in separate provisions, namely r 6.25(1) (creditors' voluntary) and r 5.6(1) (members' voluntary), although the provisions are identical.

A liquidator in voluntary winding up is only permitted to resign in those circumstances set out in r 6.25 and r 5.6 and after delivering notice to the registrar of companies (s 171(5)). These circumstances are:

- ill-health;
- an intention to cease to practise as an insolvency practitioner;
- a conflict of interest or change of personal circumstances which precludes or makes impracticable the further discharge of the duties of a liquidator;
- where two or more persons are acting as liquidator jointly and it is the opinion of both or all of them that it is no longer expedient that there should continue to be that number of joint liquidators.

In a creditors' voluntary liquidation, before resigning, a liquidator must send a notice to the creditors and invite them by a decision procedure or by deemed consent procedure to consider whether a replacement should be appointed except where the resignation is under the last of the circumstances set out above (r 6.25(2)). In a members' voluntary liquidation, before resigning, a liquidator must send a notice to the members and call a meeting of members to consider whether a replacement should be appointed except where the resignation is under the last of the circumstances set out above (r 5.6(2)).

There is no provision in the Act or Rules dealing with the refusal by the meeting of contributories or the creditors in a decision procedure to accept the resignation of the liquidator. It seems fair to say that the liquidator could apply to the court pursuant to s 112 if one of the grounds for resignation existed.

A decision procedure must be instigated under s 171(2)(b) in a creditors' voluntary liquidation for the removal of the liquidator, other than a liquidator appointed by the court under s 108, if 25% in value of the company's creditors, excluding those who are connected with the company, request it (r 15.18(4)). While decided under the previous rules, the decision in *Kean v Kevin Lucas (as Liquidator of J&R Builders (Norwich) Limited* [2016] EWHC 2684 (Ch), [2017] BPIR 128 is arguably still relevant. Applying the essential principles of the judgment, in determining whether the 25% in value of the company's creditors support the instigation of a decision procedure for the removal of the liquidator it must be noted that the scrutiny of the claims of creditors as far as their right to vote is different when compared to the scrutiny to be undertaken for other purposes. The creditors are not to be subject to strict proof of their claims. The only claims that should be discounted are those with connected party claims (as r 15.18(4) provides in any event) and any claim that appears obviously wrong or mala fide.

For the situation where a liquidator seeks to resign from multiple offices and to appoint some appropriate person in his or her stead, see rr 12.35–12.38 and the notes accompanying them. Also, see the note 'Resign' under s 172.

See the notes accompanying s 108.

**[1.224]**

## 172 Removal, etc (winding up by the court)

(1)  This section applies with respect to the removal from office and vacation of office of the liquidator of a company which is being wound up by the court, or of a provisional liquidator.

(2)  Subject as follows, the liquidator may be removed from office only by an order of the court or by a decision of the company's creditors made by a qualifying decision procedure instigated specially for that purpose in accordance with the rules; and a provisional liquidator may be removed from office only by an order of the court.

(3)  Where—

    (a)    the official receiver is liquidator otherwise than in succession under section 136(3) to a person who held office as a result of a nomination by . . . the company's creditors or contributories, or

    (b)    the liquidator was appointed by the court otherwise than under section 139(4)(a) or 140(1), or was appointed by the Secretary of State,

a qualifying decision procedure such as is mentioned in subsection (2) shall be instigated only if the liquidator thinks fit, the court so directs, or it is requested, in accordance with the rules, by not less than one-quarter, in value, of the creditors.

(4) If appointed by the Secretary of State, the liquidator may be removed from office by a direction of the Secretary of State.

(5) A liquidator or provisional liquidator, not being the official receiver, shall vacate office if he ceases to be a person who is qualified to act as an insolvency practitioner in relation to the company.

(6) A liquidator may, in the prescribed circumstances, resign his office by giving notice of his resignation to the court.

(7) Where an order is made under section 204 (early dissolution in Scotland) for the dissolution of the company, the liquidator shall vacate office when the dissolution of the company takes effect in accordance with that section.

(8) Where the liquidator has produced an account of the winding up under section 146 (final account), the liquidator vacates office as soon as the liquidator has complied with section 146(4) (requirement to send account etc to registrar and to court).

(9) . . .

(10) . . .

**Amendments**—Small Business, Enterprise and Employment Act 2015, s 126, Sch 9, Pt 1, paras 1, 43; SI 2017/702; SI 2019/146, as from IP completion day (as defined in the European Union (Withdrawal Agreement) Act 2020, s 39(1)–(5)).

**General note**—This provision accords, as far as it can, with s 171, which deals with voluntary liquidation.

Once a liquidator has vacated office under any of the provisions in this section, he or she is required to deliver up to his or her successor as liquidator all company assets, books, papers and records (r 7.73(1)).

**SECTION 172(2)**

This is in similar terms to its creditors' voluntary winding up equivalent, namely s 171(2)(b), However, there is no reference in r 15.18(4) to s 172; it only refers to s 171. It could be argued that the terms of r 15.18(4) should also apply to compulsory liquidations, as explained in the notes to s 171.

It only takes the establishing of one good ground or cause by an applicant as to why a person should be removed if the applicant to succeed. The applicant does not have 'prove everything in sight': *Shepheard v Lamey* [2001] BPIR 939.

**Removed by direction of the Secretary of State**—Before the Secretary of State decides to remove the liquidator, (s)he must notify the liquidator and the official receiver of the decision and the basis for it, and indicate a period in which the liquidator may make representations against the decision (r 7.66(1)–(3)). If the Secretary of State directs removal, then immediately (s)he is to file notice of the decision in court and send notices of the decision to both the liquidator and the official receiver (r 7.66(4)).

**Removal under section 172(2)**—for an order of removal the applicant had to satisfy the court that it was in the best interests of the liquidation to remove the liquidator: *Managa Properties Ltd v Brittain* [2009] EWHC 157 (Ch), [2009] 1 BCLC 689, [2009] BPIR 306.

**Resign**—A liquidator in compulsory winding up is only permitted to resign in prescribed circumstances (s 172(6)). Those circumstances are set out in r 7.61. Resignation is only effective after giving notice to the court (s 172(6)). The prescribed circumstances in r 7.61 are:

- ill-health;
- an intention to cease to practise as an insolvency practitioner;
- a conflict of interest or change of personal circumstances which precludes or makes impracticable the further discharge of the duties of a liquidator;
- where two or more persons are acting as liquidator jointly and it is the opinion of both or all of them that it is no longer expedient that there should continue to be that number of joint liquidators.

Before resigning, a liquidator must send a notice to the creditors and invite them by a decision procedure or by deemed consent procedure to consider whether a replacement should be appointed except where the resignation is under the last of the circumstances set out above (r 7.61(2)).

If it is clear that a liquidator should be willing to step aside if a move is made to remove him or her, but if he or she fights a resultant application for removal, indemnity costs should be awarded against the liquidator: *Shepheard v Lamey* [2001] BPIR 939. Similarly, Australian authority holds that if a liquidator resigns after opposing an application to remove him or her, the liquidator will be liable for the costs of the applicant: *Nicou v Ngan* [2005] NSWSC 446, (2005) 53 ACSR 529, NSW Sup Ct.

See the notes accompanying s 108.

*Release of liquidator*

**[1.225]**

**173 Release (voluntary winding up)**

(1)   This section applies with respect to the release of the liquidator of a company which is being wound up voluntarily.

(2)   A person who has ceased to be a liquidator shall have his release with effect from the following time, that is to say—

   (a)   in the following cases, the time at which notice is given to the registrar of companies in accordance with the rules that the person has ceased to hold office—

      (i)   the person has been removed from office by a general meeting of the company,

      (ii)   the person has been removed from office by a decision of the company's creditors and the company's creditors have not decided against the release,

      (iii)   the person has died;

   (b)   in the following cases, such time as the Secretary of State may, on the application of the person, determine—

      (i)   the person has been removed from office by a decision of the company's creditors and the company's creditors have decided against his release,

      (ii)   the person has been removed from office by the court,

      (iii)   the person has vacated office under section 171(4);

   (c)   in the case of a person who has resigned, such time as may be prescribed;

   (d)   in the case of a person who has vacated office under subsection (6) of section 171, the time at which he vacated office;

   (e)   in the case of a person who has vacated office under section 171(7)—

      (i)   if any of the company's creditors objected to the person's release before the end of the period for so objecting prescribed by the rules, such time as the Secretary of State may, on an application by that person, determine, and

      (ii)   otherwise, the time at which the person vacated office.

(2A)   Where the person is removed from office by a decision of the company's creditors, any decision of the company's creditors as to whether the person should have his release must be made by a qualifying decision procedure.

(3)   In the application of subsection (2) to the winding up of a company registered in Scotland, the references to a determination by the Secretary of State as to the time from which a person who has ceased to be liquidator shall have his release are to be read as references to such a determination by the Accountant of Court.

(4)   Where a liquidator has his release under subsection (2), he is, with effect from the time specified in that subsection, discharged from all liability both in respect of acts or omissions of his in the winding up and otherwise in relation to his conduct as liquidator.

   But nothing in this section prevents the exercise, in relation to a person who has had his release under subsection (2), of the court's powers under section 212 of this Act (summary remedy against delinquent directors, liquidators, etc).

   **Amendments**—Small Business, Enterprise and Employment Act 2015, s 126, Sch 9, Pt 1, paras 1, 44.

   **General note**—Release is available to liquidators who have resigned or been removed from office, and also to those liquidators who have ceased to be qualified insolvency practitioners, as well as those removed by the direction of the Secretary of State (r 6.33). The usual thing is that the liquidator remains in office until winding up is completed and then obtains a release. This occurs when all the property of the company (or so much as can be realised without needlessly protracting the liquidation) has been realised, the liquidator has distributed a final dividend to the creditors, adjusted the rights of contributories, and made a final return, if any, to the contributories.

It has been said that the classic case where release is designed to apply is where the liquidator has been frequently challenged and perhaps even sued by a creditor and there is every reason to think this would continue after the liquidator completed his or her work as liquidator *Re Australasian Barrister Chambers Pty Ltd* [2020] NSWSC 304, (2020) 146 ACSR 1 at [40].

### SECTION 173(2)(b)

A former liquidator must apply to the Secretary of State, who, if he or she grants a release must deliver a notice to the registrar of companies (r 6.33). In a members' voluntary a similar process and result is provided for (r 5.14). Where it is incumbent on the Secretary of State to decide the issue of release and release is granted, it may be revoked on proof that it was obtained by fraud or by suppression or concealment of any material fact: *Re Harris* [1899] 2 QB 97.

The compulsory liquidation equivalent provision is s 174.

'**Discharged from all liability**'—Although release discharges a liquidator from all liability, if a creditor, contributory or the official receiver obtains the leave of the court, an application may be made to the court for it to examine the conduct of a liquidator under s 212 (s 212(4)).

## [1.226]

### 174 Release (winding up by the court)

(1)   This section applies with respect to the release of the liquidator of a company which is being wound up by the court, or of a provisional liquidator.

(2)   Where the official receiver has ceased to be liquidator and a person becomes liquidator in his stead, the official receiver has his release with effect from the following time, that is to say—

    (a)    in a case where that person was nominated by the company's creditors or contributories, or was appointed by the Secretary of State, the time at which the official receiver gives notice to the court that he has been replaced;

    (b)    in a case where that person is appointed by the court, such time as the court may determine.

(3)   If the official receiver while he is a liquidator gives notice to the Secretary of State that the winding up is for practical purposes complete, he has his release with effect from such time as the Secretary of State may determine.

(4)   A person other than the official receiver who has ceased to be a liquidator has his release with effect from the following time, that is to say—

    (a)    in the following cases, the time at which notice is given to the court in accordance with the rules that the person has ceased to hold office—

        (i)    the person has been removed from office by a decision of the company's creditors and the company's creditors have not decided against his release,

        (ii)    the person has died;

    (b)    in the following cases, such time as the Secretary of State may, on the application of the person, determine—

        (i)    the person has been removed from office by a decision of the company's creditors and the company's creditors have decided against his release;

        (ii)    the person has been removed from office by the court or the Secretary of State;

        (iii)    the person has vacated office under section 172(5) or (7);

    (c)    in the case of a person who has resigned, such time as may be prescribed;

    (d)    in the case of a person who has vacated office under section 172(8)—

        (i)    if any of the company's creditors objected to the person's release before the end of the period for so objecting prescribed by the rules, such time as the Secretary of State may, on an application by that person, determine, and

        (ii)    otherwise, the time at which the person vacated office.

(4A)   Where a winding-up order made by the court in England and Wales is rescinded, the person (whether the official receiver or another person) who is the liquidator of the company at the time the order is rescinded has his release with effect from such time as the court may determine.

(4ZA) Where the person is removed from office by a decision of the company's creditors, any decision of the company's creditors as to whether the person should have his release must be made by a qualifying decision procedure.

(5) A person who has ceased to hold office as a provisional liquidator has his release with effect from such time as the court may, on an application by him, determine.

(6) Where the official receiver or a liquidator or provisional liquidator has his release under this section, he is, with effect from the time specified in the preceding provisions of this section, discharged from all liability both in respect of acts or omissions of his in the winding up and otherwise in relation to his conduct as liquidator or provisional liquidator.

But nothing in this section prevents the exercise, in relation to a person who has had his release under this section, of the court's powers under section 212 (summary remedy against delinquent directors, liquidators, etc).

(7) In the application of this section to a case where the order for winding up has been made by the court in Scotland, the references to a determination by the Secretary of State as to the time from which a person who has ceased to be liquidator has his release are to such a determination by the Accountant of Court.

**Amendments**—Deregulation Act 2015, s 19, Sch 6, Pt 3, paras 8, 10; Small Business, Enterprise and Employment Act 2015, s 126, Sch 9, Pt 1, paras 1, 45.

**General note**—This section is, for compulsory liquidations, the corresponding section to s 173.

See the notes accompanying s 173. Also see r 7.69 which provides, inter alia, an indication of what an application for release must contain.

CHAPTER VIII

PROVISIONS OF GENERAL APPLICATION IN WINDING UP
*Preferential Debts*

## [1.227]

### 174A  Moratorium debts etc: priority

(1) This section applies where proceedings for the winding up of a company are begun before the end of the period of 12 weeks beginning with the day after the end of any moratorium for the company under Part A1.

(2) In the winding up, the following are payable out of the company's assets (in the order of priority shown) in preference to all other claims—

    (a)    any prescribed fees or expenses of the official receiver acting in any capacity in relation to the company;

    (b)    moratorium debts and priority pre-moratorium debts.

(3) In subsection (2)(b) "priority pre-moratorium debt" means—

    (a)    any pre-moratorium debt that is payable in respect of—

        (i)    the monitor's remuneration or expenses,

        (ii)    goods or services supplied during the moratorium,

        (iii)    rent in respect of a period during the moratorium, or

        (iv)    wages or salary arising under a contract of employment, so far as relating to a period of employment before or during the moratorium,

    (b)    any pre-moratorium debt that—

        (i)    consists of a liability to make a redundancy payment, and

        (ii)    fell due before or during the moratorium, and

    (c)    any pre-moratorium debt that—

        (i)    arises under a contract or other instrument involving financial services,

        (ii)    fell due before or during the moratorium, and

        (iii)    is not relevant accelerated debt (see subsection (4)).

(4) For the purposes of subsection (3)(c)—

"relevant accelerated debt" means any pre-moratorium debt that fell due during the relevant period by reason of the operation of, or the exercise of rights under, an acceleration or early termination clause in a contract or other instrument involving financial services;

"the relevant period" means the period—

(a) beginning with the day on which the statement under section A6(1)(e) is made, and

(b) ending with the last day of the moratorium.

(5) The rules may make provision as to the order in which the debts mentioned in subsection (2)(b) rank among themselves in a case where the assets of the company are insufficient to meet them in full.

(6) The Secretary of State may by regulations made by statutory instrument amend this section for the purposes of changing the definition of "moratorium debt" or "priority pre-moratorium debt" in this section.

(7) Regulations under subsection (6) may make consequential, supplementary, incidental or transitional provision or savings.

(8) A statutory instrument containing regulations under subsection (6) may not be made unless a draft of the instrument has been laid before and approved by a resolution of each House of Parliament.

(9) For the purposes of this section proceedings for the winding up of a company are begun when—

(a) a winding-up petition is presented, or

(b) a resolution for voluntary winding up is passed.

(10) Any rules made under section A18(4) (meaning of supply of goods or services) apply also for the purposes of subsection (3)(a)(ii) of this section.

(11) In this section—

"acceleration or early termination clause", in relation to a contract or other instrument involving financial services, means a provision of the contract or other instrument—

(a) under which, on the happening of an event—

(i) a debt or other liability falls due earlier than it otherwise would, or

(ii) a debt or other liability is terminated and replaced by another debt or liability, or

(b) which confers on a party a right which, if exercised, will result in—

(i) a debt or other liability falling due earlier than it otherwise would, or

(ii) a debt or other liability being terminated and replaced by another debt or liability;

"contract or other instrument involving financial services" has the same meaning as it has for the purposes of section A18 (see Schedule ZA2);

"monitor's remuneration or expenses" has the meaning given by section A18;

"moratorium debt" has the meaning given by section A53;

"pre-moratorium debt" has the meaning given by section A53;

"redundancy payment" has the meaning given by section A18;

"wages or salary" has the meaning given by section A18.

**Amendments**—Inserted by Corporate Insolvency and Governance Act 2020, s 2(1), Sch 3, paras 1, 13.

## [1.228]

### 175 Preferential debts (general provision)

(1) In a winding up the company's preferential debts . . . shall be paid in priority to all other debts after the payment of—

(a) any liabilities to which section 174A applies, and

(b) expenses of the winding up.

(1A)   Ordinary preferential debts rank equally among themselves . . . and shall be paid in full, unless the assets are insufficient to meet them, in which case they abate in equal proportions.

(1B)   Secondary preferential debts rank equally among themselves after the ordinary preferential debts and shall be paid in full, unless the assets are insufficient to meet them, in which case they abate in equal proportions.

(2)   Preferential debts—

    (a)   . . .

    (b)   so far as the assets of the company available for payment of general creditors are insufficient to meet them, have priority over the claims of holders of debentures secured by, or holders of, any floating charge created by the company, and shall be paid accordingly out of any property comprised in or subject to that charge.

(3)   In this section "preferential debts", "ordinary preferential debts" and "secondary preferential debts" each has the meaning given in section 386 in Part 12.

**Amendments**—SI 2014/3486; Corporate Insolvency and Governance Act 2020, s 2(1), Sch 3, paras 1, 14(1).

**General note**—While subsection (1) states that the preferential debts are to be paid in priority to all other debts, subsection (2) qualifies that by indicating that the preferential debts do not rank for payment until the winding-up expenses have been satisfied in full.

Preferential debts are defined in s 386 and the kinds of debts that are preferential are enumerated in Sch 6. The types of debts that qualify have gradually been reduced over the years and since the commencement of the provisions in the Enterprise Act 2002 that deal with corporate insolvency, Crown debts no longer rank as preferential debts (Enterprise Act, s 251). Their priority status was abolished from 15 September 2003. The abolition was regarded as an integral part of the objective of government, which was to see more companies rescued. The government wanted to see the funds that would normally be swallowed up by the Crown pass on to the unsecured creditors. However, that will not always be the case because unless a charge was created post 15 September 2003, the floating chargeholder will get the benefit of the abolition of the Crown priority. From 1 December 2020 some Crown debts and notably tax and national insurance contributions deducted from employees' wages not remitted to HMRC as well as VAT that has been paid to the company and not remitted to HMRC will regain preferential status (see, ss 98 and 99 of the Finance Act 2020 and The Insolvency Act 1986 (HMRC Debts: Priority on Insolvency) Regulations 2020).

Section 754 of the Companies Act 2006 provides (if the company is not being wound up) that preferential creditors will obtain priority in relation to assets subject to a floating charge where the chargeholder takes possession of the assets. It has been held by the Court of Appeal in *HM Commissioners for Revenue and Customs v Royal Bank of Scotland* [2007] EWCA Civ 1262 that s 754's precursor provision could not apply to all payments made by a company to the credit of its account with the chargeholder, and that it was necessary to distinguish between acts which are, substantially, acts by which the chargeholder realises its security and those acts which are, substantially, no more than the ordinary discharge of a debtor's liability. The substance of each transaction had to be considered.

Until 2003 the Crown enjoyed a priority over other unsecured creditors when it came to distribution of the company's funds. The Finance Act 2020, which received Royal Assent on 22 July 2020, provided in ss 98 and 99 for the re-introduction of a priority in insolvency, from 1 December 2020, for the Crown, although the priority was not as broad in scope as that which it enjoyed pre-2003. The Crown now has priority for amounts owed to HMRC in respect of VAT and any 'relevant deduction'. Secondary legislation, in the form of reg 2 of The Insolvency Act 1986 (HMRC Debts: Priority on Insolvency) Regulations 2020 (SI 2020/983), specified what qualifies as a 'relevant deduction'; these are restricted to PAYE income tax, employee NICs, student loan repayments and construction industry scheme deductions that the company has made. See Category 9 of Sch 6, para 15D to the Act.

As regards 'winding-up' expenses, see the notes attaching to r 7.108 (compulsory liquidation) and r 6.42 (creditors' voluntary liquidation).

**Payment**—The preferential debts are paid in full, if the company's funds permit, before lower order creditors, such as the general unsecured creditors, get paid anything, and if the funds do not permit full payment the preferential debts rank equally and abate in equal proportions. Importantly, the preferential debts are paid out of the funds of the company that are subject to a floating charge, in priority to the chargeholder where the general funds of the company (that are not encumbered by the charge) are not sufficient to pay them in full (s 175(2)(b)).

**Floating charge**—As a result of the definition in s 251, a floating charge for the purposes of the Act is one that was created as a floating charge. So, any charge that was created as a floating charge and still was at the time of winding-up order is regarded as a floating charge for the purposes of the legislation and, more importantly, so is a floating charge that has crystallised before winding up commences.

A receiver appointed before winding up, and operating under a floating charge is required by s 40 to pay the preferential debts, as they exist at the time of the 'relevant date' in priority to repaying his or her appointor. The relevant date is the date of the appointment of the receiver (s 387(4)(a)). But if winding up occurs subsequent to receivership commencing, s 175 will overtake s 40: *Re Leyland DAF Ltd* [2002] 1 BCLC 571. This leads to the consequence that the receiver has to pay preferential debts that exist at the time of a different 'relevant date'. In the latter circumstance the relevant date is the date of the winding-up order or the date of the resolution to wind up (s 387(3)(b), (c)). But it was held that the assets covered by the charge could not be used by the liquidator to recoup the expenses of winding up, save where they involved the preservation and/or realisation of charged assets: *Buchler v Talbot* [2004] UKHL 9, [2004] 2 AC 298, [2004] 2 WLR 582, [2004] 1 All ER 1289. The effect of the decision was, however, overturned by s 176ZA, which was introduced by Companies Act 2006. See the notes accompanying s 176ZA.

See ss 40, 386 and Sch 6 and the notes thereto.

See Keay and Walton 'The Preferential Debts' Regime in Liquidation Law: In the Public Interest?' (1999) 3 *Company Financial and Insolvency Law Review* 84.

## [1.229]

### 176 Preferential charge on goods distrained, etc

(1)  This section applies where a company is being wound up by the court in England and Wales, and is without prejudice to section 128 (avoidance of attachments, etc).

(2)  Subsection (2A) applies where—

  (a)  any person (whether or not a landlord or person entitled to rent) has distrained upon the goods or effects of the company, or

  (b)  Her Majesty's Revenue and Customs has been paid any amount from an account of the company under Part 1 of Schedule 8 to the Finance (No 2) Act 2015 (enforcement by deduction from accounts),

in the period of 3 months ending with the date of the winding-up order.

(2A)  Where this subsection applies—

  (a)  in a case within subsection (2)(a), the goods or effects, or the proceeds of their sale, and

  (b)  in a case within subsection (2)(b), the amount in question,

is charged for the benefit of the company with the preferential debts of the company to the extent that the company's property is for the time being insufficient for meeting those debts.

(3)  Where by virtue of a charge under subsection (2A) any person surrenders any goods or effects to a company or makes a payment to a company, that person ranks, in respect of the amount of the proceeds of sale of those goods or effects by the liquidator or (as the case may be) the amount of the payment, as a preferential creditor of the company, except as against so much of the company's property as is available for the payment of preferential creditors by virtue of the surrender or payment.

**Amendments**—Finance (No 2) Act 2015, s 51, Sch 8, Pt 2, paras 26, 30.

**General note**—This provision only applies where the action of distress has not been put in force following the commencement of winding up (s 128). The age old remedy at common law of the landlord's right to distrain against a person's property has now been axed through the provisions of the Tribunals, Courts and Enforcement Act 2007 (s 71) which only came into force in 2014, and this so if even though 'distrain' is still used in the section. The right to distrain is effectively replaced with a new regime for landlords. Landlords now have the right to CRAR (commercial rent arrears recovery) as far as commercial leases are concerned. The fact that CRAR applies to this provision now can be discerned from the fact that in s 436 'distress' (the noun equivalent of distrain) includes 'the procedure in Sch 12 to the Tribunals, Courts and Enforcement Act 2007' which is an oblique reference to CRAR. Due to the coronavirus pandemic, tenants have been given greater protection from CRAR by Taking Control of Goods (Amendment) (Coronavirus) Regulations 2020 (SI 2020/1002), Taking Control of Goods and Certification of Enforcement Agents (Amendment) (No 2) (Coronavirus) Regulations 2020 (SI 2020/614), Taking Control of Goods (Amendment) (Coronavirus) Regulations 2021 (SI 2021/300), Taking Control of Goods and Certification of Enforcement Agents (Amendment) (Coronavirus) Regulations 2020 (SI 2020/451), Taking Control of Goods and Certification of Enforcement Agents (Amendment) (No 2) (Coronavirus) Regulations 2020 (SI 2020/614).

**Preferential debts**—If a landlord distrains and the tenant has a winding-up order made against it within 3 months of that occurring the landlord may lose some or all of the benefit of the distress under s 176(2A) and (3). These provisions operate where the company's estate is insufficient to meet the debts that are owed to preferential creditors. If the provisions do operate, the goods which have been distrained, or the proceeds from their sale, are charged for the benefit of the company's estate with the preferential debts. So, while a landlord obtains a form of priority he or she, does not, where s 176(2A) and (3) apply, have priority over the preferential creditors. So, while distress permits a landlord to get ahead of the general unsecured creditors, he or she falls behind the preferential creditors, in the circumstances mentioned above.

See the notes to accompany s 347.

*Non-preferential debts*

**[1.230]**

**176AZA  Non-preferential debts of financial institutions**

(1)  This section applies in the winding up of a company which is a relevant financial institution.

(2)  The company's ordinary non-preferential debts shall be paid in priority to its secondary non-preferential debts.

(3)  The company's secondary non-preferential debts—

(a)    shall be paid in priority to its tertiary non-preferential debts, and

(b)    rank equally among themselves after the ordinary non-preferential debts and shall be paid in full, unless the assets are insufficient to meet them, in which case they abate in equal proportions.

(4)  See section 387A for definitions relevant to this section.

**Amendments**—Inserted by SI 2018/1244.

*Property subject to floating charge*

**Amendments**—Cross-heading inserted by Enterprise Act 2002, s 52.

**[1.231]**

**176ZA  Payment of expenses of winding up (England and Wales)**

(1)  The expenses of winding up in England and Wales, so far as the assets of the company available for payment of general creditors are insufficient to meet them, have priority over any claims to property comprised in or subject to any floating charge created by the company and shall be paid out of any such property accordingly.

(2)  In subsection (1)—

(a)    the reference to assets of the company available for payment of general creditors does not include any amount made available under section 176A(2)(a);

(b)    the reference to claims to property comprised in or subject to a floating charge is to the claims of—

(i)      the holders of debentures secured by, or holders of, the floating charge, and

(ii)     any preferential creditors entitled to be paid out of that property in priority to them.

(3)  Provision may be made by rules restricting the application of subsection (1), in such circumstances as may be prescribed, to expenses authorised or approved—

(a)    by the holders of debentures secured by, or holders of, the floating charge and by any preferential creditors entitled to be paid in priority to them, or

(b)    by the court.

(4)  References in this section to the expenses of the winding up are to all expenses properly incurred in the winding up, including the remuneration of the liquidator.

**Amendments**—Inserted by the Companies Act 2006, s 1282(1).

**General note**—This provision was introduced by the Companies Act 2006 and came into force on 6 April 2008. The provision represents the Government's response to the decision of the House of Lords in *Buchler v Talbot* [2004] UKHL 9, [2004] 2 AC 298, [2004] 2 WLR 582, [2004] 1 All ER 1289, which held that liquidation expenses are not to be paid out of assets subject to a floating charge over company property, because where a company is in both administrative receivership and liquidation, its assets are comprised in two different funds. One fund involved some assets that were subject to a floating charge and the other fund involved assets that were just subject to the liquidation. Generally each fund bears its own costs and, as the chargeholder has no interest in the liquidation, he or she should not have to contribute towards the liquidation expenses (at [30] and [31]). This ruling severely limited liquidators as often a floating charge is granted over most, if not all, of a company's property. Hence, liquidators could not use, without the consent of the chargeholder much (or any) of the company's property to pay for litigation and other expenses. The new provision and accompanying rules acknowledge the fact that floating chargeholders (and in some cases, preferential creditors) have a special interest in the use of assets (covered by a charge) to fund litigation in the liquidation, so they are given a voice in the use of such assets.

New rules were introduced to the 1986 Rules in light of the introduction of the section, namely rr 4.218A–4.218E (inserted by the Insolvency (Amendment) Rules 2008 (SI 2008/737)), and they have been included in the Insolvency (England and Wales) Rules 2016. They have been included separately for compulsory and creditors' voluntary liquidations. The provisions are now rr 7.111–7.116 for compulsory liquidations and rr 6.42–6.48 for creditors' voluntary liquidations.

Assets that are covered by a floating charge, but which make up the prescribed part under s 176A and are payable to general creditors as a result, cannot be used to pay expenses of the winding up (s 176ZA(2)(a)).

The payment of expenses out of assets subject to a floating charge is restricted by the need for approval or authorisation to be obtained from those interested in the assets subject to the charge. The procedure for obtaining this approval or authorisation is explained in rather detailed rules, namely rr 7.111–7.116 for compulsory liquidations and rr 6.42–6.48 for creditors' voluntary liquidations. The only kind of expenses that are restricted when it comes to using charged assets for the payment of liquidation expenses are litigation expenses as defined in r 7.111(1) or r 6.44(1) (also, see r 7.112 and 6.44(2)).

See, A Keay 'Litigation Expenses in Liquidations' (2009) 22 *Insolvency Intelligence* 113.

See the detailed commentary on rr 7.111–7.116.

**[1.232]**

### 176ZB Application of proceeds of office-holder claims

(1) This section applies where—
- (a) there is a floating charge (whether created before or after the coming into force of this section) which relates to property of a company which—
  - (i) is in administration, or
  - (ii) has gone into liquidation; and
- (b) the administrator or the liquidator (referred to in this section as "the office-holder") has—
  - (i) brought a claim under any provision mentioned in subsection (3), or
  - (ii) made an assignment (or, in Scotland, assignation) in relation to a right of action under any such provision under section 246ZD.

(2) The proceeds of the claim or assignment (or, in Scotland, assignation) are not to be treated as part of the company's net property, that is to say the amount of its property which would be available for satisfaction of claims of holders of debentures secured by, or holders of, any floating charge created by the company.

(3) The provisions are—
- (a) section 213 or 246ZA (fraudulent trading);
- (b) section 214 or 246ZB (wrongful trading);
- (c) section 238 (transactions at an undervalue (England and Wales));
- (d) section 239 (preferences (England and Wales));
- (e) section 242 (gratuitous alienations (Scotland));
- (f) section 243 (unfair preferences (Scotland));
- (g) section 244 (extortionate credit transactions).

(4) Subsection (2) does not apply to a company if or in so far as it is disapplied by—
- (a) a voluntary arrangement in respect of the company, or

(b)    a compromise or arrangement agreed under Part 26 or 26A of the Companies Act 2006 (arrangements and reconstructions).

**Amendments**—Inserted by Small Business, Enterprise and Employment Act 2015, s 119. Amended by Corporate Insolvency and Governance Act 2020, s 7, Sch 9, Pt 2, paras 5, 6(1), (2).

**General note**—The provision is in force and applies in respect of a company which enters administration or goes into liquidation on or after 1 October 2015. It seeks to clarify the order of priority for the distribution of proceeds arising from an office-holder claim or from the assignment of such a claim that is covered by sub-section (3). It codifies the legal position established by case law by providing that the proceeds of these types of claim do not form part of the company's property which is available for the satisfaction of debts owed to a creditor who holds a floating charge.

## [1.233]

### 176A  Share of assets for unsecured creditors

(1)    This section applies where a floating charge relates to property of a company—
    (a)    which has gone into liquidation,
    (b)    which is in administration,
    (c)    of which there is a provisional liquidator, or
    (d)    of which there is a receiver.

(2)    The liquidator, administrator or receiver—
    (a)    shall make a prescribed part of the company's net property available for the satisfaction of unsecured debts, and
    (b)    shall not distribute that part to the proprietor of a floating charge except in so far as it exceeds the amount required for the satisfaction of unsecured debts.

(3)    Subsection (2) shall not apply to a company if—
    (a)    the company's net property is less than the prescribed minimum, and
    (b)    the liquidator, administrator or receiver thinks that the cost of making a distribution to unsecured creditors would be disproportionate to the benefits.

(4)    Subsection (2) shall also not apply to a company if or in so far as it is disapplied by—
    (a)    a voluntary arrangement in respect of the company, or
    (b)    a compromise or arrangement agreed under Part 26 or 26A of the Companies Act 2006 (arrangements and reconstructions).

(5)    Subsection (2) shall also not apply to a company if—
    (a)    the liquidator, administrator or receiver applies to the court for an order under this subsection on the ground that the cost of making a distribution to unsecured creditors would be disproportionate to the benefits, and
    (b)    the court orders that subsection (2) shall not apply.

(6)    In subsections (2) and (3) a company's net property is the amount of its property which would, but for this section, be available for satisfaction of claims of holders of debentures secured by, or holders of, any floating charge created by the company.

(7)    An order under subsection (2) prescribing part of a company's net property may, in particular, provide for its calculation—
    (a)    as a percentage of the company's net property, or
    (b)    as an aggregate of different percentages of different parts of the company's net property.

(8)    An order under this section—
    (a)    must be made by statutory instrument, and
    (b)    shall be subject to annulment pursuant to a resolution of either House of Parliament.

(9)    In this section—
"floating charge" means a charge which is a floating charge on its creation and which is created after the first order under subsection (2)(a) comes into force, and
"prescribed" means prescribed by order by the Secretary of State.

(10)   An order under this section may include transitional or incidental provision.

**Amendments**—Inserted by Enterprise Act 2002, s 252. Amended by SI 2008/948; Corporate Insolvency and Governance Act 2020, s 7, Sch 9, Pt 2, paras 5, 6(1), (3).

**General note**—This provision was introduced by the Enterprise Act 2002. It is part of the package that involved the abolition of the Crown preference. It is to be seen as a counterweight to the benefit that floating chargeholders have received from the elimination of the Crown priority. See the notes to s 175 and Sch 6.

The provision, which applies to four kinds of insolvency administration, provides for what has become known as 'top-slicing'. That is, in relation to floating charges created on or after 15 September 2003, a certain part of the net proceeds (net property) from the realisation of the property covered by floating charges must be set aside for the unsecured creditors.

A secured creditor, who has either a fixed or floating charge over company property, and whose security is not adequate to discharge his or her debt, is not permitted to share in the net property. If the net property is sufficient to pay out all unsecured creditors then the surplus may be paid out to secured creditors: *Re Airbase (UK) Ltd* [2008] EWHC 124 (Ch), [2008] 1 BCLC 437; *Re Permacell Finesse Ltd (in liq)* [2007] EWHC 3233 (Ch). But if a floating chargeholder surrendered entirely his or her security under the charge pursuant to, or in accordance with, r 14.19(2) of the Rules, received nothing pursuant to it, and is entitled to prove as if his or her debt were unsecured, the former chargeholder becomes an unsecured creditor and may share in the prescribed part: *Kelly and Sumpton v Inflexion Fund 2* 2850 Limited Partnership and Autocruise Co-Investment Limited Partnership [2010] EWHC 2850 (Ch) at [41]). HHJ Kaye QC (sitting as a High Court judge) who gave judgment in this case made the point that if the chargeholder elects to become an unsecured creditor he or she should be treated as such in relation both to proving under r 4.88(2) of the 1986 Rules (now r 14.19(2) of the 2016 Rules) and to sharing in the prescribed part (at [48]). In *Re JT Frith Ltd* [2012] EWHC 196 (Ch) it was held that if a secured creditor does not take any action to surrender its security, but lodges a proof of debt for the whole of its debt then it can be assumed that it is surrendering its security and it is entitled to share in the prescribed part, even if the proof of debt does not state that security is surrendered but where the creditor states 'None' in answer to the question in the proof 'particulars of any security held' ([29]).

This provision does not apply:

- to charges created before the commencement date (15 September 2003) (s 176A(9)) (hence, benefiting the holders of any pre 15 September 2003 charges substantially as the charges are not placed behind Crown debts and are not subject to top-slicing);
- where the company's net property is less than the prescribed minimum (at present this is £10,000 (Insolvency Act 1986 (Prescribed Part) Order 2003 (SI 2003/2097), art 2)) and the relevant office-holder thinks that the cost of making a distribution to the unsecured creditors would be disproportionate to the benefits received by the unsecured creditors (s 176A(3)(a), (b));
- where it is disapplied by a company voluntary arrangement in respect of the company or a compromise or arrangement under s 895 of the Companies Act 2006 (s 176A(4)(a), (b));
- where the office-holder applies to the court for an order, and one is granted, on the basis that the cost of making a distribution would be disproportionate to the benefits (s 176A(5)(a), (b)) (the right to a dividend was disapplied under this provision in *Re Hydroserve Ltd* [2007] EWHC 3026 (Ch), but not in either *Re Courts plc* [2008] EWHC 2339 (Ch) or *Re International Sections Ltd (in creditors' voluntary liquidation)* [2009] EWHC 137 (Ch), [2009] BPIR 297.

In the second situation just referred to, both conditions must exist if a payment is to be set aside. So, it is possible that the sum available is less than the minimum, but the office-holder thinks that it might be proportionate to make a distribution. If the minimum is exceeded, then there is no discretion in the office-holder when it comes to distribution.

In the penultimate situation referred to above, the unsecured creditors will have agreed to forego the top-slicing so as to assist the implementation of some arrangement that might benefit them more in the long run. The question is: would dissenting creditors be entitled to challenge the decision, under s 6(1) of the Insolvency Act 1986, on the basis that the arrangement unfairly prejudices his or her interests as a creditor?

The last situation mentioned above might be fulfilled where there are a huge number of creditors and making a distribution would not be worthwhile, given the attendant costs and expenses. But note the approach taken in *Re Courts plc* [2008] EWHC 2339 (Ch) and *Re International Sections Ltd (in creditors' voluntary liquidation)* [2009] EWHC 137 (Ch), [2009] BPIR 297.

As the provision does not have retrospective effect (note s 176A(9)), it might be thought that where there are any subsequent orders to the first order setting the prescribed part, they will only apply to charges created after the commencement of the respective orders (Davies et al *Insolvency and the Enterprise Act 2002* (Jordan Publishing, 2003) at 58).

'Shall not apply'—While in *Re Hydroserve Ltd* [2007] EWHC 3026 (Ch) the court was willing to disapply section 176A(2), in *Re Courts plc* [2008] EWHC 2339 (Ch) Blackburne J took the view that he was not entitled, in his discretion, to order the partial disapplication of the section, as he was asked to do by the applicant (at [15]). In the case the liquidator sought an order under s 176A(5) that s 176A(2) would not apply so as to require a distribution to those unsecured creditors who were owed less than £28,000 on the basis that to make a distribution would be disproportionate to the benefits. His Lordship rejected the application on the basis that if he were to accede to it, it would interfere with a pari passu distribution, as a minority of creditors would be able to take the whole of the prescribed part if the judge made the order sought, and unless Parliament specifically indicated that the pari passu principle should not apply then the learned judge said that it should be applied (at [16]). Furthermore, his Lordship said that if, when averaged out, a liquidator's expenses relating to the processing of each creditor's claim to a share of the prescribed part equals or exceeds the distribution to a particular creditor, that is not a relevant matter to be taken into account in consideration of the operation of this section (at [17]). The judge stated that the cost/benefit balance that is to be considered in relation to s 176A(5) is to be approached on the basis of treating creditors as a body, and one cannot look at individual creditors and see what each would actually receive ([19]). Later, in *Re International Sections Ltd (in creditors' voluntary liquidation)* [2009] EWHC 137 (Ch), [2009] BPIR 297 HHJ Purle QC (sitting as a High Court judge) also declined to disapply s 176A(2). The learned judge said that in deciding whether to disapply the section a court had to be satisfied that the cost of making a distribution would be disproportionate to the benefits, and that it was right to disapply the section on that ground. It was permissible for a court to adopt the view, even where the cost of making a distribution would be disproportionate, that unsecured creditors should still receive what remained of the prescribed part, after deducting costs. His Lordship said that the court should not be too ready to disapply the section merely because the dividend would be small. His Lordship said that the disapplication of s 176A(2) should be very much the exception, and not the rule (at [9], [15]), a position supported by Lord Glennie in the Scottish case of *Re QMD Hotels Ltd* [2010] CSOH 168 at [4]. Often liquidators and administrators may say that there should be disapplication because of the cost of dealing with the payment out of the prescribed part. Yet in *Re QMD Hotels Ltd* Lord Glennie said, in relation to the case before him, that the administrators should do no more than was necessary to effect payment of a dividend without carrying out further investigations into the merits of the claims (at [6]). In another Scottish case the court said that even if the requirement for the granting of a disapplication order was fulfilled, that is, the costs of making a distribution was disproportionate to the benefits, it might not be appropriate in the whole circumstances to exercise the power to disapply: *Re Joint Administrators of Casterbridge Plant Ltd* [2015] CSOH 165.

'Net property'—This term covers the property that would, but for this section, be available to be paid to the floating chargeholder.

'Floating charge'—See the comments relating to s 175.

'Prescribed'—The part that is set aside for unsecured creditors is prescribed by the Secretary of State. The government decided that there should be a minimum amount available to the unsecured creditors and that thereafter payment would be on a sliding scale. At present the prescribed sums are (Insolvency Act 1986 (Prescribed Part) Order 2003 (SI 2003/2097), art 3(1)(a), (b)):

- where the property's value does not exceed £10,000 in value, 50% of that;
- where the company's net property exceeds £10,000 in value, 50% of the first £10,000 in value and 20% of that part that exceeds £10,000 in value.

The above is subject to the fact that the prescribed part is not to exceed £800,000 in satisfying the debts of unsecured creditors (art 3(2)). Article 3(2) was amended by The Insolvency Act 1986 (Prescribed Part) (Amendment) Order 2020 (SI 2020/211) from 6 April 2020 so as to increase the sum to £800,000 from £600,000.

**Report to creditors**—Within 28 days of the appointment of the liquidator under s 100, in a creditors' voluntary liquidation, the liquidator is obliged to send a notice accompanied by a statement of affairs and a report to the creditors and contributories (r 6.15(1)) and in the report he or she should provide an estimate of the prescribed part, and an estimate of the value of the company's net property (r 6.15(2)).

'Created'—The charges to which the prescribed part apply are ones created after 15 September 2003. Does 'created' here mean the execution of a new document or does it cover the assignment of debenture to a new lender, who lends money on the basis of the debenture? It has been submitted that a charge is created when a debenture is assigned – the parties being the new lender and the company (Simmons 'Some Reflections on Administrations, Crown Preferences and the Ring-Fenced Sums in the Enterprise Act' [2004] JBL 423 at 434).

For further discussion, see A Keay 'The Prescribed Part: Sharing Around the Company's Funds' (2011) 24 (6) *Insolvency Intelligence* 81; P Cranston 'The unchartered shallows of the prescribed part' (2010) 5 JIBFL 278.

*Special managers*

**[1.234]**

**177 Power to appoint special manager**

(1)   Where a company has gone into liquidation or a provisional liquidator has been appointed, the court may, on an application under this section, appoint any person to be the special manager of the business or property of the company.

(2)   The application may be made by the liquidator or provisional liquidator in any case where it appears to him that the nature of the business or property of the company, or the interests of the company's creditors or contributories or members generally, require the appointment of another person to manage the company's business or property.

(3)   The special manager has such powers as may be entrusted to him by the court.

(4)   The court's power to entrust powers to the special manager includes power to direct that any provision of this Act that has effect in relation to the provisional liquidator or liquidator of a company shall have the like effect in relation to the special manager for the purposes of the carrying out by him of any of the functions of the provisional liquidator or liquidator.

(5)   The special manager shall—

  (a)   give such security or, in Scotland, caution as may be prescribed;
  (b)   prepare and keep such accounts as may be prescribed; and
  (c)   produce those accounts in accordance with the rules to the Secretary of State or to such other persons as may be prescribed.

**General note**—It is normal, where limited circumstances exist, for a court to appoint a special manager, namely if the company's business or affairs are too extensive, too remote or too specialised for the liquidator to be able to exercise personal control over their conduct or administration. For an example of an appointment, see *Re US Ltd* (1983) 1 BCC 98, 985.

The special manager is an officer of the court and under its control: *Re Walter L Jacob & Son Ltd* [1989] BCLC 345.

In its order the court is to set the duration of the appointment, which may be for a specific period of time or until the occurrence of a specified event, or alternatively the court may state that the appointment is to be subject to a further order of the court (rr 5.17, 6.37 and 7.93).

See rr 5.17–5.21, 6.37–6.41 and 7.92–7.97 for the details of practice and procedure.

**Security**—The appointment of a special manager does not take effect until the prescribed security has been given to the applicant for the appointment (rr 5.18(1), 6.38(1), 7.94(1)). The security given is not to be less than the value of the assets as estimated by the liquidator in his or her report under r 5.17(3), 6.38(3) or 7.93(3).

*Disclaimer (England and Wales only)*

**[1.235]**

**178 Power to disclaim onerous property**

(1)   This and the next two sections apply to a company that is being wound up in England and Wales.

(2)   Subject as follows, the liquidator may, by the giving of the prescribed notice, disclaim any onerous property and may do so notwithstanding that he has taken possession of it, endeavoured to sell it, or otherwise exercised rights of ownership in relation to it.

(3)   The following is onerous property for the purposes of this section—

  (a)   any unprofitable contract, and
  (b)   any other property of the company which is unsaleable or not readily saleable or is such that it may give rise to a liability to pay money or perform any other onerous act.

(4)   A disclaimer under this section—

(a)   operates so as to determine, as from the date of the disclaimer, the rights, interests and liabilities of the company in or in respect of the property disclaimed; but

(b)   does not, except so far as is necessary for the purpose of releasing the company from any liability, affect the rights or liabilities of any other person.

(5)   A notice of disclaimer shall not be given under this section in respect of any property if—

(a)   a person interested in the property has applied in writing to the liquidator or one of his predecessors as liquidator requiring the liquidator or that predecessor to decide whether he will disclaim or not, and

(b)   the period of 28 days beginning with the day on which that application was made, or such longer period as the court may allow, has expired without a notice of disclaimer having been given under this section in respect of that property.

(6)   Any person sustaining loss or damage in consequence of the operation of a disclaimer under this section is deemed a creditor of the company to the extent of the loss or damage and accordingly may prove for the loss or damage in the winding up.

**General note**—This provision, which has caused many problems over the years, permits liquidators to disclaim certain forms of property that can be regarded as onerous. In many ways s 178 closely follows the pattern set by the law of bankruptcy (see s 315) from which it is directly imported. But in bankruptcy, as the bankrupt estate vests in the trustee, the trustee will be personally liable in respect of onerous property if disclaimer does not occur (*Titterton v Cooper* (1882) 9 QBD 473), while liquidators are not liable: *Stead Hazel & Co v Cooper* [1933] 1 KB 840.

The reason for permitting disclaimer is to allow the liquidator to obtain an early closure of the liquidation (*Re Park Air Services plc* [1999] 1 BCLC 155 at 162, HL). Without disclaimer, where a lease exists, for instance, the liquidator would have to retain sufficient sums to pay the rent on the leased premises as they fell due: *Re Park Air Services plc* at 163.

The power to disclaim is available to liquidators in both compulsory and voluntary liquidations. It is a power that exists to allow a liquidator to reduce company liabilities, and thereby boost dividends paid to creditors. The power can be exercised unilaterally by the liquidator now, which differs from the previous law where a liquidator had to secure the leave of the court before he or she was able to disclaim.

Although the power to disclaim is exercised in relation to insolvent companies for the most part, it is exercisable in the case of a solvent company as well (*Re Nottingham General Cemetery Co* [1955] Ch 683; *Re Park Air Services plc* [1999] 1 BCLC 155, HL), where it might hamper the winding up of the company.

The liquidator must disclaim the whole of the property and is not entitled to disclaim just part of it (*Re Fussell* (1882) 20 ChD 341, CA).

A person who is affected by a proposed disclaimer is able to apply to the court under s 168(5) for a review of the liquidator's decision to disclaim: *Re Hans Place Ltd* [1992] BCLC 768. See the notes accompanying s 168 to see when a challenge under s 168(5) might be successful.

If a liquidator is unsure about disclaiming some property, he or she might seek directions from the court under s 112, for voluntary liquidations, and s 168(3) for compulsory liquidations.

'**Property**'—The word is defined widely in s 436 (*Bristol Airport plc v Powdrill* [1990] Ch 744, [1990] 2 WLR 1362, [1990] 2 All ER 493, [1990] BCLC 585, CA), but it is not an exhaustive definition. Leases are the kinds of property often the subject of the action of disclaimer. Property that can be disclaimed includes a cause of action: *Khan-Ghauri v Dunbar Bank* [2010] EWHC 1591 (Ch); *Fosdick v Fox* [2017] EWHC 1737 (Ch), [2017] BPIR 1194.

A licence under the Sea Fish (Conservation) Act 1992 (*Re Rae* [1995] BCC 102) and a waste management licence (*Re Celtic Extraction Ltd; Re Blue Stone Chemicals Ltd* [1999] 2 BCLC 555, CA) have been held to constitute property within s 436 of the Act and constituted onerous property within s 178, as has an interest under a chattel lease: *Bristol Airport plc v Powdrill* [1990] Ch 744, [1990] 2 WLR 1362, [1990] 2 All ER 493, [1990] BCLC 585, and a water use licence under the Water Environment (Controlled Activities) (Scotland) Regulations 2011 (SSI 2011/209): *Joint Liquidators of the Scottish Coal Co Ltd, Petitioners* 2013 SLT 1055.

Where the property consisted of permits provided under legislation, whether disclaimer was permitted would depend on the terms of the permits and the statutory provisions: *Joint Liquidators of the Scottish Coal Co Ltd, Petitioners* 2013 SLT 1055.

In *Longley v Chief Executive of Department of Environment and Heritage and Protection* [2018] QCA 32 the court said that the property that is able to be disclaimed encompassed the company's possession of a wide variety of legal rights against others in relation to some tangible or intangible property.

'**Unprofitable contract**'—A contract is unprofitable if the cost involved for the company in performing its obligations is greater than the benefit which the company will enjoy under the terms of the contract. A contract is not unprofitable if the amount of profit is small: *Re Bastable* [1901] 2 KB 518, CA, or is merely financially disadvantageous: *Squires v AIG Europe (UK) Ltd* [2006] EWCA Civ 7, [2006] Ch 610, [2006] 2 WLR 1369, [2007] 1 BCLC 29, [2006] BPIR 457. And demonstrating that a better commercial bargain could be made by the liquidator compared with the bargain that was arranged originally (prior to liquidation) does not mean that the original contract was unprofitable: *Re Bastable* [1901] 2 KB 518; *Capital Prime Properties plc v Worthgate Ltd (in liquidation)* [2000] 1 BCLC 647; *Squires v AIG Europe (UK) Ltd*. But if a contract that had been entered into before liquidation would take a significant time to complete, then it might be regarded as unprofitable: *Dekala Pty Ltd (in liquidation) v Perth Land & Leisure Ltd* (1989) 17 NSWLR 664 (contract would take 8 months to be completed). The Court of Appeal appears to see that this is a critical issue in determining that a contract was unprofitable, as the need to perform future obligations would prejudice the liquidator's responsibility to realise the company's property and pay a dividend to creditors within a reasonable period of time: *Squires v AIG Europe (UK) Ltd*.

Contracts cannot be disclaimed where the effect of disclaimer would be to undo the contract in so far as it had been performed and in so far as interests had been created under it: *Capital Prime Properties plc v Worthgate Ltd (in liquidation)* [2000] 1 BCLC 647. Also a contract cannot be disclaimed merely because the property that is the subject of the contract can be sold by a liquidator more readily and at a higher price if a contract was not in place that itself will not mean that the contract is unprofitable: *Re Blue Sennar Air Pty Ltd (in liq)* [2016] NSWSC 772.

As a liquidator is able to disclaim despite having taken possession of property, attempting to sell it, or exercising an act of ownership in relation to it (s 178(2)), it is probably the case that the right to disclaim unprofitable contracts still exists even if the company or the liquidator has attempted to assign, or has exercised rights in relation to the contract or any property to which the contract relates.

Section 178 does not apply where there is a market contract (a contract defined in s 155(2) of the Companies Act 1989) or a contract effected by the exchange or clearing house for the purpose of realising property provided as margin in relation to market contracts (s 164(1) of the Companies Act 1989), so such contracts cannot be disclaimed as unprofitable.

'**Unsaleable**'—Given more recent case law, it is probable that a liquidator is not required to show that reasonable efforts were taken to sell the property; rather, he or she can rely on his or her subjective view that the property is not readily saleable, provided that the liquidator's view is not totally unreasonable to the point of being perverse: *Re Hans Place Ltd* [1992] BCLC 768. Moreover, property can still be onerous even if one cannot establish unsaleability, such as property that requires expensive repairs before it can be sold (see s 178(3)(b)).

**Not affecting the rights or liabilities of other persons**—When disclaimer occurs, it is to do as little violence as possible to the rights and liabilities of others (*Capital Prime Properties plc v Worthgate Ltd (in liquidation)* [2000] 1 BCLC 647) and only 'to the extent necessary to achieve the primary object: the release of the company from all liability': *Hindcastle Ltd v Barbara Attenborough Associates Ltd* [1997] AC 70, [1996] 2 WLR 262, [1996] 1 All ER 737, [1996] 2 BCLC 234, [1996] BPIR 595, HL per Lord Nicholls.

**Effect**—The disclaimer of a lease (the kind of property often disclaimed) involves an extinguishing of the liability between landlord and tenant, with the consequence that the tenant's liability to pay rent ends, as does the landlord's right to receive it: *Re Park Air Services plc* [1999] 1 BCLC 155, HL. See the notes attached to s 181 for further discussion on the effects of disclaiming leases.

As in many cases, disclaimer releases the company from liability to others, with the persons who are affected by the disclaimer being given a right to prove as creditors of the company for the amount of the loss suffered together with, under s 181(2), a right to apply for a vesting order or order for delivery of the property disclaimed. In assessing damages for a landlord, where the company disclaimed a lease, the landlord should not be regarded as a secured creditor within the meaning of s 248 of the Act, and so the matter should be approached as a claim for damages for breach of contract and the appropriate principles applying in such a claim applied: *Re Park Air Services plc*. Also, the landlord's right of re-entry, which is lost on disclaimer, is not to be taken into account, and allowance should be made in favour of the company for the accelerated receipt of any sums which have not fallen due at the date of disclaimer: *Re Park Air Services plc*. Where a lease is disclaimed, the loss of the lessor will, in general terms, be the rents and other payments which will be payable pursuant to the lease for the balance of the lease period, and subtracted from that amount which the lessor will or is likely to receive by re-letting the premises, and in relation to each amount the court will build in a discount because the lessor has received the amount earlier than he or she would in the normal run of things: *Re Park Air Services plc*.

While the lessee of a lease who subleased the lease to a company that ends up in liquidation and disclaimed the lease, continued to be liable for the rent under the lease until the lease expired or is determined, because the lease continued to exist: *Hill v East & West India Dock Co* (1884) 9 App Cas 448; *Wanford Investments Ltd v Duckworth* [1979] Ch 127, [1978] 2 WLR 741; *WH Smith Ltd v Wyndram Investments Ltd* [1994] 2 BCLC 571, the enactment of the Landlord and Tenant (Covenants) Act 1995 meant that this does not apply to leases entered into after 1 January 1996. But in the scenario just set out, if the original lessee guaranteed rent payments and other covenants by the company, after disclaimer the lessee would be liable under the guarantee for any breaches: *Shaw v Doleman* [2009] EWCA Civ 279, [2009] 2 BCLC 123, [2009] BPIR 945. According to *Shaw v Doleman* the Landlord and Tenant (Covenants) Act 1995 made no difference as far as the liability of a guarantor was concerned, and the *Hindcastle* ruling applies. So, a disclaimer by a tenant company in liquidation which took an assignment of a lease will free the assignor from liability, but not if the assignor were to have given a guarantee to the landlord concerning compliance with the terms of the covenants.

While the liabilities of a company pursuant to a lease are terminated when a liquidator disclaims an interest in the lease, this does not determine the covenants in the lease for all purposes: *Hindcastle Ltd v Barbara Attenborough Associates Ltd* [1997] AC 70, [1996] 2 WLR 262, [1996] 1 All ER 737, [1996] 2 BCLC 234, [1996] BPIR 595, HL. So, if a person guaranteed the lease payments which were to be paid by the company whose liquidator has disclaimed the lease, he or she remains liable under the guarantee, because the legal rights of recourse to the guarantor could be determined without releasing the guarantor from his or her liability to the landlord (*Hindcastle Ltd*). The guarantor's liability survived the extinguishment of the guarantor's right of recourse (*Hindcastle Ltd*). The Court of Appeal applied similar reasoning in relation to a charge, which continued to exist after disclaimer of an agreement to sell the land over which the charge was held: *Groveholt Ltd v Hughes* [2005] EWCA Civ 897, [2005] BPIR 1345, [2005] 2 BCLC 421. It follows from the House of Lords' decision in *Hindcastle Ltd* that if the landlord of a disclaimed lease assigns the lease to another, the latter could enforce the obligations of any guarantors of the company's liability under the lease: *Scottish Widows plc v Tripipatkul* [2003] EWHC 1874 (Ch), [2003] BPIR 1413. But, if no vesting order is made and the landlord re-takes possession, then the obligations of persons in the position of a guarantor terminate as far as future liability is concerned (*Hindcastle Ltd*). What a guarantor needs to do when a debtor company disclaims a lease is to reduce his or her liability by finding a new tenant for the premises: *Bhogal v Mohinder Singh Cheema* [1999] BPIR 13.

Where a tenant's leasehold interest is disclaimed by a liquidator the obligation to pay rates on the property reverts to the landlord even though the tenant's obligations to pay rent were guaranteed, and even if the landlord does not actually re-take possession: *Schroder Exempt Property Unit Trust v Birmingham City Council* [2014] EWHC 2207 (Admin).

The approach taken in *Hindcastle Ltd v Barbara Attenborough Associates Ltd* has been applied in other areas. For instance, a liquidator who disclaimed a waste management licence was unable to claim any interest in a trust fund that had been established in relation to the licence: *Environment Agency v Hillridge Ltd* [2003] EWHC 3023 (Ch), [2004] BCLC 358. The fund was inextricably linked to the licence, and the company could not keep the interest in the fund and yet be freed from its liabilities under the licence.

The *Hindcastle* approach has been applied in Australia where the one disclaiming the lease is the landlord. Usually the company in liquidation wishes to disclaim a leasehold interest. If it wishes to disclaim a lease that it had granted as landlord, then according to the Australian case of *Re Wilmott Forests Ltd (in liq)* [2013] HCA 51 such disclaimer does extinguish the tenant's interest in the property. Effectively the High Court of Australia (affirming the decision of the Victorian Court of Appeal below) held that the principle in *Hindcastle* applies equally to the disclaimer of a lease by a landlord, as the disclaimer necessarily extinguishes the tenant's interest.

Unless a court makes a vesting order in relation to the interest of the company which is disclaimed, that interest vests in the Crown automatically as bona vacantia (*Re Mercer & Moore* (1880) 14 ChD 287), while rights of the company under a contract do not vest in the Crown: they terminate.

If the freehold in land is disclaimed, then the land goes to the Crown on an escheat, unless a vesting order is made in favour of some other person, and the Crown does not have to do anything for this to occur: *Scmlla Properties Ltd v Gesso Properties (BVI) Ltd* [1995] BCC 793. A legal charge and the leases of tenants would survive a disclaimer (*Scmlla Properties Ltd*).

No room exists for any rights or liabilities to be preserved by s 178(4): *Hindcastle Ltd v Barbara Attenborough Associates Ltd* [1997] AC 70 at 90, [1996] 2 WLR 262, [1996] 1 All ER 737, [1996] 2 BCLC 234, [1996] BPIR 595 HL.

**Loss**—It is necessary for the liquidator or (possibly) the court, following a disclaimer, to quantify the loss in money terms in the same way that is done where there is a breach of contract because one party to the contract has repudiated it and the other party has accepted the repudiation as ending the contract: *Re Park Air Services plc* [1999] 1 BCLC 155 at 158, HL. To determine what loss has been sustained the court must compare the pre-disclaimer position with the post-disclaimer position (*Re Park Air Services plc* at 159). The same approach that is adopted for calculating damages for a breach of contract is to be used in calculating compensation where there is a disclaimer, because a lessor is not a secured creditor within the meaning of the Act (*Re Park Air Services plc* at 162, 163–164).

Where a loss is suffered over a period in the future, the calculation has to allow for any advancement that has occurred or else the aggrieved party will be over-compensated (*Re Park Air Services plc* at 158). With disclaimers of leases, the right of the lessor to prove for loss is not a right to prove in relation to any debt due in the future, and r 11.13 IR 1986 (now r 14.14 IR 2016) does not apply (*Re Park Air Services plc* at 158–159). The lessor's compensation is for the loss of his or her right to future rent and not the rent itself, because he or she has no right to the latter anymore (*Re Park Air Services plc* at 161). The loss of a lessor is the 'aggregate of the differences between the contractual rent and the market rent over a period of the remainder of the lease discounted to allow for advancement' (*Re Park Air Services plc* at 159 per Lord Hobhouse). In calculating the loss of a lessor one has to take into account the sums he or she will be able to obtain from re-letting the premises, so that there should be a discount for early receipt by the lessor (*Re Park Air Services plc* at 161–162). In *Re Park Air Services plc* (at 166) the House of Lords held that the best evidence of the appropriate discount rate to be applied is the yield on gilt-edged securities for an equivalent term.

If a creditor is able to prove for loss as a result of a disclaimer, interest can be claimed from the time of the disclaimer (*Re Park Air Services plc*).

**Procedure**—See rr 19.2 and 19.9 and the notes relating to those rules.

See McCartney 'Disclaimer of leases and its impact: the "pecking order"' (2002) 18 IL & P 79; A Keay *McPherson and Keay's Law of Company Liquidation* (Sweet and Maxwell, 4th edn, 2018) at 587–604 for a detailed discussion.

## [1.236]

### 179 Disclaimer of leaseholds

(1)   The disclaimer under section 178 of any property of a leasehold nature does not take effect unless a copy of the disclaimer has been served (so far as the liquidator is aware of their addresses) on every person claiming under the company as underlessee or mortgagee and either—

(a)   no application under section 181 below is made with respect to that property before the end of the period of 14 days beginning with the day on which the last notice served under this subsection was served; or

(b)   where such an application has been made, the court directs that the disclaimer shall take effect.

(2)   Where the court gives direction under subsection (1)(b) it may also, instead of or in addition to any order it makes under section 181, make such orders with respect to fixtures, tenant's improvements and other matters arising out of the lease as it thinks fit.

**General note**—Disclaimer of a lease creates in the lessor of the premises that are subject to lease a right to claim loss or damage which he or she has suffered as a result of the disclaimer, the right to rent having been lost (s 178(6)): *Re Park Air Services plc* [1999] 1 BCLC 155 at 157, 158, HL.

This provision requires liquidators to serve notice on those who might wish to apply for a vesting order pursuant to s 181, namely underlessees and mortgagees.

On disclaimer of a lease, any underlease is destroyed: *Re AE Realisations (1985) Ltd* [1988] 1 WLR 200. Any underlessees have the right to remain in occupation, paying the rent and discharging the covenants required under the lease for the length of the underlease (*Re AE Realisations (1985) Ltd*).

A landlord is not obliged to mitigate his or her loss on the disclaimer of a lease: *Bhogal v Mohinder Singh Cheema* [1999] BPIR 13.

See the notes relating to s 178 and r 19.4. Also, see McCartney 'Disclaimer of leases and its impact: the "pecking order"' (2002) 18 IL & P 79; A Keay *McPherson and Keay's Law of Company Liquidation* (Sweet and Maxwell, 4th edn, 2018) at 587–604.

## [1.237]

### 180 Land subject to rentcharge

(1)   The following applies where, in consequence of the disclaimer under section 178 of any land subject to a rentcharge, that land vests by operation of law in the Crown or any other person (referred to in the next subsection as "the proprietor").

(2)   The proprietor and the successors in title of the proprietor are not subject to any personal liability in respect of any sums becoming due under the rentcharge except sums becoming due after the proprietor, or some person claiming under or through the proprietor, has taken possession or control of the land or has entered into occupation of it.

General note—This provision serves to keep anyone, including the Crown, in whom land subject to a rentcharge vests by operation of law free from personal liability in respect of any sums becoming due under the rentcharge, except sums becoming due after possession or control of the land or the entering into of occupation following the making of the vesting order.

## [1.238]

### 181  Powers of court (general)

(1)   This section and the next apply where the liquidator has disclaimed property under section 178.

(2)   An application under this section may be made to the court by—
    (a)    any person who claims an interest in the disclaimed property, or
    (b)    any person who is under any liability in respect of the disclaimed property, not being a liability discharged by the disclaimer.

(3)   Subject as follows, the court may on the application make an order, on such terms as it thinks fit, for the vesting of the disclaimed property in, or for its delivery to—
    (a)    a person entitled to it or a trustee for such a person, or
    (b)    a person subject to such a liability as is mentioned in subsection (2)(b) or a trustee for such a person.

(4)   The court shall not make an order under subsection (3)(b) except where it appears to the court that it would be just to do so for the purpose of compensating the person subject to the liability in respect of the disclaimer.

(5)   The effect of any order under this section shall be taken into account in assessing for the purpose of section 178(6) the extent of any loss or damage sustained by any person in consequence of the disclaimer.

(6)   An order under this section vesting property in any person need not be completed by conveyance, assignment or transfer.

General note—This provision empowers a court to order the vesting of property (disclaimed under s 178) in, or delivered to, a person entitled to it or a person subject to a liability because of the disclaimed property. See r 19.11 for the procedure that applies.

Applications—Applications can be made by a person who claims an interest in the disclaimed property, or a person who is under any liability in respect of the disclaimed property (not including a liability discharged by the disclaimer).—This does not include anyone who cannot demonstrate some form of proprietary interest in the disclaimed property and in relation to which a vesting order was sought: *Lloyds Bank SF Nominees v Aladdin Ltd* [1996] 1 BCLC 720 at 721, CA (a person was in occupation of premises and he had agreed to take an assignment provided that the consent of the landlord was secured, and in this case the occupier did not have a proprietary interest); *Re Ballast plc* [2006] EWHC 3189 (Ch), [2007] BPIR 117 at [42], [109]. Any right granted to an insurer by way of subrogation did not constitute a proprietary interest in any cause of action which the company (the assured) might have against another party (although it might have an interest in the proceedings of the action) until the action is assigned: *Re Ballast plc* at [41], [100]. For a critical discussion of *Re Ballast plc*, see L Ho, 'Of proprietary restitution, insurers' subrogation and insolvency set-off – the untenable case of *Re Ballast*' (2007) 23 I L & P 103.

A landlord is only able to become entitled to possession of property once all of the interests of all other relevant parties who had, or could obtain, an interest in the property had been cleared away by invoking the mechanism provided in s 182: *Re ITM Corp Ltd (in liquidation)* [1997] 2 BCLC 389.

It was held in *Re Spirit Motorsport Ltd (in liquidation)* [1996] 1 BCLC 684, [1997] BPIR 288 that the directors of a company that was in liquidation were not able to make an application as persons who were under a liability in respect of disclaimed property of their company, where the property had been disclaimed by the Crown after it had received it as bona vacantia. The directors had guaranteed the debts of the company, but this was not sufficient, as the liability was not in respect of disclaimed property.

The guarantor of the obligations that exist under a lease that has been disclaimed, as well as a lessee who assigned the lease, come within s 181(2)(b) as persons who are under a liability in respect of disclaimed property and who could apply for a vesting order, enabling them to rent out or use the premises that are the subject of the lease.

'Under a liability'—While at common law a lessee who assigns the lease is liable for the payments pursuant to the lease as well as fulfilling the covenants under the lease if the assignee disclaims the sublease (*Hindcastle Ltd v Barbara Attenborough Associates Ltd* [1997] AC 70, [1996] 2 WLR 262, [1996] 1 All ER 737, [1996] 2 BCLC 234, [1996] BPIR 595, HL), if a lease was entered into after 1 January 1996 and the assignee disclaims, then the original lessee will not be liable for future rent and meeting the covenants of the assignee as he or she is automatically discharged from such liability on assignment of the lease (Landlord and Tenant (Covenants) Act 1995, ss 1(1), (3), 5(1), (2) and 31(1)).

Vesting orders—In making a vesting order under s 181 the court has a wide discretion and it is wide enough to permit a court to order that the surplus proceeds of the sale of a lease, in which no one had an interest, be given back to the liquidator: *Lee v Lee* [2000] 1 FLR 92, [1999] BPIR 926, CA.

The power of a court to make a vesting order is restricted somewhat by s 182(1), and by the fact that it must be just made for the purpose of compensating the person who is liable following the disclaimer (s 181(4)).

## [1.239]

### 182 Powers of court (leaseholds)

(1) The court shall not make an order under section 181 vesting property of a leasehold nature in any person claiming under the company as underlessee or mortgagee except on terms making that person—

    (a)    subject to the same liabilities and obligations as the company was subject to under the lease at the commencement of the winding up, or

    (b)    if the court thinks fit, subject to the same liabilities and obligations as that person would be subject to if the lease had been assigned to him at the commencement of the winding up.

(2) For the purposes of an order under section 181 relating to only part of any property comprised in a lease, the requirements of subsection (1) apply as if the lease comprised only the property to which the order relates.

(3) Where subsection (1) applies and no person claiming under the company as underlessee or mortgagee is willing to accept an order under section 181 on the terms required by virtue of that subsection, the court may, by order under that section, vest the company's estate or interest in the property in any person who is liable (whether personally or in a representative capacity, and whether alone or jointly with the company) to perform the lessee's covenants in the lease.

The court may vest that estate and interest in such a person freed and discharged from all estates, incumbrances and interests created by the company.

(4) Where subsection (1) applies and a person claiming under the company as underlessee or mortgagee declines to accept an order under section 181, that person is excluded from all interest in the property.

General note—It has been held that s 182(4) does not apply where an application is made by statutory tenants, because the provision is limited to cases where the applicant has a proprietary interest in the land: *Re Vedmay Ltd* [1994] 1 BCLC 676.

Given what Sir William Blackburne said in *Hunt v Conwy CBC* [2013] EWHC 1154 (Ch), [2013] BPIR 790 at [48] in relation to s 320, it might be argued that a vesting of part of the property, if it is possible practically, can be valid.

See the notes accompanying s 181.

*Execution, attachment and the Scottish equivalents*

## [1.240]

### 183 Effect of execution or attachment (England and Wales)

(1) Where a creditor has issued execution against the goods or land of a company or has attached any debt due to it, and the company is subsequently wound up, he is not

entitled to retain the benefit of the execution or attachment against the liquidator unless he has completed the execution or attachment before the commencement of the winding up.

(2)  However—

(a)  if a creditor has had notice of a meeting having been called at which a resolution for voluntary winding up is to be proposed, the date on which he had notice is substituted, for the purpose of subsection (1), for the date of commencement of the winding up;

(b)  a person who purchases in good faith under a sale by the enforcement officer or other officer charged with the execution of the writ any goods of a company on which execution has been levied in all cases acquires a good title to them against the liquidator; and

(c)  the rights conferred by subsection (1) on the liquidator may be set aside by the court in favour of the creditor to such extent and subject to such terms as the court thinks fit.

(3)  For purposes of this Act—

(a)  an execution against goods is completed by seizure and sale, or by the making of a charging order under section 1 of the Charging Orders Act 1979;

(b)  an attachment of a debt is completed by receipt of the debt; and

(c)  an execution against land is completed by seizure, by the appointment of a receiver, or by the making of a charging order under section 1 of the Act above-mentioned.

(4)  In this section, "goods" includes all chattels personal; and "enforcement officer" means an individual who is authorised to act as an enforcement officer under the Courts Act 2003.

(4A)  For the purposes of this section, Her Majesty's Revenue and Customs is to be regarded as having attached a debt due to a company if it has taken action under Part 1 of Schedule 8 to the Finance (No 2) Act 2015 (enforcement by deduction for accounts) as a result of which an amount standing to the credit of an account held by the company is—

(a)  subject to arrangements made under paragraph 6(3) of that Schedule, or

(b)  the subject of a deduction notice under paragraph 13 of that Schedule.

(5)  This section does not apply in the case of a winding up in Scotland.

**Amendments**—Courts Act 2003, s 109(1), Sch 8, para 295; Finance (No 2) Act 2015, s 51, Sch 8, Pt 2, paras 26, 31.

**General note**—The thrust of the provision is that if a creditor has not completed an execution or attachment by the time winding up commences, the creditor is not entitled to retain the benefit of the execution or attachment process. The avoiding effect of the section is enhanced by s 183(2)(a), which provides that if the creditor is to be able to retain the benefit of execution, he or she must have effected completion before the creditor had notice of a meeting called to consider resolving to put the relevant company into liquidation.

The court has no jurisdiction under the section to make an order in relation to a creditor who has engaged in execution in a foreign jurisdiction, as the section has no extra-territorial effect: *Mitchell v Carter* [1997] 1 BCLC 673, [1997] BCC 907.

**'Execution' and 'attachment'**—The levying of distress is not within the meaning of execution or attachment for the purposes of this section (*Re Herbert Barry Associates Ltd v IRC* [1977] 1 WLR 1437, [1978] 1 All ER 161, HL; *Re Modern Jet Support Centre Ltd* [2005] EWHC 1611 (Ch), [2005] 1 WLR 3880, [2006] 1 BCLC 703, [2005] BPIR 1382), so if the process of distress has commenced before the date of the commencement of winding up it should be allowed to continue unless there are special circumstances, such as fraud or unfair dealing, justifying a stay, the reason being that the distress was not put in force after commencement: *Re G Winterbottom (Leeds) Ltd* [1937] 2 All ER 232; *Re Bellaglade Ltd* [1977] 1 All ER 319 at 321. Liquidation would not constitute 'special circumstances' and justify the distress being halted (*Re Bellaglade Ltd* at 321). See comments relating to s 128.

Ordinarily the word 'execution' was used to describe a process of enforcement of a judgment inter partes. However, the word could take on a broader meaning if the context clearly demanded, such as involving extra-judicial process for the recovery of a debt: *Re Modern Jet Support Centre Ltd* [2005] EWHC 1611 (Ch), [2005] 1 WLR 3880, [2006] 1 BCLC 703, [2005] BPIR 1382, at [17], [21].

## SECTION 183(1)

'Benefit'—It has been said that 'benefit' in this context means the benefit which the charge provides for the creditor as a consequence of the execution and does not mean the money received under the charge: *Re Andrew* [1937] Ch 122, CA.

The benefit of the attachment means 'the right to take the necessary steps to complete the attachment' (*Re Caribbean Products (Yam Importers Ltd)* [1966] Ch 331, CA), and so a creditor who obtained payment of a garnisheed debt after receipt of notice of the meeting called to consider a resolution to wind up was bound to account to the liquidator for the payment received (*Re Caribbean Products (Yam Importers Ltd)*).

'Completed'—In terms of execution there is a completion when there is a sale of the goods seized (*Re Standard Manufacturing Co* [1891] 1 Ch 627) or, if the execution is by the making of a charging order, completion occurs when the order is made absolute (*Clarke v Coutts & Co* [2002] BPIR 916 at 924, CA (reversing [2002] BPIR 762)), and an order will not be made absolute after the debtor company has entered liquidation (*Roberts Petroleum Ltd v Bernard Kelly Ltd* [1983] 2 AC 192 at 208). With attachments, there is completion when the debt is received (s 183(3)(b)): see *Re Walkden Sheet Metal Co Ltd* [1960] Ch 170. The point of completion where land is involved is explained by s 183(3)(c).

## SECTION 183(3)(a)

'Charging order'—A charging order nisi imposes an immediate charge, but it is defeasible until being made absolute, and the intervention of liquidation before the making of the order absolute would mean that the property charged falls into the assets subject to the liquidation: *Roberts Petroleum Ltd v Bernard Kelly Ltd* [1983] 2 AC 192 at 209. In *JGD Construction Ltd v Aaron Mills* [2013] EWHC 572 (Ch), [2013] BPIR 811 it was said that it would be very unlikely that an interim charging order would be made final where there was compelling evidence of an imminent insolvency process or of actual insolvency. The case also held that while there was no rule that no charging order could be finalised when there was a formal insolvency regime in existence, the predominant view in the cases was that the finalisation of the order would be precluded.

Court discretion—Sub-section (2)(c) gives the court the right to take no account of the liquidator's entitlement under subsection (1) if it thinks fit. The discretion in this respect is wide (*Re Grosvenor Metals Co* [1950] Ch 63 at 64), and allows the court to do what is right and fair according to the circumstances of the case: *Re Suidair International Airways Ltd* [1951] Ch 165. If, because of some deception perpetrated by the company, a creditor is induced not to proceed to execution, the creditor will be permitted by the court to retain the benefit of the execution against the liquidator (*Re Suidair International Airways Ltd*). The rights of a liquidator have been set aside where a creditor's attempts to levy execution were frustrated when the company improperly obtained leave to defend an action on a debt in respect of which it had previously admitted liability (*Re Suidair International Airways Ltd*). The same result has also occurred even where the company has not acted improperly, but persuaded a creditor to delay execution in consequence of requests and representations by the company (*Re Grosvenor Metal Co*). However, where the company has not acted fraudulently, substantial reasons must exist before the court will exercise its discretion and permit a creditor to retain the benefit of an uncompleted execution: *Re Caribbean Products (Yam Importers) Ltd* [1966] Ch 331 at 348, 354. The courts have said that they are careful to ensure that the pari passu principle is not compromised by allowing one or two creditors to benefit through execution when the rest of the creditors receive nothing. In fact, there is a strong presumption in favour of pari passu once a creditor had notice of a meeting that was to consider placing a debtor company, against which execution had been sought, in liquidation: *Re Science and Media LLP* [2014] BPIR 774.

## [1.241]

## 184 Duties of officers charged with execution of writs and other processes (England and Wales)

(1)  The following applies where a company's goods are taken in execution and, before their sale or the completion of the execution (by the receipt or recovery of the full amount of the levy), notice is served on the enforcement officer, or other officer, charged with execution of the writ or other process, that a provisional liquidator has been appointed or that a winding-up order has been made, or that a resolution for voluntary winding up has been passed.

(2)  The enforcement officer or other officer shall, on being so required, deliver the goods and any money seized or received in part satisfaction of the execution to the liquidator; but the costs of execution are a first charge on the goods or money so delivered, and the liquidator may sell the goods, or a sufficient part of them, for the purpose of satisfying the charge.

(3)   If under an execution in respect of a judgment for a sum exceeding £500 a company's goods are sold or money is paid in order to avoid sale, the enforcement officer or other officer shall deduct the costs of the execution from the proceeds of sale or the money paid and retain the balance for 14 days.

(4)   If within that time notice is served on the enforcement officer or other officer of a petition for the winding up of the company having been presented, or of a meeting having been called at which there is to be proposed a resolution for voluntary winding up, and an order is made or a resolution passed (as the case may be), the enforcement officer or other officer shall pay the balance to the liquidator, who is entitled to retain it as against the execution creditor.

(5)   The rights conferred by this section on the liquidator may be set aside by the court in favour of the creditor to such extent and subject to such terms as the court thinks fit.

(6)   In this section, "goods" includes all chattels personal; and "enforcement officer" means an individual who is authorised to act as an enforcement officer under the Courts Act 2003.

(7)   The money sum for the time being specified in subsection (3) is subject to increase or reduction by order under section 416 in Part XV.

(8)   This section does not apply in the case of a winding up in Scotland.

**Amendments**—SI 1986/1996; Courts Act 2003, s 109(1), Sch 8, para 296.

**General note**—The section follows along the same lines as some of the matters mentioned in s 183, except that it is focused on enforcement officers and the work done in the process of execution.

**'Completion'**—See the notes under 'Completed' in s 183.

**'Execution in respect of judgments exceeding £500'**—If the company pays an enforcement officer a sum, in order to avoid the sale of its assets, the money is not characterised as satisfaction of the execution: *Re Walkden Sheet Metal Co Ltd* [1960] Ch 170 at 177. The enforcement officer is bound to retain the money, less the costs of execution, for 14 days (the time runs from the time of payment – *Re Walkden Sheet Metal Co Ltd* at 178), but if no notice within s 184(4) is served in the 14 days, then the enforcement officer is at liberty to pay the money to the execution creditor.

The costs that the enforcement officer is to deduct from the proceeds of the sale or money paid does not include the creditor's costs of issuing and serving the execution process, but only costs which the enforcement officer has incurred: *Re Wood (Bristol) Ltd* [1931] 2 Ch 320.

**Court discretion**—As with s 183, the court has a wide discretion (under s 184(5)) to override the rights of a liquidator. See the comments under 'Court discretion' in the notes accompanying s 183.

## [1.242]

### 185   Effect of diligence (Scotland)

(1)   In the winding up of a company registered in Scotland, the following provisions of the Bankruptcy (Scotland) Act 2016—

  (a)   subsections (3) to (10) of section 23A (effect of sequestration on land attachment) and section 24 (effect of sequestration on diligence generally); and

  (b)   subsections (6), (7), (10) and (11) of section 109 (management and realisation of estate),

apply, so far as consistent with this Act, in like manner as they apply in the sequestration of a debtor's estate, with the substitutions specified below and with any other necessary modifications.

(2)   The substitutions to be made in those sections of the Act of 2016 are as follows—

  (a)   for references to the debtor, substitute references to the company;

  (b)   for references to the sequestration, substitute references to the winding up;

  (c)   for references to the date of sequestration, substitute references to the commencement of the winding up of the company; and

  (d)   for references to the trustee, substitute references to the liquidator.

(3)   In this section, "the commencement of the winding up of the company" means, where it is being wound up by the court, the day on which the winding-up order is made.

(4)   This section, so far as relating to any estate or effects of the company situated in Scotland, applies in the case of a company registered in England and Wales as in the case of one registered in Scotland.

**Amendments**—Bankruptcy and Diligence etc (Scotland) Act 2007, s 226(2), Sch 6, Pt 1; SI 2016/1034.

*Miscellaneous matters*

## [1.243]
### 186   Rescission of contracts by the court
(1)   The court may, on the application of a person who is, as against the liquidator, entitled to the benefit or subject to the burden of a contract made with the company, make an order rescinding the contract on such terms as to payment by or to either party of damages for the non-performance of the contract, or otherwise as the court thinks just.
(2)   Any damages payable under the order to such a person may be proved by him as a debt in the winding up.

**General note**—This provision enables an executory contract to be rescinded by court order when liquidation has occurred.

This provision does not apply where there is a market contract (a contract defined in s 155(2) of the Companies Act 1989) or a contract effected by the exchange or clearing house for the purpose of realising property provided as margin in relation to market contracts (s 164(1) of CA 1989).

## [1.244]
### 187   Power to make over assets to employees
(1)   On the winding up of a company (whether by the court or voluntarily), the liquidator may, subject to the following provisions of this section, make any payment which the company has, before the commencement of the winding up, decided to make under section 247 of the Companies Act 2006 (power to provide for employees or former employees on cessation or transfer of business).
(2)   The liquidator may, after the winding up has commenced, make any such provision as is mentioned in section 247(1) If—
   (a)   the company's liabilities have been fully satisfied and provision has been made for the expenses of the winding up,
   (b)   the exercise of the power has been sanctioned by a resolution of the company, and
   (c)   any requirements of the company's articles as to the exercise of the power conferred by section 247 (1) are complied with.
(3)   Any payment which may be made by a company under this section (that is, a payment after the commencement of its winding up) may be made out of the company's assets which are available to the members on the winding up.
(4)   On a winding up by the court, the exercise by the liquidator of his powers under this section is subject to the court's control, and any creditor or contributory may apply to the court with respect to any exercise or proposed exercise of the power.
(5)   Subsections (1) and (2) above have effect notwithstanding anything in any rule of law or in section 107 of this Act (property of company after satisfaction of liabilities to be distributed among members).

**Amendments**—SI 2007/2194; SI 2009/1941.

**General note**—The provision refers to s 247 of the Companies Act 2006 and expressly empowers a company by resolution to make provision for employees or former employees in relation to the cessation or transfer of the company's business, and this can be done even if it is not in the best interests of the company. Payments may only be made from profits available for dividend pay-outs. Section 247 effectively overruled the decision in *Parke v Daily News Ltd* [1962] Ch 927, which provided that ex gratia payments to employees were ultra vires. Section 187 complements the Companies Act in that the liquidator of a company that, prior to the commencement of winding up, resolved to make payments falling within s 247, is entitled to make those payments. But such payments can only be made from funds that would be available for the members, and this can only occur after the company's liabilities have been satisfied in full and provision has been made for the expenses relating to the winding up. Thus, payments can only be made in relation to solvent companies.

A contributory can apply to the court in relation to the exercise of the power permitted under this section, where the company is being compulsorily wound up. On what basis a contributory might succeed in having the exercise of the power halted or change the way in which the power is used is not easy to ascertain. This is especially so given the fact that s 247(2) provides that the power does not have to be exercised in accordance with s 172 of the Companies Act 2006 (duty to promote the success of the company). Perhaps, though, a claim that the power is not being used for its proper purposes, or the majority in exercising the power was acting oppressively as far as the minority is concerned, might succeed.

## [1.245]

### 188 Notification that company is in liquidation

(1) When a company is being wound up, whether by the court or voluntarily—

    (a)   every invoice, order for goods or services, business letter or order form (whether in hard copy, electronic or any other form)issued by or on behalf of the company, or a liquidator of the company, or a receiver or manager of the company's property, and

    (b)   all the company's websites,

must contain a statement that the company is being wound up.

(2) If default is made in complying with this section, the company and any of the following persons who knowingly and wilfully authorises or permits the default, namely, any officer of the company, any liquidator of the company and any receiver or manager, is liable to a fine.

**Amendments**—SI 2006/3429; SI 2008/1897.

## [1.246]

### 189 Interest on debts

(1) In a winding up interest is payable in accordance with this section on any debt proved in the winding up, including so much of any such debt as represents interest on the remainder.

(2) Any surplus remaining after the payment of the debts proved in a winding up shall, before being applied for any other purpose, be applied in paying interest on those debts in respect of the periods during which they have been outstanding since the company went into liquidation.

(3) All interest under this section ranks equally, whether or not the debts on which it is payable rank equally.

(4) The rate of interest payable under this section in respect of any debt ("the official rate" for the purposes of any provision of this Act in which that expression is used) is whichever is the greater of—

    (a)   the rate specified in section 17 of the Judgments Act 1838 on the day on which the company went into liquidation, and

    (b)   the rate applicable to that debt apart from the winding up.

(5) In the application of this section to Scotland—

    (a)   references to a debt proved in a winding up have effect as references to a claim accepted in a winding up, and

    (b)   the reference to section 17 of the Judgments Act 1838 has effect as a reference to the rules.

**General note**—Where a debt has accrued interest before the company went into liquidation, it may be proved in winding up, but interest that falls due after the company went into liquidation is not able to be claimed (r 14.23(1)), certainly as far as insolvent companies are generally concerned. Where liquidation was immediately preceded by administration interest only up to the date of the commencement of administration can be claimed. But s 189(2) provides that where there is a surplus remaining after the payment of all debts that have been proved, the first call on the surplus is for the payment of interest on those debts in relation to the period following winding up.

Section 189 and r 14.23 are a complete code for the payment of interest on proved debts. 'Its purpose is to compensate creditors for the delay occasioned by the insolvency in the payment of the proved debts which are all notionally payable as at the commencement of the insolvency. It is unconnected with any right to interest under the contract or to the lack of any such contractual right, save for the purpose of determining the rate at which statutory interest is to be paid.': *Re Lehman Brothers International (Europe): Lomas v Burlington Loan Management Ltd* [2016] EWHC 2131 (Ch) at [52] per David Richards LJ (referring to r 2.88 of the 1986 Rules and which formerly applied to administrations). This was approved of by the Supreme Court in *Joint Administrators of Lehman Brothers International (Europe) (In Administration) v Revenue and Customs Commissioners* [2019] UKSC 12, [2019] 1 WLR 2173 at [7].

Statutory interest falls within the contractual definition of 'Liabilities': *Joint Administrators of LB Holdings Intermediate 2 Ltd (In Administration) v Lomas* (on appeal from (*Re Lehman Brothers International (Europe) (No 7)*) [2015] EWCA Civ 485, [2016] Ch 50, [2015] 2 BCLC 433 at [48].

As interest payable out of the surplus in a liquidation ranks equally and does not depend on the debts being ranked equally, interest on preferential debts is paid equally with interest on the ordinary unsecured creditors' debts.

The payment of subordinated debt ranks after statutory interest that is payable under this section: *The Joint Administrators of LB Holdings Intermediate 2 Ltd v the Joint Administrators of Lehman Brothers International (Europe)* [2017] UKSC 38, [2017] 2 WLR 1497, [2017] 2 BCLC 149 at [56].

Contributories are not liable for interest payable under this section as 'section 74 only requires payment from contributories of an "amount sufficient for payment of [a company's] . . . liabilities", the section cannot be invoked to create a "surplus" from which statutory interest can then be paid. If there is a deficit, there is no liability for statutory interest, and, if there is a surplus, there is only a liability for statutory interest to the extent of the surplus. Accordingly, in the absence of a sufficient surplus to pay all the statutory interest, there is no obligation to pay all the statutory interest, and therefore there can be no "liability[y]" which a contributory could be called on to meet under section 74(1).': *The Joint Administrators of LB Holdings Intermediate 2 Ltd v the Joint Administrators of Lehman Brothers International (Europe)* [2017] UKSC 38, [2017] 2 WLR 1497, [2017] 2 BCLC 149 at [139] per Lord Neuberger.

If a company is in administration and then moves into liquidation before a creditor is paid statutory interest provided for under s 189, the creditor is not entitled to claim from the liquidator the interest that is accrued from the time of the administration commencing until the entry into liquidation as s 189(2) only refers to paying interest since the company went into liquidation, although the administrator might be liable for it if he or she distributes a surplus to members without paying such interest: *The Joint Administrators of LB Holdings Intermediate 2 Ltd v the Joint Administrators of Lehman Brothers International (Europe)* [2017] UKSC 38, [2017] 2 WLR 1497, [2017] 2 BCLC 149 at [117].

Payment of statutory interest is part of the winding-up scheme (*The Joint Administrators of LB Holdings Intermediate 2 Ltd v the Joint Administrators of Lehman Brothers International (Europe)* [2017] UKSC 38, [2017] 2 WLR 1497, [2017] 2 BCLC 149 at [48]). It is not possible for a creditor to sue the company for any failure to adhere to s 189 because the relevant claim should be against the liquidator: *Re HIH Casualty & General Insurance Ltd* [2005] EWHC 2125 (Ch), [2006] 2 All ER 671 at [115]–[121]; *The Joint Administrators of LB Holdings Intermediate 2 Ltd v the Joint Administrators of Lehman Brothers International (Europe)* [2017] UKSC 38, [2017] 2 WLR 1497, [2017] 2 BCLC 149 at [52].

**Rate of interest**—Section 189(4) does not provide a basis for those creditors receiving interest at a contractual rate for periods to which interest did not apply under the contract, that is, if no interest is contractually payable on a contingent debt until the contingency occurs, the interest at the contractual rate for any earlier period is not interest at 'the rate applicable apart from the liquidation' as mentioned in s 189(4)(b). During the period before the contingency occurs, there would have been no interest payable on the debt if there was no liquidation. But creditors would be entitled to interest at the rate prevailing under the Judgments Act 1838 (in accord with s 189(4)(a)) as from the date of liquidation: *Re Lehman Brothers International (Europe): Lomas v Burlington Loan Management Ltd* [2016] EWHC 2131 (Ch) at [34].

Debts known as deferred debts are only provable once all other creditors' claims, together with interest under s 189(2), have been paid (r 14.2(4)).

See r 14.23.

[1.247]

## 190  Documents exempt from stamp duty

(1)  In the case of a winding up by the court, or of a creditors' voluntary winding up, the following has effect as regards exemption from duties chargeable under the enactments relating to stamp duties.

(2)   If the company is registered in England and Wales, the following documents are exempt from stamp duty—

> (a)   every assurance relating solely to freehold or leasehold property, or to any estate, right or interest in, any real or personal property, which forms part of the company's assets and which, after the execution of the assurance, either at law or in equity, is or remains part of those assets, and
>
> (b)   every writ, order, certificate, or other instrument or writing relating solely to the property of any company which is being wound up as mentioned in subsection (1), or to any proceeding under such a winding up.

"Assurance" here includes deed, conveyance, assignment and surrender.

(3)   If the company is registered in Scotland, the following documents are exempt from stamp duty—

> (a)   every conveyance relating solely to property which forms part of the company's assets and which, after the execution of the conveyance, is or remains the company's property for the benefit of its creditors,
>
> (b)   any articles of roup or sale, submission and every other instrument and writing whatsoever relating solely to the company's property, and
>
> (c)   every deed or writing forming part of the proceedings in the winding up.

"Conveyance" here includes assignation, instrument, discharge, writing and deed.

## [1.248]

### 191   Company's books to be evidence

Where a company is being wound up, all books and papers of the company and of the liquidators are, as between the contributories of the company, prima facie evidence of the truth of all matters purporting to be recorded in them.

## [1.249]

### 192   Information as to pending liquidations

(1)   If the winding up of a company is not concluded within one year after its commencement, the liquidator shall, at such intervals as may be prescribed, until the winding up is concluded, send to the registrar of companies a statement in the prescribed form and containing the prescribed particulars with respect to the proceedings in, and position of, the liquidation.

(2)   If a liquidator fails to comply with this section, he is liable to a fine and, for continued contravention, to a daily default fine.

> **General note**—If the liquidator fails to comply with the section, an order may be sought from the court by a creditor, contributory or registrar of companies, and under s 170, to force the liquidator to comply. Further failure to comply will constitute a contempt of court and may lead to imprisonment: eg *Re S & A Conversions Ltd* (1988) 4 BCC 384; *Re Allan Ellis (Transport & Packing) Services Ltd* (1989) 5 BCC 835.

## [1.250]

### 193   Unclaimed dividends (Scotland)

(1)   The following applies where a company registered in Scotland has been wound up, and is about to be dissolved.

(2)   The liquidator shall lodge in an appropriate bank or institution as defined in section 228(1) of the Bankruptcy (Scotland) Act 2016 (not being a bank or institution in or of which the liquidator is acting partner, manager, agent or cashier) in the name of the Accountant of Court the whole unclaimed dividends and unapplied or undistributable balances, and the deposit receipts shall be transmitted to the Accountant of Court.

(3)   The provisions of section 150 of the Bankruptcy (Scotland) Act 2016 (so far as consistent with this Act and the Companies Acts) apply with any necessary modifications to sums lodged in a bank or institution under this section as they apply to sums deposited under section 148 of the Act first mentioned.

> **Amendments**—SI 2009/1941; SI 2016/1034.

**194**

*(Repealed)*

**Amendments**—Repealed by Small Business, Enterprise and Employment Act 2015, s 126, Sch 9, Pt 1, paras 1, 46.

## [1.251]

### 195 Court's powers to ascertain wishes of creditors or contributories
(1) The court may—

    (a)    as to all matters relating to the winding up of a company, have regard to the wishes of the creditors or contributories (as proved to it by any sufficient evidence), and

    (b)    if it thinks fit, for the purpose of ascertaining those wishes, direct qualifying decision procedures to be instigated or the deemed consent procedure to be used in accordance with any directions given by the court, and appoint a person to report the result to the court.

(2) In the case of creditors, regard shall be had to the value of each creditor's debt.

(3) In the case of contributories, regard shall be had to the number of votes conferred on each contributory.

**Amendments**—SI 2009/1941; Small Business, Enterprise and Employment Act 2015, s 126, Sch 9, Pt 1, paras 1, 47.

**General note**—As the creditors, and possibly the contributories, are the persons primarily interested in a winding up, it seems appropriate that the court has the right to ascertain the wishes of these groups in certain circumstances: see eg *Wilson v PLT Pipetech Pty Ltd* (1989) 7 ACLC 191.

Where the views of creditors and contributories are sought, then they should normally be accepted, save in exceptional circumstances (*Re Bank of Credit and Commerce International SA (No 3)* [1993] BCLC 1490).

Previously this section provided for the holding of meetings of creditors and contributories. The law that related to the calling of meetings is likely now to apply to the instigation of a decision procedure under the latest version of the section. Under case law relating to the previously drafted section, meetings were generally ordered in the context of whether or not there should be a winding up (*Re Western of Canada Oil Co* (1873) 17 Eq 1; *Re Chapel House Colliery Co* (1883) 24 ChD 259), whether it is to be compulsory or voluntary and, if voluntary (*Re City & County Bank* (1875) 10 Ch App 470), who is to be the liquidator (*Re Manmac Farmers Ltd* [1968] 1 WLR 572). So that when a winding-up petition is before the court (see *Re Western of Canada Oil Co* and *Re Chapel House Colliery Co*), the views of a meeting of creditors provide the courts with an additional source of discretionary power to refuse a winding-up order (*Re Western of Canada Oil Co* and *Re Chapel House Colliery Co*). See the notes under 'Creditor opposition to the petition' and accompanying s 125.

Where no order of winding up has been made, the court does not have power to order that a decision procedure be instigated until the court has been satisfied that a ground for winding up does in fact exist: *Re Joint Stock Coal* (1869) 8 Eq 146; *Re Langham Skating Rink* (1877) 5 ChD 669.

The court is not bound to accede to the wishes of creditors or contributories expressed by way of decision procedure that is instigated: *Re Land Development Association* [1892] WN 23.

**'The value of each creditors' debt'**—This has been held to refer to the amount of the debt and not what it may ultimately prove to be worth in a liquidation: *Re Manakau Timber Co* (1895) 13 NZLR 319.

## [1.252]

### 196 Judicial notice of court documents
In all proceedings under this Part, all courts, judges and persons judicially acting, and all officers, judicial or ministerial, of any court, or employed in enforcing the process of any court shall take judicial notice—

    (a)    of the signature of any officer of the High Court or of the county court in England and Wales, or of the Court of Session or a sheriff court in Scotland, or of the High Court in Northern Ireland, and also

    (b)    of the official seal or stamp of the several offices of the High Court in England and Wales or Northern Ireland, or of the Court of Session, appended to or impressed on any document made, issued or signed under the provisions of this Act or the Companies Acts, or any official copy of such a document.

**Amendments**—SI 2009/1941; Crime and Courts Act 2013, s 17(5), Sch 9, Pt 3, para 52(1)(b), (2).

## [1.253]

### 197 Commission for receiving evidence

(1) When a company is wound up in England and Wales or in Scotland, the court may refer the whole or any part of the examination of witnesses—

- (a) to the county court in England and Wales, or
- (b) to the sheriff principal for a specified sheriffdom in Scotland, or
- (c) to the High Court in Northern Ireland or a specified Northern Ireland County Court,

("specified" meaning specified in the order of the winding-up court).

(2) Any person exercising jurisdiction as a judge of the court to which the reference is made (or, in Scotland, the sheriff principal to whom it is made) shall then, by virtue of this section, be a commissioner for the purpose of taking the evidence of those witnesses.

(3) The judge or sheriff principal has in the matter referred the same power of summoning and examining witnesses, of requiring the production and delivery of documents, of punishing defaults by witnesses, and of allowing costs and expenses to witnesses, as the court which made the winding-up order.

These powers are in addition to any which the judge or sheriff principal might lawfully exercise apart from this section.

(4) The examination so taken shall be returned or reported to the court which made the order in such manner as that court requests.

(5) This section extends to Northern Ireland.

**Amendments**—Crime and Courts Act 2013, s 17(5), Sch 9, Pt 3, para 52(1)(b), (2).

## [1.254]

### 198 Court order for examination of persons in Scotland

(1) The court may direct the examination in Scotland of any person for the time being in Scotland (whether a contributory of the company or not), in regard to the trade, dealings, affairs or property of any company in course of being wound up, or of any person being a contributory of the company, so far as the company may be interested by reason of his being a contributory.

(2) The order or commission to take the examination shall be directed to the sheriff principal of the sheriffdom in which the person to be examined is residing or happens to be for the time; and the sheriff principal shall summon the person to appear before him at a time and place to be specified in the summons for examination on oath as a witness or as a haver, and to produce any books or papers called for which are in his possession or power.

(3) The sheriff principal may take the examination either orally or on written interrogatories, and shall report the same in writing in the usual form to the court, and shall transmit with the report the books and papers produced, if the originals are required and specified by the order or commission, or otherwise copies or extracts authenticated by the sheriff.

(4) If a person so summoned fails to appear at the time and place specified, or refuses to be examined or to make the production required, the sheriff principal shall proceed against him as a witness or haver duly cited; and failing to appear or refusing to give evidence or make production may be proceeded against by the law of Scotland.

(5) The sheriff principal is entitled to such fees, and the witness is entitled to such allowances, as sheriffs principal when acting as commissioners under appointment from the Court of Session and as witnesses and havers are entitled to in the like cases according to the law and practice of Scotland.

(6) If any objection is stated to the sheriff principal by the witness, either on the ground of his incompetency as a witness, or as to the production required, or on any other ground, the sheriff principal may, if he thinks fit, report the objection to the court, and suspend the examination of the witness until it has been disposed of by the court.

**[1.255]**

### 199 Costs of application for leave to proceed (Scottish companies)

Where a petition or application for leave to proceed with an action or proceeding against a company which is being wound up in Scotland is unopposed and is granted by the court, the costs of the petition or application shall, unless the court otherwise directs, be added to the amount of the petitioner's or applicant's claim against the company.

**[1.256]**

### 200 Affidavits etc in United Kingdom and overseas

(1) An affidavit required to be sworn under or for the purposes of this Part may be sworn in the United Kingdom, or elsewhere in Her Majesty's dominions, before any court, judge or person lawfully authorised to take and receive affidavits, or before any of Her Majesty's consuls or vice-consuls in any place outside Her dominions.

(2) All courts, judges, justices, commissioners and persons acting judicially shall take judicial notice of the seal or stamp or signature (as the case may be) of any such court, judge, person, consul or vice-consul attached, appended or subscribed to any such affidavit, or to any other document to be used for the purposes of this Part.

CHAPTER IX

Dissolution of Companies After Winding Up

**[1.257]**

### 201 Dissolution (voluntary winding up)

(1) This section applies, in the case of a company wound up voluntarily, where the liquidator has sent to the registrar of companies his final account . . . under section 94 (members' voluntary) or his final account and statement under section 106 (creditors' voluntary).

(2) The registrar on receiving the account . . . , or the account and statement, . . . shall forthwith register it or them; and on the expiration of 3 months from the registration of the account the company is deemed to be dissolved . . . .

(2A) . . .

(2B) . . .

(3) However, the court may, on the application of the liquidator or any other person who appears to the court to be interested, make an order deferring the date at which the dissolution of the company is to take effect for such time as the court thinks fit.

(4) It is the duty of the person on whose application an order of the court under this section is made within 7 days after the making of the order to deliver to the registrar a copy of the order for registration; and if that person fails to do so he is liable to a fine and, for continued contravention, to a daily default fine.

**Amendments**—SI 2006/3429; Small Business, Enterprise and Employment Act 2015, s 126, Sch 9, Pt 1, paras 1, 48; SI 2017/702; SI 2019/146, as from IP completion day (as defined in the European Union (Withdrawal Agreement) Act 2020, s 39(1)–(5)).

**General note**—This provision and ss 202–205 address dissolution. Dissolution involves the death of the company, which constitutes the termination of its existence as a legal entity (*Re Working Project Ltd* [1995] 1 BCLC 226), although in certain circumstances the company's registration might be reinstated (see ss 1024 and 1029 of the Companies Act 2006). The process of dissolution brings winding up to an end (*Re Working Project Ltd*).

Under this section a company, in voluntary liquidation, is dissolved automatically once the conditions provided for here are complied with.

As a company's affairs are able to be regarded as fully wound up in situations where there is property still retained by the liquidator, but where all that can be done has been done, it follows that once the account required by s 106 has been returned to the registrar of companies the company would be dissolved automatically: *Re Wilmott Trading Ltd (in liquidation) (No 1 and 2)*, sub nom *Henry v Environmental Agency (No 2)* [1999] 2 BCLC 541, [1999] BPIR 1021 (the continued holding of a waste management licence).

**Expiration of 3 months**—This is designed to provide time for any matters that need resolving to come to light, such as the finding of other assets, and any disagreement between the creditors and the liquidator concerning whether the latter's work is complete: *Re Working Project Ltd* [1995] 1 BCLC 226 at 231.

## [1.258]

### 202 Early dissolution (England and Wales)

(1)   This section applies where an order for the winding up of a company has been made by the court in England and Wales.

(2)   The official receiver, if—

    (a)   he is the liquidator of the company, and

    (b)   it appears to him—

        (i)   that the realisable assets of the company are insufficient to cover the expenses of the winding up, and

        (ii)   that the affairs of the company do not require any further investigation,

may at any time apply to the registrar of companies for the early dissolution of the company.

(2A)   ...

(2B)   ...

(3)   Before making an application under subsection (2), the official receiver shall give not less than 28 days' notice of his intention to do so to the company's creditors, other than opted-out creditors, and contributories and, if there is an administrative receiver of the company, to that receiver.

(4)   With the giving of that notice the official receiver ceases (subject to any directions under the next section) to be required to perform any duties imposed on him in relation to the company, its creditors or contributories by virtue of any provision of this Act, apart from a duty to make an application under subsection (2) . . ..

(5)   On the receipt of the official receiver's application under subsection (2) . . . the registrar shall forthwith register it . . . and, at the end of the period of 3 months beginning with the day of the registration of the application, the company shall be dissolved . . ..

(6)   ...

(7)   ...

(8)   However, the Secretary of State may, on the application of the official receiver or any other person who appears to the Secretary of State to be interested, give directions under section 203 at any time before the end of the period in subsection (5) . . ..

**Amendments**—Small Business, Enterprise and Employment Act 2015, s 126, Sch 9, Pt 1, paras 1, 49; SI 2017/702; SI 2019/146, as from IP completion day (as defined in the European Union (Withdrawal Agreement) Act 2020, s 39(1)–(5)).

**General note**—The provision enables a company that is being wound up compulsorily and is hopelessly insolvent to be dissolved without adding costs where it would be a waste of time and money for a company to go through the formal processes that are involved with a winding up. This procedure would not be invoked where there are suggestions of improper activity, and investigation is needed. The concern for the winding up of companies that have no assets, save expending costs, will be secondary, if there are indications of unlawful conduct in the formation or management of the company.

The section does not provide for the scenario where the official receiver is replaced by a private insolvency practitioner as liquidator and he or she finds that the company does not have the assets it was thought to have. One suspects that the appropriate course of action would be for the practitioner to resign, with the official receiver taking over because of the vacancy (s 136(3)). The official receiver could then invoke the procedure under s 202.

Where the official receiver gives notice of an intention to make an application under the section, any creditor, contributory or administrative receiver may apply to the Secretary of State for directions pursuant to s 203(1) if any of the grounds set out in s 203(2) are cited.

As under s 201, dissolution is automatic when the circumstances in subsection (5) are fulfilled.

## [1.259]

### 203 Consequence of notice under s 202

(1)   Where a notice has been given under section 202(3), the official receiver or any creditor or contributory of the company, or the administrative receiver of the company (if there is one) may apply to the Secretary of State for directions under this section.

(2)   The grounds on which that application may be made are—

(a)   that the realisable assets of the company are sufficient to cover the expenses of the winding up;

(b)   that the affairs of the company do require further investigation; or

(c)   that for any other reason the early dissolution of the company is inappropriate.

(3)   Directions under this section—

(a)   are directions making such provision as the Secretary of State thinks fit for enabling the winding up of the company to proceed as if no notice had been given under section 202(3), and

(b)   may, in the case of an application under section 202(8), include a direction deferring the date at which the dissolution of the company is to take effect for such period as the Secretary of State thinks fit.

(4)   An appeal to the court lies from any decision of the Secretary of State on an application for directions under this section.

(5)   It is the duty of the person on whose application any directions are given under this section, or in whose favour an appeal with respect to an application for such directions is determined, within 7 days after the giving of the directions or the determination of the appeal, to deliver to the registrar of companies for registration such a copy of the directions or determination as is prescribed.

(6)   If a person without reasonable excuse fails to deliver a copy as required by subsection (5), he is liable to a fine and, for continued contravention, to a daily default fine.

Amendments—SI 2017/702.

General note—This section merely provides the mechanism for certain parties to seek directions from the Secretary of State (and possibly from a court if there is an appeal from the decision of the Secretary of State) where a notice pursuant to s 202 has been given by the official receiver.

See r 7.119

## [1.260]

### 204 Early dissolution (Scotland)

(1)   This section applies where a winding-up order has been made by the court in Scotland.

(2)   If after a liquidator has been appointed under section 138 (appointment of liquidator in Scotland) it appears to the liquidator that the realisable assets of the company are insufficient to cover the expenses of the winding up, the liquidator may at any time apply to the court for an order that the company be dissolved.

(3)   Where the liquidator makes that application, if the court is satisfied that the realisable assets of the company are insufficient to cover the expenses of the winding up and it appears to the court appropriate to do so, the court shall make an order that the company be dissolved in accordance with this section.

(4)   A copy of the order shall within 14 days from its date be forwarded by the liquidator to the registrar of companies, who shall forthwith register it; and, at the end of the period of 3 months beginning with the day of the registration of the order, the company shall be dissolved.

(4A)   . . ..

(4B)   . . .

(4C) . . .

(4D) . . .

(4E) . . .

(5)   The court may, on an application by any person who appears to the court to have an interest, order that the date at which the dissolution of the company is to take effect shall be deferred for such period as the court thinks fit.

(6)   It is the duty of the person on whose application an order is made under subsection (5), within 7 days after the making of the order, to deliver to the registrar of companies such a copy of the order as is prescribed.

(7)   If the liquidator without reasonable excuse fails to comply with the requirements of subsection (4), he is liable to a fine and, for continued contravention, to a daily default fine.

(8)   If a person without reasonable excuse fails to deliver a copy as required by subsection (6), he is liable to a fine and, for continued contravention, to a daily default fine.

**Amendments**—Small Business, Enterprise and Employment Act 2015, s 126, Sch 9, Pt 1, paras 1, 50; SSI 2016/141; SI 2017/702; SI 2019/146, as from IP completion day (as defined in the European Union (Withdrawal Agreement) Act 2020, s 39(1)–(5)).

## [1.261]

### 205   Dissolution otherwise than under ss 202–204

(1)   This section applies where the registrar of companies receives—

    (a)    a final account and statement sent under section 146(4) (final account), or

    (b)    a notice from the official receiver that the winding up of a company by the court is complete.

(2)   The registrar shall, on receipt of the final account and statement or the notice . . ., forthwith register them or it; and, subject as follows, at the end of the period of 3 months beginning with the day of the registration of the final account or notice . . ., the company shall be dissolved.

(2A)   . . .

(2B)   . . .

(3)   The Secretary of State may, on the application of the official receiver or any other person who appears to the Secretary of State to be interested, give a direction deferring the date at which the dissolution of the company is to take effect for such period as the Secretary of State thinks fit.

(4)   An appeal to the court lies from any decision of the Secretary of State on an application for a direction under subsection (3).

(5)   Subsection (3) does not apply in a case where the winding-up order was made by the court in Scotland, but in such a case the court may, on an application by any person appearing to the court to have an interest, order that the date at which the dissolution of the company is to take effect shall be deferred for such period as the court thinks fit.

(6)   It is the duty of the person—

    (a)    on whose application a direction is given under subsection (3);

    (b)    in whose favour an appeal with respect to an application for such a direction is determined; or

    (c)    on whose application an order is made under subsection (5),

within 7 days after the giving of the direction, the determination of the appeal or the making of the order, to deliver to the registrar for registration such a copy of the direction, determination or order as is prescribed.

(7)   If a person without reasonable excuse fails to deliver a copy as required by subsection (6), he is liable to a fine and, for continued contravention to a daily default fine.

**Amendments**—Small Business, Enterprise and Employment Act 2015, s 126, Sch 9, Pt 1, paras 1, 51; SI 2017/702; SI 2019/146, as from IP completion day (as defined in the European Union (Withdrawal Agreement) Act 2020, s 39(1)–(5)).

General note—This provision corresponds to s 201 and relates to compulsory liquidations (note references in s 205(1) to s 172(8) and winding up by the court). Under the previous legislation, a compulsory liquidation could only be dissolved by way of court order. But this section allows for automatic dissolution, as in voluntary liquidation, at the end of a 3-month period following the registration by the registrar of companies of the receipt of either the return from a private insolvency practitioner who is acting as the liquidator that the final account required under s 146 has been has been made up and delivered or, in the case of the official receiver, notice that the winding up is complete.

Although the provision corresponds to s 201, it combines aspects of ss 202 and 203 as well as s 201, particularly in relation to applications to the Secretary of State for directions.

See r 7.119.

For a detailed discussion of dissolution, including the restoration of dissolved companies, see A Keay *McPherson and Keay's Law of Company Liquidation* (Sweet and Maxwell, 4th edn, 2018) at 1086–1105.

## CHAPTER X

### Malpractice Before and During Liquidation; Penalisation of Companies and Company Officers; Investigations and Prosecutions

[1.262]

General comment on Chapter X—This Chapter deals with wrongdoing, both before and during a liquidation, and imposes both criminal and civil sanctions.

Sections 206–211 set out specific offences and these sections provide defences to, and impose sanctions for, criminal offences which may be committed prior to or in the course of a liquidation. Notably, certain of the provisions, namely ss 206(4), 207(2)(b), 208(4) and 210(4), reverse the burden of proof from the ordinary position in criminal law whereby the prosecution is required to establish beyond reasonable doubt that a particular offence has been committed by the defendant. These provisions deem the committing of an offence in the circumstances prescribed, subject to a defendant establishing, in contrast to the usual position, that, on a balance of probabilities, any of the defences defined in the provisions are available to him or her: *Morton v Confer* [1963] 2 All ER 765 at 767 (Lord Parker CJ) and 768 (Havers and Edmund Davies JJ agreeing). In considering whether reverse burdens involve a contravention of a defendant's human rights the Court of Appeal said in *Attorney-General's Reference (No 1 of 2004); R v Edwards* [2004] EWCA Crim 1025, [2004] 1 WLR 2111, [2004] BPIR 1073 that reference should be made only to the House of Lords' decision in *R v Johnstone* [2003] 1 WLR 1736 (and see especially at 1748–1751) and the guidance the Court of Appeal gave in *R v Edwards*. In that case the Court of Appeal was dealing with reverse burden provisions relating to bankruptcy offences, but they are drafted in similar ways to the provisions mentioned above and contained in this Chapter of the Act. The court stated (at 1073) that the common law and the European Convention for the Protection of Human Rights permitted legal reverse burdens in appropriate circumstances. The court also stated (at 1073) that if an evidential reverse burden alone was invoked, and not a legal burden, there was no risk of breach of art 6(2) of the European Convention. The result is that if a defendant is able to adduce evidence supporting a statutory defence, then the burden of proof shifts onto the prosecution, which must establish the constituent parts of the offence beyond reasonable doubt. In *R v Edwards* Lord Woolf stated that insolvency offences have long been regarded as subject to special rules ([80], as the following sections and notes attest. The reason for allowing such burdens is that those involved in companies have the benefit of corporate personality and limited liability ([81]).

The remaining sections of the Chapter address such matters as misfeasance, fraudulent trading, wrongful trading, and the so-called Phoenix Syndrome.

*Offences of fraud, deception etc*

[1.263]

### 206 Fraud etc in anticipation of winding up

(1) When a company is ordered to be wound up by the court, or passes a resolution for voluntary winding up, any person, being a past or present officer of the company, is deemed to have committed an offence if, within the 12 months immediately preceding the commencement of the winding up, he has—

> (a)  concealed any part of the company's property to the value of £500 or more, or concealed any debt due to or from the company, or

(b)    fraudulently removed any part of the company's property to the value of £500 or more, or

(c)    concealed, destroyed, mutilated or falsified any book or paper affecting or relating to the company's property or affairs, or

(d)    made any false entry in any book or paper affecting or relating to the company's property or affairs, or

(e)    fraudulently parted with, altered or made any omission in any document affecting or relating to the company's property or affairs, or

(f)    pawned, pledged or disposed of any property of the company which has been obtained on credit and has not been paid for (unless the pawning, pledging or disposal was in the ordinary way of the company's business).

(2)   Such a person is deemed to have committed an offence if within the period above mentioned he has been privy to the doing by others of any of the things mentioned in paragraphs (c), (d) and (e) of subsection (1); and he commits an offence if, at any time after the commencement of the winding up, he does any of the things mentioned in paragraphs (a) to (f) of that subsection, or is privy to the doing by others of any of the things mentioned in paragraphs (c) to (e) of it.

(3)   For purposes of this section, "officer" includes a shadow director.

(4)   It is a defence—

(a)    for a person charged under paragraph (a) or (f) of subsection (1) (or under subsection (2) in respect of the things mentioned in either of those two paragraphs) to prove that he had no intent to defraud, and

(b)    for a person charged under paragraph (c) or (d) of subsection (1) (or under subsection (2) in respect of the things mentioned in either of those two paragraphs) to prove that he had no intent to conceal the state of affairs of the company or to defeat the law.

(5)   Where a person pawns, pledges or disposes of any property in circumstances which amount to an offence under subsection (1)(f), every person who takes in pawn or pledge, or otherwise receives, the property knowing it to be pawned, pledged or disposed of in such circumstances, is guilty of an offence.

(6)   A person guilty of an offence under this section is liable to imprisonment or a fine, or both.

(7)   The money sums specified in paragraphs (a) and (b) of subsection (1) are subject to increase or reduction by order under section 416 in Part XV.

**Amendments**—SI 1986/1996.

**CIGA 2020**—This provision is affected by temporary measures at Sch 10, para 11 of CIGA 2020.

**General note**—The provision was formally s 624 of the Companies Act 1985 and it deems a person to be guilty of an offence, and it is for the defendant to extricate himself or herself by establishing his or her innocence on the balance of probabilities. See the note at the commencement of the Chapter and the comments on reverse burden provisions.

Details of any offence under this section should be reported by the liquidator to the Secretary of State for Business Energy and Industrial Strategy and should include: details of the date and circumstances of the transaction(s); details of the assets/amount concerned and the director's explanations; and whether there has been a civil recovery under either s 238 or s 239 (Dear IP Millennium Edition, December 2000, chapter 20).

Where a winding-up order was made as a result of a petition presented under s 124 during the period of 27 April 2020 to 30 September 2021 on the basis that the company was unable to pay its debts, s 206(1) has effect as if the reference to 12 months immediately preceding the commencement of the winding-up were to a period which begins with whichever is the later of the day 12 months before the day on which the petition was presented, and the day 18 months before the day on which the winding-up order was made, and ends with the day on which the winding-up order was made (para 11 of Sch 10 of the Corporate Insolvency and Governance Act 2020 as amended by the Corporate Insolvency and Governance Act 2020 (Coronavirus) (Extension of the Relevant Period) Regulations 2020 (SI 2020/1031), reg 2(3), the Corporate Insolvency and Governance Act 2020 (Coronavirus) (Extension of the Relevant Period) (No 2) Regulations 2020 (SI 2020/1483), reg 2, The Corporate Insolvency and Governance Act 2020 (Coronavirus) (Extension of the Relevant Period) Regulations 2021 (SI 2021/375), reg 3(4) and The Corporate Insolvency and Governance Act 2020 (Coronavirus) (Extension of the Relevant Period) (No 2) Regulations 2021 (SI 2021/718), reg 2 ).

'Officer'—This term is defined in s 1173 of the Companies Act 2006, as incorporated by s 251. The term includes a director. According to s 251 of the Act, 'director' includes anyone occupying that position, no matter what they are called. So, a person who is a 'shadow director' falls within that term, but in any event s 206(3) actually states that a shadow director is included within the term. Section 251(1) of the Companies Act 2006 provides a definition of 'shadow director'. See the notes accompanying that term in s 251 of the Insolvency Act.

The term in s 1173 of the Companies Act 2006 also includes anyone who is a manager of the company. For the meaning of 'manager of the company', see the notes under the heading 'Involved in the management' and following s 217.

'Concealed'—In the Australian case of *Motor Auction Pty Ltd v John Joyce Wholesale Cars Pty Ltd* (1997) 15 ACLC 987 the New South Wales Supreme Court held that the word, in a similar kind of context to which it is found in s 206, included a hiding of property by a person who then deliberately disappeared so as not to be amenable to questioning concerning the property's whereabouts.

'Book or paper affecting or relating to the company's property or affairs'—Computer records are included within this expression as found in s 206(1)(c) (*R v Taylor* [2011] EWCA Civ 728, [2011] 1 WLR 1809).

'Commencement of the winding up'—This phrase is defined in s 129. See the note under this heading and accompanying s 129.

Defence—Note the burden of proof that is placed on the defendant. See the general note at the commencement of the Chapter on this subject. In the circumstances of this offence a legal burden was compatible with the Human Rights Act 1998: *Attorney-General's Reference (No 1 of 2004); R v Edwards* [2004] EWCA Crim 1025, [2004] 1 WLR 2111, [2004] BPIR 1073; *Sheldrake v DPP* [2005] 1 AC 264, HL. According to *R v Richmond Magistrates' Court* [2008] EWHC 84 (Admin), [2008] 1 BCLC 681, [2008] BPIR 468 under this provision the reverse of burden provision is to be regarded as placing a legal as well as an evidential burden on the defendant.

'Penalty'—The penalties for a breach of s 206(1), s 206(2) or s 206(5) are 7 years' imprisonment or a fine or both where the prosecution is brought on indictment (s 430 and Sch 10 to the Act). Where the prosecution is a summary one, the punishment is 6 months' imprisonment or the statutory maximum or both. The statutory maximum fine is £5,000 (Magistrates' Courts Act 1980, s 32 as amended by Criminal Justice Act 1991, s 17).

## [1.264]
### 207 Transactions in fraud of creditors

(1)   When a company is ordered to be wound up by the court or passes a resolution for voluntary winding up, a person is deemed to have committed an offence if he, being at the time an officer of the company—

    (a)    has made or caused to be made any gift or transfer of, or charge on, or has caused or connived at the levying of any execution against, the company's property, or

    (b)    has concealed or removed any part of the company's property since, or within 2 months before, the date of any unsatisfied judgment or order for the payment of money obtained against the company.

(2)   A person is not guilty of an offence under this section—

    (a)    by reason of conduct constituting an offence under subsection (1)(a) which occurred more than 5 years before the commencement of the winding up, or

    (b)    if he proves that, at the time of the conduct constituting the offence, he had no intent to defraud the company's creditors.

(3)   A person guilty of an offence under this section is liable to imprisonment or a fine, or both.

CIGA 2020—This provision is affected by temporary measures at Sch 10, para 12 of CIGA 2020.

General note—The offences now contained in s 207(1) are broadly based on those which previously appeared in s 625 of the Companies Act 1985, and deem the committing of an offence. See the general note at the commencement of the Chapter on this subject. In *R v Enver* (unreported, 20 January 2000) the defendant was prosecuted under s 207(1)(b) and it was alleged he had stripped the assets of the company in order to pay off a bank and his own company. In a far more recent case (*R v Reed* – details available at: https://www.gov.uk/government/news/taunton-boss-h anded-suspended-sentence-after-pocketing-100000) a former director of an insolvent company was found liable under s 207(1)(a) for transferring out of his company's accounts large sums of money, just before the company went into liquidation, to his own advantage and that of a company in which is wife was a director.

Details of any offence under this section should be reported by the liquidator to the Secretary of State for Business, Energy and Industrial Strategy. The details that should be included are the same as for offences under s 206. See the General note to s 206.

Where a winding-up order was made as a result of a petition presented under s 124 during the period of 27 April 2020 to 30 September 2021 on the basis that the company was unable to pay its debts, s 207(2)(a) has effect as if the reference to conduct occurring more than 5 years before the commencement of the winding up were to conduct occurring more than 5 years before the day on which the petition was presented, or if the winding-up order was made more than 6 months after the day on which the petition was presented, more than 5 years and 6 months before the day on which the winding-up order was made (para 12 of Sch 10 of the Corporate Insolvency and Governance Act 2020 and as amended by the Corporate Insolvency and Governance Act 2020 (Coronavirus) (Extension of the Relevant Period) Regulations 2020 (SI 2020/1031), reg 2(3), the Corporate Insolvency and Governance Act 2020 (Coronavirus) (Extension of the Relevant Period) (No 2) Regulations 2020 (SI 2020/1483), reg 2 and The Corporate Insolvency and Governance Act 2020 (Coronavirus) (Extension of the Relevant Period) Regulations 2021 (SI 2021/375), reg 3(4) and The Corporate Insolvency and Governance Act 2020 (Coronavirus) (Extension of the Relevant Period) (No 2) Regulations 2021 (SI 2021/718), reg 2).

'Officer'—The term is defined in Companies Act 2006, s 1173 as incorporated by s 251. It is notable, however, that in contrast to s 206(3) and s 208(3) the term 'officer' is not extended here to include a shadow director, such that the offences in this provision must be taken, for no obvious reason, as not extending to shadow directors.

'Commencement of the winding up'—This phrase is defined in s 129. See the note under this heading and accompanying s 129.

In a compulsory liquidation the 5-year period in which the offence must have occurred is reckoned from the date of presentation of the winding-up petition and not from the date of the winding-up order.

Defence—Note the burden of proof that is placed on the defendant. See the general note at the commencement of the Chapter on this subject.

This provision infers that a person is taken to have committed the actus reus of the offence with the requisite mens rea of intent to defraud the company's creditors, subject to the statutorily defined defence.

Penalty—The offence is punishable by imprisonment for 2 years or a fine or both, where proceedings have been brought by indictment, and where initiated summarily, the penalty is imprisonment for 6 months or a fine equal to the statutory maximum or both (ss 207(3) and 430, and Sch 10). The statutory maximum fine is £5,000 according to s 32 of the Magistrates' Courts Act 1980 as amended by s 17 of the Criminal Justice Act 1991.

## [1.265]

### 208 Misconduct in course of winding up

(1) When a company is being wound up, whether by the court or voluntarily, any person, being a past or present officer of the company, commits an offence if he—

(a) does not to the best of his knowledge and belief fully and truly discover to the liquidator all the company's property, and how and to whom and for what consideration and when the company disposed of any part of that property (except such part as has been disposed of in the ordinary way of the company's business), or

(b) does not deliver up to the liquidator (or as he directs) all such part of the company's property as is in his custody or under his control, and which he is required by law to deliver up, or

(c) does not deliver up to the liquidator (or as he directs) all books and papers in his custody or under his control belonging to the company and which he is required by law to deliver up, or

(d) knowing or believing that a false debt has been proved by any person in the winding up, fails to inform the liquidator as soon as practicable, or

(e) after the commencement of the winding up, prevents the production of any book or paper affecting or relating to the company's property or affairs.

(2)   Such a person commits an offence if after the commencement of the winding up he attempts to account for any part of the company's property by fictitious losses or expenses; and he is deemed to have committed that offence if he has so attempted in connection with any qualifying decision procedure or deemed consent procedure of the company's creditors within the 12 months immediately preceding the commencement of the winding up.

(3)   For purposes of this section, "officer" includes a shadow director.

(4)   It is a defence—

    (a)    for a person charged under paragraph (a), (b) or (c) of subsection (1) to prove that he had no intent to defraud, and

    (b)    for a person charged under paragraph (e) of that subsection to prove that he had no intent to conceal the state of affairs of the company or to defeat the law.

(5)   A person guilty of an offence under this section is liable to imprisonment or a fine, or both.

**Amendments**—Small Business, Enterprise and Employment Act 2015, s 126, Sch 9, Pt 1, paras 1, 52.

**CIGA 2020**—This provision is affected by temporary measures at Sch 10, para 13 of CIGA 2020.

**General note**—Formerly this provision was s 626 of the Companies Act 1985. The provision identifies the nature of seven separate offences, found in s 208(1) and (2) which may arise in the course of a liquidation, save that the second offence in s 208(2), which amounts to a deeming provision, is relevant only to the period preceding the commencement of the winding up. These notes should be read in conjunction with those in relation to the offences in s 206 and the General note to the Chapter.

Where a winding-up order was made as a result of a petition presented under s 124 during the period of 27 April 2020 to 30 September 2021 on the basis that the company was unable to pay its debts, s 208(2) has effect as if the reference to 12 months immediately preceding the commencement of the winding up were to a period which begins with whichever is the later of the day 12 months before the day on which the petition was presented, and the day 18 months before the day on which the winding-up order was made, and ends with the day on which the winding-up order was made (para 13 of Sch 10 of the Corporate Insolvency and Governance Act 2020 and as amended by the Corporate Insolvency and Governance Act 2020 (Coronavirus) (Extension of the Relevant Period) Regulations 2020 (SI 2020/1031), reg 2(3), the Corporate Insolvency and Governance Act 2020 (Coronavirus) (Extension of the Relevant Period) (No 2) Regulations 2020 (SI 2020/1483), reg 2, The Corporate Insolvency and Governance Act 2020 (Coronavirus) (Extension of the Relevant Period) Regulations 2021 (SI 2021/375), reg 3(4) and The Corporate Insolvency and Governance Act 2020 (Coronavirus) (Extension of the Relevant Period) (No 2) Regulations 2021 (SI 2021/718), reg 2 ).

The actus reus of five separate offences appear here together with, in the case of s 208(1)(d), the mens rea ('knowing or believing that a false debt has been proved by any person in the winding up') of that particular offence. Section 208(4)(a) and (b) infer that a person is taken to have committed the actus reus of the offences prescribed in s 208(1)(a), (b), (c) and (e) with the requisite intent to defraud or intent to conceal the state of affairs of the company etc, subject to the defences in s 208(4)(a) and (b).

The directors are under a continuous duty because of this section to co-operate with the liquidator and to be proactive in disclosing and delivering up company property, and the section is not triggered by the liquidator's inquiry concerning property or request for production: *R v McCredie; R v French* [2000] 2 BCLC 438 at 442, CA, Criminal Division.

As would be expected, a cheque is regarded as property for the purposes of the section (*R v McCredie* at 445). The fruits of company property as compiled by a company officer are also part of the property of a company (*R v McCredie* at 445).

In relation to s 208(1)(c) books and records may include computer disks (*McCredie*).

In relation to s 208(1)(d), in contrast to the other subparagraphs in this subsection, the burden of proof rests on the prosecution in establishing beyond reasonable doubt the knowledge or belief as to the proof of a false debt (see s 208(4)).

'**Commencement of the winding up**'—The term is defined in s 129. See the note accompanying s 129.

'**Officer**'—See the note to s 206 under the heading of 'officer'.

'**Deliver up**'—Details of any offence under s 208(1)(c) should be reported by the liquidator to the Secretary of State and should include: details of the attempts to recover records, including a copy of the correspondence with the director; the effect of the failure to deliver up the records; and the director's explanations for failing to deliver up (Dear IP Millennium Edition, December 2000, chapter 20).

**Defences**—In relation to the burden of proof, see the note at the commencement of this Chapter. Note that no defences are provided to those offences prescribed by s 208(1)(d) or s 208(2). In relation to this offence a legal burden was compatible with the Human Rights Act: *R v Richmond Magistrates' Court* [2008] EWHC 84 (Admin), [2008] 1 BCLC 681, [2008] BPIR 468) at [29]. According to this case under this section the reverse of burden provision Is to be regarded as placing a legal as well as an evidential burden on the respondent.

**Penalty**—See the note to s 206, under the heading 'penalty'. The severity of the penalty is the same as for s 206. For the imposition of a custodial sentence: see *Re Bevis* [2001] All ER (D) 09 (Jan). In this case a custodial sentence of 18 months ordered in relation to a director for failure to discover all company property to the liquidator in contravention of s 208(1) was reduced to 9 months on appeal on the basis that the offence, whilst involving an element of dishonesty (which was not a technical or administrative offence), was in fact distinguishable from fraudulent trading under the Companies Act 2006, s 993.

## [1.266]

### 209 Falsification of company's books

(1)   When a company is being wound up, an officer or contributory of the company commits an offence if he destroys, mutilates, alters or falsifies any books, papers or securities, or makes or is privy to the making of any false or fraudulent entry in any register, book of account or document belonging to the company with intent to defraud or deceive any person.

(2)   A person guilty of an offence under this section is liable to imprisonment or a fine, or both.

**General note**—Formerly this provision was s 627 of the Companies Act 1985. The offence identified in this provision is only capable of being committed 'when a company is being wound up'. For a pre-liquidation offence (which extends to concealment, which is not mentioned within the present provision), see s 206(1)(c).

Besides prosecuting officers, contributories can also be prosecuted. For a discussion of who are contributories, see the notes accompanying s 74.

The burden of proof in establishing mens rea ('intent to defraud or deceive any person') rests on the prosecution.

'**Officer**'—See the note under this heading accompanying s 206.

**Penalty**—See the note to s 206 dealing with 'Penalty'. The severity of the penalty is the same as for s 206.

## [1.267]

### 210 Material omissions from statement relating to company's affairs

(1)   When a company is being wound up, whether by the court or voluntarily, any person, being a past or present officer of the company, commits an offence if he makes any material omission in any statement relating to the company's affairs.

(2)   When a company has been ordered to be wound up by the court, or has passed a resolution for voluntary winding up, any such person is deemed to have committed that offence if, prior to the winding up, he has made any material omission in any such statement.

(3)   For purposes of this section, "officer" includes a shadow director.

(4)   It is a defence for a person charged under this section to prove that he had no intent to defraud.

(5)   A person guilty of an offence under this section is liable to imprisonment or a fine, or both.

**General note**—This provision creates two separate offences which are limited in scope to the making of any material omission in any statement relating to the company's affairs. Section 210(1) applies to material omissions made by a person 'when a company is being wound up', irrespective of whether the liquidation is compulsory or voluntary. Section 210(2) is a deeming provision which provides for the actus reus of the offence at a time 'prior to the winding up'. This provision should be read in conjunction with the notes to s 206 and the general note to s 211, which addresses false representations – apparently something distinct from omissions – to creditors.

The offence within s 210(2) involves the making of an omission which is material by a person who, at the time of the making of the omission, is or was an officer of the company in 'any statement relating to the company's affairs'. Section 210(4) infers that a person is taken to have committed the actus reus of the offence with the requisite mens rea of intent to defraud, subject to the defence in that subsection.

This offence is plainly not limited to material omissions which appear in the statement of affairs provided for in s 99 (creditors' voluntary winding up) or s 131 (winding up by the court or in provisional liquidation). The provision instead appears to be wide enough to catch omissions in any statement, whether made for the purposes of the legislation or not. Examples might include statements made to a liquidator in the course of the preparation of a statement of affairs under s 95(3) (conversion of members' voluntary winding up to creditors' voluntary winding up) or statements made to creditors or other third parties, such as those made in correspondence or circulars. There would also not appear to be any requirement that the statement from which there is an omission should be in writing, and so the offence may well catch omissions from statements made orally. The offence might also cover omissions from statements made in the course of a public or private examination (on which see s 133 and s 236, respectively), although statements made under oath in the course of such examinations will in any case be covered by s 5 of the Perjury Act 1911.

Positive misstatements relating to the company's affairs are not caught, at least not expressly, by this provision, but will be caught by s 208 and/or s 209.

The offence in s 210(2) mirrors that in s 210(1) and would appear wide enough to catch material omissions from statements made relating to the company's affairs without a requirement that such statements should relate to the winding up itself. Thus, it would follow that the provision would catch material omissions from a statement of officers prepared for the purposes of a company voluntary arrangement (seer 2.6), an administration order (para 47 of Sch B1) or administrative receivership (s 47), together with material omissions in the course of other statements made to creditors or third parties.

'**Officer**'—See the note under this heading accompanying s 206.

**Defences**—In relation to the reverse burden of proof, see the General note at the commencement of the Chapter.

**Penalty**—See the note to s 206 dealing with 'Penalty.' The severity of the penalty is the same as for s 206.

**[1.268]**

### 211 False representations to creditors

(1)  When a company is being wound up, whether by the court or voluntarily, any person, being a past or present officer of the company—

  (a)  commits an offence if he makes any false representation or commits any other fraud for the purpose of obtaining the consent of the company's creditors or any of them to an agreement with reference to the company's affairs or to the winding up, and

  (b)  is deemed to have committed that offence if, prior to the winding up, he has made any false representation, or committed any other fraud, for that purpose.

(2)  For purposes of this section, "officer" includes a shadow director.

(3)  A person guilty of an offence under this section is liable to imprisonment or a fine, or both.

*Penalisation of directors and officers*

**[1.269]**

**General note**—This provision creates two separate offences. Both are limited in scope to the making of any false representation to creditors – but not to any other third party – for the purpose of obtaining consent to an agreement 'with reference to the company's affairs or to the winding up'. Either offence may be committed 'when the company is being wound up' (in the case of s 211(1)(a)) or, by virtue of the deeming provision in s 211(1)(b), prior to the winding up.

The actus reus of each of the offences in s 211(1)(a) and (b) necessarily involves the making of a fraudulent (as opposed to a negligent or innocent) representation, given the subsequent reference to the alternative act of committing 'any other fraud' for the purpose then identified. An offence may be committed under these provisions through the silence of an officer, given that silence may, in certain circumstances, amount to a misrepresentation: see Furmston *Cheshire, Fifoot and*

*Furmston's Law of Contract* (Butterworths, 14th edn, 2001) at pp 297–298; Halson *Contract Law* (Pearson, 2001) at pp 31–34). It appears that silence may also fall susceptible to prosecution under s 210 as a material omission.

The offence does not require the obtaining of consent to an agreement on the part of one or more creditors but, rather, involves only the making of a false representation or the committing of any other fraud for that purpose.

The burden of proof in establishing fraud rests on the prosecution.

'**Officer**'—See the note under this heading accompanying s 206.

**Penalty**—See the note to s 206 dealing with 'Penalty'. The severity of the penalty is the same as for s 206.

## [1.270]

### 212 Summary remedy against delinquent directors, liquidators etc

(1)   This section applies if in the course of the winding up of a company it appears that a person who—

(a)   is or has been an officer of the company,

(b)   has acted as liquidator or administrative receiver of the company, or

(c)   not being a person falling within paragraph (a) or (b), is or has been concerned, or has taken part, in the promotion, formation or management of the company,

has misapplied or retained, or become accountable for, any money or other property of the company, or been guilty of any misfeasance or breach of any fiduciary or other duty in relation to the company.

(2)   The reference in subsection (1) to any misfeasance or breach of any fiduciary or other duty in relation to the company includes, in the case of a person who has acted as liquidator of the company, any misfeasance or breach of any fiduciary or other duty in connection with the carrying out of his functions as liquidator of the company.

(3)   The court may, on the application of the official receiver or the liquidator, or of any creditor or contributory, examine into the conduct of the person falling within subsection (1) and compel him—

(a)   to repay, restore or account for the money or property or any part of it, with interest at such rate as the court thinks just, or

(b)   to contribute such sum to the company's assets by way of compensation in respect of the misfeasance or breach of fiduciary or other duty as the court thinks just.

(4)   The power to make an application under subsection (3) in relation to a person who has acted as liquidator of the company is not exercisable, except with the leave of the court, after he has had his release.

(5)   The power of a contributory to make an application under subsection (3) is not exercisable except with the leave of the court, but is exercisable notwithstanding that he will not benefit from any order the court may make on the application.

**Amendments**—Enterprise Act 2002, ss 248(3), 278(2), Sch 17, paras 9, 18, Sch 26.

**General note**—This provision is often said to cover misfeasance (a term mentioned in s 212(2)), particularly perpetrated by directors of companies, and is often misunderstood. There is no such distinct wrongful act known to the law as misfeasance. The provision is purely procedural in effect (*Re B Johnson & Co (Builders) Ltd* [1955] Ch 634 at 647–648; *Cohen v Selby* [2001] 1 BCLC 176 at 183); its purpose is to provide a summary mode of enforcing rights which, apart from the section, could have been enforced by the company prior to liquidation. The provision is merely a gateway enabling a claim which was, but for liquidation, able to be brought by the company and so the liquidator can bring it instead: *French v Cipolletta* [2009] EWHC 223 (Ch) at [9]. The section does not affect any right of a liquidator to bring action in the ordinary way, nor does it affect the rights of the liquidator which came into existence by virtue of special statutory provisions: *Re Home & Colonial Insurance Co* [1930] 1 Ch 102 at 132. Liquidators are only able to take proceedings to enforce claims vested in the company, and not actions that vest in other persons, such as creditors: *Re Hill's Waterfall Estate and Gold Mining Co* [1896] 1 Ch 947.

The usual respondent to an action under this provision will be directors, but others as indicated in s 212(1) may be the subject of proceedings. An example of an action against a liquidator is *Centralcrest Engineering Ltd* [2000] BCC 727. It has been held in Australia that before a court will inquire into the conduct of a liquidator the complainant must make out a prima facie case that there is something which requires an inquiry to be conducted: *Vink v Tuckwell* [2008] VSC 100,

[2008] 216 FLR 309. A claim against a liquidator can be answered successfully if there is no loss sustained by the company or creditors: *Lomax Leisure Ltd v Miller* [2007] EWHC 2508 (Ch), [2007] BPIR 1615, [2008] 1 BCLC 262 at [37]. Any proceedings to be brought against administrators must be instituted under para 75 of Sch B1.

It has been held that misfeasance covers the whole spectrum of duties of directors, and the provision is not restricted to cases where the respondent is guilty of moral turpitude: *Re Westlowe Storage and Distribution Ltd* [2000] 2 BCLC 590.

In a misfeasance claim that is based on an alleged breach of duty, a respondent will not be able to escape liability even though he or she has sought and obtained professional legal advice if the advice given to the respondent was based on the respondent's wrong and inadequate instructions to his or her legal advisors: *Top Brands Ltd v Sharma* [2014] EWHC 2753 (Ch), [2015] 1 BCLC 546, [2015] BPIR 621.

A liquidator may take action under the provision as well as making application for relief on some other basis, such as wrongful trading under s 214 (*Re DKG Contractors Ltd* [1990] BCC 903; *Re Brian D Pierson (Contractors) Ltd* [2001] 1 BCLC 275, [1999] BPIR 18), or at common law (*A & J Fabrications Ltd v Grant Thornton* [1998] 2 BCLC 227).

The difficulty of obtaining summary judgment can be seen in *Phillips v McGregor-Paterson* [2009] EWHC 2385 (Ch), [2010] BPIR 239 at [37]ff. There is going to be a need for a trial very often when the questions involve consideration of whether the defendant was in breach of his or her duties as a director. There may also be the need to consider whether the defendant should be excused under s 1157 of the Companies Act 2006.

In bringing an action under the section proof of loss to the company is a necessary ingredient of a cause of action for breach of fiduciary duty or negligence. There is no basis for saying that the section justifies a laxer approach to pleading than would be called for in an ordinary action. The director is entitled to know what case is being made against him or her and it is necessary that the pleadings allege loss and make clear the types of loss that are alleged to have been caused by the breaches of duty or negligence in question: *French v Cipolletta* [2009] EWHC 223 (Ch) at [16].

Applications can be made pursuant to this provision by liquidators of limited liability partnerships. Members of LLPs were potentially subject at common law and in equity to the same duties applicable to those which apply to company directors under ss 171–187 of the Companies Act 2006 and such breaches may form the basis of a claim under s 212: *Re CJ and RA Eade LLP* [2019] EWHC 1673 (Ch), [2019] BPIR 1380.

If a liquidator were to assign a cause of action that would be able to be covered by a misfeasance claim, if action was brought by the liquidator, the assignee would not be able to use the misfeasance procedure in s 212. This is even though the liquidator could have done so unless the assignee was a person who is mentioned in s 212: *Manolete Partners Plc v Hayward And Barrett Holdings Ltd & Ors* [2021] EWHC 1481 (Ch) at [51]–[52].

**Applicants**—The usual applicant will be a liquidator for relief against a director, but the official receiver and creditors are also permitted to apply (for an instance of an application by a creditor, see *Re Loquitur Ltd* [2003] EWHC 999 (Ch), [2003] 2 BCLC 410).

Contributories may apply if they obtain the leave of the court (s 212(5)). Before the 1986 Act, contributories would not be granted leave unless they could demonstrate a real interest in the outcome of the proceedings, but this is no longer the case. It has been said that the provision enables contributories to commence direct proceedings against a director instead of derivative proceedings, which might be unavailable or difficult to institute: *Wightman v Bennett* [2005] BPIR 470 at 473. A contributory is not able to apply under s 212 after a winding-up petition has been presented, but must wait until an order has been made (*Wightman v Bennett*).

A person who made a claim against the company, and the claim had been settled, could not bring an action under s 212 as a creditor: *Re Tertiary Enterprises Ltd* (unreported, 3 August 2006, ChD, Thomas Ivory QC).

**Negligence**—Negligence is covered by s 212 (*Re D'Jan of London Ltd* [1994] 1 BCLC 561; *Centralcrest Engineering Ltd* [2000] BCC 727; *Cohen v Selby* [2001] 1 BCLC 176, CA), because the provision refers not only to misfeasance, but also 'breach of any fiduciary or other duty'. But the liquidator must establish a cause of action whereby the alleged breach of duty of care caused loss or damage: *Re Anglo-Austrian Printing & Publishing Co* [1985] 2 Ch 891.

**Contribution**—Courts have a broad discretion as to what they order should be paid by the respondent: *Re Home & Colonial Insurance Co* [1930] 1 Ch 102; *Re Westlowe Storage and Distribution Ltd* [2000] 2 BCLC 590. Courts are able to order compensation as they think fit, and a court can decide to award only part of the compensation sought (*Re Home & Colonial Insurance Co*), as was the case in *Re Loquitur Ltd* [2003] EWHC 999 (Ch), [2003] 2 BCLC 410, where the court felt that it should limit the amount to be paid. It has been said recently that the court has a discretion as to the mode and amount of repayment or compensation, and the courts are not compelled to assess that compensation by reference to any established loss to the company: *Liquidator of Glasgow and Weir Blacksmiths Ltd v David Glasgow* [2016] SCEDIN 20 at [31].

The courts have a discretion as to whether any order should be made: *Re Sunlight Incandescent Gas Lamp Co Ltd* (1900) 16 TLR 535, and there is Australian authority to the effect that in very limited circumstances the court may exonerate a liquidator for breach of duty: *Re ACN 003 671 387 and ACN 008 664 257* [2004] NSWSC 368 (sale to the liquidator's service trust), but in *Re Paycheck Services 3 Ltd* [2008] EWHC 2200 (Ch), [2008] 2 BCLC 613, Mark Cawson QC (sitting as a deputy High Court judge) doubted whether it had been intended to provide in s 212 a judicial ability to relieve from liability, given the existence of s 727 of the Companies Act 1985 (now s 1157 of the Companies Act 2006).

Most frequently a court will order the respondent to pay the amount of the loss suffered because of the misconduct: *Bishopsgate Investment Management Ltd v Maxwell (No 2)* [1993] BCLC 814 (affirmed on appeal [1994] 2 All ER 261, [1993] BCLC 1282, CA). Notwithstanding their broad discretion, courts cannot order the rescission of contracts (*Re Centrifugal Butter Co Ltd* [1913] 1 Ch 188) or order the payment of debts owed to the company (*Re Etic Ltd* [1928] Ch 861).

Before any contribution will be ordered, the applicant must demonstrate that the company has suffered loss: *Re Derek Randall Enterprises Ltd* [1991] BCLC 379, CA.

Where a claim is made pursuant to both s 212 and s 214 there would be no injustice in ordering payments under both provisions, provided that the liquidator does not recover more than what was required to satisfy the liabilities of the company: *Re Purpoint Ltd* [1991] BCLC 491.

Any contribution paid by a respondent will, following the deduction of costs of the action, be available to any holders of charges over the present and future property of the company for the discharge of their debt: *Re Anglo-Austrian Printing & Publishing Co* [1985] 2 Ch 891.

**Orders**—A court is able to order one respondent to indemnify another respondent to the proceedings: *Re Morecombe Bowling Ltd* [1969] 1 WLR 133. But third party procedure cannot be used so as to make a person contribute where he or she is not a respondent (*Re B Johnson & Co (Builders) Ltd*), and this is the case despite the fact that the latter could have been made a respondent: *Re A Singer & Co (Hat Manufacturers) Ltd* [1943] 1 Ch 121, CA.

If an application is brought by a creditor or a contributory, any order can only be made to the benefit of the company, and not to the applicant: *Oldham v Kyrris* [2003] EWCA Civ 1506, [2004] 1 BCLC 305, [2004] BPIR 165.

**'Officer'**—An auditor has been held to be within this term for the purposes of s 212 (*Re London and General Bank* [1895] 2 Ch 166, CA; *Re Thomas Gerrard & Sons Ltd* [1968] Ch 455), but other professionals who might be involved in providing advice to the company, such as a company's bankers (*Re Imperial Land Co of Marseilles* (1870) LR 10 Eq 298) and solicitors (*Re Great Western Forest of Dean Co* (1886) 31 ChD 496) are not.

De facto directors are officers for the purposes of this section: *Re Mumtaz Properties Ltd* [2011] EWCA Civ 610, [2012] 2 BCLC 109, as are shadow directors: *Re Hydrodan (Corby) Ltd* [1994] 2 BCLC 180.

The High Court of Australia has held that a person, under the Australian companies legislation which includes the Australian equivalent of s 212, does not have to have held a recognised position with rights and duties attached to it within a company for that person to be regarded as an officer: *ASIC v King* [2020] HCA 4.

**'Liquidator'**—Australian authority, *ASIC v Mack* [2019] SASC 17, has held that proceedings broadly under the equivalent of s 212 against a liquidator should be considered and conducted separately from, and will not be preempted by the existence of, prior other proceedings which may overlap with the s 212 proceedings. In the same case the court adverted to the fact that proceedings under s 212 had a public purpose.

In *Fakhry v Pagden* [2020] EWCA Civ 1207, [2021] BPIR 526 at [70] David Richards LJ said that it was uncertain whether proceedings could be brought against former liquidators while they remained in office.

**Limit on actions**—The limitation for taking proceedings would run from the time when the breach upon which the action is brought occurred or was discovered by the company. As s 212 is merely procedural in nature, it does not provide a limitation period that is independent from that applying to the claim underlying the proceedings (*Re Eurocruit Europe Ltd (in liq)* [2007] EWHC 1433 (Ch), [2007] 2 BCLC 598).

See generally, on breach of duties of directors, A Keay *Directors' Duties* (4th edn, LexisNexis, 2020).

## [1.271]

### 213 Fraudulent trading

(1)  If in the course of the winding up of a company it appears that any business of the company has been carried on with intent to defraud creditors of the company or creditors of any other person, or for any fraudulent purpose, the following has effect.

(2)   The court, on the application of the liquidator may declare that any persons who were knowingly parties to the carrying on of the business in the manner above-mentioned are to be liable to make such contributions (if any) to the company's assets as the court thinks proper.

General note—The law against fraudulent trading dates from 1928. Since then until the 1986 Act was enacted, the Companies Acts dealt with fraudulent trading and provided for both civil and criminal liability. Now s 213 deals solely with civil liability. Criminal liability is covered by s 993 of the Companies Act 2006. Sections 213 and 993 are essentially identical, with the primary difference being procedural. The former has the civil standard of proof, namely the balance of probabilities, while the standard for the criminal proceeding under s 993 remains beyond reasonable doubt. Unlike s 993, proceedings can only be brought under s 213 where the company is in liquidation, and can only be initiated by the liquidator. The corresponding provision for administrations is s 246ZA.

There are three elements that need to be established by a liquidator. These are: the business of the company in liquidation has been carried on with intent to defraud creditors or for any other fraudulent purpose; the defendant participated in the carrying of business; the defendant did so knowingly: *Re BCCI; Morris v Bank of India* [2004] 2 BCLC 236 at 243.

At one time it was generally thought that this section would not be invoked frequently, certainly given the advent of the action of wrongful trading in s 214, but while s 214 has a lower threshold of proof, and the elements of the section appear prima facie easier to establish, there were several fraudulent trading actions in the first decade of this century with a number being reported (eg *Morris v Bank of America National Trust and Savings Association* [2000] BPIR 83, [2001] 1 BCLC 771, CA; *Re Bank of Credit and Commerce International SA; Morris v State Bank of India* [2004] 2 BCLC 236; *Morphites v Bernasconi* [2003] EWCA Civ 289, CA; *Morris v Bank of India* [2004] EWHC 528 (Ch), [2004] 2 BCLC 279 and affirmed on appeal in [2005] EWCA Civ 693, [2005] 2 BCLC 328, [2005] BPIR 1067); many of them revolved around the liquidation of BCCI.

Any court award must be in favour of the liquidator for the whole body of creditors, and not an individual creditor: Re *Esal (Commodities) Ltd* [1997] 1 BCLC 705, CA. The award is to be held by a liquidator for the purpose of making a distribution to the unsecured creditors (*Re Oasis Merchandising Services Ltd* [1995] BCC 911, affirmed on appeal [1997] 1 All ER 1009, [1997] BCC 282, CA) and is, therefore, not available for a chargeholder.

It is probably in order for a liquidator to take proceedings under s 213 where a company is being wound up as an unregistered company: *Re Howard Holdings Inc* [1998] BCC 549 (involving an application under s 214). While at one time a liquidator was unable to assign an action under s 213 because it was an action given to him or her personally in the position of liquidator: *Re Oasis Merchandising Services Ltd*, now s 246ZD(2)(a) permits assignment.

Proceedings are not available under s 213 in relation to conduct that occurred between the date of the presentation of a winding-up petition and the making of a winding-up order as a company cannot be regarded as carrying on business when any transaction in the course of that business which amounts to a disposition of property is deemed to be void under s 127 of the Insolvency Act 1986 unless the court orders to the contrary (*Carman v Cronos Group SA* [2005] EWHC 2403 (Ch) at [37]–[38]). But it was held in the same case that people can be held liable under s 213 in relation to actions that occurred when the company had been dissolved at the time, but is later reinstated to the register (at [24]). This is on the basis that ss 1028(1) and 1032(1) (formerly s 653 of the Companies Act 1985) state that a dissolved company, when reinstated, is deemed to have deemed to have continued in existence as if it had not been struck off the register (at [24]).

It appears that it would be in order for a liquidator to bring an action that relied on both ss 213 and 214. There is nothing in s 213 to prevent it, and s 214(8) specifically provides that s 214 is not to prejudice s 213.

Only liquidators can bring proceedings and this does not include a provisional liquidator: *Re Overnight Ltd; Goldfarb v Higgins* [2009] EWHC 601 (Ch).

It is critical that in the claim of the liquidator there is a pleading that creditors of the company have sustained loss: *Goldfarb v Alibhai* (unrep, 11 December 2017, Business and Property Courts, Registrar Barber).

Respondents—While it is likely that directors will be the usual respondents to any fraudulent trading case, the provision is in fact quite wide, as anyone who was knowingly a party to the carrying on of a business of a company with intent to defraud creditors can be the subject of proceedings, and this can include companies: *Bank of India v Morris* [2005] EWCA Civ 693, [2005] 2 BCLC 328, [2005] BPIR 1067. The respondent does not have to be someone who performed a managerial or controlling role in the company. In fact, the language of s 213(2) might point towards persons who were not employed by the company, but were in fact outsiders: *Re BCCI; Banque Arabe Internationale D'Investissement SA v Morris* [2001] 1 BCLC 263. So, in *Re Gerald Cooper Chemicals Ltd* [1978] 2 WLR 866 a creditor was held liable, and in *Morris v*

*Bank of India* [2004] EWHC 528 (Ch), [2004] 2 BCLC 279 and affirmed on appeal [2005] EWCA (Civ) 693, [2005] 2 BCLC 328, [2005] BPIR 1067, CA, a bank was found liable. Similarly, later in *Re BCCI; Banque Arabe Internationale D'Investissement SA v Morris* the court said that a company or other entity that was involved in and assisted and benefited from the action that was fraudulent, and did so knowingly, could be a respondent. Outsider respondents need not know all of the details of any fraudulent action perpetrated by the company or how the fraud was to be carried out before they are held liable, provided that they knew, either from their own observations of what was being done or from what they were told, that the company was intending to carry out a fraud on creditors: *Re BCCI; Morris v State Bank of India* [2004] EWHC 528 (Ch), [2004] 2 BCLC 279.

Generally, employees of the company that are merely carrying out orders are not able to be made respondents: *Re BCCI; Banque Arabe Internationale D'Investissement SA v Morris* [2001] 1 BCLC 263. A company could be held liable even if none of its board members did not have knowledge of the fraudulent trading activity as that would defeat the policy behind the provision (*Bank of India v Morris* [2005] EWCA Civ 693, [2005] 2 BCLC 328, [2005] BPIR 1067 at [108], [129]). A company employee's knowledge of fraudulent trading may be attributed to his or her employer company (*Bank of India v Morris*). However, there are some circumstances where a person's knowledge of fraudulent trading should not be attributed to the company (*Bank of India v Morris* at [114], [129]).

There is a strong argument that a claim under the section would survive the death of a person allegedly liable under s 213, but who died before the initiation of proceedings, so a liquidator would be able to take proceedings against the personal representative of the deceased's estate: see *Re Sherborne Associates Ltd* [1995] BCC 40 (a s 214 claim).

The provision could be used against respondents who are foreign residents where the company was involved in trade across borders as the section had extra-territorial effect: *Bilta (UK) Ltd v Nazir* [2012] EWHC 2163 (Ch) at [44]. This judgment was confirmed on appeal both by the Court of Appeal at [2013] EWCA Civ 968, [2013] 3 WLR 1167 and the Supreme Court at [2015] UKSC 23, [2016] AC 1, [2015] 2 WLR 1168, [2015] 2 All ER 1083, [2015] 1 BCLC 443.

**Extent of liability**—The liability of those against whom a liquidator is successful is without limit. Persons who are liable must make such contributions to the company as the court thinks proper. The Court of Appeal has stated that the contribution to the assets to be shared amongst the creditors should reflect the loss which has been caused to the creditors by the carrying on of the business in the way that gives rise to the exercise of the power (*Morphites v Bernasconi* [2003] EWCA Civ 289, [2003] Ch 552, [2003] 2 WLR 1521, [2003] 2 BCLC 53, [2003] BPIR 973 at [55]). The court also said that there was no power in s 213 permitting the imposition of any punitive element in the amount of any contribution. The court added (at [55]) that the power to punish a guilty party was preserved in s 458 of the Companies Act 1985 (now s 993 of the Companies Act 2006).

**'Creditors'**—This term in s 213(1) covers future creditors, so an applicant could establish that the business of the company was carried on with intent to defraud either future creditors of the company as well as present creditors or in lieu of present creditors: *National Crime Agency v GTG Management Ltd* [2020] EWHC 963 (Ch) at [31].

**'Intent to defraud'**—This phrase has never been defined statutorily and there has been inconsistency concerning what test should be applied. The test for intent to defraud is a subjective test (*Bernasconi v Nicholas Bennett & Co* [2000] BPIR 8; *Re BCCI; Morris v Bank of India* [2004] 2 BCLC 236), namely the state of mind of the respondent at the time of the alleged fraudulent trading is the decisive factor: the respondent had to evince an intent or a reckless indifference whether creditors were defrauded (*Bernasconi v Nicholas Bennett & Co*).

While the subjective test is applied to respondents, objective considerations are not without some relevance. For instance, the circumstances pertaining to what is being alleged as fraudulent trading must be taken into account and, if a respondent's subjective view is found not to be reasonable, he or she might be found liable. But it has been said that courts must be careful in invoking the concept of the hypothetical decent honest man and what he would have done in the circumstances, as there might be a temptation to treat shortcomings by the respondent as a failure to comply with the necessary objective standard of conduct: *Aktieselskabet Dansk Skibsfinansiering v Brothers* [2001] 2 BCLC 324 at 334 (HKCFA). The Court of Appeal decision in *R v Grantham* [1984] QB 675, seems to suggest that courts can take into account objective considerations when respondents incur debts at a time when they know that their company will clearly not be able to make repayment, or where there is considerable risk that the company will not be able to repay.

The liquidator is required to demonstrate dishonesty on the part of the respondent, and it is this element which caused s 213 to be distinguishable from s 214: *Bernasconi v Nicholas Bennett & Co* [2000] BPIR 8 at 13. Whether a person is regarded as being dishonest must depend on an assessment of all of the facts (*Aktieselskabet Dansk Skibsfinansiering v Brothers*). If it was established that the respondent had knowledge of fraud, then it follows that the respondent was dishonest: *Re BCCI; Morris v State Bank of India* [2004] EWHC 528 (Ch), [2004] 2 BCLC 279.

An intent to defraud in the carrying on of business must be distinguished from misrepresentations and deception in general: *Morphites v Bernasconi* [2003] EWCA Civ 289, [2003] Ch 552, [2003] 2 WLR 1521, [2003] 2 BCLC 53, [2003] BPIR 973, CA at [43].

The payment of preferences, which are within the scope of s 239, will not generally be deemed to be fraud for the purposes of s 213: *Re Sarflax Ltd* [1979] 1 All ER 529 at 535, 545. Inaction cannot constitute fraud, as some positive action must have been taken. So, if an officer of, or adviser to, the company, were to fail to tell the directors that the company is insolvent, that person is not liable: *Re Maidstone Buildings Ltd* [1971] 1 WLR 1085. But a company outsider may be held liable even where he or she does not commit a positive act or is involved in the carrying on of business if the outsider is knowingly a party to a fraudulent act: *Re Augustus Barnett & Sons Ltd* (1986) 2 BCC 98, 904 at 98, 907. Thus, if a creditor were to be paid by the company when the creditor knew that the payment resulted from the carrying on of business with an intent to defraud, he or she might be liable: *Re Gerald Cooper Chemicals Ltd* [1978] Ch 262, [1978] 2 All ER 49.

The actual conduct that constitutes an intent to defraud must be set out clearly in any application (*Morris v Bank of America National Trust* [2001] 1 BCLC 771, [2000] BPIR 83, CA – an appeal relating to a strike out application).

See A Keay 'Fraudulent Trading: The Intent to Defraud Element' (2006) 35 *Common Law World Review* 121.

'Knowingly'—In considering whether the respondent was knowingly a party to fraud, if liquidators could demonstrate that respondents had 'blind-eye' knowledge of the intent to defraud, namely deliberately shutting their eyes to the obvious, in that it was obvious to the respondents that fraud was involved, they could succeed: *Re BCCI; Morris v Bank of India* [2004] 2 BCLC 236; *Bank of India v Morris* [2005] EWCA Civ 693, [2005] 2 BCLC 328, [2005] BPIR 1067. Blind-eye knowledge involves a suspicion that a fraud exists and a deliberate decision to avoid confirming that it exists, and that the suspicion is well-grounded (*Re BCCI; Morris v Bank of India*). To be knowingly parties to the fraud, people do not have to know every detail of the fraud or how it was to be perpetrated: *Re BCCI; Morris v Bank of India*. To be liable a person must have had the relevant knowledge contemporaneously with giving assistance to effect the fraud: *Re BCCI; Morris v Bank of India*. In *Bilta (UK) Ltd v Natwest Markets plc* ([2020] EWHC 546 (Ch) at [240]) Snowden J said that if a person fails to recognise the truth of what was occurring, namely the dishonesty, that will not mean he or she is liable, and that is the case even if in hindsight the conduct of the company was obvious.

'Fraudulent purpose'—This expression is not designed in any way to restrict the application of s 213. On the contrary, the expression is extremely wide: *R v Kemp* [1988] QB 645 at 654–655. But it should not be construed so as to stultify normal business transactions: *Re BCCI; Banque Arabe Internationale D'Investissement SA v Morris* [2001] 1 BCLC 263.

Carrying on business—Carrying on business is interpreted broadly. For fraudulent trading to have been committed, it is not necessary for the liquidator to prove that there has been a course of conduct, as a single transaction or act is able to constitute the basis for action under s 213: *Re Gerald Cooper Chemicals Ltd* [1978] Ch 262, [1978] 2 All ER 49; *Morphites v Bernasconi* [2003] EWCA Civ 289, [2003] Ch 552, [2003] 2 WLR 1521, [2003] 2 BCLC 53, [2003] BPIR 973, CA. Hence, where a company is doing nothing except collecting and distributing its assets, it can be regarded as carrying on business within s 213: *Re Sarflax Ltd* [1979] 1 All ER 529. Fraudulent trading can occur when business is being carried on to defraud just one creditor, but one cannot say that whenever a fraud on a creditor is perpetrated while carrying on business, it is inevitable that a breach of s 213 occurs; critically s 213 only applies where the business has been carried on with intent to defraud (*Morphites v Bernasconi* at [46]–[47]).

Contribution—The liquidator, in order for a contribution to be ordered, has to establish a nexus between the loss caused to creditors because of the fraudulent trading, and the contribution that is being sought from the person allegedly involved in the fraudulent trading (*Morphites v Bernasconi*).

Any order of contribution, while essentially compensatory, could only ever be a reasonable approximation of the damage that the respondent precipitated or to which he or she contributed: *Re BCCI; Morris v State Bank of India* [2004] EWHC 528 (Ch), [2004] 2 BCLC 279.

The court is entitled to determine that several persons should be held jointly and severally liable for the loss caused. As the word 'contributions' was used in the section the court is not required to order the contribution is the same for each of the respondents; the court has a wide discretion when it comes to ordering what each respondent should contribute: *Re Overnight Ltd (in liq)* [2010] EWHC 613 (Ch), [2010] 2 BCLC 186. The court held that in relation to the issue of contribution the approach utilised in cases dealing with wrongful trading should apply to s 213 as it would be surprising if different approaches were used in relation to identical wording contained in adjacent provisions of the Act.

**Directions**—If an order under s 213 is made, a court is, at its discretion, empowered to make further directions to give effect to its declaration. This is covered by s 215. See the comments attaching to that section.

**Practice**—As a successful claim under s 213 involves an allegation of dishonesty, dishonesty must be pleaded and also put to the respondent in cross-examination: *Dempster v HMRC* [2008] EWHC 63 (Ch), [2008] STC 2079, *Abbey Forwarding Ltd v Hone* [2010] EWHC 2029 (Ch).

**Limitation period**—It has been held in relation to s 214 that the application can be categorised as a claim in respect of a sum of money within the Limitation Act, and hence, a 6-year limitation period applies: *Re Farmizer (Products) Ltd* [1997] 1 BCLC 589 at 598, CA. It appears that the same comments could be applied to s 213. The limitation period would begin from the time of the resolution to wind up in voluntary liquidations, or from the date of the court order in compulsory liquidations, being the time when the cause of action accrued.

See A Keay *Company Directors' Responsibilities to Creditors* (Routledge-Cavendish, 2007), chs 3–6.

## [1.272]

### 214 Wrongful trading

(1)  Subject to subsection (3) below, if in the course of the winding up of a company it appears that subsection (2) of this section applies in relation to a person who is or has been a director of the company, the court, on the application of the liquidator, may declare that that person is to be liable to make such contribution (if any) to the company's assets as the court thinks proper.

(2)  This subsection applies in relation to a person if—

    (a)    the company has gone into insolvent liquidation,

    (b)    at some time before the commencement of the winding up of the company, that person knew or ought to have concluded that there was no reasonable prospect that the company would avoid going into insolvent liquidation or entering insolvent administration, and

    (c)    that person was a director of the company at that time;

but the court shall not make a declaration under this section in any case where the time mentioned in paragraph (b) above was before 28th April 1986.

(3)  The court shall not make a declaration under this section with respect to any person if it is satisfied that after the condition specified in subsection (2)(b) was first satisfied in relation to him that person took every step with a view to minimising the potential loss to the company's creditors as (on the assumption that he had knowledge of the matter mentioned in subsection (2)(b)) he ought to have taken.

(4)  For the purposes of subsections (2) and (3), the facts which a director of a company ought to know or ascertain, the conclusions which he ought to reach and the steps which he ought to take are those which would be known or ascertained, or reached or taken, by a reasonably diligent person having both—

    (a)    the general knowledge, skill and experience that may reasonably be expected of a person carrying out the same functions as are carried out by that director in relation to the company, and

    (b)    the general knowledge, skill and experience that that director has.

(5)  The reference in subsection (4) to the functions carried out in relation to a company by a director of the company includes any functions which he does not carry out but which have been entrusted to him.

(6)  For the purposes of this section a company goes into insolvent liquidation if it goes into liquidation at a time when its assets are insufficient for the payment of its debts and other liabilities and the expenses of the winding up.

(6A)  For the purposes of this section a company enters insolvent administration if it enters administration at a time when its assets are insufficient for the payment of its debts and other liabilities and the expenses of the administration.

(7)  In this section "director" includes a shadow director.

(8)  This section is without prejudice to section 213.

**Amendments**—Small Business, Enterprise and Employment Act 2015, s 117(1), (3).

**CIGA 2020**—This provision is affected by temporary measures at s 12(1) of CIGA 2020.

**General note**—The provision fails to specify what action will cause a director to breach it. Claims by liquidators have apparently not been plentiful and those liquidators taking proceedings have struggled to obtain judgments: see notably *Re Continental Assurance Co of London plc* [2001] BPIR 733; *The Liquidator of Marini Ltd v Dickensen* [2003] EWHC 334 (Ch). Rarely, it seems, if at all, where directors have made an effort to understand the position of their company, and where they decided to continue doing business, will they be held liable: *Re Sherborne Associates Ltd* [1995] BCC 40; *Re Continental Assurance Co of London plc*. The courts do not appear readily to impose liability on directors, and this is particularly so where the directors have sought and obtained advice from professionals. In most cases where directors have been found liable they have been found to have acted irresponsibly.

This section was introduced to stop directors from continuing to trade while their companies are on a slide into insolvency and to allow a liquidator to recoup the loss to the company caused by the actions of the directors, so as to benefit the creditors as a whole: *Re Purpoint Ltd* [1991] BCLC 491 at 499, but it has been made clear that liability is not imposed on the directors necessarily where they knew or ought to have known that the company was insolvent; it is only where the directors knew or ought to have concluded that the company could not avoid entering insolvent liquidation: *Re Hawkes Hill Publishing Co Ltd (in liq)* [2007] BPIR 1305 at [28].

Since 1 October 2015 administrators have also been given the power to claim against directors for wrongful trading. See s 246ZB.

Claims are able to be made against a director's estate in the event of his or her death: *Re Sherborne Associates Ltd* [1995] BCC 40 at 46. Where there are a number of directors, their liability is several, requiring each director's position to be considered separately and the payment by one director does not automatically discharge the other director(s): *Re Continental Assurance Co of London plc* [2001] BPIR 733 at 846–848. Nevertheless, the court has the discretion of ordering that the liability of any two or more directors is joint and several for the whole or part of the contribution that the court orders to be paid (*Re Continental Assurance Co of London plc* at 847). The courts in *Re Produce Marketing Marketing Consortium Ltd* [1989] 1 WLR 745, [1989] BCLC 520 and *Re DKG Contractors Ltd* [1990] BCC 903 at 912 held that the directors were jointly and severally liable.

Claims under s 214 against foreign directors of a foreign company that is being wound up in England or Wales can be commenced (*Re Howard Holdings Inc* [1998] BCC 549 at 552; *Stocznia Gdanska SA v Latreefers Inc (No 2)*, [2001] 2 BCLC 116 at 142, CA) but, in assessing the claims, courts must have regard for the relevant foreign law under which the directors were acting and what obligations a director had to minimise losses to the company's creditors under that law, and it might well be that if the foreign law did not impose obligations akin to s 214, the English court will decide that it is not appropriate to make an order under s 214 (*Re Howard Holdings Inc* at 554).

Once liquidators were not permitted to assign actions under s 214 because they were actions given by statute to them personally in the position of liquidator: *Re Oasis Merchandising Services Ltd* [1995] BCC 911, affirmed on appeal [1997] 1 All ER 1009, [1997] BCC 282, CA. However, now liquidators are specifically permitted to do so, by s 246ZD(2)(b).

Liability for wrongful trading might be the basis for a court making a disqualification order against the director concerned (Company Directors' Disqualification Act 1986, s 10): eg *Re Brian D Pierson (Contractors) Ltd* [2001] 1 BCLC 275, [1999] BPIR 18. It has been held that an application under s 214 may be consolidated with disqualification proceedings: *Official Receiver v Doshi* [2001] 2 BCLC 235.

Applications for summary judgment may be dealt with in relation to a claim under s 214: *Re Bangla Television Ltd (in liq)* [2009] EWHC 1632 (Ch).

Section 12 of the Corporate Insolvency and Governance Act 2020 has as its heading 'Suspension of liability for wrongful trading' and this was to be for a period, namely from 1 March 2020 until 30 September 2020. This, however, did not suspend the wrongful trading provision or liability under it. The Act actually provided in s 12(1) that a court is to assume that a director is not responsible for the worsening of a company's financial position or that of the company's creditors during this period. This 'suspension' did not apply if the company concerned was excluded from being eligible by any of the paragraphs of Sch ZA1 to the Insolvency Act 1986 listed in para (4). A further suspension of liability for the period from 26 November 2020 until 30 April 2021 was subsequently introduced, namely in reg 2 of the Corporate Insolvency and Governance Act 2020 (Coronavirus) (Suspension of Liability for Wrongful Trading and Extension of the Relevant Period) Regulations 2020 (SI 2020/1349). This left a period of about two months (30 September to 26 November 2020) where the suspension does not apply. On 21 March 2021 the Government in reg 2 of The Corporate Insolvency and Governance Act 2020 (Coronavirus) (Extension of the Relevant Period) Regulations 2021 (SI 2021/375) further extended the suspension of liability for wrongful trading to 30 June 2021. Unlike the early regulations which amended the Corporate Insolvency and Governance Act 2020 in relation to director liability under s 214, there was no inclusion of a provision that said that suspension did not apply if the company concerned was excluded from being eligible by any of the paragraphs of Sch ZA1 to the Insolvency Act 1986.

'**Contribution**'—The provision does not specify what a miscreant director is to pay; it is left to the court's discretion: *Re Produce Marketing Consortium Ltd* [1989] BCLC 520, [1989] BCLC 520. However, in relation to s 213, the Court of Appeal, when dealing with the same wording as in s 214(1), has said that the contribution to the assets to be shared amongst the creditors should reflect the loss which has been caused to the creditors by the carrying on of the business in the way that gives rise to the exercise of the power (*Morphites v Bernasconi* [2003] EWCA Civ 289, [2003] Ch 552, [2003] 2 WLR 1521, [2003] 2 BCLC 53, [2003] BPIR 973 at [55]; also see, *Re Purpoint Ltd* [1991] BCLC 491), and this appears to limit the discretion of judges, certainly when it comes to ascertaining loss. In an earlier case, while accepting that the contributions should be the amount by which the company's assets can be regarded as being depleted by the wrongful trading of the directors, the court seemed to leave open the possibility of being able to take into account the fact that a director was culpable, with the result that courts may treat directors who have been reckless more harshly than those who have acted honestly, and perhaps naively: *Re Produce Marketing Consortium Ltd* [1989] 1 WLR 745, [1989] BCLC 520. The Court of Appeal in *Morphites v Bernasconi* rejected any notion of providing for a penal award, and this does accord with the opinion of Knox J in *Re Produce Marketing Consortium Ltd* ([1989] BCLC 520 at 597) when he was dealing with s 214.

If liability is established the court must, where two or more directors have been sued, determine how much each ought to contribute individually (*Re Continental Assurance Co of London Plc* [2001] BPIR 733 at [385]). The court may in its discretion order that the directors be 'jointly and severally liable for the whole or part of whatever sum the court thinks fit to require to be contributed to the company's assets'. (at [385]). Thus, a judge can order various respondents to a liquidator's claim to pay different amounts, depending on their position, knowledge and experience (*Re Continental Assurance* at 847; *Paton, as liquidator of Ricky Martin (Racing) Limited v Kelly Martin, Elizabeth Martin, Richard John Martin* [2016] SC AIR 57.

As with s 213, courts cannot make orders in favour of particular creditors, as the objective is to benefit all of the creditors of the company: *Re Purpoint Ltd* [1991] BCLC 491 at 499. The contribution ordered to be paid by errant directors must be distributed according to the statutory scheme (pari passu after allowing for preferential creditors) among the general body of unsecured creditors and that points to the fact that the provision's purpose is not to benefit creditors differentially depending on the nature of their loss caused by the wrongful trading: *Re Ralls Builders Ltd* [2016] EWHC 243 (Ch) at [236].

Liquidators are entitled to accept property other than money from directors when the latter seek to satisfy any award against them: *Re Farmizer (Products) Ltd* [1997] 1 BCLC 589, CA.

A transfer of assets at an undervalue could constitute the basis for a contribution by the directors: *Re Bangla Television Ltd (in liq)* [2009] EWHC 1632 (Ch). In this case the directors had effected a transfer at an undervalue and the judge held that the value of the property transferred represented an increase in the net deficiency of the company's assets.

Where a claim is made pursuant to both s 212 and s 214 (which is permissible (*Re Brian D Pierson (Contractors) Ltd* [2001] BCLC 275, [1999] BPIR 18), there was no injustice in ordering payments under both provisions, provided that the liquidator did not recover more than was required to satisfy the liabilities of the company: *Re Purpoint Ltd* [1991] BCLC 491.

## SECTION 214(2)

'**At some time**'—It has been said that liquidators must nominate a point of time from which to argue that the director knew or ought to have concluded that there was no reasonable prospect of the company avoiding going into insolvent liquidation. Liquidators must stand by the date nominated and are not able to argue for wrongful trading in respect of other dates, as that would be regarded as being unfair: *Re Sherborne Associates Ltd* [1995] BCC 40 at 42. But the court appears to be able to impose its own starting point for wrongful trading: *Re Purpoint Ltd* [1991] BCLC 491. In *Re Brian D Pierson (Contractors) Ltd* [2001] BCLC 275 at 302–303 Hazel Williamson QC (sitting as a deputy High Court judge), while not disagreeing with the viewpoint expressed in *Re Sherborne Associates*, appeared to take the view that she would not rule against a liquidator being able to point to events that establish liability around about the date that has been pleaded. In *Official Receiver v Doshi* [2001] 2 BCLC 235 at 281 Hart J held that the respondent was engaging in wrongful trading from November 1992, and the fact that the liquidator had alleged that the trading had commenced on February 1992 did not seem to matter. Liquidators are not permitted to amend the date relied on if permission is sought late in the day: *Re Langreen Ltd* (unreported, 21 October 2011, ChD, Registrar Derrett). Courts do not seem to have had any concern about liquidators nominating dates in the alternative (*Roberts v Frohlich* [2011] EWHC 257 (Ch), [2011] 2 BCLC 635; *Re Kudos Business Solutions* [2011] EWHC 1436 (Ch) at [53])). Furthermore dates can be estimates. For instance, in *Roberts v Frohlich* the case pleaded was that the wrongful trading occurred 'around 1 July 2004 (or alternatively on or around 1 September 2004)' ([6]). In this case the judge found that wrongful trading had occurred by 14 September and allowed the liquidator's claim. In *Brooks v Armstrong* [2015] EWHC 2289 (Ch), [2016] BPIR 272 and applying *Re Continental Assurance*, it was said that liquidators did not always have to specify an actual date, although to do so was useful, and a case would not fail simply because a specific date was not mentioned (while the decision in *Brooks v Armstrong* was partly reversed on appeal, this view was not criticised ([2016] EWHC 2893 (Ch)).

See A Keay 'Wrongful Trading and the Point of Liability' (2006) 19 *Insolvency Intelligence* 132.

**Tests for determining liability**—Section 214(2) provides the conditions for liability. Then subsection (4) indicates how the former subsection must be interpreted and it provides for both objective and subjective tests. First, the provision sets out an objective test in that the facts that a director ought to know or ascertain, the conclusions which ought to be reached and the steps which the director ought to take are those that a reasonably diligent person would take or have taken. Then there is a subjective element concerning the general knowledge, skill and experience that may reasonably be expected of a person who carries out the same functions as are carried out by the respondent director, and, in addition, whether that person has the general knowledge, skill and experience that the respondent director has. This two-limb criterion makes life tougher for directors. For if a director is not very experienced or has qualities that do not match that of the reasonable person, he or she is not able to take advantage of that, and be protected from liability. The director will fall below that expected of the reasonable director: eg *Re DKG Contractors Ltd* [1990] BCC 903. Conversely, if an experienced and well-qualified director were to meet the standard of a reasonable person carrying out his or her functions in relation to the company, but failed to act in such a way as one would expect of someone with his or her knowledge, skill and experience, the director could be held liable under s 214.

When assessing whether a director knew or ought to have concluded that there was no reasonable prospect of avoiding insolvent liquidation, courts are not limited to taking into account the material available to the director during the time when wrongful trading is alleged to have occurred, because the court can refer to material that was able to be accessed by a person exercising reasonable diligence and an appropriate level of general knowledge: *Re Produce Marketing Consortium Ltd* [1989] 1 WLR 745, [1989] BCLC 520. Where a director performs a specialist function, such as finance director, the special skills expected of a person discharging the duties of that post are expected of the director concerned: *Re Brian D Pierson (Contractors) Ltd* [2001] BCLC 275 at 309. Courts may factor into their assessment the kind of company managed by the director, as well as the type of business in which it was involved: *Re Produce Marketing Consortium Ltd; Re Sherborne Associates Ltd* [1995] BCC 40 at 54; *Re Brian D Pierson (Contractors) Ltd* [2001] BCLC 275. Courts are careful, in assessing whether a director is liable, not to place undue emphasis on hindsight and assume that what in fact occurred was always bound to happen and was apparent to the director: *Re Sherborne Associates Ltd* [1995] BCC 40 at 54; *Re Brian D Pierson (Contractors) Ltd* [2001] BCLC 275 at 303; *Re Ralls Builders Ltd* [2016] EWHC 243 (Ch) at [173], [216].

Recent indications have been that where a company is in financial difficulty and the directors have a difficult decision as to whether they trade on or close down the company and go into liquidation, the courts will take note of the fact that the directors can be in a real and unenviable dilemma: *Re Continental Assurance Co of London plc* [2001] BPIR 733. The court will also take into account the fact that the directors have taken appropriate professional advice: *Re Hawkes Hill Publishing Co Ltd* [2007] BPIR 1305 at [45]; *Re Ralls Builders Ltd* [2016] EWHC 243 (Ch) at [176], [206].

The court had to judge objectively whether there was at the point of the alleged wrongful trading no reasonable prospect that the company would avoid insolvent liquidation: *Singla v Hedman* [2010] EWHC 902 (Ch), [2010] 2 BCLC 61.

Directors will not be able to escape liability if they acted with blind optimism: *Roberts v Frohlich* [2011] EWHC 257 (Ch), [2011] 2 BCLC 625 at [112].

It has been emphasised that the fact that a company is insolvent and the directors know that, does not mean that they will be liable: *Re Hawkes Hill Publishing Co Ltd* [2007] BPIR 1305, for the directors might properly take the view that in the interests of the company and creditors that the company could trade out of its problems (*Re C S Holidays Ltd* [1997] 1 WLR 407 at 414), but the fact that the company is hopelessly insolvent and the directors know that might be an important factor: *Re Bangla Television Ltd (in liq)* [2009] EWHC 1632 (Ch). The fact that continued trading might be expected to be profitable for the company does not mean that the directors ought not to have concluded that the company could avoid insolvent liquidation: *Re Ralls Builders Ltd* [2016] EWHC 243 (Ch) at [186]. The court in this case also indicated that it does not necessarily follow that directors should be required to make a contribution to the company's assets if they ought to have concluded that there was no reasonable prospect of the company avoiding insolvent liquidation (at [219]).

**'Insolvent liquidation'**—This is defined in terms of the balance sheet test. See comments under 'Value of assets less than liabilities' in relation to s 123.

'Director'—Only directors may be the subject of proceedings, although subsection (7) makes it plain that this includes shadow directors. But it has been held that liability may extend to de facto directors as well as de jure and shadow directors: *Re Hydrodan (Corby) Ltd* [1994] 2 BCLC 180. An insolvency practitioner who advised directors before their company entered liquidation could not be under a common liability with the directors in relation to proceedings brought against the directors (*Re International Championship Management Ltd* [2006] EWHC 768 (Ch)).

'Every step'—As part of a defence to an action under s 214, a director has to establish that he or she took every step with a view to minimising creditor losses. The phrase 'every step' is not defined in any shape or form and one cannot really ascertain what is meant by the phrase from the surrounding provisions. It is difficult for a director to know what every step is, and when he or she has completed taking all of the steps necessary. The extreme measure of entering liquidation cannot be taken by a single director of a multiple director board (*Re Instrumentation Electrical Services Ltd* [1988] BCLC 550), so a concerned director has to convince a majority of directors that liquidation is the appropriate avenue to go down. In *Re Continental Assurance*, Park J was impressed with the fact that the directors 'reduced the scale of trading to minimal and cautious levels', and eventually ceased trading when they were advised that their company was insolvent (at 769). In contrast in *Re Idessa (UK) Ltd* [2011] EWHC 804 (Ch), [2011] BPIR 957 the directors failed in their defence as they had not 'tightened the corporate belt' or encouraged cost savings or done anything differently despite the company's state (at [120]). If directors can demonstrate that they took every step etc, they avoid liability even if they do not actually succeed in minimising the potential loss to the creditors: *Re Ralls Builders Ltd* [2016] EWHC 243 (Ch) at [244].

'Every step' was intended to cover specific steps taken by directors with a view to preserving or realising assets or claims for the benefit of creditors and did not apply to the act of wrongful trading itself, even if that action was undertaken with the intention of attempting to make a profit: *Re Brian D Pierson (Contractors) Ltd* [2001] BCLC 275.

The defence in s 214(3) has to be construed strictly, such that if the directors of a company decided to continue trading when they ought to have concluded that the company was bound for insolvent liquidation and they wish to make out the defence in s 214(3) then they must show that the continuation of trading was intended to reduce the net deficiency of the company and, in addition, it was designed to minimise the risk of loss to individual creditors: *Re Ralls Builders Ltd* [2016] EWHC 243 (Ch) at [245]. In *Brooks v Armstrong* [2016] EWHC 2893 (Ch)) it was made clear that losses suffered by individual creditors would not lead to liability for the defendant directors if there was not an increase in net deficiency. In *Re Ralls Builders Ltd.* Snowden J held that the directors' failure to take steps that ought to have been taken to protect the interests of new creditors (those holding debt incurred after the point when the directors had to take every step to minimise loss) meant that they were stopped from being able to rely on the defence (at [246]).

The liquidator does not have the burden of establishing that the directors failed to take every step: *Brooks v Armstrong* [2015] EWHC 2289 (Ch) at [7] (while this decision was partly reversed on appeal, this view was not criticised ([2016] EWHC 2893 (Ch)). The directors who are respondents to s 214 claims have the burden of establishing that they took every step, and they must establish their case on the balance of probabilities, but in this regard we must note that courts have cautioned against the use of hindsight (*Re Sherborne Associates Ltd* [1995] BCC 40 at 54; *Re Brian D Pierson (Contractors) Ltd* [2001] BCLC 275 at 303; *Brooks v Armstrong* [2015] EWHC 2289 (Ch), [2016] BPIR 272), and so a determination whether a director took every step should not be considered in light of later developments that could not be reasonably foreseen by directors.

The test as to whether a director has taken every step depends on courts considering what has been done in light of the criteria contained in s 214(4).

**Not carrying out functions**—Directors can be held liable for not carrying out functions that were entrusted to them (s 214(5)). So directors are responsible if they omit to do that which they should have done.

**Loss**—Although not deciding the issue, it has been assumed that it may not be necessary to prove a causal link between the wrongful trading established, and any particular loss: *Re Simmon Box (Diamonds) Ltd* [2001] 1 BCLC 176, CA. However, subsequently in *Re Continental Assurance Co of London plc* [2001] BPIR 733 at 844 Park J said that it was necessary to establish some connection between the wrongfulness of the directors' conduct with the company's losses which the liquidator seeks to recover. Snowden J in *Re Ralls Builders Ltd* [2016] EWHC 243 (Ch) at [242] said something similar, and his Lordship added that the directors should not be responsible for losses that the company would have incurred in any event as a result of the company entering a formal insolvency procedure. This is in line with the argument that counsel for the liquidator put in *Re Produce Marketing Consortium Ltd*, an argument that appeared to have been accepted by the judge in that case, namely that the test of liability is analogous to the assessment of tortious damages, being dependent on causation. Nevertheless, Park J in *Continental Assurance* said that more had to be established than mere nexus between an incorrect decision to carry on trading and a particular loss sustained by the company (at 844). Park J pointed out that the required nexus will often be obvious, such as where a director turns a blind eye to inherent loss-making (at 844). Not all losses suffered by a company after the directors wrongly decide to continue trading can necessarily be claimed by a liquidator: *Re Continental Assurance* at 844; *The Liquidator of Marini Ltd v Dickensen* [2003] EWHC 334 (Ch) at [68]. The law will limit liability to those consequences which are attributable to the wrongful action(s) (*Re Continental Assurance* at 845). The maximum that can be ordered against the director is not the loss to the company's creditors, but the loss to the company as a result of the liquidation being delayed: *Re Continental Assurance* at [297].

Liquidators are required to show that there was a net deficiency in company assets when comparing the company's position as at the time when wrongful trading is alleged to have commenced (and trading should have stopped or every step was taken to minimize creditors' loss) and the position when trading actually ceased (perhaps on the commencement of winding up); thus it had to be proven that there was an increase in the net deficiency (*Re Continental Assurance* at 844; *The Liquidator of Marini Ltd v Dickensen* at [68]; *Brooks v Armstrong* [2016] EWHC 2893 (Ch)). These cases focused attention on the loss to the company as a result of the time in which wrongful trading was carried on and this is the basis for the amount that directors are required to pay: *Re Ralls Builders Ltd* [206] EWHC 243 (Ch) at [240], [241].

The aim of s 214 is not 'to provide differential redress for individual creditors, depending upon an assessment of the extent of their loss caused by the period of wrongful trading.' (*Re Ralls Builders Ltd* [2016] EWHC 243 (Ch) at [236]).

Even if the liquidator can prove his or her case the court may decide not to award anything: *Nicholson v Fielding* [2017] All ER (D) 156 (Oct) at [110].

**Relief from liability**—It has been held that directors cannot be excused for wrongful trading under s 1157 of the Companies Act 2006 (formerly s 727 of the Companies Act 1985), which requires directors to have acted honestly and reasonably, as this defence is incompatible with the objective nature of the test found in s 214 (*Re Produce Marketing Consortium Ltd* [1989] 1 WLR 745, (1989) 5 BCC 399; *Re Brian D Pierson (Contractors) Ltd* [2001] BCLC 275), the test under s 1157 being essentially a subjective test (*Re Produce Marketing Consortium Ltd; Bairstow v Queens Moat Houses plc* [2000] BCC 1025). Quaere whether this is correct, as s 214 (as discussed earlier) involves both subjective and objective elements, as does s 1157. Perhaps it can be argued that s 214 and s 1157 are not incompatible after all. It is notable that in *Re D'Jan of London Ltd* [1994] 1 BCLC 561 Hoffmann LJ was prepared to relieve a director from liability for breach of the director's duty of care and skill, and the test for a breach of this duty was, according to his Lordship, the same as that found in s 214. The judge in *Re DKG Contractors Ltd* [1990] BCC 903 did not exclude possible relief for a director liable under s 214. Furthermore, in Australia it has been held that the Australian counterpart of s 1157 (Corporations Act, s 1318) is able to be relied upon by a director if he or she is found guilty of engaging in insolvent trading (broadly equivalent to wrongful trading): *Kenna & Brown Ltd v Kenna* (1999) 32 ACSR 430. But see the argument against the use of s 1157 mounted by Edmunds and Lowry ('The Continuing Value of Relief for Directors' Breach of Duty' (2003) 66 MLR 195 at 211).

**Beneficiaries of any award**—The award is to be held by a liquidator for the purpose of making a distribution to the unsecured creditors (*Re Oasis Merchandising Services Ltd* [1995] 2 BCLC 493, affirmed on appeal [1997] 1 All ER 1009, CA), and is therefore not available for a chargeholder.

**Directions**—If an order under s 214 is made, a court is, at its discretion, empowered to make further directions to give effect to its declaration. This is covered by s 215. See the comments attaching to that section.

**Limitation period**—Claims under the section are regarded as claims for the recovery of sums recoverable under any enactment, so the limitation period is 6 years (Limitation Act 1989, s 9(1)), and runs from the date when the company entered insolvent liquidation (*Re Farmizer (Products) Ltd* [1997] 1 BCLC 589, CA), namely either the date of the resolution to wind up or the date of the winding-up order. In any event, unreasonable delay in initiating proceedings by a liquidator could see the proceedings struck out (*Re Farmizer (Products) Ltd*).

See A Keay *Company Directors' Responsibilities to Creditors* (Routledge-Cavendish, 2007), chs 7–10.

## [1.273]

### 214A Adjustment of withdrawals

(1)   This section has effect in relation to a person who is or has been a member of a limited liability partnership where, in the course of the winding up of that limited liability partnership, it appears that subsection (2) of this section applies in relation to that person.

(2)   This subsection applies in relation to a person if—

    (a)   within the period of two years ending with the commencement of the winding up, he was a member of the limited liability partnership who withdrew property of the limited liability partnership, whether in the form of a share of profits, salary, repayment of or payment of interest on a loan to the limited liability partnership or any other withdrawal of property, and

(b)  it is proved by the liquidator to the satisfaction of the court that at the time of the withdrawal he knew or had reasonable ground for believing that the limited liability partnership—

(i)  was at the time of the withdrawal unable to pay its debts within the meaning of section 123, or

(ii)  would become so unable to pay its debts after the assets of the limited liability partnership had been depleted by that withdrawal taken together with all other withdrawals (if any) made by any members contemporaneously with that withdrawal or in contemplation when that withdrawal was made.

(3)  Where this section has effect in relation to any person the court, on the application of the liquidator, may declare that that person is to be liable to make such contribution (if any) to the limited liability partnership's assets as the court thinks proper.

(4)  The court shall not make a declaration in relation to any person the amount of which exceeds the aggregate of the amounts or values of all the withdrawals referred to in subsection (2) made by that person within the period of two years referred to in that subsection.

(5)  The court shall not make a declaration under this section with respect to any person unless that person knew or ought to have concluded that after each withdrawal referred to in subsection (2) there was no reasonable prospect that the limited liability partnership would avoid going into insolvent liquidation.

(6)  For the purposes of subsection (5) the facts which a member ought to know or ascertain and the conclusions which he ought to reach are those which would be known, ascertained, or reached by a reasonably diligent person having both—

(a)  the general knowledge, skill and experience that may reasonably be expected of a person carrying out the same functions as are carried out by that member in relation to the limited liability partnership, and

(b)  the general knowledge, skill and experience that that member has.

(7)  For the purposes of this section a limited liability partnership goes into insolvent liquidation if it goes into liquidation at a time when its assets are insufficient for the payment of its debts and other liabilities and the expenses of the winding up.

(8)  In this section "member" includes a shadow member.

(9)  This section is without prejudice to section 214.

**Amendments**—Inserted, in so far as it applies to limited liability partnerships, by SI 2001/1090.

**CIGA 2020**—This provision is affected by temporary measures at Sch 10, para 14 of CIGA 2020.

**General note**—While somewhat analogous to s 214 and including similar sub-parts, the provision does not provide for the same claim: *Re CJ and RA Eade LLP* [2019] EWHC 1673 (Ch), [2019] BPIR 1380. The principles as to the necessary knowledge a member must have to be liable including in relation to causation and compensation were the same as applying to s 214: *Re CJ and RA Eade LLP*. But a person might be held liable under s 214A if he or she had reasonable grounds for believing that the limited liability partnership was at the time of the withdrawal unable to pay its debts within the meaning of s 123, whereas the fact that a company is unable to pay its debts is not necessarily going to see a director held liable under s 214.

There are three limbs to the provision: (1) the respondent must have been a member of the LLP within the period of two years ending on the commencement of the winding up, and he or she withdrew property (which includes money) from the LLP during that period (ss 214A(1), 214A(2)(a)); (2) the court must be satisfied that at the time of each withdrawal the respondent knew or had reasonable grounds for believing that the LLP was unable to pay its debts within the meaning of s 123 (s 214A(2)(b)(i)); (3) the court shall not make a declaration that the respondent is liable to make such contribution unless the respondent knew or ought to have concluded that after each withdrawal of property there was no reasonable prospect that the LLP would avoid going into insolvent liquidation (s 214A(5)) (*Milne v Rashid* [2018] CSOH 23, [2018] 2 BCLC 673 at [11]–[13]).

**[1.274]**

### 215 Proceedings under ss 213–214

(1)   On the hearing of an application under section 213, or 214, the liquidator may himself give evidence or call witnesses.

(2)   Where under either section the court makes a declaration, it may give such further directions as it thinks proper for giving effect to the declaration; and in particular, the court may—

- (a)   provide for the liability of any person under the declaration to be a charge on any debt or obligation due from the company to him, or on any mortgage or charge or any interest in a mortgage or charge on assets of the company held by or vested in him, or any person on his behalf, or any person claiming as assignee from or through the person liable or any person acting on his behalf, and
- (b)   from time to time make such further order as may be necessary for enforcing any charge imposed under this subsection.

(3)   For the purposes of subsection (2), "assignee"—

- (a)   includes a person to whom or in whose favour, by the directions of the person made liable, the debt, obligation, mortgage or charge was created, issued or transferred or the interest created, but
- (b)   does not include an assignee for valuable consideration (not including consideration by way of marriage or the formation of a civil partnership) given in good faith and without notice of any of the matters on the ground of which the declaration is made.

(4)   Where the court makes a declaration under either section in relation to a person who is a creditor of the company, it may direct that the whole or any part of any debt owed by the company to that person and any interest thereon shall rank in priority after all other debts owed by the company and after any interest on those debts.

(5)   Sections 213 and 214 have effect notwithstanding that the person concerned may be criminally liable in respect of matters on the ground of which the declaration under the section is to be made.

**Amendments**—Civil Partnership Act 2004, s 261(1), Sch 27, para 112.

**General note**—Where a court makes a declaration in relation to either a s 213 or s 214 application, it is, at its discretion, empowered to make further directions to give effect to its declaration. This might even involve directing that any debt or obligation owed to the respondent by his or her company is to rank after the unsecured creditors and the payment of interest (s 215(4)). According to s 246ZC this provision applies to applications made by an administrator under either 246ZA or s 246ZB claiming that respondents are liable for wrongful trading or fraudulent trading respectively, and as if references to a liquidator were references to an administrator.

**[1.275]**

### 216 Restriction on re-use of company names

(1)   This section applies to a person where a company ("the liquidating company") has gone into insolvent liquidation on or after the appointed day and he was a director or shadow director of the company at any time in the period of 12 months, ending with the day before it went into liquidation.

(2)   For the purposes of this section, a name is a prohibited name in relation to such a person if—

- (a)   it is a name by which the liquidating company was known at any time in that period of 12 months, or
- (b)   it is a name which is so similar to a name falling within paragraph (a) as to suggest an association with that company.

(3)   Except with leave of the court or in such circumstances as may be prescribed, a person to whom this section applies shall not at any time in the period of 5 years beginning with the day on which the liquidating company went into liquidation—

- (a)   be a director of any other company that is known by a prohibited name, or

(b)     in any way, whether directly or indirectly, be concerned or take part in the promotion, formation or management of any such company, or

(c)     in any way, whether directly or indirectly, be concerned or take part in the carrying on of a business carried on (otherwise than by a company) under a prohibited name.

(4)   If a person acts in contravention of this section, he is liable to imprisonment or a fine, or both.

(5)   In subsection (3) "the court" means any court having jurisdiction to wind up companies; and on an application for leave under that subsection, the Secretary of State or the official receiver may appear and call the attention of the court to any matters which seem to him to be relevant.

(6)   References in this section, in relation to any time, to a name by which a company is known are to the name of the company at that time or to any name under which the company carries on business at that time.

(7)   For the purposes of this section a company goes into insolvent liquidation if it goes into liquidation at a time when its assets are insufficient for the payment of its debts and other liabilities and the expenses of the winding up.

(8)   In this section "company" includes a company which may be wound up under Part V of this Act.

**General note**—This provision is to be read with s 217 and rr 22.1–22.7 (*ESS Production Ltd (in administration) v Sully* [2005] EWCA Civ 554, [2005] 2 BCLC 547 at [2]; s 216(3)) and is designed to prevent the re-use of the name of a company that has entered insolvent liquidation, except where the leave of the court is secured or in certain limited circumstances. This action has been taken to thwart the use of the so-called 'Phoenix syndrome' (*Re Lightning Electrical Contractors Ltd* [1996] 2 BCLC 302), defined as where a company 'trading under a particular name goes into liquidation or receivership, leaving its creditors behind, and then a new company, with much the same name and all the same assets run by the same people, takes over but shorn of its previous creditors' (*Western Intelligence Ltd v KDO Label Printing Machines Ltd* [1998] BCC 472 at 473 per Jacob J). Chadwick LJ has said, in the Court of Appeal decision of *ESS Production Ltd (in administration) v Sully* [2005] EWCA Civ 554, [2005] 2 BCLC 547, [2005] BPIR 691 at [91] that there is no breach of the section where an active company had, before the liquidation of the liquidating company, a name that suggested association with the liquidating company.

The following is the scenario that the provision seeks to prevent. An unscrupulous person who has carried on business by way of a limited liability company that had substantial debts owed to unsecured creditors, and which fails and enters liquidation, carries on the business of the company through another company after, as often occurs, the second company acquires the original company's business as a going concern (as occurred in *ESS Production Ltd (in admin) v Sully*), often at an undervalue, with the new company effectively benefiting from the goodwill of the failed company. It must be emphasised though that while s 216 has Phoenix-type situations as its principal target: *First Independent Factors & Finance v Mountford* [2008] EWHC 835 (Ch), [2008] 2 BCLC 297 at [17], [26], it can apply where the Phoenix situation is not strictly relevant, and that some Phoenix scenarios are not necessarily wrong; it has been held that the section applies to both unscrupulous and honest traders: *First Independent Factors & Finance v Mountford* at [17]. Also there have been suggestions that the section could serve to protect shareholders as well as creditors. In *Re Neath Rugby Ltd; Hawkes v Cuddy* [2007] EWHC 1789 (Ch), [2008] 1 BCLC 527 at [93], it was said that the provision was quite wide in that it 'creates a free-standing criminal offence (in s 217). It concerns the management of companies and is designed to protect anyone who is interested in or has dealings with companies from those who act as directors of liquidating companies and then seek to carry on business through another corporate vehicle bearing the same or a similar name. The principal target of s 216 was the phoenix company: but the application of the section is not confined to the phoenix phenomenon.' The court went on to say that a breach of s 216 could form the basis for a successful petition under s 459 of the Companies Act 1985 (now s 994 of the Companies Act 2006) (on appeal the Court of Appeal did not criticise this approach concerning the section: *Cuddy v Hawkes* [2007] EWCA Civ 1072, [2007] BPIR 1217).

The critical issue is the use of a name that is prohibited and not that a company that is insolvent has transferred assets to another company (*Ricketts v Ad Valorem Factors Ltd* [2004] 1 BCLC 1, CA) or that the goodwill of an insolvent has been exploited: *Thorne v Silverleaf* [1994] BCLC 637 at 642–643, CA. There is no requirement, before holding that s 216 applies, that anyone must be misled by the use of the company name (*Ricketts* at [13], [16]). According to Etherton J in *Re Bowman Power Systems (UK) Ltd* (unreported, ChD, 27 October 2004), the provision was designed to prevent the danger of the insolvent company being acquired at an undervalue and the danger that creditors might be under the misapprehension that there had been no change in the original corporate vehicle. In dealing with any cases, it is critical that the purpose behind the section is kept in mind: *ESS Production Ltd (in administration) v Sully* [2005] EWCA Civ 554, [2005] 2 BCLC 547, [2005] BPIR 691at [91].

Notwithstanding the points made at the end of the last paragraph, one of the judges in the Court of Appeal in *Ricketts* (Simon Brown LJ) was of the view that 'Draconian consequences' of the section meant that courts should 'strive to avoid adopting a construction which penalises someone where the legislator's intention to do so is doubtful' (at [30]).

Details of any offence under this section should be reported by the liquidator to the Secretary of State for Business, Energy and Industrial Strategy and should include: evidence that the successor business is using the prohibited name in cases where this is not evident from records at Companies House; and any details of any sale of the liquidated company's assets or business by the liquidator in accordance with r 22.4 of the Rules (Dear IP Millennium Edition, December 2000, chapter 20).

While the provision can apply to limited liability partnerships it does not apply to ordinary partnerships: *Newton v Secretary of State for Business, Energy and Industrial Strategy* [2016] EWHC 3068 (Ch), [2018] 1 BCLC 285.

'Insolvent liquidation'—See the comments under this heading in relation to s 214.

### SECTION 216(2)

'A prohibited name in relation to such a person'—Section 216 only stops directors and shadow directors of the company in liquidation from using the name of the insolvent company. So a company's name may be re-used, but it must not involve someone who is a prohibited person, ie anyone mentioned in s 216 ('such a person').

Similar name—When determining whether a name of a company is similar to the name of another, the matter is one of fact for the court: *Archer Structures v Christopher Griffiths* [2003] EWHC 957 (Ch), [2003] BPIR 1071 at [15]. Courts will employ an objective test (*Archer Structures* at [18]). The test that is to be used in determining similarity of names is not whether members of the public believed that the company was the same as the one that was in liquidation, but whether the similarity between the two companies is such that it is probable that members of the public, when comparing the names in the appropriate context, would associate the two companies with one another. The impact of the names on a reasonable person in the relevant commercial field, taking into account the manner in which the names were employed, the kind of customers of the companies and the context in which they would do so as well as the sorts of businesses involved, are matters to be considered by courts: *Commissioners for HM Revenue and Customs v Walsh* [2005] EWHC 1304 (Ch), [2005] BPIR 1105, [2005] 2 BCLC 455 (the two companies involved were both building and civil engineering companies); *First Independent Factors & Finance v Mountford* [2008] EWHC 835 (Ch), [2008] 2 BCLC 297 at [18]. It has been held that the addition of words such as 'Contractors' and 'Construction' when used with company names with no other differences does not stop the company names being deemed to be similar (*Archer Structures* at [21]). Hence, where the name of the insolvent company was 'MPJ Construction Ltd', and its assets were transferred to a company with the name of 'MPJ Contractors Ltd', the person prohibited to act because of s 216 had to obtain leave to be involved in the latter company, as the names were similar (*Archer Structures* at [21]). Also see *Re Lightning Electrical Contractors Ltd* [1996] 2 BCLC 302.

It is not possible to circumvent the law in relation to a company in insolvent liquidation. This is confirmed by the Court of Appeal decision in *Ricketts v Ad Valorem Factors Ltd* [2004] 1 BCLC 1. In that case the names 'Air Component Co Ltd' and 'Air Equipment Co Ltd' were regarded as being similar for the purposes of the section. The former went into liquidation and, because the latter was a similar name to the former, it was a prohibited name in the context of s 216(2)(b). The court took into account the circumstances in which the names were actually used or likely to be used, namely the types of product in which they carried on business, the location of the businesses, the types of customers, and those who were involved in the operation of the businesses. In this case all of this suggested an association between the two companies, or that they were part of the same group of companies (at [22]); see *R v Richmond Magistrates' Court* [2008] EWHC 84 (Admin), [2008] 1 BCLC 681, [2008] BPIR 468) at [9].

If the court finds that two names are similar, then it has no discretion in relation to the personal liability of the director against whom proceedings are brought (*Ricketts* at [22]).

Leave of the court—If leave of the court is granted, a person who is ordinarily prohibited by the section from using the name, may do so: eg *Re Bonus Breaks Ltd* [1991] BCC 546; *Re Lightning Electrical Contractors Ltd* [1996] 2 BCLC 302. The court may grant leave subject to conditions. While some principles have been specified by the courts, each case must be taken on its own merits. The courts will, in deciding whether or not to grant leave, examine whether there is any risk to the creditors of the new company: *Penrose v Official Receiver* [1996] 1 WLR 482 at 490. Where there is an application for leave the court should not treat the applicant, without evidence of misconduct, as if the applicant were unfit to be a director, and it would be incorrect for a court to approach the application in the same way that it would with an application for leave under the Company

Directors' Disqualification Act 1986: *Re Lightning Electrical Contractors Ltd* [1996] 2 BCLC 302; *Penrose v Official Receiver* at 489. But if the court heard evidence on a s 216 application that indicated that the applicant was, because of his or her conduct relating to the affairs of the company in liquidation, unfit to be involved in the management of a company, then the court could exercise the discretion that it possesses in accordance with the principles that operate when the court is hearing applications for leave under s 17 of the Company Directors' Disqualification Act 1986 (*Penrose v Official Receiver* at 489).

To aid its deliberations concerning an application for leave, the court may ask the liquidator of the company to provide a report detailing the circumstances of the company's insolvency and the extent (if any) of the applicant's apparent responsibility for the insolvency (r 22.3). It is likely to enable the applicant under s 216 to obtain leave if the receiver or liquidator of the company whose name is being used supports the application: *Re Lightning Electrical Contractors Ltd* [1996] 2 BCLC 302.

Leave may well be granted to those involved in a company that enters insolvent liquidation to be directors of companies with prohibited names if they were not culpable in the failing of the company: *Re Bonus Breaks Ltd* [1991] BCC 546.

See rr 22.4–22.7 and the relevant notes for three situations where the prohibition in s 216 does not apply. These situations ensure that the disposal of company property in the ordinary course of business is not restricted.

### SECTION 216(3)(b)

'concerned or take part in the . . . management'—This is not defined, but from s 217(1)(b) and s 217(4) it would seem that it would mean being involved in the management of a company. See comments under 'Involved in the management' under s 217.

### SECTION 216(3)(c)

'Indirectly'—This is obviously designed to cover the case where a person runs a company by using others who appear, prima facie, to be running the company, but who are effectively puppets, or at least dependent on the prohibited person.

**Breach**—In a prosecution mens rea in relation to a breach does not have to be proved: *R v Cole* [1998] 2 BCLC 234. The offence under this provision is one of strict liability: *R v Doring* [2002] EWCA Crim 1695, [2002] BPIR 1204; *ESS Production Ltd (in administration) v Sully* [2005] EWCA Civ 554, [2005] 2 BCLC 547, [2005] BPIR 691.

Any breach of s 216 automatically makes the respondent liable under s 217: *Thorne v Silverleaf* [1994] 1 BCLC 637, CA. A breach of s 216 by a director may be taken into account by a court in considering an application for a disqualification order pursuant to the Company Directors' Disqualification Act 1986 on the basis that the director is unfit for office: *Re Migration Services International Ltd* [2000] 1 BCLC 666.

'carrying on of a business carried on (otherwise than by a company)'—this means that the section is not confined to the situation where the defendant has been involved in carrying on a business through a company. It might apply to where he or she was carrying on business as a sole trader or in partnership: *First Independent Factors & Finance v Mountford* [2008] EWHC 835 (Ch), [2008] 2 BCLC 297 at [20].

**Penalty**—As far as the criminal penalties are concerned, see s 430 and Sch 10 to the Act. The latter provides that the penalty is imprisonment for 2 years or a fine or both where the prosecution is on indictment, and where prosecutions are initiated summarily then the penalty is imprisonment for 6 months or a statutory maximum fine (the statutory maximum is £5,000 according to s 32 of the Magistrates' Courts Act 1980 as amended by s 17 of the Criminal Justice Act 1991).

The penalty for a breach of the section was considered in *R v Enver* (20 January 2000, CA (Crim Div)). The court reduced the fine of £10,000 to £5,000 because of the respondent's previous good character and the severe personal losses that he suffered. In contrast, the defendants in *R v McCredie* [2000] 2 BCLC 438, CA (Crim Div) were subjected to community service orders of 180 and 100 hours respectively.

If the magistrates hearing a case believe that their own power in sentencing a person under this provision is too limited, they may commit a person to the Crown Court for sentencing: *R v Chelmsford Justices ex parte Lloyd* (2000) *The Times*, December 5.

Where directors trade under a company name which was prohibited, they can be held liable under the Proceeds of Crime Act 2002 s.76(2). What they are liable for is not a proportion of the sum that could be attributed to the name of the company but the full amount that the director actually received in their role as directors: *R v Weintroub* [2011] EWCA Crim 2167.

### SECTION 216(6)

'a name by which a company is known'—This could mean the registered name of the company or any other name that the company carried on business with during the 12 months prior to liquidation, including a change of name during the relevant period: *ESS Production Ltd (in administration) v Sully* [2005] EWCA Civ 554, [2005] 2 BCLC 547, [2005] BPIR 691 at [68], [70].

The reference to 'any name' indicates that a company could have more than one name in the relevant period before liquidation (*ESS Production Ltd (in administration) v Sully* at [70]).

'**carries on business**'—This covers the case where a company carries on some of its business, but not necessarily all of it, under a prohibited name (*ESS Production Ltd (in administration) v Sully* [2005] EWCA Civ 554, [2005] 2 BCLC 547, [2005] BPIR 691at [72]).

'**Company**'—This can include an unregistered company that is wound up under Part V of the Act. This would include foreign companies.

See the comments relating to s 217 and rr 22.4–22.7.

## [1.276]

### 217 Personal liability for debts, following contravention of s 216

(1)  A person is personally responsible for all the relevant debts of a company if at any time—

> (a)  in contravention of section 216, he is involved in the management of the company, or
>
> (b)  as a person who is involved in the management of the company, he acts or is willing to act on instructions given (without the leave of the court) by a person whom he knows at that time to be in contravention in relation to the company of section 216.

(2)  Where a person is personally responsible under this section for the relevant debts of a company, he is jointly and severally liable in respect of those debts with the company and any other person who, whether under this section or otherwise, is so liable.

(3)  For the purposes of this section the relevant debts of a company are—

> (a)  in relation to a person who is personally responsible under paragraph (a) of subsection (1), such debts and other liabilities of the company as are incurred at a time when that person was involved in the management of the company, and
>
> (b)  in relation to a person who is personally responsible under paragraph (b) of that subsection, such debts and other liabilities of the company as are incurred at a time when that person was acting or was willing to act on instructions given as mentioned in that paragraph.

(4)  For the purposes of this section, a person is involved in the management of a company if he is a director of the company or if he is concerned, whether directly or indirectly, or takes part, in the management of the company.

(5)  For the purposes of this section a person who, as a person involved in the management of a company, has at any time acted on instructions given (without the leave of the court) by a person whom he knew at that time to be in contravention in relation to the company of section 216 is presumed, unless the contrary is shown, to have been willing at any time thereafter to act on any instructions given by that person.

(6)  In this section "company" includes a company which may be wound up under Part V.

**General note**— This provision is to be read with s 216 and rr 22.4–22.7: *ESS Production Ltd (in administration) v Sully* [2005] EWCA Civ 554, [2005] 2 BCLC 547, [2005] BPIR 691 at [2].

While the section is primarily invoked by creditors, it has been held that it is not so limited. It simply imposes a personal liability on a director or manager who was formerly a director of a liquidating company: *Re Neath Rugby Ltd; Hawkes v Cuddy* [2007] EWHC 1789 (Ch), [2008] 1 BCLC 527 at [93].

While only directors and shadow directors can be liable under s 216, the sister provision to s 217, any person involved in the management of a company and acting on the instructions of someone who he or she knows is acting in breach of s 216, may be held liable under s 217. This provision was included in order to provide a more effective deterrent than would be provided by criminal sanctions: *Thorne v Silverleaf* [1994] 2 BCLC 637.

To assist those proceeding under s 217, there is no need for a director to be found guilty of a breach of s 216 before proceedings can be initiated under s 217. What an applicant under s 217 has to establish is that two companies traded under similar names and that the respondent was a director of one of the companies, that had gone into insolvent liquidation, and was either a director, or involved in the management, of the other company, or acted on the instructions of someone whom he or she knew was liable under s 216: *Inland Revenue Commissioners v Nash* [2003] EWHC 686 (Ch), [2003] BPIR 1138. See notes accompanying s 216.

Even if a person deals with a company that he or she knows has a person who is in breach of s 216 involved in its management, he or she is entitled to recover against the director under s 217: *Thorne v Silverleaf* [1994] 1 BCLC 637.

The section does not specify who can initiate proceedings, and creditors have done so successfully: *Archer Structures v Christopher Griffiths* [2003] EWHC 957 (Ch), [2003] BPIR 1071.

In *City of Glasgow Council v Craig* [2008] CSOH 171, [2009] 1 BCLC 742 at [20] (Lord Glennie, Outer House of the Scottish Court of Session) it was said that a director is only liable for liabilities incurred by the company that has used the prohibited name while it is carrying on business using that name, and this does not mean that there is liability for all debts of the company, however incurred.

Where an application is made against a director for a confiscation order under the Proceeds of Crimes Act 2002 in relation to a breach of s 216, the director is liable for the sums that he or she has received in his or her capacity as a director, including salaries and dividends: *R v Weintroub* [2011] EWCA Crim 2167 at [8].

'Involved in the management'—This phrase is defined in s 217(4) and includes taking part in the management of a company. It is likely that it will encompass those acting in relation to the internal workings of the company and its external relations with others: *R v Austen* (1985) 1 BCC 99,528. Each case will have to be taken on its merits. If a person acts in the capacity of an adviser to the board of a company, this conduct has been regarded as sufficient to constitute taking part in the management of a company: *R v Campbell* (1984) 80 Cr App R 47, CA (Crim Div). The appeal court in *R v Campbell* approved of a distinction drawn by the trial judge between someone involved in the central direction of the company's affairs, which involved taking part in the management of the company, and managing particular aspects of the company's trading affairs, which did not constitute taking part in the management of the company (at 98). Certainly it is not necessary to have control of the company before one can be regarded as being involved in the management of the company: *Re Market Wizard Systems (UK) Ltd* [1998] 2 BCLC 282.

In the Australian case of *Commissioner for Corporate Affairs (Vic) v Bracht* (1989) 7 ACLC 40 (referred to in *Re Market Wizard Systems (UK) Ltd*) a person was charged with breaching the Companies Code of Victoria because he was, allegedly, taking part in the management of a company while an undischarged bankrupt (equivalent to s 11 of the Company Directors' Disqualification Act 1986). Ormiston J of the Victorian Supreme Court, following, inter alia, the English case of *R v Campbell* (above), said that the size of the company should be taken into account in considering what was meant by taking part in the management of a company (at 733–734). His Honour went on to say that the concept of 'taking part in the management of a company' should be construed widely, and would include activities involving some responsibility and participation in the decision-making processes of a company related to its business affairs, but need not involve directly communicating with the board (at 733–734, 735, 736). Taking part in management would neither encompass routine clerical or administrative duties associated with management, nor activities that did not involve any significant discretion or advisory role in decision-making (at 733).

Relevant debts—'Relevant debts' are defined widely in s 217(3) and include liabilities that are not debts in the strict sense of the term. So, a damages award against the company would qualify. As a consequence of the breadth of the expression 'relevant debts' a person liable under s 217 may be liable for claims in damages, and the person is not simply liable for all debts incurred by him or her during the relevant time. Only debts that are incurred under a prohibited name (and where there is a breach of the section) are to be categorised as relevant for the purposes of the section: *ESS Production Ltd (in administration) v Sully* [2005] EWCA Civ 554, [2005] 2 BCLC 547, [2005] BPIR 691 at [75].

'A person . . . has at any time acted on instructions'—Section 217(5) provides that if a person who has been involved in the management of a company and acted at any time on instructions from someone whom he or she knew to be in breach of s 216, then he or she is presumed to have been willing at any time to act on any instructions given by the person in breach of s 216. Consequently, if it is established at one point of time that a person is willing to act on instructions from a person who breached s 216, a continuing presumption prevails that he or she is willing to act on instructions. The presumption can be rebutted.

Relief from liability—Arden LJ in *ESS Production Ltd (in administration) v Sully* [2005] EWCA Civ 554, [2005] 2 BCLC 547, [2005] BPIR 691 at [20] left unresolved whether a director might be able to be relieved from liability under s 1157 of the Companies Act 2006 (formerly s 727 of the Companies Act 1985) where he or she has acted scrupulously. But more recently Lewison J in *First Independent Factors & Finance v Mountford* [2008] EWHC 835 (Ch), [2008] 2 BCLC 297 at [33] has said that where a person is found liable under the section a court cannot give relief under s 1157 for the relieving provision is not available where a stranger is bringing proceedings (as against the situation where proceedings are brought by the company itself or someone acting for the company, such as a liquidator).

See Werner 'Phoenixing: Avoiding the Ashes' (2009) 22 Ins Intel 105.

*Investigation and prosecution of malpractice*

[1.277]

### 218 Prosecution of delinquent officers and members of company

(1) If it appears to the court in the course of a winding up by the court that any past or present officer, or any member, of the company has been guilty of any offence in relation to the company for which he is criminally liable, the court may (either on the application of a person interested in the winding up or of its own motion) direct the liquidator to refer the matter—

    (a)    in the case of a winding up in England and Wales, to the Secretary of State, and

    (b)    in the case of a winding up in Scotland, to the Lord Advocate.

(2)   . . .

(3) If in the case of a winding up by the court in England and Wales it appears to the liquidator, not being the official receiver, that any past or present officer of the company, or any member of it, has been guilty of an offence in relation to the company for which he is criminally liable, the liquidator shall report the matter to the official receiver.

(4) If it appears to the liquidator in the course of a voluntary winding up that any past or present officer of the company, or any member of it, has been guilty of an offence in relation to the company for which he is criminally liable, he shall forthwith report the matter—

    (a)    in the case of a winding up in England and Wales, to the Secretary of State, and

    (b)    in the case of a winding up in Scotland, to the Lord Advocate,

and shall furnish to the Secretary of State or (as the case may be) the Lord Advocate such information and give to him such access to and facilities for inspecting and taking copies of documents (being information or documents in the possession or under the control of the liquidator and relating to the matter in question) as the Secretary of State or (as the case may be) the Lord Advocate requires.

(5) Where a report is made to the Secretary of State under subsection (4) he may, for the purpose of investigating the matter reported to him and such other matters relating to the affairs of the company as appear to him to require investigation, exercise any of the powers which are exercisable by inspectors appointed under section 431 or 432 of the Companies Act 1985 to investigate a company's affairs.

(6) If it appears to the court in the course of a voluntary winding up that—

    (a)    any past or present officer of the company, or any member of it, has been guilty as above-mentioned, and

    (b)    no report with respect to the matter has been made by the liquidator under subsection (4),

the court may (on the application of any person interested in the winding up or of its own motion) direct the liquidator to make such a report.

On a report being made accordingly, this section has effect as though the report had been made in pursuance of subsection (4).

**Amendments**—Insolvency Act 2000, ss 10(1)–(6), 15(1), Sch 5; SI 2009/1941.

**General note**—The provision is not exhaustive and does not deal with assisting criminal investigators and prosecutors who might seek assistance from liquidators and official receivers: *R v Brady* [2004] EWCA Crim 1763, [2004] 1 WLR 3240, [2004] 3 All ER 520, [2004] BPIR 962.

**Official receiver**—If the official receiver obtains information pursuant to s 218(3), he or she is entitled to pass that on to the relevant prosecuting authority: *Re Arrows Ltd (No 4)* [1995] 2 AC 75, [1994] 3 WLR 656, [1994] 3 All ER 814, [1994] 2 BCLC 738, HL; *R v Brady* [2004] EWCA Crim 1763, [2004] 1 WLR 3240, [2004] 3 All ER 520, [2004] BPIR 962. The Court of Appeal has specifically held that the official receiver has the power to disclose any information gleaned under s 235 to the Inland Revenue if it was otherwise lawful and this information could be used to prosecute under this provision (*R v Brady*).

**References to the Secretary of State**—The powers given to the Secretary of State by s 218(5) to investigate, are wide and not restricted to undertaking inquiries related to criminal activity. Investigations are to be conducted in private, and information disclosed is not to be made public (*Re an Inquiry into Mirror Group Newspapers plc* [2000] Ch 194, [1999] 3 WLR 583, [1999] 2 All ER 641, [1999] 1 BCLC 690).

## [1.278]

### 219 Obligations arising under s 218

(1)   For the purpose of an investigation by the Secretary of State in consequence of a report made to him under section 218(4), any obligation imposed on a person by any provision of the Companies Act 1985 to produce documents or give information to, or otherwise to assist, inspectors appointed as mentioned in section 218(5) is to be regarded as an obligation similarly to assist the Secretary of State in his investigation.

(2)   An answer given by a person to a question put to him in exercise of the powers conferred by section 218(5) may be used in evidence against him.

(2A)   However, in criminal proceedings in which that person is charged with an offence to which this subsection applies—

    (a)   no evidence relating to the answer may be adduced, and

    (b)   no question relating to it may be asked,

by or on behalf of the prosecution, unless evidence relating to it is adduced, or a question relating to it is asked, in the proceedings by or on behalf of that person.

(2B)   Subsection (2A) applies to any offence other than—

    (a)   an offence under section 2 or 5 of the Perjury Act 1911 (false statements made on oath otherwise than in judicial proceedings or made otherwise than on oath), or

    (b)   an offence under section 44(1) or (2) of the Criminal Law (Consolidation) (Scotland) Act 1995 (false statements made on oath or otherwise than on oath).

(3)   Where criminal proceedings are instituted by the Director of Public Prosecutions, the Lord Advocate or the Secretary of State following any report or reference under section 218, it is the duty of the liquidator and every officer and agent of the company past and present (other than the defendant or defender) to give to the Director of Public Prosecutions, the Lord Advocate or the Secretary of State (as the case may be) all assistance in connection with the prosecution which he is reasonably able to give.

For this purpose "agent" includes any banker or solicitor of the company and any person employed by the company as auditor, whether that person is or is not an officer of the company.

(4)   If a person fails or neglects to give assistance in the manner required by subsection (3), the court may, on the application of the Director of Public Prosecutions, the Lord Advocate or the Secretary of State (as the case may be) direct the person to comply with that subsection; and if the application is made with respect to a liquidator, the court may (unless it appears that the failure or neglect to comply was due to the liquidator not having in his hands sufficient assets of the company to enable him to do so) direct that the costs shall be borne by the liquidator personally.

**Amendments**—Insolvency Act 2000, ss 10(1), (7), 11; SI 2009/1941.

**Use of evidence**—Answers given by those who are the subject of Secretary of State inquiries, may be used in subsequent civil proceedings, but not in criminal proceedings save in limited circumstances set out in s 219(2A). The bar to the use of answers in criminal proceedings would conform to the European Convention on Human Rights, which gives the right of a fair trial to people, and to ensure that this occurs they are not to be forced to give evidence that will incriminate themselves.

## PART V WINDING UP OF UNREGISTERED COMPANIES

[1.279]

**General comment on Part V**—This Part deals solely with the winding up of unregistered companies. While the term 'unregistered company' in relation to the power to wind up was originally aimed at dealing with the situation which existed in the mid-nineteenth century with some companies which had not registered pursuant to relevant companies legislation, the primary type of company to which the provisions have been applied are oversea companies, namely those that are not registered in this jurisdiction, but which have been carrying on business in Great Britain or have some other relevant connection with Great Britain: *Re Real Estate Development Co Ltd* [1991] BCLC 210. Other types that will be covered are unincorporated registered friendly societies and unincorporated building societies, as well as certain insolvent partnerships (see s 420 and arts 7 and 9 of the Insolvent Partnerships Order 1994 (SI 1994/2421).

Leaving aside oversea companies, the companies that have been wound up in the past under the precursor of this Part, are companies incorporated by special Acts of Parliament (*Re South London Fish Market* (1888) 39 ChD 324; *Re Barton-upon-Humber Water Co* (1889) 42 ChD 585) and companies incorporated by Royal Charter (*Re Oriental Bank Corporation* (1884) 28 ChD 634; *Re Bank of South Australia* [1895] 1 Ch 578).

Oversea companies are treated as unregistered companies for the purposes of British company law (see *Banco Nacional de Cuba v Cosmos Trading Corp* [2000] 1 BCLC 813 at 816–817, CA) and may be wound up by the courts of England and Wales, or Scotland. In winding up such companies, all of the provisions of the Act and the Companies Acts 1985 and 2006 relating to winding up apply to an unregistered company with the exceptions and additions mentioned in s 221.

In *Re International Tin Council* [1989] Ch 309, [1988] 3 WLR 1159, [1988] 3 All ER 257 the Court of Appeal held that English courts should not wind up a corporate body established by international treaty, as Parliament, in enacting the forerunner of s 221 (Companies Act 1985, s 665) could not have intended to subject the body to the winding-up jurisdiction of English courts.

[1.280]

### 220 Meaning of "unregistered company"

For the purposes of this Part "unregistered company" includes any association and any company, with the exception of a company registered under the Companies Act 2006 in any part of the United Kingdom.

**Amendments**—Substituted by SI 2009/1941.

**General note**—The provision defines the bodies that may be regarded as unregistered companies and wound up as such in England and Wales or Scotland.

The provision only applies to truly unregistered companies falling within the Unregistered Companies Regulations, SI 2009/2436 (see s 1043 of the Companies Act 2006 for the power to make provision in this regard): *Re National Union of Flint Glassworkers* [2006] BCC 828 at [12].

It has been held that the liquidators of a company that was registered overseas and liquidated in England as an unregistered company were able to continue to exercise their functions despite the fact that the company had been dissolved in the jurisdiction in which it had been registered: *Agrenco Madeira – Comercio Internacional LDA* [2015] BCC 300.

'**Association**'—In this context 'any' is not to be given its literal meaning, and so it is not without limit: *Re St James's Club* (1852) 2 De GM & G 383, 42 ER 920. Association is a word that has been held, in relation to earlier and different legislation, to refer only to associations which are conducted for profit or gain: see *Re St James's Club* and *Re International Tin Council* [1989] Ch 309, [1988] 3 WLR 115 (affirming [1987] 1 BCLC 272). In *Re Witney Town Football and Social Club* [1994] 2 BCLC 487 it was held that a club established solely for professional football was not an association and could not be wound up as an unregistered company within s 220. But it has been held that if a body was not an association it could be wound up by a court under its inherent jurisdiction: *Baker v West Reading Social Club* [2014] EWHC 3033 (Ch).

'**Company**'—This covers any company except for a company registered in any part of the United Kingdom under the Joint Stock Companies Act or under the legislation (past or present) relating to companies in Great Britain.

**[1.281]**

## 221 Winding up of unregistered companies

(1) Subject to the provisions of this Part, any unregistered company may be wound up under this Act; and all the provisions of this Act about winding up apply to an unregistered company with the exceptions and additions mentioned in the following subsections.

(2) If an unregistered company has a principal place of business situated in Northern Ireland, it shall not be wound up under this Part unless it has a principal place of business situated in England and Wales or Scotland, or in both England and Wales and Scotland.

(3) For the purpose of determining a court's winding-up jurisdiction, an unregistered company is deemed—

    (a)    to be registered in England and Wales or Scotland, according as its principal place of business is situated in England and Wales or Scotland, or

    (b)    if it has a principal place of business situated in both countries, to be registered in both countries;

and the principal place of business situated in that part of Great Britain in which proceedings are being instituted is, for all purposes of the winding up, deemed to be the registered office of the company.

(4) No unregistered company shall be wound up under this Act voluntarily, except in accordance with the EU Regulation.

(5) The circumstances in which an unregistered company may be wound up are as follows—

    (a)    if the company is dissolved, or has ceased to carry on business, or is carrying on business only for the purpose of winding up its affairs;

    (b)    if the company is unable to pay its debts;

    (c)    if the court is of opinion that it is just and equitable that the company should be wound up.

(6) . . .

(7) In Scotland, an unregistered company which the Court of Session has jurisdiction to wind up may be wound up by the court if there is subsisting a floating charge over property comprised in the company's property and undertaking, and the court is satisfied that the security of the creditor entitled to the benefit of the floating charge is in jeopardy.

For this purpose a creditor's security is deemed to be in jeopardy if the court is satisfied that events have occurred or are about to occur which render it unreasonable in the creditor's interests that the company should retain power to dispose of the property which is subject to the floating charge.

**Amendments**—Trustee Savings Banks Act 1985, ss 4(3), 7(3), Sch 4; SI 2002/1240; SI 2009/1941; SI 2017/702.

**CIGA 2020**—This provision is affected by temporary measures at Sch 10, paras 6(2), 6(3), 7(1)(a), 7(5)(a) and 8(1)(b) of CIGA 2020 and by the *Insolvency Practice Direction relating to the Corporate Insolvency and Governance Act 2020* [2020] BPIR 1207 (at Appendix 4 of this book).

**General note**—So as to ascertain the jurisdiction in which a company is to be wound up, an unregistered company is deemed to be registered in England and Wales or Scotland if its principal place of business is situated in either of those jurisdictions, or if it has a principal place of business in both jurisdictions (ie England and Wales as well as Scotland) and the principal place of business situated in that part of Great Britain in which proceedings are being instituted is, for all purposes of the winding up, deemed to be the registered office of the company (s 221(3)).

This section cannot be considered without taking into account the possible application of either the EU Regulation on Insolvency Proceedings or the Cross-Border Regulations 2006 applying Great Britain. Both of these pieces of legislation are set out later in the book with commentary, hence the commentary to this section does not discuss these legislative instruments in any great detail. Many of the comments provided have to be read subject to the aforementioned internationally focused legislation.

Much of the winding-up law that applies to registered companies applies equally to unregistered companies.

**Principal place of business in Northern Ireland**—A company that is an unregistered company in Northern Ireland cannot be wound up in England and Wales, unless it has its principal place of business in England and Wales (it might be wound up in Scotland if it has its principal place of business there): *Re Normandy Marketing Ltd* [1994] Ch 198, [1994] 2 WLR 438, [1994] 1 All ER 1007, [1994] 1 BCLC 565 (this case dealt with a company incorporated in Northern Ireland).

**Oversea companies**—As indicated in the introduction to this Part, s 221 is primarily used to wind up oversea companies. No definitive principles have been formulated as to when such companies will be wound up; it falls completely within the discretion of the courts. Where oversea companies can be wound up satisfactorily in their jurisdiction of incorporation, they will not usually be wound up in England and Wales: *Re Standard Contract and Debenture Corporation* (1892) 8 TLR 485; *Re Jarvis Conklin Mortgage Co* (1895) 11 TLR 373. Initially, the courts have to be satisfied that there is a sufficient connection between the company and the jurisdiction of England and Wales or Scotland before winding-up procedures can be set in train, as the company is essentially beyond the limits of its territory: *Re Real Estate Development Co Ltd* [1991] BCLC 210 at 217; *Stocznia Gdanska SA v Latreefers Inc (No 2)* [2001] 2 BCLC 116 at 140, CA. The connections with Great Britain that have been said to suffice are: a place of business (see *South India Shipping Corporation Ltd v The Export-Import Bank of Korea* [1985] 1 WLR 585); a branch office; assets within the jurisdiction (see *Banque des Marchands de Moscou (Koupetchesky) v Kindersley* [1951] Ch 112, [1950] 2 All ER 549; *Re Titan International Inc* [1998] 1 BCLC 102); the fact that if the company is wound up in England the employees of the foreign company would be entitled to receive statutory benefits on termination of their employment (*Re Eloc Electro-Optieck and Communicatie BV* [1982] Ch 43, [1981] 2 All ER 1111); and winding up in England would benefit creditors of the company: *Re a Company No 00359 of 1987*, [1987] 3 WLR 339, [1987] 3 All ER 137, [1987] BCLC 450, sub nom *International Westminster Bank plc v Okeanos Maritime Corporation* (the liquidator had claims under s 213 or s 214); *Re Paramount Airways Ltd* [1993] Ch 223 at 240, [1992] BCLC 710 at 722. In some cases, such as *Atlantic & General Investment Trust Ltd v Richbell Information Services Inc* [2000] 2 BCLC 778, the court will base its right to jurisdiction on a number of factors. In this case they were: the directors were resident in England; the company was part of a group consisting of English companies; the transaction that led to the bringing of the petition was arranged in England; the company conducted correspondence from a London address; there were assets in the UK. But just because a connection has been established, it does not necessarily mean that the English courts will accede to a petition for winding up: *Re Compania Merabello San Nicholas SA* [1973] Ch 75 at 86; *Stocznia Gdanska SA v Latreefers Inc (No 2)* [2001] 2 BCLC 116 at 140, CA. Any consideration now might well involve the court deciding where the company's centre of main interests is to be found, as required under the Cross-Border Regulations 2006 (GB).

While the presence of an asset in the jurisdiction might be a sufficient connection, in *Re OJSC ANK Yugraneft* [2008] EWHC 2614 (Ch) it was said that the fact that there was an asset within the jurisdiction to which the company laid claim was not automatically a reason for the court to exercise the winding-up jurisdiction. The asset might be so small or of such a character that the link with the jurisdiction said to be constituted by it was too tenuous to justify invoking the winding-up jurisdiction (at [58]). The asset must be one of substance and a valuable chose in action would qualify (at [41]).

If the connection with the jurisdiction is that there are assets within Great Britain, then the court must, before deciding whether to order winding up, consider whether there is any likelihood of the assets being administered by the courts of another jurisdiction: *Re Compania Merabello San Nicholas SA* [1973] Ch 75 at 86–87. This occurred in *New Hampshire Insurance Co v Rush & Tompkins Group plc* [1998] 2 BCLC 471, where the Court of Appeal refused to wind up two Dutch companies that were part of a group of companies which included English companies, all of which were being wound up compulsorily in the Netherlands.

There is nothing that requires the oversea company that is the subject of a winding-up petition ever to have had a place of business, or carried on business in England or Wales, nor to have had assets within the jurisdiction (*Re Real Estate Development Co Ltd* [1991] BCLC 210; *Re a Company No 00359 of 1987* [1988] Ch 210, [1987] 3 WLR 339, [1987] 3 All ER 137, [1987] BCLC 450, sub nom *International Westminster Bank plc v Okeanos Maritime Corporation*; *Stocznia Gdanska SA v Latreefers Inc (No 2)* [2001] 2 BCLC 116 at 140, CA), before a court will agree to order winding up: *Re Compania Merabello San Nicholas SA*. But besides requiring a sufficient connection with the jurisdiction, a court must be satisfied that making a winding-up order would benefit the petitioner (*Re Compania Merabello San Nicholas SA* [1973] Ch 75; *Re Latreefers Inc* [1999] 1 BCLC 271; *Banco Nacional de Cuba v Cosmos Trading Corp* [2000] 1 BCLC 813 at 817, CA), and that it is able to exercise jurisdiction over at least one person who has the right to share in the distribution of the company's assets: *Re Real Estate Development Co Ltd* [1991] BCLC 210.

In the situation where a foreign company has been dissolved in its home jurisdiction, it could be wound up in the UK: *Re Eurodis Electron Ltd plc* [2011] EWHC 1025 (Ch) at [22]. Where a company had been dissolved in its home jurisdiction the English courts will not make it a prerequisite for jurisdiction to wind up that the company had a branch or place of business in

Great Britain before its dissolution. In such a case it suffices if there are assets within the jurisdiction and there are creditors claiming debts owed by the company: *Banque des Marchands de Moscou (Koupetchesky) v Kindersley*.

In *Re Real Estate Development Co Ltd* Knox J laid down a three-fold test (affirmed by the Court of Appeal in *Banco Nacional de Cuba v Cosmos Trading Corp* [2000] 1 BCLC 813 at 817–818 and approved of in *Re OJSC ANK Yugraneft* [2008] EWHC 2614 (Ch) at [20] that must be satisfied for jurisdiction to exist. They are:

- a sufficient connection with England and Wales (which may include, though it is not necessary, the presence of assets within the jurisdiction);
- a reasonable possibility of benefiting those petitioning;
- one or more of the persons who would be recipients in a distribution of the company's assets had to be persons over whom the court had jurisdiction.

While it is not a requirement that assets must exist in the jurisdiction before English courts will make a winding-up order, it was said in the Court of Appeal in *Banco Nacional de Cuba v Cosmos Trading Corp* [2000] 1 BCLC 813 that the courts should hesitate before they subject foreign companies with no assets in the UK to being wound up here (at 819), and in fact caution should be shown where a company continues to trade in its place of incorporation and in other places in the world (at 819). It was said that making a winding-up order in such a situation would be 'thoroughly undesirable' (at 819).

The courts need to consider, when assessing a petition, whether there was a more appropriate jurisdiction then Britain in which a company should be wound up: *Re Buccament Bay Ltd* [2014] EWHC 4776 (Ch), [2015] 1 BCLC 646. Overall the courts, while having a broad discretion concerning whether to make a winding-up order or not, have proceeded cautiously, and on many occasions they have decided that it was more appropriate that the company be wound up in another jurisdiction: *Re a Company No 00359 of 1987* [1988] Ch 210, [1987] 3 WLR 339, [1987] 3 All ER 137, [1987] BCLC 450, sub nom *International Westminster Bank plc v Okeanos Maritime Corporation*; *Re a Company (No 003102 of 1991) ex parte Nyckeln Finance Co Ltd* [1991] BCLC 539; *Re Wallace Smith & Co Ltd* [1992] BCLC 970. With the existence of the EU Regulation on Insolvency Proceedings and the Cross-Border Regulations 2006, it is likely that this conclusion might be reached more often, at least certainly after considering where the centre of main interests of the company is.

A court has the power, where it decides to order winding up, to place conditions on the order, and this might include a provision that the winding up is to be conducted as ancillary to a main liquidation being conducted in another country: In *Re Commercial Bank of South Australia* (1886) 33 ChD 174 at 178; *Re Hibernian Merchants Ltd* [1958] Ch 76 at 80. But, of course, conditions might be inappropriate (*Re Hibernian Merchants Ltd*).

There is authority for the proposition that where the winding up of an oversea company is pending or proceeding in the place of its incorporation and base, it may be wound up in England and Wales: *Re Matheson Brothers* (1884) 27 ChD 225; *Re Commercial Bank of South Australia* (1886) 33 ChD 174; *Re Federal Bank of Australia* [1893] WN 77. However, now one must take into account the EU Regulation on Insolvency Proceedings in this regard, and in regard to all issues surrounding the winding up of companies that operate in Member States of the EU. The Regulation provides, in effect, that UK courts could make winding-up orders in relation to companies that have the centre of their main interests in the UK (Art 3(1)). An example, although addressing administration, is *Re Daisytek-Isa Ltd* [2004] BPIR 30, where the English courts were held to have jurisdiction because the company had its main centre of interests in England (Bradford). The decision was challenged in a French court, and while the French court held that Bradford was not the company's centre of main interests, on appeal a French appellate court reversed the earlier French decision and affirmed the decision of the English court: *Klempka v ISA* [2003] BCC 984 (CA of Versailles). It is likely that companies that have the centre of their main interests in the UK will have assets here. UK courts could not make winding-up orders in relation to companies that have the centre of their main interests in another Member State of the EU, even if they operate in the UK and have some connection with the jurisdiction, unless these companies possess establishments within the UK, and the UK proceedings may only affect the assets of the companies situated in the UK (Art 3(2)), whereby such proceedings in the UK would be secondary proceedings (Art 3(3)). Proceedings initiated pursuant to Art 3(2) (they will be territorial proceedings) in the UK will only be permitted in the event that proceedings cannot be opened in the Member State where the centre of the company's main interests is situated or where the opening of proceedings is requested by a creditor who has his domicile, habitual residence or registered office (if a company) in the UK where the debtor company has an establishment, or whose claim arises as a result of the operation of the establishment, such as incurring debts (Art 3(4)). It is emphasised that the Regulation only affects companies that have the centre of a company's main interests in the EU, but of course that could include companies that are incorporated outside of the Member States of the EU but conduct the substantial part of their business in one or more of the States of the EU. Nevertheless, the Regulation has the capacity to limit the number of occasions on which UK courts will assume jurisdiction and order the winding up of foreign companies. For further discussion of the Regulation and its impact, see the comments to the Regulation later in this volume.

For shareholder petitions for winding up, an extremely weighty factor, according to a recent Hong Kong decision (Court of Final Appeal) is the presence of the shareholders in the jurisdiction where the petition is presented: *Kam Leung Sui Kwan v Kam Kwan Lai* [2015] HKCFA 79, [2015] 6 HKC 644. The Court rejected the view that it would only exercise jurisdiction to wind up in very exceptional circumstances if the application was made by an aggrieved shareholder.

One must also take into account the Cross-Border Insolvency Regulations 2006 when considering the winding up of a foreign company that is registered in a non-EU Member State or in Denmark. If foreign insolvency proceedings have been opened then it would seem, because of art 28 of the Regulations, liquidation proceedings will not be permitted under s 221. But if no foreign insolvency proceedings have been instigated s 221 could be relied on.

**Voluntary winding up**—While the section provides in subsection (4) that unregistered companies cannot be wound up in voluntary liquidation, this has to be qualified, because they can be where the EU Regulation on Insolvency Proceedings applies. So companies that were, for instance, incorporated in a Member State of the EU and which have their centre of main interests in the UK will be able to wind up in voluntary liquidation here: *Re TXU Europe German Finance BV* [2005] BPIR 209. This decision also suggests that companies from outside of the EU may be wound up pursuant to the creditors' voluntary liquidation process in the UK, provided that the centre of their main interests is in the UK. This follows from the case of *Re BRAC Rent-a-car International Inc* [2003] EWHC 128 (Ch), [2003] 1 WLR 1421, [2003] 2 All ER 201, [2003] 1 BCLC 470, where a foreign non-EU company was made the subject of an administration order in England.

See s 97.

**Circumstance for winding up**—While including some of the grounds that permit the winding up of registered domestic companies, the number of grounds mentioned in subsection (5) is fewer. As for registered companies, the main ground will be that the company cannot pay its debts, ie insolvent.

See Dawson 'The Doctrine of Forum Non Conveniens and the Winding Up of Insolvent Foreign Companies' [2005] JBL 28.

## [1.282]

### 222 Inability to pay debts: unpaid creditor for £750 or more

(1) An unregistered company is deemed (for the purposes of section 221) unable to pay its debts if there is a creditor, by assignment or otherwise, to whom the company is indebted in a sum exceeding £750 then due and—

    (a)    the creditor has served on the company, by leaving at its principal place of business, or by delivering to the secretary or some director, manager or principal officer of the company, or by otherwise serving in such manner as the court may approve or direct, a written demand in the prescribed form requiring the company to pay the sum due, and

    (b)    the company has for 3 weeks after the service of the demand neglected to pay the sum or to secure or compound for it to the creditor's satisfaction.

(2) The money sum for the time being specified in subsection (1) is subject to increase or reduction by regulations under section 417 in Part XV; but no increase in the sum so specified affects any case in which the winding-up petition was presented before the coming into force of the increase.

**CIGA 2020**—This provision is affected by temporary measures at Sch 10, paras 1(2), 3(1), 6(1)(b) and 6(2) of CIGA 2020 and by the *Insolvency Practice Direction relating to the Corporate Insolvency and Governance Act 2020* [2020] BPIR 1207 (at Appendix 4 of this book).

**General note**—This provision, with some changes, replicates s 123(1)(a). Like s 123(1)(a) it allows for a company to be deemed to be unable to pay its debts. The provision, when it comes to service of the demand, provides for greater flexibility. For a discussion of the demand and the matters affecting service, see the comments applying to s 123.

As a temporary measure and to address the COVID-19 pandemic in 2020–2021, the government introduced specific provisions in the Corporate Insolvency and Governance Act 2020. If a creditor presents a petition for winding up under s 124 between 27 April 2020 and 30 September 2021 and the company is deemed unable to pay its debts on a ground specified in s 222 (as well as ss 223 or 224) and it appears to the court that coronavirus had a financial effect on the company before the presentation of the petition, the court may wind the company up under s 221(5)(b) on a ground specified in ss 222, 223 or 224(1)(a) to (c) only if the court is satisfied that the facts by reference to which that ground applies would have arisen even if coronavirus had not had a financial effect on the company. The court may wind the company up under s 221(5)(b) on the ground specified in s 224(1)(d) or (2) only if the court is satisfied that the ground would apply even if coronavirus had not had a financial effect on the company. No petition for the winding up of an unregistered company may be presented on the ground set out in s 222, where the demand referred to in the section was served during the relevant period: Sch 10, paras 1(2) and 6(1)–(3) of the Corporate Insolvency and Governance Act 2020 (as amended by Corporate Insolvency and Governance Act 2020 (Coronavirus) (Extension of the Relevant Period) Regulations 2020 (SI 2020/1031), reg 2, The Corporate Insolvency and Governance Act 2020 (Coronavirus) (Extension of the Relevant Period) (No 2) Regulations 2020 (SI 2020/1483), reg 2, The Corporate Insolvency and Governance Act 2020 (Coronavirus) (Extension of the Relevant Period) Regulations 2021 (SI 2021/375), reg 3(4) and The Corporate Insolvency and Governance Act 2020 (Coronavirus) (Extension of the Relevant Period) (No 2) Regulations 2021 (SI 2021/718), reg 2).

## [1.283]

### 223 Inability to pay debts: debt remaining unsatisfied after action brought

An unregistered company is deemed (for the purposes of section 221) unable to pay its debts if an action or other proceeding has been instituted against any member for any debt or demand due, or claimed to be due, from the company, or from him in his character of member, and—

(a) notice in writing of the institution of the action or proceeding has been served on the company by leaving it at the company's principal place of business (or by delivering it to the secretary, or some director, manager or principal officer of the company, or by otherwise serving it in such manner as the court may approve or direct), and

(b) the company has not within 3 weeks after service of the notice paid, secured or compounded for the debt or demand, or procured the action or proceeding to be stayed or sisted, or indemnified the defendant or defender to his reasonable satisfaction against the action or proceeding, and against all costs, damages and expenses to be incurred by him because of it.

**CIGA 2020**—This provision is affected by temporary measures at Sch 10, paras 3(1), 6(1)(b) and 6(2) of CIGA 2020 and by the *Insolvency Practice Direction relating to the Corporate Insolvency and Governance Act 2020* [2020] BPIR 1207 (at Appendix 4 of this book).

**General note**—This provision does not follow a corresponding provision applying to registered companies. It provides creditors of unregistered companies with greater flexibility in establishing the insolvency of a company.

See the note on s 222.

## [1.284]

### 224 Inability to pay debts: other cases

(1) An unregistered company is deemed (for purposes of section 221) unable to pay its debts—

(a) if in England and Wales execution or other process issued on a judgment, decree or order obtained in any court in favour of a creditor against the company, or any member of it as such, or any person authorised to be sued as nominal defendant on behalf of the company, is returned unsatisfied;

(b) if in Scotland the induciae of a charge for payment on an extract decree, or an extract registered bond, or an extract registered protest, have expired without payment being made;

(c) if in Northern Ireland a certificate of unenforceability has been granted in respect of any judgment, decree or order obtained as mentioned in paragraph (a);

(d) if it is otherwise proved to the satisfaction of the court that the company is unable to pay its debts as they fall due.

(2) An unregistered company is also deemed unable to pay its debts if it is proved to the satisfaction of the court that the value of the company's assets is less than the amount of its liabilities, taking into account its contingent and prospective liabilities.

**CIGA 2020**—This provision is affected by temporary measures at Sch 10, paras 3(1), 3(3), 6(1)(b), 6(2) and 6(3) of CIGA 2020 and by the *Insolvency Practice Direction relating to the Corporate Insolvency and Governance Act 2020* [2020] BPIR 1207 (at Appendix 4 of this book).

General note—This section brings into play the remaining bases in s 123 for deeming a company to be insolvent. See the comments accompanying that section.

Subsection (1) is broader than the corresponding provision in s 123 in that it permits execution against a person who represents the company to be considered.

See the note on s 222.

## [1.285]

### 225 Company incorporated outside Great Britain may be wound up though dissolved

(1) Where a company incorporated outside Great Britain which has been carrying on business in Great Britain ceases to carry on business in Great Britain, it may be wound up as an unregistered company under this Act, notwithstanding that it has been dissolved or otherwise ceased to exist as a company under or by virtue of the laws of the country under which it was incorporated.

(2) ...

Amendments—SI 2002/1240; SI 2009/1941; SI 2017/702; SI 2019/146, as from IP completion day (as defined in the European Union (Withdrawal Agreement) Act 2020, s 39(1)–(5)).

General note—This is an additional provision to s 221, which enables the court to exercise jurisdiction to wind up an oversea company. That provision permits the winding up of a company, while incorporated outside of Great Britain that has carried on business in Great Britain and has now ceased carrying on business, even though the company has been dissolved or otherwise ceased to exist as a company under the laws of the country where it was incorporated.

The power in this provision is more restricted compared with that found in s 221, and it is not as frequently invoked.

As with s 221, the provision is subject to the EU Regulation on Insolvency Proceedings. See the comments under 'Overseas companies' in relation to s 221 for further discussion of the function and operation of the Regulation.

## [1.286]

### 226 Contributories in winding up of unregistered company

(1) In the event of an unregistered company being wound up, every person is deemed a contributory who is liable to pay or contribute to the payment of any debt or liability of the company, or to pay or contribute to the payment of any sum for the adjustment of the rights of members among themselves, or to pay or contribute to the payment of the expenses of winding up the company.

(2) Every contributory is liable to contribute to the company's assets all sums due from him in respect of any such liability as is mentioned above.

(3) In the case of an unregistered company engaged in or formed for working mines within the stannaries, a past member is not liable to contribute to the assets if he has ceased to be a member for 2 years or more either before the mine ceased to be worked or before the date of the winding-up order.

(4) ...

Amendments—SI 2009/1941.

General note—This provision inserts provisions that correspond to those sections found elsewhere in the Act and relate to registered companies. It confirms the requirement of contributories to contribute to company funds in relation to what is outstanding on their shares, for instance.

Contributory—See the comments attached to s 79.

## [1.287]

### 227 Power of court to stay, sist or restrain proceedings

The provisions of this Part with respect to staying, sisting or restraining actions and proceedings against a company at any time after the presentation of a petition for winding up and before the making of a winding-up order extend, in the case of an unregistered company, where the application to stay, sist or restrain is presented by a creditor, to actions and proceedings against any contributory of the company.

General note—This provision causes provisions such as s 126 to apply to unregistered companies. See the notes accompanying that section.

**[1.288]**

### 228 Actions stayed on winding-up order

Where an order has been made for winding up an unregistered company, no action or proceeding shall be proceeded with or commenced against any contributory of the company in respect of any debt of the company, except by leave of the court, and subject to such terms as the court may impose.

General note—This provision corresponds to s 130(2) for registered companies. See the comments relating to that latter provision.

**[1.289]**

### 229 Provisions of this Part to be cumulative

(1)   The provisions of this Part with respect to unregistered companies are in addition to and not in restriction of any provisions in Part IV with respect to winding up companies by the court; and the court or liquidator may exercise any powers or do any act in the case of unregistered companies which might be exercised or done by it or him in winding up companies registered under the Companies Act 2006 in England and Wales or Scotland.

(2)   . . .

Amendments—SI 2009/1941.

General note—This provision makes it clear that provisions that apply to registered companies also can apply to unregistered companies and a liquidator is entitled to employ relevant provisions in his or her actions in the winding up of the company.

## PART VI   MISCELLANEOUS PROVISIONS APPLYING TO COMPANIES WHICH ARE INSOLVENT OR IN LIQUIDATION

**[1.290]**

Amendments—SI 2009/1941.

General comment on Part VI—This Part deals with miscellaneous provisions that are relevant to a company that is being administered pursuant to some formal insolvency regime or liquidation (if the company is not insolvent). While the provisions can be described as miscellaneous, there is very much of an emphasis on the function of office-holders. The majority of the Part focuses on provisions that can support the investigative work of office-holders as well as those that can assist in the recovery of money or property, namely the adjustment provisions (ss 238–246).

*Office-holders*

**[1.291]**

### 230 Holders of office to be qualified insolvency practitioners

(1)   . . .

(2)   Where an administrative receiver of a company is appointed, he must be a person who is so qualified.

(3)   Where a company goes into liquidation, the liquidator must be a person who is so qualified.

(4)   Where a provisional liquidator is appointed, he must be a person who is so qualified.

(5)   Subsections (3) and (4) are without prejudice to any enactment under which the official receiver is to be, or may be, liquidator or provisional liquidator.

Amendments—Enterprise Act 2002, ss 248(3), 278(2), Sch 17, paras 9, 19, Sch 26.

General note—This provision clearly states that those who act as different types of office-holders in relation to companies must be qualified to act, and the persons who are qualified are known as insolvency practitioners (see, s 388). If anyone does act as one of the office-holders mentioned in the section, and he or she is not qualified as an insolvency practitioner, that person is guilty of an offence pursuant to s 389. See the comments accompanying s 389.

It is notable that the nominee or supervisor of a company voluntary arrangement is omitted from the section, yet the person occupying this position must be qualified as an insolvency practitioner (ss 1(2), 7(5)).

**'Act as an insolvency practitioner'**—This is defined in s 388 and covers the types of office-holder mentioned in s 230 as well as supervisors of company voluntary arrangements and office-holders in relation to individual insolvent estates.

**'Qualified'**—This is explained in s 390. See the comments applying to that section.

**Official receiver**—Official receivers occupy statutory offices and in carrying out the functions of their office they are to act under the directions of the Secretary of State, and are officers of the court when exercising those functions (s 400(2)). Official receivers are not regulated by the scheme that governs insolvency practitioners as the scheme only applies to private insolvency practitioners.

## [1.292]

### 231 Appointment to office of two or more persons

(1) This section applies if an appointment or nomination of any person to the office of administrative receiver, liquidator or provisional liquidator—

    (a)    relates to more than one person, or

    (b)    has the effect that the office is to be held by more than one person.

(2) The appointment or nomination shall declare whether any act required or authorised under any enactment to be done by the administrative receiver, liquidator or provisional liquidator is to be done by all or any one or more of the persons for the time being holding the office in question.

    **Amendments**—Enterprise Act 2002, ss 248(3), 278(2), Sch 17, paras 9, 20, Sch 26.

## [1.293]

### 232 Validity of office-holder's acts

The acts of an individual as administrative receiver, liquidator or provisional liquidator of a company are valid notwithstanding any defect in his appointment, nomination or qualifications.

    **Amendments**—Enterprise Act 2002, ss 248(3), 278(2), Sch 17, paras 9, 21, Sch 26.

    **General note**—Notwithstanding the apparent breadth of the section – which may be regarded as a fair approach as a person acting as a purported agent may affect the legal position of the purported principal – there is Australian authority that indicates that it can only apply where there has been at least a purported appointment, in the form of a genuine attempt to appoint, say a liquidator (*Mercantile Bank of Australia Ltd v Dinwoodie* (1902) 28 VLR 491 at 501), and the acts of liquidators are validated only in so far as any defects in qualification or appointment are discovered after the acts in question have been done: *Re Bridport Old Brewery Co* (1867) 2 Ch App 191. This suggests that upon the discovery of any such defects, the liquidator cannot validly perform further acts in purported reliance upon this validating provision (*Re Bridport Old Brewery Co*).

    In *OBG v Allan* [2005] BPIR 928 the Court of Appeal (Peter Gibson and Carnwath LJJ, Mance LJ dissenting) held that the tort of unlawful interference with contractual relations could not be extended to an improperly appointed receiver who takes over the management of the contractual commitments of a company. Neither does English law recognise the tort of conversion of a chose in action.

*Management by administrators, liquidators etc*

## [1.294]

### 233 Supplies of gas, water, electricity, etc

(1) This section applies in the case of a company where—

    (a)    the company enters administration, or

    (b)    an administrative receiver is appointed, or

    (ba)   ...

    (c)    a voluntary arrangement approved under Part I, has taken effect, or

    (d)    the company goes into liquidation, or

    (e)    a provisional liquidator is appointed;

and "the office-holder" means the administrator, the administrative receiver, . . . the supervisor of the voluntary arrangement, the liquidator or the provisional liquidator, as the case may be.

(2)  If a request is made by or with the concurrence of the office-holder for the giving, after the effective date, of any of the supplies mentioned in the next subsection, the supplier—

(a)  may make it a condition of the giving of the supply that the office-holder personally guarantees the payment of any charges in respect of the supply, but

(b)  shall not make it a condition of the giving of the supply, or do anything which has the effect of making it a condition of the giving of the supply, that any outstanding charges in respect of a supply given to the company before the effective date are paid.

(3)  The supplies referred to in subsection (2) are—

(a)  a supply of gas by a gas supplier within the meaning of Part I of the Gas Act 1986;

(aa)  a supply of gas by a person within paragraph 1 of Schedule 2A to the Gas Act 1986 (supply by landlords etc);

(b)  a supply of electricity by an electricity supplier within the meaning of Part I of the Electricity Act 1989;

(ba)  a supply of electricity by a class of person within Class A (small suppliers) or Class B (resale) of Schedule 4 to the Electricity (Class Exemptions from the Requirement for a Licence) Order 2001 (SI 2001/3270);

(c)  a supply of water by a water undertaker or, in Scotland, Scottish Water,

(ca)  a supply of water by a water supply licensee within the meaning of the Water Industry Act 1991;

(cb)  a supply of water by a water services provider within the meaning of the Water Services etc (Scotland) Act 2005;

(cc)  a supply of water by a person who has an interest in the premises to which the supply is given;

(d)  a supply of communications services by a provider of a public electronic communications service;

(e)  a supply of communications services by a person who carries on a business which includes giving such supplies;

(f)  a supply of goods or services mentioned in subsection (3A) by a person who carries on a business which includes giving such supplies, where the supply is for the purpose of enabling or facilitating anything to be done by electronic means.

(3A)  The goods and services referred to in subsection (3)(f) are—

(a)  point of sale terminals;

(b)  computer hardware and software;

(c)  information, advice and technical assistance in connection with the use of information technology;

(d)  data storage and processing;

(e)  website hosting.

(4)  "The effective date" for the purposes of this section is whichever is applicable of the following dates—

(a)  the date on which the company entered administration,

(b)  the date on which the administrative receiver was appointed (or, if he was appointed in succession to another administrative receiver, the date on which the first of his predecessors was appointed),

(ba)  . . .

(c)  the date on which the voluntary arrangement took effect,

(d)  the date on which the company went into liquidation,

(e)  the date on which the provisional liquidator was appointed.

(5)  The following applies to expressions used in subsection (3)—

(a)  . . .

(b)   ...

(c)   ...

(d)   "communications services" do not include electronic communications services to the extent that they are used to broadcast or otherwise transmit programme services (within the meaning of the Communications Act 2003).

**Amendments**—Water Act 1989, s 190(1), Sch 25, para 78(1); Gas Act 1995 ss 16(1), 17(5), Sch 4, para 14, Sch 6; Insolvency Act 2000, s 1, Sch 1, paras 1, 8; Utilities Act 2000, s 108, Sch 6, para 47, Sch 8; Enterprise Act 2002, s 248(3), Sch 17, paras 9, 22; Communications Act 2003, s 406(1), Sch 17, para 82; SI 2004/1822; SI 2015/989; Corporate Insolvency and Governance Act 2020, s 2(1), Sch 3, paras 1, 15(1).

**General note**—This provision was introduced to stop suppliers of critical utilities refusing to continue to supply office-holders when the latter were appointed to companies, unless any charges outstanding were paid or security given in relation to them. Where the office-holder was administering a company, the supply of some or all of the utilities mentioned in the section could be critical, and the utilities had the office-holder 'over a barrel' in that the office-holder could not carry on, or even wind up, the company's business without supplies, something that the utility suppliers realised to their advantage. If the supplier refuses to supply then the office-holder may apply to the courts to obtain an order to require the supplier to furnish supplies.

The provision was amended in 2015 so as to extend it so as to include a wider list of private suppliers of gas, electricity, water or communication services including the supply of utilities from a landlord to tenant. Added to the existing list of utility supplies to which the s 233 already applies is the supply of goods or services that are for the purpose of enabling or facilitating anything done by electronic means.

The liquidator is permitted to serve an application out of the jurisdiction as the court may authorise this if the circumstances justify it, and an order could be made without notice. In this case the circumstances leading to the making of the application were of such potential gravity that justice required that permission be granted: *Official Receiver v Sahaviriya Steel Industries Public Co Ltd* [2015] EWHC 2877 (Ch), [2016] 1 BCLC 758, at [5], [9].

## [1.295]

### 233A  Further protection of essential supplies

(1)   An insolvency-related term of a contract for the supply of essential goods or services to a company ceases to have effect if—

(a)   the company enters administration, or

(b)   a voluntary arrangement approved under Part 1 takes effect in relation to the company.

(2)   An insolvency-related term of a contract does not cease to have effect by virtue of subsection (1) to the extent that—

(a)   it provides for the contract or the supply to terminate, or any other thing to take place, because the company becomes subject to an insolvency procedure other than administration or a voluntary arrangement;

(b)   it entitles a supplier to terminate the contract or the supply, or do any other thing, because the company becomes subject to an insolvency procedure other than administration or a voluntary arrangement; or

(c)   it entitles a supplier to terminate the contract or the supply because of an event that occurs, or may occur, after the company enters administration or the voluntary arrangement takes effect.

(3)   Where an insolvency-related term of a contract ceases to have effect under this section the supplier may—

(a)   terminate the contract, if the condition in subsection (4) is met;

(b)   terminate the supply, if the condition in subsection (5) is met.

(4)   The condition in this subsection is that—

(a)   the insolvency office-holder consents to the termination of the contract,

(b)   the court grants permission for the termination of the contract, or

(c)   any charges in respect of the supply that are incurred after the company entered administration or the voluntary arrangement took effect are not paid within the period of 28 days beginning with the day on which payment is due.

The court may grant permission under paragraph (b) only if satisfied that the continuation of the contract would cause the supplier hardship.

(5)  The condition in this subsection is that—

(a)  the supplier gives written notice to the insolvency office-holder that the supply will be terminated unless the office-holder personally guarantees the payment of any charges in respect of the continuation of the supply after the company entered administration or the voluntary arrangement took effect, and

(b)  the insolvency office-holder does not give that guarantee within the period of 14 days beginning with the day the notice is received.

(6)  For the purposes of securing that the interests of suppliers are protected, where—

(a)  an insolvency-related term of a contract (the "original term") ceases to have effect by virtue of subsection (1), and

(b)  the company subsequently enters administration, or a voluntary arrangement subsequently has effect in relation to it,

the contract is treated for the purposes of subsections (1) to (5) as if, immediately before the subsequent administration is entered into or the subsequent voluntary arrangement takes effect, it included an insolvency-related term identical to the original term.

(7)  A contract for the supply of essential goods or services is a contract for a supply mentioned in section 233(3).

(8)  An insolvency-related term of a contract for the supply of essential goods or services to a company is a provision of the contract under which—

(a)  the contract or the supply would terminate, or any other thing would take place, because the company enters administration or the voluntary arrangement takes effect,

(b)  the supplier would be entitled to terminate the contract or the supply, or to do any other thing, because the company enters administration or the voluntary arrangement takes effect, or

(c)  the supplier would be entitled to terminate the contract or the supply because of an event that occurred before the company enters administration or the voluntary arrangement takes effect.

(9)  In this section "insolvency office-holder" means—

(a)  in a case where a company enters administration, the administrator;

(b)  in a case where a voluntary arrangement under Part 1 takes effect in relation to a company, the supervisor of the voluntary arrangement.

(10)  Subsection (1) does not have effect in relation to a contract entered into before 1st October 2015.

**Amendments**—Inserted by SI 2015/989.

**General note**—This section causes certain 'insolvency-related terms' in contracts to cease to have effect, thus preventing a supplier from terminating a supply or contract, altering the terms of the contract or compelling higher payments for the supply, when a company enters administration or when a company voluntary arrangement is approved. The insolvency-related terms cease to have effect only in a contract for the supply of those utility and IT supplies listed under s 233. The insolvency-related terms may continue to be relied upon in relation to where the company enters any other insolvency regime. This permits a supplier to terminate a contract when a company goes into liquidation.

## [1.296]

### 233B  Protection of supplies of goods and services

(1)  This section applies where a company becomes subject to a relevant insolvency procedure.

(2)  A company becomes subject to a relevant insolvency procedure for the purposes of this section where—

(a)  a moratorium under Part A1 comes into force for the company,

(b)  the company enters administration,

(c)  an administrative receiver of the company is appointed (otherwise than in succession to another administrative receiver),

    (d)    a voluntary arrangement approved under Part 1 takes effect in relation to the company,

    (e)    the company goes into liquidation,

    (f)    a provisional liquidator of the company is appointed (otherwise than in succession to another provisional liquidator), or

    (g)    a court order is made under section 901C(1) of the Companies Act 2006 in relation to the company (order summoning meeting relating to compromise or arrangement).

(3)   A provision of a contract for the supply of goods or services to the company ceases to have effect when the company becomes subject to the relevant insolvency procedure if and to the extent that, under the provision—

    (a)    the contract or the supply would terminate, or any other thing would take place, because the company becomes subject to the relevant insolvency procedure, or

    (b)    the supplier would be entitled to terminate the contract or the supply, or to do any other thing, because the company becomes subject to the relevant insolvency procedure.

(4)   Where—

    (a)    under a provision of a contract for the supply of goods or services to the company the supplier is entitled to terminate the contract or the supply because of an event occurring before the start of the insolvency period, and

    (b)    the entitlement arises before the start of that period,

the entitlement may not be exercised during that period.

(5)   Where a provision of a contract ceases to have effect under subsection (3) or an entitlement under a provision of a contract is not exercisable under subsection (4), the supplier may terminate the contract if—

    (a)    in a case where the company has become subject to a relevant insolvency procedure as specified in subsection (2)(b), (c), (e) or (f), the office-holder consents to the termination of the contract,

    (b)    in any other case, the company consents to the termination of the contract, or

    (c)    the court is satisfied that the continuation of the contract would cause the supplier hardship and grants permission for the termination of the contract.

(6)   Where a provision of a contract ceases to have effect under subsection (3) and the company becomes subject to a further relevant insolvency procedure, the supplier may terminate the contract in accordance with subsection (5)(a) to (c).

(7)   The supplier shall not make it a condition of any supply of goods and services after the time when the company becomes subject to the relevant insolvency procedure, or do anything which has the effect of making it a condition of such a supply, that any outstanding charges in respect of a supply made to the company before that time are paid.

(8)   In this section "the insolvency period", in relation to a relevant insolvency procedure, means the period beginning when the company becomes subject to the relevant insolvency procedure and ending—

    (a)    in the case of a moratorium under Part A1, when the moratorium comes to an end,

    (b)    in the case of the company entering administration, when the appointment of the administrator ceases to have effect under—

        (i)    paragraphs 76 to 84 of Schedule B1, or

        (ii)    an order under section 901F of the Companies Act 2006,

    (c)    in the case of the appointment of an administrative receiver of the company, when the receiver or any successor to the receiver ceases to hold office without a successor being appointed,

    (d)    in the case of a voluntary arrangement approved under Part 1 taking effect in relation to the company, when the arrangement ceases to have effect,

    (e)    in the case of the company going into liquidation, when—

(i) the liquidator complies with section 94(2), 106(2) or 146(3) (duties relating to final account), or

(ii) the appointment of the liquidator ceases to have effect under an order under section 901F of the Companies Act 2006,

(f) in the case of the appointment of a provisional liquidator for the company, when the provisional liquidator or any successor to the provisional liquidator ceases to hold office without a successor being appointed, and

(g) in the case of the making of a court order under section 901C(1) of the Companies Act 2006 in relation to the company, when—

(i) an order made by the court under section 901F of that Act takes effect, or

(ii) the court decides not to make such an order.

(9) In this section "office-holder", in relation to a company which has entered into an insolvency procedure as specified in subsection (2)(b), (c), (e) or (f), means the administrator, administrative receiver, liquidator or provisional liquidator respectively.

(10) Schedule 4ZZA provides for exclusions from the operation of this section.

**Amendments**—Inserted by Corporate Insolvency and Governance Act 2020, s 14(1).

The provision prohibits clauses which allow the supplier of goods or services to terminate or do any other thing in relation to that contract if the company enters any formal insolvency procedure. The section therefore prevents suppliers from terminating a supply upon the company's insolvency but also prevent suppliers from making it a condition of continued supply that arrears incurred before the entry to the insolvency regime are paid and from making other changes to the contract such as increasing prices.

Section 233B(5) allows for a contract to be terminated by a supplier under the kind of clause referred to in the previous paragraph either where the company or office-holder consents or, on application to the court, the court is satisfied that the continuation of the contract would cause the supplier hardship, and grants permission for termination.

## [1.297]

### 233C Powers to amend section 233B and Schedule 4ZZA

(1) The Secretary of State may by regulations omit any of paragraphs (a) to (g) of section 233B(2) (relevant insolvency procedures).

(2) The Secretary of State may by regulations amend Schedule 4ZZA so as to—

(a) remove or amend any exclusion from section 233B for the time being specified there, or

(b) add further exclusions from section 233B.

(3) In subsection (2), references to exclusions from section 233B are to circumstances in which section 233B, or any provision of that section, does not apply.

(4) The circumstances referred to in subsection (3) may be framed by reference to kinds of company, supplier, contract, goods or services or in any other way.

(5) Regulations under this section may make—

(a) different provision for different purposes;

(b) consequential provision;

(c) transitional and supplementary provision.

(6) Regulations under this section made by virtue of subsection (5) may in particular make provision amending this Act or any other enactment whenever passed or made (including, if paragraph 1(1) or (2) of Schedule 4ZZA is omitted, provision omitting section 233A or 233 respectively).

(7) Regulations under subsection (1) may not omit section 233B(2)(c) unless the Secretary of State has first consulted the Scottish Ministers.

(8) In this section "enactment" includes an Act of the Scottish Parliament and an instrument made under such an Act.

(9) Regulations under this section are to be made by statutory instrument.

(10) A statutory instrument containing regulations under this section may not be made unless a draft of the instrument has been laid before and approved by a resolution of each House of Parliament.

**Amendments**—Inserted by Corporate Insolvency and Governance Act 2020, s 14(1).

**[1.298]**

**234 Getting in the company's property**

(1)   This section applies in the case of a company where—

    (a)    the company enters administration, or

    (b)    an administrative receiver is appointed, or

    (c)    the company goes into liquidation, or

    (d)    a provisional liquidator is appointed;

and "the office-holder" means the administrator, the administrative receiver, the liquidator or the provisional liquidator, as the case may be.

(2)   Where any person has in his possession or control any property, books, papers or records to which the company appears to be entitled, the court may require that person forthwith (or within such period as the court may direct) to pay, deliver, convey, surrender or transfer the property, books, papers or records to the office-holder.

(3)   Where the office-holder—

    (a)    seizes or disposes of any property which is not property of the company, and

    (b)    at the time of seizure or disposal believes, and has reasonable grounds for believing, that he is entitled (whether in pursuance of an order of the court or otherwise) to seize or dispose of that property,

the next subsection has effect.

(4)   In that case the office-holder—

    (a)    is not liable to any person in respect of any loss or damage resulting from the seizure or disposal except in so far as that loss or damage is caused by the office-holder's own negligence, and

    (b)    has a lien on the property, or the proceeds of its sale, for such expenses as were incurred in connection with the seizure or disposal.

**Amendments**—Enterprise Act 2002, s 248(3), Sch 17, paras 9, 23.

**General note**—This provision creates a summary procedure for office-holders in obtaining payment, delivery, or transfer of property, books, papers or records from any person: *Re Oakwell Collieries Co* [1879] WN 65. The purpose of this form of procedure is simply to facilitate the administrative side of an insolvency regime.

The section replaced s 551 of the Companies Act 1985, and as s 234 states that the liquidator is able to get property from 'any person', this means that it is easier for the liquidator (and now other office-holders) than under the former provision, as there is no need, as there was under s 551, to have to assert, and to establish, that the holder of the property falls into any specified categories.

The section does not give an office-holder a better right to property than that held by the company: *Re Leyland DAF Ltd* [1994] 2 BCLC 106, CA.

The application must be commenced in the office-holder's own name, and not that of the company: *Re Cosslett (Contractors) Ltd* [2001] UKHL 58, [2002] 1 AC 336, [2001] 3 WLR 1347, [2002] 1 All ER 292, [2002] 1 BCLC 77 at [32]. Applications ex parte should only be sought in exceptional circumstances: *Re First Express Ltd* [1991] BCC 782 at 785.

The provision protects the office-holder from liability if, in taking the property and disposing of it, he or she had reasonable grounds for believing that the company was entitled to it: *Euromex Ventures Ltd v BNP Paribas Real Estate Advisory and Property Management UK Ltd* [2013] EWHC 3007 (Ch).

Section 234 is directed to the recovery of the property or records to which the relevant company has an entitlement under the general law. It did not confer a power to require the delivery of any record that might shed light on the affairs of the company: *Chesterton v Emson* [2017] EWHC 3226 (Ch).

**Court's powers**—While s 234(2) refers to the court requiring a person to deliver etc property, r 7.78 makes it clear that a liquidator may invoke the power of the court. The rule applies only to a compulsory winding up; in voluntary liquidations applications under s 112 must be made to the court for it to exercise these powers.

The courts will deal with any disputes over the ownership of property covered by a s 234 demand (*Re London Iron & Steel Co Ltd* [1990] BCLC 372 (motor cars); *Euro Commercial Leasing Ltd v Cartwright & Lewis* [1995] 2 BCLC 618 (company money held by its solicitors); *Re Cosslett (Contractors) Ltd* [2001] UKHL 58, [2002] 1 AC 336, [2001] 3 WLR 1347, [2002] 1 All ER 292, [2002] 1 BCLC 77, HL (heavy plant)), but are not entitled to do so where the issue of ownership of property is subject to the jurisdiction of the courts of a foreign country: *Re Leyland DAF Ltd* [1994] 2 BCLC 106, CA.

Whilst the provision is broad, it might not be broad enough to permit office-holders to use the procedure to take proceedings that should be commenced in another manner. For instance, in *Byers v Yacht Bull Corp* [2010] EWHC 133 (Ch), [2010] 2 BCLC 169, at [11] the office-holder added ss 238 and 239 to the s 234 application as grounds for taking action yet the court indicated that the applicant could not do so until the ownership of the beneficial of the property was dealt with.

The provision does not allow a court to determine complex legal issues relating to the property in question, such as title, and any matter involving third party claims or the prosecution of a claim for specific performance: *Ezair v Conn* [2020] EWCA Civ 687 at [26]–[27]. The provision enables a liquidator to carry out his or her statutory functions by placing the apparent property of the company under the liquidator's control, but this process does not, therefore, necessarily involve any determination of title and the final resolution of such a dispute may fall to be made in subsequent proceedings: *Re Cosslett (Contractors) Ltd* [2001] UKHL 58, [2001] BCC 740 at [26]–[28], *Ezair v Conn* at [26].

### SECTION 234(2)

'**Property**'—This has the meaning that is provided for in s 436: *Everitt v Zeital* [2018] EWHC 1316 (Ch) at [66].

'**Books, papers and records**'—This phrase was wide, but it was directed to getting in the company's property and records: *Chesterton v Emson* [2017] EWHC 3226 (Ch).

Books, papers and records has been held by the Supreme Court of Appeal of South Africa in *Le Roux v Viana* 2008 (2) SA 173 in that jurisdiction's equivalent provision, to include any information relating to the company in liquidation where it is located on a computer's hard drive and where the computer is owned by a third party.

### SECTION 234(3)

'**Property**'—This does not embrace the improper seizure of choses in action, as it only covers tangible property: *Welsh Development Agency Ltd v Export Finance Co* [1992] BCLC 148 (by receivers interfering in a contract in this case).

For a discussion of whether s 234 may be used to recover debts, see A Keay 'The Office-Holder's Delivery Up Power and the Recovery of Debts' [2011] 4 *Corporate Rescue and Insolvency* 3.

## [1.299]

### 235 Duty to co-operate with office-holder

(1) This section applies as does section 234; and it also applies, in the case of a company in respect of which a winding-up order has been made by the court in England and Wales, as if references to the office-holder included the official receiver, whether or not he is the liquidator.

(2) Each of the persons mentioned in the next subsection shall—

    (a) give to the office-holder such information concerning the company and its promotion, formation, business, dealings, affairs or property as the office-holder may at any time after the effective date reasonably require, and

    (b) attend on the office-holder at such times as the latter may reasonably require.

(3) The persons referred to above are—

    (a) those who are or have at any time been officers of the company,

    (b) those who have taken part in the formation of the company at any time within one year before the effective date,

    (c) those who are in the employment of the company, or have been in its employment (including employment under a contract for services) within that year, and are in the office-holder's opinion capable of giving information which he requires,

    (d) those who are, or have within that year been, officers of, or in the employment (including employment under a contract for services) of, another company which is, or within that year was, an officer of the company in question, and

    (e) in the case of a company being wound up by the court, any person who has acted as administrator, administrative receiver or liquidator of the company.

(4)   For the purposes of subsections (2) and (3), "the effective date" is whichever is applicable of the following dates—

    (a)    the date on which the company entered administration,

    (b)    the date on which the administrative receiver was appointed or, if he was appointed in succession to another administrative receiver, the date on which the first of his predecessors was appointed,

    (c)    the date on which the provisional liquidator was appointed, and

    (d)    the date on which the company went into liquidation.

(5)   If a person without reasonable excuse fails to comply with any obligation imposed by this section, he is liable to a fine and, for continued contravention, to a daily default fine.

**Amendments**—Enterprise Act 2002, s 248(3), Sch 17, paras 9, 24.

**General note**—This section is an investigative power providing for an informal procedure to allow office-holders to obtain information: *Re Arrows Ltd (No 4)* [1995] 2 AC 75, [1994] 3 WLR 656, [1994] 3 All ER 814, [1994] 2 BCLC 738, HL. The provision was part of statutory investigative powers that had as their purpose the identification of potential criminal or other misconduct and the initiation of the relevant steps to prosecute or apply for a director's disqualification: *R v Brady* [2004] EWCA Crim 1763.

The burden of proof lies with the office-holder in establishing that he or she reasonably required what was sought in his or her application: *Re Corporate Jet Realisations Ltd* [2015] EWHC 221 (Ch), [2015] 2 BCLC 95.

Liquidators of a company are entitled under the provision to obtain information from administrative receivers who had previously been appointed in relation to the company's affairs: *Re Corporate Jet Realisations Ltd* [2015] EWHC 221 (Ch), [2015] 2 BCLC 95.

Office-holders who are permitted to obtain formal examinations under s 236 should first, ordinarily, seek to avail themselves of s 235 in order to gain information.

Any information or documents obtained pursuant to s 235 may be disclosed by the official receiver or liquidator to the Secretary of State for Business, Energy and Industrial Strategy so that a decision can be made as to whether proceedings for the disqualification of a director should be commenced: *Re Polly Peck International plc* [1994] BCC 15. It makes no difference if an undertaking was given that the information or documents would only be used for the purposes of winding up as disclosure would fall within the purposes of winding up (*Polly Peck*).

Information obtained under this provision is confidential and should only be used for the purpose for which it had been obtained (*R v Brady* [2004] EWCA Crim 1763), but the Court of Appeal has held that confidentiality was not absolute and might be outweighed by the public interest. So, the court held information could be passed to the appropriate prosecuting authority, as a matter of public interest. In that case it was said that the official receiver has the power to disclose any information gleaned under s 235 to the Inland Revenue if it was otherwise lawful (*R v Brady* at [18]). An office-holder could apply to obtain an order of the court to permit the office-holder to disclose material to another office-holder, but a court would not give a blanket order as it would wish to know what material was being disclosed: *Re Bernard L Madoff Investment Securities LLC* [2009] EWHC 442 (Ch), [2009] 2 BCLC 78 at [13].

Details of any breach of this section should be reported by the liquidator to the Secretary of State for Business, Energy and Industrial Strategy and should include: details of efforts of the liquidator to enforce co-operation by the director, officer or other person; details of any action taken by the liquidator to enforce compliance; and the consequences of non-co-operation on the part of the director, officer or other person (Dear IP, Millennium Edition, December 2000, chapter 20).

There was nothing in s 235 which limited the ability of the office-holder to have whoever he or she pleased at interview when he or she required it to be conducted under s 235: *Re Bernard L Madoff Investment Securities LLC* [2009] EWHC 442 (Ch), [2009] 2 BCLC 78 at [15].

An interviewee at an interview convened under this section could only be required to answer questions about the company to which the office-holder was appointed: *Re Bernard L Madoff Investment Securities LLC* [2009] EWHC 442 (Ch), [2009] 2 BCLC 78 at [15].

If a person fails to co-operate with the office-holder, then the latter may apply to the court under r 12.52(1)(e) for an order against the person in order to enforce compliance. In such a case the person against whom an order is made might be made liable for costs (r 12.52(3)).

## [1.300]

### 236  Inquiry into company's dealings etc

(1)   This section applies as does section 234; and it also applies in the case of a company in respect of which a winding-up order has been made by the court in England

and Wales as if references to the office-holder included the official receiver, whether or not he is the liquidator.

(2)   The court may, on the application of the office-holder, summon to appear before it—

(a)   any officer of the company,

(b)   any person known or suspected to have in his possession any property of the company or supposed to be indebted to the company, or

(c)   any person whom the court thinks capable of giving information concerning the promotion, formation, business, dealings, affairs or property of the company.

(3)   The court may require any such person as is mentioned in subsection (2)(a) to (c) to submit to the court an account of his dealings with the company or to produce any books, papers or other records in his possession or under his control relating to the company or the matters mentioned in paragraph (c) of the subsection.

(3A)   An account submitted to the court under subsection (3) must be contained in—

(a)   a witness statement verified by a statement of truth (in England and Wales), and

(b)   an affidavit (in Scotland).

(4)   The following applies in a case where—

(a)   a person without reasonable excuse fails to appear before the court when he is summoned to do so under this section, or

(b)   there are reasonable grounds for believing that a person has absconded, or is about to abscond, with a view to avoiding his appearance before the court under this section.

(5)   The court may, for the purpose of bringing that person and anything in his possession before the court, cause a warrant to be issued to a constable or prescribed officer of the court—

(a)   for the arrest of that person, and

(b)   for the seizure of any books, papers, records, money or goods in that person's possession.

(6)   The court may authorise a person arrested under such a warrant to be kept in custody, and anything seized under such a warrant to be held, in accordance with the rules, until that person is brought before the court under the warrant or until such other time as the court may order.

**Amendments**—SI 2010/18.

**General note**—This provision is to be read together with ss 235 (*Shierson v Rastogi*, sub nom *Re RGB Resources plc* [2002] EWCA Civ 1624, [2003] 1 WLR 586, [2003] BPIR 148 and 237. Sections 235 and 236 differ in that s 235 includes a mandatory requirement that officers give information that is reasonably required and s 236 gives a court a discretion as to whether there should in fact be an examination (*Shierson v Rastogi*). Section 236 provides a composite code to enable office-holders to obtain information from books, papers and records relating to the company and information from witnesses who may have relevant information to give concerning the company: *Re Trading Partners Ltd* [2002] BPIR 606, [2002] 1 BCLC 655.

The provision involves an examination in private: *Bishopsgate Investment Management Ltd (in provisional liquidation) v Maxwell* [1992] Ch 1, [1992] 2 All ER 856, [1992] BCLC 475, CA.

The power to examine privately is very broad and extraordinary: *Re British & Commonwealth Holdings plc (No 2)* [1992] Ch 342, CA (affirmed on appeal by the House of Lords [1993] AC 476). And as the power is broad the courts are concerned about possible abuse, and so they have said that the power must be exercised carefully in order to ensure that the examinee is not unfairly disadvantaged: *Re North Australian Territory Company* (1890) 45 ChD 87 at 93; *Ex parte Willey* (1883) 23 ChD 118 at 128; *Re Rolls Razor Ltd (No 2)* [1970] Ch 576 at 591, [1969] 3 All ER 1386 at 1396. The courts are careful to ensure that the rights of a person to privacy and confidentiality are not unfairly interfered with: *Hamilton v Oades* (1989) 166 CLR 486 (Australian HC). The courts have to engage in a balancing exercise between the requirements of the liquidator, to ascertain all of the relevant information about the company, and the possible oppression of the examinee: *Cloverbay Ltd (Joint Administrators) v Bank of Credit and Commerce International SA* [1991] Ch 90, [1990] 3 WLR 574, [1991] 1 All ER 894 [1991] BCLC 135, CA; *Re British and Commonwealth Holdings plc* [1993] AC 426, [1992] 3 WLR 853, [1992] 4 All ER 876, [1993] BCLC 168.

The provision binds the Crown, so an office-holder might require inspectors appointed by the Department of Business, Energy and Industrial Strategy to disclose transcripts of evidence given to them in relation to the company in winding up. In such a case, those giving evidence are to be given a right to be heard on whether disclosure should be permitted: *Soden v Burns* [1996] 1 WLR 1512, [1996] 3 All ER 967, [1996] 2 BCLC 636.

If the prospective examinee is the subject of criminal proceedings, an examination may still be held. The usual balancing exercise, to weigh up the importance to the office-holder of the information sought as against the extent of oppression likely to be suffered by the examinee, will be undertaken: *Re Arrows Ltd (No 2)* [1992] BCLC 1176; *Re British and Commonwealth Holdings plc* [1993] AC 426, [1992] 3 WLR 853, [1992] 4 All ER 876, [1993] BCLC 168, HL.

It has been held that it is not appropriate to use an examination to test the proof of debt that a liquidator has rejected: *Re BCCI (No 7)* [1994] BCLC 455.

It has been said that it is not appropriate in applications to mix up requests for information and documents without indicating clearly that 'information' cannot be sought under r 12.18(1)(b)(iv). An application to produce documents under r 12.18(1)(b)(iv) could not be used as a disguised request for information. Where information is sought a court is only able to order it to be provided by summoning a person to answer questions, ordering interrogatories or ordering the filing of witness statements, if an applicant did not know the identity of the particular documents he or she wished to see, but adequately described them by reference to the subject matter they contained, that could be sufficient for the purposes of the provision: *Re Comet Group Ltd* [2014] EWHC 3477 (Ch), [2015] BPIR 1.

**Purpose**—The purpose of private examinations is to assist a liquidator to ascertain the truth concerning the affairs of the company and obtain information concerning the company's trading and dealings. This is to be done with the object of allowing the liquidator, as effectively and as inexpensively as possible to fulfil the functions that liquidators have; to put the affairs of the company in order; and to carry out all aspects of the liquidation, including the getting in of any assets of the company: *Re Rolls Razor Ltd* [1968] 3 All ER 698 at 700 per Buckley J (approved in *Re British and Commonwealth Holdings plc* [1993] AC 426, [1992] 3 WLR 853, [1992] 4 All ER 876, [1993] BCLC 168, HL). In *Shierson v Rastogi*, sub nom *Re RGB Resources plc* [2002] EWCA Civ 1624, [2003] 1 WLR 586, [2003] BPIR 148 Peter Gibson LJ stated that: 'The primary duty of a liquidator of a company being wound up by the court is to collect its assets with a view to discharging its liabilities to the extent the assets permit. To perform that function the liquidator needs information, and the companies legislation has for very many years given the liquidator power to obtain it from those who can be expected to have relevant information' (at [23]).

In referring to examinations, some emphasis has been given to the idea that it can be a vital aspect in relation to the ascertaining and collection of the assets to which the company is entitled (*Shierson v Rastogi*). But the purpose of examinations is not limited to one purpose: *Re Pantmaenog Timber Co Ltd (in liquidation); Official Receiver v Wadge Rapps & Hunt* [2003] UKHL 49, [2003] 2 BCLC 257. In *Ezair v Conn* ([2020] EWCA Civ 687) the Court of Appeal said that s 236 was designed to assist office-holders in the carrying out of the relevant insolvency process by placing under their control the property and records to which the company appears to be entitled (at [26]). In *Official Receiver v Wadge Rapps & Hunt*, the House of Lords held that it is permissible for the official receiver to use the examination process only for the purpose of obtaining evidence to be employed in disqualification proceedings against a director of a company in liquidation (reversing *Re Pantmaenog Timber Co Ltd (in liquidation)* [2001] EWCA Civ 1227, [2002] Ch 239, [2002] 2 WLR 20, [2001] 4 All ER 588, [2001] 2 BCLC 555, CA).

Examinations are often used to enable the liquidator to ascertain whether any substantive claims can be mounted against third parties or whether there are defences against proceedings that have been brought against the company: *Re Gold Company* (1897) 12 ChD 77; *Re Castle New Homes Ltd* [1979] 2 All ER 775 at 788. Also, the objective of examinations is to permit liquidators to investigate the conduct of directors and others, where necessary (*Re Arrows Ltd (No 4)* [1995] 2 AC 75, [1994] 3 WLR 656, [1994] 3 All ER 814, [1994] 2 BCLC 738, HL; *Re Pantmaenog Timber Co Ltd (in liquidation); Official Receiver v Wadge Rapps & Hunt* [2003] UKHL 49, [2003] 2 BCLC 257) and to investigate the causes of the failure of a company (*Re Pantmaenog Timber Co Ltd (in liquidation); Official Receiver v Wadge Rapps & Hunt*).

The power to examine may not, however, be used to conduct a fishing expedition: *Re Castle New Homes Ltd* [1979] 2 All ER 775 at 790; *Re James McHale Automobiles Ltd* [1997] 1 BCLC 273. Having said that, Newey J stated in *Re Chesterfield United Inc* [2012] EWHC 244 (Ch) at [16] that within limits, s 236 can properly be used for what might be termed 'fishing,' but his Lordship did not indicate what the limits in fact were.

Where a company is in members' voluntary liquidation, an examination will not be permitted, as the examination process is designed to protect the interests of creditors and not to provide a windfall for the shareholders of the solvent company: *Re Galileo Group Ltd* [1998] 2 WLR 364, [1998] 1 BCLC 318.

Australian authority in the form of *Re Newheadspace Pty Ltd (in liq)* [2020] NSWSC 173 provides that an examination will not be permitted where it is sought to exert pressure on an alleged debtor of the company in liquidation to pay amounts owed to the company. The New South Wales Supreme Court said that it may be an abuse of process if the liquidator's predominant purpose is to pressure prospective respondents to enter into a settlement of a claim. The liquidator's communications and dealings with others can be used to enable the court to ascertain the liquidator's predominant purpose of seeking the examination. The court added that if the purpose of an examination is as a way of obtaining litigation funding for taking action against parties, that of itself is not improper.

**Court discretion**—The court has a discretion as to whether it will make the order sought (s 236(2)). However, there are some principles that must be considered by a court in arriving at its decision. Justice and fairness must demand that an order be made: *Re BCCI (No 7)* [1994] 1 BCLC 458. The discretion is to be exercised judicially and following a careful balancing of the interests and factors involved, including taking into account the purpose of the examination power and whether the making of an order would be unreasonable, unnecessary or oppressive: *Re British & Commonwealth Holdings plc* [1993] AC 426, [1992] 3 WLR 853, [1992] 4 All ER 876, [1993] BCLC 168, HL. Of the principles that must be taken into account, the overarching ones are that any examination must be necessary in the interests of the insolvency administration involved (*Re Embassy Art Products* [1988] BCLC 1), and that the liquidator has a reasonable need for the information sought (*Re Galileo Group Ltd* [1998] 2 WLR 364, [1998] 1 BCLC 318), as well as the fact that the examination should not be unreasonably oppressive as far as the examinee is concerned (*British & Commonwealth Holdings plc*). Some of the factors that a court may well consider in making their decision are: the purpose of an examination; the reasonable requirements of the liquidator to wind up the company; the oppression of the prospective examinee; and the width of the order sought (*Re British & Commonwealth Holdings plc*. An example of oppression occurred in *Re PFTZM Ltd (in liquidation)* [1995] 2 BCLC 354, where the liquidator was seeking to discover whether third parties were shadow directors of the company.

In striking the balance between permitting the promotion of the public interest of allowing examinations so as to ensure the efficient administration of an insolvency regime, on the one hand, and protecting the private interests of individual examinees, on the other, the court has to weigh up the need to uncover wrongdoing with the possible oppression of an innocent party: *Morris v European Islamic Ltd* [1999] CLY 3283, Neuberger J. The cases indicate that applications to examine insiders, namely directors and officers of the company, are treated more liberally compared with applications to examine third parties, but having said that, applications in respect of insiders can be set aside on the basis of oppression, such as where they are accused of serious wrongdoing and an examination would constitute an occasion for the office-holder to prove the case against them (*Shierson v Rastogi*, sub nom *Re RGB Resources plc* [2002] EWCA Civ 1624, [2003] 1 WLR 586, [2003] BPIR 148, CA); the fact is that the degree of possible oppression with third parties is greater than with insiders (*Shierson v Rastogi*). In *Shierson* Peter Gibson LJ indicated that requiring something that is effectively oppressive can in fact be outweighed by the legitimate requirements of the liquidator (at [39]).

The principles that govern the exercise of the court's discretion were set out in two Court of Appeal decisions, *Cloverbay Ltd (Joint Administrators) v Bank of Credit and Commerce International SA* [1991] Ch 90, [1990] 3 WLR 574, [1991] 1 All ER 894, [1991] 1 BCLC 135, and *Re British & Commonwealth Holdings plc (No 2)* [1992] Ch 342 (affirmed on appeal by the House of Lords at [1993] AC 476), which considered examinations in liquidations. In *Cloverbay* it was said that courts, in engaging in balancing the requirements of the liquidator as against the possible oppression of the examinee, should consider the importance to the office-holder of obtaining the information sought and the degree of oppression to the examinee (at 141). Browne-Wilkinson V-C stated that a court should consider, in exercising its discretion, the following points (in relation to a liquidation), but the points can, for the most part, apply to other office-holders:

- the liquidator arrives on the scene with no previous knowledge and often important documents cannot be found; but the examination process is not to put the liquidator in a better position than would have been enjoyed if liquidation had not occurred;
- the test is not whether the liquidator has an absolute need for the information, but whether obtaining the information is a reasonable requirement;
- generally, liquidators have a stronger argument for the examination of officers or former officers of the company compared with the examination of third parties;
- any order for oral examination of a person is more likely to be oppressive than an order for the production of documents.

Later, in *Re British & Commonwealth Holdings plc (No 2)* [1992] Ch 342, Ralph Gibson LJ in a judgment that was ultimately approved of by the House of Lords ([1993] AC 426), formulated the principles which should guide a court when considering the power to examine. They were (at 370–372): the court has an unfettered discretion whether or not to permit an examination; the exercise of the discretion involves balancing the liquidator's requirements as against possible oppression to the prospective examinee; the power is to enable the court to help the liquidator discharge his or her function as effectively and as speedily as possible.

It may be oppressive for a court to permit certain questions where the amount of work required to answer them is not justified by the benefit to the inquiry of the answers to be given: *Re Richbell Strategic Holdings Ltd (in liquidation) (No 2)* [2000] 2 BCLC 794. It is probably oppressive to seek an examination where the prospective examinee has already given a detailed witness statement, unless the office-holder can demonstrate that it is necessary for the examinee to come to court to be questioned: *Re Westmead Consultants Ltd (in liquidation)* [2002] 1 BCLC 384.

Liquidators of a foreign company who make an application under Art 21(1)(d) of the UNCITRAL Model Law on Cross-Border Insolvency as incorporated by the Cross-Border Insolvency Regulations 2006 can clearly obtain an order from an English court for examination of persons under s 236 (*Re Chesterfield United Inc* [2012] EWHC 244 (Ch) at [10].

**The application**—The person who applies for an examination must provide reasonable grounds for the belief that the respondent is able to provide information which may assist the applicant in carrying out his or her duties, but it is unlikely that a court will dismiss an application unless it is oppressive as far as the respondent is concerned or an abuse of process: *Re Metropolitan Bank* (1880) 15 ChD 139, CA; *Re Embassy Art Products* [1988] BCLC 1; *Re Adlards Motor Group Holdings Ltd* [1990] BCLC 68. Office-holders have the onus of establishing the need for the examination (*Re BCCI v Bank of America National Trust & Savings Association* [1997] 1 BCLC 526; *Joint Liquidators of Sasea Finance Ltd v KPMG* [1998] BCC 216), but a good deal of weight is given to the views of administrators and liquidators (*Cloverbay Ltd (Joint Administrators) v Bank of Credit and Commerce International SA* [1991] Ch 90, [1990] 3 WLR 574, [1991] 1 All ER 894, [1991] BCLC 135, CA; *Joint Liquidators of Sasea Finance Ltd v KPMG* [1998] BCC 216 at 220), and there is a general tendency for more latitude to be extended to office-holders in recent days because of the greater concern over the perpetration of fraud, particularly by company officers: *Re Arrows Ltd (No 4)* [1995] 2 AC 75, [1994] 3 WLR 656, [1994] 3 All ER 814, [1994] 2 BCLC 738, HL, per Lord Browne-Wilkinson. Consequently, office-holders do not have to demonstrate an absolute need for the information sought: *Cloverbay Ltd (Joint Administrators) v Bank of Credit and Commerce International SA*.

The required contents of an application are set out in r 12.18.

Creditors are not given the right to apply for an examination and it has been held that s 112 cannot be used in voluntary liquidations as an alternative basis for a creditor instigating the examination process: *Re James McHale Automobiles Ltd* [1997] 1 BCLC 273.

Where office-holders wish to ascertain information from a company, they are not able to ask in the application for an order to be issued against the company. The order must be directed to the proper officer, who will give evidence on behalf of the company: *Re JN Taylor Pty Ltd* [1999] 2 BCLC 256, [1998] BPIR 347.

The application is made to an ICC judge in London or a district judge where the application is made in the county court. An application will be governed by art 6 of the European Convention on Human Rights, namely the right to a fair hearing.

The Rules do permit an application to be made without notice to any other party (formerly 'ex parte') (r 12.18(3)), but it seems that now the general rule in practice is that applications must be made inter partes (*Re PFTZM Ltd (in liquidation)* [1995] 2 BCLC 354; *Re Murjani* [1996] 1 BCLC 272, [1996] BPIR 325 (a bankruptcy case)), unless there are compelling reasons for having an ex parte application. Such reasons might include: urgency or concern over the likelihood of documents disappearing: *Re Maxwell Communications Corporation plc* [1994] BCC 741 at 747; *Re PFTZM Ltd (in liquidation)*. The preference for an inter partes application is consistent with the general principle that a person is entitled to be heard before a court delivers an order that has significant impact on the person (see *Re Maxwell Communications Corporation plc* and *Re PFTZM Ltd (in liquidation)*). Such an approach seems to be in accord with art 6 of the European Convention on Human Rights, which provides persons with the right to a fair hearing.

The courts will exercise caution in making orders where the application is wide: *Chesterton v Emson* [2017] EWHC 3226 (Ch).

**Contemporaneous or contemplated proceedings**—A significant amount of litigation has resulted from office-holders seeking to examine a person who is likely to be a party to (or a witness at the hearing of) legal proceedings which the office-holder is either contemplating or has already commenced. The potential examinee's worry is that the office-holder may be able to gain significant forensic advantages in the conduct of contemplated or pending litigation.

As with any application for an examination, the courts need to engage in balancing the need of the liquidator to gain information and the possible oppression of the respondent (*Re British and Commonwealth Holdings plc* [1993] AC 426, [1992] 3 WLR 853, [1992] 4 All ER 876, [1993] BCLC 168; *Re Atlantic Computers plc* [1998] BCC 200 at 209–210; *Joint Liquidators of Sasea Finance Ltd v KPMG* [1998] BCC 216 at 220), and this is necessary even if the persons to be examined are insiders, because they can be the subject of oppression: *Shierson v Rastogi*, sub nom *Re RGB Resources plc* [2002] EWCA Civ 1624, [2003] 1 WLR 586, [2003] BPIR 148, CA.

Simply because a liquidator has decided to proceed, or has initiated proceedings, against the examinee or someone related to the examinee, does not necessarily preclude the holding of an examination (*Re Castle New Homes Ltd* [1979] 2 All ER 775 at 782; *Re British and Commonwealth Holdings plc* [1993] AC 426, [1992] 3 WLR 853, [1992] 4 All ER 876, [1993] BCLC 168) because the presiding officer at the examination can disallow questions if they are oppressive (*Shierson v Rastogi*), and an examination of insiders is particularly likely to be permitted where there are reasonable grounds for suspecting that the insiders have pocketed company funds (*Shierson v Rastogi*). Having said that, if litigation has been commenced and the examination is sought in order to improve the position of a liquidator as a litigant, this will not be permitted: *Re Spiraflite Ltd* [1979] 2 All ER 766 at 769; *Re Castle New Homes Ltd* [1979] 2 All ER 775 at 789. The purpose of the office-holder in seeking the examination might well be considered (*Re Spiraflite Ltd*). The purpose of the power to examine is to enable an office-holder to discharge his or her functions and not to improve the prospects of any litigation, so the liquidator's purpose must be the former and not the latter (*Re Spiraflite Ltd*). More recent cases have moved away from the purpose of the office-holder and focused almost totally on the balancing exercise, referred to above, but they have said that in undertaking the balancing, the court should consider the importance to the office-holder of obtaining the information sought as well as the degree of oppression to the examinee: *Cloverbay Ltd (Joint Administrators) v Bank of Credit and Commerce International SA* [1991] Ch 90, [1990] 3 WLR 574, [1991] 1 All ER 894, [1991] BCLC 135.

An examination will not be prevented merely because the office-holder has completed litigation against the examinee (*Re JT Rhodes Ltd* (1986) 2 BCC 99, 284 – but cf the view of Evans-Lombe J in *Re JN Taylor Pty Ltd* [1998] BPIR 347 at 361, where he regarded the former case as 'a case arising from unusual facts'). However, an office-holder will not be permitted to have an examination if litigation is discontinued in order to make an application for an examination: *Re Bletchley Boat Co Ltd* [1974] 1 WLR 630, [1974] 1 All ER 1225.

Where an examination is sought and the information to be given may be of assistance to the office-holder in legal proceedings already commenced, the court might permit the examination to be held if it is the case that gaining the information relevant to the proceedings is merely an incidental consequence of inquiries that are necessary to enable the office-holder to discharge his or her duties: *Re Brook Martin & Co (Nominees) Ltd* [1993] BCLC 328. This might be difficult for a court to determine.

'**Affairs or property of the company**'—It has been held in Australia that the affairs or property of a company includes the company's choses in action: *Grosvenor Hill (Qld) Pty Ltd v Barber* (1994) 120 ALR 262; *Gerah Imports Pty Ltd v The Duke Group Ltd (in liquidation)* (1994) 12 ACLC 116, (1994) 12 ACSR 513; *Re Interchase Corporation Ltd* (1996) 21 ACSR 375. It has been held that office-holders are entitled to documents relating to a trading relationship between one of the company's subsidiaries and a third party where those documents are kept by the third party, on the basis that such documents involved the affairs of the company: *Re PNC Telecom Plc* [2003] EWHC 2220 (Ch).

**Books, papers or other records**—This subsection covers information that is contained in books, papers and records that are the property of the company, whether or not still in its possession: *Re Trading Partners Ltd* [2002] BPIR 606, [2002] 1 BCLC 655. The office-holder is not limited to papers that came into existence before the advent of an insolvency administration. For example, if the company became insolvent and came under the control of administrative receivers, a subsequent liquidator is entitled to have access to papers that relate to the company's affairs even if they came into existence after the receivers took office and the papers were produced at the expense of the chargeholder who appointed the receivers: *Re Trading Partners Ltd*. In *Re Trading Partners Ltd* the court ordered the production of working and litigation papers held by the receivers. Books, papers and records has been held by the Supreme Court of Appeal of South Africa in *Le Roux v Viana* 2008 (2) SA 173 to include any information relating to the company in liquidation where it is located on a computer's hard drive and where the computer is owned by a third party. 'Documents' includes those that are in electronic form: *Re Comet Group Ltd* [2014] EWHC 3477 (Ch), [2015 BPIR 1 at [26]. In an Australian case 'books' has been interpreted to cover documents relating to any insurance policy covering an auditor in respect of his or her liability to the company in liquidation: *Re Banksia Securities Ltd* [2013] VSC 416.

If an applicant does not know the exact identity of particular documents that he or she wishes to see, it is sufficient if he or she adequately describes them by reference to the subject matter that they contained: *Re Comet Group Ltd* [2014] EWHC 3477 (Ch), [2015] BPIR 1 at [24].

It has been held that a court could order that access to emails exchanged between the administrative receivers of a company and the appointing bank before liquidation of the company could be given to the liquidators of the company. Also, administrative receivers could be ordered to produce documents issued to third parties on behalf of the company prior to liquidation: *Re Corporate Jet Realisations Ltd* [2015] EWHC 221 (Ch), [2015] 2 BCLC 95.

In seeking documents, it is not sufficient for a liquidator to state merely that the documents are needed in the winding-up process; the liquidator must state specifically why the documents are necessary: *Re XL Communications Group plc* [2005] EWHC 2413 (Ch).

Liquidators of a foreign company who make an application under Art 21(1)(g) of the UNCITRAL Model Law on Cross-Border Insolvency as incorporated by the Cross-Border Insolvency Regulations 2006 may obtain an order from an English court for disclosure of documents relating to the company under s 236: *Re Chesterfield United Inc* [2012] EWHC 244 (Ch).

It has been held that a court could exercise its discretion under s 236 to order HM Revenue and Customs to disclose information to a liquidator which had been obtained from a foreign authority under a letter of request (*XYZ v Revenue and Customs Commissioners* [2010] EWHC 1645 (Ch), [2010] BPIR 1297).

In *Re Delberry Ltd* [2008] EWHC 925, [2008] BPIR 1277 it was said that the court could consider, inter alia, the following factors when hearing an application under s 236(3): '(i) should be necessary for the liquidator to obtain the documents in the interests of the winding up; (ii) that production should not be oppressive or unfair to the respondent; (iii) the onus of establishing the need for the documents is on the office-holder (albeit a great deal of weight is to be given to the office-holder's views that production is required) and the status of the person to whom the order is addressed; (iv) if the person is a stranger to the company the court may be slower to make an order but where the person owed fiduciary duties to the company, and was an ex-officer of the company, the court may be more ready to make the order; (v) s 236 is not intended to give the office-holder special advantages in ordinary litigation and in general the court is disinclined to make an order where the office holder has commenced litigation against the respondent to the s 236 application. However, there is no hard and fast rule in relation to that issue (as held in *Chesterton v Emson* [2017] EWHC 3226 (Ch)) and (vi) the volume of documentation requested and the effort required to produce it; (vii) s 236 is not limited to documents belonging to the company in liquidation' (at [25]).

The Hong Kong Court of Appeal has said that the fact that the documents that have to be provided as relating to the affairs of the insolvent company might also relate to other persons does not prevent a court order covering production of the documents: *Liquidators of China Medical Technologies Inc v Samson Tsang Tak Yung* [2018] HKCA 252. It is unclear whether an English court would follow suit.

**The order**—In making an order, the courts have the power to limit the ambit of the examination, if they feel that it is too wide as sought in the application: In *Re Richbell Strategic Holdings Ltd (in liquidation) (No 2)* [2000] 2 BCLC 794. Alternatively, the court may restrict the material that is sought to be produced: *Re Galileo Group Ltd* [1998] 2 WLR 364, [1998] 1 BCLC 318; *Re Atlantic Computers plc* [1998] BCC 200. In *Finnigan v Ellis* [2017] NZCA 488, [2017] 2 NZLR 123, the New Zealand Court of Appeal said that an order could not require a former director of the company in liquidation to provide personal financial information to a liquidator under the New Zealand equivalent of s 236.

If an order is made that the respondent must produce documents, then the liquidator is not able to demand that he or she be given copies. The respondent's duty is to produce and let the liquidator inspect, and it is then for the liquidator to make copies at his or her expense: *Re Maxwell Communications Corporation plc (No 3)* [1995] 1 BCLC 521.

If exceptional circumstances exist, a court is able to make an order, pursuant to its powers under the Supreme Court Act 1981, preventing an examinee from absconding abroad prior to the examination and restraining the examinee from leaving the jurisdiction: *Re Oriental Credit Ltd* [1988] 2 WLR 172. A court may order, although this would be done rarely, that the examinee surrender his or her passport or order that the examinee not leave the jurisdiction pending the examination: *Daltel Europe Ltd (in liquidation) v Makki* [2005] 1 BCLC 594. If a court takes any of the foregoing actions, a person who wishes to leave the jurisdiction may obtain court permission to go, on condition that security be given, so as to ensure that the examinee will adhere to the order: *Re a Company (No 003318 of 1987)* (1987) 3 BCC 564; *Re BCCI (No 7)* [1994] 1 BCLC 455. In *Re BCCI (No 7)* an order against a person domiciled overseas, but resident in the UK, was supported by a requirement that he should give security in the amount of £500,000 before being permitted to leave the country: *Re a Company (No 003318 of 1987)* (1987) 3 BCC 564.

If the office-holder who applied for and obtained an order subsequently vacates office, the order ceases to have any force: *Re Kingscroft Insurance Co Ltd* [1994] 1 BCLC 80.

Rule 12.19 covers the rule concerning any order made for an examination.

**Rescission of order**—Where an order for examination is made, the examinee may apply, under r 12.59(1), to have the order set aside, perhaps because the examination would be unreasonable or oppressive. In hearing an application the court is required to carry out a balancing of interests, just as it did when the application for the examination was determined. If the respondent does apply, the judge may exercise a discretion, not being fettered by the earlier exercise of discretion by an ICC judge or district judge, and the judge's discretion supplants that of the ICC judge or district judge: *Re Rolls Razor Ltd (No 2)* [1970] Ch 576 at 594.

Where an application for a rescission of an order is opposed, the costs will usually be awarded against the party who loses. If that is the examinee then, unless special circumstances exist, he or she will be ordered to pay the costs of the liquidator: *Re Cloverbay Ltd* [1989] 1 BCLC 724 at 733; *Re BCCI (No 12)* [1997] BCC 561 at 579.

**Examinees**—While it is not usual, it appears that a creditor may be examined in certain circumstances (*Massey v Allen* (1878) 9 ChD 164; *Re Tyne Chemical Co* (1874) 43 LJ Ch 354), for example in relation to a proof of debt (*Bellmex International v British American Tobacco* [2001] 1 BCLC 91). But such orders should only be made when office-holders demonstrate a clear necessity for them (*Bellmex International*).

Persons who are residing in England and Wales and whose examination is sought in a letter of request from a foreign court to a court in England and Wales, under s 426, may be ordered to be examined (*Re Southern Equities Corp* [2001] Ch 419, [2000] 2 WLR 1141, [2000] 2 BCLC 21, [2000] BPIR 28, CA (a letter of request from the South Australian Supreme Court to High Court in England and Wales)), and will be summoned to appear by the court in England and Wales to be examined, provided that the examination is justified under the law of the foreign jurisdiction and notwithstanding that an order would not be granted if the request came from an office-holder administering an insolvent administration in England and Wales (*Re Southern Equities Corp*).

The provisions as far as the procedure of an examination are concerned are set out in r 12.20.

As far as costs and expenses of examinees go, see r 12.2 and the notes accompanying it.

## SECTION 236(2)

'Officer'—There are a number of definitions of 'officer' in the Act (eg ss 206(3), 208(3), 210(3) and 211(2)), as well as a definition in the Companies Act 2006 (s 1173). The latter section includes directors, managers and secretaries. 'Director' is explained in s 250 as including any person occupying the position of director by whatever name called. For the purposes of s 236, auditors of the company are also officers: *Joint Liquidators of Sasea Finance Ltd v KPMG* [1998] BCC 216 at 222.

'Person'—This has been interpreted so as to include corporate bodies, so they can be examined through their appropriate officer: *Re Highgrade Traders Ltd* [1984] BCLC 151, CA. It included a bank in *Re Omni Trustees Ltd* [2015] EWHC 2122 (Ch) where the company, a trustee company, had transferred trust funds into a bank account.

**Examinees residing outside of the jurisdiction**—Paragraph 1 of Sch 4 of the Rules provides that the Civil Procedure Rules (CPR) apply to the service of documents outside of the jurisdiction. Rule 6.38 of the CPR provides that a claimant must obtain permission to serve any document out of the jurisdiction. The effect of CPR 6.38 is to apply to applications the rules set out in CPR Pt 6 Practice Direction 6B 'Service out of the Jurisdiction.' Paragraph 3.1(20) of PD6B confers jurisdiction on the court to give permission to serve proceedings out of the jurisdiction that are brought under an enactment which allows those proceedings to be brought where those proceedings are not covered by any other grounds set out in PD6B. There has been some difference of opinion, explained in the next paragraph, as to whether this provision applies to applications made under s 236.

It has been held that a court may order the service of an order of public examination on a person who is outside the jurisdiction, whether or not that person is a British subject: *Re Seagull Manufacturing Co Ltd (in liquidation)* [1993] Ch 345, [1993] 2 WLR 872, [1993] 2 All ER 980, [1993] BCLC 1139. However, at first instance in that case, it was said that this was not the position with private examinations, and in *Re Tucker* [1990] Ch 148, [1988] 1 All ER 603 the Court of Appeal said that it would not order, under a bankruptcy equivalent of s 236, the examination in Belgium of a person if it could not compel that person to attend. But that is inconsistent with the law relating to public examinations (*Re Casterbridge Properties Ltd (in liquidation)* [2002] BPIR 428), and in the Scottish case of *McIsaac, Petitioners; Joint Liquidators of First Tokyo Index Trust Ltd* [1994] BCC 410, the Court of Session held that there was no reason why an order under s 236 could not be made in relation to a person resident in New York. The court indicated that whether or not it was proper to make an order for a person residing overseas depended, not on a consideration of s 236, but rather on whether the court could effectively invoke s 426 in obtaining assistance from the courts of the place of the person's residence. In *Re Casterbridge Properties Ltd (in liq)* Burton J doubted the correctness of the reason given in *McIsaac*. His Lordship did not have to decide whether s 236 could be used extra-territorially, although he was willing to say that s 236 had partial extra-judicial effect (at [43]). He was of the view that a summons for an examination could be served overseas and be effective if the examination was to take place where the examinee was residing (at [48]). In *Re M F Global UK Ltd* [2015] EWHC 2319 (Ch), [2015] BPIR 1208 at [32] David Richards J indicated that there was a good deal to say for concluding that the section was to have extra-territorial effect, for if it does not then it is out of line with other provisions in the Act. But his Lordship said that it was not possible to overlook the decision in *Re Tucker* and so his Lordship denied the application for the orders sought by administrators (production of documents) under the section on the basis that s 236 does not have extra-territorial effect. Then in *Re Omni Trustees Ltd; sub nom Official Receiver v Norriss* [2015] EWHC 2697 (Ch) HHJ Hodge QC (sitting as a High Court judge) declined to follow the approach in *M F Global* and said that he had been persuaded that s 236 was different from the section that was the subject of the decision in *Re Tucker*. In his Lordship's view, s 236 did have extra-territorial effect, and provided that the matters identified by the House of Lords in *Re British and Commonwealth Holdings plc* ([1993] AC 426, [1992] 3 WLR 853, [1992] 4 All ER 876, [1993] BCLC 168) were taken into account, English courts do have jurisdiction to require persons resident overseas to give an account of their dealings with the company or produce any books or papers in their possession or control that relate to the company (at [21]). Subsequently, in *Official Receiver v Sahaviriya Steel Industries Public Co Ltd* ([2015] EWHC 2877 (Ch)) HHJ Pelling QC (sitting as a High Court judge) acknowledged the divergence of opinion as to whether s 236 can be said to have extra-territorial effect, but was of the view that a liquidator is permitted to serve an application out of the jurisdiction as the court may authorise this if the circumstances justify it, but it is probably necessary that notice of the application be given to the relevant prospective examinee: at [5], [12]. Earlier, the Court of Appeal in *Re Mid-East Trading Ltd* [1998] 1 BCLC 240 said that an order under s 236 could be made in relation to documents that are held overseas. An order would only be made in circumstances where the office-holder required to see the documents in order to discharge the duties and functions of office and production of the documents did not unnecessarily or unreasonably burden the person required to produce. In *Wallace v Wallace* ([2019] EWHC 2503 (Ch) at [54]) Adam Johnson QC (sitting as a deputy High Court judge) agreed with the view expressed in *Re Omni Trustees Ltd*. *Wallace* was only concerned with s 236(3), and thus the deputy judge's comments may only be said to be obiter as far as they apply to s 236(2). The deputy judge felt that there was an important difference between applications under s 236(3) compared with those under s 236(2) as the power to order the production of documents and information was far less intrusive (at [54]). But most recently, in *Re Akkurate Limited* ([2020] EWHC 1433 (Ch)), Vos C had to deal with the issue again, after analysing the case law his Lordship held that *Re Tucker*, although dealing with different legislation, was binding on the High Court and, therefore, the decisions in *Re Omni* and *Wallace* were incorrect (at [47], [49]). The judge pointed out that *Tucker* had not been disapproved of by either the Court of Appeal or the House of Lords when the respective courts considered *Tucker* (at [51]). Also, Vos C said that *Re Mid-East Trading Ltd* did not provide any basis for departing from *Tucker* by a court of first instance as the ratio of the case did not concern the making of an order under s 236 against a person outside the jurisdiction (at [50]). Finally, the judge said that: 'the compelling reasons for thinking that section 236 ought, in the contemporary commercial environment, to have extra-territorial effect, does not affect the reasoning in *Tucker*'. (at [52]) The fact that the Chancellor's decision was given following very careful and detailed analysis of prior case law means that the chances of a party persuading another High Court judge to distinguish or disagree with the decision are very poor. All of this indicates that until the Supreme Court feels that *Tucker* should be overruled, it will now be followed in future cases in the High Court and Court of Appeal. However, in *Re Akkurate Limited* Vos C was, as had been Adam Johnson QC in *Wallace*, of the view that the jurisprudence of the Court of Justice of the European Union had made clear that the Regulation could and did extend the territoriality of purely domestic insolvency provisions, with the result that the Regulation conferred extra-territorial jurisdiction on the English court to make orders against EU residents under s 236 (at [57]–[60]).

**The examination**—A person may be examined orally or by interrogatories (see s 237(4)). See r 12.20 as to the procedure for an examination.

The judge who presides at the examination has a complete discretion in determining how the examination ought to be conducted and what questions may be put to the examinee: In *Re North Australian Territory Company* (1890) 45 ChD 87 at 93; *Re Maville Hose Ltd* [1938] 1 ChD 32 at 40; *Rottmann v Brittain* [2009] EWCA Civ 473, [2010] 1 WLR 67, [2009] BPIR 1148 at [16]). However, only relevant questions should be permitted: In *Re Pennington ex parte Pennington* (1888) 5 Mor 268 at 269.

The content of without prejudice negotiations involving the applicant for the examination and the examinee will not be able to be admitted at the examination, although a court may be advised that without prejudice negotiations have occurred: *Re Anglo-American Insurance Co Ltd* [2003] BPIR 793.

Those examined are required to provide the best answers they are able, possibly supplemented by documents where necessary: *Re Richbell Strategic Holdings Ltd (in liquidation) (No 2)* [2000] 2 BCLC 794. If the examinee refuses to answer a question then it is likely that the judge will adjourn the hearing to a judge of the High Court, who has power to commit for contempt (*Practice Direction – Insolvency Proceedings* (July 2020) [2020] BPIR 1211, para 3.2(1)) and the question may be repeated and, if not answered, the judge may make necessary punitive orders: *Re JN Taylor Pty Ltd* [1998] BPIR 347 at 349.

See r 12.20(3) and the notes accompanying that rule.

**Privilege against self-incrimination**—It has been held that an officer of an insolvent company is unable to refuse to answer questions at an examination on the basis that those answers might incriminate him or her: *Bishopsgate Investment Management Ltd (in provisional liquidation) v Maxwell* [1992] Ch 1, [1992] 2 All ER 856, [1992] BCLC 475, CA. This is because the purpose of s 236 necessitates the abrogation of the privilege, or else an officer who is examined could frustrate the purpose of the section: *Re Jeffery S Levitt Ltd* [1992] BCLC 250; *Bishopsgate Investment Management Ltd (in provisional liquidation) v Maxwell*. If the examinee refuses to answer, on the basis of self-incrimination, the examinee is in contempt of court: *Bishopsgate Investment Management Ltd (in provisional liquidation) v Maxwell*. An ICC judge or district judge cannot commit for contempt. That must be handled by a High Court judge. Even if the prospective examinee is being investigated by the Serious Fraud Office, no right to claim the privilege exists: *Re AE Farr Ltd* [1992] BCLC 333.

Any statement made that incriminates the examinee can be used in subsequent civil proceedings if the trial judge permits, but it cannot be used in any criminal proceedings, save those mentioned in s 433(3): see *R v Faryabb* [1999] BPIR 569, CA. For further details, see the notes accompanying s 433. In a civil action, if a trial judge acts in a proportionate way, that is considering the strength of the case for interference with the rights of the former examinee against the seriousness of the interference, it would appear that there would not be a breach of the rights under the European Convention on Human Rights if statements given at a s 236 hearing were admitted: Simmons and Smith 'The Human Rights Act 1998: the practical impact on insolvency' (2000) 16 IL & P 167 at 171–172.

The Court of Appeal has stated, in the context of an examination, that the privilege against self-incrimination did not apply where the criminal offence arose under the law of another country: *Rottmann v Brittain* [2009] EWCA Civ 473, [2010] 1 WLR 67, [2009] BPIR 1148.

**Legal professional privilege**—This privilege cannot be asserted by the solicitors of the company which is in liquidation in relation to documents which belonged to the company: *Re Brook Martin & Co (Nominees) Ltd* [1993] BCLC 328 at 336. Also, the company's solicitors could not assert the privilege in answer to a question relating to the company's affairs. It is not clear whether the privilege may be asserted in relation to clients other than the company. But in Australia, it has been held that a liquidator is able to claim or waive privilege on behalf of the company if it were in the interests of the company or its creditors to do so: *Re Dallhold Investments Pty Ltd* (1994) 53 FCR 339 at 348.

If solicitors for a company officer, or other person examined under s 236, are examined and asked a question, privilege is not able to be claimed if their client would be lawfully required to answer the question and divulge the information which is the subject of the question: *Re Murjani* [1996] 1 BCLC 272, [1996] BPIR 325.

**Witness immunity**—In *Mitchell v Al Jaber* ([2021] EWHC 912 (Ch), [2021] 3 WLR 15) liquidators had brought proceedings against a director based on misrepresentation, negligent misstatement and conspiracy, alleging that a company director had knowingly given false information to the liquidators in the course of a s 236 examination. The case turned on whether the director was able to rely on the witness immunity principle as far as his evidence was concerned. Joanna Smith J held at first instance that the witness did not enjoy witness immunity in relation to his evidence, as examinations are not judicial proceedings; the private examination process is deficient in various of the indicia of judicial proceedings which have been held to be important (at [92], [101], [141]). The director appealed to the Court of Appeal (*Al Jaber v Mitchell* [2021] EWCA Civ 1190) and Asplin LJ (with whom Carr LJ and Sir Nicholas Patten concurred) allowed the appeal on the basis that, inter alia: the s 236 examination must be considered not as a standalone procedure, but viewed in the context of the wider compulsory winding-up proceedings in which it arises which are commenced by an order of the court and the examination is designed to further the insolvency proceedings; an examination is conducted in court; both the judge and the liquidator enjoyed immunity at an examination and it would be odd if other participants did not.

**Requiring documents to be kept confidential**—There is Scottish authority to the effect that where a liquidator seeks production of documents under s 236, the person delivering the documents is not entitled to obtain from the liquidator an undertaking of confidentiality with respect to the documents: *McIsaac, Petitioners; Joint Liquidators of First Tokyo Index Trust Ltd* [1994] BCC 410. English courts have not gone this far, stating that the obligation of an office-holder to keep information obtained under s 236 confidential may be waived by court order if the court was satisfied that either such action enabled the purposes of the office-holder's position to be fulfilled, or it was otherwise justified by the balance of considerations of how justice was to be secured: *Re Esal (Commodities) Ltd (No 2)* [1990] BCC 708 at 723; *Re a Company (No 005374 of 1993)* [1993] BCC 734.

Information secured pursuant to an order under s 236 by a liquidator of a holding company can be disclosed to the directors and liquidators of subsidiary companies (*Re Esal (Commodities) Ltd* [1989] BCLC 59 at 65, CA), on the basis that disclosure may assist the officers of the subsidiaries getting in assets or defending actions for the ultimate benefit of the holding company.

In *Re Sandford Farm Properties Ltd* [2015] EWHC 2999 (Ch) the view was taken that an order that allowed the liquidator of a company to disclose what happened at a private examination to the assignee of claims vesting in the company should be varied to permit a second assignee to be granted disclosure.

While the application for an examination is governed by Art 6 of the European Convention on Human Rights, the examination itself is not, as it does not determine the respondent's substantive rights (see Trower 'Bringing Human Rights Home to the Insolvency Practitioner' (Part 1) (2000) 13 *Insolvency Intelligence* 41 at 43). But, as a result of the decision of the European Court of Human Rights in *Saunders v United Kingdom* [1997] EHRR 313, [1998] 1 BCLC 362, evidence given by the examinee will not be able to be used in subsequent criminal proceedings because the evidence is given under compulsion, and permitting the use of such evidence would constitute a contravention of Art 6(1) of the European Convention on Human Rights. Notwithstanding this, the court did say that testimony obtained under compulsion which appeared to be of a non-incriminating nature could later be used in criminal proceedings to contradict or cast doubt on the other statements of the person or otherwise to undermine his or her credibility.

### SECTION 236(4), (5)

**Enforcement**—Provision for enforcing an order against an examinee who fails to appear at the examination or absconds is provided for in s 236(4), (5) and (6). Also, see s 237 and rr 12.51–12.55 and the comments that accompany these provisions.

Examinees who do not attend can be held to be in contempt. In *Atkinson v Varma* ([2020] EWHC 1868 (Ch)) Judge Johns QC (sitting as a High Court judge) declined to order an examinee not attending to be in contempt because he could not be sure that he did not have a genuine reason for his non-attendance (at [68]). The examinee had underlying health issues including diabetes, although the judge was uncertain whether the medical condition really justified non-attendance. Nevertheless, he could not be sure that it did not (at [68]).

**Costs**—Rule 12.22 deals with the costs of proceedings under this section but it does not state how the issue of costs is to be dealt with. The rule does provide that where an application succeeds the court may award costs against the respondent if it is of the view that the examination was necessary because of the fact that the respondent unjustifiably refused to provide information. It would seem that the court may order payment of the costs of compliance with an order, such as locating and accumulating documents that are the subject of an order of production, unless unreasonable conduct otherwise justifies an order and that will depend on the facts, although it would appear that such orders will be rare: see *Re Harvest Finance Ltd (in liquidation)* [2014] EWHC 4237 (Ch), [2015] 2 BCLC 240, at [44]–[47]. Certainly, there is no presumption or even a principle that a respondent's costs will be paid: *Re GP Cars (Herts) Ltd* [2018] EWHC 2639 (Ch) at [95]. Also a court may order an examinee to pay the costs incurred by the office-holder in relation to the application for private examination. For instance, in *Caulfield v Al Jaber* [2017] EWHC 3678 (Ch) an order was made in favour of the liquidator where she had made extensive efforts to obtain information but had been met with a lack of co-operation from the respondent. See the notes on 'Expenses' relating to r 12.22.

For a more detailed discussion of private examinations, see A Keay *McPherson and Keay's Law of Company Liquidation* (Sweet and Maxwell, 4th edn, 2018) at 980–1019.

Also, see the comments accompanying rr 12.17–12.22.

## [1.301]

### 237 Court's enforcement powers under s 236

(1) If it appears to the court, on consideration of any evidence obtained under section 236 or this section, that any person has in his possession any property of the company, the court may, on the application of the office-holder, order that person to deliver the whole or any part of the property to the office-holder at such time, in such manner and on such terms as the court thinks fit.

(2) If it appears to the court, on consideration of any evidence so obtained, that any person is indebted to the company, the court may, on the application of the office-holder, order that person to pay to the office-holder, at such time and in such manner as the court may direct, the whole or any part of the amount due, whether in full discharge of the debt or otherwise, as the court thinks fit.

(3) The court may, if it thinks fit, order that any person who if within the jurisdiction of the court would be liable to be summoned to appear before it under section 236 or this section shall be examined in any part of the United Kingdom where he may for the time being be, or in a place outside the United Kingdom.

(4)   Any person who appears or is brought before the court under section 236 or this section may be examined on oath, either orally or (except in Scotland) by interrogatories, concerning the company or the matters mentioned in section 236(2)(c).

**Flexibility on place and mode of examination**—In an attempt to be flexible and to ensure that the powers of examination are not easily thwarted, the court is provided with a discretion to order that any person who, if within England and Wales, would be liable to be summoned to appear before it, be examined in any part of the UK where he or she may for the time being be, or in a place outside of the UK. Furthermore, the person may be examined in person or through interrogatories.

**Costs**—If a court makes orders, under either s 237(1) or s 237(2), it may order the costs to be paid by the examinee under s 236 (r 12.22(2)).

An order may be made against a non-resident under s 237(3): *Re M F Global UK Ltd* [2015] EWHC 2319 (Ch), [2015] BPIR 1208.

See rr 12.51–12.55.

*Adjustment of prior transactions (administration and liquidation)*

**[1.302]**

### 238   Transactions at an undervalue (England and Wales)

(1)   This section applies in the case of a company where—

    (a)    the company enters administration, or

    (b)    the company goes into liquidation;

and "the office-holder" means the administrator or the liquidator, as the case may be.

(2)   Where the company has at a relevant time (defined in section 240) entered into a transaction with any person at an undervalue, the office-holder may apply to the court for an order under this section.

(3)   Subject as follows, the court shall, on such an application, make such order as it thinks fit for restoring the position to what it would have been if the company had not entered into that transaction.

(4)   For the purposes of this section and section 241, a company enters into a transaction with a person at an undervalue if—

    (a)    the company makes a gift to that person or otherwise enters into a transaction with that person on terms that provide for the company to receive no consideration, or

    (b)    the company enters into a transaction with that person for a consideration the value of which, in money or money's worth, is significantly less than the value, in money or money's worth, of the consideration provided by the company.

(5)   The court shall not make an order under this section in respect of a transaction at an undervalue if it is satisfied—

    (a)    that the company which entered into the transaction did so in good faith and for the purpose of carrying on its business, and

    (b)    that at the time it did so there were reasonable grounds for believing that the transaction would benefit the company.

**Amendments**—Enterprise Act 2002, s 248(3), Sch 17, paras 9, 25.

**General note**—The section is, in many ways, to be viewed as a successor to s 42 of the Bankruptcy Act 1914, which provided for the avoidance of voluntary settlements and was, until the advent of the Insolvency Act 1986, incorporated by reference by the Companies Act. Section 42 was seen as being outmoded, not sufficiently broad and difficult to apply in relation to companies. Section 238 has its roots in the law which first provided for the avoidance of fraudulent conveyances, the Statute of Elizabeth in 1571, although there is now no need to establish fraud. Section 423 tends to be closer to the fraudulent conveyance language, although it is also related to s 238 in that both deal with transactions at an undervalue. Hence, there is some overlap between the provisions, and office-holders have, on occasions, brought proceedings under both sections. See the comments attached to s 423. Section 238 aims to prevent insolvent companies disposing of property at an undervalued amount just before winding up (as a means of asset-stripping), thereby reducing the pool of property which would be available to the liquidator to distribute to creditors.

Administrators and liquidators are able to invoke the section. The section corresponds to s 339, which relates to bankruptcy and is able to be employed by a trustee in bankruptcy.

The section only applies to a transaction entered into by the company that is in administration or liquidation, and does not cover transactions that are entered into by a party other than the company, such as the company's mortgagee: *Re Brabon* [2001] 1 BCLC 11, [2000] BPIR 537.

The burden of establishing that a transaction was entered into at an undervalue lies squarely on the shoulders of the applicant: *Stone & Rolls Ltd v Micro Communications Inc* [2005] EWHC 1052 (Ch) at [93]). However the circumstances might be such that an evidential burden is placed on the respondent: *Phillips v Brewin Dolphin Bell Lawrie Ltd* [2001] UKHL 2, [2001] 1 WLR 143, [2001] 1 All ER 673, [2001] 1 BCLC 145, [2001] BPIR 119 at [26] (HL).

There is no obligation on the applicant to prove that the insolvent company intended to sell at an undervalue or pay over the market value for an asset, but if that can be established then it may have an effect on the remedy that is ordered: *Stanley and Wood v TMK Finance Ltd* [2010] EWHC 3349 (Ch), [2011] BPIR 876 at [7].

In *Re MC Bacon Ltd* [1990] BCLC 324 at 335, a case involving an application under both s 238 and s 239, Millett J protested, in relation to arguments concerning the application of s 239, at counsel citing cases which dealt with previous preference provisions. In dealing with a transaction at an undervalue case, *Hill v Haines* [2007] EWCA Civ 1284, [2008] 2 All ER 901, [2007] BPIR 1280, the Court of Appeal did not take the same view as far as such transactions were concerned (at [18]).

It is critical that an application for a claim under s 238 pleads or defines the transaction (that is challenged) for the purpose of the provision and adequately addresses in evidence adduced the value that is alleged to flow between the company in liquidation or administration and the counter-party (*Hellard v Graiseley Investments Ltd* [2018] EWHC 2664 (Ch) at [64]).

'Relevant time'—This is defined in s 240, and involves two aspects. First, the transaction must have occurred in a particular time zone, namely the 2 years preceding the onset of insolvency. 'Onset of insolvency' is defined in s 240(3). Second, besides falling within this time zone, the transaction must have been entered into at a time when the company was unable to pay its debts within the meaning of s 123 or the entering into of the transaction resulted in the company being unable to pay its debts. The latter requirement is not relevant where the transaction was entered into with a person connected with the company (s 240(2)), although in such a case, the 2-year time period still applies. See the comments under 'Relevant time' and 'Unable to pay debts' in relation to s 240 and 'Connected person' in relation to s 249.

### SECTION 238(2)

'Any person'—While the section does not indicate that it operates extraterritorially, it has been said that the use of 'any person' should bear its literal and natural meaning: anyone, wherever he or she is situated. So s 238 could have effect outside of the country in which the court making the order is situated, and an order could be made against a foreign resident who has no place of business in the UK and who does not carry on business in the jurisdiction, provided that the court is satisfied, in exercising its discretion, that the respondent has a sufficient connection with England for it to be just and proper to make an order against the person: *Re Paramount Airways Ltd (No 2)* [1993] Ch 223, [1992] 3 WLR 690, [1992] 3 All ER 1, [1992] BCLC 710. But where a case involves a foreign element, the court will have to be persuaded that the defendant was sufficiently connected with England for it to be just and proper to make an order: *Re Paramount Airways Ltd (No 2)* at 239–240 (Ch). The court in *Paramount Airways* mentioned specific factors and in *Avonwick Holdings Ltd v Azitio Holdings Ltd* ([2018] EWHC 2458 (Comm) Cockerill J stated that the court must consider the factors mentioned in *Paramount Airways* but that others could be taken into account in undertaking a balancing exercise (at [53]). The judge opined that there were connections other than those mentioned in *Paramount Airways* that enabled her to decide the issue. In *Suppipat v Narongdej* ([2020] EWHC 3191 (Comm)) Butcher J refused a strike out application that was argued on the basis that a s 423 claim which was made against foreign defendants with no connection with England and Wales could not be brought.

'Transaction at an undervalue'—The most critical element of a s 238 action is to prove that the company entered into a transaction that involved an undervalue. The office-holder must establish that the transaction involved a gift given by the company or one where the company agrees to accept from a person consideration the value of which, in money or money's worth, is significantly less than the value, in money or money's worth, of the consideration provided by the company.

In *Re MC Bacon Ltd* [1990] BCLC 324 at 340 Millett J said that there were six elements to be established for a successful claim, namely: 'a transaction entered into by the company; for a consideration; the value of which is measured in money or money's worth; is significantly less than the value; also measured in money or money's worth; of the consideration provided by the company.' This assessment was approved of by the House of Lords in *Phillips v Brewin Dolphin Bell Lawrie Ltd* [2001] UKHL 2, [2001] 1 WLR 143, [2001] 1 All ER 673, [2001] 1 BCLC 145, [2001] BPIR 119 at [21].

'Entered into a transaction'—The Court of Appeal in *Re Ovenden Colbert Printers Ltd (in liq) (sub nom Hunt v Hosking)* [2013] EWCA Civ 1408, [2014] BPIR 285, [2014] 1 BCLC 291 stated that this expression connoted the taking of some step or act of participation by the company.

**Transaction**—'Transaction' is defined in s 436 as including 'a gift, agreement or arrangement' and it is indicated that the references to 'entering into a transaction' in the Act are to be construed accordingly. 'Transaction' is defined broadly and embraces a potentially wide range of possibilities (*Re Taylor Sinclair (Capital) Ltd* [2001] 2 BCLC 176 at 184, *Re HHO Licensing Ltd* [2007 EWHC 2953 (Ch), [2007] BPIR 1363, [2008] 1 BCLC 223 at [31]) and the courts have said that they should not strain to limit the width of the definition: *Phillips v Brewin Dolphin Bell Lawrie Ltd* [1999] 1 WLR 2052, [1999] 2 All ER 844, [1999] 1 BCLC 714, [1999] BPIR, CA (the House of Lords dismissed the appeal). For there to be a transaction under s 238 the existence of a contract is not required: *Re HHO Licensing Ltd* [2007 EWHC 2953 (Ch), [2007] BPIR 1363, [2008] 1 BCLC 223 at [31]. It is probable that something like a guarantee would constitute a transaction. The giving of security by a company to a creditor constitutes a transaction, but, the generally-held view since *Re MC Bacon Ltd* [1990] BCLC 324 is that it is not one that falls within s 238, as all that the company loses is the ability to apply the proceeds of the realisation of the security otherwise than in satisfaction of the secured debt: *Re Mistral Finance Ltd (in liquidation)* [2001] BCC 27. That is not something capable of valuation in monetary terms and is not customarily disposed of for value (*Re MC Bacon Ltd* at 340). But, in light of the comments of Arden LJ (with whom the other judges agreed on all points save the issue of the limitation period – see later) in the Court of Appeal in *Hill v Spread Trustee Company Ltd* [2006] EWCA Civ 542, [2007] 1 WLR 2404, [2006] BPIR 789, [2007] 1 All ER 1106, [2007] 1 BCLC 450 it does not follow from this that a transaction involving the grant of security can never amount to a transaction for no consideration, as such a grant is no different from any other transaction in that respect (at [93]).

The House of Lords in *Phillips v Brewin Dolphin Bell Lawrie Ltd* [2001] UKHL 2, [2001] 1 WLR 143, [2001] 1 All ER 673, [2001] 1 BCLC 145, [2001] BPIR 119 indicated that it was not necessary to search for one transaction, as inter-connected transactions could be considered in assessing whether there was a transaction at an undervalue. Their Lordships actually said that the focus should not be on finding the transaction, but on finding the consideration (if any) that is given and received. Lord Scott gave the following example (at [20]) to explain the view: 'if a company agrees to sell an asset to A on terms that B agrees to enter into some collateral agreement with the company, the consideration for the asset will, in my opinion, be the combination of the consideration, if any, expressed in the agreement with A and the value of the agreement with B.'

To claim successfully under s 238, the office-holder must be able to prove that there was some form of dealing between the company and the respondent (*Re Taylor Sinclair (Capital) Ltd* [2001] 2 BCLC 176 at 185), and this must involve an engagement between the parties (*Re Hampton's Capital Ltd* [2015] EWHC 1905 (Ch)), but indications are that it is sometimes difficult to isolate the transaction that can be challenged. The unilateral misappropriation by a director of his or her company's property does not constitute a transaction between the director and the company: *Re Ovenden Colbert Printers Ltd (sub nom Hunt v Hosking)* [2014] EWCA Civ 1408, [2014] BPIR 285, [2014] 1 BCLC 291. It was said per curiam in *Re Kiss Cards Ltd* [2016] EWHC 2176 (Ch), [2016] BPIR 1450 that the mere fact that a payment is made into a joint account does not mean, necessarily, that there was a 'transaction' between the one making the payment and all those who are account holders of the account. It may be the case that if there is no explanation for the payment it might be regarded as a gift to the account holders. But in any other circumstances it is necessary to consider the surrounding circumstances to identify whether there has been any kind of mutual dealing or arrangement that may constitute a 'transaction' and if so which if any of the account holders were parties to it (at [8]).

See Mokal and Ho 'Consideration, Characterisation and evaluation: Transactions at an Undervalue after *Phillips v Brewin Dolphin*' (2001) 1 JCLS 359.

**Undervalue**—Besides actually establishing a transaction, an undervalue element must be proved, and that can be difficult in some cases. The House of Lords in *Phillips v Brewin Dolphin Bell Lawrie Ltd* [2001] UKHL 2, [2001] 1 WLR 143, [2001] 1 All ER 673, [2001] 1 BCLC 145, [2001] BPIR 119 at [27] said that if the value of the consideration for which a company enters into a transaction is speculative, then the party who relies on the consideration is required to establish the value. Lord Scott in that case said (at [30]) that: 'The value of an asset that is being offered for sale is, prima facie, not less than the amount which a reasonably well-informed purchaser is prepared, in arm's length negotiations, to pay for it.'. His Lordship went on to consider the situation where a unique asset is involved in the transaction. Unique assets can cause valuation problems. His Lordship said (at [30]) that the price for such an asset can be presumed to be market value, and, therefore, not transferred at something other than an undervalue within the section, if it was sold after arm's length negotiations and after proper marketing and both parties acted 'knowledgeably, prudently and without compulsion.'

Any transfer that is expressed to be simply for natural love and affection will constitute a transfer at an undervalue unless there is some other explanation of it (*Simms v Oakes* [2002] EWCA Civ 8, [2002] BPIR 1244 at [5]. This is an issue that is more pertinent in relation to s 340, the personal insolvency equivalent.

If a joint tenant of property that is subject to a mortgage transfers his or her interest to the other joint tenant for no consideration except that the transferee tenant assumes sole liability under the mortgage, the transfer would be a transaction at an undervalue: *Re Kumar* [1993] 1 WLR 224.

Clearly, office-holders must establish a significant undervalue by proving the respective values of the consideration given by the parties to the transaction, and this must be done in money terms: *Re Brabon* [2000] BPIR 537 at 562.

The issue of valuation can play a significant part in establishing whether or not the required transaction was entered into. It is incumbent on the office-holder, as just indicated, to establish the respective values in money or money terms of the consideration given and received by the company and, also, to demonstrate that what it received was significantly less than what it provided: *Re MC Bacon Ltd* [1990] BCLC 324 at 340–341. So, if consideration is not able to be valued in money terms, it is not able to be considered as part of any consideration passing between the parties. In relation to a s 423 action, it has been said that when determining whether consideration received by the defendant was significantly less than the consideration passed to the debtor, the court is obliged to form the view as to the price which could be obtained in the open market in relation to the property representing the consideration given by the defendant and that given by the debtor: *National Westminster Bank plc v Jones* [2000] BPIR 1092 at 1115. It will be necessary for the court to compare the value of property in relation to the consideration given for it, and then consider 'in percentage terms, how much less the consideration is than the value' (*National Westminster Bank plc v Jones* at 1115).

It would appear that in determining whether there is an inequality of benefit, a court must be aware of all aspects of the transaction, including the totality of the benefits received in practice: see *Agricultural Mortgage Corporation v Woodward* [1995] 1 BCLC 1 (a case decided under s 423).

Value is not to be determined in the light of the debtor's subjective views. Rather, value is an objective concept and any value passed to the debtor must be determined by reference to what the debtor receives: *Lyle v Bedborough* [2021] EWHC 220 (Ch), [2021] BPIR 581 at [70].

There is nothing in the section which requires the court to ascribe a precise figure either to the outgoing value or to the incoming value relating to the relevant transaction. The provision will apply whenever the court is satisfied that, whatever the precise values may be, the incoming value is on any view 'significantly less' than the outgoing value: *Ramlort Ltd v Reid* [2004] EWCA Civ 800, [2004] BPIR 985 at [103]. Jonathan Parker LJ did accept that it was preferable if a judge could find precise figures (at [105]). His Lordship said that he could 'see no reason why the court, if it considers it appropriate to do so, should not address the issue of undervalue by taking from a range of possible values those which are most favourable to the party seeking to uphold the transaction' (at [104]). In this regard, see *Ailyan and Fry v Smith* [2010] EWHC 24 (Ch), [2010] BPIR 289 at [48]–[49].

If property was purchased by the company from a person at arm's length, and after it had been offered for sale publicly, this will suggest the price paid by the company was market value: *Re Brabon* [2000] BPIR 537.

The same valuation principles should be employed for valuing both the consideration received by the company and the consideration disposed of by the company (*Re Thoars* [2003] 1 BCLC 499). While the consideration should be valued as at the date of the transfer, in appropriate circumstances the occurrence or non-occurrence of events subsequent to the transfer that is impugned, and before the assessment of the consideration, may be considered in assessing the value of consideration in money or money's worth (*Re Thoars* at [8], [17]), an approach that the House of Lords in *Phillips v Brewin Dolphin Bell Lawrie Ltd* [2001] UKHL 2, [2001] 1 WLR 143, [2001] BPIR 119 appeared to endorse. An example of this might be where a property, when sold, was expected to receive planning permission that would boost its value and those in the market for a property with such permission might be willing to pay more for it, and the property did in fact attract the necessary permission post sale. The value of an asset that is being offered for sale is, prima facie as not less than the amount that a reasonably well informed purchaser is prepared, in arms' length negotiations, to pay for it.': *Phillips v Brewin Dolphin Bell Lawrie Ltd* [2001] UKHL 2, [2001] 1 WLR 143, [2001] 1 All ER 673, [2001] 1 BCLC 145, [2001] BPIR 119 at [30] per Lord Scott.

It has been held that the court can specifically take into account a subsequent sale of the property as the basis for establishing the value of the property at the relevant time, however this depended on the fact that there had been no significant change in market conditions and the circumstances surrounding the sale could be regarded as proving a reliable base for inferring market value at the relevant time, namely the sale from the company to the defendant: *Stanley and Wood v TMK Finance Ltd* [2010] EWHC 3349 (Ch), [2011] BPIR 876. This is not to be seen as suing hindsight to value assets.

As far as valuation goes it has been said that the question in every case would be whether there was a 'significant' disparity in the consideration moving from and to the debtor: *Ramlort v Reid* [2004] BPIR 985 at [102]–[105]).

It has been accepted that a preferential payment which is susceptible to challenge cannot amount to consideration for the purposes of this provision (or s 339): *Re Peppard* [2009] BPIR 331 at [28].

A court might say that there is an undervalue, not because the purchase price given or received is an undervalue, but because of the terms of the agreement relating to the transfer. For instance, if A Ltd was to sell a property to B for what is regarded as market value, a court might hold that the transfer is an undervalue if the purchase price was not due to be paid for 12 months and no interest component was factored in.

The compromise or release of, or forebearance to press, a valid claim, or even a doubtful or invalid claim, as long as it is not known to be invalid but is advanced in good faith, can provide good consideration in this context: *Hill v Haines* [2007] EWCA Civ 1284, [2008] 2 All ER 901, [2007] BPIR 1280, at [79].

See G Peters 'Undervalues and the Value of Creditor and Debtor Covenants: A Comparative Analysis' (2008) 21 *Insolvency Intelligence* 81.

**Defence**—Provided that the office-holder is able to establish that there was a transaction at an undervalue, that it was entered into during the 2 years before the onset of insolvency and either the company was insolvent at the time of the transaction or was made insolvent as a consequence of entering into the transaction, to resist the claim the defendant must establish a two-limbed defence. This requires proving that:

- the company entered into the transaction in good faith for the purpose of carrying on its business; *and*
- when entering the transaction there were reasonable grounds for believing that the transaction would benefit the company.

It is the company that must act in good faith, and so the mind of the respondent is not at issue: *Re Baron Manufacturing Co Ltd* [1999] 1 BCLC 740 (a case where the defence failed, even though the respondent acted in innocence). The defence is rarely successful, but was in *Levy McCallum Ltd v Allen* [2007] NICh 3, [2007] NIJB 366 (and noted in *Capper* (2008) 21 *Insolvency Intelligence* 59). In that case Treacy J found that a guarantee given by a company that ended up in liquidation was given in good faith for the purpose of carrying on the business of the company and with reasonable grounds for believing that it would benefit the company. The company had guaranteed the debt of another company (in the same corporate group) that owed it money.

The second limb introduces an objective factor. If no consideration was given to the company, the respondent has a much harder task in fulfilling this limb of the defence.

Whether or not reasonable grounds existed must be determined at the time of the transaction.

**Court order**—If a court believes that the office-holder has succeeded in proving a case under s 238, it will make a declaration to that effect. Then the court must consider what orders, if any, will be made to restore the position to what it would have been if the company had not entered the transaction (s 238(3)). Section 238(3) is a restitutionary, rather than a compensatory provision. Examples of the kinds of orders that a court might make are set out in s 241. Importantly, courts are not restricted to those orders contained in s 241, but generally one or more of them will be incorporated into the orders of courts. Where there is a transaction at an undervalue, involving the company having purchased an asset at an inflated price, often courts will order, in the terms of s 241(1)(a), that the property that is the subject of the transaction at undervalue be re-transferred to the company: eg *Re Schuppan* [1997] BPIR 271 (shares). Where the liquidator does not seek the return of the property which was transferred under the transaction challenged under s 238, or the court does not think it appropriate to order the re-transfer of the property, it is likely that the hearing of an application under s 238 will end up involving a battle of valuations by experts: *Walker v WA Personnel Ltd* [2002] BPIR 621 at 635.

See s 241 and the comments accompanying that section.

The idea that the courts can only make an order by way of monetary compensation has been expressly rejected, and it has been said that a court can order restitution of assets even where the nature and substance of the assets had changed significantly since the transfer that is under attack: *Walker v WA Personnel Ltd* [2002] BPIR 621 at 634. Courts will be slow to allow a transferee of property that is later subject to a successful claim pursuant to s 238 to retain the property and pay the difference between the purchase price and a fair value, where the transferee had notice that the transaction might be challenged by a liquidator: *Walker v WA Personnel Ltd* at 634–635. The Court of Appeal in *Ramlort Ltd v Reid* [2004] EWCA Civ 800, [2004] BPIR 985 approved of that general approach. It stated that the court is not to start with a presumption that favours monetary compensation as against a setting aside of the relevant transaction. Courts must fashion the most appropriate remedy, as far as practicable, in order to restore the position pre-transaction: *Ramlort Ltd v Reid*.

Notwithstanding the use of 'shall' in s 238(3), usually indicating something that is mandatory, there is authority that provides that a court is not obliged to make an order, if it thinks fit: *Re Paramount Airways Ltd (No 2)* [1993] Ch 223 at 229, [1992] 3 WLR 690, [1992] 3 All ER 1, [1992] BCLC 710. This is perhaps illustrated in *Re MDA Investment Management Ltd*

[2004] 1 BCLC 217 where Park J declined to make an order even though he found the elements of s 238 to be established. His Lordship said that if he were to order the position to be restored to what it was before the relevant transaction, the company in liquidation would have been in a worse position.

It has been said that it is impossible to say that delay by the office-holder can never be a factor in the exercise of discretion under this section. However, delay by itself cannot be a relevant reason for not exercising the discretion to grant relief which would otherwise seem to be appropriate: *Stonham v Ramrattan* [2010] EWHC 1033 (Ch) (Mann J) at [34].

Interest could be claimed by a successful office-holder. From what date the interest may be calculated is somewhat of a moot point. In *Re Barton Manufacturing Ltd* [1999] BCLC 740 at 747–748 the court adopted the date of the liquidation. See the comments dealing with interest under the heading 'Orders' in relation to s 239.

A third party (someone other than the respondent who was a party to the transaction) who benefited from the transaction at an undervalue might be able to secure some protection where the transaction is declared to be at an undervalue within s 238. See the comments under 'Safeguarding third parties' relating to s 241.

See the comments under 'Remedy' in s 339.

**Benefits of orders**—As far as the destination of the benefits of orders, see the comments under 'Benefits of orders' relating to s 239.

**Market contracts are exempted**—This provision is specifically disapplied in relation to market contracts if a recognised investment exchange or clearing-house is a party to those contracts, and does not affect a disposition of property in pursuance of a market contract (Companies Act 1989, ss 155, 165(1)(a), 165(3)). Similar exemptions applicable to financial and security settlements and associated security arrangements are provided for in the Financial Markets and Insolvency (Settlement Finality) Regulations 1999 (SI 1999/2979).

**Limitation period**—Actions under this section are generally to be regarded as actions on a specialty, covered by ss 8 and 9 of the Limitation Act 1980, and as a consequence there is a 12-year time period in which office-holders can commence proceedings, *provided* that the substance of the application is to set aside a transaction, and not to recover a sum that is recoverable: *Re Priory Garages (Walthamstow) Ltd* [2001] BPIR 144 at 149, 160; *Re Yates* [2005] BPIR 476. Also, see *Hill v Spread Trustee Company Ltd* [2006] EWCA Civ 542, [2007] 1 WLR 2404, [2007] 1 All ER 1106, [2007] 1 BCLC 450, [2006] BPIR 789, (discussed in the notes to s 423). If a claim for a sum is ancillary to a primary head of relief that involves the setting aside of transactions, then the time limit is 12 years (*Re Priory Garages* at 160).

For further discussion, see Parry et al, *Transaction Avoidance in Insolvencies* (OUP, 2nd edn, 2011); Armour 'Transactions at an Undervalue' in Armour and Bennett (eds) *Vulnerable Transactions in Corporate Insolvency* (Hart Publishing, 2003) at 95–122; A Keay *McPherson and Keay's Law of Company Liquidation* (Sweet and Maxwell, 4th edn, 2018) at 668–692. For a discussion of a possible challenge pursuant to the Human Rights Act 1998, see Ulph and Allen 'Transactions at an Undervalue, Purchasers and the Impact of the Human Rights Act 1998' [2004] JBL 1.

See the notes accompanying s 339.

## [1.303]

### 239 Preferences (England and Wales)

(1)  This section applies as does section 238.

(2)  Where the company has at a relevant time (defined in the next section) given a preference to any person, the office-holder may apply to the court for an order under this section.

(3)  Subject as follows, the court shall, on such an application, make such order as it thinks fit for restoring the position to what it would have been if the company had not given that preference.

(4)  For the purposes of this section and section 241, a company gives a preference to a person if—

    (a)    that person is one of the company's creditors or a surety or guarantor for any of the company's debts or other liabilities, and

    (b)    the company does anything or suffers anything to be done which (in either case) has the effect of putting that person into a position which, in the event of the company going into insolvent liquidation, will be better than the position he would have been in if that thing had not been done.

(5)   The court shall not make an order under this section in respect of a preference given to any person unless the company which gave the preference was influenced in deciding to give it by a desire to produce in relation to that person the effect mentioned in subsection (4)(b).

(6)   A company which has given a preference to a person connected with the company (otherwise than by reason only of being its employee) at the time the preference was given is presumed, unless the contrary is shown, to have been influenced in deciding to give it by such a desire as is mentioned in subsection (5).

(7)   The fact that something has been done in pursuance of the order of a court does not, without more, prevent the doing or suffering of that thing from constituting the giving of a preference.

General note—This section permits courts to adjust transactions that constitute preferences. These are transactions that involve a creditor getting paid more (the debt being paid in full or in part) than would be paid to other creditors in a winding up. If such a transaction could not be adjusted, then creditors would grab what they could as quickly as possible when there was an inkling that a company was insolvent or heading towards, insolvency, and this would affect the statutorily regulated system laid down for the payment of creditors (and, some would say, derogates from the pari passu principle). A preference is where a transaction confers a priority or advantage on a creditor in relation to past indebtedness of the insolvent company and the advantage is given at the expense of other creditors who are owed debts at the time of transaction, thus preventing a distribution of the insolvent's property amongst the creditors according to the statutory scheme.

The Insolvency Law Review Committee's *Insolvency Law and Practice* ('the Cork Report') (Cmnd 858) provided the following as examples of preferences: paying the whole or part of a debt, providing security or further security for an existing debt, and returning goods that have been delivered but not paid for (at para 1208).

Where the preference involves the creation of a security interest, orders can be made under s 239 setting aside the security interest even though another secured creditor (ranking behind the secured creditor whose security is declared to be a preference) would benefit from the action of the liquidator: *Mills v Edict Ltd* [1999] BPIR 391 at 394.

When assessing whether a transaction is a preference, the court is to have regard for the transaction as a whole, in much the same way that the House of Lords in *Phillips v Brewin Dolphin Bell Lawrie Ltd* [2001] UKHL 2, [2001] 1 WLR 143, [2001] 1 All ER 673, [2001] 1 BCLC 145, [2001] BPIR 119 approached s 238: *Damon v Widney plc* [2002] BPIR 465 at 469–470. See the comments under 'Transaction at an undervalue' in relation to s 238.

For an assignee of a liquidator's claim of a preference to be entitled to succeed in an action against a creditor for the disgorging of a payment or transfer, the assignment must state that the right of the liquidator to claim a preference is assigned: *Global Corporate Ltd v Hale* [2017] EWHC 2277 (Ch) (the judgment has been appealed).

If the debtor company authorised a payment by a third party to one of its creditors (to pay off a debt owed by the company to the creditor) the payment can constitute a preference, and this is even though the company and the third party had no arrangement where the third party paid the creditor at the direction of the debtor company: *Burness v Supaproducts Pty Ltd* [2009] FCA 893, (2009) ALR 259. But, if at no point ownership of the funds paid to the creditor by the third party actually passed to the company (and it was never entitled to the funds) then the payment is not a preference: *Rambaldi (Trustee) v Commissioner of Taxation* [2017] FCAFC 217 at [37].

The effect of a transaction being regarded as a preference is that it is voidable, but certainly not void as is the situation where a transaction falls within s 127 of the Insolvency Act: *Marks v Feldman* (1870) LR 5 QB 275, 281; *Skandinaviska Enskilda Banken AB v Conway* [2019] UKPC 36, [60].

'Relevant time'—This is defined in s 240, and involves two aspects. First, the transaction must have occurred in a particular time zone, namely either the 6 months preceding the onset of insolvency, or, where the respondent is a person connected with the company, 2 years before the onset of insolvency. 'Onset of insolvency' is defined in s 240(3). Second, besides falling within this time zone, the transaction must have been entered into at a time when the company was unable to pay its debts within the meaning of s 123 or the entering into of the transaction resulted in the company being unable to pay its debts. See the comments under 'Relevant time' and 'Unable to pay debts' in relation to s 240 and 'Connected person' in relation to s 249.

Creditors—The word 'creditor' is not defined. But taking into account rr 14.1 and 14.2, it must be someone who can prove for a debt in the winding up.

The reference to 'creditor' sought to identify the creditor in the legal sense of the word: *Re Thirty-Eight Building Ltd* [1999] 1 BCLC 416, [1999] BPIR 620.

Where a supplier delivers goods on the basis of cash-on-delivery, any payment made at the time of delivery is not able to be regarded as being a preference (*Ferrier & Knight v Civil Aviation Authority* (1994) 48 FCR 163 at 169), because the supplier was not at any time a creditor for any of the company's debts, ie there was no creditor-debtor relationship.

There is no English authority that specifically holds that a contingent creditor is a creditor for the purposes of s 239. In *Re Blackpool Motor Car Co Ltd* [1901] 1 Ch 77 it was held that a surety was a contingent creditor and was, therefore, a creditor for the purposes of the preference provisions. Now s 239 includes a surety within its terms (s 239(4)(a)). In the Australian case of *Re Timbatec Pty Ltd* (1974) 24 FLR 30 it was held that a contingent creditor was a 'creditor' for the purposes of the then Australian statutory provision that was equivalent to s 239.

See the comments under 'Creditor' relating to s 124.

**Amelioration of a creditor's position**—This is required by para 4(b) of the section and it means establishing that the respondent received more from the company before winding up than would be received if no payment were received and the respondent proved for the debt in a winding up and was given a dividend, pari passu with all of the other creditors. This assessment could be based on either what the creditor would have received if liquidation occurred at the time of the alleged preference, or what the creditor would receive in the actual winding up. The legislation does not specify the time. But it seems that the former position is correct given the wording of s 239(4)(b) and some comments in the case law: *Re FP & CH Matthews Ltd* [1982] 1 Ch 257, [1982] 2 WLR 495, CA; *Re Ledingham-Smith* [1993] BCLC 635; *Re Hawkes Hill Publishing Co Ltd (in liq)*; *Ward v Perks* [2007] BPIR 1305 at [31].

Any payments made to secured creditors who have valid security does not improve the position of the secured creditor and it does not affect the position vis-à-vis the other creditors in winding up: *National Australia Bank Ltd v KDS Construction Services Pty Ltd* (1987) 163 CLR 668 (Aust HC). It is generally acknowledged that a payment in discharge of a valid security is not a preference (*National Australia Bank Ltd v KDS Construction Services Pty* at 679), but the giving of security to cover existing indebtedness would be preferential: *Re Transworld Trading Ltd* ([1999] BPIR 628. If there was to be a change in the form of security held by the creditor, there is still no preference, for example in *Sharyn Development Co Pty Ltd (in liquidation) v Official Receiver in Bankruptcy as Trustee of the Estate of Bridgland* (1980) 5 ACLR 1 (where a registered mortgage replaced a vendor's lien for unpaid purchase money). In the case where security is created over company property in order to secure both past indebtedness and new advances, the security is able to be challenged as a preference as far as the giving of the security related to the debtor's existing indebtedness is concerned: *Burns v Stapleton* (1959) 102 CLR 97 (Aust HC); *Re Mistral Finance Ltd* [2001] BCC 27.

The Australian High Court had stated in obiter comments that payments to creditors out of assets not usually available to unsecured creditors, such as those belonging to secured creditors, can constitute preferences: *G & M Aldridge Pty Ltd v Walsh* [2002] BPIR 482, (2001) 179 ALR 416.

**Influenced by a desire to provide a preference**—Section 239(5) demands that office-holders prove, on a subjective basis (see *Re MC Bacon Ltd* [1990] BCLC 324), that the company, when deciding to give the alleged preference, desired to produce the effect of a preference, although this is not required where the defendant is a person connected to the company (s 239(6)). In this latter situation there is a presumption that the desire was present (eg *Mills v Edict Ltd* [1999] BPIR 391, sub nom *Re Shapland Inc*) unless the respondent can show the contrary.

In relation to a claim under s 340 of the Act in *Abdulali v Finnegan* [2018] EWHC 1806 (Ch), [2018] BPIR 1547 at [31], Birss J said that 'the fact that something is the inevitable consequence of an act does not mean a person has necessarily been influenced by a desire to bring it about, or that it has even occurred to them at all'. He had earlier said at [17] that 'if more than one factor was influential in the debtor's mind, it is sufficient if one of the factors which did influence them was to put one of the unsecured creditors in a better position. Furthermore if that factor is present, it does not have to be the decisive factor which caused the debtor to do what they did nor does the trustee have to prove that it is the factor which "tipped the scales" in favour of making the preference'.

In establishing the desire of the company, the office-holder need not necessarily prove that the controllers of the company knew that their company was insolvent (*Katz v McNally* [1999] BCC 291 at 296, CA), or that the controllers knew that the company would enter insolvent liquidation: *Wills v Corfe Joinery Ltd* [1998] 2 BCLC 75, [1997] BPIR 611; *Katz v McNally* at 296. But it has been suggested that knowledge of impending liquidation may assist the office-holder in establishing desire: *Re Living Images Ltd* [1996] BCC 112 at 127, and *Re Agriplant Services Ltd* [1997] 2 BCLC 598.

It has been held that it is not always necessary to adduce direct evidence of the requisite desire as a court might infer desire from the facts: *Re MC Bacon Ltd* [1990] BCLC 324 at 335–336; *Rooney v Das* [1999] BPIR 404 at 406; *Skandinaviska Enskilda Banken AB v Conway* [2019] UKPC 36. Critically, the desire must have influenced the decision of the company to enter into the transaction that is the subject of the action (*Re MC Bacon Ltd* at 335–336). There must be a nexus between the desire and the making of the transaction, but it is not necessary to prove that the requisite desire is the only or decisive factor that caused the company to give the preference, for the desire might only be one of the factors that led to the payment or transfer (*Re MC Bacon Ltd* at 336). Also, it is not necessary for the liquidator to prove that if the requisite desire had not been present then the company would not have entered into the transaction impugned (*Re MC Bacon Ltd* at 336). The point at which to assess whether the necessary desire existed is when the decision to enter the transaction was made and not when the transaction was effected (*Re MC Bacon Ltd* at 336, *Re Stealth Construction Ltd* [2011] EWHC 1305 (Ch), [2011] BPIR 1173). The question of when the decision to enter the transaction is made is a matter to be decided the facts of each case: *Re Stealth Construction Ltd* at [62]. It is clear from this decision, and others, that it is the state of mind of the directors that is critical and not the creditor who is paid or any other person.

Liquidators are not required to prove that the sole or dominant desire of the company was to effect an improvement in the position of the creditor who benefited from the preference, and it is probably sufficient if some desire to provide an improvement is established: *Re Fairway Magazines Ltd* [1993] BCLC 643.

In ascertaining the desire of a corporate entity, it has been said that it is 'necessary to explore the mind of the company which gave the preference' (*Re Transworld Trading Ltd* [1999] BPIR 628 at 629). As it is an abstraction, a company has no mind of its own, for it acts through human agents (*Tesco Supermarkets Ltd v Nattrass* [1972] AC 153 at 170; *El Ajou v Dollar Land Holdings plc* [1994] 2 All ER 685, [1994] 1 BCLC 464), and so it is necessary to ascertain the human agents whose desire needs to be considered. Usually the board of directors is given, by the articles of association, the power to manage the affairs of the company, and so the desire of the board may need to be taken into account. But it is not going to be easy, in many cases, for the liquidator to know whose desire needs to be established, and, even when that can be ascertained, how that desire is to be in fact established. In *Re Agriplant Services Ltd* [1997] 2 BCLC 598, Jonathan Parker J equated the state of mind of the director who essentially ran the company with the state of mind of the company. It is going to be easier for a liquidator to establish desire in 'one-man companies' as the desire of the controller will be attributable to the company.

Even where the director who makes the payment that is being challenged has no personal desire to improve the position of the creditor to whom the payment was made, if the controllers of the company with whom the creditor was connected were behind the payment then there would be necessary desire within s 239: *Katz v McNally* [1999] BCC 291 at 297, CA.

While it has not been judicially settled that if a director of a company omits to do something, such as preventing a regular payment arrangement to a creditor, that it can constitute desire on the part of the company in giving a preference, Marcus Smith J in *Re Paul Flatman Ltd* ([2019] EWHC 3338 (Ch)) said that an argument to that effect might well have some force (at [36]).

It is probably notable, and indicative of the difficulty of establishing a desire, that there are few reported cases in which a court has found there to be a preference in favour of a person other than a connected person: *Re Living Images Ltd* [1996] BCC 112; *Re Agriplant Services Ltd* [1997] 2 BCLC 598; *Re Mistral Finance Ltd* [2001] BCC 27.

If it can be demonstrated that in making a payment to a creditor, the company is motivated solely by commercial considerations, such as ensuring the provision of future supplies or credit, and has no desire to improve the creditor's position, there is no preference, because the company is not positively wishing that the creditor be given a preference: *Re MC Bacon Ltd* at 335, 336; *Re DKG Contractors Ltd* [1990] BCC 903, 910; *Re Fairway Magazines Ltd* [1993] BCLC 643; *Wills v Corfe Joinery Ltd (in liquidation)* [1998] 2 BCLC 75, [1997] BPIR 611. Probably the most common commercial consideration is the pressure brought to bear by a major creditor. So, if a payment is made to a creditor who threatens that if he is not paid then he will not supply the company with any raw materials that it needs to carry on its business, it is likely that a court would not rule that the payment constituted a preference, as the desire of the company, in making the payment, was not to prefer the creditor but to ensure that its business could continue. In *Re Agriplant Services Ltd* [1997] 2 BCLC 598 Jonathan Parker J found that a creditor was liable under s 239 in respect of a sum of £20,000 paid to discharge a company debt even though there was alleged pressure placed on the company to pay as the director who orchestrated the payment of the creditor was influenced by a desire to see the creditor get a preference. He had this desire because in making the payment it meant that the director's liability under a guarantee that he had given to the creditor in relation to the debt owed to it by the company was reduced. The director was ordered in turn to pay the creditor £20,000, presumably under s 241(1)(e).

It has been suggested that events subsequent to the giving of the alleged preference can be considered in determining whether there was a desire to prefer and whether that desire influenced the company to enter into the transaction: *Re Transworld Trading Ltd* [1999] BPIR 628 at 634. Such events will not be as relevant as events occurring before the transaction was entered into, and while inferences may be drawn from these subsequent events, courts must do so with care (*Re Transworld Trading Ltd*).

If the debtor company had a desire, in making a transfer, to fulfil its legal obligations to creditors, it does not mean that the company cannot be said to also desire to prefer all or any of the creditors (*Re Fowlds* [2020] EWHC 1200 (Ch) at [65]).

For further discussion of this element of preference law, see Keay 'Preferences in Liquidation Law: A Time for a Change' (1998) 2 *Company Financial and Insolvency Law Review* 198.

**Presumption**—Where connected persons are involved in a transaction, the presumption in s 239(6) comes into play. It is only in such circumstances that liquidators have experienced any real success (see, for example, *Re DKG Contractors Ltd* [1990] BCC 903; *Weisgard v Pilkington* [1995] BCC 1108; *Wills v Corfe Joinery Ltd (in liquidation)* [1998] 2 BCLC 75, [1997] BPIR 611; *Re Transworld Trading Ltd* [1999] BPIR 628; *Katz v McNally* [1999] BCC 291, CA; *Re Conegrade Ltd* [2003] BPIR 358), although in a few cases the presumption has been rebutted: *Re Fairway Magazines Ltd* [1993] BCLC 643; *Re Beacon Leisure Ltd* [1992] BCLC 565; *Green v Tai* [2015] BPIR 24. Such a rebuttal was upheld by Birss J on appeal in a personal insolvency case in *Abdulali v Finnegan* [2018] EWHC 1806 (Ch), [2018] BPIR 1547.

The rationale for this presumption is that those connected with the company are more likely to know about the financial position of the company and will seek to benefit at the expense of the general body of creditors. But the presumption does not apply to a creditor who receives a benefit only because he or she is a company employee. Most frequently, preferences have been alleged where companies have paid directors, and in such cases the liquidator is able to avail himself or herself of the benefit of the presumption: eg *Re DKG Contractors Ltd* [1990] BCC 903; *Weisgard v Pilkington* [1995] BCC 1108; *Wills v Corfe Joinery Ltd (in liquidation)* [1998] 2 BCLC 75, [1997] BPIR 611; *Re Brian D Pierson (Contractors) Ltd* [2001] 1 BCLC 75, [1999] BPIR 18.

It has been held in *Katz v McNally* [1999] BCC 291 at 295, CA that persons connected with the company are not able to rebut the presumption that the company desired to give a preference to the defendant, merely by establishing that they did not know the company was insolvent at the time of the preference being made and, therefore, could not have had the requisite desire. Also, defendants have failed to rebut the presumption where they believed that there was reason to be optimistic concerning the prospects of the company: *Re Conegrade Ltd* [2003] BPIR 358.

See the comments under 'Connected person' in relation to s 249.

**Orders**—If a court believes that the office-holder has succeeded in proving a case under s 239, it will make a declaration to that effect. Then the court must consider what orders, if any, will be made to restore the position to what it would have been if the company had not entered the transaction (s 239(3)). Section 239(3) is a restitutionary, rather than a compensatory, provision. Examples of the kinds of orders that a court might make are set out in s 241. And although courts are not restricted to those orders contained in s 241, additional orders are usually in terms of one of the paragraphs in s 241(1). For instance para (c) indicates that a court could order the release or discharge of any security given by the company as part of a preference: *Mills v Edict Ltd* [1999] BPIR 391 at 394. It is likely that most often courts will make orders pursuant to s 241(1)(d): eg *Re Conegrade Ltd* [2003] BPIR 358.

A court can, either pursuant to the Insolvency Act, or (more likely) pursuant to the Supreme Court Act 1981, award interest. Section 35A of the Supreme Court Act provides, inter alia, that in proceedings for the recovery of a debt there may be included in any sum for which judgment is given simple interest from the date on which the cause of action arose and the date of judgment, and the recovery of an amount as a preference would be regarded as the recovery of a debt: *Re FP & CH Matthews Ltd* [1982] 1 All ER 338, CA. While there is some doubt as to the date from which interest will be calculated, existing authority seems to suggest that it will be from the time of the commencement of winding up, as that is the date when the liquidator's cause of action arose (*Re FP & CH Matthews Ltd*). However, it is submitted that the time should run from the date on which the liquidator first demands repayment of the sum paid to the creditor. This view is based on the fact that, arguably, it would be unfair to make a creditor liable for interest before any demand, as the creditor cannot be sure that he or she will be pursued until that time, and until a demand is made a preferred creditor may not actually be aware that he or she is liable to disgorge benefits: see *Star v O'Brien* (1997) 15 ACLC 144. For further discussion on this point, see Keay 'The Recovery of Voidable Preferences: Aspects of Restoration' [2000] *Company Financial and Insolvency Law Review* 1 and reproduced in Francis Rose (ed) *Restitution and Insolvency* (Mansfield Press, 2000) at 237 ff.

**Benefits of orders**—Traditionally, it has been held that any benefits flowing from orders made are held on statutory trust for the benefit of the general body of creditors, not the chargeholders, as they did not exist as part of the company's property at the time of the commencement of the winding up: *Re Yagerphone* [1935] Ch 392; *Lewis v Commissioners of Inland Revenue* [2001] 3 All ER 499). It is only when the liquidator or administrator was appointed that the action under s 239 came into being, and the action is personal to the liquidator or administrator (*Re Oasis Merchandising Services Ltd* [1995] 2 BCLC 493 and affirmed on appeal: [1998] Ch 170, [1997] 2 WLR 764, [1997] 1 All ER 1009, [1997] 1 BCLC 689). But see the comments of Neuberger J in *Ciro Citterio Menswear plc v Thakrar* (unreported) 10 July 2002 (discussed in P Fleming 'Sharing the Spoils of a Preference Action: Save a Slice for the Secured Creditors' (2003) 16(5) *Insolvency Intelligence* 33). For further discussion, see Parry, 'The Destination of Proceeds of Insolvency Liquidation' (2002) 23 *Company Lawyer* 49; Armour and Walters, ''The Proceeds of Office-holder Actions under the Insolvency Act: Charged Assets of Free Estate?' [2006] LMCLQ 27.

**Limitation of action**—Actions under this section are generally to be regarded as actions on a specialty, covered by ss 8 and 9 of the Limitation Act 1980, and as a consequence there is a 12-year time period in which office-holders can commence proceedings, *provided* that the substance of the application is to set aside a transaction, and not to recover a sum that is recoverable: *Re Priory Garages (Walthamstow) Ltd* [2001] BPIR 144 at 149, 160. If a claim for a sum is ancillary to a primary head of relief that involves the setting aside of transactions, then the time limit is 12 years (*Re Priory Garages* at 160).

See the comments under 'Court orders' in relation to s 238. Also, see the comments relating to ss 240 and 241.

**Market contracts are exempted**—This provision is specifically disapplied in relation to market contracts if a recognised investment exchange or clearing-house is a party to those contracts, and does not affect a disposition of property in pursuance of a market contract (Companies Act 1989, ss 155, 165(1)(b), 165(3)). Similar exemptions applicable to financial and security settlements and associated security arrangements are provided for in the Financial Markets and Insolvency (Settlement Finality) Regulations 1999 (SI 1999/2979).

For further discussion on preferences, see Parry et al *Transaction Avoidance in Insolvencies* (OUP, 2nd edn, 2011); Walters 'Preferences' in J Armour and H Bennett (eds) *Vulnerable Transactions in Corporate Insolvency* (Hart Publishing, 2003) at 123–181; A Keay *McPherson and Keay's Law of Company Liquidation* (Sweet and Maxwell, 4th edn, 2018) at 692–725. Also, see Wilkes 'Setting aside vulnerable transactions – an update (2011) 4 *Corporate Rescue and Insolvency* 189; J Morgan 'Preference – when is the decision made?' (2011) 5 *Corporate Rescue and Insolvency* 75.

## [1.304]

### 240 "Relevant time" under ss 238, 239

(1)  Subject to the next subsection, the time at which a company enters into a transaction at an undervalue or gives a preference is a relevant time if the transaction is entered into, or the preference given—

   (a)  in the case of a transaction at an undervalue or of a preference which is given to a person who is connected with the company (otherwise than by reason only of being its employee), at a time in the period of 2 years ending with the onset of insolvency (which expression is defined below),

   (b)  in the case of a preference which is not such a transaction and is not so given, at a time in the period of 6 months ending with the onset of insolvency, . . .

   (c)  in either case, at a time between the making of an administration application in respect of the company and the making of an administration order on that application, and

   (d)  in either case, at a time between the filing with the court of a copy of notice of intention to appoint an administrator under paragraph 14 or 22 of Schedule B1 and the making of an appointment under that paragraph.

(2)  Where a company enters into a transaction at an undervalue or gives a preference at a time mentioned in subsection (1)(a) or (b), that time is not a relevant time for the purposes of section 238 or 239 unless the company—

   (a)  is at that time unable to pay its debts within the meaning of section 123 in Chapter VI of Part IV, or

   (b)  becomes unable to pay its debts within the meaning of that section in consequence of the transaction or preference;

but the requirements of this subsection are presumed to be satisfied, unless the contrary is shown, in relation to any transaction at an undervalue which is entered into by a company with a person who is connected with the company.

(3)  For the purposes of subsection (1), the onset of insolvency is—

   (a)  in a case where section 238 or 239 applies by reason of an administrator of a company being appointed by administration order, the date on which the administration application is made,

    (b)    in a case where section 238 or 239 applies by reason of an administrator of a company being appointed under paragraph 14 or 22 of Schedule B1 following filing with the court of a copy of a notice of intention to appoint under that paragraph, the date on which the copy of the notice is filed,

    (c)    in a case where section 238 or 239 applies by reason of an administrator of a company being appointed otherwise than as mentioned in paragraph (a) or (b), the date on which the appointment takes effect,

    (d)    in a case where section 238 or 239 applies by reason of a company going into liquidation . . . at the time when the appointment of an administrator ceases to have effect, the date on which the company entered administration (or, if relevant, the date on which the application for the administration order was made or a copy of the notice of intention to appoint was filed), and

    (e)    in a case where section 238 or 239 applies by reason of a company going into liquidation at any other time, the date of the commencement of the winding up.

**Amendments**—Enterprise Act 2002, ss 248(3), 278(2), Sch 17, paras 9, 26, Sch 26; SI 2017/702; SI 2019/146, as from IP completion day (as defined in the European Union (Withdrawal Agreement) Act 2020, s 39(1)–(5)).

**CIGA 2020**—This provision is affected by temporary measures at Sch 10, paras 15(2) and 15(3) of CIGA 2020.

**General note**—This section limits the actions that can be brought under either s 238 or s 239. Not all transactions at an undervalue and all preferences can be challenged. Only those transactions that occurred in the relevant time can be attacked. The provision sets out two factors that will limit the transactions that a liquidator can impugn. First, the transaction must have been effected within a certain time zone prior to liquidation or administration. Second, there is a financial restriction on the bringing of actions, for in order to succeed, a company must have been unable to pay its debts at the time of the transaction or, as a result of the transaction, the company is unable to pay its debts.

Where a winding-up order was made as a result of a petition presented under s 124 during the period of 27 April 2020 to 30 September 2021 on the basis that the company was unable to pay its debts, s 240(1)(a) has effect as if the reference to the period of two years ending with the onset of insolvency were to the period which begins with whichever is the later of the day 2 years before the day on which the petition was presented, and the day 2 years and 6 months before the day on which the winding-up order was made, and it ends with the day on which the winding-up order was made (para 15(2) of Sch 10 of the Corporate Insolvency and Governance Act 2020) (as amended by The Corporate Insolvency and Governance Act 2020 (Coronavirus) (Extension of the Relevant Period) Regulations 2020 (SI 2020/1031), reg 2, The Corporate Insolvency and Governance Act 2020 (Coronavirus) (Extension of the Relevant Period) (No 2) Regulations 2020 (SI 2020/1483), reg 2 and The Corporate Insolvency and Governance Act 2020 (Coronavirus) (Extension of the Relevant Period) Regulations 2021 (SI 2021/375), reg 3(4)). Where a winding-up order was made as a result of a petition presented under s 124 during the period of 27 April 2020 to 30 September 2021 on the basis that the company was unable to pay its debts, s 240(1)(b) has effect as if the reference to the period of 6 months ending with the onset of insolvency were to the period which begins with whichever is the later of the day 6 months before the day on which the petition was presented, and the day 12 months before the day on which the winding-up order was made, and ends with the day on which the winding-up order was made (para 15(3) of Sch 10 of the Corporate Insolvency and Governance Act 2020) (as amended by The Corporate Insolvency and Governance Act 2020 (Coronavirus) (Extension of the Relevant Period) Regulations 2020 (SI 2020/1031), reg 2, The Corporate Insolvency and Governance Act 2020 (Coronavirus) (Extension of the Relevant Period) (No 2) Regulations 2020 (SI 2020/1483), reg 2, The Corporate Insolvency and Governance Act 2020 (Coronavirus) (Extension of the Relevant Period) Regulations 2021, reg 3(4) (SI 2021/375) and The Corporate Insolvency and Governance Act 2020 (Coronavirus) (Extension of the Relevant Period) (No 2) Regulations 2021 (SI 2021/718), reg 2).

**Relevant time**—The actual time zone applicable will depend on several circumstances, including what type of transaction is alleged to have been made, but what is uniform with all transactions is that the time zone is calculated in relation to a specific date: the onset of insolvency (s 240(3)) (see below).

**Transaction at an undervalue**—For a successful action under s 238 the transaction must have taken place during the 2 years preceding the onset of insolvency (discussed below), or, where administration occurred, in the interim period between either the presentation of a petition for an administration order and the making of such an order or the filing with the court of a copy of a notice of intention to appoint an administrator pursuant to para 14 or 22 of Sch B1 and the making of the appointment.

**Preference**—For a successful action under s 238 the transaction must have taken place during the 6 months preceding the onset of insolvency, unless the recipient of the alleged preference is a connected party, and then the period is extended to 2 years, or, where administration occurred, either during the interim period between the presentation of a petition for an administration order and the making of such an order or the filing with the court of a copy of a notice of intention to appoint an administrator pursuant to para 14 or 22 of Sch B1 and the making of the appointment.

The date of payment is the critical point of time: *Wills v Corfe Joinery Ltd (in liquidation)* [1998] 2 BCLC 75, [1997] BPIR 611.

**Unable to pay debts**—While the transaction that a liquidator wants to attack occurs during the necessary time zone, s 240(2) provides that he or she will not succeed unless the debtor company was unable to pay its debts at the time of the transaction or, as a result of the transaction, the company was unable to pay its debts. 'Unable to pay its debts' means the same as the manner in which the phrase is defined in s 123. See the comments relating to s 123, and especially those under the headings: 'Unable to pay debts as they fall due'; 'Value of assets less than liabilities'. In deciding cases involving adjustment claims hindsight might be used in determining the issue of whether the company could pay its debts at the time of the entry into the impugned transaction: *Green v Tai* [2015] BPIR 24 at [82], *Watchorn v Jupiter Industries Ltd* [2014] EWHC 3003 (Ch) at [46], [47].

An important proviso is that if the respondent to a s 238 action is a person connected with the company, then the company is presumed to have been unable to pay its debts at the time or unable to pay its debts as a consequence of entering into the transaction. This exception accommodates the fact that for provisions like s 238, which are designed to prevent asset-stripping in favour of persons connected with companies, insolvency should not be a required factor, unlike with preferences where the concern is to ensure that there is a division of the assets of the company amongst creditors according to the statutory scheme. With a preference the recipient is actually entitled to be paid (even if he or she is a connected person, provided that the debt was incurred bona fide) as a debt is owed to him or her, but with a transaction at an undervalue, entered into in favour of a connected person, the recipient is not entitled to the benefit. In the majority of cases the respondent is likely to be a connected person.

See the comments under this heading and accompanying s 123.

**'Onset of insolvency'**—This is an expression which is used as a matter of convenience to establish the end point for the time zone in which transactions must occur if they are able to be challenged. The use of the expression is somewhat confusing at first blush because it does not identify the beginning of insolvency, but identifies steps in the advent of formal insolvency proceedings. Section 240(3) explains what this phrase means, where action is taken in an administration or in a liquidation. To ensure that the time zone for transactions is not unreasonably reduced when a liquidation follows an administration, the provision will not take effect at the time at which liquidation commences, but when the administration commenced. If this were not done then the onset of insolvency would not occur until the commencement of winding up (the presentation of a petition to wind up), and this might permit transactions, that would have just been in the relevant time when the administration was occurring, to 'escape'.

If the company's liquidation occurred in any circumstances, other than following administration, then the date of the commencement of the winding up is the onset of insolvency. The commencement of winding up is not really the beginning of the liquidation; it is a deemed commencement of winding up. In voluntary winding up the deemed date of commencement is at the time of the passing of the resolution for voluntary winding up (s 86). In compulsory liquidation, winding up is deemed to have commenced at the time of the presentation of the petition (s 129(2)). If a voluntary liquidation was commenced prior to the presentation of a petition on which a winding up order is subsequently made, then the commencement of winding up is deemed to be the date of the resolution to wind up (s 129(1)). If a petition is presented and then there is a substitution order made, leading to an amended petition, with a different petitioner, the date of the commencement of the winding up is deemed to be the date of the presentation of the first petition: *Re Western Welsh International System Buildings Ltd* (1985) 1 BCC 99, 296. If action is brought in a liquidation, that followed the conversion of an administration into a liquidation through the agency of Art 37 of the EU Regulation on Insolvency Proceedings, the date of the presentation of the administration petition is the date of the onset of insolvency. Article 37 provides that a liquidator in main proceedings may request that proceedings covered by the Regulation (for the UK this includes compulsory and creditors' voluntary liquidations) previously commenced in another State of the EU (secondary proceedings) be converted into winding-up proceedings if this is for the benefit of the creditors. The court may order conversion into compulsory or creditors' voluntary liquidation.

**[1.305]**

**241 Orders under ss 238, 239**

(1)  Without prejudice to the generality of sections 238(3) and 239(3), an order under either of those sections with respect to a transaction or preference entered into or given by a company may (subject to the next subsection)—

(a)  require any property transferred as part of the transaction, or in connection with the giving of the preference, to be vested in the company,

(b)  require any property to be so vested if it represents in any person's hands the application either of the proceeds of sale of property so transferred or of money so transferred,

(c)  release or discharge (in whole or in part) any security given by the company,

(d)  require any person to pay, in respect of benefits received by him from the company, such sums to the office-holder as the court may direct,

(e)  provide for any surety or guarantor whose obligations to any person were released or discharged (in whole or in part) under the transaction, or by the giving of the preference, to be under such new or revived obligations to that person as the court thinks appropriate.

(f)  provide for security to be provided for the discharge of any obligation imposed by or arising under the order, for such an obligation to be charged on any property and for the security or charge to have the same priority as a security or charge released or discharged (in whole or in part) under the transaction or by the giving of the preference, and

(g)  provide for the extent to which any person whose property is vested by the order in the company, or on whom obligations are imposed by the order, is to be able to prove in the winding up of the company for debts or other liabilities which arose from, or were released or discharged (in whole or in part) under or by, the transaction or the giving of the preference.

(2)  An order under section 238 or 239 may affect the property of, or impose any obligation on, any person whether or not he is the person with whom the company in question entered into the transaction or (as the case may be) the person to whom the preference was given; but such an order—

(a)  shall not prejudice any interest in property which was acquired from a person other than the company and was acquired in good faith and for value, or prejudice any interest deriving from such an interest, and

(b)  shall not require a person who received a benefit from the transaction or preference in good faith and for value to pay a sum to the office-holder, except where that person was a party to the transaction or the payment is to be in respect of a preference given to that person at a time when he was a creditor of the company.

(2A)  Where a person has acquired an interest in property from a person other than the company in question, or has received a benefit from the transaction or preference, and at the time of that acquisition or receipt—

(a)  he had notice of the relevant surrounding circumstances and of the relevant proceedings, or

(b)  he was connected with, or was an associate of, either the company in question or the person with whom that company entered into the transaction or to whom that company gave the preference,

then, unless the contrary is shown, it shall be presumed for the purposes of paragraph (a) or (as the case may be) paragraph (b) of subsection (2) that the interest was acquired or the benefit was received otherwise than in good faith.

(3)  For the purposes of subsection (2A)(a), the relevant surrounding circumstances are (as the case may require)—

(a)  the fact that the company in question entered into the transaction at an undervalue; or

(b)  the circumstances which amounted to the giving of the preference by the company in question;

and subsections (3A) to (3C) have effect to determine whether, for those purposes, a person has notice of the relevant proceedings.

(3A) Where section 238 or 239 applies by reason of a company's entering administration, a person has notice of the relevant proceedings if he has notice that—

 (a) an administration application has been made,

 (b) an administration order has been made,

 (c) a copy of a notice of intention to appoint an administrator under paragraph 14 or 22 of Schedule B1 has been filed, or

 (d) notice of the appointment of an administrator has been filed under paragraph 18 or 29 of that Schedule.

(3B) Where section 238 or 239 applies by reason of a company's going into liquidation at the time when the appointment of an administrator of the company ceases to have effect, a person has notice of the relevant proceedings if he has notice that—

 (a) an administration application has been made,

 (b) an administration order has been made,

 (c) a copy of a notice of intention to appoint an administrator under paragraph 14 or 22 of Schedule B1 has been filed,

 (d) notice of the appointment of an administrator has been filed under paragraph 18 or 29 of that Schedule, or

 (e) the company has gone into liquidation.

(3C) In a case where section 238 or 239 applies by reason of the company in question going into liquidation at any other time, a person has notice of the relevant proceedings if he has notice—

 (a) where the company goes into liquidation on the making of a winding-up order, of the fact that the petition on which the winding-up order is made has been presented or of the fact that the company has gone into liquidation;

 (b) in any other case, of the fact that the company has gone into liquidation.

(4) The provisions of sections 238 to 241 apply without prejudice to the availability of any other remedy, even in relation to a transaction or preference which the company had no power to enter into or give.

**Amendments**—Insolvency (No 2) Act 1994, s 1; Enterprise Act 2002, s 248(3), Sch 17, paras 9, 27.

**General note**—This provision addresses the issue of orders made in relation to ss 238 and 239 claims. If a court believes that the office holder has succeeded in proving a case under either s 238 or s 239, it will make a declaration to that effect. Then the court must consider, because of ss 238(3) and 239(3), what orders, if any, will be made to restore the position to what it would have been if the company had not entered the transaction. This does not mean that the court is limited to restoring the position of the company as it was before the dealing. Rather it has to put all the parties back into the position that they would have been in had the transaction not been entered into or the preference given: *Johnson v Arden* [2018] EWHC 1624 (Ch) at [92]. What the court is to do is restitutionary in nature, not compensatory (at [92]). In order to restore parties prior to the transaction, the court might make any order that it sees fit. If an order cannot be made that fully restores the parties to the pre-transaction position, then the court is able to make such order that restores the parties' positions as far as possible: *Chohan v Saggar* [1994] 1 BCLC 706 at 713; *Walker* v *WA Personnel Ltd* [2002] BPIR 621. Full restoration might not be possible because property is not in the hands of the party to the preference or transaction at an undervalue but has passed to an innocent third party (see below under 'Safeguarding third parties'). Whilst all of this gives the courts a wide discretion, s 241(1) provides a number of examples of orders that a court might make. The language of s 241(1) ('without prejudice to the generality of sections 238(3) and 239(3) . . . ') makes it clear that the kinds of orders set out there are not meant to be seen as exhaustive. The orders set out in s 241 merely indicate the wide range that court orders may take. Courts are able to make any of the kinds of orders set out in s 241(1) where they find that a transaction at an undervalue was entered into or a preference granted, but clearly some provisions in s 241 will be more suited to transactions at an undervalue and others more suited to preferences. In *Johnson v Arden* [2018] EWHC 1624 (Ch) the argument that the court has an unlimited jurisdiction to grant relief under s 238 or s 239 was rejected (at [91]).

The provision goes on to restrict courts in making orders where a third party might be prejudiced by the court's order.

## SECTION 241(1)

The granting of relief is at the discretion of the court and while the discretion is unfettered it must be exercised judicially within the context of the statutory provision and its purpose (*Re Fowlds* [2020] EWHC 1200 (Ch) at [12]), and a court may decline to grant relief where justice requires (*Re Paramount Airways Ltd (No 2)* [1993] Ch 223 at 229, [1992] 3 All ER 1, [1992] BCLC 710; *Singla v Brown* [2007] EWHC 405 (Ch), [2008] 1 Ch 357 at [52]).

Unfairness has been acknowledged by case law to be a possible factor in a court's exercise of discretion and in declining to grant relief (*Re Fowlds* [2020] EWHC 1200 (Ch) at [12]). But, as indicated in *Stonham v Ramrattan* [2010] EWHC 1033, [2010] BPIR 1210 at [40] 'a significant or strong or even exceptional' circumstance must arise before the court declines to exercise such discretion. In *Re Fowlds* [2020] EWHC 1200 (Ch) at [12] ICC Judge Jones said that there will have to be something unusual to justify not granting relief in favour of the successful applicant. Delay in taking proceedings to challenge a transaction would not of itself suffice for a court to decline to provide relief where it would otherwise appear to be appropriate; there would have to be other factors, but it might be taken into account in deciding whether to exercise the discretion (*Stoneham v Ramrattan* at [34]). The respondent to the action has the burden of convincing the court that it should not make an order in favour of the applicant (*Re Fowlds* [2020] EWHC 1200 (Ch) at [13]). For examples of cases where exceptional circumstances warranted the exercise of the discretion, see *Re Claridge* ([2011] EWHC 2047 (Ch), (2011) BPIR 1529; *Re Fowlds* [2020] EWHC 1200 (Ch)). In the latter case ICC Judge Jones accepted that the respondent's change of position could be a factor taken into account in a judge deciding whether to decline to grant relief to the applicant.

**The orders**—It has been said in relation to a transaction at an undervalue case (under s 339, the bankruptcy equivalent of s 238) that the court is not to start with a presumption that favours monetary compensation as against a setting aside of the relevant transaction. Courts must fashion the most appropriate remedy, as far as practicable, in order to restore the position pre-transaction: *Ramlort Ltd v Reid* [2004] EWCA Civ 800, [2004] BPIR 985. The court in *Ramlort* went on to say that when a court exercises its discretion in relation to what is the most appropriate remedy, the events subsequent to the impugned transaction will be considered.

While the examples of orders that might be made suggest that they can be made against different persons, it was held in *Johnson v Arden* [2018] EWHC 1624 (Ch) that the court does not have jurisdiction to make an order under s 238 or s 239 against a director of a company who has received no benefit from the transaction or preference and whose only role is to direct the company to enter into the transaction or to give the preference. The director has in fact nothing to 'restore'. (at [10]).

## SECTION 241(1)(a)

**Scope of provision**—This provision is most likely to be invoked with transactions at an undervalue, where the company has either purchased an asset at an inflated price or sold one of its assets for a significantly smaller sum than market value would dictate: see *Walker v WA Personnel Ltd* [2002] BPIR 621. The paragraph involves an order whereby the court requires the vesting of any property transferred in connection with the transaction at an undervalue in the company. The order could be invoked where the company, which is now in liquidation or administration, transferred property prior to its liquidation or administration to a creditor to discharge its indebtedness, with such a transfer being regarded as preferential. If the order involves the respondent having to re-transfer property to the liquidator or administrator and the property has been enhanced in value by the respondent, one would think that the court would include in the order some requirement that the respondent be paid, or allowed a sum to cover his or her expenses in enhancing the property.

## SECTION 241(1)(b)

**Scope of provision**—This provides that property is to be vested in the company where the property represents in anyone's hands the application of either the proceeds of property, or money, transferred by the company as part of the preference transaction. The order allows for tracing, and might be useful where the company made a payment or transferred property to a person who is, when proceedings are ready to be commenced, insolvent. If the money or property had been transferred to a third person, the liquidator or administrator might investigate the possibility of proceeding against that other person. Whether such action is able to succeed will depend, partly, on whether the third person can make use of the protections for third parties contained elsewhere in the section.

## SECTION 241(1)(c)

**Scope of provision**—Effectively, the order in *Mills v Edict Ltd* [1999] BPIR 391 at 394 fell within this broad category. It could be applied where a company granted a mortgage to a creditor over some property which it owns, either in exchange for some property if transferred (where a transaction at an undervalue is concerned) or in payment of a debt owed (in the case of a preference). A release or discharge would enable the company to regain the property and return it to the position it enjoyed prior to the transaction.

#### SECTION 241(1)(d)

**Scope of provision**—Commonly this will apply in preference cases and involve the creditor, who was paid by the company in relation to a debt owed by the company, being ordered to repay that sum to the liquidator or administrator. This order could also be made in a transaction at an undervalue case, where property has been transferred at an undervalue, and instead of the court ordering a re-transfer of the property, perhaps in circumstances where re-transfer is impossible, the court might order the transferee to repay the company the difference between what the respondent paid and a fair price: see *Phillips v Brewin Dolphin Bell Lawrie Ltd* 2001] UKHL 2, [2001] 1 WLR 143, [2001] 1 All ER 673, [2001] 1 BCLC 145, [2001] BPIR 119.

#### SECTION 241(1)(e)

**Scope of provision**—The order envisaged by this paragraph will visit new or revived obligations on a guarantor who was released or discharged from obligations under a transaction or as a result of the giving of a preference. This kind of order could well be coupled with a s 241(1)(d) type order. The restoration of the obligations of a guarantor may not only benefit the company. Take a situation where a director of the company in liquidation or administration guaranteed the company's debts to a creditor and ensures that the creditor is paid off before liquidation or administration ensues. This extinguishes the guarantor's obligations. The liquidator or administrator will take preference proceedings against the creditor (assuming the payment falls in the relevant time) and if he or she succeeds the creditor will be ordered to repay the payment to the liquidator. To ensure that the creditor is restored to his or her pre-preference position, an order might be made under this paragraph to provide that the director's guarantee obligations be revived and the creditor could, once again, rely on the guarantee. For an example of this, see *Re Agriplant Services Ltd* [1997] 2 BCLC 598.

#### SECTION 241(1)(f)

**Scope of provision**—This paragraph covers the case where a court makes an order which requires the provision of security for the discharge of any obligation imposed by the court's order, for the obligation to be charged on any property and for the security to have the same priority as a security released or discharged by the giving of the preference or a transaction at an undervalue.

#### SECTION 241(1)(g)

**Scope of provision**—This paragraph allows courts to limit the amount that could be proved in the winding up by a party. It is the type of order that has to be used carefully, remembering that the purpose of orders is to restore the position to what it was before the impugned transaction was entered into. The order will probably see a preferred creditor being given the right to prove in the liquidation of the insolvent company for the debt owed to him or her, and which he or she has been ordered to repay to the company.

**The safeguarding of third parties**—Section 241(2) acknowledges that court orders may affect the property of, or impose an obligation on, persons (third parties) other than the company now in liquidation or administration, and the other party to the transaction at an undervalue or the preference. In such a case the court is obliged in making its order not to prejudice the interest in property which a third party acquired from anyone other than the company and where the third party was not a party to the transaction at an undervalue or a preference. If a third party acquired property in good faith and for value, then his or her successor in title will also be safeguarded from the attack of an office-holder. All of this accords with the position at common law, where traditionally the effect of the avoidance of transactions in relation to preferences and transactions at an undervalue has been limited to immediate parties and their privies: see *Stevenson v Newnham* (1853) CB 286 at 302, (1853) 138 ER 1208 at 1215.

A third party who relies on the ground of good faith has the onus of establishing good faith. There are indications from *Re Sonatacus Ltd* [2007] EWCA Civ 31, [2007] 1 BCLC 627 at [29], that establishing good faith may not be easy. *Re Sonatacus Ltd* represents a case where the court used s 241(2) to order the repayment of a preference.

**Presumption against third parties**—But a third party, if he or she at the time of receiving a benefit from anyone other than the company had notice of both the surrounding circumstances and relevant proceedings, or he or she is a person connected with, or was an associate of, the company or the person who entered into the transaction (under challenge) with the company, a presumption exists that the third party had not acted in good faith (s 240(2A)). The presumption is rebuttable. Where the situation is not covered by any of the factors in this paragraph the onus is on the office-holder to demonstrate that the third party did not act in good faith.

**'Surrounding circumstances'**—This is defined in s 241(3) and means the fact that the company had entered into a transaction that amounted to a transaction at an undervalue or a preference. The meaning of 'relevant proceedings' is determined whether the company has entered administration, liquidation following administration or straight liquidation, and is defined in subsections (3A), (3B), and (3C) respectively.

See Keay 'The Recovery of Voidable Preferences: Aspects of Restoration' [2000] *Company Financial and Insolvency Law Review* 1 and reproduced in Francis Rose (ed) *Restitution and Insolvency*, (Mansfield Press, 2000) at 237 ff.

For a discussion of a possible challenge by third parties, who are affected by orders made as a result of a successful claim under either s 238 or s 239, pursuant to the Human Rights Act 1998, see Ulph and Allen 'Transactions at an Undervalue, Purchasers and the Impact of the Human Rights Act 1998' [2004] JBL 1.

## [1.306]

### 242 Gratuitous alienations (Scotland)

(1) Where this subsection applies and—

    (a) the winding up of a company has commenced, an alienation by the company is challengeable by –

        (i) any creditor who is a creditor by virtue of a debt incurred on or before the date of such commencement, or

        (ii) the liquidator;

    (b) a company enters administration, an alienation by the company is challengeable by the administrator.

(2) Subsection (1) applies where—

    (a) by the alienation, whether before or after 1st April 1986 (the coming into force of section 75 of the Bankruptcy (Scotland) Act 1985), any part of the company's property is transferred or any claim or right of the company is discharged or renounced, and

    (b) the alienation takes place on a relevant day.

(3) For the purposes of subsection (2)(b), the day on which an alienation takes place is the day on which it becomes completely effectual; and in that subsection "relevant day" means, if the alienation has the effect of favouring—

    (a) a person who is an associate (within the meaning of the Bankruptcy (Scotland) Act 2016) of the company, a day not earlier than 5 years before the date on which –

        (i) the winding up of the company commences, or

        (ii) as the case may be, the company enters administration; or

    (b) any other person, a day not earlier than 2 years before that date.

(4) On a challenge being brought under subsection (1), the court shall grant decree of reduction or for such restoration of property to the company's assets or other redress as may be appropriate; but the court shall not grant such a decree if the person seeking to uphold the alienation establishes—

    (a) that immediately, or at any other time, after the alienation the company's assets were greater than its liabilities, or

    (b) that the alienation was made for adequate consideration, or

    (c) that the alienation—

        (i) was a birthday, Christmas or other conventional gift, or

        (ii) was a gift made, for a charitable purpose, to a person who is not an associate of the company,

which, having regard to all the circumstances, it was reasonable for the company to make:

Provided that this subsection is without prejudice to any right or interest acquired in good faith and for value from or through the transferee in the alienation.

(5) In subsection (4) above, "charitable purpose" means any charitable, benevolent or philanthropic purpose, whether or not it is charitable within the meaning of any rule of law.

(6) For the purposes of the foregoing provisions of this section, an alienation in implementation of a prior obligation is deemed to be one for which there was no consideration or no adequate consideration to the extent that the prior obligation was undertaken for no consideration or no adequate consideration.

(7)   A liquidator and an administrator have the same right as a creditor has under any rule of law to challenge an alienation of a company made for no consideration or no adequate consideration.

(8)   This section applies to Scotland only.

**Amendments**—Enterprise Act 2002, s 248(3), Sch 17, paras 9, 28; SI 2016/1034.

**CIGA 2020**—This provision is affected by temporary measures at Sch 10, paras 16(2) and 16(3) of CIGA 2020.

## [1.307]

### 243 Unfair preferences (Scotland)

(1)   Subject to subsection (2) below, subsection (4) below applies to a transaction entered into by a company, whether before or after 1st April 1986, which has the effect of creating a preference in favour of a creditor to the prejudice of the general body of creditors, being a preference created not earlier than 6 months before the commencement of the winding up of the company or the company enters administration.

(2)   Subsection (4) below does not apply to any of the following transactions—

  (a)   a transaction in the ordinary course of trade or business;

  (b)   a payment in cash for a debt which when it was paid had become payable, unless the transaction was collusive with the purpose of prejudicing the general body of creditors;

  (c)   a transaction whereby the parties to it undertake reciprocal obligations (whether the performance by the parties of their respective obligations occurs at the same time or at different times) unless the transaction was collusive as aforesaid;the granting of a mandate by a company authorising an arrestee to pay over the arrested funds or part thereof to the arrester where –

    (i)   there has been a decree for payment or a warrant for summary diligence, and

    (ii)   the decree or warrant has been preceded by an arrestment on the dependence of the action or followed by an arrestment in execution.

(3)   For the purposes of subsection (1) above, the day on which a preference was created is the day on which the preference became completely effectual.

(4)   A transaction to which this subsection applies is challengeable by—

  (a)   in the case of a winding up—

    (i)   any creditor who is a creditor by virtue of a debt incurred on or before the date of commencement of the winding up, or

    (ii)   the liquidator; and

  (b)   where the company has entered administration, the administrator.

(5)   On a challenge being brought under subsection (4) above, the court, if satisfied that the transaction challenged is a transaction to which this section applies, shall grant decree of reduction or for such restoration of property to the company's assets or other redress as may be appropriate:

Provided that this subsection is without prejudice to any right or interest acquired in good faith and for value from or through the creditor in whose favour the preference was created.

(6)   A liquidator and an administrator have the same right as a creditor has under any rule of law to challenge a preference created by a debtor.

(7)   This section applies to Scotland only.

**Amendments**—Enterprise Act 2002, s 248(3), Sch 17, paras 9, 29.

**CIGA 2020**—This provision is affected by temporary measures at Sch 10, para 17 of CIGA 2020.

[1.308]

### 244 Extortionate credit transactions

(1) This section applies as does section 238, and where the company is, or has been, a party to a transaction for, or involving, the provision of credit to the company.

(2) The court may, on the application of the office-holder, make an order with respect to the transaction if the transaction is or was extortionate and was entered into in the period of 3 years ending with the day on which the company entered administration or went into liquidation.

(3) For the purposes of this section a transaction is extortionate if, having regard to the risk accepted by the person providing the credit—

(a) the terms of it are or were such as to require grossly exorbitant payments to be made (whether unconditionally or in certain contingencies) in respect of the provision of the credit, or

(b) it otherwise grossly contravened ordinary principles of fair dealing;

and it shall be presumed, unless the contrary is proved, that a transaction with respect to which an application is made under this section is or, as the case may be, was extortionate.

(4) An order under this section with respect to any transaction may contain such one or more of the following as the court thinks fit, that is to say—

(a) provision setting aside the whole or part of any obligation created by the transaction,

(b) provision otherwise varying the terms of the transaction or varying the terms on which any security for the purposes of the transaction is held,

(c) provision requiring any person who is or was a party to the transaction to pay to the office-holder any sums paid to that person, by virtue of the transaction, by the company,

(d) provision requiring any person to surrender to the office-holder any property held by him as security for the purposes of the transaction,

(e) provision directing accounts to be taken between any persons.

(5) The powers conferred by this section are exercisable in relation to any transaction concurrently with any powers exercisable in relation to that transaction as a transaction at an undervalue or under section 242 (gratuitous alienations in Scotland).

**Amendments**—Enterprise Act 2002, s 248(3), Sch 17, paras 9, 30.

**General note**—Effectively, the provision will allow for the re-opening of a transaction that can be deemed to be extortionate and which occurred within the stated time zone. The provision was modelled on ss 137–140 of the Consumer Credit Act 1974.

The provision's object is to ensure that the assets of a company that has gone into liquidation or administration are not reduced by reason of the company having entered into a loan arrangement for which the consideration paid by the company is excessive. The aim is not to attack loans which ultimately end up being bad bargains, but to allow for the impugning of those loans which are grossly unfair, ie loans which no reasonable company in normal circumstances would enter into except where the true intention was to confer an undue benefit on the lender.

The section does not appear as yet to have been the subject of any reported decision, suggesting that it has not been invoked frequently, or at all, by liquidators and administrators.

The powers conferred by s 244 are exercisable in relation to any transaction concurrently with any powers exercisable under s 238 (transaction at an undervalue) (s 244(5)).

In dealing with a case under the Consumer Credit Act the Court of Appeal in *Paragon Finance plc v Nash* [2001] EWCA Civ 1466, [2002] 1 WLR 685 said that the nature of the test for what is an extortionate transaction is stringent, and this was adopted in relation to a consideration of s 244 in *White v Davenham Trust Ltd* (2010) [2010] EWHC 2748 (Ch).

**Time zone**—The transaction, to be impugned, must have been entered into in the period of 3 years before the date of the administration order or the date when the company went into liquidation. Unusually, the point of time that rules this type of transaction, where liquidation has occurred, is not the commencement of winding up (as it is for transactions at an undervalue and preferences), but the going into liquidation. Going into liquidation is defined in s 247 to mean the date of the resolution to wind up, for voluntary liquidations, and the date of the winding-up order, in compulsory liquidations, and so it is submitted that these dates will be the ones from which the liquidator will calculate the 3-year time zone.

'Credit'—This is not defined, but in the Consumer Credit Act, s 9 the word is defined broadly to include 'a cash loan, and any other form of financial accommodation', and it is likely that this is the same meaning that Parliament intended to apply here as the provision is based on aspects of the Consumer Credit Act.

'Extortionate'—This word is, obviously, the critical part of the provision. Section 244(3) states what is meant by the term. 'Extortionate' does not mean unwise: *Broadwick Financial Services Ltd v Spencer* [2002] EWCA Civ 35 at [79]. It has been said, in relation to the Consumer Credit Act, that any transaction must not only be unfair but also oppressive, reflecting an imbalance in bargaining power of which the other party took improper advantage (*Wills v Wood* (1984) CCLR 7, (1984) 128 SJ 222; *Broadwick Financial Services Ltd* at [79]), while another view is that only unfairness is required (*Davies v Direct Loans Ltd* [1986] 1 WLR 823 at 831). In *Batooneh v Asombang* [2004] BPIR 1 (a case involving an allegation that a loan was extortionate under the Consumer Credit Act 1974) it was said that to be within the idea of extortionate, the loan had to be grossly exorbitant or in some other way it had to grossly contravene the principles of fair dealing.

Courts might well consider, when interpreting this provision, s 138 of the Consumer Credit Act. The latter provision states that in determining whether a bargain is extortionate, regard must be had to a number of specified matters.

**Presumption**—The office-holder is assisted by the fact that a transaction to which an application under s 244 relates is presumed, unless the contrary is proved, to be extortionate. It is unclear how much an office-holder has to establish before the presumption operates. The legislation suggests that the office-holder would merely have to prove that the company entered into a credit transaction within the 3 years of going into administration or liquidation.

**Orders**—Unlike where there are transactions at an undervalue or preferences, there is no general provision that requires the position of the parties to be restored to what they were prior to the entering into of the transaction. Rather, if a liquidator can establish that a transaction was an extortionate credit transaction, then the court may make any order it sees fit and this might contain one of the orders set out in subs (4). These orders are designed to liberate the company from the burdens associated with the transaction. As with ss 238 and 239 actions, it is assumed that the court could decline to make an order if it chooses.

These orders are somewhat similar to the powers given to courts under s 139(2) of the Consumer Credit Act.

## [1.309]

### 245 Avoidance of certain floating charges

(1)  This section applies as does section 238, but applies to Scotland as well as to England and Wales.

(2)  Subject as follows, a floating charge on the company's undertaking or property created at a relevant time is invalid except to the extent of the aggregate of—

    (a)    the value of so much of the consideration for the creation of the charge as consists of money paid, or goods or services supplied, to the company at the same time as, or after, the creation of the charge,

    (b)    the value of so much of that consideration as consists of the discharge or reduction, at the same time as, or after, the creation of the charge, of any debt of the company, and

    (c)    the amount of such interest (if any) as is payable on the amount falling within paragraph (a) or (b) in pursuance of any agreement under which the money was so paid, the goods or services were so supplied or the debt was so discharged or reduced.

(3)  Subject to the next subsection, the time at which a floating charge is created by a company is a relevant time for the purposes of this section if the charge is created—

    (a)    in the case of a charge which is created in favour of a person who is connected with the company, at a time in the period of 2 years ending with the onset of insolvency,

    (b)    in the case of a charge which is created in favour of any other person, at a time in the period of 12 months ending with the onset of insolvency,

    (c)    in either case, at a time between the making of an administration application in respect of the company and the making of an administration order on that application, or

(d)    in either case, at a time between the filing with the court of a copy of notice of intention to appoint an administrator under paragraph 14 or 22 of Schedule B1 and the making of an appointment under that paragraph.

(4)    Where a company creates a floating charge at a time mentioned in subsection (3)(b) and the person in favour of whom the charge is created is not connected with the company, that time is not a relevant time for the purposes of this section unless the company—

(a)    is at that time unable to pay its debts within the meaning of section 123 in Chapter VI of Part IV, or

(b)    becomes unable to pay its debts within the meaning of that section in consequence of the transaction under which the charge is created.

(5)    For the purposes of subsection (3), the onset of insolvency is—

(a)    in a case where this section applies by reason of an administrator of a company being appointed by administration order, the date on which the administration application is made,

(b)    in a case where this section applies by reason of an administrator of a company being appointed under paragraph 14 or 22 of Schedule B1 following filing with the court of a copy of notice of intention to appoint under that paragraph, the date on which the copy of the notice is filed,

(c)    in a case where this section applies by reason of an administrator of a company being appointed otherwise than as mentioned in paragraph (a) or (b), the date on which the appointment takes effect, and

(d)    in a case where this section applies by reason of a company going into liquidation, the date of the commencement of the winding up.

(6)    For the purposes of subsection (2)(a) the value of any goods or services supplied by way of consideration for a floating charge is the amount in money which at the time they were supplied could reasonably have been expected to be obtained for supplying the goods or services in the ordinary course of business and on the same terms (apart from the consideration) as those on which they were supplied to the company.

**Amendments**—Enterprise Act 2002, ss 248(3), 278(2), Sch 17, paras 9, 31, Sch 26.

**CIGA 2020**—This provision is affected by temporary measures at Sch 10, para 18(2) and 18(3) of CIGA 2020.

**General note**—The provision permits office-holders to take proceedings to have certain floating charges avoided. If this can be done, the chargeholders become unsecured creditors and, therefore, more funds should be available to the general body of creditors. Primarily, the section aims to prevent companies on their last legs from creating floating charges in favour of certain creditors in order to secure past debts (see *Re Orleans Motor Co* [1911] 2 Ch 41 at 45), so the purpose and effect of the provision is similar to that of s 239. The section proscribes the granting of a charge unless the chargeholder has advanced fresh value, in the form of funds, goods or services to the company. Where a charge has been given to secure past indebtedness, an office-holder could take action under s 239, but action under s 245 might be more effective. In particular, the time zone in which charges can be set aside is longer, where a non-connected party is involved, under s 245 when compared with s 239, and with s 245 there is not a requirement that the company had to have been influenced by a desire to give a preference, as there is with s 239.

The objective of s 245 is to prevent a secured creditor from gaining an unfair advantage as against unsecured creditors which would occur if the former were able to 'obtain priority for any part of the company's indebtedness to it which in substance preceded the date of the charge, or which post-dated the charge but exceeded the further value actually provided by the creditor to the company before the charge crystallised'. (*Re Peak Hotels and Resorts Ltd* [2019] EWCA Civ 345 at [33].

**Floating charge**—The floating charges that are avoided are those that were created in the relevant time (see below), but if the charge was created in favour of a non-connected person, then the company had to be insolvent at the time of the creation of the charge or became so as a result of the entering into of the charge. 'Floating charge' is defined in s 251 and provides that the phrase includes a charge that was created as a floating charge, so s 245 would apply where a floating charge covered by the section is converted into a fixed charge by crystallisation before the onset of insolvency.

**Relevant time**—As with ss 238 and 239, the provision limits the transactions that can be adjusted to those occurring within a specified time before administration or liquidation.

The time zone is defined in s 245(3). The critical thing is the time of creation of the charge. There are two time zones in which a charge may be created for it to be subject to invalidation. First, any floating charge created within the 12 months preceding the onset of insolvency may be invalid. 'Onset of insolvency' is defined in subs (5). Also, see the comments under that heading in relation to s 240. The second zone is in relation to charges created in favour of a connected person, and they may be invalidated where they were created within the period of 2 years prior to the onset of insolvency. This is designed to stop a connected person, such as a director, from taking a charge and enjoying security when the company may be on the verge of insolvency (but still technically solvent). For 'connected person', see under that heading in relation to s 249.

Where a charge is created in the 12 months prior to the onset of insolvency, and in favour of a person who is not a connected person, the charge is not created within the relevant time unless, according to s 245(4), the company is either unable to pay its debts within the meaning of s 123 or became unable to pay its debts within s 123 as a result of the entering into of the transaction under which the charge is created.

Also, the time zone covers the period between the presenting of a petition for an administration order and the making of an order on the petition.

Where a winding-up order was made as a result of a petition presented under s 124 during the period of 27 April 2020 to 30 September 2021 on the basis that the company was unable to pay its debts, s 245(3)(a) has effect as if the reference to the period of 2 years ending with the onset of insolvency were to the period which begins with whichever is the later of the day 2 years before the day on which the petition was presented, and the day 2 years and 6 months before the day on which the winding-up order was made, and ends with the day on which the winding-up order was made (para 18(2) of Sch 10 of the Corporate Insolvency and Governance Act 2020) (as amended by The Corporate Insolvency and Governance Act 2020 (Coronavirus) (Extension of the Relevant Period) Regulations 2020 (SI 2020/1031), reg 2, The Corporate Insolvency and Governance Act 2020 (Coronavirus) (Extension of the Relevant Period) (No 2) Regulations 2020 (SI 2020/1483), reg 2, The Corporate Insolvency and Governance Act 2020 (Coronavirus) (Extension of the Relevant Period) Regulations 2021 (SI 2021/375), reg 3(4) and The Corporate Insolvency and Governance Act 2020 (Coronavirus) (Extension of the Relevant Period) (No 2) Regulations 2021 (SI 2021/718), reg 2).

**Exceptions**—Section 245(2) enumerates certain cases where the charges will not be avoided. These exceptions are applicable whether the chargeholder is a connected person or not.

Paragraph (a) purports to make an exception where funds are lent in order to revitalise a failing company. The legislature wants to encourage persons who lend in such circumstances, and they should be entitled to their security. Whether there has, in fact, been money advanced by the chargeholder within para (a) is going to depend upon the circumstances, and in considering the circumstances, the courts will probably examine substance and not form: *Re Matthew Ellis Ltd* [1933] Ch 458. There have been attempts to use this exception to hide a charge that would ordinarily be avoided. These have included cases in which there appears to be a payment of money to the company, but this was really no more than a transparent subterfuge designed to secure a creditor in respect of an existing debt, such as where a loan to the company in cash is immediately repaid to the lender (*Revere Trust Ltd v Wellington Handkerchief Works Ltd* [1931] NI 55), or where directors who had guaranteed the company's bank overdraft take a floating charge over its assets in return for a payment to the company of money which was to be applied in reducing its overdraft: *Re Orleans Motor Co* [1911] 2 Ch 41.

For para (a) to operate, it is important that any cash is paid or provided to the company, becoming part of the assets of the company and available to the company to be used as it likes (*Re Fairway Magazines Ltd* [1993] BCLC 643), and not paid to a third person (*Re Orleans Motor Co*). Unless this occurs, a chargeholder might have to attempt to rely on para (b) on the basis that it discharges or reduces the liability of a debt of the company.

The meaning of 'at the same time as' in para (a) has never been interpreted in such a way as to require strict contemporaneity as far as the creation of the charge and the payment of the money is concerned; provided that the advance follows the creation of the charge there seems to be no problem. The problem is where the advance is made before the creation, for unless the advance is regarded as being made at the time of the charge's creation, the charge is not an exception within para (a): *Re Shoe Lace Ltd*, sub nom *Power v Sharp Investments Ltd* [1994] 1 BCLC 111. In recent times a fairly strict approach appears to have been applied (*Re Shoe Lace Ltd*). In *Re Shoe Lace* it was said in the Court of Appeal [1994] 1 BCLC 111 at 123, per Sir Christopher Slade) that 'no moneys paid before the execution of the debenture will qualify for exemption . . . unless the interval between payment and execution is so short that it can be regarded as minimal and payment and execution can be regarded as contemporaneous'. So, it would appear that any delay would have to be very short.

Paragraph (a) also requires that exception is to be given in relation to 'the value of so much of the consideration for the creation of the charge', and, therefore, if the chargeholder is to benefit from this exception in relation to any advance subsequent to creation of the charge, it must be established that it was in consideration of the charge. 'Consideration' here does not mean what might be regarded as good consideration in contract law, and so past consideration will suffice: *Re Yeovil Glove Co* [1965] Ch 148 at 184–185, CA.

**Value of services supplied**—In valuing under s 245(6) any services that are supplied in consideration of the granting of a charge the test was, according to Henderson LJ (with whom the other judges agreed) in *Re Peak Hotels and Resorts Ltd* ([2019] EWCA Civ 345 at [38]), objective. The Court of Appeal said that the commercial fairness underlying any agreement between the company and the service-provider was immaterial in dealing with s 245(6) and the valuation of the services which the provision required (at [36], [40]). The court went on to say that in relation to s 245(6) there has to be regard for services supplied in the ordinary course of the supplier's business, and for that purpose, it is both legitimate and helpful to examine the supplier's standard terms for guidance, although in doing so it would be in no sense conclusive, because the test is an objective one (at [41]).

**The effect**—If a charge falls foul of this section, any debt owed to the chargeholder will continue to be able to be claimed, but the claim will only be that of an unsecured creditor. The chargeholder will lose its right to priority when it comes to payment.

**For further discussion, see** A Keay *McPherson and Keay's Law of Company Liquidation* (Sweet and Maxwell, 4th edn, 2018) at 728–737.

## [1.310]

### 246 Unenforceability of liens on books etc

(1) This section applies in the case of a company where—

  (a)  the company enters administration, or

  (b)  the company goes into liquidation, or

  (c)  a provisional liquidator is appointed;

and "the office-holder" means the administrator, the liquidator or the provisional liquidator, as the case may be.

(2) Subject as follows, a lien or other right to retain possession of any of the books, papers or other records of the company is unenforceable to the extent that its enforcement would deny possession of any books, papers or other records to the office-holder.

(3) This does not apply to a lien on documents which give a title to property and are held as such.

**Amendments**—Enterprise Act 2002, s 248(3), Sch 17, paras 9, 32.

**General note**—The provision aims to stop persons, especially accountants and solicitors, from withholding documents on the basis that they have a lien over them, eg for the payment of fees, and thereby placing themselves in a formidable position as far as getting paid.

There is an equivalent provision in personal insolvency. See s 349.

'**Enforcement**'—The exercise of a right to retain property under a lien constitutes the enforcement of the security: *Bristol Airport plc v Powdrill* [1990] Ch 744 at 762, CA.

'**Documents which give a title to property and are held as such**'—This clearly permits a bank or other lender that has a fixed charge over assets of the company to retain the indicia of title, such as the title deeds to real property.

The section would cover documents like share certificates, charges over land, debentures and any other document that was evidence of possession of, or right to, land or personal property or anything covered by the definition of 'property' in s 436, but would not encompass a motor vehicle registration certificate: *Joblin v Watkins & Rosaveare (Motors) Ltd* [1949] 1 All ER 47.

The wording of s 246 as a whole is inconsistent with any requirement that for the document to be held 'as such' it had to be held so as to confer a proprietary title on the holder of the document: *Brereton v Nicholls* [1993] BCLC 593. It has been said that the words, 'as such' referred to the circumstances, manner or capacity in which the documents gave rise to the lien, in order to distinguish that situation from those where the documents were held by someone who would sometimes be entitled to assert a lien, but in the situation when a lien did not arise (*Re SEIL Trade Finance Ltd* [1992] BCC 538). This means that provided that the documents fall within subsection (3), such as debentures and share certificates, it does not matter that the only reason that the documents are being held is to obtain payment. Thus solicitors and accountants could retain such documents so as to obtain their fees.

*Administration: penalisation of directors etc*

**Amendments**—Inserted by Small Business, Enterprise and Employment Act 2015, s 117(1), (2).

**[1.311]**

**246ZA Fraudulent trading: administration**

(1) If while a company is in administration it appears that any business of the company has been carried on with intent to defraud creditors of the company or creditors of any other person, or for any fraudulent purpose, the following has effect.

(2) The court, on the application of the administrator, may declare that any persons who were knowingly parties to the carrying on of the business in the manner mentioned in subsection (1) are to be liable to make such contributions (if any) to the company's assets as the court thinks proper.

**Amendments**—Inserted by Small Business, Enterprise and Employment Act 2015, s 117(1), (2).

**General note**—This provision provides for claims by administrators in the same way as s 213 does for liquidators. In most, if not all respects, the law that has been applied in relation to s 213 will be applied in the same way as to claims made under this provision.

**[1.312]**

**246ZB Wrongful trading: administration**

(1) Subject to subsection (3), if while a company is in administration it appears that subsection (2) applies in relation to a person who is or has been a director of the company, the court, on the application of the administrator, may declare that that person is to be liable to make such contribution (if any) to the company's assets as the court thinks proper.

(2) This subsection applies in relation to a person if—

    (a)    the company has entered insolvent administration,

    (b)    at some time before the company entered administration, that person knew or ought to have concluded that there was no reasonable prospect that the company would avoid entering insolvent administration or going into insolvent liquidation, and

    (c)    the person was a director of the company at that time.

(3) The court must not make a declaration under this section with respect to any person if it is satisfied that, after the condition specified in subsection (2)(b) was first satisfied in relation to the person, the person took every step with a view to minimising the potential loss to the company's creditors as (on the assumption that the person had knowledge of the matter mentioned in subsection (2)(b)) the person ought to have taken.

(4) For the purposes of subsections (2) and (3), the facts which a director of a company ought to know or ascertain, the conclusions which the director ought to reach and the steps which the director ought to take are those which would be known or ascertained, or reached or taken, by a reasonably diligent person having both—

    (a)    the general knowledge, skill and experience that may reasonably be expected of a person carrying out the same functions as are carried out by that director in relation to the company, and

    (b)    the general knowledge, skill and experience that that director has.

(5) The reference in subsection (4) to the functions carried out in relation to a company by a director of the company includes any functions which the director does not carry out but which have been entrusted to the director.

(6) For the purposes of this section—

    (a)    a company enters insolvent administration if it enters administration at a time when its assets are insufficient for the payment of its debts and other liabilities and the expenses of the administration;

    (b)    a company goes into insolvent liquidation if it goes into liquidation at a time when its assets are insufficient for the payment of its debts and other liabilities and the expenses of the winding up.

(7) In this section "director" includes shadow director.

(8) This section is without prejudice to section 246ZA.

**Amendments**—Inserted by Small Business, Enterprise and Employment Act 2015, s 117(1), (2).

**CIGA 2020**—This provision is affected by temporary measures at s 12(1) of CIGA 2020.

**General note**—This provision provides for claims by administrators in the same way as s 214 does for liquidators. In most, if not all respects, the law that has been applied in relation to s 214 will be applied in the same way as to claims made under this provision.

## [1.313]

### 246ZC  Proceedings under section 246ZA or 246ZB

Section 215 applies for the purposes of an application under section 246ZA or 246ZB as it applies for the purposes of an application under section 213 but as if the reference in subsection (1) of section 215 to the liquidator was a reference to the administrator.

**Amendments**—Inserted by Small Business, Enterprise and Employment Act 2015, s 117(1), (2).

*Power to assign certain causes of action*

**Amendments**—Inserted by Small Business, Enterprise and Employment Act 2015, s 118.

## [1.314]

### 246ZD  Power to assign

(1)   This section applies in the case of a company where—
      (a)    the company enters administration, or
      (b)    the company goes into liquidation;
and "the office-holder" means the administrator or the liquidator, as the case may be.
(2)   The office-holder may assign a right of action (including the proceeds of an action) arising under or by virtue of any of the following—
      (za)   section A43 (challenges to monitor remuneration in subsequent insolvency proceedings);
      (a)    section 213 or 246ZA (fraudulent trading);
      (b)    section 214 or 246ZB (wrongful trading);
      (c)    section 238 (transactions at an undervalue (England and Wales));
      (d)    section 239 (preferences (England and Wales));
      (e)    section 242 (gratuitous alienations (Scotland));
      (f)    section 243 (unfair preferences (Scotland));
      (g)    section 244 (extortionate credit transactions).

**Amendments**—Inserted by Small Business, Enterprise and Employment Act 2015, s 118. Amended by Corporate Insolvency and Governance Act 2020, s 2(1), Sch 3, paras 1, 16.

**General note**—Before the advent of this provision office-holders were limited in what actions they were able to assign to others, particularly where the action was granted to the liquidator personally, such as a preference claim under s 239. This provision enhances the ability of office-holders to assign causes of action to third parties. Office-holders now can assign actions which they hold on their own behalf because of the provisions of the legislation, where previously they could not do so. Assignment will usually occur where either the office-holder is concerned that the action is too risky to pursue and another person is willing to take the action, or the office-holder does not have or cannot obtain sufficient funding to take legal proceedings and some third party does have the necessary resources and is willing to give some kind of consideration to the office-holder for the assignment.

The decision in *Re Totalbrand Ltd* ([2020] EWHC 2917 (Ch)) provides that the wording of s 246ZD(2) permits the assignment of the right of action in which all of the proceeds would go to the assignee, the creditors getting a benefit in the form of the price which the assignee will have paid to obtain the claim.

*Decisions by creditors and contributories*

**Amendments**—Inserted by Small Business, Enterprise and Employment Act 2015, s 122.

## [1.315]

### 246ZE  Decisions by creditors and contributories: general

(1)   This section applies where, for the purposes of this Group of Parts, a person ("P") seeks a decision about any matter from a company's creditors or contributories.

(2)   The decision may be made by any qualifying decision procedure P thinks fit, except that it may not be made by a creditors' meeting or (as the case may be) a contributories' meeting unless subsection (3) applies.

(3)   This subsection applies if at least the minimum number of creditors or (as the case may be) contributories make a request to P in writing that the decision be made by a creditors' meeting or (as the case may be) a contributories' meeting.

(4)   If subsection (3) applies P must summon a creditors' meeting or (as the case may be) a contributories' meeting.

(5)   Subsection (2) is subject to any provision of this Act, the rules or any other legislation, or any order of the court—

   (a)   requiring a decision to be made, or prohibiting a decision from being made, by a particular qualifying decision procedure (other than a creditors' meeting or a contributories' meeting);

   (b)   permitting or requiring a decision to be made by a creditors' meeting or a contributories' meeting.

(6)   Section 246ZF provides that in certain cases the deemed consent procedure may be used instead of a qualifying decision procedure.

(7)   For the purposes of subsection (3) the "minimum number" of creditors or contributories is any of the following—

   (a)   10% in value of the creditors or contributories;

   (b)   10% in number of the creditors or contributories;

   (c)   10 creditors or contributories.

(8)   The references in subsection (7) to creditors are to creditors of any class, even where a decision is sought only from creditors of a particular class.

(9)   In this section references to a meeting are to a meeting where the creditors or (as the case may be) contributories are invited to be present together at the same place (whether or not it is possible to attend the meeting without being present at that place).

(10)   Except as provided by subsection (8), references in this section to creditors include creditors of a particular class.

(11)   In this Group of Parts "qualifying decision procedure" means a procedure prescribed or authorised under paragraph 8A of Schedule 8.

**Amendments**—Inserted by Small Business, Enterprise and Employment Act 2015, s 122.

**General**—This is one of two relatively new provisions in the legislation that are the basis for the introduction of a new decision-making system in insolvency practice. Until recently many decisions in a liquidation had to be made by way of a vote at a creditors' or contributories' meeting. While meetings might still occur, for the most part decisions will be made by way of a qualifying decision procedure or, as provided for in s 246ZF, a deemed consent procedure. The full details concerning qualifying decision procedures are principally found in Part 15 of the IR 2016. In particular, see rr 15.2–15.6 and rr 15.8–15.16.

The provision makes it clear that meetings of creditors or contributories may still be held, but only if at least the minimum number of creditors or contributories make a request to P in writing that the decision be made by a meeting. P is the person who seeks a decision from the creditors or contributories and in the 2016 Rules he or she is known as the convener. The minimum number needed to have a meeting convened is explained in s 246ZE(7).

The use of the qualifying decision procedure is subject to any provision of the Act, the rules or any other legislation, or any order of the court:

   (a)   requiring a decision to be made, or prohibiting a decision from being made, by a particular qualifying decision procedure (other than a creditors' meeting or a contributories' meeting);

   (b)   permitting or requiring a decision to be made by a creditors' meeting or a contributories' meeting.

For a detailed discussion of the decision-making processes in liquidation, see A Keay *McPherson and Keay's Law of Company Liquidation* (Sweet and Maxwell, 4th edn, 2018) at 424–436.

## [1.316]

### 246ZF  Deemed consent procedure

(1)   The deemed consent procedure may be used instead of a qualifying decision procedure where a company's creditors or contributories are to make a decision about any matter, unless—

(a) a decision about the matter is required by virtue of this Act, the rules, or any other legislation to be made by a qualifying decision procedure, or

(b) the court orders that a decision about the matter is to be made by a qualifying decision procedure.

(2) If the rules provide for a company's creditors or contributories to make a decision about the remuneration of any person, they must provide that the decision is to be made by a qualifying decision procedure.

(3) The deemed consent procedure is that the relevant creditors (other than opted-out creditors) or (as the case may be) the relevant contributories are given notice of—

(a) the matter about which they are to make a decision,

(b) the decision that the person giving the notice proposes should be made (the "proposed decision"),

(c) the effect of subsections (4) and (5), and

(d) the procedure for objecting to the proposed decision.

(4) If less than the appropriate number of relevant creditors or (as the case may be) relevant contributories object to the proposed decision in accordance with the procedure set out in the notice, the creditors or (as the case may be) the contributories are to be treated as having made the proposed decision.

(5) Otherwise—

(a) the creditors or (as the case may be) the contributories are to be treated as not having made a decision about the matter in question, and

(b) if a decision about that matter is again sought from the creditors or (as the case may be) the contributories, it must be sought using a qualifying decision procedure.

(6) For the purposes of subsection (4) the "appropriate number" of relevant creditors or relevant contributories is 10% in value of those creditors or contributories.

(7) "Relevant creditors" means the creditors who, if the decision were to be made by a qualifying decision procedure, would be entitled to vote in the procedure.

(8) "Relevant contributories" means the contributories who, if the decision were to be made by a qualifying decision procedure, would be entitled to vote in the procedure.

(9) In this section references to creditors include creditors of a particular class.

(10) The rules may make further provision about the deemed consent procedure.

**Amendments**—Inserted by Small Business, Enterprise and Employment Act 2015, s 122.

**General**—The background to this provision is explained in the notes to the previous section. The deemed consent procedure may be used in relation to any situation where a company's creditors or contributories are to make a decision about any matter unless either any provision of the Act, the rules or any other legislation, or any order of the court provides that a decision must be effected by way of a qualifying decision procedure.

In particular, see r 15.7 and the notes accompanying it.

A Keay *McPherson and Keay's Law of Company Liquidation* (Sweet and Maxwell, 4th edn, 2018) at 424–436.

[1.317]

**246ZG Power to amend sections 246ZE and 246ZF**

(1) The Secretary of State may by regulations amend section 246ZE so as to change the definition of—

(a) the minimum number of creditors;

(b) the minimum number of contributories.

(2) The Secretary of State may by regulations amend section 246ZF so as to change the definition of—

(a) the appropriate number of relevant creditors;

(b) the appropriate number of relevant contributories.

(3) Regulations under this section may define the minimum number or the appropriate number by reference to any one or more of—

(a) a proportion in value,

(b) a proportion in number,

(c)    an absolute number,

and the definition may include alternative, cumulative or relative requirements.

(4)    Regulations under subsection (1) may define the minimum number of creditors or contributories by reference to all creditors or contributories, or by reference to creditors or contributories of a particular description.

(5)    Regulations under this section may make provision that will result in section 246ZE or 246ZF having different definitions for different cases, including—

    (a)    for creditors and for contributories,

    (b)    for different kinds of decisions.

(6)    Regulations under this section may make transitional provision.

(7)    The power of the Secretary of State to make regulations under this section is exercisable by statutory instrument.

(8)    A statutory instrument containing regulations under this section may not be made unless a draft of the instrument has been laid before, and approved by a resolution of, each House of Parliament.

**Amendments**—Inserted by Small Business, Enterprise and Employment Act 2015, s 122.

*Remote attendance at meetings*

**[1.318]**

**246A  Remote attendance at meetings**

(1)    Subject to subsection (2), this section [applies to any meeting of the members of a company summoned by the office-holder under this Act or the rules, other than a meeting of the members of the company in a members' voluntary winding up].

(2)    *This section does not apply where—*

    *(a)    a company is being wound up in Scotland, or*

    *(b)    a receiver is appointed under section 51 in Chapter 2 of Part 3.*

(3)    Where the person summoning a meeting ("the convener") considers it appropriate, the meeting may be conducted and held in such a way that persons who are not present together at the same place may attend it.

(4)    Where a meeting is conducted and held in the manner referred to in subsection (3), a person attends the meeting if that person is able to exercise any rights which that person may have to speak and vote at the meeting.

(5)    For the purposes of this section—

    (a)    a person is able to exercise the right to speak at a meeting when that person is in a position to communicate to all those attending the meeting, during the meeting, any information or opinions which that person has on the business of the meeting; and

    (b)    a person is able to exercise the right to vote at a meeting when—

        (i)    that person is able to vote, during the meeting, on resolutions put to the vote at the meeting, and

        (ii)    that person's vote can be taken into account in determining whether or not such resolutions are passed at the same time as the votes of all the other persons attending the meeting.

(6)    The convener of a meeting which is to be conducted and held in the manner referred to in subsection (3) shall make whatever arrangements the convener considers appropriate to—

    (a)    enable those attending the meeting to exercise their rights to speak or vote, and

    (b)    ensure the identification of those attending the meeting and the security of any electronic means used to enable attendance.

(7)    Where in the reasonable opinion of the convener—

    (a)    a meeting will be attended by persons who will not be present together at the same place, and

    (b)    it is unnecessary or inexpedient to specify a place for the meeting, any requirement under this Act or the rules to specify a place for the meeting may be satisfied by specifying the arrangements the convener proposes to enable persons to exercise their rights to speak or vote.

(8)   In making the arrangements referred to in subsection (6) and in forming the opinion referred to in subsection (7)(b), the convener must have regard to the legitimate interests of the [members] and others attending the meeting in the efficient despatch of the business of the meeting.

(9)   If—

(a)   the notice of a meeting does not specify a place for the meeting,

(b)   the convener is requested in accordance with the rules to specify a place for the meeting, and

(c)   that request is [made] by members representing not less than ten percent of the total voting rights of all the members having at the date of the request a right to vote at the meeting,

it shall be the duty of the convener to specify a place for the meeting.

(10)   In this section, "the office-holder", in relation to a company, means—

(za)   the monitor in relation to a moratorium under Part A1,

(a)   its liquidator, provisional liquidator, administrator, receiver (appointed under section 51) or administrative receiver, or

(b)   where a voluntary arrangement in relation to the company is proposed or has taken effect under Part 1, the nominee or the supervisor of the voluntary arrangement.

**Amendments**—Inserted by SI 2010/18. Amended by Small Business, Enterprise and Employment Act 2015, s 126, Sch 9, Pt 1, paras 1, 54; SSI 2017/209; Corporate Insolvency and Governance Act 2020, s 2(1), Sch 3, paras 1, 17.

**General**—This section and subsequent ones introduce new procedures to take into account and take advantage of the developments in technology and accessibility to that technology that has occurred in recent years. It is hoped that this will, inter alia, reduce costs and time for creditors.

*Giving of notices etc by office-holders*

**Amendments**—Small Business, Enterprise and Employment Act 2015, s 124(1), (3).

## [1.319]

### 246B   Use of websites

(1)   Subject to subsection (2), where any provision of this Act or the rules requires the office-holder to give, deliver, furnish or send a notice or other document or information to any person, that requirement is satisfied by making the notice, document or information available on a website—

(a)   in accordance with the rules, and

(b)   in such circumstances as may be prescribed.

(2)   . . .

(3)   In this section, "the office-holder" means—

(za)   the monitor in relation to a moratorium under Part A1,

(a)   the liquidator, provisional liquidator, administrator, receiver (appointed under section 51), or administrative receiver of a company, or

(b)   where a voluntary arrangement in relation to a company is proposed or has taken effect under Part 1, the nominee or the supervisor of the voluntary arrangement.

**Amendments**—Inserted by SI 2010/18. Amended by SSI 2016/141; Corporate Insolvency and Governance Act 2020, s 2(1), Sch 3, paras 1, 18.

**General note**—See rr 1.49–1.50 which deal with the use of websites.

**[1.320]**

**246C Creditors' ability to opt out of receiving certain notices**

(1)   Any provision of the rules which requires an office-holder of a company to give a notice to creditors of the company does not apply, in circumstances prescribed by the rules, in relation to opted-out creditors.

(2)   Subsection (1)—

(a)     does not apply in relation to a notice of a distribution or proposed distribution to creditors;

(b)     is subject to any order of the court requiring a notice to be given to all creditors (or all creditors of a particular category).

(3)   Except as provided by the rules, a creditor may participate and vote in a qualifying decision procedure or a deemed consent procedure even though, by virtue of being an opted-out creditor, the creditor does not receive notice of it.

(4)   In this section—

"give" includes deliver, furnish or send;

"notice" includes any document or information in any other form;

"office-holder", in relation to a company, means—

(a)     a liquidator, provisional liquidator, administrator or administrative receiver of the company,

(b)     a receiver appointed under section 51 in relation to any property of the company, or

(c)     the supervisor of a voluntary arrangement which has taken effect under Part 1 in relation to the company.

**Amendments**—Inserted by Small Business, Enterprise and Employment Act 2015, s 124(1), (3).

**General note**—See r 1.38 which gives details on opting out. Also see, rr 1.37 and 1.39 on delivery of documents and giving information to those opting out.

PART VII   INTERPRETATION FOR FIRST GROUP OF PARTS

**[1.321]**

**247 "Insolvency" and "go into liquidation"**

(1)   In this Group of Parts, except in so far as the context otherwise requires, "insolvency", in relation to a company, includes the coming into force of a moratorium for the company under Part A1, the approval of a voluntary arrangement under Part I, or the appointment of an administrator or administrative receiver.

(2)   For the purposes of any provision in this Group of Parts, a company goes into liquidation if it passes a resolution for voluntary winding up or an order for its winding up is made by the court at a time when it has not already gone into liquidation by passing such a resolution.

(3)   The reference to a resolution for voluntary winding up in subsection (2) includes a reference to a resolution which is deemed to occur by virtue of—

(a)     paragraph 83(6)(b) of Schedule B1. . .

(b)     . . ..

**Amendments**—SI 2002/1240; Enterprise Act 2002, s 248(3), Sch 17, paras 9, 33; SI 2017/702; SI 2019/146, as from IP completion day (as defined in the European Union (Withdrawal Agreement) Act 2020, s 39(1)–(5)); Corporate Insolvency and Governance Act 2020, s 2(1), Sch 3, paras 1, 19.

**General note**—The provision is a little vague in referring to 'this Group of Parts'. Undoubtedly the reference is to Parts I–VI of the Act (the Parts preceding the Part now under review), dealing with company voluntary arrangements, administration, administrative receivership and winding up, as well as some provisions that apply generally to corporate insolvency proceedings.

**'Insolvency'**—In this context it does not have the meaning suggested in s 123, but means entering one of the forms of insolvency regime set out in Parts I–III.

**'Goes into liquidation'**—This phrase signifies when a company practically enters liquidation, and is to be contrasted with 'the commencement of liquidation', although as far as voluntary liquidation is concerned the point of time when a company commences liquidation is the same as when it goes into liquidation, namely the passing of the resolution to wind up.

**Conversion under Art 37**—The meaning of s 247(3) is not clear. Let us begin with Art 37 of the EU Regulation and referred to in s 247(3)(b). It covers the case where main proceedings are initiated in a Member State, the place of the debtor's centre of main interests, when proceedings have already been commenced in another Member State. The insolvency practitioner (as the person administering the insolvent estate is generally known, no matter what kind of regime is involved (Art 2(b)) may apply to have the latter proceedings (secondary proceedings) converted into winding-up proceedings. The scenario envisaged by s 247(3) is where proceedings, such as the entering into of either a company voluntary arrangement or administration, have commenced as secondary proceedings, and liquidation has subsequently been initiated in the UK (where the company's centre of main interests exist), and the liquidator applies to have the voluntary arrangement or administration converted to winding-up proceedings. If a conversion order is made, then the company is deemed to have passed a resolution to wind up on the date of the order. It is from this date that the company goes into liquidation for the purposes of the Act, and not when the original proceedings (company voluntary arrangement or administration) were commenced.

**'Paragraph 83(6)(b)'**—Paragraph 83 is referred to in s 247(3)(a) and it deals with the conversion of administration into a creditors' voluntary liquidation. The company is to be wound up as if a resolution to wind up had been passed on the day when the administrator's notice to which para 83 applies, is registered by the registrar of companies.

## [1.322]

### 248 "Secured creditor" etc

In this Group of Parts, except in so far as the context otherwise requires—

    (a)    "secured creditor", in relation to a company, means a creditor of the company who holds in respect of his debt a security over property of the company, and "unsecured creditor" is to be read accordingly; and

    (b)    "security" means—

        (i)    in relation to England and Wales, any mortgage, charge, lien or other security, and

        (ii)    in relation to Scotland, any security (whether heritable or moveable), any floating charge and any right of lien or preference and any right of retention (other than a right of compensation or set off).

**General note**—This provision deals with the meaning of security, an important concept in Parts I–VI.

**'Secured creditor'**—The definition provides little assistance. Consideration of the case law is necessary to ascertain the scope of the expression.

A landlord is not a secured creditor within s 248, as he or she does not hold a security interest over company property: *Re Park Air Services plc* [2000] 2 AC 172, [1999] 2 WLR 396, [1999] 1 All ER 673, [1999] 1 BCLC 155, [1999] BPIR 786, HL.

**Security**—Again, the definition is of little assistance, only specifying mortgages, charges and liens as securities. One would expect these interests to have given the holders security interests. The provision, by the use of the words 'other security', obviously leaves open the fact that other kinds of security interests may well qualify. While some interests, such as retention of title rights under contracts, do not qualify as security interests, they might provide the holder with similar rights.

## [1.323]

### 248A "Opted-out creditor"

(1)   For the purposes of this Group of Parts "opted-out creditor", in relation to an office-holder of a company, means a person who—

    (a)    is a creditor of the company, and

    (b)    in accordance with the rules has elected (or is deemed to have elected) to be (and not to cease to be) an opted-out creditor in relation to the office-holder.

(2)   In this section, "office-holder", in relation to a company, means—

    (a)    a liquidator, provisional liquidator, administrator or administrative receiver of the company,

(b)  a receiver appointed under section 51 in relation to any property of the company, or

(c)  the supervisor of a voluntary arrangement which has taken effect under Part 1 in relation to the company.

**Amendments**—Inserted by Small Business, Enterprise and Employment Act 2015, s 124(1), (4).

**General note**—The provision for the category of 'opted-out creditor' means that an insolvency practitioner does not have to expend time and money involving someone in the process who has no interest in it, or has decided that it is not worth his or her while in being involved.

See r 1.38.

## [1.324]

### 249 "Connected" with a company

For the purposes of any provision in this Group of Parts, a person is connected with a company if—

(a)  he is a director or shadow director of the company or an associate of such a director or shadow director, or

(b)  he is an associate of the company;

and "associate" has the meaning given by section 435 in Part XVIII of this Act.

**General note**—The provision deals with a term that is important, particularly for the provisions that cover the adjustment of pre-administration or pre-liquidation transactions, such as preferences (s 239). The use of the term in the context of the adjustment provisions is designed to prevent persons and companies associated with the company that has subsequently entered administration or liquidation, or directors of that company, from benefiting from transactions that occurred not long before the advent of administration or liquidation, but outside of the normal time zone for the setting aside of such transactions. The Insolvency Law Review Committee, in its *Insolvency Law and Practice* report ('the Cork Report') said (at para 1033):

'If the law of insolvency is to reflect the social and economic conditions of modern society, and is to be accepted as fair and just by the general public, then it cannot treat husband and wife, or persons living together as man and wife, or other closely connected persons, as if they were unrelated parties accustomed to deal with each other at arms' length. Nor can it treat companies which are members of the same group, or other closely associated companies, as if they were wholly unrelated. Special relationships call for special provisions to be made.'

The date at which one determines whether a person is connected is the date on which the agreement that led to the transaction that is sought to be impugned is entered into and not the date when any assets are transferred pursuant to the agreement: *Breese v Hiley* [2018] EWHC 12 (Ch).

In *Re SMU Investments Ltd* ([2020] EWHC 875 (Ch)) while ICC Judge Prentis said that the test for establishing someone is a connected party is not a high one, the onus is on the person alleging a connectedness to show grounds of substance, even if they are inferential (at [38]).

The expression 'connected' is not defined simply. To appreciate the full impact of the term, one has to have reference to s 251 of the Act, as explained below. The expression has two main limbs to it. First, it covers directors and shadow directors of the company and their associates. Second, it encompasses associates of the company.

See the comments under 'Director' and 'Shadow director' in relation to s 251.

**Associate**—The expression 'associate' is defined far more fully than the other elements of s 249, but in s 435. 'Associate' includes a broad range of persons and relationships.

The expression was considered in *Mills v Edict Ltd* [1999] BPIR 391, where a Liberian company entered liquidation and its liquidator sought to attack, under s 239, security given to Edict Ltd, the only shareholder of the former company (and, therefore, the controlling shareholder). The Liberian company had borrowed money from Edict, and when it was insolvent it had created a charge in favour of Edict. It was held that Edict was connected to the Liberian company on the basis that the former was an associate of the latter, Edict having control of the Liberian company.

In *Re Dougan* [2016] NICh 19 McBride J held that a company is not an associate (under s.435(7)) of a person where the latter is not either a shareholder or director of the former, even if his or her associates have control of the company (at [28]–[29]).

See the comments under s 435.

**[1.325]**

### 250 "Member" of a company

For the purposes of any provision in this Group of Parts, a person who is not a member of a company but to whom shares in the company have been transferred, or transmitted by operation of law, is to be regarded as a member of the company, and references to a member or members are to be read accordingly.

General note—The word 'member' is defined by s 122 of the Companies Act 2006 and covers those who were the subscribers to the memorandum of association (the first members) and those who have been registered as members. This provision encompasses others, who are the owners or holders of the shares, but who are not registered as such. Prime amongst these are the personal representatives of deceased shareholders and the trustee in bankruptcy of bankrupt members.

The definition means that persons who were not registered as members may be held liable to pay contributions pursuant to s 74.

See the discussion under 'Contributory' under s 124 and the case of *Hamilton v Brown*, sub nom, *Re C and MB Holdings Ltd* [2016] EWHC 191 (Ch), [2017] 1 BCLC 269, [2016] BPIR 531 which is discussed there.

**[1.326]**

### 251 Expressions used generally

In this Group of Parts, except in so far as the context otherwise requires—
"administrative receiver" means—

    (a)    an administrative receiver as defined by section 29(2) in Chapter I of Part III, or

    (b)    a receiver appointed under section 51 in Chapter II of that Part in a case where the whole (or substantially the whole) of the company's property is attached by the floating charge;

"agent" does not include a person's counsel acting as such;

"books and papers" and "books or papers" includes accounts, deeds, writing and documents;

"business day" means any day other than a Saturday, a Sunday, Christmas Day, Good Friday or a day which is a bank holiday in any part of Great Britain;

"chattel leasing agreement" means an agreement for the bailment or, in Scotland, the hiring of goods which is capable of subsisting for more than 3 months;

"contributory" has the meaning given by section 79;

"the court", in relation to a company, means a court having jurisdiction to wind up the company;

"deemed consent procedure" means the deemed consent procedure provided for by section 246ZF;

"director" includes any person occupying the position of director, by whatever name called;

"document" includes summons, notice, order and other legal process, and registers;

. . .

"floating charge" means a charge which, as created, was a floating charge and includes a floating charge within section 462 of the Companies Act (Scottish floating charges);

"the Gazette" means—

    (a)    as respects companies registered in England and Wales, the London Gazette;

    (b)    as respects companies registered in Scotland, the Edinburgh Gazette;

. . .

. . .

"officer", in relation to a body corporate, includes a director, manager or secretary;
"the official rate", in relation to interest, means the rate payable under section 189(4);

"prescribed" means prescribed by the rules;

"qualifying decision procedure" has the meaning given by section 246ZE(11);

"receiver", in the expression "receiver or manager", does not include a receiver appointed under section 51 in Chapter II of Part III;

"retention of title agreement" means an agreement for the sale of goods to a company, being an agreement—

    (a)    which does not constitute a charge on the goods, but

    (b)    under which, if the seller is not paid and the company is wound up, the seller will have priority over all other creditors of the company as respects the goods or any property representing the goods;

"the rules" means rules under section 411 in Part XV; and

"shadow director", in relation to a company, means a person in accordance with whose directions or instructions the directors of the company are accustomed to act, but so that a person is not deemed a shadow director by reason only that the directors act—

    (a)    on advice given by that person in a professional capacity;

    (b)    in accordance with instructions, a direction, guidance or advice given by that person in the exercise of a function conferred by or under an enactment (within the meaning given by section 1293 of the Companies Act 2006);

    (c)    in accordance with guidance or advice given by that person in that person's capacity as a Minister of the Crown (within the meaning of the Ministers of the Crown Act 1975).

. . .

**Amendments**—SI 2007/2194; SI 2009/1941; Small Business, Enterprise and Employment Act 2015, ss 90, 122(1), (4); SI 2017/702; SI 2019/146, as from IP completion day (as defined in the European Union (Withdrawal Agreement) Act 2020, s 39(1)–(5)).

**General note**—The provision defines some important terms for Parts I–VI.

'**Deemed consent procedure**'—besides s 246ZF and the notes relating to it, reference should also be made to r 15.7.

'**Director**'—The definition incorporates the definition in s 250 of the Companies Act 2006. The definition means that not only de jure directors, but also de facto directors are encompassed.

There is no legislative provision that defines the term 'de facto director', but it has been used for a long time (*Re Kaytech International plc* [1999] 2 BCLC 351, CA), and covers a person who is held out as a director by the company and claims to be one and acts as a director while never being appointed according to law. A de facto director is a person who assumes the functions and status of a director (*Re Kaytech International*). A person will only be held to be a de facto director if it can be established that he or she carried out director-like functions, and they are functions that could only be discharged by a director: see *Secretary of State for Trade and Industry v Becker* [2003] 1 BCLC 555. There is not one decisive test that establishes that a person was or was not a de facto director. Courts have to take into account all relevant factors including:

- whether there was a holding out of the person as a director;
- whether the person used the title;
- whether the person had proper information on which to base decisions;
- whether the person had to make major decisions: *Secretary of State for Trade and Industry v Tjolle* [1998] 1 BCLC 333, CA.

But none of these factors are necessarily decisive on their own (eg *Secretary of State for Trade and Industry v Tjolle*), and even where a person uses the title of 'director' a court might not hold that the person is a de facto director (*Secretary of State for Trade and Industry v Tjolle*).

A person does not have to believe that he or she is a director before being regarded as a de facto director (*Re Kaytech International*).

'**Floating charge**'—See *SAW (SW) 2010 Ltd v Wilson* [2015] EWHC 4069 (Ch) where the court held that the administrators of a company who had been appointed by an alleged qualifying chargeholder had been appointed legitimately as the charge holder did have a floating charge over company property.

'**Shadow director**'—The definition incorporates that contained in s 251 of the Companies Act 2006: see *Re Hydrodam (Corby) Ltd* [1994] BCLC 180.

While professional advisers are not considered to be shadow directors, they might act in such a way that they cross the line and move from advising to instructing.

In determining whether a person is a shadow director, courts will look at the communications between the alleged shadow and the board, and ascertain, from an objective perspective, whether those communications might be able to be regarded as directions or instructions. In this regard the outcome of the communication is the important element on which to focus: *Secretary of State for Trade and Industry v Deverell* [2001] Ch 340, [2000] 2 WLR 907, [2000] 2 BCLC 133, CA. If the board is able to be characterised as subservient, that indicates shadow directorship, but it is not necessary to establish subservience before one can establish that someone is a shadow director (*Secretary of State for Trade and Industry v Deverell*). While a bank will not usually be regarded as a connected person, it might be if the liquidator can establish that it is a shadow director. The possibility of this being proven has been raised (*Re a Company (No 005009 of 1987)* [1989] BCLC 13), but banks will not be categorised as shadow directors when they merely lay down terms for continuing to provide credit for the business of a company, as these cannot be taken as instructions, for the company can take or leave the terms (*Re PFTZM Ltd* [1995] 2 BCLC 354).

It is important that one distinguishes between a shadow and a de facto director (*Re Hydrodam (Corby) Ltd*). A de facto director claims to act for the company as a director and is held out as such by the company even though he or she has never been appointed properly. In contrast, a shadow does not make such a claim; on the contrary he or she says that he or she is not a director. Shadows tend to act behind the scene (although this is not necessary) while the activity of de facto directors may well be more obvious.

THE SECOND GROUP OF PARTS
INSOLVENCY OF INDIVIDUALS; BANKRUPTCY

PART VIIA    DEBT RELIEF ORDERS

*Preliminary*

## [1.327]

**Amendments**—Inserted by Tribunals, Courts and Enforcement Act 2007, s 108(1), Sch 17.

**General note**—As concisely summarised by Baroness Hale, 'DROs are a new and simplified way of wiping the slate clean for debtors who are too poor to go bankrupt.': *R (on the application of Payne) v Secretary of State for Work and Pensions* [2011] UKSC 60, [2012] 2 AC 1, [2012] BPIR 224 at [7]. As such, DROs are only available to those with a little surplus income (maximum £50), little property (maximum £1,000) and little indebtedness (maximum £20,000): Insolvency Proceedings (Monetary Limits) Order 1986/1996 (as amended).

Reference should also be made to Schs 4ZA and 4ZB to the IA 1986, and Part 9 of the IR 2016 and the commentary thereto.

## [1.328]

### 251A  Debt relief orders

(1)    An individual who is unable to pay his debts may apply for an order under this Part ("a debt relief order") to be made in respect of his qualifying debts.

(2)    In this Part "qualifying debt" means (subject to subsection (3)) a debt which—

    (a)    is for a liquidated sum payable either immediately or at some certain future time; and

    (b)    is not an excluded debt.

(3)    A debt is not a qualifying debt to the extent that it is secured.

(4)    In this Part "excluded debt" means a debt of any description prescribed for the purposes of this subsection.

**Amendments**—Inserted by Tribunals, Courts and Enforcement Act 2007, s 108(1), Sch 17.

*Applications for a debt relief order*

## [1.329]

### 251B  Making of application

(1)    An application for a debt relief order must be made to the official receiver through an approved intermediary.

(2)    The application must include—

(a)    a list of the debts to which the debtor is subject at the date of the application, specifying the amount of each debt (including any interest, penalty or other sum that has become payable in relation to that debt on or before that date) and the creditor to whom it is owed;

(b)    details of any security held in respect of any of those debts; and

(c)    such other information about the debtor's affairs (including his creditors, debts and liabilities and his income and assets) as may be prescribed.

(3)   The rules may make further provision as to—

(a)    the form of an application for a debt relief order;

(b)    the manner in which an application is to be made; and

(c)    information and documents to be supplied in support of an application.

(4)   For the purposes of this Part an application is not to be regarded as having been made until—

(a)    the application has been submitted to the official receiver; and

(b)    any fee required in connection with the application by an order under section 415 has been paid to such person as the order may specify.

**Amendments**—Inserted by Tribunals, Courts and Enforcement Act 2007, s 108(1), Sch 17.

## [1.330]

### 251C  Duty of official receiver to consider and determine application

(1)   This section applies where an application for a debt relief order is made.

(2)   The official receiver may stay consideration of the application until he has received answers to any queries raised with the debtor in relation to anything connected with the application.

(3)   The official receiver must determine the application by—

(a)    deciding whether to refuse the application;

(b)    if he does not refuse it, by making a debt relief order in relation to the specified debts he is satisfied were qualifying debts of the debtor at the application date;

but he may only refuse the application if he is authorised or required to do so by any of the following provisions of this section.

(4)   The official receiver may refuse the application if he considers that—

(a)    the application does not meet all the requirements imposed by or under section 251B;

(b)    any queries raised with the debtor have not been answered to the satisfaction of the official receiver within such time as he may specify when they are raised;

(c)    the debtor has made any false representation or omission in making the application or on supplying any information or documents in support of it.

(5)   The official receiver must refuse the application if he is not satisfied that—

(a)    the debtor is an individual who is unable to pay his debts;

(b)    at least one of the specified debts was a qualifying debt of the debtor at the application date;

(c)    each of the conditions set out in Part 1 of Schedule 4ZA is met.

(6)   The official receiver may refuse the application if he is not satisfied that each condition specified in Part 2 of Schedule 4ZA is met.

(7)   If the official receiver refuses an application he must give reasons for his refusal to the debtor in the prescribed manner.

(8)   In this section "specified debt" means a debt specified in the application.

**Amendments**—Inserted by Tribunals, Courts and Enforcement Act 2007, s 108(1), Sch 17.

**[1.331]**

### 251D Presumptions applicable to the determination of an application

(1)  The following presumptions are to apply to the determination of an application for a debt relief order.

(2)  The official receiver must presume that the debtor is an individual who is unable to pay his debts at the determination date if—

    (a)    that appears to the official receiver to be the case at the application date from the information supplied in the application and he has no reason to believe that the information supplied is incomplete or inaccurate; and

    (b)    he has no reason to believe that, by virtue of a change in the debtor's financial circumstances since the application date, the debtor may be able to pay his debts.

(3)  The official receiver must presume that a specified debt (of the amount specified in the application and owed to the creditor so specified) is a qualifying debt at the application date if—

    (a)    that appears to him to be the case from the information supplied in the application; and

    (b)    he has no reason to believe that the information supplied is incomplete or inaccurate.

(4)  The official receiver must presume that the condition specified in paragraph 1 of Schedule 4ZA is met if—

    (a)    that appears to him to be the case from the information supplied in the application;

    (b)    any prescribed verification checks relating to the condition have been made; and

    (c)    he has no reason to believe that the information supplied is incomplete or inaccurate.

(5)  The official receiver must presume that any other condition specified in Part 1 or 2 of Schedule 4ZA is met if—

    (a)    that appears to him to have been the case as at the application date from the information supplied in the application and he has no reason to believe that the information supplied is incomplete or inaccurate;

    (b)    any prescribed verification checks relating to the condition have been made; and

    (c)    he has no reason to believe that, by virtue of a change in circumstances since the application date, the condition may no longer be met.

(6)  References in this section to information supplied in the application include information supplied to the official receiver in support of the application.

(7)  In this section "specified debt" means a debt specified in the application.

    **Amendments**—Inserted by Tribunals, Courts and Enforcement Act 2007, s 108(1), Sch 17.

*Making and effect of debt relief order*

**[1.332]**

### 251E  Making of debt relief orders

(1)  This section applies where the official receiver makes a debt relief order on determining an application under section 251C.

(2)  The order must be made in the prescribed form.

(3)  The order must include a list of the debts which the official receiver is satisfied were qualifying debts of the debtor at the application date, specifying the amount of the debt at that time and the creditor to whom it was then owed.

(4)  The official receiver must—

    (a)    give a copy of the order to the debtor; and

    (b)    make an entry for the order in the register containing the prescribed information about the order or the debtor.

(5)   The rules may make provision as to other steps to be taken by the official receiver or the debtor on the making of the order.

(6)   Those steps may include in particular notifying each creditor to whom a qualifying debt specified in the order is owed of—

    (a)    the making of the order and its effect,

    (b)    the grounds on which a creditor may object under section 251K, and

    (c)    any other prescribed information.

(7)   In this Part the date on which an entry relating to the making of a debt relief order is first made in the register is referred to as "the effective date".

**Amendments**—Inserted by Tribunals, Courts and Enforcement Act 2007, s 108(1), Sch 17.

## [1.333]

### 251F  Effect of debt relief order on other debt management arrangements

(1)   This section applies if—

    (a)    a debt relief order is made, and

    (b)    immediately before the order is made, other debt management arrangements are in force in respect of the debtor.

(2)   The other debt management arrangements cease to be in force when the debt relief order is made.

(3)   In this section "other debt management arrangements" means—

    (a)    an administration order under Part 6 of the County Courts Act 1984;

    (b)    an enforcement restriction order under Part 6A of that Act;

    (c)    a debt repayment plan arranged in accordance with a debt management scheme that is approved under Chapter 4 of Part 5 of the Tribunals, Courts and Enforcement Act 2007.

**Amendments**—Inserted by Tribunals, Courts and Enforcement Act 2007, s 108(1), Sch 17.

## [1.334]

### 251G  Moratorium from qualifying debts

(1)   A moratorium commences on the effective date for a debt relief order in relation to each qualifying debt specified in the order ("a specified qualifying debt").

(2)   During the moratorium, the creditor to whom a specified qualifying debt is owed—

    (a)    has no remedy in respect of the debt, and

    (b)    may not—

        (i)    commence a creditor's petition in respect of the debt, or

        (ii)    otherwise commence any action or other legal proceedings against the debtor for the debt,

except with the permission of the court and on such terms as the court may impose.

(3)   If on the effective date a creditor to whom a specified qualifying debt is owed has any such petition, action or other proceeding as mentioned in subsection (2)(b) pending in any court, the court may—

    (a)    stay the proceedings on the petition, action or other proceedings (as the case may be), or

    (b)    allow them to continue on such terms as the court thinks fit.

(4)   In subsection (2)(a) and (b) references to the debt include a reference to any interest, penalty or other sum that becomes payable in relation to that debt after the application date.

(5)   Nothing in this section affects the right of a secured creditor of the debtor to enforce his security.

**Amendments**—Inserted by Tribunals, Courts and Enforcement Act 2007, s 108(1), Sch 17.

**General note**—The purpose of the DRO moratorium is quite different to that of the bankruptcy moratorium as the DRO process does not entail any administration of the debtor's property to satisfy the creditors: that there is no such property is a prerequisite to the making of a DRO. The purpose of the DRO moratorium is, therefore, to allow for objections concerning the correctness of the DRO to be considered: Smith LJ in *R (on the application of Payne) v Secretary of State for Work and Pensions* [2010] EWCA Civ 1431, [2011] 1 WLR 1723, [2011] BPIR 223 at [54] (approved by the Supreme Court in *R (on the application of Payne) v Secretary of State for Work and Pensions* [2011] UKSC 60, [2012] 2 AC 1, [2012] BPIR 224 at [23].

' . . . remedy . . . '—Though the drafting of this section differs slightly from that of s 285, this is readily explicable by the antiquity of the latter and, when considering what constitutes a 'remedy', there is no reason to distinguish between the two: Baroness Hale in *R (on the application of Payne) v Secretary of State for Work and Pensions* [2011] UKSC 60, [2012] 2 AC 1, [2012] BPIR 224 at [23] (finding that the Secretary of State's powers under ss 71 and 78 of the Social Security Administration Act 1992 to recover overpayment of social security benefits and repayment of social fund loans is a remedy for the purposes of s 251G and s 285).

By seeking an order for possession of leasehold property on the basis of arrears of rent, a landlord is not exercising a remedy in respect of the debt. The object of a possession order is to restore to the landlord the right to full possession and enjoyment of the property, not to secure payment of arrears of rent at all: Etherton LJ in *Places for People Homes Ltd v Sharples* [2011] EWCA Civ 813, [2012] Ch 382, [2011] BPIR 1488 at [95].

Reference should also be made to the commentary to s 285.

## [1.335]

### 251H  The moratorium period

(1)  The moratorium relating to the qualifying debts specified in a debt relief order continues for the period of one year beginning with the effective date for the order, unless—

    (a)    the moratorium terminates early; or

    (b)    the moratorium period is extended by the official receiver under this section or by the court under section 251M.

(2)  The official receiver may only extend the moratorium period for the purpose of—

    (a)    carrying out or completing an investigation under section 251K;

    (b)    taking any action he considers necessary (whether as a result of an investigation or otherwise) in relation to the order; or

    (c)    in a case where he has decided to revoke the order, providing the debtor with the opportunity to make arrangements for making payments towards his debts.

(3)  The official receiver may not extend the moratorium period for the purpose mentioned in subsection (2)(a) without the permission of the court.

(4)  The official receiver may not extend the moratorium period beyond the end of the period of three months beginning after the end of the initial period of one year mentioned in subsection (1).

(5)  The moratorium period may be extended more than once, but any extension (whether by the official receiver or by the court) must be made before the moratorium would otherwise end.

(6)  References in this Part to a moratorium terminating early are to its terminating before the end of what would otherwise be the moratorium period, whether on the revocation of the order or by virtue of any other enactment.

**Amendments**—Inserted by Tribunals, Courts and Enforcement Act 2007, s 108(1), Sch 17.

## [1.336]

### 251I  Discharge from qualifying debts

(1)  Subject as follows, at the end of the moratorium applicable to a debt relief order the debtor is discharged from all the qualifying debts specified in the order (including all interest, penalties and other sums which may have become payable in relation to those debts since the application date).

(2)  Subsection (1) does not apply if the moratorium terminates early.

(3)  Subsection (1) does not apply in relation to any qualifying debt which the debtor incurred in respect of any fraud or fraudulent breach of trust to which the debtor was a party.

(4)  The discharge of the debtor under subsection (1) does not release any other person from—

(a)    any liability (whether as partner or co-trustee of the debtor or otherwise) from which the debtor is released by the discharge; or

(b)    any liability as surety for the debtor or as a person in the nature of such a surety.

(5)   If the order is revoked by the court under section 251M after the end of the moratorium period, the qualifying debts specified in the order shall (so far as practicable) be treated as though subsection (1) had never applied to them.

**Amendments**—Inserted by Tribunals, Courts and Enforcement Act 2007, s 108(1), Sch 17.

**General note**—Only qualifying debts in existence at the date of the DRO are discharged. New debts incurred after the DRO are not discharged at the end of the moratorium period: Lewison LJ in *Irwell Valley Housing Association Ltd v Docherty* [2012] EWCA Civ 704.

*Duties of debtor*

**[1.337]**

**251J Providing assistance to official receiver etc**

(1)   The duties in this section apply to a debtor at any time after the making of an application by him for a debt relief order.

(2)   The debtor must—

(a)    give to the official receiver such information as to his affairs,

(b)    attend on the official receiver at such times, and

(c)    do all such other things,

as the official receiver may reasonably require for the purpose of carrying out his functions in relation to the application or, as the case may be, the debt relief order made as a result of the application.

(3)   The debtor must notify the official receiver as soon as reasonably practicable if he becomes aware of—

(a)    any error in, or omission from, the information supplied to the official receiver in, or in support of, the application;

(b)    any change in his circumstances between the application date and the determination date that would affect (or would have affected) the determination of the application.

(4)   The duties under subsections (2) and (3) apply after (as well as before) the determination of the application, for as long as the official receiver is able to exercise functions of the kind mentioned in subsection (2).

(5)   If a debt relief order is made as a result of the application, the debtor must notify the official receiver as soon as reasonably practicable if—

(a)    there is an increase in his income during the moratorium period applicable to the order;

(b)    he acquires any property or any property is devolved upon him during that period;

(c)    he becomes aware of any error in or omission from any information supplied by him to the official receiver after the determination date.

(6)   A notification under subsection (3) or (5) must give the prescribed particulars (if any) of the matter being notified.

**Amendments**—Inserted by Tribunals, Courts and Enforcement Act 2007, s 108(1), Sch 17.

*Objections, investigations and revocation*

**[1.338]**

**251K Objections and investigations**

(1)   Any person specified in a debt relief order as a creditor to whom a specified qualifying debt is owed may object to—

(a)    the making of the order;

    (b)    the inclusion of the debt in the list of the debtor's qualifying debts; or

    (c)    the details of the debt specified in the order.

(2)    An objection under subsection (1) must be—

    (a)    made during the moratorium period relating to the order and within the prescribed period for objections;

    (b)    made to the official receiver in the prescribed manner;

    (c)    based on a prescribed ground;

    (d)    supported by any information and documents as may be prescribed;

and the prescribed period mentioned in paragraph (a) must not be less than 28 days after the creditor in question has been notified of the making of the order.

(3)    The official receiver must consider every objection made to him under this section.

(4)    The official receiver may—

    (a)    as part of his consideration of an objection, or

    (b)    on his own initiative,

carry out an investigation of any matter that appears to the official receiver to be relevant to the making of any decision mentioned in subsection (5) in relation to a debt relief order or the debtor.

(5)    The decisions to which an investigation may be directed are—

    (a)    whether the order should be revoked or amended under section 251L;

    (b)    whether an application should be made to the court under section 251M; or

    (c)    whether any other steps should be taken in relation to the debtor.

(6)    The power to carry out an investigation under this section is exercisable after (as well as during) the moratorium relating to the order.

(7)    The official receiver may require any person to give him such information and assistance as he may reasonably require in connection with an investigation under this section.

(8)    Subject to anything prescribed in the rules as to the procedure to be followed in carrying out an investigation under this section, an investigation may be carried out by the official receiver in such manner as he thinks fit.

**Amendments**—Inserted by Tribunals, Courts and Enforcement Act 2007, s 108(1), Sch 17.

## [1.339]

### 251L Power of official receiver to revoke or amend a debt relief order

(1)    The official receiver may revoke or amend a debt relief order during the applicable moratorium period in the circumstances provided for by this section.

(2)    The official receiver may revoke the order on the ground that—

    (a)    any information supplied to him by the debtor—

        (i)    in, or in support of, the application, or

        (ii)    after the determination date,

was incomplete, incorrect or otherwise misleading;

    (b)    the debtor has failed to comply with a duty under section 251J;

    (c)    a bankruptcy order has been made in relation to the debtor; or

    (d)    the debtor has made a proposal under Part 8 (or has notified the official receiver of his intention to do so).

(3)    The official receiver may revoke the order on the ground that he should not have been satisfied—

    (a)    that the debts specified in the order were qualifying debts of the debtor as at the application date;

    (b)    that the conditions specified in Part 1 of Schedule 4ZA were met;

    (c)    that the conditions specified in Part 2 of that Schedule were met or that any failure to meet such a condition did not prevent his making the order.

(4)    The official receiver may revoke the order on the ground that either or both of the conditions in paragraphs 7 and 8 of Schedule 4ZA (monthly surplus income and property) are not met at any time after the order was made.

For this purpose those paragraphs are to be read as if references to the determination date were references to the time in question.

(5)   Where the official receiver decides to revoke the order, he may revoke it either—

   (a)   with immediate effect, or

   (b)   with effect from such date (not more than three months after the date of the decision) as he may specify.

(6)   In considering when the revocation should take effect the official receiver must consider (in the light of the grounds on which the decision to revoke was made and all the other circumstances of the case) whether the debtor ought to be given the opportunity to make arrangements for making payments towards his debts.

(7)   If the order has been revoked with effect from a specified date the official receiver may, if he thinks it appropriate to do so at any time before that date, revoke the order with immediate effect.

(8)   The official receiver may amend a debt relief order for the purpose of correcting an error in or omission from anything specified in the order.

(9)   But subsection (8) does not permit the official receiver to add any debts that were not specified in the application for the debt relief order to the list of qualifying debts.

(10)   The rules may make further provision as to the procedure to be followed by the official receiver in the exercise of his powers under this section.

**Amendments**—Inserted by Tribunals, Courts and Enforcement Act 2007, s 108(1), Sch 17.

**General note**—There is limited jurisprudence on the circumstances and procedure to be followed where the official receiver wishes to revoke a debt relief order. In *R (on the application of Howard) v Official Receiver* [2013] EWHC 1839 (Admin), [2014] QB 930, [2014] BPIR 204, Stadlen J considered the procedure to be adopted and the nature of debt relief orders generally (see paras 60 onwards).

*Role of the court*

**[1.340]**

**251M  Powers of court in relation to debt relief orders**

(1)   Any person may make an application to the court if he is dissatisfied by any act, omission or decision of the official receiver in connection with a debt relief order or an application for such an order.

(2)   The official receiver may make an application to the court for directions or an order in relation to any matter arising in connection with a debt relief order or an application for such an order.

(3)   The matters referred to in subsection (2) include, among other things, matters relating to the debtor's compliance with any duty arising under section 251J.

(4)   An application under this section may, subject to anything in the rules, be made at any time.

(5)   The court may extend the moratorium period applicable to a debt relief order for the purposes of determining an application under this section.

(6)   On an application under this section the court may dismiss the application or do one or more of the following—

   (a)   quash the whole or part of any act or decision of the official receiver;

   (b)   give the official receiver directions (including a direction that he reconsider any matter in relation to which his act or decision has been quashed under paragraph (a));

   (c)   make an order for the enforcement of any obligation on the debtor arising by virtue of a duty under section 251J;

   (d)   extend the moratorium period applicable to the debt relief order;

   (e)   make an order revoking or amending the debt relief order;

   (f)   make an order under section 251N; or

   (g)   make such other order as the court thinks fit.

(7)   An order under subsection (6)(e) for the revocation of a debt relief order—

    (a)    may be made during the moratorium period applicable to the debt relief order or at any time after that period has ended;

    (b)    may be made on the court's own motion if the court has made a bankruptcy order in relation to the debtor during that period;

    (c)    may provide for the revocation of the order to take effect on such terms and at such a time as the court may specify.

(8)   An order under subsection (6)(e) for the amendment of a debt relief order may not add any debts that were not specified in the application for the debt relief order to the list of qualifying debts.

**Amendments**—Inserted by Tribunals, Courts and Enforcement Act 2007, s 108(1), Sch 17.

## [1.341]

### 251N Inquiry into debtor's dealings and property

(1)   An order under this section may be made by the court on the application of the official receiver.

(2)   An order under this section is an order summoning any of the following persons to appear before the court—

    (a)    the debtor;

    (b)    the debtor's spouse or former spouse or the debtor's civil partner or former civil partner;

    (c)    any person appearing to the court to be able to give information or assistance concerning the debtor or his dealings, affairs and property.

(3)   The court may require a person falling within subsection (2)(c)—

    (a)    to provide a written account of his dealings with the debtor; or

    (b)    to produce any documents in his possession or under his control relating to the debtor or to the debtor's dealings, affairs or property.

(4)   Subsection (5) applies where a person fails without reasonable excuse to appear before the court when he is summoned to do so by an order under this section.

(5)   The court may cause a warrant to be issued to a constable or prescribed officer of the court—

    (a)    for the arrest of that person, and

    (b)    for the seizure of any records or other documents in that person's possession.

(6)   The court may authorise a person arrested under such a warrant to be kept in custody, and anything seized under such a warrant to be held, in accordance with the rules, until that person is brought before the court under the warrant or until such other time as the court may order.

**Amendments**—Inserted by Tribunals, Courts and Enforcement Act 2007, s 108(1), Sch 17.

*Offences*

## [1.342]

### 251O False representations and omissions

(1)   A person who makes an application for a debt relief order is guilty of an offence if he knowingly or recklessly makes any false representation or omission in making the application or providing any information or documents to the official receiver in support of the application.

(2)   A person who makes an application for a debt relief order is guilty of an offence if—

    (a)    he intentionally fails to comply with a duty under section 251J(3) in connection with the application; or

    (b)    he knowingly or recklessly makes any false representation or omission in providing any information to the official receiver in connection with such a duty or otherwise in connection with the application.

(3)   It is immaterial for the purposes of an offence under subsection (1) or (2) whether or not a debt relief order is made as a result of the application.

(4)   A person in respect of whom a debt relief order is made is guilty of an offence if—

    (a)   he intentionally fails to comply with a duty under section 251J(5) in connection with the order; or

    (b)   he knowingly or recklessly makes any false representation or omission in providing information to the official receiver in connection with such a duty or otherwise in connection with the performance by the official receiver of functions in relation to the order.

(5)   It is immaterial for the purposes of an offence under subsection (4)—

    (a)   whether the offence is committed during or after the moratorium period; and

    (b)   whether or not the order is revoked after the conduct constituting the offence takes place.

**Amendments**—Inserted by Tribunals, Courts and Enforcement Act 2007, s 108(1), Sch 17.

## [1.343]

### 251P Concealment or falsification of documents

(1)   A person in respect of whom a debt relief order is made is guilty of an offence if, during the moratorium period in relation to that order—

    (a)   he does not provide, at the request of the official receiver, all his books, papers and other records of which he has possession or control and which relate to his affairs;

    (b)   he prevents the production to the official receiver of any books, papers or other records relating to his affairs;

    (c)   he conceals, destroys, mutilates or falsifies, or causes or permits the concealment, destruction, mutilation or falsification of, any books, papers or other records relating his affairs;

    (d)   he makes, or causes or permits the making of, any false entries in any book, document or record relating to his affairs; or

    (e)   he disposes of, or alters or makes any omission in, or causes or permits the disposal, altering or making of any omission in, any book, document or record relating to his affairs.

(2)   A person in respect of whom a debt relief order is made is guilty of an offence if—

    (a)   he did anything falling within paragraphs (c) to (e) of subsection (1) during the period of 12 months ending with the application date; or

    (b)   he did anything falling within paragraphs (b) to (e) of subsection (1) after that date but before the effective date.

(3)   A person is not guilty of an offence under this section if he proves that, in respect of the conduct constituting the offence, he had no intent to defraud or to conceal the state of his affairs.

(4)   In its application to a trading record subsection (2)(a) has effect as if the reference to 12 months were a reference to two years.

(5)   In subsection (4) "trading record" means a book, document or record which shows or explains the transactions or financial position of a person's business, including—

    (a)   a periodic record of cash paid and received,

    (b)   a statement of periodic stock-taking, and

    (c)   except in the case of goods sold by way of retail trade, a record of goods sold and purchased which identifies the buyer and seller or enables them to be identified.

(6)   It is immaterial for the purposes of an offence under this section whether or not the debt relief order in question is revoked after the conduct constituting the offence takes place (but no offence is committed under this section by virtue of conduct occurring after the order is revoked).

**Amendments**—Inserted by Tribunals, Courts and Enforcement Act 2007, s 108(1), Sch 17.

**[1.344]**

### 251Q Fraudulent disposal of property

(1)   A person in respect of whom a debt relief order is made is guilty of an offence if he made or caused to be made any gift or transfer of his property during the period between—

    (a)    the start of the period of two years ending with the application date; and

    (b)    the end of the moratorium period.

(2)   The reference in subsection (1) to making a transfer of any property includes causing or conniving at the levying of any execution against that property.

(3)   A person is not guilty of an offence under this section if he proves that, in respect of the conduct constituting the offence, he had no intent to defraud or to conceal the state of his affairs.

(4)   For the purposes of subsection (3) a person is to be taken to have proved that he had no such intent if—

    (a)    sufficient evidence is adduced to raise an issue as to whether he had such intent; and

    (b)    the contrary is not proved beyond reasonable doubt.

(5)   It is immaterial for the purposes of this section whether or not the debt relief order in question is revoked after the conduct constituting an offence takes place (but no offence is committed by virtue of conduct occurring after the order is revoked).

**Amendments**—Inserted by Tribunals, Courts and Enforcement Act 2007, s 108(1), Sch 17.

**[1.345]**

### 251R Fraudulent dealing with property obtained on credit

(1)   A person in respect of whom a debt relief order is made is guilty of an offence if during the relevant period he disposed of any property which he had obtained on credit and, at the time he disposed of it, had not paid for it.

(2)   Any other person is guilty of an offence if during the relevant period he acquired or received property from a person in respect of whom a debt relief order was made (the "debtor") knowing or believing—

    (a)    that the debtor owed money in respect of the property, and

    (b)    that the debtor did not intend, or was unlikely to be able, to pay the money he so owed.

(3)   In subsections (1) and (2) "relevant period" means the period between—

    (a)    the start of the period of two years ending with the application date; and

    (b)    the determination date.

(4)   A person is not guilty of an offence under subsection (1) or (2) if the disposal, acquisition or receipt of the property was in the ordinary course of a business carried on by the debtor at the time of the disposal, acquisition or receipt.

(5)   In determining for the purposes of subsection (4) whether any property is disposed of, acquired or received in the ordinary course of a business carried on by the debtor, regard may be had, in particular, to the price paid for the property.

(6)   A person is not guilty of an offence under subsection (1) if he proves that, in respect of the conduct constituting the offence, he had no intent to defraud or to conceal the state of his affairs.

(7)   In this section references to disposing of property include pawning or pledging it; and references to acquiring or receiving property shall be read accordingly.

(8)   It is immaterial for the purposes of this section whether or not the debt relief order in question is revoked after the conduct constituting an offence takes place (but no offence is committed by virtue of conduct occurring after the order is revoked).

**Amendments**—Inserted by Tribunals, Courts and Enforcement Act 2007, s 108(1), Sch 17.

**[1.346]**

### 251S Obtaining credit or engaging in business

(1)   A person in respect of whom a debt relief order is made is guilty of an offence if, during the relevant period—

(a)   he obtains credit (either alone or jointly with any other person) without giving the person from whom he obtains the credit the relevant information about his status; or

(b)   he engages directly or indirectly in any business under a name other than that in which the order was made without disclosing to all persons with whom he enters into any business transaction the name in which the order was made.

(2)   For the purposes of subsection (1)(a) the relevant information about a person's status is the information that—

(a)   a moratorium is in force in relation to the debt relief order,

(b)   a debt relief restrictions order is in force in respect of him, or

(c)   both a moratorium and a debt relief restrictions order is in force,

as the case may be.

(3)   In subsection (1) "relevant period" means—

(a)   the moratorium period relating to the debt relief order, or

(b)   the period for which a debt relief restrictions order is in force in respect of the person in respect of whom the debt relief order is made,

as the case may be.

(4)   Subsection (1)(a) does not apply if the amount of the credit is less than the prescribed amount (if any).

(5)   The reference in subsection (1)(a) to a person obtaining credit includes the following cases—

(a)   where goods are bailed to him under a hire-purchase agreement, or agreed to be sold to him under a conditional sale agreement;

(b)   where he is paid in advance (in money or otherwise) for the supply of goods or services.

**Amendments**—Inserted by Tribunals, Courts and Enforcement Act 2007, s 108(1), Sch 17.

**[1.347]**

### 251T Offences: supplementary

(1)   Proceedings for an offence under this Part may only be instituted by the Secretary of State or by or with the consent of the Director of Public Prosecutions.

(2)   It is not a defence in proceedings for an offence under this Part that anything relied on, in whole or in part, as constituting the offence was done outside England and Wales.

(3)   A person guilty of an offence under this Part is liable to imprisonment or a fine, or both (but see section 430).

**Amendments**—Inserted by Tribunals, Courts and Enforcement Act 2007, s 108(1), Sch 17.

*Supplementary*

**[1.348]**

### 251U Approved intermediaries

(1)   In this Part "approved intermediary" means an individual for the time being approved by a competent authority to act as an intermediary between a person wishing to make an application for a debt relief order and the official receiver.

(2)   In this section "competent authority" means a person or body for the time being designated by the Secretary of State for the purposes of granting approvals under this section.

(3)   Designation as a competent authority may be limited so as to permit the authority only to approve persons of a particular description.

(4)   The Secretary of State may by regulations make provision as to—

    (a)   the procedure for designating persons or bodies as competent authorities;

    (b)   descriptions of individuals who are ineligible to be approved under this section;

    (c)   the procedure for granting approvals under this section;

    (d)   the withdrawal of designations or approvals under this section;

and provision made under paragraph (a) or (c) may include provision requiring the payment of fees.

(5)   The rules may make provision about the activities to be carried out by an approved intermediary in connection with an application for a debt relief order, which may in particular include—

    (a)   assisting the debtor in making the application;

    (b)   checking that the application has been properly completed;

    (c)   sending the application to the official receiver.

(6)   The rules may also make provision about other activities to be carried out by approved intermediaries.

(7)   An approved intermediary may not charge a debtor any fee in connection with an application for a debt relief order.

(8)   An approved intermediary is not liable to any person in damages for anything done or omitted to be done when acting (or purporting to act) as an approved intermediary in connection with a particular application by a debtor for a debt relief order.

(9)   Subsection (8) does not apply if the act or omission was in bad faith.

(10)   Regulations under subsection (4) shall be made by statutory instrument subject to annulment in pursuance of a resolution of either House of Parliament.

**Amendments**—Inserted by Tribunals, Courts and Enforcement Act 2007, s 108(1), Sch 17.

**Designation and approval**—The relevant statutory instrument setting out the qualification requirements for both competent authorities and approved intermediaries is the Debt Relief Orders (Designation of Competent Authorities) Regulations 2009 (SI 2009/457) (as amended).

## [1.349]

### 251V  Debt relief restrictions orders and undertakings

Schedule 4ZB (which makes provision about debt relief restrictions orders and debt relief restrictions undertakings) has effect.

**Amendments**—Inserted by Tribunals, Courts and Enforcement Act 2007, s 108(1), Sch 17.

## [1.350]

### 251W  Register of debt relief orders etc

The Secretary of State must maintain a register of matters relating to—

    (a)   debt relief orders;

    (b)   debt relief restrictions orders; and

    (c)   debt relief restrictions undertakings.

**Amendments**—Inserted by Tribunals, Courts and Enforcement Act 2007, s 108(1), Sch 17.

## [1.351]

### 251X  Interpretation

(1)   In this Part—

    "the application date", in relation to a debt relief order or an application for a debt relief order, means the date on which the application for the order is made to the official receiver;

    "approved intermediary" has the meaning given in section 251U(1);

    "debt relief order" means an order made by the official receiver under this Part;

    "debtor" means—

(a)  in relation to an application for a debt relief order, the applicant; and

(b)  in relation to a debt relief order, the person in relation to whom the order is made;

"debt relief restrictions order" and "debt relief restrictions undertaking" means an order made, or an undertaking accepted, under Schedule 4ZB;

"the determination date", in relation to a debt relief order or an application for a debt relief order, means the date on which the application for the order is determined by the official receiver;

"the effective date" has the meaning given in section 251E(7);

"excluded debt" is to be construed in accordance with section 251A;

"moratorium" and "moratorium period" are to be construed in accordance with sections 251G and 251H;

"qualifying debt", in relation to a debtor, has the meaning given in section 251A(2);

"the register" means the register maintained under section 251W;

"specified qualifying debt" has the meaning given in section 251G(1).

(2)   In this Part references to a creditor specified in a debt relief order as the person to whom a qualifying debt is owed by the debtor include a reference to any person to whom the right to claim the whole or any part of the debt has passed, by assignment or operation of law, after the date of the application for the order.

**Amendments**—Inserted by Tribunals, Courts and Enforcement Act 2007, s 108(1), Sch 17.


## PART VIII   INDIVIDUAL VOLUNTARY ARRANGEMENTS

**[1.352]**

**Introductory note to Part VIII**—The individual voluntary arrangement ('IVA') was a creation of the 1986 Act and followed recommendations made by the Cork Committee which had observed that, in effect, an individual debtor in financial difficulties had no practical option between bankruptcy and an arrangement requiring registration under the Deeds of Arrangement Act 1914, a procedure which was cumbersome, if not unworkable, in a large number of cases. In *Re Bradley-Hole (a Bankrupt)* [1995] 1 WLR 1097, [1995] 2 BCLC 163 Rimer J identified at 1108–1109 (WLR) that 'the essence of a voluntary arrangement is that under it each creditor compromises or releases his right against the debtor in respect of his pre-existing debts and receives in exchange and full satisfaction whatever terms are being offered by the debtor.'

IVAs have become common in everyday insolvency practice and have doubtless provided a workable rescue mechanism and an alternative to bankruptcy in a large number of cases. One challenge in the immediate future lies in the professional bodies remaining alive to and taking steps as necessary in relation to those non-authorised undertakings which peddle the procedure as an apparently quick-fix solution to indebted individuals in circumstances where those individuals are simply passed on to a licensed practitioner for a fee, invariably payable up front, where little, if any, thought has been given to the appropriateness of the procedure. The IVA procedure is reliant on the skill and judgment of a professional individual fulfilling the roles of nominee and supervisor. It is that individual who must initially form a view as to whether the procedure is appropriate and, even if it may be, whether bankruptcy might not be an alternative which better serves the interests of both debtor and creditors.

The IVA procedure has been described variously in the authorities as a form of quasi-contract or a form of statutory binding. Whilst contractually based, the real essence of the procedure lies in what American practitioners would term a cramming down by way of the ability of a debtor and a requisite majority of creditors to reach agreement in compromising the debtor's liability whilst, at the same time, binding into the same arrangement any dissentient creditors. An aggrieved party may apply under s 262 to challenge the arrangement on the grounds of a material irregularity in relation to the approval of the proposal or on the grounds that the operation of the arrangement is unfairly prejudicial to, at least, the applicant. These matters are discussed further in the notes to s 262.

Many (although by no means all) of the statutory provisions concerning IVAs are in mirror form to those concerning the analogous company voluntary arrangement ('CVA') procedure. In such instances, cases decided under one species of voluntary arrangement are generally relevant to and are appropriately cited in respect of cases arising under the other. In the commentary to the provisions in respect of IVAs, cross-reference is made where appropriate to the equivalent provision in respect of CVAs.

*Moratorium for insolvent debtor*

[1.353]

### 252 Interim order of court

(1)   In the circumstances specified below, the court may in the case of a debtor (being an individual) make an interim order under this section.

(2)   An interim order has the effect that, during the period for which it is in force—

(a)   no bankruptcy petition relating to the debtor may be presented or proceeded with,

(aa)   no landlord or other person to whom rent is payable may exercise any right of forfeiture by peaceable re-entry in relation to premises let to the debtor in respect of a failure by the debtor to comply with any term or condition of his tenancy of such premises, except with the leave of the court, and

(b)   no other proceedings, and no execution or other legal process, may be commenced or continued and no distress may be levied against the debtor or his property except with the leave of the court.

**Amendments**—Insolvency Act 2000, s 3, Sch 3, paras 1, 2(a), 2(b).

**General note**—Prior to the introduction of s 256A, effective from 1 January 2003, the obtaining of an interim order was a prerequisite to the approval of an IVA by creditors without which any purported approved arrangement was void: *Fletcher v Vooght* [2000] BPIR 435 (Lloyd J). Section 256A removed the requirement that an interim order be obtained before invoking the procedure under Part VIII.

The moratorium provided by way of an interim order operates to confer wide-ranging protection on a debtor and his property so as to allow a debtor to formulate an IVA proposal, albeit within relatively tight time constraints. Following an application for an interim order under s 253 the protection in s 254(1) and (2) is brought into force, following which the interim order has the effect prescribed in s 252(2) upon being made. Subject to extension by the court under s 256(5), an interim order will cease to have effect at the end of the period of 14 days beginning with the day after the making of the order, by virtue of s 255(6). The tight initial 14-day period, coupled with the court's power to extend the effect of an interim order under s 256(5), has led to the common practice of the court making so-called 'concertina' orders, on which see the note under the heading 'Interim orders and the 'concertina' order' below.

For an interesting suggested use of the interim order procedure, see the decision of the Court of Appeal in *Bramston v Haut* [2012] EWCA Civ 1637, [2013] 1 WLR 1720, [2013] BPIR 25 in which Kitchin LJ considered that it was open to an undischarged bankrupt to make an application under s 252 for an interim order which would also invite the court to use s 255(4) to provide that his or her discharge from bankruptcy be suspended pending determination of the bankrupt's IVA proposal. The Court of Appeal's decision contains a useful review of the interim order procedure. The procedure in *Bramston v Haut* was applied by Barling J in *Tucker v Atkins* [2014] EWHC 4469 (Ch), [2014] BPIR 1359.

#### SECTION 252(1)

'**in the circumstances specified below**'—The eligible applicants for an interim order are as prescribed in s 253(3). An application may not be made in the circumstances identified in s 253(5). The conditions for the making of an interim order by the court are stipulated in s 255(1).

**Insolvent partnerships**—The words 'a debtor (being an individual)' refer to an individual but not a partnership, company or any other undertaking. An IVA is not available to an insolvent partnership. Although art 11 of the Insolvent Partnerships Order 1986 (SI 1986/2142), made pursuant to s 420, extended Part VIII to individual partners of insolvent partnerships where a winding-up order was made against the partnership and bankruptcy orders made against individual members, the Insolvent Partnerships Order 1994 (SI 1994/2421), which revoked the 1986 Order, only applies the CVA procedure, appropriately modified, to insolvent partnerships, on which see art 4 and Sch 1 thereto.

**Interim orders and the 'concertina' order**—Either of two forms of order are commonly made on an application for an interim order. First, the court may make a 14-day interim order with the application adjourned for a 14-day period to allow for consideration of the nominee's report. At the return hearing, the court may make an order, on consideration of the nominee's report, extending the interim order to a date 7 weeks after the date of the proposed meeting, directing a qualifying decision procedure and adjourning the hearing to a date on or around 3 weeks after the decision date. Alternatively, in cases where the nominee's report is available immediately, the court may make a 'concertina' order which combines both of those orders just mentioned. Where the papers are in order and where there is no bankruptcy order in existence and, so far as is known, there is no pending bankruptcy petition, the court may consider making any such order without the attendance of the parties, on which see para 14.1(1) of the *Practice Direction – Insolvency Proceedings* (July 2020) [2020] BPIR 1211.

Note also s 260(4), which provides for the automatic lapse of an interim order 28 days after the filing of the chairman's report with the court, subject to contrary order.

## SECTION 252(2)

**Effect of the interim order**—The scope of the moratorium in s 252(2)(aa) and (b) was bolstered by s 3 of and Sch 3 to the Insolvency Act 2000 by expressly extending the protection to forfeiture by peaceable re-entry by a landlord and the levying of distress so as to reverse the effect of previous contrary authority: see *Re A Debtor (No 13AIO and 14AIO of 1994)* [1995] 1 WLR 1127, [1996] BPIR 43 and *McMullen & Sons v Cerrone* [1994] 1 BCLC 152.

The prohibition against the presentation of or proceeding with a bankruptcy petition is absolute; in contrast to s 252(2)(aa) and (b), the court has no jurisdiction to give leave for a bankruptcy petition to proceed.

## SECTION 252(2)(aa)

**'no landlord or other person to whom rent is payable . . . '**—Subject to the leave of the court, this provision protects against the exercise of any right of forfeiture by peaceable re-entry. The protection is restricted to premises which are let to the debtor, but not necessarily occupied by the debtor. The reference to a failure by the *debtor* 'to comply with any term or condition of his tenancy' makes clear that the protection of the sub-provision extends to forfeiture by peaceable re-entry whether arising on breach of a covenant for rent or any other covenant which, but for the moratorium, would give rise to such relief. Furthermore, the draftsman's use of the words 'tenancy of such premises' provides a debtor with no protection where the substance of his or her interest amounts only to a licence: see *Street v Mountford* [1985] AC 809.

## SECTION 252(2)(b)

**'no other proceedings, and no execution or other legal process may be commenced or continued . . . except with the leave of the court'**—The term 'proceedings' is a more compendious expression than the word 'action' used previously and most recently in s 9 of the Bankruptcy Act 1914. The former term is apt to denote any legal or quasi-legal proceedings and has been held to extend to arbitration proceedings (*Bristol Airport plc v Powdrill* [1990] Ch 744, [1990] BCLC 585 (Browne-Wilkinson V-C)), proceedings before an industrial tribunal (*Carr v British International Helicopters Ltd (in administration)* [1994] 2 BCLC 474 (EAT)), a statutory adjudication process under s 108 of the Housing Grants, Construction and Regeneration Act 1996 and under cl 41A of the standard-form JCT 80 contract (*A Straume (UK) Ltd v Bradlor Developments Ltd* [2000] BCC 333 (HHJ Behrens)), criminal prosecution under the Environmental Protection Act 1990 (*Environment Agency v Clark* [2001] Ch 57, [2000] BCC 653 (Robert Walker and Henry LJJ and Scott-Baker J)) and an application by a special freight train operator for a replacement access contract under s 17 of the Railways Act 1993 (*Winsor v Special Railway Administrators of Railtrack plc* [2002] EWHC 1027 (Ch), [2002] 2 BCLC 308).

In *Re Olympia & York Canary Wharf Ltd* [1993] BCLC 453 at 457A Millett J identified that the words 'legal process' refer to a process which requires the assistance of the court and which would not, therefore, extend, for example, to the service of a contractual notice, whether or not the service of such a notice was a pre-condition to the bringing of legal proceedings. If the view is taken that a particular process does not require the assistance of the court, then careful consideration should be given to the question of whether that process falls within the scope of 'proceedings' above. It is doubtful, however, that the service of a counter-notice under Part II of the Landlord and Tenant Act 1954 for a fresh tenancy constitutes 'proceedings': *Bristol Airport plc v Powdrill* [1990] Ch 744, 766, [1990] BCLC 585 (Browne-Wilkinson V-C).

**When will leave be granted by the court?**—Although interim order cases requiring the leave of the court are necessarily decided on a case by case basis, useful guidance may be gleaned from the guidance given in the Court of Appeal in *Re Atlantic Computer Systems plc* [1992] Ch 505, [1991] BCLC 606, which is set out in full, together with further commentary, in the note to para 43 of Sch B1 (on administrations). That guidance is relevant here to the extent that the court's approach will be rooted in establishing the purpose for which the interim order has been obtained and the extent to which, if leave was granted, the assertion of third party rights would operate to undermine that purpose. In *Hall and Shivers v Van Der Heiden* [2010] EWHC 537 (TCC), [2010] BPIR 585, Coulson J was faced with a situation where a defendant debtor, on the last business day before a trial, obtained an interim order from the Swindon County Court. The claimants in the proceedings, on the first day of the trial, applied for leave to continue the proceedings. The judge held both that he had jurisdiction to make the order, and that it was appropriate to make the order. In *Stella v Harris* [2014] EWHC 4492 (Ch), [2015] BPIR 926, at [22], Mann J granted leave to a contingent creditor to enter judgment against a defendant debtor. The defendant had previously been permitted leave to defend conditional upon making a payment into court, had failed to comply with that condition, and thereafter obtained an interim order. Mann J considered that in seeking to enter judgment in advance of the creditors' meeting, the creditor was simply following through with his rights under a court order and was not stealing a march on the other creditors.

**Criminal proceedings which are not protected against by an interim order**—Certain criminal statutes allow for the making of orders against the assets of a defendant by way of charging orders, confiscation orders and the like. The effect of the making of a restraint order under s 8 of the Drug Trafficking Offences Act 1986, for example, takes effect so as to take such property out of the scope of the defendant's estate. Provisions to like effect appear in Part V of the Criminal Justice Act 1988 and the Proceeds of Crime Act 2002. In *Re M (Restraint Order)* [1992] QB 377 Otton J held that an interim order did not prevent the making of an application by the prosecuting authorities and the making of an order appointing a receiver over such property which would remain outside the scope of the defendant's estate pending the discharge of the restraint order. Neither will the interim order protect against the enforcement of an order imposed by a magistrates' court for the payment of compensation following the defendant's conviction for VAT offences, since the purpose of an IVA is to provide an alternative to bankruptcy in which a claim under a criminal compensation order is not provable: *R v Barnet Magistrates' Court ex parte Philippou* [1997] BPIR 134.

**Creditor and third party remedies not protected against by an interim order**—Like the protection of the moratorium in administration under paras 40–43 of Sch B1 – which, in substance, resembles the protection previously afforded by ss 10 and 11 – nothing within the interim order provisions suggests that the statutory protection afforded to a debtor is intended to deprive a creditor or third party from utilising any self-help remedies against the debtor, even where the effect of such remedies is harmful to the financial interests or standing of the debtor. These self-help remedies would include determination by repudiation of a contract, service of a contractual notice (such as one making time of the essence, as in *Re Olympia & York Canary Wharf Ltd* [1993] BCLC 453 (Millett J)) or forfeiture (though not by peaceable re-entry) of a lease. Neither would the protection of the moratorium appear to catch the combination of accounts, most obviously by a bank or trading customer, or an application for an extension of time for the registration of a charge over the company's property, as in *Re Barrow Borough Transport Ltd* [1990] Ch 227, [1989] BCLC 653. Since the exercise of a right of set-off cannot sensibly be characterised as proceedings, execution or other legal process, such a right – whether legal, equitable or contractual – should also remain available to a third party, in support of which proposition see *Electromagnetic (S) Ltd v Development Bank of Singapore* [1994] SLR 734, a decision of the High Court of Singapore, in which jurisdiction the administration regime had been modelled on the former English scheme. It is suggested that the service of a demand, say for the return of goods, constitutes no more than self-help and will not fall within the scope of s 252(2)(b) (on which see *Barclays Mercantile Business Finance Ltd v Sibec Developments Ltd* [1992] 1 WLR 1253, [1993] BCLC 1077), although it is arguable that the position is different where the service of such a demand or other notice is a contractual pre-condition for the taking of any step within s 252(2)(b), on which see *Re Olympia & York Canary Wharf Ltd* [1993] BCLC 453 at 454G–454H (Millett J).

**Secured creditors**—In contrast with the position under para 43 of Sch B1 in relation to company administration, the interim order in an IVA offers no protection against the enforcement of the rights of a secured creditor. Neither is an IVA capable of modifying the rights of a secured creditor, save with that creditor's consent: see s 258(4).

## [1.354]

### 253 Application for interim order

(1) Application to the court for an interim order may be made where the debtor intends to make a proposal under this Part, that is, a proposal to his creditors for a composition in satisfaction of his debts or a scheme of arrangement of his affairs (from here on referred to, in either case, as a "voluntary arrangement").

(2) The proposal must provide for some person ("the nominee") to act in relation to the voluntary arrangement either as trustee or otherwise for the purpose of supervising its implementation and the nominee must be a person who is qualified to act as an insolvency practitioner, or authorised to act as nominee, in relation to the voluntary arrangement.

(3)    Subject as follows, the application may be made—

    (a)    if the debtor is an undischarged bankrupt, by the debtor, the trustee of his estate, or the official receiver, and

    (b)    in any other case, by the debtor.

(4)    An application shall not be made under subsection (3)(a) unless the debtor has given notice of the proposal to the official receiver and, if there is one, the trustee of his estate.

(5)    . . .

**Amendments**—Insolvency Act 2000, s 3, Sch 3, paras 1, 3(a)–(c); Enterprise and Regulatory Reform Act 2013, s 71(3), Sch 19, paras 1, 2.

**General note**—An IVA backed by a moratorium is open to a debtor who has not made an application for an interim order within the 12 months ending with the day of the application (on which see s 255(1)(c)) or an undischarged bankrupt. An application may not be made in the circumstances prescribed in s 253(5). A debtor may not propose an IVA proposal to a meeting of creditors where he has received his automatic discharge from bankruptcy after the date of an interim order but before the date of the creditors' meeting: *Re Ravichandran* [2004] BPIR 814 (Registrar Nicholls). The solution in such a case is for the debtor to seek a suspension of discharge at the same as he applies for an interim order: see general note to s 252. The IVA procedure is not available to a discharged bankrupt in respect of the bankruptcy debts since those debts will have been released on discharge by operation of s 281: *Wright v Official Receiver* [2001] BPIR 196 (District Judge Caddick, Medway County Court). An IVA would, however, be available to a discharged bankrupt in respect of non-bankruptcy debts which are not released by s 281(1); in those circumstances the debtor will fall within s 253(3)(b). Equally, a discharged bankrupt would have standing to propose an IVA in respect of post-bankruptcy debts.

**The scope of the term 'creditor'**—See notes to s 1(1) (equivalent CVA provision) under this heading.

**Unliquidated debts**—See notes to s 1(1) (equivalent CVA provision) under this heading.

**Disputed debts**—See notes to s 1(1) (equivalent CVA provision) under this heading.

**Contingent debts**—See notes to s 1(1) (equivalent CVA provision) under this heading.

**Court control over the admission of creditor's proof**—See notes to s 1(1) (equivalent CVA provision) under this heading.

**The effect of the arrangement on third parties**—See notes to s 1(1) (equivalent CVA provision) under this heading.

## SECTION 253(1)

**The scope of the terms 'voluntary arrangement', 'composition', and 'scheme of arrangement'**—See notes to s 1(1) (equivalent CVA provision) under this heading.

**Proposals which do not amount to a composition or scheme of arrangement**—See notes to s 1(1) (equivalent CVA provision) under this heading.

**The court's approach to the construction of voluntary arrangements**—See notes to s 5(2) (equivalent CVA provision) under this heading.

## SECTION 253(2)

**Scope of provision**—A valid proposal is implemented on being approved under s 258(1) by a creditors' decision procedure under s 257 by the requisite majority of creditors as provided for in r 15.34(6). Thereafter, the nominee – or any person appointed in his or her stead under s 256(3) or s 258(3) – is known as the supervisor of the voluntary arrangement: see s 263(2) and the notes thereto.

**Qualifications of the nominee**—See notes to s 1(2) (equivalent CVA provision) under this heading.

**Identity of the nominee**—See notes to s 1(2) (equivalent CVA provision) under this heading.

**Role of the nominee**—See notes to s 1(2) (equivalent CVA provision) under this heading.

**Role of the supervisor**—See notes to s 1(2) (equivalent CVA provision) under this heading.

**Duties of the nominee**—See notes to s 2(2) (equivalent CVA provision) under this heading.

**The status of arrangement assets in a winding-up or bankruptcy**—See commentary to s 1(2) (equivalent CVA provision) under this heading.

## SECTION 253(4)

**Scope of provision**—Two clear days' notice must be given to the official receiver or trustee: r 8.8(4).

**[1.355]**

### 254 Effect of application

(1)  At any time when an application under section 253 for an interim order is pending,

    (a)    no landlord or other person to whom rent is payable may exercise any right of forfeiture by peaceable re-entry in relation to premises let to the debtor in respect of a failure by the debtor to comply with any term or condition of his tenancy of such premises, except with the leave of the court, and

    (b)    the court may forbid the levying of any distress on the debtor's property or its subsequent sale, or both, and stay any action, execution or other legal process against the property or person of the debtor.

(2)  Any court in which proceedings are pending against an individual may, on proof that an application under that section has been made in respect of that individual, either stay the proceedings or allow them to continue on such terms as it thinks fit.

**Amendments**—Insolvency Act 2000, s 3, Sch 3, paras 1, 4(a), (b).

**General note**—Section 254 takes effect for the period starting with the filing of an application for an interim order under s 253 and ending with either the making of an interim order or the dismissal of the application.

Subparagraphs (1)(a) and (b) provide protection very similar to that provided under an interim order in s 252(2)(aa) and (b). The protection in s 254(1)(a) arises automatically on the filing of an interim order application and may only be circumvented with leave of the court. The protection in s 254(1)(b), on the other hand, requires the intervention of either the debtor or the nominee by way of an application to court.

**SECTION 254(1)(a)**

**Scope of provision**—Subject to the leave of the court, this provision protects against the exercise of any right of forfeiture by peaceable re-entry. The protection is restricted to premises which are let to the debtor, but not necessarily occupied by the debtor. The reference to a failure by the *debtor* 'to comply with any term or condition of his tenancy' makes clear that the protection of the provision extends to forfeiture by peaceable re-entry whether arising on breach of a covenant for rent or any other covenant which, but for the moratorium, would give rise to such relief. Furthermore, the draftsman's use of the words 'tenancy of such premises' provides a debtor with no protection where the substance of his interest amounts only to a licence: see *Street v Mountford* [1985] AC 809. The extension of the provision to protection against the exercise of rights of forfeiture was effected by s 3 of the Insolvency Act 2000 and Sch 3 thereto.

**SECTION 254(1)(b)**

**Scope of provision**—This provision allows the court to prevent not only the levying of distress against the debtor's property – following amendment introduced by s 3 and Sch 3 of the Insolvency Act 2000 – but also the continuation of any distress by way of the sale of any of the debtor's property.

The reference to the court staying 'any action' in s 254(1)(b) differs from the reference in s 252(2)(b), which refers to 'proceedings'; if anything, the latter term is broader than the former, although it is doubtful that any meaningful distinction could have been intended. In any case, the reference to 'action' would allow for the stay of an extant bankruptcy petition in the absence of any specific reference to a petition as appears in s 252(2)(a). The subsection would not appear, however, to prevent the presentation of a bankruptcy petition prior to or during the period in which an application for an interim order under s 252 is pending.

For the scope of the terms 'execution or other legal process against the property or person of the debtor' see the notes under that heading to s 252(2)(b).

**SECTION 254(2)**

**The appropriate court on an application for continuance or stay**—Where proceedings are pending against an individual (ie under s 254(1)(b)) it is the court in which those proceedings have been commenced which has jurisdiction to stay the proceedings or allow them to continue, subject to any stipulated terms on being satisfied that an application has been made under s 253, very possibly in another court. The court to which the s 253 application is made does not appear capable of exercising such jurisdiction based on the wording in s 254(2). The position is different where leave of the court is sought as against the automatic bars imposed by s 254(1)(a), since the reference to 'the court' in that provision must be read as being the court to which the interim order application under s 253 is made by virtue of the definition in s 385(1).

**When will the court grant leave or allow proceedings to continue?**—The considerations here will be the same as those identified under this heading in the notes to s 252(2)(b).

**[1.356]**

## 255 Cases in which interim order can be made

(1) The court shall not make an interim order on an application under section 253 unless it is satisfied—

    (a)    that the debtor intends to make a proposal under this Part;

    (b)    that on the day of the making of the application the debtor was an undischarged bankrupt or was able to make a bankruptcy application;

    (c)    that no previous application has been made by the debtor for an interim order in the period of 12 months ending with that day; and

    (d)    that the nominee under the debtor's proposal is willing to act in relation to the proposal.

(2) The court may make an order if it thinks that it would be appropriate to do so for the purpose of facilitating the consideration and implementation of the debtor's proposal.

(3) Where the debtor is an undischarged bankrupt, the interim order may contain provision as to the conduct of the bankruptcy, and the administration of the bankrupt's estate, during the period for which the order is in force.

(4) Subject as follows, the provision contained in an interim order by virtue of subsection (3) may include provision staying proceedings in the bankruptcy or modifying any provision in this Group of Parts, and any provision of the rules in their application to the debtor's bankruptcy.

(5) An interim order shall not, in relation to a bankrupt, make provision relaxing or removing any of the requirements of provisions in this Group of Parts, or of the rules, unless the court is satisfied that that provision is unlikely to result in any significant diminution in, or in the value of, the debtor's estate for the purposes of the bankruptcy.

(6) Subject to the following provisions of this Part, an interim order made on an application under section 253 ceases to have effect at the end of the period of 14 days beginning with the day after the making of the order.

**Amendments**—Insolvency Act 2000, ss 3, 15(1), Sch 3, paras 1, 5(a), (b), Sch 5); Enterprise and Regulatory Reform Act 2013, s 71(3), Sch 19, paras 1, 3.

**General note**—There are two features to this provision. First, the first two subsections stipulate preconditions for the making of an interim order and direct the circumstances in which an order may be made respectively. Secondly, subss (3)–(5) specifically allow, where the debtor is an undischarged bankrupt, for the interim order to include provisions providing for the future conduct of the bankruptcy, the administration of the bankrupt's estate, staying of proceedings, and the modification of any statutory rules within this Group of Parts provided, in the last case, that the provision is unlikely to result in any significant reduction in the debtor's estate or the value thereof. Creative use was made of s 255(4) in *Bramston v Haut* [2012] EWCA Civ 1637, [2013] 1 WLR 1720, [2013] BPIR 25; see general note to s 252.

### SECTION 255(1)(a)

**Scope of provision**—This precondition will be satisfied by the court having sight of what appears to it to be a genuine proposal.

### SECTION 255(1)(b)

**Scope of provision**—On a literal interpretation, this condition would not appear to be met if, on the day of the application, the debtor was not an undischarged bankrupt but was unable to make an application for his own bankruptcy by reason of there being an extant bankruptcy petition against the debtor. However, this interpretation would be incompatible with s 252(2)(a), which provides that a petition may not be presented *or proceeded with* once an interim order has been obtained, demonstrating that an interim order may be obtained after a petition has been presented. This is consistent with the policy of the interim order regime, which is to prevent the frustration of a potentially viable IVA proposal by a minority creditor's insistence on bankruptcy. In practice, interim orders are often obtained by debtors immediately before the hearing of a bankruptcy petition to obtain a stay of the process, whether their IVA proposal is realistic or not.

### SECTION 255(1)(c)

**Scope of provision**—This provision requires only that an application has been made, rather than an interim order obtained, within the preceding 12-month period. In *Hurst v Bennett (No 2)* [2001] EWCA Civ 1398, [2002] BPIR 102 the Court of Appeal (Mummery and Jonathan Parker LJJ), in refusing permission to appeal, upheld the decision of Ferris J on an appeal from the registrar to the effect that it is an improper use of the review procedure under s 375(1) to challenge the dismissal of an interim order application within the preceding 12 months whilst, at the same time, seeking to advance a fresh application, albeit in relation to a reformulated proposal with the support of a new nominee.

### SECTION 255(1)(d)

**Scope of provision**—The court need only be satisfied that the nominee is willing to act in relation to the proposal. It will be necessary in any case for the nominee to be authorised to act as such.

### SECTION 255(2)

**Scope of provision**—In effect, this provision amounts to an additional precondition to the four subsections above, in that an interim order may only be made if the court 'thinks' (on the meaning of which see the commentary in the notes to para 36 in Sch B1) that the making of the order would be appropriate for facilitating 'the consideration and implementation of the debtor's proposal', being a reference to the views and decision of the creditors' meeting and the viability thereafter of the proposal. Although the provision provides that the court 'may make' – as opposed to 'may only make' – an order, it is implausible that Parliament might have intended that the court should even consider making an interim order in any circumstances other than where it would be appropriate to do so for the specific purpose identified above.

It is well established that, in determining the appropriateness of making an interim order, the court will consider whether the proposal is 'serious or viable' on which test see the notes to s 2(2). The wording of s 255(2) is apt to confer on the court a discretion as to whether to make an interim order.

In *Singh v Singh* [2013] EWHC 4783 (Ch), [2014] BPIR 1555, at [12]–[16], [22], Proudman J appeared to take the view that where it was clear that a proposal would be defeated, an interim order should not be made. Similarly, it was implicit in Asplin J's reasoning in *Tucker v Atkins* [2014] EWHC 2260 (Ch), [2014] BPIR 1569, [32]–[33], that an interim order would not be appropriate where it was 'strongly improbable' that the proposal would be approved at the creditors' meeting.

### SECTION 255(3)–(5)

**Scope of provision**—The discretion of the court and the scope of any additional provisions which may be provided for by the court is unfettered and broad. See general note to s 255.

### SECTION 255(6)

**Scope of provision**—Although an interim order would ordinarily expire 14 days from the date on which it was made, see the note headed 'Interim orders and the 'concertina' order' to s 252.

## [1.357]

### 256 Nominee's report on debtor's proposal

(1)   Where an interim order has been made on an application under section 253, the nominee shall, before the order ceases to have effect, submit a report to the court stating—

    (a)    whether, in his opinion, the voluntary arrangement which the debtor is proposing has a reasonable prospect of being approved and implemented, and

    (aa)   whether, in his opinion, the debtor's creditors should consider the debtor's proposal

    (b)    . . .

(2)   For the purpose of enabling the nominee to prepare his report the debtor shall submit to the nominee—

    (a)    a document setting out the terms of the voluntary arrangement which the debtor is proposing, and

    (b)    a statement of his affairs containing—

        (i)    such particulars of his creditors and of his debts and other liabilities and of his assets as may be prescribed, and

        (ii)   such other information as may be prescribed.

(3)   The court may—

    (a)    on an application made by the debtor in a case where the nominee has failed to submit the report required by this section or has died, or

    (b)    on an application made by the debtor or the nominee in a case where it is impracticable or inappropriate for the nominee to continue to act as such, direct that the nominee shall be replaced as such by another person qualified to act as an insolvency practitioner, or authorised to act as nominee, in relation to the voluntary arrangement.

(3A)   The court may, on an application made by the debtor in a case where the nominee has failed to submit the report required by this section, direct that the interim order shall continue, or (if it has ceased to have effect) be renewed, for such further period as the court may specify in the direction.

(4)   The court may, on the application of the nominee, extend the period for which the interim order has effect so as to enable the nominee to have more time to prepare his report.

(5)   If the court is satisfied on receiving the nominee's report that the debtor's creditors should consider the debtor's proposal, the court shall direct that the period for which the interim order has effect shall be extended, for such further period as it may specify in the direction, for the purpose of enabling the debtor's proposal to be considered by his creditors in accordance with the following provisions of this Part.

(6)   The court may discharge the interim order if it is satisfied, on the application of the nominee—

> (a)   that the debtor has failed to comply with his obligations under subsection (2), or
>
> (b)   that for any other reason it would be inappropriate for the debtor's creditors should to consider the debtor's proposal.

**Amendments**—Insolvency Act 2000, s 3, Sch 3, paras 1, 6(a), (b), 7; Small Business, Enterprise and Employment Act 2015, s 126, Sch 9, Pt 2, paras 60, 61.

**General note**—The counterpoint to s 256 appears in s 256A, which applies to cases where no interim order is sought, whether or not the debtor is an undischarged bankrupt. The detailed procedural rules governing the preparation and contents of an IVA proposal together with the preparation of the proposal and the nominee's report to the court are set out in rr 8.2–8.21.

### SECTION 256(1)

**Scope of provision**—Section 256 applies where an interim order has been made and requires action before the interim order ceases to have effect.

**The viability of the proposal and the duties of the nominee in reporting to the court**—See notes to s 2(2) (equivalent CVA provision) under this heading.

### SECTION 256(1)(a)

**'Whether . . . the proposed voluntary arrangement has a reasonable prospect of being approved and implemented'**—See notes to s 2(2) (equivalent CVA provision) under this heading.

### SECTION 256(1)(aa)

**Whether the proposal should be considered by the creditors: the 'serious and viable' test**—See notes to s 2(2) (equivalent CVA provision) under this heading.

### SECTION 256(2)

**'a document setting out the terms of the proposed voluntary arrangement'**—See notes to s 2(3) (equivalent CVA provision) under this heading.

**'a statement of . . . affairs'**—See notes to s 2(3) (equivalent CVA provision) under this heading.

**False representations etc**—See notes to s 2(3) (equivalent CVA provision) under this heading.

### SECTION 256(3)

**Scope of provision**—See notes to s 2(4)(a) and (b) (equivalent CVA provision) under this heading.

### SECTION 256(5)

It has been stated judicially that the court is not a rubber-stamp and must consider the contents of and reasons for a nominee's report and whether or not a meeting of creditors ought to be summoned: *Re a Debtor (No 140-IO-1995)* [1996] 2 BCLC 429 at 436 (Lindsay J).

If the court has not directed that a meeting of creditors ought to be summoned then any meeting of creditors convened to consider a proposal is not a statutory meeting within s 257 such that the court will be unable to entertain any complaint under s 262 in relation to it: *Vleiland-Boddy v Dexter* [2003] EWHC 2592 (Ch), [2004] BPIR 235 (Roger Kaye QC, sitting as a deputy High Court judge).

*Procedure where no interim order made*

**[1.358]**

**256A Debtor's proposal and nominee's report**

(1) This section applies where a debtor (being an individual)—

    (a) intends to make a proposal under this Part (but an interim order has not been made in relation to the proposal and no application for such an order is pending), and

    (b) if he is an undischarged bankrupt, has given notice of the proposal to the official receiver and, if there is one, the trustee of his estate.

. . .

(2) For the purpose of enabling the nominee to prepare a report under subsection (3), the debtor shall submit to the nominee—

    (a) a document setting out the terms of the voluntary arrangement which the debtor is proposing, and

    (b) a statement of his affairs containing—

        (i) such particulars of his creditors and of his debts and other liabilities and of his assets as may be prescribed, and

        (ii) such other information as may be prescribed.

(3) If the nominee is of the opinion that the debtor is an undischarged bankrupt, or is able to make a bankruptcy application, the nominee shall, within 14 days (or such longer period as the court may allow) after receiving the document and statement mentioned in subsection (2), submit a report to the debtor's creditors stating—

    (a) whether, in his opinion, the voluntary arrangement which the debtor is proposing has a reasonable prospect of being approved and implemented, and

    (b) whether, in his opinion, the debtor's creditors should consider the debtor's proposal,

    (c) . . .

(4) The court may—

    (a) on an application made by the debtor in a case where the nominee has failed to submit the report required by this section or has died, or

    (b) on an application made by the debtor or the nominee in a case where it is impracticable or inappropriate for the nominee to continue to act as such,

direct that the nominee shall be replaced as such by another person qualified to act as an insolvency practitioner, or authorised to act as nominee, in relation to the voluntary arrangement.

(5) The court may, on an application made by the nominee, extend the period within which the nominee is to submit his report.

**Amendments**—Inserted by the Insolvency Act 2000, s 3, Sch 3, paras 1, 7. Amended by SI 2010/18; Enterprise and Regulatory Reform Act 2013, s 71(3), Sch 19, paras 1, 4; Small Business, Enterprise and Employment Act 2015, s 126, Sch 9, Pt 2, paras 60, 62.

**General note**—Section 256A was introduced by s 3 of and Sch 3 to the Insolvency Act 2000 and took effect from 1 January 2003. Section 256A closely resembles s 256. The significance of the new provisions, however, lies in their facilitating the implementation of an individual debtor's IVA proposal without any requirement for an application for an interim order. Prior to the introduction of s 256A an interim order had been held to be an integral part of the IVA procedure under Part VIII and a pre-requisite for the approval of a valid IVA which could not be cured retrospectively: *Fletcher v Vooght* [2000] BPIR 435 (Lloyd J). Neither, in the absence of a provision equivalent to s 256(5), is the court under any duty to consider the report of the nominee submitted under s 256A(3) with a view to satisfying itself that a meeting of the debtor's creditors should be summoned to consider the debtor's proposal. The court will be under a duty to consider the report, however, if any application is made in relation to the debtor's proposal: see IR 2016, r 8.20.

Where the s 256A procedure is used, the requisitioning of a creditors' decision procedure by the nominee is pursuant to s 257(1) and is dependent solely on the submission to the creditors of a positive report by the nominee under s 256A(3).

**Cases in which s 256A will be of use**—IVAs implemented under the s 256A procedure will be obtainable more quickly and cheaply than under the interim order route. The real question for the debtor, and those advising him, is whether the debtor requires the protection of an interim order immediately or is likely to need such protection upon creditors becoming aware of his IVA proposal. In a borderline case where no interim order is sought in the belief that no creditor will resort to pre-emptive action, there is no reason why a debtor should not resort to the interim order procedure for protection where that belief turns out to be mistaken, subject to the restrictions imposed by s 253(3) and (5) and the conditions in s 255(1).

**Procedure**—See rr 8.19–8.20.

### SECTION 256A(2)

**Scope of provision**—See notes to s 2(3) (equivalent CVA provision) under this heading.

### SECTION 256A(3)

**Scope of provision**—The s 256A procedure is not available if the nominee is of the opinion that the debtor is a discharged bankrupt seeking to make a proposal in respect of debts released in the bankruptcy, on which see *Wright v Official Receiver* [2001] BPIR 196 and the general note to s 253. Neither may an individual propose an IVA under s 256A if a bankruptcy application made by the individual himself or herself under s 263H-O is outstanding, since in those circumstances the debtor would not be able to make an application for his or her own bankruptcy. Subject to the nominee's opinion – the absence of a reference to the nominee being 'satisfied' suggests that the nominee may take the documents submitted to him under s 256A(2) at face value without the need for further investigation, in the absence of any suspicion – that the debtor is an undischarged bankrupt or is able to petition for his or her own bankruptcy these provisions are otherwise identical to those in s 256(1), on which see the notes thereto.

### SECTION 256A(4)

**Scope of provision**—See notes to s 2(4)(a) and (b) (equivalent CVA provision) under this heading.

### SECTION 256A(5)

**Scope of provision**—The nominee's report must be submitted to the debtor's creditors of whose address the nominee is aware, if the debtor is an undischarged bankrupt to the official receiver and the trustee, and any person who has presented a bankruptcy petition against the debtor within 14 days after receiving those documents prescribed in s 256A(2): r 8.19. The court should not extend the period for the submission of the nominee's report without a proper explanation for the reasons giving rise to the need for extra time.

*Creditors' decisions*

**Amendments**—Inserted by Insolvency Act 2000, s 3, Sch 3, paras 1, 7. Amended by Small Business, Enterprise and Employment Act 2015, s 126, Sch 9, Pt 2, paras 60.

## [1.359]

### 257 Consideration of debtor's proposal by creditors

(1) This section applies where it has been reported to the court under section 256 or to the debtor's creditors under section 256A that the debtor's creditors should consider the debtor's proposal.

(2) The nominee (or the nominee's replacement under section 256(3) or 256A(4)) must seek a decision from the debtor's creditors as to whether they approve the proposed voluntary arrangement (unless, in the case of a report to which section 256 applies, the court otherwise directs).

(2A) The decision is to be made by a creditors' decision procedure.

(2B) Notice of the creditors' decision procedure must be given to every creditor of the debtor of whose claim and address the nominee (or the nominee's replacement) is aware.

(3) For this purpose the creditors of a debtor who is an undischarged bankrupt include—

    (a)    every person who is a creditor of the bankrupt in respect of a bankruptcy debt, and

    (b)    every person who would be such a creditor if the bankruptcy had commenced on the day on which notice of the creditors's decision procedure is given.

**Amendments**—Insolvency Act 2000, s 3, Sch 3, paras 1, 8(a), (b); SI 2010/18. Amended by Small Business, Enterprise and Employment Act 2015, s 126, Sch 9, Pt 2, paras 60, 64.

**General note**—See notes to s 3 (equivalent CVA provision) under this heading.

### SECTION 257(1)

**Scope of provision**—See notes to s 3(1) (equivalent CVA provision) under this heading.

**Timing of the decision date**—Where an interim order has not been obtained, r 8.22(7) provides that the decision date must be not more than 28 days from the date on which the nominee receives the document and statement referred to in s 256A(2). Where an interim order is in force, the decision date must be not less than 14 days from the date on which the nominee's report is filed in court nor more than 28 days from the date on which it is considered by the court.

The reference to 14 days' notice is to 14 days' clear notice being given to a creditor; there is no scope for arguing for 'substantial compliance' with the provision where less than 14 days' clear notice has been given: *Mytre Investments Ltd v Reynolds (No 2)* [1996] BPIR 464 at 468H–470H. This point is relevant to the question of whether a creditor can be said to have had notice of a creditors' decision procedure 'in accordance with the rules' under s 262(3)(b).

### SECTION 257(2)

**Scope of provision**—See notes to s3(3) and (4) (equivalent CVA provision) under this heading.

**The scope of the term 'creditor'**—See notes to s 3(3) and(4) (equivalent CVA provision) under this heading.

**Unliquidated debts**—See notes to s 1(1) (equivalent CVA provision) under this heading.

**Disputed debts**—See notes to s 1(1) (equivalent CVA provision) under this heading.

**Court control over the admission of creditor's proof**—See notes to s 1(1) (equivalent CVA provision) under this heading.

### SECTION 257(3)

**Scope of provision**—This subsection applies only to any proposal made by an undischarged bankrupt. Its effect is to extend the scope of creditors entitled to receive notice of a creditors' decision procedure under s 257(2) beyond the creditors in the bankruptcy so as to include post-bankruptcy creditors. The rationale behind s 257(3)(b) is self-evident. Without the subsection a debtor could not succeed in binding a post-bankruptcy creditor in any approved arrangement, with the consequence that any such creditor would remain entitled to pursue his or her debt, ultimately to a second bankruptcy.

**'bankruptcy debt'**—The scope of bankruptcy debts in delineating the creditors of a debtor under s 257(3) is as provided for in ss 382, 383 and 385.

*Consideration and implementation of debtor's proposal*

## [1.360]

### 258 Approval of debtor's proposal

(1) This section applies where under section 257 the debtor's creditors are asked to decide whether to approve the proposed voluntary arrangement.

(2) The creditors may approve the proposed voluntary arrangement with or without modifications, but shall not [approve it with modifications] unless the debtor consents to each modification.

(3) The modifications subject to which the proposed voluntary arrangement may be approved may include one conferring the functions proposed to be conferred on the nominee on another person qualified to act as an insolvency practitioner or authorised to act as nominee, in relation to the voluntary arrangement.

But they shall not include any modification by virtue of which the proposal ceases to be a proposal under this Part.

(4) The creditors shall not approve any proposal or modification which affects the right of a secured creditor of the debtor to enforce his security, except with the concurrence of the creditor concerned.

(5) Subject as follows, the creditors shall not approve any proposal or modification under which—

    (a)    any preferential debt of the debtor is to be paid otherwise than in priority to such of his debts as are not preferential debts,

    (aa)    any ordinary preferential debt of the debtor is to be paid otherwise than in priority to any secondary preferential debts that the debtor may have,

(b)    a preferential creditor of the debtor is to be paid an amount in respect of an ordinary preferential debt that bears to that debt a smaller proportion than is borne to another ordinary preferential debt by the amount that is to be paid in respect of that other debt,

(c)    a preferential creditor of the debtor is to be paid an amount in respect of a secondary preferential debt that bears to that debt a smaller proportion than is borne to another secondary preferential debt by the amount that is to be paid in respect of that other debt, or

(d)    if the debtor is a relevant financial institution (see section 387A), any non-preferential debt is to be paid otherwise than in accordance with the rules in section 328(3A) (reading references to the bankrupt as references to the debtor).

However, the creditors may approve such a proposal or modification with the concurrence of the creditor concerned.

(6) . . .

(7)   In this section "preferential debt", "ordinary preferential debt" and "secondary preferential debt" each has the meaning given by section 386 in Part XII; and "preferential creditor" is to be construed accordingly.

**Amendments**—Insolvency Act 2000, s 3, Sch 3, paras 1, 9; SI 2014/3486; Small Business, Enterprise and Employment Act 2015, s 126, Sch 9, Pt 2, paras 60, 65; SI 2018/1244.

**General note**—See notes to s 4 (equivalent CVA provision) under this heading.

## SECTION 258(1)

**Scope of provision**—A chairman may adjourn a creditors' meeting under r 15.23 without putting the IVA proposal to a vote.

## SECTION 258(2)

**Scope of provision**—This subsection should be read in conjunction with s 258(3), which limits the scope of modifications.

**'with modifications'**—In practice, proposed modifications, particularly those introduced at the last moment, can create difficulties and may prompt the chairman to consider adjourning a creditors' meeting, even for a short time, under r 15.23, where creditors require time to consider their respective positions.

Where modifications are introduced, it is prudent to include a provision of a kind frequently required as a condition of support for a proposal by Crown creditors to the effect that any modification is deemed to override any term in the original proposal where an inconsistency arises between the two.

**'unless the debtor consents to each modification'**—In contrast to the position in CVAs, where the debtor company's consent to modifications proposed by creditors is not required, in respect of an IVA, the debtor's consent is required. It now seems that the failure to obtain a debtor's consent to a modification will be no more than a material irregularity: *Narandas-Girdhar v Bradstock* [2016] EWCA Civ 88, [2016] 1 WLR 2366, [2016] BPIR 428. The former view expressed by Registrar Baister in *Re Plummer* [2004] BPIR 767 at [21]–[24] that a failure to obtain the debtor's consent to a modification rendered the purported IVA a nullity was disapproved by the Court of Appeal in *Narandas-Girdhar v Bradstock* at [53]. See general note s 3 and notes to s 6(1)(b) and 6(7).

## SECTION 258(3)

**Scope of provision**—Any modification altering the identity of the nominee squares with s 253(2) in that the amendment will not deprive the IVA proposal of its status as such.

**'. . . any modification by virtue of which the proposal ceases to be a proposal . . .'**—Section 258(2) imposes no limitation on the extent of the modifications which may be proposed, subject to the debtor's consent. In practice, such modifications are common enough and may be insisted upon by a significant creditor or creditors as the price for their support of the proposal, subject to the standing of an eligible applicant making application to the court complaining of unfair prejudice or material irregularity under s 262(1). In theory, therefore, there is no good reason why the proposal should not be modified extensively at the decision stage, provided that the modifications do not fall within the scope of challenge under s 262(1).

The specific limitation imposed by s 258(3) prevents the proposal being modified so as to deprive it of its status as a composition or a scheme of arrangement such that, if approved, the proposal would not constitute a voluntary arrangement as defined in s 253(1).

### SECTION 258(4)

**Scope of provision**—A proposal or modified proposal is incapable of affecting the rights of the secured creditor 'to enforce his security' other than with the 'concurrence' of the secured creditor. For the definition of 'secured creditor' and of 'security' see s 383.

' . . . **to enforce his security** . . . '—See notes to s 4(3) (equivalent CVA provision) under this heading.

' . . . **except with the concurrence of the creditor concerned** . . . '—See notes to s 4(3) (equivalent CVA provision) under this heading.

### SECTION 258(5)

**Scope of provision**—See notes to s 4(4) and s 4(4)(a) and (b) (equivalent CVA provision) under this heading.

### SECTION 258(6)

**Scope of provision**—For the relevant rules see rr 8.22 and 15.28–15.35. Note also rr 8.25–8.31 which relate to implementation of the arrangement.

### SECTION 258(7)

**Scope of provision**—Where the debtor is not an undischarged bankrupt, the 'relevant date' for the assessment of preferential debts is the date of any interim order made under s 252 or, where no interim order is made, the date on which the arrangement takes effect: s 387(5). Where the debtor is an undischarged bankrupt, the 'relevant date' is the date of the bankruptcy order or the date of the appointment of an interim receiver where such an appointment was made after presentation of the bankruptcy petition but prior to the bankruptcy order: s 387(6).

## [1.361]

### 259 Report of decisions to court

(1) When pursuant to section 257 the debtor's creditors have decided whether to approve the debtor's proposal (with or without modifications), the nominee (or the nominee's replacement under section 256(3) or 256A(4)) must—

    (a)    give notice of the creditors' decision to such persons as may be prescribed, and

    (b)    where the creditors considered the debtor's proposal pursuant to a report to the court under section 256(1)(aa), report the creditors' decision to the court.

(2) If the report is that the creditors have declined (with or without modifications) to approve the voluntary arrangement proposed under section 256, the court may discharge any interim order which is in force in relation to the debtor.

**Amendments**—SI 2010/18; Small Business, Enterprise and Employment Act 2015, s 126, Sch 9, Pt 2, paras 60, 66.

**General note**—The filing of the chairman's report with the court amounts to a reporting obligation only and has no substantive consequence. The IVA comes into being as a consequence of approval under s 258. The result of a creditors' decision procedure reported to the court must be taken at face value and accepted in the absence of a timely application to the court to challenge it pursuant to s 262: *Smith-Evans v Smailes* [2013] EWHC 3199 (Ch), [2014] 1 WLR 1548, [2014] BPIR 306 (HHJ Purle QC, sitting as a High Court judge, at [25]). See general note to s 257.

IR 2016, r 8.24 provides that a report of the creditors' decision concerning their consideration of the proposal is to be prepared by the chairman. Rule 8.24(2) prescribes the contents of the report. Where an interim order was obtained, the report must be filed with the court under r 8.24(3) within 4 business days of the decision date. The chairman must also send a notice of the result of the meeting – but not necessarily a copy of the chairman's report – to all those persons who were sent notice of each of the meetings summoned under s 257 and any other creditor of whom the chairman is aware, as well as the official receiver and the trustee in bankruptcy (if any) where the debtor is an undischarged bankrupt.

### SECTION 259(2)

**Scope of provision**—Although the court has an unlimited discretion under this provision, the only power conferred on the court is a power to discharge the interim order or to decline to discharge the interim order; the court has no power to extend the period for which the interim order has effect: *Re Symes* [1995] 2 BCLC 651 at 669H–670A. The practical utility in the court declining to discharge the interim order is in affording a debtor some final breathing space in appropriate circumstances or in affording protection to the debtor where the court is satisfied that the making of an application under s 262 challenging the arrangement will follow.

**[1.362]**

## 260 Effect of approval

(1)   This section has effect where pursuant to section 257 the debtor's creditors decide to approve the proposed voluntary arrangement (with or without modifications).

(2)   The approved arrangement—

  (a)   takes effect as if made by the debtor at the time the creditors decided to approve the proposal, and

  (b)   binds every person who in accordance with the rules—

   (i)   was entitled to vote at the time the creditors decided to approve the proposal, or

   (ii)   would have been so entitled if he had had notice of it,

  as if he were a party to the arrangement.

(2A)   If—

  (a)   when the arrangement ceases to have effect any amount payable under the arrangement to a person bound by virtue of subsection (2)(b)(ii) has not been paid, and

  (b)   the arrangement did not come to an end prematurely,

the debtor shall at that time become liable to pay to that person the amount payable under the arrangement.

(3)   . . .

(4)   Any interim order in force in relation to the debtor immediately before the end of the period of 28 days beginning with the day on which the report with respect to the creditors' decision was made to the court under section 259 ceases to have effect at the end of that period.

This subsection applies except to such extent as the court may direct for the purposes of any application under section 262 below.

(5)   Where proceedings on a bankruptcy petition have been stayed by an interim order which ceases to have effect under subsection (4), the petition is deemed, unless the court otherwise orders, to have been dismissed.

**Amendments**—Insolvency Act 2000, s 3, Sch 3, paras 1, 10; Deregulation Act 2015, s 19, Sch 6, Pt 1, para 2(1), (11)(a); Small Business, Enterprise and Employment Act 2015, s 126, Sch 9, Pt 2, paras 60, 67.

**General note**—Under the previous version of this section (which referred to meetings rather than decisions), it was held that this section must be read as if it referred to further meetings held under s 262 as well as meetings summoned under s 257, despite there being express reference only to the latter in the section. The Court of Appeal held in *Price v Davis* [2014] EWCA Civ 26, [2014] 1 WLR 2129, [2014] BPIR 494 at [38]–[45] that a literal interpretation of s 260(1) would create anomalies Parliament could not have intended.

An approved arrangement remains in force until either revoked by way of a modification validly approved by creditors or until the making of any order setting aside the arrangement under s 262.

## SECTION 260(1)

**Scope of provision**—see notes to s 5(1) (equivalent CVA provision) under this heading.

## SECTION 260(2)

**Scope of provision**—See notes to s 5(2) (equivalent CVA provision) under this heading.

## SECTION 260(2)(a)

**Scope of provision**—See notes to s 5(2)(a) (equivalent CVA provision) under this heading.

**The court's approach to the construction of voluntary arrangements**—See notes to s 5(2) (equivalent CVA provision) under this heading.

**The implication of terms into an arrangement**—see notes to s 5(2) (equivalent CVA provision) under this heading.

## SECTION 260(2)(b)

**The meaning of 'notice'**—See notes to s 5(2)(b) (equivalent CVA provision) under this heading.

**The two classes of person within s 260(2)(b)**—See notes to s 5(2)(b) (equivalent CVA provision) under this heading.

**Failure to give notice as ground for alleging unfair prejudice/material irregularity under s 262**—See notes to s 5(2)(b) (equivalent CVA provision) under this heading.

Unliquidated, future or contingent debts, co-debtors and third parties—See notes to s 5(2)(b) (equivalent CVA provision) under this heading.

The effect of an arrangement on assignees—See notes to s 5(2)(b) (equivalent CVA provision) under this heading.

Single creditor with a claim within and a claim outside of the arrangement—See notes to s 5(2)(b) (equivalent CVA provision) under this heading.

Single creditor pursuing only part of single debt in arrangement— see notes to s 5(2)(b) (equivalent CVA provision) under this heading

### SECTION 260(2A)

Scope of provision—See notes to s 5(2A) (equivalent CVA provision) under this heading.

### SECTION 260(4), (5)

Lapse of certain interim orders and effect on extant bankruptcy petition—In the absence of contrary order, an interim order will cease to have effect at the end of the 28-day period beginning with the day on which the chairman's report of the creditors' meeting under s 259 is filed with the court.

On the cessation of an interim order under s 260(4), any bankruptcy petition stayed by virtue of s 252(2)(a) is deemed dismissed by virtue of s 260(5), subject to contrary order of the court.

## [1.363]

### 261 Additional effect on undischarged bankrupt

(1) This section applies where—

    (a) pursuant to section 257 the debtor's creditors decide to approve the proposed voluntary arrangement (with or without modifications), and

    (b) the debtor is an undischarged bankrupt.

(2) Where this section applies the court shall annul the bankruptcy order on an application made—

    (a) by the bankrupt, or

    (b) where the bankrupt has not made an application within the prescribed period, by the official receiver.

(3) An application under subsection (2) may not be made—

    (a) during the period specified in section 262(3)(a) during which creditors' decision can be challenged by application under section 262,

    (b) while an application under that section is pending, or

    (c) while an appeal in respect of an application under that section is pending or may be brought.

(4) Where this section applies the court may give such directions about the conduct of the bankruptcy and the administration of the bankrupt's estate as it thinks appropriate for facilitating the implementation of the approved voluntary arrangement.

Amendments—Substituted by Enterprise Act 2002, s 264(1), Sch 22, para 1. Amended by Small Business, Enterprise and Employment Act 2015, s 126, Sch 9, Pt 2, paras 60, 68.

General note—This provision provides for the annulment of the bankruptcy order where a creditors' decision procedure under s 257 approves an IVA proposed by an undischarged bankrupt. The annulment is not automatic and requires an application by either the bankrupt within the prescribed period (ie 28 days) or by the official receiver, but only where the bankrupt has not made an application within the prescribed period: see s 261(2). Such an application may not be made, however, in any of the three circumstances in s 261(3) which each relate to an application or an appeal from an order under s 262.

The strategic advantage to a debtor of annulment under s 261—Annulment of a bankruptcy order is often the motive behind an undischarged bankrupt seeking approval of an IVA. Assuming the bankruptcy order to be beyond challenge under s 282(1)(a), the only other alternative route to annulment for an undischarged bankrupt is in seeking to satisfy the court under s 282(1)(b) that the bankruptcy debts and expenses of the bankruptcy have been paid or secured for. Since there is no requirement that an annulment under s 261 is dependent on unsecured creditors being paid in full in the IVA – the debtor's proposal as to dividends or returns to creditors in the IVA is a matter for the requisite majority of the unsecured creditors alone – a debtor may find an annulment via this provision less expensive than under s 282(1)(b).

An application for annulment will proceed by way of an application in the bankruptcy proceedings and will usually be issued with a witness statement or affidavit in support: see the notes to r 1.35(2). Although the legislation makes no such stipulation, it is suggested that the respondents to the application should normally include the creditor upon whose petition the bankruptcy order was made and the trustee in bankruptcy. There are also good reasons why the official receiver should at least be given notice of the application and be permitted to report to or appear before the court if the official receiver considers such action appropriate.

## [1.364]

### 262 Challenge of creditors' decision

(1)   Subject to this section, an application to the court may be made, by any of the persons specified below, on one or both of the following grounds, namely—

    (a)    that a voluntary arrangement approved by a decision of the debtor's creditors pursuant to section 257 unfairly prejudices the interests of a creditor of the debtor;

    (b)    that there has been some material irregularity in relation to a creditors' decision procedure instigated under that section.

(2)   The persons who may apply under this section are—

    (a)    the debtor;

    (b)    a person who—

        (i)    was entitled, in accordance with the rules, to vote in the creditors' decision procedure, or

        (ii)    would have been so entitled if he had had notice of it;

    (c)    the nominee (or his replacement under section 256(3), 256A(4) or 258(3)); and

    (d)    if the debtor is an undischarged bankrupt, the trustee of his estate or the official receiver.

(3)   An application under this section shall not be made—

    (a)    after the end of the period of 28 days beginning with the day on which the creditors decided whether to approve the proposed voluntary arrangement or, where a report was required to be made to the court under section 259(1)(b), the day on which the report was made, or

    (b)    in the case of a person who was not given notice of the creditors' decision procedure, after the end of the period of 28 days beginning with the day on which he became aware that a decision as to whether to approve the proposed voluntary arrangement had been made,

but (subject to that) an application made by a person within subsection (2)(b)(ii) on the ground that the arrangement prejudices his interests may be made after the arrangement has ceased to have effect, unless it has come to an end prematurely.

(4)   Where on an application under this section the court is satisfied as to either of the grounds mentioned in subsection (1), it may do one or both of the following, namely—

    (a)    revoke or suspend any approval given by a decision of the debtor's creditors;

    (b)    direct any person to seek a decision from the debtor's creditors (using a creditors' decision procedure) as to whether they approve—

        (i)    any revised proposal the debtor may make, or

        (ii)    in a case falling within subsection (1)(b), the debtor's original proposal.

(5)   Where at any time after giving a direction under subsection (4)(b) in relation to a revised proposal the court is satisfied that the debtor does not intend to submit such a proposal, the court shall revoke the direction and revoke or suspend any approval previously given by the debtor's creditors.

(6)   Where the court gives a direction under subsection (4)(b), it may also give a direction continuing or, as the case may require, renewing, for such period as may be specified in the direction, the effect in relation to the debtor of any interim order.

(7)   In any case where the court, on an application made under this section with respect to a creditors' decision, gives a direction under subsection (4)(b) or revokes or suspends an approval under subsection (4)(a) or (5), the court may give such supplemental directions as it thinks fit and, in particular, directions with respect to—

>    (a)    things done since the decision under any voluntary arrangement approved by the decision, and
>
>    (b)    such things done since the decision as could not have been done if an interim order had been in force in relation to the debtor when they were done.

(8)   Except in pursuance of the preceding provisions of this section, the approval of a voluntary arrangement by a decision of the debtor's creditors pursuant to section 257 is not invalidated by any irregularity in relation to the creditors' decision procedure by which the decision was made.

**Amendments**—Insolvency Act 2000, s 3, Sch 3, paras 1, 11(1)(a), (b), (2)(a), (b); Small Business, Enterprise and Employment Act 2015, s 126, Sch 9, Pt 2, paras 60, 69.

**General note**—See notes to s 6 (equivalent CVA provision) under this heading.

### SECTION 262(1)(a)

**Scope of provision**—See notes to s 6(1)(a) (equivalent CVA provision) under this heading.

' . . . **unfairly prejudices the interests of a creditor of the debtor**'—See notes to s 6(1)(a) (equivalent CVA provision) under this heading.

**The meaning and scope of unfair prejudice**—See notes to s 6(1)(a) (equivalent CVA provision) under this heading.

**Cases on unfair prejudice**—See notes to s 6(1)(a) (equivalent CVA provision) under this heading.

**Unfair prejudice based on lower projected dividend than in bankruptcy?**—See notes to s 6(1)(a) (equivalent CVA provision) under this heading.

### SECTION 262(1)(b)

**The meaning and scope of material irregularity**—See notes to 6(1)(b) (equivalent CVA provision) under this heading.

**The 'good faith' principle**—See notes to s 6(1)(b) (equivalent CVA provision) under this heading.

**Material irregularity and creditors for costs**—See notes to s 6(1)(b) (equivalent CVA provision) under this heading.

### SECTION 262(2)

**Scope of provision**—See notes to s 6(2) (equivalent CVA provision) under this heading.

**Eligible applicants**—Categories (a) and (b) are clear enough by reference to the two grounds in s 262(1). For the purposes of categories (c) and (d) it appears that either the nominee (or his replacement) or a trustee in bankruptcy or the official receiver (where the debtor is an undischarged bankrupt) has standing to make application under s 262(1)(a), although such an application may only proceed on the basis of alleged unfair prejudice to the interests of a creditor; as such, and in the absence of an application by either such party, such applications are unlikely. More obviously plausible are applications under s 262(1)(b), since these are not restricted to prejudice to the interests of a creditor.

**Procedure on a s 262(2) application**—See notes to s 6(2) (equivalent CVA provision) under this heading.

### SECTION 262(3)

' . . . **shall not be made** . . . **after the end of the period of 28 days** . . . '—These words are not a common formulation for the computation of time under statute. The 28-day period begins with and includes the dates specified in subsections (a) and (b). Furthermore, the 28-day period in s 262(3) is capable of extension under s 376 (time-limits): *Tager v Westpac Banking Corp* [1997] 1 BCLC 313 (HHJ Weeks QC). The position is different in CVA cases where the 28-day period in the analogous s 6(3) cannot be extended by the court in the absence of any equivalent to s 376 in Part I of the Act: *Re Bournemouth & Boscombe Athletic Football Club Co Ltd* [1998] BPIR 183 (Lloyd J). In the context of IVAs HHJ Weeks QC (sitting as a High Court judge) held in *Tager* (at 325D) that the factors relevant to the exercise of discretion and extending time are the length of delay, the reasons for the delay, the apparent merits of the underlying application and the prejudice to each side, other than the inevitable prejudice inherent in re-opening the question of approval of the arrangement. The decision in *Tager* extending time was approved of by Carnwath J in *Plant v Plant* [1998] 1 BCLC 38. In *Warley Continental Services Ltd (in liquidation) v Johal* [2002] EWHC 3247 (Ch), [2004] BPIR 353 HHJ Norris QC, sitting as a High Court judge, also identified the conduct of the parties as being of potential significance in a wide range of cases; an extension of time in that case was refused given the unjustifiable and significant delay in making the application, notwithstanding the obvious merits of the case. Plainly the 28-day period will not be extended as a matter of course without proper explanation in evidence being tendered to the court.

SECTION 262(4)

**Remedies and relief on a s 262(2) application**—See notes to s 6(4) (equivalent CVA provision) under this heading.

**The court's discretion in granting relief**—See notes to s 6(4) (equivalent CVA provision) under this heading.

SECTION 262(4)(a)

**Scope of provision**—Section 255(1)(c) prevents the grant of a further interim order where such an application has been made in the preceding 12 months, so bankruptcy may not be delayed indefinitely by repeat proposals.

See also notes to s 6(4)(a) (equivalent CVA provision) under this heading.

SECTION 262(4)(b)

**Scope of provision**—See notes to s 6(4)(b) (equivalent CVA provision) under this heading.

SECTION 262(5)

**Scope of provision**—See notes to s 6(5) (equivalent CVA provision) under this heading.

SECTION 262(6)

**Scope of provision**—This provision provides specifically for control of any interim order where a further creditors' decision procedure is ordered under s 262(4)(b). The usual course will be for the interim order to continue in effect pending the decision of the further meeting.

SECTION 262(7)

**Scope of provision**—See notes to s 6(6) (equivalent CVA provision) under this heading.

SECTION 262(8)

**Scope of provision**—See notes to s 6(7) (equivalent CVA provision) under this heading.

## [1.365]

### 262A False representations etc

(1) If for the purpose of obtaining the approval of his creditors to a proposal for a voluntary arrangement, the debtor—

    (a)    makes any false representation, or

    (b)    fraudulently does, or omits to do, anything,

he commits an offence.

(2) Subsection (1) applies even if the proposal is not approved.

(3) A person guilty of an offence under this section is liable to imprisonment or a fine, or both.

**Amendments**—Inserted by Insolvency Act 2000, s 3, Sch 3, paras 1, 12.

**General note**—See notes to s 6A (equivalent CVA provision) under this heading.

SECTION 262A(1)

**Scope of provision**—See notes to s 6A(1) (equivalent CVA provision) under this heading.

SECTION 262A(2)

**Scope of provision**—See notes to s 6A(2) (equivalent CVA provision) under this heading.

SECTION 262A(3)

**Scope of provision**—See notes to s 6A(4) (equivalent CVA provision) under this heading.

## [1.366]

### 262B Prosecution of delinquent debtors

(1) This section applies where a voluntary arrangement approved by a decision of the debtor's creditors pursuant to section 257 has taken effect.

(2) If it appears to the nominee or supervisor that the debtor has been guilty of any offence in connection with the arrangement for which he is criminally liable, he shall forthwith—

    (a)    report the matter to the Secretary of State, and

    (b)    provide the Secretary of State with such information and give the Secretary of State such access to and facilities for inspecting and taking copies of documents (being information or documents in his possession or under his control and relating to the matter in question) as the Secretary of State requires.

(3) Where a prosecuting authority institutes criminal proceedings following any report under subsection (2), the nominee or, as the case may be, supervisor shall give the authority all assistance in connection with the prosecution which he is reasonably able to give.

For this purpose, "prosecuting authority" means the Director of Public Prosecutions or the Secretary of State.

(4) The court may, on the application of the prosecuting authority, direct a nominee or supervisor to comply with subsection (3) if he has failed to do so.

**Amendments**—Inserted by Insolvency Act 2000, s 3, Sch 3, paras 1, 12. Amended by Small Business, Enterprise and Employment Act 2015, s 126, Sch 9, Pt 2, paras 60, 70.

**General note**—The heart of this provision lies in s 262B(2) in the obligation to report to the Secretary of State, which triggers the possibility of a criminal prosecution and the consequences in s 262B(3). That obligation is triggered on it appearing to the nominee or supervisor that the debtor has been guilty of an offence. The term 'appears' does not envisage steps having to be taken by the nominee or supervisor by way of investigating matters, although the office-holder may well consider such steps to be appropriate where a suspicion is aroused as to the possible commission of an offence.

Section 262B(2)(b) is unlimited in affording the Secretary of State access to and facilities for the inspection and copying of such documents as he requires. In the absence of any provision providing for the costs of such an exercise it is submitted, given the unconditional wording in s 262B(2)(b), that such costs must fall on the office-holder, who might in turn seek to recover such sums by way of an enhanced nominee's fee or as an expense or disbursement in the arrangement.

## [1.367]

### 262C Arrangements coming to an end prematurely

For the purposes of this Part, a voluntary arrangement approved by a decision of the debtor's creditors pursuant to section 257 comes to an end prematurely if, when it ceases to have effect, it has not been fully implemented in respect of all persons bound by the arrangement by virtue of section 260(2)(b)(i).

**Amendments**—Inserted by Insolvency Act 2000, s 3, Sch 3, paras 1, 12. Amended by Small Business, Enterprise and Employment Act 2015, s 126, Sch 9, Pt 2, paras 60, 71.

**General note**—For the relevance of this definition, introduced by s 3 and Sch 3 of the Insolvency Act 2000 with effect from 1 January 2003, see ss 260(2A) and 262(3).

## [1.368]

### 263 Implementation and supervision of approved voluntary arrangement

(1) This section applies where a voluntary arrangement approved by a decision of the debtor's creditors pursuant to section 257 has taken effect.

(2) The person who is for the time being carrying out, in relation to the voluntary arrangement, the functions conferred by virtue of the approval on the nominee (or his replacement under section 256(3), 256A(4) or 258(3)) shall be known as the supervisor of the voluntary arrangement.

(3) If the debtor, any of his creditors or any other person is dissatisfied by any act, omission or decision of the supervisor, he may apply to the court; and on such an application the court may—

    (a)    confirm, reverse or modify any act or decision of the supervisor,

    (b)    give him directions, or

    (c)    make such other order as it thinks fit.

(4) The supervisor may apply to the court for directions in relation to any particular matter arising under the voluntary arrangement.

(5) The court may, whenever—

    (a)    it is expedient to appoint a person to carry out the functions of the supervisor, and

(b)     it is inexpedient, difficult or impracticable for an appointment to be made without the assistance of the court,

make an order appointing a person who is qualified to act as an insolvency practitioner or authorised to act as supervisor, in relation to the voluntary arrangement, either in substitution for the existing supervisor or to fill a vacancy.

. . .

(6)   The power conferred by subsection (5) is exercisable so as to increase the number of persons exercising the functions of the supervisor or, where there is more than one person exercising those functions, so as to replace one or more of those persons.

**Amendments**—Insolvency Act 2000, s 3, Sch 3, paras 1, 13(a), (b); Deregulation Act 2015, s 19, Sch 6, Pt 1, para 2(1), (11)(b); Small Business, Enterprise and Employment Act 2015, s 126, Sch 9, Pt 2, paras 60, 72.

**General note**—See notes to s 7 (equivalent CVA provision) under this heading.

**SECTION 263(1)**

**Scope of provision**—See notes to s 7(1) (equivalent CVA provision) under this heading.

**SECTION 263(2)**

**Scope of provision**—See notes to s 7(2) (equivalent CVA provision) under this heading.

**SECTION 263(3)**

**Scope of provision**—See notes to s 7(3) (equivalent CVA provision) under this heading.

'  . . .  **any other person**  . . . '—See notes to s 7(3) (equivalent CVA provision) under this heading.

'  . . .  **is dissatisfied**  . . . '—See notes to s 7(3) (equivalent CVA provision) under this heading.

'  . . .  **by any act, omission or decision of the supervisor**  . . . '—See notes to s 7(3) (equivalent CVA provision) under this heading.

**Does s 263(3) preclude the existence of a private right of action outside of the provision in favour of a creditor?**—See notes to s 7(3) (equivalent CVA provision) under this heading.

**Is a private law remedy available against a nominee?**—See notes to s 7(3) (equivalent CVA provision) under this heading.

**SECTION 263(4)**

'  . . .  **directions in relation to any particular matter arising under the voluntary arrangement**  . . . '—See notes to s 7(4)(a) (equivalent CVA provision) under this heading.

**Supervisor's petition for bankruptcy order**—In practice, the provisions of an IVA will commonly require a supervisor either to petition or to consider petitioning for bankruptcy in the event of one or more specified defaults. The standing of a supervisor to petition is expressly provided for in s 264(1)(c). The supervisor of an IVA does not necessarily lose standing to petition by virtue of the fact that an arrangement is no longer functioning as originally envisaged. In *Re Arthur Rathbone Kitchens Ltd* [1997] 2 BCLC 280 Roger Kaye QC, sitting as deputy High Court judge, rejected submissions in a CVA case to the effect that a supervisor could not petition for winding up under s 7(4)(b) – which, in contrast to the present provisions, expressly provides a CVA supervisor with standing to petition for a winding-up order – if the CVA was not still on foot so as to deprive the supervisor of locus standi as 'supervisor' within the meaning of s 7(2). The deputy judge identified that, on the particular terms of the CVA, the arrangement had not terminated, although the company was in default, at the time of the presentation of the supervisor's petition. Neither does a supervisor lose standing to petition on the expiration of a fixed-term arrangement, provided that, at the time of presentation of the petition, the supervisor was still 'carrying out in relation to the voluntary arrangement the functions' conferred on the supervisor by virtue of s 263(2): *Harris v Gross* [2001] BPIR 586 (HHJ Maddocks sitting as a High Court judge; bankruptcy orders made on petitions presented by IVA supervisor one month after expiration of 4-year fixed term interlocking IVAs in respect of ongoing defaults committed during the fixed arrangement terms).

## 263A–263G

*(Repealed)*

**Amendments**—Inserted by Enterprise Act 2002, s 264(1), Sch 22, para 2. Repealed by Small Business, Enterprise and Employment Act 2015, s 135(1).

## PART IX   BANKRUPTCY

**[1.369]**

**General note**—Three pieces of legislation have made extensive changes to Part IX of the Insolvency Act 1986. The Enterprise and Regulatory Reform Act 2013, s 71(2) and Sch 18 inserted a new Chapter A1 which provided for a new regime by which debtors may apply by way of an out of court procedure to an adjudicator for a bankruptcy order. These sections were enacted in response to concern about court time wasted in processing uncontested petitions by debtors for their own bankruptcy. Various (and extensive) consequential amendments were made to other sections of the IA 1986 by s 71(3) and Sch 19. These amendments came fully into force on 6 April 2016.

The Small Business, Enterprise and Employment Act 2015, s 120 removed the need for trustees in bankruptcy to seek sanction to exercise the powers in Parts 1 and 2 of Sch 5 with effect from 25 May 2015. Sections 123 and 125 abolished the requirement for creditors' meetings and enable creditors to elect to opt out from receiving notices (save for those related to distribution) respectively, with consequential legislative amendments being made by s 126 and Sch 19 of that Act. Section 133 inserted a new s 291A into the Insolvency Act 1986 (effective from 6 April 2017), which provided that the official receiver becomes the trustee of a bankrupt's estate upon the making of a bankruptcy order, unless someone else is appointed, with various consequential amendments being made by Sch 10.

The Deregulation Act 2015 was intended to 'make provision for the reduction of burdens resulting from legislation for businesses or other organisations or for individuals'. Section 19 and Part 5 of Sch 6 made various miscellaneous amendments to Part IX of the Insolvency Act 1986.

## CHAPTER A1

Adjudicators: Bankruptcy Applications by Debtors and Bankruptcy Orders

**[1.370]**

**Amendments**—Inserted by Enterprise and Regulatory Reform Act 2013, s 71(2), Sch 18.
See the general note to Part IX.

**[1.371]**

**263H   Bankruptcy applications to an adjudicator**
(1)   An individual may make an application to an adjudicator in accordance with this Chapter for a bankruptcy order to be made against him or her.
(2)   An individual may make a bankruptcy application only on the ground that the individual is unable to pay his or her debts.

**Amendments**—Inserted by Enterprise and Regulatory Reform Act 2013, s 71(2), Sch 18.

**[1.372]**

**263I   Debtors against whom an adjudicator may make a bankruptcy order**
(1)   An adjudicator has jurisdiction to determine a bankruptcy application only if—
    (a)    the centre of the debtor's main interests is in England and Wales, or
    (ab)    the centre of the debtor's main interests is in a member State (other than Denmark) and the debtor has an establishment in England and Wales, or
    (b)    . . . the test in subsection (2) is met.
(2)   The test is that—
    (a)    the debtor is domiciled in England and Wales, or
    (b)    at any time in the period of three years ending with the day on which the application is made to the adjudicator, the debtor—
        (i)    has been ordinarily resident, or has had a place of residence, in England and Wales, or
        (ii)    has carried on business in England and Wales.
(3)   The reference in subsection (2) to the debtor carrying on business includes—
    (a)    the carrying on of business by a firm or partnership of which the debtor is a member, and

(b)  the carrying on of business by an agent or manager for the debtor or for such a firm or partnership.

(4)  In this section, references to the centre of the debtor's main interests have the same meaning as in Article 3 of the EC Regulation.

(5)  In this section "establishment" has the same meaning as in Article 2(10) of the EU Regulation.

**Amendments**—Inserted by Enterprise and Regulatory Reform Act 2013. Amended by SI 2017/702; SI 2019/146, as from IP completion day (as defined in the European Union (Withdrawal Agreement) Act 2020, s 39(1)–(5)).

See the general note to Part IX.

**General note**—A considerable body of case law developed under the now-repealed debtor's petition provisions concerning so-called 'bankruptcy tourism', where citizens of other member states with less debtor-friendly bankruptcy regimes sought to claim that their centre of main interests was in England and Wales in order to petition for their own bankruptcies and take advantage, in particular, of a more lenient discharge period. The courts were alive to potential abuses. In *Re Eichler (No 2)* [2011] BPIR 1293, for example, Chief Registrar Baister set out guidance as to the court's practice where there were doubts as to jurisdiction. Proudman J emphasised the importance of full disclosure where a debtor's petition was presented *ex parte* in *Die Sparkeasse Bremen AG v Armutcu* [2012] EWHC 4026 (Ch), [2013] BPIR 210. The new adjudicator regime appears to be different in a significant way. As Chief Registrar Baister noted in *Re Budniok* [2017] BPIR 521, in introducing the adjudicator regime, Parliament appears to have abandoned the concept that debtors' petitions are class proceedings. The Chief Registrar considered that, uniquely in insolvency proceedings, debtor's petitions appear now to be simply a bilateral private process between the debtor and the adjudicator, which was an unfortunate departure from a key principle. *Re Budniok* is currently the only reported judgment on the new regime and it remains to be seen how this apparently radical development will play out in practice. See further note to s 263N below.

## [1.373]

### 263J  Conditions applying to bankruptcy application

(1)  A bankruptcy application must include—

(a)  such particulars of the debtor's creditors, debts and other liabilities, and assets, as may be prescribed, and

(b)  such other information as may be prescribed.

(2)  A bankruptcy application is not to be regarded as having been made unless any fee or deposit required in connection with the application by an order under section 415 has been paid to such person, and within such period, as may be prescribed.

(3)  A bankruptcy application may not be withdrawn.

(4)  A debtor must notify the adjudicator if, at any time before a bankruptcy order is made against the debtor or the adjudicator refuses to make such an order—

(a)  the debtor becomes able to pay his or her debts, or

(b)  a bankruptcy petition has been presented to the court in relation to the debtor.

**Amendments**—Inserted by Enterprise and Regulatory Reform Act 2013, s 71(2), Sch 18.
See the general note to Part IX.

## [1.374]

### 263K  Determination of bankruptcy application

(1)  After receiving a bankruptcy application, an adjudicator must determine whether the following requirements are met—

(a)  the adjudicator had jurisdiction under section 263I to determine the application on the date the application was made,

(b)  the debtor is unable to pay his or her debts at the date of the determination,

(c)  no bankruptcy petition is pending in relation to the debtor at the date of the determination, and

(d)  no bankruptcy order has been made in respect of any of the debts which are the subject of the application at the date of the determination.

(2) If the adjudicator is satisfied that each of the requirements in subsection (1) are met, the adjudicator must make a bankruptcy order against the debtor.

(3) If the adjudicator is not so satisfied, the adjudicator must refuse to make a bankruptcy order against the debtor.

(4) The adjudicator must make a bankruptcy order against the debtor or refuse to make such an order before the end of the prescribed period ("the determination period").

**Amendments**—Inserted by Enterprise and Regulatory Reform Act 2013, s 71(2), Sch 18.
See the general note to Part IX.

## [1.375]

### 263L Adjudicator's requests for further information

(1) An adjudicator may at any time during the determination period request from the debtor information that the adjudicator considers necessary for the purpose of determining whether a bankruptcy order must be made.

(2) The adjudicator may specify a date before which information requested under subsection (1) must be provided; but that date must not be after the end of the determination period.

(3) If the rules so prescribe, a request under subsection (1) may include a request for information to be given orally.

(4) The rules may make provision enabling or requiring an adjudicator to request information from persons of a prescribed description in prescribed circumstances.

**Amendments**—Inserted by Enterprise and Regulatory Reform Act 2013, s 71(2), Sch 18.
See the general note to Part IX.

## [1.376]

### 263M Making of bankruptcy order

(1) This section applies where an adjudicator makes a bankruptcy order as a result of a bankruptcy application.

(2) The order must be made in the prescribed form.

(3) The adjudicator must—
    (a) give a copy of the order to the debtor, and
    (b) give notice of the order to persons of such description as may be prescribed.

**Amendments**—Inserted by Enterprise and Regulatory Reform Act 2013, s 71(2), Sch 18.
See the general note to Part IX.

## [1.377]

### 263N Refusal to make a bankruptcy order: review and appeal etc

(1) Where an adjudicator refuses to make a bankruptcy order on a bankruptcy application, the adjudicator must give notice to the debtor—
    (a) giving the reasons for the refusal, and
    (b) explaining the effect of subsections (2) to (5).

(2) If requested by the debtor before the end of the prescribed period, the adjudicator must review the information which was available to the adjudicator when the determination that resulted in the refusal was made.

(3) Following a review under subsection (2) the adjudicator must—
    (a) confirm the refusal to make a bankruptcy order, or
    (b) make a bankruptcy order against the debtor.

(4) Where the adjudicator confirms a refusal under subsection (3), the adjudicator must give notice to the debtor—
    (a) giving the reasons for the confirmation, and
    (b) explaining the effect of subsection (5).

(5)   If the refusal is confirmed under subsection (3), the debtor may appeal against the refusal to the court before the end of the prescribed period.

**Amendments**—Inserted by Enterprise and Regulatory Reform Act 2013, s 71(2), Sch 18. See the general note to Part IX.

**General note**—Chief Registrar Baister gave the first detailed appellate judgment from a decision of the adjudicator in *Re Budniok* [2017] BPIR 521. The Chief Registrar considered that there was nothing in a 263N(5) to indicate what kind of 'appeal' Parliament had in mind, but there were compelling reasons for treating it in the same way as similar appeals from, or challenges to, the decisions of office-holders or the official receiver, which meant fresh evidence could be adduced and cross-examination ordered. See note to s 236I above.

## [1.378]

### 263O  False representations and omissions

(1)   It is an offence knowingly or recklessly to make any false representation or omission in—

    (a)   making a bankruptcy application to an adjudicator, or

    (b)   providing any information to an adjudicator in connection with a bankruptcy application.

(2)   It is an offence knowingly or recklessly to fail to notify an adjudicator of a matter in accordance with a requirement imposed by or under this Part.

(3)   It is immaterial for the purposes of an offence under this section whether or not a bankruptcy order is made as a result of the application.

(4)   It is not a defence in proceedings for an offence under this section that anything relied on, in whole or in part, as constituting the offence was done outside England and Wales.

(5)   Proceedings for an offence under this section may only be instituted—

    (a)   by the Secretary of State, or

    (b)   by or with the consent of the Director of Public Prosecutions.

**Amendments**—Inserted by Enterprise and Regulatory Reform Act 2013, s 71(2), Sch 18. See the general note to Part IX.

## CHAPTER I

### THE COURT: BANKRUPTCY PETITIONS AND BANKRUPTCY ORDERS

**Amendments**—Substituted by Enterprise and Regulatory Reform Act 2013, s 71(3), Sch 19, paras 1, 5.

*Preliminary*

## [1.379]

### 264  Who may present a bankruptcy petition

(1)   A petition for a bankruptcy order to be made against an individual may be presented to the court in accordance with the following provisions of this Part—

    (a)   by one of the individual's creditors or jointly by more than one of them,

    (b)   . . .

    (ba)   . . .

    (bb)   . . .

    (c)   by the supervisor of, or any person (other than the individual) who is for the time being bound by, a voluntary arrangement proposed by the individual and approved under Part VIII, *or*

    (d)   *where a criminal bankruptcy order has been made against the individual, by the Official Petitioner or by any person specified in the order in pursuance of section 39(3)(b) of the Powers of Criminal Courts Act 1973.*

(2)   Subject to those provisions, the court may make a bankruptcy order on any such petition.

**Amendments**—Criminal Justice Act 1988, s 170(2), Sch 16, as from a date to be appointed; SI 2002/1240; Enterprise and Regulatory Reform Act 2013, s 71(3), Sch 19; SI 2017/702; SI 2019/146, as from IP completion day (as defined in the European Union (Withdrawal Agreement) Act 2020, s 39(1)–(5)).

**General note**—The court can only make a bankruptcy order on a petition presented by any of the class of persons in s 264(1), subject to the conditions relating to a debtor in s 265(2) in the case of a creditor's petition. The conditions in s 265 do not apply to a default petition under s 264(1)(c): *Loy v O'Sullivan* [2010] EWHC 3583 (Ch), [2011] BPIR 181.

### SECTION 264(1)(a)

**Scope of provision**—The term 'creditor' is defined in s 383(1)(a) and (b), on which see also IR 2016, r 10.6 and the general power to dismiss or stay in s 266(3). It is permissible for separate debts owed to different creditors to be joined in a single petition, provided that the combined level of such petition debts exceeds the bankruptcy level in s 267(4): *Re Allen, Re a Debtor (No 367 of 1992)* [1998] BPIR 319 at 320F–320G (Ferris J).

In *Levy v Legal Services Commission* [2000] BPIR 1065 at 1075A–1075F (Jonathan Parker LJ, Peter Gibson LJ and Waller J agreeing) the Court of Appeal held that, given that no distinction is made between provable and non-provable debts in ss 264 and 383(1), the court had jurisdiction to make a bankruptcy order upon a petition based on a non-provable debt although it would only do so in very exceptional circumstances, which, indeed, the court was unable to envisage save where a supporting creditor with a provable debt obtained a change of carriage order pursuant to IR 1986, r 6.32 (replaced by IR 2016, r 10.29).

Once s 115 of the Tribunals, Courts and Enforcement Act 2007 is commenced, an unsecured creditor with a qualifying debt will require the court's permission to present a bankruptcy petition against a debtor who has entered into a debt repayment plan in accordance with an approved scheme under that Act.

### SECTION 264(1)(b)

**Scope of provision**—Section 264(1)(b) was omitted from the Act by s 71(3) and Sch 19 of the Enterprise and Regulatory Reform Act 2013. Debtors may no longer present a petition for their own bankruptcy, and instead will apply to an adjudicator for a bankruptcy order pursuant to the out of court regime in the new Chapter A1 of Part IX. See ss 263H–263O above.

### SECTION 264(1)(c)

**Scope of provision**—Where a bankruptcy petition is presented by the supervisor of an IVA or a creditor bound by an IVA under this provision, the court may not make a bankruptcy order unless it is satisfied as to the fulfilment of any one of the three conditions in s 276(1) on which see also the notes thereto.

In *Harris v Gross* [2001] BPIR 586 at 589D–589H HHJ Maddocks, sitting as a High Court judge, held that a supervisor may present a default petition even after the expiration of any fixed term for which the arrangement subsists, although such petition must be presented within a reasonable period following expiration.

For the consequences of an order made on a supervisor's petition following the decision of the Court of Appeal in *Re NT Gallagher & Son Ltd* [2002] EWCA Civ 404, [2002] 1 WLR 2380, [2002] 2 BCLC 133 see the notes to s 2(2).

Where a voluntary arrangement fails on the making of a bankruptcy order the proper destination of funds paid into the arrangement will depend on the terms of the arrangement and the possibility of any Quistclose trust: see, for example, *Cooper v Official Receiver* [2002] EWHC 1970 (Ch), [2003] BPIR 55.

### SECTION 264(1)(d)

**Scope of provision**—This obsolete provision is to be repealed from a date to be appointed pursuant to s 170(2) of and Sch 16 to the Criminal Justice Act 1988, on which see further the general note to ss 277 and 280.

The Financial Conduct Authority may present its own petition or be heard on any other person's petition (if presented against a person who is or has been an authorised person or carrying out regulated functions in contravention of the general prohibition), on which see ss 372 and 374(2) of the Financial Services and Markets Act 2000 respectively.

**Petition deposits and court fees**—Under the Insolvency Proceedings (Fees) Order 2004 (SI 2004/593) as amended by the Insolvency Proceedings (Fees) (Amendment) Order 2015 (SI 2015/1819), with effect from 15 November 2015 the deposit payable under s 264(1)(a),(ba), (bb), (c) and (d) is £825. The court fee for issuing a bankruptcy petition is £180 if it is issued by the debtor or their personal representative and £280 if issued by a creditor or other person: Civil Proceedings Fees Order 2008 (SI 2008/1053) as amended by the Civil Proceedings Fees (Amendment) Order 2014 (SI 2014/874).

## SECTION 264(2)

**The court's discretion**—The decision whether or not to make a bankruptcy order remains a discretionary one: note the word 'may' in s 264(2). On the principles going to the exercise of the court's discretion on a creditor's petition see the notes to s 271 and the notes to r 10.24 under the sub-heading 'The court's discretion'.

On the exercise of the court's discretion on the supervisor's petition see the notes to s 276.

**Procedure**—The procedure applicable to a creditor's bankruptcy petition appears in rr 10.6–10.33.

## [1.380]

### 265 Creditor's petition: debtors against whom the court may make a bankruptcy order

(1)   A bankruptcy petition may be presented to the court under section 264(1)(a) only if—

  (a)   the centre of the debtor's main interests is in England and Wales, or

  (ab)   the centre of the debtor's main interests is in a member State (other than Denmark) and the debtor has an establishment in England and Wales, or

  (b)   . . . the test in subsection (2) is met.

(2)   The test is that—

  (a)   the debtor is domiciled in England and Wales, or

  (b)   at any time in the period of three years ending with the day on which the petition is presented, the debtor—

    (i)   has been ordinarily resident, or has had a place of residence, in England and Wales, or

    (ii)   has carried on business in England and Wales.

(3)   The reference in subsection (2) to the debtor carrying on business includes—

  (a)   the carrying on of business by a firm or partnership of which the debtor is a member, and

  (b)   the carrying on of business by an agent or manager for the debtor or for such a firm or partnership.

(4)   In this section, references to the centre of the debtor's main interests have the same meaning as in Article 3 of the EU Regulation.

(5)   In this section "establishment" has the same meaning as in Article 2(10) of the EU Regulation.

**Amendments**—Substituted by Enterprise and Regulatory Reform Act 2013, s 71(3), Sch 19. This heavily amended version of s 265 came into force on 6 April 2016. Amended by SI 2017/702; SI 2019/146, as from IP completion day (as defined in the European Union (Withdrawal Agreement) Act 2020, s 39(1)–(5)).

**General note**—In the case of a creditor's petition (but not that of an IVA supervisor: *Loy v O'Sullivan* [2010] EWHC 3583 (Ch), [2011] BPIR 181) there is a requirement that the petitioner can satisfy the court as to the debtor's geographical connection with the jurisdiction by the fulfilment of any one of what amount to the three requirements in s 265(2) and (3). There is no longer any provision referring to a debtor's presence in England and Wales, as was formerly the case with the old s 265(1)(b). Neither do the provisions make any reference to the debtor's nationality or the state of his citizenship.

## SECTION 265(1)

**Conditions for presentation of a bankruptcy petition**—Two gateways are now available to those seeking to present a bankruptcy petition. Most cases will fall under s 265(1)(a), ie where the debtor's centre of main interests ('COMI') is in England and Wales. Section 265(1)(b) will provide the basis for the making of a bankruptcy order where the EU Regulation has no application on account of the debtor having no centre of main interests within a Member State: *Geveran Trading Co v Skjevesland* [2002] EWHC 2898 (Ch), [2003] BPIR 924.

**Centre of main interests ('COMI')**—A debtor's centre of main interests is to be determined at the time when the court is first required to decide whether to open insolvency proceedings and should correspond not to the place where his debts were incurred but, rather, by reference to the place where the debtor conducted the administration of his interests so as to be ascertainable by an objective third party: *Shierson v Vlieland-Boddy* [2005] EWCA Civ 974, [2005] 1 WLR 3966, [2005] BPIR 1170 (Chadwick LJ, Longmore LJ and Sir Martin Nourse). For an example of the court refusing jurisdiction on a creditor's petition because the link between the debtor and the English jurisdiction was too tenuous, see *Anglo Irish Bank Corporation v Flannery* [2012] EWHC 4090 (Ch), [2013] BPIR 165.

**Non-COMI cases**—where a debtor does not have his COMI in England and Wales, s 265(1)(b) provides that the test in s 265(2) must be satisfied in order for a bankruptcy petition to be presented: see note to s 265(2) below.

### SECTION 265(2)

**The test referred to in s 265(1)(b)**—Each of the conditions amounts to a question of fact. This new version of s 265(2) is in a similar form to the old s 265(1), save that the former s 265(1)(b) (providing for a petition to be presented where the debtor 'is personally present in England and Wales on the day on which the petition is presented') is not replicated in the new s 265(2). For cases on the 'personally present' requirement in the former s 265(1)(b) see the 5th edition of this work.

The leading authorities on the issue of domicile in s 265(2)(a) are the Court of Appeal's decisions in *Re Bird* [1962] 1 WLR 686 and *Re Brauch (a Debtor)* [1978] Ch 316, and the decision on tax legislation in *Plummer v IRC* [1988] 1 WLR 292. Where a person abandons the domicile of choice, the domicile of origin is revived as a matter of law: *Barlow Clowes International Ltd v Henwood* [2008] EWCA Civ 577, [2008] BPIR 778 (Waller, Arden and Moore-Bick LJJ), the judgment of Arden LJ containing a useful survey of the authorities

On 'ordinarily resident' under s 265(2)(b)(i) see also the authorities mentioned above in relation to s 265(2)(a). The fact that an individual has not appealed tax assessments made against him by the Inland Revenue does not estop a debtor from disputing his or her alleged residence within the jurisdiction based on the fact of those assessments alone: *Wilkinson v IRC* [1998] BPIR 418 (HHJ Collyer QC, sitting as a deputy High Court judge).

In *Reynolds Porter Chamberlain LLP v Khan* [2016] BPIR 722 (which was a late case decided under the former s 265), Chief Registrar Baister considered the 'ordinarily resident' requirement now found in s 265(2)(b)(i) and identified at paragraph 25 a list of factors that are relevant to it. The Chief Registrar emphasised that the expression is not to be treated as a term of art and is a question of fact and degree.

On 'carried on business' now found under s 265(2)(b)(ii), in *Gate Gourmet Luxembourg IV Sarl v Morby* [2015] EWHC 1203 (Ch), [2015] BPIR 787, Registrar Briggs held that entry by a debtor into an agreement for the sale of his shareholding in a group of companies that operated in England and Wales amounted to carrying on business and that 'in my view a claim for a breach of warranty or a claim for tax would keep alive the business connection which is carrying on' ([28]) (Registrar Briggs was upheld by Edward Murray (sitting as a deputy High Court judge) [2016] EWHC 74 (Ch), [2016] BPIR 414, where this point was not appealed). On the other side of the line, Barling J allowed an appeal in *Charlton v Funding Circle Trustee Ltd* [2019] EWHC 2701 (Ch), [2020] BPIR 125 on the ground (at [24]) that the debtor's discussions with potential investors about a possible sale of his shareholding in a company did not justify a finding that he had 'carried on business'. See also *Masters v Barclays Bank plc* [2013] EWHC 2166 (Ch), [2013] BPIR 1058, where the debtor could not be shown to be carrying on a business in the jurisdiction just because he remained liable under a guarantee, although Norris J accepted that a single transaction might in certain circumstances be sufficient to demonstrate the carrying on of a business.

### SECTION 265(3)

**Scope of provision**—This new s 265(3) is in similar form to the former s 265(2). The question of whether an individual has 'carried on business' within the preceding 3-year period under s 265(2)(b)(ii) 'includes', but is not therefore limited to, those two circumstances in s 265(3). If an individual has carried on business within the jurisdiction and has left debts of the business unpaid then, notwithstanding the cessation of the business operation, the individual is deemed to continue to carry on business so as to be susceptible to a petition: *Theophile v Solicitor General* [1950] AC 186, which was followed by Hoffmann J in *Re a Debtor (No 784 of 1991)* [1992] Ch 554.

### SECTION 265(4)

See note to s 265(1) above.

## [1.381]

### 266 Other preliminary conditions

(1)   Where a bankruptcy petition relating to an individual is presented by a person who is entitled to present a petition under two or more paragraphs of section 264(1), the petition is to be treated for the purposes of this Part as a petition under such one of those paragraphs as may be specified in the petition.

(2)   A bankruptcy petition shall not be withdrawn without the leave of the court.

(3)   The court has a general power, if it appears to it appropriate to do so on the grounds that there has been a contravention of the rules or for any other reason, to dismiss a bankruptcy petition or to stay proceedings on such a petition; and, where it stays proceedings on a petition, it may do so on such terms and conditions as it thinks fit.

*(4)   Without prejudice to subsection (3), where a petition under section 264(1)(a) or (c) in respect of an individual is pending at a time when a criminal bankruptcy order is made against him, or is presented after such an order has been so made, the court may on the application of the Official Petitioner dismiss the petition if it appears to it appropriate to do so.*

**Amendments**—Criminal Justice Act 1988, s 170(2), Sch 16, as from a date to be appointed; Enterprise and Regulatory Reform Act 2013, s 71(3), Sch 19.

**General note**—The two procedural conditions in s 266(1) and (2) are conveniently located with the general power in subs (3) within this provision: see also IR 2016, r 10.24. Section 266(4) is to be repealed from a date to be appointed pursuant to s 170(2) and Sch 16 of the Criminal Justice Act 1988 with the effect of finally rendering obsolete the criminal bankruptcy regime.

## SECTION 266(1)

**Scope of provision**—The requirement that a petition must specify the ground under which the petitioner proceeds where the petitioner has standing to proceed under more than one ground serves to prevent a debtor having to deal, in effect, with more than one ground for the making of a bankruptcy order at any one time. The scheme of the legislation prevents more than one bankruptcy petition proceeding against a debtor simultaneously. In practice, however, the court may well be prepared to allow an amendment to cure any such defect, particularly where it can be shown that the debtor has placed no reliance on an omission or suffers no prejudice as a consequence of it or is plainly well aware of the ground upon which the petition has proceeded.

## SECTION 266(2)

**Withdrawal of a petition**—The effect of this provision is not only to prevent abuse of the bankruptcy procedure through the presentation of groundless petitions (which will come under the scrutiny of the court on being withdrawn) but also to allow other creditors to substitute or effect a change of carriage of the petition under IR 2016, rr 10.27 and 10.29, as appropriate. The procedure on dismissal or leave to withdraw a petition, including evidence which must support such an application, appears in IR 2016, r 10.30.

## SECTION 266(3)

**The court's general power to dismiss or stay a petition**—The court's general power to dismiss or stay arises where 'there has been a contravention of rules or for any other reason.' In *Re Micklethwait* [2002] EWHC 1123 (Ch), [2003] BPIR 101 at [11] Peter Smith J observed in relation to s 266(3) that 'Earlier cases as to when petitions have been adjourned or dismissed under such a discretionary power are of no assistance, except in drawing to my attention the fact that I have a discretionary power. It is the facts of each case which indicate how, if at all, the discretion should be exercised.' In that case his Lordship made bankruptcy orders on three petitions where the petition debts were undisputed, unpaid and longstanding and refused to grant open-ended adjournments so as to allow the debtors, who were Lloyd's names, to pursue cross-claims which faced significant procedural hurdles, even if the claims could be said to exist at all. In *TSB Bank plc v Platts* [1997] BPIR 151 HHJ Weeks QC, sitting as a High Court judge, held that s 266(3) does confer a discretion on the court to strike out a petition on the grounds of delay. Although in that case there had been delay following which the bankruptcy petition was re-listed of the court's own motion, the judge did not dismiss the petition, having taken account of the possibility of the bankruptcy proceedings starting again and the waste of costs that would entail together with the fact that the bankruptcy petition was, by that time, ready for trial.

There is no closed class of circumstances in which the court will dismiss a bankruptcy petition. The court's power, being a general one, has been held to justify dismissal where the petitioner could be shown to have been guilty of extortion or where the purpose of the proceedings is to gain some collateral advantage for himself: see *Re Majory* [1955] Ch 600 at 623, CA and compare, on its facts, *Re Malcolm Robert Ross (a Bankrupt) (No 2)* [2000] BPIR 636 at 643A–645E (Nourse LJ, Mantell LJ agreeing). The court may also dismiss a petition based on a non-provable debt, on which see the notes to s 264, or an unliquidated debt, on which see the notes to s 267 and the other examples therein. As regards going behind a judgment debt upon which a petition is based, Etherton J, following a review of the authorities, held in *Dawodu v American Express Bank* [2001] BPIR 983 at 990D–990E that: '  .  .  .   what is required before the court is prepared to investigate a judgment debt, in the absence of an outstanding appeal or an application to set it aside, is some fraud, collusion, or miscarriage of justice. The latter phrase is of course capable of wide application according to the particular circumstances of the case. What in my judgment is required is that the court be shown something from which it can conclude that had there been a properly conducted judicial process then it would have been found, or very likely would have been found, that nothing was in fact due to the claimant'. In *HMRC v Crossman* [2007] EWHC 1585 (Ch), [2007] BPIR 1068 Rimer J held that HMRC was entitled to a bankruptcy order on a petition based on the difference between unpaid duty of £343,450 and the sum of £55,965.46 paid by the debtor pursuant to a confiscation order made under s 71 of the Criminal Justice Act 1988 notwithstanding the failure of HMRC to notify the criminal court at the time of the confiscation order proceedings of the possibility of it seeking to make a civil recovery for the balance. In *Dunbar Assets Plc v Fowler* [2013] BPIR 46 (at [37]) Chief Registrar Baister indicated the section could be used to 'deal with any serious abuse that did result in prejudice to a debtor by dismissing a petition presented in circumstances that did give rise to unfairness to the debtor'.

In *Re Maud; Maud v Aabar Block SARL* [2016] EWHC 2175 (Ch), [2016] BPIR 1486, Snowden J held that even where a petition was not an abuse of process, where some creditors opposed the petition, the collective nature of bankruptcy proceedings required the court to evaluate the wishes of the creditors (both seeking and opposing a bankruptcy order) in the interests of the class ([97]). The question of abuse of process is distinct from the assessment of the class interest, which must always be undertaken where some creditors oppose the making of a bankruptcy order: see under the heading 'The court discretion' in the note to r 10.24. The test for establishing an abuse of process appears to be a high hurdle: in a subsequent hearing of the same petition (*Re Maud (No 2)*; *Aabar Block SARL v Maud* [2018] EWHC 1414 (Ch), [2019] Ch 15, [2018] BPIR 1207), Snowden J held at [79]–[82] that the test for whether or not a petition is an abuse is the same as the test for an abusive statutory demand, applying *Maud v Aabar Block Sarl and Edgeworth Capital (Luxembourg) Sarl* [2015] EWHC 1626 (Ch), [2015] BPIR 845, per Rose J, [29]. Snowden J observed that in most of the cases in which a petition has been shown to be an abuse, the petitioner has been acting for a collateral purpose that was adverse to the interests of the class. The judge accepted a submission that a petition will not be an abuse of process if, in addition to wishing to receive a dividend on his debt, the petitioner has a collateral purpose which is not shared by the other creditors, but which will not cause them any detriment if it is achieved ([82]–[83]). Snowden J did not find the petition to be an abuse and refused the debtor's application to dismiss it on that ground, but nonetheless declined to make an immediate bankruptcy order because it was not in the class interest of the creditors for an order to be made ([2018] EWHC 1414 (Ch), [140]).

There is a significant overlap between these issues and those addressed in the commentary under 'The court's discretion' in the note to r 10.24, and 'Abuse of process' and 'Creditor opposition to the petition' in the note to s 125.

**Where bankruptcy would serve no useful purpose**—Exceptionally, a court may exercise its discretion under s 266(3) not to make a bankruptcy order where it would serve 'no useful purpose'. In *Re Betts* [1897] 1 QB 50, 52, Esher MR explained:

> ' . . . I think that the law may properly be stated thus. If the Court is clearly convinced, not merely by the statement of the debtor, but from all the circumstances of the case, that there cannot be any assets or any prospect of any coming into existence, and that, if a receiving order is made, the only effect will be a mere waste of money in costs, then in such a case the Court has a discretion in the matter, and will be justified in exercising that discretion by refusing to make the order.'

The 'no assets' point also finds authority in the decision of Jules Sher QC, sitting as a deputy High Court judge, in *Re Thulin* [1995] 1 WLR 165 at 169 and in the decision of Rimer J in *HMRC v Crossman* [2007] EWHC 1585 (Ch), [2007] BPIR 1068 at [42].

More recently, HHJ Hodge QC (sitting as a High Court judge) allowed an appeal from a bankruptcy order made against a debtor with no assets in *Lock v Aylesbury Vale District Council* [2018] EWHC 2015 (Ch), [2018] BPIR 1694. The judge considered at [15] that there was no prospect of any dividend and no need for any investigation to take place: the debtor had no income, no earning capacity, rented her house from a social landlord, and her capital was less than £100. Nonetheless, Judge Hodge QC observed that a debtor who seeks to establish the 'no useful purpose' exception faces 'a heavy burden' in resisting a bankruptcy order on this ground: [35]. Sir Robert Megarry V-C had employed similar words in *Re Field (A Debtor)*, [1978] Ch 371, 375; as did Snowden J in *Maud v Aabar Block SARL* [2016] EWHC 2175 (Ch), [2016] BPIR 1486, [103]. Snowden J returned to the point in a further judgment in relation to the same debtor in *Edgeworth Capital (Luxembourg) SARL v Maud* [2020] EWHC 974 (Ch), where the need for a debtor to give a full and complete account of their affairs in order to discharge the heavy burden was given particular emphasis at [120]–[127].

It appears that it is necessary that a debtor should have no assets, rather than simply insufficient assets, before the 'no useful purpose' exception might apply. A mere insufficiency of assets, which will almost invariably be the case where a debtor cannot pay a petition debt, does not engage the principle. Cases in the 'insufficient assets' category are more likely to be offers to compound, which fall under s 271(3) of the IA 1986, and not cases of 'no assets' capable of engaging s 266(3). Compare *Cooke v Dunbar Assets plc* [2016] EWHC 579 (Ch), [2016] BPIR 576, where

Jeremy Cousins QC (sitting as a deputy High Court judge) expressed the view that, where a debtor opposed a bankruptcy order on the basis that he had offered to pay everything he had to the creditor, this amounted to an attempt to resist bankruptcy on the very ground of insolvency, which could not be right ([21]).

Moreover, the court should not dismiss a bankruptcy petition solely on the ground that a debtor has no assets, since bankruptcy is a class action which is justifiable on grounds other than the realisation and distribution of assets by way of an investigation by a trustee of the affairs of the debtor: *Shepherd v Legal Services Commission* [2003] BPIR 140 at 146F–146H, per Gabriel Moss QC, sitting as a deputy High Court judge. The cases as a whole indicate that a petitioner will only be refused a bankruptcy order on the basis of the 'no useful purpose' principle where there are both no assets and nothing to investigate or any other reason to make a bankruptcy order.

In the unusual case of *Amihyia v Official Receiver* [2004] EWHC 2617 (Ch), [2005] BPIR 264 Evans-Lombe J allowed annulment of a bankruptcy order under s 375 where the order had been made through no fault of the bankrupt's where there were no assets to realise in the bankruptcy. In *Hemsley v Bance* [2016] EWHC 1028 (Ch), [2016] BPIR 934, Registrar Jones declined to make a bankruptcy order on a petition presented in respect of a debt arising from the debtor's fraud, which had not been released on the debtor's first bankruptcy pursuant to s 281(3). Registrar Jones underlined the discretionary nature of s 266(3), which may extend even to circumstances where the statutory requirements are satisfied.

The discretion does not, however, extend to the task of ascertaining whether a bankruptcy order is a disproportionate remedy in the circumstances of the case since the question of proportionality is not appropriate to a bankruptcy petition in the absence of an unreasonable refusal by the petitioning creditor, any serious procedural defect or abuse of process: *John Lewis plc v Pearson Burton* [2004] BPIR 70 (Pumfrey J).

**Maladministration by local authorities**—There has been a number of cases in which the Local Government Ombudsman has criticised local authorities for bankrupting residents over small arrears of council tax and considered this to be maladministration causing injustice (see *Ford v Wolverhampton CC (Local Government's Ombudsman's Report)* [2008] BPIR 1304; *Report of an investigation into Complaint 07/A/12661 Against Camden LBC* [2008] BPIR 1572; Report of an Investigation in No 08002300 against Exeter City Council [2009] BPIR 598 and other LGO reports to similar effect noted in [2010] BPIR at 464, 476, 1407, 1420 and [2011] BPIR 1098). In *Hunt v Fylde* BC [2008] BPIR 1368 (an annulment case) the district judge referred ([19]) to the possibility of human rights issues arising 'as we contemplate an individual losing his home for a small tax liability when the more proportionate remedy of a charging order subject to court control is available'. The question was put off for submissions at the future hearing of the bankruptcy petition. However, the Court of Appeal in *Lonergan v Gedling Borough Council* [2009] EWCA Civ 1569, [2010] BPIR 911 considered that a local authority is entitled to present a petition in respect of a liability order and rejected arguments that the practice violated the debtor's human rights ([30]–[32]).

See further note to r 10.24.

*Creditor's petition*

**[1.382]**

**267 Grounds of creditor's petition**

(1)   A creditor's petition must be in respect of one or more debts owed by the debtor, and the petitioning creditor or each of the petitioning creditors must be a person to whom the debt or (as the case may be) at least one of the debts is owed.

(2)   Subject to the next three sections, a creditor's petition may be presented to the court in respect of a debt or debts only if, at the time the petition is presented—

    (a)    the amount of the debt, or the aggregate amount of the debts, is equal to or exceeds the bankruptcy level,

    (b)    the debt, or each of the debts, is for a liquidated sum payable to the petitioning creditor, or one or more of the petitioning creditors, either immediately or at some certain, future time, and is unsecured,

    (c)    the debt, or each of the debts, is a debt which the debtor appears either to be unable to pay or to have no reasonable prospect of being able to pay, and

    (d)    there is no outstanding application to set aside a statutory demand served (under section 268 below) in respect of the debt or any of the debts.

*(3)  A debt is not to be regarded for the purposes of subsection (2) as a debt for a liquidated sum by reason only that the amount of the debt is specified in a criminal bankruptcy order.*

(4)  "The bankruptcy level" is £5,000; but the Secretary of State may by order in a statutory instrument substitute any amount specified in the order for that amount or (as the case may be) for the amount which by virtue of such an order is for the time being the amount of the bankruptcy level.

(5)  An order shall not be made under subsection (4) unless a draft of it has been laid before, and approved by a resolution of, each House of Parliament.

**Amendments**—Criminal Justice Act 1988, s 170(2), Sch 16, as from a date to be appointed; SI 2015/922.

**General note**—The substance of this provision is in identifying the nature of the debt upon which a creditors' petition under s 264(1)(a) may be based. Section 267(3) refers to the now obsolete criminal bankruptcy regime and is to be repealed from a day to be appointed under s 171(1) of the Criminal Justice Act 1988. The bankruptcy level was increased to £5,000 in respect of petitions presented on or after 1 October 2015 by the Insolvency Act 1986 (Amendment) Order 2015 (SI 2015/922). It was formerly £750, having been fixed at that level by the Insolvency Proceedings (Increase of Monetary Limits) Regulations 1984 (SI 1984/1199).

The four conditions in s 267(2) are cumulative. If a petition debt does not fall within each of those criteria, then the court has power to dismiss the petition under s 266(3).

The words 'subject to the next three sections' in s 267(2) mean that s 267 must be read as subject to ss 268–270. Accordingly, the procedure for an expedited petition under s 270 may be engaged despite the fact of an outstanding application to set aside a statutory demand as mentioned in s 267(2)(d): *Re a Debtor (No 22 of 1993)* [1994] 1 WLR 46 (Mummery J). Further, where a statutory demand seeks payment of an unsecured debt and a secured debt and the debtor discharges the unsecured debt the petitioner is precluded from amending the petition to revalue its security where the security has become unrealisable such that the debtor is entitled to have the petition dismissed. The reference in s 267(2)(c) is to the unsecured debt alone given that s 269(2) stipulates that the secured and unsecured debts are separate debts: *Dubai Aluminium Company Ltd v Salaam* [2007] BPIR 690 (Registrar Simmonds).

**Malicious petitions**—A cause of action in tort lies in respect of injury caused by the malicious and unreasonable commencement of bankruptcy proceedings against an individual: *Gregory v Portsmouth City Council* [2000] 1 AC 419 at 427. The five elements of such an action are: (a) the presentation of a bankruptcy petition, (b) the termination of that petition in favour of the party against whom it was presented, (c) the absence of reasonable and probable cause for presentation of the petition, (d) the malicious presentation of the petition, and (e) the identification of damage caused by the malicious presentation of that petition. The authorities were considered by HHJ Peter Coulson QC, sitting as a High Court judge, in *Jacob v Vockrodt* [2007] EWHC 2403 (QB), [2007] BPIR 1568. The Privy Council has since confirmed in the corporate insolvency context in *Ebbvale Ltd v Hosking* [2013] UKPC 1, [2013] BPIR 219 that provided a winding up order is objectively likely to be of substantial advantage to the petitioner as a creditor, it is irrelevant that the petitioner's principle purpose behind presenting the petition was illegitimate; but see also *Aabar Block SARL v Maud* [2016] EWHC 2175 (Ch), [2016] BPIR 1486 and note to s 266(3) above.

**'Liquidated sum'**—A creditor's petition may only be based on a debt for a 'liquidated sum', with the consequence that a petition based on a claim for damages or a claim for an account and payment is liable to be dismissed: *Hope v Premierpace (Europe) Ltd* [1999] BPIR 695 (Rimer J). The sum must be a 'liquidated sum' at the time the statutory demand is presented. If it is not, the statutory demand is irredeemably defective and cannot be saved by the fact the debt may become liquidated by the date the petition is presented (eg by agreement with the debtor): *Orrick, Herrington and Sutcliffe (Europe) LLP v Frohlich* [2012] BPIR 169.

Where a guarantor's obligation is to pay the principal debtor's debt, or the guarantor has undertaken a concurrent obligation with the principal debtor, then the liability can be regarded as a liquidated sum: *McGuinness v Norwich & Peterborough Building Society* [2011] EWCA Civ 1286, [2012] BPIR 145 which contains a detailed discussion of the classification of different types of guarantee liability as either damages (unliquidated) or a debt (liquidated). See also *Sofaer v Anglo Irish Asset Finance plc* [2011] EWHC 1480 (Ch), [2011] BPIR 1736, *Dunbar Assets plc v Fowler* [2013] BPIR 46 and *Francis v Solomon Taylor & Shaw* [2013] EWHC 9 (Ch), [2013] BPIR 314 (in each of which the debtor's guarantee liability was held to be a liquidated sum).

Where, despite some irregularity in its signing, the court was able to order specific performance of a tenancy agreement, the rent due thereunder is a contingent debt in a liquidated sum: *Hurley v The Darjan Estate Company Plc* [2012] EWHC 189 (Ch), [2012] 1 WLR 1782, [2012] BPIR 1021.

Where a written agreement has been breached, the question whether the breach gives rise to a liquidated debt capable of supporting a petition is a matter of contractual construction in each case. In *Doherty v Fannigan Holdings Ltd* [2018] EWCA Civ 1615, [2018] 2 BCLC 623, [2018] BPIR 1266, the Court of Appeal upheld the setting aside of a statutory demand where a share sale agreement had been breached. The breach gave rise to an action for specific performance or damages, but did not give rise to a petitionable debt ([43]). In contrast, Roth J upheld the refusal of Chief ICC Judge Briggs to strike out a petition based on the breach of a settlement agreement in *Mulville v Sandelson* [2019] EWHC 3287 (Ch), [2020] BPIR 392. The question was whether the liability was independent and unqualified, which was a question of contractual construction ([3], [25]). In *Mulville*, the payment of a money sum was a discrete obligation that required no other step to be taken and, as such, was petitionable ([27]–[31]).

**Petition based on legal costs**—A sum awarded in respect of costs is capable of founding a bankruptcy petition, but only at the point at which the costs are assessed or the client is otherwise prevented from disputing them on the basis of a binding agreement or an estoppel. An interim order in respect of costs for a liquidated sum would also be capable of founding a petition. A solicitor's bill which has not been assessed is not a liquidated debt within s 267(2) such that it is incapable of founding a bankruptcy petition or a statutory demand: *Klamer v Kyrkiakides and Braier (a firm)* [2005] BPIR 1142 (Registrar Simmonds). In *Truex v Toll* [2009] EWHC 396 (Ch), [2009] 1 WLR 2121, [2009] BPIR 692 Proudman J held that a simple admission by the client of his or her costs bill, unsupported by consideration, was not sufficient to convert an unliquidated debt into a liquidated one. The client had to be bound by an agreement or an estopppel. The cost of presenting the statutory demand and petition in reliance on the admission was insufficient detriment to found an estoppel. An estoppel argument succeeded in *Moseley v Else Solicitors LLP* [2010] BPIR 1192, where the petitioning solicitors had continued work in reliance upon the debtor's representation that an invoice would be paid. An estoppel argument failed on the facts in *Wallace LLP v Yates* [2010] EWHC 1098 (Ch), [2010] BPIR 1041.

Legal costs incurred by the Law Society in the course of an intervention into a solicitor's practice were held by the Court of Appeal to be a liquidated sum in *The Law Society v Blavo* [2018] EWCA Civ 2250, [2018] BPIR 1704. Moylan LJ applied *McGuinness v Norwich & Peterborough Building Society* [2011] EWCA Civ 1286, [2012] BPIR 145 (see above) and held at [115] that para 13 of Sch 1 to the Solicitors Act 1974, which imposed liability for costs 'incurred' by the Law Society, constituted a 'pre-determined formula or machinery' within the meaning of McGuinness, which created a liquidated sum for the purposes of s 267(2)(b).

For the position on sums due in publicly funded cases see *Galloppa v Galloppa* [1999] BPIR 352 (Jonathan Parker J).

There are conflicting authorities on whether a costs liability incurred post-IVA, but arising out of an agreement entered into pre-IVA, falls into the IVA or can found a subsequent petition. It is submitted that following the Supreme Court's decision in *In re Nortel GmbH (in administration)* [2013] UKSC 52, [2014] AC 209, [2013] 2 BCLC 135 such a costs liability will usually be a debt within the IVA, even where it was entirely contingent at the date of the IVA, and will not be available to found a petition outside the IVA.

**Disputed debts**—The court will not make a bankruptcy order where the petition debt is disputed, although an order is properly made if the undisputed element of the petition debt exceeds the bankruptcy level: *TSB Bank plc v Platts (No 2)* [1998] BPIR 284 at 293A–293E (Peter Gibson and Otton LJJ and Sir John Balcombe). Where the debtor claims to have a counterclaim, set-off or cross-demand or otherwise disputes the debt, the question before the bankruptcy court is whether, on the evidence, there is a genuine triable issue. This reflects the evidential test for setting aside a statutory demand, which is essentially the same as in an application for summary judgment: see notes to r 10.5 under the heading 'The test for setting aside a statutory demand'; but see also the notes to r 10.24 under the heading 'Debtor rearguing points that have been addressed at the set-aside stage' and the notes under the heading 'Debt relied on in the petition is disputed' in s 125. It is emphasised that while the evidential standard in relation to the debt is the same, the question for a court on the hearing of a bankruptcy petition is whether a bankruptcy order should be made, which is a wider question than whether there is a debt capable of grounding a petition, see *Vieira v Revenue and Customs Commissioners* [2017] EWHC 936 (Ch), [2017] 4 WLR 86, [83]–[84].

**Statute-barred debts**—A statutory demand may not be based on a statute-barred debt (see, for example, *Mittal v RP Capital Explorer Master Fund* [2014] BPIR 1537), with the consequence that a petition based on such a debt must be dismissed. A petition based on a judgment debt, however, is not subject to the 6-year limitation period within s 24(1) of the Limitation Act 1980 since a petition is neither an action upon a judgment nor a process of execution of the judgment: *Ridgeway Motors (Isleworth) Ltd v ALTS Ltd* [2005] EWCA Civ 92, [2005] 1 WLR 2871, [2005] BPIR 423 (Brooke, Mummery and Scott Baker LJJ).

**Partnership debts**—A debt owed jointly by a partner is capable of founding a bankruptcy petition against that partner: *Schooler v Commissioners of Customs & Excise* [1996] BPIR 207 (Nourse LJ, Roch and Hobhouse LJJ agreeing).

**Payment of petition debt by date of hearing**—In *Lilley v American Express Europe Ltd* [2000] BPIR 70 John Jarvis QC, sitting as a deputy High Court judge, held that the court retained jurisdiction to make a bankruptcy order even where the debtor had reduced the outstanding petition debt to beneath the bankruptcy level by the time of the hearing of the petition. However, having made reference to IR 1986, r 6.25 (now replaced by IR 2016, r 10.24) and s 271, the deputy judge observed that this was a course which the court should approach cautiously. He went on (at 74H–75B):

> 'It seems to me clear that the court cannot make a bankruptcy order if the whole of the debt has been paid by the time it comes for hearing, but the Act says nothing to prevent a court from making an order if only part of the debt has been paid. In my judgment a court must retain a discretion as to whether or not it is proper to make an order in these circumstances. One can imagine a case where a debtor has played a cat and mouse game with the petitioning creditor and has paid off just under the bankruptcy level on a number of petitions, and one can imagine in those circumstances that a court will be reluctant to permit a bankrupt to behave in that way. It seems to me that the court would retain a discretion then to make an order in those circumstances. If, on the other hand, the case is one where there were genuine difficulties for the debtor and the debtor has made efforts to pay money in and it was not a cat and mouse game, then the court would consider carefully whether or not it should exercise its discretion to make a bankruptcy order.'

It is submitted that where the court is satisfied as to the genuine efforts of the debtor then, subject to the facts of the case, the court would be justified in adjourning the petition, albeit for a relatively short period. Notably, the deputy judge also went on (at 76D–77G) to hold that it is wrong in principle to add to a petition debt the costs of the petition to date so as to bring the petition debt above the bankruptcy level.

**Tax assessments**—The bankruptcy court has no standing to interfere with assessments made by the General Commissioner on evidence supplied by the Inland Revenue where a bankruptcy order has been made on such assessments and where the bankrupt seeks to challenge the evidence supplied by the Revenue: *Cullinane v Commissioners of Inland Revenue* [2000] BPIR 996 (Hart J) and see *Flett v HMRC* [2010] EWHC 2662 (Ch), [2010] BPIR 1075. This is not to say, however, that the fact of a tax assessment must automatically result in a bankruptcy order being made. In *Vieira v Revenue and Customs Commissioners* [2017] EWHC 936 (Ch), [2017] 4 WLR 86, [2017] BPIR 1062 Arnold J carried out a detailed review of the authorities and held that when considering a petition based on a tax assessment, the court's jurisdiction is wider than when considering whether to set aside a statutory demand, but how wide depends on the position with regard to an appeal against the assessment. Where the debtor's appeal rights are exhausted or out of time, then the court's discretion is as stated in *Lam v Inland Revenue Commissioners* [2005] EWHC 592 (Ch), [2009] BPIR 301 and *Chamberlin v Revenue and Customs Commissioners* [2011] EWCA Civ 271, [2011] BPIR 691: the court will make a bankruptcy order absent fraud, collusion or miscarriage of justice. If, however, there is an extant appeal pending against the assessment, then *Customs and Excise Commissioners v D & D Marketing (UK) Ltd* [2002] EWHC 660 (Ch), [2003] BPIR 539 shows the discretion is broader and the key factor is whether the appeal has a real prospect of success ([84]). Note that the right to appeal against a tax assessment vests in a debtor's trustee in bankruptcy: see notes to s 283(1)(a). Further, HMRC must have regard to its obligations under the Disability Discrimination Act 1995 in conducting its affairs: in *Re Haworth* [2011] EWHC 36 (Ch), [2011] BPIR 428 HHJ Pelling QC, sitting as a High Court judge, annulled a bankruptcy order made on a petition by HMRC where the debtor had lacked capacity to deal with the bankruptcy proceedings. Moreover it was held that as HMRC knew of the debtor's mental impairment it was in breach of its obligations under the Disability Discrimination Act 1995 in acting as it did. HMRC was ordered in principle to pay the fees and expenses of the bankruptcy, once they were determined. See the notes under the heading 'The kind of dispute' in s 125.

**Council tax**—A council tax liability order is a 'debt' for the purpose of s 267 (*Smolen v Tower Hamlets LBC* [2006] EWHC 3628 (Ch), [2007] BPIR 448). The Court of Appeal has confirmed that unpaid council tax arrears still constitute a debt even if no liability order has been made (*Bolsover DC v Ashfield Nominees Ltd* [2010] EWCA Civ 1129, [2011] BPIR 7). For some discussion on proportionality and bankruptcy petitions based on council tax arrears see the notes to s 266(3) under the sub-heading 'Maladministration by local authorities'.

**Debt governed by foreign law**—In *PJSC VTB Bank v Laptev* [2020] EWHC 321 (Ch), the debtor opposed a petition on the ground that, having proved for the debt in his Russian bankruptcy, the petitioner was no longer a creditor to whom the debt was payable within the meaning of s 267(2)(b) and therefore had no standing to petition in England. After a detailed analysis of the position, ICC Judge Burton concluded that the position was governed by Russian law and, while there was no Russian authority directly on point, the consistent position of the Russian courts had been to prohibit enforcement actions outside insolvency proceedings ([61]). Judge Burton dismissed the petition on the basis of jurisdiction, but pointed out that it was open to the Russian insolvency administrator to apply for recognition under the Cross-Border Insolvency Regulations 2006 ([64]).

**SECTION 267(2)(c)**
Scope of provision—See s 268 and the notes thereto.

**SECTION 267(2)(d)**
Scope of provision—The formal requirements for an application to set aside a statutory demand are at r 10.4.

There is 'no outstanding application to set aside a statutory demand' if such an application has been dismissed but is subject to an appeal at the time a petition is presented: *Ahmad v IR Commissioners* [2005] BPIR 541 ([7]–[8], Evans-Lombe J).

In the unusual case of *Regis Direct Ltd v Hakeem* [2012] EWHC 4328 (Ch), Norris J refused to set aside a bankruptcy order, even though there had been an extant application to set aside the statutory demand when the petition was presented. He considered there was no point in doing so, because the set aside application had been dismissed 3 days after the bankruptcy order had been made and there was no injustice to the debtor.

Setting aside a statutory demand—See notes to IR 2016, r 10.5(5).

## [1.383]

### 268 Definition of "inability to pay", etc; the statutory demand

(1)  For the purposes of section 267(2)(c), the debtor appears to be unable to pay a debt if, but only if, the debt is payable immediately and either—

    (a)    the petitioning creditor to whom the debt is owed has served on the debtor a demand (known as "the statutory demand") in the prescribed form requiring him to pay the debt or to secure or compound for it to the satisfaction of the creditor, at least 3 weeks have elapsed since the demand was served and the demand has been neither complied with nor set aside in accordance with the rules, or

    (b)    execution or other process issued in respect of the debt on a judgment or order of any court in favour of the petitioning creditor, or one or more of the petitioning creditors to whom the debt is owed, has been returned unsatisfied in whole or in part.

(2)  For the purposes of section 267(2)(c) the debtor appears to have no reasonable prospect of being able to pay a debt if, but only if, the debt is not immediately payable and—

    (a)    the petitioning creditor to whom it is owed has served on the debtor a demand (also known as "the statutory demand") in the prescribed form requiring him to establish to the satisfaction of the creditor that there is a reasonable prospect that the debtor will be able to pay the debt when it falls due,

    (b)    at least 3 weeks have elapsed since the demand was served, and

    (c)    the demand has been neither complied with nor set aside in accordance with the rules.

General note—This provision provides the definition relevant to s 267(2)(c) by reference to a statutory demand or an unsatisfied execution. It is not concerned with the grounds for the setting aside of a statutory demand, which are considered in IR 2016, r 10.5(5).

Form and procedure on a statutory demand—See rr 10.1–10.5.

The use of a statutory demand by a creditor constitutes a form of self-help. The statutory demand procedure does not, however, involve the court (other than where there is an application to set aside the demand) and, as such the demand does not constitute 'insolvency proceedings': *Re a Debtor (No 340 of 1992)* [1996] 2 All ER 211, CA. The court may overlook defects in the statutory demand, provided the document is not so defective that it cannot be construed as a statutory demand – on the difference, see *Agilo Ltd v Henry* [2010] EWHC 2717 (Ch), [2011] BPIR 297, per Newey J. Neither does pursuit of a statutory demand constitute 'legal proceedings' for the purposes of s 9 of the Arbitration Act 1996: *Shalson v D F Keane Ltd* [2003] EWHC 599 (Ch), [2003] BPIR 1045 at [13] (Blackburne J). In *Canning v Irwin Mitchell LLP* [2017] EWHC 718 (Ch), [2017] BPIR 934, Jeremy Cousins QC (sitting as a deputy High Court judge) granted a debtor's appeal and dismissed a bankruptcy petition where there had been a fundamental failure to effect service of a statutory demand. The deputy judge held that service of a statutory demand is a requirement to found jurisdiction to proceed to the making of a bankruptcy order and there was no discretion to cure such a fundamental defect. See also notes to rr 10.2 and 10.5.

In *Howell v Lerwick Commercial Mortgage Corp Ltd* [2015] EWHC 1177 (Ch), [2015] 1 WLR 3554, [2015] BPIR 821 Nugee J considered that a bankruptcy petition could be based upon several statutory demands for debts which in aggregate exceed the bankruptcy level (and thus refused to set aside a statutory demand where the undisputed part of the debt fell below the bankruptcy level, but where there was a suggestion of other debts which could be the subject of further statutory demands).

If the requirements of this section are satisfied, the debtor cannot avoid a bankruptcy order being made by demonstrating that he or she is solvent – if the debt which is the subject of the statutory demand is due and owing it must be paid: *Johnson v Tandridge DC* [2007] EWHC 3325 (Ch), [2008] BPIR 405.

### SECTION 268(1)(b)

' . . . execution or other process . . . returned unsatisfied in whole or in part'—Although, strictly speaking, only an execution, as opposed to any 'other process', is capable of involving anything being 'returned unsatisfied', in *Skarzynski v Chalford Property Co Ltd* [2001] BPIR 673 at [13] Jacob J held that the words 'returned unsatisfied' meant 'proof that the execution or other process failed to satisfy the debt – the upshot of the execution or other process.' As such, it is open to a creditor to go down the 'execution or other process' route and, where that route produces no money or insufficient money, to petition for bankruptcy. In that case the fact that the sheriff had failed to endorse a statement on the writ of execution had not been fatal to the writ's validity as an unsatisfied return. That decision should be read with that of the Court of Appeal in *Re a Debtor (No 340 of 1992)* [1996] 2 All ER 211, and the judgment of Millett J to which Jacob J referred. *Re a Debtor*, however, as Jacob J pointed out, was a case which involved no valid execution such that there could be no return, as opposed to the position in *Skarzynski* where there had been a valid execution but a failure by the sheriff to endorse the writ subsequently. See notes under 'Unsatisfied execution' in s 123.

Execution of foreign judgment—In *Islandsbanki HF v Stanford* [2020] EWCA Civ 480, the Court of Appeal held (at [62], on a second appeal upholding both ICC Judge Jones and Fancourt J) that where execution of a foreign judgment registered in England under the Lugano Convention had been purportedly attempted within the one month period for appeal against such registration, there had been no execution or other process capable of being returned unsatisfied for the purposes of s 268(1)(b) and the court had no jurisdiction to waive the defect.

### SECTION 268(2)

Future debts—Section 268 provides no guidance as to what a creditor must allege in respect of a future debt other than the grounds upon which it is alleged that the debtor has no reasonable prospect of paying the debt. This is a difficult ground to make out in practice. It is most likely to arise in a case where the debtor is hopelessly insolvent and/or has given an indication that he will be unable to pay in future.

## [1.384]

### 269 Creditor with security

(1) A debt which is the debt, or one of the debts, in respect of which a creditor's petition is presented need not be unsecured if either—

    (a)    the petition contains a statement by the person having the right to enforce the security that he is willing, in the event of a bankruptcy order being made, to give up his security for the benefit of all the bankrupt's creditors, or

    (b)    the petition is expressed not to be made in respect of the secured part of the debt and contains a statement by that person of the estimated value at the date of the petition of the security for the secured part of the debt.

(2) In a case falling within subsection (1)(b) the secured and unsecured parts of the debt are to be treated for the purposes of sections 267 and 270 as separate debts.

General note—The fact that a creditor holds security does not preclude the creditor from proceeding on a bankruptcy petition subject to compliance with either s 269(1)(a) or (b). The position of a secured creditor who petitions for a debtor's bankruptcy is provided for in s 383(3). Section 383(2) provides that a creditor is secured if he or she 'holds any security for the debt (whether a mortgage, charge or lien or other security) over any property of the [debtor]': see notes to s 271(1)(a) on the implications of this. On the interplay between s 269 and IR 2016, r 10.5(5)(c) (which states that the court may set aside a statutory demand if the debt is fully secured) see *1st Credit (Finance) Ltd v Bartram* [2010] EWHC 2910 (Ch), [2011] BPIR 1.

A freezing order over the debtor's assets is not security and a creditor with the benefit of such an order is not a secured creditor: *Day v Refulgent* [2016] EWHC 7 (Ch), [2016] BPIR 594.

Section 269 is available to a petitioning creditor even if the debtor has no other creditors and the petitioning creditor would otherwise be entitled to rely on its security rights: *Zandfarid v Bank of Credit & Commerce International (SA) (in liquidation)* [1996] 1 WLR 1420, [1996] BPIR 501 at 509G–509H (Jonathan Parker J).

In *Barclays Bank plc v Mogg* [2003] EWHC 2645 (Ch), [2004] BPIR 259 David Richards J held that, whilst a failure to comply with s 269 constituted a serious flaw, the proper course was to allow a petition to be amended, rather than to dismiss it, where the omission was not deliberate and where the debtor had not been misled and had suffered no prejudice as a consequence of the omission. Appeals from bankruptcy orders made on petitions that had failed to comply with s 269 were allowed in *Wave Lending Ltd v Parmar* [2017] EWHC 681, [2019] BPIR 451, with the petitions remitted to the County Court so that any application to amend may be determined. In *State Bank of India v Mallya* [2020] EWHC 96 (Ch), Chief ICC Judge Briggs referred to the discussion of these cases in the 8th edition of this work, and held that neither *Mogg* nor *Parmar* was authority for the proposition that a petition should be dismissed for a breach of s 269, although the position may be otherwise if the petition cannot be cured by amendment. Judge Briggs held that where there is a breach of s 269, the court should take account of at least the following factors in exercising its discretion: (i) the consequence of the breach; (ii) the conduct of the parties; and (iii) all the circumstances of the case ([40]–[42]).

IR 2016, rr 14.15–14.19 deal with the valuation etc of a creditor's security.

## [1.385]

### 270 Expedited petition

In the case of a creditor's petition presented wholly or partly in respect of a debt which is the subject of a statutory demand under section 268, the petition may be presented before the end of the 3-week period there mentioned if there is a serious possibility that the debtor's property or the value of any of his property will be significantly diminished during that period and the petition contains a statement to that effect.

**General note**—This provision allows for the presentation of a petition without the need for the elapse of the 3-week period mentioned in s 268(1)(a) following service of a statutory demand, but only 'if there is a serious possibility that the debtor's property or the value of any of his property will be significantly diminished during that period . . . '. The court will, therefore, require evidence of the jeopardy alleged; in keeping with the threshold applied to interim, and in particular freezing, injunctions, the court will require something over and above mere suspicion or fear.

Section 270 applies only to cases where a statutory demand has been served: *Wehmeyer v Wehmeyer* [2001] BPIR 548 (Registrar James). The fact that there is an outstanding application to set aside a statutory demand within s 267(2)(d) does not prevent the expedition of a petition: *Re a Debtor (No 22 of 1993)* [1994] 1 WLR 46 (Mummery J). Rule 10.21(2) provides that an expedited petition may be heard within the 14-day period which must ordinarily elapse following service of a bankruptcy petition. In theory at least, it would follow that, in the most extreme case, the statutory demand might be served contemporaneously with the bankruptcy petition and the matter listed immediately for hearing although in practice a creditor would usually be better proceeding directly down the petition route and seeking an expedited hearing under r 10.21(2), although a hearing would remain subject to s 271(2).

## [1.386]

### 271 Proceedings on creditor's petition

(1)   The court shall not make a bankruptcy order on a creditor's petition unless it is satisfied that the debt, or one of the debts, in respect of which the petition was presented is either—

(a)   a debt which, having been payable at the date of the petition or having since become payable, has been neither paid nor secured or compounded for, or

(b)   a debt which the debtor has no reasonable prospect of being able to pay when it falls due.

(2)   In a case in which the petition contains such a statement as is required by section 270, the court shall not make a bankruptcy order until at least 3 weeks have elapsed since the service of any statutory demand under section 268.

(3)   The court may dismiss the petition if it is satisfied that the debtor is able to pay all his debts or is satisfied—

    (a)    that the debtor has made an offer to secure or compound for a debt in respect of which the petition is presented,

    (b)    that the acceptance of that offer would have required the dismissal of the petition, and

    (c)    that the offer has been unreasonably refused;

and, in determining for the purposes of this subsection whether the debtor is able to pay all his debts, the court shall take into account his contingent and prospective liabilities.

(4)   In determining for the purposes of this section what constitutes a reasonable prospect that a debtor will be able to pay a debt when it falls due, it is to be assumed that the prospect given by the facts and other matters known to the creditor at the time he entered into the transaction resulting in the debt was a reasonable prospect.

(5)   Nothing in sections 267 to 271 prejudices the power of the court, in accordance with the rules, to authorise a creditor's petition to be amended by the omission of any creditor or debt and to be proceeded with as if things done for the purposes of those sections had been done only by or in relation to the remaining creditors or debts.

**General note**—The key provisions here are in s 271(1) and (3) which, respectively, impose two alternative conditions which arise for consideration on the hearing of the bankruptcy petition together with a single ground, made up of three cumulative criteria, which, if fulfilled, afford the court a discretion to dismiss the petition.

Section 271(1) should also be read in conjunction with IR 2016, r 10.24 which, in addition to corresponding with the former provision, adds a further fetter to the court's jurisdiction in the case of an over-stated debt in a statutory demand, as considered below. Section 271(2) should be read in conjunction with the notes to s 270.

On procedure generally on a bankruptcy petition see para 12 of the *Practice Direction – Insolvency Proceedings* (July 2020) [2020] BPIR 1211. As to circumstances which might justify the imposition of a stay pending the hearing of an appeal see *Emap Active Ltd v Hill* [2007] EWHC 1592 (Ch), [2007] BPIR 1228 (Morgan J, stay granted on undertakings where real harm would be done if the order under appeal remained in force and effect in the event that the appeal was successful). Where a bankruptcy order is successfully appealed after a trustee has been installed it is important that the appeal court be invited to address the trustee's remuneration and expenses incurred in the interim, and the court has an inherent jurisdiction to do so: *Appleyard v Wewelwala* [2012] EWHC 3302 (Ch), [2013] 1 WLR 752, [2013] BPIR 15.

### SECTION 271(1)

'the court . . . is satisfied'—In the absence of authority it is submitted that the word 'satisfied' equates to the court being satisfied on a balance of probabilities.

A debtor is not precluded from disputing that a debt is due at the petition stage if he has not challenged a statutory demand leading to the petition. In *Barnes v Whitehead* [2004] BPIR 693 at 697 HHJ Maddocks, sitting as a High Court judge, said this:

'The principle is well settled, and frequently applied in relation to company winding-up petitions, that the insolvency procedure is not the appropriate procedure for resolving disputed debts. The proper course is to issue a claim and obtain a judgment. The court does in any case have a discretion and once it appears that there is a dispute on substantial grounds it would be wrong to make a bankruptcy order. On principle therefore it would seem to me that the court would be bound to hear the case that the debt was disputed, notwithstanding the failure of the debtor to raise it by a preliminary application to set aside the demand. I would finally note that r 6.25(3) [now replaced by IR 2016, r 10.24(5)] seems to contemplate a situation in which a debt, disputed as to part, would be resolved on the hearing of the petition.'

For guidance on the circumstances in which arguments unsuccessfully deployed in an application to set aside a statutory demand might be relied on at the petition stage, see *Turner v Royal Bank of Scotland* [2000] BPIR 683. In *Harvey v Dunbar Assets plc* [2017] EWCA Civ 60, [2017] BPIR 450, the Court of Appeal reviewed the authorities on re-running arguments at different stages of the bankruptcy process and held that it would usually be an abuse of process to do so in the absence of a change of circumstances or some other special reason. See notes to r 10.24 under the heading 'Debtor rearguing points that have been addressed at the set-aside stage'.

### SECTION 271(1)(a)

'a debt which . . . has been neither paid nor secured nor compounded for'—The word 'paid' is not controversial. Either the debt has been paid or it has not, and, if paid in part, the court must be satisfied that the amount outstanding exceeds £5,000 although, even if it does not, the court retains a discretion in making an order: *Lilley v American Express Europe Ltd* [2000] BPIR 70 (John Jarvis QC sitting as a deputy High Court judge).

For debts capable of founding a bankruptcy petition see the notes to s 267.

The term 'secured' is best understood by reference to s 383(2) which provides that 'a debt is secured . . . to the extent that the person to whom the debt is owed holds any security for the debt (whether a mortgage, charge, lien or other security) over any property of the person by whom the debt is owed'. Accordingly, security over third party property (including the property of a principal debtor where a creditor seeks to bankrupt a personal guarantor) does not fall within the definition of 'security' for these purposes: *White v Davenham Trust Ltd* [2011] EWCA Civ 747, [2011] BPIR 1187; *Dunbar Assets plc v Fowler* [2013] BPIR 46. A freezing order over the debtor's assets is not security and a creditor with the benefit of such an order is not a secured creditor: *Day v Refulgent* [2016] EWHC 7 (Ch), [2016] BPIR 594.

In *Smith v Ian Simpson & Co* [2001] Ch 239, [2000] BPIR 667 (Laws LJ and Jonathan Parker J, Evans LJ dissenting on result but not reasoning) it was held that the reference to payment in s 271(1)(a) is to unconditional payment such that a payment from the debtor's funds which is liable to be avoided under s 284(1) on a bankruptcy order being made cannot constitute payment. In such circumstances the court retains the power to make a bankruptcy order, which will be relevant where a supporting creditor seeks carriage of the petition under r 10.29(1). If there are no such supporting creditors, then the court is entitled to dismiss the bankruptcy petition notwithstanding the fact that the petition debt has been discharged out of the debtor's own estate: *Re Marr (a Bankrupt)* [1990] Ch 773, CA.

For further commentary see the notes to s 123 under the heading 'Secure or compound to the reasonable satisfaction of the creditor'.

In *Marquis de Louville de Toucy v Bonhams* 1793 Ltd [2011] EWHC 3809 (Ch), [2012] BPIR 793 Vos J allowed an appeal against a bankruptcy order made against a debtor who lacked capacity to deal with his financial affairs. In the circumstances, given the incomplete nature of the information before the court, the registrar could not have been sure that the debt could not in fact have been discharged from the debtor's assets and could not have been sure whether or not s 271(1) was satisfied without investigation and hearing submissions from somebody who could represent the debtor, and the petition should have been adjourned to allow such a representative to be appointed.

The court can exercise its discretion to adjourn a petition if, although the debt remains unpaid, there is a reasonable prospect that it will be paid in a reasonable time, but there must be credible evidence in support – see *Edginton v Sekhon* [2015] EWCA Civ 816, [2015] 1 WLR 4435, [2015] BPIR 1397. In that case, the Court of Appeal upheld the decision of the district judge to make a bankruptcy order, despite the debtor having made a request for an adjournment to pay the debt at the very last minute. See further on this point the notes to r 10.24 under the sub-heading 'The court's discretion'.

## SECTION 271(1)(b)

' . . . no reasonable prospect of being able to pay when it falls due . . . '—This provision requires the court to reach a finding of fact as to whether, on the balance of probabilities, a debtor has no reasonable prospect of being able to pay a future debt when it falls due. Thus, the court must not make a bankruptcy order if satisfied that there is a 'reasonable prospect' that the debtor will be able to pay the future debt at a due date. This assessment may amount to a very difficult exercise for the court which may dictate that further evidence is required other than in extreme cases, as do arise in practice, such as where the debtor is hopelessly insolvent, where promises of future funding are unevidenced and plainly speculative or where the debtor himself has admitted that he will be unable to make payment in the future. It should also be noted that, in reaching a finding on the evidence, by virtue of s 271(4), the facts and other matters known to the creditor at the time the future debt came into being was a reasonable prospect such that the burden rests on the creditor to establish some new fact or matter which has come to his knowledge since the debt came into being which detracts from that statutorily presumed reasonable prospect.

## SECTION 271(3)

Scope of provision—The court retains a discretion to dismiss a petition in the circumstances listed within subsection (3). The fact of a debtor asserting solvency is no answer to a petition based on a debt which remains unpaid: *Johnson v Tandridge District Council* [2007] EWHC 3325 (Ch), [2008] BPIR 405 at [37] (HHJ Kaye QC, sitting as a High Court judge).

The final part of the provision requires that, in reaching its conclusion, the court must take into account both the debtor's contingent liabilities (ie those which will crystallise subject to a condition which may or may not occur) and the debtor's prospective liabilities (ie those liabilities which will crystallise at some future time). The relevant principles, which draw on the judgments of Timothy Lloyd QC, sitting as a deputy High Court judge in *Re a Debtor (No 32 of 1993)* [1994] 1 WLR 899, and of Robert Walker J in *Commissioners of Inland Revenue v the Debtor, Re a Debtor*

*(No 6349 of 1994)* [1996] BPIR 271, are summarised conveniently in the judgment of Lightman J in *HM Customs & Excise v Dougall* [2001] BPIR 269 at 272F–272H thus:

'First, the test of unreasonableness is whether an unreasonable creditor in the position of the petitioning creditor and in the light of the actual history as disclosed to the court could have reached the conclusion that the petitioning creditor reached. There may be a range of reasonable positions on the part of the hypothetical reasonable creditors and a rejection of an offer by the petitioner is only to be categorised as unreasonable if no reasonable creditor would have refused the offer and accordingly the refusal is beyond the range of reasonable responses to it. Secondly, the test is objective, namely the response of the hypothetical reasonable creditor. The court is not limited to considering the considerations that were taken into account by the petitioning creditor himself when he refused to agree to the offer. The court must look at all the relevant factors and decide what are the relevant and what impact those relevant factors would have on the hypothetical reasonable creditor. The third proposition is that the debtor must be full, frank and open and provide all the necessary information to enable an informed decision to be made by the creditor.'

The identification of the relevant principles as above is important because, whilst any reported authority on s 271(3) may illustrate the court's approach to any particular set of facts, each case may only be determined by a comparison of the response of any particular creditor to the range of reasonable positions open to a hypothetical reasonable creditor on the particular facts before the court.

The test has been elaborated upon in the detailed judgment of Chief Registrar Baister in *HMRC v Garwood* [2012] BPIR 575, which identified at [23] a comprehensive summary of the principal propositions that emerge from the authorities. In that case it was held (unusually) that HMRC had unreasonably refused an offer of security where, if it had applied thought and not acted mechanistically, it would have been clear that the offer had increased the possibility of recovering the tax due. This position can be contrasted with the prior decision *Ross v HMRC* [2010] BPIR 652, where the contrary result was reached on the facts (although the court did caution HMRC against adopting a blanket policy of refusing security in every case). The Chief Registrar's criteria in *HMRC v Garwood* were approved and applied at High Court judge level by Jeremy Cousins QC (sitting as a deputy High Court judge) in an appeal from a bankruptcy order in *Cooke v Dunbar Assets plc* [2016] EWHC 579 (Ch), [2016] BPIR 576.

For examples of cases where a debtor has unsuccessfully argued a creditor had not acted reasonably in rejecting his offer see: *Nottingham County Council v Pennant* [2009] EWHC 2437 (Ch), [2010] BPIR 430 (HHJ Purle QC, sitting as a High Court judge, held that a local authority had been entitled to reject an offer of repayment over 2 years where the debtor had defaulted on payment arrangements in the past, and the district judge had erred in treating the situation as analogous to an application in a mortgagee possession case under s 36 of the Administration of Justice Act 1970, since in bankruptcy cases an undisputed creditor was prima facie entitled to the bankruptcy order which was petitioned for); *Shrimpton v Darby's Solicitors LLP* [2011] EWHC 3796 (Ch), [2012] BPIR 631 (where the offer to pay was based upon a future income stream which was too speculative); *Cooke v Dunbar Assets plc* [2016] EWHC 579, [2016] BPIR 576 (where the subject of the debtor's offer of security was a half-share in his matrimonial home, which it was reasonable for the creditor to think might be more readily realised by a trustee in bankruptcy).

In *Dunbar Assets plc v Fowler* [2013] BPIR 46 Chief Registrar Baister was faced with the seemingly novel submission that offers made by third parties were not offers made by the debtor and did not engage s 271(3)(a). He said (at [21]) 'I venture to express the tentative view that it could be possible for an offer from the debtor to include an offer that contemplates fulfilment of some or all of what is on offer by a third party as, for example, agent of the debtor'.

The question of whether or not a creditor has unreasonably refused an offer of security for the purposes of s 271(3)(c) is to be considered at the hearing of the petition and is not a ground for setting aside a statutory demand: *In Re A Debtor (No 415-SD-1993)*, [1994] 1 WLR 917, per Jacob J.

### SECTION 271(5)

**Amendment to creditor's petition**—The only provision in the IR 2016 allowing for amendment of a bankruptcy petition appears in IR 2016, r 10.16 which, subject to the leave of the court, allows a petition to be amended 'at any time after presentation by the omission of any creditor or any debt'. The general power in the present provision allows for the omission of a creditor or a debt mentioned therein so as to allow for the continuance of the petition with the remaining creditors or debts and is not limited in scope by the narrower r 10.16: *Aspinall's Club Ltd v Halabi* [1998] BPIR 322 (John Martin QC, sitting as a deputy High Court judge, a case decided under the equivalent IR 1986, r 6.22).

. . .

**[1.387]**

**272–275A . . .**

. . .

**Amendments**—Repealed by Enterprise and Regulatory Reform Act 2013, s 71(3), Sch 19, paras 1, 9(1).

**General note**—A debtor seeking a bankruptcy order must now apply to an adjudicator for a bankruptcy order in accordance with the new procedure in Part IX Chapter 1A above.

*Other cases for special consideration*

**[1.388]**

**276 Default in connection with voluntary arrangement**

(1) The court shall not make a bankruptcy order on a petition under section 264(1)(c) (supervisor of, or person bound by, voluntary arrangement proposed and approved) unless it is satisfied—

    (a)    that the debtor has failed to comply with his obligations under the voluntary arrangement, or

    (b)    that information which was false or misleading in any material particular or which contained material omissions—

        (i)    was contained in any statement of affairs or other document supplied by the debtor under Part VIII to any person, or

        (ii)    was otherwise made available by the debtor to his creditors in connection with a creditors' decision procedure instigated under that Part, or

    (c)    that the debtor has failed to do all such things as may for the purposes of the voluntary arrangement have been reasonably required of him by the supervisor of the arrangement.

(2) Where a bankruptcy order is made on a petition under section 264(1)(c), any expenses properly incurred as expenses of the administration of the voluntary arrangement in question shall be a first charge on the bankrupt's estate.

**Amendments**—Small Business, Enterprise and Employment Act 2015, s 126, Sch 29, Pt 2, paras 60, 73.

**General note**—The three alternative conditions in s 276(1)(a)–(c) apply where the court is asked to make a bankruptcy order on a petition presented under s 264(1)(c). These conditions will not, it is submitted, apply where a person who is bound by a voluntary arrangement proceeds by way of a creditor's petition under s 264(1)(a) in respect of a debt which is not caught by the voluntary arrangement, such as, for example, fresh indebtedness arising after approval of the arrangement. Even where any of these conditions are fulfilled the court retains a discretion in making a bankruptcy order under s 264(2).

**Time for presentation of a supervisor's default petition**—The basis for the presentation of a bankruptcy petition by a supervisor will depend on the particular terms of the voluntary arrangement. Although the arrangement will often require presentation of a petition in the event of default, often following the issue of a certificate of non-compliance or default, the arrangement may confer a discretion on the supervisor as to whether or not to present. In either case a petition should be presented timeously once the requirement or the decision to present is made, particularly where the debtor may otherwise continue to make contributions to the supervisor which are capable of being ring-fenced from any ensuing bankruptcy following the decision of the Court of Appeal in *Re NT Gallagher & Son Ltd* [2002] EWCA Civ 404, [2002] 1 WLR 2380, [2002] 2 BCLC 133 (on which see the note to s 2(2)).

In *Harris v Gross* [2001] BPIR 586 at 589G HHJ Maddocks, sitting as a High Court judge, held that the standing of a supervisor to petition under s 264(1)(c) does not determine on the termination of the period of a fixed-term arrangement. HHJ Maddocks did point out (at 589G), however, that the fact of any delay in presenting a petition would be a factor which would influence the court in the exercise of its discretion in making a bankruptcy order.

**The absence of a requirement for a deliberate or culpable act by the debtor for s 276(1)(a) and (b) purposes**—In *Re Keenan* [1998] BPIR 205 Jacob J rejected submissions to the effect that s 276(1)(a) only applies where there is a culpable failure by a debtor to comply with an obligation; the test, therefore, in approaching that provision is objective. It was common ground that it did not matter whether the debtor had supplied false or misleading information intentionally or not for the purposes of s 276(1)(b), to which the approach is also objective. At 210F Jacob J employed the example of a case where a debtor had agreed to pay £1,000 per month and for some reason did not make one payment but was in a position to make and did make twice the payment the month after. In considering a bankruptcy petition his Lordship suggested that: 'that would be a failure to comply with an obligation of the agreement, but the court would not regard it as blameworthy or sufficiently important to justify the bankruptcy, save perhaps where the failure to make the first payment involved a degree of culpability . . . .'.

### SECTION 276(1)(a)

' . . . the debtor has failed to comply with his obligations . . . '—This condition requires a finding of fact as to (a) the obligations of the debtor under the voluntary arrangement, and (b) whether there has been a failure to comply with such obligations. In terms of construing the terms of any particular voluntary arrangement, some assistance may be gleaned from the extract of the judgment of Blackburne J in *Wellsby v Brelec Installations Ltd* [2000] 2 BCLC 576 as appears in the note to s 5(2).

One practical difficulty that can arise in relation to this provision comes about where the debtor is guilty of a minor or de minimis breach of obligations under an arrangement which, dependent on the terms of the arrangement, may trigger the presentation of a bankruptcy petition. Alternatively, the debtor may have committed a fundamental breach of his or her obligations through, say, a failure to make monthly contributions to the supervisor, which have been fully remedied following presentation of the petition. Unless the supervisor is empowered by the arrangement, either by an express or implied term or by a variation validly approved by creditors, to withdraw the petition, the court may find itself faced with either a petition which is resisted by the debtor or a petition which the supervisor has no real enthusiasm for prosecuting, given the remedied breach and the likelihood, as will usually have been the case at the time of approval, that the continuance of the arrangement will provide a better return for creditors. Although the decision of Neuberger J in *Carter-Knight v Peat* [2000] BPIR 968 at 971H–973D is authority for the proposition that it is not necessary on a default petition presented by a supervisor that the alleged breach of the terms of an arrangement should continue at the date of the hearing of the petition, his Lordship did identify (at 973D) that the court retains a discretion under IR 1986, r 6.25(1) (now replaced by IR 2016, r 10.24) – as also arises under s 264(2) – as to whether or not to make a bankruptcy order. It is submitted that the fact that a petition is presented by the supervisor of a voluntary arrangement should not, of itself, incline the court towards the making of an order where the court might otherwise be inclined to adjourn or even dismiss the petition. The fact that a petition is presented by a supervisor amounts to no more than the supervisor acting in accordance with the terms of an arrangement; the creditors approving the arrangement, however, can do no more than require the supervisor to seek an order, which remains entirely in the discretion of the court, through the presentation of a petition.

On the other hand, the court will plainly give weight to the seriousness of any breach and any other relevant surrounding circumstances such as a failure or repeated failure to honour any previous promise by a debtor to remedy a breach. In *Kaye v Bourne* [2004] EWHC 3236 (Ch), [2005] BPIR 590 Patten J held that, where a petition is presented by a supervisor based on defaults under an arrangement, but where the debtor is able to show that the defaults have been remedied at the date of the hearing of the petition, the court retains a discretion under s 276 to refuse a bankruptcy order and to allow the arrangement to continue if satisfied that such a course would secure a better return for creditors. Each case will be decided upon its own facts and careful consideration of the terms of the IVA.

In *Clarke v Birkin* [2006] EWHC 340 (Ch), [2006] BPIR 632 a bankruptcy order was made upon a petition brought by IVA participating creditors, despite the fact that the debtor's defaults had been partially remedied by the bankrupt who had made significant payments under the IVA. The bankrupt's appeal on the basis that his default in making payments was not a material default was dismissed by Evans-Lombe J. The IVA had contained a term making it clear that failure to pay instalments on time could not be remedied by later payment, and although the registrar had a discretion whether or not to make a bankruptcy order where a breach of the terms of the voluntary arrangement had been established (see *Re Keenan* [1998] BPIR 205), there were no grounds for interfering with the registrar's exercise of his discretion in this case.

### SECTION 276(1)(b)

' . . . **information which was false or misleading in any material particular or which contained material omissions** . . . '—Initially, what should be noted here is the scope of the documents in s 276(1)(b)(i) and the fact that s 276(1)(b)(ii) apparently extends beyond the scope of documents and might conceivably catch oral representations made at a creditors' meeting or in connection with it, say prior to it in response to an enquiry by a creditor.

In *Re Tack* [2000] BPIR 164 at 204C–204D Rimer J held that information in a proposal or statement of affairs will be false or misleading in a material way for the purposes of s 276(1)(b) if, had the truth been told, it would be likely to have made a material difference to the way in which creditors would have considered and assessed the particular arrangement to which they were being invited to agree. In *Somji v Cadbury Schweppes plc* [2001] 1 WLR 615, [2001] BPIR 172 at [25] Robert Walker LJ, in a court also comprising Judge LJ and Sir Christopher Staughton, approved of Rimer J's formulation, subject to two provisos. First, the test must be answered objectively. Secondly, it is necessary to bear in mind that any number of creditors might themselves unrepresented, having given proxies in favour of the nominee as chairman of the meeting; as such, the court should bear in mind that it would ordinarily be the chairman's duty as chairman to adjourn the meeting and to report to creditors on learning of the true position, even if such a course would mean having to obtain an extension of time under s 376. In *Somji* the Court of Appeal confirmed a bankruptcy order made in the court below by Anthony Boswood QC, sitting as a deputy High Court judge, on the basis that a secret agreement under which two creditors were to be paid sums by a third party in return for voting in support of the proposal constituted a material omission, as did non-disclosure of the fact that two previously dissentient creditors were at an advanced stage in negotiations for improved returns over any return under the arrangement in which they would not participate.

Where there is an air of suspicion as to the veracity of information or an omission, it may be appropriate to order cross-examination to confirm or dispel the suspicion: *Re A Debtor (No 574 of 1995)* [1998] 2 BCLC 124 at 130H (John Martin QC sitting as a deputy High Court judge).

### SECTION 276(1)(c)

' . . . the debtor has failed to do all such things as may . . . have been reasonably required of him by the supervisor . . . '—There is no specific statutory term requiring a debtor to do things required of him or her by a supervisor. Such an obligation would, however, appear implicit, given the present provision. Whether in any particular case a thing required by a supervisor of a debtor can be said to have been reasonably required will turn on the facts of the arrangement under consideration and the circumstances of the case in which the supervisor has come to require a particular thing to be done by the debtor.

In *Vadher v Weisgard* [1998] BPIR 295 at 298–298 Chadwick J identified that the provisions in Part VIII 'require a degree of co-operation between the debtor and the supervisor. In particular, they are provisions which require that the debtor does honour faithfully the proposals to which creditors have agreed.' So far as non-co-operation on the part of the debtor went, so as to give rise to increased time costs due to the supervisor, his Lordship went on to identify at 298 that, 'If the debtor is failing to co-operate to such an extent that the contributions are being absorbed in the supervisor's proper expenses, then the arrangements are not working and should be brought to an end.'

## [1.389]

### 277 Petition based on criminal bankruptcy order

*(1)   Subject to section 266(3), the court shall make a bankruptcy order on a petition under section 264(1)(d) on production of a copy of the criminal bankruptcy order on which the petition is based.*

*This does not apply if it appears to the court that the criminal bankruptcy order has been rescinded on appeal.*

*(2)   Subject to the provisions of this Part, the fact that an appeal is pending against any conviction by virtue of which a criminal bankruptcy order was made does not affect any proceedings on a petition under section 264(1)(d) based on that order.*

*(3)   For the purposes of this section, an appeal against a conviction is pending—*

*(a)   in any case, until the expiration of the period of 28 days beginning with the date of conviction;*

*(b)   if notice of appeal to the Court of Appeal is given during that period and during that period the appellant notifies the official receiver of it, until the determination of the appeal and thereafter for so long as an appeal to the Supreme Court is pending within the meaning of subsection (4).*

*(4)   For the purposes of subsection (3)(b) an appeal to the Supreme Court shall be treated as pending until any application for leave to appeal is disposed of and, if leave to appeal is granted, until the appeal is disposed of; and for the purposes of this subsection an application for leave to appeal shall be treated as disposed of at the expiration of the time within which it may be made, if it is not made within that time.*

**Amendments**—Prospectively repealed by Criminal Justice Act 1988, s 170(2), Sch 16, as from a date to be appointed under s 171(1) of the Criminal Justice Act 1988; Constitutional Reform Act 2005, s 40(4), Sch 9, Pt 1, para 44.

**General note**—Criminal bankruptcy orders were previously provided for under the Powers of the Criminal Courts Act 1973. The power to make such orders, which were rare in any case in practice, was abolished with effect from 3 April 1989 by s 101 of the Criminal Justice Act 1988. The standing of the Official Petitioner or any other person within s 264(1)(d) to present a bankruptcy petition where a criminal bankruptcy order has been made against an individual is therefore redundant, at least for practical purposes.

## CHAPTER 1A

### COMMENCEMENT AND DURATION OF BANKRUPTCY

**Amendments**—Substituted by Enterprise and Regulatory Reform Act 2013, s 71(3), Sch 19, paras 1, 10.

## [1.390]

### 278  Commencement and continuance

The bankruptcy of an individual against whom a bankruptcy order has been made—

    (a)    commences with the day on which the order is made, and

    (b)    continues until the individual is discharged under this Chapter.

**Amendments**—Enterprise and Regulatory Reform Act 2013, s 71(3), Sch 19, paras 1, 11.

**General note**—In contrast to a compulsory winding up under s 129(2), bankruptcy commences not with the presentation of the petition but with the day on which the order is made.

Although the bankruptcy itself ends with the discharge of the bankrupt – on which see ss 279 and 280 and the notes thereto – the effect of discharge itself is as provided for in s 281, which allows for the continuation of the functions of the trustee, the right of any creditor to prove in the bankruptcy for any debt from which the bankrupt is released, the right of any secured creditor to enforce security for the payment of a debt from which the bankrupt has been released and the continuance in effect of certain bankruptcy debts incurred through fraud, together with those particular species of debt identified in s 281(4)–(8).

**Third Parties (Rights Against Insurers) Act 1930**—It is well established that the statutory transfer to a third party of an insured's right against his insurer under s 1 of the 1930 Act takes place at the moment of the insured's bankruptcy: see *Law Society v Official Receiver* [2007] EWHC 2841 (Ch), [2009] Ch 223, [2007] BPIR 1595 at [27] and the cases cited therein.

**Procedures on the making of a bankruptcy order**—See generally Part 10 of the IR 2016.

## [1.391]

### 279  Duration

(1)  A bankrupt is discharged from bankruptcy at the end of the period of one year beginning with the date on which the bankruptcy commences.

(2)  . . .

(3)  On the application of the official receiver or the trustee of a bankrupt's estate, the court may order that the period specified in subsection (1) shall cease to run until—

    (a)    the end of a specified period, or

    (b)    the fulfilment of a specified condition.

(4)  The court may make an order under subsection (3) only if satisfied that the bankrupt has failed or is failing to comply with an obligation under this Part.

(5)  In subsection (3)(b) "condition" includes a condition requiring that the court be satisfied of something.

(6)  In the case of an individual who is made bankrupt on a petition under section 264(1)(d)—

    (a)    subsections (1) to (5) shall not apply, and

    (b)    the bankrupt is discharged from bankruptcy by an order of the court under section 280.

(7)  This section is without prejudice to any power of the court to annul a bankruptcy order.

**Amendments**—Substituted by Enterprise Act 2002, s 256(1). Amended by Enterprise and Regulatory Reform Act 2013, ss 70(3), 73, Sch 19, paras 1, 12, Sch 21, Pt 3, para 5.

**General note**—This version of s 279 was introduced by s 256 of and Sch 19 to the Enterprise Act 2002 with effect from 1 April 2004. These provisions apply to all individuals against whom a bankruptcy order is made on or after that date. The principal amendment is that the bankrupt is automatically discharged, in the absence of a contrary order under s 279(3), after a one-year period beginning with the date of the bankruptcy order, or sooner under s 279(2), on the official receiver filing a s 289 notice.

The effect of discharge is provided for in s 281.

**Suspension of discharge**—In *Shierson v Rastogi* [2007] EWHC 1266 (Ch), [2007] BPIR 891 at [65], and whilst resiling from expressing a concluded view on this issue, Morritt C opined that the purpose of s 279 in allowing for the postponement of discharge from bankruptcy lies in the continuance of the disabilities arising from an individual being an undischarged bankrupt, as opposed to the providing of an incentive to full compliance by the bankrupt with his or her statutory obligations, since otherwise Parliament might have been expected to provide that discharge was conditional upon full compliance. This distinction was not easy to draw in practice and more helpful guidance on the purpose of and ground for suspension has since been provided by the Court of Appeal in *Bramston v Haut* [2012] EWCA Civ 1637, [2013] 1 WLR 1720, [2013] BPIR 25. In *Bramston v Haut*, it was the bankrupt himself who wanted his discharge suspended so that he might put forward an IVA proposal to his creditors, the trustee being opposed to this course of action. At first instance ([2012] EWHC 1279 (Ch), [2012] BPIR 672), Arnold J had granted a period of suspension, concluding that the trustee had acted '*Wednesbury*' unreasonably and that the court should have ordered the trustee to make the application to suspend under s 303 if necessary. The Court of Appeal overturned this decision on the trustee's appeal since the bankrupt was acting for an impermissible purpose outside the scope of s 279(3). Kitchin LJ qualified Morritt C's remarks in *Shierson v Rastogi* and made clear that the power in s 279 was intended to be penal in character and used for purposes connected with getting in the estate. The trustee could not have acted perversely in refusing to authorise the bankrupt to make the application on his behalf, since the suspension was not linked to any failure by the bankrupt to comply with his obligations, nor was it made to ensure that he continued to suffer from the disabilities of being an undischarged bankrupt until he had fully complied with those obligations, nor for any other purpose that might be within s 279(3) of the 1986 Act. Penelope Reed QC (sitting as a deputy High Court judge) followed Kitchin LJ's approach in *Hellard v Kapoor* [2013] EWHC 2204 (Ch), [2013] BPIR 745 and held that incentivising the bankrupt to comply with his obligations was indeed relevant to the exercise of the power.

**Application and order that discharge period ceases to run**—An application under s 279(3) may be made either by the official receiver or by the trustee of a bankrupt's estate. The procedure on such an application is as provided for in r 10.142. The procedure on the lifting of a suspension of discharge appears in r 10.143. The lifting of a suspension of discharge is not retrospective and can only permit the period of bankruptcy to continue to run from the point at which the period was previously suspended.

In *Hardy v Focus Insurance Co Ltd* [1997] BPIR 77 at 82F–82G Robert Walker J held that the court has no jurisdiction, whether under s 303 or otherwise, to give directions to the official receiver to make an application for a suspension of discharge in the course of what amounts to his public law functions. That decision was made under the former s 279 under which the official receiver was the only eligible applicant. The amended s 279 allows for an application to be made by a trustee. While it might be thought that the jurisdiction of the court should be no different from that identified by Robert Walker J, in that an application by a trustee is hardly distinguishable from an application by the official receiver in terms of its public law function, it was taken for granted by Arnold J in *Bramston v Haut* [2012] EWHC 1279 (Ch), [2012] BPIR 672 that, in a suitable case, the court had power to direct the trustee to make an application under s 279. The Court of Appeal did not disagree, although it overturned Arnold J's decision on other grounds.

**Grounds of application**—In *Hellard v Kapoor* [2013] EWHC 2204 (Ch), [2013] BPIR 745 at [11], Penelope Reed QC (sitting as a High Court judge) accepted a bankrupt's submission that an applicant trustee was confined to reliance on the grounds actually set out in the application. But Nugee J in *Weir (as trustee in bankruptcy of Claire Elizabeth Hilsdon) v Hilsdon* [2017] EWHC 983 (Ch), [2017] BPIR 1088 expressed doubts about that approach. Nugee J favoured a more flexible approach and indicated, without expressing a concluded view, that while a trustee should not be permitted to spring an entirely new case on a bankrupt at the hearing, applications to suspend discharge often evolve between the initial application and the hearing and the judge should retain the ability to look at the situation as it stands at the time of the hearing.

**Timing of application**—Notwithstanding the requirement in r 10.142(5) that evidence in support of an application to suspend must reach the bankrupt at least 21 days before the date fixed for the suspension hearing, given the practical consequence that no action can be taken to reverse an automatic discharge from bankruptcy, the Court of Appeal has confirmed that the court has power to make an interim order on an urgent and without notice basis under r 7.4(6) of the 1986 Rules (now restated in IR 2016, r 12.10) suspending the bankrupt's automatic discharge until the substantive hearing of an application to suspend under s 279(3): *Bagnall v Official Receiver* [2003] EWCA Civ 1925, [2004] 1 WLR 2832, [2004] BPIR 445 (Arden LJ, Latham LJ agreeing). It was emphasised, however, in *Hellard v Kapoor* [2013] EWHC 2204, [2013] BPIR 745 (at [10]) by Penelope Reed QC (sitting as a deputy High Court judge) that the trustee should not wait to the last minute to seek suspension of discharge.

In *Chadwick v Nash* [2012] BPIR 70, the trustee was unsuccessful for reasons including the late stage at which the application was made. The registrar accepted that information supplied by the bankrupt was not as detailed as it might have been and that there were some omissions, inaccuracies and inconsistencies which led to suspicions and doubts. Nonetheless he did not consider this was sufficient to deprive the bankrupt of the right to automatic discharge in the circumstances (particularly, it would seem, where the trustee had not sought to meet and discuss matters with the bankrupt and had delayed in making the application until just 7 days before the scheduled discharge). A special feature of this case was that the registrar seems to have considered that the real motivation underlying the application was the pursuit by the trustee of an income payments agreement, which the bankrupt was resisting. In these circumstances the trustee should have resolved the uncertainties relating to the bankrupt's income by an application for an income payments order, not by a late application for suspension of discharge.

**Conditions applicable to a suspension order**—Section 279(3) envisages the possibility of suspension for a specified period, or subject to the fulfilment of a specified condition, such as the delivery up of particular property or answering specific questions, to the satisfaction of the trustee or the official receiver. A commonly used form of order, however, is that suspension shall continue indefinitely until the trustee has confirmed to the court in writing that the bankrupt has complied with his duties and obligations: *Mawer v Bland* [2013] EWHC 3122 (Ch), [2015] BPIR 1319 and the unsuccessful challenge to this form of order in *Wilson v Williams* [2015] EWHC 1841 (Ch), [2015] BPIR 1319. But caution should be exercised: in *Weir v Hilsdon* [2017] EWHC 983 (Ch), [2017] BPIR 1088, Nugee J reviewed all the authorities on suspension of discharge (including *Mawer v Bland* and *Wilson v Williams*) and allowed an appeal against an order in that indefinite form on the ground that, although such an order was one that it was open to the court to make and may be necessary in suitable cases, the court should always consider whether such an order is really justified on the facts of the case. It should not be treated as the default option and the court should consider whether a lesser order (such as for a fixed period or until specific questions are answered) is more suitable.

**The relevance of an application to annul a bankruptcy order**—The fact that a bankrupt has been discharged either automatically or following a suspended discharge does not affect the power of the court to annul a bankruptcy order: see also s 282(3). The court is likely to be reluctant to annul a bankruptcy order, however, where there is an outstanding application by the official receiver or a trustee to suspend discharge under s 279(3), at least not without further enquiry.

**Procedure on discharge**—IR 2016, r 11.17 the Secretary of State shall delete from the individual insolvency register all information concerning a bankruptcy where 3 months has elapsed from the date of discharge.

## [1.392]

### 280 Discharge by order of the court

(1) An application for an order of the court discharging an individual from bankruptcy in a case falling within section 279(6) may be made by the bankrupt at any time after the end of the period of 5 years beginning with the date on which the bankruptcy commences.

(2) On an application under this section the court may—

    (a)    refuse to discharge the bankrupt from bankruptcy,

    (b)    make an order discharging him absolutely, or

    (c)    make an order discharging him subject to such conditions with respect to any income which may subsequently become due to him, or with respect to property devolving upon him, or acquired by him, after his discharge, as may be specified in the order.

(3) The court may provide for an order falling within subsection (2)(b) or (c) to have immediate effect or to have its effect suspended for such period, or until the fulfilment of such conditions (including a condition requiring the court to be satisfied as to any matter), as may be specified in the order.

**Amendments**—Enterprise Act 2002, s 269, Sch 23, paras 1, 3(a), (b).

General note—This provision is now obsolete, in that it applies only where an application is made for discharge by an individual made bankrupt on a petition under s 264(1)(d) based on a criminal bankruptcy order after the end of the 5-year period commencing with the bankruptcy order. There will be no more such orders following the abolition of the court's power to make a criminal bankruptcy order with effect from 3 April 1989 by virtue of s 101 of the Criminal Justice Act 1988.

## [1.393]

### 281 Effect of discharge

(1) Subject as follows, where a bankrupt is discharged, the discharge releases him from all the bankruptcy debts, but has no effect—

   (a)   on the functions (so far as they remain to be carried out) of the trustee of his estate, or

   (b)   on the operation, for the purposes of the carrying out of those functions, of the provisions of this Part;

and, in particular, discharge does not affect the right of any creditor of the bankrupt to prove in the bankruptcy for any debt from which the bankrupt is released.

(2) Discharge does not affect the right of any secured creditor of the bankrupt to enforce his security for the payment of a debt from which the bankrupt is released.

(3) Discharge does not release the bankrupt from any bankruptcy debt which he incurred in respect of, or forbearance in respect of which was secured by means of, any fraud or fraudulent breach of trust to which he was a party.

(4) Discharge does not release the bankrupt from any liability in respect of a fine imposed for an offence or from any liability under a recognisance except, in the case of a penalty imposed for an offence under an enactment relating to the public revenue or of a recognisance, with the consent of the Treasury.

(4A) In subsection (4) the reference to a fine imposed for an offence includes a reference to—

   (a)   a charge ordered to be paid under section 46 of the Sentencing Code (criminal courts charge), whether on conviction or otherwise;

   (b)   a confiscation order under Part 2, 3 or 4 of the Proceeds of Crime Act 2002.

(5) Discharge does not, except to such extent and on such conditions as the court may direct, release the bankrupt from any bankruptcy debt which—

   (a)   consists in a liability to pay damages for negligence, nuisance or breach of a statutory, contractual or other duty, or to pay damages by virtue of Part I of the Consumer Protection Act 1987, being in either case damages in respect of personal injuries to any person, or

   (b)   arises under any order made in family proceedings or under a *maintenance assessment* maintenance calculation made under the Child Support Act 1991 . . ..

(6) Discharge does not release the bankrupt from such other bankruptcy debts, not being debts provable in his bankruptcy, as are prescribed.

(7) Discharge does not release any person other than the bankrupt from any liability (whether as partner or co-trustee of the bankrupt or otherwise) from which the bankrupt is released by the discharge, or from any liability as surety for the bankrupt or as a person in the nature of such a surety.

(8) In this section—

   "family proceedings" means—

      (a)   proceedings in the family court; and

      (b)   family proceedings within the meaning of Part V of the Matrimonial and Family Proceedings Act 1984.

   "fine" means the same as in the Magistrates' Courts Act 1980; and

   "personal injuries" includes death and any disease or other impairment of a person's physical or mental condition.

Amendments— Consumer Protection Act 1987, Children Act 1989, ss 92(11), 108(7) Sch 11, Pt II, para 11(1), (2), Sch 15; s 48, Sch 4, para 12; Child Support Act 1991, s 58(13), Sch 5, para 7;

Child Support, Pensions and Social Security Act 2000, s 26, Sch 3, para 6, partly as from a date to be appointed; Proceeds of Crime Act 2002, s 456, Sch 11, paras 1, 16(1), (2); Crime and Courts Act 2013, s 17(5), Sch 10, Pt 2, para 74; Criminal Justice and Courts Act 2015, s 54(3), Sch 12, para 6; Sentencing Act 2020, s 410, Sch 24, Pt 1, para 88.

**General note**—The most significant consequence of discharge from bankruptcy is the release of the bankrupt from bankruptcy debts, subject to the exceptions identified in this section. Discharge does not, however, operate so as to re-vest any part of the bankruptcy estate in the discharged individual, a point which can come as a surprise to some bankrupts.

The process of discharge itself has no bearing either on the conduct of the bankruptcy by the trustee, whose general functions remain as provided for under s 305, or on the procedure for the proving of debt under rr 14.2–14.11.

Discharge takes effect immediately to remove the disqualifications imposed by s 427 (membership of either House of Parliament), s 63A of the Justices of the Peace Act 1979 (Justice of the Peace) and s 11 of the Company Directors Disqualification Act 1986 (company director).

**'Discharge and the running of time for limitation period purposes'**—In *Anglo Manx Group Ltd v Aitken* [2002] BPIR 215 at [69] John Jarvis QC (sitting as a deputy High Court judge) held, following the Court of Appeal's decision in *Re Benzon, Bower v Chetwynd* [1914] 2 Ch 68, that the IA 1986 contains nothing which should detract from the earlier established principle that time does not cease to run for limitation purposes during the period of bankruptcy. This point is of particular relevance to those debts, considered under the next two sub-headings below, which are not released on discharge.

### SECTION 281(1)

' . . . the discharge releases him from all the bankruptcy debts . . . '—The term 'bankruptcy debt' is defined in s 382(1) and should be read in conjunction with s 382(2)–(4), which give the term an extremely broad scope. It includes a liability to repay overpaid benefits, so that upon discharge, this liability is released and deductions cannot be made against future benefit payments: *Secretary of State for Work and Pensions v Balding* [2007] EWCA Civ 1327, [2008] 1 WLR 564, [2007] BPIR 1669; approved by the Supreme Court in *Secretary of State for Work and Pensions v Payne* [2011] UKSC 60, [2012] 2 AC 1, [2012] BPIR 224 (which held that such deductions were a 'remedy' caught by the moratorium imposed by s 251G(2)(a) of the IA 1986 when a debt relief order was in place). A solicitor's liability to pay compensation imposed by the Legal Complaints Service was not a 'bankruptcy debt' where the matter complained of arose prior to the bankruptcy but the award was not made until afterwards, since the obligation to pay compensation could not properly be characterised as a contingent liability prior to the bankruptcy: *Casson and Wales v The Law Society* [2009] EWHC 1943 (Admin), [2010] BPIR 49. Cases limiting the scope of 'bankruptcy debt' that were decided prior to the Supreme Court's detailed consideration of this area in *In Re Nortel GmbH (in administration)* [2013] UKSC 52, [2014] AC 209, [2013] 2 BCLC 135 should be approached with some caution.

The exceptions in s 281 (3)–(7) to the general release under s 281(1) are justifiable in each case on public policy grounds and serve to avoid the abuse of the bankruptcy procedure as a means of escaping such liabilities.

The proviso in the final part of s 281(1) operates to preserve the underlying cause of action giving rise to a creditor's claim so as to allow for its proof in the bankruptcy after discharge: *Law Society v Official Receiver* [2007] EWHC 2841 (Ch), [2009] Ch 223, [2007] BPIR 1595 at [34]–[37] (Floyd J).

**The effect of discharge on debts from which a bankrupt is not released**—Discharge has a different effect on debts which are not released under s 281(1), depending on whether any such debt is provable or not provable in the bankruptcy.

IR 2016, r 14.1 provides a general rule that all claims by creditors are provable, subject to specific exceptions in r 14.2(2)-(4), which provisions extend to obligations arising under an order made in family proceedings (as defined therein) or under a maintenance assessment made under the Child Support Act 1991, a confiscation order under Parts 2, 3 or 4 of the Proceeds of Crime Act 2002 and any claim arising under s 382(1)(a) of the Financial Services and Markets Act 2000, not being a claim under s 382(1)(b) of the 2000 Act. If a debt which is not released is provable in the bankruptcy then, prior to discharge, a creditor may not commence any action or legal proceedings in respect of the debt other than with leave of the court, by virtue of s 285(3), subject to ss 346 (enforcement procedures) and 347 (limited right to distress). On the other hand, a creditor whose debt is not released, and which is not provable, is not caught by the limitations imposed by the bankruptcy procedure or by s 285(3), with the consequence that the creditor may pursue the bankrupt prior to or following discharge. Thus, in *Re X (a Bankrupt)* [1996] BPIR 494 Singer J, sitting in the Family Division of the High Court, held that a bankrupt father was not protected by his bankruptcy or by s 285(3) from a lump sum order made in favour of the mother of the bankrupt's child under para 5 of Sch 1 to the Children Act 1989, since that debt was neither provable nor released on discharge. Arrears of child support maintenance payments were, however, held to be provable in a deceased insolvent estate in *Re Tovey (deceased)* [2016] EWHC

1418 (Ch), [2016] BPIR 1256. HHJ McCahill QC (sitting as a High Court judge) took a purposive approach to the regime to reach this conclusion. The rationale for the outcome appears to have been that, by definition, a deceased debtor cannot be financially rehabilitated by bankruptcy and so the creditor has no prospect of payment from the debtor post-discharge; if the debt is not provable the creditor has no recourse and will receive nothing, which is the opposite of the policy underlying exempting certain debts from release on discharge from bankruptcy.

**The effect of discharge on after-acquired property claims under s 307 and income payments orders under s 310**—A trustee may not claim after-acquired property for the benefit of the estate after discharge: s 307(2)(c). Neither may an income payments order be made after discharge, although the period for which such an order is made may extend beyond discharge: s 310(1A)(b) and (6)(a).

### SECTION 281(3)

'**Any bankruptcy debt . . . incurred in respect of, or forbearance in respect of which was secured by means of, any fraud or fraudulent breach of trust . . .** '—In *Mander v Evans* [2001] 1 WLR 2378, [2001] BPIR 902 at [25] Ferris J held that the word 'fraud' in this provision means actual fraud in the sense explained by the House of Lords in *Derry v Peek* (1889) 14 App Cas 337. In rejecting an argument for a wider definition of the term his Lordship went on to say that he found it 'much less comprehensible that [the bankrupt] should remain liable for constructive fraud, which covers a wide range of conduct regarded by equity as unconscionable but not necessarily involving actual dishonesty.' In *Woodland-Ferrari v UCL Group Retirement Benefit Schemes* [2002] EWHC 1354 (Ch), [2003] Ch 115, [2002] BPIR 1270 Ferris J went on to identify at [37]–[50] that the term 'fraudulent breach of trust' has no wider meaning than the term 'fraud' in s 281(3) and therefore requires proof of dishonesty as an essential ingredient.

The burden of proof in establishing fraud within the meaning of *Mander v Evans* will rest on a creditor. That burden will not be discharged, however, merely by production of a foreign default judgment based purely on a single cause of action alleging fraud: *Masters v Leaver* [2000] BPIR 284 (Morritt and Thorpe LJJ and Sir Oliver Popplewell, appeal against summary judgment upheld where deputy judge below granted judgment based on a Texan default judgment which, notably, was itself based on actual fraud on the part of the bankrupt). For another example of a case where an allegation that certain of the bankrupt's debts fell within 281(3) failed on the facts see *Soutzos v Asombang* [2010] EWHC 842 (Ch), [2010] BPIR 960, where it was empahasised the burden of proof was on the creditor, and the creditors' claims against the bankrupt in deceit and the tort of conspiracy to injure by unlawful means were not made out.

The utility to defrauded creditors of this provision was tempered in *Hemsley v Bance* [2016] EWHC 1028 (Ch), [2016] BPIR 934, in which Registrar Jones declined to make a bankruptcy order and dismissed a petition presented in respect of a debt arising from the debtor's fraud, which had not been released on the debtor's first bankruptcy pursuant to s 281(3). Registrar Jones considered that if the debtor had concealed assets (as the creditor contended) then such assets continued to be caught by the first bankruptcy and therefore no purpose would be served by a second bankruptcy order.

In *The Pensions Regulator v Payae Limited* [2018] EWHC 36 (Ch), the claimant regulator brought proceedings under s 16 of the Pensions Act 2004 arising from an improper pension 'liberation' scheme. The case was deliberately advanced on the basis of dishonesty, despite there being no dishonesty requirement in the cause of action, in order to bring any judgment within the scope of s 281(3), see [5]. In making findings of dishonesty, HHJ Pelling QC (sitting as a High Court judge) applied the test for dishonesty as restated by the Supreme Court in *Ivey v Genting Casinos (UK) Ltd* [2017] UKSC 67, [2017] 3 WLR 1212, [15].

### SECTION 281(4)

**Fines and other penalties**—A fine imposed for an offence is not provable by virtue of r 14.2(2)(c). Section 281(8) provides that the term 'fine' is as defined in s 150(1) of the Magistrates' Courts Act 1980 as extended by s 281(4A) below. The term 'recognisance' may be more readily understood by English lawyers as equating to the American bail bond.

### SECTION 281(4A)

**Scope of provision**—This provision was inserted by s 456 of, and para 16 of Sch 11 to the Proceeds of Crime Act 2002 and amended by the Criminal Justice and Courts Act 2015, s 54(3), Sch 12, para 6.

### SECTION 281(5)

**The court's discretion to order release**—The discretion afforded to the court under this section to order the debtor's release from the bankruptcy debts described in s 281(5)(a) and (b) was subject to detailed examination by HHJ Pelling QC, sitting as a High Court judge, in *Hayes v Hayes* [2012] EWHC 1240 (Ch), [2012] BPIR 739 and Hildyard J in *McRoberts v McRoberts* [2012] EWHC 2966 (Ch), [2013] 1 WLR 1601, [2013] BPIR 77. These cases indicate that the discretion is unfettered, and has to be exercised by reference to all the relevant circumstances as they existed at the date when the application was determined, including: (a) any lapse of time between the date when the discharge occurred and the date of any application for release, and the reasons for any delay; (b) the future earning capacity of the applicant, the possibility of some future income or capital receipt or windfall, the prospect accordingly of the obligation being fulfilled in whole or in part if not released, and in the round whether there was any good reason for maintaining the obligation; (c) the risk of the respondent to the application using the fact of the obligation (if not released) to harass the applicant, for example by seeking to diminish the applicant in the eyes of the community, or his future prospects, by reference to the stigma still relating to bankruptcy, or by bringing new and abusive bankruptcy proceedings calculated to restrict the applicant in building a new life; and (d) the duration of time that had elapsed since the relevant obligation arose. The default position is that the obligation should remain in place and the burden is on the applicant to show the balance of prejudice favours its release.

### SECTION 281(6)

**Other bankruptcy debts as prescribed**—This provision extends to non-provable debts on which see r 10.146. Neither is liability for a student loan discharged by virtue of s 42 of the Higher Education Act 2004 and reg 5 of the Education (Student Support) (No 2) Regulations 2002 (Amendment) Regulations 2004 (SI 2004/2041).

### SECTION 281(7)

**Liability as surety etc**—Discharge only releases the bankrupt from liability and has no bearing on a partner, co-trustee, co-indemnifier or surety who is personally liable for the same debt. In the case of sureties, this provision overrides earlier authorities (as did s 28(4) of the Bankruptcy Act 1914), such as *Re Moss* [1905] 2 KB 307, in which a surety was held to have no liability for interest on a debt for which the debtor would have been liable had he or she not been made bankrupt. See *Evans v Finance-U-Ltd* [2013] EWCA Civ 869, [2013] BPIR 1001.

## [1.394]

### 281A  Post-discharge restrictions

Schedule 4A to this Act (bankruptcy restrictions order and bankruptcy restrictions undertaking) shall have effect.

**Amendments**—Inserted by Enterprise Act 2002, s 257(1).

**General note**—With effect from 1 April 2004, s 257 of and Schs 20 and 21 to the Enterprise Act 2002 introduced the new concepts of bankruptcy restriction orders ('BROs') and bankruptcy restriction undertakings ('BRUs') to which this provision gives effect. No transitional provisions govern the new provisions. However, art 7 of the Enterprise Act 2002 (Commencement No 4 and Transitional Provisions and Savings) Order 2003 (SI 2003/2093) provides that, in considering whether or not to make a BRO, the court shall not take into account any conduct of the bankrupt before 1 April 2004.

The substance of the provisions governing BROs and BRUs appears in Sch 4A, although those provisions do not prescribe the effect of a BRO, which is to be found in the amendments in Sch 21 to the Enterprise Act 2001.

In short, para 1 of Sch 4A allows for a BRO to be made on application to the Secretary of State or the official receiver acting on a direction of the Secretary of State. Paragraph 3 requires an application to be made within one year of the bankruptcy order (even, apparently, if the bankrupt is discharged within the one-year period) or later with the permission of the court. The ordinary one-year period ceases to run whilst discharge is suspended under s 279(3). In considering the making of an order para 2(1) provides that the court 'shall' grant an application for a BRO 'if it thinks it appropriate having regard to the conduct of the bankrupt (whether before or after the making of the bankruptcy order)'. Paragraph 2(2) requires that the court 'shall, in particular, take into account' any of 13 specific factors, whilst para 2(3) also requires the court to consider whether the bankrupt was an undischarged bankrupt at some time during the period of 6 years ending with the date of the bankruptcy to which the application relates. Paragraph 4 allows the court to make a BRO for a period of between 2 years and 15 years in addition to provision being made in para 5 for the making of an interim BRO pending determination of a substantive application. Paragraphs 7 and 9 provide for the entering into of BRUs. Paragraphs 10 and 11 provide for the differing effects of annulment on a BRO or BRU, depending on the provision under which the annulment is granted.

The principal restrictions imposed on a person subject to a BRO are (i) a prohibition on the obtaining of credit of more than £500 without disclosure that the individual is subject to a BRO, (ii) a prohibition against an individual acting in the promotion, formation or management of a company without permission of the court, (iii) a prohibition against trading under any name other than that in which the individual was made bankrupt without disclosure of that name, (iv) a prohibition against acting as an LPA receiver of the property of a company other than in the very unlikely circumstances of a court appointment, and (v) a prohibition against acting as an insolvency practitioner. The additional disqualifications identified in the notes to s 281 also apply, in addition to which the Secretary of State may provide for additional restrictions under s 268 of the Enterprise Act 2002.

**Exercise of the court's jurisdiction**—In *Randhawa v Official Receiver* [2006] EWHC 2946 (Ch), [2007] 1 WLR 1700, [2006] BPIR 1435, Launcelot Henderson QC, sitting as a deputy High Court judge, considered the BRO jurisdiction in some detail. The following four principles appear from the judgment. First, the purpose of a BRO is one of public protection comprising three distinct elements: (a) keeping bankrupts whose conduct warrants a BRO 'off the road'; (b) deterring such bankrupts from repeating such conduct (individual deterrence); and (c) deterring others (general deterrence): see [69] and [72]–[75]. Secondly, the jurisdiction is not one of general discretion but one entirely analogous to the regime under s 6 of the Company Directors' Disqualification Act 1986. Accordingly, the court is required to determine whether any of the conduct alleged has been established and, if so, to determine whether that conduct, viewed individually and cumulatively, and taking account of any extenuating circumstances, is such as to establish that the defendant has so seriously failed to meet the proper standards of probity and competence as fixed by courts, being the standards required of individuals in conducting their financial affairs, as to warrant the making of a BRO; if it does then the court has no discretion and is required to make an order: see [64], [65], [68] and [71]–[75]. Thirdly, although the court will consider conduct within para 2(2) of Sch 4A, and any prior bankruptcy under para 2(3), the fact of such conduct does not of itself warrant the making of a BRO. Further, conduct not falling within para 2(2) may be sufficiently serious to justify a BRO: [66]. Fourthly, the period of a BRO is in the discretion of the judge but should be fixed by reference to the principles in *Re Sevenoaks Stationers (Retail) Ltd* [1991] Ch 164, [1991] BCLC 325, at [88].

In *Official Receiver v Doganci* [2007] BPIR 87 Chief Registrar Baister, considering *Randhawa*, dismissed an application for a BRO where the sole ground relied on by the official receiver was an allegation that the debtor, made bankrupt on his own petition, had rented a piano worth over £9,000 and had failed to account satisfactorily for its disposal. Though not entirely satisfactory, the bankrupt's evidence was not unbelievable.

In *Official Receiver v Southay* [2009] BPIR 89 the court refused to make a BRO because it was not satisfied that the bankrupt had incurred a debt which he had no reasonable expectation of being able to repay – there had been a reasonable chance of repayment (albeit not a likelihood). The bankrupt had incurred debt previously which he had always managed to repay and had simply misjudged his ability to make repayment on this occasion. This conduct fell short of the relatively high threshold required for a BRO.

**Period of the BRO**—In *Jenkins v The Official Receiver* [2007] EWHC 1402 (Ch), [2007] BPIR 740 Rimer J dismissed an appeal against a BRO of 4 years imposed upon an individual who could be shown to have acted in wilful defiance of a bankruptcy restrictions undertaking entered into by the debtor who had continued to act as a company director irresponsibly and without sanction contrary to terms which had been stressed to him at the outset. It did not matter that the individual might have obtained leave to act as a director or that an order annulling the bankruptcy had been obtained.

In *Official Receiver v Pyman* [2007] EWHC 2002 (Ch), [2007] BPIR 1150 Stuart Isaacs QC, sitting as a deputy High Court judge, allowed an appeal by the official receiver against an order of a deputy district judge imposing a BRO for 4 years, extending the period to 7 years. Although necessarily fact specific, the deputy judge emphasised at [24] that, whilst the main object of making a BRO must undoubtedly be the protection of the public, the jurisdiction also had a deterrent effect which has two distinct aspects by way of, first, the deterrence of the bankrupt himself repeating the misconduct complained of and, secondly, the deterrence of others.

In *Official Receiver v Bathurst* [2008] EWHC 1724 (Ch), [2008] BPIR 1548 Morritt C allowed an appeal from a district judge and imposed a BRO for 9 years in place of the 3-year order below. In particular, the district judge had failed to take proper account of the bankrupt's failure to co-operate with the official receiver and the level of the bankrupt's personal expenditure.

Where a district judge had formed the view that a bankrupt's conduct was culpable, so as to constitute that justifying the making of a BRO, she had no discretion to refuse to make a BRO and was obliged to impose such an order for at least 2 years: *Official Receiver v May* [2008] EWHC 1778 (Ch), [2008] BPIR 1562 (Christopher Nugee QC sitting as a deputy High Court judge; BRO of 2 years and 6 months imposed on official receiver's appeal).

An 8-year BRO was successfully appealed in *Official Receiver v Going* [2011] EWHC 786 (Ch), [2011] BPIR 1069 on the basis that the conclusions reached by the district judge at first instance could not be supported on the evidence. HHJ Pelling QC, sitting as a High Court judge, rejected the OR's argument that the BRO should nevertheless be maintained (albeit for a reduced period) on the basis of additional allegations which, although set out in the allegations in the OR's report, had not been the subject of submissions and about which no findings had been made by the district judge: it was not open to an appeal court to make essentially an entirely new order by reference to issues which had not been argued before the court below.

**Time period for making an application**—An application for a BRO must be made within a year from the date of the bankruptcy or the court's permission is required. The court considered the factors to be considered in deciding whether to grant permission for a late application in *Official Recevier v Baars* [2009] BPIR 524. The main factors to be taken into account were the length of the delay, the reason for the delay and the strength of the case against the bankrupt. A failure to comply with disclosure obligations so that an asset was not discovered until after the expiry of the one-year period was an obvious circumstance when, depending on the facts, such an application should be allowed to proceed.

**The impact of the Human Rights Act 1998**—The bankrupt's challenge to the interim BRO procedure on the ground that it infringed his human rights under Art 6 of the ECHR (right to a fair trial) failed in *Michael v Official Receiver* [2010] EWHC 2246 (Ch).

## [1.395]

### 282 Court's power to annul bankruptcy order

(1) The court may annul a bankruptcy order if it at any time appears to the court—

    (a) that, on the grounds existing at the time the order was made, the order ought not to have been made, or

    (b) that, to the extent required by the rules, the bankruptcy debts and the expenses of the bankruptcy have all, since the making of the order, been either paid or secured for to the satisfaction of the court.

*(2) The court may annul a bankruptcy order made against an individual on a petition under paragraph (a) or (c) of section 264(1) or on a bankruptcy application if it at any time appears to the court, on an application by the Official Petitioner—*

    *(a) that the petition was pending or the application was ongoing at a time when a criminal bankruptcy order was made against the individual or was presented after such an order was so made, and*

    *(b) no appeal is pending (within the meaning of section 277) against the individual's conviction of any offence by virtue of which the criminal bankruptcy order was made;*

*and the court shall annul a bankruptcy order made on a petition under section 264(1)(d) if it at any time appears to the court that the criminal bankruptcy order on which the petition was based has been rescinded in consequence of an appeal.*

(3) The court may annul a bankruptcy order whether or not the bankrupt has been discharged from the bankruptcy.

(4) Where the court annuls a bankruptcy order (whether under this section or under section 261 in Part VIII)—

    (a) any sale or other disposition of property, payment made or other thing duly done, under any provision in this Group of Parts, by or under the authority of the official receiver or a trustee of the bankrupt's estate or by the court is valid, but

    (b) if any of the bankrupt's estate is then vested, under any such provision, in such a trustee, it shall vest in such person as the court may appoint or, in default of any such appointment, revert to the bankrupt on such terms (if any) as the court may direct;

and the court may include in its order such supplemental provisions as may be authorised by the rules.

(5) . . .

**Amendments**—Words in italics repealed by Criminal Justice Act 1988, s 170(2), Sch 16, as from a date to be appointed; Enterprise Act 2002, ss 269, 278(2), Sch 23, paras 1, 4(a), (b), Sch 26; Enterprise and Regulatory Reform Act 2013, s 71(3), Sch 19, paras 1, 13; Small Business, Enterprise and Employment Act 2015, 135(2)(a).

**General note**—An annulment may also be obtained under s 261(2) on the approval of an IVA proposed by an undischarged bankrupt. Alternatively, the same effect may be obtained through the rescission of a bankruptcy order under s 375(1). On the relationship between annulment under s 282(1)(a) and appeal, see the comments of HHJ Kaye QC (sitting as a High Court judge) in *Johnson v Tandridge District Council* [2007] EWHC 3325 (Ch), [2008] BPIR 405 at [29]–[32].

**Annulment and bankruptcy restrictions orders**—Where an annulment order was made under s 282(1)(b) the court retained jurisdiction to make a bankruptcy restrictions order on the same day provided the application for the BRO had been made prior to the annulment and before the one year period commencing with the date of the bankruptcy order: *Jenkins v The Official Receiver* [2007] EWHC 1402 (Ch), [2007] BPIR 740 at [12] (Rimer J).

**The court's jurisdiction to annul**—Prior to the Bankruptcy Act 1914 it had been held in *Ex parte Ashworth* (1874) LR 18 Eq 705 that, in the absence of statutory enactment, there was an inherent jurisdiction in the court to annul what was previously termed a receiving order where good reason could be established. In *Re A Debtor (No 68 of 1992), Royal Bank of Scotland v The Debtor* [1996] BPIR 478 at 479A–479D, Harman J (in the course of overturning an annulment granted by a deputy district judge) held that there is no longer a general discretion or inherent jurisdiction in the court and that the only basis for annulling a bankruptcy order – apart from the alternative methods identified in the general note above, which were not relevant – is as provided for in s 282(1)(a) and (b). Those observations were not the subject of the appeal from that decision, reported as *Royal Bank of Scotland v Farley* [1996] BPIR 638, in which appeal Hoffmann LJ identified at 640A–640D that it is appropriate for a bankruptcy court on an annulment application to go behind a default judgment: see, for example, *Hunter v Lex Vehicles Ltd* [2005] EWHC 223 (Ch), [2005] BPIR 586 (David Richards J). In *Yang v Official Receiver* [2017] EWCA Civ 1465, [2018] Ch 178, [2018] BPIR 255, Gloster LJ declined to follow Hoffmann LJ's approach in Farley, distinguished it, and at 193E expressed some doubt about it. Care should be taken in applying Farley to circumstances other than default judgment and regard should be had to *Yang*. See further notes under heading 'Interaction between annulment and rescission' below.

Since there is a single High Court, in which judges are assigned to any particular Division, each Division applies precisely the same principles on an application to annul: *Whig v Whig* [2007] EWHC 1856 (Fam), [2007] BPIR 1418 at [55]–[60] (Munby J).

**Eligible applicants**—In contrast to s 29 of the Bankruptcy Act 1914, which allowed for an application for an annulment only by 'any person interested', the present provision makes no mention of persons who might apply for an annulment. Indeed, s 282 itself makes no reference to the making of an order on an application, which might suggest that the court has jurisdiction to make an order, at least under s 282(1)(a), of its own volition. Rule 10.132 indicates that, in the case of application being made, the application need not be made by the bankrupt. In *F v F (divorce: insolvency: annulment of bankruptcy order)* [1994] 1 FLR 359, for example, the court ordered an annulment under s 282(1)(a) on the application of a bankrupt's wife who satisfied the court that the bankrupt's bankruptcy petition misrepresented his true financial circumstances. Further in *Die Sparkasse Bremen AG v Armutcu* [2012] EWHC 4026 (Ch), [2013] BPIR 210 Proudman J considered that even a secured creditor could apply for an annulment where it could show a legitimate interest in the matter, as for instance where there was likely to be a significant shortfall when the security was realised. A creditor successfully applied for annulment in *Re Leitzbach (a bankrupt)* [2018] EWHC 1544 (Ch), [2019] BPIR 1299. The court will, however, approach with some caution an application by a person with no immediately obvious interest in the annulment.

**Relevance of debtor's motive in obtaining bankruptcy order**—Where an applicant seeks an order under s 282(1)(a) the burden of proof rests on the applicant on the balance of probabilities. It had been held that, where an annulment is sought on the basis that the debtor has presented a false picture of his or her financial position in obtaining a bankruptcy order, a high standard of proof is required to reflect the gravity of the stain on the debtor's integrity: *Whig v Whig* [2007] EWHC 1856 (Fam), [2007] BPIR 1418 at [51] (Munby J) but the Court of Appeal has confirmed in *Paulin v Paulin* [2009] EWCA Civ 221, [2010] 1 WLR 1057, [2009] BPIR 572 that this reference to a higher standard should be regarded as wrong. While the onus is on the applicant to show the bankruptcy order should never have been made, the burden of proof is the ordinary burden in civil cases. Furthermore, the Court of Appeal considered that where the applicant establishes the debtor was not insolvent on a balance sheet basis, the debtor falls under an evidential burden to establish commercial insolvency (ie that nevertheless he was unable to pay his debts). Adverse inferences could be drawn against a debtor who prevaricated and failed to give a candid account of his affairs. In *Arif v Zar* [2012] EWCA Civ 986, [2012] BPIR 948 the Court of Appeal emphasised the fact that the courts should be alive to the real possibility of debtors attempting to use the protection of a bankruptcy order as a shield against ancillary relief proceedings and, where there is credible evidence of this, judges and registrars should not be afraid to use their powers of ordering full disclosure and cross examination and for this purpose it may be more cost effective to transfer the matter to be dealt with alongside the ancilliary relief proceedings.

If satisfied, however, that the debtor is, in fact, insolvent within the meaning of s 272(1) – on which see the notes thereto – the court cannot annul the bankruptcy order under s 282(1)(a), even if the debtor's purpose was corrupt or self-serving: see *Whig* at [54] and the survey of the cases at [55]–[66]. See also *Paulin v Paulin* [2009] EWCA Civ 221, [2010] 1 WLR 1057, [2009] BPIR 572 where the Court of Appeal considered that it is safe to assume that if a debtor is insolvent on the date of his or her petition (now application) its presentation is not an abuse of process (at [48]) but if, on the other hand, the debtor was solvent and the court must then go on to exercise its discretion as to whether to annul the bankruptcy, the debtor's motive in procuring bankruptcy will be a relevant factor (at [53]). For an example of a failed annulment application by a wife in respect of her estranged husband's bankruptcy see *Re Ruiz* [2011] EWHC 913 (Ch), [2011] BPIR 1139 (permission to appeal refused at a hearing before the Court of Appeal – see [2011] EWCA Civ 1646, [2012] BPIR 446).

**The court's two stage approach to a s 282(1)(a) application**—In *Society of Lloyds v Waters* [2001] BPIR 698 at 704G–705C Park J identified that s 282(1)(a) requires the court to proceed in two stages:

'First, it must ask whether, at the time that the bankruptcy order was made . . . any grounds existed on the basis of which the order ought not to have been made. If it does not appear to the court that any such grounds existed, the bankruptcy order stays in place and the second stage is not reached. If, however, it does appear to the court that such grounds existed, the second stage is reached. At that stage the court has a discretion whether or not to annul the bankruptcy. It is only a discretion, not a duty; the word is "may", not "shall".'

Park J went on in *Waters* to make the following observations as to the first of the two stages. In looking back to the time of the bankruptcy order, it does not matter that the debtor did not put before the court those grounds which existed at that time and on which the bankruptcy order ought not to have been made. In other words, it is sufficient for the debtor to put those grounds before the court on the hearing of the annulment application, provided that they can be shown to have existed at the time of the hearing of the bankruptcy petition. However, the burden of proof in establishing the existence of those grounds at the earlier time rests on the applicant; it is not good enough for the bankrupt to say that such grounds *may* have existed at that time. Furthermore, a debtor is not entitled to an annulment and must still make out his grounds in the event of a petitioning creditor's non-attendance: *Leicester v Plumtree Farms Ltd* [2003] EWHC 206 (Ch), [2004] BPIR 296, per Lloyd J. An application may in any case be open to challenge by a creditor who argues that grounds raised by the bankrupt on the annulment application were available to him at the bankruptcy hearing and, as such, constitute abuse of process. In *Crammer v West Bromwich Building Society* [2012] EWCA Civ 517, [2012] BPIR 963 the Court of Appeal confirmed that the court can take into account in the exercise of its discretion any matters which had not already been adjudicated upon, even if they could have been raised earlier, but if the creditor had acted reasonably in seeking the bankruptcy order and the debtor had failed to raise defences open to him at an earlier stage the court was not bound to grant the annulment. By contrast, it would be only in exceptional circumstances that the court would allow points already raised and rejected at the statutory demand/hearing of the petition to be re-litigated on an annulment application. The authorities in this area were reviewed by the Court of Appeal in *Harvey v Dunbar Assets plc* [2017] EWCA Civ 60, [2017] BPIR 450, which held that re-running arguments at different stages of the bankruptcy process would usually be an abuse of process in the absence of a change of circumstances or some other special reason. For an example of such exceptional circumstances see *Mowbray v Sanders* [2015] EWHC 296 (Ch), [2015] BPIR 665.

For an example of the court taking a flexible approach to late evidence, see *1st Credit (Finance) Ltd v Carr* [2013] EWHC 2318 (Ch), [2013] BPIR 1012 (an annulment was granted in respect of a debtor who had informed the court at his bankruptcy hearing that he was able to pay the debt, which unsupported suggestion had been rejected, but who later produced a bank statement showing he had had sufficient funds). On the question of the introduction of fresh evidence see also *Oraki v Dean and Dean (A Firm)* [2012] EWHC 2885 (Ch), [2013] BPIR 88 (upheld by the Court of Appeal, the evidence point not being appealed, [2013] EWCA Civ 1629, [2014] BPIR 266).

Where an application proceeds under s 282(1)(a) on the basis of the bankrupt disputing the petition debt, it has been held by Neuberger J that the appropriate test should equate to that under CPR 24.2 as to whether there is a real issue to be tried: *Guinan III v Caldwell Associates Ltd* [2003] EWHC 3348 (Ch), [2004] BPIR 531 at [32]–[33]. However, in *Flett v HMRC* [2010] EWHC 2662 (Ch), [2010] BPIR 1075 Anthony Ellray QC (sitting as a deputy High Court judge) drew a distinction between a debtor challenging the making of a bankruptcy order (where the question for the court is whether the debtor's evidence establishes a real prospect of making out the alleged defence) and a debtor making an application under s 282(1)(a), where the bankrupt is trying to establish that the bankruptcy order ought not to have been made on grounds existing at the time the order was made: 'In context it appears to me that the court hearing the application of the debtor for annulment must be satisfied as to those grounds on the balance of probability. It may not be enough in my view for a debtor to say at the time of an application for annulment: "I had an arguable defence to a given case". He should be saying: "I did not in fact owe the money for this or that reason," and it is for that reason that he now seeks the annulment of the order.' (at [46]). The conflict between the tests expounded in *Guinan* and *Flett* was considered by John Male QC (sitting as a deputy High Court judge) in *Re Payne; Woolsey v Payne* [2015] EWHC 968 (Ch), [2015]

BPIR 933, where he concluded that the approach of Neuberger J in Guinan was to be preferred and that the test was the same as for setting aside a statutory demand, namely 'was there a genuinely disputed debt?'

As regards the second stage of the process identified in *Waters*, the court retains a very wide discretion in the exercise of which some general guidance may be gleaned from some of the reported authorities. In *Askew v Peter Dominic Ltd* [1997] BPIR 163 Millett LJ (with whom Sir John Balcombe agreed) refused leave to appeal from a decision of HHJ Cooke who, on an appeal from a district judge, had refused to exercise his discretion in annulling a bankruptcy order notwithstanding the fact that Judge Cooke had described the statutory demand and the bankruptcy petition leading to the order as 'sheer nonsense', given technical defects which mis-described the source of the appellant's indebtedness but which, notably, could not possibly have misled the appellant. More importantly, however, Millett LJ identified (at 164F–164H) that, despite those observations, Judge Cooke had relied heavily upon the fact that the appellant was plainly indebted to the petitioning creditor, that the appellant did not dispute the debt and that, if sued, the appellant would have no defence to the petitioning creditor's claim. Accordingly, the only effect of annulling the bankruptcy order would have been to compel the petitioning creditor to serve a fresh statutory demand which the appellant could neither satisfy nor have set aside. *Askew* was accepted as authority for the proposition that the court may refuse to annul a bankruptcy order even if prima facie grounds to annul are made out, as held by Chief Registrar Baister in *Omokwe v HFC Bank Ltd* [2007] BPIR 1157 (at [37]–[38]). Further, in exercising its discretion the court should always have regard to the ability of a debtor to meet his or her liabilities: see, for example, *Owo-Samson v Barclays Bank* [2003] EWCA Civ 714, [2003] BPIR 1373.

A tension may be detected in the authorities concerning the extent of the discretion. In *Re Leitzbach (a bankrupt)* [2018] EWHC 1544 (Ch), [2018] BPIR 1299, HHJ Hodge QC held that where a debtor's COMI was not in England and Wales, there had been no jurisdiction to make the bankruptcy order. The judge held at [45], [84] that where a bankruptcy order is made without jurisdiction it should be annulled under s 282(1)(a) without consideration of discretionary matters. *Leitzbach* may be contrasted with *Ardawa v Uppal* [2019] EWHC 456 (Ch), [2019] BPIR 475, where a bankruptcy order had been made following service of the petition by means of a retrospective order for substituted service, for which there was no jurisdiction ([48]). Roth J held that this had been a fundamental failure regarding the rules as to service and could not be cured by r 7.55 of the IR 1986 (replaced by r 12.64 of the IR 2016). Nonetheless, the decision whether or not to annul the bankruptcy order remained a matter of discretion, despite this fundamental failing, and taking into account a series of factors, Roth J decided at [66] not to grant annulment.

In *Housiaux v HM Customs & Excise* [2003] EWCA Civ 257, [2003] BPIR 858 (at [25]–[26]) Chadwick LJ (with whom Morland J and Thorpe LJ agreed) identified bankruptcy as a class remedy which necessitated that, when asked to make an order under s 282(1)(a), a court ought to satisfy itself, by such investigation of the facts as it thinks necessary, that the bankruptcy order ought not to have been made. Accordingly, the court should not annul a bankruptcy order by consent and without investigation. Even where a petitioning creditor does not oppose an annulment of a bankruptcy order, the petitioning creditor should make it clear that he or she does not challenge the factual basis, or identified parts of the factual basis, upon which the application for annulment is made.

In *Hope v Premierpace (Europe) Ltd* [1999] BPIR 695 Rimer J held at 698E–698H, again in the course of an appeal, that a district judge had been wrong to refuse an annulment where a bankruptcy petition had been made in the debtor's absence, where the debtor's solicitor could show that he had not attended at the hearing because he had not only been told by an unidentified individual at the court that the bankruptcy hearing would not be effective but also he had subsequently confirmed to the chief clerk in writing what he had been told. That decision is also authority for the proposition that an annulment should be ordered under s 282(1)(a) where, contrary to s 267(2)(b), the petition is based on an unliquidated debt.

In *Henwood v Customs & Excise* [1998] BPIR 339 Evans and Rose LJJ gave leave to appeal against an order of Millett J which had dismissed the applicant's appeal against a refusal to annul a bankruptcy order where the applicant's solicitors had failed to appear at the bankruptcy hearing through a mix-up in relation to the solicitors and in circumstances where the bulk of the petition debt – sufficient to bring the petition debt below the statutory minimum – could be shown to be disputed on substantial grounds.

In the exercise of its discretion the court will also wish to consider any prima facie evidence requiring investigation that the bankrupt has concealed assets and the existence of other debts which make it likely that the bankrupt might be made bankrupt again: *Society of Lloyds v Reuters* [2001] BPIR 698 at 707B–707C; and see *Re a Bankrupt (No 622 of 1995)*, *Artman v Artman* [1996] BPIR 511 at 517A–517D (Robert Walker J).

For an annulment, which was not opposed by the official receiver, in very unusual circumstances where justice required such a course see *Amihyia v Official Receiver* [2004] EWHC 2617 (Ch), [2005] BPIR 264 (Evans-Lombe J). See also *Parveen v Manchester City Council* [2010] BPIR 152 (bankruptcy order should not have been made as it represented a disproportionate response to council tax arrears and caused injustice to the debtor). For another case made in good faith but too late in the day, where many creditors could not be contacted because bankruptcy records had been destroyed, see *Gill v Quinn* [2004] EWHC 883 (Ch), [2005] BPIR 129 (Mann J).

**Interaction between annulment and rescission**—The Court of Appeal considered for the first time at appellate level the ambit and interaction of s 282(1)(a) (annulment on grounds existing at the time the order was made) and s 375(1) (rescission) in *Yang v Official Receiver* [2017] EWCA Civ 1465, [2018] Ch 178, [2018] BPIR 255, 192H–193E. The appellant had been made bankrupt on liability orders arising from unpaid council tax, which were later set aside by a valuation tribunal. Gloster LJ dismissed the bankrupt's appeal from a refusal to annul her bankruptcy, holding that the liability orders had been legally enforceable statutory debts unless and until they were set aside. Certainty and expediency required that the bankruptcy court should not go behind liability orders except in the event of fraud or miscarriage of justice. The fact that the liability orders were subsequently set aside was not a ground 'existing at the time the [bankruptcy] order was made' as required by s 282(1)(a). Rescission under s 375(1), not annulment, had been the appropriate order. Gloster LJ declined to follow Hoffmann LJ in *Royal Bank of Scotland v Farley* [1996] BPIR 636, 640, where annulment had been granted in similar circumstances concerning a default judgment that was set aside post-bankruptcy. At 193E, Gloster LJ appeared to cast doubt on Hoffmann LJ's reasoning in *Farley*. In light of the discussion in *Yang*, care should be taken in applying *Farley* to circumstances other than default judgments.

**Timing**—Although the court may annul a bankruptcy order at any time, delay in making the application is a factor relevant to the exercise of the discretion: in *Taylor v The Macdonald Partnership* [2015] EWCA Civ 921 the Court of Appeal refused permission to the bankrupt to appeal the lower court's refusal to accede to an annulment application made 12 years after the bankruptcy order.

## SECTION 282(1)(b)

' . . . to the extent required by the rules, the bankruptcy debts and the expenses of the bankruptcy have all, since the making of the order, been either paid or secured for . . . '—The reference here to 'the rules' was identified by Warner J in *Re Robertson (a Bankrupt)* [1989] 1 WLR 1139 as being a reference to IR 1986, rr 6.209 and 6.211 (now replaced by IR 2016, rr 10.136 and 10.138). Following *Robertson*, it is not open to a bankrupt to argue that the term 'the bankruptcy debts' extends only to such of the bankruptcy debts in respect of which a proof has been lodged. Rather, it is a pre-condition of annulment under s 282(1)(b) that all creditors must be given an opportunity to prove following an application for annulment on that ground. IR 2016, r 10.136 provides a mechanism for such steps to be taken and for the adjournment of the application in the interim. The fact that a particular creditor may choose not to prove in the bankruptcy following notice of the application need not be fatal, although the court may, dependent on circumstances, require clarification of the position of a significant creditor. This, at least, is the theory. In practice, steps are not always taken to clarify the position with creditors who, for whatever reason, have not proved, with the consequence that the court is at risk of granting what might be an invalid annulment. See the discussion on what is required in *Salliss v Hunt* [2014] EWHC 229 (Ch), [2014] 1 WLR 2402, [2014] BPIR 754.

The term 'bankruptcy debts' is as defined in the broadest terms in s 382(1) and (2). The latter subsection begs the question as to how it might be that an unliquidated debt can be 'paid', although it is easy to see how such a debt might be secured. In practice, this 'paid' difficulty is most obviously overcome by the creditor placing an agreed figure on its claim.

The term 'paid or secured for' was considered by John Jarvis QC, sitting as a deputy High Court judge, in *Halabi v London Borough of Camden* [2008] EWHC 322 (Ch), [2008] BPIR 370. The wording in IR 1986, r 6.211(2) and (3) (now replaced by IR 2016, r 10.138(2)), as meaning that 'paid' means just that – 'A debt is either paid or not paid' – and that the words 'to the satisfaction of the court' refer to and qualify only the words 'secured for', and not the word 'paid'. As such, paid could not mean secured by an undertaking. The question of undertakings was relevant given the practice that had evolved in the county courts by which, commonly, a mortgage advance would be paid over to the bankrupt's solicitors on an undertaking that the solicitor would hold the funds in client account and would not release the funds until the making of the annulment order. This inconvenient ruling was reversed by the insertion of IR 1986, r 6.211(6) (now replaced by IR 2016, r 10.138(7)), which provides that security includes an undertaking given by a solicitor and accepted by the court.

The term 'secured for' is more flexible than the term 'paid' such that the court may make an order if satisfied that the debts and expenses cannot exceed a particular amount and that amount is fully secured: *Engel v Peri* [2002] EWHC 799 (Ch), [2002] BPIR 961 at [42]. The court may grant an annulment conditionally on payment of such sums: see, for example, *Hirani v Rendle* [2003] EWHC 2538 (Ch), [2004] BPIR 274 (Lawrence Collins J) (annulment conditional on debtor securing Inland Revenue debt and any unpaid costs and expenses of the trustee), and see *Thornhill v Atherton* [2004] EWCA Civ 1858, [2005] BPIR 437 (Waller and Jonathan Parker LJJ, Lloyd J) (appeal upholding annulment order under s 282(1)(a) on terms that order not to be perfected until order that the debtor paid the trustee-in-bankruptcy's costs and expenses in full).

**Statutory interest**—An application under s 282(1)(b) does not require the court to be satisfied that interest which would accrue on bankruptcy debts after the date of the bankruptcy order has either been paid or secured, since the term 'bankruptcy debt' does not, by reason of the reference to s 322(2) and s 382(1)(d), extend to interest payable in any period after the making of the bankruptcy order. Certainly the Court of Appeal had held in *Re A Debtor (No 37 of 1976) ex parte Taylor v the Debtor* [1980] Ch 565 that the court was entitled to grant an annulment without any provision being made for statutory interest. In *Harper v Buchler* [2004] BPIR 724 Deputy Registrar Barnett, considering *Taylor*, held that statutory interest is not a bankruptcy debt within s 382, and identified the following general principles (at 727G–728B):

> '(1) The grant of an annulment is a privilege. The court has a completely unfettered discretion in deciding whether or not to grant it. (2) In considering the exercise of its discretion the court may have regard to all of the circumstances of the matter before it. I do not think that the court is limited to an analysis of the applicant's conduct. (3) The length of time between the date of the bankruptcy order and the date of the application for the annulment of the order is one such factor that the court may take into consideration. If an application for annulment is made very promptly it may well be that the court would disregard the issue of statutory interest. Equally, if the application was not made until some years later the court may very well have regard to that. (4) The court would also have regard to the source of the funds being made available to discharge creditors and will doubtless have regard to the question of whether the bankruptcy estate, if realised, is sufficient to discharge both the principal debts and any statutory interest that would ordinarily accrue in the bankruptcy.'

By IR 2016, r 10.138(6) payment of post-commencement interest on the bankruptcy debts which have been proved is a relevant factor to the court's discretion and the court may take such payment into account if it thinks just.

**Third party funds**—Adopting the above principles in *Harper v Buchler (No 2)* [2005] BPIR 577 Registrar Derrett identified at [12] that statutory interest should be paid in circumstances where there are more than sufficient assets in the bankruptcy estate. However, where third party funds are being made available, and those funds are insufficient to meet the claims of creditors for interest in full, the burden lies on the bankrupt to show that the third party funds are in no way linked (eg by re-mortgaging) to assets within the bankruptcy estate: *Wilcock v Duckworth* [2005] BPIR 682 at [8]–[9] (Deputy Registrar Schaffer).

Annulment funding agreements have been the subject of judicial consideration in *Annulment Funding Co Ltd v Cowey* [2010] EWCA Civ 711, [2010] BPIR 1304; *Consolidated Finance Limited v Hunter* [2010] BPIR 1322; *Cook v Consolidated Finance Limited* [2010] EWCA Civ 369, [2010] BPIR 1331; *Consolidated Finance Limited v (1) Collins (2) Collins* [2013] EWCA Civ 475, [2013] BPIR 543 (loan and charge unenforceable as they did not comply with the terms of the Consumer Credit Act 1974).

If an annulment order under s 282(1)(b) is made on the basis of an undertaking to pay monies and that undertaking is not honoured then the appropriate course is to apply to set aside the annulment order, and not to present a fresh bankruptcy petition: *Inland Revenue Commissioners v Khan* [2005] BPIR 409 (Registrar Rawson).

**The effect of IR 2016, r 10.138(2)**—Rule 10.138(2) provides that 'all bankruptcy debts which have been proved must have been . . . paid in full' as one of the matters to be proved in a s 282(1)(b) application. The court, therefore, has no jurisdiction to annul an order where payment is to be made in less than full even where some or all of the creditors in the bankruptcy have expressly agreed to accept less than their full claim for the purposes of obtaining the annulment. However sympathetic the court may be to a debtor in these circumstances it remains that the term 'bankruptcy debt' is as defined in s 382(1) by reference to debt or liability and to which the debtor 'is subject' at the commencement of the bankruptcy or to which he 'may become subject' after commencement in the case of a pre-commencement obligation, together with interest. Section 282(1)(b) does not contemplate annulment on the debtor discharging anything less than the full extent of the bankruptcy debts as so defined, and the court has no jurisdiction to facilitate such a course, although payment of less than his full bankruptcy debts remains achievable by way of an IVA by a debtor.

**The effect of annulment**—The effect of an annulment is to treat the bankruptcy order as if it had never been made. Upon annulment taking effect those assets then vested in the trustee-in-bankruptcy will re-vest in the former bankrupt: see *Bell v Brown* [2007] EWHC 2788 (QB), [2008] BPIR 829 at [60] (Tugendhat J), albeit the point did not require final resolution in that case.

**Costs**—Whilst the making of an order for costs necessarily remains subject to the court's discretion on the facts of any particular case, the starting point in respect of liability for the trustee in bankruptcy's costs is with the petitioning creditor in a s 282(1)(a) case, whereas the starting point is with the debtor in a s 282(1)(b) case: *Butterworth v Soutter* [2000] BPIR 582 (Neuberger J). For a case where a different approach was taken in a s 282(1)(a) case because of delay on the part of a debtor see *Tetteh v London Borough of Lambeth* [2008] BPIR 241 (Registrar Nicholls). See also the detailed discussion in *Redbridge LBC v Mustafa* [2010] EWHC 1105 (Ch), [2010] BPIR 893 and the difficult case of *Re Haworth* [2011] EWHC 36 (Ch), [2011] BPIR 428 and *Mowbray v Sanders* [2015] EWHC 2317 (Ch). For judicial consideration of the level of expenses payable by the bankrupt seeking annulment on the s 282(1)(b) ground, see the comments of Registrar Jones in *Secondus v Atkinson* [2013] BPIR 632. A bankrupt who had been the victim of a miscarriage of justice (in that the petition debt had been procured by fraud and was not properly payable) was nonetheless required by the Court of Appeal to pay the trustee's reasonably and properly incurred costs, which would otherwise not be paid, in *Oraki v (1) Dean & Dean (2) Defty* [2013] EWCA Civ 1629, [2014] BPIR 266. This was an unfortunate outcome for the innocent bankrupt but a reassuring one for officeholders.

**Credit reference agencies**—For an interesting case where a bankrupt successfully established a cause of action in negligence and breach of statutory duty against a credit reference agency for their failure to update their records to show a bankruptcy had been stayed and then rescinded see *Smeaton v Equifax* [2013] EWCA Civ 108, [2013] BPIR 231 (principles equally applicable to an annulment).

**Procedure**—See IR 2016, rr 10.132–10.141. Mann J held that although it may be possible to effect equivalent compliance with IR 1986, r 6.209 (replaced by IR 2016, r 10.136) by way of making efforts to contact creditors in the bankruptcy, the court is very unlikely to grant an annulment where there is a significant passage of time and where records have been destroyed making such contact difficult: *Gill v Quinn* [2004] EWHC 883 (Ch), [2005] BPIR 129. In *Howard v Savage* [2006] EWHC 3693 (Ch), [2007] BPIR 1097 at [8] Lewison J identified that the Rules are silent on the position where there may be unknown creditors in the absence of a report under IR 1986, r 6.207 (replaced by IR 2016, r 10.133) that there are known creditors who have not proved. In upholding the decision of a district judge not to direct advertisement under r 6.211(4) IR 1986 (replaced by 10.138(5) IR 2016) his Lordship held (at [10]–[14]) that the decision as to whether or not advertisement is appropriate forms part of the discretion under s 282(1)(b) and amounts to a fact-sensitive exercise which depends on the particular circumstances of any case. *Howard* involved an annulment application made some 12 or 13 years after the making of the bankruptcy order and the district judge was, in those circumstances, entitled to form the view that advertisement would be pointless in terms of bringing forward unknown claims.

A bankrupt may challenge a trustee's costs, even following annulment: *Hirani v Rendle* [2003] EWHC 2538 (Ch), [2004] BPIR 274 at [65], which concerned IR 1986, r 6.214(1), replaced by IR 2016, r 10.141(1).

## CHAPTER II

### PROTECTION OF BANKRUPT'S ESTATE AND INVESTIGATION OF HIS AFFAIRS

**[1.396]**

#### 283 Definition of bankrupt's estate

(1) Subject as follows, a bankrupt's estate for the purposes of any of this Group of Parts comprises—

    (a)    all property belonging to or vested in the bankrupt at the commencement of the bankruptcy, and

    (b)    any property which by virtue of any of the following provisions of this Part is comprised in that estate or is treated as falling within the preceding paragraph.

(2) Subsection (1) does not apply to—

    (a)    such tools, books, vehicles and other items of equipment as are necessary to the bankrupt for use personally by him in his employment, business or vocation;

    (b)    such clothing, bedding, furniture, household equipment and provisions as are necessary for satisfying the basic domestic needs of the bankrupt and his family.

This subsection is subject to section 308 in Chapter IV (certain excluded property reclaimable by trustee).

(3) Subsection (1) does not apply to—

    (a)    property held by the bankrupt on trust for any other person, or

    (b)    the right of nomination to a vacant ecclesiastical benefice.

(3A) Subject to section 308A in Chapter IV, subsection (1) does not apply to—

(a)    a tenancy which is an assured tenancy or an assured agricultural occupancy, within the meaning of Part I of the Housing Act 1988, and the terms of which inhibit an assignment as mentioned in section 127(5) of the Rent Act 1977, or

(b)    a protected tenancy, within the meaning of the Rent Act 1977, in respect of which, by virtue of any provision of Part IX of that Act, no premium can lawfully be required as a condition of assignment, or

(c)    a tenancy of a dwelling-house by virtue of which the bankrupt is, within the meaning of the Rent (Agriculture) Act 1976, a protected occupier of the dwelling-house, and the terms of which inhibit an assignment as mentioned in section 127(5) of the Rent Act 1977, or

(d)    a secure tenancy, within the meaning of Part IV of the Housing Act 1985, which is not capable of being assigned, except in the cases mentioned in section 91(3) of that Act.

(4)   References in any of this Group of Parts to property, in relation to a bankrupt, include references to any power exercisable by him over or in respect of property except in so far as the power is exercisable over or in respect of property not for the time being comprised in the bankrupt's estate and—

(a)    is so exercisable at a time after either the official receiver has had his release in respect of that estate under section 299(2) in Chapter III or the trustee of that estate has vacated office under section 298(8), or

(b)    cannot be so exercised for the benefit of the bankrupt;

and a power exercisable over or in respect of property is deemed for the purposes of any of this Group of Parts to vest in the person entitled to exercise it at the time of the transaction or event by virtue of which it is exercisable by that person (whether or not it becomes so exercisable at that time).

(5)   For the purposes of any such provision in this Group of Parts, property comprised in a bankrupt's estate is so comprised subject to the rights of any person other than the bankrupt (whether as a secured creditor of the bankrupt or otherwise) in relation thereto, but disregarding—

(a)    any rights in relation to which a statement such as is required by section 269(1)(a) was made in the petition on which the bankrupt was made bankrupt, and

(b)    any rights which have been otherwise given up in accordance with the rules.

(6)   This section has effect subject to the provisions of any enactment not contained in this Act under which any property is to be excluded from a bankrupt's estate.

**Amendments**—Housing Act 1988, s 117(1); Enterprise and Regulatory Reform Act 2013, s 71(3), Sch 19, paras 1, 14; Small Business, Enterprise and Employment Act 2015, s 126, Sch 9, Pt 2, paras 60, 74.

**General note**—The definition of the bankrupt's estate identifies the scope of that property which vests automatically in a trustee or the official receiver under s 306(1). In brief terms, the bankrupt's estate includes all property to which the bankrupt is entitled legally or beneficially, save for those domestic or business assets in s 283(2), property held on trust for another and those 'personal' claims which are identified under that heading below and which, for reasons of public policy, remain vested in a debtor despite the making of a bankruptcy order against him. The bankruptcy estate is also subject to the rights, including the security rights, of third parties, save to the extent that such rights are abandoned under s 283(5). Section 283(6) expressly provides that legislation may expressly or impliedly override s 283 so as to exclude particular property from the scope of the bankrupt's estate. This point is also considered below.

Section 283 should be read in conjunction with ss 306–310, especially s 307 (after-acquired property) and s 310 (income payments orders), which are specifically concerned with property which does not fall within the definition of the bankrupt's estate under s 283 but which becomes claimable by a trustee in the course of the bankruptcy.

**Joint property**—The making of a bankruptcy order gives rise to the severance of an equitable joint tenancy to which the bankrupt is party by operation of law: *Re Dennis (a bankrupt)* [1993] Ch 72.

## SECTION 283(1)–(4)

' . . . **property** . . . '—Although it is commonly said that s 436 contains a definition of the term 'property', what appears in that provision is in fact a non-exhaustive list of certain forms of property which are included within the term. Given the breadth of the wording employed in s 436, it is difficult indeed to conceive of a form of tangible or intangible property which would not fall within its scope. The width of the definition, and the fact that it is inclusive rather than comprehensive, was emphasised by the Court of Appeal in *Gwinnutt v George* [2019] EWCA Civ 656, [2019] Ch 471, [2019] BPIR 1195 at [29]. Newey LJ held that 'property' for these purposes included a non-contractual expectation of payment under a pure honoraria, arising in respect of the unpaid fees of a bankrupt barrister.

**Contracts**—In general, contracts are 'property'. A contract for purely personal service on the part of the bankrupt will not, however, vest in the trustee: *Bailey v Thurston & Co Ltd* [1903] 1 KB 137. That exception should be narrowly construed and it is irrelevant whether or not the trustee has the necessary skills or could in fact perform the contract: *McGann v Bisping* [2021] EWHC 704 (QB), [23], [33] (Hugh Southey QC (sitting as a deputy High Court judge).

**Powers**—The bankrupt's estate will include any power exercisable by the bankrupt over property. A power which is not exercisable by the bankrupt, therefore, falls outside of the estate; equally, a power will be excluded if exercised by the bankrupt in trust for a third party: *Clarkson v Clarkson* [1996] BPIR 37 (Hoffmann LJ, Stuart-Smith and Saville LJJ agreeing). In *Tasarruf Mevduati Sigorta Fonu v Merrill Lynch Bank and Trust Company (Cayman) Ltd* [2011] UKPC 17, [2012] 1 WLR 1721, [2011] BPIR 1743, the Privy Council (reversing both the Grand Court and the Court of Appeal of the Cayman Islands) rejected a judgment debtor's submission that a power of revocation over various trusts was not property and was not susceptible to the appointment of a receiver by way of equitable execution. The Privy Council held that the power was tantamount to absolute ownership of the trust assets and a receiver was appointed.

**Privilege**—Legal professional privilege attaching to the information contained in a document is not property forming part of the bankrupt's estate and does not vest in trustees in bankruptcy, per Etherton LJ in *Avonwick Holdings Limited v Shlosberg* [2016] EWCA Civ 1138, [2017] Ch 210, [2017] BPIR 1. That principle extends both to documents relating to a bankrupt's liabilities and to documents relating to assets: *In re Lemos; Leeds v Lemos* [2017] EWHC 1825 (Ch), [2018] Ch 81, [2017] BPIR 1223, [242]. See also note to s 311(1).

If property vests in a trustee then, unless the trustee disclaims that property under s 315, the bankrupt has no standing to apply to the court for an order re-vesting such property in him: *Khan-Ghauri v Dunbar Bank plc* [2001] BPIR 618 at 622B–622G (Pumfrey J).

**Benefits arising from the use of the bankrupt's estate by third parties**—In *Trustee of FC Jones & Sons v Jones* [1997] Ch 159, [1996] BPIR 644 the Court of Appeal (Nourse, Beldam and Millett LJJ) held that a wife who had used monies to which a trustee-in-bankruptcy was entitled, and who had made substantial profits from engaging in speculation with those monies, was liable to account to the trustee on the basis of common law tracing for both the original monies and interest thereon together with the profits derived from its use. Although *Jones* was decided under the Bankruptcy Act 1914, the same principles will continue to apply under the IA 1986.

**Trust assets**—In bankruptcy, perhaps the most common example of property held on trust involves the matrimonial home. If a debtor is the sole legal owner of a property which is held on trust for himself and his wife, then the consequence of a bankruptcy order is that the trustee will acquire the legal estate and hold the beneficial interest in equity for himself and the bankrupt's wife. Where, however, the legal estate is owned by the debtor and his wife on trust for themselves, then the consequence of the bankruptcy is that the legal estate will be held by the bankrupt and his wife with the trustee and the bankrupt's wife being entitled to the beneficial interest in the property. The making of a bankruptcy order operates to sever a joint tenancy.

Property which is subject to an individual voluntary arrangement constitutes trust property, even where the arrangement contains no express trust clause. That proposition and the consequences of bankruptcy on an individual voluntary arrangement are explained in the notes to s 2(2).

For a novel case in which a bankrupt was held to hold lottery winnings on a resulting trust for an individual on whose behalf the bankrupt had purchased the lottery ticket, see *Abrahams v Trustee of Property of Abrahams* [1999] BPIR 637.

Where a trustee in bankruptcy realises an asset for the benefit of a secured creditor with the agreement of that creditor, the trustee is entitled to look to that creditor for the costs of realisation: *Re Sobey (a Bankrupt)* [1999] BPIR 1009 (Registrar Baister).

For a complex proprietary claim including discussion of the possibility of tracing by the official receiver see *KK v MA* [2012] EWHC 788 (Fam), [2012] BPIR 1137.

Property is not held on trust merely because it has been the subject of criminal conduct, but for the relationship between s 283, s 306 and forfeiture orders under the Proceeds of Crime Act 2002 see *Chief Constable of Greater Manchester v Wright* [2015] EWHC 3824 (Ch), [2016] BPIR 339.

**Pension interests**—In any case where a bankruptcy petition is presented on or after 31 May 2000, ss 11 and 12 of the Welfare Reform and Pensions Act 1999 operate so as to exclude from the scope of the bankrupt's estate any interest in a pension scheme as defined very broadly in the 1999 Act. Certain unapproved schemes and other specialist arrangements are not subject to that exclusion.

The Occupational and Personal Pension Schemes (Bankruptcy) Regulations 2002 (SI 2002/427) allow for agreement between a trustee and a bankrupt as to the exclusion of pension rights from the bankrupt's estate where such rights would otherwise vest in the estate.

'Tools . . . necessary to the bankrupt'—for detailed discussion on what constitutes a tool necessary to the bankrupt for use personally by him in his employment under s 283(2)(a), see *Official Receiver v Lloyd* [2015] BPIR 374 (a BRO case). The exemption in s 283(2) does not extend to choses in action associated with chattels that could themselves be regarded as tools of the trade. In *Mikki v Duncan* [2017] EWCA Civ 57, [2017] 1 WLR 2907, [2017] BPIR 490 a bankrupt unsuccessfully sought to claim the surplus realised on the post-bankruptcy sale of a car held by him on a hire purchase contract on the ground that he was entitled to the benefit of the contract via the tools of the trade exemption. Mann J (giving the leading judgment in the Court of Appeal, Patten and David Richards LJJ concurring) analysed the exemption at length and concluded that it was limited to physical property: 2915B–D. Guidance to the opposite effect at paragraph 30.155 of the Insolvency Service Technical Manual was not followed (2912F). In *Birdi v (1) Price (2) Pettit* [2018] EWHC 2943 (Ch), [2019] BPIR 306, HHJ Eyre QC conducted a review of the relevant authorities and set out at [58] ten principles to be applied in determining matters arising under s 283(2)(a). These include that the burden of establishing that a particular chattel falls within the exception lies on the bankrupt; the relevant questions are to be determined on the facts existing at the date of the bankruptcy; the statutory language is non-technical, the test highly fact-sensitive, and each element of the sub-section must be shown; regard must be had to the statutory purpose of the exception in rehabilitating the debtor as a useful and productive member of society; and the test is one of necessity and not of convenience. The judge further held that a trustee in bankruptcy was under no obligation to inform a bankrupt of the s 283(2)(a) exception.

## SECTION 283(5)

Secured and other third party rights—Section 283(5) is sufficiently broad so as to protect the rights of secured creditors and any party entitled to an equitable interest in property otherwise comprised in the bankrupt's estate other than to the extent that such rights or interests are waived or abandoned.

In *Mountney v Trehearne* [2002] EWCA Civ 1174, [2003] Ch 135 the Court of Appeal held that an order in ancillary relief proceedings created a specifically enforceable contract and immediate equitable interest in a property which would be sufficient to take that interest out of the estate for present purposes: to similar effect see *Roberts v Nunn and Tiffany* [2004] BPIR 623 (Nicholas Strauss QC sitting as a deputy High Court judge), and see also the notes on 'disposition' to s 284.

A trustee-in-bankruptcy assumes the rights of a bankrupt under an ancillary relief consent order for the purposes of the Trusts of Land and Appointment of Trustees Act 1996 unless the order can be shown to have some special force going beyond the agreement of the parties to it: *Avis v Turner* [2007] EWCA Civ 748, [2008] Ch 218, [2007] BPIR 663 (Ward, Chadwick and May LJJ).

Causes of action—See *Young v Hamilton* [2010] BPIR 1468 and *Young v OR* [2010] EWHC 1591 (Ch), [2010] BPIR 1477 for a discussion of the rule that bankruptcy deprives bankrupts of the right to commence or continue proceedings in their own name. Neither the English and Irish courts considered that this infringed the bankrupt's human rights under the European Convention. In *Thames Chambers Solicitors v Miah* [2013] EWHC 1245 (QB), [2013] BPIR 650 Tugendhat J upheld a wasted costs order made against solicitors who conducted proceedings on behalf of a bankrupt without the consent of the official receiver or trustee, despite being aware of the bankruptcy.

'Personal' claims which are not comprised in the bankruptcy estate—In *Heath v Tang* [1993] 1 WLR 1421 at 1423A–1423B Hoffmann LJ identified that the courts have long recognised that certain causes of action can be said to be personal to the bankrupt such that they do not vest in his trustee. Almost a century and a half earlier, Earle J indicated in *Beckham v Drake* (1849) 2 HL Cas 579 at 604 that these cases include those where 'damages are to be estimated by immediate reference to pain felt by the bankrupt in respect of his body, mind, or character, without immediate reference to his rights of property.' In recent years the courts have been busy in this area and have reached findings which extend beyond what Lord Atkinson had, in *Hollinshead v Hazelton* [1916] 1 AC 428 at 436, termed 'compassionate allowances' for the maintenance of the bankrupt. The authorities do not, however, suggest that there is any sort of trend or inclination in finding that any particular species of claim should fall inside or outside the bankrupt's estate, since each particular cause of action must be assessed according to its own characteristics.

Those causes of action which have been held to be 'personal' to the bankrupt and therefore outside of the scope of the bankrupt's estate include:

- A claim for damages for slander: *Re Wilson ex parte Vine* (1878) 8 ChD 364.

- A claim for damages for loss of reputation: *Wilson v United Counties Bank Ltd* [1920] AC 102.
- The hope or expectation of a payment by the Criminal Injuries Compensation Board which remains subject to the Board's discretion such that the hope or expectation did not exist as a right to which some future or contingent entitlement could relate: *Re Campbell (a Bankrupt)* [1997] Ch 14, [1996] BPIR 238.
- An aviation licence awarded to an individual as a fit and proper person: *Griffiths v Civil Aviation Authority* [1997] BPIR 50 (Federal Court of Australia).
- Social security benefits of an income nature: *Mulvey v Secretary of State for Social Security* [1997] BPIR 696, considered in *Secretary of State for Work and Pensions v Payne* [2011] UKSC 60, [2012] 2 AC 1, [2012] BPIR 224.
- A claim for medical negligence giving rise to personality change: *Davis v Trustee in Bankruptcy of the Estate of Davis* [1998] BPIR 572.
- A claim for damages for professional negligence in respect of conduct which gave rise to the bankruptcy of the bankrupt: *Mulkerrins v PricewaterhouseCoopers* [2003] UKHL 41, [2003] 1 WLR 1937, [2003] BPIR 1357.
- Claim for unfair dismissal under the Employment Rights Act 1996: *Grady v Prison Service* [2003] EWCA Civ 527, [2003] BPIR 823.
- A claim in tort for harassment under the Protection from Harassment Act 1997 where the harassment continued after discharge (*Grant v Hayes* [2014] EWHC 2646 (Ch), [2014] BPIR 1455). In the related case of *Hayes v Butters* [2014] EWHC 4557 (Ch), [2015] Ch 495, [2015] BPIR 287, Nugee J held that a hybrid claim for harassment seeking compensation for personal and non-personal loss vested in the estate, but a claim relating to alleged harassment post-bankruptcy did not so vest. The case provides valuable discussion of the nature of so-called hybrid claims (on which see further below) in the harassment context.

The following causes of action have been held to be within the scope of the bankrupt's estate:

- Damages for breaking, entering and damaging the property of the bankrupt: *Rogers v Spence* (1846) 12 Cl & Fin 700.
- A claim for damages for breach of a contract of employment (but not, according to a majority of the Exchequer Chamber, a claim in respect of mental suffering): *Beckham v Drake* (1849) 2 HL Cas 579.
- Damages equating to 6 months' salary in lieu of proper notice of dismissal: *Walding v Oliphant* (1875) 1 QBD 145.
- Entitlement to a licence allowing for use of registered fishing vessels: *Re Rae* [1995] BCC 102. At 113C–113D Warner J observed that, 'I am not persuaded that one can, merely from a consideration of the purposes of the Insolvency Act and the non-exhaustive nature of the definition of 'property' in s 436, reach the conclusion that any asset of the bankrupt which can be realised or turned to account is "property" within the meaning of the act.'
- Right to appeal pre-bankruptcy summary judgment: *Wordsworth v Dixon* [1997] BPIR 337. See also *Cowey v Insol Funding Ltd* [2012] EWHC 2421 (Ch), [2012] BPIR 958 for confirmation that a bankrupt has no right to appeal in his own name from a judgment against him which is enforceable only against the estate vested in his trustee.
- A claim for a grant of a new tenancy under Part II of the Landlord & Tenant Act 1954: *Saini v Petroform Ltd* [1997] BPIR 515.
- A claim under a contingency fee agreement entered into by a solicitor prior to his bankruptcy: *Royal Bank of Canada v Chetty* [1997] BPIR 137.
- Right to receive royalties from the Performing Rights Society: *Performing Rights Society v Rowland* [1998] BPIR 128.
- An award of damages to compensate the bankrupt for loss of earning capacity: *Re Bell (a Bankrupt)* [1998] BPIR 26 (British Columbia Supreme Court).
- A claim for damages for breach of joint venture agreement: *Morris v Morgan* [1998] BPIR 764.
- A claim on the critical illness element of a life assurance policy which produced a fixed sum in the event of a varying range of disabilities: *Cork v Rawlins* [2001] EWCA Civ 202, [2001] Ch 792. The judgment of Peter Gibson LJ in *Rawlins* is of note, since it draws attention to the fact that there is no authority supporting the proposition that a contractual claim is capable of remaining vested in a bankrupt.
- The entitlement to one half of the policy proceeds of a joint life policy payable upon the bankrupt's wife being diagnosed terminally ill where the joint tenancy in equity representing entitlement to the policy proceeds had been severed upon the husband's earlier bankruptcy: *Re Pritchard (a bankrupt), Williams v Pritchard* [2007] BPIR 1385 (Registrar Derrett).

- The right to challenge a tax assessment (at least where the assessment was raised prior to the bankruptcy): *R (Singh) v HMRC* [2010] BPIR 933. See also *McNulty v HMRC* [2012] STC 2110 (the right to appeal in tax cases vests in the trustee pursuant to s 306, and the bankrupt tax payer therefore has no locus standi to pursue an appeal). In *Re GP Aviation Group International Ltd* [2013] EWHC 1447 (Ch), [2014] 1 WLR 166, [2013] BPIR 576 the court accepted that only the trustee was entitled to appeal a tax assessment but considered that, for the purposes of assignment, the right to appeal was not property within the meaning of s 436 and was not capable of being sold by the liquidator.
- A payment protection insurance refund (either because it was an 'interest incidental to property', ie the policy itself, or because it was the fruit of a cause of action which was in itself property encompassed within the estate: see the definition of property in s 436): *Ward v Official Receiver* [2012] BPIR 1073.
- An equitable interest arising under a proprietary estoppel: *Walden v Atkins (Executor of the Estate of Dennis Walden)* [2013] EWHC 1387 (Ch), [2013] BPIR 943.
- A claim for professional negligence against solicitors: *Frosdick v Fox* [2017] EWHC 1737 (Ch), [2018] 1 WLR 38, [2017] BPIR 1194.

In *BPE Solicitors v Gabriel* [2015] UKSC 39, [2015] AC 1663, [2015] BPIR 779 the Supreme Court over-ruled the old case of *Borneman v Wilson* (1884) LR 28 ChD 53 and decided that, although the trustee had adopted an appeal launched by the debtor pre-bankruptcy, he should not be held personally liable for any costs incurred by the other party prior to the bankruptcy.

The fact that any particular item of property is of no value when in the hands of the bankrupt is not determinative of whether the item constitutes property: *Rothschild v Bell* [2000] QB 33, [1999] BPIR 300.

A cause of action is capable of constituting 'onerous property' and may be disclaimed under s 315: *Frosdick v Fox* [2017] EWHC 1737 (Ch), [2018] 1 WLR 38, [2017] BPIR 1194.

'Hybrid' claims—It is possible that a single cause of action will comprise two or more heads of damage in respect of loss which is respectively personal and non-personal. In *Ord v Upton* [2000] Ch 352, [2000] BPIR 104 the Court of Appeal considered a claim for medical negligence which comprised separate heads of claim for loss of earnings and pain and suffering. Aldous LJ, with whom Mantell and Kennedy LJJ agreed, held at 207J–208B that the single cause of action vested in the trustee, but that the trustee held the proceeds of the pain and suffering element of the claim on a constructive trust for the bankrupt, with the consequence that the trustee would have to account to the bankrupt for any such damages recovered. It would also, of course, be open to the trustee to consider assigning the cause of action to the bankrupt, subject to the bankrupt accounting to the trustee for the proceeds of the loss of income element of the claim. On 'hybrid claims' see also *Hayes v Butters* [2014] EWHC 4557 (Ch), [2015] Ch 495, [2015] BPIR 287 and *Hayes v Willoughby* (unreported) July 22, 2015.

Property excluded from the bankruptcy estate by other statutes—The exclusion of pensions from the scope of the bankrupt's estate is considered in the notes to s 283(1)–(4) under the heading 'Pension interests', but see also *Horton v Henry* [2016] EWCA Civ 989, [2017] 1 WLR 391, [2016] BPIR 1426 and note to s 310(7) below.

By s 417 of the Proceeds of Crime Act 2002, property which is subject to an order under that legislation is automatically excluded from the bankrupt's estate.

Under reg 80(2)(a) of the Education (Student Loans) (Repayment) Regulations 2009 (SI 2009/470) any part of a student loan received by a bankrupt after the bankruptcy is excluded from his estate.

Section 308(1)(b) allows the trustee to claim property excluded by s 283(2) (tools of trade, household effects etc) if 'it appears to the trustee that the realisable value of the whole or any part of the property exceeds the cost of a reasonable replacement for that property'.

## [1.397]

### 283A Bankrupt's home ceasing to form part of estate

(1) This section applies where property comprised in the bankrupt's estate consists of an interest in a dwelling-house which at the date of the bankruptcy was the sole or principal residence of—

    (a)   the bankrupt,

    (b)   the bankrupt's spouse or civil partner, or

    (c)   a former spouse or former civil partner of the bankrupt.

(2) At the end of the period of three years beginning with the date of the bankruptcy the interest mentioned in subsection (1) shall—

    (a)   cease to be comprised in the bankrupt's estate, and

    (b)   vest in the bankrupt (without conveyance, assignment or transfer).

(3)   Subsection (2) shall not apply if during the period mentioned in that subsection—

    (a)   the trustee realises the interest mentioned in subsection (1),
    (b)   the trustee applies for an order for sale in respect of the dwelling-house,
    (c)   the trustee applies for an order for possession of the dwelling-house,
    (d)   the trustee applies for an order under section 313 in Chapter IV in respect of that interest, or
    (e)   the trustee and the bankrupt agree that the bankrupt shall incur a specified liability to his estate (with or without the addition of interest from the date of the agreement) in consideration of which the interest mentioned in subsection (1) shall cease to form part of the estate.

(4)   Where an application of a kind described in subsection (3)(b) to (d) is made during the period mentioned in subsection (2) and is dismissed, unless the court orders otherwise the interest to which the application relates shall on the dismissal of the application—

    (a)   cease to be comprised in the bankrupt's estate, and
    (b)   vest in the bankrupt (without conveyance, assignment or transfer).

(5)   If the bankrupt does not inform the trustee or the official receiver of his interest in a property before the end of the period of three months beginning with the date of the bankruptcy, the period of three years mentioned in subsection (2)—

    (a)   shall not begin with the date of the bankruptcy, but
    (b)   shall begin with the date on which the trustee or official receiver becomes aware of the bankrupt's interest.

(6)   The court may substitute for the period of three years mentioned in subsection (2) a longer period—

    (a)   in prescribed circumstances, and
    (b)   in such other circumstances as the court thinks appropriate.

(7)   The rules may make provision for this section to have effect with the substitution of a shorter period for the period of three years mentioned in subsection (2) in specified circumstances (which may be described by reference to action to be taken by a trustee in bankruptcy).

(8)   The rules may also, in particular, make provision—

    (a)   requiring or enabling the trustee of a bankrupt's estate to give notice that this section applies or does not apply;
    (b)   about the effect of a notice under paragraph (a);
    (c)   requiring the trustee of a bankrupt's estate to make an application to the Chief Land Registrar.

(9)   Rules under subsection (8)(b) may, in particular—

    (a)   disapply this section;
    (b)   enable a court to disapply this section;
    (c)   make provision in consequence of a disapplication of this section;
    (d)   enable a court to make provision in consequence of a disapplication of this section;
    (e)   make provision (which may include provision conferring jurisdiction on a court or tribunal) about compensation.

**Amendments**—Inserted by Enterprise Act 2002, s 261(1). Amended by Civil Partnership Act 2004, s 261(1), Sch 27, para 113.

**General note**—Section 283A – together, with s 313A, the so-called 'use it or lose it' provisions – was introduced with effect from 1 April 2004 by s 261 of the Enterprise Act 2002. These provisions should be read in conjunction with s 313 (charge on bankrupt's home) and s 313A (application for sale, possession or charge of low value home) and engender Parliament's attempt at addressing the unsatisfactory practice by which a trustee could previously take no action in relation to a bankrupt's home and later, often years later, and usually to the surprise of the by now discharged bankrupt, take steps to realise not only the property but also its enhanced value over time. The new provisions require action of the trustee, irrespective of the state of the property market. This obligation, however, is subject to s 313, which permits a trustee to apply for a charge on a bankrupt's interest in a dwelling-house where 'the trustee is, for any reason, unable for the time being to realise that property.' Such a charge will secure the value of the bankrupt's interest, as assessed by the court, together with interest, and is enforceable notwithstanding the subsequent discharge of the bankrupt or the release of the trustee. On the other hand, s 313A imposes restrictions on actions by a trustee where the bankrupt's interest in a dwelling-house is of no value, as defined in that provision.

The policy underlying s 283A was discussed by Lawrence Collins J, as he then was, in *Re Byford (Deceased)* [2003] EWHC 1267 (Ch), [2003] BPIR 1089 in the context of the relevance of that policy to cases involving equitable accounting.

The mechanism employed in s 283A is to exclude any interest of the bankrupt in a dwelling-house – as defined in s 385(1) – from the scope of the bankrupt's estate, as defined in s 283, at the end of the 3-year period identified in s 283A(2), subject to extension under s 283A(5) and (6).

Section 283A has no application to a bankruptcy commenced prior to 29 December 1986 (ie under the Bankruptcy Act 1914): *Pannell v The Official Receiver* [2008] EWHC 736 (Ch), [2008] BPIR 629 (HHJ Havelock-Allan QC, sitting as a judge of the High Court).

For discussion of the transitional provisions applying to s 283A see *Stonham v Ramrattan* [2011] EWCA Civ 119, [2011] 1 WLR 1617, [2011] BPIR 518.

**Property to which s 283A applies**—Section 283A(1) defines the property or properties to which the provision applies. The provision catches any dwelling-house at the date of the bankruptcy order in which the bankrupt had a legal or beneficial interest where any such property was 'the sole or principal residence' of the bankrupt, the bankrupt's spouse, or a former spouse (without limitation in number) of the bankrupt. Although, by definition, a person may have only one sole or principal residence, s 283A(1) plainly envisages more than one property falling within its scope. Any property which is not the sole or principal residence of any of those persons mentioned in s 283A(1), such as an investment property or holiday home, will not fall within the protection of s 283A or, indeed, s 313A. Section 283A does not apply to property vested in a third party at the date of the bankruptcy but later recovered by the trustee by virtue of s 342 (orders made in respect of transactions at an undervalue and preferences): *Stonham v Ramrattan* [2011] EWCA Civ 119, [2011] 1 WLR 1617, [2011] BPIR 518.

For the position where a trustee's interest was bought out by the bankrupt and his wife and the bankrupt was then made bankrupt for a second time, see *Garwood v Ambrose* [2012] EWHC 1494 (Ch), [2012] BPIR 996, where the trustee's argument that the bankrupt's interest re-vested in him pursuant to s 283A was successful on the facts (since the evidence did not establish any agreement that the wife would solely own the property).

**The combined effect of s 283A(2)–(4)**—The starting point here lies in the automatic re-vesting of the bankrupt's interest in the bankrupt at the end of the 3-year period beginning with the date of the bankruptcy order. That period has no application, however, where the trustee realises the bankrupt's interest, by virtue of s 283A(3)(a), or reaches agreement with the bankrupt for s 283A(3)(e) purposes within the 3-year period (note the Court of Appeal's decision in *Lewis v Metropolitan Property Realisations Ltd* [2009] EWCA Civ 448, [2010] Ch 148, [2009] BPIR 820 that effecting a sale for future cash consideration does not amount to 'realisation' until the cash is actually received, differing from the view of Proudman J in the court below ([2008] EWHC 2760 (Ch), [2009] BPIR 79)). The trustee will also avoid the automatic re-vesting in the bankrupt of the bankrupt's interest if he or she 'applies' for any of the orders listed in s 283A(3)(b)–(d) within the 3-year period. In this context, 'applies' means delivers the application notice and tenders the relevant fee to the appropriate court – it does not matter if the proceedings are not actually issued by the court until later: *Sands v Singh* [2015] EWHC 2219 (Ch), [2015] BPIR 1293. On the other hand, if any such application is issued and dismissed – and only dismissed – within the 3-year period then, by virtue of s 283A(4), the interest re-vests in the bankrupt (although note *Hunt and Another v Conwy County Borough Council* [2013] EWHC 1154 (Ch), [2014] 1 WLR 254, [2013] BPIR 790, where Sir William Blackburne (sitting as a High Court judge) confirmed that where a trustee had disclaimed the property as onerous by the time his application for possession and sale was dismissed, the property did not re-vest in the bankrupt under s 283A. He did not think there was anything improper in allowing the Trustee to extend the 3-year time period by making an application within such a period to enable him or her to disclaim an asset). The onus, therefore, is squarely on the trustee to ensure that he or she has undertaken appropriate investigations into any interest to which the bankrupt's estate is entitled within the applicable time-limit, and that the application is properly prepared and technically sound. See also the comments of Morgan J in *Hunt v Withinshaw* [2015] EWHC 3072 (Ch), [2016] BPIR 59. Where the trustee has obtained an order for sale, but has not enforced it, the 3 year time limit does not apply to prevent a later application to affirm the previous order: *Re Ellis Carr (in Bankruptcy); Levy v Ellis- Carr* [2012] EWHC 63 (Ch), [2012] BPIR 347.

### SECTION 283A(5)

The period of 3 years runs from the date of the bankruptcy order only if the bankrupt notifies the trustee or official receiver of his interest in the property within 3 months of that date. Otherwise, the period runs from the date on which the trustee or official receiver becomes aware of the bankrupt's interest. For detailed discussion on s 283A(5) see *Stonham v Ramrattan* [2011] EWCA Civ 119, [2011] 1 WLR 1617, [2011] BPIR 518.

### SECTION 283A(6)

**Substitution of period exceeding three years**—The court may substitute, for the purposes of s 283A(2), 'such longer period as the court thinks just and reasonable in all the circumstances of the case' (see also IR 2016, r 10.170).

### SECTION 283A(7)

**Substitution of shorter period than three years**—IR 2016, r 10.170 allows for automatic re-vesting in the bankrupt one month from the date of a notice sent by the trustee to the bankrupt to the effect that the trustee considers that the continued vesting of the property in the bankrupt's estate is of no benefit to creditors or, alternatively, that the re-vesting in the bankrupt will facilitate a more efficient administration of the bankrupt's estate.

**Procedure**—For the notification of a property falling within s 283A, see rr 10.168, 10.169.

## [1.398]

### 284 Restrictions on dispositions of property

(1) Where a person is made bankrupt, any disposition of property made by that person in the period to which this section applies is void except to the extent that it is or was made with the consent of the court, or is or was subsequently ratified by the court.

(2) Subsection (1) applies to a payment (whether in cash or otherwise) as it applies to a disposition of property and, accordingly, where any payment is void by virtue of that subsection, the person paid shall hold the sum paid for the bankrupt as part of his estate.

(3) This section applies to the period beginning with the day of the making of the bankruptcy application or (as the case may be) the presentation of the bankruptcy petition and ending with the vesting, under Chapter IV of this Part, of the bankrupt's estate in a trustee.

(4) The preceding provisions of this section do not give a remedy against any person—

> (a) in respect of any property or payment which he received before the commencement of the bankruptcy in good faith, for value and without notice that the bankruptcy application had been made or (as the case may be) that the bankruptcy petition had been presented, or
>
> (b) in respect of any interest in property which derives from an interest in respect of which there is, by virtue of this subsection, no remedy.

(5) Where after the commencement of his bankruptcy the bankrupt has incurred a debt to a banker or other person by reason of the making of a payment which is void under this section, that debt is deemed for the purposes of any of this Group of Parts to have been incurred before the commencement of the bankruptcy unless—

> (a) that banker or person had notice of the bankruptcy before the debt was incurred, or
>
> (b) it is not reasonably practicable for the amount of the payment to be recovered from the person to whom it was made.

(6) A disposition of property is void under this section notwithstanding that the property is not or, as the case may be, would not be comprised in the bankrupt's estate; but nothing in this section affects any disposition made by a person of property held by him on trust for any other person.

**Amendments**—Enterprise and Regulatory Reform Act 2013, s 71(3), Sch 19, paras 1, 15.

**General note**—This provision renders void any disposition of property that is made between the time when a bankruptcy petition is presented and the time when a debtor's property vests in the trustee, unless court approval is obtained. Section 284 is the bankruptcy equivalent of s 127, which applies in the liquidation of companies, and basically many of the same principles will apply, or at least provide legitimate guidelines (*Re Flint* [1993] Ch 319 at 328). But s 284 is in different terms to s 127 and so one cannot approach this section with the assumption that it is designed to achieve the same outcome as s 127, and one cannot necessarily apply a case decided under one section to the other section: *Pettit v Novakovic* [2007] BPIR 1643. The aim of the provision is to ensure that the bankrupt's estate is not dissipated, between the dates mentioned above, and so prevent a rateable distribution of the bankrupt's estate amongst his or her creditors.

The provision is expressly disapplied in the case of certain financial market transactions prescribed in Companies Act 1989, ss 164(3), 173(3)–(5). Similar exemptions applicable to financial and security settlements and associated security arrangements are provided for in the

Financial Markets and Insolvency (Settlement Finality) Regulations 1999 (SI 1999/2979). These provisions seek to protect certain transactions from the normal effects of a company's insolvency.

'Disposition'—See the notes under the same heading in relation to s 127. Disposition is to be interpreted broadly in this context. It includes, as s 284(2) indicates, cash, and this would, consequently, cover things such as direct debits, cheques and the use of debit cards. For the application of s 284 to a power of attorney see *Sanders v Donovan* [2012] BPIR 219.

Whether the disposition by a debtor in the relevant time and pursuant to an order under s 24 of the Matrimonial Causes Act 1973 is a disposition within s 284 has been the subject of divergent views over the years. It was held in *Re Flint* [1993] Ch 319 that a transfer of a husband's interest in the matrimonial home, within the period mentioned in s 284, to his wife pursuant to an order (whether or not by consent) under s 24 of the Matrimonial Causes Act 1973 constitutes a disposition for the purposes of s 284. This decision was made even though the debtor had not actually effected a transfer before bankruptcy ensued, although the order of the court was made during the s 284 period. The position taken by the judge was that the court order was effectively a disposition by the debtor. This diverged from the view in *Burton v Burton* [1986] 2 FLR 419 that a transfer order is not a disposition of property, as there is not a transfer until the completion of the relevant documentation effecting it. In Australia it has been held that a disposition made under an order pursuant to the Australian Family Law Act 1975 is protected from the impact of the Australian equivalent (although Australia retains the relation back doctrine that formerly applied in England and Wales) (*Corke v Corke and Official Trustee in Bankruptcy* (1994) 121 ALR 320). *Re Flint* was not followed in *Beer v Higham* [1997] BPIR 349, where Jonathan Parker J sided with the view expressed in *Burton*. However, in *Mountney v Treharne* [2002] EWCA Civ 1174, [2003] Ch 135, [2002] BPIR 1126 at [77], a case distinguishable from *Flint*, his Lordship, who was by now Jonathan Parker LJ, accepted that his decision in *Beer* was wrong and that the view expressed in *Flint* was correct. In the decision of *Treharne v Forrester* [2003] EWHC 2784 (Ch), [2004] BPIR 338 Lindsay J followed the approach taken in *Re Flint*. As a consequence we now appear to have some certainty and can say that any disposition of a debtor's property in the time covered by s 284 will, even if it is pursuant to a court order in family law proceedings, be void. A matrimonial settlement which had not been finalised by the date of the bankruptcy petition was struck down as a void disposition by HHJ Cooke, sitting as a High Court judge, in *Warwick v Trustee of Bankruptcy of Yarwood* [2010] EWHC 2272 (Ch), [2010] BPIR 1443.

'Property'—For the purposes of s 284, 'property' means property owned beneficially by the debtor or in which the debtor held a beneficial interest. Where a business associate of a debtor paid the petitioner directly, such payment did not amount to a disposition of the debtor's property for the purposes of s 284 and was not void, despite the payment having been a loan by the associate to the debtor: *In re Hood* [2020] EWHC 3232 (Ch), [2021] Ch 125, [73]–[74] (Michael Green J).

'Void'—A disposition is not void at the point of the transaction taking place. It only becomes void once the bankruptcy order is made, because unless an order is made, the disposition cannot be impugned. The Court of Appeal analysed the position in *Re Eaitisham Ahmed* [2018] EWCA Civ 519 and held that where a transfer was made post-petition, assets were held on the following trusts: (i) contingently for the bankrupt (ie the future bankruptcy estate) in the event that a bankruptcy order was made; and (ii) if no such order was made, for the transferee as absolute owner. Upon first appointment of a trustee, the shares should be restored to the trustee in bankruptcy. See also the comments under the same heading for s 127.

'Payment'—A payment within s 284(2) could be, but was not necessarily, a disposition of property within s 284(1): *Pettit v Novakovic* [2007] BPIR 1643. Thus a payment of money which did not dispose the beneficial interest in the money (eg to an agent, to be held to the order of the bankrupt) was still caught within s 284(2).

'Consent of the court'—This can be obtained at the time of any disposition or subsequently.

Validation—Payments to solicitors and barristers by the debtor, in order to obtain advice and representation in relation to the bankruptcy petition that has been presented against him or her, may be validated by the court, even where the payments will prejudice creditors (*Re Sinclair ex parte Payne* (1885) 15 QBD 616; *Rio Properties Inc v Al-Midani* [2003] BPIR 128). But under s 284, and in order to validate payments, the court would require evidence as to the financial position of the debtor and of the grounds for validation (*Rio Properties Inc v Al-Midani* at 139). However, funds used to pay for costs related to attempts to finalise arrangements with creditors, and so avoid bankruptcy, will not be validated (*Re Spackman ex parte Foley* (1890) 24 QBD 728, distinguishing *Re Sinclair*).

The current guidelines for applications for validation are in para 12.8 of the *Practice Direction – Insolvency Proceedings* (July 2020) [2020] BPIR 1211. These provisions were considered by ICC Judge Jones in refusing to grant a validation order to enable the debtor to pay his petitioning creditor in full in *Hood v Commissioners for HMRC* [2019] EWHC 2236 (Ch), [2019] BPIR 1425. Judge Jones accepted the debtor's argument that creditors whose debts were disputed were not 'creditors' for the purposes of the words 'unsecured creditors as a class' in para 12.8.8 of the *Practice Direction* and, accordingly, their debts should not be included when considering the debtor's solvency for the purposes of validation ([36]–[41]). Validation was, nonetheless, refused because the debtor had not provided credible evidence of solvency ([55]–[56]).

See the notes under 'Validating Orders' in relation to s 127, as the validation process under s 127 has been regarded as not unlike the process under s 284 (*Treharne v Forrester* [2003] EWHC 2784 (Ch), [2004] BPIR 338 at [57]). For a detailed consideration and exposition of the authorities relevant to the validation discretion in the s 127 context, see the decision of Registrar Briggs in *Wilson v SMC Properties Ltd* [2015] EWHC 870 (Ch), [2015] 2 BCLC 173.

*Tomlinson v Bridging Finance Ltd* [2010] BPIR 759 clarified that, although s 284 only applies to a disposition made between presentation of the bankruptcy petition and the vesting of the estate in the trustee, dispositions made by the bankrupt of property within the bankruptcy estate after it had vested in the trustee are also void (see in particular [10]).

**Third party protection**—Section 284(4) protects a third party who receives property or money before the date of the bankruptcy order, provided that he or she was a bona fide purchaser without notice.

**Good faith**—This element involves the state of mind of the beneficiary of the disposition. It connotes the fact that some duty is owed, and that is to the general body of creditors. Good faith goes beyond mere personal honesty, requiring more than absence of dishonesty, and more than absence of a conscious attempt to defraud (*Re Dalton* [1963] Ch 336 at 355, dealing with the old relation back doctrine under Bankruptcy Act 1914). If a person is aware that the debtor (soon to become a bankrupt) had failed to comply with a statutory demand, then it might be that good faith would not exist for the purposes of this section. The same would occur if the person who received the disposition did not know, but shut his or her eyes to some suspicion, that the debtor was the subject of bankruptcy proceedings. For an example of an unsuccessful attempt to rely on the good faith exception, see *Sands and Treharne v Wright* [2010] BPIR 1437, where the test in *Dalton* was applied.

There is Australian authority to the effect that a person would be acting in good faith if he or she believed that the disposition was regularly and properly done (*PT Garuda Indonesia v Grellman* (1992) 107 ALR 199).

**Value**—Obviously this would rule out any disposition by way of gift. The focus of s 284(4) is on the protection of innocent third parties and to promote certainty in a bankrupt's dealings. Provided receipt is not gratuitous, value will have been provided. There is no requirement that value be received by the estate: *Edwards (trustee in bankruptcy of Wasu) v Aurora Leasing Ltd* [2021] EWHC 96 (Ch), [61]–[64] (ICC Judge Prentis).

**Deceased estates**—HHJ David Cooke, sitting as a High Court judge, considered the application of s 284 to the insolvent estate of a deceased person (see s 421) in *Williams v Lawrence* [2011] EWHC 2001 (Ch), [2011] BPIR 1761. In such estates, all payments from the date of death are rendered void by a subsequent order for administration as a deceased insolvent estate (the equivalent of a bankruptcy order in respect of estates where the debtor is deceased) irrespective of the date of the order, which may be many years later. Extreme caution must be exercised by those dealing with deceased estates of doubtful solvency.

**Remedy**—The Court of Appeal addressed remedy in *Re Eaitisham Ahmed* [2018] EWCA Civ 519. Section 284 does not provide a free-standing right to recover compensation, which is instead covered by the general law. Where assets that have been the subject of a void disposition are not restored to the estate upon first vesting in a trustee in bankruptcy, it will constitute a breach of trust and a claim for equitable compensation will be available where the asset has diminished in value. But the fact that a breach has occurred does not necessarily mean that the loss should be calculated from that date. On the evidence, the trustee in bankruptcy would have sold the shares within a three to 6–month window and loss should be calculated on that basis. Fair value, not market value, on the basis of a transaction between knowledgeable and willing parties, was appropriate.

**Foreign bankruptcy**—Where a United States bankruptcy had been recognised under The Cross-Border Insolvency Regulations 2006, the relevant date for the application of both s 284 and s 306 was the date of the presentation of the petition in the USA (which was also the date of the commencement of the bankruptcy) and not the date of the recognition order: *Moser (as Chapter 7 Bankruptcy Trustee of Tomoye) v Tomoye* [2020] EWHC 1865 (Ch), [17]–[22] (ICC Judge Jones).

**SECTION 284(5)**

**Commencement of bankruptcy**—This is the date on which the bankruptcy order is made. See s 278. See the notes accompanying s 127.

## [1.399]

### 285 Restriction on proceedings and remedies

(1) At any time when proceedings on a bankruptcy application are ongoing proceedings on a bankruptcy petition are pending or an individual has been made

bankrupt the court may stay any action, execution or other legal process against the property or person of the debtor or, as the case may be, of the bankrupt.

(2)   Any court in which proceedings are pending against any individual may, on proof that a bankruptcy application has been made or a bankruptcy petition has been presented in respect of that individual or that he is an undischarged bankrupt, either stay the proceedings or allow them to continue on such terms as it thinks fit.

(3)   After the making of a bankruptcy order no person who is a creditor of the bankrupt in respect of a debt provable in the bankruptcy shall—

(a)   have any remedy against the property or person of the bankrupt in respect of that debt, or

(b)   before the discharge of the bankrupt, commence any action or other legal proceedings against the bankrupt except with the leave of the court and on such terms as the court may impose.

This is subject to sections 346 (enforcement procedures) and 347 (limited right to distress).

(4)   Subject as follows, subsection (3) does not affect the right of a secured creditor of the bankrupt to enforce his security.

(5)   Where any goods of an undischarged bankrupt are held by any person by way of pledge, pawn or other security, the official receiver may, after giving notice in writing of his intention to do so, inspect the goods.

Where such a notice has been given to any person, that person is not entitled, without leave of the court, to realise his security unless he has given the trustee of the bankrupt's estate a reasonable opportunity of inspecting the goods and of exercising the bankrupt's right of redemption.

(6)   References in this section to the property or goods of the bankrupt are to any of his property or goods, whether or not comprised in his estate.

**Amendments**—Enterprise and Regulatory Reform Act 2013, s 71(3), Sch 19, paras 1, 16.

**General note**—Although grouped together, these provisions address distinct issues which, in the case of s 285(3), should be read in conjunction with ss 346 and 347, together with the analogous provisions in s 130 and the commentary thereto.

Section 285 is effectively disapplied in relation to action by an exchange or clearing house in the context of default proceedings by s 161(4) of the Companies Act 1989.

**Scope of provision**—Section 285(1) allows the court with bankruptcy jurisdiction over an individual to stay any action, execution or other legal process against the property or the debtor at any time when a bankruptcy petition is pending against the debtor or following the making of a bankruptcy order against him, to stay the proceedings or allow them to continue subject to such terms as the court thinks fit. The purpose of the provision lies in protecting the bankrupt's estate for the whole body of creditors and preventing unsecured creditors from taking steps to obtain advantages over other creditors following the presentation of a bankruptcy petition: *Re Smith ex parte Braintree District Council* [1990] 2 AC 215, HL. Subsection (2), on the other hand, allows *any* court in which 'proceedings' are pending against the respondent to a bankruptcy petition or an undischarged bankrupt to stay those proceedings or to allow them to continue on such terms as the court considers appropriate. The purpose behind s 285(2) is the same as that underlying s 285(1); the differences between the two lies in s 285(1) being limited to the staying of a variety of proceedings and the greater elaboration in s 285(2) on the scope of proceedings subject to that provision.

In *Kemsley v Barclays Bank Plc* [2013] EWHC 1274 (Ch), [2013] BPIR 839 at [22], Roth J indicated that this provision does not apply to foreign enforcement proceedings (although s 37 of the Senior Courts Act 1981 could be used to the same effect).

**SECTION 285(1), (2)**

'  .  .  .   **other legal process**  .  .  .  '—In *Braintree District Council* (above) the House of Lords held that a warrant of committal for non-payment of rates fell within the term 'other legal process' which the court therefore had standing to stay, consistent with the purpose of s 285(1), as identified above, notwithstanding the punitive element of the warrant.

In the important case of *Sharples v Place for People Homes Ltd* [2011] EWCA Civ 813, [2011] BPIR 1488, the Court of Appeal held that where a bankruptcy order was made against the tenant of property, the automatic stay in s 285(3) did not apply to a landlord's application for possession on the grounds of rent arrears, although it does apply to any claim for the arrears themselves (the same analysis applies in the context of debt relief orders and s 251G: *Godfrey v A2 Dominion Homes Ltd*, reported together with *Sharples*).

**By which principles, if any, should the court be guided in exercising its discretion under s 285(1) or (2)?**—Although there is no reported authority in which the exercise of the court's jurisdiction is considered by reference to any reasoned general principles, it is submitted that, certainly as regards the stay or continuance of proceedings prior to bankruptcy, the principles identified in the judgment of Lord Brandon in the Court of Appeal in *Roberts Petroleum Ltd v Bernard Kenny Ltd* [1982] 1 All ER 685 at 690F–690J in relation to the making of a charging order or garnishee order absolute will be of some assistance. Although reversed on appeal, those principles were not called into question in any of the opinions of the House of Lords in *Roberts Petroleum Ltd v Bernard Kenny Ltd* [1983] AC 192.

Consistent with the purpose of s 285(1) and (2) (see above) and, it is submitted, the principles established by Lord Brandon in *Roberts Petroleum*, the court might be expected to allow for the continuance of proceedings which advance a liability from which the bankrupt would not be released on discharge, the most obvious example being a claim for fraudulent breach of trust: see *Re Blake ex parte Coker* (1875) 10 Ch App 652. Equally, the court may be prepared to permit a claim which seeks a remedy which, in substance, will not reduce the level of assets comprised within the bankrupt's estate, such as a monetary claim which will give rise to a debt which is not provable (see, for example, *Albert v Albert* [1996] BPIR 232, CA) or a claim for specific performance or an injunction, on which see *Re Coregrange Ltd* [1984] BCLC 453 (on the former but analogous liquidation provisions). For the same reasons the court will usually be inclined to allow proceedings which are brought to obtain a judgment so as to allow the claimant to pursue the bankrupt's insurer under the Third Parties (Rights against Insurers) Act 1999, which proceedings have no effect on the bankrupt's estate itself: see *Post Office v Norwich Union* [1967] 2 QB 363 at 377–378.

There appears to be no fundamental incompatibility between a bankruptcy order and a freezing order: *Polly Peck v Nadir* [1992] BCLC 746 (Knox J). The usual 'just and convenient' course on the making of a bankruptcy order will usually be the discharge of any subsisting freezing order although, exceptionally, there may be grounds on which justice and convenience requires the continuance of the freezing order: *Eco Quest v GFI Consultants Ltd* [2014] EWHC 4329 (QB) (Mr Richard Salter QC).

While not purporting to lay down any general principles to be considered in an application for a stay under s 285, Registrar Barber gave a detailed judgment in relation to her own exercise of the discretion in *Re Mireskandari; Hellard v Chadwick* [2014] BPIR 163. The decision was upheld on appeal ([2014] EWHC 2158, [2014] BIR 1234), but Charles Hollander QC (sitting as a deputy High Court judge) appeared to take a much more restrictive view of the ambit of the court's discretion, holding that once it was concluded that the claim against the estate was for a bankruptcy debt it would need some very particular circumstances before the court would do other than grant a stay. Such circumstances can, however, arise. For example, in *Fern Advisers Ltd v Burford* [2014] EWHC 762 (QB), [2014] BPIR 581 HHJ Mackie QC treated a litigant-in-person defendant as making an application under s 285 in the face of a summary judgment application but granted summary judgment nonetheless where the defendant admitted acting dishonestly and forging documents.

In the unreported decision in *Public Joint Stock Co Aeroflot Russian Airlines v Berezovsky* (16 December 2015), Rose J considered that on an application under s 285 by trustees for a stay of litigation against the estate, the court had a broad and unfettered discretion to do what was right in the circumstances. The judge adverted to a number of considerations including the complexity and suitability of the proceedings for adjudication and the risk of inconsistent findings where there were a number of defendants, and whether there would be unfairness to other defendants if a stay were granted against the estate only.

**The scope of s 285(3) and the principles governing permission to proceed**—Section 285(3)(a) prevents a creditor with a provable debt having remedy against the property or person of the bankrupt. In *Re Heating and Electrical Piping Ltd* [2012] BPIR 1122 HHJ Peter Langan QC stressed that s 285(3)(a) does not debar the handing down of a judgment, merely the enforcement thereof. This decision was followed in *Re Mireskandari; Hellard v Chadwick* [2014] BPIR 163 by Registrar Barber who considered that 'in context, "remedy" as used in s 285(3)(a) cannot be construed so as to preclude legal proceedings down to and including declaratory relief or judgments. Enforcement is an entirely different issue' [40]. Permission of the court is not required, therefore, if a committal application is not being brought to recover damages or costs awarded by the court: see, for example, *Bayliss v Saxton* [2018] EWHC 3365 (QB), and contrast *Smith v Braintree DC* [1990] 2 AC 215 (warrant of committal used as direct means of enforcement of debt).

Section 285(3)(b) only applies where a bankruptcy order is made and a creditor with a provable debt seeks to *commence* any action or other legal proceedings – which will have the broadest scope – against the bankrupt. In *Bristol & West Building Society v Trustee of the Property of John Julius Bach (a Bankrupt) and Stuart Samuel Melinek (a Bankrupt)* [1997] BPIR 358 at 361G–362F David Young QC, sitting as a deputy High Court judge, drew on the following principles set out in the judgment of Master Lee QC in *Ex parte Walker* (1982) 6 ACLR 423 at 426 as guiding the court in the exercise of its discretion, albeit not exhaustively:

(1)     If, on the face of the matter, there is no arguable claim, leave should be refused.

(2)     There must be no prejudice to the creditors or to the orderly administration of the bankruptcy if the action is to proceed.

(3)     The claim must be of a type that should proceed by action rather than through the proofing procedure of bankruptcy.

(4)     Leave is more likely to be granted where the defendant is insured – s 285(3) is not designed to protect an insurer.

(5)     A condition is often imposed that a claimant cannot enforce any judgment against the defendant without the leave of the bankruptcy court.

(6)     Mere delay in applying for leave will not prevent leave being granted.

(7)     Leave may be granted after the expiry of the relevant period of limitation to continue an action commenced within the limitation period without the leave of the court.

See also *Avonwick Holdings Ltd v Castle Investment Fund Ltd* (unreported, 15 December 2015) where permission to add a bankrupt as a defendant to existing claims was granted, despite some suggestion that he was being added as an 'anchor defendant' in the jurisdiction to enable the other defendants to be served abroad, where the claimant was the bankrupt's largest creditor by far, other creditors would not be prejudiced if the action proceeded, the claim was arguable and the application had not been made in bad faith.

The use of the mandatory leave requirement in s 285(3) does not infringe Art 6 of the European Convention for the Protection of Human Rights for if an applicant for leave had an arguable case leave would be granted: *Seal v Chief Constable of South Wales Police* [2007] UKHL 31, [2007] BPIR 1396.

Section 285(4) specifically provides that the rights of a secured creditor are not affected by s 285(3). A secured creditor may prove for his debt subject to the valuation of the security and admission to proof by a trustee-in-bankruptcy: *Evans v Finance-U-Ltd* [2013] EWCA Civ 869, [2013] BPIR 1001 at [19] (Patten LJ). Neither does the acceptance of a dividend by a secured creditor amount to an agreement or election by the secured creditor to treat as unsecured that part of the debt in respect of which the dividend is paid: *Whitehead v Household Mortgage Corp Ltd* [2002] EWCA Civ 1657, [2003] 1 WLR 1173 at [24] (Chadwick LJ) (an IVA case in which the ethos underlying the bankruptcy code was applied).

The judgment of Lindsay J in *Bristol & West Building Society v Saunders* [1996] 3 WLR 473 is authority for the proposition that the court has jurisdiction under s 285(3) to grant leave retrospectively although *Saunders* was not followed by HHJ Kershaw, sitting as a judge of the High Court, in the doubtful decision in *Re Taylor (a bankrupt)* [2007] BPIR 175. *Saunders* was preferred by Chief Registrar Baister in *Bank of Scotland plc v Breytenbach* [2012] BPIR 1 and by David Richards J in *Bank of Ireland v Colliers International* [2012] EWHC 2942 (Ch), [2013] Ch 422, [2012] BPIR 1099.

Further assistance on leave may be gleaned from the review of the authorities on leave in the context of derivative proceedings involving a solvent company by HHJ Davis-White QC in *Wilton UK Ltd v Shuttleworth* [2017] EWHC 2195 (Ch).

**The meaning of s 285(6)**—Sections 283 and 283A define the scope of a bankrupt's estate. Subsection (6) makes clear that s 285 applies to proceedings against *any* property or goods of the bankrupt, irrespective of whether such property or goods is comprised in the bankrupt's estate, such that a creditor is susceptible to the court's control where he attacks property excluded from the scope of the bankrupt's estate, on which see s 283 and the notes thereto.

## [1.400]

### 286 Power to appoint interim receiver

(1)     The court may, if it is shown to be necessary for the protection of the debtor's property, at any time after the presentation of a bankruptcy petition and before making a bankruptcy order, appoint the official receiver or an insolvency practitioner to be interim receiver of the debtor's property.

(2)     . . .

(3)     The court may by an order appointing any person to be an interim receiver direct that his powers shall be limited or restricted in any respect; but, save as so directed, an interim receiver has, in relation to the debtor's property, all the rights, powers, duties and immunities given by the next section.

(4)     An order of the court appointing any person to be an interim receiver shall require that person to take immediate possession of the debtor's property or, as the case may be, the part of it to which his powers as interim receiver are limited.

(5)   Where an interim receiver has been appointed, the debtor shall give him such inventory of his property and such other information, and shall attend on the interim receiver at such times, as the latter may for the purpose of carrying out his functions under this section reasonably require.

(6)   Where an interim receiver is appointed, section 285(3) applies for the period between the appointment and the making of a bankruptcy order on the petition, or the dismissal of the petition, as if the appointment were the making of such an order.

(7)   A person ceases to be interim receiver of a debtor's property if the bankruptcy petition relating to the debtor is dismissed, if a bankruptcy order is made on the petition or if the court by order otherwise terminates the appointment.

(8)   References in this section to the debtor's property are to all his property, whether or not it would be comprised in his estate if he were made bankrupt.

**Amendments**—Enterprise and Regulatory Reform Act 2013, s 71(3), Sch 19, paras 1, 17; Deregulation Act 2015, s 19, Sch 6, Pt 5, paras 12, 13; Small Business, Enterprise and Employment Act 2015, s 133(2), Sch 10, paras 1, 2.

**General note**—The appointment of an interim receiver in the period between the presentation of a bankruptcy petition and the making of a bankruptcy order is a draconian measure which is designed to safeguard against the depletion of the bankruptcy estate and which finds a broad equivalent in the appointment of a provisional liquidator under s 135 in winding up. By s 286(6) the appointment of an interim receiver triggers the limitation on creditors' actions under s 285(3), which would otherwise only apply on the making of a bankruptcy order.

**The circumstances in which an interim receiver will be appointed**—The requirement that an applicant must show that the appointment of an interim receiver is 'necessary for the protection of the debtor's property' has not been the subject of reported judicial analysis. It is suggested that the test must necessarily reflect the scope for the divergence of circumstances in which such an application might be made and, as such, should equate to the requirements for the appointment of a provisional liquidator under s 135 in winding up, on which see the notes thereto.

The decision in *HMRC v Winnington Networks Ltd* [2014] EWHC 1259 (Ch) concerned an application without notice for the appointment of provisional liquidators to a company. The type of considerations in that case would apply by analogy in the appointment of an interim receiver over a personal debtor's property. In particular, Norris J gave weight to the fact that the appointment was necessary to ensure the preservation of records stored on computers and other electronic devices so as to protect against tampering with that material.

**Identity of the interim receiver**—Although an interim receiver will ordinarily be the official receiver, as provided for in s 286(1), the Court of Appeal has held that a person other than the official receiver may be appointed in an appropriate case: *Gibson Dunn & Crutcher v Rio Properties Inc* [2004] BPIR 1203. The court also retains a discretion to appoint as interim receiver an insolvency practitioner already appointed under s 273.

**Appointment of a special manager**—Given that the function of the interim receiver is essentially protective, it may be appropriate for the official receiver to consider an application under s 370(2) for the appointment of another person as special manager where the particular nature of the estate, property or business comprised in the debtor's estate or the interests of creditors generally require such an appointment to be made.

**Rights and powers of the interim receiver**—In the absence of contrary order under s 286(3), the rights and powers of the interim receiver are those set out in s 287(2) and (3). In an appropriate case, however, the court may be receptive to a submission that the provision of express powers is appropriate, as in *Re Baars* [2003] BPIR 523 at 530D–530E, where Lloyd J was prepared to declare 'that the interim receiver's powers shall extend to the powers that he would have under ss 366 and 367 [which he would have in any case] and 426 of the Insolvency Act 1986 just in case there is otherwise room for arguing that he does not have those powers.'

**Immunities of the interim receiver**—Section 286(3) provides that the interim receiver has the protection provided by s 287(4) unless the court orders otherwise.

The combined effect of s 286(4) and (8) is that the interim receiver is protected from the risk of seizing property which he reasonably believes to be the property of the debtor, or which is subject to contrary representations as to ownership by the debtor or an interested third party, or property which cannot easily be removed or separated from other property for the purpose of taking immediate possession.

**Contents of court order**—The contents of the order appointing an interim receiver are set out in r 10.51. Apart from the question of powers, the circumstances of the case may require further express provision, although the legislation makes no stipulation as to such terms. For example, an order may identify specific property which is not subject to immediate possession by the interim receiver. Further provisions might include sums to be made available to a debtor for the obtaining of legal advice, sums to be available in respect of living expenses, the sale or charge of property subject to the consent of the official receiver and, possibly, the requirement for co-operation with the interim receiver in any particular respect. It is usually the case that any appointment of a special manager is incorporated within a single order, together with any further consequential provisions such as those just mentioned. It may also be appropriate that undertakings are provided by the debtor; for example, in *Re Baars* (above) the debtor gave an undertaking that he would not gamble pending the determination of the bankruptcy petition.

The inclusion in an order allowing a debtor to expend monies on, most commonly, legal advice and living expenses mirrors a similar provision commonly found within a freezing order made under CPR, Pt 25. Where a dispute arises as to what constitutes the very common 'reasonable' provision made for such items in the context of a freezing order, the resolution of that issue is a matter for the parties to the litigation. On the other hand, in the case of an interim receiver's appointment the issue will concern the petitioner only indirectly and, ultimately, the dispute is one between the interim receiver himself and the debtor. Given the inherent difficulty that the interim receiver may not be in a position to assess what is reasonable and what is not in the circumstances of any particular case, one solution, as employed by Lloyd J in the *Re Baars* case, is for an order to impose a cap on the amount that may be spent on legal advice etc and living expenses, the interim receiver thereby being in a position to object to and refuse plainly extravagant requests for monies.

**Appointment to estate of deceased person**—The court may appoint an interim receiver in the administration of a deceased person's insolvent estate if the court considers it necessary to protect the estate's property: art 3 and Sch 1, Pt II, para 13 of the Administration of Insolvent Estates of Deceased Persons Order 1986.

**Position of interim receiver where order in effect under Proceeds of Crime Act 2002**—An interim receiver takes subject to any order made under the 2002 Act, in that the interim receiver's powers are not exercisable over property which is subject to such an order by virtue of s 417(4) of the 2002 Act.

**Procedure**—The procedure governing the appointment of an interim receiver and the giving of security appears in rr 10.49–10.54. Most significantly, eligible applicants – being a closed class of three persons, including a creditor or debtor – together with the mandatory contents of the affidavit or witness statement in support of an application appear in r 10.49. Section 286(7) identifies the three circumstances in which the appointment of an interim receiver may terminate; r 10.54(2) allows the court to give appropriate directions on termination.

Paragraph 9 of Sch 9 allows for the making of rules under s 412 as to the manner in which an interim receiver is to carry out his functions. No such rules have yet been introduced.

See notes accompanying s 135.

## [1.401]

### 287 Powers of interim receiver

(1) An interim receiver appointed under section 286 is the receiver and (subject to section 370 (special manager)) the manager of the debtor's property and is under a duty to act as such.

(2) The function of an interim receiver while acting as receiver or manager of the debtor's property under this section is to protect the property; and for this purpose—

    (a)    he has the same powers as if he were a receiver or manager appointed by the High Court, and

    (b)    he is entitled to sell or otherwise dispose of any perishable goods comprised in the property and any other goods so comprised the value of which is likely to diminish if they are not disposed of.

(3) An interim receiver while acting as receiver or manager of the debtor's property under this section—

    (a)    shall take all such steps as he thinks fit for protecting the debtor's property,

    (b)    is not required to do anything that involves his incurring expenditure, except in pursuance of directions given by—

        (i)    the Secretary of State, where the official receiver is the interim receiver, or

        (ii)    the court, in any other case,

    (c)    may, if he thinks fit (and shall, if so directed by the court) at any time seek a decision on a matter from the debtor's creditors.

(4) Where—

(a)    an interim receiver acting as receiver or manager of the debtor's property under this section seizes or disposes of any property which is not the debtor's property, and

(b)    at the time of the seizure or disposal the interim receiver believes, and has reasonable grounds for believing, that he is entitled (whether in pursuance of an order of the court or otherwise) to seize or dispose of that property,

the interim receiver is not to be liable to any person in respect of any loss or damage resulting from the seizure or disposal except in so far as that loss or damage is caused by his negligence; and he has a lien on the property, or the proceeds of its sale, for such of the expenses of the interim receivership as were incurred in connection with the seizure or disposal.

(5)    . . .

**Amendments**—Small Business, Enterprise and Employment Act 2015, ss 126, 133(2), Schs 9, 10.

**General note**—It was formerly the case that, as a general rule, the official receiver became receiver and manager of the bankrupt's estate between the making of a bankruptcy order and the time at which the bankrupt's estate vested in a trustee under s 306 on his or her appointment. Since the introduction in 2015 of the new s 291A, however, the general rule (subject to the exception in s 291A(2) where an IVA is in place) is that the official receiver becomes trustee in bankruptcy upon the making of a bankruptcy order, which vests the estate in the trustee at that moment. The scope and application of s 287 is accordingly now limited to interim receivers appointed prior to the making of a bankruptcy order under s 286.

Rules 13.1–13.4 govern the status of the official receiver.

### SECTION 287(2)

**Functions and powers of the interim receiver**—The powers of a receiver and manager appointed by the High Court are at the court's discretion and will depend on the facts of any particular case.

Section 287(2)(b) applies only to either 'perishable goods' or any other goods comprised within the estate 'the value of which is likely to diminish if they are not disposed of.' This latter reference is narrower than the scope of onerous property under s 315(2) and, in contrast to s 315(2)(b), requires the likelihood of diminishment in value as opposed to the risk that the property may give rise to a liability to pay money or perform any other onerous act which amounts to a very different requirement.

The role of the interim receiver in exercising his powers must be read in conjunction with s 287(3).

### SECTION 287(3)

**Steps towards protecting property**—The three provisions of s 287(3) are independent of each other. Section 287(3)(a) allows the interim receiver a good deal of leeway in exercising his discretion in taking steps to protect any property comprised within the scope of the bankruptcy estate without, under s 287(3)(b), being required to do anything involving the incurring of expenditure other than on the direction of the Secretary of State where the official receiver is the interim receiver. It should be noted, however, that 287(3)(b) does not require the direction of the court (or, in addition, the Secretary of State where the interim receiver is the official receiver) where the interim receiver is prepared to incur expenditure voluntarily.

Although 287(3)(c) allows for the summoning of a general meeting of creditors, such meetings are rare in practice. The provision would allow for an application to court by the interim receiver if he is uncertain as to whether or not a meeting of creditors should be summoned, or an application by a creditor where the interim receiver refuses to summon a meeting voluntarily and where the court can be satisfied that the summoning of a meeting is appropriate in the circumstances. This provision represents a marked shift from the former s 74(2) of the Bankruptcy Act 1914 which required the Official Receiver to 'consult the wishes of the creditors' with respect to the management of the debtor's property 'as far as practicable'. It would appear that one or more creditors aggrieved at a lack of consultation could apply to the court for relief, including the summoning of a creditors' meeting, under s 303(1).

### SECTION 287(4)

**Limitation on liability of the interim receiver**—Other than in a case of negligence, the interim receiver is protected from any claim for loss or damage following the seizure or disposal of property which is not comprised in the debtor's estate, subject to the interim receiver discharging the burden of proof upon him in establishing both that he believed (ie subjectively) and had reasonable grounds for believing (ie objectively) that he was entitled to seize or dispose of that property. The substance of that protection is now mirrored in s 432(2) of the Proceeds of Crime Act

2002. Provided the interim receiver is able to establish both grounds, he is equally entitled to the statutory lien created by s 287(4) in respect of expenses incurred in connection with the seizure or disposal.

**Appointment to estate of deceased person**—The court may appoint an interim receiver in the administration of a deceased person's insolvent estate if the court considers it necessary to protect the estate's property: art 3 and Sch 1, Pt II, para 13 of the Administration of Insolvent Estates of Deceased Persons Order 1986.

## [1.402]

### 288 Statement of affairs

(1)  Where a bankruptcy order has been made otherwise than on a bankruptcy application, the official receiver may at any time before the discharge of the bankrupt require the bankrupt to submit to the official receiver a statement of affairs.

(2)  The statement of affairs shall contain—

    (a)    such particulars of the bankrupt's creditors and of his debts and other liabilities and of his assets as may be prescribed, and

    (b)    such other information as may be prescribed.

(2A)  Where a bankrupt is required under subsection (1) to submit a statement of affairs to the official receiver, the bankrupt shall do so (subject to subsection (3)) before the end of the period of 21 days beginning with the day after that on which the prescribed notice of the requirement is given to the bankrupt by the official receiver.

(3)  The official receiver may, if he thinks fit—

    (a)    release a bankrupt from an obligation imposed on the bankrupt under subsection (1), or

    (b)    either when giving the notice mentioned in subsection (2A) or subsequently, extend the period mentioned in that subsection,

and where the official receiver has refused to exercise a power conferred by this section, the court, if it thinks fit, may exercise it.

(4)  A bankrupt who—

    (a)    without reasonable excuse fails to comply with an obligation imposed under this section, or

    (b)    without reasonable excuse submits a statement of affairs that does not comply with the prescribed requirements,

is guilty of a contempt of court and liable to be punished accordingly (in addition to any other punishment to which he may be subject).

**Amendments**—Enterprise and Regulatory Reform Act 2013, s 71(3), Sch 19, paras 1, 18; Deregulation Act 2015, s 19, Sch 6, Pt 5, paras 12, 15.

**General note**—This provision applies in all cases other than on a debtor's application, for which see s 263J and IR 2016, rr 10.34–10.48. The statement of affairs itself is of fundamental importance in enabling the official receiver and creditors to reach an informed assessment of the assets and liabilities in the bankruptcy. Section 433 also allows for the use of the statement in evidence against any person making or concurring with its contents. The effect of the amendments made by s 19 of and Sch 6 to the Deregulation Act 2015 are that statements of affairs are no longer compulsory. Instead, the official receiver is empowered to require the bankrupt to submit a statement of affairs at any time before discharge.

**The obligation in s 288(1) and the power of dispensation under s 288(3)**—As to the bankrupt's statement of affairs, see r 10.56. A bankrupt required to submit a statement of affairs may apply to the court for a release or extension of time, if the request is refused by the official receiver: r 10.58(2).

**Contents of the statement of affairs**—See r 10.56.

**Deceased insolvents' estates**—These provisions apply to such estates: para 15 of the Administration of Insolvent Estates of Deceased Persons Order 1986 (SI 1986/1999).

## [1.403]

### 289 Investigatory duties of official receiver

(1)  The official receiver shall—

    (a)    investigate the conduct and affairs of each bankrupt (including his conduct and affairs before the making of the bankruptcy order), and

(b)     make such report (if any) to the court as the official receiver thinks fit.

(2)   Subsection (1) shall not apply to a case in which the official receiver thinks an investigation under that subsection unnecessary.

(3)   Where a bankrupt makes an application for discharge under section 280 —

(a)     the official receiver shall make a report to the court about such matters as may be prescribed, and

(b)     the court shall consider the report before determining the application.

(4)   A report by the official receiver under this section shall in any proceedings be prima facie evidence of the facts stated in it.

**Amendments**—Enterprise Act 2002, s 258.

**General note**—Section 289 was amended by s 258 of the Enterprise Act 2002 with effect from 1 April 2004 and applies to all bankruptcies commencing after that date. The new provision represents a relaxation of the obligation under the former s 289(1) which imposed a duty on the official receiver to investigate the conduct and affairs of *every* bankrupt other than in the case of summary administration under s 275 (which has itself now been repealed). Despite this amendment, the significance of the investigatory duties imposed on the official receiver by s 289 remains as identified by the Court of Appeal in *R v Kearns* [2002] 1 WLR 2815.

**The grounds for and consequences of the official receiver thinking an investigation to be unnecessary**—The word 'shall' in s 289(1) raises a presumption that the obligations within that provision will apply to any particular bankruptcy. The presumption, however, is capable of being rebutted if the official receiver 'thinks' an investigation is unnecessary. The word 'thinks' is new: see the commentary on possible interpretation in the notes to para 3(3) of Sch B1. In the absence of any guidance – there is certainly no good reason why the grounds for the making of a bankruptcy restrictions order in Sch 4A should be of any particular relevance here – it is suggested that an investigation might only be considered unnecessary if the official receiver thinks, based on proper consideration of the information available to him, and in the absence of suspicion as to the accuracy of that information, that the time and cost likely to be involved in an investigation outweighs any practical benefit of an investigation, bearing in mind in particular the public interest element of an investigation.

Where the official receiver intends to file a notice that an investigation is unnecessary, he is obliged to give notice to that effect to all creditors and any trustee, any of whom may object within 28 days. That procedure is relevant because, in the absence of any objections, the filing of a notice by the official receiver with the court, as a general rule, has the irreversible effect of discharging the bankrupt under s 279(2) within the one-year period after which discharge is ordinarily obtained under s 279(1).

**Statements made in the report under s 289(4)**—The official receiver enjoys absolute privilege for the purpose of a claim for libel by any person named within his report: *Bottomley v Brougham* [1908] 1 KB 584; and see also *Burr v Smith* [1909] 2 KB 306.

**Deceased insolvents' estates**—These provisions apply to such estates: para 16 of the Administration of Insolvent Estates of Deceased Persons Order 1986 (SI 1986/1999); the official receiver is not under a duty to investigate the conduct of a deceased debtor but may do so if he thinks fit.

## [1.404]

### 290  Public examination of bankrupt

(1)   Where a bankruptcy order has been made, the official receiver may at any time before the discharge of the bankrupt apply to the court for the public examination of the bankrupt.

(2)   Unless the court otherwise orders, the official receiver shall make an application under subsection (1) if notice requiring him to do so is given to him, in accordance with the rules, by one of the bankrupt's creditors with the concurrence of not less than one-half, in value, of those creditors (including the creditor giving notice).

(3)   On an application under subsection (1), the court shall direct that a public examination of the bankrupt shall be held on a day appointed by the court; and the bankrupt shall attend on that day and be publicly examined as to his affairs, dealings and property.

(4)   The following may take part in the public examination of the bankrupt and may question him concerning his affairs, dealings and property and the causes of his failure, namely—

(a)　the official receiver and, in the case of an individual made bankrupt on a petition under section 264(1)(d), the Official Petitioner,

(b)　the trustee of the bankrupt's estate, if his appointment has taken effect,

(c)　any person who has been appointed as special manager of the bankrupt's estate or business,

(d)　any creditor of the bankrupt who has tendered a proof in the bankruptcy.

(5)　If a bankrupt without reasonable excuse fails at any time to attend his public examination under this section he is guilty of a contempt of court and liable to be punished accordingly (in addition to any other punishment to which he may be subject).

**Amendments**—Enterprise and Regulatory Reform Act 2013, s 71(3), Sch 19, paras 1, 19.

**General note**—The examination of bankrupts has a long lineage, going back to the Act of 1604 (1 Jac 1 c 15). Under s 15 the Bankruptcy Act 1914 a public examination of a bankrupt was obligatory in all cases save for where the bankrupt was afflicted with a physical or mental disability. The time and expense, if nothing else, was hardly justifiable in the majority of cases. There is now no obligation in any case for a public examination, other than where the court makes an order under s 290(2) on the application of the official receiver – and only the official receiver – under s 290(1). Although the official receiver must make application to the court for an examination if required to do so by at least one-half in value of the creditors, it remains open to the official receiver to seek an examination of his own volition, irrespective of the position of creditors.

Those persons in s 290(4) and, again, only those persons, may question the bankrupt in the course of the public examination as to the bankrupt's 'affairs, dealings and property and the causes of his failure.' The court will not allow an examination to stray beyond the scope of those matters.

Much of the discussion under s 133 will also apply here, although under s 290 only the bankrupt may be summoned to an examination. This contrasts with s 366 under which others may be summoned to appear for a private examination as to the bankrupt or his dealings, affairs or property.

**Persons resident outside the jurisdiction**—The power of the court to order a person resident outside the jurisdiction to attend for a public examination under s 133, as confirmed by the Court of Appeal in *Re Seagull Manufacturing Co Ltd* [1993] BCC 241 in the context of winding up, must, it is submitted, extend to bankruptcy (and see *Official Receiver v Sahaviriya Steel Industries Public Co Ltd* [2015] EWHC 2877 (Ch) (HHJ Pelling QC)).

**Fails to attend**—If a bankrupt fails to attend he or she can be held to be in contempt and imprisoned. For an instance of this, see *R v Scriven* [2004] EWCA Civ 683, [2004] BPIR 972.

**Self-incrimination**—The decision of the Court of Appeal in *Bishopsgate Investments Ltd v Maxwell* [1993] Ch 1 confirmed that a bankrupt is not entitled to refuse to answer any question on the ground of privilege against self-incrimination in the course of a public examination. This was also the position previously under the Bankruptcy Act 1914, on which see *Re Paget ex parte Official Receiver* [1927] 2 Ch 85. Refusal to answer any question within the scope of a public examination will constitute a contempt on the part of the bankrupt. Under s 433 a bankrupt's answers at his/her public examination would not generally be admissible against him in criminal proceedings. If the court is concerned about the use to which the transcript might be put in proceedings outside the English jurisdiction, it can adjourn and order proceedings to continue in private: see *Rottman v Official Receiver* [2009] BPIR 617 (affirmed on appeal).

**Deceased person's estate**—See the Administration of Insolvent Estates of Deceased Persons Order 1986 (SI 1986/1999) and *Re Jawett* [1929] 1 Ch 108.

**Procedure**—See rr 10.99–10.105.

See notes accompanying s 133.

## [1.405]

### 291 Duties of bankrupt in relation to official receiver

(1)　. . .

(2)　. . .

(3)　. . .

(4)　The bankrupt shall give the official receiver such inventory of his estate and such other information, and shall attend on the official receiver at such times, as the official receiver may reasonably require—

(a)　for a purpose of this Chapter, or

(b)　in connection with the making of a bankruptcy restrictions order.

(5)　Subsection (4) applies to a bankrupt after his discharge.

(6) If the bankrupt without reasonable excuse fails to comply with any obligation imposed by this section, he is guilty of a contempt of court and liable to be punished accordingly (in addition to any other punishment to which he may be subject).

**Amendments**—Enterprise Act 2002, s 269, Sch 23; Small Business, Enterprise and Employment Act 2015, s 133(2), Sch 10, paras 1, 4.

**General note**—In some ways parts of this section are the counterpart of s 235, which applies to company officers and others, although one must remember that in bankruptcy, unlike with company insolvency administrations, the property of the bankrupt vests in the trustee immediately on the making of a bankruptcy order. Besides this provision, s 363(2) also obliges bankrupts (discharged and undischarged) to do all such things as they may be directed to do by their trustees for the purposes of the bankruptcy or the administration of the estate. Failure to assist involves a contempt of court (s 363(4)).

### SECTION 291(4)

**Scope of provision**—This provision was revised with effect from 1 April 2004 by s 269 of and Sch 23 to the Enterprise Act 2002 so as to provide for the reference to bankruptcy restrictions orders in s 291(4)(b), on which see the notes to s 281A. Whilst the reference to 'the making' of a bankruptcy restrictions order might be read restrictively so as to limit the scope of the obligation imposed on the bankrupt, it is doubtful, if not absurd, that the bankrupt should only be obliged to provide information in connection with the making of a bankruptcy restrictions order, as opposed to having to provide information within the scope of the subsection where, most obviously, the official receiver is looking into the *possibility* of making application for such an order. Like s 333(1), the obligation to provide information survives discharge.

The purpose of the provisions is in assisting the official receiver in the discharge of his function and facilitating the mandatory investigation required by s 289(1). In its revised form, s 291(4) (see below) also anticipates that the official receiver may have an ongoing requirement for the provision of information, including information in connection with what is specifically termed 'the making' of a bankruptcy restrictions order under s 281A.

In practice, the official receiver attached to the court in which a bankruptcy order is made will, for the purpose of his investigatory duties under s 289(1), require the bankrupt to attend on him for an initial interview at which a sworn statement detailing the bankrupt's assets, liabilities and pre-bankruptcy dealings is produced, usually in a Preliminary Bankruptcy Questionnaire, Form B40.01.

**The nature of the obligations in s 291(4)**—The substance of the obligations imposed on the bankrupt by these provisions is virtually identical to those imposed by ss 312(1) and 333(1). Reference should be made to the notes to those provisions. See *DBIS v Compton* [2012] BPIR 1108 for an example of the Magistrate's practical (although perhaps surprisingly lenient) approach to the obligations of a bankrupt under s 291 in the context of criminal charges under s 356 and s 357.

## CHAPTER III

### Trustees in Bankruptcy
*Tenure of office as trustee*

**[1.406]**

#### 291A First trustee in bankruptcy

(1) On the making of a bankruptcy order the official receiver becomes trustee of the bankrupt's estate, unless the court appoints another person under subsection (2).

(2) If when the order is made there is a supervisor of a voluntary arrangement approved in relation to the bankrupt under Part 8, the court may on making the order appoint the supervisor of the arrangement as the trustee.

(3) Where a person becomes trustee of a bankrupt's estate under this section, the person must give notice of that fact to the bankrupt's creditors (or, if the court so allows, advertise it in accordance with the court's directions).

(4) A notice or advertisement given by a trustee appointed under subsection (2) must explain the procedure for establishing a creditors' committee under section 301.

**Amendments**—Inserted by Small Business, Enterprise and Employment Act 2015, s 133(1).

**General note**—This is an entirely new provision which was inserted by s 133(1) of the Small Business, Enterprise and Employment Act 2015. The official receiver is no longer the receiver and manager on the making of a bankruptcy order, but will immediately become the first trustee, unless the court decides to appoint the supervisor of an approved voluntary arrangement instead. For the general rationale behind these amendments, see the general note to Part IX.

The first decision on this provision, *Barker v Baxendale-Walker* [2018] EWHC 2518 (Ch) (Chief ICC Judge Briggs), is authority for the proposition that, despite the default provision provided for in sub-section (1), s 291A is not more restrictive than the court's former power under s 292 such that the court has jurisdiction to appoint another office-holder in place of the official receiver.

## [1.407]

### 292 Appointment of trustees: general provision

(1)   This section applies to any appointment of a person (other than the official receiver) as trustee of a bankrupt's estate.

(2)   No person may be appointed as trustee of a bankrupt's estate unless he is, at the time of the appointment, qualified to act as an insolvency practitioner in relation to the bankrupt.

(3)   Any power to appoint a person as trustee of a bankrupt's estate includes power to appoint two or more persons as joint trustees; but such an appointment must make provision as to the circumstances in which the trustees must act together and the circumstances in which one or more of them may act for the others.

(4)   The appointment of any person as trustee takes effect only if that person accepts the appointment in accordance with the rules. Subject to this, the appointment of any person as trustee takes effect at the time specified in his certificate of appointment.

(5)   . . .

**Amendments**—Enterprise Act 2002, ss 269, 278(2), Sch 23, paras 1, 6, Sch 26; Small Business, Enterprise and Employment Act 2015, s 133(2), Sch 10, paras 1, 5.

**General note**—This provision applies to both the first appointment of a trustee and the making of an appointment following death, resignation etc. The power to appoint extends to two or more joint appointees under s 292(3), subject to the requirements of the second part of that provision.

The relationship between s 292 and the new provision in s 291A is explored in the judgment of Chief ICC Judge Briggs in *Barker v Baxendale-Walker* [2018] EWHC 2518 (Ch).

Although an appointment may be made by the bankrupt's creditors, the Secretary of State or by the court in the circumstances described in s 292(1), the appointment will usually, but need not be, made by the creditors. Section 292 is not exhaustive of the circumstances in which a trustee can be appointed, for example the general powers of the court under the Insolvency Act 1986 ss 303(2) (to give directions) and 363 (to exercise control of bankruptcy proceedings) could be used to confer jurisdiction on the court to appoint trustees under a block transfer arrangement: *Donaldson v O'Sullivan* [2008] EWHC 387 (Ch), [2008] BPIR 288 (confirmed on appeal: [2008] EWCA Civ 879, [2008] BPIR 1288).

**Appointment of one or more common office-holders in relation to connected insolvency estates**—In some cases there can be an efficiency in time and cost, and the consequent convenience involved, in the appointment of one or more common office-holders to connected insolvency estates which outweighs the possibility or risk of any conflicts of interest. The practice was approved in the corporate context by Lord Hoffmann in *Parmalat Capital Finance Ltd v Food Holdings Ltd (in liquidation)* [2008] UKPC 23, [2008] BPIR 641 at [23], following *Re Maxwell Communications Corp plc* [1992] BCC 372. In *Re Schlosberg (a bankrupt)* [2017] EWHC 2446 (Ch), [2018] BPIR 182 Arnold J made an order authorising the applicants, as trustees-in-bankruptcy of the estate of a shareholder in a company, to share material obtained by compulsion with the liquidator of the company where the trustees were able to demonstrate a real, as opposed to fanciful, prospect of benefit to the shareholder's estate as a consequence. In making the order in Schlosberg, his Lordship also took account of the fact of dishonesty and other malpractice as justifying disclosure.

10.67–10.75.

### 293–295

*(Repealed)*

## [1.408]

### 296 Appointment of trustee by Secretary of State

(1)   At any time when the official receiver is the trustee of a bankrupt's estate by virtue of any provision of this Chapter he may apply to the Secretary of State for the appointment of a person as trustee instead of the official receiver.

(2)   On an application under subsection (1) the Secretary of State shall either make an appointment or decline to make one.

(3)   Such an application may be made notwithstanding that the Secretary of State has declined to make an appointment either on a previous application under subsection (1) or under section 300(4) below.

(4)   Where the trustee of a bankrupt's estate has been appointed by the Secretary of State (whether under this section or otherwise), the trustee shall give notice to the bankrupt's creditors of his appointment or, if the court so allows, shall advertise his appointment in accordance with the court's directions.

(5)   In that notice or advertisement the trustee shall explain the procedure for establishing a creditors' committee under section 301.

**Amendments**—Small Business, Enterprise and Employment Act 2015, ss 126, 133(2), Schs 9, 10.

**General note**—At any time at which the official receiver is trustee, without limitation, he may apply to the Secretary of State for the appointment of a person as trustee in his stead. The official receiver's standing in this regard is unaffected by the fact of any previous application of the kind mentioned in s 296(3). This is not surprising, since an application under s 296(1) is most likely to be made where the official receiver becomes aware of information which has a significant bearing on his perception of the nature of the bankruptcy and, for example, the need for further investigation, proceedings etc where no such action was previously considered necessary or appropriate.

Although s 296(2) allows the Secretary of State to decline to make an appointment following an application under s 296(1), the grounds giving rise to the application will usually give rise to an appointment being made.

**Procedure**—Section 296(4) and (5) are only triggered on an appointment being made by the Secretary of State under s 296(2). Subsection (5) has been amended by Sch 9 of the Small Business, Enterprise and Employment Act 2015 such that it is no longer be necessary to have a general meeting of creditors to establish a creditors' committee under s 301.

## 297

*(Repealed)*

## [1.409]

### 298  Removal of trustee; vacation of office

(1)   Subject as follows, the trustee of a bankrupt's estate may be removed from office only by an order of the court or by a decision of the bankrupt's creditors made by a creditors' decision procedure instigated specially for that purpose in accordance with the rules.

(2)   . . .

(3)   . . .

(4)   Where the official receiver is trustee by virtue of section 291A(1) or a trustee is appointed by the Secretary of State or (otherwise than under section 291A(2)) by the court, a creditors' decision procedure may be instigated for the purpose of removing the trustee only if—

    (a)    the trustee thinks fit, or

    (b)    the court so directs, or

    (c)    one of the bankrupt's creditors so requests with the concurrence of not less than one-quarter, in value, of the creditors (including the creditor making the request).

(4A)   Where the bankrupt's creditors decide to remove a trustee, they may in accordance with the rules appoint another person as trustee in his place.

(4B)   Where the decision to remove a trustee is made under subsection (4), the decision does not take effect until the bankrupt's creditors appoint another person as trustee in his place.

(5)   If the trustee was appointed by the Secretary of State, he may be removed by a direction of the Secretary of State.

(6)   The trustee (not being the official receiver) shall vacate office if he ceases to be a person who is for the time being qualified to act as an insolvency practitioner in relation to the bankrupt.

(7)   The trustee may, in the prescribed circumstances, resign his office by giving notice of his resignation to the prescribed person.

(8)   The trustee shall vacate office on giving notice to the prescribed person that the trustee has given notice under section 331(2).

(8A)   A notice under subsection (8)—

> (a)   must not be given before the end of the period prescribed by the rules as the period within which the bankrupt's creditors may object to the trustee's release, and
>
> (b)   must state whether any of the bankrupt's creditors objected to the trustee's release.

(9)   The trustee shall vacate office if the bankruptcy order is annulled.

**Amendments**—Enterprise Act 2002, ss 269, 278(2), Sch 23, paras 1, 10, Sch 26; Enterprise and Regulatory Reform Act 2013, s 71(3), Sch 19, paras 1, 23; Small Business, Enterprise and Employment Act 2015, ss 126, 133(2), Schs 9, 10.

**General note**—The principles applying to removal of a trustee by order of the court under s 298(1) are the same as those considered in the notes to the analogous provision in liquidation in s 108, and in s 171. The authorities are reviewed in detail by Adam Johnson QC in *Re Birdi (in bankruptcy), Miles v Price* [2019] EWHC 291 (Ch), [2019] BPIR 498 (application dismissed). In *Birdi*, the court refused to give a direction under s 298(4) requiring the trustee to call a meeting of creditors at which his removal could be proposed; mindful of the additional costs involved in such a direction, and the nature of the criticisms directed at the trustee by the applicant, the court is very unlikely to require the convening of such a meeting if in all likelihood, as in *Birdi*, such relief will serve no practical purpose. Although it was identified by Registrar Nicholls in *Smedley v Brittain* [2008] BPIR 219 at [16] that a bankruptcy case may not be analogous to a liquidation case to the extent that an application may be brought by a debtor in bankruptcy, whereas the authorities in liquidation are, for the most part, concerned with applications to remove by creditors, it is respectfully submitted that such a distinction is only of any practical relevance to the extent that a debtor's application in bankruptcy can be shown to serve the debtor himself, as opposed to the interests of creditors, that is, to the extent that those two sets of interest cannot be shown to coincide. *Smedley* also provides guidance at [24]–[26] upon the removal of, specifically, a trustee by the court. In particular:

> ' . . . if the trustee has gone about his or her actions effectively, honestly, reasonably, without misconduct or maladministration, the court must think carefully and long and hard before deciding to remove him or her and that is especially the case if an application is made by a debtor. It should not be seen as easy to remove a trustee because, say, one or two actions are subject to criticism and especially if that comes with hindsight . . . the test to be achieved by the debtor is a particularly high one, if he is to be successful in removing from office the trustee, and he must show a very real and substantial cause.'

See also *Doffman and Isaacs v Wood and Hellard* [2011] EWHC 4008 (Ch), [2012] BPIR 972 for an example of an unsuccessful application for removal where a conflict of interest was alleged. Proudman J considered that (1) the interests of creditors were paramount and they had no objection to the appointment which would save costs, and (2) the potential conflict could be managed on the basis of undertakings.

**Procedure**—On procedure on removal or vacation see rr 10.77–10.85.

## [1.410]

### 299   Release of trustee

(1)   Where the official receiver has ceased to be the trustee of a bankrupt's estate and a person is appointed in his stead, the official receiver shall have his release with effect from the following time, that is to say—

> (a)   where that person is appointed by the bankrupt's creditors or by the Secretary of State, the time at which the official receiver gives notice under this paragraph to the prescribed person that he has been replaced, and
>
> (b)   where that person is appointed by the court, such time as the court may determine.

(2)   If the official receiver while he is the trustee gives notice to the Secretary of State that the administration of the bankrupt's estate in accordance with Chapter IV of this Part is for practical purposes complete, he shall have his release with effect from such time as the Secretary of State may determine.

(3)   A person other than the official receiver who has ceased to be the trustee shall have his release with effect from the following time, that is to say—

   (a)    in the following cases, the time at which notice is given to the prescribed person in accordance with the rules that that person has ceased to hold office—

       (i)    the person has been removed from office by a decision of the bankrupt's creditors and the creditors have not decided against his release,

       (ii)   the person has died;

   (b)    in the following cases, such time as the Secretary of State may, on an application by the person, determine—

       (i)    the person has been removed from office by a decision of the bankrupt's creditors and the creditors have decided against his release,

       (ii)   the person has been removed from office by the court or by the Secretary of State,

       (iii)  the person has vacated office under section 298(6);

   (c)    in the case of a person who has resigned, such time as may be prescribed;

   (d)    in the case of a person who has vacated office under section 298(8)—

       (i)    if any of the bankrupt's creditors objected to the person's release before the end of the period for so objecting prescribed by the rules, such time as the Secretary of State may, on an application by that person, determine, and

       (ii)   otherwise, the time at which the person vacated office.

(3A)   Where the person is removed from office by a decision of the bankrupt's creditors, any decision of the bankrupt's creditors as to whether the person should have his release must be made by a creditors' decision procedure.

(4)   Where a bankruptcy order is annulled, the trustee at the time of the annulment has his release with effect from such time as the court may determine.

(5)   Where the official receiver or the trustee has his release under this section, he shall, with effect from the time specified in the preceding provisions of this section, be discharged from all liability both in respect of acts or omissions of his in the administration of the estate and otherwise in relation to his conduct as trustee.

But nothing in this section prevents the exercise, in relation to a person who has had his release under this section, of the court's powers under section 304.

**Amendments**—Enterprise and Regulatory Reform Act 2013, s 71(3), Sch 19, paras 1, 24; Small Business, Enterprise and Employment Act 2015, s 126, Sch 9, paras 60, 78.

**General note**—This provision deals with the timing and effect of a trustee's release. The timing of release varies depending on the circumstances in s 299(1)–(4). On release by the court see Dear IP, Issue 26 (March 2006).

The effect of release is provided for in s 299(5) and effectively exonerates a trustee from all liability save for any liability imposed by the court under s 304, which is entirely unaffected.

The effect of the provision is, as Walton J described it in *Singer v Trustee in Bankruptcy* [1981] 1 WLR 1358 at 1362G (in relation to s 93(3) of the Bankruptcy Act 1914), 'to wipe the slate completely clean so far as the trustee is concerned, so that he may thereafter pay no thought to the previous course of his actions as the trustee in bankruptcy': see to like effect *Re Borodzicz, Borodzicz v Horton* [2016] BPIR 24 at [43] (Chief Registrar Baister). There are good reasons, therefore, why the court should be cautious about granting leave under s 304 following a trustee's release given that a trustee has no control over the bankruptcy estate and the costs a former trustee will inevitably face by reason of such leave being granted.

The judgment of Proudman J in *Oraki v Bramston* [2015] EWHC 2046 (Ch), [2015] BPIR 1238 at [158]–[162] considers the nature of the release effected by s 299(5) and the relationship between that provision and s 304. The judgment of David Richards LJ in the Court of Appeal casts some doubt on that analysis as to the relationship between the two provisions, without it being necessary to determine the point: [2017] EWCA Civ 403, [2017] BPIR 1021. For further discussion on the relationship between the provisions see the judgment of HHJ Eyre QC in *Re Birdi v Price* [2019] EWHC 3943 (Ch), [2019] BPIR 306 at [92]–[104].

**[1.411]**

### 300 Vacancy in office of trustee

(1) This section applies where the appointment of any person as trustee of a bankrupt's estate fails to take effect or, such an appointment having taken effect, there is otherwise a vacancy in the office of trustee.

(2) The official receiver shall be trustee until the vacancy is filled.

(3) The official receiver may ask the bankrupt's creditors to appoint a person as trustee, and must do so if so requested by not less than one tenth in value of the bankrupt's creditors.

(3A) If the official receiver makes such a request the bankrupt's creditors may in accordance with the rules appoint a person as trustee.

(4) If at the end of the period of 28 days beginning with the day on which the vacancy first came to the official receiver's attention he has not asked, and is not proposing to ask, the bankrupt's creditors to appoint a person as trustee, he shall refer the need for an appointment to the Secretary of State.

(5) . . .

(6) On a reference to the Secretary of State under subsection (4) the Secretary of State shall either make an appointment or decline to make one.

(7) If on a reference under subsection (4) no appointment is made, the official receiver shall continue to be trustee of the bankrupt's estate, but without prejudice to his power to make a further reference.

(8) References in this section to a vacancy include a case where it is necessary, in relation to any property which is or may be comprised in a bankrupt's estate, to revive the trusteeship of that estate after the vacation of office by the trustee under section 298(8) or the giving by the official receiver of notice under section 299(2).

**Amendments**—Enterprise Act 2002, ss 269, 278(2), Sch 23, paras 1, 11(a), (b), Sch 26; Small Business, Enterprise and Employment Act 2015, s 126, Sch 9, Pt 2, paras 60, 79.

**General note**—This provision applies to a vacancy in the office of trustee as defined in s 300(1) and (8). By s 300(2) the official receiver is trustee in all cases until a vacancy is filled.

The reference to it being necessary to 'revive the trusteeship' in s 300(8) caters for the need for a trustee to be appointed following the release of the official receiver as trustee under s 299(2), or the release of a trustee following the release determined by a meeting of the bankrupt's creditors under s 331(2)(b). Such a need might arise where property enures for the benefit of the bankruptcy estate following release or, for example, where any charge on the bankrupt's home under s 313(2) becomes enforceable following release.

*Control of trustee*

**[1.412]**

### 301 Creditors' committee

(1) Subject as follows, a bankrupt's creditors may, in accordance with the rules, establish a committee (known as "the creditors' committee") to exercise the functions conferred on it by or under this Act.

(2) The bankrupt's creditors shall not establish such a committee, or confer any functions on such a committee, at any time when the official receiver is the trustee of the bankrupt's estate, except in connection with the appointment of a person to be trustee instead of the official receiver.

**Amendments**—Small Business, Enterprise and Employment Act 2015, s 126, Sch 9, Pt 2, paras 60, 80.

**General note**—A creditors' committee may be established by a meeting of creditors in any bankruptcy. Where at any time there is no creditors' committee, s 302 vests the functions of such a committee in the Secretary of State. The provisions governing the formation and function of a creditors' committee appear in rr 17.2 to 17.28. The functions of a creditors' committee are essentially in monitoring the trustee and holding him to account on matters of genuine concern with respect to the bankruptcy: see r 17.22. In addition, a creditors' committee has specific powers under certain provisions, namely s 326(2) (permission to distribute bankrupt's property in specie), and s 326(3) (retrospective permission for acts undertaken without committee's permission in certain circumstances). However, where the official receiver is trustee, the role of the committee is limited by s 301(2), other than in connection with an appointment by the meeting of creditors of a person to be trustee in the place of the official receiver. Rule 17.19 specifically provides for resolutions of the committee to be effected by post, subject to the standing of any committee member to require the trustee to summon a committee meeting. See also IR 2016, Part 17, especially rr 17.3 and 17.4.

The decision of the Court of Appeal in *Re Bulmer ex parte Greaves* [1937] Ch 499 is authority for the proposition that a member of a Committee of Inspection, as a committee was known under the Bankruptcy Act 1914, is a fiduciary in relation to the bankrupt's estate so far as a committee member deals in property comprised in the estate. Although that authority almost certainly remains good, its practical relevance is now very much limited by the fact that, in contrast with the position under the earlier legislation, the committee has no standing to direct the trustee in the conduct of the bankruptcy.

Rule 1.58 authorises a trustee to refuse inspection of a document comprising part of the records of the bankruptcy from any member of the creditors' committee if the document should be treated as confidential or its disclosure would be prejudicial to the conduct of the proceedings or might reasonably be expected to lead to violence against any person.

For the position of the Financial Services Authority, see s 374(4) of the Financial Services and Markets Act 2000.

## [1.413]

### 302 Exercise by Secretary of State of functions of creditors' committee

(1)   The creditors' committee is not to be able or required to carry out its functions at any time when the official receiver is trustee of the bankrupt's estate; but at any such time the functions of the committee under this Act shall be vested in the Secretary of State, except to the extent that the rules otherwise provide.

(2)   Where in the case of any bankruptcy there is for the time being no creditors' committee and the trustee of the bankrupt's estate is a person other than the official receiver, the functions of such a committee shall be vested in the Secretary of State, except to the extent that the rules otherwise provide.

General note—See the notes to s 301.

## [1.414]

### 303 General control of trustee by the court

(1)   If a bankrupt or any of his creditors or any other person is dissatisfied by any act, omission or decision of a trustee of the bankrupt's estate, he may apply to the court; and on such an application the court may confirm, reverse or modify any act or decision of the trustee, may give him directions or may make such other order as it thinks fit.

(2)   The trustee of a bankrupt's estate may apply to the court for directions in relation to any particular matter arising under the bankruptcy.

(2A)   Where at any time after a bankruptcy petition has been presented to the court against any person, whether under the provisions of the Insolvent Partnerships Order 1994 or not, the attention of the court is drawn to the fact that the person in question is a member of an insolvent partnership, the court may make an order as to the future conduct of the insolvency proceedings and any such order may apply any provisions of that Order with any necessary modifications.

(2B)   Where a bankruptcy petition has been presented against more than one individual in the circumstances mentioned in subsection (2A) above, the court may give such directions for consolidating the proceedings, or any of them, as it thinks just.

(2C)   Any order or directions under subsection (2A) or (2B) may be made or given on the application of the official receiver, any responsible insolvency practitioner, the trustee of the partnership or any other interested person and may include provisions as to the administration of the joint estate of the partnership, and in particular how it and the separate estate of any member are to be administered.

Amendments—SI 1994/2421.

General note—These two provisions allow matters within the scope of either to be resolved by way of the procedure provided for in Part 12 of the Insolvency (England and Wales) Rules 2016. An application will usually proceed by way of an application in the existing bankruptcy proceedings.

Although broad in scope, this section should be read in conjunction with s 363. In particular, an application by a trustee or the official receiver that an undischarged or discharged bankrupt should do as directed by the court falls within s 363(2) and not s 303(2). Reference should also be made to s 298 (removal of trustee) and the notes thereto.

In *Re Lynch, Inspiration Finance Ltd v Cadwallader* [2020] EWHC 15 (Ch) Marcus Smith J allowed an appeal from an ICC judge in the context of an application issued by a bankrupt under s 303 for an order directing his trustee to contest proceedings brought by a finance company. Rather than dealing with the s 303 application on its merits, the judge below had erred in directing that the relevant issue should be determined between the finance company and the bankrupt for the purpose of which she had directed the trustee to issue an application under s 363 for the purpose of facilitating a determination of those issues. Smith J was of the view that the judge below should have considered the issue of whether the trustee should be directed to defend the possession proceedings in the course of the s 303 application, rather than the alternative course adopted (which was not, on analysis, in law, open to her). The judgment in *Lynch* contains a useful examination of the relationship between s 303 and s 363.

Section 303 does confer the necessary jurisdiction for the court to fix a trustee's legal fees 'although the challenge to the legal fees actually incurred may well be a difficult one to make successfully'. See also *Freeburn v Hunt* [2010] BPIR 325. In *Woodbridge v Smith* [2004] BPIR 247 Registrar Baister held that the wife of a bankrupt with an interest in the matrimonial home who wished to challenge a trustee's claim to remuneration was entitled to do so pursuant to s 303.

Further commentary on a trustee's remuneration appears in the notes to s 363.

A bankrupt may not use s 303 as a means, in substance, of challenging the bankruptcy order made against him: *Canty v Boyden* [2006] EWCA Civ 194, [2006] BPIR 624.

## SECTION 303(1)

' . . . or any other person is dissatisfied . . . '—In *Port v Auger* [1994] 1 WLR 862 at 874A Harman J considered that 'a person can only be "dissatisfied" if he can show that he has some substantial interest which has been adversely affected by whatever is complained of.' A person dissatisfied may therefore include a discharged bankrupt (on which see *Osborn v Cole* [1999] BPIR 251 at 254C–254F (Registrar Baister)) or a person in respect of whom a bankruptcy order has been annulled (on which see *Engel v Peri* [2002] BPIR 961 (Ferris J)). In *Re Dennis Michael Cook* [1999] BPIR 881 at 883G Stanley Burnton QC, sitting as a deputy High Court judge, adopted a wider interpretation than that of Harman J in expressing the view at 883F–883G that the term 'dissatisfied' is no narrower than the term 'aggrieved', as employed in the former s 80 of the Bankruptcy Act 1914, and was arguably wider. Accordingly, the term should not be given a restricted interpretation and will extend to a person who has a genuine grievance whose interests are prejudicially affected by any act, omission or decision of a trustee, but will not include a mere busybody who is interfering with things which do not concern him. Following consideration of these authorities in *Woodbridge v Smith* [2004] BPIR 247 Registrar Baister held that the wife of a bankrupt with an interest in the matrimonial home who wished to challenge a trustee's claim to remuneration, apparently approved at a meeting of which proper notice had not been given, fell within the scope of s 303(1) as a person 'dissatisfied'. In *Miller v Bayliss* [2009] EWHC 2063 (Ch), [2009] BPIR 1438 a person who was an existing shareholder in a company who alleged she had a contract with a trustee to sell shares to her in the company (which assertion the trustee denied) did not fall within the meaning of a 'person dissatisfied' and therefore had no standing to challenge the trustee's conduct in relation to the shares under s 303.

' . . . by any act, omission or decision of a trustee . . . '—Unless some unnecessary overlap was intended, the terms 'decision', 'act' and 'omission' are mutually exclusive. It would follow that an omission extends to a failure to do something, say through an oversight or through ignorance, but not a failure to do something as a consequence of a conscious decision as to such inaction.

**Circumstances in which the court's jurisdiction under s 303(1) should be invoked**—Practicality and justice, including the need to protect the interests of creditors, are not always served by allowing the time and expense necessarily involved in an application challenging a trustee's conduct, however genuine the sense of grievance on the part of the applicant. It was for this reason that Harman J expressed the view in *Port v Auger* [1994] 1 WLR 862 at 873–874 that s 303(1) should not be invoked lightly, and only where the applicant can be shown to have some substantial interest (see above) which has been adversely affected by whatever conduct is under complaint. In *Engel v Peri* [2002] BPIR 961 at [18] Ferris J held that it is the establishing of this 'substantial interest' which is determinative of whether an applicant has standing to proceed under s 303(1). The judge considered, but rejected, a submission to the effect that it was also necessary for an applicant to show that there would be a surplus after all the bankruptcy debts and the expenses of the bankruptcy had been paid in full. That proposition had been based on the judgment of Charles Harman J in *Re A Debtor ex parte the Debtor v Dodwell (the Trustee)* [1949] Ch 236 at 240. Ferris J considered (at [18]) that 'While this decision will obviously be applicable to the great majority of cases where a bankrupt seeks to interfere with the day to day administration of his estate in the course of the bankruptcy, I do not think it can be shown as laying down a universal requirement that a bankrupt must show that there will or may be a surplus before he has standing to apply under s 303.'

This was confirmed with a thorough review of the authorities in *Brake & Ors v Lowes & Ors* [2020] EWCA Civ 1491, [2020] BPIR 1 where Asplin LJ found at [78] that:

' . . . there is an additional requirement before a bankrupt can seek relief against the trustee in bankruptcy under section 303(1). This is consistent with the approach in all of the cases to which I have referred and has been the case for a considerable time and was articulated in the *Dodwell* case in 1949. The very nature of the bankruptcy regime is such that the bankrupt having taken the benefit of being relieved of his debts, absent fraud, cannot have the standing to interfere with the day-to-day administration of the estate by the trustee on behalf of the creditors. He must be able to show that he has a substantial interest which has been affected by the conduct complained of and a direct interest in the relief sought. The potential existence of a surplus is one way of being able to demonstrate such a substantial interest but it seems to me that it is not the only one . . . In my judgment, therefore, although the principles in the *Dodwell* and *Deloitte* cases apply in relation to applications under section 303(1) and 168(5), the judge was wrong to apply the *Deloitte* case narrowly and to concentrate solely on whether there is a surplus in this case.'

A creditor will usually be able to establish the 'substantial interest' requirement if the decision, act or omission complained of can be shown to have a potential and real effect on the creditor's financial interest in the bankruptcy. Perhaps the most obvious form of such conduct involves the trustee in refusing to pursue a cause of action vested in the bankruptcy estate, as suggested by Hoffmann J in *Heath v Tang* [1993] 1 WLR 1421, or the taking of steps by a trustee which are indefensible on any objective scrutiny. The court will not, however, interfere with a decision of a trustee in the course of his discharging his function under s 305(2), other than where, as Registrar Baister put the matter in *Osborn v Cole* [1999] BPIR 251 at 255G–255H, following a review of the authorities, 'it can be shown that [the trustee] has acted in bad faith or so perversely that no trustee properly advised or properly instructing himself could so have acted, alternatively if he had acted fraudulently or in a manner so unreasonable and absurd that no reasonable person would have acted in that way': see to the same effect *Hamilton v The Official Receiver* [1998] BPIR 602 at 605C–606A (Laddie J) and *Re Don Basil Williams* [2003] BPIR 545 at 546A–546D (Jacob J). *Osborne v Cole* was approved in *Supperstone v Hurst (No 3)* [2006] EWHC 2147 (Ch), [2006] BPIR 1263 and in *Bank of Baroda v Patel* [2009] BPIR 255. The effect of the provision is, as Walton J described it in *Singer v Trustee in Bankruptcy* [1981] 1 WLR 1358 at 1362G (in relation to s 93(3) of the Bankruptcy Act 1914), 'to wipe the slate completely clean so far as the trustee is concerned, so that he may thereafter pay no thought to the previous course of his actions as the trustee in bankruptcy': see to like effect *Re Borodzicz, Borodzicz v Horton* [2016] BPIR 24 at [43] (Chief Registrar Baister). There are good reasons, therefore, why the court should be cautious about granting leave under s 304 following a trustee's release given that a trustee has no control over the bankruptcy estate and the costs a former trustee will inevitably face by reason of such leave being granted. Arnold J proposed a slightly more interventionist approach at first instance in *Bramston v Haut* [2012] EWHC 1279 (Ch), [2012] BPIR 672, but the Court of Appeal confirmed that the court should only intervene if the trustee's decision was 'perverse' ([2012] EWCA Civ 1637, [2013] BPIR 25, an approach noted by reference to the contrasting earlier decision of Arnold J in the decision of Barling J in *Tucker v Atkins* [2014] EWHC 4469 (Ch), [2014] BPIR 1359. It follows that an applicant is plainly at risk on costs unless he can show that he has arguable grounds for challenging a decision of a trustee, given that onerous test, and irrespective of any subjective sense of grievance on the part of the bankrupt, as in *Aslam v Finn* [2013] EWHC 3405 (Ch) (Newey J).

In *Shepherd v The Official Receiver* [2007] BPIR 101 Gabriel Moss QC, sitting as a deputy High Court judge, dismissed an application by a bankrupt under s 303 challenging the official receiver's decision not to investigate what the bankrupt had maintained tenaciously, but unreasonably, was a claim in the bankruptcy estate against the Legal Services Commission.

The court may direct a trustee to assign a cause of action against a third party although it may refuse to do so on the ground that the cause of action is doubtful or that the assignee's financial position is so weak as to pose a real risk as to a costs order being made against the trustee in any ensuing litigation: *Re Shettar* [2003] BPIR 1055 (Park J). See also *Hunt v Harb* [2011] EWCA Civ 1239, [2012] BPIR 117. For an analogous case in winding up see *Hamilton v Official Receiver* [1998] BPIR 602 in which the applicant was successful under the equivalent s 168(5) in requiring the assignment of a cause of action which the Official Receiver had no intention of pursuing, a stance characterised by Laddie J as perverse.

Neither s 303(1) nor s 303(2) confers on the court jurisdiction or power to give directions to the official receiver as to the performance of his public law functions: *Hardy v Focus Insurance Co Ltd* [1997] BPIR 77 at 82F (Robert Walker J).

Where a bankrupt is in a position to apply to court for directions under s 303 in relation to any particular matter, but does not do so, a trustee who has acted negligently in relation to that matter is not automatically absolved from liability by reason of the bankrupt's inaction, although the position will depend on the particular facts of any case: *Bramston v Oraki* [2014] EWHC 4828 (Ch), [2014] BPIR 1374 at [8] (Mr Nicholas Strauss QC).

**Applicants under s 303(2)**—Although s 303(2) only makes reference to the trustee in making an application, the judgment of Blackburne J in *Re A & C Supplies Ltd* [1998] 1 BCLC 603 at 608G – a case on block-transfer orders – is authority for the proposition that an application may be made by any person with a sufficient interest to invoke the court's jurisdiction. That decision was followed by Park J in *Supperstone v Auger* [1999] BPIR 152 at 154B–154C, another block-transfer case. In *Craig v Humberclyde Industrial Finance Group Ltd* [1999] 1 WLR 129 the Court of Appeal confirmed the approach of Chadwick J at first instance in treating an application by the official receiver under the analogous s 168(3) (in a compulsory winding-up) for directions as to whether a claim by the company in liquidation ought to be compromised or assigned to the company's directors as akin to a *Beddoe* application.

**The court is not a bomb shelter for the office-holder's commercial decisions**— The court will not allow an office-holder to abrogate the potentially demanding responsibility in making commercial and administrative decisions which properly fall to the office-holder and for which the court does not provide a bomb shelter, to use the language of Neuberger J in *Re T & D Industries plc* [2000] 1 All ER 333 at 344I (an administration case). For example, in *Re Chinn* [2016] BPIR 346 Registrar Barber refused to give directions to a trustee on the adjudication of a proof of debt where the trustee had not undertaken that exercise; the proper course was for the trustee to adjudicate, as envisaged by the legislation, so as to trigger the appeal mechanism available to creditors. Equally, the outcome of a directions application may be the subject of an appeal: see, for example, *Revenue and Customs Commissioners v Ariel* [2016] EWHC 1674 (Ch), [2016] BPIR 1144 (Mann J overturning the decision of Registrar Derrett as to the jurisdictions of the bankruptcy court and the First-tier Tax Tribunal).

In *Re Longmeade Ltd (in liquidation)* [2016] EWHC 356 (Ch), [2016] BPIR 666 Snowden J identified, in the context of the bringing of proceedings for which the court's sanction was no longer required with effect from 26 May 2015, that a decision to commence proceedings is a commercial decision for the office-holder acting in the best interests of the insolvent estate and giving appropriate weight to the reasoned views of those with an interest in the litigation. On the other hand, unusual circumstances, as in the present case, might well prompt a directions application where an office-holder was faced with a genuine dilemma in relation to which the court's assistance is genuinely and reasonably required. The judgment gives guidance as to the sorts of factors an office-holder will ordinarily wish to consider.

For a case in which HMRC successfully appealed the provision of directions by the court to a trustee-in-bankruptcy on the issue of whether or not the trustee could properly provide documents in response to a request under para 2 of Sch 36 of the Finance Act 2008: see *Revenue & Customs Commissioners v Ariel* [2016] EWHC 1674 (Ch), [2017] 1 WLR 310 (Mann J).

**The court's approach to interfering with the decisions of a trustee-in-bankruptcy**—The judgment of Chief Registrar Baister in *Re Borodzicz, Borodzicz v Horton* [2016] BPIR 24 at [33]–[40] contains an informative analysis of the case law enshrining the long-established principle that, notwithstanding every bankruptcy being under the control of the court (by reference to s 363), the court will be slow to interfere with decisions of a trustee concerning the administration of the bankruptcy with which he is charged ('the case law makes clear that an applicant has a high hurdle to overcome to obtain permission to challenge decisions of a trustee'). There is further reference to the case law under the heading 'Circumstances in which the court's jurisdiction under s 303(1) should be invoked' above.

**Section 303(2A)–(2C)**—The court has jurisdiction to give directions in relation to a partnership dissolution where the partnership is not being wound up as an unregistered company but where its two partners are subject to bankruptcy orders: *Official Receiver v Hollens* [2007] BPIR 830 (Blackburne J).

**Costs of a s 303 application**—There is no hard and fast rule as to where the costs of a s 303 application will fall. In addition to the exercise of its discretion in ordering costs against a particular party, the court may have to consider whether or not any costs should rank as an expense in the bankruptcy. In the context of a contentious application the court is perfectly entitled to take the view, in the exercise of its discretion under CPR 44.3 and 44.5, as invoked by r 12.1, that the costs of an unsuccessful party should not fall as an expense of the bankruptcy, so as to be borne, in effect, by creditors in the bankruptcy, and that an unsuccessful party should meet the cost of other litigants whose conduct in the proceedings is either proper and justifiable or of assistance to the court. In *Re Tully* [2017] NICh 18 Deeny J ordered the costs of the application to be borne by the bankruptcy estate, and not the trustee personally. On the other hand, the court must be mindful of not only the wide import of the term 'person aggrieved' but also the risk of what Mr Stanley Burnton QC (sitting as a deputy High Court judge) termed in *Re Cooke (Dennis*

*Michael)* [1999] BPIR 881 'a mere busybody who is interfering with things which do not concern him'. Although the term 'dissatisfied' in s 303 is to be attributed a wide meaning, the court retains a sanction in relation to demonstrably unmeritorious applications by requiring the applicant to pay all of the costs occasioned by his or her application on which see, for example, *Walker Morris (a firm) v Khalastchi* [2001] 1 BCLC 1 (analogous case in winding up).

## [1.415]

### 304 Liability of trustee

(1) Where on an application under this section the court is satisfied—

    (a)    that the trustee of a bankrupt's estate has misapplied or retained, or become accountable for, any money or other property comprised in the bankrupt's estate, or

    (b)    that a bankrupt's estate has suffered any loss in consequence of any misfeasance or breach of fiduciary or other duty by a trustee of the estate in the carrying out of his functions,

the court may order the trustee, for the benefit of the estate, to repay, restore or account for money or other property (together with interest at such rate as the court thinks just) or, as the case may require, to pay such sum by way of compensation in respect of the misfeasance or breach of fiduciary or other duty as the court thinks just.

This is without prejudice to any liability arising apart from this section.

(2) An application under this section may be made by the official receiver, the Secretary of State, a creditor of the bankrupt or (whether or not there is, or is likely to be, a surplus for the purposes of section 330(5) (final distribution)) the bankrupt himself.

But the leave of the court is required for the making of an application if it is to be made by the bankrupt or if it is to be made after the trustee has had his release under section 299.

(3) Where—

    (a)    the trustee seizes or disposes of any property which is not comprised in the bankrupt's estate, and

    (b)    at the time of the seizure or disposal the trustee believes, and has reasonable grounds for believing, that he is entitled (whether in pursuance of an order of the court or otherwise) to seize or dispose of that property,

the trustee is not liable to any person (whether under this section or otherwise) in respect of any loss or damage resulting from the seizure or disposal except in so far as that loss or damage is caused by the negligence of the trustee; and he has a lien on the property, or the proceeds of its sale, for such of the expenses of the bankruptcy as were incurred in connection with the seizure or disposal.

**General note**—Section 304 should be read in conjunction with s 299 (release of trustee) and the notes to that section.

The effect of s 304(1)(a) and (b) is to create two distinct statutory causes of action which may be advanced by those applicants listed in s 304(2), subject to the limitations therein. Although s 304(1) closely resembles s 212(3) (misfeasance proceedings) the latter provision does not create any cause of action but is procedural in facilitating the advancing of already existing causes of action. It is for this reason that the words 'This is without prejudice to any liability arising apart from this section' appear in s 304(1) but are absent from s 212, since s 304(1) cannot prejudice any other cause of action – for breach of trust, breach of duty etc – which may also be available to a person eligible to proceed under s 304. However, even if other causes of action co-exist with s 304, the effect of a trustee's release under s 299 exonerates a trustee from all liability, save for liability imposed by court order under s 304(1). This was confirmed by the court in *Oraki v Bramston* [2015] EWHC 2046 (Ch), [2015] BPIR 1238. There Proudman J held that no common law duty in negligence lay against a trustee in bankruptcy to the bankrupt, but a statutory duty arises where the estate proves to be solvent, as a result of the trustee's obligation to return any surplus to the bankrupt pursuant to s 330, as: 'the trustee should not ride roughshod over someone who either should obviously not have been made bankrupt in the first place or who it can be seen has assets greater than liabilities' (para 34). The judgment of David Richards J in the Court of Appeal in *Oraki v Bramston* [2017] EWCA Civ 403, [2017] BPIR 1021 casts some doubt over the view of Proudman J as to the relationship between s 299(5) and s 304, without the point being material on appeal. The analysis of Proudman J in *Oraki* is, however, consistent with that of Mr Nicholas Strauss QC, sitting as a deputy High Court judge, in an earlier judgment in the same litigation, *Bramston v Oraki* [2014] EWHC 4828 (Ch), [2014] BPIR 1374 where, at [5]–[7], the deputy judge held that, in a case where it is clear throughout that the assets of the estate far exceed the sums necessary to pay all creditors in full and the expenses of the bankruptcy, it is at least arguable that the surplus gives rise to a duty on the trustee's part to the bankrupt as the person entitled to the surplus, subject to the trustee's overriding duty (or function) as provided for in s 305(2). On release, a trustee is released from everything except the matters specifically provided for in s 304. There is a useful review of the authorities in the judgment of Chief Registrar Baister in *Re Borodzicz, Borodzicz v Horton* [2016] BPIR 24 at [36]–[44].

For examples of claims under s 304 see *Green v Satsangi* [1998] BPIR 55 (Rimer J); *A & J Fabrications Ltd v Grant Thornton* [1998] 2 BCLC 227 (a liquidation case under s 212) (Jacob J); *Brown v Beat* [2002] BPIR 421 (Hart J), as approved of by the Court of Appeal in *Parkinson Engineering Services Ltd (in liquidation) v Swan* [2010] BCLC 163; see also *Chapper v Jackson* [2012] EWHC 3897 (Ch), [2012] BPIR 257 and *McAteer v Lismore* [2012] NICh 7, [2012] BPIR 812 (dealing with the comparable provision in art 277 of the Northern Ireland Insolvency Order 1989) – cases on each side of the line as to whether a trustee had breached his duties in relation to property. In the former the trustee had not fallen short of the standard of a reasonably skilled and careful insolvency practitioner where he had refused to intervene in a court ordered sale at a price alleged to be an undervalue. A relevant but not determinative factor was that the trustee had taken and followed legal advice. In the latter the trustee was found to have breached his duty of care by failing to properly advertise a property and selling at a price deemed to be an undervalue.

As a general principle, by analogy with the authorities in relation to administration, an office-holder will not generally owe any duty of care towards an individual unsecured creditor, absent some special relationship: *Oldham v Kyrris* [2003] EWCA Civ 1506, [2004] 1 BCLC 305 (Jonathan Parker LJ, upholding the decision at first instance of HHJ Behrens) and *Peskin v Anderson* [2001] 1 BCLC 372 at [31]–[34] per Mummery LJ (on the special relationship point). *Oldham* was approved by the Privy Council in *Hague v Nam Tai Electronics* [2008] UKPC 13, [2008] BPIR 363, and applied in *Lomax Leisure Ltd v Miller* [2007] EWHC 2508 (Ch) and *Charalambous v B & C Associates* [2009] EWHC 2601 (Ch).

**Who benefits from an order under s 304(1)**—Despite the varying class of applicants in s 304(2), the words 'for the benefit of the estate' in s 304(1) must be taken, it is submitted, as meaning that the court may only make an order which results in an award being made in favour of the bankruptcy estate, and not in favour of any individual applicant or creditor. That analysis is consistent with the class nature of bankruptcy and the concept of pari passu.

**Leave under s 304(2)**—A bankrupt requires the leave of the court to proceed with a s 304 claim in all cases, irrespective of the possibility of a surplus which will, nevertheless, usually be a relevant factor: *McGuire v Rose* [2013] EWCA Civ 429. Any other person within s 304(2) requires leave of the court once the trustee has had his release under s 299. In *Brown v Beat* [2002] BPIR 421 at 424D Hart J identified that the requirement that a bankrupt requires leave under s 304(2) reflects Parliament's recognition 'that applications by bankrupts against their trustees may well have a tendency to be vexatious'. The test for permission is whether or not there is a reasonable prospect of success: *Katz v Oldham* [2016] BPIR 83 at [9] (Registrar Derrett).

In any case requiring leave, the court will wish to be satisfied that the claim advanced has at least a real prospect of succeeding. For an example of the refusal of leave see *Reynard v Fox* [2018] EWHC 2141 (Ch), [2018] BPIR 1780 (HHJ Matthews).

**SECTION 304(3)**

'. . . property . . . '—In *Welsh Development Agency v Export Finance Co Ltd* [1992] BCC 270 the Court of Appeal held, in the context of s 234, that the word 'seizes' is only capable of extending to tangible property.

For an example of the operation of s 304(3) in protecting a trustee see the decision of HHJ Eyre QC (sitting as a High Court judge) in *Birdi v Price* [2019] EWHC 2943 (Ch), [2019] BPIR 306.

## CHAPTER IV

### Administration by Trustee
### *Preliminary*

**[1.416]**

#### 305 General functions of trustee

(1) This Chapter applies in relation to any bankruptcy where either—

    (a)    the appointment of a person as trustee of a bankrupt's estate takes effect, or

(b)     the official receiver becomes trustee of a bankrupt's estate.

(2)   The function of the trustee is to get in, realise and distribute the bankrupt's estate in accordance with the following provisions of this Chapter; and in the carrying out of that function and in the management of the bankrupt's estate the trustee is entitled, subject to those provisions, to use his own discretion.

(3)   It is the duty of the trustee, if he is not the official receiver—

(a)     to furnish the official receiver with such information,

(b)     to produce to the official receiver, and permit inspection by the official receiver of, such books, papers and other records, and

(c)     to give the official receiver such other assistance,

as the official receiver may reasonably require for the purpose of enabling him to carry out his functions in relation to the bankruptcy.

(4)   The official name of the trustee shall be "the trustee of the estate of ............., a bankrupt" (inserting the name of the bankrupt); but he may be referred to as "the trustee in bankruptcy" of the particular bankrupt.

**General note**—The key provision in defining the general functions of a trustee appears in s 305(2). The powers of a trustee should, of necessity, be exercised directly or indirectly in pursuit of those general functions. Furthermore, the trustee is subject not only to the rule in *Ex parte James*, which is discussed in more detail in the notes to para 5 of Sch B1, but is also obliged to maintain independence. In the words of Lightman J in *Re Ng (a Bankrupt)* [1997] BPIR 267 at 269H–270A – words which were approved of subsequently by the Court of Appeal in *Trustee in Bankruptcy of Bukhari v Bukhari* [1999] BPIR 157 – 'A trustee in bankruptcy is not vested with the powers and privileges of his office so as to enable himself to accept engagement as a hired gun. His duty is to exercise his powers and privileges for the benefit of the creditors for whom he is appointed a trustee.'

The generality of the words in s 305(2), and the reliance of the procedure of bankruptcy on the professional judgment of a trustee-in-bankruptcy, afford the trustee a considerable breadth of discretion in discharging his functions. The court, therefore, is only likely to interfere with the trustee's conduct, perhaps in the course of an application under s 303(1), where the conduct complained of is so manifestly beyond the scope of that in which a competent and reasonable trustee might engage as to justify the court's interference – see *Oraki v Bramston* [2015] EWHC 2046 (Ch), [2015] BPIR 1238 (affirmed on appeal [2017] EWCA Civ 403, [2017] BPIR 1021). Absent such conduct, the court will not entertain complaints which amount, in substance, to a difference of opinion as between the complainant and the trustee, or complaints which are plainly frivolous or vexatious. Conversely, a trustee should not approach any given situation blindly and thereafter seek to argue that any steps taken by him were only undertaken pursuant to his functions under s 305(2); so, for example, a trustee must weigh up all relevant circumstances, including litigation risk, when making what amounts to a commercial decision as to whether proceedings should be instituted in connection with the bankruptcy.

It is no part of the trustee's function under s 305(2) to deploy the bankrupt's privilege to assist a third party in a claim against another, even if it might result in the reduction or elimination of a creditor's claim against the estate: *Avonwick Holdings Limited v Shlosberg* [2016] EWCA Civ 1138, [2017] Ch 210, [2017] BPIR 1.

As a general principle it is not unreasonable for a trustee-in-bankruptcy to retain the solicitors which acted for the petitioning creditor: *Re Schuppan (a Bankrupt) (No 1)* [1996] 2 All ER 664 (Robert Walker J), as considered with further cases in the notes to s 314 under the heading 'Employment of solicitors'.

In *Re Birchall; Bell v Birchall* [2015] EWHC 1541 (Ch), [2017] 1 WLR 667, [2015] BPIR 751 a trustee applied to the court for an order to recoup from the practice client accounts his costs and expenses incurred in preserving a bankrupt solicitor's records and files. The court held that it did not have jurisdiction to make such an order and, even if it had, it would not have exercised it in the circumstances.

For the position in relation to the Financial Conduct Authority see s 373 of the Financial Services and Markets Act 2000 ('Insolvency Practitioner's duty to report').

*Acquisition, control and realisation of bankrupt's estate*

**[1.417]**

### 306 Vesting of bankrupt's estate in trustee

(1)  The bankrupt's estate shall vest in the trustee immediately on his appointment taking effect or, in the case of the official receiver, on his becoming trustee.

(2)  Where any property which is, or is to be, comprised in the bankrupt's estate vests in the trustee (whether under this section or under any other provision of this Part), it shall so vest without any conveyance, assignment or transfer.

**General note**—For the definition of the bankrupt's estate, see s 283. The vesting of property in a trustee-in-bankruptcy on his appointment – in contrast to the position in liquidation where property remains vested in the company – is fundamental to the discharge of the trustee's functions under s 305(2). At a practical level, a trustee will also wish to ensure that adequate insurance arrangements are in place.

The fact that a third party is unaware of the trustee's entitlement to property does not excuse that third party from dealings in respect of the property. The third party will not be able to give a good receipt for property to which the trustee is entitled: *Rooney v Cardona* [1999] 1 WLR 1388, CA (bankrupt husband could not give good receipt for proceeds of life policy written by wife on her life for his benefit where wife was deceased prior to bankruptcy order, following which husband claimed and obtained policy proceeds from life assurance company which was ignorant of bankruptcy order).

Since the introduction of s 291A, the official receiver becomes trustee of the bankrupt's estate on the making of a bankruptcy order, unless the court appoints the IVA supervisor to be trustee when the bankruptcy order is made. The result is that the bankrupt's estate will vest in a trustee immediately upon the making of a bankruptcy order. Under s 300(2), the official receiver becomes trustee to fill a vacancy in that office until the vacancy is otherwise filled.

For the appointment of a trustee-in-bankruptcy see ss 291A (first trustee in bankruptcy) ss 292 (general provision) and 296 (appointment by the Secretary of State) and rr 10.67–10.76.

**Location of property comprised in the bankrupt's estate**—The definition of property in the Bankruptcy Act 1869 made no reference to the location of such property, although the definition in s 167 of the Bankruptcy Act 1914 referred to property 'whether situated in England or elsewhere'. The absence of any qualification in s 306 means that all property to which the bankrupt is legally or beneficially entitled, wherever situated in the world, will, save for those exceptions identified in the notes to s 283, vest in the trustee: see *Pollard v Ashurst* [2001] Ch 595, [2001] BPIR 131.

**Ascertaining the extent of the bankrupt's estate**—Specific provisions envisage the trustee taking steps to identify the property comprised in the bankrupt's estate as soon as practicable. First, there is an express obligation under s 311(1) to take possession of all books, papers and other records which relate to the bankrupt's estate or affairs. The trustee has a right to look at these documents, but neither this provision nor any other imports a right to waive the bankrupt's privilege in them vis a vis third parties, such privilege not being property forming part of the bankrupt's estate: *Re Shlosberg* [2016] EWCA Civ 1138, [2017] Ch 210, [2017] BPIR 1, see also *Leeds v Lemos* [2017] EWHC 1825 (Ch), [2018] Ch 81, [2017] BPIR 1223 at [260], [278]. Second, and more generally, the functions of the trustee, as defined in s 305(2), envisage the trustee exercising those powers conferred on him by s 315 and Sch 5 ' . . . to get in, realise and distribute the bankrupt's estate' as soon as is reasonably practicable in the circumstances. The trustee also has statutory powers of inquiry into the bankrupt's dealings and property in addition to his standing to enforce those duties owed to him by the bankrupt under s 333.

**Steps securing property**—Notwithstanding the automatic vesting of property in a trustee without the requirement for any further formality, a trustee may consider it prudent to take steps to secure his position by noting his title on any register maintained in respect of such property so as to give notice of his title or interest to third parties. Furthermore, whilst a trustee is not entitled to property previously transferred out of the bankruptcy estate under a transaction which is susceptible to challenge as a transaction-at-undervalue or a preference it is usually prudent to register a caution against dealings in favour of the trustee where that property comprises registered land or an equivalent entry, where title is determined by reference to a register of interests. Failure to take such steps which results in loss to the bankruptcy estate may give rise to a claim against the trustee under s 304(1).

**Shares**—Where a bankrupt owns shares and the company is regulated by Table A, reg 30 thereof allows a trustee to elect, on producing such evidence as the directors may require, to be registered as holder of the shares or to nominate some other person to be so registered. A bankrupt who remains a registered holder of shares is allowed to vote at general meetings, although a trustee may direct a bankrupt under s 333(1) as to how he should vote: *Wise v Landsell* [1921] 1 Ch 420, and – for a slightly more recent authority – *Morgan v Gray* [1953] Ch 83, [1953] 2 WLR 140.

**Registered land**—Previously a trustee obtained title to registered land automatically without the need for his entry on the title register: under s 61(5) of the Land Registration Act 1925. For the registration of a bankruptcy petition as a pending action under the Land Charges Act 1972 and the registration of a trustee as proprietor, now see s 86 of the Land Registration Act 2002. For the interaction between s 303 and the LRA 2002 see *Pick v Chief Land Registrar* [2011] EWHC 206 (Ch), [2012] Ch 564, [2011] BPIR 1090 (cf *Tomlinson v Bridging Finance Ltd* [2010] BPIR 759).

**Equity of redemption**—In respect of mortgaged property, the equity of redemption vests in the trustee on bankruptcy, such that if the mortgagee appoints receivers over the property they no longer owe a duty of care to the bankrupt and any duty is owed to the trustee: *Purewal v Countrywide Residential Lettings Ltd* [2015] EWCA Civ 1122, [2016] 4 WLR 31.

**Contractual prohibition against assignment**—A contractual prohibition preventing assignment of a thing in action does not affect the deemed assignment of such property to a trustee under s 306 and s 311(4), since vesting by reference to the latter provision is deemed to take effect without assignment: *Re Landau* [1998] Ch 223, [1997] BPIR 229 (Ferris J).

**Claims which are 'personal' to the bankrupt**—Certain causes of action which are regarded as being 'personal' to a bankrupt do not, by virtue of decisions of the court, vest in the trustee despite the fact that they would otherwise fall within the scope of the bankrupt's estate. These are considered in the notes to s 283.

**Pension rights**—The recent case law on this area is of diminishing importance, given the exclusion of the vast majority of pension interests from the scope of the bankrupt's estate by virtue of ss 11 and 12 of the Welfare Reform and Pensions Act 1999 for bankruptcies commencing after 29 May 2000. For pre-existing and ongoing cases the case law remains that in *Re Landau* [1998] Ch 223; *Krasner v Dennison* [2001] Ch 76; *Patel v Jones* [2001] BPIR 919; *Rowe v Sanders* [2002] BPIR 847; *Re the Trusts of the Scientific Investment Pension Plan* [1998] BPIR 410; and *Malcolm v Benedict Mackenzie* [2004] EWCA Civ 1748, [2005] BPIR 176.

**Proceeds of crime**—HHJ Hodge QC did not consider that the fact that property had vested in the trustee in bankruptcy pursuant to s 306 would prevent a magistrates' court from exercising its discretion to make a forfeiture order under s 298 of the Proceeds of Crime Act 2002 in an appropriate case: see *The Chief Constable of Greater Manchester v Wright* [2015] EHWC 3824 (Ch), [2016] BPIR 339 at [21] and [22].

## [1.418]
### 306A  Property subject to restraint order

(1)  This section applies where—

    (a)    property is excluded from the bankrupt's estate by virtue of section 417(2)(a) of the Proceeds of Crime Act 2002 (property subject to a restraint order),

    (b)    an order under section 50, 67A, 128, 131A, 198 or 215A of that Act has not been made in respect of the property,

    (c)    the restraint order is discharged, and

    (d)    immediately after the discharge of the restraint order the property is not detained under or by virtue of section 44A, 47J, 122A, 127J, 193A or 195J of that Act.

(2)  The property vests in the trustee as part of the bankrupt's estate.

(3)  But subsection (2) does not apply to the proceeds of property realised by a management receiver under section 49(2)(d) or 197(2)(d) of that Act (realisation of property to meet receiver's remuneration and expenses).

**Amendments**—Inserted by Proceeds of Crime Act 2002, s 456, Sch 11, paras 1, 16(1), (3). Amended by Serious Crime Act 2007, ss 74(2)(g), 92, Sch 8, Pt 7, para 151, Sch 14; Policing and Crime Act 2009, s 112(1), Sch 7, Pt 6, paras 53, 54.

**General note**—Sections 306A–306C were introduced by s 456 and paras 1 and 16 of Sch 11 to the Proceeds of Crime Act 2002 and took effect from 24 March 2003. The provisions are necessary to cater expressly for the vesting in a trustee of property which becomes available as a result of the three specific and differing circumstances identified in each of the new sections. Sections 306A(3) and 306C(3) afford protection to a management receiver appointed under the 2002 Act in respect of remuneration and expenses which may be drawn from the proceeds of property realised which would otherwise vest automatically in the trustee under ss 306A(2) or 306C(2).

Sections 306AA and 306BA were introduced by paras 55 and 57 of Sch 7 to the Policing and Crime Act 2009 and took effect from 1 June 2015. The 2009 Act sought to implement the main recommendations of the government's Asset Recovery Action Plan (2007) and to strengthen the arrangements for recovery of assets obtained through criminal means. These provisions cater expressly for the vesting of property which is released from detention (s 306AA) or, although the subject of an order authorising realisation, is surplus to what was required to satisfy a confiscation order (s 306BA).

Property subject to a restraint order, a detention order, a receivership, an administration, a realisation order or confiscation order does not comprise part of the bankruptcy estate in a subsequent bankruptcy, although those enforcement sanctions are not exercisable where the debtor has previously been made bankrupt. See *R v S* [2019] EWCA Crim 1728, [2020] 1 WLR 109, [2020] 1 Cr App R 13, [2020] BPIR 278 for a stark illustration of the effect of a prior restraint order on a bankruptcy estate, at [75] per Davis LJ. A fuller discussion of the scope of the 2002 Act (as amended) is beyond the scope of this text; further reference should be made initially to ss 50, 52, 128, 198, 200, 417, 418 and 419 of the 2002 Act.

Chief Registrar Baister gave directions on the proper construction of s 306A (in the light of s 417 of the 2002 Act), in circumstances where a restraint order had been made in *(1) Brittain (2) Stevens v (1) Whyte (2) Crown Office and Procurator Fiscal Service* [2016] BPIR 1314.

## [1.419]

### 306AA Property released from detention

(1) This section applies where—
- (a) property is excluded from the bankrupt's estate by virtue of section 417(2)(b) of the Proceeds of Crime Act 2002 (property detained under certain provisions),
- (b) no order is in force in respect of the property under section 41, 50, 120, 128, 190 or 198 of that Act, and
- (c) the property is released.

(2) The property vests in the trustee as part of the bankrupt's estate.

**Amendments**—Inserted by Policing and Crime Act 2009, s 112(1), Sch 7, Pt 6, paras 53, 55.
**General note**—See the general note to s 306A.

## [1.420]

### 306B Property in respect of which receivership or administration order made

(1) This section applies where—
- (a) property is excluded from the bankrupt's estate by virtue of section 417(2)(c) of the Proceeds of Crime Act 2002 (property in respect of which an order for the appointment of a receiver or administrator under certain provisions of that Act is in force),
- (b) a confiscation order is made under section 6, 92 or 156 of that Act,
- (c) the amount payable under the confiscation order is fully paid, and
- (d) any of the property remains in the hands of the receiver or administrator (as the case may be).

(2) The property vests in the trustee as part of the bankrupt's estate.

**Amendments**—Inserted by Proceeds of Crime Act 2002, s 456, Sch 11, paras 1, 16(1), (3). Amended by Policing and Crime Act 2009, s 112(1), Sch 7, Pt 6, paras 53, 56.
**General note**—See the general note to s 306A.

## [1.421]

### 306BA Property in respect of which realisation order made

(1) This section applies where—
- (a) property is excluded from the bankrupt's estate by virtue of section 417(2)(d) of the Proceeds of Crime Act 2002 (property in respect of which an order has been made authorising realisation of the property by an appropriate officer),
- (b) a confiscation order is made under section 6, 92 or 156 of that Act,
- (c) the amount payable under the confiscation order is fully paid, and
- (d) any of the property remains in the hands of the appropriate officer.

(2) The property vests in the trustee as part of the bankrupt's estate.

**Amendments**—Inserted by Policing and Crime Act 2009, s 112(1), Sch 7, Pt 6, paras 53, 57.
**General note**—See the general note to s 306A.

## [1.422]

**306C Property subject to certain orders where confiscation order discharged or quashed**

(1)  This section applies where—

  (a)  property is excluded from the bankrupt's estate by virtue of section 417(2)(a), (b), (c) or (d) of the Proceeds of Crime Act 2002 (property excluded from bankrupt's estate),

  (b)  a confiscation order is made under section 6, 92 or 156 of that Act, and

  (c)  the confiscation order is discharged under section 30, 114 or 180 of that Act (as the case may be) or quashed under that Act or in pursuance of any enactment relating to appeals against conviction or sentence.

(2)  Any such property vests in the trustee as part of the bankrupt's estate if it is in the hands of—

  (a)  a receiver appointed under Part 2 or 4 of that Act,

  (b)  an administrator appointed under Part 3 of that Act,

  (c)  an appropriate officer (within the meaning of section 41A, 120A or 190A of that Act).

(3)  But subsection (2) does not apply to the proceeds of property realised by a management receiver under section 49(2)(d) or 197(2)(d) of that Act (realisation of property to meet receiver's remuneration and expenses).

**Amendments**—Inserted by Proceeds of Crime Act 2002, s 456, Sch 11, paras 1, 16(1), (3). Amended by Policing and Crime Act 2009, s 112(1), Sch 7, Pt 6, paras 53, 58.
**General note**—See the general note to s 306A.

## [1.423]

### 307 After-acquired property

(1)  Subject to this section and section 309, the trustee may by notice in writing claim for the bankrupt's estate any property which has been acquired by, or has devolved upon, the bankrupt since the commencement of the bankruptcy.

(2)  A notice under this section shall not be served in respect of—

  (a)  any property falling within subsection (2) or (3) of section 283 in Chapter II,

  (aa)  any property vesting in the bankrupt by virtue of section 283A in Chapter II,

  (b)  any property which by virtue of any other enactment is excluded from the bankrupt's estate, or

  (c)  without prejudice to section 280(2)(c) (order of court on application for discharge), any property which is acquired by or, devolves upon, the bankrupt after his discharge.

(3)  Subject to subsections (4) and (4A), upon the service on the bankrupt of a notice under this section the property to which the notice relates shall vest in the trustee as part of the bankrupt's estate; and the trustee's title to that property has relation back to the time at which the property was acquired by, or devolved upon, the bankrupt.

(4)  Where, whether before or after service on the bankrupt of a notice under this section—

  (a)  a person acquires property in good faith, for value and without notice of the bankruptcy,

  (b)   . . .

the trustee is not in respect of that property entitled by virtue of this section to any remedy against that person, or any person whose title to any property derives from that person.

(4A)   Where a banker enters into a transaction before service on the banker of a notice under this section (and whether before or after service on the bankrupt of a notice under this section) the trustee is not in respect of that transaction entitled by virtue of this section to any remedy against the banker.

This subsection applies whether or not the banker has notice of the bankruptcy.

(5)   References in this section to property do not include any property which, as part of the bankrupt's income, may be the subject of an income payments order under section 310.

**Amendments**—Enterprise Act 2002, s 261(4); Deregulation Act 2015, s 19, Sch 6, Pt 5, paras 12, 16.

**General note**—Only that property comprised in the bankrupt's estate as at the date of the trustee's appointment vests in the trustee automatically under s 306. Any property which is subsequently acquired by or devolves upon the bankrupt after the commencement of the bankruptcy – as defined in s 278(a) as the date of the bankruptcy order – is property to which the bankrupt is entitled in the absence of either the trustee utilising s 307 or the court making an income payments order under s 310, or an income payments agreement being entered into under s 310A. The notes to s 310 include commentary as to the distinction between property subject to s 307 and the mutually exclusive s 310. In particular, income within the meaning of s 310(7) is incapable of being claimed as after-acquired property: see s 307(5). A single one-off payment for services rendered is capable of constituting 'income' for s 307(7) purposes: *Supperstone v Lloyd's Names Association Working Party* [1999] BPIR 832 (Evans-Lombe J).

The operation of s 307 presupposes compliance by the bankrupt with his duty under s 333(2) to give notice to the trustee within 21 days of property devolving upon him. More specifically, r 10.125 imposes a specific duty on a bankrupt to give notice to his trustee of after-acquired property. The safeguard for the trustee in the event of non-compliance by the bankrupt with his duties lies in s 309(1)(a), under which the 42-day period in which the trustee must serve a notice only commences upon the trustee obtaining knowledge of the property in question. In *Viscount St David v Lewis* [2015] EWHC 2826 (Ch), [2015] BPIR 1471 at [28]–[33] Henderson J held that where a bankrupt has failed to co-operate with his trustee in this regard, the court should be slow to accede to a self-serving claim by the bankrupt that his trustee first obtained knowledge of the acquisition at a significantly earlier date. Further, in practical terms, a trustee should normally be held to have first obtained the relevant knowledge only when it has become clear to him on cogent evidence, verified to his reasonable satisfaction that the property was acquired by the bankrupt after the commencement of the bankruptcy.

In *Wood v Baker* [2015] EWHC 2536 (Ch), [2015] BPIR 1524, the court granted a without-notice injunction to prevent dissipation of disputed after-acquired property (subject to a cross-undertaking in damages by the trustees limited to the value of assets that came under their control).

**Property to which s 307 applies**—Apart from the observations above as to income, s 307 applies to 'property' – as defined very broadly in non-exhaustive terms in s 436 – but does not catch any property which falls within the scope of the bankrupt's estate under ss 283 or 283A.

Although the general rule is that property subject to an order under the Proceeds of Crime Act 2002 will not be available in bankruptcy, s 418(3) of the 2002 Act precludes the exercise of the court's power under that statute in relation to property in respect of which a trustee may serve a notice under ss 307, 308 or 308A, but only where the notice may be served without leave of the court.

**Service of the s 307(1) notice**—In *Pike v Cork Gully* [1997] BPIR 723 the Court of Appeal (Millett and Schiemann LJJ) considered the position where a trustee had seized money in a bank account following which he served the requisite notice. At 724C–724D Millett LJ, with whom Schiemann LJ agreed, concurred with the reasoning of the judge below to the effect that, once the notice had been given, it was effective and related back to the date on which the bankrupt acquired the money such that, whilst the seizure was not proper at that time, the later service of the notice and the operation of the relation-back cured the technical defect.

**Extension of the 42-day period for service of the s 307(1) notice**—Section 309(1)(a) allows for the extension of the 42-day period after its expiration. In *Solomons v Williams* [2001] BPIR 1123 at 1136F–1136H Pumfrey J identified that 'good cause' must be established to justify extension of the period. His Lordship considered that each case must be determined on its own facts, but that relevant factors would include the period of delay both in serving the notice under s 307 and seeking the extension, the merits of the application having regard to the overall position of the bankrupt, any prejudice caused to the bankrupt by the lateness of the application and the reasons for the delay. An order should not be made, however, if it causes prejudice to the bankrupt which is disproportionate to the likely benefit conferred on the creditors. An extension was refused in *Solomons v Williams* where there was a 4 month delay in serving the s 307 notice but where the application was only made 2 years later. For a refusal on an even longer delay (7.5 years) see *Franses v Oomerjee* [2005] BPIR 1320 (Registrar Derrett). Neither is it sufficient simply for an application to be made by a trustee since the court must have evidence upon which any permissive discretion can be based: *Vickers v Mitchell* [2004] All ER (D) 414 (May) (Sir Donald Rattee). See also *Warley Continental Services Ltd v Johal* [2004] EWHC 3247 (Ch), [2004] BPIR 353 at [30]–[33] (HHJ Norris QC) on the court's approach to delay generally when considering whether to extend time limits imposed under IA 1986, and the commentary to s 376.

**Procedure**—There is no prescribed form for a s 307(1) notice. The relevant procedure appears in rr 10.125–10.126.

**Subsection (4) and (4A)**—Under the former sub-s (4)(b), where a banker entered into a transaction in good faith and without notice of the bankruptcy, the trustee was not entitled to a remedy under s 307 against the banker or any successor in title. This subsection was omitted by Deregulation Act 2015, s 19, Sch 6, Pt 5, paras 12, 16, with effect from 1 October 2015, and replaced by sub-s 4A which provides that the trustee will have no remedy against a banker in respect of a transaction entered into before service on the banker of a s 307 notice, it being irrelevant whether (i) the banker has notice of the bankruptcy and (ii) whether a s 307 notice has been served on the bankrupt.

## [1.424]

### 308 Vesting in trustee of certain items of excess value

(1) Subject to section 309, where—

    (a)    property is excluded by virtue of section 283(2) (tools of trade, household effects, etc) from the bankrupt's estate, and

    (b)    it appears to the trustee that the realisable value of the whole or any part of that property exceeds the cost of a reasonable replacement for that property or that part of it,

the trustee may by notice in writing claim that property or, as the case may be, that part of it for the bankrupt's estate.

(2) Upon the service on the bankrupt of a notice under this section, the property to which the notice relates vests in the trustee as part of the bankrupt's estate; and, except against a purchaser in good faith, for value and without notice of the bankruptcy, the trustee's title to that property has relation back to the commencement of the bankruptcy.

(3) The trustee shall apply funds comprised in the estate to the purchase by or on behalf of the bankrupt of a reasonable replacement for any property vested in the trustee under this section; and the duty imposed by this subsection has priority over the obligation of the trustee to distribute the estate.

(4) For the purposes of this section property is a reasonable replacement for other property if it is reasonably adequate for meeting the needs met by the other property.

**Amendments**—Housing Act 1988, s 140(1), Sch 17, para 73.

**General note**—The purpose of this provision lies in permitting the trustee to claim property for the benefit of the bankrupt's estate where that property is excluded by s 283(2) but where it appears that the realisable value of any part of that excluded property exceeds the cost of a reasonable replacement. It appears from *Mikki v Duncan* [2017] EWCA Civ 57, [2017] 1 WLR 2907, [2017] BPIR 490, that s 308 applies to physical property only. In that case, the benefit of a car hire purchase agreement was deemed to be a chose in action; the bankrupt had no actual right of property in the vehicle itself, and it thus did not fall within the exemption in s 283(2).

The trustee is also necessarily constrained by s 308(3), which imposes an overriding duty to apply funds in purchasing a reasonable replacement for any property claimed under this provision. Thus, s 308 will require the trustee to be satisfied that he is both able to sell a particular item of property and to replace it – within the meaning of s 308(4) – so as to produce a net benefit for the bankruptcy estate which justifies the time and cost of that exercise.

In practice, applications under s 308 are not common. Moreover, it is submitted that there is some scope for a bankrupt challenging a claim by a trustee on the basis that the term 'reasonable replacement' in s 308(1)(b) and (4) should not be construed by reference to some objective minimum standard applicable to all individuals but is capable of reflecting the particular circumstances of an individual bankrupt. In other words, what is a reasonable replacement in one case will not necessarily be a reasonable replacement in another. This approach would certainly be consistent with that adopted by the courts to the concept of reasonable domestic needs in the context of income payments order applications under s 310, on which see the notes thereto.

**Procedure**—See rr 10.106 and 10.107.

**[1.425]**

### 308A Vesting in trustee of certain tenancies

Upon the service on the bankrupt by the trustee of a notice in writing under this section, any tenancy—

(a)    which is excluded by virtue of section 283(3A) from the bankrupt's estate, and

(b)    to which the notice relates,

vests in the trustee as part of the bankrupt's estate; and, except against a purchaser in good faith, for value and without notice of the bankruptcy, the trustee's title to that tenancy has relation back to the commencement of the bankruptcy.

**Amendments**—Inserted by Housing Act 1988, s 117(2).

**[1.426]**

### 309 Time-limit for notice under s 307 or 308

(1)    Except with the leave of the court, a notice shall not be served—

(a)    under section 307, after the end of the period of 42 days beginning with the day on which it first came to the knowledge of the trustee that the property in question had been acquired by, or had devolved upon, the bankrupt;

(b)    under section 308 or section 308A, after the end of the period of 42 days beginning with the day on which the property or tenancy in question first came to the knowledge of the trustee.

(2)    For the purposes of this section—

(a)    anything which comes to the knowledge of the trustee is deemed in relation to any successor of his as trustee to have come to the knowledge of the successor at the same time; and

(b)    anything which comes (otherwise than under paragraph (a)) to the knowledge of a person before he is the trustee is deemed to come to his knowledge on his appointment taking effect or, in the case of the official receiver, on his becoming trustee.

**Amendments**—Housing Act 1988, s 117(3).
**General note**—See the notes to ss 307 and 308.

**[1.427]**

### 310 Income payments orders

(1)    The court may make an order ("an income payments order") claiming for the bankrupt's estate so much of the income of the bankrupt during the period for which the order is in force as may be specified in the order.

(1A)    An income payments order may be made only on an application instituted—

(a)    by the trustee, and

(b)    before the discharge of the bankrupt.

(2)    The court shall not make an income payments order the effect of which would be to reduce the income of the bankrupt when taken together with any payments to which subsection (8) applies below what appears to the court to be necessary for meeting the reasonable domestic needs of the bankrupt and his family.

(3)    An income payments order shall, in respect of any payment of income to which it is to apply, either—

(a)    require the bankrupt to pay the trustee an amount equal to so much of that payment as is claimed by the order, or

(b)    require the person making the payment to pay so much of it as is so claimed to the trustee, instead of to the bankrupt.

(4)    Where the court makes an income payments order it may, if it thinks fit, discharge or vary any attachment of earnings order that is for the time being in force to secure payments by the bankrupt.

(5)  Sums received by the trustee under an income payments order form part of the bankrupt's estate.

(6)  An income payments order must specify the period during which it is to have effect; and that period—

(a)  may end after the discharge of the bankrupt, but

(b)  may not end after the period of three years beginning with the date on which the order is made.

(6A)  An income payments order may (subject to subsection (6)(b)) be varied on the application of the trustee or the bankrupt (whether before or after discharge).

(7)  For the purposes of this section the income of the bankrupt comprises every payment in the nature of income which is from time to time made to him or to which he from time to time becomes entitled, including any payment in respect of the carrying on of any business or in respect of any office or employment and (despite anything in section 11 or 12 of the Welfare Reform and Pensions Act 1999) any payment under a pension scheme but excluding any payment to which subsection (8) applies.

(8)  This subsection applies to—

(a)  payments by way of guaranteed minimum pension; and

(b)    . . .

(9)  In this section, "guaranteed minimum pension" has the same meaning as in the Pension Schemes Act 1993.

**Amendments**—Pensions Act 1995, s 122, Sch 3, para 15(a), (b); Welfare Reform and Pensions Act 1999, s 18, Sch 2, para 2; Enterprise Act 2002, ss 259(1)–(4), 278(2), Sch 26; SI 2011/1730 (as amended by SI 2012/709).

**General note**—Under the former legislation – on which see *Tennant's Application* [1956] 1 WLR 874, CA and *Re Cohen* [1961] Ch 246 – s 51(2) of the Bankruptcy Act 1914 provided that 'salary and income' received or receivable by a bankrupt vested in the trustee, subject to an order of the court to the contrary and s 38(1) of the 1914 Act, which dealt with after-acquired property and provided that all such property devolved automatically on the trustee before discharge.

The income payments order is an invention of the 1986 Act. Section 310 represents a marked shift from the old law, in that income now remains vested in the bankrupt subject to the making of an income payments order which itself requires the court to safeguard the bankrupt's reasonable domestic needs. This change in the law followed recommendations in paras 591–598 of the Cork Committee Report (1982, Cmnd 8558) to the effect that, consistent with the wider principle of seeking, so far as possible, to bring about the rehabilitation of the debtor, as espoused in paras 192 and 193 of the Cork Report, whilst income should remain available for payment of creditors, the legislation should facilitate a more realistic and humane attitude being taken than previously in relation to the debtor and his family. In particular, there was no intention that earning capacity should automatically be made available for payment of debts such that 'the debtor must in no circumstances become the slave of his creditors', a point now also found in Art 3 of the European Convention on Human Rights. Nevertheless, whilst the policy of the Act appears to be to allow a bankrupt to enhance his post-bankruptcy estate by retention of his income and receipts, whether earned or not, it seems equally clear from the breadth of the definition of 'income' in s 310(7) that a trustee may lay claim to all such income and receipts, unless protected by statute, in the absence of an unconditional statutory exclusion of such income and receipts from the bankrupt's estate and the plain intention of Parliament that income should be available for distribution to creditors subject to the protection of the reasonable domestic needs of the bankrupt and his family.

**Is a trustee-in-bankruptcy obliged to make an application for an income payments order?**—A trustee has a discretion, not a duty, to make an application under s 310 in the discharge of his functions under s 305. Where no application is made in a very obvious case of surplus income over reasonable domestic needs, an aggrieved creditor might consider an application under s 303(1).

The trustee should not approach an application blindly and should give consideration to the likely benefit to creditors as against the overall cost of an application and any consequent hardship to the bankrupt and his family. The reported judgment of a district judge in *Boyden v Watson* [2004] BPIR 1131 is instructive in terms of the blistering criticism levelled at a trustee, his solicitors and counsel in relation to the apparent motives behind and conduct of what was ultimately an unsuccessful application in which the trustee's costs of the application itself amounted to one-half of the relatively modest total sum sought over a 3-year period which, costs and the bankrupt's evidence that he had no surplus income available apart, would only have produced approximately three pence in the pound, if that, for creditors over that period.

However, Newey J confirmed in *Official Receiver v Negus* [2011] EWHC 3719 (Ch), [2012] 1 WLR 1598, [2012] BPIR 382 that the court can still grant an IPO where the creditors will receive no direct benefit because the entirety of the sum generated will go to discharge bankruptcy expenses.

**Timing**—An application for an IPO must be made before the bankrupt is discharged. An application to suspend a bankrupt's discharge where the underlying motivation of the trustee appeared to be to try and facilitate an income payments arrangement attracted criticism (and was roundly rejected by Registrar Nicholls) in circumstances where action to obtain an IPO could and should have been taken much earlier in *Chadwick v Nash* [2012] BPIR 70. The same considerations do not apply, however, if the trustee was not in a position to make any such application earlier because of the bankrupt's failures to provide information (see the decision of Nugee J in *Weir v Hilsdon* [2014] EWHC 983 (Ch), [2017] BPIR 1088 at [73]–[78]).

**Income payments agreements under s 310A**—So as to avoid the cost associated with an income payments order, even one made by consent, particularly given the relatively modest amounts often involved, with effect from 1 April 2004, by virtue of s 310A as introduced by s 260 of the Enterprise Act 2002, a bankrupt may reach agreement for payments of contributions by himself or a third party to his trustee (or the official receiver, as appropriate), which agreement is enforceable as an order under s 310A(2).

The procedure governing such agreements appears in rr 10.114A–10.117.

**The inter-relationship between s 307 and s 310**—The most useful analysis of the interplay of ss 307 and 310 appears in the judgment of Chadwick LJ in *Dennison v Krasner* [2001] Ch 76, [2000] BPIR 410 at 421B–421C. After-acquired property does not automatically form part of the bankrupt's estate, as defined in s 283(1)(a), other than where a notice is served by the trustee under s 307(1). However, after-acquired property which, as part of the bankrupt's income, could be the subject of an income payments order under s 310 cannot be the subject of a notice under s 307(1), by virtue of s 307(5). In other words, ss 307 and 310 are mutually exclusive. Section 310 itself provides a separate regime in relation to after-acquired property which is in the nature of income. Such property does not, however, form part of the bankrupt's estate unless it is received by the trustee under an income payments order. Section 310 does not control and qualify the vesting provisions in ss 306 or 307 but instead supplements those provisions in that s 310 applies to property which would not otherwise fall within those provisions. Accordingly, there is no need, indeed no justification, for construing s 310 as having any application to property which has vested in the trustee on his appointment under s 306(1), on which see the finding of Ferris J in *Re Landau* [1997] BPIR 229 at 233C–234D, approved of by Chadwick LJ in *Dennison* at 421E, to the effect that contractual rights to either income or capital under a retirement annuity contract vested automatically in a trustee-in-bankruptcy under s 306 on his appointment on the basis that the future entitlement constituted an existing chose in action within the meaning of property in s 436 irrespective of whether benefits were actually in payment at the commencement of the bankruptcy. While the analysis is still of interest in other contexts, the actual effect of the decision in *Re Landau* was reversed by s 11 of the Welfare Reform and Pensions Act 1999 which provides that where a bankruptcy order is made against a person on a petition presented after the coming into force of the section, any rights of his under an approved pension arrangement are excluded from his estate.

**The approach to distinguishing between income and after-acquired property**—Nothing analogous to s 310(7) appears in s 307. Accordingly, given the observation by Chadwick LJ in *Dennison* to the effect that s 310 provides what amounts, in effect, to an exception to the after-acquired property regime under s 307 – which itself amounts to an exception to the automatic vesting rule under s 306 – it is submitted that the proper approach is to consider in the first place whether a particular payment is capable of falling within s 310 as income before falling back on the s 307 provisions.

**SECTION 310(2)**

'**the reasonable domestic needs of the bankrupt and his family**'——'Family' is defined in s 385(1). However, by reason of the discretion afforded to the court by s 310(1), the court may take into account the interests of other dependents when considering whether to make an order (*Re Fowlds (a bankrupt)* [2020] EWHC 329 (Ch), [2020] BPIR 541).

The reference in s 310(2) to 'the reasonable domestic needs of the bankrupt and his family' is not to be construed as meaning that which 'is necessary to enable the bankrupt to live' (as had been the position under the Bankruptcy Act 1914 and at common law following *Re Roberts* [1900] 1 QB 122): *Re Rayatt (a Bankrupt)* [1998] BPIR 495 at 499G–500E (Michael Hart QC, sitting as a deputy High Court judge). *Rayatt* (which concerned an unsuccessful attempt by a trustee to claim monies expended by the bankrupt on private education fees) established (at 500G–500H) a two-stage test which, it is submitted, should be adopted in relation to any particular item of expenditure challenged by the trustee as involving monies which are claimed as falling subject to an income payments order. First, can expenditure by the bankrupt on a particular item be said to constitute the meeting of a *domestic need* of the bankrupt and his family? The court should note here that the deputy judge identified (at 502F–502G) the 'implicit notion' in para 591 of the Cork Committee

Report that, given that income does not form part of the bankruptcy estate in the absence of an order under s 310, and that the bankrupt is under no legal obligation to work, 'within reasonable limits the debtor should retain some freedom of choice as to the lifestyle he adopts for himself and his family on the basis of the earnings which he is able to achieve by the deployment of his professional or other skills'. The second stage of the test involves the court establishing how much expenditure of that particular kind can be described as meeting a *reasonable* domestic need, given the particular facts of the case. This is a question of fact which, consistent with para 591 of the Cork Committee Report, necessitates the court considering the particular circumstances of the particular bankrupt and ascertaining to what the bankrupt intends applying his income and *not* what others might do with such monies (*Kilvert v Flackett* [1998] BPIR 721, Peter Scott QC, sitting as a deputy High Court judge). *Rayatt* (at 502H) is further authority for the proposition that, to the extent that an order imposes real hardship, there must be some reasonable proportionality between the hardship imposed and the benefit which will be recouped by creditors. The same point was also made subsequently in *Kilvert* (at 723H).

The term 'reasonable domestic needs' finds no elucidation in the cases. The starting point, it is submitted, lies in the non-exhaustive list of items identified in s 283(2) and other items capable of falling within those terms. Ultimately, however, it is impossible to state further items which might fall within 'reasonable domestic needs' in all cases, since each case can only be determined on its own facts. In *Rayatt*, for example, the deputy judge was satisfied that private school fees were capable of amounting to a reasonable domestic need, given medical evidence demonstrating the possible effect of removing a child from her private schooling. In *Scott v Davis* [2003] BPIR 1009 at [13] Anthony Mann QC, sitting as a deputy High Court judge, identified that there is no presumption one way or the other in relation to school fees – or, it is submitted, any particular item of expenditure – and that 'it all depends on the facts of the individual case.' In *Malcolm v Official Receiver* [1999] BPIR 97 at 100C–100E Rattee J held that it was unreasonable for a bankrupt to pay £820 on mortgage payments out of £1,100 net monthly income where the property was also occupied by the bankrupt's wife and where unsecured liabilities in the bankruptcy amounted to £144,000-odd, although the judge took the view that the bankrupt should be afforded some time to revise his domestic arrangements. See also the comments of HHJ Jarman QC in *Official Receiver v Wilson* [2013] BPIR 907 (the OR's appeal against the decision at first instance to refuse an application for an IPO was successful and the matter remitted for reconsideration where the bankrupt's joint mortgage was £1,750 per month and there was evidence that an equivalent property could be rented for £700pcm, albeit there was some uncertainty as to how difficult or otherwise it might be for the undischarged bankrupt to obtain a tenancy).

Accordingly, if it can be shown that no real benefit will enure for creditors on particular expenditure being appropriated to the bankruptcy estate, it is submitted that it will in an appropriate case be at least well arguable that monies expended on tobacco, alcohol, satellite television subscription or, say, gym membership – other than in cases of plain excess – are capable of amounting to reasonable domestic needs, not because a bankrupt can be said to be entitled to what might be called such luxury items as of right, but on the basis that the bankrupt may be able to show that his day-to-day life, which might well mean his day-to-day working life, involves and should involve any such item as a reasonable method of relaxation or spending leisure time. The court should not consider any sort of penal element in imposing an income payments order, since the provision does not feature and is not based on any punitive element or policy.

## SECTION 310(7)

' . . . income . . . '—The wording of s 310(7) expressly extends the provision beyond merely 'income' to 'every payment in the nature of income', without the limitations of the term 'salary' as appeared in s 51(2) of the Bankruptcy Act 1914 and previously in s 53(2) of the Bankruptcy Act 1883. In *Dennison v Krasner* [2000] BPIR 410 at 420E Chadwick LJ expressed the view that s 310(7) extends to income other than earnings, 'say, an allowance from a parent or other relative, or income under a discretionary trust.' It is respectfully submitted that the scope of 'payment in the nature of income' probably extends far beyond the examples given by Chadwick LJ in *Dennison* – which examples were provided in passing as illustrations on a point for which numerous other examples might have been given – to any cash or cash equivalent receipt by a bankrupt save where the payment actually forms part of the bankruptcy estate. Obvious examples would include wages, salary, commission, bonus or gratuity payments, whether or not paid regularly, or a gratuity or a payment made as compensation for loss of office, including a statutory redundancy payment, or a payment in lieu of notice.

Even though pension interests are ordinarily excluded from the scope of the bankruptcy estate where the bankruptcy commenced after 1 May 2001 by virtue of the provisions recited in s 310(7), pension income is capable of being claimed under an income payments order, subject to the exclusions in s 310(8) and (9). However, it is now settled that a trustee cannot compel a bankrupt to elect to draw down payments from his personal pension where he was eligible to make such an election but had not yet done so: *Horton v Henry* [2016] EWCA Civ 989, [2017] 1 WLR 391, [2016] BPIR 1426, at [37], [41]–[56], disapproving *Raithatha v Williamson* [2012] EWHC 909

(Ch), [2012] 1 WLR 3559, [2012] BPIR 621 in which Bernard Livesey QC (sitting as a deputy High Court judge) had held that even where the bankrupt had not made an election prior to his bankruptcy to take up his rights under a pension scheme, the payments he was entitled to receive under that scheme could nevertheless be taken into account as income under s 310.

Registrar Jones gave guidance as to the principles that apply to an application for an income payments order where a bankrupt's pension is already in drawdown in *Hinton v Wotherspoon* [2016] EWHC 621 (Ch), [2016] BPIR 944.

**The exercise of the court's discretion in making an order**—The court need not grant the specific relief sought and might even dismiss an application. In particular, the court will wish to consider the age, health and likely future earning capacity of the debtor as well as the broader issues of income and expenditure.

' . . . from time to time . . . '—The words 'from time to time' in s 310(7) equate to 'at any time' and do not envisage or necessitate periodical payments such that the provision may catch a one-off payment: *Supperstone v Lloyds Names Associations' Working Party* [1999] BPIR 832 at 840G–841G (Evans-Lombe J, one-off payment for services rendered susceptible to income payments order); and see *Kilvert v Flackettt* [1998] BPIR 721 at 722C–724D (single lump sum payment under NHS occupational pension within s 310) and *Raithatha v Williamson* [2012] EWHC 909 (Ch), [2012] 1 WLR 3559, [2012] BPIR 621 at [30] (although disapproved on other grounds – see the notes regarding 'income' above).

Further, the court confirmed in *Official Receiver v Baker* [2013] EWHC 4594 (Ch), [2014] BPIR 724 (Warren J) that an IPO can be made in respect of any income arising after the bankruptcy order, and was not restricted to income arising after the IPO was made.

**Varying an existing income payments order**—Variation of an existing order is provided for in s 310(6A).

The power to increase an income payments order under IR 2016, r 10.114 should only be exercised in the case of a material change of circumstances which can be shown by an applicant to justify such an increase (*Jones v Patel* [1999] BPIR 509 at 515D–515E). A reduction on an application by the bankrupt under the same provision will also, it is submitted, require a material change of circumstances.

In *Thomas v Edmondson* [2014] EWHC 1494 (Ch), [2015] 1 WLR 1395, [2014] BPIR 1070 Asplin J confirmed that the IPO regime under s 310 and the IPA regime under s 310A were not mutually exclusive, and the court had jurisdiction to make an order under s 310 despite the bankrupt having previously entered into an IPA under s 310A.

**Effect of second bankruptcy**—The Court of Appeal held in *Azuonye v Kent* [2019] EWCA Civ 1289, [2019] 4 WLR 101, [2019] BPIR 1317 that an income payments order could not continue to operate following a second bankruptcy, and future payments were a provable debt in the second bankruptcy, at [24]–[29], per David Richards LJ, reversing Falk J.

**Procedure**—The procedure on s 310 orders, including variations, appears in rr 10.108–10.114.

## [1.428]

### 310A Income payments agreement

(1)   In this section "income payments agreement" means a written agreement between a bankrupt and his trustee or between a bankrupt and the official receiver which provides—

(a)   that the bankrupt is to pay to the trustee or the official receiver an amount equal to a specified part or proportion of the bankrupt's income for a specified period, or

(b)   that a third person is to pay to the trustee or the official receiver a specified proportion of money due to the bankrupt by way of income for a specified period.

(2)   A provision of an income payments agreement of a kind specified in subsection (1)(a) or (b) may be enforced as if it were a provision of an income payments order.

(3)   While an income payments agreement is in force the court may, on the application of the bankrupt, his trustee or the official receiver, discharge or vary an attachment of earnings order that is for the time being in force to secure payments by the bankrupt.

(4)   The following provisions of section 310 shall apply to an income payments agreement as they apply to an income payments order—

(a)   subsection (5) (receipts to form part of estate), and

(b)   subsections (7) to (9) (meaning of income).

(5)   An income payments agreement must specify the period during which it is to have effect; and that period—

- (a) may end after the discharge of the bankrupt, but
- (b) may not end after the period of three years beginning with the date on which the agreement is made.

(6) An income payments agreement may (subject to subsection (5)(b)) be varied—

- (a) by written agreement between the parties, or
- (b) by the court on an application made by the bankrupt, the trustee or the official receiver.

(7) The court—

- (a) may not vary an income payments agreement so as to include provision of a kind which could not be included in an income payments order, and
- (b) shall grant an application to vary an income payments agreement if and to the extent that the court thinks variation necessary to avoid the effect mentioned in section 310(2).

**Amendments**—Inserted by Enterprise Act 2002, s 260.

**General note**—See the notes under the heading referring to this section in the notes to s 310 above (in particular the commentary on *Thomas v Edmondson* [2014] EWHC 1494 (Ch), [2015] 1 WLR 1395, [2014] BPIR 1070), and see also rr 10.114A–10.117. An income payments agreement is a form of contract, and can constitute a compromise agreement (see *Elston v King* [2020] EWHC 55 (Ch)).

In *Re Hargreaves (Booth v Mond)* [2010] BPIR 1111, the court considered that arrears due under an income payments agreement could rank as debts in the subsequent IVA of the former bankrupt. Since under s 310A the terms of the IPA could be varied, the trustee in bankruptcy could compromise the sums due under the IPA under an IVA.

## [1.429]

### 311 Acquisition by trustee of control

(1) The trustee shall take possession of all books, papers and other records which relate to the bankrupt's estate or affairs and which belong to him or are in his possession or under his control (including any which would be privileged from disclosure in any proceedings).

(2) In relation to, and for the purpose of acquiring or retaining possession of, the bankrupt's estate, the trustee is in the same position as if he were a receiver of property appointed by the High Court; and the court may, on his application, enforce such acquisition or retention accordingly.

(3) Where any part of the bankrupt's estate consists of stock or shares in a company, shares in a ship or any other property transferable in the books of a company, office or person, the trustee may exercise the right to transfer the property to the same extent as the bankrupt might have exercised it if he had not become bankrupt.

(4) Where any part of the estate consists of things in action, they are deemed to have been assigned to the trustee; but notice of the deemed assignment need not be given except in so far as it is necessary, in a case where the deemed assignment is from the bankrupt himself, for protecting the priority of the trustee.

(5) Where any goods comprised in the estate are held by any person by way of pledge, pawn or other security and no notice has been served in respect of those goods by the official receiver under subsection (5) of section 285 (restriction on realising security), the trustee may serve such a notice in respect of the goods; and whether or not a notice has been served under this subsection or that subsection, the trustee may, if he thinks fit, exercise the bankrupt's right of redemption in respect of any such goods.

(6) A notice served by the trustee under subsection (5) has the same effect as a notice served by the official receiver under section 285(5).

**General note**—The obligation imposed by s 311(1) should be read in conjunction with the corresponding obligation imposed on the bankrupt by s 312. The trustee's obligation is unqualified and ongoing to the extent that the collective term 'books, papers and other records' within the meaning of s 311(1) is capable of relating to property which does not form part of the bankruptcy estate at the commencement of the bankruptcy, whether or not such property is capable of being claimed by the trustee for the estate as after-acquired property under s 307. It is submitted that the trustee's obligation under s 311(1) will continue following discharge of the bankrupt as regards property forming part of the bankruptcy estate. The obligation under s 311(1) would not, however, continue beyond discharge in respect of property acquired by or devolved upon the bankrupt after discharge, since such property cannot be claimed as after-acquired property, by virtue of s 307(2)(c).

## SECTION 311(1)

' . . . books, papers and other records . . . '—The term 'records' is defined non-exhaustively in s 436 as including 'computer records and other non-documentary records'. The term would, therefore, extend to e-mail communications and web-based records.

' . . . which relate to the bankrupt's estate or affairs . . . '—These words, taken together with 'books, papers and other records', appear to impose a limitation on the scope of the records to which the trustee's obligation relates by way of excluding records which do not relate to the bankrupt's estate or affairs.

There is no requirement that the records to which s 311(1) relates should form part of the bankruptcy estate. Indeed, in *Haig v Jonathan Aitken* [2000] BPIR 462 at 470E–470F Rattee J expressed the view that s 311(1) contemplated and made express provision for records outside of the scope of the estate.

Personal correspondence, even correspondence between a famous bankrupt and parliamentary colleagues or distinguished statesmen which may be worth a considerable sum to the media, does not form part of the bankruptcy estate and cannot therefore be subject to acquisition by a trustee under s 311: see *Haig v Jonathan Aitken* [2000] BPIR 462 at 470A–470D, in which Rattee J also expressed the view that it was 'at least strongly arguable' that a contrary construction of the provision might give rise to a breach of the right of privacy under Art 8 of the European Convention on Human Rights.

' . . . which belong to him or are in his possession or under his control . . . '—As identified under the immediately preceding heading, the present provision extends to property which does not form part of the bankruptcy estate. Although the provision would not on its face appear to extend to records which are neither within the bankrupt's possession nor under his control, the court is unlikely to take anything but a dim view of any arrangement under which the bankrupt has sought to divest himself of such 'control'.

**Privileged records**—Legal professional privilege may be of significant practical relevance to an individual and is also of fundamental importance in the administration of justice: see *R v Derby Magistrates* [1995] 4 All ER 526. Notwithstanding that, it was held in *(1) Avonwick Holdings Limited (2) Willmont and Sayers v Shlosberg* [2016] EWCA Civ 1138, [2017] Ch 210, [2017] BPIR 1 that, on the proper interpretation of the relevant provisions of IA 1986, privilege is not property of a bankrupt which automatically vests in the trustee in bankruptcy [63], and thus the trustee is not entitled to waive it as of right [69] – although he is entitled to see the privileged information (see the notes to s 306, in particular the reference to *Leeds v Lemos* [2017] EWHC 1825 (Ch), [2018] Ch 81, [2017] BPIR 1223 at [260], [278]).

However, in certain cases legal professional privilege can be overridden by other factors. Thus in *Re Omar (a Bankrupt)* [1999] BPIR 1001 Jacob J considered an application for directions by a trustee as to whether he should disclose documents obtained by him under s 311(1) to the administrators of the estate of the bankrupt's deceased husband who were to take part in a proposed examination of the bankrupt by the trustee and who intended to use the documents in an action against the bankrupt in which there was strong evidence that the bankrupt fraudulently concealed monies to which the bankruptcy estate would be entitled. In authorising disclosure, subject to undertakings by administrators to use the documents only for the purposes just mentioned, Jacob J relied in particular (at 1007H) on the fact in that case of fraud on the part of the bankrupt in earlier litigation and the use by the bankrupt of her previous lawyers for the advancement of what amounted to a fraudulent defence. Given that legal professional privilege is capable of being overridden by other factors, in particular fraud, consideration should be given to an application for directions where, as in *Re Omar*, the bankrupt objects to the disclosure on the grounds of privilege.

A bankrupt is not entitled to assert legal professional privilege against a trustee to prevent the trustee taking possession of privileged documents which are in the bankrupt's control, but s 366 does not operate so as to override privilege, with the consequence that a trustee is not entitled to an order for the disclosure of privileged documents against an individual other than the bankrupt: *Re Ouvaroff (a Bankrupt)* [1997] BPIR 712 at 720C (Stanley Burnton QC, sitting as a deputy High Court judge).

See also *Re Murjani (a Bankrupt)* [1996] 1 BCLC 272 (Lightman J, a bankrupt's solicitor may not claim privilege on behalf of a bankrupt where such privilege would not have been available to the bankrupt himself). Note also the decision of the Supreme Court in *R (on the application of Prudential plc) v Special Commissioner of Income Tax* [2013] UKSC 1 on limitations to the scope of legal advice privilege (it does not apply to person other than a member of the legal profession and therefore does not cover legal advice given by accountants in relation to a tax avoidance scheme).

## SECTION 311(2)

**Trustee like receiver**—The most obvious significance of the trustee being treated as if he were a receiver of property appointed by the High Court is that the trustee acquires the protection of the law of contempt. Any proceedings for enforcement brought under s 311(2), therefore, may be accompanied with an application against the respondent for contempt of court.

'. . . **and the court may, on his application, enforce such acquisition or retention accordingly'**—Only the trustee may make an application for enforcement under this provision. An order for enforcement under s 311(2) should be distinguished from an order for enforcement under s 367 for s 366 purposes in that the present provision relates to the trustee taking possession 'of all books, papers and other records which relate to the bankrupt's estate or affairs' (which need not form part of the bankruptcy estate), whereas s 367 provides inter alia for the making of an order for delivery up of property comprised in the bankrupt's estate.

## SECTION 311(3)

**Exercise by the trustee of rights of transfer of transferable property**—Although a trustee obtains ownership of all property comprised in the bankruptcy estate automatically under s 306(1), including intangible property incapable of physical delivery, the present provision operates so as to override any external procedural mechanism which might otherwise operate to preclude the trustee from transferring property to a third party. The trustee's standing to transfer, however, which would be enforceable most obviously by way of an application for directions under s 303(2), can be no better than the position in which the bankrupt would otherwise have been. Thus, a trustee would be entitled to transfer shares in a limited company, but only subject to the articles of association.

Although a company may refuse to register a trustee as a member under the terms of its articles, the decision in *Morgan v Gray* [1953] Ch 83 is authority for the proposition that, whilst a bankrupt may exercise voting rights attached to the shares and give proxies, he may be required by the trustee to exercise the voting rights as directed. Although it was held in *Re HL Bolton Engineering Co* [1956] Ch 577 that a trustee who is not registered as a member may not petition for relief under what is now s 994 of the Companies Act 2006, there is nothing which prevents the bankrupt presenting a petition on behalf of the trustee: *Re K/9 Meat Supplies (Guildford) Ltd* [1966] 1 WLR 1112.

## SECTION 311(4)

**Things in action**—The first part of this provision repeats in substance the effect of s 306(2). A statutory deemed assignment does not contravene any contractual provision prohibiting assignment, such as a term commonly being included within private pension policies as a condition of tax approval: *Re Landau (a Bankrupt)* [1998] Ch 223 (Ferris J).

The balance of the provision provides a general rule dispensing with the need for notice of the deemed assignment. Consequently, a life insurer which is ignorant of the bankruptcy of the beneficiary of a life policy, and which makes payment of the policy proceeds to the bankrupt, remains liable to the bankrupt's trustee for an equivalent sum in the absence of the bankrupt being in a position to give a good receipt for the proceeds: *Rooney v Cardona* [1999] 1 WLR 1388, CA.

The exception to the general rule on deemed assignment arises where notice is necessary for protecting the priority of the trustee, but only where the deemed assignment is from the bankrupt to the trustee; for examples of circumstances warranting protection of a trustee see *Weddell v JEA Pearce & Major* [1988] Ch 26 at [31]–[32] on the substantively identical provision under s 48(5) of the Bankruptcy Act 1914.

## SECTION 311(5), (6)

**Goods held by pledge etc**—Prior to bankruptcy an individual in worsening financial circumstances may have chosen to pawn, pledge or use his goods as security for his debts. The present provision operates for the benefit of the bankruptcy estate to the extent that the true value of the goods is significantly in excess of the amount for which those goods were pawned etc, as is often the case in practice. Subject to the service of a notice – for which there is no prescribed form – the trustee may exercise the bankrupt's right of redemption, although it would follow that the trustee can obtain no better right than that to which the bankrupt would otherwise have been entitled.

Where a notice has been given to any person under s 285(5), that person is not entitled, without the leave of the court, to realise his security unless he has given the trustee of the bankrupt's estate a reasonable opportunity of inspecting the goods and of exercising the bankrupt's right of redemption.

**[1.430]**

### 312 Obligation to surrender control to trustee

(1)   The bankrupt shall deliver up to the trustee possession of any property, books, papers or other records of which he has possession or control and of which the trustee is required to take possession.

This is without prejudice to the general duties of the bankrupt under section 333 in this Chapter.

(2)   If any of the following is in possession of any property, books, papers or other records of which the trustee is required to take possession, namely—

    (a)    the official receiver,

    (b)    a person who has ceased to be trustee of the bankrupt's estate, or

    (c)    a person who has been the supervisor of a voluntary arrangement approved in relation to the bankrupt under Part VIII,

the official receiver or, as the case may be, that person shall deliver up possession of the property, books, papers or records to the trustee.

(3)   Any banker or agent of the bankrupt or any other person who holds any property to the account of, or for, the bankrupt shall pay or deliver to the trustee all property in his possession or under his control which forms part of the bankrupt's estate and which he is not by law entitled to retain as against the bankrupt or trustee.

(4)   If any person without reasonable excuse fails to comply with any obligation imposed by this section, he is guilty of a contempt of court and liable to be punished accordingly (in addition to any other punishment to which he may be subject).

General note—This provision should be read alongside s 333 and corresponds with but exceeds the scope of s 311, in that the present provision refers to the trustee taking possession of 'any property' in addition to books, papers and other records. The obligation in s 312(1) mirrors the duty of a bankrupt in relation to the official receiver in s 291(1). The burden on the debtor to deliver up is a heavy one: *Smedley v Brittain* [2008] BPIR 219 at [45] (Registrar Nicholls).

Related provisions—See also r 10.75 (handover of estate by official receiver to trustee) and r 10.90 (trustee's duties on vacating office).

Procedure for contempt—It was noted in *Simmonds v Pearce* [2017] EWHC 3126 (Admin), [2018] 1 WLR 1849, [2018] BPIR 206 at [28]–[32] that the appropriate procedure to be adopted in contempt cases falling under IR 1986 was unclear, and in this regard IR 2016 is unsatisfactory and unclear. Pending consideration by the Rules Committee, the procedure under CPR 81.15 should be adopted. On sanctions for contempt in this context, and the applicable principles, see *Official Receiver v Brown* [2017] EWHC 2762 (Ch), [2018] BPIR 98 (upheld on appeal [2018] EWCA Civ 303).

**[1.431]**

### 313 Charge on bankrupt's home

(1)   Where any property consisting of an interest in a dwelling house which is occupied by the bankrupt or by his spouse or former spouse or by his civil partner or former civil partner is comprised in the bankrupt's estate and the trustee is, for any reason, unable for the time being to realise that property, the trustee may apply to the court for an order imposing a charge on the property for the benefit of the bankrupt's estate.

(2)   If on an application under this section the court imposes a charge on any property, the benefit of that charge shall be comprised in the bankrupt's estate and is enforceable, up to the charged value from time to time, for the payment of any amount which is payable otherwise than to the bankrupt out of the estate and of interest on that amount at the prescribed rate.

(2A)   In subsection (2) the charged value means—

    (a)    the amount specified in the charging order as the value of the bankrupt's interest in the property at the date of the order, plus

    (b)    interest on that amount from the date of the charging order at the prescribed rate.

(2B)   In determining the value of an interest for the purposes of this section the court shall disregard any matter which it is required to disregard by the rules.

(3) An order under this section made in respect of property vested in the trustee shall provide, in accordance with the rules, for the property to cease to be comprised in the bankrupt's estate and, subject to the charge (and any prior charge), to vest in the bankrupt.

(4) Subsection (1), (2), (4), (5) and (6) of section 3 of the Charging Orders Act 1979 (supplemental provisions with respect to charging orders) have effect in relation to orders under this section as in relation to charging orders under that Act.

(5) But an order under section 3(5) of that Act may not vary a charged value.

**Amendments—** Enterprise Act 2002, s 261(2)(a)–(c); Civil Partnership Act 2004, s 261(1), Sch 27, para 114; Tribunals, Courts and Enforcement Act 2007, s 93(5).

**General note—**The circumstances in which a trustee may make an application under this provision are precisely the same as those to which s 283A applies, on which see the commentary thereto. Section 313 is of heightened relevance to a trustee, given the introduction of s 283A which requires action on the part of the trustee within a variable 3-year period, failing which the trustee's interest in a dwelling-house reverts to the bankrupt. The provision is not concerned with the extent of the interest in a dwelling-house but, rather, the realisation of that interest. Specifically, s 313(2) allows for the imposition by the court of a charge – a charging order by virtue of s 313(4) – securing the interest to which the bankrupt's estate is entitled. This will be of assistance to the trustee where, as can commonly arise in practice, there are no assets in the estate to fund litigation where the possession and sale of the property is disputed or, alternatively, where an order for possession and sale is likely to be postponed on the establishment of exceptional circumstances under either s 335A(3) or s 336(5) – see *Re Parkins* [2014] BPIR 1054.

**The 'charged value' in s 313(2A), (2B) and (5)—**These subsections were inserted with effect from 1 April 2004 by s 260 of the Enterprise Act 2002 and represent a marked shift from the previous position in favour of the bankrupt and his family. If the court grants a charge under s 313(2), then it is obliged to value the bankrupt's interest at that date under s 313(2B), which thereafter constitutes the charged value when taken together with interest on that amount from that date. Interest, for those purposes, will be the applicable rate under s 17 of the Judgments Act 1838, which at present is 8% per annum. The charged value is incapable of variation under s 3(5) of the Charging Orders Act 1979. Section 313(3) is necessary to reflect the vesting of the charged interest in the bankrupt, without which the charge would secure nothing, since the relevant interest would remain vested in the bankrupt's estate. The 'charged value', therefore, is capped as at the date of the charging order and can increase only at the applicable level of interest. In a rising property market this will be advantageous to the bankrupt and his family, although in a falling market a trustee will retain the value of his security as fixed by the court together with ongoing interest.

**Limitation—**Section 20(1) of the Limitation Act 1980 does not apply to the enforcement of a charge under s 313(2) with the consequence that enforcement will not be statute-barred 12 years after the making of such an order: *Doodes v Gotham* [2006] EWCA Civ 1080, [2006] BPIR 1178 reversing Lindsay J at [2006] BPIR 36 below. The right to receive the amounts provided for in s 313 does not accrue for the purposes of the 1980 Act until the making of an order for sale of the property by the court.

**Procedure—**See r 10.171.

## [1.432]

### 313A Low value home: application for sale, possession or charge

(1) This section applies where—

    (a) property comprised in the bankrupt's estate consists of an interest in a dwelling-house which at the date of the bankruptcy was the sole or principal residence of—

        (i) the bankrupt,

        (ii) the bankrupt's spouse or civil partner, or

        (iii) a former spouse or former civil partner of the bankrupt, and

    (b) the trustee applies for an order for the sale of the property, for an order for possession of the property or for an order under section 313 in respect of the property.

(2) The court shall dismiss the application if the value of the interest is below the amount prescribed for the purposes of this subsection.

(3) In determining the value of an interest for the purposes of this section the court shall disregard any matter which it is required to disregard by the order which prescribes the amount for the purposes of subsection (2).

Amendments—Inserted by the Enterprise Act 2002, s 261(3). Amended by Civil Partnership Act 2004, s 261(1), Sch 27, para 115.

General note—This provision can only apply on any one of the applications in s 313A(1)(b) (applications for possession and sale usually being combined) where the bankrupt's estate consists of an interest in a dwelling-house, as defined in s 385(1), within s 313A(1)(a). The concept of 'sole or principal residence' in relation to a dwelling-house is discussed in the notes to s 283A.

The purpose of the provision is in avoiding the hardship associated with the sale of a dwelling-house, even one which is not the sole or principal residence of the bankrupt himself, where the value of net realisations is modest and therefore unlikely to make any real difference to the position of unsecured creditors.

### SECTION 313A(2)

Scope of provision—The court has no discretion and must dismiss an application brought by a trustee if the value of the interest to which the application relates is below £1,000, as currently prescribed by art 2 of the Insolvency Proceedings (Monetary Limits) (Amendment) Order 2004 (SI 2004/547). In determining the value of an interest, art 3 of the 2004 Order directs, for the purposes of s 313A(3), that the court must disregard the value of the property equal to the value of any loan secured by mortgage or other charge against the property, the value of any third party interest and the value of reasonable costs of sale.

Consequences of dismissal of trustee's application—An application within s 313A(1)(b) will fall within s 283A(3)(b)–(d), with the consequence that, if dismissed, the interest will cease to be comprised in the bankrupt's estate and will vest automatically in the bankrupt, subject to contrary order of the court, by virtue of s 283A(4).

Practical considerations—Section 313A does nothing to prevent a negotiated sale of any interest vested in the bankrupt's estate. Such a course may be satisfactory to all parties where there is a genuine dispute as to valuation of the interest or where the bankrupt's estate includes two or more properties potentially within the scope of the provision.

## [1.433]

### 314 Powers of trustee

(1) The trustee may exercise any of the powers specified in Parts 1 and 2 of Schedule 5.

(2) The trustee may appoint the bankrupt—

    (a) to superintend the management of his estate or any part of it,

    (b) to carry on his business (if any) for the benefit of his creditors, or

    (c) in any other respect to assist in administering the estate in such manner and on such terms as the trustee may direct.

(3) . . .

(4) . . .

(5) Part III of Schedule 5 to this Act has effect with respect to the things which the trustee is able to do for the purposes of, or in connection with, the exercise of any of his powers under any of this Group of Parts.

(6) Where the trustee (not being the official receiver) in exercise of the powers conferred on him by any provision in this Group of Parts—

    (a) disposes of any property comprised in the bankrupt's estate to an associate of the bankrupt, or

    (b) employs a solicitor,

he shall, if there is for the time being a creditors' committee, give notice to the committee of that exercise of his powers.

(7) Without prejudice to the generality of subsection (5) and Part III of Schedule 5, the trustee may, if he thinks fit, at any time seek a decision on a matter from the bankrupt's creditors.

Subject to the preceding provisions in this Group of Parts, he shall seek a decision on a matter if he is requested to do so by a creditor of the bankrupt and the request is made with the concurrence of not less than one-tenth, in value, of the bankrupt's creditors (including the creditor making the request).

(8) Nothing in this Act is to be construed as restricting the capacity of the trustee to exercise any of his powers outside England and Wales.

Amendments—Small Business, Enterprise and Employment Act 2015, s 121(1), (2).

General note—The powers of a trustee are set out in Sch 5. Under the old s 314 (1)(b) certain powers listed in Sch 5 required sanction. This section was significantly amended by the Small

Business, Enterprise and Employment Act 2015 such that, with effect from 26 May 2015, the requirement for sanction was removed (with no transitional provisions). Thus all the powers set out in Sch 5 are now exercisable by the trustee without sanction. Although the powers in Part III of Sch 5 never required sanction, those ancillary powers could only (and still may only) be exercised for the purposes of, or in connection with, the exercise of any of the powers of the trustee under Parts VIII to XI: s 314(5) and Sch 5, para 14.

These amendments mirror, for bankruptcy, the amendments made to the liquidation regime by s 117.

**Carrying on the bankrupt's business**—Section 314(2)(b) must be read subject to Part I of Sch 5. A trustee in bankruptcy has the power under para 1 of Part I of Sch 5 to carry on the bankrupt's business 'so far as may be necessary for winding it up beneficially' and by virtue of s 314(2)(b) he has the ability to appoint the bankrupt to assist in doing so. Sch 5 does not authorise a trustee to carry on a bankrupt's business, with or without the assistance of the bankrupt, indefinitely. This point was considered in some detail by ICC Judge Barber in *Leopard (trustee in bankruptcy of Robinson) v Robinson* [2020] EWHC 2928 (Ch) at [57], [75].

**Employment of solicitors**—Section 56(3) of the Bankruptcy Act 1914 required a trustee to obtain permission before employing a solicitor (or other agent), although Scott J held in *Re a Debtor (26A of 1975)* [1985] 1 WLR 6 that the court had jurisdiction to give permission retrospectively. Section 314(6)(b) specifically sanctions the employment of solicitors without any requirement for permission, but subject to the giving of notice to any creditors' committee.

Although it is understood to be the official receiver's practice not to employ the same solicitors as a petitioning creditor, in *Re Schuppan (a Bankrupt) (No 1)* [1996] 2 All ER 664 at 668 Robert Walker J expressed the view that that practice was a 'counsel of perfection which need not necessarily be followed by all insolvency practitioners in all circumstances.' Indeed, as his Lordship went on, 'In a case where the real difficulties that are foreseen are in connection with the identification, tracing and recovery of assets for the bankrupt's estate, the retainer of solicitors who already have a good grasp of these difficulties can be of great advantage to all creditors, not just the petitioning creditor.' In particular, if the petitioning creditor is the largest creditor, and no difficulties are foreseen in quantifying the provable debts of the petitioning creditor or other creditors, the risk of a conflict of interest would appear to be, in the words of Hoffmann J in *Re Maxwell Communication Corp plc* [1992] BCLC 465 at 468, 'a mere distant possibility.' In *Re Baron Investments (Holdings) Ltd* [2000] 1 BCLC 272 (a liquidation case) Pumfrey J expressed the view that, whilst all cases must turn on their own facts, the retention of a petitioning creditors' solicitors by an office-holder contemporaneous with the employment of other solicitors in relation to particular matters in which a conflict was perceived was only justifiable where there is a reasonable apprehension of potential conflict and not a mere theoretical possibility. In dealing with potential conflicts it is necessary to adopt a pragmatic approach, although an actual conflict cannot be ignored and must be addressed with appropriate steps.

The judgment of Lord Millett in *Prince Jefri Bolkiah v KPMG (a firm)* [1999] 2 AC 222 at 234 includes a useful summary of the duties of solicitors and other fiduciaries.

**Exercise of trustee's powers outside the jurisdiction**—Section 314(8) clearly allows for the exercise of any of the trustee's powers outside England and Wales. The court must, however, consider whether, on the facts of any particular case, any application before it is concerned with English bankruptcy law or whether, in reality, the action is in substance a matter of foreign law. That issue is one determined by reference to the Civil Jurisdiction and Judgments Act 1982, which gives effect to the Convention on Jurisdiction and the Enforcement of Judgments in Civil and Commercial Matters 1968, commonly known as the Brussels Convention.

In *Re Hayward (Deceased)* [1997] Ch 45 Rattee J struck out a trustee's application, which had sought declaratory and consequential relief, including the rectification of a property register located in the foreign jurisdiction, in relation to the bankrupt's alleged beneficial half-share in a Spanish property. In distinguishing the decision of the European Court of Justice in *Webb v Webb* [1994] QB 696, his Lordship held that Art 16 of the Brussels Convention required the proceedings to proceed in the Spanish courts, since the trustee was seeking to enforce a right in rem in the land and to rectify the Spanish property register. A contrary decision on different facts was reached in *Ashurst v Pollard* [2001] BPIR 131, which followed the European court's decision in *Webb* and which required a bankrupt and his wife to transfer title in a Portuguese property to the trustee so as to allow for a sale with vacant possession, notwithstanding the fact that Art 16 of the Brussels Convention dictated that the English courts had no jurisdiction to authorise a sale by the trustee (note however that *Ashurst v Pollard* was doubted in *Magiera v Magiera* [2016] Civ 1292, [2017] Fam 327, [2017] BPIR 472 at [52]–[55]).

*Disclaimer of onerous property*

**[1.434]**

### 315 Disclaimer (general power)

(1)   Subject as follows, the trustee may, by the giving of the prescribed notice, disclaim any onerous property and may do so notwithstanding that he has taken possession of it, endeavoured to sell it or otherwise exercised rights of ownership in relation to it.

(2)   The following is onerous property for the purposes of this section, that is to say—

    (a)    any unprofitable contract, and

    (b)    any other property comprised in the bankrupt's estate which is unsaleable or not readily saleable, or is such that it may give rise to a liability to pay money or perform any other onerous act.

(3)   A disclaimer under this section—

    (a)    operates so as to determine, as from the date of the disclaimer, the rights, interests and liabilities of the bankrupt and his estate in or in respect of the property disclaimed, and

    (b)    discharges the trustee from all personal liability in respect of that property as from the commencement of his trusteeship,

but does not, except so far as is necessary for the purpose of releasing the bankrupt, the bankrupt's estate and the trustee from any liability, affect the rights or liabilities of any other person.

(4)   A notice of disclaimer shall not be given under this section in respect of any property that has been claimed for the estate under section 307 (after-acquired property) or 308 (personal property of bankrupt exceeding reasonable replacement value) or 308A, except with the leave of the court.

(5)   Any person sustaining loss or damage in consequence of the operation of a disclaimer under this section is deemed to be a creditor of the bankrupt to the extent of the loss or damage and accordingly may prove for the loss or damage as a bankruptcy debt.

**Amendments**—Housing Act 1988, s 117(4).

**General note**—The power of disclaimer can be of great practical assistance to a trustee who, unlike any ordinary person, has the ability under these provisions to disown property with the characteristics prescribed by s 315(2). The utility of the power of disclaimer lies in the trustee's ability to jettison property which might otherwise pose an unavoidable financial drain on the bankrupt's estate or which might otherwise unduly protract the administration of the bankruptcy, ultimately at the expense of creditors.

The power to disclaim is unaffected by the trustee having dealt with the relevant property: s 315(1). Further, no time limit applies to the power of disclaimer, save where the trustee is put to a decision on service of a notice under s 316.

Corresponding provisions on disclaimer in winding up appear in ss 178–182. Reference may also be made to the commentary on those provisions.

**SECTION 315(2)**

**Onerous property**—The term 'property' is defined in non-exhaustive terms in s 436.

In *Re Celtic Extraction Ltd (in liquidation)* [2001] Ch 475 the Court of Appeal (Morritt and Roch LJJ and Rattee J) upheld the decision of Neuberger J albeit on different grounds, to the effect that a waste management licence issued under the terms of the Environmental Protection Act 1990 constituted 'property', with the consequence that a liquidator was entitled to exercise his power of disclaimer in relation to it (cf the position in Scotland, see *Scottish Coal Company* [2013] CSIH 108).

The question of whether property is 'onerous' is a question of fact and one for the trustee in the discharge of his functions under s 305(2). A trustee's decision to disclaim particular property might be challenged by way of a claim under s 304(1). An eligible applicant might also consider injunctive relief so as to prevent the exercise of the power of disclaimer, which would be coupled, most obviously, with a claim under s 303(1), in an appropriate case. The court will not, however, interfere with an office-holder's decision to disclaim unless there is a challenge to the bona fides of the office-holder or a suggestion that his decision to disclaim can be categorised as perverse: *Re Hans Place Ltd* [1992] BCC 737 at 749D (Edward Evans-Lombe QC, sitting as a deputy High Court judge).

Subject to particular circumstances, examples of onerous property might include a cause of action (on which see *Khan-Ghauri v Dunbar Bank plc* [2001] BPIR 618, *Young v Hamilton* [2010] BPIR 1468, *Young v Official Receiver* [2010] BPIR 1477, and *Frosdick v Fox* [2017] EWHC 1737 (Ch), [2018] 1 WLR 38, [2017] BPIR 1194), a property giving rise to ongoing environmental or other liabilities, property for which there is no market or in respect of which the costs of marketing and sale are disproportionate to the likely proceeds of sale or an unduly onerous contract.

It was held in *Abdulla v Whelan* [2017] EWHC 605 (Ch), [2017] 1 WLR 3318, [2017] BPIR 791 that a trustee cannot disclaim property held on trust by a bankrupt, even in circumstances where the bankrupt is one of the beneficiaries of the trust.

### SECTION 315(3)

**Effect of disclaimer**—Section 315(3) provides for the determination of the rights, interests and liabilities of the bankrupt and his estate in relation to the property disclosed and, secondly, the discharge of the trustee's personal liability in respect of that property. The determination of rights etc is 'as from the date of the disclaimer' and cannot, therefore, be retrospective, although a trustee is discharged from all personal liability in respect of that property as from the date of the bankruptcy order. Furthermore, the decision of Neuberger J in *Capital Prime Properties plc v Worthgate Ltd (in liquidation)* [2000] 1 BCLC 647 is authority for the proposition that the exercise of the power of disclaimer cannot operate so as to undo contractual rights and benefits which had vested prior to that date. The following extract from the judgment, at 655B–655C, provides a useful analysis:

> 'In the context of a commercial contract, eg where A agrees to sell 1,000 tonnes of aluminium a month to B for 2 years, it seems to me that, if A went into liquidation after a year, the liquidator would be able to disclaim the contract if A did not have the aluminium and would have had to have purchased it in the market at a price considerably in excess of £1,000 a tonne. But it cannot be sensibly suggested that the effect of the disclaimer would be to undo the rights which had been acquired by B in relation to the aluminium which had already been supplied to B.'

It is not possible for a trustee to disclaim onerous liabilities for rent under a lease whilst at the same time retaining the property itself: *MEPC Ltd v Scottish Amicable* [1996] BPIR 447 at 450E–450G (Dillon LJ, Leggatt LJ agreeing).

Freehold property disclaimed by a trustee devolves on the Crown Estate.

**The effect of disclaimer on third parties**—Disclaimer affects third parties insofar as the rights, interests and liabilities of the bankrupt and his estate are determined under s 315(3) in relation to the property disclaimed, but no further. The operation of that rule is illustrated by the House of Lords' decision in *Hindcastle Ltd v Barbara Attenborough Associate*s [1997] AC 70, which held that a disclaimer does not operate so as to release a guarantor or surety for future rent and obligations under a lease from such liability where the guarantor's remedy on disclaimer is to prove in the bankruptcy in respect of the indemnity to which the guarantor is entitled by operation of law.

### SECTION 315(4)

**Leave to disclaim under s 315(4)**—The court will require a clear explanation as to the circumstances giving rise to the trustee's decision to disclaim property caught by s 315(4) where he has previously taken steps to claim that property for the benefit of the bankrupt's estate. Even if satisfied that disclaimer is appropriate, it is open to the court to take the view that the costs incurred by the trustee either in claiming and/or disclaiming the property should not rank as an expense of the bankruptcy if a trustee can be shown to have acted unreasonably in discharging his function.

**Financial markets etc**—Section 315 has no application to market contracts and the like: see s 164(1) of the Companies Act 1989.

### SECTION 315(5)

**Assessment of loss or damage**—This provision should be read in conjunction with s 320(5).

**Procedure**—See rr 19.2–19.11.

See the notes accompanying s 178.

## [1.435]

### 316 Notice requiring trustee's decision

(1) Notice of disclaimer shall not be given under section 315 in respect of any property if—

> (a) a person interested in the property has applied in writing to the trustee or one of his predecessors as trustee requiring the trustee or that predecessor to decide whether he will disclaim or not, and

(b)    the period of 28 days beginning with the day on which that application was made has expired without a notice of disclaimer having been given under section 315 in respect of that property.

(2)    The trustee is deemed to have adopted any contract which by virtue of this section he is not entitled to disclaim.

**General note**—Although the trustee's power to disclaim under s 315 is not subject to any time limit, 'a person interested in' any particular property may impose a 28-day period in which the trustee must elect whether or not to disclaim that property. Note, however, that the bankrupt is not a 'person interested in the property' for the purposes of s 316, and cannot make a valid application under s 316: *Frosdick v Fox* [2017] EWHC 1737 (Ch), [2018] 1 WLR 38, [2017] BPIR 1194 at [61]–[65]. Section 316 is not intended to protect the bankrupt, but other persons who have (or perhaps may have) an interest in the relevant property. If the bankrupt wished to challenge the disclaimer, the bankrupt would need to challenge the exercise of the trustee's discretion under s 304(2).

The 28-day period in s 316(1)(b) begins with the day on which the trustee receives that person's notice in writing (the form of which is no long prescribed under IR 2016) and follow the procedure in r 19.9(1) and 19.9(2). The 28-day period is extendable by an application to the court by the trustee under r 19.9(3) where the trustee requires leave to disclaim (on which see ss 315(4) and ss 317–321). The 28-day period is not otherwise extendable, with the consequence that the trustee will be fixed with being unable to disclaim if he does not act by disclaiming within that period following service of a notice on him.

**Procedure**—See the notes to s 315 and see rr 19.2–19.11.

## [1.436]

### 317  Disclaimer of leaseholds

(1)    The disclaimer of any property of a leasehold nature does not take effect unless a copy of the disclaimer has been served (so far as the trustee is aware of their addresses) on every person claiming under the bankrupt as underlessee or mortgagee and either—

(a)    no application under section 320 below is made with respect to the property before the end of the period of 14 days beginning with the day on which the last notice served under this subsection was served, or

(b)    where such an application has been made, the court directs that the disclaimer is to take effect.

(2)    Where the court gives a direction under subsection (1)(b) it may also, instead of or in addition to any order it makes under section 320, make such orders with respect to fixtures, tenant's improvements and other matters arising out of the lease as it thinks fit.

**General note**—This provision applies only to leasehold property which is onerous within the meaning of s 315(2) and is only triggered where the disclaimer is communicated to persons interested in compliance with IR 2016, r 19.4 and either s 317(1)(a) or (b) applies. Curiously, there is no requirement for a copy of the disclaimer to be served on the lessor or the landlord, despite the fact that either person would have standing to apply for a vesting order under s 320.

For further commentary see the notes to the analogous s 179 applicable in winding up.

**Procedure**—See the notes to s 315 and see rr 19.2–19.11.

## [1.437]

### 318  Disclaimer of dwelling house

Without prejudice to section 317, the disclaimer of any property in a dwelling house does not take effect unless a copy of the disclaimer has been served (so far as the trustee is aware of their addresses) on every person in occupation of or claiming a right to occupy the dwelling house and either—

(a)    no application under section 320 is made with respect to the property before the end of the period of 14 days beginning with the day on which the last notice served under this section was served, or

(b)    where such an application has been made, the court directs that the disclaimer is to take effect.

**General note**—This provision applies where a dwelling-house constitutes onerous property within the meaning of s 315(2), and is very similar in substance to s 317. The trustee must comply with r 19.5. The term 'dwelling-house' is defined in s 385. Notably, it is a specific requirement of s 318 that a copy of the disclaimer is served not only on every person in occupation of a dwelling-house but also on every person *claiming* a right to occupy.

Procedure—See the notes to s 315 and see rr 19.2–19.11.

## [1.438]

### 319 Disclaimer of land subject to rentcharge

(1) The following applies where, in consequence of the disclaimer under section 315 of any land subject to a rentcharge, that land vests by operation of law in the Crown or any other person (referred to in the next subsection as "the proprietor").

(2) The proprietor, and the successors in title of the proprietor, are not subject to any personal liability in respect of any sums becoming due under the rentcharge, except sums becoming due after the proprietor, or some person claiming under or through the proprietor, has taken possession or control of the land or has entered into occupation of it.

General note—This provision will most commonly be relevant on the disclaimer of freehold land where, as a consequence, the freehold vests in the Crown or some other person who, but for s 319(2), would be personally liable to pay any rent charge on the land. The term 'rent charge' is defined in s 205(1)(xxiii) of the Law of Property Act 1925. The leading case under the old law is the House of Lords' decision in *Attorney-General v Parsons* [1956] AC 421.

Procedure—See the notes to s 315 and see rr 19.2–19.11.

## [1.439]

### 320 Court order vesting disclaimed property

(1) This section and the next apply where the trustee has disclaimed property under section 315.

(2) An application may be made to the court under this section by—

    (a)    any person who claims an interest in the disclaimed property,

    (b)    any person who is under any liability in respect of the disclaimed property, not being a liability discharged by the disclaimer, or

    (c)    where the disclaimed property is property in a dwelling-house, any person who at the time when the bankruptcy application was made or (as the case may be) the bankruptcy petition was presented was in occupation of or entitled to occupy the dwelling house.

(3) Subject as follows in this section and the next, the court may, on an application under this section, make an order on such terms as it thinks fit for the vesting of the disclaimed property in, or for its delivery to—

    (a)    a person entitled to it or a trustee for such a person,

    (b)    a person subject to such a liability as is mentioned in subsection (2)(b) or a trustee for such a person, or

    (c)    where the disclaimed property is property in a dwelling-house, any person who at the time when the bankruptcy application was made or (as the case may be) the bankruptcy petition was presented was in occupation of or entitled to occupy the dwelling house.

(4) The court shall not make an order by virtue of subsection (3)(b) except where it appears to the court that it would be just to do so for the purpose of compensating the person subject to the liability in respect of the disclaimer.

(5) The effect of any order under this section shall be taken into account in assessing for the purposes of section 315(5) the extent of any loss or damage sustained by any person in consequence of the disclaimer.

(6) An order under this section vesting property in any person need not be completed by any conveyance, assignment or transfer.

Amendments—Enterprise and Regulatory Reform Act 2013, s 71(3), Sch 19, paras 1, 25.

General note—Following disclaimer under s 315, any of those persons listed in s 320(2) may apply for what is commonly termed a 'vesting order' under s 320(3). Section 320(3)(b) must be read in the light of s 320(4).

SECTION 320(2)(a)

'Any person who claims an interest . . . '—A person with a statutory charge over disclaimed property constitutes a person 'who claims an interest' in the disclaimed property: *London Borough of Hackney v Crown Estates Commissioners* [1996] BPIR 428 (Knox J). See also *Fenland DC v Shappard* [2011] EWHC 2829 (Ch), [2012] BPIR 289 (a vesting order in favour of a mortgagee will not operate to merge the freehold interest with the interest under the charge where that result was not intended). By s 320(2)(c) a person has standing to make application for a vesting order on the sole ground of being in occupation or entitled to occupy a dwelling-house at the time of the bankruptcy petition. This provision is important, since the mere fact of occupation, in the context of a person who had agreed to take an assignment subject to the consent of the landlord, does not give rise to a proprietary interest within s 181(2)(a), the liquidation equivalent of s 320(2)(a): *Lloyds Bank SF Nominees v Aladdin Ltd* [1996] 1 BCLC 720 (Leggatt and Peter Gibson LJJ).

It was held in *Re Mascall (Deceased)* [2018] EWHC 3489 (Ch), [2019] BPIR 430 that a trustee in bankruptcy who had disclaimed assets, which had then been sold and realised a surplus, had no standing to apply for a vesting order.

'Disclaimed property'—According to Sir William Blackburne in *Hunt v Conwy CBC* [2013] EWHC 1154 (Ch), [2013] BPIR 790 at [48] a vesting of part of the property can be valid. The judge also said that in relation to s 320(2)(c) he did not consider that to qualify under that provision the whole of the disclaimed property must comprise a dwelling-house (at [48]). He considered that the discretion to make a vesting order was at large in the sense that there was no statutory guidance but in the absence of some competing applicant and in the absence of some good reason to the contrary the court ought ordinarily to exercise its discretion in favour of a qualifying applicant at least in relation to a freehold (see also related proceedings in *Hunt v Withinshaw* [2015] EWHC 3072 (Ch), [2016] BPIR 59).

Procedure—See the notes to s 315 and rr 19.2–19.11, in particular r 19.11 which, in r 19.11(2), imposes a 3-month time limit for the making of an application for a vesting order.

## [1.440]

### 321 Order under s 320 in respect of leaseholds

(1)  The court shall not make an order under section 320 vesting property of a leasehold nature in any person, except on terms making that person—

    (a)    subject to the same liabilities and obligations as the bankrupt was subject to under the lease on the day the bankruptcy application was made or (as the case may be) the bankruptcy petition was presented, or

    (b)    if the court thinks fit, subject to the same liabilities and obligations as that person would be subject to if the lease had been assigned to him on that day.

(2)  For the purposes of an order under section 320 relating to only part of any property comprised in a lease, the requirements of subsection (1) apply as if the lease comprised only the property to which the order relates.

(3)  Where subsection (1) applies and no person is willing to accept an order under section 320 on the terms required by that subsection, the court may (by order under section 320) vest the estate or interest of the bankrupt in the property in any person who is liable (whether personally or in a representative capacity and whether alone or jointly with the bankrupt) to perform the lessee's covenants in the lease.

The court may by virtue of this subsection vest that estate and interest in such a person freed and discharged from all estates, incumbrances and interests created by the bankrupt.

(4)  Where subsection (1) applies and a person declines to accept any order under section 320, that person shall be excluded from all interest in the property.

Amendments—Enterprise and Regulatory Reform Act 2013, s 71(3), Sch 19, paras 1, 26.

General note—See the notes to s 320. Where the trustee of an under-lessor disclaims the head-lease, the under-lease continues to exist and remains subject to the rights of the lessor to distrain for rent or to re-enter for breach of covenant: *Re Town Investment Ltd's Under-lease* [1954] Ch 301.

*Distribution of bankrupt's estate*

## [1.441]

### 322 Proof of debts

(1) Subject to this section and the next, the proof of any bankruptcy debt by a secured or unsecured creditor of the bankrupt and the admission or rejection of any proof shall take place in accordance with the rules.

(2) Where a bankruptcy debt bears interest, that interest is provable as part of the debt except in so far as it is payable in respect of any period after the commencement of the bankruptcy.

(3) The trustee shall estimate the value of any bankruptcy debt which, by reason of its being subject to any contingency or contingencies or for any other reason, does not bear a certain value.

(4) Where the value of a bankruptcy debt is estimated by the trustee under subsection (3) or, by virtue of section 303 in Chapter III, by the court, the amount provable in the bankruptcy in respect of the debt is the amount of the estimate.

General note—A creditor 'proves' for his debt by asserting his claim by way of a document known as a 'proof'. The procedure for proving appears in rr 14.3–14.4.

A creditor bears the costs of proving its own debt: r 14.5(a).

Other than non-provable and postponed debts (see below), r 14.2(1) provides that all claims by creditors are provable as debts against a bankrupt, whether they are present or future, certain or contingent, ascertained or sounding only in damages.

SECTION 322(1)

' . . . bankruptcy debt . . . '—This term is defined very broadly in s 382.

Non-provable debts—Debts which are not provable, and postponed debts which are only provable after all other creditors have been paid in full, appear in rr 14.2(2) and (4).

Secured creditors—The term 'secured creditor' and the position of a secured creditor who petitions for a debtor's bankruptcy are provided for in s 383.

A secured creditor is entitled to rely on his security without submission of a proof. Any proof must, however, provide particulars of any security held, the date it was given and the value which the creditor puts upon it: r 14.4(1)(g). A secured creditor is entitled to alter the value which is put upon his security in his proof of debt with the agreement of the trustee or with the leave of the court, although the leave of the court must be obtained if the secured creditor has put a value on his security in the bankruptcy petition or has voted in respect of the unsecured balance of his debt: r 14.15(1) and (2).

Interest—The calculation of interest is provided for in r 14.23; and see also s 328(5).

Under s 322(2) interest is provable as part of a debt but not in respect of any period after the date of the bankruptcy order. A contractual provision for the capitalisation of interest cannot be relied upon in relation to any post-bankruptcy order period: *Re Amalgamated Investment & Property Co Ltd* [1984] BCLC 341.

SECTION 322(3), (4)

Scope of provision—The quantification of claims is a matter for the trustee. The particular rules governing discounts, debt in a foreign currency, periodical payments, interest and debts payable at a future time appear in rr 14.20–14.23 and r 14.44(1). A creditor has a right of appeal against the trustee's decision on a proof under r 14.8. Such an appeal is not a true appeal and is determined by the court on the facts before it at the date of the hearing: *Cadwell v Jackson* [2001] BPIR 966 at 967E–967F (Neuberger J).

## [1.442]

### 323 Mutual credit and set-off

(1) This section applies where before the commencement of the bankruptcy there have been mutual credits, mutual debts or other mutual dealings between the bankrupt and any creditor of the bankrupt proving or claiming to prove for a bankruptcy debt.

(2) An account shall be taken of what is due from each party to the other in respect of the mutual dealings and the sums due from one party shall be set off against the sums due from the other.

(3) Sums due from the bankrupt to another party shall not be included in the account taken under subsection (2) if that other party had notice at the time they became due

that proceedings on a bankruptcy application relating to the bankrupt were ongoing or that a bankruptcy petition relating to the bankrupt was pending.

(4)   Only the balance (if any) of the account taken under subsection (2) is provable as a bankruptcy debt or, as the case may be, to be paid to the trustee as part of the bankrupt's estate.

**Amendments**—Enterprise and Regulatory Reform Act 2013, s 71(3), Sch 19, paras 1, 27.

**General note**—The provision specifically allows set-off, which is an exception to the pari passu rule, for reasons of policy and justice.

The provision mirrors r 14.25, which applies to liquidations. There appears no good reason for the fact that set-off for liquidation is covered by the Rules and set-off for bankruptcy is dealt with by the Act.

A debt arising from a market contract cannot be set-off until the completion of default proceedings (Companies Act 1989, ss 159(4), 163(1), (2)). These are proceedings brought pursuant to the relevant investment exchange or clearing house rules, where default occurs.

**Time**—The set-off takes place, in relation to the respective parties' rights, as at the date of the bankruptcy order.

**Application of set-off**—Set-off is a statutory directive and therefore applies automatically without any action having to be taken by the bankrupt's trustee or the other party (*Stein v Blake* [1996] AC 243, [1995] BCC 543).

**'What is due from each party to the other . . . and the sums due from one party shall be set off against the sums due from the other'**—This means that the sums that are owed are treated as having been owing as at the date of bankruptcy with the benefit and estimation laid down by the bankruptcy law: *Stein v Blake* at 256 (AC).

A contingent liability that is owed to X by Y is sufficient to allow X to claim set-off if there is liability of Y to X: *Bateman v Williams* [2009] EWHC 1760 (Ch), [2009] BPIR 973 at [10].

**The effect**—Once set-off has occurred, the original choses in action of the parties cease to exist, and the party with the greater claim then has a right to the net balance (*Stein v Blake*). The right to the net balance may be assigned (*Stein v Blake*).

See the notes accompanying r 14.25, which deal with set-off in some depth.

## [1.443]

### 324 Distribution by means of dividend

(1)   Whenever the trustee has sufficient funds in hand for the purpose he shall, subject to the retention of such sums as may be necessary for the expenses of the bankruptcy, declare and distribute dividends among the creditors in respect of the bankruptcy debts which they have respectively proved.

(2)   The trustee shall give notice of his intention to declare and distribute a dividend.

(3)   Where the trustee has declared a dividend, he shall give notice of the dividend and of how it is proposed to distribute it; and a notice given under this subsection shall contain the prescribed particulars of the bankrupt's estate.

(4)   In the calculation and distribution of a dividend the trustee shall make provision—

    (a)    for any bankruptcy debts which appear to him to be due to persons who, by reason of the distance of their place of residence, may not have had sufficient time to tender and establish their proofs,

    (b)    for any bankruptcy debts which are the subject of claims which have not yet been determined, and

    (c)    for disputed proofs and claims.

**General note**—Section 324(1) imposes an unqualified duty on a trustee to declare and distribute dividends among creditors which have proved in respect of bankruptcy debts 'whenever' the trustee has sufficient funds in hand, subject to the retention of sums necessary for the expenses of the bankruptcy. It is unhelpful that the unqualified nature of the duty takes no account of the fact that in some cases the cost of distributing the dividend may be disproportionate to the level of the dividend itself.

The purpose of the giving of the notice of intention to declare and distribute a dividend under s 324(2) is to afford an opportunity to any creditor which has not proved to do so, on which see rr 14.28–14.32. There is no form prescribed for the giving of a notice of intention to pay dividends, although the notice must be in writing unless the court permits notice to be given in some other way: r 1.4(1). Even where a trustee is unable to declare any dividend, or any further dividend where an interim dividend has been paid, he must give notice of the fact to creditors: see r 14.37(1). The trustee is obliged to state that payment of a dividend will be made within a period of 2 months from the last date for proving: see rr 14.29 and 14.30. A dividend may be distributed simultaneously with the notice declaring it: r 14.35(2).

**Undistributed and unclaimed dividends**—See regs 23 and 31 of the Insolvency Regulations 1994.

**Procedure**—See the detailed provisions in rr 14.26–14.45.

## [1.444]

### 325  Claims by unsatisfied creditors

(1)   A creditor who has not proved his debt before the declaration of any dividend is not entitled to disturb, by reason that he has not participated in it, the distribution of that dividend or any other dividend declared before his debt was proved, but—

(a)   when he has proved that debt he is entitled to be paid, out of any money for the time being available for the payment of any further dividend, any dividend or dividends which he has failed to receive; and

(b)   any dividend or dividends payable under paragraph (a) shall be paid before that money is applied to the payment of any such further dividend.

(2)   No action lies against the trustee for a dividend, but if the trustee refuses to pay a dividend the court may, if it thinks fit, order him to pay it and also to pay, out of his own money—

(a)   interest on the dividend, at the rate for the time being specified in section 17 of the Judgments Act 1838, from the time it was withheld, and

(b)   the costs of the proceedings in which the order to pay is made.

**General note**—The two subsections in this provision deal with very different situations.

#### SECTION 325(1)

**Scope of provision**—This subsection is only triggered where a creditor who has not proved his debt before the declaration of any dividend but subsequently proves. In those circumstances, whilst the late creditor is not entitled to disturb any dividend previously made, he obtains a right to be paid his original dividend, effectively as if he had proved on time, from any monies available for the payment of any future dividend.

#### SECTION 325(2)

**Scope of provision**—This subsection insulates a trustee from personal liability for any claim in relation to a dividend, although the court may, if it thinks fit, order the trustee to pay any dividend which he *refuses* to pay; that is, from the fund available to the trustee for the payment of dividends. In those circumstances, however, the trustee may be made personally liable for interest on any such dividend and the costs of any proceedings in which the order to pay is made.

## [1.445]

### 326  Distribution of property in specie

(1)   Without prejudice to sections 315 to 319 (disclaimer), the trustee may, with the permission of the creditors' committee, divide in its existing form amongst the bankrupt's creditors, according to its estimated value, any property which from its peculiar nature or other special circumstances cannot be readily or advantageously sold.

(2)   A permission given for the purposes of subsection (1) shall not be a general permission but shall relate to a particular proposed exercise of the power in question; and a person dealing with the trustee in good faith and for value is not to be concerned to enquire whether any permission required by subsection (1) has been given.

(3)   Where the trustee has done anything without the permission required by subsection (1), the court or the creditors' committee may, for the purpose of enabling him to meet his expenses out of the bankrupt's estate, ratify what the trustee has done. But the committee shall not do so unless it is satisfied that the trustee acted in a case of urgency and has sought its ratification without undue delay.

**General note**—A distribution of property in specie is only permitted where the property to be distributed cannot be readily or advantageously sold on account of its 'peculiar nature', such as perishable goods or goods for which the market is so specialised that the costs of realisation are disproportionate to the likely proceeds of sale, or 'other special circumstances' which are not defined. Such special circumstances might include the absence of any ready market for the property in question.

Permission of and ratification by the creditors' committee—The distribution of property in specie is subject to the permission of the creditors' committee. That permission may only be given in relation to particular proposed exercise of the power to distribute in specie and must not be general. Section 326(3) permits the creditors' committee to ratify the act of a trustee in distributing in specie without permission – without which permission the trustee would not be entitled to recover the expense of the distribution exercise as an expense of the bankrupt's estate – but only if the committee is satisfied that the trustee acted in a case of urgency and that ratification was sought without undue delay.

## [1.446]

### 327  Distribution in criminal bankruptcy

*Where the bankruptcy order was made on a petition under section 264(1)(d) (criminal bankruptcy), no distribution shall be made under sections 324 to 326 so long as an appeal is pending (within the meaning of section 277) against the bankrupt's conviction of any offence by virtue of which the criminal bankruptcy order on which the petition was based was made.*

Amendments—Prospectively repealed by Criminal Justice Act 1988, s 170(2), Sch 16, as from a date to be appointed.

General note—This provision is now obsolete and is to be repealed from a date to be appointed by virtue of s 170(2) of Sch 16 to the Criminal Justice Act 1988.

## [1.447]

### 328  Priority of debts

(1)  In the distribution of the bankrupt's estate, his preferential debts shall be paid in priority to other debts.

(1A)  Ordinary preferential debts rank equally among themselves after the expenses of the bankruptcy and shall be paid in full, unless the bankrupt's estate is insufficient to meet them, in which case they abate in equal proportions between themselves.

(1B)  Secondary preferential debts rank equally among themselves after the ordinary preferential debts and shall be paid in full, unless the bankrupt's estate is insufficient to meet them, in which case they abate in equal proportions between themselves.

(2)  ...

(3)  Debts which are neither preferential debts nor debts to which the next section applies also rank equally between themselves and, after the preferential debts, shall be paid in full unless the bankrupt's estate is insufficient for meeting them, in which case they abate in equal proportions between themselves.

(3A)  If the bankrupt is a relevant financial institution, subsection (3) does not apply but—

(a)  the bankrupt's ordinary non-preferential debts shall be paid in priority to the bankrupt's secondary non-preferential debts,

(b)  the bankrupt's ordinary non-preferential debts rank equally among themselves after the secondary preferential debts and shall be paid in full, unless the bankrupt's estate is insufficient to meet them, in which case they abate in equal proportions,

(c)  the bankrupt's secondary non-preferential debts shall be paid in priority to the bankrupt's tertiary non-preferential debts, and

(d)  the bankrupt's secondary non-preferential debts rank equally among themselves after the ordinary non-preferential debts and shall be paid in full, unless the bankrupt's estate is insufficient to meet them, in which case they abate in equal proportions.

See section 387A for definitions relevant to this subsection.

(4)  Any surplus remaining after the payment of the debts—

(a)  where subsection (3) applies, that are preferential or rank equally under that subsection, or

(b)  where subsection (3A) applies, that are preferential or are referred to in that subsection, shall be applied in paying interest on those debts in respect of the periods during which they have been outstanding since the commencement of the bankruptcy; and interest on preferential debts ranks equally with interest on debts other than preferential debts.

(5) The rate of interest payable under subsection (4) in respect of any debt is whichever is the greater of the following—

    (a)    the rate specified in section 17 of the Judgments Act 1838 at the commencement of the bankruptcy, and

    (b)    the rate applicable to that debt apart from the bankruptcy.

(6) This section and the next are without prejudice to any provision of this Act or any other Act under which the payment of any debt or the making of any other payment is, in the event of bankruptcy, to have a particular priority or to be postponed.

(7) In this section "preferential debts", "ordinary preferential debts" and "secondary preferential debts" each has the meaning given in section 386 in Part 12.

**Amendments**—SI 2014/3486; SI 2018/1244. Note the insertion of s 328(3A), with effect from 19 December 2018.

**General note**—The priority of debts in bankruptcy is as follows:
- Expenses of the bankruptcy (on which see r 10.149).
- Preferential claims (which abate in equal proportions between themselves, and on which see the commentary to Sch 6).
- Unsecured claims (which abate in equal proportions between themselves).
- Interest on preferential and unsecured claims from the date of the bankruptcy order (such claims for interest being treated as a single class). On 328(5), see *KK v MA* [2012] EWHC 788 (Ch), [2012] BPIR 1137, at [79].

Section 328(6) allows for other legislation varying the above priority regime. Examples include postponed debts under ss 2 and 3 of the Partnership Act 1890 and fees paid to a bankrupt by an apprentice or clerk under s 348.

## [1.448]

### 329 Debts to spouse or civil partner

(1) This section applies to bankruptcy debts owed in respect of credit provided by a person who (whether or not the bankrupt's spouse or civil partner at the time the credit was provided) was the bankrupt's spouse or civil partner at the commencement of the bankruptcy.

(2) Such debts—

    (a)    rank in priority after the interest required to be paid in pursuance of section 328(4), and

    (b)    are payable with interest at the rate specified in section 328(5) in respect of the period during which they have been outstanding since the commencement of the bankruptcy;

and the interest payable under paragraph (b) has the same priority as the debts on which it is payable.

**Amendments**—Civil Partnership Act 2004, s 261(1), Sch 27, para 116; SI 2018/1244.

**General note**—These provisions are limited to the priority of a debt owed by the bankrupt to an individual who was the bankrupt's spouse at the commencement of the bankruptcy, as defined at the date of the bankruptcy order by s 278(a), irrespective of whether that creditor was the bankrupt's spouse at the time that the credit was provided or, indeed, whether or not that individual was the bankrupt's spouse at the date at which the priority of debts comes to be assessed.

The effect of s 329(2) is to subordinate a debt to which the provision applies to interest ranking within s 328(4).

## [1.449]

### 330 Final distribution

(1) When the trustee has realised all the bankrupt's estate or so much of it as can, in the trustee's opinion, be realised without needlessly protracting the trusteeship, he shall give notice in the prescribed manner either—

    (a)    of his intention to declare a final dividend, or

    (b)    that no dividend, or further dividend, will be declared.

(1A)   A notice under subsection (1)(b) need not be given to opted-out creditors.

(2)   The notice under subsection (1) shall contain the prescribed particulars and shall require claims against the bankrupt's estate to be established by a date ("the final date") specified in the notice.

(3)   The court may, on the application of any person, postpone the final date.

(4)   After the final date, the trustee shall—

    (a)    defray any outstanding expenses of the bankruptcy out of the bankrupt's estate, and

    (b)    if he intends to declare a final dividend, declare and distribute that dividend without regard to the claim of any person in respect of a debt not already proved in the bankruptcy.

(5)   If a surplus remains after payment in full and with interest of all the bankrupt's creditors and the payment of the expenses of the bankruptcy, the bankrupt is entitled to the surplus.

(6)   ...

**Amendments**—SI 2002/1240; Small Business, Enterprise and Employment Act 2015, s 126, Sch 9, Pt 2, paras 60, 82; SI 2017/702; SI 2019/146, as from IP completion day (as defined in the European Union (Withdrawal Agreement) Act 2020, s 39(1)–(5)).

**General note**—These provisions govern the closure of the bankruptcy and should be read in conjunction with s 331 (final meeting) below. Although s 305(2) provides that the function of a trustee includes the realisation and distribution of the bankrupt's estate, the trustee is permitted by s 330(1) to give notice of his intention to declare a final dividend etc where he is of the opinion that any remaining part of the bankrupt's estate is incapable of being realised without needlessly protracting the trusteeship. This squares with s 331(1) which is triggered where it appears to the trustee that the administration of a bankrupt's estate 'is for practical purposes complete'.

The 'final date' identified in s 330(2) is of significance since its passing allows the trustee to take those steps in s 330(4) without regard to the claim of any person who has not already proved in the bankruptcy.

For the purpose of any surplus payable under s 330(5) – which very rarely arises in practice – the term 'expenses' is as defined in r 10.148. For the duties of a trustee in a case where it becomes evident that there will be a surplus, see *Oraki v Bramston* [2017] EWCA Civ 403, [2018] Ch 469, [2017] BPIR 1021.

Unclaimed dividends are subject to regs 23 and 31 of the Insolvency Regulations 1994.

Although the class of persons eligible to apply to postpone the final date of the bankruptcy under s 330(3) is not defined, it is unlikely that the court would entertain an application by any person other than one with a financial interest in the outcome of the bankruptcy.

## [1.450]

### 331 Final report

(1)   Subject as follows in this section and the next, this section applies where—

    (a)    it appears to the trustee that the administration of the bankrupt's estate in accordance with this Chapter is for practical purposes complete, and

    (b)    the trustee is not the official receiver.

(2)   The trustee must give the bankrupt's creditors (other than opted-out creditors) notice that it appears to the trustee that the administration of the bankrupt's estate is for practical purposes complete.

(2A)   The notice must—

    (a)    be accompanied by a report of the trustee's administration of the bankrupt's estate;

    (b)    explain the effect of section 299(3)(d) and how the creditors may object to the trustee's release.

**Amendments**—Small Business, Enterprise and Employment Act 2015, s 126, Sch 9, Pt 2, paras 60, 83.

**General note**—Section 331(1) comes into operation where the trustee is not the official receiver and it appears to the trustee that the administration of the estate 'is for practical purposes complete'. As identified in the general note to s 330, the trustee does not therefore have to be satisfied that the entirety of the assets comprised in the bankrupt's estate have been realised but, rather, that there is nothing further which is capable of practical completion. The calling of a meeting under s 331 is subject to s 332.

The practical significance of the final meeting of creditors lies in the general meeting receiving the trustee's report of his administration of the estate and the determination by the meeting of whether the trustee should have his release under s 299. The time of the trustee's release is determined by s 299(3)(d). Furthermore, s 298(8) provides that the trustee shall vacate office on giving notice to the court that a final meeting has been held under s 331, although, it should be noted, that notice will not affect the release of the trustee under s 299(3)(d).

## [1.451]

### 332 Saving for bankrupt's home

(1)  This section applies where—

    (a)    there is comprised in the bankrupt's estate property consisting of an interest in a dwelling house which is occupied by the bankrupt or by his spouse or former spouse or by his civil partner or former civil partner, and

    (b)    the trustee has been unable for any reason to realise that property.

(2)  The trustee shall not give notice under section 331(2) unless either—

    (a)    the court has made an order under section 313 imposing a charge on that property for the benefit of the bankrupt's estate, or

    (b)    the court has declined, on an application under that section, to make such an order, or

    (c)    the Secretary of State has issued a certificate to the trustee stating that it would be inappropriate or inexpedient for such an application to be made in the case in question.

**Amendments**—Civil Partnership Act 2004, s 261(1), Sch 27, para 117; Small Business, Enterprise and Employment Act 2015, s 126, Sch 9, Pt 2, paras 60, 83.

**General note**—The effect of this provision is to preclude the giving of notice under s 331 in the circumstances set out in s 332(1), subject to the exceptions in s 332(2).

Further assistance may be found in the commentary to ss 313, 336 and 337. The term 'dwelling-house' is defined in s 385 and extends under s 322(1)(a) not only to a dwelling-house occupied by the bankrupt or an interest therein, but also to any dwelling-house occupied by the bankrupt's spouse or one occupied by the bankrupt's former spouse.

*Supplemental*

## [1.452]

### 333 Duties of bankrupt in relation to trustee

(1)  The bankrupt shall—

    (a)    give to the trustee such information as to his affairs,

    (b)    attend on the trustee at such times, and

    (c)    do all such other things,

as the trustee may for the purposes of carrying out his functions under any of this Group of Parts reasonably require.

(2)  Where at any time after the commencement of the bankruptcy any property is acquired by, or devolves upon, the bankrupt or there is an increase of the bankrupt's income, the bankrupt shall, within the prescribed period, give the trustee notice of the property or, as the case may be, of the increase.

(3)  Subsection (1) applies to a bankrupt after his discharge.

(4)  If the bankrupt without reasonable excuse fails to comply with any obligation imposed by this section, he is guilty of a contempt of court and liable to be punished accordingly (in addition to any other punishment to which he may be subject).

**General note**—Section 333(1) sets out the duties owed by a bankrupt to his trustee. These duties apply to a bankrupt both before and after discharge (emphasised by Registrar Nicholls in *Chadwick v Nash* [2012] BPIR 70 at [13]). Broadly, these duties correspond with the duties of a bankrupt in relation to the official receiver under s 291. The duties owed to both previously appeared in rather more elaborate terms in s 22 of the Bankruptcy Act 1914. In *Morris v Murjani* [1996] BPIR 458 at 462H–463A Peter Gibson LJ (with whom Buxton J and Hirst LJ agreed) observed that there is no corporate insolvency equivalent to s 333, with the consequence that decisions on corporate cases, including decisions made under s 561 of the Companies Act 1985, should not be treated as binding in a s 333 case.

Section 333 should also be read in conjunction with s 312 (which gives rise to an independent obligation to surrender control of property, books etc to the trustee), and s 307 (standing of trustee to claim after-acquired property) with which s 333(2) corresponds.

**The scope of the trustee's duties under s 333(1)**—In *Murjani* Peter Gibson LJ identified the nature of s 333(1) as follows (at 462B–462D):

' . . . it is not in dispute that s 333(1) has imposed a type of public duty on the bankrupt, though not one, in my view, such as would be enforceable only at the suit of the Attorney-General. The duties are owed, as [counsel for the bankrupt] accepts, to the trustee who is the person designated as being able to require the performance and determine the content of that duty and who can enforce it. A trustee has the right, and in appropriate circumstances it may be said that he also has the duty, to enforce the statutory duty owed by the bankrupt. The bankrupt's estate has become vested in the trustee as a result of the adjudication [bankruptcy] order made by the court. The trustee must therefore collect the assets of the estate as speedily as possible, which may require the obtaining of information in order to trace the relevant assets. His ultimate object is to make a distribution in accordance with the statutory scheme. The duties imposed on the bankrupt are all plainly designed to assist the trustee in the performance by him of his statutory functions.'

The final two sentences of the above extract, it is submitted, provide the benchmark against which any application by a trustee to enforce the bankrupt's duties should be tested. Relief should be granted only if what is required of the bankrupt is necessary to assist a trustee in the performance by him of his statutory functions, as identified in s 305(2). The question of enforcement of the s 333(1) duties is dealt with below.

The requirement that a bankrupt shall '(c) do all such other things' as his trustee may reasonably require extends to a duty to execute any document necessary for the discharge of the trustee's functions. Where a bankrupt is in default of that obligation, as can arise where a bankrupt refuses to execute a transfer or conveyance of property which the bankrupt holds as co-trustee or co-owner in law, a registrar or district judge has power under s 39(1) of the Supreme Court Act 1981 to execute the document in the name of the bankrupt: *Savage v Norton* [1908] 1 Ch 290. By parity of reasoning it would follow that the court would have jurisdiction to execute any document, such as a power of attorney or other written authority, reasonably required by the trustee to discharge his functions in the face of the bankrupt's refusal to do so.

**The position of the bankrupt**—A bankrupt should be extremely cautious in refusing to comply with the reasonable requirements of a trustee under s 333(1), given the public nature of the bankrupt's duties as identified in *Murjani* (above) and the risk of the bankrupt's liability for contempt of court under s 333(4) (see below). As noted above, the court has the ability in any case to execute documents in the name of the bankrupt under s 39(1) of the Senior Courts Act 1981.

In a judgment handed down on 19 July 1984 in relation to the former but analogous s 22(3) of the Bankruptcy Act 1914 the Court of Appeal (Oliver LJ and Balcombe J) held in *Fryer and Thompson v Brooke* [1998] BPIR 687 that the nature of the bankrupt's duties precludes him from raising against the trustee some personal right of occupation in property so as to impede and inhibit the sale of the property at its best value where the bankrupt's estate was also entitled to an interest in the property which was capable of being realised for the purpose of paying off creditors. In *Christofi v Barclays Bank plc* [2000] 1 WLR 937 the Court of Appeal (Stuart-Smith and Chadwick LJJ) affirmed the decision of Lawrence Collins QC, sitting as a deputy High Court judge, to the effect that an instruction by a bankrupt to his bank to have no contact with and provide no information to his trustee (who, in that case, was investigating pre-bankruptcy transactions) would constitute a breach of the bankrupt's duties. Further, the bank would be justified, notwithstanding the bankrupt's instructions, to respond to the trustee's legitimate enquiries in connection with an account in which the bankrupt had an interest and of which the bank had every reason to suppose the trustee was already aware: see *Tournier v National Provincial & Union Bank of England* [1924] 1 KB 461.

A transaction entered into for the illegal purpose of enabling a bankrupt to escape his disclosure obligations under s 333(2) cannot be used to assert a proprietary claim and is liable to be struck out: *Barrett v Barrett* [2008] EWHC 1061 (Ch), [2008] BPIR 817 (David Richards J).

**Enforcement of the s 333(1) duties**—A trustee may enforce the bankrupt's duties by seeking an order under s 366 or, it is submitted, by an application under s 363(2). Further, or in the alternative, a trustee might institute contempt proceedings under s 333(4). In an appropriate case the court may also grant an injunction ordering the bankrupt not to leave the jurisdiction and to deliver up his passport, as in *Murjani*. As Peter Gibson LJ observed in that case (at 462F), 'It would be extraordinary if the trustee could obtain an order for the arrest of the bankrupt but could not obtain a less severe remedy restraining the bankrupt from leaving the jurisdiction.' Failure to comply with s 333 duties will also often form the basis for an application for suspension of the bankrupt's discharge under s 279 eg *Hellard v Kapoor* [2013] EWHC 2204 (Ch), [2013] BPIR 745; and *Keely v Bell* [2016] EWHC 308 (Ch), [2016] BPIR 653 (see also the cases in the notes to s 279).

For an example of a case where the court was prepared to grant an ex parte injunction which pierced the corporate veil between the bankrupt and the respondent companies where there was evidence the bankrupt was treating the company accounts as his own, and had failed to disclose them pursuant to s 333, see *Wood v Baker* [2015] EWHC 2536 (Ch), [2015] BPIR 1524. This case also contains a useful commentary on the extent of the cross undertaking in damages in a case involving an office holder applicant.

In *Re M (a minor) (contact order: committal)* (1998) *The Times*, December 31 the Court of Appeal gave guidance, albeit in the context of a claim under the Children Act 1989, on the exercise of the power of committal for non-compliance with a court order; in particular, it is inadvisable that the judge initiating the committal procedure should also rule on the decision to commit.

In finding that a bankrupt was in contempt it lies within the court's inherent jurisdiction to regulate or stay any proceedings pursued by the bankrupt until further order or until the contempt is purged.

**Procedure**—On s 333(2) see the 21-day period in r 10.125(1).

## [1.453]

### 334 Stay of distribution in case of second bankruptcy

(1)   This section and the next apply where a bankruptcy order is made against an undischarged bankrupt; and in both sections—

    (a)    "the later bankruptcy" means the bankruptcy arising from that order,

    (b)    "the earlier bankruptcy" means the bankruptcy (or, as the case may be, most recent bankruptcy) from which the bankrupt has not been discharged at the commencement of the later bankruptcy, and

    (c)    "the existing trustee" means the trustee (if any) of the bankrupt's estate for the purposes of the earlier bankruptcy.

(2)   Where the existing trustee has been given the prescribed notice of the making of the application or (as the case may be) the presentation of the petition for the later bankruptcy, any distribution or other disposition by him of anything to which the next subsection applies, if made after the giving of the notice, is void except to the extent that it was made with the consent of the court or is or was subsequently ratified by the court. This is without prejudice to section 284 (restrictions on dispositions of property following bankruptcy order).

(3)   This subsection applies to—

    (a)    any property which is vested in the existing trustee under section 307(3) (after-acquired property);

    (b)    any money paid to the existing trustee in pursuance of an income payments order under section 310; and

    (c)    any property or money which is, or in the hands of the existing trustee represents, the proceeds of sale or application of property or money falling within paragraph (a) or (b) of this subsection.

**Amendments**—Enterprise and Regulatory Reform Act 2013, s 71(3), Sch 19, paras 1, 28.

**General note**—These provisions must be read in conjunction with s 335 and are only triggered where a bankruptcy order is made against an undischarged bankrupt.

The purpose of the provisions is in protecting the assets in what is termed 'the earlier bankruptcy' so as to allow for the adjustment between the earlier bankruptcy and the later bankruptcy under s 335.

**SECTION 334(2)**

'Where the existing trustee has been given a prescribed notice . . . '—It is not clear whether the notice is to be given by the petitioning creditor or the existing trustee. In either case, however, it is the giving of the prescribed notice which brings s 334(2) into operation. A disposition will not be rendered void by s 334(2) until such notice is given.

**Property subject to s 334(2)**—Although the wording in the opening of s 334(3) might suggest that only the property listed within that provision is subject to s 334(2), this is not the case. Section 334(2) applies not only to the property listed in s 334(3) but also to all of the property comprised in the bankrupt's estate in the earlier bankruptcy. Subsection (3) appears to have been included in the provisions for the avoidance of any doubt which might otherwise have arisen.

The effect of a void disposition—Any property which is lost to the bankruptcy estate under a disposition rendered void by s 334(2) may be recovered by the trustee in the earlier bankruptcy or, it is submitted, the trustee in the later bankruptcy. The principles applicable to such a void disposition are the same as those which apply to any void disposition under s 127 or s 284.

Procedure—See rr 10.150–10.153 which provide, in r 10.150(1), for the general duty of the existing trustee in the event of a second bankruptcy.

## [1.454]

### 335 Adjustment between earlier and later bankruptcy estates

(1) With effect from the commencement of the later bankruptcy anything to which section 334(3) applies which, immediately before the commencement of that bankruptcy, is comprised in the bankrupt's estate for the purposes of the earlier bankruptcy is to be treated as comprised in the bankrupt's estate for the purposes of the later bankruptcy and, until there is a trustee of that estate, is to be dealt with by the existing trustee in accordance with the rules.

(2) Any sums which in pursuance of an income payments order under section 310 are payable after the commencement of the later bankruptcy to the existing trustee shall form part of the bankrupt's estate for the purposes of the later bankruptcy; and the court may give such consequential directions for the modification of the order as it thinks fit.

(3) Anything comprised in a bankrupt's estate by virtue of subsection (1) or (2) is so comprised subject to a first charge in favour of the existing trustee for any bankruptcy expenses incurred by him in relation thereto.

(4) Except as provided above and in section 334, property which is, or by virtue of section 308 (personal property of bankrupt exceeding reasonable replacement value) or section 308A (vesting in trustee of certain tenancies) is capable of being, comprised in the bankrupt's estate for the purposes of the earlier bankruptcy, or of any bankruptcy prior to it, shall not be comprised in his estate for the purposes of the later bankruptcy.

(5) The creditors of the bankrupt in the earlier bankruptcy and the creditors of the bankrupt in any bankruptcy prior to the earlier one, are not to be creditors of his in the later bankruptcy in respect of the same debts; but the existing trustee may prove in the later bankruptcy for—

   (a)   the unsatisfied balance of the debts (including any debt under this subsection) provable against the bankrupt's estate in the earlier bankruptcy;

   (b)   any interest payable on that balance; and

   (c)   any unpaid expenses of the earlier bankruptcy.

(6) Any amount provable under subsection (5) ranks in priority after all the other debts provable in the later bankruptcy and after interest on those debts and, accordingly, shall not be paid unless those debts and that interest have first been paid in full.

Amendments—Housing Act 1988, s 140, Sch 17, Part I, para 74.

General note—These provisions must be read in conjunction with s 334, and apply where a bankruptcy order is made in respect of an undischarged bankrupt. Their effect is to denude an earlier bankruptcy of property comprised in that bankruptcy estate, together with any income payments order, save to the extent of property within ss 308 or 308A, in favour of the later bankruptcy. In addition, s 335(6) confers priority on creditors in the later bankruptcy over creditors in the earlier bankruptcy whose claims may only be advanced under s 335(5) by the existing trustee for the unsatisfied balance in the earlier bankruptcy and interest thereon together with any unpaid expenses of the earlier bankruptcy. Notably, s 335(3) confers the benefit of a statutory first charge in favour of the existing trustee for any bankruptcy expenses incurred by him in relation to the earlier bankruptcy estate.

Income payments orders—An income payments order does not survive the making of a second bankruptcy and is provable in that second bankruptcy. There is no other way for the first trustee to enforce future IPO payments against the bankrupt: *Azuonye v Kent* [2019] EWCA Civ 1289, [2019] 4 WLR 101, [2019] BPIR 1317, at [24]–[29], per David Richards LJ (reversing Falk J).

Procedure—See rr 10.150–10.153 which provide, in r 10.151(1), for the general duty of the existing trustee in the event of the second bankruptcy.

## CHAPTER V

### Effect of Bankruptcy on Certain Rights, Transactions, Etc
*Rights under trusts of land*

**[1.455]**

### 335A  Rights under trusts of land

(1)   Any application by a trustee of a bankrupt's estate under section 14 of the Trusts of Land and Appointment of Trustees Act 1996 (powers of court in relation to trusts of land) for an order under that section for the sale of land shall be made to the court having jurisdiction in relation to the bankruptcy.

(2)   On such an application the court shall make such order as it thinks just and reasonable having regard to—

    (a)    the interests of the bankrupt's creditors;

    (b)    where the application is made in respect of land which includes a dwelling house which is or has been the home of the bankrupt or the bankrupt's spouse or civil partner or former spouse or former civil partner—

        (i)    the conduct of the spouse, civil partner, former spouse or former civil partner, so far as contributing to the bankruptcy,

        (ii)    the needs and financial resources of the spouse, civil partner, former spouse or former civil partner, and

        (iii)    the needs of any children; and

    (c)    all the circumstances of the case other than the needs of the bankrupt.

(3)   Where such an application is made after the end of the period of one year beginning with the first vesting under Chapter IV of this Part of the bankrupt's estate in a trustee, the court shall assume, unless the circumstances of the case are exceptional, that the interests of the bankrupt's creditors outweigh all other considerations.

(4)   The powers conferred on the court by this section are exercisable on an application whether it is made before or after the commencement of this section.

**Amendments**—Inserted by the Trusts of Land and Appointment of Trustees Act 1996, s 25(1), Sch 3, para 23; Civil Partnership Act 2004, s 261(1), Sch 27, para 118.

**General note**—Section 335A was inserted by s 25(1) of and Sch 3 to the Trusts of Land and Appointment of Trustees Act 1996 and took effect from 1 January 1997. The new provision replaced s 336(3) and disapplied s 336(4) to cases involving trusts of land.

Sections 14 and 15 of the 1996 Act replaced s 30 of the Law of Property Act 1925. Section 15 of the 1996 Act, however, is disapplied by s 15(4) thereof if s 335A is applicable. Section 335A(1) expressly provides that an application for the sale of land is made to the court having jurisdiction in relation to the bankruptcy. The issue of court jurisdiction is dealt with in ss 373 and 374 and the notes thereto.

**Application of s 335A**—Despite the reference to the bankrupt's 'spouse', 'civil partner', 'former spouse' or 'former civil partner' in s 335A(2), it is clear from s 335A(1) that the section applies in any case where a trustee applies for an order under s 14 of the 1996 Act. The provision will, therefore, apply to *any* trust of land under which the bankrupt has an interest, irrespective of whether the beneficial co-owner is a spouse, a civil partner, a former spouse, a former civil partner, an unmarried co-habitee or any other person.

Section 335A only applies to applications made under s 14 of the 1996 Act and therefore is not engaged where the property of which the trustee seeks possession and sale is solely owned by the bankrupt (in such cases it is s 363 which is engaged) (*Holtham v Kelmanson* [2006] EWHC 2588 (Ch), [2006] BPIR 1422 at [15]–[16]; *Carter v Hewitt* [2019] EWHC 3729 (Ch) at [17]–[20]).

**Other statutory considerations**—Regard should be had initially to s 283A (bankrupt's home ceasing to form part of bankrupt's estate at the end of the period of three years beginning with the date of the bankruptcy unless the trustee takes one of the steps in s 283A(3) towards realising the interest in it) and s 313A (low value home) and, in particular, s 313A(2) which requires the court to dismiss an application for possession and sale etc if the value of the trustee's interest in the dwelling-house is below the £1,000 figure presently prescribed under that provision.

**The court's approach to a s 335A case**—Section 335A does not, of course, create a new cause of action but, rather, provides for the position where an application is made for an order for sale by a trustee under s 14 of the 1996 Act. The introduction of the 1996 Act represented a change in the law from the former law under s 30 of the Law of Property Act 1925. Under the former law, there was no difference in treatment of applications by trustees in bankruptcy and applications by chargees; the normal rule being that, save in exceptional circumstances, the wish of the person wanting the sale would prevail over the interests of children and families in occupation (*Mortgage Corporation plc v Shaire* [2001] Ch 743, [2000] BPIR 483 at 757D; *Re Citro* [1991] Ch 142; *Lloyds Bank plc v Byrne & Byrne* [1993] 1 FLR 369). Following the introduction of the 1996 Act, s 15 of the 1996 Act applies to applications by chargees whilst s 335A applies to applications by trustees in bankruptcy. In *Mortgage Corporation v Shaire*, Neuberger J (at 758F–761C) concluded that, on applications by chargees, the introduction of s 15 of the 1996 Act gave courts greater flexibility as to how to exercise their jurisdiction with it being a matter for the court what weight to give each relevant factor (rather than the interest of the chargee being the most important as under the former law) and therefore that, whilst it would be wrong to have no regard to earlier cases, they had to be treated with caution and in many cases they are unlikely to be of great assistance. It is submitted that, on applications by trustees in bankruptcy made after the period of one year beginning with the vesting of the bankrupt's estate in the trustee, the earlier cases will still be of relevance since s 335A(3) essentially codifies the presumption that the interests of the bankrupt's creditors will outweigh all other considerations absent exceptional circumstances (*Barca v Mears* [2004] EWHC 2170 (Ch), [2005] BPIR 15 at [23]). Further, it is submitted that, given the difference between s 15 of the 1996 and s 335A, caution should be exercised before relying on any case law dealing with s 15 of the 1996 Act on any application involving s 335A. The relationship between the two provisions was considered by Jeremy Cousins QC (sitting as a High Court judge) in *Cooke v Dunbar Assets plc* [2016] EWHC 579 (Ch), [2016] BPIR 576, where it was concluded that a creditor could well, and reasonably, reach the conclusion that it could be more confident of a sooner realisation of a debtor's property if an application were made by a trustee in bankruptcy rather than by the creditor under the 1996 Act (paras [24]–[26], [42]–[43]).

Once an order for possession has been made the court will not direct the trustee to delay implementation of the order, although it is within the trustee's powers to consider doing so if there is a reasonable prospect of the bankruptcy debts and expenses being paid: *Awoyemi v Bowell* [2006] BPIR 1 (Evans-Lombe J).

A custodial 6-month prison sentence for contempt of court by way of wilful breach of a possession order (in addition to breach of obligations under ss 313, 333 and 363) was not manifestly excessive: *Boyden v Canty (No 2)* [2007] BPIR 299 (Chadwick and Lloyd LJJ).

**Factors considered under s 335A(2)**—The court must make such order as it thinks just and reasonable having regard to those factors specifically identified within s 335A(2)(a)-(b) together with all the circumstances of the case other than the needs of the bankrupt (s 335A(2)(c)). Accordingly, the court may not have regard for the need of the bankrupt, say, to use the property in issue for earning his livelihood, or evidence that the bankrupt may suffer some adverse mental or physical consequence as a result of the property being sold.

Section 335A(2)(b)(i) is broad enough to include excessive or irresponsible spending on the part of a spouse or former spouse or, it is submitted, a refusal by a spouse or former spouse to assist the bankrupt in avoiding bankruptcy from assets available to that individual.

In *Grant v Baker* [2016] EWHC 1782 (Ch), [2016] BPIR 1409 Henderson J held (at [30]) that the 'needs of any children' in s 335A(2)(b)(iii) was not confined to their needs whilst under the age of 18 and, in that case, included the needs of an adult child with disabilities who was cared for in the property.

In *Everitt v Budhram* [2009] EWHC 1219 (Ch), [2010] Ch 170 Henderson J noted that the term 'needs' in s 335A(2)(c) was to be more widely defined than merely encompassing financial needs.

## SECTION 335A(3)

'. . . **unless the circumstances of the case are exceptional** . . . '—Following the expiration of one year from the vesting of the bankrupt's estate in a trustee s 335A(3) raises a rebuttable presumption that the interests of the bankrupt's creditors outweigh all other considerations such that an order for sale should be made. The interests of the bankrupt's creditors will normally require that the property be sold so that the bankrupt's share in it can be realised. Consequently, any successful defence to an application for sale brought about after the expiry of the one year period will normally depend on establishing that the circumstances of the case are exceptional (*Grant v Baker* at [25]). In seeking to establish exceptional circumstances two points should be borne in mind. First, as appears from the authorities (see below) the court will not be receptive to arguments which, in substance, are based on nothing more than inconvenience and the like. Secondly, each case must be determined on its own facts such that the *facts* of any other reported decision will be of very limited use, since each case necessarily involves a weighing-up exercise on a case-by-case basis.

The principles which the court should follow when considering whether the circumstances of the case are exceptional were conveniently summarised by Lawrence Collins J in *Dean v Stout (The Trustee in Bankruptcy of Dean)* [2004] EWHC 3315 (Ch), [2005] BPIR 1113 at [6]–[11]:

'[6] . . . First, the presence of exceptional circumstances is a necessary condition to displace the presumption that the interests of the creditors outweigh all other considerations, but the presence of exceptional circumstances does not debar the court from making an order for sale.

[7] Secondly, typically the exceptional circumstances in the modern cases relate to the personal circumstances of one of the joint owners, such as a medical or mental condition.

[8] Thirdly, the categories of exceptional circumstances are not to be categorised or defined and the court makes a value judgment after looking at all the circumstances.

[9] Fourthly, the circumstances must be exceptional and this expression was intended to apply the same test as the pre-Insolvency Act 1986 decisions on bankruptcy (see in *Re Citro (Domenico) (A Bankrupt)* [1991] Ch 142, [1991] 1 FLR 71 at 159/160 and 84 respectively), that is to say exceptional or special circumstances which are outside the usual "melancholy consequences of debt and improvidence" (in the words of Nourse LJ) or (in the words of Bingham LJ) "compelling reasons not found in the ordinary run of cases".

[10] Fifthly, it is not uncommon for a wife with children to be faced with eviction in circumstances where the realisation of her beneficial interest will not produce enough to buy a comparable home in the same neighbourhood or, indeed, elsewhere. Such circumstances, while engendering a natural sympathy, cannot be described as exceptional, and it was in that context that Nourse LJ referred to the "melancholy consequences of debt and improvidence" with which every civilised society has been familiar (see 157 and 82 respectively).

[11] Sixthly, for the purposes of weighing the interests of the creditors, the creditors have an interest in the order for sale being made, even if the whole of the net proceeds will go towards the expenses of the bankruptcy, and the fact that they will be swallowed up in paying those expense is not an exceptional circumstance justifying the displacement of the presumption that the interests of the creditors outweigh all other considerations.'

In *Hosking v Michaelides* [2006] BPIR 1192 Paul Morgan QC, sitting as a deputy High Court judge, adopted the definition given by the Court of Appeal of the term 'exceptional' in *R v Kelly (Edward)* [2000] 1 QB 198 as meaning ' . . . a circumstance . . . which is out of the ordinary course, or unusual, or special or uncommon. To be exceptional, a circumstance need not be unique, unprecedented or very rare, but it cannot be one that is regularly or routinely encountered'.

Examples of cases where medical conditions have amounted to exceptional circumstances include *Grant v Baker* (bankrupt's disabled adult child who was cared for at home), *Pickard v Constable* [2017] EWHC 2475 (Ch), [2018] BPIR 140 (the bankrupt's husband suffered from a serious auto-immune condition) and *Re Haghighat* [2009] EWHC 90 (Ch), [2009] BPIR 268 (involving a very severely disabled child – although this was, in fact, a case decided with reference to ss 336 and 337). *Re Haghighat* was unsuccessfully appealed as *Brittain v Haghighat* [2010] EWCA Civ 1521, [2011] BPIR 328. Examples of cases where exceptional circumstances were found not to exist are *Barca v Mears* ([2004] EWHC 2170 (Ch), [2005] BPIR 15 and *Lyle v Bedborough* [2021] EWHC 220 (Ch), [2021] BPIR 581. In *Barca v Mears* Nicholas Strauss QC (sitting as a deputy High Court judge), applying *Re Citro* [1991] Ch 142), concluded that the bankrupt's son's special educational needs were not sufficient to amount to exceptional circumstances. In *Lyle v Bedborough*, Judge Jonathan Richards (sitting as a deputy High Court judge) rejected submissions that the use of the property for the bankrupt's business which would not be practicable in a smaller property and that the bankrupt's wife's diagnosis of polymyalgia were exceptional circumstances. The judge held that the business issues were ordinary consequences of a sale following bankruptcy of a co-owner and that the bankrupt's wife would suffer the symptoms wherever she lived and there was no suggestion that the property had been specially adapted (at [101]–[102]).

The fact that it may well be possible for a debtor to make full repayment, including statutory interest, over a period of time does not of itself constitute exceptional circumstances: *Donohoe v Ingram* [2006] BPIR 417 (Stuart Isaacs QC sitting as a deputy High Court judge). Neither is the court concerned with the degree of interest displayed by the bankrupt's creditors in pursuing their debts in bankruptcy; rather, the interest of the bankrupt's creditors is a reference to the creditors' legal rights to be paid the debts due to them: *Foyle v Turner* [2007] BPIR 43 (HHJ Norris QC (sitting as a High Court judge); order for sale sought (and obtained) 13 years after bankruptcy orders).

In *Martin-Sklan v White* [2007] BPIR 76 Evans-Lombe J upheld on appeal a decision of a district judge that, for the purposes of the equivalent provision in s 337(6), the bankrupt's partner's alcoholism and the support network available through neighbours and a relative living locally for two children aged 10 and 14 together with the poor state of the property (valued at £120,000 and subject to a mortgage of £41,000) constituted exceptional circumstances justifying postponement of an order for sale for a period of some 6 years and 10 months.

Exceptional circumstances were not established in *Turner v Avis* [2008] BPIR 1143 (HHJ Pelling QC (sitting as a High Court judge)) based on a wife's reliance on the terms of an ancillary relief order and an allegation of delay in bringing the possession proceedings.

In *Foenander v Allan* [2006] EWHC 2101 (Ch), [2006] BPIR 1392 Nicholas Strauss QC (sitting as a deputy High Court judge) held that a potential insurance claim arising from subsidence at the property which may have resulted in the insurers repairing the property increasing its value might amount to an exceptional circumstance albeit there was insufficiently clear evidence as to the insurance position for a decision to be reached.

The presence of exceptional circumstances displaces the presumption in s 335A(3) that the interests of creditors outweighs all other considerations. However it does not debar the court from making an order for sale (*Dean v Stout* [2005] BPIR 1113 at [6]). Where exceptional circumstances exist, the court must exercise its powers in accordance with s 335A(2) (*Pickard v Constable* at [10]). Consequently, where exceptional circumstances exist, the interests of the bankrupt's creditors is one factor which must be taken into account but the appropriate weight to attach to this will be in the discretion of the court (*Grant v Baker* [2016] EWHC 1782 (Ch), [2016] BPIR 1409 at [25]).

**Appeals on decisions on exceptional circumstances**—The application of s 335A requires a value judgement, requiring the court to look at all the circumstances and consider whether or not they are exceptional. Such process leaves little scope for interference by an appellate court albeit there will be cases where an appellate court should interfere, for example, where there is an error of law appearing on the face of the judgment or where the conclusion reached is so plainly wrong as to raise the inference that in reaching its conclusion the court somehow misdirected itself in law (Jonathan Parker J in *Claughton v Charalambous* [1998] BPIR 558 at 562H).

Where exceptional circumstances had not been raised at the hearing, nor in the grounds of appeal or skeleton argument, the court indicated that it 'would take a lot of convincing that it was right to allow the point to be argued' at the permission hearing, but indicated if there was an obvious case of exceptional circumstances, it might have been persuaded to take a more indulgent attitude: *Begum v Cockerton* [2015] EWHC 2042 (Ch).

**Human rights**—In *Barca v Mears*, at [33]–[43], the deputy judge considered, but left open, the question of whether the narrow approach to exceptional circumstances in *Re Citro* (on which see *Dean v Stout* at [9]–[10] quoted above) is consistent with Art 8 of the European Convention for the Protection of Human Rights (right to respect for private family life and home). The point was, however, engaged by HHJ Norris QC (sitting as a High Court judge) in *Foyle v Turner* [2007] BPIR 43. *Foyle* is authority for the proposition (at [16]–[19]) that, in light of the decision of the House of Lords in *Kay v London Borough of Lambeth* [2006] UKHL 10, s 335A is compliant with Convention rights in that Art 8 of the Convention added nothing to the substance of the protection already provided by domestic law on the provision and does not require any modification to the approach of the courts (as set out above) to exceptional circumstances: see also to the same effect the decision of Paul Morgan QC (sitting as a deputy High Court judge) in *Nicholls v Lan* [2006] EWHC 1255 (Ch), [2006] BPIR 1243 at [43] and *Turner v Avis* [2008] BPIR 1143 in which HHJ Pelling QC adopted the analysis of HHJ Norris QC in *Foyle*. In *Ford v Alexander* [2012] EWHC 266 (Ch), [2012] BPIR 528 (at [49]), Peter Smith J came to the view that the s 335A procedure was compliant with Art 8. In the Northern Irish case of *Official Receiver for Northern Ireland v O'Brien* [2012] NICh 12, [2012] BPIR 826, however, Deeny J accepted that an argument based on Art 6 and Art 8 from a co-owner defeated the Official Receiver's claim for sale. Weir J similarly accepted human rights arguments under Art 6 and Art 8 in *Official Receiver for Northern Ireland v Rooney and Paulson* [2008] NICh 22, [2009] BPIR 536. Both of these cases were ones in which there had been very considerable delay. However those cases concerned s 4 of the Partition Act 1868 without the protection afforded by s 283A IA 1986 and a delay in issuing of almost 12 years and therefore it is submitted that they are of little, if any relevance, to an application concerning s 335A.

**Postponement of an order for possession and sale**—Where an order for possession and sale is made, the court has the power to postpone the date for possession and/or sale if warranted by the circumstances. However, an indefinite suspension, for a period measured in decades, is incompatible with the underlying purpose of the bankruptcy code (to enable the bankrupt's interests in property to be realised and made available for distribution to his creditors) and in all save the most truly exceptional circumstances, the underlying purpose of the code requires realisation within a time frame normally to be measured in months rather than years (*Grant v Baker* at [45]).

In *Grant v Baker* Henderson J allowed an appeal against a decision that the sale be postponed until the bankrupt's disabled adult child no longer lived there (with no long stop date) instead ordering a postponement of 12 months which would allow a suitable replacement property to be found on the rental market and for the move to be prepared with the child's welfare and best interests at heart. In *Pickard v Constable* Warren J allowed an appeal against a decision that the sale be postponed until the death or earlier vacation of the property by the bankrupt's husband who suffered from an auto-immune condition instead ordering a postponement of 12 months with liberty to apply to vary the date for possession and rely on further evidence. In both cases, the judges stressed the need for cogent evidence in support of requests for postponement whether that be medical evidence or evidence of non-availability of alternative accommodation. In *Re Haghighat*, where the bankrupt's child was severely disabled and cared for by the bankrupt's wife and there was evidence from the local authority that providing alternative accommodation would be difficult and take time, possession was postponed for 3 years or, if sooner, 3 months after the child ceased to permanently reside at the property, to allow the local authority to make provision for the bankrupt's wife and child to be rehoused in accommodation suitable to their needs and an orderly change to be effected in the child's care arrangements.

However, in appropriate cases circumstances may be such as to justify indefinite postponement until an occupant either dies or vacates the property (see for example *Claughton v Charalambous* where the bankrupt's wife was in poor health, suffering from chronic renal failure and chronic osteoarthritis, could only walk with great difficulty with the aid of a zimmer frame and needed a wheelchair, was 60 years old and had a reduced life expectancy and *Re Bremner (A Bankrupt)* [1999] BPIR 185 (a case under s 336 IA 1986) where the needs of the bankrupt's wife were sufficiently exceptional for indefinite postponement to three months after the bankrupt's death in circumstances where he had inoperable cancer with a life expectancy of probably less than six months, his wife was his carer, his wife had no beneficial interest and there was sufficient equity in the property to pay all creditors in full (with some but not full statutory interest).

It is not appropriate to suspend an order for sale to allow a period for payment of a specific figure in circumstances where the evidence indicates that the figure in question is uncertain or not up-to-date; such an approach not being in the interests of creditors. The court ought to make an unconditional possession order to take effect on a fixed date and if, in the meantime sufficient funds are raised to pay off or secure the debts, costs and expenses, the bankrupt can apply for an annulment (per HHJ Purle QC sitting as a High Court judge in *Pick v Sumpter* [2010] EWHC 685 (Ch), [2010] BPIR 638).

**Equitable accounting**—Equitable accounting is not to be confused with an enquiry into the extent of the parties' respective beneficial interests in the property concerned and can only be undertaken once such interests have been determined, since the requirement to account (where it exists) is a reflection of and derives from those beneficial interests. The appropriate date for the commencement of equitable accounting, assuming it is appropriate at all, depends upon the facts of each case. In an ordinary cohabitation case it is only likely to come into play in respect of the period following the termination of the relationship between the co-owners, but this is not an absolute rule (*Wilcox v Tait* [2006] EWCA Civ 1867, [2007] BPIR 262). The court has a broad equitable jurisdiction to do justice between the co-owners on the facts of each case: *Re Pavlou* [1993] 1 WLR 1046 (Millett J), *Re Byford (Deceased)* [2003] BPIR 1089 (Lawrence Collins J) and *Brassford v Patel* [2007] BPIR 1049 (Richard Sheldon QC sitting as a deputy High Court judge), *Davis v Jackson* [2017] EWHC 698 (Ch), [2017] 1 WLR 4005, [2017] BPIR 950, *Shilabeer v Lanceley* [2019] EWHC 3380 (QB). In *Davis v Jackson*, Snowden J held that the court was entitled to have regard to the position prior to the bankruptcy, including any agreements or understandings between the co-owners and concluded that it would not be equitable for the trustee to be allowed an occupation rent where the bankrupt had never occupied, and was never intended to occupy, the property as his home. In *Shilabeer v Lanceley* [2019] EWHC 3380 (QB) (in a non-bankruptcy context) Foster J, in refusing an appeal against a finding that an occupation rent was payable, rejected the submission that *Davis v Jackson* had changed the landscape, concluding that it did not alter the underlying principles and was a case with unusual facts which made it readily distinguishable from authorities which had preceded it.

The consequence of the decision of the House of Lords in *Stack v Dowden* [2007] UKHL 17, [2007] 2 WLR 831 is that the court's power to order payment by a beneficiary in occupation of occupation rent to a beneficiary who has been excluded from the property is no longer governed by the doctrine of equitable accounting as developed by the courts but, rather, by the statutory provisions now laid down in ss 12–15 of the 1996 Act (on which see, in particular, the speech of Baroness Hale in *Stack v Dowden* at [12]) (as identified by the Court of Appeal in *Murphy v Gooch* [2007] EWCA Civ 603, [2007] BPIR 1123 at [11]). Consequently, in such circumstances, cases such as *Re Pavlou* [1993] 1 WLR 1046 (Millett J), *Re Byford (Deceased)* [2003] BPIR 1089 (Lawrence Collins J) and *Brassford v Patel* [2007] BPIR 1049 (Richard Sheldon QC sitting as a deputy High Court judge) no longer govern the position. The difference between the two approaches lies in the equitable doctrine developed in the case law concerning itself with the achievement of a just result between the parties as compared with the statutory provisions by which s 15 stipulates matters to which the court must give its consideration. However, it was observed by Lord Neuberger in *Stack v Dowden* at [150] that it would be a rare case in which the application of the equitable and statutory principles would produce a different result. Further, in *French v Barcham* [2008] EWHC 1505 (Ch), [2009] 1 WLR 1124, [2008] BPIR 857 (at [18]–[21]) and *Davis v Jackson* [2017] EWHC 698 (Ch) (at [47]–[48]), Blackburne J and Snowden J respectively held that the doctrine of equitable accounting continued to apply in the bankruptcy context as ss 12–15 of the 1996 Act did not provide an exhaustive regime for compensation for exclusion of a beneficiary from occupation of property held subject to a trust of land and would not apply (so far as claiming occupation rent was concerned) in the case of a trustee in bankruptcy since he was not a person entitled to occupy property pursuant to s 12 of the 1996 Act. In *French v Barcham* Blackburne J held that whilst the trustee had no statutory right to occupy, it was wrong (as the district judge below had held) that the bankrupt's co-owning spouse was not liable to be charged an occupation rent (or equitable compensation) for her occupation from the time the bankrupt's interest in the property vested in his trustee because it was not reasonable to expect the trustee to exercise the right of occupation attaching to his interest in the property. This conclusion was entirely consistent with the line of authorities on equitable accounting culminating in *Re Byford (Deceased)* [2003] BPIR 1089 which remained good law notwithstanding the explanation of ss 12–15 of the 1996 Act by the House of Lords in *Stack v Dowden* [2007] AC 423.

As to the reasoning in *Stack v Dowden* generally as regards the beneficial interests of co-owners, see also *Jones v Kernott* [2011] UKSC 53, [2012] 1 AC 776. It was emphasised in *Erlam v Rahman* [2016] EWHC 111(Ch), [2016] BPIR 856 that where the joint intention of the parties was to acquire the property for a commercial or business purpose such as letting, the *Stack v Dowden* approach was not apposite and a stricter resulting trust analysis should be applied, which turned upon the extent of the claimant's contribution to the purchase price. Adverse inferences were drawn in that case from the failure of the claimant to place before the court evidence of historic contributions relied on to found their alleged beneficial interest without adequate explanation.

Equitable accounting can also work against a trustee in bankruptcy, for example, where the non-bankrupt co-owner has spent monies on improving the property: see *Lyle v Bedborough* [2021] EWHC 220 (Ch), [2021] BPIR 581 where such a claim was rejected, the court finding that it was entitled to infer that, while the co-owners lived together at the property, there was no common intention that either should have to account for sums spent on the property for the co-owners' joint benefit and that the evidence did not upset that inference (at [93]–[96]).

**Equity of exoneration**—For the application of this equitable principle in a bankruptcy context see *Re Pittortou* [1985] 1 WLR 58; *Re Chawda* [2014] BPIR 49; *Cadlock (Trustee in Bankruptcy of Dunn) v Dunn* [2015] EWHC 1318 (Ch), [2015] BPIR 739 and *Armstrong v Onyearu* [2015] EWHC 1937 (Ch) (at first instance) and on appeal at [2017] EWCA Civ 268, [2018] Ch 137 (particularly David Richard LJ's helpful summary of the principles at [43]).

*Rights of occupation*

**[1.456]**

### 336 Rights of occupation etc of bankrupt's spouse or civil partner

(1)   Nothing occurring in the initial period of the bankruptcy (that is to say, the period beginning with the day of the making of the bankruptcy application or (as the case may be) the presentation of the bankruptcy petition and ending with the vesting of the bankrupt's estate in a trustee) is to be taken as having given rise to any home rights under Part IV of the Family Law Act 1996 in relation to a dwelling house comprised in the bankrupt's estate.

(2)   Where a spouse's or civil partner's home rights under the Act of 1996 are a charge on the estate or interest of the other spouse or civil partner, or of trustees for the other spouse or civil partner, and the other spouse or civil partner is made bankrupt—

    (a)    the charge continues to subsist notwithstanding the bankruptcy and, subject to the provisions of that Act, binds the trustee of the bankrupt's estate and persons deriving title under that trustee, and

    (b)    any application for an order under section 33 of that Act shall be made to the court having jurisdiction in relation to the bankruptcy.

(3)   . . .

(4)   On such an application as is mentioned in subsection (2) the court shall make such order under section 33 of the Act of 1996 as it thinks just and reasonable having regard to—

    (a)    the interests of the bankrupt's creditors,

    (b)    the conduct of the spouse or former spouse or civil partner or former civil partner, so far as contributing to the bankruptcy,

    (c)    the needs and financial resources of the spouse or former spouse or civil partner or former civil partner,

    (d)    the needs of any children, and

(e)     all the circumstances of the case other than the needs of the bankrupt.

(5)   Where such an application is made after the end of the period of one year beginning with the first vesting under Chapter IV of this Part of the bankrupt's estate in a trustee, the court shall assume, unless the circumstances of the case are exceptional, that the interests of the bankrupt's creditors outweigh all other considerations.

**Amendments**—Family Law Act 1996, s 66(1), Sch 8, para 57(2), (3)(a), (b), (4); Trusts of Land and Appointment of Trustees Act 1996, s 25(2), Sch 4; Civil Partnership Act 2004, s 82, Sch 9; Enterprise and Regulatory Reform Act 2013, s 71(3), Sch 19, paras 1, 29.

**General note**—This provision applies where a bankrupt's spouse or civil partner asserts matrimonial home rights under the Family Law Act 1996, as opposed to rights under a trust of land in which case s 335A will apply. The present provisions specifically provide for the relevant court and the factors to be considered by the court on an application being made under s 33 of the 1996 Act for what is commonly termed an 'occupation order'. Such an application may be made by the trustee (ie so as to require the bankrupt's non-owning spouse or civil partner to vacate the dwelling-house) or by a non-owning spouse or civil partner seeking to assert her matrimonial home rights under the 1996 Act which amount to a charge on the state or interest of the bankrupt, or of trustees for the bankrupt: see s 336(2).

**Other statutory considerations**—Regard should be had initially to s 283A (bankrupt's home ceasing to form part of bankrupt's estate in certain circumstances) and s 313A (low value home) and, in particular, s 313A(2) which requires the court to dismiss an application for possession and sale etc if the value of the trustee's interest in the dwelling-house is below the £1,000 figure currently prescribed under that provision.

**Definitions**—The terms 'family' and 'dwelling-house' are defined in s 385.

**The spouse or civil partner's rights of occupation as a charge on the bankrupt's estate**—Section 336(1) precludes anything giving rise to any matrimonial home rights under the 1996 Act in favour of the bankrupt's non-owning spouse or civil partner in the period between the presentation of the petition and the vesting of the bankrupt's estate in the trustee under s 306, although s 336(1) does nothing to inhibit matrimonial home rights which came into existence prior to the presentation of the petition. Such rights continue to bind the bankrupt's estate by virtue of s 336(2)(a), but do not take the home permanently beyond the reach of creditors, as made clear in *Mekarska v Ruiz* [2011] EWHC 913 (Fam), [2011] 2 FCR 608 (permission to appeal was not granted (*Re Ruiz* [2011] EWCA Civ 1646, [2012] BPIR 446). A trustee in bankruptcy may apply to the bankruptcy court to terminate the spouse or civil partner's right of occupation under s 33 of the 1996 Act (*Ruiz* at [23]).

**The appropriate court for an application under s 33 of the 1996 Act**—Irrespective of the provisions of the 1996 Act, the application is made to the court having jurisdiction in relation to the bankruptcy: s 336(2)(b). Sections 373 and 374 and the notes thereto deal with the bankruptcy court having jurisdiction.

SECTION 336(4)

**Scope of provision**—Section 336(4) requires the court to make an order 'as it thinks just and reasonable' having regard to the four specific factors in s 336(4)(a)–(d) and the particular circumstances of the case in (e) which, notably, do not include the needs of the bankrupt. Accordingly, the court should not take account of any particular need of the bankrupt in relation to the dwelling-house other than to the extent that such needs might have a bearing on those factors in (c) or (d). For the purposes of (b) the court will be justified in taking into account any conduct on the part of a spouse or former spouse which might properly be said to have contributed to the bankruptcy such as an excessive level of personal expenditure or, arguably, a refusal to assist the bankrupt in his financial difficulties from assets available to the spouse or former spouse.

Section 336(5)

' . . .   **unless the circumstances of the case are exceptional** . . . '—See the notes on exceptional circumstances to s 335A.

## [1.457]

### 337 Rights of occupation of bankrupt

(1)   This section applies where—

(a)     a person who is entitled to occupy a dwelling house by virtue of a beneficial estate or interest is made bankrupt, and

(b)     any persons under the age of 18 with whom that person had at some time occupied that dwelling house had their home with that person at the time when the bankruptcy application was made or (as the case may be) the bankruptcy petition was presented and at the commencement of the bankruptcy.

(2)   Whether or not the bankrupt's spouse or civil partner (if any) has home rights under Part IV of the Family Law Act 1996—

(a)    the bankrupt has the following rights as against the trustee of his estate—

(i)     if in occupation, a right not to be evicted or excluded from the dwelling house or any part of it, except with the leave of the court,

(ii)    if not in occupation, a right with the leave of the court to enter into and occupy the dwelling house, and

(b)    the bankrupt's rights are a charge, having the like priority as an equitable interest created immediately before the commencement of the bankruptcy, on so much of his estate or interest in the dwelling house as vests in the trustee.

(3)   The Act of 1996 has effect, with the necessary modifications, as if—

(a)    the rights conferred by paragraph (a) of subsection (2) were home rights under that Act,

(b)    any application for such leave as is mentioned in that paragraph were an application for an order under section 33 of that Act, and

(c)    any charge under paragraph (b) of that subsection on the estate or interest of the trustee were a charge under that Act on the estate or interest of a spouse or civil partner.

(4)   Any application for leave such as is mentioned in subsection (2)(a) or otherwise by virtue of this section for an order under section 33 of the Act of 1996 shall be made to the court having jurisdiction in relation to the bankruptcy.

(5)   On such an application the court shall make such order under section 33 of the Act of 1996 as it thinks just and reasonable having regard to the interests of the creditors, to the bankrupt's financial resources, to the needs of the children and to all the circumstances of the case other than the needs of the bankrupt.

(6)   Where such an application is made after the end of the period of one year beginning with the vesting (under Chapter IV of this Part) of the bankrupt's estate in a trustee, the court shall assume, unless the circumstances of the case are exceptional, that the interests of the bankrupt's creditors outweigh all other considerations.

**Amendments**—Family Law Act 1996, s 66(1), Sch 8, para 58(2)–(4); Civil Partnership Act 2004, s 82, Sch 9; Enterprise and Regulatory Reform Act 2013, S 71(3), Sch 19, paras 1, 30.

For the rationale behind this prospective amendment, see the general note to Part IX.

**General note**—This provision applies where, on the making of a bankruptcy order, a bankrupt is entitled to occupy a dwelling-house (as defined in s 385) by virtue of a beneficial estate or interest where, at the time of the presentation of the bankruptcy petition *and* on the making of the bankruptcy order, a minor had his home with the bankrupt at that dwelling-house. Section 337(1) makes no mention of, and is therefore not concerned with, the presence of a spouse, former spouse, civil partner, former civil partner or co-habitee, or any rights of occupation in favour of such an individual, although s 337(2) makes clear that nothing within s 337 should be understood as detracting from any such rights of occupation. The provision therefore most obviously addresses the position of a single, separated or divorced bankrupt who occupies a dwelling-house with one or more minors at the relevant times.

## SECTION 337(1), (2), (3)

**Scope of provision**—Where the conditions in s 337(1) are met, the bankrupt acquires those rights identified in s 337(2)(a), dependent on whether or not the bankrupt is in occupation of the dwelling-house, which take effect under s 337(2)(b) as a statutory charge enforceable against the trustee with the priority of an equitable interest created immediately prior to the making of the bankruptcy order. Section 337(3) then takes effect by treating the rights in s 337(2)(a) as matrimonial home rights under the Family Law Act 1996, enforceable by way of an occupation order under s 33 of that Act, and the statutory charge encapsulating those rights under s 337(2)(b) as a charge on the estate or interest of a spouse for the purposes of the 1996 Act.

Notably, s 337 creates no specific rights in favour of a minor (or, indeed, any other person).

As with applications under s 335A or s 336, an application for an occupation order under s 33 of the 1996 Act is made to the court having bankruptcy jurisdiction. Bankruptcy court jurisdiction is dealt with in ss 373 and 374 and the notes thereto.

## SECTION 337(5)

**Factors to be considered by the court**—The court must make such occupation order as it thinks just and reasonable having regard to those factors in s 337(5).

SECTION 337(6)

' . . . unless the circumstances of the case are exceptional . . . '—See the note on exceptional circumstances to s 335A.

## [1.458]

### 338 Payments in respect of premises occupied by bankrupt

Where any premises comprised in a bankrupt's estate are occupied by him (whether by virtue of the preceding section or otherwise) on condition that he makes payments towards satisfying any liability arising under a mortgage of the premises or otherwise towards the outgoings of the premises, the bankrupt does not, by virtue of those payments, acquire any interest in the premises.

**General note**—If, by virtue of the making of an occupation order under s 33 of the Family Law Act 1996 or otherwise, premises forming part of the bankrupt's estate are occupied by the bankrupt on condition that the bankrupt makes payment towards any liability arising under a mortgage of those premises or otherwise on the outgoings of the premises, then the bankrupt acquires no interest in the premises by the fact of making such payments.

It would follow from the prohibition on the bankrupt acquiring any interest in premises, that any benefit which might accrue as a consequence of such payments, say on the reduction of capital liability under a mortgage, must accrue for the benefit of the bankrupt's estate. Certainly it would not seem possible for any such interest to be claimed by the trustee as after-acquired property since s 338 specifically precludes the possibility of such property being acquired by or devolving upon the bankrupt, as a consequence of which such property cannot fall within the scope of s 307(1).

*Adjustment of prior transactions, etc*

## [1.459]

### 339 Transactions at an undervalue

(1) Subject as follows in this section and sections 341 and 342, where an individual is made bankrupt and he has at a relevant time (defined in section 341) entered into a transaction with any person at an undervalue, the trustee of the bankrupt's estate may apply to the court for an order under this section.

(2) The court shall, on such an application, make such order as it thinks fit for restoring the position to what it would have been if that individual had not entered into that transaction.

(3) For the purposes of this section and sections 341 and 342, an individual enters into a transaction with a person at an undervalue if—

    (a)    he makes a gift to that person or he otherwise enters into a transaction with that person on terms that provide for him to receive no consideration,

    (b)    he enters into a transaction with that person in consideration of marriage or the formation of a civil partnership, or

    (c)    he enters into a transaction with that person for a consideration the value of which, in money or money's worth, is significantly less than the value, in money or money's worth, of the consideration provided by the individual.

**Amendments**—Civil Partnership Act 2004, s 261(1), Sch 27, para 119; Enterprise and Regulatory Reform Act 2013, s 71(3), Sch 19, paras 1, 31.

**General note**—This is equivalent to s 238, which deals with companies. The provision is almost identical save for the fact that, in addition to the transaction covered by s 238, transactions in consideration of marriage (s 339(3)(b)) may be caught by the section. The inclusion of this category is probably to address the fact that in equity marriage constitutes valid consideration (*Attorney-General v Jacobs Smith* [1895] 2 QB 341) and also under the previous legislation (Bankruptcy Act 1914, s 42) marriage could render an otherwise voidable transaction valid.

There is no equivalent to the defence that is potentially available in cases involving corporate insolvency under s 238(5). Also, the 'relevant time' that is explained in s 341 is different in some cases from that applying to s 238. See the comments accompanying s 341.

The fact that there is no mental element required for s 339 (as opposed to s 423, transactions defrauding creditors) was underlined in *Bramston v Riaz* [2014] BPIR 42 (at [11]).

**Matrimonial proceedings**—In something of a controversial decision, the Court of Appeal, in reversing the decision at first instance ([2007] EWHC 1012 (Ch)), held in *Hill v Haines* [2007]

EWCA Civ 1284, [2007] BPIR 1280, that a transfer made pursuant to an ancillary order for relief granted by the court under the Matrimonial Causes Act 1973, in relation to a divorce, was not a transaction at an undervalue. The Court held that the order did constitute consideration for the purposes of s 339. Inter alia, the property adjustment order made by the court involved the husband transferring his property to his wife. After the order the husband became bankrupt. The Court of Appeal held that s 339(3)(a) was inapplicable as the wife was deemed to have given consideration, namely that her claim had been turned into financial provision by the husband, and consequently the husband received consideration. Effectively, the order of the court quantifies the value of the wife's statutory right by reference to the value of the money or property thereby ordered to be paid or transferred by the husband to the wife (at [35] also, see [79]). Additionally, s 339(3)(c) was not applicable as the consideration provided by the wife constituted money's worth and its value was not less than the value of the consideration provided by the husband whether significantly or at all. This was the case whether an order was made with or without consent, absent fraud, mistake, misrepresentation or other vitiating factor (at [35], [47]). If a transfer occurs as a result of the couple colluding, dishonestly, it could be regarded as a transaction at an undervalue (at [46]). In *Re Jones* [2008] BPIR 1051, Chief Registrar Baister rejected the notion that any agreement between spouses that placed one of them ahead of creditors was collusive and dishonest ([64]). See also *Sands v Singh* [2016] EWHC 636 (Ch), [2016] BPIR 737. The Chief Registrar said that what was needed to establish collusion and dishonesty was evidence that the spouses had sought to put assets out of the reach of a trustee in bankruptcy (at [64]). The Court of Appeal in *Hill v Haines* could not accept that it was Parliament's intention that one of the most common orders made in matrimonial matters could be nullified by the action of a trustee in bankruptcy (at [36]). Leave to appeal to the House of Lords was refused.

Giving up a right to pursue a claim can be valuable consideration but only where it is given up in an enforceable way; there is no valuable consideration if only an unenforceable assurance is given or the right in question is simply not exercised subsequently (per Fancourt J in *Gendrot v Chadwick* [2018] EWHC 48 (Ch), [2018] BPIR 423 at [18]).

See J Briggs 'Haines v Hill: Where Does This Leave a Trustee in Bankruptcy?' (2008) 21 *Insolvency Intelligence* 90.

See *Hargreaves v Salt* [2010] EWHC 3549 (Fam), [2011] BPIR 656 for a case where the court dealt with a s 339 application alongside an application under s 37 of the Matrimonial Causes Act 1973, both arising as a result of the same transaction.

**Consideration and 'undervalue'**—The 'value' is to be assessed objectively by reference to what the debtor receives rather than what the counterparty gives up (*Lyle v Bedborough* [2021] EWHC 220 (Ch), [2021] BPIR 581 at [69]–[70] citing *Ramlort Ltd v Reid* [2004] EWCA Civ 800, [2005] 1 BCLC 331, [2004] BPIR 985).

In the Northern Irish case of *Official Receiver for Northern Ireland v Stranaghan* [2010] NICh 8, [2010] BPIR 928, the grant of a mortgage security for an existing loan was held to be void as a transaction at an undervalue where it was entered into only for the past consideration represented by the existing loan. See also *Re Peppard* [2009] BPIR 331, where various claimed elements of consideration were rejected by the court in the context of a transfer between family members. In particular the argument that good consideration could be given by a transferee by waiving repayment of a debt, repayment of which could have been challenged as a preference, was rejected.

In *Ailyan v Smith* [2010] EWHC 24 (Ch), [2010] BPIR 289 the requirements for a transaction at an undervalue were found to have been met in the context of investments in an alleged pyramid scheme. HHJ David Cooke sitting as a High Court judge held that, in assessing the value of an asset, the court has to assess as best it can on the evidence what the asset's value in money or money's worth would be to a rational and reasonably well-informed purchaser, having knowledge of the actual characteristics of what it is he is buying (at [69]).

In *Tailby v HSBC Bank plc, Re Anwar Ul-Haq Rashid* [2015] BPIR 143 Registrar Derrett gave detailed consideration to whether a guarantee given by a director of a small company in return for business finance for that company amounted to a transaction at an undervalue, and concluded it did not. A guarantee involved a two-way flow of rights and obligations. The director obtained personal benefit from the finance afforded to the Company. The company was solvent when the guarantee was given, the risk of the guarantor being called upon was minimal and he had a valuable right of indemnity from the company. The case also contains an interesting discussion of past consideration and the position on 'linked agreements', on which see also *Bramston v Riaz* [2014] BPIR 42.

In *Durkan v Patel* [2018] EWHC 3231 (Ch) payments by a bankrupt towards a mortgage secured on a property which had been transferred into the sole name of his wife were not transactions at undervalue where the bankrupt had remained jointly and severally liable to the mortgagee to repay the secured loan and interest.

On the interaction between transactions at undervalue and bankruptcy debts (s 382) debt see *Hellard v Chadwick* [2014] EWHC 2158 (Ch), [2014] BPIR 1234.

**Remedy**—A (non-exhaustive) menu of remedial orders is set out in s 342. A court has the discretion to make no remedial order even if a transaction falls foul of s 339, where justice requires: *Singla v Brown* [2007] EWHC 405 (Ch), [2008] Ch 357, [2007] BPIR 424 at [52]; *Trustee in Bankruptcy of Claridge v Claridge* [2011] EWHC 2047 (Ch), [2011] BPIR 1529 at [41]. The cases indicate that such action is likely to be something that is out of the ordinary (*Singla v Brown* at [59]) and it would only be in exceptional circumstances that a court would be justified in withholding relief to which the trustee in bankruptcy otherwise would seem to be entitled: *Stonham v Ramrattan* [2010] EWHC 1033 (Ch), [2010] BPIR 1210 at [40] (appeal to the Court of Appeal was dismissed ([2011] EWCA Civ 119, [2011] 1 WLR 1617), *Trustee in Bankruptcy of Claridge v Claridge*. No order was made in *Re Fowlds*; *Bucknall v Wilson* [2020] EWHC 1200 (Ch), where ICC Judge Jones held that justice and fairness required no order to be made, despite a preference within the meaning of s 340 having been established. Judge Jones emphasised that something out of the norm was required for no order to be made and identified as a 'prerequisite' the requirement that the recipient should no longer have the asset or its proceeds (at [87]) and had no actual or constructive notice that the payment was a preference (at [101]). As well as these factors, either a change of position or disproportionate consequences had to be shown and, on the facts, both had been proved (at [102]–[103]).

Any exercise of such discretion must explain why the circumstances of the case should not lead to the usual result of an order being made (*Lyle v Bedborough* [2021] EWHC 220 (Ch), [2021] BPIR 581 at [78]). In *Lyle v Bedborough* Judge Jonathan Richards (sitting as a deputy High Court judge) rejected submissions that the discretion should be exercised in circumstances where: (i) the relevant property could have been transferred to the transferee without falling foul of s 339 if the transferor and transferee had taken different actions, holding that this would be to insulate the parties from the consequences of their own decisions and visiting the associated consequences on the creditors (at [79]); and (ii) the transaction only just fell within the relevant period, holding that Parliament had specified 'bright line' deadlines which applied even to transactions implemented relatively close to those deadlines (at [80]).

In *Re Jones* [2008] BPIR 1051, Chief Registrar Baister said that a court will take into account, where a claim originates from an order relating to a dissolution of marriage, the personal effect of a restitutionary order (at [68]). In that case the Chief Registrar would have taken into account, if the section applied, the fact that an order in favour of the trustee would have made homeless a man in serious ill health and who had a child living with him. He also would have taken into account the fact that he was not satisfied that the creditors would receive a real, tangible benefit after the trustee's costs had been paid (at [68]). As far as delay in taking action is concerned, it alone cannot be a relevant reason for not exercising the discretion to grant relief which would otherwise seem to be appropriate: *Stonham v Ramrattan* [2010] EWHC 1033 (Ch), [2010] BPIR 1210, per Mann J at [34] (not relevant to the issue before the Court of Appeal ([2011] EWCA Civ 119, [2011] 1 WLR 1617 at [55]).

**Limitation period**—As with actions under s 238 in relation to companies, actions under this section are generally to be regarded as actions on a specialty, covered by ss 8 of the Limitation Act 1980, and as a consequence there is a 12-year time period in which office-holders can commence proceedings, *provided* that the substance of the application is to set aside a transaction: *Segal v Pasram* [2007] EWHC 3448 (Ch), [2007] BPIR 881. Where, however, it can be fairly said that the substance or essential nature of the application is to recover a sum recoverable by virtue of s 339 (such as where the transaction to be set aside is a simple payment of a sum of money), the limitation period will be six years by virtue of ss 8(2) and 9(1) of the Limitation Act 1980 (*Re Priory Garage (Walthamstow) Limited* [2001] BPIR 144 at 160).

See also the notes to s 238.

## [1.460]

### 340 Preferences

(1) Subject as follows in this and the next two sections, where an individual is made bankrupt and he has at a relevant time (defined in section 341) given a preference to any person, the trustee of the bankrupt's estate may apply to the court for an order under this section.

(2) The court shall, on such an application, make such order as it thinks fit for restoring the position to what it would have been if that individual had not given that preference.

(3) For the purposes of this and the next two sections, an individual gives a preference to a person if—

> (a) that person is one of the individual's creditors or a surety or guarantor for any of his debts or other liabilities, and

    (b)    the individual does anything or suffers anything to be done which (in either case) has the effect of putting that person into a position which, in the event of the individual's bankruptcy, will be better than the position he would have been in if that thing had not been done.

(4) The court shall not make an order under this section in respect of a preference given to any person unless the individual who gave the preference was influenced in deciding to give it by a desire to produce in relation to that person the effect mentioned in subsection (3)(b) above.

(5) An individual who has given a preference to a person who, at the time the preference was given, was an associate of his (otherwise than by reason only of being his employee) is presumed, unless the contrary is shown, to have been influenced in deciding to give it by such a desire as is mentioned in subsection (4).

(6) The fact that something has been done in pursuance of the order of a court does not, without more, prevent the doing or suffering of that thing from constituting the giving of a preference.

**Amendments**—Enterprise and Regulatory Reform Act 2013, s 71(3), Sch 19, paras 1, 32.

**General note**—This is equivalent to s 239, which deals with companies, and is generally identical.

See the comments attaching to s 239.

**Matrimonial proceedings**—In *Re Jones* [2008] BPIR 1051, Chief Registrar Baister rejected the argument that the spouse who benefitted under an ancillary relief order could be regarded, for the purposes of the IA 1986, as a creditor of the spouse who had to make good on the relief, and who subsequently became a bankrupt. Hence a claim for a preference failed. However in reaching this decision the Chief Registrar drew parallels between an order for ancillary relief and a prospective claim for costs and placed reliance on the line of authorities following *Glenister v Rowe* [2000] Ch 76, [1999] BPIR 674, where it had been held that a claim for costs was not a contingent liability and therefore that the litigant with an arguable claim for costs was not a creditor. Reliance was also placed on *R (on the application of Steele) v Birmingham City Council* [2005] EWCA Civ 1824, [2006] BPIR 856 in which the possibility that the Secretary of State might make a repayment determination under the Social Security Administration Act 1992 was held not to constitute a contingent liability. The Chief Registrar found that a claimant for ancillary relief, being in a similar position to a litigant with an arguable claim for costs or the litigant in Steele (requiring an exercise of the court's discretion in their favour to succeed), was therefore also not a creditor for the purposes of s 340. However, *Glenister v Rowe* and *Steele* were overruled by the Supreme Court in *Re Nortel* [2013] UKSC 52, [2014] AC 209, [2013] 2 BCLC 135 on this point. Accordingly the finding in *Re Jones* that a spouse who benefitted under an ancillary relief order is not a creditor must now be open to doubt.

**Influenced by a desire to provide a preference**—This requirement is the same as in s 239, but it might be a little easier for a trustee to establish the desire of the bankrupt than a liquidator to try to establish the desire of a corporate body. However, after saying that, as with liquidators claiming preferences in relation to the corporate equivalent (s 239), trustees in bankruptcy have had little success in impugning transactions as preferences where the recipient of the alleged preference is not connected with the bankrupt (eg *Rooney v Das* [1999] BPIR 404; *Re Ledingham-Smith* [1993] BCLC 635). *Abdulali v Finnegan* [2018] EWHC 1806 (Ch), [2018] BPIR 1547 is an example of an associate of the bankrupt rebutting the presumption in s 340(5). The repayment of a loan by the bankrupt to his brother-in-law was motivated by a desire to secure a greater loan from a company controlled by the brother-in-law which would 'keep the ship afloat' before the bankrupt's business ventures came good and not a desire to prefer him over other unsecured creditors.

See the notes under the same heading in relation to s 239.

## [1.461]

### 341 "Relevant time" under ss 339, 340

(1) Subject as follows, the time at which an individual enters into a transaction at an undervalue or gives a preference is a relevant time if the transaction is entered into or the preference given—

    (a)    in the case of a transaction at an undervalue, at a time in the period of 5 years ending with the day of the making of the bankruptcy application as a result of which, or (as the case may be) the presentation of the bankruptcy petition on which, the individual is made bankrupt,

(b)    in the case of a preference which is not a transaction at an undervalue and is given to a person who is an associate of the individual (otherwise than by reason only of being his employee), at a time in the period of 2 years ending with that day, and

(c)    in any other case of a preference which is not a transaction at an undervalue, at a time in the period of 6 months ending with that day.

(2)    Where an individual enters into a transaction at an undervalue or gives a preference at a time mentioned in paragraph (a), (b) or (c) of subsection (1) (not being, in the case of a transaction at an undervalue, a time less than 2 years before the end of the period mentioned in paragraph (a)), that time is not a relevant time for the purposes of sections 339 and 340 unless the individual—

(a)    is insolvent at that time, or

(b)    becomes insolvent in consequence of the transaction or preference;

but the requirements of this subsection are presumed to be satisfied, unless the contrary is shown, in relation to any transaction at an undervalue which is entered into by an individual with a person who is an associate of his (otherwise than by reason only of being his employee).

(3)    For the purposes of subsection (2), an individual is insolvent if—

(a)    he is unable to pay his debts as they fall due, or

(b)    the value of his assets is less than the amount of his liabilities, taking into account his contingent and prospective liabilities.

*(4)    A transaction entered into or preference given by a person who is subsequently adjudged bankrupt on a petition under section 264(1)(d) (criminal bankruptcy) is to be treated as having been entered into or given at a relevant time for the purposes of sections 339 and 340 if it was entered into or given at any time on or after the date specified for the purposes of this subsection in the criminal bankruptcy order on which the petition was based.*

*(5)    No order shall be made under section 339 or 340 by virtue of subsection (4) of this section where an appeal is pending (within the meaning of section 277) against the individual's conviction of any offence by virtue of which the criminal bankruptcy order was made.*

**Amendments**—Subsections (4), (5) prospectively repealed by Criminal Justice Act 1988, s 170(2), Sch 16, as from a date to be appointed; Enterprise and Regulatory Reform Act 2013, s 71(3), Sch 19, paras 1, 33.

**General note**—This is equivalent to s 240, which applies to companies. One major difference is that while s 240 only provides for a 2-year time zone prior to the onset of insolvency for transactions at an undervalue, s 341 provides for an extended period of 5 years prior to the date of the presentation of the petition which led to the debtor's bankruptcy. Another difference is that if it can be established in a bankruptcy that the transaction at an undervalue was effected in the 2 years before the presentation of the bankruptcy petition or the making of a bankruptcy application, then there is no requirement to prove that the debtor was insolvent at the time of the transaction or became insolvent as a consequence of the entering into of the transaction.

**Insolvent**—Apart from where a transaction at an undervalue within the 2-year period preceding the presentation of the petition is alleged, the trustee must establish either that the bankrupt was insolvent at the time of the transaction or that he or she became insolvent as a result of the transaction. Insolvency here means either cash flow or balance sheet insolvency, as set out in s 123(1)(e) and s 123(2), whereas, where a company is involved, insolvency can be in terms of any of the provisions in s 123. For a discussion of insolvency, see the comments under the heading 'Unable to pay debts' relating to s 123. As to the presumption of insolvency under s 341(2) in relation to an associate, see *Re Calder; Salter v Wetton* [2011] EWHC 3192 (Ch), [2012] BPIR 63 in which Briggs J accepted a submission that, despite the statutory presumption placing the burden of proving that the bankrupt was not insolvent at the time on the respondent, where the trustee had relied solely on one alleged debt in relation to insolvency in his evidence, it was sufficient to rebut the presumption for the respondent to simply deal with the case advanced by the trustee ie prove that debt was not due (at [21]–[24]). However it should be noted that Briggs J stated that if the trustee had presented his case on the basis of the presumption, even in the alternative, this may not have been sufficient.

**Associate**—For the definition of 'associate' see s 435.

See also the notes to s 240.

**[1.462]**

### 342 Orders under ss 339, 340

(1)  Without prejudice to the generality of section 339(2) or 340(2), an order under either of those sections with respect to a transaction or preference entered into or given by an individual who is subsequently made bankrupt may (subject as follows)—

   (a)  require any property transferred as part of the transaction, or in connection with the giving of the preference, to be vested in the trustee of the bankrupt's estate as part of that estate;

   (b)  require any property to be so vested if it represents in any person's hands the application either of the proceeds of sale of property so transferred or of money so transferred;

   (c)  release or discharge (in whole or in part) any security given by the individual;

   (d)  require any person to pay, in respect of benefits received by him from the individual, such sums to the trustee of his estate as the court may direct;

   (e)  provide for any surety or guarantor whose obligations to any person were released or discharged (in whole or in part) under the transaction or by the giving of the preference to be under such new or revived obligations to that person as the court thinks appropriate;

   (f)  provide for security to be provided for the discharge of any obligation imposed by or arising under the order, for such an obligation to be charged on any property and for the security or charge to have the same priority as a security or charge released or discharged (in whole or in part) under the transaction or by the giving of the preference; and

   (g)  provide for the extent to which any person whose property is vested by the order in the trustee of the bankrupt's estate, or on whom obligations are imposed by the order, is to be able to prove in the bankruptcy for debts or other liabilities which arose from, or were released or discharged (in whole or in part) under or by, the transaction or the giving of the preference.

(2)  An order under section 339 or 340 may affect the property of, or impose any obligation on, any person whether or not he is the person with whom the individual in question entered into the transaction or, as the case may be, the person to whom the preference was given; but such an order—

   (a)  shall not prejudice any interest in property which was acquired from a person other than that individual and was acquired in good faith and for value, or prejudice any interest deriving from such an interest, and

   (b)  shall not require a person who received a benefit from the transaction or preference in good faith and for value to pay a sum to the trustee of the bankrupt's estate, except where he was a party to the transaction or the payment is to be in respect of a preference given to that person at a time when he was a creditor of that individual.

(2A)  Where a person has acquired an interest in property from a person other than the individual in question, or has received a benefit from the transaction or preference, and at the time of that acquisition or receipt—

   (a)  he had notice of the relevant surrounding circumstances and of the relevant proceedings, or

   (b)  he was an associate of, or was connected with, either the individual in question or the person with whom that individual entered into the transaction or to whom that individual gave the preference,

then, unless the contrary is shown, it shall be presumed for the purposes of paragraph (a) or (as the case may be) paragraph (b) of subsection (2) that the interest was acquired or the benefit was received otherwise than in good faith.

(3)  Any sums required to be paid to the trustee in accordance with an order under section 339 or 340 shall be comprised in the bankrupt's estate.

(4)  For the purposes of subsection (2A)(a), the relevant surrounding circumstances are (as the case may require)—

(a)    the fact that the individual in question entered into the transaction at an undervalue; or

(b)    the circumstances which amounted to the giving of the preference by the individual in question.

(5)  For the purposes of subsection (2A)(a), a person has notice of the relevant proceedings if he has notice—

(a)    of the fact that the bankruptcy application as a result of which, or (as the case may be) the bankruptcy petition on which, the individual in question is made bankrupt has been made or presented; or

(b)    of the fact that the individual in question has been made bankrupt.

(6)  Section 249 in Part VII of this Act shall apply for the purposes of subsection (2A)(b) as it applies for the purposes of the first Group of Parts.

**Amendments**—Insolvency (No 2) Act 1994, s 2(1)–(3); Enterprise and Regulatory Reform Act 2013, s 71(3), Sch 19, paras 1, 34.

**General note**—This is equivalent to s 241, which deals with companies. Just like ss 238(3) and 239(3), with successful proceedings under either s 339 or s 340 the court is required to restore the position to what it would have been had the transaction that is adjusted had not been entered into (ss 339(2), 340(2)), but s 342 sets out some examples of orders that the court can make. As with s 241, courts are not limited to what is enumerated in s 342. The primary differences between s 342 and s 241 turn on the fact that the latter is dealing with companies.

The court is not limited to restoring the position of the debtor as it was before the dealing. Rather it has to put all the parties back into the position that they would have been in had the transaction not been entered into or the preference given. The exercise is restitutionary in its nature not compensatory (*Johnson v Arden* [2018] EWHC 1624 (Ch), [2019] 2 BCLC 215, [2019] BPIR 901, at [92] (approved by Bryan J in *National Bank Trust v Yurov* [2020] EWHC 100 (Comm)).

**Vesting**—Several of the orders refer to property vesting in the trustee in bankruptcy. This is because the bankrupt's estate vests in the trustee in bankruptcy at the date of the appointment of the trustee (s 306), so orders involving the re-transfer of a bankrupt's property will involve providing that the property will vest in the trustee. In liquidation, by contrast, the property is transferred to the company, as usually the company property is not vested in the liquidator. As to the interaction between s 283A, s 339 and s 342, see *Stonham v Ramrattan* [2011] EWCA Civ 119, [2011] 1 WLR 1617, referred to above in relation to s 339.

See the comments under s 241 and those on relief under s 339.

## [1.463]

### 342A Recovery of excessive pension contributions

(1)  Where an individual who is made bankrupt—

(a)    has rights under an approved pension arrangement, or

(b)    has excluded rights under an unapproved pension arrangement,

the trustee of the bankrupt's estate may apply to the court for an order under this section.

(2)  If the court is satisfied—

(a)    that the rights under the arrangement are to any extent, and whether directly or indirectly, the fruits of relevant contributions, and

(b)    that the making of any of the relevant contributions ("the excessive contributions") has unfairly prejudiced the individual's creditors,

the court may make such order as it thinks fit for restoring the position to what it would have been had the excessive contributions not been made.

(3)  Subsection (4) applies where the court is satisfied that the value of the rights under the arrangement is, as a result of rights of the individual under the arrangement or any other pension arrangement having at any time become subject to a debit under section 29(1)(a) of the Welfare Reform and Pensions Act 1999 (debits giving effect to pension-sharing), less than it would otherwise have been.

(4)  Where this subsection applies—

(a)    any relevant contributions which were represented by the rights which became subject to the debit shall, for the purposes of subsection (2), be taken to be contributions of which the rights under the arrangement are the fruits, and

(b) where the relevant contributions represented by the rights under the arrangement (including those so represented by virtue of paragraph (a)) are not all excessive contributions, relevant contributions which are represented by the rights under the arrangement otherwise than by virtue of paragraph (a) shall be treated as excessive contributions before any which are so represented by virtue of that paragraph.

(5) In subsections (2) to (4) "relevant contributions" means contributions to the arrangement or any other pension arrangement—

(a) which the individual has at any time made on his own behalf, or

(b) which have at any time been made on his behalf.

(6) The court shall, in determining whether it is satisfied under subsection (2)(b), consider in particular—

(a) whether any of the contributions were made for the purpose of putting assets beyond the reach of the individual's creditors or any of them, and

(b) whether the total amount of any contributions—

(i) made by or on behalf of the individual to pension arrangements, and

(ii) represented (whether directly or indirectly) by rights under approved pension arrangements or excluded rights under unapproved pension arrangements,

is an amount which is excessive in view of the individual's circumstances when those contributions were made.

(7) For the purposes of this section and sections 342B and 342C ("the recovery provisions"), rights of an individual under an unapproved pension arrangement are excluded rights if they are rights which are excluded from his estate by virtue of regulations under section 12 of the Welfare Reform and Pensions Act 1999.

(8) In the recovery provisions—

"approved pension arrangement" has the same meaning as in section 11 of the Welfare Reform and Pensions Act 1999;

"unapproved pension arrangement" has the same meaning as in section 12 of that Act.

**Amendments**—Substituted by Welfare Reform and Pensions Act 1999, s 15. Amended by Enterprise and Regulatory Reform Act 2013, s 71(3), Sch 19, paras 1, 35.

**General note**—Sections 342A to 342F came into force on 29 May 2000 and were introduced by Sch 12 to the Welfare Reform and Pensions Act 1999 and the Welfare Reform and Pensions Act 1999 (Commencement No 7) Order 2000 (SI 2000/1382).

These new provisions are necessary, given ss 11 and 12 of the 1999 Act which, in effect, exclude pension rights from the scope of the bankrupt's estate, subject to certain but uncommon exceptions. The consequence of those provisions is that a pension arrangement, as defined, represents a vehicle to which an individual in financial difficulties facing bankruptcy might be tempted to transfer assets with a view to those assets escaping the scope of the bankruptcy. These provisions, framed, as they are, in necessarily technical language, provide the basis by which a trustee might seek to challenge such conduct on the part of a bankrupt. In *Stanley v Wilson* [2017] BPIR 227 HHJ Mark Raeside QC held that s 342A required a two-step process. First consideration of the 'purpose' of the payments and second consideration of whether the payments were 'excessive'. 'Purpose' meant 'substantial purpose'. Dishonesty was not required and inferences could be drawn from evidence before, at the time of, and after the payments. 'Excessive' had not been defined and whether a payment was 'excessive' was a question of fact for the trial judge and for the trustee to prove on the balance of probabilities. The obvious evidential ingredient would, of necessity, include consideration of the source of the money and the ability of the bankrupt to make such payment. HHJ Raeside QC held that both limbs must be proven as a matter of law before it is established that 'unfairness' arises. However in *Re Henry* [2016] EWCA Civ 989, [2017] 1 WLR 391, [2016] BPIR 1426 Gloster LJ (with whom McFarlane LJ and Sir Stanley Burton agreed) held (obiter) that these two considerations were merely matters which the court is required to consider for the purpose of deciding whether payment of the contributions has unfairly prejudiced the bankrupt's creditors and that, even if they are not established, the court may nonetheless be entitled to conclude that the excessive contributions have unfairly prejudiced the bankrupt's creditors and make an appropriate order restoring the position to what it would have been had the excessive contributions not been made.

**[1.464]**

### 342B Orders under section 342A

(1) Without prejudice to the generality of section 342A(2), an order under section 342A may include provision—

    (a)    requiring the person responsible for the arrangement to pay an amount to the individual's trustee in bankruptcy,

    (b)    adjusting the liabilities of the arrangement in respect of the individual,

    (c)    adjusting any liabilities of the arrangement in respect of any other person that derive, directly or indirectly, from rights of the individual under the arrangement,

    (d)    for the recovery by the person responsible for the arrangement (whether by deduction from any amount which that person is ordered to pay or otherwise) of costs incurred by that person in complying in the bankrupt's case with any requirement under section 342C(1) or in giving effect to the order.

(2) In subsection (1), references to adjusting the liabilities of the arrangement in respect of a person include (in particular) reducing the amount of any benefit or future benefit to which that person is entitled under the arrangement.

(3) In subsection (1)(c), the reference to liabilities of the arrangement does not include liabilities in respect of a person which result from giving effect to an order or provision falling within section 28(1) of the Welfare Reform and Pensions Act 1999 (pension sharing orders and agreements).

(4) The maximum amount which the person responsible for an arrangement may be required to pay by an order under section 342A is the lesser of—

    (a)    the amount of the excessive contributions, and

    (b)    the value of the individual's rights under the arrangement (if the arrangement is an approved pension arrangement) or of his excluded rights under the arrangement (if the arrangement is an unapproved pension arrangement).

(5) An order under section 342A which requires the person responsible for an arrangement to pay an amount ("the restoration amount") to the individual's trustee in bankruptcy must provide for the liabilities of the arrangement to be correspondingly reduced.

(6) For the purposes of subsection (5), liabilities are correspondingly reduced if the difference between—

    (a)    the amount of the liabilities immediately before the reduction, and

    (b)    the amount of the liabilities immediately after the reduction,

is equal to the restoration amount.

(7) An order under section 342A in respect of an arrangement—

    (a)    shall be binding on the person responsible for the arrangement, and

    (b)    overrides provisions of the arrangement to the extent that they conflict with the provisions of the order.

**Amendments**—Substituted by Welfare Reform and Pensions Act 1999, s 15.

**[1.465]**

### 342C Orders under section 342A: supplementary

(1) The person responsible for—

    (a)    an approved pension arrangement under which a bankrupt has rights,

    (b)    an unapproved pension arrangement under which a bankrupt has excluded rights, or

    (c)    a pension arrangement under which a bankrupt has at any time had rights,

shall, on the bankrupt's trustee in bankruptcy making a written request, provide the trustee with such information about the arrangement and rights as the trustee may reasonably require for, or in connection with, the making of applications under section 342A.

(2) Nothing in—

(a) any provision of section 159 of the Pension Schemes Act 1993 or section 91 of the Pensions Act 1995 (which prevent assignment and the making of orders that restrain a person from receiving anything which he is prevented from assigning),

(b) any provision of any enactment (whether passed or made before or after the passing of the Welfare Reform and Pensions Act 1999) corresponding to any of the provisions mentioned in paragraph (a), or

(c) any provision of the arrangement in question corresponding to any of those provisions,

applies to a court exercising its powers under section 342A.

(3) Where any sum is required by an order under section 342A to be paid to the trustee in bankruptcy, that sum shall be comprised in the bankrupt's estate.

(4) Regulations may, for the purposes of the recovery provisions, make provision about the calculation and verification of—

(a) any such value as is mentioned in section 342B(4)(b);

(b) any such amounts as are mentioned in section 342B(6)(a) and (b).

(5) The power conferred by subsection (4) includes power to provide for calculation or verification—

(a) in such manner as may, in the particular case, be approved by a prescribed person; or

(b) in accordance with guidance from time to time prepared by a prescribed person.

(6) References in the recovery provisions to the person responsible for a pension arrangement are to—

(a) the trustees, managers or provider of the arrangement, or

(b) the person having functions in relation to the arrangement corresponding to those of a trustee, manager or provider.

(7) In this section and sections 342A and 342B—

"prescribed" means prescribed by regulations;

"the recovery provisions" means this section and sections 342A and 342B;

"regulations" means regulations made by the Secretary of State.

(8) Regulations under the recovery provisions may—

(a) make different provision for different cases;

(b) contain such incidental, supplemental and transitional provisions as appear to the Secretary of State necessary or expedient.

(9) Regulations under the recovery provisions shall be made by statutory instrument subject to annulment in pursuance of a resolution of either House of Parliament.

**Amendments**—Substituted by Welfare Reform and Pensions Act 1999, s 15; Pensions Act 2007, s 17, Sch 5, para 3.

**General note**—See the general note to s 342A.

**Subordinate legislation**—Occupational and Personal Pension Schemes (Bankruptcy) (No 2) Regulations 2002, SI 2002/836 (made under sub-ss (4)(a), (7)–(9)).

## [1.466]

### 342D Recovery of excessive contributions in pension-sharing cases

(1) For the purposes of sections 339, 341 and 342, a pension-sharing transaction shall be taken—

(a) to be a transaction, entered into by the transferor with the transferee, by which the appropriate amount is transferred by the transferor to the transferee; and

(b) to be capable of being a transaction entered into at an undervalue only so far as it is a transfer of so much of the appropriate amount as is recoverable.

(2) For the purposes of sections 340 to 342, a pension-sharing transaction shall be taken—

(a) to be something (namely a transfer of the appropriate amount to the transferee) done by the transferor; and

(b) to be capable of being a preference given to the transferee only so far as it is a transfer of so much of the appropriate amount as is recoverable.

(3) If on an application under section 339 or 340 any question arises as to whether, or the extent to which, the appropriate amount in the case of a pension-sharing transaction is recoverable, the question shall be determined in accordance with subsections (4) to (8).

(4) The court shall first determine the extent (if any) to which the transferor's rights under the shared arrangement at the time of the transaction appear to have been (whether directly or indirectly) the fruits of contributions ("personal contributions")—

(a) which the transferor has at any time made on his own behalf, or

(b) which have at any time been made on the transferor's behalf,

to the shared arrangement or any other pension arrangement.

(5) Where it appears that those rights were to any extent the fruits of personal contributions, the court shall then determine the extent (if any) to which those rights appear to have been the fruits of personal contributions whose making has unfairly prejudiced the transferor's creditors ("the unfair contributions").

(6) If it appears to the court that the extent to which those rights were the fruits of the unfair contributions is such that the transfer of the appropriate amount could have been made out of rights under the shared arrangement which were not the fruits of the unfair contributions, then the appropriate amount is not recoverable.

(7) If it appears to the court that the transfer could not have been wholly so made, then the appropriate amount is recoverable to the extent to which it appears to the court that the transfer could not have been so made.

(8) In making the determination mentioned in subsection (5) the court shall consider in particular—

(a) whether any of the personal contributions were made for the purpose of putting assets beyond the reach of the transferor's creditors or any of them, and

(b) whether the total amount of any personal contributions represented, at the time the pension-sharing transaction was made, by rights under pension arrangements is an amount which is excessive in view of the transferor's circumstances when those contributions were made.

(9) In this section and sections 342E and 342F—

"appropriate amount", in relation to a pension-sharing transaction, means the appropriate amount in relation to that transaction for the purposes of section 29(1) of the Welfare Reform and Pensions Act 1999 (creation of pension credits and debits);

"pension-sharing transaction" means an order or provision falling within section 28(1) of the Welfare Reform and Pensions Act 1999 (orders and agreements which activate pension-sharing);

"shared arrangement", in relation to a pension-sharing transaction, means the pension arrangement to which the transaction relates;

"transferee", in relation to a pension-sharing transaction, means the person for whose benefit the transaction is made;

"transferor", in relation to a pension-sharing transaction, means the person to whose rights the transaction relates.

**Amendments**—Inserted by Welfare Reform and Pensions Act 1999, s 84(1), Sch 12, Pt II, paras 70, 71.

**General note**—See the general note to s 342A.

## [1.467]

### 342E Orders under section 339 or 340 in respect of pension-sharing transactions

(1) This section and section 342F apply if the court is making an order under section 339 or 340 in a case where—

    (a)    the transaction or preference is, or is any part of, a pension-sharing transaction, and

    (b)    the transferee has rights under a pension arrangement ("the destination arrangement", which may be the shared arrangement or any other pension arrangement) that are derived, directly or indirectly, from the pension-sharing transaction.

(2)   Without prejudice to the generality of section 339(2) or 340(2), or of section 342, the order may include provision—

    (a)    requiring the person responsible for the destination arrangement to pay an amount to the transferor's trustee in bankruptcy,

    (b)    adjusting the liabilities of the destination arrangement in respect of the transferee,

    (c)    adjusting any liabilities of the destination arrangement in respect of any other person that derive, directly or indirectly, from rights of the transferee under the destination arrangement,

    (d)    for the recovery by the person responsible for the destination arrangement (whether by deduction from any amount which that person is ordered to pay or otherwise) of costs incurred by that person in complying in the transferor's case with any requirement under section 342F(1) or in giving effect to the order,

    (e)    for the recovery, from the transferor's trustee in bankruptcy, by the person responsible for a pension arrangement, of costs incurred by that person in complying in the transferor's case with any requirement under section 342F(2) or (3).

(3)   In subsection (2), references to adjusting the liabilities of the destination arrangement in respect of a person include (in particular) reducing the amount of any benefit or future benefit to which that person is entitled under the arrangement.

(4)   The maximum amount which the person responsible for the destination arrangement may be required to pay by the order is the smallest of—

    (a)    so much of the appropriate amount as, in accordance with section 342D, is recoverable,

    (b)    so much (if any) of the amount of the unfair contributions (within the meaning given by section 342D(5)) as is not recoverable by way of an order under section 342A containing provision such as is mentioned in section 342B(1)(a), and

    (c)    the value of the transferee's rights under the destination arrangement so far as they are derived, directly or indirectly, from the pension-sharing transaction.

(5)   If the order requires the person responsible for the destination arrangement to pay an amount ("the restoration amount") to the transferor's trustee in bankruptcy it must provide for the liabilities of the arrangement to be correspondingly reduced.

(6)   For the purposes of subsection (5), liabilities are correspondingly reduced if the difference between—

    (a)    the amount of the liabilities immediately before the reduction, and

    (b)    the amount of the liabilities immediately after the reduction,

is equal to the restoration amount.

(7)   The order—

    (a)    shall be binding on the person responsible for the destination arrangement, and

    (b)    overrides provisions of the destination arrangement to the extent that they conflict with the provisions of the order.

**Amendments**—Inserted by Welfare Reform and Pensions Act 1999, s 84(1), Sch 12, Pt II, paras 70, 71.

**General note**—See the general note to s 342A.

[1.468]

### 342F Orders under section 339 or 340 in pension-sharing cases: supplementary

(1)   On the transferor's trustee in bankruptcy making a written request to the person responsible for the destination arrangement, that person shall provide the trustee with such information about—

(a)   the arrangement,

(b)   the transferee's rights under it, and

(c)   where the destination arrangement is the shared arrangement, the transferor's rights under it,

as the trustee may reasonably require for, or in connection with, the making of applications under sections 339 and 340.

(2)   Where the shared arrangement is not the destination arrangement, the person responsible for the shared arrangement shall, on the transferor's trustee in bankruptcy making a written request to that person, provide the trustee with such information about—

(a)   the arrangement, and

(b)   the transferor's rights under it,

as the trustee may reasonably require for, or in connection with, the making of applications under sections 339 and 340.

(3)   On the transferor's trustee in bankruptcy making a written request to the person responsible for any intermediate arrangement, that person shall provide the trustee with such information about—

(a)   the arrangement, and

(b)   the transferee's rights under it,

as the trustee may reasonably require for, or in connection with, the making of applications under sections 339 and 340.

(4)   In subsection (3) "intermediate arrangement" means a pension arrangement, other than the shared arrangement or the destination arrangement, in relation to which the following conditions are fulfilled—

(a)   there was a time when the transferee had rights under the arrangement that were derived (directly or indirectly) from the pension-sharing transaction, and

(b)   the transferee's rights under the destination arrangement (so far as derived from the pension-sharing transaction) are to any extent derived (directly or indirectly) from the rights mentioned in paragraph (a).

(5)   Nothing in—

(a)   any provision of section 159 of the Pension Schemes Act 1993 or section 91 of the Pensions Act 1995 (which prevent assignment and the making of orders which restrain a person from receiving anything which he is prevented from assigning),

(b)   any provision of any enactment (whether passed or made before or after the passing of the Welfare Reform and Pensions Act 1999) corresponding to any of the provisions mentioned in paragraph (a), or

(c)   any provision of the destination arrangement corresponding to any of those provisions,

applies to a court exercising its powers under section 339 or 340.

(6)   Regulations may, for the purposes of sections 339 to 342, sections 342D and 342E and this section, make provision about the calculation and verification of—

(a)   any such value as is mentioned in section 342E(4)(c);

(b)   any such amounts as are mentioned in section 342E(6)(a) and (b).

(7)   The power conferred by subsection (6) includes power to provide for calculation or verification—

(a)   in such manner as may, in the particular case, be approved by a prescribed person; or

(b)   in accordance with guidance from time to time prepared by a prescribed person.

(8)   In section 342E and this section, references to the person responsible for a pension arrangement are to—

    (a)    the trustees, managers or provider of the arrangement, or

    (b)    the person having functions in relation to the arrangement corresponding to those of a trustee, manager or provider.

(9)   In this section—

    "prescribed" means prescribed by regulations;

    "regulations" means regulations made by the Secretary of State.

(10)   Regulations under this section may—

    (a)    make different provision for different cases;

    (b)    contain such incidental, supplemental and transitional provisions as appear to the Secretary of State necessary or expedient.

(11)   Regulations under this section shall be made by statutory instrument subject to annulment in pursuance of a resolution of either House of Parliament.

**Amendments**—Inserted by Welfare Reform and Pensions Act 1999, s 84(1), Sch 12, Pt II, paras 70, 71. Amended by Pensions Act 2007, s 17, Sch 5, para 4.

**General note**—See the general note to s 342A.

## [1.469]

### 343 Extortionate credit transactions

(1)   This section applies where a person is made bankrupt who is or has been a party to a transaction for, or involving, the provision to him of credit.

(2)   The court may, on the application of the trustee of the bankrupt's estate, make an order with respect to the transaction if the transaction is or was extortionate and was not entered into more than 3 years before the commencement of the bankruptcy.

(3)   For the purposes of this section a transaction is extortionate if, having regard to the risk accepted by the person providing the credit—

    (a)    the terms of it are or were such as to require grossly exorbitant payments to be made (whether unconditionally or in certain contingencies) in respect of the provision of the credit, or

    (b)    it otherwise grossly contravened ordinary principles of fair dealing;

and it shall be presumed, unless the contrary is proved, that a transaction with respect to which an application is made under this section is or, as the case may be, was extortionate.

(4)   An order under this section with respect to any transaction may contain such one or more of the following as the court thinks fit, that is to say—

    (a)    provision setting aside the whole or part of any obligation created by the transaction;

    (b)    provision otherwise varying the terms of the transaction or varying the terms on which any security for the purposes of the transaction is held;

    (c)    provision requiring any person who is or was party to the transaction to pay to the trustee any sums paid to that person, by virtue of the transaction, by the bankrupt;

    (d)    provision requiring any person to surrender to the trustee any property held by him as security for the purposes of the transaction;

    (e)    provision directing accounts to be taken between any persons.

(5)   Any sums or property required to be paid or surrendered to the trustee in accordance with an order under this section shall be comprised in the bankrupt's estate.

(6)   The powers conferred by this section are exercisable in relation to any transaction concurrently with any powers exercisable under this Act in relation to that transaction as a transaction at an undervalue.

**Amendments**—Consumer Credit Act 2006, s 70, Sch 4; Enterprise and Regulatory Reform Act 2013, s 71(3), Sch 19, paras 1, 36.

**General note**—These provisions allow a trustee to apply to the court for relief under s 343(2) and (4) in relation to any credit transaction entered into by the bankrupt in the 3 years prior to the making of the bankruptcy order on the grounds that the transaction is or was extortionate. As such, these provisions bear a close resemblance to the former s 139(1)(a) of the Consumer Credit Act 1974 which allowed a debtor to apply to the court to re-open a credit agreement on the grounds that what is termed therein a 'credit bargain' is extortionate (now repealed and replaced by a new regime governing 'unfair consumer credit relationships' in ss 140A–140C of the Consumer Credit Act 1974 inserted by the Consumer Credit Act 2006, s 19).

It appears from *Davies v Directloans Ltd* [1986] 1 WLR 823 (a case decided under the Consumer Credit Act 1974) that the court is limited to having regard to those factors in s 343(3) alone in assessing whether a transaction is extortionate. In reversing the usual position the subsection places the burden of proof on the other party to the transaction in establishing that the transaction was not extortionate.

Section 343(6) confirms that, notwithstanding s 343, a trustee retains standing to challenge a credit transaction as a transaction-at-undervalue under s 339, but not, apparently, as a preference under s 340.

The commentary on the analogous provision in s 244, applicable in liquidations, should also be considered here.

## [1.470]

### 344 Avoidance of general assignment of book debts

(1)   The following applies where a person engaged in any business makes a general assignment to another person of his existing or future book debts, or any class of them, and is subsequently made bankrupt.

(2)   The assignment is void against the trustee of the bankrupt's estate as regards book debts which were not paid before the making of the bankruptcy application or (as the case may be) the presentation of the bankruptcy petition, unless the assignment has been registered under the Bills of Sale Act 1878.

(3)   For the purposes of subsections (1) and (2)—

   (a)   "assignment" includes an assignment by way of security or charge on book debts, and

   (b)   "general assignment" does not include—

      (i)   an assignment of book debts due at the date of the assignment from specified debtors or of debts becoming due under specified contracts, or

      (ii)   an assignment of book debts included either in a transfer of a business made in good faith and for value or in an assignment of assets for the benefit of creditors generally.

(4)   For the purposes of registration under the Act of 1878 an assignment of book debts is to be treated as if it were a bill of sale given otherwise than by way of security for the payment of a sum of money; and the provisions of that Act with respect to the registration of bills of sale apply accordingly with such necessary modifications as may be made by rules under that Act.

**Amendments**—Enterprise and Regulatory Reform Act 2013, s 71(3), Sch 19, paras 1, 37.

**General note**—This provision renders void a general assignment of book debts, a term which includes an assignment by way of security or charge of book debts, to the extent that such book debts were not paid before the making of the bankruptcy application or the presentation of a bankruptcy petition other than where the assignment was registered under the Bills of Sale Act 1878. A specific assignment of particular debts falls outside of the provision, as does an assignment effected in the transfer of a business made in good faith or an assignment for the benefit of creditors generally, as might arise in the context of an IVA: s 344(3).

If, prior to bankruptcy, an individual enters into a general assignment of book debts and subsequently enters into a specific assignment of particular book debts, then s 344 will render the general assignment void but will not affect the specific assignment: *Hill v Alex Lawrie Factors* [2000] BPIR 1038 (Jacob J).

## [1.471]

### 345 Contracts to which bankrupt is a party

(1)   The following applies where a contract has been made with a person who is subsequently made bankrupt.

(2) The court may, on the application of any other party to the contract, make an order discharging obligations under the contract on such terms as to payment by the applicant or the bankrupt of damages for non-performance or otherwise as appear to the court to be equitable.

(3) Any damages payable by the bankrupt by virtue of an order of the court under this section are provable as a bankruptcy debt.

(4) Where an undischarged bankrupt is a contractor in respect of any contract jointly with any person, that person may sue or be sued in respect of the contract without the joinder of the bankrupt.

**Amendments**—Enterprise and Regulatory Reform Act 2013, s 71(3), Sch 19, paras 1, 38.

**General note**—It is a long-established rule at common law that a contract is not determined by the bankruptcy of one of the parties to the agreement: *Ex parte Chalmers* (1873) LR 8 Ch App 289, CA. Whilst a trustee might disclaim a contract as onerous property under s 315(2), the present provision allows the other party to the contract to make an application to court for an order discharging obligations under the contract on terms envisaged by s 345(2). Subsection (3) then permits that party to prove for any damages payable by virtue of the court's order as a bankruptcy debt.

In practice, s 345 will often have no application, particularly where the parties contract on the basis of detailed standard form terms, since commercial contracts frequently provide for automatic termination, together with the agreed consequences thereof, on bankruptcy or even the presentation of a bankruptcy petition or, equally commonly, stipulated events in connection with an IVA proposal.

## [1.472]

### 346 Enforcement procedures

(1) Subject to section 285 in Chapter II (restrictions on proceedings and remedies) and to the following provisions of this section, where the creditor of any person who is made bankrupt has, before the commencement of the bankruptcy—

    (a)    issued execution against the goods or land of that person, or

    (b)    attached a debt due to that person from another person,

that creditor is not entitled, as against the official receiver or trustee of the bankrupt's estate, to retain the benefit of the execution or attachment, or any sums paid to avoid it, unless the execution or attachment was completed, or the sums were paid, before the commencement of the bankruptcy.

(1A) For the purposes of this section, Her Majesty's Revenue and Customs is to be regarded as having attached a debt due to a person if it has taken action under Part 1 of Schedule 8 to the Finance (No 2) Act 2015 (enforcement by deduction from accounts) as a result of which an amount standing to the credit of an account held by that person is—

    (a)    subject to arrangements made under paragraph 6(3) of that Schedule, or

    (b)    the subject of a deduction notice under paragraph 13 of that Schedule.

(2) Subject as follows, where any goods of a person have been taken in execution, then, if before the completion of the execution notice is given to the enforcement officer or other officer charged with the execution that that person has been made bankrupt—

    (a)    the enforcement officer or other officer shall on request deliver to the official receiver or trustee of the bankrupt's estate the goods and any money seized or recovered in part satisfaction of the execution, but

    (b)    the costs of the execution are a first charge on the goods or money so delivered and the official receiver or trustee may sell the goods or a sufficient part of them for the purpose of satisfying the charge.

(3) Subject to subsection (6) below, where—

    (a)    under an execution in respect of a judgment for a sum exceeding such sum as may be prescribed for the purposes of this subsection, the goods of any person are sold or money is paid in order to avoid a sale, and

    (b)    before the end of the period of 14 days beginning with the day of the sale or payment the enforcement officer or other officer charged with the execution is given notice that a bankruptcy application has been made or a bankruptcy petition has been presented in relation to that person, and

    (c)    a bankruptcy order is or has been made as a result of that application or on that petition,

the balance of the proceeds of sale or money paid, after deducting the costs of execution, shall (in priority to the claim of the execution creditor) be comprised in the bankrupt's estate.

(4) Accordingly, in the case of an execution in respect of a judgment for a sum exceeding the sum prescribed for the purposes of subsection (3), the enforcement officer or other officer charged with the execution—

    (a)    shall not dispose of the balance mentioned in subsection (3) at any time within the period of 14 days so mentioned or while proceedings on a bankruptcy application are ongoing or (as the case may be) there is pending a bankruptcy petition of which he has been given notice under that subsection, and

    (b)    shall pay that balance, where by virtue of that subsection it is comprised in the bankrupt's estate, to the official receiver or (if there is one) to the trustee of that estate.

(5) For the purposes of this section—

    (a)    an execution against goods is completed by seizure and sale or by the making of a charging order under section 1 of the Charging Orders Act 1979;

    (b)    an execution against land is completed by seizure, by the appointment of a receiver or by the making of a charging order under that section;

    (c)    an attachment of a debt is completed by the receipt of the debt.

(6) The rights conferred by subsections (1) to (3) on the official receiver or the trustee may, to such extent and on such terms as it thinks fit, be set aside by the court in favour of the creditor who has issued the execution or attached the debt.

(7) Nothing in this section entitles the trustee of a bankrupt's estate to claim goods from a person who has acquired them in good faith under a sale by an enforcement officer or other officer charged with an execution.

(8) Neither subsection (2) nor subsection (3) applies in relation to any execution against property which has been acquired by or has devolved upon the bankrupt since the commencement of the bankruptcy, unless, at the time the execution is issued or before it is completed—

    (a)    the property has been or is claimed for the bankrupt's estate under section 307 (after-acquired property), and

    (b)    a copy of the notice given under that section has been or is served on the enforcement officer or other officer charged with the execution.

(9) In this section "enforcement officer" means an individual who is authorised to act as an enforcement officer under the Courts Act 2003.

**Amendments**—Courts Act 2003, s 109(1), Sch 8, para 297(1)–(4); Enterprise and Regulatory Reform Act 2013, s 71(3), Sch 19, paras 1, 39; Finance (No 2) Act 2015, s 51, Sch 8, Pt 2, paras 26, 32.

**General note**—These provisions provide, in fairly elaborate terms, for the circumstances in which a creditor is entitled to retain the benefit of an execution or attachment where the execution was issued or debt due attached prior to the commencement of the bankruptcy (ie the date of the bankruptcy order: s 278(a)). The court may also stay an execution under s 285(1) or (2). Section 285(3)(a) expressly provides that a creditor has no remedy against the property or person of a bankrupt after the making of a bankruptcy order, a provision which, in contrast to s 285(3)(b), is not subject to contrary leave of the court.

The commentary on the analogous provisions in liquidation in ss 183 and 184 will also be of assistance here albeit it should be noted that in liquidation the 'commencement' of the winding up means the date of presentation of the petition (s 129) not the date of the order as in bankruptcy.

See *State Bank of India v Mallya* [2019] EWHC 995 (QB) where Master Cook adjourned an application for an interim third party debt order to be made final where a bankruptcy petition had been presented, holding that the existence of the bankruptcy petition was relevant to the court's discretion to make the order final.

**The sum prescribed for the purposes of s 346(3) and (4)**—With effect from 1 April 2004 the sum prescribed is £1,000 by virtue of the Insolvency Proceedings (Monetary Limits) (Amendment) Order 2004 (SI 2004/547).

**Challenge to execution or attachment completed before the commencement of the bankruptcy**—Despite the terms of s 346(1), a trustee may challenge a charging order absolute or a garnishee order absolute, particularly where any such order was obtained only a short period prior to the making of the bankruptcy order, as can arise in practice where a bankruptcy petition is not presented in the same court as that in which the order absolute is obtained. The trustee's standing to challenge an order absolute arises under CPR 40.9: *Industrial Diseases Compensation Ltd v Marrons* [2001] BPIR 600 at 606C–606F (HHJ Behrens sitting as a High Court judge) and/or s 3(5) of the Charging Orders Act 1979 (*Nationwide Building Society v Wright* [2009] EWCA Civ 811, [2010] Ch 318, [2009] 2 BCLC 695). On an application to set aside an order absolute, the legislative intention which underlies s 346(1) should be borne in mind: that a judgment creditor who has obtained a final charging order before the making of a bankruptcy order is not to be deprived of his security by reason of the bankruptcy alone. Some additional feature is needed before it could be appropriate for a court to exercise its discretion to set aside the order (*Nationwide Building Society v Wright*).

**Application by creditor to set aside rights conferred on official receiver or trustee under s 346(6)**—See *Tagore Investments SA v Official Receiver* [2008] EWHC 3495 (Ch), [2009] BPIR 392 – this jurisdiction should only be exercised in exceptional cases owing to the need to respect the pari passu rule. The onus of proving that exceptional circumstances exist that produce unfairness which is a heavy burden, lies on the applicant. On the exceptional facts of the case (bankrupt had misled the court prior to judgment, his petition for bankruptcy was a pre-planned act of manipulation, the applicant had not delayed in enforcing judgment and there were few unsecured creditors) the application was granted.

**Procedure**—The assessment of a sheriff's bill for the purposes of s 346(2) or (3) is governed by r 12.44.

## [1.473]

### 347 Distress, etc

(1)   CRAR (the power of commercial rent arrears recovery under section 72(1) of the Tribunals, Courts and Enforcement Act 2007) is exercisable where the tenant is an undischarged bankrupt (subject to sections 252(2)(b) and 254(1) above and subsection (5) below) against goods and effects comprised in the bankrupt's estate, but only for 6 months' rent accrued due before the commencement of the bankruptcy.

(2)   Where CRAR has been exercised to recover rent from an individual to whom a bankruptcy application or a bankruptcy petition relates and a bankruptcy order is subsequently made as a result of that application or on that petition, any amount recovered by way of CRAR which—

    (a)    is in excess of the amount which by virtue of subsection (1) would have been recoverable after the commencement of the bankruptcy, or

    (b)    is in respect of rent for a period or part of a period after goods were taken control of under CRAR,

shall be held for the bankrupt as part of his estate.

(3)   Subsection (3A) applies where—

    (a)    any person (whether or not a landlord or person entitled to rent) has distrained upon the goods or effects of an individual who is adjudged bankrupt before the end of the period of 3 months beginning with the distraint, or

    (b)    Her Majesty's Revenue and Customs has been paid any amount from an account of an individual under Part 1 of Schedule 8 to the Finance (No 2) Act 2015 (enforcement by deduction from accounts) and the individual is adjudged bankrupt before the end of the period of 3 months beginning with the payment.

(3A)   Where this subsection applies—

    (a)    in a case within subsection (3)(a), the goods or effects, or the proceeds of their sale, and

    (b)    in a case within subsection (3)(b), the amount in question,

is charged for the benefit of the bankrupt's estate with the preferential debts of the bankrupt to the extent that the bankrupt's estate is for the time being insufficient for meeting them.

(4)   Where by virtue of any charge under subsection (3A) any person surrenders any goods or effects to the trustee of a bankrupt's estate or makes a payment to such a

trustee, that person ranks, in respect of the amount of the proceeds of the sale of those goods or effects by the trustee or, as the case may be, the amount of the payment, as a preferential creditor of the bankrupt, except as against so much of the bankrupt's estate as is available for the payment of preferential creditors by virtue of the surrender or payment.

(5)   CRAR is not exercisable at any time after the discharge of a bankrupt against any goods or effects comprised in the bankrupt's estate.

(6)   . . .

(7)   . . .

(8)   Subject to sections 252(2)(b) and 254(1) above nothing in this Group of Parts affects any right to distrain otherwise than for rent; and any such right is at any time exercisable without restriction against property comprised in a bankrupt's estate, even if that right is expressed by any enactment to be exercisable in like manner as a right to distrain for rent.

(9)   Any right to distrain against property comprised in a bankrupt's estate is exercisable notwithstanding that the property has vested in the trustee.

(10)   The provisions of this section are without prejudice to a landlord's right in a bankruptcy to prove for any bankruptcy debt in respect of rent.

(11)   . . .

**Amendments**—Insolvency Act 2000, s 3, Sch 3, paras 1, 14(a), (b); Courts Act 2003, s 109(1), (4), Sch 8, para 298(1)–(3); Tribunals, Courts and Enforcement Act 2007, ss 86, 146, Sch 14, para 44, Sch 23, Pt 4; Enterprise and Regulatory Reform Act 2013, s 71(3), Sch 19, paras 1, 40; Finance (No 2) Act 2015, s 51, Sch 8, Pt 2, paras 26, 33.

**General note**—These intricate provisions provide, essentially, in s 347(1), that bankruptcy has no effect on the right of a landlord or other person to whom rent is payable to distrain upon the goods and effects of an undischarged bankrupt, save that the distraint is limited to 6 months' rent accrued due before the bankruptcy order. The fact that the bankrupt's estate will have vested in the trustee under s 306, or conceivably under ss 307 or 310, is immaterial: s 347(9). Sections 347(2)–(10) follow from the basic rule in s 347(1). Three particular points warrant mention. First, the combined effect of s 347(3) and (4) is to create a statutory charge to secure preferential debts over the goods or effects distrained upon, or the proceeds of sale thereof, consequential upon which the landlord or person entitled to rent is subrogated to the position of the preferential creditors so secured for an equivalent sum. Secondly, the discharge of a bankrupt terminates the right of a landlord or other person to distrain upon any goods or effects comprised in the bankrupt's estate: s 347(5). Thirdly, s 347(10) makes clear that a landlord retains standing to prove for outstanding rent as a bankruptcy debt. However, whilst a landlord is not precluded from distraining by virtue of submitting a proof in respect of rent, the landlord is put to election as between a dividend and distraint at the time the dividend becomes payable: *Holmes v Watt* [1935] 2 KB 300, CA.

**[1.474]**

## 348 Apprenticeships, etc

(1)   This section applies where—

(a)   a bankruptcy order is made in respect of an individual to whom another individual was an apprentice or articled clerk at the time when the application for the order was made or (as the case may be) the petition for the order was presented, and

(b)   the bankrupt or the apprentice or clerk gives notice to the trustee terminating the apprenticeship or articles.

(2)   Subject to subsection (6) below, the indenture of apprenticeship or, as the case may be, the articles of agreement shall be discharged with effect from the commencement of the bankruptcy.

(3)   If any money has been paid by or on behalf of the apprentice or clerk to the bankrupt as a fee, the trustee may, on an application made by or on behalf of the apprentice or clerk, pay such sum to the apprentice or clerk as the trustee thinks reasonable, having regard to—

(a)   the amount of the fee,

(b)    the proportion of the period in respect of which the fee was paid that has been served by the apprentice or clerk before the commencement of the bankruptcy, and

(c)    the other circumstances of the case.

(4)   The power of the trustee to make a payment under subsection (3) has priority over his obligation to distribute the bankrupt's estate.

(5)   Instead of making a payment under subsection (3), the trustee may, if it appears to him expedient to do so on an application made by or on behalf of the apprentice or clerk, transfer the indenture or articles to a person other than the bankrupt.

(6)   Where a transfer is made under subsection (5), subsection (2) has effect only as between the apprentice or clerk and the bankrupt.

**Amendments**—Enterprise and Regulatory Reform Act 2013, s 71(3), Sch 19, paras 1, 41.

**General note**—These provisions are more or less self-explanatory and are rarely applicable in practice. For the payment to an apprentice or articled clerk from the National Insurance Fund see ss 182 and 184 of the Employment Rights Act 1996.

## [1.475]

### 349 Unenforceability of liens on books, etc

(1)   Subject as follows, a lien or other right to retain possession of any of the books, papers or other records of a bankrupt is unenforceable to the extent that its enforcement would deny possession of any books, papers or other records to the official receiver or the trustee of the bankrupt's estate.

(2)   Subsection (1) does not apply to a lien on documents which give a title to property and are held as such.

**General note**—See commentary on s 246, which is identical in substance to s 349.

## [1.476]

### 349A Arbitration agreements to which bankrupt is party

(1)   This section applies where a bankrupt had become party to a contract containing an arbitration agreement before the commencement of his bankruptcy.

(2)   If the trustee in bankruptcy adopts the contract, the arbitration agreement is enforceable by or against the trustee in relation to matters arising from or connected with the contract.

(3)   If the trustee in bankruptcy does not adopt the contract and a matter to which the arbitration agreement applies requires to be determined in connection with or for the purposes of the bankruptcy proceedings—

(a)    the trustee with the consent of the creditors' committee, or

(b)    any other party to the agreement,

may apply to the court which may, if it thinks fit in all the circumstances of the case, order that the matter be referred to arbitration in accordance with the arbitration agreement.

(4)   In this section—

"arbitration agreement" has the same meaning as in Part I of the Arbitration Act 1996; and

"the court" means the court which has jurisdiction in the bankruptcy proceedings.

**Amendments**—Inserted by Arbitration Act 1996, s 107(1), Sch 3, para 46.

## CHAPTER VI

### BANKRUPTCY OFFENCES

## [1.477]

Reference should be had to the introduction to Chapter X of Part IV of the Act.

*Preliminary*

**[1.478]**

**350 Scheme of this Chapter**

(1) Subject to section 360(3) below, this Chapter applies—

    (a)    where an adjudicator has made a bankruptcy order as a result of a bankruptcy application, or

    (b)    where the court has made a bankruptcy order on a bankruptcy petition.

(2) This Chapter applies whether or not the bankruptcy order is annulled, but proceedings for an offence under this Chapter shall not be instituted after the annulment.

(3) Without prejudice to his liability in respect of a subsequent bankruptcy, the bankrupt is not guilty of an offence under this Chapter in respect of anything done after his discharge; but nothing in this Group of Parts prevents the institution of proceedings against a discharged bankrupt for an offence committed before his discharge.

(3A) Subsection (3) is without prejudice to any provision of this Chapter which applies to a person in respect of whom a bankruptcy restrictions order is in force.

(4) It is not a defence in proceedings for an offence under this Chapter that anything relied on, in whole or in part, as constituting that offence was done outside England and Wales.

(5) Proceedings for an offence under this Chapter or under the rules shall not be instituted except by the Secretary of State or by or with the consent of the Director of Public Prosecutions.

(6) A person guilty of an offence under this Chapter is liable to imprisonment or a fine, or both.

**Amendments**—Enterprise Act 2002, s 257(3), Sch 21, para 2; Enterprise and Regulatory Reform Act 2013, s 71(3), Sch 19, paras 1, 42.

**General note**—This provision, together with the definitions in s 351, relates to those offences in ss 353–360.

Under s 350(2) proceedings for an offence are not affected by an annulment provided that the proceedings are instituted prior to the annulment. On the other hand, by virtue of s 350(3), proceedings may be instituted irrespective of discharge, but only in respect of an offence committed prior to discharge.

**Human rights**—On the question of whether the Human Rights Act 1998 can operate in a retrospective way to render unsafe convictions which were unimpeachable at the date of trial see the survey of the law expressed in the opinions of the House of Lords in *R v Kansal* [2001] UKHL 62, [2002] BPIR 370.

**Documentary evidence relied upon by the Crown**—In *Re Attorney General's Reference (No 7 of 2000)* [2001] EWCA Crim 888, [2001] 1 WLR 1879, [2001] BPIR 953 the Criminal Division of the Court of Appeal held that a bankrupt's right to a fair trial under Art 6 of the European Convention on Human Rights was not breached where the Crown relied upon documents which had been delivered to the official receiver under s 291(1)(b) (duties of bankrupt in relation to official receiver) where the delivery up had been made under compulsion but where the documents did not contain any statement made by the bankrupt under compulsion.

**Other offences**—Rule 1.56 of and Sch 3 to IR 2016 (formerly r 12.18 and Sch 5, IR 1986) creates a further offence of falsely claiming to be a creditor, member or contributory of a company entitled to inspection of a document to gain sight of it.

**Penalties**—See s 430 and Sch 10. For consideration of sentencing: see *R v Theivendran (Sundranpillai)* (1992) 13 Cr App R(S) 601 and *R v Claire Elizabeth Hilsdon* [2021] EWCA Crim 52 – if a contravention is flagrant, a custodial sentence would in principle be appropriate. Rule 0.6 of and Sch 3 to IR 2016 deal with the punishment of offences under the rules.

**[1.479]**

**351 Definitions**

In the following provisions of this Chapter—

    (a)    references to property comprised in the bankrupt's estate or to property possession of which is required to be delivered up to the official receiver or the trustee of the bankrupt's estate include any property which would be such property if a notice in respect of it were given under section 307 (after-acquired property), section 308 (personal property and effects of bankrupt having more than replacement value) or section 308A (vesting in trustee of certain tenancies);

(b) "the initial period" means the period between the making of the bankruptcy application or (as the case may be) the presentation of the bankruptcy petition and the commencement of the bankruptcy;

(c) . . .

**Amendments**—Housing Act 1988, s 140, Sch 17, Part I; Enterprise and Regulatory Reform Act 2013, s 71(3), Sch 19, paras 1, 43.

**General note**—The offences in ss 353–359 should be read with references to these definitions. The definition in s 351(a) extends the basic definition of the bankruptcy estate in s 283(1).

## [1.480]

### 352 Defence of innocent intention

Where in the case of an offence under any provision of this Chapter it is stated that this section applies, a person is not guilty of the offence if he proves that, at the time of the conduct constituting the offence, he had no intent to defraud or to conceal the state of his affairs.

**General note**—The effect of this provision is to bring the availability of the defence of innocent intention into play in the case of any of the offences in ss 353–359 in which reference to s 352 is made. The defence will not, therefore, be available to defendants in proceedings instituted under ss 354(3), 356(2), 359(2) and 360(1).

**The burden of proof**—In *R v Daniel* [2002] EWCA Crim 959, [2002] BPIR 1193 the Court of Appeal (Auld LJ, Newman and Roderick-Evans JJ) held at [31] and [36] that, in the context of an appeal against conviction under s 354(1)(b), the burden of proof in establishing concealment rests with the prosecution but, once discharged, and for the purpose of the defence of innocent intention, the burden of proof then switches to the defendant, who must establish on the balance of probabilities that he did not intend to conceal the property. Whether s 352 imposes a legal burden or an evidential burden depends on which provision in ss 353–360 it is being applied to because, whilst the ordinary meaning is to impose a legal burden, this must be read down as imposing only an evidential burden where imposing a legal burden would infringe Article 6(2) of the European Convention on Human Rights: *Attorney-General's Reference (No 1 of 2004)*; *R v Edwards* [2004] EWCA Crim 1025, [2004] BPIR 1073 (which can be said to be supported by comments in *Sheldrake v DPP* [2004] UKHL 43, [2005] 1 AC 264 and in particular those of Lord Bingham). In *Attorney-General's Reference (No 1 of 2004)* the Court of Appeal held that when applied in the context of an offence under s 353(1)(b) it imposes a legal burden but in the context of an offence under s 357 it imposes only an evidential burden. In *R v Daniel* the Court of Appeal held that when applied in the context of s 354(1)(b) it would only impose an evidential burden but only because it felt bound to follow the decision in *R v Carass* [2001] EWCA Crim 2845. Since *R v Carass* was impliedly overruled in *Attorney-General's Reference (No 1 of 2004)* and disapproved in *Sheldrake v DPP* it is submitted that the burden imposed in the context of s 354(1)(b) is legal. In *Department of Business, Innovation and Skills v Compton* [2012] BPIR 1108, the magistrates' court held that s 352 imposed an evidential burden when applied to s 357(1) but a legal burden when applied to s 356(1).

*Wrongdoing by the bankrupt before and after bankruptcy*

## [1.481]

### 353 Non-disclosure

(1) The bankrupt is guilty of an offence if—

(a) he does not to the best of his knowledge and belief disclose all the property comprised in his estate to the official receiver or the trustee, or

(b) he does not inform the official receiver or the trustee of any disposal of any property which but for the disposal would be so comprised, stating how, when, to whom and for what consideration the property was disposed of.

(2) Subsection (1)(b) does not apply to any disposal in the ordinary course of a business carried on by the bankrupt or to any payment of the ordinary expenses of the bankrupt or his family.

(3)   Section 352 applies to this offence.

General note—This provision reproduces the provision in s 154(1) of the Bankruptcy Act 1914. For convictions under ss 353 and 354 see *R v Edwards* [2010] EWCA Crim 1682 where the bankrupt was convicted for the non-disclosure of a credit balance in a current account. Note *Williams v Mohammed* [2011] EWHC 3293 (Ch), [2011] BPIR 1787 where HHJ Hodge QC upheld an order that the bankrupt deliver up an attendance note of a meeting between himself and his solicitor on the basis that the usual privilege attaching to the document had been abrogated by the iniquity exception: the bankrupts underlying purpose in seeking advice at the meeting was to attempt to conceal from the trustee assets comprised in his estate (contrary to s 353 and s 354).

The judgment in *Re Bolus* (1870) 23 LT 339 considers the phrase 'in the ordinary course of business' in the context of the now repealed s 11 of the Debtors Act 1969, although the antiquity of that authority and the new legislative code in the 1986 Act, as amended, really call for a more contemporary judicial view on the point.

Defence of innocent intention—See the notes to s 352. See also *R v Edwards* [2010] EWCA Crim 1682 where the defence was not established.

## [1.482]

### 354   Concealment of property

(1)   The bankrupt is guilty of an offence if—

- (a)   he does not deliver up possession to the official receiver or trustee, or as the official receiver or trustee may direct, of such part of the property comprised in his estate as is in his possession or under his control and possession of which he is required by law so to deliver up,
- (b)   he conceals any debt due to or from him or conceals any property the value of which is not less than the prescribed amount and possession of which he is required to deliver up to the official receiver or trustee, or
- (c)   in the 12 months before the making of the bankruptcy application or (as the case may be) the presentation of the bankruptcy petition, or in the initial period, he did anything which would have been an offence under paragraph (b) above if the bankruptcy order had been made immediately before he did it.

Section 352 applies to this offence.

(2)   The bankrupt is guilty of an offence if he removes, or in the initial period removed, any property the value of which was not less than the prescribed amount and possession of which he has or would have been required to deliver up to the official receiver or the trustee.

Section 352 applies to this offence.

(3)   The bankrupt is guilty of an offence if he without reasonable excuse fails, on being required to do so by the official receiver, the trustee or the court—

- (a)   to account for the loss of any substantial part of his property incurred in the 12 months before the making of the bankruptcy application or (as the case may be) the presentation of the bankruptcy petition or in the initial period, or
- (b)   to give a satisfactory explanation of the manner in which such a loss was incurred.

Amendments—Enterprise Act 2002, s 269, Sch 23, paras 1, 12; Enterprise and Regulatory Reform Act 2013, s 71(3), Sch 19, paras 1, 44.

General note—The offences within this provision are closely related to those in s 353 and references should be made to the notes thereto. See also the notes accompanying s 206. For the purposes of the Human Rights Act 1998 s 354 is indistinguishable from s 206: *R v Daniel* [2002] EWCA Crim 959).

'conceals'—See the note to s 206.

The direction of the jury in a s 354(2) case—Using assets which ought to have been delivered up to pay a debt which is not provable would be committing an offence under s 354(2): *Woodley v Woodley (No 2)* [1994] 1 WLR 1167.

### SECTION 354(2)

'  . . .   the prescribed amount   . . . '—With effect from 1 April 2004 the prescribed amount was increased from £500 to £1,000 under the Insolvency Proceedings (Monetary Limits) (Amendment) Order 2004 (SI 2004/547).

SECTION 354(3)

**Failure to account for loss**—In the words of Sachs LJ in *R v Salter* [1968] 2 QB 793 at 809, in commenting on the similarly worded predecessor to s 354(2), this provision:

'intends to and does, in the interests of the business community as a whole, put in peril the man who goes bankrupt without having so conducted his affairs as to be able satisfactorily to explain why some substantial loss has been incurred. It is as well to make it plain, as the offence is absolute, it follows that, once a prosecution has been initiated, no issue arises before verdict as to the reason why the failure has occurred or as to any motive which led to that failure.'

A jury should be directed that an offence has been committed if they are satisfied, as regards the total sum of money constituting the loss of any substantial part of his estate, that the bankrupt had not at the time of the alleged failure given, with such reasonable details as was appropriate in the circumstances, an explanation which is both reasonably clear and true of how such sum was made up (as the loss may be composed of more than one component), of how it came to be lost, and where the money has gone. The degree of particularity required of the bankrupt will depend on the facts of the case and may vary greatly between cases.

**Human rights**—Given the public interest served by the investigation and realisation of assets caught by the bankruptcy estate, the Court of Appeal held in *R v Kearns* [2002] EWCA Crim 748, [2002] 1 WLR 2815 that s 354(3) is proportionate to the extent that a bankrupt is deprived of his right to silence or a right against self-incrimination, with the consequence that a prosecution under that provision does not violate an individual's right to a fair trial under Art 6 of the European Convention on Human Rights.

**Defence of innocent intention in s 354(1) and (2)**—See the notes to s 352.

## [1.483]

### 355 Concealment of books and papers; falsification

(1) The bankrupt is guilty of an offence if he does not deliver up possession to the official receiver or the trustee, or as the official receiver or trustee may direct, of all books, papers and other records of which he has possession or control and which relate to his estate or his affairs.

Section 352 applies to this offence.

(2) The bankrupt is guilty of an offence if—

    (a)    he prevents, or in the initial period prevented, the production of any books, papers or records relating to his estate or affairs;

    (b)    he conceals, destroys, mutilates or falsifies, or causes or permits the concealment, destruction, mutilation or falsification of, any books, papers or other records relating to his estate or affairs;

    (c)    he makes, or causes or permits the making of, any false entries in any book, document or record relating to his estate or affairs; or

    (d)    in the 12 months before the making of the bankruptcy application or (as the case may be) the presentation of the bankruptcy petition, or in the initial period, he did anything which would have been an offence under paragraph (b) or (c) above if the bankruptcy order had been made before he did it.

Section 352 applies to this offence.

(3) The bankrupt is guilty of an offence if—

    (a)    he disposes of, or alters or makes any omission in, or causes or permits the disposal, altering or making of any omission in, any book, document or record relating to his estate or affairs, or

    (b)    in the 12 months before the making of the bankruptcy application or (as the case may be) the presentation of the bankruptcy petition, or in the initial period, he did anything which would have been an offence under paragraph (a) if the bankruptcy order had been made before he did it.

Section 352 applies to this offence.

(4) In their application to a trading record subsections (2)(d) and (3)(b) shall have effect as if the reference to 12 months were a reference to two years.

(5) In subsection (4) "trading record" means a book, document or record which shows or explains the transactions or financial position of a person's business, including—

    (a)    a periodic record of cash paid and received,

(b)    a statement of periodic stock-taking, and

(c)    except in the case of goods sold by way of retail trade, a record of goods sold and purchased which identifies the buyer and seller or enables them to be identified.

**Amendments**—Enterprise Act 2002, s 269, Sch 23, paras 1, 13; Enterprise and Regulatory Reform Act 2013, s 71(3), Sch 19, paras 1, 45.

**General note**—Section 355(4) and (5) took effect from 1 April 2004 and were introduced by s 269 of and Sch 23 to the Enterprise Act 2002. 'Books', 'papers' and 'records' extends to electronic records (s 436B and *R v Taylor* [2011] EWCA Crim 728, [2011] 1 WLR 1809 which dealt with the corporate equivalent in s 206(1)(c).

'**conceals**'—See the note to s 206.

**Defence of innocent intention in s 356(1)**—See the notes to s 352.

## [1.484]

### 356 False statements

(1)   The bankrupt is guilty of an offence if he makes or has made any material omission in any statement made under any provision in this Group of Parts and relating to his affairs.

Section 352 applies to this offence.

(2)   The bankrupt is guilty of an offence if—

(a)    knowing or believing that a false debt has been proved by any person under the bankruptcy, he fails to inform the trustee as soon as practicable; or

(b)    he attempts to account for any part of his property by fictitious losses or expenses; or

(c)    in connection with any creditors' decision procedure or deemed consent procedure in the 12 months before the making of the bankruptcy application or (as the case may be) the presentation of the bankruptcy petition or (whether or not in connection with such a procedure) at any time in the initial period, he did anything which would have been an offence under paragraph (b) if the bankruptcy order had been made before he did it; or

(d)    he is, or at any time has been, guilty of any false representation or other fraud for the purpose of obtaining the consent of his creditors, or any of them, to an agreement with reference to his affairs or to his bankruptcy.

**Amendments**—Enterprise and Regulatory Reform Act 2013, s 71(3), Sch 19, paras 1, 46; Small Business, Enterprise and Employment Act 2015, s 126, Sch 9, Pt 2, paras 60, 85.

**General note**—The defence of innocent intention under s 352 is not available in relation to any of the four offences provided for in s 356(2).

The offence in s 356(1) extends beyond bankruptcy to 'any statement made under any provision in this group of Parts' which relates to the bankrupt's affairs. It follows that a prosecution under s 356(1) may be instituted in relation to any material omission in any statement made in connection with the proposal for or approval of an individual voluntary arrangement under Part VIII.

Omissions from the statement of affairs required by s 288(1) are not actionable under s 5 of the Perjury Act 1911, which relates only to the making of a 'false statement'. Such omissions may, however, be actioned under s 356(1).

In *Re Johnson* (unreported, 12 April 2013, Bristol Crown Court) the bankrupt was sentenced to 4 months imprisonment, suspended for 18 months for a breach of s 356(2)(b).

See *DBIS v Compton* [2012] BPIR 1108 (DJ Davison sitting in the magistrates' court) for an example of how charges under this provision (and s 357) are dealt with by the criminal courts and discussion of the burden of proof.

In *R v Hussain* [2013] EWCA Crim 2243, [2014] 2 Cr App R (S) 15, the Court of Appeal held that a sentence of 8 months' imprisonment (reduced to six months for a guilty plea) was appropriate for a bankrupt who, in breach of ss 356 and 357, had transferred his residential property (worth £69,000) to his wife for no consideration less than 6 months before he petitioned for his own bankruptcy and failed to disclose the transfer in his statement of affairs.

**[1.485]**

### 357 Fraudulent disposal of property

(1) The bankrupt is guilty of an offence if he makes or causes to be made, or has in the period of 5 years ending with the commencement of the bankruptcy made or caused to be made, any gift or transfer of, or any charge on, his property.
Section 352 applies to this offence.

(2) The reference to making a transfer of or charge on any property includes causing or conniving at the levying of any execution against that property.

(3) The bankrupt is guilty of an offence if he conceals or removes, or has at any time before the commencement of the bankruptcy concealed or removed, any part of his property after, or within 2 months before, the date on which a judgment or order for the payment of money has been obtained against him, being a judgment or order which was not satisfied before the commencement of the bankruptcy.
Section 352 applies to this offence.

**General note**—Two separate offences are provided for in s 357(1) and (3). Section 357(2) refers to s 357(1).

At a practical level it is difficult to imagine proceedings being instituted under s 357(1) in the absence of civil proceedings alleging a transaction-at-undervalue and/or a preference under s 339 and/or s 340 or a transaction defrauding creditors under s 423, although any such civil claim is plainly not a prerequisite to criminal proceedings.

The burden that was placed on the bankrupt was evidential and not legal: *Attorney-General's Reference (No 1 of 2004); R v Edwards* [2004] EWCA Crim 1025, [2004] 1 WLR 2111, [2004] BPIR 1073. See also *DBIS v Compton* [2012] BPIR 1108 and the note to s 352.

**Penalties**—These are as provided for in ss 350 and 430 and Sch 10. In *R v Mungroo* [1998] BPIR 784 the Criminal Division of the Court of Appeal (McCowan LJ, Ognall and Sedley JJ) had no difficulty in upholding a short custodial sentence of 2 months imposed by a recorder in the Crown Court against a 44-year-old man of previously excellent character with a 20-year exemplary army career who had received a gratuity of £31,000 on leaving the service and who had used those monies to pay off debts, including gambling debts, debts due to family members and a debt incurred in putting an extension onto the family home, and who thereafter failed to provide information concerning the gratuity to the official receiver following a bankruptcy order based on a judgment debt which pre-dated the payment out of the gratuity. Giving the judgment of the court Ognall J pointed out at 78D–78E that, notwithstanding evidence of good character, in all normal circumstances conduct in contravention of s 357 crosses the custody threshold.

In *R v Hussain* [2013] EWCA Crim 2243, [2014] 2 Cr App R (S) 15, the Court of Appeal held that a sentence of 8 months' imprisonment (reduced to 6 months for a guilty plea) was appropriate for a bankrupt who, in breach of ss 356 and 357 had transferred his residential property (worth £69,000) to his wife for no consideration less than 6 months before he petitioned for his own bankruptcy and failed to disclose the transfer in his statement of affairs.

**Defence of innocent intention in s 357(1) and (3)**—See the notes to s 352.

**[1.486]**

### 358 Absconding

The bankrupt is guilty of an offence if—

(a) he leaves, or attempts or makes preparations to leave, England and Wales with any property the value of which is not less than the prescribed amount and possession of which he is required to deliver up to the official receiver or the trustee, or

(b) in the 6 months before the making of the bankruptcy application or (as the case may be) the presentation of the bankruptcy petition, or in the initial period, he did anything which would have been an offence under paragraph (a) if the bankruptcy order had been made immediately before he did it.

Section 352 applies to this offence.

**Amendments**—Enterprise and Regulatory Reform Act 2013, s 71(3), Sch 19, paras 1, 47.

**General note**—Despite its heading, it is sufficient for the commission of this offence that the bankrupt merely 'attempts or makes preparations' to leave the jurisdiction with property of the prescribed value. Under s 358(b) the offence may be committed in the 6-month period preceding presentation of the bankruptcy petition.

' . . . prescribed amount . . . '—The figure is modest. With effect from 1 April 2004 the amount was increased from £500 to £1,000 by the Insolvency Proceedings (Monetary Limits) (Amendment) Order 2004 (SI 2004/547).

**Defence of innocent intention**—See the notes to s 352.

## [1.487]

### 359 Fraudulent dealing with property obtained on credit

(1)   The bankrupt is guilty of an offence if, in the 12 months before the making of the bankruptcy application or (as the case may be) the presentation of the bankruptcy petition, or in the initial period, he disposed of any property which he had obtained on credit and, at the time he disposed of it, had not paid for.
Section 352 applies to this offence.

(2)   A person is guilty of an offence if, in the 12 months before the making of the bankruptcy application or (as the case may be) the presentation of the bankruptcy petition or in the initial period, he acquired or received property from the bankrupt knowing or believing—

    (a)    that the bankrupt owed money in respect of the property, and

    (b)    that the bankrupt did not intend, or was unlikely to be able, to pay the money he so owed.

(3)   A person is not guilty of an offence under subsection (1) or (2) if the disposal, acquisition or receipt of the property was in the ordinary course of a business carried on by the bankrupt at the time of the disposal, acquisition or receipt.

(4)   In determining for the purposes of this section whether any property is disposed of, acquired or received in the ordinary course of a business carried on by the bankrupt, regard may be had, in particular, to the price paid for the property.

(5)   In this section references to disposing of property include pawning or pledging it; and references to acquiring or receiving property shall be read accordingly.

**Amendments**—Enterprise and Regulatory Reform Act 2013, s 71(3), Sch 19, paras 1, 48.

**General note**—The purpose of the offences created by and sanctions imposed under this provision is in seeking to prevent an individual in financial difficulties, other than a person acting in the ordinary course of business, from obtaining property on credit and then disposing of that property – within the broad scope of s 359(5) – without paying for it. Those acquiring or receiving property from a bankrupt, subject to proof of the relevant state of mind in subsection (2), are also caught by the provisions.

Section 359(1) provides for an offence which may be committed by the bankrupt in the period commencing 12 months prior to presentation of the petition and ending with the bankruptcy order. Section 359(2) provides for a separate offence which comprises the actus reus of acquiring or receiving property from a bankrupt together with the mens rea of knowledge or belief as to those two matters in s 359(2)(a) and (b). No offence may be committed if the bankrupt acts in the ordinary course of business, as defined in s 359(3) and qualified in s 359(4).

**Defence of innocent intention in s 359(1)**—See the notes to s 352.

## [1.488]

### 360 Obtaining credit; engaging in business

(1)   The bankrupt is guilty of an offence if—

    (a)    either alone or jointly with any other person, he obtains credit to the extent of the prescribed amount or more without giving the person from whom he obtains it the relevant information about his status; or

    (b)    he engages (whether directly or indirectly) in any business under a name other than that in which he was made bankrupt without disclosing to all persons with whom he enters into any business transaction the name in which he was so made.

(2)   The reference to the bankrupt obtaining credit includes the following cases—

    (a)    where goods are bailed to him under a hire-purchase agreement, or agreed to be sold to him under a conditional sale agreement, and

    (b)    where he is paid in advance (whether in money or otherwise) for the supply of goods or services.

(3)   A person whose estate has been sequestrated in Scotland, or who has been adjudged bankrupt in Northern Ireland, is guilty of an offence if, before his discharge, he does anything in England and Wales which would be an offence under subsection (1) if he were an undischarged bankrupt and the sequestration of his estate or the adjudication in Northern Ireland were an adjudication under this Part.

(4)   For the purposes of subsection (1)(a), the relevant information about the status of the person in question is the information that he is an undischarged bankrupt or, as the case may be, that his estate has been sequestrated in Scotland and that he has not been discharged.

(5)   This section applies to the bankrupt after discharge while a bankruptcy restrictions order is in force in respect of him.

(6)   For the purposes of subsection (1)(a) as it applies by virtue of subsection (5), the relevant information about the status of the person in question is the information that a bankruptcy restrictions order is in force in respect of him.

**Amendments**—Enterprise Act 2002, s 257(3), Sch 21, para 3; Enterprise and Regulatory Reform Act 2013, s 71(3), Sch 19, paras 1, 49.

**General note**—There are two distinct offences in s 360(1)(a) and (b). The purpose of the provision in the former case is in affording protection to any third party advancing credit meeting the prescribed amount (see below) to whom a bankrupt must disclose his status. The latter provision also provides protection to third parties, in that a bankrupt is prohibited from engaging in business under any name other than that in which he was adjudged bankrupt without disclosing that name 'to all persons with whom he enters into any business transaction'. Strictly speaking, s 360(1)(b) does not preclude a bankrupt from engaging in business under a name other than his bankruptcy name, in that the disclosure obligation is only triggered on the entry into a business transaction.

No equivalent offences apply to a debtor subject to an individual voluntary arrangement.

**SECTION 360(1)**
'  . . .  **the prescribed amount**   . . .  '—With effect from 1 April 2004 the amount is £500 by virtue of the Insolvency Proceedings (Monetary Limits) (Amendment) Order 2004 (SI 2004/547).

**SECTION 360(1)(a)**
'  . . .  **the relevant information about his status**   . . .  '—The relevant information is that prescribed in s 360(4) and, perhaps surprisingly, given the form of words employed here, requires no more than the disclosure of the fact that the bankrupt is an undischarged bankrupt, or its Scottish equivalent.

**SECTION 360(1)(b)**
'  . . .  **any business transaction**   . . .  '—This term is not specifically defined in the legislation, although the term 'transaction' is defined in very broad, non-exhaustive terms in s 436 as including a gift, agreement or arrangement.

**Strict liability**—The predecessor to s 360(1), in the substantially similar s 155 of the Bankruptcy Act 1914, provided offences of strict liability: see *R v Duke of Leinster* [1924] 1 KB 311. The offence under s 360(1) is an absolute offence and does not require proof of dishonesty (*R v Mohammed Ramzan* [1998] 2 Cr App R 328). In *R v Scott* [1998] BPIR 471 the Supreme Court of South Australia, the Court of Criminal Appeal (Doyle CJ, Cox and Matheson JJ) held that an offence under s 369(1)(a) or (b) of the Australian Bankruptcy Act 1966, which creates offences very similar to those in s 360(1), were offences of strict liability. Consequently, all that was required was that the appellant had failed to disclose her status as an undischarged bankrupt to the provider of credit in that case. It was immaterial that the lender knew that she was an undischarged bankrupt, just as it was no defence for the appellant to say that she believed that the credit provider was aware that she was an undischarged bankrupt.

**SECTION 360(2)**
'  . . .  **obtaining credit**   . . .  '—Section 360(2) does no more than identify two forms of agreement and one form of arrangement, albeit in very general terms, which fall within the scope of the term 'obtaining credit'. Given the purpose of the provision, identified in the general note above, it is submitted that, subject to the prescribed amount, s 360(1)(a) will extend to the obtaining of any credit whatsoever. The absence of any express exclusion from the scope of the provision militates against any argument that any particular form of credit, say credit obtained in the course of the conduct of a bank account in overdraft, will fall outside the provision.

**Section 360(5) and (6)**—These provisions were introduced with effect from 1 April 2004 by s 257 of and Sch 21 to the Enterprise Act 2002; for commentary on BROs see the notes to s 281A.

## 361

*(Repealed)*

**General note**—This provision provided for offences in relation to a failure to maintain accounting records and was repealed with effect from 1 April 2004 by s 263 of the Enterprise Act 2002. The court may, however, take into account such conduct under para 2(2)(a) of Sch 4A in considering the making of a bankruptcy restrictions order under para 1 thereof, as discussed in the notes to s 281A, where such conduct is perpetrated on or after 1 April 2004.

## 362

*(Repealed)*

**General note**—This provision provided for offences in relation to gambling and to rash and hazardous speculations and was repealed with effect from 1 April 2004 by s 263 of the Enterprise Act 2002. The court may, however, take into account such conduct under para 2(2)(j) of Sch 4A in considering the making of a bankruptcy restrictions order under para 1 thereof, as discussed in the notes to s 281A, where such conduct is perpetrated on or after 1 April 2004.

## CHAPTER VII

### POWERS OF COURT IN BANKRUPTCY

**[1.489]**

### 363 General control of court

(1) Every bankruptcy is under the general control of the court and, subject to the provisions in this Group of Parts, the court has full power to decide all questions of priorities and all other questions, whether of law or fact, arising in any bankruptcy.

(2) Without prejudice to any other provision in this Group of Parts, an undischarged bankrupt or a discharged bankrupt whose estate is still being administered under Chapter IV of this Part shall do all such things as he may be directed to do by the court for the purposes of his bankruptcy or, as the case may be, the administration of that estate.

(3) The official receiver or the trustee of a bankrupt's estate may at any time apply to the court for a direction under subsection (2).

(4) If any person without reasonable excuse fails to comply with any obligation imposed on him by subsection (2), he is guilty of a contempt of court and liable to be punished accordingly (in addition to any other punishment to which he may be subject).

**General note**—These provisions subject all bankruptcies to the power of 'the court', as defined in s 385(1), and on which see ss 373 and 374 and the notes thereto. Section 363 allows for an application to court only by the official receiver or a trustee for the determination of issues within the very broadly cast s 363(1) or so as to require action of an undischarged or discharged bankrupt under s 363(2). The class of eligible applicants has nevertheless been held to be wider in scope: *Hardy v Buchler* [1997] BPIR 643. Subsection (1) should be read in conjunction with s 303(2). The former provision alone anticipates determination of any question of priorities of law or fact. Nothing equivalent to s 363(2) appears in s 303. Furthermore, only s 303(1) provides for an application by a dissatisfied bankrupt or any of his or her creditors.

As with s 303, the court's jurisdiction under s 363 is exercisable irrespective of whether a bankrupt is undischarged or discharged, or whether the bankruptcy has been annulled: *Engel v Peri* [2002] EWHC 799 (Ch), [2002] BPIR 961 (Ferris J).

A number of cases have considered the ambit of the court's 'full power' under s 363. Typically, s 363 provides a mechanism for the determination by the court of common issues as to, say, the ranking or validity of security, the extent of any particular interest in property comprised in the bankrupt's estate or issues of disputed fact relevant to the administration of the bankruptcy. In general, the ambit is very wide. Chief ICC Judge Briggs held in *Barker v Baxendale-Walker* [2018] EWHC 2518 (Ch) at [36] that it may even include contradicting language in the IA 1986 if to do so is just and convenient in aid of controlling the bankruptcy process.

**Examples of matters within s 363(1)**—

*Appointment.* The provision also extends to the appointment of an additional trustee: *Clements v Udal* [2001] BPIR 454. The court may appoint an insolvency practitioner to act as first trustee in bankruptcy (overriding the automatic appointment of the official receiver under s 291A of the IA 1986) provided that the court is satisfied that doing so will be beneficial to the creditors as a class: *Barker v Baxendale-Walker* [2018] EWHC 2518 (Ch) at [39]–[40] (Chief ICC Judge Briggs).

*Remuneration.* The court has jurisdiction under s 363(1), and under its inherent jurisdiction, to fix a trustee's remuneration although it is doubtful that s 303(2) extends to such an application: *Engel v Peri* [2002] BPIR 961 at [33] (Ferris J). For guidance on the proper approach to the fixing of remuneration (in an administration case) see *Re Cabletel Installation Ltd* [2005] BPIR 28 (Chief Registrar Baister) and the review of the English authorities in the judgment of Weatherup J in the decision of the Northern Ireland High Court in *Re Cooper (a bankrupt), Houston v Finnegan* [2007] BPIR 1206 at [9] and [10]. In the wake of *Cabletel* the *Practice Statement: The Fixing and Approval of the Remuneration of Appointees* was brought into force in relation to the vast majority of applications to fix remuneration brought after 1 October 2004. The Practice Statement prescribes information which should be provided by an office-holder for the purposes of fixing remuneration (see paras 5.2 and 5.3) together with guiding principles in relation to the Practice Statement's main objective of ensuring that remuneration fixed by the court 'is fair, reasonable and commensurate with the nature and extent of the work properly undertaken by the appointee in any given case and is fixed and approved by reference to a process which is consistent and predictable' (see para 3). The Court of Appeal reviewed the Practice Statement in *Brook v Reid* [2011] EWCA Civ 331, [2012] 1 WLR 419, [2011] BPIR 583, which contains an excellent summary and analysis of the case law relating to office holders' remuneration. The 2004 Practice Statement has been replaced numerous times and the most recent version is the *Practice Direction – Insolvency Proceedings* [2020] BPIR 1211 (in effect from 3 July 2020), which appears at APPENDIX 2 of this work. The importance of the guidelines now contained in Pt V in all cases where remuneration is being questioned was reiterated by the Chancellor of the High Court, Sir Terence Etherton in *Salliss v Hunt* [2014] EWHC 229 (Ch), [2014] 1 WLR 2402, [2014] BPIR 754.

It has been suggested (obiter) that s 363(1) would provide the court with power to make a summary assessment of the legal costs recoverable by a trustee, *Ardawa v Uppal* [2019] EWHC 1663 (Ch), [2019] Bus LR 1943, [2019] BPIR 1086 (Roth J) at [37]–[38].

*Cabletel* is authority for the proposition that the court should only interfere with a trustee's decision as to the taking of and paying for legal advice if the trustee acts unreasonably and outside the generous scope of his or her discretion: *Barker v Bajjon* [2008] BPIR 771 at [17] (Chief Registrar Baister).

*Sale of bankrupt's home.* In *Holtham v Kelmanson* [2006] EWHC 2588 (Ch), [2006] BPIR 1422 the court indicated that, where a bankrupt is the absolute owner of land (and therefore there is no trust of land), he could be ordered to deliver it up to the trustee under this provision, with no need for an application under s 335A or s 14 of the Trusts of Land and Appointment of Trustees Act 1996. Further, in *Re Gonsalves* [2011] BPIR 419 the court held that under s 363, every bankruptcy was under the general control of the court and the court had full power to decide all questions of priorities and all other questions, whether of law or fact, arising in any bankruptcy including the right to suspend an order for sale made under s 363. On the interrelation between s 363, Part 7 and Part 55 possession proceedings against former tenants/trespassers occupying property which has vested in the trustee, see *Garwood v Bolter* [2015] EWHC 3619 (Ch), [2016] BPIR 367. In exercising its discretion to make an order for the sale of the bankrupt's property pursuant to s 363, it may be necessary for the court to take into account considerations similar to those set out in s 335A(2) even though there is no trust of land, *Carter v Hewitt* [2019] EWHC 3729 (Ch) (Andrew Hochhauser QC (sitting as a deputy High Court judge) at [20].

*Dismissal of petition.* In *Dunbar Assets Plc v Fowler* [2013] BPIR 46 (at para 37) Chief Registrar Baister indicated the section might perhaps be used to dismiss a bankruptcy petition presented in circumstances that gave rise to unfairness to the debtor.

*Directing trustees.* In *Re Young* [2014] EWHC 4315 (Ch) the court confirmed that it had power under s 303 and s 363 to direct the trustees not to convene a meeting for the purpose of removing a trustee, but accepted the submissions that the circumstances had to be 'unusual' and that it had to be established that 'the proposed removal could have a "dramatically inconvenient effect" on the outcome of the bankruptcy'.

**Examples of matters not within s 363(1)—**

The court does not have the power under s 363(2) to compel a bankrupt to elect to receive payments from a pension in order to enable the trustee to claim the payments by way of income payments order under s 310: *Horton v Henry* [2016] EWCA Civ 989, [2017] 1 WLR 391, [2016] BPIR 1426.

In *Leeds v Lemos* [2017] EWHC 1825 (Ch), [2018] Ch 81, [2017] BPIR 1223, HHJ Hodge QC (sitting as a High Court judge) (at [279] and [280]) held that legal privilege was not property of the bankrupt and so does not vest in the trustee upon bankruptcy. As a matter of jurisdiction, therefore, the court cannot compel a bankrupt to waive legal privilege in documents to assist the trustee in bankruptcy in making an application pursuant to s 423. The judge found that, if he was wrong and the court had a discretion to order the waiver of privilege, a very powerful case indeed would have to be made out before the court would exercise such a discretion.

The court has no jurisdiction to determine whether or not a creditor properly holds security for its debt under s 363 as this is not a matter arising in or under the bankruptcy but concerns the existence of proprietary rights acquired independently of the bankruptcy: *Inspiration Finance v Cadwallader & Lynch* [2020] EWHC 15 (Ch) (Marcus Smith J) at [40].

### SECTION 363(4)

**Contempt**—In *Re M (a minor) (contact order: committal)* [1999] 2 WLR 810 the Court of Appeal gave guidance, albeit in the context of a claim under the Children Act 1989, on the exercise of the power of committal for non-compliance with a court order; in particular, it is inadvisable that the judge initiating the committal procedure should also rule on the decision to commit. In finding that a bankrupt is in contempt it lies within the court's inherent jurisdiction to regulate or stay any proceedings pursued by the bankrupt until further order or until the contempt is purged.

One bankrupt was, on the application of the official receiver, imprisoned for 20 months for a number of defalcations in assisting his trustee and failing to adhere to orders and undertakings, including consistently refusing to answer questions put to him properly by the official receiver in and out of court, not complying with court orders, lying on oath in court in the course of applications relating to the administration of the bankrupt estate, and falsely excusing himself from attending court on the basis of false grounds of ill health (*Official Receiver v Cummings-John* [2000] BPIR 320).

In *Simmonds v Pearce (A Bankrupt)* [2017] EWHC 3126 (Admin), [2018] 1 WLR 1849, [2018] BPIR 206, the court was asked to commit a bankrupt to prison for various breaches of the IA 1986. Andrews J held that, though the current state of the law is unsatisfactory and unclear, the procedure set out by r 81.15 of the CPR ought to be adopted for all applications for committal flowing from breaches of the IA 1986 (at [28]). Such applications for committal should be issued in the Business and Property Courts of England and Wales and dealt with by a judge of that court (at [30]). Andrews J was mindful of the difficulties and delays that this could cause in court centres outside London but, at present, found that this was the best way forward until the issue could be properly considered by the Rules Committee (at [31]).

In finding that a bankrupt is in contempt it lies within the court's inherent jurisdiction to regulate or stay any proceedings pursued by the bankrupt until further order or until the contempt is purged.

## [1.490]

### 364 Power of arrest

(1)   In the cases specified in the next subsection the court may cause a warrant to be issued to a constable or prescribed officer of the court—

  (a)    for the arrest of a debtor to whom a bankruptcy application or a bankruptcy petition relates or of an undischarged bankrupt, or of a discharged bankrupt whose estate is still being administered under Chapter IV of this Part, and

  (b)    for the seizure of any books, papers, records, money or goods in the possession of a person arrested under the warrant,

and may authorise a person arrested under such a warrant to be kept in custody, and anything seized under such a warrant to be held, in accordance with the rules, until such time as the court may order.

(2)   The powers conferred by subsection (1) are exercisable in relation to a debtor or undischarged or discharged bankrupt if, at any time after the making of the bankruptcy application or the presentation of the bankruptcy petition relating to him or the making of the bankruptcy order against him, it appears to the court—

  (a)    that there are reasonable grounds for believing that he has absconded, or is about to abscond, with a view to avoiding or delaying the payment of any of his debts or his appearance to a bankruptcy petition or to avoiding, delaying or disrupting any proceedings in bankruptcy against him or any examination of his affairs, or

  (b)    that he is about to remove his goods with a view to preventing or delaying possession being taken of them by the official receiver or the trustee of his estate, or

  (c)    that there are reasonable grounds for believing that he has concealed or destroyed, or is about to conceal or destroy, any of his goods or any books, papers or records which might be of use to his creditors in the course of his bankruptcy or in connection with the administration of his estate, or

(d)      that he has, without the leave of the official receiver or the trustee of his estate, removed any goods in his possession which exceed in value such sum as may be prescribed for the purposes of this paragraph, or

(e)      that he has failed, without reasonable excuse, to attend any examination ordered by the court.

**Amendments**—Enterprise and Regulatory Reform Act 2013, s 71(3), Sch 19, paras 1, 50.

**General note**—These provisions should be read along with s 366(3) and (4) and the potential liability of a bankrupt for contempt under ss 291(6) and 333(4).

This provision is triggered if, following presentation of a bankruptcy petition against a debtor or the making of a bankruptcy order against an undischarged bankrupt, and without any requirement for the petition to be served on the debtor or the bankrupt to be made aware of the order, 'it appears to the court' that any of the five circumstances listed in s 364(2) have arisen, with the consequence that the court 'may cause a warrant' to be issued for the arrest of a debtor 'and' the seizure of any books, papers, records etc 'in the possession of a person arrested under the warrant', together with the discretion to authorise those further steps identified in the latter part of s 364(1).

The powers exercisable under s 364(1) expressly extend to a discharged bankrupt whose estate continues to be administered under Chapter IV (ie ss 305–335): see *Oakes v Simms* [1997] BPIR 499. The section can apply to a discharged bankrupt: *Oakes v Simms*. There needs to be a distinction drawn, when it comes to the issue of arrest warrants, where the bankrupt absents himself or herself because the bankrupt believes the bankruptcy proceedings to be at an end (where he or she has been discharged), on the one hand, and, on the other, where a bankrupt absconds so as to delay the examination of his or her affairs (*Oakes v Simms* [1997] BPIR 499 at 503).

**SECTION 364(2)(b)**

**Scope of provision**—The word 'goods' is used here, and not the broader term 'property'. The word 'his' goods cannot be taken as applying to 'goods' which form part of the bankrupt's estate under s 283 vesting in a trustee under s 306 following the making of a bankruptcy order, although the term would catch goods subsequently acquired by or devolved upon a bankrupt which have yet to be claimed as after-acquired property under s 307. It also appears doubtful that the words 'his goods' can apply to items of excess value which do not form part of the bankrupt's estate under s 308, but which are claimable by a trustee.

**SECTION 364(2)(c)**

**Scope of provision**—For the term 'records' see the definition of s 436.

**SECTION 364(2)(d)**

**Scope of provision**—Compare the requirement here for an individual to have 'removed any goods in his possession' with the requirement under s 364(2)(b), 'he is about to remove his goods', with a view to the consequences identified therein.

The sum prescribed for the purposes of s 364(2)(d) is £1,000 with effect from 1 April 2004 by virtue of the Insolvency Proceedings (Monetary Limits) Order 1986 (SI 1986/1996) (as amended).

**Procedure**—In relation to enforcement procedures, see generally rr 12.51–12.57.

Although Art 5 of the European Convention on Human Rights does not require notice of an application to commit under s 364, the evidence in support of such an application must make clear why a without notice application is said to be justified as an exception to the normal rule: *Hickling v Baker* [2007] EWCA Civ 287, [2007] 1 WLR 2386, [2007] BPIR 346.

## [1.491]

### 365  Seizure of bankrupt's property

(1)  At any time after a bankruptcy order has been made, the court may, on the application of the official receiver or the trustee of the bankrupt's estate, issue a warrant authorising the person to whom it is directed to seize any property comprised in the bankrupt's estate which is, or any books, papers or records relating to the bankrupt's estate or affairs which are, in the possession or under the control of the bankrupt or any other person who is required to deliver the property, books, papers or records to the official receiver or trustee.

(2)  Any person executing a warrant under this section may, for the purpose of seizing any property comprised in the bankrupt's estate or any books, papers or records relating to the bankrupt's estate or affairs, break open any premises where the bankrupt or anything that may be seized under the warrant is or is believed to be and any receptacle of the bankrupt which contains or is believed to contain anything that may be so seized.

(3)   If, after a bankruptcy order has been made, the court is satisfied that any property comprised in the bankrupt's estate is, or any books, papers or records relating to the bankrupt's estate or affairs are, concealed in any premises not belonging to him, it may issue a warrant authorising any constable or prescribed officer of the court to search those premises for the property, books, papers or records.

(4)   A warrant under subsection (3) shall not be executed except in the prescribed manner and in accordance with its terms.

**General note**—These provisions, which are capable of being triggered only after a bankruptcy order has been made, are draconian in nature and allow not only for the issue of a warrant authorising the seizure of any property comprised in a bankrupt's estate or any books, papers or records relating to the bankrupt's estate or affairs from either the bankrupt or a third party, but also the breaking open of any premises and any receptacle which contains 'or is believed to contain' (ie believed subjectively but reasonably by the trustee or his or her agent) anything capable of seizure. As such, case law has established that this is a remedy of last resort. The power to authorise a search under s 365(3) is independent of s 365(1) and (2). These powers are still perhaps rather under-used in practice. For a thorough review of the law and practice relating to applications under s 365, reference should be made to the decision of ICC Judge Jones in *Lasytsya v Koumettou* [2020] EWHC 660 (Ch). The judge dealt with the required content of an application and the duty of full and frank disclosure in making the application (at [28], [31]–[33]), the test to be applied by the court in considering an application under s 365 (at [22]–[26]), the content of the court order and warrant (at [29]), and the types of safeguard that the court will expect either to be included in the draft order or for the parties to have provided an explanation for their absence (at [30]).

For discussion of the test to be applied to an application under this section, see *Williams v Mohammed* (No 2) [2012] BPIR 238. HHJ Hodge QC (sitting as a High Court judge) considered the relevant questions are threefold: (i) Is there a real risk that the respondent's possessions might be dissipated, destroyed or otherwise disposed of unless the warrant was issued? (ii) Does the value of the property liable to be seized justify the grant of such a draconian remedy? (iii) Can the rights of third parties be respected as far as possible? The task of the court was to find a balance between such rights and the need to advance the bankruptcy in the interests of the creditors. The court must also bear in mind the principle that a trustee should not take advantage of his legal rights if it is unfair to do so (*Re Condon ex p James* (1873–74) LR 9 Ch App 609). See also *Nicholson v Fayinka* [2014] BPIR 692 (Chief Registrar Baister).

It is submitted that the nature of the powers in s 365(1)–(3) is so serious that the court will not engage such extreme measures lightly, and certainly not without a very detailed consideration of the evidence and the grounds upon which it is alleged that such steps should be taken. For example, the court is very unlikely to exercise its power under s 365(3) without clear evidence, which extends beyond mere suspicion, as to the specific property or books, papers etc which are alleged to be subject to concealment. Furthermore, the court will not exercise any of its powers in a vacuum and will wish to be satisfied that the likely benefit to creditors' consequent, directly or indirectly, upon the exercise of its discretion is proportionate to the very extreme remedy or remedies which the court is being asked to grant.

An order under s 365 was made by Chief Registrar Baister in favour of a German insolvency administrator in *Re A Bankrupt* [2012] BPIR 469.

**Procedure**—In relation to enforcement procedures, see generally rr 12.51–12.57.

## [1.492]

### 366 Inquiry into bankrupt's dealings and property

(1)   At any time after a bankruptcy order has been made the court may, on the application of the official receiver or the trustee of the bankrupt's estate, summon to appear before it—

    (a)    the bankrupt or the bankrupt's spouse or former spouse or civil partner or former civil partner,

    (b)    any person known or believed to have any property comprised in the bankrupt's estate in his possession or to be indebted to the bankrupt,

    (c)    any person appearing to the court to be able to give information concerning the bankrupt or the bankrupt's dealings, affairs or property.

The court may require any such person as is mentioned in paragraph (b) or (c) to submit a witness statement verified by a statement of truth to the court containing an account of his dealings with the bankrupt or to produce any documents in his possession or under his control relating to the bankrupt or the bankrupt's dealings, affairs or property.

(2) Without prejudice to section 364, the following applies in a case where—

    (a)    a person without reasonable excuse fails to appear before the court when he is summoned to do so under this section, or

    (b)    there are reasonable grounds for believing that a person has absconded, or is about to abscond, with a view to avoiding his appearance before the court under this section.

(3) The court may, for the purpose of bringing that person and anything in his possession before the court, cause a warrant to be issued to a constable or prescribed officer of the court—

    (a)    for the arrest of that person, and

    (b)    for the seizure of any books, papers, records, money or goods in that person's possession.

(4) The court may authorise a person arrested under such a warrant to be kept in custody, and anything seized under such a warrant to be held, in accordance with the rules, until that person is brought before the court under the warrant or until such other time as the court may order.

**Amendments**—Civil Partnership Act 2004, s 261(1), Sch 27, para 120; SI 2010/18.

**General note**—This is the bankruptcy equivalent of s 236 and much of what is included in the comments relating to s 236 can be applied to this section.

The court has a discretion whether or not to order an examination and this will depend on the circumstances.

A bankrupt can be required to be examined even after he or she has obtained a discharge: *Oakes v Simms* [1997] BPIR 499 at 501–502, CA (trustee seeking to ascertain whether the bankrupt had concealed assets). Further, an order can be made under s 366 so as to obtain information which only came into existence after the discharge: *Brake v Guy* [2021] EWHC 671 (Ch), per HHJ Paul Matthews (sitting as a High Court judge) at [283].

**Extraterritorial effect**—Decisions at first instance concerning s 236 (the equivalent provision to s 366 for corporate insolvency) have reached inconsistent conclusions on whether the provision has extraterritorial effect. In *Re MF Global UK Ltd (in special administration) (No 7)* [2015] EWHC 2319 (Ch), [2016] Ch 325, [2015] BPIR 1208 David Richards J held that there was no extraterritorial effect. The judge held that the earlier decision of the Court of Appeal in *Re Tucker (a bankrupt)* [1990] Ch 148, which had concerned the substantially similar s 25 of the Bankruptcy Act 1914, was authoritative on the successor provisions in the IA 1986. Just two months later, however, HHJ Hodge QC (sitting as a High Court judge) declined to follow *Re MF Global* in *Re Omni Trustees Ltd (in Liquidation) (No 2)* [2015] EWHC 2697 (Ch), [2016] BPIR 188. The approach of the court in *Re Omni* was followed by Adam Johnson QC (sitting as a deputy High Court judge) in *Re Carna Meats (UK) Ltd*; *Wallace v Wallace* [2019] EWHC 2503 (Ch), [2020] 1 WLR 1176, [2020] BPIR 299 at [54]. *Re Omni* and *Re Carna Meats* drew a distinction between the power under s 236(2) (to summon appearance before the court) and the power under s 236(3) (to submit an account and produce books, papers or other records): even if the power to summon a person before the court was confined to persons within the jurisdiction, the power to require the production of documents and information was not. That approach was rejected by Vos C in *Re Akkurate Limited (in liquidation)* [2020] EWHC 1433 (Ch). Vos C (sitting as a judge of first instance) observed that much confusion had been caused by the competing decisions and regarded the matter as one that must be determined by the strict application of precedent ([21]). Vos C concluded (as had David Richards J in *Re MF Global*) that *Re Tucker* was binding authority, and further held that *Re Omni* was wrongly decided and the reasoning in *Re Carna Meats* on the point was incorrect ([54]). While a Supreme Court decision is required to put the point beyond doubt, it is submitted that courts of first instance are likely to follow *Re MF Global* and *Re Akkurate* until then. See the comments under 'Examinees residing out of the jurisdiction' in relation to s 236.

Where the potential examinee resides within an EU member state, an order under s 366 falls within the automatic jurisdiction and enforcement provisions of the EU Regulation on Insolvency Proceedings 2015/848: *Re Shlosberg* [2018] EWHC 603 (Ch) at [17] (Clive Freedman QC sitting as a deputy High Court judge); *Re Akkurate Limited (in liquidation)* [2020] EWHC 1433 (Ch), at [58]–[60] (Vos C).

**Any such person**—If an application were made in relation to anyone who is abroad the court would take into account the need for that person to comply with obligations under local laws: *Buchler v Al-Midani* [2005] EWHC 3183 (Ch), [2006] BPIR 867. For an example of the enforcement of an order made under s 366 by an English Court abroad see *Handelsveem BV v Hill* [2011] BPIR 1024 (enforcement by the Dutch Supreme Court).

**Affidavit containing an account of his dealings with the bankrupt**—If an order is made that a person covered by s 366 is to provide an affidavit of his dealings with the bankrupt, he or she is expected to take reasonable steps to ascertain the true facts. If he fails to do so and does not provide an accurate explanation, he or she is in contempt of court (*Bird v Hadkinson* [1999] BPIR 653). If the person does take reasonable steps and provides information honestly, then if it is inaccurate he will not be in contempt of court (*Bird v Hadkinson*).

**Legal professional privilege**—If solicitors of a bankrupt, or other persons who can be examined under s 366 are examined, they are not able to rely on the privilege in circumstances where it would be incumbent on their client to reveal the information which is the subject of the question (*Re Murjani* [1996] 1 WLR 1498, [1996] 1 BCLC 272, [1996] BPIR 325). See also the discussion on the interaction between s 366 and legal professional privilege in *Hooper v Duncan Lewis (Solicitors) Ltd* [2010] BPIR 591 and *Leeds v Lemos* [2017] EWHC 1825 (Ch), [2018] Ch 81, [2017] BPIR 1223.

**Use of material obtained pursuant to s 366**—In *Re Webinvest Ltd (in Liquidation)* [2017] EWHC 2446 (Ch), [2018] BPIR 182, Arnold J held that material obtained pursuant to s 366 could be shared with other office-holders of related insolvency proceedings in certain circumstances. The first is where an office-holder appointed to a shareholder passes material to a liquidator of the company, and there is a real, as opposed to fanciful, prospect of a surplus arising in the liquidation. Presumably this would also apply to an administrator but, because generally there is no concept of a solvent administration in the same way that an MVL is a solvent liquidation, this is much less likely to occur. The second circumstance is where the sharing of information would facilitate the discovery of dishonesty or malpractice by bankrupts or officers of insolvent companies. For an office-holder to share information for this reason, it is necessary to obtain the permission of the court.

See the notes relating to s 236.

## [1.493]

### 367 Court's enforcement powers under s 366

(1)  If it appears to the court, on consideration of any evidence obtained under section 366 or this section, that any person has in his possession any property comprised in the bankrupt's estate, the court may, on the application of the official receiver or the trustee of the bankrupt's estate, order that person to deliver the whole or any part of the property to the official receiver or the trustee at such time, in such manner and on such terms as the court thinks fit.

(2)  If it appears to the court, on consideration of any evidence obtained under section 366 or this section, that any person is indebted to the bankrupt, the court may, on the application of the official receiver or the trustee of the bankrupt's estate, order that person to pay to the official receiver or trustee, at such time and in such manner as the court may direct, the whole or part of the amount due, whether in full discharge of the debt or otherwise as the court thinks fit.

(3)  The court may, if it thinks fit, order that any person who if within the jurisdiction of the court would be liable to be summoned to appear before it under section 366 shall be examined in any part of the United Kingdom where he may be for the time being, or in any place outside the United Kingdom.

(4)  Any person who appears or is brought before the court under section 366 or this section may be examined on oath, either orally or by interrogatories, concerning the bankrupt or the bankrupt's dealings, affairs and property.

**General note**—This is the bankruptcy counterpart to s 237. See the comments relating to s 237.

## [1.494]

### 368 Provision corresponding to s 366, where interim receiver appointed

Sections 366 and 367 apply where an interim receiver has been appointed under section 286 as they apply where a bankruptcy order has been made, as if—

    (a)    references to the official receiver or the trustee were to the interim receiver, and

    (b)    references to the bankrupt and to his estate were (respectively) to the debtor and his property.

General note—This provides for private examinations to be conducted where a bankruptcy order has not been made against a person, but an interim receiver has been appointed (under s 286) over his or her estate before the hearing of a bankruptcy petition, but after the presentation of the petition. This is usually done to protect the estate for the benefit of creditors. See the comments accompanying s 286.

## [1.495]

### 369 Order for production of documents by inland revenue

(1)   For the purposes of an examination under section 290 (public examination of bankrupt) or proceedings under sections 366 to 368, the court may, on the application of the official receiver or the trustee of the bankrupt's estate, order an inland revenue official to produce to the court—

-   (a)   any return, account or accounts submitted (whether before or after the commencement of the bankruptcy) by the bankrupt to any inland revenue official,
-   (b)   any assessment or determination made (whether before or after the commencement of the bankruptcy) in relation to the bankrupt by any inland revenue official, or
-   (c)   any correspondence (whether before or after the commencement of the bankruptcy) between the bankrupt and any inland revenue official.

(2)   Where the court has made an order under subsection (1) for the purposes of any examination or proceedings, the court may, at any time after the document to which the order relates is produced to it, by order authorise the disclosure of the document, or of any part of its contents, to the official receiver, the trustee of the bankrupt's estate or the bankrupt's creditors.

(3)   The court shall not address an order under subsection (1) to an inland revenue official unless it is satisfied that that official is dealing, or has dealt, with the affairs of the bankrupt.

(4)   Where any document to which an order under subsection (1) relates is not in the possession of the official to whom the order is addressed, it is the duty of that official to take all reasonable steps to secure possession of it and, if he fails to do so, to report the reasons for his failure to the court.

(5)   Where any document to which an order under subsection (1) relates is in the possession of an inland revenue official other than the one to whom the order is addressed, it is the duty of the official in possession of the document, at the request of the official to whom the order is addressed, to deliver it to the official making the request.

(6)   In this section "inland revenue official" means any inspector or collector of taxes appointed by the Commissioners of Inland Revenue or any person appointed by the Commissioners to serve in any other capacity.

(7)   This section does not apply for the purposes of an examination under sections 366 and 367 which takes place by virtue of section 368 (interim receiver).

General note—The power of the court to make and direct an order under s 369(1) to a particular Inland Revenue official or officials is rather more restricted than might at first appear, for two reasons. First, the court's power is not independent and free-standing and may only be exercised in the course of a public examination under s 290 or inquiries under ss 366 and 367, but not such inquiries undertaken by an interim receiver where no bankruptcy order will have been made. Secondly, the court's power extends, at least in the first instance, only to the production of documents to the court. As a second stage to the exercise of this power s 369(2) then empowers the court to authorise the disclosure of any such document to the official receiver or the trustee or the bankrupt's creditors, who are apparently not caught by an order for disclosure in favour of the trustee under this provision.

Procedure—See rr 10.118–10.120.

## [1.496]

### 370 Power to appoint special manager

(1)   The court may, on an application under this section, appoint any person to be the special manager—

(a)     of a bankrupt's estate, or

(b)     of the business of an undischarged bankrupt, or

(c)     of the property or business of a debtor in whose case an interim receiver has been appointed under section 286.

(2)   An application under this section may be made by the interim receiver or the trustee of the bankrupt's estate in any case where it appears to the interim receiver or trustee that the nature of the estate, property or business, or the interests of the creditors generally, require the appointment of another person to manage the estate, property or business.

(3)   A special manager appointed under this section has such powers as may be entrusted to him by the court.

(4)   The power of the court under subsection (3) to entrust powers to a special manager includes power to direct that any provision in this Group of Parts that has effect in relation to the official receiver, interim receiver or trustee shall have the like effect in relation to the special manager for the purposes of the carrying out by the special manager of any of the functions of the official receiver, interim receiver or trustee.

(5)   A special manager appointed under this section shall—

(a)     give such security as may be prescribed,

(b)     prepare and keep such accounts as may be prescribed, and

(c)     produce those accounts in accordance with the rules to the Secretary of State or to such other persons as may be prescribed.

**Amendments**—Deregulation Act 2015, s 19, Sch 6, Pt 5, paras 12, 14.

**General note**—For the purposes of s 370(1) the power of the court to appoint a special manager arises under s 286(1) or (2), s 287(1), or on an application by a trustee.

Although the court retains a discretion to make an appointment under s 370(1), the court is very likely to weigh heavily the fact that, for the purposes of s 370(2), it 'appears' to the official receiver or trustee that the circumstances of the case require the appointment of another person as special manager. In practice, the requirement for a special manager most commonly arises where the nature of any business or assets comprised in the bankrupt's estate is particularly specialist or idiosyncratic and where it is inappropriate to involve the bankrupt in the management of such business or assets. Inevitably, the court will, in the exercise of its discretion, be concerned that the benefit to creditors consequent upon the appointing of a special manager is proportionate to the likely costs of such an appointment.

**SECTION 370(3)**

**Powers of a special manger**—As in the case of a court appointed receiver, the court's order should expressly provide for the powers of a special manager. The court will not confer powers which exceed those reasonably required by a special manager, dependent on the facts of any particular case, although the court will be equally alive to the risk of unduly restricting its appointee and the time and expense involved in an application to extend such powers. The powers listed in Sch 5, free of the restrictions imposed as to sanction, may provide a useful starting point for the selection of appropriate powers.

**Procedure**—See r 10.94.

For the cost of the security of the special manager where a bankruptcy order is made see r 10.149(f). The remuneration of a special manager is governed by para 20 of Sch 9.

## [1.497]

### 371 Re-direction of bankrupt's letters, etc

(1)   Where a bankruptcy order has been made, the court may from time to time, on the application of the official receiver or the trustee of the bankrupt's estate, order a postal operator (within the meaning of Part 3 of the Postal Services Act 2011) to re-direct and send or deliver to the official receiver or trustee or otherwise any postal packet (within the meaning of that Act) which would otherwise be sent or delivered by the operator concerned to the bankrupt at such place or places as may be specified in the order.

(2)   An order under this section has effect for such period, not exceeding 3 months, as may be specified in the order.

**Amendments**—Postal Services Act 2000, s 127(4), Sch 8, para 20(a)–(c); Postal Services Act 2011, s 91(1), (2), Sch 12, Pt 3, paras 124, 125.

**General note**—The exercise of the court's power under this provision constitutes a serious intrusion into a bankrupt's privacy. In *Foxley v United Kingdom* [2000] BPIR 1009 the European Court of Human Rights held that, whilst the interception of mail clearly interfered with the right of privacy under Art 8 of the European Convention on Human Rights, interference sanctioned by court order was 'in accordance with the law' of the United Kingdom jurisdiction and fell within the margin of appreciation afforded to a Member State in determining the level of interference permissible. However, the continued interception of mail after a 3-month period stipulated in the court's order was not in accordance with the law. Neither was the opening and copying of mail from the bankrupt's legal advisers justified at any time as a proportionate response or 'necessary in a democratic society' within the terms of Art 8.2 of the Convention. For an opposite finding in relation to the law of Finland, see *Narinen v Finland* [2004] BPIR 914. In *Smedley v Brittain* [2008] BPIR 219 at [67] and [68] Registrar Nicholls identified, in the context of Art 8 of the Convention, that the reasonableness of a trustee-in-bankruptcy seeking and obtaining an order for re-direction would necessarily be determined by reference to the conduct of and approach adopted by the debtor. On the evidence in that case there had been no breach of Art 8 in the trustee obtaining a re-direction order in accordance with the legislation.

Section 371 has no application to mail of any sort emanating from a bankrupt.

**Duration of order**—Although s 371(2) envisages an order not exceeding 3 months in duration, the words 'from time to time' would allow the court to make a fresh order for up to 3 months following the expiration of a previous order.

**Procedure**—Whilst the procedure governing redirection of a bankrupt's mail may be made without notice and need only be supported by a letter setting out the grounds upon which the order is sought, in *Singh v Official Receiver* [1997] BPIR 530 Sir Richard Scott V-C expressed concern at those requirements and commented (at 532A–532C):

' . . . in any event in my view all applications to the court ought to be supported by something more substantial than merely a letter informing the courts that the order was being sought on the grounds of non-co-operation or whatever. The material ought to give chapter and verse of the non-co-operation relied on. In the case of applications under s 279 rules have been prescribed which provide for the official receiver to lodge with the court a report, a copy of which is then to be supplied to the respondent bankrupt, in which the details of the non-co-operation relied on for the purposes of the application are set out. In my view a similar procedure ought to be introduced for the purposes of applications under s 371. I think it is unreasonable for an application to be made in circumstances where the substantive allegations on which the application are based are not set out in some written form available to be provided to the bankrupt respondent.'

Chief Registrar Baister made an order under s 371 in favour of a German insolvency administrator (pursuant to the co-operation mechanisms in Art 25 of the EC Regulation on Insolvency Proceedings (1346/2000) in *Re A Bankrupt* [2012] BPIR 469.

## PART X   INDIVIDUAL INSOLVENCY: GENERAL PROVISIONS

**[1.498]**

### 372 Supplies of gas, water, electricity, etc

(1)   This section applies where on any day ("the relevant day")—

    (a)    a bankruptcy order is made against an individual or an interim receiver of an individual's property is appointed, or

    (b)    a voluntary arrangement proposed by an individual is approved under Part VIII,

    (c)    . . .

and in this section "the office-holder" means the official receiver, the trustee in bankruptcy, the interim receiver, or the supervisor of the voluntary arrangement, as the case may be.

(2)   If a request falling within the next subsection is made for the giving after the relevant day of any of the supplies mentioned in subsection (4), the supplier—

    (a)    may make it a condition of the giving of the supply that the office-holder personally guarantees the payment of any charges in respect of the supply, but

    (b)    shall not make it a condition of the giving of the supply, or do anything which has the effect of making it a condition of the giving of the supply, that any outstanding charges in respect of a supply given to the individual before the relevant day are paid.

(3)   A request falls within this subsection if it is made—
    (a)    by or with the concurrence of the office-holder, and
    (b)    for the purposes of any business which is or has been carried on by the individual, by a firm or partnership of which the individual is or was a member, or by an agent or manager for the individual or for such a firm or partnership.

(4)   The supplies referred to in subsection (2) are—
    (a)    a supply of gas by a gas supplier within the meaning of Part I of the Gas Act 1986;
    (aa)    a supply of gas by a person within paragraph 1 of Schedule 2A to the Gas Act 1986 (supply by landlords etc);
    (b)    a supply of electricity by an electricity supplier within the meaning of Part I of the Electricity Act 1989;
    (ba)    a supply of electricity by a class of person within Class A (small suppliers) or Class B (resale) of Schedule 4 to the Electricity (Class Exemptions from the Requirement for a Licence) Order 2001 (SI 2001/3270);
    (c)    a supply of water by a water undertaker,
    (ca)    a supply of water by a water supply licensee within the meaning of the Water Industry Act 1991;
    (cb)    a supply of water by a person who has an interest in the premises to which the supply is given;
    (d)    a supply of communications services by a provider of a public electronic communications service.
    (e)    a supply of communications services by a person who carries on a business which includes giving such supplies;
    (f)    a supply of goods or services mentioned in subsection (4A) by a person who carries on a business which includes giving such supplies, where the supply is for the purpose of enabling or facilitating anything to be done by electronic means.

(4A)   The goods and services referred to in subsection (4)(f) are—
    (a)    point of sale terminals;
    (b)    computer hardware and software;
    (c)    information, advice and technical assistance in connection with the use of information technology;
    (d)    data storage and processing;
    (e)    website hosting.

(5)   The following applies to expressions used in subsection (4)—
    (a)    . . .
    (b)    . . .
    (c)    "communications services" do not include electronic communications services to the extent that they are used to broadcast or otherwise transmit programme services (within the meaning of the Communications Act 2003).

**Amendments**—Water Act 1989, s 190(1), Sch 25, para 78(1); Gas Act 1995, ss 16(1), 17(5), Sch 4, para 14(3), (4), Sch 6; Utilities Act 2000, s 108, Sch 6, Pt III, para 47(1), (3)(a), (b), Sch 8; Communications Act 2003, s 406(1), Sch 17, para 82(1), (3)(a), (b); Deregulation Act 2015, s 19, Sch 6, Pt 1, para 2(1), (11)(d); SI 2015/989.

**General note**—These provisions apply in any of the three circumstances set out in s 372(1) and, in effect, prohibit any supplier of utilities within the meaning of s 372(4) from imposing conditions in relation to outstanding utility charges for the continued supply of utilities or extracting any personal guarantee relating to the payment of outstanding or future charges. Amendments were made to s 372(4)(d) and (5)(c) by the Broadcasting Act 2003.

Further commentary appears in the notes to s 233 which applies in corporate insolvencies and which provision corresponds in substance with s 372.

**[1.499]**

### 372A Further protection of essential supplies

(1) An insolvency-related term of a contract for the supply of essential goods or services to an individual ceases to have effect if—

    (a)    a voluntary arrangement proposed by the individual is approved under Part 8, and

    (b)    the supply is for the purpose of a business which is or has been carried on by the individual, by a firm or partnership of which the individual is or was a member, or by an agent or manager for the individual or for such a firm or partnership.

(2 An insolvency-related term of a contract does not cease to have effect by virtue of subsection (1) to the extent that—

    (a)    it provides for the contract or the supply to terminate, or any other thing to take place, because the individual becomes subject to an insolvency procedure other than a voluntary arrangement;

    (b)    it entitles a supplier to terminate the contract or the supply, or do any other thing, because the individual becomes subject to an insolvency procedure other than a voluntary arrangement; or

    (c)    it entitles a supplier to terminate the contract or the supply because of an event that occurs, or may occur, after the voluntary arrangement proposed by the individual is approved.

(3) Where an insolvency-related term of a contract ceases to have effect under this section the supplier may—

    (a)    terminate the contract, if the condition in subsection (4) is met;

    (b)    terminate the supply, if the condition in subsection (5) is met.

(4) The condition in this subsection is that—

    (a)    the supervisor of the voluntary arrangement consents to the termination of the contract,

    (b)    the court grants permission for the termination of the contract, or

    (c)    any charges in respect of the supply that are incurred after the voluntary arrangement is approved are not paid within the period of 28 days beginning with the day on which payment is due.

The court may grant permission under paragraph (b) only if satisfied that the continuation of the contract would cause the supplier hardship.

(5) The condition in this subsection is that—

    (a)    the supplier gives written notice to the supervisor of the voluntary arrangement that the supply will be terminated unless the supervisor personally guarantees the payment of any charges in respect of the continuation of the supply after the arrangement was approved, and

    (b)    the supervisor does not give that guarantee within the period of 14 days beginning with the day the notice is received.

(6) For the purposes of securing that the interests of suppliers are protected, where—

    (a)    an insolvency-related term of a contract (the "original term") ceases to have effect by virtue of subsection (1), and

    (b)    a subsequent voluntary arrangement proposed by the individual is approved,

the contract is treated for the purposes of subsections (1) to (5) as if, immediately before the subsequent voluntary arrangement proposed by the individual is approved, it included an insolvency-related term identical to the original term.

(7) A contract for the supply of essential goods or services is a contract for a supply mentioned in section 372(4).

(8) An insolvency-related term of a contract for the supply of essential goods or services to an individual is a provision of the contract under which—

    (a)    the contract or the supply would terminate, or any other thing would take place, because the voluntary arrangement proposed by the individual is approved,

> (b)   the supplier would be entitled to terminate the contract or the supply, or to do any other thing, because the voluntary arrangement proposed by the individual is approved, or
>
> (c)   the supplier would be entitled to terminate the contract or the supply because of an event that occurred before the voluntary arrangement proposed by the individual is approved.

(9)   Subsection (1) does not have effect in relation to a contract entered into before 1 October 2015.

**Amendments**—Inserted by SI 2015/989.

**General note**—this is a new, self-explanatory, provision which seeks to protect a debtor who has entered into a voluntary arrangement from the termination of a contract for the supply of essential goods or services (as defined in s 372(4)) for the purpose of that debtor's business.

## [1.500]

### 373 Jurisdiction in relation to insolvent individuals

(1)   The High Court and the county court have jurisdiction throughout England and Wales for the purposes of the Parts in this Group.

(2)   For the purposes of those Parts, the county court has, in addition to its ordinary jurisdiction, all the powers and jurisdiction of the High Court; and the orders of the court may be enforced accordingly in the prescribed manner.

(3)   Jurisdiction for the purposes of those Parts is exercised—

> (a)   by the High Court or the county court in relation to the proceedings which, in accordance with the rules, are allocated to the London insolvency district, and
>
> (b)   by the county court in relation to the proceedings which are so allocated to any other insolvency district.

(4)   Subsection (3) is without prejudice to the transfer of proceedings from one court to another in the manner prescribed by the rules; and nothing in that subsection invalidates any proceedings on the grounds that they were initiated or continued in the wrong court.

**Amendments**—SI 2011/761; Crime and Courts Act 2013, s 17(5), Sch 9, Pt 3, paras 52, 93.

**General note**—Section 373(1) confers co-existing bankruptcy jurisdiction on the High Court and the county courts of England and Wales. Section 373(2) is necessary to bring the powers and jurisdiction of a county court into line with those of the High Court. Notwithstanding the co-existing jurisdiction of the High Court and the county courts, s 373(3) allocates jurisdiction in bankruptcy cases between the High Court, which exercises jurisdiction in relation to the London bankruptcy district as defined in s 374(4)(a), and the county court exercising jurisdiction in relation to that court's insolvency district as defined in s 374(4)(b) and (c); see the decision of Morritt C in *HMRC v Earley* [2011] EWHC 1783 (Ch), [2011] BPIR 1590 on the jurisdiction of the High Court.

**Distribution of business**—Para 3 of *Practice Direction – Insolvency Proceedings* (July 2020) [2020] BPIR 1211 sets out detailed provisions in relation to the appropriate distribution of insolvency work between the High Court, the County Court and the District Registries. A failure to comply with the requirement to transfer an opposed bankruptcy petition in accordance with those provisions was found by HHJ David Cooke (sitting as a High Court judge) to have been a serious procedural error in *Siddiqi v Taparis Ltd* [2019] EWHC 417 (Ch), [2019] BPIR 1025 ([7]–[8], [28]–[29]). However, given that the failure to issue in the correct court does not invalidate the proceedings, the court may take a pragmatic view of the relevant requirements so as to dispose of cases efficiently where the circumstances are just: *IV Fund Limited SAC v Mountain* [2021] EWHC 738 (Ch), per Deputy ICC Judge Barnett at [17].

**Transfer of proceedings**—Rules 12.30–12.38 deal with the transfer of proceedings between courts; see the commentary to those provisions.

## [1.501]

### 374 Insolvency districts

(1)   The Lord Chancellor may, with the concurrence of the Lord Chief Justice, by order designate the areas which are for the time being to be comprised, for the purposes of the Parts in this Group, in the London Insolvency district and the insolvency district, or districts, of the county court.

(2)   An order under this section may contain such incidental, supplemental and transitional provisions as may appear to the Lord Chancellor and the Lord Chief Justice necessary or expedient.

(3)   An order under this section shall be made by statutory instrument and, after being made, shall be laid before each House of Parliament.

(4)   Subject to any order under this section—

    (a)   the district which, immediately before the appointed day, is the London bankruptcy district becomes, on that day, the London insolvency district;

    (b)   any district which immediately before that day is the bankruptcy district of a county court becomes, on that day, the insolvency district of that court, and

    (c)   any county court which immediately before that day is excluded from having jurisdiction in bankruptcy is excluded, on and after that day, from having jurisdiction for the purposes of the Parts in this Group.

(5)   The Lord Chief Justice may nominate a judicial office holder (as defined in section 109(4) of the Constitutional Reform Act 2005) to exercise his functions under this section.

**Amendments**—Constitutional Reform Act 2005, s 15(1), Sch 4; Crime and Courts Act 2013, s 17(5), Sch 9, Pt 3, para 93.

**General note**—See the commentary to s 373.

## [1.502]

### 375 Appeals etc from courts exercising insolvency jurisdiction

(1)   Every court having jurisdiction for the purposes of the Parts in this Group may review, rescind or vary any order made by it in the exercise of that jurisdiction.

(2)   An appeal from a decision made in the exercise of jurisdiction for the purposes of those Parts by the county court or by a registrar in bankruptcy of the High Court lies to a single judge of the High Court; and an appeal from a decision of that judge on such an appeal lies to the Court of Appeal.

(3)   The county court is not, in the exercise of its jurisdiction for the purposes of those Parts, to be subject to be restrained by the order of any other court, and no appeal lies from its decision in the exercise of that jurisdiction except as provided by this section.

**Amendments**—Access to Justice Act 1999, s 106, Sch 15, Pt III; Crime and Courts Act 2013, s 17(5), Sch 9, Pt 3, para 52(1), (2).

**General note**—Section 375 corresponds in substance with IR 2016, r 12.59 which applies to court orders in corporate insolvency. (Rule 12.59(3) finds no counterpart in s 375.) The commentary to r 12.59, which includes reference to the authorities decided under s 375, may also be read as a commentary to the present provision. This section only applies to orders of the 'court' and, therefore, offers no jurisdiction to review decisions of an adjudicator: *Re Budniok* [2017] EWHC 368 (Ch), [2017] BPIR 521.

**Review of bankruptcy order**—In *Crammer v West Bromwich Building Society* [2012] EWCA Civ 517, [2012] BPIR 963 (at [7] to [8]) Patten LJ considered it to be 'well established' that, as a matter of discretion in principle, a bankruptcy order could only be reviewed pursuant to s 375 in circumstances where there was new material and/or a material change of circumstances and not to allow bankrupt to merely re-argue points already decided at the original bankruptcy hearing. Snowden J added in *Re Maud* [2020] EWHC 1469 (Ch) that the power to review, rescind or vary under s 375 is plainly not intended to be an alternative to or to subvert the proper processes of an appeal (at [24]). It was undesirable for there to be a parallel appeal and an application under s 375, which would be confusing, wasteful of the time and resources of the parties and the court, and in an extreme scenario might even lead to inconsistent decisions (at [27]). An application cannot be brought under s 375 to re-run the case itself, even where there is fresh material or new arguments which were previously overlooked or not thought to have a sufficient prospect of success to be run at the original hearing: *Discovery (Northampton) Ltd v Debenhams Retail Ltd* [2020] EWHC 260, per Sir Alastair Norris (sitting as a High Court judge) at [13].

The court may consider there to be a change in circumstances where facts which did exist at the time a bankruptcy order was made have subsequently come to light: Gloster LJ in *Yang v Official Receiver* [2017] EWCA Civ 1465, [2018] 2 WLR 307, [2018] BPIR 255 at [53].

**Review of appellate decisions**—The jurisdiction under s 375(1) is not limited to the review of orders made by the court when sitting at first instance. The High Court and the Court of Appeal may review orders made on appeal under this provision: *Sands v Layne* [2016] EWCA Civ 1159,

[2017] 1 WLR 1782, [2017] BPIR 215. Nevertheless, it must be shown that there is some justification for the court reviewing its previous order other than a desire to re-argue that which was argued on the former occasion such as a material change of circumstances or where the court was then acting under material misapprehension as to the true facts: *Adetula v Barking and Dagenham LBC* (unreported), 9 November 2017, ChD.

**Stay of bankruptcy order pending appeal**—It is well-established that a stay of a bankruptcy order will not usually be granted while a challenge is made to it, in order to avoid prejudice to existing creditors in relation to securing the estate or to persons with whom the bankrupt may deal if the challenge to the bankruptcy fails: *Howell v Hughes* [2019] EWHC 1559 (Ch), [2019] BPIR 1211, [12].

**Costs**—In *Cooke v Dunbar Assets plc* [2016] EWHC 1888 (Ch), [2016] BPIR 1339, Jeremy Cousins QC (sitting as a deputy High Court judge) rejected a debtor's submission that the creditor's costs of successfully resisting the debtor's appeal from a bankruptcy order (separately reported at [2016] EWHC 579 (Ch), [2016] BPIR 576) were necessarily either a cost and expense of the bankruptcy or, alternatively, a provable debt. The deputy judge agreed with the creditor that the costs liability did not fall into the bankruptcy and the court retained its usual discretion on costs. It was appropriate to order that the bankrupt pay the costs as a post-bankruptcy debt and, to the extent the costs were not recovered from the bankrupt, they could be treated as a cost and expense of the bankruptcy. The principles relating to the correct approach to costs when a bankruptcy order is rescinded under s 375 are the same that apply in cases of annulment under s 282 (in particular, those principles set out in *London Borough of Redbridge v Mustafa* [2010] EWHC 1105 (Ch)): Nugee J in *Amin v London Borough of Redbridge* [2018] EWHC 3100 (Ch). For an explanation of those principles, see the commentary to s 282 above.

**Procedure**—See generally rr 12.58–12.62. In *Sands v Layne* [2016] EWCA Civ 1159, [2017] 1 WLR 1782, [2017] BPIR 215 at [51], Arden LJ held that the trustee in bankruptcy should be joined to an application pursuant to s 375 so that: (i) provision can be made for his or her costs and expenses; and (ii) the risk that he or she is not aware that the bankruptcy order is set aside is minimised. In *Re Oraki* [2017] EWHC 11 (Ch), [2017] BPIR 750, Robert Ham QC (sitting as a deputy High Court judge) held that the trustee in bankruptcy should be joined in any event so that he or she can assist the court.

## [1.503]

### 376  Time-limits

Where by any provision in this Group of Parts or by the rules the time for doing anything (including anything in relation to a bankruptcy application) is limited, the court may extend the time, either before or after it has expired, on such terms, if any, as it thinks fit.

**Amendments**—Enterprise and Regulatory Reform Act 2013, s 71(3), Sch 19, paras 1, 51.

For the rationale behind this prospective amendment, see the general not to Part IX above.

**General note**—Section 376 has its origins in s 105(4) of the Bankruptcy Act 1883 and applies to any time-limit for the doing of anything imposed by 'any provision in this Group of Parts' (ie the Second Group of Parts, being ss 252–385) or 'by the rules' (ie seemingly the entirety of the IR 2016, without limitation). The power of the court lies in its discretion to extend time either prospectively or retrospectively, and subject to any terms the court considers appropriate.

Formerly s 376 corresponded in substance with IR 1986, r 12.9(2) which applied to the extension or shortening of time for anything to be done under the rules. Rule 12.9(2) was replaced by r 12A.55(2) (introduced by the Insolvency (Amendment) Rules 2010 (SI 2010/686)) which has itself been replaced by r 1.3 and Sch 5 to the IR 2016 which provides the provisions of CPR 3.1(2)(a) (the court's general powers of management) apply so as to enable the court to extend or shorten the time limit for compliance with anything required or authorised to be done by the rules.

A party seeking to extend time under s 376 does not also need to apply for relief from sanction pursuant to CPR 3.9. The court may, in certain circumstances, take into account matters that may be relevant to an application under CPR 3.9 in the balancing exercise to be carried out in the exercise of its discretion: *Rankin v Dissington Lending Company Ltd* [2021] EWHC 172 (Ch), per Deputy ICC Judge Kyriakides at [10].

**Procedure**—In the Royal Courts of Justice, an officer acting on behalf of the Operations Manager or chief clerk was authorised under para 13.1(1) of the *Practice Direction – Insolvency Proceedings* [2012] BPIR 409 to extend time for the hearing of a petition on an application by a petitioning creditor. There is no similar provision in the *Practice Direction – Insolvency Proceedings* (July 2020) [2020] BPIR 1211.

**Discretion**—Section 376 gives the court an unfettered discretion to extend time limits either before or after the prescribed time has expired. In exercising this discretion, the court must consider all the circumstances, including the purpose of the prescribed time-limit, the merits of the underlying case, the reasons for not having taken the required step in-time, any prejudice that might be suffered if time is not extended, and any prejudice that might be suffered if time is extended: *Rankin v Dissington Lending Company Ltd* [2021] EWHC 172 (Ch), per Deputy ICC Judge Kyriakides at [9].

## [1.504]

### 377 Formal defects

The acts of a person as the trustee of a bankrupt's estate or as a special manager, and the acts of the creditors' committee established for any bankruptcy, are valid notwithstanding any defect in the appointment, election or qualifications of the trustee or manager or, as the case may be, of any member of the committee.

General note—The substance of this provision in relation to the acts of a trustee, special manager or a creditors' committee in bankruptcy is precisely the same as s 232, which operates in relation to the office-holders identified therein, and para 104 of Sch B1 in relation to administrators. Reference should be made to the commentary to s 232.

Section 377, like, s 232 and para 104 of Sch B1, is concerned with the acts of an office-holder, as well as the acts of a creditors' committee. Unlike its predecessor in s 147(1) of the Bankruptcy Act 1914, no cure is provided for formal defects or irregularities in insolvency proceedings. Such a provision, however, does appear in IR 2016, r 12.64.

## [1.505]

### 378 Exemption from stamp duty

Stamp duty shall not be charged on—

(a) any document, being a deed, conveyance, assignment, surrender, admission or other assurance relating solely to property which is comprised in a bankrupt's estate and which, after the execution of that document, is or remains at law or in equity the property of the bankrupt or of the trustee of that estate,

(b) any writ, order, certificate or other instrument relating solely to the property of a bankrupt or to any bankruptcy proceedings.

General note—Documents relating to bankruptcy matters are exempt from stamp duty. Section 378 is a simplified version of the former provision in s 148 of the Bankruptcy Act 1914.

## [1.506]

### 379 Annual report

As soon as practicable after the end of 1986 and each subsequent calendar year, the Secretary of State shall prepare and lay before each House of Parliament a report about the operation during that year of so much of this Act as is comprised in this Group of Parts.

Amendments—Deregulation Act 2015, s 19, Sch 6, Pt1, para 2(1), (11)(e).

General note—This provision provides for the laying before Parliament of an annual report by the Secretary of State which extends to proceedings under the Deeds of Arrangement Act 1914.

*Creditors' decisions*

Amendments—Inserted by Small Business, Enterprise and Employment Act 2015, s 123(1), (2).

## [1.507]

### 379ZA Creditors' decisions: general

(1) This section applies where, for the purposes of this Group of Parts, a person ("P") seeks a decision from an individual's creditors about any matter.

(2) The decision may be made by any creditors' decision procedure P thinks fit, except that it may not be made by a creditors' meeting unless subsection (3) applies.

(3) This subsection applies if at least the minimum number of creditors request in writing that the decision be made by a creditors' meeting.

(4) If subsection (3) applies, P must summon a creditors' meeting.

(5)   Subsection (2) is subject to any provision of this Act, the rules or any other legislation, or any order of the court—

(a)   requiring a decision to be made, or prohibiting a decision from being made, by a particular creditors' decision procedure (other than a creditors' meeting);

(b)   permitting or requiring a decision to be made by a creditors' meeting.

(6)   Section 379ZB provides that in certain cases the deemed consent procedure may be used instead of a creditors' decision procedure.

(7)   For the purposes of subsection (3) the "minimum number" of creditors is any of the following—

(a)   10% in value of the creditors;

(b)   10% in number of the creditors;

(c)   10 creditors.

(8)   The references in subsection (7) to creditors are to creditors of any class, even where a decision is sought only from creditors of a particular class.

(9)   In this section references to a meeting are to a meeting where the creditors are invited to be present together at the same place (whether or not it is possible to attend the meeting without being present at that place).

(10)   Except as provided by subsection (8), references in this section to creditors include creditors of a particular class.

(11)   In this Group of Parts "creditors' decision procedure" means a procedure prescribed or authorised under paragraph 11A of Schedule 9.

**Amendments**—Inserted by Small Business, Enterprise and Employment Act 2015, s 123(1), (2).

**General note**—This new section abolishes the requirement for creditors' decisions to be made at creditors meetings unless 10% by value or in number or 10 creditors request in writing that the decision be made a creditors' meeting. Instead the decision may be made by any 'creditors' decision procedure' the person seeking the decision sees fit, except by creditors' meeting.

The provision is equivalent to s 246ZE that applies to companies. See the notes accompanying that provision.

## [1.508]

### 379ZB   Deemed consent procedure

(1)   The deemed consent procedure may be used instead of a creditors' decision procedure where an individual's creditors are to make a decision about any matter, unless—

(a)   a decision about the matter is required by virtue of this Act, the rules or any other legislation to be made by a creditors' decision procedure, or

(b)   the court orders that a decision about the matter is to be made by a creditors' decision procedure.

(2)   If the rules provide for an individual's creditors to make a decision about the remuneration of any person, they must provide that the decision is to be made by a creditors' decision procedure.

(3)   The deemed consent procedure is that the relevant creditors (other than opted-out creditors) are given notice of—

(a)   the matter about which the creditors are to make a decision,

(b)   the decision the person giving the notice proposes should be made (the "proposed decision"),

(c)   the effect of subsections (4) and (5), and

(d)   the procedure for objecting to the proposed decision.

(4)   If less than the appropriate number of relevant creditors object to the proposed decision in accordance with the procedure set out in the notice, the creditors are to be treated as having made the proposed decision.

(5)   Otherwise—

(a)   the creditors are to be treated as not having made a decision about the matter in question, and

(b)   if a decision about that matter is again sought from the creditors, it must be sought using a creditors' decision procedure.

(6)   For the purposes of subsection (4) the "appropriate number" of relevant creditors is 10% in value of those creditors.

(7)   "Relevant creditors" means the creditors who, if the decision were to be made by a creditors' decision procedure, would be entitled to vote in the procedure.

(8)   In this section references to creditors include creditors of a particular class.

(9)   The rules may make further provision about the deemed consent procedure.

**Amendments**—Inserted by Small Business, Enterprise and Employment Act 2015, s 123(1), (2).

**General note**—The provision is equivalent to s 246ZF that applies to companies. See the notes accompanying that provision.

## [1.509]

### 379ZC  Power to amend sections 379ZA and 379ZB

(1)   The Secretary of State may by regulations amend section 379ZA so as to change the definition of the minimum number of creditors.

(2)   The Secretary of State may by regulations amend section 379ZB so as to change the definition of the appropriate number of relevant creditors.

(3)   Regulations under this section may define the minimum number or the appropriate number by reference to any one or more of—

    (a)    a proportion in value,

    (b)    a proportion in number,

    (c)    an absolute number,

and the definition may include alternative, cumulative or relative requirements.

(4)   Regulations under subsection (1) may define the minimum number of creditors by reference to all creditors, or by reference to creditors of a particular description.

(5)   Regulations under this section may make provision that will result in section 379ZA or 379ZB having different definitions for different cases, including for different kinds of decisions.

(6)   Regulations under this section may make transitional provision.

(7)   The power of the Secretary of State to make regulations under this section is exercisable by statutory instrument.

(8)   A statutory instrument containing regulations under this section may not be made unless a draft of the instrument has been laid before, and approved by a resolution of, each House of Parliament.

**Amendments**—Inserted by Small Business, Enterprise and Employment Act 2015, s 123(1), (2).

### 379A

*(Repealed)*

**Amendments**—Repealed by Small Business, Enterprise and Employment Act 2015, s 126, Sch 9, Pt 2, paras 60, 88, partly as from 26 May 2015, fully as from 6 April 2017, in relation to England and Wales and partly as from a date to be appointed in relation to Scotland.

*Giving of notices etc by office-holders*

**Amendments**—Inserted by SI 2010/18. Substituted by Small Business, Enterprise and Employment Act 2015, s 125(1), (2), partly as from 26 May 2015, fully as from 6 April 2017, in relation to England and Wales and partly as from a date to be appointed in relation to Scotland.

## [1.510]

### 379B  Use of websites

(1)   This section applies where—

    (a)    a bankruptcy order is made against an individual or an interim receiver of an individual's property is appointed, or

    (b)    a voluntary arrangement in relation to an individual is proposed or is approved under Part 8, and "the office-holder" means the official receiver, the trustee in bankruptcy, the interim receiver, the nominee or the supervisor of the voluntary arrangement, as the case may be.

(2)   Where any provision of this Act or the rules requires the office-holder to give, deliver, furnish or send a notice or other document or information to any person, that requirement is satisfied by making the notice, document or information available on a website—

> (a)    in accordance with the rules, and
> (b)    in such circumstances as may be prescribed.

**Amendments**—Inserted by SI 2010/18.

**General note**—This self-explanatory provision mirrors s 246B. See also IR 2016, rr 1.47 and 1.49.

## [1.511]

### 379C   Creditors' ability to opt out of receiving certain notices

(1)   Any provision of the rules which requires an office-holder to give a notice to creditors of an individual does not apply, in circumstances prescribed by the rules, in relation to opted-out creditors.

(2)   Subsection (1)—

> (a)    does not apply in relation to a notice of a distribution or proposed distribution to creditors;
> (b)    is subject to any order of the court requiring a notice to be given to all creditors (or all creditors of a particular category).

(3)   Except as provided by the rules, a creditor may participate and vote in a creditors' decision procedure or a deemed consent procedure even though, by virtue of being an opted-out creditor, the creditor does not receive notice of it.

(4)   In this section—

> "give" includes deliver, furnish or send;
> "notice" includes any document or information in any other form; "office-holder", in relation to an individual, means—
>> (a)    where a bankruptcy order is made against the individual, the official receiver or the trustee in bankruptcy;
>> (b)    where an interim receiver of the individual's property is appointed, the interim receiver;
>> (c)    the supervisor of a voluntary arrangement approved under Part 8 in relation to the individual.

**Amendments**—Inserted by Small business, Enterprise and Employment Act 2015, s 125(1), (3).

**General note**—See the general note to Part IX.

## PART XI   INTERPRETATION FOR SECOND GROUP OF PARTS

## [1.512]

**Introduction to Part XI**—This Part includes just five sections and these provisions define words and expressions used in what is called 'the Second Group of Parts'. The provisions covered in the Second Group of Parts are ss 254–379, being provisions that deal with individual insolvency, including bankruptcy.

## [1.513]

### 380   Introductory

The next five sections have effect for the interpretation of the provisions of this Act which are comprised in this Group of Parts; and where a definition is provided for a particular expression, it applies except so far as the context otherwise requires.

**General note**—In addition to ss 381–385 a number of useful definitions relating to bankruptcy appear r 1.2 and in Part X of the IR 2016.

**[1.514]**

### 381 "Bankrupt" and associated terminology

(1) "Bankrupt" means an individual who has been made bankrupt and, in relation to a bankruptcy order, it means the individual made bankrupt by that order.

(1A) "Bankruptcy application" means an application to an adjudicator for a bankruptcy order.

(2) "Bankruptcy order" means an order making an individual bankrupt.

(3) "Bankruptcy petition" means a petition to the court for a bankruptcy order.

**Amendments**—Enterprise and Regulatory Reform Act 2013, s 71(3), Sch 19, paras 1, 52.

**[1.515]**

### 382 "Bankruptcy debt", 'liability'

(1) "Bankruptcy debt", in relation to a bankrupt, means (subject to the next subsection) any of the following—

(a) any debt or liability to which he is subject at the commencement of the bankruptcy,

(b) any debt or liability to which he may become subject after the commencement of the bankruptcy (including after his discharge from bankruptcy) by reason of any obligation incurred before the commencement of the bankruptcy,

*(c) any amount specified in pursuance of section 39(3)(c) of the Powers of Criminal Courts Act 1973 in any criminal bankruptcy order made against him before the commencement of the bankruptcy, and*

(d) any interest provable as mentioned in section 322(2) in Chapter IV of Part IX.

(2) In determining for the purposes of any provision in this Group of Parts whether any liability in tort is a bankruptcy debt, the bankrupt is deemed to become subject to that liability by reason of an obligation incurred at the time when the cause of action accrued.

(3) For the purposes of references in this Group of Parts to a debt or liability, it is immaterial whether the debt or liability is present or future, whether it is certain or contingent or whether its amount is fixed or liquidated, or is capable of being ascertained by fixed rules or as a matter of opinion; and references in this Group of Parts to owing a debt are to be read accordingly.

(4) In this Group of Parts, except in so far as the context otherwise requires, "liability" means (subject to subsection (3) above) a liability to pay money or money's worth, including any liability under an enactment, any liability for breach of trust, any liability in contract, tort or bailment and any liability arising out of an obligation to make restitution.

(5) Liability under the Child Support Act 1991 to pay child support maintenance to any person is not a debt or liability for the purposes of Part 8.

**Amendments**—Subsection (1)(c) prospectively repealed by Criminal Justice Act 1988, s 170(2), Sch 16, as from a date to be appointed; Welfare Reform Act 2012, s 142(1), (2).

**General note**—The provision explains what constitutes a bankruptcy debt, namely a debt that permits a creditor to petition for bankruptcy, although a bankruptcy debt is not necessarily provable. In theory, a creditor can base a petition on a non-provable debt: *Levy v Legal Services Commission* [2001] 1 All ER 895, [2000] BPIR 1065. See IR 2016, r 14.2 and the comments applying to it for consideration of the debts which are provable.

The definition of 'bankruptcy debt' has most obvious significance to s 281(1), by which the effect of discharge is to release a bankrupt from all such debts.

The scope of the term 'bankruptcy debt', which extends not only to debts but also to 'liability', on which see s 382(3) and (4), is extremely broad and extends to all manner of unliquidated claims.

A liability to repay benefit overpayments (in respect of income support) arising on a decision by the Secretary of State to recover such an overpayment made prior to the recipient's bankruptcy, and in the absence of fraud, constitutes a bankruptcy debt from which the recipient is released on discharge: *Secretary of State for Work and Pensions v Balding* [2007] EWCA Civ 1327, [2008] 1 WLR 564, [2007] BPIR 1669 (Mummery, Thomas and Lloyd LJJ). *Balding* was approved by the

Supreme Court in *Secretary of State for Work and Pensions v Payne* [2011] UKSC 60, [2012] 2 AC 1, [2012] BPIR 224. It was held in *Steele v Birmingham City Council* [2005] EWCA Civ 1824, [2006] 1 WLR 2380, [2006] BPIR 856 that the liability will not constitute a bankruptcy debt and will not therefore be released on discharge if the decision to recover the overpayment is made after the commencement of the bankruptcy, but that case was held by the Supreme Court to have been wrongly decided in *In re Nortel GmbH (in administration)* [2013] UKSC 52, [2013] 3 WLR 504, [2013] BPIR 866 (per Lord Neuberger PSC, [91]). Post-*Nortel*, it appears that the liability will be provable whether the decision is made before or after the commencement of the bankruptcy, as long as the relevant 'obligation' giving rise to the decision was incurred before the bankruptcy. See note to r 14.1.

In *Jones v Revenue and Customs Commissioners* [2017] UKFTT 567 (TC) (FTT (Tax)) Tribunal, Judge Barbara Mosedale held that tax liabilities related to assessments carried out prior to the taxpayer becoming bankrupt were bankruptcy debts.

Income payment orders made during a first bankruptcy will be bankruptcy debts and provable in a subsequent bankruptcy: *Azuonye v Kent* [2019] EWCA Civ 1289, [2019] 4 WLR 101, [2019] BPIR 1317 (per David Richards LJ, reversing Falk J).

Section 382(1)(c), which is obsolete in any case, is to be repealed from a date to be appointed by virtue of s 170(2) and Sch 16 to the Criminal Justice Act 1988.

For the purposes of s 382(3) a liability is contingent if it arises out of an existing legal commitment or state of affairs but which is dependent on the happening or non-happening of a stipulated event: *Re Sutherland* [1963] AC 235, HL.

In *Glenister v Rowe* [2000] Ch 76, [1999] BPIR 674 the Court of Appeal held that liability for an opposing party's costs in proceedings commenced prior to the making of a bankruptcy order did not constitute a contingent liability, since an order for costs remains a matter for the court's discretion and, until that discretion is exercised, there cannot be said to be a contingency in the *Sutherland* sense. Lord Neuberger PSC held in *In re Nortel GmbH (in administration)* [2013] UKSC 52, [2013] 3 WLR 504, [2013] BPIR 866 that *Glenister v Rowe* (like *Steele v Birmingham City Council* referred to above) was wrongly decided (per Lord Neuberger, [91]). Any pre-*Nortel* decision taking a restrictive view of 'bankruptcy debt' should now be approached with caution. See note to r 14.1.

'Contingent'—See under the heading 'Contingent or prospective creditors' in relation to s 124.

## [1.516]

### 383 "Creditor", "security", etc

(1) "Creditor"—

    (a)    in relation to a bankrupt, means a person to whom any of the bankruptcy debts is owed *(being, in the case of an amount falling within paragraph (c) of the definition in section 382(1) of "bankruptcy debt", the person in respect of whom that amount is specified in the criminal bankruptcy order in question)*, and

    (b)    in relation to an individual to whom a bankruptcy application or bankruptcy petition relates, means a person who would be a creditor in the bankruptcy if a bankruptcy order were made on that application or petition.

(2) Subject to the next two subsections and any provision of the rules requiring a creditor to give up his security for the purposes of proving a debt, a debt is secured for the purposes of this Group of Parts to the extent that the person to whom the debt is owed holds any security for the debt (whether a mortgage, charge, lien or other security) over any property of the person by whom the debt is owed.

(3) Where a statement such as is mentioned in section 269(1)(a) in Chapter I of Part IX has been made by a secured creditor for the purposes of any bankruptcy petition and a bankruptcy order is subsequently made on that petition, the creditor is deemed for the purposes of the Parts in this Group to have given up the security specified in the statement.

(4) In subsection (2) the reference to a security does not include a lien on books, papers or other records, except to the extent that they consist of documents which give a title to property and are held as such.

**Amendments**—Subsection (1)(a) prospectively repealed by Criminal Justice Act 1988, s 170(2), Sch 16, as from a date to be appointed; Enterprise and Regulatory Reform Act 2013, s 71(3), Sch 19, paras 1, 53.

**General note**—Apart from the definition of the term 'creditor' in s 383(1), s 383(2) and (3) are most obviously relevant to s 269, which deals with a petitioning creditor with security. In addition to the more common mortgage or charge, a debt may be secured by 'lien or other security' such as a trust arrangement as arises in favour of the Law Society under the Solicitors Act 1974 following an intervention, but not including a landlord's right of re-entry: *Razzaq v Pala* [1997] 1 WLR 1336, [1997] BPIR 726. For commentary on the two lines of authority as to whether money in court is capable of constituting security see the Court of Appeal's judgment in *Flightline Ltd v Edwards* [2003] EWCA Civ 63, [2003] 1 WLR 1200, [2003] 1 BCLC 427, [2003] BPIR 549 at [23].

**Secured creditor**—On the court's approach to the definition of a secured creditor in insolvency proceedings, reference should also be made to the commentary to ss 248, 269 and r 10.5(5)(c).

As one would expect, a creditor is only a secured creditor if he or she holds security over the property of a debtor who becomes bankrupt, and not if security is held over the property of a third party: *Re A Debtor (No 310 of 1988)* [1989] 1 WLR 452. However, where a guarantor both guarantees and grants security in respect of the principal debt, the creditor stands as a secured creditor both in respect of the principal debt and the guarantor's liability under the guarantee – each £1 recovered by the creditor under the charge would pro rata reduce the liability under the guarantee, *Promontoria (Chestnut) Limited v Bell & Bell* [2019] EWHC 1581 (Ch), [2019] BPIR 1241, (Zacaroli J) at [41]–[54].

A landlord who has a right to distrain is not a secured creditor: *Re Coal Consumers' Association* (1876–1877) 4 ChD 625; *Re Bridgewater Engineering Co* (1879) 12 ChD 181 at 186.

**Security and surrender**—Section 383(3) relates to s 269(1)(a) which provides that if a petitioning creditor bases a bankruptcy petition on a secured debt, he or she must be ready to surrender security for the benefit of all creditors of the debtor, if a bankruptcy order is made. See also the note to s 269(1)(a).

## [1.517]

### 383A "Opted-out creditor"

(1) For the purposes of this Group of Parts "opted-out creditor" in relation to an office-holder for an individual means a person who—

    (a)    is a creditor of the individual, and

    (b)    in accordance with the rules has elected (or is deemed to have elected) to be (and not to cease to be) an opted-out creditor in relation to the office-holder.

(2) In this section, "office-holder", in relation to an individual, means—

    (a)    where a bankruptcy order is made against the individual, the official receiver or the trustee in bankruptcy;

    (b)    where an interim receiver of the individual's property is appointed, the interim receiver;

    (c)    the supervisor of a voluntary arrangement approved under Part 8 in relation to the individual.

**Amendments**—Inserted by Small Business, Enterprise and Employment Act 2015, s 125(1), (4).

## [1.518]

### 384 "Prescribed" and "the rules"

(1) Subject to the next subsection and sections 342C(7) and 342F(9) in Chapter V of Part IX, "prescribed" means prescribed by the rules; and "the rules" means rules made under section 412 in Part XV.

(2) References in this Group of Parts to the amount prescribed for the purposes of any of the following provisions—

    section 251S(4);

    section 273;

    section 313A;

    section 346(3);

    section 354(1) and (2);

    section 358;

    section 360(1);

    section 361(2);

section 364(2)(d),

paragraphs 6 to 8 of Schedule 4ZA,

and references in those provisions to the prescribed amount are to be read in accordance with section 418 in Part XV and orders made under that section.

**Amendments**—Welfare Reform and Pensions Act 1999, s 84(1), Sch 12, Pt II, paras 70, 72; Enterprise Act 2002, s 261(5); Tribunals, Courts and Enforcement Act 2007, s 108(3), Sch 20, Pt 1, paras 1, 4.

'Debt'—This will include (because of the reference to s 382(3)) future and contingent claims.

## [1.519]

### 385 Miscellaneous definitions

(1) The following definitions have effect—

"adjudicator" means a person appointed by the Secretary of State under section 398A;

"the court", in relation to any matter, means the court to which, in accordance with section 373 in Part X and the rules, proceedings with respect to that matter are allocated or transferred;

"creditors' decision procedure" has the same meaning given by section 379ZA(11);

"creditor's petition" means a bankruptcy petition under section 264(1)(a);

*"criminal bankruptcy order" means an order under section 39(1) of the Powers of Criminal Courts Act 1973;*

"debt" is to be construed in accordance with section 382(3);

"the debtor"—

    (za)    in relation to a debt relief order or an application for such an order, has the same meaning as in Part 7A,

    (a)    in relation to a proposal for the purposes of Part VIII, means the individual making or intending to make that proposal, and

    (b)    in relation to a bankruptcy application or a bankruptcy petition, means the individual to whom the application or petition relates;

. . .

"debt relief order" means an order made by the official receiver under Part 7A

"deemed consent procedure" means the deemed consent procedure provided for by section 379ZB;

"determination period" has the meaning given in section 263K(4);

"dwelling house" includes any building or part of a building which is occupied as a dwelling and any yard, garden, garage or outhouse belonging to the dwelling house and occupied with it;

"estate", in relation to a bankrupt is to be construed in accordance with section 283 in Chapter II of Part IX;

"family", in relation to a bankrupt, means the persons (if any) who are living with him and are dependent on him;

"insolvency administration order" means an order for the administration in bankruptcy of the insolvent estate of a deceased debtor (being an individual at the date of his death);

"insolvency administration petition" means a petition for an insolvency administration order;

"the Rules" means the Insolvency (England and Wales) Rules 2016.

"secured" and related expressions are to be construed in accordance with section 383; and

"the trustee", in relation to a bankruptcy and the bankrupt, means the trustee of the bankrupt's estate.

(2) References in this Group of Parts to a person's affairs include his business, if any.

**Amendments**—SI 1986/1999; Criminal Justice Act 1988, s 170(2), Sch 16 as from a date to be appointed; Tribunals, Courts and Enforcement Act 2007, s 108(3), Sch 20, Pt 1, paras 1, 5;

Enterprise and Regulatory Reform Act 2013, s 71(3), Sch 19, paras 1, 55; Small Business, Enterprise and Employment Act 2015, s 123(1), (4)(a); SI 2017/369.

**General note**—On the meaning of the 'court' and questions of jurisdiction see *Hall and Shivers v Van Der Heiden* [2010] EWHC 537 (TCC), [2010] BPIR 585. In the context of an application for an income payments order under s 310, it was common ground that a bankrupt's estranged wife did not come within the statutory definition of 'family', *Re Fowlds* [2020] EWHC 329 (Ch), [2020] BPIR 541, Marcus Smith J at [13].

**Dwelling house**—The definition was considered in detail by HHJ Paul Matthews (sitting as a High Court judge) in *Brake v Swift* [2020] EWHC 1810 (Ch), [2020] 4 WLR 113 at [186]–[187]. He held that a 'yard, garden etc' will 'belong' to a dwelling house where it is useful to or serves the dwelling house – it is not required to be in the same ownership. However, the idea of occupation 'with' the dwelling house refers to occupation of the same quality by the same persons.

## THIRD GROUP OF PARTS
## MISCELLANEOUS MATTERS BEARING ON BOTH COMPANY AND INDIVIDUAL INSOLVENCY; GENERAL INTERPRETATION; FINAL PROVISIONS

### PART XII   PREFERENTIAL DEBTS IN COMPANY AND INDIVIDUAL INSOLVENCY

**[1.520]**

**General comment on Part XII**—This Part only consists of three sections. The first two sections simply deal with one topic, namely preferential debts that can be claimed in both corporate and personal insolvency. The provisions also apply to limited liability partnerships through reg 5(1)(b) of the Limited Liability Partnerships Regulations 2001 (SI 2001/1090) (operative from 6 April 2001) and insolvent partnerships due to arts 8, 10 and 11 and Sch 7 (paras 1 and 23) of the Insolvent Partnerships Order 1994 (SI 1994/2421).

The scheme provided by this Part (and Sch 6) allows certain unsecured creditors to get a right to payment in priority to other unsecured creditors, and, in relation to companies that have given floating charges, priority over a secured creditor. See the notes accompanying s 107 in relation to the position where a company is subject to a floating charge.

At one time there were two main preferential creditors, namely employees of the debtor and the Crown. The Crown's right to recover unremitted taxes and duties was gradually eroded in the latter part of the twentieth century, until s 251 of the Enterprise Act 2002 abolished Crown priority totally (in accord with the actions of a number of countries, such as Austria, Australia and Germany). However, Crown priority was reintroduced in part, with effect from 1 December 2020, by amendments to s 386 and the addition of para 15D of Sch 16 by s 98 of the Finance Act 2020 and the Insolvency Act 1986 (HMRC Debts: Priority on Insolvency) Regulations 2020 (SI 2020/ 983). Consequently HMRC is a secondary preferential creditor in respect of specified taxes; being sums collected or deducted from employees and customers (VAT, PAYE Income Tax, employee National Insurance Contributions and Construction Industry Scheme deductions) where the relevant date is 1 December 2020 or later. The rules for 'business taxes' (eg corporation tax or employer National Insurance Contributions) remain unchanged. A large number of countries around the world still retain priority for debts owed to government. Spain, France, Italy and South Africa are examples.

See the notes accompanying Sch 6 and s 175.

See A Keay *McPherson and Keay's Law of Company Liquidation* (Sweet and Maxwell, 4th edn, 2018), Ch 13 for a detailed discussion of the preferential debts scheme.

The third section was introduced by the Banks and Building Societies (Priorities on Insolvency) Order 2018 (SI 2018/1244) and deals with non-preferential debts of relevant financial institutions. See the notes to s 387A.

**[1.521]**

**386 Categories of preferential debts**

(1)   A reference in this Act to the preferential debts of a company or an individual is to the debts listed in Schedule 6 to this Act (contributions to occupational pension schemes; remuneration, &c of employees; levies on coal and steel production; debts owed to the Financial Services Compensation Scheme; deposits covered by Financial Services Compensation Scheme; other deposits; certain HMRC debts); and references to preferential creditors are to be read accordingly.

(1A) A reference in this Act to the "ordinary preferential debts" of a company or an individual is to the preferential debts listed in any of paragraphs 8 to 15B of Schedule 6 to this Act.

(1B) A reference in this Act to the "secondary preferential debts" of a company or an individual is to the preferential debts listed in paragraph 15BA, 15BB or 15D of Schedule 6 to this Act.

(2) In Schedule 6 "the debtor" means the company or the individual concerned.

(3) Schedule 6 is to be read with Schedule 4 to the Pension Schemes Act 1993 (occupational pension scheme contributions).

**Amendments**—Pension Schemes Act 1993, s 190, Sch 8, para 18; Enterprise Act 2002, s 251(3); Financial Services (Banking Reform) Act 2013, s 13(2); SI 2014/3160; SI 2014/3486; SI 2015/486; Finance Act 2020, s 98(1)(a).

**General note**—See Sch 6 for the debts that are preferential. Also, see the notes accompanying that Schedule for more details. See general commentary to Pt XII above for discussion on Crown preference.

## [1.522]

### 387 "The relevant date"

(1) This section explains references in Schedule 6 to the relevant date (being the date which determines the existence and amount of a preferential debt).

(2) For the purposes of section 4 in Part I (consideration of company voluntary arrangement), the relevant date in relation to a company which is not being wound up is—

    (a)    if the company is in administration, the date on which it entered administration, and

    (b)    if the company is not in administration, the date on which the voluntary arrangement takes effect.

(2A) . . .

(3) In relation to a company which is being wound up, the following applies—

    (a)    if the winding up is by the court, and the winding-up order was made immediately upon the discharge of an administration order, the relevant date is the date on which the company entered administration;

    (aa)    *if the winding up is by the court and the winding-up order was made following conversion of administration into winding up by virtue of Article 51 of the EU Regulation, the relevant date is the date on which the company entered administration;*

    (ab)    *if the company is deemed to have passed a resolution for voluntary winding up by virtue of an order following conversion of administration into winding up under Article 51 of the EU Regulation, the relevant date is the date on which the company entered administration;*

    (b)    if the case does not fall within paragraph (a), *(aa)* or *(ab)* and the company—

        (i)    is being wound up by the court, and

        (ii)    had not commenced to be wound up voluntarily before the date of the making of the winding-up order,

the relevant date is the date of the appointment (or first appointment) of a provisional liquidator or, if no such appointment has been made, the date of the winding-up order;

    (ba)    if the case does not fall within paragraph (a), *(aa)*, *(ab)* or (b) and the company is being wound up following administration pursuant to paragraph 83 of Schedule B1, the relevant date is the date on which the company entered administration;

    (c)    if the case does not fall within paragraph (a), *(aa)*, *(ab)*, (b) or (ba), the relevant date is the date of the passing of the resolution for the winding up of the company.

(3A)   In relation to a company which is in administration (and to which no other provision of this section applies) the relevant date is the date on which the company enters administration.

(4)   In relation to a company in receivership (where section 40 or, as the case may be, section 59 applies), the relevant date is—

    (a)    in England and Wales, the date of the appointment of the receiver by debenture-holders, and

    (b)    in Scotland, the date of the appointment of the receiver under section 53(6) or (as the case may be) 54(5).

(5)   For the purposes of section 258 in Part VIII (individual voluntary arrangements), the relevant date is, in relation to a debtor who is not an undischarged bankrupt—

    (a)    where an interim order has been made under section 252 with respect to his proposal, the date of that order, and

    (b)    in any other case, the date on which the voluntary arrangement takes effect.

(6)   In relation to a bankrupt, the following applies—

    (a)    where at the time the bankruptcy order was made there was an interim receiver appointed under section 286, the relevant date is the date on which the interim receiver was first appointed after the making of the bankruptcy application or (as the case may be) the presentation of the bankruptcy petition;

    (b)    otherwise, the relevant date is the date of the making of the bankruptcy order.

**Amendments**—Insolvency Act 2000, s 1, Sch 1, paras 1, 9; Enterprise Act 2002, s 248(3), Sch 17, paras 9, 34; SI 2002/1240; Enterprise and Regulatory Reform Act 2013, s 71(3), Sch 19, paras 1, 56; Small Business, Enterprise and Employment Act 2015, s 126, Sch 9, Pt 1, paras 1, 55; SI 2017/702; SI 2019/146, as from IP completion day (as defined in the European Union (Withdrawal Agreement) Act 2020, s 39(1)–(5)); Corporate Insolvency and Governance Act 2020, s 2(1), Sch 3, paras 1, 20.

**General note**—The section explains what 'relevant date' means for the various insolvency regimes. The expression is used frequently in Sch 6 and is the point used for determining and quantifying a preferential debt. The reintroduction in part of Crown preference in s 386 does not apply where the relevant date is before 1 December 2020 (s 98(7) of the Finance Act 2020 – see commentary to Pt XII above for discussion on Crown preference.

Paragraph 23 of Sch 7 of the Insolvent Partnerships Order 1994 (SI 1994/2421) modifies s 387 as far as it applies to insolvent partnerships.

## [1.523]

### 387A   Financial institutions and their non-preferential debts

(1)   In this Act "relevant financial institution" means any of the following—

    (a)    a credit institution,

    (b)    an investment firm,

    (c)    a financial holding company,

    (d)    a mixed financial holding company,

    (e)    a financial institution which is—

        (i)    a subsidiary of an entity referred to in sub-paragraphs (a) to (d), and

        (ii)    covered by the supervision of that entity on a consolidated basis in accordance with Articles 6 to 17 of Regulation (EU) No 575/2013, or

    (f)    a mixed-activity holding company.

(2)   The definitions in Article 4 of Regulation (EU) No 575/2013 apply for the purposes of subsection (1).

(3)   In this Act, in relation to a relevant financial institution—

    (a)    "ordinary non-preferential debts" means non-preferential debts which are neither secondary non-preferential debts nor tertiary non-preferential debts;

(b) "secondary non-preferential debts" means non-preferential debts issued under an instrument where—

    (i) the original contractual maturity of the instrument is of at least one year,

    (ii) the instrument is not a derivative and contains no embedded derivative, and

    (iii) the relevant contractual documentation and where applicable the prospectus related to the issue of the debts explain the priority of the debts under this Act, and

(c) "tertiary non-preferential debts" means all subordinated debts, including (but not limited to) debts under Common Equity Tier 1 instruments, Additional Tier 1 instruments and Tier 2 instruments (all within the meaning of Part 1 of the Banking Act 2009).

(4) In subsection (3)(b), "derivative" has the same meaning as in Article 2(5) of Regulation (EU) No 648/2012.

(5) For the purposes of subsection (3)(b)(ii) an instrument does not contain an embedded derivative merely because—

(a) it provides for a variable interest rate derived from a broadly used reference rate, or

(b) it is not denominated in the domestic currency of the person issuing the debt (provided that the principal, repayment and interest are denominated in the same currency).

**Amendments**—Inserted by SI 2018/1244.

**General note**—This section was inserted by the Banks and Buildings Societies (Priorities on Insolvency) Order 2018 and applies to insolvency proceedings commenced on or after 19 December 2018. It implements obligations in the Bank Creditor Hierarchy Directive 2017/2399/EU amending the Banking Recovery and Resolution Directive 2014/59/EU as regards the ranking of unsecured debt instruments in insolvency.

The Directive provides organisations with an alternative to existing options to meet their Minimum Requirement for own funds and Eligible Liabilities (MREL) requirement. MREL comprises the organisation's regulatory capital and debt instruments that meet certain eligibility criteria and is the loss absorbing capacity that EU banks are required to hold to bear losses in resolution. The purpose of MREL is to help ensure that if organisations fail, the resolution authority (the Bank of England in the UK) can use these financial resources to absorb losses and recapitalise the continuing business.

The Directive provides for a new class of non-preferred debt to be issued by specified 'relevant financial institutions'. In insolvency proceedings such debts rank below ordinary unsecured debts but above own funds, investments and subordinated liabilities that do not qualify as own funds instruments.

## PART XIII INSOLVENCY PRACTITIONERS AND THEIR QUALIFICATION

## [1.524]

**General comment on Part XIII**—The Insolvency Law Review Committee's Report, entitled *Insolvency Law and Practice* (and known as 'the Cork Report') (Cmnd 8558, 1982), acknowledged that the success of an insolvency regime was heavily dependent on those who administer it, namely the insolvency practitioners in private practice who did the work of liquidators, receivers, trustees and so on (at para 732). At the time of the Cork Committee's review of insolvency law and practice, insolvency practitioners were not required to have any particular qualifications, and this was identified by many as a major shortcoming in the system (at para 735). There was general recognition in the commercial world that there were some persons who were acting as insolvency practitioners, who might be termed 'cowboys', and who were not really qualified to act, and who engaged in questionable activities in administering the affairs of the insolvent. The Cork Committee agreed with the need for regulation and standards for qualification as an insolvency practitioner. This Part seeks to fulfil many of the Cork Committee's recommendations, with the heart of the Part being the requirement that practitioners should be members of professional bodies that regulate and discipline their members. The aim of the Part is to ensure that there is a qualified, independent and competent insolvency profession that is marked by integrity. Under this Part, insolvency practitioners are authorised and regulated by 'Recognised Professional Bodies' (see s 391) and people unhappy with the actions of insolvency practitioners should initially complain to those bodies. If no satisfaction is obtained, the person should then go to the Department for Business, Energy and Industrial Strategy.

To assist practitioners the Insolvency Service issues what are known as 'Dear IP' letters. Further guidance for practitioners may be found in the 'Statements of Insolvency Practice' ('SIPs'), issued and updated from time to time under procedures agreed between the Recognised Professional Bodies, acting through the Joint Insolvency Committee. According to SIP 1, the SIPs set principles and key compliance standards with which insolvency practitioners are required to comply and are intended to apply in parallel to the prevailing statutory framework. The latest versions of the SIPs may be found at APPENDIX 1 to this work.

Besides being members of Recognised Professional Bodies, many practitioners have become members of R3 (the Association for Business Recovery Professionals, formerly the Society for Practitioners of Insolvency). R3 (standing for Rescue, Recovery and Renewal) is involved in training practitioners, representing the interests of insolvency practitioners, and acts as the trade association for the UK insolvency and restructuring industry.

The Insolvency Practitioners Regulations 2005 (SI 2005/524) set out the requirements for a person to be authorised as an insolvency practitioner. The Regulations prescribe rules in relation to education, practical training and experience. The Insolvency Practitioners Regulations 1990 (SI 1990/439) (and amended by SI 1993/221) apply to applications for authorisation under s 393 to act as an insolvency practitioner made before 1 April 2005 (Insolvency Practitioners Regulations 2005, reg 4(2)), as well as cases in which an insolvency practitioner was appointed before that date (reg 4(3)).

In the following commentary, unless it is indicated to the contrary, the term 'insolvency practitioner' refers to licensed insolvency practitioners carrying out any of the following roles: liquidator, provisional liquidator, administrator, administrative receiver, a supervisor of a company voluntary arrangement, trustee in bankruptcy, interim receiver and a supervisor of an individual voluntary arrangement.

As from 1 October 2015, s 17 and Part 6 of Sch 6 of the Deregulation Act 2015 made substantial changes to the regime for authorisation of insolvency practitioners in Part XIII. From the same date, Part 10 of the Small Business, Enterprise and Employment Act 2015 also made substantial changes to Part XIII of the Act, in relation notably to the Recognised Professional Bodies.

*Restrictions on unqualified persons acting as liquidator, trustee in bankruptcy, etc*

## [1.525]

### 388 Meaning of "act as insolvency practitioner"

(1) A person acts as an insolvency practitioner in relation to a company by acting—

    (a) as its liquidator, provisional liquidator, administrator, administrative receiver or monitor, or

    (b) where a voluntary arrangement in relation to the company is proposed or approved under Part I, as nominee or supervisor.

(2) A person acts as an insolvency practitioner in relation to an individual by acting—

    (a) as his trustee in bankruptcy or interim receiver of his property or as trustee (or interim trustee) in the sequestration of his estate; or

    (b) as trustee under a deed which is . . ., in Scotland, a trust deed for his creditors; or

    (c) where a voluntary arrangement in relation to the individual is proposed or approved under Part VIII, as nominee or supervisor

    (d) in the case of a deceased individual to the administration of whose estate this section applies by virtue of an order under section 421 (application of provisions of this Act to insolvent estates of deceased persons), as administrator of that estate.

(2A) A person acts as an insolvency practitioner in relation to an insolvent partnership by acting—

    (a) as its liquidator, provisional liquidator or administrator, or

    (b) as trustee of the partnership under article 11 of the Insolvent Partnerships Order 1994, or

    (c) where a voluntary arrangement in relation to the insolvent partnership is proposed or approved under Part I of the Act, as nominee or supervisor.

(2B)   In relation to a voluntary arrangement proposed under Part I or VIII, a person acts as nominee if he performs any of the functions conferred on nominees under the Part in question.

(3)   References in this section to an individual include, except in so far as the context otherwise requires, references ... to any debtor within the meaning of the Bankruptcy (Scotland) Act 2016.

(4)   In this section—

"administrative receiver" has the meaning given by section 251 in Part VII;

"company" means—

(a)   a company registered under the Companies Act 2006 in England and Wales or Scotland, or

(b)   a company that may be wound up under Part 5 of this Act (unregistered companies);

"monitor" has the same meaning as in Part A1 (moratorium);

"sequestration" means sequestration under the Bankruptcy (Scotland) Act 2016.

(5)   Nothing in this section applies to anything done by—

(a)   the official receiver; or

(b)   the Accountant in Bankruptcy (within the meaning of the Bankruptcy (Scotland) Act 2016).

(6)   Nothing in this section applies to anything done (whether in the United Kingdom or elsewhere) in relation to insolvency proceedings under the EU Regulation in a member State other than the United Kingdom.

**Amendments**—Bankruptcy (Scotland) Act 1993, s 11(1); SI 1994/2421; Insolvency Act 2000, s 4(1), (2); SI 2002/1240; SI 2002/2708; SI 2009/1941; Deregulation Act 2015, s 19, Sch 6, Pt 1, para 2(1), (11)(f); SI 2016/1034; SI 2017/702; SI 2019/146, as from IP completion day (as defined in the European Union (Withdrawal Agreement) Act 2020, s 39(1)–(5)); Corporate Insolvency and Governance Act 2020, s 2(1), Sch 3, paras 1, 21(1).

**General note**—The provision explains what acting as an insolvency practitioner entails. This is done by setting out the fact that acting in certain roles means one is acting as an insolvency practitioner. This is important, as it is acting as an insolvency practitioner that is regarded as an offence (see s 389). Official receivers are not required to be qualified insolvency practitioners (s 388(5)(a)). Their work is, of course, monitored in different ways within the civil service and by the courts.

Section 388(2A)(c) was amended by the Insolvent Partnerships (Amendment) (No 2) Order 2002 (SI 2002/2708).

## [1.526]

### 389 Acting without qualification an offence

(1)   A person who acts as an insolvency practitioner in relation to a company or an individual at a time when he is not qualified to do so is liable to imprisonment or a fine, or to both.

(1A)   . . .

(2)   This section does not apply to the official receiver or the Accountant in Bankruptcy (within the meaning of the Bankruptcy (Scotland) Act 2016).

**Amendments**—Bankruptcy (Scotland) Act 1993, s 11(2); Insolvency Act 2000, s 4(1), (3); Deregulation Act 2015, s 19, Sch 6, Pt 6, paras 17, 18; SI 2016/1034.

**General note**—This provision gives the bite to the whole regime for insolvency practitioners, making it a criminal offence to act as an insolvency practitioner when not authorised to do so. Schedule 10 to the Act sets out the penalty for breaching this provision. It can be severe with, in a trial on indictment, a prison sentence of up to 2 years and/or a fine.

### 389A

*(Repealed)*

**[1.527]**

### 389B Official receiver as nominee or supervisor

(1) The official receiver is authorised to act as nominee or supervisor in relation to a voluntary arrangement approved under Part VIII provided that the debtor is an undischarged bankrupt when the arrangement is proposed.

(2) The Secretary of State may by order repeal the proviso in subsection (1).

(3) An order under subsection (2)—

    (a)    must be made by statutory instrument, and

    (b)    shall be subject to annulment in pursuance of a resolution of either House of Parliament.

**Amendments**—Inserted by Enterprise Act 2002, s 264(1), Sch 22, para 3.

**General note**—Originally official receivers could not act in relation to IVAs, but this provision, part of the Enterprise Act 2002 reforms, permits official receivers to act in relation to so-called 'fast track' IVAs under s 263A. See that section and the notes accompanying it.

*The requisite qualification, and the means of obtaining it*

**[1.528]**

### 390 Persons not qualified to act as insolvency practitioners

(1) A person who is not an individual is not qualified to act as an insolvency practitioner.

(2) A person is not qualified to act as an insolvency practitioner at any time unless at that time that person is appropriately authorised under section 390A.

(3) A person is not qualified to act as an insolvency practitioner in relation to another person at any time unless—

    (a)    there is in force at that time security or, in Scotland, caution for the proper performance of his functions, and

    (b)    that security or caution meets the prescribed requirements with respect to his so acting in relation to that other person.

(4) A person is not qualified to act as an insolvency practitioner at any time if at that time—

    (a)    he has been made bankrupt under this Act or the Insolvency (Northern Ireland) Order 1989 or sequestration of his estate has been awarded and (in either case) he has not been discharged,

    (aa)    a moratorium period under a debt relief order under this Act or the Insolvency (Northern Ireland) Order 1989 applies in relation of him,

    (b)    he is subject to a disqualification order made or a disqualification undertaking accepted under the Company Directors Disqualification Act 1986 or the Company Directors Disqualification (Northern Ireland) Order 2002,

    (c)    he is a patient within the meaning of section 329(1) of the Mental Health (Care and Treatment) (Scotland) Act 2003 or has had a guardian appointed to him under the Adults with Incapacity (Scotland) Act 2000 (asp 4), or

    (d)    he lacks capacity (within the meaning of the Mental Capacity Act 2005) to act as an insolvency practitioner.

(5) A person is not qualified to act as an insolvency practitioner while there is in force in respect of that person—

    (a)    a bankruptcy restrictions order under this Act, the Bankruptcy (Scotland) Act 1985 or the Bankruptcy (Scotland) Act 2016 or the Insolvency (Northern Ireland) Order 1989, or

    (b)    a debt relief restrictions order under this Act or that Order.

**Amendments**—Insolvency Act 2000, s 8, Sch 4, paras 1, 16; Adults with Incapacity (Scotland) Act 2000, s 88(2), Sch 5, para 18; Enterprise Act 2002, s 257(3), Sch 21, para 4; SI 2004/1941; SI 2005/2078; Mental Capacity Act 2005, s 67(1), (2), Sch 6, para 31(1), (3), Sch 7; Tribunals, Courts and Enforcement Act 2007, s 108(3), Sch 20, Pt 1, paras 1, 6; SI 2009/1941; SI 2009/3081;

Enterprise and Regulatory Reform Act 2013, s 71(3), Sch 19, paras 1, 58; Deregulation Act 2015, s 17(1), (2); Small Business, Enterprise and Employment Act 2015, s 115(a)(i); SI 2016/1034.

**General note**—The provision explains who is not qualified to act as an insolvency practitioner, and implicitly indicates what must be done to act legitimately.

**Authorisation**—See ss 390A and 391 and the notes accompanying them.

**Security**—The requirement in s 390(3) is designed to safeguard the positions of creditors where an insolvency practitioner has acted in such a way as to cause loss to creditors. See Insolvency Practitioners Regulations 2005 (SI 2005/524), Sch 2, paras 2–8 for the details of any security bond. The Regulations provide that the surety under the bond that is given undertakes to be jointly and severally liable with the insolvency practitioner for the proper performance by the practitioner of the duties and obligations imposed upon the practitioner.

## [1.529]

### 390A Authorisation

(1)  In this Part—

"partial authorisation" means authorisation to act as an insolvency practitioner—

(a)  only in relation to companies, or

(b)  only in relation to individuals;

"full authorisation" means authorisation to act as an insolvency practitioner in relation to companies, individuals and insolvent partnerships;

"'partially authorised" and "fully authorised" are to be construed accordingly.

(2)  A person is fully authorised under this section to act as an insolvency practitioner—

(a)  by virtue of being a member of a professional body recognised under section 391(1) and being permitted to act as an insolvency practitioner for all purposes by or under the rules of that body, or

(b)  by holding an authorisation granted by the Department of Enterprise, Trade and Investment in Northern Ireland under Article 352 of the Insolvency (Northern Ireland) Order 1989.

(3)  A person is partially authorised under this section to act as an insolvency practitioner—

(a)  by virtue of being a member of a professional body recognised under section 391(1) and being permitted to act as an insolvency practitioner in relation only to companies or only to individuals by or under the rules of that body, or

(b)  by virtue of being a member of a professional body recognised under section 391(2) and being permitted to act as an insolvency practitioner by or under the rules of that body.

**Amendments**—Inserted by Deregulation Act 2015, s 17(1), (3).

## [1.530]

### 390B Partial authorisation: acting in relation to partnerships

(1)  A person who is partially authorised to act as an insolvency practitioner in relation to companies may nonetheless not accept an appointment to act in relation to a company if at the time of the appointment the person is aware that the company—

(a)  is or was a member of a partnership, and

(b)  has outstanding liabilities in relation to the partnership.

(2)  A person who is partially authorised to act as an insolvency practitioner in relation to individuals may nonetheless not accept an appointment to act in relation to an individual if at the time of the appointment the person is aware that the individual—

(a)  is or was a member of a partnership other than a Scottish partnership, and

(b)  has outstanding liabilities in relation to the partnership.

(3)  Subject to subsection (9), a person who is partially authorised to act as an insolvency practitioner in relation to companies may nonetheless not continue to act in relation to a company if the person becomes aware that the company—

(a)    is or was a member of a partnership, and

(b)    has outstanding liabilities in relation to the partnership,

unless the person is granted permission to continue to act by the court.

(4)    Subject to subsection (9), a person who is partially authorised to act as an insolvency practitioner in relation to individuals may nonetheless not continue to act in relation to an individual if the person becomes aware that the individual—

(a)    is or was a member of a partnership other than a Scottish partnership, and

(b)    has outstanding liabilities in relation to the partnership,

unless the person is granted permission to continue to act by the court.

(5)    The court may grant a person permission to continue to act for the purposes of subsection (3) or (4) if it is satisfied that the person is competent to do so.

(6)    A person who is partially authorised and becomes aware as mentioned in subsection (3) or (4) may alternatively apply to the court for an order (a "replacement order") appointing in his or her place a person who is fully authorised to act as an insolvency practitioner in relation to the company or (as the case may be) the individual.

(7)    A person may apply to the court for permission to continue to act or for a replacement order under—

(a)    where acting in relation to a company, this section or, if it applies, section 168(5B) (member of insolvent partnership: England and Wales);

(b)    where acting in relation to an individual, this section or, if it applies, section 303(2C) (member of insolvent partnership: England and Wales).

(8)    A person who acts as an insolvency practitioner in contravention of any of subsections (1) to (4) is guilty of an offence under section 389 (acting without qualification).

(9)    A person does not contravene subsection (3) or (4) by continuing to act as an insolvency practitioner during the permitted period if, within the period of 7 business days beginning with the day after the day on which the person becomes aware as mentioned in the subsection, the person—

(a)    applies to the court for permission to continue to act, or

(b)    applies to the court for a replacement order.

(10)    For the purposes of subsection (9)—

"business day" means any day other than a Saturday, a Sunday, Christmas Day, Good Friday or a day which is a bank holiday in any part of Great Britain;

"permitted period" means the period beginning with the day on which the person became aware as mentioned in subsection (3) or (4) and ending on the earlier of—

(a)    the expiry of the period of 6 weeks beginning with the day on which the person applies to the court as mentioned in subsection (9)(a) or (b), and

(b)    the day on which the court disposes of the application (by granting or refusing it);

"replacement order" has the meaning given by subsection (6).

**Amendments**—Inserted by Deregulation Act 2015, s 17(1), (3).

## [1.531]

### 391 Recognised professional bodies

(1)    The Secretary of State may by order declare a body which appears to the Secretary of State to meet the requirements of subsection (4) to be a recognised professional body which is capable of providing its insolvency specialist members with full authorisation or partial authorisation.

(2)    The Secretary of State may by order declare a body which appears to the Secretary of State to meet the requirements of subsection (4) to be a recognised professional body which is capable of providing its insolvency specialist members with partial authorisation only.

(3)   An order under subsection (2) must state whether the partial authorisation relates to companies or to individuals.

(4)   The requirements are that the body—

    (a)   regulates the practice of a profession, and,

    (b)   maintains and enforces rules for securing that its insolvency specialist members—

        (i)   are fit and proper persons to act as insolvency practitioners, and

        (ii)   meet acceptable requirements as to education and practical training and experience.

(5)   The Secretary of State may make an order revoking an order under subsection (1) or (2) in relation to a professional body if it appears to the Secretary of State that the body no longer meets the requirements of subsection (4).

(6)   The Secretary of State may make an order revoking an order under subsection (1) and replacing it with an order under subsection (2) in relation to a professional body if it appears to the Secretary of State that the body is capable of providing its insolvency specialist members with partial authorisation only.

(7)   An order of the Secretary of State under this section has effect from such date as is specified in the order.

(8)   An order revoking an order made under subsection (1) or (2) may make provision whereby members of the body in question continue to be treated as fully or partially authorised to act as insolvency practitioners (as the case may be) for a specified period after the revocation takes effect.

(9)   In this section—

    (a)   references to members of a recognised professional body are to persons who, whether members of that body or not, are subject to its rules in the practice of the profession in question (and the references in section 390A to members of a recognised professional body are to be read accordingly);

    (b)   references to insolvency specialist members of a professional body are to members who are permitted by or under the rules of the body to act as insolvency practitioners.]

**Amendments**—Substituted by the Deregulation Act 2015, s 17(1), (4).

**General note**—The Secretary of State is granted the power under this provision to declare bodies to be recognised professional bodies, to which a person who wishes to act as an insolvency practitioner must belong.

**Recognised professional bodies**—Bodies that have been recognised for the purposes of s 391 as being ones that were professional and able to discipline and regulate members. The recognised professional bodies (RPBs) number four and are the Institute of Chartered Accountants in England and Wales, the Institute of Chartered Accountants of Scotland, the Institute of Chartered Accountants in Ireland, and the Insolvency Practitioners' Association (Insolvency Practitioners (Recognised Professional Bodies) Order 1986 (SI 1986/1764)). The Law Society and the Law Society of Scotland were RPBs until their status was revoked (at their own request) in 2016. Until 1 March 2021 the Association of Certified Chartered Accountants (ACCA) (formerly the Chartered Association of Certified Accountants) was also an RPB but its recognition was revoked with effect from 1 March 2021 at the ACCA's request; all IPs previously licenced by the ACCA now being licenced by one of the four RPBs above. While the professional bodies that are recognised exercise control over their own qualified members, there is governmental monitoring, as the Insolvency Service supervises the regulatory process, conducts regular visits to all of the professional bodies and endeavours to ensure that necessary standards are maintained. Besides being a member of a professional body that is recognised, a person must also satisfy other requirements in order to be able to practise as an insolvency practitioner. These requirements include passing examinations and practical experience. Hence, the mere fact that one is a member of one of the professional bodies does not mean that one is qualified to practise as an insolvency practitioner. In July 2019, the Insolvency Service launched a call for evidence in relation to the future of insolvency practitioner regulation, including the possibility of moving from multiple RPBs to a single regulator. At the time of writing (June 2021) the evidence remains under consideration.

The professional bodies must determine whether a member is a fit and proper person to act as an insolvency practitioner. The bodies operate various processes to control and correct those acting improperly, with revocation of a practitioner's licence to operate as an insolvency practitioner as one critical measure that can be taken. Obviously, if this were done, the practitioner would no longer be qualified to act as an insolvency practitioner. Bodies may withdraw a licence with immediate effect and before the exhausting of the appeal process, if it is deemed necessary in order to protect the public (*R (on the application of Eliades) v Institute of Chartered Accountants* [2001] BPIR 363 at [33], a case concerning an application for judicial review in relation to the withdrawal of an insolvency practitioner's licence to act).

## [1.532]

### 391A  Application for recognition as recognised professional body

(1)  An application for an order under section 391(1) or (2) must—

    (a)    be made to the Secretary of State in such form and manner as the Secretary of State may require,

    (b)    be accompanied by such information as the Secretary of State may require, and

    (c)    be supplemented by such additional information as the Secretary of State may require at any time between receiving the application and determining it.

(2)  The requirements which may be imposed under subsection (1) may differ as between different applications.

(3)  The Secretary of State may require information provided under this section to be in such form, and verified in such manner, as the Secretary of State may specify.

(4)  An application for an order under section 391(1) or (2) must be accompanied by—

    (a)    a copy of the applicant's rules,

    (b)    a copy of the applicant's policies and practices, and

    (c)    a copy of any guidance issued by the applicant in writing.

(5)  The reference in subsection (4)(c) to guidance issued by the applicant is a reference to guidance or recommendations which are—

    (a)    issued or made by it which will apply to its insolvency specialist members or to persons seeking to become such members,

    (b)    relevant for the purposes of this Part, and

    (c)    intended to have continuing effect,

including guidance or recommendations relating to the admission or expulsion of members.

(6)  The Secretary of State may refuse an application for an order under section 391(1) or (2) if the Secretary of State considers that recognition of the body concerned is unnecessary having regard to the existence of one or more other bodies which have been or are likely to be recognised under section 391.

(7)  Subsection (8) applies where the Secretary of State refuses an application for an order under section 391(1) or (2); and it applies regardless of whether the application is refused on the ground mentioned in subsection (6), because the Secretary of State is not satisfied as mentioned in section 391(1) or (2) or because a fee has not been paid (see section 415A(1)(b)).

(8)  The Secretary of State must give the applicant a written notice of the Secretary of State's decision; and the notice must set out the reasons for refusing the application.

**Amendments**—Sections 391 and 391A substituted for s 391 by Small Business, Enterprise and Employment Act 2015, s 137(1).

### *Regulatory objectives*

**Amendments**—Inserted by Small Business, Enterprise and Employment Act 2015, s 138(1).

## [1.533]

### 391B  Application of regulatory objectives

(1)  In discharging regulatory functions, a recognised professional body must, so far as is reasonably practicable, act in a way—

    (a)    which is compatible with the regulatory objectives, and

    (b)    which the body considers most appropriate for the purpose of meeting those objectives.

(2)   In discharging functions under this Part, the Secretary of State must have regard to the regulatory objectives.

**Amendments**—Inserted by Small Business, Enterprise and Employment Act 2015, s 138(1).

## [1.534]

### 391C  Meaning of "regulatory functions" and "regulatory objectives"

(1)   This section has effect for the purposes of this Part.

(2)   "Regulatory functions", in relation to a recognised professional body, means any functions the body has—

    (a)   under or in relation to its arrangements for or in connection with—

        (i)   authorising persons to act as insolvency practitioners, or

        (ii)   regulating persons acting as insolvency practitioners, or

    (b)   in connection with the making or alteration of those arrangements.

(3)   "Regulatory objectives" means the objectives of—

    (a)   having a system of regulating persons acting as insolvency practitioners that—

        (i)   secures fair treatment for persons affected by their acts and omissions,

        (ii)   reflects the regulatory principles, and

        (iii)   ensures consistent outcomes,

    (b)   encouraging an independent and competitive insolvency-practitioner profession whose members—

        (i)   provide high quality services at a cost to the recipient which is fair and reasonable,

        (ii)   act transparently and with integrity, and

        (iii)   consider the interests of all creditors in any particular case,

    (c)   promoting the maximisation of the value of returns to creditors and promptness in making those returns, and

    (d)   protecting and promoting the public interest.

(4)   In subsection (3)(a), "regulatory principles" means—

    (a)   the principles that regulatory activities should be transparent, accountable, proportionate, consistent and targeted only at cases in which action is needed, and

    (b)   any other principle appearing to the body concerned (in the case of the duty under section 391B(1)), or to the Secretary of State (in the case of the duty under section 391B(2)), to lead to best regulatory practice.

**Amendments**—Inserted by Small Business, Enterprise and Employment Act 2015, s 138.

*Oversight of recognised professional bodies*

**Amendments**—Inserted by Small Business, Enterprise and Employment Act 2015, s 139.

## [1.535]

### 391D  Directions

(1)   This section applies if the Secretary of State is satisfied that an act or omission of a recognised professional body (or a series of such acts or omissions) in discharging one or more of its regulatory functions has had, or is likely to have, an adverse impact on the achievement of one or more of the regulatory objectives.

(2)   The Secretary of State may, if in all the circumstances of the case satisfied that it is appropriate to do so, direct the body to take such steps as the Secretary of State considers will counter the adverse impact, mitigate its effect or prevent its occurrence or recurrence.

(3)   A direction under this section may require a recognised professional body—

    (a)   to take only such steps as it has power to take under its regulatory arrangements;

(b)  to take steps with a view to the modification of any part of its regulatory arrangements.

(4)  A direction under this section may require a recognised professional body—

(a)  to take steps with a view to the institution of, or otherwise in respect of, specific regulatory proceedings;

(b)  to take steps in respect of all, or a specified class of, such proceedings.

(5)  For the purposes of this section, a direction to take steps includes a direction which requires a recognised professional body to refrain from taking a particular course of action.

(6)  In this section "regulatory arrangements", in relation to a recognised professional body, means the arrangements that the body has for or in connection with—

(a)  authorising persons to act as insolvency practitioners, or

(b)  regulating persons acting as insolvency practitioners.

**Amendments**—Inserted by Small Business, Enterprise and Employment Act 2015, s 139.

## [1.536]

### 391E  Directions: procedure

(1)  Before giving a recognised professional body a direction under section 391D, the Secretary of State must give the body a notice accompanied by a draft of the proposed direction.

(2)  The notice under subsection (1) must—

(a)  state that the Secretary of State proposes to give the body a direction in the form of the accompanying draft,

(b)  specify why the Secretary of State has reached the conclusions mentioned in section 391D(1) and (2), and

(c)  specify a period within which the body may make written representations with respect to the proposal.

(3)  The period specified under subsection (2)(c)—

(a)  must begin with the date on which the notice is given to the body, and

(b)  must not be less than 28 days.

(4)  On the expiry of that period, the Secretary of State must decide whether to give the body the proposed direction.

(5)  The Secretary of State must give notice of that decision to the body.

(6)  Where the Secretary of State decides to give the proposed direction, the notice under subsection (5) must—

(a)  contain the direction,

(b)  state the time at which the direction is to take effect, and

(c)  specify the Secretary of State's reasons for the decision to give the direction.

(7)  Where the Secretary of State decides to give the proposed direction, the Secretary of State must publish the notice under subsection (5); but this subsection does not apply to a direction to take any step with a view to the institution of, or otherwise in respect of, regulatory proceedings against an individual.

(8)  The Secretary of State may revoke a direction under section 391D; and, where doing so, the Secretary of State—

(a)  must give the body to which the direction was given notice of the revocation, and

(b)  must publish the notice and, if the notice under subsection (5) was published under subsection (7), must do so (if possible) in the same manner as that in which that notice was published.

**Amendments**—Inserted by Small Business, Enterprise and Employment Act 2015, s 139.

## [1.537]

### 391F  Financial penalty

(1)  This section applies if the Secretary of State is satisfied—

    (a)    that a recognised professional body has failed to comply with a requirement to which this section applies, and

    (b)    that, in all the circumstances of the case, it is appropriate to impose a financial penalty on the body.

(2)   This section applies to a requirement imposed on the recognised professional body—

    (a)    by a direction given under section 391D, or

    (b)    by a provision of this Act or of subordinate legislation under this Act.

(3)   The Secretary of State may impose a financial penalty, in respect of the failure, of such amount as the Secretary of State considers appropriate.

(4)   In deciding what amount is appropriate, the Secretary of State—

    (a)    must have regard to the nature of the requirement which has not been complied with, and

    (b)    must not take into account the Secretary of State's costs in discharging functions under this Part.

(5)   A financial penalty under this section is payable to the Secretary of State; and sums received by the Secretary of State in respect of a financial penalty under this section (including by way of interest) are to be paid into the Consolidated Fund.

(6)   In sections 391G to 391I, "penalty" means a financial penalty under this section.

**Amendments**—Inserted by Small Business, Enterprise and Employment Act 2015, s 139.

## [1.538]

### 391G Financial penalty: procedure

(1)   Before imposing a penalty on a recognised professional body, the Secretary of State must give notice to the body—

    (a)    stating that the Secretary of State proposes to impose a penalty and the amount of the proposed penalty,

    (b)    specifying the requirement in question,

    (c)    stating why the Secretary of State is satisfied as mentioned in section 391F(1), and

    (d)    specifying a period within which the body may make written representations with respect to the proposal.

(2)   The period specified under subsection (1)(d)—

    (a)    must begin with the date on which the notice is given to the body, and

    (b)    must not be less than 28 days.

(3)   On the expiry of that period, the Secretary of State must decide—

    (a)    whether to impose a penalty, and

    (b)    whether the penalty should be the amount stated in the notice or a reduced amount.

(4)   The Secretary of State must give notice of the decision to the body.

(5)   Where the Secretary of State decides to impose a penalty, the notice under subsection (4) must—

    (a)    state that the Secretary of State has imposed a penalty on the body and its amount,

    (b)    specify the requirement in question and state—

        (i)    why it appears to the Secretary of State that the requirement has not been complied with, or

        (ii)   where, by that time, the requirement has been complied with, why it appeared to the Secretary of State when giving the notice under subsection (1) that the requirement had not been complied with, and

    (c)    specify a time by which the penalty is required to be paid.

(6)   The time specified under subsection (5)(c) must be at least three months after the date on which the notice under subsection (4) is given to the body.

(7)   Where the Secretary of State decides to impose a penalty, the Secretary of State must publish the notice under subsection (4).

(8)   The Secretary of State may rescind or reduce a penalty imposed on a recognised professional body; and, where doing so, the Secretary of State—
- (a)     must give the body notice that the penalty has been rescinded or reduced to the amount stated in the notice, and
- (b)     must publish the notice; and it must (if possible) be published in the same manner as that in which the notice under subsection (4) was published.

**Amendments**—Inserted by Small Business, Enterprise and Employment Act 2015, s 139.

## [1.539]

### 391H  Appeal against financial penalty

(1)   A recognised professional body on which a penalty is imposed may appeal to the court on one or more of the appeal grounds.
(2)   The appeal grounds are—
- (a)     that the imposition of the penalty was not within the Secretary of State's power under section 391F;
- (b)     that the requirement in respect of which the penalty was imposed had been complied with before the notice under section 391G(1) was given;
- (c)     that the requirements of section 391G have not been complied with in relation to the imposition of the penalty and the interests of the body have been substantially prejudiced as a result;
- (d)     that the amount of the penalty is unreasonable;
- (e)     that it was unreasonable of the Secretary of State to require the penalty imposed to be paid by the time specified in the notice under section 391G(5)(c).

(3)   An appeal under this section must be made within the period of three months beginning with the day on which the notice under section 391G(4) in respect of the penalty is given to the body.
(4)   On an appeal under this section the court may—
- (a)     quash the penalty,
- (b)     substitute a penalty of such lesser amount as the court considers appropriate, or
- (c)     in the case of the appeal ground in subsection (2)(e), substitute for the time imposed by the Secretary of State a different time.

(5)   Where the court substitutes a penalty of a lesser amount, it may require the payment of interest on the substituted penalty from such time, and at such rate, as it considers just and equitable.
(6)   Where the court substitutes a later time for the time specified in the notice under section 391G(5)(c), it may require the payment of interest on the penalty from the substituted time at such rate as it considers just and equitable.
(7)   Where the court dismisses the appeal, it may require the payment of interest on the penalty from the time specified in the notice under section 391G(5)(c) at such rate as it considers just and equitable.
(8)   In this section, "the court" means the High Court or, in Scotland, the Court of Session.

**Amendments**—Inserted by Small Business, Enterprise and Employment Act 2015, s 139.

## [1.540]

### 391I  Recovery of financial penalties

(1)   If the whole or part of a penalty is not paid by the time by which it is required to be paid, the unpaid balance from time to time carries interest at the rate for the time being specified in section 17 of the Judgments Act 1838 (but this is subject to any requirement imposed by the court under section 391H(5), (6) or (7)).
(2)   If an appeal is made under section 391H in relation to a penalty, the penalty is not required to be paid until the appeal has been determined or withdrawn.

(3)   Subsection (4) applies where the whole or part of a penalty has not been paid by the time it is required to be paid and—

(a)   no appeal relating to the penalty has been made under section 391H during the period within which an appeal may be made under that section, or

(b)   an appeal has been made under that section and determined or withdrawn.

(4)   The Secretary of State may recover from the recognised professional body in question, as a debt due to the Secretary of State, any of the penalty and any interest which has not been paid.

**Amendments**—Inserted by Small Business, Enterprise and Employment Act 2015, s 139.

## [1.541]

### 391J Reprimand

(1)   This section applies if the Secretary of State is satisfied that an act or omission of a recognised professional body (or a series of such acts or omissions) in discharging one or more of its regulatory functions has had, or is likely to have, an adverse impact on the achievement of one or more of the regulatory objectives.

(2)   The Secretary of State may, if in all the circumstances of the case satisfied that it is appropriate to do so, publish a statement reprimanding the body for the act or omission (or series of acts or omissions).

**Amendments**—Inserted by Small Business, Enterprise and Employment Act 2015, s 139.

## [1.542]

### 391K Reprimand: procedure

(1)   If the Secretary of State proposes to publish a statement under section 391J in respect of a recognised professional body, it must give the body a notice—

(a)   stating that the Secretary of State proposes to publish such a statement and setting out the terms of the proposed statement,

(b)   specifying the acts or omissions to which the proposed statement relates, and

(c)   specifying a period within which the body may make written representations with respect to the proposal.

(2)   The period specified under subsection (1)(c)—

(a)   must begin with the date on which the notice is given to the body, and

(b)   must not be less than 28 days.

(3)   On the expiry of that period, the Secretary of State must decide whether to publish the statement.

(4)   The Secretary of State may vary the proposed statement; but before doing so, the Secretary of State must give the body notice—

(a)   setting out the proposed variation and the reasons for it, and

(b)   specifying a period within which the body may make written representations with respect to the proposed variation.

(5)   The period specified under subsection (4)(b)—

(a)   must begin with the date on which the notice is given to the body, and

(b)   must not be less than 28 days.

(6)   On the expiry of that period, the Secretary of State must decide whether to publish the statement as varied.

**Amendments**—Inserted by Small Business, Enterprise and Employment Act 2015, s 139.

*Revocation etc of recognition*

**Amendments**—Inserted by Small Business, Enterprise and Employment Act 2015, s 140.

**[1.543]**

### 391L Revocation of recognition at instigation of Secretary of State

(1)  An order under section 391(1) or (2) in relation to a recognised professional body may be revoked by the Secretary of State by order if the Secretary of State is satisfied that—

    (a)    an act or omission of the body (or a series of such acts or omissions) in discharging one or more of its regulatory functions has had, or is likely to have, an adverse impact on the achievement of one or more of the regulatory objectives, and

    (b)    it is appropriate in all the circumstances of the case to revoke the body's recognition under section 391.

(2)  If the condition set out in subsection (3) is met, an order under section 391(1) in relation to a recognised professional body may be revoked by the Secretary of State by an order which also declares the body concerned to be a recognised professional body which is capable of providing its insolvency specialist members with partial authorisation only of the kind specified in the order (see section 390A(1)).

(3)  The condition is that the Secretary of State is satisfied—

    (a)    as mentioned in subsection (1)(a), and

    (b)    that it is appropriate in all the circumstances of the case for the body to be declared to be a recognised professional body which is capable of providing its insolvency specialist members with partial authorisation only of the kind specified in the order.

(4)  In this Part—

    (a)    an order under subsection (1) is referred to as a "revocation order";

    (b)    an order under subsection (2) is referred to as a "partial revocation order".

(5)  A revocation order or partial revocation order—

    (a)    has effect from such date as is specified in the order, and

    (b)    may make provision for members of the body in question to continue to be treated as fully or partially authorised (as the case may be) to act as insolvency practitioners for a specified period after the order takes effect.

(6)  A partial revocation order has effect as if it were an order made under section 391(2).

**Amendments**—Inserted by Small Business, Enterprise and Employment Act 2015, s 140.

**[1.544]**

### 391M Orders under section 391L: procedure

(1)  Before making a revocation order or partial revocation order in relation to a recognised professional body, the Secretary of State must give notice to the body—

    (a)    stating that the Secretary of State proposes to make the order and the terms of the proposed order,

    (b)    specifying the Secretary of State's reasons for proposing to make the order, and

    (c)    specifying a period within which the body, members of the body or other persons likely to be affected by the proposal may make written representations with respect to it.

(2)  Where the Secretary of State gives a notice under subsection (1), the Secretary of State must publish the notice on the same day.

(3)  The period specified under subsection (1)(c)—

    (a)    must begin with the date on which the notice is given to the body, and

    (b)    must not be less than 28 days.

(4)  On the expiry of that period, the Secretary of State must decide whether to make the revocation order or (as the case may be) partial revocation order in relation to the body.

(5)  The Secretary of State must give notice of the decision to the body.

(6)  Where the Secretary of State decides to make the order, the notice under subsection (5) must specify—

(a)    when the order is to take effect, and

(b)    the Secretary of State's reasons for making the order.

(7)    A notice under subsection (5) must be published; and it must (if possible) be published in the same manner as that in which the notice under subsection (1) was published.

Amendments—Inserted by Small Business, Enterprise and Employment Act 2015, s 140.

## [1.545]

### 391N Revocation of recognition at request of body

(1)    An order under section 391(1) or (2) in relation to a recognised professional body may be revoked by the Secretary of State by order if—

(a)    the body has requested that an order be made under this subsection, and

(b)    the Secretary of State is satisfied that it is appropriate in all the circumstances of the case to revoke the body's recognition under section 391.

(2)    An order under section 391(1) in relation to a recognised professional body may be revoked by the Secretary of State by an order which also declares the body concerned to be a recognised professional body which is capable of providing its insolvency specialist members with partial authorisation only of the kind specified in the order (see section 390A(1)) if—

(a)    the body has requested that an order be made under this subsection, and

(b)    the Secretary of State is satisfied that it is appropriate in all the circumstances of the case for the body to be declared to be a recognised professional body which is capable of providing its insolvency specialist members with partial authorisation only of the kind specified in the order.

(3)    Where the Secretary of State decides to make an order under this section the Secretary of State must publish a notice specifying—

(a)    when the order is to take effect, and

(b)    the Secretary of State's reasons for making the order.

(4)    An order under this section—

(a)    has effect from such date as is specified in the order, and

(b)    may make provision for members of the body in question to continue to be treated as fully or partially authorised (as the case may be) to act as insolvency practitioners for a specified period after the order takes effect.

(5)    An order under subsection (2) has effect as if it were an order made under section 391(2).

Amendments—Inserted by Small Business, Enterprise and Employment Act 2015, s 140.

*Court sanction of insolvency practitioners in public interest cases*

Amendments—Inserted by Small Business, Enterprise and Employment Act 2015, s 141.

## [1.546]

### 391O Direct sanctions orders

(1)    For the purposes of this Part a "direct sanctions order" is an order made by the court against a person who is acting as an insolvency practitioner which—

(a)    declares that the person is no longer authorised (whether fully or partially) to act as an insolvency practitioner;

(b)    declares that the person is no longer fully authorised to act as an insolvency practitioner but remains partially authorised to act as such either in relation to companies or individuals, as specified in the order;

(c)    declares that the person's authorisation to act as an insolvency practitioner is suspended for the period specified in the order or until such time as the requirements so specified are complied with;

(d)   requires the person to comply with such other requirements as may be specified in the order while acting as an insolvency practitioner;

(e)   requires the person to make such contribution as may be specified in the order to one or more creditors of a company, individual or insolvent partnership in relation to which the person is acting or has acted as an insolvency practitioner.

(2)   Where the court makes a direct sanctions order, the relevant recognised professional body must take all necessary steps to give effect to the order.

(3)   A direct sanctions order must not be made against a person whose authorisation to act as an insolvency practitioner was granted by the Department of Enterprise, Trade and Investment in Northern Ireland (see section 390A(2)(b)).

(4)   A direct sanctions order must not specify a contribution as mentioned in subsection (1)(e) which is more than the remuneration that the person has received or will receive in respect of acting as an insolvency practitioner in the case.

(5)   In this section and section 391P—

"the court" means the High Court or, in Scotland, the Court of Session;

"relevant recognised professional body", in relation to a person who is acting as an insolvency practitioner, means the recognised professional body by virtue of which the person is authorised so to act.

**Amendments**—Inserted by Small Business, Enterprise and Employment Act 2015, s 141.

## [1.547]

### 391P  Application for, and power to make, direct sanctions order

(1)   The Secretary of State may apply to the court for a direct sanctions order to be made against a person if it appears to the Secretary of State that it would be in the public interest for the order to be made.

(2)   The Secretary of State must send a copy of the application to the relevant recognised professional body.

(3)   The court may make a direct sanctions order against a person where, on an application under this section, the court is satisfied that condition 1 and at least one of conditions 2, 3, 4 and 5 are met in relation to the person.

(4)   The conditions are set out in section 391Q.

(5)   In deciding whether to make a direct sanctions order against a person the court must have regard to the extent to which—

(a)   the relevant recognised professional body has taken action against the person in respect of the failure mentioned in condition 1, and

(b)   that action is sufficient to address the failure.

**Amendments**—Inserted by Small Business, Enterprise and Employment Act 2015, s 141.

## [1.548]

### 391Q  Direct sanctions order: conditions

(1)   Condition 1 is that the person, in acting as an insolvency practitioner or in connection with any appointment as such, has failed to comply with—

(a)   a requirement imposed by the rules of the relevant recognised professional body;

(b)   any standards, or code of ethics, for the insolvency-practitioner profession adopted from time to time by the relevant recognised professional body.

(2)   Condition 2 is that the person—

(a)   is not a fit and proper person to act as an insolvency practitioner;

(b)   is a fit and proper person to act as an insolvency practitioner only in relation to companies, but the person's authorisation is not so limited; or

(c)   is a fit and proper person to act as an insolvency practitioner only in relation to individuals, but the person's authorisation is not so limited.

(3)   Condition 3 is that it is appropriate for the person's authorisation to act as an insolvency practitioner to be suspended for a period or until one or more requirements are complied with.

(4)   Condition 4 is that it is appropriate to impose other restrictions on the person acting as an insolvency practitioner.

(5)   Condition 5 is that loss has been suffered as a result of the failure mentioned in condition 1 by one or more creditors of a company, individual or insolvent partnership in relation to which the person is acting or has acted as an insolvency practitioner.

(6)   In this section "relevant recognised professional body" has the same meaning as in section 391O.

**Amendments**—Inserted by Small Business, Enterprise and Employment Act 2015, s 141.

## [1.549]
### 391R   Direct sanctions direction instead of order

(1)   The Secretary of State may give a direction (a "direct sanctions direction") in relation to a person acting as an insolvency practitioner to the relevant recognised professional body (instead of applying, or continuing with an application, for a direct sanctions order against the person) if the Secretary of State is satisfied that—

    (a)    condition 1 and at least one of conditions 2, 3, 4 and 5 are met in relation to the person (see section 391Q), and

    (b)    it is in the public interest for the direction to be given.

(2)   But the Secretary of State may not give a direct sanctions direction in relation to a person without that person's consent.

(3)   A direct sanctions direction may require the relevant recognised professional body to take all necessary steps to secure that—

    (a)    the person is no longer authorised (whether fully or partially) to act as an insolvency practitioner;

    (b)    the person is no longer fully authorised to act as an insolvency practitioner but remains partially authorised to act as such either in relation to companies or individuals, as specified in the direction;

    (c)    the person's authorisation to act as an insolvency practitioner is suspended for the period specified in the direction or until such time as the requirements so specified are complied with;

    (d)    the person must comply with such other requirements as may be specified in the direction while acting as an insolvency practitioner;

    (e)    the person makes such contribution as may be specified in the direction to one or more creditors of a company, individual or insolvent partnership in relation to which the person is acting or has acted as an insolvency practitioner.

(4)   A direct sanctions direction must not be given in relation to a person whose authorisation to act as an insolvency practitioner was granted by the Department of Enterprise, Trade and Investment in Northern Ireland (see section 390A(2)(b)).

(5)   A direct sanctions direction must not specify a contribution as mentioned in subsection (3)(e) which is more than the remuneration that the person has received or will receive in respect of acting as an insolvency practitioner in the case.

(6)   In this section "relevant recognised professional body" has the same meaning as in section 391O.

**Amendments**—Inserted by Small Business, Enterprise and Employment Act 2015, s 141.

*General*

**Amendments**—Inserted by Small Business, Enterprise and Employment Act 2015, s 142.

**[1.550]**

### 391S  Power for Secretary of State to obtain information

(1)   A person mentioned in subsection (2) must give the Secretary of State such information as the Secretary of State may by notice in writing require for the exercise of the Secretary of State's functions under this Part.

(2)   Those persons are—

- (a)   a recognised professional body;
- (b)   any individual who is or has been authorised under section 390A to act as an insolvency practitioner;
- (c)   any person who is connected to such an individual.

(3)   A person is connected to an individual who is or has been authorised to act as an insolvency practitioner if, at any time during the authorisation—

- (a)   the person was an employee of the individual;
- (b)   the person acted on behalf of the individual in any other way;
- (c)   the person employed the individual;
- (d)   the person was a fellow employee of the individual's employer;
- (e)   in a case where the individual was employed by a firm, partnership or company, the person was a member of the firm or partnership or (as the case may be) a director of the company.

(4)   In imposing a requirement under subsection (1) the Secretary of State may specify—

- (a)   the time period within which the information in question is to be given, and
- (b)   the manner in which it is to be verified.

**Amendments**—Inserted by Small Business, Enterprise and Employment Act 2015, s 142.

**[1.551]**

### 391T  Compliance orders

(1)   If at any time it appears to the Secretary of State that—

- (a)   a recognised professional body has failed to comply with a requirement imposed on it by or by virtue of this Part, or
- (b)   any other person has failed to comply with a requirement imposed on the person by virtue of section 391S,

the Secretary of State may make an application to the court.

(2)   If, on an application under this section, the court decides that the body or other person has failed to comply with the requirement in question, it may order the body or person to take such steps as the court considers will secure that the requirement is complied with.

(3)   In this section, "the court" means the High Court or, in Scotland, the Court of Session.

**Amendments**—Inserted by Small Business, Enterprise and Employment Act 2015, s 143.

**392–398**

*(Repealed)*

## PART XIV   PUBLIC ADMINISTRATION (ENGLAND AND WALES)

**[1.552]**

**General comment on Part XIV**—This Part deals with the public administration of insolvency law and practice. Its primary focus is on the office of official receiver and the financing and accounting arrangements in the Insolvency Service for monies held in insolvent estates.

*Adjudicators*

**[1.553]**

### 398A Appointment etc of adjudicators and assistants

(1)  The Secretary of State may appoint persons to the office of adjudicator.

(2)  A person appointed under subsection (1)—

    (a)  is to be paid out of money provided by Parliament such salary as the Secretary of State may direct,

    (b)  holds office on such other terms and conditions as the Secretary of State may direct, and

    (c)  may be removed from office by a direction of the Secretary of State.

(3)  A person who is authorised to act as an official receiver may not be appointed under subsection (1).

(4)  The Secretary of State may appoint officers of the Secretary of State's department to assist adjudicators in the carrying out of their functions.

**Amendments**—Inserted by Enterprise and Regulatory Reform Act 2013, s 71(1).

**General note**—Section 398A gives the Secretary of State power to appoint individuals to the office of 'adjudicator'. Where an individual wishes to apply to be made bankrupt, their application is now not heard by the court but by an adjudicator: see Chapter A1 of Part IX. By s 263K, an adjudicator now has power to make a bankruptcy order in respect of an individual. In the case of *Re Budniok; Budniok v Adjudicator* [2017] EWHC 368 (Ch), [2017] BPIR 521, Chief Registrar Baister reviewed the nature and role of an adjudicator in the context of an appeal by an individual against a decision refusing to make a bankruptcy order.

*Official receivers*

**[1.554]**

### 399  Appointment etc of official receivers

(1)  For the purposes of this Act the official receiver, in relation to any bankruptcy, winding up, individual voluntary arrangement, debt relief order or application for such an order, is any person who by virtue of the following provisions of this section or section 401 below is authorised to act as the official receiver in relation to that bankruptcy, winding up, individual voluntary arrangement, debt relief order or application for such an order.

(2)  The Secretary of State may (subject to the approval of the Treasury as to numbers) appoint persons to the office of official receiver, and a person appointed to that office (whether under this section or section 70 of the Bankruptcy Act 1914)—

    (a)  shall be paid out of money provided by Parliament such salary as the Secretary of State may with the concurrence of the Treasury direct,

    (b)  shall hold office on such other terms and conditions as the Secretary of State may with the concurrence of the Treasury direct, and

    (c)  may be removed from office by a direction of the Secretary of State.

(3)  Where a person holds the office of official receiver, the Secretary of State shall from time to time attach him either to the High Court or to the county court.

(4)  Subject to any directions under subsection (6) below, an official receiver attached to a particular court is the person authorised to act as the official receiver in relation to every bankruptcy, winding up, individual voluntary arrangement, debt relief order or application for such an order falling within the jurisdiction of that court.

(5)  The Secretary of State shall ensure that there is, at all times, at least one official receiver attached to the High Court and at least one attached to the county court; but he may attach the same official receiver to both courts.

(6)  The Secretary of State may give directions with respect to the disposal of the business of official receivers, and such directions may, in particular—

    (a)  authorise an official receiver attached to one court to act as the official receiver in relation to any case or description of cases falling within the jurisdiction of the other court;

(b)    provide, where there is more than one official receiver authorised to act as the official receiver in relation to cases falling within the jurisdiction of any court, for the distribution of their business between or among themselves.

(7)   A person who at the coming into force of section 222 of the Insolvency Act 1985 (replaced by this section) is an official receiver attached to a court shall continue in office after the coming into force of that section as an official receiver attached to that court under this section.

**Amendments**—Enterprise Act 2002, s 269, Sch 23, paras 1, 14; Tribunals, Courts and Enforcement Act 2007, s 108(3), Sch 20, Pt 1, paras 1, 7; Crime and Courts Act 2013, s 17(5), Sch 9, Pt 3, para 93.

**General note**—Official receivers carry out an important role in relation to many aspects of insolvency law, including acting as the first liquidator in compulsory windings up (s 136(2)) and as first trustee in bankruptcy in bankruptcies (s 291A) and investigating the causes of failure of insolvents (ss 132 and 289). Before being appointed as official receivers, such persons have usually occupied positions as civil servants within the Department of Business, Energy and Industrial Strategy, but when appointed as official receivers they cease 'to be civil servants in the proper sense of servants of the Crown employed in the business of government within (in this case) a department of state' (*Re Minotaur Data Systems Ltd* [1999] 2 BCLC 766 at 772, per Aldous LJ). Because Beldam LJ in *Mond v Hyde* [1999] 2 WLR 499 at 516, [1998] 2 BCLC 340 at 357 was of the view that the relationship between the Department of Trade and Industry (as the relevant government department was then known) and official receivers was not that of master and servant, each official receiver is entitled to initiate legal proceedings in his or her own name, and has a right of audience before the court to which he or she is attached.

See *Re Minotaur Data Systems Ltd* [1999] 1 WLR 1129, [1999] 2 BCLC 766, [1999] BPIR 560 for a judicial discussion of the nature of the office of official receiver.

## [1.555]

### 400 Functions and status of official receivers

(1)   In addition to any functions conferred on him by this Act, a person holding the office of official receiver shall carry out such other functions as may from time to time be conferred on him by the Secretary of State.

(2)   In the exercise of the functions of his office a person holding the office of official receiver shall act under the general directions of the Secretary of State and shall also be an officer of the court in relation to which he exercises those functions.

(3)   Any property vested in his official capacity in a person holding the office of official receiver shall, on his dying, ceasing to hold office or being otherwise succeeded in relation to the bankruptcy or winding up in question by another official receiver, vest in his successor without any conveyance, assignment or transfer.

**Officers of the court**—Because official receivers have the status of officers of the court in carrying out their functions, if there is any interference with their work, it could constitute a contempt of court. See *Mond v Hyde* [1999] QB 1097, [1998] 2 BCLC 340 on the position of official receivers' immunity from suit where a claim by a trustee in bankruptcy in respect of loss suffered as a result of a negligent statement made by the official receiver was dismissed on the basis that the official receiver, as an officer of the court, was immune from suit.

## [1.556]

### 401 Deputy official receivers and staff

(1)   The Secretary of State may, if he thinks it expedient to do so in order to facilitate the disposal of the business of the official receiver attached to any court, appoint an officer of his department to act as deputy to that official receiver.

(2)   Subject to any directions given by the Secretary of State under section 399 or 400, a person appointed to act as deputy to an official receiver has, on such conditions and for such period as may be specified in the terms of his appointment, the same status and functions as the official receiver to whom he is appointed deputy.

Accordingly, references in this Act (except section 399(1) to (5)) to an official receiver include a person appointed to act as his deputy.

(3)   An appointment made under subsection (1) may be terminated at any time by the Secretary of State.

(4)   The Secretary of State may, subject to the approval of the Treasury as to numbers and remuneration and as to the other terms and conditions of the appointments, appoint officers of his department to assist official receivers in the carrying out of their functions.

*The Official Petitioner*

## [1.557]

### 402   Official Petitioner

*(1)   There continues to be an officer known as the Official Petitioner for the purpose of discharging, in relation to cases in which a criminal bankruptcy order is made, the functions assigned to him by or under this Act; and the Director of Public Prosecutions continues, by virtue of his office, to be the Official Petitioner.*

*(2)   The functions of the Official Petitioner include the following—*

    *(a)   to consider whether, in a case in which a criminal bankruptcy order is made, it is in the public interest that he should himself present a petition under section 264(1)(d) of this Act;*

    *(b)   to present such a petition in any case where he determines that it is in the public interest for him to do so;*

    *(c)   to make payments, in such cases as he may determine, towards expenses incurred by other persons in connection with proceedings in pursuance of such a petition; and*

    *(d)   to exercise, so far as he considers it in the public interest to do so, any of the powers conferred on him by or under this Act.*

*(3)   Any functions of the Official Petitioner may be discharged on his behalf by any person acting with his authority.*

*(4)   Neither the Official Petitioner nor any person acting with his authority is liable to any action or proceeding in respect of anything done or omitted to be done in the discharge, or purported discharge, of the functions of the Official Petitioner.*

*(5)   In this section "criminal bankruptcy order" means an order under section 39(1) of the Powers of Criminal Courts Act 1973.*

**Amendments**—Prospectively repealed by Criminal Justice Act 1998, s 170(2), Sch 16, as from a date to be appointed.

*Insolvency Service finance, accounting and investment*

## [1.558]

### 403   Insolvency Services Account

(1)   All money received by the Secretary of State in respect of proceedings under this Act as it applies to England and Wales shall be paid into the Insolvency Services Account kept by the Secretary of State with the Bank of England; and all payments out of money standing to the credit of the Secretary of State in that account shall be made by the Bank of England in such manner as he may direct.

(2)   Whenever the cash balance standing to the credit of the Insolvency Services Account is in excess of the amount which in the opinion of the Secretary of State is required for the time being to answer demands in respect of bankrupts' estates or companies' estates, the Secretary of State shall—

    (a)   notify the excess to the National Debt Commissioners, and

    (b)   pay into the Insolvency Services Investment Account ("the Investment Account") kept by the Commissioners with the Bank of England the whole or any part of the excess as the Commissioners may require for investment in accordance with the following provisions of this Part.

(3)   Whenever any part of the money so invested is, in the opinion of the Secretary of State, required to answer any demand in respect of bankrupt's estates or companies'

estates, he shall notify to the National Debt Commissioners the amount so required and the Commissioners—

    (a)    shall thereupon repay to the Secretary of State such sum as may be required to the credit of the Insolvency Services Account, and

    (b)    for that purpose may direct the sale of such part of the securities in which the money has been invested as may be necessary.

## [1.559]

### 404 Investment Account

Any money standing to the credit of the Investment Account (including any money received by the National Debt Commissioners by way of interest on or proceeds of any investment under this section) may be invested by the Commissioners, in accordance with such directions as may be given by the Treasury, in any manner for the time being specified in Part II of Schedule 1 to the Trustee Investments Act 1961.

### 405

*(Repealed)*

## [1.560]

### 406 Interest on money received by liquidators or trustees in bankruptcy and invested

Where under rules made by virtue of paragraph 16 of Schedule 8 to this Act (investment of money received by company liquidators) or paragraph 21 of Schedule 9 to this Act (investment of money received by trustee in bankruptcy) a company or a bankrupt's estate has become entitled to any sum by way of interest, the Secretary of State shall certify that sum and the amount of tax payable on it to the National Debt Commissioners; and the Commissioners shall pay, out of the Investment Account—

    (a)    into the Insolvency Services Account, the sum so certified less the amount of tax so certified, and

    (b)    to the Commissioners of Inland Revenue, the amount of tax so certified.

**Amendments**—Insolvency Act 2000, s 13(2).

## [1.561]

### 407 Unclaimed dividends and undistributed balances

(1)    The Secretary of State shall from time to time pay into the Consolidated Fund out of the Insolvency Services Account so much of the sums standing to the credit of that Account as represents—

    (a)    dividends which were declared before such date as the Treasury may from time to time determine and have not been claimed, and

    (b)    balances ascertained before that date which are too small to be divided among the persons entitled to them.

(2)    For the purposes of this section the sums standing to the credit of the Insolvency Services Account are deemed to include any sums paid out of that Account and represented by any sums or securities standing to the credit of the Investment Account.

(3)    The Secretary of State may require the National Debt Commissioners to pay out of the Investment Account into the Insolvency Services Account the whole or part of any sum which he is required to pay out of that account under subsection (1); and the Commissioners may direct the sale of such securities standing to the credit of the Investment Account as may be necessary for that purpose.

## [1.562]

### 408 Adjustment of balances

(1)    The Treasury may direct the payment out of the Consolidated Fund of sums into—

    (a)    the Insolvency Services Account;

    (b)    the Investment Account.

(2)   The Treasury shall certify to the House of Commons the reason for any payment under subsection (1).

(3)   The Secretary of State may pay sums out of the Insolvency Services Account into the Consolidated Fund.

(4)   The National Debt Commissioners may pay sums out of the Investment Account into the Consolidated Fund.

**Amendments**—Substituted by Enterprise Act 2002, s 272(2).

**General note**—This provision was amended by the Enterprise Act 2002, s 272(2) and became operative from 1 April 2004.

## [1.563]

### 409  Annual financial statement and audit

(1)   The National Debt Commissioners shall for each year ending on 31 March prepare a statement of the sums credited and debited to the Investment Account in such form and manner as the Treasury may direct and shall transmit it to the Comptroller and Auditor General before the end of November next following the year.

(2)   The Secretary of State shall for each year ending 31st March prepare a statement of the sums received or paid by him under section 403 above in such form and manner as the Treasury may direct and shall transmit each statement to the Comptroller and Auditor General before the end of November next following the year.

(3)   Every such statement shall include such additional information as the Treasury may direct.

(4)   The Comptroller and Auditor General shall examine, certify and report on every such statement and shall lay copies of it, and of his report, before Parliament.

*Supplementary*

## [1.564]

### 410  Extent of this Part

This Part of this Act extends to England and Wales only.

PART XV    SUBORDINATE LEGISLATION

## [1.565]

**General comment on Part XV**—This Part deals with subordinate legislation that can be enacted to make the insolvency process work, and includes: the power to make rules and orders; provision for fees; and the power to make regulations for insolvency practice.

*General insolvency rules*

## [1.566]

### 411  Company insolvency rules

(1)   Rules may be made—

  (a)    in relation to England and Wales, by the Lord Chancellor with the concurrence of the Secretary of State and, in the case of rules that affect court procedure, with the concurrence of the Lord Chief Justice, or

  (b)    in relation to Scotland, by the Secretary of State,

for the purpose of giving effect to Parts A1 to VII of this Act or the EU Regulation.

(1A)   Rules may also be made for the purpose of giving effect to Part 2 of the Banking Act 2009 (bank insolvency orders); and rules for that purpose shall be made—

  (a)    in relation to England and Wales, by the Lord Chancellor with the concurrence of—

    (i)    the Treasury, and

        (ii)    in the case of rules that affect court procedure, the Lord Chief Justice, or

    (b)    in relation to Scotland, by the Treasury.

(1B)   Rules may also be made for the purpose of giving effect to Part 3 of the Banking Act 2009 (bank administration); and rules for that purpose shall be made—

    (a)    in relation to England and Wales, by the Lord Chancellor with the concurrence of—

        (i)    the Treasury, and

        (ii)    in the case of rules that affect court procedure, the Lord Chief Justice, or

    (b)    in relation to Scotland, by the Treasury.

(2)   Without prejudice to the generality of subsection (1), (1A) or (1B) or to any provision of those Parts by virtue of which rules under this section may be made with respect to any matter, rules under this section may contain—

    (a)    any such provision as is specified in Schedule 8 to this Act or corresponds to provision contained immediately before the coming into force of section 106 of the Insolvency Act 1985 in rules made, or having effect as if made, under section 663(1) or (2) of the Companies Act 1985 (old winding-up rules), and

    (b)    such incidental, supplemental and transitional provisions as may appear to the Lord Chancellor or, as the case may be, the Secretary of State or the Treasury necessary or expedient.

(2A)   For the purposes of subsection (2), a reference in Schedule 8 to this Act to doing anything under or for the purposes of a provision of this Act includes a reference to doing anything under or for the purposes of the EU Regulation (in so far as the provision of this Act relates to a matter to which the EU Regulation applies).

(2B)   Rules under this section for the purpose of giving effect to the EU Regulation may not create a new relevant offence.

(2C)   For the purposes of subsection (2), a reference in Schedule 8 to this Act to doing anything under or for the purposes of a provision of this Act includes a reference to doing anything under or for the purposes of Part 2 of the Banking Act 2009.

(2D)   For the purposes of subsection (2), a reference in Schedule 8 to this Act to doing anything under or for the purposes of a provision of this Act includes a reference to doing anything under or for the purposes of Part 3 of the Banking Act 2009.

(3)   In Schedule 8 to this Act "liquidator" includes a provisional liquidator or bank liquidator or administrator; and references above in this section to Parts A1 to VII of this Act or Part 2 or 3 of the Banking Act 2009 are to be read as including the Companies Acts so far as relating to, and to matters connected with or arising out of, the insolvency or winding up of companies.

(3A)   In this section references to Part 2 or 3 of the Banking Act 2009 include references to those Parts as applied to building societies (see section 90C of the Building Societies Act 1986).

(4)   Rules under this section shall be made by statutory instrument subject to annulment in pursuance of a resolution of either House of Parliament.

(5)   Regulations made by the Secretary of State or the Treasury under a power conferred by rules under this section shall be made by statutory instrument and, after being made, shall be laid before each House of Parliament.

(6)   Nothing in this section prejudices any power to make rules of court.

(7)   The Lord Chief Justice may nominate a judicial office holder (as defined in section 109(4) of the Constitutional Reform Act 2005) to exercise his functions under this section.

**Amendments**—SI 2002/1037; Constitutional Reform Act 2005, s 15(1), Sch 4; SI 2007/2194; Banking Act 2009, ss 125, 160; SI 2009/805; SI 2009/1941; SI 2017/702; SI 2019/146, as from IP completion day (as defined in the European Union (Withdrawal Agreement) Act 2020, s 39(1)–(5)); Corporate Insolvency and Governance Act 2020, s 2(1), Sch 3, paras 1, 22(1).

**General note**—This provision only deals with corporate insolvency (Parts I–VII of the Act) and the EU Regulation on Insolvency Proceedings.

Section 411(2A) and (2B) were introduced by reg 3 of the Insolvency Act 1986 (Amendment) Regulations 2002 (SI 2002/1037) to accommodate the advent of the EC Regulation on Insolvency Proceedings and amended by the Insolvency Amendment (EU 2015/848) Regulations 2017 (SI 2017/702) to accommodate the Recast EU Regulation 2015/848. Section 411(2B) was further amended by the Insolvency (Amendment) (EU Exit) Regulations 2019 (SI 2019/146) to address issues arising from the UK's withdrawal from the European Union; the reference to an offence of a kind referred to in para 1(1) of Sch 2 to the European Communities Act 1972 was replaced with a reference to a new relevant offence as provided for by a newly inserted s 422A.

## [1.567]

### 412 Individual insolvency rules (England and Wales)

(1) The Lord Chancellor may, with the concurrence of the Secretary of State and, in the case of rules that affect court procedure, with the concurrence of the Lord Chief Justice, make rules for the purpose of giving effect to Parts 7A to 11 of this Act or the EU Regulation.

(2) Without prejudice to the generality of subsection (1), or to any provision of those Parts by virtue of which rules under this section may be made with respect to any matter, rules under this section may contain—

(a) any such provision as is specified in Schedule 9 to this Act or corresponds to provision contained immediately before the appointed day in rules made under section 132 of the Bankruptcy Act 1914; and

(b) such incidental, supplemental and transitional provisions as may appear to the Lord Chancellor necessary or expedient.

(2A) For the purposes of subsection (2), a reference in Schedule 9 to this Act to doing anything under or for the purposes of a provision of this Act includes a reference to doing anything under or for the purposes of the EU Regulation (in so far as the provision of this Act relates to a matter to which the EU Regulation applies).

(2B) Rules under this section for the purpose of giving effect to the EU Regulation may not create a new relevant offence.

(3) Rules under this section shall be made by statutory instrument subject to annulment in pursuance of a resolution of either House of Parliament.

(4) Regulations made by the Secretary of State under a power conferred by rules under this section shall be made by statutory instrument and, after being made, shall be laid before each House of Parliament.

(5) Nothing in this section prejudices any power to make rules of court.

(6) The Lord Chief Justice may nominate a judicial office holder (as defined in section 109(4) of the Constitutional Reform Act 2005) to exercise his functions under this section.

**Amendments**—SI 2002/1037; Constitutional Reform Act 2005, s 15(1), Sch 4; Tribunals, Courts and Enforcement Act 2007, s 108(3), Sch 20, Pt 1, paras 1, 8; SI 2017/702; SI 2019/146, as from IP completion day (as defined in the European Union (Withdrawal Agreement) Act 2020, s 39(1)–(5)).

**General note**—This provision is the personal insolvency equivalent of s 411.

Section 412(2A) and (2B) were introduced by reg 3 of the Insolvency Act 1986 (Amendment) Regulations 2002 (SI 2002/1037) to accommodate the advent of the EC Regulation on Insolvency Proceedings and amended by the Insolvency Amendment (EU 2015/848) Regulations 2017 (SI 2017/702) to accommodate the Recast EU Regulation 2015/848. Section 412(2B) was further amended by the Insolvency (Amendment) (EU Exit) Regulations 2019 (SI 2019/146) to address issues arising from the UK's withdrawal from the European Union; the reference to an offence of a kind referred to in para 1(1) of Sch 2 to the European Communities Act 1972 was replaced with a reference to a new relevant offence as provided for by a newly inserted s 422A.

## [1.568]

### 413 Insolvency Rules Committee

(1) The committee established under section 10 of the Insolvency Act 1976 (advisory committee on bankruptcy and winding-up rules) continues to exist for the purpose of being consulted under this section.

(2) The Lord Chancellor shall consult the committee before making any rules under section 411 or 412 other than rules which contain a statement that the only provision made by the rules is provision applying rules made under section 411, with or without modifications, for the purposes of provision made by any of sections 23 to 26 of the Water Industry Act 1991 or Schedule 3 to that Act or by any of sections 59 to 65 of, or Schedule 6 or 7 to, the Railways Act 1993.

(3) Subject to the next subsection, the committee shall consist of—

(a) a judge of the High Court attached to the Chancery Division;

(b) a circuit judge;

(c) a registrar in bankruptcy of the High Court:

(d) a district judge;

(e) a practising barrister;

(f) a practising solicitor; and

(g) a practising accountant;

and the appointment of any person as a member of the committee shall be made in accordance with subsection (3A) or (3B).

(3A) The Lord Chief Justice must appoint the persons referred to in paragraphs (a) to (d) of subsection (3), after consulting the Lord Chancellor.

(3B) The Lord Chancellor must appoint the persons referred to in paragraphs (e) to (g) of subsection (3), after consulting the Lord Chief Justice.

(4) The Lord Chancellor may appoint as additional members of the committee any persons appearing to him to have qualifications or experience that would be of value to the committee in considering any matter with which it is concerned.

(5) The Lord Chief Justice may nominate a judicial office holder (as defined in section 109(4) of the Constitutional Reform Act 2005) to exercise his functions under this section.

**Amendments**—Water Act 1989, s 190(1), Sch 25, para 78(2); Water Consolidation (Consequential Provisions) Act 1991, s 2(1), Sch 1, para 46; Railways Act 1993, s 152(1), Sch 12, para 25; Constitutional Reform Act 2005, s 15(1), Sch 4; Crime and Courts Act 2013, s 17(5), Sch 9, Pt 3, para 93.

*Fees orders*

**[1.569]**

**414 Fees orders (company insolvency proceedings)**

(1) There shall be paid in respect of—

(a) proceedings under any of Parts A1 to VII of this Act, and

(b) the performance by the official receiver or the Secretary of State of functions under those Parts,

such fees as the competent authority may with the sanction of the Treasury by order direct.

(2) That authority is—

(a) in relation to England and Wales, the Lord Chancellor, and

(b) in relation to Scotland, the Secretary of State.

(3) The Treasury may by order direct by whom and in what manner the fees are to be collected and accounted for.

(4) The Lord Chancellor may, with the sanction of the Treasury, by order provide for sums to be deposited, by such persons, in such manner and in such circumstances as may be specified in the order, by way of security for fees payable by virtue of this section.

(5) An order under this section may contain such incidental, supplemental and transitional provisions as may appear to the Lord Chancellor, the Secretary of State or (as the case may be) the Treasury necessary or expedient.

(6) An order under this section shall be made by statutory instrument and, after being made, shall be laid before each House of Parliament.

(7) Fees payable by virtue of this section shall be paid into the Consolidated Fund.

(8)   References in subsection (1) to Parts A1 to VII of this Act are to be read as including the Companies Acts so far as relating to, and to matters connected with or arising out of, the insolvency or winding up of companies.

(8A)   This section applies in relation to Part 2 of the Banking Act 2009 (bank insolvency) as in relation to Parts I to VII of this Act.

(8B)   This section applies in relation to Part 3 of the Banking Act 2009 (bank administration) as in relation to Parts I to VII of this Act.

(8C)   In subsections (8A) and (8B) the reference to Parts 2 and 3 of the Banking Act 2009 include references to those Parts as applied to building societies (see section 90C of the Building Societies Act 1986).

(9)   *Nothing in this section prejudices any power to make rules of court; and the application of this section to Scotland is without prejudice to section 2 of the Courts of Law Fees (Scotland) Act 1895.*

**Amendments**—SI 2007/2194; Banking Act 2009, ss 126, 161; SI 2009/805; words in italics repealed in relation to Scotland, by SSI 2015/150; Corporate Insolvency and Governance Act 2020, s 2(1), Sch 3, paras 1, 23(1).

**General note**—See the Insolvency Proceedings (Fees) Order 2016 (SI 2016/692) (replacing the Insolvency Proceedings (Fees) Order 2004 (SI 2004/593)).

## [1.570]

### 415 Fees orders (individual insolvency proceedings in England and Wales)

(1)   There shall be paid in respect of—

>   (za)   the costs of persons acting as approved intermediaries under Part 7A,
>
>   (a)   proceedings under Parts 7A to 11 of this Act,
>
>   (b)   the performance by the official receiver or the Secretary of State of functions under those Parts, and
>
>   (c)   the performance by an adjudicator of functions under Part 9 of this Act,

such fees as the Lord Chancellor may with the sanction of the Treasury by order direct.

(1A)   An order under subsection (1) may make different provision for different purposes, including by reference to the manner or form in which proceedings are commenced.

(2)   The Treasury may by order direct by whom and in what manner the fees are to be collected and accounted for.

(3)   The Lord Chancellor may, with the sanction of the Treasury, by order provide for sums to be deposited, by such persons, in such manner and in such circumstances as may be specified in the order, by way of security for—

>   (a)   fees payable by virtue of this section, and
>
>   (b)   fees payable to any person who has prepared an insolvency practitioner's report under section 274 in Chapter I of Part IX.

(4)   An order under this section may contain such incidental, supplemental and transitional provisions as may appear to the Lord Chancellor or, as the case may be, the Treasury, necessary or expedient.

(5)   An order under this section shall be made by statutory instrument and, after being made, shall be laid before each House of Parliament.

(6)   Fees payable by virtue of this section shall be paid into the Consolidated Fund.

(7)   Nothing in this section prejudices any power to make rules of court.

**Amendments**—Tribunals, Courts and Enforcement Act 2007, s 108(3), Sch 20, Pt 1, paras 1, 9; Enterprise and Regulatory Reform Act 2013, s 71(3), Sch 19, paras 1, 59.

**General note**—See the Insolvency Proceedings (Fees) Order 2016 (SI 2016/692) (replacing the Insolvency Proceedings (Fees) Order 2004 (SI 2004/593)).

## [1.571]

### 415A Fees orders (general)

(A1)   The Secretary of State—

(a)    may by order require a person or body to pay a fee in connection with the grant or maintenance of a designation of that person or body as a competent authority under section 251U, and

(b)    may refuse to grant, or may withdraw, any such designation where a fee is not paid.

(1)   The Secretary of State—

(a)    may by order require a body to pay a fee in connection with the grant or maintenance of recognition of the body under section 391, and

(b)    may refuse recognition, or revoke an order of recognition under section 391(1) or (2) by a further order, where a fee is not paid.

(1A)   Fees under subsection (1) may vary according to whether the body is recognised under section 391(1) (body providing full and partial authorisation) or under section 391(2) (body providing partial authorisation).

(1B)   In setting under subsection (1) the amount of a fee in connection with maintenance of recognition, the matters to which the Secretary of State may have regard include, in particular, the costs of the Secretary of State in connection with any functions under sections 391D, 391E, 391J, 391K and 391N.

(2)   . . .

(3)   The Secretary of State may by order require the payment of fees in respect of—

(a)    the operation of the Insolvency Services Account;

(b)    payments into and out of that Account.

(4)   The following provisions of section 414 apply to fees under this section as they apply to fees under that section –

(a)    subsection (3) (manner of payment),

(b)    subsection (5) (additional provision),

(c)    subsection (6) (statutory instrument),

(d)    subsection (7) (payment into Consolidated Fund), and

(e)    subsection (9) (saving for rules of court).

(5)   Section 391M applies for the purposes of an order under subsection (1)(b) as it applies for the purposes of a revocation order made under section 391L.

**Amendments**—Inserted by Enterprise Act 2002, s 270(1). Amended by Tribunals, Courts and Enforcement Act 2007, s 108(3), Sch 20, Pt 1, paras 1, 10; Deregulation Act 2015, s 17(5); Small Business, Enterprise and Employment Act 2015, s 139(2).

**General note**—The provision allows for the making of orders that provide for the payment of fees. It was introduced by Enterprise Act 2002, s 270. The Insolvency Practitioners and Insolvency Services Account (Fees) Order 2003 (SI 2003/3363) was made pursuant to the provision.

## [1.572]

### 415B Monetary limits (company moratorium)

(1)   The Secretary of State may by regulations increase or reduce any of the money sums for the time being specified in the following provisions of Part A1—

(a)    section A25(1) (maximum amount of credit which company may obtain without disclosing moratorium);

(b)    section A28(2) (maximum amount for certain payments without obtaining monitor consent etc);

(c)    section A46(2) (minimum value of company property concealed or fraudulently removed, affecting criminal liability of company's officer).

(2)   Regulations under this section may contain such transitional provisions as may appear to the Secretary of State necessary or expedient.

(3)   Regulations under this section are to be made by statutory instrument subject to annulment in pursuance of a resolution of either House of Parliament.

**Amendments**—Inserted by the Corporate Insolvency and Governance Act 2020, s 2(1), Sch 3, paras 1, 24.

*Specification, increase and reduction of money sums relevant in the operation of this Act*

[1.573]

### 416 Monetary limits (companies winding up)

(1) The Secretary of State may by order in a statutory instrument increase or reduce any of the money sums for the time being specified in the following provisions in the first Group of Parts—

> section 117(2) (amount of company's share capital determining whether county court has jurisdiction to wind it up);
>
> section 120(3) (the equivalent as respects sheriff court jurisdiction in Scotland);
>
> section 123(1)(a) (minimum debt for service of demand on company by unpaid creditor);
>
> section 184(3) (minimum value of judgment, affecting sheriff's duties on levying execution);
>
> section 206(1)(a) and (b) (minimum value of company property concealed or fraudulently removed, affecting criminal liability of company's officer).

(2) An order under this section may contain such transitional provisions as may appear to the Secretary of State necessary or expedient.

(3) No order under this section increasing or reducing any of the money sums for the time being specified in section 117(2), 120(3) or 123(1)(a) shall be made unless a draft of the order has been laid before and approved by a resolution of each House of Parliament.

(4) A statutory instrument containing an order under this section, other than an order to which subsection (3) applies, is subject to annulment in pursuance of a resolution of either House of Parliament.

**Subordinate Legislation**—Insolvency Proceedings (Monetary Limits) Order 1986 (SI 1986/1996).

[1.574]

### 417 Money sum in s 222

The Secretary of State may by regulations in a statutory instrument increase or reduce the money sum for the time being specified in section 222(1) (minimum debt for service of demand on unregistered company by unpaid creditor); but such regulations shall not be made unless a draft of the statutory instrument containing them has been approved by resolution of each House of Parliament.

### 417A

*(Repealed)*

**Amendments**—Inserted by Insolvency Act 2000, s 1, Sch 1, paras 1, 10. Repealed by Corporate Insolvency and Governance Act 2020, s 2(1), Sch 3, paras 1, 25.

[1.575]

### 418 Monetary limits (bankruptcy)

(1) The Secretary of State may by order prescribe amounts for the purposes of the following provisions in the second Group of Parts—

> section 251S(4) (maximum amount of credit which a person in respect of whom a debt relief order is made may obtain without disclosure of his status);
>
> section 273 (minimum value of debtor's estate determining whether immediate bankruptcy order should be made; small bankruptcies level);
>
> section 313A (value of property below which application for sale, possession or charge to be dismissed);
>
> section 346(3) (minimum amount of judgment, determining whether amount recovered on sale of debtor's goods is to be treated as part of his estate in bankruptcy);

section 354(1) and (2) (minimum amount of concealed debt, or value of property concealed or removed, determining criminal liability under the section);

section 358 (minimum value of property taken by a bankrupt out of England and Wales, determining his criminal liability);

section 360(1) (maximum amount of credit which bankrupt may obtain without disclosure of his status);

section 361(2) (exemption of bankrupt from criminal liability for failure to keep proper accounts, if unsecured debts not more than the prescribed minimum);

section 364(2)(d) (minimum value of goods removed by the bankrupt, determining his liability to arrest);

paragraphs 6 to 8 of Schedule 4ZA (maximum amount of a person's debts monthly surplus income and property for purposes of obtaining a debt relief order);

and references in the second Group of Parts to the amount prescribed for the purposes of any of those provisions, and references in those provisions to the prescribed amount, are to be construed accordingly.

(2)   An order under this section may contain such transitional provisions as may appear to the Secretary of State necessary or expedient.

(3)   An order under this section shall be made by statutory instrument subject to annulment in pursuance of a resolution of either House of Parliament.

**Amendments**—Enterprise Act 2002, s 261(6); Tribunals, Courts and Enforcement Act 2007, s 108(3), Sch 20, Pt 1, paras 1, 11.

**Subordinate legislation**—Insolvency Proceedings (Monetary Limits) Order 1986 (SI 1986/1996) (as amended).

*Insolvency practice*

## [1.576]

### 419  Regulations for purposes of Part XIII

(1)   The Secretary of State may make regulations for the purpose of giving effect to Part XIII of this Act; and "prescribed" in that Part means prescribed by regulations made by the Secretary of State.

(2)   Without prejudice to the generality of subsection (1) or to any provision of that Part by virtue of which regulations may be made with respect to any matter, regulations under this section may contain—

(a)   provision as to the matters to be taken into account in determining whether a person is a fit and proper person to act as an insolvency practitioner;

(b)   provision prohibiting a person from so acting in prescribed cases, being cases in which a conflict of interest will or may arise;

(c)   provision imposing requirements with respect to—

  (i)   the preparation and keeping by a person who acts as an insolvency practitioner of prescribed books, accounts and other records, and

  (ii)   the production of those books, accounts and records to prescribed persons;

(d)   provision conferring power on prescribed persons –

  (i)   to require any person who acts or has acted as an insolvency practitioner to answer any inquiry in relation to a case in which he is so acting or has so acted, and

  (ii)   to apply to a court to examine such a person or any other person on oath concerning such a case;

(e)   provision making non-compliance with any of the regulations a criminal offence; and

(f)   such incidental, supplemental and transitional provisions as may appear to the Secretary of State necessary or expedient.

(3)   Any power conferred by Part XIII or this Part to make regulations, rules or orders is exercisable by statutory instrument subject to annulment by resolution of either House of Parliament.

(4)   Any rule or regulation under Part XIII or this Part may make different provision with respect to different cases or descriptions of cases, including different provision for different areas.

(5)   In making regulations under this section, the Secretary of State must have regard to the regulatory objectives (as defined by section 391C(3)).

**Amendments**—Small Business, Enterprise and Employment Act 2015, s 138(2).

**General note**—This provision enables the Secretary of State to make regulations to effect the objectives of the section that deal with the qualification of insolvency practitioners. See Insolvency Practitioners Regulations 2005 (SI 2005/524) (as amended).

*Other order-making powers*

## [1.577]

### 420   Insolvent partnerships

(1)   The Lord Chancellor may, by order made with the concurrence of the Secretary of State and the Lord Chief Justice, provide that such provisions of this Act as may be specified in the order shall apply in relation to insolvent partnerships with such modifications as may be so specified.

(1A)   An order under this section may make provision in relation to the EU Regulation.

(1B)   But provision made by virtue of this section in relation to the EU Regulation may not create a new relevant offence.

(2)   An order under this section may make different provision for different cases and may contain such incidental, supplemental and transitional provisions as may appear to the Lord Chancellor and the Lord Chief Justice necessary or expedient.

(3)   An order under this section shall be made by statutory instrument subject to annulment in pursuance of a resolution of either House of Parliament.

(4)   The Lord Chief Justice may nominate a judicial office holder (as defined in section 109(4) of the Constitutional Reform Act 2005) to exercise his functions under this section.

**Amendments**—SI 2002/1037; Constitutional Reform Act 2005, s 15(1), Sch 4; SI 2017/702; SI 2019/146, as from IP completion day (as defined in the European Union (Withdrawal Agreement) Act 2020, s 39(1)–(5)).

**General note**—The Insolvent Partnerships Orders are instances of the use of this power. The Insolvent Partnerships Order 1994 (SI 1994/2421) governs insolvent partnerships at present (replacing Insolvent Partnerships Order 1986 (SI 1986/2142)).

Section 420(1A) and (1B) were introduced by reg 3 of the Insolvency Act 1986 (Amendment) Regulations 2002 (SI 2002/1037) to accommodate the commencement of the EC Regulation on Insolvency Proceedings and were amended by the Insolvency Amendment (EU 2015/848) Regulations 2017 (SI 2017/702) to accommodate the Recast EU Regulation 2015/848. Section 420(1B) was further amended by the Insolvency (Amendment) (EU Exit) Regulations 2019 (SI 2019/146) to address issues arising from the UK's withdrawal from the European Union; the reference to an offence of a kind referred to in para 1(1) of Sch 2 to the European Communities Act 1972 was replaced with a reference to a new relevant offence as provided for by a newly inserted s 422A.

## [1.578]

### 421   Insolvent estates of deceased persons

(1)   The Lord Chancellor may, by order made with the concurrence of the Secretary of State and the Lord Chief Justice, provide that such provisions of this Act as may be specified in the order shall apply in relation to the administration of the insolvent estates of deceased persons with such modifications as may be so specified.

(1A)   An order under this section may make provision in relation to the EU Regulation.

(1B)   But provision made by virtue of this section in relation to the EU Regulation may not create a new relevant offence.

(2)   An order under this section may make different provision for different cases and may contain such incidental, supplemental and transitional provisions as may appear to the Lord Chancellor and the Lord Chief Justice necessary or expedient.

(3)   An order under this section shall be made by statutory instrument subject to annulment in pursuance of a resolution of either House of Parliament.

(4)   For the purposes of this section the estate of a deceased person is insolvent if, when realised, it will be insufficient to meet in full all the debts and other liabilities to which it is subject.

(5)   The Lord Chief Justice may nominate a judicial office holder (as defined in section 109(4) of the Constitutional Reform Act 2005) to exercise his functions under this section.

**Amendments**—Insolvency Act 2000, s 12(2); SI 2002/1037; Constitutional Reform Act 2005, s 15(1), Sch 4; SI 2017/702; SI 2019/146, as from IP completion day (as defined in the European Union (Withdrawal Agreement) Act 2020, s 39(1)–(5)).

**General note**—The Administration of Insolvent Estates of Deceased Persons Order 1986 (SI 1986/1999), an example of the power to make orders under this section, deals with many of the issues relating to insolvent estates of deceased debtors. This Order, which applies to England and Wales, specifies the provisions of the Insolvency Act 1986 which apply to the administration in bankruptcy of the insolvent estates of deceased persons and the modifications to those provisions. Such provisions apply with the modifications specified in the Order and any further modifications as may be necessary to render them applicable to the estate of a deceased person and the provisions of IR 2016 and any order made under s 415 shall apply accordingly (art 3(1)). If there is any inconsistency between the Order and IR 2016, the former shall prevail (art 3(2)). The Order applies to the estates of persons who die before the presentation of a bankruptcy petition or making a bankruptcy application. If a person dies after the presentation of a petition or the making of a bankruptcy application, the proceedings continue just as if the person remained alive (Administration of Insolvent Estates of Deceased Persons Order 1986, art 5(1)).

The Order has been amended by the Administration of Insolvent Estates of Deceased Persons (Amendment) Order 2002 (SI 2002/1309) to provide for the operation of the EC Regulation on Insolvency Proceedings and by the Insolvency (Miscellaneous Amendments) Regulations 2017/1119.

Section 421(1A) and (1B) were introduced by reg 3 of the Insolvency Act 1986 (Amendment) Regulations 2002 (SI 2002/1037) to accommodate the commencement of the EC Regulation on Insolvency Proceedings and were amended by the Insolvency Amendment (EU 2015/848) Regulations 2017 (SI 2017/702) to accommodate the Recast EU Regulation 2015/848. Section 421(1B) was further amended by the Insolvency (Amendment) (EU Exit) Regulations 2019 (SI 2019/146) to address issues arising from the UK's withdrawal from the European Union; the reference to an offence of a kind referred to in para 1(1) of Sch 2 to the European Communities Act 1972 was replaced with a reference to a new relevant offence as provided for by a newly inserted s 422A.

**[1.579]**

**421A Insolvent estates: joint tenancies**

(1)   This section applies where—

   (a)   an insolvency administration order has been made in respect of the insolvent estate of a deceased person,

   (b)   the petition for the order was presented after the commencement of this section and within the period of five years beginning with the day on which he died, and

   (c)   immediately before his death he was beneficially entitled to an interest in any property as joint tenant.

(2)   For the purpose of securing that debts and other liabilities to which the estate is subject are met, the court may, on an application by the trustee appointed pursuant to the insolvency administration order, make an order under this section requiring the survivor to pay to the trustee an amount not exceeding the value lost to the estate.

(3)   In determining whether to make an order under this section, and the terms of such an order, the court must have regard to all the circumstances of the case, including the

interests of the deceased's creditors and of the survivor; but, unless the circumstances are exceptional, the court must assume that the interests of the deceased's creditors outweigh all other considerations.

(4) The order may be made on such terms and conditions as the court thinks fit.

(5) Any sums required to be paid to the trustee in accordance with an order under this section shall be comprised in the estate.

(6) The modifications of this Act which may be made by an order under section 421 include any modifications which are necessary or expedient in consequence of this section.

(7) In this section, "survivor" means the person who, immediately before the death, was beneficially entitled as joint tenant with the deceased or, if the person who was so entitled dies after the making of the insolvency administration order, his personal representatives.

(8) If there is more than one survivor—

    (a)    an order under this section may be made against all or any of them, but

    (b)    no survivor shall be required to pay more than so much of the value lost to the estate as is properly attributable to him.

(9) In this section—

    "insolvency administration order" has the same meaning as in any order under section 421 having effect for the time being,

    "value lost to the estate" means the amount which, if paid to the trustee, would in the court's opinion restore the position to what it would have been if the deceased had been made bankrupt immediately before his death.

**Amendments**—Inserted by the Insolvency Act 2000, s 12(1); Enterprise and Regulatory Reform Act 2013, s 71(3), Sch 19, paras 1, 60.

**General note**—This provision overcomes the common law to the effect that where a person dies insolvent his or her interest in a joint tenancy passed automatically to the other joint tenant and could not be regarded as part of the insolvent's estate. Under this provision the surviving joint tenant can be ordered by a court, on the application of the trustee in bankruptcy, to pay to the bankrupt estate an amount up to the value that the estate has lost. The value is defined in s 421A(9). For the meaning of exceptional circumstances see notes to s 335A.

## [1.580]

### 422 Formerly authorised banks

(1) The Secretary of State may by order made with the concurrence of the Treasury and after consultation with the Financial Conduct Authority and the Prudential Regulation Authority provide that specified provisions in the first Group of Parts shall apply with specified modifications in relation to any person who—

    (a)    has a liability in respect of a deposit which he accepted in accordance with the Banking Act 1979 (c. 37) or 1987 (c. 22), but

    (b)    does not have permission under Part 4A of the Financial Services and Markets Act 2000 (c. 8) (regulated activities) to accept deposits.

(1A) Subsection (1)(b) shall be construed in accordance with—

    (a)    section 22 of the Financial Services and Markets Act 2000 (classes of regulated activity and categories of investment),

    (b)    any relevant order under that section, and

    (c)    Schedule 2 to that Act (regulated activities).

(2) An order under this section may make different provision for different cases and may contain such incidental, supplemental and transitional provisions as may appear to the Secretary of State necessary or expedient.

(3) An order under this section shall be made by statutory instrument subject to annulment in pursuance of a resolution of either House of Parliament.

**Amendments**—Enterprise Act 2002, s 248(3), Sch 17, paras 9, 35; SI 2002/1555; Financial Services Act 2012, s 114(1), Sch 18, Pt 2, paras 51, 53.

**[1.581]**

### 422A Meaning of "relevant offence"

In this Part "relevant offence" means a criminal offence punishable with imprisonment for more than two years or punishable on summary conviction with imprisonment for more than three months or with a fine of more than level 5 on the standard scale (if not calculated on a daily basis) or with a fine of more than £100 a day.

**Amendments**—Inserted by SI 2019/146, as from IP completion day (as defined in the European Union (Withdrawal Agreement) Act 2020, s 39(1)–(5)).

**General note**—This provision introduces the concept of 'relevant offence' referred to in amendments to ss 411, 412, 420 and 421 in place of references to offences referred to in the European Communities Act 1972 in the previous versions of those sections.

## PART XVI   PROVISIONS AGAINST DEBT AVOIDANCE (ENGLAND AND WALES ONLY)

**[1.582]**

### 423 Transactions defrauding creditors

(1)   This section relates to transactions entered into at an undervalue; and a person enters into such a transaction with another person if—

    (a)    he makes a gift to the other person or he otherwise enters into a transaction with the other on terms that provide for him to receive no consideration;

    (b)    he enters into a transaction with the other in consideration of marriage or the formation of a civil partnership; or

    (c)    he enters into a transaction with the other for a consideration the value of which, in money or money's worth, is significantly less than the value, in money or money's worth, of the consideration provided by himself.

(2)   Where a person has entered into such a transaction, the court may, if satisfied under the next subsection, make such order as it thinks fit for—

    (a)    restoring the position to what it would have been if the transaction had not been entered into, and

    (b)    protecting the interests of persons who are victims of the transaction.

(3)   In the case of a person entering into such a transaction, an order shall only be made if the court is satisfied that it was entered into by him for the purpose—

    (a)    of putting assets beyond the reach of a person who is making, or may at some time make, a claim against him, or

    (b)    of otherwise prejudicing the interests of such a person in relation to the claim which he is making or may make.

(4)   In this section "the court" means the High Court or—

    (a)    if the person entering into the transaction is an individual, any other court which would have jurisdiction in relation to a bankruptcy petition relating to him;

    (b)    if that person is a body capable of being wound up under Part IV or V of this Act, any other court having jurisdiction to wind it up.

(5)   In relation to a transaction at an undervalue, references here and below to a victim of the transaction are to a person who is, or is capable of being, prejudiced by it; and in the following two sections the person entering into the transaction is referred to as "the debtor".

**Amendments**—Civil Partnership Act 2004, s 261(1), Sch 27, para 121.

**General note**—Whilst an action to avoid transactions entered into in fraud of creditors was first introduced by statute in the so-called Statute of Elizabeth 1571 (which rendered transactions 'clearly and utterly void, frustrated and of no effect' and which remained in force until replaced by the Law of Property Act 1925, s 172), the common law had also previously recognised a similar action, analogous to the actio Pauliana available to creditors under Roman law: see *Cadogen v Kennett* (1776) 2 Cowp 432 at 434. Section 172 of the 1925 Act provided a remedy in respect of so-called 'fraudulent conveyance' in that ' . . . every conveyance of property, made whether before or after commencement of this Act, with intent to defraud creditors, shall be voidable at the instance of any person thereby prejudiced'.

The heading 'Transactions defrauding creditors' is incorrect as that suggests that there must be some fraud or dishonesty perpetrated by the respondent for a claim to succeed, but that is not the case: *Watchorn v Jupiter Industries Ltd* [2014] EWHC 3003 (Ch), [3].

Section 423 of the 1986 Act makes four significant points. First, even if the requisite element in s 423(3) can be satisfied, a transaction is only capable of being avoided if it meets the definition of a transaction-at-undervalue in s 423(1). Secondly, s 423(3) provides that the transaction under challenge must have been entered into by the transferor 'for the purpose' of putting assets beyond the reach of actual or potential claimants or otherwise prejudicing the interests of any such person. Thirdly, unlike the fraudulent conveyance, transactions under s 423 are subject to the remedial powers of the court pursuant to s 423(2), and not void. Fourthly, the new provision attributes no relevance to the state of mind of the counterparty, an approach adopted by Mervyn Davies J in *Moon v Franklin* [1996] BPIR 196 at 202 in ignoring a wife's evidence to the effect that she did not attribute any value to benefits transferred to her by her husband. It remains, however, that it is open to the court to draw inferences from the evidence of the counterparty or, indeed, the evidence of any other party, in construing as a matter of fact the mind of the transferor at the relevant time. This appears to be confirmed both by the Court of Appeal in *Hashmi v Inland Revenue* [2002] EWCA Civ 981, [2002] 2 BCLC 489, [2002] BPIR 974 in upholding the making of an inference made by the judge at first instance, and again, by the Court of Appeal, albeit obliquely, in *JSC BTA Bank v Ablyazov* [2018] EWCA Civ 1176 at [15].

Whilst s 423 allows not only office-holders under the legislation but also 'victims' of transactions (on which see the note to s 423(3) below) to challenge transactions without any time-limit of the sort imposed in the case of transactions-at-undervalue and preferences, the applicant carries the evidential burden in establishing the transferor's purpose. No presumption operates in favour of an applicant, even when a transaction is effected in favour of a connected party. Whilst each case must turn on its own facts, the court will not entertain speculative claims, particularly where the allegations reach back many years: see, for example, the Court of Appeal's dismissal of a claim under CPR, Pt 24 (reversing Hart J below) in *Law Society v Southall* [2002] BPIR 336, in which Peter Gibson LJ identified that the allegation of an attempt to defeat creditors over 30 years previously was 'mere speculation' and that it was 'wishful thinking on the [applicant's] part that the pre-trial procedures, or cross-examination, would yield valuable support for its case' (at [52]).

Any application brought under this provision is brought on behalf of all victims of the impugned transaction: *Hill v Spread Trustee Company Ltd* [2006] EWCA Civ 542, [2007] 1 WLR 2404, [2007] 1 All ER 1106, [2007] 1 BCLC 450, [2006] BPIR 789 at [104].

The overriding objective of the section is to recover assets for the victims so as to protect their interests: *BTI 2014 LLC v Sequana SA* [2017] EWHC 211 (Ch) at [25] (upheld by the Court of Appeal [2019] EWCA Civ 112, [2019] 1 BCLC 347).

It is not necessary for the claimant to establish that when the transaction impugned was effected the debtor was engaging, or about to engage, in risky or hazardous business: *Midland Bank v Wyatt* [1997] 1 BCLC 242; *Sands v Clitheroe* [2006] BPIR 1000. Engaging in such activity was merely a factor which might well justify the court making an inference that the debtor's intention was to put assets beyond the reach of creditors.

For liability to be imposed on a debtor it is not necessary to establish that the debtor was insolvent or on the verge of insolvency: *BTI 2014 LLC v Sequana SA* [2016] EWHC 1686 (Ch), [2017] 1 BCLC 453 at [494] (upheld by the Court of Appeal [2019] EWCA Civ 112, [2019] 1 BCLC 347).

### SECTION 423(1)

**Scope of provision**—This subsection reproduces the definition of a transaction-at-undervalue as it appears in s 339(3) (bankruptcy) and, in substantially similar terms, in s 238(4) (winding up): see further the notes to those sections.

**'Transaction'**—A critical thing with the provision is that there must be an entering into of a transaction. The idea of transaction is broadly interpreted. 'Transaction' is defined in s 436 and is not exhaustive. It includes gifts, agreements and arrangements. According to *Defra v Feakins* [2004] EWHC 2735 (Ch), [2005] BPIR 292, entering into a transaction includes participating in an arrangement. This was upheld on appeal ([2005] EWCA Civ 1513, [2006] BPIR 895) and the court said that the word 'arrangement' was to be given its natural meaning, and included an agreement or understanding, whether formal or informal, oral or in writing. Hence the term, 'transaction' is broad: *Griffin v Awoderu* [2008] EWHC 349 (Ch) at [25].

In recent times transaction for the purposes of s 423(1) has been held to encompass a payment of a dividend by a company (if it was made when the debtor had the purpose mentioned in s 423(3)) (*BTI 2014 LLC v Sequana SA* [2016] EWHC 1686 (Ch) at [502], affirmed by the Court of Appeal, [2019] EWCA Civ 112, [2019] 1 BCLC 347) as, according to the Court of Appeal, it cannot be said that the distributing company receives consideration for the payment of a dividend (at [50]).

The Court of Appeal went on to say that a dividend is able to be considered to be a 'transaction' within s 423(1) and it could constitute a transaction even if there was not an arrangement between the company and the shareholders (at [58], [63]). The Court of Appeal's decision on this point has been appealed to the Supreme Court and judgment is awaited at the time of writing. Also, a transaction involving the buying back by a company debtor of its own shares from shareholders is a transaction at an undervalue (*Dickinson v NAL Realisations (Staffordshire) Ltd* [2017] EWHC 28 (Ch) at [111]).

It has been held that there is no policy reason that confines 'transaction' within s 423(1) to gifts and bilateral transactions. Something that involves a unilateral act can constitute a transaction: *BTI 2014 LLC v Sequana SA* [2019] EWCA Civ 112, [2019] 1 BCLC 347.

'Value' – see the notes accompanying s 238. In considering a transaction under s 423 the court is to look at the value received from the point of view of the debtor *(Re MC Bacon Limited* [1991] Ch 127 and affirmed in *Delaney v Chen* [2010] EWCA Civ 1455, [2011] BPIR 39 at [15].

A spouse's forbearance in not petitioning for divorce and seeking a property order in return for the impugned transfer could constitute consideration: *Papanicola v Fagan* [2008] EWHC 3348 (Ch) at [29]–[30]; *Bataillon and Macquarie v Shone* [2016] EWHC 1174 (QB) at [18].

## SECTION 423(2)

**Scope of provision**—This provision makes it plain that a court has a discretion as to whether or not to make any order and this discretion permits a court to make no order, where justice requires, even if exceptional circumstances do not exist (*Moffat v Moffat* [2021] NICh 17 at [51]). Although s 423(2)(a) mirrors ss 238(3) and 339(2) (both addressing transactions-at-undervalue) in identifying the end to which the powers of the court under s 423 should be directed, s 423(2)(b) adds an additional purpose which should also feature in the mind of the court for the purposes of the discretion exercised by it in granting relief. These two paragraphs must be read conjunctively so that ' . . . Any order made under [s 423(2)] must seek, so far as practicable, both to restore the position to what it would have been if the transaction had not been entered into and to protect the victims of it': *Chohan v Saggar* [1994] 1 BCLC 706 at 714 (per Nourse LJ, with Balcombe and Waite LJJ agreeing in varying the trial judge's order on the basis that it had given insufficient protection to victims of the transaction so as to restore the full net value lost to it by way of impugned transaction). In other words, the restorative purpose in s 423(2)(a) is not pursued by way of an order under s 423 in isolation; rather, the court should restore the position so far as is necessary to protect the interests of creditors. In *Moon v Franklin* [1996] BPIR 196, for example, the respondent had sold his accountancy practice for £65,000 and gifted the bulk of the proceeds to his wife at a time when the respondent was facing a possible professional negligence claim. The husband subsequently transferred the beneficial interest in the couple's joint property to his wife. Whilst the professional negligence proceedings were pending Mervyn Davies J (whilst, unhelpfully, construing paragraphs (a) and (b) disjunctively, at 205) declared the gift of the practice proceeds and the transfer of the matrimonial home interest to be in contravention of s 423, whilst requiring the wife to repay only the £5,000 of the proceeds remaining in her hands and ordering that there be no further dealings in the matrimonial property. For an order in a case where improper transfers from one trading company L, to another, F, were impugned, see *Arbuthnot Leasing International Ltd v Havelet Leasing (No 2)* [1990] BCC 636 at 645 where it was said by Scott J:

> 'The mechanics of the reversal must take into account that since the date of the transfer F has been carrying on business on its own account and will have creditors who are not creditors of L and who have become its creditors since the date of the transfers. Those creditors are entitled prima facie to look at the assets standing in the name of F for payment of the debts due to them. Accordingly, it seems to me that I ought to order that the business and assets of F, including the sums held on its behalf by H, are held by F, upon trust for L but without prejudice to the claims of creditors of F who have become creditors since the date of the transfers.'

Section 423(2) differs from ss 238(3) and 339(2) in its use of the word 'may' as opposed to 'shall'. This would appear definitely to allow the court some scope for making an order which seeks to protect the interests, even where it is not possible to restore by order the pre-transaction position.

Relief granted under s 423(2) by way of an order and s 425 does not invalidate the transaction attacked in the applicant's claim, although it may do so. Rather, an order pursuant to s 423(2) requires the counterparty to the transaction challenged to confer on the transferor's estate the benefit received by it unjustly on a restitutionary basis, subject to the protection afforded to bona fide third parties by s 425(2).

## SECTION 423(3)

**Scope of provision**—As a pre-condition of the granting of any relief by order, this provision imposes a requirement that the court makes a finding of fact as to either of those matters set out in s 423(3)(a) or (b).

Reliance on legal advice will not necessarily provide a transferor with a defence to a s 423 claim, although it is a point which the court may consider on the facts: *Arbuthnot Leasing International Ltd v Havelet Leasing Ltd (No 2)* [1990] BCC 636 at 644B–644D.

In *Barclays Bank v Eustice* [1995] 2 BCLC 630 the Court of Appeal upheld the decision of the judge below in granting specific discovery of documents which would otherwise be protected by legal professional privilege on the basis that privilege did not protect communications between client and legal advisers where there was strong evidence of a s 423 transaction. The scope of those persons referred to in s 423(3)(a) and (b) are considered in the notes to s 423(6) below.

'Purpose'—As a matter of law the term 'purpose' has been the subject of some judicial consideration. The point is not an issue where the transferor can be shown to have acted only for either of the purposes in s 423(3)(a) or (b) where the transferor is unable to offer some legitimate and credible explanation for his actions, as in *Barclays Bank v Eustice* [1995] 2 BCLC 630 (assignment of agricultural tenancy and equipment at nominal rate without disclosure to a bank one week following Inland Revenue distraint and one week before the bank appointed receivers upheld by Court of Appeal as disclosing strong prima facie case); *Midland Bank v Wyatt* [1997] 1 BCLC 242 (protection of assets where transferor executed voluntary settlement of his interest in matrimonial property in favour of daughters at a time when the transferor was contemplating setting up his own business); or *Hashmi v Inland Revenue* [2002] EWCA Civ 981, [2002] 2 BCLC 489, [2002] BPIR 974 (Court of Appeal upheld inferences drawn by Hart J at first instance to the effect that a deceased shopkeeper who defrauded Revenue and who transferred interest in commercial property to his son did so to put assets beyond the reach of creditors, given likelihood of substantial tax claims against him): see also *Aiglon Ltd v Gau Shan Co Ltd* [1993] BCLC 1321 (Hirst J) and *Agricultural Mortgage Corporation v Woodward* [1995] 1 BCLC 1, [1996] 1 FLR 226, CA. The Court of Appeal in *Williams v Taylor* [2012] EWCA Civ 1443, [2013] BPIR 133 at [30] provided that the required intention to defraud might be based on objective factors that are in evidence. Neither is s 423 intended to catch only transactions where either of the statutory purposes in s 423(3) is capable of being shown to be the sole purpose of the transferor: *Royscott Spa Leasing Ltd v Lovett* [1995] BCC 502 at 507. Indeed, it is the question of mixed purposes which poses the real difficulty in construing s 423(3). After several first instance decisions that took different approaches, some saying the purpose of the debtor required by the section had to be his or her dominant purpose while others saying it only had to be a substantial purpose for liability, the Court of Appeal's judgment in *Hashmi v Inland Revenue* [2002] EWCA Civ 981, [2002] BPIR 974, [2002] 2 BCLC 489 seemed to resolve things to a large degree. There Arden LJ, after considering the authorities, opined that s 423 does not require proof of a dominant purpose, only 'a real substantial purpose' (at [23]–[25]): 'It is sufficient if the statutory purpose can properly be described as a purpose, and not merely as a consequence . . . Moreover, I agree with the observation of [Hart J below] that it will often be the case that the motive to defeat creditors and the motive to secure family protection will co-exist in such a way that even the transferor himself may be unable to say what was uppermost in his mind'; and see to like effect the comments of Laws LJ at [32]–[33]. The following caveat of Simon Brown LJ (who agreed that the arguments supporting a test involving substantial purpose rather than a test of dominant purpose were compelling) must not be ignored. If a judge '[W]ere to find in any given case that the transaction is one which the debtor might well have entered into in any event, he should not then too readily infer that the debtor also had the substantial purpose of escaping his liabilities.' (at [40]). In a more recent Court of Appeal decision, *JSC BTA Bank v Ablyazov* [2018] EWCA Civ 1176 Leggatt LJ (with whom the other judges agreed) explained what he felt Simon Brown LJ was seeking to emphasise in the aforementioned comment and that was that if a judge finds 'that the transaction is one which the debtor might well have entered into in any event, then that is a matter which tells against concluding that the debtor had the prohibited purpose. Whether such an inference should nevertheless be drawn must depend on all the relevant circumstances.' (at [25]).

In *JSC BTA Bank v Ablyazov* [2018] EWCA Civ 1176 in the Court of Appeal Leggatt LJ (with whom Coulson and Gloster LJJ agreed) cast doubt on the formulation in *Hashmi* concerning the need for there to be a substantial purpose and said that:

'The description of the requisite purpose as a "substantial" purpose was not necessary to the decision of the Court of Appeal in the Hashmi case and to my mind it risks causing confusion. The word "substantial" is not used in section 423 and I can see no necessity or warrant for reading this (or any other) adjective into the wording of the section. At best it introduces unnecessary complication and at worst introduces an additional requirement which makes the test stricter than Parliament intended.' (at [14]).

His Lordship went on to say that:

'It is sufficient simply to ask whether the transaction was entered into by the debtor for the prohibited purpose. If it was, then the transaction falls within section 423(3), even if it was also entered into for one or more other purposes. The test is no more complicated than that.' (at [14]).

In *BTI 2014 LLC v Sequana SA* [2016] EWHC 1686 (Ch) at [502] Rose J said that the: 'The purpose of a person in entering into a transaction is a matter of the subjective intention of that person: what did he aim to achieve?' This was affirmed by the Court of Appeal, [2019] EWCA Civ 112, [2019] 1 BCLC 347, at [66]).

A person can be said to have the necessary purpose even if he or she is mistaken as to whether the entering into of the transaction challenged can have the effect of being detrimental to the interests of a victim: *Hill v Spread Trustee Company Ltd* [2006] EWCA Civ 542, [2007] 1 WLR 2404, [2007] 1 All ER 1106, [2007] 1 BCLC 450, [2006] BPIR 789 at [102]. Also, if a person knows that the entering into of a transaction alone will not cause prejudice, but some other event must also occur for that to happen, that will not save the transaction from successful attack, provided that the person had the necessary purpose; this is because it is the entering into of the transaction that is critical for a successful s 423 action: *Hill v Spread Trustee Company Ltd* at [102].

The first limb of the purpose, namely putting assets beyond the reach of someone who had made or may make a claim, has inherent in it the assumption that following the transaction that is impugned, the respondent to a s 423 claim does not have adequate funds left to pay an actual or potential claim against the respondent, whereas if the respondent has adequate funds remaining after entering into the transaction then the respondent could not have had the requisite purpose: *BTI 2014 LLC v Sequana SA* [2016] EWHC 1686 (Ch) at [517].

In prosecuting an action, it is not enough to be successful under s 423 to establish that the transaction had the consequence of putting assets of the debtor beyond the reach of creditors. That is so, even if the consequence was foreseeable or was actually foreseen by the debtor at the time of entering into the transaction. If there is evidence that the debtor believed that the transaction would result in putting assets beyond the reach of creditors that may support an inference that the transaction was entered into for the purpose of doing so, but it is not possible to say that believing the transaction would put assets beyond the reach of creditors means that the debtor had the necessary purpose: *JSC BTA Bank v Ablyazov* [2018] EWCA Civ 1176 at [15]. Leggatt LJ (with whom the other judges agreed) in this case went on to say that a consequence is more likely to be perceived as positively intended if there is reason to think that it is something which was desired. His Lordship said (at [16]) that: 'a person who has entered into a transaction at an undervalue foresaw that the result would be to put assets out of reach of creditors and desired that result [it] might lead the court to infer that the transaction was entered into for that purpose. But such a conclusion is not a logical or legal necessity. It is a judgment which has to be based on an evaluation of all the relevant facts of the particular case.' His Lordship also said that if a judge finds 'that the transaction is one which the debtor might well have entered into in any event, then that is a matter which tells against concluding that the debtor had the prohibited purpose. Whether such an inference should nevertheless be drawn must depend on all the relevant circumstances.' (at [25]).

It has been said that the necessary purpose could be inferred where a debtor had entered into a deed of trust which conferred the beneficial interest of his property to his wife but he had not had the transfer registered publicly: *Swift Advances Plc v Ahmed* [2015] EWHC 3265 (Ch).

The Court of Appeal has said that there is no rule of law that if the debtor knew at the time of entering into the transaction that he or she was facing claims, the court must find that the transaction was entered into for the prohibited purpose unless the debtor adduces evidence to show otherwise; there is no presumption found in s 423 of the same ilk as that in s 239(5): *JSC BTA Bank v Ablyazov* [2018] EWCA Civ 1176 at [28].

For companies it is sufficient to make a claim successfully under the section if the claimant is able to demonstrate that a majority of the directors acted with the necessary purpose: *BTI 2014 LLC v Sequana SA* [2016] EWHC 1686 (Ch) at [494].

See A Keay 'Transactions Defrauding Creditors: The Problem of Purpose Under Section 423 of the Insolvency Act' [2003] *The Conveyancer and Property Lawyer* 272.

## SECTION 423(4)

**Scope of provision**—This provision is determinative of the courts having jurisdiction to deal with a s 423 claim. For further guidance, see the notes on 'Forms and procedure' below.

## SECTION 423(5)

**'Victim'**—The term 'victim' is employed here as shorthand for the purposes of the three categories of persons eligible to bring a claim under s 423 by s 424(1). The term is used to characterise those persons who are capable of being prejudiced by the transaction-at-undervalue defined in s 423(1) and who fall within either s 423(3)(a) or (b).

The concept of a 'victim' here is a wide one and deliberately so, and the status of 'victim' is not made to depend on whether the victim has suffered quantifiable loss as a result of the transaction that is impugned: *Gordian Holdings Limited v Sofroniou* [2021] EWHC 235 (Comm) at [16], [20].

The definition of 'victim' by its indirect reference to the persons within the scope of s 423(3) is broad and extends to existing and future creditors, including putative – further unascertained – creditors. Thus, whilst the term 'victim' will catch unsecured creditors (*Re Ayala Holdings Ltd*

[1993] BCLC 256 (Chadwick J)), members as creditors (*Soden v British and Commonwealth Holdings plc* [1998] AC 298, [1997] 3 WLR 840, [1997] 4 All ER 353, [1997] 2 BCLC 501), a mortgagee (*Agricultural Mortgage Corporation plc v Woodward* [1995] 1 BCLC 1, [1996] 1 FLR 226) or a claimant or prospective claimant in litigation (as in *Moon v Franklin* [1996] BPIR 196), an individual with no creditors at the time of a transaction may face a claim in future on the basis that the debtor may be construed as having entered into the transaction at issue for the purpose of defeating future claims, even if he or she was solvent at that time. In *Sands v Clitheroe* [2006] BPIR 1000 it was indicated that a person could be regarded as a victim provided that he or she could prove to have been prejudiced by the transaction; victims were not limited to those who became creditors as a consequence of the activity that the debtor had in mind when entering into the transaction (at [18]–[20]). It was made clear in *Clydesdale Financial Services Ltd v Smailes* [2009] EWHC 3190 (Ch) that 'victim' is a term that is wider than creditors; the critical thing is that the applicant can demonstrate that he or she was capable of being prejudiced by the transaction. If a person's interests are prejudiced (or capable of being prejudiced) by a transaction as soon as it occurs, then that person is within the definition of 'victim'. The person does not lose that status by reason of something else which may subsequently be unilaterally done by the debtor: *Gordian Holdings Limited v Sofroniou* [2021] EWHC 235 (Comm) at [20].

Whilst the recommendation of the Cork Committee in para 1215(b) of its Report to the effect that a debtor may be taken to have acted for the purpose of prejudicing victims where that consequence was a reasonably foreseeable (ie natural and probable) consequence, given the debtor's knowledge of his financial circumstances at the time of the transaction, was not enacted in express terms, the authorities do actually generally bear out such an approach to s 423(3), although the decision of the Court of Appeal in *JSC BTA Bank v Ablyazov* [2018] EWCA Civ 1176 (at [15] might require those authorities to be re-visited. There is first instance authority in which the court has accepted the pre-1986 Act proposition, established in *Mackay v Douglas* (1872) 14 Eq 106, and *Re Butterworth ex parte Russell* (1882) 19 ChD 588, to the effect that, in circumstances in which a transferor has no creditors at the time of a disposition but is contemplating a new business venture, the court will more readily infer the requisite intention (or purpose), the more hazardous the business contemplated: *Midland Bank v Wyatt* [1997] 1 BCLC 242 at 255. Specifically the Court of Appeal has stated that a victim might be someone who may not have been the person within the purpose of the person entering into the impugned transaction; in fact the person entering into the transaction may not have been aware of the victim's existence: *Hill v Spread Trustee Company Ltd* [2006] EWCA Civ 542, [2007] 1 WLR 2404, [2007] 1 All ER 1106, [2007] 1 BCLC 450, [2006] BPIR 789 at [101]. In *Fortress Value Recovery Fund I LLC v Blue Skye Special Opportunites Fund LP* [2013] EWHC 14 (Comm) at [110] Flaux J said that the scope of persons falling within s 423(3), namely those who are making or may at some time make a claim, is to be given a broad interpretation and is not necessarily limited to 'victims' under s 423(5).

It has been held that s 423(3) does not require that the transaction sought to be impugned was entered into in order to prejudice the particular person now bringing the claim. It is enough that the transferor acted with the purpose of defrauding any person who had made or might make a claim against him: *4 Eng v Harper* [2009] EWHC 2633 (Ch), [2010] 1 BCLC 176, [2010] BPIR 1 at [22], *Fortress Value Recovery Fund I LLC v Blue Skye Special Opportunities Fund LP* [2013] EWHC 14 (Comm) at [111].

**Forms and procedure**—It has been held that a claim under s 423 does not constitute 'insolvency proceedings': *J Syke Bank Ltd v Spieldnaes* [1999] 2 BCLC 101 at 124 (Evans-Lombe J, referring to an unreported interim application on 5 October 1998); *Re Baillies Ltd* [2012] EWHC 285 (Ch), [2012] BPIR 665; *Manolete Partners v Hayward and Barrett Holdings Ltd* [2021] EWHC 1481 at [27]). However, *Practice Direction – Insolvency Proceedings* (July 2020) [2020] BPIR 1211 provides that insolvency proceedings means (inter alia): 'in an insolvency context an application made pursuant to s 423 of the Act' (para 1.6(c)). While the Practice Direction is not able to overrule precedent the existence of para 1.6(c) does cause some uncertainty. Section 423 claims are now subject to para 1 of Sch 4 of the 2016 Rules (service outside the jurisdiction) which provides in para 1(8) that Part 6 of the CPR applies to the service of documents outside the jurisdiction with such modifications as the court may approve or direct. The Court of Appeal held in *Orexim Trading Ltd v Mahvir Port and Terminal Private Ltd* [2018] EWCA Civ 1660, [2018] BPIR 1432 at [47] that the court has power under the jurisdictional 'gateway' in para 3.1(20) of PD6B of the CPR to permit service of a claim under s 423 outside England and Wales. The Court said that the effect of s 423 was to confer on the court power to make orders against persons and property outside of England and Wales although this was subject to the fact that there had to be a sufficient connection between the claim and England and Wales (at [55]). The claimant has the burden of establishing the fact that there was a sufficient connection and this would only be achieved if the claimant persuades the court not merely that England and Wales is the appropriate forum but that this is clearly so (at [63] and applying *Spiliada Maritime Corpn v Cansulex Ltd* [1987] AC 460, at 480H–481E). When it came to sufficient connection with the jurisdiction, the Court of Appeal in the s 238 case of *Re Paramount Airways Ltd (No 2)* ([1993] Ch 223, [1992] 3 WLR 690, [1992]

3 All ER 1, [1992] BCLC 710) mentioned specific factors, and in *Avonwick Holdings Ltd v Azitio Holdings Ltd* ([2018] EWHC 2458 (Comm), a s 423 case, Cockerill J stated that the court must consider the factors mentioned in *Paramount Airways* but she also said that others could be taken into account in undertaking a balancing exercise (at [53]). The judge opined that there were connections other than those mentioned in *Paramount Airways* that enabled her to decide the issue. In *Suppipat v Narongdej* ([2020] EWHC 3191 (Comm)) Butcher J refused a strike out an application that was argued on the basis that a s 423 claim which was made against foreign defendants with no connection with England and Wales could not be brought.

Insofar as actions do not seek the recovery of a sum recoverable by virtue of an enactment within s 9 of the Limitation Act 1980, they are actions for a specialty: *Hill v Spread Trustee Company Ltd* [2006] EWCA Civ 542, [2007] 1 WLR 2404, [2007] 1 All ER 1106, [2007] 1 BCLC 450, [2006] BPIR 789 at [116].

A claim under s 423 may be commenced in any Division of the High Court. The 2016 Rules do not apply to a s 423 claim other than where the claim is brought in existing proceedings in the Business and Property Courts: *TSB Bank v Katz* [1997] 147 at 149–150.

A claimant under s 423 may also consider seeking declaratory and consequential relief alleging that a transaction constitutes a sham, as identified by Diplock LJ in *Snook v London and West Riding Investments Ltd* [1967] 2 QB 786 at 802, on which see further the comments of David Young QC (sitting as a deputy judge of the High Court) in *Midland Bank v Wyatt* [1997] 1 BCLC 242 at 245 as to the need for any common intention between the parties to the sham transaction.

**Limitation period**—It was generally accepted that pre-1986 Act claims alleging a fraudulent conveyance were not subject to a limitation period on the basis that such conveyances were rendered void. Notwithstanding the apparent presumption in earlier cases that no statutory limitation period applied to actions under s 423 (for example, *Law Society v Southall* [2001] EWCA Civ 2001, [2002] BPIR 336), the Court of Appeal has now ruled that there is: *Hill v Spread Trustee Company Ltd* [2006] EWCA Civ 542, [2007] 1 WLR 2404, [2007] 1 All ER 1106, [2007] 1 BCLC 450, [2006] BPIR 789 at [117]–[118], [143]. The period is 12 years if s 9 of the Limitation Act 1980 applies (actions upon a specialty), and 6 years if s 8 of that Act applies (a claim for monetary relief): *Hill v Spread* at [116]. It was accepted in *Hill v Spread* that there could be separate limitation periods for different applicants (at [149]). For instance, where the applicant was a bankruptcy trustee the period would not start to run until the making of a bankruptcy order (applied in *Rubin v Dweck* [2012] BPIR 854), for it was not until then that the applicant could bring proceedings; the appointment of the trustee is an ingredient in the cause of action (see at [150], Arden LJ dissenting on this point at [120]–[122]). It was held that it was of no consequence that at the time of the bringing of an action by a trustee in bankruptcy there might be creditors whose action under s 423 was statute-barred and who would benefit from the trustee's action ([150]).

The Court of Appeal allowed the extension of the limitation period in the case of *Giles v Rhind* [2008] EWCA Civ 118, [2008] BPIR 342, [2008] 2 BCLC 1. Arden LJ (with whom the other judges agreed) held that a claim under s 423 could be within the expression, 'breach of duty,' in s 32(2) of the Limitation Act 1980, as 'breach of duty' bears a wide meaning. Section 32(2) provides that the deliberate commission of a breach of duty in circumstances in which it is unlikely to be discovered for some time amounts to a deliberate concealment of the facts and the deliberate concealing of facts permits, according to s 32(1) of the Limitation Act 1980, a court to extend time (at [38]–[39]. The time runs from the time the applicant discovers that the improper action occurred. Her Ladyship noted that a transaction covered by s 423 is the kind of transaction of which there was likely to be concealment and 'thus there would be a heightened policy reason for the application of s 32(2) to claims under that section.' (at [54]).

Generally, see R Stubbs 'Section 423 of the Insolvency Act in Practice' (2008) 21 *Insolvency Intelligence* 17; A Keay, *McPherson and Keay's Law of Company Liquidation* (Sweet and Maxwell, 4th edn, 2018), 737–752.

## [1.583]

### 424 Those who may apply for an order under s 423

(1)  An application for an order under section 423 shall not be made in relation to a transaction except—

    (a)    in a case where the debtor has been made bankrupt or is a body corporate which is being wound up or is in administration, by the official receiver, by the trustee of the bankrupt's estate or the liquidator or administrator of the body corporate or (with the leave of the court) by a victim of the transaction;

(b)     in a case where a victim of the transaction is bound by a voluntary arrangement approved under Part I or Part VIII of this Act, by the supervisor of the voluntary arrangement or by any person who (whether or not so bound) is such a victim; or

(c)     in any other case, by a victim of the transaction.

(2)     An application made under any of the paragraphs of subsection (1) is to be treated as made on behalf of every victim of the transaction.

**Amendments**—Enterprise Act 2002, s 248(3), Sch 17, paras 9, 36; Enterprise and Regulatory Reform Act 2013, s 71(3), Sch 19, paras 1, 61.

**General note**—This provision provides distinct categories of claimant who are deemed by s 424(2) to proceed on behalf of every victim of the particular transaction challenged. For the standing of the Financial Conduct Authority to make application in an appropriate case, see s 375 of the Financial Services and Markets Act 2000. In *Schmitt v Deichmann* [2012] EWHC 62 (Ch), [2014] 1 BCLC 663 a German administrator of a German company was allowed to bring proceedings under s 423.

## SECTION 424(1)(a)

**Scope of provision**—Where any of the insolvency procedures specified in this provision are in place the cause of action under s 423 falls to the office-holder such that a victim of the transaction requires leave of the court to enable him or her to bring proceedings. Section 424(1) recognises that in cases where the debtor is bankrupt, in liquidation or in administration the office-holder is the most appropriate persons to bring s 423 proceedings: *Lemos v Church Bay Trust Company Limited* [2021] EWHC 1157 (Ch) at [57], [59]. Leave should ordinarily be given to a victim by the court where the claim is plainly arguable on its face and where the incumbent office-holder consents. Such consent might be forthcoming where there are no assets in the estate to fund the proceedings, as in *Re Ayala Holdings* [1993] BCLC 256 at 266–267. Where the debtor has been adjudged bankrupt or entered a formal corporate insolvency regime after proceedings have been instituted under s 423, the claimant does not need to obtain leave of the court: *Godfrey v Torpy* [2007] EWHC 919 (Ch), [2007] BPIR 1538 at [39]. In any event, if leave is required in such a situation it can be granted retrospectively by the court: *Godfrey v Torpy* at [43].

An office-holder may be joined by court order to proceedings commenced by a victim who has been granted leave to bring proceedings against the debtor: *Lemos v Church Bay Trust Company Limited* [2021] EWHC 1157 (Ch). In *Lemos* at [59], ICC Judge Barber said that she was not convinced that it was it is necessary, in order to clear the jurisdictional threshold of CPR 19.2(2)(a), to demonstrate that the party seeking joinder can actively assist the court. Where a victim has commenced proceedings with leave, it is open to office-holders to require the victim to discontinue his or her claim and to commence their own proceedings under s 423 instead (provided that the limitation period had not expired): *Lemos* at [70].

Where a claimant does require leave and the office-holder has declined to bring proceedings under s 423 then the claimant must demonstrate that he or she has a realistic prospect of establishing: the transaction is covered by s 423; the claimant was a victim of the transaction within s 423; and there is a good reason why he or she should bring proceedings when the liquidator had not: *Re Simon Carves Ltd* [2013] EWHC 685 (Ch) at [27].

**The nature of the court's relief**—The court's remedial power is, it is submitted, restitutionary and not compensatory in nature. The proceeds of a s 423 action will in any case enure for the benefit of the insolvent estate, irrespective of the identity of the claimant, since, whilst in contrast to s 238(3), which concerns the making of an order for the purpose of restoring the pre-transaction position, s 423(2) admits of the court also seeking to protect the interests of the victims of a challenged transaction. Accordingly, the position should only be returned to what it would have been by way of the court asking what is necessary to restore what has been lost to the debtor, albeit by allowing for the restoration of assets to the debtor so as to make those assets available for execution by victims: see *Chohan v Saggar* [1994] BCLC 706 at 714.

## SECTION 424(1)(b)

**Scope of provision**—Where a voluntary arrangement is in place, the claim may be pursued by the supervisor, an arrangement creditor, or a non-arrangement creditor – provided either is a victim as defined in s 423(5) – without any requirement for the leave of the court.

## SECTION 424(1)(c)

**Scope of provision**—A victim may proceed with a claim without a requirement for leave if none of the preceding circumstances apply. Such a claim will be available where a debtor company is in receivership (of any form) or subject to a company voluntary arrangement, although a CVA backed by a moratorium will ordinarily prevent such proceedings.

**[1.584]**

**425 Provision which may be made by order under s 423**

(1) Without prejudice to the generality of section 423, an order made under that section with respect to a transaction may (subject as follows)—

(a) require any property transferred as part of the transaction to be vested in any person, either absolutely or for the benefit of all the persons on whose behalf the application for the order is treated as made;

(b) require any property to be so vested if it represents, in any person's hands, the application either of the proceeds of sale of property so transferred or of money so transferred;

(c) release or discharge (in whole or in part) any security given by the debtor;

(d) require any person to pay to any other person in respect of benefits received from the debtor such sums as the court may direct;

(e) provide for any surety or guarantor whose obligations to any person were released or discharged (in whole or in part) under the transaction to be under such new or revived obligations as the court thinks appropriate;

(f) provide for security to be provided for the discharge of any obligation imposed by or arising under the order, for such an obligation to be charged on any property and for such security or charge to have the same priority as a security or charge released or discharged (in whole or in part) under the transaction.

(2) An order under section 423 may affect the property of, or impose any obligation on, any person whether or not he is the person with whom the debtor entered into the transaction; but such an order—

(a) shall not prejudice any interest in property which was acquired from a person other than the debtor and was acquired in good faith, for value and without notice of the relevant circumstances, or prejudice any interest deriving from such an interest, and

(b) shall not require a person who received a benefit from the transaction in good faith, for value and without notice of the relevant circumstances to pay any sum unless he was a party to the transaction.

(3) For the purposes of this section the relevant circumstances in relation to a transaction are the circumstances by virtue of which an order under section 423 may be made in respect of the transaction.

(4) In this section "security" means any mortgage, charge, lien or other security.

**General note**—For the purpose of orders under s 425(1) see s 423(2) and the notes thereto.

It has been held that the nature and the extent of relief should take into account the mental state of either the transferee of the property that is the subject of the impugned transaction or any other person against whom an order is sought, as well as their involvement in the scheme of the debtor to put assets out of the reach of creditors: *4Eng Ltd v Harper* [2009] EWHC 2633 (Ch), [2010] 1 BCLC 176, [2010] BPIR 1, at [11], [13]. Sales J in this case said that where a person receives property in good faith and he or she has changed his or her position as a result, then it would not be appropriate to require the transferee to return the property ([14]). The decision is analysed and criticised in Morgan, '*4Eng Ltd v Harper* – an unjustified change?' (2010) 3(1) CRI 5. The decision has been the subject of reasonably wide criticism (eg Goode *Principles of Corporate Insolvency Law* (Sweet and Maxwell, 4th edn 2011) at 633–634), although in *BTI 2014 LLC v Sequana SA* [2016] EWHC 1686 (Ch) Rose J did not criticise it; while she said change of position did not provide a complete defence to the claim under s 423, she considered that it was relevant to the question of the appropriate relief to be granted (at [523]). In fact in a later hearing involving this litigation her Ladyship said that court is entitled to take into account all the circumstances of the different parties involved in the process of fashioning a just and appropriate remedy: *BTI 2014 LLC v Sequana SA* [2017] EWHC 211 (Ch) at [24]. These decisions by Rose J were upheld by the Court of Appeal at [2019] EWCA Civ 112, [2019] 1 BCLC 347.

The court, in formulating an order, is not limited to restoring the position of the debtor as it was before the dealing. Rather it has to put all the parties back into the position that they would have been in had the transaction not been entered into (*Johnson v Arden* [2018] EWHC 1624 (Ch) at [92]). What the court is to do is restitutionary in nature, not compensatory (at [92]).

### SECTION 425(1)

**Scope of provision**—Judges are granted wide discretion when it comes to ordering relief: *Griffin v Awoderu* [2008] EWHC 349 (Ch) at [40], *4Eng Ltd v Harper* [2009] EWHC 2633 (Ch) at [9], *BTI 2014 LLC v Sequana SA* [2017] EWHC 211 (Ch) at [23] (upheld by the Court of Appeal [2019] EWCA Civ 112, [2019] 1 BCLC 347 at [88]), although it cannot be said that the court has an unlimited jurisdiction to grant relief (*Johnson v Arden* [2018] EWHC 1624 (Ch) at [91]). The range of orders in s 425(1)(a)–(f) closely resemble those in ss 241(1) and 342(1), save that those sections feature an additional sub-para (g) which allows the court to control proofs in a winding up or bankruptcy. This range of orders is, however, no more than illustrative of the types of orders, singly or in any combination, which the court may choose to make in its discretion under s 423(2) in meeting the two purposes in that subsection. Neither does the range of orders set out here limit the scope of the court's power given the words 'without prejudice to the generality of Section 423 . . . '. There are some circumstances in which the court can decide that it is not appropriate for there to be any remedy imposed, but this would only be in an exceptional case: *Chohan v Saggar* [1994] BCLC 706, *BTI 2014 LLC v Sequana SA* [2017] EWHC 211 (Ch) at [24]. It would only be in exceptional circumstances as the purpose of the provision was to recover assets for victims and generally override the interests of the transferee. Thus far the range of considerations which may lead a court to refrain from granting relief where the claimant had proved his or her case has not been authoritatively determined (*Payroller Ltd v Little Panda Consultants Ltd* [2018] EWHC 3161 (QB), [2019] BPIR 205 at [30]). See the comments accompanying the heading 'Section 241(1)' in the notes accompanying 241.

What relief is ordered is heavily dependent on the facts. The provision allows for flexibility in tailoring orders to permit justice to be done. Hard and fast rules cannot be laid down: *4Eng Ltd v Harper* [2009] EWHC 2633 (Ch), [2010] 1 BCLC 176, [2010] BPIR 1 at [16]. If a debtor can establish that he or she has had a change of position then this might be taken into account by a court in determining what relief should be ordered: *BTI 2014 LLC v Sequana SA* [2016] EWHC 1686 (Ch), [2017] 1 BCLC 453 at [523] (upheld by the Court of Appeal [2019] EWCA Civ 112, [2019] 1 BCLC 347). According to Rose J in a later case, it is not correct to say that the remedy under the section cannot go further 'than the value of any obligations of the transferor to the victims at the time when the court comes to consider the imposition of the remedy. Such a principle would risk creating an unfairness to the victims where, as here, a substantial period of time has elapsed between the date of the impugned transaction and the date when the remedy is devised and where the relationship between the various parties has changed in ways which have, at the least, been influenced by the fact that the impugned transaction took place.': *BTI 2014 LLC v Sequana SA* [2017] EWHC 211 (Ch) at [39]. Change of position was one of several factors that were taken into account by ICC Judge Jones in *Re Fowlds* ([2020] EWHC 1200 (Ch)) when deciding not to give relief to an applicant who had successfully established that a preference had been given.

It is not necessary for a claimant to establish bad faith on the part of the respondent in the sense of recklessness or sharp practice before a remedy under s 425 can be awarded: *BTI 2014 LLC v Sequana SA* [2016] EWHC 1686 (Ch), [2017] 1 BCLC 453 at [523].

Where property has been transferred to a person who had no knowledge of the transferor's intention to put assets out of the reach of creditors and the transferee had simply held the property then the appropriate order should normally be one that transfers the property either to the creditors or the transferor: *4Eng Ltd v Harper* [2009] EWHC 2633 (Ch), [2010] 1 BCLC 176, [2010] BPIR 1 at [14]. The court in this case said that there was no obligation on the court to inquire, when providing for relief, into the need to maintain the standard of living of the transferee.

The court does not have jurisdiction to make an order under s 423 against a director of a debtor company, who has received no benefit from the transaction and whose only role was to direct the company to enter into the transaction or to give the preference. The director has in fact nothing to 'restore': *Johnson v Arden* [2018] EWHC 1624 (Ch), [2019] 2 BCLC 215 at [10]).

### SECTION 425(2), (3)

**Scope of provision**—Whilst it is open to the court to upset third party rights, s 425(2) provides mandatory protection for two categories of bona fide purchasers for value without notice of the relevant circumstances defined in s 425(3). (Compare here the more complex third party protection provisions in ss 241(2)–(3) and 341(2)–(3).)

For an example of protection of third party rights, see the order of Scott J in *Arbuthnot Leasing International Ltd v Havelet Leasing Ltd (No 2)* [1990] BCC 636, noted above, to s 423(2).

## PART XVII   MISCELLANEOUS AND GENERAL

## [1.585]

**General comment on Part XVII**—This Part covers a number of diverse matters including provisions for: co-operation with overseas courts exercising insolvency jurisdiction; dealing with

Members of Parliaments and Assemblies who are subject to bankruptcy restriction orders or undertakings; penalties for breach of the Insolvency Act; and the admissibility of certain statements in evidence.

**[1.586]**

**426 Co-operation between courts exercising jurisdiction in relation to insolvency**

(1)   An order made by a court in any part of the United Kingdom in the exercise of jurisdiction in relation to insolvency law shall be enforced in any other part of the United Kingdom as if it were made by a court exercising the corresponding jurisdiction in that other part.

(2)   However, without prejudice to the following provisions of this section, nothing in subsection (1) requires a court in any part of the United Kingdom to enforce, in relation to property situated in that part, any order made by a court in any other part of the United Kingdom.

(3)   The Secretary of State, with the concurrence in relation to property situated in England and Wales of the Lord Chancellor, may by order make provision for securing that a trustee or assignee under the insolvency law of any part of the United Kingdom has, with such modifications as may be specified in the order, the same rights in relation to any property situated in another part of the United Kingdom as he would have in the corresponding circumstances if he were a trustee or assignee under the insolvency law of that other part.

(4)   The courts having jurisdiction in relation to insolvency law in any part of the United Kingdom shall assist the courts having the corresponding jurisdiction in any other part of the United Kingdom or any relevant country or territory.

(5)   For the purposes of subsection (4) a request made to a court in any part of the United Kingdom by a court in any other part of the United Kingdom or in a relevant country or territory is authority for the court to which the request is made to apply, in relation to any matters specified in the request, the insolvency law which is applicable by either court in relation to comparable matters falling within its jurisdiction.

In exercising its discretion under this subsection, a court shall have regard in particular to the rules of private international law.

(6)   Where a person who is a trustee or assignee under the insolvency law of any part of the United Kingdom claims property situated in any other part of the United Kingdom (whether by virtue of an order under subsection (3) or otherwise), the submission of that claim to the court exercising jurisdiction in relation to insolvency law in that other part shall be treated in the same manner as a request made by a court for the purpose of subsection (4).

(7)   Section 38 of the Criminal Law Act 1977 (execution of warrant of arrest throughout the United Kingdom) applies to a warrant which, in exercise of any jurisdiction in relation to insolvency law, is issued in any part of the United Kingdom for the arrest of a person as it applies to a warrant issued in that part of the United Kingdom for the arrest of a person charged with an offence.

(8)   Without prejudice to any power to make rules of court, any power to make provision by subordinate legislation for the purpose of giving effect in relation to companies or individuals to the insolvency law of any part of the United Kingdom includes power to make provision for the purpose of giving effect in that part to any provision made by or under the preceding provisions of this section.

(9)   An order under subsection (3) shall be made by statutory instrument subject to annulment in pursuance of a resolution of either House of Parliament.

(10)   In this section "insolvency law" means—

(a)     in relation to England and Wales, provision extending to England and Wales and made by or under this Act or sections 1A, 6 to 10, 12 to 15, 19(c) and 20 (with Schedule 1), of the Company Directors Disqualification Act 1986 and sections 1 to 17 of that Act as they apply for the purposes of those provisions of that Act;

(b)     in relation to Scotland, provision extending to Scotland and made by or under this Act, sections 1A, 6 to 10, 12 to 15, 19(c) and 20 (with Schedule 1) of the Company Directors Disqualification Act 1986 and sections 1 to

17 of that Act as they apply for the purposes of those provisions of that Act, Part XVIII of the Companies Act or the Bankruptcy (Scotland) Act 2016;

(c)    (*not reproduced*)

(d)    in relation to any relevant country or territory, so much of the law of that country or territory as corresponds to provisions falling within any of the foregoing paragraphs;

and references in this subsection to any enactment include, in relation to any time before the coming into force of that enactment the corresponding enactment in force at that time.

(11)   In this section "relevant country or territory" means—

(a)    any of the Channel Islands or the Isle of Man, or

(b)    any country or territory designated for the purposes of this section by the Secretary of State by order made by statutory instrument.

(12)   In the application of this section to Northern Ireland—

(a)    for any reference to the Secretary of State there is substituted a reference to the Department of Economic Development in Northern Ireland;

(b)    in subsection (3) for the words "another part of the United Kingdom" and the words "that other part" there are substituted the words "Northern Ireland";

(c)    for subsection (9) there is substituted the following subsection—

"(9)   An order made under subsection (3) by the Department of Economic Development in Northern Ireland shall be a statutory rule for the purposes of the Statutory Rules (Northern Ireland) Order 1979 and shall be subject to negative resolution within the meaning of section 41(6) of the Interpretation Act (Northern Ireland) 1954.".

(13)   Section 129 of the Banking Act 2009 provides for provisions of that Act about bank insolvency to be "insolvency law" for the purposes of this section.

(14)   Section 165 of the Banking Act 2009 provides for provisions of that Act about bank administration to be "insolvency law" for the purposes of this section.

**Amendments**—SI 1989/2405; Insolvency Act 2000, s 8, Sch 4, paras 1, 16; Banking Act 2009, ss 129, 165; SI 2016/1034.

**General note**—This provision is designed to promote co-operation between the UK courts and the courts of certain other designated countries and territories. It permits the UK courts to give assistance to a foreign court in an insolvency matter. Only countries or territories that are designated for the purposes of s 426 may apply and they are known as 'relevant countries or territories': s 426(11). At the present time they are: Anguilla, Australia, the Bahamas, Bermuda, Botswana, Canada, Cayman Islands, Falkland Islands, Gibraltar, Hong Kong, the Republic of Ireland, Montserrat, New Zealand, St Helena, Turks and Caicos Islands, Tuvalu and the Virgin Islands. These were designated by the Co-operation of Insolvency Courts (Designation of Relevant Countries and Territories) Order 1986 (SI 1986/2123). Subsections (4), (5), (10) and (11) of s 426 now apply to the Bailiwick of Guernsey by Insolvency Act 1986 (Guernsey) Order 1989 (SI 1989/2409). Malaysia and the Republic of South Africa were added to the list by SI 1996/253, and Brunei was the last country to be designated by SI 1998/2766. This means that, although the purpose of s 426 is to encourage co-operation, only a very limited number of countries can ask for assistance, thereby limiting the utility of the provision. Nevertheless, the UK has ceased to be an EU Member State and, as presently understood, the Insolvency Regulation 2015/848 will generally cease to apply to the UK except where main insolvency proceedings have already been opened before the Brexit implementation period completion day, which is scheduled to be 31 December 2020 at 11 pm. Therefore, there may be scope for arguing that EU Member States should be added to the list of designated countries for the purposes of 426. The powers of the UK courts may be greater under s 426 than they are under the UK Model Law on Cross Border Insolvency, in particular by allowing for the application of foreign insolvency law in certain circumstances.

The UNCITRAL Model Law, which has been brought into effect in Great Britain by s 14 of the Insolvency Act 2000 through the Cross-Border Insolvency Regulations 2006 (SI 2006/1030) is relevant to the application of s 426. The aim of the Model Law is to foster the efficient administration of cross-border insolvency proceedings where there is an international element. One great benefit of the Model Law is that, its effects are not limited to specific countries, as is the case with s 426 and the EU Regulation 2015/848. However this also means that there is the potential for conflict between s 426 and the Model Law. Where an insolvency proceeding is connected to a country that is designated under s 426(11), an application may still be made under the Model Law. Under Article 7 of schedule 1 of the Cross-Border Insolvency Regulations 2006 it is stated that any additional assistance that may be forthcoming under the laws of Great Britain may be given in conjunction with assistance under the Model Law.

See also the introduction to the Cross-Border Insolvency Regulations 2006.

## SECTION 426(1), (2)

**Reciprocal enforcement of orders within the UK**—Sections 426(1) and (2) state that any court order made in relation to insolvency law in any part of the UK is enforceable throughout the UK, except with regard to orders relating to property.

## SECTION 426(3), (9)

**Rights to property**—Sections 426(3) and (9) permit the Secretary of State to make an order by statutory instrument which gives a trustee or liquidator the same rights with regard to property situated in another part of the UK, as a trustee or assignee would have in that other part. By virtue of s 426(6) a trustee or liquidator is able to claim property situated in any other part of the UK by asking for assistance from the UK court with jurisdiction over the property. The request is to be treated in the same way as a request under s 426(4).

## SECTION 426(4)

**The jurisdiction of the UK courts – the discretion to grant a request**—It is fair to say that, although cross-border insolvency has become increasingly important in recent times, there has not been a deluge of cases under these provisions. This may be because of the countries and territories that have been designated as there are significant omissions, such as the USA and Japan. However, there have been a number of cases that have clarified the court's approach to its jurisdiction under s 426.

It is possible to put into administration, or apply the CVA procedure to, a foreign company. See *Re Dallhold Estates (UK) Ltd* [1992] 1 BCLC 621, where an Australian company was put into administration, and *Re Television Trade Rentals Ltd* [2002] BPIR 859, where the CVA procedure was applied to companies incorporated in the Isle of Man.

It was held by the Court of Appeal in *HSBC v Tambrook Jersey Ltd* [2013] EWCA Civ 576, [2014] Ch 242 that there need not be any 'substantive' insolvency proceedings in motion in the relevant foreign jurisdiction or the intention to institute such proceedings before the UK court could accept a request for assistance. In this case, a Jersey court had issued a letter of request asking an English court to put a Jersey registered company into administration in England. There was no such procedure in Jersey and it was considered that an English administration would produce the best outcome for creditors and other stakeholders. At first instance – [2013] EWHC 866 (Ch) – it was held that since insolvency proceedings in Jersey were neither in progress nor contemplated, there was nothing to assist, and the English court lacked jurisdiction to grant the request. The Court of Appeal took a different view holding that the Jersey court, by hearing the application and issuing the letter of request, was exercising its insolvency jurisdiction. In its view, that was sufficient to fulfil the requirements of s 426 and nothing more by way of formal insolvency proceedings was needed. Davis LJ observed at para 37: 'I would be prepared to accept that s 426 would not in itself empower the courts to issue or act upon a request in respect of a matter unrelated to insolvency . . . But, that said, I do not think that the courts should be astute to equate "having" jurisdiction with "exercising" jurisdiction in the sense of connoting a requirement for the existence of some formal insolvency proceedings in the requesting state.'

Section 426(4) states that the UK courts 'shall assist' any other UK court or any 'relevant country or territory' (defined in s 426(11)) with regard to insolvency law.

It was held by the Court of Appeal in *HSBC v Tambrook Jersey Ltd* [2013] EWCA Civ 576, [2013] BPIR 484 that there need not be any 'substantive' insolvency proceedings in motion in the relevant foreign jurisdiction or the intention to institute such proceedings before the UK court could accept the request for assistance. In this case, a Jersey court had issued a letter of request asking an English court to put a Jersey registered company into administration in England. There was no such procedure in Jersey and it was considered that an English administration would produce the best outcome for creditors and other stakeholders. At first instance it was held that since insolvency proceedings in Jersey were neither in progress nor contemplated, there was nothing to assist, and the English court lacked jurisdiction to grant the request. The Court of Appeal took a different view holding that the Jersey court, by hearing the application and issuing the letter of request, was exercising its insolvency jurisdiction. In its view, that was sufficient to fulfil the requirements of s 426 and nothing more by way of formal insolvency proceedings was needed. Davis LJ observed (at para 37):

> 'I would be prepared to accept that s 426 would not in itself empower the courts to issue or act upon a request in respect of a matter unrelated to insolvency . . . But, that said, I do not think that the courts should be astute to equate "having" jurisdiction with "exercising" jurisdiction in

the sense of connoting a requirement for the existence of some formal insolvency proceedings in the requesting state.'

The apparently mandatory words of s 426(5) have not been interpreted as meaning that the UK courts have to assist in every case. Instead, in *Hughes v Hannover* [1997] BCLC 497, the Court of Appeal stated that the court has a discretion to refuse to give assistance where it is appropriate. The case involved an insurance company being wound up in Bermuda. The defendants were re-insurers of the company and sought arbitration under the re-insurance contracts. A letter of request from the Bermudan court sought a worldwide injunction restraining any actions or proceedings being commenced against the company. The court did refuse assistance in this case because the circumstances, had changed by the time the court came to make its decision.

In setting down guidelines for deciding whether assistance should be given, Morritt LJ referred with approval to early cases involving s 426, eg *Re Dallhold Estates (UK) Ltd* [1992] 1 BCLC 621 and *Re Focus Insurance Co Ltd* [1997] 1 BCLC 219, in which the judges concerned acknowledged that assistance was not to be granted automatically: rather the courts had a discretion to determine whether to accede to a letter of request. Assistance should be given if, in accordance with the law to be applied, the relief sought may be properly granted. Public policy might be a reason for refusing to give assistance, but it is not the only one. He stressed that the fact that a request has been made is a weighty factor to be taken into account in deciding whether to grant the assistance sought; nevertheless it is not in itself conclusive that assistance should be given. Furthermore, Jonathan Parker LJ in *England v Smith (Re Southern Equities Corp)* [2001] Ch 419 (see below) stated that since countries and territories are specifically designated for the purpose of s 426, this indicated that public policy favours the giving of assistance. He then went on to say that the court would not make an order if it considered that such action would be oppressive.

In *Centaur Litigation SPC v Terrill* [2015] EWHC 3420 (Ch), [2015] All ER (D) 52 (Dec) at para 28 Norris J said that s 426(5) undoubtedly confers a discretion on the court whose assistance is requested but in this case the discretion was exercised in favour of giving assistance.

The case of *Hughes v Hannover* makes clear that in deciding whether to give assistance the courts may apply their own inherent jurisdiction, English insolvency law, or the insolvency law of the foreign jurisdiction applying for assistance. In that case the court could have granted a worldwide injunction only under its general jurisdiction, as both of the relevant insolvency provisions of England and Bermuda were limited territorially in their scope.

In *Re Focus Insurance Co Ltd* [1996] BCC 659 Scott VC declined to make an order for the assistance of foreign liquidators in the recovery of English assets in an English bankruptcy where the liquidators were the petitioning creditors in the bankruptcy and the relief sought could be obtained in the bankruptcy proceedings by the trustee in bankruptcy. The same judge also held in *Re BCCI (No 11)* [1997] 1 BCLC 80 that s 426 assistance could not be given where its effect would be to disapply the mandatory English set off rules prescribed by the Insolvency Rules.

### SECTION 426(5)

An English court under s 426 may provide any form of assistance comparable to that given in English insolvency proceedings, whether the assistance takes the form of an order under the Insolvency Act or pursuant to the court's general equitable jurisdiction. The available forms of assistance include an order for examination of a company officer pursuant to s 236 Insolvency Act 1986; an injunction to restrain the institution or continuation of proceedings against the debtor company; a declaration recognising the right and title of a foreign representative and the appointment of a receiver over the company's assets within the jurisdiction. In *Centaur Litigation SPC v Terrill* [2015] EWHC 3420 (Ch), [2015] All ER (D) 52 (Dec). The assistance granted to the Cayman court took the form of a worldwide freezing order in respect of the assets of a director of the debtor company who may have been implicated in wrongdoing.

It has been held that assistance can take the form of making an administration order in relation to a foreign insolvent company that had a place of business in this country where the order would preserve economic value for the benefit of parties interested in the foreign liquidation or restructuring.

**Application of foreign law**—In a Court of Appeal case, *England v Smith (Re Southern Equities Corp)* [2001] Ch 419, Morritt LJ, giving the leading judgment, stated that an examination under Australian law would be permitted pursuant to a request under s 426. (Under s 426(5) the UK court is permitted to apply the law of the foreign court making the request.) The English provision, IA 1986, s 236 identified s 596B as a provision of the Australian Corporations Law. But once the decision to apply provisions of the foreign law has been made, any corresponding English provisions cease to have any relevance.

So, despite the fact the Australian law pertaining to examinations was different to English law and under the latter provisions the examination could not have gone ahead, that was no reason to refuse to grant assistance. The object of s 426 was to provide reciprocal assistance in insolvencies; it would be inconsistent with the need for comity if the English courts stigmatised the law of the requesting court as oppressive because it did not correspond to English law. Both the Australian and English provisions were interpreted to avoid oppression, but this was achieved in different ways. By acknowledging that a provision of the insolvency law of the foreign court should not be divorced from the principles and practice by which the provision is applied in that jurisdiction, s 426 could be given full effect. In the alternative, if the English court applied a foreign provision only when it corresponded to English law, there would have been little point in the legislature giving the court the power to apply foreign law. In so deciding, the Court of Appeal disapproved of *Re JN Taylor Finance Pty Ltd* [1999] 2 BCLC 256, where a similar request to that in *England v Smith* was made for an examination under Australian law. The request was refused because the examination could not go ahead under English law.

In insolvency matters where choice of law is concerned, there has been a traditional emphasis placed on the law of the place of the forum (the lex fori) and the power to apply foreign law is at variance with this traditional emphasis. In deciding what law to apply, s 426(5) provides that an English court 'shall have regard, in particular' to the rules of private international law. It is not entirely clear what this statement is intended to imply. In *Re Television Trade Rentals Ltd* [2002] BPIR 859 Lawrence Collins J while suggesting that the provision was 'obscure and ill thought out' also expressed the view that the requested court should take the foreign elements into account in deciding what law to apply. (See also Lord Neuberger in *RE HIH Casualty and General Insurance Ltd* [2008] 1 WLR 852 at para 81 talking about the reference as 'slightly mystifying'.) Where these elements point to the application of the foreign law, this may influence the court in deciding to apply that law, although courts would seem still to have a discretion to disregard the English conflicts rule in an appropriate case. This view suggests that in applying s 426, an English court should not regard common law rules of jurisdiction and recognition as inhibiting its statutory power to give assistance if, in the circumstances, it is considered appropriate to offer the assistance requested.

Others have suggested however, that s 426(5) should be accorded a more decisive meaning and for a variant on this view see Carnwath LJ in *Re HIH Casualty and General Insurance Ltd* [2007] 1 All ER 177 at para 71 who suggested that it was for those seeking to justify a departure from English principles, to show that there is some rule of Private International Law which so requires. In other words, and as a matter of principle, when a court is confronted with a choice between the provisions of two different systems of law from which to derive the basis for its decision, it should select the rule contained within that system which, according to the rules of private international law, is properly applicable to the issue which forms the subject matter of the request to which the court is responding.

For a discussion see in I Fletcher *Insolvency in Private International Law* 2nd edn (Oxford, 2005) at pp 236–237 and the comments of Lord Hodge in *UBS AG New York v Fairfield Sentry Ltd* [2019] UKPC 20 who observed at para 15 that it was 'not uncommon for the courts in one country to apply the insolvency laws of another when giving assistance to the latter country'.

**Handing over assets to a foreign liquidator**—An English ancillary liquidation is conducted in accordance with English insolvency rules in deciding, for example, what proofs can be admitted and what counts as a preferential debt but once secured and preferential debts have been paid off it is common to remit the remaining assets to the jurisdiction where the principal liquidation is taking place. In *Re HIH Casualty and General Insurance Ltd* [2008] 1 WLR 852 the question arose whether this power to remit assets should be exercised where the foreign law of distribution does not coincide with English law. The case concerned the liquidation of an Australian insurance company where the assets of the company would be distributed on a different basis from that in an English liquidation to the disadvantage of certain creditors. Under Australian law insurance creditors were treated better and non-insurance creditors worse than under English law. As Lord Hoffmann pointed out at para 32 English law has now adopted a regime for the winding-up of insurance companies which gives preference to insurance creditors – reg 21(2) of the Insurers (Reorganisation and Winding Up) Regulations 2004 (SI 2004/353) giving effect to Directive 2001/17/EC on the reorganisation and winding up of insurance companies. At first instance, David Richards J held that ([2006] 2 All ER 671 at para 8): 'in an English liquidation of a foreign company, the court has no power to direct the liquidator to transfer funds for distribution in the principal liquidation, if the scheme for pari passu distribution in that liquidation is not substantially the same as under English law.'

The decision was confirmed by the Court of Appeal, which, nevertheless, did introduce some qualifications to this general statement of principle. Morritt VC said ([2007] 1 All ER 177 at) para 41:

'There may be circumstances in which it is for the benefit of the creditors that a transfer should be made, notwithstanding that their interests in the liquidation in England, when viewed in isolation would be adversely affected. For example, the savings in cost by avoiding duplication may offset any reduction in prospective dividend. Similarly a loss of priority may be sufficiently offset by an increase in the pool available for distribution to those whose priority was changed. The admission of further creditors may be offset by an increase in the pool available for distribution to that class of creditor. In such cases it may be that an order sanctioning the transfer may properly be made.'

The Court of Appeal pointed to *Daewoo Motor Co Ltd* [2006] BPIR 415 as an example of the operation of this qualification in practice. In that case Lewison J authorised the transfer of the assets collected by provisional liquidators to a receiver appointed by a Korean court. The transfer was ordered because it was being done with the consent of the three creditors whose interests might be prejudiced and to the overall advantage of all the others.

In *Re HIH Casualty and General Insurance Ltd* the request to transfer assets came from an Australian court pursuant to s 426 of the Insolvency Act 1986 rather than at common law and the House of Lords overturned the Court of Appeal holding that it failed to take sufficient heed of the section. Lord Hoffmann said that the section should not be deprived of its intended potential to enable a single universal scheme for insolvency distribution to be achieved. Australia was a designated country for s 426 purposes and there was nothing unacceptably discriminatory or otherwise contrary to public policy in the Australian insolvency provisions. Lord Neuberger said a fundamental principle of English insolvency law would not be offended or unfairness perpetrated by the application of the Australian insolvency regime.

Lord Hoffmann was prepared to go further placing greater emphasis on the principle of universalism and suggesting that a remission of assets to Australia could be ordered at common law. The differences between English and foreign systems of distribution were relevant only to discretion and in this case the application of Australian law to the distribution of all the assets was more likely to give effect to the expectations of creditors as a whole than the distribution of some of the assets according to English law.

English courts now also have discretionary power to order the transfer of assets to a foreign insolvency representative power under Art 21(2) of the UNCITRAL Model Law on Cross-Border Insolvency as implemented in the UK by the Cross-Border Insolvency Regulations 2006. There is however a proviso that the interests of domestic creditors should be 'adequately protected'.

It may be noted that the UNCITRAL Model Law has also been implemented in the US by Chapter 15 of the Bankruptcy Abuse Prevention and Consumer Protection Act 2005, superseding s 304 of the US Bankruptcy Code under which a US bankruptcy court could exercise various powers in a 'case ancillary to a foreign proceeding'. The substance of the old s 304 is, however, preserved in the new s 1507. US courts can authorise the transfer of assets to foreign insolvency representatives provided that the interests of the creditors and other interested parties, including the debtor, are 'sufficiently protected'. The UNCITRAL Model Law itself uses the expression 'adequately protected' and the legislative wording it seems was changed in the US to avoid confusion with a traditional and well-used expression under US bankruptcy jurisprudence.

It is a moot point to what extent 'sufficient protection' differs from 'adequate protection' under the UK Cross Border Insolvency Regulations.

Morritt VC in *Re HIH Casualty and General Insurance Ltd* [2006] EWCA Civ 732, [2007] 1 All ER 177 at [54]: 'This is not the occasion on which to determine what degree of protection would be "adequate". Nor are we concerned with whether that test is the same as that contained in the US Bankruptcy Code which requires the protection to be "sufficient"'. See also David Richards J at first instance – [2005] EWHC 2125 (Ch) at [147], [2006] 2 All ER 671 at 671h-e.

There was some consideration of Art 21(2) in *Bakhshiyeva v Sberbank of Russia* [2018] EWCA Civ 2802. The Court of Appeal suggested (at [95]) that in exercising the powers to remit assets to a foreign liquidator, it might be appropriate to exercise powers under the Model Law so as to achieve the discharge or variation of an English law right in a way that was tantamount to the application of a foreign law.

### SECTION 426(10)

**Meaning of insolvency law**—Insolvency law is defined under this provision and in *Hughes v Hannover* [1997] BCLC 49, where the court asserted that s 426(10) states what insolvency law means, not what it includes.

There may be difficulties with the application of the 'correspondence' test to foreign schemes of arrangement as these may or may not be equivalent to company voluntary arrangements under Part 1 Insolvency Act 1986. The point however was glossed over in *Re Business City Express Ltd* [1997] BCC 826 where a scheme of arrangement entered into pursuant to the Irish examinership procedures was made binding on English creditors.

The matter was recently addressed by Quinn J in Ireland in *Re Arctic Aviation Assets* [2021] IEHC 268. Quinn J suggested that the dearth of recent authorities on recognition of Irish restructuring and insolvency proceedings pursuant to s 426 was largely due to the fact that the European Insolvency Regulation had been in force and has governed insolvency proceedings regarding companies having their centre of main interests in either England or Ireland. Nonetheless, the persuasive authority of the decision in *Re Business City Express Limited* was undiminished. Quinn J accepted expert evidence on the UK practice to the effect that 'The authorities suggest that a broad approach should be taken to the meaning of "corresponds" and that it is not necessary that the foreign law be the same as the 1986 Act provisions, or, at least, to involve the same approach or procedure. I say "suggest" because little judicial consideration appears to have been given to the meaning of "corresponds to" within the meaning of s 426 (10)(d)' ([277]). At [279] Quinn J said: 'The question of recognition and enforceability of an order made was considered by Snowden J in *Re Noble Group Ltd* [2018] EWHC 3092 (Ch) where he quoted from a prior judgment of his own in *Re Van Gansewinkel Groep BV* [2015] EWHC 2151 (Ch) as follows: "The English court does not need certainty as to the position under foreign law - but it ought to have some credible evidence to the effect that it would not be acting in vain"' ([279]).

### SECTION 426(11)

**Countries and territories to which s 426 applies**—Any of the Channel Islands, the Isle of Man and any place designated by statutory instrument can be a relevant country or territory for the purposes of making a request to the UK courts: see s 426(11). Section 426 applies to Northern Ireland by virtue of s 426(12). It should be noted that although s 426 applies in Northern Ireland, the Cross-Border Insolvency Regulations 2006 (SI 2006/1030) apply within Great Britain.

See the general note for a list of those countries or territories that are currently designated.

## [1.587]

### Disqualification from Parliament (England and Wales and Northern Ireland)

(1) A person in respect of whom a bankruptcy restrictions order or a debt relief restrictions order has effect shall be disqualified—

(a) from membership of the House of Commons,

(b) from sitting or voting in the House of Lords, and

(c) from sitting or voting in a committee of the House of Lords or a joint committee of both Houses.

(2) If a member of the House of Commons becomes disqualified under this section, his seat shall be vacated.

(3) If a person who is disqualified under this section is returned as a member of the House of Commons, his return shall be void.

(4) No writ of summons shall be issued to a member of the House of Lords who is disqualified under this section.

(5) If a court makes a bankruptcy restrictions order or interim order, or a debt relief restrictions order or an interim debt relief restrictions order, in respect of a member of the House of Commons or the House of Lords the court shall notify the Speaker of that House.

(6) If the Secretary of State accepts a bankruptcy restrictions undertaking or a debt relief restrictions undertaking made by a member of the House of Commons or the House of Lords, the Secretary of State shall notify the Speaker of that House.

(7) If the Department of Enterprise, Trade and Investment for Northern Ireland accepts a bankruptcy restrictions undertaking made by a member of the House of Commons or the House of Lords under Schedule 2A to the Insolvency (Northern Ireland) Order 1989, the Department shall notify the Speaker of that House.

(8) In this section a reference to a bankruptcy restrictions order or an interim order includes a reference to a bankruptcy restrictions order or an interim order made under Schedule 2A to the Insolvency (Northern Ireland) Order 1989.

**Amendments**—Inserted by Enterprise Act 2002, s 266(1); Tribunals, Courts and Enforcement Act 2007, s 108(3), Sch 20, Pt 1, paras 1, 12; SI 2012/1544.

## [1.588]

### 426B Devolution

(1) If a court in England and Wales makes a bankruptcy restrictions order or interim order in respect of a member of the Scottish Parliament, the Northern Ireland Assembly or the National Assembly for Wales, or makes a debt relief restrictions order or interim debt relief restrictions order in respect of such a member, the court shall notify the presiding officer of that body.

(1A) If the High Court in Northern Ireland makes a bankruptcy restrictions order or interim order under Schedule 2A to the Insolvency (Northern Ireland) Order 1989 in respect of a member of the Scottish Parliament or the National Assembly for Wales, the Court shall notify the presiding officer of that body.

(2) If the Secretary of State accepts a bankruptcy restrictions undertaking or a debt relief restrictions undertaking made by a member of the Scottish Parliament, the Northern Ireland Assembly or the National Assembly for Wales, the Secretary of State shall notify the presiding officer of that body.

(3) If the Department of Enterprise, Trade and Investment for Northern Ireland accepts a bankruptcy restrictions undertaking made by a member of the Scottish Parliament or the National Assembly for Wales under Schedule 2A to the Insolvency (Northern Ireland) Order 1989, the Department shall notify the presiding officer of that body.

**Amendments**—Inserted by Enterprise Act 2002, s 266(1); Tribunals, Courts and Enforcement Act 2007, s 108(3), Sch 20, Pt 1, paras 1, 13; SI 2012/1544.

## [1.589]

### 426C Irrelevance of privilege

(1) An enactment about insolvency applies in relation to a member of the House of Commons or the House of Lords irrespective of any Parliamentary privilege.

(2) In this section "enactment" includes a provision made by or under—

    (a)    an Act of the Scottish Parliament, or

    (b)    Northern Ireland legislation.

**Amendments**—Inserted by Enterprise Act 2002, s 266(1).

## [1.590]

### 427 Disqualification from Parliament (Scotland . . .)

(1) Where . . . a court in Scotland awards sequestration of an individual's estate, the individual is disqualified—

    (a)    for sitting or voting in the House of Lords,

    (b)    for being elected to, or sitting or voting in, the House of Commons, and

    (c)    for sitting or voting in a committee of either House.

(2) Where an individual is disqualified under this section, the disqualification ceases—

    (a)    except where the award is recalled or reduced without the individual having been first discharged, on the discharge of the individual, and

    (b)    in the excepted case, on the . . .recall or reduction, as the case may be.

(3) No writ of summons shall be issued to any lord of Parliament who is for the time being disqualified under this section for sitting and voting in the House of Lords.

(4) Where a member of the House of Commons who is disqualified under this section continues to be so disqualified until the end of the period of 6 months beginning with the day of the . . . award, his seat shall be vacated at the end of that period.

(5) A court which makes an . . . award such as is mentioned in subsection (1) in relation to any lord of Parliament or member of the House of Commons shall forthwith certify the . . .award to the Speaker of the House of Lords or, as the case may be, to the Speaker of the House of Commons.

(6) Where a court has certified an . . . award to the Speaker of the House of Commons under subsection (5), then immediately after it becomes apparent which of the following certificates is applicable, the court shall certify to the Speaker of the House of Commons—

    (a)    that the period of 6 months beginning with the day of the . . . award has expired without the . . . award having been . . .recalled or reduced, or

    (b)    that the . . . award has been . . .recalled or reduced before the end of that period.

(6A) Subsections (4) to (6) have effect in relation to a member of the Scottish Parliament but as if—

    (a)    references to the House of Commons were to the Parliament and references to the Speaker were to the Presiding Officer, and

(b)     in subsection (4), for "under this section" there were substituted "under section 15(1)(b) of the Scotland Act 1998 by virtue of this section".

(6B)   Subsections (4) to (6) have effect in relation to a member of the National Assembly for Wales but as if—

(a)     references to the House of Commons were to the Assembly and references to the Speaker were to the presiding officer, and

(b)     in subsection (4), for "under this section" there were substituted "under section 16(A1)(a) of the Government of Wales Act 2006 and paragraph 4 of Schedule 1A to that Act".

(6C)   Subsections (4) to (6) have effect in relation to a member of the Northern Ireland Assembly but as if—

(a)     references to the House of Commons were to the Assembly and references to the Speaker were to the Presiding Officer; and

(b)     in subsection (4), for "under this section" there were substituted "under section 36(4) of the Northern Ireland Act 1998 by virtue of this section".

(7) . . .

**Amendments**—Government of Wales Act 2006, s160 (1); Enterprise Act 2002, ss 266(1)–(2)(b), 278(2), Sch 26; Scotland Act 1998, s 125, Sch 8, para 23(6); Government of Wales Act 1998, s 125, Sch 12, para 24; Northern Ireland Act 1998, s 99, Sch 13, para 6; SI 2012/1544; Senedd and Elections (Wales) Act 2020, s 35(1).

**General note**—While a Member of the UK Parliament was disqualified from his or her position if he or she became bankrupt, now, as a result of changes brought about by the Enterprise Act 2002, that does not apply in relation to Members who have been adjudged bankrupt in England and Wales.

## [1.591]

### 428  Exemptions from Restrictive Trade Practices Act

(1)  . . .

(2)  . . .

(3)  In this section "insolvency services" means the services of persons acting as insolvency practitioners or carrying out under the law of Northern Ireland functions corresponding to those mentioned in section 388(1) or (2) in Part XIII, in their capacity as such.

**Amendments**—SI 2000/311.

## [1.592]

### 429  Disabilities on revocation of administration order against an individual

*(1)   The following applies where a person fails to make any payment which he is required to make by virtue of an administration order under Part VI of the County Courts Act 1984.*

*(2)   The court which is administering that person's estate under the order may, if it thinks fit—*

*(a)     revoke the administration order, and*

*(b)     make an order directing that this section and section 12 of the Company Directors Disqualification Act 1986 shall apply to the person for such period, not exceeding one year, as may be specified in the order.*

(1)   This section applies if the county court revokes an administration order made in respect of an individual ("the debtor") on one of the relevant grounds.

(2)   The court may, at the time it revokes the administration order, make an order directing that this section and section 12 of the Company Directors Disqualification Act 1986 shall apply to the debtor for such period, not exceeding one year, as may be specified in the order.

(2A)   Each of the following is a relevant ground—

(a)     he debtor had failed to make two payments (whether consecutive or not) required by the order;

(b)     at the time the order was made—

(i)    the total amount of the debtor's qualifying debts was more than the prescribed maximum for the purposes of Part 6 of the 1984 Act, but

(ii)    because of information provided, or not provided, by the debtor, that amount was thought to be less than, or the same as, the prescribed maximum.

(3)    *A person* An individual to whom this section so applies shall not—

(a)    either alone or jointly with another person, obtain credit to the extent of the amount prescribed for the purposes of section 360(1)(a) or more, or

(b)    enter into any transaction in the course of or for the purposes of any business in which he is directly or indirectly engaged,

without disclosing to the person from whom he obtains the credit, or (as the case may be) with whom the transaction is entered into, the fact that this section applies to him.

(4)    The reference in subsection (3) to *a person* an individual obtaining credit includes—

(a)    a case where goods are bailed or hired to him under a hire-purchase agreement or agreed to be sold to him under a conditional sale agreement, and

(b)    a case where he is paid in advance (whether in money or otherwise) for the supply of goods or services.

(5)    *A person* An individual who contravenes this section is guilty of an offence and liable to imprisonment or a fine, or both.

**Amendments**—Enterprise Act 2002, s 269, Sch 23, paras 1, 15; words in italics repealed and words in square brackets inserted by Tribunals, Courts and Enforcement Act 2007, s 106, Sch 16, para 3, as from a date to be appointed (words in square brackets in sub-s (1) (as substituted by the Tribunals, Courts and Enforcement Act 2007, s 106, Sch 16, paras 3(1), (2)) substituted by the Crime and Courts Act 2013, s 17(5), Sch 9, Pt 3, para 52(1)(b), (2)).

**General note**—This provision covers the situation where a person has neglected to adhere to the terms of an administration order that has been given pursuant to the County Courts Act 1984. The administration order may be revoked and the debtor will be subject to some of the restrictions that are imposed on a bankrupt.

The penalty for contravention of any restrictions placed on a debtor is set out in Sch 10 to the Insolvency Act 1986.

## [1.593]

### 430 Provision introducing Schedule of punishments

(1)    Schedule 10 to this Act has effect with respect to the way in which offences under this Act are punishable on conviction.

(2)    In relation to an offence under a provision of this Act specified in the first column of the Schedule (the general nature of the offence being described in the second column), the third column shows whether the offence is punishable on conviction on indictment, or on summary conviction, or either in the one way or the other.

(3)    The fourth column of the Schedule shows, in relation to an offence, the maximum punishment by way of fine or imprisonment under this Act which may be imposed on a person convicted of the offence in the way specified in relation to it in the third column (that is to say, on indictment or summarily) a reference to a period of years or months being to a term of imprisonment of that duration.

(4)    The fifth column shows, (in relation to an offence for which there is an entry in that column) that a person convicted of the offence after continued contravention is liable to a daily default fine; that is to say, he is liable on a second or subsequent conviction of the offence to the fine specified in that column for each day on which the contravention is continued (instead of the penalty specified for the offence in the fourth column of the Schedule).

(4A)    In relation to an offence committed before section 154(1) of the Criminal Justice Act 2003 comes into force, a reference in Schedule 10 to 12 months on summary conviction in England and Wales is to be read as a reference to 6 months.

(5)    For the purpose of any enactment in this Act whereby an officer of a company who is in default is liable to a fine or penalty, the expression "officer who is in default" means

any officer of the company who knowingly and wilfully authorises or permits the default, refusal or contravention mentioned in the enactment.

**Amendments**—Corporate Insolvency and Governance Act 2020, s 2(1), Sch 3, paras 1, 26.

**General note**—The section indicates that Sch 10 to the Act sets out the penalties for offences against sections of the Act. Schedule 5 to the IR 1986 sets out the penalties for breaching the Rules.

'**Officer who is in default**'—This expression is identical to that used in the equivalent provision in the Companies Act 2006 (s 1121(1)).

## [1.594]

### 431 Summary proceedings

(1) Summary proceedings for any offence under any of Parts A1 to VII of this Act may (without prejudice to any jurisdiction exercisable apart from this subsection) be taken against a body corporate at any place at which the body has a place of business, and against any other person at any place at which he is for the time being.

(2) Notwithstanding anything in section 127(1) of the Magistrates' Courts Act 1980, an information relating to such an offence which is triable by a magistrates' court in England and Wales may be so tried if it is laid at any time within 3 years after the commission of the offence and within 12 months after the date on which evidence sufficient in the opinion of the Director of Public Prosecutions or the Secretary of State (as the case may be) to justify the proceedings comes to his knowledge.

(3) Summary proceedings in Scotland for such an offence shall not be commenced after the expiration of 3 years from the commission of the offence.

Subject to this (and notwithstanding anything in section 136 of the Criminal Procedure (Scotland) Act 1995), such proceedings may (in Scotland) be commenced at any time within 12 months after the date on which evidence sufficient in the Lord Advocate's opinion to justify the proceedings came to his knowledge or, where such evidence was reported to him by the Secretary of State, within 12 months after the date on which it came to the knowledge of the latter; and subsection (3) of that section applies for the purpose of this subsection as it applies for the purpose of that section.

(4) For purposes of this section, a certificate of the Director of Public Prosecutions, the Lord Advocate or the Secretary of State (as the case may be) as to the date on which such evidence as is referred to above came to his knowledge is conclusive evidence.

**Amendments**—Criminal Procedure (Consequential Provisions) (Scotland) Act 1995, s 5, Sch 4, para 61; Corporate Insolvency and Governance Act 2020, s 2(1), Sch 3, paras 1, 27.

**Summary proceedings in Scotland**—The court is not entitled to go behind a certificate from the Lord Advocate provided for the purposes of s 431(4) (*Roberts v Procurator Fiscal, Kilmarnock* [2019] SAC (Crim) 10).

## [1.595]

### 432 Offences by bodies corporate

(1) This section applies to offences under this Act other than those excepted by subsection (4).

(2) Where a body corporate is guilty of an offence to which this section applies and the offence is proved to have been committed with the consent or connivance of, or to be attributable to any neglect on the part of, any director, manager, secretary or other similar officer of the body corporate or any person who was purporting to act in any such capacity he, as well as the body corporate, is guilty of the offence and liable to be proceeded against and punished accordingly.

(3) Where the affairs of a body corporate are managed by its members, subsection (2) applies in relation to the acts and defaults of a member in connection with his functions of management as if he were a director of the body corporate.

(4) The offences excepted from this section are those under sections A19(5), A25(3), A26(4), A27(1), A28(5), A29(6), A30(2), A31(10), A32(4), 30, 39, 51, 53, 54, 62, 64, 66, 85, 89, 164, 188, 201, 206, 207, 208, 209, 210 and 211 . . ..

**Amendments**—Insolvency Act 2000, s 1, Sch 1, paras 1, 11; Corporate Insolvency and Governance Act 2020, s 2(1), Sch 3, paras 1.

**General note**—This mirrors former s 733 of the Companies Act 1985.

## [1.596]

### 433 Admissibility in evidence of statements of affairs, etc

(1)  In any proceedings (whether or not under this Act)—

(a)  a statement of affairs prepared for the purposes of any provision of this Act which is derived from the Insolvency Act 1985,

(aa)  a statement made in pursuance of a requirement imposed by or under Part 2 of the Banking Act 2009 (bank insolvency),

(ab)  a statement made in pursuance of a requirement imposed by or under Part 3 of that Act (bank administration), and

(b)  any other statement made in pursuance of a requirement imposed by or under any such provision or by or under rules made under this Act,

may be used in evidence against any person making or concurring in making the statement.

(2)  However, in criminal proceedings in which any such person is charged with an offence to which this subsection applies—

(a)  no evidence relating to the statement may be adduced, and

(b)  no question relating to it may be asked,

by or on behalf of the prosecution, unless evidence relating to it is adduced, or a question relating to it is asked, in the proceedings by or on behalf of that person.

(3)  Subsection (2) applies to any offence other than—

(a)  an offence under section 22(6), 47(6), 48(8), 66(6), 67(8), 95(8), 99(3), 131(7), 192(2), 208(1)(a) or (d) or (2), 210, 235(5), 353(1), 354(1)(b) or (3) or 356(1) or (2)(a) or (b) or paragraph 4(3)(a) of Schedule 7;

(b)  an offence which is—

(i)  created by rules made under this Act, and

(ii)  designated for the purposes of this subsection by such rules or by regulations made by the Secretary of State;

(c)  an offence which is—

(i)  created by regulations made under any such rules, and

(ii)  designated for the purposes of this subsection by such regulations;

(d)  an offence under section 1, 2 or 5 of the Perjury Act 1911 (false statements made on oath or made otherwise than on oath); or

(e)  an offence under section 44(1) or (2) of the Criminal Law (Consolidation) (Scotland) Act 1995 (false statements made on oath or otherwise than on oath).

(4)  Regulations under subsection (3)(b)(ii) shall be made by statutory instrument and, after being made, shall be laid before each House of Parliament.

**Amendments**—Youth Justice and Criminal Evidence Act 1999, s 59, Sch 3, para 7; Banking Act 2009, ss 128, 162; Small Business, Enterprise and Employment Act 2015, s 126, Sch 9, Pt 1, paras 1, 56.

**General note**—The provision was added to, but the effect of it was circumscribed, as a result of the enactment of the Youth Justice and Criminal Evidence Act 1999. Section 59 and Sch 3, para 7(1) of that Act introduced sub-ss (2)–(4) of s 433. The section now drafted means that statements obtained by compulsion cannot be used in most criminal proceedings, ie those not mentioned in s 433(3). It was held, however, in *Simmonds v Pearce* [2017] EWHC 3126 (Admin), [2018] 1 WLR 1849, [2018] BPIR 206 that evidence of statements made under compulsion in a bankruptcy examination can be adduced in proceedings for contempt of court.

The changes made to s 433 resulted from the decision of the European Court of Human Rights in *Saunders v United Kingdom* (1997) 23 EHRR 313, [1998] 1 BCLC 362, [1997] BCC 872, where it was held that the use of evidence that was obtained by company inspectors from persons who were compelled to answer was a contravention of the right to a fair trial under Art 6(1) of the European Convention on Human Rights.

**[1.597]**

### 434 Crown application

For the avoidance of doubt it is hereby declared that provisions of this Act which derive from the Insolvency Act 1985 and Part A1 and sections 233A and 233B and Schedule 4ZZA bind the Crown so far as affecting or relating to the following matters, namely—

(a)    remedies against, or against the property of, companies or individuals;

(b)    priorities of debts;

(c)    transactions at an undervalue or preferences;

(d)    voluntary arrangements approved under Part I or Part VIII, and

(e)    discharge from bankruptcy.

**Amendments**—Corporate Insolvency and Governance Act 2020, s 2(1), Sch 3, paras 1, 28.

### PART XVIIA    SUPPLEMENTARY PROVISIONS

**[1.598]**

### 434A Introductory

The provisions of this Part have effect for the purposes of—

(a)    the First Group of Parts, and

(b)    sections 411, 413, 414, 416 and 417 in Part 15.

**Amendments**—Inserted by SI 2008/948.

**[1.599]**

### 434B Representation of corporations in decision procedures and at meetings

(1)   If a corporation is a creditor or debenture-holder, it may by resolution of its directors or other governing body authorise a person or persons to act as its representative or representatives—

(a)    in a qualifying decision procedure, held in pursuance of this Act or of rules made under it, by which a decision is sought from the creditors of a company, or

(b)    at any meeting of a company held in pursuance of the provisions contained in a debenture or trust deed.

(2)   Where the corporation authorises only one person, that person is entitled to exercise the same powers on behalf of the corporation as the corporation could exercise if it were an individual creditor or debenture-holder.

(3)   Where the corporation authorises more than one person, any one of them is entitled to exercise the same powers on behalf of the corporation as the corporation could exercise if it were an individual creditor or debenture-holder.

(4)   Where the corporation authorises more than one person and more than one of them purport to exercise a power under subsection (3)—

(a)    if they purport to exercise the power in the same way, the power is treated as exercised in that way;

(b)    if they do not purport to exercise the power in the same way, the power is treated as not exercised.

**Amendments**—Inserted by SI 2008/948. Amended by Small Business, Enterprise and Employment Act 2015, s 126, Sch 9, Pt 1, paras 1, 57.

**[1.600]**

### 434C Legal professional privilege

In proceedings against a person for an offence under this Act nothing in this Act is to be taken to require any person to disclose any information that he is entitled to refuse to disclose on grounds of legal professional privilege (in Scotland, confidentiality of communications).

**Amendments**—Inserted by SI 2008/948.

**[1.601]**

### 434D Enforcement of company's filing obligations

(1)  This section applies where a company has made default in complying with any obligation under this Act—

(a)  to deliver a document to the registrar, or

(b)  to give notice to the registrar of any matter.

(2)  The registrar, or any member or creditor of the company, may give notice to the company requiring it to comply with the obligation.

(3)  If the company fails to make good the default within 14 days after service of the notice, the registrar, or any member or creditor of the company, may apply to the court for an order directing the company, and any specified officer of it, to make good the default within a specified time.

(4)  The court's order may provide that all costs (in Scotland, expenses) of or incidental to the application are to be borne by the company or by any officers of it responsible for the default.

(5)  This section does not affect the operation of any enactment imposing penalties on a company or its officers in respect of any such default.

**Amendments**—Inserted by SI 2009/1941.

**[1.602]**

### 434E Application of filing obligations to overseas companies

The provisions of this Act requiring documents to be forwarded or delivered to, or filed with, the registrar of companies apply in relation to an overseas company that is required to register particulars under section 1046 of the Companies Act 2006 as they apply in relation to a company registered under that Act in England and Wales or Scotland.

**Amendments**—Inserted by SI 2009/1941.

## PART XVIII   INTERPRETATION

**[1.603]**

**General comment on Part XVIII**—This Part explains the meaning of certain expressions.

**[1.604]**

### 435 Meaning of "associate"

(1)  For the purposes of this Act any question whether a person is an associate of another person is to be determined in accordance with the following provisions of this section (any provision that a person is an associate of another person being taken to mean that they are associates of each other).

(2)  A person is an associate of an individual if that person is—

(a)  the individual's husband or wife or civil partner,

(b)  a relative of—

(i)  the individual, or

(ii)  the individual's husband or wife or civil partner, or

(c)  the husband or wife or civil partner of a relative of—

(i)  the individual, or

(ii)  the individual's husband or wife or civil partner.

(3)  A person is an associate of any person with whom he is in partnership, and of the husband or wife or civil partner or a relative of any individual with whom he is in partnership; and a Scottish firm is an associate of any person who is a member of the firm.

(4)  A person is an associate of any person whom he employs or by whom he is employed.

(5)  A person in his capacity as trustee of a trust other than—

(a)    a trust arising under any of the second Group of Parts or the Bankruptcy (Scotland) Act 2016, or

(b)    a pension scheme or an employees' share scheme,

is an associate of another person if the beneficiaries of the trust include, or the terms of the trust confer a power that may be exercised for the benefit of, that other person or an associate of that other person.

(6)    A company is an associate of another company—

(a)    if the same person has control of both, or a person has control of one and persons who are his associates, or he and persons who are his associates, have control of the other, or

(b)    if a group of two or more persons has control of each company, and the groups either consist of the same persons or could be regarded as consisting of the same persons by treating (in one or more cases) a member of either group as replaced by a person of whom he is an associate.

(7)    A company is an associate of another person if that person has control of it or if that person and persons who are his associates together have control of it.

(8)    For the purposes of this section a person is a relative of an individual if he is that individual's brother, sister, uncle, aunt, nephew, niece, lineal ancestor or lineal descendant, treating—

(a)    any relationship of the half blood as a relationship of the whole blood and the stepchild or adopted child of any person as his child, and

(b)    an illegitimate child as the legitimate child of his mother and reputed father;

and references in this section to a husband or wife include a former husband or wife and a reputed husband or wife and references to a civil partner include a former civil partner and a reputed civil partner.

(9)    For the purposes of this section any director or other officer of a company is to be treated as employed by that company.

(10)    For the purposes of this section a person is to be taken as having control of a company if—

(a)    the directors of the company or of another company which has control of it (or any of them) are accustomed to act in accordance with his directions or instructions, or

(b)    he is entitled to exercise, or control the exercise of, one third or more of the voting power at any general meeting of the company or of another company which has control of it;

and where two or more persons together satisfy either of the above conditions, they are to be taken as having control of the company.

(11)    In this section "company" includes any body corporate (whether incorporated in Great Britain or elsewhere); and references to directors and other officers of a company and to voting power at any general meeting of a company have effect with any necessary modifications.

**Amendments**—Civil Partnership Act 2004, s 261(1), Sch 27, para 122; SI 2005/3129; SI 2009/1941; SI 2016/1034.

**General note**—The provision deals, in great detail, with the meaning of 'associate', and covers relatives, companies, employment and trusts. It is clear that if A is associated with B, and B is associated with C, it does not follow that A is necessarily also associated with C.

The term is of particular importance in relation to claims to adjust preferential transfers under s 239 or s 340. It is integral to the meaning of 'connected person' in s 249. 'Connected person' is used in relation to the adjustment provisions in Part IV of the Act, but also in several other places in the First Group of Parts of the Act. It was held in *Darty Holdings SAS v Carton-Kelly* [2021] EWHC 1018 (Ch) that there is nothing in the wording of s 435 to indicate that it should be read restrictively so as to exclude cases where the 'association' was intended to come to an end shortly after the relevant transaction, or, moreover, so as to exclude cases where the transaction in question was part of a wider arm's length deal.

See the comments accompanying s 249 and specifically under the heading 'associate'.

**[1.605]**

**436 Expressions used generally**

(1)  In this Act, except in so far as the context otherwise requires (and subject to Parts VII and XI)—

"the appointed day" means the day on which this Act comes into force under section 443;

"associate" has the meaning given by section 435;

"body corporate" includes a body incorporated outside Great Britain, but does not include—

  (a)  a corporation sole, or

  (b)  a partnership that, whether or not a legal person, is not regarded as a body corporate under the law by which it is governed;

"business" includes a trade or profession;

  . . .

"the Companies Acts" means the Companies Acts (as defined in section 2 of the Companies Act 2006) as they have effect in Great Britain;

"conditional sale agreement" and "hire-purchase agreement" have the same meanings as in the Consumer Credit Act 1974;

"distress" includes use of the procedure in Schedule 12 to the Tribunals, Courts and Enforcement Act 2007, and references to levying distress, seizing goods and related expressions shall be construed accordingly;

  . . .

"EEA State" means a state that is a Contracting Party to the Agreement on the European Economic Area signed at Oporto on 2nd May 1992 as adjusted by the Protocol signed at Brussels on 17th March 1993;

"employees' share scheme" means a scheme for encouraging or facilitating the holding of shares in or debentures of a company by or for the benefit of—

  (a)  the bona fide employees or former employees of—

    (i)   the company,

    (ii)  any subsidiary of the company, or

    (iii) the company's holding company or any subsidiary of the company's holding company, or

  (b)  the spouses, civil partners, surviving spouses, surviving civil partners, or minor children or step-children of such employees or former employees;

"the EU Regulation" means Regulation (EU) 2015/848 of the European Parliament and of the Council of 20 May 2015 on insolvency proceedings as it forms part of domestic law on and after exit day;

"modifications" includes additions, alterations and omissions and cognate expressions shall be construed accordingly;

"property" includes money, goods, things in action, land and every description of property wherever situated and also obligations and every description of interest, whether present or future or vested or contingent, arising out of, or incidental to, property;

"records" includes computer records and other non-documentary records;

"subordinate legislation" has the same meaning as in the Interpretation Act 1978; and

"transaction" includes a gift, agreement or arrangement, and references to entering into a transaction shall be construed accordingly.

(2)  The following expressions have the same meaning in this Act as in the Companies Acts—

"articles", in relation to a company (see section 18 of the Companies Act 2006);

"debenture" (see section 738 of that Act);

"holding company" (see sections 1159 and 1160 of, and Schedule 6 to, that Act);

"the Joint Stock Companies Acts" (see section 1171 of that Act);

"overseas company" (see section 1044 of that Act);

"paid up" (see section 583 of that Act);

"private company" and "public company" (see section 4 of that Act);

"registrar of companies" (see section 1060 of that Act);

"share" (see section 540 of that Act);

"subsidiary" (see sections 1159 and 1160 of, and Schedule 6 to, that Act).

**Amendments**—SI 2002/1037; SI 2005/879; SI 2007/2194; SI 2009/1941; Tribunals, Courts and Enforcement Act 2007, s 62(3), Sch 13, para 85; SI 2017/702; SI 2019/146, as from IP completion day (as defined in the European Union (Withdrawal Agreement) Act 2020, s 39(1)–(5)).

**'Property'**—The provision defines 'property' very broadly. In *Bristol Airport plc v Powdrill* [1990] Ch 744 at 759, Sir Nicholas Browne-Wilkinson said, in relation to the definition, that: 'It is hard to think of a wider definition of property.' An obligation to repay a loan is not 'property', however (*Re Hood (A Debtor)* [2020] EWHC 3232 (Ch), [2021] Ch 125).

A licence under the Sea Fish (Conservation) Act 1992 (*Re Rae* [1995] BCC 102) and a waste management licence (*Re Celtic Extraction Ltd; Re Blue Stone Chemicals Ltd* [1999] 2 BCLC 555, CA) have been held to constitute property within s 436. More recently, the Court of Appeal confirmed that barristers' non-contractual fees are 'property' for the purposes of IA 1986, stating that the definition set out in s 436 is 'inclusive rather than comprehensive': *Gwinnutt v George* [2019] EWCA Civ 656, [2019] Ch 471, [2019] BPIR 1195.

In *Re The Estate of Bertha Hemming* [2008] EWHC 2731 (Ch) it was held that a residuary legatee's entitlement to receive assets that comprise the residue in the future of a deceased estate, and the right to compel due administration of the estate, constituted a chose in action which was transmissible to the legatee's trustee in bankruptcy and so was property for the purposes of this section.

But, a right of appeal against a tax assessment has been held not to be property and could not be assigned by a liquidator: *Re GP Aviation Group International (in liq)* [2013] EWHC 1447 (Ch), [2013] BPIR 576.

See notes to s 283.

**'Transaction'**—This also is a very widely defined term (see *Phillips v Brewin Dolphin Lawrie Bell Ltd* [1999] BCC 557 at 565, CA). It was stressed in *BTI 2014 LLC v Sequana SA* [2019] EWCA Civ 112, [2019] 1 BCLC 347 at [58] that the definition is inclusive rather than exhaustive, and can include the payment of an otherwise lawful dividend.

## 436A

*(Repealed)*

**Amendments**—Inserted by SI 2002/1240; SI 2017/702. Repealed by SI 2019/146, as from IP completion day (as defined in the European Union (Withdrawal Agreement) Act 2020, s 39(1)–(5)).

## [1.606]

### 436B References to things in writing

(1)   A reference in this Act to a thing in writing includes that thing in electronic form.

(2)   Subsection (1) does not apply to the following provisions—

   (a)   section 53 (mode of appointment by holder of charge),

   (b)   *section 67(2) (report by receiver),*

   (c)   section 70(4) (reference to instrument creating a charge),

   (d)   section 111(2) (dissent from arrangement under s 110),

   (e)   *in the case of a winding up of a company registered in Scotland, section 111(4),*

   (f)   section 123(1) (definition of inability to pay debts),

   (g)   section 198(3) (duties of sheriff principal as regards examination),

   (h)   section 222(1) (inability to pay debts: unpaid creditor for £750 or more), and

   (i)   section 223 (inability to pay debts: debt remaining unsatisfied after action brought).

**Amendments**—Inserted by SI 2010/18; SSI 2016/141.

## PART XIX   FINAL PROVISIONS

**[1.607]**

### 437 Transitional provisions, and savings

The transitional provisions and savings set out in Schedule 11 to this Act shall have effect, the Schedule comprising the following Parts—

> Part I: company insolvency and winding up (matters arising before appointed day, and continuance of proceedings in certain cases as before that day);
>
> Part II: individual insolvency (matters so arising, and continuance of bankruptcy proceedings in certain cases as before that day);
>
> Part III: transactions entered into before the appointed day and capable of being affected by orders of the court under Part XVI of this Act;
>
> Part IV: insolvency practitioners acting as such before the appointed day; and
>
> Part V: general transitional provisions and savings required consequentially on, and in connection with, the repeal and replacement by this Act and the Company Directors Disqualification Act 1986 of provisions of the Companies Act 1985, the greater part of the Insolvency Act 1985 and other enactments.

**[1.608]**

### 438 Repeals

The enactments specified in the second column of Schedule 12 to this Act are repealed to the extent specified in the third column of that Schedule.

**Amendments**—SI 2009/1941.

**General note**—Schedule 12, to which the section makes reference, provides primarily for the repeal of a number of sections in the Companies Act 1985 (those dealing with insolvency and insolvency-related matters that are now covered in the Act) and most of the Insolvency Act 1985. For a brief explanation of the reason for these repeals and how they relate to the advent of the 1986 Act, see the Introduction to the Insolvency Legislation at the beginning of the book.

**[1.609]**

### 439 Amendment of enactments

(1)   The Companies Act is amended as shown in Parts I and II of Schedule 13 to this Act, being amendments consequential on this Act and the Company Directors Disqualification Act 1986.

(2)   The enactments specified in the first column of Schedule 14 to this Act (being enactments which refer, or otherwise relate, to those which are repealed and replaced by this Act or the Company Directors Disqualification Act 1986) are amended as shown in the second column of that Schedule.

(3)   The Lord Chancellor may by order make such consequential modifications of any provision contained in any subordinate legislation made before the appointed day and such transitional provisions in connection with those modifications as appear to him necessary or expedient in respect of—

> (a)   any reference in that subordinate legislation to the Bankruptcy Act 1914;
>
> (b)   any reference in that subordinate legislation to any enactment repealed by Part III or IV of Schedule 10 to the Insolvency Act 1985; or
>
> (c)   any reference in that subordinate legislation to any matter provided for under the Act of 1914 or under any enactment so repealed.

(4)   An order under this section shall be made by statutory instrument subject to annulment in pursuance of a resolution of either House of Parliament.

**[1.610]**

### 440 Extent (Scotland)

(1)   Subject to the next subsection, provisions of this Act contained in the first Group of Parts extend to Scotland except where otherwise stated.

(2)   The following provisions of this Act do not extend to Scotland—
  (a)   in the first Group of Parts—
        section 43;
        sections 238 to 241; and
        section 246;
  (b)   the second Group of Parts;
  (c)   in the third Group of Parts—
        sections 399 to 402,
        sections 412, 413, 415, 415A(3), 418, 420 and 421,
        sections 423 to 425, and
        *section 429(1) and (2)* section 429(1) to (2A); and
  (d)   in the Schedules—
        Parts II and III of Schedule 11; and
        Schedules 12 and 14 so far as they repeal or amend enactments which
        extend to England and Wales only.

**Amendments**—Enterprise Act 2002, s 270(4); Tribunals, Courts and Enforcement Act 2007, s 106, Sch 16, para 4, as from a date to be appointed.

## [1.611]

### 441  Extent (Northern Ireland)
(1)   The following provisions of this Act extend to Northern Ireland—
  (a)   sections 197, 426, , 426B, 427 and 428; and
  (b)   so much of section 439 and Schedule 14 as relates to enactments which
        extend to Northern Ireland.
(2)   Subject as above, and to any provision expressly relating to companies incorporated elsewhere than in Great Britain, nothing in this Act extends to Northern Ireland or applies to or in relation to companies registered or incorporated in Northern Ireland.

**Amendments**—SI 2012/1544.

## [1.612]

### 442  Extent (other territories)
Her Majesty may, by Order in Council, direct that such of the provisions of this Act as are specified in the Order, being provisions formerly contained in the Insolvency Act 1985, shall extend to any of the Channel Islands or any colony with such modifications as may be so specified.

## [1.613]

### 443  Commencement
This Act comes into force on the day appointed under section 236(2) of the Insolvency Act 1985 for the coming into force of Part III of that Act (individual insolvency and bankruptcy), immediately after that Part of that Act comes into force for England and Wales.

## [1.614]

### 444  Citation
This Act may be cited as the Insolvency Act 1986.

SCHEDULE ZA1

MORATORIUM: ELIGIBLE COMPANIES

Section A2

## [1.615]

**Amendments**—Inserted by Corporate Insolvency and Governance Act 2020, s 1(2), Sch 1.

**1** *Eligible companies*

A company is "eligible" for the purposes of this Part unless it is excluded from being eligible by any of the following—

    paragraph 2 (current or recent insolvency procedure);

    paragraph 2A (private registered providers of social housing);

    paragraph 2B (a registered social landlord under Part 2 of the Housing (Scotland) Act 2010);

    paragraph 3 (insurance companies);

    paragraph 4 (banks);

    paragraph 5 (electronic money institutions);

    paragraph 6 (investment banks and investment firms);

    paragraph 7 (market contracts, market charges, etc);

    paragraph 8 (participants in designated systems);

    paragraph 9 (payment institutions);

    paragraph 10 (operators of payment systems, infrastructure providers etc);

    paragraph 11 (recognised investment exchanges, clearing houses and CSDs);

    paragraph 12 (securitisation companies);

    paragraph 13 (parties to capital market arrangements);

    paragraph 15 (public-private partnership project companies);

    paragraph 18 (certain overseas companies).

**2 Companies subject to, or recently subject to, moratorium or an insolvency procedure**

(1)   A company is excluded from being eligible if—

    (a)    on the filing date, a moratorium for the company is in force, or

    (b)    at any time during the period of 12 months ending with the filing date, a moratorium for the company was in force (but see section A42(6) for power of the court to modify the effect of this paragraph).

(2)   A company is excluded from being eligible if—

    (a)    on the filing date, the company is subject to an insolvency procedure, or

    (b)    at any time during the period of 12 months ending with the filing date, the company was subject to an insolvency procedure within sub-paragraph (3)(a) or (b).

(3)   For the purposes of sub-paragraph (2), a company is subject to an insolvency procedure at any time if at that time—

    (a)    a voluntary arrangement has effect in relation to the company,

    (b)    the company is in administration,

    (c)    paragraph 44 of Schedule B1 applies in relation to the company (administration: interim moratorium),

    (d)    there is an administrative receiver of the company,

    (e)    there is a provisional liquidator of the company,

    (f)    the company is being wound up, or

    (g)    a relevant petition for the winding up of the company has been presented and has not been withdrawn or determined.

(4)   In sub-paragraph (3)(g) "relevant petition" means a petition under—

    (a)    section 124A (winding up on grounds of public interest),

    (b)    section 124B (winding up of SE), or

    (c)    section 124C (winding up of SCE).

*Private registered providers of social housing*

**2A**

A company is excluded from being eligible if it is a private registered provider of social housing.

*Insurance companies*

**2B  Registered social landlord under Part 2 of the Housing (Scotland) Act 2010**

A company is excluded from being eligible if it is a registered social landlord under Part 2 of the Housing (Scotland) Act 2010.]

**3**

(1)  A company is excluded from being eligible if—

    (a)    it carries on the regulated activity of effecting or carrying out contracts of insurance, and

    (b)    it is not an exempt person in relation to that activity.

(2)  In this paragraph—

"exempt person", in relation to a regulated activity, has the meaning given by section 417 of the Financial Services and Markets Act 2000;

"regulated activity" has the meaning given by section 22 of that Act, taken with Schedule 2 to that Act and any order under that section.

**4  Banks**

(1)  A company is excluded from being eligible if—

    (a)    it has permission under Part 4A of the Financial Services and Markets Act 2000 to carry on the regulated activity of accepting deposits,

    (b)    it is a banking group company within the meaning of Part 1 of the Banking Act 2009 (see section 81D of that Act), or

    (c)    it has a liability in respect of a deposit which it accepted in accordance with the Banking Act 1979 or the Banking Act 1987.

(2)  In sub-paragraph (1)(a) "regulated activity" has the meaning given by section 22 of the Financial Services and Markets Act 2000, taken with Schedule 2 to that Act and any order under that section.

**5  Electronic money institutions**

A company is excluded from being eligible if it is an electronic money institution within the meaning of the Electronic Money Regulations 2011 (SI 2011/99) (see regulation 2 of those Regulations).

**6  Investment banks and investment firms**

(1)  A company is excluded from being eligible if it is an investment bank or an investment firm.

(2)  In this paragraph—

"investment bank" means a company that has permission under Part 4A of the Financial Services and Markets Act 2000 to carry on the regulated activity of—

    (a)    safeguarding and administering investments,

    (b)    managing an AIF or a UCITS,

    (c)    acting as trustee or depositary of an AIF or a UCITS,

    (d)    dealing in investments as principal, or

    (e)    dealing in investments as agent,

    but does not include a company that has permission to arrange for one or more others to carry on the activity mentioned in paragraph (a) if it does not otherwise have permission to carry on any of the activities mentioned in paragraphs (a) to (e);

"investment firm" has the same meaning as in the Banking Act 2009 (see section 258A of that Act), disregarding any order made under section 258A(2)(b) of that Act;

"regulated activity" has the meaning given by section 22 of the Financial Services and Markets Act 2000, taken with Schedule 2 to that Act and any order under that section.

**7  Companies that are party to market contracts or subject to market charges, etc**

(1)  A company is excluded from being eligible if it is a party to a market contract for the purposes of Part 7 of the Companies Act 1989 (see section 155 of that Act).

(2)   A company is excluded from being eligible if any of its property is subject to a market charge for the purposes of Part 7 of the Companies Act 1989 (see section 173 of that Act).

(3)   A company is excluded from being eligible if any of its property is subject to a charge that is a system-charge, within the meaning of the Financial Markets and Insolvency Regulations 1996 (SI 1996/1469) (see regulation 2 of those Regulations).

## 8  Participants in designated systems

A company is excluded from being eligible if—

    (a)    it is a participant in a designated system, within the meaning of the Financial Markets and Insolvency (Settlement Finality) Regulations 1999 (SI 1999/2979) (see regulation 2 of those Regulations), or

    (b)    any of its property is subject to a collateral security charge within the meaning of those Regulations (see regulation 2 of those Regulations).

## 9  Payment institutions

A company is excluded from being eligible if it is an authorised payment institution, a small payment institution or a registered account information service provider within the meaning of the Payment Services Regulations 2017 (SI 2017/752) (see regulation 2 of those Regulations).

## 10  Operators of payment systems, infrastructure providers etc

A company is excluded from being eligible if—

    (a)    it is the operator of a payment system or an infrastructure provider within the meaning of Part 5 of the Financial Services (Banking Reform) Act 2013 (see section 42 of that Act), or

    (b)    it is an infrastructure company, within the meaning of Part 6 of that Act (see section 112 of that Act).

## 11  Recognised investment exchanges, clearing houses and CSDs

A company is excluded from being eligible if it is a recognised investment exchange, a recognised clearing house or a recognised CSD within the meaning of the Financial Services and Markets Act 2000 (see section 285 of that Act).

## 12  Securitisation companies

A company is excluded from being eligible if it is a securitisation company within the meaning of the Taxation of Securitisation Companies Regulations 2006 (SI 2006/3296) (see regulation 4 of those Regulations).

## 13  Parties to capital market arrangements

(1)   A company is excluded from being eligible if, on the filing date—

    (a)    it is a party to an agreement which is or forms part of a capital market arrangement (see sub-paragraph (2)),

    (b)    a party has incurred, or when the agreement was entered into was expected to incur, a debt of at least £10 million under the arrangement (at any time during the life of the capital market arrangement), and

    (c)    the arrangement involves the issue of a capital market investment (see paragraph 14).

(2)   For the purposes of this paragraph, an arrangement is a "capital market arrangement" if any of the following applies—

    (a)    it involves a grant of security to a person holding it as trustee for a person who holds a capital market investment issued by a party to the arrangement;

    (b)    at least one party guarantees the performance of obligations of another party;

    (c)    at least one party provides security in respect of the performance of obligations of another party;

    (d)    the arrangement involves an investment of a kind described in articles 83 to 85 of the Financial Services and Markets Act 2000 (Regulated Activities) Order 2001 (SI 2001/544) (options, futures and contracts for differences).

(3)   For the purposes of sub-paragraph (2)—

(a)    a reference to holding a security as trustee includes a reference to holding it as nominee or agent,

(b)    a reference to holding for a person who holds a capital market investment includes a reference to holding for a number of persons at least one of whom holds a capital market investment, and

(c)    a reference to holding a capital market investment is to holding a legal or beneficial interest in it.

(4)   For the purposes of sub-paragraph (1)(b), where a debt is denominated wholly or partly in a foreign currency, the sterling equivalent is to be calculated as at the time when the arrangement is entered into.

**14**

(1)   For the purposes of paragraph 13 an investment is a "capital market investment" if condition A or B is met.

(2)   Condition A is that the investment—

(a)    is within article 77 or 77A of the Financial Services and Markets Act 2000 (Regulated Activities) Order 2001 (SI 2001/544) (debt instruments), and

(b)    is rated, listed or traded or designed to be rated, listed or traded.

(3)   In sub-paragraph (2)—

"listed" means admitted to the official list within the meaning given by section 103(1) of the Financial Services and Markets Act 2000 (interpretation);

"rated" means rated for the purposes of investment by an internationally recognised rating agency;

"traded" means admitted to trading on a market established under the rules of a recognised investment exchange or on a foreign market.

(4)   In sub-paragraph (3)—

"foreign market" has the same meaning as "relevant market" in article 67(2) of the Financial Services and Markets Act 2000 (Financial Promotion) Order 2005 (SI 2005/1529) (foreign markets);

"recognised investment exchange" has the meaning given by section 285 of the Financial Services and Markets Act 2000 (recognised investment exchange).

(5)   Condition B is that the investment consists of a bond or commercial paper issued to one or more of the following—

(a)    an investment professional within the meaning of article 19(5) of the Financial Services and Markets Act 2000 (Financial Promotion) Order 2005 (SI 2005/1529);

(b)    a person who, when the agreement mentioned in paragraph 13(1) is entered into, is a certified high net worth individual in relation to a communication within the meaning of article 48(2) of that Order;

(c)    a person to whom article 49(2) of that Order applies (high net worth company, etc);

(d)    a person who, when the agreement mentioned in paragraph 13(1) is entered into, is a certified sophisticated investor in relation to a communication within the meaning of article 50(1) of that Order;

(e)    a person in a State other than the United Kingdom who under the law of that State is not prohibited from investing in bonds or commercial paper.

(6)   For the purposes of sub-paragraph (5)—

(a)    in applying article 19(5) of the Financial Services and Markets Act 2000 (Financial Promotion) Order 2005—

(i)    in article 19(5)(b), ignore the words after "exempt person",

(ii)    in article 19(5)(c)(i), for the words from "the controlled activity" to the end substitute "a controlled activity", and

(iii)    in article 19(5)(e), ignore the words from "where the communication" to the end;

(b)    in applying article 49(2) of that Order, ignore article 49(2)(e);

(c)    "bond" means—

        (i)     a bond that is within article 77(1) of the Financial Services and Markets Act 2000 (Regulated Activities) Order 2001, or

        (ii)    an alternative finance investment bond within the meaning of article 77A of that Order;

    (d)    "commercial paper" has the meaning given by article 9(3) of that Order.

### 15 Public-private partnership project companies

(1)   A company is excluded from being eligible if. . ., it is a project company of a project which—

    (a)    is a public-private partnership project (see paragraph 16), and

    (b)    includes step-in rights (see paragraph 17).

(2)   For the purposes of this paragraph a company is a "project company" of a project if any of the following applies—

    (a)    it holds property for the purpose of the project;

    (b)    it has sole or principal responsibility under an agreement for carrying out all or part of the project;

    (c)    it is one of a number of companies which together carry out the project;

    (d)    it has the purpose of supplying finance to enable the project to be carried out;

    (e)    it is the holding company of a company within any of paragraphs (a) to (d).

(3)   But a company is not a "project company" of a project if—

    (a)    it performs a function within sub-paragraph (2)(a) to (d) or is within sub-paragraph (2)(e), but

    (b)    it also performs a function which is not—

        (i)     within sub-paragraph (2)(a) to (d),

        (ii)    related to a function within sub-paragraph (2)(a) to (d), or

        (iii)   related to the project.

(4)   For the purposes of this paragraph a company carries out all or part of a project whether or not it acts wholly or partly through agents.

### 16

(1)   For the purposes of paragraph 15 "public-private partnership project" means a project—

    (a)    the resources for which are provided partly by one or more public bodies and partly by one or more private persons, or

    (b)    which is designed wholly or mainly for the purpose of assisting a public body to discharge a function.

(2)   In sub-paragraph (1) "public body" means—

    (a)    a body which exercises public functions,

    (b)    a body specified for the purposes of this paragraph by the Secretary of State, or

    (c)    a body within a class specified for the purposes of this paragraph by the Secretary of State.

(3)   In sub-paragraph (1)(a) "resources" includes—

    (a)    funds (including payment for the provision of services or facilities);

    (b)    assets;

    (c)    professional skill;

    (d)    the grant of a concession or franchise;

    (e)    any other commercial resource.

(4)   A specification under sub-paragraph (2) may be—

    (a)    general, or

    (b)    for the purpose of the application of paragraph 15 to a specified case.

### 17

(1)   For the purposes of paragraph 15 a project has "step-in rights" if a person who provides finance in connection with the project has a conditional entitlement under an agreement to—

    (a)    assume sole or principal responsibility under an agreement for carrying out all or part of the project, or

    (b)    make arrangements for carrying out all or part of the project.

(2)   In sub-paragraph (1) a reference to the provision of finance includes a reference to the provision of an indemnity.

## 18 Overseas companies with corresponding functions

A company is excluded from being eligible if its registered office or head office is outside the United Kingdom and—

    (a)    its functions correspond to those of a company mentioned in any of the previous paragraphs of this Schedule apart from paragraphs 2 and 2A and, if it were a company registered under the Companies Act 2006 in England and Wales or Scotland, it would be excluded from being eligible by that paragraph, or

    (b)    it has entered into a transaction or done anything else that, if done in England and Wales or Scotland by a company registered under the Companies Act 2006 in England and Wales or Scotland, would result in the company being excluded by any of the previous paragraphs of this Schedule apart from paragraphs 2 and 2A.

## 19 Interpretation of Schedule

(1)   This paragraph applies for the purposes of this Schedule.

(2)   "Agreement" includes any agreement or undertaking effected by—

    (a)    contract,

    (b)    deed, or

    (c)    any other instrument intended to have effect in accordance with the law of England and Wales, Scotland or another jurisdiction.

(3)   "The filing date" means the date on which documents are filed with the court under section A3, A4 or A5.

(4)   "Party" to an arrangement includes a party to an agreement which—

    (a)    forms part of the arrangement,

    (b)    provides for the raising of finance as part of the arrangement, or

    (c)    is necessary for the purposes of implementing the arrangement.

## 20 Powers to amend Schedule

(1)   The Secretary of State may by regulations amend this Schedule, apart from paragraph 2, so as to alter the circumstances in which a company is "eligible" for the purposes of this Part.

(2)   Regulations under this paragraph are subject to the affirmative resolution procedure.

## 21

(1)   The Welsh Ministers may by regulations amend this Schedule—

    (a)    so as to provide that a social landlord registered under Part 1 of the Housing Act 1996 is excluded from being "eligible" for the purposes of this Part;

    (b)    so as to reverse the effect of any provision made under paragraph (a).

(2)   Regulations under this paragraph extend to England and Wales only.

(3)   A statutory instrument containing regulations under this paragraph may not be made unless a draft of the statutory instrument containing them has been laid before and approved by a resolution of Senedd Cymru.

## 22

(1)   The Scottish Ministers may by regulations amend this Schedule—

    (a)    so as to provide that a social landlord registered under Part 2 of the Housing (Scotland) Act 2010 (asp 17) is excluded from being "eligible" for the purposes of this Part;

    (b)    so as to reverse the effect of any provision made under paragraph (a).

(2)   Regulations under this paragraph extend to Scotland only.

(3)   Regulations under this paragraph are subject to the affirmative procedure (see section 29 of the Interpretation and Legislative Reform (Scotland) Act 2010 (asp 10)).

**Amendments**—Inserted by Corporate Insolvency and Governance Act 2020, s 1(2), Sch 1; Amended by SI 2020/652; SSI 2020/338.

**CIGA 2020**—Para 2 of this Schedule is affected by temporary measures at Sch 4, paras 6(1)(c), 7(b) of CIGA 2020; paras 13 and 15 are affected by temporary measures at s 12(5)(a) of CIGA 2020; para 18 is affected by temporary measures at s 12(5)(b) of CIGA 2020.

## SCHEDULE ZA2
### MORATORIUM: CONTRACT OR OTHER INSTRUMENT INVOLVING FINANCIAL SERVICES

Section A18

**[1.616]**

**Amendments**—Inserted by Corporate Insolvency and Governance Act 2020, s 1(3), Sch 2.

**1 Introductory**

For the purposes of section A18 "contract or other instrument involving financial services" means a contract or other instrument to which any of the following paragraphs applies.

**2 Financial contracts**

(1)   This paragraph applies to a financial contract.

(2)   "Financial contract" means—

 (a)   a contract for the provision of financial services consisting of—

  (i)   lending (including the factoring and financing of commercial transactions),

  (ii)   financial leasing, or

  (iii)   providing guarantees or commitments;

 (b)   a securities contract, including—

  (i)   a contract for the purchase, sale or loan of a security, group or index of securities;

  (ii)   an option on a security or group or index of securities;

  (iii)   a repurchase or reverse repurchase transaction on any such security, group or index;

 (c)   a commodities contract, including—

  (i)   a contract for the purchase, sale or loan of a commodity or group or index of commodities for future delivery;

  (ii)   an option on a commodity or group or index of commodities;

  (iii)   a repurchase or reverse repurchase transaction on any such commodity, group or index;

 (d)   a futures or forwards contract, including a contract (other than a commodities contract) for the purchase, sale or transfer of a commodity or property of any other description, service, right or interest for a specified price at a future date;

 (e)   a swap agreement, including—

  (i)   a swap or option relating to interest rates, spot or other foreign exchange agreements, currency, an equity index or equity, a debt index or debt, commodity indexes or commodities, weather, emissions or inflation;

  (ii)   a total return, credit spread or credit swap;

  (iii)   any agreement or transaction that is similar to an agreement that is referred to in sub-paragraph (i) or (ii) and is the subject of recurrent dealing in the swaps or derivatives markets;

 (f)   an inter-bank borrowing agreement where the term of the borrowing is three months or less;

 (g)   a master agreement for any of the contracts or agreements referred to in paragraphs (a) to (f).

(3)   For the purposes of this paragraph "commodities" includes—

    (a)    units recognised for compliance with the requirements of EU Directive 2003/87/EC establishing a scheme for greenhouse gas emission allowance trading,

    (b)    allowances under paragraph 5 of Schedule 2 to the Climate Change Act 2008 relating to a trading scheme dealt with under Part 1 of that Schedule (schemes limiting activities relating to emissions of greenhouse gas), and

    (c)    renewables obligation certificates issued—

        (i)    by the Gas and Electricity Markets Authority under an order made under section 32B of the Electricity Act 1989, or

        (ii)    by the Northern Ireland Authority for Utility Regulation under the Energy (Northern Ireland) Order 2003 (SI 2003/419 (NI 6)) and pursuant to an order made under Articles 52 to 55F of that Order.

### 3  Securities financing transactions

(1)   This paragraph applies to—

    (a)    a securities financing transaction, and

    (b)    a master agreement for securities financing transactions.

(2)   "Securities financing transaction" has the meaning given by Article 3(11) of Regulation (EU) 2015/2365 on the transparency of securities financing transactions.

(3)   But for the purposes of that Article as it applies for the purposes of this paragraph, references to "commodities" in that Regulation are to be taken as including the units, allowances and certificates referred to in paragraph 2(3)(a), (b) and (c).

### 4  Derivatives

(1)   This paragraph applies to—

    (a)    a derivative, and

    (b)    a master agreement for derivatives.

(2)   "Derivative" has the meaning given by Article 2(5) of Regulation (EU) No 648/2012.

### 5  Spot contracts

(1)   This paragraph applies to—

    (a)    a spot contract, and

    (b)    a master agreement for spot contracts.

(2)   "Spot contract" has the meaning given by Article 7(2) or 10(2) of Commission Delegated Regulation of 25.4.2016 supplementing Directive 2014/65/EU of the European Parliament and of the Council as regards organisational requirements and operating conditions for investment firms and defined terms for the purposes of that Directive.

### 6  Capital market investments

(1)   This paragraph applies to an agreement which is, or forms part of, an arrangement involving the issue of a capital market investment.

(2)   "Capital market investment" has the meaning given by paragraph 14 of Schedule ZA1.

### 7  Contracts forming part of a public-private partnership

This paragraph applies to a contract forming part of a public-private partnership project within the meaning given by paragraph 16 of Schedule ZA1.

### 8  Market contracts

This paragraph applies to a market contract within the meaning of Part 7 of the Companies Act 1989 (see section 155 of that Act).

### 9  Qualifying collateral arrangements and qualifying property transfers

This paragraph applies to qualifying collateral arrangements and qualifying property transfers within the meaning of Part 7 of the Companies Act 1989 (see section 155A of that Act).

### 10  Contracts secured by certain charges or arrangements

This paragraph applies to a contract where any obligation under the contract is—

   (a)    secured by a market charge within the meaning of Part 7 of the Companies Act 1989 (see section 173 of that Act),

   (b)    secured by a system-charge within the meaning of the Financial Markets and Insolvency Regulations 1996 (SI 1996/1469) (see regulation 2 of those Regulations), or

   (c)    secured or otherwise covered by a financial collateral arrangement within the meaning of the Financial Collateral Arrangements (No 2) Regulations 2003 (SI 2003/3226) (see regulation 3 of those Regulations).

**11 Default arrangements and transfer orders**

This paragraph applies to a contract which is included in default arrangements, or a transfer order, within the meaning of the Financial Markets and Insolvency (Settlement Finality) Regulations 1999 (SI 1999/2979) (see regulation 2 of those Regulations).

**12 Card-based payment transactions**

This paragraph applies to a contract to accept and process card-based payment transactions within the meaning given by Regulation (EU) 2015/751 of the European Parliament and of the Council of 29th April 2015 on interchange fees for card-based payment transactions.

**13 Power to amend Schedule**

(1)   The Secretary of State may by regulations amend this Schedule so as to change the meaning of "contract or other instrument involving financial services" for the purposes of section A18.

(2)   Regulations under this paragraph are subject to the affirmative resolution procedure.

**Amendments**—Inserted by Corporate Insolvency and Governance Act 2020, s 1(3), Sch 2.

## SCHEDULE A1

. . .

**Amendments**—Repealed by Corporate Insolvency and Governance Act 2020, s 2(1), Sch 3, paras 1, 30.

## SCHEDULE B1
## ADMINISTRATION

### ARRANGEMENT OF SCHEDULE

| | |
|---|---|
| Nature of administration | Paragraphs 1 to 9 |
| Appointment of administrator by court | Paragraphs 10 to 13 |
| Appointment of administrator by holder of floating charge | Paragraphs 14 to 21 |
| Appointment of administrator by company or directors | Paragraphs 22 to 34 |
| Administration application – special cases | Paragraphs 35 to 39 |
| Effect of administration | Paragraphs 40 to 45 |
| Process of administration | Paragraphs 46 to 58 |
| Functions of administrator | Paragraphs 59 to 75 |
| Ending administration | Paragraphs 76 to 86 |
| Replacing administrator | Paragraphs 87 to 99 |
| General | Paragraphs 100 to 116 |

**[1.617]**

. . .

**Amendments**—Inserted by Enterprise Act 2002, s 248(2), Sch 16.

**Introductory notes regarding administration**—Administration was a regime first introduced by Part II of the 1986 Act. Whilst that regime provided a workable mechanism for rescue or, at least, asset maximisation, it was not without its difficulties. First, the procedure was expensive and was not therefore readily available to small or even medium sized concerns, which would have no option but to go into liquidation or seek to pursue an unprotected CVA. Secondly, the original administration procedure was more unwieldy than was strictly necessary for achieving the end objective envisaged by the Cork Committee whose recommendations had led to the new provisions.

The new regime in Sch B1, introduced in 2003, sought to address these difficulties and introduced a reformulated procedure incorporating the enforcement of floating charge security, subject to certain qualifications, which security would otherwise have allowed for the appointment of an administrative receiver if created prior to 15 September 2003: see s 72A. Judicial analysis and development of Sch B1 has continued apace since its inception. The annotations and commentary which follow seek to provide some detailed elaboration in particular on the new statutory purpose (para 3), the new extendable time constraints (paras 4 and 76), the alternative methods of appointment (paras 10, 13, 14 and 22) and the wide procedure governing the conduct of administration, together with the various remedies available to dissatisfied creditors and third parties, including the new provisions in para 74 which allow the creditor or member to challenge the administrator's conduct of the administration.

With the implementation of Sch B1 the DTI issued Explanatory Notes to the new provisions which, whilst not having statutory force, are of some practical assistance and are referred to in the text which follows. These remain relevant but should not necessarily be used as an aid to interpretation or the way in which a court will construe any particular provision.

**Practice Direction – Insolvency Proceedings (July 2020) [2020] BPIR 1211**—Para 8 of this Practice Direction is concerned with administration. The Practice Direction is supplemented by the Temporary Insolvency Practice Direction that came into force on 30 June 2021 and at the time of writing is due to remain in force until 30 September 2021, as appears at Appendix 3 of this work.

**The Corporate Insolvency and Governance Act 2020 (CIGA 2020)**—This significant new piece of legislation, which was introduced into Parliament on 20 May 2020 before receiving the Royal Assent on 25 June 2020, introduced two new, free-standing insolvency procedures – the moratorium procedure under the newly inserted Part A1 of the 1986 Act, and the restructuring plan procedure by way of a newly introduced Part 26A of the Companies Act 2006 (Arrangements and Reconstructions for Companies in Financial Difficulty) – which complement administration as a rescue mechanism, as well as amending a small number of the existing provisions in Sch B1, most notably paras 64 to 66. The CIGA 2020 appears elsewhere in this work. The Practice Direction, *Practice Direction (Insolvency) Relating to the Corporate Insolvency and Governance Act 2020* [2020] BPIR 1207, appears at Appendix 4 of this work.

**Pre-pack sales**—So-called pre-packaged or pre-pack sales, by which the whole or part of a company's business is sold on by an administrator, usually immediately upon the appointment being made or shortly thereafter, and often involving pre-appointment negotiations, commonly arise in practice. This technique of preserving or rescuing a business is both a matter of controversy in some quarters because it carries the potential for abuse where, in reality, the real purpose of the sale out of administration is the thwarting of creditor claims coupled with the appropriation of debt and liability free assets into a new entity.

The review undertaken by Teresa Graham CBE into how pre-packs are working in practice was published on 16 June 2014. The report identified the utility of the procedure as a rescue mechanism but also made observations as to the potential for abuse and the need for increased transparency.

The latest version of SIP 16, version 3, effective from 1 November 2015, provides guidance specifically on pre-pack sales out of administration. A new version of SIP 13 (now entitled *Disposal of assets to connected parties in an insolvency process*) was published on 4 November 2016, effective from 1 December 2016. SIP 13 is not restricted to administration but has an obvious significance to, and overlap with, SIP 16.

On 27 July 2015 the Pension Protection Fund published guidance on pre-packs and their potential abuse as a mechanism in avoiding company pension liabilities, PPF Restructuring and Insolvency Team: Guidance note 2: Pre-packaged administration. On the day following the inception of the above-mentioned third version of SIP 16, the Insolvency Service launched the so-called Pre-pack Pool, an independent body of practitioners established to scrutinise sales to connected parties on pre-packs. The Pre-pack Pool is run by a private company which charges £800 + VAT per application.

On 12 December 2017 the Insolvency Service announced its intention to assess the impact of the voluntary measures identified above in seeking to improve the transparency of connected party pre-pack sales.

The Insolvency Service operates a hotline for the reporting of suspected abuse of the pre-pack procedure, 0845 6013546.

Para 60A, effective from 26 May 2015, empowers the Secretary of State to make regulations prohibiting or imposing requirements or conditions in relation to the disposal, hire out or sale of property of a company by an administrator to a connected person. That power expired on 26 May 2020 but was revived by the provisions of the Corporate Insolvency and Governance Act 2020.

In *DKLL Solicitors v HM Revenue and Customs* [2007] EWHC 2067 (Ch), [2007] BCC 908, two equity partners in an insolvent firm of solicitors which was a limited liability partnership applied for an administration order in relation to the partnership where the proposal was to effect a pre-pack sale of the partnership's business immediately upon the appointment of the administrators without the necessity of the approval by a creditors' meeting. The proposal was opposed by HMRC, the partnership's majority creditor, which had presented a winding up petition. Nevertheless, Andrew Simmonds QC (sitting as a deputy High Court judge) granted an administration order.

In *Re Kayley Vending Limited* [2009] BCC 578, HHJ Cooke, sitting as a High Court judge, held that in exercising its discretion in pre-pack cases, the court must be alert to see, so far as it could, that the procedure was at least not being obviously abused to the disadvantage of creditors. If it was, or may be, the court may conclude that it was inappropriate to give the pre-pack the apparent blessing conferred by making the administration order. Accordingly, in most cases the information required by SIP 16 should be included in the administration application.

In *Re Hellas Telecommunications (Luxembourg) II SCA* [2009] EWHC 3199 (Ch), [2010] BCC 295 Lewison J made an administration order but also provided liberty to the administrators to enter into a pre-pack sale pursuant to the only bid that, on the evidence, would command the consent of creditors entitled to consent to a sale. The judge observed at [8] that it is not entirely easy to see precisely where in the statutory structure the court is concerned with the merits of a pre-pack sale which, ultimately, and generally, are for the administrator to deal with subject to sufficiently aggrieved creditors having a remedy in the course of the administration in challenging any such decision:

> 'It may on the evidence be obvious that a pre-pack sale is an abuse of the administrator's powers, in which event the court could refuse to make the administration order or could direct the administrators not to complete a pre-pack sale. At the other end of the spectrum it may be that it is obvious that a particular pre-pack is on the evidence the only real way forward, in which case the court could give the administrators liberty to enter into the pre-pack, leaving open the possibility that a sufficiently aggrieved creditor could nevertheless challenge the administrators' decision ex post facto.'

Where the position is not clear, the judge also identified that the making of an administration order should not be taken as giving the court's blessing to a pre-pack sale which, ultimately, remains a commercial judgment for, and the responsibility of, the administrator.

In *Re UK Steelfixers Ltd* [2012] EWHC 2409 (Ch), [2012] BCC 751 the court was satisfied as to the insolvency of the company and that there was evidence 'of the usual quality that the result of an administration [would] be better than a liquidation.' HHJ Purle QC, sitting as a High Court judge, nevertheless declined to exercise his discretion in making an administration order and instead made a winding-up order thereby allowing post-petition transactions to be considered against the background of s 127. The significance of that order was in frustrating a proposed pre-pack in favour of a company owned and controlled by an employee of the company in the face of a winding-up petition presented by HMRC.

In *Capital for Enterprise Fund A LP v Bibby Financial Services Ltd* [2015] EWHC 2593 (Ch) a creditor challenged the pre-pack sale by the company in administration to another company with a common controlling director, alleging that the director had acted in breach of duty and claiming damages for conspiracy. HHJ Pelling QC, sitting as a High Court judge, upheld the validity of the pre-pack sale and dismissed the claim on the basis that, despite certain elements of the conspiracy claim being established, there could be no loss or damage by reason of the conspiracy because there was no prospect of the debtor company in administration having been capable of sale to a third-party purchaser as would have enabled the creditor to recover its debt.

*VE Vegas Investors IV LLC and others v Shinners and others* [2018] EWHC 186 (Ch) involved an application for removal of administrators due to a conflict of interest that arose in respect of a pre-pack sale to the company's management team. Registrar Jones considered the issue of the conflict of interest that arose was clear, and it was for the administrators to have effectively addressed the conflict through the appointment of independent administrators to deal with the investigation of the sale. Since the administrators had failed even to acknowledge, let alone address, the conflict, their conduct was serious enough as to justify an order for their removal. The question was not whether the administrators had acted improperly; rather, the issue was whether the administrators ought to be removed in the face of the conflict of interest manifested by the need to investigate potential claims and the failure to act appropriately in response.

The decision of HHJ Eyre QC, sitting as a High Court judge, in *Re Moss Groundworks Ltd* [2019] EWHC 3079 (Ch), in which an administration order was made following an adjournment, days previously before Snowden J, contains a valuable analysis of the authorities concerning the making of an administration order to facilitate a proposed pre-pack sale, the quality of the evidence the court can expect, including marketing activity and compliance with SIP 16, and the need for caution given the risk of abuse.

**The Administration (Restrictions on Disposals etc to Connected Parties) Regulations 2021 (SI 2021/427)**—These provisions came into force on 30 April 2021. The new provisions follow recommendations in the Insolvency Service's *Pre-pack sales in administration report* (8 October 2020) following media attention drawing attention to the potential abuse perpetrated by a sale of a company's business or assets out of administration before an administrator's proposals are considered by creditors. They require that a person intending to acquire a business or assets from a company in administration within the first eight weeks of administration – that is, any 'substantial disposal' to a 'connected person', as defined in the Regulations and the IA 1986, and not only 'pre-pack' arrangements (a term not defined in any event in law) – must seek an independent opinion on the purchase if that person is connected to the insolvent company unless the sale has been approved by creditors. An evaluator must evaluate whether the consideration payable and the grounds for the sale are reasonable in the circumstances and express a view as to whether a case has been made out for the purchase to complete. If the evaluator's opinion is that such a case has not been made out, the sale may still proceed with the connected party provided that an explanation is furnished as to why that course has been adopted in the face of the evaluator's adverse view. Amendments to SIP 13 and SIP 16 consequent upon the new Regulations took effect on 30 April 2021.

**Pre-appointment costs**—The former r 2.67(1)(c) of the IR 1986 provided that where an administration order is made, the costs of the applicant are payable as an administration expenses. The former r 2.67A, which dealt with pre-appointment costs, effective from 6 April 2010, was brought into force in response to two decisions.

In *Re Kayley Vending* [2009] EWHC 904 (Ch), the court held it was not appropriate to hold that an administrator's pre-appointment costs were in all cases part of the costs of the applicant that must be allowed under the former IR 1986, r 2.67(1)(c). Rather, it was appropriate to use the general power under para 13(1)(f) to order on a discretionary basis that the pre-appointment costs of the proposed administrator be treated as an expense of the administration where the court was satisfied that the balance of benefit arising from the incurring of pre-appointment costs was in favour of the creditors rather than the management as potential purchasers of the business.

In contrast, in *Re Johnson Machine and Tool Co Ltd* [2010] EWHC 582 (Ch), [2010] BCC 382, the directors of a company applied for an administration order. It was proposed that following the administrator's appointment there would be an immediate pre-pack sale of the company's business and assets to a connected company. Following the making of an administration order, HHJ Purle QC, sitting as a High Court judge, declined to allow the administrator's pre-appointment costs to be treated as an administration expense. Although he was satisfied that the pre-pack sale would result in a better return for creditors if the company were placed into liquidation, he noted that where the directors (or a company which they control or have a substantial connection with) are the purchasers, it is rarely possible to establish clearly that the balance of advantage is in the creditors' favour.

Pre-appointment costs are now governed by rr 3.35(10), 3.36 and 3.52 of the IR 2016. The second of those provisions provides a detailed list of what must be included in an administrator's proposals relating to a claim for pre-administration costs. As a matter of practice, the Insolvency Service's Dear IP letter, September 2014, directs that the approval of payment of pre-administration costs should be identified as a separate resolution in any notice to creditors.

**TUPE Regulations 2006**—The Transfer of Undertakings (Protection of Employment) Regulations 2006 (SI 2006/246) give statutory protection to employees by providing that where a company transfers a business situated immediately before the transfer in the United Kingdom to another person where there is a transfer of an economic entity which retains its identity, the contract of employment of any person employed by the company in relation to that business will have effect after the transfer as if originally made between the employee and the transferee. However, reg 8(7) provides that these regulations do not apply if at the time of a relevant transfer the transferor is subject to 'bankruptcy proceedings or any analogous insolvency proceedings which have been instituted with a view to the liquidation of the assets of the transferor and are under the supervision of an insolvency practitioner'.

In *Oakland v Wellswood (Yorkshire) Limited* [2009] EWCA Civ 1094, [2010] BCC 263, the Court of Appeal held that whether or not an administration falls within the terms of reg 8(7) will depend upon the purpose of the administration.

However, in *OTG Limited v Barke* [2011] BCC 608, the Employment Appeals Tribunal rejected this approach and held that reg 8(7) applies to all administrations. This was affirmed by the Court of Appeal in *Key2Law (Surrey) LLP v De'Antiquis* [2011] EWCA Civ 1567, [2012] BCC 375: to like effect see *Spaceright Europe Ltd v Baillavoine* [2011] EWCA Civ 1565, [2012] ICR 520 and *Crystal Palace FC Ltd v Kavanagh* [2013] EWCA Civ 1410.

In consequence, where the administrators transfer the company's business as a going concern, its employees will be entitled to the statutory protection of TUPE.

**Partnerships**—A partnership may be placed into administration under the Insolvent Partnerships (Amendment) Order 2005 (SI 2005/1516), effective from 1 July 2005.

An administration application in respect of a partnership must be made by all the partners unanimously: *In re Brake, Patley Wood Farm LLP v Brake* [2016] EWHC 1688 (Ch), [2017] 1 WLR 343 (Jeremy Cousins QC, leaving open at [52] the position where a partnership deed expressly permitted a majority of members to make an administration application, the preferable conclusion, it is submitted, in line with the deputy judge's view, being that nothing short of unanimity will suffice).

**Special administration regimes**—The legislation provides an expanding number of special administration regimes in relation to companies engaging in certain activities. These include: investment banks (see Pt 5, Ch 3 of the Investment Bank Special Administration (England and Wales) Rules 2011 (SI 2011/1301), under which see the approval by Arnold J of a distribution plan in *Re Beaufort Asset Clearing Services Ltd (in special administration)* [2018] EWHC 2287 (Ch)) and the plan approved by Henry Carr J in *Re Strand Capital Ltd* [2019] EWHC 1449 (Ch)); insurance companies (see the Financial Services and Markets Act 2000 (Administration Orders Relating to Insurers) Order 2010 (SI 2010/3023)); banks and other entities identified in s 422(1) which are companies within the meaning of ss 1 and 1171 of the Companies Act 2006 (see the Banks (Former Authorised Institutions) (Insolvency) Order 2006 (SI 2006/3107)); financial market infrastructure (FMI) companies (see Pt 6 of the Financial Services (Banking Reform) Act 2013 and the Financial Market Infrastructure Administration (England and Wales) Rules 2018 (SI 2018/833)); energy companies (see s 159 and Schs 20 and 21 of the Energy Act 2004, as amended by ss 93 to 102 of the Energy Act 2011 and the decision in *Gas and Electricity Markets Authority v GB Energy Supply Ltd* [2016] EWHC 3341 (Ch) (order made on basis of urgent telephone application made on Saturday evening) and the Energy Supply Company Administration Rules 2013 (SI 2013/1046)); companies designated under s 35 of the Postal Services Act 2011 (see the Postal Administration Rules 2013 (SI 2013/3208)); private registered providers of social housing (see the Housing and Planning Act 2016 (Commencement No 9 and Transitional and Saving Provisions) Regulations 2018 (SI 2018/805)); benefit societies and credit unions (see the Co-operative and Community benefit Societies and Credit Unions (Arrangements, Reconstruction and Administration) (Amendment) Order 2014 (SI 2014/1822)); and companies carrying on as further education institutions in England and Wales (see Pt 2, Ch 4 of the Technical and Further Education Act 2017 and the Education Administration Rules 2018 (SI 2018/1135) under which the first order was made by Chief ICCJ Briggs on 19 May 2019 on the application of the Secretary of State for Education in the matter of Hadlow College, Kent: [2019] EWHC 2035 (Ch))).

**Stay of special administration proceedings**—In *Bundeszentralamt v Heis and others (as special administrators of MF Global UK Ltd)* [2019] EWHC 705 (Ch), [2020] 1 BCLC 649 it was held that appeals against administrators' rejection of proofs of debt by the German tax authorities should be stayed pending proceedings by the German Federal tax Office being determined by the German courts. On the facts, an application for the same relief by Deutsche Bank in respect of differently constituted debts was dismissed.

**Winding up in special administration cases**—In *Re Beaufort Asset Clearing Services Ltd* [2020] EWHC 3627 Miles J held (at [56]) that the administrators of an investment bank in special administration had standing to seek the compulsory winding-up of the company under para 79 of Sch B1 at the same time as the application for the cessation of their appointments and discharge from liability in the absence of anything in the Investment Bank Special Administration Regulations 2011 (SI 2011/246) (the IBSA Regulations) suggesting that such a course was not open to the administrators. The point had arisen because, although regs 20 and 21 of the IBSA Regulations provide routes out of an investment bank special administration, neither provision applied in the present case because the company retained client assets and money which it had proved not possible for the administrators to return. (Winding-up orders were also considered appropriate on winding-up petitions presented in respect of two wholly owned nominee subsidiaries which were not in administration.) It is likely that the court will adopt a similar approach to the application of para 79 in other special administration regimes in the absence of any express or implied bar to such relief being sought.

**Power for administrator to bring claim for fraudulent or wrongful trading**—Section 117 of the Small Business, Enterprise and Employment Act 2015 inserts new ss 246ZA and 264ZB into the 1986 Act which provide provisions equivalent to those available to a liquidator under ss 213 and 214 of the Act.

**Power for administrator to assign statutory causes of action**—Section 118 of the Small Business, Enterprise and Employment Act 2015 inserts a new s 246ZD into the 1986 Act which provides a power for an administrator (or liquidator) to assign a statutory right of action (including the proceeds of an action) for fraudulent trading, wrongful trading, transactions at an undervalue, preferences, gratuitous alienations (Scotland), unfair preferences (Scotland) and extortionate credit transactions.

**Assignment of causes of action**—For the proper approach to the assignment of a cause of action by an administrator, including the position where there are competing interested parties, see *LF2 Ltd v Supperstone* [2018] EWHC 1776 (Ch) (Morgan J).

An office-holder should ensure that the methodology employed in the decision-making process to assign a cause of action does not run the risk of attack on the grounds that it is so utterly unreasonable or absurd that it is properly to be regarded as perverse, a test derived from the decision in *Leon v York-o-Matic Ltd* [1966] 1 WLR 1450, as applied to administrators in *Davey v Money* [2018] EWHC 766 (Ch) at [255] (Snowden J).

**A statutory trust?**—There is no authority as to whether a statutory trust arises over the assets of a company in administration or, if so, what the scope and implications of that trust might be. The Court of Appeal found it unnecessary to determine the issue in *Harms Offshore AHT 'Taurus' GmbH and Co KG* [2009] EWCA Civ 632 at [24] and [27]. Based on the observations of Hildyard J in *Re Lehman Bros Europe Ltd (in administration)* [2017] EWHC 2031 (Ch) at [84], the obvious distinctions between the position of a company in administration and in liquidation render a so-called statutory trust inapposite in the case of administration.

Generally, see A Keay 'A Comparative Analysis of the Administration Regimes in Australia and the United Kingdom' in P Omar (ed) *International Insolvency Law: Themes and Perspectives* (Aldershot, Ashgate, 2008), at 105ff.

## NATURE OF ADMINISTRATION

**[1.618]**

### 1 Administration

(1) For the purposes of this Act "administrator" of a company means a person appointed under this Schedule to manage the company's affairs, business and property.

(2) For the purposes of this Act—

    (a)    a company is "in administration" while the appointment of an administrator of the company has effect,

    (b)    a company "enters administration" when the appointment of an administrator takes effect,

    (c)    a company ceases to be in administration when the appointment of an administrator of the company ceases to have effect in accordance with this Schedule, and

    (d)    a company does not cease to be in administration merely because an administrator vacates office (by reason of resignation, death or otherwise) or is removed from office.

**General note**—The practical significance of these provisions is in the change of language adopted by the draftsman over that employed in the former administration provisions in Part II.

'**administrator**'—This term refers to an appropriately qualified individual (on which see para 6) who is appointed administrator by one of the three alternative methods identified in para 2.

'**enters administration**'—A company cannot be 'in administration' (see below) until such time as it 'enters administration'. The term 'enters administration' is defined by reference to the appointment of an administrator taking effect, as opposed to the time of any administration application or the taking of preparatory steps to effect an out-of-court appointment. A company may enter administration in one of three ways: first, on the making of an administration order under paras 10 and 13(1)(a), secondly, on the satisfaction of the requirements of para 18 on an out-of-court appointment by a floating charge holder under para 14 (see para 19) or, thirdly, on the satisfaction of the requirements of para 29 in an out-of-court appointment by a company or its directors under para 22 (see para 31).

**Motive**—'If the directors have active for an improper purpose, or are otherwise in breach of their duty to the company in making the decision to appoint an administrator, that is something that may give rise to a claim against them. When they have made that decision, it seems to me, the responsibility on the prospective administrator in considering whether the statement as to the statutory purpose can be made is to look ahead of this at what will or may happen during the administration if he is appointed, and not behind at the motives which may have led the directors to choose to make the appointment': *Re BW Estates Ltd* [2015] EWHC 517 (Ch) at [28] (HHJ David Cooke, sitting as a High Court judge) (overturned on appeal on other grounds: [2017] EWCA Civ 1201).

A distinction is to be drawn between, on the one hand, the directors of a company having a particular motive in placing the company into administration, and, on the other hand, an appointment effected under a qualifying floating charge caused to have been created by way of an improper motive on the part of a de facto director for the purpose of effecting an appointment of an administrator and thereafter influencing the insolvency process, as in *Re CA & T Developments Ltd, Koon v Bowes* [2019] EWHC 3455 (Ch) (order under para 81(1) providing for the appointment of the administrators to cease to have effect).

'in administration'—Once a company 'enters administration' (as defined in para 1(2)(b)) the company remains 'in administration' until such time as the appointment of the administrator ceases to have effect. The new terminology should be contrasted with that employed under the former Part II under which a company was deemed to be in administration on the making of an administration order under s 8(2) until such time as the court made an order discharging the administration order under s 18(3).

Once a company is in administration, the assets owned by it, legally or beneficially, fall to be managed in the administration. However, an administrator may seek an order for payment of his or her proper expenses and remuneration out of property held by the company, but not owned by it, with which the administrator has dealt in the course of the administration, based on the principle in *Re Berkeley Applegate (Investment Consultants) Ltd (No 2)* [1989] Ch 32. For a case in which the court recognised the principle in relation to administrators but refused the application on its facts see *Gillan v HEC Enterprises Ltd* [2016] EWHC 3179 (Ch), the judgment of Morgan J containing a penetrating analysis of the genesis of the principle, its development and scope at [71]–[89].

'a company'—The term 'company' is as defined in para 111(1A) and see para 111A (non-UK companies).

In *Re Eurodis Electron Plc (in Administration)* [2011] EWHC 1025 (Ch), [2011] BPIR 1372 an administration order was made in respect of a company incorporated in Belgium which had its centre of main interests in England. Subsequently, the company was wound up and dissolved in Belgium. Mann J held that once the company had been dissolved it was not possible for the administration to continue.

A company incorporated in Gibraltar was a company in respect of which the English court had jurisdiction to make an administration order on the basis that it fell within the definition of 'company' under para 111(1A)(c) notwithstanding the fact that the company's centre of main interests was in Gibraltar: *Re Nektan (Gibraltar) Ltd* [2020] EWHC 65 (Ch).

Do a director's duties to the company survive the company's entry into administration?—In *Hunt v Michie* [2020] EWHC 54 (Ch) the respondents raised belated and perhaps surprising submissions to the effect that the general duties of a director, as codified under ss 171–177 of the Companies Act 2006, survive only in respect of any exercise by a director qua director of powers preserved by, or permitted in accordance with, the Insolvency Act 1986. Notwithstanding limited argument as a result of the late introduction of the issue, ICCJ Barber rejected the respondents' submission on five separate grounds. The duties owed by a director to the company and its creditors survive the company's entry into administration (or voluntary liquidation) and are independent of, and run parallel with, the separate duties owed by an administrator or liquidator to the company. The contraction of a director's managerial powers consequent upon an insolvency procedure do not derogate from the continued nature of his or her duties. In addition, the first and foremost of a director's duties in the insolvency context remains the duty to have regard to the interests of the creditors as a whole, as is expressly preserved by s 172(3) of the 2006 Act.

When does the appointment of an administrator cease to have effect for the purposes of para 1(2)(c)?—The starting point here is para 1(2)(d) which provides that a company does not cease to be in administration by reason of an administrator vacating or being removed from office. Thus, despite para 1(2), a company will remain 'in administration' during the period in which no administrator remains in office following the vacation or removal of an administrator pending the appointment of a replacement. The appointment of an administrator 'ceases to have effect' for the purposes of para 1(2)(c) in any one of seven circumstances, namely:

(a)     under para 76(1) at the end of the period of one year beginning with the date of the appointment of the administrator, subject to extension of the one-year period under para 76(2);

(b)     by order of the court on the application of an administrator under para 79(1);

(c)     under para 80(3) on the filing of the prescribed forms where the administrator thinks that the purpose of an administration has been sufficiently achieved;

(d)     by order of the court on the application of a creditor under para 81(1);

(e)     under para 82(3)(a) by order of the court following the presentation of a public interest winding-up petition;

(f)     under para 83(6)(a) following the registration of the requisite notice by an administrator prior to the company moving into creditors' voluntary liquidation;

(g)     under para 84(4) on the registration of the requisite notice by the administrator prior to a company moving to dissolution.

**Consequences of a court order providing for the appointment of an administrator to cease to have effect where the administrator was appointed by an administration order**—In these circumstances the court is obliged to discharge the administration order under para 85(2).

**The scope of the rule in** *Re Condon, ex parte James* (1874) LR Ch App 609 **in the context of creditor claims**—The authorities starting with *ex parte James* provide no justification for an administrator being ordered to change the ranking of a particular debt simply because the statutory ranking appears unattractive (in the case in point because the particular debt in issue ranked lower than other unsecured debts): *In Re Nortel GmbH (in administration)* [2013] UKSC 52, [2014] AC 209 at [123]. On the contrary, observations in the first instance decision in *In Re Lune Metal Products Ltd* [2007] Bus LR 589 at [35] to [38] tend to support the notion that the court cannot sanction a course which would be outside an administrator's statutory powers.

The rule in *ex parte James* is considered further in the notes to para 5 below.

**Does the rule in** *ex parte James* **apply in a creditors' voluntary liquidation following administration?**—In *Re Agrimarche Ltd (in creditors' voluntary liquidation)* [2010] EWHC 1655 (Ch) at [25] Lewison LJ 'left to a case in which it matters' the question of whether the principle in *Re Condon, ex parte James* is excluded in the context of a creditors' voluntary liquidation following administration on the ground that the Court of Appeal held in *Re TH Knitwear (Wholesale) Ltd* [1988] Ch 275 that a liquidator in a CVL is not an officer of the court. Respectfully, there is much to be said for the judge's view that it would be odd if moving from administration to creditors' voluntary liquidation radically altered the standard of conduct to be expected from the office-holder, particularly where (as is usual) there is no change in the identity of the office-holder.

## [1.619]

**2**

A person may be appointed as administrator of a company—

    (a)    by administration order of the court under paragraph 10,

    (b)    by the holder of a floating charge under paragraph 14, or

    (c)    by the company or its directors under paragraph 22.

**General note**—This provision identifies the three possible methods by which an administrator of a company may be appointed. Note, however, that despite such a purported appointment, in or out of court, the appointment may be invalidated by any of those general restrictions in paras 6–9.

## [1.620]

### 3 Purpose of administration

(1)   The administrator of a company must perform his functions with the objective of—

    (a)    rescuing the company as a going concern, or

    (b)    achieving a better result for the company's creditors as a whole than would be likely if the company were wound up (without first being in administration), or

    (c)    realising property in order to make a distribution to one or more secured or preferential creditors.

(2)   Subject to sub-paragraph (4), the administrator of a company must perform his functions in the interests of the company's creditors as a whole.

(3)   The administrator must perform his functions with the objective specified in sub-paragraph (1)(a) unless he thinks either—

    (a)    that it is not reasonably practicable to achieve that objective, or

    (b)    that the objective specified in sub-paragraph (1)(b) would achieve a better result for the company's creditors as a whole.

(4)   The administrator may perform his functions with the objective specified in sub-paragraph (1)(c) only if—

    (a)    he thinks that it is not reasonably practicable to achieve either of the objectives specified in sub-paragraph (1)(a) and (b), and

    (b)    he does not unnecessarily harm the interests of the creditors of the company as a whole.

**General note**—This key provision identifies, in para 3(1), the purpose – or, rather, a hierarchy of three specific purposes – in all administrations, whether instigated by an out of court appointment or by a court order. This approach represents a marked shift from that in the formerly operative s 8(3) under which the court could make an order providing for any one or more of the four purposes specified therein.

It will be seen that the hierarchy of purposes mentioned above is established by sub-paras 3(3) and 3(4). The provisions draw a distinction between the obligation of an administrator pursuing the objectives in sub-para 3(1)(a) and (b), which involve an obligation to perform his or her functions in the interests of creditors as a whole, and the obligation of the administrator pursuing the objective in sub-para 3(1)(c), which is prohibited unless the administrator does not unnecessarily harm the interests of the creditors of the company as a whole.

### PARAGRAPH 3(1)

Scope of provision—These provisions place greater emphasis than previously on company rescue. Paragraph 3(1) provides a hierarchy of objectives, which, as provided for in para 3(3) and (4), and subject to the provisos therein, an administrator *must* pursue in turn unless the administrator forms the view that the achievement of any particular objective is not reasonably practicable.

'The administrator of a company must perform his functions with the objective of . . . '—These words suggest that the exercise of any power under Sch 1 or those powers identified in the notes to para 60 must be exercised, and only exercised, in pursuit of such objective as the administrator considers to be reasonably practicably capable of achievement.

The above words impose a positive obligation which do not permit an administrator to perform any of his or her functions on the basis that doing so does not conflict with the statutory purpose of the administration. Parliament has not so legislated. Rather, the provision is clear (as with para 68(1)) that any performance of an administrator's function must be performed for, and only for, the purpose of the administration: *In the matter of Lehman Bros Europe Ltd (in administration)* [2017] EWHC 2031 (Ch) at [64] (Hildyard J).

See also here the notes to para 11(b) below on the court's approach to pursuit of the statutory purpose encapsulating the three distinct objectives in para 3(1)(a)–(c).

### PARAGRAPH 3(1)(a)

'Rescuing the company as a going concern . . . '—An administrator must pursue the primary objective of rescuing the company as a going concern unless, according to para 3(3), either it is not reasonably practicable to achieve that purpose or the achievement of the purpose in para 3(1)(b) would bring about a better result for the company's creditors as a whole.

The term 'rescuing the company as a going concern' contrasts with that in the former s 8(3)(a) which referred to 'the survival of the company, and the whole or any part of its undertaking, as a going concern'. In *Re Rowbotham Baxter Ltd* [1990] BCC 113 at 115E–115F Harman J held, in construing the wording in s 8(3)(a), that the subsection required the survival of the company itself together with all or part of its undertaking as a going concern, an outcome which was incapable of being achieved through what is commonly termed the hiving down of the company's business into a new company. Hiving down might, however, have led to the achievement of the purpose in the former s 8(3)(d), which corresponds in substance with the sub-purpose now found in para 3(1)(b).

The wording now employed in para 3(1)(a), it is submitted, should be construed as having the same meaning as that under the former s 8(3)(a) as interpreted in *Rowbotham Baxter*. That approach finds support in para 647 of the DTI's Explanatory Notes which indicates that the objective of rescuing the company as a going concern 'is intended to mean the company and as much of its business as possible'. The survival of a company intact, but with no subsisting going concern undertaking, would not fall within the scope of para 3(1)(a) since, in line with para 649 of the DTI's Explanatory Notes, a proposal resulting in nothing more than a 'shell' company does not constitute a rescue. Such an outcome might, however, fall within para 3(1)(b).

In considering the prospects of achievement of the sub-purpose in para 3(1)(a), as with sub-paras (1)(b) and (c), the court is concerned with the weighing up of evidence, and not mere assertions. For example, in *Doltable Ltd v Lexi Holdings plc* [2005] EWHC 1804 (Ch), [2006] 1 BCLC 384 Mann J refused to make an administration order in the absence of evidence that, in a liquidation, creditors would be no worse off, nor indeed any better off, than in an administration. On the other hand, in considering whether the statement as to statutory purpose can be made, the responsibility on the prospective administrator is to look ahead at what will or may happen during the administration if appointed and not behind at the motives which may have led the directors to choose to make the appointment: *Re BW Estates Ltd, Randhawa v Turpin* [2015] EWHC 517 (Ch) (HHJ David Cooke, sitting as a High Court judge) (application by creditors under the former IR 1986, r 2.109 for order disallowing company's administrators remuneration dismissed). After making reference to the decision in *Doltable*, the judge observed at [24] that it does not follow that a process in which the assets of the company are managed whilst its liabilities or potential liabilities are explored, which may lead to the position that when the true level of liabilities is established they can be satisfied out of the assets, leaving assets with which the company can continue its business, cannot be described as 'rescuing the company as a going concern'. In other words, the word 'rescue' does not imply that the administrators must themselves do or achieve something which could not otherwise happen, but only that the administration should enable a going concern to be preserved when it otherwise would or might not be. Consistent with this view, in *Davey v Money* [2018] EWHC 766 (Ch), Snowden J made clear at [283] that the objective in para 3(1)(a) was not achieved by successfully realising a company's assets so that a distribution could be made to shareholders after paying creditors in full, so that the company can properly continue to trade as a going concern. Instead, para 3(1)(a) connoted the retention of all, or a material part, of a company's business, together with its restoration to solvency. Snowden J's approach was applied by Henry Carr J in *Zinc Hotels (Investment) Ltd v Beveridge* [2018] EWHC 1936 (Ch) at [25].

**DTI's examples of para 3(1)(a) rescue**—By way of illustration, the DTI's Explanatory Notes suggest that a hypothetical example of a reasonably practicable rescue for para 3(1)(a) purposes would include the following. Company A is operating at a profit and has excellent products, a loyal customer base and a healthy order book. However, major investment in a new IT system, which is late and over budget, has knocked the company off its business plan, its cash flow has suffered and it is unable to pay its debts. The company has been placed in administration and the administrator has had an offer for its business that would provide sufficient funds to pay the secured creditors and give 35p in the pound for unsecured creditors. However, the administrator determines that the problems are short-term and they can be resolved and will not have any ongoing effect. The company's bankers have given their support to the administrator's plans to continue trading, the company's business is profitable and the administrator is confident that the company can be rescued by trading its way out of its current financial difficulties and provide 65p in the pound return for unsecured creditors within 12 months. Whilst no exit route is suggested in this hypothetical example, para 649 of the DTI's Explanatory Notes suggests that company rescue is most likely to involve creditors agreeing to a CVA or a scheme of arrangement under Part 26 of the Companies Act 2006.

The DTI's Explanatory Notes go on to provide the following as a hypothetical example of a case where a rescue would not be reasonably practicable. A company is in financial difficulties and it is clear that the only viable options depend on the continuing support of the company's bankers. The administrator knows that this support will not be forthcoming and that there is no alternative means of financing the company.

In the above circumstances it would follow that the administrator would be required to consider the purpose in para 3(1)(b) upon forming the view that the rescue purpose in para 3(1)(a) is not reasonably practicably capable of achievement. If that purpose, or that in para 3(1)(c) is not, in the opinion of the administrator, reasonably practicably capable of achievement, then the administrator would necessarily have to consider terminating the administration under para 79(2).

## PARAGRAPH 3(1)(b)

'Achieving a better result for the company's creditors as a whole than would be likely if the company were wound up (without first being in administration)'—This objective only comes into play where either of the two conditions in para 3(3) is satisfied.

Paragraph 3(1)(b) is substantially equivalent to the purpose in the former s 8(3)(d). What is envisaged here is the sale of a company's business or businesses as a going concern or concerns to one or more buyers, including a so-called 'pre-pack' sale, or a sale other than on a going concern basis as might arise where, for example, an administrator has been unable to sustain a going concern business through lack of funding or in the absence of a ready and willing purchaser.

In *Logitech UK Ltd* [2004] EWHC 2899 (Ch), [2005] 1 BCLC 326 Lindsay J was prepared to make an administration order where a non-trading, insolvent company had no assets save for a number of potential causes of action for transaction-at-undervalue and breach of directors' duties where the applicant, a substantial creditor, was prepared to fund those claims to the tune of £50,000 in administration, but not in liquidation, so as to produce a better projected outcome in administration.

**DTI example of para 3(1)(b) case**—Paragraph 650 of the DTI's Explanatory Notes provides the following hypothetical example of the para 3(1)(b) objective being achieved. Company B has good products and a sound customer base. The company is making losses, its plant and machinery are outdated, and its overheads and debts have been rising for some time. The company has been placed in administration and the administrator has determined that there are no funds available to maintain its entire trading operation or invest in new machinery and it is therefore not reasonably practicable to rescue the company. The administrator has reviewed the company and determined that a sale of its business on a going concern basis would provide a better return than a break-up sale of its assets. The administrator markets the businesses and the best offer he or she receives would provide sufficient funds to pay the secured creditors and give 40p in the pound for unsecured creditors. The administrator reports to the creditors at a meeting and explains why it was not reasonably practicable to rescue the company.

**PARAGRAPH 3(1)(c)**

'Realising property in order to make a distribution to one or more secured or preferential creditors'—This objective only comes into play on the two conditions in para 3(4) being satisfied.

The wording in this provision envisages no distribution being made to unsecured creditors, although an administrator may properly pursue this objective even if unsecured creditors might also receive a distribution: *Re Taylor Pearson (Construction) Ltd (in administration)* [2020] EWHC 2933 (Ch), [2021] 1 BCLC 725 at [80]–[82] (HHJ Davis-White QC). Although in practice this objective will usually involve a company which is not viable with no business that can be sold as a going concern, there is no reason why the sale of a company's assets and/or business as a going concern should not be effected pursuant to the achievement of this objective.

DTI example of a para 3(1)(c) case—Paragraph 651 of the DTI's Explanatory Notes provides the following hypothetical example of the achievement of this objective. Company C is a service company whose business and reputation were built around its excellent standards of customer service. But a number of key personnel have recently left, the quality of the company's service and its reputation have suffered badly, customers have become dissatisfied and the company is no longer able to attract and retain business. It has been making losses for a number of months and is unable to pay its debts. The company is then placed in administration. The administrator reviews the company and concludes that its business is not viable and a sale is not possible. The administrator markets the company's assets and realises funds that are sufficient to make a part-payment to the secured creditors, and there are no funds available to pay unsecured creditors, except for those resulting from the operation of the ring-fence (ie under s 176A). The administrator reports to the creditors and explains why it was not reasonably practicable to achieve either a company rescue or a better return for unsecured creditors.

**PARAGRAPH 3(2)**

The requirement that an administrator performs his functions in the interests of the company's creditors as a whole—This provision encapsulates the distinction between the office of administrator and that of the virtually abolished administrative receiver. A receiver managing mortgaged property primarily owes duties to the appointing charge holder and anyone else with an interest in the equity of redemption, the primary duty of the receiver being to try to bring about a situation in which interest on the secured debt can be paid and the debt itself repaid: *Medforth v Blake* [1999] 2 BCLC 221 at 237A–237D (Sir Richard Scott V-C, Swinton Thomas and Tuckey LJJ agreeing). Neither is a receiver under any general duty to carry on a business on the mortgaged premises as previously carried on by the mortgagor: (*Medforth v Blake*). The effect of para 3(2) is that an administrator – even one appointed under para 14 by the holder of a qualifying floating charge – must perform his or her functions in the interests of the company's creditors (ie unsecured, secured and preferential creditors) as a whole. An administrator must not merely have regard to or consider the interests of creditors, or purport to do so, but, rather, is required to perform his or her functions with the interests of unsecured creditors weighing equally with those of preferential and secured creditors. This is a significant step and one by which the legislation has substantially altered the position as it was (and remains) under the general law governing receivership. The most obvious practical consequence of the provision is that an administrator will be obliged to *consider* objectives (a) and (b) in all cases, even where the level of secured indebtedness exceeds the value of secured assets. Paragraph 3(4)(b) expressly provides that even where the achievement of the objectives in para 3(1)(a) and (b) is not reasonably practicable – such that consideration will necessarily have to be given to the enforcement of any security for the purpose of making a distribution to any secured creditor – the administrator may only pursue the objective in para 3(1)(c) provided 'he does not unnecessarily harm the interests of the creditors of the company as a whole'. The differences between receivers and administrators in the context of para 3 were considered in detail by Snowden J in *Davey v Money* [2018] EWHC 766 (Ch) at [254], [381]–[393].

Given the conflict between the interests of a secured creditor and unsecured creditors generally where a company is or is likely to become unable to pay its debts (on which see para 11(a)) it remains to be seen whether the concept of 'the interests of the company's creditors as a whole', in the context of administration, is sufficient in itself in providing a workable basis for disgruntled unsecured creditors to mount a challenge, most obviously under para 74, to the actions or proposed conduct of an administrator, and in particular one appointed by a floating charge holder whose appointee appears disinclined to pursue either of the objectives in para 3(1)(a) and (b) without justification. The administrator is in any case required to nail his or her colours firmly to the mast at an early stage, in that the administrator's statement of proposals under para 49(1) must contain a statement of how it is envisaged the purpose of the administration will be achieved whilst, more specifically, para 49(2)(b) requires an explanation to be included within the statement as to why the administrator thinks that the objective in para 3(1)(a) or (b) cannot be achieved. It should also be noted that each of the examples drawn from paras 650 and 651 of the DTI's Explanatory Notes, above, envisages the administrator reporting to creditors and explaining why the achievement of any particular objective was not reasonably practicable.

**PARAGRAPH 3(3)**
' . . . **unless he thinks** . . . '—The use of the verb 'thinks' on the part of the administrator – a term which also appears in paras 49, 52, 79, 80, 83 and 84 – is interesting in that the draftsman has not employed the more common 'considers', 'is satisfied' or 'in his opinion'. Parliament must be taken as imposing a subjective requirement on an insolvency practitioner which must be rational in terms of being gauged against the objective test of the range of conclusions which might be reached by a hypothetical reasonable and reputable insolvency practitioner acting in the particular circumstances of the case. Indeed the Government's suggestion was that it was not seeking to apply any other test than expecting the court to assess whether the administrator has been 'rational' – see *Hansard*, 21 October 2002, col 1105.

In *Unidare plc v Cohen and Power* [2005] EWHC 1410 (Ch), [2005] BPIR 1472, a case in part concerning the word 'thinks' as it appears in para 83(1), Lewison J, at [71], said, 'I accept that the process of thinking involves a rational thought process; but I do not accept that what the administrator thinks is subject to any form of test by reference to an objective *standard*' (emphasis added). In practice, an administrator should not derogate from the obtaining of such information as can reasonably be obtained in the circumstances of any particular case for the purpose of enabling the administrator to make an appropriate assessment of the course to be adopted in the discharge of his or her functions.

Snowden J held that an administrator's decision as to which objective to pursue was open to challenge only on grounds of lack of good faith or irrationality in *Davey v Money* [2018] EWHC 766 (Ch) at [255]; applied by Henry Carr J in *Zinc Hotels (Investments) Ltd v Beveridge* [2018] EWHC 1936 (Ch) at [98]. In *Davey*, Snowden J attributed significant importance to Parliament's use of the word 'thinks', as it suggested clearly that a degree of latitude should be given to an administrator in deciding upon the objective to be pursued. The court was sympathetic to the practical need for an objective to be identified quickly after appointment, often with an administrator acting on less than full information. Clearly the administrator's original view was properly subject to change as matters developed and information became fuller. Accordingly, the court's intervention necessitated the establishment of a lack of good faith or rationality in the decision taken by the administrator.

**PARAGRAPH 3(3)(a)**
' . . . **that it is not reasonably practicable to achieve that objective** . . . '—It would appear that the achievement of an objective, or sub-purpose, is not reasonably practicable either if it is incapable of achievement or if it is capable of achievement, but not reasonably so, by reference to the net effect on creditors of the time and/or cost reasonably anticipated as being necessary for the achievement of that objective.

**PARAGRAPH 3(3)(b)**
Scope of provision—See the note to para 3(1)(b) above.

**PARAGRAPH 3(3), (5)**
Is an administrator obliged to take steps in seeking to achieve each of the sub-purposes in para 3(1) in turn?—There is nothing in para 3 which requires the administrator to take steps in all cases to seek to achieve, in turn, the three objectives within para 3(1). In some cases it will be obvious from the outset that objective (a) or objectives (a) and (b) cannot be achieved within the reasonably practicable test identified in the note to para 3(3)(a) above. In those circumstances the administrator is required to pursue either sub-purpose (b) or (c) as appropriate, subject to the requirement under para 3(4)(b) in the latter case that the administrator must not unnecessarily harm the interests of creditors of the company as a whole.

See here also the notes to para 11(b) below and in particular the judgment of Rimer LJ in *Key2 Law (Surrey) LLP v De'Antiquis* [2011] EWCA Civ 1567 at [98].

What is of practical importance, most obviously in the event of a subsequent challenge, is that an administrator is able to evidence his reasoning, objectively speaking, as to his or her reasoning as to achievement of the statutory purpose and the facts and opinions upon which that decision is based. See the note to 3(2) above.

**PARAGRAPH 3(4)(a)**
Scope of provision—See the notes to paras 3(3)(a) and (b) above.

**PARAGRAPH 3(4)(b)**
' . . . **he does not unnecessarily harm the interests of the creditors of the company as a whole**'— This provision is closely related to para 3(2). Its purpose is to provide protection to unsecured, preferential and any secured creditor which is junior to any one or more secured creditors to whom an administrator proposes making a distribution following the realisation of property on the pursuit of the objective in para 3(1)(c). An administrator, therefore, in contrast to a receiver appointed pursuant to security, is not subject to an overarching duty to consider or have regard to the interests of the company's secured (or preferential) creditors; rather, his obligation is

to the interests of the company's creditors as a whole. Although the separate classes of 'protected' creditor are grouped together in the present provisions, it is difficult to envisage how an unsecured creditor might have grounds to complain of an administrator's performance given that, by definition, the objective in para 3(1)(c) does not envisage any distribution being made to unsecured creditors. On the other hand, a junior ranking secured creditor with an interest in the equity of redemption in secured assets might conceivably allege that the administrator has placed the value of that equity in jeopardy through his conduct of the administration. Notably, such a claim would be available to a junior ranking secured creditor against a receiver who owes duties in managing mortgaged property not only to the mortgagor but also to anyone else with an interest in the equity of redemption: *Medforth v Blake* [1999] 2 BCLC 221 at 237A (Sir Richard Scott V-C). Snowden J explained the scope and extent of an administrator's duties in this respect in *Davey v Money* [2018] EWHC 766 (Ch) at [381]–[393].

If administration is more costly than liquidation then, on its face, that might amount to there being unnecessary harm to creditors as a whole, but that harm might not be unnecessary harm if the potential benefits in administration outweigh the additional costs of liquidation: *Baltic House Development Ltd v Wing Keung Cheung* [2018] EWHC 1525 (Ch) at [30] (HHJ Eyre QC). For a case where the court made a winding-up order where the financial advantage of administration was trivial in comparison with liquidation and the facts justified the creditors having the benefit of '*the complete independence and objectivity of the official receiver*' as office-holder see *Abdul Ghani El-Ajou v Dollar Land (Manhattan) Ltd* [2007] BCC 953 (Warren J).

Although para 3(4)(b), like para 3(2), makes reference to the interests of the creditors of the company 'as a whole', any claim by a creditor alleging a breach of para 3(4)(b) will, under para 74(1), require that the administrator is, has or proposes to act so as to unfairly harm the interests of the applicant, whether alone or in common with some or all other members or creditors.

' . . . **harm** . . . '—The term 'harm' appears both in this provision and, in the same context, in para 74(1). Although there is an obvious and neat question as to whether the term 'harm' means the same as the more commonly employed 'prejudice', as appeared in s 27 in Part II coupled with the word 'unfair', recourse to the Parliamentary debates on the terms of the Enterprise Act 2002 reveals that no such distinction was intended. On 21 October 2002, in resisting an amendment from 'harm' to 'prejudice', Lord McIntosh stated (HL Deb, col 1120), 'For the purposes of *Pepper v Hart*, I am advised that there is no distinction between "harm" and "prejudice" – but "harm" is a common word and more understandable to lawyers.' At the third reading of the Bill in the House of Lords Lord McIntosh went on to say that '"harm" is a word more likely to be understood not only by the courts and practitioners but also by professional advisers and above all by the public' (HL Deb, col 84 (28 October 2002)).

See also here the notes to para 74.

## [1.621]

4

The administrator of a company must perform his functions as quickly and efficiently as is reasonably practicable.

**General note**—This provision corresponds with the time-constricting provisions in paras 76 and 77, which provide for the automatic ending of administration after one year, subject to extension of that period by the court or creditors subject to the limitations prescribed therein. What is now expressly stipulated, however, would almost certainly have been implicit in any case, since it could hardly have been the case that an administrator might not have been obliged to perform his or her functions as quickly and efficiently as is reasonably practicable in the circumstances of any particular case. In remains, however, that in practice not all administrations under the former Part II were conducted with as much expedition as might in fact have been reasonably achievable.

It is doubtful that para 4 creates any fresh duty in favour of an individual creditor on account of the specific cause of action provided for in para 74(2) which allows a creditor or member to apply to the court claiming that an administrator is not performing his or her functions in accordance with this provision. The relief available on such an application, as provided for in para 74(4), does not appear sufficiently broad to allow the court to make an order for damages or other financial recompense arising as a consequence of a breach of para 4. It appears that a claim may be made in respect of loss so arising on behalf of the company in administration by an applicant eligible to bring a misfeasance claim under para 75(3)(c) on the basis that para 4 amounts to an 'other duty', if not a fiduciary duty, in relation to the company.

**[1.622]**

### 5 Status of administrator

An administrator is an officer of the court (whether or not he is appointed by the court).

**General note**—Under the former administration regime under Part II an administrator was an officer of the court: *Re Atlantic Computer Systems plc* [1992] Ch 505. Paragraph 5 confirms that position, even where an administrator is appointed out-of-court. Whilst this provision will avoid any suggestion that an out-of-court appointee is not an officer of the court, particularly in light of the decision of the Court of Appeal in *Re TH Knitwear (Wholesale) Ltd* [1988] Ch 275, which is authority for the proposition that a liquidator in a voluntary liquidation is not an officer of the court, its real significance lies in ensuring that an out-of-court appointee is treated as a court appointee for the purposes of the EC Regulation on Insolvency Proceedings (1346/2000) (now replaced by Regulation (EU) 2015/848) (of which see Article 1 thereof and Annex A thereto).

**The consequences of the administrator's status as an officer of the court**—There are three obvious consequences which follow from the administrator's status as an officer of the court.

First, an administrator is subject to the rule in *Re Condon ex parte James* (1874) 9 Ch App 609. The elusive and difficult principle enshrined in that rule was identified in *Re Tyler* [1907] 1 KB 865 at 871 as being based on morality and requires that an officer of the court should behave in a high-minded and honourable way. More recently, the matter was identified by His Honour Judge Weeks QC, sitting as a High Court judge, in the following terms in *Re South West Car Sales Ltd (in liquidation)* (1998) BCC 163 at 170, 'The principle underlying the rule in *Ex parte James* is that officers of the court should behave decently and honourably and not retain money which a decent and honourable man would think it dishonest to keep.' In *Re Condon* a trustee-in-bankruptcy was ordered to restore monies paid to him under a mistake of law and which would otherwise have been irrecoverable from him. However, following the decision in *Re Tyler* [1907] 1 KB 865, the courts have extended the application of the rule beyond the recovery of payments made pursuant to a mistake of law to cases which turn on the enrichment of the bankruptcy estate, irrespective of how the enrichment came about: see, for example, *Green v Satangi* [1998] BPIR 55. Indeed, in *Re Clarke* [1975] 1 WLR 559 at 563 Walton J identified the requirement for some form of enrichment of the insolvent estate as being the universal characteristic of all of the cases in which the rule had been applied, in addition to establishing the further conditions required for the rule to operate. Subsequent authorities, however, militate against an inflexible approach to the scope of the rule: see, for example, *Re T H Knitwear (Wholesale) Ltd* [1988] Ch 275 at 289 per Slade LJ, 'The entire basis of the principle, as I discern it from the cases, is that the court will not allow its own officer to behave in a dishonourable manner. There is no doubt much to be said in favour of the principle'. It is suggested that there is much to be said for the subsuming of the rule in *ex parte James* into the law of restitution, since the courts could then be seen to be applying the rule on a legal basis, as opposed to the less predictable basis of morality, given that the enforcement of the rule relies on the court reaching a finding of unfairness or inequity. This matter is developed further in Dawson 'The Administrator, Morality and the Court' [1996] JBL 437 at 454. For the application and further elaboration on the development of the rule see *Scranton's Trustee v Pearce* [1922] 2 Ch 87 (trustee not permitted to recover unenforceable gambling debts); *Re Wyvern Developments Ltd* [1974] 1 WLR 1097; *Re Multi-Guarantee Co Ltd* [1987] BCLC 257, CA; *Re Thellusson* [1919] 2 KB 735 (trustee required to repay monies loaned to bankrupt in ignorance of receiving order having been made); *Re Japan Leasing (Europe) plc* [1999] BPIR 911; *Re Spring Valley Properties Ltd* [2001] BCC 793; *Allen (trustee in bankruptcy of Young) v Young* [2017] All ER (D) 65 (Apr) (trustee not entitled to claim assets under binding agreement between bankrupt and trustee where assets constituted trust assets under life policy outside of the scope of the bankruptcy estate as would therefore have resulted in unjust enrichment of bankruptcy estate). For the restrictive approach to the scope of the rule in Australia see the commentary in A Keay *McPherson and Keay's Law of Company Liquidation* (Sweet and Maxwell, 4th edn, 2018) at 585–586. It will be apparent from the above analysis that the rule in *ex parte James* can only operate subject to relatively exacting requirements and does not amount to some generally applicable ground upon which all manner of complaints against an office-holder might be advanced. In practice, the rule has been rarely invoked with success. Dishonourable conduct is frequently not actually the real issue under complaint; many complaints are really concerned with outcomes with which applicants are dissatisfied. It should also be borne in mind that specific statutory provisions are cast generally in affording the court a wide jurisdiction to determine questions arising in the course of an insolvency, including issues arising out of or relating to decision-making. Paragraph 63 of Sch B1 serves that purpose in administration. The judgment of Hildyard J in *Lehman Brothers Australia Ltd (in liquidation) v Lomas* [2018] EWHC 2783 (Ch) at [38]–[72] contained an incisive analysis of the development and scope of the rule in *ex parte James*. His Lordship emphasised that the rule ought not to be used to interfere with contractual rights freely entered into, but might be engaged where it can be shown that the implementation of a relevant decision would amount to dishonourable conduct by the office-holder: see *Re TH Knitwear (Wholesale) Ltd* [1988] Ch 275 at 290 (a case in which the Court of Appeal confirmed that a liquidator in a voluntary liquidation is not caught by the rule in *Ex parte James*). In allowing the appeal of the applicant creditor, the Court of Appeal in *Lehman Brothers* identified that there was no authority requiring that the exercise of the court's inherent jurisdiction to control its officers in accordance with the rule should depend on unconscionable, as opposed to unfair, conduct on the part of the court's officer: [2020] EWCA Civ 321 at [64]–[69]. The court rejected the concern of the judge at first instance that a test based on unfairness would become 'an unruly horse'. Fairness represented an objective standard and was one the courts were very familiar with in its application in relation to different concepts and contexts. The fundamental principle was that the court would not permit its officers to act in a way which would be clearly wrong for the court itself to act by reference to the standard of the right-thinking person, subject to each case necessarily being fact specific.

The second consequence of an administrator being an officer of the court is that an officer of the court has access to the court for the provision of directions. In administration such a facility is in any case expressly provided for in paras 63 and 68(2), on which see the notes thereto. An officer of the court is also subject to the direction of the court by way of the court's inherent jurisdiction: *Re Sabre International Products Ltd* [1991] BCC 694.

Finally, an officer of the court enjoys the very useful protection of the law of contempt from interference with the performance of his or her duties: see *Bristol Airport plc v Powdrill* [1990] Ch 744 and *Re Sabre International Products Ltd* [1991] BCC 694.

## [1.623]

### 6 General restrictions

A person may be appointed as administrator of a company only if he is qualified to act as an insolvency practitioner in relation to the company.

**General note**—An administrator must be both 'qualified to act as an insolvency practitioner' (on which see ss 388(1)(a) and 390) and eligible to act as such in relation to any particular company.

## [1.624]

### 7

A person may not be appointed as administrator of a company which is in administration (subject to the provisions of paragraphs 90 to 97 and 100 to 103 about replacement and additional administrators).

**General note**—This provision expressly precludes the contemporaneous appointment of two or more administrators, in or out of court, save for the appointment of joint, replacement and additional administrators.

Save for the overriding rights of a qualifying charge holder – on which see para 12(2) – the race for appointment will go to the quicker or quickest appointor.

## [1.625]

### 8

(1) A person may not be appointed as administrator of a company which is in liquidation by virtue of—

    (a)    a resolution for voluntary winding up, or

    (b)    a winding-up order.

(2) Sub-paragraph (1)(a) is subject to paragraph 38.

(3) Sub-paragraph (1)(b) is subject to paragraphs 37 and 38.

**General note**—Subject to one very limited exception, a person may not be appointed as administrator of a company which is in liquidation. Contemporaneous liquidation and administration may come about in a single and, in practice, relatively rare case, namely where a winding-up order is made on a public interest petition presented under s 124A or on a petition presented by the Financial Services Authority under s 367 of the Financial Services and Markets Act 2000 – neither of which is precluded by the moratorium in administration, as to which see para 40(2) – where the court makes an order that the appointment of the administrator shall continue to have effect under para 82(3)(b).

Paragraph 37 allows the court to discharge a winding-up order, together with the giving of appropriate directions on the making of an administration application by a qualifying floating charge holder. Paragraph 38 also enables the court to make such an order on the making of an administration application by a liquidator.

In *Hooley Ltd v Victoria Jute Co Ltd* [2016] CSOH 141 a company incorporated in Scotland was placed into administration by the Scottish court without the court being aware that a winding-up order had previously been made against the company in India, a non-EU jurisdiction where the company's trading activities and assets were located. In a pragmatic decision, the Court of Session, applying the principle of modified universalism, held that the winding-up proceedings in India were ancillary to the administration proceedings in Scotland where the company was incorporated. Accordingly, the administrator was validly appointed and was not constrained in the exercise of powers as such by the Indian winding-up.

**[1.626]**

9

(1)   A person may not be appointed as administrator of a company which—

    (a)    has a liability in respect of a deposit which it accepted in accordance with the Banking Act 1979 or 1987, but

    (b)    is not an authorised deposit taker.

(2)   A person may not be appointed as administrator of a company which effects or carries out contracts of insurance.

(3)   But sub-paragraph (2) does not apply to a company which—

    (a)    is exempt from the general prohibition in relation to effecting or carrying out contracts of insurance, or

    (b)    is an authorised deposit taker effecting or carrying out contracts of insurance in the course of a banking business.

(4)   In this paragraph—

    "authorised deposit taker" means a person with permission under Part IV of the Financial Services and Markets Act 2000 to accept deposits, and

    "the general prohibition" has the meaning given by section 19 of that Act.

(5)   This paragraph shall be construed in accordance with—

    (a)    section 22 of the Financial Services and Markets Act 2000 (classes of regulated activity and categories of investment),

    (b)    any relevant order under that section, and

    (c)    Schedule 2 to that Act (regulated activities).

**General note**—These provisions re-enact the general bar excluding banks and insurance companies from the previous Part II of the 1986 Act, and the concessions thereto.

For the continued relevance of Part II of the 1986 Act in relation to certain undertakings see the note to para 10 below.

**Special administration regimes**—The specific provisions relevant to paras 9 and 10 in those specialist regimes identified in the introductory notes to Sch B1 under this heading should be considered on any such court application.

## APPOINTMENT OF ADMINISTRATOR BY COURT

**[1.627]**

### 10 Administration order

An administration order is an order appointing a person as the administrator of a company.

**General note**—An administration order may only be made by the court under para 13(1)(a) on the making of an administration application by any one or more of those applicants identified in para 12(1)(a)–(d).

**Administration applications by parties eligible to appoint out of court**—There is nothing to prevent the holder of a qualifying floating charge, the company or its directors making an application for an administration order notwithstanding the right of any such party to effect an out-of-court appointment under paras 14 or 22. Such an application may be considered appropriate by an applicant who perceives a wide degree of interest on the part of third parties, as well as creditors, in a company's affairs and/or who wishes to avoid the potentially adverse impression conveyed by an out-of-court appointment with the attendant lack of publicity. Administration orders made in respect of Football League clubs post 15 September 2003 provide good examples of such court appointments.

Moreover, given the continuing uncertainty surrounding the effect of formal defects on the validity of out-of-court appointments (see notes to para 26), an application for an administration order may be perceived to be a 'safer' route. An eligible applicant may also opt for a court appointment where, for commercial reasons, an out-of-court appointment is at risk of criticism, often for perceived reasons of non-transparency.

An applicant for an administration order who is entitled to appoint out-of-court will nevertheless remain subject to the burden of proof under para 11(b) in satisfying the court that an administration order is reasonably likely to achieve the purpose of administration. Self-evidently, a court application is not merely an exercise in the court 'rubber stamping' the application. Paragraph 11 places the requirement for satisfaction as to the fulfilment of the conditions therein squarely on the court, although the court will no doubt have regard to the opinion expressed by the proposed administrator in conjunction with the evidence in support. Such an opinion, however, is not always conclusive. For example, in *Re Rowbotham Baxter Ltd* [1990] BCC 113 Harman J dismissed a petition for an administration order despite giving 'considerable weight' to the proposed administrator's opinion that the making of an administration order carried with it the real prospect of the approval of a company voluntary arrangement. Neither will, or should, the court necessarily accept the view of a proposed administrator, or his appreciation of the administration procedure. For example, the judgment of Jacob J in *Re Colt Telecom Group plc* [2003] BPIR 324, a case under the former Part II, features serious criticism of both the contents of the (former) r 2.2 report produced by a proposed administrator and that individual's apparent lack of understanding of the (former) administration regime.

**Undertakings to which the former Part II of the 1986 Act continues to apply**—There are three categories of undertaking to which the original Part II provisions continue to apply. First, and in theory, any company in respect of which an administration order was made prior to 15 September 2003 will remain subject to the former regime pending discharge of the order. There is, it should be noted, no scope for the two regimes applying contemporaneously to a single undertaking. Secondly, Part II continues to apply to those special cases identified in s 249(1) of the Enterprise Act 2002 (ie appointed water and sewerage undertakers, a protected railway company, a licensed air traffic services company, certain public-private partnership companies and building societies within the meaning of s 119 of the Building Societies Act 1986), by virtue of s 249(2) of the 2002 Act). Thirdly, by virtue of reg 5(2)–(4) of the Insolvency (Amendment) Rules 2003 (SI 2003/1730), certain applications remain subject to Part II, namely those made under the Insolvent Partnerships Order 1994, the Limited Liability Partnerships Regulations 2001 and the Financial Services and Markets Act 2002 (Administration Orders Relating to Insurers) Order 2002 (SI 2002/1242, as amended by SI 2003/2134 and reg 52 of SI 2004/353, effective from 18 February 2004).

## [1.628]

### 11 Conditions for making order

The court may make an administration order in relation to a company only if satisfied—

    (a)    that the company is or is likely to become unable to pay its debts, and

    (b)    that the administration order is reasonably likely to achieve the purpose of administration.

**General note**—These two conditions for the making of an administration order mirror those which appeared previously in s 8(1)(a) and (b).

Where the holder of a qualifying floating charge makes an application to court for the appointment of an administrator, in circumstances where the charge holder could appoint an administrator out of court under para 14, para 35(2)(a) effectively disapplies the requirement in para 11(a) that the company is or is likely to become unable to pay its debts.

**'The court may make an administration order'**—The use of the word 'may' indicates that the court is not required to make an administration order, even if satisfied of the two pre-conditions in para 11. In some cases the court may prefer, exceptionally, to adjourn the hearing of the application, conditionally or unconditionally, most obviously to allow for the filing of further evidence under para 13(1)(c), where the court harbours concerns as to the material presented to it. The nature of the administration regime, however, with its emphasis on the relevance of time, dictates that such an adjournment would ordinarily be for only a short period, typically a period of days.

In *Re Information Governance Limited; Hall v Popham* [2013] EWHC 2611 (Ch), the sole director of a company applied for an administration order. Prior to the hearing of the application, the respondents exercised their rights under a shareholder agreement to appoint themselves as directors and opposed the application. Although the conditions in para 11 were satisfied, David Richards J held it was not appropriate for the court to exercise its discretion to make an administration order. For further case examples see the notes to para 13(1)(a) below.

**PARAGRAPH 11(a)**

**Threshold test**—The wording here is identical to that in the former s 8(1)(a). The analysis of that former provision provided by Jacob J, as he then was, in *Re Colt Telecom Group plc* [2003] BPIR 324 will continue to be of relevance here. In *Colt* Jacob J drew a distinction between the evidential test applicable to the two pre-conditions in s 8(1). The two were not the same. In the case of establishing that a company is or is likely to become unable to pay its debts the burden rests on the applicant in satisfying the court on a balance of probabilities that the requirement is met. This differs from the less onerous 'real prospect' test applicable to the second purpose pre-condition, on which see the note to para 11(b) below.

In *Fieldfisher LLP v Pennyfeathers Ltd* [2016] EWHC 566 (Ch), [2016] BCC 697 a firm of solicitors applied for an administration order in relation to a company for which it had acted in litigation under the terms of a conditional fee agreement containing a mediation and arbitration clause. Whilst satisfied that there was a good arguable case that the solicitors were currently owed large sums and were, therefore, a creditor within the meaning outlined in *Hammonds (a firm) v Pro-Fit USA Ltd* [2007] EWHC 1998 (Ch). Nugee J refused the application on the grounds that the court could not be satisfied on the para 11(a) ground without embarking on enquiries given the company's dispute as to the entirety of the solicitors' claims for fees. Such enquiries would be contrary to the policy underlying the Arbitration Act 1996, namely that parties which have agreed to arbitrate should not be able to bypass the arbitration process through court proceedings.

' . . . is or is likely to become unable to pay its debts'—The term 'unable to pay its debts' has the meaning given by s 123: para 111(1). Section 123 provides either a 'cash-flow' or a 'balance sheet' test of insolvency. For the term 'debts' see r 14.1(3).

In *BNY Corporate Trustee Services Limited v Eurosail-UK 2007–3BL PLC* [2013] UKSC 28, the Supreme Court confirmed that the cash-flow test is concerned both with presently-due debts and with debts falling due from time to time in the 'reasonably near' future (which will depend on all the circumstances, but especially on the nature of the company's business). Beyond the reasonably near future any attempt to apply a cash-flow test is completely speculative, and a comparison of present assets with present and future liabilities (discounted for contingencies and deferment) becomes the only sensible test, although it is far from an exact science. See comments accompanying s 123.

In *Green v Gigi Brooks Ltd* [2015] EWHC 961 (Ch) Hildyard J refused to make an administration order on the application of a former director and shareholder who had been excluded from the company's business. The application was refused on the grounds that the court could not be satisfied either as to para 11(a) or para 11(b). As regards the former, the company was a start-up and had not filed audited accounts at Companies House. The management accounts available to the applicant and relied upon in the course of the application were out of date such that the current cash flow and balance sheet positions were unclear. Although the court gave weight to the fact that the applicant and another creditor appeared to be unpaid, such that the company's financial position was not entirely secure, the threshold test in para 11(a) was held not to be met.

Although the vast majority of cases involve companies which are insolvent, in common with Chapter 11 proceedings in the US, an administration application may be made in respect of a company which is solvent but which is likely to become unable to pay its debts.

**PARAGRAPH 11(b)**

**'that the administration order is reasonably likely to achieve the purpose of administration'**—An analysis of para 11(b) warrants consideration of the threshold test established under the former administration provisions under Part II, which continues to be of relevance. In *Re Harris Simons Construction Ltd* [1989] 5 BCC 11 Hoffmann J held (at 13H–14A) that the requirements of the former s 8(1)(b) were satisfied if the court considered there to be a 'real prospect' that one or more of the former purposes might be achieved. This relatively low threshold, it should be noted, was lower than that adopted by Peter Gibson J in *Re Consumer & Industrial Press Ltd* (1988) 4 BCC 68 at 70, which had pitched the requirement as being above 50%. Although Hoffmann J accepted in *Harris Simons* that terms such as 'real prospect' might be said to lack precision, he likened such phrases to tempo markings in music; thus, 'although there is inevitably a degree of subjectivity in the way they are interpreted, they are nonetheless meaningful and useful.' In *Re Lomax Leisure Ltd* [2000] BCC 352 Neuberger J, as he then was, confirmed (at 363H) that the 'real prospect' test expounded in *Harris Simons* 'is now well established'.

The wording in para 11(b) is not identical to the equivalent provision in the form of s 8(1)(b). Whereas the former provision required that the court 'considers' that the making of an administration order would be 'likely' to achieve one or more of the former statutory purposes, the new provision requires the court to be 'satisfied' that the administration order is 'reasonably likely' to achieve the purpose of administration. Those differences, however, raise no practical distinction. In keeping with the standard established under the former legislation, the decision of Lewison J in *Re AA Mutual International Insurance Co Ltd* [2005] 2 BCLC 8, a Sch B1 case, is authority for the propositions that 'reasonably likely' requires the court to be satisfied that there is a real prospect that a particular objective will be achieved and that real prospect does not equate to more than a 50% probability: to like effect see also *Re C:4net* [2005] BCC 277. For further discussion see the notes to para 13(1)(a) below.

For para 11(b) purposes it is now well established that, as with the previous test applicable to Part II, the court must be satisfied that there is a real prospect that the purpose of administration may be achieved, and not that the applicant can demonstrate a greater than 50% chance that the purpose will be achieved: *Hammonds (a firm) v Pro-Fit USA Ltd* [2007] EWHC 1998 (Ch), [2008] 2 BCLC 159 at [24] (Warren J).

In *Auto Management Services Ltd v Oracle Fleet UK Ltd* [2007] EWHC 392 (Ch), [2008] BCC 761 at [3], Warren J suggested that if an administration can be shown in all but the most unlikely circumstances to produce a result no worse than a liquidation and there are reasonably likely circumstances where the result will be better, that will be significant in influencing the court towards making an order. In *Baltic House Developments Ltd v Wing Keung Cheung* [2018] EWHC 1525 (Ch) at [28], in the face of counsel agreeing that Warren J's formulation encapsulated the correct approach, HHJ Eyre QC, sitting as a High Court judge concluded, on the authorities, that a real prospect of achievement of the statutory purpose needs to be shown, otherwise the court has no jurisdiction to make an order. It is then a matter of discretion as to whether an order ought to be made, including the giving weight, if applicable on the facts, to the factors identified in *Auto Management*.

It is not necessary to identify in advance with certainty which of the statutory objectives is intended to be attained: *Hammonds (a firm) v Pro-fit USA Ltd* [2007] EWHC 1998 (Ch), [2008] 2 BCLC 159 at [20] (Warren J). That point was explained further in the judgment of Rimer LJ in *Key2 Law (Surrey) LLP v De'Antiquis* [2011] EWCA Civ 1567 at [98]. The purpose of an administration order is not in the achievement of any particular objective, even where such a particular objective is identified at the outset; rather, an administration order keeps the administrator's options open so as to allow an administrator to change tack and seek to achieve the statutory purpose in another way. The Court of Appeal endorsed that approach in *R (on the application of Monarch Airlines Ltd (in administration)) v Airport Coordination Ltd* [2017] EWCA Civ 1892 at [56].

In *Green v Gigi Brooks Ltd* [2015] EWHC 961 (Ch) Hildyard J was not satisfied that the para 11(b) test was met on the basis of evidence comprising no more than a letter from a potential funder of the applicant in seeking to acquire the company's business, a brief estimate of the administrators' projected costs and a bare statement by the proposed administrators that the purpose of administration could be achieved. Such thin evidence is unlikely in practice to meet the para 11(b) threshold other perhaps than in the most basic, uncontroversial and unopposed case.

For cases where the court has refused to make an administration order as a matter of discretion see the notes to para 13(1)(a) below.

## [1.629]

### 12 Administration application

(1)   An application to the court for an administration order in respect of a company (an "administration application") may be made only by—

  (a)   the company,

  (b)   the directors of the company,

  (c)   one or more creditors of the company,

  (d)   the designated officer for a magistrates' court in the exercise of the power conferred by section 87A of the Magistrates' Courts Act 1980 (fine imposed on company), or

  (e)   a combination of persons listed in paragraphs (a) to (d).

(2)   As soon as is reasonably practicable after the making of an administration application the applicant shall notify—

  (a)   any person who has appointed an administrative receiver of the company,

  (b)   any person who is or may be entitled to appoint an administrative receiver of the company,

  (c)   any person who is or may be entitled to appoint an administrator of the company under paragraph 14, and

  (d)   such other persons as may be prescribed.

(3)   An administration application may not be withdrawn without the permission of the court.

(4)   In sub-paragraph (1) "creditor" includes a contingent creditor and a prospective creditor.

(5)   Sub-paragraph (1) is without prejudice to section 7(4)(b).

**Amendments**—Courts Act 2003, s 109(1), Sch 6, para 299; Enterprise Act 2002, s 249(2), Sch 16 (as amended by SI 2003/2096).

**General note**—Although certain of the eligible applicants for an administration order appear in para 12(1)(a)–(d), it should be noted that there are three further eligible applicants, namely (a) a liquidator under para 38(1), (b) a supervisor of a company voluntary arrangement under s 7(4)(b) (and see also para 12(5)), and (c) the Financial Services Authority under s 359 of the Financial Services and Markets Act 2000, as amended by para 55 of Sch 17 of the Enterprise Act 2002.

The restricted list of applicants does nothing to preclude the court from considering joinder to proceedings in the administration of a party with a sufficient interest to justify its involvement: see, for example, *LB Holdings Intermediate 2 Ltd (in administration)* [2018] EWHC 2017 (Ch) (Mann J, joinder application by two companies to proceedings concerning proper distribution of assets in administration of Lehman Brothers group company; one application granted on the basis that that party had something new to add to the application in assisting the court, the other refused).

**Conduct of applications**—In *Re Nationwide Accident Repair Centres Ltd* [2020] EWHC 2420 (Ch) at [19]–[22] Fancourt J was critical of the conduct of administration urgent applications in the context of a pre-pack sale and expressed the unacceptability of parties negotiating terms 'that have the effect of presenting the Court with an ultimatum and require important matters affecting the livelihoods of thousands of people to be decided under pressure of time . . . The exercise of the Court's discretion in such important matters is not to be treated as if it were a rubber stamp. Intending applicants must expect that time required properly to prepare and conduct a fair hearing and reach a decision will not be abridged solely to accommodate their preferences'.

For the need for intelligent and proactive remote hearing bundle management by the parties see the comments of HHJ Hodge QC, sitting as a High Court judge, in *Re TPS Investments Ltd (in administration)* [2020] EWHC 1135 (Ch) and those of Mr Philip Marshall QC, sitting as a deputy High Court judge, in *Re Burningnight Ltd (in administration), Re Crowdstacker Ltd (in administration), Mackenzie v Crowdstacker Corporate Services Ltd* [2020] EWHC 2663 (Ch), [2021] 1 BCLC 557.

## PARAGRAPH 12(1)(a)

**'the company'**—In *Re Frontsouth (Witham) Ltd (In Administration)* [2011] EWHC 1668 (Ch), [2011] BPIR 1382 Henderson J held (obiter) that where the company's articles included reg 70 of Table A, which provides that 'the business of the company shall be managed by the directors who may exercise all the powers of the company', as a matter of general company law the decision whether or not to place the company into administration is one to be taken by the directors. The decision cannot be taken by an ordinary resolution of the shareholders, although by a special resolution they may direct the board to take such a step. This may significantly reduce the utility of para 12(1)(a).

**Partnership**—Paragraph 12 is modified to apply to partnerships by the Insolvent Partnership Order 1994, art 5, Sch 2, para 6, as substituted by the Insolvent Partnerships (Amendment) Order 2005, arts 3 and 7, Sch 1. An administration application in respect of a partnership must be made by all the partners unanimously: *In re Brake, Patley Wood Farm LLP v Brake* [2016] EWHC 1688 (Ch), [2017] 1 WLR 343 (Jeremy Cousins QC, leaving open at [52] the position where a partnership deed expressly permitted a majority of members to make an administration application; the preferable view, it is submitted, in line with the deputy judge's view, being that nothing short of unanimity will suffice).

## PARAGRAPH 12(1)(b)

**'the directors of the company'**—Paragraph 105 specifically provides that 'something done by the directors of a company' includes 'the same thing done by a majority of the directors of a company'. Accordingly, the directors may act by a simple majority. However, in *Minmar (929) Ltd v Khalastchi* [2011] EWHC 1159 (Ch), [2011] BCC 485, Sir Andrew Morritt C held that an out-of-court appointment purportedly made with the informal consent of a majority of directors was invalid; a board resolution was required. It is suggested that the same approach applies to an application under para 12. *Re Brickvest Ltd* [2019] EWHC 3084 (Ch) raised what Marcus Smith J called 'a rather difficult question of construction' in considering (at [13]–[21]) an administration application made by the company's sole director where there was doubt as to the sole director's standing to appoint administrators out-of-court and where the terms of the company's article of association cast doubt as to the sole director's standing to appoint. His Lordship considered that, where there could be shown to be a real benefit to a company in making an administration order, but where there is also a serious question over the director's standing to make an administration, the application should be considered in the first instance as a matter of discretion. In particular, there was nothing in para 12(1)(b) which raised a jurisdictional question as to which the court had to be satisfied on a mandatory basis as a pre-condition of an application proceeding. In the circumstances of the case, where the applicant director had been left as sole director by reason of the recent resignation of two other directors, the refusal to entertain the director's standing and make the order sought would amount to 'conduct capable of grave injustice' (at [20]). For the future, Smith J also commented that an irregularity of the sort giving rise to the perceived need for the application might be better dealt with under IR r 12.65 by way of an application on-notice to all interested parties. The approach taken in *Brickvest* was followed by Fancourt J in *Re Nationwide Accident Repair Centres Ltd* [2020] EWHC 2420 (Ch) at [15] who, as well as pointing out that s 6 of the Interpretation Act 1978 provides that the plural will include the singular, identified that, as a matter of principle, a single director may make an application to the court as 'the directors of the company' if he is the sole director or where to treat a sole director applicant otherwise would be an impediment to the court in making an order where it would otherwise be appropriate to do so, such as where (see [16]) by reason of the internal governance provisions of the company the applicant could not alone pass a resolution of the company to make such an application.

### PARAGRAPH 12(1)(c)

'one or more creditors of the company'—This class will include a secured creditor, including the holder of a qualifying floating charge. In *Bank of Scotland Plc v Targetfollow Properties Holdings Limited* [2010] EWHC 3606 (Ch), a qualifying charge holder chose to apply for an administration order where another secured creditor claimed that under the terms of an inter-creditor deed it had a contractual right to consultation as a pre-condition to the out-of-court appointment of administrators.

The term 'creditor' includes a contingent or prospective creditor: see para 12(4). See 'contingent or prospective creditors' in the notes accompanying s 124.

A creditor will include a former administrator with a claim for fees unpaid in the original administration: *Re Elgin Legal Ltd* [2016] EWHC 2523 (Ch) (Snowden J), and to like effect see *Bennett v Bosco Investments Ltd* [2018] EWHC 2901 (Ch), [2019] BPIR 33 at [12]–[16] (HHJ Matthews, administration order made).

Practice where dispute as to standing of applicant as creditor of the company—There is no established practice in relation to administration applications which equates to the practice on a disputed winding-up petition. The practice in relation to winding-up petitions is one of practice, not jurisdiction. In an administration case the court will have to be satisfied, save in an exceptional case, that the applicant is in fact a creditor, and the court will take account of the same sort of factors it would consider in a winding-up case, although a 'bona fide and substantial' cross-claim need not preclude the making of an order if the overall circumstances require an administration order to be made: *Hammonds (a firm) v Pro-Fit USA Ltd* [2008] 2 BCLC 159 at [49]–[57] (Warren J); compare to like effect the comments on Carnwath J in *Re MGI Trading Systems Ltd (in administration)* [1998] 2 BCLC 246 (under the former Part II regime) to the effect that the 1986 Act calls for a realistic interpretation and that, particularly where there is a need for an administration order to be made urgently, it would frustrate the purpose of the provisions if any dispute as to locus or jurisdiction had to be decided before an order could be made. In *Re Berkshire Homes (Northern) Ltd, Newbury Venture Capital Ltd (in liquidation) v Berkshire Homes (Northern) Ltd* [2018] EWHC 938 (Ch) HHJ Hodge QC, sitting as a High Court judge, made an administration order where the debt by reference to which the applicant, acting by its joint liquidators, claimed to be a creditor was disputed but where the respondent had not produced sufficient satisfactory evidence (notwithstanding a schedule produced by its accountant) to demonstrate that there was no sum owing to the applicant. The judge considered *Hammonds* (above) and *Pennyfeathers* (below) and identified that the applicant had to prove that it was a creditor by way of a debt that was undisputed on the balance of probabilities, that test being in sharp contrast with the test applicable to a disputed debt in the context of a winding-up petition on which see the notes headed 'Debt relied on in the petition is disputed' to s 125.

A party will not have standing if its claim on the company is subject to a binding arbitration clause in the face of a genuine dispute as to the debt alleged due: *Fieldfisher LLP v Pennyfeathers Ltd* [2016] EWHC 566 (Ch).

### PARAGRAPH 12(2)

Notification of application to floating charge holders and others—Paragraph 12(2)(a) and (b) require notification of an application to be given to any person who was appointed an administrative receiver (ie where the administrative receiver remains in office) or any person who is or may be entitled to effect such an appointment. For the definition of an administrative receiver see s 29(2) and the notes thereto. There is a requirement for notification to the holder of requisite security for the appointment of an administrative receiver, since Sch B1 does nothing to prevent the appointment of an administrative receiver in the case of security granted prior to 15 September 2003 or in any of those excepted cases in ss 72B–72GA. Paragraph 39 provides that the court must dismiss an administration application where an administrative receiver is appointed prior to or following the making of an administration application other than in specified circumstances.

Paragraph 12(2)(c) operates so as to give notice to the holder of a qualifying floating charge – who may no longer prevent appointment of an administrator by appointing an administrative receiver: see s 72A – and who may take any of three steps on receipt of an administration application. First, the floating charge holder may effect an out-of-court appointment under para 14. Secondly, the charge holder may intervene in the administration application by way of an application under para 36 for the purpose of seeking the appointment of an administrator other than the person proposed by the administration applicant. The third option involves the charge holder simply acquiescing to the administration application.

### PARAGRAPH 12(3)

**Withdrawal of application only with permission of the court**—The purpose of this provision is in guarding against unmeritorious administration applications of the kind which might be made for the sole purpose of obtaining the temporary protection of the statutory moratorium and which, as such, would constitute an abuse of process. The making of an administration application is a significant step, and the court will invariably require an explanation as to why an application has to be aborted.

### PARAGRAPH 12(5)

**A supervisor's application**—An application by a supervisor is treated as if it were an application by the company: r 3.5 and r 3.6(1)(a).

## [1.630]

### 13 Powers of court

(1)   On hearing an administration application the court may—

(a)     make the administration order sought;

(b)     dismiss the application;

(c)     adjourn the hearing conditionally or unconditionally;

(d)     make an interim order;

(e)     treat the application as a winding-up petition and make any order which the court could make under section 125;

(f)     make any other order which the court thinks appropriate.

(2)   An appointment of an administrator by administration order takes effect—

(a)     at a time appointed by the order, or

(b)     where no time is appointed by the order, when the order is made.

(3)   An interim order under sub-paragraph (1)(d) may, in particular—

(a)     restrict the exercise of a power of the directors or the company;

(b)     make provision conferring a discretion on the court or on a person qualified to act as an insolvency practitioner in relation to the company.

(4)   This paragraph is subject to paragraph 39.

**General note**—The court has the widest jurisdiction in making an order on the hearing or at an adjourned hearing of an administration application. The practical relevance of para 13(2) lies in para 1(2)(a) which provides that a company is 'in administration' while the appointment of an administrator of the company has effect: see further the notes to para 13(2) below.

An administration order cannot be made by consent and is a matter for the court's discretion: *Libyan Foreign Bank v International Mining and Infrastructure Corp* [2018] EWHC 1315 (Ch) at [12] (Amanda Tipples QC).

The proposed administrator's statement of opinion as to the achievement of the purpose of administration – see r 3.2(1)(h) – should not be treated lightly. In *Re Integral Ltd* [2013] EWHC 164 (Ch) at [69], Mr Richard Snowden QC, sitting as a deputy High Court judge, identified the fundamental importance of any insolvency practitioner, as an officer of the court nominated as a potential administrator, who ventures his opinion to the court as to the prospects for an administration 'should do so carefully, with an independent mind, and on the basis of a critical assessment of the position of the company and the proposals put forward'.

**Eligible applicants**—In addition to the classes of person identified in para 12(1) an application for an administration order may also be made by the holder of a qualifying floating charge where the company is in compulsory liquidation – but not, for any obviously good reason, where the company is in voluntary liquidation – under para 37(2) or by a liquidator under para 38(1). An application may also be made by the supervisor of a CVA under s 7(4)(b) (on which see para 12(5)) or the Financial Services Authority under s 359 of the Financial Services and Markets Act 2000.

The Financial Services (now the Financial Conduct Authority (FCA)) also has standing to be heard on an application under s 362(2)(a) of the Financial Services and Markets Act 2000. For a case where the court refused to make an administration order or an interim administration order in relation to an e-commerce company, where the FCA had presented a winding-up petition under s 367 of the Financial Services and Markets Act 2000 and applied for the appointment of a provisional liquidator, see *Khawaja v FCA* [2019] EWHC 2909 (Ch). For a case where the court refused to make an administration order on the application of the company (an electronic money institution) and appointed provisional liquidators on the application of the FCA, see *Financial Conduct Authority v Allied Wallet Ltd* [2019] EWHC 2808 (Ch).

Where an applicant for an administration order is a qualifying floating charge-holder, with standing to apply for an order under para 35 without having to establish that it is more probable than not that the company is insolvent, the issue of insolvency is likely to be one which is highly relevant to the exercise of discretion in making the order sought: *Hellenic Capital Investments Ltd v Trainfx Ltd* [2015] EWHC 3713 (Ch) at [11] (HHJ Pelling QC, sitting as a High Court judge): see also *Re High Street Rooftop Holdings Ltd* [2020] EWHC 2572 (Ch) (Mr Andrew Sutcliffe QC) (noted further below).

### PARAGRAPH 13(1)(a)

' . . . make the administration order sought . . . '—In considering the making of an administration order the court will wish to consider not only the interests of all of the company's creditors as a whole, as well as the particular interests of secured, preferential and unsecured creditors, but also the attitude of creditors generally to the administration. The interests of any secured creditor will weigh less heavily where that creditor is fully secured: *Re Consumer & Industrial Press Ltd* [1988] BCLC 177 at 181A (Peter Gibson J) and *Re Imperial Motors (UK) Ltd* [1990] BCLC 29. The court is unlikely to make an administration order if satisfied that a majority of creditors are either opposed to the order or are unlikely to support the administrator's proposals: *Re Arrows Ltd (No 3)* [1992] BCLC 555; and see *Re Stalton Distribution Ltd* [2002] BCC 486, and *Re West Park Golf & Country Club* [1997] 1 BCLC 20, but compare *Re Structures and Computers Ltd* [1998] 1 BCLC 292 and see the notes to para 55 and the cases cited therein. An order was made in *Re DKLL Solicitors* [2008] 1 BCLC 112 (Andrew Simmonds QC, sitting as a deputy High Court judge) where, notwithstanding the opposition of the Revenue as a creditor for some £1.7m of total debts of approximately £2.4m, the order would allow for a pre-pack sale of a firm of solicitors' business which would operate to save more than 50 employees' jobs, minimise disruption to clients' affairs and avoid a Law Society intervention. The fact that an administration order is sought by directors prompted by an ulterior motive did not preclude the making of an order by Blackburne J in *Re Dianoor Jewels Ltd* [2001] 1 BCLC 450 where a former wife alleged that a petition had been instituted by her managing director husband in an attempt to scupper ancillary relief proceedings. Opposition to an application on the grounds that incumbent management or owners of a company claim to be able to achieve an outcome equivalent to any of the statutory purposes at a reduced cost should ordinarily, it is submitted, be attributed only modest weight, if any.

In *Rowntree Ventures Ltd v Oak Property Partners Ltd* [2017] EWCA Civ 1944, in overturning the decision of Mann J in refusing to make an administration order, Vos C (David Richards LJ and Asplin J agreeing) emphasised the unconstrained discretion provided in para 13 with the consequence that a multitude of factors may properly be taken into account in deciding in any particular case whether it is appropriate to make an administration order when the two statutory preconditions in para 11 have been held to be fulfilled ('The circumstances are likely to be infinitely variable. The interests of secured creditors, preferential creditors, unsecured creditors and the company itself will change from case to case'). The reversal of Mann J's refusal to make an administration order turned on the weight attributed to the possibility of a turnaround absent administration, as will often exist in some measure and the possibility of which does not always militate against an administration order. The Court of Appeal held as 'logically fallacious' a positive finding on the statutory precondition for insolvency coupled with the exercise of discretion against an administration order on the basis that the company may have fared better in the future under its current management. Whilst acknowledging that there is no 'normal case', the judge at first instance had attached too much weight to the possibility of a turnaround so as to justify interference with the exercise of discretion on the appeal by way of the making of an administration order.

The decision of Warren J in *El Ajou v Dollar Land (Manhattan) Ltd* [2007] BCC 953 involved the question of whether the court should make an administration order on the application of the company (which was no longer trading) or a winding-up order on a petition presented by a creditor based on a judgment debt which was subject to an outstanding appeal by the company. Adopting the view that the outstanding appeal did not affect the judgment creditor's status as a creditor, and whilst ultimately a matter of discretion on the facts of the case, his Lordship, in making a winding-up order, took particular notice of the fact that there was no ongoing business on which a winding-up order could have any serious effect, that the official receiver would take office as liquidator subject to any replacement being subject to the control of creditors generally and that the only advantage of administration appeared to be a saving of some £2,000 in costs which, in the circumstances, was trivial.

In *Brockstone Ltd v Force India Formula One Team Ltd* [2018] EWHC 3852 (Ch) Barling J made an administration order in respect of a company trading as a Formula One racing team against which a winding-up petition had been presented by HMRC. Insolvency was not in issue. In making an administration order the court found there to be no point in a 'wait and see' approach given that promised funding, even if received, would likely have made no significant difference. There was a prospect of sale as a going concern, administration would not preclude participation in the remainder of the racing season, a number of substantial creditors (including suppliers) supported administration and the court had no confidence that existing management would alter course from a failure to properly preserve the position of creditors if an order was not made.

For a refusal, on the unusual facts of separate proceedings for circa £238m under a term facility loan brought against a high street retailer to amend the grounds of an administration application to allow for the earlier resolution of issues already being litigated in the Financial List, but without keeping the applicants out of those additional grounds, see the judgment of Marcus Smith J in *Debussy DTC plc v Solutus Advisors Ltd* [2019] EWHC 1035 (Ch). The same judge had previously declined an application by the creditor claimant for the administration order application and the Financial List proceedings to be managed together: *Re Toys R Us Properties (UK) Ltd* [2018] EWHC 3848 (Ch).

For another unusual case (because the administration application was made by the one director who was on the board at the time of the application which was opposed by two of the three persons who, by the time of the hearing, had been appointed directors) in which the court was satisfied that the company was probably insolvent and that administration was reasonably likely to achieve the purpose of a better result than in a winding-up, but where the court refused to exercise its discretion in making an administration order see *Re Information Governance Ltd* [2013] EWHC 2611 (Ch), [2015] BCC 277 (David Richards J). It was not appropriate to grant an administration order where the other two directors opposing the application believed that there was a prospect of sufficient business to enable the company to trade and meet its liabilities.

In *Re High Street Rooftop Holdings Ltd* [2020] EWHC 2572 (Ch), [2020] Bus LR 2127, on an application resisted by the company and made by a QFC holder under para 35 (under which realistic prospect of achievement of purpose of administration must also be demonstrated), Mr Andrew Sutcliffe QC made an administration order in what reads as a finely balanced case taking into account factors which do arise from time to time in practice. Having found at [60] that, on a balance of probabilities, the company was presently insolvent (to the extent that it was not even able to demonstrate an ability to meet ongoing debt interest payments), the deputy judge went on, '... a return to secured creditors is more likely to be achieved if licensed insolvency practitioners (rather than existing management) are in control of the company who can seek to ascertain full information regarding the financial position of the company and take informed commercial decisions about safeguarding the company's assets and achieving a return for creditors'.

The court's exercise of discretion in making an administration order (or not) is necessarily fact specific on a case by case basis. Even if the conditions in para 11(a) and (b) are met, the court retains a discretion in refusing to make an order. Where the court does not make an administration order or a winding-up order in the alternative, one significant ramification which ought usually to feature in the court's exercise of discretion is the fact that the company will be returned, unchecked by any insolvency process, to incumbent management who, often, are the individuals responsible as directors for the company's financial difficulties. In *Re UK Steelfixers Ltd* [2012] EWHC 2409 (Ch) HHJ Purle QC, sitting as a High Court judge, was so satisfied as to the para 11 conditions, but declined to make an administration order; instead, the court made a winding-up order to allow for post-winding-up transactions to be considered against the background of s 127 where the proposed administration envisaged a pre-pack sale in favour of a company owned and controlled by an employee in the face of a winding-up petition presented by HMRC. For further examples of the exercise of discretion, see *Re Information Governance Ltd* [2013] EWHC 2611 (Ch); *Re Brown Bear Foods Ltd* [2014] EWHC 1132 (Ch) (order refused, notwithstanding court accepting that an administration order was likely to provide a better result for company's creditors in the face of a winding-up petition; the refusal of the order was based on a number of matters not satisfactorily explained, including a substantial payment made to connected parties for reasons not apparently related to the company's business dealings); *Re Christophorus 3 Ltd* [2014] EWHC 1162 (Ch) (order made, only feasible alternative to liquidation); *Re VST Enterprises* [2021] EWHC 887 (Ch) (application by contingent creditor representing small fraction of unsecured creditors so as to raise real question as to whether applicant had genuine financial interest in administration; settlement agreement relating to earlier debt construed to preclude action including administration application; no evidence of support or opposition from significant number of other unsecured creditors; and no evidence of continuation of earlier conduct as to unsubstantiated and outlandish statements made to prospective investors to attract subscription for shares, despite which the effect of the dismissal of the application was the return of control of the company to a chief executive officer responsible for those statements). *VST* is presently subject to an application to the Court of Appeal for permission to appeal.

For a case where the court treated the application as a winding-up petition where there was no evidence that the company had ever traded at a profit such that the court was not satisfied as to the reasonable likelihood of the achievement of any of the purposes of administration in para 3(1) see *Data Power Systems Ltd v Safehosts (London) Ltd* [2013] EWHC 2479 (Ch).

**Retrospective administration orders**—The decision of Hart J reported in *Re G-Tech Construction Ltd* [2007] BPIR 1275 survives only by way of a draft judgment which had not received formal judicial approval by the late judge who was in the process of preparing a reasoned judgment which was never completed. The fact that the reported judgment is in draft is apparent from a reading of it and, therefore, respectfully, the judgment should be treated with some care. The *ratio* of the decision (or, at least, as close as the draft judgment gets to a *ratio*) appears at [20]–[21] in observing that the statute does not say that an administration order cannot be made retrospectively and that, in the late judge's view, the wording in para 13 is wide enough to provide such jurisdiction without doing violence to the language used. Although the *G-Tech* decision has been of considerable utility, especially in facilitating the cure of otherwise technically defective appointments, there have been clear expressions of concern in later cases as to the basis of the jurisdiction notwithstanding the practical assistance it has provided: see, for example, *Re Derfshaw* [2011] EWHC 1565 (Ch), [2011] BCC 485 (Morgan J), *Re Frontsouth (Witham) Ltd (in administration)* [2011] EWHC 1668 (Ch), [2011] BPIR 1382 (Henderson J) and *Re Care Matters Partnership Ltd (in administration)* [2011] EWHC 2672 (Ch), [2011] BCC 963 at [3] where Norris J observed that retrospective applications appeared to be 'increasingly treated as a matter of routine'. Interestingly, in *Care Matters* Norris J gave permission to appeal 'without hesitation' on the basis that the jurisdictional foundation of *G-Tech* was in need of definitive determination in a case fully argued on both sides. It is certainly questionable that *G-Tech* should distinguish the earlier judgment of Lewison J in *Darrell v Miller* [2003] EWHC 2811 (Ch), [2004] BPIR 470 in which an application to backdate an administration order under the former Part II of the 1986 Act was refused on the grounds that the court had no jurisdiction to make such a retrospective order because the CPR governed the order and did not permit an order with retrospective effect. The more fundamental concern over the judgment in *G-Tech*, however, must lie in how paras 13(1) and 13(2) of Sch B1 can be read as being capable of having retrospective effect in the absence of express language to that effect. This is problematic because there is well established authority at the highest level to the effect that it is contrary to principle to construe a statute as having retrospective operation in the absence of clear wording supportive of such a conclusion: see, for example, *Sunshine Porcelain Potteries Pty Ltd v Nash* [1961] AC 927 at 938 per Lord Reid and the judgment of Lord Brightman in the Privy Council to like effect in *Yew Bon Tew alias Young Boon Tiew v Kenderann Bas Mara* [1983] 1 AC 553 at 557. *G-Tech* involved representation by counsel for the applicant only, and it does not appear from the draft judgment that these authorities, or the principle just mentioned for which they stand, were drawn to the judge's attention. Despite the fact that the draft judgment identifies (at [20]) that the retrospective jurisdiction must be exercised 'with extreme caution', the underlying basis of the decision, it is submitted, is flawed and is only justifiable in future on a rational basis through amendment to the wording in paras 13(1) and 13(2). In the absence of such statutory intervention, the courts at first instance seem likely to continue to rely upon the fragile basis of *G-Tech* in the absence of an appeal which serves to shine light on the unsustainable platform the decision rests upon.

In *Mond v Synergi Partners Ltd* [2015] EWHC 964 (Ch), HHJ Hodge QC, sitting as a High Court judge, refused to make an administration order backdated for a period in excess of 4 years on the application of joint CVL liquidators which order was sought to cure a defect in their appointment which had arisen by reason of the late filing of the then requisite form 2.34B upon the company previously having been moved from administration, purportedly to CVL (such that the applicant joint liquidators had been acting without standing in the name of the company for a period in excess of 4 years and in the course of which they had investigated and served letters before claim on the company's former directors for wrongful trading). In observing that the authorities confirmed that a retrospective administration order cannot be backdated in any event for more than one year, the judge was not satisfied that the purpose of administration could be achieved by way of the order sought. The court was, however, prepared of its own volition, acceded to by the applicants, to make a compulsory winding-up order under para 13(1)(e).

The court's continued willingness to rely on the *G-Tech* jurisdiction is apparent from the decision of Snowden J in *Re Elgin Legal Ltd* [2016] EWHC 2523 (Ch). Following a review of the authorities, including the survey in *Synergi Partners* (above), Snowden J expressed concerns as to the jurisdiction to make a retrospective order but did so in light of the authorities and the unfairness that not making an order would create as regards creditors. To like effect see the judgment of Mann J in *Pettit v Bradford Bulls (Northern) Ltd* [2016] EWHC 3557 (Ch), [2017] BCC 50 in which a retrospective administration order was made to cure a doubtful appointment made previously out-of-court. In *Pettit* Mann J expressed the view that, if there is to be a challenge to the G-Tech jurisdiction, then it should now be raised in the Court of Appeal, a view with which HHJ Davis-White QC concurred in *Gregory v A.R.G. (Mansfield) Ltd* [2020] EWHC 1133 (Ch) at [122].

In *Biomethane (Castle Easton) Ltd, Baker v Biomethane (Castle Easton) Ltd* [2019] EWHC 3298 (Ch) at [18] Norris J observed, 'I think the time has come where it must be regarded as settled at first instance (i) that the [G-Tech] jurisdiction is available (ii) that extreme caution is required before its exercise and (iii) that frequently, as a matter of discretion, an exercise of the jurisdiction will be withheld. It is undoubtedly the case that the jurisdiction provides a pragmatic and convenient solution to multiple problems which can be occasioned by defective appointments of administrators. There will come a time where the competing arguments are addressed at a full adversarial hearing, either at first instance or on appeal, but until that occurs, I regard the practice is established at first instance that would treat the jurisdiction as existing and consider, principally, whether to exercise it or not . . . '.

In *Strategic Advantage SPC v ARL O09 Ltd* [2020] EWHC 3350 (Ch) Mr Andrew Sutcliffe QC, sitting as a deputy High Court judge, made administration orders in relation to three linked companies, and acceded to an application, 'having given the matter very careful consideration' to make a retrospective order dating back two months to the defective appointment, noting, at [71], Norris J's warning in Biomethane (above) that it is necessary to exercise extreme caution in such a course.

In *Re Wolf International Ltd* [2021] 1 WLUK 104, Deputy ICCJ Baister, in the context of a specialist fishing rod business run by a father and son between whom tensions had arisen, and following *Pettit* (above) and the principle that it would is unnecessary to consider whether the administrator has been appointed validly if a clear answer can be achieved by a retrospective appointment, the court made such an order to the appointment two months previously by the father, out-of-court on the basis that it was arguable that the father was a creditor entitled to effect that appointment and was therefore entitled to apply to court for an appointment, the company was cash flow insolvent and that one of the statutory purposes of administration was likely to be achieved. There was nothing to warrant a review of the administrators' conduct to date so as to justify the appointment of a further joint appointment on the application by the son, in addition to the additional cost involved; neither did the court consider that it would be assisted by the cross-examination of the administrators by or on behalf of the son.

A defective appointee has no standing to apply for a retrospective administration order; the application must be made by an eligible applicant under para 12(1).

**Should the court ratify or validate the act of an administrator undertaken pursuant to a defective appointment where the appointment is cured by a retrospective administration order?**—In *Adjei v Law for All* [2011] EWHC 2672 (Ch), [2012] 2 BCLC 317 at [19] Norris J, in making a retrospective order, expressed the view that there 'is no need' for the court to ratify or declare valid the earlier acts of the administrators or to declare that they are entitled to receive remuneration for their services. The judge went on to say that the fact that the court does not know in detail what acts the administrators have done or what remuneration they claim was a strong reason why the court should not do so in case there is a party aggrieved by what has occurred and has a proper ground for challenge or complaint. That approach was followed by HHJ Davis-White QC in *Gregory v A.R.G. (Mansfield) Ltd* [2020] EWHC 1133 (Ch) at [123] ('There is a difference between making the acts and decisions ones quae administrators, and in that sense validating them, and going beyond that and saying that the acts and decisions have been correctly made'). Following both decisions, Mr Andrew Sutcliffe QC, sitting as a deputy High Court judge in *Strategic Advantage SPC v ARL O09 Ltd* [2020] EWHC 3350 (Ch) at [71] explained that, 'The sole effect of making the order retrospective is that any act done by the [defectively appointed administrators whose appointment was proposed on the retrospective order] in this intervening period will be treated as having been done as administrators appointed by the court rather than as trespassers'.

**Identity of the administrator**—There may be a conflict as to the choice of administrator. In *Re World Class Homes Ltd* [2005] 2 BCLC 1 a petitioning creditor had presented a winding-up petition following which the debtor company made an application for an administration order. The petitioning creditor argued that its nominee should be appointed administrator because the majority of creditors favoured his appointment and had lost confidence in the company's nominees on account of their refusal to provide relevant information to the petitioning creditor and because of doubts as to their ability to obtain the best possible price for the company's assets. In upholding the company's choice of administrators (and refusing the petitioning creditor's nominees' costs of attendance) Lindsay J held that there was no substance to the petitioning creditor's objections and that the unwillingness to disclose information was explicable on the ground that the company's nominees had not yet been appointed with the consequence that there were no grounds for a lack of confidence and concern as to the independence of professional individuals who already had some acquaintance with the company's affairs.

In *The Oracle (North West) Ltd v Pinnacle Services (UK) Ltd* [2008] EWHC 1920 the directors of the company applied for an administration order in response to which a winding-up petitioner, which was also the largest unsecured creditor, made its own cross-application. Whilst it was not in issue that the making of an administration order was appropriate, each party sought the appointment of different office-holders and made allegations as to the motives of the other as to their proposed appointees. In considering that a joint appointment as between the two sets of proposed administrators was inappropriate (in the absence of evidence as to an agreed strategy), and taking account of the facts that the secured creditor remained neutral and that the winding-up petitioner applicant (who was supported by the next most significant creditor) would effectively control a creditors' meeting, Patten J held that where significant creditors have a clear preference for one administrator over another, and the secured and other creditors remain neutral, the court should ordinarily give effect to the wishes of those creditors given that administration is intended to operate for the benefit of creditors.

In *Healthcare Management Services Ltd v Caremark Properties Ltd* [2012] EWHC 1693 (Ch) the conflict as to the choice of administrator arose between the applicant creditor and another creditor. Morgan J held that in the ordinary case where the conflict was between the views of one group of creditors and the views of a rival group of creditors, the majority in terms of value would prevail as between the creditors, although the majority view did not bind a court which has the final say.

In *Re Japanese Koi Co Ltd*, unreported, 13 July 2016 Snowden J appointed independent administrators and capped the costs of the dispute leading to the court application by which a director and a creditor had insisted on the appointment of different administrators.

### PARAGRAPH 13(1)(c)

There is no limit to the scope of the conditions upon which the court may adjourn an administration application. Conceivably, especially where the adjournment is granted on the application of the applicant and with any degree of reluctance on the part of the court, such conditions might require that the application is withdrawn, dismissed or moved at the adjourned hearing.

Generally speaking, the court is unlikely to grant a lengthy adjournment or repeated adjournments given the exceptional nature of the interim moratorium and its effect upon the legitimate rights of third parties.

### PARAGRAPH 13(1)(d)

' . . . make an interim order . . . '—No indication appears in Sch B1 as to the scope of an interim order, which was also available to the court previously under s 9(4). Such an order may only be made on the hearing of an administration application – and therefore cannot be sought in the period between presentation of the application and its hearing unless the court is prepared to abridge time for the hearing of the application – and, by its nature, will take effect where the hearing of the application is adjourned under para 13(1)(c). However, in *Re Switch Services Ltd (in administration), SB Corporate Solutions Ltd v Prescott* [2012] Bus LR D91, HHJ McCahill QC (sitting as a High Court judge) held that the court had the power to grant interim relief prior to a formal application being issued and without written evidence. Such a course will usually require exceptional circumstances.

The purpose of an interim order will usually be something analogous to an interim injunction so as to hold the proverbial ring pending the determination of the administration application. This is envisaged in the terms of para 13(3) which reflects orders made in the earlier case law. For example, in *Re a Company (No 00175 of 1987)* (1987) 3 BCC 124 Vinelott J made an interim order appointing an insolvency practitioner to take control of a company's property and manage its affairs pending the adjourned hearing and identified that appointment as something akin to a receiver appointed over disputed property which was in jeopardy. In addition to such an appointment, or as an alternative to it, as in *Re Gallidoro Trawlers Ltd* [1991] BCC 691, the court may make an order which restricts the powers of a company's directors so far as deemed necessary pending the hearing of the application. There is also no good reason why the court should not make an interim order which restricts the enforcement of security over the company's property and undertaking where the validity or enforceability of that security can be called into question on genuinely arguable grounds, for the purposes of para 39(1) or otherwise, and where such enforcement might otherwise have a prejudicial effect on the administration application. In *Zinc Hotels (Investment) Limited v Beveridge* [2018] EWHC 1936 (Ch), [2018] BCC 968 Henry Carr J held at [47]–[52] that *Re a Company (No 00175 of 1987)* and *Re Gallidoro Trawlers* were authority for the proposition that there was no power to appoint a *provisional* administrator, ie to make an interim appointment prior to a company's entry into administration. There was, however, power for the court to appoint an additional or replacement administrator on an interim basis once a company was in administration, which derived from para 7 of Sch B1.

If the court makes an interim order under para 13(1)(d), then r 3.15(3) requires that the court give directions as to the persons to whom, and how, notice of that order is to be given. The interim order need not follow any prescribed form.

### PARAGRAPH 13(1)(e)

' . . . treat the application as a winding-up petition . . . '—This provision allows the court to make any order available to it under s 125, most obviously a winding-up order notwithstanding the absence of a winding-up petition (other than where such a petition is extant but stayed by para 42(3)). Previously, it had been held that the court could only make a winding-up order on a winding-up petition: *Re Brooke Marine Ltd* [1988] BCLC 546. Para 13(1)(e) is a useful facility which effectively allows for the avoidance of the time and expense of instituting the winding-up procedure where the court is satisfied that there is no real prospect of an administration application succeeding and where the court takes the view that it is appropriate on the facts for a formal insolvency procedure to be put in place, as in practice can arise in the course of the hearing of the application without winding-up relief being sought in the application. Winding-up orders were made in *Re UK Steelfixers Limited* [2012] EWHC 2409 (Ch); *Re Bowen Travel* [2012] EWHC 3405 (Ch), [2013] BCC 182, *Re Integral Limited* [2013] EWHC 164 (Ch), and *Mond v Synergi Partners Ltd* [2015] EWHC 964 (Ch).

A contributory does not apparently have standing under para 13(1)(e) unless, in common with the winding-up jurisdiction, the contributory can demonstrate that there would likely be a surplus in a winding-up accruing for his benefit; neither can it have been Parliament's intention to enlarge the jurisdiction under para 13(1)(e) beyond that in s 125 and consideration of the alternative remedies available to the contributory under the latter provision: *Re One World Logistics Freight Ltd* [2018] EWHC 264 (Ch) (Alison Foster QC).

Alternatively, the court might be prepared to resile from the making of a winding-up order, so as to avoid the DTI levy in a compulsory liquidation, on being given suitable undertakings for the placing of the company into voluntary liquidation.

Although the usual practice in the Companies Court on the making of a winding-up order is for the petitioner's costs to be paid by the company, the usual order on the making of a winding-up order under para 13(1)(e) should, in line with the former Part II practice, provide that the costs of an administration application be treated as costs in the winding up where a winding-up order is made under para 13(1)(e): see *Re Gosscott (Groundworks) Ltd* [1988] BCLC 363. That general rule does not apply, however, where an administrator is appointed out-of-court under para 14 so as to trigger the dismissal of the winding-up petition, although the costs of the winding-up petitioner may rank as an expense of the liquidation: *Re Portsmouth City Football Club Ltd* [2013] EWCA Civ 916, [2014] 1 All ER 12 at [41] (Mummery LJ), affirming the decision of Morgan J below, and see now r 3.51(2)(c) and (d).

For the commencement of the winding-up in a para 13(1)(e) case see s 129(1A).

### PARAGRAPH 13(1)(f)

' . . . any other order which the court thinks appropriate'—An order under this provision will be one falling outside the scope of para 13(1)(a)–(e). Such an order would include one appointing an administrator other than the appointee proposed by an applicant where other creditors, who will in the ordinary course face an uphill struggle, are able to convince the court that an alternative appointee is more appropriate. Paragraph 13(1)(f) would also extend to the provision of directions under para 68(2). The utility of the former provision lies in the court having the widest discretion to tailor its order to meet the particular facts of a case.

In *Re MBI Hawthorn Care Ltd* [2019] EWHC 2365 (Ch) Norris J considered that a court making an administration order had a discretion under para 13(1)(f) sufficiently broad to allow for the removal of a subsidiary's director if that was conducive to achieving the statutory objectives.

It is doubtful that para 13(1)(f) allows for the making of an order providing for the costs of a winding-up petition, or any other costs consequent, to rank as an expense of the administration upon an out-of-court appointment of an administrator being made: see the notes to r 3.51.

### PARAGRAPH 13(2)

Scope of the provision—Note (j) to the former prescribed form of administration order in Form 2.4B allowed for the inclusion of the time at which the order was made. No form of order is prescribed by the IR 2016; rather, r 3.13 prescribes the content of an order. Rule 3.13(1)(j) provides for 'the date of the order (and if the court so orders the time)'. Paragraph 13(2)(b) implies the time of the order in the event that no time is so stipulated. It appears, however, that the court has power under para 13(2)(a) to provide that an order takes effect at a time other than when the order is made. It is not at all clear why the court should wish an appointment to take effect after the making of an administration order, although it is conceivable that such an order might be desirable in a case where other administration-type applications are pursued in other jurisdictions in respect of other group or associated companies and where there can be shown to be good commercial reasons for the synchronizing of the effect of such orders. Nevertheless, it is even less clear upon what basis the court might order, as appears possible from the wording employed, that the appointment is to take effect at a time *before* the order is made. Until an appointment takes effect the administrator has no standing to exercise any of his or her statutory powers, as identified in the note to para 60, such that the court should give consideration in such circumstances to the making of an interim order under para 13(1)(d) for the intervening period.

As noted in relation to para 13(1)(a) above ('Retrospective administration orders'), in *Re G-Tech Construction Ltd* [2007] BPIR 1275, Hart J held that the wording of para 13 was wide enough to give the court jurisdiction to make an administration order with retrospective effect. However, the court may only make a retrospective order if the conditions in para 11 are satisfied at the time when the order is made: *Re Care Matters Partnership Limited* [2011] EWHC 2543 (Ch), [2011] BCC 957. This jurisdiction has been used extensively in recent times in cases where a purported out-of-court appointment has subsequently been discovered to be invalid as a result of a technical defect (eg *Re Derfshaw Limited* [2011] EWHC 1565 (Ch)).

### PARAGRAPH 13(4)

**The effect of para 39**—The court must dismiss an administration application under para 39(1) where an administrative receiver has been appointed before or after the making of an administration application unless any of the four exceptions in that provision apply. Where any of the four circumstances in para 39(1) are alleged, it is submitted that the court should not undertake a detailed and rigorous examination of the challenge to the security, but should adopt an approach of the sort suggested in the notes to para 38. On the other hand, the court may take the view that it is possible to resolve the issue finally in the course of a short hearing after a relatively brief adjournment allowing for the filing of any evidence without undermining the essential element of speed and economy at the heart of the administration regime.

## APPOINTMENT OF ADMINISTRATOR BY HOLDER OF FLOATING CHARGE

### [1.631]

### 14 Power to appoint

(1)   The holder of a qualifying floating charge in respect of a company's property may appoint an administrator of the company.

(2)   For the purposes of sub-paragraph (1) a floating charge qualifies if created by an instrument which—

(a)   states that this paragraph applies to the floating charge,

(b)   purports to empower the holder of the floating charge to appoint an administrator of the company,

(c)   purports to empower the holder of the floating charge to make an appointment which would be the appointment of an administrative receiver within the meaning given by section 29(2), or

(d)   purports to empower the holder of a floating charge in Scotland to appoint a receiver who on appointment would be an administrative receiver.

(3)   For the purposes of sub-paragraph (1) a person is the holder of a qualifying floating charge in respect of a company's property if he holds one or more debentures of the company secured—

(a)   by a qualifying floating charge which relates to the whole or substantially the whole of the company's property,

(b)   by a number of qualifying floating charges which together relate to the whole or substantially the whole of the company's property, or

(c)   by charges and other forms of security which together relate to the whole or substantially the whole of the company's property and at least one of which is a qualifying floating charge.

**Notice of appointment**—There is no longer a prescribed form for the notice of appointment. Rather, r 3.17(1) prescribes the contents of a notice which must be headed 'Notice of appointment of an administrator by holder of a qualifying floating charge'.

**Consent of the Financial Conduct Authority (FCA)**—In the case of a company regulated by the FCA, see the notes to para 29.

**Electronic filing**—See notes to para 29; an out-of-court appointment by the holder of a qualifying floating charge is permissible.

**General note**—The basis of the power of the holder of a qualifying floating charge – the term 'floating charge' being defined in para 111 – to appoint an administrator lies in para 14(1) which is provisoed by paras 14(2), 14(3) and 16. Paragraph 16 provides that 'an administrator may not be appointed under para 14 while a floating charge on which the appointment relies is not enforceable'. A proper understanding of the two provisions requires a distinction to be drawn between a purported power to appoint an administrator (under para 14(2)), the property comprised in the charge holder's security (under para 14(3)) and the enforceability of the floating charge pursuant to which the appointment of the administrator is to be made (see para 16).

The validity of an instrument as a floating charge, at the time of its creation, is not dependent upon the existence of uncharged assets of the company creating it, or upon a power in the company to acquire assets in the future, free from any fixed charge arising from the crystallisation of a prior floating charge: *SAW (W) 2010 Ltd v Wilson* [2017] EWCA Civ 1001 at [24] and [25] (Briggs LJ, Arden LJ agreeing). The reasoning of Vinelott J in *Re Croftbell Ltd* [1990] BCC 781 at 786 on s 29(2) (administrative receivership) as to the validity and utility of a so-called lightweight floating charge remains applicable.

A floating charge that had been signed by a company director and a company secretary, but not dated until 3 months later when the director was no longer a director, complied with the execution requirements in s 44 of the Companies Act 2006. Accordingly, the floating charge was valid and allowed a para 14 appointment pursuant to it: *Re Armstrong Brands Ltd* [2015] EWHC 3303 (Ch) (HHJ Purle QC, sitting as a High Court judge).

Paragraph 14(2) is concerned with the existence of a purported power to appoint. *Prima facie* it is the existence of such a purported power by which a floating charge 'qualifies' as a qualifying floating charge for the purpose of para 14(1) although, for the reasons identified below in relation to para 14(3), the floating charge must also meet one of the conditions in that provision so as to qualify as a floating charge, in addition to the charge being enforceable for the purposes of para 16. If the floating charge pursuant to which the appointment is made comprises a purported power to appoint which, it is argued, has not been triggered then, it is submitted, para 16 would come into operation given that the *purported* power to appoint requirement in para 14(2) could be shown to have been met.

The wording in the opening part of para 14(3) is less clear than it might have been since the impression is conveyed that the holder of the security defined within the provision 'is the holder of a qualifying floating charge' whereas para 14(2) stipulates that the floating charge comprising such security only 'qualifies' subject to its terms. The position might have been made clearer by omitting the word 'qualifying' from the opening part of para 14(3) or, alternatively, by reading para 14(1) as being expressly subject to para 14(2) and omitting the mechanism by which 'a floating charge qualifies' from that latter provision.

The following commentary should be read in conjunction with the notes to para 16.

**Security enforcement as alternatives to administration**—The holder of security meeting the requirements of s 29(2)(a) remains entitled to appoint an administrative receiver within the meaning of s 29(2) where the requisite floating charge element of that security was created prior to 15 September 2003: see s 72A(4)(a). Irrespective of the date of its creation, the holder of a fixed charge, or a floating charge which does not meet any of the para 14(3) requirements, may appoint a non-administrative or LPA receiver pursuant to that security. There are also certain exceptional cases provided for in s 72B–72GA which allow for the appointment of an administrative receiver, irrespective of the date of the creation of the requisite security. An administrative receiver must, however, vacate office on the appointment of an administrator (para 41(1)), as must a non-administrative/LPA receiver, but only if the administrator requires him or her to do so (para 41(2)).

**No insolvency requirement on appointment of administrator by holder of floating charge out-of-court**—In the case of an out-of-court appointment by a floating charge holder there is no requirement that the company is or is likely to become unable to pay its debts as there is where the court makes an administration order (see para 11(a)) or where an out-of-court appointment is effected by a company or its directors (see para 27(2)). Neither is there such a requirement where a floating charge holder seeks an administration order under para 35, subject to the conditions therein.

**The triggering of the statutory moratorium**—The moratorium provided for in paras 40–43 will only trigger in a para 14 appointment case when the requirements of para 18 are satisfied. In practice, whilst the para 18 formalities go rather beyond the more basic steps necessary to effect the appointment of an administrative receiver, compliance with the statutory requirements should be capable of being met within a very short period of time in most cases, at least where speed is a factor; furthermore, provision is made for a para 14 appointment taking place out of court business hours by faxing the notice of appointment to the court: see para 29.

Where there exists a prior floating charge holder entitled to notice of intention to appoint under para 15(1)(a), an interim moratorium – equivalent in substance to paras 42 and 43, but operating so as to dismiss any winding-up petition under para 40 – is triggered on the filing of a copy of the notice of intention to appoint. The interim moratorium is effective until the appointment of the administrator takes effect or upon the expiration of 5 days beginning with the date of filing: para 44(2)–(5).

**Appointment where QFC comprised in deceased estate**—In *Re Secure Mortgage Corporation Limited; Secure Mortgage Corporation Limited v Harold* [2020] EWHC 1364 (Ch), HHJ Halliwell (sitting as a High Court judge) held that a purported appointment under para 14 by the executors of a deceased estate was invalid because the executors could not demonstrate that the qualifying floating charge relied upon comprised an asset of the deceased estate and, in any event, absent a grant of probate, the executors were unable to establish their title to the estate under the Land Transfer Act 1897 and Administration of Estates Act 1925. The grounds apart, the court found that the appointment would have been invalid in any event on the basis of non-compliance with the statutory declaration requirement in the notice of appointment for para 18 purposes. The gravity of the matters raised on the successful challenge to the appointment warranted a costs order on the indemnity basis against the unlawfully appointed administrator and those responsible for the purported appointment: [2020] EWHC 1780 (Ch).

## PARAGRAPH 14(1)

'**The holder of a qualifying floating charge . . . may appoint an administrator of the company**'—As noted in the introductions to Sch B1 and Part III on receiverships, the holder of a floating charge compliant with s 29(2)(a) but created on or after 15 September 2003 may no longer appoint an administrative receiver other than in those excepted cases identified in ss 72B to 72GA. Such a charge holder is specifically entitled by virtue of this provision to appoint an administrator. The position of the charge-holder may, however, be said to be significantly weaker than previously, since the out-of-court appointee is obliged, in common with any other administrator, to perform functions with the objectives identified in para 3(1). From a practical perspective, an administrator appointed out-of-court by a qualifying floating charge holder will be obliged at least to consider whether it is reasonably practicable to achieve the objectives in para 3(1)(a) or (b), even when, in reality, the real wish on the part of the charge holder is to realise its security. Further commentary on this issue appears in the notes to para 3.

An out of court appointment of an administrator pursuant to para 14 amounts to enforcement of a floating charge: *SAW (SW) 2010 Ltd v Wilson* [2017] EWCA Civ 1001, [2018] Ch 213. The point may be relevant in the context of any contractual agreement, such as a deed of priority requiring consent for appointment by a subordinate QFC holder, as to whether enforcement has or is to be effected.

**So-called lightweight floating charges**—The validity of an instrument as a floating charge, at the time of its creation, is not dependent upon the existence of uncharged assets of the company creating it, or upon a power in the company to acquire assets in the future, free from any fixed charge arising from the crystallisation of a prior floating charge: *SAW (SW) 2010 Ltd v Wilson* [2017] EWCA Civ 1001 at [24] and [25] (Briggs LJ, Arden LJ agreeing), applying *Re Croftbell Ltd* [1990] BCC 781 at 786 (Vinelott J). *Croftbell* demonstrates that a company may wish to grant a floating charge for the purpose of setting itself up in business by borrowing working capital, before it has any significant assets to which a floating charge may attach. Equally, a prior fixed charge over all or part of the company's assets nonetheless leaves a subsequent floating charge to attach to the company's equity of redemption under the fixed charge. The question is not whether the company is inhibited in some way from dealing with its assets under the floating charge, but whether the company is inhibited by the terms of the instrument by which the floating charge is created.

**Floating charge security created in favour of a trustee**—Where loan notes to the value of over £440m were secured by a company in favour of a note trustee under a note trust deed which provided that the note trustee was the holder of the requisite qualifying floating charge, a purported appointment by the holder of a substantial amount of the notes, but not by the note trustee, was void and of no effect: *Fairhold Securitisation Ltd v Clifden IoM No 1 Ltd* [2018] 8 WLUK 114. The beneficiary under such a trust arrangement would usually have standing to require the trustee to make an application (as the judge considered in *Fairhold*).

## PARAGRAPH 14(2)

'**. . . floating charge qualifies if created by an instrument which . . .** '—There are four separate grounds upon which a floating charge 'qualifies' for the purpose of para 14(1). Although only para 14(2)(b)–(d) make express reference to the instrument purporting to empower the floating charge holder to make an appointment, para 14(2)(a) is to the same effect (given the heading 'power to appoint' to para 14). Whilst in practice it would not strictly be necessary, for the purposes of para 14(2)(a), for an instrument to expressly make reference to a power to appoint (it being apparently sufficient for the instrument merely to make reference to para 14 alone, without more), a well-drawn, standard-form debenture or other instrument will invariably, if only for the avoidance of doubt and clarity, make specific reference to a power to appoint.

In the cases of para 14(2)(b)–(d) the purported power to appoint must relate to the specific type of office-holder identified in each provision.

Paragraph 14(2)(c) relates to a floating charge created prior to 15 September 2003 which is compliant with para 14(3).

## PARAGRAPH 14(3)

'**. . . is the holder of a qualifying floating charge in respect of a company's property if he holds one or more debentures of the company secured . . .** '—There are three alternative scenarios by any of which a charge holder may qualify as the holder of a floating charge within this provision. The language used and the substance of the three subparagraphs, it should be noted, very closely resemble, but are not identical to, the language employed in the definition of an administrative receiver in s 29(2)(a) ('a receiver or manager of the whole (or substantially the whole) of a company's property appointed by or on behalf of the holders of any debentures of the company secured by a charge which, as created, was a floating charge, or by such a charge and one or more other securities').

There are two requirements common to each of the four constituent elements in para 14(3), namely (i) the requirement that the security is constituted by a floating charge (ie as defined in para 111(1)) or charges, and (ii) the requirement that the requisite security (ie a single floating charge or number of floating charges which, whether or not in combination, extend to the whole or substantially the whole of the company's property). The words 'one or more debentures' means that there is no requirement that the requisite security is created by a single instrument or provided for in a single security document.

Paragraph 14(3)(b) differs from the substance of s 29(2) in that the former provision now allows the charge holder to meet the requisite security requirements if two or more floating charges, taken together, constitute security over the whole or substantially the whole of the company's property. Although it was held in *Re Croftbell Ltd* [1990] BCLC 844 by Vinelott J that a floating charge remains a valid basis for the appointment of an administrative receiver for the purposes of s 29(2), notwithstanding the fact that the security actually catches on no assets (so as to constitute a so-called 'lightweight floating charge'), such a position is highly unlikely in practice since a floating charge is usually framed in terms so as to catch any assets not subject to any fixed charge such that the floating charge would catch nothing on crystallisation only if the debtor company had no assets whatsoever or if the entirety of the company's assets were subject to a valid fixed charge.

Paragraph 14(3)(c) addresses the position where the charge holder holds two or more 'charges and other forms of security' of which at least one constitutes a qualifying floating charge. However, in such a case the presence of the qualifying floating charge itself would appear to entitle the charge holder to qualify as a floating charge holder under para 14(3)(a), such that the existence of charges and other forms of security which do not constitute a qualifying floating charge would appear irrelevant. In *Meadrealm Ltd* (unreported, Chancery Division, 29 November 1991) Vinelott J held that a receiver could not amount to an administrative receiver where appointed pursuant to a fixed charge only when the appointor was the holder of a floating charge and a fixed charge – including a lightweight floating charge that catches no company assets – but which securities extended cumulatively to the whole or substantially the whole of the company's assets. The substance of the decision must be questionable to the extent that nothing in s 29(2) requires an appointment of an administrative receiver to be effected pursuant to any particular security. Rather, the provision is concerned with the substance of the security held by a debenture holder. Paragraph 14(3) adopts precisely the same approach. In both provisions, the common requirement is for a floating charge (or two or more such charges in the case of para 14(3)) which extends to the whole or substantially the whole of the assets of the company. Although para 14(2) does make reference to the existence of a purported power to appoint, there is no requirement that the appointment of an administrator should actually be effected pursuant to that power provided that, by way of substance over form, the requirements in both para 14(2) and (3), contrary to the form over substance approach in *Meadrealm*, are met.

**The inter-relationship between para 14(1), (2) and (3)**—The appointment of an administrator under para 14(1) requires an intended appointor and the security held by the intended appointor to come within both para 14(3) and (2) respectively.

The language used in the three subparagraphs is not as straightforward or as clear as it might have been. The starting point lies in para 14(3) which, though determinative of the appointor's status as the 'holder' of a qualifying floating charge, is actually concerned with the substance of the appointor's security, as discussed under the heading immediately above. Paragraph 14(2), on the other hand, determines whether a floating charge constitutes a qualifying floating charge not by reference to the substance of the security itself (which, of course, is addressed by para 14(2)), but by reference (and no more) to either, in the case of para 14(1), the label (and no more) attached to the instrument by which the floating charge is created or, in the case of each of the subparas (b)–(d), the existence of a purported power to appoint.

An appointment under para 14(1) will not be possible where the intended appointor's security does not meet the requirements in para 14(3), even though either of the requirements in para 14(2) can be met, since, in those circumstances, the intended appointor would not be the 'holder' of a qualifying floating charge, and only such a 'holder . . . may appoint an administrator . . . ' under para 14(1).

[1.632]

### 15 Restrictions on power to appoint

(1) A person may not appoint an administrator under paragraph 14 unless—

    (a) he has given at least two business days' written notice to the holder of any prior floating charge which satisfies paragraph 14(2), or

(b) the holder of any prior floating charge which satisfies paragraph 14(2) has consented in writing to the making of the appointment.

(2) One floating charge is prior to another for the purposes of this paragraph if—

 (a) it was created first, or

 (b) it is to be treated as having priority in accordance with an agreement to which the holder of each floating charge was party.

(3) Sub-paragraph (2) shall have effect in relation to Scotland as if the following were substituted for paragraph (a)—

  "(a) it has priority of ranking in accordance with section 464(4)(b) of the Companies Act 1985,".

**General note**—This provision operates as a further pre-condition to a valid appointment under para 14, although it only arises where the security of the intending appointor under para 14(3) ranks subject to any prior floating charge – of which there may be more than one – which meets the appointment criteria in para 14(2).

The obvious purpose of para 15 is to enable the holders of prior floating charges to appoint their chosen administrators, should they wish to do so, in preference to those selected by the holder of a subordinate charge. The reason why para 15 only requires notice to, or consent from, the holder of a prior floating charge is because it is floating rather than fixed chargees who have the right to appoint administrators out-of-court: *SAW (SW) 2010 Ltd v Wilson* [2017] EWCA Civ 1001 at [32] (Briggs LJ, Arden LJ agreeing).

The intending appointor must give at least 2 business days' written notice of the intention to appoint to the senior charge holder(s) under para 15(1)(a). Where the senior charge holder is content with the identity of the proposed appointee, the senior charge holder may consent in writing to the making of the appointment under para 15(1)(b). In the first of these two cases the senior charge holder(s) has no standing to prevent the proposed appointment proceeding other than where a challenge is made to the enforceability of the intending appointor's security, say on grounds of illegality in the creation of the charge. Instead, the giving of the relatively short period of notice of intention to appoint is designed to provide a senior qualifying floating charge holder the opportunity to effect an appointment of its own administrator, whether by court order or out-of-court, thereby guaranteeing an appointee of its choice and precluding the appointment by the junior charge holder on the basis that only one administrator, or joint appointees, may hold office at any one time.

In *Re Eco Link Resources Ltd (in CVL)* [2012] BCC 731, HHJ David Cooke (sitting as a High Court judge) held that failure to comply with para 15 is a defect which renders an appointment by a second charge holder invalid from the beginning and is not capable of being cured retrospectively.

In contrast, in *Re Care People Limited* [2013] EWHC 1734 (Ch), HHJ Purle QC (sitting as a High Court judge) held that an appointment which was made before a floating charge had become enforceable (ie in breach of para 16) was not a nullity; the defect was capable of cure under r 12.64.

Applying the approach in *Re Tokenhouse VB Ltd (formerly Vat Bridge 7) Ltd* [2020] EWHC 3171 (Ch), in which ICCJ Jones considered whether the failure to comply with the notice requirements in para 26 of Sch B1 inevitably invalidated the appointment out-of-court of an administrator, following *Ceart Risk Services Limited* [2012] EWHC 1178 (Ch), [2012] BCC 592 in which Arnold J considered that 'the law must now be taken as settled at first instance' that the failure to comply with para 26(2) was not fatal, and *Re Skeggs Beef* [2019] EWHC 2607 (Ch) (Marcus Smith J), Deputy ICCJ Frith held in *Re NMUL Realisations Ltd (in administration)* [2021] EWHC 94 (Ch) that failure by a debenture holder to serve a notice of intention to appoint on the holder of prior ranking security under para 15 of Sch B1 was an irregularity capable of cure by r 12.64 with the consequence that the appointment was not invalidated from the outset.

**PARAGRAPH 15(1)(a)**

' . . . **written notice** . . . '—Strictly speaking, there is no requirement that written notice is given in the prescribed notice since, although any document accompanying the notice of appointment for the purpose of filing with the court under para 18(1) 'must be in the prescribed form' by virtue of para 18(5), there is no requirement for the filing of the actual notice of intention to appoint.

' . . . **the holder of any prior floating charge which satisfies para 14(2)**'—In identifying the party or parties entitled to written notice a junior intending appointor is apparently only concerned with the senior charge holder's ability to appoint under para 14(2) without any consideration as to the extent of the senior security for the purposes of para 14(3). The giving of notice is required without regard to the question of whether the standing to appoint has arisen or, it seems, any other question as to the enforceability of the senior ranking security. (This analysis was approved of by HHJ Hodge QC, sitting as a High Court judge, in *Re OMP Leisure Ltd* [2008] BCC 67 at [6]). In practice it is very unlikely that the ability of the senior charge holder to effect an appointment will be apparent from a search of Companies House since such information does not fall within the scope of the prescribed particulars necessary on the registration of a debenture although, in theory, such additional information may be included within the statutory form by which registration of a charge is effected. In the interests of certainty a junior charge holder should consider giving notice to all senior ranking charge holders, including fixed charge holders, whose security, particularly over intangibles, receivables and movables, might well, on closer analysis, not in fact have been created as such so as to constitute a floating charge within the para 111(1) definition: see now in particular the decision of the House of Lords in *National Westminster Bank plc v Spectrum Plus Ltd* [2005] UKHL 41 in relation to charges over book debts.

In practice, where an apparently senior charge holder can be shown to have been discharged the court may be prepared to make the order sought subject to granting the senior charge holder liberty to apply.

**Priority of floating charges for the purposes of para 15(2)**—This provision gives statutory effect to floating charges ranking chronologically in time, save that effect is given to any agreement varying that priority, such as a subrogation or subordination agreement, to which the intending appointor must have been party. Paragraph 15(1)(a) and (b) each make reference to 'the holder of any prior floating charge which satisfied para 14(2)'. In the absence of express provision there appears to be no basis to read into the provisions a requirement that the holder of a qualifying floating charge ranking equally with the intending appointor should be afforded notice of intention to appoint. As such, the appointment will go to the quicker of any two (or more) equal ranking and eligible appointors.

**[1.633]**

**16**

An administrator may not be appointed under paragraph 14 while a floating charge on which the appointment relies is not enforceable.

**General note**—Like para 15, this provision operates as a further pre-condition to a valid appointment under para 14. The language employed precludes an appointment where the underlying floating charge 'is not enforceable', as a consequence of which the appointment itself would be 'invalid', to use the language employed in para 21(1) (invalid appointment: indemnity). The enforceability of a floating charge under foreign law is irrelevant to the issue of whether the floating charge holder falls within the statutory definition: *Hooley Ltd v Victoria Jute Co Ltd* [2016] CSOH 141 at [16] (charge created by Scottish registered company over assets in India).

The requirement that the floating charge relied upon for the appointment of administrators is enforceable 'is concerned with the question whether the chargee has a right to enforce, rather than with the question whether there are free assets to which the chargee can have recourse for the purposes of enforcement. A floating charge is in my judgment enforceable if any condition precedent to enforcement has been satisfied (such as an event of default) and there remains a debt for which the floating charge may stand as security': *SAW (SW) 2010 Ltd v Wilson* [2017] EWCA Civ 1001 at [33] (Briggs LJ, Arden LJ agreeing).

Quite apart from the possibility of a floating charge being 'not enforceable' – say, through a failure of consideration (on which see s 245) – this provision raises the specific question of whether a floating charge on which an appointment relies is 'not enforceable' by virtue of the power to appoint an administrator, as identified in para 14(2), having yet to arise. Whilst in most cases that power will almost always have arisen, at least under the terms of a well-drawn standard form debenture, the point warrants confirmation since the term 'enforceable' in para 16 appears to require that the floating charge holder must be entitled to enforce its security, of which a power to appoint within the meaning of para 14(2) is plainly a constituent part.

In *Lovett v Carson Country Homes Limited* [2009] EWHC 1143 (Ch), the administrators of a company applied to court to determine if they were properly appointed after it was discovered that the signature of one of the company's directors on a debenture in favour of a bank under which the bank appointed the administrators had been forged. Davis J held that the bank was entitled to assume that the debenture had been validly executed by virtue of s 44 of the Companies Act 2006.

In *Re Care People Limited* [2013] EWHC 1734 (Ch), HHJ Purle QC (sitting as a High Court judge) held that para 16 is not of such fundamental importance that an appointment made shortly before the charge had become enforceable was rendered a nullity. In that case a floating charge became enforceable if a written demand was not met in full. The chargeholder served a demand upon the company and purported to appoint an administrator without having given the company an opportunity to comply with the demand. The appointment was therefore premature. However, there was no evidence to suggest that the company could comply with the demand. It was held that the premature appointment was properly characterised as a defective exercise of an undoubted power of appointment, which was procedural in nature but not fundamental to the existence of the power. In the circumstances, the defect could be cured under r 12.64.

The appointment of administrators was held by ICCJ Jones to be incapable of cure under r 12.64, on its facts, for breach of para 16 of Sch B1 in *Re Glint Pay Ltd (in administration)* [2020] EWHC 3078 (Ch), following a review by the same judge of the authorities in *Re Tokenhouse VB (formerly Vat Bridge 7) Ltd* [2020] EWHC 3171 (Ch) at [40]–[41].

In *Arlington Infrastructure Ltd (in administration) v Woolrych* [2020] EWHC 3123 (Ch) Mr Andrew Sutcliffe QC, sitting as a deputy High Court judge, held that an out of court appointment under para 14 was a nullity by reason of para 16 because the appointing QFC had failed to obtain the prior written consent of senior creditors, as required. By a deed of priority. Because appointment under para 14 amounts to enforcement of a charge, it would make no sense for para 16 to provide than an administrator could not be appointed under para 14 while the floating charge on which the appointment relied was not enforceable. As such, the appointment was void from the outset and was incapable of cure.

In keeping with the former position under Part II, the appointment of an administrator under Sch B1 is not rendered invalid because of the existence of a bona fide dispute as to the enforceability of the security pursuant to which an administrator is appointed: *BCPMS (Europe) Ltd v GMAC Commercial Finance* [2006] All ER (D) 285 (Lewison J).

## [1.634]

**17**

An administrator of a company may not be appointed under paragraph 14 if—

   (a)    a provisional liquidator of the company has been appointed under section 135, or

   (b)    an administrative receiver of the company is in office.

**General note**—Paragraph 17(a) and (b) constitute the only circumstances preventing an out-of-court appointment of an administrator by the holder of a qualifying floating charge. In contrast to an out-of-court appointment by a company or its directors under para 22 the existence of an outstanding winding-up petition or administration application presents no bar to an appointment: see para 25 and the notes thereto. A provisional liquidator may only be removed from office by an order of the court under r 7.39, the holder of a floating charge having standing to make such an application under r 7.33(1)(b). In those circumstances, however, the court would be concerned at maintaining the preservation and custody of the company's assets if those factors were relevant, as will invariably be the case, on the appointment of the provisional liquidator. An administrative receiver may only vacate office on removal by order of the court or on resigning in compliance with s 45(1) or on the making of an administration order under para 13(1): see para 41(1). The holder of a qualifying floating charge has standing to seek an administration order by virtue of para 12(1)(c).

In contrast to the position on the making of an administration order, which has the effect of dismissing a winding-up petition, an appointment under para 14 only suspends a winding-up petition for the period of the administration other than in the case of a public interest or Financial Services Authority petition which is unaffected by such an appointment: see paras 40(1)(b) and 40(2) and the notes thereto.

## [1.635]

**18 Notice of appointment**

(1)   A person who appoints an administrator of a company under paragraph 14 shall file with the court—

   (a)    a notice of appointment, and

   (b)    such other documents as may be prescribed.

(2)   The notice of appointment must include a statutory declaration by or on behalf of the person who makes the appointment—

   (a)    that the person is the holder of a qualifying floating charge in respect of the company's property,

   (b)    that each floating charge relied on in making the appointment is (or was) enforceable on the date of the appointment, and

   (c)    that the appointment is in accordance with this Schedule.

(3)   The notice of appointment must identify the administrator and must be accompanied by a statement by the administrator—

   (a)    that he consents to the appointment,

  (b)    that in his opinion the purpose of administration is reasonably likely to be achieved, and

  (c)    giving such other information and opinions as may be prescribed.

(4)    For the purpose of a statement under sub-paragraph (3) an administrator may rely on information supplied by directors of the company (unless he has reason to doubt its accuracy).

(5)    The notice of appointment and any document accompanying it must be in the prescribed form.

(6)    A statutory declaration under sub-paragraph (2) must be made during the prescribed period.

(7)    A person commits an offence if in a statutory declaration under sub-paragraph (2) he makes a statement—

  (a)    which is false, and

  (b)    which he does not reasonably believe to be true.

**General note**—These provisions prescribe the formalities necessary to give effect to the appointment of an administrator, on which see para 19 and the notes thereto. A purported appointment in *Re Secure Mortgage Corporation Limited; Secure Mortgage Corporation Limited v Harold* [2020] EWHC 1364 (Ch) would have been invalid for a failure to comply with para 18, had it not also been invalid on the independent ground that the purported appointer was not entitled to exercise the statutory power of appointment in para 14(1), at [31]–[35].

As to the date and time of filing, see the notes to para 29.

**PARAGRAPH 18(1)**
**Documents for filing with the court**—The notice of appointment incorporates a statutory declaration (required under para 18(2)) which must be made not more than 5 business days before the form is filed with the court. The reference in para 18(1)(b) to 'other documents as may be prescribed' is to those identified in r 3.17, being (a) the administrator's written statement of consent to act); (b) evidence of the giving of any notice required by para 15(1)(a) or copies of the written consent of those required to give consent under para 15(1)(b); and (c) a statement of those matters provided for in para 100(2) (joint and concurrent administrators).

Paragraph 18(5) stipulates that the notice of appointment and any document appointing it must be in the prescribed form, in default of which the requirements of para 18 cannot be said to be satisfied for the purpose of para 19.

**PARAGRAPH 18(7)**
**Criminal liabilities**—The penalties provided for in s 430 and Sch 10 are also provided for in s 5 of the Perjury Act 1911.

**The obtaining of advice on the validity of the administrator's appointment**—The statutory declaration made by or on behalf of the appointing charge holder carries with it potential criminal liability where any statement therein is false and is not reasonably believed to be true by the maker: see para 18(7). Despite the statutory indemnity to which an invalidly appointed appointee might have recourse under para 21, an administrator appointed by the holder of a qualifying floating charge will usually wish to seek legal advice on the validity of the appointment.

**Appointment of administrator taking place**—See rr 3.16–3.20.

## [1.636]

### 19 Commencement of appointment

The appointment of an administrator under paragraph 14 takes effect when the requirements of paragraph 18 are satisfied.

**General note**—This provision predicates the effectiveness of a para 14 appointment on satisfaction of the requirements in para 18. It is at this point, and no sooner, that the administrator becomes entitled to exercise those statutory powers identified in the note to para 60.

The reference in para 19 is to 'paragraph 18', and not merely para 18(1); consequently, an appointment is not effective unless there is strict compliance with paras 18(2), (3), (5) and (6): *Fliptex Ltd v Hogg* [2004] EWHC 1280 (Ch) (Peter Smith J). Despite any defects in the appointment in relation to those provisions, however, para 104 would operate to render valid any act on the part of the administrator, although that provision does not operate to validate the defective appointment itself, which might be remedied either through the taking of the administrative step necessary to secure compliance with para 18 or, in an appropriate case, through an application to court for an appropriate direction under para 63. It is also arguable that a defective appointment might be capable of being cured under r 12.64, since out-of-court appointments constitute 'insolvency proceedings' for the purpose of that provision, given that such appointments are attributed a case number, title and court file and, by virtue of para 5, out-of-court appointees are officers of the court. A challenge to the validity of an administrator's appointment may also be subject to estoppel arguments: see the comments of Peter Smith J in *Fliptex* (above).

The appointment of the administrator does not take effect until the filing of the notice of appointment with the court: *Re Spaces London Bridge Ltd* [2018] EWHC 3099 (Ch), [2019] BCC 280 (Nugee J) (a decision made under the analogous para 31): see the notes to r 3.24.

The effectiveness of a para 14 appointment is unaffected by any non-compliance with para 20(a).

## [1.637]

### 20

A person who appoints an administrator under paragraph 14—

- (a) shall notify the administrator and such other persons as may be prescribed as soon as is reasonably practicable after the requirements of paragraph 18 are satisfied, and
- (b) commits an offence if he fails without reasonable excuse to comply with paragraph (a).

**General note**—This provision imposes notice obligation on the appointing holder of a qualifying floating charge. Notice obligations are also imposed by para 46(2) on the administrator following appointment.

Non-compliance with para 20(a) will not affect the validity of the appointment of an administrator or his or her standing to act as such, the sanction for default lying in the criminal penalties under para 20(b), on which see s 430, Sch 10 and the daily default fine imposed by para 106(2)(a).

## [1.638]

### 21 Invalid appointment: indemnity

(1) This paragraph applies where—

- (a) a person purports to appoint an administrator under paragraph 14, and
- (b) the appointment is discovered to be invalid.

(2) The court may order the person who purported to make the appointment to indemnify the person appointed against liability which arises solely by reason of the appointment's invalidity.

**General note**—This provision appears identical in substance to that in s 34 which provides for an indemnity by court order where the appointment of a receiver and manager appointed out-of-court is discovered to be invalid. The authorities considered below arise in relation to s 34 but, by analogy, will apply equally here.

#### PARAGRAPH 21(1)(a), (b)

**Scope of the provision**—The power of the court to make an order under para 21(2) only arises where both para 21(a) and (b) are met and, as a separate matter, can only extend to liability which arises solely by reason of the invalidity of the appointment. There is nothing in the language employed in the provision to suggest that the invalidity of the appointment, for the purposes of para 21(b), should arise solely by virtue of any lack of standing to appoint under para 14.

**Invalid and defective appointments distinguished**—A distinction is drawn between invalidity in appointment under this provision, say where there is no power to appoint or no substantive appointment (on which see *Morris v Kanssen* [1946] AC 459 in relation to a receivership appointment), and mere defects in the formalities or procedure by which appointment is effected, which defects may be cured by para 104.

#### PARAGRAPH 21(2)

' . . . **liability which arises solely by reason of the appointment's invalidity** . . . '—These words appear wide enough to cover liabilities flowing solely from the invalidity of the appointment which are incurred by the appointee either to the company itself, say for wrongful interference with goods or conversion, or to a third party with whom the appointee has had dealings as receiver. Such liability would not appear to arise 'solely' from any invalidity in appointment where the liability is incurred by the appointee contracting with personal liability on the basis of an indemnity from the company's assets (which indemnity would be lost by virtue of the invalidity of the appointment).

The exercise of the court's discretion under this provision – which arises through the use of the word 'may' in para 21(2) – will depend on the extent to which the appointor and appointee can each be shown to have been aware of the invalidity of the appointment or capable of establishing such invalidity on reasonable investigation.

**Invalidly appointed administrator agent of appointor?**—In the case of an invalidly appointed administrator, quite apart from para 21, the appointor will be vicariously liable for the acts of his or her agent, the purported administrator, where the purported administrator acts on the instructions or directions of the appointor: *Standard Chartered Bank v Walker* [1982] 1 WLR 1410 at 1416A, CA (a receivership case). Paragraph 21 does not appear to preclude the existence of such an agency relationship; compare the reasoning of Walton J in *Bank of Baroda v Panessar* [1986] 3 All ER 751 to the opposite effect. However, neither does the mere fact of appointment automatically trigger an agency relationship between appointor and appointee in the usual absence of a provision to such effect in the debenture pursuant to which an administrator may be appointed: *National Bank of Greece v Pinios* [1990] 1 AC 637 at 648–649 (Lloyd LJ).

**Indemnities beyond para 21**—The statutory indemnity provided for in para 21 is also discrete from any indemnity which may be claimed by an administrator who incurs liability to the chargor company or any third party in the course of acting on the instructions of his appointor: *Re B Johnson & Co (Builders) Ltd* [1955] Ch 634 at 647–648 (Evershed MR, a receivership case).

Where there are concerns over the validity of an appointment, a prospective appointee may seek a contractual indemnity, usually in the form of a deed, from the appointor to cover consequential liabilities as a condition of his or her appointment. The provision of indemnities very much varies in practice. An indemnity will ordinarily only protect an administrator from liability arising from invalidity in the debenture or in the form of appointment.

There is no good reason why the court's discretion should not be invoked under para 21 notwithstanding the existence of a contractual indemnity between an appointor and appointee.


## APPOINTMENT OF ADMINISTRATOR BY COMPANY OR DIRECTORS

**[1.639]**

### 22 Power to appoint

(1)   A company may appoint an administrator.

(2)   The directors of a company may appoint an administrator.

**General note**—Subject to the conditions identified below, either a company or its directors may appoint an administrator out-of-court, though such standing does not affect the entitlement of either party to make an application for an administration order under para 12(1). Neither a company nor its directors has standing to appoint an administrator out of court business hours, as in the case of the holder of a qualifying floating charge.

**The decision of the directors**—The requirement for a shareholders' resolution will generally be met by either an ordinary resolution or a unanimous informal agreement which is equivalent to such a resolution, either at common law or under ss 288–289 of the Companies Act 2006. However, in *Re Frontsouth (Witham) Ltd (In Administration)* [2011] EWHC 1668 (Ch), [2011] BPIR 1382 Henderson J held that where the company's articles included reg 70 of Table A, which provides that 'the business of the company shall be managed by the directors who may exercise all the powers of the company', as a matter of general company law the decision whether or not to place the company into administration is one to be taken by the directors. Under Table A such a decision cannot be taken by an ordinary resolution of the shareholders, although by a special resolution they may direct the board to take such a step.

The former r 2.22 of the 1986 Rules referred not to a 'resolution' (as in the case of a company) but 'a record of the decision of the directors' to appoint. Para 105 (which provides that a decision of the directors may be made by a majority of the board under para 105), does not apply to para 22: *Minmar (929) Ltd v Khalastchi* [2011] EWHC 1159 (Ch), [2011] BCC 485.

In *Re Melodious Corp, Pui-Kwan v Kam-Ho* [2015] EWHC 621 (Ch), [2015] 1 BCLC 518, in which *Minmar* was noted, the meeting of directors at which a resolution purporting to appoint an administrator was inquorate with the consequence that the resolution was not a valid resolution for para 22(2) purposes. As a consequence, the company could not be said to have entered into administration. The procedural defect was incapable of cure under the former IR 1986, r 7.55 (now r 12.64) because that provision applies only to defects or irregularities in insolvency proceedings; no such relevant insolvency proceedings had come into existence if the company had never gone into administration. Those two decisions were followed by ICCJ Prentis in *Re Sprout Land Holdings Ltd (in administration)* [2019] EWHC 807 (Ch) (appointment invalid, administration ceased). Conversely, a directors' appointment of administrators is not invalid by reason of a procedural irregularity at board level in the appointment capable of cure by reference to the principle in *Re Duomatic Ltd* [1969] 2 Ch 365. In *Re BW Estates Ltd, Randhawa v Turpin* [2016] EWHC 2156 (Ch), [2016] BCC 814 HHJ Cooke, sitting as a High Court judge, held that where a director's appointment had been made at a board meeting at which only one director was present, where the company's articles of association provided that two or more directors were required for a meeting to be quorate, the *Duomatic* principle allowed for an effective variation of the company's articles, either by a consistent course of conduct which had informally sanctioned the exercise of all the directors' powers by one director alone, or by the sole director being authorised to put the company into administration. That decision was overturned on appeal on the basis that, on the facts, the *Duomatic* principle was inapplicable (because one of its registered members was neither notified of the proposal to appoint nor assented to such a course) such that the company's articles had not been complied with. Vos C expressed the view that para 22(2) is insufficient in itself to override the provisions of a company's articles, finding agreement in the reasoning of Sir Andrew Morritt C in *Minmar (929) Ltd v Khalastchi* [2011] EWHC 1159 (Ch) at [49]–[52] to the effect that there is no notion of informality in para 22 allowing the directors of a company to appoint an administrator: *Randhawa v Turpin* [2017] EWCA Civ 1201 at [78].

**Alleged improper motive in effecting an appointment**—In *Re Hat and Mitre plc (in administration)* [2020] EWHC 2649 (Ch) Trower J dismissed an application for declarations that a directors' appointment under para 22 was a nullity where the statutory requirements had been complied with, but the appointment had been made for the improper purpose of furthering their interests as minority shareholders to the disadvantage of the majority shareholders and contrary to the company's best interest. On the evidence, the directors had been entitled to form the view that the company was or was likely to become cash-flow insolvent ([101]–[102], [106] and [125]). As to improper purpose, despite the reliance on s 171(b) of the Companies Act 2006 and the nullifying effect on improper purpose transactions, the proper approach was to identify the source of the power and the context in which it was exercised before considering the consequences of exercise for a purpose other than that for which the power was conferred. Crucially, the judge was of the view that the scheme of Sch B1 contemplated the court being entitled to proceed and uphold the validity of an appointment, even in circumstances in which the vitiating factor (here of improper purpose) was said to, or would otherwise, nullify the appointment. On the evidence, the applicants could not make out the fact of improper motive on the part of the appointors and, even if they could, the challenge came more than a year after the appointment which had been followed by the applicants engaging with the administrators as if validly appointed; a party challenging an appointment must take steps as soon as practicable: [139], [142], [150], [172] and [174]). The administrators could not be shown to have caused unfair harm to the applicants as members in approaching what had been a difficult administration; where there is more than one way forward, administrators ought to adopt a course most likely to be in the interests of the members as a whole: [200], [204], [207].

**Consent of the Financial Conduct Authority (FCA)**—In the case of a company regulated by the FCA, see the notes to para 29.

**Conditions for out-of-court appointment by company or directors**—An out-of-court appointment may only be made by the company or its directors if all of the following five conditions are satisfied:

(a)    the company has not been in administration following an out-of-court appointment effected by the company or its directors – the fact of any administration application or order on any such application being irrelevant – nor subject to a moratorium in respect of a failed CVA under Sch A1 in the previous 12 months: see paras 23(2) and 24(1) and (3) and the differing dates therein on which the 12-month period is to commence;

(b)    the company is or is likely to become unable to pay its debts: see para 27(2)(a) and the definition in para 111(1) by reference to s 123;

(c)    there is no outstanding winding-up petition or application for an administration order in respect of the company: see para 25(a) and (b);

(d)    the company is not in liquidation: see para 8(1)(a) and (b); and

(e)    there is no administrator or administrative receiver in office: see paras 7 and 25(c).

## [1.640]

### 23 Restrictions on power to appoint

(1)    This paragraph applies where an administrator of a company is appointed—

    (a)    under paragraph 22, or

    (b)    on an administration application made by the company or its directors.

(2)    An administrator of the company may not be appointed under paragraph 22 during the period of 12 months beginning with the date on which the appointment referred to in sub-paragraph (1) ceases to have effect.

**General note**—See here para 22 and the notes thereto.

These restrictions apply only to an out-of-court appointment under para 22; they do not restrict the company or its directors in making an application for an administration order.

**24**

*(Repealed)*

**Amendments**—Repealed by Corporate Insolvency and Governance Act 2020, s 2(1), Sch 3, paras 1, 31(1), (2).

**[1.641]**

**25**

An administrator of a company may not be appointed under paragraph 22 if—

(a)     a petition for the winding up of the company has been presented and is not yet disposed of,

(b)     an administration application has been made and is not yet disposed of, or

(c)     an administrative receiver of the company is in office.

**General note**—See here paras 22 and 23 and the notes thereto.

A winding-up petition is presented for the purposes of para 25(a) upon its presentation to the court, and not upon its issue by the court: *Re Blights Builders Ltd* [2008] 1 BCLC 245 (HHJ Norris QC, sitting as a High Court judge; para 22 appointment held invalid where made on 24 July 2006 in ignorance of creditor's winding-up petition presented on 5 July 2006 but only issued by the court on 25 July 2006).The restrictions in para 25 apply only to an out-of-court appointment under para 22. They do not prevent the company or its directors from making an application for an administration order, although, where there is an administrative receiver in office, whether appointed before or after the making of the administration application, the court must dismiss the application unless any of the four conditions in para 39(1) are satisfied.

Paragraph 5 of Sch 6 to the Deregulation Act 2015 provided for the implementation of para 25A (below). This provision has significant practical consequences in permitting the filing of a notice of intention to appoint under para 27 provided (a) any winding-up petition was presented after the filing of that notice, and (b) the petition is not one mentioned in para 42(4).

These restrictions on a para 22 appointment are more extensive than those imposed by para 17 in relation to a para 14 appointment. The major practical difference between paras 17 and 25 is that the former does not prevent the holder of a qualifying floating charge from making an out-of-court appointment following the presentation of a winding-up petition or an administration application. Such an appointment would also have the effect of suspending a winding-up petition under para 40(1)(b), subject to those exceptional cases in para 40(2), as well as preventing the appointment of an administrator on the hearing of an administration application. Subject to the general restriction in para 39, on the other hand, para 25 does nothing to prevent a company and/or its directors from making an administration application under para 12(1)(a) and/or (b) where a winding-up petition or an administration application presented by a third party is on foot.

If a winding up petition is presented after a notice of intention to appoint has been filed, although the petition was not a nullity, it was prohibited by the interim moratorium. In the circumstances, para 25(a) did not prevent the appointment of an administrator: *Re Ramora UK Ltd* [2011] EWHC 3959 (Ch).

**[1.642]**

**25A**

(1)   Paragraph 25(a) does not prevent the appointment of an administrator of a company if the petition for the winding up of the company was presented after the person proposing to make the appointment filed the notice of intention to appoint with the court under paragraph 27.

(2)   But sub-paragraph (1) does not apply if the petition was presented under a provision mentioned in paragraph 42(4).

**Amendments**—Inserted by Deregulation Act 2015, s 19, Sch 6, Pt 2, paras 4, 5, effective from 26 May 2015.

**[1.643]**

### 26 Notice of intention to appoint

(1) A person who proposes to make an appointment under paragraph 22 shall give at least five business days' written notice to—

    (a)    any person who is or may be entitled to appoint an administrative receiver of the company, and

    (b)    any person who is or may be entitled to appoint an administrator of the company under paragraph 14.

(2) A person who gives notice of intention to appoint under sub-paragraph (1) shall also give such notice as may be prescribed to such other persons as may be prescribed.

(3) A notice under this paragraph must—

    (a)    identify the proposed administrator, and

    (b)    be in the prescribed form.

**Amendments**—Deregulation Act 2015, s 19, Sch 6, Pt 2, paras 4, 6.

**General note**—Paragraph 28 prohibits an out-of-court appointment by a company and/or its directors under para 22 where there has been a failure to comply with any requirement in paras 26 and 27.

The purpose behind para 26(1) differs from that behind para 26(2). The former provision affords any person who is or may be entitled to appoint an administrative receiver or an administrator to a minimum of 5 business days' written notice of the intention to appoint. Any such person is thereby afforded the opportunity to effect its own appointment within that 5-day period, failing which the company and/or its directors are able to effect an appointment of which notice must be given in the period commencing with the expiry of the 5 business days' written notice and ending with the 10 business days period prescribed in para 28(2). The purpose behind para 26(2) would appear to be in affording those four classes of person identified in r 3.23(4) notice of the intended appointment so as to avoid an inadvertent contempt through an innocent breach of the interim moratorium triggered under para 44(4) on a copy of the notice of intention to appoint being filed with the court under para 27(1). A submission to that effect, however, was rejected by Warren J in *Westminster Bank plc v Msaada Group* [2011] EWHC 3423 (Ch), [2012] 2 BCLC 342 at [32], although the judge did not identify what other purpose might be served by the provision.

The contrast between the purpose of these two provisions was recognised by HHJ McCahill QC (sitting as a High Court judge) in *Hill v Stokes plc* [2010] EWHC 3726 (at [51].

**Repeated and invalid para 26 notices of intention to appoint**—The repeated service of a notice of intention to appoint, without an appointment being made, but nevertheless invoking the protection of the interim moratorium, constitutes an abuse which should be capable of control by the court. In *Re Cornercare Ltd* [2010] EWHC 893 (Ch), [2010] BCC 592, HHJ Purle QC, sitting as a High Court judge, suggested that this could be achieved either by restraining the lodging of further notices of intention to appoint unless followed by an actual appointment or even, in an extreme case, vacating and removing from the file under its inherent jurisdiction any abusive notice of intention to appoint, coupled with a blanket order for permission under para 43 during the unexpired period of the illicit moratorium.

It is a pre-requisite of a valid para 26(1) notice of intention to appoint that the proposing appointor has a settled intention to appoint; a conditional proposal to appoint, by which the appointment is a possibility only, is insufficient such that the notice so filed is liable to be removed from the court file: *JCAM Commercial Real Estate Property XV Ltd v Davis Haulage Ltd* [2017] EWCA Civ 267 (David Richards LJ, Jackson and Flaux LJJ agreeing). The practice of filing a notice of intention to appoint, so as to trigger the protection of the statutory moratorium, where administration is only a possibility amongst other options (such as the approval of a CVA) is therefore outlawed. (In *JCAM* the Court of Appeal, like the court below, entertained discussion as to whether it had become common practice to give and file one or more notices of intention to appoint in order to obtain a moratorium while a company proposes a CVA or some other solution to its financial problems, but without the court coming to any concluded view in the absence of generally available material to that effect). There is either a settled intention to appoint an administrator, or there is not. The Court of Appeal's reference to 'settled intention' would appear to require that the intention is not simply transient – as in, for example, 'I held that intention at the time the notice was filed but changed my mind immediately afterwards' – but has a permanence to it by reference to the considerations giving rise to it and an unequivocal resolution to appoint. On the other hand, there does seem to be room for argument that a settled intention does not necessarily preclude a subsequent change of mind.

*Re Seabrook Road Ltd* [2021] EWHC 436 (Ch) involved receivers appointed by a security trustee and QFC holder on 7 December 2020. Upon being given notice of that appointment, the company notified the receivers and the security trustee that it had filed a para 26 notice of intention to appoint with the court on 27 November 2020, but without the notice being served on the security trustee as QFC. Subsequently, it transpired that the company had filed four such notices previously between 3 November and 10 December 2020, each stating that notice had been given to the QFC holder when, in fact, it had not. Miles J inferred that the notices had been served for the purpose of invoking the para 43 interim moratorium so as to provide the company with negotiation leverage in the face of a receiver appointment or other enforcement being pursued by the security trustee. On the basis that the notices misrepresented the fact of notice having been given to the security trustee as QFC alone, the notices were each held to constitute an abuse of process. Further, applying *JCAM* (above), Miles J was satisfied that the company had not held an unconditional intention to appoint at the time of any of the notices. Accordingly, the judge held the notices to be invalid such that the interim moratorium had never come into effect. The judge also ordered the removal of the notices from the court file and declared the appointment of the receivers valid.

## PARAGRAPH 26(1)

' . . . is or may be entitled to appoint . . . '—The use of the words 'or may be' requires notice to be given to a person whose security is not presently enforceable or whose security is challenged as void or voidable where that challenge is disputed on genuinely arguable grounds. It follows that the holder of a floating charge within the meaning of s 29(2) or the holder of a qualifying floating charge is entitled to notice, even where the charge presently secures no presently outstanding indebtedness. This is an important point, because in practice the view is sometimes taken that it is unnecessary to serve such a charge-holder. The notes to para 15(1) provide further commentary relevant here.

In *Adjei v Law for All* [2011] EWHC 2672 (Ch), [2011] BCC 963, it was accepted that the failure by the directors to give notice of intention to appoint to the holder of a qualifying floating charge rendered the subsequent appointment of administrators invalid notwithstanding that the debt had been discharged in full and the continued registration of the debenture had merely been overlooked.

## PARAGRAPH 26(2)

Paragraph 26(2) was amended by para 6 of Sch 6 to the Deregulation Act 2015, effective from 26 May 2015. The trigger for the giving of notice under that provision is the giving of notice of intention to appoint under para 26(1).

The effect of a failure to give notice—The requirement to serve notice of intention to appoint on those persons specified in r 3.23(4) prior to appointment where there is no person entitled to notice under para 26(1) has been the subject of detailed consideration. Unhelpfully, there is a clear divergence of judicial opinion.

In *Hill v Stokes plc* [2010] EWHC 3726, [2011] BCC 473, the directors failed to give notice of intention to appoint to landlords who, to their knowledge, had distrained against the company's property (as required by IR 1986, r 3.23(4)(b)). HHJ McCahill QC (sitting as a High Court judge) held that the reference in para 28(1) to compliance with 'any requirement of paragraphs 26 and 27' should be read as 'any requirement of paragraphs 26(1) and 27'. Alternatively, the requirements of paragraph 26(2) should be construed as 'non-fundamental', such that non-compliance was not necessarily fatal to the validity of appointment.

In contrast, in *Minmar (929) Ltd v Khalastchi* [2011] EWHC 1159 (Ch), [2011] BCC 485, the Chancellor held that the failure by directors to give notice of intention to appoint to the company (as required by the former IR 1986, r 2.20(2)(d), now r 3.23(4)(d)) caused the appointment to be invalid. The requirement in para 26(2) that notice 'also' be given to such persons as may be prescribed made it plain that it was an additional obligation.

Although *Hill v Stokes plc* was decided before *Minmar*, it was not reported until afterwards. It was not therefore referred to by the Chancellor in his judgment.

Subsequently, there have been a number of decisions in which the court has adopted differing approaches. The lack of resulting lack of clarity is starkly illustrated by the fact that on 21 December 2011 two directly conflicting judgments were handed down by the High Court. In *Westminster Bank plc v Msaada Group* [2011] EWHC 3423 (Ch), Warren J followed the reasoning in *Minmar*, holding that the failure to give notice of intention to appoint to the company invalidated the subsequent appointment. In contrast, in *Re Virtualpurple Professional Services Ltd* [2011] EWHC 3487 (Ch), Norris J followed *Hill v Stokes plc* in reaching the opposite conclusion. *Virtualpurple* contains the most extensive discussion and reasoning in the authorities as to whether the intention of the legislature could have been for total invalidity in the absence of notice being given.

In *Re BXL Services* [2012] EWHC 1877 (Ch), [2012] BCC 657, HHJ Purle QC, sitting as a High Court judge, held that in light of the fact that Arnold J had followed *Virtualpurple* in *Re Ceart Risk Services Limited* [2012] EWHC 1178 (Ch), [2012] BCC 592, 'the law must now be taken as settled at first instance' that the failure to comply with para 26(2) was not fatal.

In *Re Tokenhouse VB Ltd (formerly Vat Bridge 7) Ltd* [2020] EWHC 3171 (Ch) ICCJ Jones considered whether the failure to comply with the notice requirements in para 26 of Sch B1 inevitably invalidated the appointment out-of-court of an administrator or was capable of cure under r 12.64. Applying *Ceart* (above) and *Re Skeggs Beef* [2019] EWHC 2607 (Ch) (Marcus Smith J), the task of the court was, first, to identify the purpose of the provision breached, and, secondly, to identify the consequences of non-compliance. Following some discussion (at [42]–[54]) the failure to give notice was held to be non-fundamental such that the validity of the appointment stood. However, the court considered appropriate an order appointing the preferred choice of office-holders of the applicant, the largest creditor. *Tokenhouse* and *Re NMUL Realisations Ltd (in administration)* [2021] EWHC 94 (Ch) (Deputy ICCJ Frith, para 15 defect not fatal) were followed by Mr Stuart Isaacs QC, sitting as a deputy High Court judge, in *Re Zoom UK Distribution Ltd (in administration)* [2021] EWHC 800 (Ch) where failure by directors to provide written notice to a floating charge holder of an intention to appoint under para 26 was held not to be fundamental where no injustice resulted from the breach such that the defect was capable of cure under r 12.64.

## [1.644]

27

(1)   A person who gives notice of intention to appoint under paragraph 26 shall file with the court as soon as is reasonably practicable a copy of—

(a)   the notice, and

(b)   any document accompanying it.

(2)   The copy filed under sub-paragraph (1) must be accompanied by a statutory declaration made by or on behalf of the person who proposes to make the appointment—

(a)   that the company is or is likely to become unable to pay its debts,

(b)   that the company is not in liquidation, and

(c)   that, so far as the person making the statement is able to ascertain, the appointment is not prevented by paragraphs 23 to 25, and

(d)   to such additional effect, and giving such information, as may be prescribed.

(3)   A statutory declaration under sub-paragraph (2) must—

(a)   be in the prescribed form, and

(b)   be made during the prescribed period.

(4)   A person commits an offence if in a statutory declaration under sub-paragraph (2) he makes a statement—

(a)   which is false, and

(b)   which he does not reasonably believe to be true.

**General note**—Paragraph 28 prohibits an out-of-court appointment by a company and/or its directors under para 22 where there has been a failure to comply with any requirement in paras 26 and 27.

The filing of the notice of intention to appoint with the court under para 27(1), but not apparently any other document required under r 3.23(2), triggers the interim moratorium in para 44(4).

During the currency of the interim moratorium, it will not be possible for the directors of the company to resolve to put the company into creditors' voluntary liquidation. Any such purported resolution is invalid and incapable of retrospective validation: *Re Business Dream Limited* [2011] EWHC 2860 (Ch).

**PARAGRAPH 27(2)**

**Statutory declaration**—The notice of intention to appoint, as provided for in r 3.16, does not incorporate a statutory declaration which, by this provision, must accompany the notice.

**PARAGRAPH 27(3)(b)**

'  . . .   **the prescribed period** . . .  '—Rule 3.25(4)(b) provides that the statutory declaration must not be made more than 5 business days before the notice of intention to appoint is filed with the court.

**PARAGRAPH 27(4)**

**Criminal liabilities under para 27(4)**—The penalties prescribed by s 430 and Sch 10 are also provided for in s 5 of the Perjury Act 1911.

**[1.645]**

**28**

(1)   An appointment may not be made under paragraph 22 unless the person who makes the appointment has complied with any requirement of paragraphs 26 and 27 and—

(a)   the period of notice specified in paragraph 26(1) has expired, or

(b)   each person to whom notice has been given under paragraph 26(1) has consented in writing to the making of the appointment.

(2)   An appointment may not be made under paragraph 22 after the period of ten business days beginning with the date on which the notice of intention to appoint is filed under paragraph 27(1).

**General note**—The words in para 28(1) that 'an appointment may not be made' suggest that a purported appointment made under para 22 in the absence of compliance with paras 26 and 27 will be void ab initio and, it is submitted, as such will be incapable of cure under para 104.

**Consent in writing of person given notice under para 26(1)**—There is no form prescribed for the giving of consent in writing. The former Form 2.8B envisaged consent being endorsed on the form before being returned to the company or its directors.

**The position where no person is entitled to notice under para 26(1)**—Paragraph 30 provides that para 28 has no application where there is no person entitled to notice of intention to appoint under para 26(1). In *Hill v Stokes plc* [2010] EWHC 3726, [2011] BCC 473, it was held that the reference in para 28(1) to 'Paragraph 26' should be read as a reference to 'Paragraph 26(1)'. It would follow that the 10 business days time limit imposed by para 28(2) will not apply where any person is entitled to notice of intention to appoint under para 26(2), but not under para 26(1).

**'The period of 10 business days' in para 28(2)**—The period of 10 days commences on the date on which the notice of intention to appoint is filed with the court (after which an appointment may not be made): *Re Statebourne (Cryogenic) Ltd* [2020] EWHC 231 (Zacaroli J). *Statebourne* (at [11] to [14]) doubts the correctness of the expansive approach taken in the decision of HHJ Hodge QC in *Re Keyworker Homes (North West) Ltd* [2019] EWHC 3499 (Ch) holding that the 10-day period begins on the first working day after the date on which the notice of intention to appoint is filed. Zacaroli J pointed out that the two previous decisions relied upon in *Keyworker* in support of that conclusion did not concern the interpretation of the time period required by para 28(2).

**The effect of the expiry of the relevant period**—In *Re Cornercare Ltd* [2010] EWHC 893 (Ch), [2010] BCC 592, HHJ Purle QC, sitting as a High Court judge, held that para 28(2) does not prevent a fresh notice of intention to appoint from being served and filed, resulting in a fresh 10-day appointment window. However, the court has the power to prevent this where it would amount to an abuse of process (see the notes to para 26 above).

Moreover, an appointment of an administrator made after the expiry of the prescribed period in para 28(2) does not automatically invalidate the appointment but should be treated as a curable irregularity under the former IR 1986, r 7.55 (now r 12.64): *Re Euromaster Limited* [2012] EWHC 2356 (Ch), [2012] BCC 754.

**[1.646]**

**29 Notice of appointment**

(1)   A person who appoints an administrator of a company under paragraph 22 shall file with the court—

(a)   a notice of appointment, and

(b)   such other documents as may be prescribed.

(2)   The notice of appointment must include a statutory declaration by or on behalf of the person who makes the appointment—

(a)   that the person is entitled to make an appointment under paragraph 22,

(b)   that the appointment is in accordance with this Schedule, and

(c)   that, so far as the person making the statement is able to ascertain, the statements made and information given in the statutory declaration filed with the notice of intention to appoint remain accurate.

(3)   The notice of appointment must identify the administrator and must be accompanied by a statement by the administrator—

(a)   that he consents to the appointment,

    (b)    that in his opinion the purpose of administration is reasonably likely to be achieved, and

    (c)    giving such other information and opinions as may be prescribed.

(4)    For the purpose of a statement under sub-paragraph (3) an administrator may rely on information supplied by directors of the company (unless he has reason to doubt its accuracy).

(5)    The notice of appointment and any document accompanying it must be in the prescribed form.

(6)    A statutory declaration under sub-paragraph (2) must be made during the prescribed period.

(7)    A person commits an offence if in a statutory declaration under sub-paragraph (2) he makes a statement—

    (a)    which is false, and

    (b)    which he does not reasonably believe to be true.

**General note**—Compliance with these provisions is of more than administrative importance, in that an appointment under para 22 will not take effect by virtue of para 33(a) if an administration order or an appointment under para 14 is made before the requirements of para 29 are satisfied. Paragraph 31 provides that the appointment of an administrator under para 22 only takes effect when the requirements of para 29 are satisfied.

These provisions correspond with those in para 18 which apply in a para 14 appointment case, although there is no facility for an out-of-court business hours appointment to be made under para 22.

**Consent of the Financial Conduct Authority (FCA)**—A company regulated by the FCA can only be put into administration with the FCA's consent by virtue of s 362A of the Financial Services and Markets Act 2000. In *Re ARG (Mansfield) Ltd* [2020] EWHC 1133 (Ch) HHJ Davis-White QC (sitting as a High Court judge), was asked to consider the making of a retrospective administration order to cure the fact of the consent of the FCA not having been obtained for the purpose of an appointment by the directors under para 22. (Although a search of the FCA register had been conducted, no record had been found.) The court considered the conflicting approach taken in the earlier High Court decisions, *Re MTB Motors Ltd (in administration)* [2010] EWHC 3751 (Ch) (in which the failure to obtain the FCA's consent was held to be a fatal flaw rendering the purported appointment a nullity so as to require a retrospective appointment) and *Re Ceart Risk Services Ltd* [2012] EWHC 1178 (Ch) (in which *MTB* had not been brought to the court's attention and which held that the defect in the appointment process was procedural only and did not invalidate the appointment which took effect from the date on which the FCA ultimately gave its consent). Following *Pettit v Bradford Bulls (Northern) Ltd (in administration)* [2016] EWHC 3357 (Ch), applying *MTB* and not following *Ceart*, and considering the approach in *R v Soneji* [2005] UKHL 49, [2006] 1 AC 340 (court asking itself whether Parliament had intended that the consequence of non-compliance should be the nullification of the appointment), the court found in *ARG* that the requirement for regulator consent defined the circumstances in which the power to appoint arose with the consequence that the original appointment had been a nullity but was capable of cure by way of a retrospective appointment on the grounds that the breach was inadvertent, that retrospective validation would not appear to cause any specific prejudice and the administration appeared to be for the benefit of creditors (at [121]–[125]).

**Electronic filing**—On 29 January 2020, Sir Geoffrey Vos C issued guidance in the form of a *Practice Note* [2020] BCC 211 indicating that amendments to the IR 2016 are anticipated which will clarify the position pending which any Notice of Appointment filed by way of the CE-File outside court hours by a company or its directors or by a qualifying floating charge-holder is to be referred at the first possible opportunity to a High Court judge for the purpose of determining the validity of the appointment and, if appropriate, the time at which the appointment takes effect, either on paper or following a short hearing, for which the judge may request written or oral submissions. Following such a referral, in *Re Symm & Co Ltd* [2020] EWHC 317 (Ch) at [37]–[41] Zacaroli J held that, pending the anticipated amendment to the IR 2016, and following the decisions of ICCJ Burton in *Re S J Henderson & Co Ltd* [2019] EWHC 2742 (Ch) and Marcus Smith J in *Re Skeggs Beef Ltd* [2019] EWHC 2607 (Ch), para 2.1 of the CPR PD 51O (Electronic Working Pilot Scheme) does not apply to any notice of appointment of an administrator outside court opening hours with the consequence that it is not permissible for the company or its directors to effect such an appointment which is capable of being made only by the holder of a qualifying floating charge. In the case of a company or director appointment, rather than holding that the appointment was effective under IR 2016, r 12.64 at the time the notice of appointment was purportedly filed by CE-File (as was the appropriate course in *Skeggs Beef* which involved an appointment by a qualifying floating charge-holder), the better approach was to cure the defect by treating the notice as filed at the time the court opened for business on the next working day, thereby treating the CE-filing after hours as an analogous to a hard-copy notice being left on the (closed) counter of the court awaiting the court office opening.

Where an administrative error had occurred in the course of electronic filing of a Notice of Appointment, in the form of an indication being given on a drop-down box that the case was not an existing but a new case, the error was capable of cure under CPR PD 51O, para 5.3(2) and CPR 3.10(b) with effect from the time of the original inadvertent filing: *Re Carter Moore Solicitors Ltd* [2020] EWHC 186 (Ch) (Snowden J).

'the date and time of the appointment'—The date and time of the appointment are amongst the prescribed (IR 2016, r 3.24(1)(j)) contents of a Notice of Appointment. One novel practical problem to which that requirement gave rise was the potential for a disparity between the date and time inserted in the notice and the date and time at which the notice was filed with the court. That anomaly was the subject of an impressive analysis by HHJ Klein in *Re NJM Clothing Ltd, Ross v Fashion Design Solutions Ltd* [2018] EWHC 2388 (Ch), as followed by HHJ Matthews in *Re Towcester Racecourse Co Ltd (in administration)* [2018] EWHC 2902 (Ch). The issue was laid to rest by the judgment of Nugee J in *Re Spaces London Bridge Ltd* [2018] EWHC 3099 (Ch) which held that an appointment is effective from the date and time at which the Notice of Appointment is filed, irrespective of the date and time endorsed in advance, but reflecting the usual practice of the court endorsing the Notice with the date and time of filing upon filing.

See also the notes to IR, r 3.24.

### PARAGRAPH 29(5)

Former effect of failure to use prescribed form—In *Re Kaupthing Capital Partners II Master LP Inc (in administration); Pillar Securitisation SARL v Spicer* [2010] EWHC 836 (Ch), [2011] BCC 338, Proudman J held that the use of the wrong prescribed form rendered the appointment invalid and was not capable of cure under the former IR 1986, r 7.55 (now r 12.64).

There is no longer a prescribed form for the notice of appointment; rather, r 3.24(1) prescribes the content of a notice of appointment after notice of intention to appoint, and r 3.25(2) sets out the corresponding requirements in a case without prior notice of intention to appoint. It seems likely and justifiable that the court would adopt a similar approach to that in *Kaupthing* (above) where those requirements are not met.

### PARAGRAPH 29(7)

Penalties—The penalties prescribed by s 430 and Sch 10 are also provided for in s 5 of the Perjury Act 1911.

## [1.647]

### 30

In a case in which no person is entitled to notice of intention to appoint under paragraph 26(1) (and paragraph 28 therefore does not apply)—

    (a)    the statutory declaration accompanying the notice of appointment must include the statements and information required under paragraph 27(2), and

    (b)    paragraph 29(2)(c) shall not apply.

General note—These provisions are triggered where no person is entitled to notice of intention to appoint under para 26(1). That position is unchanged where any person is entitled to notice under para 26(2) for the reasons set out in the notes to para 28.

## [1.648]

### 31 Commencement of appointment

The appointment of an administrator under paragraph 22 takes effect when the requirements of paragraph 29 are satisfied.

General note—This provision predicates the effectiveness of a para 22 appointment on satisfaction of the requirements in para 29. It is at this point, and no sooner, that the administrator becomes entitled to exercise those statutory powers identified in the note to para 60.

The reference in para 31 is to 'paragraph 29', and not merely para 29(1), as a consequence of which it would appear that an appointment is not effective unless there is strict compliance with para 29(2), (3), (5) and (6). Despite any such defects in appointments, however, para 104 would operate to render valid any act on the part of the administrator, although that provision does not operate to validate the defective appointment itself, which might be remedied either through the administrative step necessary to secure compliance with para 29 or, in an appropriate case, through an application to court for an appropriate direction under para 63. It is also arguable that a defective appointment might be capable of being cured under r 12.64, since out-of-court appointments constitute 'insolvency proceedings' for the purpose of that provision, given that such appointments are attributed a case number, title and court file and, by virtue of para 5, out-of-court appointees are officers of the court.

The effectiveness of a para 22 appointment is unaffected by any non-compliance with para 32(a).

The appointment of the administrator does not take effect until the filing of the notice of appointment with the court: *Re Spaces London Bridge Ltd* [2018] EWHC 3099 (Ch), [2019] BCC 280 (Nugee J): see the notes to r 3.24.

## [1.649]

**32**

A person who appoints an administrator under paragraph 22—

    (a)    shall notify the administrator and such other persons as may be prescribed as soon as is reasonably practicable after the requirements of paragraph 29 are satisfied, and

    (b)    commits an offence if he fails without reasonable excuse to comply with paragraph (a).

**General note**—This provision imposes notice obligations on the person appointing an administrator under para 22. Notice obligations are also imposed by para 46(2) on the administrator himself following appointment. No 'other persons' have been prescribed for the purposes of para 32(a).

Non-compliance with para 32(a) will not affect the validity of the appointment of an administrator or his or her standing to act as such, the sanction for default lying in the criminal penalties under para 32(b), on which see s 430, Sch 10 and the daily default fine imposed by para 106(2)(b).

## [1.650]

**33**

If before the requirements of paragraph 29 are satisfied the company enters administration by virtue of an administration order or an appointment under paragraph 14—

    (a)    the appointment under paragraph 22 shall not take effect, and

    (b)    paragraph 32 shall not apply.

**General note**—This provision should be read in conjunction with the general note to para 29. As defined in para 1(2)(b) a company 'enters administration' when the appointment of an administrator takes effect, on which see para 13 in the case of an administration order and para 19 in the case of a para 14 appointment.

## [1.651]

**34 Invalid appointment: indemnity**

(1)    This paragraph applies where—

    (a)    a person purports to appoint an administrator under paragraph 22, and

    (b)    the appointment is discovered to be invalid.

(2)    The court may order the person who purported to make the appointment to indemnify the person appointed against liability which arises solely by reason of the appointment's invalidity.

**General note**—This provision appears identical in substance to s 34 which provides for an indemnity by court order where the appointment of a receiver and manager appointed out-of-court is discovered to be invalid. The commentary to the identical para 21 (which applies to an out-of-court appointment by a qualifying floating charge holder) applies equally to para 34.

ADMINISTRATION APPLICATION – SPECIAL CASES

**[1.652]**

**35 Application by holder of floating charge**

(1) This paragraph applies where an administration application in respect of a company—

   (a)    is made by the holder of a qualifying floating charge in respect of the company's property, and

   (b)    includes a statement that the application is made in reliance on this paragraph.

(2) The court may make an administration order—

   (a)    whether or not satisfied that the company is or is likely to become unable to pay its debts, but

   (b)    only if satisfied that the applicant could appoint an administrator under paragraph 14.

**General note**—This provision allows the holder of a qualifying floating charge to make application for an administration order without the requirement of proof that the company is or is likely to become unable to pay its debts otherwise required by para 11(a). Subject to the application including a statement that it is made in reliance on para 35, the court will only make an order if satisfied that the applicant could appoint out-of-court under para 14: see paras 14–17 and the notes thereto. In addition, an applicant under para 35 must demonstrate that there is a real prospect of achieving the purpose of administration: *Re High Street Rooftop Holdings Ltd* [2020] EWHC 2572 (Ch) at [13] (Mr Andrew Sutcliffe QC, sitting as a deputy High Court judge).

In *Re St John Spencer Estates & Development Ltd; AIB Group (UK) plc v St John Spencer Estates & Development Ltd* [2012] EWHC 2317 (Ch), [2013] 1 BCLC 718, Robert Ham QC (sitting as a deputy High Court judge) noted that the purpose of the para 35 procedure was to provide secured lenders with a simple and assured route to realise their security where the company was in default, and to enable any doubts as to the enforceability of the security to be determined in advance without the administrators being exposed to any risk that an appointment out of court was invalid. In that case, at [39], the deputy judge accepted a submission on behalf of the applicant bank to the effect that, given that it held a demonstrably enforceable debenture comprising the requisite floating charge security, the applicant had a prima facie right to an administration order under para 35 in the absence of countervailing considerations. The deputy judge in *High Street Rooftop* (above) observed at [13] that, in so doing, the deputy judge in *John Spencer* was not addressing the issue of the applicant demonstrating a real prospect of the purpose of administration being achieved, as remained a requirement in a para 35 case just as much as it was under para 11.

In *Barclays Bank Plc v Choicezone Ltd* [2011] EWHC 1303 (Ch), [2012] BCC 767, Newey J held that the fact that a company had cross-claims against the floating charge holder which exceeded the amount of the debt owed by the company could not detract from the enforceability of the charge.

If the holder of a floating charge is unable to satisfy the court, for the purposes of para 35(2)(b), of its standing to appoint under para 14, then the charge holder would remain entitled to pursue an administration order, conceivably in the same application, as a creditor under para 12(1)(c), but subject to meeting both conditions in para 11.

The holder of a floating charge was granted an administration order on a para 11 application in *Re Trainfx Ltd, Hellenic Capital Investments Ltd v Trainfx Ltd* [2015] EWHC 3713 (Ch) (HHJ Pelling QC, sitting as a High Court judge) on the basis of the strength of the applicant's case, the company's technical insolvency and the standing of the applicant to effect an appointment out-of-court. The application was made because of the proposed administrator's reluctance to accept an appointment out-of-court given the stance adopted by the respondent company in opposing the appointment.

**[1.653]**

**36 Intervention by holder of floating charge**

(1) This paragraph applies where—

   (a)    an administration application in respect of a company is made by a person who is not the holder of a qualifying floating charge in respect of the company's property, and

(b) the holder of a qualifying floating charge in respect of the company's property applies to the court to have a specified person appointed as administrator (and not the person specified by the administration applicant).

(2) The court shall grant an application under sub-paragraph (1)(b) unless the court thinks it right to refuse the application because of the particular circumstances of the case.

General note—This provision serves to confer a level of priority on the holder of a qualifying floating charge by allowing the charge holder to nominate its own administrator on the hearing of an administration application. The wording in para 36(1)(b) does not require the charge-holder to be represented at the hearing, although this will be preferable to both the charge holder and the court, where the alternative proposed appointee is opposed by the applicant.

The use of the word 'shall' in para 36(2) requires the court to give effect to the alternative appointment proposed by the holder of a qualifying floating charge unless the court thinks it right to confirm the applicant's proposed appointment 'because of the particular circumstances of the case'. Those circumstances might include proof of a previous professional relationship giving rise to a conflict of interests or the applicant establishing to the court's satisfaction that its proposed appointee has engaged in significant work prior to the application so as to be far more readily familiar with the company's affairs – a point most obviously demonstrated by reference to the preparation of the affidavit and/or report in support of the application – in comparison with the charge holder's proposed appointee whose appointment might be shown to involve an avoidable duplication of such work and associated professional costs.

The fact of an administration application does not affect the standing of the holder of a qualifying floating charge effecting an out-of-court appointment of its chosen appointee under para 14.

' . . . **the court thinks** . . . '—The same words also appear in paras 13(1)(f), 39(1)(b)–(d) and 68(3)(c) and (d). The proper interpretation of the verb 'thinks' was not originally clear, but see now the notes to para 3. Unless what is intended is nothing more than what might be thought by the draftsman to be plain, unambiguous language with no real change in substance from earlier formulations, it appears more likely that what is intended is something other than the court being 'satisfied' of something, since that term is used in paras 11 and 95(a) where the word 'thinks' might otherwise have been employed. The key distinction between the word 'thinks' and the court being 'satisfied' appears to be the former term requiring an exercise of mind in the formation of a view or opinion without any requirement for that view or opinion being conclusive. The term 'satisfied', on the other hand, calls for a determinative judgment to be made on a balance of probabilities. This approach would square with the use of 'thinks' in paras 36(2) and 68(3)(c) and (d) which each involve the court in an exercise of discretion dependent on the circumstances of any case without, it seems, any strict need for findings of fact to be made. The same approach to para 39(1)(b)–(d) would also avoid the obvious difficulty, by what might otherwise quite properly be regarded as a determination for the purposes of any of the transaction avoidance provisions mentioned within those subparagraphs, which might otherwise arise if reference to the court being 'satisfied' had been utilised by the draftsman. As such, the term 'thinks' is open to interpretation as shorthand for 'has considered and is of the view that, without necessarily reaching a final determination on any issue of fact and/or law' whereas the term 'satisfied' is a convenient substitute for 'satisfied on a balance of probabilities'.

**[1.654]**

### 37 Application where company in liquidation

(1) This paragraph applies where the holder of a qualifying floating charge in respect of a company's property could appoint an administrator under paragraph 14 but for paragraph 8(1)(b).

(2) The holder of the qualifying floating charge may make an administration application.

(3) If the court makes an administration order on hearing an application made by virtue of sub-paragraph (2)—

(a) the court shall discharge the winding-up order,

(b) the court shall make provision for such matters as may be prescribed,

(c) the court may make other consequential provision,

(d) the court shall specify which of the powers under this Schedule are to be exercisable by the administrator, and

(e)     this Schedule shall have effect with such modifications as the court may specify.

**General note**—Where the holder of a qualifying floating charge is precluded from effecting an out-of-court appointment under para 14 by virtue of the company being in compulsory liquidation (to which para 8(1)(b) refers) this provision allows the charge holder to make an administration application which, if successful, has the consequence of requiring the court to discharge the winding-up order and to comply with those matters in para 37(3)(b) and (d).

For no obviously good reason there is no provision by which the holder of a qualifying floating charge might seek an administration order where a company is in voluntary liquidation, although a liquidator might pursue such an order, irrespective of whether the company is in voluntary or compulsory liquidation, under para 38.

In a voluntary liquidation there is also no good reason why the holder of a qualifying floating charge should not present a winding-up petition, having waived its security to the extent of the petition debt, with a view to obtaining a winding-up order so as to facilitate the appointment of an administrator under para 37. As a matter of discretion, however, the court may not be inclined to make a winding-up order in the face of such a tactical ploy.

**Cases in which an order might be made under para 37**—Although liquidation is a terminal procedure, the fact of liquidation is not necessarily inconsistent with the court being satisfied, for para 11(b) purposes, that the making of an administration order is reasonably likely to achieve the purpose of administration. The 'purpose of administration', of course, is made up of the hierarchy of the three objectives in para 3(1). In the vast majority of liquidations the business of a company is not carried on as a going concern, although this can arise in a voluntary liquidation where the carrying on of business can be shown to be for the benefit of the winding up. The objective in para 3(1)(a) is, therefore, unlikely to feature in a para 37 application, although this possibility cannot be discounted, subject to the proviso that there will usually be a need to act with some speed so as to avoid the loss of goodwill or the adverse reaction of third parties to a winding up. Far more likely in a para 37 application is the charge holder's assertion that the achievement of either of the objectives in para 3(1)(b) or (c) is reasonably practicable although, particularly where the business of the company is incapable of being continued or wound down as a going concern, the burden on the applicant will be in substantiating why either objective should produce a more advantageous outcome than would otherwise arise in the liquidation, taking account of the likely cost of each alternative procedure, which should always be provided so as to facilitate an informed comparative assessment by the court. An order might also be made under para 37 where a qualifying floating charge holder has appointed an administrative receiver whose agency for the company is terminated upon the making of a winding-up order.

Some judges will not automatically accept an unsubstantiated assertion, even one advanced by an experienced and qualified valuer, as can arise in practice, to the effect that the estimated realisation value of a particular asset, on either an open market or forced sale basis, is necessarily higher in administration than in liquidation. On the facts, there may be a basis for such a disparity, but there is no universally accepted general principle to that effect.

**PARAGRAPH 37(3)(a)**

The discharge of a winding-up order is not the same as rescission and means only that for the future the order shall cease to have effect; as a consequence, any disposition between the presentation of the winding-up order and its discharge under para 37(3)(a) will be void in the absence of a validating order for the purposes of s 127: *Re Albany Building Ltd* [2007] BCC 591 at [5] and [6] (HHJ Norris QC sitting as a High Court judge; validating order made on application of joint administrators).

**[1.655]**

**38**

(1)   The liquidator of a company may make an administration application.

(2)   If the court makes an administration order on hearing an application made by virtue of sub-paragraph (1)—

(a)     the court shall discharge any winding-up order in respect of the company,

(b)     the court shall make provision for such matters as may be prescribed,

(c)     the court may make other consequential provision,

(d)     the court shall specify which of the powers under this Schedule are to be exercisable by the administrator, and

(e)     this Schedule shall have effect with such modifications as the court may specify.

**General note**—This provision is very similar to para 37, save that it allows a liquidator – in either a voluntary or compulsory liquidation – to make an administration application. The commentary and procedure outlined in the notes to para 37 apply equally here.

It is understood that an administration order on the application of a liquidator was granted by Hart J on 25 September 2003 in an unreported case, albeit in rather unusual circumstances. The case involved a winding-up order which was made many months after the presentation of a petition by the Inland Revenue. The directors had caused the company to make payments to the Revenue following presentation of the petition in the belief that a winding-up order would not be made. The directors were oblivious to the order as, apparently, was the company's bank, which had not frozen the company's account. On informing the directors that the company was in liquidation the official receiver identified that the company was solvent on its balance sheet and that it retained a strong order book. Within 2 weeks of the speedy appointment of an insolvency practitioner as liquidator by the Secretary of State the administration order was obtained.

**Consequential provisions in a voluntary liquidation case**—In contrast to a compulsory winding up, there is no provision for the court to discharge a voluntary winding up. Given that administration and liquidation must, by the nature of each, be seen as mutually exclusive, practical necessity and good order would dictate the making of an order by the court under s 147(1) staying a voluntary winding up from the time of the making of the administration order. On the other hand, it might be argued that the making of an administration order on an application under para 38 is capable of operating to eradicate a preceding creditors' voluntary liquidation. That may matter in practical terms where, for example, a viable business in liquidation becomes the subject of a para 38 application for the purpose of rescuing the company's business, where the business is subsequently capable of being returned to the directors of the company; in such a case, the viability of the company post-administration may be severely hampered by the apparently permanent existence of a stayed liquidation, an outcome hardly consistent with a rescue operation.

## [1.656]

### 39 Effect of administrative receivership

(1) Where there is an administrative receiver of a company the court must dismiss an administration application in respect of the company unless—

    (a) the person by or on behalf of whom the receiver was appointed consents to the making of the administration order,

    (b) the court thinks that the security by virtue of which the receiver was appointed would be liable to be released or discharged under sections 238 to 240 (transaction at undervalue and preference) if an administration order were made,

    (c) the court thinks that the security by virtue of which the receiver was appointed would be avoided under section 245 (avoidance of floating charge) if an administration order were made, or

    (d) the court thinks that the security by virtue of which the receiver was appointed would be challengeable under section 242 (gratuitous alienations) or 243 (unfair preferences) or under any rule of law in Scotland.

(2) Sub-paragraph (1) applies whether the administrative receiver is appointed before or after the making of the administration application.

**General note**—Administrative receivership and administration are mutually exclusive regimes. The starting point is in the requirement that the court must dismiss an administration application where an administrative receiver is in office unless one of the four conditions in para 39(1)(a)–(d) is met. The status or former status of the company as a private or public company is irrelevant: *Chesterton International Group plc v Deka Immobilien Inv Gmbh* [2005] BPIR 1103. For the purposes of para 39(1)(a) there will usually be no incentive for the appointor of an administrative receiver to consent to the making of an administration order. By virtue of the words 'the court thinks' – on which see the note under that heading to para 36 – para 39(1)(b)–(d) do not require the court to come to a final determination under any of the transaction avoidance provisions mentioned therein.

It is irrelevant whether an administrative receiver was appointed prior to or following the issue of the administration application: para 39(2). An administrative receiver – as defined in para 111(1) by reference to s 251 – may be appointed pursuant to floating charge security satisfying s 29(2)(a) which was created prior to 15 September 2003 or in any of the seven exceptional cases identified in ss 72B–72GA.

For the effect of the making of an administration order on an administrative receiver or a non-administrative or LPA receiver see para 41.

EFFECT OF ADMINISTRATION

**[1.657]**

## 40 Dismissal of pending winding-up petition

(1) A petition for the winding up of a company—

   (a)    shall be dismissed on the making of an administration order in respect of the company, and

   (b)    shall be suspended while the company is in administration following an appointment under paragraph 14.

(2) Sub-paragraph (1)(b) does not apply to a petition presented under—

   (a)    section 124A (public interest),

   (aa)   section 124B (SEs), or

   (b)    section 367 of the Financial Services and Markets Act 2000 (petition by Financial Conduct Authority or Prudential Regulation Authority).

(3) Where an administrator becomes aware that a petition was presented under a provision referred to in sub-paragraph (2) before his appointment, he shall apply to the court for directions under paragraph 63.

**Amendments**—SI 2004/2326; Financial Services Act 2012, s 114(1), Sch 18, Pt 2, paras 51, 55.

**General note**—This provision is concerned only with a winding-up petition which is extant on the making of an administration order or at the time of the appointment of an administrator by a qualifying floating charge holder under para 14. Paragraph 25(1) prohibits an out-of-court appointment of an administrator by a company or its directors under para 22 where a winding-up petition has been presented but is not yet disposed of.

### PARAGRAPH 40(1)

'A petition . . . (a) shall be dismissed . . . '—The dismissal of a winding-up petition takes effect automatically by virtue of para 40(1)(a). Nevertheless, it is useful to record the fact of the dismissal within the body of the administration order. The court will also usually be prepared to order that the costs of the winding-up petition shall rank as an expense in the administration, although any costs order must necessarily turn on the facts of any particular case.

### PARAGRAPH 40(1)(b)

'A petition . . . (b) shall be suspended . . . '—The suspension of a winding-up petition is a new and innovative concept. Suspension, as opposed to dismissal, retains a petition before the court, albeit temporarily inert, in part to reserve the position of the petitioner in the event of the administration ceasing and in part to guard against the scope for abuse of the moratorium provisions, for example through the tactical appointment of an administrator by a qualifying floating charge holder. A suspended petition remains live or effective, so as not to require revival or awakening, once the respondent company is no longer in administration: *Harlow (Administrator of Blak Pearl Ltd) v Creative Staging Ltd* [2014] EWHC 2787 (Ch). Suspension also provides a benefit to creditors in any ensuing liquidation by fixing the starting point for the periods in which transactions might be challenged by a liquidator under ss 238 and 239 at the earliest possible time: see ss 129(2) and 240(3)(e).

Paragraph 55(2)(d) specifically empowers the court to make an order on a suspended winding-up petition where an administrator reports to the court that creditors have failed to approve proposals or revised proposals.

**Is a validation order under s 127 necessary where a winding-up petition is suspended under para 40(1)(b)?**—Section 127, as amended by para 15 of Sch 17 to the Enterprise Act 2002, is disapplied in respect of anything done by an administrator whilst a winding-up petition is suspended. The effect of the amendment appears to have been overlooked in *Re J Smiths Haulage Ltd* [2007] BCC 135 at [5] (HHJ Norris QC, sitting as a High Court judge), though the same conclusion was reached as provided for in the amendment. The amendment does not, however, affect the period between the presentation of a winding-up petition and the appointment of an administrator such that dispositions of company property during that period will continue to require validation by the court.

### PARAGRAPH 40(2)

**Public interest and Financial Services Authority winding-up petitions**—Either variety of winding-up petition identified in para 40(2) is unaffected by the making of an administration order or the appointment of an administrator by a qualifying floating charge holder under para 14. A winding-up order may also be made in respect of either petition where a company is in administration: see para 42(3) and the notes thereto.

The requirement in para 40(3) that an administrator makes an application for directions is mandatory. Any hearing on such an application should take account of the possible orders available to the court on a winding-up order being made under para 82(3) and (4).

## [1.658]

### 41 Dismissal of administrative or other receiver

(1) When an administration order takes effect in respect of a company any administrative receiver of the company shall vacate office.

(2) Where a company is in administration, any receiver of part of the company's property shall vacate office if the administrator requires him to.

(3) Where an administrative receiver or receiver vacates office under sub-paragraph (1) or (2)—

    (a)    his remuneration shall be charged on and paid out of any property of the company which was in his custody or under his control immediately before he vacated office, and

    (b)    he need not take any further steps under section 40 or 59.

(4) In the application of sub-paragraph (3)(a)—

    (a)    "remuneration" includes expenses properly incurred and any indemnity to which the administrative receiver or receiver is entitled out of the assets of the company,

    (b)    the charge imposed takes priority over security held by the person by whom or on whose behalf the administrative receiver or receiver was appointed, and

    (c)    the provision for payment is subject to paragraph 43.

**General note**—Paragraph 41(1) applies only where an administration order 'takes effect' and requires the vacation of office of any administrative receiver. That provision applies only to administration orders, since the fact of an administrative receiver holding office is a bar to any out-of-court appointment by virtue of paras 17(b) and 25(c).

Both sub-paras 41(1) and (2) require the incumbent receiver to vacate office, but only if requested in the latter case. There is no automatic removal. Neither provision imposes a timescale for such vacation. Given the function of an administrator it must be implicit that vacation will be effected as soon as reasonably practicable or with some broadly equivalent level of expedition. It is conceivable that, notwithstanding the directive nature of these provisions, a receiver might refuse to vacate office if there are genuine grounds upon which the validity of the appointment of the administrator is challenged because, first, the provision appears to be predicated on the effectiveness of a valid appointment and, secondly, a requirement for mandatory vacation of office in the absence of a valid administrator appointment must be doubtful.

An administrative receiver vacating office 'on completion of the administrative receivership' must give notice to those parties identified in r 4.20.

For para 41(2) purposes, no form of administration affects the appointment of a receiver of part of the company's property – that is, any receiver appointed out of court who does not meet the criteria in s 29(2)(a) – unless the administrator requires the receiver to vacate office under para 41(2). In practice, an administrator will usually require such a receiver to vacate office other than, for example, where the receiver's task is all but complete and the remaining conduct of the receivership is unlikely to affect the administration of the company and is to be carried out expeditiously and on clearly defined terms, invariably in practice against a background of co-operation between office-holders.

On vacation of office a receiver should surrender property in his custody or under his control to the administrator; the receiver may also consider it appropriate to seek an acknowledgement of the existence and extent of the statutory charge in his favour under para 41(3)(a).

### PARAGRAPH 41(3), (4)

**The charge in favour of the receiver**—The statutory charge created by para 41(3)(a) is distinct from any lien which exists in favour of a receiver and bites only on property within that provision. The sum secured will, by virtue of the definition of 'remuneration' in para 41(4)(a), extend not only to fees properly due to the receiver but also disbursements and expenses properly incurred, such as fees due to solicitors and agents, and indemnity rights. The charge so created is not expressed as dependent on the receiver retaining possession of the assets so secured although the risk of a receiver releasing such assets is that a bona fide purchaser for value without notice of the statutory charge would not be bound by it.

**Paragraph 41(3)(b)**—The effect of this provision is that an administrative receiver or receiver vacating office is no longer under any duty to pay preferential debts. The provision reads as forward looking such that preferential distributions already made are unaffected, at least by this provision.

**PARAGRAPH 41(4)(c)**

'The provision for payment is subject to paragraph 43'—There is some ambiguity here. Paragraph 43 is concerned with the imposition of a general bar against various forms of legal process. The draftsman's approach in casting para 41(4)(c) appears to be predicated upon the assumption that any payment due to a former receiver must involve the enforcement of the statutory charge created under para 41(3)(a), an assumption that will not apply if the payment of a secured debt does not involve the enforcement of the underlying security. Caution, at least, dictates that an outgoing receiver should not draw 'remuneration' due to him without the consent of the administrator or the permission of the court under para 43(2).

## [1.659]

### 42 Moratorium on insolvency proceedings

(1) This paragraph applies to a company in administration.

(2) No resolution may be passed for the winding up of the company.

(3) No order may be made for the winding up of the company.

(4) Sub-paragraph (3) does not apply to an order made on a petition presented under—

    (a)    section 124A (public interest), or

    (aa)   section 124B (SEs),

    (b)    section 367 of the Financial Services and Markets Act 2000 (petition by Financial Conduct Authority or Prudential Regulation Authority).

(5) If a petition presented under a provision referred to in sub-paragraph (4) comes to the attention of the administrator, he shall apply to the court for directions under paragraph 63.

Amendments—SI 2004/2326; Financial Services Act 2012, s 114(1), Sch 18, Pt 2, paras 51, 55.

General note—This provision, which should be read in conjunction with para 40, provides that, save in the exceptional case of an order made under a winding-up petition within para 42(4), a company in administration, as defined in para 1(2)(a), may not be placed into voluntary or compulsory liquidation. Paragraph 42 does nothing, however, to prevent the *presentation* of a winding-up petition. Any resolution for voluntary winding up in contravention of para 42(2) will be a nullity and of no effect.

Orders made on a public interest or Financial Services Authority winding-up petition—Paragraph 82 enables the court either to order that the appointment of the administrator shall cease to have effect or that the appointment shall continue subject to the court specifying the powers and role of the administrator.

Paragraph 42(5)—The application for directions by the administrator in the specified circumstances is a mandatory requirement.

## [1.660]

### 43 Moratorium on other legal process

(1) This paragraph applies to a company in administration.

(2) No step may be taken to enforce security over the company's property except—

    (a)    with the consent of the administrator, or

    (b)    with the permission of the court.

(3) No step may be taken to repossess goods in the company's possession under a hire-purchase agreement except—

    (a)    with the consent of the administrator, or

    (b)    with the permission of the court.

(4) A landlord may not exercise a right of forfeiture by peaceable re-entry in relation to premises let to the company except—

    (a)    with the consent of the administrator, or

    (b)    with the permission of the court.

(5)   In Scotland, a landlord may not exercise a right of irritancy in relation to premises let to the company except—

   (a)   with the consent of the administrator, or

   (b)   with the permission of the court.

(6)   No legal process (including legal proceedings, execution, distress and diligence) may be instituted or continued against the company or property of the company except—

   (a)   with the consent of the administrator, or

   (b)   with the permission of the court.

(6A)   An administrative receiver of the company may not be appointed.

(7)   Where the court gives permission for a transaction under this paragraph it may impose a condition on or a requirement in connection with the transaction.

(8)   In this paragraph "landlord" includes a person to whom rent is payable.

**Amendments**—Enterprise Act 2002, s 248(2), Sch 16 (as amended by SI 2003/2096).

**General note**—The various forms of protection within this provision very closely resemble those made available previously under ss 10(1) and 11(3) in Part II. Given that the purpose of both moratoria is the same in facilitating the achievement of the purpose or purposes of administration, the commentary below draws on authorities decided under the previous regime which are of continued relevance. As previously, there is nothing within the provisions to suggest that Parliament's intention was the statutory interference with the substantive rights or interests of creditors or third parties; rather the moratorium protects against the exercise or enforcement of such rights.

Paragraph 43(1) makes clear that the provisions are only effective on a company being 'in administration', a term defined in para 1(2) by reference to the appointment of an administrator.

Where the English courts recognise foreign proceedings under the Cross Border Insolvency Regulations 2006, and those foreign proceedings are more akin in nature to administration than liquidation, it has become customary for the English court exercise its power under reg 21 to align the moratorium arising automatically upon recognition with that under para 43 of Sch B1: *Re NMC Healthcare Ltd (in administration)* [2021] EWHC 1806 (Ch) (Sir Alastair Norris; recognition of administration order under Abu Dhabi Global Market Insolvency Regulations 2015; moratorium granted binding secured creditors).

**The Financial Collateral Arrangements (No 2) Regulations 2003**—These Regulations (SI 2003/3226) came into effect on 26 December 2003 and operate by way of disapplying certain domestic insolvency legislation as would otherwise apply to financial collateral arrangements so as to give effect to EU Directive 2002/47. The Regulations have potentially far-reaching consequences in that they afford priority to close-out netting provisions under such arrangements in place of the mandatory set-off provisions applicable in administration and winding-up. Whilst not of any great significance to traditional security taking under English law, the Regulations are of some relevance in administration in that they will preclude the operation of the statutory moratorium where, in an applicable arrangement, A takes fixed security over cash (or cash equivalent) held by B when B goes into administration and A wishes to enforce its security.

**'(a) with the consent of the administrator   . . . '** —The consent of the administrator is envisaged in sub-para (a) of sub-paras 43(2) to (6). The permission of the court can be granted retrospectively: *Re Colliers International UK plc (in administration)* [2012] EWHC 2942 (Ch), [2013] 1 Ch 422. At [32] David Richards J expressed the view that, 'I can think of no convincing reason why an administrator should not be permitted to grant retrospective consent'. The same view was adopted in the Northern Irish jurisdiction in relation to analogous legislation by Horner J in *Fulton v AIB Group (UK) plc* [2014] NI Ch 8, [2014] BPIR 1169 at [5].

**PARAGRAPH 43(2)**

**'No step   . . . '**—In *Bristol Airport plc v Powdrill* [1990] BCC 130 at 151E–151F Browne-Wilkinson V-C held that, at least in the case of an ordinary possessory lien, the assertion by the lien holder of a right to retain the property constituted the taking of a 'step' to enforce security which would, therefore, in the absence of the administrator's agreement, require the leave of the court. More generally, what appears to be required in the taking of a 'step' is an unqualified assertion of the barred rights, but not a mere threat or hypothesis which of itself will not breach the statutory moratorium.

For a case where the applicant was granted permission to enforce security against the assets of a company in administration, see *Re UK Housing Alliance (North West) Ltd (in administration), Mackay (as joint administrators) v Kaupthing Singer & Friedlander Ltd (in administration)* [2013] EWHC 2553 (Ch), [2013] BCC 752. In so deciding, Martin Mann QC, sitting as a deputy High Court judge, observed (at [75]) that, in considering whether or not to exercise its discretion to grant permission to enforce securities, the court is required to balance the interests of the secured and unsecured creditors only if the relevant property is required for the purposes of the administration, and in any event normally permission will be given if significant loss would be caused by a refusal. For a fact-specific case in which the Technology and Construction Court would have given permission to enforce an adjudicator's decision see *South Coast Construction Ltd v Iverson Road Ltd* [2017] EWHC 61 (TCC).

'No step may be taken to enforce security . . . '—The term 'security' is defined very broadly in s 248(b) in non-exhaustive terms as 'any mortgage, charge, lien or other security'.

## PARAGRAPH 43(3)

'No step . . . '—See the note to para 43(2) above.

' . . . to repossess goods in the company's possession under a hire-purchase agreement . . . '—As under the previous provisions, reference to a 'hire-purchase agreement' includes a conditional sale agreement, a chattel leasing agreement and a retention of title agreement: see para 111(1).

Since the protection in para 43(3) is expressly dependent on the relevant goods being 'in the company's possession' the burden rests on the office-holder not only in ensuring that the company has possession, but also that such possession can be evidenced. Note here that para 67 imposes a general duty on an administrator on his appointment to take custody or control of all property to which he thinks the company is entitled.

## PARAGRAPH 43(4)

'A landlord may not exercise . . . '—Paragraph 43(8) provides that the term 'landlord' includes a person to whom rent is payable, and so the term must be read as including any subsequent assignee entitled to receive rent.

' . . . a right of forfeiture by peaceable re-entry in relation to premises let to the company . . . '—Subject to the leave of the court, this provision protects against the exercise of any right of forfeiture by peaceable re-entry. The protection is restricted to premises which are let to the company, but not necessarily occupied by it. The protection afforded by the subparagraph applies generally and draws no distinction between the grounds giving rise to the exercise of the right of forfeiture such that it will be immaterial whether the right arises on breach of a covenant for payment of rent or any other covenant which, but for the moratorium, would give rise to such relief.

In *Re SSRL Realisations Ltd (in administration), Lazari Investments Ltd v Saville* [2015] EWHC 2590 (Ch), [2016] 1 P&CR 2 the court allowed an application by a landlord for permission to forfeit a lease by peaceable re-entry. In reaching that conclusion, Richard Spearman QC, sitting as a deputy High Court judge, took the view that permission would not impede the purpose of the administration order against the tenant company, and there were no grounds for believing that the administrators would be able to achieve a premium on assigning the lease.

## PARAGRAPH 43(6)

'No legal process (including legal proceedings, execution, distress and diligence) may be instituted or continued against the company or property of the company'—This form of words is the one for which the draftsman has opted to replace the words 'no other proceedings and no execution or other legal process' which had appeared in ss 10(1)(c) and 11(3)(d) and which remain in s 252(2)(b) in the case of an IVA interim order. The change in wording is not problematic, however, since the term 'legal process' plainly now includes 'legal proceedings' and must be taken as a more precise term than 'proceedings' (to use the former terminology) which had been held to extend to either legal proceedings or quasi-legal proceedings. Certainly it is inconceivable that Parliament might have intended to reduce substantially the protection offered by the moratorium in the administration regime through the use of the term 'legal proceedings'. One potential problem, however, in the terms used in para 43(6) lies in the use of the word 'legal process' as a generic term, which is apparently wider than, but encompasses, the term 'legal proceedings'. The difficulty lies in the fact that the term 'legal process' had previously been held by Millett J in *Re Olympia & York Canary Wharf Ltd* [1993] BCLC 453 at 457A, relatively restrictively, as meaning a process which requires the assistance of the court. Given the breadth of the term 'legal proceedings' – identified in the next section below by reference to the term 'proceedings' under Part II – it is difficult to see how that narrow interpretation of 'legal process' can survive the implementation of Sch B1. It is suggested that the term requires a purposive interpretation by the court so as to catch all forms of legal and quasi-legal proceedings and enforcements, extending beyond court processes, but extending to any form of process in which the court or court procedures play a necessary part, on which see the commentary attaching to s 130.

Consistent with the above, in *Re Frankice (Golders Green) Ltd (in administration) and others* [2010] EWHC 1229 (Ch), [2010] Bus LR 1608, Norris J held that a proposed review hearing before a regulatory panel of the Gambling Commission to consider whether to revoke or suspend the operating licences of three companies in administration fell within the description of 'legal process'.

'legal proceedings'—As suggested above, the term 'legal proceedings' should be attributed the meaning formerly attributed to the term 'proceedings' under Part II. The term 'proceedings' is a more compendious expression than the word 'action' which had been used previously in s 9 of the Bankruptcy Act 1914. The term 'proceedings' is apt to denote any legal or quasi-legal proceedings and has been held to extend to arbitration proceedings (*Bristol Airport plc v Powdrill* [1990] Ch 744 (Browne-Wilkinson V-C)), proceedings before an industrial tribunal (*Carr v British International Helicopters Ltd (in administration)* [1994] 2 BCLC 474 (EAT)), a statutory adjudication process under s 108 of the Housing Grants, Construction and Regeneration Act 1996 and under cl 41A of the standard form JCT 80 building contract (*A Straume (UK) Ltd v Bradlor Developments Ltd* [2000] BCC 333 (HHJ Behrens, sitting as a High Court judge)), criminal prosecution under the Environmental Protection Act 1990 (*Environment Agency v Clark* [2000] BCC 653 (Robert Walker and Henry LJJ and Scott-Baker J)) and, but not without some degree of doubt given the diametrically opposed views of Sir Andrew Morritt V-C and Lord Woolf (with whom Waller and Robert Walker LJJ agreed), an application by a special freight train operator for a replacement access contract under s 17 of the Railways Act 1993 in *Winsor v Special Railway Administrators of Railtrack plc* [2002] 2 BCLC 308. On the other hand, it is doubtful that the service of a counter-notice under Part II of the Landlord and Tenant Act 1954 for a fresh tenancy constitutes 'proceedings': *Bristol Airport plc v Powdrill* [1990] Ch 744 at 766 (Browne-Wilkinson V-C). The conclusion of the Scottish Court of Session in *Air Ecosse Ltd v Civil Aviation Authority* [1987] 3 BCC 492 to the effect that the words 'other proceedings . . . against the company' in the former s 11(3)(d) were confined to the activities of creditors and did not extend to actions which might be open to persons who were not creditors, such as competitors asserting rights under different statutes, is now extremely doubtful given the later authorities which construe the term far more broadly.

In *Re Olympia & York Canary Wharf Ltd* [1993] BCLC 453 at 457A Millett J identified that the words 'legal process' refer to a process which requires the assistance of the court and which would not, therefore, extend to the service of a contractual notice, whether or not the service of such a notice was a pre-condition to the bringing of legal proceedings. This interpretation may, however, require revision for the purposes of Sch B1 for the reasons set out above, on which see the commentary attaching to s 130.

A simple money claim will fall within the scope of the term 'legal proceedings'.

**Territorial limitations of the moratorium**—The prohibition on legal process in para 43(6) does not have extraterritorial effect (ie it does not extend to proceedings brought in foreign courts): *Bloom and others v Harms Offshore AHT 'Taurus' GmbH & Co KG and another* [2009] EWCA Civ 632, [2010] Ch 187. However, the court has jurisdiction to prevent a creditor from taking advantage of a foreign attachment by granting an anti-suit injunction, although the comity owed by the courts of different jurisdictions to each other will normally make it inappropriate for the court to grant injunctive relief affecting procedures in a court of foreign jurisdiction.

**The permission of the court**—In *Metro Nominees (Wandsworth) (No 1) Limited v Rayment* [2008] BCC 40, HHJ Norris QC, sitting as a High Court judge, held that general rule in the normal case for permission for peaceable re-entry or to commence legal proceedings was that if a creditor sought to exercise a proprietary right that was unlikely to impede the achievement of the purpose for which the administration was being pursued, then leave should normally be given. Where that was not the case (so that there was a likelihood that the proprietary right would impede the achievement of the purpose) then the court has to carry out a balancing exercise, balancing the legitimate interest of the lessor and the legitimate interests of the other creditors. In carrying out that balancing exercise, great importance or weight was normally given to the proprietary interests of the lessor (the underlying principle being that an administration for the benefit of unsecured creditors should not be conducted at the expense of those who have proprietary rights, save to the extent that this was unavoidable).

In *Magical Marking Ltd v Phillips* [2008] EWHC 1640 (Pat), [2008] FSR 36, Norris J granted permission to the claimant to continue a breach of copyright claim.

In *Somerfield Stores Ltd v Spring (Sutton Coldfield) Ltd* [2009] EWHC 2384 (Ch), [2010] 2 BCLC 452, where a landlord company opposed the tenant's application for a new tenancy under Part II of the Landlord and Tenant Act 1954 on the ground that it intended to redevelop the property but was unable to do so by reason of subsequently being put into administration, and the administrators required 6–12 months to put in place a viable scheme for redevelopment for the benefit of the sole secured creditor, HHJ Purle QC (sitting as a High Court judge) granted permission to the tenant under para 43(6) to continue the application for a new tenancy.

In *Innovate Logistics Ltd v Sunberry Properties Ltd* [2008] EWHC 2450 (Ch), [2009] BCC 164, the Court of Appeal refused to grant permission to a landlord to seek repossession of premises which were necessary for the continuation of the company's business during the administration.

In *Re Nortel Networks UK Ltd: Unite The Union v Nortel Networks UK Ltd* [2010] EWHC 826 (Ch), [2010] BPIR 1003, Norris J refused permission to employees of a company in administration and a trade union for permission under para 43(6) to institute legal proceedings against the company in relation to the termination of employment contracts by the administrators. Paragraph 43(6) imposed a general rule that those with monetary claims against the company may not pursue them. The employees and the trade union could not demonstrate that their case was exceptional. Consistent with this approach, the decision of the Employment Appeal Tribunal in *Ince Gordon Dadds LLP v Tunstall* [2020] ICR 124 (EAT) affirmed the decision below of the Employment Tribunal in refusing permission for the continuation of unfair dismissal claims against two defendants which had been placed into administration before the hearing of the preliminary hearing in the claims. The Employment Tribunal had considered the possibility of vicarious liability on the part of the two defendants in administration in relation to the claims which were free to continue as freestanding claims against the other defendants.

The court has jurisdiction to grant retrospective permission for the commencement of legal proceedings under para 43(6): *Bank of Ireland v Colliers International UK Plc* [2012] EWHC 2942 (Ch), [2013] Ch 422. In addition, the court has jurisdiction to grant permission once administration had ended in an appropriate case, although it will be rarely exercised: *Gaardsoe v Optimal Wealth Management Ltd (in liquidation)* [2012] EWHC 3266 (Ch), [2013] Ch 298.

## PARAGRAPH 43(6A)

**Scope of provision**—In contrast with the position under para 41(1) where an incumbent administrative receiver must vacate office on the making of an administration order, the fact of a company being in administration operates as an absolute bar against such an appointment being made. For the term 'administrative receiver' see s 29(2) and the general prohibition and excepted cases in ss 72A–72GA.

## PARAGRAPH 43(7)

**When will leave be granted by the court, on conditions or otherwise?**—The decision by a third party to seek leave of the court should ordinarily follow the third party's confirmation that the administrator is not prepared to consent to the particular enforcement, repossession, exercise of right etc. An administrator should, however, take care to ensure that his refusal of consent is justifiable, and certainly in practice he should give reasons for his refusing consent, since the guidance set out below indicates that a costs consequence may follow if such consent is unreasonably withheld. In *Re Atlantic Computer Systems plc* [1992] Ch 505 Nicholls LJ, in giving the judgment of the court also comprising Neill and Staughton LJJ, albeit with some reluctance, acceded to an invitation by the parties to give guidance on the principles to be applied on an application for the grant of leave under the former s 11, in the absence of any guidance in the 1986 Act as to when the administrator or the court should allow the moratorium to be lifted in favour of a particular claim. Those principles formed the cornerstone of many subsequent applications in which leave was sought, not only on the issue of leave but also the more subtle question of the imposition of conditions, most commonly the requirement that an administrator makes a rental payment in respect of any particular item as an expense of the administration for the period of its use. There is no reason to suppose that the new administration regime should involve differing principles on the question of leave. What follows therefore is the relevant extract of Nicholls LJ's judgment in full (at 542–544) which concerned claims to repossess computer equipment and enforce the security constituted by the assignment of the benefit of subleases but which should be read as conveying general observations regarding cases where leave is sought to exercise existing proprietary rights, including security rights, against the company in administration:

'(1) It is in every case for the person who seeks leave to make out a case for him to be given leave.

(2) The prohibition in section 11(3)(c) and (d) is intended to assist the company, under the management of the administrator, to achieve the purpose for which the administration order was made. If granting leave to a lessor of land or the hirer of goods (a "lessor") to exercise his proprietary rights and repossess his land or goods is unlikely to impede the achievement of that purpose, leave should normally be given.

(3) In other cases where a lessor seeks possession the court has to carry out a balancing exercise, balancing the legitimate interests of the lessor and the legitimate interests of the other creditors of the company: see *per* Peter Gibson J in *Royal Trust Bank v Buchler* [1989] BCLC 130, 135. The metaphor employed here, for want of a better term, is that of scales and weights. Lord Wilberforce averted to the limitations of this metaphor in *Science Research Council v Nassé* [1980] AC 1028, 1067. It must be kept in mind that the exercise under section 11 is not a mechanical one; each case calls for an exercise in judicial judgment, in which the court seeks to give effect to the purpose of the statutory provisions, having regard to the parties' interests and all the circumstances of the case. As already noted, the purpose of the prohibition is to enable or assist the company to achieve the object for which the administration order was made. The purpose of the power to give leave is to enable the court to relax the prohibition where it would be inequitable for the prohibition to apply.

(4) In carrying out the balancing exercise great importance, or weight, is normally to be given to the proprietary interests of the lessor. Sir Nicholas Browne-Wilkinson V-C observed in *Bristol Airport Plc v Powdrill* [1990] Ch 744, 767D–767E that, so far as possible, the administration procedure should not be used to prejudice those who were secured creditors when the administration order was made in lieu of a winding-up order. The same is true regarding the proprietary interests of a lessor. The underlying principle here is that an administration for the benefit of unsecured creditors should not be conducted at the expense of those who have proprietary rights which they are seeking to exercise, save to the extent that this may be unavoidable and even then this will usually be acceptable only to a strictly limited extent.

(5) Thus it will normally be a sufficient ground for the grant of leave if significant loss would be caused to the lessor by a refusal. For this purpose loss comprises any kind of financial loss, direct or indirect, including loss by reason of delay, and may extend to loss which is not financial. But if substantially greater loss would be caused to others by the grant of leave, or loss which is out of all proportion to the benefit which leave would confer on the lessor, that may outweigh the loss to the lessor caused by a refusal. Our formulation was criticised in the course of the argument, and we certainly do not claim for it the status of a rule in those terms. At present we say only that it appears to us the nearest we can get to a formulation of what Parliament had in mind.

(6) In assessing these respective losses the court will have regard to matters such as the financial position of the company, its ability to pay the rental arrears and the continuing rentals, the administrator's proposals, the period for which the administration order has already been in force and is expected to remain in force, the effect on the administration if leave were given, the effect on the applicant if leave were refused, the end result sought to be achieved by the administration, the prospects of that result being achieved, and the history of the administration so far.

(7) In considering these matters it will often be necessary to assess how probable the suggested consequences are. Thus if loss to the applicant is virtually certain if leave is refused, and loss to others a remote possibility if leave is granted, that will be a powerful factor in favour of granting leave.

(8) This is not an exhaustive list. For example, the conduct of the parties may also be a material consideration in a particular case, as it was in the *Bristol Airport* case. There leave was refused on the ground that the applicants had accepted benefits under the administration, and had only sought to enforce their security at a later stage: indeed, they have only acquired their security as a result of the operations of the administrators. It behoves a lessor to make his position clear to the administrator at the outset of the administration and, if it should become necessary, to apply to the court promptly.

(9) The above considerations may be relevant not only to the decision whether leave should be granted or refused, but also to a decision to impose terms if leave is granted.

(10) The above considerations will also apply to a decision on whether to impose terms as a condition for refusing leave. Section 11(3)(c) and (d) makes no provision for terms being imposed if leave is refused, but the court has power to achieve that result. It may do so directly, by giving directions to the administrator; for instance, under section 17, or in response to an application by the administrator under section 14(3), or in exercise of its control over an administrator as an officer of the court. Or it may do so indirectly, by ordering that the applicant shall have leave unless the administrator is prepared to take this or that step in the conduct of the administration. Cases where leave is refused but terms are imposed can be expected to arise frequently. For example, the permanent loss to a lessor flowing from his inability to recover his property will normally be small if the administrator is required to pay the current rent. In most cases this should be possible, since if the administration order has been rightly made the business should generally be sufficiently viable to hold down current outgoings. Such a term may therefore be a normal term to impose.

(11) The above observations are directed at a case such as the present where a lessor of land or the owner of goods is seeking to repossess his land or goods because of non-payment of rentals. A broadly similar approach will be applicable on many applications to enforce a security: for instance, an application by a mortgagee for possession of land. On such applications an important consideration will often be whether the applicant is fully secured. If he is, delay in enforcement is likely to be less prejudicial than in cases where his security is insufficient.

(12) In some cases there will be a dispute over the existence, validity or nature of the security which the applicant is seeking leave to enforce. It is not for the court on the leave application to seek to adjudicate upon that issue, unless (as in the present case, on the fixed or floating charge point) the issue raises a short point of law which it is convenient to determine without further ado. Otherwise the court needs to be satisfied only that the applicant has a seriously arguable case.'

The authorities demonstrate that the approach to permission turns on both the nature of the claim asserted and the facts of the case. At a general level, however, it can be said that, first, the burden rests on the applicant in demonstrating why the moratorium should be lifted, and, secondly, the burden extends to establishing that the applicant's underlying claim is seriously arguable. The court should not make an order in vain: *Re Algrave Ltd and other companies, Safe Business Solutions Ltd (in liquidation) v Cohen* [2017] EWHC 145 (Ch) at [24] (Chief Registrar Briggs).

Cases for leave to enforce proprietary rights will necessarily turn on their own facts and require the court to identify the relevant facts and to weigh those matters in the balance; for examples see *Re Neesam Investments Ltd* [1988] 4 BCC 788 (fixed charge over office building where charge-holder concerned that amount of debt secured by charge would exceed value of security in course of administration); *Bristol Airport plc v Powdrill* [1990] Ch 744 (court refused leave to airport authorities to exercise statutory right of detention on aircraft under s 88 of the Civil Aviation Act 1982 in respect of airport costs due); *Re David Meek Plant Ltd* [1994] 1 BCLC 680 (leave to possess goods on hire purchase refused to a number of finance companies but granted to two companies which had sought to repossess the day before presentation of the administration petition); *Re Divine Solutions UK Ltd* [2003] EWHC 1931 (Ch), [2004] 1 BCLC 373 (application for leave to proceed with proceedings before employment tribunal dismissed where administration order made for period of only one year and where little evidence adduced by applicant to substantiate claim of unfair dismissal); and *Metro Nominees (Wandsworth) Ltd (No 1) v Rayment* [2008] BCC 40 (permission to enforce terms of lease by proceedings but not immediate physical re-entry notwithstanding service of 'unimpeachable' notice under s 146 of the Law of Property Act 1925 and offer to pay rent by administrators). *Promontoria (Chestnut) Limited v Craig and another* [2017] EWHC 2405 (Ch) involved somewhat unusual facts and a novel para 43 application. A secured creditor which had appointed LPA receivers challenged the decision of joint administrators to remove the receivers the day after the administrators were appointed and to replace them with more expensive property agents. The applicant also sought permission to enforce its security under para 43 by reappointment of the receivers. On the first point HHJ Hodge QC, sitting as a High Court judge, held that the administrators' conduct was unreasonable and improper and was not amenable to a plea of having exercised commercial judgment in good faith. The para 43 issue was also resolved in favour of the applicant following the guidance in *Re UK Housing Alliance (North West) Limited* [2013] BCC 752. The administrators were found to have acted irrationally and were ordered to pay the costs of the application personally without reimbursement as an expense.

Permission to commence a simple money claim, rather than allow an administration to run its course, will be granted only in the most exceptional of cases: *AES Barry Ltd v TXU Europe Energy Trading Ltd* [2005] 2 BCLC 22 at [24] (Patten J). In *Fashoff (UK) Ltd v Linton* [2008] 2 BCLC 362 at [97]–[108] HHJ Toulmin QC, sitting as a High Court judge, held that, in light of the creditor's obligation to act promptly in seeking leave (by virtue of guideline (8) above), a creditor with proprietary rights under a retention of title clause which had delayed by some 8 months in applying to court following an administrator's refusal to consent to the recovery of goods would be refused leave where the creditor's conduct had prevented and continued to prevent a distribution to creditors in the administration.

In *BAE Systems Pension Funds Trustees Ltd v Bowmer and Kirkland Ltd* [2017] EWHC 1222 (TCC) the Technology and Construction Court considered an application for permission to continue proceedings for damages in excess of £10 million and to join the defendant's insurer as co-defendant. O'Farrell J identified at [17] that permission will only be granted in exceptional circumstances where the claim is a monetary claim, as opposed to a proprietary claim, and that the court should consider at what stage the substantive proceedings had reached when the application for permission to continue was made, and in particular whether allowing the action to proceed would significantly impede the objective of the administration by reference to *Magical Marking Ltd v Philips* [2008] FSR 36 at [21]. For that purpose the court has to have regard to the likely commercial judgment of the administrators and the impact that permission would have on unsecured creditors, as well as any delay in making the application. On the facts, the court adjourned the application in order to allow the defendant to carry out a full and proper investigation into its position regarding substantive defences and jurisdiction whilst protecting the claimant from any potential limitation defence by incorporating into the order an undertaking on behalf of the defendant (which had been volunteered) that it agreed not to rely on any limitation defence in any jurisdiction arising out of the adjournment down to determination of the issue.

In *The Funding Corp Block Discounting Ltd v Lexi Holdings plc (in administration)* [2008] 2 BCLC 596 at [5] and [6] Briggs J equated the task of the court under guideline 12 above with that in proceedings against a company not in administration where that company made an application for defendant's summary judgment under CPR Pt 24.

As well as the *Atlantic Computer* guidelines identified above, and in addition to distinguishing between proprietary and monetary claims, relevant factors on permission will usually include the state of the proceedings at the time of any application (on which see *Ronelp Marine Ltd v STX*

*Offshore & Shipbuilding Co Ltd* [2016] EWHC 2228 (Ch) in which Norris J said that 'The nearer the outcome of the proceedings, the greater the weight to be attached to that factor') and conduct on both sides (on which see *X-Fab Semiconductor Foundries AG v Plessey Semiconductors Ltd* [2014] EWHC 3190 in which HHJ Seymour QC, sitting as a High Court judge, took account of the fact that the respondent was 'playing fast and loose with the claimant and this court', and *Re Kornercare Ltd* [2010] EWHC 893 (Ch) in which HHJ Purle QC, sitting as a High Court judge, observed that the issuing of repeated notices of intention to appoint could amount to a potential abuse of process with the consequence that the court could 'act accordingly'). In *South Coast Construction Ltd v Iverson Road Ltd* [2017] EWHC 61 (TCC) Coulson J placed significant weight on the defendant's behaviour in issuing serial notices of intention to appoint so as to trigger repeatedly the interim moratorium, conduct 'which should not be rewarded by the court' (and on which practice see the notes to para 26). Coulson J also granted permission in another money claim application in *Bernard Sport Surfaces Ltd v Astrosoccer4U Ltd* [2017] EWHC 2425 (TCC) where at [29] the judge characterised the case as 'a classic example of two directors endeavouring to use Victorian company legislation to avoid paying a due debt' coupled with the unusual factor of the connivance of the respondent company's solicitors.

If the purpose of administration has been achieved then the court need not carry out the balancing exercise identified above, and no prejudice could be caused by the court granting permission: *Re Algrave Ltd, Safe Business Solutions International Ltd v Cohen* [2017] EWHC 145 (Ch). In *Re Algrave* Chief Registrar Briggs observed that Briggs J in *Lazari v Jervis* [2012] EWHC 1466 had had no difficulty in lifting the moratorium so that a landlord could re-enter as the purpose of administration had been achieved at the time a pre-pack sale had been completed such that, strictly speaking, there was no need to engage in the balancing exercise required as the administrators had not identified any prejudice to the administration if permission to forfeit were to be granted, in addition to which the landlords were able to demonstrate that they would lose the opportunity to secure a new lease for a higher rent if permission were not granted.

**Creditor and third party self-help remedies which are not protected against by the statutory moratorium in administration**—Nothing within the moratorium provisions suggests that the statutory protection afforded to a debtor is intended as depriving a creditor or third party from utilising any self-help remedies against the debtor company, even where the effect of such remedies is harmful to the financial interests or standing of the company in administration.

These self-help remedies would include repudiation for breach of contract, service of a contractual notice (such as one making time of the essence, as in *Re Olympia & York Canary Wharf Ltd* [1993] BCLC 453 (Millett J) or forfeiture (though not by peaceable re-entry) of a lease. Neither would the protection of the moratorium appear to catch a combination of accounts, most obviously by a bank or trading customer, or an application for an extension of time for the registration of a charge over the company's property, as in *Re Barrow Borough Transport Ltd* [1990] Ch 227. It is suggested that the filing and service of a defence to a claim commenced by a company under the protection of the moratorium would amount to the legitimate exercise of a self-help remedy, whereas the filing and service of a counterclaim with the defence would contravene para 43(6), but not to the extent that the counterclaim was relied on solely for the purpose of a defence by way of set-off, on which see CPR 16.6.

Since the exercise of a right of set-off cannot be characterised as constituting proceedings, execution or other legal process, such a right – whether legal equitable, contractual or otherwise – will, other than where the set-off falls within the scope of r 14.24, remain available to a third party, for which proposition see *Electromagnetic (S) Ltd v Development Bank of Singapore* [1994] SLR 734, a decision of the High Court of Singapore in which jurisdiction the administration regime had been modelled on the former English provisions in Part II.

It would follow that the service of a demand, say for the return of goods, constitutes no more than self-help and will not fall within the scope of para 43(6) (on which see *Barclays Mercantile Business Finance Ltd v Sibec Developments Ltd* [1992] 1 WLR 1253), although it is arguable that the position is different where the service of such a demand or other notice is a contractual pre-condition for the taking of any step protected against by s 43(2)–(6A), on which see *Re Olympia & York Canary Wharf Ltd* [1993] BCLC 453 at 454G–454H. The service of a statutory demand, however, constitutes a 'legal process': *Fulton v AIB Group (UK) plc* [2014] NI Ch 8, [2014] BPIR 1169.

**'transaction'**—See the very broad and non-exhaustive definition in s 436 which identifies a 'transaction' as extending to something less than contractual agreement.

## [1.661]

### 44 Interim moratorium

(1) This paragraph applies where an administration application in respect of a company has been made and—

     (a)     the application has not yet been granted or dismissed, or

    (b)    the application has been granted but the administration order has not yet taken effect.

(2)   This paragraph also applies from the time when a copy of notice of intention to appoint an administrator under paragraph 14 is filed with the court until—

    (a)    the appointment of the administrator takes effect, or

    (b)    the period of five business days beginning with the date of filing expires without an administrator having been appointed.

(3)   Sub-paragraph (2) has effect in relation to a notice of intention to appoint only if it is in the prescribed form.

(4)   This paragraph also applies from the time when a copy of notice of intention to appoint an administrator is filed with the court under paragraph 27(1) until—

    (a)    the appointment of the administrator takes effect, or

    (b)    the period specified in paragraph 28(2) expires without an administrator having been appointed.

(5)   The provisions of paragraphs 42 and 43 shall apply (ignoring any reference to the consent of the administrator).

(6)   If there is an administrative receiver of the company when the administration application is made, the provisions of paragraphs 42 and 43 shall not begin to apply by virtue of this paragraph until the person by or on behalf of whom the receiver was appointed consents to the making of the administration order.

(7)   This paragraph does not prevent or require the permission of the court for—

    (a)    the presentation of a petition for the winding up of the company under a provision mentioned in paragraph 42(4),

    (b)    the appointment of an administrator under paragraph 14,

    (c)    the appointment of an administrative receiver of the company, or

    (d)    the carrying out by an administrative receiver (whenever appointed) of his functions.

**General note**—The interim moratorium, which is provided for in all court and out-of-court appointments, is very similar in substance to, but quite distinct from, the moratorium protection in paras 42 and 43 which is triggered only on a company being 'in administration'.

**The period for which the interim moratorium takes effect**—In the case of an administration application the interim protection is triggered once the application 'has been made': para 44(1). In the absence of any express stipulation for the filing of the application and all supporting documents, the interim moratorium protection is obtained automatically at the moment at which the application itself is filed with the court. In certain cases it might be thought appropriate to give notice and provide evidence of the operation of the moratorium to a pressing creditor.

In the case of an out-of-court appointment under paras 14 or 22 the interim moratorium is obtained from the time at which a copy of the notice of intention to appoint is filed with the court.

In the case of an administration application the interim moratorium endures until the application has been dismissed or, alternatively, until an administration order is made, in which case there is a seamless triggering of the moratorium under paras 42 and 43. As a further alternative, the interim moratorium will continue under para 44(1) where the court has made an interim order under para 13(1)(d) or some other order under para 13(1)(f) which accedes to the application but which amounts in substance to something less than the making of an administration order: see the notes to para 13(1).

In a para 14 case the interim protection will automatically end after the 5 business days period stipulated in para 44(2)(b) in the absence of an appointment having been effected. The same rule applies in a para 22 case in which the relevant period is 10 business days: see the reference to para 28(2) in para 44(4)(b).

If no person is entitled to service of a notice of intention to appoint under para 15(1) (in a para 14 case) or under para 26(1) (in a para 22 case) then, subject to compliance with the pre-conditions applicable to either case, the holder of a qualifying floating charge, or the company or its directors, may proceed to an immediate appointment so as to render the interim moratorium irrelevant.

### PARAGRAPH 44(5)–(7)

**The protective nature of the interim moratorium**—The effect of para 44(5) is, in effect, to replicate paras 42 and 43 for the purpose of defining the scope of the interim moratorium save, of course, that there will be no administrator in office who might consent to those steps otherwise prevented by paras 43(2)–(6). One effect of the application of paras 42 and 43 is that, during the period of the interim moratorium, the court may give permission for what is termed 'a transaction' which would otherwise be prohibited by para 43, subject to any condition or other requirement which the court might impose.

Paragraph 44(6) only applies where an administrative receiver is in office at the time of the making of an administration order, although the provision has no application in a para 14 or para 22 case. Save where the court thinks the security pursuant to which an administrative receiver has been appointed is susceptible under the statutory provisions identified in para 39(1)(b)–(d) the court may not make an administration order where an administrative receiver is in office other than in the scenario where the receiver's appointor consents to the making of an administration order under para 39(1)(a). In the absence of such consent the interim moratorium, by way of its application of paras 42 and 43, has no application. Even where such consent is given, para 44(7)(d) allows for the continued carrying out by the administrative receiver of his functions pending the making of an administration order.

In contrast with the prohibitions imposed by para 43, para 44(7) allows for the presentation of a winding-up petition – but not the making of a winding-up order – on the grounds in para 42(4), the appointment of an administrator by the holder of a qualifying floating charge under para 14, the appointment of an administrative receiver and the carrying out by an administrative receiver of his or her functions.

## [1.662]

### 45 Publicity

(1)   While a company is in administration, every business document issued by or on behalf of the company or the administrator, and all the company's websites, must state—

    (a)    the name of the administrator, and

    (b)    that the affairs, business and property of the company are being managed by the administrator.

(2)   Any of the following persons commits an offence if without reasonable excuse the person authorises or permits a contravention of sub-paragraph (1)—

    (a)    the administrator,

    (b)    an officer of the company, and

    (c)    the company.

(3)   In sub-paragraph (1) "'business document" means—

    (a)    an invoice,

    (b)    an order for goods or services,

    (c)    a business letter, and

    (d)    an order form,

whether in hard copy, electronic or any other form.

**Amendments**—Substituted by SI 2008/1897.

**General note**—The substance of these publicity requirements is common to those under the former administration regime under s 12, receivership under s 39 and liquidation under s 188.

It is common practice and advisable for an administrator to include on all business documents an express statement to the effect that the administrator contracts as agent of the company only and without personal liability, notwithstanding the fact that a provision to that effect appears in any case in para 69.

### PROCESS OF ADMINISTRATION

## [1.663]

### 46 Announcement of administrator's appointment

(1)   This paragraph applies where a person becomes the administrator of a company.

(2)   As soon as is reasonably practicable the administrator shall—

    (a)    send a notice of his appointment to the company, and

    (b)    publish a notice of his appointment in the prescribed manner.

(3)   As soon as is reasonably practicable the administrator shall—

    (a)    obtain a list of the company's creditors, and

(b)     send a notice of his appointment to each creditor of whose claim and address he is aware.

(4)  The administrator shall send a notice of his appointment to the registrar of companies before the end of the period of 7 days beginning with the date specified in sub-paragraph (6).

(5)  The administrator shall send a notice of his appointment to such persons as may be prescribed before the end of the prescribed period beginning with the date specified in sub-paragraph (6).

(6)  The date for the purpose of sub-paragraphs (4) and (5) is—

    (a)     in the case of an administrator appointed by administration order, the date of the order,

    (b)     in the case of an administrator appointed under paragraph 14, the date on which he receives notice under paragraph 20, and

    (c)     in the case of an administrator appointed under paragraph 22, the date on which he receives notice under paragraph 32.

(7)  The court may direct that sub-paragraph (3)(b) or (5)—

    (a)     shall not apply, or

    (b)     shall apply with the substitution of a different period.

(8)  A notice under this paragraph must—

    (a)     contain the prescribed information, and

    (b)     be in the prescribed form.

(9)  An administrator commits an offence if he fails without reasonable excuse to comply with a requirement of this paragraph.

**General note**—This provision, as with paras 47 and 48, applies to all administrations and provides the procedural steps by which the process of administration is commenced.

Although the rules here are administrative in nature, they are nonetheless of practical importance so far as concerns the giving of notice to third parties such that non-compliance without reasonable excuse constitutes an offence under para 46(9). In *Re All Leisure Holidays Ltd (in administration)* [2017] EWHC 870 (Ch), [2017] BCC 354, HHJ Purle QC, sitting as a High Court judge, adopted the approach he had taken previously in *Re Advent Computer Trading* [2010] EWHC 459 (Ch) in permitting a single notice to all creditors, together with a link to relevant documents, without the need for the sending out of all notices to all customers separately on the ground of unnecessary and wasteful cost. *All Leisure* was concerned with the former provisions in IR 1986, rr 12A.10–12.A.13: see now IR 2016, rr 1.45–1.53 and, in particular, the deemed consent to electronic delivery in r 1.45(4). The broad approach in *Advent Computer* and *All Leisure* is likely to continue in cases concerning the new provisions.

In *Re Advent Computer Training Ltd* [2010] EWHC 1042 (Ch) it was held that notice of appointment and statement of proposals could be sent to creditors by e-mail. The earlier decision in *Re Sporting Options plc* [2005] BPIR 435 (in which Mann J was not prepared to direct that those documents be sent by e-mail to the creditors of a company which carried on a gaming business on the internet and where confirmation of bets (but not the placing of bets) was notified by e-mail) was distinguished on its facts, the court noting that e-mail communication had moved on in the 5 years since that decision.

## [1.664]

### 47 Statement of company's affairs

(1)  As soon as is reasonably practicable after appointment the administrator of a company shall by notice in the prescribed form require one or more relevant persons to provide the administrator with a statement of the affairs of the company.

(2)  The statement must—

    (a)     be verified by a statement of truth in accordance with Civil Procedure Rules,

    (b)     be in the prescribed form,

    (c)     give particulars of the company's property, debts and liabilities,

    (d)     give the names and addresses of the company's creditors,

    (e)     specify the security held by each creditor,

    (f)     give the date on which each security was granted, and

    (g)     contain such other information as may be prescribed.

(3)   In sub-paragraph (1) "relevant person" means—
- (a)   a person who is or has been an officer of the company,
- (b)   a person who took part in the formation of the company during the period of one year ending with the date on which the company enters administration,
- (c)   a person employed by the company during that period, and
- (d)   a person who is or has been during that period an officer or employee of a company which is or has been during that year an officer of the company.

(4)   For the purpose of sub-paragraph (3) a reference to employment is a reference to employment through a contract of employment or a contract for services.

(5)   In Scotland, a statement of affairs under sub-paragraph (1) must be a statutory declaration made in accordance with the Statutory Declarations Act 1835 (and sub-paragraph (2)(a) shall not apply).

**General note**—This provision applies in all administrations.

The statement of affairs is a key document, which will be of fundamental importance to the formulation of the administrator's proposals for para 49 purposes. In producing the statement, the 'relevant persons' (see below), and those advising them, should bear in mind that the statement must be verified by a statement of truth (compliant with Part 22 of the CPR).

In practice, an administrator will frequently have had some insight prior to appointment into those matters set out in the statement of affairs. The veracity of what is presented to the office-holder should not in any case be taken at face value without consideration or relevant and obvious inquiry. Neither should the administrator be accepting of any reticence on the part of any relevant person in producing or submitting the statement of affairs, given the statutory obligation to do so under paras 47 and 48. An administrator has specific standing under r 12.52(2)(a) to make application to court for an order enforcing para 47 together with an order for costs. Failure to comply with a requirement by an administrator under para 47(1) constitutes an offence under para 48(4), on which see s 430, Sch 10 and the daily default fine under para 106(2)(d).

**PARAGRAPH 47(2)**

**Scope of provision**—The statement of affairs shall be in the prescribed form. A statement of concurrence may be considered appropriate where, for example, the administrator has doubts or concerns as to the information set out in the statement of affairs where the individual from whom the statement of concurrence is required is properly able, given the information to which that individual has access or the level of knowledge attributed to that individual, to concur or otherwise comment on the contents of the statement of affairs.

'relevant person'—For the scope of the term 'officer' in para 47(3)(a) see the definition in s 1121 of the Companies Act 2006 which extends to a director, manager or secretary of the company, and see also the notes to s 206(3). The reference in para 47(4) to a contract for services means that, subject to evidence of such a contract, those providing services to the company, most obviously its solicitors, accountants or auditors, might be called on to submit a statement of affairs or a statement of concurrence. Such requests are, however, very rare in practice.

## [1.665]

**48**

(1)   A person required to submit a statement of affairs must do so before the end of the period of 11 days beginning with the day on which he receives notice of the requirement.

(2)   The administrator may—
- (a)   revoke a requirement under paragraph 47(1), or
- (b)   extend the period specified in sub-paragraph (1) (whether before or after expiry).

(3)   If the administrator refuses a request to act under sub-paragraph (2)—
- (a)   the person whose request is refused may apply to the court, and
- (b)   the court may take action of a kind specified in sub-paragraph (2).

(4)   A person commits an offence if he fails without reasonable excuse to comply with a requirement under paragraph 47(1).

**General note**—This provision applies in all administrations.

The standing of a person to apply to court under para 48(3) is conditional on the administrator refusing a request to act under para 48(2).

**Procedure**—A release from duty to submit a statement of affairs might be granted or be sought by a relevant person in the event of genuine illness and disability or, possibly, say, through a prolonged and unavoidable absence overseas which precludes access to the company's books and records.

## [1.666]

### 49 Administrator's proposals

(1)   The administrator of a company shall make a statement setting out proposals for achieving the purpose of administration.

(2)   A statement under sub-paragraph (1) must, in particular—

    (a)    deal with such matters as may be prescribed, and

    (b)    where applicable, explain why the administrator thinks that the objective mentioned in paragraph 3(1)(a) or (b) cannot be achieved.

(3)   Proposals under this paragraph may include—

    (a)    a proposal for a voluntary arrangement under Part I of this Act (although this paragraph is without prejudice to section 4(3));

    (b)    a proposal for a compromise or arrangement to be sanctioned under Part 26 or 26A of the Companies Act 2006 (arrangements and reconstructions).

(4)   The administrator shall send a copy of the statement of his proposals—

    (a)    to the registrar of companies,

    (b)    to every creditor of the company, other than an opted-out creditor, of whose claim and address he is aware, and

    (c)    to every member of the company of whose address he is aware.

(5)   The administrator shall comply with sub-paragraph (4)—

    (a)    as soon as is reasonably practicable after the company enters administration, and

    (b)    in any event, before the end of the period of eight weeks beginning with the day on which the company enters administration.

(6)   The administrator shall be taken to comply with sub-paragraph (4)(c) if he publishes in the prescribed manner a notice undertaking to provide a copy of the statement of proposals free of charge to any member of the company who applies in writing to a specified address.

(7)   An administrator commits an offence if he fails without reasonable excuse to comply with sub-paragraph (5).

(8)   A period specified in this paragraph may be varied in accordance with paragraph 107.

**Amendments**—SI 2008/948; Small Business, Enterprise and Employment Act 2015, s 126, Sch 9, Pt 1, paras 1, 10; Corporate Insolvency and Governance Act 2020, s 7, Sch 9, Pt 2, paras 5, 7(1), (2).

**General note**—The statement of the administrator's proposals is produced for consideration by creditors at the initial creditors' meeting under para 51 or para 52(2).

In *Re Advent Computer Training Ltd* [2010] EWHC 459 (Ch) HHJ Purle QC (sitting as a High Court judge) held that notice of appointment and statement of proposals could be sent to creditors by e-mail. The earlier decision in *Re Sporting Options plc* [2005] BPIR 435 (in which Mann J was not prepared to direct that those documents be sent by e-mail to the creditors of a company which carried on a gaming business on the internet and where confirmation of bets (but not the placing of bets) was notified by e-mail) was distinguished on its facts, the court noting that e-mail communication had moved on in the 5 years since that decision.

The court has power to dispense with the obligations under paras 49 and 51 if the circumstances justify. Where the company was about to enter creditors' voluntary liquidation with the consequence that the company would no longer be in administration by the time of the envisaged meeting of creditors, it was appropriate to dispense with those requirements: *In the matter of UK Coal Operations Ltd* [2013] EWHC 2581 (Ch).

#### PARAGRAPH 49(2)

**The altered approach under Sch B1 to the formulation of the administrator's proposals**—The former Part II made no specific stipulation as to the contents of the statement of an administrator's proposals under s 23(1). Rule 3.35, formerly IR 1986, r 2.33(2), read together with para 49(2) and the scope of that provision as identified above, represents a marked shift from that position. Under the former law it was not uncommon, particularly in the case of an administration instituted hastily, to find that an administrator's proposals were cast in the most general of terms, which would often not extend beyond proposing that creditors simply approve the continued management of the affairs of the company for the purpose or purposes for which the order was granted and that the administrator be authorised to market or sell the assets of the company on receiving a suitable offer, together with equally general proposals as to reporting to creditors. That former practice, it is submitted, is inconsistent with the new provisions which, amongst other specific matters, impose a positive duty on the administrator under r 3.35(1)(j)(i) to set out how it is envisaged that the purpose of the administration will be achieved and how it is proposed, in specific terms, that the administration shall end. On the other hand, it is, in practical terms, something of a counsel of perfection to expect that all administrators in all cases will be in a position to map out with unfailing accuracy how the conduct of the administration is to evolve. This necessitates some sense of commercial balance. What should be expected, it is submitted, is the administrator's best assessment of the way forward. It should also be borne in mind here that, despite the requirement for a relative degree of precision, para 54(1) specifically allows for the revision of an administrator's proposals but does not apparently require creditors' approval for such revision other than where, as para 54(1)(c) provides, 'the administrator thinks that the proposed revision is substantial'. This point is discussed further in the notes to para 52.

The administrator's proposals will, of necessity, have to take into account the purpose of administration in para 3(1). In particular, para 49(2)(b) reinforces the point made in the commentary to para 3(1) to the effect that the administrator must be able to present cogent and objectively sound reasons as to why the sub-purposes in either para 3(1)(a) and/or (b) cannot be achieved. The importance of this requirement was emphasised Snowden J in *Davey v Money* [2018] EWHC 766 (Ch) at [316]-[324]. An explicit explanation for a decision not to pursue the objectives in para 3(1)(a) or (b) is required. Snowden J was critical of the administrators' statement in that case, although the defects did not invalidate the actions of the administrators altogether.

**Further limitations on the administrator's proposals**—Paragraph 73(1) provides that an administrator's statement of proposals – which, by virtue of para 73(3), includes a revised or modified statement – may not include any action which affects the right of a secured creditor of the company to enforce its security, would result in a preferential debt being paid otherwise than in priority to a non-preferential debt, or would result in one preferential creditor being paid a smaller proportion of his or her debt than another. Those limitations do not apply in the circumstances set out in para 73(2), namely where the relevant secured creditor consents in the case of a CVA under Part 1 (subject, again, to the relevant secured creditor consenting to any variation of secured rights) or on a proposal for sanction for a compromise or arrangement under Part 26 or Part 26A (restructuring plan) of the Companies Act 2006.

### PARAGRAPH 49(3)

**Proposals including a CVA proposal or a proposal under Part 26 or Part 26A of the Companies Act 2006**—A CVA or a scheme of arrangement will commonly provide the mechanism by which an administrator seeks to rescue a company as a going concern by way of creditors agreeing to accept less than full payment of their debts. In the case of a CVA, s 4(3) protects the right of a secured creditor to enforce the security other than where the creditor consents to any variation of such rights. In the case of a scheme of arrangement or restructuring plan, the protection of secured (and preferential) rights will be achieved by the obligation under ss 895–901 of the Companies Act 2006 and the restructuring plan provisions in Part 26A of the 2006 Act respectively to place such creditors in a separate class or classes for voting purposes.

**The sending out of copies of the administrator's statement of proposals**—In keeping with the increased emphasis in Sch B1 on administration being as speedy a process as practicably possible, para 49(5) should be read as imposing a requirement for compliance 'as soon as is reasonably practicable'. The period of 8 weeks mentioned in para 49(5)(b) is not to be read as the ordinary rule in all cases and, indeed, is only relevant if it is not reasonably practicable to send out the statement within that period. Paragraph 107 allows for the extension of the 8-week time period by the court on the application of the administrator, more than once and retrospectively, although the court will ordinarily require a clear explanation in evidence as to the reasons for any such application being made to it. An extension is also possible with the consent of creditors under para 108, albeit in more limited circumstances. In the event of a time extension for para 49(5) purposes the administrator must notify all those persons set out in para 49(4) as soon as reasonably practicable.

**Paragraph 49(7) penalties**—See s 430, Sch 10 and the daily default fine in para 106(2)(e).

### 50

*(Repealed)*

**[1.667]**

### 51 Consideration of administrator's proposals by creditors

(1)  The administrator must seek a decision from the company's creditors as to whether they approve the proposals set out in the statement made under paragraph 49(1).

(2)  The initial decision date for that decision must be within the period of 10 weeks beginning with the day on which the company enters administration.

(3)  The "initial decision date" for that decision—

    (a)    if the decision is initially sought using the deemed consent procedure, is the date on which a decision will be made if the creditors by that procedure approve the proposals, and

    (b)    if the decision is initially sought using a qualifying decision procedure, is the date on or before which a decision will be made if it is made by that qualifying decision procedure (assuming that date does not change after the procedure is instigated).

(4)  A period specified in this paragraph may be varied in accordance with paragraph 107.

(5)  An administrator commits an offence if he fails without reasonable excuse to comply with a requirement of this paragraph.

**Amendments**—Small Business, Enterprise and Employment Act 2015, s 126, Sch 9, Pt 1, paras 1, 10.

**General note**—Paragraph 53(1) provides that the business of what is defined here as the 'initial creditors' meeting' is the approval or rejection by creditors of the administrator's proposals or, alternatively, approval of the proposals with modifications to which the administrator consents. Literally construed, para 53(1) does not actually provide for the rejection of proposals, although para 55(1)(a) plainly envisages such rejection or, rather, as it is put, a failure to approve, which must be read into para 53(1).

It is not possible for the creditors to approve modifications upon which they insist but to which the administrator is not prepared to give consent.

**Options where the administrator's proposals are not approved**—If the administrator's proposals are not approved at the initial meeting, then the administrator must report the matter to the court (and others) under para 53(2) and may then proceed in one of four ways. If the administrator considers that approval might be obtained to revised proposals then, consequent on para 55(1)(a), he or she might invite the court to direct the summoning of a further creditors' meeting under para 55(2)(e) (or para 56(1)(b)), together with appropriate consequential provisions which, it is suggested, would include a direction consistent with para 49 for the circulation of the revised proposals. Alternatively, the administrator might invite the court to make an order under para 55(2)(a) terminating the appointment with any other appropriate order within the scope of para 55(2)(b)–(e). The administrator's third alternative is to proceed without the court's involvement where he considers that revised proposals are capable of obtaining approval.

**Cases in which there is no requirement for an initial creditors' meeting**—Whilst mandatory in all other cases, an administrator may dispense with an initial creditors' meeting where he intends to apply to the court or file a notice under para 80(2) for the administration to cease at a time before he has sent a statement of his proposals to creditors. Neither will the obligation to convene the initial meeting arise where the administrator sends a notice under para 84(1) to the Registrar of Companies, with the consequence that the company moves from administration to dissolution under that provision. Furthermore, no initial meeting is required where the administrator's statement of proposals fulfils the criteria in para 52(1) other than where at least 10% of the creditors request the summoning of such a meeting under para 52(2).

**Time limit for the initial creditors' meeting**—The 10-week period referred to in para 51(2)(b) refers to the date of the meeting itself, and not the date by which the administrator's proposals are to be sent to creditors. Furthermore, para 51(2)(a) raises a rebuttable presumption that it will be reasonably practicable in all cases to hold the initial meeting within 10 weeks. Very often it will be reasonably practicable to hold the meeting sooner, and sometimes very much sooner.

Paragraphs 107 and 108 allow for the extension of the 10-week period by the court or creditors, subject to the limitations therein.

**Is it possible to hold a 'further creditors' meeting' prior to an 'initial creditors' meeting'?**—The limit on the scope of the business conducted at the initial creditors' meeting as imposed by para 53(1) is predicated upon the assumption that a first meeting of creditors will only ever be required to consider the administrator's proposals. Whilst in practice this is usually the case, there is no good reason why in appropriate circumstances a meeting should not be summoned if requested or directed under para 56(1) (despite that provision being headed 'Further creditors' meetings') or by the administrator himself or herself under para 62 prior to the initial creditors' meeting. This might arise in a case of urgency or one in which the weighing up of creditors' views at an early stage and on a formal basis is deemed necessary by the administrator to assess the viability of the administration.

**Penalties**—On penalties see s 430, Sch 10 and the daily default fine provided for in para 106(2)(f).

## [1.668]

**52**

(1)   Paragraph 51(1) shall not apply where the statement of proposals states that the administrator thinks—

>   (a)     that the company has sufficient property to enable each creditor of the company to be paid in full,

>   (b)     that the company has insufficient property to enable a distribution to be made to unsecured creditors other than by virtue of section 176A(2)(a), or

>   (c)     that neither of the objectives specified in paragraph 3(1)(a) and (b) can be achieved.

(2)   But the administrator shall seek a decision from the company's creditors as to whether they approve the proposals set out in the statement made under paragraph 49(1) if requested to do so—

>   (a)     by creditors of the company whose debts amount to at least 10% of the total debts of the company,

>   (b)     in the prescribed manner, and

>   (c)     in the prescribed period.

(3)   Where a decision is sought by virtue of sub-paragraph (2) the initial decision date (as defined in paragraph 51(3)) must be within the prescribed period.

(4)   The period prescribed under sub-paragraph (3) may be varied in accordance with paragraph 107.

**Amendments**—Small Business, Enterprise and Employment Act 2015, s 126, Sch 9, Pt 1, paras 1, 10.

**General note**—The obligation requiring an administrator's statement of proposals to be accompanied by an invitation to an initial creditors' meeting under para 51(1) does not apply if the statement of proposals states that the administrator thinks that any of the three circumstances in para 52(1) arises, since unsecured creditors will, in such a case, have no financial interest in the administration. Where an administrator pursues the purpose in para 3(1)(c) but there is a possibility that unsecured creditors may nevertheless receive a distribution as a consequence, para 52(1)(c) remains effective: *Re Taylor Pearson (Construction) Ltd (in administration)* [2020] EWHC 2933 (Ch), [2021] 1 BCLC 725 at [83]–[84] (HHJ Davis-White QC sitting as a High Court judge).

Paragraph 52(2)(d) was inserted by para 2, as amended, of the Schedule to the Financial Services and Markets Act 2000 (Administration Orders Relating to Insurers) Order 2000 (SI 2002/1242).

Where proposals are not approved see r 3.38 and *Re Taylor Pearson (Construction) Ltd (in administration)* [2020] EWHC 2933 (Ch), [2021] BCLC 725 (HHJ Davis-White QC).

## [1.669]

### 53 Creditors' decision

(1)   The company's creditors may approve the administrator's proposals—

>   (a)     without modification, or

>   (b)     with modification to which the administrator consents.

(2)   The administrator shall as soon as is reasonably practicable report any decision taken by the company's creditors to—

>   (a)     the court,

>   (b)     the registrar of companies, and

>   (c)     such other persons as may be prescribed.

(3)   An administrator commits an offence if he fails without reasonable excuse to comply with sub-paragraph (2).

**Amendments**—Small Business, Enterprise and Employment Act 2015, s 126, Sch 9, Pt 1, paras 1, 10.

**General note**—The formal business of the initial creditors' meeting is restricted in scope by para 53(1). In addition to considering and approving the proposals, subject to any modifications to which the administrator consents, the meeting might also vote so as to reject the proposals, a point implicit in para 55(1). In practice, the initial creditors' meeting is also the most likely forum for argument, debate and the expression of views upon which the administrator might form a view as to the possibility and nature of any revisions to his or her proposals or even an adjournment of the meeting under IR 2016, r 15.23(2).

The approval of the administrator's proposals binds the administrator to them by virtue of para 68(1), subject to para 68(2).

**The report of 'any decision' under para 53(2)**—In addition to the court and the Registrar of Companies the persons prescribed for para 53(2)(c) purposes are those creditors identified in r 3.41.

There will not be 'any decision' to report under para 53(2) where the creditors' meeting is adjourned without a resolution approving or rejecting the proposals, although a reportable decision will have been made if the adjournment is granted on the basis of a resolution of the meeting. If the meeting is adjourned by the chairman without any resolution then, other than where the adjournment is for a very short period, or one which is so short as to preclude effective notice being given by post, the administrator may wish to consider giving notice to creditors in any case since, although there is technically not 'any decision' to report, creditors may have legitimate grounds for complaint if they are not notified of the fact of the adjournment, and possibly the circumstances giving rise to it.

**PARAGRAPH 53(2)**

**Scope of provision**—The Financial Services Authority is also entitled to notice in an appropriate case by virtue of s 362(3) of the Financial Services and Markets Act 2000.

**Penalties**—See s 430, Sch 10 and the daily default fine in para 106(2)(g).

## [1.670]

### 54 Revision of administrator's proposals

(1)    This paragraph applies where—

    (a)    an administrator's proposals have been approved (with or without modification) by the company's creditors,

    (b)    the administrator proposes a revision to the proposals, and

    (c)    the administrator thinks that the proposed revision is substantial.

(2)    The administrator shall—

    (a)    . . .

    (b)    send a statement in the prescribed form of the proposed revision to each creditor who is not an opted-out creditor,

    (c)    send a copy of the statement, within the prescribed period, to each member of the company of whose address he is aware, and

    (d)    seek a decision from the company's creditors as to whether they approve the proposed revision.

(3)    The administrator shall be taken to have complied with sub-paragraph (2)(c) if he publishes a notice undertaking to provide a copy of the statement free of charge to any member of the company who applies in writing to a specified address.

(4)    A notice under sub-paragraph (3) must be published—

    (a)    in the prescribed manner, and

    (b)    within the prescribed period.

(5)    The company's creditors may approve the proposed revision—

    (a)    without modification, or

    (b)    with modification to which the administrator consents.

(6)    The administrator shall as soon as is reasonably practicable report any decision taken by the company's creditors to—

    (a)    the court,

    (b)    the registrar of companies, and

    (c)    such other persons as may be prescribed.

(7) An administrator commits an offence if he fails without reasonable excuse to comply with sub-paragraph (6).

**Amendments**—Small Business, Enterprise and Employment Act 2015, s 126, Sch 9, Pt 1, paras 1, 10.

**General note**—This provision only operates where the administrator's proposals have been approved, with or without modification, at an initial creditors' meeting and the administrator proposes a revision to the proposals and 'thinks' – a term discussed in the notes to para 3(3) – that the proposed revision is substantial. Once that view is formed the procedure in para 54(2)–(6) is triggered.

The approval of revised proposals, or the insubstantial revision of proposals, binds the administrator by virtue of para 68(1), subject to para 68(2).

' . . . **the proposed revision is substantial**'—What is 'substantial' will inevitably vary from case to case. However, since insolvency procedures, and certainly administration, are mechanisms in which creditor interests are central, and given that those interests are essentially measured in financial terms, it is submitted that a revision will be 'substantial' if, measured in financial terms, the likely consequence for creditors generally would be regarded by an honest and reasonable hypothetical creditor as being substantial. Alternatively, a revision might be regarded as substantial if the methodology or strategy to be employed in the conduct of the administration differs significantly from that originally approved, even where the likely outcome for creditors in financial terms is no different or not substantially different from that contained in the original proposal.

**Alternatives to the para 54 procedure**—The timescales involved in the convening of a meeting under para 54 may render that procedure unworkable in a time-critical or urgent case. In those circumstances it is open to the administrator to make an application to court for directions sanctioning the proposed revision under para 68(2) on the grounds set out in para 68(3)(c). Alternatively, approved proposals now frequently contain a standard-form provision which, as approved at the initial creditors' meeting, allows the administrator to implement revisions either at his own discretion or, for example, with the permission of any creditors' committee, a practice approved of by Neuberger J in *Re Dana (UK) Ltd* [1999] 2 BCLC 239.

**Revisions in a para 52 case**—Where the administrator's proposals contain a statement in accordance with any of the three grounds in para 52(1), then there is no requirement for an initial creditors' meeting to consider the proposals under paras 51 and 53 unless at least 10% in value of the creditors of the company request such a meeting under para 52(2). If no such initial meeting is requested, then the administration simply proceeds in accordance with the administrator's statement of proposals. If the administrator then proposes a substantial revision to those proposals, the mechanism in para 54(2)–(6) and rr 3.41, 3.42 and 3.43 would not appear to trigger since there could not be said to have been administrator's proposals which had been 'approved (with or without modification) at an initial creditors' meeting' for the purposes of para 54(1)(a). This is unlikely to be problematic where the original proposals contained a statement for the purposes of either para 52(1)(b) or (c) since in neither case would unsecured creditors have had any legitimate expectation of financial participation in the administration. A difficulty might arise in a para 52(1)(a) case where the original proposals anticipated all creditors being paid in full but where, on account of the revision to the proposals, unsecured creditors are to receive less, even substantially less, than payment in full. It would be odd indeed if in those circumstances the administrator was not under any obligation to seek the approval of unsecured creditors. In the event of a proposed substantial revision to proposals in a para 52(1)(a) case the administrator should either convene a meeting of creditors of his own volition under para 62 or, at the very least, in keeping with the approach apparent in para 52(2), notify creditors of the position and propose summoning a creditors' meeting should at least 10% in value of creditors so request.

**PARAGRAPH 54(6)**

**Scope of provision**—The Financial Services Authority is also entitled to notice in an appropriate case by virtue of s 362(3) of the Financial Services and Markets Act 2000.

**[1.671]**

### 55 Failure to obtain approval of administrator's proposals

(1) This paragraph applies where an administrator—

    (a) reports to the court under paragraph 53 that a company's creditors have failed to approve the administrator's proposals, or

    (b) reports to the court under paragraph 54 that a company's creditors have failed to approve a revision of the administrator's proposals.

(2) The court may—

    (a) provide that the appointment of an administrator shall cease to have effect from a specified time;

(b)     adjourn the hearing conditionally or unconditionally;

(c)     make an interim order;

(d)     make an order on a petition for winding up suspended by virtue of paragraph 40(1)(b);

(e)     make any other order (including an order making consequential provision) that the court thinks appropriate.

**Amendments**—Small Business, Enterprise and Employment Act 2015, s 126, Sch 9, Pt 1, paras 1, 10(17).

**General note**—This provision applies where the administrator's report to the court under para 53(2)(a) or para 54(6)(a) confirms those matters in para 55(1)(a) and (b) respectively. No report will be necessary in the event of an adjournment of any creditors' meeting at which no decision is made as to the administrator's proposals or revised proposals.

In *Re BTR (UK) Ltd; Lavin v Swindell* [2012] EWHC 2398 (Ch), [2012] BCC 864, HHJ Behrens (sitting as a High Court judge) held that it was implicit from the language of para 55(2) that where para 55(1) applies an application must be made to the court for directions. That application should ordinarily be made by the administrator, but if he does not make the application, it can be made by a creditor. In *Lavin* the judge made a winding-up order. For a case in which Judge Behrens made an order placing the company into CVL where the administrators' proposals had been rejected, and where the administrators would not agree the capping of their fees and pre-administration costs at £75,000, see *Re Pudsey Steel Services Ltd* [2015] BPIR 1459. In *Pudsey Steel* the judge observed that it was implicit in the judgment of Sales J in *Re Stanleybet UK Investments Ltd* [2011] EWHC 2820 (Ch), [2012] BCC 550, where the court had ordered a CVL in the course of identifying the view of responsible administrators as carrying considerable weight, that the court has power to allow an administrator to continue with proposals not approved of by creditors. It is apparent from the judgment that the cases identified in the final paragraph of this section below (to precisely that effect) were not cited to HHJ Behrens in *Pudsey Steel* despite those authorities providing for such a course where exceptional circumstances so justify.

Without casting any doubt on the decision of HHJ Behrens in *Lavin*, in *Re Parmeko Holdings Ltd (in administration)* [2014] BCC 159, HHJ David Cooke, sitting as a High Court judge, held that an application for directions under para 55(2) is only necessary where a creditors' meeting has failed to approve an administrator's proposals and there is some real question as to the course that the administrator should follow. If no useful purpose would be served by an application – in *Parmkeo* the only choice the court was being asked to exercise was whether or not to put the company immediately into liquidation in circumstances in which the administrator did not propose that and could continue trading – then the administrator should simply indicate that when making his report to the court under para 55(1).

In *Re Fortuna Fix Ltd (in administration)* [2020] EWHC 2369 (Ch) ICCJ Jones determined that, although the court had jurisdiction to authorise the implementation of a rejected proposal despite opposition from a majority of creditors, it would not exercise its discretion to do so with the consequence that directions would not be given for the convening of a creditors' meeting to consider replacement of the administrators as that would serve no useful purpose. The court considered that it had jurisdiction to make a winding-up order under para 55(2)(e) in the absence of a winding-up petition but granted an adjournment to allow non-party creditors to consider the position.

**Action by the court on receipt of a report**—Although para 55(2) appears to envisage the court exercising its discretion of its own volition without the need for any application before it, in *Re ML Design Group Ltd* [2006] EWHC 2224, [2006] All ER (D) 75 Richard Sheldon QC, sitting as a deputy High Court judge, held that, where an initial meeting had failed to approve proposals within para 55(1)(a), the administrators should be required to comply with r 3.57 (the judge referring to the former IR 1986, r 2.114(1) and (3)) by way of a procedure analogous to that under para 79. Accordingly, a progress report should be attached to an application for termination and creditors given notice of the application. On the facts of that case, the administrators were also directed to notify creditors that an application for the fixing of remuneration would be made to the court.

Nothing in para 55(2) can be read as precluding an administrator from formulating and presenting revised or further revised proposals to creditors, although it would be prudent to appraise the court of that position on the filing of the administrator's report. In an appropriate, albeit exceptional, case the court retains a discretion, as it did under the former law, to make an order under para 55(2)(e) that proposals which have not been approved by creditors are nevertheless carried into effect: *Re Maxwell Communication Corp plc* [1992] BCLC 465 at 467G–467I (Hoffmann J) and *Re Structures & Computers Ltd* [1998] 1 BCLC 292 at 297G–298C (Neuberger J): compare *SCL Building Services* [1990] BCLC 98 (Peter Gibson J), and *Re Land and Property Trust Co plc (No 2)* [1991] BCLC 849 (Harman J). The key point demonstrated by the first mentioned of these authorities is that even a majority creditor does not have a right of veto on the implementation of an administrator's proposals, although the fact of such opposition will invariably weight as a factor in the exercise of the court's discretion: *Re DKLL Solicitors* [2008] 1 BCLC 112 at [17]–[20] (Andrew Simmonds QC sitting as a deputy High Court judge; partnership administration order made in respect of firm of solicitors notwithstanding opposition of Revenue with £1.7m debt of total £2.4m liabilities).

## [1.672]

### 56 Further creditors' decisions

(1) The administrator of a company shall seek a decision from the company's creditors on a matter if—

    (a)    it is requested in the prescribed manner by creditors of the company whose debts amount to at least 10% of the total debts of the company, or

    (b)    he is directed by the court to do so.

(2) An administrator commits an offence if he fails without reasonable excuse to seek a decision from the company's creditors on a matter as required by this paragraph.

**Amendments**—Small Business, Enterprise and Employment Act 2015, s 126, Sch 9, Pt 1, paras 1, 10(18)-(20).

**General note**—Although an administrator may call a meeting of members or creditors or otherwise seek a decision from creditors under para 62, he may be required to summon a meeting or seek a decision of creditors either by the requisite level of creditors or at the court's direction. As noted in the commentary to para 51 there is no good reason why in an appropriate case such a meeting should not be summoned prior to the initial creditors' meeting.  .

**Penalties**—See s 430, Sch 10 and the daily default fine in para 106(2)(j).

## [1.673]

### 57 Creditors' committee

(1) The company's creditors may, in accordance with the rules, establish a creditors' committee.

(2) A creditors' committee shall carry out functions conferred on it by or under this Act.

(3) A creditors' committee may require the administrator—

    (a)    to attend on the committee at any reasonable time of which he is given at least seven days' notice, and

    (b)    to provide the committee with information about the exercise of his functions.

**Amendments**—Small Business, Enterprise and Employment Act 2015, s 126, Sch 9, Pt 1, paras 1, 10(21).

**General note**—The formation of a creditors' committee is at the option of any creditors' meeting, but usually the initial creditors' meeting. A creditors' committee will often act as a brake or monitor on the administrator on behalf of creditors generally and to that end may call the administrator to account under para 57(3). The administrator should also place an appropriate degree of weight on the views of the creditors' committee, whether expressed informally or by way of a vote, subject to he or she retaining sole responsibility for the discharge of functions in the management of the affairs, business and property of the company; whilst bearing in mind that the court will only authorise an administrator to act contrary to a resolution of a creditors' committee in 'very exceptional circumstances': *Re CE King Ltd* [2000] 2 BCLC 297 at 306B–306C (Neuberger J).

**PARAGRAPH 57(2)**

' . . . functions conferred on it by or under this Act'—The following matters also fall to the creditors' committee. The committee may apply to court under para 91(1)(a) in an administration order case for the replacement of an administrator on a vacancy arising under para 90. In an out-of-court appointment case the committee may also resolve on the time from which an administrator is discharged (previously released under s 20) from liability under para 98(2)(b). The division of unsold assets in specie is subject to the permission of the creditors' committee, which is also responsible for the fixing of the basis for the administrator's remuneration and is entitled to notice of any application by the administrator to the court for an increase in the amount or rate of his remuneration as fixed. The committee is also subject to a duty to review the adequacy of an administrator's security for the proper performance of his functions.

**58**

*(Repealed)*

## FUNCTIONS OF ADMINISTRATOR

**[1.674]**

### 59 General powers

(1)   The administrator of a company may do anything necessary or expedient for the management of the affairs, business and property of the company.

(2)   A provision of this Schedule which expressly permits the administrator to do a specified thing is without prejudice to the generality of sub-paragraph (1).

(3)   A person who deals with the administrator of a company in good faith and for value need not inquire whether the administrator is acting within his powers.

**General note**—Paragraph 59(1) and (2), which correspond with the former s 14(1)(a) and (b), should be read in the context of the administrator's powers, which are considered in the commentary to para 60 below. The general power to do anything within the scope of para 59(1) is deemed by para 111(3) to include inaction. The implication from the use of the word 'or' in para 59(1) is that action by an administrator need be 'necessary', but not necessarily 'expedient', and vice versa. The use of the word 'or' might also have been more appropriate in place of the word 'and' in para 59(1), since the reference to 'the management of the affairs, business and property' must be a reference to any or all of those matters.

**Disclaimer**—An administrator has no statutory powers to disclaim onerous or leasehold property analogous to those available to a liquidator under ss 178 and 179. Given the specific terms in which the powers identified in the commentary to para 60 are cast, there is no basis for reading such a power of disclaimer into Sch B1.

**PARAGRAPH 59(1)**

**Scope of the provision**—In what the court termed 'a highly unusual application', in *Re Inspired Asset Management Ltd* [2019] EWHC 3301 (Ch) the ICC judge held that para 59(1) conferred jurisdiction on administrators to remove the sole director of eight wholly-owned subsidiary companies, and to appoint replacement directors, thereby sidestepping the relevant provisions in the Companies Act 2006, in particular s 168. The court sanctioned the removal on being satisfied that removal would facilitate the statutory objective of the administration, in particular by allowing the administrators to protect the assets of the company in administration and to realise them. The orders were made, however, without prejudice to any right of the removed director to claim compensation consequent upon removal given the judge's concern that the exercise of the court's jurisdiction ought not, so far as possible, infringe existing rights.

In *Re MBI Hawthorn Care Ltd* [2019] EWHC 2365 (Ch) Norris J considered that a court making an administration order had a discretion under para 13(1)(f) sufficiently broad to allow for the removal of a subsidiary's director if that was conducive to achieving the statutory objectives.

**PARAGRAPH 59(3)**

**Third parties dealing with the administrator**—Paragraph 59(3) corresponds with the former s 14(6) which referred to 'a person dealing with the administrator' who was 'not concerned to inquire' whether the administrator was acting within his or her powers. Nothing turns on the minor linguistic changes in the new provision which is itself almost certainly superfluous in any case, given the protection afforded to such a third party by s 39 of the Companies Act 2006 and the general law of agency. A third party need not inquire whether the administrator is acting within powers and will also be unaffected by any constructive knowledge of a breach of any fiduciary duty on the part of an administrator.

**[1.675]**

### 60

(1)   The administrator of a company has the powers specified in Schedule 1 to this Act.

(2)   But the power to sell, hire out or otherwise dispose of property is subject to any regulations that may be made under paragraph 60A.

**Amendments**—Small Business, Enterprise and Employment Act 2015, s 129.

**General note**—The powers in Sch 1 are extremely broad and comprise 22 specific powers and a twenty-third general power enabling the office-holder 'to do all other things incidental to the exercise of the foregoing powers.' As identified in the note to para 69, however, the powers of an administrator as agent of the company cannot extend beyond those of the company as principal. Conversely, the scope of Sch 1 means that an administrator may exercise any power which would have been available to the directors prior to the appointment of the administrator: *Denny v Yeldon* [1995] 1 BCLC 560 at 564A–564F (Jacob J, permitting an administrator to procure the amendment of a company's pension scheme trust deed).

**Sales to connected parties**—Paragraph 60 was amended by s 129 of the Small Business, Enterprise and Employment Act 2015. The amendment by way of para 60A (below) provides a reserve power permitting the Secretary of State to create regulations either to prohibit administration sales to connected parties or to impose conditions or requirements to allow a connected party administration sale to proceed. That amendment is wide enough to catch a connected 'pre-pack' sale. This reserve power (which lapses 5 years after commencement) will only be utilised if the voluntary measures arising from the Graham Review into pre-pack administrations prove unsuccessful.

The exercise of any power under Sch 1 must be within the scope of para 59(1) as 'anything necessary or expedient for the management of the affairs, business and property of the company', an observation consistent with para 59(2).

An administrator also has powers to remove or appoint a director under para 61, to call meetings of members or creditors under para 62, to apply to the court for directions under paras 63 and 68(2), to make a distribution to a creditor under para 65(1) and to make payments under para 66 other than in accordance with para 65 or para 13 of Sch 1.

## [1.676]

**60A**

(1)  The Secretary of State may by regulations make provision for—
>  (a)  prohibiting, or
>  (b)  imposing requirements or conditions in relation to,

the disposal, hiring out or sale of property of a company by the administrator to a connected person in circumstances specified in the regulations.

(2)  Regulations under this paragraph may in particular require the approval of, or provide for the imposition of requirements or conditions by—
>  (a)  creditors of the company,
>  (b)  the court, or
>  (c)  a person of a description specified in the regulations.

(3)  In sub-paragraph (1), "connected person", in relation to a company, means—
>  (a)  a relevant person in relation to the company, or
>  (b)  a company connected with the company.

(4)  For the purposes of sub-paragraph (3)—
>  (a)  "relevant person", in relation to a company, means—
>>    (i)  a director or other officer, or shadow director, of the company;
>>    (ii)  a non-employee associate of such a person;
>>    (iii)  a non-employee associate of the company;
>  (b)  a company is connected with another if any relevant person of one is or has been a relevant person of the other.

(5)  In sub-paragraph (4), "non-employee associate" of a person means a person who is an associate of that person otherwise than by virtue of employing or being employed by that person.

(6)  Subsection (10) of section 435 (extended definition of company) applies for the purposes of sub-paragraphs (3) to (5) as it applies for the purposes of that section.

(7)  Regulations under this paragraph may—
>  (a)  make different provision for different purposes;
>  (b)  make incidental, consequential, supplemental and transitional provision.

(8)  Regulations under this paragraph are to be made by statutory instrument.

(9)  Regulations under this paragraph may not be made unless a draft of the statutory instrument containing the regulations has been laid before Parliament and approved by a resolution of each House of Parliament.

(10)  This paragraph expires at the end of June 2021 unless the power conferred by it is exercised before then.

**Amendments**—Inserted by Small Business, Enterprise and Employment Act 2015, s 129. Revived and amended by Corporate Insolvency and Governance Act 2020, s 8.

**General note**—This new provision creates a power to enact secondary legislation giving force of law to what are presently voluntary requirements for best practice in relation to pre-pack administration sales following the recommendations of the Graham Report (on which see the introductory notes to Sch B1). The regulation-making power in para 60A expired on 26 May 2020, but was capable of being renewed by way of further legislation. Paragraph 60A was revived by the Corporate Insolvency and Governance Act 2020, which received the Royal Assent on 25 June 2020 and came into force on 26 June 2020. The revived power enables the Secretary of State to make regulations to prohibit or impose requirements or conditions in relation to the disposal, hiring out or sale of property of a company by an administrator to a person connected with the company in circumstances specified in the regulations, provided the power is used before the end of June 2021: see the Administration (Restrictions on Disposals etc to Connected Parties) Regulations 2021 (SI 2021/427), effective 30 April 2021.

## [1.677]

### 61

The administrator of a company—

    (a)    may remove a director of the company, and

    (b)    may appoint a director of the company (whether or not to fill a vacancy).

**General note**—The power to remove a director under para 61(a) is most likely to be of use where, despite the limitation on the exercise of management power by a company in administration or any officer under para 64, a director purports to exercise such management power or otherwise interferes in the conduct of the administration. The removal of a director in breach of any contract under which he or she holds office will give rise to a claim in damages against the company, but not the administrator, for loss arising as a foreseeable consequence of the breach, irrespective of the fact that the removal was effected under a statutory power: *Southern Foundries (1926) Ltd v Shirlaw* [1940] AC 701 and *Shindler v Northern Raincoat Co Ltd* [1960] 1 WLR 1038.

The appointment of a director under para 61(b) is unlikely other than where the appointment serves the interests of the administration, as discussed in the notes to para 64 below, or possibly where the appointment is necessary to ensure compliance with the company's articles of association.

## [1.678]

### 62

The administrator of a company may—

    (a)    call a meeting of members of the company;

    (b)    seek a decision on any matter from the company's creditors.

**Amendments**—Small Business, Enterprise and Employment Act 2015, s 126, Sch 9, Pt 1, paras 1, 10(23).

**General note**—The administrator's power to call a meeting of members or creditors is unlimited. It is submitted, however, that this power may only be exercised properly if incidental or pursuant to the general power in para 59(1).

## [1.679]

### 63

The administrator of a company may apply to the court for directions in connection with his functions.

**General note**—As an officer of the court – on which see para 5 and the notes thereto – an administrator would have standing to make an application to the court for directions even in the absence of this provision: *Re Rover Espana SA* [2006] BCC 599 at [18]. In addition to paras 63 and 68(2), an administrator is obliged to seek directions or permission from the court in a range of circumstances prescribed by paras 40(3), 42(5), 53(2)(a), 54(6)(a), 55, 65(3), 71, 72, 76(2)(a), 79, rr 3.44-48 and rr 18.24(b) and 18.28.

Although the wording of para 63 is less specific than the former s 14(3) which allowed for an application 'in relation to any particular matter arising in connection with the carrying out of [the administrator's] functions', its substance is the same. Under para 68(2) the court may give directions in connection with any aspect of the management of the company's affairs, business or property, but, in the case of the latter provision, only in any of the four circumstances identified therein. The scope of the words 'in connection with his functions' is extremely broad and, in practice, will catch an almost endless range of circumstances, depending on the facts of any particular case. Obvious examples include directions as to whether pre-administration payments were susceptible as preferences, as in *Re Lewis's of Leicester* [1995] BCC 514; directions as to the enforceability of a contract, or the true construction of the terms and conditions of contracts between the company in administration and third parties: *Re Fundingsecure Ltd (in administration)* [2021] EWHC 798 (Ch) (which involved the common issue of whether the applicant administrators were neutral and entitled to protect their positions or, as the respondents alleged, in substance, partisan); a direction for the removal of a delinquent co-appointee under para 88 and his or her replacement under para 91: see *Re Fox Street Village Ltd (in administration)* [2020] EWHC 2541 (Ch) (HHJ Halliwell, sitting as a High Court judge) and the note to r 3.62; a direction that administrators were entitled to apply to the French court for a stay or dismissal of proceedings against them relating to pre-packs, and the incidence of costs: *Re Blue Co London LLP (in administration)* [2020] EWHC 2385 (Ch).

In *Re Nortel Networks SA (in administration)* [2018] EWHC 1812 (Ch) Snowden J held that para 63 extends to the provision of directions to assist administrators in ascertaining which liabilities of the company rank as administration expenses by the stipulation of notification of such claims by an expense bar date, and authorising the distribution of assets to unsecured creditors who ranked lower in order of priority in the statutory waterfall without regard to administration expenses not notified by the bar date.

Paragraph 63 extends to an application for directions by an administrator appointed under the Investment Bank Special Administration Regulations 2011: *Re Worldspreads Ltd (in special administration)* [2015] EWHC 1719 (Ch).

Any application for directions should not put the court in a difficult or embarrassing position by failing to raise a particular and clear issue or issues. The application should set out the directions sought and, if possible, the alternatives, even though the court may ultimately grant relief other than the relief or the alternatives put forward: *Re Synthetic Technology Ltd* [1990] BCLC 378 at 380F–380H (Harman J). Neither should an administrator employ an application for directions as a means of avoiding what amounts in substance to a matter of commercial judgment by seeking to place the burden of such a decision on the court. As Neuberger J observed in *Re T & D Industries plc* [2000] 1 All ER 333 at 344J, ' . . . a person appointed to act as an administrator may be called upon to make important and urgent decisions. He has a responsible and potentially demanding role. Commercial and administrative decisions are for him and the court is not there to act as a sort of bomb shelter for him.' His Lordship later held that, as a matter of principle, the court will not interfere with a commercial decision on the part of an administrator unless what was proposed was a course based on a wrong application of the law and/or was conspicuously unfair to a particular creditor, although the court would not second guess an issue which an administrator was far better placed to resolve: *Re CE King Ltd (in administration)* [2000] 2 BCLC 297 at 306C–306G: see also *MTI Trading Systems Ltd v Winter* [1998] BCC 591. Inappropriate applications to the court will almost inevitably be met with hostile orders for costs: *Re CE King Ltd* at 303E. Accordingly, the court may, in an appropriate case, decline to give directions on all or part of the matters before it, particularly where the evidence before the court is incomplete and not all parties with an interest in the matter in issue are before the court, as in *Re NS Distribution Ltd* [1990] BCLC 169 at 171E–171F (Harman J, refusal to sanction sale of single asset at good price: 'It is not in my view right for the court to be asked to bless all such steps. If it were, the court would be inundated with applications of this sort'). On the other hand, there may be cases, albeit uncommon, where the administrators surrender their discretion to the court and stand by the court's decision or invite the court to give direction as to how the administrators are to go about the task of exercising their judgment: see, for example, the requirement for administrators to make a value judgment as to whether a CVA ought to become effective where the CVA was based on unanticipated claims emerging after approval of the CVA in *Heis v Financial Services Compensation* [2018] EWCA Civ 1327, [2018] BCC 921 (at [58], 'the exercise that is required is not one of commercial judgment. It is rather a case of the court being required to identify the nature of the judgment that requires to be exercised, and exercising it fairly by reference to the scope, purpose and the relevant facts').

For the exercise of the court's jurisdiction in giving approval for joint administrators to perform, or to procure the relevant companies in administration to perform, a complicated agreement settling various legal claims see *Nortel Networks UK Ltd* [2014] EWHC 2614 (Ch) (HHJ Hodge QC, sitting as a High Court judge) on the court being satisfied that the administrators, with the benefit of legal advice, genuinely and properly believed that the agreement was in the best interests of the companies and their creditors. At [33] the judge, in addressing the settlement of certain of the claims, expressed himself thus: ' . . . I am not myself forming any view in the matter. I am concerned to satisfy myself that the decision which the Joint Administrators have reached to enter into the settlement of [the claims] is a reasonable decision, taken on proper grounds, and with full regard to all the relevant considerations, and not ignoring any such considerations'. At [37], and by reference to the decision of Sir Andrew Morritt C in *Tamlin v Edgar* [2011] EWHC 3949 (Ch), the judge bore in mind the limited extent of the court's role on such an application. The court need only be satisfied that performance of the agreement is both rational and a decision honestly reached and that full and frank disclosure has been made to the court of all relevant facts and circumstances. 'The court is not a rubber stamp, and the parties and their advisers must be astute not to appear to treat the court as such'. The court again approved a global settlement agreement with creditors and 19 of the group companies in *Re Nortel Networks UK Ltd* [2016] EWHC 2769 (Ch). Such an application was akin to an application for directions by a trustee and required caution in the court's approach. Although approval was not to be withheld merely because the court would not have exercised the administrators' power in the way proposed under the settlement, the court should be anxious to ascertain that the proposed exercise was within the administrators' powers, that the administrators genuinely believed that the proposal would benefit the company and its creditors, and that the administrators were acting rationally and absent any conflict of interest in reaching that view. The proposed settlement was approved despite the fact that certain creditors might have obtained a greater return through continued litigation, but where the outcome of such litigation was uncertain and would necessarily incur additional time and cost.

An administrator appointed under Sch B1 may sell the assets of a company without the need for the approval of the court under para 63 or para 68: *Re Transbus International Ltd (in administration)* [2004] EWHC 932 (Ch), [2004] BCLC 550 (Lawrence Collins J, expressly adopting in relation to Sch B1 administrations the principles identified in *Re T & D Industries* (above)).

**Distribution plans**—Para 63 is broad enough in terms of jurisdiction to allow the court to give directions with respect to monies held on statutory trust by a company, even though those monies do not form part of the company's assets: *Re Allanfield Property Insurance Services Ltd (in administration), Allanfield Property Insurance Services Ltd (in administration) v Aviva Insurance Ltd* [2015] EWHC 3721 (Ch) (HHJ Keyser QC, sitting as a High Court judge). *Allanfield* is also authority for the proposition that, in principle, the court's inherent jurisdiction extends to approval of the administrator's proposals to establish a scheme of distribution for the monies subject to the statutory trust. In *Re Supercapital Ltd (in administration)* [2020] EWHC 1685 (Ch), [2020] 1 BCLC 355 Deputy ICCJ Agnello QC approved an application for a distribution plan concerning funds held on clients' behalf by way of a statutory trust by a failed provider of international payment services. The judgment considers the authorities that provide the court with such jurisdiction. For a similar judicial exercise see *Re Beaufort Asset Clearing Services Ltd (in special administration)* [2020] EWHC 2309 (Ch). In *Re Hyde (Joint Administrators of Betindex Ltd)* [2021] EWHC 1542 (Ch) Mr Robin Vos, sitting as a deputy High Court judge, gave directions for the distribution of funds held on trust for customers of a betting operator in a client money bank account, including fixing of entitlements, date(s) of distributions, the application of any surplus, costs and the applicant administrators' fees. See the notes to r 3.50 for the applicability of the principle in *Berkeley Applegate* to the fees and expenses associated with dealing with trust assets and administering the trust out of trust assets.

**Time for the making of an application for directions**—An administrator may seek directions at any time during the course of office or on the hearing of the administration application, at which time directions may be given under para 13(1)(f).

**Applications for directions by parties other than the administrator**—Although para 63 only envisages an application by an administrator for directions it is suggested that the position under Sch B1 will remain as it did under Part II such that the court retains an inherent power to give directions, albeit not under para 63, to an administrator as an officer of the court on the application of a third party capable of demonstrating a genuine and legitimate interest in the directions sought. Such an application is capable of being made by a creditor, as in *Re Mirror Group (Holdings) Ltd* [1992] BCC 972 at 976G–976H (Sir Donald Nicholls V-C) or by a third party, say as to the terms upon which an administrator might continue to make use of the third party's goods for the benefit of the administration, as in *Barclays Mercantile Business Finance Ltd* [1992] 1 WLR 1253 at 1259D–1259G (Millett J).

Where the court is prepared to give directions, say in directing that an administrator could dispose of company assets without the leave of the court prior to a meeting of the company's creditors, as in the *T & D Industries* case (above), the court's direction in approving any particular course of action is not to be taken as absolving an administration of any liability if the proposed course turns out to have been negligent in some way: ibid at 346B–346C. A creditor or member might pursue such a complaint under para 74 or a claim may be available under para 75.

**[1.680]**

**64**

(1)   A company in administration or an officer of a company in administration may not exercise a management power without the consent of the administrator.

(2)   For the purpose of sub-paragraph (1)—

(a)   "management power" means a power which could be exercised so as to interfere with the exercise of the administrator's powers,

(b)   it is immaterial whether the power is conferred by an enactment or an instrument, and

(c)   consent may be general or specific.

**General note**—The appointment of an administrator does not of itself affect the status of a director as such. The powers of the directors, however, are curtailed on the administrator's appointment. In contrast to the position in receivership, which is discussed in the notes to s 42, para 64(1) prohibits the exercise of a 'management power' without the consent of the administrator. It is submitted that the hypothesis introduced by the use of the words 'could be' in the definition of the term 'management power' in para 64(2)(a), together with the express powers conferred on the administrator under Sch 1 and the provisions in paras 59(1) and (2) and 68(1), effectively precludes the exercise of any power whatsoever by the directors or any of them without the consent of the administrator. An errant director runs the risk of being removed under para 61(a).

The judgment of ICC Judge Jones in *Re ASA Resource Group plc, Dearing v Skelton* [2020] EWHC 1370 (Ch) contains a useful analysis of the extent to which an administrator might allow a director to exercise management powers in the course of the administration. Ordinarily, the procedural route for the resolution of issues arising in that context is under para 63.

In *Re Lehman Brothers (International) Europe Ltd (in administration)* [2020] EWHC 1932 (Ch) Sir Geoffrey Vos C directed administrators, on a para 63 application, to accede to a request by the company's directors under para 64 to distribute surplus funds to the company's sole shareholder. It did not have to be shown that the exercise of the administrators' functions and powers would advance in a commercially appropriate way the para 3(1)(a) purpose of rescuing the company as a going concern in a definable way, but neither was there a need for every exercise of every function to be shown to be tied in a causative sense to the purpose of administration being pursued. It was sufficient that acceding to the request was within the administrators' powers and that the purpose was being pursued overall.

A director of a company in administration who acts in breach of his fiduciary duties and duties of skill and care is also likely to have acted in breach of para 64(1): *McTear v Englehard* [2014] EWHC 1056 (Ch). It appears that the remedies for breach of duty and para 64(1) will be the same.

Paragraph 64 has no effect on the power of directors to challenge the appointment of an administrator: *Closegate Hotel Development (Durham) Ltd v McLean* [2013] EWHC 3237 (Ch).

The appointment of an administrator has no bearing on the statutory duties of the directors to convene an annual general meeting and to file accounts and an annual return with the Registrar of Companies. This, at least, is the theory. In fact, directors rarely comply with such obligations, in the main, it is thought, because they are oblivious to the continuance of their duty to do so. As a matter of practice, neither does the Registrar of Companies enforce such obligations in any case.

An administrator will not ordinarily consent in either general or specific terms to the exercise of a management power by a company or its officers. In an appropriate case, however, the administrator may consider it appropriate, expedient or even necessary to consent, invariably subject to agreed terms, to the continued management role, in whole or part, of some or all of the directors. This all assumes, of course, the continuing co-operation and willingness to act on the part of any one or more of the directors. Perhaps the most obvious example of a director engaging in management in administration will arise in a trading administration where the nature of the company's business is idiosyncratic, as in the case of a football club, or otherwise highly specialist in nature. The administrator must bear in mind in all cases that what is termed his 'consent' in para 64 will usually amount to a delegation of his responsibilities and that responsibility for the conduct of the administration rests with him or her alone, given the provisions mentioned in the opening paragraph above. Furthermore, for both the purposes of third party perception and the need for ongoing, pro-active monitoring, the administrator will also have to be mindful that those to whom he chooses to delegate may well have held office during the financial demise leading to the company's administration such that it will usually be prudent for an appropriate member of the administrator's staff, at the very least, to be in situ during the period of the administrator's consent.

Although an administrator might consider the making of an application for directions as to the extent of his delegation of management powers, it is submitted that, in all but the most exceptional of cases, the court is likely to view such a decision as commercial or administrative in nature so as to remain a matter for the administrator alone: see para 63 and the notes thereto.

## [1.681]

### 64A Distribution

(1) This paragraph applies where a company enters administration before the end of the period of 12 weeks beginning with the day after the end of any moratorium for the company under Part A1.

(2) The administrator must make a distribution to the creditors of the company in respect of—

    (a)    moratorium debts (within the meaning given by section 174A), and

    (b)    priority pre-moratorium debts (within the meaning given by section 174A).

(3) A sum payable under sub-paragraph (2) is to be paid in priority to—

    (a)    any security to which paragraph 70 applies or paragraph 115(1) applies;

    (b)    any sums payable under paragraph 99.

(4) The administrator must realise any property necessary to comply with sub-paragraph (2).

(5) The rules may make provision as to the order in which the moratorium and priority pre-moratorium debts rank among themselves for the purposes of this paragraph in a case where the assets of the company are insufficient to meet them in full.

**Amendments**—Inserted by Corporate Insolvency and Governance Act 2020, s 2(1), Sch 3, paras 1, 31(1), (3).

## [1.682]

### 65

(1) If the assets of a company are sufficient to meet any debts or other liabilities payable under paragraph 64A in full, the administrator of the company may make a distribution to any other creditor of the company.

(2) Sections 175 and 176AZA shall apply in relation to a distribution under this paragraph as they apply in relation to a winding up.

(3) A payment may not be made by way of distribution under this paragraph to a creditor of the company who is neither secured nor preferential unless—

    (a)    the distribution is made by virtue of section 176A(2)(a), or

    (b)    the court gives permission.

**Amendments**—Small Business, Enterprise and Employment Act 2015, s 128; SI 2018/1244. Paragraphs 64A and 65(1) were inserted and substituted by Sch 3, para 31 of the Corporate Insolvency and Governance Act 2020, in force from 26 June 2020. Those provisions give effect to the super-priority afforded to moratorium debts and priority pre-moratorium debts (as defined in para 64A(2)) where a company enters administration before the end of the period of 12 weeks beginning with the day after the end of any moratorium for the company under Part A1. That super-priority status would afford such creditors standing ahead of the costs and expenses of the administrator or liquidator and the costs and expenses of the administration or liquidation.

**General note**—Paragraph 65 finds no equivalent in the former Part II provisions. Although there appear to have been a number of unreported cases under the former law in which the court was prepared to sanction the making of a distribution to pre-administration unsecured creditors, in *Re The Designer Room Ltd* [2004] EWHC 720 Rimer J held the general rule to be that in an ordinary case an administrator had no power to make such a distribution since, in the absence of an express provision, such action could not be construed as necessary or incidental to the functions of the administrator, even where the making of a distribution would have been cheaper and more convenient that on a liquidation. Rimer J took account of and accepted that in *Re WBSL Realisations (1992) Ltd* [1995] 2 BCLC 576 Knox J had permitted payments to be made under para 13 of Sch 1 on being satisfied that those payments were necessary to preserve the goodwill of the company's business in the course of the administrators seeking to achieve a survival of the company and its business as a going concern, but only on terms that any distribution was brought into account on any subsequent liquidation so as to achieve parity between all creditors. That decision, however, and that of Pumfrey J in *Rolph v AY Bank Ltd* [2002] BPIR 1231 which followed it, in similar circumstances, were decided on very unusual facts and, as such, were capable of being distinguished from the general rule in *Designer Room*.

The absence of a power to distribute in an ordinary Part II case meant that the only way of effecting a distribution to creditors was to discharge the administration order under s 18 and to place the company into liquidation, thereby incurring the DTI levy applicable in a compulsory liquidation or, alternatively, by engaging the cumbersome requirements associated with placing the company into voluntary liquidation following *Re Mark One (Oxford St) plc* [1999] 1 WLR 1445. Paragraph 65 overcomes that practical difficulty and radically alters the complexion of administration by allowing distribution to all species of pre-administration creditor, subject to the court's permission in the case of an unsecured creditor: see *Re Lune Metal Products* [2007] 2 BCLC 746 at [6] (Neuberger LJ). The new position is not only justifiable on account of savings in time and expense but also because Sch B1 now envisages the possibility of an administration being conducted, in effect, as a form of quasi-liquidation, given the machinery for the proving of debts etc in IR 2016, rr 14.26–14.44 and the specific provision in para 84 for the seamless movement from administration to dissolution without an intervening liquidation.

**Amendment to para 65(3)**—Section 128 of the Small Business, Enterprise and Employment Act 2015 amended para 65(3) (and 83(1)(b) and (2)(b)) so as to dispense with the requirement for the permission of the court where the administrator makes a payment of the prescribed part under s 176A to unsecured creditors. Previously, permission was not required only where a distribution was made to secured or preferential creditors.

## PARAGRAPH 65(1)

' . . . a distribution to a creditor of the company'—A post-administration creditor is only capable of being eligible for the making of a payment – as opposed to a 'distribution' – under para 66. The term 'creditor' will extend to preferential and secured creditors as at the date on which the company entered into administration, on which see s 387(3A) on preferential debts. The position of unsecured creditors is considered in the notes to para 66(3) below.

In *Re Lehman Bros International (Europe) (in administration)* [2014] EWHC 704 (Ch), [2015] Ch 1 David Richards J held that the contributory rule applies only in liquidation, not in administration, such that there is no provision for calls on contributories to be made by administrators of the sort provided for in s 74(1). In addition, the equitable rule in *Cherry v Boultbee*, allowing for the netting-off of reciprocal money obligations, does not apply in administration. That view was upheld in the Court of Appeal [2015] EWCA Civ 485, [2015] 3 WLR 1205 (Moore-Bick LJ, Lewison LJ, Briggs LJ). As such, the foreign currency creditors in that case were entitled to claim against the company without the imposition of the rules just mentioned as would prevent such claims in liquidation. That conclusion, however, is apparently wrong according to the judgment of the Supreme Court in *Joint Administrators of LB Holdings Intermediate No 2 Ltd v Joint Administrators of Lehman Bros International (Europe)* [2017] UKSC 38, [2017] 2 WLR 1497. The court's conclusion was that the application of the contributory rule in liquidation was capable of extension to administration because the rule was rooted not in the insolvency legislation but in the court's development of general equitable principles applicable to insolvency. The extension of the rule to administration could be justified if it was capable of application in a practical and principled fashion.

Although envisaging insolvency, the court has jurisdiction to make an order under para 65, by way of directions under para 63, to allow for the distribution of a surplus while the company remains in administration: *In the matter of Lehman Bros Europe Ltd (in administration)* [2017] EWHC 2031 (Ch) (Hildyard J) (a distribution to sole member of company itself in administration).

## PARAGRAPH 65(2)

**The effect of s 175**—The effect of para 65(2) is to impose on an administrator a statutory duty, akin to that imposed on a receiver by s 40, to pay preferential creditors, as defined in s 386(1) and Sch 6 and assessed in accordance with s 387(3A), in priority to the holder of any floating charge or unsecured creditors to whom a distribution would otherwise be made.

The holder of a valid fixed charge retains priority over preferential claims. In addition, by virtue of s 175(2)(a) the expenses of an administration rank ahead of preferential claims.

The claim of a floating charge holder caught by para 70, and, therefore, unsecured claims, is also subject to an administrator's claim for remuneration and expenses under para 99(3) and debts or liabilities arising out of any contract entered into by an administrator under para 99(4).

Paragraph 99(3)(b) affords the administrator's claims priority over the claims of the floating charge holder and which finds no equivalent in liquidation. Whilst s 175(2)(b) (applicable in liquidation) is framed in terms of property comprised in or subject to a floating charge, para 99(3)(b) creates a specific statutory charge which is distinct from and ranks in priority to any floating charge under para 70. It is the operation of that statutory charge which effectively removes the assets subject to it from the scope of any floating charge.

In *Re Collins & Aikman Europe SA* [2007] 1 BCLC 182 at [27] Lindsay J identified that the words 'under this paragraph' in para 65(2) refer to a distribution under either para 65(2) or para 65(3) and appear to require that any such distribution 'shall be subject to those creditors characterised under *English* law as preferential creditors being paid (or at least with such provision for them that their payment could be expected would not be jeopardised, either in amount or at all, by the proposed distribution) before the distribution under para 65 is made.' It is plain, however, from para [29] of the judgment that Lindsay J was not reaching any final determination on the point, particularly given his Lordship's reference to the judgment of HHJ Norris QC (sitting as a High Court judge) in *Re MG Rover Belux SA/NV* [2006] EWHC 3618 (Ch) where, as appears from the report of that case, the judge was prepared to give permission for a distribution under para 65(3) on being satisfied that preferential creditors under local law (ie Belgian law) were provided for without enquiry into the position of English preferential creditors. There is much, it is submitted, to be said for Lindsay J's preliminary view since the words 'under this paragraph' (and not 'under this sub-paragraph') in para 65(2) must be a reference to para 65 generally, and not to any sub-paragraph thereof, which cannot avoid the reference to s 175 which itself (in s 175(1)) makes specific reference to 'preferential debts' within the meaning of s 386.

The notes to ss 40, 107 and 175 include commentary on the consequences of a breach of the statutory duty to preferential creditors now imposed on an administrator under para 65.

**The court's permission under para 65(3) for a distribution to a creditor of the company**—The legislation gives no guidance as to when permission might be granted by the court under para 65(3). It is suggested, however, at least as a starting point, that only in very exceptional circumstances will the court be prepared to detract from the pari passu principle embodied in r 14.12(2). Nevertheless, it remains that para 65 contains no express bar on a distribution which involves an inequality of treatment as between the same class of creditors. Neither is there any compelling reason why there should be. Support for this analysis appears in the judgment of HHJ Norris QC, sitting as a High Court judge, in *Re HPJ UK Ltd (in administration)* [2007] BCC 284 in which the court was asked to sanction a distribution to unsecured creditors which involved a payment of £2.25m to HMRC in respect of an undisputed claim of £1.2m in respect of PAYE, NIC, corporation tax and VAT and in full and final settlement of an assessed claim for £7.2m for corporation tax in respect of a US agency together with an interim distribution of between 62p and 81p (subject to the conclusion of the administration) in the pound to the remaining 1.2% of unsecured creditors. In granting permission for the distribution his Lordship observed (at [11]):

'In my judgment paragraph 65 is sufficiently flexible to enable administrators to make a distribution in respect of a compromised claim of exactly the type which has been negotiated in the present circumstances. The plain words of the paragraph are sufficiently broad to encompass the proposal in the present case. I do not think it can be said that "a distribution" must of necessity be a rateable payment. There is no policy reason why the court should obstruct a carefully negotiated compromise achieved between parties of equal power, the outcome of which has received the unanimous approval of the creditors.'

In *Re GHE Realisations Ltd* [2006] BCC 139 at [7] and [8] Rimer J identified four specific factors as being material, but not necessarily conclusive, on the issue of whether the court should grant permission for a distribution under para 65. First, does the administrator have sufficient funds to make the distribution proposed? Secondly, the administrator should not propose to exit the administration by moving to creditors' voluntary liquidation under para 83 (in which a distribution to creditors would be possible). Thirdly, do the administrator's proposals, as approved by creditors, include a proposal to make a distribution of the sort proposed? Fourthly, is the proposed distribution consistent with the administrator's functions and duties and any actual or intended proposals to creditors? Having adopted the guidance in *GHE Realisations*, and having observed that, given the width of the discretion in para 65(3), it is doubtful that it is possible to draw up a definitive list of considerations relevant to all cases, in *Re MG Rover Belux SA/NV (in administration)* [2007] BCC 446 at [7] and [8] HHJ Norris QC, sitting as a High Court judge, identified the following considerations as relevant to the facts of that case (which, it is suggested, in whole or part, are capable of have some general significance to other cases):

'(a)   The matter is to be judged at the time when permission is sought;

(b)   the court must at that time be satisfied that the proposed distribution is conducive to the achievement of the then current objectives of the administration;

(c)   the court must be satisfied that the distribution is in the interests of the company's creditors as a whole (because para 3(2) of Sch B1 says that the administrator must perform his functions in that manner);

(d)   the court must be satisfied that proper provision has been made for secured and preferential creditors (for the requirement to obtain the permission of the court seems to be directed at their protection);

(e)   the court must consider what are the realistic alternatives to the proposed distribution sought by the administrators, consider the merits and demerits of adopting a course other than that proposed by the administrators and assess whether the proposed distribution adversely affects the entitlement of others (when compared with their entitlement if one of the other realistic alternatives were to be adopted);

(f) the court must take into account the basis on which the administration has been conducted so far as the creditors are concerned (under the original proposals, any modification to those original proposals, or any indications given in any reports to creditors), and in particular whether the creditors have approved (or not objected to) any proposal concerning the relevant distribution;

(g) the court must consider the nature and terms of the distribution; and

(h) the court must consider the impact of the distribution upon any proposed exit route from the administration.'

To all of these considerations, the following two considerations might also be added in an appropriate case. First, the court should exercise its discretion on the basis of evidence as to the likely level of distribution or distributions to be made, and the source thereof, mindful that any recipient might seek to rely on the court's order as a defence to a claim for overpayment. Secondly, any permission should be specific, so far as practicable, as to the level of any distribution, as opposed to a general, non-specific form of permission.

In *Re Nortel Networks UK Ltd* [2015] EWHC 2506 (Ch) Snowden J gave permission for administrators to make distributions under para 65(3) to the company's unsecured non-preferential creditors as they thought fit. In making that order, the court found that such distributions would be conducive to the objectives of the administration at the time the para 65(3) application was made. In addition, the court was satisfied that the distributions would be in the interests of the creditors as a whole and would take account of the position of the secured and preferential creditors.

It is possible as a matter of jurisdiction, subject to discretion as to whether it is appropriate, for the court to give directions under para 63 for a regime that involves a distribution to unsecured creditors under para 65(3), even though the approved regime carries a risk that, at the end of the administration, insufficient assets might have been retained to enable a late expense claimant to be paid under para 99(3): *Re Nortel Networks UK Ltd* [2017] EWHC 1429 (Ch) at [87] (Snowden J). The court does not, however, have a residual discretion to change the priority rules set out in the insolvency legislation: *Bloom v Pensions Regulator* [2013] UKSC 52, [2014] AC 209 at [115]–[127] (Lord Neuberger). That is, the court may not extinguish statutory rights to priority or promote lower ranking creditors to a higher order of priority in the statutory waterfall. The application in *Nortel* is an example of the court exercising its discretion in approving a regime, having regard to the need to protect the interests of persons who might have expense claims, but also recognising the need to facilitate an efficient conclusion to the insolvency process.

Unsecured claims will not be relevant in a para 3(1)(c) case unless there is a surplus achieved on realisations, as can happen: *Re Taylor Pearson (Construction) Ltd (in administration)* [2020] EWHC 2933 (Ch), [2021] 1 BCLC 725 at [80]–[82] (HHJ Davis-White QC (sitting as a High Court judge)). The most likely scenario in which para 65(3) will be relevant is in avoiding the time and expense of a liquidation where the only practical purpose of the liquidation would be the distribution of assets by way of dividend to unsecured creditors. Where there are no assets remaining for distribution to creditors in the administration the duty in para 84(1) (moving from administration to dissolution) will be engaged, subject to disapplication under para 84(2). If assets do remain for distribution to unsecured creditors then para 83 becomes available.

## [1.683]

**66**

If the debts and other liabilities payable under paragraph 64A have been met, the administrator of a company may make a payment otherwise than in accordance with paragraph 65 or paragraph 13 of Schedule 1 if he thinks it likely to assist achievement of the purpose of administration.

**Amendments**—See the note on amendments to para 65 following the enactment of the Corporate Insolvency and Governance Act 2020.

**General note**—Paragraph 13 of Sch 1 confers a power on an administrator 'to make any payment which is necessary or incidental to the performance of his functions', a phrase broad enough to extend to either pre- or post-administration liabilities or a payment to a party who is not a creditor but who requires payment as a pre-condition of providing a supply of goods or services. Paragraph 66 finds no counterpart in the former Part II and amounts to a power to make a payment which is not within para 13 of Sch 1, or para 65, but which the administrator 'thinks is likely to assist achievement of the purpose of administration'. (The word 'thinks' is discussed in the notes to para 3(3) and, apparently envisages a subjective view subject to objective reasonability.) The quandary as to how a payment might fall outside para 13 of Sch 1 but still be likely to assist achievement of the purpose of administration may be one with no satisfactory solution. Neither do the DTI's Explanatory Notes cast any light on the matter. All that may be gleaned from para 66 is that Parliament intended to confer the widest possible power on an administrator in making payments so as to assist in the achievement of the purpose of administration. Certainly para 66 contains none of the limits relating to the payment of secured or preferential creditors as appear in para 65(2) and (3): *Re Collins v Aikman Europe SA* [2007] 1 BCLC 182 at [30] (Lindsay J). Whether exercised under para 66 or para 13 of Sch 1 an administrator would, therefore, be entitled to discharge pre-administration liabilities, say to a key employee or an essential supplier where there is a real risk of discontinued service or supply on non-payment, or a party with whom a liability has been incurred in the course of the administration, whether or not entitled to such payments under English law. Any such payment would remain possible, certainly under para 66, even if it contravened the strict ranking of claims in administration, provided the administrator 'thinks' that the payment is likely to assist achievement of the broader purpose of administration: *Re MG Rover Espana* [2005] BPIR 1162 at [13] (HHJ Norris QC sitting as a High Court judge).

An administrator should always consider making an application to court for directions under para 63 so as to sanction any payment. The judgment of Peter Smith J in *Re TXU UK Ltd* [2003] 2 BCLC 341 at [18]–[19] contains a useful discussion of the proper approach to payments made under para 13 of Sch 1, where such payments can be said to be for the overall benefit of the administration, and suggests that 'administrators would be unwise to make such a decision (as to payment) without applying to the court because they may face retrospective challenge.' Those guidelines, it is submitted, will apply equally to para 66. The court may also direct that a payment ranks as an expense of the administration: see *Re Atlantic Computer Systems plc* [1992] Ch 505 at 528 (Nicholls LJ); see also r 3.51(2).

## [1.684]

### 67 General duties

The administrator of a company shall on his appointment take custody or control of all the property to which he thinks the company is entitled.

**General note**—This provision imposes an unqualified obligation on an administrator which resembles that found previously in s 17(1). However, the reference in para 67 is now to property 'to which [the administrator] thinks the company is entitled', and not property 'to which the company is or appears to be entitled', as previously.

The term 'thinks' is new (and is discussed in the notes to para 3(3)) with the consequence that the present provision relies on the administrator's subjective view with the proviso that that view must be objectively reasonable.

In *Sandhu v Jet Star Retail Ltd (in administration)* [2011] EWCA Civ 459 the Court of Appeal dismissed a claim in conversion by a fashion clothing manufacturer which had supplied goods to a retailer under the terms of a contract which the retailer had not paid for and which had been sold by the administrators following the retailer's administration. The manufacturer submitted that the company's authority to dispose of the goods extended only to the ordinary course of its business which had ceased upon the company entering into administration. The court found that the parties had clearly had in mind that the retailer could deal with the goods even after it had become insolvent or gone into administration. The supplier's contractual protection depended on it withdrawing the company's authority to deal with the goods. As such, having regard to the commercial considerations and the language of the contract between the parties, the company's authority to dispose of goods subject to the retention of title clause could not be said to be limited to disposals in the ordinary course of business. It was the manufacturer which had reserved the right to decide whether, and when, to intervene in order to preserve his interest in goods for which payment had not been made.

The judgment of HHJ McCahill QC, sitting as a High Court judge, in *Blue Monkey Gaming Ltd v Hudson* [2014] 4 All ER (D) 222 contains a detailed analysis of the duties and position of administrators and claimants in retention of title claims in the context of a claim for conversion brought against administrators by the supplier of asserts subject to such a contractual provision. Broadly, an administrator is not under an obligation to do the job of the party seeking to rely on the retention of title clause; rather, it is the claimant asserting title that carries the responsibility for being clear and specific as to the goods to which it asserts ownership.

## [1.685]

### 68

(1) Subject to sub-paragraph (2), the administrator of a company shall manage its affairs, business and property in accordance with—

   (a)     any proposals approved under paragraph 53,

   (b)     any revision of those proposals which is made by him and which he does not consider substantial, and

(c)     any revision of those proposals approved under paragraph 54.

(2)   If the court gives directions to the administrator of a company in connection with any aspect of his management of the company's affairs, business or property, the administrator shall comply with the directions.

(3)   The court may give directions under sub-paragraph (2) only if—

    (a)     no proposals have been approved under paragraph 53,

    (b)     the directions are consistent with any proposals or revision approved under paragraph 53 or 54,

    (c)     the court thinks the directions are required in order to reflect a change in circumstances since the approval of proposals or a revision under paragraph 53 or 54, or

    (d)     the court thinks the directions are desirable because of a misunderstanding about proposals or a revision approved under paragraph 53 or 54.

**General note**—The powers of an administrator under Sch 1 and as identified in the note to para 60 arise automatically on his appointment. Under the former provisions – on which see *Re Charnley Davies Ltd* [1990] BCC 605 (Vinelott J); *NS Distribution Ltd* [1990] BCLC 169 (Harman J); *Re Consumer & Industrial Press Ltd (No 2)* (1988) 4 BCC 72 (Peter Gibson J); *Re Montin Ltd* [1999] 1 BCLC 663; *Re Osmosis Group Ltd* [1999] 2 BCLC 329; *Re PD Fuels Ltd* [1999] BCC 450; and *Re Harris Bus Co Ltd* [2000] BCC 1, 151 (Rattee J) – there was a divergence of opinion as to whether or not an administrator could not exercise his statutory powers prior to the approval of his proposals under the former s 23 without a direction from the court under the former s 17(2)(a). In *Re T & D Industries plc* [2000] BCC 956 Neuberger J engaged in an extensive review of the authorities and held that the exercise of powers under the former s 14 was not subject to a direction under the former s 17(2)(a). As such, the administrator was entitled to exercise his or her statutory powers to sell the company's assets prior to the approval of proposals by creditors. Neuberger J's conclusion was subject to a number of provisos. First, administrators should never act for the purpose of avoiding consideration of their proposals. Secondly, if circumstances allow, administrators should formulate their proposals and either call the creditors' meeting as soon as reasonably practicable or seek a direction from the court for the summoning of a meeting on short notice. Thirdly, in very urgent cases, where such steps were not possible, administrators should at least seek to consult with the major creditors of the company prior to completing any sale.

Paragraph 68 does not appear to alter the position from that identified above. As such, an administrator seems to be at liberty to exercise all of his or her statutory powers immediately following appointment and in the absence of the approval of proposals under paras 53 or 54. Consistent with that view, the former r 2.33(6) of the IR 1986 specifically envisaged an application by an administrator for the cessation of the administration prior to his having sent a statement of his proposals to creditors in accordance with para 49. Furthermore, there is nothing in the wording in para 68 to suggest that the exercise of any statutory power prior to the approval of the administrator's proposals is conditional upon a direction from the court under para 68(2). The administrator remains, however, under the obligation in para 49(5)(a) to send out his statement of proposals 'as soon as is reasonably practicable after the company enters administration.' The guidance provided by Neuberger J in the *T & D* case as to regard being had to an application to court, the convening of a creditors' meeting on short notice or at least liaison with major creditors, will also remain relevant. As discussed in the notes to para 63, the court will also have little enthusiasm for what amounts to a commercial decision which falls to the administrator alone or a hearing which is of little practical use in the absence of third parties who might reasonably be expected to advance arguments contrary to the administrator's proposed course of action. Conversely, there is an inherent risk in employing administration as a convenient device for the effecting of a so-called 'pre-pack' sale, particularly one entered into with the former owners or directors of the company in administration, other than where the administrator can be confident on reasonable, objective grounds that the sale could be said to be in the best interests of the creditors as a whole. In some cases, however, such a sale is either the only viable way forward or is genuinely the most effective course for maximising realisations for the benefit of creditors. Schedule B1 does nothing to intrude on an administrator's standing to opt for such a course.

Paragraph 68(1) contains a positive obligation on an administration to 'manage [the company's] affairs, business and property in accordance with . . . [the] proposals' (subject to any permissible revision of the proposals or directions of the court). For this purpose it is not sufficient for an administrator generally (and absent directions of the court) to perform his or her functions merely in a way that does not cut across the proposals; rather, the administrator's function is subject to a positive obligation with the objective of the statutory purpose: *In the matter of Lehman Bros Europe Ltd (in administration)* [2017] EWHC 2031 (Ch) at [7] (Hildyard J).

Nothing in para 68 imposes a requirement for the approval of the court where an administrator proposes selling the assets of a company prior to the meeting of creditors under para 53 to consider the administrator's proposals: *Re Transbus Ltd (in administration)* [2004] EWHC 932 (Ch), [2004] 2 BCLC 550. The position therefore remains as it was held to be under the former Part II of the 1986 Act, on which see the commentary to para 63 and, in particular, the responsibility of the administrator for such a decision to sell.

In *Re London Oil & Gas Ltd (in administration)* [2019] EWHC 3675 (Ch) the claimant sought an injunction prohibiting the defendant administrators from accessing, reviewing or making use of privileged documents on an electronic database. The court gave directions aimed at ensuring that privileged documents should be permanently removed from the database and delivered up to the claimants. The issue at the heart of the claim was how the court might best provide directions for the identification of which, if any, documents were privileged and should be returned to the claimants. In practice, this is not an uncommon scenario and one which ought to be resolved ordinarily by way of an application for directions under para 68(2) and/or the court's inherent jurisdiction (see [7]–[8] and [14]). The judgment in *London Oil* contains a useful survey of the options available to the court and the methodology intended to ensure the protection of privilege whilst, at the same time, ensuring that such protection did not interfere with the administration and its purposes, applying the most cost and time-effective solution (see especially [60]–[64]).

### PARAGRAPH 68(3)

**The grounds for the provision of directions under para 68(2)**—Ground (a) is most likely to arise in a case of urgency, typically where an administrator seeks sanction for a sale of the company's business and assets or seeks a direction for the convening of a creditors' meeting on short notice to that end. Even where no proposals have been approved the court may wish to consider the basis of and the evidence supporting any administration application on which an administration order was made under para 13(1)(a).

The significance of ground (b) is that the court has no jurisdiction to give directions which are inconsistent with any proposals or revised proposals which have been approved by creditors other than in the limited circumstances in grounds (c) and (d). This represents a marked shift from the position under the former law where such jurisdiction, albeit one exercised only in exceptional cases, did exist: see *Re Smallman Construction Ltd* [1989] BCLC 420 (Knox J). The terms of para 68(3)(b) might suggest that no jurisdiction can exist under para 68 by which the court might give directions which are inconsistent with any proposals or revised proposals approved by creditors, but see the cases cited in the notes to para 55 to contrary effect.

Although the words 'only if' appear in the opening to para 68(3), the wording in para 68(2) is itself positive in nature and does not prescribe that no directions may be given by the court other than in relation to the company's affairs, business or property such that an inherent jurisdiction in the court survives: Re *Collins & Aikman Europe SA* [2007] 1 BCLC 182 at [37] (Lindsay J).

**Eligible applicants**—Unlike para 63, para 68 makes no reference to the parties eligible to make application for directions under para 68(2). It is suggested that the eligible class of persons would extend beyond the administrator himself or herself so as to catch third parties, and most obviously creditors, with a genuine and legitimate interest in the directions sought: see further the notes to para 63.

### PARAGRAPH 68(3)(c), (d)

' . . . the court thinks . . . '—See the commentary on this term in the notes to para 36(2).

**Time for the making of an application for directions**—An administrator may seek directions at any time during the course of his office, even if simultaneous with or on the hearing of the administration application under para 13(1)(f).

## [1.686]

### 69 Administrator as agent of company

In exercising his functions under this Schedule the administrator of a company acts as its agent.

**General note**—This provision repeats the substance of the former s 14(5).

Notwithstanding para 69, like the former s 14(5), the question of an administrator's agency is one of substance not form. Not every act or omission on the part of an administrator is necessarily taken as the company's agent. So, in *SNR Denton UK LLP v Kirwan* [2013] ICR 101, [2012] IRLR 968 (Langstaff J), the Employment Appeal Tribunal held that solicitors engaged to act for the administrators had been retained by the administrators personally, and not on behalf of the company in administration notwithstanding the fact that the administrator and the company would often have a common purpose. The para 69 agency is an agency of a design peculiar to its purpose. In *Wright Hassall LLP v Morris* [2012] EWCA Civ 1472, [2013] BCC 192 the Court of Appeal reversed a decision of the High Court which had held that an administrator was not personally liable for fees alleged as being owed by two companies in administration. The administrator had signed conditional fee agreements and was sued personally on them (the companies in administration not being parties to those proceedings). There is no authority that limited the liability of the defendant sued in his representative form so that he was not personally liable on a judgment against him. Neither is there any authority that naming a defendant as an individual 'as administrator' recognises that he or she is sued as an agent rather than in a personal capacity. (For a finding to like effect in the context of a CFA entered into by a liquidator, who was held to be personally liable on it, see *Stevensdrake Ltd t/a Stevensdrake Solicitors v Hunt* [2015] EWHC 1527 (Ch), [2015] BPIR 1462 (HHJ Purle QC, sitting as a High Court judge), and see [2016] EWHC 342 (Ch).)

**The scope of the administrator's power as agent**—The status of an administrator as agent means that, irrespective of the considerable breadth of the powers in Sch 1, an administrator can have no greater power than the company itself as principal under the scope of the company's objects clause provisions in its memorandum of association: *Re Home Treat Ltd* [1991] BCLC 705 at 706I–707B (Harman J). Should such an issue arise, s 39 of the Companies Act 2006 may be of assistance to a bona fide third party. Paragraph 59(3) also provides that a person who deals with an administrator in good faith and for value need not enquire whether the administrator is acting within his powers.

**Contracts entered into by the administrator as agent**—Other than in the unlikely event of express agreement to the contrary, any contract entered into by the administrator as agent will be binding on the company, but not on the administrator personally: *Re Atlantic Computer Systems plc* [1992] Ch 505 at 526D–526E (Nicholls LJ).

Paragraph 99(4) creates a statutory charge in respect of a debt or liability arising out of a contract entered into by an administrator: see the notes to para 99.

**Contracts adopted by an administrator**—The term 'adopted' is discussed in the commentary to s 44, which will apply equally here. The statutory charge under para 99(4) extends, by virtue of para 99(5), to liability under a contract of employment adopted by an administrator.

**Tax liability**—With effect from 15 September 2003 the appointment of an administrator closes an old accounting period and starts a new accounting period by virtue of s 12(7ZA) of the Income and Corporation Taxes Act 1988 as amended by para 1 of Part V, Sch 41 of the Finance Act 2003. As the proper officer for the company for tax purposes the administrator is required to pay tax on account as required and to give notification and make returns to the Inland Revenue in respect of taxable income or capital gains. The status of the administrator as agent of the company, however, means that the administrator cannot be assessed for corporation tax personally, which post-administration liability remains the liability of the company. Certainly this analysis accords with the Inland Revenue's practice, as notified previously in the ICAEW Technical Release 799 of June 1990. The former IR 1986, r 2.67(1)(j), now r 3.51(2)(j), made express provision for corporation tax on chargeable gains accruing on the realisation of any asset of the company as an expense of the administration.

Neither does an administrator have any liability for pre-administration corporation tax. If an administrator refuses to discharge such liability as an expense of the administration, then the Inland Revenue may have no alternative but to make application to the court under para 43(6)(b) for permission to levy distress. Alternatively, it might be possible to obtain a direction from the court under para 68(2) that the liability be discharged as an expense of the administration, on which jurisdiction see *Re Atlantic Computer Systems plc* [1992] Ch 505 at 528C–528G (Nicholls LJ).

**Tort liability**—In *John Smith & Co (Edinburgh) Ltd v Hill* [2010] EWHC 1016 (Ch), [2010] 2 BCLC 556, Briggs J dismissed an administrator's application for summary judgment in a claim against him by a reversioner on the basis that on the basis that the administrator's decision to allow scaffolding to remain around a building leased by the company constituted a breach of the covenant of quiet enjoyment and was interfering with its attempts to assign the sublease.

**Potential liability of purchaser from administrator**—A purchaser from administrators who knowingly bought property in breach of a third party's rights was held liable for damages in the tort of procuring a breach of contract in *Lictor Anstalt v Mir Steel UK Ltd* [2014] EWHC 3316 (Ch), [2014] 6 Costs LO 918 (Asplin J). The case involved two companies which had knowingly procured a breach of contract by entering into a hive-down agreement and thereafter executing a transfer of land in circumstances where both knew that a third party asserted contractual rights over a hot strip steel mill located on the land.

## [1.687]

### 70 Charged property: floating charge

(1) The administrator of a company may dispose of or take action relating to property which is subject to a floating charge as if it were not subject to the charge.

(2) Where property is disposed of in reliance on sub-paragraph (1) the holder of the floating charge shall have the same priority in respect of acquired property as he had in respect of the property disposed of.

(3)   In sub-paragraph (2) "acquired property" means property of the company which directly or indirectly represents the property disposed of.

**General note**—This provision relates only to property which is subject to a floating charge, as defined in para 111(1), and, by para 70(1), allows the administrator to deal with such property irrespective of the security rights of the holder of the charge, which will almost certainly have crystallised. Paragraph 70(1) will not, however, permit such dealing where the property in question is subject to a valid fixed charge, in which case the administrator may consider an application to court under para 71(1).

**The effect of para 70(2)**—Any floating charge property which is disposed of by an administrator other than with the express consent of the floating charge-holder must, it is submitted, be disposed of in reliance on para 70(1). In those circumstances the security rights of the floating charge holder are deemed to attach to what is termed the 'acquired property' (see below). The security rights of the charge holder in respect of the acquired property will be the same as those which attached to the property disposed of by the administrator under para 70(1). Those rights will, however, remain subject to the statutory charge created under para 99(3) in relation to a former administrator's remuneration and expenses, and any debt or liability falling within para 99(4).

It should also be noted that the holder of a floating charge is in a weaker position than the holder of non-floating security, not only because of the autonomy granted in favour of the administrator by para 70(1) but also because para 70 contains nothing equivalent to para 71(3) which, in effect, provides the holder of non-floating security with a statutory right to the value of any property disposed of by an administrator as would be realised on a hypothetical sale of the property at market value.

**'acquired property'**—The most obvious example of 'acquired property' directly representing floating charge property will be the proceeds of sale or other consideration representing the price of that property. Property will indirectly represent the property disposed of if the proceeds of sale, or other consideration provided on the disposal of the floating charge property, is then converted into some other property to which the floating charge holder's security rights will apply under para 70(2).

**Market contracts etc**—This provision does not apply to market contracts and the like by virtue of para 47 of Sch 17 to the Enterprise Act 2002.

## [1.688]

### 71  Charged property: non-floating charge

(1)   The court may by order enable the administrator of a company to dispose of property which is subject to a security (other than a floating charge) as if it were not subject to the security.

(2)   An order under sub-paragraph (1) may be made only—

    (a)    on the application of the administrator, and

    (b)    where the court thinks that disposal of the property would be likely to promote the purpose of administration in respect of the company.

(3)   An order under this paragraph is subject to the condition that there be applied towards discharging the sums secured by the security—

    (a)    the net proceeds of disposal of the property, and

    (b)    any additional money required to be added to the net proceeds so as to produce the amount determined by the court as the net amount which would be realised on a sale of the property at market value.

(4)   If an order under this paragraph relates to more than one security, application of money under sub-paragraph (3) shall be in the order of the priorities of the securities.

(5)   An administrator who makes a successful application for an order under this paragraph shall send a copy of the order to the registrar of companies before the end of the period of 14 days starting with the date of the order.

(6)   An administrator commits an offence if he fails to comply with sub-paragraph (5) without reasonable excuse.

**General note**—The substance of this provision is mutually exclusive with para 70 and is similar to the provisions in the former s 15 and s 43. Reference should be made to the commentary on the latter provision, which will apply here, in addition to the following. For an example of the court's exercise of discretion, see: *Re MBI Clifton Moor Ltd (in administration)* [2020] EWHC 1835 (Ch) (ICC Judge Jones); *Re Fox Street Village Ltd (in administration)* [2020] EWHC 2541 (Ch) (HHJ Halliwell (sitting as a High Court judge), sale of freehold properties sanctioned based on independent valuation advice notwithstanding creditor opposition, and guidance given on management of potential for conflict by administrators).

For an example of a case in which the Court of Appeal upheld the decision of Warren J to allow the sale of assets under para 71 on an urgent basis see *Re Musion Systems Ltd (in administration), O'Connell v Rollings* [2014] EWCA Civ 639. Although Kitchin LJ identified at [39] that the judge below had observed that 'the balance could not be finer' in considering the application, the judge had been correct in satisfying himself that the proposed sale was at a proper price before undertaking the appropriate balancing exercise and, in so doing, the judge had had proper regard to the prejudice suffered by the chargeholder if the order were made and the prejudice that would be suffered by all those interested in the promotion of the purposes of the administration if he did not, applying *Re ARV Aviation Ltd* (1988) 4 BCC 708. Although a para 71 order amounts to a significant interference with the chargeholder's rights in realising his or her security at a time and in a manner of his or her own choosing, that interference was inevitable where the chargeholder objected to the sale but was a consequence that had to be balanced against the wider interests of those interested in the promotion of the purposes of the administration. In addition, the judge had been entitled to proceed to hear the application pending the creditors' meeting ([76]–[77]).

For a further order under para 71 allowing administrators of a company, whose property development had been halted through lack of funding, to promote the achievement of the purpose of administration by disposing of land and sale proceeds free of the security interests of most off-plan purchasers who thereby lost their deposits see *Williams v Broadoak Private Finance Ltd* [2018] EWHC 1107 (Ch) (HHJ Hodge QC). For a successful application opposed by unsecured creditors to sell a nursing home property, as would further the purpose of administration and allow for a distribution to a secured creditor see *Re MBI Clifton Moor Ltd (in administration)* [2020] EWHC 1835 (Ch) (ICCJ Jones). The same judge dismissed an opposed para 71 application in *Re Sky Building Ltd* [2020] EWHC 3139 (Ch) where the administrators sought permission to sell a development property as if not subject to a purchaser's lien. The court could not be satisfied as to the market value of the property on the untested valuation evidence relied on by the applicants such that it could not be satisfied that the condition in para 71(3)(b) was met.

In *Re Capitol Films Ltd, Rubin v Cobalt Pictures Limited* [2010] EWHC 3223 (Ch), [2011] BPIR 334, Richard Snowden QC held that conduct of the administrators of a film company in administration had been unreasonable to such an extent that it was appropriate to make an order for them to pay the costs of their application under para 71 personally and on the indemnity basis.

Paragraph 71 has no application to the enforcement of a security interest under a financial collateral arrangement: see reg 8(1)(b) of the Financial Collateral Arrangements (No 2) Regulations 2003 (SI 2003/3226).

### PARAGRAPH 71(1)

' . . . property which is subject to a security (other than a floating charge) . . . '— The term 'security' is not defined in Sch B1, but is defined in s 248(b)(i), albeit for the purpose of the First Group of Parts in ss 1–251, as meaning 'any mortgage, charge, lien or other security'. The distinction between the enforcement of security under para 43(2) and the reference to the exercise by a landlord of a right of forfeiture by peaceable re-entry in para 43(4) suggests, in keeping with the decision of Lightman J in *Razzaq v Pala* [1998] BCC 66, that the latter form of right does not constitute a security. The reference to security is to be distinguished from goods in the possession of a company under a hire-purchase agreement. That term is defined in para 111(1) as including a conditional sale agreement, a chattel leasing agreement and a retention of title agreement. Hire purchase property is addressed specifically by para 72. The term 'security' would appear to extend not only to a valid fixed charge but also to a lien and any other security rights precluding dealings in the underlying property by an administrator other than rights arising under a hire-purchase agreement.

### PARAGRAPH 71(2)(b)

' . . . where the court thinks . . . '—See the commentary in the notes to para 36.

' . . . would be likely . . . '—This term, it is submitted, must be taken as meaning 'more likely than not'.

### PARAGRAPH 71(3)(a)

'the net proceeds . . . '—Prior to payment over to a chargeholder, an administrator is entitled to deduct all proper costs, charges and expenses reasonably incurred in the preservation and realisation of the relevant property, including the administrator's related remuneration: *Re James Rose Projects Ltd (in administration), Townsend v Biscoe* [2010] WL 3166608 (Registrar Simmonds).

### PARAGRAPH 71(3)(b)

'Market value'—This term is defined in para 111(1) as 'the amount which would be realised on a sale of property in the open market by a willing vendor'. It is submitted, however, that, in context, that definition can only mean the amount which would be raised in the open market by a willing vendor *administrator* in the particular circumstances of the case since a contrary, literal reading would potentially entitle the security holder under para 71 to a windfall since the amount to which the security holder would be entitled on a true, administration-free market could well exceed, perhaps significantly, the market price obtainable by an administrator.

Whilst an application should be supported by appropriate valuation evidence the court may adjourn an application to allow for an inquiry where there is a dispute or difficulty in fixing valuation: *Re ARV Aviation Ltd* (1988) 4 BCC 708 (Knox J, a decision on the similarly worded s 15). Where the court is presented with two conflicting valuations it is inappropriate for the court to determine valuation by splitting the difference between the two: *Stanley J Holmes & Sons Ltd v Davenham Trust plc* [2006] EWCA Civ 1568, [2007] BCC 485 (Tuckey, Arden, Lloyd LJJ).

**Market contracts etc**—This provision does not apply to market contracts and the like by virtue of para 47 of Sch 17 to the Enterprise Act 2002.

**Penalties**—See s 430, Sch 10 and the daily default find in para 106(2)(j).

## [1.689]

### 72 Hire-purchase property

(1)   The court may by order enable the administrator of a company to dispose of goods which are in the possession of the company under a hire-purchase agreement as if all the rights of the owner under the agreement were vested in the company.

(2)   An order under sub-paragraph (1) may be made only—

    (a)     on the application of the administrator, and

    (b)     where the court thinks that disposal of the goods would be likely to promote the purpose of administration in respect of the company.

(3)   An order under this paragraph is subject to the condition that there be applied towards discharging the sums payable under the hire-purchase agreement—

    (a)     the net proceeds of disposal of the goods, and

    (b)     any additional money required to be added to the net proceeds so as to produce the amount determined by the court as the net amount which would be realised on a sale of the goods at market value.

(4)   An administrator who makes a successful application for an order under this paragraph shall send a copy of the order to the registrar of companies before the end of the period of 14 days starting with the date of the order.

(5)   An administrator commits an offence if he fails without reasonable excuse to comply with sub-paragraph (4).

**General note**—See the notes to para 71 above.

## [1.690]

### 73 Protection for priority creditor

(1)   An administrator's statement of proposals under paragraph 49 may not include any action which—

    (a)     affects the right of a secured creditor of the company to enforce his security,

    (b)     would result in a preferential debt of the company being paid otherwise than in priority to its non-preferential debts, . . .

    (bb)    would result in an ordinary preferential debt of the company being paid otherwise than in priority to any secondary preferential debts that it may have,

    (c)     would result in one preferential creditor of the company being paid a smaller proportion of an ordinary preferential debt than another, . . .

    (d)     would result in one preferential creditor of the company being paid a smaller proportion of a secondary preferential debt than another, or

    (e)     if the company is a relevant financial institution (see section 387A), would result in any non-preferential debt being paid otherwise than in accordance with the rules in section 176AZA(2) or (3).

(2)   Sub-paragraph (1) does not apply to—

    (a)     action to which the relevant creditor consents,

> (b) a proposal for a voluntary arrangement under Part I of this Act (although this sub-paragraph is without prejudice to section 4(3)), . . .
>
> (c) a proposal for a compromise or arrangement to be sanctioned under Part 26 or 26A of the Companies Act 2006 (arrangements and reconstructions), . . .
>
> (d) . . ..

(3) The reference to a statement of proposals in sub-paragraph (1) includes a reference to a statement as revised or modified.

**Amendments**—SI 2007/2974; SI 2008/948; SI 2014/3486; SI 2018/1244; SI 2019/348 having effect from IP completion day (as defined in the European Union (Withdrawal Agreement) Act 2020, s 39(1)–(5)); Corporate Insolvency and Governance Act 2020, s 7, Sch 9, Pt 2, paras 5, 7(1), (3).

**General note**—These provisions should be read in the context of para 49, on which see the commentary thereto. Further commentary also appears in the notes to s 4(3) and (4), which apply equally here.

For the purposes of paras 73(1)(a) and 73(2)(a) the term 'secured creditor' is not defined in Sch B1, but is defined in s 248(a), but only for the purposes of ss 1–251, as a creditor who holds in respect of his debt a security over property of the company. A landlord does not constitute a secured creditor by virtue of a right of forfeiture by peaceable re-entry, on which see the distinction drawn between para 43(2) and (4) and the decision of Lightman J in *Razzaq v Pala* [1998] BCC 66.

## [1.691]

### 74 Challenge to administrator's conduct of company

(1) A creditor or member of a company in administration may apply to the court claiming that—

> (a) the administrator is acting or has acted so as unfairly to harm the interests of the applicant (whether alone or in common with some or all other members or creditors), or
>
> (b) the administrator proposes to act in a way which would unfairly harm the interests of the applicant (whether alone or in common with some or all other members or creditors).

(2) A creditor or member of a company in administration may apply to the court claiming that the administrator is not performing his functions as quickly or as efficiently as is reasonably practicable.

(3) The court may—

> (a) grant relief;
>
> (b) dismiss the application;
>
> (c) adjourn the hearing conditionally or unconditionally;
>
> (d) make an interim order;
>
> (e) make any other order it thinks appropriate.

(4) In particular, an order under this paragraph may—

> (a) regulate the administrator's exercise of his functions;
>
> (b) require the administrator to do or not do a specified thing;
>
> (c) require a decision of the company's creditors to be sought on a matter;
>
> (d) provide for the appointment of an administrator to cease to have effect;
>
> (e) make consequential provision.

(5) An order may be made on a claim under sub-paragraph (1) whether or not the action complained of—

> (a) is within the administrator's powers under this Schedule;
>
> (b) was taken in reliance on an order under paragraph 71 or 72.

(6) An order may not be made under this paragraph if it would impede or prevent the implementation of—

> (a) a voluntary arrangement approved under Part I,
>
> (b) a compromise or arrangement sanctioned under Part 26 or 26A of the Companies Act 2006 (arrangements and reconstructions), . . .
>
> (ba) . . .

(c)     proposals or a revision approved under paragraph 53 or 54 more than 28 days before the day on which the application for the order under this paragraph is made.

**Amendments**—SI 2007/2974; SI 2008/948; Small Business, Enterprise and Employment Act 2015, s 126, Sch 9, Pt 1, paras 1, 10(24); SI 2019/348 having effect from IP completion day (as defined in the European Union (Withdrawal Agreement) Act 2020, s 39(1)–(5)); Corporate Insolvency and Governance Act 2020, s 7, Sch 9, Pt 2, paras 5, 7(1), (4).

**General note**—This provision bears some resemblance to the former s 27 which did not play a significant part in advancing the interests of creditors or members in administration, at least by reference to the reported authorities. The provision might initially be read as being extremely broad in scope. Certainly it has been suggested that para 74(1) and (2) permits the court to make an order providing for the appointment of an administrator to cease to have effect (on which see para 88): *SISU Capital Fund Ltd v Tucker* [2006] BPIR 154 at [88] (Warren J). Paragraph 74 remains, however, subject to a number of limitations identified below.

Paragraph 74 is concerned with the management of an administration, not claims for liability post-administration: *Re Glint Pay Services Ltd* [2020] EWHC 3078 (Ch) (ICCJ Jones).

**Eligible applicants**—Paragraph 74 is only available to 'a creditor or member of a company in administration . . . '. An application may, however, be brought after the administration has come to an end: *Re Coniston Hotel (Kent) LLP* [2013] EWHC 93 (Ch).

In *PJSC Uralkali v Rowley* [2020] EWHC 3442 (Ch) an unsuccessful bidder in an administration sales process, which was not a shareholder or creditor, was outside of the scope of para 74 and failed in fact-heavy claims for negligent misstatement and breach of confidence and was held not to benefit from a direct duty of care owed by the administrators: see further the note to para 75 below.

Irrespective of para 74(1), the Financial Services Authority has standing to make an application by virtue of s 362(4) of the Financial Services and Markets Act 2000, as does a Member State liquidator, whose standing is equivalent to that of a creditor, by virtue of Art 32(3) of the EU Regulation on Insolvency Proceedings.

**The distinction between paras 74 and 75**—Paras 74 and 75 are not identical. The former is concerned with management whereas the latter is concerned with misconduct. Further, under para 74 there is at least the possibility of arguing for relief on an individual basis whereas under para 75 the relief available is directed to restoring the administration estate for the benefit of all members of the relevant class (secured creditors, unsecured creditors or contributories): *Re Coniston Hotel (Kent) LLP (in liquidation), Berntsen v Tait* [2013] EWHC 93 (Ch), [2015] BCC 1 at [69] (Norris J), a point undisturbed on appeal [2015] EWCA Civ 1001.

**Assignment of a para 74 claim**—In *LF2 v Supperstone* [2018] EWHC 1776 (Ch), [2019] 1 BCLC 38 Morgan J found the most helpful guidance to be adopted by administrators asked to assign a para 74 claim to be the decision of the Federal Court of Australia in *Citicorp Australia v Official Trustee in Bankruptcy* [1996] FCA 1115 which is authority for the proposition that the burden rests on the party objecting to any proposed assignment to demonstrate that the claim has no prospect of success. Except where it is clearly hopeless, an administrator should be prepared to investigate whether a claim should be preserved and pursued and to give proper consideration to its assignment, including the inviting of competing bids or auctioning the claim. On an application under para 74(1)(a) for an order requiring administrators to assign a cause of action to the applicant, the burden rests on the applicant to demonstrate that any refusal by the administrators to assign is harmful to the applicant's interests, as requires the applicant establishing a real prospect of success on the claim of which assignment is sought: *Re L&ND Development and Design Ltd* [2020] EWHC 2803 (Ch) (ICCJ Mullen).

**PARAGRAPH 74(1)**

**Unfairness as an ingredient of the cause of action**—In order to succeed in such application, it will be necessary for the applicant to demonstrate both that the action complained of is or will be causative of harm to its interests and that that harm is unfair; harm alone is not enough: *Re Lehman Brothers International (Europe) (in admin)*; *Four Private Investment Funds v Lomas* [2008] EWHC 2869 (Ch), [2009] BCC 632.

Action taken by administrators in the interests of the creditors as a whole is not open to challenge simply because it affects an individual creditor differently: *Re Zegna III Holdings Inc* [2009] EWHC 2994 (Ch), [2010] BPIR 277.

In *Re London & Westcountry Estates Ltd, Hockin v Marsden* [2014] EWHC 763 (Ch), [2014] BPIR 637 the applicant creditors applied for an order under para 74 directing the respondent administrators to assign them certain potential claims against the company's bank for mis-selling an interest rate swap agreement. In granting the application the deputy judge refused to adopt the test of perversity in place of the statutory test of unfair harm and observed that para 74 caters not merely for a challenge to an individual decision of an administrator but also a challenge to a course of conduct (at [16]). Differential treatment was not the only form of unfairness capable of satisfying para 74; a lack of commercial justification for a decision causing harm to the creditors as a whole might be unfair in the sense that the harm was not one which they should be expected to suffer (at [19]–[20]). Although the administrators' decision not to pursue the claims against the bank was reasonable, the real question was not whether it was justifiable to decline to pursue the claims, but, rather, whether it was justifiable also to decline to assign them with the consequence that the claims would be lost. If the claims were successful then the creditors would benefit. If the claims failed then the creditors would have suffered no prejudice. It would unfairly harm the creditors if all the claims were simply lost (at [51]).

In *Re ASA Resource Group plc (in administration)*, *Dearing v Skelton* [2020] EWHC 1370 (Ch) ICC Judge Jones rejected an allegation of unfairness levelled at administrators for refusing to agree with the applicant director that additional directors ought to be appointed for the remaining period of the administration of the company. Although it was open to an administrator to leave part of a business to the management of directors, subject to supervision and provided that such delegation did not adversely affect the purposes of the administration in line with the administrators' proposals, a refusal to agree with incumbent management did not necessarily connote unfairness.

'. . . **unfairly to harm the interests of the applicant** . . . '—In *Coniston Hotel (Kent) LLP* [2013] 2 BCLC 405 at [36] Norris J said, 'Paragraph 74 does not exist to enable individually disgruntled creditors to pursue administrators for compensation. Its focus is, "unfair harm": and that, I think, will ordinarily mean unequal or differential treatment to the disadvantage of the applicant (or applicant class) which cannot be justified by reference to the interests of the creditors as a whole or to achieving the objective of the administration. (The reference to an administrator acting unfairly to harm the interests of "all other members or creditors", so that unequal or differential treatment had not occurred, would (I think) only arise in relation to issues concerning the expenses of the administration, or where the administrator was also an office holder in another insolvency and acted unfairly prejudicially as regards the stakeholders in Company A in promoting the interests [of] the stakeholders in company B)'. This approach was followed In the High Court in Northern Ireland by McCloskey J in *Re Sheridan Millennium Ltd*, *Curistan v Keenan* [2013] NICh 13. Subsequently, in *Hockin v Marsden* [2014] 2 BCLC 531 at [19] Nicholas le Poidevin QC, sitting as a deputy High Court judge, after referring to *Coniston* and *Sheridan*, queried why the requisite unfairness must necessarily be found in an unjustifiable discrimination. The deputy judge went on, 'A lack of commercial justification for a decision causing harm to the creditors as a whole may be unfair in the sense that the harm is not one which they should be expected to suffer. I am not sure that Norris J had such a case in mind in the passage quoted from the *Coniston* case. In the *Coniston* case, the applicants (who appear to have been acting in person earlier in the proceedings) had muddled claims for professional negligence against the administrators for acts before the administration commenced with claims for harm suffered by them as members or creditors and the decision, given on a striking out application, was one of case management.' The deputy judge also identified the obvious dangers in introducing jurisprudence derived from other provisions in considering the specific wording in para 74 and its focus on the context of unfair harm. The deputy judge's approach found agreement in the judgment of David Halpern QC, sitting as a deputy High Court judge, in *Re Meem SL Ltd (in administration)*, *Goel v Grant* [2017] EWHC 2688 at [34]. In holding that the term 'unfair' is not limited to cases of unequal treatment but is capable of including conduct which is unfair to everybody within the class, it was also pointed out that the predecessor to para 74, in s 27 of the 1986 Act, referred to unfair prejudice but that that wording does not appear in the present provision. Neither is there any limitation by which para 74 cannot be invoked in a case which also falls within para 81 (court ending administration on application of creditor). The paradigm case under para 74 arises where the administrator treats the applicant (either along or together with further creditors) less favourably than another creditor or creditors. This constitutes harm, but it is not necessarily unfair harm. In order to be unfair, the applicant has to show that the decision cannot be justified by reference to the interests of the creditors as a whole or to achieving the objective of the administration. The deputy judge in *Meem* resisted, at [44], reaching any concluded view as to whether unfair harm which consists of differential treatment has to be perverse so as to be actionable.

Respectfully, there is no good reason why in all cases discrimination as between creditors ought to be a pre-requisite of a finding of unfairness for the purposes of para 74, as envisaged in *Hockin* by reference to the authorities identified above. Although a successful challenge to an administrator's exercise of powers may often feature discrimination between creditors, it is equally possible that unfairness on the part of an administrator might be founded instead, not on a footing of discrimination, but on a failure on the part of the administrator to act in accordance with his or her duties under Sch B1 – see the approach of Blackburne J in *Four Private Investment Funds v Lomas* [2008] EWHC 2869 (Ch), as approved of by the Court of Appeal in *Fraser Turner Ltd v PwC LLP* [2019] EWCA Civ 1290 at [76] – as might also attract a challenge to a decision on the grounds that the administrator has acted in a manner that is so utterly unreasonable or absurd that it is to be characterised as perverse and set aside (on which, in the context of administration, see *Davey v Money* [2018] EWHC 766 (Ch) at [255] (Snowden J)). In *Lehman Bros Australia Ltd (in liquidation) v MacNamara* [2020] EWCA Civ 321 at [83]–[85] the Court of Appeal expressed the view that, whilst discriminatory conduct can certainly amount to unfairness, there is no reason for confining para 74 to such cases because discrimination is not a mandatory qualification found within the provision.

In *Cheshire West and Chester BC, Petitioners* [2010] CSOH 115, [2011] BCC 174, the Court of Session (Outer House) held that administrators had caused unfair harm to the council as landlord to the company by the non-payment of rent after the appointment of the administrators.

### PARAGRAPH 74(2)

**Scope of provision**—Paragraph 74(2) should be read in conjunction with paras 4 and 76 and the notes thereto. The provision envisages a claim on the basis of either a failure in terms of speed or efficiency on the part of the administrator by reference to what is 'reasonably practicable'. In practice, it is very doubtful that the court will be sympathetic to an application which amounts in substance to nothing more than a difference of opinion between the applicant and the administrator as to the past, present or proposed conduct of the administration. On the other hand, the court will always be alive to properly evidenced complaints where an administrator can be shown to be lacking in speed or efficiency by reference to the objective benchmark of what is 'reasonably practicable'. It is submitted that, whilst an applicant under para 74(2) need not establish as a prerequisite any actual or prospective harm to the applicant in terms of his financial participation in the administration (or, it is submitted, any ensuing liquidation), it is doubtful that the court will be receptive to an application where the applicant has no prospect of a financial participation in the administration.

**Alternative courses of action**—Before embarking on a claim under para 74 a creditor should also consider the possibility of seeking relief by way of permission to take action otherwise prevented by the moratoria and related provisions in paras 40–43. Certainly, para 74(5)(b) anticipates an application by the holder of fixed or other non-floating security or the owner of goods under a hire-purchase agreement. Other possibilities are also mentioned in the next section.

### PARAGRAPH 74(3), (4)

**Relief available**—Subject to the limitations imposed by para 74(6), the scope of the relief open to the court is cast in the broadest possible terms. There is, it is submitted, a danger in drawing analogies between para 74 and the relief granted by the court in petitions brought under s 994 of the Companies Act 2006. In cases where the substance of what is alleged is nothing short of professional misconduct or negligence, consideration should be given to the making of an application by a creditor under para 81 for an order ending the administration or an application under para 88 removing the administrator from office, or an action in misfeasance proceedings under para 75.

Relief under para 74 is not precluded by a company having been placed into liquidation. The court may still grant relief under para 74 even though the administration has come to an end: *Re Coniston Hotel (Kent) LLP (in liquidation), Berntsen v Tait* [2013] EWHC 93 (Ch), [2015] BCC 1 at [68] (Norris J) undisturbed on appeal, [2015] EWCA Civ 1001. In *Coniston* at [35] Norris J drew attention to the argument that para 74 is sufficiently broad to allow the court to order compensation or damages but without deciding the point.

## [1.692]

### 75 Misfeasance

(1) The court may examine the conduct of a person who—

    (a)    is or purports to be the administrator of a company, or

    (b)    has been or has purported to be the administrator of a company.

(2) An examination under this paragraph may be held only on the application of—

    (a)    the official receiver,

    (b)    the administrator of the company,

    (c)    the liquidator of the company,

    (d)    a creditor of the company, or

    (e)    a contributory of the company.

(3) An application under sub-paragraph (2) must allege that the administrator—

    (a)    has misapplied or retained money or other property of the company,

    (b)    has become accountable for money or other property of the company,

    (c)    has breached a fiduciary or other duty in relation to the company, or

    (d)    has been guilty of misfeasance.

(4) On an examination under this paragraph into a person's conduct the court may order him—

(a)    to repay, restore or account for money or property;

(b)    to pay interest;

(c)    to contribute a sum to the company's property by way of compensation for breach of duty or misfeasance.

(5)  In sub-paragraph (3) "administrator" includes a person who purports or has purported to be a company's administrator.

(6)  An application under sub-paragraph (2) may be made in respect of an administrator who has been discharged under paragraph 98 only with the permission of the court.

General note—With effect from 15 September 2003 all references to administrators were removed from s 212 (summary remedy against delinquent directors and office-holders) by virtue of para 18 of Sch 17 to the Enterprise Act 2002. Paragraph 75 is dedicated specifically to any so-called misfeasance claim against an administrator appointed under Sch B1. Although the notes to s 212 will be of continuing relevance to claims pursued under the procedure in para 75, three specific changes should also be considered. First, para 75 is not dependent on a company being in liquidation. Secondly, para 75(1) now extends not only to an administrator or a former administrator but also to the conduct of a person who 'has purported to be the administrator of a company' – words also used in para 75(5) – which would catch an individual whose appointment was actually invalid or void. Thirdly, by virtue of para 75(3), there is now a specific procedural requirement for the specifics of the allegation or allegations.

Paragraph 75 allows causes of action vested in the insolvent company's estate, representing a collective remedy for the benefit of creditors generally, subject to effective floating charge security, to be actioned by those categories of person listed in para 75(2). The parties in para 75(2) do not include the company itself which cannot therefore avail itself of the para 75 procedure in the face of an invalid appointment: *Re Glint Pay Ltd (in administration)* [2020] EWHC 3078 (Ch) (ICCJ Jones).

Save where a special relationship is made out founding a duty owed to an individual creditor (see next section below), the financial interests of creditors in a company in liquidation or administration are mediated through the office-holder's duties to the company. It would appear to follow that, other than where the cause of action has been assigned to a third party, para 75, like s 212, cannot facilitate the actioning of a cause of action vested in a party other than the insolvent company. A claim vested in a party other than the insolvent company would be capable of action against an administrator or former administrator (subject to discharge under para 98) either by way of a CPR Pt 7 claim or, conceivably, by way of an insolvency application for directions under para 63. In *PJSC Uralkali v Rowley* [2020] EWHC 3442 (Ch) an unsuccessful bidder in an administration sales process, which was not a shareholder or creditor, was outside of the scope of para 75 and failed in fact-heavy claims for negligent misstatement and breach of confidence and was held not to benefit from a direct duty of care owed by the administrators. The judgment of Miles J acknowledged the challenging role of an office-holder ('The task of administrators is demanding and exacting enough without requiring them to have to look over their shoulders for personal claims by bidders. I consider that the imposition of a personal duty of care on the administrators on facts such as the present case would be inimical to the single-minded duty placed on administrators to act in the interests of the company's creditors').

The reference to 'an administrator who has been discharged under para 98' in para 75(6) equates to the *release* of an administrator under the former s 20.

For examples of professional negligence claims against administrators see *Davey v Money* [2018] EWHC 766 (Ch) (unsuccessful contributory claim); *Brewer v Iqbal* [2019] EWHC 182 (Ch) (successful liquidator claim); *Re One Blackfriars Ltd* [2021] EWHC 684 (Ch) (unsuccessful liquidator claim).

**Assignment of para 75 claim**—If a para 75 claim is capable of valid assignment see the procedural difficulties posed by *Manolete Partners plc v Hayward and Barrett Holdings Ltd* [2021] EWHC 1481 (Ch) (assignment of s 212 claim in context of hybrid claim) and the notes to s 212 and r 1.35.

**The nature of the duties of an administrator**—The duties of an administrator, and the procedural way in which a claim may be brought against an administrator, are based in statute. In *Davey v Money* [2018] EWHC 766 (Ch) Snowden J rejected the applicant's submissions that the former administrators were to be characterised as fiduciaries whose duties were the same as or equivalent to those owed by express trustees by way of a 'custodial' or 'management stewardship duty', as described by Lord Toulson JSC in *AIB Group (UK) plc v Mark Redler & Co* [2014] UKSC 58, [2015] AC 1503 at [51]. Although Snowden J accepted that administrators owe fiduciary duties to a company, the substance of those duties comprises no more and no less than a duty to exercise powers in good faith and for a proper purpose, and not irrationally. That conclusion was based on the judgment of Millett LJ in *Bristol & West Building Society v Mothew* [1998] Ch 1, [1997] 2 WLR 436, CA which had relied heavily upon the speech of Lord Browne-Wilkinson in *Henderson* *v Merrett Syndicates (No 1)* [1995] 2 AC 145 at 205, [1994] 3 WLR 761, HL in characterising the duties undertaken using skill and care as being other than fiduciary in nature. Snowden J also rejected the applicants' submissions that an administrator acts as a fiduciary and, as a consequence, in the sale of property as an office-holder, should be regarded as owing the same equitable duties as a trustee. In reaching that conclusion, Snowden J quoted a passage from the judgment of Millett J in *Re Charnley Davies Ltd (No 2)* [1990] BCLC 760 which best characterises the obligation of an administrator in the sale of an asset: '[I]t is not an absolute duty to obtain the best price that circumstances permit but only to take reasonable care to do so, and in my judgment that means the best price that circumstances as he reasonably perceives to be permit. He is not to be made liable because his perception is wrong, unless it is unreasonable . . . .'.

Applying *Oldham v Kyrris* [2003] EWCA Civ 1506 (administrator owes no general duty of care to individual creditor absent special relationship), in *Charalambous v B&C Associates* [2009] EWHC 2601 (Ch), [2009] 43 EG 105 (CS), Michael Furness QC, sitting as a deputy High Court judge, granted the administrators' application to strike out a claim against them pursuant to para 75 on the basis that, absent some special relationship (which did not arise on the facts), an administrator owed no general common law duty of care to specific unsecured creditors in relation to the conduct of the administration. See also *Hague v Nam Tai Electronics* [2008] UKPC 13.

In *Re Coniston Hotel (Kent) LLP* [2013] EWHC 93 (Ch), Norris J held that the court could not order a wrongdoing administrator to pay equitable compensation for breach of fiduciary duty to an individual creditor. If there was a deficiency in the insolvency then the payment was for the benefit of the creditors as a class. The Court of Appeal dismissed the creditor's appeal as having no prospect of success in what would have been costly legal proceedings: [2015] EWCA Civ 1001.

For a successful para 75 claim by liquidators against a former administrator for breach of fiduciary duty (failure to obtain proper valuation or test the market for agreements to use electronic programming guides before selling them) see *Brewer v Iqbal* [2019] EWHC 182 (Ch), [2019] 1 BCLC 487 (Chief ICC Judge Briggs). See *Fraser Turner Ltd v PricewaterhouseCoopers LLP* [2019] EWCA Civ 1290 on the sale by administrators of an insolvent mining company and the issue of whether the purchaser ought to meet royalty obligations attached to the asset.

**Para 75(6)**—The requirement for permission arises because a former office-holder no longer has the assets of the company in his hands from which to indemnify himself in respect of unmeritorious claims: *Re Hellas Telecommunications (Luxembourg) II SCA* [2011] EWHC 3176 (Ch) at [96] (Sales J). The test for whether permission ought to be granted under para 75(6) is, first, whether a reasonable meritorious cause of action has been shown, and, secondly, whether giving permission for its prosecution is reasonably likely to result in benefit to the estate: *Katz v Oldham* [2016] BPIR 83 at [5]–[7] (Registrar Derrett). In concluding on the same test in *Re One Blackfriars Ltd, Hyde v Bannon* [2018] EWHC 901 (Ch) at [30], William Trower QC, sitting as a deputy High Court judge, said that reasonably meritorious equates to having a proper foundation, and that the test applicable in most cases is the same as asking whether a reasonable litigant would commence and pursue the claim.

## ENDING ADMINISTRATION

### [1.693]

### 76 Automatic end of administration

(1)   The appointment of an administrator shall cease to have effect at the end of the period of one year beginning with the date on which it takes effect.

(2)   But—

    (a)    on the application of an administrator the court may by order extend his term of office for a specified period, and

    (b)    an administrator's term of office may be extended for a specified period not exceeding one year by consent.

**Amendments**—Small Business, Enterprise and Employment Act 2015, s 127.

**General note**—Paragraph 76 applies to all administrations under Sch B1 and raises a rebuttable presumption in all cases that an administration will be conducted to its conclusion within the period of one year beginning with the date on which the company enters administration, as defined in para 1(2)(b) and ending one year thereafter. In *Re Property Professionals + Limited* [2013] EWHC 1903 (Ch) HHJ Purle QC (sitting as a High Court judge) held that this period should be calculated from the precise time at which the administration order was made. Accordingly, where administrators were appointed at 2.13pm on 3 February 2010, their term of office terminated just before 2.13pm on 3 February 2011.

In *Re Taylor Made Foods plc* (unreported, 28 February 2010), where the administrators' term of office had terminated at a weekend, Henderson J allowed an application for an extension to be made on the next day that the Court Office was open.

The one-year period in para 76(1) significantly exceeds the unworkable 3-month period originally proposed, but still represents a marked shift from the position under the former Part II which imposed no such time limit, with the consequence that, in some cases at least, there was no real incentive for the administrator to conduct the administration with the degree of vigour which might otherwise have been the case, or to apply for a discharge of the order in accordance with the duty in s 18(2) in a timely fashion. The imposition of a time limit, albeit one capable of extension, also squares with the administrator's duty under para 4 to perform his functions as quickly and efficiently as is reasonably practicable.

Under the Part II of the 1986 Act, the practice adopted by judges in the Chancery Division varied on the making of an administration order as regards the perceived need to monitor the conduct of an administration. It was common enough that an administration order was made for a fixed period of time, at the expiry of which the matter would come back to court, particularly where the petition was advanced on grounds that a sale of the company's business and/or assets might be achieved within a stipulated period. Less commonly, an order would require that an administrator should make an application for directions within a fixed period for the further conduct of the administration. In cases where such an order was not made, there would be no reason why the matter should come back before the court at any time prior to the application for discharge under s 18, in the absence of an application by the administrator for directions or a contentious application in the administration by a third party. Despite the imposition of the one-year period in para 76(1) there will continue to be cases under Sch B1 where the court may wish to review the continuance of the order within a far shorter timescale and to impose any such consequential order as is considered appropriate under para 13(1)(f), although there is no mechanism for such an order in an out-of-court appointment case under paras 14 or 22. Further, there is no good reason why in an appropriate out-of-court appointment case an aggrieved creditor should not make an application to court for directions under para 68(2) or on the basis identified in the notes to para 63, where it is alleged that the administrator is in breach of his duty under para 4, even though that duty is only likely to be owed to the company itself.

The period by which an administrator's term of office may be extended by consent in para 76(2)(b) was extended from 6 months to one year by s 127 of the Small Business, Enterprise and Employment Act 2015.

Paragraph 76(2)(a) is now supplemented by r 3.54 which, by sub-rules (2) and (5), requires an application to state the reasons why an administrator is seeking an extension and requires the administrator to deliver to creditors as soon as reasonably practicable a notice of the order and the administrator's reasons given in the application for seeking the extension

**Extending the one-year period in para 76(1)**—The presumption identified in the general note above is capable of rebuttal so as to allow for the extension of the administrator's term of office either by the court for an unlimited but specified period under para 76(2)(a) or with the consent of the company's creditors, as defined and qualified in para 78(1)–(3), for a period not exceeding 6 months under para 76(2). In practice, the administrator may have to do very little to procure the consent of creditors. It is curious that, close on to 13 years since the first one-year periods of administration would have fallen to expire or require extension under the new Sch B1 regime, there is no reported authority which deals squarely with the test applicable to an application to extend the period of administration. In an article by Philip Ridgeway and Ryan Beckwith (Insolv Int 2005, 18(2), 25–28) reference is made to an unreported decision called *Re Trident Fashions (No 3) (in administration)*, in which the High Court apparently accepted that the appropriate test is whether the extension of the administration is reasonably likely to achieve the purpose of administration, the authors noting that, in granting the one-year extension sought, the court considered it unlikely that creditors would suffer prejudice as a result of the extension and that the secured creditor, shareholder and key funders had consented to the extension sought. It is respectfully suggested here that the test so identified in *Trident* is correct but that factors such as the unlikelihood of prejudice to creditors and the consent or support of any interested party (as with opposition by such a party) can only be factors relevant to the exercise of the court's discretion in granting or refusing an extension, without those factors necessarily being determinative. Further, given that an extension constitutes a derogation from the statutory one-year (maximum) period of administration, and the statutory duty imposed on an administrator by para 4 of Sch B1 to, the evidential burden must rest with the applicant administrators in establishing to the court's satisfaction that there is a reasonable likelihood that the purpose of the particular administration before the court will be achieved. It is one thing for administrators to make such an assertion, but another for the administrators to discharge the test identified above in evidence, especially (as often arises in practice) where the extension is sought on the basis of pursuing further a single activity such as continuation of a claim in litigation, the sale of a property or properties or the collection of book debts. The projected costs of extending the administration will often be key here. The evidence in support of the extension application will usually require the administrators to set out the likely cost of extending the administration (which the court may want to consider in light of the costs to date) and the anticipated benefit of those costs being expended together with a comparison of the administration not being extended, most obviously by the company being placed into liquidation. The expressed position of creditors as regards the extension sought will also usually be a material factor relevant to the exercise of the court's discretion.

The judgment of Snowden J in *Re Nortel Networks Ltd* [2017] EWHC 3299 (Ch) identifies at [22] that the discretion under para 76(2)(a) is not circumscribed in any express way before broad factors relevant to discretion and the significance of alternative outcomes if an extension is not granted. On the facts, the administration was extended again but not beyond 29 March 2019 due to uncertainty over Brexit.

In *Re Burningnight Ltd (in administration), Re Crowdstacker Ltd (in administration), Mackenzie v Crowdstacker Corporate Services Ltd* [2020] EWHC 2663 (Ch), [2021] 1 BCLC 557 Mr Philip Marshall QC, sitting as a deputy High Court judge, in the context of opposed extension applications in respect of parent and wholly-owned subsidiary companies, the extension was refused in respect of the parent on the basis that any outstanding matters could be dealt with in liquidation. In relation to the insolvent parent, in which the opposing respondent was the only creditor with any potential financial interest and was pressing for liquidation, the judge applied *Lancefield v Lancefield* [2002] BPIR 1108 (Ch) and exercised the exceptional jurisdiction allowing for a winding-up order in the absence of a petition (the presentation of which would involve needless expense and delay), to take effect from the time of the termination of the administrators' appointment, with a view to the appointment of an independent liquidator to investigate matters given the respondent's concerns as to conduct of the administration, including a pre-pack sale. The judge extended the period of administration for six-months in respect of the subsidiary (although another judge subsequently extended that period by a further six months given the subsequent listing for trial of the ongoing litigation in which the administrators were applicants, and which ultimately settled), applying *Biomethane and Nortel* (above). The basis of the extension was in avoiding the disruption consequent upon a more immediate termination, the fact that there still appeared to be a real prospect of achieving the purpose of a better realisation by reference to the completion of sale of a hotel and four separate insolvency proceedings instituted by the administrator and the existence of other potentially financially interested unsecured creditors who did not oppose the extension notwithstanding the opposition of the respondent.

Where an administration order was made with retrospective effect after the close of the transition period for the UK's withdrawal from the EU, the proceedings were opened on the date of that order, and not from the retrospective date from which the order took effect. Accordingly, such an order has to contain the recitals specified by r 3.13, as amended by the Insolvency (Amendment) (EU Exit) Regulations 2019 (SI 2019/146): *Re Mederco (Cardiff) Ltd* [2021] EWHC 386 (Ch) (HHJ Davis-White QC (sitting as a High Court judge), observations made without the benefit of full argument).

The large scale and complex debt arrangements between companies can justify extensions for periods of years: see, for example, *Re Lehman Brothers Holdings plc (in administration)* [2020] EWHC 3449 (Ch) (Hildyard J).

**The proper time for an application for extension**—Paragraph 8.3 of the *Practice Direction – Insolvency Proceedings* (July 2020) [2020] BPIR 1211 provides that, in the absence of special circumstances, an application for the extension of an administration should be made not less than one month before the end of the administration. The evidence in support of any later application must explain why the application is being made late. The court will consider whether any part of the costs should be disallowed where an application is made less than one month before the end of the administration.

**Circumstances in which an extension of the period of administration may not be obtained**—Paragraph 78(4) provides that an extension by consent of creditors may only be obtained once, and not after any extension by order of the court. There is no limitation on the number of times that an extension may be granted by order of the court, irrespective of the fact of any previous extension by consent of creditors, by virtue of para 77(1)(a).

Once expired, whether at the end of the statutory one-year period or any extended period, paras 77(1)(b) and 78(4)(c) expressly provide that an administrator's term of office is incapable of being extended retrospectively by the court or with creditor consent. Schedule B1 provides no solution to this problem, which dictates that an administrator must be resolute in monitoring the period of the term of office, given his or her potential personal liability for trespass to or inference with the company's property and/or a claim for breach of duty in misfeasance proceedings under para 75 arising out of failure to conduct the administration appropriately where he or she fails to apprehend the end of the term of office and to seek any extension necessary.

In an appropriate case where an administration is in its later stages the administrator might couple an application for extension to court with an application for permission under para 65(3) to make a distribution to unsecured creditors.

Following expiry of the term of an administration the former administrator will have no standing to exercise any of the powers under paras 59–64, including the power to apply to the court for directions, or to discharge those duties referred to in paras 67 and 68, although the former administrator's remuneration and expenses would remain protected by the statutory charge created by para 99(3). On expiry of the term of the administration the control and management of the assets of the company would appear to revert to the company acting by its directors. The former administrator would also appear to be under a duty to give actual notice of that position, and the circumstances giving rise to it, to the directors and all creditors of the company.

The position where an application for extension is filed with the court before the end of the one-year period, but only comes on for hearing after its expiry, was considered by HHJ Norris QC, sitting as a High Court judge, in *Re TT Industries Ltd* [2006] BCC 373. Identifying the problem as one of jurisdiction, as opposed to procedure, the judge took the view that any lapse of time after the end of the statutory one-year period could not be cured under para 107 of Sch B1, s 376 of IA 1986, r 12.9(2) of IR 1986 (now repealed) or CPR 40.7 (at [6]). Despite the wording in para 77(1) the judge took the view (at [14]) that that provision does not deprive the court of standing to make an extending order where: (a) the application is made after the administrator's term of office has expired; and (b) there is a real possibility that the court itself had contributed to the matter not coming on for hearing before expiry of the term (as the judge found to be the case), since the court's jurisdiction allowed it to extend an order on the ground that unavoidable delays in the administration of justice should not interfere with the rights of parties: see *Re Keystone Knitting Mill's Trade Mark* [1929] 1 Ch 92. Given that this issue had not apparently come before the court previously the judge went on to draw attention to the proper procedure available in some courts (the *TT Industries* case proceeded in the Birmingham District Registry of the High Court, Chancery Division) in which it was apparent to court staff that an administration order was about to lapse, the matter would be placed before the judge for immediate consideration on paper (and for the judge to grant a short extension pending a hearing if there was insufficient time for a proper consideration of the matter); to issue strong guidance to practitioners to draw attention (on the face of the application and a covering letter) to the fact that an order was required by a specified date; to remind practitioners that a Chancery (Section 9 or High Court) judge may not be immediately available to consider cases (even on paper); and to give a clear warning that applications lodged within the last few days of a current administration (where no satisfactory reason was given for the lateness) and with which the court could not deal during the currency of the administration were likely to be treated as cases where the order has not been obtained through the default of the administrator.

## [1.694]

**77**

(1)  An order of the court under paragraph 76—
- (a)  may be made in respect of an administrator whose term of office has already been extended by order or by consent, but
- (b)  may not be made after the expiry of the administrator's term of office.

(2)  Where an order is made under paragraph 76 the administrator shall as soon as is reasonably practicable notify the registrar of companies.

(3)  An administrator who fails without reasonable excuse to comply with sub-paragraph (2) commits an offence.

**General note**—These provisions should be read in conjunction with para 76, on which see the notes thereto.

**Penalties**—See s 430, Sch 10 and the daily default fine in para 106(2)(l).

## [1.695]

**78**

(1)  In paragraph 76(2)(b) "consent" means consent of—
- (a)  each secured creditor of the company, and
- (b)  if the company has unsecured debts, the unsecured creditors of the company.

(2)  But where the administrator has made a statement under paragraph 52(1)(b) "consent" means—
- (a)  consent of each secured creditor of the company, or
- (b)  if the administrator thinks that a distribution may be made to preferential creditors, consent of—

      (i)     each secured creditor of the company, and

      (ii)    the preferential creditors of the company.

(2A)   Whether the company's unsecured creditors or preferential creditors consent is to be determined by the administrator seeking a decision from those creditors as to whether they consent.

(3)   . . .

(4)   An administrator's term of office—

      (a)    may be extended by consent only once,

      (b)    may not be extended by consent after extension by order of the court, and

      (c)    may not be extended by consent after expiry.

(5)   Where an administrator's term of office is extended by consent he shall as soon as is reasonably practicable—

      (a)    file notice of the extension with the court, and

      (b)    notify the registrar of companies.

(6)   An administrator who fails without reasonable excuse to comply with sub-paragraph (5) commits an offence.

**Amendments**—Small Business, Enterprise and Employment Act 2015, s 126, Sch 9, Pt 1, paras 1, 10(25)–(28).

**General note**—For the relevance of 'consent' see para 76(2)(b). An extension of an administrator's term of office through the consent of creditors may only be effected once. It is not, therefore, open to an administrator to seek a further extension where a first extension by creditors was for a period of less than 6 months.

   **The three alternative meanings of 'consent'**—'Consent' means either:

   (a)    the consent of those creditors identified in para 78(1)(a) and (b). The wording employed in both paras 78(1)(b) and 78(2)(b)(ii) means that consent depends on the consent of more than 50% of the particular class of creditor who respond to an invitation to give or withhold consent. Since the exclusion of votes under para 78(1)(b) is dependent on a non-response to an invitation, it would follow that a response conveying an abstention should be taken into account; or

   (b)    if the administrator has made a para 52(1)(b) statement (ie in his statement of proposals to the effect that the company has insufficient property to enable a distribution to be made to unsecured creditors other than by virtue of the 'prescribed part' provisions in s 176A(2)(a)) the consent of each secured creditor of the company; or

   (c)    if the administrator has made a para 52(1)(b) statement, and the administrator thinks that a distribution may be made to preferential creditors, the consent of each secured creditor of the company and those preferential creditors identified in para 78(2)(b)(ii).

**Consent under para 78(3)**—Written consent may involve a saving of the cost involved in the convening of a creditors' meeting although, as a matter of good practice, an administrator may consider this a false economy if he perceives some obvious level of dissent between a significant number of creditors in value despite written consent apparently being obtainable. Written consent may include such consent in electronic form by virtue of para 111(2).

**Extension of administrator's term of office**—See paras 76 and 77 and the notes to para 76.

**Penalties**—See s 430, Sch 10 and para 106(2)(m).

## [1.696]

### 79 Court ending administration on application of administrator

(1)   On the application of the administrator of a company the court may provide for the appointment of an administrator of the company to cease to have effect from a specified time.

(2)   The administrator of a company shall make an application under this paragraph if—

      (a)    he thinks the purpose of administration cannot be achieved in relation to the company,

      (b)    he thinks the company should not have entered administration, or

      (c)    the company's creditors decide that he must make an application under this paragraph.

(3)   The administrator of a company shall make an application under this paragraph if—

      (a)    the administration is pursuant to an administration order, and

(b)    the administrator thinks that the purpose of administration has been sufficiently achieved in relation to the company.

(4)   On an application under this paragraph the court may—

(a)    adjourn the hearing conditionally or unconditionally;

(b)    dismiss the application;

(c)    make an interim order;

(d)    make any order it thinks appropriate (whether in addition to, in consequence of or instead of the order applied for).

**Amendments**—Small Business, Enterprise and Employment Act 2015, s 126, Sch 9, Pt 1, paras 1, 10(29).

**General note**—Paragraph 79(1) applies in all administrations. Paragraphs 79(2) and 79(3) prescribe circumstances in which an application under para 79(1) is mandatory. Whilst paras 79(2) and 79(3) subject the administrator to an obligation to make an application under para 89(1) in those circumstances, the administrator is not precluded from making such an application in other circumstances: *Re TM Kingdom Ltd (in administration)* [2007] BCC 480 at [16] (HHJ Norris QC, sitting as a High Court judge; para 79(1) application approved to allow company to be placed into CVL to avoid ad valorem charges on compulsory winding up and unoccupied business rates then ranking as an expense of an administration but not of a liquidation). Although para 79(2) applies to all administrations (most obviously under para 79(2)(b) where the administrator becomes aware of something which fundamentally alters his perception of the basis upon which the company was put into administration), para 79(3) is restricted to those cases in which an administration order has been made, given that an out-of-court appointee may file a notice under para 80(2) where he thinks that the purpose of administration has been sufficiently achieved.

For an example of court termination of appointments (in the context of discharge from liability and remuneration following conclusion of a CVA, anticipated dissolution and the transfer of remaining assets to a French parent company against Brexit-related considerations) see *Re Nortel Networks France SAS* [2019] EWHC 2447 (Ch).

### PARAGRAPH 79(1)

**Administrator's appointment ceasing to take effect**—A company is no longer in administration once an administrator's appointment ceases to take effect: see para 1(2)(a) and (c) and the notes to para 1.

### PARAGRAPH 79(2)–(4)

**'thinks . . . '**—For commentary on the meaning of the term 'thinks' see the notes to para 3.

**The court's discretion under para 79(4)**—It is apparent from para 79(4)(d) that the court need not grant the specific relief sought in a para 79(1) application. The fact that proposals under para 49 have not been sent out to creditors does not inhibit the exercise of the court's discretion, although the procedures identified below provide for the provision of information to creditors in such a case.

Even if the creditors require an administrator to make an application for a termination order under para 79(1), the discretion as to whether to make such an order is a matter for the court, not the creditors: *Re Fox Street Village Ltd (in administration)* [2020] EWHC 2541 (Ch) at [58]–[60] (HHJ Halliwell, sitting as a High Court judge). In *Fox*, which concerned a partly completed and significant development in Liverpool, there were no substantial grounds for terminating the administration. Further, given that the administrators were able to dispose of the property as a whole free of a purchaser's lien, by way of a successful para 71 application, and that the purpose of administration was still reasonably capable of achievement, there was no good reason to make a termination order under para 79(1) despite the opposition of the majority of creditors.

Under Sch B1, as with the former Part II, an administrator is not obliged to seek the winding up of a company at the end of his term of office. Under the former provisions it was very common for an administrator to couple an application for discharge of an administration order under s 18 with a petition for winding up, or for the court to accept undertakings pursuant to which the company was placed into voluntary liquidation. A similar practice should be adopted by office-holders and by the court under the new provisions in light of the approval of the Court of Appeal (Chadwick, Rix and Arden LJJ) in *Oakley Smith v Greenberg* [2003] EWCA Civ 1217, [2003] BPIR 709 at [31] and of the view expressed by Millett J in *Re Barrow Borough Transport Ltd* [1990] Ch 227, to the effect that the court should not sanction the cessation of an administration in the absence of proposals for the realisation and distribution of the assets of the company, which could include moving the company into a CVL under para 83, other than where it is intended to return control of the company and its assets to the company's directors.

The wording of para 79(4)(d) appears sufficiently broad to allow the court to make a winding-up order and an order for the appointment of a liquidator notwithstanding the absence of a winding-up petition or, it seems, where there is already an extant winding-up petition which is not before the court at that time. Such an order was made in *Re Graico Property Ltd* [2016] EWHC 2827 (Ch), [2017] BCC 15. That case was followed in *Re West End Quay Estate Management*, 6 February 2017, unreported, where the court was not prepared to return control of the company to its directors and instead appointed the company's administrators, who were familiar with the nuances of the case, as liquidators upon the winding-up order being made in the interests of saving time and costs. In *Pettit v Bradford Bulls (Northern) Ltd* [2016] EWHC 3357 (Ch) the court, in considering an out-of-court appointment of doubtful validity, proceeded as if the applicant administrators had applied for their purported appointments to come to an end, discharged those administrators insofar as they had been validly appointed, and made a fresh appointment by court order backdated to the date of the purported out-of-court appointment, all notwithstanding the absence of an application for the original out-of-court appointments to come to an end. If the court makes an order under para 79(1) providing for the appointment of an administrator to cease to have effect, then the court is obliged to discharge any administration order under para 85(2). In *Re West End Quay Estate Management Ltd (in administration)* [2017] EWHC 958 (Ch) the court considered an application for the discharge of administrators on the ground that the purpose of administration could not be achieved. There was no money to fund the ongoing costs of the administration. Rather than handing the company back to its directors, the court made a winding-up order in the absence of a winding-up petition, further to the jurisdiction explained by Norris J in *Re Graico Property Co Ltd (in administration)* [2016] EWHC 2827 (Ch), and appointed the former administrators to be liquidators, holding over the discharge of the administrators in the face of an objection by an interested party.

Paragraph 86 applies where a court order provides for the appointment of an administrator to cease to have effect.

## [1.697]

### 80 Termination of administration where objective achieved

(1)   This paragraph applies where an administrator of a company is appointed under paragraph 14 or 22.

(2)   If the administrator thinks that the purpose of administration has been sufficiently achieved in relation to the company he may file a notice in the prescribed form—

    (a)   with the court, and

    (b)   with the registrar of companies.

(3)   The administrator's appointment shall cease to have effect when the requirements of sub-paragraph (2) are satisfied.

(4)   Where the administrator files a notice he shall within the prescribed period send a copy to every creditor of the company, other than an opted-out creditor, of whose claim and address he is aware.

(5)   The rules may provide that the administrator is taken to have complied with sub-paragraph (4) if before the end of the prescribed period he publishes in the prescribed manner a notice undertaking to provide a copy of the notice under sub-paragraph (2) to any creditor of the company who applies in writing to a specified address.

(6)   An administrator who fails without reasonable excuse to comply with sub-paragraph (4) commits an offence.

**Amendments**—Small Business, Enterprise and Employment Act 2015, s 126, Sch 9, Pt 1, paras 1, 10(30).

**General note**—The termination of the administrator's office under this provision is permitted only on the single ground in para 80(2). An administrator in such a case remains obliged to make an application to court under para 79(2) in any of the three circumstances mentioned therein and, furthermore, may make an application under para 79(1) in any other circumstances.

For the approach taken where the company had been placed into administration for the purpose of realising property in order to make a distribution to secured and preferential creditors but where sufficient monies were realised to discharge creditors in full and return control of the company, such that the administrators were permitted to terminate without leave of the court, but subject to first convening a meeting under para 54 so as to obtain approval for a change of the administration purpose originally proposed, see the decision of the Scottish Court of Session (Outer House), and the detailed directions provided for therein, in *Joint Administrators of Station Properties, Nimmo and Fraser* [2013] CSOH 120, 2013 GWD 25–504.

**PARAGRAPH 80(2)**

'if the administrator thinks   . . . '—For commentary on the term 'thinks' see the notes to para 3(3).

PARAGRAPH 80(3)

**Administrator's appointment ceasing to take effect**—A company is no longer in administration once an administrator's appointment ceases to take effect: see para 1(2)(a) and (c) and the notes to para 1.

The termination of the administrator's appointment under para 80(3) is expressly stated as being subject to satisfaction of the requirements in para 80(2) which requires the appropriate notice to be served on only the court and the Registrar of Companies, but not creditors for whom notice is afforded in IR 1986, r 3.56(6). Creditors, therefore, are not guaranteed any effective means of preventing termination under para 80(2). Furthermore, neither para 80 nor, indeed, Sch B1 or the IR 2016 provide any mechanism for the prevention or undoing of a termination effected of the administrator's own volition. The termination will not, however, affect the administrator's personal liability, which will remain subject to para 98(2).

Where an administrator proposes invoking the procedure under para 80, then he should remain mindful of the practice approved of by the Court of Appeal in *Oakley-Smith v Greenberg* [2003] EWCA Civ 1217, [2003] BPIR 709 at [31], as noted in the commentary to para 79.

The discharge from liability – equivalent to what was formerly termed 'release' from liability under s 20 – of an administrator whose office is terminated under para 80 is determined in accordance with para 98(2).

**Penalties**—See s 430, Sch 10 and the daily default fine in para 106(2)(n).

## [1.698]

### 81 Court ending administration on application of creditor

(1)   On the application of a creditor of a company the court may provide for the appointment of an administrator of the company to cease to have effect at a specified time.

(2)   An application under this paragraph must allege an improper motive—

   (a)   in the case of an administrator appointed by administration order, on the part of the applicant for the order, or

   (b)   in any other case, on the part of the person who appointed the administrator.

(3)   On an application under this paragraph the court may—

   (a)   adjourn the hearing conditionally or unconditionally;

   (b)   dismiss the application;

   (c)   make an interim order;

   (d)   make any order it thinks appropriate (whether in addition to, in consequence of or instead of the order applied for).

**General note**—Save to the extent that under the former s 19(1) the court retained a general power to remove an administrator from office 'at any time', this provision finds no equivalent in the former Part II so far as it confers standing specifically on a creditor to apply for the cessation of the appointment of an administrator on the grounds of 'improper motive' in the appointment of the administrator in para 81(2).

The specific terms of this provision are necessary so as to allow a creditor without notice of an out-of-court appointment to challenge the appointment in an appropriate case. It is clear from para 81(2), however, that the provision applies to both out-of-court and court appointments since, whilst in theory a creditor might appear and be heard at the hearing of the administration application, in practice any unsecured creditor is not entitled to notice of the application and may therefore only be in a position to raise a challenge to the court appointment after the event.

If nothing else, the drafting of para 81 is curious. Although para 81(2) requires an allegation of improper motive by the applicant creditor it is by no means clear from the wording of the provision that an order under para 81(1) is conditional upon a finding as to such improper motive. The view taken here is that a substantive order under para 81(1) must be taken as being so conditional since otherwise the requirement for the applicant's allegation of improper motive would be rendered meaningless. It is further suggested that an order is capable of being made under para 81(1) where a finding of improper motive is made without that finding necessarily relating to the particular improper motive alleged. It is also clear enough, it is suggested, that an order under para 81(3), in contrast to para 81(2), is conditional upon neither an allegation nor a finding of improper motive.

PARAGRAPH 81(1)

'  . . . the court may provide for the appointment of an administrator of the company to cease to have effect  . . . '—This wording reflects the formula provided for in para 1(2)(a) whereby a company is 'in administration' while the appointment of an administrator of the company has effect. This would suggest that a successful application under para 81(1) would result in a company no longer being 'in administration'. However, it is submitted that there is no good reason why, in an appropriate case, the court should not make a consequential order under para 81(3)(d) for the appointment of a replacement administrator. Such a replacement appointment would suppose that the court had reached a finding of 'improper motive' for the purposes of para 81(2) but nonetheless considered it justifiable, most likely but not necessarily with the support of the applicant creditor, to continue the administration under the control of a replacement office-holder. Equally, it is conceivable that the court could reach a finding of improper motive for para 81(2) purposes and yet decline both to terminate the administration and to replace the incumbent office-holder, most likely on the grounds of economy and/or the wishes and/or the interests of creditors.

For a case where the court made an order under para 81(1) providing for the appointment of administrators to cease to have effect, see *Re CA & T Developments Ltd, Koon v Bowes* [2019] EWHC 3455 (Ch) (appointment attributable to de facto director's improper motive in causing the company to create debenture in his favour for purpose of effecting appointment and thereafter influencing insolvency process).

## PARAGRAPH 81(2)

**'improper motive'**—This term does not appear elsewhere in the legislation. Improper motive is the only ground upon which the court may terminate an administration under this provision. It is submitted that the proper approach on the part of the court to the term involves a two-stage process. First, that the court should be concerned in establishing, as a matter of fact, the motive on the part of the applicant for an administration order or the appointor in an out-of-court appointment; secondly, it falls to the court to consider whether, in the particular circumstances of a case, that motive is improper. There is scope, however, for the court further restricting the potential usage of the provision. In particular, it is submitted, the proper use of para 81 should address clear, or at least obvious, impropriety and, just as importantly, should not be capable of deployment as a weapon in seeking to frustrate an administration where the achievement of the statutory purpose is reasonably likely to be achieved.

The establishing in evidence of an improper motive does no more than engage the court's jurisdiction, but it does not follow from such proof that the court will exercise its discretion in ordering a cessation of the administration: *Thomas v Frogmore Real Estate Partners GP1 Ltd* [2017] EWHC 25 (Ch), following the reasoning of the High Court of Northern Ireland in *Cursitan v Keenan* [2011] NICh 23. Neither does it follow that a motive not in harmony with the statutory purpose of administration and causative of the decision to appoint the administrator will dictate cessation of the appointment, especially where the statutory purpose could properly be achieved, irrespective of motive. If the appointor's motive and the statutory purpose of administration are in harmony then it is difficult to characterise the appointor's motive as improper so as to justify the termination of the appointment. Moreover, before ordering a termination of appointment following proof of improper motive, the court, in exercising its discretion, will necessarily have regard to the class nature of administration and its potential implications for other parties.

Although para 81(2) imposes a requirement for an allegation of improper motive, a bare allegation in isolation is unlikely to be of assistance to the court. What the provision should be read as calling for is an allegation of improper motive which is supported by particulars in support of the allegation, whether in evidence or points of claim, depending on the form of the application and any directions given by the court. An application which fails to allege improper motive in contravention of para 81(2), and, arguably, an application which fails to give proper particulars of that allegation, is defective and may be susceptible to being struck out by the court under any of the grounds in CPR 3.4(2) or under CPR 24(2) (summary judgment).

## PARAGRAPH 81(3)

**Further orders**—The scope of the orders available to the court under this provision is unfettered, particularly given para 81(3)(d). Such orders may be tailored to the particular circumstances of the case, most obviously where the court is minded on the initial return date of the application to give directions for the filing of further evidence and where there is a need to regulate or limit the scope of the administration pending the matter coming back before the court. Unlike para 81(2) the making of an order under para 81(3) is not subject to the requirement for the establishment of improper motive, as discussed in the General Note above.

Paragraph 86 applies where a court order provides for the appointment of an administrator to cease to have effect.

**Costs**—The fact that para 81 application is rendered otiose by an administrator making an application for his or her appointment to cease and for a winding-up order prior to the para 81 application coming on for hearing does not prevent the court from ordering the costs of the para 81 application against the administrator if the circumstances justify: *Coyne v DRC Distribution Ltd* [2008] BCC 612 (Ward, Jacob and Rimer LJJ: costs order by judge justified where creditor made para 81 application following administrator's failure to take steps to recover assets transferred away pre-administration).

**[1.699]**

### 82 Public interest winding-up

(1) This paragraph applies where a winding-up order is made for the winding up of a company in administration on a petition presented under—

    (a)    section 124A (public interest), or

    (aa)    section 124B (SEs),

    (b)    section 367 of the Financial Services and Markets Act 2000 (petition by Financial Conduct Authority or Prudential Regulation Authority).

(2) This paragraph also applies where a provisional liquidator of a company in administration is appointed following the presentation of a petition under any of the provisions listed in sub-paragraph (1).

(3) The court shall order—

    (a)    that the appointment of the administrator shall cease to have effect, or

    (b)    that the appointment of the administrator shall continue to have effect.

(4) If the court makes an order under sub-paragraph (3)(b) it may also—

    (a)    specify which of the powers under this Schedule are to be exercisable by the administrator, and

    (b)    order that this Schedule shall have effect in relation to the administrator with specified modifications.

**Amendments**—SI 2004/2326; Financial Services Act 2012, s 11(2), Sch 18, Pt 2, paras 51, 55(1), (4).

**General note**—Paragraph 42(2) and (3) imposes a general bar on the placing of a company into liquidation where that company is in administration. That general bar is subject to the making of a winding-up order on a public interest or Financial Services Authority petition by virtue of para 42(4) or the appointment of a provisional liquidator following presentation of such a petition by virtue of para 82(2).

On the making of a permitted winding-up order – paras 40(3) and 42(5) envisaging an application for directions by the administrator under para 63 in the interim – the court must decide whether the appointment of the administrator should cease or continue. In the latter case, the wording employed in para 82(4) suggests that, whilst both the administrator and the liquidator are each to hold office contemporaneously, it is the scope of the administration which should be restricted so as to allow for the proper conduct of the winding-up petition.

**PARAGRAPH 82(3)**

**Scope of provision**—A company is no longer in administration once an administrator's appointment ceases to take effect: see para 1(2)(a) and (c) and the notes to para 1.

**Procedure**—Paragraph 86 applies where a court order provides for the appointment of an administrator to cease to have effect.

**[1.700]**

### Moving from administration to creditors' voluntary liquidation

### 83

(1) This paragraph applies in England and Wales where the administrator of a company thinks—

    (a)    that the total amount which each secured creditor of the company is likely to receive has been paid to him or set aside for him, and

    (b)    that a distribution will be made to unsecured creditors of the company (if there are any) which is not a distribution by virtue of section 176A(2)(a).

(2) This paragraph applies in Scotland where the administrator of a company thinks—

    (a)    that each secured creditor of the company will receive payment in respect of his debt, and

    (b)    that a distribution will be made to unsecured creditors (if there are any) which is not a distribution by virtue of section 176A(2)(a).

(3) The administrator may send to the registrar of companies a notice that this paragraph applies.

(4) On receipt of a notice under sub-paragraph (3) the registrar shall register it.

(5)  If an administrator sends a notice under sub-paragraph (3) he shall as soon as is reasonably practicable—

- (a)  file a copy of the notice with the court, and
- (b)  send a copy of the notice to each creditor, other than an opted-out creditor, of whose claim and address he is aware.

(6)  On the registration of a notice under sub-paragraph (3)—

- (a)  the appointment of an administrator in respect of the company shall cease to have effect, and
- (b)  the company shall be wound up as if a resolution for voluntary winding up under section 84 were passed on the day on which the notice is registered.

(7)  The liquidator for the purposes of the winding up shall be—

- (a)  a person nominated by the creditors of the company in the prescribed manner and within the prescribed period, or
- (b)  if no person is nominated under paragraph (a), the administrator.

(8)  In the application of Part IV to a winding up by virtue of this paragraph—

- (a)  section 85 shall not apply,
- (b)  section 86 shall apply as if the reference to the time of the passing of the resolution for voluntary winding up were a reference to the beginning of the date of registration of the notice under sub-paragraph (3),
- (c)  section 89 does not apply,
- (d)  sections 99 and 100 shall not apply,
- (e)  section 129 shall apply as if the reference to the time of the passing of the resolution for voluntary winding up were a reference to the beginning of the date of registration of the notice under sub-paragraph (3), and
- (f)  any creditors' committee which is in existence immediately before the company ceases to be in administration shall continue in existence after that time as if appointed as a liquidation committee under section 101.

**Amendments**—Small Business, Enterprise and Employment Act 2015, ss 126, 128, Sch 9, Pt 1, paras 1, 10(31), (32).

**General note**—This provision finds no equivalent in the former Part II and enables an administrator to procure a seamless transition from administration to creditors' voluntary liquidation without the need for meetings of members and creditors as envisaged by s 98(1). There is no provision for a move from administration to a members' voluntary liquidation. The para 83 procedure is not dependent upon the method of appointment of the administrator seeking to invoke it; nor does para 83 require the making of an order under paras 79 or 85: *Re Ballast plc (in administration)* [2005] BCLC 446 at [21] (Blackburne J).

One practical advantage of a CVL over a compulsory liquidation is the saving of the ad valorem levy, which applies in compulsory liquidation only.

Where a CVL is envisaged as the exit route from an administration, there was a requirement under the former IR 1986, r 2.33(2)(m) for the administrator's proposals under para 49 to include a statement of the proposed liquidator and a statement in accordance with para 83(7) and the former r 2.117(3). Where, however, the move to a CVL is only considered subsequent to the initial creditors' meeting which approved the administrator's proposals under para 53(1), it will be necessary to put the matter to creditors as a revision to the administrator's proposals under para 54(1) since the former r 2.33(2)(m) appeared to deem that move to be something substantial. On the other hand, it will not be necessary to put the matter to creditors as a substantial revision where the original statement of proposals includes a statement under para 52(1)(b), since in those circumstances para 54 is inoperative in the absence of an initial creditors' meeting under para 54(1)(a). It would appear that where a para 52(1)(b) statement has been made, but grounds subsequently arise which cause the administrator to think that a distribution will be made to unsecured creditors, so as to bring the administration within para 83(1)(b), it will be unnecessary for the administrator to put the proposed move to a CVL to creditors since para 54 will not apply in the absence of an initial creditors' meeting under para 54(1)(a). If that analysis is correct, then it gives rise to a further anomaly identified in the note on procedure below.

Other than in a case where a company is to be handed back into the control of its directors, an administrator is obliged, on the grounds identified in the notes to para 79, to make provision for the distribution of free assets following the termination of his or her term of office.

In a case where there are no assets for distribution to creditors, whether or not following a distribution under para 65, the duty in para 84(1) will trigger subject to disapplication under para 84(2): *Re GHE Realisations Ltd* [2006] BCC 139 at [24] (where the approach of the administrators was to realise the company's assets, to pay preferential creditors in full, to make a distribution to unsecured creditors without first placing the company into voluntary liquidation).

The only means of challenging the procedure under para 83 is by an application under para 74 which will require a causative link between the action challenged as being unfair – which, it is submitted, might bring in the issue of what the administrator 'thinks' and the basis for such thinking – and the alleged harm to creditors' interests: *Unidare plc v Cohen and Power* [2005] BPIR 1472 at [65]–[66] (Lewison J).

### PARAGRAPH 83(1), (2)

' . . . the administrator . . . thinks'—The term 'thinks' is considered in the notes to para 3(3).

### PARAGRAPH 83(3)–(6)

Scope of provision—It is the registration by the Registrar of Companies of the notice sent by the administrator which triggers the move from administration to voluntary liquidation under para 83(6). The word 'may' in that provision, however, makes clear that the para 83 procedure remains optional in all cases within the scope of para 83(1).

Provided that the notice under para 83(3) is sent to the registrar whilst he or she remains in office, it is immaterial to the operation of para 83(6)(a) that the administrator's term of office has lapsed before registration of the notice by the registrar, as where an out of court appointment was effected on 31 January 2005, a para 83(3) notice was stamped as received by the registrar on 28 January 2006 but the notice was not registered until 1 February 2006: *Re E-Squared Ltd* [2006] BCC 379 (David Richards J). In such a case the company is wound up at the date of the registration and the former administrator takes office as liquidator.

A notice under para 83(3) takes effect only on its registration by the Registrar of Companies, not on the date when the registrar receives it. An administrator's term of office is by implication from the words of para 83(6) extended by filing a conversion notice, from the date on which it would otherwise expire by effluxion of time until para 83(6) comes into effect on registration of the notice, unless in the interim he or she resigns, dies, is removed from office or ceases to be qualified to act: *Re Globespan Airways Ltd; Cartwright and another v Registrar of Companies* [2012] EWCA Civ 1159, [2013] 1 WLR 1122; *Re Property Professionals + Limited* [2013] EWHC 1903 (Ch).

If an administrator or members of staff erroneously files the requisite form under para 83 in a case to which para 83(1) applies, then the subsequent commencement of a CVL under para 83(6) is irreversible, even apparently on an application to the court, and is not in any way dependent on or affected by the state of mind or intention of the administrator.

### PARAGRAPH 83(6)

Administrator's appointment ceasing to take effect—A company is no longer in administration once an administrator's appointment ceases to take effect: see para 1(2)(a) and (c) and the notes to para 1.

Preferential creditors—In a para 83 case s 387(3)(ba) preserves the position of preferential creditors by fixing the relevant date for determining the existence and amount of preferential debts as that on which the company entered administration.

Time limits applicable to transaction-at-undervalue and preference claims in liquidation—The 'relevant time' under ss 238 and 239 is fixed by s 240(3)(d) in a para 83 case as the date on which the company entered administration.

Paragraph 86 applies where a court order provides for the appointment of an administrator to cease to have effect.

## [1.701]

### 84 Moving from administration to dissolution

(1)   If the administrator of a company thinks that the company has no property which might permit a distribution to its creditors, he shall send a notice to that effect to the registrar of companies.

(1A)   . . .

(1B)   . . .

(2)   The court may on the application of the administrator of a company disapply sub-paragraph (1) in respect of the company.

(3)   On receipt of a notice under sub-paragraph (1) . . . the registrar shall register it . . ..

(4)   On the registration of a notice in respect of a company under sub-paragraph (1) the appointment of an administrator of the company shall cease to have effect.

(5) If an administrator sends a notice under sub-paragraph (1) he shall as soon as is reasonably practicable—

(a)     file a copy of the notice with the court, and

(b)     send a copy of the notice to each creditor, other than an opted-out creditor, of whose claim and address he is aware.

(6) At the end of the period of three months beginning with the date of registration of a notice in respect of a company under sub-paragraph (1) the company is deemed to be dissolved . . ..

(6A) . . .

(6B) . . .

(7) On an application in respect of a company by the administrator or another interested person the court may—

(a)     extend the period specified in sub-paragraph (6) . . .,

(b)     suspend that period, or

(c)     disapply sub-paragraph (6) . . ..

(8) Where an order is made under sub-paragraph (7) in respect of a company the administrator shall as soon as is reasonably practicable notify the registrar of companies.

(9) An administrator commits an offence if he fails without reasonable excuse to comply with sub-paragraph (5).

**Amendments**—Small Business, Enterprise and Employment Act 2015, s 126, Sch 9, Pt 1, paras 1, 10(33); SI 2017/702; SI 2019/146, as from IP completion day (as defined in the European Union (Withdrawal Agreement) Act 2020, s 39(1)–(5)).

**General note**—These provisions find no counterpart in the former Part II, although they find an equivalent in ss 202 and 203 which provide for early dissolution in company liquidation in similar circumstances.

The duty imposed on an administrator by para 84(1) by the use of the word 'shall', and the consequent duty imposed on the Registrar of Companies under para 84(3), are only triggered where the administrator 'thinks that the company has no property which might permit a distribution to its creditors'. The reference to 'creditors' is not limited to unsecured creditors. Consequently, para 84 can have no application where the administrator thinks that there might be even the smallest distribution to any class of creditor. The provision in para 84(1) will, therefore, be triggered either where the administrator forms the view that the company has no property for distribution to creditors or where no such property remains following a distribution under para 65. Accordingly, para 84 provides a convenient and straightforward enough procedure for bringing the existence of a company to an end through dissolution where an intervening winding up would serve no useful purpose. The mandatory application of the scheme in the circumstances prescribed in para 84(1), however, is capable of disapplication by the court, but only on the application of the administrator, under para 84(2), perhaps most obviously where a winding-up might serve a useful purpose by way of investigations undertaken by a liquidator, regardless, it is submitted, of whether those investigations might lead to the recovery of property for the benefit of the company.

**PARAGRAPH 84(1)**

**'If the administrator . . . thinks . . . '**—For commentary on the meaning of the term 'thinks' see the notes to para 3(3). The requirement is for the administrator to form the requisite view only at the time para 84(1) applies: *Re GHE Realisations Ltd* [2006] BCC 139 at [24] (Rimer J).

**' . . . that the company has no property which might permit a distribution to the creditors . . . '**—This condition is met once the administrator forms the view that there are no assets remaining which allow for a distribution: *Re Preston & Duckworth Ltd* [2006] BCC 133 (Mr Recorder Hodge QC sitting as a deputy High Court judge). The contrary view, expressed obiter, by Blackburne J in *Re Ballast plc (in administration)* [2005] 1 WLR 1928 at [20], to the effect that para 84(1) only applies where the company in administration has no property at any time during the administration which might permit a distribution, is wrong and should not be followed: *Re GHE Realisations Ltd* [2006] BCC 139 at [23] (Rimer J). Although a company with no assets will not usually be eligible for administration, this might arise where an individual company with no assets enters administration with the other members of a group of companies.

**The effects of para 84(1) being triggered**—The wording in para 84(2) allows for the disapplication of para 84(1) on an application by an administrator prior to the sending of a notice under para 84(1). On receipt of the notice the registrar is under an unconditional obligation to register it under para 84(3), which gives rise to the termination of the administrator's appointment as such. (Despite the cessation of his appointment the administrator will, however, only be discharged from liability – being the equivalent of release under the former s 20 – under para 98(2) which operates quite independently of para 84.) The dissolution of the company follows automatically under para 84(6), subject to para 84(7), on the expiration of the 3-month period commencing with registration of the para 84(1) notice. Paragraph 84(5) is administrative in nature and does not affect the consequences of termination of appointment and dissolution under para 84(4) and (6), although an administrator will face liability for default under para 84(9).

A move from administration to dissolution does not require the obtaining of an order under paras 79 or 85: *Re Ballast (in administration)* [2005] 1 WLR 1928 at [21] (Blackburne J), followed in *Re GHE Realisations Ltd* [2006] BCC 139 at [25] (Rimer J).

**Possible action following dissolution**—Once para 84(4) takes effect, para 84 provides the court with no power to restore the administration, although para 84(7) does allow for the suspension or total disapplication of the subsequent dissolution under para 84(6).

However, s 1029(1)(b) of the Companies Act 2006 expressly provides that an application may be made to the court to restore to the register a company that is deemed to have been dissolved under para 84(6).

Although s 1029(2) does not specifically list an administrator in the list of persons who may make such application (in contrast s 1029(2)(j) expressly refers to 'any former liquidator of the company'), it is submitted that an administrator will constitute 'a person appearing to the court to have an interest in the matter'. Applications under s 1029 are commonly made where it transpires that a company was, in fact, legally or beneficially entitled to property at the date of dissolution or for the purpose of facilitating a claim against the company's insurers under the Third Parties (Right Against Insurers) Act 1999.

Deemed dissolution under para 84(6) does not affect the jurisdiction of the appropriate court to determine director disqualification proceedings: *Secretary of State for Trade and Industry v Arnold* [2008] BCC 119 (HHJ Pelling QC, sitting as a High Court judge).

### PARAGRAPH 84(4)

The effect of the registration of a notice under para 84(4) is the cessation of the appointment of an administrator. By reference to the definition in para 1(2)(a) the company would thereafter no longer be 'in administration'. It would follow, therefore, that in the period between registration of the notice and the end of the 3-month period provided for in para 84(6), or any extended period under para 84(7), the company would be neither in administration nor in dissolution. It would appear quite extraordinary in these circumstances if the company was to revert to the control of its directors in this interim period, and it seems most unlikely that this is what Parliament could have intended. Accordingly, during such an interim period, and despite the fact that the company is no longer in administration, by virtue of the appointment of the administrators ceasing to have effect, the company seems likely to remain subject to the powers of the administrator on a residual basis pending dissolution, rather than reverting to the control of its directors (who would not have been removed as such merely by the fact of the company being in administration) or existing in some other undefined state of limbo.

### PARAGRAPH 84(6)

Following dissolution, a former administrator may be entitled either to bring an application for restoration as 'any other person appearing to the court to have an interest in the matter' within s 1029(2) of the Companies Act 2006 or to object to such an application brought by another eligible party. Such standing, however, is not automatic and is dependent on the circumstances: *Barclays Bank plc v Registrar of Companies* [2015] EWHC 2806 (Ch) (Norris J). In that case the former administrator was held to have an interest in the matter by way of her seeking to supplement or correct evidence before the court. Neither was restoration held to be at odds with the company having been dissolved in accordance with the administrator's original approved proposals, even where the applicant for restoration was party to the approval of those proposals. Norris J's judgment includes a very useful analysis of the effect on transaction avoidance time limits following restoration. Although the judge was prepared to restore the company, and accepted that there was jurisdiction to backdate the winding-up petition also presented by the applicant bank, following the decision in *Davy v Pickering* [2015] EWHC 380 (Ch), [2015] 2 BCLC 116, such backdating was not appropriate in the absence of fuller information about what transactions might be under challenge or any explanation as to why the bank had not applied to suspend dissolution or petition for winding-up before dissolution. Neither had the counterparties to the potentially affected transactions been notified.

Although a company is deemed to have continued in existence as if it had not been dissolved upon being restored to the register, it is not possible to grant additional relief through the retrospective extension of an administration order: *Re People's Restaurant Group Ltd, RLoans LLP v Registrar of Companies* [2013] All ER (D) 180 (May), ChD (Registrar Jones).

For an example of restoration following dissolution and the retrospective re-creation and re-vesting in the company of a freehold that was then caught by the applicant bank's legal charge see *Re Fivestar Properties Ltd* [2015] EWHC 2782 (Ch) (HHJ Cooke, sitting as a High Court judge).

Norris J drew attention in the *Barclays Bank plc case* (above) to the uncertainties posed by the 3-month hiatus period provided for in para 84(6) and the apparent uncertainty as to the status of the company during that period, on which see the notes to para 84(4) above.

### PARAGRAPH 84(7)

There is no provision pursuant to para 84(7) for restoring to office an administrator whose appointment has terminated: *Re People's Restaurant Group Ltd, RLoans LLP v Registrar of Companies* [2013] All ER (D) 180 (May), ChD (Registrar Jones). Neither can the court extend the period of administration on the basis of the court's power to restore a company to the register under s 1032 of the Companies Act 2006. (The issue arose because the applicant wished for liquidation to commence at the time the appointment of the administrators was terminated so as to facilitate a preference claim that was otherwise statute-barred).

**Penalties**—See s 430, Sch 10 and the daily default fine in para 106(2)(o).

## [1.702]

### 85 Discharge of administration order where administration ends

(1)   This paragraph applies where—

    (a)   the court makes an order under this Schedule providing for the appointment of an administrator of a company to cease to have effect, and

    (b)   the administrator was appointed by administration order.

(2)   The court shall discharge the administration order.

**General note**—This provision applies only to cases in which an administration order is made and should be read in conjunction with para 79(1), (3) and (4) and the notes thereto. Discharge under para 85 equates to discharge of an administration order under the former s 18(1). Discharge now follows mandatorily from an order under para 79(1). The cessation of an administrator's term of office as administrator does not, however, automatically release him or her from liability, which remains subject to para 98(2).

## [1.703]

### 86 Notice to Companies Registrar where administration ends

(1)   This paragraph applies where the court makes an order under this Schedule providing for the appointment of an administrator to cease to have effect.

(2)   The administrator shall send a copy of the order to the registrar of companies within the period of 14 days beginning with the date of the order.

(3)   An administrator who fails without reasonable excuse to comply with sub-paragraph (2) commits an offence.

**General note**—This is an administrative provision which applies in all cases where the court makes an order under Sch B1 terminating the appointment of an administrator, a class of cases not necessarily limited to those in which an administration order is made by the court. Paragraph 86 will therefore apply to paras 79(1), 81(1), 82(3) and 83(6) and any order made under any other provision in Sch B1 by which the appointment of an administrator ceases to have effect, but the wording in para 86(1) makes clear that the provision will not apply to any such order made under any provision other than those in Sch B1.

**Penalties**—See s 430, Sch 10 and the daily default fine in para 106(2)(p).

## REPLACING ADMINISTRATOR

## [1.704]

### 87 Resignation of administrator

(1)   An administrator may resign only in prescribed circumstances.

(2)   Where an administrator may resign he may do so only—

    (a)   in the case of an administrator appointed by administration order, by notice in writing to the court,

(b)    in the case of an administrator appointed under paragraph 14, by notice in writing to the holder of the floating charge by virtue of which the appointment was made,

(c)    in the case of an administrator appointed under paragraph 22(1), by notice in writing to the company, or

(d)    in the case of an administrator appointed under paragraph 22(2), by notice in writing to the directors of the company.

**Amendments**—Enterprise Act 2002, s 248(2), Sch 16 (as amended by SI 2003/2096).

**General note**—This provision should be read in conjunction with paras 90–95 which deal with the appointment of a new administrator where there is a vacancy in office. In *Re Alt Landscapes Ltd* [1999] BPIR 459 at 461D–461H Lloyd J held that the term 'impracticable', in the context of the then (and former) analogous IR 1986, r 6.126(3) in bankruptcy, connoted something more than inexpedient and undesirable and came to something not far short of impossible.

In any case where an administrator may resign, he may do so only subject to compliance with the giving of notice in writing in the circumstances prescribed in para 87(2).

Creditors cannot require an administrator to seek permission to resign under para 87; if creditors wish to have an administrator removed then the proper course is an application under para 88: *Re Fox Street Village Ltd (in administration)* [2020] EWHC 2541 (Ch) at [48]–[52] (HHJ Halliwell, sitting as a High Court judge) and see the note to r 3.62.

Paragraph 1(2)(b) provides that a company does not cease to be in administration merely because an administrator vacates or is removed from office without being replaced. As a matter of professional conduct an outgoing administrator should satisfy himself as to arrangements for his replacement before vacating office.

**Costs**—The fact that an application is rendered otiose by an administrator making an application for his or her appointment to cease and for a winding-up order does not prevent the court from ordering the costs of the application against the administrator if the circumstances justify: *Coyne v DRC Distribution Ltd* [2008] BCC 612 (Ward, Jacob and Rimer LJJ: costs order by judge justified where the creditor made para 81 application following administrator's failure to take steps to recover assets transferred away pre-administration).

## [1.705]

### 88 Removal of administrator from office

The court may by order remove an administrator from office.

**General note**—Paragraph 88 should be read in conjunction with paras 90–95. The provision imposes no requirement for removal of an administrator by the court from office being conditional on 'cause shown', as is expressly provided for in s 108(2) and implied, on the authorities, into s 172(2) in liquidation. In *SISU Capital Fund Ltd v Tucker* [2006] BPIR 154 at [88] Warren J considered that, like Nourse LJ addressing s 172(2) in *Re Edennote Ltd* [1996] 2 BCLC 389 at 397H–397I and 398F, 'it is not easy to think of any circumstances (that is to say, I cannot at present think of any circumstances) in which the court would remove a liquidator under para 88 [*Editorial Note*: presumably, his Lordship intended to refer to an administrator] without cause being shown'.

In *Clydesdale Financial Services Ltd v Smailes* [2009] EWHC 1745 (Ch), [2009] BCC 810, David Richards J granted an application to remove the administrators of an insolvent solicitors' practice where they and their firm had been so closely involved in negotiations for the sale of the firm's business immediately prior to their appointment that they could not be expected to conduct an independent review of the transaction. It was noted that on such application, the court will have regard to, but will certainly not be bound by, the wishes of the majority of creditors.

Applying both *SISU Capital Fund* and *Clydesdale v Smailes*, Registrar Jones held *in Re Ve Interactive Ltd (in administration)* [2018] EWHC 186 (Ch) that the test for removal is whether or not there is a 'serious issue for investigation', not whether the claims identified for investigation have merit, [18]. *Re Ve* and *Clydesdale v Smailes* were, however, distinguished by Henry Carr J from the case before him in *Zinc Hotels (Investment) Ltd v Beveridge* [2018] EWHC 1936 (Ch) at [67], on the ground that those cases concerned pre-pack sales where the administrators were unable to investigate their own conduct in arranging such sales. No such conflict was apparent in *Zinc Hotels*.

Where an application to remove an office-holder is forced by that office-holder's refusal to resign voluntarily where the circumstances would justify such resignation, the court may make a costs order of the application against the outgoing office-holder on the indemnity basis: *Shepheard v Lamey* [2001] BPIR 939 (Jacob J, a liquidation case). The outgoing administrators in *Re Ve Interactive Ltd (in administration)* [2018] EWHC 186 (Ch) were also refused the ability to recover certain costs and expenses, including their remuneration, insofar as it was rendered unnecessary or wasted by their decision not to resign voluntarily until the trial of the removal application was underway, [41].

Creditors cannot require an administrator to seek permission to resign under para 87; if creditors wish to have an administrator removed then the proper course is an application under para 88: *Re Fox Street Village Ltd (in administration)* [2020] EWHC 2541 (Ch) at [48]–[52] (HHJ Halliwell, sitting as a High Court judge) and see the note to r 3.62.

In *Re St Georges Property Services (London) Ltd, Finnerty v Clark* [2010] EWHC 2538 (Ch), [2011] BPIR 242 the two shareholders of a company (who were also substantial unsecured creditors) applied under para 88 for the removal of administrators who were unwilling to seek to challenge the default rate of interest charged by the company's secured lenders pursuant to s 244 as an extortionate credit transaction. The Chancellor held that if an administrator is unbiased and entitled on the material before him to reach a relevant conclusion his decision should be respected unless and until the court concludes otherwise. The fact that another mind might reach a different conclusion may be a reason to challenge the administrator's decision but cannot be a good reason to remove him altogether. The decision was upheld by the Court of Appeal ([2011] EWCA Civ 858, [2011] BPIR 1514).

A company continues to be in administration notwithstanding the removal from office of an administrator: see para 1(2)(d).

**Eligible applicants**—No provision is made for the class of persons eligible to make an application under para 88. Other than in a block transfer-type case, where the applicant and respondent are, very commonly, partners or co-office-holders with the outgoing individual, the court will, it is submitted, require an applicant to establish a genuine and legitimate interest in the discontinuance of the administrator's term of office. In an ordinary case this will not extend to a creditor with no prospect of receiving a distribution in the administration or any subsequent liquidation or a third party seeking to interfere in the administration for personal reasons: *Deloitte & Touche AG v Johnson* [2000] 1 BCLC 485, PC.

In *Re Angel Group Ltd, Davey v Croxen* [2015] EWHC 2372 (Ch) the respondent administrators to an application for removal were denied disclosure by the applicant on the basis that it was open to the trial judge to draw adverse inferences if the applicant had failed to give full and frank disclosure with the collateral advantage of saving undue cost to the parties.

**Costs**—The fact that an application is rendered otiose by an administrator making an application for the appointment to cease and for a winding-up order does not prevent the court from ordering the costs of the application against the administrator if the circumstances justify: *Coyne v DRC Distribution Ltd* [2008] BCC 612 (Ward, Jacob and Rimer LJJ: costs order by judge justified where the creditor made para 81 application following administrator's failure to take steps to recover assets transferred away pre-administration).

## [1.706]

### 89 Administrator ceasing to be qualified

(1)   The administrator of a company shall vacate office if he ceases to be qualified to act as an insolvency practitioner in relation to the company.

(2)   Where an administrator vacates office by virtue of sub-paragraph (1) he shall give notice in writing—

    (a)   in the case of an administrator appointed by administration order, to the court,

    (b)   in the case of an administrator appointed under paragraph 14, to the holder of the floating charge by virtue of which the appointment was made,

    (c)   in the case of an administrator appointed under paragraph 22(1), to the company, or

    (d)   in the case of an administrator appointed under paragraph 22(2), to the directors of the company.

(3)   An administrator who fails without reasonable excuse to comply with sub-paragraph (2) commits an offence.

**Amendments**—Enterprise Act 2002, s 248(2), Sch 16 (as amended by SI 2003/2096).

**General note**—The vacation of office under para 89(1) is automatic and requires no further action such that there is no requirement for an application under para 88(1): *Re Stella Metals Ltd* [1997] BCC 626 (Knox J).

**Penalties**—See s 430, Sch 10 and the daily default fine in para 106(2)(q).

**[1.707]**

### 90 Supplying vacancy in office of administrator

Paragraphs 91 to 95 apply where an administrator—

    (a)    dies,

    (b)    resigns,

    (c)    is removed from office under paragraph 88, or

    (d)    vacates office under paragraph 89.

**General note**—Paragraphs 91–95 apply only to the filling of a vacancy in office which arises in any of the four circumstances identified therein. Paragraphs 96 and 97, on the other hand, allow for the substitution of a replacement administrator in the circumstances prescribed therein. Paragraphs 100–103 allow for the appointment of an additional administrator or administrators and the joint and concurrent status of appointees.

As a general rule, the approach taken in paras 91–95 is to confer on the person responsible for the administrator's appointment primary responsibility for his or her replacement subject, in the cases of paras 93 and 94, to the prior rights of a qualifying floating charge holder in the case of an out-of-court appointment and, in the cases covered by paras 93–95, any order of the court.

**[1.708]**

### 91

(1)   Where the administrator was appointed by administration order, the court may replace the administrator on an application under this sub-paragraph made by—

    (a)    a creditors' committee of the company,

    (b)    the company,

    (c)    the directors of the company,

    (d)    one or more creditors of the company, or

    (e)    where more than one person was appointed to act jointly or concurrently as the administrator, any of those persons who remains in office.

(2)   But an application may be made in reliance on sub-paragraph (1)(b) to (d) only where—

    (a)    there is no creditors' committee of the company,

    (b)    the court is satisfied that the creditors' committee or a remaining administrator is not taking reasonable steps to make a replacement, or

    (c)    the court is satisfied that for another reason it is right for the application to be made.

**General note**—This provision only applies where the administrator was appointed by court order. An application may only be made by any of those persons listed in paras 91(1)(b)–(d) where any of the three circumstances in para 91(2) arise. Paragraphs 91(2)(b) or (c) might apply where the court can be provided with credible evidence that a creditors' committee is dilatory in replacing a sole appointee or where a remaining administrator is guilty of such conduct in replacing an outgoing co-appointee subject, in the latter case, to the court being satisfied that the appointment of a replacement co-appointee is appropriate.

In contrast to paras 92–94 cases, para 95 does not provide a fall-back position to those persons listed in para 91(1) in a para 91 case, since para 95 applies only to out-of-court appointment cases under paras 92–94, whereas para 91 is concerned only with cases where an administrator is appointed by court order.

**Applications by an outgoing administrator or his partners**—Paragraph 91(1)(e) is insufficiently broad in scope to catch an outgoing administrator. Neither will that provision extend to an outgoing administrator's partners save to the extent that any such partner remains in office as co-administrator. The court could in any case regard an application by an outgoing administrator as being made under para 63 which, it is submitted, is sufficiently broad so as to allow for the appointment of a replacement administrator, but only where the application by the outgoing office-holder was made prior to the termination of office as such.

**[1.709]**

### 92

Where the administrator was appointed under paragraph 14 the holder of the floating charge by virtue of which the appointment was made may replace the administrator.

**General note**—This provision is only exercisable in the circumstances listed in para 90. No limitation is imposed on the holder of the floating charge by virtue of which the appointment was made in effecting the appointment of a replacement. See *Zinc Hotels (Investment) Ltd v Beveridge* [2018] EWHC 1936 (Ch), where the primacy of the qualifying floating chargeholder's rights were considered in detail. Neither is there any bar to the replacement being effected by an assignee of the floating charge pursuant to which the original appointment was made. Given the breadth of the provision and the commercial self-interest in the holder of a floating charge effecting a replacement speedily, it is very difficult to envisage circumstances in which the court might engage its power under para 95(b). See also note to para 103.

## [1.710]

**93**

(1)　Where the administrator was appointed under paragraph 22(1) by the company it may replace the administrator.

(2)　A replacement under this paragraph may be made only—

(a)　with the consent of each person who is the holder of a qualifying floating charge in respect of the company's property, or

(b)　where consent is withheld, with the permission of the court.

**General note**—Paragraph 93 can only operate in the circumstances listed in para 90. In such circumstances a company has an unfettered power in replacing a vacancy in office subject to the consent of any person who is a holder of a qualifying floating charge, as defined in para 14. Even where such consent is withheld, the court has power under para 93(2)(b) to give permission for the company's proposed replacement. It is submitted that the court will grant such permission where the consent of any holder of a qualifying floating charge is, objectively construed, unreasonably withheld in the circumstances of the case.

The court is unlikely to consider an application where the relevant charge holder or holders have not been served with the application.

## [1.711]

**94**

(1)　Where the administrator was appointed under paragraph 22(2) the directors of the company may replace the administrator.

(2)　A replacement under this paragraph may be made only—

(a)　with the consent of each person who is the holder of a qualifying floating charge in respect of the company's property, or

(b)　where consent is withheld, with the permission of the court.

**General note**—The commentary to para 93 above is equally applicable where the outgoing administrator was appointed by the directors of the company under para 22.

## [1.712]

**95**

The court may replace an administrator on the application of a person listed in paragraph 91(1) if the court—

(a)　is satisfied that a person who is entitled to replace the administrator under any of paragraphs 92 to 94 is not taking reasonable steps to make a replacement, or

(b)　that for another reason it is right for the court to make the replacement.

**General note**—The power of the court is only exercisable in cases under paras 92–94, although eligible applicants are defined by reference to those persons listed in para 91(1) to which para 95 is otherwise inapplicable.

The provision will only operate where a vacancy in office arises in those circumstances listed in para 90 and is most likely to be of practical use where either the person entitled to appoint a replacement under the relevant provision is dilatory in making an appointment (as in para 95(a)) or proposes or appoints a replacement who is manifestly unsuitable to act in the best interests of the administrator (as in para 95(b)).

**[1.713]**

**96 Substitution of administrator: competing floating charge-holder**

(1) This paragraph applies where an administrator of a company is appointed under paragraph 14 by the holder of a qualifying floating charge in respect of the company's property.

(2) The holder of a prior qualifying floating charge in respect of the company's property may apply to the court for the administrator to be replaced by an administrator nominated by the holder of the prior floating charge.

(3) One floating charge is prior to another for the purposes of this paragraph if—

    (a)    it was created first, or

    (b)    it is to be treated as having priority in accordance with an agreement to which the holder of each floating charge was party.

(4) Sub-paragraph (3) shall have effect in relation to Scotland as if the following were substituted for paragraph (a)—

    "(a)    it has priority of ranking in accordance with section 464(4)(b) of the Companies Act 1985,".

General note—This provision is not concerned with a replacement in office where a vacancy arises, as in the circumstances listed in para 90, but allows for the holder of a prior ranking qualifying floating charge, as defined in para 96(3), to apply to the court to replace an administrator appointed by the holder of a junior ranking floating charge.

The approach of the court to a para 96 application—There would appear to be a two-stage approach to a para 96 application. First, the court will be concerned with the enforceability of the prior ranking qualifying floating charge under paras 14, 16 and 17, on which see the notes thereto. The question of enforceability should be assessed as at the time of the application, since nothing in para 96(2) suggests that the prior ranking charge need have been enforceable at the time of the original appointment under the junior ranking security. If satisfied as to enforceability the court should then go on to consider the merits of the application. Despite the prior ranking of the applicant's security, the court may require some persuasion in acceding to a substitution where the prior ranking charge holder was given notice of the earlier appointment and consented to it in writing under para 15, the more so where the substitution would lead to the administration bearing an additional and avoidable level of expense and delay where the conduct of the administration has been progressed in some real way. At the other extreme, the court is likely to have considerable sympathy with an application made at a very early stage where it can be evidenced that the prior ranking charge holder was not given notice under para 15 and reacted expeditiously on becoming aware of the position.

**[1.714]**

**97 Substitution of administrator appointed by company or directors: creditors' decision**

(1) This paragraph applies where—

    (a)    an administrator of a company is appointed by a company or directors under paragraph 22, and

    (b)    there is no holder of a qualifying floating charge in respect of the company's property.

(2) The administrator may be replaced by a decision of the creditors made by a qualifying decision procedure.

(3) The decision has effect only if, before the decision is made, the new administrator has consented to act in writing.

Amendments—Small Business, Enterprise and Employment Act 2015, s 126, Sch 9, Pt 1, paras 1, 10(34), (35).

General note—As with para 96, this provision is concerned with the substitution of an administrator for another in the prescribed circumstances, and not with the filling of a vacancy arising under the circumstances listed in para 90. In contrast to para 96, however, para 97 does not involve the court and allows a creditors' meeting to substitute its choice of administrator for one appointed by a company or its directors under para 22, but only where there is no holder of a qualifying floating charge as defined in para 14. The standing of the creditors' meeting to replace the company or directors' choice of administrator is unqualified and reflects the priority status afforded to the wishes of creditors by the provisions, irrespective of the bona fide status and intentions of the incumbent administrator and his appointor.

**[1.715]**

**98 Vacation of office: discharge from liability**

(1)   Where a person ceases to be the administrator of a company (whether because he vacates office by reason of resignation, death or otherwise, because he is removed from office or because his appointment ceases to have effect) he is discharged from liability in respect of any action of his as administrator.

(2)   The discharge provided by sub-paragraph (1) takes effect—

    (a)    in the case of an administrator who dies, on the filing with the court of notice of his death,

    (b)    in the case of an administrator appointed under paragraph 14 or 22 who has not made a statement under paragraph 52(1)(b), at a time appointed by resolution of the creditors' committee or, if there is no committee, by decision of the creditors,

    (ba)    in the case of an administrator appointed under paragraph 14 or 22 who has made a statement under paragraph 52(1)(b), at a time decided by the relevant creditors, or

    (c)    in any case, at a time specified by the court.

(3)   For the purposes of sub-paragraph (2)(ba), the "relevant creditors" of a company are—

    (a)    each secured creditor of the company, or

    (b)    if the administrator has made a distribution to preferential creditors or thinks that a distribution may be made to preferential creditors—

        (i)    each secured creditor of the company, and

        (ii)    the preferential creditors of the company.

(3A)   In a case where the administrator is removed from office, a decision of the creditors for the purposes of sub-paragraph (2)(b), or of the preferential creditors for the purposes of sub-paragraph (2)(ba), must be made by a qualifying decision procedure.

(4)   Discharge—

    (a)    applies to liability accrued before the discharge takes effect, and

    (b)    does not prevent the exercise of the court's powers under paragraph 75.

**Amendments**—Deregulation Act 2015, s 19, Sch 6, Pt 2, paras 4, 7; Small Business, Enterprise and Employment Act 2015, s 126, Sch 9, Pt 1, paras 1, 10(36)–(38).

**General note**—Broadly speaking, para 98 finds its former equivalent in s 20. The former provision provided for the 'release' of an administrator, a term which meant, by virtue of s 20(2) and (3), that a former administrator was thereafter discharged from all liability both in respect of his acts or omissions in the administration and otherwise in relation to his conduct as administrator save to the extent of any order of the court under s 212 in misfeasance proceedings. There is an avoidable confusion in para 98 referring not to release but to 'discharge', given that the draftsman has also employed the term 'discharge' in relation to the wholly different matter of the discharge of an administration order under para 85. It is also clear from Sch B1 that a discharge from liability under para 98 is something quite distinct from the appointment of an administrator ceasing to have effect under paras 76, 79–81, 83 or 84 or the provisions on replacement, disqualification or substitution under paras 87–97. A cessation in office will, of itself, do nothing to discharge an administrator from personal liability from what is termed in para 98(1) 'any action of his as administrator', a phrase which will also extend to inaction by virtue of para 111(3).

The reason for the discharge of administrators was explained by Sales J in *Re Hellas Telecommunications (Luxembourg) II SCA (in administration)* [2013] 1 BCLC 426 at [96]. It is unfair to leave an outgoing administrator on risk generally; accordingly, it is important that some discipline is exercised over the conduct of nominated liquidators intimating a claim against the outgoing administrators so as to ensure that matters are investigated promptly and efficiently and to guard against open-ended liability: *In the matter of Angel Group Ltd* [2015] EWHC 3624 (Ch) at [36] and [46] (Rose J).

For an unsuccessful challenge to an order discharging administrators see *Re Paragon Offshore Ltd (in liquidation)* [2020] EWHC 1925 (Ch) (Deputy ICCJ Agnello QC).

**The time for discharge under para 98(2)**—Paragraph 98(2)(a) is self-explanatory. In a para 14 or para 22 case, then, unless a resolution can be obtained from any creditors' committee or the creditors – subject to the strict requirements of para 98(3) in a para 52(1)(b) case – it will be necessary to obtain discharge by order of the court under para 98(2)(c). Discharge from liability is only available from the court under that provision in an administration order case. In practice, an administrator's proposals under para 49 may include a resolution providing for the release of the administrator. The court will commonly grant discharge relief if creditors have been given advance notice of the intention to seek it and have given their approval: *Green v SCL Group Ltd* [2019] EWHC 954 (Ch) at [98] (Norris J) and see the observations in the General note above.

The words 'in any case' in para 98(2)(c) indicate that the jurisdiction of the court arises in *all* administrations in providing for the time at which discharge takes effect or, perhaps more importantly, in preventing discharge as it would otherwise arise under para 98(2)(a) or (b), most obviously where a creditor or creditors object to such discharge by making an application to the court. Thus, as under the former s 20, the court is empowered to suspend discharge for a sufficient period as to allow for an appropriate level of investigation into the conduct of an administrator against whom legitimate complaint is raised, or even to allow for the institution of proceedings against an administrator, although in the latter case the court will no doubt wish to take into account the new provision in para 98(4)(a), which finds no counterpart in s 20, and which preserves any pre-discharge liability in any case.

The exercise of the court's discretion is case specific and will ultimately turn on individual facts and the court's perception of the level of compulsion, as opposed to genuine but misplaced sense of grievance, in a complainant's case. For example, in *Re Exchange Travel (Holdings) Ltd* [1992] BCC 954 Mr Edward Evans-Lombe QC, sitting as a deputy High Court judge, suspended the administrators' discharge under s 20 IA 1986 for 3 months so as to allow for investigation of the administrator's conduct. In *Green v SCL Group Ltd* [2019] EWHC 954 (Ch) at [100] Norris J directed that the outgoing administrator's discharge would take place 28 days after the date of their final report to creditors, so as to allow creditors the opportunity to raise questions of the administrators but without the need to formulate any allegation of misfeasance; the court rejected a suggestion of discharge 3 months following the end of the administration. The court will usually prescribe a time for discharge taking effect which provides an opportunity for objection to the discharge or to the effective date for discharge to be raised before the court, as opposed to an order excluding from the effect of discharge any claim issued or notified before the effective time specified; whilst practice may vary on a case by case basis, the normal order is for discharge 28 days after the administrator has filed his or her final report: *Re Glint Pay Ltd (in administration)* [2020] EWHC 3078 (Ch) at [43] (ICCJ Jones). On the hearing of a discharge application, the court should have evidence from the applicant administrator explaining what steps have been taken to make creditors and any other potentially interested party aware of the application and (assuming this to be the case) that no objection has been raised or relevant liability identified: *Re Nortel Networks France SAS* [2019] EWHC 2447 at [19]–[20] (Snowden J, discharge on the later of two dates which depended on the date of filing of the administrators' final receipts and payments account as part of their final progress report).

In *Re Lehman Bros Europe Ltd (in administration)* [2020] EWHC 1369 (Ch) the former administrators sought discharge from liability on the basis of an application to be dealt with on paper without an oral hearing. The company had entered liquidation without the administrators obtaining their discharge, but all creditors had been paid in full with statutory interest in addition to which a return had been made to shareholders. All interested parties were invited by the former administrators to notify them of any objection to the application, but no interested party responded. Hildyard J granted the application; because there were no longer any creditors of the company, and the creditors' committee had been disbanded, the only means of providing for the taking effect of the discharge was by an order under para 98(2)(c).

**The scope of the administrator's discharge**—Para 98(4) leaves pre-discharge liability unaffected by the operation of para 98(2). Neither does discharge affect any power exercised by the court in misfeasance proceedings under para 75. Although para 75, like s 212, is procedural in the sense that those provisions provide a convenient and workable procedural gateway for substantive claims against office-holders, the reference in para 98(4)(b) to 'the exercise of the court's powers' means that discharge does not exonerate a former administrator from liability arising on an order of the court which is itself only capable of being made on a *substantive* cause of action.

**[1.716]**

### 99 Vacation of office: charges and liabilities

(1) This paragraph applies where a person ceases to be the administrator of a company (whether because he vacates office by reason of resignation, death or otherwise, because he is removed from office or because his appointment ceases to have effect).

(2) In this paragraph—

"the former administrator" means the person referred to in sub-paragraph (1), and "cessation" means the time when he ceases to be the company's administrator.

(3)   The former administrator's remuneration and expenses shall be—

    (a)   charged on and payable out of property of which he had custody or control immediately before cessation, and

    (b)   payable in priority to any security to which paragraph 70 applies.

(4)   A sum payable in respect of a debt or liability arising out of a contract entered into by the former administrator or a predecessor before cessation shall be—

    (a)   charged on and payable out of property of which the former administrator had custody or control immediately before cessation, and

    (b)   payable in priority to any charge arising under sub-paragraph (3).

(5)   Sub-paragraph (4) shall apply to a liability arising under a contract of employment which was adopted by the former administrator or a predecessor before cessation; and for that purpose—

    (a)   action taken within the period of 14 days after an administrator's appointment shall not be taken to amount or contribute to the adoption of a contract,

    (b)   no account shall be taken of a liability which arises, or in so far as it arises, by reference to anything which is done or which occurs before the adoption of the contract of employment, and

    (c)   no account shall be taken of a liability to make a payment other than wages or salary.

(6)   In sub-paragraph (5)(c) "wages or salary" includes—

    (a)   a sum payable in respect of a period of holiday (for which purpose the sum shall be treated as relating to the period by reference to which the entitlement to holiday accrued),

    (b)   a sum payable in respect of a period of absence through illness or other good cause,

    (c)   a sum payable in lieu of holiday,

    (d)   . . . and

    (e)   a contribution to an occupational pension scheme.

**Amendments**—Deregulation Act 2015, s 19, Sch 6, Pt 2, paras 24, 27.

**General note**—The scheme of this provision is similar in substance to the former s 19. Although s 19 was frequently referred to as creating a statutory charge in favour of an administrator, the former provision, as now with para 99(3) and (4), actually envisaged two specific statutory charges, each in favour of what is termed 'the former administrator', of which that in para 99(4) takes priority over that under para 99(3). The scope of those charges is considered below. Furthermore, whilst the heading to para 99 and the use of the term 'the former administrator' might suggest that the remuneration and expenses and sums payable under para 99(3) and (4) respectively are only payable on an administrator vacating office so as to trigger the creation of the statutory charges therein, it was held under s 19, and, it is submitted, remains the case under para 99, that those items are payable in the course of an administration such that the statutory charges only trigger so as to secure any such sums which remain outstanding on an administrator vacating office. This point is also considered below.

**The circumstances in which para 99 operates**—In addition to any of those circumstances in which an administrator vacates office under paras 87–89 or 91–97, para 99 will also apply where the appointment of an administrator ceases to have effect under paras 79–81 or 83 or 84. The operative parts of the provision are in para 99(3) and (4), which apply automatically on a person ceasing to be the administrator of a company.

**The enforcement of the charges created at para 99(3) and (4)**—In *Re MK Airlines Ltd, Katz v Bradney* [2012] EWHC 1018 (Ch), [2014] BCC 87 at [25] Sir Andrew Morritt C expressed surprise at the fact that both the Act and Sch B1 are entirely silent as to the consequences if a para 99 charge is created but not duly discharged. The conclusion reached (at [26]) was that, if no other means are available, the charges imposed by para 99 are enforceable by the appointment of a receiver whose powers and remuneration could be fixed by the court. The decision in *Re MK Airlines* was applied by HHJ Purle QC, sitting as a High Court judge, in *Re Hotel Company 42 The Calls Ltd: Whitfield v Al Jaber* [2013] EWHC 3925 (Ch). Any sale will be subject to the court's directions and may be on terms that remuneration is to be paid from the sale proceeds. In *Hotel Company 42* the judge identified that the statutory charge amounts to an interest affecting the registered estate which would be capable of registration as an agreed notice capable of protecting the administrator's priority. The nature of the statutory charge was also analysed in *Walker v National Westminster Bank plc* [2015] EWHC 315 (Ch), [2016] BCC 355. The rights of the holder of the charge are limited to enforcement by order of the court and confer no entitlement on the chargeholder to deal with the charged asset direct.

The scope of **'property of which [he/former administrator] had custody or control immediately before cessation' for the purposes of the para 99(3) and (4) charges**—The words 'custody or control' do not require administrators to take steps to obtain physical custody or control of the item or property in question. Rather, the property right subject to the charge remains vested in the company but its custody and control passes from the directors to the administrators on appointment automatically. The relevant test of custody or control, therefore, is entitlement to property or entitlement to the property from which it was derived: *Re MK Airlines Ltd, Katz v Bradney* [2012] EWHC 1018 (Ch), [2014] BCC 87 at [14] and [15] (Sir Andrew Morritt C). Property held on a bare trust by the company, such that the company has no interest in those assets so held, is not property to which para 99 applies such that an administrator cannot avail himself or herself of such assets in meeting charges and liabilities: *Gillan v HEC Enterprises Ltd* [2016] EWHC 3179 (Ch) (Morgan J).

### PARAGRAPH 99(3)

**Scope of the charge**—Paragraph 99(3) very closely resembles the former s 19(4). Blackburne J observed in *Re Salmet International Ltd* [2001] BCC 796 at 803B–803D, in relation to the analogous s 19(4) and by reference to an extract from the judgment of Dillon LJ in *Re Paramount Airways Ltd (No 3), Powdrill v Watson* [1994] BCC 172 at 180G–180H, noted below, that:

' . . . the sub-section is not to be understood as empowering the administrator to draw his remuneration and discharge any expenses properly incurred by him only at the time he ceases to be administrator. The sub-section does not prohibit payment of remuneration or expenses during the course of the administration. Many an administration would be quite impossible if expenses could only be discharged out of the company's property at the time that the administrator ceases to act. In my view, its purpose is to make clear that when the administrator leaves office he will be entitled to deduct his (undrawn) remuneration and pay any expenses properly incurred by him (but not hitherto provided for) out of any property of the company in his custody or under his control in priority to the floating charge holder's rights. It is necessary so to provide because a person may cease to be an administrator before his remuneration has been drawn and any expenses properly incurred by him have been paid.'

Precisely the same analysis ought to apply to para 99(3). The reference to para 70 in para 99(3)(b) is to a floating charge, as defined in para 111(1).

The statutory charge created under para 99(3) is subject to any charge under para 99(4), an order of priority which is incapable of variation given the unqualified words relating to payment pursuant to such security in para 99(4)(b). As regards payment of any debt or liability otherwise secured by the para 99(4) charge, Dillon LJ observed in *Powdrill v Watson* (see above) in connection with the former but analogous s 19(5) that:

'Although strictly sums payable are, under s 19(5), only payable when the administrator vacates office, it is well understood that administrators will, in the ordinary way, pay expenses of the administration including salaries and other payments to employees as they arise during the continuance of the administration. There is no need to wait until the end, and it would be impossible as a practical matter to do that. What is picked up at the end are those matters which fall within the phrase, but have not been paid.'

Given the resemblance between the former and present provisions, the above reasoning ought to apply in relation to para 99(4).

The fact that an administrator has the benefit of security under para 99(3) does not preclude the administrator from presenting a petition for winding-up: *Re Lafayette Electronics Europe Ltd* [2007] BCC 890 (HHJ Norris QC, sitting as a High Court judge).

The operation of the charge created by para 99(3), subject to that provided for in para 99(4), survives liquidation and the handing over of assets to a liquidator: *Re Sheridan Securities Ltd* (1988) 4 BCC 200 at 203 (Mervyn Davies J).

### PARAGRAPH 99(4)

**Scope of the charge**—Paragraph 99(4) applies to contracts entered into by 'the former administrator', or his predecessor, and extends to any contract of employment adopted by such an office-holder, as qualified in para 99(5) and (6). The term 'adopted' here should be understood by reference to the commentary to s 44 on administrative receivership, which applies equally to an administrator.

Where administrators had incurred liabilities caught by para 99(4), had made part-payment of those liabilities and had subsequently been replaced, those part-payments did not form part of the company's estate and were not to be taken into account for the purposes of pari passu distribution as between all creditors entitled to the benefit of the para 99(4) charge; in addition, the new administrators were also entitled to a reasonable sum in respect of their costs of administering that fund on the basis of *Re Berkeley Applegate (Investment Consultants) Ltd* (1988) 4 BCC 279: *Re Sports Betting Media Ltd (in administration)* [2008] BCC 177 (Briggs J).

Whether a debt or liability 'arises out of a contract' is fact specific: see, for example, *Centre Reinsurance International Co v Freakley* [2006] UKHL 45, [2007] 1 BCLC 85 (claims-handling expenses not liabilities within the meaning of the former but analogous s 19(5)).

In *Re Nortel Companies* [2013] UKSC 52, the Supreme Court held that a financial support direction issued by the Pensions Regulator to a company after it had entered insolvent administration was to be treated as a provable debt and would rank pari passu with other unsecured debts.

## PARAGRAPH 99(5), (6)

'Wages or salary', protective awards, payments in lieu and redundancy payments—A protective award does not fall within the ambit of para 99(6)(d) and is therefore outside of the scope of para 99(5)(c) and the super-priority status conferred by para 99(5); likewise, payments in lieu, as categorised by Lord Browne-Wilkinson in *Delaney v Staples* [1992] 1 AC 687 at 692D–692H, do not fall within para 99(5): *Re Huddersfield Fine Worsteds Ltd* [2005] EWCA Civ 1072, [2005] BCC 916 (Neuberger, Clarke and Jacob LJJ), reversing a decision of Peter Smith J and affirming a decision of Etherton J below to the effect that 'wages or salary' are conferred a 'super priority' status as part of the rescue culture encouraged by the new administration regime. That decision confirms the position as it was understood to be prior to the implementation of Sch B1. In *Re Allders Department Stores Ltd* [2005] EWHC 172 (Ch), [2005] BCC 289 Lawrence Collins J held that both statutory redundancy payments and claims for unfair dismissal were each outside of the scope of para 99(5). Neither were such payments within the scope of necessary disbursements under IR 1986, r 2.67(1)(f) (now r 3.51(2)(e)). This decision also reflects the pre-Sch B1 position as it was understood in practice. In *Re Leeds United Association Football Club Ltd (in administration)* [2008] BCC 11 Pumfrey J again identified that the words 'wages or salary' in paras 99(5) and (6) were to be attributed their normal meaning (in accordance with *Delaney v Staples* as consideration for work done or to be done under a contract of employment. Accordingly, following the decision in *Huddersfield Fine Worsteds*, a payment by an employer for wrongful dismissal following termination by the employer in respect of a period following termination was not a payment of wages since the employee was not under an obligation to render services during that period. An administrator could therefore adopt a contract of employment but subsequently dismiss the employee without the damages payable as a consequence of the dismissal ranking as 'wages or salary'. Following the decision in *Allders Department Stores*, with which David Richards J had also agreed in *Exeter City Council v Bairstow* [2007] BCC 236 at [77], Pumfrey J further rejected a submission that liabilities for wrongful dismissal could rank as necessary disbursements.

Furloughed workers under the Coronavirus Job Retention Scheme (CJRS)—In *Re Carluccio's Ltd (in administration)* [2020] EWHC 886 (Ch) the joint administrators of a restaurant chain applied for directions as to the availability and consequences of placing a company's employees on furlough under the CJRS. In the absence of employees or interested parties appearing on the application, by reason of time constraints, Snowden J proceeded on the basis that the court should do what it could on the legal issues in seeking to assist the administrators. The CJRS Scheme Guidance indicated that the scheme was available 'if there is a reasonable likelihood of re-hiring the workers. For instance . . . as a result of an administration and pursuit of a sale of the business'. The administrators required a mechanism under the legislation to justify the making of payments to furloughed employees from monies claimed by the employer under the CJRS. Paragraph 99 of Sch B1, which deals with the administrator's adoption of contracts of employment, was the starting point. The court rejected an argument by the administrators that sub-para 99(5) applied only where employees actually rendered services to the company in administration and could not, as a consequence, apply to furlough for the reason that furloughed employees were being paid not to render such services. Further, if Parliament had intended to limit super-priority for wages and salaries to cases where services were actually rendered, it could have provided so in terms. Following the House of Lords' decision in *Powdrill v Watson* [1995] 2 AC 394, sub-para 99(5) was to be interpreted so as to permit the CJRS to be given effect with a view to supporting the rescue culture and the Government's attempts at dealing with the economic consequences of the Covid-19 pandemic. It followed that employees would have super-priority status ahead of the administrators' fees and expenses, floating charge creditors and unsecured creditors such that payments could be made to employees as and when the administrators were put in funds under the CJRS.

Four days after the handing down of judgment in *Carluccio's*, Trower J gave judgment in *Re Debenhams Retail Ltd (in administration)* [2020] EWHC 921 (Ch) on the application of the administrators of a chain of department stores for directions under para 63 as to the proposed actions of the administrators in participating in the CJRS and paying sums received under the scheme to furloughed employees. The application was concerned, in particular, with the issue as to whether such conduct would amount to adoption of the contracts of those employees for the purposes of para 99. Trower J was troubled by the fact that it had not been possible for any representative employees or other interested parties to be joined to the application with the consequence that the directions would not be binding as to the relevant law. Following *Powdrill*, His Lordship took the view that an employee being continued in employment for more than 14 days after the appointment of the administrators was sufficient to constitute adoption for the purposes of para 99. An absence of services being provided under subsisting contracts of employment was not of itself a good reason to find that the contracts had not been adopted ([51]–[59]). The fact of the administrators causing the company to apply under the CJRS and make payment to furloughed employees under the scheme constituted positive conduct on the part of the administrators which was predicated on the continued existence of the contracts of employment of those employees. Irrespective of that conduct, the payment to those employees of wages from monies received under the CJRS would alone, following *Re Antal International Ltd* [2003] EWHC 1339 (Ch), [2003] 2 BCLC 406, constitute the adoption of the contracts of furloughed employees. Further, it would not be possible for the administrators to participate in the CJRS without electing first to treat the relevant contracts of employment as continuing, and thereby adopted. The obligation to pay the employee an amount equivalent to that received under the CJRS arose out of the continued contract of employment which the company in administration was required to honour as a condition of participation in the CJRS. The administrators appealed. Following *Carluccio's*, in a judgment handed down on 6 May 2020 ([2020] EWCA Civ 600), the Court of Appeal rejected the administrators' argument that they had not adopted the employment contracts of furloughed employees to whom they were paying remuneration from monies recovered under the CJRS on the grounds that adoption of the employment contracts necessitated words or conduct which, objectively construed, evidenced an election by the administrators to treat the liabilities arising under the employment contracts as enjoying super-priority status. The Court of Appeal (Vos C, Bean and David Richards LJJ) refuted any requirement for evidence of a what amounted to a self-generated need election on the part of the administrators by their conduct. What mattered was the objective question of whether or not the administrators had 'continued' the employment of the relevant employees, irrespective of the administrators' intentions. The administrators had misunderstood what had been said in *Powdrill*. The reference in the House of Lords' judgment to 'some conduct by the administrator . . . which amounts to an election to treat the continued contract of employment as giving rise' to super-priority raised only the objective issue as to whether or not the facts supported the conclusion that the administrators had continued the employment of the furloughed employees. An election of the sort envisaged before Trower J was not necessary. On the facts, and considering *Carluccio's* (see [61], [63] and [70]), the administrators had adopted the contracts of the furloughed employees. That separate liability to an employee enjoyed super-priority status (see [54]–[55] and [63]–[64]).

GENERAL

[1.717]

### 100 Joint and concurrent administrators

(1)   In this Schedule—

(a)   a reference to the appointment of an administrator of a company includes a reference to the appointment of a number of persons to act jointly or concurrently as the administrator of a company, and

(b)   a reference to the appointment of a person as administrator of a company includes a reference to the appointment of a person as one of a number of persons to act jointly or concurrently as the administrator of a company.

(2)   The appointment of a number of persons to act as administrator of a company must specify—

(a)   which functions (if any) are to be exercised by the persons appointed acting jointly, and

(b)   which functions (if any) are to be exercised by any or all of the persons appointed.

General note—This provision is cast more elaborately than s 231 which governed joint appointments under Part II. Paragraph 100(1) sets up para 100(2) by providing a default rule that the reference to the appointment of any two or more persons as administrators of a company is to be taken as meaning that any or all may act jointly or concurrently as administrator. Paragraph 100(2) then requires the appointment to specify which functions (if any) are to be exercised by the appointees acting jointly and those to be exercised by any or all (which might include some but not all) of those persons. The practical implication of para 100(2) is the requirement for a statement of the position, be it in an administration order or a statement attached to a notice of appointment.

Paragraphs 101 and 102 provide further and rather lengthy definitions and dealing provisions on joint and concurrent appointments. Paragraph 103 governs the procedure on the appointment of an additional office-holder following administration, subject to the overriding consent of the person or persons then acting: see para 103(6).

## [1.718]

**101**

(1) This paragraph applies where two or more persons are appointed to act jointly as the administrator of a company.

(2) A reference to the administrator of the company is a reference to those persons acting jointly.

(3) But a reference to the administrator of a company in paragraphs 87 to 99 of this Schedule is a reference to any or all of the persons appointed to act jointly.

(4) Where an offence of omission is committed by the administrator, each of the persons appointed to act jointly—

    (a)    commits the offence, and

    (b)    may be proceeded against and punished individually.

(5) The reference in paragraph 45(1)(a) to the name of the administrator is a reference to the name of each of the persons appointed to act jointly.

(6) Where persons are appointed to act jointly in respect of only some of the functions of the administrator of a company, this paragraph applies only in relation to those functions.

## [1.719]

**102**

(1) This paragraph applies where two or more persons are appointed to act concurrently as the administrator of a company.

(2) A reference to the administrator of a company in this Schedule is a reference to any of the persons appointed (or any combination of them).

## [1.720]

**103**

(1) Where a company is in administration, a person may be appointed to act as administrator jointly or concurrently with the person or persons acting as the administrator of the company.

(2) Where a company entered administration by administration order, an appointment under sub-paragraph (1) must be made by the court on the application of—

    (a)    a person or group listed in paragraph 12(1)(a) to (e), or

    (b)    the person or persons acting as the administrator of the company.

(3) Where a company entered administration by virtue of an appointment under paragraph 14, an appointment under sub-paragraph (1) must be made by—

    (a)    the holder of the floating charge by virtue of which the appointment was made, or

    (b)    the court on the application of the person or persons acting as the administrator of the company.

(4) Where a company entered administration by virtue of an appointment under paragraph 22(1), an appointment under sub-paragraph (1) above must be made either by the court on the application of the person or persons acting as the administrator of the company or—

    (a)    by the company, and

(b)      with the consent of each person who is the holder of a qualifying floating charge in respect of the company's property or, where consent is withheld, with the permission of the court.

(5)  Where a company entered administration by virtue of an appointment under paragraph 22(2), an appointment under sub-paragraph (1) must be made either by the court on the application of the person or persons acting as the administrator of the company or—

(a)      by the directors of the company, and

(b)      with the consent of each person who is the holder of a qualifying floating charge in respect of the company's property or, where consent is withheld, with the permission of the court.

(6)  An appointment under sub-paragraph (1) may be made only with the consent of the person or persons acting as the administrator of the company.

**General note**—Although the former legislation included no express power to appoint an additional administrator, the court had been prepared to make such an appointment on the basis of its inherent jurisdiction: see, for example, *Clements v Udal* [2002] 2 BCLC 606 (Neuberger J). The power to appoint an additional administrator is now put in express terms. In *Re Zinc Hotels (Holdings) Ltd* [2018] EWHC 1936 (Ch), [2018] BCC 968 shareholders applied to appoint interim additional joint administrators and for an injunction restraining administrators from effecting a sale of assets on the basis that there had not been a formal valuation and the administrators lacked independence with certain creditors. Henry Carr J held that there is no inherent jurisdiction in the court to appoint an additional administrator given para 103 which, by reference to para 7, stipulates the conditions for appointment once a company is in administration. On the facts, these were not met. The principles identified by the judge at [62] do not allow for the appointment of a provisional administrator pre-administration.

For commentary on each of the circumstances in para 103(2)–(5) see the notes to paras 91, 92, 93 and 94.

In *Re BHS Ltd* [2016] EWHC 1965 (Ch) Snowden J ordered the appointment of concurrent administrators on the basis that it was in the best interests of creditors for the existing administrators to trade down the business and the concurrently appointed administrators to investigate possible claims against current and former directors. The concurrent appointment was also viewed as facilitating the conclusion of the company's trading in administration without it being envisaged that there would be a significant increase in the overall cost of the administration caused by the division of work.

## [1.721]

### 104 Presumption of validity

An act of the administrator of a company is valid in spite of a defect in his appointment or qualification.

**General note**—Although the reference to an administrator in s 232 was removed by para 21 of Sch 17 to the Enterprise Act 2002 in anticipation of the implementation of Sch B1, the substance of para 104 remains as under the previous provision, on which see the notes thereto.

Paragraph 104 should be read in conjunction with r 12.64 and the notes thereto.

**Defective administration appointments**—In *Re Blights Builders* [2008] 1 BCLC 245, administrators were (invalidly) appointed under para 22 when there was an extant winding up petition against the company. HHJ Norris QC, sitting as a High Court judge, held that the appointment was incapable of cure under IR 1986, r 7.55 (now r 12.64) (at the time of the hearing, the decision of Hart J in *Re G-Tech Construction Limited* [2007] BPIR 1275, in which it was held that the court had the power to make a retrospective administration order, had not been reported). Accordingly, he made a fresh administration order and declared that pursuant to para 104, their acts as joint administrators were to be treated as valid in spite of the defect in their appointment.

However, in *Re Kaupthing Capital Partners II Master LP Inc (in administration); Pillar Securitisation SARL v Spicer* [2010] EWHC 836 (Ch), [2011] BCC 338, Proudman J held that the use of the wrong prescribed form was a fundamental flaw going to the validity of the appointment itself and was not capable of cure under para 104.

In *Re Care Matters Partnership Ltd* [2011] BCC 957, Norris J, in considering whether or not the actions of an administrator could be validated under para 104 distinguished between cases where there was simply no power to appoint because, for example, there was no valid charge in respect of which the power under para 14 could be exercised, or the persons purporting to appoint an administrator under para 22 were not directors at all, and a case where there is power to make an appointment but the power has been defectively exercised through some irregularity in procedure.

He ruled that in the latter case para 104 was available. The same approach was applied in the Chancery Division in Northern Ireland in *Re Cloughvalley Stores (NI) Ltd (in administration)* [2018] NICh 4 (Treacy J).

**[1.722]**

**105  Majority decision of directors**

A reference in this Schedule to something done by the directors of a company includes a reference to the same thing done by a majority of the directors of a company.

General note—This provision is of significant practical utility. Previously it was common practice to exhibit to an affidavit or witness statement in support of an administration petition a resolution of the board confirming the decision to seek an administration order and related matters. Difficulties could arise from time to time where it was impractical to convene a board meeting. All that is now required for 'something done by the directors' – being a reference to the decision of the directors – is a majority decision for which evidence – most obviously in writing – will be required without the need for a formal board meeting, unanimity amongst the directors, or even a formal board resolution. This new approach is not without its potential difficulties, however, in that the validity of a majority decision for the purposes of this provision might be capable of challenge, notwithstanding para 105, where the wishes of that majority in number are outweighed either by the express wishes of a dissenting director or directors, or directors with weighted board voting rights.

Para 105 does not apply to para 22: *Minmar (929) Ltd v Khalastchi* [2011] EWHC 1159 (Ch), [2011] BCC 485.

**[1.723]**

**106  Penalties**

(1)  A person who is guilty of an offence under this Schedule is liable to a fine (in accordance with section 430 and Schedule 10).

(2)  A person who is guilty of an offence under any of the following paragraphs of this Schedule is liable to a daily default fine (in accordance with section 430 and Schedule 10)—

|      |                  |
| ---- | ---------------- |
| (a)  | paragraph 20,    |
| (b)  | paragraph 32,    |
| (c)  | paragraph 46,    |
| (d)  | paragraph 48,    |
| (e)  | paragraph 49,    |
| (f)  | paragraph 51,    |
| (g)  | paragraph 53,    |
| (h)  | paragraph 54,    |
| (i)  | paragraph 56,    |
| (j)  | paragraph 71,    |
| (k)  | paragraph 72,    |
| (l)  | paragraph 77,    |
| (m)  | paragraph 78,    |
| (n)  | paragraph 80,    |
| (o)  | paragraph 84,    |
| (p)  | paragraph 86, and |
| (q)  | paragraph 89.    |

General note—The amount of any daily default fine is as provided for in Sch 10.

**[1.724]**

**107  Extension of time limit**

(1)  Where a provision of this Schedule provides that a period may be varied in accordance with this paragraph, the period may be varied in respect of a company—

(a)    by the court, and

(b)    on the application of the administrator.

(2)  A time period may be extended in respect of a company under this paragraph—

    (a)    more than once, and

    (b)    after expiry.

**General note**—The reference to any provision which 'provides that a period may be varied in accordance with this paragraph' is to para 49(8) (administrator's proposals), para 50(2) (notice of creditors' meeting) and para 51(4) (time for initial creditors' meeting). The draftsman appears to have made specific provision for the extension of the time limits within those provisions on the application of the administrator alone by reference to para 107 on account of the central procedural importance in administration of the giving of notice and convening of the creditors' meeting, default in relation to two of the provisions giving rise to potential criminal liability. That approach should not be seen as implying that other time limits within Sch B1 are of any lesser importance, only that the court may vary such other time limits as empowered under particular paragraphs or by way of consequential order.

In *Re Advent Computer Training Ltd* [2010] EWHC 459 (Ch), [2011] BCC 44, HHJ Purle QC, sitting as a High Court judge, held that the power in paras 49(8) and 107 of to vary the period can properly be construed as empowering the court to vary the period in relation to some only of the prescribed matters.

## [1.725]

### 108

(1)   A period specified in paragraph 49(5) or 51(2) may be varied in respect of a company by the administrator with consent.

(2)   In sub-paragraph (1) "consent" means consent of—

    (a)    each secured creditor of the company, and

    (b)    if the company has unsecured debts, the unsecured creditors of the company.

(3)   But where the administrator has made a statement under paragraph 52(1)(b) "consent" means—

    (a)    consent of each secured creditor of the company, or

    (b)    if the administrator thinks that a distribution may be made to preferential creditors, consent of—

        (i)    each secured creditor of the company, and

        (ii)   the preferential creditors of the company.

(3A)   Whether the company's unsecured creditors or preferential creditors consent is to be determined by the administrator seeking a decision from those creditors as to whether they consent.

(4)   . . .

(5)   The power to extend under sub-paragraph (1)—

    (a)    may be exercised in respect of a period only once,

    (b)    may not be used to extend a period by more than 28 days,

    (c)    may not be used to extend a period which has been extended by the court, and

    (d)    may not be used to extend a period after expiry.

**Amendments**—Small Business, Enterprise and Employment Act 2015, s 126, Sch 9, Pt 1, paras 1, 10(39)-(43).

**General note**—The periods capable of extension, as provided for in para 108(1), may only be varied – invariably, in practice, meaning extended – by the administrator with the consent of those creditors identified in para 108(2) or, where the administrator has made a statement that the company has insufficient property to enable a distribution to be made to unsecured creditors other than by virtue of s 176A(2)(a) (prescribed part for unsecured debts), as identified in para 108(3).

By virtue of s 436B, a written consent may be by electronic communication for the purposes of para 108(1).

Paragraph 108(5) imposes relatively stringent limits on the extension of the prescribed periods. An extension is permissible only once, and then by not more than 28 days, but not where a period has already been extended by the court, even, it seems, where the court's extension was for a period of less than 28 days. Retrospective extension is not permissible by virtue of the express provision in sub-para 108(5)(d).

PARAGRAPH 108(4)(a)

'written'—For the extension of the scope of 'a thing in writing' to a thing in electronic form – most obviously e-mail – see para 111(2).

## [1.726]

### 109

Where a period is extended under paragraph 107 or 108, a reference to the period shall be taken as a reference to the period as extended.

## [1.727]

### 110  Amendment of provision about time

(1)  The Secretary of State may by order amend a provision of this Schedule which—

    (a)    requires anything to be done within a specified period of time,

    (b)    prevents anything from being done after a specified time, or

    (c)    requires a specified minimum period of notice to be given.

(2)  An order under this paragraph—

    (a)    must be made by statutory instrument, and

    (b)    shall be subject to annulment in pursuance of a resolution of either House of Parliament.

**General note**—To date no order has been made by the Secretary of State under this provision.

## [1.728]

### 111  Interpretation

(1)  In this Schedule—

"administrative receiver" has the meaning given by section 251,

"administrator" has the meaning given by paragraph 1 and, where the context requires, includes a reference to a former administrator,

. . .

. . .

. . .

"enters administration" has the meaning given by paragraph 1,

"floating charge" means a charge which is a floating charge on its creation,

"in administration" has the meaning given by paragraph 1,

"hire-purchase agreement" includes a conditional sale agreement, a chattel leasing agreement and a retention of title agreement,

"holder of a qualifying floating charge" in respect of a company's property has the meaning given by paragraph 14,

"market value" means the amount which would be realised on a sale of property in the open market by a willing vendor,

"the purpose of administration" means an objective specified in paragraph 3, and

"unable to pay its debts" has the meaning given by section 123.

(1A)  In this Schedule, "company" means—

    (a)    a company registered under the Companies Act 2006 in England and Wales or Scotland,

    (b)    a company incorporated in an EEA State . . ., or

    (c)    a company not incorporated in an EEA State but having its centre of main interests in a member State (other than Denmark) or in the United Kingdom.

(1B)  In sub-paragraph (1A), in relation to a company, "centre of main interests" has the same meaning as in Article 3 of the EU Regulation.

(2)  . . .

(3)  In this Schedule a reference to action includes a reference to inaction.

**Amendments**—SI 2005/879; SI 2009/1941; SI 2010/18; Small Business, Enterprise and Employment Act 2015, s 126, Sch 9, Pt 1, paras 1, 10(44); SI 2017/702; SI 2019/146, as from IP completion day (as defined in the European Union (Withdrawal Agreement) Act 2020, s 39(1)–(5)).

'company'—See para 111A and the note to EU Regulation, Art 3.

The decision in *Re The Salvage Association* [2003] BCC 504 to the effect that a company incorporated by Royal Charter may be placed into administration gave rise to some confusion as to whether the EC Regulation (since replaced by the recast EU Regulation) permitted an unincorporated entity to enter administration or a company voluntary arrangement. The effect of that decision was effectively reversed by statute with effect from 13 April 2005 by way of the Insolvency Act 1986 (Amendment) Regulations 2005 (SI 2005/879) which amends ss 1(4) and 436 and para 111 and inserts para 111A so as to provide that only companies as defined in s 735(1) of the Companies Act 1985 (now s 1(1) of the Companies Act 2006) and certain companies formed or incorporated outside the United Kingdom which may enter administration or a CVA.

In *Re Hellas Telecommunications (Luxembourg) II SCA* [2009] EWHC 3199 (Ch), [2010] BCC 295, Lewison J held that an entity that was a combination of a joint stock company and a limited partnership registered in Luxembourg, with a separate legal personality, a constitution and shareholders, was within the definition of a 'company'.

In *Re Dairy Farmers of Britain Limited* [2009] EWHC 1389 (Ch), [2010] Ch 63, Henderson J held that an industrial and provident society was not a 'company' within the meaning of para 111(1A).

Similarly, in *Pantner v Rowellian Football Social Club* [2011] EWHC 1301 (Ch), [2012] Ch 125, HHJ Behrens, sitting as a High Court judge, held that an unassociated football and social club was not a 'company'. Since the club's rules contained provisions for election, a management committee, subscriptions and expulsion, the club was a members' club and not an 'association' within s 220. The club had none of the usual attributes of a company and, given that it was not susceptible to compulsory winding up, there was no reason why Parliament should have intended it to be subject to the administration regime.

A Northern Irish company may no longer apply for an administration order in England and Wales: for commentary see Moss 'Jurisdiction over Northern Ireland Company – the Comi in England Heresy' (2005) 18(7) Insolv Int 107–108.

'correspondence'—This term will extend to fax or other electronic communication, most obviously e-mail.

'floating charge'—The definition of this term here has no different meaning from that in s 251. For a comparison of the nature of a floating charge over a fluctuating body of assets and a legal possessory lien created by contract over stock coupled with a right to sell and use proceeds see *Re Hamlet International plc (in administration)* [1999] 2 BCLC 506 (Mummery LJ, Chadwick and Henry LJJ agreeing).

A floating charge that had been signed by a company director and a company secretary, but not dated until 3 months later when the director was no longer a director, complied with the execution requirements in s 44 of the Companies Act 2006. Accordingly, the floating charge was valid and allowed a para 14 appointment pursuant to it: *Re Armstrong Brands Ltd* [2015] EWHC 3303 (Ch) (HHJ Purle QC, sitting as a High Court judge).

## [1.729]

### 111A Non-UK companies

A company incorporated outside the United Kingdom that has a principal place of business in Northern Ireland may not enter administration under this Schedule unless it also has a principal place of business in England and Wales or Scotland (or both in England and Wales and in Scotland).

Amendments—Inserted by SI 2005/879.

General note—See the note under the heading 'company' to para 111 above.

## [1.730]

### 112 Scotland

In the application of this Schedule to Scotland—

    (a)    a reference to filing with the court is a reference to lodging in court, and

    (b)    a reference to a charge is a reference to a right in security.

**[1.731]**

**113**

Where property in Scotland is disposed of under paragraph 70 or 71, the administrator shall grant to the disponee an appropriate document of transfer or conveyance of the property, and—

(a) that document, or

(b) recording, intimation or registration of that document (where recording, intimation or registration of the document is a legal requirement for completion of title to the property),

has the effect of disencumbering the property of or, as the case may be, freeing the property from, the security.

**[1.732]**

**114**

In Scotland, where goods in the possession of a company under a hire-purchase agreement are disposed of under paragraph 72, the disposal has the effect of extinguishing as against the disponee all rights of the owner of the goods under the agreement.

**[1.733]**

**115**

(1) In Scotland, the administrator of a company may make, in or towards the satisfaction of the debt secured by the floating charge, a payment to the holder of a floating charge which has attached to the property subject to the charge.

(1A) In Scotland, sub-paragraph (1B) applies in connection with the giving by the court of permission as provided for in paragraph 65(3)(b).

(1B) On the giving by the court of such permission, any floating charge granted by the company shall, unless it has already so attached, attach to the property which is subject to the charge.

(2) In Scotland, where the administrator thinks that the company has insufficient property to enable a distribution to be made to unsecured creditors other than by virtue of section 176A(2)(a), he may file a notice to that effect with the registrar of companies.

(3) On delivery of the notice to the registrar of companies, any floating charge granted by the company shall, unless it has already so attached, attach to the property which is subject to the charge.

(4) Attachment of a floating charge under sub-paragraph (1B) or (3) has effect as if the charge is a fixed security over the property to which it has attached.

**Amendments**—Small Business, Enterprise and Employment Act 2015, s 130(1)–(4).

**[1.734]**

**116**

In Scotland, the administrator in making any payment in accordance with paragraph 115 shall make such payment subject to the rights of any of the following categories of persons (which rights shall, except to the extent provided in any instrument, have the following order of priority)—

(a) the holder of any fixed security which is over property subject to the floating charge and which ranks prior to, or pari passu with, the floating charge,

(b) creditors in respect of all liabilities and expenses incurred by or on behalf of the administrator,

(c) the administrator in respect of his liabilities, expenses and remuneration and any indemnity to which he is entitled out of the property of the company,

(d) the preferential creditors entitled to payment in accordance with paragraph 65,

(e) the holder of the floating charge in accordance with the priority of that charge in relation to any other floating charge which has attached, and

(f) the holder of a fixed security, other than one referred to in paragraph (a), which is over property subject to the floating charge.

**Amendments**—Inserted by Enterprise Act 2002, s 248(2), Sch 16. Amended by Enterprise Act 2002, s 248(2), Sch 16; SI 2003/2096; SI 2004/2326; SI 2005/879.

## SCHEDULE 1
### POWERS OF ADMINISTRATOR OR ADMINISTRATIVE RECEIVER
Sections 14, 42

**[1.735]**

**1**

Power to take possession of, collect and get in the property of the company and, for that purpose, to take such proceedings as may seem to him expedient.

**2**

Power to sell or otherwise dispose of the property of the company by public auction or private contract or, in Scotland, to sell, hire out or otherwise dispose of the property of the company by public group or private bargain.

**3**

Power to raise or borrow money and grant security therefore over the property of the company.

**4**

Power to appoint a solicitor or accountant or other professionally qualified person to assist him in the performance of his functions.

**5**

Power to bring or defend any action or other legal proceedings in the name and on behalf of the company.

**6**

Power to refer to arbitration any question affecting the company.

**7**

Power to effect and maintain insurances in respect of the business and property of the company.

**8**

Power to use the company's seal.

**9**

Power to do all acts and to execute in the name and on behalf of the company any deed, receipt or other document.

**10**

Power to draw, accept, make and endorse any bill of exchange or promissory note in the name and on behalf of the company.

**11**

Power to appoint any agent to do any business which he is unable to do himself or which can more conveniently be done by an agent and power to employ and dismiss employees.

**12**

Power to do all such things (including the carrying out of works) as may be necessary for the realisation of the property of the company.

**13**

Power to make any payment which is necessary or incidental to the performance of his functions.

**14**

Power to carry on the business of the company.

**15**

Power to establish subsidiaries of the company.

**16**

Power to transfer to subsidiaries of the company the whole or any part of the business and property of the company.

**17**

Power to grant or accept a surrender of a lease or tenancy of any of the property of the company, and to take a lease or tenancy of any property required or convenient for the business of the company.

**18**

Power to make any arrangement or compromise on behalf of the company.

**19**

Power to call up any uncalled capital of the company.

**20**

Power to rank and claim in the bankruptcy, insolvency, sequestration or liquidation of any person indebted to the company and to receive dividends, and to accede to trust deeds for the creditors of any such person.

**21**

Power to present or defend a petition for the winding up of the company.

**22**

Power to change the situation of the company's registered office.

**23**

Power to do all other things incidental to the exercise of the foregoing powers.

> **Amendments**—Abolition of Feudal Tenure etc (Scotland) Act 2000, s 76(2), Sch 13, Pt 1.
>
> **General note**—These powers should be read against s 42 (administrative receivers), para 60 of Sch B1 (administrators) and the notes thereto.

## SCHEDULE 2
## POWERS OF A SCOTTISH RECEIVER (ADDITIONAL TO THOSE CONFERRED ON HIM BY THE INSTRUMENT OF CHARGE)

Section 55

**[1.736]**

**1**

Power to take possession of, collect and get in the property from the company or a liquidator thereof or any other person, and for that purpose, to take such proceedings as may seem to him expedient.

**2**

Power to sell, hire out or otherwise dispose of the property by public roup or private bargain and with or without advertisement.

**3**

Power to raise or borrow money and grant security therefor over the property.

**4**

Power to appoint a solicitor or accountant or other professionally qualified person to assist him in the performance of his functions.

**5**

Power to bring or defend any action or other legal proceedings in the name and on behalf of the company.

**6**

Power to refer to arbitration all questions affecting the company.

**7**

Power to effect and maintain insurances in respect of the business and property of the company.

**8**

Power to use the company's seal.

**9**

Power to do all acts and to execute in the name and on behalf of the company any deed, receipt or other document.

**10**

Power to draw, accept, make and endorse any bill of exchange or promissory note in the name and on behalf of the company.

**11**

Power to appoint any agent to do any business which he is unable to do himself or which can more conveniently be done by an agent, and power to employ and dismiss employees.

**12**

Power to do all such things (including the carrying out of works), as may be necessary for the realisation of the property.

**13**

Power to make any payment which is necessary or incidental to the performance of his functions.

**14**

Power to carry on the business of the company or any part of it.

**15**

Power to grant or accept a surrender of a lease or tenancy of any of the property, and to take a lease or tenancy of any property required or convenient for the business of the company.

**16**

Power to make any arrangement or compromise on behalf of the company.

**17**

Power to call up any uncalled capital of the company.

**18**

Power to establish subsidiaries of the company.

**19**

Power to transfer to subsidiaries of the company the business of the company or any part of it and any of the property.

**20**

Power to rank and claim in the bankruptcy, insolvency, sequestration or liquidation of any person or company indebted to the company and to receive dividends, and to accede to trust deeds for creditors of any such person.

**21**

Power to present or defend a petition for the winding up of the company.

**22**

Power to change the situation of the company's registered office.

**23**

Power to do all other things incidental to the exercise of the powers mentioned in section 55(1) of this Act or above in this Schedule.

**Amendments**—Abolition of Feudal Tenure etc (Scotland) Act 2000, s 76(2), Sch 13, Pt 1.

### SCHEDULE 2A
### EXCEPTIONS TO PROHIBITION ON APPOINTMENT OF ADMINISTRATIVE RECEIVER: SUPPLEMENTARY PROVISIONS

Section 72H(1)

**[1.737]**

**Amendments**—Inserted by Enterprise Act 2002, s 250(2), Sch 18.

**1 Capital market arrangement**

(1) For the purposes of section 72B an arrangement is a capital market arrangement if—

    (a)    it involves a grant of security to a person holding it as trustee for a person who holds a capital market investment issued by a party to the arrangement, or

    (aa)    it involves a grant of security to—

        (i)    a party to the arrangement who issues a capital market investment, or

        (ii)    a person who holds the security as trustee for a party to the arrangement in connection with the issue of a capital market investment, or

    (ab)    it involves a grant of security to a person who holds the security as trustee for a party to the arrangement who agrees to provide finance to another party, or

    (b)    at least one party guarantees the performance of obligations of another party, or

    (c)    at least one party provides security in respect of the performance of obligations of another party, or

    (d)    the arrangement involves an investment of a kind described in articles 83 to 85 of the Financial Services and Markets Act 2000 (Regulated Activities) Order 2001 (SI 2001/544) (options, futures and contracts for differences).

(2) For the purposes of sub-paragraph (1)—

    (a)    a reference to holding as trustee includes a reference to holding as nominee or agent,

    (b)    a reference to holding for a person who holds a capital market investment includes a reference to holding for a number of persons at least one of whom holds a capital market investment, and

    (c)    a person holds a capital market investment if he has a legal or beneficial interest in it; and

    (d)    the reference to the provision of finance includes the provision of an indemnity.

(3) In section 72B(1) and this paragraph "party" to an arrangement includes a party to an agreement which—

    (a)    forms part of the arrangement,

    (b)    provides for the raising of finance as part of the arrangement, or

    (c)    is necessary for the purposes of implementing the arrangement.

## 2 Capital market investment

(1)    For the purposes of section 72B an investment is a capital market investment if it—

    (a)    is within article 77 or 77A of the Financial Services and Markets Act 2000 (Regulated Activities) Order 2001 (SI 2001/544) (debt instruments), and

    (b)    is rated, listed or traded or designed to be rated, listed or traded.

(2)    In sub-paragraph (1)—

    "rated" means rated for the purposes of investment by an internationally recognised rating agency,

    "listed" means admitted to the official list within the meaning given by section 103(1) of the Financial Services and Markets Act 2000 (interpretation), and

    "traded" means admitted to trading on a market established under the rules of a recognised investment exchange or on a foreign market.

(3)    In sub-paragraph (2)—

    "recognised investment exchange" has the meaning given by section 285 of the Financial Services and Markets Act 2000 (recognised investment exchange), and

    "foreign market" has the same meaning as "relevant market" in article 67(2) of the Financial Services and Markets Act 2000 (Financial Promotion) Order 2001 (SI 2001/1335) (foreign markets).

## 3

(1)    An investment is also a capital market investment for the purposes of section 72B if it consists of a bond or commercial paper issued to one or more of the following—

    (a)    an investment professional within the meaning of article 19(5) of the Financial Services and Markets Act 2000 (Financial Promotion) Order 2001,

    (b)    a person who is, when the agreement mentioned in section 72B(1) is entered into, a certified high net worth individual in relation to a communication within the meaning of article 48(2) of that order,

    (c)    a person to whom article 49(2) of that order applies (high net worth company, etc),

    (d)    a person who is, when the agreement mentioned in section 72B(1) is entered into, a certified sophisticated investor in relation to a communication within the meaning of article 50(1) of that order, and

    (e)    a person in a State other than the United Kingdom who under the law of that State is not prohibited from investing in bonds or commercial paper.

(2)    In sub-paragraph (1)—

    "bond" shall be construed in accordance with article 77 of the Financial Services and Markets Act 2000 (Regulated Activities) Order 2001 (SI 2001/544), and includes any instrument falling within article 77A of that Order, and

    "commercial paper" has the meaning given by article 9(3) of that order.

(3)    For the purposes of sub-paragraph (1)—

    (a)    in applying article 19(5) of the Financial Promotion Order for the purposes of sub-paragraph (1)(a)—

        (i)    in article 19(5)(b), ignore the words after "exempt person",

        (ii)    in article 19(5)(c)(i), for the words from "the controlled activity" to the end substitute "a controlled activity", and

        (iii)    in article 19(5)(e) ignore the words from "where the communication" to the end, and

    (b)    in applying article 49(2) of that order for the purposes of sub-paragraph (1)(c), ignore article 49(2)(e).

**Amendments**—SI 2010/86.

## 4 "Agreement"

For the purposes of sections 72B and 72E and this Schedule "agreement" includes an agreement or undertaking effected by—

(a)    contract,

(b)    deed, or

(c)    any other instrument intended to have effect in accordance with the law of England and Wales, Scotland or another jurisdiction.

## 5 Debt

The debt of at least £50 million referred to in section 72B(1)(a) or 72E(2)(a)—

(a)    may be incurred at any time during the life of the capital market arrangement or financed project, and

(b)    may be expressed wholly or partly in foreign currency (in which case the sterling equivalent shall be calculated as at the time when the arrangement is entered into or the project begins).

## 6 Step-in rights

(1)    For the purposes of sections 72C to 72E a project has "step-in rights" if a person who provides finance in connection with the project has a conditional entitlement under an agreement to—

(a)    assume sole or principal responsibility under an agreement for carrying out all or part of the project, or

(b)    make arrangements for carrying out all or part of the project.

(2)    In sub-paragraph (1) a reference to the provision of finance includes a reference to the provision of an indemnity.

## 7 Project company

(1)    For the purposes of sections 72C to 72E a company is a "project company" of a project if—

(a)    it holds property for the purpose of the project,

(b)    it has sole or principal responsibility under an agreement for carrying out all or part of the project,

(c)    it is one of a number of companies which together carry out the project,

(d)    it has the purpose of supplying finance to enable the project to be carried out, or

(e)    it is the holding company of a company within any of paragraphs (a) to (d).

(2)    But a company is not a "project company" of a project if—

(a)    it performs a function within sub-paragraph (1)(a) to (d) or is within sub-paragraph (1)(e), but

(b)    it also performs a function which is not—

(i)    within sub-paragraph (1)(a) to (d),

(ii)    related to a function within sub-paragraph (1)(a) to (d), or

(iii)    related to the project.

(3)    For the purposes of this paragraph a company carries out all or part of a project whether or not it acts wholly or partly through agents.

## 8 "Resources"

In section 72C "resources" includes—

(a)    funds (including payment for the provision of services or facilities),

(b)    assets,

(c)    professional skill,

(d)    the grant of a concession or franchise, and

(e)    any other commercial resource.

## 9 "Public body"

(1)    In section 72C "public body" means—

(a)    a body which exercises public functions,

(b)    a body specified for the purposes of this paragraph by the Secretary of State, and

(c)    a body within a class specified for the purposes of this paragraph by the Secretary of State.

(2)    A specification under sub-paragraph (1) may be—

(a)    general, or

(b)    for the purpose of the application of section 72C to a specified case.

**10 Regulated business**

(1)   For the purposes of section 72D a business is regulated if it is carried on—

    (a)    . . .

    (b)    in reliance on a licence under section 7, 7A or 7B of the Gas Act 1986 (c 44) (transport and supply of gas),

    (c)    in reliance on a licence granted by virtue of section 41C of that Act (power to prescribe additional licensable activity),

    (d)    in reliance on a licence under section 6 of the Electricity Act 1989 (c 29) (supply of electricity),

    (e)    by a water undertaker,

    (f)    by a sewerage undertaker,

    (g)    by a universal service provider within the meaning of Part 3 of the Postal Services Act 2011,

    (h)    by a Post Office company within the meaning of Part 1 of that Act,

    (i)    . . .

    (j)    in reliance on a licence under section 8 of the Railways Act 1993 (c 43) (railway services),

    (k)    in reliance on a licence exemption under section 7 of that Act (subject to sub-paragraph (2) below),

    (l)    by the operator of a system of transport which is deemed to be a railway for a purpose of Part I of that Act by virtue of section 81(2) of that Act (tramways, &c), . . .

    (m)    by the operator of a vehicle carried on flanged wheels along a system within paragraph (l) or

    (n)    in reliance on a railway undertaking licence granted pursuant to the Railway (Licensing of Railway Undertakings) Regulations 2005.

(2)   Sub-paragraph (1)(k) does not apply to the operator of a railway asset on a railway unless on some part of the railway there is a permitted line speed exceeding 40 kilometres per hour.

(2A)   For the purposes of section 72D a business is also regulated to the extent that it consists in the provision of a public electronic communications network or a public electronic communications service.

(2B)  . . .

**Amendments**—SI 2019/700 having effect from IP completion day (as defined in the European Union (Withdrawal Agreement) Act 2020, s 39(1)–(5)): see SI 2019/700, reg 1(2).

**11 "Person"**

A reference to a person in this Schedule includes a reference to a partnership or another unincorporated group of persons.

**Amendments**—Inserted by Enterprise Act 2002, s 250(2), Sch 18. Amended by Communications Act 2003, s 406(1), (7), Sch 17, para 82(1), (4), Sch 19(1); SI 2003/1468; SI 2005/3050; SI 2010/86; Postal Services Act 2011, s 91(1), (2), Sch 12, Pt 3, paras 124, 126; SI 2012/2400; SI 2016/645.

**General note**—See the note on ss 72A–72H in the introductory note to receivership preceding s 28.

SCHEDULE 3
ORDERS IN COURSE OF WINDING UP PRONOUNCED IN VACATION
(SCOTLAND)
Section 162

PART I   ORDERS WHICH ARE TO BE FINAL
**[1.738]**

Orders under section 153, as to the time for proving debts and claims.
Orders under section 195 as to meetings for ascertaining wishes of creditors or contributories.
Orders under section 198, as to the examination of witnesses in regard to the property or affairs of a company.

PART II   ORDERS WHICH ARE TO TAKE EFFECT UNTIL MATTER DISPOSED
OF BY INNER HOUSE
**[1.739]**

Orders under section 126(1), 130(2) or (3), 147, 227 or 228, restraining or permitting the commencement or the continuance of legal proceedings.
Orders under section 135(5), limiting the powers of provisional liquidators.
Orders under section 108, appointing a liquidator to fill a vacancy.
Orders under section 158, as to the arrest and detention of an absconding contributory and his property.

**Amendments**—Small Business, Enterprise and Employment Act 2015, s 120(1), (5).

SCHEDULE 4
POWERS OF LIQUIDATOR IN A WINDING UP
Sections 165, 167

**[1.740]**

**General comment on Schedule 4**—This Schedule deals with the powers that are given to liquidators of companies. The powers are not exhaustive. Besides the powers set out here and in the Act, liquidators are able to do other things which do not affect the assets or liabilities of the company. As far as powers are concerned, particular reference should be had to s 168 where supplementary powers for liquidators are mentioned. Liquidators of voluntary liquidations are given powers in ss 165 and 166. Other provisions in the Act, such as s 236 (power to apply for examinations), set out specific powers given to liquidators. The Schedule does not apply to provisional liquidators, but courts have the power, in their discretion, to grant provisional liquidators particular powers when appointing them. See the notes accompanying s 135.

Generally on liquidator powers, see A Keay *McPherson and Keay's Law of Company Liquidation* (Sweet and Maxwell, 4th edn, 2018) at 527–550.

PART I
**[1.741]**

**Amendments**—Part heading repealed by Small Business, Enterprise and Employment Act 2015, s 120(1), (6)(c).

**General comment on Part 1**—To exercise the powers in this Part, previously liquidators needed to have the sanction of the court or the liquidation committee in a court winding up, but that has now been changed and no sanction is required (see s 167(1)).

In members' voluntary liquidations, previously the sanction of an extraordinary meeting of the company was required, but that is no longer the case (see s 165(2)).

Many of the cases deal with the law when liquidators needed exercise of the powers sanctioned and address whether a liquidator was entitled to have exercise of the power sanctioned. The principles which they provide can be applied to assist a liquidator to know whether he or she should exercise the power and also applied where an application is made to have exercise of the powers reviewed.

While the liquidator has more unfettered power, it may well be wise for him or her to seek approval in certain cases, such as where proposed litigation might be very expensive or involving significant risk. In *Re Longmeade Ltd* [2016] EWHC 356 (Ch), [2017] 1 BCLC 605, [2016] BPIR 666 Snowden J set out the principles that should be applied by a liquidator in relation to the exercise of powers in situations where sanction was previously required. These are as follows:

- the institution of legal proceedings in a compulsory liquidation and in the name of the company was essentially a commercial decision;
- in taking that decision, the liquidators had to act in what they believed to be the best interests of the insolvent company and all those who had an interest in its estate;
- liquidators could, but were not obliged to, consult the creditors (or contributories) who had an interest in the estate;
- the liquidators should normally give weight to the reasoned views of the majority of such creditors (or contributories), provided that those views were uninfluenced by extraneous considerations;
- if all those who were interested in the insolvent estate are fully informed and were unanimously of the same view, the liquidators should ordinarily give effect to their wishes;
- the court should not generally interfere with a commercial or administrative decision of liquidators after the event, unless it was a decision that was taken in bad faith or was a decision that no reasonable liquidator could have taken (at [66]).

**1**

Power to pay any class of creditors in full.

**2**

Power to make any compromise or arrangement with creditors or persons claiming to be creditors, or having or alleging themselves to have any claim (present or future, certain or contingent, ascertained or sounding only in damages) against the company, or whereby the company may be rendered liable.

**General note**—The power to effect compromises is wide, and wide enough to permit the liquidator to enter into any compromise arrangement with creditors that might have been entered into by the company itself: *Re Bank of Credit and Commerce International SA (No 2)* [1993] BCLC 1490.

The main concern for a court, in deciding whether or not to overturn a compromise in relation to an insolvent company or whether to approve a compromise where it is sought by the liquidator, is whether the compromise benefits and serves the interest of the creditors in the funds of the company: *Re Edennote Ltd (No 2)* [1997] 2 BCLC 89; *Re Greenhaven Motors Ltd* [1999] 1 BCLC 635, CA. It has been held that just because the liquidator might benefit personally from a compromise, namely relief from liability in costs, a compromise will not be interfered with: *Re Greenhaven Motors Ltd* [1999] 1 BCLC 635, CA.

Courts, when hearing applications seeking the overturning of a compromise or a liquidator's application for sanction, will not consider all of the issues considered by the liquidator in coming to his or her decision about the compromise proposal. The role of the court is not to evaluate whether a proposal is commercially sound, as that is the function of the liquidator. Rather, the court's function is to review the proposal, consider the liquidator's commercial judgment and knowledge of the liquidation, and ensure that it is satisfied that the liquidator has not committed an error of law in law or principle, there is some real and substantive ground for questioning the proposal, or that there is any ground for suspecting bad faith or impropriety: *State Bank of New South Wales v Turner Corporation Ltd* (1994) 14 ACSR 480 at 483; *Corporate Affairs Commission v ASC Timber Pty Ltd* (1998) 16 ACLC 1642 at 1650. If a party alleges a lack of good faith etc, then the burden that is on that party is not light, as the liquidator is regarded as being generally in the best position to assess whether a proposal is in the best interests of the creditors: *Re Geelong Building Society* (1996) 14 ACLC 334 at 338. The English courts have taken a similar approach as is evidenced by the decision of Snowden J in *Re Longmeade Ltd* [2016] EWHC 356 (Ch), [2017] 1 BCLC 605, [2016] BPIR 666. While the court is not bound by the views of the liquidator it should not conduct a mini-trial of the merits of the issues that relate to the claim that is being compromised: *Rubin v Coote* [2009] EWHC 2266 (Ch), [2010] BPIR 262 (appeal dismissed: [2011] EWCA Civ 106).

In considering whether to overturn a compromise or whether to give sanction to a compromise on the liquidator's application, it has been said in the Australian case of *Re S & D International Pty Ltd (in liquidation) (No 7)* [2012] VSC 551 that the following questions should be considered: Is the compromise of debt proposed by the liquidator in the best interests of creditors? Has the liquidator made a proper assessment of prospects and recovery of the debt? Are there any concerns about future claims by creditors against the liquidators in relation to the debt? Is the proposed compromise in good faith and for a proper purpose? Has there been full and frank disclosure to the Court/creditors of all matters relevant to the debt and the proposed compromise?

**3**

Power to compromise, on such terms as may be agreed—

(a) all calls and liabilities to calls, all debts and liabilities capable of resulting in debts, and all claims (present or future, certain or contingent, ascertained or sounding only in damages) subsisting or supposed to subsist between the company and a contributory or alleged contributory or other debtor or person apprehending liability to the company, and

(b) all questions in any way relating to or affecting the assets or the winding up of the company,

and take any security for the discharge of any such call, debt, liability or claim and give a complete discharge in respect of it.

**Amendments**—SI 2010/18; Small Business, Enterprise and Employment Act 2015, s 120(1), (6)(a).

**3A**

Power to bring legal proceedings under section 213, 214, 238, 239, 242, 243 or 423.

**Amendments**—Inserted by Enterprise Act 2002, s 253.

**General note**—Previously liquidators were required to obtain sanction before initiating proceedings under the relevant sections mentioned in the paragraph. Now the liquidator does not need to seek sanction for the bringing of legal proceedings but he or she might do so. The occasions when it is likely to be done is where proceedings will involve substantial costs and risk.

For a discussion of the issues relevant to the bringing of proceedings, see A Keay *McPherson and Keay's Law of Company Liquidation* (Sweet and Maxwell, 4th edn, 2018) at 532–543.

## PART II

**Amendments**—Part heading repealed by Small Business, Enterprise and Employment Act 2015, s 120(1), (6)(c).

**[1.742]**

**4**

Power to bring or defend any action or other legal proceeding in the name and on behalf of the company.

**General note**—The liquidator used to have to obtain the sanction of the court to bring proceedings in the name of the company, but that is no longer the case. However, the liquidator may seek to obtain court sanction in certain situations.

ICC Judge Barber said in *Hellard v Graiseley Investments Ltd* ([2018] EWHC 2664 (Ch)) that a liquidator's position was no different from that of other parties to litigation. Hence, they could be the subject of adverse costs orders, as for instance, in *Hosking v Apax Partners LLP* ([2018] EWHC 2732 (Ch), [2019] 1 WLR 3347).

For a discussion of the issues relevant to the bringing or defending of proceedings, see A Keay *McPherson and Keay's Law of Company Liquidation* (Sweet and Maxwell, 4th edn, 2018) at 532–543.

**5**

Power to carry on the business of the company so far as may be necessary for its beneficial winding up.

**General note**—A voluntary liquidator, who does not get leave to carry on business, must be aware that he or she needs to have reasonable grounds for believing that carrying on the business is beneficial or else he or she may be held personally liable for any loss sustained: *Re Centralcast Engineering Ltd* [2000] BCC 727.

While in *Re Wreck Recovery & Salvage Co* (1880) 15 ChD 353 at 362) Thesiger LJ said that the liquidator's statutory authority to carry on business is to be construed liberally, the power is only to be exercised where it is clearly necessary and will benefit the winding up, and it does not cover activity that involves speculation with the assets in the hope of making a profit for the benefit of the creditors or shareholders. In this context 'necessary' means something more than beneficial, and it will be determined by the court, having regard to all the circumstances of the case: *Re Wreck Recovery & Salvage Co* at 360. The power confines a liquidator to acts relating to the business of the company as it existed when the winding up commenced: *Re Crouch* [2007] NSWSC 1055, (2007) 214 FLR 244 at [23].

When hearing applications by creditors or others complaining about the liquidator's decision to carry on business, courts will not decide on whether a liquidator acted improperly in carrying on a business by making a judgment from hindsight; a court will not chastise a liquidator who, at the relevant time, acted bona fide, and reasonably formed the opinion that it was necessary to carry on the business for the benefit of winding up or disposal of the company's business: *Re Great Eastern Electric Co* [1941] Ch 241.

The liquidator is permitted to carry on the business so that it can be sold as a going concern at a higher price than would be received for the assets in a liquidation sale: *Re Skay Fashions Pty Ltd (in liq)* (1986) 10 ACLR 743; *Warne v GDK Financial Solutions Pty Ltd* [2006] NSWSC 464, (2006) 233 ALR 181 at [49]. The courts have placed no specific time limit on the period for which a liquidator is permitted to carry on business as all companies will be different. In *Re Batey; Ex p Emmanuel* ((1881) 17 Ch D 35), the court said that 12 months was a long period but it was not necessarily inappropriate (at 39).

## PART III

Amendments—Part heading repealed by Small Business, Enterprise and Employment Act 2015, s 120(1), (6)(c).

**[1.743]**

6

Power to sell any of the company's property by public auction or private contract with power to transfer the whole of it to any person or to sell the same in parcels.

General note—There are a number of methods of selling the assets of the company, including private contract, public auction, tender and clearance sale. The liquidator must choose the method and price which will give maximum benefit to the creditors. The liquidator has a wide discretion in selling assets. The court will only interfere with sales if the liquidator has not acted as a reasonable liquidator would act: *Leon v York-O-Matic Ltd* [1966] 1 WLR 1450, [1966] 3 All ER 277.

'Property' here includes causes of action vested in the company at the time of the liquidation (*Seear v Lawson* (1880) 15 ChD 426 at 432–433; *Grovewood Holdings plc v James Capel & Co Ltd* [1995] Ch 80, [1995] 2 WLR 70, [1994] 4 All ER 417, [1994] 2 BCLC 782). In the past the question whether a liquidator has been entitled to assign a cause of action, part of it, or the proceeds of a cause of action has been the subject of concern. Now this has been resolved to a large degree by the fact that s 246ZD permits a liquidator to assign a right of action, including the proceeds of the action, where it arises under any of: ss 213, 214, 238, 239, 242, 243 and 244 and this can be done without sanction.

It has been held by the New South Wales Court of Appeal that where the company, before liquidation, had agreed that particular property was incapable of being assigned, the power in this paragraph does not enable the liquidator to assign the property provided that the agreement not to assign was valid in law: *Owners of Strata Plan 5290 v CGS & Co Pty Ltd* [2011] NSWCA 168 at [64].

Where a liquidator is considering making an assignment of a cause of action, he or she, if not a lawyer, should not proceed on the basis of his or her own valuation: *Ultraframe (UK) Ltd v Rigby* [2005] EWCA Civ 276 at [52].

The power to disclaim is able to be covered by this paragraph: *Re Business Dream Ltd* [2011] EWHC 2860 (Ch), [2013] 1 BCLC 456, [2012] BPIR 490 at [36].

6A

*(Repealed)*

Amendments—Inserted by SI 2010/18. Repealed by Small Business, Enterprise and Employment Act 2015, s 120(1), (6)(b).

General note—Prior to the enactment of this provision liquidators had to secure the sanction of the court.

**7**

Power to do all acts and execute, in the name and on behalf of the company, all deeds, receipts and other documents and for that purpose to use, when necessary, the company's seal.

General note—If liquidators enter into contracts on behalf of the company, they do not become liable if they make it clear to the other parties that they are acting on behalf of the company: *Stead Hazel & Co v Cooper* [1933] 1 KB 840.

**8**

Power to prove, rank and claim in the bankruptcy, insolvency or sequestration of any contributory for any balance against his estate, and to receive dividends in the bankruptcy, insolvency or sequestration in respect of that balance, as a separate debt due from the bankrupt or insolvent, and rateably with the other separate creditors.

**9**

Power to draw, accept, make and indorse any bill of exchange or promissory note in the name and on behalf of the company, with the same effect with respect to the company's liability as if the bill or note had been drawn, accepted, made or indorsed by or on behalf of the company in the course of its business.

General note—When exercising this power a liquidator should sign as the liquidator as well as for and on behalf of the company in order to avoid personal liability on the cheque or other instrument involved: *Rolfe Lubell & Co v Keith* [1979] 1 All ER 860.

**10**

Power to raise on the security of the assets of the company any money requisite.

General note—If a liquidator raises money as against company property, which is used as security, the security granted is subject to the rights of existing secured creditors whose rights are fixed: *Re Regent's Canal Ironworks Co* (1875) 3 ChD 411.

**11**

Power to take out in his official name letters of administration to any deceased contributory, and to do in his official name any other act necessary for obtaining payment of any money due from a contributory or his estate which cannot conveniently be done in the name of the company.

In all such cases the money due is deemed, for the purpose of enabling the liquidator to take out the letters of administration or recover the money, to be due to the liquidator himself.

**12**

Power to appoint an agent to do any business which the liquidator is unable to do himself.

**13**

Power to do all such other things as may be necessary for winding up the company's affairs and distributing its assets.

General note—This is known as the incidental power, or even a 'mopping-up provision' (*Re Phoenix Oil and Transport Co Ltd (No 2)* [1958] Ch 565, [1958] 1 All ER 158). The power is extremely broad (*Re Cambrian Mining Co* (1882) 48 LT 114 at 116), and relies on the professionalism and competence of the liquidator. It permits the liquidator to do anything which may be thought expedient with reference to the property of the company (*Re Cambrian Mining Co* at 116). Australian authorities have provided that the power allows a liquidator to lease company property (*Re Premier Permanent Building Society* (1890) 16 VLR 643) or purchase property for the purpose of resale: *Re Bairnsdale Food Products Ltd* [1948] VLR 624.

The power to disclaim is able to be covered by this paragraph: *Re Business Dream Ltd* [2011] EWHC 2860 (Ch), [2013] 1 BCLC 456, [2012] BPIR 490 at [36].

SCHEDULE 4ZZA
PROTECTION OF SUPPLIES UNDER SECTION 233B: EXCLUSIONS
Section 233B

## PART 1   ESSENTIAL SUPPLIES

*Essential supplies*

**[1.744]**

**1**

(1)   Section 233B(3) and (4) do not apply in relation to provision of a contract if—

    (a)   the company becomes subject to a relevant insolvency procedure as specified in section 233B(2)(b) or (d), and

    (b)   the provision of the contract ceases to have effect under section 233A(1).

(2)   Section 233B(7) does not apply in relation to a supply to the company if—

    (a)   the company becomes subject to a relevant insolvency procedure as specified in section 233B(2)(b) to (f), and

    (b)   the supply is a supply mentioned in section 233(3).

## PART 2   PERSONS INVOLVED IN FINANCIAL SERVICES

*Introductory*

**[1.745]**

**2**

Section 233B does not apply in relation to a contract for the supply of goods or services to a company ("the company") where any of paragraphs 3 to 11 applies.

*Insurers*

**3**

(1)   This paragraph applies where either the company or the supplier—

    (a)   carries on the regulated activity of effecting or carrying out contracts of insurance, and

    (b)   is not an exempt person in relation to that activity.

(2)   In this paragraph—

"exempt person", in relation to a regulated activity, has the meaning given by section 417 of the Financial Services and Markets Act 2000;

"regulated activity" has the meaning given by section 22 of that Act, taken with Schedule 2 to that Act and any order under that section.

*Banks*

**4**

(1)   This paragraph applies where either the company or the supplier—

    (a)   has permission under Part 4A of the Financial Services and Markets Act 2000 to carry on the regulated activity of accepting deposits,

    (b)   is a banking group company within the meaning of Part 1 of the Banking Act 2009 (see section 81D of that Act), or

    (c)   has a liability in respect of a deposit which it accepted in accordance with the Banking Act 1979 or the Banking Act 1987.

(2) In sub-paragraph (1)(a) "regulated activity" has the meaning given by section 22 of the Financial Services and Markets Act 2000 2000, taken with Schedule 2 to that Act and any order under that section.

*Electronic money institutions*

5

This paragraph applies where either the company or the supplier is an electronic money institution within the meaning of the Electronic Money Regulations 2011 (SI 2011/99) (see regulation 2 of those Regulations).

*Investment banks and investment firms*

6

(1) This paragraph applies where either the company or the supplier is an investment bank or an investment firm.

(2) In this paragraph—

"investment bank" means a company or other entity that has permission under Part 4A of the Financial Services and Markets Act 2000 to carry on the regulated activity of—

    (a) safeguarding and administering investments,

    (b) managing an AIF or a UCITS,

    (c) acting as trustee or depositary of an AIF or a UCITS,

    (d) dealing in investments as principal, or

    (e) dealing in investments as agent;

"investment firm" has the same meaning as in the Banking Act 2009 (see section 258A of that Act), disregarding any order made under section 258A(2)(b) of that Act;

"regulated activity" has the meaning given by section 22 of the Financial Services and Markets Act 2000, taken with Schedule 2 to that Act and any order under that section.

*Payment institutions*

7

This paragraph applies where either the company or the supplier is an authorised payment institution, a small payment institution or a registered account information service provider within the meaning of the Payment Services Regulations 2017 (SI 2017/752) (see regulation 2 of those Regulations).

*Operators of payment systems, infrastructure providers etc*

8

This paragraph applies where either the company or the supplier is—

    (a) the operator of a payment system or an infrastructure provider within the meaning of Part 5 of the Financial Services (Banking Reform) Act 2013 (see section 42 of that Act), or

    (b) an infrastructure company within the meaning of Part 6 of that Act (see section 112 of that Act).

*Recognised investment exchanges etc*

9

This paragraph applies where either the company or the supplier is a recognised investment exchange, a recognised clearing house or a recognised CSD within the meaning of the Financial Services and Markets Act 2000 (see section 285 of that Act).

*Securitisation companies*

**10**

This paragraph applies where either the company or the supplier is a securitisation company within the meaning of the Taxation of Securitisation Companies Regulations 2006 (SI 2006/3296) (see regulation 4 of those Regulations).

*Overseas activities*

**11**

This paragraph applies where either the company or the supplier does or has done anything outside the United Kingdom which, if done in the United Kingdom, would cause any of the preceding paragraphs of this Part of this Schedule to apply.

## PART 3   CONTRACTS INVOLVING FINANCIAL SERVICES

*Introductory*

**[1.746]**

**12**

To the extent that anything to which any of paragraphs 13 to 18 applies is a contract for the supply of goods or services, section 233B does not apply in relation to it.

*Financial contracts*

**13**

(1) This paragraph applies to a financial contract.

(2) "Financial contract" means—

    (a) a contract for the provision of financial services consisting of—

        (i) lending (including the factoring and financing of commercial transactions),

        (ii) financial leasing, or

        (iii) providing guarantees or commitments;

    (b) a securities contract, including—

        (i) a contract for the purchase, sale or loan of a security or group or index of securities;

        (ii) an option on a security or group or index of securities;

        (iii) a repurchase or reverse repurchase transaction on any such security, group or index;

    (c) a commodities contract, including—

        (i) a contract for the purchase, sale or loan of a commodity or group or index of commodities for future delivery;

        (ii) an option on a commodity or group or index of commodities;

        (iii) a repurchase or reverse repurchase transaction on any such commodity, group or index;

    (d) a futures or forwards contract, including a contract (other than a commodities contract) for the purchase, sale or transfer of a commodity or property of any other description, service, right or interest for a specified price at a future date;

    (e) a swap agreement, including—

        (i) a swap or option relating to interest rates, spot or other foreign exchange agreements, currency, an equity index or equity, a debt index or debt, commodity indexes or commodities, weather, emissions or inflation;

        (ii) a total return, credit spread or credit swap;

        (iii)    any agreement or transaction similar to an agreement that is referred to in sub-paragraph (i) or (ii) and is the subject of recurrent dealing in the swaps or derivatives markets;

    (f)    an inter-bank borrowing agreement where the term of the borrowing is three months or less;

    (g)    a master agreement for any of the contracts or agreements referred to in paragraphs (a) to (f).

(3)    For the purposes of this paragraph "commodities" includes—

    (a)    units recognised for compliance with the requirements of EU Directive 2003/87/EC establishing a scheme for greenhouse gas emission allowance trading,

    (b)    allowances under paragraph 5 of Schedule 2 to the Climate Change Act 2008 relating to a trading scheme dealt with under Part 1 of that Schedule (schemes limiting activities relating to emissions of greenhouse gas), and

    (c)    renewables obligation certificates issued—

        (i)    by the Gas and Electricity Markets Authority under an order made under section 32B of the Electricity Act 1989, or

        (ii)    by the Northern Ireland Authority for Utility Regulation under the Energy (Northern Ireland) Order 2003 (SI 2003/419 (NI 6)) and pursuant to an order made under Articles 52 to 55F of that Order.

*Securities financing transactions*

**14**

(1)    This paragraph applies to—

    (a)    a securities financing transaction, and

    (b)    a master agreement for securities financing transactions.

(2)    "Securities financing transaction" has the meaning given by Article 3(11) of Regulation (EU) 2015/2365 on the transparency of securities financing transactions.

(3)    But for the purposes of that Article as it applies for the purposes of this paragraph, references to "commodities" in that Regulation are to be taken as including the units, allowances and certificates referred to in paragraph 13(3)(a) to (c).

*Derivatives*

**15**

(1)    This paragraph applies to—

    (a)    a derivative, and

    (b)    a master agreement for derivatives.

(2)    "Derivative" has the meaning given by Article 2(5) of Regulation (EU) No 648/2012.

*Spot contracts*

**16**

(1)    This paragraph applies to—

    (a)    a spot contract, and

    (b)    a master agreement for spot contracts.

(2)    "Spot contract" has the meaning given by Article 7(2) or 10(2) of Commission Delegated Regulation of 25.4.2016 supplementing Directive 2014/65/EU of the European Parliament and of the Council as regards organisational requirements and operating conditions for investment firms and defined terms for the purposes of that Directive.

*Capital market investments*

**17**

(1)   This paragraph applies to an agreement which is, or forms part of, an arrangement involving the issue of a capital market investment.

(2)   "Capital market investment" has the meaning given by paragraph 14 of Schedule ZA1.

*Contracts forming part of a public-private partnership*

**18**

This paragraph applies to a contract forming part of a public-private partnership project within the meaning given by paragraph 16 of Schedule ZA1.

## PART 4   OTHER EXCLUSIONS

*Financial markets and insolvency*

**[1.747]**

**19**

Nothing in section 233B affects the operation of—

(a)   Part 7 of the Companies Act 1989 (financial markets and insolvency),

(b)   the Financial Markets and Insolvency Regulations 1996 (SI 1996/1469),

(c)   the Financial Markets and Insolvency (Settlement Finality) Regulations 1999 (SI 1999/2979), or

(d)   the Financial Collateral Arrangements (No 2) Regulations 2003 (SI 2003/3226).

*Set-off and netting*

**20**

Nothing in section 233B affects any set-off or netting arrangements (within the meanings given by section 48(1)(c) and (d) of the Banking Act 2009).

*Aircraft equipment*

**21**

Nothing in section 233B affects the International Interests in Aircraft Equipment (Cape Town Convention) Regulations 2015 (SI 2015/912).

## SCHEDULE 4ZA
## CONDITIONS FOR MAKING A DEBT RELIEF ORDER

Amendments—Inserted by Tribunals, Courts and Enforcement Act 2007, s 108(1), Sch 18.

## PART 1   CONDITIONS WHICH MUST BE MET

**[1.748]**

**1 Connection with England and Wales**

(1)   The debtor—

(a)   is domiciled in England and Wales on the application date; or

(b)   at any time during the period of three years ending with that date—

(i)   was ordinarily resident, or had a place of residence, in England and Wales; or

      (ii)    carried on business in England and Wales.

(2)   The reference in sub-paragraph (1)(b)(ii) to the debtor carrying on business includes—

    (a)    the carrying on of business by a firm or partnership of which he is a member;

    (b)    the carrying on of business by an agent or manager for him or for such a firm or partnership.

## 2 Debtor's previous insolvency history

The debtor is not, on the determination date—

    (a)    an undischarged bankrupt;

    (b)    subject to an interim order or voluntary arrangement under Part 8; or

    (c)    subject to a bankruptcy restrictions order or a debt relief restrictions order.

## 3

A bankruptcy application under Part 9—

    (a)    has not been made before the determination date; or

    (b)    has been so made, but proceedings on the application have been finally disposed of before that date.

**Amendments**—Substituted by Enterprise and Regulatory Reform Act 2013, s 71(3), Sch 19, paras 1, 62.

## 4

A creditor's petition for the debtor's bankruptcy under Part 9—

    (a)    has not been presented against the debtor at any time before the determination date;

    (b)    has been so presented, but proceedings on the petition have been finally disposed of before that date; or

    (c)    has been so presented and proceedings in relation to the petition remain before the court at that date, but the person who presented the petition has consented to the making of an application for a debt relief order.

## 5

A debt relief order has not been made in relation to the debtor in the period of six years ending with the determination date.

## 6 Limit on debtor's overall indebtedness

(1)   The total amount of the debtor's debts on the determination date, other than unliquidated debts and excluded debts, does not exceed the prescribed amount.

(2)   For this purpose an unliquidated debt is a debt that is not for a liquidated sum payable to a creditor either immediately or at some future certain time.

## 7 Limit on debtor's monthly surplus income

(1)   The debtor's monthly surplus income (if any) on the determination date does not exceed the prescribed amount.

(2)   For this purpose "monthly surplus income" is the amount by which a person's monthly income exceeds the amount necessary for the reasonable domestic needs of himself and his family.

(3)   The rules may—

    (a)    make provision as to how the debtor's monthly surplus income is to be determined;

    (b)    provide that particular descriptions of income are to be excluded for the purposes of this paragraph.

## 8 Limit on value of debtor's property

(1)   The total value of the debtor's property on the determination date does not exceed the prescribed amount.

(2)   The rules may—

    (a)    make provision as to how the value of a person's property is to be determined;

    (b)    provide that particular descriptions of property are to be excluded for the purposes of this paragraph.

**Amendments**—Inserted by Tribunals, Courts and Enforcement Act 2007, s 108(1), Sch 18.

## PART 2  OTHER CONDITIONS

**[1.749]**

9

(1)   The debtor has not entered into a transaction with any person at an undervalue during the period between—

    (a)    the start of the period of two years ending with the application date; and

    (b)    the determination date.

(2)   For this purpose a debtor enters into a transaction with a person at an undervalue if—

    (a)    he makes a gift to that person or he otherwise enters into a transaction with that person on terms that provide for him to receive no consideration;

    (b)    he enters into a transaction with that person in consideration of marriage or the formation of a civil partnership; or

    (c)    he enters into a transaction with that person for a consideration the value of which, in money or money's worth, is significantly less than the value, in money or money's worth, of the consideration provided by the individual.

10

(1)   The debtor has not given a preference to any person during the period between—

    (a)    the start of the period of two years ending with the application date; and

    (b)    the determination date.

(2)   For this purpose a debtor gives a preference to a person if—

    (a)    that person is one of the debtor's creditors to whom a qualifying debt is owed or is a surety or guarantor for any such debt, and

    (b)    the debtor does anything or suffers anything to be done which (in either case) has the effect of putting that person into a position which, in the event that a debt relief order is made in relation to the debtor, will be better than the position he would have been in if that thing had not been done.

**Amendments**—Inserted by Tribunals, Courts and Enforcement Act 2007, s 108(1), Sch 18.

## SCHEDULE 4ZB
## DEBT RELIEF RESTRICTIONS ORDERS AND UNDERTAKINGS

**Amendments**—Inserted by Tribunals, Courts and Enforcement Act 2007, s 108(1), Sch 18.

**[1.750]**

**1 Debt relief restrictions order**

(1)   A debt relief restrictions order may be made by the court in relation to a person in respect of whom a debt relief order has been made.

(2)   An order may be made only on the application of—

    (a)    the Secretary of State, or

    (b)    the official receiver acting on a direction of the Secretary of State.

**2 Grounds for making order**

(1)   The court shall grant an application for a debt relief restrictions order if it thinks it appropriate to do so having regard to the conduct of the debtor (whether before or after the making of the debt relief order).

(2)   The court shall, in particular, take into account any of the following kinds of behaviour on the part of the debtor—

(a) failing to keep records which account for a loss of property by the debtor, or by a business carried on by him, where the loss occurred in the period beginning two years before the application date for the debt relief order and ending with the date of the application for the debt relief restrictions order;

(b) failing to produce records of that kind on demand by the official receiver;

(c) entering into a transaction at an undervalue in the period beginning two years before the application date for the debt relief order and ending with the date of the determination of that application;

(d) giving a preference in the period beginning two years before the application date for the debt relief order and ending with the date of the determination of that application;

(e) making an excessive pension contribution;

(f) a failure to supply goods or services that were wholly or partly paid for;

(g) trading at a time, before the date of the determination of the application for the debt relief order, when the debtor knew or ought to have known that he was himself to be unable to pay his debts;

(h) incurring, before the date of the determination of the application for the debt relief order, a debt which the debtor had no reasonable expectation of being able to pay;

(i) failing to account satisfactorily to the court or the official receiver for a loss of property or for an insufficiency of property to meet his debts;

(j) carrying on any gambling, rash and hazardous speculation or unreasonable extravagance which may have materially contributed to or increased the extent of his inability to pay his debts before the application date for the debt relief order or which took place between that date and the date of the determination of the application for the debt relief order;

(k) neglect of business affairs of a kind which may have materially contributed to or increased the extent of his inability to pay his debts;

(l) fraud or fraudulent breach of trust;

(m) failing to co-operate with the official receiver.

(3) The court shall also, in particular, consider whether the debtor was an undischarged bankrupt at some time during the period of six years ending with the date of the application for the debt relief order.

(4) For the purposes of sub-paragraph (2)—

"excessive pension contribution" shall be construed in accordance with section 342A;

"preference" shall be construed in accordance with paragraph 10(2) of Schedule 4ZA;

"undervalue" shall be construed in accordance with paragraph 9(2) of that Schedule.

### 3 Timing of application for order

An application for a debt relief restrictions order in respect of a debtor may be made—

(a) at any time during the moratorium period relating to the debt relief order in question, or

(b) after the end of that period, but only with the permission of the court.

### 4 Duration of order

(1) A debt relief restrictions order—

(a) comes into force when it is made, and

(b) ceases to have effect at the end of a date specified in the order.

(2) The date specified in a debt relief restrictions order under sub-paragraph (1)(b) must not be—

(a) before the end of the period of two years beginning with the date on which the order is made, or

(b) after the end of the period of 15 years beginning with that date.

**5 Interim debt relief restrictions order**

(1)  This paragraph applies at any time between—

   (a)   the institution of an application for a debt relief restrictions order, and

   (b)   the determination of the application.

(2)  The court may make an interim debt relief restrictions order if the court thinks that—

   (a)   there are prima facie grounds to suggest that the application for the debt relief restrictions order will be successful, and

   (b)   it is in the public interest to make an interim debt relief restrictions order.

(3)  An interim debt relief restrictions order may only be made on the application of—

   (a)   the Secretary of State, or

   (b)   the official receiver acting on a direction of the Secretary of State.

(4)  An interim debt relief restrictions order—

   (a)   has the same effect as a debt relief restrictions order, and

   (b)   comes into force when it is made.

(5)  An interim debt relief restrictions order ceases to have effect—

   (a)   on the determination of the application for the debt relief restrictions order,

   (b)   on the acceptance of a debt relief restrictions undertaking made by the debtor, or

   (c)   if the court discharges the interim debt relief restrictions order on the application of the person who applied for it or of the debtor.

**6**

(1)  This paragraph applies to a case in which both an interim debt relief restrictions order and a debt relief restrictions order are made.

(2)  Paragraph 4(2) has effect in relation to the debt relief restrictions order as if a reference to the date of that order were a reference to the date of the interim debt relief restrictions order.

**7 Debt relief restrictions undertaking**

(1)  A debtor may offer a debt relief restrictions undertaking to the Secretary of State.

(2)  In determining whether to accept a debt relief restrictions undertaking the Secretary of State shall have regard to the matters specified in paragraph 2(2) and (3).

**8**

A reference in an enactment to a person in respect of whom a debt relief restrictions order has effect (or who is "the subject of" a debt relief restrictions order) includes a reference to a person in respect of whom a debt relief restrictions undertaking has effect.

**9**

(1)  A debt relief restrictions undertaking—

   (a)   comes into force on being accepted by the Secretary of State, and

   (b)   ceases to have effect at the end of a date specified in the undertaking.

(2)  The date specified under sub-paragraph (1)(b) must not be—

   (a)   before the end of the period of two years beginning with the date on which the undertaking is accepted, or

   (b)   after the end of the period of 15 years beginning with that date.

(3)  On an application by the debtor the court may—

   (a)   annul a debt relief restrictions undertaking;

   (b)   provide for a debt relief restrictions undertaking to cease to have effect before the date specified under sub-paragraph (1)(b).

**10 Effect of revocation of debt relief order**

Unless the court directs otherwise, the revocation at any time of a debt relief order does not—

   (a)   affect the validity of any debt relief restrictions order, interim debt relief restrictions order or debt relief restrictions undertaking which is in force in respect of the debtor;

   (b)     prevent the determination of any application for a debt relief restrictions order, or an interim debt relief restrictions order, in relation to the debtor that was instituted before that time;

   (c)     prevent the acceptance of a debt relief restrictions undertaking that was offered before that time; or

   (d)     prevent the institution of an application for a debt relief restrictions order or interim debt relief restrictions order in respect of the debtor, or the offer or acceptance of a debt relief restrictions undertaking by the debtor, after that time.

**Amendments**—Inserted by Tribunals, Courts and Enforcement Act 2007, s 108(1), Sch 18.
**General note**–See also IR 2016 rr 11.1–11.9.

SCHEDULE 4A
BANKRUPTCY RESTRICTIONS ORDER AND UNDERTAKING
Section 281A

**Amendments**—Inserted by Enterprise Act 2002, s 257(2), Sch 20.

## [1.751]

**1 Bankruptcy restrictions order**
(1)   A bankruptcy restrictions order may be made by the court.
(2)   An order may be made only on the application of—
   (a)     the Secretary of State, or
   (b)     the official receiver acting on a direction of the Secretary of State.

**2 Grounds for making order**
(1)   The court shall grant an application for a bankruptcy restrictions order if it thinks it appropriate having regard to the conduct of the bankrupt (whether before or after the making of the bankruptcy order).
(2)   The court shall, in particular, take into account any of the following kinds of behaviour on the part of the bankrupt—

   (a)     failing to keep records which account for a loss of property by the bankrupt, or by a business carried on by him, where the loss occurred in the period beginning 2 years before the making of the bankruptcy application or (as the case may be) the presentation of the bankruptcy petition and ending with the date of the application for the bankruptcy restrictions order;

   (b)     failing to produce records of that kind on demand by the official receiver or the trustee;

   (c)     entering into a transaction at an undervalue;

   (d)     giving a preference;

   (e)     making an excessive pension contribution;

   (f)     a failure to supply goods or services which were wholly or partly paid for which gave rise to a claim provable in the bankruptcy;

   (g)     trading at a time before commencement of the bankruptcy when the bankrupt knew or ought to have known that he was himself to be unable to pay his debts;

   (h)     incurring, before commencement of the bankruptcy, a debt which the bankrupt had no reasonable expectation of being able to pay;

   (i)     failing to account satisfactorily to the court, the official receiver or the trustee for a loss of property or for an insufficiency of property to meet bankruptcy debts;

   (j)     carrying on any gambling, rash and hazardous speculation or unreasonable extravagance which may have materially contributed to or increased the extent of the bankruptcy or which took place between the making of the bankruptcy application or (as the case may be) the presentation of the bankruptcy petition and commencement of the bankruptcy;

(k)    neglect of business affairs of a kind which may have materially contributed to or increased the extent of the bankruptcy;

(l)    fraud or fraudulent breach of trust;

(m)    failing to cooperate with the official receiver or the trustee.

(3)    The court shall also, in particular, consider whether the bankrupt was an undischarged bankrupt at some time during the period of six years ending with the date of the bankruptcy to which the application relates.

(4)    For the purpose of sub-paragraph (2)—

"excessive pension contribution" shall be construed in accordance with section 342A,

"preference" shall be construed in accordance with section 340, and

"undervalue" shall be construed in accordance with section 339.

**Amendments**—Enterprise and Regulatory Reform Act 2013, s 71(3), Sch 19, paras 1, 63(1), (3). See also IR 2016, rr 11.10–11.12.

### 3 Timing of application for order

(1)    An application for a bankruptcy restrictions order in respect of a bankrupt must be made—

(a)    before the end of the period of one year beginning with the date on which the bankruptcy commences, or

(b)    with the permission of the court.

(2)    The period specified in sub-paragraph (1)(a) shall cease to run in respect of a bankrupt while the period set for his discharge is suspended under section 279(3).

### 4 Duration of order

(1)    A bankruptcy restrictions order—

(a)    shall come into force when it is made, and

(b)    shall cease to have effect at the end of a date specified in the order.

(2)    The date specified in a bankruptcy restrictions order under sub-paragraph (1)(b) must not be—

(a)    before the end of the period of two years beginning with the date on which the order is made, or

(b)    after the end of the period of 15 years beginning with that date.

### 5 Interim bankruptcy restrictions order

(1)    This paragraph applies at any time between—

(a)    the institution of an application for a bankruptcy restrictions order, and

(b)    the determination of the application.

(2)    The court may make an interim bankruptcy restrictions order if the court thinks that—

(a)    there are prima facie grounds to suggest that the application for the bankruptcy restrictions order will be successful, and

(b)    it is in the public interest to make an interim order.

(3)    An interim order may be made only on the application of—

(a)    the Secretary of State, or

(b)    the official receiver acting on a direction of the Secretary of State.

(4)    An interim order—

(a)    shall have the same effect as a bankruptcy restrictions order, and

(b)    shall come into force when it is made.

(5)    An interim order shall cease to have effect—

(a)    on the determination of the application for the bankruptcy restrictions order,

(b)    on the acceptance of a bankruptcy restrictions undertaking made by the bankrupt, or

(c)    if the court discharges the interim order on the application of the person who applied for it or of the bankrupt.

**6**

(1)   This paragraph applies to a case in which both an interim bankruptcy restrictions order and a bankruptcy restrictions order are made.

(2)   Paragraph 4(2) shall have effect in relation to the bankruptcy restrictions order as if a reference to the date of that order were a reference to the date of the interim order.

## 7 Bankruptcy restrictions undertaking

(1)   A bankrupt may offer a bankruptcy restrictions undertaking to the Secretary of State.

(2)   In determining whether to accept a bankruptcy restrictions undertaking the Secretary of State shall have regard to the matters specified in paragraph 2(2) and (3).

**8**

A reference in an enactment to a person in respect of whom a bankruptcy restrictions order has effect (or who is "the subject of" a bankruptcy restrictions order) includes a reference to a person in respect of whom a bankruptcy restrictions undertaking has effect.

**9**

(1)   A bankruptcy restrictions undertaking—

    (a)     shall come into force on being accepted by the Secretary of State, and

    (b)     shall cease to have effect at the end of a date specified in the undertaking.

(2)   The date specified under sub-paragraph (1)(b) must not be—

    (a)     before the end of the period of two years beginning with the date on which the undertaking is accepted, or

    (b)     after the end of the period of 15 years beginning with that date.

(3)   On an application by the bankrupt the court may—

    (a)     annul a bankruptcy restrictions undertaking;

    (b)     provide for a bankruptcy restrictions undertaking to cease to have effect before the date specified under sub-paragraph (1)(b).

## 10 Effect of annulment of bankruptcy order

Where a bankruptcy order is annulled under section 282(1)(a) or (2)—

    (a)     any bankruptcy restrictions order, interim order or undertaking which is in force in respect of the bankrupt shall be annulled,

    (b)     no new bankruptcy restrictions order or interim order may be made in respect of the bankrupt, and

    (c)     no new bankruptcy restrictions undertaking by the bankrupt may be accepted.

**11**

Where a bankruptcy order is annulled under section 261 or 282(1)(b)—

    (a)     the annulment shall not affect any bankruptcy restrictions order, interim order or undertaking in respect of the bankrupt,

    (b)     the court may make a bankruptcy restrictions order in relation to the bankrupt on an application instituted before the annulment,

    (c)     the Secretary of State may accept a bankruptcy restrictions undertaking offered before the annulment, and

    (d)     an application for a bankruptcy restrictions order or interim order in respect of the bankrupt may not be instituted after the annulment.

**Amendments**—Small Business, Enterprise and Employment Act 2015, s 135(2)(b).

## 12 Registration

The Secretary of State shall maintain a register of—

    (a)     bankruptcy restrictions orders,

    (b)     interim bankruptcy restrictions orders, and

    (c)     bankruptcy restrictions undertakings.

**General note**—See s 281A and the notes thereto.
See also IR 2016, rr 11.10–11.12.

## SCHEDULE 5

## POWERS OF TRUSTEE IN BANKRUPTCY

Section 314

**[1.752]**

**General note**—See s 314 and the notes thereto. For commentary on the exercise of powers in winding up see the notes to Sch 4 above.

## PART I

**Amendments**—Part heading repealed by Small Business, Enterprise and Employment Act 2015, s 121(1), (3).

**[1.753]**

**1**

Power to carry on any business of the bankrupt so far as may be necessary for winding it up beneficially and so far as the trustee is able to do so without contravening any requirement imposed by or under any enactment.

**2**

Power to bring, institute or defend any action or legal proceedings relating to the property comprised in the bankrupt's estate.

**2A**

Power to bring legal proceedings under section 339, 340 or 423.

**Amendments**—Inserted by SI 2010/18.

**3**

Power to accept as the consideration for the sale of any property comprised in the bankrupt's estate a sum of money payable at a future time subject to such stipulations as to security or otherwise as the creditors' committee or the court thinks fit.

**4**

Power to mortgage or pledge any part of the property comprised in the bankrupt's estate for the purpose of raising money for the payment of his debts.

**5**

Power, where any right, option or other power forms part of the bankrupt's estate, to make payments or incur liabilities with a view to obtaining, for the benefit of the creditors, any property which is the subject of the right, option or power.

**6**

*(Repealed)*

**Amendments**—Repealed by SI 2010/18.

**7**

Power to make such compromise or other arrangement as may be thought expedient with creditors, or persons claiming to be creditors, in respect of bankruptcy debts.

**8**

Power to make such compromise or other arrangement as may be thought expedient with respect to any claim arising out of or incidental to the bankrupt's estate made or capable of being made on the trustee by any person.

**Amendments**—SI 2010/18.

## PART II

**Amendments**—Part heading repealed by Small Business, Enterprise and Employment Act 2015, s 121(1), (3).

**[1.754]**

**9**

Power to sell any part of the property for the time being comprised in the bankrupt's estate, including the goodwill and book debts of any business.

**9A**

Power to refer to arbitration, or compromise on such terms as may be agreed, any debts, claims or liabilities subsisting or supposed to subsist between the bankrupt and any person who may have incurred any liability to the bankrupt.

**9B**

Power to make such compromise or other arrangement as may be thought expedient with respect to any claim arising out of or incidental to the bankrupt's estate made or capable of being made by the trustee on any person.

**10**

Power to give receipts for any money received by him, being receipts which effectually discharge the person paying the money from all responsibility in respect of its application.

**11**

Power to prove, rank, claim and draw a dividend in respect of such debts due to the bankrupt as are comprised in his estate.

**12**

Power to exercise in relation to any property comprised in the bankrupt's estate any powers the capacity to exercise which is vested in him under Parts VIII to XI of this Act.

**13**

Power to deal with any property comprised in the estate to which the bankrupt is beneficially entitled as tenant in tail in the same manner as the bankrupt might have dealt with it.

## PART III

Amendments—Part heading repealed by Small Business, Enterprise and Employment Act 2015, s 121(1), (3).

**[1.755]**

**14**

For the purposes of, or in connection with, the exercise of any of his powers under Parts VIII to XI of this Act, the trustee may, by his official name—
- (a) hold property of every description,
- (b) make contracts,
- (c) sue and be sued,
- (d) enter into engagements binding on himself and, in respect of the bankrupt's estate, on his successors in office,
- (e) employ an agent,
- (f) execute any power of attorney, deed or other instrument;

and he may do any other act which is necessary or expedient for the purposes of or in connection with the exercise of those powers.

General note—See s 314 and the notes thereto.

## SCHEDULE 6
## THE CATEGORIES OF PREFERENTIAL DEBTS
Section 386

**[1.756]**

**General comment on Schedule 6**—This Schedule applies to all insolvencies. It has been added to in recent years, in particular by the insertion of paras 15B and 15C (with effect from 31 December 2014), and 15BA and 15BB (which introduced a category of 'secondary preferential debts' for insolvencies commencing after 1 January 2015), and the insertion of Category 6A from 26 March 2015.

It was also changed in a significant way by the Enterprise Act 2002, in order to accommodate the abolition of the Crown's right to be counted as a preferential creditor. This strategy was part of the Government's attempt to promote corporate rescue and the use of administration as the formal way of dealing with an insolvent company's financial problems. As a result of the commencement of the corporate insolvency provisions in the Enterprise Act, the number of categories of preferential debts was reduced significantly. Until that time, the majority of provisions in Sch 6 related to debts owed to the Crown, and notably tax deducted from employees' income and not remitted to the revenue authorities, and Value Added Tax due to HM Customs (formerly paras 1 and 3).

However, Crown preference has returned for insolvencies commencing on or after 1 December 2020, by way of para 15D. VAT and 'relevant deductions' are given secondary preferential status. Relevant deductions are set out in The Insolvency Act 1986 (HMRC Debts: Priority on Insolvency) Regulations 2020 (SI 2020/983), and include PAYE Income Tax, employee National Insurance contributions, Student Loan repayments, and Construction Industry Scheme deductions.

Debts under paras 8–15B are 'ordinary preferential debts', and those listed in paras 15BA, 15BB and 15D are 'secondary preferential debts' (see s 386(1A) and (1B)).

There are several references to 'the relevant date' in the Schedule. This expression is explained in s 387. See the notes accompanying that section.

### 1–7 *Category 1: Debts due to Inland Revenue*
*(Repealed by Enterprise Act 2002, ss 251(1), 278(2), Sch 26)*

### 8 Category 4: Contributions to occupational pension schemes, etc
Any sum which is owed by the debtor and is a sum to which Schedule 4 to the Pension Schemes Act 1993 applies (contributions to occupational pension schemes and state scheme premiums).

**Amendments**—Pension Scheme Act 1993, s 190, Sch 8, para 18.

### 9 Category 5: Remuneration, etc, of employees
So much of any amount which—

(a)    is owed by the debtor to a person who is or has been an employee of the debtor, and

(b)    is payable by way of remuneration in respect of the whole or any part of the period of 4 months next before the relevant date,

as does not exceed so much as may be prescribed by order made by the Secretary of State.

### 10
An amount owed by way of accrued holiday remuneration, in respect of any period of employment before the relevant date, to a person whose employment by the debtor has been terminated, whether before, on or after that date.

### 11
So much of any sum owed in respect of money advanced for the purpose as has been applied for the payment of a debt which, if it had not been paid, would have been a debt falling within paragraph 9 or 10.

### 12
So much of any amount which—

(a)    is ordered (whether before or after the relevant date) to be paid by the debtor under the Reserve Forces (Safeguard of Employment) Act 1985, and

    (b)    is so ordered in respect of a default made by the debtor before that date in the discharge of his obligations under that Act,

as does not exceed such amount as may be prescribed by order made by the Secretary of State.

**13 Interpretation for Category 5**

(1)    For the purposes of paragraphs 9 to 12, a sum is payable by the debtor to a person by way of remuneration in respect of any period if—

    (a)    it is paid as wages or salary (whether payable for time or for piece work or earned wholly or partly by way of commission) in respect of services rendered to the debtor in that period, or

    (b)    it is an amount falling within the following sub-paragraph and is payable by the debtor in respect of that period.

(2)    An amount falls within this sub-paragraph if it is—

    (a)    a guarantee payment under Part III of the Employment Rights Act 1996 (employee without work to do);

    (b)    any payment for time off under section 53 (time off to look for work or arrange training) or section 56 (time off for ante-natal care) of that Act or under section 169 of the Trade Union and Labour Relations (Consolidation) Act 1992 (time off for carrying out trade union duties etc);

    (c)    remuneration on suspension on medical grounds, or on maternity grounds, under Part VII of the Employment Rights Act 1996; or

    (d)    remuneration under a protective award under section 189 of the Trade Union and Labour Relations (Consolidation) Act 1992 (redundancy dismissal with compensation).

**Amendments**—Employment Rights Act 1996, s 240, Sch 1, para 29.

**14**

(1)    This paragraph relates to a case in which a person's employment has been terminated by or in consequence of his employer going into liquidation or being made bankrupt or (his employer being a company not in liquidation) by or in consequence of—

    (a)    a receiver being appointed as mentioned in section 40 of this Act (debenture-holders secured by floating charge), or

    (b)    the appointment of a receiver under section 53(6) or 54(5) of this Act (Scottish company with property subject to floating charge), or

    (c)    the taking of possession by debenture-holders (so secured), as mentioned in section 754 of the Companies Act 2006.

(2)    For the purposes of paragraphs 9 to 12, holiday remuneration is deemed to have accrued to that person in respect of any period of employment if, by virtue of his contract of employment or of any enactment that remuneration would have accrued in respect of that period if his employment had continued until he became entitled to be allowed the holiday.

(3)    The reference in sub-paragraph (2) to any enactment includes an order or direction made under an enactment.

**Amendments**—SI 2008/948; Enterprise and Regulatory Reform Act 2014, s 71(3), Sch 19, paras 1, 64.

**15**

Without prejudice to paragraphs 13 and 14—

    (a)    any remuneration payable by the debtor to a person in respect of a period of holiday or of absence from work through sickness or other good cause is deemed to be wages or (as the case may be) salary in respect of services rendered to the debtor in that period,

    (b)    . . .

**Amendments**—Deregulation Act 2015, s 19, Sch 6, Pt 7, paras 24, 28.

**General comment on Category 5**—Category 5 will have to be taken into account in most insolvencies. The primary focus is on paras 9 and 10, which relate to the remuneration and holiday pay of employees of the insolvent.

Who is an employee for the purposes of this category has been a vexed issue, and the case law is difficult to synthesise. The fact that a director is the majority shareholder of a company does not of itself prevent a contract of employment arising (*Clark v Clark Construction Initiatives Ltd* [2008] ICR 635, [2008] IRLR 364 (involving a claim against dismissal from a solvent company) (an appeal to the Court of Appeal was dismissed ([2008] EWCA Civ 1446). The Court of Appeal in *Secretary of State for Employment v Bottrill* [1999] BCC 177, [1999] ICR 592, [1999] IRLR 326 said that the fact that a director holds a controlling interest in the company was only one factor in the equation, albeit probably a significant factor. The leading case on the subject is now *Secretary of State for Business Enterprise and Regulatory Reform v Neufeld* [2009] EWCA Civ 280. The judgment of the court was that there was no reason in principle why a person who was the controlling shareholder and a director of a company could not be an employee. Rimer LJ said that in the situation where the contract is a valid one, was in writing and sufficiently explicit to establish its content, he could not see the relevance of the power of the shareholder/director in making a determination as to whether the director was or was not an employee. His Lordship said that if: 'the contract was not in writing, or was expressed only in short form, so that it is necessary to examine the conduct of the parties in order to deduce the content of the contract, the position of the individual and manner in which the company's affairs were conducted provide the factual setting for the inquiry.' (at [61]). The Court said that there are two issues that have to be considered by a court. First, whether the contract is a genuine contract or a sham. Second, if the contract is genuine, does it amount to a contract of employment ([81]). In considering the second issue various matters might be of relevance including the fact of the director's control of the company. But it would not go against a director merely because he or she had capital invested in the company.

Paragraphs 9, 10 and 12 enable employees to claim: remuneration in respect of the whole or any part of the 4 months before the relevant date, not exceeding the prescribed amount (at present this is £800); accrued holiday pay for the period of employment before the relevant date (this is also payable to former employees and those whose employment was terminated at or after the relevant date); any amount which is ordered to be paid by the company under the Reserve Forces (Safeguard of Employment) Act 1985, and it is ordered in respect of a default by the company in respect of the employee's obligations under the said Act, not exceeding the prescribed sum (at present it is £800).

The monetary limits mentioned above are prescribed by order of the Secretary of State and at present they are set out in Insolvency Proceedings (Monetary Limits) Order 1986 (SI 1986/1996).

To safeguard employees, because they could be waiting a significant amount of time before they receive their entitlements in an insolvent estate, there is a scheme provided under the Employment Rights Act 1996. Pursuant to this scheme, payments are made to employees by the Secretary of State out of the National Insurance Fund, according to the entitlements that employees have. The Secretary of State is then subrogated to the employees' rights to the extent that the payments made are in respect of the insolvent employers' liabilities, which have preferential status under the Act.

Paragraph 11 covers the situation where a third party advances money to the company for the payment of remuneration or holiday pay of employees. If this is done the third party is entitled to be subrogated to the rights which would be given to the employees. But the right under this paragraph does not exist where an advance is made for general purposes, or the person advancing the money does not specify that it be used for the payment of employees.

See Keay and Walton 'The Preferential Debts' Regime in Liquidation Law: In the Public Interest?' (1999) 3 *Company Financial and Insolvency Law Review* 84; A Keay *McPherson's Law of Company Liquidation* (Sweet and Maxwell, 4th edn, 2018).

### 15A  Category 6: Levies on coal and steel production

Any sums due at the relevant date from the debtor in respect of—

(a)  the levies on the production of coal and steel referred to in Articles 49 and 50 of the ECSC Treaty, or

(b)  any surcharge for delay provided for in Article 50(3) of that Treaty and Article 6 of Decision 3/52 of the High Authority of the Coal and Steel Community.

**Amendments**—Inserted by SI 1987/2093.

### 15AA  Category 6A: Debts owed to the Financial Services Compensation Scheme

Any debt owed by the debtor to the scheme manager of the Financial Services Compensation Scheme under section 215(2A) of the Financial Services and Markets Act 2000.

**Amendments**—Inserted by SI 2015/486.

**15B Category 7: Deposits covered by Financial Services Compensation Scheme**
So much of any amount owed at the relevant date by the debtor in respect of an eligible deposit as does not exceed the compensation that would be payable in respect of the deposit under the Financial Services Compensation Scheme to the person or persons to whom the amount is owed.

Amendments—Inserted by Financial Services (Banking Reform) Act 2013, s 13(1).

**15BA Category 8: Other deposits**
So much of any amount owed at the relevant date by the debtor to one or more eligible persons in respect of an eligible deposit as exceeds any compensation that would be payable in respect of the deposit under the Financial Services Compensation Scheme to that person or those persons.

Amendments—Inserted by SI 2014/3486.

**15BB**
An amount owed at the relevant date by the debtor to one or more eligible persons in respect of a deposit that—

   (a)    was made through a non-UK branch of a credit institution authorised by the competent authority of the United Kingdom, and

   (b)    would have been an eligible deposit if it had been made through a UK branch of that credit institution.

Amendments—Inserted by SI 2014/3486. Amended by SI 2018/1394, as from IP completion day (as defined in the European Union (Withdrawal Agreement) Act 2020, s 39(1)–(5)).

**15C Interpretation for Categories 6A, 7 and 8**
(A1)  In paragraph 15AA "the scheme manager" has the meaning given in section 212(1) of the Financial Services and Markets Act 2000.

(1)  In paragraphs 15B to 15BB "eligible deposit" means a deposit in respect of which the person, or any of the persons, to whom it is owed would be eligible for compensation under the Financial Services Compensation Scheme.

(2)  For the purposes of those paragraphs and this paragraph a "deposit" means rights of the kind described in—

   (a)    paragraph 22 of Schedule 2 to the Financial Services and Markets Act 2000 (deposits), or

   (b)    section 1(2)(b) of the Dormant Bank and Building Society Accounts Act 2008 (balances transferred under that Act to authorised reclaim fund).

(3)  In paragraphs 15BA and 15BB, "eligible person" means—

   (a)    an individual, or

   (b)    any micro, small and medium-sized enterprise, as defined with regard to the annual turnover criterion referred to in Article 2(1) of the Annex to Commission recommendation 2003/361/EC.

(4)  In paragraph 15BB—

   (a)    "credit institution" has the meaning given in Article 4.1(1) of the capital requirements regulation;

   (b)    "non-UK branch" means a branch, as defined in Article 4.1(17) of the capital requirements regulation, which is established outside the United Kingdom;

   (c)    "UK branch" means a branch, as so defined, which is established in the United Kingdom,

and for this purpose "the capital requirements regulation" means Regulation (EU) No 575/2013 of the European Parliament and of the Council of 26th June 2013 on prudential requirements for credit institutions and investment firms and amending Regulation (EU) No 648/2012, as it had effect on the day on which the Bank Recovery and Resolution and Miscellaneous Provisions (Amendment) (EU Exit) Regulations 2018 were made.

Amendments—Inserted by Financial Services (Banking Reform) Act 2013, s 13(1). Amended by SI 2014/3486; SI 2015/486; SI 2018/1394, partly as from 21 December 2018 and fully as from IP completion day (as defined in the European Union (Withdrawal Agreement) Act 2020, s 39(1)–(5)).

**15D Category 9: Certain HMRC debts**

(1) Any amount owed at the relevant date by the debtor to the Commissioners in respect of—

    (a) value added tax, or

    (b) a relevant deduction.

(2) In sub-paragraph (1), the reference to "any amount" is subject to any regulations under section 99(1) of the Finance Act 2020.

(3) For the purposes of sub-paragraph (1)(b) a deduction is "relevant" if—

    (a) the debtor is required, by virtue of an enactment, to make the deduction from a payment made to another person and to pay an amount to the Commissioners on account of the deduction,

    (b) the payment to the Commissioners is credited against any liabilities of the other person, and

    (c) the deduction is of a kind specified in regulations under section 99(3) of the Finance Act 2020.

(4) In this paragraph "the Commissioners" means the Commissioners for Her Majesty's Revenue and Customs.

**Amendments**—Inserted by Finance Act 2020, s 98(2).

**16 Orders**

An order under paragraph 9 or 12—

    (a) may contain such transitional provisions as may appear to the Secretary of State necessary or expedient;

    (b) shall be made by statutory instrument subject to annulment in pursuance of a resolution of either House of Parliament.

SCHEDULE 7

*(Repealed)*

**Amendments**—Repealed by Deregulation Act 2015, s 19, Sch 6, Pt 6, paras 17, 21.

SCHEDULE 8

PROVISIONS CAPABLE OF INCLUSION IN COMPANY INSOLVENCY RULES

Section 411

**[1.757]**

**General comment on Schedule 8**—The Schedule sets out many areas of insolvency law that can be the subject of the Insolvency Rules. It does enable flexibility; for instance, para 28 permits the passing of rules relating to the conferring of a discretion on the court, but there are a number of matters that have been included in the Rules that arguably should have been included in the Act, eg the rules on set-off in IR 2016, r 14.25 (formerly IR 1986, r 4.90). Many of the matters upon which Rules can be passed have in fact been addressed in the Rules.

'**Liquidator**'—This word when used in this Schedule includes a provisional liquidator (s 411(3)), notwithstanding the specific mention of provisional liquidator in para 7, a paragraph that deals with a matter peculiar to provisional liquidators.

**1 Courts**

Provision for supplementing, in relation to the insolvency or winding up of companies, any provision made by or under section 117 of this Act (jurisdiction in relation to winding up).

**2**

(1) Provision for regulating the practice and procedure of any court exercising jurisdiction for the purposes of Parts A1 to VII of this Act or the Companies Acts so far as relating to, and to matters connected with or arising out of, the insolvency or winding up of companies, being any provision that could be made by rules of court.

(2) Rules made by virtue of this paragraph about the consequence of failure to comply with practice or procedure may, in particular, include provision about the termination of administration.

**Amendments**—Enterprise Act 2002, s 248(8), Sch 17, paras 9, 38; SI 2007/2194; Corporate Insolvency and Governance Act 2020, s 2(1), Sch 3, paras 1, 32(1), (2).

## 3 Notices etc

Provision requiring notice of any proceedings in connection with or arising out of the insolvency or winding up of a company to be given or published in the manner prescribed by the rules.

## 4

Provision with respect to the form, manner of serving, contents and proof of any petition, application, order, notice, statement or other document required to be presented, made, given, published or prepared under any enactment or subordinate legislation relating to, or to matters connected with or arising out of, the insolvency or winding up of companies.

## 5

Provision specifying the persons to whom any notice is to be given.

## 5A

Provision for enabling a creditor of a company to elect to be, or to cease to be, an opted-out creditor in relation to an office-holder of the company (within the meaning of section 248A), including, in particular, provision—

    (a)    for requiring an office-holder to provide information to creditors about how they may elect to be, or cease to be, opted-out creditors;

    (b)    for deeming an election to be, or cease to be, an opted-out creditor in relation to a particular office-holder of a company to be such an election also in relation to any other office-holder of the company.

**Amendments**—Inserted by Small Business, Enterprise and Employment Act 2015, s 124(1), (5).

## 6 Registration of voluntary arrangements

Provision for the registration of voluntary arrangements approved under Part I of this Act, including provision for the keeping and inspection of a register.

## 7 Provisional liquidator

Provision as to the manner in which a provisional liquidator appointed under section 135 is to carry out his functions.

## 8 Conduct of insolvency

Provision with respect to the certification of any person as, and as to the proof that a person is, the monitor in relation to a moratorium under Part A1 or the liquidator, administrator or administrative receiver of a company.

**Amendments**—Corporate Insolvency and Governance Act 2020, s 2(1), Sch 3, paras 1, 32(1), (3).

## 8A

(1) Provision about the making of decisions by creditors and contributories, including provision—

    (a)    prescribing particular procedures by which creditors and contributories may make decisions;

    (b)    authorising the use of other procedures for creditors and contributories to make decisions, if those procedures comply with prescribed requirements.

(2) Provision under sub-paragraph (1) may in particular include provision about—

    (a)    how creditors and contributories may request that a creditors' meeting or a contributories' meeting be held,

    (b)    the rights of creditors, contributories and others to be given notice of, and participate in, procedures,

    (c)    creditors' and contributories' rights to vote in procedures,

    (d)    the period within which any right to participate or vote is to be exercised,

(e)     the proportion of creditors or contributories that must vote for a proposal for it to be approved,

(f)     how the value of any debt or contribution should be determined,

(g)     the time at which decisions taken by a procedure are to be treated as having been made.

**Amendments**—Inserted by Small Business, Enterprise and Employment Act 2015, s 122(1), (3).

**9**

The following provision with respect to meetings of a company's creditors contributories or members—

(a)     provision as to the manner of summoning a meeting (including provision as to how any power to require a meeting is to be exercised, provision as to the manner of determining the value of any debt or contribution for the purposes of any such power and provision making the exercise of any such power subject to the deposit of a sum sufficient to cover the expenses likely to be incurred in summoning and holding a meeting);

(b)     provision specifying the time and place at which a meeting may be held and the period of notice required for a meeting;

(c)     provision as to the procedure to be followed at a meeting (including the manner in which decisions may be reached by a meeting and the manner in which the value of any vote at a meeting is to be determined);

(d)     provision for requiring a person who is or has been an officer of the company to attend a meeting;

(e)     provision creating, in the prescribed circumstances, a presumption that a meeting has been duly summoned and held;

(f)     provision as to the manner of proving the decisions of a meeting.

**9A**

Provision about how a company's creditors may nominate a person to be liquidator, including in the case of a voluntary winding up provision conferring functions on the directors of the company.

**Amendments**—Inserted by Small Business, Enterprise and Employment Act 2015, s 126, Sch 9, Pt 1, paras 1, 58.

**10**

(1)    Provision as to the establishment, functions, membership and proceedings of a committee provided for by section 49, 68, 101, 141 or 142 of, or paragraph 57 of Schedule B1 to, this Act.

(2)    The following provision with respect to the establishment of a committee under section 101, 141 or 142 of this Act, that is to say—

(a)     provision for resolving differences between the company's creditors and its contributories or members;

(b)     provision authorising the establishment of the committee without seeking a decision from contributories in a case where a company is being wound up on grounds including its inability to pay its debts; and

(c)     provision modifying the requirements of this Act with respect to the establishment of the committee in a case where a winding-up order has been made immediately upon the discharge of an administration order.

**Amendments**—Enterprise Act 2002, s 248(3), Sch 17, paras 9, 38(1), (3); Small Business, Enterprise and Employment Act 2015, s 126, Sch 9, Pt 1, paras 1, 59.

**11**

Provision as to the manner in which any requirement that may be imposed on a person under any of Parts I to VII of this Act by the official receiver, the liquidator, administrator or administrative receiver of a company or a special manager appointed under section 177 is to be so imposed.

**12**

Provision as to the debts that may be proved in a winding up, as to the manner and conditions of proving a debt and as to the manner and expenses of establishing the value of any debt or security.

**13**

Provision with respect to the manner of the distribution of the property of a company that is being wound up, including provision with respect to unclaimed funds and dividends.

**13A**

Provision for a creditor who has not proved a small debt to be treated as having done so for purposes relating to the distribution of a company's property (and for provisions of, or contained in legislation made under, this Act to apply accordingly).

**Amendments**—Inserted by Small Business, Enterprise and Employment Act 2015, s 131.

**14**

Provision which, with or without modifications, applies in relation to the winding up of companies any enactment contained in Parts VIII to XI of this Act or in the Bankruptcy (Scotland) Act 2016.

**Amendments**—SI 2016/1034.

**14A**

Provision about the application of section 176A of this Act which may include, in particular—

    (a)    provision enabling a receiver to institute winding up proceedings;

    (b)    provision requiring a receiver to institute winding up proceedings.

**Amendments**—Inserted by Enterprise Act 2002, s 248(3), Sch 17, paras 9, 38(1), (4).

**14B  Administration**

Provision which—

    (a)    applies in relation to administration, with or without modifications, a provision of Parts IV to VII of this Act, or

    (b)    serves a purpose in relation to administration similar to a purpose that may be served by the rules in relation to winding up by virtue of a provision of this Schedule.

**Amendments**—Inserted by Enterprise Act 2002, s 248(3), Sch 17, paras 9, 38(1), (5).

**15  Financial provisions**

Provision as to the amount, or manner of determining the amount, payable to the liquidator, administrator or administrative receiver of a company or a special manager appointed under section 177, by way of remuneration for the carrying out of functions in connection with or arising out of the insolvency or winding up of a company.

**16**

Provision with respect to the manner in which moneys received by the liquidator of a company in the course of carrying out his functions as such are to be invested or otherwise handled and with respect to the payment of interest on sums which, in pursuance of rules made by virtue of this paragraph, have been paid into the Insolvency Services Account.

**16A**

Provision enabling the Secretary of State to set the rate of interest paid on sums which have been paid into the Insolvency Services Account.

**Amendments**—Inserted by Enterprise Act 2002, s 271(1).

**17**

Provision as to the fees, costs, charges and other expenses that may be treated as the expenses of a winding up.

**General comment**—The use of 'may' was considered in *Re Toshoku Finance UK plc*, sub nom

*Kahn v Commissioners of Inland Revenue* [2002] 1 WLR 671 at [17], HL.

**18**

Provision as to the fees, costs, charges and other expenses that may be treated as properly incurred by the administrator or administrative receiver of a company.

**19**

Provision as to the fees, costs, charges and other expenses that may be incurred for any of the purposes of Part I of this Act or in the administration of any voluntary arrangement approved under that Part.

**20 Information and records**

Provision requiring registrars and other officers of courts having jurisdiction in England and Wales in relation to, or to matters connected with or arising out of, the insolvency or winding up of companies—

    (a)    to keep books and other records with respect to the exercise of that jurisdiction, and

    (b)    to make returns to the Secretary of State of the business of those courts.

**21**

Provision requiring a creditor, member or contributory, or such a committee as is mentioned in paragraph 10 above, to be supplied (on payment in prescribed cases of the prescribed fee) with such information and with copies of such documents as may be prescribed.

**22**

Provision as to the manner in which public examinations under sections 133 and 134 of this Act and proceedings under sections 236 and 237 are to be conducted, as to the circumstances in which records of such examinations or proceedings are to be made available to prescribed persons and as to the costs of such examinations and proceedings.

**23**

Provision imposing requirements with respect to—

    (a)    the preparation and keeping by the liquidator, administrator or administrative receiver of a company, or by the supervisor of a voluntary arrangement approved under Part I of this Act, of prescribed books, accounts and other records;

    (b)    the production of those books, accounts and records for inspection by prescribed persons;

    (c)    the auditing of accounts kept by the liquidator, administrator or administrative receiver of a company, or the supervisor of such a voluntary arrangement; and

    (d)    the issue by the administrator or administrative receiver of a company of such a certificate as is mentioned in section 22(3)(b) of the Value Added Tax Act 1983 (refund of tax in cases of bad debts) and the supply of copies of the certificate to creditors of the company.

**24**

Provision requiring the person who is the supervisor of a voluntary arrangement approved under Part I, when it appears to him that the voluntary arrangement has been fully implemented and that nothing remains to be done by him under the arrangement—

    (a)    to give notice of that fact to persons bound by the voluntary arrangement, and

    (b)    to report to those persons on the carrying out of the functions conferred on the supervisor of the arrangement.

**25**

Provision as to the manner in which the liquidator of a company is to act in relation to the books, papers and other records of the company, including provision authorising their disposal.

**26**

Provision imposing requirements in connection with the carrying out of functions under section 7A of the Company Directors Disqualification Act 1986 (including, in particular, requirements with respect to the making of periodic returns).

**Amendments**—SI 2016/481.

**27 General**

Provision conferring power on the Secretary of State or the Treasury to make regulations with respect to so much of any matter that may be provided for in the rules as relates to the carrying out of the functions of the liquidator, administrator or administrative receiver of a company.

**Amendments**—Banking Act 2009, s 125(7).

**28**

Provision conferring a discretion on the court.

**29**

Provision conferring power on the court to make orders for the purpose of securing compliance with obligations imposed by or under section 47, 66, 131, 143(2) or 235 of, or paragraph 47 of Schedule B1 to, this Act or section 7(4) of the Company Directors Disqualification Act 1986.

**Amendments**—Inserted by Enterprise Act 2002, s 248(3), Sch 17, paras 9, 38(1), (6).

**30**

Provision making non-compliance with any of the rules a criminal offence.

**31**

Provision making different provision for different cases or descriptions of cases, including different provisions for different areas.

SCHEDULE 9

PROVISIONS CAPABLE OF INCLUSION IN INDIVIDUAL INSOLVENCY RULES
Section 412

**[1.758]**

**1 Courts**

Provision with respect to the arrangement and disposition of the business under Parts 7A to 11 of this Act of courts having jurisdiction for the purpose of those Parts, including provision for the allocation of proceedings under those Parts to particular courts and for the transfer of such proceedings from one court to another.

**Amendments**—Tribunals, Courts and Enforcement Act 2007, s 108(3), Sch 20, Pt 1, paras 1, 14.

**2**

Provision for enabling an insolvency and companies court judge to exercise such of the jurisdiction conferred for those purposes on the High Court as may be prescribed.

**Amendments**—Crime and Courts Act 2013, s 17(5), Sch 9, Pt 3, para 93(l).

**3**

Provision for regulating the practice and procedure of any court exercising jurisdiction for the purposes of those Parts, being any provision that could be made by rules of court.

**4**

Provision conferring rights of audience, in courts exercising jurisdiction for the purposes of those Parts, on the official receiver and on solicitors.

**4A Adjudicators**

Provision for regulating the practice and procedure of adjudicators in the discharge of functions for the purposes of Part 9 of this Act.

**Amendments**—Inserted by Enterprise and Regulatory Reform Act 2013, s 71(3), Sch 19, paras 1, 65.

**4B**

Provision about the form and content of a bankruptcy application (including an application for a review of an adjudicator's determination).

**Amendments**—Inserted by Enterprise and Regulatory Reform Act 2013, s 71(3), Sch 19, paras 1, 65.

**4C Appeals against determinations by adjudicators**

Provision about the making and determining of appeals to the court against a determination by an adjudicator, including provision—

  (a)  enabling the court to make a bankruptcy order on such an appeal, and
  (b)  about where such appeals lie.

**Amendments**—Inserted by Enterprise and Regulatory Reform Act 2013, s 71(3), Sch 19, paras 1, 65.

**5 Notices, etc**

Provision requiring notice of any proceedings under Parts 7A to 11 of this Act or of any matter relating to or arising out of a proposal under Part VIII or a bankruptcy to be given or published in the prescribed manner.

**Amendments**—Tribunals, Courts and Enforcement Act 2007, s 108(3), Sch 20, Pt 1, paras 1, 14.

**6**

Provision with respect to the form, manner of serving, contents and proof of any petition, application, order, notice, statement or other document required to be presented, made, given, published or prepared under any enactment contained in Parts 7A to 11 or subordinate legislation under those Parts or Part XV (including provision requiring prescribed matters to be verified by affidavit).

**Amendments**—Tribunals, Courts and Enforcement Act 2007, s 108(3), Sch 20, Pt 1, paras 1, 14.

**7**

Provision specifying the persons to whom any notice under Parts VIII to XI is to be given.

**7A**

Provision for enabling a creditor of an individual to elect to be, or to cease to be, an opted-out creditor in relation to an office-holder for the individual (within the meaning of section 383A), including, in particular, provision—

  (a)  for requiring an office-holder to provide information to creditors about how they may elect to be, or cease to be, opted-out creditors;
  (b)  for deeming an election to be, or cease to be, an opted-out creditor in relation to a particular office-holder for an individual to be such an election also in relation to any other office-holder for the individual.

**Amendments**—Inserted by Small Business, Enterprise and Employment Act 2015, s 125(5). Note this is not an error. There are two paragraphs numbered 7A in this Schedule.

**7A Debt relief orders**

Provision as to the manner in which the official receiver is to carry out his functions under Part 7A.

**Amendments**—Inserted by Tribunals, Courts and Enforcement Act 2007, s 108(3), Sch 20, Pt 1, paras 1, 14.

**7B**

Provision as to the manner in which any requirement that may be imposed by the official receiver on a person under Part 7A is to take effect.

**Amendments**—Inserted by Tribunals, Courts and Enforcement Act 2007, s 108(3), Sch 20, Pt 1, paras 1, 14.

**7C**

Provision modifying the application of Part 7A in relation to an individual who has died at a time when a moratorium period under a debt relief order applies in relation to him.

**Amendments**—Inserted by Tribunals, Courts and Enforcement Act 2007, s 108(3), Sch 20, Pt 1, paras 1, 14.

**7D Debt relief restrictions orders and undertakings**

Provision about debt relief restrictions orders, interim orders and undertakings, including provision about evidence.

**Amendments**—Inserted by Tribunals, Courts and Enforcement Act 2007, s 108(3), Sch 20, Pt 1, paras 1, 14.

**7E Register of debt relief orders and debt relief restrictions orders etc**

Provision about the register required to be maintained by section 251W and the information to be contained in it, including provision—

(a)     enabling the amalgamation of the register with another register;

(b)     enabling inspection of the register by the public.

**Amendments**—Inserted by Tribunals, Courts and Enforcement Act 2007, s 108(3), Sch 20, Pt 1, paras 1, 14.

**7F**

Provision for enabling a creditor of an individual to elect to be, or to cease to be, an opted-out creditor in relation to an office-holder for the individual (within the meaning of section 383A), including, in particular, provision—

(a)     for requiring an office-holder to provide information to creditors about how they may elect to be, or cease to be, opted-out creditors;

(b)     for deeming an election to be, or cease to be, an opted-out creditor in relation to a particular office-holder for an individual to be such an election also in relation to any other office-holder for the individual.

**Amendments**—Inserted by Small Business, Enterprise and Employment Act 2015, s 125(1), (5).

**8 Registration of voluntary arrangements**

Provision for the registration of voluntary arrangements approved under Part VIII of this Act, including provision for the keeping and inspection of a register.

**Amendments**—Enterprise Act 2002, ss 269, 271(2), Sch 23, paras 1, 16(1), (2).

**8A Official receiver acting on voluntary arrangement**

Provision about the official receiver acting as nominee or supervisor in relation to a voluntary arrangement under Part VIII of this Act, including—

(a)     provision requiring the official receiver to act in specified circumstances;

(b)     provision about remuneration;

(c)     provision prescribing terms or conditions to be treated as forming part of a voluntary arrangement in relation to which the official receiver acts as nominee or supervisor;

(d)     provision enabling those terms or conditions to be varied or excluded, in specified circumstances or subject to specified conditions, by express provision in an arrangement.

**Amendments**—Inserted by Enterprise Act 2002, s 269, Sch 23, paras 1, 16(1), (2).

**9 Interim receiver**

Provision as to the manner in which an interim receiver appointed under section 286 is to carry out his functions, including any such provision as is specified in relation to the trustee of a bankrupt's estate in paragraph 21 or 27 below.

**10**

*(Repealed)*

**Amendments**—Repealed by Small Business, Enterprise and Employment Act 2015, s 133(2), Sch 10, paras 1, 10.

### 11 Administration of individual insolvency

Provision with respect to the certification of the appointment of any person as trustee of a bankrupt's estate and as to the proof of that appointment.

### 11A

(1)  Provision about the making of decisions by creditors, including provision—
    (a)    prescribing particular procedures by which creditors may make decisions;
    (b)    authorising the use of other procedures for creditors to make decisions, if those procedures comply with prescribed requirements.

(2)  Provision under sub-paragraph (1) may in particular include provision about—
    (a)    how creditors may request that a creditors' meeting be held,
    (b)    the rights of creditors and others to be given notice of, and participate in, procedures,
    (c)    creditors' rights to vote in procedures,
    (d)    the period within which any right to participate or vote is to be exercised,
    (e)    the proportion of creditors that must vote for a proposal for it to be approved,
    (f)    how the value of any debt should be determined,
    (g)    the time at which decisions taken by a procedure are to be treated as having been made.

**Amendments**—Inserted by Small Business, Enterprise and Employment Act 2015, s 123(1), (3).

### 12

The following provision with respect to meetings of creditors—
    (a)    provision as to the manner of summoning a meeting (including provision as to how any power to require a meeting is to be exercised, provision as to the manner of determining the value of any debt for the purposes of any such power and provision making the exercise of any such power subject to the deposit of a sum sufficient to cover the expenses likely to be incurred in summoning and holding a meeting);
    (b)    provision specifying the time and place at which a meeting may be held and the period of notice required for a meeting;
    (c)    provision as to the procedure to be followed at such a meeting (including the manner in which decisions may be reached by a meeting and the manner in which the value of any vote at a meeting is to be determined);
    (d)    provision for requiring a bankrupt or debtor to attend a meeting;
    (e)    provision creating, in the prescribed circumstances, a presumption that a meeting has been duly summoned and held; and
    (f)    provision as to the manner of proving the decisions of a meeting.

### 12A

Provision about how a bankrupt's creditors may appoint a person as trustee.

**Amendments**—Inserted by Small Business, Enterprise and Employment Act 2015, s 126, Sch 9, Pt 2, paras 60, 86.

### 13

Provision as to the establishment, functions, membership and proceedings of a creditors' committee provided for by section 301.

**Amendments**—Small Business, Enterprise and Employment Act 2015, s 126, Sch 9, Pt 2, paras 60, 87.

### 14

Provision as to the manner in which any requirement that may be imposed on a person under Parts VIII to XI of this Act by the official receiver, the trustee of a bankrupt's estate or a special manager appointed under section 370 is to be so imposed and, in the case of any requirement imposed under section 305(3) (information etc to be given by the trustee to the official receiver), provision conferring power on the court to make orders for the purpose of securing compliance with that requirement.

**15**

Provision as to the manner in which any requirement imposed by virtue of section 310(3) (compliance with income payments order) is to take effect.

**16**

Provision as to the terms and conditions that may be included in a charge under section 313 (dwelling house forming part of bankrupt's estate).

**17**

Provision as to the debts that may be proved in any bankruptcy, as to the manner and conditions of proving a debt and as to the manner and expenses of establishing the value of any debt or security.

**18**

Provision with respect to the manner of the distribution of a bankrupt's estate, including provision with respect to unclaimed funds and dividends.

**18A**

Provision for a creditor who has not proved a small debt to be treated as having done so for purposes relating to the distribution of a bankrupt's estate (and for provisions of, or contained in legislation made under, this Act to apply accordingly).

**Amendments**—Inserted by Small Business, Enterprise and Employment Act 2015, s 132.

**19**

Provision modifying the application of Parts VIII to XI of this Act in relation to a debtor or bankrupt who has died.

**20 Financial provisions**

Provision as to the amount, or manner of determining the amount, payable to an interim receiver, the trustee of a bankrupt's estate or a special manager appointed under section 370 by way of remuneration for the performance of functions in connection with or arising out of the bankruptcy of any person.

**21**

Provision with respect to the manner in which moneys received by the trustee of a bankrupt's estate in the course of carrying out his functions as such are to be invested or otherwise handled and with respect to the payment of interest on sums which, in pursuance of rules made by virtue of this paragraph, have been paid into the Insolvency Services Account.

**Amendments**—Insolvency Act 2000, s 13(1).

**21A**

Provision enabling the Secretary of State to set the rate of interest paid on sums which have been paid into the Insolvency Services Account.

**Amendments**—Inserted by Enterprise Act 2002, s 271(2).

**22**

Provision as to the fees, costs, charges and other expenses that may be treated as the expenses of a bankruptcy.

**23**

Provision as to the fees, costs, charges and other expenses that may be incurred for any of the purposes of Part VIII of this Act or in the administration of any voluntary arrangement approved under that Part.

**24 Information and records**

Provision requiring registrars and other officers of courts having jurisdiction for the purposes of Parts VIII to XI—

    (a)    to keep books and other records with respect to the exercise of that jurisdiction, and

    (b)    to make returns to the Secretary of State of the business of those courts.

**Amendments**—Deregulation Act 2015, s 19, Sch 6, Pt 1, para 2(1), (11)(g).

**24A**

Provision requiring adjudicators—

    (a)    to keep files and other records relating to bankruptcy applications and bankruptcies resulting from bankruptcy applications,

    (b)    to make files and records available for inspection by persons of a prescribed description, and

    (c)    to provide files and records, or copies of them, to persons of a prescribed description.

**Amendments**—Inserted by Enterprise and Regulatory Reform Act 2013, s 71(3), Sch 19, paras 1, 65(1), (4).

**24B**

Provision requiring an adjudicator to make returns to the Secretary of State of the adjudicator's business under Part 9 of this Act.

**Amendments**—Inserted by Enterprise and Regulatory Reform Act 2013, s 71(3), Sch 19, paras 1, 65(1), (4).

**24C**

Provision requiring official receivers—

    (a)    to keep files and other records relating to bankruptcy applications and bankruptcies resulting from bankruptcy applications, and

    (b)    to make files and records available for inspection by persons of a prescribed description.

**Amendments**—Inserted by Enterprise and Regulatory Reform Act 2013, s 71(3), Sch 19, paras 1, 65(1), (4).

**24D**

Provision requiring a person to whom notice is given under section 293(2), 295(3), 298(7) or (8) or section 299(1)(a) or (3)(a)—

    (a)    to keep files and other records of notices given under the section in question, and

    (b)    to make files and records available for inspection by persons of a prescribed description.

**Amendments**—Inserted by Enterprise and Regulatory Reform Act 2013, s 71(3), Sch 19, paras 1, 65(1), (4).

**25**

Provision requiring a creditor or a committee established under section 301 to be supplied (on payment in prescribed cases of the prescribed fee) with such information and with copies of such documents as may be prescribed.

**26**

Provision as to the manner in which public examinations under section 290 and proceedings under sections 366 to 368 are to be conducted, as to the circumstances in which records of such examinations and proceedings are to be made available to prescribed persons and as to the costs of such examinations and proceedings.

**27**

Provision imposing requirements with respect to—

    (a)    the preparation and keeping by the trustee of a bankrupt's estate, or the supervisor of a voluntary arrangement approved under Part VIII, of prescribed books, accounts and other records;

    (b)    the production of those books, accounts and records for inspection by prescribed persons; and

    (c)    the auditing of accounts kept by the trustee of a bankrupt's estate or the supervisor of such a voluntary arrangement.

**28**

Provision requiring the person who is the supervisor of a voluntary arrangement approved under Part VIII, when it appears to him that the voluntary arrangement has been fully implemented and that nothing remains to be done by him under it—

(a) to give notice of that fact to persons bound by the voluntary arrangement, and

(b) to report to those persons on the carrying out of the functions conferred on the supervisor of it.

**29**

Provision as to the manner in which the trustee of a bankrupt's estate is to act in relation to the books, papers and other records of the bankrupt, including provision authorising their disposal.

**29A  Bankruptcy restrictions orders and undertakings**

Provision about bankruptcy restrictions orders, interim orders and undertakings, including—

(a) provision about evidence;

(b) provision enabling the amalgamation of the register mentioned in paragraph 12 of Schedule 4A with another register;

(c) provision enabling inspection of that register by the public.

**Amendments**—Inserted by Enterprise Act 2002, s 269, Sch 23, paras 1, 16(1), (3).

**30  General**

Provision conferring power on the Secretary of State to make regulations with respect to so much of any matter that may be provided for in the rules as relates to the carrying out of the functions of an interim receiver appointed under section 286 or of a trustee of a bankrupt's estate.

**Amendments**—Small Business, Enterprise and Employment Act 2015, s 133(2), Sch 10, paras 1, 11.

**31**

Provision conferring a discretion on the court.

**32**

Provision making non-compliance with any of the rules a criminal offence.

**33**

Provision making different provision for different cases, including different provision for different areas.

## SCHEDULE 10
## PUNISHMENT OF OFFENCES UNDER THIS ACT

Section 430

**[1.759]**

General comment on Schedule 10—This Schedule lists the offences that are mentioned in the Act and sets out: the mode of prosecution; the punishment; and any daily default that might be applicable. Many of the offences may be the subject of summary prosecution only, while some can be prosecuted summarily or on indictment. The punishment for some offences is simply by fine. The punishment for others is by either a term of imprisonment or a fine or both.

Where offences are punishable by fine, the fine is expressed as a fraction of the statutory maximum. The statutory maximum fine in England and Wales is at present £5,000 according to s 32 of the Magistrates' Courts Act 1980 as amended by s 17 of the Criminal Justice Act 1991.

| Section (Section of Act creating offence) | General nature of offence | Mode of prosecution | Punishment | Daily default fine (where applicable) |
|---|---|---|---|---|
| A8(4) | Directors failing to notify monitor of beginning of moratorium. | 1. On indictment. 2. Summary. | 2 years or a fine or both. On conviction in England and Wales: 12 months or a fine or both. On conviction in Scotland: 12 months or the statutory maximum or both. | |
| A8(5) | Monitor failing to notify creditors etc of beginning of moratorium. | Summary. | Level 3 on the standard scale. | |
| A17(6) | Directors failing to notify monitor of change in end of moratorium. | 1. On indictment. 2. Summary. | 2 years or a fine or both. On conviction in England and Wales: 12 months or a fine or both. On conviction in Scotland: 12 months or the statutory maximum or both. | |
| A17(7) | Monitor failing to notify creditors etc of change in end of moratorium. | Summary. | Level 3 on the standard scale. | |
| A19(5) | Company or officer failing to state in correspondence etc that moratorium in force. | Summary. | Level 3 on the standard scale. | |

| Section (Section of Act creating offence) | General nature of offence | Mode of prosecution | Punishment | Daily default fine (where applicable) |
|---|---|---|---|---|
| A24(4) | Directors failing to notify monitor of insolvency proceedings etc. | 1. On indictment. 2. Summary. | 2 years or a fine or both. On conviction in England and Wales: 12 months or a fine or both. On conviction in Scotland: 12 months or the statutory maximum or both. | |
| A25(3)(a) | Company obtaining credit without disclosing existence of moratorium. | 1. On indictment. 2. Summary. | A fine. On conviction in England and Wales: a fine. On conviction in Scotland: the statutory maximum. | |
| A25(3)(b) | Obtaining credit for company without disclosing existence of moratorium. | 1. On indictment. 2. Summary. | 2 years or a fine or both. On conviction in England and Wales: 12 months or a fine or both. On conviction in Scotland: 12 months or the statutory maximum or both. | |
| A26(4)(a) | Company granting security without monitor's consent. | 1. On indictment. 2. Summary. | A fine. On conviction in England and Wales: a fine. On conviction in Scotland: the statutory maximum. | |

| Section (Section of Act creating offence) | General nature of offence | Mode of prosecution | Punishment | Daily default fine (where applicable) |
|---|---|---|---|---|
| A26(4)(b) | Authorising or permitting company to do so. | 1. On indictment 2. Summary. | 2 years or a fine or both. On conviction in England and Wales: 12 months or a fine or both. On conviction in Scotland: 12 months or the statutory maximum. | |
| A27(1)(a) | Company entering into market contract, etc. | 1. On indictment. 2. Summary. | A fine. On conviction in England and Wales: a fine. On conviction in Scotland: the statutory maximum. | |
| A27(1)(b) | Authorising or permitting company to do so. | 1. On indictment. 2. Summary. | 2 years or a fine or both. On conviction in England and Wales: 12 months or a fine or both. On conviction in Scotland: 12 months or the statutory maximum or both. | |
| A28(5)(a) | Company making unauthorised payments. | 1. On indictment. 2. Summary. | A fine. On conviction in England and Wales: a fine. On conviction in Scotland: the statutory maximum. | |

| Section (Section of Act creating offence) | General nature of offence | Mode of prosecution | Punishment | Daily default fine (where applicable) |
|---|---|---|---|---|
| A28(5)(b) | Authorising or permitting company to do so. | 1. On indictment.<br>2. Summary. | 2 years or a fine or both. On conviction in England and Wales: 12 months or a fine or both. On conviction in Scotland: 12 months or the statutory maximum or both. | |
| A29(6)(a) | Company making unauthorised disposal of property. | 1. On indictment<br>2. Summary. | A fine. On conviction in England and Wales: a fine. On conviction in Scotland: the statutory maximum. | |
| A29(6)(b) | Authorising or permitting such a disposal. | 1. On indictment.<br>2. Summary. | 2 years or a fine or both. On conviction in England and Wales: 12 months or a fine or both. On conviction in Scotland: 12 months or the statutory maximum or both. | |
| A30(2)(a) | Unauthorised disposal of hire-purchase property. | 1. On indictment.<br>2. Summary. | A fine. On conviction in England and Wales: a fine. On conviction in Scotland: the statutory maximum. | |

| Section (Section of Act creating offence) | General nature of offence | Mode of prosecution | Punishment | Daily default fine (where applicable) |
|---|---|---|---|---|
| A30(2)(b) | Authorising or permitting such a disposal. | 1. On indictment. 2. Summary. | 2 years or a fine or both. On conviction in England and Wales: 12 months or a fine or both. On conviction in Scotland: 12 months or the statutory maximum or both. | |
| A31(8) | Directors failing to send to registrar copy of court order permitting disposal of charged property. | Summary. | Level 3 on the standard scale. | |
| A31(10)(a) | Company failing to comply with requirements relating to disposal of charged property. | 1. On indictment.A fine. 2. Summary. | A fine. On conviction in England and Wales: a fine. On conviction in Scotland: the statutory maximum. | |
| A31(10)(b) | Authorising or permitting such a failure. | 1. On indictment. 2. Summary. | 2 years or a fine or both. On conviction in England and Wales: 12 months or a fine or both. On conviction in Scotland: 12 months or the statutory maximum or both. | |

| Section (Section of Act creating offence) | General nature of offence | Mode of prosecution | Punishment | Daily default fine (where applicable) |
|---|---|---|---|---|
| A32(4)(a) | Company failing to comply with requirements relating to disposal of hire-purchase property. | 1. On indictment. 2. Summary. | A fine. On conviction in England and Wales: a fine. On conviction in Scotland: the statutory maximum. | |
| A32(4)(b) | Authorising or permitting such a failure. | 1. On indictment. 2. Summary. | 2 years or a fine or both. On conviction in England and Wales: 12 months or a fine or both. On conviction in Scotland: 12 months or the statutory maximum or both. | |
| A32(6) | Directors failing to send to registrar copy of court order permitting disposal of hire-purchase property. | Summary. | Level 3 on the standard scale. | |
| A39(9) | Monitor failing to notify creditors etc of change in monitor. | Summary. | Level 3 on the standard scale. | |
| A46(1) | Fraud or privity to fraud during or in anticipation of moratorium. | 1. On indictment. 2. Summary. | 2 years or a fine or both. On conviction in England and Wales: 12 months or a fine or both. On conviction in Scotland: 12 months or the statutory maximum or both. | |

| Section (Section of Act creating offence) | General nature of offence | Mode of prosecution | Punishment | Daily default fine (where applicable) |
|---|---|---|---|---|
| A46(4) | Knowingly taking in pawn or pledge, or otherwise receiving, company property. | 1. On indictment. 2. Summary. | 2 years or a fine or both. On conviction in England and Wales: 12 months or a fine or both. On conviction in Scotland: 12 months or the statutory maximum or both. | |
| A47(1) | False representation or fraud for purpose of obtaining or extending moratorium. | 1. On indictment. 2. Summary. | 2 years or a fine or both. On conviction in England and Wales: 12 months or a fine or both. On conviction in Scotland: 12 months or the statutory maximum or both. | |
| A49(5) | Directors failing to notify regulator of qualifying decision procedure in relation to regulated company. | 1. On indictment. 2. Summary. | 2 years or a fine or both. On conviction in England and Wales: 12 months or a fine or both. On conviction in Scotland: 12 months or the statutory maximum or both. | |

| Section (Section of Act creating offence) | General nature of offence | Mode of prosecution | Punishment | Daily default fine (where applicable) |
|---|---|---|---|---|
| 6A(1) | False representation or fraud for purpose of obtaining members' or creditors' approval of proposed voluntary arrangement. | 1 On indictment | 7 years or a fine, or both. | |
| | | 2 Summary | 6 months or the statutory maximum, or both. | |
| 12(2) | ... | ... | ... | |
| 15(8) | ... | ... | ... | ... |
| 18(5) | ... | ... | ... | ... |
| 21(3) | ... | ... | ... | ... |
| 22(6) | ... | ... | ... | |
| | | ... | ... | ... |
| 23(3) | ... | ... | ... | ... |
| 24(7) | ... | ... | ... | ... |
| 27(6) | ... | ... | ... | ... |
| 30 | Body corporate acting as receiver. | 1 On indictment | A fine. | |
| | | 2 Summary | The statutory maximum. | |
| 31 | ... Bankrupt or person in respect of whom a debt relief order is made acting as receiver or manager. | 1 On indictment | 2 years or a fine, or both. | |
| | | 2 Summary | 6 months or the statutory maximum, or both. | |
| 38(5) | Receiver failing to deliver accounts to registrar. | Summary | One-fifth of the statutory maximum. | One-fiftieth of the statutory maximum. |

| Section (Section of Act creating offence) | General nature of offence | Mode of prosecution | Punishment | Daily default fine (where applicable) |
|---|---|---|---|---|
| 39(2) | Company and others failing to state in correspondence that receiver appointed. | Summary | One-fifth of the statutory maximum. | |
| 43(6) | Administrative receiver failing to file copy of order permitting disposal of charged property. | Summary | One-fifth of the statutory maximum. | One-fiftieth of the statutory maximum. |
| 45(5) | Administrative receiver failing to file notice of vacation of office. | Summary | One-fifth of the statutory maximum. | *One-fiftieth of the statutory maximum.* |
| 46(4) | Administrative receiver failing to give notice of his appointment. | Summary | One-fifth of the statutory maximum. | One-fiftieth of the statutory maximum. |
| 47(6) | Failure to comply with provisions relating to statement of affairs, where administrative receiver appointed. | 1 On indictment | A fine. | |
| | | 2 Summary | The statutory maximum. | One-tenth of the statutory maximum. |
| 48(8) | Administrative receiver failing to comply with requirements as to his report. | Summary | One-fifth of the statutory maximum. | One-fiftieth of the statutory maximum. |
| 51(4) | Body corporate or Scottish firm acting as receiver. | 1 On indictment | A fine. | |
| | | 2 Summary | The statutory maximum. | |

| Section (Section of Act creating offence) | General nature of offence | Mode of prosecution | Punishment | Daily default fine (where applicable) |
|---|---|---|---|---|
| 51(5) | Undischarged bankrupt acting as receiver (Scotland). | 1 On indictment | 2 years or a fine, or both. | |
| | | 2 Summary | 6 months or the statutory maximum, or both. | |
| 53(2) | Failing to deliver to registrar copy of instrument of appointment of receiver. | Summary | One-fifth of the statutory maximum. | *One-fiftieth of the statutory maximum.* |
| 54(3) | Failing to deliver to registrar the court's interlocutor appointing receiver. | Summary | One-fifth of the statutory maximum. | *One-fiftieth of the statutory maximum.* |
| 61(7) | Receiver failing to send to registrar certified copy of court order authorising disposal of charged property. | Summary | One-fifth of the statutory maximum. | One-fiftieth of the statutory maximum. |
| 62(5) | Failing to give notice to registrar of cessation or removal of receiver. | Summary | One-fifth of the statutory maximum. | *One-fiftieth of the statutory maximum.* |
| 64(2) | Company and others failing to state on correspondence etc that receiver appointed. | Summary | One-fifth of the statutory maximum. | |
| 65(4) | Receiver failing to send or publish notice of his appointment. | Summary | One-fifth of the statutory maximum. | One-fiftieth of the statutory maximum. |

| Section (Section of Act creating offence) | General nature of offence | Mode of prosecution | Punishment | Daily default fine (where applicable) |
|---|---|---|---|---|
| 66(6) | Failing to comply with provisions concerning statement of affairs, where receiver appointed. | 1 On indictment | A fine. | |
| | | 2 Summary | The statutory maximum. | One-tenth of the statutory maximum. |
| 67(8) | Receiver failing to comply with requirements as to his report. | Summary | One-fifth of the statutory maximum. | One-fiftieth of the statutory maximum. |
| 85(2) | Company failing to give notice in Gazette of resolution for voluntary winding up. | Summary | One-fifth of the statutory maximum. | One-fiftieth of the statutory maximum. |
| 89(4) | Director making statutory declaration of company's solvency without reasonable grounds for his opinion. | 1 On indictment | 2 years or a fine, or both. | |
| | | 2 Summary | 6 months or the statutory maximum, or both. | |
| 89(6) | Declaration under section 89 not delivered to registrar within prescribed time. | Summary | One-fifth of the statutory maximum. | One-fiftieth of the statutory maximum. |
| 92A(2) | Liquidator failing to send progress report to members ... | Summary | Level 3 on the standard scale. | |
| 93(3) | ... | ... | ... | |

| Section (Section of Act creating offence) | General nature of offence | Mode of prosecution | Punishment | Daily default fine (where applicable) |
|---|---|---|---|---|
| 94(4) | Liquidator failing to send to company members a copy of account of winding up. | Summary | Level 3 on the standard scale. | |
| 94(5) | Liquidator failing to send to registrar a copy of account of winding up. | Summary | Level 3 on the standard scale. | One tenth of level 3 on the standard scale. |
| 95(8) | Liquidator failing to comply with s 95(1) to (4A), where company insolvent. | Summary | The statutory maximum. | |
| 98(6) | . . . | . . . . . . | . . . . . . | |
| 99(3) | Directors failing to send statement in prescribed form to creditors. | 1 On indictment | A fine. | |
| | | 2 Summary | The statutory maximum. | |
| 104A(2) | Liquidator failing to send progress report to members and creditors . . . | Summary | Level 3 on the standard scale. | |
| 105(3) | . . . | . . . | . . . | |
| 106(5) | Liquidator failing to send to company members and creditors a copy of account of winding up. | Summary | Level 3 on the standard scale. | |
| 106(6) | Liquidator failing to send to registrar a copy of account of winding up. | Summary | Level 3 on the standard scale. | One tenth of level 3 on the standard scale. |

| Section (Section of Act creating offence) | General nature of offence | Mode of prosecution | Punishment | Daily default fine (where applicable) |
|---|---|---|---|---|
| 109(2) | Liquidator failing to publish notice of his appointment. | Summary | One-fifth of the statutory maximum. | One-fiftieth of the statutory maximum. |
| 114(4) | Directors exercising powers in breach of s 114, where no liquidator. | Summary | The statutory maximum. | |
| 131(7) | Failing to comply with requirements as to statement of affairs, where liquidator appointed. | 1 On indictment | A fine. | |
| | | 2. Summary | The statutory maximum. | One-tenth of the statutory maximum. |
| 164 | Giving, offering etc corrupt inducement affecting appointment of liquidator. | 1 On indictment | A fine. | |
| | | 2 Summary | The statutory maximum. | |
| 166(7) | Liquidator failing to comply with requirements of s 166 in creditors' voluntary winding up. | Summary | The statutory maximum. | |
| 188(2) | Default in compliance with s 188 as to notification that company being wound up. | Summary | One-fifth of the statutory maximum. | |
| 192(2) | Liquidator failing to notify registrar as to progress of winding up. | Summary | One-fifth of the statutory maximum. | One-fiftieth of the statutory maximum. |

| Section (Section of Act creating offence) | General nature of offence | Mode of prosecution | Punishment | Daily default fine (where applicable) |
|---|---|---|---|---|
| 201(4) | Failing to deliver to registrar copy of court order deferring dissolution. | Summary | One-fifth of the statutory maximum. | One-fiftieth of the statutory maximum. |
| 203(6) | Failing to deliver to registrar copy of directions or result of appeal under s 203. | Summary | One-fifth of the statutory maximum. | One-fiftieth of the statutory maximum. |
| 204(7) | Liquidator failing to deliver to registrar copy of court order for early dissolution. | Summary | One-fifth of the statutory maximum. | One-fiftieth of the statutory maximum. |
| 204(8) | Failing to deliver to registrar copy of court order deferring early dissolution. | Summary | One-fifth of the statutory maximum. | One-fiftieth of the statutory maximum. |
| 205(7) | Failing to deliver to registrar copy of Secretary of State's directions or court order deferring dissolution. | Summary | One-fifth of the statutory maximum. | One-fiftieth of the statutory maximum. |
| 206(1) | Fraud etc in anticipation of winding up. | 1 On indictment | 7 years or a fine, or both. | |
| | | 2 Summary | 6 months or the statutory maximum, or both. | |
| 206(2) | Privity to fraud in anticipation of winding up; fraud, or privity to fraud, after commencement of winding up. | 1 On indictment | 7 years or a fine, or both. | |

| Section (Section of Act creating offence) | General nature of offence | Mode of prosecution | Punishment | Daily default fine (where applicable) |
|---|---|---|---|---|
| | | 2 Summary | 6 months or the statutory maximum, or both. | |
| 206(5) | Knowingly taking in pawn or pledge, or otherwise receiving, company property. | 1 On indictment | 7 years or a fine, or both. | |
| | | 2 Summary | 6 months or the statutory maximum, or both. | |
| 207 | Officer of company entering into transaction in fraud of company's creditors. | 1 On indictment | 2 years or a fine, or both. | |
| | | 2 Summary | 6 months or the statutory maximum, or both. | |
| 208 | Officer of company misconducting himself in course of winding up. | 1 On indictment | 7 years or a fine, or both. | |
| | | 2 Summary | 6 months or the statutory maximum, or both. | |
| 209 | Officer or contributory destroying, falsifying, etc company's books. | 1 On indictment | 7 years or a fine, or both. | |
| | | 2 Summary | 6 months or the statutory maximum, or both. | |

| Section (Section of Act creating offence) | General nature of offence | Mode of prosecution | Punishment | Daily default fine (where applicable) |
|---|---|---|---|---|
| 210 | Officer of company making material omission from statement relating to company's affairs. | 1 On indictment | 7 years or a fine, or both. | |
| | | 2 Summary | 6 months or the statutory maximum, or both. | |
| 211 | False representation or fraud for purpose of obtaining creditors' consent to an agreement in connection with winding up. | 1 On indictment | 7 years or a fine, or both. | |
| | | 2 Summary | 6 months or the statutory maximum, or both. | |
| 216(4) | Contravening restrictions on re-use of name of company in insolvent liquidation. | 1 On indictment | 2 years or a fine, or both. | |
| | | 2 Summary | 6 months or the statutory maximum, or both. | |
| 235(5) | Failing to co-operate with office-holder. | 1 On indictment. | A fine. | |
| | | 2 Summary | The statutory maximum. | One-tenth of the statutory maximum. |
| 251O(1) | False representations or omissions in making an application for a debt relief order. | 1 On indictment | 7 years or a fine, or both. | |

| Section (Section of Act creating offence) | General nature of offence | Mode of prosecution | Punishment | Daily default fine (where applicable) |
|---|---|---|---|---|
|  |  | 2 Summary | 12 months or the statutory maximum, or both. |  |
| 251O(2)(a) | Failing to comply with duty in connection with an application for a debt relief order. | 1 On indictment | 2 years or a fine, or both. |  |
|  |  | 2 Summary | 12 months or the statutory maximum, or both. |  |
| 251O(2)(b) | False representations or omissions in connection with duty in relation to an application for a debt relief order. | 1 On indictment | 7 years or a fine, or both. |  |
|  |  | 2 Summary | 12 months or the statutory maximum, or both. |  |
| 251O(4)(a) | Failing to comply with duty in connection with a debt relief order. | 1 On indictment | 2 years or a fine, or both. |  |
|  |  | 2 Summary | 12 months or the statutory maximum, or both. |  |
| 251O(4)(b) | False representations or omissions in connection with a duty in relation to a debt relief order. | 1 On indictment | 7 years or a fine, or both. |  |
|  |  | 2 Summary | 12 months or the statutory maximum, or both. |  |

| Section (Section of Act creating offence) | General nature of offence | Mode of prosecution | Punishment | Daily default fine (where applicable) |
|---|---|---|---|---|
| 251P(1) | Failing to deliver books, records and papers to official receiver, concealing or destroying them or making false entries in them by person in respect of whom a debt relief order is made. | 1 On indictment | 7 years or a fine, or both. | |
| | | 2 Summary | 12 months or the statutory maximum, or both. | |
| 251P(2) | Person in respect of whom debt relief order is made doing anything falling within paragraphs (c) to (e) of section 251P(1) during the period of 12 months ending with the application date or doing anything falling within paragraphs (b) to (e) of section 251P(1) after that date but before the effective date. | 1 On indictment | 7 years or a fine, or both. | |
| | | 2 Summary | 12 months or the statutory maximum, or both. | |

| Section (Section of Act creating offence) | General nature of offence | Mode of prosecution | Punishment | Daily default fine (where applicable) |
|---|---|---|---|---|
| 251Q(1) | Fraudulent disposal of property by person in respect of whom a debt relief order is made. | 1 On indictment | 2 years or a fine, or both. | |
| | | 2 Summary | 12 months or the statutory maximum, or both. | |
| 251R(1) | Disposal of property that is not paid for by person in respect of whom a debt relief order is made. | 1 On indictment | 7 years or a fine, or both. | |
| | | 2 Summary | 12 months or the statutory maximum, or both. | |
| 251R(2) | Obtaining property in respect of which money is owed by a person in respect of whom a debt relief order is made. | 1 On indictment | 7 years or a fine, or both. | |
| | | 2 Summary | 12 months or the statutory maximum, or both. | |
| 251S(1) | Person in respect of whom a debt relief order is made obtaining credit or engaging in business without disclosing his status or name. | 1 On indictment | 2 years or a fine, or both. | |
| | | 2 Summary | 12 months or the statutory maximum, or both. | |

| Section (Section of Act creating offence) | General nature of offence | Mode of prosecution | Punishment | Daily default fine (where applicable) |
|---|---|---|---|---|
| 262A(1) | False representation or fraud for purpose of obtaining creditors' approval of proposed voluntary arrangement. | 1 On indictment | 7 years or a fine, or both. | |
| | | 2 Summary | 6 months or the statutory maximum, or both. | |
| 263O | False representations or omissions in connection with a bankruptcy application. | 1 On indictment | 1 7 years or a fine, or both. | |
| | | 2 Summary | 2 12 months or the statutory maximum, or both. | |
| 353(1) | Bankrupt failing to disclose property or disposals to official receiver or trustee. | 1 On indictment | 7 years or a fine, or both. | |
| | | 2 Summary | 6 months or the statutory maximum, or both. | |
| 354(1) | Bankrupt failing to deliver property to, or concealing property from, official receiver or trustee. | 1 On indictment | 7 years or a fine, or both. | |
| | | 2 Summary | 6 months or the statutory maximum, or both. | |
| 354(2) | Bankrupt removing property which he is required to deliver to official receiver or trustee. | 1 On indictment | 7 years or a fine, or both. | |

| Section (Section of Act creating offence) | General nature of offence | Mode of prosecution | Punishment | Daily default fine (where applicable) |
|---|---|---|---|---|
| | | 2 Summary | 6 months or the statutory maximum, or both. | |
| 354(3) | Bankrupt failing to account for loss of substantial part of property. | 1 On indictment | 2 years or a fine, or both. | |
| | | 2 Summary | 6 months or the statutory maximum, or both. | |
| 355(1) | Bankrupt failing to deliver books, papers and records to official receiver or trustee. | 1 On indictment | 7 years or a fine, or both. | |
| | | 2 Summary | 6 months or the statutory maximum, or both. | |
| 355(2) | Bankrupt concealing, destroying etc books, papers or records, or making false entries in them. | 1 On indictment | 7 years or a fine, or both. | |
| | | 2 Summary | 6 months or the statutory maximum, or both. | |
| 355(3) | Bankrupt disposing of, or altering, books, papers or records relating to his estate or affairs. | 1 On indictment | 7 years or a fine, or both. | |
| | | 2 Summary | 6 months or the statutory maximum, or both. | |

| Section (Section of Act creating offence) | General nature of offence | Mode of prosecution | Punishment | Daily default fine (where applicable) |
|---|---|---|---|---|
| 356(1) | Bankrupt making material omission in statement relating to his affairs. | 1 On indictment | 7 years or a fine, or both. | |
| | | 2 Summary | 6 months or the statutory maximum, or both. | |
| 356(2) | Bankrupt making false statement, or failing to inform trustee, where false debt proved. | 1 On indictment | 7 years or a fine, or both. | |
| | | 2 Summary | 6 months or the statutory maximum, or both. | |
| 357 | Bankrupt fraudulently disposing of property. | 1 On indictment | 2 years or a fine, or both. | |
| | | 2 Summary | 6 months or the statutory maximum, or both. | |
| 358 | Bankrupt absconding with property he is required to deliver to official receiver or trustee. | 1 On indictment | 2 years or a fine, or both. | |
| | | 2 Summary | 6 months or the statutory maximum, or both. | |
| 359(1) | Bankrupt disposing of property obtained on credit and not paid for. | 1 On indictment | 7 years or a fine, or both. | |
| | | 2 Summary | 6 months or the statutory maximum, or both. | |

| Section (Section of Act creating offence) | General nature of offence | Mode of prosecution | Punishment | Daily default fine (where applicable) |
|---|---|---|---|---|
| 359(2) | Obtaining property in respect of which money is owed by a bankrupt. | 1 On indictment | 7 years or a fine, or both. | |
| | | 2 Summary | 6 months or the statutory maximum, or both. | |
| 360(1) | Bankrupt obtaining credit or engaging in business without disclosing his status or name in which he was made bankrupt. | 1 On indictment | 2 years or a fine, or both. | |
| | | 2 Summary | 6 months or the statutory maximum, or both. | |
| 360(3) | Person made bankrupt in Scotland or Northern Ireland obtaining credit, etc in England and Wales. | 1 On indictment | 2 years or a fine, or both. | |
| | | 2 Summary | 6 months or the statutory maximum, or both. | |
| 361(1) | . . . | . . . | . . . | |
| | | . . . | . . . | |
| 362 | . . . | . . . | . . . | |
| | | . . . | . . . | |
| 389 | Acting as insolvency practitioner when not qualified. | 1 On indictment | 2 years or a fine, or both. | |
| | | 2 Summary | 6 months or the statutory maximum or both. | |

| Section (Section of Act creating offence) | General nature of offence | Mode of prosecution | Punishment | Daily default fine (where applicable) |
|---|---|---|---|---|
| 429(5) | Contravening s 429 in respect of disabilities imposed by county court on revocation of administration order. | 1 On indictment | 2 years or a fine, or both. | |
| | | 2 Summary | 6 months or the statutory maximum, or both. | |
| . . . | . . . | . . . | . . . | |
| Sch B1, para 18(7) | Making false statement in statutory declaration where administrator appointed by holder of floating charge. | 1 On indictment | 2 years, or a fine or both. | |
| | | 2 Summary | 6 months, or the statutory maximum or both. | |
| Sch B1, para 20 | Holder of floating charge failing to notify administrator or others of commencement of appointment. | 1 On indictment | 2 years, or a fine or both. | |
| | | 2 Summary | 6 months, or the statutory maximum or both. | One-tenth of the statutory maximum. |
| Sch B1, para 27(4) | Making false statement in statutory declaration where appointment of administrator proposed by company or directors. | 1 On indictment | 2 years, or a fine or both. | |

| Section (Section of Act creating offence) | General nature of offence | Mode of prosecution | Punishment | Daily default fine (where applicable) |
|---|---|---|---|---|
| | | 2 Summary | 6 months, or the statutory maximum or both. | |
| Sch B1, para 29(7) | Making false statement in statutory declaration where administrator appointed by company or directors. | 1 On indictment | 2 years, or a fine or both. | |
| | | 2 Summary | 6 months, or the statutory maximum or both. | |
| Sch B1, para 32 | Company or directors failing to notify administrator or others of commencement of appointment. | 1 On indictment | 2 years, or a fine or both. | One-tenth of the statutory maximum. |
| | | 2 Summary | 6 months, or the statutory maximum or both. | |
| Sch B1, para 45(2) | Administrator, company or officer failing to state in business document that administrator appointed. | Summary | One-fifth of the statutory maximum. | |
| Sch B1, para 46(9) | Administrator failing to give notice of his appointment. | Summary | One-fifth of the statutory maximum. | One-fiftieth of the statutory maximum. |
| Sch B1, para 48(4) | Failing to comply with provisions about statement of affairs where administrator appointed. | 1 On indictment | A fine. | |

| Section (Section of Act creating offence) | General nature of offence | Mode of prosecution | Punishment | Daily default fine (where applicable) |
|---|---|---|---|---|
| | | 2 Summary | The statutory maximum. | One-tenth of the statutory maximum. |
| Sch B1, para 49(7) | Administrator failing to send out statement of his proposals. | Summary | One-fifth of the statutory maximum. | One-fiftieth of the statutory maximum. |
| Sch B1, para 51(5) | Administrator failing to seek creditors' decision. | Summary | One-fifth of the statutory maximum. | One-fiftieth of the statutory maximum. |
| Sch B1, para 53(3) | Administrator failing to report decision taken by creditors. | Summary | One-fifth of the statutory maximum. | One-fiftieth of the statutory maximum. |
| Sch B1, para 54(7) | Administrator failing to report creditors' decision on revised proposal. | Summary | One-fifth of the statutory maximum. | One-fiftieth of the statutory maximum. |
| Sch B1, para 56(2) | Administrator failing to seek creditors' decision. | Summary | One-fifth of the statutory maximum. | One-fiftieth of the statutory maximum. |
| Sch B1, para 71(6) | Administrator failing to file court order enabling disposal of charged property. | Summary | One-fifth of the statutory maximum. | One-fiftieth of the statutory maximum. |
| Sch B1, para 72(5) | Administrator failing to file court order enabling disposal of hire-purchase property. | Summary | One-fifth of the statutory maximum. | One-fiftieth of the statutory maximum. |
| Sch B1, para 77(3) | Administrator failing to notify Registrar of Companies of automatic end of administration. | Summary | One-fifth of the statutory maximum. | One-fiftieth of the statutory maximum. |

| Section (Section of Act creating offence) | General nature of offence | Mode of prosecution | Punishment | Daily default fine (where applicable) |
|---|---|---|---|---|
| Sch B1, para 78(6) | Administrator failing to give notice of extension by consent of term of office. | Summary | One-fifth of the statutory maximum. | One-fiftieth of the statutory maximum. |
| Sch B1, para 80(6) | Administrator failing to give notice of termination of administration where objective achieved. | Summary | One-fifth of the statutory maximum. | One-fiftieth of the statutory maximum. |
| Sch B1, para 84(9) | Administrator failing to comply with provisions where company moves to dissolution. | Summary | One-fifth of the statutory maximum. | One-fiftieth of the statutory maximum. |
| Sch B1, para 86(3) | Administrator failing to notify Registrar of Companies where court terminates administration. | Summary | One-fifth of the statutory maximum. | One-fiftieth of the statutory maximum. |
| Sch B1, para 89(3) | Administrator failing to give notice on ceasing to be qualified. | Summary | One-fifth of the statutory maximum. | One-fiftieth of the statutory maximum. |
| Sch 7, para 4(3) | ... | ... | ... | |

**Amendments**—Companies Act 1989, s 212, Sch 24, as from a date to be appointed; Statute Law (Repeals) Act 1993, s 1(1), Sch 1, Pt IV; Insolvency Act 2000, ss 2, 3, Sch 2, paras 1, 12, Sch 3, paras 1, 16; Enterprise Act 2002, ss 248(3), 269, 278(2), Sch 17, paras 9, 39, Sch 23, paras 1, 17(a), Sch 26; Tribunals, Courts and Enforcement Act 2007, s 108(3), Sch 20, Pt 1, paras 1, 15; SI 2009/1941; SI 2010/18; Enterprise and Regulatory Reform Act 2013, s 71(3), Sch 19, paras 1, 66(1), as from a date to be appointed; Deregulation Act 2015, s 19, Sch 6, Pt 6, para 22(1), (5)(b); Small Business, Enterprise and Employment Act 2015, ss 126, 136(1), (4)(a), (b), Sch 9, Pt 1, paras 1, 11(1)–(5), 53(1)–(6); SI 2015/1329; SI 2016/1020; Corporate Insolvency and Governance Act 2020, s 2(1), Sch 3, paras 1, 33(1), (3); SS 2016/141.

## SCHEDULE 11
## TRANSITIONAL PROVISIONS AND SAVINGS
Section 437

### PART I   COMPANY INSOLVENCY AND WINDING UP

**[1.760]**

### 1  Administration orders

(1)   Where any right to appoint an administrative receiver of a company is conferred by any debentures or floating charge created before the appointed day, the conditions precedent to the exercise of that right are deemed to include the presentation of a petition applying for an administration order to be made in relation to the company.

(2)   "Administrative receiver" here has the meaning assigned by section 251.

### 2  Receivers and managers (England and Wales)

(1)   In relation to any receiver or manager of a company's property who was appointed before the appointed day, the new law does not apply; and the relevant provisions of the former law continue to have effect.

(2)   "The new law" here means Chapter I of Part III, and Part VI, of this Act; and "the former law" means the Companies Act 1985 and so much of this Act as replaces provisions of that Act (without the amendments in paragraphs 15 to 17 of Schedule 6 to the Insolvency Act 1985, or the associated repeals made by that Act), and any provision of the Insolvency Act 1985 which was in force before the appointed day.

(3)   This paragraph is without prejudice to the power conferred by this Act under which rules under section 411 may make transitional provision in connection with the coming into force of those rules; and such provision may apply those rules in relation to the receiver or manager of a company's property notwithstanding that he was appointed before the coming into force of the rules or section 411.

Amendments—SI 2009/1941.

### 3  Receivers (Scotland)

(1)   In relation to any receiver appointed under section 467 of the Companies Act 1985 before the appointed day, the new law does not apply and the relevant provisions of the former law continue to have effect.

(2)   "The new law" here means Chapter II of Part III, and Part VI, of this Act; and "the former law" means the Companies Act 1985 and so much of this Act as replaces provisions of that Act (without the amendments in paragraphs 18 to 22 of Schedule 6 to the Insolvency Act 1985 or the associated repeals made by that Act), and any provision of the Insolvency Act 1985 which was in force before the appointed day.

(3)   This paragraph is without prejudice to the power conferred by this Act under which rules under section 411 may make transitional provision in connection with the coming into force of those rules; and such provision may apply those rules in relation to a receiver appointed under section 467 notwithstanding that he was appointed before the coming into force of the rules or section 411.

Amendments—SI 2009/1941.

### 4  Winding up already in progress

(1)   In relation to any winding up which has commenced, or is treated as having commenced, before the appointed day, the new law does not apply, and the former law continues to have effect, subject to the following paragraphs.

(2)   "The new law" here means any provisions in the first Group of Parts of this Act which replace sections 66 to 87 and 89 to 105 of the Insolvency Act 1985; and "the former law" means Parts XX and XXI of the Companies Act 1985 (without the amendments in paragraphs 23 to 52 of Schedule 6 to the Insolvency Act 1985, or the associated repeals made by that Act).

Amendments—SI 2009/1941.

## 5 Statement of affairs

(1) Where a winding up by the court in England and Wales has commenced, or is treated as having commenced, before the appointed day, the official receiver or (on appeal from a refusal by him) the court may, at any time on or after that day—

    (a) release a person from an obligation imposed on him by or under section 528 of the Companies Act 1985 (statement of affairs), or

    (b) extend the period specified in subsection (6) of that section.

(2) Accordingly, on and after the appointed day, section 528(6) has effect in relation to a winding up to which this paragraph applies with the omission of the words from "or within" onwards.

**Amendments—**SI 2009/1941.

## 6 Provisions relating to liquidator

(1) This paragraph applies as regards the liquidator in the case of a winding up by the court in England and Wales commenced, or treated as having commenced, before the appointed day.

(2) The official receiver may, at any time when he is liquidator of the company, apply to the Secretary of State for the appointment of a liquidator in his (the official receiver's) place; and on any such application the Secretary of State shall either make an appointment or decline to make one.

(3) Where immediately before the appointed day the liquidator of the company has not made an application under section 545 of the Companies Act 1985 (release of liquidators), then—

    (a) except where the Secretary of State otherwise directs, sections 146(1) and (2) and 172(8) of this Act apply, and section 545 does not apply, in relation to any liquidator of that company who holds office on or at any time after the appointed day and is not the official receiver;

    (b) section 146(3) applies in relation to the carrying out at any time after that day by any liquidator of the company of any of his functions; and

    (c) a liquidator in relation to whom section 172(8) has effect by virtue of this paragraph has his release with effect from the time specified in section 174(4)(d) of this Act.

(4) Subsection (6) of section 174 of this Act has effect for the purposes of sub-paragraph (3)(c) above as it has for the purposes of that section, but as if the reference to section 212 were to section 631 of the Companies Act 1985.

(5) The liquidator may employ a solicitor to assist him in the carrying out of his functions without the permission of the committee of inspection; but if he does so employ a solicitor he shall inform the committee of inspection that he has done so.

**Amendments—**SI 2009/1941.

## 7 Winding up under supervision of the court

The repeals in Part II of Schedule 10 to the Insolvency Act 1985 of references (in the Companies Act 1985 and elsewhere) to a winding up under the supervision of the court do not affect the operation of the enactments in which the references are contained in relation to any case in which an order under section 606 of the Companies Act 1985 (power to order winding up under supervision) was made before the appointed day.

**Amendments—**SI 2009/1941.

## 8 Saving for power to make rules

(1) Paragraphs 4 to 7 are without prejudice to the power conferred by this Act under which rules made under section 411 may make transitional provision in connection with the coming into force of those rules.

(2) Such provision may apply those rules in relation to a winding up notwithstanding that the winding up commenced, or is treated as having commenced, before the coming into force of the rules or section 411.

## 9 Setting aside of preferences and other transactions

(1) Where a provision in Part VI of this Act applies in relation to a winding up or in relation to a case in which an administration order has been made, a preference given,

floating charge created or other transaction entered into before the appointed day shall not be set aside under that provision except to the extent that it could have been set aside under the law in force immediately before that day, assuming for this purpose that any relevant administration order had been a winding-up order.

(2)   The references above to setting aside a preference, floating charge or other transaction include the making of an order which varies or reverses any effect of a preference, floating charge or other transaction.

## PART II   INDIVIDUAL INSOLVENCY

**[1.761]**

### 10  Bankruptcy (general)

(1)   Subject to the following provisions of this Part of this Schedule, so much of this Act as replaces Part III of the Insolvency Act 1985 does not apply in relation to any case in which a petition in bankruptcy was presented, or a receiving order or adjudication in bankruptcy was made, before the appointed day.

(2)   In relation to any such case as is mentioned above, the enactments specified in Schedule 8 to that Act, so far as they relate to bankruptcy, and those specified in Parts III and IV of Schedule 10 to that Act, so far as they so relate, have effect without the amendments and repeals specified in those Schedules.

(3)   Where any subordinate legislation made under an enactment referred to in sub-paragraph (2) is in force immediately before the appointed day, that subordinate legislation continues to have effect on and after that day in relation to any such case as is mentioned in sub-paragraph (1).

### 11

(1)   In relation to any such case as is mentioned in paragraph 10(1) the references in any enactment or subordinate legislation to a petition, order or other matter which is provided for under the Bankruptcy Act 1914 and corresponds to a petition, order or other matter provided for under provisions of this Act replacing Part III of the Insolvency Act 1985 continue on and after the appointed day to have effect as references to the petition, order or matter provided for by the Act of 1914; but otherwise those references have effect on and after that day as references to the petition, order or matter provided for by those provisions of this Act.

(2)   Without prejudice to sub-paragraph (1), in determining for the purposes of section 279 of this Act (period of bankruptcy) or paragraph 13 below whether any person was an undischarged bankrupt at a time before the appointed day, an adjudication in bankruptcy and an annulment of a bankruptcy under the Act of 1914 are to be taken into account in the same way, respectively, as a bankruptcy order under the provisions of this Act replacing Part III of the Insolvency Act 1985 and the annulment under section 282 of this Act of such an order.

### 12

Transactions entered into before the appointed day have effect on and after that day as if references to acts of bankruptcy in the provisions for giving effect to those transactions continued to be references to acts of bankruptcy within the meaning of the Bankruptcy Act 1914, but as if such acts included failure to comply with a statutory demand served under section 268 of this Act.

### 13  Discharge from old bankruptcy

(1)   Where a person—

    (a)    was adjudged bankrupt before the appointed day or is adjudged bankrupt on or after that day on a petition presented before that day, and

    (b)    that person was not an undischarged bankrupt at any time in the period of 15 years ending with the adjudication,

that person is deemed (if not previously discharged) to be discharged from his bankruptcy for the purposes of the Bankruptcy Act 1914 at the end of the discharge period.

(2)   Subject to sub-paragraph (3) below, the discharge period for the purposes of this paragraph is—
   (a)   in the case of a person adjudged bankrupt before the appointed day, the period of 3 years beginning with that day, and
   (b)   in the case of a person who is adjudged bankrupt on or after that day on a petition presented before that day, the period of 3 years beginning with the date of the adjudication.

(3)   Where the court exercising jurisdiction in relation to a bankruptcy to which this paragraph applies is satisfied, on the application of the official receiver, that the bankrupt has failed, or is failing, to comply with any of his obligations under the Bankruptcy Act 1914, any rules made under that Act or any such rules as are mentioned in paragraph 19(1) below, the court may order that the discharge period shall cease to run for such period, or until the fulfilment of such conditions (including a condition requiring the court to be satisfied as to any matter) as may be specified in the order.

### 14 Provisions relating to trustee

(1)   This paragraph applies as regards the trustee in the case of a person adjudged bankrupt before the appointed day, or adjudged bankrupt on or after that day on a petition presented before that day.

(2)   The official receiver may at any time when he is the trustee of the bankrupt's estate apply to the Secretary of State for the appointment of a person as trustee instead of the official receiver; and on any such application the Secretary of State shall either make an appointment or decline to make one.

(3)   Where on the appointed day the trustee of a bankrupt's estate has not made an application under section 93 of the Bankruptcy Act 1914 (release of trustee), then—
   (a)   except where the Secretary of State otherwise directs, sections 298(8), 304 and 331(1) to (3) of this Act apply, and section 93 of the Act of 1914 does not apply, in relation to any trustee of the bankrupt's estate who holds office on or at any time after the appointed day and is not the official receiver;
   (b)   section 331(4) of this Act applies in relation to the carrying out at any time on or after the appointed day by the trustee of the bankrupt's estate of any of his functions; and
   (c)   a trustee in relation to whom section 298(8) of this Act has effect by virtue of this paragraph has his release with effect from the time specified in section 299(3)(d).

(4)   Subsection (5) of section 299 has effect for the purposes of sub-paragraph (3)(c) as it has for the purposes of that section.

(5)   In the application of subsection (3) of section 331 in relation to a case by virtue of this paragraph, the reference in that subsection to section 330(1) has effect as a reference to section 67 of the Bankruptcy Act 1914.

(6)   The trustee of the bankrupt's estate may employ a solicitor to assist him in the carrying out of his functions without the permission of the committee of inspection; but if he does so employ a solicitor, he shall inform the committee of inspection that he has done so.

### 15 Copyright

Where a person who is adjudged bankrupt on a petition presented on or after the appointed day is liable, by virtue of a transaction entered into before that day, to pay royalties or a share of the profits to any person in respect of any copyright or interest in copyright comprised in the bankrupt's estate, section 60 of the Bankruptcy Act 1914 (limitation on trustee's powers in relation to copyright) applies in relation to the trustee of that estate as it applies in relation to a trustee in bankruptcy under the Act of 1914.

### 16 Second bankruptcy

(1)   Sections 334 and 335 of this Act apply with the following modifications where the earlier bankruptcy (within the meaning of section 334) is a bankruptcy in relation to which the Act of 1914 applies instead of the second Group of Parts in this Act, that is to say—

(a)  references to property vested in the existing trustee under section 307(3) of this Act have effect as references to such property vested in that trustee as was acquired by or devolved on the bankrupt after the commencement (within the meaning of the Act of 1914) of the earlier bankruptcy; and

(b)  references to an order under section 310 of this Act have effect as references to an order under section 51 of the Act of 1914.

(2)   Section 39 of the Act of 1914 (second bankruptcy) does not apply where a person who is an undischarged bankrupt under that Act is adjudged bankrupt under this Act.

**17  Setting aside of preferences and other transactions**

(1)   A preference given, assignment made or other transaction entered into before the appointed day shall not be set aside under any of sections 339 to 344 of this Act except to the extent that it could have been set aside under the law in force immediately before that day.

(2)   References in sub-paragraph (1) to setting aside a preference, assignment or other transaction include the making of any order which varies or reverses any effect of a preference, assignment or other transaction.

**18  Bankruptcy offences**

(1)   Where a bankruptcy order is made under this Act on or after the appointed day, a person is not guilty of an offence under Chapter VI of Part IX in respect of anything done before that day; but, notwithstanding the repeal by the Insolvency Act 1985 of the Bankruptcy Act 1914, is guilty of an offence under the Act of 1914 in respect of anything done before the appointed day which would have been an offence under that Act if the making of the bankruptcy order had been the making of a receiving order under that Act.

(2)   Subsection (5) of section 350 of this Act applies (instead of sections 157(2), 158(2), 161 and 165 of the Act of 1914) in relation to proceedings for an offence under that Act which are instituted (whether by virtue of sub-paragraph (1) or otherwise) after the appointed day.

**19  Power to make rules**

(1)   The preceding provisions of this Part of this Schedule are without prejudice to the power conferred by this Act under which rules under section 412 may make transitional provision in connection with the coming into force of those rules; and such provision may apply those rules in relation to a bankruptcy notwithstanding that it arose from a petition presented before either the coming into force of the rules or the appointed day.

(2)   Rules under section 412 may provide for such notices served before the appointed day as may be prescribed to be treated for the purposes of this Act as statutory demands served under section 268.


PART III   TRANSITIONAL EFFECT OF PART XVI


**[1.762]**

**20**

(1)   A transaction entered into before the appointed day shall not be set aside under Part XVI of this Act except to the extent that it could have been set aside under the law in force immediately before that day.

(2)   References above to setting aside a transaction include the making of any order which varies or reverses any effect of a transaction.

## PART IV INSOLVENCY PRACTITIONERS

**[1.763]**

**21**

Where an individual began to act as an insolvency practitioner in relation to any person before the appointed day, nothing in section 390 (2) or (3) prevents that individual from being qualified to act as an insolvency practitioner in relation to that person.

## PART V GENERAL TRANSITIONAL PROVISIONS AND SAVINGS

**[1.764]**

### 22 Interpretation for this Part

In this Part of this Schedule, "the former enactments" means so much of the Companies Act 1985 as is repealed and replaced by this Act, the Insolvency Act 1985 and the other enactments repealed by this Act.

Amendments—SI 2009/1941.

### 23 General saving for past acts and events

So far as anything done or treated as done under or for the purposes of any provision of the former enactments could have been done under or for the purposes of the corresponding provision of this Act, it is not invalidated by the repeal of that provision but has effect as if done under or for the purposes of the corresponding provision; and any order, regulation, rule or other instrument made or having effect under any provision of the former enactments shall, insofar as its effect is preserved by this paragraph, be treated for all purposes as made and having effect under the corresponding provision.

### 24 Periods of time

Where any period of time specified in a provision of the former enactments is current immediately before the appointed day, this Act has effect as if the corresponding provision had been in force when the period began to run; and (without prejudice to the foregoing) any period of time so specified and current is deemed for the purposes of this Act—

    (a)    to run from the date or event from which it was running immediately before the appointed day, and

    (b)    to expire (subject to any provision of this Act for its extension) whenever it would have expired if this Act had not been passed;

and any rights, priorities, liabilities, reliefs, obligations, requirements, powers, duties or exemptions dependent on the beginning, duration or end of such a period as above mentioned shall be under this Act as they were or would have been under the former enactments.

### 25 Internal cross-references in this Act

Where in any provision of this Act there is a reference to another such provision, and the first-mentioned provision operates, or is capable of operating, in relation to things done or omitted, or events occurring or not occurring, in the past (including in particular past acts of compliance with any enactment, failures of compliance, contraventions, offences and convictions of offences), the reference to the other provision is to be read as including a reference to the corresponding provision of the former enactments.

### 26 Punishment of offences

(1) Offences committed before the appointed day under any provision of the former enactments may, notwithstanding any repeal by this Act, be prosecuted and punished after that day as if this Act had not passed.

(2) A contravention of any provision of the former enactments committed before the appointed day shall not be visited with any severer punishment under or by virtue of this Act than would have been applicable under that provision at the time of the contravention; but where an offence for the continuance of which a penalty was

provided has been committed under any provision of the former enactments, proceedings may be taken under this Act in respect of the continuance of the offence on and after the appointed day in the like manner as if the offence had been committed under the corresponding provision of this Act.

### 27 References elsewhere to the former enactments

(1) A reference in any enactment, instrument or document (whether express or implied, and in whatever phraseology) to a provision of the former enactments (including the corresponding provision of any yet earlier enactment) is to be read, where necessary to retain for the enactment, instrument or document the same force and effect as it would have had but for the passing of this Act, as, or as including, a reference to the corresponding provision by which it is replaced in this Act.

(2) The generality of the preceding sub-paragraph is not affected by any specific conversion of references made by this Act, nor by the inclusion in any provision of this Act of a reference (whether express or implied, and in whatever phraseology) to the provision of the former enactments corresponding to that provision, or to a provision of the former enactments which is replaced by a corresponding provision of this Act.

### 28 Saving for power to repeal provisions in section 51

The Secretary of State may by order in a statutory instrument repeal subsections (3) to (5) of section 51 of this Act and the entries in Schedule 10 relating to subsections (4) and (5) of that section.

### 29 Saving for Interpretation Act 1978, ss 16, 17

Nothing in this Schedule is to be taken as prejudicing sections 16 and 17 of the Interpretation Act 1978 (savings from, and effect of, repeals); and for the purposes of section 17(2) of that Act (construction of references to enactments repealed and replaced etc), so much of section 18 of the Insolvency Act 1985 as is replaced by a provision of this Act is deemed to have been repealed by this Act and not by the Company Directors Disqualification Act 1986.

# INSOLVENCY (ENGLAND AND WALES) RULES 2016

## INSOLVENCY (ENGLAND AND WALES) RULES 2016

### SI 2016/1024

#### ARRANGEMENT OF RULES

##### Introductory Rules

| | | |
|---|---|---|
| 1 | Citation and commencement | 2.1 |
| 2 | Revocations | 2.2 |
| 3 | Extent and application | 2.3 |
| 4 | Transitional and savings provisions | 2.4 |
| 5 | Power of the Secretary of State to regulate certain matters | 2.5 |
| 6 | Punishment of offences | 2.6 |
| 7 | Review | 2.7 |

#### PART 1
#### SCOPE, INTERPRETATION, TIME AND RULES ABOUT DOCUMENTS

##### CHAPTER 1
##### SCOPE OF THESE RULES

| | | |
|---|---|---|
| 1.1 | Scope | 2.8 |

##### CHAPTER 2
##### INTERPRETATION

| | | |
|---|---|---|
| Note | | 2.9 |
| 1.2 | Defined terms | 2.10 |
| 1.3 | Calculation of time periods | 2.11 |

##### CHAPTER 3
##### FORM AND CONTENT OF DOCUMENTS

| | | |
|---|---|---|
| 1.4 | Requirement for writing and form of documents | 2.12 |
| 1.5 | Authentication | 2.13 |
| 1.6 | Information required to identify persons and proceedings etc | 2.14 |
| 1.7 | Reasons for stating whether proceedings are or will be COMI proceedings, establishment proceedings etc | 2.15 |
| 1.8 | Prescribed format of documents | 2.16 |
| 1.9 | Variations from prescribed contents | 2.17 |

##### CHAPTER 4
##### STANDARD CONTENTS OF GAZETTE NOTICES AND THE GAZETTE AS EVIDENCE ETC

| | | |
|---|---|---|
| Note | | 2.18 |
| 1.10 | Contents of notices to be gazetted under the Act or Rules | 2.19 |
| 1.11 | Standard contents of all notices | 2.20 |
| 1.12 | Gazette notices relating to a company | 2.21 |
| 1.13 | Gazette notices relating to a bankruptcy | 2.22 |
| 1.14 | The Gazette: evidence, variations and errors | 2.23 |

CHAPTER 5

STANDARD CONTENTS OF NOTICES ADVERTISED OTHERWISE THAN IN
THE GAZETTE

| | | |
|---|---|---|
| Note | | 2.24 |
| 1.15 | Standard contents of notices advertised otherwise than in the Gazette | 2.25 |
| 1.16 | Non-Gazette notices relating to a company | 2.26 |
| 1.17 | Non-Gazette notices relating to a bankruptcy | 2.27 |
| 1.18 | Non-Gazette notices: other provisions | 2.28 |

CHAPTER 6

STANDARD CONTENTS OF DOCUMENTS TO BE DELIVERED TO THE REGISTRAR
OF COMPANIES

| | | |
|---|---|---|
| Note | | 2.29 |
| 1.19 | Standard contents of documents delivered to the registrar of companies | 2.30 |
| 1.20 | Registrar of companies: covering notices | 2.31 |
| 1.21 | Standard contents of all documents | 2.32 |
| 1.22 | Standard contents of documents relating to the office of office-holders | 2.33 |
| 1.23 | Standard contents of documents relating to other documents | 2.34 |
| 1.24 | Standard contents of documents relating to court orders | 2.35 |
| 1.25 | Standard contents of returns or reports of decisions | 2.36 |
| 1.26 | Standard contents of returns or reports of matters considered by company members by correspondence | 2.37 |
| 1.27 | Standard contents of documents relating to other events | 2.38 |

CHAPTER 7

STANDARD CONTENTS OF NOTICES FOR DELIVERY TO OTHER PERSONS ETC

| | | |
|---|---|---|
| Note | | 2.39 |
| 1.28 | Standard contents of notices to be delivered to persons other than the registrar of companies | 2.40 |
| 1.29 | Standard contents of all notices | 2.41 |
| 1.30 | Standard contents of notices relating to the office of office-holders | 2.42 |
| 1.31 | Standard contents of notices relating to documents | 2.43 |
| 1.32 | Standard contents of notices relating to court proceedings or orders | 2.44 |
| 1.33 | Standard contents of notices of the results of decisions | 2.45 |
| 1.34 | Standard contents of returns or reports of matters considered by company members by correspondence | 2.46 |

CHAPTER 8

APPLICATIONS TO THE COURT

| | | |
|---|---|---|
| Note | | 2.47 |
| 1.35 | Standard contents and authentication of applications to the court under Parts 1 to 11 of the Act | 2.48 |

CHAPTER 9

DELIVERY OF DOCUMENTS AND OPTING OUT (SECTIONS 246C, 248A, 379C AND 383A)

| | | |
|---|---|---|
| 1.36 | Application of Chapter | 2.49 |
| 1.37 | Delivery to the creditors and opting out | 2.50 |
| 1.38 | Creditor's election to opt out | 2.51 |
| 1.39 | Office-holder to provide information to creditors on opting-out | 2.52 |
| 1.40 | Delivery of documents to authorised recipients | 2.53 |
| 1.41 | Delivery of documents to joint office-holders | 2.54 |
| 1.42 | Postal delivery of documents | 2.55 |
| 1.43 | Delivery by document exchange | 2.56 |
| 1.44 | Personal delivery of documents | 2.57 |
| 1.45 | Electronic delivery of documents | 2.58 |
| 1.46 | Electronic delivery of documents to the court | 2.59 |
| 1.47 | Electronic delivery of notices to enforcement officers | 2.60 |
| 1.48 | Electronic delivery by office-holders | 2.61 |
| 1.49 | Use of website by office-holder to deliver a particular document (sections 246B and 379B) | 2.62 |
| 1.50 | General use of website to deliver documents | 2.63 |
| 1.51 | Retention period for documents made available on websites | 2.64 |
| 1.52 | Proof of delivery of documents | 2.65 |

1.53          Delivery of proofs and details of claims                                    2.66

CHAPTER 10

INSPECTION OF DOCUMENTS, COPIES AND PROVISION OF INFORMATION

1.54          Right to copies of documents                                                2.67
1.55          Charges for copies of documents provided by the office-holder               2.68
1.56          Offence in relation to inspection of documents                             2.69
1.57          Right to list of creditors                                                  2.70
1.58          Confidentiality of documents: grounds for refusing inspection              2.71

PART 2

COMPANY VOLUNTARY ARRANGEMENTS (CVA)

CHAPTER 1

PRELIMINARY

2.1           Interpretation                                                              2.72

CHAPTER 2

THE PROPOSAL FOR A CVA (SECTION 1)

Note                                                                                      2.73
2.2           Proposal for a CVA: general principles and amendment                        2.74
2.3           Proposal: contents                                                          2.75

CHAPTER 3

PROCEDURE FOR A CVA WITHOUT A MORATORIUM

Note                                                                                      2.76
2.4           Procedure for proposal where the nominee is not the liquidator or the
              administrator (section 2)                                                   2.77
2.5           Information for the official receiver                                       2.78
2.6           Statement of affairs (section 2(3))                                         2.79
2.7           Application to omit information from statement of affairs delivered to
              creditors                                                                   2.80
2.8           Additional disclosure for assistance of nominee where the nominee is not
              the liquidator or administrator                                             2.81
2.9           Nominee's report on proposal where the nominee is not the liquidator or
              administrator (section 2(2))                                                2.82
2.10          Replacement of nominee (section 2(4))                                       2.83

CHAPTER 4

PROCEDURE FOR A CVA WITH A MORATORIUM

Note                                                                                      2.84
2.11          Statement of affairs (paragraph 6(1)(b) of Schedule A1)                     2.85
2.12          Application to omit information from a statement of affairs                 2.86
2.13          The nominee's statement (paragraph 6(2) of Schedule A1)                     2.87
2.14          Documents filed with court to obtain a moratorium (paragraph 7(1) of
              Schedule A1)                                                                2.88
2.15          Notice and advertisement of beginning of a moratorium                      2.89
2.16          Notice of continuation of a moratorium where physical meeting of
              creditors is summoned (paragraph 8(3B) of Schedule A1)                      2.90
2.17          Notice of decision extending or further extending a moratorium (para-
              graph 36 of Schedule A1)                                                    2.91
2.18          Notice of court order extending or further extending or continuing or
              renewing a moratorium (paragraph 34(2) of Schedule A1)                      2.92
2.19          Advertisement of end of a moratorium (paragraph 11(1) of Schedule A1)       2.93
2.20          Disposal of charged property etc during a moratorium                       2.94
2.21          Withdrawal of nominee's consent to act (paragraph 25(5) of Schedule
              A1)                                                                         2.95
2.22          Application to the court to replace the nominee (paragraph 28 of
              Schedule A1)                                                                2.96
2.23          Notice of appointment of replacement nominee                               2.97
2.24          Applications to court to challenge nominee's actions etc (paragraphs 26
              and 27 of Schedule A1)                                                      2.98

CHAPTER 5

CONSIDERATION OF THE PROPOSAL BY THE COMPANY MEMBERS AND CREDITORS

| | | |
|---|---|---|
| Note | | 2.99 |
| 2.25 | Consideration of proposal: common requirements (section 3) | 2.100 |
| 2.26 | Members' consideration at a meeting | 2.101 |
| 2.27 | Creditors' consideration by a decision procedure | 2.102 |
| 2.28 | Timing of decisions on proposal | 2.103 |
| 2.29 | Creditors' approval of modified proposal | 2.104 |
| 2.30 | Notice of members' meeting and attendance of officers | 2.105 |
| 2.31 | Requisition of physical meeting by creditors | 2.106 |
| 2.32 | Non-receipt of notice by members | 2.107 |
| 2.33 | Proposal for alternative supervisor | 2.108 |
| 2.34 | Chair at meetings | 2.109 |
| 2.35 | Members' voting rights | 2.110 |
| 2.36 | Requisite majorities of members | 2.111 |
| 2.37 | Notice of order made under section 4A(6) or paragraph 36(5) of Schedule A1 | 2.112 |
| 2.38 | Report of consideration of proposal under section 4(6) and (6A) or paragraph 30(3) and (4) of Schedule A1 | 2.113 |

CHAPTER 6

ADDITIONAL MATTERS CONCERNING AND FOLLOWING APPROVAL OF CVA

| | | |
|---|---|---|
| Note | | 2.114 |
| 2.39 | Hand-over of property etc to supervisor | 2.115 |
| 2.40 | Revocation or suspension of CVA | 2.116 |
| 2.41 | Supervisor's accounts and reports | 2.117 |
| 2.42 | Production of accounts and records to the Secretary of State | 2.118 |
| 2.43 | Fees and expenses | 2.119 |
| 2.44 | Termination or full implementation of CVA | 2.120 |

CHAPTER 7

TIME RECORDING INFORMATION

| | | |
|---|---|---|
| Note | | 2.121 |
| 2.45 | Provision of information | 2.122 |

PART 3

ADMINISTRATION

CHAPTER 1

INTERPRETATION FOR THIS PART

| | | |
|---|---|---|
| Note | | 2.123 |
| 3.1 | Interpretation for Part 3 | 2.124 |
| 3.2 | Proposed administrator's statement and consent to act | 2.125 |

CHAPTER 2

APPOINTMENT OF ADMINISTRATOR BY COURT

| | | |
|---|---|---|
| Note | | 2.126 |
| 3.3 | Administration application (paragraph 12 of Schedule B1) | 2.127 |
| 3.4 | Administration application made by the directors | 2.128 |
| 3.5 | Administration application by the supervisor of a CVA | 2.129 |
| 3.6 | Witness statement in support of administration application | 2.130 |
| 3.7 | Filing of application | 2.131 |
| 3.8 | Service of application | 2.132 |
| 3.9 | Notice to enforcement agents charged with distress or other legal process, etc | 2.133 |
| 3.10 | Notice of other insolvency proceedings | 2.134 |
| 3.11 | Intervention by holder of qualifying floating charge (paragraph 36(1)(b) of Schedule B1) | 2.135 |
| 3.12 | The hearing | 2.136 |
| 3.13 | The order | 2.137 |
| 3.14 | Order on an application under paragraph 37 or 38 of Schedule B1 | 2.138 |
| 3.15 | Notice of administration order | 2.139 |

## CHAPTER 3
### APPOINTMENT OF ADMINISTRATOR BY HOLDER OF FLOATING CHARGE

| | | |
|---|---|---|
| Note | | 2.140 |
| 3.16 | Notice of intention to appoint | 2.141 |
| 3.17 | Notice of appointment | 2.142 |
| 3.18 | Filing of notice with the court | 2.143 |
| 3.19 | Appointment by floating charge holder after administration application made | 2.144 |
| 3.20 | Appointment taking place out of court business hours: procedure | 2.145 |
| 3.21 | Appointment taking place out of court business hours: content of notice | 2.146 |
| 3.22 | Appointment taking place out of court business hours: legal effect | 2.147 |

## CHAPTER 4
### APPOINTMENT OF ADMINISTRATOR BY COMPANY OR DIRECTORS

| | | |
|---|---|---|
| Note | | 2.148 |
| 3.23 | Notice of intention to appoint | 2.149 |
| 3.24 | Notice of appointment after notice of intention to appoint | 2.150 |
| 3.25 | Notice of appointment without prior notice of intention to appoint | 2.151 |
| 3.26 | Notice of appointment: filing with the court | 2.152 |

## CHAPTER 5
### NOTICE OF ADMINISTRATOR'S APPOINTMENT

| | | |
|---|---|---|
| Note | | 2.153 |
| 3.27 | Publication of administrator's appointment | 2.154 |

## CHAPTER 6
### STATEMENT OF AFFAIRS

| | | |
|---|---|---|
| Note | | 2.155 |
| 3.28 | Interpretation | 2.156 |
| 3.29 | Statement of affairs: notice requiring and delivery to the administrator (paragraph 47(1) of Schedule B1) | 2.157 |
| 3.30 | Statement of affairs: content (paragraph 47 of Schedule B1) | 2.158 |
| 3.31 | Statement of affairs: statement of concurrence | 2.159 |
| 3.32 | Statement of affairs: filing | 2.160 |
| 3.33 | Statement of affairs: release from requirement and extension of time | 2.161 |
| 3.34 | Statement of affairs: expenses | 2.162 |

## CHAPTER 7
### ADMINISTRATOR'S PROPOSALS

| | | |
|---|---|---|
| Note | | 2.163 |
| 3.35 | Administrator's proposals: additional content | 2.164 |
| 3.36 | Administrator's proposals: statement of pre-administration costs | 2.165 |
| 3.37 | Advertising administrator's proposals and notices of extension of time for delivery of proposals (paragraph 49 of Schedule B1) | 2.166 |
| 3.38 | Seeking approval of the administrator's proposals | 2.167 |
| 3.39 | Invitation to creditors to form a creditors' committee | 2.168 |
| 3.40 | Notice of extension of time to seek approval | 2.169 |
| 3.41 | Notice of the creditors' decision on the administrator's proposals (paragraph 53(2)) | 2.170 |
| 3.42 | Administrator's proposals: revision | 2.171 |
| 3.43 | Notice of result of creditors' decision on revised proposals (paragraph 54(6)) | 2.172 |

## CHAPTER 8
### LIMITED DISCLOSURE OF STATEMENTS OF AFFAIRS AND PROPOSALS

| | | |
|---|---|---|
| Note | | 2.173 |
| 3.44 | Application of Chapter | 2.174 |
| 3.45 | Orders limiting disclosure of statement of affairs etc | 2.175 |
| 3.46 | Order for disclosure by administrator | 2.176 |
| 3.47 | Rescission or amendment of order for limited disclosure | 2.177 |
| 3.48 | Publication etc of statement of affairs or statement of proposals | 2.178 |

## CHAPTER 9
### DISPOSAL OF CHARGED PROPERTY

| | | |
|---|---|---|
| Note | | 2.179 |
| 3.49 | Disposal of charged property | 2.180 |

## CHAPTER 10
### EXPENSES OF THE ADMINISTRATION

| | | |
|---|---|---|
| Note | | 2.181 |
| 3.50 | Expenses | 2.182 |
| 3.51 | Order of priority | 2.183 |
| 3.52 | Pre-administration costs | 2.184 |

## CHAPTER 11
### EXTENSION AND ENDING OF ADMINISTRATION

| | | |
|---|---|---|
| Note | | 2.185 |
| 3.53 | Interpretation | 2.186 |
| 3.54 | Application to extend an administration and extension by consent (paragraph 76(2) of Schedule B1) | 2.187 |
| 3.55 | Notice of automatic end of administration (paragraph 76 of Schedule B1) | 2.188 |
| 3.56 | Notice of end of administration when purposes achieved (paragraph 80(2) of Schedule B1) | 2.189 |
| 3.57 | Administrator's application for order ending administration (paragraph 79 of Schedule B1) | 2.190 |
| 3.58 | Creditor's application for order ending administration (paragraph 81 of Schedule B1) | 2.191 |
| 3.59 | Notice by administrator of court order | 2.192 |
| 3.60 | Moving from administration to creditors' voluntary winding up (paragraph 83 of Schedule B1) | 2.193 |
| 3.61 | Moving from administration to dissolution (paragraph 84 of Schedule B1) | 2.194 |

## CHAPTER 12
### REPLACING THE ADMINISTRATOR

| | | |
|---|---|---|
| Note | | 2.195 |
| 3.62 | Grounds for resignation | 2.196 |
| 3.63 | Notice of intention to resign | 2.197 |
| 3.64 | Notice of resignation (paragraph 87 of Schedule B1) | 2.198 |
| 3.65 | Application to court to remove administrator from office | 2.199 |
| 3.66 | Notice of vacation of office when administrator ceases to be qualified to act | 2.200 |
| 3.67 | Deceased administrator | 2.201 |
| 3.68 | Application to replace | 2.202 |
| 3.69 | Appointment of replacement or additional administrator | 2.203 |
| 3.70 | Administrator's duties on vacating office | 2.204 |

## PART 4
### RECEIVERSHIP

| | | |
|---|---|---|
| Note | | 2.205 |

## CHAPTER 1
### APPOINTMENT OF JOINT RECEIVERS OR MANAGERS TO WHOM PART 3 OF THE ACT APPLIES (OTHER THAN THOSE APPOINTED UNDER SECTION 51 (SCOTTISH RECEIVERSHIPS))

| | | |
|---|---|---|
| Note | | 2.206 |
| 4.1 | Receivers or managers appointed under an instrument: acceptance of appointment (section 33) | 2.207 |

## CHAPTER 2
### ADMINISTRATIVE RECEIVERS (OTHER THAN IN SCOTTISH RECEIVERSHIPS)

| | | |
|---|---|---|
| Note | | 2.208 |

| | | |
|---|---|---|
| 4.2 | Application of Chapter 2 | 2.209 |
| 4.3 | Interpretation | 2.210 |
| 4.4 | Administrative receiver's security | 2.211 |
| 4.5 | Publication of appointment of administrative receiver (section 46(1)) | 2.212 |
| 4.6 | Requirement to provide a statement of affairs (section 47(1)) | 2.213 |
| 4.7 | Statement of affairs: contents and delivery of copy (section 47(2)) | 2.214 |
| 4.8 | Statement of affairs: statement of concurrence | 2.215 |
| 4.9 | Statement of affairs: retention by administrative receiver | 2.216 |
| 4.10 | Statement of affairs: release from requirement and extension of time (section 47(5)) | 2.217 |
| 4.11 | Statement of affairs: expenses | 2.218 |
| 4.12 | Limited disclosure | 2.219 |
| 4.13 | Administrative receiver's report to the registrar of companies and secured creditors (section 48(1)) | 2.220 |
| 4.14 | Copy of report for unsecured creditors (section 48(2)) | 2.221 |
| 4.15 | Invitation to creditors to form a creditors' committee | 2.222 |
| 4.16 | Disposal of charged property (section 43(1)) | 2.223 |
| 4.17 | Summary of receipts and payments | 2.224 |
| 4.18 | Resignation | 2.225 |
| 4.19 | Deceased administrative receiver | 2.226 |
| 4.20 | Other vacation of office | 2.227 |
| 4.21 | Notice to registrar of companies (section 45(4)) | 2.228 |

CHAPTER 3

NON-ADMINISTRATIVE RECEIVERS AND THE PRESCRIBED PART

| | | |
|---|---|---|
| Note | | 2.229 |
| 4.22 | Application of Chapter 3 | 2.230 |
| 4.23 | Report to creditors | 2.231 |
| 4.24 | Receiver to deal with prescribed part | 2.232 |

PART 5

MEMBERS' VOLUNTARY WINDING UP

CHAPTER 1

STATUTORY DECLARATION OF SOLVENCY (SECTION 89)

| | | |
|---|---|---|
| Note | | 2.233 |
| 5.1 | Statutory declaration of solvency: requirements additional to those in section 89 | 2.234 |

CHAPTER 2

THE LIQUIDATOR

| | | |
|---|---|---|
| Note | | 2.235 |
| 5.2 | Appointment by the company | 2.236 |
| 5.3 | Meetings in members' voluntary winding up of authorised deposit-takers | 2.237 |
| 5.4 | Appointment by the court (section 108) | 2.238 |
| 5.5 | Cost of liquidator's security (section 390(3)) | 2.239 |
| 5.6 | Liquidator's resignation | 2.240 |
| 5.7 | Removal of liquidator by the court | 2.241 |
| 5.8 | Removal of liquidator by company meeting | 2.242 |
| 5.9 | Delivery of proposed final account to members (section 94) | 2.243 |
| 5.10 | Final account prior to dissolution (section 94) | 2.244 |
| 5.11 | Deceased liquidator | 2.245 |
| 5.12 | Loss of qualification as insolvency practitioner | 2.246 |
| 5.13 | Liquidator's duties on vacating office | 2.247 |
| 5.14 | Application by former liquidator to the Secretary of State for release (section 173(2)(b)) | 2.248 |
| 5.15 | Power of court to set aside certain transactions entered into by liquidator | 2.249 |
| 5.16 | Rule against improper solicitation by or on behalf of the liquidator | 2.250 |

CHAPTER 3

SPECIAL MANAGER

| | | |
|---|---|---|
| Note | | 2.251 |
| 5.17 | Application for and appointment of special manager (section 177) | 2.252 |

| | | |
|---|---|---|
| 5.18 | Security | 2.253 |
| 5.19 | Failure to give or keep up security | 2.254 |
| 5.20 | Accounting | 2.255 |
| 5.21 | Termination of appointment | 2.256 |

CHAPTER 4

CONVERSION TO CREDITORS' VOLUNTARY WINDING UP

| | | |
|---|---|---|
| 5.22 | Statement of affairs (section 95(3)) | 2.257 |

PART 6

CREDITORS' VOLUNTARY WINDING UP

CHAPTER 1

APPLICATION OF PART 6

| | | |
|---|---|---|
| 6.1 | Application of Part 6 | 2.259 |

CHAPTER 2

STATEMENT OF AFFAIRS AND OTHER INFORMATION

| | | |
|---|---|---|
| Note | | 2.260 |
| 6.2 | Statement of affairs made out by the liquidator under section 95(1A) | 2.261 |
| 6.3 | Statement of affairs made out by the directors under section 99(1) | 2.262 |
| 6.4 | Additional requirements as to statements of affairs | 2.263 |
| 6.5 | Statement of affairs: statement of concurrence | 2.264 |
| 6.6 | Order limiting disclosure of statement of affairs etc | 2.265 |
| 6.7 | Expenses of statement of affairs and decisions sought from creditors | 2.266 |
| 6.8 | Delivery of accounts to liquidator (section 235) | 2.267 |
| 6.9 | Expenses of assistance in preparing accounts | 2.268 |

CHAPTER 3

NOMINATION AND APPOINTMENT OF LIQUIDATORS AND INFORMATION TO CREDI-TORS

| | | |
|---|---|---|
| Note | | 2.269 |
| 6.10 | Application of the rules in this Chapter | 2.270 |
| 6.11 | Nomination of liquidator and information to creditors on conversion from members' voluntary winding up (section 96) | 2.271 |
| 6.12 | Creditors' decision on appointment other than at a meeting (conversion from members' voluntary winding up) | 2.272 |
| 6.13 | Information to creditors and contributories (conversion of members' voluntary winding up into creditors' voluntary winding up) | 2.273 |
| 6.14 | Information to creditors and appointment of liquidator | 2.274 |
| 6.15 | Information to creditors and contributories | 2.275 |
| 6.16 | Further information where administrator becomes liquidator (paragraph 83(3) of Schedule B1) | 2.276 |
| 6.17 | Report by director etc | 2.277 |
| 6.18 | Decisions on nomination | 2.278 |
| 6.19 | Invitation to creditors to form a liquidation committee | 2.279 |

CHAPTER 4

THE LIQUIDATOR

| | | |
|---|---|---|
| Note | | 2.280 |
| 6.20 | Appointment by creditors or by the company | 2.281 |
| 6.21 | Power to fill vacancy in office of liquidator | 2.282 |
| 6.22 | Appointment by the court (section 100(3) or 108) | 2.283 |
| 6.23 | Advertisement of appointment | 2.284 |
| 6.24 | Cost of liquidator's security (section 390(3)) | 2.285 |
| 6.25 | Liquidator's resignation and replacement | 2.286 |
| 6.26 | Removal of liquidator by creditors | 2.287 |
| 6.27 | Removal of liquidator by the court | 2.288 |
| 6.28 | Final account prior to dissolution (section 106) | 2.289 |
| 6.29 | Deceased liquidator | 2.290 |
| 6.30 | Loss of qualification as insolvency practitioner | 2.291 |
| 6.31 | Vacation of office on making of winding-up order | 2.292 |
| 6.32 | Liquidator's duties on vacating office | 2.293 |
| 6.33 | Application by former liquidator for release (section 173(2)(b)) | 2.294 |
| 6.34 | Power of court to set aside certain transactions | 2.295 |

| | | |
|---|---|---|
| 6.35 | Rule against improper solicitation | 2.296 |
| 6.36 | Permission for exercise of powers by liquidator | 2.297 |

CHAPTER 5
SPECIAL MANAGER

| | | |
|---|---|---|
| Note | | 2.298 |
| 6.37 | Application for and appointment of special manager (section 177) | 2.299 |
| 6.38 | Security | 2.300 |
| 6.39 | Failure to give or keep up security | 2.301 |
| 6.40 | Accounting | 2.302 |
| 6.41 | Termination of appointment | 2.303 |

CHAPTER 6
PRIORITY OF PAYMENT OF COSTS AND EXPENSES, ETC

| | | |
|---|---|---|
| 6.42 | General rule as to priority | 2.305 |
| 6.43 | Saving for powers of the court | 2.306 |

CHAPTER 7
LITIGATION EXPENSES AND PROPERTY SUBJECT TO A FLOATING CHARGE

| | | |
|---|---|---|
| Note | | 2.307 |
| 6.44 | Interpretation | 2.308 |
| 6.45 | Requirement for approval or authorisation | 2.309 |
| 6.46 | Request for approval or authorisation | 2.310 |
| 6.47 | Grant of approval or authorisation | 2.311 |
| 6.48 | Application to the court by the liquidator | 2.312 |

PART 7
WINDING UP BY THE COURT

CHAPTER 1
APPLICATION OF PART

| | | |
|---|---|---|
| 7.1 | Application of Part 7 | 2.314 |

CHAPTER 2
THE STATUTORY DEMAND (SECTIONS 123(1)(A) AND 222(1)(A))

| | | |
|---|---|---|
| 7.2 | Interpretation | 2.315 |
| 7.3 | The statutory demand | 2.316 |

CHAPTER 3
PETITION FOR WINDING-UP ORDER

| | | |
|---|---|---|
| Note | | 2.317 |
| 7.4 | Application of this Chapter | 2.318 |
| 7.5 | Contents of petition | 2.319 |
| 7.6 | Verification of petition | 2.320 |
| 7.7 | Petition: presentation and filing | 2.321 |
| 7.8 | Court to which petition is to be presented where the company is subject to a CVA or is in administration | 2.322 |
| 7.9 | Copies of petition to be served on company or delivered to other persons | 2.323 |
| 7.10 | Notice of petition | 2.324 |
| 7.11 | Persons entitled to request a copy of petition | 2.325 |
| 7.12 | Certificate of compliance | 2.326 |
| 7.13 | Permission for the petitioner to withdraw | 2.327 |
| 7.14 | Notice by persons intending to appear | 2.328 |
| 7.15 | List of appearances | 2.329 |
| 7.16 | Witness statement in opposition | 2.330 |
| 7.17 | Substitution of creditor or contributory for petitioner | 2.331 |
| 7.18 | Order for substitution of petitioner | 2.332 |
| 7.19 | Notice of adjournment | 2.333 |
| 7.20 | Order for winding up by the court | 2.334 |
| 7.21 | Notice to official receiver of winding-up order | 2.335 |
| 7.22 | Delivery and notice of the order | 2.336 |
| 7.23 | Petition dismissed | 2.337 |
| 7.24 | Injunction to restrain presentation or notice of petition | 2.338 |

CHAPTER 4

PETITION BY A CONTRIBUTORY OR A RELEVANT OFFICE-HOLDER

| | | |
|---|---|---:|
| Note | | 2.339 |
| 7.25 | Interpretation and application of rules in Chapter 3 | 2.340 |
| 7.26 | Contents of petition for winding-up order by a contributory | 2.341 |
| 7.27 | Petition presented by a relevant office-holder | 2.342 |
| 7.28 | Verification of petition | 2.343 |
| 7.29 | Presentation and service of petition | 2.344 |
| 7.30 | Request to appoint former administrator or supervisor as liquidator (section 140) | 2.345 |
| 7.31 | Hearing of petition | 2.346 |
| 7.32 | Order for winding up by the court of a company in administration or where there is a supervisor of a CVA in relation to the company | 2.347 |

CHAPTER 5

PROVISIONAL LIQUIDATOR

| | | |
|---|---|---:|
| Note | | 2.348 |
| 7.33 | Application for appointment of provisional liquidator (section 135) | 2.349 |
| 7.34 | Deposit by applicant | 2.350 |
| 7.35 | Order of appointment of provisional liquidator | 2.351 |
| 7.36 | Notice of appointment of provisional liquidator | 2.352 |
| 7.37 | Security | 2.353 |
| 7.38 | Remuneration | 2.354 |
| 7.39 | Termination of appointment | 2.355 |

CHAPTER 6

STATEMENT OF AFFAIRS AND OTHER INFORMATION

| | | |
|---|---|---:|
| Note | | 2.356 |
| 7.40 | Notice requiring statement of affairs (section 131) | 2.357 |
| 7.41 | Statement of affairs | 2.358 |
| 7.42 | Statement of affairs: statement of concurrence | 2.359 |
| 7.43 | Order limiting disclosure of statement of affairs etc | 2.360 |
| 7.44 | Release from duty to submit statement of affairs: extension of time (section 131) | 2.361 |
| 7.45 | Statement of affairs: expenses | 2.362 |
| 7.46 | Delivery of accounts to official receiver | 2.363 |
| 7.47 | Further disclosure | 2.364 |

CHAPTER 7

REPORTS AND INFORMATION TO CREDITORS AND CONTRIBUTORIES

| | | |
|---|---|---:|
| Note | | 2.365 |
| 7.48 | Reports by official receiver | 2.366 |
| 7.49 | Reports by official receiver: estimate of prescribed part | 2.367 |
| 7.50 | Further information where winding up follows administration | 2.368 |
| 7.51 | Notice of stay of winding up | 2.369 |

CHAPTER 8

THE LIQUIDATOR

| | | |
|---|---|---:|
| Note | | 2.370 |
| 7.52 | Choosing a person to be liquidator | 2.371 |
| 7.53 | Appointment of liquidator by creditors or contributories | 2.372 |
| 7.54 | Decision on nomination | 2.373 |
| 7.55 | Invitation to creditors and contributories to form a liquidation committee | 2.374 |
| 7.56 | Appointment by the court | 2.375 |
| 7.57 | Appointment by the Secretary of State | 2.376 |
| 7.58 | Cost of liquidator's security (section 390(3)) | 2.377 |
| 7.59 | Appointment to be gazetted and notice given to registrar of companies | 2.378 |
| 7.60 | Hand-over of assets by official receiver to liquidator | 2.379 |
| 7.61 | Liquidator's resignation | 2.380 |
| 7.62 | Notice to official receiver of intention to vacate office | 2.381 |
| 7.63 | Decision of creditors to remove liquidator | 2.382 |
| 7.64 | Procedure on removal by creditors | 2.383 |

| 7.65 | Removal of liquidator by the court (section 172(2)) | 2.384 |
| 7.66 | Removal of liquidator by the Secretary of State (section 172(4)) | 2.385 |
| 7.67 | Deceased liquidator | 2.386 |
| 7.68 | Loss of qualification as insolvency practitioner | 2.387 |
| 7.69 | Application by liquidator for release (section 174(4)(b) or (d)) | 2.388 |
| 7.70 | Release of official receiver | 2.389 |
| 7.71 | Final account prior to dissolution (section 146) | 2.390 |
| 7.72 | Relief from, or variation of, duty to report | 2.391 |
| 7.73 | Liquidator's duties on vacating office | 2.392 |
| 7.74 | Power of court to set aside certain transactions | 2.393 |
| 7.75 | Rule against improper solicitation | 2.394 |

CHAPTER 9

DUTIES AND POWERS OF LIQUIDATOR

| Note | | 2.395 |
| 7.76 | General duties of liquidator | 2.396 |
| 7.77 | Permission for exercise of powers by liquidator | 2.397 |
| 7.78 | Enforced delivery up of company's property (section 234) | 2.398 |

CHAPTER 10

SETTLEMENT OF LIST OF CONTRIBUTORIES

| Note | | 2.399 |
| 7.79 | Delegation to liquidator of power to settle list of contributories | 2.400 |
| 7.80 | Duty of liquidator to settle list (section 148) | 2.401 |
| 7.81 | Contents of list | 2.402 |
| 7.82 | Procedure for settling list | 2.403 |
| 7.83 | Application to court for variation of the list | 2.404 |
| 7.84 | Variation of, or addition to, the list | 2.405 |
| 7.85 | Costs of applications to vary etc the list of contributories | 2.406 |

CHAPTER 11

CALLS ON CONTRIBUTORIES

| Note | | 2.407 |
| 7.86 | Making of calls by the liquidator (sections 150 and 160) | 2.408 |
| 7.87 | Sanction of the liquidation committee for making a call | 2.409 |
| 7.88 | Application to court for permission to make a call (sections 150 and 160) | 2.410 |
| 7.89 | Order giving permission to make a call | 2.411 |
| 7.90 | Making and enforcement of the call | 2.412 |
| 7.91 | Court order to enforce payment of call by a contributory | 2.413 |

CHAPTER 12

SPECIAL MANAGER

| Note | | 2.414 |
| 7.92 | Application of this Chapter and interpretation | 2.415 |
| 7.93 | Appointment and remuneration of special manager (section 177) | 2.416 |
| 7.94 | Security | 2.417 |
| 7.95 | Failure to give or keep up security | 2.418 |
| 7.96 | Accounting | 2.419 |
| 7.97 | Termination of appointment | 2.420 |

CHAPTER 13

PUBLIC EXAMINATION OF COMPANY OFFICERS AND OTHERS (SECTION 133)

| Note | | 2.421 |
| 7.98 | Applications relating to promoters, past managers etc (section 133(1)(c)) | 2.422 |
| 7.99 | Request by a creditor for a public examination (section 133(2)) | 2.423 |
| 7.100 | Request by a contributory for a public examination | 2.424 |
| 7.101 | Further provisions about requests by a creditor or contributory for a public examination | 2.425 |
| 7.102 | Order for public examination | 2.426 |
| 7.103 | Notice of the public examination | 2.427 |
| 7.104 | Examinee unfit for examination | 2.428 |
| 7.105 | Procedure at public examination | 2.429 |
| 7.106 | Adjournment | 2.430 |

| | | |
|---|---|---|
| 7.107 | Expenses of examination | 2.431 |

CHAPTER 14

PRIORITY OF PAYMENT OF COSTS AND EXPENSES, ETC

| | | |
|---|---|---|
| 7.108 | General rule as to priority | 2.433 |
| 7.109 | Winding up commencing as voluntary | 2.434 |
| 7.110 | Saving for powers of the court (section 156) | 2.435 |

CHAPTER 15

LITIGATION EXPENSES AND PROPERTY SUBJECT TO A FLOATING CHARGE

| | | |
|---|---|---|
| Note | | 2.436 |
| 7.111 | Interpretation | 2.437 |
| 7.112 | Priority of litigation expenses | 2.438 |
| 7.113 | Requirement for approval or authorisation of litigation expenses | 2.439 |
| 7.114 | Requests for approval or authorisation | 2.440 |
| 7.115 | Grant of approval or authorisation | 2.441 |
| 7.116 | Application to the court by the liquidator | 2.442 |

CHAPTER 16

MISCELLANEOUS RULES

| | | |
|---|---|---|
| Note | | 2.443 |

*Sub-division A: Return of capital*

| | | |
|---|---|---|
| 7.117 | Application to court for order authorising return of capital | 2.444 |
| 7.118 | Procedure for return | 2.445 |

*Sub-division B: Dissolution after winding up*

| | | |
|---|---|---|
| 7.119 | Secretary of State's directions under sections 203 and 205 and appeal | 2.446 |

PART 8

INDIVIDUAL VOLUNTARY ARRANGEMENTS (IVA)

CHAPTER 1

PRELIMINARY

| | | |
|---|---|---|
| 8.1 | Interpretation | 2.447 |

CHAPTER 2

PREPARATION OF THE DEBTOR'S PROPOSAL FOR AN IVA

| | | |
|---|---|---|
| Note | | 2.448 |
| 8.2 | Proposal for an IVA: general principles and amendment | 2.449 |
| 8.3 | Proposal: contents | 2.450 |
| 8.4 | Notice of nominee's consent | 2.451 |
| 8.5 | Statement of affairs (section 256 and 256A) | 2.452 |
| 8.6 | Application to omit information from statement of affairs delivered to creditors | 2.453 |
| 8.7 | Additional disclosure for assistance of nominee | 2.454 |

CHAPTER 3

CASES IN WHICH AN APPLICATION FOR AN INTERIM ORDER IS MADE

| | | |
|---|---|---|
| Note | | 2.455 |
| 8.8 | Application for interim order | 2.456 |
| 8.9 | Court in which application is to be made | 2.457 |
| 8.10 | Order granting a stay | 2.458 |
| 8.11 | Hearing of the application | 2.459 |
| 8.12 | The interim order | 2.460 |
| 8.13 | Action to follow making of an interim order | 2.461 |
| 8.14 | Order extending period of an interim order (section 256(4)) | 2.462 |
| 8.15 | Nominee's report on the proposal | 2.463 |
| 8.16 | Order extending period of interim order to enable the creditors to consider the proposal (section 256(5)) | 2.464 |
| 8.17 | Replacement of the nominee (section 256(3)) | 2.465 |
| 8.18 | Consideration of the nominee's report | 2.466 |

CHAPTER 4

CASES WHERE NO INTERIM ORDER IS TO BE OBTAINED

| | | |
|---|---|---|
| Note | | 2.467 |
| 8.19 | Nominee's report (section 256A) | 2.468 |
| 8.20 | Court or hearing centre to which applications must be made where no interim order | 2.469 |
| 8.21 | Replacement of the nominee (section 256A(4)) | 2.470 |

CHAPTER 5

CONSIDERATION OF THE PROPOSAL BY THE CREDITORS

| | | |
|---|---|---|
| Note | | 2.471 |
| 8.22 | Consideration of the proposal | 2.472 |
| 8.23 | Proposals for an alternative supervisor | 2.473 |
| 8.24 | Report of the creditors' consideration of a proposal | 2.474 |

CHAPTER 6

ACTION FOLLOWING APPROVAL OF AN IVA

| | | |
|---|---|---|
| Note | | 2.475 |
| 8.25 | Hand-over of property, etc to supervisor | 2.476 |
| 8.26 | Report to the Secretary of State of the approval of an IVA | 2.477 |
| 8.27 | Revocation or suspension of an IVA (section 262) | 2.478 |
| 8.28 | Supervisor's accounts and reports | 2.479 |
| 8.29 | Production of accounts and records to the Secretary of State | 2.480 |
| 8.30 | Fees and expenses | 2.481 |
| 8.31 | Termination or full implementation of the IVA | 2.482 |

CHAPTER 7

APPLICATIONS TO ANNUL BANKRUPTCY ORDERS UNDER SECTION 261(2)(A) AND (B)

| | | |
|---|---|---|
| Note | | 2.483 |
| 8.32 | Application by the bankrupt to annul the bankruptcy order (section 261(2)(a)) | 2.484 |
| 8.33 | Application by the official receiver to annul the bankruptcy order (section 261(2)(b)) | 2.485 |
| 8.34 | Order annulling bankruptcy | 2.486 |
| 8.35 | Notice of order | 2.487 |
| 8.36 | Advertisement of order | 2.488 |
| 8.37 | Trustee's final account | 2.489 |

CHAPTER 8

TIME RECORDING INFORMATION

| | | |
|---|---|---|
| Note | | 2.490 |
| 8.38 | Provision of information | 2.491 |

PART 9

DEBT RELIEF ORDERS

CHAPTER 1

INTERPRETATION

| | | |
|---|---|---|
| Note | | 2.492 |
| 9.1 | Debtor's family | 2.493 |
| 9.2 | Excluded debts | 2.494 |

CHAPTER 2

APPLICATION FOR A DEBT RELIEF ORDER

| | | |
|---|---|---|
| Note | | 2.495 |
| 9.3 | Application for a debt relief order: information required in the application | 2.496 |
| 9.4 | Delivery of application | 2.497 |
| 9.5 | Role of approved intermediary | 2.498 |

CHAPTER 3

VERIFYING THE APPLICATION AND DETERMINING THE DEBTOR'S INCOME AND PROPERTY

| | | |
|---|---|---|
| 9.6 | Prescribed verification checks: conditions in paragraphs 1 to 8 of Schedule 4ZA of the Act | 2.499 |
| 9.7 | Determination of debtor's monthly surplus income | 2.500 |
| 9.8 | Determination of value of the debtor's property (paragraph 8 of Schedule 4ZA) | 2.501 |
| 9.9 | Property to be excluded in determining the value of a debtor's property | 2.502 |

CHAPTER 4

MAKING OR REFUSAL OF A DEBT RELIEF ORDER

| | | |
|---|---|---|
| Note | | 2.503 |
| 9.10 | Contents of debt relief order | 2.504 |
| 9.11 | Other steps to be taken by official receiver or debtor upon making of the order | 2.505 |
| 9.12 | Prescribed information for creditors on making of debt relief order | 2.506 |
| 9.13 | Refusal of application for debt relief order | 2.507 |

CHAPTER 5

OBJECTION AND REVOCATION

| | | |
|---|---|---|
| Note | | 2.508 |
| 9.14 | Meaning of "creditor" | 2.509 |
| 9.15 | Creditor's objection to a debt relief order (section 251K) | 2.510 |
| 9.16 | Official receiver's response to objection under section 251K | 2.511 |
| 9.17 | Creditor's request that a debt relief order be revoked (section 251L(4)) | 2.512 |
| 9.18 | Procedure in revoking or amending a debt relief order (section 251L) | 2.513 |
| 9.19 | Debtor's notification of official receiver of matters in section 251J(3) or (5) | 2.514 |
| 9.20 | Death of debtor during a moratorium period under a debt relief order | 2.515 |

CHAPTER 6

APPLICATIONS TO THE COURT

| | | |
|---|---|---|
| Note | | 2.516 |
| 9.21 | Notice of application to court under section 251M | 2.517 |
| 9.22 | Court in which applications under sections 251M or 251N are to be made | 2.518 |
| 9.23 | Creditor's bankruptcy petition: creditor consents to making application for a debt relief order | 2.519 |
| 9.24 | Extension of moratorium period | 2.520 |

CHAPTER 7

PERMISSION TO ACT AS A DIRECTOR, ETC

| | | |
|---|---|---|
| Note | | 2.521 |
| 9.25 | Application for permission under the Company Directors Disqualification Act 1986 | 2.522 |
| 9.26 | Report of official receiver | 2.523 |
| 9.27 | Court's order on application | 2.524 |

PART 10

BANKRUPTCY

CHAPTER 1

THE STATUTORY DEMAND

| | | |
|---|---|---|
| Note | | 2.525 |
| 10.1 | The statutory demand (section 268) | 2.526 |
| 10.2 | Service of statutory demand | 2.527 |
| 10.3 | Proof of service of statutory demand | 2.528 |
| 10.4 | Application to set aside statutory demand | 2.529 |
| 10.5 | Hearing of application to set aside | 2.530 |

## CHAPTER 2
### CREDITORS' BANKRUPTCY PETITIONS
*Preliminary*

| | | |
|---|---|---|
| Note | | 2.531 |
| 10.6 | Application and interpretation | 2.532 |
| 10.7 | Contents of petition | 2.533 |
| 10.8 | Identification of debtor | 2.534 |
| 10.9 | Identification of debt | 2.535 |
| 10.10 | Verification of petition | 2.536 |
| 10.11 | Court in which petition is to be presented | 2.537 |
| 10.12 | Procedure for presentation and filing of petition | 2.538 |
| 10.13 | Application to Chief Land Registrar to register petition | 2.539 |
| 10.14 | Service of petition and delivery of copies | 2.540 |
| 10.15 | Death of debtor before service | 2.541 |
| 10.16 | Amendment of petition | 2.542 |
| 10.17 | Security for costs | 2.543 |
| 10.18 | Debtor's notice of opposition to petition | 2.544 |
| 10.19 | Notice by persons intending to appear | 2.545 |
| 10.20 | List of appearances | 2.546 |
| 10.21 | Hearing of petition | 2.547 |
| 10.22 | Postponement of hearing | 2.548 |
| 10.23 | Adjournment of the hearing | 2.549 |
| 10.24 | Decision on the hearing | 2.550 |
| 10.25 | Vacating registration on withdrawal of petition | 2.551 |
| 10.26 | Non-appearance of petitioning creditor | 2.552 |
| 10.27 | Substitution of petitioner | 2.553 |
| 10.28 | Order for substitution of petitioner | 2.554 |
| 10.29 | Change of carriage of petition | 2.555 |
| | | |
| Note | | 2.556 |
| 10.30 | Petitioner seeking dismissal or permission to withdraw | 2.557 |
| 10.31 | Contents of bankruptcy order | 2.558 |
| 10.32 | Delivery and notice of the order | 2.559 |
| 10.33 | Application to Chief Land Registrar to register bankruptcy order | 2.560 |

## CHAPTER 3
### DEBTORS' BANKRUPTCY APPLICATIONS

| | | |
|---|---|---|
| Note | | 2.561 |
| 10.34 | Preliminary | 2.562 |
| 10.35 | Bankruptcy application for a bankruptcy order | 2.563 |
| 10.36 | Procedure for making a bankruptcy application and communication with the adjudicator | 2.564 |
| 10.37 | Application to the Chief Land Registrar to register a bankruptcy application | 2.565 |
| 10.38 | Verification checks | 2.566 |
| 10.39 | Determination of the bankruptcy application | 2.567 |
| 10.40 | The determination period | 2.568 |
| 10.41 | Settlement and contents of bankruptcy order | 2.569 |
| 10.42 | Refusal to make a bankruptcy order and contents of notice of refusal | 2.570 |
| 10.43 | Review of refusal to make a bankruptcy order | 2.571 |
| 10.44 | Appeal to the court following a review of refusal to make a bankruptcy order | 2.572 |
| 10.45 | Action to follow making of order | 2.573 |
| 10.46 | Application to the Chief Land Registrar | 2.574 |
| 10.47 | The bankruptcy file | 2.575 |
| 10.48 | Court to which applications are to be made | 2.576 |

## CHAPTER 4
### THE INTERIM RECEIVER

| | | |
|---|---|---|
| Note | | 2.577 |
| 10.49 | Application for appointment of interim receiver (section 286) | 2.578 |
| 10.50 | Deposit | 2.579 |
| 10.51 | Order of appointment | 2.580 |

| 10.52 | Security | 2.581 |
| 10.53 | Remuneration | 2.582 |
| 10.54 | Termination of appointment | 2.583 |

CHAPTER 5

DISCLOSURE OF THE BANKRUPT'S AFFAIRS

| Note | | 2.584 |

*Sub-division A: creditor's petition*

| 10.55 | Notice requiring statement of affairs (section 288) | 2.585 |
| 10.56 | Statement of affairs | 2.586 |
| 10.57 | Limited disclosure | 2.587 |
| 10.58 | Requirement to submit statement of affairs and extension of time (section 288(3)) | 2.588 |
| 10.59 | Expenses of assisting bankrupt to prepare statement of affairs | 2.589 |
| 10.60 | Delivery of accounts to official receiver | 2.590 |
| 10.61 | Further disclosure | 2.591 |

*Sub-division B: Bankruptcy application*

| 10.62 | Preliminary | 2.592 |
| 10.63 | Delivery of accounts to official receiver | 2.593 |
| 10.64 | Expenses of preparing accounts | 2.594 |
| 10.65 | Further disclosure | 2.595 |

*Sub-division C: Reports by the official receiver*

| 10.66 | Reports by the official receiver | 2.596 |

CHAPTER 6

THE TRUSTEE IN BANKRUPTCY

| Note | | 2.597 |

*Sub-division A: appointment and associated formalities*

| 10.67 | Appointment by creditors of new trustee | 2.598 |
| 10.68 | Certification of appointment | 2.599 |
| 10.69 | Cost of the trustee's security (section 390(3)) | 2.600 |
| 10.70 | Creditors' decision to appoint a trustee | 2.601 |
| 10.71 | Appointment by the court (section 291A(2)) | 2.602 |
| 10.72 | Appointment by the Secretary of State | 2.603 |
| 10.73 | Authentication of trustee's appointment | 2.604 |
| 10.74 | Appointment to be gazetted | 2.605 |
| 10.75 | Hand-over of bankrupt's estate by official receiver to trustee | 2.606 |
| 10.76 | Invitation to creditors to form a creditors' committee | 2.607 |

*Sub-division B: resignation and removal*

| 10.77 | Trustee's resignation and appointment of replacement (section 298(7)) | 2.608 |
| 10.78 | Decision of creditors to remove trustee (section 298(1)) | 2.609 |
| 10.79 | Procedure on removal by creditors | 2.610 |
| 10.80 | Removal of trustee by the court (section 298(1)) | 2.611 |
| 10.81 | Removal of trustee by the Secretary of State (section 298(5)) | 2.612 |
| 10.82 | Notice of resignation or removal | 2.613 |
| 10.83 | Release of removed trustee (section 299) | 2.614 |
| 10.84 | Deceased trustee | 2.615 |
| 10.85 | Loss of qualification as insolvency practitioner (section 298(6)) | 2.616 |

*Sub-division C: release on completion of administration of bankrupt's estate*

| 10.86 | Release of official receiver on completion of administration (section 299) | 2.617 |
| 10.87 | Vacation of office on completion of bankruptcy (sections 298(8) and 331) | 2.618 |
| 10.88 | Rule as to reporting | 2.619 |
| 10.89 | Notice to official receiver of intention to vacate office | 2.620 |
| 10.90 | Trustee's duties on vacating office | 2.621 |
| 10.91 | Power of the court to set aside certain transactions | 2.622 |
| 10.92 | Rule against improper solicitation | 2.623 |
| 10.93 | Enforcement of trustee's obligations to official receiver (section 305(3)) | 2.624 |

CHAPTER 7
SPECIAL MANAGER

| | | |
|---|---|---|
| Note | | 2.625 |
| 10.94 | Application for and order of appointment of special manager (section 370) | 2.626 |
| 10.95 | Security | 2.627 |
| 10.96 | Failure to give or keep up security | 2.628 |
| 10.97 | Accounting | 2.629 |
| 10.98 | Termination of appointment | 2.630 |

CHAPTER 8
PUBLIC EXAMINATION OF BANKRUPT

| | | |
|---|---|---|
| Note | | 2.631 |
| 10.99 | Order for public examination of bankrupt | 2.632 |
| 10.100 | Notice of public examination | 2.633 |
| 10.101 | Order for public examination requested by creditors | 2.634 |
| 10.102 | Bankrupt unfit for examination | 2.635 |
| 10.103 | Procedure at public examination | 2.636 |
| 10.104 | Adjournment | 2.637 |
| 10.105 | Expenses of examination | 2.638 |

CHAPTER 9
REPLACEMENT OF EXEMPT PROPERTY

| | | |
|---|---|---|
| 10.106 | Purchase of replacement property | 2.639 |
| 10.107 | Money provided in lieu of sale | 2.640 |

CHAPTER 10
INCOME PAYMENTS ORDERS

| | | |
|---|---|---|
| Note | | 2.641 |
| 10.108 | Interpretation | 2.642 |
| 10.109 | Application for income payments order (section 310) | 2.643 |
| 10.110 | Order for income payments order | 2.644 |
| 10.111 | Action to follow making of order | 2.645 |
| 10.112 | Variation of order | 2.646 |
| 10.113 | Order to payer of income: administration | 2.647 |
| 10.114 | Review of order | 2.648 |

CHAPTER 11
INCOME PAYMENTS AGREEMENTS

| | | |
|---|---|---|
| Note | | 2.649 |
| 10.114A | Interpretation | 2.650 |
| 10.115 | Approval of income payments agreements | 2.651 |
| 10.116 | Acceptance of income payments agreements | 2.652 |
| 10.117 | Variation of income payments agreements | 2.653 |

CHAPTER 12
APPLICATIONS FOR PRODUCTION OF DOCUMENTS BY HER MAJESTY'S REVENUE AND CUSTOMS (SECTION 369)

| | | |
|---|---|---|
| Note | | 2.654 |
| 10.118 | Application for order | 2.655 |
| 10.119 | Making and service of the order | 2.656 |
| 10.120 | Custody of documents | 2.657 |

CHAPTER 13
MORTGAGED PROPERTY

| | | |
|---|---|---|
| Note | | 2.658 |
| 10.121 | Interpretation | 2.659 |
| 10.122 | Claim by mortgagee of land | 2.660 |
| 10.123 | Power of court to order sale | 2.661 |
| 10.124 | Proceeds of sale | 2.662 |

## CHAPTER 14
### AFTER-ACQUIRED PROPERTY

| | | |
|---|---|---|
| 10.125 | Duties of bankrupt in relation to after-acquired property | **2.663** |
| 10.126 | Trustee's recourse to person to whom property disposed | **2.664** |

## CHAPTER 15
### PERMISSION TO ACT AS DIRECTOR, ETC

| | | |
|---|---|---|
| Note | | **2.665** |
| 10.127 | Interpretation | **2.666** |
| 10.128 | Application for permission | **2.667** |
| 10.129 | Report of official receiver | **2.668** |
| 10.130 | Court's order on application | **2.669** |
| 10.131 | Costs under this Chapter | **2.670** |

## CHAPTER 16
### ANNULMENT OF BANKRUPTCY ORDER

| | | |
|---|---|---|
| Note | | **2.671** |
| 10.132 | Application for annulment | **2.672** |
| 10.133 | Report by trustee | **2.673** |
| 10.134 | Applicant's claim that remuneration or expenses are excessive | **2.674** |
| 10.135 | Power of court to stay proceedings | **2.675** |
| 10.136 | Notice to creditors who have not proved | **2.676** |
| 10.137 | The hearing | **2.677** |
| 10.138 | Matters to be proved under section 282(1)(b) | **2.678** |
| 10.139 | Notice to creditors | **2.679** |
| 10.140 | Other matters arising on annulment | **2.680** |
| 10.141 | Trustee's final account | **2.681** |

## CHAPTER 17
### DISCHARGE

| | | |
|---|---|---|
| Note | | **2.682** |
| 10.142 | Application for suspension of discharge | **2.683** |
| 10.143 | Lifting of suspension of discharge | **2.684** |
| 10.144 | Certificate of discharge from bankruptcy order made otherwise than on a bankruptcy application | **2.685** |
| 10.145 | Certificate of discharge from bankruptcy order made on a bankruptcy application | **2.686** |
| 10.146 | Bankrupt's debts surviving discharge | **2.687** |
| 10.147 | Costs under this Chapter | **2.688** |

## CHAPTER 18
### PRIORITY OF PAYMENT OF COSTS ETC OUT OF THE BANKRUPT'S ESTATE

| | | |
|---|---|---|
| Note | | **2.689** |
| 10.148 | Expenses | **2.690** |
| 10.149 | General rule as to priority | **2.691** |

## CHAPTER 19
### SECOND BANKRUPTCY

| | | |
|---|---|---|
| Note | | **2.692** |
| 10.150 | Scope of this Chapter | **2.693** |
| 10.151 | General duty of existing trustee | **2.694** |
| 10.152 | Delivery up to later trustee | **2.695** |
| 10.153 | Existing trustee's expenses | **2.696** |

## CHAPTER 20
### CRIMINAL BANKRUPTCY

| | | |
|---|---|---|
| Note | | **2.697** |
| 10.153A | Application | **2.698** |
| 10.154 | Contents of petition | **2.699** |
| 10.155 | Status and functions of Official Petitioner | **2.700** |
| 10.156 | Interim receivership | **2.701** |
| 10.157 | Proof of bankruptcy debts and notice of order | **2.702** |

| | | |
|---|---|---|
| 10.158 | Rules not applying in criminal bankruptcy | 2.703 |
| 10.159 | Annulment of criminal bankruptcy order | 2.704 |
| 10.160 | Application by bankrupt for discharge | 2.705 |
| 10.161 | Report of official receiver | 2.706 |
| 10.162 | Order of discharge | 2.707 |
| 10.163 | Deferment of issue of order pending appeal | 2.708 |
| 10.164 | Costs under this Chapter | 2.709 |

CHAPTER 21
MISCELLANEOUS RULES IN BANKRUPTCY

| | | |
|---|---|---|
| Note | | 2.710 |
| 10.165 | Amendment of title of proceedings | 2.711 |
| 10.166 | Application for redirection order | 2.712 |
| 10.167 | Bankrupt's home: property falling within section 283A | 2.713 |
| 10.168 | Application in relation to the vesting of an interest in a dwelling-house (registered land) | 2.714 |
| 10.169 | Vesting of bankrupt's interest (unregistered land) | 2.715 |
| 10.170 | Vesting of bankrupt's estate: substituted period | 2.716 |
| 10.171 | Charging order | 2.717 |

PART 11
BANKRUPTCY AND DEBT RELIEF RESTRICTIONS ORDERS AND UNDERTAKINGS AND THE INSOLVENCY REGISTERS

CHAPTER 1
INTERPRETATION

| | | |
|---|---|---|
| 11.1 | References to the Secretary of State | 2.718 |

CHAPTER 2
BANKRUPTCY AND DEBT RELIEF RESTRICTIONS ORDERS (SCHEDULES 4ZB AND 4A)

| | | |
|---|---|---|
| Note | | 2.719 |
| 11.2 | Application for a bankruptcy or debt relief restrictions order | 2.720 |
| 11.3 | Service of the application on the bankrupt or debtor | 2.721 |
| 11.4 | The bankrupt's or debtor's evidence opposing an application | 2.722 |
| 11.5 | Making a bankruptcy or debt relief restrictions order | 2.723 |

CHAPTER 3
INTERIM BANKRUPTCY AND DEBT RELIEF RESTRICTIONS ORDERS

| | | |
|---|---|---|
| Note | | 2.724 |
| 11.6 | Application for an interim bankruptcy or debt relief restrictions order | 2.725 |
| 11.7 | Making an interim bankruptcy or debt relief restrictions order | 2.726 |
| 11.8 | Application to set aside an interim order | 2.727 |
| 11.9 | Order setting aside an interim order | 2.728 |

CHAPTER 4
BANKRUPTCY RESTRICTIONS AND DEBT RELIEF RESTRICTIONS UNDERTAKINGS

| | | |
|---|---|---|
| Note | | 2.729 |
| 11.10 | Acceptance of a bankruptcy restrictions or a debt relief restrictions undertaking | 2.730 |
| 11.11 | Notification | 2.731 |
| 11.12 | Application to annul a bankruptcy restrictions or a debt relief restrictions undertaking | 2.732 |

CHAPTER 5
INSOLVENCY REGISTERS: GENERAL

| | | |
|---|---|---|
| 11.13 | Maintenance of the registers and inspection | 2.733 |

CHAPTER 6
INDIVIDUAL INSOLVENCY REGISTER

| | | |
|---|---|---|
| 11.14 | Entry of information on the individual insolvency register: IVAs | 2.734 |
| 11.15 | Deletion of information from the individual insolvency register: IVAs | 2.735 |
| 11.16 | Entry of information on to the individual insolvency register: bankruptcy orders | 2.736 |

| | | |
|---|---|---|
| 11.17 | Deletion of information from the individual insolvency register: bankruptcy orders | 2.737 |
| 11.18 | Entry of information on to the individual insolvency register: debt relief orders | 2.738 |
| 11.19 | Deletion of information from the individual insolvency register: debt relief orders | 2.739 |

CHAPTER 7

BANKRUPTCY AND DEBT RELIEF RESTRICTIONS REGISTER

| | | |
|---|---|---|
| 11.20 | Bankruptcy restrictions and debt relief restrictions orders and undertakings: entry of information on the registers | 2.740 |
| 11.21 | Deletion of information from the registers | 2.741 |

CHAPTER 8

RECTIFICATION OF REGISTERS AND DEATH OF PERSONS ON REGISTER

| | | |
|---|---|---|
| 11.22 | Rectification of the registers | 2.742 |
| 11.23 | Death of a person about whom information is held on a register | 2.743 |

PART 12

COURT PROCEDURE AND PRACTICE

CHAPTER 1

GENERAL

*Application of the Civil Procedure Rules 1998*

| | | |
|---|---|---|
| 12.1 | Court rules and practice to apply | 2.744 |
| 12.2 | Performance of functions by the Court | 2.745 |

CHAPTER 2

COMMENCEMENT OF INSOLVENCY PROCEEDINGS IN THE COUNTY COURT

| | | |
|---|---|---|
| Note | | 2.746 |
| 12.3 | Commencement of insolvency proceedings under Parts 1 to 7 of the Act (corporate insolvency proceedings) | 2.747 |
| 12.4 | Commencement of insolvency proceedings under Parts 7A to 11 of the Act (personal insolvency proceedings; bankruptcy) | 2.748 |
| 12.5 | Allocation of proceedings to the London Insolvency District | 2.749 |

CHAPTER 3

MAKING APPLICATIONS TO COURT: GENERAL

| | | |
|---|---|---|
| Note | | 2.750 |
| 12.6 | Preliminary | 2.751 |
| 12.7 | Filing of application | 2.752 |
| 12.8 | Fixing the venue | 2.753 |
| 12.9 | Service or delivery of application | 2.754 |
| 12.10 | Hearing in urgent case | 2.755 |
| 12.11 | Directions | 2.756 |
| 12.12 | Hearing and determination without notice | 2.757 |
| 12.13 | Adjournment of the hearing of an application | 2.758 |

CHAPTER 4

MAKING APPLICATIONS TO COURT: SPECIFIC APPLICATIONS

| | | |
|---|---|---|
| Note | | 2.759 |

*Sub-division A: Applications in connection with section 176A (prescribed part)*

| | | |
|---|---|---|
| 12.14 | Applications under section 176A(5) to disapply section 176A | 2.760 |
| 12.15 | Notice of application under section 176A(5) | 2.761 |
| 12.16 | Notice of an order under section 176A(5) | 2.762 |

*Sub-division B: Applications for private examination (sections 236, 251N and 366)*

| | | |
|---|---|---|
| Note | | 2.763 |
| 12.17 | Application of this sub-division and interpretation | 2.764 |
| 12.18 | Contents of application | 2.765 |
| 12.19 | Order for examination etc | 2.766 |
| 12.20 | Procedure for examination | 2.767 |
| 12.21 | Record of examination | 2.768 |

| | | |
|---|---|---|
| 12.22 | Costs of proceedings under sections 236, 251N and 366 | 2.769 |

*Sub-division C--persons unable to manage own property or affairs*

| | | |
|---|---|---|
| 12.23 | Application and interpretation | 2.771 |
| 12.24 | Appointment of another person to act | 2.772 |
| 12.25 | Witness statement in support of application | 2.773 |
| 12.26 | Service of notices following appointment | 2.774 |

CHAPTER 5

OBTAINING INFORMATION AND EVIDENCE

| | | |
|---|---|---|
| Note | | 2.775 |
| 12.27 | Further information and disclosure | 2.776 |
| 12.28 | Witness statements and reports | 2.777 |
| 12.29 | Evidence provided by the official receiver, an insolvency practitioner or a special manager | 2.778 |

CHAPTER 6

TRANSFER OF PROCEEDINGS

| | | |
|---|---|---|
| Note | | 2.779 |

*Sub-division A: General*

| | | |
|---|---|---|
| 12.30 | General power of transfer | 2.780 |
| 12.31 | Proceedings commenced in the wrong court | 2.781 |
| 12.32 | Applications for transfer | 2.782 |
| 12.33 | Procedure following order for transfer | 2.783 |
| 12.34 | Consequential transfer of other proceedings | 2.784 |

*Sub-division B: Block transfer of cases where insolvency practitioner has died etc*

| | | |
|---|---|---|
| 12.35 | Interpretation | 2.786 |
| 12.36 | Power to make a block transfer order | 2.787 |
| 12.37 | Application for a block transfer order | 2.788 |
| 12.38 | Action following application for a block transfer order | 2.789 |

CHAPTER 7

THE COURT FILE

| | | |
|---|---|---|
| Note | | 2.790 |
| 12.39 | The court file | 2.791 |
| 12.40 | Office copies of documents | 2.792 |

CHAPTER 8

COSTS

| | | |
|---|---|---|
| Note | | 2.793 |
| 12.41 | Application of Chapter and interpretation | 2.794 |
| 12.42 | Requirement to assess costs by the detailed procedure | 2.795 |
| 12.43 | Procedure where detailed assessment is required | 2.796 |
| 12.44 | Costs of officers charged with execution of writs or other process | 2.797 |
| 12.45 | Petitions presented by insolvent companies | 2.798 |
| 12.46 | Costs paid otherwise than out of the insolvent estate | 2.799 |
| 12.47 | Awards of costs against an office-holder, the adjudicator or the official receiver | 2.800 |
| 12.48 | Applications for costs | 2.801 |
| 12.49 | Costs and expenses of petitioners and other specified persons | 2.802 |
| 12.50 | Final costs certificate | 2.803 |

CHAPTER 9

ENFORCEMENT PROCEDURES

| | | |
|---|---|---|
| Note | | 2.804 |
| 12.51 | Enforcement of court orders | 2.805 |
| 12.52 | Orders enforcing compliance | 2.806 |
| 12.53 | Warrants (general provisions) | 2.807 |
| 12.54 | Warrants under sections 134 and 364 | 2.808 |
| 12.55 | Warrants under sections 236, 251N and 366 | 2.809 |
| 12.56 | Warrants under section 365 | 2.810 |
| 12.57 | Execution overtaken by judgment debtor's insolvency | 2.811 |

CHAPTER 10
APPEALS

| | | |
|---|---|---|
| Note | | 2.812 |
| 12.58 | Application of Chapter | 2.813 |
| 12.59 | Appeals and reviews of court orders in corporate insolvency | 2.814 |
| 12.60 | Appeals in bankruptcy by the Secretary of State | 2.815 |
| 12.61 | Procedure on appeal | 2.816 |
| 12.62 | Appeals against decisions of the Secretary of State or official receiver | 2.817 |

CHAPTER 11
COURT ORDERS, FORMAL DEFECTS AND SHORTHAND WRITERS

| | | |
|---|---|---|
| Note | | 2.818 |
| 12.63 | Court orders | 2.819 |
| 12.64 | Formal defects | 2.820 |
| 12.65 | Shorthand writers: nomination etc | 2.821 |

PART 13
OFFICIAL RECEIVERS

| | | |
|---|---|---|
| 13.1 | Official receivers in court | 2.822 |
| 13.2 | Persons entitled to act on official receiver's behalf | 2.823 |
| 13.3 | Application for directions | 2.824 |
| 13.4 | Official receiver's expenses | 2.825 |
| 13.5 | Official receiver not to be appointed liquidator or trustee | 2.826 |

PART 14
CLAIMS BY AND DISTRIBUTIONS TO CREDITORS IN ADMINISTRATION, WINDING UP
AND BANKRUPTCY

CHAPTER 1
APPLICATION AND INTERPRETATION

| | | |
|---|---|---|
| 14.1 | Application of Part 14 and interpretation | 2.827 |

CHAPTER 2
CREDITORS' CLAIMS IN ADMINISTRATION, WINDING UP AND BANKRUPTCY

| | | |
|---|---|---|
| Note | | 2.828 |
| 14.2 | Provable debts | 2.829 |
| 14.3 | Proving a debt | 2.830 |
| 14.4 | Requirements for proof | 2.831 |
| 14.5 | Costs of proving | 2.832 |
| 14.6 | Allowing inspection of proofs | 2.833 |
| 14.7 | Admission and rejection of proofs for dividend | 2.834 |
| 14.8 | Appeal against decision on proof | 2.835 |
| 14.9 | Office-holder not liable for costs under rule 14.8 | 2.836 |
| 14.10 | Withdrawal or variation of proof | 2.837 |
| 14.11 | Exclusion of proof by the court | 2.838 |
| 14.12 | Administration and winding up by the court: debts of insolvent company to rank equally | 2.839 |
| 14.13 | Administration and winding up: division of unsold assets | 2.840 |
| 14.14 | Administration and winding up: estimate of value of debt | 2.841 |
| 14.15 | Secured creditor: value of security | 2.842 |
| 14.16 | Secured creditor: surrender for non-disclosure | 2.843 |
| 14.17 | Secured creditor: redemption by office-holder | 2.844 |
| 14.18 | Secured creditor: test of security's value | 2.845 |
| 14.19 | Realisation or surrender of security by creditor | 2.846 |
| 14.20 | Discounts | 2.847 |
| 14.21 | Debts in foreign currency | 2.848 |
| 14.22 | Payments of a periodical nature | 2.849 |
| 14.23 | Interest | 2.850 |
| 14.24 | Administration: mutual dealings and set-off | 2.851 |
| 14.25 | Winding up: mutual dealings and set-off | 2.852 |

CHAPTER 3
DISTRIBUTION TO CREDITORS IN ADMINISTRATION, WINDING UP AND
BANKRUPTCY

| | | |
|---|---|---|
| Note | | 2.853 |
| 14.26 | Application of Chapter to a particular class of creditors and to distributions | 2.854 |
| 14.27 | Declaration and distribution of dividends in a winding up | 2.855 |
| 14.28 | Gazette notice of intended first dividend or distribution | 2.856 |
| 14.29 | Individual notices to creditors etc of intended dividend or distribution | 2.857 |
| 14.30 | Contents of notice of intention to declare a dividend or make a distribution | 2.858 |
| 14.31 | Further contents of notice to creditors owed small debts etc | 2.859 |
| 14.32 | Admission or rejection of proofs following last date for proving | 2.860 |
| 14.33 | Postponement or cancellation of dividend | 2.861 |
| 14.34 | Declaration of dividend | 2.862 |
| 14.35 | Notice of declaration of a dividend | 2.863 |
| 14.36 | Last notice about dividend in a winding up | 2.864 |
| 14.37 | Contents of last notice about dividend (administration, winding up and bankruptcy) | 2.865 |
| 14.38 | Sole or final dividend | 2.866 |
| 14.39 | Administration and winding up: provisions as to dividends | 2.867 |
| 14.40 | Supplementary provisions as to dividends and distributions | 2.868 |
| 14.41 | Secured creditors | 2.869 |
| 14.42 | Disqualification from dividend | 2.870 |
| 14.43 | Assignment of right to dividend | 2.871 |
| 14.44 | Debt payable at future time | 2.872 |
| 14.45 | Administration and winding up: non-payment of dividend | 2.873 |

PART 15
DECISION MAKING

CHAPTER 1
APPLICATION OF PART

| | | |
|---|---|---|
| 15.1 | Application of Part | 2.875 |

CHAPTER 2
DECISION PROCEDURES

| | | |
|---|---|---|
| Note | | 2.876 |
| 15.2 | Interpretation | 2.877 |
| 15.3 | The prescribed decision procedures | 2.878 |
| 15.4 | Electronic voting | 2.879 |
| 15.5 | Virtual meetings | 2.880 |
| 15.6 | Physical meetings | 2.881 |
| 15.7 | Deemed consent (sections 246ZF and 379ZB) | 2.882 |

CHAPTER 3
NOTICES, VOTING AND VENUES FOR DECISIONS

| | | |
|---|---|---|
| Note | | 2.883 |
| 15.8 | Notices to creditors of decision procedure | 2.884 |
| 15.9 | Voting in a decision procedure | 2.885 |
| 15.10 | Venue for decision procedure | 2.886 |
| 15.11 | Notice of decision procedures or of seeking deemed consent: when and to whom delivered | 2.887 |
| 15.12 | Notice of decision procedure by advertisement only | 2.888 |
| 15.13 | Gazetting and advertisement of meeting | 2.889 |
| 15.14 | Notice to company officers, bankrupts etc in respect of meetings | 2.890 |
| 15.15 | Non-receipt of notice of decision | 2.891 |
| 15.16 | Decisions on remuneration and conduct | 2.892 |

CHAPTER 4
DECISION MAKING IN PARTICULAR PROCEEDINGS

| | | |
|---|---|---|
| Note | | 2.893 |
| 15.17 | Decisions in winding up of authorised deposit-takers | 2.894 |

CHAPTER 5
REQUISITIONED DECISIONS

| | | |
|---|---|---|
| Note | | 2.895 |
| 15.18 | Requisitions of decision | 2.896 |
| 15.19 | Expenses and timing of requisitioned decision | 2.897 |

CHAPTER 6
CONSTITUTION OF MEETINGS

| | | |
|---|---|---|
| 15.20 | Quorum at meetings | 2.898 |
| 15.21 | Chair at meetings | 2.899 |
| 15.22 | The chair--attendance, interventions and questions | 2.900 |

CHAPTER 7
ADJOURNMENT AND SUSPENSION OF MEETINGS

| | | |
|---|---|---|
| 15.23 | Adjournment by chair | 2.901 |
| 15.24 | Adjournment of meetings to remove a liquidator or trustee | 2.902 |
| 15.25 | Adjournment in absence of chair | 2.903 |
| 15.26 | Proofs in adjournment | 2.904 |
| 15.27 | Suspension | 2.905 |

CHAPTER 8
CREDITORS' VOTING RIGHTS AND MAJORITIES

| | | |
|---|---|---|
| Note | | 2.906 |
| 15.28 | Creditors' voting rights | 2.907 |
| 15.29 | Scheme manager's voting rights | 2.908 |
| 15.30 | (*Revoked*) | |
| 15.31 | Calculation of voting rights | 2.909 |
| 15.32 | Calculation of voting rights: special cases | 2.910 |
| 15.33 | Procedure for admitting creditors' claims for voting | 2.911 |
| 15.34 | Requisite majorities | 2.912 |
| 15.35 | Appeals against decisions under this Chapter | 2.913 |

CHAPTER 9
EXCLUSIONS FROM MEETINGS

| | | |
|---|---|---|
| Note | | 2.914 |
| 15.36 | Action where person excluded | 2.915 |
| 15.37 | Indication to excluded person | 2.916 |
| 15.38 | Complaint | 2.917 |

CHAPTER 10
CONTRIBUTORIES' VOTING RIGHTS AND MAJORITIES

| | | |
|---|---|---|
| 15.39 | Contributories' voting rights and requisite majorities | 2.918 |

CHAPTER 11
RECORDS

| | | |
|---|---|---|
| 15.40 | Record of a decision | 2.919 |

CHAPTER 12
COMPANY MEETINGS

| | | |
|---|---|---|
| 15.41 | Company meetings | 2.920 |
| 15.42 | Remote attendance: notification requirements | 2.921 |
| 15.43 | Location of company meetings | 2.922 |
| 15.44 | Action where person excluded | 2.923 |
| 15.45 | Indication to excluded person | 2.924 |
| 15.46 | Complaint | 2.925 |

PART 16
PROXIES AND CORPORATE REPRESENTATION

| | | |
|---|---|---|
| Note | | 2.926 |
| 16.1 | Application and interpretation | 2.927 |
| 16.2 | Specific and continuing proxies | 2.928 |
| 16.3 | Blank proxy | 2.929 |
| 16.4 | Use of proxies | 2.930 |
| 16.5 | Use of proxies by the chair | 2.931 |

| 16.6 | Right of inspection and retention of proxies | 2.932 |
| 16.7 | Proxy-holder with financial interest | 2.933 |
| Note | | 2.934 |
| 16.8 | Corporate representation: bankruptcy and IVA | 2.935 |
| 16.9 | Instrument conferring authorisation to represent corporation | 2.936 |

### PART 17
### CREDITORS' AND LIQUIDATION COMMITTEES

#### CHAPTER 1
#### INTRODUCTORY

| 17.1 | Scope and interpretation | 2.937 |

#### CHAPTER 2
#### FUNCTIONS OF A COMMITTEE

| 17.2 | Functions of a committee | 2.938 |

#### CHAPTER 3
#### MEMBERSHIP AND FORMALITIES OF FORMATION OF A COMMITTEE

| Note | | 2.939 |
| 17.3 | Number of members of a committee | 2.940 |
| 17.4 | Eligibility for membership of creditors' or liquidation committee | 2.941 |
| 17.5 | Establishment of committees | 2.942 |
| 17.6 | Liquidation committee established by contributories | 2.943 |
| 17.7 | Notice of change of membership of a committee | 2.944 |
| 17.8 | Vacancies: creditor members of creditors' or liquidation committee | 2.945 |
| 17.9 | Vacancies: contributory members of liquidation committee | 2.946 |
| 17.10 | Resignation | 2.947 |
| 17.11 | Termination of membership | 2.948 |
| 17.12 | Removal | 2.949 |
| 17.13 | Cessation of liquidation committee in a winding up when creditors are paid in full | 2.950 |

#### CHAPTER 4
#### MEETINGS OF COMMITTEE

| Note | | 2.951 |
| 17.14 | Meetings of committee | 2.952 |
| 17.15 | The chair at meetings | 2.953 |
| 17.16 | Quorum | 2.954 |
| 17.17 | Committee-members' representatives | 2.955 |
| 17.18 | Voting rights and resolutions | 2.956 |
| 17.19 | Resolutions by correspondence | 2.957 |
| 17.20 | Remote attendance at meetings of committee | 2.958 |
| 17.21 | Procedure for requests that a place for a meeting should be specified | 2.959 |

#### CHAPTER 5
#### SUPPLY OF INFORMATION BY THE OFFICE-HOLDER TO THE COMMITTEE

| Note | | 2.960 |
| 17.22 | Notice requiring office-holder to attend the creditors' committee (administration and administrative receivership) (paragraph 57(3)(a) of Schedule B1 and section 49(2)) | 2.961 |
| 17.23 | Office-holder's obligation to supply information to the committee (winding up and bankruptcy) | 2.962 |

#### CHAPTER 6
#### MISCELLANEOUS

| Note | | 2.963 |
| 17.24 | Expenses of members etc | 2.964 |
| 17.25 | Dealings by committee members and others | 2.965 |
| 17.26 | Dealings by committee members and others: administration and administrative receivership | 2.966 |
| 17.27 | Formal defects | 2.967 |

17.28      Special rule for winding up by the court and bankruptcy: functions vested in the Secretary of State      2.968

CHAPTER 7

WINDING UP BY THE COURT FOLLOWING AN ADMINISTRATION

Note      2.969
17.29      Continuation of creditors' committee      2.970

PART 18

REPORTING AND REMUNERATION OF OFFICE-HOLDERS

Note      2.971

CHAPTER 1

INTRODUCTORY

18.1      Scope of Part 18 and interpretation      2.972

CHAPTER 2

PROGRESS REPORTS

Note      2.973
18.2      Reporting by the office-holder      2.974
18.3      Contents of progress reports in administration, winding up and bankruptcy      2.975
18.4      Information about remuneration      2.976
18.5      Information about pre-administration costs      2.977
18.6      Progress reports in administration: timing      2.978
18.7      Progress reports in voluntary winding up: timing      2.979
18.8      Progress reports in winding up by the court and bankruptcy: timing      2.980
18.9      Creditors' and members' requests for further information in administration, winding up and bankruptcy      2.981
18.10      Administration, creditors' voluntary liquidation and compulsory winding up: reporting distribution of property to creditors under rule 14.13      2.982
18.11      Voluntary winding up: reporting arrangement under section 110      2.983
18.12      Members' voluntary winding up: reporting distribution to members other than under section 110      2.984
18.13      Bankruptcy proceedings: reporting distribution of property to creditors under section 326      2.985

CHAPTER 3

FINAL ACCOUNTS IN WINDING UP AND FINAL REPORTS IN BANKRUPTCY

Note      2.986
18.14      Contents of final account (winding up) and final report (bankruptcy)      2.987

CHAPTER 4

REMUNERATION AND EXPENSES IN ADMINISTRATION, WINDING UP AND BANKRUPTCY

Note      2.988
18.15      Application of Chapter      2.989
18.16      Remuneration: principles      2.990
18.17      Remuneration of joint office-holders      2.991
18.18      Remuneration: procedure for initial determination in an administration      2.992
18.19      Remuneration: procedure for initial determination in a members' voluntary winding up      2.993
18.20      Remuneration: procedure for initial determination in a creditors' voluntary winding up or a winding up by the court      2.994
18.21      Remuneration: procedure for initial determination in a bankruptcy      2.995
18.22      Application of scale fees where creditors fail to fix the basis of the office-holder's remuneration      2.996
18.23      Remuneration: application to the court to fix the basis      2.997
18.24      Remuneration: administrator, liquidator or trustee seeking increase etc      2.998
18.25      Application for an increase etc in remuneration: the general rule      2.999
18.26      First exception: administrator has made a statement under paragraph 52(1)(b) of Schedule B1      2.1000

| | | |
|---|---|---|
| 18.27 | Second exception: administrator who had applied for increase etc under rule 18.24 becomes liquidator | **2.1001** |
| 18.28 | Remuneration: recourse by administrator, liquidator or trustee to the court | **2.1002** |
| 18.29 | Remuneration: review at request of administrator, liquidator or trustee | **2.1003** |
| 18.30 | Remuneration: exceeding the fee estimate | **2.1004** |
| 18.31 | Remuneration: new administrator, liquidator or trustee | **2.1005** |
| 18.32 | Remuneration: apportionment of set fees | **2.1006** |
| 18.33 | Remuneration: variation of the application of rules 18.29, 18.30 and 18.32 | **2.1007** |
| 18.34 | Remuneration and expenses: application to court by a creditor or member on grounds that remuneration or expenses are excessive | **2.1008** |
| 18.35 | Remuneration and expenses: application to court by a bankrupt on grounds that remuneration or expenses are excessive | **2.1009** |
| 18.36 | Applications under rules 18.34 and 18.35 where the court has given permission for the application | **2.1010** |
| 18.37 | Applications under rule 18.34 where the court's permission is not required for the application | **2.1011** |
| 18.38 | Remuneration of a liquidator or trustee who realises assets on behalf of a secured creditor | **2.1012** |

PART 19
DISCLAIMER IN WINDING UP AND BANKRUPTCY

| | | |
|---|---|---|
| Note | | **2.1013** |
| 19.1 | Application of this Part | **2.1014** |
| 19.2 | Notice of disclaimer (sections 178 and 315) | **2.1015** |
| 19.3 | Notice of disclaimer to interested persons (sections 178 and 315) | **2.1016** |
| 19.4 | Notice of disclaimer of leasehold property (sections 179 and 317) | **2.1017** |
| 19.5 | Notice of disclaimer in respect of a dwelling house (bankruptcy) (section 318) | **2.1018** |
| 19.6 | Additional notices of disclaimer | **2.1019** |
| 19.7 | Records | **2.1020** |
| 19.8 | Application for permission to disclaim in bankruptcy (section 315(4)) | **2.1021** |
| 19.9 | Application by interested party for decision on disclaimer (sections 178(5) and 316) | **2.1022** |
| 19.10 | Disclaimer presumed valid and effective | **2.1023** |
| 19.11 | Application for exercise of court's powers under section 181 (winding up) or section 320 (bankruptcy) | **2.1024** |

PART 20
DEBTORS AND THEIR FAMILIES AT RISK OF VIOLENCE: ORDERS NOT TO DISCLOSE CURRENT ADDRESS

| | | |
|---|---|---|
| Note | | **2.1025** |
| 20.1 | Application of this Part and interpretation | **2.1026** |
| 20.2 | Proposed IVA (order for non-disclosure of current address) | **2.1027** |
| 20.3 | IVA (order for non-disclosure of current address) | **2.1028** |
| 20.4 | Debt relief application (order for non-disclosure of current address) | **2.1029** |
| 20.5 | Bankruptcy application (order for non-disclosure of current address) | **2.1030** |
| 20.6 | Bankruptcy and debt relief proceedings (order for non-disclosure of current address) | **2.1031** |
| 20.7 | Additional provisions in respect of orders under rule 20.6(4) | **2.1032** |

PART 21
THE EU REGULATION

| | | |
|---|---|---|
| Note | | **2.1033** |
| 21.1–21.2 | (Revoked) | |
| | | |
| Note (Revoked) | | |
| 21.3 | (Revoked) | |
| 21.4 | Confirmation of creditors' voluntary winding up: application | **2.1035** |
| 21.5 | Confirmation of creditors' voluntary winding up: court order | **2.1036** |
| 21.6–21.8 | (Revoked) | |
| | | |
| Note (Revoked) | | |
| 21.9–21.17 | (Revoked) | |

PART 22
PERMISSION TO ACT AS DIRECTOR ETC OF COMPANY WITH A PROHIBITED NAME
(SECTION 216)

| | | |
|---|---|---|
| Note | | **2.1037** |
| 22.1 | Preliminary | **2.1038** |
| 22.2 | Application for permission under section 216(3) | **2.1039** |
| 22.3 | Power of court to call for liquidator's report | **2.1040** |
| 22.4 | First excepted case | **2.1041** |
| 22.5 | Statement as to the effect of the notice under rule 22.4(2) | **2.1042** |
| 22.6 | Second excepted case | **2.1043** |
| 22.7 | Third excepted case | **2.1044** |
| | Schedules | |
| | Schedule 1 Revocations | **2.1045** |
| | Schedule 2 Transitional and Savings Provisions | **2.1046** |
| | Schedule 3 Punishment of Offences under These Rules | **2.1047** |
| | Schedule 4 Service of Documents | **2.1048** |
| | Schedule 5 Calculation of Time Periods | **2.1049** |
| | Schedule 6 Insolvency Jurisdiction of County Court Hearing Centres | **2.1050** |
| | Schedule 7 Information to be Provided in the Bankruptcy Application | **2.1051** |
| | Schedule 8 Additional Information to be Provided in the Bankruptcy Application | **2.1053** |
| | Schedule 9 Information to be Given to Creditors | **2.1054** |
| | Schedule 10 Destination of Appeals from Decisions of District Judges in Corporate Insolvency Matters | **2.1055** |
| | Schedule 11 Determination of Insolvency Office-Holder's Remuneration | **2.1056** |

## INTRODUCTORY RULES

**[2.1]**

**1 Citation and commencement**

These Rules may be cited as the Insolvency (England and Wales) Rules 2016 and come into force on 6th April 2017.

**Derivation**—This rule derived from the Insolvency Rules 1986, SI 1986/1925, r 0.1.

**[2.2]**

**2 Revocations**

The Rules listed in Schedule 1 are revoked.

**[2.3]**

**3 Extent and application**

(1)   These Rules extend to England and Wales only.

(2)   These Rules as they relate to company voluntary arrangements under Part 1 of the Act, administration under Part 2 of the Act and winding up under Parts 4 and 5 of the Act apply in relation to companies which the courts in England and Wales have jurisdiction to wind up.

(3)   These Rules do not apply to receivers appointed under section 51 (Scottish receivership).

**Derivation**—This rule derived from the Insolvency Rules 1986, SI 1986/1925, r 0.3.

**[2.4]**

**4 Transitional and savings provisions**

The transitional and savings provisions set out in Schedule 2 have effect.

**Derivation**—This rule derived from the Insolvency Rules 1986, SI 1986/1925, r 13.14.

[2.5]

**5 Power of the Secretary of State to regulate certain matters**

(1)   Under paragraph 27 of Schedule 8 and paragraph 30 of Schedule 9 to the Act, the Secretary of State may, subject to the Act and the Rules made under it, make regulations with respect to any matter provided for in the Rules relating to the carrying out of the functions of—

(a)   a liquidator, provisional liquidator, administrator or administrative receiver of a company;

(b)   an interim receiver appointed under section 286; and

(c)   a trustee of a bankrupt's estate.

(2)   The regulations that may be made may include, without prejudice to the generality of paragraph (1), provision with respect to the following matters arising in companies winding up and individual bankruptcy—

(a)   the preparation and keeping by liquidators, trustees, provisional liquidators, interim receivers and the official receiver, of books, accounts and other records, and their production to such persons as may be authorised or required to inspect them;

(b)   the auditing of liquidators' and trustees' accounts;

(c)   the manner in which liquidators and trustees are to act in relation to the insolvent company's or bankrupt's books, papers and other records, and the manner of their disposal by the responsible office-holder or others;

(d)   the supply of copies of documents relating to the insolvency and the affairs of the insolvent company or individual (on payment, in such cases as may be specified by the regulations, of the specified fee)—

(i)   by the liquidator in company insolvency to creditors and members of the company, contributories in its winding up and the liquidation committee; and

(ii)   by the trustee in bankruptcy to creditors and the creditors' committee;

(e)   the manner in which insolvent estates are to be distributed by liquidators and trustees, including provision with respect to unclaimed funds and dividends;

(f)   the manner in which moneys coming into the hands of a liquidator or trustee in the course of the administration of the proceedings are to be handled and invested, and the payment of interest on sums which, have been paid into the Insolvency Services Account under regulations made by virtue of this sub-paragraph;

(g)   the amount (or the manner of determining the amount) to be paid to the official receiver as remuneration when acting as provisional liquidator, liquidator, interim receiver or trustee.

(3)   Regulations made under this rule may—

(a)   confer a discretion on the court;

(b)   make non-compliance with any of the regulations a criminal offence;

(c)   make different provision for different cases, including different provision for different areas; and

(d)   contain such incidental, supplemental and transitional provisions as may appear to the Secretary of State necessary or expedient.

Derivation—This rule derived from the Insolvency Rules 1986, SI 1986/1925, r 12.1.

[2.6]

**6 Punishment of offences**

Schedule 3 sets out the punishments for certain contraventions of these Rules.

Derivation—This rule derived from the Insolvency Rules 1986, SI 1986/1925, r 12.21, Sch 5.

**[2.7]**

**7 Review**

(1)   The Secretary of State must from time to time—
  (a)     carry out a review of these Rules;
  (b)     set out the conclusions of the review in a report; and
  (c)     publish the report.

(2)   The report must in particular—
  (a)     set out the objectives intended to be achieved by the regulatory system established by these Rules;
  (b)     assess the extent to which those objectives are achieved; and
  (c)     assess whether those objectives remain appropriate and, if so, the extent to which they could be achieved with a system that imposes less regulation.

(3)   The first report under this rule must be published before the end of the period of five years beginning with the day on which these Rules come into force.

(4)   Reports under this rule are afterwards to be published at intervals not exceeding five years.

PART 1   SCOPE, INTERPRETATION, TIME AND RULES ABOUT DOCUMENTS

CHAPTER 1

SCOPE OF THESE RULES

**[2.8]**

**1.1 Scope**

(1)   These Rules are made to give effect to Parts 1 to 11 of the Insolvency Act 1986 and to the EU Regulation.

(2)   Consequently references to insolvency proceedings and requirements relating to such proceedings are, unless the context requires otherwise, limited to proceedings in respect of Parts 1 to 11 of the Act and the EU Regulation (whether or not court proceedings).

  Derivation—This rule derived from the Insolvency Rules 1986, SI 1986/1925, r 13.7.
  Amendments—SI 2017/1115.

CHAPTER 2

INTERPRETATION

**[2.9]**

Note
[Note: the terms which are defined in rule 1.2 include some terms defined by the Act for limited purposes which are applied generally by these Rules. Such terms have the meaning given by the Act for those limited purposes.]

**[2.10]**

**1.2 Defined terms**

(1)   In these Rules, unless otherwise stated, a reference to a Part or a Schedule is to a Part of, or Schedule to, these Rules.

(2)   In these Rules—
    "the Act" means the Insolvency Act 1986, and—
      (a)     a reference to a numbered section without mention of another Act is to that section of the Act; and
      (b)     a reference to Schedule A1, B1, 4ZA, 4ZB or 4A is to that Schedule to the Act;

"appointed person" means a person as described in paragraph (3) who is appointed by an office-holder (other than the official receiver);

"Article 1.2 undertaking" means one of the following within the meaning of Article 1.2 of Regulation (EU) 2015/848 of the European Parliament and of the Council" ("the EU Regulations")—

    (a)    an insurance undertaking;

    (b)    a credit institution;

    (c)    an investment undertaking which provides services involving the holding of funds or securities for third parties;

    (d)    a collective investment undertaking;

Note: "associate" is defined by section 435;

"attendance" and "attend" a person attends, or is in attendance at, a meeting who is present or attends remotely in accordance with section 246A or rule 15.6, or who participates in a virtual meeting, whether that person attends the meeting or virtual meeting in person, by proxy, or by corporate representative (in accordance with section 434B or section 323 of the Companies Act, as applicable);

"authenticate" means to authenticate in accordance with rule 1.5;

"authorised deposit-taker" means a person with permission under Part 4A of the Financial Services and Markets Act 2000 to accept deposits; this definition must be read with—

    (a)    section 22 of that Act and any relevant order under that section; and

    (b)    Schedule 2 to that Act;

Note: "bankrupt's estate" is defined in section 283;

"bankruptcy application" means the bankruptcy application submitted by the debtor to the adjudicator requesting the making of a bankruptcy order against the debtor;

"bankruptcy file" means the file opened by the adjudicator in accordance with rule 10.47;

"bankruptcy restrictions register" means the register referred to in rule 11.13(2) of matters relating to bankruptcy restrictions orders, interim bankruptcy restrictions orders and bankruptcy restrictions undertakings;

"business day" means, for the purposes of these Rules as they relate to Parts 7A to 10 of the Act (insolvency of individuals; bankruptcy), any day other than a Saturday, a Sunday, Christmas Day, Good Friday or a day which is a bank holiday in England and Wales Note: for the purposes of these Rules as they relate to Parts 1 to 7 of the Act (company insolvency; company winding up) section 251 defines "business day" as including additionally a day which is a bank holiday in Scotland;

"centre of main interests" has the same meaning as in the EU Regulation;

"certificate of service" means a certificate of service which complies with the requirements in Schedule 4;

"COMI proceedings" means insolvency proceedings in England and Wales to which the EU Regulation applies where the centre of the debtor's main interests is in the United Kingdom;

"Companies Act" means the Companies Act 2006;

Note: the term "connected" used of a person in relation to a company is defined in section 249 of the Act;

"consumer" means an individual acting for purposes that are wholly or mainly outside that individual's trade, business, craft or profession;

Note: "contributory" is defined by section 79;

"convener" means an office-holder or other person who seeks a decision in accordance with Part 15 of these Rules;

Note: "the court" is defined by section 251 for the purposes of these Rules as they relate to Parts 1 to 7 of the Act (company insolvency; company winding up) and by section 385(1) for the purposes of these Rules as they relate to Parts 7A to 10 of the Act (insolvency of individuals; bankruptcy);

"CPR" means the Civil Procedure Rules 1998;

"credit reference agency" means a person authorised or permitted by the Financial Conduct Authority to carry on the regulated activity of providing credit references;

"CVA" means a voluntary arrangement in relation to a company under Part 1 of the Act;

"debt" is defined in rule 14.1(3) for the purposes of administration and winding up and "small debt" is also defined in rule 14.1(3) for administration, winding up and bankruptcy Note: debt is defined in section 385(1) for the purposes of these Rules as they relate to Parts 7A to 10 of the Act (insolvency of individuals; bankruptcy);

"debt relief restrictions register" means the register referred to in rule 11.13(2) of matters relating to debt relief restrictions orders and debt relief restrictions undertakings;

"decision date" and "decision procedure" are to be interpreted in accordance with rule 15.2 and Part 15;

"decision procedure" means a decision procedure prescribed by rule 15.3;

Note: "deemed consent procedure" is defined in section 246ZF for corporate insolvency and 379ZB for individual insolvency; rule 15.7 makes further provision about deemed consent;

"deliver" and "delivery" are to be interpreted in accordance with Chapter 9 of Part 1;

"deliver to the creditors" and similar expressions in these Rules and the Act are to be interpreted in accordance with rule 1.37;

Note: "distress" is defined in section 436 as including the procedure in Schedule 12 to the Tribunals, Courts and Enforcement Act 2007 (c 15), and references to levying distress, seizing goods and related expressions are to be construed accordingly;

"document" includes a written notice or statement or anything else in writing capable of being delivered to a recipient;

Note: EU Regulation is defined for the purposes of these Rules by section 436 of the Act as Regulation (EU) 2015/848 of the European Parliament and of the Council;

"enforcement agent" means a person authorised by section 63(2) of the Tribunals, Courts and Enforcement Act 2007 to act as an enforcement agent;

"enforcement officer" means an individual who is authorised to act as an enforcement officer under the Courts Act 2003;

"establishment" has the same meaning as in Article 2(10) of the EU Regulation;

"establishment proceedings" means insolvency proceedings in England and Wales to which the EU Regulation applies where the debtor has an establishment in the United Kingdom;

"fees estimate" means a written estimate that specifies—

    (a)    details of the work the insolvency practitioner ("the IP") and the IP's staff propose to undertake;

    (b)    the hourly rate or rates the IP and the IP's staff propose to charge for each part of that work;

    (c)    the time the IP anticipates each part of that work will take;

    (d)    whether the IP anticipates it will be necessary to seek approval or further approval under Chapter 4 of Part 18; and

    (e)    the reasons it will be necessary to seek such approval under these Rules;

"file with the court" and similar expressions in these Rules means deliver to the court for filing and such references are to be read as including "submit" and "submission" to the court in the Act (except in sections 236 and 366);

"the Gazette", which has the meaning given in section 251 for the purposes of these Rules as they relate to Parts 1 to 7 of the Act (company insolvency; company winding up), has that meaning for the purposes of these Rules as they relate to Parts 7A to 10 of the Act;

"Gazette notice" means a notice which is, has been or is to be gazetted;

"to gazette" means to advertise once in the Gazette;

"general regulations" means regulations made by the Secretary of State under introductory rule 5;

"hearing centre" means a hearing centre of the County Court;

Note: "hire-purchase agreement" is defined by section 436(1) as having the same meaning as in the Consumer Credit Act 1974 for the purposes of the Act and by paragraph 1 of Schedule A1 (company voluntary arrangement) for the purposes of that Schedule and by paragraph 111(1) of Schedule B1 (administration) for the purposes of that Schedule;

"identification details" and similar references to information identifying persons, proceedings, etc are to be interpreted in accordance with rule 1.6;

"individual insolvency register" means the register referred to in rule 11.13(1) of matters relating to bankruptcies, debt relief orders and IVAs;

"individual register" has the meaning given by rule 217(1) of the Land Registration Rules 2003;

"insolvent estate" means—

    (a)    in relation to a company insolvency, the company's assets;

    (b)    in relation to a bankruptcy, a petition or an application for bankruptcy, the bankrupt's estate (as defined in section 283);

    (c)    or otherwise the debtor's property;

"IP number" means the number assigned to an office-holder as an insolvency practitioner by the Secretary of State;

"IVA" means a voluntary arrangement in relation to an individual under Part 8 of the Act;

"judge" includes an Insolvency and Companies Court Judge unless the context otherwise requires;

"London Insolvency District" has the meaning given by section 374 of the Act and the London Insolvency District (County Court at Central London) Order 2014;

. . .

"meeting" in relation to a person's creditors or contributories means either a "physical meeting" or a "virtual meeting" as defined in rule 15.2, unless the contrary intention is given;

. . .

"nominated person" means a person who has been required under section 47 or 131 to make out and submit a statement as to the affairs of a company in administrative receivership or being wound up by the court;

Note: "nominee" is defined in section 1(2) in relation to company voluntary arrangements and section 253(2) in relation to individual voluntary arrangements;

. . .

"office-holder" means a person who under the Act or these Rules holds an office in relation to insolvency proceedings and includes a nominee;

"permission" of the court is to be read as including "leave of the court" in the Act and in the Company Directors' Disqualification Act 1986;

"petitioner" or "petitioning creditor" includes a person who has been substituted as such or has been given carriage of the petition;

"physical meeting" means a meeting as described in section 246ZE(9) or 379ZA(9);

"Practice Direction" means a direction as to the practice and procedure of a court within the scope of the CPR;

"prescribed order of priority" means the order of priority of payments of expenses set out in—

    (a)    Chapter 10 of Part 3 for administration proceedings;

    (b)    Chapter 6 of Part 6 for creditors' voluntary winding up proceedings;

    (c)    Chapter 14 of Part 7 for winding up by the court proceedings; and

    (d)    Chapter 18 of Part 10 for bankruptcy proceedings;

"prescribed part" has the same meaning as in section 176A(2)(a) and the Insolvency Act 1986 (Prescribed Part) Order 2003;

"progress report" means a report which complies with Chapter 2 of Part 18;

Note: "property" is defined by section 436(1) of the Act;

"prove" and "proof" have the following meaning—

    (a)    a creditor who claims for a debt in writing is referred to as proving that debt;

    (b)    the document by which the creditor makes the claim is referred to as that creditor's proof; and

    (c)    for the purpose of voting, or objecting to a deemed consent, in an administration, an administrative receivership, a creditors' voluntary winding up, a CVA or an IVA, the requirements for a proof are satisfied by the convener or chair having been notified by the creditor in writing of a debt;

"proxy" and "blank proxy" are to be interpreted in accordance with Part 16;

"qualified to act as an insolvency practitioner" in relation to a company, debtor or bankrupt has the meaning given by section 390 of the Act;

Note: "records" are defined in section 436(1) of the Act

"registered land" has the meaning given by section 132(1) of the Land Registration Act 2002;

"registrar" means an Insolvency and Companies Court Judge and unless the context requires otherwise includes a District Judge—

    (a)    in a District Registry of the High Court; and

    (b)    in a hearing centre with relevant insolvency jurisdiction;

"residential address" means the current residential address of an individual or, if that is not known, the last known residential address;

. . .

"serve" and "service" are to be interpreted in respect of a particular document by reference to Schedule 4;

"solicitor" means a solicitor of the Senior Courts and, in relation to England and Wales, includes any other person who, for the purpose of the Legal Services Act 2007 is an authorised person in relation to an activity which constitutes the conduct of litigation (within the meaning of that Act);

"standard contents" means—

    (a)    for a Gazette notice, the standard contents set out in Chapter 4 of this Part;

    (b)    for a notice to be advertised other than in the Gazette, the standard contents set out in Chapter 5 of Part 1;

    (c)    for a document to be delivered to the registrar of companies, the standard contents set out in Chapter 6 of Part 1;

    (d)    for notices to be delivered to other persons, the standard contents set out in Chapter 7 of Part 1;

    (e)    for applications to the court the standard contents set out in Chapter 8 of Part 1;

"standard fee for copies" means 15 pence per A4 or A5 page or 30 pence per A3 page;

"statement of proposals" means a statement made by an administrator under paragraph 49 of Schedule B1 setting out proposals for achieving the purpose of an administration;

"statement of truth" means a statement of truth made in accordance with Part 22 of the CPR;

. . .

. . .

"trustee" has the same meaning throughout these Rules as they relate to the insolvency of individuals as it has for bankruptcy in section 385(1);

"venue" in relation to any proceedings, attendance before the court, decision procedure or meeting means the time, date and place or platform for the proceedings, attendance, decision procedure or meeting;

"virtual meeting" has the meaning given by rule 15.2(2);

"winding up by the court" means a winding up under section 122(1), 124A or 221;

"witness statement" means a witness statement verified by a statement of truth made in accordance with Part 32 of the CPR;

Note: "writing": section 436B(1) of the Act provides that a reference to a thing in writing includes that thing in electronic form; subsection (2) excludes certain documents from the application of subsection (1); and

"written resolution" in respect of a private company refers to a written resolution passed in accordance with Chapter 2 of Part 13 of the Companies Act.

(3) An appointed person in relation to a company, debtor or bankrupt must be—
 (a) qualified to act as an insolvency practitioner in relation to that company, debtor or bankrupt; or
 (b) a person experienced in insolvency matters who is—
  (i) a member or employee of the office-holder's firm, or
  (ii) an employee of the office-holder.

(4) A fee or remuneration is charged when the work to which it relates is done.

**Derivation**—This rule derived from the Insolvency Rules 1986, SI 1986/1925, r 12A.55.

**Amendments**—SI 2017/366; SI 2017/702; SI 2017/1115; SI 2018/130; SI 2019/146, as from IP completion day (as defined in the European Union (Withdrawal Agreement) Act 2020, s 39(1)–(5)).

## [2.11]

### 1.3 Calculation of time periods

The rules set out in Schedule 5 apply to the calculation of the beginning and end of time periods under these Rules.

**Derivation**—This rule derived from the Insolvency Rules 1986, SI 1986/1925, r 12A.55.

CHAPTER 3

FORM AND CONTENT OF DOCUMENTS

## [2.12]

### 1.4 Requirement for writing and form of documents

(1) A notice or statement must be in writing unless the Act or these Rules provide otherwise.

(2) A document in electronic form must be capable of being—
 (a) read by the recipient in electronic form; and
 (b) reproduced by the recipient in hard-copy form.

**Derivation**—This rule derived from the Insolvency Rules 1986, SI 1986/1925, r 12A.7.

## [2.13]

### 1.5 Authentication

(1) A document in electronic form is sufficiently authenticated—
 (a) if the identity of the sender is confirmed in a manner specified by the recipient; or
 (b) where the recipient has not so specified, if the communication contains or is accompanied by a statement of the identity of the sender and the recipient has no reason to doubt the truth of that statement.

(2) A document in hard-copy form is sufficiently authenticated if it is signed.

(3) If a document is authenticated by the signature of an individual on behalf of—
 (a) a body of persons, the document must also state the position of that individual in relation to the body;

    (b)    a body corporate of which the individual is the sole member, the document must also state that fact.

**Derivation**—This rule derived from the Insolvency Rules 1986, SI 1986/1925, r 12A.9.

## [2.14]

### 1.6 Information required to identify persons and proceedings etc

(1)   Where the Act or these Rules require a document to identify, or to contain identification details in respect of, a person or proceedings, or to provide contact details for an office-holder, the information set out in the table must be given.

(2)   Where a requirement relates to a proposed office-holder, the information set out in the table in respect of an office-holder must be given with any necessary adaptations.

| | |
|---|---|
| Bankrupt | (a)  full name; and |
| | (b)  residential address (subject to any order for limited disclosure made under Part 20). |
| Company where it is the subject of the proceedings | In the case of a registered company— |
| | (c)  the registered name; |
| | (d)  for a company incorporated in England and Wales under the Companies Act or a previous Companies Act, its registered number; |
| | (e)  for a company incorporated outside the United Kingdom— |
| |     (i)  the country or territory in which it is incorporated, |
| |     (ii)  the number, if any, under which it is registered, and |
| |     (iii) the number, if any, under which it is registered as an overseas company under Part 34 of the Companies Act. |
| | In the case of an unregistered company— |
| | (f)  its name; and |
| | (g)  the postal address of any principal place of business. |
| Company other than one which is the subject of the proceedings | In the case of a registered company— |
| | (h)  the registered name; |
| | (i)  for a company incorporated in any part of the United Kingdom under the Companies Act or a previous Companies Act, its registered number; |
| | (j)  for a company incorporated outside the United Kingdom— |
| |     (i)  the country or territory in which it is incorporated, |
| |     (ii)  the number, if any, under which it is registered; and |
| | (k)  the number, if any, under which it is registered as an overseas company under Part 34 of the Companies Act; |
| | (l)  In the case of an unregistered company— |
| |     (i)  its name, and |
| |     (ii)  the postal address of any principal place of business. |
| Debtor | (m) full name; and |
| | (n)  residential address (subject to any order for limited disclosure made under Part 20). |
| Office-holder | (o)  the name of the office-holder; and |
| | (p)  the nature of the appointment held by the office-holder. |

| Contact details for an office-holder | (q) | a postal address for the office-holder; and |
|---|---|---|
| | (r) | either an email address, or a telephone number, through which the office-holder may be contacted. |
| Proceedings | (s) | for proceedings relating to a company, the information identifying the company; |
| | (t) | for proceedings relating to an individual, the full name of the bankrupt or debtor; |
| | (u) | the full name of the court or hearing centre in which the proceedings are, or are to be, conducted or where documents relating to the proceedings have been or will be filed; and, if applicable, |
| | (v) | any number assigned to those proceedings by the court, the hearing centre or the adjudicator. |

## [2.15]

### 1.7 Reasons for stating whether proceedings are or will be COMI proceedings, establishment proceedings etc

Where these Rules require reasons to be given for a statement that proceedings are or will be COMI proceedings, establishment proceedings or proceedings to which the EU Regulation as it has effect in the law of the United Kingdom does not apply, the reasons must include as applicable—

    (a)    for a company—

        (i)    the centre of main interests,

        (ii)    the place of the registered office within the meaning of Article 3(1) of the EU Regulation and where appropriate an explanation why this is not the same as the centre of main interests, . . .

        (iia)    the place where there is an establishment within the jurisdiction, or

        (iii)    that there is no registered office if that be the case in proceedings to which the EU Regulation as it has effect in the law of the United Kingdom does not apply;

    (b)    for a debtor—

        (i)    the centre of main interests, or

        (ii)    the place where there is an establishment within the jurisdiction.

**Amendments**—SI 2017/1115; SI 2019/146, as from IP completion day (as defined in the European Union (Withdrawal Agreement) Act 2020, s 39(1)–(5)).

## [2.16]

### 1.8 Prescribed format of documents

(1) Where a rule sets out requirements as to the contents of a document any title required by the rule must appear at the beginning of the document.

(2) Any other contents required by the rule (or rules where more than one apply to a particular document) must be provided in the order listed in the rule (or rules) or in another order which the maker of the document considers would be convenient for the intended recipient.

**General note**—Insolvency forms were formerly prescribed by IR 1986, r 12A.30, which referred to Sch 4 of those rules and required the use of the forms set out therein. A transitional provision appears at para 15 of Sch 2 to the IR 2016, which applies where applications were made or petitions presented prior to the commencement date. The IR 2016 do not otherwise prescribe any forms. Although non-mandatory, a suite of acceptable forms has been made freely available by HM Courts & Tribunals Service https://www.gov.uk/government/collections/bankruptcy-and-insolvency-forms.

**[2.17]**

### 1.9 Variations from prescribed contents

(1)   Where a rule sets out the required contents of a document, the document may depart from the required contents if—

    (a)    the circumstances require such a departure (including where the requirement is not applicable in the particular case); or

    (b)    the departure (whether or not intentional) is immaterial.

(2)   However this rule does not apply to the required content of a statutory demand on a company set out in rule 7.3 and on an individual set out in rule 10.1.

CHAPTER 4

STANDARD CONTENTS OF GAZETTE NOTICES AND THE GAZETTE AS EVIDENCE ETC

**[2.18]**

### Note

[Note: (1) the requirements in Chapter 4 must be read with rule 1.6 which sets out the information required to identify an office-holder, a company etc;

(2)   this Chapter does not apply to the notice of a liquidator's appointment prescribed under section 109 by SI 1987/752.]

**[2.19]**

### 1.10  Contents of notices to be gazetted under the Act or Rules

(1)   Where the Act or these Rules require or permit a notice to be gazetted, the notice must also contain the standard contents set out in this Chapter in addition to any content specifically required by the Act or any other provision of these Rules.

(2)   Information which this Chapter requires to be included in a Gazette notice may be omitted if it is not reasonably practicable to obtain it.

  **Derivation**—This rule derived from the Insolvency Rules 1986, SI 1986/1925, rr 12A.33, 12A.36.

**[2.20]**

### 1.11  Standard contents of all notices

(1)   A notice must identify the proceedings, if it is relevant to the particular notice, identify the office-holder and state—

    (a)    the office-holder's contact details;

    (b)    the office-holder's IP number (except for the official receiver);

    (c)    the name of any person other than the office-holder who may be contacted about the proceedings; and

    (d)    the date of the office-holder's appointment.

(2)   This rule does not apply to a notice under rule 22.4(3) (Permission to act as a director: first excepted case).

  **Derivation**—This rule derived from the Insolvency Rules 1986, SI 1986/1925, rr 12A.33, 12A.36.

**[2.21]**

### 1.12  Gazette notices relating to a company

(1)   A notice relating to a registered company must also state—

    (a)    its registered office;

    (b)    any principal trading address if this is different from its registered office;

    (c)    any name under which it was registered in the period of 12 months before the date of the commencement of the proceedings which are the subject of the Gazette notice; and

    (d)    any other name or style (not being a registered name)—

      (i)      under which the company carried on business, and

      (ii)     in which any debt owed to a creditor was incurred.

(2)   A notice relating to an unregistered company must also identify the company and specify any name or style—

     (a)    under which the company carried on business; and

     (b)    in which any debt owed to a creditor was incurred.

**Derivation**—This rule derived from the Insolvency Rules 1986, SI 1986/1925, rr 12A.33, 12A.36.

## [2.22]

### 1.13 Gazette notices relating to a bankruptcy

A notice relating to a bankruptcy must also identify the bankrupt and state—

     (a)    any other address at which the bankrupt has resided in the period of 12 months before the making of the bankruptcy order;

     (b)    any principal trading address if different from the bankrupt's residential address;

     (c)    the bankrupt's date of birth;

     (d)    the bankrupt's occupation;

     (e)    any other name by which the bankrupt has been known; and

     (f)    any name or style (other than the bankrupt's own name) under which—

        (i)    the bankrupt carried on business, and

        (ii)   any debt owed to a creditor was incurred.

**Derivation**—This rule derived from the Insolvency Rules 1986, SI 1986/1925, rr 12A.35, 12A.36.

## [2.23]

### 1.14 The Gazette: evidence, variations and errors

(1)   A copy of the Gazette containing a notice required or permitted by the Act or these Rules to be gazetted is evidence of any facts stated in the notice.

(2)   Where the Act or these Rules require an order of the court or of the adjudicator to be gazetted, a copy of the Gazette containing the notice may be produced in any proceedings as conclusive evidence that the order was made on the date specified in the notice.

(3)   Where an order of the court or of the adjudicator which is gazetted has been varied, or any matter has been erroneously or inaccurately gazetted, the person whose responsibility it was to gazette the order or other matter must as soon as is reasonably practicable cause the variation to be gazetted or a further entry to be made in the Gazette for the purpose of correcting the error or inaccuracy.

**Derivation**—This rule derived from the Insolvency Rules 1986, SI 1986/1925, r 12A.37.

CHAPTER 5

STANDARD CONTENTS OF NOTICES ADVERTISED OTHERWISE THAN IN THE GAZETTE

## [2.24]

**Note**

[Note: the requirements in Chapter 5 must be read with rule 1.6 which sets out the information required to identify an office-holder, a company etc]

## [2.25]

### 1.15 Standard contents of notices advertised otherwise than in the Gazette

(1)   Where the Act or these Rules provide that a notice may be advertised otherwise than in the Gazette the notice must contain the standard contents set out in this Chapter

(in addition to any content specifically required by the Act or any other provision of these Rules).

(2)   A notice must, if it is relevant to the particular notice, identify the office-holder and specify the office-holder's contact details.

(3)   Information which this Chapter requires to be included in a notice may be omitted if it is not reasonably practicable to obtain it.

   **Derivation**—This rule derived from the Insolvency Rules 1986, SI 1986/1925, rr 12A.38, 12A.41.

## [2.26]

### 1.16 Non-Gazette notices relating to a company

A notice relating to a company must also identify the proceedings and state—

    (a)    the company's principal trading address;

    (b)    any name under which the company was registered in the 12 months before the date of the commencement of the proceedings which are the subject of the notice; and

    (c)    any name or style (not being a registered name) under which—

        (i)    the company carried on business, and

        (ii)    any debt owed to a creditor was incurred.

   **Derivation**—This rule derived from the Insolvency Rules 1986, SI 1986/1925, rr 12A.39, 12A.41.

## [2.27]

### 1.17 Non-Gazette notices relating to a bankruptcy

A notice relating to a bankruptcy must also identify the proceedings, identify the bankrupt and state—

    (a)    any other address at which the bankrupt has resided in the period of 12 months before the making of the bankruptcy order;

    (b)    any principal trading address if different from the bankrupt's residential address;

    (c)    the bankrupt's date of birth;

    (d)    the bankrupt's occupation;

    (e)    any other name by which the bankrupt has been known; and

    (f)    any name or style (other than the bankrupt's own name) under which—

        (i)    the bankrupt carried on business, and

        (ii)    any debt owed to a creditor was incurred.

   **Derivation**—This rule derived from the Insolvency Rules 1986, SI 1986/1925, rr 12A.40, 12A.41.

## [2.28]

### 1.18 Non-Gazette notices: other provisions

Information which this Chapter requires to be stated in a notice must be included in an advertisement of that notice in a way that is clear and comprehensible.

   **Derivation**—This rule derived from the Insolvency Rules 1986, SI 1986/1925, r 12A.41.

### CHAPTER 6

STANDARD CONTENTS OF DOCUMENTS TO BE DELIVERED TO THE REGISTRAR
OF COMPANIES

## [2.29]

### Note

[Note: the requirements in Chapter 6 must be read with rule 1.6 which sets out the information required to identify an office-holder, a company etc]

**[2.30]**

### 1.19 Standard contents of documents delivered to the registrar of companies

(1) Where the Act or these Rules require a document to be delivered to the registrar of companies the document must contain the standard contents set out in this Chapter (in addition to any content specifically required by the Act or any other provision of these Rules).

(2) A document of more than one type must satisfy the requirements which apply to each.

(3) However requirements as to the contents of a document which is to be delivered to another person at the same time as the registrar of companies, may be satisfied by delivering to that other person a copy of the document delivered to the registrar.

**Derivation**—This rule derived from the Insolvency Rules 1986, SI 1986/1925, rr 12A.42, 12A.43.

**[2.31]**

### 1.20 Registrar of companies: covering notices

(1) This rule applies where the Act or these Rules require an office-holder to deliver any of the following documents to the registrar of companies—

    (a) an account (including a final report) or a summary of receipts and payments;

    (b) an administrative receiver's report under section 48(1);

    (c) a court order;

    (d) a declaration of solvency;

    (e) a direction of the Secretary of State under section 203 or 205;

    (f) a notice of disclaimer;

    (g) a statement of administrator's proposals (including a statement of revised proposals);

    (h) a statement of affairs;

    (i) a statement of concurrence;

    (j) a notice of an administrator's resignation under paragraph 87(2) of Schedule B1;

    (k) a notice of a liquidator's death which the official receiver is required to deliver under rule 7.67(3)(b);

    (l) a notice that a liquidator has vacated office on loss of qualification to act which the official receiver is required to deliver under rule 7.68(4)(b);

    (m) any report including—

        (i) a final report,

        (ii) a progress report (including a final progress report),

        (iii) a report of a creditors' decision under paragraph 53(2) or 54(6) of Schedule B1, and

        (iv) a report of a decision approving a CVA under section 4(6) and (6A) or paragraph 30(3) and (4) of Schedule A1 to the Act;

    (n) a copy of the notice that a CVA has been fully implemented or terminated that the supervisor is required to deliver under rule 2.44(3);

    (o) . . ..

(2) The office-holder must deliver to the registrar of companies with a document mentioned in paragraph (1) a notice containing the standard contents required by this Part.

(3) Such a notice may relate to more than one document where those documents relate to the same proceedings and are delivered together to the registrar of companies.

**Amendments**—SI 2017/366; SI 2017/702; SI 2019/146, as from IP completion day (as defined in the European Union (Withdrawal Agreement) Act 2020, s 39(1)–(5)).

**[2.32]**

**1.21 Standard contents of all documents**

(1)   A document to be delivered to the registrar of companies must—

    (a)   identify the company;

    (b)   state—

        (i)   the nature of the document,

        (ii)   the section of the Act, the paragraph of Schedule A1 or B1 or the rule under which the document is delivered,

        (iii)   the date of the document,

        (iv)   the name and address of the person delivering the document, and

        (v)   the capacity in which that person is acting in relation to the company; and

    (c)   be authenticated by the person delivering the document.

(2)   Where the person delivering the document is the office-holder, the address may be omitted if it has previously been notified to the registrar of companies in the proceedings and is unchanged.

**Derivation**—This rule derived from the Insolvency Rules 1986, SI 1986/1925, r 12A.43.

**[2.33]**

**1.22 Standard contents of documents relating to the office of office-holders**

(1)   A document relating to the office of the office-holder must also identify the office-holder and state—

    (a)   the date of the event of which notice is delivered or of the notice (as applicable);

    (b)   where the document relates to an appointment, the person, body or court making the appointment;

    (c)   where the document relates to the termination of an appointment, the reason for that termination; and

    (d)   the contact details for the office-holder.

(2)   Where the person delivering the document is the office-holder, the address may be omitted if it has previously been notified to the registrar of companies in the proceedings and is unchanged.

**Derivation**—This rule derived from the Insolvency Rules 1986, SI 1986/1925, r 12A.44.

**[2.34]**

**1.23 Standard contents of documents relating to other documents**

A document relating to another document must also state—

    (a)   the nature of the other document;

    (b)   the date of the other document; and

    (c)   where the other document relates to a period of time, the period of time to which it relates.

**Derivation**—This rule derived from the Insolvency Rules 1986, SI 1986/1925, r 12A.45.

**[2.35]**

**1.24 Standard contents of documents relating to court orders**

A document relating to a court order must also specify—

    (a)   the nature of the order; and

    (b)   the date of the order.

**Derivation**—This rule derived from the Insolvency Rules 1986, SI 1986/1925, r 12A.46.

**[2.36]**

**1.25 Standard contents of returns or reports of decisions**
A return or report of a decision procedure, deemed consent procedure or meeting must also state—

    (a)    the purpose of the procedure or meeting;

    (b)    a description of the procedure or meeting used;

    (c)    in the case of a decision procedure or meeting, the venue;

    (d)    whether, in the case of a meeting, the required quorum was in place;

    (e)    the outcome (including any decisions made or resolutions passed); and

    (f)    the date of any decision made or resolution passed.

**Derivation**—This rule derived from the Insolvency Rules 1986, SI 1986/1925, r 12A.47.

**[2.37]**

**1.26 Standard contents of returns or reports of matters considered by company members by correspondence**
A return or report of a matter, consideration of which has been sought from the members of a company by correspondence, must also state—

    (a)    the purpose of the consideration; and

    (b)    the outcome of the consideration (including any resolutions passed or deemed to be passed).

**Derivation**—This rule derived from the Insolvency Rules 1986, SI 1986/1925, r 12A.47.

**[2.38]**

**1.27 Standard contents of documents relating to other events**
A document relating to any other event must also state—

    (a)    the nature of the event, including the section of the Act, the paragraph of Schedule A1 or B1 or the rule under which it took place; and

    (b)    the date on which the event occurred.

**Derivation**—This rule derived from the Insolvency Rules 1986, SI 1986/1925, r 12A.48.

CHAPTER 7

STANDARD CONTENTS OF NOTICES FOR DELIVERY TO OTHER PERSONS ETC

**[2.39]**

Note
[Note: the requirements in Chapter 7 must be read with rule 1.6 which sets out the information required to identify an office-holder, a company etc]

**[2.40]**

**1.28 Standard contents of notices to be delivered to persons other than the registrar of companies**
(1)   Where the Act or these Rules require a notice to be delivered to a person other than the registrar of companies in respect of proceedings under Parts 1 to 11 of the Act or the EU Regulation, the notice must contain the standard contents set out in this Chapter (in addition to any content specifically required by the Act or another provision of these Rules).
(2)   A notice of more than one type must satisfy the requirements which apply to each.
(3)   However, the requirements in respect of a document which is to be delivered to another person at the same time as the registrar of companies may be satisfied by delivering to that other person a copy of the document delivered to the registrar.

**Amendments**—SI 2017/1115.

**[2.41]**

**1.29 Standard contents of all notices**

A notice must—

> (a) state the nature of the notice;
>
> (b) identify the proceedings;
>
> (c) in the case of proceedings relating to an individual, identify the bankrupt or debtor;
>
> (d) state the section of the Act, the paragraph of Schedule A1 or B1 or the rule under which the notice is given; and
>
> (e) in the case of a notice delivered by the office-holder, state the contact details for the office-holder.

**[2.42]**

**1.30 Standard contents of notices relating to the office of office-holders**

A notice relating to the office of the office-holder must also identify the office-holder and state—

> (a) the date of the event of which notice is delivered;
>
> (b) where the notice relates to an appointment, the person, body or court making the appointment; and
>
> (c) where the notice relates to the termination of an appointment, the reason for that termination.

**[2.43]**

**1.31 Standard contents of notices relating to documents**

A notice relating to a document must also state—

> (a) the nature of the document;
>
> (b) the date of the document; and
>
> (c) where the document relates to a period of time the period of time to which the document relates.

**[2.44]**

**1.32 Standard contents of notices relating to court proceedings or orders**

A notice relating to court proceedings must also identify those proceedings and if the notice relates to a court order state—

> (a) the nature of the order; and
>
> (b) the date of the order.

**[2.45]**

**1.33 Standard contents of notices of the results of decisions**

A notice of the result of a decision procedure, deemed consent procedure or meeting must also state—

> (a) the purpose of the procedure or meeting;
>
> (b) a description of the procedure or meeting used;
>
> (c) in the case of a decision procedure or meeting, the venue;
>
> (d) whether, in the case of a meeting, the required quorum was in place; and
>
> (e) the outcome (including any decisions made or resolutions passed).

**[2.46]**

**1.34 Standard contents of returns or reports of matters considered by company members by correspondence**

A return or report of a matter, consideration of which has been sought from the members of a company by correspondence, must also specify—

> (a) the purpose of the consideration; and

(b)    the outcome of the consideration (including any resolutions passed or deemed to be passed).

## CHAPTER 8

### APPLICATIONS TO THE COURT

**[2.47]**

**Note**

[Note: the requirements in Chapter 8 must be read with rule 1.6 which sets out the information required to identify an office-holder, a company etc]

**[2.48]**

**1.35  Standard contents and authentication of applications to the court under Parts 1 to 11 of the Act**

(1)   This rule applies to applications to court under Parts 1 to 11 of the Act (other than an application for an administration order, a winding up petition or a bankruptcy petition).

(2)   The application must state—

(a)    that the application is made under the Act or these Rules (as applicable);

(b)    the section of the Act or paragraph of a Schedule to the Act or the number of the rule under which it is made;

(c)    the names of the parties;

(d)    the name of the bankrupt, debtor or company which is the subject of the insolvency proceedings to which the application relates;

(e)    the court (and where applicable, the division or district registry of that court) or hearing centre in which the application is made;

(f)    where the court has previously allocated a number to the insolvency proceedings within which the application is made, that number;

(g)    the nature of the remedy or order applied for or the directions sought from the court;

(h)    the names and addresses of the persons on whom it is intended to serve the application or that no person is intended to be served;

(i)    where the Act or Rules require that notice of the application is to be delivered to specified persons, the names and addresses of all those persons (so far as known to the applicant); and

(j)    the applicant's address for service.

(3)   The application must be authenticated by or on behalf of the applicant or the applicant's solicitor.

**Derivation**—This rule derived from the Insolvency Rules 1986, SI 1986/1925, r 7.3.

**General note**—Prior to the revocation of IR 1986, r 7.2, applicants were required to use a single form of insolvency application notice in Form 7.1A. As noted in the general note to r 1.8, there are no longer any forms prescribed by IR 2016. Most practitioners continue, however, to make to make applications in a form resembling the old Form 7.1A. An acceptable, but non-mandatory, template can be freely accessed at https://www.gov.uk/government/publications/apply-to-the-cour t-about-an-insolvency-issue-form-iaa.

Further procedural guidance is contained in the *Practice Direction – Insolvency Proceedings* (July 2020) [2020] BPIR 1211. Paragraph 4 of the Practice Direction governs court documents and provides appropriate guidance.

**Scope of insolvency applications**—Chief ICC Judge Briggs held in *Manolete Partners Plc v Hayward and Barrett Holdings Ltd* [2021] EWHC 1481 (Ch) that only applications arising under Pts 1 to 11 of the IA 1986 could be included within an insolvency application. Other claims are required to be commenced separately by way of a claim under Pt 7 of the CPR, even where these are brought at the same time as matters arising under Pts 1 to 11. On the facts of that case, an assignee of the causes of action of a company in liquidation was unable to pursue company claims (which could have been brought under s 212 by the liquidator had they not been assigned) by way of an insolvency application alongside preference claims under s 239. This decision appears to have far-reaching implications for insolvency practice, as it also affects s 423 claims arising under

Part 16 of the IA 1986, which are frequently brought by way of insolvency application, either on their own or with other claims arising under Pts 1 to 11. See notes to s 423.

**Does the court have jurisdiction to strike out an insolvency application?**—In *Port v Auger* [1994] 1 WLR 862, in a judgment critical of the confusion potentially created by the use of the former terms 'originating application' and 'ordinary application', Harman J held that the court had no jurisdiction to strike out an originating or ordinary application (now an insolvency application) under the former Ord 18, r 19 of the former Rules of the Supreme Court on the grounds that any such application did not constitute what was formerly termed a 'pleading'. Apart from its inherent jurisdiction, the court's jurisdiction to strike out is now contained in CPR 3.4(2), which refers to 'statement of case' as defined in CPR 2.3. In *Re John Holmes, Sadler v Holmes* (unreported) 20 February 2006, ChD, Registrar Jaques held that the reasoning in *Port v Auger* will continue to apply following the advent of the CPR, since the purpose of both an originating and ordinary application (now an insolvency application) remains in identifying the issues to which the court is addressed together with the relief sought by an applicant, as opposed to disclosing anything by way of the detailed particulars of claim. However, it appears that CPR 3.4(2) will apply where the court has directed service of particulars or points of claim, points of defence etc, provided that the court is satisfied that those points meet the definition of a statement of case in CPR 2.3, given Harman J's view (at 866B–F) that the former Ord 18, r 19 would have had application to what were previously termed 'pleadings'. Equally, as Harman J identified at 874G–H, the court retains an inherent power to strike out an originating or ordinary application – whether or not supported by evidence and whether or not elaborated upon by particulars or points of claim, points of defence etc – where the court is satisfied that the application constitutes an abuse of process or is vexatious or frivolous in the sense that the claim, on its face, appears to be wholly unfounded upon legally recognisable principles. When striking out under its inherent jurisdiction, the court's approach is not in weighing up the truth of any party's evidence but is instead in assessing the substance of the allegation or case advanced whilst accepting the truthfulness of any supporting particulars or evidence.

Apart from the striking out jurisdictions identified above it is also now open to an applicant or respondent in insolvency proceedings to seek summary judgment under CPR 24.2 which applies and involves a 'no real prospect' test.

CHAPTER 9

DELIVERY OF DOCUMENTS AND OPTING OUT (SECTIONS 246C, 248A, 379C AND 383A)

**[2.49]**

**1.36 Application of Chapter**
[Note: the registrar's rules include provision for the electronic delivery of documents.]
(1) This Chapter applies where a document is required under the Act or these Rules to be delivered, filed, forwarded, furnished, given, sent, or submitted in respect of proceedings under Parts 1 to 11 of the Act or the EU Regulation unless the Act, a rule or an order of the court makes different provision including one requiring service of the document.
(2) However in respect of delivery of a document to the registrar of companies—
    (a)    subject to sub-paragraph (b) only the following rules in this Chapter apply: rules 1.42 (postal delivery of documents), 1.43 (delivery by document exchange), 1.44 (personal delivery) and 1.52 (proof of delivery of documents);
    (b)    the registrar's rules made under sections 1068 and 1117 of the Companies Act apply to determine the date when any document is received by the registrar of companies.

Amendments—SI 2017/1115.

**[2.50]**

**1.37 Delivery to the creditors and opting out**
(1) Where the Act or a rule requires an office-holder to deliver a document to the creditors, or the creditors in a class, the requirement is satisfied by the delivery of the document to all such creditors of whose address the office-holder is aware other than opted-out creditors unless the opt out does not apply.

(2) Where a creditor has opted out from receiving documents, the opt out does not apply to—

    (a)    a notice which the Act requires to be delivered to all creditors without expressly excluding opted-out creditors;

    (b)    a notice of a change in the office-holder or the contact details for the office-holder;

    (c)    a notice as provided for by sections 246C(2) or 379C(2) (notices of distributions, intended distributions and notices required to be given by court order); or

    (d)    a document which these Rules requires to accompany a notice within sub-paragraphs (a) to (c).

(3) The office-holder must begin to treat a creditor as an opted-out creditor as soon as reasonably practicable after delivery of the creditor's election to opt out.

(4) An office-holder in any consecutive insolvency proceedings of a different kind under Parts 1 to 11 of the Act in respect of the same company or individual who is aware that a creditor was an opted-out creditor in the earlier proceedings must treat the creditor as an opted out creditor in the consecutive proceedings.

**Derivation**—This rule derived from the Insolvency Rules 1986, SI 1986/1925, rr 4.44, 6.74.
**Amendments**—SI 2017/366.

## [2.51]

### 1.38 Creditor's election to opt out

(1) A creditor may at any time elect to be an opted-out creditor.

(2) The creditor's election to opt out must be by a notice in writing authenticated and dated by the creditor.

(3) The creditor must deliver the notice to the office-holder.

(4) A creditor becomes an opted-out creditor when the notice is delivered to the office-holder.

(5) An opted-out creditor—

    (a)    will remain an opted-out creditor for the duration of the proceedings unless the opt out is revoked; and

    (b)    is deemed to be an opted-out creditor in respect of any consecutive insolvency proceedings under Parts 1 to 11 of the Act of a different kind relating to the same company or individual.

(6) The creditor may at any time revoke the election to opt out by a further notice in writing, authenticated and dated by the creditor and delivered to the office-holder.

(7) The creditor ceases to be an opted-out creditor from the date the notice is received by the office-holder.

## [2.52]

### 1.39 Office-holder to provide information to creditors on opting-out

(1) The office-holder must, in the first communication with a creditor, inform the creditor in writing that the creditor may elect to opt out of receiving further documents relating to the proceedings.

(2) The communication must contain—

    (a)    identification and contact details for the office-holder;

    (b)    a statement that the creditor has the right to elect to opt out of receiving further documents about the proceedings unless—

        (i)    the Act requires a document to be delivered to all creditors without expressly excluding opted-out creditors,

        (ii)    it is a notice relating to a change in the office-holder or the office-holder's contact details, or

        (iii)    it is a notice of a dividend or proposed dividend or a notice which the court orders to be sent to all creditors or all creditors of a particular category to which the creditor belongs;

    (c)    a statement that opting-out will not affect the creditor's entitlement to receive dividends should any be paid to creditors;

    (d)    a statement that unless these Rules provide to the contrary opting-out will not affect any right the creditor may have to vote in a decision procedure or a participate in a deemed consent procedure in the proceedings although the creditor will not receive notice of it;

    (e)    a statement that a creditor who opts out will be treated as having opted out in respect of any consecutive insolvency proceedings of a different kind in respect of the same company or individual; and

    (f)    information about how the creditor may elect to be or cease to be an opted-out creditor.

**[2.53]**

### 1.40 Delivery of documents to authorised recipients

Where under the Act or these Rules a document is to be delivered to a person (other than by being served on that person), it may be delivered instead to any other person authorised in writing to accept delivery on behalf of the first-mentioned person.

Derivation—This rule derived from the Insolvency Rules 1986, SI 1986/1925, r 12A.5.

**[2.54]**

### 1.41 Delivery of documents to joint office-holders

Where there are joint office-holders in insolvency proceedings, delivery of a document to one of them is to be treated as delivery to all of them.

Derivation—This rule derived from the Insolvency Rules 1986, SI 1986/1925, r 12A.15.

**[2.55]**

### 1.42 Postal delivery of documents

(1)    A document is delivered if it is sent by post in accordance with the provisions of this rule.

(2)    First class or second class post may be used to deliver a document except where these Rules require first class post to be used.

(3)    Unless the contrary is shown—

    (a)    a document sent by first class post is treated as delivered on the second business day after the day on which it is posted;

    (b)    a document sent by second class post is treated as delivered on the fourth business day after the day on which it is posted;

    (c)    where a post-mark appears on the envelope in which a document was posted, the date of that post-mark is to be treated as the date on which the document was posted.

(4)    In this rule "post-mark" means a mark applied by a postal operator which records the date on which a letter entered the postal system of the postal operator.

Derivation—This rule derived from the Insolvency Rules 1986, SI 1986/1925, r 12A.3.

**[2.56]**

### 1.43 Delivery by document exchange

(1)    A document is delivered to a member of a document exchange if it is delivered to that document exchange.

(2)    Unless the contrary is shown, a document is treated as delivered—

    (a)    one business day after the day it is delivered to the document exchange where the sender and the intended recipient are members of the same document exchange; or

    (b)    two business days after the day it is delivered to the departure facility of the sender's document exchange where the sender and the intended recipient are members of different document exchanges.

**[2.57]**

### 1.44 Personal delivery of documents

A document is delivered if it is personally delivered in accordance with the rules for personal service in CPR Part 6.

Derivation—This rule derived from the Insolvency Rules 1986, SI 1986/1925, r 12A.2.

**[2.58]**

### 1.45 Electronic delivery of documents

(1)  A document is delivered if it is sent by electronic means and the following conditions apply.

(2)  The conditions are that the intended recipient of the document has—

(a)   given actual or deemed consent for the electronic delivery of the document;

(b)   not revoked that consent before the document is sent; and

(c)   provided an electronic address for the delivery of the document.

(3)  Consent may relate to a specific case or generally.

(4)  For the purposes of paragraph (2)(a) an intended recipient is deemed to have consented to the electronic delivery of a document by the office-holder where the intended recipient and the person who is the subject of the insolvency proceedings had customarily communicated with each other by electronic means before the proceedings commenced.

(5)  Unless the contrary is shown, a document is to be treated as delivered by electronic means to an electronic address where the sender can produce a copy of the electronic communication which—

(a)   contains the document; and

(b)   shows the time and date the communication was sent and the electronic address to which it was sent.

(6)  Unless the contrary is shown, a document sent electronically is treated as delivered to the electronic address to which it is sent at 9.00 am on the next business day after it was sent.

Derivation—This rule derived from the Insolvency Rules 1986, SI 1986/1925, r 12A.10.

**[2.59]**

### 1.46 Electronic delivery of documents to the court

(1)  A document may not be delivered to a court by electronic means unless this is expressly permitted by the CPR, a Practice Direction, or these Rules.

(2)  A document delivered by electronic means is to be treated as delivered to the court at the time it is recorded by the court as having been received or otherwise as the CPR, a Practice Direction or these Rules provide.

Derivation—This rule derived from the Insolvency Rules 1986, SI 1986/1925, r 12A.14.

General note—See *Practice Note* [2020] BCC 211 and under the heading 'Electronic filing' in the note to para 29 of Sch B1 for guidance on out-of-hours administration appointments using CE-File.

**[2.60]**

### 1.47 Electronic delivery of notices to enforcement officers

Where anything in the Act or these Rules provides for the delivery of a notice to an enforcement officer or enforcement agent, it may be delivered by electronic means to a person who has been authorised to receive such a notice on behalf of a specified enforcement officer or enforcement agent or on behalf of enforcement officers or enforcement agents generally.

Derivation—This rule derived from the Insolvency Rules 1986, SI 1986/1925, r 12A.29.

## [2.61]

### 1.48 Electronic delivery by office-holders

(1)   Where an office-holder delivers a document by electronic means, the document must contain, or be accompanied by, a statement that the recipient may request a hard copy of the document and a telephone number, email address and postal address that may be used to make that request.

(2)   An office-holder who receives such a request must deliver a hard copy of the document to the recipient free of charge within five business days of receipt of the request.

Derivation—This rule derived from the Insolvency Rules 1986, SI 1986/1925, r 12A.11.

## [2.62]

### 1.49 Use of website by office-holder to deliver a particular document (sections 246B and 379B)

[Note: rule 3.54(3) allows notice of an extension to an administration to be given on a website, and rules 2.25(6) and 8.22(5) do likewise in respect of notice of the result of the consideration of a proposal for a CVA and an IVA respectively.]

(1)   This rule applies for the purposes of sections 246B and 379B (use of websites).

(2)   An office-holder who is required to deliver a document to any person may (except where personal delivery is required) satisfy that requirement by delivering a notice to that person which contains—

   (a)   a statement that the document is available for viewing and downloading on a website;

   (b)   the website's address and any password necessary to view and download the document; and

   (c)   a statement that the person to whom the notice is delivered may request a hard copy of the document with a telephone number, email address and postal address which may be used to make that request.

(3)   An office-holder who receives such a request must deliver a hard copy of the document to the recipient free of charge within five business days of receipt of the request.

(4)   A document to which a notice under paragraph (2) relates must—

   (a)   remain available on the website for the period required by rule 1.51; and

   (b)   be in a format that enables it to be downloaded within a reasonable time of an electronic request being made for it to be downloaded.

(5)   A document which is delivered to a person by means of a website in accordance with this rule, is deemed to have been delivered—

   (a)   when the document is first made available on the website; or

   (b)   when the notice under paragraph (2) is delivered to that person, if that is later.

Derivation—This rule derived from the Insolvency Rules 1986, SI 1986/1925, r 12A.12.

## [2.63]

### 1.50 General use of website to deliver documents

(1)   The office-holder may deliver a notice to each person to whom a document will be required to be delivered in the insolvency proceedings which contains—

   (a)   a statement that future documents in the proceedings other than those mentioned in paragraph (2) will be made available for viewing and downloading on a website without notice to the recipient and that the office-holder will not be obliged to deliver any such documents to the recipient of the notice unless it is requested by that person;

   (b)   a telephone number, email address and postal address which may be used to make a request for a hard copy of a document;

   (c)   a statement that the recipient of the notice may at any time request a hard copy of any or all of the following—

      (i)     all documents currently available for viewing on the website,

      (ii)    all future documents which may be made available there, and

    (d)    the address of the website, any password required to view and download a relevant document from that site.

(2)   A statement under paragraph (1)(a) does not apply to the following documents—

    (a)    a document for which personal delivery is required;

    (b)    a notice under rule 14.29 of intention to declare a dividend; and

    (c)    a document which is not delivered generally.

(3)   A document is delivered generally if it is delivered to some or all of the following classes of persons—

    (a)    members,

    (b)    contributories,

    (c)    creditors;

    (d)    any class of members, contributories or creditors.

(4)   An office-holder who has delivered a notice under paragraph (1) is under no obligation—

    (a)    to notify a person to whom the notice has been delivered when a document to which the notice applies has been made available on the website; or

    (b)    to deliver a hard copy of such a document unless a request is received under paragraph (1)(c).

(5)   An office-holder who receives such a request—

    (a)    in respect of a document which is already available on the website must deliver a hard copy of the document to the recipient free of charge within five business days of receipt of the request; and

    (b)    in respect of all future documents must deliver each such document in accordance with the requirements for delivery of such a document in the Act and these Rules.

(6)   A document to which a statement under paragraph (1)(a) applies must—

    (a)    remain available on the website for the period required by rule 1.51; and

    (b)    must be in such a format as to enable it to be downloaded within a reasonable time of an electronic request being made for it to be downloaded.

(7)   A document which is delivered to a person by means of a website in accordance with this rule, is deemed to have been delivered—

    (a)    when the relevant document was first made available on the website; or

    (b)    if later, when the notice under paragraph (1) was delivered to that person.

(8)   Paragraph (7) does not apply in respect of a person who has made a request under paragraph (1)(c)(ii) for hard copies of all future documents.

**Derivation**—This rule derived from the Insolvency Rules 1986, SI 1986/1925, r 12A.13.

## [2.64]

### 1.51 Retention period for documents made available on websites

(1)   This rule applies to a document which is made available on a website under rules 1.49, 1.50, 2.25(6) (notice of the result of the consideration of a proposal for a CVA), 3.54(3) (notice of an extension to an administration) and 8.22(4) (notice of the result of the consideration of a proposal for an IVA).

(2)   Such a document must continue to be made available on the website until two months after the end of the particular insolvency proceedings or the release of the last person to hold office as the office-holder in those proceedings.

**Derivation**—This rule derived from the Insolvency Rules 1986, SI 1986/1925, rr 12A.12, 12A.13.

**[2.65]**

**1.52 Proof of delivery of documents**

(1)   A certificate complying with this rule is proof that a document has been duly delivered to the recipient in accordance with this Chapter unless the contrary is shown.

(2)   A certificate must state the method of delivery and the date of the sending, posting or delivery (as the case may be).

(3)   In the case of the official receiver or the adjudicator the certificate must be given by—

    (a)   the official receiver or the adjudicator; or

    (b)   a member of the official receiver's or adjudicator's staff.

(4)   In the case of an office-holder other than the official receiver or the adjudicator the certificate must be given by—

    (a)   the office-holder;

    (b)   the office-holder's solicitor; or

    (c)   a partner or an employee of either of them.

(5)   In the case of a person other than an office-holder the certificate must be given by that person and must state—

    (a)   that the document was delivered by that person; or

    (b)   that another person (named in the certificate) was instructed to deliver it.

(6)   A certificate under this rule may be endorsed on a copy of the document to which it relates.

**Derivation**—This rule derived from the Insolvency Rules 1986, SI 1986/1925, r 12A.8.

**[2.66]**

**1.53 Delivery of proofs and details of claims**

(1)   Once a proof has, or details of a claim have, been delivered to an office-holder in accordance with these Rules that proof or those details need not be delivered again; and accordingly, where a provision of these Rules requires delivery of a proof or details of a claim by a certain time, that requirement is satisfied if the proof has or the details have already been delivered.

(2)   Paragraph (1) also applies to those cases set out in rule 14.3(2)(a) and (b) where a creditor who has proved in insolvency proceedings is deemed to have proved in an insolvency proceedings which immediately follows that proceeding.

**Derivation**—This rule derived from the Insolvency Rules 1986, SI 1986/1925, rr 4.54, 6.81.

CHAPTER 10

INSPECTION OF DOCUMENTS, COPIES AND PROVISION OF INFORMATION

**[2.67]**

**1.54 Right to copies of documents**

Where the Act, in relation to proceedings under Parts 1 to 11 of the Act, or these Rules give a person the right to inspect documents, that person has a right to be supplied on request with copies of those documents on payment of the standard fee for copies.

**Derivation**—This rule derived from the Insolvency Rules 1986, SI 1986/1925, r 12A.52.

**[2.68]**

**1.55 Charges for copies of documents provided by the office-holder**

Except where prohibited by these Rules, an office-holder is entitled to require the payment of the standard fee for copies of documents requested by a creditor, member, contributory or member of a liquidation or creditors' committee.

**Derivation**—This rule derived from the Insolvency Rules 1986, SI 1986/1925, r 12A.53.

**[2.69]**

### 1.56 Offence in relation to inspection of documents

(1) It is an offence for a person who does not have a right under these Rules to inspect a relevant document falsely to claim to be a creditor, a member of a company or a contributory of a company with the intention of gaining sight of the document.

(2) A relevant document is one which is on the court file, the bankruptcy file or held by the office-holder or any other person and which a creditor, a member of a company or a contributory of a company has the right to inspect under these Rules.

(3) A person guilty of an offence under this rule is liable to imprisonment or a fine, or both.

**Derivation**—This rule derived from the Insolvency Rules 1986, SI 1986/1925, r 12.18.

**General note**—The penalty for breaching this rule is, on indictment, imprisonment for 2 years or a fine or both, and on summary hearing it is imprisonment for 6 months or a fine or both (Sch 3).

**[2.70]**

### 1.57 Right to list of creditors

(1) This rule applies to—
- (a) administration;
- (b) creditors' voluntary winding up;
- (c) winding up by the court; and
- (d) bankruptcy.

(2) A creditor has the right to require the office-holder to provide a list of the names and addresses of the creditors and the amounts of their respective debts unless—
- (a) a statement of affairs has been filed with the court or delivered to the registrar of companies; or
- (b) the information is available for inspection on the bankruptcy file.

(3) The office-holder on being required to provide such a list—
- (a) must deliver it to the person requiring the list as soon as reasonably practicable; and
- (b) may charge the standard fee for copies for a hard copy.

(4) The office-holder may omit the name and address of a creditor if the office-holder thinks its disclosure would be prejudicial to the conduct of the proceedings or might reasonably be expected to lead to violence against any person.

(5) In such a case the list must include—
- (a) the amount of that creditor's debt; and
- (b) a statement that the name and address of the creditor has been omitted for that debt.

**Derivation**—This rule derived from the Insolvency Rules 1986, SI 1986/1925, r 12A.54.

**Sub-paragraph (3)(b)**—The amount that can be charged as the standard fee is set out in r 1.2(2).

**'Winding up'**—The rule does not apply to companies where a winding-up petition is pending: *Equitas Ltd v Jacob* [2005] EWHC 1440 (Ch), [2005] BPIR 1312.

**[2.71]**

### 1.58 Confidentiality of documents: grounds for refusing inspection

(1) Where an office-holder considers that a document forming part of the records of the insolvency proceedings—
- (a) should be treated as confidential; or
- (b) is of such a nature that its disclosure would be prejudicial to the conduct of the proceedings or might reasonably be expected to lead to violence against any person;

the office-holder may decline to allow it to be inspected by a person who would otherwise be entitled to inspect it.

(2) The persons to whom the office-holder may refuse inspection include members of a liquidation committee or a creditors' committee.

(3)   Where the office-holder refuses inspection of a document, the person wishing to inspect it may apply to the court which may reconsider the office-holder's decision.

(4)   The court's decision may be subject to such conditions (if any) as it thinks just.

Derivation—This rule derived from the Insolvency Rules 1986, SI 1986/1925, r 12A.51.

## PART 2   COMPANY VOLUNTARY ARRANGEMENTS (CVA)

### CHAPTER 1

#### PRELIMINARY

**[2.72]**

**2.1 Interpretation**

In this Part—

"nominee" and "supervisor" include the proposed nominee or supervisor in relation to a proposal for a CVA; and

"proposal" means a proposal for a CVA.

### CHAPTER 2

#### THE PROPOSAL FOR A CVA (SECTION 1)

**[2.73]**

**Note**

[Note: (1) section 1 of the Act sets out who may propose a CVA;

(2)   a document required by the Act or these Rules must also contain the standard contents set out in Part 1.]

**[2.74]**

**2.2 Proposal for a CVA: general principles and amendment**

(1)   A proposal must—

(a)   contain identification details for the company;

(b)   explain why the proposer thinks a CVA is desirable;

(c)   explain why the creditors are expected to agree to a CVA; and

(d)   be authenticated and dated by the proposer.

(2)   The proposal may be amended with the nominee's agreement in writing in the following cases.

(3)   The first case is where—

(a)   no steps have been taken to obtain a moratorium;

(b)   the nominee is not the liquidator or administrator of the company; and

(c)   the nominee's report has not been filed with the court under section 2(2).

(4)   The second case is where—

(a)   the proposal is made with a view to obtaining a moratorium; and

(b)   the nominee's statement under paragraph 6(2) of Schedule A1 (nominee's opinion on prospects of CVA being approved etc) has not yet been submitted to the directors.

Derivation—This rule derived from the Insolvency Rules 1986, SI 1986/1925, r 1.3.

RULE 2.2(2)

Scope of provision—Nominees will invariably be heavily involved in assisting in the drafting of the directors' proposal. Indeed, in practice, the proposal is usually produced by nominees themselves, or their firm, following the provision of information by the directors and/or their advisors or the company's advisors. The amendment of a proposal is therefore most likely to arise from observations made by nominees themselves, or others who may be assisting in the preparation of the proposal, following an analysis of its contents, or, alternatively, following an unexpected change of circumstances.

**RULES 2.2(3) AND 2.2(4)**

Scope of provision—In a departure from the position which prevailed prior to the introduction of the Insolvency (England and Wales) Rules 2016, the rules now provide for two specific situations in which a proposal can be amended. The rules contain specific requirements which will need to be met in each of the two situations.

**[2.75]**

## 2.3 Proposal: contents

(1)   The proposal must set out the following so far as known to the proposer—

| | |
|---|---|
| Assets | (a) the company's assets, with an estimate of their respective values;<br>(b) which assets are charged and the extent of the charge;<br>(c) which assets are to be excluded from the CVA; and<br>(d) particulars of any property to be included in the CVA which is not owned by the company, including details of who owns such property, and the terms on which it will be available for inclusion; |
| Liabilities | (e) the nature and amount of the company's liabilities;<br>(f) how the company's liabilities will be met, modified, postponed or otherwise dealt with by means of the CVA and in particular—<br>(i) how preferential creditors and creditors who are, or claim to be, secured will be dealt with,<br>(ii) how creditors who are connected with the company will be dealt with,<br>(iii) if the company is not in administration or liquidation whether, if the company did go into administration or liquidation, there are circumstances which might give rise to claims under section 238 (transactions at an undervalue), section 239 (preferences), section 244 (extortionate credit transactions), or section 245 (floating charges invalid), and<br>(iv) where there are circumstances that might give rise to such claims, whether, and if so what, provision will be made to indemnify the company in respect of them; |
| Nominee's fees and expenses | (g) the amount proposed to be paid to the nominee by way of fees and expenses; |
| Supervisor | (h) identification and contact details for the supervisor;<br>(i) confirmation that the supervisor is qualified to act as an insolvency practitioner in relation to the company and the name of the relevant recognised professional body which is the source of the supervisor's authorisation;<br>(j) how the fees and expenses of the supervisor will be determined and paid;<br>(k) the functions to be performed by the supervisor;<br>(l) where it is proposed that two or more supervisors be appointed a statement whether acts done in connection with the CVA may be done by any one or more of them or must be done by all of them; |
| Guarantees and proposed guarantees | (m) whether any, and if so what, guarantees have been given in respect of the company's debts, specifying which of the guarantors are persons connected with the company;<br>(n) whether any, and if so what, guarantees are proposed to be offered for the purposes of the CVA and, if so, by whom and whether security is to be given or sought; |
| Timing | (o) the proposed duration of the CVA;<br>(p) the proposed dates of distributions to creditors, with estimates of their amounts; |
| Type of proceedings | (q) whether the proceedings will be COMI proceedings, establishment proceedings or proceedings to which the EU Regulation as it has effect in the law of the United Kingdom does not apply with reasons; |

| Conduct of the business | (r) how the business of the company will be conducted during the CVA; |
|---|---|
| Further credit facilities | (s) details of any further proposed credit facilities for the company, and how the debts so arising are to be paid; |
| Handling of funds arising | (t) the manner in which funds held for the purposes of the CVA are to be banked, invested or otherwise dealt with pending distribution to creditors; <br> (u) how funds held for the purpose of payment to creditors, and not so paid on the termination of the CVA, will be dealt with; <br> (v) how the claim of any person bound by the CVA by virtue of section 5(2)(b)(ii) or paragraph 37(2)(b)(ii) of Schedule A1 will be dealt with; |
| Address (where moratorium proposed) | (w) where the proposal is made in relation to a company that is eligible for a moratorium (in accordance with paragraphs 2 and 3 of Schedule A1) with a view to obtaining a moratorium under Schedule A1, the address to which the documents referred to in paragraph 6(1) of that Schedule must be delivered; and |
| Other matters | (x) any other matters that the proposer considers appropriate to enable members and creditors to reach an informed decision on the proposal. |

(2)   Where the proposal is made by the directors, an estimate so far as known to them of—

(a)   the value of the prescribed part if the proposal for the CVA is not accepted and the company goes into liquidation (whether or not the liquidator might be required under section 176A to make the prescribed part available for the satisfaction of unsecured debts); and

(b)   the value of the company's net property (as defined by section 176A(6)) on the date that the estimate is made.

(3)   Where the proposal is made by the administrator or liquidator the following so far as known to the office-holder—

(a)   an estimate of—

(i)   the value of the prescribed part (whether or not the administrator or liquidator might be required under section 176A to make the prescribed part available for the satisfaction of unsecured debts), and

(ii)   the value of the company's net property (as defined by section 176A(6)); and

(b)   a statement as to whether the administrator or liquidator proposes to make an application to the court under section 176A(5) and if so the reasons for the application; and

(c)   details of the nature and amount of the company's preferential creditors.

(4)   Information may be excluded from an estimate under paragraph (2) or (3)(a) if the inclusion of the information could seriously prejudice the commercial interests of the company.

(5)   If the exclusion of such information affects the calculation of the estimate, the proposal must include a statement to that effect.

**Amendments**—SI 2017/1115; SI 2019/146, as from IP completion day (as defined in the European Union (Withdrawal Agreement) Act 2020, s 39(1)–(5)).

**Derivation**—This rule derived from the Insolvency Rules 1986, SI 1986/1925, r 1.3.

**General note**—The detailed disclosure requirements in r 2.3 are intended to enable members and, more especially, creditors to make an informed assessment of what is proposed. To that end, these disclosure requirements should not be read as exhaustive as a matter of course. The proposal should, for example, address what might otherwise be plainly unanswered questions as to the underlying basis of or the specific content of the proposal. The notes to s 2(3) suggest the type of additional terms which might be included in a proposal.

For the court's approach to the construction of the terms of a voluntary arrangement see the notes to s 5(2).

**RULES 2.3(2) AND 2.3(3)**

**Scope of provision**—For the nature of the so-called reserved fund for unsecured creditors see the notes to s 176A.

**RULE 2.3(1)(p)**

**Scope of provision**—This item must raise consideration of whether creditors are able to make an informed assessment of the proposal if a statement appears in the proposal to the effect that estimated distributions are subject to professional costs where no indication or meaningful basis for the calculation of such costs is apparent from the proposal, on which see r 2.3(1)(j).

**RULE 2.3(1)(g)**

**Scope of provision**—In *Re Julie O'Sullivan* [2001] BPIR 534 HHJ Maddocks, sitting as a High Court judge, dismissed an appeal from the decision of a district judge which had refused an interim order in connection with an IVA on the grounds that the nominee's fee of £2,000 was excessive set against the relatively modest level of assets and liabilities disclosed in the proposal. The decision is authority for the proposition that the court has jurisdiction to interfere with the proposed level of nominee's fees, even though such fees would otherwise be a matter for consideration by creditors. Although leave to appeal to the Court of Appeal was granted by HHJ Maddocks, the appeal did not proceed.

**RULE 2.3(1)(u)**

**Scope of provision**—For the effect of the Court of Appeal's decision in *Re Gallagher (NT) & Son Ltd* [2002] 2 BCLC 133, and the effect of liquidation on any trust created under the arrangement, see the notes under that heading to s 1.

CHAPTER 3

PROCEDURE FOR A CVA WITHOUT A MORATORIUM

**[2.76]**

**Note**

[Note: a document required by the Act or these Rules must also contain the standard contents set out in Part 1.]

**[2.77]**

**2.4 Procedure for proposal where the nominee is not the liquidator or the administrator (section 2)**

(1)   This rule applies where the nominee is not the same person as the liquidator or the administrator.

(2)   A nominee who consents to act must deliver a notice of that consent to the proposer as soon as reasonably practicable after the proposal has been submitted to the nominee under section 2(3).

(3)   The notice must state the date the nominee received the proposal.

(4)   The period of 28 days in which the nominee must submit a report to the court under section 2(2) begins on the date the nominee received the proposal as stated in the notice.

Derivation—This rule derived from the Insolvency Rules 1986, SI 1986/1925, r 1.4.

**[2.78]**

**2.5 Information for the official receiver**

Where the company is being wound up by the court, the liquidator must deliver to the official receiver—

(a)   a copy of the proposal; and

(b)   the name and address of the nominee (if the nominee is not the liquidator).

Derivation—This rule derived from the Insolvency Rules 1986, SI 1986/1925, r 1.10.

**[2.79]**

**2.6 Statement of affairs (section 2(3))**

(1)   The statement of the company's affairs required by section 2(3) must contain the following—

- (a)   a list of the company's assets, divided into such categories as are appropriate for easy identification, and with each category given an estimated value;
- (b)   in the case of any property on which a claim against the company is wholly or partly secured, particulars of the claim, and of how and when the security was created;
- (c)   the names and addresses of the preferential creditors, with the amounts of their respective claims;
- (d)   the names and addresses of the unsecured creditors with the amounts of their respective claims;
- (e)   particulars of any debts owed by the company to persons connected with it;
- (f)   particulars of any debts owed to the company by persons connected with it;
- (g)   the names and addresses of the company's members, with details of their respective shareholdings; and
- (h)   any other particulars that the nominee in writing requires to be provided for the purposes of making the nominee's report on the proposal to the court.

(2)   The statement must be made up to a date not earlier than two weeks before the date of the proposal.

(3)   However the nominee may allow the statement to be made up to an earlier date (but not more than two months before the date of the proposal) where that is more practicable.

(4)   Where the statement is made up to an earlier date, the nominee's report to the court on the proposal must explain why.

(5)   The statement of affairs must be verified by a statement of truth made by the proposer.

(6)   Where the proposal is made by the directors, only one director need make the statement of truth.

**Derivation**—This rule derived from the Insolvency Rules 1986, SI 1986/1925, r 1.5.

**General note**—Typically in practice, so as to assist creditors in the making of an informed assessment as to the merits of the proposal, a comparative statement will accompany the statement of affairs which shows the projected outcome in alternative insolvency procedures, most obviously a creditors' voluntary liquidation and/or compulsory liquidation.

For the contents and certification of the company's statement of affairs where it is intended or proposed to obtain a moratorium under  Sch A1, see the notes to  r 2.11 and see  r 2.14.

**[2.80]**

**2.7 Application to omit information from statement of affairs delivered to creditors**

The nominee, the directors or any person appearing to the court to have an interest, may apply to the court for a direction that specified information be omitted from the statement of affairs as delivered to the creditors where disclosure of that information would be likely to prejudice the conduct of the CVA or might reasonably be expected to lead to violence against any person.

**Derivation**—This rule derived from the Insolvency Rules 1986, SI 1986/1925, r 1.56.

**[2.81]**

**2.8 Additional disclosure for assistance of nominee where the nominee is not the liquidator or administrator**

(1)   This rule applies where the nominee is not the administrator or the liquidator of the company.

(2)   If it appears to the nominee that the nominee's report to the court cannot properly be prepared on the basis of information in the proposal and statement of affairs, the nominee may require the proposer to provide—

(a)   more information about the circumstances in which, and the reasons why, a CVA is being proposed;

(b)   particulars of any previous proposals which have been made in relation to the company under Part 1 of the Act; and

(c)   any further information relating to the company's affairs which the nominee thinks necessary for the purposes of the report.

(3)   The nominee may require the proposer to inform the nominee whether, and if so in what circumstances, any person who is, or has been at any time in the two years before the date the nominee received the proposal, a director or officer of the company has—

(a)   been concerned in the affairs of any other company (whether or not incorporated in England and Wales) or limited liability partnership which has been the subject of insolvency proceedings;

(b)   been made bankrupt;

(c)   been the subject of a debt relief order; or

(d)   entered into an arrangement with creditors.

(4)   The proposer must give the nominee such access to the company's accounts and records as the nominee may require to enable the nominee to consider the proposal and prepare the nominee's report.

**Derivation**—This rule derived from the Insolvency Rules 1986, SI 1986/1925, r 1.6.

**General note**—The standing of the nominee to request further information of the sort identified here should be considered against the duties of the nominee as identified in the notes to s 2(2).

## [2.82]

### 2.9 Nominee's report on proposal where the nominee is not the liquidator or administrator (section 2(2))

(1)   The nominee's report must be filed with the court under section 2(2) accompanied by—

(a)   a copy of the report;

(b)   a copy of the proposal (as amended under rule 2.2(2), if that is the case); and

(c)   a copy of the statement of the company's affairs or a summary of it.

(2)   The report must state—

(a)   why the nominee considers the proposal does or does not have a reasonable prospect of being approved and implemented; and

(b)   why the members and the creditors should or should not be invited to consider the proposal.

(3)   The court must endorse the nominee's report and the copy of it with the date of filing and deliver the copy to the nominee.

(4)   The nominee must deliver a copy of the report to the company.

**Derivation**—This rule derived from the Insolvency Rules 1986, SI 1986/1925, r 1.7.

## [2.83]

### 2.10 Replacement of nominee (section 2(4))

(1)   A person (other than the nominee) who intends to apply to the court under section 2(4) for the nominee to be replaced must deliver a notice that such an application is intended to be made to the nominee at least five business days before filing the application with the court.

(2)   A nominee who intends to apply under that section to be replaced must deliver a notice that such an application is intended to be made to the person intending to make the proposal, or the proposer, at least five business days before filing the application with the court.

(3)   The court must not appoint a replacement nominee unless a statement by the replacement nominee has been filed with the court confirming that person—

(a)   consents to act; and

(b)   is qualified to act as an insolvency practitioner, in relation to the company.

Derivation—This rule derived from the Insolvency Rules 1986, SI 1986/1925, r 1.8.

General note—These provisions anticipate either a friendly or hostile replacement of the nominee.

## CHAPTER 4

### PROCEDURE FOR A CVA WITH A MORATORIUM

**[2.84]**

Note

[Note: a document required by the Act or these Rules must also contain the standard contents set out in Part 1.]

**[2.85]**

**2.11  Statement of affairs (paragraph 6(1)(b) of Schedule A1)**

(1)   The statement of affairs required by paragraph 6(1)(b) of Schedule A1 must contain the same information as is required by rule 2.6.

(2)   The statement must be made up to a date not earlier than two weeks before the date of the proposal.

(3)   However the nominee may allow the statement to be made up to an earlier date (but not more than two months before the proposal) where that is more practicable.

(4)   Where the statement is made up to an earlier date, the nominee's statement to the directors on the proposal must explain why.

(5)   The statement of affairs must be verified by a statement of truth made by at least one director.

Derivation—This rule derived from the Insolvency Rules 1986, SI 1986/1925, r 1.37.

General note—For guidance see the notes to r 2.6. Although there is no equivalent to r 2.8 (additional disclosure for assistance of nominee) within the Rules governing a CVA moratorium case, a provision to similar effect does appear in para 6(1)(c) of Sch A1.

**[2.86]**

**2.12  Application to omit information from a statement of affairs**

The nominee, the directors or any person appearing to the court to have an interest, may apply to the court for a direction that specified information be omitted from the statement of affairs as delivered to the creditors where disclosure of that information would be likely to prejudice the conduct of the CVA or might reasonably be expected to lead to violence against any person.

Derivation—This rule derived from the Insolvency Rules 1986, SI 1986/1925, r 1.56.

**[2.87]**

**2.13  The nominee's statement (paragraph 6(2) of Schedule A1)**

(1)   The nominee must submit to the directors the statement required by paragraph 6(2) of Schedule A1 within 28 days of the submission to the nominee of the proposal.

(2)   The statement must—

(a)   include the name and address of the nominee; and

(b)   be authenticated and dated by the nominee.

(3)   A statement which contains an opinion on all the matters referred to in paragraph 6(2) must—

(a)   explain why the nominee has formed that opinion; and

(b) if the nominee is willing to act, be accompanied by a statement of the nominee's consent to act in relation to the proposed CVA.

(4) The statement of the nominee's consent must—

(a) include the name and address of the nominee;

(b) state that the nominee is qualified to act as an insolvency practitioner in relation to the company; and

(c) be authenticated and dated by the nominee.

**Derivation**—This rule derived from the Insolvency Rules 1986, SI 1986/1925, r 1.38.

**General note**—This provision governs the nominee's response to the directors' proposal and has no equivalent where no moratorium is sought in support of the CVA. For further comment on the statement required by para 6(2) of Sch A1 see the notes to that provision.

## [2.88]

**2.14 Documents filed with court to obtain a moratorium (paragraph 7(1) of Schedule A1)**

(1) The statement of the company's affairs which the directors file with the court under paragraph 7(1)(b) of Schedule A1 must be the same as the statement they submit to the nominee under paragraph 6(1)(b) of that Schedule.

(2) The statement required by paragraph 7(1)(c) of that Schedule that the company is eligible for a moratorium must—

(a) be made by the directors;

(b) state that the company meets the requirements of paragraph 3 of Schedule A1 and is not a company which falls within paragraph 2(2) of that Schedule;

(c) confirm that the company is not ineligible for a moratorium under paragraph 4 of that Schedule; and

(d) be authenticated and dated by the directors.

(2A) A statement from the nominee whether the proceedings will be COMI proceedings, establishment proceedings or proceedings to which the EU Regulation as it has effect in the law of the United Kingdom does not apply with the reasons for so stating must also be filed with the court.

(3) The statement required by paragraph 7(1)(d) of that Schedule that the nominee has consented to act must be in the same terms as the statement referred to in rule 2.13(3)(b) and (4).

(4) The statement of the nominee's opinion required by paragraph 7(1)(e) of that Schedule—

(a) must be the same as the statement of opinion required by paragraph 6(2) of that Schedule; and

(b) must be filed with the court not later than ten business days after it was submitted to the directors.

(5) The documents filed with the court under paragraph 7(1) of that Schedule must be accompanied by four copies of a schedule, authenticated and dated by the directors, identifying the company and listing all the documents filed.

(6) The court must endorse the copies of the schedule with the date on which the documents were filed and deliver three copies of the endorsed schedule to the directors.

**Amendments**—SI 2017/702; SI 2017/1115; SI 2019/146, as from IP completion day (as defined in the European Union (Withdrawal Agreement) Act 2020, s 39(1)–(5)).

**Derivation**—This rule derived from the Insolvency Rules 1986, SI 1986/1925, r 1.39.

**General note**—The submission of documents to the court in accordance with this rule is of significant practical importance in that the moratorium – the nature of which is provided for in paras 12–19 of Sch A1 – comes into effect from the time at which each of those documents listed in para 7(1)(a)–(e) is filed with the court by virtue of para 8(1). The endorsement by the court of the date on which the documents were filed will provide clear evidence of the day on which the moratorium came into effect.

**The coming into effect of the moratorium and its extension**—In contrast to an IVA pursued with the protection of an interim order, the court is not involved in the making of an order for the moratorium provided for under Sch A1 in the case of a CVA. By virtue of para 8(1)–(3) of Sch A1 a moratorium ordinarily lasts for a 28-day period, although the period is capable of extension, or further extension, by meetings of the company and creditors by operation of paras 29 and 32, provision also being made on such an extension for the appointment of a new nominee under para 33

**Notice and advertisement of the moratorium**—The coming into effect of the moratorium imposes an obligation on the directors, on pain of criminal sanction, to notify the nominee of that fact forthwith, subject to which the nominee is obliged, again on pain of criminal sanction, to advertise – in accordance with r 2.15(2) – the fact of the moratorium and to give notice to the Registrar of Companies, the company and the petitioner on any extant winding-up petition presented prior to the moratorium coming into effect: see paras 9 and 10 of Sch A1. Notice of the coming into force of the moratorium must also be given to those persons specified in r 2.15(4) and (6). The nominee is also under an obligation by virtue of para 11(1) to advertise – in accordance with r 2.19 – and to give notice to those parties just mentioned of the fact of the moratorium coming to an end, on which see para 8(4)–(8).

## [2.89]

### 2.15 Notice and advertisement of beginning of a moratorium

(1) The directors must as soon as reasonably practicable after delivery to them of the endorsed copies of the schedule deliver two copies of the schedule to the nominee and one to the company.

(2) After delivery of the copies of the schedule, the nominee—

    (a) must as soon as reasonably practicable gazette a notice of the coming into force of the moratorium; and

    (b) may advertise the notice in such other manner as the nominee thinks fit.

(3) The notice must specify—

    (a) the nature of the business of the company;

    (b) that a moratorium under section 1A has come into force; and

    (c) the date on which it came into force.

(4) The nominee must as soon as reasonably practicable deliver a notice of the coming into force of the moratorium to—

    (a) the registrar of companies;

    (b) the company; and

    (c) any petitioning creditor of whose address the nominee is aware.

(5) The notice must specify—

    (a) the date on which the moratorium came into force; and

    (b) the court with which the documents to obtain the moratorium were filed.

(6) The nominee must deliver a notice of the coming into force of the moratorium and the date on which it came into force to—

    (a) any enforcement agent or other officer who to the knowledge of the nominee is charged with distress or other legal process, against the company or its property; and

    (b) any person who to the nominee's knowledge has distrained against the company or its property.

**Derivation**—This rule derived from the Insolvency Rules 1986, SI 1986/1925, r 1.40.

**General note**—See the notes to r 2.14.

Notice is required to be given to those parties under r 2.15(6) to prevent any inadvertent contempt which might otherwise come about as a consequence of any person so notified taking steps which would breach the statutory moratorium provided for in paras 12–19 of Sch A1.

## [2.90]

### 2.16 Notice of continuation of a moratorium where physical meeting of creditors is summoned (paragraph 8(3B) of Schedule A1)

(1) This rule applies where under paragraph 8(3B)(b) and (3C) of Schedule A1 the moratorium continues after the initial period of 28 days referred to in paragraph 8(3) of that Schedule because a physical meeting of the company's creditors is first summoned to take place after the end of that period.

(2)   The nominee must file with the court and deliver to the registrar of companies a notice of the continuation as soon as reasonably practicable after summoning such a meeting of the company's creditors.

(3)   The notice must—
- (a)   identify the company;
- (b)   give the name and address of the nominee;
- (c)   state the date on which the notice of the meeting was sent to the creditors under rule 15.6;
- (d)   state the date for which the meeting is summoned;
- (e)   state that under paragraph 8(3B)(b) and (3C) of Schedule A1 the moratorium will be continued to that date; and
- (f)   be authenticated and dated by the nominee.

## [2.91]

### 2.17 Notice of decision extending or further extending a moratorium (paragraph 36 of Schedule A1)

(1)   This rule applies where the moratorium is extended, or further extended by a decision which takes effect under paragraph 36 of Schedule A1.

(2)   The nominee must, as soon as reasonably practicable, file with the court and deliver to the registrar of companies a notice of the decision.

(3)   The notice must—
- (a)   identify the company;
- (b)   give the name and address of the nominee;
- (c)   state the date on which the moratorium was extended or further extended;
- (d)   state the new expiry date of the moratorium; and
- (e)   be authenticated and dated by the nominee.

**Derivation**—This rule derived from the Insolvency Rules 1986, SI 1986/1925, r 1.41.
**General note**—See the notes to r 2.14.

## [2.92]

### 2.18 Notice of court order extending or further extending or continuing or renewing a moratorium (paragraph 34(2) of Schedule A1)

Where the court makes an order extending, further extending, renewing or continuing a moratorium, the nominee must, as soon as reasonably practicable, deliver to the registrar of companies a notice stating the new expiry date of the moratorium.

**Derivation**—This rule derived from the Insolvency Rules 1986, SI 1986/1925, r 1.41.
**General note**—See the notes to r 2.14.

## [2.93]

### 2.19 Advertisement of end of a moratorium (paragraph 11(1) of Schedule A1)

(1)   After the moratorium ends, the nominee—
- (a)   must, as soon as reasonably practicable, gazette a notice of its coming to an end; and
- (b)   may advertise the notice in such other manner as the nominee thinks fit.

(2)   The notice must state—
- (a)   the nature of the company's business;
- (b)   that a moratorium under section 1A has ended; and
- (c)   the date on which it came to an end.

(3)   The nominee must, as soon as reasonably practicable—
- (a)   file with the court a notice specifying the date on which the moratorium ended; and
- (b)   deliver such a notice to—
  - (i)   the registrar of companies,
  - (ii)   the company, and

        (iii)   the creditors.

(4)  The notice to the court must—

    (a)    identify the company;

    (b)    give the name and address of the nominee; and

    (c)    be authenticated and dated by the nominee.

**Derivation**—This rule derived from the Insolvency Rules 1986, SI 1986/1925, r 1.42.
**General note**—See the notes to r 2.14.

## [2.94]

### 2.20 Disposal of charged property etc during a moratorium

(1)  This rule applies where the company applies to the court under paragraph 20 of Schedule A1 for permission to dispose of—

    (a)    property subject to a security; or

    (b)    goods under a hire-purchase agreement.

(2)  The court must fix a venue for hearing the application.

(3)  The company must as soon as reasonably practicable deliver a notice of the venue to the holder of the security or the owner of the goods under the agreement.

(4)  If an order is made, the court must deliver two sealed copies of the order to the company and the company must deliver one of them to the holder or owner as soon as reasonably practicable.

**Derivation**—This rule derived from the Insolvency Rules 1986, SI 1986/1925, r 1.43.

**General note**—The object of this rule is to facilitate the purpose of a CVA by providing a procedure, set out in para 20 of Sch A1, by which, as a statutory exception to the ordinary position, the company may dispose of charged assets without the consent of the charge-holder or a lessor under a hire-purchase agreement. For further guidance see the notes to para 20 of Sch A1.

## [2.95]

### 2.21 Withdrawal of nominee's consent to act (paragraph 25(5) of Schedule A1)

(1)  A nominee who withdraws consent to act, must file with the court and otherwise deliver a notice under paragraph 25(5) of Schedule A1 as soon as reasonably practicable.

(2)  The notice filed with the court must—

    (a)    identify the company;

    (b)    give the name and address of the nominee;

    (c)    specify the date on which the nominee withdrew consent;

    (d)    state, with reference to the reasons at paragraph 25(2) of that Schedule, why the nominee withdrew consent; and

    (e)    be authenticated and dated by the nominee.

**Derivation**—This rule derived from the Insolvency Rules 1986, SI 1986/1925, r 1.44.

**General note**—The impression conveyed by this rule on its face is that a nominee is free to withdraw his consent or act in any circumstances. Paragraph 25(1) of Sch A1, however, provides that a nominee 'may only withdraw his consent to act in the circumstances mentioned in this paragraph'. Those circumstances relate to the prospects of the proposed arrangement being implemented, the sufficiency of funding for business operations, the ineligibility of the company for a moratorium, or the failure on the part of the directors to furnish the nominee with the information necessary for monitoring the company's affairs during the moratorium. By virtue of para 25(4) the moratorium comes to an end if the nominee withdraws consent to act.

The withdrawal of the nominee's consent to act should be distinguished from his or her replacement, on his or her own application or that of the directors, under r 2.22. The replacement of the nominee by the court under that rule will not affect the operation of the moratorium.

## [2.96]

### 2.22 Application to the court to replace the nominee (paragraph 28 of Schedule A1)

(1)  Directors who intend to make an application under paragraph 28 of Schedule A1 for the nominee to be replaced must deliver a notice of the intention to make the

application to the nominee at least five business days before filing the application with the court.

(2)   A nominee who intends to make an application under that paragraph to be replaced must deliver notice of the intention to make the application to the directors at least five business days before filing the application with the court.

(3)   The court must not appoint a replacement nominee unless a statement by the replacement nominee has been filed with the court confirming that person—

(a)      consents to act; and

(b)      is qualified to act as an insolvency practitioner in relation to the company.

Derivation—This rule derived from the Insolvency Rules 1986, SI 1986/1925, r 1.45.

## [2.97]

### 2.23  Notice of appointment of replacement nominee

(1)   A person appointed as a replacement nominee must as soon as reasonably practicable deliver a notice of the appointment to the registrar of companies and the former nominee and, where the appointment is not by the court, file a notice of the appointment with the court.

(2)   The notice filed with the court must—

(a)      identify the company;

(b)      give the name and address of the replacement nominee;

(c)      specify the date on which the replacement nominee was appointed to act; and

(d)      be authenticated and dated by the replacement nominee.

Derivation—This rule derived from the Insolvency Rules 1986, SI 1986/1925, r 1.46.
General note—This provision has no equivalent where no moratorium is in force.

## [2.98]

### 2.24  Applications to court to challenge nominee's actions etc (paragraphs 26 and 27 of Schedule A1)

A person intending to make an application to the court under paragraph 26 or 27 of Schedule A1 must deliver a notice of the intention to make the application to the nominee at least five business days before filing the application with the court.

Derivation—This rule derived from the Insolvency Rules 1986, SI 1986/1925, r 1.47.

CHAPTER 5

CONSIDERATION OF THE PROPOSAL BY THE COMPANY MEMBERS AND CREDITORS

## [2.99]

### Note

[Note: a document required by the Act or these Rules must also contain the standard contents set out in Part 1.]

## [2.100]

### 2.25  Consideration of proposal: common requirements (section 3)

(1)   The nominee must invite the members of the company to consider a proposal by summoning a meeting of the company as required by section 3.

(2)   The nominee must invite the creditors to consider the proposal by way of a decision procedure.

(2A)   The nominee must examine whether there is jurisdiction to open the proceedings and must specify in the nominee's comments on the proposal required by paragraphs (3)(d)(iii) and (5)(a)(iii) whether the proceedings will be COMI proceedings, establishment proceedings or proceedings to which the EU Regulation as it has effect in the law of the United Kingdom does not apply with the reasons for so stating.

(3)   In the case of the members, the nominee must deliver to every person whom the nominee believes to be a member a notice which must—
  (a)   identify the proceedings;
  (b)   state the venue for the meeting;
  (c)   state the effect of the following—
      (i)   rule 2.35 about members' voting rights,
      (ii)   rule 2.36 about the requisite majority of members for passing resolutions, and
      (iii)   rule 15.35 about rights of appeal; and
  (d)   be accompanied by—
      (i)   a copy of the proposal,
      (ii)   a copy of the statement of affairs, or if the nominee thinks fit a summary including a list of creditors with the amounts of their debts,
      (iii)   the nominee's comments on the proposal, unless the nominee is the administrator or liquidator in which case the comments required are limited to stating whether the proceedings will be main, secondary, territorial or non-EU proceedings with the reasons for so stating, and
      (iv)   details of each resolution to be voted on.
(4)   In the case of the creditors, the nominee must deliver to each creditor a notice in respect of the decision procedure which complies with rule 15.8 so far as is relevant.
(5)   The notice must also—
  (a)   be accompanied by—
      (i)   a copy of the proposal,
      (ii)   a copy of the statement of affairs, or if the nominee thinks fit a summary including a list of creditors with the amounts of their debts, and
      (iii)   the nominee's comments on the proposal, unless the nominee is the administrator or liquidator; and
  (b)   state how a creditor may propose a modification to the proposal, and how the nominee will deal with such a proposal for a modification.
(6)   The notice may also state that the results of the consideration of the proposal will be made available for viewing and downloading on a website and that no other notice will be delivered to the creditors or members (as the case may be).
(7)   Where the results of the consideration of the proposal are to be made available for viewing and downloading on a website the nominee must comply with the requirements for use of a website to deliver a document set out in rule 1.49(2)(a) to (c), (3) and (4) with any necessary adaptations and rule 1.49(5)(a) applies to determine the time of delivery of the document.

**Amendments**—SI 2017/702; SI 2019/146, as from IP completion day (as defined in the European Union (Withdrawal Agreement) Act 2020, s 39(1)–(5)).

**Derivation**—This rule derived from the Insolvency Rules 1986, SI 1986/1925, rr 1.9, 1.11, 1.48.

'**The nominee must**'—The word 'must' as used in r 2.25(1) and (2) denotes a mandatory obligation for inviting creditors and members to consider the proposals. There are no grounds justifying a decision to withhold an invitation to any member or creditor, even where the directors give instructions to that effect. For the effect of a voluntary arrangement on a person entitled to have been invited to participate in a decision procedure see s 5(2)(b) and the notes thereto. For complaints of material irregularity at or in relation to a members' or creditors' meetings or decision procedures, see s 6(1)(b) and the notes thereto.

[2.101]

### 2.26 Members' consideration at a meeting

(1)   Where the nominee invites the members to consider the proposal at a meeting the notice to members under rule 2.25(3) must also—
  (a)   specify the purpose of and venue for the meeting; and
  (b)   be accompanied by a blank proxy.

(2)   The nominee must have regard to the convenience of those invited to attend when fixing the venue for a meeting (including the resumption of an adjourned meeting).

(3)   The date of the meeting (except where the nominee is the administrator or liquidator of the company) must not be more than 28 days from the date on which—

    (a)   the nominee's report is filed with the court under rule 2.9; or

    (b)   the moratorium came into force.

**Derivation**—This rule derived from the Insolvency Rules 1986, SI 1986/1925, rr 1.9, 1.11, 1.48.

## [2.102]

### 2.27  Creditors' consideration by a decision procedure

Where the nominee is inviting the creditors to consider the proposal by a decision procedure, the decision date must be not less than 14 days from the date of delivery of the notice and not more than 28 days from the date—

    (a)   the nominee's report is filed with the court under rule 2.9; or

    (b)   the moratorium came into force.

**Derivation**—This rule derived from the Insolvency Rules 1986, SI 1986/1925, rr 1.9, 1.11, 1.48.

## [2.103]

### 2.28  Timing of decisions on proposal

(1)   The decision date for the creditors' decision procedure may be on the same day as, or on a different day to, the meeting of the company.

(2)   But the creditors' decision on the proposal must be made before the members' decision.

(3)   The members' decision must be made not later than five business days after the creditors' decision.

(4)   For the purpose of this rule, the timing of the members' decision is either the date and time of the meeting of the company or, where the nominee invites members to consider the proposal by correspondence, the deadline for receipt of members' votes.

**Derivation**—This rule derived from the Insolvency Rules 1986, SI 1986/1925, r 1.13.

## [2.104]

### 2.29  Creditors' approval of modified proposal

(1)   This rule applies where a decision is sought from the creditors following notice to the nominee of proposed modifications to the proposal from the company's directors under paragraph 31(7) of Schedule A1.

(2)   The decision must be sought by a decision procedure with a decision date within 14 days of the date on which the directors gave notice to the nominee of the modifications.

(3)   The creditors must be given at least seven days' notice of the decision date.

## [2.105]

### 2.30  Notice of members' meeting and attendance of officers

(1)   A notice under rule 2.25(3) summoning a meeting of the company must be delivered at least 14 days before the day fixed for the meeting to all the members and to—

    (a)   every officer or former officer of the company whose presence the nominee thinks is required; and

    (b)   all other directors of the company.

(2)   Every officer or former officer who receives such a notice stating that the nominee thinks that person's attendance is required is required to attend the meeting.

**Derivation**—This rule derived from the Insolvency Rules 1986, SI 1986/1925, rr 1.9, 1.11, 1.48.

**Amendments**—SI 2017/1115.

**General note**—Rule 2.30 confers a power on the convener to give at least 14 days' notice to the directors or officers or former officers of the company requiring them to attend the meeting. It seems that the meeting which the rule is referring to is the meeting of the members, and not a creditors' meeting. It is not clear what sanction is engaged in the event of an officer or former officer of the company failing to attend the meeting.

**[2.106]**

### 2.31 Requisition of physical meeting by creditors

(1)   This rule applies where the creditors requisition a physical meeting to consider a proposal (with or without modifications) in accordance with section 246ZE and rule 15.6.

(2)   The meeting must take place within 14 days of the date on which the prescribed proportion of creditors have required the meeting to take place.

(3)   A notice summoning a meeting of the creditors must be delivered to the creditors at least seven days before the day fixed for the meeting.

Amendments—SI 2017/366.

**[2.107]**

### 2.32 Non-receipt of notice by members

Where in accordance with the Act or these Rules the members are invited to consider a proposal, the consideration is presumed to have duly taken place even if not everyone to whom the notice is to be delivered receives it.

Derivation—This rule derived from the Insolvency Rules 1986, SI 1986/1925, r 12A.4.

**[2.108]**

### 2.33 Proposal for alternative supervisor

(1)   If in response to a notice inviting—

    (a)    members to consider the proposal by correspondence; or

    (b)    creditors to consider the proposal other than at a meeting,

a member or creditor proposes that a person other than the nominee be appointed as supervisor, that person's consent to act and confirmation of being qualified to act as an insolvency practitioner in relation to the company must be delivered to the nominee by the deadline in the notice of the decision by correspondence or by the decision date (as the case may be).

(2)   If, at either a meeting of the company or the creditors to consider the proposal, a resolution is moved for the appointment of a person other than the nominee to be supervisor, the person moving the resolution must produce to the chair at or before the meeting—

    (a)    confirmation that the person proposed as supervisor is qualified to act as an insolvency practitioner in relation to the company; and

    (b)    that person's written consent to act (unless that person is present at the meeting and there signifies consent to act).

Derivation—This rule derived from the Insolvency Rules 1986, SI 1986/1925, r 1.22.

**[2.109]**

### 2.34 Chair at meetings

The chair of a meeting under this Part must be the nominee or an appointed person.

Derivation—This rule derived from the Insolvency Rules 1986, SI 1986/1925, r 1.14.

**[2.110]**

### 2.35 Members' voting rights

(1)   A member is entitled to vote according to the rights attaching to the member's shares in accordance with the articles of the company.

(2)   A member's shares include any other interest that person may have as a member of the company.

(3) The value of a member for the purposes of voting is determined by reference to the number of votes conferred on that member by the company's articles.

**Derivation**—This rule derived from the Insolvency Rules 1986, SI 1986/1925, rr 1.18, 1.51.

**General note**—Voting rights include not only the voting rights attaching to a member's shares under the company's articles of association but also any other voting rights arising under any other interest which that member has as a member of the company, but only as a member of the company.

See also r 2.36 on the calculation of requisite majorities.

**[2.111]**

### 2.36 Requisite majorities of members

(1) A resolution is passed by members by correspondence or at a meeting of the company when a majority (in value) of those voting have voted in favour of it.

(2) This is subject to any express provision to the contrary in the articles.

(3) A resolution is not passed by correspondence unless at least one member has voted in favour of it.

**Derivation**—This rule derived from the Insolvency Rules 1986, SI 1986/1925, rr 1.20, 1.53.

**RULE 2.36(1)**

' . . . majority . . . '—The requirement for the passing of a resolution is for a simple majority 'in value' of members who vote on the resolution.

' . . . in value . . . '—The term 'in value' refers to the number of votes conferred on each member by the company's articles of association. According to r 2.35 a member will not be entitled to vote, and will therefore carry no 'value' for the purposes of r 2.36(1), if no voting rights attach to his or her shares.

**[2.112]**

### 2.37 Notice of order made under section 4A(6) or paragraph 36(5) of Schedule A1

(1) This rule applies where the court makes an order under section 4A(6) or paragraph 36(5) of Schedule A1.

(2) The member who applied for the order must deliver a sealed copy of it to—

    (a) the proposer; and

    (b) the supervisor (if there is one different to the proposer).

(3) If the directors are the proposer a single copy may be delivered to the company at its registered office.

(4) The supervisor, or the proposer where there is no supervisor, must as soon as reasonably practicable deliver a notice that the order has been made to every person who had received a notice to vote on the matter or who is affected by the order.

(5) The member who applied for the order must, within five business days of the order, deliver a copy to the registrar of companies.

**Derivation**—This rule derived from the Insolvency Rules 1986, SI 1986/1925, r 1.22A.

**General note**—Orders under s 4A(6) will be rare in practice.

**[2.113]**

### 2.38 Report of consideration of proposal under section 4(6) and (6A) or paragraph 30(3) and (4) of Schedule A1

(1) A report or reports as the case may be must be prepared of the consideration of a proposal under section 4(6) and (6A) or paragraph 30(3) and (4) of Schedule A1 by the convener or, in the case of a meeting, the chair.

(2) The report must—

    (a) state whether the proposal was approved or rejected and whether by the creditors alone or by both the creditors and members and, in either case, whether any approval was with any modifications;

    (b) list the creditors and members who voted or attended or who were represented at the meeting or decision procedure (as applicable) used to consider the proposal, setting out (with their respective values) how they voted on each resolution or whether they abstained;

(c)    identify which of those creditors were considered to be connected with the company;

(d)    if the proposal was approved, state with reasons whether the proceedings are COMI proceedings, establishment proceedings or proceedings to which the EU Regulation as it has effect in the law of the United Kingdom does not apply; and

(e)    include such further information as the nominee or the chair thinks it appropriate to make known to the court.

(3)   A copy of the report must be filed with the court, within four business days of . . . the date of the company meeting.

(4)   The court must endorse the copy of the report with the date of filing.

(5)   The chair (in the case of a company meeting) or otherwise the convener must give notice of the result of the consideration of the proposal to everyone who was invited to consider the proposal or to whom notice of a decision procedure or meeting was delivered as soon as reasonably practicable after a copy of the report is filed with the court.

(6)   Where the decision approving the CVA has effect under section 4A or paragraph 36 of Schedule A1 with or without modifications, the supervisor must as soon as reasonably practicable deliver a copy of the convener's report or, in the case of a meeting, the chair's report to the registrar of companies.

**Derivation**—This rule derived from the Insolvency Rules 1986, SI 1986/1925, r 1.24.

**Amendments**—SI 2017/366; SI 2017/1115; SI 2019/146, as from IP completion day (as defined in the European Union (Withdrawal Agreement) Act 2020, s 39(1)–(5)).

**General note**—Rules 2.38(1), 2.38(2)(b) and 2.38(3) have been amended by the Insolvency (England and Wales) (Amendment) Rules 2017 which came into force on 6 April 2017. SIP 12 which governed the records of meetings in formal insolvency proceedings is withdrawn with effect from 6 April 2017 and is replaced by a new SIP 6 ('Deemed Consent and Decision Procedures in Insolvency Proceedings') which has effect as from 1 January 2018.

**RULE 2.38(1)**

**Scope of provision**—The obligation for the preparation of the reports of the meetings falls on the person who actually chaired the meetings or the convener.

## CHAPTER 6

### Additional Matters Concerning and Following Approval of CVA

## [2.114]

**Note**

[Note: a document required by the Act or these Rules must also contain the standard contents set out in Part 1.]

## [2.115]

### 2.39 Hand-over of property etc to supervisor

(1)   Where the decision approving a CVA has effect under section 4A or paragraph 36 of Schedule A1, and the supervisor is not the same person as the proposer, the proposer must, as soon as reasonably practicable, do all that is required to put the supervisor in possession of the assets included in the CVA.

(2)   Where the company is in administration or liquidation and the supervisor is not the same person as the administrator or liquidator, the supervisor must—

(a)    before taking possession of the assets included in the CVA, deliver to the administrator or liquidator an undertaking to discharge the balance referred to in paragraph (3) out of the first realisation of assets; or

(b)    upon taking possession of the assets included in the CVA, discharge such balance.

(3)   The balance is any balance due to the administrator or liquidator, or to the official receiver not acting as liquidator—

(a)   by way of fees or expenses properly incurred and payable under the Act or these Rules; and

(b)   on account of any advances made in respect of the company together with interest on such advances at the rate specified in section 17 of the Judgments Act 1838 at the date on which the company entered administration or went into liquidation.

(4)   The administrator or liquidator, or the official receiver not acting as liquidator, has a charge on the assets included in the CVA in respect of any sums comprising such balance, subject only to the deduction from realisations by the supervisor of the proper costs and expenses of such realisations.

(5)   The supervisor must from time to time out of the realisation of assets—

(a)   discharge all guarantees properly given by the administrator or liquidator for the benefit of the company; and

(b)   pay all the expenses of the administrator or liquidator or of the official receiver not acting as liquidator.

(6)   Sums due to the official receiver take priority over those due to any other person under this rule.

**Derivation**—This rule derived from the Insolvency Rules 1986, SI 1986/1925, rr 1.23, 1.54.

## RULE 2.39(1)

**Scope of provision**—This subrule operates independently of any provision within the approved arrangement and involves three distinct parts.

'**as soon as reasonably practicable**'—It is submitted that this term, in context, means 'forthwith' as opposed to the less exacting requirement of 'as soon as practicable'.

'**do all that is required**'—The logical sense of this phrase is that it refers to 'all that is required' by the supervisor. It is suggested that the onus under this provision rests on the supervisor to notify the proposer of such steps as he requires to be taken.

'**to put the supervisor in possession of the assets included in the CVA**'—There is no requirement here for the transfer of the assets to the supervisor. It is submitted that the term 'possession', properly construed, refers to possession in the sense of control of the arrangement assets, since the supervisor will hardly wish to be in physical possession of assets where, say, those assets are extensive and continue to be used on a day-to-day basis by the company in a trading arrangement.

**The status of arrangement assets as trust assets**—Assets comprised within a voluntary arrangement are impressed with a trust in favour of creditors bound by the voluntary arrangement: see the notes to  s 1(2) and the authorities cited therein. It is submitted that the status of arrangement assets as trust assets is not affected in any way by the absence of any requirement for the transfer of the assets to the supervisor under  r 2.39(1) since, according to the reasoning of Harman J in  *Re Leisure Study Group Ltd* [1994] 2 BCLC 65, the trust comes into being by operation of law under  s 1(2) (or  s 253(2) in the case of an IVA). This position, it is suggested, is unchanged even if the purpose of the voluntary arrangement is the reduction or rescheduling of the liabilities of the debtor.

## RULE 2.39(2)

**Scope of provision**—It is clear from the wording of  s 5(3) that a company may enter into a CVA whilst in administration or liquidation. Whilst, in those circumstances, the court may bring the administration to an end, it may be preferable to allow the administration to continue where the voluntary arrangement is to be employed as an exit route from that procedure. Equally, but far less commonly, a voluntary arrangement may be employed to serve the best interests of creditors where the company is subject to a winding-up order, say, with a view to the company trading through the voluntary arrangement so as to mitigate tax liabilities.

## RULE 2.39(2), (3), (4), (5), (6)

**Scope of provision**—Rules 2.39(2) and (3) impose a mandatory obligation on the supervisor to discharge fees 'due' or expenses 'properly incurred and payable under the Act or these Rules' and any balance on account of any advances made in respect of the company by an administrator or a liquidator. The obligation arises on taking possession of the assets within the CVA, or pursuant to an undertaking to be given by the supervisor before taking possession of the assets. The supervisor's undertaking is plainly envisaged as being personal and being enforceable as such. It is suggested that the obligation to provide a written undertaking will only bite where there are not sufficient realisations to meet fees, costs and any advances due to the liquidator or administrator. Where any realisations are available, then the obligation to discharge under r 2.39(2)(b) will bind the supervisor.

The statutory charge under r 2.39(4) would provide a basis upon which a claim for outstanding fees, costs and advances might be enforced by a liquidator or administrator against a supervisor, subject only to the supervisor's claim for the proper costs and expenses of any realisations of arrangement assets.

The liability of a liquidator or administrator under any guarantee given for the benefit of the company does not, it is suggested, fall within the scope of r 2.39(3)(a) or (b), given the separate treatment of any such liability in r 2.39(5), but this appears to be the case only where any guarantee liability is not crystallised at the time at which the supervisor takes possession of the arrangement assets for the purposes of r 2.39(2).

Where a liquidator or administrator has incurred and discharged any such guarantee liability at the time of the supervisor taking possession, it would be open to the liquidator or administrator to claim such liability as an expense properly incurred and payable by him under r 7.108(4)(a) or (r) in liquidation or para 99(3) of Sch B1 in administration (equating to the formerly operative s 19(4)). Given the priority afforded by r 2.28(2) and (3) to a liquidator or administrator in relation to arrangement assets it would seem anomalous if guarantee liabilities were not accorded equivalent priority, despite the separate treatment of such liabilities in r 2.39(5) and the apparent fact of the charge in r 2.39(4) not extending to such liabilities.

## [2.116]

### 2.40  Revocation or suspension of CVA

(1)  This rule applies where the court makes an order of revocation or suspension under section 6 or paragraph 38 of Schedule A1.

(2)  The applicant for the order must deliver a sealed copy of it to—

    (a)    the proposer; and

    (b)    the supervisor (if different).

(3)  If the directors are the proposer a single copy of the order may be delivered to the company at its registered office.

(4)  If the order includes a direction by the court under section 6(4)(b) or (c) or under paragraph 38(4)(b) or (c) of Schedule A1 for action to be taken, the applicant for the order must deliver a notice that the order has been made to the person who is directed to take such action.

(5)  The proposer must—

    (a)    as soon as reasonably practicable deliver a notice that the order has been made to all of those persons to whom a notice to consider the matter was delivered or who appear to be affected by the order;

    (b)    within five business days of delivery of a copy of the order (or within such longer period as the court may allow), deliver (if applicable) a notice to the court advising that it is intended to make a revised proposal to the company and its creditors, or to invite re-consideration of the original proposal.

(6)  The applicant for the order must deliver a copy of the order to the registrar of companies within five business days of the making of the order with a notice which must contain the date on which the voluntary arrangement took effect.

**Derivation**—This rule derived from the Insolvency Rules 1986, SI 1986/1925, r 1.25.
**Amendments**—SI 2017/366.

## [2.117]

### 2.41  Supervisor's accounts and reports

(1)  The supervisor must keep accounts and records where the CVA authorises or requires the supervisor—

    (a)    to carry on the business of the company;

    (b)    to realise assets of the company; or

    (c)    otherwise to administer or dispose of any of its funds.

(2)   The accounts and records which must be kept are of the supervisor's acts and dealings in, and in connection with, the CVA, including in particular records of all receipts and payments of money.

(3)   The supervisor must preserve any such accounts and records which were kept by any other person who has acted as supervisor of the CVA and are in the supervisor's possession.

(4)   The supervisor must deliver reports on the progress and prospects for the full implementation of the CVA to—

  (a)   the registrar of companies;

  (b)   the company;

  (c)   the creditors bound by the CVA;

  (d)   subject to paragraph (10) below, the members; and

  (e)   if the company is not in liquidation, the company's auditors (if any) for the time being.

(5)   The notice which accompanies the report when delivered to the registrar of companies must contain the date on which the voluntary arrangement took effect.

(6)   The first report must cover the period of 12 months commencing on the date on which the CVA was approved and a further report must be made for each subsequent period of 12 months.

(7)   Each report must be delivered within the period of two months after the end of the 12 month period.

(8)   Such a report is not required if the obligation to deliver a final report under rule 2.44 arises in the two month period.

(9)   Where the supervisor is authorised or required to do any of the things mentioned in paragraph (1), the report must—

  (a)   include or be accompanied by a summary of receipts and payments required to be recorded by virtue of paragraph (2); or

  (b)   state that there have been no such receipts and payments.

(10)   The court may, on application by the supervisor, dispense with the delivery of such reports or summaries to members, either altogether or on the basis that the availability of the report to members is to be advertised by the supervisor in a specified manner.

**Derivation**—This rule derived from the Insolvency Rules 1986, SI 1986/1925, r 1.26A.
**Amendments**—SI 2017/366.

## [2.118]

### 2.42 Production of accounts and records to the Secretary of State

(1)   The Secretary of State may during the CVA, or after its full implementation or termination, require the supervisor to produce for inspection (either at the premises of the supervisor or elsewhere)—

  (a)   the supervisor's accounts and records in relation to the CVA; and

  (b)   copies of reports and summaries prepared in compliance with rule 2.41.

(2)   The Secretary of State may require the supervisor's accounts and records to be audited and, if so, the supervisor must provide such further information and assistance as the Secretary of State requires for the purposes of audit.

**Derivation**—This rule derived from the Insolvency Rules 1986, SI 1986/1925, r 1.27.

**General note**—This provision is designed to allow for investigation of a supervisor by the Secretary of State by way of a power for the production and inspection of records, accounts etc relating to a voluntary arrangement. The power is unfettered in that there is no requirement for proof by the Secretary of State of 'reasonable cause' or the like, although in practice the power is only likely to be invoked where the Secretary of State has credible evidence giving rise to obvious suspicion as to the state of veracity of the supervisor's records. One ground for such suspicion may be repeated default under the filing obligations in r 2.41.

Although s 3(3) of the Company Directors Disqualification Act 1986 does not refer specifically to a supervisor – the provision extends only to receivers, managers and liquidators – it might be argued that a supervisor falls within the scope of s 3 of that Act as 'a person' who has persistently been in default of a provision requiring information to be given to the Registrar of Companies in an appropriate case. In the case of default or persistent default there is also the potential for disciplinary action by a professional regulating body.

## [2.119]

### 2.43 Fees and expenses

The fees and expenses that may be incurred for the purposes of the CVA are—

(a) fees for the nominee's services agreed with the company (or, as the case may be, the administrator or liquidator) and disbursements made by the nominee before the decision approving the CVA takes effect under section 4A or paragraph 36 of Schedule A1;

(b) fees or expenses which—

(i) are sanctioned by the terms of the CVA, or

(ii) where they are not sanctioned by the terms of the CVA would be payable, or correspond to those which would be payable, in an administration or winding up.

**Derivation**—This rule derived from the Insolvency Rules 1986, SI 1986/1925, r 1.28.

**General note**—The underlying purpose of this provision is to limit the scope of the disbursements and fees which may be incurred by a nominee, or the fees or expenses which may be incurred by a supervisor in connection with a voluntary arrangement.

#### RULE 2.43(a)

**Scope of provision**—Subparagraph (a) suggests that the remuneration of a nominee is usually a matter of agreement between the nominee and the company. Such remuneration is, however, commonly approved by a meeting of creditors considering a proposal and is also an item for specific disclosure in the proposal under r 2.3(1)(g). The decision of the High Court in *Re Julie O'Sullivan* [2001] BPIR 534, noted in r 2.3(1)(g), suggests that, whilst ordinarily a matter for agreement with creditors, the court itself has jurisdiction to interfere with the level of a nominee's fees (the district judge's objection in that case was to the nominee's proposed fee of £2,000 in the context of a relatively modest IVA involving non-trade debts of around £10,000, thereby justifying the refusal of an interim order under s 255).

#### RULE 2.43(b)

**Scope of provision**—In practice, an approved proposal will invariably include an express provision sanctioning the fees, costs, charges and expenses of a supervisor. Fees are almost always provided for on a time/cost basis SIP 9 commonly being provided to creditors with the proposal for guidance on the issue of remuneration etc.

In the unlikely case that fees, costs, charges or expenses are not expressly sanctioned by an arrangement, the supervisor has recourse to draw such items under r 2.43(b)(ii) as if he or she were an administrator or liquidator.

## [2.120]

### 2.44 Termination or full implementation of CVA

(1) Not more than 28 days after the full implementation or termination of the CVA the supervisor must deliver a notice that the CVA has been fully implemented or terminated to all the members and those creditors who are bound by the arrangement.

(2) The notice must state the date the CVA took effect and must be accompanied by a copy of a report by the supervisor which—

(a) summarises all receipts and payments in relation to the CVA;

(b) explains any departure from the terms of the CVA as it originally had effect;

(c) if the CVA has terminated, sets out the reasons why; and

(d) includes (if applicable) a statement as to the amount paid to any unsecured creditors by virtue of section 176A.

(3) The supervisor must within the 28 days mentioned above send to the registrar of companies and file with the court a copy of the notice to creditors and of the supervisor's report.

(4) The supervisor must not vacate office until after the copies of the notice and report have been delivered to the registrar of companies and filed with the court.

**Derivation**—This rule derived from the Insolvency Rules 1986, SI 1986/1925, r 1.29.

**General note**—These provisions concern the reporting obligations of the supervisor following 'full implementation or termination', for differing terms on which see the note to r 2.44(1) below.

**RULE 2.44(1)**

'**not more than 28 days after** . . . '—This period, and the period of 28 days referred to in r 2.44(3), will be extendable by the court in an appropriate case under para 3 of Sch 5 to the Rules.

' . . . **the full implementation or termination of the CVA** . . . '—The terms 'full implementation' and 'termination' do not, apparently, necessarily have the same meaning. The former, it is suggested, refers to total completion as envisaged in the proposal, whereas the latter refers to an arrangement coming to an end on any other grounds, most obviously on the intervention of a supervisor.

If an arrangement does not refer specifically to 'full implementation' or 'termination' then it will be necessary to construe the terms of the arrangement to examine whether the arrangement actually provides for the happening of such events, words or phrases such as 'breach', 'failure of the scheme' or 'failure of the arrangement' being common enough in practice. Evidence of final completion or termination may also be found through the issue by a supervisor of what are commonly termed 'certificate of due completion' or 'certificate of non-compliance', although confusion may arise from the issue of the latter in that the terms of an arrangement may provide for the issue of such a certificate as a means of giving notice to the debtor of the fact of a breach without that breach itself necessarily amounting to termination of the arrangement. Certificates of due completion, non-compliance and the like are mechanisms which derive from approved arrangements and are not referred to anywhere in the legislation. For the court's approach to the construction of a voluntary arrangement see the notes to s 5(2).

**RULE 2.44(2)**

**Scope of provision**—The report must include a statement as to any amount paid by virtue of s 176A: see r 2.44(2)(d).

**RULE 2.44(4)**

**Scope of provision**—A supervisor may not vacate office as such until after copies of the notice and report under r 2.44(2) have been sent to the Registrar of Companies and to the court.

CHAPTER 7

TIME RECORDING INFORMATION

## [2.121]

Note

[Note: a document required by the Act or these Rules must also contain the standard contents set out in Part 1.]

## [2.122]

### 2.45 Provision of information

(1) This rule applies where the remuneration of the nominee or the supervisor has been fixed on the basis of the time spent.

(2) A person who is acting, or has acted within the previous two years, as—

    (a)    a nominee in relation to a proposal; or

    (b)    the supervisor in relation to a CVA;

must, within 28 days of receipt of a request from a person mentioned in paragraph (3), deliver free of charge to that person a statement complying with paragraphs (4) and (5).

(3) The persons are—

    (a)    any director of the company; and

    (b)    where the proposal has been approved, any creditor or member.

(4) The statement must cover the period which—

    (a)    in the case of a person who has ceased to act as nominee or supervisor in relation to a company, begins with the date of appointment as nominee or supervisor and ends with the date of ceasing to act; and

    (b)    in any other case, consists of one or more complete periods of six months beginning with the date of appointment and ending most nearly before the date of receiving the request.

(5) The statement must set out—

(a)   the total number of hours spent on the matter during that period by the nominee or supervisor, and any staff;

(b)   for each grade of staff engaged on the matter, the average hourly rate at which work carried out by staff in that grade is charged; and

(c)   the number of hours spent on the matter by each grade of staff during that period.

**Derivation**—This rule derived from the Insolvency Rules 1986, SI 1986/1925, r 1.55.

# PART 3   ADMINISTRATION

## CHAPTER 1

### INTERPRETATION FOR THIS PART

## [2.123]

**Note**

[Note: a document required by the Act or these Rules must also contain the standard contents set out in Part 1.]

## [2.124]

### 3.1  Interpretation for Part 3

In this Part—

"pre-administration costs" means fees charged, and expenses incurred by the administrator, or another person qualified to act as an insolvency practitioner in relation to the company, before the company entered administration but with a view to it doing so; and

"unpaid pre-administration costs" means pre-administration costs which had not been paid when the company entered administration.

**Derivation**—This rule derived from the Insolvency Rules 1986, SI 1986/1925, r 2.33(2A).

## [2.125]

### 3.2  Proposed administrator's statement and consent to act

(1)   References in this Part to a consent to act are to a statement by a proposed administrator headed "Proposed administrator's statement and consent to act" which contains the following—

(a)   identification details for the company immediately below the heading;

(b)   a certificate that the proposed administrator is qualified to act as an insolvency practitioner in relation to the company;

(c)   the proposed administrator's IP number;

(d)   the name of the relevant recognised professional body which is the source of the proposed administrator's authorisation to act in relation to the company;

(e)   a statement that the proposed administrator consents to act as administrator of the company;

(f)   a statement whether or not the proposed administrator has had any prior professional relationship with the company and if so a short summary of the relationship;

(g)   the name of the person by whom the appointment is to be made or the applicant in the case of an application to the court for an appointment; and

(h)   a statement that the proposed administrator is of the opinion that the purpose of administration is reasonably likely to be achieved in the particular case.

(2)   The statement and consent to act must be authenticated and dated by the proposed administrator.

(3)   Where a number of persons are proposed to be appointed to act jointly or concurrently as the administrator of a company, each must make a separate statement and consent to act.

**Derivation**—This rule derived from the Insolvency Rules 1986, SI 1986/1925, Sch 4, Fm 2.2.

**General note**—In keeping with the approach adopted in the IR 2016, no form for the statement and consent to act is prescribed; rather, the provision prescribes the content of the statement.

**Rule 3.2(1)(f)**—It might be considered anomalous for a proposed administrator to omit the fact of his or her (or his or her firm) having advised the company in relation to the proposed administration itself, even if the proposed administrator does not consider such a professional relationship to be material in the context of other historic professional associations with the company.

**Rule 3.2(1)(h)**—The proposed administrator's statement of opinion should not be treated lightly. In *Re Integral Ltd* [2013] EWHC 164 (Ch) at [69], Mr Richard Snowden QC, sitting as a deputy High Court judge, identified the fundamental importance of any insolvency practitioner, as an officer of the court nominated as a potential administrator, who ventures his opinion to the court as to the prospects for an administration 'should do so carefully, with an independent mind, and on the basis of a critical assessment of the position of the company and the proposals put forward'.

## CHAPTER 2

### APPOINTMENT OF ADMINISTRATOR BY COURT

**[2.126]**

**Note**

[Note: a document required by the Act or these Rules must also contain the standard contents set out in Part 1.]

**[2.127]**

**3.3  Administration application (paragraph 12 of Schedule B1)**

(1)   An administration application in relation to a company must be headed "Administration application" and must identify the company immediately below the heading.

(2)   The application must contain—

    (a)     the name of the applicant;

    (b)     a statement whether the application is being made by—

        (i)      the company under paragraph 12(1)(a) of Schedule B1,

        (ii)     the directors of the company under paragraph 12(1)(b) of Schedule B1,

        (iii)    a single creditor under paragraph 12(1)(c) of Schedule B1,

        (iv)    a creditor under paragraph 12(1)(c) of Schedule B1 on behalf of that creditor and others,

        (v)     the holder of a qualifying floating charge under paragraph 35 or 37 of Schedule B1 (specifying which),

        (vi)    the liquidator of the company under paragraph 38 of Schedule B1,

        (vii)   the supervisor of a CVA under section 7(4)(b), or

        (viii)  a designated officer of a magistrates' court under section 87A of the Magistrates' Courts Act 1980;

    (c)     if the application is made by a creditor on behalf of that creditor and others, the names of the others;

    (d)     if the application is made by the holder of a qualifying floating charge, details of the charge including the date of the charge, the date on which it was registered and the maximum amount if any secured by the charge;

    (e)     if the company is registered under the Companies Act—

   (i)  any issued and called-up capital, the number of shares into which the capital is divided, the nominal value of each share and the amount of capital paid up or treated as paid up; or

   (ii)  that it is a company limited by guarantee;

 (f)  particulars of the principal business carried on by the company;

 (g)  a statement whether the company is an Article 1.2 undertaking;

 (h)  a statement whether the proceedings flowing from the appointment will be COMI proceedings, establishment proceedings or proceedings to which the EU Regulation as it has effect in the law of the United Kingdom does not apply and that the reasons for the statement are set out in the witness statement in support of the application made under rule 3.6;

 (i)  except where the applicant is the holder of a qualifying floating charge and is making the application under paragraph 35 of Schedule B1, a statement that the applicant believes, for the reasons set out in the witness statement in support of the application that the company is, or is likely to become, unable to pay its debts;

 (j)  the name and address of the proposed administrator;

 (k)  the address for service of the applicant;

 (l)  the statement that the applicant requests the court—

   (i)  to make an administration order in relation to the company,

   (ii)  to appoint the proposed person to be administrator, and

   (iii)  to make such ancillary order as the applicant may request, and such other order as the court thinks appropriate.

(3) The application must be authenticated by the applicant or the applicant's solicitor and dated.

**Derivation**—This rule derived from the Insolvency Rules 1986, SI 1986/1925, Sch 4, Fm 2.1.

**Amendments**—SI 2017/1115; SI 2019/146, as from IP completion day (as defined in the European Union (Withdrawal Agreement) Act 2020, s 39(1)–(5)).

**Application by company or directors**—In *Re Frontsouth (Withan) Ltd* [2011] EWHC 1668 (Ch), [2011] BCC 635 at [31] Henderson J was of the view that, where a company's articles of association confer management of the company's business exclusively on the board of directors (as under reg 70 of table A and art 3 of the Model Articles of Association (SI 2008/3229)), ' . . . The decision [whether or not to place the company into administration] cannot be taken by an ordinary resolution of the shareholders, although by a special resolution they may direct the board to take such a step'. Although that observation was obiter, and Henderson J noted (at [32]) that he had not heard detailed argument on the point, the observation must be doubtful, not least because it would render paras 12(1)(a) and 22(1) of Sch B1 (court and out-of-court appointments by company) meaningless other than where, somewhat unusually, a company's articles did not confer exclusive powers of management on the board. In practice, appointments effected by shareholders are far less common than appointments by directors.

Somewhat controversially, in *Minmar (929) Ltd v Khalastchi* [2011] EWHC 1159 (Ch), [2011] BCC 485 Morritt C held that, in the case of an appointment by directors, nothing less than compliance with the provisions of the company's articles relating to matters of internal management will suffice. Thus, the court set aside the appointment of administrators under para 22 of Sch B1 where the decision to appoint the administrators had been taken by a single director at an inquorate meeting, contrary to the company's articles. Paragraph 105 of Sch B1 (majority decision of directors) was of no assistance because, as the Chancellor put it at [50] 'The terms of para 105 give to an act of the majority the same validity as would be accorded to an act of the directors as a whole but if the act in question must still be an act of the majority of such directors, I see no reason why the reduction in the requisite number of directors should also dispense with the usual rules of internal management'. The Chancellor was at pains to point out, at [51], that the previous case law on the former Part II of the Act, on which see the decision of Millett J in *Re Equiticorp International plc* [1989] 1 WLR 1010 as to a dissentient minority being bound notwithstanding the absence of a formal resolution, went no further than recognizing a majority decision of the board which had nonetheless failed to comply with the usual formalities of a board resolution.

**Application by qualifying floating charge-holder in reliance on paragraph 35**—In a case of this sort there is no requirement to demonstrate the applicant's belief as to the company's insolvent status although the alternative basis must be provided, such as particulars of the (non-insolvency) default event(s) by reference to which the floating charge is enforceable.

**RULE 3.3(2)(i)**

**Inability to pay debts**—See the decision of the Supreme Court in *BNY Corporate Trustee Services Ltd v Eurosail-UK 2007–3 BL plc* [2013] UKSC 28, [2013] 1 WLR 1408 affirming the decision of the Court of Appeal to the effect that, for the purposes of the 'balance-sheet' insolvency test in s 123(2), the ability of a company to meet its liabilities, both prospective and contingent, is to be determined on the balance of probabilities with the burden of proof on the party asserting balance-sheet insolvency.

**[2.128]**

**3.4 Administration application made by the directors**

After an application by the directors for an administration order is filed it is to be treated for all purposes as an application by the company.

**Derivation**—This rule derived from the Insolvency Rules 1986, SI 1986/1925, r 2.3(2).

**General note**—Under the former Part II of the Act, the fact of the directors' application being treated as an application by the company did not protect the directors from personal liability for costs incurred in respect of an administration petition: *Re WF Fearman Ltd (No 2)* (1988) 4 BCC 141.

**[2.129]**

**3.5 Administration application by the supervisor of a CVA**

After an application by the supervisor of a CVA for an administration order in respect of the company has been served on the company as required by rule 3.8(3)(d) it is to be treated for all purposes as an application by the company.

**Derivation**—This rule derived from the Insolvency Rules 1986, SI 1986/1925, r 2.2(4).

**[2.130]**

**3.6 Witness statement in support of administration application**

(1)  If an administration application is to be made by—

    (a)    the company, a witness statement must be made by one of the following stating that the person making the statement does so on behalf of the company—

        (i)    one of the directors,

        (ii)    the secretary of the company, or

        (iii)    the supervisor of a CVA;

    (b)    the company's directors, a witness statement must be made by one of the following stating that the person making it does so on behalf of the directors—

        (i)    one of the directors, or

        (ii)    the secretary of the company;

    (c)    a single creditor, a witness statement must be made by—

        (i)    that creditor, or

        (ii)    a person acting under that creditor's authority;

    (d)    two or more creditors, a witness statement must be made by a person acting under the authority of them all, whether or not one of their number.

(2)  In a case falling within paragraph (1)(c)(ii) or (d), the witness statement must state the nature of the authority of the person making it and the means of that person's knowledge of the matters to which the witness statement relates.

(3)  The witness statement must contain—

    (a)    a statement of the company's financial position, specifying (to the best of the applicant's knowledge and belief) the company's assets and liabilities, including contingent and prospective liabilities;

    (b)    details of any security known or believed to be held by creditors of the company, and whether in any case the security is such as to confer power on the holder to appoint an administrative receiver or to appoint an administrator under paragraph 14 of Schedule B1;

    (c)    a statement that an administrative receiver has been appointed if that is the case;

    (d)    details of any insolvency proceedings in relation to the company, including any petition that has been presented for the winding up of the company so far as known to the applicant;

    (e)    where it is intended to appoint a number of persons as administrators, a statement of the matters relating to the exercise of their functions set out in paragraph 100(2) of Schedule B1;

    (f)    the reasons for the statement that the proceedings will be COMI proceedings, establishment proceedings or proceedings to which the EU Regulation as it has effect in the law of the United Kingdom does not apply; and

    (g)    any other matters which, in the applicant's opinion, will assist the court in deciding whether to make such an order.

(4)    Where the application is made by the holder of a qualifying floating charge under paragraph 35 or 37 of Schedule B1, the witness statement must give sufficient details to satisfy the court that the applicant is entitled to appoint an administrator under paragraph 14 of Schedule B1.

(5)    Where the application is made under paragraph 37 or 38 of Schedule B1 in relation to a company in liquidation, the witness statement must also contain—

    (a)    details of the existing insolvency proceedings, the name and address of the liquidator, the date the liquidator was appointed and by whom;

    (b)    the reasons why it has subsequently been considered appropriate that an administration application should be made; and

    (c)    any other matters that would, in the applicant's opinion, assist the court in deciding whether to make provision in relation to matters arising in connection with the liquidation.

**Derivation**—This rule derived from the Insolvency Rules 1986, SI 1986/1925, rr 2.2–2.4, 2.11.

**Amendments**—SI 2017/1115; SI 2019/146, as from IP completion day (as defined in the European Union (Withdrawal Agreement) Act 2020, s 39(1)–(5)).

**General note**—Schedule B1 contains no express requirement for a report of the sort previously required under the former r 2.2. All that is required of a proposed administrator is a statement and consent to act, which must state those matters in r 3.2(1). An administration application to court must, however, be supported with a witness statement compliant with r 3.6. Those matters of detail prescribed in r 3.6(3)(a)–(f) may not serve to convey much by persuading the court that there is a reasonable likelihood of the purpose of administration (on which see Sch B1, para 3 and the notes thereto) being achieved. Neither is the court likely to be won over by the mere fact of a statement by a proposed administrator that in his opinion it is reasonably likely that the purpose of administration will be achieved. Attention, therefore, is drawn to r 3.6(3)(g). In practice, an administration application will often be supported by a statement or report produced by, or with the assistance of, a proposed administrator and which includes much of the same sort of financial information as appeared in a r 2.2 report. In para 3(1)(b) cases the court will be assisted by an estimated statement of affairs together with an estimated outcome statement which provides for a comparison of outcomes in administration and liquidation. An estimated outcome statement should also include provision for the estimated costs of each procedure, particularly where there is likely to be a difference between the two. The court may also wish to be apprised of the strategy to be adopted by a proposed administrator, at least other than in the most straightforward case. In a trading administration the court may also wish to have sight of cash flow projections and an indication of the funding position.

## RULE 3.6(3)

**Witness statements**—Apart from information prescribed by this rule, in practice an administration application will often be supported by a statement or report produced by, or with the assistance of, the proposed administrator which may include the sort of information which would have appeared previously in what was commonly known as the r 2.2 report. In para 3(1)(b) cases the court will often be assisted by an estimated statement of affairs together with an estimated outcome statement providing for a comparison of outcomes in administration and liquidation. An estimated outcome statement will also often include provision for the estimated costs of each procedure (without which a meaningful comparison of the procedures is often impossible). The court may also wish to be apprised of the strategy to be adopted by a proposed administrator, at least other than in the most straightforward case. In a trading administration the court may also be assisted by a cash-flow projection and an indication of the source of any funding.

**RULE 3.6(3)(e)**

**Pre-pack cases**—In *Re Kayley Vending Ltd* [2009] EWHC 904 (Ch), [2009] BCC 578 at [24] HHJ Cooke observed, 'It seems to me that in exercising its discretion in pre-pack cases, the court must be alert to see, so far as it can, that the procedure is at least not being obviously abused to the disadvantage of creditors in any of the ways outlined above. If it is, or may be, the court may conclude that it is inappropriate to give the pre-pack the apparent blessing conferred by making the administration order. In reaching that decision, it is likely to be assisted by the provision of information in relation to the pre-pack transaction and its background, and to that extent the provision of such information falls within r 2.4(2)(e) of the Insolvency Rules 1986. While it is primarily a matter for the applicant to identify what information is likely to assist the court, and that information may not be limited to the matters identified in SIP 16, it seems to me likely that in most cases the information required by SIP 16, insofar as known or ascertainable at the date of the application, would fall within the requirement I have referred to and so ought to be included in the application . . . It should not normally be unduly burdensome or costly for it to be so included, and no doubt if there are special reasons why it cannot readily be provided in a particular case this can be explained'. For a case in which the court accepted the SIP 16 material annexed to the report of the proposed administrators in circumstances where an out-of-court appointment could have been effected the following week in the absence of an order (' . . . it seems churlish of me to cavil at what seems in the particular circumstances to be an entirely proper transaction'), see *Re Cornercare Ltd* [2010] EWHC 893 (Ch), [2010] BCC 592 at [15] (HHJ Purle QC).

**RULE 3.6(3)(f)**

For the application of the EU Regulation and the distinct forms of proceedings thereby provided for see Art 3 of the EU Regulation and Part 21 of the IR 2016.

## [2.131]

### 3.7 Filing of application

(1)   The application must be filed with the court together with the witness statement in support and the proposed administrator's consent to act.

(2)   The court must fix a venue for the hearing of the application.

(3)   There must also be filed, at the same time as the application or at any time after that, a sufficient number of copies of the application and the statement for service in accordance with rule 3.8.

(4)   Each of the copies filed must—

    (a)   have applied to it the seal of the court;

    (b)   be endorsed with—

        (i)   the date and time of filing, and

        (ii)   the venue fixed by the court; and

    (c)   be delivered by the court to the applicant.

**Derivation**—This rule derived from the Insolvency Rules 1986, SI 1986/1925, r 2.5.

## [2.132]

### 3.8 Service of application

(1)   In this rule, references to the application are to a copy of the application and witness statement delivered by the court under rule 3.7(4)(c).

(2)   Notification for the purposes of paragraph 12(2) of Schedule B1 must be by service of the application.

(3)   The applicant must serve the application on the following (in addition to serving it on the persons referred to in paragraph 12(2)(a) to (c) of Schedule B1)—

    (a)   any administrative receiver of the company;

    (b)   if there is a petition pending for the winding up of the company on—

        (i)   the petitioner, and

        (ii)   any provisional liquidator;

    (c)   . . .

    (d)   the company, if the application is made by anyone other than the company or its directors;

    (e)   any supervisor of a CVA in relation to the company; and

    (f)   the proposed administrator.

(4) The certificate of service must be filed with the court as soon as reasonably practicable after service and in any event not later than the business day before the hearing of the application.

**Derivation**—This rule derived from the Insolvency Rules 1986, SI 1986/1925, r 2.6.

**Amendments**—SI 2019/146, as from IP completion day (as defined in the European Union (Withdrawal Agreement) Act 2020, s 39(1)–(5)).

**General note**—See the notes to para 12 of Sch B1.

Although the service obligation under para 12(2) and r 3.8(4) requires service as soon as is reasonably practicable after the making of an administration application, an applicant, so as to best protect its position, would ordinarily be well advised to notify any of the classes of persons entitled to service of the application if the applicant only becomes aware of their existence subsequently. Such a post-issue continuing obligation is imposed by r 3.10, albeit in relation to the court and in the context of other insolvency proceedings.

For details of the location of service of the application see Sch 4, para 3 of the IR 2016.

For service on a company see *Re Bezier Acquisitions Ltd* [2011] EWHC 3299 (Ch) (service of application on solicitor authorised to accept delivery deemed good service).

## [2.133]

### 3.9 Notice to enforcement agents charged with distress or other legal process, etc

The applicant must as soon as reasonably practicable after filing the application deliver a notice of its being made to—

    (a)    any enforcement agent or other officer who to the knowledge of the applicant is charged with distress or other legal process against the company or its property; and

    (b)    any person who to the knowledge of the applicant has distrained against the company or its property.

**Derivation**—This rule derived from the Insolvency Rules 1986, SI 1986/1925, r 2.7.

**General note**—See the notes to para 12 of Sch B1. The purpose of this provision is not only to seek to prevent action which might frustrate the purpose of a pending administration but also to warn the classes of person entitled to notice of the application so as to prevent an inadvertent breach of the statutory moratorium and the contempt of court consequent upon such a breach.

## [2.134]

### 3.10 Notice of other insolvency proceedings

After the application has been filed and until an order is made, it is the duty of the applicant to file with the court notice of the existence of any insolvency proceedings in relation to the company, as soon as the applicant becomes aware of them—

    (a)    anywhere in the world, in the case of a company registered under the Companies Act in England and Wales;

    (b)    in any EEA State . . ., in the case of a company incorporated in an EEA State . . .; or

    (c)    in any member State other than Denmark, in the case of a company not incorporated in an EEA State.

**Derivation**—This rule derived from the Insolvency Rules 1986, SI 1986/1925, r 2.5.

**Amendments**—SI 2019/146, as from IP completion day (as defined in the European Union (Withdrawal Agreement) Act 2020, s 39(1)–(5)).

**General note**—This is a continuing obligation. The leading authority is that of the Court of Appeal in *Re Stanford International Bank (in receivership)* [2011] Ch 33: see also *Re Hans Brochier Holdings Ltd* [2007] BCC 127 (administrators appointed out-of-court) and *Re Hellas Telecommunications (Luxembourg) II SCA* [2010] BCC 295 (English court administration order in respect of combination of joint stock company and limited partnership registered in Luxembourg).

**[2.135]**

**3.11 Intervention by holder of qualifying floating charge (paragraph 36(1)(b) of Schedule B1)**

(1)   Where the holder of a qualifying floating charge applies to the court under paragraph 36(1)(b) of Schedule B1 to have a specified person appointed as administrator, the holder must produce to the court—

(a)     the written consent of the holder of any prior qualifying floating charge;

(b)     the proposed administrator's consent to act; and

(c)     sufficient evidence to satisfy the court that the holder is entitled to appoint an administrator under paragraph 14 of Schedule B1.

(2)   If an administration order is made appointing the specified person, the costs of the person who made the administration application and of the applicant under paragraph 36(1)(b) of Schedule B1 are, unless the court orders otherwise, to be paid as an expense of the administration.

Derivation—This rule derived from the Insolvency Rules 1986, SI 1986/1925, r 2.10.

**[2.136]**

**3.12 The hearing**

(1)   At the hearing of the administration application, any of the following may appear or be represented—

(a)     the applicant;

(b)     the company;

(c)     one or more of the directors;

(d)     any administrative receiver;

(e)     any person who has presented a petition for the winding up of the company;

(f)     the proposed administrator;

(g)     . . .

(h)     the holder of any qualifying floating charge;

(i)     any supervisor of a CVA;

(j)     with the permission of the court, any other person who appears to have an interest which justifies appearance.

(2)   If the court makes an administration order, the costs of the applicant, and of any other person whose costs are allowed by the court, are payable as an expense of the administration.

Derivation—This rule derived from the Insolvency Rules 1986, SI 1986/1925, r 2.12.

Amendments—SI 2019/146, as from IP completion day (as defined in the European Union (Withdrawal Agreement) Act 2020, s 39(1)–(5)).

General note—See the notes to paras 10 and 13 of Sch B1. If an administration order is made under para 13(1)(a) of Sch B1 then, by virtue of para 13(2), the appointment of the administrator takes effect at the time appointed by the order or, when no time is appointed, when the order is made, as does the commencement of the administration by virtue of para 1(2)(b).

For an example of the exercise of permission under r 3.12(1)(j) see *Strategic Advantage SPC v ARL O09 Ltd* [2020] EWHC 3350 (Ch) (Mr Andrew Sutcliffe QC).

Costs and r 3.12(2)—See also here the note to r 3.51. In *Irish Reel Productions Ltd v Capitol Films Ltd* [2010] EWHC 180 (Ch) Briggs J acknowledged that the payment of the costs of a winding-up petition dismissed on the making of an administration order was an established practice of the Companies Court. At [8] his Lordship identified the jurisdiction for such an order to lie in the phrase 'the costs  . . .  of any person whose costs are allowed by the court' which comprehends not merely that person's costs of appearing at the hearing of an administration application, but that person's costs of any petition which is dismissed at the same time, where the court thinks fit to make such an order. The remaining words of r 3.12(2) then automatically provide for such costs to be payable as an expense of the administration, and fall within the words in r 3.51(2)(c) 'the costs of  . . .  any person appearing on the hearing of the application  . . . .'. Briggs J declined to make an order pursuant to what is now r 3.51(3) ranking the costs of the dismissed winding-up petition in priority to other administration expenses in the extremely unlikely event of a deficiency in meeting the costs of the petition.

Where a party unsuccessfully opposes an administration order it will not ordinarily be entitled to its costs as an expense of the administration. Exceptionally, however, in *Re Structures & Computers Ltd* [1998] BCC 348 at 358 Neuberger J (as he then was) allowed a majority creditor opposing the administration petition its costs of doing so as an expense of the administration on the grounds of the unusual circumstances of the case, including the assistance provided to the court by the majority creditor despite its opposition, and because it was having to bear the majority of the shortfall in the administration. To make any other costs order would have been unjust: see also *Re A Company (No 005174 of 1999)* [2000] 1 BCLC 593.

In *Re Professional Computer Group Ltd* [2008] EWHC 1541 (Ch), in a judgment dealing only with costs following the making of an administration order, Morgan J, having considered the decision in *Structures*, held that it would not be just to make an order for the costs of root and branch opposition by a creditor – Mountain – to be paid as an expense of the administration. Mountain's opposition had increased the company's costs. If the court did not give the company its costs against Mountain, then it followed that Mountain's unsuccessful opposition had increased the burden of costs on the company, and as a result, on its creditors. Whatever the debt due from the company to Mountain turned out to be, Mountain was not the only creditor and making an order for costs in favour of Mountain would adversely impact on other creditors. Mountain had been unsuccessful in relation to all of the principal submissions made in relation to the application for an administration order. As an unsuccessful litigant, it would require something out of the ordinary to justify an order which would provide for its costs to be paid as an expense of the administration. The fact that the unsuccessful litigant caused the court to have doubts, which the court overcame, about whether to make the administration order was not enough of a reason to give the creditor its costs as an expense of the administration. In a case which was neither unusual nor exceptional, an opposing creditor should not expect that it will automatically obtain an order for its costs as an expense of the administration. Ordering Mountain to pay the company's costs was governed not by r 2.12(3) of the IR 1986 (now r 3.12(2) of the IR 2016 2016) but by s 51 of the Supreme Court (now Senior Courts) Act 1981 for the purposes of which the court joined Mountain as a party under CPR 48.2. In all the circumstances it was just to make an order against Mountain that it should pay the costs of the company on the standard basis to the extent that those costs had been increased by Mountain's unsuccessful opposition. There was no pre-condition of such liability that the creditor should have advance notice of the possible costs consequences of its actions and there was no settled practice preventing such an order.

In *WF Fearman Ltd (No 2)* [1988] BCC 141 the directors of the applicant company were ordered by Harman J to pay the costs of an unsuccessful administration petition personally and not as an expense in the winding-up ordered notwithstanding, first, the court accepting that the directors had acted in good faith, and, secondly, the former provision to the effect that a petition presented by directors was to be treated as a petition of the company. On very similar facts, in *Re Gosscott (Groundworks) Ltd* [1988] 4 BCC 372 Mervyn Davies J ordered that the costs of the company's failed administration petition ranked as an expense in the winding-up ordered. In *Re Land & Property Trust Co plc (No 2)* [1993] BCC 462 the Court of Appeal confirmed the jurisdiction to make such an order personally against directors although, on the facts, discharged the order to that effect made below. Such orders are appropriate in exceptional cases and not where the directors have proceeded in good faith and on the basis of professional advice, even if that advice was erroneous. In [1996] BCC 386 at 374–375 Mr Martin Mann QC, sitting as a Deputy High Court judge, held that, in imposing what amounts to a non-party costs order against directors, reason and justice would not usually require that directors of a company be ordered to pay costs personally unless it could be established summarily that they had caused costs to be incurred for an improper purpose which justified piercing the corporate veil.

For an order capping costs treated as an administration expense by reason of the parties' unreasonable behaviour where a director and a creditor each proposed a different administrator resulting in the court appointing independent administrators see *Re Japanese Koi Co Ltd* (unreported, 13 July 2016) (Snowden J).

## [2.137]

### 3.13 The order

(1) Where the court makes an administration order the court's order must be headed "Administration order" and must contain the following—

(a) identification details for the proceedings;

(b) the name and title of the judge making the order;

(c) the address for service of the applicant;

(d) details of any other parties (including the company) appearing and by whom represented;

(e)    an order that during the period the order is in force the affairs, business and property of the company is to be managed by the administrator;

(f)    the name of the person appointed as administrator;

(g)    an order that that person is appointed as administrator of the company;

(h)    a statement that the court is satisfied either that the EU Regulation as it has effect in the law of the United Kingdom does not apply or that it does;

(i)    where the EU Regulation does apply, a statement whether the proceedings are COMI proceedings or establishment proceedings;

(j)    the date of the order (and if the court so orders the time); and

(k)    such other provisions if any as the court thinks just.

(2)    Where two or more administrators are appointed the order must also specify (as required by paragraph 100(2) of Schedule B1)—

(a)    which functions (if any) are to be exercised by those persons acting jointly; and

(b)    which functions (if any) are to be exercised by any or all of those persons.

**Derivation**—This rule derived from the Insolvency Rules 1986, SI 1986/1925, r 2.13, Sch 4, Fm 2.4B.

**Amendments**—SI 2017/1115; SI 2019/146, as from IP completion day (as defined in the European Union (Withdrawal Agreement) Act 2020, s 39(1)–(5)).

**General note**—Where an administration order is made with retrospective effect after the close of the transition period for the UK's withdrawal from the EU, the proceedings were opened on the date of that order, and not from the retrospective date from which the order took effect. Accordingly, such an order has to contain the recitals specified by r 3.13, as amended by the Insolvency (Amendment) (EU Exit) Regulations 2019 (SI 2019/146): *Re Mederco (Cardiff) Ltd* [2021] EWHC 386 (Ch) (HHJ Davis-White QC, observations made without the benefit of full argument).

## [2.138]

### 3.14 Order on an application under paragraph 37 or 38 of Schedule B1

Where the court makes an administration order in relation to a company on an application under paragraph 37 or 38 of Schedule B1, the court must also include in the order—

(a)    in the case of a liquidator appointed in a voluntary winding up, the removal of that liquidator from office;

(b)    provision for payment of the expenses of the winding up;

(c)    such provision as the court thinks just relating to—

    (i)    any indemnity given to the liquidator,

    (ii)    the release of the liquidator,

    (iii)    the handling or realisation of any of the company's assets in the hands of or under the control of the liquidator, and

    (iv)    other matters arising in connection with the winding up; and

(d)    such other provisions if any as the court thinks just.

**Derivation**—This rule derived from the Insolvency Rules 1986, SI 1986/1925, r 2.13.

## [2.139]

### 3.15 Notice of administration order

(1)    If the court makes an administration order, it must as soon as reasonably practicable deliver two sealed copies of the order to the applicant.

(2)    The applicant must as soon as reasonably practicable deliver a sealed copy of the order to the person appointed as administrator.

(3)    If the court makes an order under sub-paragraph (d) or (f) of paragraph 13(1) of Schedule B1, it must give directions as to the persons to whom, and how, notice of that order is to be delivered.

**Derivation**—This rule derived from the Insolvency Rules 1986, SI 1986/1925, r 2.14.

CHAPTER 3

APPOINTMENT OF ADMINISTRATOR BY HOLDER OF FLOATING CHARGE

**[2.140]**

Note

[Note: a document required by the Act or these Rules must also contain the standard contents set out in Part 1.]

**[2.141]**

**3.16 Notice of intention to appoint**

(1)   This rule applies where the holder of a qualifying floating charge ("the appointer") gives a notice under paragraph 15(1)(a) of Schedule B1 of intention to appoint an administrator under paragraph 14 and files a copy of the notice with the court under paragraph 44(2).

(2)   The notice filed with the court must be headed "Notice of intention to appoint an administrator by holder of qualifying floating charge" and must contain the following—

- (a)   identification details for the proceedings;
- (b)   the name and address of the appointer;
- (c)   a statement that the appointer intends to appoint an administrator of the company;
- (d)   the name and address of the proposed administrator;
- (e)   a statement that the appointer is the holder of the qualifying floating charge in question and that it is now enforceable;
- (f)   details of the charge, the date upon which it was registered and the maximum amount if any secured by the charge;
- (g)   a statement that the notice is being given in accordance with paragraph 15(1)(a) of Schedule B1 to the holder of every prior floating charge which satisfies paragraph 14(2) of that Schedule;
- (h)   the names and addresses of the holders of such prior floating charges and details of the charges;
- (i)   a statement whether the company is or is not subject to insolvency proceedings at the date of the notice, and details of the proceedings if it is;
- (j)   a statement whether the company is an Article 1.2 undertaking; and
- (k)   a statement whether the proceedings flowing from the appointment will be COMI proceedings, establishment proceedings or proceedings to which the EU Regulation as it has effect in the law of the United Kingdom does not apply with reasons for the statement.

(3)   The notice must be authenticated by the appointer or the appointer's solicitor and dated.

(4)   The filing of the copy with the court under paragraph 44(2) of Schedule B1 must be done at the same time as notice is given in accordance with paragraph 15(1)(a).

(5)   The giving of notice under paragraph 15(1)(a) must be by service of the notice.

**Derivation**—This rule derived from the Insolvency Rules 1986, SI 1986/1925, r 2.15, Sch 4, Fm 2.5B.

**Amendments**—SI 2017/1115; SI 2019/146, as from IP completion day (as defined in the European Union (Withdrawal Agreement) Act 2020, s 39(1)–(5)).

**General note**—The notice of intention to appoint must comply with the requirements of r 3.16(2) and (3) if the qualifying floating charge holder wishes to invoke the interim moratorium under para 44(2) of Sch B1. Taken together, r 3.16(1)–(4) suggest that the qualifying floating charge holder may elect to give notice of intention to appoint other than in the prescribed form so as to avoid triggering the interim moratorium. The interim moratorium provisions are not engaged where there is no chargee ranking in priority to the qualifying floating charge holder intending to appoint because in those circumstances there is no party upon which service of a notice of intention to appoint is required such that the charge holder is entitled to proceed directly with the filing of a notice of appointment under r 3.17.

**[2.142]**

### 3.17 Notice of appointment

(1) Notice of an appointment under paragraph 14 of Schedule B1 must be headed "Notice of appointment of an administrator by holder of a qualifying floating charge" and must contain—

(a) identification details for the proceedings;

(b) the name and address of the appointer;

(c) a statement that the appointer has appointed the person named as administrator of the company;

(d) the name and address of the person appointed as administrator;

(e) a statement that a copy of the administrator's consent to act accompanies the notice;

(f) a statement that the appointer is the holder of the qualifying floating charge in question and that it is now enforceable;

(g) details of the charge including the date of the charge, the date on which it was registered and the maximum amount if any secured by the charge;

(h) one of the following statements—

   (i) that notice has been given in accordance with paragraph 15(1)(a) of Schedule B1 to the holder of every prior floating charge which satisfies paragraph 14(2) of that Schedule, that two business days have elapsed from the date the last such notice was given (if more than one) and—

      (aa) that a copy of every such notice was filed with the court under paragraph 44(2) of Schedule B1, and the date of that filing (or the latest date of filing if more than one), or

      (bb) that a copy of every such notice accompanies the notice of appointment but was not filed with the court under paragraph 44(2) of Schedule B1,

   (ii) that the holder of every such floating charge to whom notice was given has consented in writing to the making of the appointment and that a copy of every consent accompanies the notice of appointment,

   (iii) that the holder of every such floating charge has consented in writing to the making of the appointment without notice having been given to all and that a copy of every consent accompanies the notice of appointment, or

   (iv) that there is no such floating charge;

(i) a statement whether the company is or is not subject to insolvency proceedings at the date of the notice, and details of the proceedings if it is;

(j) a statement whether the company is an Article 1.2 undertaking;

(k) a statement whether the proceedings flowing from the appointment will be COMI proceedings, establishment proceedings or proceedings to which the EU Regulation as it has effect in the law of the United Kingdom does not apply and the reasons for so stating; and

(l) a statement that the appointment is in accordance with Schedule B1.

(2) Where two or more administrators are appointed the notice must also specify (as required by paragraph 100(2) of Schedule B1)—

(a) which functions (if any) are to be exercised by those persons acting jointly; and

(b) which functions (if any) are to be exercised by any or all of those persons.

(3) The statutory declaration included in the notice in accordance with paragraph 18(2) of Schedule B1 must be made not more than five business days before the notice is filed with the court.

**Derivation**—This rule derived from the Insolvency Rules 1986, SI 1986/1925, r 2.16, Sch 4, Fm 2.6B.

**Amendments**—SI 2017/1115; SI 2019/146, as from IP completion day (as defined in the European Union (Withdrawal Agreement) Act 2020, s 39(1)–(5)).

**General note**—Para 19 of Sch B1 provides that an appointment under para 14 only takes effect when the requirements of para 18 are met, being the filing of the notice of appointment and 'such other documents as may be prescribed', being those provided for in this Rule (which include a statutory declaration which must be dated). It is clear from the judgment of Peter Smith J in *Fliptex Ltd v Hogg* [2004] BCC 870 that there is no distinction between an appointment being made by a charge holder and the appointment taking effect under para 19 of Sch B1 provided the power of appointment has arisen upon para 19 taking effect. As his Lordship put it at [32]:

'Paragraph 19 plainly indicates that the appointment is only effective when para 18 is satisfied. That makes sound sense. Where out of court appointments take place there will be no clear mechanism identifying the date and time when an appointment takes effect (contrast court appointments). It is therefore logical to dictate that the appointment is only effective when the conditions of para 18 are satisfied. All documents executed before that date are executed subject to a condition that the appointment would become effective . . . The appointment only becomes effective for all purposes when the conditions in para 19 are satisfied and it is then unconditional. That gives a clear date when everybody knows that all the conditions have been satisfied and the appointment then becomes effective. The idea that there is an appointment made, but not effective, but nevertheless is treated as having an effect is not a result that the draftsman of the schedule could have contemplated.'

The decision of the Court of Appeal in *Byblos Bank SAL v Al-Khudhairy* [1986] 2 BCC 99, 549 is authority for the proposition that a charge holder may rely upon an event of default (ie justifying appointment) that would have been available to the charge holder at the relevant time had the charge holder had knowledge of it.

## [2.143]

### 3.18 Filing of notice with the court

(1) Three copies of the notice of appointment must be filed with the court, accompanied by—

    (a)    the administrator's consent to act; and

    (b)    either—

        (i)    evidence that the appointer has given notice as required by paragraph 15(1)(a) of Schedule B1; or

        (ii)    copies of the written consent of all those required to give consent in accordance with paragraph 15(1)(b) of Schedule B1.

(2) The court must apply the seal of the court to the copies of the notice, endorse them with the date and time of filing and deliver two of the sealed copies to the appointer.

(3) The appointer must as soon as reasonably practicable deliver one of the sealed copies to the administrator.

(4) This rule is subject to rules 3.20 and 3.21 (appointment made out of court business hours).

**Derivation**—This rule derived from the Insolvency Rules 1986, SI 1986/1925, r 2.17.

## [2.144]

### 3.19 Appointment by floating charge holder after administration application made

(1) This rule applies where the holder of a qualifying floating charge, after receiving notice that an administration application has been made, appoints an administrator under paragraph 14 of Schedule B1.

(2) The holder must as soon as reasonably practicable deliver a copy of the notice of appointment to—

    (a)    the person making the administration application; and

    (b)    the court in which the application has been made.

**Derivation**—This rule derived from the Insolvency Rules 1986, SI 1986/1925, r 2.18.

## [2.145]

### 3.20 Appointment taking place out of court business hours: procedure

(1) When (but only when) the court is closed, the holder of a qualifying floating charge may file a notice of appointment with the court by—

    (a)    faxing it to a designated telephone number; or

    (b)    emailing it, or attaching it to an email, to a designated email address.

(2)   The notice must specify the name of the court (and hearing centre if applicable) that has jurisdiction.

(3)   The Lord Chancellor must designate the telephone number and email address.

(4)   The Secretary of State must publish the designated telephone number and email address on the Insolvency Service webpages and deliver notice of them to any person requesting them from the Insolvency Service.

(5)   The appointer must ensure that—

    (a)    a fax transmission report giving the time and date of the fax transmission and the telephone number to which the notice was faxed and containing a copy of the first page (in part or in full) of the document faxed is created by the fax machine that is used to fax the notice; or

    (b)    a hard copy of the email is created giving the time and date of the email and the address to which it was sent.

(6)   The appointer must retain the fax transmission report or hard copy of the email.

(7)   The appointer must deliver a notice to the administrator of the filing of the notice of appointment as soon as reasonably practicable.

(8)   The copy of the faxed or emailed notice of appointment as received by the Courts Service must be delivered by the Lord Chancellor as soon as reasonably practicable to the court specified in the notice as the court having jurisdiction in the case, to be placed on the relevant court file.

(9)   The appointer must take to the court on the next occasion that the court is open for business—

    (a)    three copies of the faxed or emailed notice of appointment;

    (b)    the fax transmission report or hard copy required by paragraph (5);

    (c)    all supporting documents referred to in the notice in accordance with rule 3.21(1) which are in the appointer's possession; and

    (d)    a statement providing reasons for the out-of-hours filing of the notice of appointment, including why it would have been damaging to the company or its creditors not to have so acted.

(10)   The copies of the notice must be sealed by the court and endorsed with—

    (a)    the date and time when, according to the appointer's fax transmission report or hard copy of the email, the notice was faxed or sent; and

    (b)    the date when the notice and accompanying documents were delivered to the court.

(11)   The court must deliver two of the sealed copies of the notice of appointment to the appointer.

(12)   The appointer must, as soon as reasonably practicable, deliver one of the copies to the administrator.

(13)   The reference—

    (a)    to the Insolvency Service in paragraph (4) means the Secretary of State acting by means of the Insolvency Service; and

    (b)    to the Courts Service in paragraph (8) means the Lord Chancellor acting by means of Her Majesty's Courts and Tribunals Service.

**Derivation**—This rule derived from the Insolvency Rules 1986, SI 1986/1925, r 2.19.

**General note**—In certain cases of urgency there will be a genuine need for the holder of a qualifying floating charge to effect the appointment of an administrator when the court office is closed, say in ensuring the custody or preservation of assets which might otherwise be lost or jeopardised or in obtaining protection from a threatening creditor or creditors so as to facilitate the performance of a contract.

First, the procedural requirements are strict and, in relation to the physical delivery ('the appointer must take') of the prescribed documents to the court on the next business day, carry a draconian sanction in that r 3.22(2)(b) provides that the administrator's appointment 'ceases to have effect if the requirements of rule 3.20(9) are not completed on the next occasion the court is open for business'. For the purposes of r 3.20(1)(a), the fax number is currently 0870 761 7716, the fax number being published on the Insolvency Service's website at http://www.bis.gov.uk/inso lvency; the e-mail address in England and Wales is rcjcompanies.orders@hmcts.gsi.gov.uk; the fax number of any court to which a notice of appointment should be faxed directly in Scotland is available on the Scottish court's website at www.scotcourts.gov.uk from which the current e-mail address may also be obtained.

Secondly, the decision to appoint out of business hours may be subject to objective scrutiny in the event of the propriety of the appointment being challenged subsequently. Specifically, r 3.20(9)(d) requires the appointing charge holder to take to the court on the next occasion that the court is open for business a statement providing reasons for the out-of-hours filing of the notice of appointment, including why it would have been damaging to the company or its creditors not to have so acted. This requirement is justifiable, other, arguably, than in a case where it is not reasonably practicable for the administrator to achieve either of the objectives in para 3(1)(a) or (b) from the outset, on the basis that both the company and certainly its creditors – neither of which has standing to appoint out of court business hours – have a direct interest in an administration and its conduct, including its commencement. Like the court, the company and its creditors are properly entitled to an explanation as to how their interests might otherwise have been damaged but for the intervention of a charge holder. Any suggestion that a charge holder should indulge in providing the court with anything less than full and frank reasons for the out of hours appointment has nothing whatsoever to commend it.

Thirdly, these provisions provide an alternative procedure only, as r 3.20(1) provides, 'When the court is closed (and only when it is closed)'. Any suggestion that this alternative procedure is available 'out of business hours' is not strictly correct since it is only closure of the court which triggers the availability of the provisions. The reason that the court is closed is apparently irrelevant.

## [2.146]

### 3.21 Appointment taking place out of court business hours: content of notice

(1) Notice of an appointment filed in accordance with rule 3.20 must be headed "Notice of appointment of an administrator by holder of a qualifying floating charge", identify the company immediately below the heading and must contain—

- (a) the name and address of the appointer;
- (b) a statement that the appointer has appointed the person named as administrator of the company;
- (c) the name and address of the person appointed as administrator;
- (d) a statement that the appointer is the holder of the qualifying floating charge in question and that it is now enforceable;
- (e) details of the charge, the date upon which it was registered and the maximum amount secured by the charge;
- (f) one of the following statements—
  - (i) that notice has been given in accordance with paragraph 15(1)(a) of Schedule B1 to the holder of every prior floating charge which satisfies paragraph 14(2) of that Schedule, that a copy of every such notice was filed with the court under paragraph 44(2) of that Schedule, the date of that filing (or the latest date of filing if more than one) and that two business days have elapsed since notice was given under paragraph 15(1)(a) of Schedule B1,
  - (ii) that notice has been given in accordance with paragraph 15(1)(a) of Schedule B1 to the holder of every prior floating charge which satisfies paragraph 14(2) of that Schedule and that a copy of every such notice is in the appointer's possession but was not filed with the court under paragraph 44(2) of that Schedule,
  - (iii) that the holder of every such floating charge to whom notice was given has consented to the making of the appointment and that a copy of every consent in writing is in the appointer's possession,
  - (iv) that the holder of every such floating charge has consented to the making of the appointment without notice having been given to all and that a copy of every consent in writing is in the appointer's possession, or
  - (v) that there is no such floating charge;
- (g) a statement whether the company is or is not subject to insolvency proceedings at the date of the notice, and details of the proceedings if it is;
- (h) a statement whether the company is an Article 1.2 undertaking . . .;

    (i)      a statement whether the proceedings flowing from the appointment will be COMI proceedings, establishment proceedings or proceedings to which the EU Regulation as it has effect in the law of the United Kingdom does not apply and that a statement of the reasons for stating this is in the appointer's possession;

    (j)      an undertaking that the following will be delivered to the court on the next occasion on which the court is open—

        (i)      any document referred to in the notice in accordance with rule 3.20 as being in the appointer's possession,

        (ii)     the fax transmission report or hard copy of the email, and

        (iii)    the statement of reasons for out-of-hours filing;

    (k)     a statement that the proposed administrator consents to act; and

    (l)      a statement that the appointment is in accordance with Schedule B1.

(2)   Where two or more administrators are appointed the notice must also specify (as required by paragraph 100(2) of Schedule B1)—

    (a)    which functions (if any) are to be exercised by those persons acting jointly; and

    (b)    which functions (if any) are to be exercised by any or all of those persons.

(3)   The statutory declaration included in the notice in accordance with paragraph 18(2) of Schedule B1 must be made not more than five business days before the notice is filed with the court.

    **Derivation**—This rule derived from the Insolvency Rules 1986, SI 1986/1925, r 2.19(1), Sch 4, Fm 2.7B.

    **Amendments**—SI 2017/366; SI 2017/1115; SI 2019/146, as from IP completion day (as defined in the European Union (Withdrawal Agreement) Act 2020, s 39(1)–(5)).

## [2.147]

### 3.22 Appointment taking place out of court business hours: legal effect

(1)   The filing of a notice in accordance with rule 3.20 has the same effect for all purposes as the filing of a notice of appointment in accordance with rule 3.18.

(2)   The appointment—

    (a)    takes effect from the date and time of the fax transmission or sending of the email; but

    (b)    ceases to have effect if the requirements of rule 3.20(9) are not completed on the next occasion the court is open for business.

(3)   Where any question arises in relation to the date and time that the notice of appointment was filed with the court, it is a presumption capable of rebuttal that the date and time shown on the appointer's fax transmission report or hard copy of the email is the date and time at which the notice was filed.

    **Derivation**—This rule derived from the Insolvency Rules 1986, SI 1986/1925, r 2.19(2).

    See also *Practice Note* [2020] BCC 211 and the notes to para 29 under the heading 'Electronic filing'.

CHAPTER 4

APPOINTMENT OF ADMINISTRATOR BY COMPANY OR DIRECTORS

## [2.148]

### Note

[Note: a document required by the Act or these Rules must also contain the standard contents set out in Part 1.]

**[2.149]**

### 3.23 Notice of intention to appoint

(1) If paragraph 26 of Schedule B1 requires a notice of intention to appoint an administrator under paragraph 22 of that Schedule then the notice must be headed "Notice of intention to appoint an administrator by company or directors" and must contain the following—

    (a)    identification details for the proceedings;

    (b)    a statement that the company or the directors, as the case may be, intend to appoint an administrator of the company;

    (c)    the name and address of the proposed administrator;

    (d)    the names and addresses of the persons to whom notice is being given in accordance with paragraph 26(1) of Schedule B1;

    (e)    a statement that each of those persons is or may be entitled to appoint—

        (i)    an administrative receiver of the company, or

        (ii)    an administrator of the company under paragraph 14 of Schedule B1;

    (f)    a statement that the company has not within the preceding 12 months been—

        (i)    in administration;

        (ii)    the subject of a moratorium under Schedule A1 which ended on a date when no CVA was in force; or

        (iii)    the subject of a CVA which was made during a moratorium under Schedule A1 and which ended prematurely within the meaning of section 7B;

    (g)    a statement that in relation to the company there is no—

        (i)    petition for winding up which has been presented but not yet disposed of,

        (ii)    administration application which has not yet been disposed of, or

        (iii)    administrative receiver in office;

    (h)    a statement whether the company is an Article 1.2 undertaking;

    (i)    a statement whether the proceedings flowing from the appointment will be COMI proceedings, establishment proceedings or proceedings to which the EU Regulation as it has effect in the law of the United Kingdom does not apply and the reasons for so stating;

    (j)    a statement that the notice is accompanied (as appropriate) by either—

        (i)    a copy of the resolution of the company to appoint an administrator, or

        (ii)    a record of the decision of the directors to appoint an administrator; and

    (k)    a statement that if a recipient of the notice who is named in paragraph (e) wishes to consent in writing to the appointment that person may do so but that after five business days have expired from delivery of the notice the appointer may make the appointment although such a recipient has not replied.

(2) The notice must be accompanied by—

    (a)    a copy of the resolution of the company to appoint an administrator, where the company intends to make the appointment, or

    (b)    a record of the decision of the directors, where the directors intend to make the appointment.

(3) The giving of notice under paragraph 26(1) of Schedule B1 must be by service of the notice.

(4) If notice of intention to appoint is given under paragraph 26(1) of Schedule B1, a copy of the notice under paragraph 26(2) must be sent at the same time to—

    (a)    any enforcement agent or other officer who, to the knowledge of the person giving the notice, is charged with distress or other legal process against the company;

    (b)    any person who, to the knowledge of the person giving the notice, has distrained against the company or its property;

    (c)    any supervisor of a CVA; and

    (d)    the company, if the company is not intending to make the appointment.

(5) The giving of notice under paragraph 26(2) of Schedule B1 must be by service of the notice.

(6) The statutory declaration accompanying the notice in accordance with paragraph 27(2) of Schedule B1 must—

    (a)    if it is not made by the person making the appointment, indicate the capacity in which the person making the declaration does so; and

    (b)    be made not more than five business days before the notice is filed with the court.

**Derivation**—This rule derived from the Insolvency Rules 1986, SI 1986/1925, r 2.20, Sch 4, Fm 2.8B.

**Amendments**—SI 2017/366; SI 2017/1115; SI 2019/146, as from IP completion day (as defined in the European Union (Withdrawal Agreement) Act 2020, s 39(1)–(5)).

**General note**—If no party is entitled to notice of intention to appoint under para 26 of Sch B1 then the company or directors are entitled to proceed directly to effecting an appointment by way of filing a notice of appointment in accordance with r 3.25.

On the issue of the obtaining of an interim moratorium by way of the filing of a notice of intention to appoint where no party is entitled to service of such notice see the notes to para 26 of Sch B1.

## [2.150]

### 3.24 Notice of appointment after notice of intention to appoint

(1) Notice of an appointment under paragraph 22 of Schedule B1 (when notice of intention to appoint has been given under paragraph 26) must be headed "Notice of appointment of an administrator by a company (where a notice of intention to appoint has been given)" or "Notice of appointment of an administrator by the directors of a company (where a notice of intention to appoint has been given)" and must contain—

    (a)    identification details for the company immediately below the heading;

    (b)    a statement that the company has, or the directors have, as the case may be, appointed the person named as administrator of the company;

    (c)    the name and address of the person appointed as administrator;

    (d)    a statement that a copy of the administrator's consent to act accompanies the notice;

    (e)    a statement that the company is, or the directors are, as the case may be, entitled to make an appointment under paragraph 22 of Schedule B1;

    (f)    a statement that the appointment is in accordance with Schedule B1;

    (g)    a statement whether the company is an Article 1.2 undertaking;

    (h)    a statement whether the proceedings flowing from the appointment will be COMI proceedings, establishment proceedings or proceedings to which the EU Regulation as it has effect in the law of the United Kingdom does not apply and the reasons for so stating;

    (i)    a statement that the company has, or the directors have, as the case may be, given notice of their intention to appoint in accordance with paragraph 26(1) of Schedule B1, that a copy of the notice was filed with the court, the date of that filing and either—

        (i)    that five business days have elapsed since notice was given under paragraph 26(1) of Schedule B1, or

        (ii)    that each person to whom the notice was given has consented to the appointment; and

    (j)    the date and time of the appointment.

(2) Where two or more administrators are appointed the notice must also specify (as required by paragraph 100(2) of Schedule B1)—

    (a)    which functions (if any) are to be exercised by those persons acting jointly; and

(b)    which functions (if any) are to be exercised by any or all of those persons.
(3)   The statutory declaration included in the notice in accordance with paragraph 29(2) of Schedule B1 must be made not more than five business days before the notice is filed with the court.
(4)   If the statutory declaration is not made by the person making the appointment it must indicate the capacity in which the person making the declaration does so.

**Derivation**—This rule derived from the Insolvency Rules 1986, SI 1986/1925, r 2.23, 2.24, Sch 4, Fm 2.9B.

**Amendments**—SI 2017/366; SI 2017/1115; SI 2019/146, as from IP completion day (as defined in the European Union (Withdrawal Agreement) Act 2020, s 39(1)–(5)).

**General note**—In *Re Spaces London Bridge Limited* [2018] EWHC 3099 (Ch) Nugee J held that the requirement under r 3.24 for a notice of appointment to contain the time and date of the appointment means the time and date that the notice is filed (ie as opposed to some earlier time at which the resolution to appoint was passed). In following the reasoning of HHJ Klein in *Re NJM Clothing Ltd (in administration)* [2018] EWHC 2388 (Ch) the judge took the view that that the IR 2016 envisaged the appointment by the company or its directors would precede the appointment becoming effective upon the relevant filing requirements being met. However, Nugee J also considered that the exact date and time of the resolution to appoint was 'a matter of supreme irrelevance' because that appointment was in itself almost meaningless, in comparison with the position once the appointment took effect upon the notice of appointment being filed. In considering the requirement in r 3.24(1)(j) for the insertion in the notice of the time and date of the appointment, Nugee J observed that, if that actually required the insertion of the actual resolution to appoint, then that was capable of producing an outcome that was misleading to third parties because it might give the impression that a fully effective appointment of an administrator had been made prior to the filing of the notice. On the other hand, a reference in the notice to the time of the actual filing would amount to construing the statutory provision as duplicative (to use the judge's terminology) but not potentially misleading. The judge recognised that this second approach would mean construing the wording of r 3.24 as otiose but the judge preferred that outcome as an alternative to providing a potentially misleading date. The utility of Spaces London lies in the guidance given to office-holders on completion of the notice of appointment. On the facts of the case the notice had been completed to provide that 'the directors of the company . . . hereby appoint the following named persons as administrators of the company . . . and notice of the appointment is hereby given'. The conclusion reached was that this wording was sufficient to meet the requirements of r 3.24(1)(j). The judge did go on to suggest that better practice might be to use the words 'This appointment will take effect at the time and date specified below as the date and time when the notice is filed', although the judge did not consider that a failure to use this precise wording was in any way fatal. The judge also considered that any defect there might have been in the appointment was a defect only and curable under r 12.64 of the IR 2016 (previously r 7.55 of the IA 1986) (formal defects).

## [2.151]

### 3.25  Notice of appointment without prior notice of intention to appoint

(1)   Notice of an appointment under paragraph 22 of Schedule B1 (when notice of intention to appoint has not been given under paragraph 26) must be headed "Notice of appointment of an administrator by a company (where a notice of intention to appoint has not been given)" or "Notice of appointment of an administrator by the directors of a company (where a notice of intention to appoint has not been given)" and must identify the company immediately below the heading.
(2)   The notice must state the following—
    (a)    that the company has, or the directors have, as the case may be, appointed the person specified under sub-paragraph (b) as administrator of the company;
    (b)    the name and address of the person appointed as administrator;
    (c)    that a copy of the administrator's consent to act accompanies the notice;
    (d)    that the company is or the directors are, as the case may be, entitled to make an appointment under paragraph 22 of Schedule B1;
    (e)    that the appointment is in accordance with Schedule B1;
    (f)    that the company has not within the preceding 12 months been—
        (i)    in administration,

   (ii)  the subject of a moratorium under Schedule A1 which ended on a date when no CVA was in force, or

   (iii)  the subject of a CVA which was made during a moratorium under Schedule A1 and which ended prematurely within the meaning of section 7B;

 (g)  that in relation to the company there is no—

   (i)  petition for winding up which has been presented but not yet disposed of,

   (ii)  administration application which has not yet been disposed of, or

   (iii)  administrative receiver in office;

 (h)  whether the company is an Article 1.2 undertaking;

 (i)  whether the proceedings flowing from the appointment will be COMI proceedings, establishment proceedings or proceedings to which the EU Regulation as it has effect in the law of the United Kingdom does not apply and the reasons for so stating;

 (j)  that the notice is accompanied by—

   (i)  a copy of the resolution of the company to appoint an administrator, or

   (ii)  a record of the decision of the directors to appoint an administrator; and

 (k)  the date and time of the appointment.

(3) Where two or more administrators are appointed the notice must also specify (as required by paragraph 100(2) of Schedule B1)—

 (a)  which functions (if any) are to be exercised by those persons acting jointly; and

 (b)  which functions (if any) are to be exercised by any or all of those persons.

(4) The statutory declaration included in the notice in accordance with paragraphs 29(2) and 30 of Schedule B1 must—

 (a)  if the declaration is made on behalf of the person making the appointment, indicate the capacity in which the person making the declaration does so; and

 (b)  be made not more than five business days before the notice is filed with the court.

**Derivation**—This rule derived from the Insolvency Rules 1986, SI 1986/1925, r 2.25, Sch 4, Fm 2.8B.

**Amendments**—SI 2017/1115; SI 2019/146, as from IP completion day (as defined in the European Union (Withdrawal Agreement) Act 2020, s 39(1)–(5)).

## [2.152]

### 3.26 Notice of appointment: filing with the court

(1) Three copies of the notice of appointment must be filed with the court, accompanied by—

 (a)  the administrator's consent to act; and

 (b)  the written consent of all those persons to whom notice was given in accordance with paragraph 26(1) of Schedule B1 unless the period of notice set out in paragraph 26(1) has expired.

(2) Where a notice of intention to appoint an administrator has not been given, the copies of the notice of appointment must also be accompanied by—

 (a)  a copy of the resolution of the company to appoint an administrator, where the company is making the appointment; or

 (b)  a record of the decision of the directors, where the directors are making the appointment.

(3) The court must apply to the copies the seal of the court, endorse them with the date and time of filing and deliver two of the sealed copies to the appointer.

(4) The appointer must as soon as reasonably practicable deliver one of the sealed copies to the administrator.

**Derivation**—This rule derived from the Insolvency Rules 1986, SI 1986/1925, r 2.26.

See also *Practice Note* [2020] BCC 211 and the notes to para 29 under the heading 'Electronic filing'.

CHAPTER 5

NOTICE OF ADMINISTRATOR'S APPOINTMENT

## [2.153]

Note

[Note: a document required by the Act or these Rules must also contain the standard contents set out in Part 1.]

## [2.154]

**3.27 Publication of administrator's appointment**

(1) The notice of appointment, to be published by the administrator as soon as reasonably practicable after appointment under paragraph 46(2)(b) of Schedule B1, must be gazetted and may be advertised in such other manner as the administrator thinks fit.

(2) The notice of appointment must state the following—

- (a)    that an administrator has been appointed;
- (b)    the date of the appointment; and
- (c)    the nature of the business of the company.

(3) The administrator must, as soon as reasonably practicable after the date specified in paragraph 46(6) of Schedule B1, deliver a notice of the appointment—

- (a)    if a receiver or an administrative receiver has been appointed, to that person;
- (b)    if there is pending a petition for the winding up of the company, to the petitioner (and also to the provisional liquidator, if any);
- (c)    to any enforcement officer, enforcement agent or other officer who, to the administrator's knowledge, is charged with distress or other legal process against the company or its property;
- (d)    to any person who, to the administrator's knowledge, has distrained against the company or its property; and
- (e)    any supervisor of a CVA.

(4) Where, under Schedule B1 or these Rules, the administrator is required to deliver a notice of the appointment to the registrar of companies or any other person, it must be headed "Notice of administrator's appointment" and must contain—

- (a)    the administrator's name and address and IP number;
- (b)    identification details for the proceedings; and
- (c)    a statement that the administrator has been appointed as administrator of the company;

(5) The notice must be authenticated and dated by the administrator.

**Derivation**—This rule derived from the Insolvency Rules 1986, SI 1986/1925, r 2.27.

**Gazetted notices**—See rr 1.10—1.12.

**Form**—The notice of appointment delivered to the registrar should be in Form AM01.

CHAPTER 6

STATEMENT OF AFFAIRS

## [2.155]

Note

[Note: a document required by the Act or these Rules must also contain the standard contents set out in Part 1.]

**[2.156]**

### 3.28 Interpretation

In this Chapter—

"nominated person" means a relevant person who has been required by the administrator to make out and deliver to the administrator a statement of affairs; and

"relevant person" means a person mentioned in paragraph 47(3) of Schedule B1.

**Derivation**—This rule derived from the Insolvency Rules 1986, SI 1986/1925, r 2.28(1).

**[2.157]**

### 3.29 Statement of affairs: notice requiring and delivery to the administrator (paragraph 47(1) of Schedule B1)

[Note: see section 234(1) and 235(1) for the application of section 235 to administrators.]

(1) A requirement under paragraph 47(1) of Schedule B1 for one or more relevant persons to provide the administrator with a statement of the affairs of the company must be made by a notice delivered to each such person.

(2) The notice must be headed "Notice requiring statement of affairs" and must—

    (a) require each nominated person to whom the notice is delivered to prepare and submit to the administrator a statement of the affairs of the company;

    (b) inform each nominated person of—

        (i) the names and addresses of all others (if any) to whom the same notice has been delivered,

        (ii) the requirement to deliver the statement of affairs to the administrator no later than eleven days after receipt of the notice requiring the statement of affairs, and

        (iii) the effect of paragraph 48(4) of Schedule B1 (penalty for non-compliance) and section 235 (duty to co-operate with the office-holder).

(3) The administrator must inform each nominated person to whom notice is delivered that a document for the preparation of the statement of affairs capable of completion in compliance with rule 3.30 will be supplied if requested.

(4) The nominated person (or one of them, if more than one) must deliver the statement of affairs to the administrator with the statement of truth required by paragraph 47(2)(a) of Schedule B1 and a copy of each statement.

**Derivation**—This rule derived from the Insolvency Rules 1986, SI 1986/1925, r 2.28, Sch 4, Fm 2.14B.

**Amendments**—SI 2017/366.

**[2.158]**

### 3.30 Statement of affairs: content (paragraph 47 of Schedule B1)

[Note: paragraph 47(2)(a) of Schedule B1 requires the statement of affairs to be verified by a statement of truth.]

(1) The statement of the company's affairs must be headed "Statement of affairs" and must—

    (a) identify the company immediately below the heading; and

    (b) state that it is a statement of the affairs of the company on a specified date, being the date on which it entered administration.

(2) The statement of affairs must contain (in addition to the matters required by paragraph 47(2) of Schedule B1)—

    (a) a summary of the assets of the company, setting out the book value and the estimated realisable value of—

        (i) any assets subject to a fixed charge,

        (ii) any assets subject to a floating charge,

      (iii)    any uncharged assets, and

      (iv)    the total value of all the assets available for preferential creditors;

(b)    a summary of the liabilities of the company, setting out—

      (i)    the amount of preferential debts,

      (ii)    an estimate of the deficiency with respect to preferential debts or the surplus available after paying the preferential debts,

      (iii)    an estimate of the prescribed part, if applicable,

      (iv)    an estimate of the total assets available to pay debts secured by floating charges,

      (v)    the amount of debts secured by floating charges,

      (vi)    an estimate of the deficiency with respect to debts secured by floating charges or the surplus available after paying the debts secured by fixed or floating charges,

      (vii)    the amount of unsecured debts (excluding preferential debts),

      (viii)    an estimate of the deficiency with respect to unsecured debts or the surplus available after paying unsecured debts,

      (ix)    any issued and called-up capital, and

      (x)    an estimate of the deficiency with respect to, or surplus available to, members of the company;

(c)    a list of the company's creditors with the further particulars required by paragraph (3) indicating—

      (i)    any creditors under hire-purchase, chattel leasing or conditional sales agreements, and

      (ii)    any creditors claiming retention of title over property in the company's possession; and

(d)    the name and address of each member of the company and the number, nominal value and other details of the shares held by each member.

(3)    The list of creditors required by paragraph 47(2) of Schedule B1 and paragraph (2)(c) of this rule must contain the details required by paragraph (4) except where paragraphs (5) and (6) apply.

(4)    The particulars required by paragraph (3) are as follows—

(a)    the name and postal address of the creditor;

(b)    the amount of the debt owed to the creditor;

(c)    details of any security held by the creditor;

(d)    the date on which the security was given; and

(e)    the value of any such security.

(5)    Paragraph (6) applies where the particulars required by paragraph (4) relate to creditors who are either—

(a)    employees or former employees of the company; or

(b)    consumers claiming amounts paid in advance for the supply of goods or services.

(6)    Where this paragraph applies—

(a)    the statement of affairs itself must state separately for each of paragraph (5)(a) and (b) the number of such creditors and the total of the debts owed to such them; and

(b)    the particulars required by paragraph (4) must be set out in separate schedules to the statement of affairs for each of paragraphs (5)(a) and (b).

**Derivation**—This rule derived from the Insolvency Rules 1986, SI 1986/1925, r 2.29, Sch 4, Fm 2.14B.

**General note**—For commentary on the statement of affairs see the notes to paras 47 and 49 of Sch B1.

[2.159]

### 3.31 Statement of affairs: statement of concurrence

(1)    The administrator may require a relevant person to deliver to the administrator a statement of concurrence.

(2) A statement of concurrence is a statement, verified by a statement of truth, that that person concurs in the statement of affairs submitted by a nominated person.

(3) The administrator must inform the nominated person who has been required to submit a statement of affairs that the relevant person has been required to deliver a statement of concurrence.

(4) The nominated person must deliver a copy of the statement of affairs to every relevant person who has been required to submit a statement of concurrence.

(5) A statement of concurrence—

    (a)    must identify the company; and

    (b)    may be qualified in relation to matters dealt with in the statement of affairs where the relevant person—

        (i)    is not in agreement with the statement of affairs,

        (ii)    considers the statement of affairs to be erroneous or misleading, or

        (iii)    is without the direct knowledge necessary for concurring with it.

(6) The relevant person must deliver the required statement of concurrence together with a copy to the administrator before the end of the period of five business days (or such other period as the administrator may agree) beginning with the day on which the relevant person receives the statement of affairs.

**Derivation**—This rule derived from the Insolvency Rules 1986, SI 1986/1925, r 2.29(2).

## [2.160]

### 3.32 Statement of affairs: filing

(1) The administrator must as soon as reasonably practicable deliver to the registrar of companies a copy of—

    (a)    the statement of affairs; and

    (b)    any statement of concurrence.

(2) However, the administrator must not deliver to the registrar of companies with the statement of affairs any schedule required by rule 3.30(6)(b).

(3) The requirement to deliver the statement of affairs is subject to any order of the court made under rule 3.45 that the statement of affairs or a specified part must not be delivered to the registrar of companies.

**Derivation**—This rule derived from the Insolvency Rules 1986, SI 1986/1925, r 2.29(7).

**Form**—The notice to the registrar should be in Form AM02 with the statement of affairs and statement of concurrence attached.

**General note**—In *Re Peter Jones (China) Ltd, Smith v Registrar of Companies* [2021] EWHC 215 (Ch) administrators mistakenly lodged with the Registrar of Companies schedules required by r 3.30(6)(b). The Registrar registered those schedules along with the statement of affairs filed pursuant to r 3.32(1)(a). HHJ Davis-White QC held that the Registrar was in error in refusing to remove from the company file the schedules erroneously filed. The Registrar had a discretion under s 1094 of the Companies 2006 to remove the schedules, which were readily separable from the document as a whole, and had been wrong to insist on a court order before doing so. The view of the judge was that the erroneously filed schedules were 'unnecessary material' such that, under s 1074 of the 2006 Act, the non-compliant statement of affairs was not improperly delivered and the Registrar had a discretion whether to register that document in its complete state as delivered or with the unnecessary material removed. If he had exercised that discretion then, in the circumstances, he had done so irrationally or unreasonably. If the IR 2016 prohibited delivery of certain schedules to the Registrar, it was difficult to see how it could be lawful for him to register them: see [24] and [30]–[33].

## [2.161]

### 3.33 Statement of affairs: release from requirement and extension of time

(1) The power of the administrator under paragraph 48(2) of Schedule B1 to revoke a requirement to provide a statement of affairs or to extend the period within which it must be submitted may be exercised upon the administrator's own initiative or at the request of a nominated person who has been required to provide it.

(2) The nominated person may apply to the court if the administrator refuses that person's request for a revocation or extension.

(3) On receipt of an application, the court may, if it is satisfied that no sufficient cause is shown for it, dismiss it without giving notice to any party other than the applicant.

(4) Unless the application is dismissed, the court must fix a venue for it to be heard.

(5) The applicant must, at least 14 days before any hearing, deliver to the administrator a notice stating the venue with a copy of the application and of any evidence on which the applicant intends to rely.

(6) The administrator may do either or both of the following—

    (a) file a report of any matters which the administrator thinks ought to be drawn to the court's attention; or

    (b) appear and be heard on the application.

(7) If a report is filed, the administrator must deliver a copy of it to the applicant not later than five business days before the hearing.

(8) Sealed copies of any order made on the application must be delivered by the court to the applicant and the administrator.

(9) On an application under this rule, the applicant's costs must be paid by the applicant in any event, but the court may order that an allowance of all or part of them be payable as an expense of the administration.

**Derivation**—This rule derived from the Insolvency Rules 1986, SI 1986/1925, r 2.31.

## [2.162]

### 3.34 Statement of affairs: expenses

(1) The expenses of a nominated person which the administrator considers to have been reasonably incurred in making a statement of affairs or of a relevant person in making a statement of concurrence must be paid by the administrator as an expense of the administration.

(2) A decision by the administrator that expenses were not reasonably incurred (and are therefore not payable as an expense of the administration) may be appealed to the court.

**Derivation**—This rule derived from the Insolvency Rules 1986, SI 1986/1925, r 2.32.

CHAPTER 7

ADMINISTRATOR'S PROPOSALS

## [2.163]

**Note**

[Note: a document required by the Act or these Rules must also contain the standard contents set out in Part 1.]

## [2.164]

### 3.35 Administrator's proposals: additional content

(1) The administrator's statement of proposals made under paragraph 49 of Schedule B1 (which is required by paragraph 49(4) to be delivered to the registrar of companies, creditors and members) must identify the proceedings and, in addition to the matters set out in paragraph 49, contain—

    (a) any other trading names of the company;

    (b) details of the administrator's appointment, including—

        (i) the date of appointment,

        (ii) the person making the application or appointment, and

        (iii) where a number of persons have been appointed as administrators, details of the matters set out in paragraph 100(2) of Schedule B1 relating to the exercise of their functions;

    (c) the names of the directors and secretary of the company and details of any shareholdings in the company which they may have;

(d)  an account of the circumstances giving rise to the appointment of the administrator;

(e)  the date the proposals are delivered to the creditors;

(f)  if a statement of the company's affairs has been submitted—

    (i)  a copy or summary of it, except so far as an order under rule 3.45 or 3.46 limits disclosure of it, and excluding any schedule referred to in rule 3.30(6)(b), or the particulars relating to individual creditors contained in any such schedule,

    (ii)  details of who provided the statement of affairs, and

    (iii)  any comments which the administrator may have upon the statement of affairs;

(g)  if an order under rule 3.45 or 3.46 has been made—

    (i)  a statement of that fact, and

    (ii)  the date of the order;

(h)  if no statement of affairs has been submitted—

    (i)  details of the financial position of the company at the latest practicable date (which must, unless the court orders otherwise, be a date not earlier than that on which the company entered administration), and

    (ii)  an explanation as to why there is no statement of affairs;

(i)  a full list of the company's creditors in accordance with paragraph (2) if either—

    (i)  no statement of affairs has been submitted, or

    (ii)  a statement of affairs has been submitted but it does not include such a list, or the administrator believes the list included is less than full;

(j)  a statement of—

    (i)  how it is envisaged the purpose of the administration will be achieved, and

    (ii)  how it is proposed that the administration will end, including, where it is proposed that the administration will end by the company moving to a creditors' voluntary winding up—

        (aa)  details of the proposed liquidator,

        (bb)  where applicable, the declaration required by section 231, and

        (cc)  a statement that the creditors may, before the proposals are approved, nominate a different person as liquidator in accordance with paragraph 83(7)(a) of Schedule B1 and rule 3.60(6)(b);

(k)  a statement of either—

    (i)  the method by which the administrator has decided to seek a decision from creditors as to whether they approve the proposals, or

    (ii)  the administrator's reasons for not seeking a decision from creditors;

(l)  the manner in which the affairs and business of the company—

    (i)  have, since the date of the administrator's appointment, been managed and financed, including, where any assets have been disposed of, the reasons for the disposals and the terms upon which the disposals were made, and

    (ii)  will, if the administrator's proposals are approved, continue to be managed and financed;

(m)  a statement whether the proceedings are COMI proceedings, establishment proceedings or proceedings to which the EU Regulation as it has effect in the law of the United Kingdom does not apply; and

(n)  any other information that the administrator thinks necessary to enable creditors to decide whether or not to approve the proposals.

(2)  The list of creditors required by paragraph (1)(i) must contain the details required by sub-paragraph (3) except where paragraphs (4) and (5) apply;

(3)  The particulars required by paragraph (2) are as follows and must be given in this order—

  (a)   the name and postal address of the creditor;

  (b)   the amount of the debt owed to the creditor;

  (c)   details of any security held by the creditor;

  (d)   the date on which any such security was given; and

  (e)   the value of any such security;

(4)  This paragraph applies where the particulars required by paragraph (3) relate to creditors who are either—

  (a)   employees or former employees of the company; or

  (b)   consumers claiming amounts paid in advance for the supply of goods and services.

(5)  Where paragraph (4) applies—

  (a)   the list of creditors required by paragraph (1)(i) must state separately for each of paragraphs (4)(a) and (b) the number of the creditors and the total of the debts owed to them; and

  (b)   the particulars required by paragraph (3) in respect of such creditors must be set out in separate schedules to the list of creditors for each of sub-paragraphs (4)(a) and (b); and

  (c)   the administrator must not deliver any such schedule to the registrar of companies with the statement of proposals.

(6)  Except where the administrator proposes a CVA in relation to the company, the statement made by the administrator under paragraph 49 of Schedule B1 must also include—

  (a)   to the best of the administrator's knowledge and belief, an estimate of the value of—

    (i)    the prescribed part (whether or not the administrator might be required under section 176A to make the prescribed part available for the satisfaction of unsecured debts), and

    (ii)   the company's net property (as defined by section 176A(6)); and

  (b)   a statement whether the administrator proposes to make an application to the court under section 176A(5) and if so the reason for the application.

(7)  The administrator may exclude from an estimate under paragraph (6)(a) information the disclosure of which could seriously prejudice the commercial interests of the company.

(8)  If the exclusion of such information affects the calculation of an estimate, the report must say so.

(9)  The document containing the statement of proposals must include a statement of the basis on which it is proposed that the administrator's remuneration should be fixed by a decision in accordance with Chapter 4 of Part 18 of these Rules.

(10)  Where applicable the document containing the statement of proposals must include—

  (a)   a statement of any pre-administration costs charged or incurred by the administrator or, to the administrator's knowledge, by any other person qualified to act as an insolvency practitioner in relation to the company;

  (b)   a statement that the payment of any unpaid pre-administration costs as an expense of the administration is—

    (i)    subject to approval under rule 3.52, and

    (ii)   not part of the proposals subject to approval under paragraph 53 of Schedule B1.

**Derivation**—This rule derived from the Insolvency Rules 1986, SI 1986/1925, r 2.33.

**Amendments**—SI 2017/1115; SI 2019/146, as from IP completion day (as defined in the European Union (Withdrawal Agreement) Act 2020, s 39(1)–(5)).

**General note**—On the administrator's proposals, revisions thereto and approval thereof see Sch B1, paras 49–55 and the notes thereto.

**Method of communicating proposals**—Notification of proposals, as with notification of appointment, should be by post, and not e-mail, although a postal notice may give details of any website at which proposals may be accessed: *Re Sporting Options plc* [2004] EWHC 3128 (Ch), [2005] BPIR 435 (Mann J). *In Sporting Options* Mann J refused to allow the notice of appointment to be sent by e-mail given that e-mail communications to creditors had 'bounced' and the risk of e-mail addresses changing. In *Re Advent Computer Training Ltd* [2010] EWHC 459 (Ch) HHJ Purle QC held that in *Sporting Options* Mann J had not laid down a general rule excluding the dissemination of a notice of appointment by e-mail but had based his decision on the particular facts of that case. In *Advent Computer Training* the use of e-mail was permitted on the footing that student-creditors of the company had been required to use e-mail in communicating with the company and to notify the company immediately of any change in e-mail address. The judge also noted that there appeared to be fewer problems with e-mail communication failure in the case before him, some 5 years after the decision in *Sporting Options*, although the judge indicated that the administrators should seek further directions in the event of significant e-mail failure.

**The r 3.35(1)(j)(i) statement as to achievement of purpose of administration**—The guidance provided by the Insolvency Service in its Dear IP letters is that an administrator should make an attempt to identify which objective is pursued in any particular case, rather than including all three sub-purposes 'blindly' in the proposals. On the other hand, it is not necessary to identify in advance with certainty which of the statutory objectives is intended to be achieved: *Hammonds (a firm) v Pro-fit USA Ltd* [2007] EWHC 1998 (Ch), [2008] 2 BCLC 159 (Warren J) on which issue see further the notes to Sch B1, paras 12 and 13. In practice, the administrator should be able to demonstrate that he has addressed his mind to the question of purpose so far as that is reasonably possible in what in practice are not always black and white circumstances. See notes to paras 3 and 49 of Sch B1 and comments of Snowden J in *Davey v Money* [2018] EWHC 766 (Ch) at [316]–[324].

**Statement of pre-administration costs**—Rule 3.35(10)(a) is plainly limited in scope to 'pre-administration costs' although, notwithstanding the earlier judgment in *Re Johnson Machine and Tool Co Ltd* [2010] BCC 382, that rule does not read as excluding from its scope the costs of considering and arranging a pre-pack sale, at least not one which is to follow in the very early course of the administration.

Rule 3.52 now provides the procedure for the authorisation of payment of pre-administration expenses.

**[2.165]**

### 3.36 Administrator's proposals: statement of pre-administration costs

A statement of pre-administration costs under rule 3.35(10)(a) must include—

(a) details of any agreement under which the fees were charged and expenses incurred, including the parties to the agreement and the date on which the agreement was made;

(b) details of the work done for which the fees were charged and expenses incurred;

(c) an explanation of why the work was done before the company entered administration and how it had been intended to further the achievement of an objective in paragraph 3(1) of Schedule B1 in accordance with sub-paragraphs (2) to (4) of that paragraph;

(d) a statement of the amount of the pre-administration costs, setting out separately—

    (i) the fees charged by the administrator,

    (ii) the expenses incurred by the administrator,

    (iii) the fees charged (to the administrator's knowledge) by any other person qualified to act as an insolvency practitioner in relation to the company (and, if more than one, by each separately), and

    (iv) the expenses incurred (to the administrator's knowledge) by any other person qualified to act as an insolvency practitioner in relation to the company (and, if more than one, by each separately);

(e) a statement of the amounts of pre-administration costs which have already been paid (set out separately as under sub-paragraph (d));

    (f)    the identity of the person who made the payment or, if more than one person made the payment, the identity of each such person and of the amounts paid by each such person set out separately as under sub-paragraph (d); and

    (g)    a statement of the amounts of unpaid pre-administration costs (set out separately as under sub-paragraph (d)).

**Derivation**—This rule derived from the Insolvency Rules 1986, SI 1986/1925, r 2.33(2A), (2B).

**General note**—This provision should be read in conjunction with r 3.52 (pre-administration costs).

## [2.166]

### 3.37 Advertising administrator's proposals and notices of extension of time for delivery of proposals (paragraph 49 of Schedule B1)

(1) A notice published by the administrator under paragraph 49(6) of Schedule B1 must—

    (a)    identify the proceedings and contain the registered office of the company;

    (b)    be advertised in such manner as the administrator thinks fit; and

    (c)    be published as soon as reasonably practicable after the administrator has delivered the statement of proposals to the company's creditors but no later than eight weeks (or such other period as may be agreed by the creditors or as the court may order) from the date on which the company entered administration.

(2) Where the court orders, on an application by the administrator under paragraph 107 of Schedule B1, an extension of the period in paragraph 49(5) of Schedule B1 for delivering copies of the statement of proposals, the administrator must as soon as reasonably practicable after the making of the order deliver a notice of the extension to—

    (a)    the creditors of the company;

    (b)    the members of the company of whose address the administrator is aware; and

    (c)    the registrar of companies.

(3) The notice must—

    (a)    identify the proceedings;

    (b)    state the date to which the court has ordered an extension; and

    (c)    contain the registered office of the company.

(4) The administrator is taken to comply with paragraph (2)(b) if the administrator publishes a notice complying with paragraph (5).

(5) The notice must—

    (a)    contain the information required by paragraph (3);

    (b)    be advertised in such manner as the administrator thinks fit;

    (c)    state that members may request in writing a copy of the notice of the extension, and state the address to which to write; and

    (d)    be published as soon as reasonably practicable after the administrator has delivered the notice of the extension to the company's creditors.

**Derivation**—This rule derived from the Insolvency Rules 1986, SI 1986/1925, r 2.33.

**Amendments**—SI 2017/1115.

**Form**—Form AM03 is prescribed for the notice of proposals, with the statement attached. Form AM04 is prescribed for the notice of extension of time: see rr 1.15, 1.16 and 1.18 for the standard content of notices other than gazetted notices.

## [2.167]

### 3.38 Seeking approval of the administrator's proposals

(1) This rule applies where the administrator is required by paragraph 51 of Schedule B1 to seek approval from the company's creditors of the statement of proposals made under paragraph 49 of that Schedule.

(2)   The statement of proposals delivered under paragraph 49(4) of Schedule B1 must be accompanied by a notice to the creditors of the decision procedure in accordance with rule 15.8.

(3)   The administrator may seek a decision using deemed consent in which case the requirements in rule 15.7 also apply to the notice.

(4)   Where the administrator has made a statement under paragraph 52(1) of Schedule B1 and has not sought a decision on approval from creditors, the proposal will be deemed to have been approved unless a decision has been requested under paragraph 52(2) of Schedule B1.

(5)   Where under paragraph (4) the proposal is deemed to have been approved the administrator must, as soon as reasonably practicable after the expiry of the period for requisitioning a decision set out in rule 15.18(2), deliver a notice of the date of deemed approval to the registrar of companies, the court and any creditor to whom the administrator has not previously delivered the proposal.

(6)   The notice must contain—
    (a)    identification details for the proceedings;
    (b)    the name of the administrator;
    (c)    the date the administrator was appointed; and
    (d)    the date on which the statement of proposals was delivered to the creditors.

(7)   A copy of the statement of proposals, with the statements required by rule 3.35(5), must accompany the notice given to the court and to any creditors to whom a copy of the statement of proposals has not previously been delivered.

**Derivation**—This rule derived from the Insolvency Rules 1986, SI 1986/1925, r 2.34.

**Rule 3.38(4)**—See *Promontoria (Chestnut) Ltd v Craig* [2017] EWHC 2405 (Ch). For the application of r 3.38(4) and (5) see *Re Taylor Pearson (Construction) Ltd (in administration)* [2020] EWHC 2933 (Ch), [2021] BCC 217 (HHJ Davis-White QC).

**Form**—Form AM06 is prescribed for the purposes of r 3.38(5).

## [2.168]

### 3.39 Invitation to creditors to form a creditors' committee

(1)   Where the administrator is required to seek a decision from the company's creditors under rule 3.38, the administrator must at the same time deliver to the creditors a notice inviting them to decide whether a creditors' committee should be established if sufficient creditors are willing to be members of the committee.

(2)   The notice must also invite nominations for membership of the committee, such nominations to be received by the administrator by a date to be specified in the notice.

(3)   The notice must state that any nominations—
    (a)    must be delivered to the administrator by the specified date; and
    (b)    can only be accepted if the administrator is satisfied as to the creditor's eligibility under rule 17.4.

(4)   A notice under this rule must also be delivered to the creditors at any other time when the administrator seeks a decision from creditors and a creditors' committee has not already been established at that time.

**General note**—On creditors' committees generally see Part 17 of the 2016 Rules.

## [2.169]

### 3.40 Notice of extension of time to seek approval

(1)   Where the court orders an extension to the period set out in paragraph 51(2) of Schedule B1, the administrator must deliver a notice of the extension as soon as reasonably practicable to each person mentioned in paragraph 49(4) of Schedule B1.

(2)   The notice must contain identification details for the proceedings and the date to which the court has ordered an extension.

(3)   The administrator is taken to have complied with paragraph (1) as regards members of the company if the administrator publishes a notice complying with paragraph (4).

(4)   The notice must—
- (a)   be advertised in such manner as the administrator thinks fit;
- (b)   state that members may request in writing a copy of the notice of the extension, and state the address to which to write; and
- (c)   be published as soon as reasonably practicable after the administrator has delivered the notice of the extension to the company's creditors.

**Derivation**—This rule derived from the Insolvency Rules 1986, SI 1986/1925, r 2.34.
**Form**—Form AM05 is prescribed.

## [2.170]

**3.41 Notice of the creditors' decision on the administrator's proposals (paragraph 53(2))**
(1)   In addition to delivering a report to the court and the registrar of companies (in accordance with paragraph 53(2) of Schedule B1) the administrator must deliver a report to—
- (a)   the company's creditors (accompanied by a copy of the statement of proposals, with the statement required by rule 3.35(10)(a) and (b), if it has not previously been delivered to the creditor); and
- (b)   every other person to whom a copy of the statement of proposals was delivered.

(2)   A report mentioned in paragraph (1) must contain—
- (a)   identification details for the proceedings;
- (b)   details of decisions taken by the creditors including details of any modifications to the proposals which were approved by the creditors; and
- (c)   the date such decisions were made.

(3)   A copy of the statement of proposals, with any statements required by rule 3.35(9) and (10), must accompany the report to the court.

**Derivation**—This rule derived from the Insolvency Rules 1986, SI 1986/1925, r 2.46.
**Form**—Form AM07 is prescribed.

## [2.171]

**3.42 Administrator's proposals: revision**
(1)   Where paragraph 54(1) of Schedule B1 applies, the statement of the proposed revision which is required to be delivered to the creditors must be delivered with a notice of the decision procedure in accordance with rule 15.8.
(2)   The statement must identify the proceedings and include—
- (a)   any other trading names of the company;
- (b)   details of the administrator's appointment, including—
  - (i)   the date of appointment, and
  - (ii)   the person making the application or appointment;
- (c)   the names of the directors and secretary of the company and details of any shareholdings in the company which they may have;
- (d)   a summary of the original proposals and the reason or reasons for proposing a revision;
- (e)   details of the proposed revision, including details of the administrator's assessment of the likely impact of the proposed revision upon creditors generally or upon each class of creditors;
- (f)   where the proposed revision relates to the ending of the administration by a creditors' voluntary winding up and the nomination of a person to be the proposed liquidator of the company—
  - (i)   details of the proposed liquidator,
  - (ii)   where applicable, the declaration required by section 231, and
  - (iii)   a statement that the creditors may, before the proposals are approved, nominate a different person as liquidator in accordance with paragraph 83(7)(a) of Schedule B1 and rule 3.60(6)(b); and

(g)     any other information that the administrator thinks necessary to enable creditors to decide whether or not to vote for the proposed revisions.

(3)   The administrator may seek a decision using deemed consent in which case the requirements in rule 15.7 also apply to the notice.

(4)   The period within which, subject to paragraph 54(3) of Schedule B1, the administrator must send a copy of the statement to every member of the company of whose address the administrator is aware is five business days after sending the statement of the proposed revision to the creditors.

(5)   Notice under paragraph 54(3) and (4) of Schedule B1 must—

(a)     be advertised in such manner as the administrator thinks fit as soon as reasonably practicable after the administrator has sent the statement to the creditors; and

(b)     state that members may request in writing a copy of the proposed revision, and state the address to which to write.

(6)   A copy of the statement of revised proposals under rule 3.43(3) must be delivered to the registrar of companies not later than five days after the report under rule 3.43(1) is delivered.

**Derivation**—This rule derived from the Insolvency Rules 1986, SI 1986/1925, r 2.45.
**Amendments**—SI 2017/366.
**Form**—Form AM08 is prescribed.

## [2.172]

**3.43 Notice of result of creditors' decision on revised proposals (paragraph 54(6))**
(1)   In addition to delivering a report to the court and the registrar of companies (in accordance with paragraph 54(6) of Schedule B1) the administrator must deliver a report to—

(a)     the company's creditors (accompanied by a copy of the original statement of proposals and the revised statement of proposals if the administrator had not delivered notice of the decision procedure or deemed consent procedure to the creditor); and

(b)     every other person to whom a copy of the original statement of proposals was delivered.

(2)   A report mentioned in paragraph (1) must contain—

(a)     identification details for the proceedings;

(b)     the date of the revised proposals;

(c)     details of decisions taken by the creditors including details of any modifications to the revised proposals which were approved by the creditors; and

(d)     the date such decisions were made.

(3)   A copy of the statement of revised proposals must accompany the notice to the court.

**Derivation**—This rule derived from the Insolvency Rules 1986, SI 1986/1925, r 2.46.
**Form**—Form AM09 is prescribed.

CHAPTER 8

LIMITED DISCLOSURE OF STATEMENTS OF AFFAIRS AND PROPOSALS

## [2.173]

**Note**
[Note: a document required by the Act or these Rules must also contain the standard contents set out in Part 1.]

**[2.174]**

### 3.44 Application of Chapter

This Chapter applies to the disclosure of information which would be likely to prejudice the conduct of the administration or might reasonably be expected to lead to violence against any person.

Derivation—This rule derived from the Insolvency Rules 1986, SI 1986/1925, r 2.30.

**[2.175]**

### 3.45 Orders limiting disclosure of statement of affairs etc

(1)   If the administrator thinks that the circumstances in rule 3.44 apply in relation to the disclosure of—

    (a)    the whole or part of the statement of the company's affairs;

    (b)    any of the matters specified in rule 3.35(1)(h) and (i) (administrator's proposals); or

    (c)    a statement of concurrence,

the administrator may apply to the court for an order in relation to the particular document or a specified part of it.

(2)   The court may order that the whole of or a specified part of a document referred to in paragraph (1)(a) to (c) must not be delivered to the registrar of companies or, in the case of the statement of proposals, to creditors or members of the company.

(3)   The administrator must as soon as reasonably practicable deliver to the registrar of companies—

    (a)    a copy of the order;

    (b)    the statement of affairs, statement of proposals and any statement of concurrence to the extent provided by the order; and

    (c)    if the order relates to the statement of proposals, an indication of the nature of the matter in relation to which the order was made.

(4)   If the order relates to the statement of proposals, the administrator must as soon as reasonably practicable also deliver to the creditors and members of the company—

    (a)    the statement of proposals to the extent provided by the order; and

    (b)    an indication of the nature of the matter in relation to which the order was made.

Derivation—This rule derived from the Insolvency Rules 1986, SI 1986/1925, rr 2.30, 2.33A.

General note—In Registrar of Companies v Swarbrick (Joint Administrators of Gardenprime Ltd (in administration)) [2014] EWHC 1466 (Ch), [2014] Bus LR 625 Richard Spearman QC, sitting as a deputy judge of the High Court, held that r 2.33A of the IR 1986 (replaced by IR 2016, r 3.45) conferred jurisdiction on the court to limit disclosure of certain matters in the para 49 statement lodged with the registrar, even after the statement had been lodged. The issue arose upon the administrators applying to replace the filed proposals with amended proposals which omitted certain material following the administrators becoming aware that the company had breached a contractual obligation to keep certain information confidential by virtue of the statement being lodged with the registrar. The deputy judge took the view that the correct construction of r 2.33A was that the provision was not exhausted the moment the para 49 statement had been sent. As such, an application for such an order could be made after the event, and an order could be made with retrospective effect such that the registrar was bound by an order made under the formerly operative r 2.33A of the IR 1986 even if it was not made until after the statement had been sent to him. The order placed an obligation on the registrar to place the redacted version of the statement on the register. For the purposes of s 1080 of the Companies Act 2006, the original statement was no longer properly capable of being regarded as a document 'delivered to the registrar under any enactment' and was replaced for those purposes by the redacted version.

For an example of a case where the court ordered limited disclosure in the statement of affairs see *Re All Leisure Holidays Ltd* [2017] EWHC 870 (Ch) (disclosure of names and addresses and debts of all creditors capable of prejudicing the administration given risk of competitors taking commercial advantage of such information).

Form—Form AM12 is prescribed. The statements of affairs, proposals and concurrence and the court's order should be attached.

**[2.176]**

### 3.46 Order for disclosure by administrator

(1)   A creditor may apply to the court for an order that the administrator disclose any of the following in relation to which an order has been made under rule 3.45(2)—

    (a)    a statement of affairs;

    (b)    a specified part of it;

    (c)    a part of a statement of proposals; or

    (d)    statement of concurrence.

(2)   The application must be supported by a witness statement.

(3)   The applicant must deliver to the administrator notice of the application at least three business days before the hearing.

(4)   In an order for disclosure, the court may include conditions as to confidentiality, duration, the scope of the order in the event of any change of circumstances or such other matters as it thinks just.

Derivation—This rule derived from the Insolvency Rules 1986, SI 1986/1925, r 2.30(4).

**[2.177]**

### 3.47 Rescission or amendment of order for limited disclosure

(1)   If there is a material change in circumstances rendering an order for limited disclosure under rule 3.45(2) wholly or partially unnecessary, the administrator must, as soon as reasonably practicable after the change, apply to the court for the order to be rescinded or amended.

(2)   If the court makes such an order, the administrator must as soon as reasonably practicable deliver to the registrar of companies—

    (a)    a copy of the order; and

    (b)    the statement of affairs, the statement of proposals and any statement of concurrence to the extent provided by the order.

(3)   If the order relates to the statement of proposals, the administrator must as soon as reasonably practicable also deliver to the creditors and members the statement of proposals to the extent allowed by the order.

Derivation—This rule derived from the Insolvency Rules 1986, SI 1986/1925, r 2.30(7).

General note—For exercise of the court's power with retrospective effect where document which should not have been disclosed was delivered to the registrar and filed see *Registrar of Companies v Swarbrick* [2014] EWHC 1466 (Ch).

Form—Form AM13 is prescribed. The statements of affairs, proposals and concurrence and the court's order should be attached.

**[2.178]**

### 3.48 Publication etc of statement of affairs or statement of proposals

(1)   CPR Part 31 does not apply to an application under rule 3.45, 3.46 or 3.47.

(2)   If, after the administrator has sent a statement of proposals under paragraph 49(4) of Schedule B1, a statement of affairs is delivered to the registrar of companies in accordance with rule 3.47(2) as the result of the rescission or amendment of an order, the administrator must deliver to the creditors a copy or summary of the statement of affairs as delivered to the registrar of companies.

(3)   The administrator is taken to comply with the requirements for delivery to members of the company in rule 3.45(4) or 3.47(3) if the administrator publishes the required notice.

(4)   The required notice must—

    (a)    be advertised in such manner as the administrator thinks fit;

    (b)    state that members can request in writing—

        (i)    a copy of the statement of proposals to the extent provided by the order, and

        (ii)    an indication of the nature of the matter in relation to which the order was made;

(c)     state the address to which to such a written request is to be made; and

(d)     be published as soon as reasonably practicable after the administrator has delivered the statement of proposals to the extent provided by the order to the company's creditors.

Derivation—This rule derived from the Insolvency Rules 1986, SI 1986/1925, r 2.30(8)–(10).

## CHAPTER 9

### DISPOSAL OF CHARGED PROPERTY

**[2.179]**

Note

[Note: a document required by the Act or these Rules must also contain the standard contents set out in Part 1.]

**[2.180]**

**3.49  Disposal of charged property**
(1)   This rule applies where the administrator applies to the court under paragraph 71 or 72 of Schedule B1 for authority to dispose of—

(a)     property which is subject to a security other than a floating charge; or

(b)     goods in the possession of the company under a hire-purchase agreement.

(2)   The court must fix a venue for the hearing of the application.
(3)   As soon as reasonably practicable after the court has done so, the administrator must deliver notice of the venue to the holder of the security or the owner of the goods.
(4)   If an order is made under paragraph 71 or 72 of Schedule B1, the court must deliver two sealed copies to the administrator.
(5)   The administrator must deliver—

(a)     one of the sealed copies to the holder of the security or the owner of the goods; and

(b)     a copy of the sealed order to the registrar of companies.

Derivation—This rule derived from the Insolvency Rules 1986, SI 1986/1925, r 2.66.
General note—See the notes to paras 71 and 72 to Sch B1 IA 1986. The court's authority to dispose of property is not required where the property is subject to a floating charge.
Form—Form AM14 is prescribed. The court's order should be attached.
'Hire purchase agreement'—See the definition in para 111(1) of Sch B1.

## CHAPTER 10

### EXPENSES OF THE ADMINISTRATION

**[2.181]**

Note

[Note: a document required by the Act or these Rules must also contain the standard contents set out in Part 1.]

**[2.182]**

**3.50  Expenses**
(1)   All fees, costs, charges and other expenses incurred in the course of the administration are to be treated as expenses of the administration.
(2)   The expenses associated with the prescribed part must be paid out of the prescribed part.
(3)   The cost of the security required by section 390(3) for the proper performance of the administrator's functions is an expense of the administration.
(4)   For the purposes of paragraph 99 of Schedule B1, a former administrator's remuneration and expenses comprise all the items in rule 3.51(2).

**Derivation**—This rule derived from the Insolvency Rules 1986, SI 1986/1925, rr 2.67, 12.2.

**General note**—In *Re Hyde* [2021] EWHC 1542 (Ch), in the context of a para 63 application for directions concerning the distribution of funds held on trust in the client money bank account of a betting operator, Mr Robin Vos, sitting as a deputy High Court judge, accepted at [92] that the broad effect of rr 3.50 and 3.51 is the same as s 115 IA 1986. Interestingly, at [93] and [94], the deputy judge took the view that the jurisdiction in *Re Berkeley Applegate (Investment Consultants) Limited (No 2)* [1988] 4 BCC 279 (Mr Edward Nugee QC, sitting as a deputy High Court judge) did not lay down a principle that the inherent jurisdiction of the court extends only to authorising remuneration where a claim is made by beneficiaries to give effect to their equitable interests (see *Berkeley Applegate*, especially at 291). In the present case, although the beneficiaries were not seeking to enforce their beneficial interests in the sense that no beneficiary had made a claim, the purpose of the work done by the applicant administrators in relation to the trust assets was undoubtedly intended to give effect to the equitable interests of the beneficiaries in the trust. The view of the deputy judge was that, whilst *Berkeley Applegate* is commonly directed at the remuneration of a trustee, it is hard to see why the same principle should not apply where the work is done by someone other than the trustee. Accordingly, the administrators were entitled to be paid their fees and expenses for dealing with the trust assets and administering the trust out of the trust assets.

On administration expenses see *Re International Sections Ltd* [2009] BCC 574 at [16] (HHJ Purle QC) and *Re Nortel Networks UK Ltd* [2017] EWHC 1429 (Ch) (Snowden J).

## [2.183]

### 3.51 Order of priority

(1)   Where there is a former administrator, the items in paragraph 99 of Schedule B1 are payable in priority to the expenses in this rule.

(2)   Subject to paragraph (1) and to any court order under paragraph (3) the expenses of the administration are payable in the following order of priority—

    (a)    expenses properly incurred by the administrator in performing the administrator's functions;

    (b)    the cost of any security provided by the administrator in accordance with the Act or these Rules;

    (c)    where an administration order was made, the costs of the applicant and any person appearing on the hearing of the application whose costs were allowed by the court;

    (d)    where the administrator was appointed otherwise than by order of the court—

        (i)    the costs and expenses of the appointer in connection with the making of the appointment, and

        (ii)    the costs and expenses incurred by any other person in giving notice of intention to appoint an administrator;

    (e)    any amount payable to a person in respect of assistance in the preparation of a statement of affairs or statement of concurrence;

    (f)    any allowance made by order of the court in respect of the costs on an application for release from the obligation to submit a statement of affairs or deliver a statement of concurrence;

    (g)    any necessary disbursements by the administrator in the course of the administration (including any . . . expenses incurred by members of the creditors' committee or their representatives and allowed for by the administrator under rule 17.24, but not including any payment of corporation tax in circumstances referred to in sub-paragraph (j) below);

    (h)    the remuneration or emoluments of any person who has been employed by the administrator to perform any services for the company, as required or authorised under the Act or these Rules;

    (i)    the administrator's remuneration the basis of which has been fixed under Part 18 and unpaid pre-administration costs approved under rule 3.52; and

    (j)    the amount of any corporation tax on chargeable gains accruing on the realisation of any asset of the company (irrespective of the person by whom the realisation is effected).

(3)   If the assets are insufficient to satisfy the liabilities, the court may make an order as to the payment out of the assets of the expenses incurred in the administration in such order of priority as the court thinks just.

**Derivation**—This rule derived from the Insolvency Rules 1986, SI 1986/1925, r 2.67.

**Amendments**—SI 2017/702; SI 2019/146, as from IP completion day (as defined in the European Union (Withdrawal Agreement) Act 2020, s 39(1)–(5)).

**General note**—This rule should be read in conjunction with para 99 of Sch B1 and the notes thereto.

See also the General note to r 3.50.

**Order of priority**—The order of priority for administration expenses in r 2.67(1) of the Insolvency Rules 1986 is substantively reproduced in r 3.51(2).

**Costs of winding-up petition**—See also here the notes to r 3.12(2). Following *Irish Reel Productions Ltd v Capitol Films Ltd* [2010] BCC 588, the usual order where an administration order is made in the face of an extant winding-up petition is for the costs of the petition to be ordered as an expense of the administration. The same is true of the costs associated with the defence of a winding-up petition where an administration application is made subsequently to the presentation of the petition and culminates in an administration order being made: *Re Record Tennis Centres Ltd* [1991] 1 WLR 1003. The Court of Appeal pointed out in *Re Portsmouth City Football Club* [2013] EWCA Civ 916, [2014] 1 BCLC 1 that there is an anomaly in the IR 2016 in that such costs do not appear to fall within the ambit of r 3.51 in the case of an out-of-court administrator appointment; neither is there any suggestion in r 3.12 of jurisdiction to make such an order in those circumstances. In the absence of such express provision in rr 3.12 or 3.51, no such order (including one consequent upon the displacement an out-of-court appointed administrator) would appear to be within the scope of para 13(1)(f) of Sch B1.

**Non-domestic rates for unoccupied premises**—With effect from 1 April 2008 the rating legislation was amended in England by way of the Non-Domestic Rating (Unoccupied Property) (England) Regulations 2008 (SI 2008/386) to reverse the decision of David Richards J in *Exeter City Council v Bairstow, Re Trident Fashions* [2007] EWHC 400 (Ch) which had held that non-domestic rates are payable as an administration expense under r 2.67(1)(f) (now r 3.51(2)(g)) irrespective of whether the premises were occupied by the company in administration or unoccupied. The amendments extend to companies in administration the same relief from liability in respect of unoccupied premises as continues to be available in liquidations. Equivalent amendments applicable to Wales were brought into effect from 1 November 2008 by virtue of the Non-Domestic Rating (Unoccupied Property) (Wales) Regulations 2008 (SI 2008/2499).

**Varying the order of priority under r 3.51(3)**—In exercising its discretion, the court must be persuaded that there is a good or sufficient reason to make an order varying the priority in which expenses are provided for in r 3.51(2): see *Irish Reel Productions Ltd v Capitol Films Ltd* [2010] EWHC 180 (Ch) at [10] (Briggs J, refusing to make an order that the costs of a substituted petitioner on a winding-up petition dismissed on the making of an administration order should be paid out of the assets of the company in priority to the administrator's expenses and the costs of any security provided by the administrators).

In *Neumans LLP (a firm) v Andronikou* [2013] EWCA Civ 916 the Court of Appeal (Mummery LJ, Rimer and Underhill LJJ agreeing) dismissed an appeal against the decision of Morgan J ([2012] EWHC 3088 (Ch)) which had refused an application by a firm of solicitors for payment of their legal fees and disbursements, incurred in acting for a company in connect with its opposition to a winding-up petition, as an expense of an out-of-court administration. In upholding the judgment of Morgan J as 'dead on' (at [33]) the Court of Appeal held that the judge had been right in law to hold that the solicitors' fees in relation to the company's defence of the winding-up petition were payable as an expense of the liquidation, but not as an expense in the out-of-court administration. The judge had also been correct to dismiss the argument that solicitors acting for the company should not be treated on the same footing as unsecured creditors in the case of an appointment of administrators out-of-court given that it was open to solicitors acting for an insolvent or potentially insolvent company to protect their position by seeking to arrange for indemnities or third-party funding for those behind the company or associated with it. At [41] of the Court of Appeal's judgment appears a very useful summary of the legal position regarding solicitors' fees in the context of administration and liquidation expenses.

For a case in which the costs of creditors on an administration application were given priority where the application was overtaken by an out-of-court appointment see *Re Bickland Ltd, Rohl v Bickland Ltd* [2012] EWHC 706 (Ch) (Mann J).

**Rent as an expense in administration**—See *Re Goldacre (Officers) Ltd v Nortel Networks UK Ltd* [2009] EWHC 3389 (Ch), [2010] Ch 455; *Leisure (Norwich) II Ltd v Luminar Lava Ignite Ltd* [2012] EWHC 951 (Ch), [2013] 2 BCLC 115. Both of those decisions have now been overruled by the Court of Appeal in *Re Game Station Limited, Pillar v Jervis* [2014] EWCA Civ 180 (days in occupation only for purpose of administration to rank as an expense). The Court of

Appeal held that the equitable principle of salvage does not create or transfer any liabilities. Instead, its effect is to treat part of a liability as an insolvency expense. As an equitable principle, the salvage principle is not dependent on the question of whether the liability arose before or after the company entered into administration. Instead, the principle takes effect from the time when the office-holder retains beneficial possession of the property for the purposes of administration. The application of the salvage principle overruled the decision in *Luminar* which had held that an instalment of rent payable in advance could not be treated as an expense. *Goldacre* was overruled on the basis that the correct application of the salvage principle to advance payments falling due during the period of beneficial retention was on the basis of the so-called 'wait and see' approach and was not, as *Goldacre* had held, dependent on the principle of adoption.

Rent which falls due prior to the commencement of administration constitutes a provable debt and does not rank as an administration expense: *Re Luminar* (above).

**Solicitors' costs during freezing order pending consideration of application for administration order**—In *Appleyard v Reflex Recordings Ltd* [2013] EWHC 4514 (Ch) the costs of a company's solicitors during the period in which a freezing injunction was in force pending consideration of an application for an administration order were held not to constitute an expense of the administration. Those costs arose in relation to two without notice applications brought against the company. The court did, however, order that sums held in the company's bank account, which represented the company's reasonable costs in responding to the without notice applications, should be transferred to the company's solicitors prior to the administration order being made.

The decision of the Supreme Court in *Re Nortel GmbH (in administration): Re Lehman Bros International (Europe) (in administration)* [2013] UKSC 52 concerned the proper characterisation of the liability of target companies to provide financial support to under-resourced pension schemes under financial support directions and contribution notices ('FSDs') issued by the Pensions Regulator under powers contained in the Pensions Act 2004 after the administration of the target companies. At first instance Briggs J held that such a liability constituted an administration expense and could not therefore rank as provable debt within r 13.12 because the liability could not be said to have arisen out of a pre-administration liability. That decision was upheld, essentially for the reasons given below by Briggs J, in the Court of Appeal (Lloyd LJ, Rimer and Laws JJ agreeing). In overturning the decision of the Court of Appeal the Supreme Court held that the liabilities were properly characterised as provable debts with ranked pari passu with other unsecured liabilities for the purposes of a distribution in administration. Although cautious as to the risk of expressing a universally applicable formula, Lord Neuberger suggested (at [77]) that three elements would ordinarily have to be present before a company could be found to have incurred an 'obligation' under a statute which obligation could validly be the subject of a later proof. First, the company must have taken, or been subject to, 'some step or combination of steps which had some legal effect (such as putting it under some legal duty or into some legal relationship)'. Secondly, those steps must have 'resulted in it being vulnerable to the specific liability in question, such that there would be a real prospect of that liability being incurred'. Thirdly, and more generally, the obligation must also be consistent with the statute under which liability is imposed to conclude that the steps taken by the company gave rise to an obligation susceptible to proof. If these three elements could be made out, it would not matter that the liability in issue was subject to any number of contingencies before arising, and the liability would be susceptible to proof in the same way as a contingent liability arising by consent or under contract. Applying that three-element test to the facts in *Nortel*, Lord Neuberger concluded that the liability of the target companies under the FSDs (which were not issued until after the commencement of the administration in each case) would be susceptible to proof as an unsecured liability (so as to align the characterisation of liabilities arising out of FSDs issued after the commencement of administration with those issued pre-administration). As Lord Neuberger pointed out, at [61], an alternative conclusion ran the risk of incentivising the Pensions Regulator to hold off on the issue of FSDs until after the commencement of the administration. The decision also serves the interests of unsecured creditors generally who, at least in some cases, would otherwise be subject to a significant expenses-priority claim by the Pensions Regulator.

**Liability under s 59 of the Environmental Protection Act 1990**—The Scottish decision in *Joint Liquidators of Doonin Plant Ltd, Noters* [2018] CSOH 89, [2019] BCC 217 held that the liability of a company in liquidation in complying with a notice served under s 59 of the 1990 Act was an expense 'properly chargeable or incurred by the liquidator in carrying out his functions in the liquidation' for the purposes of the Scottish Rules which are substantially the same in terms as r 3.51(2)(a).

**[2.184]**

### 3.52 Pre-administration costs

(1)   Where the administrator has made a statement of pre-administration costs under rule 3.35(10)(a), the creditors' committee may determine whether and to what extent the unpaid pre-administration costs set out in the statement are approved for payment.

(2)   Paragraph (3) applies where—

    (a)   there is no creditors' committee;

    (b)   there is a creditors' committee but it does not make the necessary determination; or

    (c)   the creditors' committee does make the necessary determination but the administrator or other insolvency practitioner who has charged fees or incurred expenses as pre-administration costs considers the amount determined to be insufficient.

(3)   When this paragraph applies, determination of whether and to what extent the unpaid pre-administration costs are approved for payment must be—

    (a)   by a decision of the creditors through a decision procedure; or

    (b)   in a case where the administrator has made a statement under paragraph 52(1)(b) of Schedule B1, by—

        (i)   the consent of each of the secured creditors, or

        (ii)   if the administrator has made, or intends to make, a distribution to preferential creditors, by—

            (aa)   the consent of each of the secured creditors, and

            (bb)   a decision of the preferential creditors in a decision procedure.

(4)   The administrator must call a meeting of the creditors' committee or seek a decision of creditors by a decision procedure if so requested for the purposes of paragraphs (1) to (3) by another insolvency practitioner who has charged fees or incurred expenses as pre-administration costs; and the administrator must deliver notice of the meeting or decision procedure within 28 days of receipt of the request.

(5)   The administrator (where the fees were charged or expenses incurred by the administrator) or other insolvency practitioner (where the fees were charged or expenses incurred by that practitioner) may apply to the court for a determination of whether and to what extent the unpaid pre-administration costs are approved for payment if either—

    (a)   there is no determination under paragraph (1) or (3); or

    (b)   there is such a determination but the administrator or other insolvency practitioner who has charged fees or incurred expenses as pre-administration costs considers the amount determined to be insufficient.

(6)   Where there is a creditors' committee the administrator or other insolvency practitioner must deliver at least 14 days' notice of the hearing to the members of the committee; and the committee may nominate one or more of its members to appear, or be represented, and to be heard on the application.

(7)   If there is no creditors' committee, notice of the application must be delivered to such one or more of the company's creditors as the court may direct, and those creditors may nominate one or more of their number to appear or be represented, and to be heard on the application.

(8)   The court may, if it appears to be a proper case, order the costs of the application, including the costs of any member of the creditors' committee appearing or being represented on it, or of any creditor so appearing or being represented, to be paid as an expense of the administration.

(9)   Where the administrator fails to call a meeting of the creditors' committee or seek a decision from creditors in accordance with paragraph (4), the other insolvency practitioner may apply to the court for an order requiring the administrator to do so.

**Derivation**—This rule derived from the Insolvency Rules 1986, SI 1986/1925, r 2.67A.

**General note**—This rule should be read in conjunction with r 3.1 which defines pre-administration costs.

An administrator's pre-administration costs are specifically provided for in r 3.51(2)(i). The definition of pre-administration costs in r 3.1 appears to exclude fees and expenses incurred other than in connection with the administration; there is no reason, on that approach, why in principle the costs associated with the arrangement of a pre-pack sale of the company's business and assets to be effected in the very early course of the administration should not constitute pre-administration costs.

## CHAPTER 11

### EXTENSION AND ENDING OF ADMINISTRATION

**[2.185]**

**Note**
[Note: a document required by the Act or these Rules must also contain the standard contents set out in Part 1.]

**[2.186]**

**3.53 Interpretation**
"Final progress report" means in this Chapter, and in Part 18 in so far as it relates to final progress reports in an administration, a progress report which includes a summary of—

    (a)    the administrator's proposals;

    (b)    any major amendments to, or deviations from, those proposals;

    (c)    the steps taken during the administration; and

    (d)    the outcome.

**Derivation**—This rule derived from the Insolvency Rules 1986, SI 1986/1925, r 2.110.

**[2.187]**

**3.54 Application to extend an administration and extension by consent (paragraph 76(2) of Schedule B1)**
(1)   This rule applies where an administrator makes an application to the court for an order, or delivers a notice to the creditors requesting their consent, to extend the administrator's term of office under paragraph 76(2) of Schedule B1.

(2)   The application or the notice must state the reasons why the administrator is seeking an extension.

(3)   A request to the creditors may contain or be accompanied by a notice that if the extension is granted a notice of the extension will be made available for viewing and downloading on a website and that no other notice will be delivered to the creditors.

(4)   Where the result of a request to the creditors is to be made available for viewing and downloading on a website, the notice must comply with the requirements for use of a website to deliver documents set out in rule 1.49(2)(a) to (c), (3) and (4) with any necessary modifications and rule 1.49(5)(a) applies to determine the time of delivery of the document.

(5)   Where the court makes an order extending the administrator's term of office, the administrator must as soon as reasonably practicable deliver to the creditors a notice of the order together with the reasons for seeking the extension given in the application to the court.

(6)   Where the administrator's term of office has been extended with the consent of creditors, the administrator must as soon as reasonably practicable deliver a notice of the extension to the creditors except where paragraph (3) applies.

(7)   The notices which paragraph 78(5)(b) of Schedule B1 require to be delivered to the registrar of companies must also identify the proceedings.

**Derivation**—This rule derived from the Insolvency Rules 1986, SI 1986/1925, r 2.112.
**Form**—Form AM19 is prescribed.

**[2.188]**

**3.55 Notice of automatic end of administration (paragraph 76 of Schedule B1)**

(1)  This rule applies where—

(a)  the appointment of an administrator has ceased to have effect; and

(b)  the administrator is not required by any other rule to give notice of that fact.

(2)  The former administrator must, as soon as reasonably practicable, and in any event within five business days of the date on which the appointment has ceased, deliver to the registrar of companies and file with the court a notice accompanied by a final progress report.

(3)  The notice must be headed "Notice of automatic end of administration" and identify the company immediately below the heading.

(4)  The notice must contain—

(a)  identification details for the proceedings;

(b)  the former administrator's name and address;

(c)  a statement that that person had been appointed administrator of the company;

(d)  the date of the appointment;

(e)  the name of the person who made the appointment or the administration application, as the case may be;

(f)  a statement that the appointment has ceased to have effect;

(g)  the date on which the appointment ceased to have effect; and

(h)  a statement that a copy of the final progress report accompanies the notice.

(5)  The notice must be authenticated by the administrator and dated.

(6)  A copy of the notice and accompanying final progress report must be delivered as soon as reasonably practicable to—

(a)  the directors of the company; and

(b)  all other persons to whom notice of the administrator's appointment was delivered.

(7)  A former administrator who makes default in complying with this rule is guilty of an offence and liable to a fine and, for continued contravention, to a daily default fine.

**Derivation**—This rule derived from the Insolvency Rules 1986, SI 1986/1925, r 2.111.

**Form**—Form AM20 is prescribed, to which the report should be attached.

**[2.189]**

**3.56 Notice of end of administration when purposes achieved (paragraph 80(2) of Schedule B1)**

(1)  Where an administrator who was appointed under paragraph 14 or 22 of Schedule B1 thinks that the purpose of administration has been sufficiently achieved, the notice ("notice of end of administration") which the administrator may file with the court and deliver to the registrar of companies under paragraph 80(2) of Schedule B1 must be headed "Notice of end of administration" and identify the company immediately below the heading.

(2)  The notice must contain—

(a)  identification details for the proceedings;

(b)  the administrator's name and address;

(c)  a statement that that person has been appointed administrator of the company;

(d)  the date of the appointment;

(e)  the name of the person who made the appointment or the administration application, as the case may be;

(f)  a statement that the administrator thinks that the purpose of the administration has been sufficiently achieved;

(g)  a statement that a copy of the final progress report accompanies the notice; and

(h)    a statement that the administrator is filing the notice with the court and delivering a copy to the registrar of companies.

(3)   The notice must be authenticated by the administrator and dated.

(4)   The notice must be accompanied by a final progress report.

(5)   The notice filed with the court must also be accompanied by a copy of the notice.

(6)   The court must endorse the notice and the copy with the date and time of filing, seal the copy and deliver it to the administrator.

(7)   The prescribed period within which the administrator, under paragraph 80(4) of Schedule B1, must send a copy of the notice to the creditors is five business days from the filing of the notice.

(8)   The copy notice sent to creditors must be accompanied by the final progress report.

(9)   The administrator must within the same period deliver a copy of the notice and the final progress report to all other persons (other than the creditors and the registrar of companies) to whom notice of the administrator's appointment was delivered.

(10)   The administrator is taken to have complied with the requirement in paragraph 80(4) of Schedule B1 to give notice to the creditors if, within five business days of filing the notice with the court, the administrator gazettes a notice which—

    (a)    states that the administration has ended, and the date on which it ended;

    (b)    undertakes that the administrator will provide a copy of the notice of end of administration to any creditor of the company who applies in writing; and

    (c)    specifies the address to which to write.

(11)   The Gazette notice may be advertised in such other manner as the administrator thinks fit.

**Derivation**—This rule derived from the Insolvency Rules 1986, SI 1986/1925, r 2.113.

**Form**—Form AM21 is prescribed, to which the report should be attached.

## [2.190]

### 3.57 Administrator's application for order ending administration (paragraph 79 of Schedule B1)

(1)   An application to court by the administrator under paragraph 79 of Schedule B1 for an order ending an administration must be accompanied by—

    (a)    a progress report for the period since—

        (i)    the last progress report (if any), or

        (ii)    if there has been no previous progress report, the date on which the company entered administration;

    (b)    a statement indicating what the administrator thinks should be the next steps for the company (if applicable); and

    (c)    where the administrator makes the application because of a requirement decided by the creditors, a statement indicating with reasons whether or not the administrator agrees with the requirement.

(2)   Where the application is made other than because of a requirement by a decision of the creditors—

    (a)    the administrator must, at least five business days before the application is made, deliver notice of the administrator's intention to apply to court to—

        (i)    the person who made the administration application or appointment, and

        (ii)    the creditors; and

    (b)    the application must be accompanied by—

        (i)    a statement that notice has been delivered to the creditors, and

        (ii)    copies of any response from creditors to that notice.

(3)   Where the application is in conjunction with a petition under section 124 for an order to wind up the company, the administrator must, at least five business days before the application is filed, deliver notice to the creditors as to whether the administrator intends to seek appointment as liquidator.

Derivation—This rule derived from the Insolvency Rules 1986, SI 1986/1925, r 2.114.

## [2.191]

### 3.58 Creditor's application for order ending administration (paragraph 81 of Schedule B1)

(1)  Where a creditor applies to the court under paragraph 81 of Schedule B1 for an order ending an administration, a copy of the application must be delivered, not less than five business days before the date fixed for the hearing, to—

    (a)    the administrator;

    (b)    the person who made the administration application or appointment; and

    (c)    where the appointment was made under paragraph 14 of Schedule B1, the holder of the floating charge by virtue of which the appointment was made (if different to (b)).

(2)  Any of those persons may appear at the hearing of the application.

(3)  Where the court makes an order under paragraph 81 ending the administration, the court must deliver a copy of the order to the administrator.

Derivation—This rule derived from the Insolvency Rules 1986, SI 1986/1925, r 2.115.

General note—See the notes to Sch B1, para 81.

Presumably, under its powers of case management in CPR Part 3, by operation of r 12.1(1), the court is not restricted by r 3.58(2) from permitting the appearance of persons other than those listed in that provision at the hearing of the application.

## [2.192]

### 3.59 Notice by administrator of court order

Where the court makes an order ending the administration, the administrator must as soon as reasonably practicable deliver a copy of the order and of the final progress report to—

    (a)    the registrar of companies;

    (b)    the directors of the company; and

    (c)    all other persons to whom notice of the administrator's appointment was delivered.

Derivation—This rule derived from the Insolvency Rules 1986, SI 1986/1925, r 2.116.

Form—Form AM25 should be used, to which the court's order should be attached.

## [2.193]

### 3.60 Moving from administration to creditors' voluntary winding up (paragraph 83 of Schedule B1)

[Note: the information referred to in paragraph (5) is required to be included in the first progress report of the liquidator. See rule 18.3(5).]

(1)  This rule applies where the administrator delivers to the registrar of companies a notice under paragraph 83(3) of Schedule B1 of moving from administration to creditors' voluntary winding up.

(2)  The notice must contain—

    (a)    identification details for the proceedings;

    (b)    the name of the person who made the appointment or the administration application, as the case may be; and

    (c)    the name and IP number of the proposed liquidator.

(3)  The notice to the registrar of companies must be accompanied by a copy of the administrator's final progress report.

(4)  A copy of the notice and the final progress report must be sent as soon as reasonably practicable after delivery of the notice to all those persons to whom notice of the administrator's appointment was delivered in addition to the creditors (as required by paragraph 83(5)(b)).

(5)  The person who ceases to be administrator on the registration of the notice must inform the person who becomes liquidator of anything which happens after the date of

the final progress report and before the registration of the notice which the administrator would have included in the final report had it happened before the date of the report.

(6)   For the purposes of paragraph 83(7)(a) of Schedule B1, a person is nominated by the creditors as liquidator by—

(a)   their approval of the statement of the proposed liquidator in the administrator's proposals or revised proposals; or

(b)   their nomination of a different person, through a decision procedure, before their approval of the proposals or revised proposals.

(7)   Where the creditors nominate a different person, the nomination must, where applicable, include the declaration required by section 231.

Derivation—This rule derived from the Insolvency Rules 1986, SI 1986/1925, r 2.117A.
Form—Form AM22 is prescribed, to which the report should be attached.

## [2.194]

### 3.61 Moving from administration to dissolution (paragraph 84 of Schedule B1)

(1)   This rule applies where the administrator delivers to the registrar of companies a notice under paragraph 84(1) of Schedule B1 of moving from administration to dissolution.

(2)   The notice must identify the proceedings.

(3)   As soon as reasonably practicable after sending the notice, the administrator must deliver a copy of the notice to all persons to whom notice of the administrator's appointment was delivered (in addition to the creditors mentioned in paragraph 84(5)(b) but excluding opted-out creditors).

(4)   A final progress report must accompany the notice to the registrar of companies and every copy filed or otherwise delivered.

(5)   Where a court makes an order under paragraph 84(7) of Schedule B1 it must, where the applicant is not the administrator, deliver a copy of the order to the administrator.

(6)   The administrator must deliver a copy of the order to the registrar of companies with the notice required by paragraph 84(8).

Derivation—This rule derived from the Insolvency Rules 1986, SI 1986/1925, r 2.118.
Amendments—SI 2017/1115.
Forms—Form AM23 and AM24 are prescribed, to which the report and court order respectively should be attached.

## CHAPTER 12

### REPLACING THE ADMINISTRATOR

## [2.195]

**Note**
[Note: a document required by the Act or these Rules must also contain the standard contents set out in Part 1.]

## [2.196]

### 3.62 Grounds for resignation

(1)   The administrator may resign—

(a)   on grounds of ill health;

(b)   because of the intention to cease to practise as an insolvency practitioner; or

(c)   because the further discharge of the duties of administrator is prevented or made impractical by—

(i)   a conflict of interest, or

(ii)   a change of personal circumstances.

(2) The administrator may, with the permission of the court, resign on other grounds.

**Derivation**—This rule derived from the Insolvency Rules 1986, SI 1986/1925, r 2.119.

**General note**—The correct procedure to be used by an administrator wishing to resign from office under this and the following Rule is explained in *VE Vegas Investors IV LLC v Shinners* [2018] EWHC 186 (Ch) (Registrar Jones).

In *Re Fox Street Village Ltd (in administration)* [2020] EWHC 2541 (Ch), [2021] BCC 89 at [52] HHJ Halliwell, sitting as a High Court judge, observed that it is for an administrator himself to determine whether to resign on any of the grounds in r 3.62(1). That is a decision for the administrator himself, and not for creditors. As regards the permission of the court to resign on other grounds, under r 3.62(2), creditors have no standing to require an administrator to seek the court's permission to resign. Rather, the proper course is for creditors to seek to have an administrator removed from office, as they are entitled to apply for under para 88 of Sch B1.

**[2.197]**

### 3.63 Notice of intention to resign

(1) The administrator must give at least five business days' notice of intention—
- (a) to resign in a case falling within rule 3.62(1); or
- (b) to apply for the court's permission to resign in a case falling within rule 3.62(2).

(2) The notice must contain—
- (a) identification details for the proceedings;
- (b) the date of the appointment of the administrator;
- (c) the name of the person who made the appointment or the administration application, as the case may be.

(3) The notice must also contain—
- (a) the date with effect from which the administrator intends to resign; or
- (b) where the administrator was appointed by an administration order, the date on which the administrator intends to file with the court an application for permission to resign.

(4) The notice must be delivered—
- (a) to any continuing administrator of the company;
- (b) to the creditors' committee (if any);
- (c) if there is neither a continuing administrator nor a creditors' committee, to—
  - (i) the company, and
  - (ii) the company's creditors;
- (d) . . .
- (e) where the administrator was appointed by the holder of a qualifying floating charge under paragraph 14 of Schedule B1, to—
  - (i) the person who appointed the administrator, and
  - (ii) all holders of prior qualifying floating charges;
- (f) where the administrator was appointed by the company or the directors of the company under paragraph 22 of Schedule B1, to—
  - (i) the appointer, and
  - (ii) all holders of qualifying floating charges.

(5) The notice must be accompanied by a summary of the administrator's receipts and payments.

**Derivation**—This rule derived from the Insolvency Rules 1986, SI 1986/1925, r 2.120.

**Amendments**—SI 2019/146, as from IP completion day (as defined in the European Union (Withdrawal Agreement) Act 2020, s 39(1)–(5)).

**[2.198]**

### 3.64 Notice of resignation (paragraph 87 of Schedule B1)

(1) A resigning administrator must, within five business days of delivering the notice under paragraph 87(2) of Schedule B1, deliver a copy of the notice to—
- (a) the registrar of companies;

(b)    all persons, other than the person who made the appointment, to whom notice of intention to resign was delivered under rule 3.63; and

(c)    except where the appointment was by administration order, file a copy of the notice with the court.

(2)   The notice must contain—

(a)    identification details for the proceedings;

(b)    the date of the appointment of the administrator; and

(c)    the name of the person who made the appointment or the administration application, as the case may be.

(3)   The notice must state—

(a)    the date from which the resignation is to have effect; and

(b)    where the resignation is with the permission of the court, the date on which permission was given.

(4)   Where an administrator was appointed by an administration order, notice of resignation under paragraph 87(2)(a) of Schedule B1 must be given by filing the notice with the court.

**Derivation**—This rule derived from the Insolvency Rules 1986, SI 1986/1925, r 2.121.

**Form**—Form AM15 is prescribed for the giving of notice of resignation. Where a company is moved from administration to creditors' voluntary liquidation Form 600 is prescribed for the notice of appointment of liquidator. That form must be filed after the registration of Form AM22 (notice of move from administration to CVL). The registration of Form AM22 is determinative of both the termination of the administration and the commencement of the liquidation.

## [2.199]

### 3.65 Application to court to remove administrator from office

(1)   An application for an order under paragraph 88 of Schedule B1 that the administrator be removed from office must state the grounds on which the order is requested.

(2)   A copy of the application must be delivered, not less than five business days before the date fixed for the hearing—

(a)    to the administrator;

(b)    to the person who—

    (i)    made the application for the administration order, or

    (ii)   appointed the administrator;

(c)    to the creditors' committee (if any);

(d)    to any continuing administrator appointed to act jointly or concurrently; and

(e)    where there is neither a creditors' committee nor a continuing administrator appointed, to the company and the creditors, including any floating charge holders.

(3)   The court must deliver to the applicant a copy of any order removing the administrator.

(4)   The applicant must deliver a copy—

(a)    as soon as reasonably practicable, and in any event within five business days of the copy order being delivered, to the administrator; and

(b)    within five business days of the copy order being delivered, to—

    (i)    all other persons to whom notice of the application was delivered, and

    (ii)   the registrar of companies.

**Derivation**—This rule derived from the Insolvency Rules 1986, SI 1986/1925, r 2.122.

**General note**—In *Clydesdale Financial Services Ltd v Smailes* [2009] BCC 810, it was held that the court had the power to dispense with any failure to serve the application on all creditors in accordance with r 2.122(2) of the IR 1986, which was in substantially the same terms as r 3.65(2).

[2.200]

**3.66 Notice of vacation of office when administrator ceases to be qualified to act**
An administrator who has ceased to be qualified to act as an insolvency practitioner in relation to the company and gives notice in accordance with paragraph 89 of Schedule B1 must also deliver notice to the registrar of companies.

Derivation—This rule derived from the Insolvency Rules 1986, SI 1986/1925, r 2.123.

## [2.201]

**3.67 Deceased administrator**
(1) If the administrator dies a notice of the fact and date of death must be filed with the court.
(2) The notice must be filed as soon as reasonably practicable by one of the following—
  (a) a surviving administrator;
  (b) a member of the deceased administrator's firm (if the deceased was a member or employee of a firm);
  (c) an officer of the deceased administrator's company (if the deceased was an officer or employee of a company); or
  (d) a personal representative of the deceased administrator.
(3) If such a notice has not been filed within the 21 days following the administrator's death then any other person may file the notice.
(4) The person who files the notice must also deliver a notice to the registrar of companies which contains—
  (a) identification details for the proceedings;
  (b) the name of the person who made the appointment or the administration application, as the case may be;
  (c) the date of the appointment of the administrator; and
  (d) the fact and date of death.

Derivation—This rule derived from the Insolvency Rules 1986, SI 1986/1925, r 2.124.

## [2.202]

**3.68 Application to replace**
(1) Where an application to court is made under paragraph 91(1) or 95 of Schedule B1 to appoint a replacement administrator, the application must be accompanied by the proposed replacement administrator's consent to act.
(2) Where the application is made under paragraph 91(1), a copy of the application must be delivered—
  (a) to the person who made the application for the administration order;
  (b) to any person who has appointed an administrative receiver of the company;
  (c) to any person who is or may be entitled to appoint an administrative receiver of the company;
  (d) to any person who is or may be entitled to appoint an administrator of the company under paragraph 14 of Schedule B1;
  (e) to any administrative receiver of the company;
  (f) if there is pending a petition for the winding up of the company, to—
    (i) the petitioner, and
    (ii) any provisional liquidator;
  (g) . . .
  (h) to the company, if the application is made by anyone other than the company;
  (i) to any supervisor of any CVA in relation to the company; and
  (j) to the proposed administrator.

(3) Where the application is made under paragraph 95, the application must be accompanied by a witness statement setting out the applicant's belief as to the matters set out in that paragraph.

(4) Rules 3.12, 3.13, and 3.15(1) and (2) apply to applications made under paragraph 91(1) and 95 of Schedule B1, with any necessary modifications.

**Derivation**—This rule derived from the Insolvency Rules 1986, SI 1986/1925, r 2.125.

**Amendments**—SI 2019/146, as from IP completion day (as defined in the European Union (Withdrawal Agreement) Act 2020, s 39(1)–(5)).

**[2.203]**

**3.69 Appointment of replacement or additional administrator**
Where a replacement administrator is appointed or an additional administrator is appointed to act—
- (a) the following apply—
  - (i) rule 3.17 (notice of appointment) the requirement as to the heading in paragraph (1) and paragraphs (1)(a) to (f), and (2),
  - (ii) rule 3.18 (filing of notice with court) paragraphs (1)(a) and (b)(ii), (2) and (3),
  - (iii) rule 3.24 (notice of appointment after notice of intention to appoint) paragraphs (1)(a) to (d) and (2),
  - (iv) rule 3.25 (notice of appointment without prior notice of intention to appoint) paragraphs (1), (2)(a) to (c) and (3),
  - (v) rule 3.26 (notice of appointment: filing with the court) paragraphs (1)(a), (3) and (4), and
  - (vi) rule 3.27 (publication of administrator's appointment) paragraphs (1), (2)(a) and (b), (3) and (4);
- (b) the replacement or additional administrator must deliver notice of the appointment to the registrar of companies; and
- (c) all documents must clearly identify the appointment as of a replacement administrator or an additional administrator.

**Derivation**—This rule derived from the Insolvency Rules 1986, SI 1986/1925, rr 2.126–2.128.

**[2.204]**

**3.70 Administrator's duties on vacating office**
(1) An administrator who ceases to be in office as a result of removal, resignation or ceasing to be qualified to act as an insolvency practitioner in relation to the company must as soon as reasonably practicable deliver to the person succeeding as administrator—
- (a) the assets (after deduction of any expenses properly incurred and distributions made by the departing administrator);
- (b) the records of the administration, including correspondence, proofs and other documents relating to the administration while it was within the responsibility of the departing administrator; and
- (c) the company's records.

(2) An administrator who makes default in complying with this rule is guilty of an offence and liable to a fine and, for continued contravention, to a daily default fine.

**Derivation**—This rule derived from the Insolvency Rules 1986, SI 1986/1925, r 2.129.

PART 4   RECEIVERSHIP

**[2.205]**

**Note**
[Note: for the application of this Part see introductory rule 3.]

CHAPTER 1

APPOINTMENT OF JOINT RECEIVERS OR MANAGERS TO WHOM PART 3 OF THE ACT APPLIES (OTHER THAN THOSE APPOINTED UNDER SECTION 51 (SCOTTISH RECEIVERSHIPS))

**[2.206]**

Note

[Note: a document required by the Act or these Rules must also contain the standard contents set out in Part 1.]

**[2.207]**

**4.1 Receivers or managers appointed under an instrument: acceptance of appointment (section 33)**

(1)   This Chapter applies to all receivers to whom Part 3 of the Act applies (other than those appointed under section 51 (Scottish Receiverships)).

(2)   Where two or more persons are appointed as joint receivers or managers of a company's property under powers contained in an instrument—

    (a)    each of them must accept the appointment in accordance with section 33 as if each were a sole appointee;

    (b)    the joint appointment takes effect only when all of them have accepted; and

    (c)    the joint appointment is deemed to have been made at the time at which the instrument of appointment was received by or on behalf of all of them.

(3)   A person who is appointed as the sole or joint receiver or manager of a company's property under powers contained in an instrument and accepts the appointment in accordance with section 33(1)(a), but not in writing, must confirm the acceptance in writing to the person making the appointment within five business days.

(4)   The written acceptance or confirmation of acceptance must contain—

    (a)    the name and address of the appointer;

    (b)    the name and address of the appointee;

    (c)    the name of the company concerned;

    (d)    the time and date of receipt of the instrument of appointment; and

    (e)    the time and date of acceptance.

(5)   Acceptance or confirmation of acceptance of appointment as a receiver or manager of a company's property, whether under the Act or these Rules, may be given by any person (including, in the case of a joint appointment, any joint appointee) duly authorised for that purpose on behalf of the receiver or manager.

    Derivation—This rule derived from the Insolvency Rules 1986, SI 1986/1925, r 3.1.
    Amendments—SI 2017/366.
    General note—These provisions correspond with s 33.

CHAPTER 2

ADMINISTRATIVE RECEIVERS (OTHER THAN IN SCOTTISH RECEIVERSHIPS)

**[2.208]**

Note

[Note: a document required by the Act or these Rules must also contain the standard contents set out in Part 1.]

**[2.209]**

**4.2  Application of Chapter 2**

This Chapter applies to administrative receivers (other than those appointed under section 51 (Scottish receiverships)).

General note—See s 29(2) for the definition of administrative receivers.

**[2.210]**

### 4.3 Interpretation

In this Chapter—

"nominated person" means a relevant person who has been required by the administrative receiver to make out and deliver to the administrative receiver a statement of affairs; and

"relevant person" means a person mentioned in section 47(3).

**[2.211]**

### 4.4 Administrative receiver's security

The cost of the administrative receiver's security required by section 390(3) for the proper performance of the administrative receiver's functions is an expense of the administrative receivership.

Derivation—This rule derived from the Insolvency Rules 1986, SI 1986/1925, r 12A.56.

General note—See s 390(3) for the provision which sets out the need for security to be given by insolvency practitioners.

**[2.212]**

### 4.5 Publication of appointment of administrative receiver (section 46(1))

(1)   The notice which an administrative receiver is required by section 46(1) to send to the company and the creditors on being appointed must contain—

  (a)   identification details for the company;

  (b)   any other registered name of the company in the 12 months before the date of the appointment;

  (c)   any name under which the company has traded at any time in those 12 months, if substantially different from its then registered name;

  (d)   the name and address of the person appointed;

  (e)   the date of the appointment;

  (f)   the name of the person who made the appointment;

  (g)   the date of the instrument conferring the power under which the appointment was made;

  (h)   a brief description of the instrument; and

  (i)   a brief description of any assets of the company in relation to which the appointment is not made.

(2)   The notice which an administrative receiver is required by section 46(1) to publish—

  (a)   must be gazetted;

  (b)   may be advertised in such other manner as the administrative receiver thinks fit; and

  (c)   must state—

    (i)   that an administrative receiver has been appointed,

    (ii)   the date of the appointment,

    (iii)   the name of the person who made the appointment, and

    (iv)   the nature of the business of the company.

Derivation—This rule derived from the Insolvency Rules 1986, SI 1986/1925, r 3.2.

General note—These provisions correspond with s 46. An administrative receiver may form the view that, in addition to the mandatory advertisement in the London Gazette, a further advertisement in a local newspaper is appropriate, say where creditors are predominantly located in a particular area and are not otherwise likely to become aware of his appointment.

**[2.213]**

**4.6 Requirement to provide a statement of affairs (section 47(1))**

[Note: see sections 234(1) and 235(1) for the application of section 235 to administrative receivers.]

(1) A requirement under section 47(1) for a nominated person to make out and submit to the administrative receiver a statement of the affairs of the company must be made by a notice delivered to such a person.

(2) The notice must be headed "Notice requiring statement of affairs" and must—

    (a) identify the company immediately below the heading;

    (b) require the recipient to prepare and submit to the administrative receiver a statement of the affairs of the company; and

    (c) inform each recipient of—

        (i) the name and address of any other nominated person to whom a notice has been delivered,

        (ii) the date by which the statement must be delivered to the administrative receiver, and

        (iii) the effect of sections 47(6) (penalty for non-compliance) and 235 (duty to co-operate with the office-holder).

(3) The administrative receiver must inform each nominated person that a document for the preparation of the statement of affairs capable of completion in compliance with rule 4.7 can be supplied if requested.

**Derivation**—This rule derived from the Insolvency Rules 1986, SI 1986/1925, r 3.3.

**General note**—See the notes to s 47.

**[2.214]**

**4.7 Statement of affairs: contents and delivery of copy (section 47(2))**

[Note: section 47(2) requires the statement of affairs to be verified by a statement of truth.]

(1) The statement of affairs must be headed "Statement of affairs" and must state that it is a statement of the affairs of the company on a specified date, being the date on which the administrative receiver was appointed.

(2) The statement of affairs must contain, in addition to the matters required by section 47(2)—

    (a) a summary of the assets of the company, setting out the book value and the estimated realisable value of—

        (i) any assets subject to a fixed charge,

        (ii) any assets subject to a floating charge,

        (iii) any uncharged assets, and

        (iv) the total assets available for preferential creditors;

    (b) a summary of the liabilities of the company, setting out—

        (i) the amount of preferential debts,

        (ii) an estimate of the deficiency with respect to preferential debts or the surplus available after paying the preferential debts,

        (iii) an estimate of the prescribed part, if applicable,

        (iv) an estimate of the total assets available to pay debts secured by floating charges,

        (v) the amount of debts secured by floating charges,

        (vi) an estimate of the deficiency with respect to debts secured by floating charges or the surplus available after paying the debts secured by floating charges,

        (vii) the amount of unsecured debts (excluding preferential debts and any deficiency with respect to debts secured by floating charges),

        (viii) an estimate of the deficiency with respect to unsecured debts or the surplus available after paying unsecured debts (excluding preferential debts and any deficiency with respect to debts secured by fixed and floating charges),

  (ix) any issued and called-up capital, and

  (x) an estimate of the deficiency with respect to, or surplus available to, members of the company;

 (c) a list of the company's creditors with the further particulars required by paragraph (3) indicating—

  (i) any creditors under hire-purchase, chattel leasing or conditional sale agreements,

  (ii) any creditors who are consumers claiming amounts paid in advance for the supply of goods or services, and

  (iii) any creditors claiming retention of title over property in the company's possession.

(3) The particulars required by section 47(2) and paragraph (2)(c) of this rule to be included in the statement of affairs relating to each creditor are as follows—

 (a) the name and postal address;

 (b) the amount of the debt owed to the creditor;

 (c) details of any security held by the creditor;

 (d) the date the security was given; and

 (e) the value of any such security.

(4) Paragraph (5) applies where the particulars required by paragraph (3) relate to creditors who are either—

 (a) employees or former employees of the company; or

 (b) consumers claiming amounts paid in advance for the supply of goods or services.

(5) Where this paragraph applies—

 (a) the statement of affairs must state separately for each of paragraphs (4)(a) and (b) the number of such creditors and the total of the debts owed to them; and

 (b) the particulars required by paragraph (3) must be set out in separate schedules to the statement of affairs for each of paragraphs (4)(a) and (b).

(6) The nominated person who makes the statement of truth required by section 47(2) (or if more than one, by one of them,) must deliver the statement of affairs together with a copy to the administrative receiver.

**Derivation**—This rule derived from the Insolvency Rules 1986, SI 1986/1925, r 3.4(1), Sch 4, Fm 3.2.

**General note**—See the notes to s 47.

## [2.215]

### 4.8 Statement of affairs: statement of concurrence

(1) The administrative receiver may require a relevant person to deliver to the administrative receiver a statement of concurrence.

(2) A statement of concurrence is a statement, verified by a statement of truth, that that person concurs in the statement of affairs submitted by a nominated person.

(3) The administrative receiver must inform the nominated person who has been required to submit a statement of affairs that the relevant person has been required to deliver a statement of concurrence.

(4) The nominated person must deliver a copy of the statement of affairs to every relevant person who has been required to deliver a statement of concurrence.

(5) A statement of concurrence—

 (a) must identify the company; and

 (b) may be qualified in relation to matters dealt with in the statement of affairs where the relevant person—

  (i) is not in agreement with the statement of affairs,

  (ii) considers the statement to be erroneous or misleading, or

  (iii) is without the direct knowledge necessary for concurring in it.

(6)   The relevant person must deliver the required statement of concurrence together with a copy to the administrative receiver before the end of the period of five business days (or such other period as the administrative receiver may agree) beginning with the day on which the relevant person receives the statement of affairs.

Derivation—This rule derived from the Insolvency Rules 1986, SI 1986/1925, r 3.4(2)–(5).

## [2.216]
### 4.9 Statement of affairs: retention by administrative receiver
The administrative receiver must retain the verified statement of affairs and each statement of concurrence as part of the records of the receivership.

Derivation—This rule derived from the Insolvency Rules 1986, SI 1986/1925, r 3.4(6).

## [2.217]
### 4.10 Statement of affairs: release from requirement and extension of time (section 47(5))
(1)   The administrative receiver may exercise the power in section 47(5) to release a person from an obligation to submit a statement of affairs imposed under section 47(1) or (2), or to grant an extension of time, either on the administrative receiver's own discretion or at the request of a nominated person.

(2)   A nominated person may apply to the court if the administrative receiver refuses that person's request.

(3)   On receipt of an application, the court may, if it is satisfied that no sufficient cause is shown for it, dismiss it without giving notice to any party other than the applicant.

(4)   The applicant must, at least 14 days before any hearing, deliver to the administrative receiver a notice stating the venue with a copy of the application and of any evidence on which the applicant intends to rely.

(5)   The administrative receiver may do either or both of the following—

(a)   file a report of any matters which the administrative receiver thinks ought to be drawn to the court's attention; or

(b)   appear and be heard on the application.

(6)   If a report is filed, the administrative receiver must deliver a copy of it to the applicant not later than five business days before the hearing.

(7)   Sealed copies of any order made on the application must be delivered by the court to the applicant and the administrative receiver.

(8)   On any application under this rule, the applicant's costs must be paid by the applicant in any event; but the court may order that an allowance of all or part of them be payable out of the assets under the administrative receiver's control.

Derivation—This rule derived from the Insolvency Rules 1986, SI 1986/1925, r 3.6.
General note—See the notes to s 47(5).

## [2.218]
### 4.11 Statement of affairs: expenses
(1)   The administrative receiver must pay, out of the assets under the administrative receiver's control, the expenses which the administrative receiver considers to have been reasonably incurred by—

(a)   a nominated person in making a statement of affairs and statement of truth; or

(b)   a relevant person in making a statement of concurrence.

(2)   Any decision by the administrative receiver under this rule is subject to appeal to the court.

Derivation—This rule derived from the Insolvency Rules 1986, SI 1986/1925, r 3.7.
General note—See the notes to s 47.

**[2.219]**

#### 4.12 Limited disclosure

(1) This rule applies where the administrative receiver thinks that disclosure of the whole or part of a statement of the company's affairs or a statement of concurrence would be likely to prejudice the conduct of the receivership or might reasonably be expected to lead to violence against any person.

(2) The administrative receiver may apply to the court for an order in respect of—

    (a)    the statement of affairs; or

    (b)    a statement of concurrence;

and the court may order that the whole or any specified part of the statement of affairs or a statement of concurrence must not be open to inspection except with permission of the court.

(3) The court's order may include directions regarding the delivery of documents to the registrar of companies and the disclosure of relevant information to other persons.

**Derivation**—This rule derived from the Insolvency Rules 1986, SI 1986/1925, r 3.5.

**General note**—See the notes to s 48(6).

**[2.220]**

#### 4.13 Administrative receiver's report to the registrar of companies and secured creditors (section 48(1))

(1) The report which under section 48(1) an administrative receiver is to send to the registrar of companies must be accompanied by a copy of any statement of affairs under section 47 and any statement of concurrence under rule 4.8.

(2) However the administrative receiver must not deliver to the registrar of companies with the statement of affairs any schedule required by rule 4.7(5)(b).

(3) The duty to send a copy of the report to the registrar of companies is subject to any order for limited disclosure made under rule 4.12.

(4) If a statement of affairs or statement of concurrence is submitted to the administrative receiver after the report is sent to the registrar of companies, the administrative receiver must deliver a copy of it to the registrar of companies as soon as reasonably practicable after its receipt by the administrative receiver.

(5) The report must contain (in addition to the matters required by section 48(1)) estimates to the best of the administrative receiver's knowledge and belief of—

    (a)    the value of the prescribed part (whether or not the administrative receiver might be required under section 176A to make the prescribed part available for the satisfaction of unsecured debts); and

    (b)    the value of the company's net property (as defined by section 176A(6)).

(6) The administrative receiver may exclude from an estimate under paragraph (5) information the disclosure of which could seriously prejudice the commercial interests of the company.

(7) If the exclusion of such information affects the calculation of an estimate, the report must say so.

(8) If the administrative receiver proposes to make an application to court under section 176A(5) the report must say so and give the reason for the application.

**Derivation**—This rule derived from the Insolvency Rules 1986, SI 1986/1925, r 3.8.

**General note**—See the notes to s 48.

Rule 4.13(5)–(7) are relevant to the special reserve fund (the 'prescribed part') created for unsecured creditors by s 176A, on which see also rr 4.23 and 4.24.

**[2.221]**

#### 4.14 Copy of report for unsecured creditors (section 48(2))

A notice under section 48(2)(b) stating an address to which unsecured creditors should write for copies of an administrative receiver's report under that section—

    (a)    must be gazetted;

(b)    may be advertised in such other manner as the administrative receiver thinks fit; and

(c)    must be accompanied by a notice under rule 4.15.

**Derivation**—This rule derived from the Insolvency Rules 1986, SI 1986/1925, r 3.8.

**General note**—See the notes to s 48.

## [2.222]

### 4.15  Invitation to creditors to form a creditors' committee

(1)    An administrative receiver must deliver to the creditors with the report under section 48(1) a notice inviting the creditors to decide whether a creditors' committee should be established if sufficient creditors are willing to be members of the committee.

(2)    The notice must also invite nominations for membership of the committee, such nominations to be received by the administrative receiver by a date to be specified in the notice.

(3)    The notice must state that any nominations—

(a)    must be delivered to the administrative receiver by the specified date; and

(b)    can only be accepted if the administrative receiver is satisfied as to the creditor's eligibility under rule 17.4.

## [2.223]

### 4.16  Disposal of charged property (section 43(1))

(1)    This rule applies where an administrative receiver applies to the court under section 43(1) for authority to dispose of property of the company which is subject to a security.

(2)    The court must fix a venue for the hearing of the application.

(3)    As soon as reasonably practicable after the court has fixed the venue, the administrative receiver must deliver notice of the venue to the person who is the holder of the security.

(4)    If an order is made under section 43(1), the court must deliver two sealed copies to the administrative receiver and the administrative receiver must deliver one of them to the holder of the security.

**Derivation**—This rule derived from the Insolvency Rules 1986, SI 1986/1925, r 3.31.

## [2.224]

### 4.17  Summary of receipts and payments

(1)    The administrative receiver must deliver a summary of receipts and payments as receiver to the registrar of companies, the company and to the person who made the appointment, and to each member of the creditors' committee.

(2)    The notice delivered to the registrar of companies under rule 1.20 must contain the date of the appointment of the administrative receiver.

(3)    The summary must be delivered to those persons within two months after—

(a)    the end of the period of 12 months from the date of being appointed;

(b)    the end of every subsequent period of 12 months; and

(c)    ceasing to act as administrative receiver (unless there is a joint administrative receiver who continues in office).

(4)    The summary must show receipts and payments—

(a)    during the relevant period of 12 months; or

(b)    where the administrative receiver has ceased to act, during the period—

(i)    from the end of the last 12-month period to the time when the administrative receiver so ceased, or

(ii)    if there has been no previous summary, since being appointed.

(5)    This rule is without prejudice to the administrative receiver's duty to produce proper accounts otherwise than as above.

(6)   An administrative receiver who makes default in complying with this rule is guilty of an offence and liable to a fine and, for continued contravention, to a daily default fine.

Derivation—This rule derived from the Insolvency Rules 1986, SI 1986/1925, r 3.32.

## [2.225]

### 4.18  Resignation

(1)   An administrative receiver must deliver notice of intention to resign at least five business days before the date the resignation is intended to take effect to—

    (a)    the person by whom the appointment was made;

    (b)    the company or, if it is then in liquidation, the liquidator; and

    (c)    the members of the creditors' committee.

(2)   The notice must specify the date on which the administrative receiver intends the resignation to take effect.

Derivation—This rule derived from the Insolvency Rules 1986, SI 1986/1925, r 3.33.

## [2.226]

### 4.19  Deceased administrative receiver

(1)   If the administrative receiver dies a notice of the fact and date of death must be delivered as soon as reasonably practicable to—

    (a)    the person by whom the appointment was made;

    (b)    the registrar of companies;

    (c)    the company or, if it is in liquidation, the liquidator; and

    (d)    the members of the creditors' committee.

(2)   The notice must be delivered by one of the following—

    (a)    a surviving joint administrative receiver;

    (b)    a member of the deceased administrative receiver's firm (if the deceased was a member or employee of a firm);

    (c)    an officer of the deceased administrative receiver's company (if the deceased was an officer or employee of a company); or

    (d)    a personal representative of the deceased administrative receiver.

(3)   If such a notice has not been delivered within 21 days following the administrative receiver's death then any other person may deliver the notice.

Derivation—This rule derived from the Insolvency Rules 1986, SI 1986/1925, r 3.34.

## [2.227]

### 4.20  Other vacation of office

An administrative receiver, on vacating office on completion of the administrative receivership, or in consequence of ceasing to be qualified to act as an insolvency practitioner in relation to the company, must as soon as reasonably practicable deliver a notice of doing so to—

    (a)    the person by whom the appointment was made;

    (b)    the company or, if it is then in liquidation, the liquidator; and

    (c)    the members of the creditors' committee.

Derivation—This rule derived from the Insolvency Rules 1986, SI 1986/1925, r 3.35.

## [2.228]

### 4.21  Notice to registrar of companies (section 45(4))

Where an administrative receiver's office is vacated other than by death, the notice to the registrar of companies required by section 45(4) may be given by delivering to the registrar of companies the notice required by section 859K(3) of the Companies Act.

Derivation—This rule derived from the Insolvency Rules 1986, SI 1986/1925, r 3.35(2).

CHAPTER 3

NON-ADMINISTRATIVE RECEIVERS AND THE PRESCRIBED PART

**[2.229]**

Note

[Note: a document required by the Act or these Rules must also contain the standard contents set out in Part 1.]

**[2.230]**

#### 4.22  Application of Chapter 3

This Chapter applies where a receiver (other than an administrative receiver) is appointed by the court or otherwise under a charge which was created as a floating charge; and section 176A applies.

Derivation—This rule derived from the Insolvency Rules 1986, SI 1986/1925, r 3.39.

**[2.231]**

#### 4.23  Report to creditors

(1)   Within three months (or such longer period as the court may allow) of the date of the appointment, the receiver must deliver to the creditors—

(a)   a notice of the appointment; and

(b)   a report.

(2)   The report must contain estimates to the best of the receiver's knowledge and belief of—

(a)   the value of the prescribed part (whether or not the receiver might be required under section 176A to make the prescribed part available for the satisfaction of unsecured debts); and

(b)   the value of company's net property (as defined by section 176A(6)).

(3)   The receiver may exclude from an estimate under paragraph (2) information the disclosure of which could seriously prejudice the commercial interests of the company.

(4)   If the exclusion of such information affects the calculation of an estimate, the report must say so.

(5)   If the receiver proposes to make an application to court under section 176A(5) the report must say so and give the reason for the application.

(6)   The report must also state whether, and if so why, the receiver proposes to present a petition for the winding up of the company.

(7)   The receiver may, instead of delivering the report under paragraph (1), cause a notice to be gazetted and may advertise that notice in such other manner as the receiver thinks fit where—

(a)   full details of the unsecured creditors of the company are not available to the receiver; or

(b)   the receiver thinks it is otherwise impracticable to deliver such a report.

(8)   A notice under paragraph (7) must contain the matters required to be included in the receiver's report.

Derivation—This rule derived from the Insolvency Rules 1986, SI 1986/1925, r 3.39.

**[2.232]**

#### 4.24  Receiver to deal with prescribed part

(1)   The receiver—

(a)   may present a petition for the winding up of the company if the ground of the petition is that in section 122(1)(f); and

(b)   must deliver to any administrator or liquidator the sums representing the prescribed part.

(2)   If there is no administrator or liquidator the receiver must—

(a) apply to the court for directions as to the manner in which to discharge the duty under section 176A(2)(a); and

(b) act in accordance with any directions given.

**Derivation**—This rule derived from the Insolvency Rules 1986, SI 1986/1925, r 3.40.

## PART 5   MEMBERS' VOLUNTARY WINDING UP

### CHAPTER 1

#### STATUTORY DECLARATION OF SOLVENCY (SECTION 89)

**[2.233]**

**Note**

[Note: a document required by the Act or these Rules must also contain the standard contents set out in Part 1.]

General note—Under the previous rules the various kinds of liquidation were not divided into separate Parts. Now the Rules that were put in force on 6 April 2017 provide for three separate Parts for members' voluntary liquidations (Part 5), creditors' voluntary liquidations (Part 6) and compulsory (court) liquidations (Part 7). This obviates the need, as was the situation in Part 4 of the previous rules, for notes in individual rules to indicate that they were not applicable to either creditors' voluntary liquidations or were so applicable. This makes it easier to discern which rules apply to each kind of winding up. It does mean that there are some overlaps in the provisions contained in the respective Parts.

**[2.234]**

**5.1 Statutory declaration of solvency: requirements additional to those in section 89**

[Note: the "official rate" referred to in paragraph (1)(b) is defined in section 251 as being the rate referred to in section 189(4).]

(1) The statutory declaration of solvency required by section 89 must identify the company and state—

(a) the name and a postal address for each director making the declaration (which may be the director's service address provided for by section 163 of the Companies Act);

(b) either—

(i) that all of the directors, or

(ii) that a majority of the directors,

have made a full inquiry into the company's affairs and that, having done so, they have formed the opinion that the company will be able to pay its debts in full together with interest at the official rate within a specified period (which must not exceed 12 months) from the commencement of the winding up; and

(c) that the declaration is accompanied by a statement of the company's assets and liabilities as at a date which is stated (being the latest practicable date before the making of the declaration as required by section 89(2)(b)).

(2) The statement of the company's assets and liabilities must contain—

(a) the date of the statement;

(b) a statement that the statement shows the assets of the company at estimated realisable values and liabilities of the company expected to rank as at the date referred to in sub-paragraph (1)(c);

(c) a summary of the assets of the company, setting out the estimated realisable value of—

(i) any assets subject to a fixed charge,

(ii) any assets subject to a floating charge,

(iii) any uncharged assets; and

(iv) the total value of all the assets available to preferential creditors;

(d) the value of each of the following secured liabilities of the company expected to rank for payment—

(i)    liabilities secured on specific assets, and

(ii)    liabilities secured by floating charges;

(e)    a summary of the unsecured liabilities of the company expected to rank for payment;

(f)    the estimated costs of the winding up and other expenses;

(g)    the estimated amount of interest accruing until payment of debts in full; and

(h)    the estimated value of any surplus after paying debts in full together with interest at the official rate.

**Derivation**—This rule derived from the Insolvency Rules 1986, SI 1986/1925, Sch 4, Fm 4.70.
**General note**—See the notes accompanying s 89.

## CHAPTER 2

### The Liquidator

**[2.235]**

**Note**
[Note: a document required by the Act or these Rules must also contain the standard contents set out in Part 1.]

**[2.236]**

#### 5.2 Appointment by the company

(1)   This rule applies where the liquidator is appointed by the company.

(2)   The chair of the meeting, or a director or the secretary of the company in the case of a written resolution of a private company, must certify the appointment when the appointee has provided to the person certifying the appointment a statement to the effect that the appointee is an insolvency practitioner qualified under the Act to be the liquidator and consents to act.

(3)   The certificate must be authenticated and dated by the person who certifies the appointment and must contain—

(a)    identification details for the company;

(b)    identification and contact details for the person appointed as liquidator;

(c)    the date the liquidator was appointed; and

(d)    a statement that the appointee—

(i)    provided a statement of being qualified to act as an insolvency practitioner in relation to the company,

(ii)    has consented to act, and

(iii)    was appointed liquidator of the company.

(4)   Where two or more liquidators are appointed the certificate must also specify (as required by section 231) whether any act required or authorised under any enactment to be done by the liquidator is to be done by all or any one or more of them.

(5)   The person who certifies the appointment must deliver the certificate as soon as reasonably practicable to the liquidator, who must keep it as part of the records of the winding up.

(6)   Not later than 28 days from the liquidator's appointment, the liquidator must deliver notice of the appointment to the creditors of the company.

**Derivation**—This rule derived from the Insolvency Rules 1986, SI 1986/1925, r 4.139.

**[2.237]**

#### 5.3 Meetings in members' voluntary winding up of authorised deposit-takers

(1)   This rule applies to a meeting of the members of an authorised deposit-taker at which it is intended to propose a resolution for its winding up.

(2)   Notice of such a meeting of the company must be delivered by the directors to the Financial Conduct Authority and to the scheme manager established under section 212(1) of the Financial Services and Markets Act 2000.

(3)   The notice to the Financial Conduct Authority and the scheme manager must be the same as delivered to members of the company.

(4)   The scheme manager is entitled to be represented at any meeting of which it is required by this rule to be given notice.

Derivation—This rule derived from the Insolvency Rules 1986, SI 1986/1925, r 4.72.

## [2.238]

### 5.4  Appointment by the court (section 108)

(1)   This rule applies where the liquidator is appointed by the court under section 108.

(2)   The order of the court must contain—

    (a)   the name of the court (and hearing centre if applicable) in which the order is made;

    (b)   the name and title of the judge making the order;

    (c)   identification details for the company;

    (d)   the name and address of the applicant;

    (e)   the capacity in which the applicant made the application;

    (f)   identification details for the proposed liquidator;

    (g)   a statement that the appointee has filed with the court a statement to the effect that the appointee is an insolvency practitioner qualified to act as the liquidator and consents to act;

    (h)   an order that the proposed liquidator, having filed a statement of being qualified to act as an insolvency practitioner in relation to the company and having consented to act, is appointed liquidator of the company from the date of the order, or such other date as the court orders; and

    (i)   the date of the order.

(3)   Where two or more liquidators are appointed the order must also specify (as required by section 231) whether any act required or authorised under any enactment to be done by the liquidator is to be done by all or any one or more of them.

(4)   The court must deliver a sealed copy of the order to the liquidator, whose appointment takes effect from the date of the order or from such other date as the court orders.

(5)   Not later than 28 days from the liquidator's appointment, the liquidator must deliver notice of the appointment to the creditors of the company.

Derivation—This rule derived from the Insolvency Rules 1986, SI 1986/1925, r 4.140.
See, in particular, the notes attaching to s 108 of the 1986 Act.

## [2.239]

### 5.5  Cost of liquidator's security (section 390(3))

The cost of the liquidator's security required by section 390(3) for the proper performance of the liquidator's functions is an expense of the winding up.

Derivation—This rule derived from the Insolvency Rules 1986, SI 1986/1925, r 12A.56.
General note—Section 390(3) is the provision that sets out the need for insolvency practitioners to provide security.

## [2.240]

### 5.6  Liquidator's resignation

(1)   A liquidator may resign only—

    (a)   on grounds of ill health;

    (b)   because of the intention to cease to practise as an insolvency practitioner;

    (c)   because the further discharge of the duties of liquidator is prevented or made impractical by—

          (i)     a conflict of interest, or

          (ii)    a change of personal circumstances;

  (d)     where two or more persons are acting as liquidator jointly and it is the opinion of both or all of them that it is no longer expedient that there should continue to be that number of joint liquidators.

(2)  Before resigning, the liquidator must deliver a notice to the members of the company—

  (a)     stating the liquidator's intention to resign; and

  (b)     calling a meeting for the members to consider whether a replacement should be appointed;

except where the resignation is under sub-paragraph (1)(d).

(3)  The notice must be accompanied by a summary of the liquidator's receipts and payments.

(4)  The notice may suggest the name of a replacement liquidator.

(5)  The date of the meeting must be not more than five business days before the date on which the liquidator intends to give notice of resignation to the registrar of companies under section 171(5).

(6)  The resigning liquidator's release is effective 21 days after the date of delivery of the notice of resignation to the registrar of companies under section 171(5), unless the court orders otherwise.

    **Derivation**—This rule derived from the Insolvency Rules 1986, SI 1986/1925, r 4.142(3).

    **General note**—See comments accompanying s 171.

## [2.241]

### 5.7 Removal of liquidator by the court

(1)  This rule applies where an application is made to the court for the removal of the liquidator, or for an order directing the liquidator to summon a company meeting for the purpose of removing the liquidator.

(2)  On receipt of an application, the court may, if it is satisfied that no sufficient cause is shown for it, dismiss it without giving notice to any party other than the applicant.

(3)  Unless the application is dismissed, the court must fix a venue for it to be heard.

(4)  The applicant must, at least 14 days before any hearing, deliver to the liquidator a notice stating the venue with a copy of the application and of any evidence on which the applicant intends to rely.

(5)  A respondent may apply for security for the costs of the application and the court may make such an order if it is satisfied, having regard to all the circumstances of the case, that it is just to make such an order.

(6)  The liquidator may do either or both of the following at such a hearing—

  (a)     file a report of any matters which the liquidator thinks ought to be drawn to the court's attention; or

  (b)     appear and be heard on the application.

(7)  On a successful application the court's order must contain the following—

  (a)     the name of the court (and hearing centre if applicable) in which the order is made;

  (b)     the name and title of the judge making the order;

  (c)     identification details for the company;

  (d)     the name and address of the applicant;

  (e)     the capacity in which the applicant made the application;

  (f)     identification and contact details for the liquidator (or former liquidator);

  (g)     an order either—

          (i)     that the liquidator is removed from office, or

          (ii)    that the liquidator must summon a company meeting on or before a date which is stated in the order for the purpose of considering the liquidator's removal from office; and

  (h)     the date of the order.

(8)   The order of the court may include such provision as the court thinks just relating to matters arising in connection with the removal.

(9)   The costs of the application are not payable as an expense of the winding up unless the court orders otherwise.

(10)   Where the court removes the liquidator—

    (a)   it must deliver the sealed order of removal to the former liquidator; and

    (b)   the former liquidator must deliver a copy of the order to the registrar of companies as soon as reasonably practicable.

(11)   If the court appoints a new liquidator, rule 5.4 applies.

**Derivation**—This rule derived from the Insolvency Rules 1986, SI 1986/1925, r 4.143.

**Amendments**—SI 2017/366.

**General note**—See the comments accompanying ss 108 and 171.

## [2.242]

### 5.8  Removal of liquidator by company meeting

A liquidator removed by a meeting of the company must as soon as reasonably practicable deliver notice of the removal to the registrar of companies.

**Derivation**—This rule derived from the Insolvency Rules 1986, SI 1986/1925, r 4.142.

**General note**—See the comments accompanying s 171.

## [2.243]

### 5.9  Delivery of proposed final account to members (section 94)

(1)   The liquidator must deliver a notice to the members accompanied by the proposed final account required by section 94(1) and rule 18.14 giving them a minimum of eight weeks' notice of a specified date on which the liquidator intends to deliver the final account as required by section 94(2).

(2)   The notice must inform the members that when the company's affairs are fully wound up—

    (a)   the liquidator will make up the final account and deliver it to the members; and

    (b)   when the final account is delivered to the registrar of companies the liquidator will be released under section 171(6).

(3)   The affairs of the company are not fully wound up until the latest of—

    (a)   the period referred to in paragraph (1) having expired without the liquidator receiving any request for information under rule 18.9 or the filing of any application to court under that rule or under rule 18.34 (application to court on the grounds that the liquidator's remuneration or expenses are excessive);

    (b)   any request for information under rule 18.9 having been finally determined (including any applications to court under that rule); or

    (c)   any application to the court under rule 18.34 having been finally determined.

(4)   However the liquidator may conclude that the company's affairs are fully wound up before the period referred to in paragraph (1) has expired if every member confirms in writing to the liquidator that they do not intend to make any such request or application.

**Derivation**—This rule derived from the Insolvency Rules 1986, SI 1986/1925, r 4.126A.

**General note**—Previously a final meeting was necessary (see s 94 as it was previously drafted). See comments to s 94 as it now stands.

## [2.244]

### 5.10  Final account prior to dissolution (section 94)

(1)   The contents of the final account which the liquidator is required to make up under section 94 must comply with the requirements of rule 18.14.

(2) When the account is delivered to the members under section 94(2) it must be accompanied by a notice which states that—

    (a)    the company's affairs are fully wound up;

    (b)    the liquidator having delivered copies of the account to the members must, within 14 days of the date on which the account is made up, deliver a copy of the account to the registrar of companies; and

    (c)    the liquidator will vacate office and be released under section 171 on delivering the final account to the registrar of companies.

(3) The copy of the account which the liquidator must deliver to the registrar of companies under section 94(3) must be accompanied by a notice stating that the liquidator has delivered the final account of the winding up to the members in accordance with section 94(2).

Derivation—This rule derived from the Insolvency Rules 1986, SI 1986/1925, r 4.126A.

## [2.245]

### 5.11 Deceased liquidator

(1) If the liquidator dies a notice of the fact and date of death must be delivered as soon as reasonably practicable to—

    (a)    one of the company's directors; and

    (b)    the registrar of companies.

(2) One of the following must deliver the notice—

    (a)    a surviving joint liquidator;

    (b)    a member of the deceased liquidator's firm (if the deceased was a member or employee of a firm);

    (c)    an officer of the deceased liquidator's company (if the deceased was an officer or employee of a company); or

    (d)    a personal representative of the deceased liquidator.

(3) If such notice has not been delivered within the 21 days following the liquidator's death then any other person may deliver the notice.

Derivation—This rule derived from the Insolvency Rules 1986, SI 1986/1925, r 4.145.

## [2.246]

### 5.12 Loss of qualification as insolvency practitioner

(1) This rule applies where the liquidator vacates office on ceasing to be qualified to act as an insolvency practitioner in relation to the company.

(2) A notice of the fact must be delivered as soon as reasonably practicable to the registrar of companies and the Secretary of State by one of the following—

    (a)    the liquidator who has vacated office;

    (b)    a continuing joint liquidator; or

    (c)    the recognised professional body which was the source of the vacating liquidator's authorisation to act in relation to the company.

(3) Each notice must be authenticated and dated by the person delivering the notice.

Derivation—This rule derived from the Insolvency Rules 1986, SI 1986/1925, r 4.146.

## [2.247]

### 5.13 Liquidator's duties on vacating office

A liquidator who ceases to be in office as a result of removal, resignation or ceasing to be qualified to act as an insolvency practitioner in relation to the company, must as soon as reasonably practicable deliver to the succeeding liquidator—

    (a)    the assets (after deduction of any expenses properly incurred, and distributions made, by the former liquidator);

    (b)    the records of the winding up, including correspondence, proofs and other documents relating to the winding up; and

    (c)    the company's documents and other records.

**Derivation**—This rule derived from the Insolvency Rules 1986, SI 1986/1925, r 4.148.

**[2.248]**

### 5.14 Application by former liquidator to the Secretary of State for release (section 173(2)(b))

(1)    This rule applies to a liquidator who—

    (a)    is removed by the court;

    (b)    vacates office on ceasing to be qualified to act as an insolvency practitioner in relation to the company; or

    (c)    vacates office in consequence of the court making a winding-up order against the company.

(2)    Where the former liquidator applies to the Secretary of State for release the application must contain—

    (a)    identification details for the former liquidator;

    (b)    identification details for the company;

    (c)    the circumstances under which the former liquidator ceased to act as liquidator; and

    (d)    a statement that the former liquidator is applying to the Secretary of State for release.

(3)    The application must be authenticated and dated by the former liquidator.

(4)    When the Secretary of State gives a release, the Secretary of State must deliver—

    (a)    a certificate of the release to the former liquidator; and

    (b)    a notice of the release to the registrar of companies.

(5)    Release is effective from the date of the certificate or such other date as the certificate specifies.

**Derivation**—This rule derived from the Insolvency Rules 1986, SI 1986/1925, rr 4.144(2), 4.147.

**General note**—See the notes accompanying s 173 of the 1986 Act.

**[2.249]**

### 5.15 Power of court to set aside certain transactions entered into by liquidator

(1)    If in dealing with the estate the liquidator enters into any transaction with a person who is an associate of the liquidator, the court may, on the application of any interested person, set the transaction aside and order the liquidator to compensate the company for any loss suffered in consequence of it.

(2)    This does not apply if either—

    (a)    the transaction was entered into with the prior consent of the court; or

    (b)    it is shown to the court's satisfaction that the transaction was for value, and that it was entered into by the liquidator without knowing, or having any reason to suppose, that the person concerned was an associate.

(3)    Nothing in this rule is to be taken as prejudicing the operation of any rule of law or equity relating to a liquidator's dealings with trust property, or the fiduciary obligations of any person.

**Derivation**—This rule derived from the Insolvency Rules 1986, SI 1986/1925, r 4.149.

**General note**—'Associate' is defined in s 435. See the notes accompanying that section.

**[2.250]**

### 5.16 Rule against improper solicitation by or on behalf of the liquidator

(1)    Where the court is satisfied that any improper solicitation has been used by or on behalf of the liquidator in obtaining proxies or procuring the liquidator's appointment, it may order that no remuneration be allowed as an expense of the winding up to any person by whom, or on whose behalf, the solicitation was exercised.

(2)    An order of the court under this Rule overrides any resolution of the members, or any other provision of these Rules relating to the liquidator's remuneration.

Derivation—This rule derived from the Insolvency Rules 1986, SI 1986/1925, r 4.150.

General note—See s 164 which provides, inter alia, that a person who offers a bribe to secure his or her appointment as a liquidator of a company is liable to a fine.

## CHAPTER 3

### SPECIAL MANAGER

## [2.251]

### Note
[Note: a document required by the Act or these Rules must also contain the standard contents set out in Part 1.]

## [2.252]

### 5.17 Application for and appointment of special manager (section 177)
(1) An application by the liquidator under section 177 for the appointment of a special manager must be supported by a report setting out the reasons for the application.

(2) The report must include the applicant's estimate of the value of the business or property in relation to which the special manager is to be appointed.

(3) The court's order appointing a special manager must have the title "Order of Appointment of Special Manager" and must contain—

    (a) the name of the court (and hearing centre if applicable) in which the order is made;

    (b) the name and title of the judge making the order;

    (c) identification details for the proceedings;

    (d) the name and address of the applicant;

    (e) the name and address of the proposed special manager;

    (f) an order that the proposed special manager is appointed as special manager of the company;

    (g) details of the special manager's responsibility over the company's business or property;

    (h) the powers to be entrusted to the special manager under section 177(3);

    (i) the time allowed for the special manager to give the required security for the appointment;

    (j) the duration of the special manager's appointment, being one of the following—

        (i) for a fixed period stated in the order;

        (ii) until the occurrence of a specified event; or

        (iii) until the court makes a further order;

    (k) the order that the special manager's remuneration will be fixed from time to time by the court; and

    (l) the date of the order and the date on which it takes effect if different.

(4) The appointment of the special manager may be renewed by order of the court.

(5) The acts of the special manager are valid notwithstanding any defect in the special manager's appointment or qualifications.

Derivation—This rule derived from the Insolvency Rules 1986, SI 1986/1925, r 4.206.
Amendments—SI 2017/366.

## [2.253]

### 5.18 Security
(1) The appointment of the special manager does not take effect until the person appointed has given (or, if the court allows, undertaken to give) security to the liquidator for the appointment.

(2)   A person appointed as special manager may give security either specifically for a particular winding up, or generally for any winding up in relation to which that person may be appointed as special manager.

(3)   The amount of the security must be not less than the value of the business or property in relation to which the special manager is appointed, as estimated in the liquidator's report which accompanied the application for appointment.

(4)   When the special manager has given security to the liquidator, the liquidator must file with the court a certificate as to the adequacy of the security.

(5)   The cost of providing the security must be paid in the first instance by the special manager, but the special manager is entitled to be reimbursed as an expense of the winding up.

Derivation—This rule derived from the Insolvency Rules 1986, SI 1986/1925, r 4.207.

## [2.254]

### 5.19   Failure to give or keep up security

(1)   If the special manager fails to give the required security within the time stated in the order of appointment, or any extension of that time that may be allowed, the liquidator must report the failure to the court, which may discharge the order appointing the special manager.

(2)   If the special manager fails to keep up the security, the liquidator must report the failure to the court, which may remove the special manager, and make such order as it thinks just as to costs.

(3)   If the court discharges the order appointing the special manager, or makes an order removing the special manager, the court must give directions as to whether any, and if so what, steps should be taken for the appointment of another special manager.

Derivation—This rule derived from the Insolvency Rules 1986, SI 1986/1925, r 4.208.

## [2.255]

### 5.20   Accounting

(1)   The special manager must produce accounts, containing details of the special manager's receipts and payments, for the approval of the liquidator.

(2)   The accounts must be for—

  (a)   each three month period for the duration of the special manager's appointment; and

  (b)   any shorter period ending with the termination of the special manager's appointment.

(3)   When the accounts have been approved, the special manager's receipts and payments must be added to those of the liquidator.

Derivation—This rule derived from the Insolvency Rules 1986, SI 1986/1925, r 4.209.

## [2.256]

### 5.21   Termination of appointment

(1)   If the liquidator thinks that the appointment of the special manager is no longer necessary or beneficial for the company, the liquidator must apply to the court for directions, and the court may order the special manager's appointment to be terminated.

(2)   The liquidator must also make such an application if the members pass a resolution requesting that the appointment be terminated.

Derivation—This rule derived from the Insolvency Rules 1986, SI 1986/1925, r 4.210.

## CHAPTER 4

### CONVERSION TO CREDITORS' VOLUNTARY WINDING UP

**[2.257]**

**5.22 Statement of affairs (section 95(3))**

The rules in Chapter 2 of Part 6 apply to the statement of affairs made out by the liquidator under section 95(1A) where the liquidator is of the opinion that the company will be unable to pay its debts in full (together with interest at the official rate) within the period stated in the directors' declaration under section 89.

Derivation—This rule derived from the Insolvency Rules 1986, SI 1986/1925, r 4.34.

General note—See the comments under s 95. Also, see s 96 and the notes accompanying it for further discussion of this kind of winding up process.

## PART 6  CREDITORS' VOLUNTARY WINDING UP

**[2.258]**

General note—Under the previous rules the various kinds of liquidation were not divided into separate Parts. Now the Rules that were put in force on 6 April 2017 provide for three separate Parts for members' voluntary liquidations (Part 5), creditors' voluntary liquidations (Part 6) and compulsory (court) liquidations (Part 7). This obviates the need, as was the situation in Part 4 of the previous rules, for notes in individual rules to indicate that they were not applicable to either creditors' voluntary liquidations or were so applicable. This makes it easier to discern which rules apply to each kind of winding up. It does mean that there are some overlaps in the provisions contained in the respective Parts.

## CHAPTER 1

### APPLICATION OF PART 6

**[2.259]**

**6.1 Application of Part 6**

(1)   This Part applies to a creditors' voluntary winding up.

(2)   However where a company moves from administration to creditors' voluntary winding up by the registration of a notice under paragraph 83(3) of Schedule B1 the following rules do not apply—

> 6.2 to 6.7 (statement of affairs etc);
>
> 6.11 to 6.15 (information to creditors and contributories and appointment of liquidator);
>
> 6.17 (report by directors etc);
>
> 6.18 (decisions on nomination);
>
> 6.20 (appointment by creditors or by the company);
>
> 6.22 (appointment by the court (section 100(3) or 108), other than in respect of appointments under section 108); and
>
> 6.23 (advertisement of appointment).

Derivation—This rule derived from the Insolvency Rules 1986, SI 1986/1925, r 4.1(6).

## CHAPTER 2

### STATEMENT OF AFFAIRS AND OTHER INFORMATION

**[2.260]**

**Note**

[Note: a document required by the Act or these Rules must also contain the standard contents set out in Part 1.]

**[2.261]**

**6.2 Statement of affairs made out by the liquidator under section 95(1A)**
[Note: (1) section 95(4A) requires the statement of affairs to be verified by a statement of truth;
(2) the "official rate" referred to in paragraph (2)(c) is defined in section 251 as being the rate referred to in section 189(4)).]
(1) This rule applies to the statement of affairs made out by the liquidator under section 95(1A) (effect of company's insolvency in members' voluntary winding up).
(2) The statement of affairs must be headed "Statement of affairs" and must contain—

- (a) identification details for the company;
- (b) a statement that it is a statement of the affairs of the company on a date which is specified, being the date of the opinion formed by the liquidator under section 95(1);
- (c) a statement that as at that date, the liquidator formed the opinion that the company would be unable to pay its debts in full (together with interest at the official rate) within the period stated in the directors' declaration of solvency made under section 89; and
- (d) the date it is made.

(3) The statement of affairs must be delivered by the liquidator to the registrar of companies within five business days after the completion of the decision procedure or deemed consent procedure referred to in rule 6.11 in respect of the appointment of the liquidator.
(4) However the liquidator must not deliver to the registrar of companies with the statement of affairs any schedule required by rule 6.4(4)(b).

**Derivation**—This rule derived from the Insolvency Rules 1986, SI 1986/1925, r 4.34, Sch 4, Fm 4.18.

See the notes accompanying s 95.

**[2.262]**

**6.3 Statement of affairs made out by the directors under section 99(1)**
[Note: section 99(2A) requires the statement of affairs to be verified by a statement of truth.]
(1) This rule applies to the statement of affairs made out by the directors under section 99(1).
(2) The statement of affairs must be headed "Statement of affairs" and must contain—

- (a) identification details for the company;
- (b) a statement that it is a statement of the affairs of the company on a date which is specified, being a date not more than 14 days before the date of the resolution for winding up; and
- (c) the date it is made.

(3) If a creditor requests a copy of the statement of affairs at a time when no liquidator is appointed the directors must deliver a copy to the creditor.
(4) The directors must deliver the statement of affairs to the liquidator as soon as reasonably practicable after the liquidator is appointed.
(5) The liquidator must deliver the statement of affairs to the registrar of companies within five business days after the completion of the decision procedure or deemed consent procedure referred to in rule 6.14 in respect of the appointment of the liquidator.
(6) However the liquidator must not deliver to the registrar of companies with the statement of affairs any schedule required by rule 6.4(4)(b).

**Derivation**—This rule derived from the Insolvency Rules 1986, SI 1986/1925, r 4.34, Sch 4, Fm 4.19.

**General note**—See the comments accompanying s 99.

[2.263]

**6.4 Additional requirements as to statements of affairs**

(1)   A statement of affairs under section 95(1A) or 99(1) must also contain—

    (a)    a list of the company's shareholders, with the following details about each shareholder—

        (i)     name and postal address,

        (ii)    the type of shares held,

        (iii)   the nominal amount of the shares held,

        (iv)   the number of shares held,

        (v)    the amount per share called up, and

        (vi)   the total amount called up;

    (b)    the total amount of shares called up held by all shareholders;

    (c)    a summary of the assets of the company, setting out the book value and estimated realisable value of—

        (i)     any assets subject to a fixed charge,

        (ii)    any assets subject to a floating charge,

        (iii)   any uncharged assets, and

        (iv)   the total value of all the assets available for preferential creditors;

    (d)    a summary of the liabilities of the company, setting out—

        (i)     the amount of preferential debts,

        (ii)    an estimate of the deficiency with respect to preferential debts or the surplus available after paying the preferential debts,

        (iii)   an estimate of the prescribed part, if applicable,

        (iv)   an estimate of the total assets available to pay debts secured by floating charges,

        (v)    the amount of debts secured by floating charges,

        (vi)   an estimate of the deficiency with respect to debts secured by floating charges or the surplus available after paying the debts secured by fixed or floating charges,

        (vii)   the amount of unsecured debts (excluding preferential debts),

        (viii)  an estimate of the deficiency with respect to unsecured debts or the surplus available after paying unsecured debts,

        (ix)   any issued and called-up capital, and

        (x)    an estimate of the deficiency with respect to, or surplus available to, members of the company;

    (e)    a list of the company's creditors with the further particulars required by paragraph (2) indicating—

        (i)     any creditors under hire-purchase, chattel leasing or conditional sale agreements,

        (ii)    any creditors who are consumers claiming amounts paid in advance of the supply of goods or services, and

        (iii)   any creditors claiming retention of title over property in the company's possession.

(2)   The further particulars required by this paragraph relating to each creditor are as follows—

        (i)     the name and postal address,

        (ii)    amount of the debt owed to the creditor, (as required by section 95(4) or 99(2)),

        (iii)   details of any security held by the creditor,

        (iv)   the date the security was given, and

        (v)    the value of any such security.

(3)   Paragraph (4) applies where the particulars required by paragraph (2) relate to creditors who are either—

    (a)    employees or former employees of the company; or

(b)     consumers claiming amounts paid in advance for the supply of goods or services.

(4)   Where this paragraph applies—

(a)     the statement of affairs must state separately for each of paragraphs (3)(a) and (b) the number of such creditors and the total of the debts owed to them; and

(b)     the particulars required by paragraph (2) must be set out in separate schedules to the statement of affairs for each of paragraphs (3)(a) and (b).

Derivation—This rule derived from the Insolvency Rules 1986, SI 1986/1925, Sch 4, Fms 4.18, 4.19.

## [2.264]

### 6.5  Statement of affairs: statement of concurrence

(1)   The liquidator may require a director ("the relevant person") to deliver to the liquidator a statement of concurrence.

(2)   A statement of concurrence is a statement that the relevant person concurs in the statement of affairs submitted by another director.

(3)   The liquidator must inform the director who has been required to submit a statement of affairs that the relevant person has been required to deliver a statement of concurrence.

(4)   The director who has been required to submit the statement of affairs must deliver a copy to every relevant person who has been required to submit a statement of concurrence.

(5)   A statement of concurrence—

(a)     must identify the company; and

(b)     may be qualified in relation to matters dealt with in the statement of affairs, where the maker of the statement of concurrence—

(i)     is not in agreement with the statement of affairs,

(ii)     considers the statement of affairs to be erroneous or misleading, or

(iii)     is without the direct knowledge necessary for concurring with it.

(6)   The relevant person must deliver the required statement of concurrence, verified by a statement of truth, to the liquidator together with a copy before the end of the period of five business days (or such other period as the liquidator may agree) beginning with the day on which the relevant person receives the statement of affairs.

(7)   The liquidator must deliver the verified statement of concurrence to the registrar of companies.

Derivation—This rule derived from the Insolvency Rules 1986, SI 1986/1925, r 4.34(5).

## [2.265]

### 6.6  Order limiting disclosure of statement of affairs etc

(1)   Where the liquidator thinks that disclosure of the whole or part of the statement of affairs or of any statement of concurrence would be likely to prejudice the conduct of the winding up or might reasonably be expected to lead to violence against any person, the liquidator may apply to the court for an order that the statement of affairs, statement of concurrence or any specified part of them must not be delivered to the registrar of companies.

(2)   The court may order that the whole or a specified part of the statement of affairs or a statement of concurrence must not be delivered to the registrar of companies.

(3)   The liquidator must as soon as reasonably practicable deliver to the registrar of companies a copy of the order, the statement of affairs and any statement of concurrence to the extent allowed by the order.

Derivation—This rule derived from the Insolvency Rules 1986, SI 1986/1925, r 4.35.

**[2.266]**

### 6.7 Expenses of statement of affairs and decisions sought from creditors

(1)   Any reasonable and necessary expenses of preparing the statement of affairs under section 99 may be paid out of the company's assets, either before or after the commencement of the winding up, as an expense of the winding up.

(2)   Any reasonable and necessary expenses of the decision procedure or deemed consent procedure to seek a decision from the creditors on the nomination of a liquidator under rule 6.14 may be paid out of the company's assets, either before or after the commencement of the winding up, as an expense of the winding up.

(3)   Where payment under paragraph (1) or (2) is made before the commencement of the winding up, the directors must deliver to the creditors with the statement of affairs a statement of the amount of the payment and the identity of the person to whom it was made.

(4)   The liquidator appointed under section 100 may make such a payment, but if there is a liquidation committee, the liquidator must deliver to the committee at least five business days' notice of the intention to make it.

(5)   However such a payment may not be made to the liquidator, or to any associate of the liquidator, otherwise than with the approval of the liquidation committee, the creditors, or the court.

(6)   This is without prejudice to the court's powers under rule 7.109 (voluntary winding up superseded by winding up by the court).

Derivation—This rule derived from the Insolvency Rules 1986, SI 1986/1925, r 4.38.

General note—In dealing with the precursor rule to this rule it was said in *Re Central A1 Ltd* [2017] EWHC 220 (Ch) at [18] that it is plain from a natural reading of s 115 of the 1986 Act and r 4.38 of the 1986 Rules that expenses should only be paid, whether before or after commencement of the winding up, if they are reasonable and necessary. The case went on to say that the court has jurisdiction upon an application for directions under s 112 of the Act to decide any dispute of reasonableness or necessity under r 4.38 (at [20]). This will be applied to r 6.7.

The expenses under this rule are not to be paid as a super-priority, that is, before the other matters referred to in r 6.42: *Re Central A1 Ltd* [2017] EWHC 220 (Ch) at [27]. The expenses covered by this rule will fall under r 6.42(4)(d) as far as the issue of priority is concerned ([39]–[41]). See r 6.42 and accompanying notes.

**[2.267]**

### 6.8 Delivery of accounts to liquidator (section 235)

(1)   A person who is specified in section 235(3) must deliver to the liquidator accounts of the company of such nature, as at such date, and for such period, as the liquidator requires.

(2)   The period for which the liquidator may require accounts may begin from a date up to three years before the date of the resolution for winding up, or from an earlier date to which audited accounts of the company were last prepared.

(3)   The accounts must, if the liquidator so requires, be verified by a statement of truth.

(4)   The accounts (verified by a statement of truth if so required) must be delivered to the liquidator within 21 days from the liquidator's request, or such longer period as the liquidator may allow.

Derivation—This rule derived from the Insolvency Rules 1986, SI 1986/1925, r 4.40.

General note—The person mentioned in s 235(3) are: those who are or have at any time been officers of the company, those who have taken part in the formation of the company at any time within one year before the effective date, those who are in the employment of the company, or have been in its employment within that year, and are in the office-holder's opinion capable of giving information which he or she requires, those who are, or have within that year been, officers of, or in the employment of, another company which is, or within that year was, an officer of the company in question, and in the case of a company being wound up by the court, any person who has acted as administrator, administrative receiver or liquidator of the company.

**[2.268]**

### 6.9 Expenses of assistance in preparing accounts

(1)  Where the liquidator requires a person to deliver accounts under rule 6.8 the liquidator may, with the approval of the liquidation committee (if there is one) and as an expense of the winding up, employ a person or firm to assist that person in the preparation of the accounts.

(2)  The person who is required to deliver accounts may request an allowance of all or part of the expenses to be incurred in employing a person or firm to assist in preparing the accounts.

(3)  A request for an allowance must be accompanied by an estimate of the expenses involved.

(4)  The liquidator must only authorise the employment of a named person or a named firm approved by the liquidator.

(5)  The liquidator may, with the approval of the liquidation committee (if there is one), authorise such an allowance, payable as an expense of the winding up.

Derivation—This rule derived from the Insolvency Rules 1986, SI 1986/1925, r 4.41.

General note—Given the decision in *Re Central A1 Ltd* [2017] EWHC 220 (Ch) which dealt with the precursor rule to r 6.7 (r 4.38 of the 1986 Rules) expenses should only be sanctioned if they are reasonable and necessary (at [18]). It is likely that the expenses covered by this rule will be paid under r 6.42(4)(d) in the same way that those covered by r 6.7 are. See the notes accompanying the latter rule.

## CHAPTER 3

### Nomination and Appointment of Liquidators and Information to Creditors

**[2.269]**

### Note

[Note: a document required by the Act or these Rules must also contain the standard contents set out in Part 1.]

**[2.270]**

### 6.10 Application of the rules in this Chapter

(1)  The rules in this Chapter apply as follows.

(2)  Rules 6.11 to 6.13 only apply to a conversion from a members' voluntary winding up to a creditors' voluntary winding up.

(3)  Rule 6.16 only applies where the administrator becomes the liquidator in a voluntary winding up which follows an administration.

(4)  Rules 6.14, 6.15 and 6.17 only apply to a creditors' voluntary winding up which has not been commenced by a conversion from a members' voluntary winding up or an administration.

(5)  Rules 6.18 and 6.19 apply to all creditors' voluntary windings up.

**[2.271]**

### 6.11 Nomination of liquidator and information to creditors on conversion from members' voluntary winding up (section 96)

(1)  This rule applies in respect of the conversion of a members' voluntary winding up to a creditors' voluntary winding up under section 96.

(2)  The liquidator must seek a nomination from the creditors for a liquidator in the creditors' voluntary winding up by—

    (a)    a decision procedure; or

    (b)    the deemed consent procedure.

(3)  The liquidator must deliver to the creditors a copy of the statement of affairs required by section 95(1A) and Chapter 2 of this Part together with a notice which complies with rules 15.7 or 15.8 so far as are relevant.

(4)   The notice must also contain—

    (a)   identification and contact details for the existing liquidator; and

    (b)   a statement that if no person is nominated by the creditors then the existing liquidator will be the liquidator in the creditors' voluntary winding up.

(5)   The decision date in the notice must be not later than 28 days from the date under section 95(1) that the liquidator formed the opinion that the company will be unable to pay its debts in full.

(6)   Subject to paragraph (9), the creditors must be given at least 14 days' notice of the decision date.

(7)   Paragraph (8) applies where—

    (a)   the liquidator has sought a decision from creditors on the nomination of a liquidator by the deemed consent procedure; but

    (b)   the level of objections to the proposed nomination have meant, under section 246ZF, that no nomination is deemed to have been made.

(8)   Where this paragraph applies, the liquidator must seek a nomination from creditors by way of a decision procedure in accordance with this rule, the decision date to be as soon as reasonably practicable, but no more than 28 days from the date that the level of objections had the effect that no nomination was deemed to have been made.

(9)   Where paragraph (8) applies, the creditors must be given at least seven days' notice of the decision date.

(10)   Where the liquidator is required by rule 15.6 to summon a physical meeting as a result of requests from creditors received in response to a notice delivered under this rule, the physical meeting must be summoned to take place—

    (a)   within 28 days of the date on which the threshold for requiring a physical meeting was met; and

    (b)   with at least 14 days' notice.

**General note**—Unlike most of the rules in Part 6, this rule is not derived from a rule in the 1986 Rules.

See s 96 and accompanying notes.

**RULE 6.11(2)**

For an explanation of the decision procedure and the deemed consent procedure, see ss 246ZE and 246ZF and Chapters 1–3 of Part 15 of the Rules, and the notes accompanying those provisions.

See s 100 and the notes accompanying that section. This section explains the process for the appointment of the liquidator.

## [2.272]

### 6.12 Creditors' decision on appointment other than at a meeting (conversion from members' voluntary winding up)

(1)   This rule applies where the creditors' decision on the nomination of a liquidator in a conversion of a members' into a creditors' voluntary winding up is intended to be sought otherwise than through a meeting or through the deemed consent procedure, including where the conditions in rule 6.11(7) are met and the liquidator, under rule 6.11(8), goes on to seek a nomination from creditors by way of a decision procedure other than a meeting.

(2)   Instead of delivering a notice of the decision procedure or deemed consent procedure under rule 6.11, the liquidator must deliver a notice to creditors inviting them to make proposals for the nomination of a liquidator.

(3)   Such a notice must—

    (a)   identify any liquidator for whom a proposal which is in compliance with paragraph 4 has already been received;

    (b)   explain that the liquidator is not obliged to seek the creditors' views on any proposal that does not meet the requirements of paragraphs (4) and (5); and

    (c)   be accompanied by the statement of affairs unless that has previously been delivered to the creditor.

(4) Any proposal must state the name and contact details of the proposed liquidator, and contain a statement that the proposed liquidator is qualified to act as an insolvency practitioner in relation to the company and has consented to act as liquidator of the company.

(5) Any proposal must be received by the liquidator within five business days of the date of the notice under paragraph (2).

(6) Within two business days of the end of the period referred to in paragraph (5), the liquidator must send a notice to creditors of a decision procedure under rule 6.11.

Amendments—SI 2017/366.

General note—Unlike most of the rules in Part 6, this rule is not derived from a rule in the 1986 Rules.

The rule covers the situation where the creditors' view on the nomination of a liquidator is not to be obtained via a meeting or through the deemed consent procedure. There are various means of obtaining a decision from the creditors, besides a physical meeting.

'Decision procedure' is defined in r 15.1(1). The kind of procedures that may be used are set out in r 15.3.

## [2.273]

### 6.13 Information to creditors and contributories (conversion of members' voluntary winding up into creditors' voluntary winding up)

(1) The liquidator must deliver to the creditors and contributories within 28 days of the conversion of a members' voluntary winding up into a creditors' voluntary winding up under section 96 a notice which must contain—

    (a) the date the winding up became a creditors' voluntary winding up;

    (b) a report of the decision procedure or deemed consent procedure which took place under rule 6.11; and

    (c) the information required by paragraph (3).

(2) The notice must be accompanied by a copy of the statement of affairs or a summary except where the notice is being delivered to a creditor to whom a copy of the statement of affairs has previously been delivered under section 95(1A).

(3) The required information is an estimate to the best of the liquidator's knowledge and belief of—

    (a) the value of the prescribed part (whether or not the liquidator might be required under section 176A to make the prescribed part available for the satisfaction of unsecured debts); and

    (b) the value of the company's net property (as defined by section 176A(6)).

(4) The liquidator may exclude from an estimate under paragraph (3) information the disclosure of which could seriously prejudice the commercial interests of the company.

(5) If the exclusion of such information affects the calculation of an estimate, the report must say so.

(6) If the liquidator proposes to make an application to court under section 176A(5) the report must say so and give the reason for the application.

Derivation—This rule derived from the Insolvency Rules 1986, SI 1986/1925, r 4.49.
Amendments—SI 2017/366.
General note—See s 176A and the comments accompanying it.

## [2.274]

### 6.14 Information to creditors and appointment of liquidator

(1) This rule applies in respect of the appointment of a liquidator under section 100.

(2) The directors of the company must deliver to the creditors a notice seeking their decision on the nomination of a liquidator by—

    (a) the deemed consent procedure; or

    (b) a virtual meeting.

(3) The decision date for the decision of the creditors on the nomination of a liquidator must be not earlier than three business days after the notice under

paragraph (2) is delivered but not later than 14 days after the resolution is passed to wind up the company.

(4)   Where the directors have sought a decision from the creditors through the deemed consent procedure under paragraph (2)(a) but, pursuant to section 246ZF(5)(a) (deemed consent procedure), more than the specified number of creditors object so that the decision cannot be treated as having been made, the directors must then seek a decision from the creditors on the nomination of a liquidator by holding a physical meeting under rule 15.6 (physical meetings) as if a physical meeting had been required under section 246ZE(4) (decisions by creditors and contributories: general).

(5)   Where paragraph (4) applies, the meeting must not be held earlier than three business days after the notice under rule 15.6(3) is delivered or later than 14 days after the level of objections reach that described in paragraph (4).

(6)   A request for a physical meeting under section 246ZE must be made in accordance with rule 15.6 except that—

> (a)   such a request may be made at any time between the delivery of the notice under paragraph (2) and the decision date under paragraph (3); and
>
> (b)   the decision date where this paragraph applies must be not earlier than three business days after the notice under rule 15.6(3) is delivered and not later than 14 days after the level of requests reach that described in section 246ZE.

(7)   The directors must deliver to the creditors a copy of the statement of affairs required under section 99 of the Act not later than on the business day before the decision date.

(8)   A notice delivered under paragraph (2), in addition to the information required by rules 15.7 (deemed consent) and 15.8 (notices to creditors of decision procedure), must contain—

> (a)   the date the resolution to wind up is to be considered or was passed;
>
> (b)   identification and contact details of any liquidator nominated by the company;
>
> (c)   a statement of either—
>
>> (i)   the name and address of a person qualified to act as an insolvency practitioner in relation to the company who during the period before the decision date, will furnish creditors free of charge with such information concerning the company's affairs as they may reasonably require, or
>>
>> (ii)   a place in the relevant locality where, on the two business days falling next before the decision date, a list of the names and addresses of the company's creditors will be available for inspection free of charge; and
>
> (d)   where the notice is sent to creditors in advance of the copy of the statement of affairs, a statement that the directors, before the decision date and before the end of the period of seven days beginning with the day after the day on which the company passed a resolution for winding up, are required by section 99 of the Insolvency Act 1986—
>
>> (i)   to make out a statement in the prescribed form as to the affairs of the company, and
>>
>> (ii)   send the statement to the company's creditors.

(9)   Where the company's principal place of business in England or Wales was situated in different localities at different times during the relevant period, the duty imposed by sub-paragraph (8)(c)(ii) above applies separately in relation to each of those localities.

(10)   Where the company had no place of business in England or Wales during the relevant period, the reference in paragraph (9) to the company's principal place of business in England or Wales are replaced by references to its registered office.

(11)   In paragraph (9), "the relevant period" means the period of six months immediately preceding the day on which the notices referred to in paragraph (2) were delivered.

(12)   Where a virtual or physical meeting is held under this rule and a liquidator has already been nominated by the company, the liquidator or an appointed person must

attend any meeting held under this rule and report on any exercise of the liquidator's powers under section 112, 165 or 166 of the Act.

(13)   A director who is in default in seeking a decision on the nomination of a liquidator in accordance with this rule is guilty of an offence and is liable to a fine.

Derivation—This rule derived from the 1986 Rules, SI 1986/1925, r 4.49.

General note—Where a virtual or physical meeting is held under r 6.14 and a liquidator has already been nominated by the company, the liquidator or an appointed person must attend any meeting held under this rule and report on any exercise of the liquidator's powers under ss 112, 165 or 166 of the 1986 Act.

A decision on who is to be nominated as liquidator must be made through the deemed consent procedure or by a virtual meeting, unless in relation to where a decision is sought by way of the former mechanism under s 246ZF(5)(a), and 10 per cent in value of the creditors (taking the value of the debts owed to creditors) object to a decision being made this way, whereby a physical meeting must be held (see, s 246ZF(6)).

'Deemed consent procedure' is provided for in s 246ZF and r 15.7. See the notes accompanying those provisions

'Virtual meeting' is defined in r 15.1(1) and further explained in r 15.5. Effectively it means a meeting where the creditors will not be physically present.

Generally see the notes accompanying s 100 and particularly the reference to the decision in *Cash Generator Ltd v Fortune* [2018] EWHC 674 (Ch), where there was no compliance with this rule.

## [2.275]

### 6.15  Information to creditors and contributories

(1)   The liquidator must deliver to the creditors and contributories within 28 days of the appointment of the liquidator under section 100 a notice which must—

(a)   be accompanied by a statement of affairs or a summary where the notice is delivered to any contributory or creditor to whom the notice under rule 6.14 was not delivered;

(b)   be accompanied by a report on the decision procedure or deemed consent procedure under rule 6.14; and

(c)   be accompanied by the information required by paragraph (2).

(2)   The required information is an estimate to the best of the liquidator's knowledge and belief of—

(a)   the value of the prescribed part (whether or not the liquidator might be required under section 176A to make the prescribed part available for the satisfaction of unsecured debts); and

(b)   the value of the company's net property (as defined by section 176A(6)).

(3)   The liquidator may exclude from an estimate under paragraph (2) information the disclosure of which could seriously prejudice the commercial interests of the company.

(4)   If the exclusion of such information affects the calculation of an estimate, the report must say so.

(5)   If the liquidator proposes to make an application to court under section 176A(5) the report must say so and give the reason for the application.

Derivation—This rule derived from the Insolvency Rules 1986, SI 1986/1925, r 4.49.

Amendments—SI 2017/1115.

General note—See the commentary accompanying s 100 which seeks to give a broader picture of the process.

## [2.276]

### 6.16  Further information where administrator becomes liquidator (paragraph 83(3) of Schedule B1)

(1)   This rule applies where an administrator becomes liquidator on the registration of a notice under paragraph 83(3) of Schedule B1, and becomes aware of creditors not formerly known to that person as administrator.

(2)   The liquidator must deliver to those creditors a copy of any statement delivered by the administrator to creditors in accordance with paragraph 49(4) of Schedule B1 and rule 3.35.

Derivation—This rule derived from the Insolvency Rules 1986, SI 1986/1925, r 4.49A.

## [2.277]

### 6.17  Report by director etc

(1)   Where the statement of affairs sent to creditors under section 99(1) does not, or will not, state the company's affairs at the decision date for the creditors' nomination of a liquidator, the directors of the company must cause a report (written or oral) to be made to the creditors in accordance with this rule on any material transactions relating to the company occurring between the date of the making of the statement and the decision date.

(2)   In the case of a decision being taken through a meeting, the report must be made at the meeting by the director chairing the meeting or by another person with knowledge of the relevant matters.

(3)   Where the deemed consent procedure is used, the report must be delivered to creditors as soon as reasonably practicable after the material transaction takes place in the same manner as the deemed consent procedure.

(4)   Where the decision date is within the period of three business days from the delivery of a report under paragraph (3), this rule extends the decision date until the end of that period notwithstanding the requirement in rule 6.14(3) relating to the timing of the decision date.

(5)   On delivery of a report under paragraph (3), the directors must notify the creditors of the effects of paragraph (4).

(6)   A report under this rule must be recorded in the record of the decision under rule 15.40.

Derivation—This rule derived from the Insolvency Rules 1986, SI 1986/1925, r 4.53B.
General note—See the comments accompanying s 99.

## [2.278]

### 6.18  Decisions on nomination

(1)   In the case of a decision on the nomination of a liquidator—

  (a)   if on any vote there are two nominees, the person who obtains the most support is appointed;

  (b)   if there are three or more nominees, and one of them has a clear majority over both or all the others together, that one is appointed; and

  (c)   in any other case, the convener or chair must continue to take votes (disregarding at each vote any nominee who has withdrawn and, if no nominee has withdrawn, the nominee who obtained the least support last time) until a clear majority is obtained for any one nominee.

(2)   In the case of a decision being made at a meeting, the chair may at any time put to the meeting a resolution for the joint nomination of any two or more nominees.

Derivation—This rule derived from the Insolvency Rules 1986, SI 1986/1925, r 4.63.

## [2.279]

### 6.19  Invitation to creditors to form a liquidation committee

(1)   Where any decision is sought from the company's creditors—

  (a)   in a creditors' voluntary winding up; or

  (b)   where a members' voluntary winding up is converting in a creditors' voluntary winding up;

the convener of the decision must at the same time deliver to the creditors a notice inviting them to decide whether a liquidation committee should be established if sufficient creditors are willing to be members of the committee.

(2)   The notice must also invite nominations for membership of the committee, such nominations to be received by a date specified in the notice.

(3)   The notice must state that nominations—

(a)   must be delivered to the convener by the specified date; and

(b)   can only be accepted if the convener is satisfied as to the creditor's eligibility under rule 17.4.

General note—Unlike most of the rules in Part 6, this was not derived from the Insolvency Rules 1986. It is related to s 101. See the notes accompanying that provision.

In a creditors' voluntary winding up, the committee must have three members before it can be established (r 17.3(2)).

Part 17 of the Rules addresses the details of liquidation committees.

## CHAPTER 4

### THE LIQUIDATOR

**[2.280]**

**Note**

[Note: a document required by the Act or these Rules must also contain the standard contents set out in Part 1.]

**[2.281]**

**6.20  Appointment by creditors or by the company**

(1)   This rule applies where a person is appointed as liquidator by creditors or the company.

(2)   The liquidator's appointment takes effect from the date of the passing of the resolution of the company or, where the creditors decide to appoint a person who is not the person appointed by the company, from the relevant decision date.

(3)   Their appointment must be certified by—

(a)   the convener or chair of the decision procedure or deemed consent procedure; or

(b)   in respect of an appointment by the company the chair of the company meeting or a director or the secretary of the company (in the case of a written resolution).

(4)   The person who certifies the appointment must not do so unless and until the proposed liquidator ("the appointee") has provided that person with a statement of being an insolvency practitioner qualified under the Act to be the liquidator and of consenting to act.

(5)   The certificate must be authenticated and dated by the person who certifies the appointment and must contain—

(a)   identification details for the company;

(b)   identification and contact details for the person appointed as liquidator;

(c)   the date of the meeting of the company or conclusion of the decision procedure or deemed consent procedure when the liquidator was appointed;

(d)   a statement that the appointee—

(i)   has provided a statement of being qualified to act as an insolvency practitioner in relation to the company,

(ii)   has consented to act, and

(iii)   was appointed liquidator of the company.

(6)   Where two or more liquidators are appointed the certificate must also specify (as required by section 231) whether any act required or authorised under any enactment to be done by the liquidator is to be done by all or any one or more of them.

(7)   The person who certifies the appointment must deliver the certificate as soon as reasonably practicable to the liquidator, who must keep it as part of the records of the winding up.

**Derivation**—This rule derived from the Insolvency Rules 1986, SI 1986/1925, r 4.101.
**Amendments**—SI 2017/366.
**General note**—See s 100 and accompanying comments.

**[2.282]**

### 6.21 Power to fill vacancy in office of liquidator

Where a vacancy in the office of liquidator occurs in the manner mentioned in section 104 a decision procedure to fill the vacancy may be initiated by any creditor or, if there was more than one liquidator, by the continuing liquidator or liquidators.

**Derivation**—This rule derived from the Insolvency Rules 1986, SI 1986/1925, r 4.101A.
**General note**—See s 104.

**[2.283]**

### 6.22 Appointment by the court (section 100(3) or 108)

(1) This rule applies where the liquidator is appointed by the court under section 100(3) or 108.

(2) The court's order must not be made unless and until the proposed liquidator has filed with the court a statement of being qualified under the Act to act as an insolvency practitioner in relation to the company and of consenting to act.

(3) The order of the court must contain—

    (a) the name of the court (and hearing centre if applicable) in which the order is made;

    (b) the name and title of the judge making the order;

    (c) the date on which it is made;

    (d) identification details for the company;

    (e) the name and postal address of the applicant;

    (f) the capacity in which the applicant made the application;

    (g) identification details for the proposed liquidator; and

    (h) an order that the proposed liquidator, having filed a statement of being qualified to act as an insolvency practitioner in relation to the company and having consented to act, is appointed liquidator of the company from the date of the order, or such other date as the court orders.

(4) Where two or more liquidators are appointed the order must also specify (as required by section 231) whether any act required or authorised under any enactment to be done by the liquidator is to be done by all or any one or more of them.

(5) The court must deliver a sealed copy of the order to the liquidator.

(6) Within 28 days from appointment, the liquidator must—

    (a) deliver a notice of the appointment to creditors of the company; or

    (b) advertise the appointment in accordance with any directions given by the court.

**Derivation**—This rule derived from the Insolvency Rules 1986, SI 1986/1925, r 4.103.

**[2.284]**

### 6.23 Advertisement of appointment

(1) A liquidator appointed in a voluntary winding up in addition to delivering a notice of the appointment in accordance with section 109(1) may advertise the notice in such other manner as the liquidator thinks fit.

(2) The notice must state—

    (a) that a liquidator has been appointed; and

    (b) the date of the appointment.

(3) The liquidator must initially bear the expense of giving notice under this rule but is entitled to be reimbursed for the expenditure as an expense of the winding up.

**Derivation**—This rule derived from the Insolvency Rules 1986, SI 1986/1925, r 4.106A.

**[2.285]**

### 6.24  Cost of liquidator's security (section 390(3))

The cost of the liquidator's security required by section 390(3) for the proper performance of the liquidator's functions is an expense of the winding up.

Derivation—This rule derived from the Insolvency Rules 1986, SI 1986/1925, r 12A.56.

**[2.286]**

### 6.25  Liquidator's resignation and replacement

(1)  A liquidator may resign only—

- (a)  on grounds of ill health;
- (b)  because of the intention to cease to practise as an insolvency practitioner;
- (c)  because the further discharge of the duties of liquidator is prevented or made impractical by—
  - (i)  a conflict of interest, or
  - (ii)  or a change of personal circumstances; or
- (d)  where two or more persons are acting as liquidator jointly and it is the opinion of both or all of them that it is no longer expedient that there should continue to be that number of joint liquidators.

(2)  Before resigning the liquidator must invite the creditors by a decision procedure, or by deemed consent, to consider whether a replacement should be appointed except where the resignation is under paragraph (1)(d).

(3)  The notice of the decision procedure or of deemed consent must—

- (a)  state the liquidator's intention to resign;
- (b)  state that under rule 6.25(7) of these Rules the liquidator will be released 21 days after the date of delivery of the notice of resignation to the registrar of companies under section 171(5), unless the court orders otherwise; and
- (c)  comply with rules 15.7 and 15.8 so far as are relevant.

(4)  The notice may suggest the name of a replacement liquidator.

(5)  The notice must be accompanied by a summary of the liquidator's receipts and payments.

(6)  The decision date must be not more than five business days before the date on which the liquidator intends to give notice of resignation to the registrar of companies under section 171(5).

(7)  The resigning liquidator's release is effective 21 days after the date of delivery of the notice of resignation to the registrar of companies under section 171(5), unless the court orders otherwise.

Derivation—This rule derived from the Insolvency Rules 1986, SI 1986/1925, r 4.108.

General note—See the comments under 'Resign' accompanying s 172 and also those under s 171.

**[2.287]**

### 6.26  Removal of liquidator by creditors

(1)  Where the creditors decide that the liquidator be removed, the convener of the decision procedure or the chair of the meeting (as the case may be) must as soon as reasonably practicable deliver the certificate of the liquidator's removal to the removed liquidator.

(2)  The removed liquidator must deliver a notice of the removal to the registrar of companies as soon as reasonably practicable.

Derivation—This rule derived from the Insolvency Rules 1986, SI 1986/1925, r 4.117.

**[2.288]**

### 6.27 Removal of liquidator by the court

(1)   This rule applies where an application is made to the court for the removal of the liquidator, or for an order directing the liquidator to initiate a decision procedure of creditors for the purpose of removing the liquidator.

(2)   On receipt of an application, the court may, if it is satisfied that no sufficient cause is shown for it, dismiss it without giving notice to any party other than the applicant.

(3)   Unless the application is dismissed, the court must fix a venue for it to be heard.

(4)   The applicant must, at least 14 days before any hearing, deliver to the liquidator a notice stating the venue with a copy of the application and of any evidence on which the applicant intends to rely.

(5)   A respondent may apply for security for the costs of the application and the court may make such an order if it is satisfied, having regard to all the circumstances of the case, that it is just to make such an order.

(6)   The liquidator may do either or both of the following—

    (a)   file a report of any matters which the liquidator thinks ought to be drawn to the court's attention; or

    (b)   appear and be heard on the application.

(7)   The costs of the application are not payable as an expense of the winding up unless the court orders otherwise.

(8)   On a successful application the court's order must contain the following—

    (a)   the name of the court (and hearing centre if applicable) in which the order is made;

    (b)   the name and title of the judge making the order;

    (c)   identification details for the company;

    (d)   the name and postal address of the applicant;

    (e)   the capacity in which the applicant made the application;

    (f)   identification and contact details for the liquidator;

    (g)   an order either—

        (i)   that the liquidator is removed from office from the date of the order (unless the order specifies otherwise), or

        (ii)   that the liquidator must initiate a decision procedure of the company's creditors (specifying which procedure is to be used) on or before a date stated in the order for the purpose of considering the liquidator's removal from office; and

    (h)   the date of the order.

(9)   Where the court removes the liquidator—

    (a)   it must deliver the sealed order of removal to the former liquidator; and

    (b)   the former liquidator must deliver a copy of the order to the registrar of companies as soon as reasonably practicable.

(10)   If the court appoints a new liquidator rule 6.22 applies.

**Derivation**—This rule derived from the Insolvency Rules 1986, SI 1986/1925, r 4.120.

**General note**—There was no established practice concerning the use of the precursor of r 6.27(5), namely r 4.120(3) of the 1986 Rules: *Re Buildlead Ltd* [2003] EWHC 1981 (Ch), [2003] 4 All ER 864, [2004] 1 BCLC 83. The power to require a deposit or to give security is permissive (*Re Buildlead Ltd*). Like its precursor, r 6.27(5) is designed to winnow out claims to remove liquidators which have little chance of success (*Buildlead* at [9]). In some cases an order given under r 6.27(5) and requiring money to be brought into court by an applicant would stand, in doubtful cases, to protect a liquidator from loss sustained in defending an application to remove (*Buildlead* at [9]).

For substantive discussion concerning removal, see notes accompanying s 108. Also, see the notes accompanying s 172, which does apply to compulsory liquidations only.

**[2.289]**

### 6.28 Final account prior to dissolution (section 106)

(1)   The final account which the liquidator is required to make up under section 106(1) and deliver to members and creditors must comply with the requirements of rule 18.14.

(2)   When the account is delivered to the creditors it must be accompanied by a notice which states—

    (a)    that the company's affairs are fully wound up;

    (b)    that the creditors have the right to request information from the liquidator under rule 18.9;

    (c)    that the creditors have the right to challenge the liquidator's remuneration and expenses under rule 18.34;

    (d)    that a creditor may object to the release of the liquidator by giving notice in writing to the liquidator before the end of the prescribed period;

    (e)    that the prescribed period is the period ending at the later of—

        (i)    eight weeks after delivery of the notice, or

        (ii)    if any request for information under rule 18.9 or any application to court under that rule or rule 18.34 is made when that request or application is finally determined;

    (f)    that the liquidator will vacate office under section 171 on delivering to the registrar of companies the final account and notice saying whether any creditor has objected to release; and

    (g)    that the liquidator will be released under section 173 at the same time as vacating office unless any of the company's creditors objected to the liquidator's release.

(3)   The copy of the account which the liquidator delivers to the registrar of companies under section 106(3) must be accompanied by a notice containing the statement required by section 106(3)(a) of whether any creditors have objected to the liquidator's release.

(4)   Where a creditor has objected to the liquidator's release rule 6.33 applies to an application by the liquidator to the Secretary of State for release.

(5)   The liquidator is not obliged to prepare or deliver any progress report which may become due under these Rules in the period between the date to which the final account is made up and the date when the account is delivered to the registrar of companies under section 106(3)(a).

    **Derivation**—This rule derived from the Insolvency Rules 1986, SI 1986/1925, r 4.126.

    **General note**—The precursor to this rule, r 4.126 of the 1986 Rules, required a final meeting, but that is no longer required and that is in line with the vast reduction in the need for creditors' meetings during a liquidation.

    See s 106 and the comments accompanying it.

**[2.290]**

### 6.29 Deceased liquidator

(1)   If the liquidator dies a notice of the fact and date of death must be delivered as soon as reasonably practicable—

    (a)    where there is a liquidation committee, to the members of that committee; and

    (b)    to the registrar of companies.

(2)   The notice must be delivered by one of the following—

    (a)    a surviving joint liquidator;

    (b)    a member of the deceased liquidator's firm (if the deceased was a member or employee of a firm);

    (c)    an officer of the deceased liquidator's company (if the deceased was an officer or employee of a company); or

    (d)    a personal representative of the deceased liquidator.

(3)   If such a notice has not been delivered within the 21 days following the liquidator's death then any other person may deliver the notice.

Derivation—This rule derived from the Insolvency Rules 1986, SI 1986/1925, r 4.133.

**[2.291]**

### 6.30 Loss of qualification as insolvency practitioner

(1) This rule applies where the liquidator vacates office on ceasing to be qualified to act as an insolvency practitioner in relation to the company.

(2) A notice of the fact must be delivered as soon as reasonably practicable to the registrar of companies and the Secretary of State by one of the following—

    (a)   the liquidator who has vacated office;

    (b)   a continuing joint liquidator;

    (c)   the recognised professional body which was the source of the vacating liquidator's authorisation to act in relation to the company.

(3) Each notice must be authenticated and dated by the person delivering the notice.

Derivation—This rule derived from the Insolvency Rules 1986, SI 1986/1925, r 4.135.

**[2.292]**

### 6.31 Vacation of office on making of winding-up order

Where the liquidator vacates office in consequence of the court making a winding-up order against the company, rule 6.33 applies in relation to the application to the Secretary of State for release of the liquidator.

Derivation—This rule derived from the Insolvency Rules 1986, SI 1986/1925, r 4.136.

**[2.293]**

### 6.32 Liquidator's duties on vacating office

A liquidator who ceases to be in office in consequence of removal, resignation or ceasing to be qualified as an insolvency practitioner in relation to the company, must as soon as reasonably practicable deliver to the succeeding liquidator—

    (a)   the assets (after deduction of any expenses properly incurred, and distributions made, by the former liquidator);

    (b)   the records of the winding up, including correspondence, proofs and other documents; and

    (c)   the company's records.

Derivation—This rule derived from the Insolvency Rules 1986, SI 1986/1925, r 4.138.

**[2.294]**

### 6.33 Application by former liquidator for release (section 173(2)(b))

(1) An application to the Secretary of State by a former liquidator for release under section 173(2)(b) must contain—

    (a)   identification and contact details for the former liquidator;

    (b)   identification details for the company;

    (c)   details of the circumstances under which the liquidator has ceased to act as liquidator;

    (d)   a statement that the former liquidator of the company is applying to the Secretary of State for a certificate of release as liquidator as a result of the circumstances specified in the application.

(2) The application must be authenticated and dated by the former liquidator.

(3) When the Secretary of State releases the former liquidator, the Secretary of State must certify the release and deliver the certificate to the former liquidator whose release is effective from the date of the certificate or such other date as the certificate specifies.

(4) The Secretary of State must deliver a notice of the release to the registrar of companies.

Derivation—This rule derived from the Insolvency Rules 1986, SI 1986/1925, r 4.122(3), Sch 4, Fm 4.41.

General note—See s 173 and the accompanying comments. Also, see r 6.29 which covers the situation where a liquidator dies while in office.

**[2.295]**

### 6.34 Power of court to set aside certain transactions

(1)   If in dealing with the insolvent estate the liquidator enters into any transaction with a person who is an associate of the liquidator, the court may, on the application of any interested person, set the transaction aside and order the liquidator to compensate the company for any loss suffered in consequence of it.

(2)   This does not apply if either—

- (a)   the transaction was entered into with the prior consent of the court; or
- (b)   it is shown to the court's satisfaction that the transaction was for value, and that it was entered into by the liquidator without knowing, or having any reason to suppose, that the person concerned was an associate.

(3)   Nothing in this rule is to be taken as prejudicing the operation of any rule of law or equity relating to a liquidator's dealings with trust property or the fiduciary obligations of any person.

Derivation—This rule derived from the Insolvency Rules 1986, SI 1986/1925, r 4.149.

General note—'Associate' is defined in s 435. See the notes accompanying that section.

**[2.296]**

### 6.35 Rule against improper solicitation

(1)   Where the court is satisfied that any improper solicitation has been used by or on behalf of the liquidator in obtaining proxies or procuring the liquidator's appointment, it may order that no remuneration be allowed as an expense of the winding up to any person by whom, or on whose behalf, the solicitation was exercised.

(2)   An order of the court under this rule overrides any resolution of the liquidation committee or the creditors, or any other provision of these Rules relating to the liquidator's remuneration.

Derivation—This rule derived from the Insolvency Rules 1986, SI 1986/1925, r 4.150.

General note—See s 164 which provides, inter alia, that a person who offers a bribe to secure his or her appointment as a liquidator of a company is liable to a fine.

**[2.297]**

### 6.36 Permission for exercise of powers by liquidator

(1)   Where these Rules require permission for the liquidator to exercise a power any permission given must not be a general permission but must relate to a particular proposed exercise of the liquidator's power.

(2)   A person dealing with the liquidator in good faith and for value is not concerned to enquire whether any such permission has been given.

(3)   Where the liquidator has done anything without such permission, the court or the liquidation committee may, for the purpose of enabling the liquidator to meet the liquidator's expenses out of the assets, ratify what the liquidator has done; but neither may do so unless satisfied that the liquidator has acted in a case of urgency and has sought ratification without undue delay.

(4)   In this rule "permission" includes "sanction".

Derivation—This rule derived from the Insolvency Rules 1986, SI 1986/1925, r 4.184.

General note—In *Gresham International Ltd v Moonie* [2009] EWHC 1093 (Ch), [2010] Ch 285, [2010] 2 WLR 362 [2009] 2 BCLC 256, [2010] BPIR 122 the court considered the precursor provision of r 6.36, r 4.184 of the 1986 Rules, in light of an application for retrospective sanctioning of proceedings by a liquidator. In this case it was said that the court had the power under its supervisory role of compulsory winding up to grant retrospective sanction despite the statutory requirements not being made out. The decision is likely to apply to the new rule.

CHAPTER 5

SPECIAL MANAGER

**[2.298]**

Note
[Note: a document required by the Act or these Rules must also contain the standard contents set out in Part 1.]

**[2.299]**

**6.37 Application for and appointment of special manager (section 177)**
(1)   An application by the liquidator under section 177 for the appointment of a special manager must be supported by a report setting out the reasons for the application.
(2)   The report must include the applicant's estimate of the value of the business or property in relation to which the special manager is to be appointed.
(3)   The court's order appointing a special manager must have the title "Order of Appointment of Special Manager" and must contain—

    (a)    the name of the court (and hearing centre if applicable) in which the order is made;

    (b)    the name and title of the judge making the order;

    (c)    identification details for the proceedings;

    (d)    the name and address of the applicant;

    (e)    the name and address of the proposed special manager;

    (f)    the order that that the proposed special manager is appointed as special manager of the company from the date of the order (or otherwise as the order provides);

    (g)    details of the special manager's responsibility over the company's business or property;

    (h)    the powers entrusted to the special manager under section 177(3);

    (i)    the time allowed for the special manager to give the required security for the appointment;

    (j)    the duration of the special manager's appointment, being one of the following—

        (i)    for a fixed period stated in the order,

        (ii)    until the occurrence of a specified event, or

        (iii)    until the court makes a further order;

    (k)    the order that the special manager's remuneration will be fixed from time to time by the court; and

    (l)    the date of the order.

(4)   The appointment of the special manager may be renewed by order of the court.
(5)   The acts of the special manager are valid notwithstanding any defect in the special manager's appointment or qualifications.

   **Derivation**—This rule derived from the Insolvency Rules 1986, SI 1986/1925, r 4.206.
   **Amendments**—SI 2017/366.

**[2.300]**

**6.38 Security**
(1)   The appointment of the special manager does not take effect until the person appointed has given (or, if the court allows, undertaken to give) security to the applicant for the appointment.
(2)   A person appointed as special manager may give security either specifically for a particular winding up, or generally for any winding up in relation to which that person may be appointed as special manager.

(3) The amount of the security must be not less than the value of the business or property in relation to which the special manager is appointed, as estimated in the applicant's report which accompanied the application for appointment.

(4) When the special manager has given security to the applicant, the applicant must file with the court a certificate as to the adequacy of the security.

(5) The cost of providing the security must be paid in the first instance by the special manager; but the special manager is entitled to be reimbursed as an expense of the winding up, in the prescribed order of priority.

Derivation—This rule derived from the Insolvency Rules 1986, SI 1986/1925, r 4.207.

## [2.301]

### 6.39 Failure to give or keep up security

(1) If the special manager fails to give the required security within the time stated in the order of appointment, or any extension of that time that may be allowed, the liquidator must report the failure to the court which may discharge the order appointing the special manager.

(2) If the special manager fails to keep up the security, the liquidator must report the failure to the court, which may remove the special manager, and make such order as it thinks just as to costs.

(3) If the court discharges the order appointing the special manager or makes an order removing the special manager, the court must give directions as to whether any, and if so what, steps should be taken for the appointment of another special manager.

Derivation—This rule derived from the Insolvency Rules 1986, SI 1986/1925, r 4.208.

## [2.302]

### 6.40 Accounting

(1) The special manager must produce accounts, containing details of the special manager's receipts and payments, for the approval of the liquidator.

(2) The account must be for—
    (a)    each three month period for the duration of the special manager's appointment;
    (b)    any shorter period ending with the termination of the special manager's appointment.

(3) When the accounts have been approved, the special manager's receipts and payments must be added to those of the liquidator.

Derivation—This rule derived from the Insolvency Rules 1986, SI 1986/1925, r 4.209.

## [2.303]

### 6.41 Termination of appointment

(1) If the liquidator thinks that the employment of the special manager is no longer necessary or beneficial for the company, the liquidator must apply to the court for directions, and the court may order the special manager's appointment to be terminated.

(2) The liquidator must also make such an application if the creditors decide that the appointment should be terminated.

Derivation—This rule derived from the Insolvency Rules 1986, SI 1986/1925, r 4.210.

CHAPTER 6

PRIORITY OF PAYMENT OF COSTS AND EXPENSES, ETC

## [2.304]

General comment on Chapter 6—This Chapter deals with what payments constitute liquidation expenses as well as setting out the order in which the expenses are to be paid from company assets.

This is necessary as there might not be sufficient assets in the company to pay all of the costs and expenses of a liquidation.

## [2.305]

### 6.42 General rule as to priority

(1) All fees, costs, charges and other expenses incurred in the course of the winding up are to be treated as expenses of the winding up.

(2) The expenses of the winding up are payable out of—

    (a) assets of the company available for the payment of general creditors, including—

        (i) proceeds of any legal action which the liquidator has power to bring in the liquidator's own name or in the name of the company,

        (ii) proceeds arising from any award made under any arbitration or other dispute resolution procedure which the liquidator has power to bring in the liquidator's own name or in the name of the company,

        (iii) any payments made under any compromise or other agreement intended to avoid legal action or recourse to arbitration or to any other dispute resolution procedure, and

        (iv) payments made as a result of an assignment or a settlement of any such action, arbitration or other dispute resolution procedure in lieu of or before any judgment being given or award being made; and

    (b) subject as provided in rules 6.44 to 6.48, property comprised in or subject to a floating charge created by the company.

(3) The expenses associated with the prescribed part must be paid out of the prescribed part.

(4) Subject as provided in rules 6.44 to 6.48, the expenses are payable in the following order of priority—

    (a) expenses which are properly chargeable or incurred by the liquidator in preserving, realising or getting in any of the assets of the company or otherwise in the preparation, conduct or assignment of any legal proceedings, arbitration or other dispute resolution procedures, which the liquidator has power to bring in the liquidator's own name or bring or defend in the name of the company or in the preparation or conduct of any negotiations intended to lead or leading to a settlement or compromise of any legal action or dispute to which the proceedings or procedures relate;

    (b) the cost of any security provided by the liquidator or special manager under the Act or these Rules;

    (c) the remuneration of the special manager (if any);

    (d) any amount payable to a person employed or authorised, under Chapter 2 of this Part, to assist in the preparation of a statement of affairs or of accounts;

    (e) the costs of employing a shorthand writer on the application of the liquidator;

    (f) any necessary disbursements by the liquidator in the course of the administration of the winding up (including any . . . expenses incurred by members of the liquidation committee or their representatives and allowed by the liquidator under rule 17.24, but not including any payment of corporation tax in circumstances referred to in sub-paragraph (i));

    (g) the remuneration or emoluments of any person who has been employed by the liquidator to perform any services for the company, as required or authorised by or under the Act or these Rules;

    (h) the remuneration of the liquidator, up to an amount not exceeding that which is payable under Schedule 11 (determination of insolvency office-holder's remuneration);

(i)       the amount of any corporation tax on chargeable gains accruing on the realisation of any asset of the company (irrespective of the person by whom the realisation is effected);

(j)       the balance, after payment of any sums due under sub-paragraph (h) above, of any remuneration due to the liquidator; and

(k)      any other expenses properly chargeable by the liquidator in carrying out the liquidator's functions in the winding up.

**Derivation**—This rule is derived from the Insolvency Rules 1986, SI 1986/1925, rr 4.218, 12.2.

**Amendments**—SI 2017/702; SI 2019/146, as from IP completion day (as defined in the European Union (Withdrawal Agreement) Act 2020, s 39(1)–(5)).

**General note**—Under the previous rules only one rule covered both creditors' voluntary and compulsory liquidations. Now they are separated, although they are similar insofar as they address the same kinds of expenses. The main differences are the numbering of the paragraphs, there is no reference to some expenses such as a provisional liquidator's remuneration and expenses or the expenses of the official receiver in relation to voluntary liquidations (as they are not relevant as they are peculiar to compulsory liquidation), and some arrangement in the wording. Hence there is a lot of overlap between r 6.42(4) and r 7.108(4). The matters that were covered under the previous rules are essentially dealt with here. The rule does not cover anything that is not addressed in r 7.108.

See the detailed notes accompanying r 7.108.

**[2.306]**

### 6.43 Saving for powers of the court

Nothing in these Rules—

(a)      applies to or affects the powers of any court, in proceedings by or against the company, to order costs to be paid by the company, or the liquidator; or

(b)      affects the rights of any person to whom such costs are ordered to be paid.

**Derivation**—This rule derived from the Insolvency Rules 1986, SI 1986/1925, r 4.220.

**General note**—The discretion of the court is unfettered, but there are well-settled principles which will usually guide the courts in the exercise of their discretion: *Re Massey* (1870) 9 Eq 367. The court may apportion the assets in payment of expenses: *Re Dominion of Canada Plumbago Co* (1884) 27 ChD 33.

In making its determination the courts will only give a liquidator priority for his or her remuneration over liquidation expenses that would normally rank ahead of it where there are exceptional circumstances: *Re Linda Marie Ltd (in liquidation)* (1988) 4 BCC 463 at 472.

'**proceedings . . . against the company**'—Includes litigation with the company through its liquidators (*Unadkat & Co (Accountants) Ltd v Bhardwaj* [2006] EWHC 2785 (Ch), [2007] BCC 452 at [15]).

See the comments relating to s 156.

## CHAPTER 7

### LITIGATION EXPENSES AND PROPERTY SUBJECT TO A FLOATING CHARGE

**[2.307]**

**Note**

[Note: a document required by the Act or these Rules must also contain the standard contents set out in Part 1.]

**[2.308]**

### 6.44 Interpretation

(1)   In this Chapter—

        "approval" and "authorisation" respectively mean—

          (a)    where yet to be incurred, the approval; and

          (b)    where already incurred, the authorisation;

        of expenses specified in section 176ZA(1);

"the creditor" means—

    (a)    a preferential creditor of the company; or

    (b)    a holder of a debenture secured by, or a holder of, a floating charge created by the company;

"legal proceedings" means—

    (a)    proceedings under sections 212, 213, 214, 238, 239, 244 and 423 and any arbitration or other dispute resolution proceedings invoked for purposes corresponding to those to which the sections relate and any other proceedings, including arbitration or other dispute resolution procedures, which a liquidator has power to bring in the liquidator's own name for the purpose of preserving, realising, or getting in any of the assets of the company;

    (b)    legal actions and proceedings, arbitration or any other dispute resolution procedures which a liquidator has power to bring or defend in the name of the company; and

    (c)    negotiations intended to lead or leading to a settlement or compromise of any action, proceeding or procedure to which sub-paragraphs (a) or (b) relate;

"litigation expenses" means expenses of a winding up which—

    (a)    are properly chargeable or incurred in the preparation or conduct of any legal proceedings; and

    (b)    as expenses in the winding up, exceed, or in the opinion of the liquidator are likely to exceed (and only in so far as they exceed or are likely to exceed), in the aggregate £5,000; and

"specified creditor" means a creditor identified under rule 6.45(2).

(2)    Litigation expenses will not have the priority provided by section 176ZA over any claims to property comprised in or subject to a floating charge created by the company and must not be paid out of any such property unless and until approved or authorised in accordance with rules 6.45 to 6.48.

**Derivation**—This rule derived from the Insolvency Rules 1986, SI 1986/1925, r 4.218A.

**Amendments**—SI 2017/366.

**General note**—Rules 6.44–6.48 are equivalent to rr 7.111–7.116. The main difference is that r 6.45(2) is a separate rule in Part 7 (r 7.112) The precursors to rr 6.44–6.48, namely rr 4.218B–4.218E, were introduced to supplement s 176ZA, a provision enacted to overcome the House of Lords decision of *Buchler v Talbot* [2004] UKHL 9, [2004] 2 AC 298 that held that assets covered by a floating charge could not be used to pay expenses in the liquidation. The rules provide that a liquidator needs to obtain approval or authorisation for the use of charged assets for certain expenditure and then sets out the procedure to be followed. Reference should be had to the notes accompanying s 176ZA.

Essentially, this rule provides in para (2) that litigation expenses incurred by a liquidator (in relation to legal proceedings) will not have priority over the claims of a floating chargeholder unless approval (sought before the incurring of expenditure) or authorisation (sought after the incurring of expenditure) is obtained. It also acts as a definition provision for the following rules, which set out the procedure for the obtaining of the approval or authorisation.

'Creditor'—covers not only floating chargeholders, but also preferential creditors, who, according to s 176ZA, might be entitled to be paid out of the assets subject to a floating charge.

'legal proceedings'—means those which are initiated by liquidators in either their own name or on behalf of the company in order to recover assets or money so as to swell the size of the insolvent estate, and proceedings brought against the company and defended by the liquidator. Also, legal proceedings covers any negotiations which are designed to lead to a compromise or settlement of proceedings initiated by, or those defended by, the liquidator. It is only litigation expenses that are incurred in relation to legal proceedings, as defined, that must be approved or authorised. It is assumed that where other expenses are incurred in the legal process, such as seeking directions from the courts, will not have to be approved or authorised. It would also seem that expenses incurred by a liquidator in obtaining and being represented at a private examination under s 236 are not subject to the restrictions under these rules.

The rule does not cover legal proceedings under ss 242 and 243 as those sections only apply in Scotland, and the rule is limited to England and Wales.

See G Fidler 'Leyland Daf reversal and proposed new SI' (2007) 23 I L & P 181. Also, see A Keay, 'Litigation Expenses in Liquidations' (2009) 22 Insol Int 13.

[2.309]

### 6.45 Requirement for approval or authorisation

(1) Subject to rules 6.46 to 6.48, either paragraphs (3) and (4) apply or paragraph (5) applies where, in the course of winding up a company, the liquidator—

    (a)    ascertains that property is comprised in or subject to a floating charge;

    (b)    has personally instituted or proposes to institute or continue legal proceedings or is in the process of defending or proposes to defend any legal proceeding brought or likely to be brought against the company; and

    (c)    before or at any stage in those proceedings, is of the opinion that—

        (i)    the assets of the company available for payment of general creditors are or will be insufficient to pay litigation expenses; and

        (ii)    in order to pay litigation expenses the liquidator will have to have recourse to property comprised in or subject to a floating charge created by the company.

(2) As soon as reasonably practicable after the date on which the liquidator forms the opinion referred to in paragraph (1), the liquidator must identify the creditor who, in the liquidator's opinion at that time—

    (a)    has a claim to property comprised in or subject to a floating charge created by the company; and

    (b)    taking into account the value of that claim and any subsisting property then comprised in or secured by such a charge, appears to the liquidator to be the creditor most immediately likely of any persons having such claims to receive some payment in respect of a claim but whose claim would not be paid in full.

(3) The liquidator must request from the specified creditor the approval or authorisation of such amount for litigation expenses as the liquidator thinks fit.

(4) Where the liquidator identifies two or more specified creditors, the liquidator must seek from each of them approval or authorisation of such amount of litigation expenses as the liquidator thinks fit, apportioned between them ("the apportioned amount") according to the value of the property to the extent covered by their charges.

(5) For so long as the conditions specified in paragraph (1) subsist, the liquidator may, in the course of a winding up, make such further requests to the specified creditor or creditors for approval or authorisation of such further amount for litigation expenses as the liquidator thinks fit to be paid out of property comprised in or subject to a floating charge created by the company, taking into account any amount for litigation expenses previously approved or authorised and the value of the property comprised in or subject to the floating charge.

**Derivation**—This rule derived from the Insolvency Rules 1986, SI 1986/1925, r 4.218B.

**General note**—The rule explains that the liquidator, who has instituted or proposes to institute or continue legal proceedings or is in the process of defending or proposes to defend any legal proceeding brought or likely to be brought against the company must, as soon as reasonably practicable after determining that he or she will need to have recourse to assets subject to a floating charge, request from the creditor(s) with a claim over the assets approval or authorisation such amount for litigation expenses as he or she thinks necessary.

#### RULE 6.45(1)(b)(c)

These parts of the rule presuppose, inter alia, that the liquidator might have instituted proceedings and then ascertains that the proceedings are likely to lead to the incurring of greater expense than first thought.

**'Specified creditor'**—this person is mentioned in several paragraphs and is defined in r 6.45(2) as a creditor who appears to have a claim to the property. This covers chargeholders under the charge and also, possibly, preferential creditors, although the focus is on chargeholders. 'The specified creditor' is a person, who, according to s 176ZA(2), might be entitled to be paid out of the assets subject to a floating charge) and taking into account the value of that claim appears to the liquidator to be the creditor most immediately likely to receive some payment in respect of his or her claim but whose claim would not be paid in full.

#### RULE 6.45(5)

The paragraph makes it clear that the liquidator is entitled to make any number of requests for approval or authorisation, but the paragraph also appears to indicate that, given the words 'further amount' he or she is not permitted to go back to the creditors and request approval or authorisation for amounts that have been rejected earlier. In other words the liquidator cannot seek to wear down the creditors by repeated requests in relation to the same expenses.

## [2.310]

### 6.46 Request for approval or authorisation

(1)   All requests made by the liquidator for approval or authorisation must include the following—

(a)   a statement describing the nature of the legal proceedings, including, where relevant, the statutory provision under which proceedings are or are to be brought and the grounds upon which the liquidator relies;

(b)   a statement specifying the amount or apportioned amount of litigation expenses for which approval or authorisation is sought ("the specified amount");

(c)   notice that approval or authorisation or other reply to the request must be made in writing within 28 days from the date of its being received ("the specified time limit"); and

(d)   a statement explaining the consequences of a failure to reply within the specified time limit.

(2)   Where anything in paragraph (1) requires the inclusion of any information, the disclosure of which could be seriously prejudicial to the winding up of the company, the liquidator may—

(a)   exclude such information from any of the above statements or notices if accompanied by a statement to that effect; or

(b)   include it on terms—

(i)    that bind the creditor to keep the information confidential; and

(ii)   that include an undertaking on the part of the liquidator to apply to the court for an order that so much of the information as may be kept in the files of the court is not to be open to public inspection.

(3)   The creditor may within the specified time limit apply to the liquidator in writing for such further particulars as is reasonable and in such a case, the time limit specified in paragraph (1)(c) will apply from the date of the creditor's receipt of the liquidator's response to any such request.

(4)   Where the liquidator requires the approval or authorisation of two or more creditors, the liquidator must deliver a request to each creditor, containing the matters listed in paragraph (1) and also giving—

(a)   the number of creditors concerned;

(b)   the total value of their claims, or if not known, as it is estimated to be by the liquidator immediately before delivering any such request; and

(c)   to each preferential creditor, notice that approval or authorisation of the specified amount will be taken to be given where a majority in value of those preferential creditors who respond within the specified time limit are in favour of it; or

(d)   where rule 6.45 applies, notice to the specified creditors that the amount of litigation expenses will be apportioned between them in accordance with that rule and notice of the value of the portion allocated to, and the identity of, the specified creditors affected by that apportionment.

**Derivation**—This rule derived from the Insolvency Rules 1986, SI 1986/1925, r 4.218C.

**General note**—the rule and the succeeding one set out the contents of any request made to a creditor for approval or authorisation. The rule is nearly the same as r 4.218C. Rule 4.218C(2)(b) was not included as part of r 6.46. This is because r 4.218C(2)(b) referred to the time when under a previous version of Sch 4 of the Act when liquidators needed to obtain other approvals before initiating certain kinds of proceedings.

**'value of their claims'** (r 6.42(4)(b))—it is likely to be not uncommon that creditors will take issue with the amount which the liquidator states is the value of their claims. There is no procedure for determining any dispute. One would think that the parties have to try and resolve it, and if they cannot, it might be a matter to be decided by the court if the liquidator has to end up applying to the court for approval under r 6.48. One would think that a creditor would be able to apply under s 112.

## [2.311]

### 6.47 Grant of approval or authorisation

(1) Where the liquidator fails to include in the liquidator's request any one of the matters, statements or notices required to be specified by paragraph (1) or paragraphs (1) and (4), of rule 6.46, the request for approval or authorisation will be treated as not having been made.

(2) Subject to paragraphs (3), (4) and (5), approval or authorisation will be taken to have been given where the specified amount has been requested by the liquidator, and—

    (a) that amount is approved or authorised within the specified time limit; or

    (b) a different amount is approved or authorised within the specified time limit and the liquidator considers it sufficient.

(3) Where the liquidator requires the approval or authorisation of two or more preferential creditors, approval or authorisation will be taken to be given where a majority in value of those who respond within the specified time limit approve or authorise—

    (a) the specified amount; or

    (b) a different amount which the liquidator considers sufficient.

(4) Where a majority in value of two or more preferential creditors propose an amount other than that specified by the liquidator, they will be taken to have approved or authorised an amount equal to the lowest of the amounts so proposed.

(5) In any case in which there is no response in writing within the specified time limit to the liquidator's request—

    (a) at all, or

    (b) at any time following the liquidator's provision of further particulars under rule 6.46(3),

the liquidator's request will be taken to have been approved or authorised from the date of the expiry of that time limit.

**Derivation**—This rule derived from the Insolvency Rules 1986, SI 1986/1925, r 4.218D.

**General note**—The rule duplicates r 4.218D of the previous rules. It provides the mechanics involved in the granting of approval or authorisation at the request of the liquidator.

**RULE 6.47(2)(3)**

Creditors might decide not to approve the amount sought by the liquidator and propose a lower amount, and if that occurs and the liquidator accepts that the amount is sufficient, approval or authorisation is deemed to be granted. This might mean that liquidators will seek an ambit amount knowing that creditors might seek to reduce the amount for approval or authorisation.

**RULE 6.47(5)**

Importantly if creditors who have claims in the charged assets do not respond to the liquidator's request at all or within 28 days of the date on which the request is received, then the request is deemed to be approved or authorised (r 6.46(1)(c) and (3)).

## [2.312]

### 6.48 Application to the court by the liquidator

(1) In the circumstances specified below the court may, on the application of the liquidator, approve or authorise such amount of litigation expenses as it thinks just.

(2) Except where paragraph (3) applies, the liquidator may apply to the court for an order approving or authorising an amount for litigation expenses only where the specified creditor (or, if more than one, any one of them)—

    (a) is or is intended to be a defendant in the legal proceedings in relation to which the litigation expenses have been or are to be incurred; or

    (b) has been requested to approve or authorise the amount specified under rule 6.46(1)(b) and has—

    (i)     declined to approve or authorise, as the case may be, the specified amount;

    (ii)    approved or authorised an amount which is less than the specified amount and which lesser amount the liquidator considers insufficient; or

    (iii)   made such application for further particulars or other response to the liquidator's request as is, in the liquidator's opinion, unreasonable.

(3)   Where the liquidator thinks that circumstances are such that the liquidator requires urgent approval or authorisation of litigation expenses, the liquidator may apply to the court for approval or authorisation either—

    (a)   without seeking approval or authorisation from the specified creditor; or

    (b)   if sought, before the expiry of the specified time limit.

(4)   The court may grant such application for approval or authorisation—

    (a)   if the liquidator satisfies the court of the urgency of the case; and

    (b)   subject to such terms and conditions as the court thinks just.

(5)   The liquidator must, at the same time as making any application to the court under this rule, deliver copies of it to the specified creditor, unless the court orders otherwise.

(6)   The specified creditor (or, if more than one, any one of them) is entitled to be heard on any such application unless the court orders otherwise.

(7)   The court may grant approval or authorisation subject to such terms and conditions as it may think just, including terms and conditions relating to the amount or nature of the litigation expenses and as to any obligation to make further applications to the court under this rule.

(8)   The costs of the liquidator's application under this rule, including the costs of any specified creditor appearing or represented on it, are an expense of the winding up unless the court orders otherwise.

**Derivation**—This rule derived from the Insolvency Rules 1986, SI 1986/1925, r 4.218E.

**General note**—The rule duplicates r 4.218E of the previous rules, for the most part, with some structural differences. It provides a liquidator with the right to apply for the approval or authorisation of the court in certain circumstances, and one would expect that this will usually be where the creditors, with claims over the charged assets, refuse to approve or authorise the amount requested by the liquidator at all or where the amount suggested by the creditors is not acceptable to the liquidator. The rule goes on to explain the procedure and process involved.

The court had a discretion to order the dispensing of service on, and the attendance of, a creditor who is or intended to be a defendant in proceedings brought by the liquidator, but the default position was that the creditor should be served and entitled to be heard as it is fundamental to English law that both sides are heard. A court should not entertain an application where no notice has been given except where either the giving of notice would enable the defendant to defeat the purpose of the application or there had not been sufficient time to give notice before the application was required in order to prevent the commission of a wrongful act: *Re Premier Motor Auctions Leeds Ltd (in liq)* [2015] EWHC 3568 (Ch) at [31]–[33]. In this case the creditor had a serious financial interest in the result of the application made under this rule for if the liquidators were successful their legal expenses would take priority over the creditor's rights under its floating charge.

'Costs'—There is no indication whether the costs of any appeal from the original hearing, by either the liquidator or the creditor(s), will be covered by para (8).

## PART 7   WINDING UP BY THE COURT

**[2.313]**

**General note**—Under the previous rules the various kinds of liquidation were not divided into separate Parts. Now the Rules that were put in force on 6 April 2017 provide for three separate Parts for members' voluntary liquidations (Part 5), creditors' voluntary liquidations (Part 6) and compulsory (court) liquidations (Part 7). This obviates the need, as was the situation in Part 4 of the previous rules, for notes in individual rules to indicate that they were not applicable to either creditors' voluntary liquidations or were so applicable. This makes it easier to discern which rules apply to each kind of winding up. It does mean that there are some overlaps in the provisions contained in the respective Parts.

## CHAPTER 1

### APPLICATION OF PART

**[2.314]**

#### 7.1 Application of Part 7
This Part applies to winding up by the court.

## CHAPTER 2

### THE STATUTORY DEMAND (SECTIONS 123(1)(A) AND 222(1)(A))

**[2.315]**

#### 7.2 Interpretation
A demand served by a creditor on a company under section 123(1)(a) (registered companies) or 222(1)(a) (unregistered companies) is referred to in this Part as "a statutory demand".

**Derivation**—This rule derived from the Insolvency Rules 1986, SI 1986/1925, r 4.4.

**General note**—The failure to comply with a statutory demand used to be the most frequent way of establishing a company's inability to pay its debts under s 123. Now effectively establishing that the company is unable to pay its debts as they fall due is employed more often, but demands are still employed. See s 122(1)(e).

Unlike the procedure provided for in bankruptcy, there is no provision in the Act or Rules for the company to apply to the court for the setting aside of a demand. A company should, if it wishes to resist the demand, apply to the court for an injunction which restrains the presentation of a petition while the issue of indebtedness is resolved.

**[2.316]**

#### 7.3 The statutory demand
(1) A statutory demand must be headed either "Statutory Demand under section 123(1)(a) of the Insolvency Act 1986" or "Statutory Demand under section 222(1)(a) of the Insolvency Act 1986" (as applicable) and must contain—

    (a)    identification details for the company;

    (b)    the registered office of the company (if any);

    (c)    the name and address of the creditor;

    (d)    either a statement that the demand is made under section 123(1)(a) or a statement that it is made under section 222(1)(a);

    (e)    the amount of the debt and the consideration for it (or, if there is no consideration, the way in which it arises);

    (f)    if the demand is founded on a judgment or order of a court, details of the judgment or order;

    (g)    if the creditor is entitled to the debt by way of assignment, details of the original creditor and any intermediary assignees;

    (h)    a statement that the company must pay the debt claimed in the demand within 21 days of service of the demand on the company after which the creditor may present a winding-up petition unless the company offers security for the debt and the creditor agrees to accept security or the company compounds the debt with the creditor's agreement;

    (i)    the name of an individual with whom an officer or representative of the company may communicate with a view to securing or compounding the debt to the creditor's satisfaction;

    (j)    the named individual's address, electronic address and telephone number (if any);

    (k)    a statement that the company has the right to apply to the court for an injunction restraining the creditor from presenting or advertising a petition for the winding up of the company; and

(l)    the name of the court (and hearing centre if applicable) to which, according to the present information, the company must make the application (i.e. the High Court, the County Court at Central London or a named hearing centre of the County Court, as the case may be).

(2)    The following must be separately identified in the demand (if claimed) with the amount or rate of the charge and the grounds on which payment is claimed—

(a)    any charge by way of interest of which notice had not previously been delivered to the company as included in its liability; and

(b)    any other charge accruing from time to time.

(3)    The amount claimed for such charges must be limited to that which has accrued due at the date of the demand.

(4)    The demand must be dated, and authenticated either by the creditor, or a person authorised to make the demand on the creditor's behalf.

(5)    A demand which is authenticated by a person other than the creditor must state that the person is authorised to make the demand on the creditor's behalf and state the person's relationship to the creditor.

**Derivation**—This rule derived from the Insolvency Rules 1986, SI 1986/1925, rr 4.5, 4.6, Sch 4, Fm 4.1.

**General note**—The statutory demand is not a court document (*Practice Direction – Insolvency Proceedings* (July 2020) [2020] BPIR 1211, para 5.5). There is no prescribed form for use. But the rule sets out the contents of the demand. According to *Practice Direction – Insolvency Proceedings* (July 2020) [2020] BPIR 1211, the statutory demand must contain the information set out in this rule (para 9.1). The Practice Direction provides that the demand should, as far as possible, follow the form which appears at a specified website address. The address given in the Practice Direction is longer operative, but an HMCTS approved form may be found either at https://www.gov.uk/government/collections/bankruptcy-and-insolvency-forms, or https://www.gov.uk/government/publications/demand-immediate-payment-of-a-debt-from-a-limited-company-form-sd1.

The details to be contained in the demand are more than what was included in the previous rules. This is partly due to the fact that there is no longer any prescribed form (former Form 4.1 used to be required) as there was under the previous rules, but as mentioned above the Practice Direction does specify a form that should be followed. Creditors must ensure that those matters referred to in r 7.3 are contained in the demand.

**Defects**—The cases which have been decided under the Act indicate a more liberal approach taken by the courts as far as defects in the demand are concerned. If a demand overstates the amount owed by a debtor to a creditor, it has been held in *Re A Debtor (No 490/SD/91)* [1992] 1 WLR 507, [1992] 2 All ER 664, [1993] BCLC 164, that the demand was not necessarily invalid as the debtor could have avoided the presumption of insolvency by paying what he admitted was owing and taking issue with the demand concerning the balance. The demand will remain valid if the amount which is undisputedly owed exceeds £750.

**RULE 7.3(1)(k)**

The right mentioned in this paragraph may provide a debtor with the means by which to oppose the demand. The right is discussed in the notes relating to r 7.24.

**RULE 7.3(4)**

The statutory demand must be authenticated by the creditor or someone authorised by him or her. But if only one of two trustees of a trust that is owed money by the debtor company authenticate the demand, it will not be effective unless the non-authenticating trustee gave authority to the other to make the demand: *115 Constitution Road Pty Ltd v Downey* [2008] NSWSC 997.

See s 123(1)(a) and the notes accompanying s 123.

See, A Keay *McPherson and Keay's Law of Company Liquidation* (Sweet and Maxwell, 4th edn, 2018) at 117–130 in particular.

## CHAPTER 3

### PETITION FOR WINDING-UP ORDER

**[2.317]**

**Note**

[Notes: (1) for petitions by a contributory or relevant office-holder (an administrator, administrative receiver or supervisor of a CVA) see Chapter 4;

(2) a document required by the Act or these Rules must also contain the standard contents set out in Part 1.]

**[2.318]**

### 7.4 Application of this Chapter

(1) This Chapter applies subject to rule 7.25 to—
- (a) a petition for winding up presented by a contributory; or
- (b) a petition for winding up presented by a relevant office-holder of the company.

(2) "Relevant office-holder" in this Part means an administrator, administrative receiver and supervisor of a CVA.

**General note**—The petition is the court document that sees the commencement of winding-up proceedings in the courts. Most petitions are presented by creditors who have not been paid by the debtor company. Petitions might be presented by other parties, and they are given this right under s 124 of the Act, some other provision in the Act or in the provisions of other legislation. The following rules apply to a petition presented to the courts. Some do not apply to petitions presented by a contributory or an office-holder. Rule 7.25 indicates the provisions of Chapter 3 of Part 4 that in fact do apply to petitions presented by a contributory or an office-holder and with modifications. Chapter 4 focuses on petitions presented by a contributory or an office-holder. All of the rules in Chapter 3 apply to the most prevalent petitions, namely those presented by creditors.

**[2.319]**

### 7.5 Contents of petition

(1) The petition must contain—
- (a) the name of the court (and hearing centre if applicable);
- (b) the name and address of the petitioner;
- (c) identification details for the company subject to the petition;
- (d) the company's registered office (if any);
- (e) the date the company was incorporated and the enactment under which it was incorporated;
- (f) the total number of issued shares of the company and the manner in which they are divided up;
- (g) the aggregate nominal value of those shares;
- (h) the amount of capital paid up or credited as paid up;
- (i) a statement of the nature of the company's business if known;
- (j) the grounds on which the winding-up order is sought;
- (k) where the ground for the winding-up order is section 122(1)(a), a statement that the company has by special resolution resolved that the company be wound up by the court and the date of such resolution;
- (l) where the ground for the winding-up order is section 122(1)(f) or 221(5)(b) and a statutory demand has been served on the company, a statement that such a demand has been served and the date of service and that the company is insolvent and unable to pay its debts;
- (m) a statement whether the company is an Article 1.2 undertaking;
- (n) a statement whether the proceedings will be COMI proceedings, establishment proceedings or proceedings to which the EU Regulation as it has effect in the law of the United Kingdom does not apply and that the reasons for so stating are given in a witness statement;
- (o) a statement that in the circumstances it is just and equitable that the company should be wound up;
- (p) a statement that the petitioner therefore applies for an order that the company may be wound up by the court under the Act, or that such other order may be made as the court thinks just;
- (q) the name and address of any person on whom the petitioner intends to serve the petition; and
- (r) the contact details of the petitioner's solicitor (if any).

(2) The petition must also contain a blank box for the court to complete with the details of the venue for hearing the petition.

**Derivation**—This rule derived from the Insolvency Rules 1986, SI 1986/1925, Sch 4, Fm 4.2.

**Amendments**—SI 2017/1115; SI 2019/146, as from IP completion day (as defined in the European Union (Withdrawal Agreement) Act 2020, s 39(1)–(5)).

**CIGA 2020**—This provision is affected by temporary measures at Sch 10, para 19(3) of CIGA 2020 and by the *Insolvency Practice Direction relating to the Corporate Insolvency and Governance Act 2020* [2020] BPIR 1207 (at Appendix 4 of this book).

**General note**—The rule sets out the contents of the petition and was newly introduced by the 2016 Rules. Before these Rules were introduced there was a prescribed form to be used for petitions and it included the matters that were necessary for a petition.

For a form of the petition, see: https://www.gov.uk/government/collections/bankruptcy-and-ins olvency-forms.

According to para 9.5 of the *Practice Direction: Insolvency Proceedings* (July 2020) [2020] BPIR 1211), where, in the usual case involving a creditor's petition, the petitioning creditor relies on failure to pay a debt, details of the debt relied on should be given in the petition (whether or not they have been given in any statutory demand served in respect of the debt), including the amount of the debt, its nature and the date or dates on or between which it was incurred.

If the petition is brought in relation to a company that has been struck off the register, the petition should state that the company has been struck off and the petition should include as part of the prayer for relief a request for an order that the company be restored to the register (*Practice Direction: Insolvency Proceedings* (July 2020) [2020] BPIR 1211 at para 9.7).

## [2.320]

### 7.6 Verification of petition

(1) The petition must be verified by a statement of truth.

(2) Where the petition is in respect of debts due to different creditors then the debt to each creditor must be verified separately.

(3) A statement of truth which is not contained in or endorsed upon the petition must identify the petition and must contain—

    (a)    identification details for the company;

    (b)    the name of the petitioner; and

    (c)    the name of the court (and hearing centre if applicable) in which the petition is to be presented.

(4) The statement of truth must be authenticated and dated by or on behalf of the petitioner.

(5) Where the person authenticating the statement of truth is not the petitioner, or one of the petitioners, the statement of truth must state—

    (a)    the name and postal address of the person making the statement;

    (b)    the capacity in which, and the authority by which, the person authenticates the statement; and

    (c)    the means of that person's knowledge of the matters verified in the statement of truth.

(6) If the petition is based on a statutory demand, and more than four months have elapsed between the service of the demand and the presentation of the petition, a witness statement must explain the reasons for the delay.

(7) A statement of truth verifying more than one petition must include in its title the names of the companies to which it relates and must set out, in relation to each company, the statements relied on by the petitioner; and a clear and legible photocopy of the statement of truth must be filed with each petition which it verifies.

(8) The witness statement must give the reasons for the statement that the proceedings will be COMI proceedings, establishment proceedings or proceedings to which the EU Regulation as it has effect in the law of the United Kingdom does not apply.

**Derivation**—This rule derived from the Insolvency Rules 1986, SI 1986/1925, r 4.12.

**Amendments**—SI 2017/1115; SI 2019/146, as from IP completion day (as defined in the European Union (Withdrawal Agreement) Act 2020, s 39(1)–(5)).

**General note**—The statement of truth must be made after the petition has been prepared: *Re Western Building Benefit Society* (1864) 33 Beav 368; 55 ER 409; *Re E McCurdy Ltd* [1957] NZLR 752 at 753.

In circumstances where someone other than the petitioner authenticates the statement of truth, it is likely that he or she must state that he or she believes the debt on which the petition relies is owed, but if he or she does not in fact hold that belief, and can be said to be acting unreasonably, then the person may be held personally liable for costs incurred by the company: *Re A Company (No 006798 of 1995)* [1996] 2 All ER 417.

A form for verification is available at: https://www.gov.uk/government/collections/bankruptcy-and-insolvency-forms.

**RULE 7.6(6)**

If a petition is not presented within a reasonable time following the service of a statutory demand there might be some concern that the debtor should not be deemed to be unable to pay its debts. The requirement for the explanation of the delay in presenting is possibly to prevent a creditor from allowing a demand to hang over the head of a debtor for a long period and for the creditor to use that as a reserve measure for a long period in which to coerce payment of the debt owed. The winding-up process is not to be seen as a substitute for debt collection action: *Re Lympne Investments Pty Ltd* [1972] 1 WLR 523 at 527; *Re A Company (No 001573 of 1983)* (1983) 1 BCC 98, 937 at 98, 939; *Re A Company (No 0010656 of 1990)* [1991] BCLC 464 at 467.

The statement of truth verifying the petition should be made no more than 10 business days before the date of issue of the petition: *Practice Direction – Insolvency Proceedings* (July 2018) [2018] BPIR 1465, para 9.6.

## [2.321]

### 7.7 Petition: presentation and filing

(1)   The petition must be filed with the court.

(2)   A petition may not be filed unless—

    (a)   a receipt for the deposit payable to the official receiver is produced on presentation of the petition; or

    (b)   the Secretary of State has given notice to the court that the petitioner has made suitable alternative arrangements for the payment of the deposit and that notice has not been revoked.

(3)   A notice of alternative arrangements for the deposit may be revoked by a further notice filed with the court.

(4)   The court must fix a venue for hearing the petition, and this must be endorsed on the petition and the copies.

(5)   Each copy of the petition must have the seal of the court applied to it, and must be delivered to the petitioner.

**Derivation**—This rule derived from the Insolvency Rules 1986, SI 1986/1925, r 4.7.

**General note**—Section 124 sets out the persons who may present a petition, although other legislation may grant others power to do so, eg, Minister for Agriculture (Agricultural Marketing Act 1958).

There are two steps to the presentation of a petition. First, there is the delivery of the petition to the court (filing). The second part is the issue of the petition by the court: *Re Blights Builders Ltd* [2006] EWHC 3549 (Ch), [2007] 3 All ER 776; [2008] 1 BCLC 245.

**The petition**—There is now no prescribed form for the petition. A petition must include those matters specified in r 7.5.

The *Practice Direction – Insolvency Proceedings* (July 2020) [2020] BPIR 1211 makes the point that before presenting a winding up petition, the creditor who is petitioning must conduct a search to ensure that no petition is pending. Save in exceptional circumstances a second winding up petition should not be presented whilst a prior petition is pending. A petitioner who presents a petition while another petition is pending does so at risk as to costs (para 9.2).

Not infrequently, petitions suffer from some defect. A petition will not be held to be invalid due to formal defects or any irregularity unless the court takes the view that substantial injustice has been caused by the defect or irregularity, and the injustice is unable to be remedied by court order (see r 12.64 and the notes accompanying it). Traditionally permission is given to correct spelling (eg *Re J & P Sussmann Ltd* [1958] 1 WLR 519) and other trivial errors (*Re Army & Navy Hotel Ltd* (1886) 31 ChD 644) by amendment (*Re Vidiofusion Ltd* [1974] 1 WLR 1548), although sometimes the petition will be ordered to stand over while the giving of notice (re-advertisement) takes place. It has been said that if the following apply, then any error in spelling will be able to be corrected:

- No other company is on the register with any similar name;
- The correct and erroneous names have, substantially, the same pronunciation.
- There is no marked difference between the spellings of the correct and erroneous names.
- The error does not materially affect the alphabetical order of the names (*Re Vidiofusion Ltd* at 1549) (see r 12.64 and notes under the heading, 'Curing defects in winding-up (and bankruptcy) petitions').

Where companies are petitioners and it is intended to present at the High Court, they must instruct solicitors to present the petitions: *Re a Company (No 001029 of 1990)* [1991] BCLC 567. This does not apply in relation to petitions presented in the county court: *Charles P Kinnel and Co Ltd Harding, Wace and Co* [1918] 1 KB 405.

Where petitions are founded on a judgment relating to a debt owed to the petitioning creditor, they used to have to be presented within 6 years of the judgment becoming enforceable or else the proceedings were statue-barred under s 24 of the Limitation Act 1980 (*Re a Debtor (No 50A SD of 1995)* [1997] 1 BCLC 280). More recently it has been held that a judgment debt which is more than 6 years old may, however, form the basis for a petition: *Ridgeway Motors (Isleworth) Ltd v Altis Ltd* [2004] EWHC 1535 (Ch), [2004] BPIR 1323 and the Court of Appeal has upheld that decision ([2005] EWCA Civ 92, [2005] 1 WLR 2871, [2005] 2 All ER 304, [2005] 2 BCLC 61; [2005] BPIR 423).

If a company wishes to resist a petition, it will often consider making an application to have the court restrain the presentation of the petition. See r 7.24 and the accompanying notes.

**The deposit**—Unless the petition is one in respect of which r 7.7(2)(b) applies, a petition will not be treated as having been presented until the court fee and official receiver's deposit have been paid (*Practice Direction – Insolvency Proceedings* (July 2020) [2020] BPIR 1211 at para 9.3.1). The details concerning payment are set out in paras 9.3.2 to 9.3.4 of the Practice Direction. The paragraphs deal with the situation where a petition is filed electronically.

If a winding up order is made but subsequently rescinded the petitioner was entitled to be repaid the deposit provided that the assets available to the company were insufficient to discharge the official receiver's administration fee: *Re Direct Affinity Events Ltd* [2019] EWHC 3063 (Ch) at [47].

## [2.322]

### 7.8 Court to which petition is to be presented where the company is subject to a CVA or is in administration

(1)  A petition which is filed in relation to a company for which there is in force a CVA must be presented to the court or hearing centre to which the nominee's report under section 2 was submitted or where the documents for a moratorium under section 1A were filed.

(2)  A petition which is filed in relation to a company which is in administration must be presented to the court or hearing centre of the court having jurisdiction for the administration.

**Derivation**—This rule derived from the Insolvency Rules 1986, SI 1986/1925, r 4.7.

**General note**—This used to be part of the rule which is now r 7.7, but now it is contained in its own rule.

This rule, with the necessary modifications, applies to petitions presented by contributories or relevant office-holders: r 7.25(1). Also, see r 7.4.

## [2.323]

### 7.9 Copies of petition to be served on company or delivered to other persons

(1)  Where this rule requires the petitioner to serve a copy of the petition on the company or deliver a copy to another person the petitioner must, when filing the petition with the court, file an additional copy with the court for each such person.

(2)  Where the petitioner is not the company the petitioner must serve a sealed copy of the petition on the company in accordance with Schedule 4.

(3)  If, to the petitioner's knowledge—

    (a)    the company is in the course of being wound up voluntarily, the petitioner must deliver a copy of the petition to the liquidator;

    (b)    an administrative receiver has been appointed in relation to the company, or the company is in administration, the petitioner must deliver a copy of the petition to the receiver or the administrator; or

(c)     there is in force for the company a CVA, the petitioner must deliver a copy of the petition to the supervisor of the CVA; . . .

(d)     . . ..

(4)   If either the Financial Conduct Authority or Prudential Regulation Authority is entitled to be heard at the hearing of the petition in accordance with section 371 of the Financial Services and Markets Act 2000, the petitioner must deliver a copy of the petition to the Financial Conduct Authority or Prudential Regulation Authority (as appropriate).

(5)   Where this rule requires the petitioner to deliver a copy of the petition to any other person that copy must be delivered within three business days after the day on which the petition is served on the company or where the petitioner is the company within three business days of the company receiving the sealed petition.

**Derivation**—This rule derived from the Insolvency Rules 1986, SI 1986/1925, r 4.10.

**Amendments**—SI 2019/146, as from IP completion day (as defined in the European Union (Withdrawal Agreement) Act 2020, s 39(1)–(5)).

**CIGA 2020**—This provision is affected by temporary measures in the *Insolvency Practice Direction relating to the Corporate Insolvency and Governance Act 2020* [2020] BPIR 1207 (at APPENDIX 4 of this book).

**General note**—Rule 7.9(1), (4) and (5), with the necessary modifications, apply to petitions presented by contributories or relevant office-holders: r 7.25(1). Also, see r 7.4.

If a petition is not served correctly then any winding-up order made on the petition is a nullity and the court is able to rescind it (*Southbourne Trading Co Ltd v HMRC* [2017] EWHC 3737 (Ch), [2018] BCC 604).

## [2.324]

### 7.10 Notice of petition

(1)   Unless the court otherwise directs, the petitioner must give notice of the petition.

(2)   The notice must state—

(a)     that a petition has been presented for the winding up of the company;

(b)     in the case of an overseas company, the address at which service of the petition was effected;

(c)     the name and address of the petitioner;

(d)     the date on which the petition was presented;

(e)     the venue fixed for the hearing of the petition;

(f)      the name and address of the petitioner's solicitor (if any); and

(g)     that any person intending to appear at the hearing (whether to support or oppose the petition) must give notice of that intention in accordance with rule 7.14.

(3)   The notice must be gazetted.

(4)   The notice must be made to appear—

(a)     if the petitioner is the company itself, not less than seven business days before the day appointed for the hearing; and

(b)     otherwise, not less than seven business days after service of the petition on the company, nor less than seven business days before the day appointed for the hearing.

(5)   The court may dismiss the petition if notice of it is not given in accordance with this rule.

**Derivation**—This rule derived from the Insolvency Rules 1986, SI 1986/1925, r 4.11.

**CIGA 2020**—This provision is affected by temporary measures at Sch 10, para 19(2) of CIGA 2020 and the amendments to Sch 10 in The Corporate Insolvency and Governance Act 2020 (Coronavirus) (Extension of the Relevant Period) Regulations 2020 (SI 2020/1031), regs 1, 2(3), The Corporate Insolvency and Governance Act 2020 (Coronavirus) (Extension of the Relevant Period) (No 2) Regulations 2020 (SI 2020/1483), reg 2 and The Corporate Insolvency and Governance Act 2020 (Coronavirus) (Extension of the Relevant Period) Regulations 2021, reg 3(4) (SI 2021/375)). The CIGA 2020 as amended provides that the requirement to give notice in relation to a petition presented between 27 April 2020 and 30 June 2021 does not apply until such time as the court has made a determination in relation to the question of whether it is likely that the court will be able to make an order under s 122(1)(f) (as amended by The Corporate Insolvency and Governance Act 2020 (Coronavirus) (Extension of the Relevant Period) Regulations 2020 (SI 2020/1031), regs 1, 2(3), The Corporate Insolvency and Governance Act 2020 (Coronavirus) (Extension of the Relevant Period) (No 2) Regulations 2020 (SI 2020/1483), reg 2 and The Corporate Insolvency and Governance Act 2020 (Coronavirus) (Extension of the Relevant Period) Regulations 2021 (SI 2021/375), reg 3(4)).

**General note**—Until the enactment of the Insolvency (Amendment) Rules 2009 (SI 2009/642) this rule and related ones referred to the advertisement of the petition. Now reference is made to the giving of notice of the petition. The existing case law on advertising is likely to be applied to the changed rule. The giving of notice of the petition is an important step for two critical reasons. First, it enables other creditors and the contributories an opportunity of supporting or opposing winding up and, secondly, it acts as a notification to the public that a petition has been presented: *Applied Data Base Ltd v Secretary of State* [1995] 1 BCLC 272. The latter reason encompasses putting on notice persons who might trade with the company during the period between the time of the presentation of the petition and the time when the petition is determined by a court, as such persons might be affected by s 127: *Re a Company (No 007923 of 1994)* [1995] 1 WLR 953, [1995] BCLC 440, CA. See the discussion accompanying s 127.

The company has the onus of establishing that notice of the giving of the petition should not be in accordance with the specific process set out in the rule: *Re Normandy Marketing Ltd* [1994] Ch 198; *Re a Company (No 007923 of 1994)* [1995] 1 WLR 953, [1995] BCLC 440.

The court can exercise its discretion in r 7.10(1) and dispense with the giving of notice. A reasonably recent example of a case where the court did dispense with the need to give notice was *Secretary of State for Business Innovation and Skills v APW Asset Management Ltd* [2015] All ER (D) 160 (Apr).

On some occasions in the past re-advertisement of a petition, where the petition was defective, has been dispensed with (*Re Vidiofusion Ltd* [1974] 1 WLR 1548, [1974] 1 All ER 76) (see r 12.64 and notes under the heading 'Curing defects in winding-up (and bankruptcy) petitions'), though this is not usually done unless: the error in the petition is of a trifling kind, and one that is not likely to mislead (*Re J & P Sussman Ltd* [1958] 1 WLR 519); and the company itself does not oppose the petition: *Re Worthing Royal Sea House Hotel Co* (1872) WN 74; *Re McLean & Co* [1887] WN 8. There is an Australian authority that has held that a winding-up order may be made where the breach of the rules on advertising is unintentional and inadvertent and where the company has demonstrated no interest in opposing the proceedings: *Melcann Ltd v Marmlon Holdings* (1991) 9 ACLC 678.

**Gazetted**—*Practice Direction – Insolvency Proceedings* (July 2020) [2020] BPIR 1211 at para 9.8 states that copies of every notice gazetted in connection with a winding up petition must be lodged with the court as soon as possible after publication and in any event not later than 5 business days before the hearing of the petition. This direction applies even if the notice is defective in any way (eg is published on a date not in accordance with the Insolvency Rules, or omits or misprints some important words) or if the petitioner decides not to pursue the petition (eg on receiving payment).

**Timing of the giving of notice**—The fact that giving of notice before the elapse of 7 business days after service of the petition is not allowed is to provide the company with time in which either to pay the debt if it is not disputed, or to make an application for an injunction to prevent the giving of the notice of the petition to wind up: *Re Signland Ltd* [1982] 2 All ER 609; *Secretary of State for Trade and Industry v North West Holdings plc* [1999] 1 BCLC 425, CA. The time delay also gives the company an opportunity to apply for an order pursuant to s 127 validating transactions occurring after the presentation of a petition: *Re Bill Hennessey Associates Ltd* [1992] BCC 386; *Re a Company (No 0013925 of 1991)* [1992] BCLC 562. The giving of notice before the time that the application is served on the company is clearly premature and a serious breach of the rules: *Re Signland Ltd* [1982] 2 All ER 609 at 610. It may well lead to the dismissal of the petition: r 7.10(5). This occurred in *HMRC v Green Eye Events Ltd* [2010] EWHC 1403 (Ch), under the precursor to r 7.10(5), when the process server delivered the petition to the wrong address and the petition did not come to the notice of the company until the date before the giving of notice.

It would seem that the reference to 'giving notice' in r 7.9 is only to the giving of notice in the Gazette, so that it is only the premature giving of notice of the petition in the Gazette that would cause a court to dismiss it pursuant to r 7.9(5) (which provides that the court may dismiss a petition if notice is not duly given according to the Rules): *Secretary of State for Trade and Industry v North West Holdings plc* [1999] 1 BCLC 425, CA. In this case the court declined to dismiss the petition where press releases from the petitioner, the Department of Trade and Industry, were issued about the fact that a petition had been presented, before the petition was advertised in the Gazette. Nevertheless, the court said that premature advertising of the petition could be regarded generally as an abuse and the petition could be dismissed by the court on the basis that the court has the inherent power to control its own proceedings. In this case the Court of Appeal appeared to be influenced in deciding not to strike out the petition by the fact that the company was subject to provisional liquidation when the press releases were issued.

In *Australian Beverage Distributors Pty Ltd v Evans & Tate Premium Wines Pty Ltd* [2007] NSWCA 51, the New South Wales Court of Appeal took the view that the issuing of a press release by the petitioner on the day of the service of the petition on the company was able to be regarded as an irregularity that did not lead to the dismissal of the application. However, because the action in this case was intended to cause harm, the court held that a dismissal order should be made.

In coming to a decision on whether there has been an abuse, the court may take cognisance of the petitioner's conduct prior to, and following, the petition's presentation (*Re Doreen Boards Ltd* [1996] 1 BCLC 501 (the petitioner advised creditors that she intended to present a petition against the company and informed the Inland Revenue once the petition had been presented, but before formal advertisement of the petition). It is likely that the kind of circumstances where the court would find that there was an abuse of process occurred in *Re a Company (No 007020 of 1996)* [1998] 2 BCLC 54 where the creditor undertook not to advertise the petition until after 13 January, the date on which the hearing of an application to restrain the presentation of a petition was listed. The court did not get to the application on 13 January and was listed for the following day. In the afternoon of 13 January the creditor proceeded to advertise the petition in the London Gazette on January 14, on the basis that the undertaking expired at midnight on January 13, informing S when it was too late to prevent publication.

Another instance where a court is likely to hold that the premature giving of notice was an abuse is where the petitioner is acting so as exert as much pressure as possible on the company to pay the petitioner: *Re a Company (No 0013925 of 1991)* [1992] BCLC 562.

There are instances where courts have decided not to penalise petitioners where the reason for the failure to comply with the Rules was not their fault, but that of their solicitors: *Re Corbenstoke Ltd* [1989] BCLC 496; *Re Garton (Western) Ltd* [1989] BCLC 304.

If a petition is struck out because the petitioner acted improperly in giving notice of the petition, the courts might also be inclined to restrain the presentation of another petition based on the same debt: *Re a Company (No 001127 of 1992)* [1992] BCC 477 at 479.

The courts will ordinarily dismiss a petition (under r 7.10(5) and see *Practice Direction – Insolvency Proceedings* (July 2020) [2020] BPIR 1211 at para 9.8.1) as an abuse of process where the petitioner has intentionally flouted the procedural rules relating to the winding-up proceedings, and particularly where it involves breaching the rules on giving notice: *Re Free of Ties Leases Ltd* [2015] EWHC 3974 (Ch). The courts have a discretion as to whether a petition of which notice has not been duly given is struck out. There may be cases where the courts do not dismiss the petition. For instance, in *Re Roselmar Properties Ltd* (1986) 2 BCC 99,156 there was no striking out even though the petition had been advertised only 4 days after service. The reason for the decision of the court was that: the company was not able to pay the debt; it was already in voluntary liquidation; and, as the company was already in liquidation, notice of the company's liquidation had already been advertised. The court took the view that there was likely to be no or little damage to the company. But the court felt it appropriate to penalise the petitioner by indicating that the cost of giving notice would not be allowed as part of the petitioner's costs. Courts might take the same view where the non-compliance with the rules causes no prejudice to the company: *Dikwa Holdings Pty Ltd v Oakbury Pty Ltd* (1992) 10 ACLC 925. The court may decide to adjourn the hearing of the petition to enable notice to be given according to the Rules, but no further adjournment will normally be granted (*Practice Direction – Insolvency Proceedings* (July 2020) [2020] BPIR 1211 at para 9.8.1).

**Applying to restrain giving of notice**—If a company wishes to resist a petition, it will often consider making an application to restrain either the presentation or the giving of notice of the petition, because the company may be concerned that if the petition is presented, and (even more so) when notice of it is given, it is likely to damage the company's business. This has been recognised by the courts as a reasonable concern: *Mann v Goldstein* [1968] 1 WLR 1091; *Coulson Sanderson & Ward Ltd v Ward* (1986) 2 BCC 99,207; *Re a Company (No 007923 of 1994)* [1995] 1 WLR 953; [1995] 1 BCLC 440. For a discussion of this, see the notes accompanying r 7.24.

## [2.325]

### 7.11 Persons entitled to request a copy of petition

If a director, contributory or creditor requests a hard copy of the petition from the solicitor for the petitioner, or the petitioner, if acting in person, and pays the standard fee for copies the solicitor or petitioner must deliver the copy within two business days.

**Derivation**—This rule derived from the Insolvency Rules 1986, SI 1986/1925, r 4.13.

**General note**—This rule, with the necessary modifications, applies to petitions presented by contributories or relevant office-holders: r 7.25(1). Also, see r 7.4.

## [2.326]

### 7.12 Certificate of compliance

(1) The petitioner or the petitioner's solicitor must, at least five business days before the hearing of the petition, file with the court a certificate of compliance with rules 7.9 and 7.10 relating to service and notice of the petition.

(2) The certificate must be authenticated and dated by the petitioner or the petitioner's solicitor and must state—

 (a) the date of presentation of the petition;

 (b) the date fixed for the hearing; and

 (c) the date or dates on which the petition was served and notice of it was given in compliance with rules 7.9 and 7.10.

(3) A copy of or, where that is not reasonably practicable, a statement of the content of, any notice given must be filed with the court with the certificate.

(4) The court may, if it thinks just, dismiss the petition if this rule is not complied with.

**Derivation**—This rule derived from the Insolvency Rules 1986, SI 1986/1925, r 4.14.

**General note**—For a suggested form of the certificate, see https://www.gov.uk/government/colle ctions/bankruptcy-and-insolvency-forms.

## [2.327]

### 7.13 Permission for the petitioner to withdraw

(1) The court may order that the petitioner has permission to withdraw the petition on such terms as to costs as the parties may agree if at least five business days before the first hearing the petitioner, on an application without notice to any other party, satisfies the court that—

 (a) notice of the petition has not been given under rule 7.10;

 (b) no notices in support or in opposition to the petition have been received by the petitioner; and

 (c) the company consents to an order being made under this rule.

(2) The order must contain—

 (a) identification details for the company;

 (b) the date the winding-up petition was presented;

 (c) the name and postal address of the applicant;

 (d) a statement that upon the application made without notice to any other party by the applicant named in the order the court is satisfied that notice of the petition has not been given, that no notices in support of or in opposition to the petition have been received by the petitioner and that the company consents to this order; and

 (e) an order that, with the permission of the court, the petition is withdrawn.

**Derivation**—This rule derived from the Insolvency Rules 1986, SI 1986/1925, r 4.15.

**General note**—An application to withdraw should be supported by a witness statement stating the reasons for the withdrawal and stating that notice of the petition has not been given and no notices (whether in support or in opposition) have been received by the petitioner with reference to the petition (Chief Registrar Baister 'The hearing of the petition' (2008) CRI 115 at 115). The court also must be satisfied that the company consents to an order.

Where leave is granted to withdraw on an incorrect basis, then the petition may, subsequently, be restored: *Re Wavern Engineering Co Ltd* (1987) 3 BCC 3.

Petitioners who withdraw their petitions other than pursuant to this rule, unless they have a good reason, such as they have been paid their debt (*Re Tyneside Permanent Benefit Building Society* [1885] WN 148), will be ordered to pay the costs of all those who have given notice of an intention to appear: *Re Home Assurance Association* (1871) LR 12 Eq 59.

## [2.328]

### 7.14 Notice by persons intending to appear

(1) A creditor or contributory who intends to appear on the hearing of the petition must deliver a notice of intention to appear to the petitioner.

(2) The notice must contain—

(a)     the name and address of the creditor or contributory, and any telephone number and reference which may be required for communication with that person or with any other person (also to be specified in the notice) authorised to speak or act on the creditor's or contributory's behalf;

(b)     the date of the presentation of the petition and a statement that the notice relates to the matter of that petition;

(c)     the date of the hearing of the petition;

(d)     for a creditor, the amount and nature of the debt due from the company to the creditor;

(e)     for a contributory, the number of shares held in the company;

(f)     a statement whether the creditor or contributory intends to support or oppose the petition;

(g)     where the creditor or contributory is represented by a solicitor or other agent, the name, postal address, telephone number and any reference number of that person and details of that person's position with or relationship to the creditor or contributory; and

(h)     the name and postal address of the petitioner.

(3) The notice must be authenticated and dated by or on behalf of the creditor or contributory delivering it.

(4) Where the person authenticating the notice is not the creditor or contributory the notice must state the name and postal address of the person making the statement and the capacity in which, and the authority by which, the person authenticates the notice.

(5) The notice must be delivered to the petitioner or the petitioner's solicitor at the address shown in the court records, or in the notice of the petition required by rule 7.10.

(6) The notice must be delivered so as to reach the petitioner (or the petitioner's solicitor) not later than 4pm on the business day before that which is appointed for the hearing (or, where the hearing has been adjourned, for the adjourned hearing).

(7) A person who fails to comply with this rule may appear on the hearing of the petition only with the permission of the court.

**Derivation**—This rule derived from the Insolvency Rules 1986, SI 1986/1925, r 4.16.

**General note**—As liquidation is a collective remedy secured on behalf of the creditors as a whole, creditors are given the opportunity of indicating whether they support or oppose the petition. See the comments under 'Creditor opposition to the petition' in relation to s 125.

Rule 7.14 applies equally to the hearing of an application for review of the making of a winding-up order under r 12.59 as it does to the original winding-up hearing: *Re Dollar Land (Feltham) Ltd* [1995] 2 BCLC 370.

Secured creditors are entitled to give notice of their intention to appear, and they may appear without having to elect at this stage whether they are going to rely on their security or whether they will surrender security: *Re Carmarthenshire Anthracite Coal and Iron Co* (1875) 45 LJ Ch 200.

If the petitioner has been informed by a creditor that he or she has no intention of appearing, this should be stated in the list of appearances: *Re Australasian Alkaline Reduction and Smelting Syndicate Ltd* (1891) 36 SJ 139.

**Appear**—If notices of appearance are not filed according to this rule, then leave of the court must be obtained in order to appear. A person who has not given the requisite notice, or obtained leave, may attend the hearing but not appear and address the court, notwithstanding the fact that a court should have regard for the known views of creditors concerning the petition: *Re Piccadilly Property Management Ltd* [1999] 2 BCLC 145, [1999] BPIR 260. The view of the person could be put before the court in some other way: *Re Piccadilly Property Management Ltd*. The effect of this rule and r 7.15 are that anyone who does give notice of appearance will be entitled to appear (*Re Piccadilly Property Management Ltd*).

**Leave**—For an instance where leave was granted to creditors, see *Re Dollar Land (Feltham) Ltd* [1995] 2 BCLC 370 (discussed in relation to r 12.59). The court in this case said that leave should be granted where either the court is satisfied as to the reasons why the notice was not given in time or the court believes the case is one where it is of particular importance that the views of creditors be considered.

An instance of an appropriate notice is to be found at: https://www.gov.uk/government/collections/bankruptcy-and-insolvency-forms.

This rule, with the necessary modifications, applies to petitions presented by contributories or relevant office-holders: r 7.25(1). Also, see r 7.4.

**[2.329]**

### 7.15  List of appearances

(1)   The petitioner must prepare for the court a list of the creditors and contributories who have given notice under rule 7.14.

(2)   The list must contain—

- (a)   the date of the presentation of the petition;
- (b)   the date of the hearing of the petition;
- (c)   a statement that the creditors and contributories listed have delivered notice that they intend to appear at the hearing of the petition;
- (d)   their names and addresses;
- (e)   the amount each creditor claims to be owed;
- (f)   the number of shares claimed to be held by each contributory;
- (g)   the name and postal address of any solicitor for a person listed; and
- (h)   whether each person listed intends to support the petition, or to oppose it.

(3)   On the day appointed for the hearing of the petition, a copy of the list must be handed to the court before the hearing commences.

(4)   If the court gives a person permission to appear under rule 7.14(7), then the petitioner must add that person to the list with the same particulars.

**Derivation**—This rule derived from the Insolvency Rules 1986, SI 1986/1925, r 4.17.

**General note**—The company may be represented by counsel, a solicitor, one of its directors or a duly authorised employee.

A notice should be handed over by the petitioner even if there has been no receipt of notices. If this latter situation is in fact the case then on the form should be written 'the list is negative' (Chief Registrar Baister 'The hearing of the petition' (2008) CRI 115 at 115).

A form for the list is to be found at: https://www.gov.uk/government/collections/bankruptcy-an d-insolvency-forms.

This rule, with the necessary modifications, applies to petitions presented by contributories or relevant office-holders: r 7.25(1). Also, see r 7.4.

**[2.330]**

### 7.16  Witness statement in opposition

(1)   If the company intends to oppose the petition, it must not later than five business days before the date fixed for the hearing—

- (a)   file with the court a witness statement in opposition; and
- (b)   deliver a copy of the witness statement to the petitioner or the petitioner's solicitor.

(2)   The witness statement must contain—

- (a)   identification details for the proceedings;
- (b)   a statement that the company intends to oppose the making of a winding-up order; and
- (c)   a statement of the grounds on which the company opposes the making of the order.

**Derivation**—This rule derived from the Insolvency Rules 1986, SI 1986/1925, r 4.18.

**General note**—The rule does not apply to creditors opposing the petition: *Re Piccadilly Property Management Ltd* [1999] 2 BCLC 145, [1999] BPIR 260.

In practice the court will normally permit a company, where it has not filed a witness statement in opposition, to defend the petition where it submits that the debt on which the petition is founded is in dispute.

**[2.331]**

### 7.17  Substitution of creditor or contributory for petitioner

(1)   This rule applies where the petitioner—

- (a)   is subsequently found not to have been entitled to present the petition;
- (b)   fails to give notice of the petition in accordance with rule 7.10;

(c) consents to withdraw the petition, or to allow it to be dismissed, consents to an adjournment, or fails to appear in support of the petition when it is called on in court on the day originally fixed for the hearing, or on a day to which it is adjourned; or

(d) appears, but does not apply for an order in the terms requested in the petition.

(2) The court may, on such terms as it thinks just, substitute as petitioner—

(a) a creditor or contributory who in its opinion would have a right to present a petition and who wishes to prosecute it; . . .

(b) . . ..

**Derivation**—This rule derived from the Insolvency Rules 1986, SI 1986/1925, r 4.19.

**Amendments**—SI 2019/146, as from IP completion day (as defined in the European Union (Withdrawal Agreement) Act 2020, s 39(1)–(5)).

**General note**—In deciding whether to exercise the discretion given by r 7.17 to permit substitution, the courts must strike a balance between two policies: one is that companies that are clearly insolvent should not be allowed to continue to trade so that they might prejudice both existing and future creditors; they should be wound up, or at least subject to some form of administration; the other is that creditors should not be able to invoke winding-up proceedings for debt-collection purposes or as an instrument of oppression, where the debt relied on by a creditor is subject to genuine dispute: *Mann v Goldstein* [1968] 1 WLR 1091.

There is Australian authority to the effect that if there is any objection to a creditor being able to substitute, this must be raised at the hearing of the application to substitute, and not later at the hearing of the winding-up petition: *Kelvingrove (1993) Pty Ltd v Paratoo Pty Ltd* (1998) 16 ACLC 964 at 966.

If the court decides to make a substitution order, it will order that the petition be amended, re-verified, re-served and the petition is adjourned (in order to permit the other matters to be attended to).

Courts have, on the basis of saving costs, where there is no opposition to the petition and the making of a winding-up order, agreed to dispense with the need to re-serve and re-advertise (as occurred in *Re Commercial and Industrial Insulations Ltd* (1986) 2 BCC 98, 901), except where there may be the chance of a creditor coming forward with a substantial reason that would militate against the making of a winding-up order (*Re Commercial and Industrial Insulations Ltd*).

While at one time it appeared that it was possible for creditors to be substituted on a contributory's petition (*Re Creative Handbook Ltd* [1985] BCLC 1, 128 Sol Jo 645), it seems that there can be no substitution now in relation to a petition presented by a contributory. The reason is that r 7.25 provides that only specified rules in Chapter 3 will apply to petitions presented by contributories or relevant office-holders and the rules listed do not include r 7.17. This leads us to conclude that where r 7.17(2) provides that any creditor or contributory can be substituted, this can only apply in relation to a creditor's petition.

Successive substitutions on the one petition may be allowed: *Re Bostals Ltd* [1968] 1 Ch 346 at 350. If a winding-up order is set aside on appeal, then another person may apply to be substituted in relation to the original petition and the court hearing the appeal against the winding-up order may order substitution: *Re Goldthorpe and Lacey Ltd* (1987) 3 BCC 595, CA.

Where there is more than one applicant for substitution the court will usually grant an order to the creditor with the largest debt, or a creditor whose debt is not disputed (Chief Registrar Baister 'The hearing of the petition' (2008) CRI 115 at 116).

**Who can be substituted?**—Paragraph (2) indicates that the person to be substituted is a creditor or contributory who would have the right to petition. Does this mean that the person seeking to be substituted must have had the right to petition at the time of the presentation of the petition by the original petitioner, or when the application to substitute is made? The Rules suggest the latter and this certainly accords with the case law: see *Perak Pioneer Ltd v Petroliam Nasional* [1986] AC 849, PC. But this would mean that if the claim of an applicant for substitution has become statute-barred between the time of the presentation and the time of the substitution application, he or she is not able to succeed.

**The substitution order**—Where a court decides that it is willing to permit substitution, it should allow the petition to be amended by substituting the creditor who wishes to proceed and then direct that the petition be adjourned in order to permit the substituting petitioner to file a verifying statement of truth: *Re Invicta Works* [1894] WN 39, (1894) 38 Sol Jo 290. The substituted petitioner is to file a certificate of compliance as required by r 7.12.

**[2.332]**

### 7.18 Order for substitution of petitioner

An order for substitution of a petitioner must contain—

    (a)    identification details for the proceedings;

    (b)    the name of the original petitioner;

    (c)    the name of the creditor, or contributory . . . ("the named person") who is substituted as petitioner;

    (d)    a statement that the named person has requested to be substituted as petitioner under rule 7.17;

    (e)    the following orders—

        (i)    either—

            (aa)    that the named person must pay the statutory deposit to the court and that, upon such payment being made, the statutory deposit paid by the original petitioner is to be repaid to the original petitioner by the official receiver, or

            (bb)    where the named person is the subject of a notice to the court by the Secretary of State under rule 7.7(2)(b) (notice of alternative arrangements for the payment of deposit) that the statutory deposit paid by the original petitioner is to be repaid to the original petitioner by the official receiver;

        (ii)    that the named person be substituted as petitioner in place of the original petitioner and that the named person may amend the petition accordingly,

        (iii)    that the named person must within a period specified in the order file a statement of truth of the statements in the amended petition,

        (iv)    that not later than before the adjourned hearing of the petition, by a date specified in the order, the named person must serve a sealed copy of the amended petition on the company and deliver a copy to any other person to whom the original petition was delivered,

        (v)    that the hearing of the amended petition be adjourned to the venue specified in the order, and

        (vi)    that the question of the costs of the original petitioner and of the statutory deposit (if appropriate) be reserved until the final determination of the amended petition;

    (f)    the venue of the adjourned hearing; and

    (g)    the date of the order.

**Amendments**—SI 2019/146, as from IP completion day (as defined in the European Union (Withdrawal Agreement) Act 2020, s 39(1)–(5)).

**[2.333]**

### 7.19 Notice of adjournment

(1)    If the court adjourns the hearing of the petition the petitioner must as soon as reasonably practicable deliver a notice of the making of the order of adjournment and of the venue for the adjourned hearing to—

    (a)    the company; and

    (b)    any creditor or contributory who has given notice under rule 7.14 but was not present at the hearing.

(2)    The notice must identify the proceedings.

**Derivation**—This rule derived from the Insolvency Rules 1986, SI 1986/1925, r 4.18A.

**General note**—The court is specifically given the power under s 125 to adjourn the hearing of a petition.

This rule, with the necessary modifications, applies to petitions presented by contributories or relevant office-holders: r 7.25(1). Also, see r 7.4.

**[2.334]**

### 7.20 Order for winding up by the court

(1)   An order for winding-up by the court must contain—

(a)   identification details for the proceedings;

(b)   the name and title of the judge making the order;

(c)   the name and postal address of the petitioner;

(d)   the nature of the petitioner which entitles that person to present the petition (eg the company, a creditor, or a regulator);

(e)   the date of presentation of the petition;

(f)   an order that the company be wound up by the court under the Act;

(g)   a statement whether the proceedings are COMI proceedings, establishment proceedings or proceedings to which the EU Regulation as it has effect in the law of the United Kingdom does not apply;

(h)   an order that the petitioner's costs of the petition be paid out of the assets of the company (unless the court determines otherwise);

(i)   if applicable, an order that the costs of other persons as specified in the order be paid out of the assets of the company;

(j)   the date of the order; and

(k)   a statement that an official receiver attached to the court is by virtue of the order liquidator of the company, or

(2)   The order may contain such additional terms concerning costs as the court thinks just.

**Amendments**—SI 2017/1115; SI 2019/146, as from IP completion day (as defined in the European Union (Withdrawal Agreement) Act 2020, s 39(1)–(5)).

**General note**—This rule, with the necessary modifications, applies to petitions presented by contributories or relevant office-holders: r 7.25(1). Also, see r 7.4.

Where there are defects found in the petition after the making of a winding-up order the petitioner should make an application for permission to amend the errors to the member of Court staff in charge of the winding up list in the Royal Courts of Justice or to a district judge sitting in a District Registry or district judge (*Practice Direction – Insolvency Proceedings* (July 2020) [2018] BPIR 1211, para 9.9.1).

**[2.335]**

### 7.21 Notice to official receiver of winding-up order

(1)   When a winding-up order has been made, the court must deliver notice of the fact to the official receiver as soon as reasonably practicable.

(2)   The notice must have the title "Notice to Official Receiver of Winding-up Order" and must contain—

(a)   identification details for the proceedings;

(b)   the company's registered office;

(c)   the date of presentation of the petition;

(d)   the date of the winding-up order; and

(e)   the name and postal address of the petitioner or the petitioner's solicitor.

**Derivation**—This rule derived from the Insolvency Rules 1986, SI 1986/1925, r 4.20, Sch 4, Fm 4.13.

**General note**—This rule, with the necessary modifications, applies to petitions presented by contributories or relevant office-holders: r 7.25(1). Also, see r 7.4.

**[2.336]**

### 7.22 Delivery and notice of the order

(1)   As soon as reasonably practicable after making a winding-up order, the court must deliver to the official receiver two copies of the order sealed with the seal of the court.

(2)   The official receiver must deliver—

(a)   a sealed copy of the order to the company; and

    (b)    a copy of the order to the registrar of companies (in compliance with section 130(1)).

(3)   As an alternative to delivering a sealed copy of the order to the company, the court may direct that the sealed copy be delivered to such other person or persons, as the court directs.

(4)   The official receiver—

    (a)    must cause a notice of the order to be gazetted as soon as reasonably practicable; and

    (b)    may advertise a notice of the order in such other manner as the official receiver thinks fit.

(5)   The notice must state—

    (a)    that a winding-up order has been made in relation to the company; and

    (b)    the date of the order.

**Derivation**—This rule derived from the Insolvency Rules 1986, SI 1986/1925, r 4.21.

**General note**—This rule, with the necessary modifications, applies to petitions presented by contributories or relevant office-holders: r 7.25(1). Also, see r 7.4.

## [2.337]

### 7.23 Petition dismissed

(1)   Unless the court otherwise directs, when a petition is dismissed the petitioner must give a notice of the dismissal as soon as reasonably practicable.

(2)   The notice must be—

    (a)    gazetted; or

    (b)    advertised in accordance with any directions of the court.

(3)   The notice must contain—

    (a)    a statement that a petition for the winding up of the company has been dismissed;

    (b)    in the case of an overseas company, the address at which service of the petition was effected;

    (c)    the name and address of the petitioner;

    (d)    the date on which the petition was presented;

    (e)    the date on which the petition was gazetted or otherwise advertised; and

    (f)    the date of the hearing at which the petition was dismissed.

(4)   The company may itself gazette notice of the dismissal where—

    (a)    the petitioner is not the company; and

    (b)    the petitioner has not given notice in accordance with paragraphs (1) to (3) within 21 days of the date of the hearing at which the petition was dismissed.

**Derivation**—This rule derived from the Insolvency Rules 1986, SI 1986/1925, r 4.21B.

**General note**—Giving notice of the dismissal of a petition can be a critically important event for a company as it broadcasts the fact officially that the company is no longer subject to winding-up action.

## [2.338]

### 7.24 Injunction to restrain presentation or notice of petition

(1)   An application by a company for an injunction restraining a creditor from presenting a petition for the winding up of the company must be made to a court having jurisdiction to wind up the company.

(2)   An application by a company for an injunction restraining a creditor from giving notice of a petition for the winding up of a company must be made to the court or hearing centre in which the petition is pending.

**Derivation**—This rule derived from the Insolvency Rules 1986, SI 1986/1925, r 4.6A.

**General note**—To resist claims by creditors a company may, if it is aware that a petition is likely to be presented against it (possibly where a statutory demand has been served under s 123(1)(a) of the 1986 Act), seek to prevent presentation, or if a petition has been presented against it, it may seek to restrain the giving of notice of it. Until recent years the giving of notice was referred to as the advertising of the petition and is sometimes still so referred. It has been made clear in *Harper v London Borough of Camden Council* ([2020] EWHC 1001 at [16]) that only a company may apply under this rule; a shareholder or director of a company may not do so (at [19]).

The courts are to be cautious in granting an injunction on the basis of unsubstantiated and imprecise assertions; applicants must provide sufficiently precise factual evidence (*Re Hong Kong Investments Group Ltd* [2018] HKCFI 984; *Addchance Ltd v Herojoy Trading Ltd* [2019] HKCFI 1147).

**Presenting a petition**—The principles that apply usually to injunctions and found in *American Cyanamid* do not apply here as the hearing for an injunction to prevent presentation finally disposes of the matter that is in dispute: *Bryanston Finance Ltd v De Vries (No 2)* [1976] 1 Ch 63 at 80–81.

The Court of Appeal has said that for restraint of the presentation of the petition the court must be presented with prima facie evidence that the company would succeed in establishing that the proceedings constitute an abuse of process: *Re a Company (No 007923 of 1994)* [1995] 1 WLR 953, [1995] 1 BCLC 440.

The power to grant an injunction is to be exercised circumspectly and with regard to the justice of the case on each side: *Bryanston Finance Ltd v De Vries (No 2)* [1976] 1 Ch 63 at 78.

A petition founded on a debt that was disputed on genuine and substantial grounds was an abuse of process and would lead to the making of an injunction restraining presentation: *Coilcolor Ltd v Camtrex Ltd* [2015] EWHC 3202 (Ch), [2016] BPIR 1129; *Sell Your Car With Us Ltd v Sareen* [2019] EWHC 2332 (Ch). For abuse the prospective petitioner must have understood that the debt is disputed on substantial grounds or can be assumed to know this given the facts of which he or she was aware: *Hung Yip (HK) Engineering Company Ltd v Kinli Civil Engineering Ltd* [2021] HKCFI 153 at [14].

The Court of Appeal has indicated that it is well established that the threshold for establishing that a debt is disputed on substantial grounds in the context of a winding-up petition is not a high one for restraining the presentation of the winding-up petition, and may be reached even if the defence could be regarded to be 'shadowy': *Tallington Lakes Ltd v South Kesteven District Council* [2012] EWCA Civ 443.

If a creditor serves a demand and the company applies to restrain the presentation of a winding-up petition leading to the creditor agreeing not to present a petition because of the evidence put before it, the creditor will not be entitled to its costs: *Re Cannon Screen Entertainment Ltd* [1989] BCLC 660.

The court may award indemnity costs against the sole director of the petitioning creditor in the situation where the presentation of the petition is restrained: *Mulalley and Company Ltd v Regent Building Services Ltd* [2017] EWHC 2962 (Ch).

**Giving notice of (advertising) a petition**—Unless the company can persuade a court that a petitioner should not give notice of the petition, then the company cannot succeed; the default position was that notice of the petition should be given: *Re A Company* (unreported, ChD, Tim Kerr QC, 13 November 2014). The Court of Appeal has said that where the application is brought to restrain the advertising of a petition, the court is concerned with attempting to strike a fair balance between two public policy matters. These are: concern that proceedings be brought to the attention of all who might be interested in resisting or supporting them, as well as those who might be going to deal with the company in the ordinary course of business; and the serious consequences for the company's reputation which can result from the advertising of a petition to wind up: *Re a Company (No 007923 of 1994)* [1995] 1 WLR 953, [1995] 1 BCLC 440. The court said that if a company was to succeed in having the advertising of a petition restrained, it had to demonstrate that the advertisement of the petition would cause it serious damage (*Re a Company (No 007923 of 1994)*).

The jurisdiction to restrain the giving of notice of petitions is used sparingly, and an applicant for a restraining order must establish that there are clear and persuasive grounds for the order sought: *Bryanston Finance Pty Ltd v De Vries (No 2)* [1976] Ch 63 at 78; *Coulson Sanderson & Ward Ltd v Ward* (1986) 2 BCC 99,207 at 99,214 at 99,215; *Re Normandy Marketing Ltd* [1994] Ch 198; *Re a Company (No 007923 of 1994)* [1995] 1 WLR 953, [1995] BCLC 440. It has been held that restraint of the giving of notice of a petition will be ordered if the giving of notice would constitute an abuse of process (*James Dolman and Co Ltd v Pedley* [2003] EWCA Civ 1686; [2004] BPIR 290), but earlier it was held that a court hearing an application for the restraint of a petition's advertisement is only required to determine whether there was a substantial case to be argued concerning the petition, and not to make a finding of fact: *Re a Company (No 00962 of 1991)* [1992] BCLC 248.

The courts will restrain the prospective or actual petitioner in circumstances where a petition for an administration order is pending: *Re a Company (No 001992 of 1988)* (1988) 4 BCC 451. Also, there will be a restraint of the giving of notice even where no petition for an administration order is pending, but where such a petition is being considered and the company gives an undertaking to the court to present forthwith: *Re a Company (No 001448 of 1989)* [1989] BCLC 715. It is, therefore, possible that courts will restrain the giving of notice of a petition to wind up where it has been indicated to them that the directors or a substantial charge holder are proposing to appoint an administrator extra-judicially. Furthermore, a restraint of giving notice may be granted where the petitioner knows that the company has a defence on which it intends to rely at the hearing of the petition: *Re a Company (No 0012209 of 1991)* [1992] 1 WLR 351, [1992] 2 All ER 797, [1992] BCLC 865; *Re a Company (No 004502 of 1988)* [1992] BCLC 701.

A court may decide, as it did in *Re a Company* (unreported, ChD, David Foxton QC, 13 July 2016), to grant an injunction under the equivalent of this rule but require the company to pay a substantial amount into court as a condition of the order.

It does not matter if there is uncertainty relating to the precise sum that is payable to the petitioning creditor, as the court is merely to decide, in an application to restrain, whether the petitioner is indisputably a creditor in a sum exceeding £750: *Angel Group Ltd v British Gas Trading Ltd* [2012] EWHC 2702 (Ch) at [29]. On this note, the relevant matter in an application is whether the company is able to dispute the fact that a sum is owed to the petitioner, and it is not necessary for the company to adduce evidence of solvency at this point. The absence of evidence of solvency might lead the court to consider carefully the genuineness of the alleged dispute, but the lack of such evidence was not a reason to strike out the application to restrain the giving of notice: *Global Acquirers Ltd v Laycatelcom LDA* (unreported, 2 July 2014, ChD, Anthony Elleray QC).

If an application has been unsuccessful in having the giving of notice of a petition restrained, the court will not make an order on a second application where it is based on the same grounds: *Re Portedge Ltd* [1997] BCC 23, affirmed on appeal *RWH Enterprises Ltd v Portedge Ltd* [1998] BCC 556, CA.

See, S Lee, 'The Court's Jurisdiction to Restrain a Creditor from Presenting a Winding Up Petition Where a Cross-Claim Exists' (2010) 69 CLJ 113; A Keay *McPherson and Keay's Law of Company Liquidation* (Sweet and Maxwell, 4th edn, 2018) at 130–137.

## CHAPTER 4

### PETITION BY A CONTRIBUTORY OR A RELEVANT OFFICE-HOLDER

## [2.339]

### Note

[Note: (1) "relevant office-holder" is defined in rule 7.4(2);

(2) a document required by the Act or these Rules must also contain the standard contents set out in Part 1.]

**General note**—Rule 7.25 indicates the provisions of Chapter 3 of Part 4 apply to petitions presented by a contributory or an office-holder with modifications, but Chapter 4 focuses on petitions presented by a contributory or an office-holder.

## [2.340]

### 7.25 Interpretation and application of rules in Chapter 3

(1) The following rules in Chapter 3 apply subject to paragraph (2), with the necessary modifications, to a petition under this Chapter by a contributory or a relevant office-holder—

rule 7.8 (court to which petition is to be presented where the company is subject to a CVA or is in administration);

rule 7.9(1), (4) and (5) (copies of petition to be served on other persons);

rule 7.11 (persons entitled to request a copy of petition);

rule 7.14 (notice by persons intending to appear);

rule 7.15 (list of appearances);

rule 7.19 (notice of adjournment);

rule 7.20 (order for winding up by the court) except where rule 7.32 applies (petition by administrator or where there is a supervisor);

rule 7.21 (notice to official receiver of winding-up order); and

rule 7.22 (delivery and notice of the order).

(2) The following rules apply to petitions under this Chapter presented by a relevant office-holder—

rule 7.23 (petition dismissed); and

rule 7.24 (injunction to restrain presentation or notice of petition).

**Derivation**—This rule derived from the Insolvency Rules 1986, SI 1986/1925, r 4.24.

**General note**—The rule provides that several rules in Chapter 3 will apply to petitions presented by contributories or relevant office-holders. 'Relevant office-holder' is defined in r 7.4.

## [2.341]

### 7.26 Contents of petition for winding-up order by a contributory

(1)  A petition presented by a contributory must contain—

    (a)    the name of the court (and hearing centre if applicable);

    (b)    the name and postal address of the petitioner;

    (c)    identification details for the company subject to the petition;

    (d)    the company's registered office (if any);

    (e)    the date the company was incorporated and the enactment under which it was incorporated;

    (f)    the total number of issued shares of the company and the manner in which they are divided up;

    (g)    the aggregate nominal value of those shares;

    (h)    the amount of capital paid up or credited as paid up;

    (i)    a statement of the nature of the company's business if known;

    (j)    the number and total value of the shares held by the petitioner;

    (k)    a statement whether the shares held by the petitioner—

        (i)    were allotted to the petitioner on the incorporation of the company,

        (ii)    have been registered in the name of the petitioner for more than six months in the last 18 months, or

        (iii)    devolved upon the petitioner through the death of the former holder of the shares;

    (l)    the grounds on which the winding-up order is sought;

    (m)    a statement whether the company is an Article 1.2 undertaking;

    (n)    a statement whether the proceedings will be COMI proceedings, establishment proceedings or proceedings to which the EU Regulation as it has effect in the law of the United Kingdom does not apply and that the reasons for so stating are given in the form of a witness statement;

    (o)    a statement that in the circumstances it is just and equitable that the company should be wound up;

    (p)    a statement that the petitioner therefore applies for an order that the company may be wound up by the court under the Act, or that such other order may be made as the court thinks just;

    (q)    the name and postal address of any person on whom the petitioner intends to serve the petition; and

    (r)    the contact details of the petitioner's solicitor (if any).

(2)  The petition must also contain a blank box for the court to complete with the details of the venue for hearing the petition.

**Derivation**—This rule derived from the Insolvency Rules 1986, SI 1986/1925, Sch 4, Fm 4.14.

**Amendments**—SI 2017/1115; SI 2019/146, as from IP completion day (as defined in the European Union (Withdrawal Agreement) Act 2020, s 39(1)–(5)).

**General note**—Most frequently contributory petitions have involved the use of the ground mentioned in r 7.26(1)(o). See s 122(1)(g) and the notes accompanying it and A Keay *McPherson and Keay's Law of Company Liquidation* (Sweet and Maxwell, 4th edn, 2018) at 239–257.

## [2.342]

### 7.27 Petition presented by a relevant office-holder

(1)  A petition by a relevant office-holder must be expressed to be the petition of the company by the office-holder.

(2)   The petition must contain the particulars required by rule 7.26 (other than paragraph (1)(j) and (k) and the following (as applicable)—

(a)   identification details for the office-holder;

(b)   the full name of the court or hearing centre in which the proceedings are being conducted or where documents relating to the proceedings are filed;

(c)   the court case number;

(d)   the date the insolvency proceedings in respect of which the office-holder holds office commenced; and

(e)   where the office-holder is an administrator, an application under paragraph 79 of Schedule B1, requesting that the appointment of the administrator should cease to have effect.

**Derivation**—This rule derived from the Insolvency Rules 1986, SI 1986/1925, r 4.7.

**General note**—'Relevant office-holder' is defined in r 7.4 and means an administrator, administrative receiver or supervisor of a CVA.

## [2.343]

### 7.28  Verification of petition

(1)   The petition must be verified by a statement of truth.

(2)   A statement of truth which is not contained in or endorsed upon the petition must identify the petition and must contain—

(a)   identification details for the company;

(b)   the name of the petitioner; and

(c)   the name of the court (and hearing centre if applicable) in which the petition is to be presented.

(3)   The statement of truth must be authenticated and dated by or on behalf of the petitioner.

(4)   Where the person authenticating the statement of truth is not the petitioner, or one of the petitioners, the statement of truth must state—

(a)   the name and postal address of the person making the statement;

(b)   the capacity in which, and the authority by which, the person authenticates the statement; and

(c)   the means of the person's knowledge of the matters verified in the statement of truth.

(5)   A statement of truth verifying more than one petition must include in its title the names of the companies to which it relates and must set out, in relation to each company, the statements relied on by the petitioner; and a clear and legible photocopy of the statement of truth must be filed with each petition which it verifies.

(6)   The reasons for the statement that the proceedings will be COMI proceedings, establishment proceedings or proceedings to which the EU Regulation as it has effect in the law of the United Kingdom does not apply must be given in a witness statement.

**Derivation**—This rule derived from the Insolvency Rules 1986, SI 1986/1925, Sch 4, Fm 4.14.

**Amendments**—SI 2017/1115; SI 2019/146, as from IP completion day (as defined in the European Union (Withdrawal Agreement) Act 2020, s 39(1)–(5)).

**General note**—This is equivalent to r 7.6, which applies to all other petitions presented to the court, and in very similar terms. See the note accompanying r 7.6.

## [2.344]

### 7.29  Presentation and service of petition

(1)   The petition with one copy must be filed with the court.

(2)   The petition may not be filed unless a receipt for the deposit payable to the official receiver is produced on presentation of the petition.

(3)   The court must fix a hearing for a return day on which, unless the court otherwise directs, the petitioner and the company must attend before the court for—

(a)   directions to be given in relation to the procedure on the petition; or

(b)   the hearing of the petition where—

      (i)     it is presented by a relevant office-holder, and

      (ii)    the court considers it just in all the circumstances.

(4)  On fixing the return day, the court must deliver to the petitioner a sealed copy of the petition endorsed with the return day and time of hearing.

(5)  The petitioner must serve a sealed copy of the petition on the company at least 14 days before the return day.

(6)  . . ..

    **Derivation**—This rule derived from the Insolvency Rules 1986, SI 1986/1925, r 4.22.

    **Amendments**—SI 2019/146, as from IP completion day (as defined in the European Union (Withdrawal Agreement) Act 2020, s 39(1)–(5)).

    **General note**—One important difference between the procedures for contributories' and office-holders' petitions as against creditors' petitions, is that with the former two the court requires the petitioner and the company to attend a directions' hearing. The court will make directions concerning the procedure to be followed (r 7.29(3)). The matters that are to be the subject of directions are set out in r 7.31. Such hearings are particularly important in petitions launched under s 122(1)(g)) by contributories (just and equitable ground).

## [2.345]

### 7.30 Request to appoint former administrator or supervisor as liquidator (section 140)

(1)  This rule applies where a petition requests under section 140 the appointment of a former administrator or supervisor as liquidator.

(2)  The person whose appointment is sought ("the appointee") must, not less than two business days before the return day fixed under rule 7.29(3), file with the court a report including particulars of—

    (a)    the date on which the appointee delivered notice to creditors of the company, of the appointee's intention to seek appointment as liquidator, such date to be at least seven business days before the day on which the report is filed; and

    (b)    details of any response from creditors to that notice, including any objections to the proposed appointment.

    **Derivation**—This rule derived from the Insolvency Rules 1986, SI 1986/1925, r 4.7.

## [2.346]

### 7.31 Hearing of petition

(1)  On the return day, or at any time after it, the court—

    (a)    must, where the petition is presented by a person who is not a relevant office-holder, give directions;

    (b)    may, in any other case, give directions; or

    (c)    may, in either case, make any such order as it sees fit.

(2)  In particular, the court may give directions relating to the following matters—

    (a)    service or delivery of the petition, whether in connection with the venue for a further hearing, or for any other purpose;

    (b)    whether particulars of claim and defence are to be delivered, and generally as to the procedure on the petition;

    (c)    whether and if so by what means, notice of the petition is to be given;

    (d)    the manner in which any evidence is to be provided at any hearing before the judge and in particular (but without prejudice to the generality of the above) as to—

      (i)     the taking of evidence wholly or in part by witness statement or orally,

      (ii)    the cross-examination of any person who has made a witness statement, and

      (iii)   the matters to be dealt with in evidence; and

    (e)    any other matter affecting the procedure on the petition or in connection with the hearing and disposal of the petition.

(3) In giving directions the court must consider whether a copy of the petition should be served on or delivered to any of the persons specified in rule 7.9.

**Derivation**—This rule derived from the Insolvency Rules 1986, SI 1986/1925, r 4.23.

**General note**—This rule details those matters that should be considered in the court's directions for the litigation. For petitions presented by non-relevant office-holders directions must be given, although the nature of the directions are at the discretion of the court. In relation to petitions presented by relevant office-holders directions are discretionary.

**Giving notice**—Unlike with creditors' petitions, there is no pre-determined rule on giving notice in relation to the petition. The terms of giving notice are to be the subject of the directions of the court. If notice of the petition is given before the time that is set, the court may order that the petition by struck out on the basis of an abuse of process: *Re a Company (No 007020 of 1996)* [1998] 2 BCLC 54. The giving of notice of the petition outside of the requirements of the Rules is an abuse as it prevents the court having the opportunity to decide whether there should be, under this rule, any giving of notice at all; there should be no notice given before the return day set for the petition: *Re Doreen Boards Ltd* [1996] 1 BCLC 501 at 505.

## [2.347]

### 7.32 Order for winding up by the court of a company in administration or where there is a supervisor of a CVA in relation to the company

(1) An order for winding-up by the court of a company in administration or where there is a supervisor of a CVA in relation to the company must contain—

  (a) identification details for the proceedings;

  (b) the name and title of the judge making the order;

  (c) the name and postal address of the administrator or supervisor of the company;

  (d) the date of the administrator's or supervisor's appointment;

  (e) the date of presentation of the petition;

  (f) where there is an administrator, an order that the administrator's appointment ceases to have effect;

  (g) an order that the company be wound up by the court under the Act;

  (h) a statement whether the proceedings are COMI proceedings, establishment proceedings or proceedings to which the EU Regulation as it has effect in the law of the United Kingdom does not apply; and

  (i) the name and address of the person appointed as liquidator of the company (if applicable);

  (j) an order that—

    (i) an official receiver attached to the court is by virtue of the order liquidator of the company, or

    (ii) that the administrator or the supervisor (as the case may be) specified in the order is appointed liquidator of the company; and

  (k) the date of the order.

(2) The order may contain such additional terms as to the costs as the court thinks just.

(3) Where the court appoints the former administrator or the supervisor as liquidator paragraphs (3)(c), (4), (7), (8) and (9) of rule 7.56 apply.

**Derivation**—This rule derived from the Insolvency Rules 1986, SI 1986/1925, r 4.20, Sch 4, Fm 4.12.

**Amendments**—SI 2017/1115; SI 2019/146, as from IP completion day (as defined in the European Union (Withdrawal Agreement) Act 2020, s 39(1)–(5)).

CHAPTER 5

PROVISIONAL LIQUIDATOR

**[2.348]**

**Note**

[Note: a document required by the Act or these Rules must also contain the standard contents set out in Part 1.]

General comment on Chapter 5—This Chapter deals with the appointment of a provisional liquidator and issues surrounding that. Such an appointment is similar to the appointment of an interim receiver in bankruptcy; see s 286. See the comments accompanying s 135, the provision that provides for the appointment of a provisional liquidator in the 1986 Act.

**[2.349]**

**7.33 Application for appointment of provisional liquidator (section 135)**

(1)   An application to the court for the appointment of a provisional liquidator under section 135 may be made by—

    (a)    the petitioner;

    (b)    a creditor of the company;

    (c)    a contributory;

    (d)    the company;

    (e)    the Secretary of State;

    (f)    a temporary administrator; or

    (g)    . . .

    (h)    any person who under any enactment would be entitled to present a petition for the winding up of the company.

(2)   The application must be supported by a witness statement stating—

    (a)    the grounds on which it is proposed that a provisional liquidator should be appointed;

    (b)    if some person other than the official receiver is proposed to be appointed, that that person has consented to act and, to the best of the applicant's belief, is qualified to act as an insolvency practitioner in relation to the company;

    (c)    whether or not the official receiver has been informed of the application and, if so, whether a copy of it has been delivered to the official receiver;

    (d)    whether to the applicant's knowledge—

        (i)    there has been proposed or is in force for the company a CVA;

        (ii)    an administrator or administrative receiver is acting in relation to the company; or

        (iii)    a liquidator has been appointed for its voluntary winding up; and

    (e)    the applicant's estimate of the value of the assets in relation to which the provisional liquidator is to be appointed;

    (f)    a statement whether the proceedings will be COMI proceedings, establishment proceedings or proceedings to which the EU Regulation as it has effect in the law of the United Kingdom does not apply with the reasons for so stating.

(3)   The applicant must deliver copies of the application and the witness statement in support to the official receiver, who may attend the hearing and make any representations which the official receiver thinks appropriate.

(4)   If for any reason it is not practicable to deliver copies of the application and statement to the official receiver before the hearing, the applicant must inform the official receiver of the application in sufficient time for the official receiver to be able to attend.

(5)   If satisfied that sufficient grounds are shown for the appointment the court may appoint a provisional liquidator on such terms as it thinks just.

**Derivation**—This rule derived from the Insolvency Rules 1986, SI 1986/1925, r 4.25.

**Amendments**—SI 2017/1115; SI 2017/702; SI 2019/146, as from IP completion day (as defined in the European Union (Withdrawal Agreement) Act 2020, s 39(1)–(5)).

**General note**—Someone other than the official receiver may be appointed. This person must be, according to s 135, 'any other fit person'.

See s 135 and the notes accompanying it.

## [2.350]

### 7.34 Deposit by applicant

(1)   An applicant for an order appointing the official receiver as provisional liquidator must, before the order is made, deposit with the official receiver, or otherwise secure to the official receiver's satisfaction, such sum as the court directs to cover the official receiver's remuneration and expenses.

(2)   If the sum deposited or secured proves to be insufficient, the court may, on the application of the official receiver, order the applicant for the appointment to deposit or secure an additional sum.

(3)   If such additional sum is not deposited or secured within two business days after service of the order on the applicant then the court may discharge the order appointing the official receiver as provisional liquidator.

(4)   If a winding-up order is made after a provisional liquidator has been appointed, any money deposited under this rule must (unless it is required because the assets are insufficient to pay the remuneration and expenses of the provisional liquidator) be repaid to the person depositing it (or as that person may direct) as an expense of the winding up, in the prescribed order of priority.

**Derivation**—This rule derived from the Insolvency Rules 1986, SI 1986/1925, r 4.27.

## [2.351]

### 7.35 Order of appointment of provisional liquidator

(1)   The order appointing the provisional liquidator must have the title "Order of appointment of Provisional Liquidator" and contain—

- (a)   the name of the court (and hearing centre if applicable) in which the order is made;
- (b)   the name and title of the judge making the order;
- (c)   the name and postal address of the applicant;
- (d)   identification details for the company;
- (e)   the statement that the court is satisfied—
  - (i)   that the company is unable to pay its debts (if applicable), and
  - (ii)   that the proceedings are COMI proceedings, establishment proceedings or proceedings to which the EU Regulation as it has effect in the law of the United Kingdom does not apply, as the case may be;
- (f)   an order either that—
  - (i)   upon the sum, which is specified in the order, being deposited by the applicant with the official receiver, the official receiver is appointed provisional liquidator of the company, or
  - (ii)   the person specified in the order is appointed provisional liquidator of the company;
- (g)   identification and contact details for the provisional liquidator, where the provisional liquidator is not the official receiver;
- (h)   details of the functions to be carried out by the provisional liquidator in relation to the company's affairs;
- (i)   a notice to the officers of the company that they are required by section 235 to give the provisional liquidator all the information the provisional liquidator may reasonably require relating to the company's property and affairs and to attend upon the provisional

liquidator at such times as the provisional liquidator may reasonably require; and

(j)     the date of the order.

(2)   Where two or more provisional liquidators are appointed the order must also specify (as required by section 231) whether any act required or authorised under any enactment to be done by the provisional liquidator is to be done by all or any one or more of them.

(3)   The court must, as soon as reasonably practicable after the order is made, deliver copies of the order as follows—

(a)     if the official receiver is the provisional liquidator, two sealed copies to the official receiver;

(b)     if another person is appointed as provisional liquidator—

(i)       two sealed copies to that person, and

(ii)      one copy to the official receiver;

(c)     if there is an administrative receiver acting in relation to the company, one sealed copy to the administrative receiver.

(4)   The official receiver or other person appointed as provisional liquidator must as soon as reasonably practicable deliver a sealed copy of the order to either—

(a)     the company, or

(b)     the liquidator, if a liquidator was appointed for the company's voluntary winding-up.

(5)   The official receiver or other person appointed as provisional liquidator must as soon as reasonably practicable deliver a copy of the order to the registrar of companies.

**Derivation**—This rule derived from the Insolvency Rules 1986, SI 1986/1925, r 4.26, Sch 4, Fm 4.15.

**Amendments**—SI 2017/1115; SI 2019/146, as from IP completion day (as defined in the European Union (Withdrawal Agreement) Act 2020, s 39(1)–(5)).

**General note**—The requirement that the functions of the provisional liquidator are set out is particularly important now that the provisional liquidator is a 'liquidator' within the meaning of that word in the EU Regulation on Insolvency Proceedings. Also, the inclusion of the details of the functions to be carried out by the provisional liquidator in relation to the company's affairs (r 7.35(1)(h) is particularly important so that the provisional liquidator has the judicial authority to carry out functions).

See A Keay *McPherson and Keay's Law of Company Liquidation* (Sweet and Maxwell, 4th edn, 2018), Ch 6.

## [2.352]

### 7.36  Notice of appointment of provisional liquidator

(1)   The provisional liquidator must as soon as reasonably practicable after receipt of the copy of the order of appointment give notice of appointment unless the court directs otherwise.

(2)   The notice—

(a)     must be gazetted; and

(b)     may be advertised in such other manner as the provisional liquidator thinks fit.

(3)   The notice must state—

(a)     that a provisional liquidator has been appointed; and

(b)     the date of the appointment.

**Derivation**—This rule derived from the Insolvency Rules 1986, SI 1986/1925, r 4.25A.

## [2.353]

### 7.37  Security

(1)   This rule applies where an insolvency practitioner is appointed as provisional liquidator.

(2)   The cost of providing the security required under the Act must be paid in the first instance by the provisional liquidator, however—

(a) if a winding-up order is not made, the person appointed is entitled to be reimbursed out of the property of the company, and the court may make an order on the company accordingly; and

(b) if a winding-up order is made, the person appointed is entitled to be reimbursed as an expense of the winding up in the prescribed order of priority.

(3) If the provisional liquidator fails to give or keep up the required security, the court may remove the provisional liquidator, and make such order as it thinks just as to costs.

(4) If an order is made under this rule removing the provisional liquidator, or discharging the order appointing the provisional liquidator, the court must give directions as to whether any, and if so what, steps should be taken for the appointment of another person in the place of the removed or discharged provisional liquidator.

**Derivation**—This rule derived from the Insolvency Rules 1986, SI 1986/1925, rr 4.28, 4.29.

## [2.354]

### 7.38 Remuneration

(1) The remuneration of the provisional liquidator (other than the official receiver) is to be fixed by the court from time to time on the application of the provisional liquidator.

(2) In fixing the remuneration of the provisional liquidator, the court must take into account—

(a) the time properly given by the provisional liquidator and the staff of the provisional liquidator in attending to the company's affairs;

(b) the complexity of the case;

(c) any respects in which, in connection with the company's affairs, there falls on the provisional liquidator any responsibility of an exceptional kind or degree;

(d) the effectiveness with which the provisional liquidator appears to be carrying out, or to have carried out, the duties of the provisional liquidator; and

(e) the value and nature of the property with which the provisional liquidator has to deal.

(3) Without prejudice to any order the court may make as to costs, the remuneration of the provisional liquidator (whether the official receiver or another) must be paid to the provisional liquidator, and the amount of any expenses incurred by the provisional liquidator (including the remuneration and expenses of any special manager appointed under section 177) reimbursed—

(a) if a winding-up order is not made, out of the property of the company;

(b) if a winding-up order is made, as an expense of the winding up, in the prescribed order of priority; and

(c) in either case (if the relevant funds are insufficient), out of the deposit under rule 7.34.

(4) Unless the court otherwise directs, where a winding up order is not made, the provisional liquidator may retain out of the company's property such sums or property as are or may be required for meeting the remuneration and expenses of the provisional liquidator.

(5) Where a person other than the official receiver has been appointed provisional liquidator, and the official receiver has taken any steps for the purpose of obtaining a statement of affairs or has performed any other duty under these Rules, the provisional liquidator must pay the official receiver such sum (if any) as the court may direct.

**Derivation**—This rule derived from the Insolvency Rules 1986, SI 1986/1925, r 4.30.

**General note**—Remuneration of provisional liquidators has to be approved of by a court, on the application of the liquidator. Such applications may be opposed or unopposed. Where a provisional liquidator does some work in good faith and after doing that work a court holds that the order of appointment was incorrectly made, the provisional liquidator is still entitled to claim remuneration according to the normal terms: *Re Joseph Phillips Ltd* [1964] 1 WLR 369, [1964] 1 All ER 441. Provisional liquidators who undertake a substantial amount of work which proves to be abortive may claim for it as long as the work was not necessary because of the liquidator's own error: *Re UOC Corporation, Alipour v UOC Corporation* [1997] 2 BCLC 569.

Normally, the court will not order an unsuccessful petitioner to pay the costs of the provisional liquidator: *Re Walter L Jacob & Co Ltd* (1987) 3 BCC 532. However, in *Re Secure & Provide plc* [1992] BCC 405 the court did make an order against the Secretary of State where a s 124A petition that had been presented by the Secretary of State failed and on the basis that there was no justification for the application ex parte for the appointment of a provisional liquidator and such an order ought not to have been made without first giving the company an opportunity to be heard.

The official receiver's remuneration is determined according to reg 35 of the Insolvency Regulations 1994 (SI 1994/2507). Possibly because the official receiver would not be realising assets and distributing dividends to creditors, remuneration is calculated on an hourly basis where the official receiver operates as a provisional liquidator (reg 35(1)). This provides that the official receiver shall be entitled to remuneration calculated in accordance with the applicable hourly rates set out in paragraph (2) for services provided by him (or any of his or her officers) in relation to, inter alia, the performance by him of any functions where he or she acts as provisional liquidator.

If a provisional liquidator were to instruct an independent contractor to provide services, the service provider is not to be regarded as a member of the liquidator's staff for the purposes of the liquidator's remuneration, and, therefore, there could be no mark up by the provisional liquidator on the provider's fees: *Jacobs v UIC Insurance Co Ltd* [2006] EWHC 2717 (Ch), [2007] 2 BCLC 46, [2007] BPIR 494 at [69]. In the same case it was said that the success of the provisional liquidator's work is to be taken into account in determining remuneration, but it was held that a liquidator was not entitled to a success fee over and above reasonable remuneration. In such a case, a court is likely to be more ready to award the remuneration claimed, but not more than reasonable remuneration (at [90]). The liquidator has to point to, and prove, what he or she did that in fact led to the success (at [91]).

Remuneration is to be paid as part of the order of priorities in r 7.108 (see r 7.108(4)(f)).

**Expenses**—The expenses of a provisional liquidator are paid out of the assets of the company in the prescribed order and set out in r 7.108 (see r 7.108(4)(a)(i)). Where assets are insufficient to do so, they are paid out of the deposit lodged, pursuant to r 7.34, by the applicant for the appointment of the provisional liquidator. It has been held that this will only cover expenses paid from the provisional liquidator's own resources and for which the liquidator is personally liable: in *Re Grey Marlin Ltd* [1999] 2 BCLC 658 at 662.

The court retains the power to examine all aspects of the expenses of provisional liquidators including their own remuneration, the remuneration of their partners and staff, if appropriate, and their disbursements in respect of third parties: *Jacobs v UIC Insurance Co Ltd* [2006] EWHC 2717 (Ch), [2007] 2 BCLC 46, [2007] BPIR 494 at [80].

Where a party has paid the fees and other costs incurred by provisional liquidators pursuant to a funding agreement, the party might be granted a court order of reimbursement according to the remedy of subrogation and under r 7.38(3) if the circumstances were such that if there was no reimbursement the company in provisional liquidation would be unjustly enriched, such as where the petition for winding up and the order appointing the provisional liquidators are dismissed: *Re Beppler & Jacobson Ltd; TOC Investments Corporation v Beppler & Jacobson Ltd* [2016] EWHC 20 (Ch). According to this case the reimbursement could be ordered even if the parties funding the provisional liquidation had advanced the funds in provisional liquidation and not to the provisional liquidators themselves.

## [2.355]

### 7.39 Termination of appointment

(1) The appointment of the provisional liquidator may be terminated by the court on the application of the provisional liquidator, or a person specified in rule 7.33(1).

(2) If the provisional liquidator's appointment terminates, in consequence of the dismissal of the winding-up petition or otherwise, the court may give such directions as it thinks just relating to the accounts of the provisional liquidator's administration or any other matters which it thinks appropriate.

(3) The provisional liquidator must give notice of termination of the appointment as provisional liquidator, unless the termination is on the making of a winding-up order or the court directs otherwise.

(4) The notice referred to in paragraph (3)—

(a) must be delivered to the registrar of companies as soon as reasonably practicable;

(b) must be gazetted as soon as reasonably practicable; and

    (c)    may be advertised in such other manner as the provisional liquidator thinks fit.

(5)   The notice under paragraph (3) must state—

    (a)    that the appointment as provisional liquidator has been terminated;

    (b)    the date of that termination; and

    (c)    that the appointment terminated otherwise than on the making of a winding-up order.

**Derivation**—This rule derived from the Insolvency Rules 1986, SI 1986/1925, r 4.31.

**General note**—If a provisional liquidator is removed before the petition for winding up is heard, the court may order that the remuneration of the provisional liquidator be paid out of the company's assets: *Re UOC Corporation, Alipour v UOC Corporation* [1997] 2 BCLC 569.

## CHAPTER 6

### STATEMENT OF AFFAIRS AND OTHER INFORMATION

**[2.356]**

**Note**

[Note: a document required by the Act or these Rules must also contain the standard contents set out in Part 1.]

**General comment on Chapter 6**—The Chapter deals with the rules governing: the statement of affairs which the official receiver may, on the making of a winding-up order, require, by notice, some or all of the persons referred to in s 131(3) to make out and submit to him or her a statement of affairs of the company (s 131(1)) (referred to in the rules as 'the nominated person'), a statement of concurrence and the submission of accounts requested under s 235.

See the comments under 'Statement of affairs' accompanying s 131.

**[2.357]**

**7.40 Notice requiring statement of affairs (section 131)**

(1)   Where, under section 131, the official receiver requires a nominated person to provide the official receiver with a statement of the affairs of the company, the official receiver must deliver a notice to that person.

(2)   The notice must be headed "Notice requiring statement of affairs" and must—

    (a)    identify the company immediately below the heading;

    (b)    require a nominated person to prepare and submit to the official receiver a statement of affairs of the company;

    (c)    inform the nominated person—

        (i)    of the names and addresses of any other nominated person to whom such a notice has been delivered, and

        (ii)   of the date by which the statement must be delivered; and

    (d)    state the effect of section 131(7) (penalty for non-compliance) and section 235 (duty to co-operate) as it applies to the official receiver.

(3)   The official receiver must inform the nominated person that a document for the preparation of the statement of affairs capable of completion in compliance with rule 7.41 can be supplied by the official receiver if requested.

**Derivation**—This rule derived from the Insolvency Rules 1986, SI 1986/1925, r 4.32.

**[2.358]**

**7.41 Statement of affairs**

(1)   The statement of affairs must be headed "Statement of affairs" and must contain—

    (a)    identification details for the company;

    (b)    a statement that it is a statement of the affairs of the company on a date which is specified, being—

        (i)    the date of the winding-up order, or

        (ii)    the date directed by the official receiver;

    (c)    a list of the company's shareholders with the following information about each one—

        (i)    name and postal address,

        (ii)    the type of shares held,

        (iii)    the nominal amount of the shares held,

        (iv)    the number of shares held,

        (v)    the amount per share called up, and

        (vi)    the total amount of shares called up;

    (d)    the total amount of shares called up held by all shareholders;

    (e)    a summary of the assets of the company, setting out the book value and estimated realisable value of—

        (i)    any assets subject to a fixed charge,

        (ii)    any assets subject to a floating charge,

        (iii)    any uncharged assets, and

        (iv)    the total value of all the assets available for preferential creditors;

    (f)    a summary of the liabilities of the company, setting out—

        (i)    the amount of preferential debts,

        (ii)    an estimate of the deficiency with respect to preferential debts or the surplus available after paying the preferential debts,

        (iii)    an estimate of the prescribed part, if applicable,

        (iv)    an estimate of the total assets available to pay debts secured by floating charges,

        (v)    the amount of debts secured by floating charges,

        (vi)    an estimate of the deficiency with respect to debts secured by floating charges or the surplus available after paying the debts secured by fixed or floating charges,

        (vii)    the amount of unsecured debts (excluding preferential debts),

        (viii)    an estimate of the deficiency with respect to unsecured debts or the surplus available after paying unsecured debts,

        (ix)    any issued and called-up capital, and

        (x)    an estimate of the deficiency with respect to, or surplus available to, members of the company;

    (g)    a list of the company's creditors (as required by section 131(2)) with the following particulars required by paragraph (2) indicating—

        (i)    any creditors under hire-purchase, chattel leasing or conditional sale agreements,

        (ii)    any creditors who are consumers claiming amounts paid in advance of the supply of goods or services, and

        (iii)    any creditors claiming retention of title over property in the company's possession.

(2)   The particulars required by this paragraph are as follows—

        (i)    the name and postal address,

        (ii)    the amount of the debt owed to the creditor,

        (iii)    details of any security held by the creditor,

        (iv)    the date the security was given, and

        (v)    the value of any such security.

(3)   Paragraph (4) applies where the particulars required by paragraph (2) relate to creditors who are either—

    (a)    employees or former employees of the company; or

    (b)    consumers claiming amounts paid in advance for the supply of goods or services.

(4)   Where this paragraph applies—

    (a)    the statement of affairs itself must state separately for each of paragraph (3)(a) and (b) the number of such creditors and the total of the debts owed to them; and

(b)    the particulars required by paragraph (2) in respect of those creditors must be set out in separate schedules to the statement of affairs for each of paragraph (3)(a) and (b).

(5)   The statement of affairs must be verified by a statement of truth by the nominated person, or all of them if more than one, making the statement of affairs.

(6)   The nominated person (or one of them, if more than one) must deliver the statement of affairs verified as required by paragraph (5) to the official receiver together with a copy.

(7)   The official receiver must deliver the verified copy of the statement of affairs and any statements of concurrence delivered under rule 7.42 to the registrar of companies.

(8)   However the official receiver must not deliver to the registrar of companies with the statement of affairs any schedule required by paragraph (4)(b).

**Derivation**—This rule derived from the Insolvency Rules 1986, SI 1986/1925, Sch 4, Fm 4.17.

**General note**—Under the previously applicable rule a prescribed form had to be completed. Most of the matters required to be included in the statement were required to be inserted in the prescribed form.

The Insolvency Service has provided a template for the statement: https://www.gov.uk/governm ent/publications/rule-741-statement-of-affairs-company-winding-up.

## [2.359]

### 7.42 Statement of affairs: statement of concurrence

(1)   The official receiver may require a person mentioned in section 131(3) ("a relevant person") to deliver to the official receiver a statement of concurrence.

(2)   A statement of concurrence is a statement, verified by a statement of truth, that that person concurs in the statement of affairs submitted by a nominated person.

(3)   The official receiver must inform the nominated person who has been required to submit a statement of affairs that the relevant person has been required to deliver a statement of concurrence.

(4)   The nominated person must deliver a copy of the statement of affairs to every relevant person who has been required to submit a statement of concurrence.

(5)   A statement of concurrence—

    (a)    must identify the company; and

    (b)    may be qualified in relation to matters dealt with in the statement of affairs, where the relevant person—

        (i)    is not in agreement with the statement of affairs,

        (ii)    considers the statement of affairs to be erroneous or misleading, or

        (iii)    is without the direct knowledge necessary for concurring in it.

(6)   The relevant person must deliver the required statement of concurrence (with a copy) to the official receiver before the end of the period of five business days (or such other period as the official receiver may agree) beginning with the day on which the relevant person receives the statement of affairs.

**Derivation**—This rule derived from the Insolvency Rules 1986, SI 1986/1925, r 4.33.

The Insolvency Service has provided a template for the statement: https://www.gov.uk/governm ent/publications/rule-742-statement-of-affairs-statement-of-concurrence-company-winding-up.

## [2.360]

### 7.43 Order limiting disclosure of statement of affairs etc

(1)   Where the official receiver thinks that disclosure of the whole or part of the statement of affairs or of any statement of concurrence would be likely to prejudice the conduct of the winding up or might reasonably be expected to lead to violence against any person, the official receiver may apply to the court for an order that the statement of affairs, statement of concurrence or any specified part of them must not be filed with the registrar of companies.

(2)   The court may order that the whole or a specified part of the statement of affairs or of a statement of concurrence must not be delivered to the registrar of companies.

(3)   The official receiver must as soon as reasonably practicable deliver to the registrar of companies a copy of the order, and the statement of affairs and any statement of concurrence to the extent allowed by the order.

**Derivation**—This rule derived from the Insolvency Rules 1986, SI 1986/1925, r 4.35.

## [2.361]

### 7.44   Release from duty to submit statement of affairs: extension of time (section 131)

(1)   The official receiver may exercise the power in section 131(5) to release a person from an obligation to submit a statement of affairs imposed under section 131(1) or (2), or to grant an extension of time, either at the official receiver's own discretion, or at the request of a nominated person.

(2)   A nominated person may apply to the court for a release or an extension of time if the official receiver refuses that person's request.

(3)   On receipt of an application, the court may, if it is satisfied that no sufficient cause is shown for it, dismiss it without giving notice to any party other than the applicant.

(4)   Unless the application is dismissed, the court must fix a venue for it to be heard.

(5)   The applicant must, at least 14 days before any hearing, deliver to the official receiver a notice stating the venue with a copy of the application and of any evidence on which the applicant intends to rely.

(6)   The official receiver may do either or both of the following—

(a)      file a report of any matters which the official receiver thinks ought to be drawn to the court's attention; or

(b)      appear and be heard on the application.

(7)   If a report is filed, the official receiver must deliver a copy of it to the applicant not later than five business days before the hearing.

(8)   The court must deliver sealed copies of any order made on the application to the nominated person and the official receiver.

(9)   The applicant must pay the applicant's own costs in any event and, unless and to the extent that the court orders otherwise those costs will not be an expense of the winding up.

**Derivation**—This rule derived from the Insolvency Rules 1986, SI 1986/1925, r 4.36.

## [2.362]

### 7.45   Statement of affairs: expenses

(1)   If a nominated person cannot personally prepare a proper statement of affairs, the official receiver may, as an expense of the winding up, employ a person or firm to assist in the preparation of the statement.

(2)   At the request of a nominated person, made on the grounds that the nominated person cannot personally prepare a proper statement, the official receiver may authorise an allowance, payable as an expense of the winding up, of all or part of the expenses to be incurred by the nominated person in employing a person or firm to assist the nominated person in preparing it.

(3)   Any such request by the nominated person must be accompanied by an estimate of the expenses involved; and the official receiver must only authorise the employment of a named person or a named firm, approved by the official receiver.

(4)   An authorisation given by the official receiver under this rule must be subject to such conditions (if any) as the official receiver thinks fit to impose relating to the manner in which any person may obtain access to relevant documents and other records.

(5)   Nothing in this rule relieves a nominated person from any obligation relating to the preparation, verification and submission of the statement of affairs, or to the provision of information to the official receiver or the liquidator.

(6)   Any payment made as an expense of the winding up under this rule must be made in the prescribed order of priority.

(7)   Paragraphs (2) to (6) of this rule may be applied, on application to the official receiver by any nominated person, in relation to the making of a statement of concurrence.

Derivation—This rule derived from the Insolvency Rules 1986, SI 1986/1925, r 4.37.

General note—See the comments accompanying r 6.7.

## [2.363]

### 7.46  Delivery of accounts to official receiver

(1)   Any of the persons specified in section 235(3) must, at the request of the official receiver, deliver to the official receiver accounts of the company of such nature, as at such date, and for such period, as the official receiver may specify.

(2)   The period specified may begin from a date up to three years before the date of the presentation of the winding-up petition, or from an earlier date to which audited accounts of the company were last prepared.

(3)   The court may, on the official receiver's application, require accounts for any earlier period.

(4)   Rule 7.45 applies (with the necessary modifications) in relation to accounts to be delivered under this rule as it applies in relation to the statement of affairs.

(5)   The accounts must, if the official receiver so requires, be verified by a statement of truth and (whether or not so verified) be delivered to the official receiver within 21 days of the request under paragraph (1), or such longer period as the official receiver may allow.

Derivation—This rule derived from the Insolvency Rules 1986, SI 1986/1925, r 4.39.

## [2.364]

### 7.47  Further disclosure

(1)   The official receiver may at any time require a nominated person to deliver (in writing) further information amplifying, modifying or explaining any matter contained in the statement of affairs, or in accounts delivered under the Act or these Rules.

(2)   The information must, if the official receiver so directs, be verified by a statement of truth, and (whether or not so verified) be delivered to the official receiver within 21 days of the requirement under paragraph (1), or such longer period as the official receiver may allow.

Derivation—This rule derived from the Insolvency Rules 1986, SI 1986/1925, r 4.42.

## CHAPTER 7

### REPORTS AND INFORMATION TO CREDITORS AND CONTRIBUTORIES

## [2.365]

### Note

[Note: a document required by the Act or these Rules must also contain the standard contents set out in Part 1.]

General comment on Chapter 7—The rules in this Chapter are aimed at making sure that the creditors and contributories are informed about the position of the company's affairs.

## [2.366]

### 7.48  Reports by official receiver

(1)   The official receiver must deliver a report on the winding up and the state of the company's affairs to the creditors and contributories at least once after the making of the winding-up order.

(2)   The report must contain—

    (a)    identification details for the proceedings;

    (b)    contact details for the official receiver;

    (c)    a summary of the assets and liabilities of the company as known to the official receiver at the date of the report;

    (d)    such comments on the summary and the company's affairs as the official receiver thinks fit; and

    (e)    any other information of relevance to the creditors or contributories.

(3)   The official receiver may apply to the court to be relieved of any duty imposed by this rule or to be authorised to carry out the duty in another way.

(4)   On such an application the court must have regard to the cost of carrying out the duty, to the amount of the assets available, and to the extent of the interest of creditors or contributories, or any particular class of them.

(5)   If proceedings in a winding-up are stayed by order of the court any duty of the official receiver to deliver a report under this rule ceases.

    **Derivation**—This rule derived from the Insolvency Rules 1986, SI 1986/1925, rr 4.43, 4.45, 4.46.

## [2.367]

### 7.49  Reports by official receiver: estimate of prescribed part

(1)   The official receiver must include in a report under rule 7.48(1) estimates to the best of the official receiver's knowledge and belief of the value of—

    (a)    the prescribed part (whether or not the official receiver might be required under section 176A to make the prescribed part available for the satisfaction of unsecured debts); and

    (b)    the company's net property (as defined by section 176A(6)).

(2)   If the official receiver (as liquidator) proposes to make an application to court under section 176A(5) the report must say so and give the reason for the application.

(3)   The official receiver may exclude from an estimate under paragraph (1) information the disclosure of which could seriously prejudice the commercial interests of the company.

(4)   If the exclusion of such information affects the calculation of the estimate, the report must say so.

    **Derivation**—This rule derived from the Insolvency Rules 1986, SI 1986/1925, r 4.43.

    **General note**—For a consideration of the prescribed part, see s 176A and the notes accompanying it.

## [2.368]

### 7.50  Further information where winding up follows administration

(1)   This rule applies where an administrator is appointed by the court under section 140 as the company's liquidator and becomes aware of creditors not formerly known to that person as administrator.

(2)   The liquidator must deliver to those creditors a copy of any statement previously sent by the administrator to creditors in accordance with paragraph 49(4) of Schedule B1 and rule 3.35.

    **Derivation**—This rule derived from the Insolvency Rules 1986, SI 1986/1925, r 4.49A.

## [2.369]

### 7.51  Notice of stay of winding up

Where the court grants a stay in a winding up it may include in its order such requirements on the company as it thinks just with a view to bringing the stay to the notice of creditors and contributories.

    **Derivation**—This rule derived from the Insolvency Rules 1986, SI 1986/1925, r 4.48(2).

CHAPTER 8

THE LIQUIDATOR

[2.370]

Note

[Note: a document required by the Act or these Rules must also contain the standard contents set out in Part 1.]

General comment on Chapter 11—This part of the Rules covers the process and procedures that relate to the appointment of liquidators who follow the official receiver as the first liquidator of a company and the resignation, removal and release of appointed liquidators.

[2.371]

7.52  Choosing a person to be liquidator

(1)   This rule applies where nominations are sought by the official receiver from the company's creditors and contributories under section 136 for the purpose of choosing a person to be liquidator of the company in place of the official receiver.

(2)   The official receiver must deliver to the creditors and contributories a notice inviting proposals for a liquidator.

(3)   The notice must explain that the official receiver is not obliged to seek the creditors' views on any proposals that do not meet the requirements of paragraphs (4) and (5).

(4)   A proposal must state the name and contact details of the proposed liquidator, and contain a statement that the proposed liquidator is qualified to act as an insolvency practitioner in relation to the company and has consented to act as liquidator of the company.

(5)   A proposal must be received by the official receiver within five business days of the date of the notice under paragraph (2).

(6)   Following the end of the period for inviting proposals under paragraph (2), where any proposals are received the official receiver must seek a decision on the nomination of a liquidator from the creditors (on any proposals received from creditors) and from the contributories (on any proposals received from contributories) by—

    (a)    a decision procedure; or

    (b)    the deemed consent procedure.

(7)   Where a decision is sought under paragraph (6) following the official receiver's decision under section 136(5)(a) to seek a nomination, the decision date must be not more than four months from the date of the winding-up order.

(8)   Where the official receiver is required under section 136(5)(c) to seek such a decision, the official receiver must send a notice to the creditors and contributories which complies with rule 15.7 or 15.8 so far as relevant.

(9)   The notice must also—

    (a)    identify any liquidator proposed to be nominated by a creditor (in the case of a notice to creditors) or by a contributory (in the case of a notice to contributories) in accordance with this rule; and

    (b)    contain a statement explaining the effect of section 137(2) (duty of official receiver to consider referral of need for appointment of liquidator to the Secretary of State where no person is chosen to be liquidator).

(10)   The decision date in the notice must be no later than 21 days after the date for receiving proposals has passed.

(11)   The creditors and contributories must be given at least 14 days' notice of the decision date.

(12)   Where no proposal is received by the official receiver under paragraph (2), the official receiver has no obligation to seek a decision from creditors or contributories on a liquidator.

(13)   Nothing in this rule affects the official receiver's ability under section 137(1), at any time when liquidator of the company, to apply to the Secretary of State to appoint a liquidator in place of the official receiver.

**Derivation**—This rule derived from the Insolvency Rules 1986, SI 1986/1925, r 4.50.
**Decision procedure**—See s 246ZE and Chapter 2 of Part 15.
**Deemed consent procedure**—See s 246ZF and r 15.7.
See s 136 and the notes accompanying it.

**[2.372]**

**7.53  Appointment of liquidator by creditors or contributories**
(1)   This rule applies where a person is appointed as liquidator by the creditors or contributories.
(2)   The convener of the decision procedure or deemed consent procedure, or the chair in the case of a meeting must certify the appointment, but not unless and until the appointee has provided to the convener or the chair a statement to the effect that the appointee is an insolvency practitioner qualified under the Act to be the liquidator and consents to act.
(3)   The certificate must be authenticated and dated by the convener or chair and must—

    (a)   identify the company;
    (b)   identify and provide contact details for the person appointed as liquidator;
    (c)   state the date on which the liquidator was appointed;
    (d)   state that the appointee—
        (i)   has provided a statement of being qualified to act as an insolvency practitioner in relation to the company,
        (ii)   has consented to act, and
        (iii)   was appointed as liquidator of the company.

(4)   Where two or more liquidators are appointed the certificate must also specify (as required by section 231) whether any act required or authorised under any enactment to be done by the liquidator is to be done by all or any one or more of them.
(5)   The liquidator's appointment is effective from the date on which the appointment is certified, that date to be endorsed on the certificate.
(6)   The convener or chair (if that person is not the official receiver) must deliver the certificate to the official receiver.
(7)   The official receiver must in any case deliver the certificate to the liquidator.

**Derivation**—This rule derived from the Insolvency Rules 1986, SI 1986/1925, r 4.100.

**[2.373]**

**7.54  Decision on nomination**
(1)   In the case of a decision on the nomination of a liquidator—

    (a)   if on any vote there are two nominees, the person who obtains the most support is appointed;
    (b)   if there are three or more nominees, and one of them has a clear majority over both or all the others together, that one is appointed; and
    (c)   in any other case, the convener or chair must continue to take votes (disregarding at each vote any nominee who has withdrawn and, if no nominee has withdrawn, the nominee who obtained the least support last time) until a clear majority is obtained for any one nominee.

(2)   In the case of a decision being made at a meeting, the chair may at any time put to the meeting a resolution for the joint nomination of any two or more nominees.

**Derivation**—This rule derived from the Insolvency Rules 1986, SI 1986/1925, r 4.63.

**[2.374]**

### 7.55 Invitation to creditors and contributories to form a liquidation committee

(1)   Where a decision is sought from the company's creditors and contributories on the appointment of a liquidator, the convener of the decision must at the same time deliver to the creditors and contributories a notice inviting them to decide whether a liquidation committee should be established if sufficient creditors are willing to be members of the committee.

(2)   The notice must also invite nominations for membership of the committee, such nominations to be received by a date specified in the notice.

(3)   The notice must—

    (a)    state that nominations must be delivered to the convener by the specified date;

    (b)    state, in the case of creditors, that nominations can only be accepted if the convener is satisfied as to the creditors' eligibility under rule 17.4; and

    (c)    explain the effect of section 141(2) and (3) on whether a committee is to be established under Part 17.

**[2.375]**

### 7.56 Appointment by the court

(1)   This rule applies where the liquidator is appointed by the court under section 139(4) (different persons nominated by creditors and contributories) or section 140 (winding up following administration or CVA).

(2)   The court must not make the order unless and until the person being appointed has filed with the court a statement to the effect that that person is an insolvency practitioner, duly qualified under the Act to be the liquidator, and consents to act.

(3)   The order of the court must contain—

    (a)    identification details for the proceedings;

    (b)    the name and title of the judge making the order;

    (c)    the name and postal address of the applicant;

    (d)    the capacity in which the applicant made the application;

    (e)    identification and contact details for the proposed liquidator;

    (f)    a statement that the proposed liquidator has filed—

        (i)    a statement of qualification to act as an insolvency practitioner in relation to the company, and

        (ii)    a consent to act;

    (g)    the order that the proposed liquidator is appointed liquidator of the company; and

    (h)    the date on which the order is made.

(4)   Where two or more liquidators are appointed the order must also specify (as required by section 231) whether any act required or authorised under any enactment to be done by the liquidator is to be done by all or any one or more of them.

(5)   The court must deliver two copies of the order to the official receiver one of which must be sealed.

(6)   The official receiver must deliver the sealed copy of the order to the person appointed as liquidator.

(7)   The liquidator's appointment takes effect from the date of the order or such other date as the court orders.

(8)   Within 28 days from appointment, the liquidator must—

    (a)    deliver notice of the appointment to the creditors and to the contributories of the company of whom the liquidator is aware; or

    (b)    advertise the appointment in accordance with any directions given by the court.

(9)   In the notice under this rule the liquidator must—

    (a)    state whether the liquidator proposes to seek decisions from creditors and contributories for the purpose of establishing a liquidation committee, or proposes only to seek a decision from creditors for that purpose; and

(b)     if the liquidator does not propose to seek any such decision, set out the powers of the creditors under the Act to require the liquidator to seek one.

Derivation—This rule derived from the Insolvency Rules 1986, SI 1986/1925, r 4.102.

## [2.376]

### 7.57  Appointment by the Secretary of State

(1)   This rule applies where the official receiver applies to the Secretary of State to appoint a liquidator in place of the official receiver, or refers to the Secretary of State the need for an appointment.

(2)   If the Secretary of State makes an appointment, the Secretary of State must deliver a copy of the certificate of appointment to the official receiver, who must deliver it to the person appointed.

(3)   The certificate must specify the date from which the liquidator's appointment is to be effective.

Derivation—This rule derived from the Insolvency Rules 1986, SI 1986/1925, r 4.104.
General note—See s 137 and the notes accompanying it.

## [2.377]

### 7.58  Cost of liquidator's security (section 390(3))

The cost of the liquidator's security required by section 390(3) for the proper performance of the liquidator's functions is an expense of the winding up.

Derivation—This rule derived from the Insolvency Rules 1986, SI 1986/1925, r 12A.56.
General note—See s 390(3) of the Act which is the provision which sets out the need for security to be given by insolvency practitioners.

## [2.378]

### 7.59  Appointment to be gazetted and notice given to registrar of companies

(1)   The liquidator—

(a)     must gazette a notice of the appointment as soon as reasonably practicable after appointment; and

(b)     may advertise the notice in such other manner as the liquidator thinks fit.

(2)   The notice must state—

(a)     that a liquidator has been appointed; and

(b)     the date of the appointment.

(3)   As soon as reasonably practicable the liquidator must deliver notice of the appointment to the registrar of companies.

Derivation—This rule derived from the Insolvency Rules 1986, SI 1986/1925, r 4.106A.

## [2.379]

### 7.60  Hand-over of assets by official receiver to liquidator

(1)   This rule only applies where the liquidator is appointed in succession to the official receiver acting as liquidator.

(2)   When the liquidator's appointment takes effect, the official receiver must as soon as reasonably practicable do all that is required for putting the liquidator into possession of the assets.

(3)   On taking possession of the assets, the liquidator must discharge any balance due to the official receiver on account of—

(a)     expenses properly incurred by the official receiver and payable under the Act or these Rules; and

(b)     any advances made by the official receiver in respect of the assets, together with interest on such advances at the rate specified in section 17 of the Judgments Act 1838 at the date of the winding-up order.

(4)   Alternatively, the liquidator may (before taking office) give to the official receiver a written undertaking to discharge any such balance out of the first realisation of assets.

(5)   The official receiver has a charge on the assets in respect of any sums due to the official receiver under paragraph (3) until they have been discharged, subject only to the deduction from realisations by the liquidator of the proper costs and expenses of such realisations.

(6)   The liquidator must from time to time out of the realisation of assets discharge all guarantees properly given by the official receiver for the benefit of the insolvent estate, and must pay all the official receiver's expenses.

(7)   The official receiver must give to the liquidator all such information relating to the affairs of the company and the course of the winding up as the official receiver considers to be reasonably required for the effective discharge by the liquidator of the liquidator's duties.

(8)   The official receiver must also deliver to the liquidator a copy of any report made by the official receiver under Chapter 7 of Part 7.

**Derivation**—This rule derived from the Insolvency Rules 1986, SI 1986/1925, r 4.107.

## [2.380]

### 7.61  Liquidator's resignation

(1)   A liquidator may resign only—
  (a)   on grounds of ill health;
  (b)   because of the intention to cease to practise as an insolvency practitioner;
  (c)   because the further discharge of the duties of liquidator is prevented or made impracticable by—
    (i)   a conflict of interest, or
    (ii)   a change of personal circumstances;
  (d)   where two or more persons are acting as liquidator jointly, and it is the opinion of both or all of them that it is no longer expedient that there should continue to be that number of joint liquidators.

(2)   Before resigning, the liquidator must deliver a notice to creditors, and invite the creditors by a decision procedure, or by deemed consent procedure, to consider whether a replacement should be appointed, except where the resignation is under sub-paragraph (1)(d).

(3)   The notice must—
  (a)   state the liquidator's intention to resign;
  (b)   state that under rule 7.61(7) of these Rules the liquidator will be released 21 days after the date of delivery of the notice of resignation to the court under section 172(6), unless the court orders otherwise; and
  (c)   comply with rule 15.7 or 15.8 so far as applicable.

(4)   The notice may suggest the name of a replacement liquidator.

(5)   The notice must be accompanied by a summary of the liquidator's receipts and payments.

(6)   The decision date must be not more than five business days before the date on which the liquidator intends to give notice under section 172(6).

(7)   The resigning liquidator's release is effective 21 days after the date on which the notice of resignation under section 172(6) is filed with the court.

**Derivation**—This rule derived from the Insolvency Rules 1986, SI 1986/1925, r 4.108(4).

**General note**—The courts have been ready, on occasions in the past, to permit a practitioner to resign in circumstances where a practitioner is holding multiple appointments (perhaps across a number of different insolvency regimes) and to transfer them to another practitioner by way of a block transfer. The 2016 Rules provide specific provisions to deal with this in rr 12.36–12.38.

See the extensive comments under the heading of 'Resign' in relation to s 172.

## [2.381]

### 7.62  Notice to official receiver of intention to vacate office

(1)   This rule applies where the liquidator intends to vacate office, whether by resignation or otherwise, and as a result there will be a vacancy in the office of

liquidator (so that by virtue of section 136(3) the official receiver is liquidator until the vacancy is filled).

(2)   The liquidator must deliver notice of that intention to the official receiver at least 21 days before the liquidator intends to vacate office.

(3)   The liquidator must include in the notice to the official receiver the following details of any property of the company which has not been realised, applied, distributed or otherwise fully dealt with in the winding up—

    (a)    the nature of the property;

    (b)    its value (or the fact that it has no value);

    (c)    its location;

    (d)    any action taken by the liquidator to deal with the property or any reason for the liquidator not dealing with it; and

    (e)    the current position in relation to it.

**Derivation**—This rule derived from the Insolvency Rules 1986, SI 1986/1925, r 4.137.

## [2.382]

### 7.63  Decision of creditors to remove liquidator

(1)   This rule applies where the convener of the decision procedure or chair of the meeting (as the case may be) is other than the official receiver, and a decision is made, using a decision procedure, to remove the liquidator

(2)   The convener or chair must within three business days of the decision to remove the liquidator deliver a certificate to that effect to the official receiver.

(3)   If the creditors decided to appoint a new liquidator, the certificate of the new liquidator's appointment must also be delivered to the official receiver within that time; and the certificate must comply with the requirements in rule 7.53.

(4)   The certificate of the liquidator's removal must—

    (a)    identify the company;

    (b)    identify and provide contact details for the removed liquidator;

    (c)    state that the creditors of the company decided on the date specified in the certificate that the liquidator specified in the certificate be removed from office as liquidator of the company;

    (d)    state the decision procedure used, and the decision date;

    (e)    state that the creditors either—

        (i)    did not decide against the liquidator being released, or

        (ii)    decided that the liquidator should not be released; and

    (f)    be authenticated and dated by the convener or chair.

(5)   The liquidator's removal is effective from the date of the certificate of removal.

**Derivation**—This rule derived from the Insolvency Rules 1986, SI 1986/1925, r 4.113.

## [2.383]

### 7.64  Procedure on removal by creditors

(1)   Where the creditors have decided that the liquidator be removed, the official receiver must file the certificate of removal with the court.

(2)   The official receiver must deliver a copy of the certificate as soon as reasonably practicable to the removed liquidator and deliver a notice of the removal to the registrar of companies.

**Derivation**—This rule derived from the Insolvency Rules 1986, SI 1986/1925, r 4.116.

## [2.384]

### 7.65  Removal of liquidator by the court (section 172(2))

(1)   This rule applies where an application is made to the court under section 172(2) for the removal of the liquidator, or for an order directing the liquidator to initiate a decision procedure of creditors for the purpose of removing the liquidator.

(2)   On receipt of an application, the court may, if it is satisfied that no sufficient cause is shown for it, dismiss it without giving notice to any party other than the applicant.

(3)   Unless the application is dismissed, the court must fix a venue for it to be heard.

(4)   The applicant must, at least 14 days before any hearing, deliver to the liquidator and the official receiver a notice stating the venue with a copy of the application and of any evidence on which the applicant intends to rely.

(5)   A respondent may apply for security for costs of the application and the court may make such an order if it is satisfied, having regard to all the circumstances of the case, that it is just to make such an order.

(6)   The liquidator and the official receiver may do either or both of the following—

> (a)   file a report of any matters which the liquidator or the official receiver thinks ought to be drawn to the court's attention; or
>
> (b)   appear and be heard on the application.

(7)   On a successful application the court's order must contain—

> (a)   the name of the court (and hearing centre if applicable) in which the order is made;
>
> (b)   the name and title of the judge making the order;
>
> (c)   the name and postal address of the applicant;
>
> (d)   the capacity in which the applicant made the application;
>
> (e)   identification and contact details for the liquidator;
>
> (f)   identification details for the company;
>
> (g)   an order either—
>
>> (i)   that that the liquidator is removed from office; or
>>
>> (ii)   that the liquidator must initiate a decision procedure of the company's creditors (specifying which procedure is to be used) on or before the date specified in the order for the purpose of considering the liquidator's removal from office; and
>
> (h)   the date the order is made.

(8)   The costs of the application are not payable as an expense of the winding up unless the court orders otherwise.

(9)   Where the court removes the liquidator—

> (a)   it must deliver the sealed order of removal to the former liquidator and a copy of the order to the official receiver; and
>
> (b)   the former liquidator must deliver a copy of the order to the registrar of companies as soon as reasonably practicable.

(10)   If the court appoints a new liquidator, rule 7.56 applies.

**Derivation**—This rule derived from the Insolvency Rules 1986, SI 1986/1925, r 4.119.

**General note**—For substantive discussion concerning removal, see the notes accompanying s 172. Also, see the notes accompanying s 108, which applies to creditors' voluntary liquidations but the case law is relevant in considering removal in compulsory liquidations.

## [2.385]

### 7.66  Removal of liquidator by the Secretary of State (section 172(4))

(1)   This rule applies where the Secretary of State decides to direct under section 172(4) the removal of a liquidator appointed by the Secretary of State.

(2)   Before doing so the Secretary of State must deliver to the liquidator and the official receiver a notice of the Secretary of State's decision and the grounds for the decision.

(3)   The notice must specify a period within which the liquidator may make representations against implementation of the decision.

(4)   If the Secretary of State directs the removal of the liquidator, the Secretary of State must as soon as reasonably practicable—

> (a)   deliver notice of the Secretary of State's decision to the registrar of companies, the liquidator and the official receiver; and
>
> (b)   file notice of the decision with the court.

(5)   Where the Secretary of State directs the liquidator be removed the court may make any order that it could have made if the liquidator had been removed by the court.

Derivation—This rule derived from the Insolvency Rules 1986, SI 1986/1925, r 4.123.

**[2.386]**

### 7.67 Deceased liquidator

(1) If the liquidator (not being the official receiver) dies a notice of the fact and date of death must be delivered to the official receiver by one of the following—

    (a)    a surviving joint liquidator;

    (b)    a member of the deceased liquidator's firm (if the deceased was a member or employee of a firm);

    (c)    an officer of the deceased liquidator's company (if the deceased was an officer or employee of a company);

    (d)    a personal representative of the deceased liquidator.

(2) If no such notice has been delivered within the 21 days following the liquidator's death then any other person may deliver the notice.

(3) The official receiver must—

    (a)    file notice of the death with the court, for the purpose of fixing the date of the deceased liquidator's release under section 174(4)(a); and

    (b)    deliver a copy of the notice to the registrar of companies.

Derivation—This rule derived from the Insolvency Rules 1986, SI 1986/1925, r 4.132.

**[2.387]**

### 7.68 Loss of qualification as insolvency practitioner

(1) This rule applies where the liquidator vacates office on ceasing to be qualified to act as an insolvency practitioner in relation to the company.

(2) A notice of the fact must be delivered as soon as reasonably practicable to the official receiver by one of the following—

    (a)    the liquidator who has vacated office;

    (b)    a continuing joint liquidator;

    (c)    the recognised professional body which was the source of the vacating liquidator's authorisation to act in relation to the company.

(3) The notice must be authenticated and dated by the person delivering the notice.

(4) The official receiver must—

    (a)    deliver a notice of receiving such a notice to the Secretary of State; and

    (b)    deliver a copy to the registrar of companies.

Derivation—This rule derived from the Insolvency Rules 1986, SI 1986/1925, r 4.134.

General note—See s 390 concerning the qualifications that apply to liquidators and other office-holders.

**[2.388]**

### 7.69 Application by liquidator for release (section 174(4)(b) or (d))

(1) An application by a liquidator to the Secretary of State for release under section 174(4)(b) or (d) must contain—

    (a)    identification details for the proceedings;

    (b)    identification and contact details for the liquidator;

    (c)    a statement that the liquidator of the company is applying to the Secretary of State to grant the liquidator with a certificate of the liquidator's release as liquidator as a result of the circumstances specified in the application;

    (d)    details of the circumstances referred to in sub-paragraph (c) under which the liquidator has ceased to act as liquidator.

(2) The application must be authenticated and dated by the liquidator.

(3) When the Secretary of State releases the former liquidator, the Secretary of State must certify the release and deliver the certificate to the former liquidator whose release is effective from the date of the certificate or such other date as the certificate specifies.

(4)   The Secretary of State must deliver notice of the release to the registrar of companies.

Derivation—This rule derived from the Insolvency Rules 1986, SI 1986/1925, r 4.121.

General note—The Insolvency Service has provided a template for applications: https://www.go
v.uk/government/publications/rule-769-liquidators-application-to-the-secretary-of-state-for-releas
e-person-other-than-official-receiver-company-winding-up.

## [2.389]

### 7.70  Release of official receiver

(1)   The official receiver must, before giving notice to the Secretary of State under section 174(3) (that the winding up is for practical purposes complete), deliver notice of intention to do so to the creditors.

(2)   The notice must be accompanied by a summary of the official receiver's receipts and payments as liquidator.

(3)   The summary of receipts and payments must also include a statement as to the amount paid to unsecured creditors under section 176A (prescribed part).

(4)   When the Secretary of State has determined the date from which the official receiver's release is to be effective, the Secretary of State must—

    (a)   notify the official receiver of the release; and

    (b)   deliver a notice of the release to the registrar of companies accompanied by the summary of the official receiver's receipts and payments.

Derivation—This rule derived from the Insolvency Rules 1986, SI 1986/1925, r 4.124.

## [2.390]

### 7.71  Final account prior to dissolution (section 146)

(1)   The final account which the liquidator is required to make up under section 146(2) and deliver to creditors must comply with the requirements of rule 18.14.

(2)   When the account is delivered to the creditors it must be accompanied by a notice which states—

    (a)   that the company's affairs are fully wound up;

    (b)   that the creditor has the right to request information from the liquidator under rule 18.9;

    (c)   that a creditor has the right to challenge the liquidator's remuneration and expenses under rule 18.34;

    (d)   that a creditor may object to the release of the liquidator by giving notice in writing to the liquidator before the end of the prescribed period;

    (e)   that the prescribed period is the period ending at the later of—

        (i)   eight weeks after delivery of the notice, or

        (ii)   if any request for information under rule 18.9 or any application to court under that rule or rule 18.34 is made when that request or application is finally determined;

    (f)   that the liquidator will vacate office under section 172(8) as soon as the liquidator has complied with section 146(4) by filing with the court and delivering to the registrar of companies the final account and notice containing the statement required by section 146(4)(b) of whether any creditors have objected to the liquidator's release; and

    (g)   that the liquidator will be released under section 174(4)(d)(ii) at the same time as vacating office unless any of the creditors objected to the release.

(3)   The liquidator must deliver a copy of the notice under section 146(4) to the Secretary of State.

(4)   Rule 7.69 applies to an application by the liquidator to the Secretary of State for release.

Derivation—This rule derived from the Insolvency Rules 1986, SI 1986/1925, r 4.125.

General note—This represents quite a different rule from its precursor, r 4.125. This is because final meetings, which were required under r 4.125, are no longer necessary when a liquidation is finalised.

## [2.391]

### 7.72 Relief from, or variation of, duty to report

(1) The court may, on the application of the liquidator or the official receiver, relieve the liquidator or official receiver of any duty imposed on the liquidator or official receiver by rule 7.70 or rule 7.71, or authorise the liquidator or official receiver to carry out the duty in a way other than required by either of those rules.

(2) In considering whether to act under this rule, the court must have regard to the cost of carrying out the duty, to the amount of the assets available, and to the extent of the interest of creditors or contributories, or any particular class of them.

Derivation—This rule derived from the Insolvency Rules 1986, SI 1986/1925, r 4.125A.

## [2.392]

### 7.73 Liquidator's duties on vacating office

(1) A liquidator who ceases to be in office in consequence of removal, resignation or ceasing to be qualified to act as an insolvency practitioner in relation to the company, must as soon as reasonably practicable deliver to the successor as liquidator—

    (a)    the assets (after deduction of any expenses properly incurred, and distributions made, by the previous liquidator);

    (b)    the records of the winding up, including correspondence, proofs and other documents relating to the winding up while it was within the former liquidator's responsibility; and

    (c)    the company's documents and other records.

(2) Where the liquidator vacates office under section 172(8) (final report to creditors), the liquidator must deliver to the official receiver the company's documents and other records which have not already been disposed of in accordance with general regulations in the course of the winding up.

Derivation—This rule derived from the Insolvency Rules 1986, SI 1986/1925, r 4.138.

## [2.393]

### 7.74 Power of court to set aside certain transactions

(1) If in dealing with the insolvent estate the liquidator enters into any transaction with a person who is an associate of the liquidator, the court may, on the application of any interested person, set the transaction aside and order the liquidator to compensate the company for any loss suffered in consequence of it.

(2) This does not apply if either—

    (a)    the transaction was entered into with the prior consent of the court; or

    (b)    it is shown to the court's satisfaction that the transaction was for value, and that it was entered into by the liquidator without knowing, or having any reason to suppose, that the person concerned was an associate.

(3) Nothing in this rule is to be taken as prejudicing the operation of any rule of law or equity relating to a liquidator's dealings with trust property, or the fiduciary obligations of any person.

Derivation—This rule derived from the Insolvency Rules 1986, SI 1986/1925, r 4.149.

General note—'Associate' is defined in s 435. See the notes accompanying that section.

## [2.394]

### 7.75 Rule against improper solicitation

(1) Where the court is satisfied that any improper solicitation has been used by or on behalf of the liquidator in obtaining proxies or procuring the liquidator's appointment, it may order that no remuneration be allowed as an expense of the winding up to any person by whom, or on whose behalf, the solicitation was exercised.

(2) An order of the court under this rule overrides any resolution of the liquidation committee or the creditors, or any other provision of these Rules relating to the liquidator's remuneration.

**Derivation**—This rule derived from the Insolvency Rules 1986, SI 1986/1925, r 4.150.

**General note**—See s 164 which provides, inter alia, that a person who offers a bribe to secure his or her appointment as a liquidator of a company is liable to a fine.

## CHAPTER 9

### DUTIES AND POWERS OF LIQUIDATOR

**[2.395]**

Note

[Note: a document required by the Act or these Rules must also contain the standard contents set out in Part 1.]

**[2.396]**

#### 7.76 General duties of liquidator

(1) The duties which the Act imposes on the court relating to the collection of the company's assets and their application in discharge of the company's liabilities are discharged by the liquidator as an officer of the court subject to its control.

(2) In the discharge of the liquidator's duties, the liquidator, for the purposes of acquiring and retaining possession of the company's property, has the same powers as a receiver appointed by the High Court, and the court may on the application of the liquidator enforce such acquisition or retention accordingly.

**Derivation**—This rule derived from the Insolvency Rules 1986, SI 1986/1925, r 4.179.

**General note**—Rule 7.76(1) reflects the common law rule that liquidators in compulsory liquidations are officers of the court: *Re Contract Corp; Gooch's Case* (1871) 7 Ch App 207 at 211.

The liquidator is a representative of the court and entrusted with the reputation of the court to carry out his or her duties impartially: *Re Timberland Ltd; Corporate Affairs Commission v Harvey* (1979) 4 ACLR 259 at 286. The position of the liquidator means that he or she must at all times act in an honest, impartial, and high-minded fashion, and is directly accountable to the court for how he or she performs the duties of a liquidator (*Re Contract Corp; Gooch's Case; Re Timberland Ltd; Corporate Affairs Commission v Harvey*).

See, A Keay *McPherson and Keay's Law of Company Liquidation* (Sweet and Maxwell, 4th edn, 2018) at 562–606 for a discussion of the duties of directors.

**[2.397]**

#### 7.77 Permission for exercise of powers by liquidator

(1) Where the Act or these Rules require permission for the liquidator to exercise a power any permission given must not be a general permission but must relate to a particular proposed exercise of the liquidator's power.

(2) A person dealing with the liquidator in good faith and for value is not concerned to enquire whether any such permission has been given.

(3) Where the liquidator has done anything without such permission, the court or the liquidation committee may, for the purpose of enabling the liquidator to meet the liquidator's expenses out of the assets, ratify what the liquidator has done; but neither must do so unless satisfied that the liquidator has acted in a case of urgency and has sought ratification without undue delay.

(4) In this rule "permission" includes "sanction".

**Derivation**—This rule derived from the Insolvency Rules 1986, SI 1986/1925, r 4.184.

**General note**—In *Gresham International Ltd v Moonie* [2009] EWHC 1093 (Ch), [2009] 2 BCLC 256, [2010] BPIR 122 the court considered the provision in light of an application for retrospective sanctioning of proceedings by a liquidator.

This rule is not so much of an issue now that liquidators do not need permission to employ powers contained in Sch 4 to the Act. But there are still occasions where the liquidator requires permission to do certain things, eg under s 160(2) where the making of a call from a contributory requires either the sanction of the liquidation committee or the court's special permission.

**[2.398]**

### 7.78 Enforced delivery up of company's property (section 234)

(1) The powers conferred on the court by section 234 (enforced delivery of company property) are exercisable by the liquidator or, where a provisional liquidator has been appointed, by the provisional liquidator.

(2) Any person on whom a requirement under section 234(2) is imposed by the liquidator or provisional liquidator must, without avoidable delay, comply with it.

Derivation—This rule derived from the Insolvency Rules 1986, SI 1986/1925, r 4.185.

General note—See the comments accompanying s 234. The right to delegate to the liquidator the power contained in s 234 is found in s 160(1)(c). A liquidator under a voluntary liquidation has to obtain a court order as the s 234 power is not given to him or her. He or she could apply under s 112.

## CHAPTER 10

### SETTLEMENT OF LIST OF CONTRIBUTORIES

**[2.399]**

#### Note

[Note: a document required by the Act or these Rules must also contain the standard contents set out in Part 1.]

**[2.400]**

### 7.79 Delegation to liquidator of power to settle list of contributories

(1) The duties of the court under section 148 in relation to settling the list of contributories are, by virtue of these Rules and in accordance with section 160, delegated to the liquidator.

(2) The liquidator's duties in settling the list of contributories are performed as an officer of the court subject to the court's control.

Derivation—This rule derived from the Insolvency Rules 1986, SI 1986/1925, r 4.195.

General note—The power of the court to delegate to the liquidator the power to settle a list is conferred by this rule and by s 160(1)(b). The obligation of the court to settle a list is found in s 148. See the comments that relate to that section.

The liquidator of a voluntary liquidation is also given the power to settle the list (s 165(4)).

**[2.401]**

### 7.80 Duty of liquidator to settle list (section 148)

The liquidator must, as soon as reasonably possible after the liquidator's appointment, exercise the court's power to settle a list of the company's contributories for the purposes of section 148 and, with the court's approval, rectify the register of members.

Derivation—This rule derived from the Insolvency Rules 1986, SI 1986/1925, r 4.196.

General note—See s 148 and the notes accompanying it.

Also, see, A Keay *McPherson and Keay's Law of Company Liquidation* (Sweet and Maxwell, 4th edn, 2018) at 639–646 for a discussion of the power of the liquidator to settle a list and the process involved in making calls (dealt with in Chapter 11 of this Part of the Rules).

**[2.402]**

### 7.81 Contents of list

(1) The list must identify—

    (a) the several classes of the company's shares (if more than one); and

  (b) the several classes of contributories, distinguishing between those who are contributories in their own right and those who are so as representatives of, or liable for the debts of, others.

(2) In the case of each contributory the list must state—

  (a) the address of the contributory;

  (b) the number and class of shares, or the extent of any other interest to be attributed to the contributory; and

  (c) if the shares are not fully paid up, the amounts which have been called up and paid in respect of them (and the equivalent, if any, where the interest of the contributory is other than shares).

**Derivation**—This rule derived from the Insolvency Rules 1986, SI 1986/1925, r 4.197.

## [2.403]

### 7.82 Procedure for settling list

(1) Having settled the list, the liquidator must as soon as reasonably practicable deliver a notice, to each person included in the list, that this has been done.

(2) The notice given to each person must state—

  (a) in what character, and for what number of shares or what interest, that person is included in the list;

  (b) what amounts have been called up and paid up in respect of the shares or interest; and

  (c) that in relation to any shares or interest not fully paid up, that person's inclusion in the list may result in the unpaid capital being called.

(3) The notice must inform a person to whom it is given that, if that person objects to any entry in, or omission from, the list, that person should so inform the liquidator in writing within 21 days from the date of the notice.

(4) On receipt of an objection, the liquidator must within 14 days deliver a notice to the objector either—

  (a) that the liquidator has amended the list (specifying the amendment); or

  (b) that the liquidator considers the objection to be not well-founded and declines to amend the list.

(5) The notice must in either case inform the objector of the effect of rule 7.83.

**Derivation**—This rule derived from the Insolvency Rules 1986, SI 1986/1925, r 4.198.

## [2.404]

### 7.83 Application to court for variation of the list

(1) If a person ("the objector") objects to any entry in, or exclusion from, the list of contributories as settled by the liquidator and, notwithstanding notice by the liquidator declining to amend the list, the objector maintains the objection, the objector may apply to the court for an order removing the entry objected to or (as the case may be) otherwise amending the list.

(2) The application must be made within 21 days of the delivery to the applicant of the liquidator's notice under rule 7.82(4).

**Derivation**—This rule derived from the Insolvency Rules 1986, SI 1986/1925, r 4.199.

**General note**—See *Re Pinecord Ltd (in liquidation)* [1995] 2 BCLC 57 for an instance of an application under the precursor of this rule (r 4.199). The application in this case sought an order that the list be amended to show the shares held by the applicants to be fully paid-up.

A liquidator is not able to circumvent the procedure in this rule and the previous rule by applying to the court for a declaration that a contributory ought to be placed on the list: *Re Nathan Newman & Co* (1887) 35 ChD 1.

**[2.405]**

### 7.84 Variation of, or addition to, the list

The liquidator may from time to time vary or add to the list of contributories as previously settled by the liquidator, but subject in all respects to the preceding rules in this Chapter.

Derivation—This rule derived from the Insolvency Rules 1986, SI 1986/1925, r 4.200.

**[2.406]**

### 7.85 Costs of applications to vary etc the list of contributories

Where a person applies to set aside or vary any act or decision of the liquidator in settling the list of contributories then—

(a) the liquidator (if other than the official receiver) is not liable for any costs incurred by that person in relation to the application unless the court makes an order to that effect; and

(b) the official receiver is not personally liable for such costs.

Derivation—This rule derived from the Insolvency Rules 1986, SI 1986/1925, r 4.201.

CHAPTER 11

CALLS ON CONTRIBUTORIES

**[2.407]**

Note

[Note: a document required by the Act or these Rules must also contain the standard contents set out in Part 1.]

**[2.408]**

### 7.86 Making of calls by the liquidator (sections 150 and 160)

(1) Subject as follows the powers relating to the making of calls on contributories are exercisable by the liquidator as an officer of the court.

(2) However as provided by section 160(2) the making of a call requires either the sanction of the liquidation committee or the court's special permission.

Derivation—This rule derived from the Insolvency Rules 1986, SI 1986/1925, r 4.202.

General note—The liquidator is delegated the power to make calls on behalf of the court (in whom the power resides) by this rule and s 160(1)(d). Liquidators in voluntary liquidations are also delegated the power, and that is done by virtue of s 165(4)(b).

**[2.409]**

### 7.87 Sanction of the liquidation committee for making a call

(1) Where the liquidator proposes to make a call, and there is a liquidation committee, the liquidator may summon a meeting of the committee for the purpose of obtaining its sanction.

(2) The liquidator must deliver a notice of the meeting to each member of the committee giving at least five business days' notice of the meeting.

(3) The notice must state the purpose of making the call and the proposed amount of the call.

Derivation—This rule derived from the Insolvency Rules 1986, SI 1986/1925, r 4.203.

**[2.410]**

### 7.88 Application to court for permission to make a call (sections 150 and 160)

(1) Where the liquidator proposes to make a call the liquidator may apply to the court without notice to any other party for permission to make a call on any contributories of the company.

(2)   The application must state the amount of the proposed call, and the contributories on whom it is to be made.

(3)   The application must be supported by a witness statement accompanied by a schedule.

(4)   The witness statement must have the title "Witness statement of liquidator in support of application for call" and must contain—

    (a)   identification and contact details for the liquidator;

    (b)   identification details for the company;

    (c)   the number of persons on the list of contributories settled by the liquidator;

    (d)   the total number of shares to which the proposed call relates;

    (e)   the statement that in addition to the amount of the assets of the company mentioned in the schedule the liquidator believes a further sum will be required to satisfy the debts and liabilities of the company, and pay the expenses of and incidental to the winding up;

    (f)   the additional sum required;

    (g)   a statement that in order to provide the additional sum it is necessary to make a call upon the persons on the settled list of contributories, and that as it is probable that some of those contributories will partly or wholly fail to pay the amount of the call, the liquidator believes that it is necessary that a call of a specified amount per share be made in order to realise the amount required;

    (h)   the specified amount per share.

(5)   The accompanying schedule must show—

    (a)   the amount due in respect of debts already proved;

    (b)   the estimated amount of—

        (i)    further liabilities of the company, and

        (ii)   the expenses of the winding up;

    (c)   the total of the amounts referred to in sub-paragraphs (a) and (b); and

    (d)   a list of the assets in hand belonging to the company with their total value.

(6)   The schedule must be verified by a statement of truth made by the liquidator.

    **Derivation**—This rule derived from the Insolvency Rules 1986, SI 1986/1925, r 4.204, Sch 4, Fm 4.56.

    **General note**—Where there is no liquidation committee, special leave of the court is required in order to make a call (s 160(2)) and this rule provides the procedure. Unlike its predecessor (r 4.204) the contents of the witness statement that is to support an application are set out.

    If the court approves a call, it may permit the contributory to make payment by instalment: *Re Law Guarantee Society* (1910) 26 TLR 565.

## [2.411]

### 7.89   Order giving permission to make a call

(1)   The court's order giving permission to make a call must have the title "Order giving permission to make a call" and must contain—

    (a)   the name of the court (and hearing centre if applicable) in which the order is made;

    (b)   the name and title of the judge making the order;

    (c)   identification and contact details for the liquidator;

    (d)   identification details for the company;

    (e)   an order that the liquidator may make a call of the amount per share specified in the order on the contributories who are specified in the order;

    (f)   the amount per share of the call;

    (g)   the names of the contributories of the company on whom the liquidator is to make the call;

    (h)   an order that each such contributory must on or before the date specified in the order pay to the liquidator of the company the amount due from that contributory in respect of the call; and

(i)    the date of the order.

(2)   The court may direct that notice of the order be delivered to the contributories concerned, or to other contributories, or may direct that the notice be publicly advertised.

**Derivation**—This rule derived from the Insolvency Rules 1986, SI 1986/1925, Sch 4, Fm 4.57.

## [2.412]
### 7.90  Making and enforcement of the call

(1)   The liquidator must deliver a notice of the call to each of the contributories concerned.

(2)   The notice must contain—

(a)    identification details for the company;

(b)    identification and contact details for the liquidator;

(c)    a statement that a call on the contributories specified in the notice of the amount per share stated in the notice was sanctioned by—

(i)    a resolution of the liquidation committee of the company passed on the date which is stated in the notice, or

(ii)    an order of the court named in the notice on the date which is stated in the notice;

(d)    the amount per share of the call;

(e)    the amount or balance due from the contributory to whom the notice is addressed in respect of the call;

(f)    the date by which the sum must be paid;

(g)    a warning to the contributory that, if the required sum is not paid by the date specified in the notice, interest at the rate specified in the notice will be charged on the unpaid amount from that date until payment; and

(h)    the specified annual interest rate.

(3)   The notice must be accompanied by a copy of the resolution of the liquidation committee sanctioning the call or of the court's order giving permission as the case may be.

**Derivation**—This rule derived from the Insolvency Rules 1986, SI 1986/1925, r 4.205, Sch 4, Fm 4.58.

**General note**—Unlike its predecessor (r 4.205) the contents of the notice of call are set out in the rule (previously a prescribed form set out the necessary contents). The rule, again unlike its predecessor, provides that the notice must be accompanied by a copy of the resolution of the liquidation committee sanctioning the call or the court's order giving permission, as the case may be.

## [2.413]
### 7.91  Court order to enforce payment of call by a contributory

(1)   The court may make an order to enforce payment of the amount due from a contributory.

(2)   The order must have the title "Order for payment of call due from contributory" and must contain—

(a)    the name of the court (and hearing centre if applicable) in which the order is made;

(b)    identification and contact details for the liquidator who made the application;

(c)    the name and title of the judge making the order;

(d)    identification details for the company;

(e)    the name and postal address of the contributory who is the subject of the order;

(f)    the amount per share of the call;

(g)    an order that the contributory pay the liquidator the sum stated in the order in respect of the call on or before the date stated in the order or within four business days after service of the order whichever is the later;

(h)    an order that the contributory pay the liquidator interest at the rate stated in the order for the period commencing from the date specified in the order to the date of payment;

(i)    an order that the contributory pay the liquidator a stated sum in respect of the liquidator's costs of the application within the same period as the amount of the call must be paid;

(j)    a warning to the contributory that if the required sums are not paid within the time specified in the order further steps will be taken to compel the contributory to comply with the order; and

(k)    the date of the order.

**Derivation**—This rule derived from the Insolvency Rules 1986, SI 1986/1925, r 4.205, Sch 4, Fm 4.59.

**General note**—Unlike its predecessor (r 4.205) the contents of the order to make a call are set out.

CHAPTER 12

SPECIAL MANAGER

**[2.414]**

**Note**

[Note: a document required by the Act or these Rules must also contain the standard contents set out in Part 1.]

**General comment on Chapter 12**—Liquidators are able to apply, under s 177, to the courts for the appointment of a special manager so that he or she can secure some assistance in managing company property. This chapter lays out the procedure for this and what has to be done, procedurally, by a special manager. See the comments accompanying s 177.

**[2.415]**

**7.92 Application of this Chapter and interpretation**

This Chapter applies to applications for the appointment of a special manager by a liquidator and by a provisional liquidator (where one has been appointed), and so references to the liquidator are to be read as including a provisional liquidator.

**[2.416]**

**7.93 Appointment and remuneration of special manager (section 177)**

(1) An application made by the liquidator under section 177 for the appointment of a special manager must be supported by a report setting out the reasons for the application.

(2) The report must include the applicant's estimate of the value of the business or property in relation to which the special manager is to be appointed.

(3) The court's order appointing the special manager must have the title "Order of appointment of special manager" and must contain—

(a)    identification details for the proceedings;

(b)    the name and address of the person who made the application;

(c)    the name and title of the judge making the order;

(d)    the name and address of the proposed special manager;

(e)    the order that the proposed special manager is appointed as special manager of the company;

(f)    details of the special manager's responsibility over the company's business or property;

(g)    the powers to be entrusted to the special manager under section 177(3);

(h)    the time allowed for the special manager to give the required security for the appointment;

(i)    the duration of the special manager's appointment being one of the following—

      (i)     for a fixed period stated in the order,

      (ii)    until the occurrence of a specified event, or

      (iii)   until the court makes a further order;

    (j)    an order that the special manager's remuneration will be fixed from time to time by the court; and

    (k)    the date of the order.

(4)   The appointment of a special manager may be renewed by order of the court.

(5)   The special manager's remuneration will be fixed from time to time by the court.

(6)   The acts of the special manager are valid notwithstanding any defect in the special manager's appointment or qualifications.

**Derivation**—This rule derived from the Insolvency Rules 1986, SI 1986/1925, r 4.206.

**Amendments**—SI 2017/366.

**General note**—Unlike its predecessor (r 4.206) the contents of the order made appointing a special manager are set out in the rule.

## [2.417]

### 7.94 Security

(1)   The appointment of the special manager does not take effect until the person appointed has given (or, if the court allows, undertaken to give) security to the applicant for the appointment.

(2)   A person appointed as a special manager may give security either specifically for a particular winding up, or generally for any winding up in relation to which that person may be employed as special manager.

(3)   The amount of the security must be not less than the value of the business or property in relation to which the special manager is appointed, as estimated in the applicant's report which accompanied the application for appointment.

(4)   When the special manager has given security to the applicant that person must file with the court a certificate as to the adequacy of the security.

(5)   The cost of providing the security must be paid in the first instance by the special manager; but—

    (a)    where a winding-up order is not made, the special manager is entitled to be reimbursed out of the property of the company, and the court may order accordingly; and

    (b)    where a winding-up order is made, the special manager is entitled to be reimbursed as an expense of the winding up in the prescribed order of priority.

**Derivation**—This rule derived from the Insolvency Rules 1986, SI 1986/1925, r 4.207.

**General note**—Where a winding up has been ordered a special manager is able to claim his or her remuneration and expenses as a priority under r 7.108(4)(i).

## [2.418]

### 7.95 Failure to give or keep up security

(1)   If the special manager fails to give the required security within the time allowed for that purpose by the order of appointment, or any extension of that time that may be allowed, the liquidator must report the failure to the court, which may discharge the order appointing the special manager.

(2)   If the special manager fails to keep up the security, the liquidator must report the failure to the court, which may remove the special manager, and make such order as it thinks just as to costs.

(3)   If the court discharges the order appointing the special manager or makes an order removing the special manager, the court must give directions as to whether any, and if so what, steps should be taken for the appointment of another special manager.

**Derivation**—This rule derived from the Insolvency Rules 1986, SI 1986/1925, r 4.208.

[2.419]

### 7.96 Accounting

(1) The special manager must produce accounts, containing details of the special manager's receipts and payments, for the approval of the liquidator.

(2) The accounts must be for—

    (a) each three month period for the duration of the special manager's appointment; or

    (b) any shorter period ending with the termination of the special manager's appointment.

(3) When the accounts have been approved, the special manager's receipts and payments must be added to those of the liquidator.

**Derivation**—This rule derived from the Insolvency Rules 1986, SI 1986/1925, r 4.209.

[2.420]

### 7.97 Termination of appointment

(1) The special manager's appointment terminates—

    (a) if the winding-up petition is dismissed; or

    (b) in a case where a provisional liquidator was appointed under section 135, if the appointment is discharged without a winding-up order having been made.

(2) If the liquidator is of the opinion that the employment of the special manager is no longer necessary or beneficial for the company, the liquidator must apply to the court for directions, and the court may order the special manager's appointment to be terminated.

(3) The liquidator must make the same application if the creditors decide that the appointment should be terminated.

**Derivation**—This rule derived from the Insolvency Rules 1986, SI 1986/1925, r 4.210.

CHAPTER 13

PUBLIC EXAMINATION OF COMPANY OFFICERS AND OTHERS (SECTION 133)

[2.421]

### Note

[Note: a document required by the Act or these Rules must also contain the standard contents set out in Part 1.]

**General comment on Chapter 13**—These rules provide the procedure that relates to the public examination (under s 133) of company officers and those involved in the life of the company in some way. See the comments accompanying s 133.

For the rules applying to private examinations, see rr 12.17–12.22 and the notes accompanying them.

See A Keay, *McPherson and Keay's Law of Company Liquidation* (Sweet and Maxwell, 4th edn, 2018) at 969–980 for a general discussion of public examinations.

[2.422]

### 7.98 Applications relating to promoters, past managers etc (section 133(1)(c))

(1) An application under section 133(1) for the public examination of a person falling within paragraph (c) of subsection (1) (promoters, past managers, etc) must be accompanied by a report by the official receiver indicating—

    (a) the grounds on which the official receiver thinks the person is within that paragraph; and

    (b) whether the official receiver thinks it is likely that the order can be served on the person at a known address and, if so, by what means.

(2)  If the official receiver thinks that there is no reasonable certainty that service at a known address will be effective, the court may direct that the order be served by some means other than, or in addition to, service in such manner.

**Derivation**—This rule derived from the Insolvency Rules 1986, SI 1986/1925, r 4.211.

## [2.423]
### 7.99  Request by a creditor for a public examination (section 133(2))
(1)  A request made under section 133(2) by a creditor to the official receiver for the public examination of a person must contain—
- (a)   identification details for the company;
- (b)   the name and postal address of the creditor;
- (c)   the name and postal address of the proposed examinee;
- (d)   a description of the relationship which the proposed examinee has, or has had, with the company;
- (e)   a request by the creditor to the official receiver to apply to the court for a public examination of the proposed examinee under section 133(2);
- (f)   the amount of the creditor's claim in the winding up;
- (g)   a statement that the total amount of the creditor's and any concurring creditors' claims is believed to represent not less than one-half in value of the debts of the company;
- (h)   a statement that the creditor understands the requirement to deposit with the official receiver such sum as the official receiver may determine to be appropriate by way of security for the expenses of holding a public examination; and
- (i)   a statement that the creditor believes that a public examination is required for the reason stated in the request.

(2)  The request must be authenticated and dated by the creditor.
(3)  The request must be accompanied by—
- (a)   a list of the creditors concurring with the request and the amounts of their respective claims in the winding up, with their respective values; and
- (b)   from each concurring creditor, confirmation of the creditor's concurrence.

**Derivation**—This rule derived from the Insolvency Rules 1986, SI 1986/1925, r 4.213.
**General note**—The previous rules had, in one combined rule (r 4.213), a provision that deals with requests of both creditors and contributories. Now the requests are under separate rules.
 The Insolvency Service has provided a template for requests: https://www.gov.uk/government/p ublications/rule-799-request-by-a-creditor-for-a-public-examination-company-winding-up-notice -to-official-receiver.

## [2.424]
### 7.100  Request by a contributory for a public examination
(1)  A request made under section 133(2) by a contributory to the official receiver for the public examination of a person must contain—
- (a)   identification details for the company;
- (b)   the name and postal address of the contributory;
- (c)   the name and postal address of the proposed examinee;
- (d)   a description of the relationship which the proposed examinee has, or has had, with the company;
- (e)   a request by the contributory to the official receiver to apply to the court for a public examination of the proposed examinee under section 133(2);
- (f)   the number of shares held in the company by the contributory;
- (g)   the number of votes to which the contributory is entitled;
- (h)   a statement that the total amount of the contributory's and any concurring contributories' shares and votes is believed to represent not less than three-quarters in value of the company's contributories;

(i) a statement that the contributory understands the requirement to deposit with the official receiver such sum as the official receiver may determine to be appropriate by way of security for the expenses of holding a public examination; and

(j) a statement that the contributory believes that a public examination is required for the reason specified in the request.

(2) The request must be authenticated and dated by the contributory.

(3) The request must be accompanied by—

(a) a list of the contributories concurring with the request and the number of shares and votes each holds in the company; and

(b) from each concurring contributory, confirmation of the concurrence and of the number of shares and votes held in the company.

**Derivation**—This rule derived from the Insolvency Rules 1986, SI 1986/1925, r 4.213.

**General note**—The previous rules had, in one combined rule (r 4.213), a provision that dealt with requests of both creditors and contributories. Now the requests are under separate rules.

The Insolvency Service has provided a template for requests: https://www.gov.uk/government/p ublications/rule-7100-request-by-a-contributory-for-a-public-examination-company-winding-up-notice-to-official-receiver.

## [2.425]

### 7.101 Further provisions about requests by a creditor or contributory for a public examination

(1) A request by a creditor or contributory for a public examination does not require the support of concurring creditors or contributories if the requisitioning creditor's debt or, as the case may be, requisitioning contributory's shares, is sufficient alone under section 133(2).

(2) Before the official receiver makes the requested application, the creditor or contributory requesting the examination must deposit with the official receiver such sum (if any) as the official receiver determines is appropriate as security for the expenses of the public examination (if ordered).

(3) The official receiver must make the application for the examination—

(a) within 28 days of receiving the creditor's or contributory's request (if no security is required under paragraph (2)); or

(b) within 28 days of the creditor or contributory (as the case may be) depositing the required security.

(4) However if the official receiver thinks the request is unreasonable, the official receiver may apply to the court for an order to be relieved from making the application.

(5) If the application for an order under paragraph (4) is made without notice to any other party and the court makes such an order then the official receiver must deliver a notice of the order as soon as reasonably practicable to the creditors or contributories who requested the examination.

(6) If the court dismisses the official receiver's application under paragraph (4), the official receiver must make the application under section 133(2) as soon as reasonably practicable.

**Derivation**—This rule derived from the Insolvency Rules 1986, SI 1986/1925, rr 4.213(3), (4), (5).

## [2.426]

### 7.102 Order for public examination

(1) An order for a public examination must have the title "Order for Public Examination" and must contain the following—

(a) identification details for the proceedings;

(b) the name and title of the judge making the order;

(c) the name and postal address of the person to be examined;

(d) the venue for the public examination;

(e) the order that the person named in the order must attend the specified venue for the purpose of being publicly examined;

(f) the date of the order; and

(g) a warning to the person to be examined that failure without reasonable excuse to attend the public examination at the time and place specified in the order will make the person liable to be arrested without further notice under section 134(2); and that the person will also be guilty of contempt of court under section 134(1) and be liable to be committed to prison or fined.

(2) The official receiver must serve a copy of the order on the person to be examined as soon as reasonably practicable after the order is made.

(3) The court must rescind an order for the public examination of a person who was said to fall within section 133(1)(c) if that person satisfies the court that it is not so.

[Note: rule 81.9 (as amended) of the CPR requires a warning as mentioned in paragraph (1)(g) to be displayed prominently on the front of the order.]

**Derivation**—This rule derived from the Insolvency Rules 1986, SI 1986/1925, r 4.211, Sch 4, Fm 4.61.

**General note**—The order of the court summoning a person to be examined is to be served on the examinee as soon as reasonably practicable (r 7.102(2)). This was provided for under the previous rule (r 4.211), for although it said that service was to be undertaken forthwith the case law stated that it meant that service was to be effected as soon as is reasonably practicable: *Re Seagull Manufacturing Co Ltd (in liquidation)* [1993] Ch 345 at 359.

**Rescission of order**—For discussion of when this can occur, see comments under 'Rescission of order' in the notes accompanying s 236, which although addressing private examinations can be applied to public examinations, for the most part.

## [2.427]

### 7.103 Notice of the public examination

(1) The official receiver must give at least 14 days' notice of the public examination to—

(a) the liquidator (if a liquidator has been nominated or appointed);

(b) the special manager (if a special manager has been appointed); and

(c) the creditors and all the contributories of the company who are known to the official receiver (subject to any contrary direction of the court).

(2) Where the official receiver thinks fit additional notice of the order may be given by gazetting the notice.

(3) The official receiver may in addition to gazetting the notice advertise it in such other manner as the official receiver thinks fit;

(4) The notice must state—

(a) the purpose of the public examination; and

(b) the venue.

(5) Unless the court directs otherwise, the official receiver must not give notice under paragraph (2) of an order relating to a person falling within section 133(1)(c) until at least five business days have elapsed since the examinee was served with the order.

**Derivation**—This rule derived from the Insolvency Rules 1986, SI 1986/1925, r 4.212.

**General note**—The gazetting and giving notice of the examination is designed to bring notice of the examination to the public, and in particular any creditors. Rule 7.103(5) provides that, unless the court otherwise directs, there is to be no giving of notice before at least 5 business days have elapsed since the examinee is served with the order, thus giving the examinee time in which to apply to have the examination order rescinded, and before the examination becomes public knowledge.

## [2.428]

### 7.104 Examinee unfit for examination

(1) Where the examinee is a person who lacks capacity within the meaning of the Mental Capacity Act 2005 or is unfit to undergo or attend for public examination, the court may—

(a) stay the order for the examinee's public examination; or

    (b)    order that it is to be conducted in such manner and at such place as it thinks just.

(2)    The applicant for an order under paragraph (1) must be—

    (a)    a person who has been appointed by a court in the United Kingdom or elsewhere to manage the affairs of, or to represent, the examinee;

    (b)    a person who appears to the court to be a suitable person to make the application; or

    (c)    the official receiver.

(3)    Where the application is made by a person other than the official receiver, then—

    (a)    the application must, unless the examinee is a person who lacks capacity within the meaning of the Mental Capacity Act 2005, be supported by the witness statement of a registered medical practitioner as to the examinee's mental and physical condition;

    (b)    at least five business days' notice of the application must be given to the official receiver and the liquidator (if other than the official receiver); and

    (c)    before any order is made on the application, the applicant must deposit with the official receiver such sum as the latter certifies to be necessary for the additional expenses of an examination.

(4)    An order must contain—

    (a)    identification details for the proceedings;

    (b)    the name and postal address of the applicant;

    (c)    the name and title of the judge making the order;

    (d)    the capacity in which the applicant (other than the official receiver) made the application;

    (e)    the name and postal address of the examinee;

    (f)    the date of the order for the examinee's public examination ("the original order");

    (g)    a statement that the court is satisfied that the examinee specified in the order lacks capacity within the meaning of the Mental Capacity Act 2005 to manage and administer the examinee's property and affairs or is unfit to undergo a public examination;

    (h)    an order that—

        (i)    the original order is to be stayed on the grounds that the examinee is unfit to undergo a public examination, or

        (ii)    the original order is varied (as specified in this order) on the grounds that the examinee is unfit to attend the public examination fixed by the original order; and

    (i)    the date of the order.

(5)    Where a person other than the official receiver makes the application, the court may order that some or all of the expenses of the examination are to be payable out of the deposit under paragraph (3)(c), instead of as an expense of the winding up.

(6)    Where the application is made by the official receiver it may be made without notice to any other party, and may be supported by evidence set out in a report by the official receiver to the court.

**Derivation**—This rule derived from the Insolvency Rules 1986, SI 1986/1925, r 4.214.

**[2.429]**

### 7.105 Procedure at public examination

(1)    At the public examination the examinee must—

    (a)    be examined on oath; and

    (b)    answer all the questions which the court puts, or allows to be put.

(2)    A person allowed by section 133(4) to question the examinee may—

    (a)    with the approval of the court appear by an appropriately qualified legal representative; or

    (b)    in writing authorise another person to question the examinee on that person's behalf.

(3)   The examinee may at the examinee's own expense employ an appropriately qualified legal representative, who may put to the examinee such questions as the court may allow for the purpose of enabling the examinee to explain or qualify any answers given by the examinee, and may make representations on behalf of the examinee.

(4)   The court must have such record made of the examination as the court thinks proper.

(5)   The record may, in any proceedings (whether under the Act or otherwise) be used as evidence of any statement made by the examinee in the course of the public examination.

(6)   If criminal proceedings have been instituted against the examinee, and the court is of the opinion that continuing the hearing might prejudice a fair trial of those proceedings, the hearing may be adjourned.

**Derivation**—This rule derived from the Insolvency Rules 1986, SI 1986/1925, r 4.215.

**General note**—See comments under 'Examinations' in the notes accompanying s 133.

While the court that orders an examination may give a direction as to the hearing, a judge presiding at the examination has, under this rule, a number of broad discretions, the primary one being to allow or disallow questions: *Re Richbell Strategic Holdings Ltd (in liquidation) (No 2)* [2000] 2 BCLC 794. It has been said that questions must be relevant if they are to be permitted (*In Re Pennington ex parte Pennington* (1888) 5 Mor 268 at 269), but more recent authority suggests that such questions can be allowed provided they are not oppressive (*Re Transworld Payments UK Ltd* [2020] EWHC 115, [2021] BPIR 469 at [9]). A judge should disallow those questions which have been asked previously, or which are asked maliciously or not for the benefit of the creditors, contributories or the public: *Re London & Globe Finance Co* [1902] WN 16. One assumes that such questions would fall into the oppression category. In answering questions examinees are obliged to provide the best answers they are able, supplemented by documents where necessary: *Re Richbell Strategic Holdings Ltd (in liq) (No 2)* [2000] 2 BCLC 794.

## [2.430]

### 7.106 Adjournment

[Note: rule 81.9 (as amended) of the CPR requires a warning as mentioned in paragraph (3) to be displayed prominently on the front of the order.]

(1)   The court may adjourn the public examination from time to time, either to a fixed date or generally.

(2)   Where the examination has been adjourned generally, the court may at any time on the application of the official receiver or of the examinee—

    (a)    fix a venue for the resumption of the examination; and

    (b)    give directions as to the manner in which, and the time within which, notice of the resumed public examination is to be given to persons entitled to take part in it.

(3)   An order adjourning the public examination to a fixed date must contain a warning to the examinee that failure without reasonable excuse to attend the public examination at the time and place specified in the order will make the examinee liable to be arrested without further notice under section 134(2); and that the examinee will also be guilty of contempt of court under section 134(1) and be liable to be committed to prison or fined.

(4)   Where an application to resume an examination is made by the examinee, the court may grant it on terms that the examinee must pay the expenses of giving the notices required by paragraph (2) and that, before a venue for the resumed public examination is fixed, the examinee must deposit with the official receiver such sum as the official receiver considers necessary to cover those expenses.

**Derivation**—This rule derived from the Insolvency Rules 1986, SI 1986/1925, r 4.216.

## [2.431]

### 7.107 Expenses of examination

(1)   Where a public examination of the examinee has been ordered by the court on a request by a creditor under rule 7.99 or by a contributory under rule 7.100, the court

may order that some or all of the expenses of the examination are to be paid out of the deposit required under those rules, instead of as an expense of the winding up.

(2) The costs and expenses of a public examination do not fall on the official receiver personally.

Derivation—This rule derived from the Insolvency Rules 1986, SI 1986/1925, r 4.217.

CHAPTER 14

PRIORITY OF PAYMENT OF COSTS AND EXPENSES, ETC

[2.432]

General comment on Chapter 14—This Chapter deals with what payments constitute liquidation expenses as well as setting out the order in which the expenses are to be paid from company assets. This is necessary as there might not be sufficient assets in the company to pay the costs and expenses of a liquidation.

[2.433]

7.108 General rule as to priority

(1) All fees, costs, charges and other expenses incurred in the course of the winding up are to be treated as expenses of the winding up.

(2) The expenses of the winding up are payable out of—

(a) assets of the company available for the payment of general creditors, including—

(i) proceeds of any legal action which the liquidator has power to bring in the liquidator's own name or in the name of the company;

(ii) proceeds arising from any award made under any arbitration or other dispute resolution procedure which the liquidator has power to bring in the liquidator's own name or in the name of the company;

(iii) any payments made under any compromise or other agreement intended to avoid legal action or recourse to arbitration or to any other dispute resolution procedure;

(iv) payments made as a result of an assignment or a settlement of any such action, arrangement or procedure in lieu of or before any judgment being given or award being made; and

(b) subject as provided in rules 7.111 to 7.116, property comprised in or subject to a floating charge created by the company.

(3) The expenses associated with the prescribed part must be paid out of the prescribed part.

(4) Subject as provided in rules 7.112 to 7.116, the expenses are payable in the following order of priority—

(a) the following expenses, which rank equally in order of priority—

(i) expenses that are properly chargeable or incurred by the provisional liquidator in carrying out the functions conferred on the provisional liquidator by the court,

(ii) expenses that are properly chargeable or incurred by the official receiver or the liquidator in preserving, realising or getting in any of the assets of the company or otherwise in the preparation, conduct or assignment of any legal proceedings, arbitration or other dispute resolution procedures, which the official receiver or liquidator has power to bring in the official receiver's or liquidator's own name or bring or defend in the name of the company or in the preparation or conduct of any negotiations intended to lead or leading to a settlement or compromise of any legal action or dispute to which the proceedings or procedures relate,

> (iii)   expenses that relate to the employment of a shorthand writer, if appointed by an order of the court made at the instance of the official receiver in connection with an examination, and
>
> (iv)   expenses that are incurred in holding a hearing under rule 7.104 (examinee unfit) where the application for it was made by the official receiver;

(b)   any other expenses incurred or disbursements made by the official receiver or under the official receiver's authority, including those incurred or made in carrying on the business of the company;

(c)   the fees payable under any order made under section 414 or section 415A, including those payable to the official receiver (other than the fee referred to in sub-paragraph (d)), and any remuneration payable to the official receiver under general regulations;

(d)   the fee payable under any order made under section 414 for the performance by the official receiver of the general duties of the official receiver and any repayable sum deposited under any such order as security for the fee;

(e)   the cost of any security provided by a provisional liquidator, liquidator or special manager in accordance with the Act or these Rules;

(f)   the remuneration of the provisional liquidator (if any);

(g)   any sum deposited on an application for the appointment of a provisional liquidator;

(h)   the costs of the petitioner, and of any person appearing on the petition whose costs are allowed by the court;

(i)   the remuneration of the special manager (if any);

(j)   any amount payable to a person employed or authorised, under Chapter 6 of this Part, to assist in the preparation of a statement of affairs or of accounts;

(k)   any allowance made, by order of the court, in respect of costs on an application for release from the obligation to submit a statement of affairs, or for an extension of time for submitting such a statement;

(l)   the costs of employing a shorthand writer in any case other than one appointed by an order of the court at the instance of the official receiver in connection with an examination;

(m)   any necessary disbursements by the liquidator in the course of the administration of the winding up (including any . . . expenses incurred by members of the liquidation committee or their representatives and allowed by the liquidator under rule 17.24, but not including any payment of corporation tax in circumstances referred to in sub-paragraph (p));

(n)   the remuneration or emoluments of any person who has been employed by the liquidator to perform any services for the company, as required or authorised by or under the Act or these Rules;

(o)   the remuneration of the liquidator, up to an amount not exceeding that which is payable under Schedule 11 (determination of insolvency office-holder's remuneration);

(p)   the amount of any corporation tax on chargeable gains accruing on the realisation of any asset of the company (irrespective of the person by whom the realisation is effected);

(q)   the balance, after payment of any sums due under sub-paragraph (o) above, of any remuneration due to the liquidator; and

(r)   any other expenses properly chargeable by the liquidator in carrying out the liquidator's functions in the winding up.

**Derivation**—This rule derived from the Insolvency Rules 1986, SI 1986/1925, rr 4.218, 12.2.

**Amendments**—SI 2017/366; SI 2017/702; SI 2019/146, as from IP completion day (as defined in the European Union (Withdrawal Agreement) Act 2020, s 39(1)–(5)).

**General note**—The rule is based substantially on its precursor, r 4.218, although it is structured a little differently. Rule 7.108(4) is virtually the same as r 4.218(3). One difference in wording is mentioned below in relation to para (4)(a). The rule consists of four paragraphs, but divided into many subparagraphs. Rule 7.108 is a definitive statement of the liquidation expenses, subject to some express qualifications included in the Rules (eg r 7.109), as to what is to be regarded as an expense of a liquidation; there are no implied qualifications and no discretions in the courts (save for the limited discretion pursuant to s 156 to change the order of priority): *Kahn v Commissioners of Inland Revenue*, also known as *Toshoku Finance UK Plc* [2002] UKHL 6, [2002] 1 WLR 671 at [10]–[13], [17] and [38], HL.

Rule 7.108(4) overlaps significantly with r 6.42(4), which addresses creditors' voluntary liquidations. The main difference is that the former includes possible extra expenses that are peculiar to compulsory liquidations, such as the expenses of a provisional liquidator.

In relation to the expenses of the official receiver, litigation costs will normally be regarded as 'expenses' (*Re Transworld Payments UK Ltd* [2020] EWHC 115 at [51]).

**Expenses of the provisional liquidator**—It was held, relying on s 156 (allowing courts to order the priority of payments in a liquidation where there are insufficient assets), that the expenses of a provisional liquidator should be paid in priority to other expenses falling under the precursor of this rule, namely r 4.218(1)(a) (expenses incurred by the liquidator in the preserving, realising and getting in of company assets) (in *Re Grey Marlin Ltd*). The reason for this approach was that the rules give a provisional liquidator a higher priority over a liquidator for payment of remuneration, so a provisional liquidator should enjoy a higher priority for the repayment of expenses (in *Re Grey Marlin Ltd*). However, r 7.108(4)(a) provides that the provisional liquidator's expenses will rank equally with the other expenses mentioned in r 7.108(4)(a) so they no longer enjoy a higher priority to other liquidation expenses incurred by the liquidator and covered by r 7.108(4)(a)(ii).

Any expenses or costs awarded to a successful litigant against the company in liquidation or its liquidator were at common law (*Re London Metallurgical Company* [1895] 1 Ch 758; *Re MT Realisations Ltd* [2003] EWHC 2895 (Ch), [2004] 1 BCLC 119; *Re Toshoku Finance (UK) plc* [2002] UKHL 6, [2002] 1 WLR 671, [2002] 3 All ER 961, [2002] 1 BCLC 598, [2002] BPIR 790, HL) to be paid in priority to the general expenses and costs of the liquidation and any subsequent priority claims, such as preferential creditor claims. Also, the liquidator's own legal expenses in taking action under adjustment actions (such as preference claims) or wrongful trading proceedings could not be claimed out of the company's funds under this rule: *Re Floor Fourteen Ltd* [2001] 3 All ER 499, [2001] 2 BCLC 392, CA. This is still the case for liquidations entered into prior to 1 January 2003. But for those occurring after this date r 7.108(2), as it now stands, certainly means that the liquidator's own expenses of running litigation rank with the liquidation costs and expenses. Whether this is the case concerning an adverse costs order made against the liquidator or the company is not clear. It might be submitted that to include adverse costs orders within the general term of 'expenses' is unfair as far as the party who succeeds against the liquidator is concerned; such a party should be paid before the r 7.108 expenses. It might also be notable that r 7.110(2) has not amended the previous rule (r 4.220(2)), in that it continues to state that 'Nothing in those Rules [meaning rr 7.108 and 7.109] . . . affect the rights of any person to whom such costs are ordered to be paid'. Further, it would seem that the amendment to the Rules in 2002 which is incorporated in the 2016 Rules, was intended to overcome decisions like *Re MC Bacon Ltd (No 2)* [1991] Ch 127 and *Re Floor Fourteen Ltd*, where the liquidator was not entitled to recover *his own* legal expenses from company funds under this rule. Thus, someone with an adverse costs order is entitled to be paid in priority to liquidation expenses. See the arguments mounted in Gleghorn 'Re MT Realisations Ltd; recovering costs from an insolvent company' (2004) 20 IL & P 105 against the amendment to the Rules covering adverse costs orders.

A problem might have existed at one time in relation to the recovery of costs by liquidators who recover awards in relation to proceedings brought in their own name, such as under s 214, but have no company assets out of which they can recover their costs of the proceedings. See Gregorian and Butler 'Liquidators litigation expenses, funding arrangements and the amendment to rule 4.218' (2004) 20 IL & P 151, where the authors explore ways that might assist the liquidator.

Certainly as far as liquidations before 1 January 2003 are concerned, liquidators must ensure that they do not distribute company funds in priority to a costs' order against them or the company, or else they could be liable personally pursuant to s 212. If it is thought that the rule does not cover adverse costs orders, then the same would apply to all liquidations, whenever commenced.

Where the claim of a post-liquidation creditor comes within the category of the expenses of the winding up, the creditor should be paid by the liquidator, who has the right to be indemnified from the company's assets. If the liquidator neglects to satisfy a post-liquidation creditor, then he or she is entitled to recover the claim from company assets: *Stead Hazel & Co v Cooper* [1933] 1 KB 840. The claim, to be a winding-up expense, must be seen to be related to the winding up (*Re Denton Subdivisions Pty Ltd (in liquidation)* (1968) 89 WN (NSW) (Pt 1) 231), and must be adopted by the liquidator.

It is to be noted that r 7.108(2)(b) permits, subject to rr 7.111–7.116, expenses to be paid out of property subject to a floating charge. This is tied to s 176ZA, which was included in the Insolvency

Act 1986 in order to overcome the decision in *Buchler v Talbot* [2004] UKHL 9, [2004] 2 AC 298, [2004] 2 WLR 582, [2004] 1 All ER 1289. Reference should be had to rr 7.111–7.116 and the notes accompanying them, together with the notes relating to s 176ZA.

**The expenses associated with the prescribed part**—Unlike its precursor, r 4.218, r 7.108 provides in r 7.108(3) that these expenses are to be paid out of the prescribed part, if there is any prescribed part.

**Rule 7.108(4)(a)**—The words 'the following expenses, which rank equally in order of priority' causes some uncertainty at first blush. It would seem that the expenses contained in the paragraph are to be paid equally and if there is not enough to go around they abate equally. However, the use of the words, 'in order of priority' does cast some doubt on this view. But it would seem that the original assertion is correct given the fact that r 7.108(4)(a) has several heads of expenses adumbrated under separate paragraphs. The equivalent provision for creditors' voluntary liquidations, r 6.42, simply provides that the equivalent expenses to those found in r 7.108(4)(a) are to be paid in order of priority; there is no mention of ranking equally. But r 6.42 is different from r 7.108 in that it does not include all of the expenses referred to in r 7.108(4)(a), as some are specific to compulsory liquidations, and it does not include the same wording as r 7.108(4).

**Expenses**—All fees, costs, charges and expenses incurred in the course of winding up are to be regarded as expenses of the winding up. The term 'expenses' covers all different kinds of debts and liabilities incurred during the course of the winding up in the process of carrying on the business of the company (*Re Davis & Co* [1945] Ch 402; *Re Mawcon Ltd* [1969] 1 WLR 78), such as salaries and wages of employees, and any tax owed in respect of profits earned during the winding up: *Re Beni-Felkai Mining Co* [1934] Ch 406; *Re Toshoku Finance UK plc* [2000] 1 BCLC 683 at 699, CA.

The breadth of the expression has been extended over time so as to apply also to the recovery of expenses and costs associated with the preparation of any legal proceedings, as well as the conduct of those proceedings. Now expenses can be paid out of proceeds from any awards made under arbitration or dispute resolution procedures or of any compromise or settlement of any legal action or dispute reached prior to a judgment or award being made. Also included as costs or expenses of a liquidation are those properly incurred in the preparation or conduct of arbitration or dispute resolution procedures and negotiations leading to a settlement or compromise of any legal action or dispute.

The question as to whether rent, which becomes due during the liquidation, is a liquidation expense is not a clear matter. In relation to a pre-liquidation lease, the landlord is able to prove in the liquidation, because of r 14.1, for rent which is owed in relation to a period prior to the liquidation: *Leisure (Norwich) II Ltd v Luminar Lava Ignite Ltd* [2012] EWHC 951 (Ch), [2013] 2 BCLC 115. But what about rent due before liquidation but relating to the period post-liquidation and rent due post-liquidation? It has now been determined by the Court of Appeal in *Re Game Station Ltd* [2014] EWCA Civ 180; [2015] Ch 87, [2014] 3 WLR 901, [2014] 3 All ER 519, [2014] 2 BCLC 204 that rent payable in advance and before the liquidation can be apportioned on a day-to-day basis pursuant to the salvage principle. According to the Court of Appeal, common sense or ordinary justice should not be defeated by the happenstance that a rent day occurred immediately before the date of entry into liquidation. So, where rent received before liquidation related to a period of time after liquidation then that could be claimed as an expense of the liquidation: *Re Game Station Ltd*. As Lord Hoffmann recognised in *Kahn v Commissioners of Inland Revenue* [2002] 1 WLR 671 (at [25]–[27]) claims like rent owing post-liquidation have been allowed by courts (such as in *Re Lundy Granite Co* (1870) LR 6 Ch App 462) to be treated, on a just and equitable basis, as if it were a liquidation expense. To be treated as a liquidation expense the premises would have to be used for the benefit of the liquidation of the company: *Re Kensington Co-operative Stores* (1881) 17 ChD 161; *Re ABC Coupler & Engineering Co Ltd (No 3)* [1970] 1 WLR 702; *Re Downer Enterprises Ltd* [1974] 1 WLR 1460. The liquidator would be required to pay rent as an expense of the liquidation on a day to day basis while he or she retained the premises for the benefit of the liquidation: *Re Game Station Ltd* [2014] EWCA Civ 180, [2015] Ch 87, [2014] 3 WLR 901, [2014] 3 All ER 519, [2014] 2 BCLC 204. Leaving stock or equipment at premises could be regarded as retaining premises even if the company was not operating from the premises. According to the decision of the Court of Appeal in *Re Game Station Ltd* until the liquidator vacates the premises rent could be claimed as an expense of the liquidation as the landlord could not re-let. The landlord will have to prove as a creditor in the liquidation once the liquidator has halted his or her use of the premises and has vacated: *Re Game Station Ltd*. The situation with rates can be very different. Provided that the company remains in possession post-liquidation, rates constitute a liquidation expense (*Re National Arms & Ammunition Co* (1885) 28 ChD 474; *Re Wearmouth Crown Glass Co* (1882) 19 ChD 640; *Kahn* at [34]). Rates which were fixed before winding up, but not due until after the start of the winding up are able to be classified as liquidation expenses: *Re Nolton Business Centres Ltd* [1996] 1 BCLC 400.

The Supreme Court in *Re Nortel GmbH* [2013] UKSC 52, [2014] AC 209, [2013] 3 WLR 504 (an administration case but applicable to liquidations as far as the following discussion is concerned) allowed an appeal from the Court of Appeal ([2011] EWCA Civ 1124) on which that court had held that *Kahn v Commissioners of Inland Revenue (Re Toshoku Finance (UK) plc* [2002] 1 WLR 671) had established that where Parliament imposed a liability that was not a provable debt on a company in an insolvency process then, unless it constituted an expense under another provision of the expenses regimes for administration and liquidation, it would constitute a necessary disbursement (at [96], [99]). The result of the appeal meant that where an insolvent company employed persons and there is a shortfall in an occupational pension's fund assets, if the Pensions Regulator issues financial support directions and, if they are not complied with, a contribution notice issued pursuant to ss 43 and 47 respectively of the Pensions Act 2004 after the commencement of winding up means that the liability ensuing from these procedures is a provable debt and would rank pari passu with other unsecured debts and is not payable as an expense by the liquidator (or an administrator in administration) (as determined by the court at first instance and in the Court of Appeal). The Regulator can defer issuing the directives and the making of the contribution notice until after the commencement of winding up. The Regulator is required to have consideration for the interests of the creditors (s 100 of the Pensions Act), but in *Re Nortel* it had not stopped the Regulator seeking the payment of the shortfall as an expense of the liquidation under this rule. This, of course, would give the liability for the shortfall super-priority status. The administrators had originally sought directions from the courts as to how the contribution notices should be treated. The Supreme Court unanimously allowed the appeal from the Court of Appeal. In giving the leading judgment, Lord Neuberger said that the claim could be characterised as a provable debt within rr 12.3 (now r 14.2) and 13.12 (now r 14.1). For further consideration of the case, see the notes to r 14.1.

Any charges for the supply of gas and electricity under deemed contracts (that is, not express contracts but deemed under the Gas Act 1986 or the Electricity Act 1989) that are incurred after a company has entered liquidation are not expenses of the liquidation, but are provable debts under r 14.1: *Laverty v British Gas Trading Ltd* [2014] EWHC 2721 (Ch), [2015] 2 All ER 430, [2015] 1 BCLC 295.

While it appears not to have been decided, the liquidator's costs and expenses related to any proceedings brought to stay or terminate a winding up may well not fall within r 7.108(4)(a)(ii). If not, then they would probably fall under r 7.108(4)(m).

'Assets'—As far as the scope of 'assets' in r 7.108(2) is concerned, it was held for many years, as a result of the decision of the Court of Appeal in *Re Barleycorn Enterprises Ltd* [1970] Ch 465, that the word includes those assets that are subject to a floating charge. But, the House of Lords in *Buchler v Talbot* [2004] UKHL 9, [2004] 2 WLR 582, [2004] 1 All ER 1289, held that this was not the case. As a consequence, liquidation expenses were not to be paid out of assets subject to the charge unless the expenses relate to the charged property. However, the decision has been overcome to a great degree by s 176ZA and rr 7.111–7.116. Where there are liquidations pre-dating the enactment of s 176ZA the decision of *Buchler* will hold sway. See r 7.108(2)(e).

### RULE 7.108(4)(h)

If solicitors act for a company that is the subject of a winding-up petition and the petition is suspended upon the appointment of an administrator the fees of the solicitors in relation to the petition are payable under this paragraph if the company eventually ends up in liquidation on the basis that they are an expense of the liquidation: *Re Portsmouth City Football Club* [2012] EWHC 3088 (Ch) and confirmed on appeal ([2013] EWCA Civ 916, [2014] 1 All ER 12; [2014] 1 BCLC 1). The Court of Appeal said that fees owing to solicitors by a company, for which they have acted in unsuccessfully opposing a winding-up petition against it, may be payable as an expense of the subsequent liquidation of the company (at [41]). The Court went on to say that the court may allow payment of particular items of solicitors' fees as expenses of the liquidation, whether they were incurred by the company in unsuccessfully opposing the winding-up petition or in unsuccessfully seeking to strike it out (ibid).

### RULE 7.108(4)(m)

**Any necessary disbursements**—Corporation tax due because of chargeable gains on the realisation of assets after the start of the liquidation was a necessary disbursement, even where the company in liquidation actually did not receive any benefits from the realisations: *Kahn v Commissioners of Inland Revenue* [2002] UKHL 6, [2002] 1 WLR 671, HL.

**Remuneration of liquidator**—The court in *Re Berkeley Applegate (Investment Consultants) Ltd (No 2)* (1988) 4 BCC 279 held that the liquidator was entitled to claim for preliminary work done, before the advent of winding up, from assets which the liquidator could not reasonably have known were held by a company on trust for another.

See Moss and Segal 'Insolvency Proceedings: Contract and Financing' (1997) 1 *Company Finance and Insolvency Law Review* 1; Gleghorn 'Out of pocket? Prioritising costs orders' (2004) 154 NLJ 85 (23 January 2004); A Keay, *McPherson and Keay's Law of Company Liquidation* (Sweet and Maxwell, 4th edn, 2018) at 886–904.

**[2.434]**

### 7.109 Winding up commencing as voluntary

Where the winding up by the court immediately follows a voluntary winding up (whether members' voluntary or creditors' voluntary), such remuneration of the voluntary liquidator and costs and expenses of the voluntary winding up as the court may allow are to rank in priority with the expenses specified in rule 7.108(4)(a).

**Derivation**—This rule derived from the Insolvency Rules 1986, SI 1986/1925, r 4.219.

**General note**—Courts have tended to permit the costs and expenses of a former voluntary liquidator to rank in priority to expenses under the precursor of r 7.108, r 4.218, except where there was a good reason, relating to the conduct of the liquidator in office, not to do so: *Re Tony Rowse NMC Ltd* [1996] 2 BCLC 225 at 233.

**[2.435]**

### 7.110 Saving for powers of the court (section 156)

(1) The priorities laid down by rules 7.108 and 7.109 are subject to the power of the court to make orders under section 156, where the assets are insufficient to satisfy the liabilities.

(2) Nothing in those rules—

(a) applies to or affects the power of any court, in proceedings by or against the company, to order costs to be paid by the company, or the liquidator; or

(b) affects the rights of any person to whom such costs are ordered to be paid.

**Derivation**—This rule derived from the Insolvency Rules 1986, SI 1986/1925, r 4.220.

**General note**—The discretion of the court is unfettered, but there are well-settled principles which will usually guide the courts in the exercise of their discretion: *Re Massey* (1870) 9 Eq 367. The court may apportion the assets in payment of expenses: *Re Dominion of Canada Plumbago Co* (1884) 27 ChD 33.

In making its determination the courts will only give a liquidator priority for his or her remuneration over liquidation expenses that would normally rank ahead of it where there are exceptional circumstances: *Re Linda Marie Ltd (in liquidation)* (1988) 4 BCC 463 at 472.

**'proceedings . . . against the company'**—Includes litigation that is taken against the company through its liquidators (*Unadkat & Co (Accountants) Ltd v Bhardwaj* [2006] EWHC 2785 (Ch) at [15].

See the comments relating to s 156.

## CHAPTER 15

### Litigation Expenses and Property Subject to a Floating Charge

**[2.436]**

**Note**

[Note: a document required by the Act or these Rules must also contain the standard contents set out in Part 1.]

**General note**—This Chapter (based on rr 4.218B–4.218E of the previous rules) supplements s 176ZA, a provision enacted to overcome the House of Lords decision of *Buchler v Talbot* [2004] UKHL 9, [2004] 2 AC 298 that held that assets covered by a floating charge could not be used to pay expenses in the liquidation. The rules in Chapter 15 provide that a liquidator needs to obtain approval or authorisation for the use of charged assets for certain expenditure and then sets out the procedure to be followed. Reference should be had to the notes accompanying s 176ZA.

**[2.437]**

### 7.111 Interpretation

In this Chapter—

"approval" and "authorisation" respectively mean—

(a) where yet to be incurred, the approval, and

(b) where already incurred, the authorisation,

of expenses specified in section 176ZA(3);

"the creditor" means—

    (a)    a preferential creditor of the company; or

    (b)    a holder of a debenture secured by, or a holder of, a floating charge created by the company;

"legal proceedings" means—

    (a)    proceedings under sections 212, 213, 214, 238, 239, 244 and 423 and any arbitration or other dispute resolution proceedings invoked for purposes corresponding to those to which the sections relate and any other proceedings, including arbitration or other dispute resolution procedures, which a liquidator has power to bring in the liquidator's own name for the purpose of preserving, realising, or getting in any of the assets of the company;

    (b)    legal actions and proceedings, arbitration or any other dispute resolution procedures which a liquidator has power to bring or defend in the name of the company; and

    (c)    negotiations intended to lead or leading to a settlement or compromise of any action, proceeding or procedure to which sub-paragraphs (a) or (b) relate;

"litigation expenses" means expenses of a winding up which—

    (a)    are properly chargeable or incurred in the preparation or conduct of any legal proceedings; and

    (b)    as expenses in the winding up, exceed, or in the opinion of the liquidator are likely to exceed (and only in so far as they exceed or are likely to exceed), in the aggregate £5,000; and

"specified creditor" means a creditor identified under rule 7.113(2).

**Derivation**—This rule derived from the Insolvency Rules 1986, SI 1986/1925, r 4.218A.

**General note**—This rule provides the definitions that are employed in rr 7.112–7.116.

'Creditor'—covers not only floating chargeholders, but also preferential creditors, who, according to s 176ZA, might be entitled to be paid out of the assets that are subject to a floating charge.

'legal proceedings'—means those which are initiated by liquidators in either their own name or on behalf of the company in order to recover assets or money so as to swell the size of the insolvent estate, and proceedings brought against the company and defended by the liquidator. Also, legal proceedings covers any negotiations which are designed to lead to a compromise or settlement of proceedings initiated by, or those defended by, the liquidator. It is only litigation expenses that are incurred in relation to legal proceedings, as defined, that must be approved or authorized. It is assumed that where other expenses are incurred in the legal process, such as seeking directions from the courts will not have to be approved or authorised. It would also seem that expenses incurred by a liquidator in obtaining and being represented at a private examination under s 236 are not subject to the restrictions under these rules.

The rule does not cover legal proceedings under ss 242 and 243 as those sections only apply in Scotland, and the rule is limited to England and Wales.

See G Fidler 'Leyland Daf reversal and proposed new SI' (2007) 23 I L & P 181. Also, see A Keay, 'Litigation Expenses in Liquidations' (2009) 22 Insol Int 13.

## [2.438]

### 7.112 Priority of litigation expenses

Litigation expenses will not have the priority provided by section 176ZA over any claims to property comprised in or subject to a floating charge created by the company and must not be paid out of any such property unless and until approved or authorised in accordance with rules 7.113 to 7.116.

**Derivation**—This rule derived from the Insolvency Rules 1986, SI 1986/1925, r 4.218A(2).

**General note**—Essentially, this rule provides that litigation expenses incurred by a liquidator (in relation to legal proceedings) will not have priority over the claims of a floating chargeholder unless approval (sought before the incurring of expenditure) or authorisation (sought after the incurring of expenditure) is obtained. It also acts as a definition provision for the following rules, which set out the procedure for the obtaining of the approval or authorisation.

**[2.439]**

### 7.113 Requirement for approval or authorisation of litigation expenses

(1) Subject to rules 7.114 to 7.116 either paragraphs (3) and (4) apply or paragraph (5) applies where, in the course of winding up a company, the liquidator—

    (a)    ascertains that property is comprised in or subject to a floating charge;

    (b)    has personally instituted or proposes to institute or continue legal proceedings or is in the process of defending or proposes to defend any legal proceeding brought or likely to be brought against the company; and

    (c)    before or at any stage in those proceedings, is of the opinion that—

        (i)    the assets of the company available for payment of general creditors are or will be insufficient to pay litigation expenses, and

        (ii)    in order to pay litigation expenses the liquidator will have to have recourse to property comprised in or subject to a floating charge created by the company.

(2) As soon as reasonably practicable after the date on which the liquidator forms the opinion referred to in paragraph (1), the liquidator must identify the creditor who, in the liquidator's opinion at that time—

    (a)    has a claim to property comprised in or subject to a floating charge created by the company; and

    (b)    taking into account the value of that claim and any subsisting property then comprised in or secured by such a charge, appears to the liquidator to be the creditor most immediately likely of any persons having such claims to receive some payment in respect of a claim but whose claim would not be paid in full.

(3) The liquidator must request from the specified creditor the approval or authorisation of such amount for litigation expenses as the liquidator thinks fit.

(4) Where the liquidator identifies two or more specified creditors, the liquidator must seek from each of them approval or authorisation of such amount of litigation expenses as the liquidator thinks fit, apportioned between them ("the apportioned amount") according to the value of the property to the extent covered by their charges.

(5) For so long as the conditions specified in paragraph (1) subsist, the liquidator may, in the course of a winding up, make such further requests to the specified creditor or creditors for approval or authorisation of such further amount for litigation expenses as the liquidator thinks fit to be paid out of property comprised in or subject to a floating charge created by the company, taking into account any amount for litigation expenses previously approved or authorised and the value of the property comprised in or subject to the floating charge.

**Derivation**—This rule derived from the Insolvency Rules 1986, SI 1986/1925, r 4.218B.

**General note**—The rule explains that the liquidator, who has instituted or proposes to institute or continue legal proceedings or is in the process of defending or proposes to defend any legal proceeding brought or likely to be brought against the company must, as soon as reasonably practicable after determining that he or she will need to have recourse to assets subject to a floating charge, request from the creditor(s) with a claim over the assets approval or authorisation such amount for litigation expenses as he or she thinks necessary.

**'Specified creditor'**—this person is mentioned in several paragraphs, first in r 7.111, and is defined in r 7.113(2) as a creditor who appears to have a claim to the property. This covers chargeholders under the charge and also, possibly, preferential creditors, although the focus is on chargeholders. The specified creditor is a person, who, according to s 176ZA(2), might be entitled to be paid out of the assets subject to a floating charge) and taking into account the value of that claim appears to the liquidator to be the creditor most immediately likely to receive some payment in respect of his or her claim but whose claim would not be paid in full. Reference is made to the term 'specified creditor' in r 7.113(3), (4).

#### RULE 7.113(1)(b), (c)

These parts of the rule presuppose, inter alia, that the liquidator might have instituted proceedings and then ascertains that the proceedings are likely to lead to the incurring of greater expense than first thought.

RULE 7.113(5)

The paragraph makes it clear that the liquidator is entitled to make any number of requests for approval or authorisation, but the paragraph also appears to indicate that, given the words 'further amount' he or she is not permitted to go back to the creditors and request approval or authorisation for amounts that have been rejected earlier. In other words the liquidator cannot seek to wear down the creditors by repeated requests in relation to the same expenses.

## [2.440]

### 7.114 Requests for approval or authorisation

(1)   All requests made by the liquidator for approval or authorisation must include the following—

- (a)   a statement describing the nature of the legal proceedings, including, where relevant, the statutory provision under which proceedings are or are to be brought and the grounds upon which the liquidator relies;
- (b)   a statement specifying the amount or apportioned amount of litigation expenses for which approval or authorisation is sought ("the specified amount");
- (c)   notice that approval or authorisation or other reply to the request must be made in writing within 28 days from the date of its being received ("the specified time limit"); and
- (d)   a statement explaining the consequences of a failure to reply within the specified time limit.

(2)   Where anything in paragraph (1) requires the inclusion of any information, the disclosure of which could be seriously prejudicial to the winding up of the company, the liquidator may—

- (a)   exclude such information from any of the above statements or notices if accompanied by a statement to that effect; or
- (b)   include it on terms—
  - (i)    that bind the creditor to keep the information confidential, and
  - (ii)   that include an undertaking on the part of the liquidator to apply to the court for an order that so much of the information as may be kept in the files of the court, is not be open to public inspection.

(3)   The creditor may within the specified time limit apply to the liquidator in writing for such further particulars as is reasonable and in such a case, the time limit specified in paragraph (1)(c) will apply from the date of the creditor's receipt of the liquidator's response to any such request.

(4)   Where the liquidator requires the approval or authorisation of two or more creditors, the liquidator must deliver a request to each creditor, containing the matters listed in paragraph (1) and also giving—

- (a)   the number of creditors concerned;
- (b)   the total value of their claims, or if not known, as it is estimated to be by the liquidator immediately before delivering any such request; and
- (c)   to each preferential creditor, notice that approval or authorisation of the specified amount will be taken to be given where a majority in value of those preferential creditors who respond within the specified time limit are in favour of it; or
- (d)   where rule 7.113 applies, notice to the specified creditors that the amount of litigation expenses will be apportioned between them in accordance with that rule and notice of the value of the portion allocated to, and the identity of, the specified creditors affected by that apportionment.

**Derivation**—This rule derived from the Insolvency Rules 1986, SI 1986/1925, r 4.218C.

**General note**—The rule and the succeeding one set out the contents of any request made to a creditor for approval or authorisation. The terms of r 4.218C(2)(b) are not included in r 7.114. This is because r 4.218C(2)(b) referred to the time when, under a previous version of Sch 4 of the Act, liquidators needed to obtain other approvals before initiating certain kinds of proceedings.

**'value of their claims'**—It is likely that it will not be uncommon for creditors to take issue with the amount which the liquidator states is the value of their claims. There is no procedure for determining any dispute. One would think that the parties have to try and resolve it, and if they cannot, it might be a matter to be decided by the court if the liquidator has to end up applying to the court for approval under r 7.116. A creditor would be able to apply under s 168(5).

**[2.441]**

### 7.115  Grant of approval or authorisation

(1)   Where the liquidator fails to include in the liquidator's request any one of the matters, statements or notices required by paragraph (1) or paragraphs (1) and (4), of rule 7.114, the request for approval or authorisation will be treated as not having been made.

(2)   Subject to paragraphs (3), (4) and (5), approval or authorisation will be taken to have been given where the specified amount has been requested by the liquidator, and—

(a)     that amount is approved or authorised within the specified time limit; or

(b)     a different amount is approved or authorised within the specified time limit and the liquidator considers it sufficient.

(3)   Where the liquidator requires the approval or authorisation of two or more preferential creditors, approval or authorisation will be taken to be given where a majority in value of those who respond within the specified time limit approve or authorise—

(a)     the specified amount; or

(b)     a different amount which the liquidator considers sufficient.

(4)   Where a majority in value of two or more preferential creditors propose an amount other than that specified by the liquidator, they will be taken to have approved or authorised an amount equal to the lowest of the amounts so proposed.

(5)   In any case in which there is no response in writing within the specified time limit to the liquidator's request—

(a)     at all; or

(b)     at any time following the liquidator's provision of further particulars under rule 7.114(3);

the liquidator's request will be taken to have been approved or authorised from the date of the expiry of that time limit.

   **Derivation**—This rule derived from the Insolvency Rules 1986, SI 1986/1925, r 4.218D.

   **General note**—The rule is in the same terms as its predecessor, r 4.218D. The rule provides the mechanics involved in the granting of approval or authorisation at the request of the liquidator.

#### RULE 7.115(2), (3)

   Creditors might decide not to approve the amount sought by the liquidator and propose a lower amount, and if that occurs and the liquidator accepts that the amount is sufficient, approval or authorisation is deemed to be granted. This might mean that liquidators will seek an ambit amount knowing that creditors might seek to reduce the amount for approval or authorisation.

#### RULE 7.115(5)

   Importantly if creditors who have claims in the charged assets do not respond to the liquidator's request at all or within 28 days of the date on which the request is received, then there is deemed to be approved or authorised (r 7.114(1)(d) and (3)) and thus this prevents creditors ignoring requests or procrastinating.

**[2.442]**

### 7.116  Application to the court by the liquidator

(1)   In the circumstances specified below the court may, upon the application of the liquidator, approve or authorise such amount of litigation expenses as it thinks just.

(2)   Except where paragraph (3) applies, the liquidator may apply to the court for an order approving or authorising an amount for litigation expenses only where the specified creditor (or, if more than one, any of them)—

(a)     is or is intended to be a defendant in the legal proceedings in relation to which the litigation expenses have been or are to be incurred; or

(b)     has been requested to approve or authorise the amount specified under rule 7.114(1)(b) and has—

  (i)  declined to approve or authorise, as the case may be, the specified amount,

  (ii)  approved or authorised an amount which is less than the specified amount and which lesser amount the liquidator considers insufficient, or

  (iii)  made such application for further particulars or other response to the liquidator's request as is, in the liquidator's opinion, unreasonable.

(3) Where the liquidator thinks that circumstances are such that the liquidator requires urgent approval or authorisation of litigation expenses, the liquidator may apply to the court for approval or authorisation either—

  (a)  without seeking approval or authorisation from the specified creditor; or

  (b)  if sought, before the expiry of the specified time limit.

(4) The court may grant such application for approval or authorisation—

  (a)  if the liquidator satisfies the court of the urgency of the case; and

  (b)  subject to such terms and conditions as the court thinks just.

(5) The liquidator must, at the same time as making any application to the court under this rule, deliver copies of it to the specified creditor, unless the court orders otherwise.

(6) The specified creditor (or, if more than one, any of them) is entitled to be heard on any such application unless the court orders otherwise.

(7) The court may grant approval or authorisation subject to such terms and conditions as it may think just, including terms and conditions relating to the amount or nature of the litigation expenses and as to any obligation to make further applications to the court under this rule.

(8) The costs of the liquidator's application under this rule, including the costs of any specified creditor appearing or represented on it, will be an expense of the winding up unless the court orders otherwise.

**Derivation**—This rule derived from the Insolvency Rules 1986, SI 1986/1925, r 4.218E.

**General note**—The rule is almost identical, with a few minor structural and wording changes, to its predecessor, r 4.218E. The rule provides a liquidator with the right to apply for the approval or authorisation of the court in certain circumstances, and one would expect that this will usually be where the creditors, with claims over the charged assets, refuse to approve or authorise the amount requested by the liquidator at all or where the amount suggested by the creditors is not acceptable to the liquidator. The rule goes on to explain the procedure and process involved.

The court had a discretion to order the dispensing of service on, and the attendance of, a creditor who is or intended to be a defendant in proceedings brought by the liquidator, but the default position was that the creditor should be served and entitled to be heard as it is fundamental to English law that both sides are heard. A court should not entertain an application where no notice has been given except where either the giving of notice would enable the defendant to defeat the purpose of the application or there had not been sufficient time to give notice before the application was required in order to prevent the commission of a wrongful act: *Re Premier Motor Auctions Leeds Ltd (in liq)* [2015] EWHC 3568 (Ch) at [31]–[33]. In this case the creditor had a serious financial interest in the result of the application made under this rule, for if the liquidators were successful their legal expenses would take priority over the creditor's rights under its floating charge.

'**Costs**'—There is no indication whether the costs of any appeal from the original hearing, by either the liquidator or the creditor(s), will be covered by para (8).

## CHAPTER 16

### Miscellaneous Rules

**[2.443]**

**Note**

[Note: a document required by the Act or these Rules must also contain the standard contents set out in Part 1.]

*Sub-division A: Return of capital*

**[2.444]**

**7.117 Application to court for order authorising return of capital**
(1) This rule applies where the liquidator intends to apply to the court for an order authorising a return of capital.
(2) The application must be accompanied by a list of the persons to whom the return is to be made.
(3) The list must include the same details of those persons as appears in the settled list of contributories, with any necessary alterations to take account of matters after settlement of the list, and the amount to be paid to each person.
(4) Where the court makes an order authorising the return, it must deliver a sealed copy of the order to the liquidator.

Derivation—This rule derived from the Insolvency Rules 1986, SI 1986/1925, r 4.221.
General—See the discussion under s 154.

**[2.445]**

**7.118 Procedure for return**
(1) The liquidator must inform each person to whom a return is made of the rate of return per share, and whether it is expected that any further return will be made.
(2) Any payments made by the liquidator by way of the return may be delivered by post, unless for any reason another method of making the payment has been agreed with the payee.

Derivation—This rule derived from the Insolvency Rules 1986, SI 1986/1925, r 4.222.

*Sub-division B: Dissolution after winding up*

**[2.446]**

**7.119 Secretary of State's directions under sections 203 and 205 and appeal**
(1) This rule applies where the Secretary of State gives a direction under—
    (a)    section 203 (where official receiver applies to the registrar of companies for a company's early dissolution); or
    (b)    section 205 (application by interested person for postponement of dissolution).
(2) The Secretary of State must deliver the direction to the applicant for it.
(3) The applicant must deliver a copy of the direction to the registrar of companies, to comply with section 203(5) or, as the case may be, section 205(6).
(4) Following an appeal under section 203(4) or 205(4) (against a decision of the Secretary of State under the applicable section) the court must deliver a sealed copy of its order to the person in whose favour the appeal was determined.
(5) That person must deliver a copy to the registrar of companies to comply with section 203(5) or, as the case may be, section 205(6).

Derivation—This rule derived from the Insolvency Rules 1986, SI 1986/1925, rr 4.224, 4.225.

PART 8   INDIVIDUAL VOLUNTARY ARRANGEMENTS (IVA)

CHAPTER 1

PRELIMINARY

**[2.447]**

**8.1 Interpretation**
In this Part—
> "authorised person" means the official receiver where the official receiver is authorised to act as nominee or supervisor under section 389B(1) of the Act;
> "nominee" and "supervisor" include the proposed nominee or supervisor in relation to a proposal for an IVA; and
> "proposal" means a proposal for an IVA.

CHAPTER 2

PREPARATION OF THE DEBTOR'S PROPOSAL FOR AN IVA

**[2.448]**

**Note**
[Note: a document required by the Act or these Rules must also contain the standard contents set out in Part 1.]

**[2.449]**

**8.2 Proposal for an IVA: general principles and amendment**
(1)   A proposal must—
    (a)    identify the debtor;
    (b)    explain why the debtor thinks an IVA is desirable;
    (c)    explain why the creditors are expected to agree to an IVA; and
    (d)    be authenticated and dated by the debtor.
(2)   The proposal may be amended with the nominee's agreement in writing at any time up to the filing of the nominee's report with the court under section 256, or the submission of the nominee's report to the creditors under section 256A.

> **Derivation**—This rule derived from the Insolvency Rules 1986, SI 1986/1925, r 5.3.
> **General note**—For commentary see the notes to s 256.

**[2.450]**

**8.3 Proposal: contents**
The proposal must set out the following so far as known to the debtor—

| Assets | (a) | the debtor's assets, with an estimate of their respective values; |
|---|---|---|
| | (b) | which assets are charged and the extent of the charge; |
| | (c) | which assets are to be excluded from the IVA; and |
| | (d) | particulars of any property to be included in the IVA which is not owned by the debtor including details of who owns such property and the terms on which it will be available for inclusion; |
| Liabilities | (e) | the nature and amount of the debtor's liabilities; |
| | (f) | how the debtor's liabilities will be met, modified, postponed or otherwise dealt with by means of the IVA and, in particular— |

| | | (i) | how preferential creditors and creditors who are, or claim to be, secured will be dealt with, |
|---|---|---|---|
| | | (ii) | how creditors who are associates of the debtor will be dealt with, |
| | | (iii) | if the debtor is an undischarged bankrupt, whether any claim has been made under section 339 (transactions at an undervalue), section 340 (preferences), or section 343 (extortionate credit transactions) and, if it has, whether, and if so what, provision is being made to indemnify the bankrupt's estate in respect of such a claim; and |
| | | (iv) | if the debtor is not an undischarged bankrupt whether there are circumstances which might give rise to a claim as referred to in sub-paragraph (iii) if the debtor were made bankrupt and, where there are such circumstances, whether and, if so what, provision will be made to indemnify the bankrupt's estate in respect of such a claim; |
| Nominee's fees and expenses | (g) | | the amount proposed to be paid to the nominee by way of fees and expenses; |
| Supervisor | (h) | | identification and contact details for the supervisor; |
| | (i) | | confirmation that the supervisor is qualified to act as an insolvency practitioner (or is an authorised person) in relation to the debtor and the name of the relevant recognised professional body which is the source of the supervisor's authorisation; |
| | (j) | | how the fees and expenses of the supervisor will be determined and paid; |
| | (k) | | the functions to be undertaken by the supervisor; |
| | (l) | | where it is proposed that two or more supervisors be appointed, a statement whether acts done in connection with the IVA may be done by any one or more of them or must be done by all of them; |
| Guarantees and proposed guarantees | (m) | | whether any, and if so what, guarantees have been given in respect of the debtor's debts, specifying which of the guarantors are associates of the debtor; |
| | (n) | | whether any guarantees are proposed to be offered for the purposes of the IVA, and if so what, by whom and whether security is to be given or sought; |
| Timing | (o) | | the proposed duration of the IVA; |
| | (p); | | the proposed dates of distributions to creditors, with estimates of their amounts; |
| Type of proceedings | (q) | | whether the proceedings will be COMI proceedings, establishment proceedings or proceedings to which the EU Regulation as it has effect in the law of the United Kingdom does not apply with reasons; |
| Conduct of business | (r) | | if the debtor has any business, how that business will be conducted during the IVA; |
| Further credit facilities | (s) | | details of any further proposed credit facilities for the debtor and how the debts so arising are to be paid; |
| Handling of funds arising | (t) | | the manner in which funds held for the purposes of the IVA are to be banked, invested or otherwise dealt with pending distribution to creditors; |
| | (u) | | how funds held for the purpose of payment to creditors, and not so paid on the termination of the IVA, will be dealt with; |
| | (v) | | how the claim of any person bound by the IVA by virtue of section 260(2)(b)(ii) will be dealt with; |

| Other proposals | (w) | | whether another proposal in relation to the debtor has been submitted within the 24 months before the date of the submission of the proposal to the nominee— | | |
|---|---|---|---|---|---|
| | | (i) | | for approval by the creditors and, if so, | |
| | | | (aa) | whether that proposal was approved or rejected, | |
| | | | (bb) | whether, if approved, the IVA was completed or was terminated, and | |
| | | | (cc) | in what respects such a proposal, where rejected, differs from the current proposal; | |
| | | (ii) | | to the court in connection with an application for an interim order under section 253 and, if so, whether the interim order was made; | |
| Other matters | (x) | | any other matters which the debtor considers appropriate to enable creditors to reach an informed decision on the proposal. | | |

**Derivation**—This rule derived from the Insolvency Rules 1986, SI 1986/1925, r 5.3.

**Amendments**—SI 2017/1115; SI 2019/146, as from IP completion day (as defined in the European Union (Withdrawal Agreement) Act 2020, s 39(1)–(5)).

**General note**—For commentary see the notes to s 256.

## [2.451]

### 8.4 Notice of nominee's consent

(1)   A nominee who consents to act must deliver a notice of that consent to the debtor as soon as reasonably practicable after the proposal has been submitted to the nominee under section 256(2) or 256A(2).

(2)   The notice must state the date the nominee received the proposal.

**Derivation**—This rule derived from the Insolvency Rules 1986, SI 1986/1925, r 5.4.

**General note**—Notice of the proposal by the debtor to the nominee is necessary for the purpose of the nominee's report on the proposal under s 256 or s 256A and the triggering of the interim order procedure (under s 253) and the consideration of a debtor's proposal (under s 257).

## [2.452]

### 8.5 Statement of affairs (section 256 and 256A)

(1)   The statement of affairs which the debtor is required to submit to the nominee under either section 256(2) or 256A(2) must contain—

(a)   a list of the debtor's assets, divided into such categories as are appropriate for easy identification, and with each category given an estimated value;

(b)   in the case of any property on which a claim against the debtor is wholly or partly secured, particulars of the claim and of how and when the security was created;

(c)   the names and addresses of the preferential creditors with the amounts of their respective claims;

(d)   the names and addresses of the unsecured creditors, with the amounts of their respective claims;

(e)   particulars of any debts owed by the debtor to persons who are associates of the debtor;

(f)   particulars of any debts owed to the debtor by persons who are associates of the debtor; and

(g)   any other particulars that the nominee in writing requires to be provided for the purposes of making the nominee's report on the proposal to the court or to the creditors (as the case may be).

(2)   The statement must be made up to a date not earlier than two weeks before the date of the proposal.

(3)   However the nominee may allow the statement to be made up to a date that is earlier than two weeks (but no earlier than two months) before the date of the proposal where that is more practicable.

(4)   If the statement is made up to an earlier date the nominee's report must explain why an earlier date was allowed.

(5)   The statement must be verified by a statement of truth made by the debtor.

(6)   Where the debtor is an undischarged bankrupt and has already delivered a statement of affairs under section 288 the debtor need not submit a statement of affairs to the nominee under section 256(2) or 256A(2) unless the nominee requires a further statement of affairs to supplement or amplify the earlier one.

**Derivation**—This rule derived from the Insolvency Rules 1986, SI 1986/1925, r 5.5.

**General note**—See the note to r 8.4.

## [2.453]

### 8.6   Application to omit information from statement of affairs delivered to creditors

The nominee, the debtor or any person appearing to the court to have an interest may, if any information in the statement of affairs would be likely to prejudice the conduct of the IVA or might reasonably be expected to lead to violence against any person, apply to the court for an order that specified information be omitted from any statement of affairs required to be delivered to the creditors.

**Derivation**—This rule derived from the Insolvency Rules 1986, SI 1986/1925, r 5.68.

## [2.454]

### 8.7   Additional disclosure for assistance of nominee

(1)   If it appears to the nominee that the report to the court under section 256(1) or to the creditors under section 256A(3) cannot properly be prepared on the basis of information in the proposal and statement of affairs, the nominee may require the debtor to provide—

<ul>
<li>(a)    more information about the circumstances in which, and the reasons why, an IVA is being proposed;</li>
<li>(b)    more information about any proposals of the kind referred to in rule 8.3(w);</li>
<li>(c)    information about any proposals which have at any time been made by the debtor under Part 8 of the Act; and</li>
<li>(d)    any further information relating to the debtor's affairs which the nominee thinks necessary for the purposes of the report.</li>
</ul>

(2)   The nominee may require the debtor to inform the nominee whether and in what circumstances the debtor has at any time—

<ul>
<li>(a)    been concerned in the affairs of a company wherever incorporated or limited liability partnership which has become the subject of insolvency proceedings;</li>
<li>(b)    been made bankrupt;</li>
<li>(c)    been the subject of a debt relief order; or</li>
<li>(d)    entered into an arrangement with creditors.</li>
</ul>

(3)   The debtor must give the nominee such access to the debtor's accounts and records as the nominee requires to enable the nominee to consider the debtor's proposal and prepare the report on it.

**Derivation**—This rule derived from the Insolvency Rules 1986, SI 1986/1925, r 5.6.

**General note**—See the notes to s 256 and s 256A, as appropriate.

CHAPTER 3

CASES IN WHICH AN APPLICATION FOR AN INTERIM ORDER IS MADE

### [2.455]

**Note**

[Note: a document required by the Act or these Rules must also contain the standard contents set out in Part 1.]

### [2.456]

#### 8.8 Application for interim order

(1) An application to the court for an interim order under Part 8 of the Act must be accompanied by a witness statement containing—

    (a)    the reasons for making the application;

    (b)    information about any action, execution, other legal process or the levying of any distress which, to the debtor's knowledge, has been commenced against the debtor or the debtor's property;

    (c)    a statement that the debtor is an undischarged bankrupt or is able to make a bankruptcy application;

    (d)    a statement that no previous application for an interim order has been made by or in relation to the debtor in the period of 12 months ending with the date of the witness statement; and

    (e)    a statement that a person named in the witness statement is willing to act as nominee in relation to the proposal and is qualified to act as an insolvency practitioner (or is an authorised person) in relation to the debtor.

(2) The witness statement must be accompanied by a copy of—

    (a)    the proposal; and

    (b)    the notice of the nominee's consent to act.

(3) When the application and the witness statement have been filed, the court must fix a venue for the hearing of the application.

(4) The applicant must deliver a notice of the hearing and the venue at least two business days before the hearing to—

    (a)    the nominee;

    (b)    the debtor, the official receiver or the trustee (whichever is not the applicant) where the debtor is an undischarged bankrupt; and

    (c)    any creditor who (to the debtor's knowledge) has presented a bankruptcy petition against the debtor where the debtor is not an undischarged bankrupt.

(5) A notice under section 253(4) must contain the name and address of the nominee.

Derivation—This rule derived from the Insolvency Rules 1986, SI 1986/1925, r 5.7.

### [2.457]

#### 8.9 Court in which application is to be made

(1) An application must be made—

    (a)    to the court (and hearing centre if applicable), if any, which has the conduct of the bankruptcy, where the debtor is an undischarged bankrupt; or

    (b)    to the court (and hearing centre if applicable) determined in accordance with rule 10.48.

(2) The application must contain sufficient information to establish that it is made to the appropriate court or hearing centre.

Derivation—This rule derived from the Insolvency Rules 1986, SI 1986/1925, r 5.8.

General note—See s 253 and the notes thereto. Sections 252, 254 and 255 and the commentary to those provisions may also provide assistance here.

**[2.458]**

### 8.10 Order granting a stay

A court order under section 254(1)(b) granting a stay pending hearing of an application must identify the proceedings and contain—

   (a)   the section number of the Act under which it is made;
   (b)   details of the action, execution or other legal process which is stayed;
   (c)   the date on which the application for an interim order will be heard; and
   (d)   the date that the order granting the stay is made.

Derivation—This rule derived from the Insolvency Rules 1986, SI 1986/1925, Sch 4, Fm 5.1.

**[2.459]**

### 8.11 Hearing of the application

(1)   A person to whom a notice of the hearing of the application for an interim order was (or should have been) delivered under rule 8.8(4) may appear or be represented at the hearing.

(2)   The court must take into account any representations made by or on behalf of such a person (in particular, as to whether an order should contain such provision as is referred to in section 255(3) (provisions as to the conduct of the bankruptcy etc) and (4) (provisions staying proceedings in bankruptcy etc).

(3)   If the court makes an interim order, it must fix a venue for consideration of the nominee's report for a date no later than the date on which the order ceases to have effect.

Derivation—This rule derived from the Insolvency Rules 1986, SI 1986/1925, r 5.9.

**[2.460]**

### 8.12 The interim order

An interim order must contain—

   (a)   identification details for the proceedings;
   (b)   the section number of the Act under which it is made;
   (c)   a statement that the order has effect from its making until the end of the period of 14 days beginning on the day after the date on which it is made;
   (d)   particulars of the effect of the order (as set out in section 252(2));
   (e)   an order that the report of the nominee be delivered to the court no later than two business days before the date fixed for the court's consideration of the report;
   (f)   particulars of any orders made under section 255(3) and (4);
   (g)   where the debtor is an undischarged bankrupt and the applicant is not the official receiver, an order that the applicant delivers, as soon as reasonably practicable, a copy of the interim order to the official receiver;
   (h)   the venue for the court's consideration of the nominee's report; and
   (i)   the date of the order.

Derivation—This rule derived from the Insolvency Rules 1986, SI 1986/1925, Sch 4, Fm 5.2.

**[2.461]**

### 8.13 Action to follow making of an interim order

(1)   The court must deliver at least two sealed copies of the interim order to the applicant.

(2)   As soon as reasonably practicable, the applicant must deliver—

   (a)   one copy to the nominee and, where the debtor is an undischarged bankrupt, another copy to the official receiver (unless the official receiver was the applicant); and
   (b)   a notice that the order has been made to any other person to whom a notice of the hearing of the application for an interim order was (or should

have been) delivered under rule 8.8(4) and who was not in attendance or represented at the hearing.

Derivation—This rule derived from the Insolvency Rules 1986, SI 1986/1925, r 5.10.

## [2.462]

### 8.14 Order extending period of an interim order (section 256(4))

An order under section 256(4) extending the period for which an interim order has effect must contain—

- (a) identification details for the proceedings;
- (b) a statement that the application is that of the nominee for an extension of the period under section 256(4) for which an interim order is to have effect;
- (c) an order that the period for which the interim order has effect is extended to a specified date;
- (d) particulars of the effect (as set out in section 252(2)) of the interim order;
- (e) an order that the report of the nominee be delivered to the court no later two business days before the date fixed for the court's consideration of the nominee's report;
- (f) particulars of any orders made under section 255(3) or (4);
- (g) where the debtor is an undischarged bankrupt and the applicant is not the official receiver, an order that the applicant deliver, as soon as reasonably practicable, a copy of the order to the official receiver;
- (h) the venue for the court's consideration of the report; and
- (i) the date of the order.

Derivation—This rule derived from the Insolvency Rules 1986, SI 1986/1925, Sch 4, Fm 5.3.

## [2.463]

### 8.15 Nominee's report on the proposal

(1) The nominee's report under section 256 must be filed with the court not less than two business days before the interim order ceases to have effect, accompanied by—

- (a) a copy of the report;
- (b) a copy of the proposal (as amended, if applicable, under rule 8.2(2); and
- (c) a copy of any statement of affairs or a summary of such a statement.

(2) The nominee must also deliver a copy of the report to the debtor.

(3) The nominee's report must explain whether or not the nominee considers that the proposal has a reasonable prospect of being approved and implemented and whether or not creditors should be invited to consider the proposal.

(4) The court must endorse the nominee's report and the copy of it with the date on which they were filed and return the copy to the nominee.

(5) Where the debtor is an undischarged bankrupt, the nominee must deliver to the official receiver and any trustee, a copy of—

- (a) the proposal;
- (b) the nominee's report; and
- (c) any statement of affairs or summary of such a statement.

(6) Where the debtor is not an undischarged bankrupt, the nominee must deliver a copy of each of those documents to any person who has presented a bankruptcy petition against the debtor.

Derivation—This rule derived from the Insolvency Rules 1986, SI 1986/1925, r 5.11.

General note—See s 256 and s 256A and the commentary thereto.

**[2.464]**

**8.16 Order extending period of interim order to enable the creditors to consider the proposal (section 256(5))**

An order under section 256(5) extending the period for which an interim order has effect to enable creditors to consider the proposal must contain—

    (a)    identification details for the proceedings;

    (b)    the section number of the Act under which it is made;

    (c)    the date that the nominee's report was filed;

    (d)    a statement that for the purpose of enabling the creditors to consider the proposal, the period for which the interim order has effect is extended to a specified date;

    (e)    a statement that the nominee will be inviting the creditors to consider the proposal and details of the decision procedure the nominee intends to use;

    (f)    where the debtor is an undischarged bankrupt and the nominee is not the official receiver, an order that the nominee deliver, as soon as reasonably practicable, a copy of the order to the official receiver; and

    (g)    the date of the order.

**Derivation**—This rule derived from the Insolvency Rules 1986, SI 1986/1925, Sch 4, Fm 5.3.

**[2.465]**

**8.17 Replacement of the nominee (section 256(3))**

(1) A debtor who intends to apply under section 256(3)(a) or (b) for the nominee to be replaced must deliver a notice to the nominee that such an application is intended to be made at least five business days before filing the application with the court.

(2) A nominee who intends to apply under section 256(3)(b) to be replaced must deliver a notice to the debtor that such an application is intended to be made at least five business days before filing the application with the court.

(3) The court must not appoint a replacement nominee unless the replacement nominee has filed with the court a statement confirming—

    (a)    that person is qualified to act as an insolvency practitioner (or is an authorised person) in relation to the debtor; and

    (b)    that person's consent to act.

**Derivation**—This rule derived from the Insolvency Rules 1986, SI 1986/1925, r 5.12.

**General note**—Section 256(3) provides for the replacement of a nominee.

**[2.466]**

**8.18 Consideration of the nominee's report**

(1) A person to whom a notice was (or should have been) delivered under rule 8.8(4) may appear or be represented at the court's hearing to consider the nominee's report.

(2) Rule 8.13 applies to any order made by the court at the hearing.

**Derivation**—This rule derived from the Insolvency Rules 1986, SI 1986/1925, r 5.13.

**General note**—Para (1) appears to contemplate that in cases where an interim order is obtained no creditors' decision procedure should occur unless and until the court has positively considered the nominee's report and reached a concluded view on it.

CHAPTER 4

CASES WHERE NO INTERIM ORDER IS TO BE OBTAINED

**[2.467]**

**Note**

[Note: a document required by the Act or these Rules must also contain the standard contents set out in Part 1.]

## [2.468]

**8.19 Nominee's report (section 256A)**

(1)   The nominee's report under section 256A(3) must explain whether or not the nominee considers that the proposal has a reasonable prospect of being approved and implemented and whether or not creditors should be invited to consider the proposal.

(1A)   The nominee must examine whether there is jurisdiction to open the proceedings and must specify in the nominee's report whether the proceedings will be COMI proceedings, establishment proceedings or proceedings to which the EU Regulation as it has effect in the law of the United Kingdom does not apply with the reasons for so stating.

(2)   The report must contain sufficient information to enable a person to identify (in accordance with rule 8.20) the appropriate court or hearing centre in which to file an application relating to the proposal or the IVA.

(3)   The nominee must also deliver a copy of the report to the debtor.

(4)   Where the nominee gives an opinion in the affirmative on the matters referred to in section 256A(3)(a) and (b), the copy of the report delivered by the nominee to each of the creditors must be accompanied by—

(a)   a statement that an application for an interim order under section 253 is not being made;

(b)   a copy of the proposal (as amended, if applicable, under rule 8.2(2));

(c)   a copy of any statement of affairs or a summary of such a statement; and

(d)   a copy of the notice of the nominee's consent to act.

(5)   In such a case the nominee must also deliver those documents within 14 days (or such longer period as the court may allow) of receipt of the document and statement referred to in section 256A(2) to—

(a)   the official receiver and any trustee, where the debtor is an undischarged bankrupt; and

(b)   any person who has presented a bankruptcy petition against the debtor.

(6)   Where the nominee gives an opinion in the negative on the matters referred to in section 256A(3)(a) and (b) the nominee must within 14 days (or such longer period as the court may allow) of receipt of the document and statement referred to in section 256A(2)—

(a)   deliver a copy of the report to the creditors; and

(b)   give the reasons for that opinion to the debtor.

**Derivation**—This rule derived from the Insolvency Rules 1986, SI 1986/1925, r 5.14A.

**Amendments**—SI 2017/702; SI 2019/146, as from IP completion day (as defined in the European Union (Withdrawal Agreement) Act 2020, s 39(1)–(5)).

## [2.469]

**8.20 Court or hearing centre to which applications must be made where no interim order**

(1)   This rule applies where the nominee has made a report under section 256A(3).

(2)   Any application relating to a proposal or an IVA must be made—

(a)   to the court or hearing centre, if any, which has the conduct of the bankruptcy, where the debtor is an undischarged bankrupt; or

(b)   to the court or hearing centre determined in accordance with rule 10.48.

(3)   The application must contain sufficient information to establish that it is made to the appropriate court or hearing centre.

(4)   The applicant must file with the court (in addition to the documents in support of the application) such other documents required by this Part as the applicant considers may assist the court in determining the application.

**Derivation**—This rule derived from the Insolvency Rules 1986, SI 1986/1925, r 5.14B.

**[2.470]**

**8.21 Replacement of the nominee (section 256A(4))**

(1) A debtor who intends to apply under section 256A(4)(a) or (b) for the nominee to be replaced must deliver a notice of the intention to make the application to the nominee at least five business days before filing the application with the court.

(2) A nominee who intends to apply under section 256A(4)(b) to be replaced must deliver a notice of the intention to make such an application to the debtor at least five business days before filing the application with the court.

(3) The court must not appoint a replacement nominee unless the replacement nominee has filed with the court a statement confirming—

    (a)    that person is qualified to act as an insolvency practitioner (or is an authorised person) in relation to the debtor; and

    (b)    that person's consent to act.

**Derivation**—This rule derived from the Insolvency Rules 1986, SI 1986/1925, r 5.14B.

CHAPTER 5

CONSIDERATION OF THE PROPOSAL BY THE CREDITORS

**[2.471]**

**Note**

[Note: a document required by the Act or these Rules must also contain the standard contents set out in Part 1.]

**[2.472]**

**8.22 Consideration of the proposal**

(1) This rule applies where the nominee is required to seek a decision from the debtor's creditors as to whether they approve the debtor's proposal.

(2) The nominee must deliver to each creditor a notice which complies with rule 15.8 so far as is relevant.

(3) The notice must also contain—

    (a)    identification details for the proceedings;

    (b)    where an interim order has not been obtained, details of the court or hearing centre to which an application relating to the proposal or the IVA must be made under rule 8.20(2);

    (c)    where an interim order is in force, details of the court or hearing centre in which the nominee's report on the debtor's proposal has been filed under section 256;

    (d)    a statement as to how a person entitled to vote for the proposal may propose a modification to it, and how the nominee will deal with such a proposal for a modification.

(4) The notice may contain or be accompanied by a notice that the results of the consideration of the proposal will be made available for viewing and downloading on a website and that no other notice will be delivered to the creditors to whom the notice under this rule was sent.

(5) Where the results of the consideration of the proposal are to be made available for viewing and downloading on a website the nominee must comply with the requirements for use of a website to deliver a document set out in rule 1.49(2)(a) to (c), (3) and (4) with any necessary adaptations and rule 1.49(5)(a) applies to determine the time of delivery of the document.

(6) The notice must be accompanied by the following (unless they have been delivered already under rule 8.19)—

    (a)    a copy of the proposal;

    (b)    a copy of the statement of affairs, or a summary including a list of creditors with the amounts of their debts; and

    (c)    a copy of the nominee's report on the proposal.

(7)   The decision date must be not less than 14 days from the date of delivery of the notice and not more than 28 days from the date on which—

(a)   the nominee received the document and statement of affairs referred to in section 256A(2) in a case where an interim order has not been obtained; or

(b)   the nominee's report was considered by the court in a case where an interim order is in force.

Derivation—This rule derived from the Insolvency Rules 1986, SI 1986/1925, r 5.17.

## [2.473]

### 8.23 Proposals for an alternative supervisor

(1)   If in response to a notice of a decision procedure to consider the proposal other than at a meeting, a creditor proposes that a person other than the nominee be appointed as supervisor, that person's consent to act and confirmation of being qualified to act as an insolvency practitioner (or being an authorised person) in relation to the debtor must be delivered to the nominee by the creditor.

(2)   If at a creditors' meeting to consider the proposal a resolution is moved for the appointment of a person other than the nominee to be supervisor, that person must produce to the chair at or before the meeting—

(a)   confirmation of being qualified to act as an insolvency practitioner (or being an authorised person) in relation to the debtor; and

(b)   written consent to act (unless the person is present at the meeting and signifies consent).

Derivation—This rule derived from the Insolvency Rules 1986, SI 1986/1925, r 5.25.

## [2.474]

### 8.24 Report of the creditors' consideration of a proposal

(1)   A report of the creditors' consideration of a proposal must be prepared by the convener or, if the proposal is considered at a meeting, by the chair.

(2)   The report must—

(a)   state whether the proposal was approved or rejected and, if approved, with what (if any) modifications;

(b)   list the creditors who voted or attended or who were represented at the meeting or decision procedure (as applicable) used to consider the proposal, setting out (with their respective values) how they voted on each resolution or whether they abstained;

(c)   if the proposal was approved, state whether the proceedings are main, territorial or non-EU proceedings and the reasons for so stating; and

(d)   include such further information as the nominee or the chair thinks appropriate.

(3)   Where an interim order was obtained a copy of the report must be filed with the court, within four business days of the decision date.

(4)   The court must endorse the copy of the report with the date of filing.

(5)   The nominee must give notice of the result of the consideration to—

(a)   everyone who was invited to consider the proposal and to whom notice of the decision procedure was delivered;

(b)   any other creditor; and

(c)   where the debtor is an undischarged bankrupt, the official receiver and any trustee.

(6)   The notice must be given—

(a)   where an interim order was obtained, as soon as reasonably practicable after a copy of the report is filed with the court; or

(b)   where an interim order was not obtained, within four business days of the decision date.

Derivation—This rule derived from the Insolvency Rules 1986, SI 1986/1925, r 5.27.
Amendments—SI 2017/366; SI 2017/1115.

General note—See s 259 and the commentary thereto.

## CHAPTER 6

### ACTION FOLLOWING APPROVAL OF AN IVA

**[2.475]**

**Note**

[Note: a document required by the Act or these Rules must also contain the standard contents set out in Part 1.]

**[2.476]**

**8.25 Hand-over of property, etc to supervisor**

(1)   As soon as reasonably practicable after the IVA is approved, the debtor or, where the debtor is an undischarged bankrupt, the official receiver or any trustee must do all that is required to put the supervisor in possession of the assets included in the IVA.

(2)   Where the debtor is an undischarged bankrupt, the supervisor must—

　　(a)　before taking possession of the assets included in the IVA, deliver to the official receiver or any trustee an undertaking to discharge the balance due to the official receiver or trustee out of the first realisation of the assets; or

　　(b)　upon taking possession of the assets included in the IVA, discharge such balance.

(3)   The balance is any balance due to the official receiver or any trustee—

　　(a)　by way of fees or expenses properly incurred and payable under the Act or these Rules; and

　　(b)　on account of any advances made in respect of the bankrupt's estate, together with interest on such advances at the rate specified in section 17 of the Judgments Act 1838 at the date of the bankruptcy order.

(4)   Where the debtor is an undischarged bankrupt, the official receiver and any trustee have a charge on the assets included in the IVA in respect of any sums comprising such balance, subject only to the deduction by the supervisor from realisations of the proper costs and expenses of realisation.

(5)   Any sums due to the official receiver take priority over those due to any trustee.

(6)   The supervisor must from time to time out of the realisation of assets—

　　(a)　discharge all guarantees properly given by the official receiver or any trustee for the benefit of the bankrupt's estate; and

　　(b)　pay the expenses of the official receiver and any trustee.

Derivation—This rule derived from the Insolvency Rules 1986, SI 1986/1925, r 5.26.

**[2.477]**

**8.26 Report to the Secretary of State of the approval of an IVA**

(1)   After the creditors approve an IVA the nominee, appointed person or the chair must deliver a report containing the required information to the Secretary of State.

(2)   The report must be delivered as soon as reasonably practicable, and in any event within 14 days after the report that the creditors have approved the IVA has been filed with the court under rule 8.24(3) or the notice that the creditors have approved the IVA has been sent to the creditors under rule 8.24(5) as the case may be.

(3)   The required information is—

　　(a)　identification details for the debtor;

　　(b)　the debtor's gender;

　　(c)　the debtor's date of birth;

　　(d)　any name by which the debtor was or is known, not being the name in which the debtor has entered into the IVA;

　　(e)　the date on which the IVA was approved by the creditors; and

　　(f)　the name and address of the supervisor.

(4)   A person who is appointed to act as a supervisor as a replacement of another person, or who vacates that office must deliver a notice of that fact to the Secretary of State as soon as reasonably practicable.

Derivation—This rule derived from the Insolvency Rules 1986, SI 1986/1925, r 5.29.

## [2.478]

### 8.27   Revocation or suspension of an IVA (section 262)

(1)   This rule applies where the court makes an order of revocation or suspension under section 262.

(2)   The applicant for the order must deliver a sealed copy of it to—

    (a)   the debtor (if different from the applicant);

    (b)   the supervisor; and

    (c)   where the debtor is an undischarged bankrupt, the official receiver and any trustee (in either case, if different from the applicant).

(3)   If the order includes a direction by the court under section 262(4)(b) for a matter to be considered further by a decision procedure, the applicant for the order must deliver a notice that the order has been made to the person who is directed to take such action.

(4)   The debtor, or the trustee (if the debtor is an undischarged bankrupt) must—

    (a)   as soon as reasonably practicable deliver a notice that the order has been made to everyone to whom a notice to consider the matter by a decision procedure was delivered or who appears to be affected by the order; and

    (b)   within five business days of delivery of a copy of the order (or within such longer period as the court may allow), deliver, if applicable, a notice to the court advising that it is intended to make a revised proposal to the creditors, or to invite re-consideration of the original proposal.

(5)   The applicant for the order must, within five business days of the making of the order deliver a notice of the order to the Secretary of State.

(6)   The applicant for the order must, within five business days of the expiry of any order of suspension, deliver a notice of the expiry to the Secretary of State.

Derivation—This rule derived from the Insolvency Rules 1986, SI 1986/1925, r 5.30.

General note—Section 262(4)(a) allows for the revocation or suspension of an IVA by the court. See the notes to that section for further commentary.

## [2.479]

### 8.28   Supervisor's accounts and reports

(1)   The supervisor must keep accounts and records where the IVA authorises or requires the supervisor—

    (a)   to carry on the business of the debtor or trade on behalf of or in the name of the debtor;

    (b)   to realise assets of the debtor or, where the debtor is an undischarged bankrupt, belonging to the bankrupt's estate; or

    (c)   otherwise to administer or dispose of any funds of the debtor or the bankrupt's estate.

(2)   The accounts and records which must be kept are of the supervisor's acts and dealings in, and in connection with, the IVA, including in particular records of all receipts and payments of money.

(3)   The supervisor must preserve any such accounts and records which were kept by any other person who has acted as supervisor of the IVA and are in the supervisor's possession.

(4)   The supervisor must deliver reports on the progress and prospects for the full implementation of the IVA to—

    (a)   the debtor; and

    (b)   the creditors bound by the IVA.

(5)   The first report must cover the period of 12 months commencing on the date on which the IVA was approved and a further report must be made for each subsequent period of 12 months.

(6)   Each report must be delivered within the period of two months after the end of the 12 month period.

(7)   Such a report is not required if an obligation to deliver a report under rule 8.31 arises in the two months after the end of the period.

(8)   Where the supervisor is authorised or required to do any of the things mentioned in paragraph (1), the report—

    (a)    must include or be accompanied by a summary of receipts and payments which paragraph (2) requires to be recorded; or

    (b)    where there have been no such receipts and payments, must say so.

**Derivation**—This rule derived from the Insolvency Rules 1986, SI 1986/1925, r 5.31A.
**Amendments**—SI 2017/366.

## [2.480]

### 8.29  Production of accounts and records to the Secretary of State

(1)   The Secretary of State may during the IVA or after its full implementation or termination require the supervisor to produce for inspection (either at the supervisor's premises or elsewhere)—

    (a)    the supervisor's accounts and records in relation to the IVA; and

    (b)    copies of reports and summaries prepared in compliance with rule 8.28.

(2)   The Secretary of State may require any accounts and records produced under this rule to be audited and, if so, the supervisor must provide such further information and assistance as the Secretary of State requires for the purposes of the audit.

**Derivation**—This rule derived from the Insolvency Rules 1986, SI 1986/1925, r 5.32.

## [2.481]

### 8.30  Fees and expenses

The fees and expenses that may be incurred for the purposes of the IVA are—

    (a)    fees for the nominee's services agreed with the debtor, the official receiver or any trustee;

    (b)    disbursements made by the nominee before the approval of the IVA; and

    (c)    fees or expenses which—

        (i)    are sanctioned by the terms of the IVA, or

        (ii)    where they are not sanctioned by the terms of the IVA, would be payable, or correspond to those which would be payable, in the debtor's bankruptcy.

**Derivation**—This rule derived from the Insolvency Rules 1986, SI 1986/1925, r 5.33.

## [2.482]

### 8.31  Termination or full implementation of the IVA

(1)   Not more than 28 days after the full implementation or termination of the IVA the supervisor must deliver a notice that the IVA has been fully implemented or terminated to the debtor and the creditors bound by the IVA.

(2)   The notice must state the date the IVA took effect.

(3)   The notice must be accompanied by a copy of a report by the supervisor which—

    (a)    summarises all receipts and payments in relation to the IVA;

    (b)    explains any departure from the terms of the IVA as approved by the creditors; and

    (c)    if the IVA has terminated, sets out the reasons why.

(4)   The supervisor must within the 28 days mentioned above—

    (a)    deliver a copy of the notice and report to the Secretary of State; and

    (b)    if the creditors were invited to consider the proposal following a report under section 256(1)(aa), file a copy of the notice and report with the court.

(5)  The supervisor must not vacate office until the notice and report have been delivered to the Secretary of State.

**Derivation**—This rule derived from the Insolvency Rules 1986, SI 1986/1925, r 5.34.

**General note**—Registrar Briggs explained in *Franses v Hay* [2015] EWHC 3468 (Ch), [2016] BPIR 355, [39]–[41] that an IVA had not ended for all purposes on the issue of a certificate of termination and would not do so until the supervisor had completed the secondary contractual duties now set out in r 8.31(1). The arrangement could be resurrected during this 'twilight period'. In *Green v Wright* [2017] EWCA Civ 111, [2017] BPIR 430, the Court of Appeal (reversing the decisions of the County Court and the Chancery Division below) held that the trusts of the debtor's assets constituted by the IVA did not come to an end on successful completion (now known as 'full implementation' under the IR 2016) of the IVA. This meant that the proceeds of claims that had been assets of the arrangement, but which only paid out after the notice of completion had been given, were to be distributed to creditors in accordance with the terms of the IVA. The earlier decision of the Court of Appeal in *N T Gallagher & Sons Ltd* [2002] EWCA Civ 404, [2002] 1 WLR 2380, [2002] 2 BCLC 133 (a CVA case), which dealt with the statutory trusts of arrangement assets in liquidation where the arrangement had failed, was applied. See further notes to s 1(2) for further discussion of that case.

## CHAPTER 7

Applications to Annul Bankruptcy Orders under Section 261(2)(a) and (b)

### [2.483]

**Note**

[Note: a document required by the Act or these Rules must also contain the standard contents set out in Part 1.]

### [2.484]

**8.32 Application by the bankrupt to annul the bankruptcy order (section 261(2)(a))**
(1)  An application by bankrupt to the court under section 261(2)(a) must be supported by a witness statement stating—

    (a)    that the IVA has been approved by the creditors;

    (b)    the date of the approval; and

    (c)    that the 28 day period in section 262(3)(a) for applications to be made under section 262(1) has expired and no applications or appeals remain to be disposed of.

(2)  The application and witness statement must be filed with the court and the court must deliver a notice of the venue for the hearing to the bankrupt.

(3)  Not less than five business days before the date of the hearing, the bankrupt must deliver a notice of the venue, with a copy of the application and witness statement, to—

    (a)    the official receiver;

    (b)    any trustee (if different to the official receiver); and

    (c)    the supervisor.

(4)  The official receiver, any such trustee and the supervisor may attend the hearing or be represented and bring to the court's attention any matters which seem to them to be relevant.

**Derivation**—This rule derived from the Insolvency Rules 1986, SI 1986/1925, rr 5.51, 5.52.

### [2.485]

**8.33 Application by the official receiver to annul the bankruptcy order (section 261(2)(b))**
(1)  An application by the official receiver to the court under section 261(2)(b) to annul a bankruptcy order must be supported by a report stating—

    (a)    the grounds on which it is made;

(b)    that the time period in paragraph (2) has expired; and

(c)    that the official receiver is not aware that any application under section 262 or appeal remains to be disposed of.

(2)   The official receiver must not make such an application before the expiry of the period of 42 days beginning with the day on which—

(a)    the nominee filed the report of the creditors' consideration with the court, where the creditors considered the proposal under section 257 following a report to a court under section 256(1)(aa); or

(b)    the nominee delivered a notice to the creditors of the result of their consideration, where the creditors considered the proposal under section 257 following a report to the creditors under section 256A(3).

(3)   The application and the report must be filed with the court and the court must deliver a notice of the venue for the hearing to the official receiver.

(4)   Not less than five business days before the date of the hearing, the official receiver must deliver a notice of the venue, with a copy of the application and the report, to the bankrupt.

**Derivation**—This rule derived from the Insolvency Rules 1986, SI 1986/1925, rr 5.54, 5.55.

## [2.486]

### 8.34  Order annulling bankruptcy

(1)   An order under section 261(2) annulling a bankruptcy order must contain—

(a)    identification details the proceedings;

(b)    the section number of the Act under which the order is made;

(c)    the name and address of the applicant;

(d)    a statement that it appears that an IVA under section 258 has been approved and implemented and the date of approval;

(e)    a statement that there has been no application under section 262 for the revocation or suspension of the IVA and that the time period for making such an application has expired;

(f)    where the applicant is the official receiver under section 261(2)(b) that the time period in rule 8.33(2) has expired;

(g)    the order that the relevant bankruptcy order, identified by its date and the name of the bankrupt as set out in the bankruptcy order, be annulled;

(h)    if appropriate, an order that the relevant bankruptcy petition (identified by the date of its presentation) or the relevant bankruptcy application (identified by the date it was made) (as the case may be), be dismissed;

(i)    where there is a trustee, an order in respect of the trustee's release, having regard to rule 8.37;

(j)    an order that the registration of the bankruptcy petition or bankruptcy application as a pending action at the Land Charges Department of HM Land Registry be vacated (identified by the date of registration and reference number);

(k)    an order that the registration of the bankruptcy order on the register of writs and orders affecting land at the Land Charges Department of HM Land Registry be vacated (identified by date of registration and reference number);

(l)    the date the order is made;

(m)    a notice to the effect that if the former bankrupt requires notice of the order to be gazetted and advertised in the same manner as the bankruptcy order was advertised, the bankrupt must deliver a notice to the official receiver within 28 days; and

(n)    a notice to the effect that it is the responsibility of the former bankrupt and in the former bankrupt's interest to ensure that any registration of the petition or bankruptcy application and of the bankruptcy order at the Land Charges Department of HM Land Registry and any entries relating to the petition or bankruptcy application and bankruptcy order in any registered titles at HM Land Registry are cancelled (such a notice giving relevant HM Land Registry contact details and referring to relevant Registry guidance).

(2)  The court must deliver a sealed copy of the order to—

  (a)  the former bankrupt;

  (b)  the official receiver;

  (c)  any trustee (if different to the official receiver); and

  (d)  the supervisor.

**Derivation**—This rule derived from the Insolvency Rules 1986, SI 1986/1925, Sch 4, Fm 5.7.

## [2.487]

### 8.35  Notice of order

(1)  An official receiver, who has delivered a notice of the debtor's bankruptcy to the creditors, must, as soon as reasonably practicable, deliver a notice of an annulment under section 261(2) to them.

(2)  Expenses incurred by the official receiver in delivering a notice under this rule are a charge in the official receiver's favour on the property of the former bankrupt, whether or not actually in the hands of the former bankrupt.

(3)  Where any such property is in the hands of any person other than the former bankrupt, the official receiver's charge is valid subject only to any costs that may be incurred by that person in effecting realisation of the property for the purpose of satisfying the charge.

**Derivation**—This rule derived from the Insolvency Rules 1986, SI 1986/1925, rr 5.53, 5.56.

## [2.488]

### 8.36  Advertisement of order

(1)  The former bankrupt may in writing within 28 days of the date of an order for annulment under section 261(2) require the official receiver—

  (a)  to cause a notice of the order to be gazetted; and

  (b)  to advertise the order in the same manner as the bankruptcy order was advertised.

(2)  The official receiver must comply with any such requirement as soon as reasonably practicable.

(3)  The notice must state—

  (a)  the name of the former bankrupt;

  (b)  the date on which the bankruptcy order was made;

  (c)  that the bankruptcy order has been annulled;

  (d)  the date of the annulment order; and

  (e)  the grounds of the annulment.

(4)  Where the former bankrupt has died, or is a person lacking capacity to manage the person's own affairs (within the meaning of the Mental Capacity Act 2005), the references to the former bankrupt in paragraph (1) are to be read as references to the personal representative of the same or, as the case may be, a person appointed by the court to represent or act for the former bankrupt.

**Derivation**—This rule derived from the Insolvency Rules 1986, SI 1986/1925, r 5.60.

**General note**—These provisions give the debtor a right, without incurring the costs of advertisement, to require notification of the appointment, subject to the 28-day time limit therein.

## [2.489]

### 8.37  Trustee's final account

(1)  The making of an order under section 261(2) does not of itself release the trustee from any duty or obligation imposed by or under the Act or these Rules to account for all of the trustee's transactions in connection with the former bankrupt's estate.

(2)  As soon as reasonably practicable after the making of an order, the trustee must—

(a)  deliver a copy of the final account of the trustee to the Secretary of State; and

(b)  file a copy of that account with the court.

(3)  The final account must include a summary of the trustee's receipts and payments.

(4)  The trustee is released from such time as the court may determine, having regard to whether paragraph (2) of this rule has been complied with.

Derivation—This rule derived from the Insolvency Rules 1986, SI 1986/1925, r 5.61.

## CHAPTER 8

### Time Recording Information

**[2.490]**

**Note**

[Note: a document required by the Act or these Rules must also contain the standard contents set out in Part 1.]

**[2.491]**

### 8.38  Provision of information

(1)  This rule applies where the remuneration of the nominee or the supervisor has been fixed on the basis of time spent.

(2)  A person who is acting, or has acted within the previous two years as—

(a)  a nominee in relation to a proposal; or

(b)  the supervisor in relation to an IVA;

must, within 28 days of receipt of a request from a person mentioned in paragraph (3), deliver free of charge to that person a statement complying with paragraph (4) and (5).

(3)  The persons are—

(a)  the debtor; and

(b)  where the proposal has been approved, a creditor bound by the IVA.

(4)  The statement must cover the period which—

(a)  in the case of a person who has ceased to act as nominee or supervisor in relation to an IVA, begins with the date of that person's appointment as nominee or supervisor and ends with the date of ceasing to act; and

(b)  in any other case, consists of one or more complete periods of six months beginning with the date of appointment and ending most nearly before the date of receiving the request.

(5)  The statement must set out—

(i)  the total number of hours spent on the matter during that period by the nominee or supervisor, and by any staff,

(ii)  for each grade of staff engaged on the matter, the average hourly rate at which work carried out by staff in that grade is charged, and

(iii)  the number of hours spent on the matter by each grade of staff during that period.

Derivation—This rule derived from the Insolvency Rules 1986, SI 1986/1925, r 5.66.

PART 9   DEBT RELIEF ORDERS

CHAPTER 1

INTERPRETATION

**[2.492]**

**Note**

[Notes: (1) a debt relief order under Part 7A of the Act may be made in respect of "qualifying debts" (as defined in section 251A(2)); these do not include "excluded debts" which are prescribed by rule 9.2 for the purposes of section 251A(4).

(2) "approved intermediaries" and "competent authority" are defined in section 251U of the Act for purposes of Part 7A of the Act.]

**[2.493]**

**9.1 Debtor's family**

In this Part the expression "debtor's family" has the same meaning in relation to a debtor as it has in section 385(1) in relation to a bankrupt.

**[2.494]**

**9.2 Excluded debts**

(1)   For the purposes of Part 7A of the Act debts of the following descriptions are prescribed under section 251A(4) as "excluded debts"—

(a)     any fine imposed for an offence and any obligation (including an obligation to pay a lump sum or to pay costs) arising under an order made in family proceedings or any obligation arising under a maintenance assessment or maintenance calculation made under the Child Support Act 1991;

(b)     any debt or liability to which a debtor is or may become subject in respect of any sum paid or payable to the debtor as a student by way of a loan and which the debtor receives whether before or after the debt relief order is made;

(c)     any obligation arising under a confiscation order made under section 1 of the Drug Trafficking Offences Act 1986, section 1 of the Criminal Justice (Scotland) Act 1987, section 71 of the Criminal Justice Act 1988, or Parts 2, 3 or 4 of the Proceeds of Crime Act 2002;

(d)     any debt which consists of a liability to pay damages for negligence, nuisance or breach of a statutory, contractual or other duty, or to pay damages by virtue of Part 1 of the Consumer Protection Act 1987, being in either case damages in respect of the death of or personal injury (including any disease or other impairment of physical or mental condition) to any person; and

(e)     any obligation arising from a payment out of the social fund under section 138(1)(b) of the Social Security Contributions and Benefits Act 1992 by way of crisis loan or budgeting loan.

(2)   In paragraph (1)(a) "family proceedings" and "fine" have the meanings given by section 281(8) (which applies the Magistrates' Courts Act 1980 and the Matrimonial and Family Proceedings Act 1984).

(3)   In paragraph (1)(b) "loan" means a loan made under—

(a)     regulations made under section 22(1) of the Teaching and Higher Education Act 1998; or

(b)     the Education (Student Loans) Act 1990, or that Act as it continues in force by virtue of any savings made, in connection with its repeal by the Teaching and Higher Education Act 1998, by an order made under section 46(4) of that Act;

and includes any interest on the loan and any penalties or charges incurred in connection with it.

**Derivation**—This rule derived from the Insolvency Rules 1986, SI 1986/1925, r 5A.2. **Amendments**—SI 2017/366.

CHAPTER 2

APPLICATION FOR A DEBT RELIEF ORDER

## [2.495]

**Note**
[Note: a document required by the Act or these Rules must also contain the standard contents set out in Part 1.]

## [2.496]

### 9.3 Application for a debt relief order: information required in the application

(1) An application for a debt relief order under section 251A must state the matters set out in paragraphs (2) to (9) (which are prescribed for the purposes of section 251B(2)(c)) as they are at the date of the application as well as the matters referred to in section 251B(2)(a) (list of the debtor's debts at the date of the application) and 251B(2)(b) (details of any security held in respect of those debts).

(2) The application must identify the debtor and state—

    (a) the debtor's occupation (if any);

    (b) the debtor's gender;

    (c) the debtor's date of birth;

    (d) the debtor's places of residence during the three years before the date of the application;

    (e) any other name used by the debtor for any purpose;

    (f) the name, address and nature of any business carried on by the debtor, including any business carried on by—

        (i) a firm or partnership of which the debtor is a member;

        (ii) an agent or manager for the debtor or for such firm or partnership;

    (g) any other liabilities (including those imposed by an order of the court) to which the debtor is subject;

    (h) the address of the creditor to whom each debt is owed;

    (i) the total amount of the debtor's monthly income from all sources (see rule 9.7(1));

    (j) the sources of that income and the amount from each source;

    (k) particulars of the expenditure which the debtor claims is necessary to meet the monthly reasonable domestic needs of the debtor and the debtor's family, including the purpose and the amount of that expenditure;

    (l) the total amount available from any source to meet the claimed monthly reasonable domestic needs of the debtor and the debtor's family (see rule 9.7(2)); and

    (m) particulars of the debtor's property and its total estimated value (see rules 9.8 and 9.9).

(3) The debtor must also state in the application—

    (a) whether or not at the date of the application the debtor—

        (i) has given a preference to any person during the period of two years ending with the application date,

        (ii) has entered into a transaction with any person at an undervalue during the period of two years ending with the application date,

        (iii) is domiciled in England and Wales,

        (iv) at any time during the period of three years ending with the application date—

            (aa) was resident,

        (bb)    had a place of residence, or

        (cc)    carried on business,

in England and Wales,

    (v)      is an undischarged bankrupt,

    (vi)    is subject to a debt relief order,

    (vii)   has been subject to a debt relief order in the six years ending with the application date,

    (viii)  is subject to an interim order or an IVA under Part 8 of the Act, or

    (ix)    is subject to a bankruptcy restrictions order or undertaking or debt relief restrictions order or undertaking; and

  (b)    whether at the date of the application—

    (i)      a bankruptcy petition has been presented against the debtor,

    (ii)    a bankruptcy application has been made by the debtor,

    (iii)   any debt management arrangements (see section 251F) are in force in relation to the debtor, and

    (iv)   any other legal action has been taken against the debtor in relation to any of the debtor's existing debts.

(4)   In the application, the debtor must deduct from each debt all trade and other discounts which are available to the debtor, except any discount for immediate or early settlement.

(5)   Where any debts were incurred or are payable in a foreign currency, the amount of those debts must be converted into sterling at a single exchange rate for that currency prevailing on the relevant date.

(6)   A creditor who considers that the rate is unreasonable may apply to the court.

(7)   If the court finds that the rate is unreasonable it may itself determine the rate.

(8)   Where a debt consists of unpaid payments of a periodical nature, the amount of the debt will consist of any amounts due and unpaid up to the application date.

(9)   Where at the application date any payment was accruing due, the amount of the debt will be so much as would have fallen due at that date, if accruing from day to day.

(10)  A debtor may include a debt of which payment is not yet due at the date of the application if it is for a liquidated sum payable at some certain future time.

(11)  In the application, the debtor must also—

  (a)    consent to the official receiver making checks for the purpose of verifying that the debtor complies with the conditions to which the making of a debt relief order is subject;

  (b)    state that the debtor is unable to pay the debts;

  (c)    request a debt relief order; and

  (d)    indicate the date on which the application is completed.

(12)  The debtor must deliver to the approved intermediary such information and such documents as will enable the intermediary to substantiate the information in the application, including information about each debt, the amount of the debt and the name and address of the creditor.

**Derivation**—This rule derived from the Insolvency Rules 1986, SI 1986/1925, r 5A.3.

## [2.497]

### 9.4 Delivery of application

(1)   An application for a debt relief order must be completed and delivered to the official receiver in electronic form and by electronic means.

(2)   The preconditions for delivering a document electronically set out in rule 1.45(2) do not apply to applications for debt relief orders.

(3)   In the event of any malfunction or error in the operation of the electronic form or means of delivery, the official receiver must inform the competent authorities and approved intermediaries—

  (a)    that approved intermediaries may complete and deliver applications in hard copy for a specified period; and

(b)    of the postal address to which such applications are to be delivered and of any terms or conditions to which the use of the address is subject.

(4)    Such an application completed in hard copy may not be delivered by fax.

**Derivation**—This rule derived from the Insolvency Rules 1986, SI 1986/1925, r 5A.4.

## [2.498]

### 9.5 Role of approved intermediary

(1)    The approved intermediary, through whom the application for a debt relief order is to be made, must create an application for a debt relief order in the name of the debtor as soon as reasonably practicable after being asked by the debtor to do so.

(2)    The approved intermediary may assist the debtor—

(a)    to identify what information is required to complete the application;

(b)    based upon the documentation and information supplied by the debtor, to ascertain whether—

(i)    the debtor appears to have debts not exceeding the prescribed amount,

(ii)   the debtor's surplus income does not exceed the prescribed amount, and

(iii)  the value of the debtor's property does not exceed the prescribed amount; and

(c)    to ensure that the application (if made) is completed in full.

(3)    The approved intermediary must draw the debtor's attention to—

(a)    all the conditions to which an application for, and the making of, a debt relief order is subject;

(b)    the possible consequences of the debtor making any false representation or omission in the application; and

(c)    the fact that verification checks will be made for the purpose of verifying that the debtor complies with the conditions to which the making of a debt relief order is subject and the requirement for the debtor to consent to such checks being made.

(4)    The approved intermediary must deliver the application to the official receiver as soon as reasonably practicable after being instructed by the debtor to do so.

**Derivation**—This rule derived from the Insolvency Rules 1986, SI 1986/1925, r 5A.5.

CHAPTER 3

VERIFYING THE APPLICATION AND DETERMINING THE DEBTOR'S INCOME
AND PROPERTY

## [2.499]

### 9.6 Prescribed verification checks: conditions in paragraphs 1 to 8 of Schedule 4ZA of the Act

(1)    For the purposes of section 251D(4) and (5) and the conditions in paragraphs 1 to 8 of Schedule 4ZA of the Act, the prescribed verification checks are those searches or enquiries specified in this rule.

(2)    For the purpose of verifying a debtor's connection with England and Wales on the application date, verification checks made in, or with, one or more of the following—

(a)    the electoral registers for the areas in England and Wales in which the debtor claims to reside or to carry on business or to have resided or carried on business at the date of the application;

(b)    the individual insolvency register;

(c)    the bankruptcy restrictions register;

(d)    the debt relief restrictions register;

(e)    a credit reference agency.

(3)   Verification checks made in one or more of the registers specified in paragraph (4), for the purpose of verifying that a debtor—

    (a)   is not, on the determination date—

        (i)    an undischarged bankrupt,

        (ii)   subject to a bankruptcy restrictions order or undertaking,

        (iii)  subject to a debt relief restrictions order or undertaking,

        (iv)  subject to an IVA; or

    (b)   has not been the subject of a debt relief order in the period of six years ending with the determination date.

(4)   The registers referred to in paragraph (3) are—

    (a)   the individual insolvency register;

    (b)   the bankruptcy restrictions register; and

    (c)   the debt relief restrictions register.

(5)   Verification checks made in, or with, one or more of the sources specified in paragraph (6) for the purpose of verifying—

    (a)   that the debtor is not subject to an interim order on the determination date;

    (b)   whether a creditor's bankruptcy petition has been presented against the debtor before the determination date;

    (c)   whether the debtor has made a bankruptcy application before the determination date;

    (d)   whether proceedings in relation to any such bankruptcy application have finally been disposed of before the determination date;

    (e)   where a creditor's bankruptcy petition has been presented against the debtor before the determination date, the status of the proceedings in relation to the petition and whether the person who presented the petition has consented to the making of the application for a debt relief order.

(6)   The sources are—

    (a)   the individual insolvency register;

    (b)   county or other court records;

    (c)   a credit reference agency.

(7)   Verification checks made with a credit reference agency, for the purpose of verifying that each of the following does not exceed the prescribed amount—

    (a)   the amount of the debtor's overall indebtedness;

    (b)   the amount of the debtor's monthly surplus income; or

    (c)   the total value of the debtor's property.

**Derivation**—This rule derived from the Insolvency Rules 1986, SI 1986/1925, r 5A.7.

## [2.500]

### 9.7 Determination of debtor's monthly surplus income

(1)   For the purposes of this Part, the income of a debtor comprises every payment in the nature of income which is from time to time made to the debtor or to which the debtor from time to time becomes entitled, including any payment in respect of the carrying on of a business or in respect of an office or employment and any payment under a pension scheme.

(2)   In determining the monthly surplus income of a debtor, the official receiver must take into account any contribution made by a member of the debtor's family to the amount necessary for the reasonable domestic needs of the debtor and the debtor's family.

**Derivation**—This rule derived from the Insolvency Rules 1986, SI 1986/1925, r 5A.8.

**[2.501]**

### 9.8 Determination of value of the debtor's property (paragraph 8 of Schedule 4ZA)

(1)   The official receiver in determining the total value of the debtor's property for the purposes of determining whether the condition in paragraph 8 of Schedule 4ZA is met must treat as a debtor's property for the purposes of this Part—

(a)     all property belonging to or vested in the debtor on the determination date; and

(b)     any property which by virtue of any of the following provisions of this Part is comprised in or is treated as falling within the preceding sub-paragraph.

(2)   For the purposes of this Part—

(a)     property, in relation to a debtor, includes references to any power exercisable by the debtor over or in relation to property except in so far as the power is exercisable over or in relation to property which is not or is deemed not for the time being to be the property of the debtor and cannot be exercised for the benefit of the debtor;

(b)     a power exercisable over or in relation to property is deemed for the purposes of this Part to vest in the person entitled to exercise it at the time of the transaction or event by virtue of which it is exercisable by that person (whether or not it becomes so exercisable at that time);

(c)     property belonging to or vested in the debtor so belongs or vests in the debtor subject to the rights of any person other than the debtor (whether as a secured creditor of the debtor or otherwise).

(3)   In determining the value of the debtor's property the descriptions of property set out in rule 9.9 must be excluded.

 **Derivation**—This rule derived from the Insolvency Rules 1986, SI 1986/1925, r 5A.9.

**[2.502]**

### 9.9 Property to be excluded in determining the value of a debtor's property

(1)   For the purposes of determining the value of a person's property under rule 9.8, the official receiver must disregard—

(a)     a single domestic motor vehicle belonging to or vested in the debtor if—

(i)     it has been especially adapted for use by the debtor because of a physical impairment that has a substantial and long-term adverse effect on the debtor's ability to carry out normal day-to-day activities, subject to paragraph (2), or

(ii)     the maximum potential realisable value of the vehicle is less than £1,000 (the prescribed amount);

(b)     subject to paragraph (3), such tools, books and other items of equipment as are necessary to the debtor for use personally in the debtor's employment, business or vocation;

(c)     subject to paragraph (3), such clothing, bedding, furniture, household equipment and provisions as are necessary for satisfying the basic domestic needs of the debtor and the debtor's family;

(d)     property held by the debtor on trust for any other person;

(e)     the right of nomination to a vacant ecclesiastical benefice;

(f)     a tenancy which is an assured tenancy or an assured agricultural occupancy, within the meaning of Part 1 of the Housing Act 1988, and the terms of which inhibit an assignment as mentioned in section 127(5) of the Rent Act 1977;

(g)     a protected tenancy, within the meaning of the Rent Act 1977, in relation to which, by virtue of any provision of Part 9 of that Act, no premium can lawfully be required as a condition of assignment;

(h)     a tenancy of a dwelling-house by virtue of which the debtor is, within the meaning of the Rent (Agriculture) Act 1976, a protected occupier of the dwelling-house, and the terms of which inhibit an assignment as mentioned in section 127(5) of the Rent Act 1977;

(i)    a secure tenancy, within the meaning of Part 4 of the Housing Act 1985, which is not capable of being assigned, except in the cases mentioned in section 91(3) of that Act; and

(j)    any right of the debtor under an approved pension arrangement (as defined by section 11 of the Welfare Reform and Pensions Act 1999).

(2)   The amount the official receiver must disregard under paragraph (1)(a)(i) is limited to the value of a reasonable replacement where it appears to the official receiver that the realisable value of the vehicle to be disregarded exceeds the cost of a reasonable replacement for it.

(3)   The amount the official receiver must disregard under paragraph (1)(b) or (c) is limited to the value of a reasonable replacement where it appears to the official receiver that the realisable value of the whole or a part of the property to be disregarded exceeds the cost of a reasonable replacement for that property or that part.

(4)   A vehicle or other property is a reasonable replacement if it is reasonably adequate for meeting the needs met by the other vehicle or other property.

Derivation—This rule derived from the Insolvency Rules 1986, SI 1986/1925, r 5A.10.

CHAPTER 4

MAKING OR REFUSAL OF A DEBT RELIEF ORDER

**[2.503]**

Note
[Note: a document required by the Act or these Rules must also contain the standard contents set out in Part 1.]

**[2.504]**

**9.10  Contents of debt relief order**
A debt relief order must contain—

(a)    the debtor's identification details;

(b)    the date of, and the reference number allocated to, the debtor's application;

(c)    a list of the debtor's qualifying debts as at the application date, specifying the amount owed and the creditor's name, address and reference (if any); and

(d)    the date on which the order was made.

Derivation—This rule derived from the Insolvency Rules 1986, SI 1986/1925, r 5A.11.

**[2.505]**

**9.11  Other steps to be taken by official receiver or debtor upon making of the order**
(1)   In addition to delivering a copy of the order to the debtor under section 251E, the official receiver must—

(a)    deliver a notice of the making and date of the order to the approved intermediary through whom the debtor's application was made; and

(b)    cause an entry to be made in the individual insolvency register in accordance with rule 11.18.

(2)   If there are other debt management arrangements or an attachment of earnings order in force in relation to the debtor, the official receiver must deliver a notice of the making of the debt relief order to the court, or the body, as the case may be, responsible for making the debt management arrangements or order.

Derivation—This rule derived from the Insolvency Rules 1986, SI 1986/1925, r 5A.12.

**[2.506]**

### 9.12 Prescribed information for creditors on making of debt relief order

The official receiver must deliver a notice to each creditor to whom a qualifying debt specified in the order is owed, of—

 (a)   the making, the date and the reference number of the order;

 (b)   the effect of the order;

 (c)   the matters to which a creditor may object under section 251K; and

 (d)   the name, address and telephone number of the official receiver delivering the notice and the address to which any objection under that section may or must be delivered.

 Derivation—This rule derived from the Insolvency Rules 1986, SI 1986/1925, r 5A.13.

**[2.507]**

### 9.13 Refusal of application for debt relief order

If the official receiver refuses an application for a debt relief order, the official receiver must deliver a notice to the debtor stating that the official receiver refused the application, and the reason why it has been refused.

 Derivation—This rule derived from the Insolvency Rules 1986, SI 1986/1925, r 5A.6.

### CHAPTER 5

#### OBJECTION AND REVOCATION

**[2.508]**

**Note**

[Note: a document required by the Act or these Rules must also contain the standard contents set out in Part 1.]

**[2.509]**

### 9.14 Meaning of "creditor"

In this Chapter, "creditor" means a person specified in a debt relief order as a creditor to whom a qualifying debt is owed.

 Derivation—This rule derived from the Insolvency Rules 1986, SI 1986/1925, r 5A.14.

**[2.510]**

### 9.15 Creditor's objection to a debt relief order (section 251K)

(1)   The prescribed period under section 251K(2)(a) for a creditor to object to a debt relief order during the moratorium period is within 30 days of the date on which a notice of the making of the order was delivered to the creditor.

(2)   The objection must be made in writing to the official receiver and must contain—

 (a)   the name and address of the creditor;

 (b)   the name of the debtor and the reference number of the order;

 (c)   the matters under section 251K to which the creditor objects;

 (d)   a statement of which of the prescribed grounds for objection the creditor relies upon;

 (e)   a statement of the facts on which the creditor relies; and

 (f)   information and documents in support of the grounds and the facts on which the creditor relies.

(3)   The prescribed grounds for objection are that—

 (a)   there is an error in, or an omission from, something specified in the debt relief order;

 (b)   a bankruptcy order has been made in relation to the debtor;

 (c)   the debtor has made a proposal under Part 8 of the Act;

(d)    the official receiver should not have been satisfied that—

    (i)    the debts specified in the order were qualifying debts of the debtor as at the application date,

    (ii)    the conditions specified in Part 1 of Schedule 4ZA were met, or

    (iii)    the conditions specified in Part 2 of that Schedule were met; or

(e)    the official receiver should have been satisfied that the official receiver was permitted to make an order in spite of any failure to meet the conditions referred to in sub-paragraphs (d)(ii) and (iii).

**Derivation**—This rule derived from the Insolvency Rules 1986, SI 1986/1925, r 5A.14.

## [2.511]

### 9.16 Official receiver's response to objection under section 251K

(1) After considering a creditor's objection to a debt relief order in accordance with section 251K, the official receiver, if minded to revoke or amend the debt relief order, must deliver to the debtor—

(a)    particulars of the objection;

(b)    the grounds and facts upon which the creditor relies;

(c)    an invitation to the debtor to deliver any comments on them to the official receiver within 21 days of delivery of the particulars; and

(d)    the address to which the debtor's comments must be delivered.

(2) Before deciding whether to revoke or amend the debt relief order, the official receiver must consider any comments made by the debtor provided they are received within the 21 day period.

(3) After coming to a decision on the objection the official receiver must deliver a notice of the decision to the creditor within 14 days.

(4) If the official receiver has decided to make an application under section 251M(2) then the official receiver must treat the creditor as a person interested in the application under rule 9.21(3)(b) (if the creditor would not otherwise be such).

**Derivation**—This rule derived from the Insolvency Rules 1986, SI 1986/1925, r 5A.15.

## [2.512]

### 9.17 Creditor's request that a debt relief order be revoked (section 251L(4))

(1) A creditor may request that the official receiver revoke a debt relief order under section 251L(4) because either or both of the conditions in paragraphs 7 and 8 of Schedule 4ZA are not met at any time after the debt relief order was made.

(2) The request must contain—

(a)    the name and address of the creditor;

(b)    the name of the debtor and the reference number of the order;

(c)    which of the conditions under paragraph 7 and 8 of Schedule 4ZA are not met;

(d)    a statement of the facts on which the creditor relies; and

(e)    information and documents supporting the facts which are relied upon.

(3) After coming to a decision on the request the official receiver must deliver a notice of the decision to the creditor within 14 days.

(4) If the official receiver has decided to make an application under section 251M(2) then the official receiver must treat the creditor as a person interested in the application under rule 9.21(3)(b) (if the creditor would not otherwise be such).

**Derivation**—This rule derived from the Insolvency Rules 1986, SI 1986/1925, r 5A.16.

## [2.513]

### 9.18 Procedure in revoking or amending a debt relief order (section 251L)

(1) The official receiver must as soon as reasonably practicable after deciding to revoke a debt relief order under section 251L deliver notice of the decision to the debtor and the creditors.

(2)   The notice must contain—
   (a)   identification details for the debtor;
   (b)   the date and reference number of the debt relief order;
   (c)   the reasons for revocation; and
   (d)   the date (under subsection (5) or (7) of section 251L) on or from which the revocation has effect.

(3)   Where the official receiver—
   (a)   has delivered notices under paragraph (1) of the revocation of a debt relief order from a specified date; and
   (b)   thinks it appropriate under section 251L(7) to revoke the debt relief order with immediate effect before the specified date;
the official receiver must deliver a notice of the new date to anyone who previously received a notice under paragraph (1).

(4)   The official receiver must cause the entry in the individual insolvency register relating to the order to be amended so far as information concerning the order has not already been deleted under rule 11.19.

(5)   Where the debtor has died during the moratorium period rule 9.20 applies.

(6)   The official receiver must as soon as reasonably practicable after amending a debt relief order deliver a notice of the amendment to the debtor and the creditors.

(7)   The notice must contain—
   (a)   identification details for the debtor and the date and reference number of the debt relief order;
   (b)   the amendment;
   (c)   the date on which the amendment was made; and
   (d)   the reasons for it.

(8)   The official receiver must as soon as reasonably practicable cause the entry in the individual insolvency register relating to the amended debt relief order to be amended accordingly.

**Derivation**—This rule derived from the Insolvency Rules 1986, SI 1986/1925, r 5A.16.

## [2.514]

### 9.19  Debtor's notification of official receiver of matters in section 251J(3) or (5)

(1)   The debtor must deliver a notice to the official receiver as soon as reasonably practicable after the debtor becomes aware of an error in, or omission from, the information supplied to the official receiver in, or in support of, the application.

(2)   The notice must state the nature of the error or omission and the reason for it.

(3)   The debtor must deliver a notice to the official receiver as soon as reasonably practicable after the debtor becomes aware of a change in the debtor's circumstances between the application date and the determination date that would affect (or would have affected) the determination of the application.

(4)   The notice must state the nature of the change and the date of the change.

(5)   Where a debt relief order is made and—
   (a)   the debtor's income increases during the moratorium period applicable to the order, the debtor must as soon as reasonably practicable after the date of the increase deliver a notice to the official receiver stating—
      (i)   the amount of the increase,
      (ii)   the reason for it,
      (iii)   the date of the increase, and
      (iv)   its expected duration;
   (b)   the debtor acquires property or property is devolved upon the debtor during that period, the debtor must as soon as reasonably practicable after the date of the acquisition or devolution deliver a notice to the official receiver stating—
      (i)   the nature of the acquisition or devolution,
      (ii)   the date of the acquisition or devolution,

        (iii)    the reason for it, and

        (iv)    its value;

  (c)    the debtor becomes aware of any error in or omission from any information supplied by the debtor to the official receiver after the determination date, the debtor must as soon as reasonably practicable after the date on which the debtor becomes aware of it deliver a notice to the official receiver, stating—

        (i)    the nature of the error or omission,

        (ii)    the reason for it, and

        (iii)    the date on which the debtor became aware of it.

**Derivation**—This rule derived from the Insolvency Rules 1986, SI 1986/1925, r 5A.17.

## [2.515]

**9.20 Death of debtor during a moratorium period under a debt relief order**

(1)   This rule applies where a debtor dies during a moratorium period under a debt relief order.

(2)   The official receiver must, as soon as reasonably practicable after being informed of the death of the debtor—

  (a)    cause a note of the fact and the date of the death to be entered on the individual insolvency register under rule 11.23;

  (b)    revoke the debt relief order; and

  (c)    deliver a notice of the revocation to—

        (i)    the creditors, and

        (ii)    the personal representatives of the debtor.

(3)   The notice of revocation must—

  (a)    state the reason for the revocation; and

  (b)    specify the date on which the revocation took effect.

**Derivation**—This rule derived from the Insolvency Rules 1986, SI 1986/1925, r 5A.27.

CHAPTER 6

APPLICATIONS TO THE COURT

## [2.516]

**Note**

[Note: a document required by the Act or these Rules must also contain the standard contents set out in Part 1.]

## [2.517]

**9.21 Notice of application to court under section 251M**

(1)   This rule applies to applications to the court under section 251M.

(2)   Where the application is made by a person who is dissatisfied by an act, omission or decision of the official receiver in connection with a debt relief order or an application for a debt relief order the applicant must deliver a notice—

  (a)    if the applicant is the debtor, to the official receiver and any creditor specified in the debt relief order or in the application for the debt relief order; or

  (b)    if the applicant is a person other than the debtor, to the official receiver and the debtor.

(3)   Where the application is made by the official receiver for directions or an order in relation to a matter arising in connection with a debt relief order or an application for such an order, the official receiver must deliver notice to—

  (a)    the debtor; and

  (b)    any person appearing to the official receiver to have an interest in the application.

**Derivation**—This rule derived from the Insolvency Rules 1986, SI 1986/1925, r 5A.19.

**[2.518]**

### 9.22 Court in which applications under sections 251M or 251N are to be made

(1)   An application to the court under section 251M or 251N must be made to—

    (a)    the County Court at Central London, where the proceedings are allocated to the London Insolvency District under rule 12.5(a)(i) to (iv);

    (b)    the High Court, where the proceedings are allocated to the London Insolvency District under rule 12.5(a)(v);

    (c)    the debtor's own hearing centre as determined under paragraph (3) (subject to paragraph (4)), in any other case where the debtor is resident in England and Wales.

(2)   The application may be filed either with the debtor's own hearing centre or with the High Court if—

    (a)    the debtor is not resident in England and Wales but was resident or carried on business in England and Wales within the six months immediately before the application is filed with the court; and

    (b)    the proceedings are not allocated to the London Insolvency District.

(3)   In this rule the debtor's own hearing centre is—

    (a)    where the debtor has carried on business in England and Wales within the six months immediately before the application is filed with the court, the hearing centre which serves the insolvency district where for the longest period during those six months—

        (i)    the debtor carried on business, or

        (ii)    the principal place of business was located, if business was carried on in more than one insolvency district; or

    (b)    where the debtor has not carried on business in England and Wales within the six months immediately before the application is filed with the court, the hearing centre which serves the insolvency district where the debtor resided for the longest period during those six months.

(4)   Where, for whatever reason, it is not possible for the application to be filed with the debtor's own hearing centre, the applicant may, with a view to expediting the application, file the application—

    (a)    where paragraph (3)(a) applies, with—

        (i)    the hearing centre for the insolvency district in which the debtor resides, or

        (ii)    the hearing centre specified in Schedule 6 as the nearest full-time hearing centre to the hearing centre specified in paragraph (3)(a), or paragraph (i) as the case may be; or

    (b)    where paragraph (3)(b) applies, with the hearing centre specified in Schedule 6 as being the nearest full-time hearing centre to that specified in paragraph (3)(b).

(5)   The application must contain sufficient information to establish that it is brought in the appropriate court, and where the application is made to the County Court, the appropriate hearing centre.

**Derivation**—This rule derived from the Insolvency Rules 1986, SI 1986/1925, r 5A.21.

**[2.519]**

### 9.23 Creditor's bankruptcy petition: creditor consents to making application for a debt relief order

(1)   This rule applies where before the determination of an application for a debt relief order, a creditor's petition for bankruptcy has been presented against a debtor and the proceedings in relation to the petition remain before the court.

(2)   In this rule "the debt" means the debt to which the creditor's bankruptcy petition relates.

(3)   If, on the hearing of the petition, the petitioner consents to the debtor making an application for a debt relief order in relation to the debt the court must—

    (a)    refer the debtor to an approved intermediary for the purpose of making an application for a debt relief order in relation to the debtor and the debt noting the consent of the creditor on the order for referral; and

    (b)    stay the proceedings on the petition in relation to the debt on such terms and conditions as it thinks just.

(4)   The debtor must deliver to the approved intermediary as soon as reasonably practicable after the making of the order of referral—

    (a)    a sealed copy of the order; and

    (b)    copies of the petition and the creditor's statutory demand (if there was one).

(5)   The approved intermediary must, on receipt of the order and the copies, as soon as reasonably practicable after the application for a debt relief order has been made, deliver them to the official receiver endorsed with the name of the debtor and the number of the application to which they relate.

(6)   If, following the reference by the court, a debt relief order is made in relation to the debt, the petition must be dismissed in relation to it unless the court otherwise directs.

**Derivation**—This rule derived from the Insolvency Rules 1986, SI 1986/1925, r 5A.23.

**[2.520]**

### 9.24 Extension of moratorium period

Where the moratorium period applicable to a debt relief order is extended—

    (a)    notice of the extension, and the period of extension must be delivered—

        (i)    where extended by the court, to the official receiver, who must deliver a copy to the debtor and to the creditors specified in the debt relief order,

        (ii)    where extended by the official receiver, to the debtor and to the creditors specified in the debt relief order; and

    (b)    the official receiver must cause to be entered in the individual insolvency register—

        (i)    that such an extension has been made in relation to the debtor,

        (ii)    the date on which the extension was made,

        (iii)    its duration, and

        (iv)    the date of the anticipated end of the moratorium period.

**Derivation**—This rule derived from the Insolvency Rules 1986, SI 1986/1925, r 5A.20.

CHAPTER 7

PERMISSION TO ACT AS A DIRECTOR, ETC

**[2.521]**

### Note

[Note: a document required by the Act or these Rules must also contain the standard contents set out in Part 1.]

**[2.522]**

### 9.25 Application for permission under the Company Directors Disqualification Act 1986

(1)   This rule relates to an application for permission under section 11 of the Company Directors Disqualification Act 1986, to act as director of, or to take part or be concerned in the promotion, formation or management of a company by a person—

    (a)    in relation to whom a moratorium period under a debt relief order applies; or

(b)    in relation to whom a debt relief restrictions order or undertaking is in force.

(2)   The application must be supported by a witness statement which must contain identification details for the company and specify—

(a)    the nature of its business or intended business, and the place or places where that business is, or is to be, carried on;

(b)    in the case of a company which has not yet been incorporated, whether it is, or is to be, a private or a public company;

(c)    the persons who are, or are to be, principally responsible for the conduct of its affairs (whether as directors, shadow directors, managers or otherwise);

(d)    the manner and capacity in which the applicant for permission proposes to take part or be concerned in the promotion or formation of the company or, as the case may be, its management; and

(e)    the emoluments and other benefits to be obtained by virtue of the matters referred to in paragraph (d).

(3)   The court must fix a venue for the hearing of the application, and must deliver a notice to the applicant for permission accordingly.

**Derivation**—This rule derived from the Insolvency Rules 1986, SI 1986/1925, r 5A.24.

## [2.523]

### 9.26 Report of official receiver

(1)   The applicant for permission must, not less than 28 days before the date fixed for the hearing, deliver to the official receiver, notice of the venue, accompanied by copies of the application and the witness statement under rule 9.25.

(2)   The official receiver may, not less than 14 days before the date fixed for the hearing, file with the court a report of any matters which the official receiver considers ought to be drawn to the court's attention.

(3)   A copy of the report must be delivered by the official receiver, as soon as reasonably practicable after it is filed, to the applicant for permission.

(4)   The applicant for permission may, not later than five business days before the date of the hearing, file with the court a notice specifying any statements in the official receiver's report which are to be denied or disputed.

(5)   If a notice is filed under paragraph (4), the applicant for permission must deliver copies of it, not less than three business days before the date of the hearing, to the official receiver.

(6)   The official receiver may appear on the hearing of the application, and may make representations and put to the applicant for permission such questions as the court may allow.

**Derivation**—This rule derived from the Insolvency Rules 1986, SI 1986/1925, r 5A.25.

## [2.524]

### 9.27 Court's order on application

(1)   If the court grants the application for permission under section 11 of the Company Directors Disqualification Act 1986, its order must specify that which by virtue of the order the applicant has permission to do.

(2)   The court may at the same time, having regard to any representations made by the official receiver on the hearing of the application, exercise in relation to the moratorium period or the debt relief order to which the applicant for permission is subject, any power which it has under section 251M.

(3)   Whether or not the application is granted, copies of the order must be delivered by the court to the applicant and the official receiver.

**Derivation**—This rule derived from the Insolvency Rules 1986, SI 1986/1925, r 5A.26.

PART 10  BANKRUPTCY

CHAPTER 1

THE STATUTORY DEMAND

**[2.525]**

Note

[Note: a document required by the Act or these Rules must also contain the standard contents set out in Part 1.]

**[2.526]**

**10.1  The statutory demand (section 268)**

(1)  A statutory demand under section 268 must contain—

    (a)    the heading either "Statutory demand under section 268(1) (debt payable immediately) of the Insolvency Act 1986" or "Statutory demand under section 268(2) (debt not immediately payable)";

    (b)    identification details for the debtor;

    (c)    the name and address of the creditor;

    (d)    a statement of the amount of the debt, and the consideration for it (or, if there is no consideration, the way in which it arises);

    (e)    if the demand is made under section 268(1) and founded on a judgment or order of a court, the date of the judgment or order and the court in which it was obtained;

    (f)    if the demand is made under section 268(2), a statement of the grounds on which it is alleged that the debtor appears to have no reasonable prospect of paying the debt;

    (g)    if the creditor is entitled to the debt by way of assignment, details of the original creditor and any intermediary assignees;

    (h)    a statement that if the debtor does not comply with the demand bankruptcy proceedings may be commenced;

    (i)    the date by which the debtor must comply with the demand, if bankruptcy proceedings are to be avoided;

    (j)    a statement of the methods of compliance which are open to the debtor;

    (k)    a statement that the debtor has the right to apply to the court to have the demand set aside;

    (l)    a statement that rule 10.4(4) of the Insolvency (England and Wales) Rules 2016 states to which court such an application must be made; and name the court or hearing centre of the County Court to which, according to the present information, the debtor must make the application (i.e. the High Court, the County Court at Central London or a named hearing centre of the County Court as the case may be);

    (m)    a statement that any application to set aside the demand must be made within 18 days of service on the debtor; and

    (n)    a statement that if the debtor does not apply to set aside the demand within 18 days or otherwise deal with this demand within 21 days after its service the debtor could be made bankrupt and the debtor's property and goods taken away.

(2)  Where the statutory demand is served by a Minister of the Crown or a Government Department the statutory demand must explain that the debtor may alternatively apply to set aside the demand to the High Court or the County Court at Central London (as the case may be) if the Minister or Department intends to present a bankruptcy petition to one of them.

(3)  A demand must name one or more individuals with whom the debtor may communicate with a view to—

    (a)    securing or compounding the debt to the satisfaction of the creditor; or

    (b)    establishing to the creditor's satisfaction that there is a reasonable prospect that the debt will be paid when it falls due.

(4)    The postal address, electronic address and telephone number (if any) of the named individual must be given.

(5)    A demand must be dated and authenticated either by the creditor or by a person who is authorised to make the demand on the creditor's behalf.

(6)    A demand which is authenticated by a person other than the creditor must state that the person is authorised to make the demand on the creditor's behalf and state the person's relationship to the creditor.

(7)    If the amount claimed in the demand includes—

    (a)    any charge by way of interest of which notice had not previously been delivered to the debtor as a liability of the debtor's; or

    (b)    any other charge accruing from time to time,

the amount or rate of the charge must be separately identified, and the grounds on which payment of it is claimed must be stated.

(8)    The amount claimed for such charges must be limited to that which has accrued at the date of the demand.

(9)    If the creditor holds any security in respect of the debt, the full amount of the debt must be specified, but—

    (a)    the demand must specify the nature of the security, and the value which the creditor puts upon it at the date of the demand; and

    (b)    the demand must claim payment of the full amount of the debt, less the specified value of the security.

(10)    When the statutory demand is to be served out of the jurisdiction, the time limits of 18 days and 21 days referred to in sub-paragraphs 10.1(1)(m) and (n) above must be amended as follows—

    (a)    for any reference to 18 days there must be substituted the number of days which is the appropriate number of days set out in the table accompanying the Practice Direction supplementing Section IV of CPR Part 6 plus 4 days; and

    (b)    for any reference to 21 days there must be substituted the number of days which is the appropriate number of days set out in the table accompanying the Practice Direction supplementing Section IV of CPR Part 6 plus 7 days.

**Derivation**—This rule derived from the Insolvency Rules 1986, SI 1986/1925, rr 6.1, 6.2.

**Amendments**—SI 2017/1115.

**General note**—See ss 268 and 269 in the context of s 267(2), together with the notes thereto.

**Content, not form**—Under the IR 1986, the statutory demand was in a prescribed form (Form 6.1, 6.2 or 6.3, depending on the circumstances of the case). Under the IR 2016, the form is no longer prescribed, but the contents required of a statutory demand are set out in the rule itself at r 10.1(1). Even when the form was prescribed, the position was that, unless it was liable to mislead, the fact that a creditor had not served a correct form of statutory demand would not constitute a ground for setting the demand aside: *Cartwright v Staffordshire and Moorlands District Council* [1998] BPIR 328 (Morritt LJ, Evans LJ agreeing).

## [2.527]

### 10.2 Service of statutory demand

A creditor must do all that is reasonable to bring the statutory demand to the debtor's attention and, if practicable in the particular circumstances, serve the demand personally.

**Derivation**—This rule derived from the Insolvency Rules 1986, SI 1986/1925, r 6.3.

**General note**—Whilst there is an obligation to cause personal service to be effected if practicable, the primary obligation is to do all that is reasonable to bring the statutory demand to the debtor's attention. Paragraphs 11.2 and 12.7 of the *Practice Direction – Insolvency Proceedings* (July 2020) [2020] BPIR 1211 set out those steps which will normally be held to suffice for that purpose: see *Omokwe v HFC Bank* [2007] BPIR 1157 at [28] (Chief Registrar Baister, involving an earlier version of the Practice Direction).

Proper service had been effected on a debtor where, following the making of three liability orders for unpaid council tax including one made in the debtor's presence: (i) a process server attended at the debtor's address and thereafter sent an appointment letter to which the debtor responded confirming he or she lived at that address but refusing the appointment; (ii) the process server attended at the address and effected substituted service by placing the statutory demand in a sealed envelope through the post box; and (iii) the letter was not returned through the post: *Takavarasha v Newham Borough Council* [2006] BPIR 311 (Nicholas Warren QC sitting as a deputy High Court judge).

It is important to distinguish between irregular service capable of cure under IR 2016, r 12.64 (formerly r 7.55 IR 1986) and a fundamental failure to effect service. In *Canning v Irwin Mitchell LLP* [2017] EWHC 718 (Ch), [2017] BPIR 934, Jeremy Cousins QC (sitting as a deputy High Court judge) dismissed a bankruptcy petition where there had been a fundamental failure to effect service of a statutory demand. The deputy judge distinguished between circumstances where the document in question reached or 'at least came within the dominion' of the debtor (which is capable of cure), from the case before him where there had in no meaningful sense been service. See also notes to s 268 and 10.14.

## [2.528]

### 10.3 Proof of service of statutory demand

(1)   Where section 268 requires a statutory demand to be served before the petition, a certificate of service of the demand must be filed with the court with the petition.

(2)   The certificate must be verified by a statement of truth and be accompanied by a copy of the demand served.

(3)   If the demand has been served personally on the debtor, the statement of truth must be made by the person who served the demand unless service has been acknowledged in writing by the debtor or a person authorised to accept service.

(4)   If service has been acknowledged in writing either by—

(a)   the debtor; or

(b)   a person who is authorised to accept service on the debtor's behalf and who has stated that this is the case in the acknowledgement of service;

then the certificate of service must be authenticated either by the creditor or by a person acting on the creditor's behalf, and the acknowledgement of service must accompany the certificate.

(5)   If the demand has been served other than personally and there is no acknowledgement of service, the certificate must be authenticated by a person or persons having direct personal knowledge of the means adopted for serving the statutory demand, and must contain the following information—

(a)   the steps taken to serve the demand; and

(b)   a date by which, to the best of the knowledge, information and belief of the person authenticating the certificate, the demand will have come to the debtor's attention.

(6)   Where paragraph (5) applies the statutory demand is deemed to have been served on the debtor on the date referred to in paragraph (5)(b) unless the court determines otherwise.

**Derivation**—This rule derived from the Insolvency Rules 1986, SI 1986/1925, r 6.11.

**General note**—In keeping with the general approach of the IR 2016, there are no longer prescribed forms for the certificate of service (formerly prescribed Forms 6.11, 6.12 or 6.13 under the IR 1986).

## [2.529]

### 10.4 Application to set aside statutory demand

(1)   The debtor may apply to the court for an order setting aside the statutory demand.

(2)   The application must be made within 18 days from the date of the service of the statutory demand.

(3)   The application must—

(a)   identify the debtor;

(b)   state that the application is for an order that the statutory demand be set aside;

(c)   state the date of the statutory demand; and

    (d)    be dated and authenticated by the debtor, or by a person authorised to act on the debtor's behalf.

(4)    The application must be made to the court or hearing centre—

    (a)    determined in accordance with rule 10.48; or

    (b)    to which rule 10.11(1) requires a petition to be presented if—

        (i)    the creditor serving the statutory demand is a Minister of the Crown or a government Department,

        (ii)    the debt in respect of which the statutory demand is made, or part of it equal to or exceeding the bankruptcy level (within the meaning of section 267), is the subject of a judgment or order of a court, and

        (iii)    the statutory demand—

            (aa)    specifies the date of the judgment or order and the court in which it was obtained, and

            (bb)    indicates the creditor's intention to present a bankruptcy petition against the debtor in the High Court or the County Court at Central London as the case may be.

(5)    The time within which the debtor must comply with the statutory demand ceases to run on the date the application is filed with the court, subject to any order of the court under rule 10.5.

(6)    The debtor's application must be accompanied by a copy of the statutory demand, where it is in the debtor's possession, and supported by a witness statement containing the following—

    (a)    the date on which the debtor became aware of the statutory demand;

    (b)    the grounds on which the debtor claims that it should be set aside; and

    (c)    any evidence in support of the application.

**Derivation**—This rule derived from the Insolvency Rules 1986, SI 1986/1925, r 6.4.

**General note**—See the notes to r 10.5. On 1 October 2015, the bankruptcy level increased from £750 to £5,000.

**Content, not form**—Under the IR 1986, the form of an application to set aside a statutory demand was prescribed (Form 6.4), as was the witness statement (Form 6.5). Under the IR 2016, there is no prescribed form, but the matters to be included in the application are set out in r 10.4(3) above, and those to be set out in the accompanying witness statement are at r 10.4(6) above.

**Extension of time**—The court has an unfettered discretion under s 376 to extend time to file both an application to set aside a statutory demand and the evidence in support, either before or after the time limit has expired. An application to extend time is not an application for relief from sanction, as no sanction is expressly or impliedly imposed: *Rankin v Dissington Lending Company Ltd* [2021] EWHC 172 (Ch), [7]–[9], [42] (Deputy ICC Judge Kyriakides). In practice, debtors tend to be given considerable latitude in relation to these and other procedural requirements.

## [2.530]

### 10.5 Hearing of application to set aside

(1)    On receipt of an application to set aside a statutory demand, the court may, if satisfied that no sufficient cause is shown for it, dismiss it without giving notice of the application to the creditor.

(2)    The time for complying with the statutory demand runs again from the date the application is dismissed under paragraph (1).

(3)    Unless the application is dismissed under paragraph (1), the court must fix a venue for it to be heard, and must give at least five business days' notice to—

    (a)    the debtor or, if the debtor's application was made by a solicitor acting for the debtor, to the solicitor;

    (b)    the creditor; and

    (c)    whoever is named in the statutory demand as the person with whom the debtor may communicate about the demand (or the first such if more than one).

(4)   On the hearing of the application, the court must consider the evidence then available to it, and may either determine the application or adjourn it, giving such directions as it thinks appropriate.

(5)   The court may grant the application if—

    (a)   the debtor appears to have a counterclaim, set-off or cross demand which equals or exceeds the amount of the debt specified in the statutory demand;

    (b)   the debt is disputed on grounds which appear to the court to be substantial;

    (c)   it appears that the creditor holds some security in relation to the debt claimed by the demand, and either rule 10.1(9) is not complied with in relation to it, or the court is satisfied that the value of the security equals or exceeds the full amount of the debt; or

    (d)   the court is satisfied, on other grounds, that the demand ought to be set aside.

(6)   An order setting aside a statutory demand must contain—

    (a)   identification details for the debtor;

    (b)   the date of the hearing of the application;

    (c)   the date of the statutory demand;

    (d)   an order that the statutory demand be set aside;

    (e)   details of any further order in the matter; and

    (f)   the date of the order.

(7)   Where the creditor holds some security in relation to the debt and has complied with rule 10.1(9) but the court is satisfied that the statutory demand undervalues the security, the court may order the creditor to amend the demand (but without prejudice to the creditor's right to present a bankruptcy petition by reference to the original demand as so amended).

(8)   If the court dismisses the application, it must make an order authorising the creditor to present a bankruptcy petition either as soon as reasonably practicable, or on or after a date specified in the order.

(9)   The court must deliver a copy of any order under paragraphs (6) to (8) to the creditor as soon as reasonably practicable.

**Derivation**—This rule derived from the Insolvency Rules 1986, SI 1986/1925, r 6.5.

**General note**—Applications to set aside statutory demands are perhaps the single most commonly encountered piece of litigation in personal insolvency. The statutory demand is of crucial importance in bankruptcy. As the matter was put by Peter Gibson LJ, delivering the judgment of the court in *TSB Bank plc v Platts (No 2)* [1998] 2 BCLC 1 at [6]–[7]:

> 'It is accordingly quite different from a statutory demand in the field of company law which merely provides one means of establishing a company's inability to pay its debts, the usual ground on which a company is wound up compulsorily. In contrast in bankruptcy, it is not the debtor's general inability to pay his debts that is crucial but the apparent inability to pay the debt in the statutory demand, and at the hearing of the bankruptcy petition the failure to pay or secure or compound for that debt.'

The same decision (at [8]) is authority for the proposition that a creditor is not entitled to rely at the petition hearing on a debt which is not included in the statutory demand – in *Platts*, the overall state of the account between the bank and the debtor – since this would undermine the statutory scheme which allows the debtor to challenge only that debt with which he is faced in a statutory demand by applying to set it aside. As Peter Gibson LJ identified:

> 'A creditor faced with a cross-claim after service of the statutory demand but who has a further debt on which he can rely can always serve a further statutory demand and petition on the greater debt.'

Service of a statutory demand is a requirement to found jurisdiction to proceed to the making of a banking order: *Canning v Irwin Mitchell LLP* [2017] EWHC 718 (Ch), [2017] BPIR 934, Jeremy Cousins QC (sitting as a deputy High Court judge). See note to r 10.2.

Formal defects in the statutory demand itself, however, will tend not to prove fatal where there is no prejudice to the debtor. In *Re a Debtor (No 1 of 1987)* [1989] 1 WLR 271 Nicholls LJ, with whom Glidewell LJ and Sir Stephen Brown P agreed, expressed the view that the IA 1986 and the

IR 1986 introduced a new code governing statutory demands which must be construed unfettered by the technicalities of the old bankruptcy law. Furthermore (at 280C–280E):

'The new statutory code affords the court a desirable degree of flexibility when confronted with an application to set aside a statutory demand containing one or more defects. This is not to be taken by banks or others as a charter for the slipshod preparation of statutory demands. The making of a bankruptcy order remains a serious step so far as a debtor is concerned, and the prescribed preliminaries are intended to afford protection to him. If a statutory demand is served in an excessive amount or is otherwise defective, the court will be alert to see whether those mistakes have caused or will cause any prejudice to the debtor. In the present case no prejudice has resulted, or will result, and hence it is right that the statutory demand should be allowed to stand. But if there had been prejudice, the bank would only have itself to blame if the court had set aside the statutory demand.'

But the 'absence of prejudice' approach cannot be pushed too far. In *Agilo Ltd v Henry* [2010] EWHC 2717 (Ch), [2011] BPIR 297, Newey J dismissed a creditor's appeal against the setting aside of purported statutory demands. Newey J held at [16] that there was a distinction to be drawn between cases where creditors had served defective statutory demands and cases where it was arguable that no demand at all had been served. See also note to r 10.2 for the limits of the court's ability to cure defects in service of the statutory demand.

The commentary which follows seeks to identify the points of general principle governing an application to set aside a statutory demand. Whilst there is an ever-increasing number of reported cases dealing with such applications, many such decisions are of very limited, if any, assistance to other cases, since they illustrate nothing more than the exercise of the court's discretion on the particular facts before it.

**The test for setting aside a statutory demand**—Unlike its predecessors, the *Practice Direction – Insolvency Proceedings* (July 2020) [2020] BPIR 1211 does not make any comment on the test to be applied by the court in deciding whether or not to grant an application to set aside a statutory demand. The test is, however, well-established in the case law ('genuine triable issue') and its absence from the Practice Direction is unlikely to change that. It is essentially the same test as that applied in an application for summary judgment. In short, can the issue be resolved without the need for a trial, or does the debtor have a real prospect of successfully resisting the creditor's claim?

In *Kellar v BBR Graphic Engineers (Yorks) Ltd* [2002] BPIR 544 (a case decided under IR 1986, r 6.5(4)(b), which was in substantially the same terms as IR 2016, r 10.5(5)(b)), Roger Kaye QC (sitting as a deputy High Court judge) held at 551E–F that the 'genuine triable issue' test found in para 12.4 of the former practice direction was intended to impose a lower threshold than the 'no real prospect' test for summary judgment under CPR 24.2. That approach was rejected by the Court of Appeal in *Ashworth v Newnote* [2007] EWCA Civ 793, [2007] BPIR 1012. At [33], Lawrence Collins LJ, with whom Buxton LJ agreed, considered that there was 'no practical difference between' the two tests. That view was subsequently endorsed in *Collier v P & MJ Wright (Holdings) Ltd* [2007] EWCA Civ 1329, [2008] 1 WLR 643. Arden LJ (with whom Longmore and Mummery LJJ agreed) held at 652H that the distinction drawn between the two formulations in *Kellar v BBR Graphic Engineers* should not be followed.

The court should not conduct a mini-trial, although that should not preclude the court from undertaking a proportionate investigation of the points advanced if such an investigation appears likely to be capable of resolving matters raised by the debtor in challenging the statutory demand. As the Court of Appeal explained in *ICI Chemicals & Polymers Ltd v TTE Training Ltd* [2007] EWCA Civ 725, at [12] (a case concerning summary judgment under CPR 24.2), if the court is satisfied that it has all the evidence necessary for the proper determination of the question, then it should grasp the nettle and decide it.

It should be noted that the court's approach to setting aside a statutory demand is not the same as that for dismissal of a bankruptcy petition. The statutory demand stage concerns the existence of a debt that may found a petition; the petition stage concerns whether a bankruptcy order should be made. See discussion in *Vieira v Revenue and Customs Commissioners* [2017] EWHC 936 (Ch), [2017] 4 WLR 86, [83]–[84]. Jacob J held in *re A Debtor (No 415-SD-1993)* [1994] 1 WLR 917 that the issue of whether or not a creditor has unreasonably refused an offer of security for the purposes of s 271(3)(c) is to be considered at the hearing of the petition and is not a ground for setting aside a statutory demand. See further notes to r 10.24 under the sub-heading 'The court's discretion' concerning the court's approach to the making of a bankruptcy order.

**Approach to evidence on an application to set aside a statutory demand**—As on any summary disposal where there is no opportunity to test evidence by means of cross-examination, reasonable evidential presumptions will be made in favour of an applicant. But only reasonable ones. There is considerable authority indicating that the court must apply critical scrutiny to assertions made. For instance, in *Ashworth v Newnote* [2007] EWCA Civ 793, [2007] BPIR 1012, Lawrence Collins LJ observed at [34] that 'In each case it is open to the court to reject evidence because of its inherent implausibility or because it is contradicted by or not supported by the documents.' Arden LJ held in *Collier v P & MJ Wright Ltd* [2007] EWCA Civ 1329, [2008] 1 WLR 643, 653B-C, that 'There has to be something to suggest that the assertion is sustainable. The best evidence would be incontrovertible evidence to support the applicant's case, but this is rarely available. It would in general be enough if there were some evidence to support the applicant's version of the facts, such as a witness statement or a document, although it would be open to the court to reject that evidence if it were inherently implausible or if it were contradicted, or were not supported, by contemporaneous documentation'.

A mere evidential dispute is not, however, sufficient to set aside a statutory demand: any dispute must be capable of giving rise to a defence. Norris J held in *Macpherson v Wise* [2011] BPIR 472 at [19] (permission to appeal refused by Patten LJ [2011] EWCA Civ 399, [2011] BPIR 824) that 'A consideration of whether there are substantial grounds for disputing the debt does not mean that the court is simply bound to accept that if, in respect of any issue, there is a dispute on the evidence, then the matter must go to trial.' Having identified a dispute, the court must go on and ask itself whether that dispute is capable of giving rise to a defence. In *Dunbar Assets plc v Butler* [2015] EWHC 2546 (Ch), [2015] BPIR 1358, Jeremy Cousins QC (sitting as a deputy High Court judge) allowed an appeal and dismissed an application to set aside a statutory demand on the basis that the deputy registrar below had not adequately considered whether the factual issues raised were capable of affording the debtor an answer to the creditor's claim. Having considered the evidence, the deputy judge considered that the factual dispute did not disclose a defence.

### RULE 10.5(1)

**Right to set aside summary dismissal of application**—An order made pursuant to r 10.5(1) does not have to contain a statement, such as that for which CPR 3.3(5) provides, that a party affected by the order may apply to have it set aside, varied or stayed: *Clarke v Cognita Schools Limited* [2015] EWHC 932 (Ch), [2015] 1 WLR 3776 (a case decided under IR 1986, r 6.5(1) which was in substantially similar terms).

### RULE 10.5(4)

**Procedure at the hearing**—Rule 10.5(4) requires the court to consider the evidence available to it subsequent to which the court may move to determining the application or adjourning it with appropriate directions.

In considering an adjournment the court must inevitably consider the grounds advanced for the adjournment and the potential consequences or prejudice to either party as a result of an adjournment being granted. Of course, it remains open to the court to visit costs on any party consequent upon any adjournment being granted. In practice, applications are usually listed for a short first hearing, at which directions for further evidence and a longer hearing are likely to be given in all but the simplest or most clear-cut cases.

### RULE 10.5(5)(a)

' . . . the debtor appears to have a counterclaim, set-off or cross demand'—In *Garrow v Society of Lloyd's* [1999] BPIR 885 the Court of Appeal (Morritt, Brooke and Robert Walker LJJ) refused to interfere with the decision of Jacob J ([1999] BPIR 668), to the effect that, on proper scrutiny of the debtor's case, it was appropriate to set aside a statutory demand if the debtor had a sufficiently large cross-claim to equal or exceed the amount of the demand. Neither was the judge below wrong in holding that the debtor was entitled to assert his or her cross-claim despite the presence of a 'pay now sue later' provision, since the cross-claim could still be said to be raised 'in connection with' the creditor's claim. Although the judgment of Robert Walker LJ (at 891E–891F) noted that there were a number of differences between the individual and corporate insolvency regimes, the Court of Appeal did not find Jacob J to be in error in drawing on the headnote of the decision of the Court of Appeal in *Re Bayoil SA* [1999] 1 BCLC 62 (a disputed winding-up petition case) to the extent that the rule identified in the headnote to that case provides that, subject to the judge's residual discretion exercisable in special circumstances, the creditor's claim should not proceed where the cross-claim is genuine and serious and one of substance and in an amount exceeding the amount of the petitioner's debt. Certainly Neuberger J had accepted the applicability of the rule in *Bayoil* in bankruptcy cases in *Hofer v Strawson* [1999] BPIR 501 (a case in which it was also held that the cheque rule preventing a cross-claim or set-off being asserted on a claim based on a dishonoured cheque did not apply in a statutory demand case).

In *Hurst v Bennett* [2001] EWCA Civ 182, [2001] BPIR 287, the Court of Appeal (Peter Gibson and Arden LJJ and Sir Christopher Staughton) held that there is a requirement that a counterclaim or cross-demand must be raised in the same legal character as that in which the creditor's claim was asserted, so as to impose a requirement for mutuality as is ordinarily required under the law of set-off: compare CPR 16.6 and see also *Chan Sui v Appasamy* [2005] EWHC 3519 (Ch), [2008] BPIR 18 at [30]–[37] (HHJ Weeks QC sitting as a High Court judge). This mutuality requirement apart, however, it is to be noted that the reference in the provision is to 'counterclaim, set-off or cross demand' alike such that a successful application is not dependent on an application establishing that the cross-claim relied upon would give rise to a set-off so as to provide a defence to the claim; neither can an applicant be kept out of a cross-claim by virtue of a contractual provision requiring payment without set-off since a contractual provision cannot override the statutory scheme:

*McAllister v The Society of Lloyd's* [1999] BPIR 548 at [19] (Carnwath J) and *Stone v Vallance* [2008] BPIR 236 (Registrar Simmonds) to like effect.

Rule 10.5(5)(a) only engages when the value of the counterclaim equals or exceeds the debt in the statutory demand. In *Howell v Lerwick Commercial Mortgage Corp Ltd* [2015] EWHC 1177 (Ch), [2015] 1 WLR 3554, Nugee J held that the court should not set aside a statutory demand if the debtor's cross-claim is less than the undisputed element of the creditor's debt, even if the difference between the two debts is less than the bankruptcy level. This does not mean that a bankruptcy order will be made on the hearing of the petition; if at the hearing of the petition it remained the case that the only claims between the parties were the debt and the cross-claim, the court would probably dismiss the petition.

For further commentary on cross-claims see the notes to s 125.

## RULE 10.5(5)(b)

For commentary on disputed debts see the notes to s 125.

For debts capable and incapable of founding a bankruptcy petition see s 267(1)(a)–(c) and the notes thereto; a demand based on a solicitor's bill which is unassessed should be set aside under this subrule or subrule (d) below: *Klamer v Kyriakides and Braier (a firm)* [2005] BPIR 1142 (Registrar Simmonds).

As regards a statutory demand which overstated the indebtedness of the debtor, in *Re a Debtor (No 490/SD/91) ex parte the Debtor v Printline (Offset) Ltd* [1993] BCLC 164 Hoffmann J, having made reference to the judgment of Nicholls LJ in *Re a Debtor (No 1 of 1987)* [1989] 1 WLR 271, held that a statutory demand will not necessarily be set aside merely because the demand overstates the amount of the debt. As his Lordship put it at 166F–166G, 'There is no reason why the debtor should not be able to avoid the statutory presumption by complying with the demand as to the part which he admits he owes and then having it set aside on the ground that all the rest is disputed.'

In *Owen v Her Majesty's Revenue & Customs* [2007] EWHC 395 (Ch), [2008] BPIR 164 Lewison J dismissed an appeal against a district judge's refusal to set aside a statutory demand bought on the ground that the debtor was suffering from mild to moderate, as opposed to severe, depression and could not instruct professionals to deal with his outstanding tax returns upon which assessments had been made – and which Lewison J would not go behind following *Cullinane v Commissioners of Inland Revenue* [2000] BPIR 996 (Hart J) – in circumstances where the debtor had conducted the appeal before Lewison J in person, including production by the debtor of a 12-page skeleton argument which was well reasoned, cogent and cross-referenced to the 165-page appeal bundle.

Paragraph 11.4.4 of the *Practice Direction – Insolvency Proceedings* (July 2020) [2020] BPIR 1211 also warrants attention. This provides that, where a demand is based on a judgment, order, liability order, costs certificate, tax assessment or decision of a tribunal, the court will not at the set-aside stage inquire into the validity of the debt; neither, as a general rule, will the court adjourn the application to await the result of any application to set aside the judgment or order. That rule embodies what had previously become the firm practice of the bankruptcy court following the Bankruptcy Act 1914 and should, it is submitted, only be departed from by the court in very exceptional circumstances, such as where there is credible evidence that the judgment or order upon which the statutory demand is based was obtained through fraud or duress of which the court giving the judgment or making the order could not have been aware. See notes to s 267 under the heading 'Tax assessments'. For a detailed examination of this principle, and an example of the court's refusal to depart from the practice identified in para 11.4.4 of the Practice Direction, see *Vieira v Revenue and Customs Commissioners* [2017] EWHC 936 (Ch), [2017] 4 WLR 86. The position is different at the petition stage; for example r 10.24(2) provides for the court to stay or dismiss a petition where the petition debt is subject to appeal.

In *Howell v Lerwick Commercial Mortgage Corp Ltd* [2015] EWHC 1177 (Ch), [2015] 1 WLR 3554, Nugee J held that the court should not necessarily set aside a partially disputed statutory demand if the undisputed element of the demand is less than the bankruptcy level. This is because a bankruptcy petition can be based on more than one debt, provided that the aggregate amount of the debts is equal to or exceeds the bankruptcy level: s 267(2)(a). The earlier decision of the Court of Appeal. In *re a Debtor (Nos 49 and 50 of 1992)* [1995] Ch 66 (in which a partially disputed demand was set aside because the undisputed element of the demand was less than the bankruptcy level) could be distinguished on the basis that there was no suggestion in that case that the creditor had other debts, or might join forces with other creditors. The question of what order the court should make pursuant to the predecessor of r 10.5(8) (formerly IR 1986, r 6.5(6)) in such a case was expressly left open.

## RULE 10.5(5)(c)

**A creditor holding security**—Rule 10.5(5)(c) allows the debtor to challenge a fully secured creditor. The term 'security' is as defined in s 383(2). Security held over the property of a third party (ie someone other than the debtor) will not fall within that definition: see the notes to s 383 and the notes to s 271(1)(a). See *Re a Debtor (No 310 of 1988)* [1989] 1 WLR 452, per Knox J; and *Promontoria (Chestnut) Ltd v Bell* [2019] EWHC 1581 (Ch), [2019] BPIR 1241, [26]–[28], per Zacaroli J.

Where the valuation of security is in dispute, the appropriate method of valuation is on a forced sale basis, the burden of proof in establishing that the creditor is fully secured resting on the debtor: *Platts v Western Trust & Savings Ltd* [1996] BPIR 339 (Sir Christopher Slade, Nourse and Butler-Sloss LJJ agreeing). For r 10.5(5)(c) purposes the value of security should not include any estimated value for the associated costs of enforcing the security, even if such costs are provided for under the terms of the security itself: *Owo-Samson v Barclays Bank* [2003] EWCA Civ 714, (2003) *The Times*, May 27.

On appeal, the court should consider the adequacy of the creditor's security with the most up to date and reliable facts available, so long as those facts are really probative of the matter in issue. It may therefore be appropriate to permit the parties to adduce fresh evidence: *Ludsin Overseas Limited v Maggs* [2014] EWHC 3566 (Ch), [2015] BPIR 59.

## RULE 10.5(5)(d)

'the court is satisfied, on other grounds . . .'—The scope and nature of the residual ground in r 10.5(5)(d) was identified in the judgment of Nicholls LJ in *Re a Debtor (No 1 of 1987)* [1989] 1 WLR 271 at 271D–271F (decided under IR 1986, r 6.5(4)(d), which was in substantially the same terms) as follows:

'When therefore the rules provide, as does rule 6.5(4)(d), for the court to have a residual discretion to set aside a statutory demand, the circumstances which normally will be required before a court can be satisfied that the demand 'ought' to be set aside, are circumstances which would make it unjust for the statutory demand to give rise to those consequences in the particular case. The court's intervention is called for to prevent that injustice. This approach to subpara (d) is in line with the particular ground specified in subparas (a)–(c) of r 6.5(4). Normally it would be unjust that an individual should be regarded as unable to pay a debt if the debt is disputed on substantial grounds: subpara (b). Likewise, if the debtor has a counterclaim, set-off or cross-demand which equals or exceeds the amount of the debt: subpara (a). Again, if the creditor is fully secured: subpara (c).'

His Lordship went on to reject a submission that it was open to the court to set aside a statutory demand on the basis that the demand was calculated to perplex, as would have been arguable under the former law. In identifying that the new bankruptcy code does not adopt the same approach as under the previous law Nicholls LJ went on to hold (at 280A–280C) that, although the statutory demand was confusing and the amount specified as being due was incorrect in that case, there was neither evidence of prejudice to the debtor nor an indication that he would have taken steps to comply with a non-defective demand, with the consequence that, in the absence of injustice to the debtor, the court should not exercise its discretion in setting the demand aside.

In *Budge v AF Budge (Contractors) Ltd* [1997] BPIR 366 Peter Gibson LJ expressed the view at 371C that it would be 'quite impossible' to foresee all the circumstances which may arise and which may justify the proper application of (the predecessor of) r 10.5(5)(d). What was required (at 371G) was a substantial reason to set aside the demand which was comparable in scope with the reasons set out in r 10.5(5)(a), (b) and (c). The following extract from that judgment (at 371C–371E) repays consideration:

'There is no point in setting aside a statutory demand for defects in the statutory demand which are not so substantial as to leave the debtor truly perplexed by its contents. Similarly, in my view, there is no point in setting aside a statutory demand and requiring a creditor to litigate his claim that he is owed money by the debtor if it cannot be foreseen that there will be any ground on which the creditor will be denied his claim were the matter to be litigated. That would only be to increase costs to no purpose whatever. It also has to be borne in mind when exercising the statutory discretion that an application to set aside comes at an early state in proceedings for bankruptcy. At the hearing of the petition it must be established to the satisfaction of the court hearing the petition that the statutory conditions for making an adjudication are satisfied, and evidence that comes to light after an application to set aside can in my view properly be relied on without there being any danger of some sort of estoppel.'

In *Chan Sui v Appasamy* [2005] EWHC 3519 (Ch), [2008] BPIR 18 at [14] HHJ Weeks QC, sitting as a High Court judge, formulated the test on the authorities under the predecessor to r 10.5(5)(d) to be 'whether there are circumstances which would make it unjust for the statutory demand to give rise to insolvency consequences in the particular case'.

In *City Electrical Factors Ltd v Hardingham* [1996] BPIR 541 James Munby QC, sitting as a deputy High Court judge, was concerned with an appeal from a district judge who had set aside a demand for £756.96 on the basis of the debtor indicating, at the district judge's invitation, that he was in a position to pay £10 immediately so as to reduce the demand below the (then) bankruptcy level of £750. In dismissing the appeal the deputy judge held that it was proper for the district judge to have based his decision on what he properly foresaw would happen immediately after the hearing and that he was entitled to anticipate that event by intervening summarily and setting aside the demand. It has to be said that in cases involving amounts which exceed the bankruptcy level by only a modest amount, and where the parties, or either of them, appear to the court to be engaging in a form of skirmishing, the court may well be minded to visit costs on one or both parties, which costs are likely in themselves to exceed the amount in issue.

The court may set aside a demand under r 10.5(5)(d) where insolvency proceedings are pursued in respect of an undisputed debt for an improper collateral purpose. This will occur in two situations. The first is where the petitioner does not really want to obtain the bankruptcy of the debtor at all, but issues or threatens to issue the proceedings to put pressure on the debtor to take some other action which the debtor is otherwise unwilling to take. The second is where the petitioner does want to achieve the relief sought but he is not acting in the interests of the class of creditors of which he or she is one or where the success of his or her petition will operate to the disadvantage of the body of creditors. However, the court will not generally enter into a detailed investigation of the petitioner's motives: *Maud v Aabar Block Sarl and Edgeworth Capital (Luxembourg) Sarl* [2015] EWHC 1626 (Ch), [2015] BPIR 845, per Rose J, [29].

**Debtor rearguing points that have been addressed at the set-aside stage**—See note to r 10.24 under this sub-heading.

**Procedure**—See rr 10.1–10.5.

## CHAPTER 2

### CREDITORS' BANKRUPTCY PETITIONS

### PRELIMINARY

**[2.531]**

**Note**

[Note: a document required by the Act or these Rules must also contain the standard contents set out in Part 1.]

**[2.532]**

**10.6 Application and interpretation**

(1) This Chapter relates to a creditor's petition and making a bankruptcy order on such a petition.

(2) In this Chapter "the debt" means the debt in relation to which the petition is presented.

(3) This Chapter also applies to a petition under section 264(1)(c) by a supervisor of, or person bound by, an IVA, with any necessary modifications.

**Derivation**—This rule derived from the Insolvency Rules 1986, SI 1986/1925, r 6.6.

**[2.533]**

**10.7 Contents of petition**

(1) The petition must state—

    (a)    the name and postal address of the petitioner;

    (b)    where the petitioner is represented by a solicitor, the name, postal address and telephone number of the solicitor;

    (c)    that the petitioner requests that the court make a bankruptcy order against the debtor;

    (d)    whether—

        (i)    the centre of the debtor's main interests is within the United Kingdom or is within a member State;

        (ii)    the centre of the debtor's main interests is neither within the United Kingdom nor a member State;

        (iii)    the debtor has an establishment within the United Kingdom;

        (iv)    the debtor carries on business as an Article 1.2 undertaking;

    (e)    whether the debtor—

        (i)    is resident in England and Wales, or

      (ii)    is not resident in England and Wales;

    (f)    whether the petition is presented to—

      (i)    the High Court,

      (ii)    the County Court at Central London, or

      (iii)    a specified hearing centre; and

    (g)    the reasons why the court or hearing centre to which the petition is presented is the correct court or hearing centre under rule 10.11.

(2)   If the petition is based on a statutory demand, and more than four months have elapsed between the service of the demand and the presentation of the petition, the petition must explain the reasons for the delay.

(3)   The petition must also contain a blank box for the court to complete with the details of the venue for hearing the petition.

**Derivation**—This rule derived from the Insolvency Rules 1986, SI 1986/1925, Sch 4, Fms 6.7–6.10.

**Amendments**—SI 2019/146, as from IP completion day (as defined in the European Union (Withdrawal Agreement) Act 2020, s 39(1)–(5)).

## [2.534]

### 10.8 Identification of debtor

(1)   The petition must state the following matters about the debtor, so far as they are within the petitioner's knowledge—

    (a)    the debtor's identification details;

    (b)    the occupation (if any) of the debtor;

    (c)    the name or names in which the debtor carries on business, if other than the name of the debtor, and whether, in the case of any business of a specified nature, the debtor carries it on alone or with others;

    (d)    the nature of the debtor's business, and the address or addresses at which it is carried on;

    (e)    any name or names, other than the name of the debtor, in which the debtor has carried on business at or after the time when the debt was incurred, and whether the debtor has done so alone or with others;

    (f)    any address or addresses at which the debtor has resided or carried on business at or after that time, and the nature of that business; and

    (g)    whether the centre of main interests or an establishment of the debtor (as defined in Article 2(10) of the EU Regulation) is in the UK or a member State.

(2)   The particulars of the debtor given under this rule determine the title of the proceedings.

(3)   If to the petitioner's knowledge the debtor has used any name other than the one specified under paragraph (1)(a), that fact must be stated in the petition.

**Derivation**—This rule derived from the Insolvency Rules 1986, SI 1986/1925, r 6.7.

**Amendments**—SI 2017/1115; SI 2019/146, as from IP completion day (as defined in the European Union (Withdrawal Agreement) Act 2020, s 39(1)–(5)).

## [2.535]

### 10.9 Identification of debt

(1)   The petition must state for each debt in relation to which it is presented—

    (a)    the amount of the debt, the consideration for it (or, if there is no consideration, the way in which it arises) and the fact that it is owed to the petitioner;

    (b)    when the debt was incurred or became due;

    (c)    if the amount of the debt includes any charge by way of interest not previously notified to the debtor as a liability of the debtor's, the amount or rate of the charge (separately identified);

    (d)    if the amount of the debt includes any other charge accruing from time to time, the amount or rate of the charge (separately identified);

(e) the grounds on which any such a charge is claimed to form part of the debt, provided that the amount or rate must, in the case of a petition based on a statutory demand, be limited to that claimed in the demand;

(f) that the debt is unsecured (subject to section 269); and

(g) either—

(i) that the debt is for a liquidated sum payable immediately, and the debtor appears to be unable to pay it, or

(ii) that the debt is for a liquidated sum payable at some certain, future time (that time to be specified), and the debtor appears to have no reasonable prospect of being able to pay it.

(2) Where the debt is one for which, under section 268, a statutory demand must have been served on the debtor, the petition must—

(a) specify the date and manner of service of the statutory demand; and

(b) state that, to the best of the creditor's knowledge and belief—

(i) the demand has been neither complied with nor set aside in accordance with these Rules, and

(ii) that no application to set it aside is outstanding.

(3) If the case is within section 268(1)(b) (unsatisfied execution or process in respect of judgment debt, etc) the petition must state which court issued the execution or other process and give particulars of the return.

(4) The court may decline to file the petition if not satisfied that the creditor has discharged the obligation imposed by rule 10.2.

**Derivation**—This rule derived from the Insolvency Rules 1986, SI 1986/1925, r 6.8.
**Amendments**—SI 2017/1115.

## [2.536]

### 10.10 Verification of petition

(1) The petition must be verified by a statement of truth.

(2) If the petition relates to debts to different creditors, the debt to each creditor must be separately verified.

(3) A statement of truth which is not contained in or endorsed upon the petition which it verifies must be sufficient to identify the petition and must contain—

(a) the name of the debtor;

(b) the name of the petitioner; and

(c) the court or hearing centre in which the petition is to be presented.

(4) The statement of truth must be authenticated and dated by or on behalf of the petitioner.

(5) Where the person authenticating the statement of truth is not the petitioner, or one of the petitioners, the statement of truth must state—

(a) the name and postal address of the authenticating person;

(b) the capacity in which, and the authority by which, that person authenticates the statement of truth; and

(c) the means of the authenticating person's knowledge of the matters verified.

**Derivation**—This rule derived from the Insolvency Rules 1986, SI 1986/1925, r 6.12.

## [2.537]

### 10.11 Court in which petition is to be presented

(1) Where the proceedings are allocated to the London Insolvency District under rule 12.5(a)(i) to (iv) or (b), the creditor must present the petition to—

(a) the High Court where the debt is £50,000 or more; or

(b) the County Court at Central London where the debt is less than £50,000.

(2) Where the proceedings are allocated to the London Insolvency District under rule 12.5(a)(v), (c) or (d), the creditor must present the petition to the High Court.

(3)   Where the debtor is resident in England and Wales and the proceedings are not allocated to the London Insolvency District, the creditor must present the petition to the debtor's own hearing centre.

(4)   The debtor's own hearing centre is—

    (a)   where the debtor has carried on business in England and Wales within the six months immediately preceding the presentation of the petition, the hearing centre for the insolvency district where for the longest period during those six months—

        (i)    the debtor carried on business, or

        (ii)   the principal place of business was located, if business was carried on in more than one insolvency district; or

    (b)   where the debtor has not carried on business in England and Wales within the six months immediately preceding the presentation of the petition, the hearing centre for the insolvency district where the debtor resided for the longest period during those six months.

(5)   If the debtor is not resident in England and Wales but was resident or carried on business in England and Wales within the six months immediately preceding the presentation of the petition and the proceedings are not allocated to the London Insolvency District, the petition may be presented either to the debtor's own hearing centre or to the High Court.

(6)   Unless paragraph (2) applies, where to the petitioner's knowledge there is in force for the debtor an IVA under Part 8 of the Act, the petition must be presented to the court or hearing centre—

    (a)   to which the nominee's report under section 256 was submitted;

    (b)   to which an application has been made, where a nominee has made a report under section 256A(3); or

    (c)   as determined under paragraphs (1) to (5) in any other case.

(7)   The petition must contain sufficient information to establish that it is presented in the appropriate court and, where the court is the County Court, the appropriate hearing centre.

**Derivation**—This rule derived from the Insolvency Rules 1986, SI 1986/1925, r 6.9A.

## [2.538]

### 10.12   Procedure for presentation and filing of petition

(1)   The petition must be filed with the court.

(2)   A petition may not be filed unless—

    (a)   a receipt for the deposit payable to the official receiver is produced on presentation of the petition; or

    (b)   the Secretary of State has given notice to the court that the petitioner has made suitable alternative arrangements in accordance with an order made under section 415(3) for the payment of the deposit and that notice has not been revoked.

(3)   A notice of alternative arrangements for the deposit may be revoked by a further notice filed with the court.

(4)   The following copies of the petition must also be filed with the court with the petition—

    (a)   one for service on the debtor; and

    (b)   one copy for the supervisor, if to the petitioner's knowledge there is in force for the debtor an IVA under Part 8 of the Act, and the petitioner is not the supervisor of the IVA; . . .

    (c)   . . ..

(5)   The date and time of filing the petition must be endorsed on the petition and on the copies.

(6)   The court must fix a venue for hearing the petition, and this must also be endorsed on the petition and the copies.

(7)   Each copy of the petition must have the seal of the court applied to it and must be delivered to the petitioner.

**Derivation**—This rule derived from the Insolvency Rules 1986, SI 1986/1925, r 6.10.

**Amendments**—SI 2019/146, as from IP completion day (as defined in the European Union (Withdrawal Agreement) Act 2020, s 39(1)–(5)).

## [2.539]

### 10.13  Application to Chief Land Registrar to register petition

(1)   When the petition is filed, the court must as soon as reasonably practicable deliver to the Chief Land Registrar an application for registration of the petition in the register of pending actions.

(2)   The application must contain—

    (a)   a statement that the court is applying for registration of a petition in bankruptcy proceedings as a pending action with the Chief Land Registrar under section 5 of the Land Charges Act 1972;

    (b)   the debtor's name;

    (c)   the debtor's gender, if known;

    (d)   details of the debtor's trade, profession or occupation, including any trading name and, in the case of a partnership, the name and gender, if known, of each of the other partners;

    (e)   the postal address for each known place of residence of the debtor, including the debtor's business address where the court considers it to be appropriate for the purpose of the notice;

    (f)   the relevant key number allocated by the Land Charges Department;

    (g)   the name of the court (and hearing centre if applicable);

    (h)   the number and date of the petition; and

    (i)   the name and postal address of the petitioner.

(3)   The application must be sealed and dated by the court.

(4)   A separate application must be completed for each debtor and for any alternative name by which the debtor has been or is known (other than any trading name).

**Derivation**—This rule derived from the Insolvency Rules 1986, SI 1986/1925, r 6.13.

## [2.540]

### 10.14  Service of petition and delivery of copies

(1)   The petitioner must serve the petition on the debtor in accordance with Schedule 4 (Service of documents).

(2)   If to the petitioner's knowledge there is in force for the debtor an IVA , and the petitioner is not the supervisor of the IVA, a copy of the petition must be delivered by the petitioner to the supervisor.

(3)   . . .

**Derivation**—This rule derived from the Insolvency Rules 1986, SI 1986/1925, r 6.14.

**Amendments**—SI 2019/146, as from IP completion day (as defined in the European Union (Withdrawal Agreement) Act 2020, s 39(1)–(5)).

**General note**—Edward Murray (sitting as a deputy High Court judge) found in *Morby v Gate Gourmet Luxembourg IV Sarl* [2016] EWHC 74 (Ch), [2016] BPIR 414 that there had been personal service where a petition had been handed to the debtor's friend in his presence and at his suggestion, but had been put in a bin without coming into the debtor's physical possession. Had it been necessary, the deputy judge would have found any irregularity capable of cure under IR 1986, r 7.55 (replaced by IR 2016, r 12.64). This is to be contrasted with the position in *Canning v Irwin Mitchell LLP* [2017] EWHC 718 (Ch), [2017] BPIR 934 (concerning service of a statutory demand) where there had been no service at all, on which see notes to r 10.2 and s 268.

See also para.12.7 of the *Practice Direction – Insolvency Proceedings* (July 2020) [2020] BPIR 1211 concerning substituted service of bankruptcy petitions.

**[2.541]**

### 10.15 Death of debtor before service

If the debtor dies before service of the petition, the court may order service to be effected on the debtor's personal representative, or on such other person as it thinks just.

**Derivation**—This rule derived from the Insolvency Rules 1986, SI 1986/1925, r 6.16.

**[2.542]**

### 10.16 Amendment of petition

The petition may be amended at any time after presentation with the court's permission.

**Derivation**—This rule derived from the Insolvency Rules 1986, SI 1986/1925, r 6.22.

**General note**—The reference in s 271(5) to 'the rules' is to this provision. Rule 10.16, however, does not provide an exclusive regime for amendment, with the consequence that the court would in any case under CPR 17.1 (previously RSC Ord 20, r 8) have jurisdiction to amend a petition beyond the scope of those provisions just mentioned: *Aspinalls Club Ltd v Somone Halarbi* [1998] BPIR 322 (John Martin QC, sitting as a deputy High Court judge, and considering the predecessor rule, IR 1986, r 6.22, which was in substantially the same terms).

**[2.543]**

### 10.17 Security for costs

(1) This rule applies where the debt is a liquidated sum payable at some future time, it being claimed in the petition that the debtor appears to have no reasonable prospect of being able to pay it.

(2) The debtor may apply for an order that the petitioning creditor give security for the debtor's costs.

(3) The nature and amount of the security to be ordered is in the court's discretion.

(4) If an order for security is made then the petition may not be heard until the whole amount of the security has been given.

**Derivation**—This rule derived from the Insolvency Rules 1986, SI 1986/1925, r 6.17.

**General note**—See s 268(2) and the notes thereto.

**[2.544]**

### 10.18 Debtor's notice of opposition to petition

(1) A debtor who intends to oppose the making of a bankruptcy order must not less than five business days before the day fixed for the hearing—

    (a) file a notice with the court; and

    (b) deliver a copy of the notice to the petitioning creditor or the petitioner's solicitor.

(2) The notice must—

    (a) identify the proceedings;

    (b) state that the debtor intends to oppose the making of a bankruptcy order; and

    (c) state the grounds on which the debtor opposes the making of the order.

**Derivation**—This rule derived from the Insolvency Rules 1986, SI 1986/1925, r 6.21.

**General note**—It is common for debtors who wish to resist a bankruptcy order either to serve their notice of opposition late or not at all. There is a settled practice to consider any indication of opposition by a debtor, whether or not given in time under this rule, even if it is given for the first time at the hearing itself. That practice applies whether those matters are strictly defences, or go to the separate discretion to adjourn to allow a reasonable time to pay. The test for considering whether a petition is opposed for the purposes of adjournment is 'very low indeed': *Siddiqi v Taparis Ltd* [2019] EWHC 417 (Ch), [2019 BPIR 1025, [11], [18]–[20], [25], per HHJ David Cooke (sitting as a High Court judge).

**[2.545]**

### 10.19 Notice by persons intending to appear

(1)   A creditor . . . who intends to appear on the hearing of the petition must deliver a notice of intention to appear to the petitioner.

(2)   The notice must contain the following—

(a)   the name and address of the person, and any telephone number and reference which may be required for communication with that creditor or with any other person (also to be specified in the notice) authorised to speak or act on the person's behalf;

(b)   the date of the presentation of the bankruptcy petition and a statement that the notice relates to the matter of that petition;

(c)   the date of the hearing of the petition;

(d)   in the case of a creditor, the amount and nature of the debt due from the debtor to the creditor;

(e)   whether the person intends to support or oppose the petition;

(f)   where the person is represented by a solicitor or other agent, the name, postal address, telephone number and reference number (if any) of that person and details of that person's position with or relationship to the creditor . . .; and

(g)   the name and postal address of the petitioner.

(3)   The notice must be authenticated and dated by the person delivering it.

(4)   The notice must be delivered to the petitioner or the petitioner's solicitor at the address shown in the court records.

(5)   The notice must be delivered so as to reach the petitioner (or the petitioner's solicitor) not later than 4pm on the business day before that which is appointed for the hearing (or, where the hearing has been adjourned, for the adjourned hearing).

(6)   A person who fails to comply with this rule may appear and be heard on the hearing of the petition only with the permission of the court.

   **Derivation**—This rule derived from the Insolvency Rules 1986, SI 1986/1925, r 6.23.

   **Amendments**—SI 2019/146, as from IP completion day (as defined in the European Union (Withdrawal Agreement) Act 2020, s 39(1)–(5)).

**[2.546]**

### 10.20  List of appearances

(1)   The petitioner must prepare for the court a list of the persons who have delivered a notice under rule 10.19 of their intention to appear.

(2)   The list must contain—

(a)   the date of the presentation of the bankruptcy petition;

(b)   the date of the hearing of the petition;

(c)   a statement that the persons listed have delivered notice that they intend to appear at the hearing of the petition;

(d)   the name and address of each person who has delivered notice of intention to appear;

(e)   in the case of creditors, the amount owed to each such creditor;

(f)   the name and postal address of any solicitor for a person listed; and

(g)   whether each person listed intends to support the petition, or to oppose it.

(3)   On the day appointed for hearing the petition, a copy of the list must be handed to the court before the hearing commences.

(4)   If the court gives a person permission to appear under rule 10.19(6) then the petitioner must add that person to the list with the same particulars.

   **Derivation**—This rule derived from the Insolvency Rules 1986, SI 1986/1925, r 6.24 and Form 6.21.

**[2.547]**

### 10.21 Hearing of petition

(1)   The petition may not be heard until at least 14 days have elapsed since it was served on the debtor.

(2)   However the court may, on such terms as it thinks just, hear the petition at an earlier date, if—

    (a)   it appears that the debtor has absconded;

    (b)   the court is satisfied that it is a proper case for an expedited hearing; or

    (c)   the debtor consents to a hearing within the 14 days.

(3)   The following persons may appear and be heard—

    (a)   the petitioning creditor;

    (b)   the debtor;

    (c)   the supervisor of any IVA in force for the debtor; and

    (d)   any person who has delivered a notice under rule 10.19.

    **Derivation**—This rule derived from the Insolvency Rules 1986, SI 1986/1925, r 6.18.

**[2.548]**

### 10.22 Postponement of hearing

(1)   The petitioner may, if the petition has not been served, apply to the court to appoint another day for the hearing.

(2)   The application must state the reasons why the petition has not been served.

(3)   Costs of the application may not be allowed in the proceedings except by order of the court.

(4)   If the court appoints another day for the hearing, the petitioner must as soon as reasonably practicable deliver notice of that day to any person who delivered notice of intention to appear under rule 10.19 and to any person who must be served with a copy of the petition under rule 10.14.

    **Derivation**—This rule derived from the Insolvency Rules 1986, SI 1986/1925, r 6.28.

    **General note**—Note here, s 270 (expedited hearing) and the notes thereto.

**[2.549]**

### 10.23 Adjournment of the hearing

(1)   This rule applies if the court adjourns the hearing of a bankruptcy petition.

(2)   The order of adjournment must identify the proceedings and contain—

    (a)   the date of the presentation of the petition;

    (b)   the order that the further hearing of the petition be adjourned to the venue specified in the order;

    (c)   the venue of the adjourned hearing; and

    (d)   the date of the order.

(3)   Unless the court otherwise directs, the petitioner must as soon as reasonably practicable deliver a notice of the order of adjournment to—

    (a)   the debtor; and

    (b)   any person who has delivered a notice of intention to appear under rule 10.19 but was not present at the hearing.

(4)   The notice of the order of adjournment must identify the proceedings and—

    (a)   contain—

        (i)    the date of the presentation of the petition,

        (ii)   the date the order of adjournment was made, and

        (iii)  the venue for the adjourned hearing; and

    (b)   be authenticated and dated by the petitioner or the petitioner's solicitor.

    **Derivation**—This rule derived from the Insolvency Rules 1986, SI 1986/1925, r 6.29.

    **General note**—The factors relevant to adjournment are dealt with under the heading 'The court's discretion' under the note to r 10.24.

**[2.550]**

## 10.24 Decision on the hearing

(1)   On the hearing of the petition, the court may make a bankruptcy order if satisfied that the statements in the petition are true, and that the debt on which it is founded has not been paid, or secured or compounded.

(2)   If the petition is brought in relation to a judgment debt, or a sum ordered by any court to be paid, the court may stay or dismiss the petition on the ground that an appeal is pending from the judgment or order, or that execution of the judgment has been stayed.

(3)   An order dismissing or giving permission to withdraw a bankruptcy petition must contain—

| | |
|---|---|
| (a) | identification details for the proceedings; |
| (b) | the date of the presentation of the bankruptcy petition; |
| (c) | the name, postal address and description of the applicant; |
| (d) | a statement that the petition has been heard; |
| (e) | the order that the petition be dismissed or that, with the permission of the court, the petition is withdrawn; |
| (f) | details of any further terms of the order; |
| (g) | the date and reference number of the registration of the petition as a pending action with the Chief Land Registrar; |
| (h) | an order that the entry relating to the petition in the register of pending actions be vacated on the debtor's application; and |
| (i) | the date of the order. |

(4)   The order must notify the debtor that it is the debtor's responsibility and in the debtor's interest to ensure that the registration of the petition as an entry, both with the Chief Land Registrar and in the title register of any property owned by the debtor, is cancelled.

(5)   In the case of a petition preceded by a statutory demand, the petition will not be dismissed on the ground only that the amount of the debt was over-stated in the demand, unless the debtor, within the time allowed for complying with the demand, delivered a notice to the creditor disputing the validity of the demand on that ground; but, in the absence of such notice, the debtor is deemed to have complied with the demand if the correct amount is paid within the time allowed.

**Derivation**—This rule derived from the Insolvency Rules 1986, SI 1986/1925, r 6.25.

**General note**—The court's approach when deciding whether or not to make a bankruptcy order is not the same as when considering an application to set aside a statutory demand. The statutory demand stage concerns the existence of a debt that may found a petition; the petition stage concerns whether or not a bankruptcy order should be made. See discussion in *Vieira v Revenue and Customs Commissioners* [2017] EWHC 936 (Ch), [2017] 4 WLR 86, [83]–[84]. The test for considering whether a petition is opposed for the purposes of adjournment is opposed is 'very low indeed', whether the opposition relates to matters that are strictly defences, or to the separate discretion to adjourn to allow a reasonable time to pay: *Siddiqi v Taparis Ltd* [2019] EWHC 417 (Ch), [2019] BPIR 1025, [11], [18]–[20], [25], per HHJ David Cooke (sitting as a High Court judge).

**The court's discretion**—The decision whether or not to make a bankruptcy order remains a discretionary one: note the word 'may' in r 10.24(1). The starting point is that a petitioning creditor with an undisputed debt is entitled to an order *ex debito justitiae* ('out of the obligation of justice'): *Re Leigh Estates (UK) Ltd* [1994] BCC 292, 294, per Mr Richard Sykes QC (sitting as a deputy High Court judge); applied with approval in the personal insolvency context by Snowden J in *Maud v Aabar Block Sarl* [2016] EWHC 2175 (Ch), [2016] BPIR 1486, [81]–[82]. That starting point may, however, yield to other considerations. Such considerations are non-exhaustively summarised below.

First, and in practice by far the most usual way for a debtor to avoid an immediate bankruptcy order in relation to an undisputed debt, is for the debtor to show credible evidence of a reasonable prospect of payment within a reasonable time: see *Maud v Aabar Block Sarl* [2016] EWHC 2175 (Ch), [2016] BPIR 1486, [99] (Snowden J); and *Sekhon v Edginton* [2015] EWCA Civ 816, [2015] 1 WLR 4435, [2015] BPIR 1397, [18]–[19]. Payment for these purposes means payment in full: see *Ross v Revenue and Customs Commissioners* [2010] EWHC 13 (Ch), [2010] BPIR 652, [72] (Henderson J). To justify adjournment on this basis, the debtor must demonstrate a reasonable prospect of paying the petitioning creditor as well as any undisputed debts owed to supporting creditors: *Robertson v Wojakovski* [2020] EWHC 2737 (Ch), [2021] BPIR 178, [14]–[15] (Zacaroli J). The length of the adjournment, and how many the debtor might obtain, will depend on the circumstances and the evidence.

Secondly, a debtor may obtain an adjournment of a petition where he or she wishes to have an opportunity to put forward a proposal for an individual voluntary arrangement. Such a debtor can avoid the risk of the court making an immediate bankruptcy order on a petition by obtaining an interim order with its associated moratorium under s 252 of the IA 1986. But even where the debtor does not obtain an interim order, in practice courts will frequently be prepared to grant an adjournment of a bankruptcy petition, particularly at a first hearing, to give a debtor an opportunity to explore an IVA. Marcus Smith J indicated in *Gertner v CFL Finance Ltd* [2020] EWHC 1241 (Ch), [93] (undisturbed on appeal [2021] EWCA Civ 228, [2021] BPIR 487), that the court's discretion is significantly circumscribed where a creditor having control of the votes necessary to approve an IVA seeks a stay of the petition so that a creditors' meeting can take place and the arrangement approved. Where that is the case, the judge is obliged to grant the stay unless the 'good faith' principle is engaged, on which see notes to s 6.

Thirdly, a creditor's right to a bankruptcy order is a class right and, as such, the views of creditors other than the petitioner must be considered: *In re Crigglestone Coal Co Ltd* [1906] 2 Ch 327, 331-332. Where there are creditors who oppose the making of an immediate bankruptcy order, the interests of the class must be considered and the views of creditors on both sides weighed. This is not part of the same exercise as considering whether the debtor has demonstrated a reasonable prospect of payment within a reasonable time: *Maud v Aabar Block Sarl* [2016] EWHC 2175 (Ch), [2016] BPIR 1486, Snowden J, [99], [124]. See further judgments by Snowden J giving detailed analysis to the class interest in relation to the same debtor in *Re Maud (No 2)*; *Aabar Block SARL v Maud* [2018] EWHC 1414 (Ch), [2019] Ch 15, [2018] BPIR 1207 (where the court was not satisfied that the interests of the creditors as a class would be served by an immediate bankruptcy order: [140]) and *Re Maud*; *Edgeworth Capital (Luxembourg) SARL v Maud* [2020] EWHC 974 (Ch) (by which time the weight of votes and reasons given by members of the class led 'inexorably to the conclusion that a bankruptcy order should now be made': [112]). Evaluating the class interest is not simply a matter of counting heads; the quality of the creditors and their motives must be considered: *In Re P & J Macrae Ltd* [1961] 1 WLR 229, 238-239. These principles were to the fore in *Digby-Rogers v Speechly Bircham LLP* [2019] EWHC 1568 (Ch), [2019] BPIR 1108, [35]–[44], where the critical importance to giving proper consideration to the class interest was emphasised. Mr Mark Anderson QC (sitting as a deputy High Court judge) allowed an appeal from a bankruptcy order, despite five prior adjournments in relation to an undisputed judgment debt, in circumstances where the district judge had firmly but wrongly taken the view that bankruptcy was not a class remedy ([18]). Having considered only whether there was credible evidence of payment within a reasonable time and not undertaken the 'separate and prior' exercise of evaluating the views of the 87% of creditors by value who opposed the petition ([35]–[36]), the judge at first instance had omitted a 'critical stage' and misdirected himself in law ([41]).

Fourthly, a debtor with no assets may show that a bankruptcy order would serve 'no useful purpose'. This is a high hurdle for the debtor and is considered further in the note to s 266(3) under the sub-heading 'Where bankruptcy would serve no useful purpose'.

See further commentary to s 125.

**Debtor rearguing points that have been addressed at the statutory demand stage**—The following extract from the judgment of Chadwick LJ in *Turner v Royal Bank of Scotland* [2000] BPIR 683 at 694A–694D, though obiter, confirms authoritatively the view expressed by Vinelott J in *Re a Debtor (No 27 of 1990)*, *Brillouet v Hachette Magazines Ltd* [1996] BPIR 518 at 520B–520D, that it is not open to a debtor to expect in a normal case to be able to advance arguments at the set-aside stage and then, if unsuccessful, to advance precisely the same arguments on the hearing of the bankruptcy petition:

'Rule 6.25 of the 1986 Rules [replaced by IR 2016, r 10.31] provides that on the hearing of the petition, the court may make a bankruptcy order if satisfied that the statements in the petition are true and that the debt on which it is founded has not been paid or secured or compounded for. So the court is not bound to make a bankruptcy order; there is a residual discretion in the court to decide on the hearing of the petition whether or not to make the bankruptcy order. But it cannot have been intended, as it seems to me, that when exercising the discretion (which it undoubtedly has under r 6.25), whether or not to make a bankruptcy order at the hearing of the petition, the court is required to revisit the arguments which have already been advanced on the hearing of the application to set aside the statutory demand, and which have already been rejected at that hearing. As Vinelott J pointed out in the *Brillouet* case, the debtor cannot go back and reargue the very grounds on which he unsuccessfully sought to have the statutory demand set aside. It will require some change of circumstance between the unsuccessful attempt to set aside the statutory demand and the hearing of the petition before the court (on the hearing of the petition) can be asked to go into the question which has already been determined at the hearing of the statutory demand. To hold otherwise would be to encourage a waste of court time, and a waste of the parties' money, and would defeat the obvious purpose of the statutory scheme.'

As Chadwick LJ identified in *Coulter v Dorset Police (No 2)* [2006] BPIR 10, a case in which re-argument was not permitted, the principle identified in *Turner* goes beyond estoppel and res judicata and enshrines '(i) that it is indeed a waste of the court's time and the parties' money to rehearse arguments which have already been run and failed; and (ii) that, in circumstances where it is desired to run arguments which have not already been run, then (as HHJ Maddocks (sitting as a High Court judge) pointed out in *Barnes v Whitehead* [2004] BPIR 693) the court will inquire why those arguments were not run at the time they could, and should, have been run (at [10]).

The Court of Appeal revisited the issue on the highly unusual facts of *Harvey v Dunbar Assets plc* [2017] EWCA Civ 60, [2017] BPIR 450, in which a debtor sought on an application to set aside a second statutory demand to re-argue a point that had failed in an application to set aside a previous statutory demand for the same debt, where the first demand had been set aside on a different ground that was no longer available to the debtor by the time the second statutory demand was served. The Court of Appeal held that the principle in *Turner v Royal Bank of Scotland* was not based on estoppel but on the principle that it is a waste of the court's time and the parties' money to rehearse arguments that have already been run and have failed. The principle was not confined simply to re-running arguments at the petition stage that had been run on a previous application to set aside a statutory demand. Instead, the principle was capable of general application through the various stages of the bankruptcy process ([48]–[49]).

Whether or not a debtor will be permitted to raise matters at the petition stage may depend on the nature of the proceedings at the statutory demand stage. If there has not been a hearing at the statutory demand stage, either because an application to set aside was not actually made or because the application was dismissed for procedural reasons without determination of the issues, the court's discretion under s 271 would almost invariably result in the non-application of the principle in *Brillouet* and *Turner*: see *Adams v Mason Bullock* [2004] EWHC 2910 (Ch), [2005] BPIR 241 at [28] (Bernard Livesey QC sitting as a deputy High Court judge). Marcus Smith J made the same point in a different way in *Gertner v CFL Finance Ltd* [2020] EWHC 1241 (Ch), at [51]–[52], observing that where no application to set aside had been made, there was nothing to suggest that the debtor was precluded from taking a point at the petition stage and no basis for the application of the *Turner* principle. If there is no reasoned determination at the earlier stage and an application is struck out on the ground of a formal defect then the principle in *Turner* is also not engaged: *Commissioners of Inland Revenue v Lee-Phipps* [2003] BPIR 803 (Launcelot Henderson QC, sitting as a deputy High Court judge). Where it had been argued on an application to set aside a statutory demand that the petitioner sought to bankrupt the debtor for illegitimate private purposes rather than for the benefit of the class of creditors as a whole, there was no reason why those questions should not be revisited at the petition stage when raised by opposing creditors who had not been involved in the set aside application: *In re Maud (No 2); Aabar Block SARL v Maud* [2018] EWHC 1414 (Ch), [2019] Ch 15, [2018] BPIR 1207, [64]–[68].

It should also be borne in mind that neither the test nor the matters in issue will necessarily be exactly the same at the petition stage as at the statutory demand stage: see note to r 10.5 above under the heading 'The test for setting aside a statutory demand'.

### RULE 10.24(2)

**Judgment debts—** This provision highlights one of the differences between the test applied by the court when considering an application to set aside a statutory demand compared with the test for whether or not a bankruptcy order should be made. Compare para 11.4.4 of the *Practice Direction – Insolvency Proceedings* (July 2020) [2020] BPIR 1211 with r 10.24(2), and see note to r 10.5(5)(b) above. Chief ICC Judge Briggs gave detailed consideration to this provision in *Barker v Baxendale-Walker* [2018] EWHC 1681 (Ch) and declined to stay or dismiss the petition, despite an application for permission to appeal the judgment debt to the Supreme Court having been made.

## [2.551]

### 10.25 Vacating registration on withdrawal of petition

If the petition is withdrawn by permission of the court, the court must deliver to the debtor two sealed copies of the order (one for the Chief Land Registrar).

**Derivation—**This rule derived from the Insolvency Rules 1986, SI 1986/1925, r 6.27.

**[2.552]**

### 10.26 Non-appearance of petitioning creditor

A petitioning creditor who fails to appear on the hearing of the petition may not present a petition either alone or jointly with any other person against the same debtor in respect of the same debt without the permission of the court to which the previous petition was presented.

**Derivation**—This rule derived from the Insolvency Rules 1986, SI 1986/1925, r 6.26.

**General note**—See s 271 and the notes thereto.

The judgment of Anthony Mann QC (sitting as a deputy High Court judge), in *Omgate Ltd v Gordon* [2001] BPIR 909 at [10] sets out the relevant principles and guidelines which should be applied when the court considers the exercise of its discretion under r 10.26 (the case was decided under the predecessor rule IR 1986, r 6.26, which was in substantially similar terms).

**[2.553]**

### 10.27 Substitution of petitioner

(1)   This rule applies where the petitioner—

    (a)    is subsequently found not to have been entitled to present the petition;

    (b)    consents to withdraw the petition or to allow it to be dismissed;

    (c)    consents to an adjournment;

    (d)    fails to appear in support of the petition when it is called on in court on the day originally fixed for the hearing, or on a day to which it is adjourned; or

    (e)    appears, but does not apply for an order in the terms of the petition.

(2)   The court may, on such terms as it thinks just, substitute as petitioner a person who—

    (a)    has delivered a notice under rule 10.19 of intention to appear at the hearing;

    (b)    is willing to prosecute the petition; and

    (c)    was, in the case of a creditor, at the date on which the petition was presented, in such a position in relation to the debtor as would have enabled the creditor on that date to present a bankruptcy petition in relation to a debt or debts owed to that creditor by the debtor, paragraphs (a) to (d) of section 267(2) being satisfied in relation to that debt or those debts.

**Derivation**—This rule derived from the Insolvency Rules 1986, SI 1986/1925, r 6.30.

**General note**—See s 266 and the notes thereto. For further commentary see also the notes to r 7.17.

Consistent with the principle that a bankruptcy petition is a class remedy, the legislation, rules and court practice are generally based on the notion that there should only be one petition against a debtor at any one time: *Edgeworth Capital (Luxembourg) SARL v Maud* [2020] EWHC 1469 (Ch), per Snowden J, [98]. The ability to seek substitution under r 10.27, like the ability to seek change of carriage under r 10.29, reflects that principle. Para 12.3 of *Practice Direction – Insolvency Proceedings* (July 2020) [2020] BPIR 1211 requires a petitioning creditor to certificate before presenting a petition that a search has been conducted within 7 days preceding presentation and either (a) no other petition is believed to be pending; or (b) if a prior petition is pending, the petition is presented at risk as to costs. That being the case, without a provision to permit substitution, a creditor who would have presented their own petition but for the prior presentation of another petition would unjustly lose the benefit of an earlier presentation date if the debt for which the existing petition had been presented was for some reason successfully challenged or fell away.

ICC Judge Jones discussed the foregoing aspects of the *Practice Direction* in *Islandsbanki HF v Stanford* [2019] EWHC 595 (Ch), [2019] BPIR 876 (upheld on two subsequent appeals, with no further discussion of this point) and observed (at [6]) that a second petition is not prohibited and that a creditor might be willing to take the risk in costs of presentation of such a petition because they know they will not be in a position to ask for change of carriage of the petition (see r 10.29) and substitution may not be available for the reasons discussed above.

In practice, applications for substitution are rare, because substitution is only available to a creditor who could have presented their own petition on the date that the existing petition was presented. That requires the creditor seeking substitution to have satisfied s 267(2)(c) on the date of presentation, which requires under s 268(1) service of a statutory demand at least three weeks before, or attempted execution.

Substitution and change of carriage were compared and explained by Michael Green J in *In re Hood (a debtor)* [2020] EWHC 3232 (Ch), [2021] Ch 125, [75]–[77]. See r 10.30 on change of carriage.

## [2.554]

### 10.28 Order for substitution of petitioner

The order for substitution of a petitioner must contain—

(a) identification details for the proceedings;

(b) the date of the hearing of the petition;

(c) the name of the original petitioner;

(d) the name of the person who is willing to prosecute the petition ("the named person");

(e) a statement that the named person meets the requirements of rule 10.27(2);

(f) details of the statutory demand or return of the enforcement officer or enforcement agent;

(g) the following orders—

    (i) that upon payment by the named person of the statutory deposit to the court the statutory deposit paid by the original petitioner to the court be repaid to the original petitioner by the official receiver,

    (ii) that the named person be substituted as petitioner in place of the original petitioner and that the relevant person may amend the petition accordingly,

    (iii) that the named person must within five business days from the date of the order file a copy of the amended petition together with a statement of truth verifying the amended petition,

    (iv) that at least 14 days before the date of the adjourned hearing of the petition the named person must serve upon the debtor a sealed copy of the amended petition,

    (v) that the hearing of the amended petition be adjourned to the venue specified in the order, and

    (vi) that the question of the costs of the original petitioner and of the statutory deposit (if appropriate) be reserved until the final determination of the amended petition;

(h) the venue of the adjourned hearing; and

(i) the date of the order.

**Derivation**—This rule derived from the Insolvency Rules 1986, SI 1986/1925, Sch 4, Fm 6.24A. It sets out the information required, which was previously set out in prescribed form 6.24A.

## [2.555]

### 10.29 Change of carriage of petition

(1) On the hearing of the petition, a person who has delivered notice under rule 10.19 of intention to appear at the hearing, may apply to the court for an order giving that person carriage of the petition in place of the petitioner, but without requiring any amendment of the petition.

(2) The court may, on such terms as it thinks just, make a change of carriage order if satisfied that—

(a) the applicant is an unpaid and unsecured creditor of the debtor . . .; and

(b) the petitioner either—

    (i) intends by any means to secure the postponement, adjournment, dismissal or withdrawal of the petition, or

    (ii) does not intend to prosecute the petition, either diligently or at all.

(3)   The court must not make such an order if satisfied that the petitioner's debt has been paid, secured or compounded by means of—

    (a)    a disposition of property made by some person other than the debtor; or

    (b)    a disposition of the debtor's own property made with the approval of, or ratified by, the court.

(4)   A change of carriage order may be made whether or not the petitioner appears at the hearing.

(5)   If the order is made, the person given the carriage of the petition is entitled to rely on all evidence previously provided in the proceedings.

(6)   The change of carriage order will contain—

    (a)    identification details for the proceedings;

    (b)    the date of the hearing of the petition;

    (c)    the name of the person who is willing to be given carriage of the petition ("the relevant person");

    (d)    a statement that the relevant person is a creditor of the debtor . . .;

    (e)    the name of the original petitioner;

    (f)    a statement that the relevant person has applied for an order under this rule to have carriage of the petition in place of the original petitioner;

    (g)    the order that the relevant person must within a period which is specified in the order serve upon the debtor and the original petitioner a sealed copy of the order;

    (h)    the order that the further hearing of the petition be adjourned to the venue specified in the order;

    (i)    the venue of the adjourned hearing;

    (j)    the order that the question of the costs of the original petitioner be reserved until the final determination of the petition; and

    (k)    the date of the order.

**Derivation**—This rule derived from the Insolvency Rules 1986, SI 1986/1925, r 6.31.

**Amendments**—SI 2019/146, as from IP completion day (as defined in the European Union (Withdrawal Agreement) Act 2020, s 39(1)–(5)).

**General note**—See s 266 and the notes thereto. Note that formal amendment of the petition is not required on change of carriage. Like substitution under r 10.27, change of carriage is seldom sought in practice. See note to r 10.27 above.

**'Disposition of property made by some person other than the debtor'**—Change of carriage could not be ordered where a business associate of the debtor directly paid the petitioning creditor, despite the fact that the payment had been made by way of a loan by the associate to the debtor, which the debtor became liable to repay. There had been no disposition of property by the debtor and the payment was not void under s 284: *In re Hood (a debtor)* [2020] EWHC 3232 (Ch), [2021] Ch 125, [78] (Michael Green J).

## [2.556]

### Note

[Note. See rule 10.24 for the contents of an order dismissing or giving permission to withdraw a petition.]

## [2.557]

### 10.30 Petitioner seeking dismissal or permission to withdraw

(1)   Where the petitioner applies to the court for the petition to be dismissed, or for permission to withdraw it, the petitioner must file with the court a witness statement specifying the grounds of the application and the circumstances in which it is made if —

    (a)    a person has delivered notice under rule 10.19 of intention to appear at the hearing of the petition; or

    (b)    the court so orders.

(2)   If any payment has been made to the petitioner since the petition was filed by way of settlement (in whole or in part) of the debt or any arrangement has been entered into for securing or compounding the debt, the witness statement must also state—

(a)    what dispositions of property have been made for the purposes of the settlement or arrangement;

(b)    whether, in the case of any disposition, it was property of the debtor, or of some other person; and

(c)    whether, if it was property of the debtor, the disposition was made with the approval of, or has been ratified by, the court (if so, specifying the relevant court order).

(3)   An order giving permission to withdraw a petition must not be made before the petition is heard.

(4)   The order of dismissal or granting permission to withdraw a bankruptcy petition must contain—

(a)    identification details for the proceedings;

(b)    the date of the filing of the bankruptcy petition;

(c)    the name, postal address and description of the applicant;

(d)    a statement that the petition has been heard;

(e)    the order that the petition be dismissed or that, with the permission of the court, the petition is withdrawn;

(f)    details of any further terms of the order;

(g)    the date and reference number of the registration of the petition as a pending action with the Chief Land Registrar;

(h)    an order that the entry relating to the petition in the register of pending actions be vacated on the debtor's application; and

(i)    the date of the order.

**Derivation**—This rule derived from the Insolvency Rules 1986, SI 1986/1925, r 6.32.

## [2.558]

### 10.31 Contents of bankruptcy order

(1)   The bankruptcy order must identify the proceedings and contain—

(a)    the name and address of the petitioner;

(b)    the date of the presentation of the petition;

(c)    the details of the debtor as provided under rule 10.8(1)(a) to (g);

(d)    the order that the person named is made bankrupt;

(e)    the order either—

    (i)    that the court, being satisfied that the EU Regulation as it has effect in the law of the United Kingdom applies, declares that the proceedings are COMI proceedings or establishment proceedings, or

    (ii)    that the court is satisfied that the EU Regulation does not apply in relation to the proceedings;

(f)    a statement that the official receiver (or one of them) attached to the court is by virtue of the order trustee of the bankrupt's estate;

(g)    a notice of the bankrupt's duties in relation to the official receiver under section 291, and in particular to the bankrupt's duty to give the official receiver such inventory of the bankrupt's estate and such other information, and to attend on the official receiver at such times, as the official receiver may reasonably require; and

(h)    the date and time of the order.

(2)   If the petitioner is represented by a solicitor the order is to be endorsed with the name, address, telephone number and reference of the solicitor.

(3)   Subject to section 346 (effect of bankruptcy on enforcement procedures), the order may include provision staying any action or proceeding against the bankrupt.

**Derivation**—This rule derived from the Insolvency Rules 1986, SI 1986/1925, r 6.33.

**Amendments**—SI 2017/1115; SI 2019/146, as from IP completion day (as defined in the European Union (Withdrawal Agreement) Act 2020, s 39(1)–(5)).

**[2.559]**

### 10.32 Delivery and notice of the order

(1)   As soon as reasonably practicable after making a bankruptcy order the court must deliver two sealed copies of the order to the official receiver.

(2)   The official receiver must as soon as reasonably practicable deliver a sealed copy of the order to the bankrupt.

(3)   On receipt of the sealed copies of the bankruptcy order the official receiver—

    (a)   must as soon as reasonably practicable—

        (i)   deliver an application for registration of the order containing the particulars specified in rule 10.33 to the Chief Land Registrar, for registration in the register of writs and orders affecting land, and

        (ii)   cause notice of the order to be gazetted;

    (b)   must cause an entry to be made in the individual insolvency register in accordance with rule 11.16; and

    (c)   may cause notice of the order to be advertised in such other manner as the official receiver thinks fit.

(4)   The notice to be gazetted and any notice to be advertised must state—

    (a)   that a bankruptcy order has been made against the bankrupt;

    (b)   the date and time of the making of the bankruptcy order;

    (c)   the name and address of the petitioning creditor; and

    (d)   the date of presentation of the petition.

(5)   The court may, on the application of the bankrupt or a creditor, order the official receiver to suspend action under paragraph (3) and rule 11.16, pending a further order of the court.

(6)   An application for such action to be suspended must be supported by a witness statement stating the grounds on which it is made.

(7)   Where an order to suspend such action is made, the applicant must deliver a copy of the order to the official receiver as soon as reasonably practicable.

**Derivation**—This rule derived from the Insolvency Rules 1986, SI 1986/1925, r 6.34.

**General note**—The court's discretion under r 10.32(5) to suspend notification to the Land Registry and publication in the Gazette was considered by Fancourt J in *Howell v Hughes* [2019] EWHC 1559 (Ch), [2019] BPIR 1211. The judge refused both a general stay of the bankruptcy order and any exercise of the power under r 10.32(5), because there was no persuasive evidence that permanent harm would be done to the applicant's interests ([28]–[31]).

**[2.560]**

### 10.33 Application to Chief Land Registrar to register bankruptcy order

(1)   The application for registration of the bankruptcy order delivered to the Chief Land Registrar under rule 10.32 must contain—

    (a)   identification details for the proceedings;

    (b)   a statement that the official receiver is applying for registration of a bankruptcy order in the register of writs and orders under section 6 of the Land Charges Act 1972;

    (c)   the name of the bankrupt;

    (d)   the bankrupt's gender, if known;

    (e)   details of the bankrupt's trade, profession or occupation, including any trading name and, in the case of a partnership, the name and gender, if known, of each of the other partners;

    (f)   the postal address for each known place of residence of the bankrupt, including the bankrupt's business address where the official receiver considers it to be appropriate for the purpose of the notice;

    (g)   the relevant key number allocated by the Chief Land Registrar;

    (h)   the date of the bankruptcy order; and

    (i)   the name and postal address of the petitioner.

(2)   The application must be authenticated and dated by the official receiver.

(3) A separate application must be completed for each address and for any alternative name by which the bankrupt has been or is known (other than any trading name).

Derivation—This rule derived from the Insolvency Rules 1986, SI 1986/1925, Sch 4, Fm 6.26 and sets out the content of the Chief Land Registrar which was previously prescribed in Form 6.26.

CHAPTER 3

DEBTORS' BANKRUPTCY APPLICATIONS

**[2.561]**

**Note**

[Note: a document required by the Act or these Rules must also contain the standard contents set out in Part 1.]

**[2.562]**

**10.34 Preliminary**

This Chapter relates to a debtor's bankruptcy application and the making of a bankruptcy order on the application of a debtor.

Derivation—This rule derived from the Insolvency Rules 1986, SI 1986/1925, r 6.37.

**[2.563]**

**10.35 Bankruptcy application for a bankruptcy order**

(1) In the bankruptcy application the debtor must—

- (a) state that the debtor is unable to pay the debtor's debts;
- (b) request that the adjudicator make a bankruptcy order against the debtor;
- (c) state that the debtor is not aware of any pending bankruptcy petition;
- (d) state whether a bankruptcy order has been made in respect of any of the debts which are the subject of the bankruptcy application;
- (e) state whether the debtor has taken debt advice before completing the bankruptcy application;
- (f) consent to verification checks being made by the adjudicator;
- (g) provide the information set out in Schedule 7;
- (h) provide the additional information set out in Schedule 8;
- (i) state that the information provided in accordance with this rule is accurate and up-to-date at the date of the bankruptcy application; and
- (j) state that the prescribed fee and deposit have been paid in full.

(2) The bankruptcy application must be authenticated by the debtor.

Derivation—This rule derived from the Insolvency Rules 1986, SI 1986/1925, r 6.38, Schs 2A, 2B.

**[2.564]**

**10.36 Procedure for making a bankruptcy application and communication with the adjudicator**

(1) The bankruptcy application must be completed in accordance with these Rules in electronic form and delivered to the adjudicator by electronic means unless otherwise agreed with the adjudicator in accordance with paragraph (4).

(2) For the purposes of rule 10.35(1)(i) the date of the bankruptcy application is the date that the debtor submits the bankruptcy application to the adjudicator under these Rules.

(3) A bankruptcy application is made when its receipt has been acknowledged by the adjudicator by electronic or other means.

(4) In the event of any malfunction or error in the operation of the electronic form or means of delivery, the adjudicator must—

(a) agree that debtors may, for a specified period, complete and deliver bankruptcy applications in another format; and

(b) provide an alternative means of delivery for the bankruptcy application and details of any terms or conditions to which their use is subject.

(5) If a bankruptcy application is completed in hard copy, it may not be delivered by fax.

(6) Where the debtor has given an electronic address in the bankruptcy application, the adjudicator must so far as reasonably practicable communicate with the debtor by electronic means.

(7) Unless the contrary is shown, a document (other than a bankruptcy application) is to be treated as delivered by electronic means to an electronic address where the sender can produce a copy of the electronic communication which—

(a) contains the document; and

(b) shows the time and date the communication was sent and the electronic address to which it was sent.

(8) Unless the contrary is shown, a document (other than a bankruptcy application) is to be treated as delivered to the electronic address to which it is sent at 9.00am on the next business day after it was sent.

(9) Rule 1.45 does not apply to electronic delivery of documents between a debtor and the adjudicator.

**Derivation**—This rule derived from the Insolvency Rules 1986, SI 1986/1925, r 6.39.

## [2.565]

**10.37 Application to the Chief Land Registrar to register a bankruptcy application**

(1) When a bankruptcy application is made, the adjudicator must as soon as reasonably practicable deliver to the Chief Land Registrar an application for registration of the bankruptcy application, in the register of pending actions.

(2) The application must contain—

(a) a statement that the adjudicator is applying for registration of a bankruptcy application as a pending action under section 5 of the Land Charges Act 1972;

(b) the debtor's name and any alternative name by which the debtor has been or is known;

(c) the debtor's date of birth;

(d) the debtor's gender, if known;

(e) the debtor's occupation, including any trading name;

(f) the postal address for each known place of residence of the debtor;

(g) the debtor's business address where the adjudicator considers it appropriate for the purpose of the application;

(h) the relevant key number allocated by the Chief Land Registrar;

(i) the reference allocated to the bankruptcy application; and

(j) the date of the bankruptcy application.

(3) The application must be authenticated and dated by the adjudicator.

**Derivation**—This rule derived from the Insolvency Rules 1986, SI 1986/1925, r 6.40.

## [2.566]

**10.38 Verification checks**

For the purpose of determining whether the adjudicator can make a bankruptcy order, verification checks may be made in, or with, one or more of the following—

(a) the electoral registers for such districts in England and Wales as the adjudicator considers appropriate to determine the identity and residence of the debtor;

(b) the individual insolvency register;

(c) the official receiver; or

(d) a credit reference agency.

**Derivation**—This rule derived from the Insolvency Rules 1986, SI 1986/1925, r 6.41.

## [2.567]

### 10.39 Determination of the bankruptcy application

(1)   The adjudicator must determine whether to make a bankruptcy order within the determination period referred to in rule 10.40.

(2)   In reaching a determination, the adjudicator must have regard to whether the requirements of section 263K of the Act are met.

(3)   During the determination period the adjudicator may request such further information from the debtor as the adjudicator considers is necessary in order to make the determination, such information to be provided in writing or at the request of the adjudicator, to be provided orally.

(4)   Subject to paragraph (5), the adjudicator must make a determination from the information provided under rule 10.35(1)(g), any further information provided under paragraph (3) and from the verification checks.

(5)   Before determining that the requirements of section 263K are not met, the adjudicator must have regard to the additional information provided under rule 10.35(1)(h).

**Derivation**—This rule derived from the Insolvency Rules 1986, SI 1986/1925, r 6.42.

## [2.568]

### 10.40 The determination period

(1)   The determination period is 28 days from the date the bankruptcy application is made.

(2)   Where the adjudicator requests further information from the debtor more than 14 days after the date the bankruptcy application is made, the determination period is extended by 14 days.

(3)   A failure to make a determination within the determination period is a refusal.

**Derivation**—This rule derived from the Insolvency Rules 1986, SI 1986/1925, r 6.43.

## [2.569]

### 10.41 Settlement and contents of bankruptcy order

(1)   The bankruptcy order must be settled by the adjudicator.

(2)   The bankruptcy order must contain—

    (a)   the information set out in Part 1 of Schedule 7;

    (b)   the date of delivery of the bankruptcy application on which the order is made;

    (c)   the order that upon reading the application it is ordered that person named be made bankrupt;

    (d)   the order either—

        (i)   that the adjudicator, being satisfied that the EU Regulation as it has effect in the law of the United Kingdom applies, declares that the proceedings are COMI proceedings or establishment proceedings, or

        (ii)   that the adjudicator is satisfied that the EU Regulation does not apply in relation to the proceedings;

    (e)   a statement that the official receiver (or one of them) attached to the court is, by virtue of the order, trustee of the bankrupt's estate; and

    (f)   a notice of the bankrupt's duties in relation to the official receiver under section 291(4) (duties of bankrupt in relation to the official receiver), and in particular to the bankrupt's duty to give the official receiver such inventory of the bankrupt's estate and such other information, and to attend on the official receiver at such times, as the official receiver may reasonably require.

**Derivation**—This rule derived from the Insolvency Rules 1986, SI 1986/1925, r 6.44.

**Amendments**—SI 2017/1115; SI 2019/146, as from IP completion day (as defined in the European Union (Withdrawal Agreement) Act 2020, s 39(1)–(5)).

**[2.570]**

### 10.42 Refusal to make a bankruptcy order and contents of notice of refusal

(1) Where the adjudicator determines that the requirements of section 263K are not met, the adjudicator must refuse to make a bankruptcy order.

(2) The adjudicator must deliver notice of the refusal to make a bankruptcy order to the debtor as soon as reasonably practicable after the refusal to make the bankruptcy order under paragraph (1) or under rule 10.40(3).

(3) The notice of refusal must state—

    (a) the reason or reasons for the refusal to make a bankruptcy order;

    (b) that the debtor may request that the adjudicator review the decision to refuse to make a bankruptcy order within 14 days from the date of delivery of the notice of refusal;

    (c) that where a review is requested it will be a review of the information that was available to the adjudicator at the date when the adjudicator refused to make a bankruptcy order;

    (d) that following a review, the adjudicator must either—

        (i) confirm the refusal to make a bankruptcy order; or

        (ii) make a bankruptcy order against the debtor; and

    (e) where the adjudicator confirms the refusal following a review, that the debtor may appeal to the court against the decision within 28 days from the date of delivery of the notice of confirmation of the refusal.

**Derivation**—This rule derived from the Insolvency Rules 1986, SI 1986/1925, r 6.45.

**[2.571]**

### 10.43 Review of refusal to make a bankruptcy order

(1) The debtor may request the adjudicator to review the decision to refuse to make a bankruptcy order within 14 days from the date of delivery of the notice of refusal.

(2) The debtor must give reasons for requesting a review but the request may not include additional information that was not available to the adjudicator when the determination was made.

(3) Where the adjudicator makes a bankruptcy order following a review, the bankruptcy order must be settled by the adjudicator in accordance with rule 10.41.

(4) Where the adjudicator confirms the refusal to make a bankruptcy order, the adjudicator must deliver notice to the debtor as soon as reasonably practicable.

(5) The notice will state—

    (a) the reason or reasons for confirming the refusal to make the bankruptcy order; and

    (b) that the debtor may appeal to the court against the decision within 28 days from the date of delivery of the confirmation of the notice of refusal.

**Derivation**—This rule derived from the Insolvency Rules 1986, SI 1986/1925, r 6.46.

**[2.572]**

### 10.44 Appeal to the court following a review of refusal to make a bankruptcy order

(1) Following a decision by the adjudicator to confirm the refusal to make a bankruptcy order, a debtor may appeal the decision to the court.

(2) An appeal under this rule must be made within 28 days from the date of delivery of the confirmation of the notice of refusal.

(3) The appeal must set out the grounds for the appeal.

(4) The court must either—

    (a) dismiss the application; or

    (b) make a bankruptcy order against the debtor.

(5) The bankruptcy order must contain—

(a) the information set out in Part 1 of Schedule 7;

(b) the date of delivery of the bankruptcy application on which the order is made;

(c) the date and time of the making of the order; and

(d) a statement that the order has been made following an appeal to the court under this rule.

(6) The adjudicator is not personally liable for costs incurred by any person in respect of an application under this rule.

(7) As soon as reasonably practicable after the making of the bankruptcy order the court must deliver sealed copies of the order to the debtor and the official receiver.

**Derivation**—This rule derived from the Insolvency Rules 1986, SI 1986/1925, r 6.47.

## [2.573]

### 10.45 Action to follow making of order

(1) As soon as reasonably practicable following the making of the bankruptcy order the adjudicator must deliver copies of the bankruptcy order to the debtor and the official receiver.

(2) On the application of the bankrupt to the official receiver, the official receiver must deliver to the bankrupt a hard copy of the bankruptcy order.

(3) Subject to paragraph (5), on receipt of the bankruptcy order, the official receiver—

(a) must as soon as reasonably practicable—

(i) deliver an application to the Chief Land Registrar for registration of the bankruptcy order in the register of writs and orders affecting land, and

(ii) must cause notice of the bankruptcy order to be gazetted;

(b) may cause notice of the bankruptcy order to be advertised in such other manner as the official receiver thinks fit; and

(c) must cause an entry to be made in the individual insolvency register in accordance with rule 11.16.

(4) The notice to be gazetted under paragraph (3)(a)(ii) and any notice to be advertised under paragraph (3)(b) must state—

(a) that a bankruptcy order has been made against the bankrupt;

(b) the date of the bankruptcy order;

(c) that the bankruptcy order was made on the debtor's own bankruptcy application; and

(d) the date of delivery of the bankruptcy application.

(5) The court may, on the application of the bankrupt or a creditor, order the official receiver to suspend action under paragraph (3), pending a further order of the court.

(6) An application for such action to be suspended must be supported by a witness statement stating the grounds on which it is made.

(7) Where an order is made to suspend such action, the applicant must deliver a copy of it to the official receiver as soon as reasonably practicable.

**Derivation**—This rule derived from the Insolvency Rules 1986, SI 1986/1925, r 6.48.

## [2.574]

### 10.46 Application to the Chief Land Registrar

(1) The application to the Chief Land Registrar for registration of the bankruptcy order under rule 10.45 must contain—

(a) a statement that the official receiver is applying for registration of a bankruptcy order made by the adjudicator in the register of writs and orders under section 6 of the Land Charges Act 1972;

(b) the bankrupt's name and any alternative names by which the bankrupt has been or is known;

(c) the bankrupt's date of birth;

(d) the bankrupt's gender, if known;

    (e)    the bankrupt's occupation including any trading name;

    (f)    the postal address for each known place of residence of the bankrupt;

    (g)    the bankrupt's business address where the official receiver considers it appropriate for the purpose of the application;

    (h)    the relevant key number allocated by the Chief Land Registrar;

    (i)    the reference allocated to the bankruptcy order; and

    (j)    the date of the bankruptcy order.

(2)   The application must be authenticated and dated by the official receiver.

Derivation—This rule derived from the Insolvency Rules 1986, SI 1986/1925, r 6.49.

## [2.575]

### 10.47 The bankruptcy file

(1)   On receipt of a bankruptcy application, the adjudicator must open a file on which the adjudicator must place the bankruptcy application and any documents which are filed with the adjudicator under this Chapter.

(2)   As soon as reasonably practicable following the making of the bankruptcy order the adjudicator must deliver the bankruptcy file to the official receiver.

(3)   The official receiver must place on the bankruptcy file—

    (a)    any documents delivered to the official receiver by the court; and

    (b)    any notices delivered to the official receiver under these Rules.

(4)   The following persons may inspect the bankruptcy file—

    (a)    the court;

    (b)    the trustee;

    (c)    the Secretary of State; and

    (d)    the bankrupt.

(5)   Following the making of a bankruptcy order, a creditor may inspect the following information and documents filed on the bankruptcy file—

    (a)    the information provided to the adjudicator and set out in Schedule 9;

    (b)    the bankruptcy order; and

    (c)    directions and orders of the court, if any.

(6)   The right to inspect the bankruptcy file may be exercised on that person's behalf by a person authorised to do so by that person.

(7)   Any person who is not otherwise entitled to inspect the bankruptcy file (or any part of it) may do so if the court gives permission.

(8)   The court may direct that the bankruptcy file, a document (or part of it) must not be made available under this rule without the permission of the court.

(9)   An application for a direction to withhold the bankruptcy file, a document (or part of it) may be made by—

    (a)    the official receiver;

    (b)    the trustee; or

    (c)    any person appearing to the court to have an interest.

(10)   An application under this rule for—

    (a)    permission to inspect the bankruptcy file; or

    (b)    a direction to withhold the bankruptcy file, a document (or part of it),

may be made without notice to any other party, but the court may direct that notice must be delivered to any person who would be affected by its decision.

Derivation—This rule derived from the Insolvency Rules 1986, SI 1986/1925, r 6.50.

## [2.576]

### 10.48 Court to which applications are to be made

(1)   An application to the court under this Chapter must be made to the debtor's own hearing centre where the debtor is resident in England and Wales.

(2)   If the debtor is not resident in England and Wales but was resident or carried on business in England and Wales within the six months immediately preceding the making

of the bankruptcy application, an application may be made to the debtor's own hearing centre or to the High Court.

(3)  In this rule the debtor's own hearing centre is—

    (a)    where the debtor has carried on business in England and Wales within the six months immediately preceding the filing with the court of the application, the hearing centre for the insolvency district where for the longest period during those six months—

        (i)    the debtor carried on business, or

        (ii)    the principal place of business was located, if business was carried on in more than one insolvency district; or

    (b)    where the debtor has not carried on business in England and Wales within the six months immediately before making the application to the court, the hearing centre for the insolvency district where the debtor resided for the longest period during those six months.

(4)  Where, for whatever reason, it is not possible for the application to be made to the debtor's own hearing centre, the applicant may, with a view to expediting the application, make the application—

    (a)    where paragraph (3)(a) applies, to—

        (i)    the hearing centre for the insolvency district in which the debtor resides, or

        (ii)    whichever court or hearing centre is specified in Schedule 6 as being the nearest full-time court or hearing centre in relation to—

            (aa)    the hearing centre in paragraph (3)(a), or

            (bb)    the hearing centre in paragraph (4)(a)(i); or

    (b)    where paragraph (3)(b) applies, whichever court or hearing centre is specified in Schedule 6 as being the nearest full-time court or hearing centre in relation to the court in that paragraph.

(5)  The application must contain sufficient information to establish that it is brought in the appropriate court or hearing centre.

**Derivation**—This rule derived from the Insolvency Rules 1986, SI 1986/1925, r 6.50A.

CHAPTER 4

THE INTERIM RECEIVER

**[2.577]**

**Note**

[Note: a document required by the Act or these Rules must also contain the standard contents set out in Part 1.]

**[2.578]**

**10.49  Application for appointment of interim receiver (section 286)**

(1)  An application to the court under section 286 for the appointment of the official receiver or an insolvency practitioner as interim receiver may be made by—

    (a)    a creditor;

    (b)    the debtor; or

    (c)    a temporary administrator; . . .

    (d)    . . ..

(2)  The application must be supported by a witness statement stating—

    (a)    the grounds on which it is proposed that the interim receiver should be appointed;

    (b)    whether or not the official receiver has been informed of the application and, if so, whether a copy of it has been delivered to that person;

    (c)    if the proposed interim receiver is an insolvency practitioner, that the insolvency practitioner has consented to act;

    (d)    whether to the applicant's knowledge there has been proposed or is in force an IVA; and

    (e)    the applicant's estimate of the value of the property or business in relation to which the interim receiver is to be appointed;

    (f)    a statement whether the proceedings will be COMI proceedings, establishment proceedings or proceedings to which the EU Regulation as it has effect in the law of the United Kingdom does not apply with the reasons for so stating.

(3)   The applicant must deliver copies of the application and the witness statement to the proposed interim receiver and to the official receiver.

(4)   If for any reason it is not practicable to deliver a copy of the application to the proposed interim receiver that person must be informed of the application in sufficient time to be able to be present at the hearing.

(5)   The official receiver may attend the hearing of the application and make representations.

(6)   If satisfied that sufficient grounds are shown for the appointment, the court may appoint an interim receiver on such terms as it thinks just.

    **Derivation**—This rule derived from the Insolvency Rules 1986, SI 1986/1925, r 6.51.

    **Amendments**—SI 2017/702; SI 2019/146, as from IP completion day (as defined in the European Union (Withdrawal Agreement) Act 2020, s 39(1)–(5)).

    **General note**—These procedural provisions should be read in light of s 286 and the commentary thereto.

## [2.579]

### 10.50 Deposit

(1)   An applicant for an order appointing the official receiver as interim receiver must, before the order is made, deposit with the official receiver, or otherwise secure to the official receiver's satisfaction, such sum as the court directs to cover the official receiver's remuneration and expenses.

(2)   If the sum proves to be insufficient, the court may, on the application of the official receiver, order the applicant to deposit or secure an additional sum.

(3)   If such additional sum is not deposited or secured within two business days after service of the order on the applicant the court may discharge the order appointing the official receiver as interim receiver.

(4)   If a bankruptcy order is made after an interim receiver has been appointed, any money deposited under this rule must (unless it is required because the assets are insufficient to pay the remuneration and expenses of the interim receiver, or the deposit was made by the debtor out of the debtor's own property) be repaid to the person depositing it (or as that person may direct) out of the bankrupt's estate, in the prescribed order of priority.

    **Derivation**—This rule derived from the Insolvency Rules 1986, SI 1986/1925, r 6.53.

## [2.580]

### 10.51 Order of appointment

(1)   The order appointing the interim receiver must contain—

    (a)    identification details for the proceedings;

    (b)    the name and title of the judge making the order;

    (c)    the name and postal address of the applicant;

    (d)    identification details for the debtor;

    (e)    the statement that the court is satisfied—

        (i)    that the debtor is unable to pay the debtor's debts, and

        (ii)    that the proceedings are COMI proceedings, establishment proceedings or proceedings to which the EU Regulation as it has effect in the law of the United Kingdom does not apply (as the case may be);

    (f)    the order either that—

     (i)    upon the applicant depositing the sum specified in the order with the official receiver, the official receiver is appointed interim receiver of the property of the debtor, or

     (ii)    the person specified in the order is appointed interim receiver of the property of the debtor;

  (g)    identification and contact details for the interim receiver, where the interim receiver is not the official receiver;

  (h)    details of the nature, together with a short description, of the property of which the interim receiver is to take possession;

  (i)    details of the duties to be carried out by the interim receiver in relation to the debtor's affairs;

  (j)    a notice to the debtor stating that the debtor must give the interim receiver all the information about the debtor's property that the interim receiver may require in order to carry out the functions imposed on the interim receiver by the order; and

  (k)    the date of the order.

(2)   The court must, as soon as reasonably practicable after the order is made, deliver two sealed copies of the order to the person appointed interim receiver.

(3)   The interim receiver must as soon as reasonably practicable deliver a sealed copy of the order to the debtor.

**Derivation**—This rule derived from the Insolvency Rules 1986, SI 1986/1925, r 6.52, Sch 4, Fm 6.32.

**Amendments**—SI 2017/1115; SI 2019/146, as from IP completion day (as defined in the European Union (Withdrawal Agreement) Act 2020, s 39(1)–(5)).

**[2.581]**

### 10.52 Security

(1)   This rule applies where an insolvency practitioner is appointed as interim receiver under section 286.

(2)   The cost of providing the security required under the Act must be paid in the first instance by the interim receiver.

(3)   If a bankruptcy order is not made, the person so appointed is entitled to be reimbursed out of the property of the debtor, and the court may make an order on the debtor accordingly.

(4)   If a bankruptcy order is made, the person so appointed is entitled to be reimbursed out of the bankrupt's estate in the prescribed order of priority.

(5)   If the interim receiver fails to give or keep up the required security, the court may remove the interim receiver, and make such order as it thinks just as to costs.

(6)   If an order is made under this rule removing the interim receiver, or discharging the order appointing the interim receiver, the court must give directions as to whether any, and if so what, steps should be taken for the appointment of another person as interim receiver.

**Derivation**—This rule derived from the Insolvency Rules 1986, SI 1986/1925, r 6.54.

**[2.582]**

### 10.53 Remuneration

(1)   The remuneration of an interim receiver (other than the official receiver) must be fixed by the court from time to time on application of the interim receiver.

(2)   In fixing the remuneration of the interim receiver, the court must take into account—

  (a)    the time properly given by the interim receiver and staff of the interim receiver in attending to the debtor's affairs;

  (b)    the complexity of the case;

  (c)    any respects in which, in connection with the debtor's affairs, there falls on the interim receiver any responsibility of an exceptional kind or degree;

    (d)    the effectiveness with which the interim receiver appears to be carrying out, or to have carried out, the duties of the interim receiver; and

    (e)    the value and nature of the property with which the interim receiver has to deal.

(3)  Without prejudice to any order the court may make as to costs, the interim receiver's remuneration (whether the official receiver or another) must be paid to the interim receiver, and the amount of any expenses incurred by the interim receiver (including the remuneration and expenses of any special manager appointed under section 370) reimbursed—

    (a)    if a bankruptcy order is not made, out of the property of the debtor; and

    (b)    if a bankruptcy order is made, out of the bankrupt's estate in the prescribed order of priority; or

    (c)    in either case (the relevant funds being insufficient), out of any deposit under rule 10.50.

(4)  Unless the court otherwise directs, if a bankruptcy order is not made, the interim receiver may retain out of the debtor's property such sums or property as are or may be required for meeting the remuneration and expenses of the interim receiver.

(5)  Where a person other than the official receiver has been appointed interim receiver, and the official receiver has taken any steps for the purpose of obtaining a statement of affairs or has performed any other duty under these Rules, the interim receiver must pay the official receiver such sum (if any) as the court may direct.

**Derivation**—This rule derived from the Insolvency Rules 1986, SI 1986/1925, r 6.56.

## [2.583]

### 10.54 Termination of appointment

(1)  The appointment of the interim receiver may be terminated by the court on the application of the interim receiver, or a person specified in rule 10.49(1).

(2)  If the interim receiver's appointment terminates, in consequence of the dismissal of the bankruptcy petition or otherwise, the court may give such directions as it thinks just relating to the accounts of the interim receiver's administration and any other matters which it thinks appropriate.

**Derivation**—This rule derived from the Insolvency Rules 1986, SI 1986/1925, r 6.57.

CHAPTER 5

DISCLOSURE OF THE BANKRUPT'S AFFAIRS

## [2.584]

### Note

[Note: a document required by the Act or these Rules must also contain the standard contents set out in Part 1.]

*Sub-division A: creditor's petition*

## [2.585]

### 10.55 Notice requiring statement of affairs (section 288)

(1)  Where, under section 288, the official receiver requires a bankrupt to provide the official receiver with a statement of affairs, the official receiver must deliver a notice to the bankrupt.

(2)  The notice must be headed "Notice requiring statement of affairs" and must—

    (a)    require the bankrupt to prepare and submit to the official receiver a statement of affairs;

    (b)    inform the bankrupt of the date by which the statement must be delivered; and

    (c)    state the effect of section 288(4) (penalty for non-compliance) and section 291 (duty to co-operate).

(3) The official receiver must deliver instructions for the preparation of the statement of affairs with the notice.

Derivation—This rule derived from the Insolvency Rules 1986, SI 1986/1925, r 6.58.

**[2.586]**

**10.56 Statement of affairs**

(1) The statement of affairs must contain—

    (a)    identification details for the proceedings;

    (b)    identification details for the bankrupt;

    (c)    the date of the bankruptcy order;

    (d)    a list of the bankrupt's secured creditors giving in relation to each—

        (i)    the name and postal address,

        (ii)    the amount owed to the creditor, and

        (iii)    particulars of the property of the bankrupt which is claimed by the creditor to clear or reduce the creditor's debt and the value of that property;

    (e)    a list of unsecured creditors giving in relation to each—

        (i)    the name and postal address of the creditor,

        (ii)    the amount the creditor claims the bankrupt owes to that creditor, and

        (iii)    the amount the bankrupt thinks is owed by the bankrupt to that creditor;

    (f)    a list of the bankrupt's total assets (which must include anything not previously mentioned in the statement of affairs which may be of value) divided into the following categories and giving the value of each asset listed—

        (i)    cash at the bank or building society,

        (ii)    household furniture and belongings,

        (iii)    life policies,

        (iv)    money owed to the bankrupt,

        (v)    stock in trade,

        (vi)    motor vehicles, and

        (vii)    other property; and

    (g)    the total value of the assets listed under paragraph (f).

(2) The bankrupt must authenticate and date each page of the statement of affairs.

(3) The statement of affairs must be verified by a statement of truth and delivered to the official receiver, together with one copy.

(4) The official receiver must file the verified statement with the court.

Derivation—This rule derived from the Insolvency Rules 1986, SI 1986/1925, rr 6.59, 6.60, Sch 4, Fm 6.33A.

**[2.587]**

**10.57 Limited disclosure**

Where the official receiver thinks that disclosure of the whole or part of the statement of affairs would be likely to prejudice the conduct of the bankruptcy or might reasonably be expected to lead to violence against any person, the official receiver may apply to the court for an order that the statement of affairs or any specified part of it either—

    (a)    must not be filed with the court; or

    (b)    must be filed separately and not open to inspection otherwise than with permission of the court.

Derivation—This rule derived from the Insolvency Rules 1986, SI 1986/1925, r 6.61.

**[2.588]**

**10.58 Requirement to submit statement of affairs and extension of time (section 288(3))**

(1)   The official receiver may exercise the power in section 288(3) to require the bankrupt to submit a statement of affairs under section 288(3) and to grant an extension of time, either on the official receiver's own initiative, or at the bankrupt's request.

(2)   A bankrupt required to submit a statement of affairs under paragraph (1) may apply to the court for a release or extension of time, if the official receiver has refused to release the bankrupt from that requirement or grant an extension.

(3)   On receipt of an application, the court may, if it is satisfied that no sufficient cause is shown for it, dismiss it without giving notice to any party other than the applicant.

(4)   Unless the application is dismissed, the court must fix a venue for it to be heard.

(5)   The applicant must, at least 14 days before any hearing, deliver to the official receiver a notice stating the venue with a copy of the application and any evidence on which the applicant intends to rely.

(6)   The official receiver may do either or both of the following—

    (a)    file a report of any matters which the official receiver thinks ought to be drawn to the court's attention; or

    (b)    appear and be heard on the application.

(7)   If such a report is filed, the official receiver must deliver a copy of it to the bankrupt not later than five business days before the hearing.

(8)   The court must deliver sealed copies of any order made on the application to the bankrupt and the official receiver.

(9)   The bankrupt must pay the bankrupt's costs of the application in any event and, unless and to the extent the court orders otherwise, no allowance in respect of them will be made out of the bankrupt's estate.

Derivation—This rule derived from the Insolvency Rules 1986, SI 1986/1925, r 6.62.
General note—See the notes to s 288.

**[2.589]**

**10.59 Expenses of assisting bankrupt to prepare statement of affairs**

(1)   If the bankrupt cannot personally prepare a proper statement of affairs, the official receiver may, at the expense of the bankrupt's estate, employ a person or firm to assist in the preparation of the statement.

(2)   At the request of the bankrupt, made on the grounds that the bankrupt cannot personally prepare a proper statement, the official receiver may authorise an allowance payable out of the bankrupt's estate (in accordance with the prescribed order of priority) of all or part of the expenses to be incurred by the bankrupt in employing a person or firm to assist the bankrupt in preparing it.

(3)   The bankrupt's request must be accompanied by an estimate of the expenses involved, and the official receiver must only authorise the employment of a named person or named firm approved by the official receiver.

(4)   The official receiver may make the authorisation subject to such conditions (if any) as the official receiver thinks fit relating to the manner in which any person may obtain access to relevant documents and other records.

(5)   Nothing in this rule relieves the bankrupt from any obligation relating to the preparation, verification and submission of a statement of affairs, or to the provision of information to the official receiver or the trustee.

Derivation—This rule derived from the Insolvency Rules 1986, SI 1986/1925, r 6.63.

**[2.590]**

### 10.60 Delivery of accounts to official receiver

(1)   The bankrupt must, at the request of the official receiver, deliver to the official receiver accounts relating to the bankrupt's affairs of such nature, as at such date and for such period as the official receiver may specify.

(2)   The period specified may begin from a date up to three years before the date of the presentation of the bankruptcy petition.

(3)   The court may, on the official receiver's application, require accounts for any earlier period.

(4)   Rule 10.59 (expenses of assisting bankrupt to prepare statement of affairs) applies to accounts to be delivered under this rule as it applies to the statement of affairs.

(5)   The accounts must, if the official receiver so requires, be verified by a statement of truth, and (whether or not so verified) delivered to the official receiver within 21 days of the request, or such longer period as the official receiver may allow.

Derivation—This rule derived from the Insolvency Rules 1986, SI 1986/1925, rr 6.64, 6.65.

**[2.591]**

### 10.61 Further disclosure

(1)   The official receiver may at any time require the bankrupt to deliver in writing further information amplifying, modifying or explaining any matter contained in the bankrupt's statement of affairs, or in accounts delivered under the Act or these Rules.

(2)   The information must, if the official receiver directs, be verified by a statement of truth, and (whether or not verified) delivered to the official receiver within 21 days from the date of the requirement, or such longer period as the official receiver may allow.

Derivation—This rule derived from the Insolvency Rules 1986, SI 1986/1925, r 6.66.

*Sub-division B: Bankruptcy application*

**[2.592]**

### 10.62 Preliminary

The rules in this sub-division apply in relation to further disclosure which is required of a bankrupt where the bankruptcy order was made on a bankruptcy application.

Derivation—This rule derived from the Insolvency Rules 1986, SI 1986/1925, r 6.67.

**[2.593]**

### 10.63 Delivery of accounts to official receiver

(1)   The bankrupt must, at the request of the official receiver, deliver to the official receiver accounts relating to the bankrupt's affairs of such nature, as at such date and for such period as the official receiver may specify.

(2)   The specified period may begin from a date up to three years preceding the date of the bankruptcy application.

(3)   The accounts must, if the official receiver so requires, be verified by a statement of truth, and (whether or not so verified) be delivered to the official receiver within 21 days of the request or such longer period as the official receiver may allow.

(4)   The court may, on the official receiver's application, require accounts in respect of any earlier period.

Derivation—This rule derived from the Insolvency Rules 1986, SI 1986/1925, rr 6.69, 670.

**[2.594]**

### 10.64 Expenses of preparing accounts

(1)   If the bankrupt cannot personally prepare adequate accounts under rule 10.63, the official receiver may, at the expense of the bankrupt's estate, employ a person or firm to assist in their preparation.

(2)   At the request of the bankrupt, made on the grounds that the bankrupt cannot personally prepare the accounts, the official receiver may authorise an allowance payable out of the bankrupt's estate (in accordance with the prescribed order of priority) of all or part of the expenses to be incurred by the bankrupt in employing a person or firm to assist the bankrupt in their preparation.

(3)   The bankrupt's request must be accompanied by an estimate of the expenses involved; and the official receiver must only authorise the employment of a named person or a named firm, being in either case approved by the official receiver.

(4)   The official receiver may make the authorisation subject to such conditions (if any) as the official receiver thinks fit relating to the manner in which any person may obtain access to relevant documents and other records.

(5)   Nothing in this rule relieves the bankrupt from any obligation relating to the preparation and delivery of accounts, or to the provision of information to the official receiver or the trustee.

Derivation—This rule derived from the Insolvency Rules 1986, SI 1986/1925, r 6.71.

## [2.595]

### 10.65 Further disclosure

(1)   The official receiver may at any time require the bankrupt to deliver in writing further information amplifying, modifying or explaining any matter contained in the bankruptcy application, or in accounts delivered under the Act or these Rules.

(2)   The information must, if the official receiver so directs, be verified by a statement of truth, and (whether or not so verified) delivered to the official receiver within 21 days from the date of the requirement, or such longer period as the official receiver may allow.

Derivation—This rule derived from the Insolvency Rules 1986, SI 1986/1925, r 6.72.

*Sub-division C: Reports by the official receiver*

## [2.596]

### 10.66 Reports by the official receiver

(1)   The official receiver must deliver a report on the bankruptcy and the bankrupt's affairs to the creditors at least once after the making of the bankruptcy order.

(2)   The report must contain—

(a)   identification details for the proceedings;

(b)   contact details for the official receiver;

(c)   a summary of the assets and liabilities of the bankrupt as known to the official receiver at the date of the report;

(d)   such comments on the summary and the bankrupt's affairs as the official receiver thinks fit; and

(e)   any other information of relevance to the creditors.

(3)   The official receiver may apply to the court to be relieved of any duty imposed by this rule or to be authorised to carry out the duty in another way.

(4)   On such an application the court must have regard to the cost of carrying out the duty, to the amount of the assets available, and to the extent of the interest of creditors or any particular class of them.

(5)   If a bankruptcy order is annulled, any duty of the official receiver to deliver a report under this rule ceases.

Derivation—This rule derived from the Insolvency Rules 1986, SI 1986/1925, rr 6.73, 6.75–678.

CHAPTER 6

THE TRUSTEE IN BANKRUPTCY

**[2.597]**

Note

[Note: a document required by the Act or these Rules must also contain the standard contents set out in Part 1.]

*Sub-division A: appointment and associated formalities*

**[2.598]**

**10.67 Appointment by creditors of new trustee**

(1)   This rule applies where the bankrupt's creditors decide to remove a trustee in bankruptcy under section 298 but do not, as part of the decision procedure to remove the trustee, appoint a new trustee.

(2)   The existing trustee must send the creditors a notice inviting proposals for a new trustee.

(3)   The notice must contain a statement explaining the effect of section 298(4B) (decision of creditors to remove a trustee does not take effect until creditors appoint another trustee).

(4)   The notice must also explain that the existing trustee is not obliged to seek the creditors' views on any proposals that do not meet the requirements of paragraphs (5) and (6).

(5)   Any proposal must state the name and contact details of the proposed trustee, and contain a statement that the proposed trustee is qualified to act as an insolvency practitioner in relation to the bankrupt and has consented to act as trustee.

(6)   Any proposal must be received by the existing trustee within five business days of the date of the notice.

(7)   Following the end of the period for inviting proposals under paragraph (2) of this rule, where any proposals are received the existing trustee must seek a decision from the creditors on the appointment of a replacement trustee by—

> (a)    a decision procedure; or
>
> (b)    the deemed consent procedure.

(8)   Where paragraph (7) applies, the existing trustee must send the creditors a notice which complies with rules 15.7 and 15.8 so far as are relevant.

(9)   The notice must also identify any person proposed to be nominated as trustee in accordance with this rule.

(10)   The decision date in the notice must be no later than 14 days after the date for receiving proposals has passed.

(11)   The creditors must be given at least seven days' notice of the decision date.

(12)   A notice inviting proposals for a new trustee under paragraph (2) may be sent before or after the date of the decision to remove the trustee.

(13)   Nothing in this rule affects the official receiver's ability under section 296(1), at any time when trustee, to apply to the Secretary of State to appoint a trustee instead of the official receiver.

**Derivation**—This rule is largely new, but partially derived from the Insolvency Rules 1986, SI 1986/1925, r 6.120.

**[2.599]**

**10.68 Certification of appointment**

(1)   This rule applies where a person has been appointed as trustee by a decision of the creditors.

(2)   The convener or the chair (as the case may be) must certify the appointment, but not unless and until the appointee has delivered to the convener or chair a statement

that the appointee is an insolvency practitioner qualified to act as trustee in relation to the bankrupt and consents to act.

(3)   The trustee's appointment takes effect from the date on which the appointment is certified, that date to be endorsed on the certificate.

(4)   The certificate must contain—

    (a)   identification details for the proceedings;

    (b)   identification details for the bankrupt;

    (c)   identification and contact details for the person appointed as trustee;

    (d)   the date on which the creditors made the appointment; and

    (e)   the statement that the appointee—

        (i)   has provided a statement of being qualified to act as an insolvency practitioner in relation to the bankrupt,

        (ii)   has consented to act, and

        (iii)   was appointed trustee of the bankrupt's estate.

(5)   The certificate must be authenticated and dated by the person who certifies the appointment.

(6)   Where two or more trustees are appointed the certificate must also specify (as required by section 292(3)) the circumstances in which the trustees must act together and the circumstances in which one or more of them may act for the others.

(7)   The convener or chair (if that person is not the official receiver) must deliver the certificate to the official receiver.

(8)   The official receiver must in any case deliver the certificate to the trustee.

**Derivation**—This rule derived from the Insolvency Rules 1986, SI 1986/1925, r 6.120, Sch 4, Fms 6.40, 6.41.

## [2.600]

### 10.69   Cost of the trustee's security (section 390(3))

The cost of the trustee's security required by section 390(3) for the proper performance of the trustee's functions is an expense of the bankruptcy.

**Derivation**—This rule derived from the Insolvency Rules 1986, SI 1986/1925, r 12A.56.

**General note**—See s 390(3) for the provision which sets out the need for security to be given by insolvency practitioners.

## [2.601]

### 10.70   Creditors' decision to appoint a trustee

(1)   In the case of a decision on the appointment of a trustee—

    (a)   if on any vote there are two nominees for appointment, the person who obtains the most support is appointed;

    (b)   if there are three or more nominees, and one of them has a clear majority over both or all the others together, that one is appointed; and

    (c)   in any other case the convener or chair must continue to take votes (disregarding at each vote any nominee who has withdrawn and, if no nominee has withdrawn, the nominee who obtained the least support last time) until a clear majority is obtained for any one nominee.

(2)   In the case of a decision being made at a meeting, the chair may at any time put to the meeting a resolution for the joint appointment of any two or more nominees.

**Derivation**—This rule derived from the Insolvency Rules 1986, SI 1986/1925, r 6.88.

## [2.602]

### 10.71   Appointment by the court (section 291A(2))

(1)   This rule applies where the court appoints the trustee under section 291A(2).

(2)   The court's order must not be made unless and until the proposed appointee has filed with the court a statement that the proposed appointee is an insolvency

practitioner, qualified to act as the trustee in relation to the bankrupt and consents to act.

(3)  The order of the court must contain—

    (a)    identification details the proceedings;

    (b)    the name and title of the judge making the order;

    (c)    the name and postal address of the applicant;

    (d)    the capacity in which the applicant made the application;

    (e)    identification and contact details for the person appointed as trustee;

    (f)    a statement that that the appointee has filed a statement of qualification to act as an insolvency practitioner in relation to the bankrupt and of consent to act;

    (g)    the order that the appointee is appointed trustee of the bankrupt's estate; and

    (h)    the date of the order.

(4)  Where two or more trustees are appointed the order must also specify (as required by section 292(3)) the circumstances in which the trustees must act together and the circumstances in which one or more of them may act for the others.

(5)  The court must deliver two copies of the order, one of which must be sealed, to the official receiver.

(6)  The official receiver must deliver the sealed copy of the order to the person appointed as trustee.

(7)  The trustee's appointment takes effect from the date of the order.

  **Derivation**—This rule derived from the Insolvency Rules 1986, SI 1986/1925, r 6.121, Sch 4, Fms 6.42, 6.43.

  **General note**—See s 297(3)–(5) and the notes thereto.

## [2.603]

### 10.72  Appointment by the Secretary of State

(1)  This rule applies where the official receiver—

    (a)    refers the need for an appointment of a trustee to the Secretary of State under section 300(4); or

    (b)    applies to the Secretary of State under section 296 to make the appointment.

(2)  If the Secretary of State makes an appointment the Secretary of State must deliver a copy of the certificate of appointment to the official receiver, who must deliver it to the person appointed.

(3)  The certificate must specify the date from which the trustee's appointment is to be effective.

  **Derivation**—This rule derived from the Insolvency Rules 1986, SI 1986/1925, r 6.122.

  **General note**—See ss 295, 296 and 300 and the notes thereto.

## [2.604]

### 10.73  Authentication of trustee's appointment

Where a trustee is appointed under any of rules 10.70, 10.71 or 10.72, a sealed copy of the order of appointment or (as the case may be) a copy of the certificate of the trustee's appointment may in any proceedings be adduced as proof that the trustee is duly authorised to exercise the powers and perform the duties of trustee of the bankrupt's estate.

  **Derivation**—This rule derived from the Insolvency Rules 1986, SI 1986/1925, r 6.123.

  **General note**—HHJ Simon Barker QC (sitting as a High Court judge) referred to this provision in the course of dealing with misguided challenges to trustees' authority in the long-running *Oraki v Hall* proceedings, [2019] EWHC 1515 (Ch), at [72].

**[2.605]**

### 10.74 Appointment to be gazetted

(1)   As soon as reasonably practicable after appointment a trustee appointed by a decision of the bankrupt's creditors—

(a)   must gazette a notice of the appointment; and

(b)   may advertise the notice in other such manner as the trustee thinks fit.

(2)   The notice must state—

(a)   that a trustee has been appointed by a decision of creditors; and

(b)   the date of the appointment.

Derivation—This rule derived from the Insolvency Rules 1986, SI 1986/1925, r 6.124.

**[2.606]**

### 10.75 Hand-over of bankrupt's estate by official receiver to trustee

(1)   This rule applies where a trustee is appointed in succession to the official receiver acting as trustee.

(2)   When the trustee's appointment takes effect, the official receiver must as soon as reasonably practicable do all that is required for putting the trustee into possession of the bankrupt's estate.

(3)   On taking possession of the bankrupt's estate, the trustee must discharge any balance due to the official receiver on account of—

(a)   expenses properly incurred by the official receiver and payable under the Act or these Rules; and

(b)   any advances made by the official receiver in respect of the bankrupt's estate, together with interest on such advances at the rate specified in section 17 of the Judgments Act 1838 on the date of the bankruptcy order.

(4)   Alternatively, the trustee may (before taking office) deliver to the official receiver a written undertaking to discharge any such balance out of the first realisation of assets.

(5)   The official receiver has a charge on the bankrupt's estate in respect of any sums due under paragraph (3) until they have been discharged, subject only to the deduction from realisations by the trustee of the costs and expenses of such realisations.

(6)   The trustee must from time to time out of the realisation of assets discharge all guarantees properly given by the official receiver for the benefit of the bankrupt's estate, and must pay all the official receiver's expenses.

(7)   The official receiver must give to the trustee all the information relating to the affairs of the bankrupt and the course of the bankruptcy which the official receiver considers to be reasonably required for the effective discharge by the trustee of the trustee's duties in relation to the bankrupt's estate.

(8)   The official receiver must also deliver to the trustee any report of the official receiver under rule 10.66.

Derivation—This rule derived from the Insolvency Rules 1986, SI 1986/1925, r 6.125.
General note—These provisions supplement ss 287 and 306.

**[2.607]**

### 10.76 Invitation to creditors to form a creditors' committee

(1)   Where the trustee seeks any decision from the bankrupt's creditors, the trustee must at the same time deliver to the creditors a notice inviting them to decide whether a creditors' committee should be established if sufficient creditors are willing to be members of the committee.

(2)   The notice must also invite nominations for membership of the committee, such nominations to be received by a date specified in the notice.

(3)   The notice must state that nominations—

(a)   must be delivered to the trustee by the specified date; and

(b)   can only be accepted if the convener is satisfied as to the creditors' eligibility under rule 17.4.

**General note**—Previously the invitation to join a creditors committee would form part of the initial meeting process which was dealt with in Part 2, Ch 7 of the IR 1986. One of the functions of the IR 2016 was to abolish the requirement for meetings, and therefore a new process is required to invite creditors to participate and allow creditors to vote on those volunteering to take part – that process is the giving of notice under r 10.76.

*Sub-division B: resignation and removal*

**[2.608]**

**10.77 Trustee's resignation and appointment of replacement (section 298(7))**

(1)   A trustee may resign under section 298(7) only—

    (a)    on grounds of ill health;

    (b)    because of the intention to cease to practise as an insolvency practitioner;

    (c)    because the further discharge of the duties of trustee is prevented or made impracticable by—

        (i)    a conflict of interest, or

        (ii)    a change of personal circumstances; or

    (d)    where two or more persons are acting as trustee jointly, and it is the opinion of both or all of them that it is no longer expedient that there should continue to be that number of joint trustees.

(2)   Before resigning, the trustee must invite the creditors to consider, either by a decision procedure or by the deemed consent procedure, whether a replacement should be appointed except where the resignation is under sub-paragraph (1)(d).

(3)   The notice to the creditors must—

    (a)    state the trustee's intention to resign;

    (b)    state that under rule 10.77(8) of the Insolvency (England and Wales) Rules 2016, the trustee will be released 21 days after the date of delivery of the notice of resignation to the prescribed person under section 298(7), unless the court orders otherwise; and

    (c)    comply with rule 15.7 or 15.8 so far as applicable.

(4)   The notice may suggest the name of a replacement trustee.

(5)   The notice must be accompanied by a summary of the trustee's receipts and payments.

(6)   The decision date must be not more than five business days before the date on which the trustee intends to give notice under section 298(7).

(7)   The trustee must deliver a copy of the notice to the official receiver and the bankrupt.

(8)   The resigning trustee's release is effective 21 days after the date on which the notice of resignation under section 298(7) is filed with the court in a bankruptcy based on a petition or, delivered to the official receiver in a bankruptcy based on a debtor's application.

**Derivation**—This rule derived from the Insolvency Rules 1986, SI 1986/1925, r 6.126.

**Release**—Note that r 10.77(3)(b) allows for the resigning trustee to obtain an automatic release unless the court orders otherwise, whereas the previous position under IR 1986, r 6.135(3) was that an application to the Secretary of State for release would have been required in these circumstances.

**[2.609]**

**10.78 Decision of creditors to remove trustee (section 298(1))**

(1)   Where the convener of the decision procedure or chair of a meeting of creditors is other than the official receiver, and a decision is taken to remove the trustee, the convener or chair must, within three business days, deliver a certificate to that effect to the official receiver.

(2)   If the creditors have decided to appoint a new trustee, the certificate of the new trustee's appointment must also be delivered to the official receiver within three business

days from the date of that decision and rule 10.68 must be complied with in relation to it.

(3)  The certificate of the trustee's removal must be authenticated and dated by the convener or chair and—

(a)  identify the bankrupt;

(b)  identify and provide contact details for the removed trustee;

(c)  state that the creditors decided that the trustee specified in the certificate be removed from office as trustee of the bankrupt's estate;

(d)  state the decision date and the decision procedure used; and

(e)  state that the creditors either—

(i)  did not decide against the trustee being released, or

(ii)  decided that the trustee should not be released.

(4)  The trustee's removal is effective from the date of the certificate of removal.

Derivation—This rule derived from the Insolvency Rules 1986, SI 1986/1925, rr 6.127, 6.129.

## [2.610]

### 10.79  Procedure on removal by creditors

(1)  Where the creditors have decided that the trustee be removed, the official receiver must in a bankruptcy based on a petition file the certificate of removal with the court.

(2)  The official receiver must deliver a copy of the certificate to the removed trustee.

Derivation—This rule derived from the Insolvency Rules 1986, SI 1986/1925, r 6.131.

## [2.611]

### 10.80  Removal of trustee by the court (section 298(1))

(1)  This rule applies where an application is made to the court under section 298(1) for the removal of the trustee, or for an order directing the trustee to initiate a creditors' decision procedure for the purpose of removing the trustee.

(2)  On receipt of an application, the court may, if it is satisfied that no sufficient cause is shown for it, dismiss it without giving notice to any party other than the applicant.

(3)  Unless the application is dismissed, the court must fix a venue for it to be heard.

(4)  The applicant must, at least 14 days before any hearing, deliver to the trustee and the official receiver a notice stating the venue with a copy of the application and of any evidence on which the applicant intends to rely.

(5)  A respondent may apply for security for the costs of the application and the court may make such an order if it is satisfied, having regard to all the circumstances of the case, that it is just to make such an order.

(6)  The trustee and the official receiver may do either or both of the following—

(a)  file a report of any matters which the trustee or the official receiver thinks ought to be drawn to the court's attention; or

(b)  appear and be heard on the application.

(7)  The costs of the application are not payable as an expense of the bankruptcy unless the court orders otherwise.

(8)  On a successful application the court's order must contain—

(a)  identification details for the proceedings;

(b)  the name and title of the judge making the order;

(c)  the name and postal address of the applicant;

(d)  a statement as to the capacity in which the applicant made the application;

(e)  identification and contact details for the trustee;

(f)  an order that either—

(i)  the trustee is removed from office, or

(ii)  the trustee must instigate a creditors' decision procedure on or before the date specified in the order for the purpose of considering the trustee's removal from office;

(g)  details of any further order in the matter; and

    (h)    the date of the order.

(9)   Where the court removes the trustee it must deliver a sealed copy of the order of removal to the trustee and a copy to the official receiver.

(10)   If the court appoints a new trustee, rule 10.71 applies.

**Derivation**—This rule derived from the Insolvency Rules 1986, SI 1986/1925, r 6.132.

## [2.612]

### 10.81 Removal of trustee by the Secretary of State (section 298(5))

(1)   This rule applies where the Secretary of State decides to remove a trustee appointed by the Secretary of State.

(2)   Before doing so the Secretary of State must deliver to the trustee and the official receiver a notice of the Secretary of State's decision and the grounds for the decision.

(3)   The notice must specify a period within which the trustee may make representations against implementation of the decision.

(4)   If the Secretary of State directs the removal of the trustee, the Secretary of State must as soon as reasonably practicable—

    (a)    deliver the notice to the trustee and the official receiver; and

    (b)    where the bankruptcy was based upon a petition, file a notice of the decision with the court.

(5)   Where the Secretary of State directs the trustee be removed, the court may make any order that it could have made if the trustee had been removed by the court.

**Derivation**—This rule derived from the Insolvency Rules 1986, SI 1986/1925, r 6.133.

## [2.613]

### 10.82 Notice of resignation or removal

Where a new trustee is appointed in place of one who has resigned or been removed, the new trustee must, in the notice of appointment, state that the predecessor trustee has resigned or, as the case may be, been removed and (if it be the case) has been given release.

**Derivation**—This rule derived from the Insolvency Rules 1986, SI 1986/1925, r 6.134.

## [2.614]

### 10.83 Release of removed trustee (section 299)

(1)   Where the trustee is removed by a creditors' decision procedure the certificate of removal must state whether or not the creditors decided against the trustee's release.

(2)   Where the creditors decided against release, the trustee's application to the Secretary of State for release under subsection 299(3)(b) must—

    (a)    identify the proceedings;

    (b)    identify the bankrupt;

    (c)    identify and provide contact details for the trustee;

    (d)    provide details of the circumstances under which the trustee has ceased to act as trustee;

    (e)    state that the trustee is applying to the Secretary of State for a certificate of the trustee's release as a trustee as a result of the circumstances specified in the application; and

    (f)    be authenticated and dated by the trustee.

(3)   When the Secretary of State gives the release, the Secretary of State must certify it accordingly and file the certificate with the court in a bankruptcy based on a creditor's petition.

(4)   The Secretary of State must deliver a copy of the certificate to the official receiver and former trustee whose release is effective from the date of the certificate or such other date as the certificate specifies.

**Derivation**—This rule derived from the Insolvency Rules 1986, SI 1986/1925, r 6.135.

**[2.615]**

**10.84 Deceased trustee**

(1)   If the trustee (not being the official receiver) dies, notice of the fact and date of death must be delivered to the official receiver by one of the following—

(a)   a surviving joint trustee;

(b)   a member or partner in the deceased trustee's firm (if the deceased was a member, partner or employee of a firm);

(c)   an officer of the deceased trustee's company (if the deceased was an officer or employee of a company); or

(d)   a personal representative of the deceased trustee.

(2)   If no such notice has been delivered within 21 days following the trustee's death then any other person may deliver the notice.

(3)   In a bankruptcy based on a creditor's petition the official receiver must file notice of the death with the court.

(4)   The date of the deceased trustee's release under section 299(3)(a) is—

(a)   the date of the filing of the notice with the court where the bankruptcy is based on a creditor's petition; or

(b)   the date of delivery of the notice under paragraph (1) to the official receiver where the bankruptcy is based on a debtor's application.

Derivation—This rule derived from the Insolvency Rules 1986, SI 1986/1925, r 6.143.

**[2.616]**

**10.85   Loss of qualification as insolvency practitioner (section 298(6))**

(1)   This rule applies where the trustee vacates office under section 298(6), on ceasing to be qualified to act as an insolvency practitioner in relation to the bankrupt.

(2)   A notice of the fact must be delivered as soon as reasonably practicable to the official receiver by one of the following—

(a)   the trustee who has vacated office;

(b)   a continuing joint trustee;

(c)   the recognised professional body which was the source of the vacating trustee's authorisation to act in relation to the bankrupt.

(3)   The notice must be authenticated and dated by the person delivering the notice.

(4)   On receiving such a notice the official receiver must—

(a)   deliver a copy of the notice to the Secretary of State; and

(b)   file a copy of the notice with the court where the bankruptcy was based on a creditor's petition.

(5)   Rule 10.83(2) to (4) applies in relation to the trustee's application for release under section 299(3)(b).

Derivation—This rule derived from the Insolvency Rules 1986, SI 1986/1925, r 6.144.

*Sub-division C: release on completion of administration of bankrupt's estate*

**[2.617]**

**10.86   Release of official receiver on completion of administration (section 299)**

(1)   Before giving a notice that the administration of the bankrupt's estate is for practical purposes complete to the Secretary of State under section 299(2), the official receiver must deliver a notice of intention to do so to the creditors and to the bankrupt.

(2)   The notice must be accompanied by a summary of the official receiver's receipts and payments as trustee.

(3)   When the Secretary of State has determined the date from which the official receiver's release is effective, the Secretary of State must—

(a)   where the bankruptcy was based on a bankruptcy application, deliver a notice of release to the official receiver; or

(b)   in all other cases, file a notice of the release with the court.

(4)   The Secretary of State's notice to the court must be accompanied by the summary of the official receiver's receipts and payments.

Derivation—This rule derived from the Insolvency Rules 1986, SI 1986/1925, r 6.136.

## [2.618]

**10.87  Vacation of office on completion of bankruptcy (sections 298(8) and 331)**
(1)   The report which the trustee is required to make under section 331(2A)(a) must comply with the requirements of rule 18.14.
(2)   A copy of the notice and report that is sent to creditors under section 331(2) and (2A) must be sent to the bankrupt as soon as is reasonably practicable after notice is given to creditors under that provision.
(3)   The notice under section 331(2) must also state—

(a)   that the creditors have the right to request information from the trustee under rule 18.9;

(b)   that the creditors have the right to challenge the trustee's remuneration and expenses under rule 18.34;

(c)   that the bankrupt has a right to challenge the trustee's remuneration and expenses under rule 18.35;

(d)   that the creditors may object to the trustee's release by giving notice in writing to the trustee before the end of the prescribed period;

(e)   that the prescribed period is the period ending at the later of—

(i)   eight weeks after delivery of the notice; or

(ii)   if any request for information under rule 18.9 or any application to the court under that rule, rule 18.34 or rule 18.35 is made when that request or application is finally determined;

(f)   that the trustee will vacate office under section 298(8) when, after the end of the prescribed period, the trustee files with the court a notice that the trustee has given notice to the creditors under section 331; and

(g)   that the trustee will be released under section 299(3)(d) at the same time as vacating office unless any of the creditors objected to the trustee's release.

(4)   The notice under section 298(8) must be authenticated and dated by the trustee.
(5)   The notice must be accompanied by a copy of the final report.
(6)   The trustee must deliver a copy of the notice under section 298(8) to—

(a)   the Secretary of State; and

(b)   the official receiver.

(7)   Rule 10.83(2) to (4) applies to an application by the trustee to the Secretary of State for release.

Derivation—This rule derived from the Insolvency Rules 1986, SI 1986/1925, r 6.137.
General note—This rule replaces IR 1986, r 6.127 which dealt with the final meeting of creditors. Creditors meetings are not a feature of the IR 2016 and alternative processes have been put in place for decisions which would otherwise have been taken at those meetings.

## [2.619]

**10.88  Rule as to reporting**
(1)   The court may, on the application of the trustee or official receiver, relieve the applicant of any duty imposed on the applicant by rule 10.86 and 10.87 and rule 18.14 (contents of final report), or authorise the applicant to carry out the duty in any other way.
(2)   In considering whether to relieve the applicant, the court must have regard to the cost of carrying out the duty, to the amount of the funds available in the bankrupt's estate, and to the extent of the interest of creditors or any particular class of them.

Derivation—This rule derived from the Insolvency Rules 1986, SI 1986/1925, r 6.137A.

**[2.620]**

**10.89 Notice to official receiver of intention to vacate office**
(1)   This rule applies where the trustee intends to vacate office, whether by resignation or otherwise, and as a result there will be a vacancy in the office of trustee (so that by virtue of section 300 the official receiver is trustee until the vacancy is filled).
(2)   The trustee must deliver notice of that intention to the official receiver at least 21 days before the trustee intends to vacate office.
(3)   The notice must include the following details of any property which has not been realised, applied, distributed or otherwise fully dealt with in the bankruptcy—
    (a)    the nature of the property;
    (b)    its value (or that it has no value);
    (c)    its location;
    (d)    any action taken by the trustee to deal with the property or any reason for the trustee not dealing with it; and
    (e)    the current position in relation to it.

Derivation—This rule derived from the Insolvency Rules 1986, SI 1986/1925, r 6.145.

**[2.621]**

**10.90 Trustee's duties on vacating office**
A trustee who ceases to be in office in consequence of removal, resignation or ceasing to be qualified to act as an insolvency practitioner in relation to the bankrupt, must as soon as reasonably practicable deliver to the successor as trustee—
    (a)    the assets of the bankrupt's estate (after deduction of any expenses properly incurred, and distributions made, by the trustee);
    (b)    the records of the bankruptcy, including correspondence, proofs and other documents relating to the bankruptcy while it was within the trustee's responsibility, and
    (c)    the bankrupt's documents and other records.

Derivation—This rule derived from the Insolvency Rules 1986, SI 1986/1925, r 6.146.

**[2.622]**

**10.91 Power of the court to set aside certain transactions**
(1)   If in dealing with the bankrupt's estate the trustee enters into any transaction with a person who is an associate of the trustee, the court may, on the application of any interested person, set the transaction aside and order the trustee to compensate the bankrupt's estate for any loss suffered in consequence of it.
(2)   This does not apply if either—
    (a)    the transaction was entered into with the prior consent of the court; or
    (b)    it is shown to the court's satisfaction that the transaction was for value, and that it was entered into by the trustee without knowing, or having any reason to suppose, that the person concerned was an associate.
(3)   Nothing in this rule is to be taken as prejudicing the operation of any rule of law or equity relating to a trustee's dealings with trust property, or the fiduciary obligations of any person.

Derivation—This rule derived from the Insolvency Rules 1986, SI 1986/1925, r 6.147.

**[2.623]**

**10.92 Rule against improper solicitation**
(1)   Where the court is satisfied that any improper solicitation has been used by or on behalf of the trustee in obtaining proxies or procuring the trustee's appointment, it may order that no remuneration be allowed out of the bankrupt's estate to any person by whom, or on whose behalf, the solicitation was exercised.

(2) An order of the court under this rule overrides any decision of the creditors' committee or the creditors, or any other provision of these Rules relating to the trustee's remuneration.

Derivation—This rule derived from the Insolvency Rules 1986, SI 1986/1925, r 6.148.

## [2.624]

### 10.93 Enforcement of trustee's obligations to official receiver (section 305(3))

(1) On the application of the official receiver, the court may make such orders as it thinks necessary to enforce the duties of the trustee under section 305(3).

(2) An order of the court under this rule may provide that all costs of and incidental to the official receiver's application must be borne by the trustee.

Derivation—This rule derived from the Insolvency Rules 1986, SI 1986/1925, r 6.149.

## CHAPTER 7

### SPECIAL MANAGER

## [2.625]

**Note**

[Note: a document required by the Act or these Rules must also contain the standard contents set out in Part 1.]

## [2.626]

### 10.94 Application for and order of appointment of special manager (section 370)

[Note: section 377 provides that the acts of the special manager are valid notwithstanding any defect in the special manager's appointment or qualifications.]

(1) An application by the interim receiver or trustee under section 370 for the appointment of a special manager must be supported by a report setting out the reasons for the application. The report must include the applicant's estimate of the value of the bankrupt's estate, property or business in relation to which the special manager is to be appointed.

(2) The court's order appointing the special manager must contain—

    (a)    identification details for the proceedings;

    (b)    the name and title of the judge making the order;

    (c)    the name and postal address of the applicant;

    (d)    the name and postal address of the proposed special manager;

    (e)    an order that the proposed special manager is appointed as special manager;

    (f)    details of the special manager's responsibility over the debtor's property or the bankrupt's estate;

    (g)    the powers entrusted to the special manager under section 370(4);

    (h)    the time allowed for the special manager to give the required security for the appointment;

    (i)    the duration of the special manager's appointment, being one of the following—

        (i)    for a fixed period stated in the order,

        (ii)    until the occurrence of a specified event, or

        (iii)    until the court makes a further order;

    (j)    an order that the special manager's remuneration will be fixed from time to time by the court; and

    (k)    the date of the order.

(3) The appointment of a special manager may be renewed by order of the court.

Derivation—This rule derived from the Insolvency Rules 1986, SI 1986/1925, r 6.167, Sch 4, Fm 6.54.

**[2.627]**

**10.95 Security**

(1) The appointment of the special manager does not take effect until the person appointed has given (or, if the court allows, undertaken to give) security to the applicant for the appointment.

(2) A person appointed as special manager may give security either specifically for a particular bankruptcy, or generally for any bankruptcy in relation to which that person may be appointed as special manager.

(3) The amount of the security must be not less than the value of the bankrupt's estate, property or business in relation to which the special manager is appointed, as estimated in the applicant's report which accompanied the application for appointment.

(4) When the special manager has given security to the applicant, the applicant must file with the court a certificate as to the adequacy of the security.

(5) The cost of providing the security must be paid in the first instance by the special manager; but—

    (a)    where a bankruptcy order is not made, the special manager is entitled to be reimbursed out of the property of the debtor, and the court may order accordingly; and

    (b)    where a bankruptcy order is made, the special manager is entitled to be reimbursed out of the bankrupt's estate in the prescribed order of priority.

**Derivation**—This rule derived from the Insolvency Rules 1986, SI 1986/1925, r 6.168.

**[2.628]**

**10.96 Failure to give or keep up security**

(1) If the special manager fails to give the required security within the time stated for that purpose by the order of appointment, or any extension of that time that may be allowed, the interim receiver or trustee (as the case may be) must report the failure to the court, which may discharge the order appointing the special manager.

(2) If the special manager fails to keep up the security, the interim receiver or trustee must report the failure to the court, which may remove the special manager, and make such order as it thinks just as to costs.

(3) If the court discharges the order appointing the special manager or makes an order removing the special manager, the court must give directions as to whether any, and if so what, steps should be taken for the appointment of another special manager.

**Derivation**—This rule derived from the Insolvency Rules 1986, SI 1986/1925, r 6.169.

**[2.629]**

**10.97 Accounting**

(1) The special manager must produce accounts, containing details of the special manager's receipts and payments, for the approval of the trustee.

(2) The accounts must be for—

    (a)    each three month period for the duration of the special manager's appointment; or

    (b)    any shorter period ending with the termination of the special manager's appointment.

(3) When the accounts have been approved, the special manager's receipts and payments must be added to those of the trustee.

**Derivation**—This rule derived from the Insolvency Rules 1986, SI 1986/1925, r 6.170.

**[2.630]**

**10.98 Termination of appointment**

(1) The special manager's appointment terminates if—

    (a)    the bankruptcy petition is dismissed; or

(b)    in a case where an interim receiver was appointed under section 286, the appointment is discharged without a bankruptcy order having been made.

(2)   If the interim receiver or the trustee thinks that the appointment of the special manager is no longer necessary or beneficial to the bankrupt's estate, the interim receiver or the trustee must apply to the court for directions, and the court may order the special manager's appointment to be terminated.

(3)   The interim receiver or the trustee must make such an application if the creditors decide that the appointment should be terminated.

Derivation—This rule derived from the Insolvency Rules 1986, SI 1986/1925, r 6.171.

## CHAPTER 8

### PUBLIC EXAMINATION OF BANKRUPT

**[2.631]**

Note

[Note: a document required by the Act or these Rules must also contain the standard contents set out in Part 1.]

**[2.632]**

### 10.99  Order for public examination of bankrupt

[Note: rule 81.9 (as amended) of the CPR requires a warning as mentioned in paragraph (2)(f) to be displayed prominently on the front of the order.]

(1)   This rule applies to a court order for the public examination of a bankrupt made on an application by the official receiver under section 290.

(2)   The order must have the title "Order for public examination" and contain—

(a)    identification details for the proceedings;

(b)    the name and the title of the judge making the order;

(c)    an order that the bankrupt must attend the venue specified in the order for the purpose of being publicly examined;

(d)    the venue for the public examination;

(e)    the date of the order; and

(f)    a warning that if the bankrupt fails without reasonable excuse to attend the public examination at the time and place specified in the order the bankrupt will be liable to be arrested without further notice under section 364(1) and may be held to be in contempt of court under section 290(5) and imprisoned or fined.

(3)   The official receiver must serve a copy of the court's order on the bankrupt as soon as reasonably practicable after the order is made.

Derivation—This rule derived from the Insolvency Rules 1986, SI 1986/1925, r 6.172, Sch 4, Fm 6.55.

**[2.633]**

### 10.100  Notice of public examination

(1)   The official receiver must deliver at least 14 days' notice of the public examination to—

(a)    any trustee or special manager; and

(b)    subject to any contrary direction of the court, every creditor of the bankrupt who is known to the official receiver.

(2)   Where the official receiver thinks fit, a notice of the order must be gazetted not less than 14 days before the day fixed for the hearing.

(3)   The official receiver may advertise the notice in such other manner as the official receiver thinks fit.

(4)   The notice must state the purpose of the examination hearing and the venue.

Derivation—This rule derived from the Insolvency Rules 1986, SI 1986/1925, r 6.172.

**[2.634]**

**10.101 Order for public examination requested by creditors**

(1) A notice by a creditor to the official receiver, under section 290(2), requesting the bankrupt to be publicly examined must be accompanied by—

(a) a list of the creditors concurring with the request with the name and postal address of each and the amount of their respective claims; and

(b) confirmation by each creditor of that creditor's concurrence; and

(c) a statement of the reasons why the public examination is requested.

(2) The request must be authenticated and dated by the creditor giving the notice.

(3) A list of concurring creditors is not required if the requisitioning creditor's debt alone is at least one half in value of the bankrupt's creditors.

(4) Before the official receiver makes the requested application, the creditor requesting the examination must deposit with the official receiver such sum (if any) as the official receiver determines is appropriate as security for the expenses of the public examination, if ordered.

(5) The official receiver must make the application for the examination—

(a) within 28 days of receiving the creditor's request (if no security is required under paragraph (4)); or

(b) within 28 days of the creditor depositing such security if security is requested.

(6) However, if the official receiver thinks the request is unreasonable, the official receiver may apply to the court for an order to be relieved from making the application.

(7) If the court so orders, and the application for the order was made without notice to any other party, the official receiver must deliver a copy of the order as soon as reasonably practicable to the requisitionist.

(8) If such an application is dismissed, the official receiver's application under section 290(2) must be made as soon as reasonably practicable on conclusion of the hearing of the application first mentioned.

Derivation—This rule derived from the Insolvency Rules 1986, SI 1986/1925, r 6.173.

**[2.635]**

**10.102 Bankrupt unfit for examination**

[Note: rule 81.9 (as amended) of the CPR requires a warning as mentioned in paragraph (6) to be displayed prominently on the front of the order.]

(1) Where the bankrupt is a person who lacks capacity within the meaning of the Mental Capacity Act 2005 or is unfit to undergo or attend for public examination, the court may—

(a) stay the order for the bankrupt's public examination; or

(b) direct that it will be conducted in a manner and place the court thinks just.

(2) An application for an order under paragraph (1) must be made—

(a) by a person who has been appointed by a court in the United Kingdom or elsewhere to manage the affairs of, or to represent, the bankrupt;

(b) by a person who appears to the court to be a suitable person to make the application; or

(c) by the official receiver.

(3) Where an application is made by a person other than the official receiver, then—

(a) the application must, unless the bankrupt is a person who lacks capacity within the meaning of the Mental Capacity Act 2005, be supported by a witness statement by a registered medical practitioner as to the bankrupt's mental and physical condition;

(b) at least five business days' notice of the application must be delivered to the official receiver and the trustee (if one is appointed); and

(c) before any order is made on the application, the applicant must deposit with the official receiver such sum as the official receiver determines is necessary for the additional expenses of an examination.

(4)    The court may order that some or all of the expenses of the examination are to be payable out of the deposit under paragraph (3)(c), instead of out of the bankrupt's estate.

(5)    The order must contain—

    (a)    identification details for the proceedings;

    (b)    the name and title of the judge making the order;

    (c)    the date of the original order for the public examination of the bankrupt;

    (d)    the name and postal address of the applicant;

    (e)    a statement as to the capacity in which the applicant (other than the official receiver) made the application;

    (f)    a statement that the court is satisfied that the bankrupt is a person who lacks capacity within the meaning of the Mental Capacity Act 2005 to manage and administer the bankrupt's property and affairs or is unfit to undergo a public examination;

    (g)    an order either that—

        (i)    the original order is stayed on the grounds that the bankrupt is unfit to undergo a public examination, or

        (ii)    the original order is varied (as specified in this order) on the grounds that the bankrupt is unfit to attend the public examination fixed by the original order; and

    (h)    the date of the order.

(6)    If the original order is varied, the order must also contain a warning to the bankrupt, which must be displayed prominently on the front page of the order, stating that if the bankrupt fails without reasonable excuse to attend the public examination at the time and place set out in the order the bankrupt—

    (a)    may be arrested without further notice under section 364(1); and

    (b)    may be held to be in contempt of court under section 290(5) and imprisoned or fined.

(7)    Where the application is made by the official receiver, it may be made without notice to any other party, and may be supported by evidence set out in a report by the official receiver to the court.

**Derivation**—This rule derived from the Insolvency Rules 1986, SI 1986/1925, r 6.174.

**[2.636]**

**10.103  Procedure at public examination**

(1)    At the public examination the bankrupt must—

    (a)    be examined on oath; and

    (b)    answer all the questions the court puts, or allows to be put.

(2)    A person allowed by section 290(4) to question the bankrupt may—

    (a)    with the approval of the court be represented by an appropriately qualified legal representative;

    (b)    in writing authorise another person to question the bankrupt on that person's behalf.

(3)    The bankrupt may at the bankrupt's own expense instruct an appropriately qualified legal representative, who may put such questions as the court may allow to the bankrupt for the purpose of enabling the bankrupt to explain or qualify any answers given by the bankrupt, and may make representations on the bankrupt's behalf.

(4)    The court must have such record made of the examination as the court thinks proper.

(5)    The record may, in any proceedings (whether under the Act or otherwise) be used as evidence of any statement made by the bankrupt in the course of the bankrupt's public examination.

(6)    If criminal proceedings have been instituted against the bankrupt, and the court is of the opinion that the continuance of the hearing might prejudice a fair trial of those proceedings, the hearing may be adjourned.

**Derivation**—This rule derived from the Insolvency Rules 1986, SI 1986/1925, r 6.175.

**[2.637]**

**10.104 Adjournment**

[Note: rule 81.9 (as amended) of the CPR requires a warning as mentioned in paragraph (2) to be displayed prominently on the front of the order.]

(1)   The court may adjourn the public examination from time to time, either to a fixed date or generally.

(2)   The order of adjournment of the public examination to a fixed date must contain a warning to the bankrupt, which must be displayed prominently on the front page of the order, stating that if the bankrupt fails without reasonable excuse to attend the public examination at the time and place set out in the order the bankrupt—

    (a)    may be arrested without further notice under section 364(1); and

    (b)    may be held to be in contempt of court under section 290(5) and imprisoned or fined.

(3)   Where the examination has been adjourned generally, the court may at any time on the application of the official receiver or of the bankrupt—

    (a)    fix a venue for the resumption of the examination; and

    (b)    give directions as to the manner in which, and the time within which, notice of the resumed public examination is to be given to persons entitled to take part in it.

(4)   Where such an application is made by the bankrupt, the court may grant it on terms that the expenses of giving the notices required by that paragraph must be paid by the bankrupt and that, before a venue for the resumed public examination is fixed, the bankrupt must deposit with the official receiver such sum as the official receiver considers necessary to cover those expenses.

(5)   Where the examination is adjourned, the official receiver may, there and then, make an application under section 279(3) (suspension of automatic discharge).

(6)   If the court makes such an order suspending the bankrupt's discharge, then the court must deliver copies of the order to the official receiver, the trustee and the bankrupt.

**Derivation**—This rule derived from the Insolvency Rules 1986, SI 1986/1925, r 6.176.

**[2.638]**

**10.105 Expenses of examination**

(1)   Where a public examination of the bankrupt has been ordered by the court on a creditor's request under rule 10.101, the court may order that some or all of the expenses of the examination are to be paid out of the deposit under rule 10.101, instead of out of the bankrupt's estate.

(2)   The costs and expenses of a public examination do not fall on the official receiver personally.

**Derivation**—This rule derived from the Insolvency Rules 1986, SI 1986/1925, r 6.177.

CHAPTER 9

REPLACEMENT OF EXEMPT PROPERTY

**[2.639]**

**10.106 Purchase of replacement property**

(1)   A purchase of replacement property under section 308(3) may be made either before or after the realisation by the trustee of the value of the property vesting in the trustee under the section.

(2)   The trustee is under no obligation to apply funds to the purchase of a replacement for property vested in the trustee, unless and until the trustee has sufficient funds in the bankrupt's estate for that purpose.

**Derivation**—This rule derived from the Insolvency Rules 1986, SI 1986/1925, r 6.187.
**General note**—See s 308 and the notes thereto.

**[2.640]**

### 10.107 Money provided in lieu of sale

(1) The following applies where a third party proposes to the trustee that the third party should provide the bankrupt's estate with a sum of money enabling the bankrupt to be left in possession of property which would otherwise be made to vest in the trustee under section 308.

(2) The trustee may accept that proposal, if satisfied that it is a reasonable one, and that the bankrupt's estate will benefit to the extent of the value of the property in question less the cost of a reasonable replacement.

Derivation—This rule derived from the Insolvency Rules 1986, SI 1986/1925, r 6.188.

General note—See s 308 and the notes thereto.

CHAPTER 10

INCOME PAYMENTS ORDERS

**[2.641]**

Note

[Note: a document required by the Act or these Rules must also contain the standard contents set out in Part 1.]

**[2.642]**

### 10.108 Interpretation

In this Chapter the "permitted fee" means the amount which is prescribed for the purposes of section 7(4)(a) of the Attachment of Earnings Act 1971.

**[2.643]**

### 10.109 Application for income payments order (section 310)

(1) Where the trustee applies for an income payments order under section 310, the court must fix a venue for the hearing of the application.

(2) Notice of the application and the venue must be delivered by the trustee to the bankrupt at least 28 days before the day fixed for the hearing, together with a copy of the trustee's application and a short statement of the grounds on which it is made.

(3) The notice must inform the bankrupt that—

    (a)    the bankrupt is required to attend the hearing unless at least five business days before the date fixed for the hearing the bankrupt files with the court and delivers to the trustee, consent to an order being made in the terms of the application; and

    (b)    if the bankrupt attends, the bankrupt will be given an opportunity to show cause why the order should not be made, or why a different order should be made to that applied for by the trustee.

(4) The notice must be authenticated and dated by the trustee.

Derivation—This rule derived from the Insolvency Rules 1986, SI 1986/1925, r 6.189.

**[2.644]**

### 10.110 Order for income payments order

An order under section 310 must have the title "Income Payments Order" and must contain—

    (a)    identification details for the proceedings;

    (b)    identification and contact details for the trustee;

    (c)    a statement that the bankrupt has or has not consented to the order (as the case may be);

(d) the order that it appears to the court that the sum which is specified in the order should be paid to the trustee in accordance with the payments schedule detailed in the order until the date specified in the order;

(e) the order that the bankrupt must pay to the trustee the sum referred to in paragraph (e) in accordance with the payments schedule out of the bankrupt's income, the first of such instalments to be made on or before the date specified in the order; and

(f) the date of the order.

**Derivation**—This rule derived from the Insolvency Rules 1986, SI 1986/1925, Sch 4, Fms 6.65, 6.66 and sets out the contents of an income payments order formerly set out in the prescribed Forms (Form 6.65 and 6.66) under IR 1986.

## [2.645]

### 10.111 Action to follow making of order

(1) Where the court makes an income payments order, the trustee must deliver a sealed copy of the order to the bankrupt as soon as reasonably practicable after it is made.

(2) If the order is made under section 310(3)(b), a sealed copy of the order must also be delivered by the trustee to the person to whom the order is directed.

**Derivation**—This rule derived from the Insolvency Rules 1986, SI 1986/1925, r 6.190.

## [2.646]

### 10.112 Variation of order

(1) If an income payments order is made under section 310(3)(a), and the bankrupt does not comply with it, the trustee may apply to the court for the order to be varied, so as to take effect under section 310(3)(b) as an order to the payer of the relevant income.

(2) The trustee's application under this rule may be made without notice to any other party.

(3) The order must contain—

(a) identification details for the proceedings;

(b) identification and contact details for the trustee who made the application;

(c) the name and address of the payer;

(d) a statement that the applicant is the trustee of the bankrupt;

(e) the date of the income payments order;

(f) a statement that it appears to the court that the bankrupt has failed to comply with the income payments order;

(g) the order that the income payments order be varied to the effect that the payer specified in this order do take payment in accordance with the payments schedule detailed in this order out of the bankrupt's income and that the first instalment must be paid on the date specified in the order; and that the payer must deliver the sums deducted to the trustee; and

(h) the date of the order.

(4) The court must deliver sealed copies of any order made on the application to the trustee and the bankrupt as soon as reasonably practicable after the order is made.

(5) In the case of an order varying or discharging an income payments order made under section 310(3)(b), the court must deliver an additional sealed copy of the order to the trustee, for delivery as soon as reasonably practicable to the payer of the relevant income.

**Derivation**—This rule derived from the Insolvency Rules 1986, SI 1986/1925, r 6.191, Sch 4, Fm 6.67.

## [2.647]

### 10.113 Order to payer of income: administration

(1) Where a person receives notice of an income payments order under section 310(3)(b), with reference to income otherwise payable by that person to the

bankrupt, that person ("the payer") must make the necessary arrangements for compliance with the order as soon as reasonably practicable.

(2)   When making any payment to the trustee, the payer may deduct the permitted fee towards the clerical and administrative costs of compliance with the income payments order.

(3)   The payer must give to the bankrupt a statement of any amount deducted by the payer under paragraph (2).

(4)   Where a payer receives notice of an income payments order imposing on the payer a requirement under section 310(3)(b), and either—

    (a)    the payer is then no longer liable to make to the bankrupt any payment of income; or

    (b)    having made payments in compliance with the order, the payer ceases to be so liable;

the payer must as soon as reasonably practicable deliver notice of that fact to the trustee.

**Derivation**—This rule derived from the Insolvency Rules 1986, SI 1986/1925, r 6.192.

## [2.648]

### 10.114  Review of order

(1)   Where an income payments order is in force, either the trustee or the bankrupt may apply to the court for the order to be varied or discharged.

(2)   If the application is made by the trustee, rule 10.109 applies (with any necessary modification) as in the case of an application for an income payments order.

(3)   If the application is made by the bankrupt, it must be accompanied by a short statement of the grounds on which it is made.

(4)   On receipt of an application, the court may, if it is satisfied that no sufficient cause is shown for it, dismiss it without giving notice to any party other than the applicant.

(5)   Unless the application is dismissed, the court must fix a venue for it to be heard.

(6)   The applicant must, at least 28 days before any hearing, deliver to the trustee or the bankrupt (whichever of them is not the applicant) a notice stating the venue with—

    (a)    a copy of the application; and

    (b)    where the applicant is the bankrupt, a copy of the statement of the grounds for the application referred to in paragraph (3).

(7)   The trustee may do either or both of the following—

    (a)    file a report of any matters which the trustee thinks ought to be drawn to the court's attention; or

    (b)    appear and be heard on the application.

(8)   The trustee must file a copy of a report under paragraph (7)(a) with the court not less than five business days before the date fixed for the hearing and must deliver a copy of it to the bankrupt.

(9)   The court order must contain—

    (a)    identification details for the proceedings;

    (b)    the name and title of the judge making the order;

    (c)    the name and postal address of the applicant;

    (d)    an order that the income payments order specified is varied as specified;

    (e)    the date of the income payments order referred to in paragraph (d);

    (f)    details of how the income payments order is varied by this order; and

    (g)    the date of the order.

(10)   Sealed copies of any order made on the application must be delivered by the court to the trustee, the bankrupt and the payer (if other than the bankrupt) as soon as reasonably practicable after the order is made.

**Derivation**—This rule derived from the Insolvency Rules 1986, SI 1986/1925, r 6.193, Fm 6.68.

## CHAPTER 11

### INCOME PAYMENTS AGREEMENTS

**[2.649]**

**Note**

[Note: a document required by the Act or these Rules must also contain the standard contents set out in Part 1.]

**[2.650]**

**10.114A Interpretation**

In this Chapter, the "permitted fee" means the amount which is prescribed for the purposes of section 7(4)(a) of the Attachment of Earnings Act 1971.

**Amendments**—Inserted by SI 2017/366.

**[2.651]**

**10.115 Approval of income payments agreements**

(1) An income payments agreement can only be entered into before the bankrupt's discharge.

(2) The official receiver or trustee must provide a draft of the agreement to the bankrupt for the bankrupt's approval.

(3) Within 14 days or such longer period as may be specified by the official receiver or trustee from the date on which the income payments agreement was delivered, the bankrupt must—

    (a)    if the bankrupt decides to approve the agreement, authenticate the agreement and return it to the official receiver or trustee; or

    (b)    if the bankrupt decides not to approve the agreement, deliver a notice of that decision specifying the bankrupt's reasons for not approving the agreement to the official receiver or trustee.

**Derivation**—This rule derived from the Insolvency Rules 1986, SI 1986/1925, r 6.193A.

**[2.652]**

**10.116 Acceptance of income payments agreements**

(1) On receipt by the official receiver or trustee of the authenticated income payments agreement, the official receiver or trustee must authenticate and date it at which time it will come into force and a copy must be delivered to the bankrupt.

(2) Where the agreement provides for payments by a third person in accordance with section 310A(1)(b), a notice of the agreement must be delivered by the official receiver or trustee to that person.

(3) The notice must—

    (a)    identify the bankrupt;

    (b)    state that an income payments agreement has been made, the date of it, and that it provides for the payment by the third person of sums owed to the bankrupt (or a part of those sums) to be paid to the official receiver or trustee;

    (c)    state the name and address of the third person;

    (d)    state the amount of money to be paid to the official receiver or trustee from the bankrupt's income, the period over which the payments are to be made, and the intervals at which the sums are to be paid; and

    (e)    identify and provide contact details for the official receiver or trustee and details of how and where the sums are to be paid.

(4) When making any payment to the official receiver or the trustee a person who has received notice of an income payments agreement with reference to income otherwise payable by that person to the bankrupt may deduct the permitted fee towards the clerical and administrative costs of compliance with the income payments agreement.

(5)   The payer must give to the bankrupt a statement of any amount deducted by the payer under paragraph (4).

Derivation—This rule derived from the Insolvency Rules 1986, SI 1986/1925, r 6.193B.

**[2.653]**

### 10.117 Variation of income payments agreements

(1)   Where an application is made to court for variation of an income payments agreement, the application must be accompanied by a copy of the agreement.

(2)   Where the bankrupt applies to the court for variation of an income payments agreement under section 310A(6)(b), the bankrupt must deliver a copy of the application and notice of the venue to the official receiver or trustee (whichever is appropriate) at least 28 days before the date fixed for the hearing.

(3)   When the official receiver or trustee applies to the court for variation of an income payments agreement under section 310A(6)(b), the official receiver or trustee must deliver a copy of the application and notice of the venue to the bankrupt at least 28 days before the date fixed for the hearing.

(4)   The court may order the variation of an income payments agreement under section 310A.

(5)   The court order must contain—

    (a)   identification details for the proceedings;

    (b)   the name and title of the judge making the order;

    (c)   the name and postal address of the applicant

    (d)   the order that the income payments agreement be varied as specified;

    (e)   the date of the income payments agreement referred to in paragraph (d);

    (f)   details of how the income payments agreement is varied by the order; and

    (g)   the date of the order.

(6)   Where the court orders an income payments agreement under section 310A(1)(a) to be varied, so as to be an agreement under section 310A(1)(b) providing that a third person is to make payments to the trustee or the official receiver, the official receiver or trustee must deliver a notice of the agreement to that person in accordance with rule 10.116(2).

(7)   A person who has received notice of an income payments agreement relating to income otherwise payable by that person to the bankrupt may deduct the permitted fee towards the clerical and administrative costs of compliance with the agreement when making any payment to the official receiver or the trustee.

(8)   The payer must give the bankrupt a statement of any amount deducted under paragraph (7).

Derivation—This rule derived from the Insolvency Rules 1986, SI 1986/1925, Sch 4, Fm 6.81.

CHAPTER 12

APPLICATIONS FOR PRODUCTION OF DOCUMENTS BY HER MAJESTY'S REVENUE AND CUSTOMS (SECTION 369)

**[2.654]**

**Note**

[Note: a document required by the Act or these Rules must also contain the standard contents set out in Part 1.]

**[2.655]**

### 10.118 Application for order

(1)   An application by the official receiver or the trustee for an order under section 369 (order for production of documents) must specify (with such details as will enable the order, if made, to be most easily complied with) the documents the production of which is sought, naming the official to whom the order is to be addressed.

(2) The court must fix a venue for the hearing of the application.

(3) The applicant must deliver notice of the venue, accompanied by a copy of the application to the Commissioners for Her Majesty's Revenue and Customs ("the Commissioners") at least 28 days before the hearing.

(4) The notice must require the Commissioners, not later than five business days before the date fixed for the hearing of the application, to inform the court whether they consent or object to the making of an order.

(5) If the Commissioners consent to the making of an order, the statement must include the name of the official to whom the order should be addressed, if other than the one named in the application.

(6) If the Commissioners object to the making of an order, they must file with the court a statement of their grounds of objection not less than five business days before the hearing of the application and must ensure that an official of theirs attends the hearing.

(7) The Commissioners must deliver a copy of the statement of objections to the applicant as soon as reasonably practicable.

Derivation—This rule derived from the Insolvency Rules 1986, SI 1986/1925, r 6.194.

## [2.656]

### 10.119 Making and service of the order

(1) The court may make the order applied for, with any modifications which appear appropriate, having regard to any representations made on behalf of the Commissioners.

(2) The order—

(a) may be addressed to an official of Her Majesty's Revenue and Customs other than the one named in the application;

(b) must specify a time, not less than 28 days after service on the official to whom the order is addressed, within which compliance is required; and

(c) may include requirements as to the manner in which documents to which the order relates are to be produced.

(3) A sealed copy of the order must be served by the applicant on the official to whom it is addressed.

(4) If the official is unable to comply with the order because the relevant documents are not in the possession of the official, and the official has been unable to obtain possession of them, the official must file with the court a statement as to the reasons for the official's non-compliance.

(5) The official must deliver a copy of the statement referred to in paragraph (4) to the applicant as soon as reasonably practicable.

Derivation—This rule derived from the Insolvency Rules 1986, SI 1986/1925, r 6.195.

## [2.657]

### 10.120 Custody of documents

When, in compliance with an order under section 369, original documents are produced, any person who, by order of the court under section 369(2), has possession or custody of those documents is responsible to the court for their safe keeping as, and return when, directed.

Derivation—This rule derived from the Insolvency Rules 1986, SI 1986/1925, r 6.196.

CHAPTER 13

Mortgaged Property

## [2.658]

### Note

[Note: a document required by the Act or these Rules must also contain the standard contents set out in Part 1.]

**[2.659]**

### 10.121 Interpretation

For the purposes of this Chapter "land" includes any interest in, or right over, land.

Derivation—This rule derived from the Insolvency Rules 1986, SI 1986/1925, r 6.197.

**[2.660]**

### 10.122 Claim by mortgagee of land

(1) Any person claiming to be the legal or equitable mortgagee of land belonging to the bankrupt may apply to the court for an order directing that the land be sold.

(2) The court, if satisfied as to the applicant's title, may direct accounts to be taken and enquiries made to ascertain—

    (a)    the principal, interest and costs due under the mortgage; and

    (b)    where the mortgagee has been in possession of the land or any part of it, the rents and profits, dividends, interest, or other proceeds received by the mortgagee or on the mortgagee's behalf.

(3) The court may also give directions in relation to any mortgage (whether prior or subsequent) on the same property, other than that of the applicant.

(4) For the purpose of those accounts and enquiries, and of making title to the purchaser, any of the parties may be examined by the court, and must produce on oath before the court all such documents in their custody or under their control relating to the bankrupt's estate as the court may direct.

(5) The court may under paragraph (4) order any of the parties to clarify any matter which is in dispute in the proceedings or give additional information in relation to any such matter and CPR Part 18 (further information) applies to any such order.

(6) In any proceedings between a mortgagor and mortgagee, or the trustee of either of them, the court may order accounts to be taken and enquiries made in like manner as in the Chancery Division of the High Court.

Derivation—This rule derived from the Insolvency Rules 1986, SI 1986/1925, r 6.197.

**[2.661]**

### 10.123 Power of court to order sale

(1) The court may order that the land, or any specified part of it, be sold and any party bound by the order and in possession of the land or part, or in receipt of the rents and profits from it, may be ordered to deliver possession or receipt to the purchaser or to such other person as the court may direct.

(2) The court may—

    (a)    permit the person having the conduct of the sale to sell the land in such manner as that person thinks fit; or

    (b)    direct that the land be sold as directed by the order.

(3) The court's order may contain directions—

    (a)    appointing the person to have the conduct of the sale;

    (b)    fixing the manner of sale (whether by contract conditional on the court's approval, private treaty, public auction, or otherwise);

    (c)    settling the particulars and conditions of sale;

    (d)    for obtaining evidence of the value of the property and for fixing a reserve or minimum price;

    (e)    requiring particular persons to join in the sale and conveyance;

    (f)    requiring the payment of the purchase money into court, or to trustees or others; or

    (g)    if the sale is to be by public auction, fixing the security (if any) to be given by the auctioneer, and the auctioneer's remuneration.

(4) The court may direct that, if the sale is to be by public auction, the mortgagee may bid on the mortgagee's own behalf.

(5) Nothing in this rule or rule 10.124 affects the rights in rem of creditors or third parties protected under Article 8 of the EU Regulation.

Derivation—This rule derived from the Insolvency Rules 1986, SI 1986/1925, r 6.198.
Amendments—SI 2017/1115.

**[2.662]**

**10.124 Proceeds of sale**

(1) The proceeds of sale must be applied as follows—

    (a)    first in payment of—

        (i)    the trustee's expenses in relation to the application to the court,

        (ii)    the trustee's expenses of the sale and attendance at it, and

        (iii)    any costs of the trustee arising from the taking of accounts, and making of enquiries, as directed by the court under rule 10.122;

    (b)    secondly, in payment of the amount found due to any mortgagee, for principal, interest and costs; and

    (c)    the balance must be retained by or paid to the trustee.

(2) Where the proceeds of the sale are insufficient to pay in full the amount found due to any mortgagee, the mortgagee is entitled to prove as a creditor for any deficiency, and to receive dividends rateably with other creditors, but not so as to disturb any dividend already declared.

Derivation—This rule derived from the Insolvency Rules 1986, SI 1986/1925, r 6.199.

CHAPTER 14

AFTER-ACQUIRED PROPERTY

**[2.663]**

**10.125 Duties of bankrupt in relation to after-acquired property**

(1) The notice to be given by the bankrupt to the trustee, under section 333(2), of property acquired by, or devolving upon, the bankrupt, or of any increase of the bankrupt's income, must be given within 21 days of the bankrupt becoming aware of the relevant facts.

(2) The bankrupt must not, without the trustee's consent in writing, dispose of such property or income within the period of 42 days beginning with the date of giving the notice.

(3) If the bankrupt disposes of property before giving the notice required by this rule or contrary to paragraph (2), it is the bankrupt's duty as soon as reasonably practicable to disclose to the trustee the name and address of the person to whom the property was disposed, and to provide any other information which may be necessary to enable the trustee to trace the property and recover it for the bankrupt's estate.

(4) Paragraphs (1) to (3) do not apply to property acquired by the bankrupt in the ordinary course of a business carried on by the bankrupt.

(5) A bankrupt who carries on a business must, when required by the trustee, deliver to the trustee—

    (a)    information about the business, showing the total of goods bought and sold and services supplied and the profit or loss arising from the business; and

    (b)    fuller details including accounts of the business.

Derivation—This rule derived from the Insolvency Rules 1986, SI 1986/1925, r 6.200.

**[2.664]**

**10.126 Trustee's recourse to person to whom property disposed**

(1) Where property has been disposed of by the bankrupt, before giving the notice required by section 333(2) or otherwise in contravention of rule 10.125, the trustee may serve notice on the person to whom the property was disposed, claiming the property as part of the bankrupt's estate by virtue of section 307.

(2) The trustee's notice must be served within 28 days of the trustee becoming aware of the identity of the person to whom the property was disposed and an address at which that person can be served.

Derivation—This rule derived from the Insolvency Rules 1986, SI 1986/1925, r 6.201.

## CHAPTER 15

### PERMISSION TO ACT AS DIRECTOR, ETC

**[2.665]**

#### Note

[Note: a document required by the Act or these Rules must also contain the standard contents set out in Part 1.]

**[2.666]**

#### 10.127 Interpretation

In this Chapter a bankrupt includes a person in relation to whom a bankruptcy restrictions order is in force.

Derivation—This rule derived from the Insolvency Rules 1986, SI 1986/1925, r 6.202A.

**[2.667]**

#### 10.128 Application for permission

(1) An application under section 11 of the Company Directors Disqualification Act 1986 by the bankrupt for permission to act as director of, or to take part or be concerned in the promotion, formation or management of a company, must be supported by a witness statement.

(2) The witness statement must identify the company and specify—

    (a)    the nature of its business or intended business, and the place or places where that business is, or is to be, carried on;

    (b)    whether it is, or in the case of a company which has not yet been incorporated is to be, a private or a public company;

    (c)    the persons who are, or are to be, principally responsible for the conduct of its affairs (whether as directors, shadow directors, managers or otherwise);

    (d)    the manner and capacity in which the applicant proposes to take part or be concerned in the promotion or formation of the company or, as the case may be, its management; and

    (e)    the emoluments and other benefits to be obtained from the directorship.

(3) The court must fix a venue for hearing the bankrupt's application and deliver notice of the hearing to the bankrupt.

Derivation—This rule derived from the Insolvency Rules 1986, SI 1986/1925, r 6.203.

**[2.668]**

#### 10.129 Report of official receiver

(1) The bankrupt must, not less than 28 days before the date fixed for the hearing, deliver to the official receiver and the trustee (if different) notice of the venue, accompanied by copies of the application and the witness statement under rule 10.128.

(2) The official receiver may, not less than 14 days before the date fixed for the hearing, file with the court a report of any matters which the official receiver considers ought to be drawn to the court's attention.

(3) The official receiver must deliver a copy of the report to the bankrupt and to the trustee (if not the official receiver) as soon as reasonably practicable after it is filed.

(4) Where a copy of the report is delivered by post under paragraph (3) it must be delivered by first class post.

(5)   The bankrupt may, not later than five business days before the date of the hearing, file with the court a notice specifying any statements in the official receiver's report which the bankrupt intends to deny or dispute.

(6)   If the bankrupt files such a notice, the bankrupt must deliver copies of it, not less than three business days before the date of the hearing, to the official receiver and the trustee.

(7)   The official receiver and the trustee may appear on the hearing of the application, and may make representations and put to the bankrupt such questions as the court may allow.

Derivation—This rule derived from the Insolvency Rules 1986, SI 1986/1925, r 6.204.

## [2.669]

### 10.130   Court's order on application

(1)   A court order granting the bankrupt permission under section 11 of the Company Directors Disqualification Act 1986 must specify what the bankrupt has permission to do.

(2)   The court, having regard to any representations made by the trustee on the hearing of the application, may—

    (a)    include in the order provision varying an income payments order or an income payments agreement already in force in relation to the bankrupt; or

    (b)    if no income payments order is in force, make one.

(3)   Whether or not the application is granted, copies of the order must be delivered by the court to the bankrupt, the official receiver and the trustee (if different).

Derivation—This rule derived from the Insolvency Rules 1986, SI 1986/1925, r 6.205.

## [2.670]

### 10.131   Costs under this Chapter

In no case do any costs or expenses arising under this Chapter fall on the official receiver personally.

Derivation—This rule derived from the Insolvency Rules 1986, SI 1986/1925, r 6.222.

CHAPTER 16

ANNULMENT OF BANKRUPTCY ORDER

## [2.671]

### Note

[Note: a document required by the Act or these Rules must also contain the standard contents set out in Part 1.]

## [2.672]

### 10.132   Application for annulment

(1)   An application to the court under section 282(1) for the annulment of a bankruptcy order must specify whether it is made—

    (a)    under subsection (1)(a) (claim that the order ought not to have been made); or

    (b)    under subsection (1)(b) (debts and expenses of the bankruptcy all paid or secured).

(2)   The application must be supported by a witness statement stating the grounds on which it is made.

(3)   Where the application is made under section 282(1)(b), the witness statement must contain all the facts by reference to which, under the Act and these Rules, the court may

be satisfied that the condition in section 282(1)(b) applies before annulling the bankruptcy order.

(4)   A copy of the application and the witness statement in support must be filed with the court.

(5)   The court must deliver notice of the venue fixed for the hearing to the applicant.

(6)   Where the application is made under section 282(1)(a) the applicant must deliver notice of the venue, accompanied by copies of the application and the supporting witness statement, to the official receiver, the trustee (if different), and the person on whose petition the bankruptcy order was made in sufficient time to enable them to be present at the hearing.

(7)   Where the application is made under section 282(1)(b) the applicant must deliver notice of the venue, accompanied by copies of the application and the supporting witness statement, to the official receiver and the trustee (if different) not less than 28 days before the hearing.

(8)   Where the applicant is not the bankrupt, all notices, documents and evidence required by this Chapter to be delivered to another party by the applicant must also be delivered to the bankrupt.

**Derivation**—This rule derived from the Insolvency Rules 1986, SI 1986/1925, r 6.206.

**General note**—See the notes to s 282.

## [2.673]

### 10.133  Report by trustee

(1)   The following applies where the application is made under section 282(1)(b) (debts and expenses of the bankruptcy all paid or secured).

(2)   Not less than 21 days before the date fixed for the hearing, the trustee must file with the court a report relating to the following matters—

  (a)   the circumstances leading to the bankruptcy;

  (b)   a summary of the bankrupt's assets and liabilities at the date of the bankruptcy order and at the date of the application;

  (c)   details of any creditors who are known to the trustee to have claims, but have not proved; and

  (d)   such other matters as the person making the report considers to be, in the circumstances, necessary for the information of the court.

(3)   Where the trustee is other than the official receiver, the report must also include a statement of—

  (a)   the trustee's remuneration;

  (b)   the basis fixed for the trustee's remuneration under rule 18.16; and

  (c)   the expenses incurred by the trustee.

(4)   The report must include particulars of the extent to which, and the manner in which, the debts and expenses of the bankruptcy have been paid or secured.

(5)   In so far as debts and expenses are unpaid but secured, the person making the report must state in it whether and to what extent that person considers the security to be satisfactory.

(6)   A copy of the report must be delivered to the applicant as soon as reasonably practicable after it is filed with the court and the applicant may file a further witness statement in answer to statements made in the report.

(7)   Copies of any such witness statement must be delivered by the applicant to the official receiver and the trustee (if different).

(8)   If the trustee is other than the official receiver, a copy of the trustee's report must be delivered to the official receiver at least 21 days before the hearing.

(9)   The official receiver may then file an additional report, a copy of which must be delivered to the applicant and the trustee (if not the official receiver) at least five business days before the hearing.

**Derivation**—This rule derived from the Insolvency Rules 1986, SI 1986/1925, r 6.207.

**[2.674]**

**10.134 Applicant's claim that remuneration or expenses are excessive**

(1)   Where the trustee is other than the official receiver and application for annulment is made under section 282(1)(b), the applicant may also apply to the court for one or more of the orders in paragraph (4) on the ground that the remuneration charged, or expenses incurred, by the trustee are in all the circumstances excessive.

(2)   Application for such an order must be made no later than five business days before the date fixed for the hearing of the application for annulment and be accompanied by a copy of any evidence which the applicant intends to provide in support.

(3)   The applicant must deliver a copy of the application and of any evidence accompanying it to the trustee as soon as reasonably practicable after the application is made.

(4)   If the court annuls the bankruptcy order under section 282(1)(b) and considers the application to be well-founded, it must also make one or more of the following orders—

    (a)    an order reducing the amount of remuneration which the trustee was entitled to charge;

    (b)    an order that some or all of the remuneration or expenses in question be treated as not being bankruptcy expenses;

    (c)    an order that the trustee or the trustee's personal representative pay to the applicant the amount of the excess of remuneration or expenses or such part of the excess as the court may specify; and

    (d)    any other order that the court thinks just.

**Derivation**—This rule derived from the Insolvency Rules 1986, SI 1986/1925, r 6.207A.

**[2.675]**

**10.135 Power of court to stay proceedings**

(1)   The court may, in advance of the hearing, make an order staying any proceedings which it thinks ought, in the circumstances of the application, to be stayed.

(2)   Except in relation to an application for an order staying all or any part of the proceedings in the bankruptcy, application for an order under this rule may be made without notice to any other party.

(3)   Where an application is made under this rule for an order staying all or any part of the proceedings in the bankruptcy, the applicant must deliver copies of the application to the official receiver and the trustee, if other than the official receiver, in sufficient time to enable them to be present at the hearing and make representations.

(4)   Where the court makes an order under this rule staying all or any part of the proceedings in the bankruptcy, the rules in this Chapter nevertheless continue to apply to any application for, or other matters in connection with, the annulment of the bankruptcy order.

(5)   If the court makes an order under this rule, it must deliver copies of the order to the applicant, the official receiver and the trustee (if different).

**Derivation**—This rule derived from the Insolvency Rules 1986, SI 1986/1925, r 6.208.

**[2.676]**

**10.136 Notice to creditors who have not proved**

Where the application for annulment is made under section 282(1)(b) and it has been reported to the court under rule 10.133(2)(c) that there are known creditors of the bankrupt who have not proved, the court may—

    (a)    direct the trustee or, if no trustee has been appointed, the official receiver to deliver notice of the application to such of those creditors as the court thinks ought to be informed of it, with a view to their proving for their debts within 21 days;

    (b)    direct the trustee or, if no trustee has been appointed, the official receiver to advertise the fact that the application has been made, so that creditors who have not proved may do so within a specified time; and

    (c)    adjourn the application meanwhile, for any period not less than 35 days.

**Derivation**—This rule derived from the Insolvency Rules 1986, SI 1986/1925, r 6.209.

## [2.677]

### 10.137 The hearing

(1)   The trustee must attend the hearing of the application under section 282 unless the court directs otherwise.

(2)   The official receiver, if not the trustee, may attend, but is not required to do so unless the official receiver has filed a report under rule 10.133.

(3)   If the court makes an order on the application or on an application under rule 10.134, it must deliver copies of the order to the applicant, the official receiver and (if other) the trustee.

(4)   An order of annulment under section 282 must contain—

    (a)    identification details for the proceedings;

    (b)    the name and address of the applicant;

    (c)    the date of the bankruptcy order;

    (d)    the date of the filing of the bankruptcy petition or the making of the bankruptcy application;

    (e)    the date and reference number of the registration of the bankruptcy petition or bankruptcy application as a pending action with the Chief Land Registrar;

    (f)    the date and reference number of the registration of the bankruptcy order on the register of writs and orders affecting land with the Chief Land Registrar;

    (g)    a statement that it appears to the court that—

        (i)    the bankruptcy order ought not to have been made, or

        (ii)    the bankruptcy debts and expenses of the bankruptcy have all been paid or secured to the satisfaction of the court;

and that under section 282(2) the bankruptcy order ought to be annulled;

    (h)    an order—

        (i)    that the bankruptcy order specified in the order is annulled,

        (ii)    that the bankruptcy petition or bankruptcy application specified in the order be dismissed, and

        (iii)    that the registration of the petition or the bankruptcy application as a pending action with the Chief Land Registrar and of the bankruptcy order with the Chief Land Registrar specified in the order be vacated upon application made by the bankrupt; and

    (i)    the date of the order.

(5)   The order must contain a notice to the bankrupt stating—

    (a)    should the bankrupt require notice of the order to be gazetted and to be advertised in the same manner as the bankruptcy order was advertised, the bankrupt must within 28 days deliver notice of that requirement to the official receiver; and

    (b)    it is the bankrupt's responsibility and in the bankrupt's interest to ensure that the registration of the petition or bankruptcy application and of the bankruptcy order with the Chief Land Registrar are cancelled.

(6)   The adjudicator is not in any event to be liable for costs arising on an application under section 282.

**Derivation**—This rule derived from the Insolvency Rules 1986, SI 1986/1925, r 6.210.
**Amendments**—SI 2017/366.

## [2.678]

### 10.138 Matters to be proved under section 282(1)(b)

(1)   This rule applies in relation to the matters which—

(a)   must, in an application under section 282(1)(b), be proved to the satisfaction of the court; and

(b)   may be taken into account by the court on hearing such an application.

(2)   Subject to the following paragraph, all bankruptcy debts which have been proved must have been—

(a)   paid in full; or

(b)   secured in full to the satisfaction of the court.

(3)   If a debt is disputed, or a creditor who has proved can no longer be traced, the bankrupt must have given such security (in the form of money paid into court, or a bond entered into with approved sureties) as the court considers adequate to satisfy any sum that may subsequently be proved to be due to the creditor concerned and (if the court thinks just) costs.

(4)   Where such security has been given in the case of an untraced creditor, the court may direct that particulars of the alleged debt, and the security, be advertised in such manner as it thinks just.

(5)   If the court directs such advertisement and no claim on the security is made within 12 months from the date of the advertisement (or the first advertisement, if more than one), the court must, on application, order the security to be released.

(6)   In determining whether to annul a bankruptcy order under section 282(1)(b), the court may, if it thinks just and without prejudice to the generality of its discretion under section 282(1), take into account whether any sums have been paid or payment of any sums has been secured in respect of post-commencement interest on the bankruptcy debts which have been proved.

(7)   For the purposes of paragraphs (2) and (6), security includes an undertaking given by a solicitor and accepted by the court.

(8)   For the purposes of paragraph (6), "post-commencement interest" means interest on the bankruptcy debts at the rate specified in section 328(5) in relation to periods during which those debts have been outstanding since the commencement of the bankruptcy.

**Derivation**—This rule derived from the Insolvency Rules 1986, SI 1986/1925, r 6.211.

## [2.679]

### 10.139 Notice to creditors

(1)   Where the official receiver has delivered notice of the debtor's bankruptcy to the creditors and the bankruptcy order is annulled, the official receiver must as soon as reasonably practicable deliver notice of the annulment to them.

(2)   Expenses incurred by the official receiver in delivering such notice are a charge in the official receiver's favour on the property of the former bankrupt, whether or not the property is actually in the official receiver's hands.

(3)   Where any property is in the hands of a trustee or any person other than the former bankrupt, the official receiver's charge is subject to any costs that may be incurred by the trustee or that other person in effecting realisation of the property for the purpose of satisfying the charge.

**Derivation**—This rule derived from the Insolvency Rules 1986, SI 1986/1925, r 6.212.

## [2.680]

### 10.140 Other matters arising on annulment

(1)   Within 28 days of the making of an order under section 282, the former bankrupt may require the official receiver to publish a notice of the making of the order in accordance with paragraphs (2) and (3).

(2)   As soon as reasonably practicable the notice must be—

(a)   gazetted; and

(b)   advertised in the same manner as the bankruptcy order to which it relates was advertised.

(3)   The notice must state—

(a)   the name of the former bankrupt;

(b)    the date on which the bankruptcy order was made;

(c)    that the bankruptcy order against the former bankrupt has been annulled under section 282(1); and

(d)    the date of the annulment.

(4)  Where the former bankrupt—

(a)    has died; or

(b)    is a person lacking capacity to manage the person's own affairs (within the meaning of the Mental Capacity Act 2005);

the reference to the former bankrupt in paragraph (1) is to be read as referring to the former bankrupt's personal representative or, as the case may be, a person appointed by the court to represent or act for the former bankrupt.

**Derivation**—This rule derived from the Insolvency Rules 1986, SI 1986/1925, r 6.213.

## [2.681]

### 10.141 Trustee's final account

(1)  Where a bankruptcy order is annulled under section 282, this does not of itself release the trustee from any duty or obligation, imposed on the trustee by or under the Act or these Rules, to account for all of the trustee's transactions in connection with the former bankrupt's estate.

(2)  The trustee must deliver a copy of the trustee's final account to the Secretary of State as soon as practicable after the court's order annulling the bankruptcy order.

(3)  The trustee must file a copy of the final account with the court.

(4)  The final account must include a summary of the trustee's receipts and payments in the administration, and contain a statement to the effect that the trustee has reconciled the account with that which is held by the Secretary of State in respect of the bankruptcy.

(5)  The trustee is released from such time as the court may determine, having regard to whether—

(a)    the trustee has delivered the final accounts under paragraph (2); and

(b)    any security given under rule 10.138 has been, or will be, released.

**Derivation**—This rule derived from the Insolvency Rules 1986, SI 1986/1925, r 6.214.

CHAPTER 17

DISCHARGE

## [2.682]

### Note

[Note: a document required by the Act or these Rules must also contain the standard contents set out in Part 1.]

## [2.683]

### 10.142 Application for suspension of discharge

(1)  The following applies where the official receiver or trustee (if different) applies to the court for an order under section 279(3) (suspension of automatic discharge), but not where the official receiver makes that application under rule 10.104 on the adjournment of the bankrupt's public examination.

(2)  The official receiver or trustee must file, with the application, evidence in support setting out the reasons why it appears that such an order should be made.

(3)  The court must fix a venue for the hearing of the application, and deliver notice of it to the official receiver, the trustee, and the bankrupt.

(4)  Copies of the official receiver's report under this rule must be delivered by the official receiver to the bankrupt and any trustee who is not the official receiver, so as to reach them at least 21 days before the date fixed for the hearing.

(5)   Copies of the trustee's evidence in support of the application must be delivered by the trustee to the official receiver and the bankrupt at least 21 days before the date fixed for the hearing.

(6)   If the bankrupt intends to deny or dispute any statements in the official receiver's or trustee's evidence in support then the bankrupt must not later than five business days before the date of the hearing, file with the court a notice specifying the statements which the bankrupt intends to deny or dispute.

(7)   If the bankrupt files such a notice under paragraph (6), the bankrupt must deliver copies of it, not less than three business days before the date of the hearing, to the official receiver and any trustee.

(8)   If the court makes an order suspending the bankrupt's discharge, copies of the order must be delivered by the court to the official receiver, any trustee and the bankrupt.

(9)   An order of suspension of discharge under section 279(3) must be headed "Suspension of Discharge" and must contain—

    (a)    identification details for the proceedings;

    (b)    the name and title of the judge making the order;

    (c)    identification and contact details for the applicant who will be the official receiver or the trustee;

    (d)    the date of the bankruptcy order;

    (e)    a statement that it appears to the court that the bankrupt has failed or is failing to comply with the bankrupt's obligations under the Act for the reasons specified in the order;

    (f)    a statement in what respect the bankrupt has failed to comply with the bankrupt's obligations under the Act;

    (g)    an order that the relevant period for the purpose of section 279 will cease to run for either—

        (i)    a specified period, or

        (ii)    until specified conditions have been fulfilled;

    (h)    the period or conditions referred to in paragraph (g); and

    (i)    the date of the order.

**Derivation**—This rule derived from the Insolvency Rules 1986, SI 1986/1925, r 6.215.

**[2.684]**

### 10.143   Lifting of suspension of discharge

(1)   Where the court has made an order under section 279(3) that the period specified in section 279(1) will cease to run, the bankrupt may apply to it for the order to be discharged.

(2)   The court must fix a venue for the hearing of the application and deliver notice of it to the bankrupt.

(3)   The bankrupt must, not less than 28 days before the date fixed for the hearing, deliver notice of the venue with a copy of the application to the official receiver and any trustee.

(4)   The official receiver and the trustee may appear and be heard on the bankrupt's application.

(5)   Whether or not they appear, the official receiver and trustee may file with the court a report containing evidence in support of any matters which either of them considers ought to be drawn to the court's attention.

(6)   If the court made an order under section 279(3)(b), the court may request a report from the official receiver or the trustee as to whether or not the condition specified in the order has been fulfilled.

(7)   Copies of a report filed under paragraph (5) or requested by the court under paragraph (6) must be delivered by the official receiver or trustee to the bankrupt and to either the official receiver or trustee (depending on which has filed the report), not later than 14 days before the hearing.

(8) The bankrupt may, not later than five business days before the date of the hearing, file with the court a notice specifying any statements in the official receiver's or trustee's report which the bankrupt intends to deny or dispute.

(9) If the bankrupt files such a notice, the bankrupt must deliver copies of it to the official receiver and the trustee not less than three business days before the date of the hearing.

(10) If on the bankrupt's application the court discharges the order under section 279(3) (being satisfied that the period specified in section 279(1) should begin to run again), it must deliver to the bankrupt a certificate that it has done so, and must deliver copies of the certificate to the official receiver and the trustee (if different).

(11) The court's order lifting the suspension of discharge must contain—

    (a)    identification details for the proceedings;

    (b)    the name and title of the judge making the order;

    (c)    the date and terms of the order made under section 279;

    (d)    a statement that the bankrupt specified in the order has made the application;

    (e)    a statement whether or not the court has taken into consideration the report of the official receiver or of the trustee or both in this matter;

    (f)    an order discharging the order suspending discharge; and

    (g)    state the date of the order.

(12) The certificate that the order suspending discharge has been lifted must contain—

    (a)    identification details for the proceedings;

    (b)    the date of the bankruptcy order;

    (c)    the date of the order suspending discharge;

    (d)    a statement that the court has made—

        (i)    the bankruptcy order specified in this order against the bankrupt specified in this order, and

        (ii)    the order suspending the bankrupt's discharge specified in this order;

    (e)    a statement that it is certified that the order of suspension of discharge was lifted on the date specified in this order; and

    (f)    the date of the certificate.

**Derivation**—This rule derived from the Insolvency Rules 1986, SI 1986/1925, r 6.216.

## [2.685]

### 10.144 Certificate of discharge from bankruptcy order made otherwise than on a bankruptcy application

(1) A bankrupt may apply to the court for a certificate of discharge where the bankruptcy order was made otherwise than on a bankruptcy application.

(2) Where it appears to the court that the bankrupt is discharged, whether by expiration of time or otherwise, the court must deliver a certificate of discharge to the former bankrupt.

(3) The certificate of discharge must be headed "Certificate of Discharge" and must contain—

    (a)    identification details for the proceedings;

    (b)    the date of the bankruptcy order;

    (c)    the statement that the former bankrupt was discharged from bankruptcy;

    (d)    the date of discharge from bankruptcy; and

    (e)    the date of the certificate.

(4) The certificate must also state—

    (a)    that the former bankrupt may request in writing notice of the discharge to be gazetted and advertised in the same manner as the bankruptcy order; and

    (b)    that such a request must be delivered to the official receiver within 28 days of the making of the certificate of discharge.

(5)   As soon as reasonably practicable after delivery of such a request to the official receiver the notice of discharge must be gazetted, and advertised in the same manner as the bankruptcy order.

(6)   The notice must contain—

    (a)   the name of the former bankrupt;

    (b)   the date of the bankruptcy order;

    (c)   the statement that a certificate of discharge has been delivered to the former bankrupt;

    (d)   the date of the certificate; and

    (e)   the date from which the discharge is effective.

(7)   An application for a notice of discharge and a request in writing that the notice be gazetted and advertised may be made by the former bankrupt's personal representative or, as the case may be, a person appointed by the court to represent or act for the former bankrupt where the former bankrupt—

    (a)   has died; or

    (b)   is a person lacking capacity to manage the person's own affairs (within the meaning of the Mental Capacity Act 2005).

**Derivation**—This rule derived from the Insolvency Rules 1986, SI 1986/1925, rr 6.219(3), 6.220.

[2.686]

### 10.145 Certificate of discharge from bankruptcy order made on a bankruptcy application

(1)   A bankrupt may apply to the official receiver for a certificate of discharge where the bankruptcy order was made on a bankruptcy application.

(2)   The bankrupt must send the application to the official receiver with the prescribed fee.

(3)   Where it appears to the official receiver that the bankrupt is discharged, the official receiver must deliver a certificate of discharge to the former bankrupt by electronic means.

(4)   The certificate of discharge must be headed "Certificate of Discharge" and must contain—

    (a)   identification details for the former bankrupt;

    (b)   the date of the bankruptcy order;

    (c)   a statement that the former bankrupt was discharged from bankruptcy;

    (d)   the date of discharge from the bankruptcy; and

    (e)   the date of the certificate.

(5)   The certificate must also state—

    (a)   that the former bankrupt may request in writing notice of the discharge to be gazetted and advertised in the same manner as the bankruptcy order; and

    (b)   that such a request must be delivered to the official receiver within 28 days of the making of the certificate of discharge.

(6)   As soon as reasonably practicable after delivery of such a request to the official receiver the notice of discharge must be gazetted, and advertised in the same manner as the bankruptcy order.

(7)   The notice must contain—

    (a)   the name of the former bankrupt;

    (b)   the date of the bankruptcy order;

    (c)   the statement that a certificate of discharge has been delivered to the former bankrupt;

    (d)   the date of the certificate; and

    (e)   the date from which the discharge is effective.

(8)   An application for a notice of discharge and a request in writing that the notice be gazetted and advertised may be made by the former bankrupt's personal representative

or, as the case may be, a person appointed by the court to represent or act for the former bankrupt where the former bankrupt—

    (a)    has died; or

    (b)    is a person lacking capacity to manage the person's own affairs (within the meaning of the Mental Capacity Act 2005).

**Derivation**—This rule derived from the Insolvency Rules 1986, SI 1986/1925, rr 6.219(3), 6.220.

## [2.687]

### 10.146 Bankrupt's debts surviving discharge

[Note: see also section 281 (effect of discharge).]

Discharge does not release the bankrupt from any obligation arising—

    (a)    under a confiscation order made under section 1 of the Drug Trafficking Offences Act 1986;

    (b)    under a confiscation order made under section 1 of the Criminal Justice (Scotland) Act 1987;

    (c)    under a confiscation order made under section 71 of the Criminal Justice Act 1988;

    (d)    under a confiscation order made under Parts 2, 3 or 4 of the Proceeds of Crime Act 2002; or

    (e)    from a payment out of the social fund under section 138(1)(b) of the Social Security Contributions and Benefits Act 1992 by way of crisis loan or budgeting loan.

**Derivation**—This rule derived from the Insolvency Rules 1986, SI 1986/1925, r 6.223.

## [2.688]

### 10.147 Costs under this Chapter

In no case do any costs or expenses arising under this Chapter fall on the official receiver personally.

**Derivation**—This rule derived from the Insolvency Rules 1986, SI 1986/1925, r 6.222.

CHAPTER 18

PRIORITY OF PAYMENT OF COSTS ETC OUT OF THE BANKRUPT'S ESTATE

## [2.689]

### Note

[Note: a document required by the Act or these Rules must also contain the standard contents set out in Part 1.]

## [2.690]

### 10.148 Expenses

All fees, costs, charges and other expenses incurred in the course of the bankruptcy are to be treated as expenses of the bankruptcy.

**Derivation**—This rule derived from the Insolvency Rules 1986, SI 1986/1925, r 12.2.

**Trustee's costs of a bankrupt's appeal**—While costs incurred in the appeal of a bankruptcy order are expenses of the bankruptcy, that does not preclude the court from making a costs order that primary liability for the payment of costs fall elsewhere than the estate, such as on the bankrupt personally, if appropriate: *Cooke v Dunbar Assets plc* [2016] EWHC 1888 (Ch), [2016] BPIR 1339.

**Court's power to assess trustee's litigation costs**—Roth J rejected a trustee in bankruptcy's submission in *Ardawa v Uppal* [2019] EWHC 1663 (Ch), [2019] BPIR 1086 that rr 10.148 and 10.149 were an exhaustive code governing a trustee's costs of legal proceedings. The trustee submitted that was the case 'however excessive or exorbitant the court may think those costs are', with the debtor's right of challenge determined by r 18.35. The judge held that the fact that a trustee's costs of legal proceedings are payable out of the estate determines the source from which the funds will come, but does not remove the normal role of the court in assessing those costs (at [33]–[34]). In *Ardawa*, subject to the question of costs there was a likely surplus for the bankrupt, and as the costs related to an unsuccessful appeal the bankrupt had brought, he was in the best position to present arguments opposing the costs sought by the trustee and as a consequence was entitled to be heard on the point (at [10]).

**[2.691]**

### 10.149 General rule as to priority

The expenses of the bankruptcy are payable out of the bankrupt's estate in the following order of priority—

(a) expenses or costs which—

    (i) are properly chargeable or incurred by the official receiver or the trustee in preserving, realising or getting in any of the assets of the bankrupt or otherwise relating to the conduct of any legal proceedings which the official receiver or the trustee has power to bring (whether the claim on which the proceedings are based forms part of the bankrupt's estate or otherwise) or defend,

    (ii) relate to the employment of a shorthand writer, if appointed by an order of the court made at the instance of the official receiver in connection with an examination, or

    (iii) are incurred in holding an examination under rule 10.102 (examinee unfit) where the application was made by the official receiver;

(b) any other expenses incurred or disbursements made by the official receiver or under the official receiver's authority, including those incurred or made in carrying on the business of a debtor or bankrupt;

(c) the fees payable under any order made under section 415 or 415A, including those payable to the official receiver (other than the fee referred to in sub-paragraph (d)), and any remuneration payable to the official receiver under general regulations;

(d) the fee payable under any order made under section 415 for the performance by the official receiver of the general duties of the official receiver and any repayable sum deposited under any such order as security for the fee;

(e) . . .

(f) the cost of any security provided by an interim receiver, trustee or special manager in accordance with the Act or these Rules;

(g) the remuneration of the interim receiver (if any);

(h) any sum deposited on an application for the appointment of an interim receiver;

(i) the costs of the petitioner, and of any person appearing on the petition whose costs are allowed by the court;

(j) the remuneration of the special manager (if any);

(k) any amount payable to a person or firm employed or authorised, under rules 10.59, 10.60 or 10.64, to assist in the preparation of a statement of affairs or of accounts;

(l) any allowance made, by order of the court, in respect of costs on an application for release from the obligation to submit a statement of affairs, or for an extension of time for submitting such a statement;

(m) the costs of employing a shorthand writer in any case other than one appointed by an order of the court at the instance of the official receiver in connection with an examination;

(n) any necessary disbursements by the trustee in the course of the trustee's administration (including any . . . expenses incurred by members of the creditors' committee or their representatives and allowed by the trustee under rule 17.24, but not including any payment of capital gains tax in circumstances referred to in sub-paragraph (q));

(o)    the remuneration or emoluments of any person (including the bankrupt) who has been employed by the trustee to perform any services for the bankrupt's estate, as required or authorised by or under the Act or these Rules;

(p)    the remuneration of the trustee, up to any amount not exceeding that which is payable under Schedule 11;

(q)    the amount of any capital gains tax on chargeable gains accruing on the realisation of any asset of the bankrupt (irrespective of the person by whom the realisation is effected);

(r)    the balance, after payment of any sums due under sub-paragraph (p), of any remuneration due to the trustee; and

(s)    any other expenses properly chargeable by the trustee in carrying out the trustee's functions in the bankruptcy.

**Derivation**—This rule derived from the Insolvency Rules 1986, SI 1986/1925, r 6.224.

**Amendments**—SI 2017/366; SI 2017/1115; SI 2019/146, as from IP completion day (as defined in the European Union (Withdrawal Agreement) Act 2020, s 39(1)–(5)).

**General note**—These provisions correspond with and are analogous to those in r 3.51 (administration), r 6.42 (creditors' voluntary winding up) and r 7.108 (compulsory winding up). For commentary see the notes to those provisions. The expenses of the bankruptcy should not be concerned with the priority of debts therein, as provided for in s 328.

As to r 10.149(i), in *Edgeworth Capital (Luxembourg) SARL v Maud* [2020] EWHC 1469 (Ch), Snowden J declined to award costs as an expense of the bankruptcy (and doubted he had jurisdiction to do so) to a creditor who had presented a second petition against the bankrupt and on which no order was ultimately made. By analogy with r 7.108, the list of expenses in r 10.149 must be taken to be exhaustive, with the court having no inherent jurisdiction to enlarge them. Snowden J emphasised that this was not a simple question of deciding the incidence of costs as between parties to litigation, but an application to award such costs *and* to order that those costs should be paid in priority to the ordinary unsecured creditors in the bankruptcy ([91]–[105]).

CHAPTER 19

SECOND BANKRUPTCY

**[2.692]**

**Note**

[Note: a document required by the Act or these Rules must also contain the standard contents set out in Part 1.]

**[2.693]**

**10.150 Scope of this Chapter**

[Note: "the earlier bankruptcy", "the existing trustee" and "the later bankruptcy" are defined in section 334(1).]

The rules in this Chapter relate to the manner in which, in the case of a second bankruptcy, the existing trustee is to deal with property and money to which section 334(3) applies until there is a trustee of the bankrupt's estate in the later bankruptcy.

**Derivation**—This rule derived from the Insolvency Rules 1986, SI 1986/1925, r 6.225.

**General note**—See s 334 and s 335 and the notes thereto.

**[2.694]**

**10.151 General duty of existing trustee**

(1)   The existing trustee must take into custody or under control the property and money to which section 334(3) applies so far as this has not already been done in the earlier bankruptcy.

(2)   Where any of that property consists of perishable goods, or goods the value of which is likely to diminish if they are not disposed of, the existing trustee has power to sell or otherwise dispose of those goods.

(3) The proceeds of such a sale or disposal must be held, under the existing trustee's control, with the other property and money comprised in the bankrupt's estate.

Derivation—This rule derived from the Insolvency Rules 1986, SI 1986/1925, r 6.226.

General note—See s 334 and s 335 and the notes thereto.

## [2.695]

### 10.152 Delivery up to later trustee

The existing trustee must, if requested by the later trustee for the purposes of the later bankruptcy, deliver to the later trustee as soon as reasonably practicable all the property and money in the existing trustee's custody or under the existing trustee's control under rule 10.151.

Derivation—This rule derived from the Insolvency Rules 1986, SI 1986/1925, r 6.227.

## [2.696]

### 10.153 Existing trustee's expenses

Any expenses incurred by the existing trustee in compliance with section 335(1) and this Chapter must be paid out of, and are a charge on, all of the property and money referred to in section 334(3), whether in the hands of the existing trustee or of the later trustee for the purposes of the later bankruptcy.

Derivation—This rule derived from the Insolvency Rules 1986, SI 1986/1925, r 6.228.

CHAPTER 20

CRIMINAL BANKRUPTCY

## [2.697]

Note

[Note: a document required by the Act or these Rules must also contain the standard contents set out in Part 1.]

## [2.698]

### 10.153A Application

The rules in this chapter apply to proceedings arising out of criminal bankruptcy orders.

Amendments—Inserted by SI 2017/366.

## [2.699]

### 10.154 Contents of petition

The petition must contain—

- (a) identification details for the debtor;
- (b) the name and postal address of the petitioner if other than the Official Petitioner;
- (c) the occupation (if any) of the debtor;
- (d) any other address at which the debtor has resided at or after the time the petition debt was incurred;
- (e) any other name by which the debtor is or has been known;
- (f) the trading name, business address and nature of the business of any business carried on by the debtor;
- (g) details of any other businesses which have been carried on by the debtor at or after the time the petition debt was incurred;
- (h) a statement that the petitioner requests that court make a bankruptcy order against the debtor;

(i)   a statement that a criminal bankruptcy order was made against the debtor at the court specified in this petition and that an office copy of the order accompanies the petition;

(j)   the name of the court that made the criminal bankruptcy order;

(k)   a statement that the criminal bankruptcy order—

  (i)   remains in force, or

  (ii)  was amended by the Court of Appeal on the date specified in this petition, that an office copy of the order of the Court of Appeal accompanies the petition and that the order as amended by the Court of Appeal remains in force;

(l)   a statement that according to the criminal bankruptcy order the debtor is indebted to the persons specified in this petition as having suffered loss or damage in the aggregate sum of the amount of loss or damage suffered specified in this petition;

(m)  the names and addresses of the persons referred to in paragraph (k); and

(n)   the amount of loss or damage suffered referred to in paragraph (k).

**Derivation**—This rule derived from the Insolvency Rules 1986, SI 1986/1925, Sch 4, Fm 6.79.

## [2.700]

### 10.155  Status and functions of Official Petitioner

(1)   The Official Petitioner is to be treated for all purposes of the Act and these Rules as a creditor of the bankrupt.

(2)   The Official Petitioner may attend or be represented at any meeting of creditors, and is to be given any notice under the Act or these Rules which is required or authorised to be delivered to creditors; and the requirements of these Rules as to the delivery and use of proxies do not apply to the Official Petitioner.

**Derivation**—This rule derived from the Insolvency Rules 1986, SI 1986/1925, r 6.230.

## [2.701]

### 10.156  Interim receivership

The rules in Chapter 4 of this Part about the appointment of an interim receiver apply in criminal bankruptcy only in so far as they provide for the appointment of the official receiver as interim receiver.

**Derivation**—This rule derived from the Insolvency Rules 1986, SI 1986/1925, r 6.231.

## [2.702]

### 10.157  Proof of bankruptcy debts and notice of order

(1)   The making of a bankruptcy order on a criminal bankruptcy petition does not affect the right of creditors to prove for their debts arising otherwise than in consequence of the criminal proceedings.

(2)   A person specified in a criminal bankruptcy order as having suffered loss or damage must be treated as a creditor of the bankrupt; and a copy of the order is sufficient evidence of that person's claim, subject to its being shown by any party to the bankruptcy proceedings that the loss or damage actually suffered was more or (as the case may be) less than the amount specified in the order.

(3)   The requirements of these Rules about proofs do not apply to the Official Petitioner.

(4)   In criminal bankruptcy, notice of the making of the bankruptcy order and blank proofs must be delivered by the official receiver to every creditor who is known to the official receiver within 12 weeks from the making of the bankruptcy order.

**Derivation**—This rule derived from the Insolvency Rules 1986, SI 1986/1925, r 6.232.

**[2.703]**

### 10.158 Rules not applying in criminal bankruptcy

The following rules do not apply in criminal bankruptcy—

    (a)    (*revoked*)

    (b)    Chapter 6 of this Part, except rules 10.86 (release of official receiver) and 10.91 (power of court to set aside transactions);

    (c)    rule 15.21(a) and (b) (chair at meetings); and

    (d)    Part 17 (creditors' and liquidation committees).

Derivation—This rule derived from the Insolvency Rules 1986, SI 1986/1925, r 6.234.
Amendments—SI 2017/366.

**[2.704]**

### 10.159 Annulment of criminal bankruptcy order

Chapter 16 of this Part (annulment of bankruptcy order) applies to an application to the court under section 282(2) as it applies to an application under section 282(1), with any necessary modifications.

Derivation—This rule derived from the Insolvency Rules 1986, SI 1986/1925, r 6.234(3).

**[2.705]**

### 10.160 Application by bankrupt for discharge

(1)   A bankrupt who applies under section 280 for an order of discharge must deliver notice of the application to the official receiver, and deposit with the official receiver such sum as the official receiver may require for the purpose of covering the costs of the application.

(2)   The court, if satisfied that the bankrupt has complied with paragraph (1), must fix a venue for the hearing of the application, and give at least 42 days' notice of it to the official receiver and the bankrupt.

(3)   The official receiver must deliver notice of the application and venue to—

    (a)    the trustee; and

    (b)    every creditor who, to the official receiver's knowledge, has a claim outstanding against the bankrupt's estate which has not been satisfied.

(4)   These notices must be delivered not later than 14 days before the date fixed for the hearing of the bankrupt's application.

Derivation—This rule derived from the Insolvency Rules 1986, SI 1986/1925, r 6.217.

**[2.706]**

### 10.161 Report of official receiver

(1)   Where the bankrupt makes an application under section 280, the official receiver must, at least 21 days before the date fixed for the hearing of the application, file with the court a report containing—

    (a)    particulars of any failure by the bankrupt to comply with the bankrupt's obligations under Parts 8 to 11 of the Act;

    (b)    the circumstances surrounding the present bankruptcy, and those surrounding any previous bankruptcy of the bankrupt;

    (c)    the extent to which, in the present and in any previous bankruptcy, the bankrupt's liabilities have exceeded the bankrupt's assets; and

    (d)    particulars of any distribution which has been, or is expected to be, made to creditors in the present bankruptcy or, if such is the case, that there has been and is to be no distribution; and

    (e)    any other matters which in the official receiver's opinion ought to be brought to the court's attention.

(2)   The official receiver must deliver a copy of the report to the bankrupt and the trustee, so as to reach them at least 14 days before the date of the hearing of the application under section 280.

(3)   The bankrupt may, not later than five business days before the date of the hearing, file with the court a notice specifying any statements in the official receiver's report which the bankrupt intends to deny or dispute.

(4)   Such a notice must be authenticated and dated by the bankrupt and must contain the bankrupt's name and postal address.

(5)   The bankrupt must deliver copies of such a notice to the official receiver and the trustee not less than three business days before the date of the hearing.

(6)   The official receiver, the trustee and any creditor may appear on the hearing of the bankrupt's application, and may make representations and put to the bankrupt such questions as the court allows.

Derivation—This rule derived from the Insolvency Rules 1986, SI 1986/1925, r 6.218.

## [2.707]

### 10.162  Order of discharge

(1)   An order of the court under section 280(2)(b) (discharge absolutely) or (c) (discharge subject to conditions relating to income or property) must contain—

(a)   the name of the court;

(b)   identification details for the bankrupt;

(c)   the date of the bankruptcy order;

(d)   the date of the report of the official receiver in the matter;

(e)   the statement that the court has taken into consideration the report of the official receiver specified in the order as to the bankrupt's conduct and affairs, including the bankrupt's conduct during the bankruptcy;

(f)   an order—

(i)   that the bankrupt be discharged absolutely, or

(ii)   that the bankrupt be discharged but that the bankrupt's discharge be suspended until the conditions specified in the order are fulfilled;

(g)   the date on which the order is made;

(h)   the date on which the order takes effect; and

(i)   any conditions required to be fulfilled for discharge.

(2)   Copies of any order made on an application by the bankrupt for discharge under section 280 must be delivered by the court to the bankrupt, the trustee and the official receiver.

(3)   The order must contain a notice to the bankrupt stating that should the bankrupt require notice of the order to be gazetted and to be advertised in the same manner as the bankruptcy order was advertised, then the bankrupt must within 28 days deliver a notice of that requirement to the official receiver.

Derivation—This rule derived from the Insolvency Rules 1986, SI 1986/1925, r 6.219.

## [2.708]

### 10.163  Deferment of issue of order pending appeal

An order made by the court on an application by the bankrupt for discharge under section 280 must not be drawn up or gazetted until the time allowed for appealing has expired or, if an appeal is entered, until the appeal has been determined.

Derivation—This rule derived from the Insolvency Rules 1986, SI 1986/1925, r 6.221.

## [2.709]

### 10.164  Costs under this Chapter

In no case do any costs or expenses arising under this Chapter fall on the official receiver personally.

## CHAPTER 21

### MISCELLANEOUS RULES IN BANKRUPTCY

**[2.710]**

**Note**

[Note: a document required by the Act or these Rules must also contain the standard contents set out in Part 1.]

**[2.711]**

#### 10.165 Amendment of title of proceedings

(1)   At any time after the making of a bankruptcy order, the official receiver may amend the title of the proceedings.

(2)   An official receiver who amends the title of proceedings must as soon as reasonably practicable—

(a)   where the bankruptcy is on the petition of a creditor, file a notice of the amendment with the court;

(b)   where the bankruptcy is on the application of a debtor, file a notice of the amendment on the bankruptcy file; and

(c)   make an application to the Chief Land Registrar to amend the register of writs and orders.

(3)   If the official receiver thinks fit to gazette the amendment then it must be gazetted as soon as reasonably practicable, and may be advertised in such other manner as the official receiver thinks fit.

(4)   The notice must—

(a)   state that the title of the proceedings has been amended; and

(b)   specify the amendment.

*Derivation*—This rule derived from the Insolvency Rules 1986, SI 1986/1925, r 6.35.

**[2.712]**

#### 10.166 Application for redirection order

(1)   This rule applies where the official receiver or trustee other than the official receiver makes an application to the court under section 371(1) (re-direction of bankrupt's letters etc).

(2)   The application must be made without notice to the bankrupt or any other person, unless the court directs otherwise.

(3)   Where the applicant is the official receiver the applicant must file with the court with the application a report setting out the reasons why the order is sought.

(4)   Where the applicant is the trustee the applicant must file with the court a witness statement setting out the reasons why the order is sought.

(5)   The court must fix a venue for the hearing of the application if the court thinks just and deliver notice to the applicant.

(6)   The court may make an order on such conditions as it thinks just.

(7)   The order must identify the person on whom it is to be served, and need not be served on the bankrupt unless the court so directs.

*Derivation*—This rule derived from the Insolvency Rules 1986, SI 1986/1925, r 6.235A.

**[2.713]**

#### 10.167 Bankrupt's home: property falling within section 283A

(1)   Where it appears to a trustee that section 283A(1) applies, the trustee must deliver notice as soon as reasonably practicable to—

(a)   the bankrupt;

(b)   the bankrupt's spouse or civil partner (in a case falling within section 283A(1)(b)); and

(c)      the former spouse or former civil partner of the bankrupt (in a case falling within section 283A(1)(c)).

(2)   Such a notice must contain—

     (a)      the name of the bankrupt;

     (b)      the address of the dwelling-house;

     (c)      if the dwelling-house is registered land, the title number; and

     (d)      the date by which the trustee must have delivered the notice.

(3)   A trustee must not deliver such a notice any later than 14 days before the third anniversary of the bankruptcy order or, 14 days before the third anniversary of when the official receiver or trustee became aware of the property.

**Derivation**—This rule derived from the Insolvency Rules 1986, SI 1986/1925, r 6.237.

## [2.714]

### 10.168 Application in relation to the vesting of an interest in a dwelling-house (registered land)

(1)   This rule applies where—

     (a)      the bankrupt's estate includes an interest in a dwelling-house which at the date of bankruptcy was the sole or principal residence of—

         (i)      the bankrupt,

         (ii)      the bankrupt's spouse or civil partner, or

         (iii)      a former spouse or former civil partner of the bankrupt; and

     (b)      the dwelling-house is registered land; and

     (c)      an entry has been made relating to the bankruptcy in the individual register of the dwelling-house or the register has been altered to reflect the vesting of the bankrupt's interest in a trustee in bankruptcy.

(2)   Where such an interest ceases to be comprised in the bankrupt's estate and vests in the bankrupt under either section 283A(2) or 283A(4) of the Act, or under section 261(8) of the Enterprise Act 2002, the trustee must, within five business days of the vesting, make such application to the Chief Land Registrar as is necessary to show in the individual register of the dwelling-house that the interest has vested in the bankrupt.

(3)   The trustee's application must be made in accordance with the Land Registration Act 2002 and must be accompanied by—

     (a)      evidence of the trustee's appointment (where not previously provided to the Chief Land Registrar); and

     (b)      a certificate from the trustee stating that the interest has vested in the bankrupt under section 283A(2) or 283A(4) of the Act or section 261(8) of the Enterprise Act 2002 (whichever is appropriate).

(4)   As soon as reasonably practicable after making such an application, the trustee must deliver notice of the application—

     (a)      to the bankrupt; and

     (b)      to the bankrupt's spouse, former spouse, civil partner or former civil partner if the dwelling-house was the sole or principal residence of that person.

(5)   The trustee must deliver notice of the application to every person who (to the trustee's knowledge) claims an interest in, or is under any liability in relation to, the dwelling-house.

**Derivation**—This rule derived from the Insolvency Rules 1986, SI 1986/1925, r 6.237A.

## [2.715]

### 10.169 Vesting of bankrupt's interest (unregistered land)

(1)   Where an interest in a dwelling-house which at the date of the bankruptcy was the sole or principal residence of—

     (a)      the bankrupt;

     (b)      the bankrupt's spouse or civil partner; or

     (c)      a former spouse or former civil partner of the bankrupt;

ceases to be comprised in the bankrupt's estate and vests in the bankrupt under either section 283A(2) or 283A(4) of the Act or section 261(8) of the Enterprise Act 2002 and the dwelling-house is unregistered land, the trustee must as soon as reasonably practicable deliver to the bankrupt a certificate as to the vesting.

(2)   Such a certificate is conclusive proof that the interest mentioned in paragraph (1) has vested in the bankrupt.

(3)   As soon as reasonably practicable after delivering the certificate, the trustee must deliver a copy of the certificate to the bankrupt's spouse, former spouse, civil partner or former civil partner if the dwelling-house was the sole or principal residence of that person.

(4)   The trustee must deliver a copy of the certificate to every person who (to the trustee's knowledge) claims an interest in, or is under any liability relating to, the dwelling-house.

Derivation—This rule derived from the Insolvency Rules 1986, SI 1986/1925, r 6.237B.

## [2.716]

### 10.170  Vesting of bankrupt's estate: substituted period

[Note: section 283A(6)(b) gives the court the power to impose a longer period than the three years mentioned in section 283A(2) in such circumstances as the court thinks appropriate.]

(1)   For the purposes of section 283A(2) the period of one month is substituted for the period of three years set out in that section where the trustee has delivered notice to the bankrupt that the trustee considers—

    (a)    the continued vesting of the property in the bankrupt's estate to be of no benefit to creditors; or

    (b)    the re-vesting to the bankrupt will make dealing with the bankrupt's estate more efficient.

(2)   The one month period starts from the date of the notice.

Derivation—This rule derived from the Insolvency Rules 1986, SI 1986/1925, rr 6.237C, 6.237CA.

## [2.717]

### 10.171  Charging order

(1)   This rule applies where the trustee applies to the court under section 313 for an order imposing a charge on property consisting of an interest in a dwelling-house.

(2)   The respondents to the application must be—

    (a)    any spouse or former spouse or civil partner or former civil partner of the bankrupt having or claiming to have an interest in the property;

    (b)    any other person appearing to have an interest in the property; and

    (c)    such other persons as the court may direct.

(3)   The trustee must make a report to the court, containing the following particulars—

    (a)    the extent of the bankrupt's interest in the property;

    (b)    the amount which, at the date of the application, remains owing to unsecured creditors of the bankrupt; and

    (c)    an estimate of the cost of realising the interest.

(4)   The terms of the charge to be imposed must be agreed between the trustee and the bankrupt or in the absence of an agreement must be settled by the court.

(5)   The rate of interest applicable under section 313(2) is the rate specified in section 17 of the Judgments Act 1838 on the day on which the charge is imposed, and the rate must be stated in the court's order imposing the charge.

(6)   The court's order must also—

    (a)    describe the property to be charged;

    (b)    state whether the title to the property is registered and, if it is, specify the title number;

(c)  set out the extent of the bankrupt's interest in the property which has vested in the trustee;

(d)  indicate by reference to any, or the total, amount which is payable otherwise than to the bankrupt out of the bankrupt's estate and of interest on that amount, how the amount of the charge to be imposed is to be ascertained;

(e)  set out the conditions (if any) imposed by the court under section 3(1) of the Charging Orders Act 1979; and

(f)  identify the date any property charged under section 313 will cease to be comprised in the bankrupt's estate and will, subject to the charge (and any prior charge), vest in the bankrupt.

(7)  The date referred to in paragraph (6)(f) must be that of the registration of the charge in accordance with section 3(2) of the Charging Orders Act 1979 unless the court is of the opinion that a different date is appropriate.

(8)  Where the court order is capable of giving rise to an application under the Land Charges Act 1972 or the Land Registration Act 2002 the trustee must, as soon as reasonably practicable after the making of the court order or at the appropriate time, make the appropriate application to the Chief Land Registrar.

(9)  The appropriate application is—

(a)  an application under section 6(1)(a) of the Land Charges Act 1972 (application for registration in the register of writs and orders affecting land); or

(b)  an application under the Land Registration Act 2002 for an entry in the register in relation to the charge imposed by the order; and such application under that Act as is necessary to show in the individual register or registers of the dwelling-house that the interest has vested in the bankrupt.

(10)  In determining the value of the bankrupt's interest for the purposes of paragraph (6)(c), the court must disregard that part of the value of the property in which the bankrupt's interest subsists which is equal to the value of—

(a)  any loans secured by mortgage or other charge against the property;

(b)  any other third party interest; and

(c)  the reasonable costs of sale.

**Derivation**—This rule derived from the Insolvency Rules 1986, SI 1986/1925, r 6.237D, Sch 4, Fm 6.79A.

PART 11  BANKRUPTCY AND DEBT RELIEF RESTRICTIONS ORDERS AND UNDERTAKINGS AND THE INSOLVENCY REGISTERS

CHAPTER 1

INTERPRETATION

**[2.718]**

**11.1  References to the Secretary of State**

References to the Secretary of State in Chapters 2 and 3 include the official receiver acting on the direction of the Secretary of State in making an application for—

(a)  a bankruptcy restrictions order or an interim bankruptcy restrictions order in accordance with paragraph 1(2)(b) or 5(3)(b) respectively of Schedule 4A; or

(b)  a debt relief restrictions order or an interim debt relief restrictions order in accordance with paragraph 1(2)(b) or 5(3)(b) respectively of Schedule 4ZB.

**Derivation**—This rule derived from the Insolvency Rules 1986, SI 1986/1925, rr 6.240, 6.252.

CHAPTER 2

BANKRUPTCY AND DEBT RELIEF RESTRICTIONS ORDERS (SCHEDULES 4ZB AND 4A)

**[2.719]**

Note

[Note: a document required by the Act or these Rules must also contain the standard contents set out in Part 1.]

**[2.720]**

**11.2 Application for a bankruptcy or debt relief restrictions order**

(1)   An application by the Secretary of State to the court for a bankruptcy restrictions order under paragraph 1 of Schedule 4A, or for a debt relief restrictions order under paragraph 1 of Schedule 4ZB, must be supported by a report by the Secretary of State.

(2)   The report must—

(a)   set out the conduct which the Secretary of State thinks justifies making a bankruptcy restrictions order or a debt relief restrictions order; and

(b)   contain the evidence on which the Secretary of State relies in support of the application.

(3)   Any evidence in support of the application provided by a person other than the Secretary of State must be given in a witness statement.

(4)   The date for the hearing must be at least eight weeks after the date when the court fixes the venue for the hearing.

Derivation—This rule derived from the Insolvency Rules 1986, SI 1986/1925, rr 6.241, 6.253.

**[2.721]**

**11.3 Service of the application on the bankrupt or debtor**

(1)   The Secretary of State must serve a notice of the application and the venue on the bankrupt or debtor not more than 14 days after the application is filed with the court.

(2)   The notice must be accompanied by—

(a)   a copy of the application;

(b)   a copy of the Secretary of State's report;

(c)   a copy of any other evidence filed in support of the application; and

(d)   a document for completion as an acknowledgement of service.

(3)   The bankrupt or debtor must file the acknowledgement of service, indicating whether or not the application is contested, not more than 14 days after service of the application.

(4)   A bankrupt or debtor who fails to file an acknowledgement of service within that time may attend the hearing of the application but may not take part in the hearing unless the court gives permission.

Derivation—This rule derived from the Insolvency Rules 1986, SI 1986/1925, rr 6.242, 6.254.

**[2.722]**

**11.4 The bankrupt's or debtor's evidence opposing an application**

(1)   A bankrupt or debtor who wishes to oppose the application must—

(a)   file with the court any evidence for the court to take into consideration within 28 days of service of the application; and

(b)   serve a copy of it on the Secretary of State within three business days of filing the evidence with the court.

(2)   The Secretary of State must file with the court any evidence in reply within 14 days from receiving the copy of the bankrupt's or debtor's evidence, and must serve a copy of that evidence on the bankrupt or debtor as soon as reasonably practicable.

Derivation—This rule derived from the Insolvency Rules 1986, SI 1986/1925, rr 6.243, 6.255.

**[2.723]**

**11.5 Making a bankruptcy or debt relief restrictions order**

(1) The court may make a bankruptcy restrictions order or a debt relief restrictions order whether or not the bankrupt or debtor appears or has filed evidence.

(2) Where the court makes such an order, it must deliver two sealed copies to the Secretary of State as soon as reasonably practicable.

(3) As soon as reasonably practicable after receiving the sealed copies, the Secretary of State must deliver one of them to the bankrupt or debtor.

Derivation—This rule derived from the Insolvency Rules 1986, SI 1986/1925, rr 6.244, 6.256.

CHAPTER 3

INTERIM BANKRUPTCY AND DEBT RELIEF RESTRICTIONS ORDERS

**[2.724]**

**Note**

[Note: a document required by the Act or these Rules must also contain the standard contents set out in Part 1.]

**[2.725]**

**11.6 Application for an interim bankruptcy or debt relief restrictions order**

(1) An application by the Secretary of State to the court for an interim bankruptcy restrictions order under paragraph 5 of Schedule 4A or an interim debt relief restrictions order under paragraph 5 of Schedule 4ZB, must be supported by a report by the Secretary of State.

(2) The report must—

(a) set out the conduct which the Secretary of State thinks justifies making an interim bankruptcy restrictions order or an interim debt relief restrictions order; and

(b) contain the evidence on which the Secretary of State relies in support of the application including evidence of why it would be in the public interest to make such an order.

(3) Any evidence in support of the application provided by a person other than the Secretary of State must be given in a witness statement.

(4) The Secretary of State must deliver a notice of the application to the bankrupt or debtor at least two business days before the date set for the hearing unless the court directs otherwise.

(5) The notice must be accompanied by—

(a) a copy of the application;

(b) a copy of the Secretary of State's report;

(c) a copy of any other evidence filed in support of the application; and

(d) a document for completion as an acknowledgement of service.

(6) The bankrupt or debtor may file with the court evidence for the court to take into consideration and may appear at the hearing.

Derivation—This rule derived from the Insolvency Rules 1986, SI 1986/1925, rr 6.245, 6.246, 6.257, 6.258.

**[2.726]**

**11.7 Making an interim bankruptcy or debt relief restrictions order**

(1) The court may make an interim bankruptcy restrictions order or interim debt relief restrictions order whether or not the bankrupt or debtor appears or has filed evidence.

(2) Where the court makes such an order, it must deliver two sealed copies of the order to the Secretary of State as soon as reasonably practicable.

(3) As soon as reasonably practicable after receiving the sealed copies, the Secretary of State must deliver one of them to the bankrupt or debtor.

Derivation—This rule derived from the Insolvency Rules 1986, SI 1986/1925, rr 6.247, 6.259.

**[2.727]**

### 11.8 Application to set aside an interim order

(1)   A bankrupt subject to an interim bankruptcy restrictions order or a debtor subject to an interim debt relief restrictions order may apply to the court to set the order aside.

(2)   The application must be supported by a witness statement stating the grounds on which it is made.

(3)   The bankrupt or debtor must deliver to the Secretary of State, not less than five business days before the hearing—

  (a)   a notice of the venue;

  (b)   a copy of the application; and

  (c)   a copy of the supporting witness statement.

(4)   The Secretary of State may attend the hearing and call the attention of the court to any matter which seems to be relevant, and may give evidence or call witnesses.

Derivation—This rule derived from the Insolvency Rules 1986, SI 1986/1925, rr 6.248, 6.260.

**[2.728]**

### 11.9 Order setting aside an interim order

(1)   Where the court sets aside an interim bankruptcy restrictions order or an interim debt relief restrictions order, it must deliver two sealed copies of the order to the Secretary of State as soon as reasonably practicable.

(2)   As soon as reasonably practicable after receiving the sealed copies, the Secretary of State must deliver one of them to the bankrupt or debtor.

Derivation—This rule derived from the Insolvency Rules 1986, SI 1986/1925, rr 6.248(5), (6), 260(5), (6).

CHAPTER 4

BANKRUPTCY RESTRICTIONS AND DEBT RELIEF RESTRICTIONS UNDERTAKINGS

**[2.729]**

Note

[Note: a document required by the Act or these Rules must also contain the standard contents set out in Part 1.]

**[2.730]**

### 11.10 Acceptance of a bankruptcy restrictions or a debt relief restrictions undertaking

(1)   A bankruptcy restrictions undertaking authenticated by the bankrupt is accepted by the Secretary of State for the purposes of paragraph 9 of Schedule 4A when the Secretary of State authenticates the undertaking.

(2)   A debt relief restrictions undertaking authenticated by a person in relation to whom a debt relief order has been made is accepted by the Secretary of State for the purposes of paragraph 9 of Schedule 4ZB when the Secretary of State authenticates the undertaking.

Derivation—This rule derived from the Insolvency Rules 1986, SI 1986/1925, rr 6.249, 6.261.

**[2.731]**

### 11.11 Notification

(1)   The Secretary of State must, as soon as reasonably practicable after accepting a bankruptcy restrictions undertaking or a debt relief restrictions undertaking, deliver copies to the person who offered the undertaking and to the official receiver.

(2) In the case of a bankruptcy restrictions undertaking the Secretary of State must also file a copy with the court in the case of a creditor's bankruptcy petition or on the bankruptcy file in the case of a debtor's bankruptcy application.

**Derivation**—This rule derived from the Insolvency Rules 1986, SI 1986/1925, rr 6.250, 6.262.

## [2.732]

### 11.12 Application to annul a bankruptcy restrictions or a debt relief restrictions undertaking

(1) An application by a bankrupt or debtor to annul or vary an undertaking under paragraph 9(3)(a) or (b) of Schedule 4A or paragraph 9(3)(a) or (b) of Schedule 4ZB must be supported by a witness statement stating the grounds on which the application is made.

(2) The bankrupt or debtor must, at least 28 days before the date fixed for the hearing, deliver to the Secretary of State—

    (a) a notice of the venue;

    (b) a copy of the application; and

    (c) a copy of the supporting witness statement.

(3) The Secretary of State may attend the hearing and call the attention of the court to any matter which seems to be relevant, and may give evidence or call witnesses.

(4) Where the court annuls or varies a bankruptcy restrictions undertaking or debt relief restrictions undertaking, it must deliver two sealed copies of the order to the Secretary of State as soon as reasonably practicable.

(5) As soon as reasonably practicable after receiving the sealed copies, the Secretary of State must deliver one of them to the bankrupt or debtor.

**Derivation**—This rule derived from the Insolvency Rules 1986, SI 1986/1925, rr 6.251, 6.263.

## CHAPTER 5

### Insolvency Registers: General

## [2.733]

### 11.13 Maintenance of the registers and inspection

(1) The Secretary of State must maintain the individual insolvency register of matters relating to bankruptcies, debt relief orders and IVAs in accordance with Chapter 6.

(2) The Secretary of State must maintain the bankruptcy restrictions register and the debt relief restrictions register in accordance with Chapter 7.

(3) The registers must be available to be searched electronically by members of the public at any time unless there is malfunction or error in the electronic operation of the registers.

(4) Any person may request the official receiver to make a search of the registers on any business day between 9am and 5pm.

(5) An obligation under this Part to enter information on, or delete information from, a register, must be performed as soon as is reasonably practicable after it arises.

**Derivation**—This rule derived from the Insolvency Rules 1986, SI 1986/1925, r 6A.1.

## CHAPTER 6

### Individual Insolvency Register

## [2.734]

### 11.14 Entry of information on the individual insolvency register: IVAs

(1) This rule applies where—

    (a) an IVA has been accepted by the debtor's creditors; and

    (b) the Secretary of State receives any of the following—

        (i) a report under rule 8.26 (report on approval of IVA), or

> > (ii)   a notice under rules 8.27(5) (notice of revocation or suspension of IVA), 8.27(6) (notice of expiry of suspension) or 8.31 (notice that the IVA has been terminated or fully implemented).

(2)   The Secretary of State must enter the following on the individual insolvency register—

> (a)   the debtor's identification details;
> (b)   the debtor's date of birth;
> (c)   the date on which the IVA was approved by the creditors;
> (d)   the debtor's gender;
> (e)   any name other than the name in which the debtor entered into IVA by which the debtor was or is known;
> (f)   a statement as to whether the IVA has been—
>> (i)   completed in accordance with its terms,
>> (ii)   terminated, or
>> (iii)   revoked; and
> (g)   the name and address of the supervisor.

(3)   This rule is subject to any court order for the non-disclosure of the debtor's current address made under rule 20.2 (debtors at risk of violence: proposed IVA) or 20.3 (debtors at risk of violence: IVA).

**Derivation**—This rule derived from the Insolvency Rules 1986, SI 1986/1925, r 6A.2A.

## [2.735]

**11.15  Deletion of information from the individual insolvency register: IVAs**
The Secretary of State must delete from the individual insolvency register all information concerning an IVA three months after receiving one of the following—

> (a)   a notice under rule 8.27(5) of the making of a revocation order in relation to the IVA; or
> (b)   a notice under rule 8.31(3) of the termination or full implementation of the IVA.

**Derivation**—This rule derived from the Insolvency Rules 1986, SI 1986/1925, r 6A.3.

## [2.736]

**11.16  Entry of information on to the individual insolvency register: bankruptcy orders**
(1)   Where the official receiver receives a copy of a bankruptcy order from the court under rule 10.32, or from the adjudicator under rule 10.45, the official receiver must cause the following to be entered on the individual insolvency register—

> (a)   the matters listed in rules 10.8 or the information set out in Part 1 of Schedule 7, relating to the debtor as they are stated in the bankruptcy petition or bankruptcy application;
> (b)   the date of the bankruptcy order; and
> (c)   identification details for the proceedings.

(2)   The official receiver must cause to be entered on to the individual insolvency register the following information—

> (a)   the bankrupt's identification details and date of birth;
> (b)   the bankrupt's gender and occupation (if any);
> (c)   the date of a previous bankruptcy order or debt relief order (if any) made against the bankrupt in the period of six years before the latest bankruptcy order (if there is more than one such previous order only the latest and excluding any bankruptcy order that was annulled or any debt relief order that was revoked);
> (d)   any name by which the bankrupt was known, not being the name in which the individual was made bankrupt;
> (e)   the address of any business carried on by the bankrupt and the name in which that business was carried on if carried on in a name other than the name in which the individual was made bankrupt;

(f)     the name and address of any insolvency practitioner appointed to act as trustee in bankruptcy;

(g)     the address at which the official receiver may be contacted;

(h)     the automatic discharge date under section 279; and

(i)     where a bankruptcy order is annulled or rescinded by the court, the fact that such an order has been made, the date on which it is made and (if different) the date on which it has effect.

(3)   Where the official receiver receives a copy of an order under rule 10.104(6) or 10.142(8) suspending the bankrupt's discharge the official receiver must cause to be entered on to the individual insolvency register—

(a)     the fact that such an order has been made; and

(b)     the period for which the discharge has been suspended or that the relevant period has ceased to run until the fulfilment of conditions specified in the order.

(4)   Where the official receiver receives under rule 10.143(10) a copy of a certificate of the discharge of an order under section 279(3) the official receiver must cause the following to be entered on the individual insolvency register—

(a)     that the court has discharged the order made under section 279(3); and

(b)     the new date of discharge of the bankrupt.

(5)   Where the order discharging the order under section 279(3) is subsequently rescinded by the court, the official receiver must cause the register to be amended accordingly.

(6)   Where a bankrupt is discharged from bankruptcy under section 279(1), the official receiver must cause the fact and date of such discharge to be entered in the individual insolvency register.

(7)   This rule is subject to any court order for the non-disclosure of the debtor's current address made under rule 20.5 (persons at risk of violence: bankruptcy application) or 20.6 (debtors at risk of violence: bankruptcy and debt relief proceedings).

**Derivation**—This rule derived from the Insolvency Rules 1986, SI 1986/1925, r 6A.4.

## [2.737]

**11.17 Deletion of information from the individual insolvency register: bankruptcy orders**

The Secretary of State must delete from the individual insolvency register all information concerning a bankruptcy where—

(a)     the bankruptcy order has been annulled under section 261(2)(a), 261(2)(b) or section 282(1)(b) and a period of three months has elapsed since a notice of the annulment was delivered to the official receiver;

(b)     the bankrupt has been discharged from the bankruptcy and a period of three months has elapsed from the date of discharge;

(c)     the bankruptcy order is annulled under section 282(1)(a) and 28 days have elapsed since a notice of the annulment was delivered to the official receiver under rule 10.137(3); or

(d)     an order has been made by the court under section 375 rescinding the bankruptcy order and 28 days have elapsed since receipt by the official receiver.

**Derivation**—This rule derived from the Insolvency Rules 1986, SI 1986/1925, r 6A.5.

## [2.738]

**11.18 Entry of information on to the individual insolvency register: debt relief orders**

(1)   The official receiver must cause to be entered on to the individual insolvency register after the making of a debt relief order the following information relating to the order or the debtor—

(a)     as they are stated in the debtor's application—

(i)     the debtor's identification details and date of birth,

(ii)    the debtor's gender and occupation (if any),

(iii)    the name or names in which the debtor has carried on business, if other than the debtor's true name, and

(iv)    the nature of the debtor's business and the address or addresses at which the debtor carries or has carried it on and whether alone or with others;

(b)    the date of the debt relief order;

(c)    the reference number of the order;

(d)    the date of the end of the moratorium period; and

(e)    the date of a previous bankruptcy order or a debt relief order (if any) made against the debtor in the period of six years before the latest debt relief order (if there is more than one such order only the latest and excluding any bankruptcy order that was annulled or debt relief order that was revoked).

(2)   Except where information concerning a debt relief order has been deleted under rule 11.19, the official receiver must also cause to be entered on the register in relation to the order—

(a)    where the moratorium period is terminated early, the fact that such has happened, the date of early termination and whether the early termination is on revocation of the debt relief order or by virtue of any other enactment;

(b)    where the moratorium period is extended, the fact that such has happened, the date on which the extension was made, its duration and the date of the new anticipated end of the moratorium period; or

(c)    where the debtor is discharged from all qualifying debts, the date of such discharge.

(3)   This rule is subject to any court order for the non-disclosure of the debtor's current address made under rule 20.4 (debtors at risk of violence: debt relief application) or 20.6 (debtors at risk of violence: bankruptcy and debt relief proceedings).

**Derivation**—This rule derived from the Insolvency Rules 1986, SI 1986/1925, r 6A.5A.

## [2.739]

### 11.19 Deletion of information from the individual insolvency register: debt relief orders

The Secretary of State must delete from the individual insolvency register all information concerning a debt relief order where three months have elapsed from the date on which—

(a)    the debt relief order has been revoked; or

(b)    the debtor has been discharged from the qualifying debts.

**Derivation**—This rule derived from the Insolvency Rules 1986, SI 1986/1925, r 6A.5B.

CHAPTER 7

BANKRUPTCY AND DEBT RELIEF RESTRICTIONS REGISTER

## [2.740]

### 11.20 Bankruptcy restrictions and debt relief restrictions orders and undertakings: entry of information on the registers

(1)   Where any of the following orders are made against a bankrupt or a debtor the Secretary of State must enter on the bankruptcy restrictions register or debt relief restrictions register as appropriate the specified information—

(a)    an interim bankruptcy restrictions order;

(b)    a bankruptcy restrictions order;

(c)    an interim debt relief restrictions order; or

(d)    a debt relief restrictions order.

(2)   The specified information is—

(a)    the bankrupt's or debtor's identification details;

(b)    the bankrupt's or debtor's gender;

(c)    the bankrupt's or debtor's occupation (if any);

(d)    a statement that an interim bankruptcy restrictions order, a bankruptcy restrictions order, an interim debt relief restrictions order or a debt relief restrictions order has been made against the bankrupt or debtor;

(e)    the date of the order;

(f)    the court in which the order was made and the court or order reference number; and

(g)    the duration of the order.

(3)   Where a bankruptcy restrictions undertaking is given by a bankrupt or a debt relief restrictions undertaking is given by a debtor, the Secretary of State must enter on to the bankruptcy restrictions or debt relief restrictions register—

(a)    the bankrupt's or debtor's identification details;

(b)    the bankrupt's or debtor's gender;

(c)    the bankrupt's or debtor's occupation (if any);

(d)    a statement that a bankruptcy restrictions undertaking or debt relief restrictions undertaking has been given;

(e)    the date of the acceptance of the bankruptcy restrictions undertaking or debt relief restrictions undertaking by the Secretary of State; and

(f)    the duration of the bankruptcy restrictions undertaking or debt relief restrictions undertaking.

(4)   This rule is subject to any court order for the non-disclosure of the debtor's current address made under rules 20.6 (debtors at risk of violence: bankruptcy and debt relief proceedings) or 20.7 (additional provisions in respect of order under rule 20.6(4)).

**Derivation**—This rule derived from the Insolvency Rules 1986, SI 1986/1925, rr 6A.6, 6A.7A.

## [2.741]

### 11.21 Deletion of information from the registers

The Secretary of State must delete from the bankruptcy restrictions register or debt relief restrictions register all information relating to an interim bankruptcy restrictions order, bankruptcy restrictions order, interim debt relief restrictions order, debt relief restrictions order, bankruptcy restrictions undertaking or debt relief restrictions undertaking after—

(a)    receipt of notice that the order or undertaking has ceased to have effect; or

(b)    the expiry of the order or undertaking.

**Derivation**—This rule derived from the Insolvency Rules 1986, SI 1986/1925, rr 6A.7, 6A.7B.

CHAPTER 8

RECTIFICATION OF REGISTERS AND DEATH OF PERSONS ON REGISTER

## [2.742]

### 11.22 Rectification of the registers

Where the Secretary of State becomes aware of an inaccuracy in information on the individual insolvency register, the bankruptcy restrictions register or the debt relief restrictions register, the Secretary of State must rectify the inaccuracy as soon as reasonably practicable.

**Derivation**—This rule derived from the Insolvency Rules 1986, SI 1986/1925, r 6A.8.

## [2.743]

### 11.23 Death of a person about whom information is held on a register

Where the Secretary of State receives notice of the date of the death of a person in relation to whom information is held on any of the registers, the Secretary of State must cause the fact and date of the person's death to be entered on to the register.

**Derivation**—This rule derived from the Insolvency Rules 1986, SI 1986/1925, r 6A.8(2).

## PART 12 COURT PROCEDURE AND PRACTICE

**General note**—See *Practice Direction - Insolvency Proceedings* (July 2020) [2020] BPIR 1211 and, in response to the Covid-19 pandemic, *Temporary Insolvency Practice Direction Supporting the Insolvency Practice Direction*, presently extended to 30 September 2021 (subject to possible further extension). See Appendix 2 and Appendix 3, respectively, to this work.

### CHAPTER 1

#### General
*Application of the Civil Procedure Rules 1998*

### [2.744]

#### 12.1 Court rules and practice to apply

(1) The provisions of the CPR (including any related Practice Directions) apply for the purposes of proceedings under Parts 1 to 11 of the Act with any necessary modifications, except so far as disapplied by or inconsistent with these Rules.

(2) All insolvency proceedings must be allocated to the multi-track for which CPR Part 29 makes provision, and accordingly those provisions of the CPR which provide for directions questionnaires and track allocation do not apply.

(3) CPR Part 32 applies to a false statement in a document verified by a statement of truth made under these Rules as it applies to a false statement in a document verified by a statement of truth made under CPR Part 22.

**Derivation**—This rule derived from the Insolvency Rules 1986, SI 1986/1925, r 7.51A.

**General note**—Like the former r 7.51A(1), r 12.1 integrates the CPR into insolvency proceedings with necessary modifications and except so far as inconsistent with the Rules. By way of an example under the former provision, in *Thakerer v Lynch Hall & Hornby (No 2) (Practice Note)* [2005] EWHC 2752 (Ch), [2006] 1 WLR 1513 Lewison J held that a Bankruptcy Registrar had jurisdiction to make a third party debt order under CPR Pt 72. Likewise, a provision as important but relatively uncommonly relied upon such as CPR 21.3(3) which, where a party lacks capacity, prevents any party from taking any step in proceedings without permission of the court until the protected party has a litigation friend, will apply in insolvency proceedings by operation of IR 2016, r 12.1: *Kumar v Hellard* [2021] EWHC 181 (Ch). The inconsistency between the CPR and the IR 1986 is not always obvious and is likely to require continuing resolution by the court. For example, in *Hayes v Hayes* [2014] EWHC 2694 (Ch), [2014] BPIR 1212 Nugee J held that CPR, r 32.5 (use at trial of witness statements which have been served) was inconsistent with the 1986 Rules or was something that required a necessary modification for the purposes of the former r 7.51A in the context of disputed petition debts or cross-claims. It seems very likely that the costs provisions in CPR Pt 44 are invoked into insolvency proceedings by r 12.1(1) subject to express exceptions such as, for example, r 15.35(6) (no personal liability for costs on part of convenor or chair or creditors' meeting where decision overruled).

At an overarching level, what r 12.1 seeks to do, like the former r 7.51A, is to provide a degree of uniformity with the now well embedded CPR provisions, including the tenets of efficient case management (on which see the observations of David Richards J in *Re Lehman Bros International (Europe)* [2014] EWHC 1687 (Ch), [2014] BPIR 1259), whilst, at the same time, preserving certain procedural aspects peculiar to insolvency. This is not so much a matter of linkage as it is co-existence and interaction. The courts will have to continue to resolve the priority of one regime over another in working out that inter-relationship over time.

In the absence of any inconsistency between CPR 3.4 and the IR 2016, the court has power to strike out an unarguable bankruptcy petition: *Sandelson v Mulville* [2019] EWHC 1620 (Ch) at [2] (Chief ICCJ Briggs) in which the parties were in agreement on the proposition just mentioned. Adopting the same reasoning, the same principle ought to extend to any form of unarguable insolvency litigation under the IA 1986 or the IR 2016, absent inconsistency with CPR 3.4.

**Sub-rule 12.1(3)**—See *Atkinson v Varma* [2020] EWHC 1868 (Ch) and *Varma v Atksinon* [2020] EWCA Civ 1602 on criminal sanctions under CPR 32.14 (false statements).

**[2.745]**

**12.2 Performance of functions by the Court**

(1)   Anything to be done under or by virtue of the Act or these Rules by, to or before the court may be done by, to or before a judge, District Judge or a registrar.

(2)   The registrar or District Judge may authorise any act of a formal or administrative character which is not by statute that person's responsibility to be carried out by the chief clerk or any other officer of the court acting on that person's behalf, in accordance with directions given by the Lord Chancellor.

(3)   The hearing of an application must be in open court unless the court directs otherwise.

**Derivation**—This rule derived from the Insolvency Rules 1986, SI 1986/1925, r 7.6A.

**General note**—Rules 12.2(1) and (3) override contrary provisions in the CPR.

CHAPTER 2

COMMENCEMENT OF INSOLVENCY PROCEEDINGS IN THE COUNTY COURT

**[2.746]**

**Note**

[A document required by the Act or these Rules must also contain the standard contents set out in Part 1.]

**[2.747]**

**12.3 Commencement of insolvency proceedings under Parts 1 to 7 of the Act (corporate insolvency proceedings)**

(1)   Where section 117 of the Act, as extended in its application by section 251, gives jurisdiction to the County Court in respect of proceedings under Parts 1 to 7 of the Act any such proceedings when they are commenced in the County Court may only be commenced in the hearing centre which serves the area in which the company's registered office is situated.

(2)   However if the registered office is situated in an area served by a hearing centre for which Schedule 6 lists an alternative court or hearing centre then any such proceedings in the County Court may only be commenced in that alternative court or hearing centre.

**Derivation**—This rule derived from the Insolvency (Commencement of Proceedings) and Insolvency Rules 1986 (Amendment) Rules 2014, SI 2014/817, r 2.

**[2.748]**

**12.4 Commencement of insolvency proceedings under Parts 7A to 11 of the Act (personal insolvency proceedings; bankruptcy)**

(1)   Proceedings under Parts 7A to 11 of the Act that are allocated in accordance with rule 12.5 to the London Insolvency District when they are commenced in the County Court may only be commenced in the County Court at Central London.

(2)   Elsewhere such proceedings when they are commenced in the County Court may only be commenced in the hearing centre determined in accordance with these Rules.

(3)   However if the hearing centre so determined is one for which Schedule 6 lists an alternative hearing centre then such proceedings when they are commenced in the County Court may only be commenced in that alternative hearing centre.

**Derivation**—This rule derived from the Insolvency (Commencement of Proceedings) and Insolvency Rules 1986 (Amendment) Rules 2014, SI 2014/817, r 3.

**[2.749]**

**12.5 Allocation of proceedings to the London Insolvency District**

The following proceedings are allocated to the London Insolvency District—

(a) bankruptcy petitions or applications in relation to a debt relief order under section 251M (powers of court in relation to debt relief orders) or 251N (inquiry into debtor's dealings and property) where—

    (i) the debtor is resident in England and Wales and within the six months immediately preceding the presentation of the petition or the making of the application the debtor carried on business within the area of the London Insolvency District—

      (aa) for the greater part of those six months, or

      (bb) for a longer period in those six months than in any other insolvency district,

    (ii) the debtor is resident in England and Wales and within the six months immediately preceding the presentation of the petition or the making of the application the debtor did not carry on business in England and Wales but resided within the area of the London Insolvency District for—

      (aa) the greater part of those six months, or

      (bb) a longer period in those six months than in any other insolvency district,

    (iii) the debtor is not resident in England and Wales but within the six months immediately preceding the presentation of the petition or the making of the application carried on business within the area of the London Insolvency District,

    (iv) the debtor is not resident in England and Wales and within the 6 months immediately preceding the presentation of the petition or the making of the application did not carry on business in England and Wales but resided within the area of the London Insolvency District, or

    (v) the debtor is not resident in England and Wales and within the 6 months immediately preceding the presentation of the petition or the making of the application the debtor neither carried on business nor resided in England and Wales;

(b) creditors' bankruptcy petitions presented by a Minister of the Crown or a Government Department, where either—

    (i) in any statutory demand on which the petition is based the creditor has indicated the intention to present a bankruptcy petition to a court exercising jurisdiction in relation to the London Insolvency District, or

    (ii) the petition is presented under section 267(2)(c) on the grounds specified in section 268(1)(b);

(c) bankruptcy petitions—

    (i) where the petitioner is unable to ascertain the place where the debtor resides or, if the debtor carries on business in England and Wales, both where the debtor resides and where the debtor carries on business, or

    (ii) where the debtor is a member of a partnership and—

      (aa) the partnership is being wound up by the High Court sitting in London; or

      (bb) a petition for the winding up of the partnership has been presented to the High Court sitting in London and at the time of the presentation of the bankruptcy petition, the petition for the winding up of the partnership has not been fully disposed of; and

(d) bankruptcy petitions based on criminal bankruptcy orders under section 264(1)(d).

**Derivation**—This rule derived from the Insolvency Rules 1986, SI 1986/1925, r 7.10ZA.

CHAPTER 3

MAKING APPLICATIONS TO COURT: GENERAL

**[2.750]**

Note

[Note: (1) a document required by the Act or these Rules must also contain the standard contents set out in Part 1 and an application to court must also contain the standard contents set out in rule 1.35;

(2) Paragraphs 3 and 4 of Schedule 5 make provision in relation to the court's power to extend the time for doing anything required by these Rules;

(3) the rules about the applications referred to in rule 12.6 are found in Chapter 2 of Part 3 (administration applications); Chapter 3 of Part 7 (petition for winding up order by creditor) and Chapter 4 of Part 7 (petition for winding up by contributory or office-holder) and Chapter 2 of Part 10 (creditor's bankruptcy petitions).]

**[2.751]**

**12.6 Preliminary**

This Chapter applies to an application made to the court except—

(a)   an administration application under Part 2 of the Act;

(b)   a petition for a winding-up order under Part 4 of the Act; and

(c)   a creditor's petition for a bankruptcy order under Part 9 of the Act.

**Derivation**—This rule derived from the Insolvency Rules 1986, SI 1986/1925, r 7.1.

**General note**—Other than the application and two forms of petition specifically identified in this rule, all other proceedings under the legislation are to be initiated or continued by means of an insolvency application notice.

**Claim under s 423 alleging transaction defrauding creditors**—Proceedings under s 423 do not constitute insolvency proceedings and may be commenced in any Division of the High Court or, as is less commonly the case, in the county court: *TSB Bank plc v Katz* [1997] BPIR 147 (Arden J, as she then was). To like effect see *Jyske Bank (Gibraltar) Ltd v Spjeldnaes* [2000] BCC 16 and *Fourie v Le Rou* [2004] EWHC 2557 (Ch), [2005] BPIR 779. Accordingly, therefore, a s 423 claim is capable of being commenced not only by way of an insolvency application but also by way of claim form under Part 7 of the CPR or, theoretically, but as would be far less likely given the almost inevitable disputes of fact involved, under Part 8 of the CPR.

**Hybrid and assigned claims**—In *Manolete Partners plc v Hayward and Barrett Holdings Ltd* [2021] EWHC 1481 (Ch) Chief ICCJ Briggs concluded, with some reluctance, that a misfeasance claim under s 212 pursued by a litigation funder as assignee from a liquidator, ought not to have been included in an application pursuing causes of action within s 246ZD issued by way of an insolvency application notice in Form IAA, as provided for in IR 2016, r 1.35. Rather, the s 212 claim should have been issued as a CPR Pt 7 claim because the assignee of the claim did not have standing for the purposes of s 212 as a liquidator, official receiver, contributory or creditor, and the office of liquidator was not capable of assignment. (The s 212 claim was allowed to proceed subject to payment of the £10,000 issue fee payable in respect of a Part 7 claim for the minimum sum claimed.) The judge's conclusion was despite the fact that, as is very commonly the case in practice, the factual background to each of the claims was identical or substantially similar and the self-evident advantage in having all claims arising out of the same facts pursued by the same party or parties brought in a single set of proceedings. At [60] the judge observed that the conclusion to which he was forced did 'not promote a convenient or sensible or economical use of court resources' and that an office-holder and assignee would be forced, as a consequence, to issue claims from an insolvency using different procedures in different lists of the Business and Property Courts with the attendant risk that, without transfer, such claims would fall subject to case management by different judges. The mischief identified by Judge Briggs might be cured by an amendment to r 1.35 extending the scope of the provision to any claim within the scope of the causes of action envisaged by s 212 but presently outside the scope of that provision in terms of standing.

**[2.752]**

**12.7 Filing of application**

[Note: see rule 1.46 for electronic delivery of documents to the court.]

An application filed with the court in hard-copy form must be accompanied by one copy and a number of additional copies equal to the number of persons who are to be served with the application.

**Derivation**—This rule derived from the Insolvency Rules 1986, SI 1986/1925, r 7.4(1).

## [2.753]

### 12.8 Fixing the venue

When an application is filed the court must fix a venue for it to be heard unless—
- (a) it considers it is not appropriate to do so;
- (b) the rule under which the application is brought provides otherwise; or
- (c) the case is one to which rule 12.12 applies.

**Derivation**—This rule derived from the Insolvency Rules 1986, SI 1986/1925, r 7.4(2).

## [2.754]

### 12.9 Service or delivery of application

(1) The applicant must serve a sealed copy of the application, endorsed with the venue for the hearing, on the respondent named in the application unless the court directs or these Rules provide otherwise.

(2) The court may also give one or more of the following directions—
- (a) that the application be served upon persons other than those specified by the relevant provision of the Act or these Rules;
- (b) that service upon, or the delivery of a notice to any person may be dispensed with;
- (c) that such persons be notified of the application and venue in such other a way as the court specifies; or
- (d) such other directions as the court sees fit.

(3) A sealed copy of the application must be served, or notice of the application and venue must be delivered, at least 14 days before the date fixed for its hearing unless—
- (a) the provision of the Act or these Rules under which the application is made makes different provision;
- (b) the case is urgent and the court acts under rule 12.10; or
- (c) the court extends or abridges the time limit.

**Derivation**—This rule derived from the Insolvency Rules 1986, SI 1986/1925, r 7.4(3)–(5).

**CIGA 2020**—This provision is affected by temporary measures at Sch 4, para 47 of CIGA 2020.

**General note**—For the inter-relationship between the predecessor to this rule and CPR 7.5 and 7.6 (service and extension of time for service of a claim) see *Re Kelcrown Ltd (in liq), Hunt v Dolan* [2017] EWHC 537 (Ch) (notwithstanding CPR imposing fixed period for service following issue and IR 2016 requiring service 14 days before hearing date, like principles applied in exercise of discretion as to whether to adjourn (which, on facts, had effect of extending time for service)).

**Rule 12.9(3)**—According to the decision of HHJ Paul Matthews in *Bell v Ide* [2020] EWHC 230 (Ch), a failure to serve a sealed copy of an application at least 14 days before the date fixed and endorsed on the application was not fatal and did not lead to the application being liable to be struck out. The point mattered because the respondents seeking striking out submitted that the adjournment of the original fixed hearing and its re-listing had the effect of extending time for service with the consequence that those respondents were deprived of a limitation defence that they would have had if the application had been rendered invalid for non-compliance with r 12.9(3) and the applicant trustees made to issue a fresh application. The judge considered that the limitation issue did not arise even if the limitation period had expired by the time of the application for an adjournment so as to require re-listing; Judge Matthews considered the contrary decision of Deputy ICCJ Prentis in *Re H S Works Ltd* [2018] EWHC 1405 (Ch) was wrong. In the Court of Appeal, *Re Ide (in bankruptcy)* [2020] EWCA Civ 1469 at [55] to [65], applying *Re Kelcrown* (see General note above), the decision of Judge Matthews was reversed. Having concluded that there is no difference in substance between a claim form not served in accordance with CPR 7.5 and an insolvency application notice not served in accordance with r 12.9, Nugee LJ could discern no difference in the approach in principle – that is, as established under the CPR - that ought to be taken to the application for an extension of time required to be made if either such proceedings were to continue. Nugee LJ pointed out at [63] that in cases where limitation is engaged upon the proceedings not being served in a timely fashion, limitation becomes a defence, not merely a procedural matter. There is no good reason why an application under the insolvency legislation should not be subject to the strictures applicable to claims under the CPR in that a defendant may expect a claimant to have to demonstrate exceptional circumstances in obtaining an extension of a limitation period where a claim form has not been served within the 4-month period for service.

**Assignment of claim by administrators**—Where administrators propose to assign a cause of action against a third party, the court applies the principles identified in *Citicorp Australia v Official Trustee in Bankruptcy* [1996] FCA 1115; *LF2 Ltd v Supperstone* [2018] EWHC 1776 (Ch), [2018] BPIR 1320 (para 74 claim). It is the objecting party, not the assignee, on which the burden rests in demonstrating that the claim has no prospect of success.

## [2.755]

### 12.10 Hearing in urgent case

(1) Where the case is urgent, the court may (without prejudice to its general power to extend or abridge time limits) hear the application immediately with or without notification to, or the attendance of, other parties.

(2) The application may be heard on terms providing for the filing or service of documents, notification, or the carrying out of other formalities as the court thinks just.

**Derivation**—This rule derived from the Insolvency Rules 1986, SI 1986/1925, r 7.4(6).

**General note**—The making of an insolvency application direct to the court without allowing for the usual first return date is usually inappropriate, save where justified by special facts or exceptional circumstances: *Re Cunningham* [2002] BPIR 302 at 307F–307H (Neuberger J).

## [2.756]

### 12.11 Directions

The court may at any time give such directions as it thinks just as to—

- (a) service or notice of the application on or to any person;
- (b) whether particulars of claim and defence are to be delivered and generally as to the procedure on the application including whether a hearing is necessary;
- (c) the matters to be dealt with in evidence; and
- (d) the manner in which any evidence is to be provided and in particular as to—
  - (i) the taking of evidence wholly or partly by witness statement or orally,
  - (ii) any report to be made by an office-holder, and
  - (iii) the cross-examination of the maker of a witness statement or of a report.

**Derivation**—This rule derived from the Insolvency Rules 1986, SI 1986/1925, r 7.10(3).

**General note**—These broad provisions provide for case management in insolvency proceedings, which powers may be exercised by the court at any stage of the proceedings. In practice, the provision of such directions at a first return date is very common, as is the agreement of directions between the parties in advance. The particular directions given by the court will necessarily turn on the factual and legal issues particular to a case and will require active case management by the court, assisted by the parties. For an example of the directions as to statements of case and witness evidence given in the context of an application by a liquidator under s 112 which raised complex issues of law and fact for the purposes of jurisdiction relevant to the Brussels Convention and proceedings issues in Italy see *Re Cover Europe Ltd* [2002] BPIR 931 at [42] (Leslie Kosmin QC sitting as a deputy High Court judge), a case in which remitting the matter to the Queen's Bench Division of the High Court was not considered appropriate.

## [2.757]

### 12.12 Hearing and determination without notice

(1) Where the Act and these Rules do not require service of a sealed copy of the application on, or notice of it to be delivered to, any person, the court may—

- (a) hear the application as soon as reasonably practicable;
- (b) fix a venue for the application to be heard, in which case rule 12.9 applies to the extent that it is relevant; or

     (c)    determine the application without a hearing.

(2)  However nothing in the Act or these Rules is to be taken as prohibiting the applicant from giving notice.

**Derivation**—This rule derived from the Insolvency Rules 1986, SI 1986/1925, r 7.5A.

## [2.758]

### 12.13 Adjournment of the hearing of an application

(1)  The court may adjourn the hearing of an application on such terms as it thinks just.

(2)  The court may give directions as to the manner in which any evidence is to be provided at a resumed hearing and in particular as to—

     (a)    the taking of evidence wholly or partly by witness statement or orally;

     (b)    the cross-examination of the maker of a witness statement; or

     (c)    any report to be made by an office-holder.

**Derivation**—This rule derived from the Insolvency Rules 1986, SI 1986/1925, r 7.10(1), (2).

**General note**—The decision in *Re Gunningham* [2002] BPIR 302, which addressed the former r 7.10(2) under the 1986 Rules, informs r 12.13(2). Rule 12.13(2) is not general in nature but is tied to any adjournment under r 12.13(1). The more general powers in r 12.11 may be of assistance.

As an example of the r 12.13(1) jurisdiction see *Brooker v Advanced Industrial Technology Corp Ltd* [2019] EWHC 3160 (Ch) (application by absent appellant debtors for adjournment of appeal against bankruptcy order made on the day of the appeal hearing, on the grounds of permitting the appellant debtors time to appoint solicitors dismissed given ample time previously to organise representation). A case management-type decision such as a decision to adjourn will face significant difficulties if appealed unless demonstrably perverse.

For an extraordinary case concerning adjournment in the context of counsel not attending court on grounds of professional difficulty arising out of a judge's refusal to recuse himself see *Axnoller Events Ltd v Brake* [2021] EWHC 828 (Ch).

## CHAPTER 4

MAKING APPLICATIONS TO COURT: SPECIFIC APPLICATIONS

## [2.759]

**Note**

[Note: a document required by the Act or these Rules must also contain the standard contents set out in Part 1.]

**General note**—Rules 12.14–12.26 are concerned with the mandatory and specific requirements of three classes of case (sub-divisions A to C below).

*Sub-division A: Applications in connection with section 176A (prescribed part)*

## [2.760]

### 12.14 Applications under section 176A(5) to disapply section 176A

(1)  An application under section 176A(5) must be accompanied by a witness statement of the liquidator, administrator or receiver.

(2)  The witness statement must state—

     (a)    the type of insolvency proceedings in which the application arises;

     (b)    a summary of the financial position of the company;

     (c)    the information substantiating the applicant's view that the cost of making a distribution to unsecured creditors would be disproportionate to the benefits; and

     (d)    whether any other office-holder is acting in relation to the company and, if so, that office-holder's address.

**Derivation**—This rule derived from the Insolvency Rules 1986, SI 1986/1925, r 7.3A.

**[2.761]**

### 12.15 Notice of application under section 176A(5)

(1) An application under section 176A(5) may be made without the application being served upon, or notification to any other party.

(2) However the office-holder making the application must notify any other office-holder who is acting in relation to the company . . . .

Derivation—This rule derived from the Insolvency Rules 1986, SI 1986/1925, r 7.4A.

Amendments—SI 2019/146, as from IP completion day (as defined in the European Union (Withdrawal Agreement) Act 2020, s 39(1)–(5)).

General note—The court will not grant an application on the sole ground that a dividend will be small. For discussion see *Re Hydroserve Ltd* [2008] BCC 175; *Re International Sections Ltd* [2009] BCC 574; *Blair Carnegie Nimmo, Gerard Anthony Friar the joint administrators of Castlebridge Plant Ltd (in administration)* [2015] CSOH 165 (Court of Session, Outer House).

**[2.762]**

### 12.16 Notice of an order under section 176A(5)

(1) Where the court makes an order under section 176A(5), the court must, as soon as reasonably practicable, deliver the sealed order to the applicant and a sealed copy to any other office-holder.

(2) The liquidator, administrator or receiver must, as soon as reasonably practicable, deliver notice of the order to each creditor unless the court directs otherwise.

(3) The court may direct that the requirement in paragraph (2) is complied with if a notice is published by the liquidator, administrator or receiver which states that the court has made an order disapplying the requirement to set aside the prescribed part.

(4) As soon as reasonably practicable the notice—
    (a)    must be gazetted; and
    (b)    may be advertised in such other manner as the liquidator, administrator, or receiver thinks fit.

(5) The liquidator, administrator or receiver must deliver a copy of the order to the registrar of companies as soon as reasonably practicable after the making of the order.

Derivation—This rule derived from the Insolvency Rules 1986, SI 1986/1925, r 12A.57.

Forms—The notice in r 12.16(2) and (4) is in Companies House Form NCOP.

*Sub-division B: Applications for private examination (sections 236, 251N and 366)*

**[2.763]**

### Note

[Note: for rules about public examinations see Chapter 13 of Part 7 and Chapter 8 of Part 10.]

General note—For general discussion in relation to the former but substantially identical IR 1986 r 9.2, see *Re Comet Group Ltd, Khan v Whirlpool UK Ltd* [2014] EWHC 3477 (Ch), [2015] BPIR 1.

**[2.764]**

### 12.17 Application of this sub-division and interpretation

(1) The rules in this sub-division apply to applications to the court for an order under—
    (a)    section 236 (inquiry into company's dealings);
    (b)    section 251N (debt relief orders—inquiry into dealings and property of debtor); and
    (c)    section 366 (inquiry into bankrupt's dealings and property) including section 366 as it applies by virtue of section 368.

(2) In this sub-division—
        "applicable section" means section 236, 251N or 366; and

"the insolvent" means the company, the debtor or the bankrupt as the case may be.

**Derivation**—This rule derived from the Insolvency Rules 1986, SI 1986/1925, r 9.1.

**The applicant**—The application is made by the incumbent office-holder: *Re Maxwell Communications Corp plc* [1994] BCC 741.

## [2.765]

### 12.18  Contents of application

(1)  An application to the court under section 236, 251N or 366 must state—

    (a)    the grounds on which it is made; and

    (b)    which one or more of the following orders is sought—

        (i)    for the respondent to appear before the court,

        (ii)    for the respondent to clarify any matter which is in dispute in the proceedings or to give additional information in relation to any such matter (if so Part 18 CPR (further information) applies to any such order),

        (iii)    for the respondent to submit witness statements (if so, particulars must be given of the matters to be included), or

        (iv)    for the respondent to produce books, papers or other records (if so, the items in question to be specified).

(2)  An application under an applicable section may be made without notice to any other party.

(3)  The court may, whatever the order sought in the application, make any order which it has power to make under the applicable section.

**Derivation**—This rule derived from the Insolvency Rules 1986, SI 1986/1925, r 9.2.

**General note**—On the nature of circumstances justifying an order under r 12.18(2) see *Hill v Van der Merwe* [2007] EWHC 1613 (Ch), [2007] BPIR 1562.

Under the former r 9.2 of the IR 1986 there was a requirement for a separate statement in the form of a sworn affidavit, setting out the grounds on which the application was made. Under the IR 2016 there is no requirement for a sworn statement. The statement in support of an application is confidential: *Re Aveling Barford Ltd* [1989] 1 WLR 360. Contrary to the pre-IA 1986 position where a statement was not filed or made available to the proposed examinee, following *Re British & Commonwealth Holdings plc* [1992] BCC 65 CA (and see *(No 2)* [1993] AC 426 HL), as a matter of practice, the court may order that the statement is disclosable, in whole or part, to the person against whom the order is sought where disclosure is necessary to enable the court to dispose fairly of an application to resist or set aside an order under s 236 in which circumstances the burden will shift to the office-holder in demonstrating a need to keep the statement confidential: *Re Murjani (a bankrupt)* [1996] 1 WLR 1498 at 1507D–1509A (Lightman J), a decision under the analogous s 366 IA 1986. Such an order is fact specific: see further the notes to s 236. In practice, the court and the other parties may be assisted by the placing of the confidential material of which the office-holder seeks to resist disclosure in a separate annex or attachment to the statement in support.

**Rule 12.18(1)(b)(i) to (iii)**—These provisions require particularity. An application, or order made on an application, may be open to challenge by way of striking out or dismissal on the basis that the application or order lacks the precision required by those provisions, such as where the case the examinee has to meet is not reasonably clear: *Re Aveling Barford Ltd* [1989] 1 WLR 360.

**Rule 12.18(2) – On notice or without notice?**—Although in keeping with the former practice, sub-rule (2) allows for the making of an application without notice, following the rejection of that approach, the usual way of making such an application is on notice: *Re Maxwell Communications Corp plc* [1994] BCC 741 at 747 and 752 (Vinelott J) and *Re Murjani* (above) at 1509D. A without notice application may, however, be justifiable on the facts. *Hill* (above) is also authority for the proposition that an application may be justified on a without notice basis where the examinee is implicated in large scale fraud and has proved uncooperative. Like a without notice application, an on-notice application carries an obligation of disclosure of all material facts on the part of the office-holder: *Re John T Rhodes (No 2)* (1987) 3 BCC 588 at 593. Such full disclosure does not, however, extend to without prejudice material: *Re Anglo American Insurance Co Ltd* [2002] BCC 715.

**Rule 12.18(3) and third parties**—Where an order is sought requiring a respondent to disclose material belonging to a third party, as a general rule the third party should be joined as a party to the application: *Re Murjani (a bankrupt)* [1996] 1 WLR 1498 at 1510H (Lightman J).

**[2.766]**

### 12.19 Order for examination etc

(1) Where the court orders the respondent to appear before it, it must specify the venue for the appearance.

(2) The date must not be less than 14 days from the date of the order.

(3) If the respondent is ordered to file with the court a witness statement or a written account, the order must specify—

    (a)    the matters which are to be dealt with in it; and

    (b)    the time within which it is to be delivered.

(4) If the order is to produce documents or other records, the time and manner of compliance must be specified.

(5) The applicant must serve a copy of the order on the respondent as soon as reasonably practicable.

**Derivation**—This rule derived from the Insolvency Rules 1986, SI 1986/1925, r 9.3.

**[2.767]**

### 12.20 Procedure for examination

(1) The applicant may attend an examination of the respondent, in person, or be represented by an appropriately qualified legal representative, and may put such questions to the respondent as the court may allow.

(2) Unless the applicant objects, the following persons may attend the examination with the permission of the court and may put questions to the respondent (but only through the applicant)—

    (a)    any person who could have applied for an order under the applicable section; and

    (b)    any creditor who has provided information on which the application was made under section 236 or 366.

(3) If the respondent is ordered to clarify any matter or to give additional information, the court must direct the respondent as to the questions which the respondent is required to answer, and as to whether the respondent's answers (if any) are to be made in a witness statement.

(4) The respondent may employ an appropriately qualified legal representative at the respondent's own expense, who may—

    (a)    put to the respondent such questions as the court may allow for the purpose of enabling the respondent to explain or qualify any answers given by the respondent; and

    (b)    make representations on the respondent's behalf.

(5) Such written record of the examination must be made as the court thinks proper and such record must be read either to or by the respondent and authenticated by the respondent at a venue fixed by the court.

(6) The record may, in any proceedings (whether under the Act or otherwise), be used as evidence against the respondent of any statement made by the respondent in the course of the respondent's examination.

**Derivation**—This rule derived from the Insolvency Rules 1986, SI 1986/1925, r 9.4.

**General note**—Albeit provided under the compulsion of a court order, the provision of information by an examinee to an office-holder amounts to the discharge of a public duty: see generally *Re Harvest Finance Ltd (in liquidation)* [2014] EWHC 4237 (Ch), [2015] 2 BCLC 240 (Registrar Jones; costs of compliance with order to deliver up documents under s 236 declined). Although an examinee will ordinarily be very unlikely to benefit from an award of costs, the issue remains open to argument: see *Morris v Bank of America National Trust & Saving Association* [1997] BCC 651 (Robert Walker J) and the conflicting decision in *Re Cloverbay Ltd (No 1)* [1989] 5 BCC 732 (Vinelott J).

**[2.768]**

### 12.21 Record of examination

(1) Unless the court otherwise directs, the record of questions put to the respondent, the respondent's answers and any witness statement or written account delivered to the court by the respondent in compliance with an order of the court under the applicable section are not to be filed with the court.

(2) The documents listed in paragraph (3) may not be inspected without the permission of the court, except by—

(a) the applicant for an order under the applicable section; or

(b) any person who could have applied for such an order in relation to the affairs of the same insolvent.

(3) The documents are—

(a) the record of the respondent's examination;

(b) copies of questions put to the respondent or proposed to be put to the respondent and answers to questions given by the respondent;

(c) any witness statement by the respondent; and

(d) any document on the court file that shows the grounds for the application for the order.

(4) The court may from time to time give directions as to the custody and inspection of any documents to which this rule applies, and as to the provision of copies of, or extracts from, such documents.

**Derivation**—This rule derived from the Insolvency Rules 1986, SI 1986/1925, r 9.5.

**General note**—For commentary on the exercise of discretion under what is now r 12.21(4) see *Re Arrows Ltd (No 4), Hamilton v Naviede* [1995] 2 AC 75; *Miller v Bain* [2002] BCC 899; *Hunt v Renzland* [2008] BPIR 1380; *Re Arrowfield Services Ltd* [2015] EWHC 3046 (Ch).

**[2.769]**

### 12.22 Costs of proceedings under sections 236, 251N and 366

(1) Where the court has ordered an examination of a person under an applicable section, and it appears to it that the examination was made necessary because information had been unjustifiably refused by the respondent, it may order that the respondent pay the costs of the examination.

(2) Where the court makes an order against a person under—

(a) section 237(1) or 367(1) (to deliver up property in any person's possession which belongs to the insolvent estate); or

(b) section 237(2) or 367(2) (to pay any amount in discharge of a debt due to the insolvent);

the costs of the application for the order may be ordered by the court to be paid by the respondent.

(3) Subject to paragraphs (1) and (2), the applicant's costs must, unless the court orders otherwise, be paid—

(a) in relation to a company insolvency, as an expense of the insolvency proceedings; and

(b) in relation to an individual insolvency, but not in proceedings relating to debt relief orders or applications for debt relief orders, out of the bankrupt's estate or (as the case may be) the debtor's property.

(4) A person summoned to attend for examination must be tendered a reasonable sum for travelling expenses incurred in connection with that person's attendance but any other costs falling on that person are at the court's discretion.

(5) Where the examination is on the application of the official receiver otherwise than in the capacity of liquidator or trustee, no order may be made for the payment of costs by the official receiver.

**Derivation**—This rule derived from the Insolvency Rules 1986, SI 1986/1925, r 9.6.

**General note**—There are two elements to the costs associated with r 12.22; first, are the costs of obtaining the order for the private examination and, secondly, the costs associated with the examination itself: *Hunt v Renzland* [2008] BPIR 1380.

The costs envisaged under r 12.22(2) are limited in scope to the costs of the application, and should not extend to costs incurred through some alternative method of the applicant gathering information: *Akers v Hayley* [2017] BPIR 1700.

*Sub-division C—persons unable to manage own property or affairs*

**[2.770]**

**General note**—These provisions are capable of being invoked by the court of its own volition: *Hunt v Fylde BC* [2008] BPIR 1368.

**[2.771]**

**12.23 Application and interpretation**
(1)  This sub-division applies where it appears to the court in insolvency proceedings that a person affected by the proceedings is unable to manage and administer that person's own property and affairs by reason of—
    (a)    lacking capacity within the meaning of the Mental Capacity Act 2005;
    (b)    suffering from a physical affliction; or
    (c)    disability.
(2)  Such a person is referred to in this sub-division as "the incapacitated person".

**Derivation**—This rule derived from the Insolvency Rules 1986, SI 1986/1925, r 7.43.

**[2.772]**

**12.24 Appointment of another person to act**
(1)  The court may appoint such person as it thinks just to appear for, represent or act for the incapacitated person.
(2)  The appointment may be made either generally or for the purpose of a particular application or proceeding, or for the exercise of particular rights or powers which the incapacitated person might have exercised but for that person's incapacity.
(3)  The court may make the appointment either of its own motion or on application by—
    (a)    a person who has been appointed by a court in the United Kingdom or elsewhere to manage the affairs of, or to represent, the incapacitated person;
    (b)    any person who appears to the court to be a suitable person to make the application;
    (c)    the official receiver; or
    (d)    the office-holder.
(4)  An application may be made without notice to any other party.
(5)  However the court may require such notice of the application as it thinks necessary to be delivered to the incapacitated person, or any other person, and may adjourn the hearing of the application to enable the notice to be delivered.

**Derivation**—This rule derived from the Insolvency Rules 1986, SI 1986/1925, r 7.43.

**[2.773]**

**12.25 Witness statement in support of application**
An application under rule 12.24(3) must be supported by a witness statement made by a registered medical practitioner as to the mental or physical condition of the incapacitated person.

**Derivation**—This rule derived from the Insolvency Rules 1986, SI 1986/1925, r 7.45A.

**[2.774]**

**12.26 Service of notices following appointment**
Any notice served on, or sent to, a person appointed under rule 12.24 has the same effect as if it had been served on, or delivered to, the incapacitated person.

Derivation—This rule derived from the Insolvency Rules 1986, SI 1986/1925, r 7.46.

## CHAPTER 5

### OBTAINING INFORMATION AND EVIDENCE

**[2.775]**

**Note**
[Note: a document required by the Act or these Rules must also contain the standard contents set out in Part 1.]

**[2.776]**

### 12.27 Further information and disclosure
(1)   A party to insolvency proceedings in court may apply to court for an order—
   (a)   that in accordance with CPR Part 18 (further information) another party—
      (i)   clarify a matter that is in dispute in the proceedings, or
      (ii)   give additional information in relation to such a matter; or
   (b)   for disclosure from any person in accordance with CPR Part 31 (disclosure and inspection of documents).
(2)   An application under this rule may be made without notice to any other party.

Derivation—This rule derived from the Insolvency Rules 1986, SI 1986/1925, r 7.60.

General note—This provision formalises the availability of CPR, Parts 18 and 31 in insolvency proceedings. Note, however, that r 12.27(1)(b) does not impose disclosure and inspection automatically as a stage in insolvency proceedings. Rather, the provision makes available an application for disclosure and inspection to a party to insolvency proceedings. An order could be made for disclosure and inspection in the course of directions under r 12.11, specifically r 12.11(b).

In *Elation Capital Ltd v Hoffgen* [2021] 6 WLUK 480, an order for disclosure against a company petitioning for a bankruptcy order in favour of the respondent, a former director and shareholder, requiring the company to disclose documents and laptop records apparently necessary to allow for the construction of a timeline to demonstrate work done in consideration for the outstanding indebtedness of circa £11,000 was set aside. An order for disclosure in bankruptcy proceedings is unusual and there was no good reason on the facts to make such an order: see generally on disclosure in insolvency proceedings *Highberry Ltd v Colt Telecom Group plc* [2002] EWHC 2503 (Ch), [2003] BPIR 311. The proper course, on the facts, was for the respondent to write to the petitioner asking for documents relating to his work. If such documents were not provided, it was open to the court to draw appropriate inferences: *Re Angel Group Ltd* [2015] EWHC 2372 (Ch).

**[2.777]**

### 12.28 Witness statements and reports
(1)   Where the Act or these Rules require evidence as to a matter, such evidence may be given by witness statement unless—
   (a)   in a specific case a rule or the Act makes different provision; or
   (b)   the court otherwise directs.
(2)   Unless either the provision of the Act or rule under which the application is made provides otherwise, or the court directs otherwise—
   (a)   if the applicant intends to rely at the first hearing on evidence in a witness statement or report, the applicant must file the witness statement or report with the court and serve a copy of it on the respondent not less than 14 days before the date fixed for the hearing; and
   (b)   where the respondent intends to oppose the application and rely for that purpose on evidence contained in a witness statement or report, the respondent must file the witness statement or report with the court and serve a copy on the applicant not less than five business days before the date fixed for the hearing.

(3) The court may order a person who has made a witness statement or report to attend for cross-examination.

(4) Where a person who has been ordered to attend fails to do so the witness statement or report must not be used in evidence without the court's permission.

Derivation—This rule derived from the Insolvency Rules 1986, SI 1986/1925, rr 7.7A, 7.8.

**RULE 12.28(3)**

**Ordering a person to attend for cross-examination**—Historically, under the Practice Direction (1943) WN 246, a party had to give notice to the other side's witnesses to attend for cross-examination. The matter is now one for the court alone: see r 12.28(3).

There is no rule of universal application that, in the absence of some contrary sworn evidence, cross-examination of a deponent will not be ordered: *Re Bank of Credit and Commerce International SA (No 6)* [1994] 1 BCLC 450 at 453F–I (Sir Donald Nicholls V-C). However, an order for cross-examination should only be made where cross-examination is necessary, in the particular circumstances of any case, for fairly disposing of a particular issue. The court therefore retains the widest discretion in making such an order.

The exercise by the court of its power to order cross-examination under the former r 7.7(1), as with the power to make orders for disclosure under the former r 7.60, was held not to be appropriate to an application for an administration order save in exceptional circumstances, given the nature and purpose of an administration application and the usual degree of urgency inherent in such an application: *Highberry Ltd v Colt Telecom Group plc* [2003] 1 BCLC 290 (Lawrence Collins J, commenting at [28] that the application before him for cross-examination was unprecedented and at [46] that certain of the unjustified requests for disclosure were 'breathtaking'). The court's approach to cross-examination is unlikely to differ under the 2016 Rules.

As regards winding-up and bankruptcy petitions, the general rule is that cross-examination is inappropriate to such petitions and should ordinarily be refused: *Re Amadeus Trading Ltd (No 1), Moscow Savings Bank and the Russian Federation v Amadeus Trading Ltd* (1997) March 26, Robert Walker J (unreported) (a winding-up case; 'I cannot possibly adjudicate on that issue [as to an allegation of forgery] without both cross-examination and expert evidence from document examiners, neither of which is appropriate on the hearing of a winding-up petition' (at p 18 of the transcript)). On the other hand, the court may, albeit in an exceptional case, take the view in an appropriate case that cross-examination is necessary to determine factual issues on which a petition is fundamentally reliant and without which it is liable to be dismissed: see, for example, *Wilkinson v IRC* [1998] BPIR 418. In *Hayes v Hayes* [2014] EWHC 2694 (Ch), [2014] BPIR 1212 Nugee J considered an appeal from the decision of Registrar Jones dismissing a bankruptcy petition on the basis that there was a genuine and substantial dispute as to a cross-claim. Having identified that the practice in insolvency proceedings before the inception of the CPR was that questions as to whether the petition debt or a cross-claim was the subject of a genuine and serious dispute were to be decided without any cross-examination (by reference to the *Amadeus Trading* case above), Nugee J held (at [25]) that CPR, r 32.5 (use at trial of witness statements which have been served) is 'inconsistent' with the former r 7.51A(2) (which invoked into insolvency proceedings the provisions of the CPR; see now r 12.1)) such that the pre-CPR practice of the registrars of determining petition debts or cross-claims without cross-examination remains unchanged. His Lordship observed, 'The insolvency court must have an inherent power to give directions for the hearing of the petition and it may be appropriate in certain circumstances to require cross-examination. That is something that should be determined by an application for directions rather than being dictated by the CPR.' In dismissing the appeal against the registrar's refusal to provide for cross-examination, Nugee J expressed agreement (at [27]) with para 25 of the registrar's judgment which provided: 'The starting point is that this court will not normally hear cross-examination because it is only deciding the question whether there is a genuine and substantial dispute not the dispute itself. This normally can and should be decided upon the written evidence because that evidence will provide the answer to that question. Cross-examination will not be allowed to trespass into evidence relevant to determining the dispute when the decision to be made is whether there is one.'

**[2.778]**

**12.29 Evidence provided by the official receiver, an insolvency practitioner or a special manager**

(1) Where in insolvency proceedings a witness statement is made by an office-holder, the office-holder must state—

    (a)    the capacity in which the office-holder is acting; and

    (b)    the office-holder's address.

(2)   The following may file a report with the court instead of a witness statement in all insolvency proceedings—
- (a)   the official receiver; and
- (b)   the adjudicator.

(3)   The following may file a report with the court instead of a witness statement unless the application involves other parties or the court otherwise directs—
- (a)   an administrator;
- (b)   a provisional liquidator;
- (c)   a liquidator;
- (d)   an interim receiver;
- (e)   a trustee; and
- (f)   a special manager.

(4)   Where a report is filed instead of a witness statement, the report must be treated for the purpose of rule 12.28 and any hearing before the court as if it were a witness statement.

**Derivation**—This rule derived from the Insolvency Rules 1986, SI 1986/1925, r 7.9.

**CIGA 2020**—This provision is affected by temporary measures at Sch 4, para 47 of CIGA 2020.

**General note**—The absence of a statement of truth on an application for a bankruptcy restriction order and reports filed in support by the Official Receiver does not unduly disadvantage a bankrupt or constitutes a breach of the Art 6 ECHR (right to a fair trial): *Official Receiver v Bayliss* (Edwin Johnson QC).

CHAPTER 6

TRANSFER OF PROCEEDINGS

**[2.779]**

**Note**

[Note: a document required by the Act or these Rules must also contain the standard contents set out in Part 1.]

*Sub-division A: General*

**[2.780]**

**12.30  General power of transfer**

(1)   The High Court may order insolvency proceedings which are pending in that court to be transferred to a specified hearing centre.

(2)   The County Court may order insolvency proceedings which are pending in a hearing centre to be transferred either to the High Court or another hearing centre.

(3)   A judge of the High Court may order insolvency proceedings which are pending in the County Court to be transferred to the High Court.

(4)   The court may order a transfer of proceedings—
- (a)   of its own motion;
- (b)   on the application of the official receiver; or
- (c)   on the application of a person appearing to the court to have an interest in the proceedings.

(5)   Winding-up proceedings may only be transferred to a hearing centre in which proceedings to wind up companies may be commenced under the Act or to the County Court at Central London.

(6)   Bankruptcy proceedings or proceedings relating to a debt relief order may only be transferred to a hearing centre in which bankruptcy proceedings may be commenced under the Act.

(7)   A case in a schedule under rule 12.37(8) may be transferred solely for the purposes of rule 12.38 (action following application for a block transfer order) by—
- (a)   the registrar to or from the High Court; and
- (b)   the District Judge of the hearing centre to which the application is made, to or from that hearing centre.

**Derivation**—This rule derived from the Insolvency Rules 1986, SI 1986/1925, r 7.11.

**General note**—Rule 12.30 extends to 'insolvency proceedings' whereas its forerunner in IR 1986, r 7.11 made only express mention of winding-up, bankruptcy proceedings or proceedings relating to a debt relief order (although that provision almost certainly extended beyond those procedures). The power of transfer is of great practical utility. Whilst capable of being exercised on an application by the official receiver or a person with an interest in the proceedings under r 12.30(4)(b) and (c), the need for an application is avoided if the court exercises the power of its own volition under r 12.30(4)(a). In an appropriate case, the power to transfer of the court's own motion will allow the court to transfer a matter to itself for the purposes of a particular application, particularly in a case of urgency, before re-transferring the matter back to the proceedings' 'home' court. In such a case the transferring court will usually be assisted with full details of the documents on the home court file if timescale precludes the obtaining of the file itself.

**Transfer of part only of proceedings from the County Court to the High Court**—In *Re Ide (in bankruptcy)* [2020] EWCA Civ 1469 at [37]–[39] (Nugee LJ) the Court of Appeal upheld the decision of HHJ Matthews to the effect that r 12.30(2) enables the County Court to transfer a particular application in bankruptcy to the High Court without having to transfer the whole of the bankruptcy proceedings. This would allow, for example, for the transfer of a complex claim (such as a preference claim) to the High Court whilst retaining a more straightforward claim (such as possession and sale of the bankrupt's house) in the County Court.

**Transfers between the county court or between divisions of the High Court**—Rule 12.30 does not provide for transfers between Divisions of the High Court. Such transfers may be effected by way of a transfer order pursuant to CPR 30.2 and 30.5 respectively, which will apply to proceedings within the scope of r 12.30 by virtue of r 12.1.

## [2.781]

### 12.31 Proceedings commenced in the wrong court

Where insolvency proceedings are commenced in the wrong court or hearing centre, that court may order—

(a)    the proceedings be transferred to the court or hearing centre in which they ought to have been commenced;

(b)    the proceedings be continued in the court in which they have been commenced; or

(c)    the proceedings be struck out.

**Derivation**—This rule derived from the Insolvency Rules 1986, SI 1986/1925, r 7.12.

**General note**—This provision is virtually identical to CPR 30.2(2). The court's discretion in striking out wrongly commenced proceedings is only likely to be exercised in extreme cases, given the overriding objective in CPR 1.2, on which see r 12.1. The issue of proceedings in the wrong court should ordinarily be treated as a procedural error of an administrative nature, which does not invalidate the substantive validity of the proceedings.

Rule 12.31 is not capable of saving proceedings wrongly commenced in the High Court to remove the supervisor of an individual voluntary arrangement which subsisted in the county court: *Re Sankey Furniture Ltd* [1995] 2 BCLC 594 (Chadwick J, as he then was).

## [2.782]

### 12.32 Applications for transfer

(1)    An application by the official receiver for proceedings to be transferred must be accompanied by a report by the official receiver.

(2)    The report must set out the reasons for the transfer, and include a statement either that—

(a)    the petitioner, or the debtor in proceedings relating to a debt relief order, consents to the transfer; or

(b)    the petitioner or such a debtor has been given at least 14 days' notice of the official receiver's application.

(3)    If the court is satisfied from the report that the proceedings can be conducted more conveniently in another court or hearing centre, it must order that the proceedings be transferred to that court or hearing centre.

(4)    A person other than the official receiver who applies for the transfer of winding up or bankruptcy proceedings or proceedings relating to a debt relief order must deliver a

notice that such an application is intended to be made at least 14 days' before filing the application with the court to—

    (a)    the official receiver attached to the court or hearing centre in which the proceedings are pending; and

    (b)    the official receiver attached to the court or hearing centre to which it is proposed that they should be transferred.

**Derivation**—This rule derived from the Insolvency Rules 1986, SI 1986/1925, r 7.13.

## [2.783]

### 12.33 Procedure following order for transfer

(1) Where a court makes an order for the transfer of proceedings under rule 12.30 (other than paragraph (7) of that rule), it must as soon as reasonably practicable deliver to the transferee court or hearing centre a sealed copy of the order, and the file of the proceedings.

(2) A transferee court (or hearing centre) which receives such an order and the file in winding up or bankruptcy proceedings or proceedings relating to a debt relief order must, as soon as reasonably practicable, deliver notice of the transfer to the official receiver attached to that court or hearing centre and the transferor court respectively.

(3) Where the High Court makes a transfer order under rule 12.30(7)—

    (a)    it must deliver sealed copies of the order—

        (i)    to the hearing centre from which the proceedings are transferred, and

        (ii)    in winding up or bankruptcy proceedings or proceedings relating to a debt relief order, to the official receiver attached to that hearing centre and the High Court respectively; and

    (b)    the hearing centre must deliver the file of the proceedings to the High Court.

**Derivation**—This rule derived from the Insolvency Rules 1986, SI 1986/1925, r 7.14.
**General note**—It would not appear possible to transfer any part of proceedings.

## [2.784]

### 12.34 Consequential transfer of other proceedings

(1) This rule applies where—

    (a)    the High Court has—

        (i)    made a winding-up order,

        (ii)    appointed a provisional liquidator,

        (iii)    made a bankruptcy order, or

        (iv)    appointed an interim receiver; or

    (b)    winding-up or bankruptcy proceedings have been transferred to the High Court from the County Court.

(2) A judge of any division of the High Court may, of that judge's own motion, order the transfer to that division of any such proceedings as are mentioned below and are pending against the company or individual concerned ("the insolvent") either in another division of the High Court or in a court in England and Wales other than the High Court.

(3) Paragraph (2) is subject to rule 30.5(4) CPR (transfer between divisions and to and from a specialist list).

(4) The proceedings which may be transferred are those brought by or against the insolvent for the purpose of enforcing a claim against the insolvent estate, or brought by a person other than the insolvent for the purpose of enforcing any such claim (including in either case proceedings of any description by a debenture-holder or mortgagee).

(5) Where any such proceedings are transferred, they must be listed before a registrar for directions or final disposal as the registrar sees fit.

**Derivation**—This rule derived from the Insolvency Rules 1986, SI 1986/1925, r 7.15.

**General note**—An annulment application will not fall within r 12.34(4) by reference to the decision of the Court of Appeal in *Arif v Zar* [2012] EWCA Civ 986 at [26] which concerned the identical provision within the former IR 1986, r 7.15(3).

*Sub-division B: Block transfer of cases where insolvency practitioner has died etc*

**[2.785]**

**General note**—The court has no inherent jurisdiction to modify approved fee and disbursement levels in the course of a block transfer application: *Re A Block Transfer by Kaye and Morgan* [2010] BPIR 602 (HHJ Pelling QC).

The court will not proceed with a transfer to the transferee named by the outgoing office-holder without scrutiny: see *ACCA v Koumettou* [2012] EWHC 1265 (Ch).

**[2.786]**

**12.35 Interpretation**
In this Sub-division—
    "outgoing office-holder" has the meaning given in rule 12.36(1);
    "replacement office-holder" has the meaning given in rule 12.36(1);
    "block transfer order" has the meaning given in rule 12.36(2);
    "substantive application" is that part of the application in rule 12.37(1)(c) and (d).

**Derivation**—This rule derived from the Insolvency Rules 1986, SI 1986/1925, r 7.10A.

**[2.787]**

**12.36 Power to make a block transfer order**
(1)   This rule applies where an office-holder ('the outgoing office-holder')—
    (a)    dies;
    (b)    retires from practice; or
    (c)    is otherwise unable or unwilling to continue in office;
and it is expedient to transfer some or all of the cases in which the outgoing office-holder holds office to one or more office-holders ('the replacement office-holder') in a single transaction.
(2)   In a case to which this rule applies the court has the power to make an order ('a block transfer order') appointing a replacement office-holder in the place of the outgoing office-holder to be—
    (a)    liquidator in any winding up (including a case where the official receiver is the liquidator by virtue of section 136);
    (b)    administrator in any administration;
    (c)    trustee in a bankruptcy (including a case where the official receiver is the trustee by virtue of section 300); or
    (d)    supervisor of a CVA or an IVA.
(3)   The replacement office-holder must be—
    (a)    qualified to act as an insolvency practitioner in relation to the company or bankrupt; or
    (b)    where the replacement office-holder is to be appointed supervisor of an IVA—
        (i)    qualified to act as an insolvency practitioner in relation to the debtor, or
        (ii)    a person authorised so to act.

**Derivation**—This rule derived from the Insolvency Rules 1986, SI 1986/1925, r 7.10B.
**CIGA 2020**—This provision is affected by temporary measures at Sch 4, para 47 of CIGA 2020.

**[2.788]**

**12.37 Application for a block transfer order**
(1)   An application for a block transfer order may be made to the registrar or District Judge for—

(a)    the transfer to the High Court of the cases specified in the schedule to the application under paragraph (8);

(b)    the transfer of the cases back to the court or hearing centre from which they were transferred when a replacement office-holder has been appointed;

(c)    the removal of the outgoing office-holder by the exercise of any of the powers in paragraph (2);

(d)    the appointment of a replacement office-holder by the exercise of any of the powers in paragraph (3); or

(e)    such other order or direction as may be necessary or expedient in connection with any of the matters referred to above.

(2)   The powers referred to in paragraph (1)(c) are those in—

    (a)    section 7(5) and paragraph 39(6) of Schedule A1 (CVA);

    (b)    section 19, paragraph 88 of Schedule B1 and rule 12.36(2) (administration);

    (c)    section 108 (voluntary winding up);

    (d)    section 172(2) and rule 12.36(2) (winding up by the court);

    (e)    section 263(5) (IVA); and

    (f)    section 298 and rule 12.36(2) (bankruptcy).

(3)   The powers referred to in paragraph (1)(d) are those in—

    (a)    section 7(5) and paragraph 39(6) of Schedule A1 (CVA);

    (b)    section 13, paragraphs 63, 91 and 95 of Schedule B1 and rule 12.36(2) (administration);

    (c)    section 108 (voluntary winding up);

    (d)    section 168(3) and (5) and rule 12.36(2) (winding up by the court);

    (e)    section 263(5) (IVA); and

    (f)    sections 298 and 303(2) and rule 12.36(2) (bankruptcy).

(4)   Subject to paragraph (5), the application may be made by any of the following—

    (a)    the outgoing office-holder (if able and willing to do so);

    (b)    any person who holds office jointly with the outgoing office-holder;

    (c)    any person who is proposed to be appointed as the replacement office-holder;

    (d)    any creditor in a case subject to the application;

    (e)    the recognised professional body which was the source of the outgoing office-holder's authorisation; or

    (f)    the Secretary of State.

(5)   Where one or more outgoing office-holder in the schedule under paragraph (8) is an administrator, an application may not be made unless the applicant is a person permitted to apply to replace that office-holder under section 13 or paragraph 63, 91 or 95 of Schedule B1 or such a person is joined as applicant in relation to the replacement of that office-holder.

(6)   An applicant (other than the Secretary of State) must deliver a notice of the intended application to the Secretary of State on or before the date the application is made.

(7)   The following must be made a respondent to the application and served with it—

    (a)    the outgoing office-holder (if not the applicant or deceased);

    (b)    any person who holds office jointly with the outgoing office-holder; and

    (c)    such other person as the registrar or District Judge directs.

(8)   The application must contain a schedule setting out—

    (a)    identification details for the proceedings; and

    (b)    the capacity in which the outgoing office-holder was appointed.

(9)   The application must be supported by evidence—

    (a)    setting out the circumstances as a result of which it is expedient to appoint a replacement office-holder; and

    (b)    exhibiting the consent to act of each person who is proposed to be appointed as replacement office-holder.

(10) Where all the cases in the schedule under paragraph (8) are in the County Court—

    (a)    the application may be made to a District Judge of a convenient hearing centre in which insolvency proceedings of such type may be commenced; and

    (b)    this rule applies with appropriate modifications.

**Derivation**—This rule derived from the Insolvency Rules 1986, SI 1986/1925, r 7.10C.

**CIGA 2020**—This provision is affected by temporary measures at Sch 4, para 47 of CIGA 2020.

## [2.789]

### 12.38 Action following application for a block transfer order

(1)   The registrar or District Judge may in the first instance consider the application without a hearing and make such order as the registrar or District Judge thinks just.

(2)   In the first instance, the registrar or District Judge may do any of the following—

    (a)    make an order directing the transfer to the High Court of those cases not already within its jurisdiction for the purpose only of the substantive application;

    (b)    if the documents are considered to be in order and the matter is considered straightforward, make an order on the substantive application;

    (c)    give any directions which are considered to be necessary including (if appropriate) directions for the joinder of any additional respondents or requiring the service of the application on any person or requiring additional evidence to be provided; or

    (d)    if an order is not made on the substantive application, give directions for the further consideration of the substantive application by the registrar or District Judge or a judge of the Chancery Division.

(3)   The applicant must ensure that a sealed copy of every order transferring any case to the High Court and of every order which is made on a substantive application is filed with the court having jurisdiction over each case affected by such order.

(4)   In any case other than an application relating to the appointment of an administrator, in deciding to what extent (if any) the costs of making an application under this rule should be paid as an expense of the insolvency proceedings to which the application relates, the factors to which the court must have regard include—

    (a)    the reasons for the making of the application;

    (b)    the number of cases to which the application relates;

    (c)    the value of assets comprised in those cases; and

    (d)    the nature and extent of the costs involved.

(5)   Where an application relates to the appointment of an administrator and is made by a person under section 13 or paragraph 63, 91 or 95 of Schedule B1, the costs of making that application are to be paid as an expense of the administration to which the application relates unless the court directs otherwise.

(6)   Notice of any appointment made under this rule must be delivered—

    (a)    to the Secretary of State as soon as reasonably practicable; and

    (b)    to—

        (i)    the creditors, and

        (ii)    such other persons as the court may direct, in such manner as the court may direct.

(7)   Where the application was made to the District Judge under rule 12.37(10) this rule applies with appropriate modifications.

**Derivation**—This rule derived from the Insolvency Rules 1986, SI 1986/1925, r 7.10D.

**Practice concerning costs**—Dear IP (Issue 82, November 2018) reminds practitioners of the terms of r 12.38(4) and the appropriateness of bringing to the attention of the court the proposed costs associated with the transfer, as in practice these are often not contained in the application itself but in the body of supporting schedules.

CHAPTER 7

THE COURT FILE

[2.790]

**Note**
[Note: a document required by the Act or these Rules must also contain the standard contents set out in Part 1.]

[2.791]

**12.39 The court file**
(1)   Where documents are filed with the court under the Act or these Rules, the court must open and maintain a court file and place those documents on the file.
(2)   However where a bankruptcy file has been opened under rule 10.47, documents filed with the court under the Act or these Rules must be placed on the bankruptcy file.
(3)   The following may inspect the court file, or obtain from the court a copy of the court file, or of any document in the court file—
    (a)    the office-holder in the proceedings;
    (b)    the Secretary of State; and
    (c)    a creditor who provides the court with a statement confirming that that person is a creditor of the company or the individual to whom the proceedings relate.
(4)   The same right to inspect and obtain copies is exercisable—
    (a)    in proceedings under Parts 1 to 7 of the Act, by—
        (i)    an officer or former officer of the company to which the proceedings relate, or
        (ii)    a member of the company or a contributory in its winding up;
    (b)    in proceedings relating to an IVA, by the debtor;
    (c)    in bankruptcy proceedings, by—
        (i)    the bankrupt,
        (ii)    a person against whom a bankruptcy petition has been presented, or
        (iii)    a person who has been served with a statutory demand under section 268;
    (d)    in proceedings relating to a debt relief order, by the debtor.
(5)   The right to inspect and obtain copies may be exercised on a person's behalf by someone authorised to do so by that person.
(6)   Other persons may inspect the file or obtain copies if the court gives permission.
(7)   The right to a copy of a document is subject to payment of the fee chargeable under an order made under section 92 of the Courts Act 2003.
(8)   Inspection of the file, with permission if required, may be at any reasonable time.
(9)   The court may direct that the file, a document (or part of it) or a copy of a document (or part of it) must not be made available under paragraph (3), (4) or (5) without the permission of the court.
(10)   An application for a direction under paragraph (9) may be made by—
    (a)    the official receiver;
    (b)    the office-holder in the proceedings; or
    (c)    any person appearing to the court to have an interest.
(11)   The following applications may be made without notice to any other party, but the court may direct that notice must be delivered to any person who would be affected by its decision—
    (a)    an application for permission to inspect the file or obtain a copy of a document under paragraph (6); and
    (b)    an application for a direction under paragraph (9).

(12) If, for the purposes of powers conferred by the Act or these Rules, the Secretary of State or the official receiver makes a request to inspect or requests the transmission of the file of insolvency proceedings, the court must comply with the request (unless the file is for the time being in use for the court's own purposes).

**Derivation**—This rule derived from the Insolvency Rules 1986, SI 1986/1925, r 7.31A.

**CIGA 2020**—This provision is affected by temporary measures at Sch 10, para 19(4) of CIGA 2020.

**General note**—Rule 12.39 derives significantly from the previous r 7.31A of the Insolvency Rules 1986. The case law referred to below was decided under that provision and its predecessor r 7.28. Note, however, the observations below as to the potential difficulties arising out of the differing scope and meanings of the court file, as opposed to the court record or register(s).

There is no provision expressly providing for the title of proceedings. Paragraph 4.1 of the *Practice Direction – Insolvency Proceedings* (July 2020) [2020] BPIR 1211 provides that, 'All insolvency proceedings should be commenced and applications in insolvency proceedings should be made using the information prescribed by the Act, Insolvency Rules, the Business and Property Courts Practice Direction and/or other legislation under which the same is or are brought or made . . . ' The provision goes on to make reference to https://www.gov.uk/government/collec tions/bankruptcy-and-insolvency-forms at which some forms relating to insolvency proceedings may be found.

The obligation on the court to open and maintain a file is only activated under r 12.39(1) where documents are filed with it under the Act or the Rules.

**The scope of r 12.39 and the implications of CPR 5.4**—Rule 12.39 is limited in its scope to governing the inspection of the court file. There is a danger in confusing, on the one hand, documents on the court file with, on the other hand, the court record. The two are not the same, and this is not mere semantics. The IR 2016 say nothing in terms about the court record; neither have the Rules done so since at least 2010. In contrast with this, CPR 5.4 draws a distinction between the court record (by way of that provision's reference to the court's registers) and the court file. What is now CPR 5.4A–5.4D deal only with searches of the court's registers (ie the court record). By operation of IR r 12.1(1), and in the absence of anything in the IR 2016 disapplying or being inconsistent with CPR 5.4, it would now seem that CPR 5.4 provides for and governs applications for searches of the register or registers of insolvency proceedings, as previously regulated by r 7.28 of the IR 1986 (which finds no equivalent under the IR 2016, so as to invoke the operation of CPR 5.4). Inspection or searches of the register or registers of insolvency proceedings appears to be something quite distinct from inspection of the court file under r 12.39. The implications of this are considered below.

**Applications to inspect the court register(s) or record**—As above, inspection of the court registers or record (as opposed to the court file) now appears to be governed by CPR 5.4, as previously provided for in r 7.28 of the IR 1986. Under the forerunner r 7.28(2) to the previous r 7.31A of the IR 1986, the registrar was entitled to refuse an application for inspection if 'not satisfied as to the propriety of the purpose for which inspection is required'. The applicant was then permitted to apply forthwith and without notice to the judge who could refuse inspection or allow it on such terms as he thought fit, the judge's decision in that regard being final by virtue of the former r 7.28(3). In *Re an application pursuant to r 7.28 of the Insolvency Rules 1986* [1994] BCC 369 Millett J held that an 'insolvency consultant' searching the records of insolvency proceedings at the Bankruptcy Registry for the names and addresses of potential customers for his services was not inspecting the records for a proper purpose within the meaning of the former r 7.28. Accordingly, the application was refused. The application had come about following queries raised by the Bankruptcy Registry staff with one of the applicant's representatives, which revealed that the applicant was in the habit of making multiple searches against the names of all individuals who had had a bankruptcy petition presented against them with a view to offering the applicant's services. Millett J held that, whilst the records of insolvency proceedings are available for public inspection, the word 'propriety' in the former r 7.28(2) requires that the registrar must be satisfied that inspection is required for a legitimate purpose having regard to the purpose for which statute made the records available for inspection, namely to enable persons who have a legitimate interest in a particular insolvency proceeding to discover what has taken place. As noted above, although the word 'propriety' does not appear in r 12.39, the court's approach (albeit in relation to the court file, not the court record or register) under that provision is likely to include at least having regard for the propriety of the applicant's purpose. Neither does CPR 5.4 say anything about propriety. Creditors, though not only creditors, obviously have a legitimate purpose in inspecting the record of insolvency proceedings which relate to their debtor, but CPR 5.4 is not trammelled even to this extent. Millett J also expressed the view that in a case of wide public interest the press may also have a legitimate interest in the proceedings.

In *Re Austintel Ltd* [1996] 1 WLR 1291 Jonathan Parker J, as he then was, refused applications by a firm of insolvency practitioners and others to make multiple searches of the court registers relating to company or bankruptcy petitions, identifying (at 1299) the mischief in allowing, in effect, duplicate registers to be made available outside of the control of the court. Although, on appeal, the Court of Appeal held that it had no jurisdiction to entertain such an appeal (on which see the former r 7.28(3)) the judgment of Ward LJ did indicate that certain types of search might be properly conducted. Again, however, this was a case decided under the now inoperative r 7.28 of the IR 1986 which finds no equivalent provision in the IR 2016 so as to invoke CPR 5.4.

In *Re Haines Watts* [2004] EWHC 1970 (Ch), [2005] BPIR 798 Sir Andrew Morritt VC made orders reinstating earlier orders, subject to eleven undertakings annexed to the judgment, allowing for multiple searches by the applicant, a substantial firm of chartered accountants and insolvency practitioners, following breaches of earlier undertakings, upon which the earlier orders were made, on the court being satisfied that the breaches were not deliberate. For the first test case on the former r 7.31A(6) see the decision of Chief Bankruptcy Registrar Baister in *Times Newspapers Ltd v McNamara* [2013] BPIR 1092. *McNamara* identified a general principle of open justice that extends to documents put before a judge, even if not read out in open court. The court's task is in balancing any privacy expectations against the presumption of access. The burden of establishing a departure from the presumption of open access lies on the party asserting the need for such a departure. On the facts of *McNamara* there was a legitimate public interest in Ireland for serious journalistic discussion of the facts behind the debtor's bankruptcy, especially given the level of the debts involved. There was also a legitimate interest in a number of other legal jurisdictions for public discussion of the phenomenon of bankruptcy tourism. Accordingly, the application by the journalist working for the Sunday Times newspaper in Ireland for access to the court file was granted notwithstanding the opposition of the debtor who filed witness statements in opposition but who did not appear at the hearing of the application.

One obvious difficulty with the above authorities is that CPR 5.4 is far broader and less restrictive than the previous r 7.28 of the 1986 Rules. In particular, there is no express power in CPR 5.4 for the court to refuse a search on the ground of impropriety. The single restriction to access lies only in the requirement for payment of 'the prescribed fee'. As above, it is possible that an applicant could seek to sidestep any restriction to the court record by pointing to the fact that the present r 12.39 is restricted to inspection of the court file, which is something other than the court record or registers. If that is correct, then it gives rise to the obvious problem that r 12.39 provides the court with no power to prevent access to the court record or registers. It would also appear to follow that parties would have open access to the court record or registers for the purpose of obtaining information for use in commercial purposes regarded as improper by the above authorities.

For the above reasons, what may require revisiting is the scope of r 12.39 and reconsideration of whether what is presently termed 'the court file' is broad enough to catch the court record or registers (which appears not to be the case).

The Royal Courts of Justice Registers of Petitions for Companies and Individuals comprises both 'Home' and 'Foreign' lists (the judgment and undertakings in *Re Haines Watts* (above) relating to both).

As a matter of practice, it is understood from *Dear IP No 30, March 1994* that the High Court destroys bankruptcy files after 20 years without regard to the possibility of extant proceedings or the release of the trustee, although it is also understood that the court will retain a file upon a request from the Official Receiver.

**Applications to inspect the court file under r 12.39**—In *LB Holdings Intermediate 2 Ltd (in admin)* [2017] EWHC 2032 (Ch) the court made an order under r 12.39(9) that an exhibit should not be open for inspection without permission of the court against the background of the other parties supporting the administrators' application for such an order where those other parties had also agreed confidentiality as between themselves in relation to a substantial part of the material contained in the exhibit. Implicit in the decision is the assumption that the material subject to the order was part of the court file, as opposed to the court record or register(s), which would appear correct.

For an example of the lifting of a restriction order in the interests of open justice see *Carton-Kelly v Edwards* [2020] EWHC 131 (Ch) (Deputy ICC Judge Frith).

**[2.792]**

## 12.40 Office copies of documents

(1) The court must provide an office copy of a document from the court file to a person who has under these Rules the right to inspect the court file where that person has requested such a copy and paid the appropriate fee under rule 12.39(7).

(2) A person's right under this rule may be exercised on that person's behalf by someone authorised to do so by that person.

(3) An office copy must be in such form as the registrar or District Judge thinks appropriate, and must bear the court's seal.

**Derivation**—This rule derived from the Insolvency Rules 1986, SI 1986/1925, r 7.61.

## CHAPTER 8

### Costs

**[2.793]**

**Note**

[Note: a document required by the Act or these Rules must also contain the standard contents set out in Part 1.]

**[2.794]**

**12.41 Application of Chapter and interpretation**
(1) This Chapter applies to costs of and in connection with insolvency proceedings.
(2) In this Chapter "costs" includes charges and expenses.
(3) CPR Parts 44 and 47 (which relate to costs) apply to such costs.

**Derivation**—This rule derived from the Insolvency Rules 1986, SI 1986/1925, r 7.33A.

**[2.795]**

**12.42 Requirement to assess costs by the detailed procedure**
(1) Where the costs of any person are payable as an expense out of the insolvent estate, the amount payable must be decided by detailed assessment unless agreed between the office-holder and the person entitled to payment.
(2) In the absence of agreement, the office-holder—
    (a) may serve notice requiring the person entitled to payment to commence detailed assessment proceedings in accordance with CPR Part 47; and
    (b) must serve such notice (except in an administrative receivership) where a liquidation or creditors' committee formed in relation to the insolvency proceedings resolves that the amount of the costs must be decided by detailed assessment.
(3) Detailed assessment proceedings must be commenced in the court to which the insolvency proceedings are allocated or, where in relation to a company there is no such court, any court having jurisdiction to wind up the company.
(4) Where the costs of any person employed by an office-holder in insolvency proceedings are required to be decided by detailed assessment or fixed by order of the court, the office-holder may make payments on account to such person in respect of those costs if that person undertakes in writing—
    (a) to repay as soon as reasonably practicable any money which may, when detailed assessment is made, prove to have been overpaid; and
    (b) to pay interest on any such sum as is mentioned in sub-paragraph (a) at the rate specified in section 17 of the Judgments Act 1838 on the date payment was made and for the period beginning with the date of payment and ending with the date of repayment.
(5) In any proceedings before the court (including proceedings on a petition), the court may order costs to be decided by detailed assessment.
(6) Unless otherwise directed or authorised, the costs of a trustee in bankruptcy or a liquidator are to be allowed on the standard basis for which provision is made in—
    (a) CPR rule 44.3 (basis of assessment); and
    (b) CPR rule 44.4 (factors to be taken into account when deciding the amount of costs).

**Derivation**—This rule derived from the Insolvency Rules 1986, SI 1986/1925, r 7.34A.

**General note**—Rule 12.42 is virtually identical to the former r 7.34A in the Insolvency Rules 1986. In *Hosking v Slaughter & May* [2014] EWHC 1390 (Ch) HHJ David Cooke dismissed an appeal from the decision of Registrar Jones to refuse an order for assessment (under the former r 7.34, the forerunner to the former r 7.34A) of the fees payable to Slaughter & May solicitors because the former administrators had agreed those fees. At [22] Judge Cooke expressed the view that the change in the insolvency rules, whether looked at in the 1986 version or the version in force in 2009, was substantial and plainly intended to introduce an alternative means by which the amount of costs of solicitors and others payable from the estate could be determined. The power to decide whether the costs should be agreed or assessed is clearly given to the responsible insolvency practitioner, and the change in the legislation would be of little if any purpose if it did not mean that a decision to agree costs (ie by the former administrators) would have a binding effect (ie on the subsequently appointed liquidators). Although the registrar below had considered that the court retains an inherent jurisdiction to direct an assessment, he was not prepared to exercise it on the facts of the case, and (at [50]) Judge Cooke could identify no error in that conclusion so as to warrant interference with it.

Rule 12.42 is applicable to the costs of a trustee-in-bankruptcy associated with an unsuccessful application for annulment: *Ardawa v Uppal* [2019] EWHC 1663 (Ch), [2019] BPIR 1086 (Roth J), following *Hosking*.

**[2.796]**

### 12.43 Procedure where detailed assessment is required

(1)   The costs officer must require a certificate of employment before making a detailed assessment of the costs of a person employed in insolvency proceedings by the office-holder.

(2)   The certificate must be endorsed on the bill and signed by the office-holder and must include—

    (a)    the name and address of the person employed;

    (b)    details of the functions to be carried out under the employment; and

    (c)    a note of any special terms of remuneration which have been agreed.

(3)   A person whose costs in insolvency proceedings are required to be decided by detailed assessment must, on being required in writing to do so by the office-holder, commence detailed assessment proceedings in accordance with CPR Part 47 (procedure for detailed assessment of costs and default provisions).

(4)   If that person does not commence such proceedings within 3 months of being required to do so under paragraph (3), or within such further time as the court, on application, may permit, the office-holder may deal with the insolvent estate without regard to any claim for costs by that person, whose claim is forfeited by such failure to commence proceedings.

(5)   Where in any such case such a claim for costs lies additionally against an office-holder in the office-holder's personal capacity, that claim is also forfeited by such failure to commence proceedings.

(6)   Where costs have been incurred in insolvency proceedings in the High Court and those proceedings are subsequently transferred to the County Court, all costs of those proceedings directed by the court or otherwise required to be assessed may nevertheless, on the application of the person who incurred the costs, be ordered to be decided by detailed assessment in the High Court.

**Derivation**—This rule derived from the Insolvency Rules 1986, SI 1986/1925, r 7.35.

**General note**—Note the 3-month limitation imposed by r 12.43(4).

**[2.797]**

### 12.44 Costs of officers charged with execution of writs or other process

(1)   This rule applies where an enforcement officer, or other officer charged with execution of the writ or other process—

    (a)    is required under section 184(2) or 346(2) to deliver up goods or money; or

    (b)    has under section 184(3) or 346(3) deducted costs from the proceeds of an execution or money paid to that officer.

(2)   The office-holder may require in writing that the amount of the enforcement officer's or other officer's bill of costs be decided by detailed assessment and where such

a requirement is made rule 12.43 (procedure where detailed assessment is required) applies.

(3) Where, in the case of a deduction of the kind mentioned in paragraph (1)(b), any amount deducted is disallowed at the conclusion of the detailed assessment proceedings, the enforcement officer must as soon as reasonably practicable pay a sum equal to that disallowed to the office-holder for the benefit of the insolvent estate.

Derivation—This rule derived from the Insolvency Rules 1986, SI 1986/1925, r 7.36.

General note—The reference to 'enforcement officer' replaces previous references to 'sheriff'.

## [2.798]

### 12.45 Petitions presented by insolvent companies

(1) This rule applies where a winding-up petition is presented by a company against itself.

(2) A solicitor acting for the company must in the solicitor's bill of costs give credit for any sum or security received by the solicitor as a deposit from the company on account of the costs and expenses to be incurred in respect of the filing and prosecution of the petition and the deposit must be noted by the costs officer on the final costs certificate.

(3) Where an order is made on a petition presented by the company and before the presentation of that petition a petition had been presented by a creditor, no costs are to be allowed to the company or that company's solicitor out of the insolvent estate unless the court considers that—

    (a)    the insolvent estate has benefited by the company's conduct; or

    (b)    there are otherwise special circumstances justifying the allowance of costs.

Derivation—This rule derived from the Insolvency Rules 1986, SI 1986/1925, r 7.37A.

## [2.799]

### 12.46 Costs paid otherwise than out of the insolvent estate

Where the amount of costs is decided by detailed assessment under an order of the court directing that those costs are to be paid otherwise than out of the insolvent estate, the costs officer must note on the final costs certificate by whom, or the manner in which, the costs are to be paid.

Derivation—This rule derived from the Insolvency Rules 1986, SI 1986/1925, r 7.38.

## [2.800]

### 12.47 Awards of costs against an office-holder, the adjudicator or the official receiver

Without prejudice to any provision of the Act or Rules by virtue of which the official receiver or the adjudicator is not in any event to be liable for costs and expenses, where an office-holder, the adjudicator or the official receiver (where the official receiver is not acting as an office-holder) is made a party to any proceedings on the application of another party to the proceedings, the office-holder, the adjudicator or official receiver is not to be personally liable for the costs unless the court otherwise directs.

Derivation—This rule derived from the Insolvency Rules 1986, SI 1986/1925, r 7.39.

General note—Rule 12.47 is in identical terms to the former IR 1986, r 7.39. In *Re Mordant, Mordant v Halls* [1996] BPIR 302 Sir Donald Nicholls V-C (as he then was) held at 313A–313C that, as a matter of principle, the former r 7.39 represented a starting point by which an office-holder incurs no personal liability for costs unless 'there is good reason to direct otherwise'. On appeal against the Vice-Chancellor's costs order, which had not provided for personal liability on the part of a trustee in bankruptcy, Roche LJ, with whom Hobhouse LJ and Nourse LJ agreed, held at 322E–322G, following submissions on the authorities governing non-party costs orders under what is now s 51 of the Senior Courts Act 1981, that there was no authority to support the proposition that there must exist an exceptional circumstance or circumstances before a judge was able to embark on the balancing exercise which should be performed before making any order for costs, including one imposing personal liability on an office-holder under the former r 7.39. The criterion in making such an order is whether it is just and reasonable to make the order and the approach to such application should be one of caution. As such, it could not be said that the Vice-

Chancellor was plainly wrong in refusing to render the trustee in bankruptcy personally liable; on the contrary, on the facts of *Mordant*, that decision had plainly been right.

For a decision of the Commercial Court, which involved an Israeli trustee-in-bankruptcy's unsuccessful resistance to an anti-suit injunction justifying indemnity costs, which proceedings were incapable of characterisation as insolvency proceedings or as having any connection with English bankruptcy, in which the normal order required the defendant trustee to meet those costs personally to the extent there was a shortfall in the estate: see *Bannai v Erez* [2013] EWHC 4287 (Comm), [2014] BPIR 1369 (Burton J).

In *Appleyard Ltd v Ritecrown Ltd* [2007] EWHC 3515 (Ch), [2009] BPIR 235 at [55] Lewison J, as he then was, refused, on the facts, to displace the rule provided for in the former r 7.39 as against a CVA supervisor who had come to the court seeking declaratory relief which had not been granted. The judge was, however, prepared to ameliorate the effect of refusing the successful respondent its costs against the applicant supervisor personally by directing that certain sums were to be payable from the CVA to the respondent in priority to further payments to the supervisor in respect of his costs.

**The immunity of the official receiver from suit**—In *Mond v Hyde* [1998] 2 BCLC 340, in affirming the decision of Sir Richard Scott V-C below, the Court of Appeal (Beldam LJ, Aldous and Ward LJJ agreeing) held that the official receiver is immune from suit in respect of statements made by him in the course of proceedings which are within the scope of his powers and duties, against the background of the extensive inquiries which fall to be undertaken by him as an officer of the court and the need on the part of the official receiver to be able to state clearly and frankly all those matters which he might have ascertained in the course of discharging his function. The immunity extends not only to statements made in the course of court proceedings, but also to statements made for that purpose. The reasoning in *Mond* may well be open to challenge in the Court of Appeal or in the Supreme Court in due course.

## [2.801]

### 12.48 Applications for costs

(1) This rule applies where a party to, or person affected by, any proceedings in an insolvency applies to the court for an order allowing their costs, or part of them, of or incidental to the proceedings, and that application is not made at the time of the proceedings.

(2) The applicant must serve a sealed copy of the application—

    (a)    in proceedings other than proceedings relating to a debt relief order—

        (i)    on the office-holder, and

        (ii)    in a winding up by the court or a bankruptcy, on the official receiver; or

    (b)    in proceedings relating to a debt relief order, on the official receiver.

(3) The office-holder and, where appropriate, the official receiver may appear on an application to which paragraph (2)(a) applies.

(4) The official receiver may appear on an application to which paragraph (2)(b) applies.

(5) No costs of or incidental to the application are to be allowed to the applicant unless the court is satisfied that the application could not have been made at the time of the proceedings.

**Derivation**—This rule derived from the Insolvency Rules 1986, SI 1986/1925, r 7.40.

**CIGA 2020**—This provision is affected by temporary measures at Sch 4, para 47 of CIGA 2020.

**Rule 12.48(1)**—For discussion as to the nature of r 12.48(1) and the scope of 'person affected by' see the judgment of Morgan J in *LF2 Ltd v Supperstone* [2018] EWHC 1776 (Ch), [2018] BPIR 1320.

## [2.802]

### 12.49 Costs and expenses of petitioners and other specified persons

(1) The petitioner is not to receive an allowance as a witness for attending the hearing of the petition.

(2) However the costs officer may allow that person's expenses of travelling and subsistence in attending the hearing.

(3)  The bankrupt, the debtor or an officer of the insolvent company to which the proceedings relate is not to receive an allowance as a witness in an examination or other proceedings before the court except as directed by the court.

Derivation—This rule derived from the Insolvency Rules 1986, SI 1986/1925, r 7.41.

**[2.803]**

**12.50  Final costs certificate**
(1)  A final costs certificate of the costs officer is final and conclusive as to all matters which have not been objected to in the manner provided for under the rules of the court.
(2)  Where it is proved to the satisfaction of a costs officer that a final costs certificate has been lost or destroyed, the costs officer may issue a duplicate.

Derivation—This rule derived from the Insolvency Rules 1986, SI 1986/1925, r 7.42.

CHAPTER 9

ENFORCEMENT PROCEDURES

**[2.804]**

**Note**
[Note: a document required by the Act or these Rules must also contain the standard contents set out in Part 1.]

**[2.805]**

**12.51  Enforcement of court orders**
(1)  In any insolvency proceedings, orders of the court may be enforced in the same manner as a judgment to the same effect.
(2)  Where an order in insolvency proceedings is made, or any process is issued, by the County Court, the order or process may be enforced, executed and dealt with by any hearing centre, as if it had been made or issued for the enforcement of a judgment or order to the same effect made by that hearing centre.
(3)  Paragraph (2) applies whether or not the other hearing centre is one in which such insolvency proceedings may be commenced.
(4)  Where a warrant for the arrest of a person is issued by the High Court, the warrant may be discharged by the County Court where the person who is the subject of the warrant—
    (a)    has been brought before a hearing centre in which insolvency proceedings may be commenced; and
    (b)    has given to the County Court a satisfactory undertaking to comply with the obligations that apply to that person under the Act or these Rules.

Derivation—This rule derived from the Insolvency Rules 1986, SI 1986/1925, r 7.19.

**[2.806]**

**12.52  Orders enforcing compliance**
(1)  The court may, on application by the competent person, make such orders as it thinks necessary for the enforcement of obligations falling on any person in accordance with—
    (a)    paragraph 47 of Schedule B1 (duty to submit statement of affairs in administration);
    (b)    section 47(duty to submit statement of affairs in administrative receivership);
    (c)    section 131 (duty to submit statement of affairs in a winding up);
    (d)    section 143(2) (liquidator to furnish information, books, papers, etc); or
    (e)    section 235 (duty of various persons to co-operate with office-holder).
(2)  The competent person for this purpose is—

(a)    under paragraph 47 of Schedule B1, the administrator;

(b)    under section 47, the administrative receiver;

(c)    under section 131 or 143(2), the official receiver; and

(d)    under section 235, the official receiver, the administrator, the administrative receiver, the liquidator or the provisional liquidator, as the case may be.

(3)   An order of the court under this rule may provide that all costs of and incidental to the application for it are to be borne by the person against whom the order is made.

**Derivation**—This rule derived from the Insolvency Rules 1986, SI 1986/1925, r 7.20.

**General note**—For examples of enforcement under this provision see *Re Corporate Jet Realisations Ltd* [2015] BCC 625; *Re Wallace S Smith Trust Co Ltd* [1992] BCC 707.

**[2.807]**

### 12.53 Warrants (general provisions)

(1)   A warrant issued by the court under any provision of the Act must be addressed to such officer of the High Court or of the County Court as the warrant specifies, or to any constable.

(2)   The persons referred to in sections 134(2), 236(5), 251N(5), 364(1), 365(3) and 366(3) (court's powers of enforcement) as the prescribed officer of the court are—

(a)    in the case of the High Court, the tipstaff and the tipstaff's assistants of the court; and

(b)    in the case of the County Court, a bailiff.

(3)   In this Chapter references to property include books, papers and other documents and records.

**Derivation**—This rule derived from the Insolvency Rules 1986, SI 1986/1925, r 7.21.

**[2.808]**

### 12.54 Warrants under sections 134 and 364

When a person ("the arrested person") is arrested under a warrant issued by the court under section 134 (officer of company failing to attend for public examination), or section 364 (arrest of debtor or bankrupt)—

(a)    the arresting officer must give the arrested person into the custody of—

        (i)    the court in a case where the court is ready and able to deal with the arrested person, or

        (ii)   where the court is not ready and able, the governor of the prison named in the warrant (or where that prison is not able to accommodate the arrested person, the governor of such other prison with appropriate facilities which is able to accommodate the arrested person), who must keep the arrested person in custody until such time as the court orders otherwise and must produce that person before the court at its next sitting; and

(b)    any property in the arrested person's possession which may be seized must, as directed by the warrant, be—

        (i)    delivered to whoever is specified in the warrant as authorised to receive it, or otherwise dealt with in accordance with the directions in the warrant, or

        (ii)   kept by the officer seizing it pending the receipt of written orders from the court as to its disposal.

**Derivation**—This rule derived from the Insolvency Rules 1986, SI 1986/1925, r 7.22.

**[2.809]**

### 12.55 Warrants under sections 236, 251N and 366

(1)   When a person is arrested under a warrant issued under section 236 (inquiry into insolvent company's dealings), 251N (the equivalent in relation to debt relief orders) or

366 (the equivalent in bankruptcy), the arresting officer must as soon as reasonably practicable bring the arrested person before the court issuing the warrant in order that the arrested person may be examined.

(2) If the arrested person cannot immediately be brought up for examination, the officer must deliver that person into the custody of the governor of the prison named in the warrant (or where that prison is not able to accommodate the arrested person, the governor of such other prison with appropriate facilities which is able to accommodate the arrested person), who must keep the arrested person in custody and produce that person before the court as it may from time to time direct.

(3) After arresting the person named in the warrant, the officer must as soon as reasonably practicable report to the court the arrest or delivery into custody (as the case may be) and apply to the court to fix a venue for the arrested person's examination.

(4) The court must appoint the earliest practicable time for the examination, and must—

(a) direct the governor of the prison to produce the arrested person for examination at the time and place appointed; and

(b) as soon as reasonably practicable deliver notice of the venue to the applicant for the warrant.

(5) Where any property in the arrested person's possession is seized, the property must, as directed by the warrant, be—

(a) delivered to whoever is specified in the warrant as authorised to receive it, or otherwise dealt with in accordance with the directions in the warrant; or

(b) kept by the officer seizing it pending the receipt of written orders from the court as to its disposal.

**Derivation**—This rule derived from the Insolvency Rules 1986, SI 1986/1925, r 7.23.

## [2.810]

### 12.56 Warrants under section 365

(1) A warrant issued under section 365(3) (search of premises not belonging to the bankrupt) must authorise any person executing it to seize any property of the bankrupt found as a result of the execution of the warrant.

(2) Any property seized under a warrant issued under section 365(2) or (3) must, as directed by the warrant, be—

(a) delivered to whoever is specified in the warrant as authorised to receive it, or otherwise dealt with in accordance with the directions in the warrant; or

(b) kept by the officer seizing it pending the receipt of written orders from the court as to its disposal.

**Derivation**—This rule derived from the Insolvency Rules 1986, SI 1986/1925, r 7.25.

## [2.811]

### 12.57 Execution overtaken by judgment debtor's insolvency

(1) This rule applies where execution has been taken out against property of a judgment debtor, and notice is delivered to the enforcement officer or other officer charged with the execution—

(a) under section 184(1) (that a winding-up order has been made against the debtor, or that a provisional liquidator has been appointed, or that a resolution for voluntary winding up has been passed);

(b) under section 184(4) (that a winding-up petition has been presented, or a winding-up order made, or that a meeting has been called at which there is to be proposed a resolution for voluntary winding up, or that such a resolution has been passed);

(c) under section 346(2) (that a judgment debtor has been made bankrupt); or

(d) under section 346(3)(b) (that a bankruptcy petition has been presented or a bankruptcy application has been made in relation to the debtor).

(2)   Subject to paragraph (3) and rule 1.47, the notice must be delivered to the office of the enforcement officer or of the officer charged with the execution—

    (a)    by hand; or

    (b)    by any other means of delivery which enables proof of receipt of the document at the relevant address.

(3)   Where the execution is in the County Court then if—

    (a)    there is filed with the hearing centre in charge of such execution in relation to the judgment debtor a winding-up or bankruptcy petition; or

    (b)    there is made by the hearing centre in charge of such execution in relation to the judgment debtor a winding-up order or an order appointing a provisional liquidator, or a bankruptcy order or an order appointing an interim receiver;

section 184 or 346 is deemed satisfied in relation to the requirement of a notice to be served on, or delivered to, the officer in charge of the execution.

**Derivation**—This rule derived from the Insolvency Rules 1986, SI 1986/1925, r 12A.28.

CHAPTER 10

APPEALS

## [2.812]

### Note

[Note: a document required by the Act or these Rules must also contain the standard contents set out in Part 1.]

## [2.813]

### 12.58  Application of Chapter

CPR Part 52 (appeals) applies to appeals under this Chapter as varied by any applicable Practice Direction.

**Derivation**—This rule derived from the Insolvency Rules 1986, SI 1986/1925, r 7.49A.

**General note**—For routes of appeal, permission to appeal and the filing of appeals see *Practice Direction – Insolvency Proceedings* (July 2020) [2020] BPIR 1211, paras [17]–[19].

## [2.814]

### 12.59  Appeals and reviews of court orders in corporate insolvency

(1)   Every court having jurisdiction for the purposes of Parts 1 to 7 of the Act and the corresponding Parts of these Rules, may review, rescind or vary any order made by it in the exercise of that jurisdiction.

(2)   Appeals in civil matters in proceedings under Parts 1 to 7 of the Act and the corresponding Parts of these Rules lie as follows—

    (a)    where the decision appealed against is made by a District Judge sitting in a hearing centre specified in the first column of the table in Schedule 10—

        (i)    to a High Court Judge sitting in a district registry, or

        (ii)    to an Insolvency and Companies Court Judge;

    as specified in the second column of the table;

    (b)    to a High Court Judge where the decision appealed against is made by—

        (i)    a Circuit Judge sitting in the County Court,

        (ii)    a Master,

        (iii)    an Insolvency and Companies Court Judge, if that decision is made at first instance, or

        (iv)    a District Judge sitting in a district registry;

    (c)    to the Civil Division of the Court of Appeal where the decision appealed against is made by an Insolvency and Companies Court Judge, if that decision is an appeal from a decision made by a District Judge; and

(d)    to the Civil Division of the Court of Appeal where the decision is made by a High Court Judge.

(3)    Any application for the rescission of a winding-up order must be made within five business days after the date on which the order was made.

(4)    In this rule—

"Circuit Judge sitting in the county court" means a judge sitting pursuant to section 5(1)(a) of the County Courts Act 1984;

"Civil Division of the Court of Appeal" means the division of the Court of Appeal established by section 3(1) of the Senior Courts Act 1981;

"county court" means the court established by section A1 of the County Courts Act 1984;

"District Judge" means a person appointed a District Judge under section 6(1) of the County Courts Act 1984;

"District Judge sitting in a district registry" means a District Judge sitting in an assigned district registry as a District Judge of the High Court under section 100 of the Senior Courts Act 1981;

"district registry" means a district registry of the High Court under section 99 of the Senior Courts Act 1981;

"High Court Judge" means a judge listed in section 4(1) of the Senior Courts Act 1981;

"Insolvency and Companies Court Judge" means a person appointed to the office of Insolvency and Companies Court Judge under section 89(1) of the Senior Courts Act 1981;

"Master" means a person appointed to the office of Master, Chancery Division under section 89(1) of the Senior Courts Act 1981;

and for the purposes of each definition a person appointed to act as a deputy for any person holding that office is included.

**Derivation**—This rule derived from the Insolvency Rules 1986, SI 1986/1925, r 7.47.

**Amendments**—SI 2017/366; SI 2018/130.

**General note**—Rule 12.59(1), like its predecessor in r 7.47(1) of the Insolvency Rules 1986, is concerned with the court's exceptional jurisdiction to 'review, rescind or vary any order made by it' within the prescribed jurisdiction. Rule 12.59(2) is concerned with the pathway of appeals although the provision says nothing about permission to appeal on which see r 12.61.

The provisions in r 12.59(1) mirror those in s 375, which applies in bankruptcy. The authorities are treated here as being of equal application to both bankruptcy and winding up. The differences between an appeal and a s 375 review were explained in *Raguz v Scottish & Newcastle Ltd* [2010] BPIR 945: see also *Jacob v UIC Insurance Co Ltd* [2006] EWHC 2717 (Ch); [2007] BCC 167 at [31] (Peter Smith J). An appeal is limited to a review of the decision of the lower court unless either a practice direction makes different provision for a particular category of appeal or the court considers in the circumstances of an individual appeal it would be in the interests of justice to hold a re-hearing.

In *Wilson v The Spector Partnership* [2007] EWHC 133 (Ch), [2007] BPIR 649 at [25] Mann J pointed out that there is no general jurisdiction in the court for the setting aside of its own order although there are established bases, such as the obtaining of an order by fraud, as well as the statutory basis in s 375 and the former r 7.47. It is fundamental, therefore, that an applicant can bring itself within a jurisdictional basis to the satisfaction of the court prior to any question of discretion as to substantive relief.

**CPR 40.9**—CPR 40.9 contains a potentially useful provision in that 'a person who is not a party but who is directly affected by a judgment or order may apply to have the judgment or order set aside or varied', on which see the decision of His Honour Judge Behrens, sitting as a High Court judge, in *Industrial Diseases Compensation Ltd v Marrons* [2001] BPIR 600 (trustee-in-bankruptcy had standing to apply to set aside charging orders absolute made in the period prior to the making of a bankruptcy order where the court making the charging orders was unaware of the extant bankruptcy petition). It is submitted that, given r 12.1, r 12.59(1) will override CPR 40.9, save that the latter provision will remain available to a non-party where the order attacked is outside of the scope of the jurisdiction prescribed by the former provision, as was the case in *Marrons*.

**Review and the slip rule**—There is no inconsistency between r 12.59(1) and the 'slip rule' in CPR 40.12 (correction of errors in judgments and orders) such that either provision might be employed to correct an error in an order: *Re Brian Sheridan Cars Ltd* [1995] BCC 1035 at 1038H (David Neuberger QC sitting as a deputy High Court judge)). The slip rule, however, does not confer a review jurisdiction on the court and applies only to an accidental slip or omission in a judgment or order. Neither does CPR 40.12 enable the court to reconsider or add to an original order. Even if r 12.59 or CPR 40.12 cannot be invoked, the court retains an inherent jurisdiction to alter its own order in certain cases: *Re Brian Sheridan Cars Ltd* [1995] BCC 1035 at 1041C–1041E, and on the same point see the decision in the family case *Thynne v Thynne* [1955] P 272 at 307 and 313.

RULE 12.59(1)

Scope of provision—Any judge of the High Court may review, rescind or vary his own order or an order made by any other judge sitting as a judge of the High Court: *Re W & A Glaser Ltd* [1994] BCC 199 at 206C–206D (Harman J). The same principle applies in the county court. The provision extends to 'any order' made by a court having jurisdiction to wind up companies under the 1986 Act where the order challenged is made in the exercise of that jurisdiction. The provision will, therefore, extend not only to winding-up orders but also to any order made in the context of insolvency proceedings: *Papanicola v Humphreys* [2005] 2 All ER 418 (Laddie J, as he then was, application – which failed on its merits – to review income payments order in bankruptcy). It would appear to follow that the court would have jurisdiction to review, rescind or vary an administration order made under para 13(1)(a) of Sch B1, say where the court was kept out of or mistaken as to material facts relevant to discretion (the decision in *Re Sharps of Truro Ltd* [1990] BCC 94 being authority for the proposition that the duty of disclosure on a without notice application for an administration order applies with more force than usual in the absence of a provision for a dissenting creditor to apply for setting side), although the more obvious way of challenging an administration order in such circumstances would now be under para 81 of Sch B1, subject to the limitation in that provision which restricts applications to creditors. For a case in which an application for a review of an order discharging company administrators from liability under para 98 of Sch B1 was dismissed see *Paragon Offshore plc (in liquidation)* [2020] EWHC 2740 (Ch) (Deputy ICCJ Agnello QC). The refusal was founded on the applicant re-running arguments deployed previously at the discharge hearing in the absence of any change in circumstances. If the applicant's complaint was that that judge hearing the discharge application had failed to deal with any point or was wrong in his conclusions, the proper procedural way forward was an appeal, not a review.

A High Court judge has no jurisdiction to review, rescind or vary an order made by a county court judge or a registrar (or district judge) of the High Court; strictly speaking, a challenge to such an order may only come before a High Court judge on appeal under r 12.59(2): *Re SN Group plc* [1994] 1 BCLC 319 at 322E (Jonathan Parker J, as he then was). However, in practice a review application from a registrar or district judge will come before a High Court judge, when coupled with a r 12.59(2) appeal, or during vacation. Although such applications are commonly considered by the judge, it must be doubtful that such review jurisdiction exists. Commentary appears in the section below on the coupling of an appeal with a review application.

Rule 12.59(1) applies only to court orders and does not, therefore, confer jurisdiction in relation to a director disqualification undertaking: *Eastaway v Secretary of State for Trade and Industry* [2007] BCC 550, CA.

An application to set aside a judgment entered in insolvency proceedings in the absence of the respondent is governed by r 12.59(1), and not CPR, r 39.3(5): *Re Broadside Colours & Chemicals Ltd* [2012] EWHC 195 (Ch) (HHJ Behrens).

In *Appleyard v Wewelwala* [2012] EWHC 3302 (Ch), [2013] BPIR 15 at [16] Briggs J held that s 375(1) (bankruptcy equivalent to what is now r 12.59(1)) contemplates review, at first instance, of the exercise of jurisdiction at first instance only: 'It would be surprising if it contemplated review, at first instance, of the exercise of appellate jurisdiction since, on its language, it would then permit a Bankruptcy Registrar [now an ICC Judge] (for example) to review the decision of a High Court judge on appeal.'

The court's approach to the exercise of its discretion—Before considering the exercise of its discretion, the court must be satisfied that there are proper grounds for reviewing, rescinding or varying the order under challenge. In particular, the court should approach with considerable caution an application under r 12.59(1) which is coupled with an appeal which proceeds in a higher court. The approach, therefore, it is submitted, is in two stages. Are there proper grounds for the court considering the application and, if so, should the court exercise its discretion? It should be remembered that the jurisdiction of one judge to review the decision of a judge of coordinate jurisdiction is exceptional and is not merely an alternative form of appeal to an unsatisfied party to insolvency proceedings.

As a general proposition, the appropriate test on a review 'is not whether the original order ought to have been made upon the material then before [the original tribunal] but whether that order ought to remain in force *in the light either of changed circumstances or in the light of fresh evidence*, whether or not it might have been obtained at the time of the original hearing' (emphasis added): *Re A Debtor (No 32/SD/91)* [1993] 2 All ER 991 at 995G (Millett J, as he then was, in considering the analogous s 375(1)). Millett J's formulation was followed by Hazel

Williamson QC, sitting as a deputy High Court judge, in *Re Thirty-Eight Building Ltd (No 2)* [2000] 1 BCLC 201 at 206C–206D – and see to similar effect *Fitch v Official Receiver* [1996] 1 WLR 242 at 246 (Millett LJ, as he then was) – where the deputy judge added that, whilst unrestricted, the jurisdiction under the provision must be exercised 'extremely cautiously' but may be available, as an additional ground to those identified by Millett J, 'in very exceptional circumstances where it might be necessary to correct an obvious injustice.'

As a matter of principle, the submission by counsel for the unsuccessful applicant liquidators in *Re Thirty-Eight Building Ltd (No 2)* [2000] 1 BCLC 201 at 204G–204H, to the effect that in considering new evidence which casts doubt on a previous decision the court should receive all arguments which might affect the court's confidence in the previous order, would appear correct.

The review jurisdiction should not be employed as what amounts in substance to an appeal out of time: *Re Mid-East Trading Ltd* [1997] 3 All ER 481 at 490A (Evans-Bombe J, applying *Re Cohen* [1950] 2 All ER 36, CA; application under s 108(1) of the Bankruptcy Act 1914 to rescind bankruptcy (receiving) order 6 weeks after order and out of time dismissed). In the context of the authorities identified in the preceding paragraphs, Evans-Lombe J identified the decision in *Cohen* as authority for the proposition that: 'On an application to review, new material tending to show the original order ought not to have been made and which was not before the court on the making of the order, must be demonstrated'. With respect, it is submitted that that proposition, with its express requirement for fresh evidence, goes too far and construes the scope of the review provision too narrowly, since a change of circumstances or the need to correct an obvious injustice may alone justify the making of an order. The essential point, as identified in *Papanicola v Humphreys* [2005] 2 All ER 418 at [26] is that there is something which has changed, and which, as such, constitutes exceptional circumstances, such that it is appropriate that the court reconsiders its own earlier order; if there is no such change in circumstances then the only way to challenge the order is by appeal.

**A summary of the propositions relating to review applications under r 12.59 (formerly r 7.47(1)) and s 375(1)**—The judgment of Laddie J, in *Papanicola v Humphreys* [2005] 2 All ER 418 at [25]–[28] contains the following useful summary of a number of propositions which can be formulated in relation to s 375, and which will apply equally to r 12.59(1), some of which are derived from the authorities considered within the judgment:

'(1) The section gives the court a wide discretion to review, vary or rescind *any* order made in the exercise of the bankruptcy jurisdiction.

(2) The onus is on the applicant to demonstrate the existence of circumstances which justify exercise of the discretion in his favour.

(3) Those circumstances must be exceptional.

(4) The circumstances relied on must involve a material difference to what was before the court which made the original order. In other words there must be something new to justify the overturning of the original order.

(5) There is no limit to the factors which may be taken into account. They can include, for example, changes which have occurred since the making of the original order and significant facts which, although in existence at the time of the order, were not brought to the court's attention at that time.

(6) Where the new circumstances relied on consist of or include new evidence which could have been made available at the original hearing, that, and any explanation the applicant gives for the failure to produce it then or any lack of such explanation, are factors which can be taken into account in the exercise of the discretion.'

In relation to proposition (1) Laddie J had previously identified (at [22]) that the fact that the court has a wide discretion does not throw light on how the jurisdiction should be exercised; neither did the judge consider (at [23]) that there was anything in the wording of the provision which suggested that it should be applied in a significantly different way in different cases. In relation to proposition (2) Laddie J identified that the absence of a change of circumstances precludes the availability of a review application: 'The court is not to review its order simply on the basis that the applicant wants to present essentially the same facts and the same arguments but more forcefully or attractively [by reference to a passage in the judgment of Millett LJ, as he then was, to that effect in *Fitch v Official Receiver* [1996] 1 WLR 242 at 246G–H]'. It is fair to say that, on the authorities, the court's discretion in review cases will be exercised only sparingly, and certainly not as a matter of course: see *Scottish & Newcastle Ltd v Raguz* [2010] BPIR 945; *Re Switch Services Ltd (in administration)* [2012] Bus LR D91.

In *Ahmed v Mogul Foods* [2005] EWHC 3532 (Ch), [2007] BPIR 975 at [23], having referred to Laddie J's formulation of the relevant principles in *Papanicola*, Patten J, as he then was, elaborated on the proper approach of the court in the following terms:

'Although there are references in these cases to what are described as exceptional circumstances, the essential point that emerges from these authorities is that if nothing has changed in the nature of the material before the court on the annulment or rescission application, then the court will not entertain it. The proper course in those circumstances is for the bankrupt to have appealed the original order. But if the court, on a consideration of the application, is satisfied that it has been presented with new material, which was not before the judge who made the bankruptcy order, and perhaps was not even available at that time, then in my judgment, the court is entitled to exercise its discretion and in appropriate cases, to decide to entertain the application and review the earlier decision.'

In *HM Revenue and Customs v Cassells* [2008] EWHC 3180 (Ch), [2009] BPIR 284 at [2] Morritt C emphasised the point made in paragraph (2) of Laddie J's formulation which echoes that in the dictum of Millett LJ, as he then was, in *Fitch v Official Receiver* [1996] 1 WLR 242 at 249A–249B, namely that the circumstance must be one which justifies the exercise of the statutory discretion in favour of the applicant.

In *Re Metrocab Ltd; Re Frazer Nash Technology Ltd* [2010] EWHC 1317 (Ch), [2010] BPIR 1368 at [36] Philip Marshall QC, sitting as a deputy High Court judge, provided a useful summary of the combined authorities on r 7.47 and the analogous bankruptcy provision in s 375. By reference to *Metrocab* and the authorities cited therein, the principles discernible from the authorities were re-stated by Barling J in *Credit Lucky Ltd and Gui Hui Dong v National Crime Agency (formerly the Serious Organised Crime Agency)* [2014] EWHC 83 (Ch) at [31] as follows:

'(1) the power to rescind is discretionary and is only to be exercised with caution;

(2) the onus is on the applicant to satisfy the court that it is an Appropriate case in which to exercise the discretion;

(3) it will only be an appropriate case where the circumstances are exceptional and those circumstances must involve a material difference from those before the court that made the original order;

(4) there is no limit to the factors that the court can take into account, and they may include changes since the original order was made, and significant facts which, although in existence at the time of the original order, were not brought to the court's attention at that time; but where that evidence could have been made available, any explanation the applicant gives for the failure to produce it then or any lack of such an explanation, are factors to be taken into account;

(5) the circumstances in which the court's power will be exercised will vary but generally where the rescission application involved dismissal of the winding-up petition, so that the company is free to resume trading, the court will wish to be satisfied:

(a)     that the debt of the petitioning creditor has been paid, or will be paid, that the costs of the Official Receiver or any liquidator can be paid, and that the company is insolvent at least on the basis that it can pay its debts as they fall due;

(b)     that the application has not been presented in a misleading way and the court is in possession of all the material facts and has not been left in doubt;

(c)     that the trading operations of the company have been fair and above board, and there is nothing that requires investigation of the affairs of the company.'

In very broad summary, therefore, and subject to the guidance in the above authorities, the two key questions are: Is the court's jurisdiction engaged? If so, should the court exercise its discretion?

**The court's approach to the rescission of winding-up orders**—In addition to the points identified in the preceding section, a number of particular observations arise in relation to winding-up orders. Where the rescission of a winding-up order is pursued so as to allow a company to continue trading, the court will 'ordinarily and possibly invariably' require proof that (a) the debt of the petitioning creditor has been paid, or will be paid on rescission, (b) the company is solvent, at least on the basis that it can pay its debts as and when they fall due, and (c) that the official receiver is satisfied that there is nothing in the affairs of the company that requires investigation and that his costs will be paid: *Re Dollar Land (Feltham) Ltd* [1995] BCC 740 at 478D–478E (Blackburne J, eight winding-up orders rescinded to allow for adjournment of the petitions for a period of 28 days – refused by the registrar on the making of the winding-up orders – so as to allow for consideration of CVA proposal where it was foreseeable that creditors might vote in favour of the CVA). It follows that it is possible for the court to rescind a winding-up order even if no ground existed upon which an appeal against the order might be pursued. These requirements mirror those factors identified previously by Peter Gibson J (as he then was) in *Re Virgo Systems Ltd* [1989] 5 BCC 833 at 835A (application to rescind winding-up order granted where company able to evidence solvency on balance sheet, so as to be able to meet all creditor claims and liquidator's remuneration in full, where company ignorant of winding-up petition on account of service at registered office which had remained that of original company formation agents).

The requirements identified in *Re Dollar Land* do not apparently arise where an order is sought other than to allow continued trading. Certainly it was observed by His Honour Judge Collyer QC, sitting as a High Court judge, in *Re Piccadilly Property Management Ltd* [1999] 2 BCLC 145 at 166B–166C that Blackburne J's test is not of universal application. In *Piccadilly* the judge observed (at 163H–163I), in what amounts to a further gloss on the test identified by Millett J in *Re A Debtor (No 32/SD/91)* [1993] 2 All ER 991, that the applicant must demonstrate very cogent reasons for the exercise of the discretion to rescind in the absence of cogent reasons for refusing to make the order.

Where the court rescinds a winding-up order made through a genuine mistake, the practice is for the Registrar of Companies to remove the winding-up and stay orders on the company's file and to replace the orders with a note saying, 'Winding-up order made in error and subsequent stay of that order removed from the file' or words to that effect: *Re Calmex Ltd* [1988] 4 BCC 761 at 764 (Hoffmann J, as he then was).

For a full review of the principles governing the exercise of discretion under r 12.59(1) see *Credit Lucky Ltd and Gui Hui Dong v National Crime Agency* [2014] EWHC 83 (Ch) (Barling J, refusal to rescind or stay winding-up order). Contrast the rescission of a winding-up order on terms given the exceptional circumstances in *Diamond Hangar Ltd v Abacus Lighting Ltd* [2019] EWHC 224 (Ch).

For the official fee consequences under the Insolvency Fees Order 2016 where a winding-up order is rescinded, see *HMRC v Direct Affinity Events Ltd* [2019] EWHC 3063 (Ch) (Deputy ICCJ Frith).

**Appeal coupled with review application**—In *Re Piccadilly Property Management Ltd* [1999] 2 BCLC 145, in the course of the relevant part of the judgment at 159C–160D, Judge Collyer QC expressed the view that 'double-barrelled appeals-cum applications to review should be discouraged in every possible way.' Nevertheless, certain 'double-barrelled' applications/appeals, albeit in rare and very exceptional cases, might be justifiable, provided that the applicant is both able to establish the requisite change of circumstances necessary for a review application and is absolutely candid with the review court as to any separately pursued appeal, as well as providing good reasons to the court as to the justification for the contemporaneous review and appeal applications. In such cases, the review court will, however, plainly be mindful of the obvious danger of the review court and the appeal court reaching contradictory conclusions such that it might be thought necessary for arrangements to be made for one hearing to await the outcome of the other.

**Fresh evidence on a review application**—On a review application, an applicant is at liberty to adduce fresh evidence, although the burden will lie on the applicant in satisfying the court as to why such fresh evidence was not before the court at the original hearing: *Re A Debtor (No 32/SD/91)* [1993] 1 WLR 314 at 318–319 (Millett J, as he then was). This position is in stark contrast to that on an appeal, where the general rule is that fresh evidence is not admissible, subject to the court's discretion, on which see now the approach of the court in *Hertfordshire Investments Ltd v Bubb* [2000] 1 WLR 2318. In *Ahmed v Mogul Foods* [2005] EWHC 3532 (Ch), [2007] BPIR 975 at [24] (a s 375 application) Patten J firmly regarded the approach of Millett J in *Re A Debtor* as correct.

## RULE 12.59(3)

**Application for rescission of winding-up order**—Prior to the coming into force of the former r 7.47 of the Insolvency Rules 1986, a winding-up order could only be rescinded if application was made before the order was drawn up, usually a period of a few days from the making of the order. The 5-day time limit in r 12.59(3) envisages that an order may be rescinded notwithstanding sealing by the court.

The five-day time limit imposed by this provision is peculiar to winding-up orders. The period is deliberately tight but designed to provide as reasonably short a period as might be necessary to avoid substantive injustice. Although the court has jurisdiction to extend the five-day period, an extension, and certainly an extension of any significant period beyond the statutory five-day period, is unlikely to be granted if cogent reasons cannot be advanced explaining any significant delay in the bringing of the application: *Re Mid-East Trading Ltd* [1997] 3 All ER 481 at 489G–490C (Evans-Lombe J, refusal to extend time for application seeking rescission of winding-up order made 14 months previously); see also *Re Calmex Ltd* [1988] 4 BCC 761 at 762–763 (Hoffmann J, as he then was); and compare *Re Virgo Systems Ltd* [1989] 5 BCC 833 (Peter Gibson J, as he then was, time extended where application made promptly where company unaware of petition). In *Re Oakwood Storage Services Ltd* [2003] EWHC 2807 (Ch), [2004] 2 BCLC 404 Hart J commented that the fact that an application might have been successful had it been made in time is not a sufficient ground in itself for extending time. His Lordship went on at [28]:

'The fact is that the time-limit in [the former r 7.47(4)] is put there for the very good reason that a winding-up order affects more persons than simply the petitioning creditor and the company itself. It has long been the case for that reason, the court is extremely guarded in the exercise of its jurisdiction to review or rescind a winding-up order and has always insisted on very strict time-limits for the making of such an application.'

In *Wilson v The Specter Partnership* [2007] EWHC 133 (Ch), [2007] BPIR 649 Mann J identified the court's discretion to extend the time limit in what is now r 12.59(3) after the event where any delay was capable of proper and reasonable explanation. In *Re Metrocab Ltd; Re Frazer Nash Technology Ltd* [2010] EWHC 1317 (Ch), [2010] BPIR 1368 (applications for rescissions dismissed on facts) Philip Marshall QC, sitting as a deputy High Court judge, held at [15], in applying the decision of the Court of Appeal in *Sayers v Clarke Walker (a firm)* [2002] 1 WLR 3095, that, where an application for an extension of time is sought to set aside a winding-up order under the former r 7.47, in a case of any complexity the 'checklist' in the previous form of CPR, r 3.9 (relief from sanctions) applies. The relevant principles are set out at para [36] of the deputy judge's judgment and were adopted by Barling J in *Credit Lucky Ltd v National Crime Agency* [2014] EWHC 83 (Ch) at [31]. In *Re Sarjanda Ltd* [2021] EWHC 210 (Ch) HHJ Cooke dismissed an application for extension of time of the five-day period in r 12.59(3) where the winding-up order had been made more than two years previously. The fact that the delay had been caused by the company negotiating to pay its debts with the petitioning creditor was not a good reason for the breach justifying an extension. The Judge noted that, although bankruptcy involved a jurisdiction to allow for annulment where all proven debts had been discharged, there was no such mechanism in winding up, something that no doubt constituted a deliberate policy choice by the legislature.

The winding-up order in *Diamond Hangar Ltd v Abacus Lighting Ltd* [2019] EWHC 224 (Ch) was rescinded in what HHJ Worster described as an exceptional case involving a material change in the facts presented to the court.

**Procedure**—Prior to the implementation of the former r 7.47(4), an application to rescind a winding-up did not require the issue of an application on the basis that the petition was merely restored before the court. However, para 9.10.1 of the *Practice Direction – Insolvency Proceedings* (July 2020) [2020] BPIR 1211 now provides that an application to rescind a winding-up order 'must be made by application'. Paragraph 9.10.2 provides that, if not made within the 5 business days after the date on which the winding-up order was made (in which period the application should normally be made), the application should also include an application to extend time. The same provision provides that notice of any such application must be given to the petitioning creditor, any supporting or opposing creditor and the official receiver. By para 9.10.3 applications will only be entertained by the court if made (a) by a creditor, or (b) by a contributory, or (c) by the company jointly with a creditor or with a contributory. The application must be supported by a witness statement which should include details of assets and liabilities and (where appropriate) reasons for any failure to apply within 5 business days. The Practice Direction, therefore, provides for a wider class of applicant than that envisaged in the judgment of Evans-Lombe J in *Re Mid-East Trading Ltd* [1997] 3 All ER 481 which held that only a party able to appear on the petition to wind up the company has standing to apply to rescind any winding-up order made.

Paragraph 9.10.4 of the Practice Direction (above) provides that, on an unsuccessful application for rescission the usual costs order ('normally') will require the costs of the petitioning creditor, supporting creditors and the costs of the official receiver to be met by the creditor or the contributory joining in the application with the company so as to avoid those costs falling unfairly on the general body of creditors

## [2.815]

### 12.60 Appeals in bankruptcy by the Secretary of State
In bankruptcy proceedings, an appeal lies at the instance of the Secretary of State from any order of the court made on an application for the rescission or annulment of a bankruptcy order, or for the bankrupt's discharge.

**Derivation**—This rule derived from the Insolvency Rules 1986, SI 1986/1925, r 7.48.

**General note**—By reference to its predecessor in r 7.48 of the IR 1986, an appeal under this provision is a 'true appeal' and not a re-hearing: *Re A Debtor (2389 of 1989)* [1991] Ch 326 (Vinelott J), following *Re Gilmartin (a bankrupt)* [1989] 1 WLR 513 (Harman J). A first appeal is subject to the permission requirement in r 12.61.

## [2.816]

### 12.61 Procedure on appeal
(1) An appeal against a decision at first instance may be brought only with the permission of the court which made the decision or of the court that has jurisdiction to hear the appeal.

(2) An appellant must file an appellant's notice within 21 days after the date of the decision of the court that the appellant wishes to appeal.

**Derivation**—This rule derived from the Insolvency Rules 1986, SI 1986/1925, r 7.49A.

**General note**—This provision is supplemented by Part Four of the *Practice Direction – Insolvency Proceedings* (July 2020) [2020] BPIR 1211. Those provisions import the practice and procedure of CPR Part 52 into insolvency proceedings, as now provided for in r 12.58.

## [2.817]

**12.62 Appeals against decisions of the Secretary of State or official receiver**
An appeal under the Act or these Rules against a decision of the Secretary of State or the official receiver must be brought within 28 days of delivery of notice of the decision.

**Derivation**—This rule derived from the Insolvency Rules 1986, SI 1986/1925, r 7.50.

### CHAPTER 11

#### Court Orders, Formal Defects and Shorthand Writers

## [2.818]

**Note**
[Note: a document required by the Act or these Rules must also contain the standard contents set out in Part 1.]

## [2.819]

**12.63 Court orders**
Notwithstanding any requirement in these Rules as to the contents of a court order the court may make such other order or in such form as the court thinks just.

## [2.820]

**12.64 Formal defects**
No insolvency proceedings will be invalidated by any formal defect or any irregularity unless the court before which objection is made considers that substantial injustice has been caused by the defect or irregularity and that the injustice cannot be remedied by any order of the court.

**Derivation**—This rule derived from the Insolvency Rules 1986, SI 1986/1925, r 7.55.

**General note**—This provision repeats the former r 7.55 of the IR 1986 and reproduces s 147(1) of the Bankruptcy Act 1914 but is applicable to all insolvency proceedings.

**The structure of r 12.64**—The starting point in understanding r 12.64 lies in its opening phrase, which provides that, in the absence of any objection and without any requirement for any further step, any formal defect or irregularity does not operate so as to invalidate insolvency proceedings. The jurisdiction of the court arises under the second and third parts of the provision ('unless the court . . . ') but can only be read as coming into operation upon objection being made before the court to a formal defect or irregularity capable of invalidating the particular insolvency proceedings.

The power of the court lies in its ability, in effect, to disapply the first part of the provision, with the consequence that the formal defect or irregularity to which objection has been made is allowed to operate so as to invalidate the proceedings. That power is only capable of being exercised, however, where two specific conditions are met. First, the court must be satisfied 'that substantial injustice has been caused by the defect or irregularity'; secondly, the court must consider that 'the injustice cannot be remedied by any order of the court', such as in *Re Continental Assurance Co (in liquidation) (No 2)* [1998] 1 BCLC 583 (Evans-Lombe J) in which an application by a liquidator alleging wrongful trading in a creditor's voluntary liquidation had been issued as (what was then) an ordinary, as opposed to an originating, application.

The very broad scope of the discretion in r 12.64 gives no indication as to how the discretion should be exercised and, taken together with the widely varying circumstances of particular cases, dictates that the application of the provision must be considered on a case-by-case basis.

Although ordinarily r 12.64 should be invoked by way of an on-notice application to affected parties, in an appropriate case the court may apply the provision of its own volition and exercise its discretion in seeking to further the interests of justice: see, for example, *Re Brickvest Ltd*, *Lumineau v Berlin Hyp AG* [2019] EWHC 3084 (Ch) (non-compliance with company articles disregarded).

**The true nature of the formal defect—is the defect or irregularity a nullity? — and the application of the provision**—The fundamental question which dictates whether or not it is appropriate for the court to exercise its power under r 12.64 lies in determination of the true nature of the 'formal defect' or 'irregularity' in issue, since the provision cannot extend to any form of defect or irregularity which constitutes a nullity. In *Re Euromaster Ltd* [2012] EWHC 2356 (Ch), [2012] BCC 754) at [17] Norris J identified, drawing on the opinion expressed by the House of Lords in *R v Soneji* [2005] UKHL 49, [2006] 1 AC 340 that the proper approach to whether a defect or irregularity constitutes a nullity (ie so as to be void) is 'to focus on the consequences of non-compliance and, taking into account those consequences, to consider whether Parliament intended the outcome of non-compliance to be total invalidity; in short, to ask whether it was a purpose of the legislation that an appointment [made in breach of paragraph 28 of Schedule B1] should be null'. *Euromaster* was concerned with the validity of an administrator's appointment, but the approach adopted by Norris J will be relevant to the analysis of all forms or defect or irregularity. If the court forms the view that a defect does not render the appointment a nullity then the court can proceed to consider the provisions of what is now r 12.64 and its potentially curative effect: see, for example, *Re Statebourne (Cryogenic) Ltd* [2020] EWHC 231 (Ch) (Zacaroli J). Conversely, a nullity is incapable of such cure. Cases demonstrating this distinction appear in the paragraphs below.

In *Re A Debtor (No 340 of 1992) ex parte the debtor v First National Commercial Bank plc* [1996] 2 All ER 211 the Court of Appeal considered a case in which a petitioning creditor had sought to rely on a return made by a sheriff which merely asserted that on an unstated number of occasions, at unstated hours, and in unstated circumstances, the sheriff had failed to obtain access to the debtor's property in establishing inability to pay, for the purposes of a bankruptcy petition under s 268(1)(b). In refusing to strike out the bankruptcy petition on the ground that none of the pre-conditions for the service of a bankruptcy petition required by s 267 had been fulfilled, the district judge had held that, whilst the sheriff's return was defective, the defect was nonetheless a formal defect or irregularity for the purposes of the former r 7.55; he also held that the petition should be allowed to proceed on the basis that the appellant would not be prejudiced. On appeal, Aldous J, as he then was, overturned the district judge's decision and held that the appellant petitioner's failure to prove the respondent's inability to pay his debts as required by s 268(1)(b) was neither a formal defect nor an irregularity of the kind to which the former r 7.55 related. That approach was affirmed by the Court of Appeal (at 218H–218J, Millett LJ, Waite and Stuart-Smith LJJ agreeing). A very similar approach was adopted in *Re Awan* [2000] BPIR 241, where His Honour Judge Boggis QC, sitting as a High Court judge, refused to invoke r 7.55 to cure a failure on the part of a petitioning creditor to effect personal or substituted service of a bankruptcy petition (at 244H: 'I am not prepared to apply that rule to waive a defect in proof of service of a bankruptcy petition . . . '): see to like effect *Ardawa v Uppal* [2019] EWHC 456 (Ch). In *Canning v Irwin Mitchell LLP* [2017] EWHC 718 (Ch), [2017] BPIR 934 improper service of a statutory demand was held to be incapable of cure, distinguishing *Gate Gourmet Luxembourg IV SARL v Morby* [2015] EWHC 1203 (Ch), [2015] BPIR 787 and the appeal at [2016] EWHC 74 (Ch).

For an example of the approach to costs on a defective petition on which payment was made so as to bring about the dismissal of the petition see *Oben v Blackman* [2000] BPIR 302 (Stanley Burnton QC, sitting as a deputy High Court judge).

In *Foenander v Allan* [2006] BPIR 1392 Nicholas Strauss QC, sitting as a deputy High Court judge, considered that the former r 7.55 was capable of validating proceedings commenced by a trustee in bankruptcy where the proceedings had not been sanctioned by virtue of a defect in the qualifications of the members of the creditors' committee.

In *Phillips v McGregor-Paterson* [2009] EWHC 2385 (Ch), [2010] 1 BCLC 72 Henderson J considered the application of r 7.55 to claims brought against company directors by liquidators which ought to have been commenced by way of an ordinary application (the forerunner to what is now an insolvency application notice) but which had been instituted by way of a CPR Part 7 claim form. At [25] Henderson J said this:

> ' . . . the present proceedings are plainly insolvency proceedings . . . by virtue of the fact that they are brought under various provisions of the Insolvency Act 1986. Accordingly, they are proceedings to which Part 7 of the Insolvency Rules applies, and the use of the wrong form of application is in my judgment a "formal defect" which is capable of being cured under Rule 7.55. If that is right, the effect of Rule 7.55 is that the present proceedings are not to be invalidated by the formal defect unless the court considers that substantial injustice has been caused by it, and that the injustice cannot be remedied by any order of the court.'

In *Re Anderson Owen Ltd* [2009] EWHC 2837 (Ch), [2010] BPIR 37 at [23] Norris J held that the former r 7.55 did apply to defective service of proceedings under s 212 where the service was technically defective in that it did not comply with the EU Service Regulation in circumstances where the defective service did not occasion any substantial injustice.

In *Re Baillies (in liquidation)* [2012] EWHC 285 (Ch), [2012] BPIR 665 at [16] HHJ Purle QC doubted, on an issue of service, that the Insolvency Rules, and specifically the former r 7.55, could displace the EC Regulation and, in particular, the imperative requirements of the EC Service Regulation. That position will remain unchanged under the 2016 Rules.

In *Loy v O'sullivan* [2010] EWHC 3583 (Ch), [2011] BPIR 181 HHJ McCahill QC, sitting as a High Court judge, had no difficulty in considering the former r 7.55 applicable to the cure of errors in a bankruptcy order in the absence of injustice to the debtor.

Breach of the former r 6.26 (permission required for presentation of second petition in respect of same debt where petitioning creditor fails to appear on hearing of first petition) is capable of cure under the former r 7.55: *Kasumu v Arrow Global (Guernsey) Ltd* [2013] EWHC 789 (Ch), [2013] BPIR 1047 at [20] (Asplin J).

**Administrator appointments under Sch B1**—The provision has no relevance where the appointment is found by the court to be valid, as in *Re Spaces London Bridge Ltd* [2018] EWHC 3099 (Ch), [2019] BPIR 660, [2019] BCC 280 (Nugee J); cf *Re NJM Clothing Ltd, Ross v Fashion Design Solutions* [2018] EWHC 2388 (Ch), [2018] BCC 875 (HHJ Klein).

Rule 12.64, like its predecessor, has no application to the appointment of an administrator out-of-court under para 22 of Sch B1: *Re G-Tech Construction Ltd* [2007] BPIR 1275 (Hart J); see also *Re Blights Builders Ltd* [2006] EWHC 3549 (Ch), [2007] BCC 712 (Norris J) and *Re Frontsouth (Witham) Ltd* [2011] EWHC 1668 (Ch), [2011] BPIR 1382 (Henderson J). The provision is available, however, to cure an impermissible out-of-hours electronic filing appointment by declaring that the appointment is effective as from the time when the court office next opens subject to an absence of substantial injustice consequent upon the irregularity: see *Symm & Co Ltd* [2020] EWHC 317 (Ch) (Zacaroli J). In *Re SJ Henderson & Co Ltd; Re Triumph Furniture Ltd* [2019] EWHC 2742 (Ch), in which the purported out-of-court appointments by the directors were only received by the court after its counters had shut, ICCJ Burton held, in a judgment departing from the decision of Barling J in *HMV Ecommerce Ltd* [2019] EWHC 903 (Ch), that there is no basis for such an out-of-hours appointment by directors or the company. Adopting a pragmatic approach however, the court held that the appointment took effect from the time at which the courts next opened.

Where there are no such insolvency proceedings, the validating effect of what is now r 12.64 has been held to be unavailable: *Re Frontsouth (Witham) Ltd* [2011] EWHC 1668 (Ch), [2011] BPIR 1382 (Henderson J). Frontsouth is authority for the proposition that, where an appointment under the IA 1986 is conditional on certain consents being given, r 12.64 cannot cure the fundamental defect manifested by the absence of any such consent. In *Re Care Matters Partnership Ltd (in administration)* [2011] EWHC 2543 (Ch) at [6] Norris J indicated that the agreed view of the judges of the Chancery Division was that the former r 7.55 could not operate to cure a fundamental defect – as opposed to what might be termed some administrative slip - in the appointment of an administrator. This differs from the view expressed in other decisions, such as that of HHJ Purle QC in *Re Assured Logistics Ltd* [2012] BCC 541 at [35], where the focus has been on the nature of the defect consequent upon which a view can be taken as to whether the curative effect of r 7.55 operates. The issue is discussed further below under the heading 'The true nature of the formal defect'.

The difficulty with defective administrator appointments stems from the decision of Morritt C in *Minmar (929) Ltd v Khalastchi* [2011] EWHC 1159 (Ch) where an administrator appointment had been effected by a single director without a resolution of the board and without notice to the company. Failure to give notice was held to be fatal to the appointment which was incurable. *Minmar* was decided after *Hill v Stokes plc* [2010] EWHC 3726 (a decision of HHJ McCahill QC which was not cited in *Minmar*) in which a QFC consented to the appointment but where a person who had distrained against the company entitled to notice was not given notice. The judge considered that notice not to be mandatory such that its omission was not fatal but instead a defect capable of waiver. In *National Westminster Bank plc v Masada Group* [2012] BCC 226 Warren J followed *Minmar* and considered (at [29]) *Stokes* to be clearly wrong. The subsequent authorities – none of which have reached the Court of Appeal for a fully ventilated overall view of the area – have taken a far less exacting approach than *Minmar*, the most detailed analysis appearing in the judgment of Norris J in *Re Virtualpurple Professional Services Ltd* [2011] EWHC 3487 (Ch) in which it was held that a failure to give a company notice of an intention to appoint an administrator was not fatal to the appointment on the ground that such notice could not be said to be a fundamental requirement of the appointment. It appears, therefore, that certain defects in an administrator's appointment are curable; less clear is whether the appointment remains ineffective until any such defect is cured.

In *Re Tokenhouse VB Ltd (formerly Vat Bridge 7) Ltd* [2020] EWHC 3171 (Ch) ICCJ Jones considered whether the failure to comply with the notice requirements in para 26 of Sch B1 inevitably invalidated the appointment out-of-court of an administrator. Applying *Ceart* (above) and *Re Skeggs Beef* [2019] EWHC 2607 (Ch) (Marcus Smith J), the task of the court was, first, to identify the purpose of the provision breached, and, secondly, to identify the consequences of non-compliance. Following some discussion (at [42]–[54]) the failure to give notice was held to be non-fundamental such that the validity of the appointment stood. However, the court considered appropriate an order appointing the preferred choice of office-holders of the applicant, the largest creditor. That approach to validity of appointment was followed by Deputy ICCJ Frith in *Re NMUL Realisations Ltd (in administration)* [2021] EWHC 94 (Ch) where the failure of a debenture holder to serve a notice of intention to appoint on the holder of prior ranking security under para 15 of Sch B1 was held to be an irregularity capable of being cured by r 12.64 with the consequence that the appointment was not invalidated from the outset. *Tokenhouse* and *NMUL* were followed by Mr Stuart Isaacs QC, sitting as a deputy High Court judge, in *Re Zoom UK Distribution Ltd (in administration)* [2021] EWHC 800 (Ch). For a further case in which the appointment of administrators was held to be incapable of cure, on its facts, for breach of para 16 of Sch B1 see *Re Glint Pay Ltd (in administration)* [2020] EWHC 3078 (Ch) (ICCJ Jones).

On administrator appointments see further *Re Euromaster Ltd* [2012] EWHC 2356 (Ch), [2012] BCC 754 (Norris J, r 7.55 applied); *Re Eco Link Resources Ltd* [2012] BCC 731 and *Re MTB Motors Ltd* [2010] EWHC 3751 (Ch), [2012] BCC 601 (HHJ Hodge QC, failure to give notice to the FSA under s 362A FSMA 2000 fatal and incapable of cure, retrospective administration order made); *Re Ceart Risk Services Ltd* [2012] BCC 592 (Arnold J, appointment valid notwithstanding failure to give notice to the FSA, but only from date of FSA consent obtained and filed, *Re MTB Motors* not cited); *Re ARG (Mansfield) Ltd* [2020] EWHC 1133 (Ch) (HHJ Davis-White QC, *MTB* followed, *Ceart* wrongly decided, administrator appointment a nullity in absence of statutory notice to the FSA): more generally on administrator appointments see also *Re Care People Ltd* [2013] EWHC 1734 (Ch) (HHJ Purle QC) and *Re Harlequin Management Services Ltd* [2013] EWHC 1926 (Ch) (Arnold J).

Where a defective administrator appointment is held to be beyond cure, one technique commonly adopted is to grant a retrospective administration order using the so-called *G-Tech* jurisdiction (on which, see the notes to para 13 of Sch B1). Such orders commonly provide for the express validation of the acts of the invalidly appointed administrators from the date of their purported appointed, as subject to the retrospective order, and the time and date of the order. In *Re Care Matters Partnership Ltd (in administration)* (above), in which a retrospective administration order was refused, Norris J warned that the question of whether a retrospective administration order should be made at all should not be confused with the question of the time at which any such order ought to take effect. In that case, the only useful purpose of a retrospective administration order would have been to allow the office-holders to draw their fees which the judge did not consider to be a proper ground for the making of an administration order. Although Norris J unhesitatingly granted the applicants permission to appeal, ultimately the appeal was not pursued.

**Curing defects in winding-up (and bankruptcy) petitions**—For the purposes of defects in winding-up petitions some guidance may be gleaned from the pre-1986 authorities. In particular, in *Re Vidiofusion Ltd* [1974] 1 WLR 1548 Megarry J refused to consider the advertisement of a winding-up petition invalid where the advertisement had made reference to 'Videofusion Ltd' (as opposed to 'Vidiofusion Ltd'). In his judgment (at 1549), and without stipulating any hard and fast rule, his Lordship identified four conditions which would ordinarily allow for the waiver of an error in or in relation to a petition. First, there should not be any other company on the register with any similar name. Secondly, the correct and erroneous names should have substantially the same pronunciation. Thirdly, there should not be any marked difference between the spellings of the correct and erroneous names. Fourthly, the error should not materially affect the alphabetical order of the names.

For further examples see *Re Army & Navy Hotel Ltd* (1886) 31 ChD 644 (inclusion of 'Co' entitled to petition); *Re J & P Sussmann Ltd* [1958] 1 WLR 519 (omission of final 'n'); *Re Manual Work Services (Construction) Ltd* [1975] 1 WLR 341.

**CPR Part 7 and 8 claims issued in error in Form IAA, and vice versa**—In *Re Taunton Logs Ltd (in administration)* [2020] EWHC 3480 (Ch), [2021] BPIR 427 administrators, prior to the company being moved into liquidation, had caused to be issued erroneously an Insolvency Act Application Notice in Form IAA under r 1.35 where, as HHJ Cawson QC, sitting as a High Court judge held at [31], the nature of the claim for unpaid share capital was in substance a simple debt claim by virtue of s 33 of the Companies Act 2006 so as to be inappropriate to insolvency proceedings but actionable as such under CPR Part 7. In the face of an application to strike out by the respondents to the application, and applying the judgment of Henderson J in *Philips v McGregor-Paterson* [2009] EWHC 2385 (Ch), [2010] BCLC 72 at [34]–[35] (in which case what were insolvency proceedings had been issued in CPR Part 7 form so as to be capable of cure under the predecessor to r 12.64 (IR 1986 r 7.55)), the proceedings ought to be treated as proceedings that fell within the scope of the CPR and the use of the wrong form treated as an 'error of procedure' capable of remedy under CPR 3.10, as opposed to amounting to a nullity (see [37]-[39] and [43]). Having regard to the seriousness and significance of the procedural error, why it had occurred and the wider circumstances of the case, the court exercised its discretion to cure the procedural error and to direct that the proceedings continue as if commenced under CPR Part 7 (with directions for statements of case and a CCMC being provided (at [55]), subject to the balance of the appropriate issue fee being paid. The judge reached his conclusion because there had been no abuse of process, the respondents were not prejudiced in any significant way and striking out would be grossly disproportionate (at [45] and [54]). Contrary to the administrators' submissions as to the applicability of r 12.64, by analogy with *Philips*, CPR 3.10 is the appropriate curative provision where the substance of the underlying claim is one actionable under the CPR, as the counterpart to the reverse position in *Philips* (above). Neither was some alternative procedural route under ss 140-150 IA 1986 argued for available to the liquidators in the circumstances.

The decisions in *Philips* and *Taunton* Logs do not, of course, provide hard and fast rules. The court will necessarily exercise its discretion on a case-by-case basis. The two authorities do, however, give an indication that the court is likely to favour cure over outright dismissal where such an outcome furthers the overriding objective and the interests of justice, especially given the court's accompanying discretion on costs.

See also here the notes to s 212 and r 12.6 under the heading 'Hybrid and assigned claims' and the commentary on the judgment in *Manolete Partners plc v Hayward and Barrett Holdings Ltd* [2021] EWHC 1481 (Ch) by which Chief ICCJ Briggs concluded at [60], 'with regret' in the face of well-founded criticisms of the present procedural framework, that a misfeasance claim under s 212 pursued by a litigation funder as assignee from a liquidator ought not to be included in an application pursuing causes of action within s 246ZD issued by way of an insolvency application notice in Form IAA, as provided for in IR 2016, r 1.35, but is amenable instead only to pursuit separately by way of a CPR Part 7 claim.

## [2.821]

### 12.65 Shorthand writers: nomination etc

(1) The court may in writing nominate a person to be official shorthand writer to the court.

(2) The court may, at any time in the course of insolvency proceedings, appoint a shorthand writer to take down evidence of a person examined under section 133, 236, 251N, 290 or 366.

(3) Where the official receiver applies to the court for an order appointing a shorthand writer, the official receiver must name the person the official receiver proposes for the appointment.

(4) The remuneration of a shorthand writer appointed in insolvency proceedings must be paid by the party at whose instance the appointment was made, or out of the insolvent estate, or otherwise, as the court may direct.

(5) Any question arising as to the rates of remuneration payable under this rule must be determined by the court.

**Derivation**—This rule derived from the Insolvency Rules 1986, SI 1986/1925, rr 7.16, 7.17.

## PART 13   OFFICIAL RECEIVERS

## [2.822]

### 13.1 Official receivers in court

(1) Judicial notice must be taken of the appointment under sections 399 to 401 of official receivers and deputy official receivers.

(2) Official receivers and deputy official receivers have a right of audience in insolvency proceedings, whether in the High Court or the County Court.

**Derivation**—This rule derived from the Insolvency Rules 1986, SI 1986/1925, r 10.1.

**General note**—As judicial notice is taken concerning the appointment of official receivers under ss 399–401, there is no need to prove appointment.

## [2.823]

### 13.2 Persons entitled to act on official receiver's behalf

(1) In the absence of the official receiver authorised to act in a particular case, an officer authorised in writing for the purpose by the Secretary of State, or by the official

receiver, may with the permission of the court, act on the official receiver's behalf and in the official receiver's place—

    (a)    in any examination under section 133, 236, 251N, 290 or 366; and

    (b)    in relation to any application to the court.

(2)   In case of emergency, where there is no official receiver capable of acting, anything to be done by, to or before the official receiver may be done by, to or before the registrar or District Judge.

**Derivation**—This rule derived from the Insolvency Rules 1986, SI 1986/1925, r 10.2.

## [2.824]

### 13.3 Application for directions

The official receiver may apply to the court for directions in relation to any matter arising in insolvency proceedings.

**Derivation**—This rule derived from the Insolvency Rules 1986, SI 1986/1925, r 10.3.

This provision reflects the supervisory role of the court over liquidations (whether compulsory or not). Applications for directions are not limited to minor procedural directions: see for example *Re Transworld Payment Solutions UK Ltd (in liquidation)* [2020] EWHC 115 (Ch) where the OR applied for a direction as to whether applications that the OR had brought for public examination of individuals pursuant to s 133(2) IA 1986 upon the request of a creditor of the company should be discontinued. This was where the intended examinees asserted that the creditor concerned had improper or collateral purposes but the OR was not able to conclude that the applications should be discontinued, as the disputes were largely outside the OR's compass.

## [2.825]

### 13.4 Official receiver's expenses

(1)   Any expenses (including damages) incurred by the official receiver (in whatever capacity the official receiver may be acting) in connection with proceedings taken against the official receiver in insolvency proceedings are to be treated as expenses of the insolvency proceedings.

(2)   The official receiver has a charge on the insolvent estate in respect of any sums due to the official receiver under paragraph (1) in connection with insolvency proceedings other than proceedings relating to debt relief orders or applications for debt relief orders.

**Derivation**—This rule derived from the Insolvency Rules 1986, SI 1986/1925, r 10.4.

## [2.826]

### 13.5 Official receiver not to be appointed liquidator or trustee

The official receiver may not be appointed as liquidator or trustee by any decision of creditors or (in a winding up) contributories or the company.

**Derivation**—This rule derived from the Insolvency Rules 1986, SI 1986/1925, r 4.101B.

PART 14   CLAIMS BY AND DISTRIBUTIONS TO CREDITORS IN ADMINIS-
TRATION, WINDING UP AND BANKRUPTCY

CHAPTER 1

APPLICATION AND INTERPRETATION

## [2.827]

### 14.1 Application of Part 14 and interpretation

[Note: "bankruptcy debt" and related expressions are defined in relation to bankruptcy in section 382.]

(1)   This Part applies to administration, winding up and bankruptcy proceedings.

(2)   The definitions in this rule apply to administration, winding up and bankruptcy proceedings except as otherwise stated.

(3)   "Debt", in relation to winding up and administration, means (subject to the next paragraph) any of the following—

(a)     any debt or liability to which the company is subject at the relevant date;

(b)     any debt or liability to which the company may become subject after the relevant date by reason of any obligation incurred before that date;

(c)     any interest provable as mentioned in rule 14.23;

"small debt" means a debt (being the total amount owed to a creditor) which does not exceed £1,000 (which amount is prescribed for the purposes of paragraph 13A of Schedule 8 to the Act and paragraph 18A of Schedule 9 to the Act);

"dividend", in relation to a members' voluntary winding up, includes a distribution;

"provable debt" has the meaning given in rule 14.2; and

"relevant date" means—

(a)     in the case of an administration which was not immediately preceded by a winding up, the date on which the company entered administration,

(b)     in the case of an administration which was immediately preceded by a winding up, the date on which the company went into liquidation,

(c)     in the case of a winding up which was not immediately preceded by an administration, the date on which the company went into liquidation,

(d)     in the case of a winding up which was immediately preceded by an administration, the date on which the company entered administration, and

(e)     in the case of a bankruptcy, the date of the bankruptcy order.

(4)   For the purposes of any provision of the Act or these Rules about winding up or administration, any liability in tort is a debt provable in the winding up or administration, if either—

(a)     the cause of action has accrued at the relevant date; or

(b)     all the elements necessary to establish the cause of action exist at that date except for actionable damage.

(5)   For the purposes of references in any provision of the Act or these Rules about winding up or administration to a debt or liability, it is immaterial whether the debt or liability is present or future, whether it is certain or contingent, or whether its amount is fixed or liquidated, or is capable of being ascertained by fixed rules or as a matter of opinion; and references in any such provision to owing a debt are to be read accordingly.

(6)   In any provision of the Act or these Rules about winding up or administration, except in so far as the context otherwise requires, "liability" means (subject to paragraph (4)) a liability to pay money or money's worth, including any liability under an enactment, a liability for breach of trust, any liability in contract, tort or bailment, and any liability arising out of an obligation to make restitution.

**Derivation**—This rule derived from the Insolvency Rules 1986, SI 1986/1925, r 13.12.

**General note**—Part 14 of the IR 2016 applies to administrations, winding up and bankruptcies (but not to company voluntary arrangements, for which, surprisingly, there are no corresponding definitions in the Act or the Rules). It is one of a number of provisions that deals with the meaning of 'debt' (see also s 382 in the bankruptcy context) and r 14.2 (provable debts).

**'Debt'**—This has a broad ambit. In *Tottenham Hotspur plc v Edennote plc* [1995] 1 BCLC 65 it was said that if a person obtains an order for costs then that constitutes a debt within what is now r 14.1(3)(b) and can form the basis for the presentation of a petition to wind up.

The Supreme Court in *Re Nortel GmbH* [2013] UKSC 52, [2014] AC 209 (an administration case but applicable equally to liquidations as far as the following discussion is concerned) dealt with an appeal relating to an insolvent company where there was a shortfall in the occupational pension fund assets. The Pensions Regulator issued financial support directions, which led (after the commencement of the winding up) to the issue of contribution notices pursuant to ss 43 and 47 respectively of the Pensions Act 2004. The Court had to decide whether the liability under the contribution notices was a provable debt (which would rank pari passu with other unsecured debts) or whether it was payable as an expense by the liquidator. At first instance and in the Court of Appeal it was held that the liability constituted an expense. The Supreme Court unanimously allowed the appeal from the decision of the Court of Appeal and held that the liability was a provable debt. In giving the leading judgment, Lord Neuberger said that the claim could be characterised as a provable debt within what is now r 14.1(3)(b). Lord Neuberger said that there was no overlap between the definition of debt in sub-paras (a) and (b) - each rule has to be read in a sensible and coherent way, and one has to read paras (a) and (b) so that they work together: 'Paragraph (a) is concerned with liabilities to which the company "is subject" at the date of the insolvency event, whereas paragraph (b) is directed to those liabilities to which it "may become subject" subsequent to that date' (at [70]). Lord Neuberger said that the claim at hand fell within para (b), as it is a 'liability under an enactment' and the liability arose 'by reason of any obligation incurred before' the insolvency event ([72]–[86]). His Lordship said that, normally, in order for a company to have incurred a liability under (b) it must have taken, or been subjected to, some step or combination of steps which (a) had some legal effect (such as putting it under some legal duty or into some legal relationship), and which (b) resulted in it being vulnerable to the specific liability in question, such that there would be a real prospect of that liability being incurred. If those two requirements were satisfied, it is then relevant to consider (c) whether it would be consistent with the regime under which the liability is imposed to conclude that the step or combination of steps gave rise to an obligation under rule 14.1(3)(b) (at [77]). In *Discovery (Northampton) Ltd v Debenhams Retail Ltd* [2019] EWHC 2441 (Ch), [2020] BCC 9, Norris J held that an existing lease precisely fits this profile, that future rent fits the description of a future liability to which the company may become subject by reason of it and therefore that future rent fell within the extended meaning of the term 'debt' (albeit not a provable one due to r 14.22) (at [50], [52] and [58]–[59]). In *Re North Point Global Ltd* [2020] EWHC 1648 (Ch), [2020] 2 BCLC 676, [2020] BPIR 1170 a preference claim of liquidators of a company against another company was held to have been a contingent debt (which would fall within r 14.1(3)(b)) even before the liquidators had been appointed (ie when there was not yet anyone able to pursue such a claim) for the purposes of the other company's CVA (at [113]). In *Re Paperback Collection and Recycling Ltd (in liquidation)* [2020] EWHC 1601 (Ch), [2020] BPIR 1200 a fine imposed on a company in criminal proceedings which was triggered by criminal offences prior to the entry into liquidation was held to be a contingent or future debt or liability (at [23]).

The word 'any' in r 14.1(3)(b) means that the provision is wide: *Haine v Day* [2008] EWCA Civ 626 at [77]. A liability that is contingent on the making of an award after the commencement of liquidation is covered by the rule: *Haine v Day* (a protective award under the Trade Union and Labour Relations (Consolidation) Act 1992 was a contingent liability within this rule).

For further reading, see G Moss, 'Proof Positive – Supreme Court Expands Scope of Provable Contingent Liabilities' (2013) 26 Ins Intel 108.

'**small debt**'—A new concept introduced by IR 2016 – see the simplified procedure for proving for the purpose of payment of a dividend in r 14.3(3).

## RULE 14.1(4)

'**Liability in tort**'—The Insolvency (Amendment) Rules 2006 amended this rule (so as to overturn the effect of the judgment in *Re T & N Ltd* [2005] EWHC 2870 (Ch), [2006] 1 WLR 1728, [2006] 2 BCLC 374) with the effect of extending the claims that can be included as tort claims that can constitute debt in a winding up or administration. Now debt includes not only tort claims where all elements for a tort action exist against the company when it entered winding up or administration, but also all claims where all elements exist save for the fact that the claimant has not suffered any damage.

## RULE 14.1(5)

'**Contingent**'—See under the heading 'Contingent or prospective creditors' in relation to s 124.

## CHAPTER 2

### CREDITORS' CLAIMS IN ADMINISTRATION, WINDING UP AND BANKRUPTCY

## [2.828]

**Note**

[Note: a document required by the Act or these Rules must also contain the standard contents set out in Part 1.]

**General note on rules 14.3–14.11**—These rules sensibly bring together in one place the provisions on proof of debt for each insolvency process (previously repeated throughout the old rules within the sections dealing with each individual process).

**[2.829]**

**14.2 Provable debts**

(1)   All claims by creditors except as provided in this rule, are provable as debts against the company or bankrupt, whether they are present or future, certain or contingent, ascertained or sounding only in damages.

(2)   The following are not provable—

    (a)    an obligation arising under a confiscation order made under—

        (i)      section 1 of the Drug Trafficking Offences Act 1986,

        (ii)     section 1 of the Criminal Justice (Scotland) Act 1987,

        (iii)   section 71 of the Criminal Justice Act 1988, or

        (iv)   Parts 2, 3 or 4 of the Proceeds of Crime Act 2002;

    (b)    an obligation arising from a payment out of the social fund under section 138(1)(b) of the Social Security Contributions and Benefits Act 1992 by way of crisis loan or budgeting loan.

    (c)    in bankruptcy—

        (i)      a fine imposed for an offence,

        (ii)     an obligation (other than an obligation to pay a lump sum or to pay costs) arising under an order made in family proceedings, or

        (iii)   an obligation arising under a maintenance assessment made under the Child Support Act 1991.

(3)   In paragraph (2)(c), "fine" and "family proceedings" have the meanings given by section 281(8) (which applies the Magistrates Courts Act 1980 and the Matrimonial and Family Proceedings Act 1984).

(4)   The following claims are not provable until after all other claims of creditors have been paid in full with interest under sections 189(2) (winding up), section 328(4) (bankruptcy) and rule 14.23 (payment of interest)—

    (a)    a claim arising by virtue of section 382(1)(a) of the Financial Services and Markets Act 2000 (restitution orders), unless it is also a claim arising by virtue of sub-paragraph (b) of that section (a person who has suffered loss etc); or

    (b)    in administration and winding up, a claim which by virtue of the Act or any other enactment is a claim the payment of which in a bankruptcy, an administration or a winding up is to be postponed.

(5)   Nothing in this rule prejudices any enactment or rule of law under which a particular kind of debt is not provable, whether on grounds of public policy or otherwise.

**Derivation**—This rule derived from the Insolvency Rules 1986, SI 1986/1925, r 12.3.

**General note**—Rule 14.2(1) sets out what is provable and r 14.2(2) what is not provable. It has been said that the policy behind what is now r 14.2 requires one to read the limitation in r 14.2(2), setting out what is not provable, narrowly: *Cadwell v Jackson* [2001] BPIR 966 at 974. The rule is not to be read in isolation and the definition of 'debt' in what is now r 14.1 must also be considered: *Re T & N Ltd* [2005] EWHC 2870 (Ch), [2006] 1 WLR 1728, [2006] 2 BCLC 374. The definition of provable debt is, according to the Supreme Court in *Re Nortel GmbH* [2013] UKSC 52, [2014] AC 209 at [66], 'strikingly wide', particularly when read with what is now r 14.1. Lord Neuberger (giving the leading judgment) said that if a claim is not a liability within what is now r 14.1 then it cannot come within what is now r 14.2 and cannot be a provable debt (at [66]). See the notes under r 14.1 for a discussion of the case.

For further reading, see G Moss, 'Proof Positive – Supreme Court Expands Scope of Provable Contingent Liabilities' (2013) 26 Ins Intel 108.

**'Claims'**—This term is used here rather than debts, as the law allows parties to claim for broader things than traditional debts. A preference claim is a provable debt: *Re North Point Global Ltd* [2020] EWHC 1648 (Ch), [2020] 2 BCLC 676, [2020] BPIR 1170 at [113].

**'Future'**—Clearly this aims to refer to demands that are in liquidated form and which have not become due and payable at the commencement of the insolvency regime. See r 14.22 for proving in respect of payments of a periodic nature. See r 14.44 and the notes thereto, which explain that to offset the benefit given to creditors in relation to future claims there is a discount, calculated in accordance with r 14.44(2).

'Contingent'—See under the heading 'Contingent or prospective creditors' in relation to s 124.

'Fine'—It is only in bankruptcy that fines are not regarded as provable debts. The same does not apply in liquidation. In *Re Paperback Collection and Recycling Ltd (in liquidation)* [2020] EWHC 1601 (Ch), [2020] BPIR 1200 a fine imposed on a company in criminal proceedings which was triggered by criminal offences prior to the entry into liquidation was held to be a provable debt even where the fine was not imposed until after the onset of insolvency (at [23]).

The term 'fine' is defined in s 281(8) by reference to s 150(1) of the Magistrates' Courts Act 1980 which is limited to a fine imposed by a criminal court as a result of a criminal conviction, as opposed to a penalty imposed by, say, a professional body (which would be provable): *Marcus v Institute of Chartered Accountants* [2004] EWHC 3010 (Ch), [2005] BPIR 413 (Evans-Lombe J). So a criminal compensation order would not be provable: *R v Barnet Magistrates Court, ex p Phillippou* [1997] BPIR 134. Tax penalties are provable: *Count Artsrunik v Waller* [2005] BPIR 82.

**Order made in family proceedings**—The rule as it applies to orders in family proceedings has had several manifestations, meaning that different versions apply according to when the bankruptcy petition or order was made. For bankruptcies where the bankruptcy petition leading to the order was presented before 28 December 1986, any obligation to pay a lump sum or costs constituted provable debts, and a debtor was released from them on discharge. For bankruptcy orders made as a result of petitions presented after 28 December 1986 and bankruptcies where the order was made before 1 April 2005, lump sums and costs awarded against a person in relation to family proceedings were not provable in a bankruptcy of that person: see *Levy v Legal Services Commission* [2000] BPIR 1065; *Wehmeyer v Wehmeyer* [2001] BPIR 548; *Ram v Ram* [2005] BPIR 616. But now, according to r 14.2(2)(c)(ii), since its predecessor's amendment by the Insolvency (Amendment) Rules 2005 (SI 2005/527), they are provable, as far as bankruptcy orders made on or after 1 April 2005 are concerned. On the other hand, obligations, such as maintenance orders are not provable.

The position in relation to maintenance orders made in family proceedings held in a foreign jurisdiction is not clear. It was held in *Wehmeyer v Wehmeyer* [2001] BPIR 548 at 551 that such maintenance orders are not provable. But, shortly before *Wehmeyer* was decided, in *Cadwell v Jackson* [2001] BPIR 966, a case involving quite different facts, Neuberger J was of the view that any proceedings outside of the UK could not come within the expression 'family proceedings' found in this rule (at 970–971). Although his Lordship was dealing with a lump sum judgment, he indicated that what he had to say applied to foreign maintenance orders except where they were registered in the UK (at 972–973). Registrar James, who decided *Wehmeyer*, did not refer to *Cadwell* and one assumes that he was not referred to the decision. In a subsequent Court of Appeal decision (*Cartwright v Cartwright* [2002] BPIR 895 at 901) the court referred to both *Wehmeyer* and *Cadwell*, but refrained from commenting on whether either was correct. However, Arden LJ in delivering the leading judgment did state, in effect, that a maintenance order needs to be registered if it is to fall within r 12.3(2)(a) of the IR 1986 (replaced by r 14.2(2)(c) of the IR 2016). This all suggests that a maintenance order in family proceedings held in a foreign jurisdiction constitutes a non-provable debt only where the order is registered in the UK. However, in *Cartwright*, the payments due pursuant to the foreign maintenance order were not provable pursuant to r 12.3(3) IR 1986 (replaced by r 14.2(5) IR 2016) as the order was variable by the Hong Kong court and therefore unenforceable in England at common law because it was not final and conclusive.

**Income payments agreement/order**—Both arrears and future amounts payable under an income payments agreement or income payments order are provable debts in bankruptcy: *Booth v Mond* [2010] EWHC 1576 (Ch), [2010] BPIR 1111; *Azuonye v Kent* [2019] EWCA Civ 1289, [2019] 4 WLR 101, [2019] BPIR 1317.

**Claim by employees**—A claim by an employee for breach of contract, unfair dismissal and discrimination is a provable debt without the requirement of the obtaining of a judgment: *Unite the Union v Nortel Networks UK Ltd* [2010] EWHC 826 (Ch), [2010] 2 BCLC 674, [2010] BPIR 1003.

**Contractual subordination**—Where a provision is effective to subordinate a debt (ie a simple contractual subordination), then it means that the subordinated debt ranks below other obligations that would themselves ordinarily fall below it in the statutory waterfall. Such a clause renders the subordinated creditor unable to prove at least until the obligations prior to that debt have been satisfied in full. However, this does not cause the subordinated debt to lose its status as a provable debt or to become an unprovable obligation; it simply compels the creditor to lodge the proof late (after all prior obligations have been satisfied): *Re LB Holdings Intermediate 2 Ltd (in Administration)* [2020] EWHC 1681 at [122].

**[2.830]**

### 14.3 Proving a debt

(1)   A creditor wishing to recover a debt must submit a proof to the office-holder unless—

(a)   this rule or an order of the court provides otherwise; or

(b)   it is a members' voluntary winding up in which case the creditor is not required to submit a proof unless the liquidator requires one to be submitted.

(2)   A creditor is deemed to have proved—

(a)   in a winding up immediately preceded by an administration, where the creditor has already proved in the administration; or

(b)   in an administration immediately preceded by a winding up, where the creditor has already proved in the winding up.

(3)   A creditor is deemed to have proved for the purposes of determination and payment of a dividend but not otherwise where—

(a)   the debt is a small debt;

(b)   a notice has been delivered to the creditor of intention to declare a dividend or make a distribution under rule 14.29 which complies with rule 14.31 (further contents of notice to creditors owed small debts); and

(c)   the creditor has not advised the office-holder that the debt is incorrect or not owed in response to the notice.

**Derivation**—This rule derived from the Insolvency Rules 1986, SI 1986/1925, rr 2.72, 4.73, 6.96.

**General note**—Under IR 1986 there was a distinction in the rules for proving in compulsory, and the rules for proving in voluntary (both creditors' and members'), liquidation, with the former requiring claims to be proved formally but the latter giving discretion to the liquidator as to whether they required a claim to be submitted in writing (r 4.73(1) and (2) IR 1986). However, under r 14.3 IR 2016, the distinction is between compulsory and creditors' voluntary liquidations on the one hand and members' voluntary liquidations on the other hand. It is only in members' voluntary liquidations that a creditor is not required to submit a proof unless the liquidator requires one to be submitted. In compulsory liquidations and creditors' voluntary liquidations, creditors must submit a proof unless the creditor is deemed to have proved by virtue of r 14.3(2) or (3) or the court provides otherwise.

**RULE 14.3(3)**

This new provision simplifies the process for proving 'small debts' (defined in r 14.1(3)) for the purpose of payment of a dividend. The threshold is currently £1,000.

**[2.831]**

### 14.4 Requirements for proof

(1)   A proof must—

(a)   be made out by, or under the direction of, the creditor and authenticated by the creditor or a person authorised on the creditor's behalf;

(b)   state the creditor's name and address;

(c)   if the creditor is a company, identify the company;

(d)   state the total amount of the creditor's claim (including any value added tax) as at the relevant date, less any payments made after that date in relation to the claim, any deduction under rule 14.20 and any adjustment by way of set-off in accordance with rules 14.24 and 14.25;

(e)   state whether or not the claim includes any outstanding uncapitalised interest;

(f)   contain particulars of how and when the debt was incurred by the company or the bankrupt;

(g)   contain particulars of any security held, the date on which it was given and the value which the creditor puts on it;

(h)   provide details of any reservation of title in relation to goods to which the debt relates;

    (i)     provide details of any document by reference to which the debt can be substantiated;

    (j)     be dated and authenticated; and

    (k)    state the name, postal address and authority of the person authenticating the proof (if someone other than the creditor).

(2)   Where sub-paragraph (i) applies the document need not be delivered with the proof unless the office-holder has requested it.

(3)   The office-holder may call for the creditor to produce any document or other evidence which the office-holder considers is necessary to substantiate the whole or any part of a claim.

**Derivation**—This rule derived from the Insolvency Rules 1986, SI 1986/1925, rr 2.72(3), 4.73, 4.75, 6.96, 6.98.

Rule 14.4(1)(d) requires a proof by a creditor to acknowledge an undisputed cross-claim (*Bresco Electrical Services Ltd (in liquidation) v Michael J Lonsdale (Electrical Ltd)* [2020] UKSC 25, [2020] 2 BCLC 147, [2020] BPIR 1078 at [31]).

## [2.832]

### 14.5  Costs of proving

Unless the court orders otherwise—

    (a)    each creditor bears the cost of proving for that creditor's own debt, including costs incurred in providing documents or evidence under rule 14.4 (3);

    (b)    in an administration or winding up, costs incurred by the office-holder in estimating the value of a debt under rule 14.14 are payable out of the assets as an expense of the administration or winding up; and

    (c)    in a bankruptcy, costs incurred by the office-holder in estimating the value of a debt under section 322(3) fall on the bankrupt's estate as an expense of the bankruptcy.

**Derivation**—This rule derived from the Insolvency Rules 1986, SI 1986/1925, rr 2.74, 4.78, 6.100.

## [2.833]

### 14.6  Allowing inspection of proofs

The office-holder must, so long as proofs delivered to the office-holder are in the possession of the office-holder, allow them to be inspected, at all reasonable times on any business day, by the following—

    (a)    a creditor who has delivered a proof (unless the proof has been wholly rejected for purposes of dividend or otherwise, or withdrawn);

    (b)    a member or contributory of the company or, in the case of a bankruptcy, the bankrupt; and

    (c)    a person acting on behalf of any of the above.

**Derivation**—This rule derived from the Insolvency Rules 1986, SI 1986/1925, rr 2.75, 4.79, 6.101.

**General note**—The right of inspection is restricted to the proof itself and does not include the documentation submitted in support of the proof: *MG Rover Dealer Properties Ltd v Hunt* [2012] BPIR 590. Inspection need only be permitted if the creditor, member, contributory or person acting on their behalf can show a legitimate interest in inspection: *Burnden Group Holdings Ltd v Hunt* [2018] EWHC 463 (Ch), [2018] 2 BCLC 122.

## [2.834]

### 14.7  Admission and rejection of proofs for dividend

(1)   The office-holder may admit or reject a proof for dividend (in whole or in part).

(2)   If the office-holder rejects a proof in whole or in part, the office-holder must deliver to the creditor a statement of the office-holder's reasons for doing so, as soon as reasonably practicable.

**Derivation**—This rule derived from the Insolvency Rules 1986, SI 1986/1925, rr 2.77, 4.82, 6.104.

**General note**—The process of proof is (by comparison with litigation or arbitration) relatively light-tough and inquisitorial, and the outcome is only provisionally binding, in the sense that both the proving creditor and any other creditor may challenge the office-holder's ruling by proceedings in court, in which the issues are addressed de novo: see discussion by Lord Briggs JSC at paras [31]–[34] in *Bresco Electrical Services Limited (in liquidation) v Michael J Lonsdale (Electrical) Limited* [2020] UKSC 25, [2020] 2 BCLC 147, [2020] BPIR 1078.

Office-holders are obliged to make a decision on a proof of debt one way or another (unless the parties agree for the proof to be withdrawn or varied) regardless of whether the company had assets to make this a worthwhile exercise (*Re Burnden Group Ltd* [2017] EWHC 406 (Ch), [2017] BPIR 585 at [26]). In determining whether a proof should be admitted or rejected in a winding up, the liquidator is acting in a quasi-judicial capacity: *Re Menastar Finance Ltd* [2002] EWHC 2610 (Ch), [2003] 1 BCLC 338 at [44]. The task of the liquidator is to ensure that the assets of the company are distributed amongst those who are justly and properly creditors of that company, and so the liquidator is to satisfy himself or herself that there is adequate evidence that the debt on which the proof is based is a real one (*Re Menastar Finance Ltd* at [46]–[47]; *Nimat Halal Food Limited v Patel* [2020] EWHC 734 (Ch) at [14]). It is incumbent on the liquidator to examine every proof lodged, as far as concerns the grounds of the debt and any possible right of set-off (*Re National Wholemeal Bread & Biscuit Co* [1892] 2 Ch 457). The fact that a proof is based on a judgment does not prevent or relieve the liquidator from performing this duty. In discharging the duty to adjudicate on claims an office-holder may question and investigate but where evidence has been submitted he must examine it (*Re JPF Clarke (Construction) Ltd* [2020] BPIR 194 at [10]). If a liquidator is not convinced by a proof, he or she is to reject it, and not to conduct an examination of the creditor: *Bellmex International v British American Tobacco* [2001] 1 BCLC 91, Evans-Lombe J.

In considering whether to admit a creditor's proof that is based on a judgment debt, courts may, where appropriate, go behind the judgment and examine the circumstances surrounding the judgment and see whether the debt was truly due (*Re Menastar Finance Ltd* at [50]). Before doing this, and where there is no outstanding appeal or application to set aside, there must be some suggestion of fraud, collusion or miscarriage of justice, or else the judgment is to be taken as conclusive (*Re AMF International Ltd (No 2)* [1996] 2 BCLC 9; *Re Menastar Finance Ltd; Re Shruth Ltd* [2005] EWHC 1293 (Ch), [2006] 1 BCLC 294, [2005] BPIR 1455 at [31]). In this context 'miscarriage of justice' is given a wide application and it means 'something from which it can be concluded that had there been a properly conducted judicial process it would have been found or very likely could have been found that nothing was in fact due to the claimant': *Dawodu v American Express Bank* [2001] BPIR 983 at 990. The expression would include the situation where the substance of the claim leading to the judgment is able to be questioned, such as where a default judgment is granted: *Re Shruth Ltd* at [31]–[32]. In going behind a judgment, a liquidator is not limited to the evidence that was presented at the original hearing (*Re Menastar Finance Ltd* at [45]). In *Re Menastar Finance Ltd* the liquidator was held to be entitled to refuse to go behind a judgment obtained in proceedings which were uncontested by the company on the basis that the company and its parent had themselves effectively engineered a situation whereby the company did not contest the claim.

In *Re Lehman Brothers International (Europe) (In Administration) (No 4)* [2017] UKSC 38, [2018] AC 465, [2017] 2 BCLC 149 (SC), the Supreme Court held that it is not open to a creditor to lodge a proof in respect of a subordinated debt until the non-provable liabilities have been paid in full or at least until it is clear that, after meeting that proof in full and paying any statutory interest due on it, the non-provable liabilities could be met in full. Further, Lord Neuberger expressed the view that it may be that a subordinated debt was a non-provable debt which ranked after all other non-provable liabilities therefore requiring no proof, but left the point open. However, the point arose for determination in *Re LB Holdings Intermediate 2 Ltd (in Administration)* [2020] EWHC 1681 where Marcus Smith J held (at [122]) that a claim subordinated by a contingency did not lose its status as a provable debt or become an unprovable obligation; it simply compelled the creditor to lodge a late proof (after all prior obligations had been satisfied – see further, discussion under r 14.2).

To constitute a rejection, only basic reasons for the rejection need to be given by the liquidator: *Managa Properties Ltd v Brittain* [2009] EWHC 157 (Ch), [2009] 1 BCLC 689, [2009] BPIR 306 at [32].

In *Re RJH Stanhope Ltd* [2020] EWHC 2808 (Ch) HHJ Saffman QC (sitting as a High Court judge), held that the adjudication of a proof of debt by a company's liquidators did not bind the court when considering an application under s 212 in respect of alleged misfeasance/breach of duty by the respondent director in which the loss was quantified by reference to the proof of debt even where the respondent could have challenged the adjudication. The purpose of the liquidators' adjudication and the court's obligation were different; the former represented what the liquidators' accepted as the company's debt to the creditor whilst the purpose of the latter was to assess the loss to the company.

## [2.835]

### 14.8 Appeal against decision on proof

(1) If a creditor is dissatisfied with the office-holder's decision under rule 14.7 in relation to the creditor's own proof (including a decision whether the debt is preferential), the creditor may apply to the court for the decision to be reversed or varied.

(2) The application must be made within 21 days of the creditor receiving the statement delivered under rule 14.7(2).

(3) A member, a contributory, any other creditor or, in a bankruptcy, the bankrupt, if dissatisfied with the office-holder's decision admitting, or rejecting the whole or any part of, a proof or agreeing to revalue a creditor's security under rule 14.15, may make such an application within 21 days of becoming aware of the office-holder's decision.

(4) The court must fix a venue for the application to be heard.

(5) The applicant must deliver notice of the venue to the creditor who delivered the proof in question (unless it is the applicant's own proof) and the office-holder.

(6) The office-holder must, on receipt of the notice, file the relevant proof with the court, together (if appropriate) with a copy of the statement sent under rule 14.7(2).

(7) After the application has been heard and determined, a proof which was submitted by the creditor in hard copy form must be returned by the court to the office-holder.

**Derivation**—This rule derived from the Insolvency Rules 1986, SI 1986/1925, rr 2.78, 4.83, 6.105.

**General note**—If a creditor is unhappy with the decision of a liquidator to reject a proof, he or she must lodge an appeal under this rule as the debt cannot be pursued against the liquidator through other avenues: *BCCI v Habib Bank Ltd* [1999] 1 WLR 42, [1999] BPIR 1.

Someone who is a former liquidator, wishing to take issue with what the present liquidator has admitted to proof, is not able to apply to the court under this rule, as he or she is not a contributory or a creditor: *Re AMF International Ltd (No 2)* [1996] 1 WLR 77, [1996] 2 BCLC 9.

An appeal against the liquidator's rejection of a proof involves a rehearing de novo (*Re Trepca Mines Ltd* [1960] 1 WLR 1273 and see *Cadwell v Jackson* [2001] BPIR 966), and this enables either party to adduce fresh evidence in support of his or her case (*Re a Company (No 004539 of 1993); [1995] 1 BCLC 459; Re Menastar Finance Ltd* [2002] EWHC 2610 (Ch), [2003] 1 BCLC 338 at [45]; *Re Shruth Ltd* [2005] EWHC 1293 (Ch), [2005] BPIR 1455, [2006] 1 BCLC 294 at [26]). The burden of proof is on the applicant to the civil standard and not the office-holder (*Re The Burnden Group Limited (in liquidation)* [2017] EWHC 247 (Ch), [2017] BPIR 554). It is not for the court to review the decision of the office-holder to decide if the decision was correct, rather the court has to determine, on the evidence before it, whether the claim should be admitted and in what amount (*Lynch v Cadwallader* [2021] EWHC 328 (Ch) at [82]; *McCarthy v Tan* [2015] EWHC 2049 (Ch)), [2015] BPIR 1224 at [11]–[13]; *Re a Company (No 004539 of 1993)* [1995] 1 BCLC 459). Where necessary to dispose of a matter, courts may permit the cross-examination of a claimant on the evidence filed by the claimant in support of his or her claim against the company: *Re BCCI (No 6)* [1994] 1 BCLC 450; *Re The Burnden Group Limited (in liquidation)*. It has been held that cross-examination is necessary in a case where there was no documentary evidence of any kind submitted in order to support the contention by a person who claimed to hold money in bank accounts on behalf of the claimant (*Re BCCI (No 6)*). Although the matter is always highly fact-sensitive and no hard and fast rule can be laid down, in general, in the absence of cross-examination, the benefit of the doubt must be given to the witness, and his or her evidence should only be disbelieved if it can properly be regarded as incredible (*Re The Burnden Group Limited (in liquidation)*). Disclosure may be ordered if necessary for fairly disposing of the issue for example where the office-holder does not have the requisite knowledge for evidence to be challenged in cross-examination without disclosure (*Re BCCI (No 6)*).

Where an appeal is commenced against the decision of a liquidator concerning a proof, the role of the liquidator changes. The liquidator no longer exercises the quasi-judicial power, but in fact becomes a litigant in defending his or her decision: *Tanning Research Laboratories Inc v O'Brien* (1990) 169 CLR 332, (1990) 8 ACLC 248. If the liquidator rejected the proof, he or she is able to raise any defences that would have been available to the company had no liquidation been initiated: *Re Kentwood Constructions Ltd* [1960] 1 WLR 646; *Tanning Research Laboratories Inc v O'Brien*. However, where an office-holder adopted a neutral approach to an application where the debt arose out of a highly contentious dispute arising from an unfair prejudice petition, it was held that he had acted appropriately and with integrity (*Nimat Halal Food Limited v Patel* [2020] EWHC 734 (Ch) at [45]).

If a liquidator rejects a proof and the pertinent creditor appeals, it would seem, on the basis of Australian authority, that another creditor could not be joined as a party to the appeal on the basis that, if the rejection was overturned, it would receive a smaller dividend: *Australian Consolidated Investments Ltd v Woodings* (1996) 14 ACLC 1187.

As indicated in the notes to the previous rule, a liquidator can only go behind the judgment on which a creditor relies if there is evidence of fraud, collusion or miscarriage of justice. Where the court making the judgment has ample evidence before it from which to make the decision that it has, the judgment should stand: *Re Shruth Ltd* [2005] EWHC 1293 (Ch), [2005] BPIR 1455, [2006] 1 BCLC 294.

If a creditor is late in appealing he or she may seek an extension of time. In considering whether to grant an extension of time the court will, at least in complex cases, have regard to CPR 3.9 and apply the three stage process that is employed in applications for relief from sanctions under that rule as provided for in *Denton v TH Waite Ltd* [2014] EWCA Civ 906 (*Re Legal and Equitable Securities plc* [2010] EWHC 2046 (Ch), [2011] BCC 354; *McCarthy v Tann* [2016] EWHC 542 (Ch)). In *McCarthy v Tann* the registrar only got to the point of considering the first stage, that is, was the breach serious and significant, and did not need to proceed to consider the other two stages (whether there was a good reason for the default and whether the extension should be granted in all the circumstances in order to deal with the case justly). The registrar granted an extension of time for the filing of the appeal as it was not serious or significant because: the breach was for a short time; a trial date was not going to be lost; the hearing under consideration was not a final hearing; neither the conduct of any litigation nor the liquidation were going to be disrupted; there was no causal link between the application for an extension and any significant increase in costs; the liquidators held the assets of the company on a statutory trust for the benefit of the creditors and contributories and as there were no creditors, they must act in the interests of the contributories as a class; there were very few interested parties and no third parties; this was a solvent liquidation in which the liquidators would be able to recoup their fees and remuneration subject to a proper account and compliance with the relevant practice direction (at [36]). In *Re Legal and Equitable Securities plc* Lewison J upheld a decision to refuse an extension of time where it had been impossible for the registrar to have formed a view about the underlying merits of the claim on the evidence and held that, in any event, even a strong claim on the merits is outweighed by significant delay for which there is no satisfactory explanation. The 21-day period for an appeal starts from when the applicant becomes 'aware' of the decision. Where there is a dispute as to when the applicant became aware and therefore whether the application is time-barred, this issue may be usefully determined as a preliminary issue (*Wentworth Sons Sub-Debt SARL v Lomas* [2017] EWHC 3158 (Ch), [2018] 2 BCLC 696 at [119]).

**Contributory applying**—There is no longer an express requirement (corresponding to r 4.83(4A) of the IR 1986) that a court is not to disallow a creditor's proof on the application of a contributory unless the latter is able to show that there is, or would be if the creditor's proof were disallowed, surplus assets in the liquidation, although common sense dictates this will continue to be an important consideration for the court in considering such an application.

**Costs**—See general note to r 14.9 for the approach to a successful applicant's costs.

## [2.836]

### 14.9 Office-holder not liable for costs under rule 14.8

(1) The official receiver is not personally liable for costs incurred by any person in respect of an application under rule 14.8.

(2) An office-holder other than the official receiver is not personally liable for costs incurred by any person in respect of an application under rule 14.8 unless the court orders otherwise.

**Derivation**—This rule derived from the Insolvency Rules 1986, SI 1986/1925, rr 2.78(6), 4.83(6), 6.105(6).

**General Note**—The costs of a successful appeal against a liquidator's decision rejecting a proof are usually directed to be paid out of the company's assets (*Re National Wholemeal Bread & Biscuit Co* [1892] 2 Ch 457) and not by the liquidator personally, unless it is expressly so ordered. In *Re The Burnden Group Limited (in liquidation); Fielding v Hunt* [2017] EWHC 406 (Ch), [2017] BPIR 585 HHJ Stephen Davies (sitting as a High Court judge) dismissed a claim that a liquidator should be personally liable for the costs of unsuccessfully resisting an appeal against rejection of a proof. The court held that a court would not direct so save in a 'special case' or for 'good reason'. Something more than unsuccessfully resisting an appeal against a rejection of a proof of debt was needed for the court to make an order for personal liability. For example where a liquidator acted for his personal advantage in relation to an appeal, he ought to be ordered to pay the costs personally. In that case there was no evidence the liquidator was acting for his personal advantage rather than pursuing his general functions as liquidator. In *Nimat Halal Food Limited v Patel* [2020] EWHC 734 (Ch) Chief ICC Judge Briggs held that something more relating to the conduct of an office holder was required for an order against an office-holder personally and that the degree of conduct deserving of such an order would depend on the circumstances of each case; a mere mistake or acting in a neutral manner on an appeal from a rejection of proof is unlikely to be sufficient but acting for a personal advantage in resisting an appeal is very likely to lead to a personal costs order (at [13]). Further, the reasons given for a rejection must be considered holistically rather than picking apart each ground of rejection in an attempt to demonstrate unreasonable and unwarranted conduct (at [42]). In refusing to grant a costs order in that case, Judge Briggs held that the court would take account of the duties imposed upon an office holder to investigate the proof and took into account that the administrator in that case was entitled to and should have probed the proof of debt claim and that his actions were entirely consistent with carrying out his duty to investigate and obtain satisfactory evidence (at [36]–[37]). In *Bhogal v Knight* [2018] EWHC 2952 (Ch), [2019] BPIR 41, Falk J dismissed an appeal against a decision to make no order as to costs following a successful challenge to the rejection of the applicants' claim in an individual voluntary arrangement where the applicants had been slow in making their claim clear and in providing further information to the office-holder before their claim was rejected. Falk J held that the first instance judge had not exceeded the ambit of his discretion on costs.

## [2.837]

### 14.10 Withdrawal or variation of proof

(1)   A creditor may withdraw a proof at any time by delivering a written notice to the office-holder.

(2)   The amount claimed by a creditor's proof may be varied at any time by agreement between the creditor and the office-holder.

**Derivation**—This rule derived from the Insolvency Rules 1986, SI 1986/1925, rr 2.79, 4.84, 6.106.

**General note**—In the situation where one claim had been submitted Warren J said in *Meisels v Martin* [2005] EWHC 845 (Ch), [2005] BPIR 1151, that it was probably correct that that claim could only be increased by variation of the original proof and not by submission of a new proof. Where the only proof of debt in a bankruptcy has been withdrawn, the debt does not need to be paid in full, or at all, before the court can annul the bankruptcy pursuant to s 282(1)(b); if the trustee in bankruptcy and creditor both assert that the proof has been withdrawn by agreement no more is required in way of evidence as to the current position and, the court can proceed on the basis that the proof has been properly, validly and effectively withdrawn and there is no subsisting debt (*Official Receiver v McKay* [2009] EWCA Civ 467, [2010] Ch 303, [2009] BPIR 1061).

In *Lehman Brothers Australia Ltd (in liquidation) v McNamara* [2020] EWCA Civ 321, [2021] Ch 1, [2021] 1 BCLC 29, the Court of Appeal allowed an appeal against the dismissal of an application by a creditor for a direction that the administrators of a company increase the creditor's proof of debt where this had been agreed via a claims determination deed entered into by the company (acting by its administrators) and the creditor (acting by its liquidators) but the amount agreed was understated due to a mutual mistake. It was held that no statutory purpose was served by not correcting the error, which would mean that the creditor would be deprived of its true entitlement and the estate given a windfall (at [95]). Accordingly, the creditor was entitled to the relief sought both under para 74 of Sch B1 and by application of the principle in *Ex parte James*. In reaching this conclusion the Court of Appeal rejected the submission that *Ex parte James* required unconscionable conduct; the principle was that a court would not permit its officers to act in a way that it would be clearly wrong for the court itself to act, judged by the standard of the right-thinking person representing the current view of society; this encompassed unfairness and not just conscionability (at [68]).

See also s 324 and the notes thereto.

## [2.838]

### 14.11 Exclusion of proof by the court

(1)   The court may exclude a proof or reduce the amount claimed—

   (a)     on the office-holder's application, where the office-holder thinks that the proof has been improperly admitted, or ought to be reduced; or

   (b)     on the application of a creditor, a member, a contributory or a bankrupt, if the office-holder declines to interfere in the matter.

(2)   Where application is made under paragraph (1), the court must fix a venue for the application to be heard.

(3)   The applicant must deliver notice of the venue—

(a)   in the case of an application by the office-holder, to the creditor who submitted the proof; and

(b)   in the case of an application by a creditor, a member, a contributory or a bankrupt, to the office-holder and to the creditor who made the proof (if not the applicant).

**Derivation**—This rule derived from the Insolvency Rules 1986, SI 1986/1925, rr 2.80, 4.85, 6.107.

**General note**—Contrary to the position under IR 1986, the bankrupt may now apply to exclude a proof or reduce the amount claimed under r 14.11(1)(b).

'Office-holder' in what is now r 14.11(1)(a) does not include a former liquidator: *Re Mama Milla Ltd* [2014] EWCA Civ 761, [2015] BPIR 590.

Once a proof has been admitted, anyone who applies to have the proof expunged has the burden of proving, on the balance of probabilities, that the proof should not have been admitted: *Re Globe Legal Services Ltd* [2002] BCC 858; *Re Allard Holdings Ltd* [2001] 1 BCLC 404. But the applicant does not have to allege or establish impropriety, if he or she is to succeed (*Re Allard Holdings Ltd*).

### [2.839]

### 14.12  Administration and winding up by the court: debts of insolvent company to rank equally

[Note: for the equivalent rule for voluntary liquidation see section 107 of the Act and for bankruptcy section 328 of the Act.]

(1)   This rule applies in an administration and a winding up by the court.

(2)   Debts other than preferential debts rank equally between themselves and, after the preferential debts, must be paid in full unless the assets are insufficient for meeting them, in which case they abate in equal proportions between themselves.

**Derivation**—This rule derived from the Insolvency Rules 1986, SI 1986/1925, rr 2.69, 4.181.

**General note**—This applies the pari passu principle. But see s 387A IA 1986 which provides for different classes of non-preferred debts in relation to 'relevant financial institutions'.

Whilst unsecured creditor claims rank equally by law, a debtor and creditor can agree to vary the ranking of that creditor's claims but only so as to demote that creditor's interests in relation to other creditors (see *LB Holdings Intermediate 2 Ltd (in administration)* [2020] EWHC 1681 (Ch) where Marcus Smith J was required to determine issues concerning the priority of various subordinated debts for the purposes of distribution). See also notes under rr 14.2 and 14.7 on subordinated debts.

### [2.840]

### 14.13  Administration and winding up: division of unsold assets

[Note: in respect of bankruptcy see section 326 (distribution of property in specie).]

(1)   This rule applies in an administration or in a winding up of a company (other than a members' voluntary winding up) to any property which from its peculiar nature or other special circumstances cannot be readily or advantageously sold.

(2)   The office-holder may with the required permission divide the property in its existing form among the company's creditors according to its estimated value.

(3)   The required permission is—

(a)   the permission of the creditors' committee in an administration or, if there is no creditors' committee, the creditors; and

(b)   the permission of the liquidation committee in a winding up, or, if there is no liquidation committee, the creditors (without prejudice to provisions of the Act about disclaimer).

**Derivation**—This rule derived from the Insolvency Rules 1986, SI 1986/1925, rr 2.71, 4.183.

**[2.841]**

### 14.14 Administration and winding up: estimate of value of debt

(1)   In an administration or in a winding up, the office-holder must estimate the value of a debt that does not have a certain value because it is subject to a contingency or for any other reason.

(2)   The office-holder may revise such an estimate by reference to a change of circumstances or to information becoming available to the office-holder.

(3)   The office-holder must inform the creditor of the office-holder's estimate and any revision.

(4)   Where the value of a debt is estimated under this rule or by the court under section 168(3) or (5), the amount provable in the case of that debt is that of the estimate for the time being.

Derivation—This rule derived from the Insolvency Rules 1986, SI 1986/1925, rr 2.81, 4.86.

General note—In *Re Danka Business Systems Plc* [2012] EWHC 579 (Ch) it was held that the predecessor of this rule (r 4.86 IR 1986) imposed an obligation on a liquidator to place an estimated value on a contingent liability with an uncertain value to which the company is subject, and this is to be done however difficult that might be; there was no room for some claims being dealt with by the liquidator retaining funds as a reserve for a potentially indeterminate future period. This was approved of on appeal: [2013] EWCA Civ 92, [2013] BPIR 432, [2013] BCC 450. The Court of Appeal made it plain that once a liquidator has estimated the value of a contingent debt for the debtor to be admitted to proof, then he or she had to distribute, and this was particularly the case where the contingency was not imminent. The appeal court indicated that if the contingency was imminent then the liquidator could wait and see rather than spending time and costs on valuing the liability. The overall approach prescribed by the court was to be followed even though the effect of the winding up was to defeat the claim of the contingent creditor. This approach was to be employed for both solvent and insolvent companies, and so the existence of a contingent liability would not preclude the use of a members' voluntary liquidation process. The valuation of the contingent liability was to be based on a fair and genuine assessment of the chances of the liability occurring. This involved the liquidator using his or her own expertise and that of any appropriate advisers. If a liquidator makes an estimate and the creditor is aggrieved by the decision, an appeal to the court may be instituted under s 168(5).

**[2.842]**

### 14.15 Secured creditor: value of security

(1)   A secured creditor may, with the agreement of the office-holder or the permission of the court, at any time alter the value which that creditor has put upon a security in a proof.

(2)   Paragraph (3) applies where a secured creditor—

    (a)   being the applicant for the administration order or the appointer of the administrator, has in the application or the notice of appointment put a value on the security;

    (b)   being the petitioner in winding-up or bankruptcy proceedings, has put a value on the security in the petition; or

    (c)   has voted in respect of the unsecured balance of the debt.

(3)   Where this paragraph applies—

    (a)   the secured creditor may re-value the security only with the agreement of the office-holder or the permission of the court; and

    (b)   where the revaluation was by agreement, the office-holder must deliver a notice of the revaluation to the creditors within five business days after the office-holder's agreement.

Derivation—This rule derived from the Insolvency Rules 1986, SI 1986/1925, rr 2.90, 4.95, 6.115.

General note—This only affects the value for the purposes of the insolvency and not the actual value of the security (*W v G (Financial Provision) (Conditional Order for Sale: Equitable Interest)* [2016] EWHC 2965 (Fam), [2017] 4 WLR 80 at [105]).

**[2.843]**

### 14.16 Secured creditor: surrender for non-disclosure

(1)   If a secured creditor fails to disclose a security in a proof, the secured creditor must surrender that security for the general benefit of creditors, unless the court, on application by the secured creditor, relieves the secured creditor from the effect of this rule on the grounds that the omission was inadvertent or the result of honest mistake.

(2)   If the court grants that relief, it may require or allow the creditor's proof to be amended, on such terms as may be just.

(3)   . . ..

**Derivation**—This rule derived from the Insolvency Rules 1986, SI 1986/1925, rr 2.91, 4.96, 6.116.

**Amendments**—SI 2017/1115; SI 2019/146, as from IP completion day (as defined in the European Union (Withdrawal Agreement) Act 2020, s 39(1)–(5)).

**General note** –Where a creditor states in his proof that he has no security, he has lost the right to rely on his security and is to be treated as an unsecured creditor subject only to the court's power to grant relief: *Re JT Frith Ltd* [2012] EWHC 196 (Ch), [2012] BCC 634.

The intention of the secured creditor is the critical thing in determining whether he or she has abandoned security. This intention could be determined by correspondence in which the secured creditor engaged: *LCP Retail Ltd v Segal* [2006] EWHC 2087 (Ch), [2007] BCC 584. In this case a landlord's failure to state the right of distress in the proof of debt form was evidence of an intention to abandon it, in the absence of evidence of inadvertence or honest mistake (*LCP Retail Ltd v Segal* at [23]).

Where a creditor proves for his whole debt as if it were unsecured but does disclose the security in its proof of debt albeit not its value, he does not voluntarily surrender his security for the general benefit of creditors: *C & W Berry Ltd v Armstrong-Moakes* [2007] EWHC 2101 (QB) at [15].

In *Candey Ltd v Crumpler* [2020] EWCA Civ 26, the Court of Appeal held that the deputy judge had been wrong to say that all persons aware of litigation are to be treated as being on notice of a solicitor's right to a lien for unpaid fees such that in normal circumstances a solicitor's proof of debt was not required to spell out the right to a lien. Since the point was not determinative of the appeal (the lien had been otherwise waived by the solicitor entering into a deed of charge that was inconsistent with such a lien with no reservation of rights: [96]), the Court of Appeal left the point open ([86]–[87]). Permission has been granted to appeal to the Supreme Court.

**[2.844]**

### 14.17 Secured creditor: redemption by office-holder

(1)   The office-holder may at any time deliver a notice to a creditor whose debt is secured that the office-holder proposes, at the expiration of 28 days from the date of the notice, to redeem the security at the value put upon it in the creditor's proof.

(2)   The creditor then has 21 days (or such longer period as the office-holder may allow) in which to alter the value of the security in accordance with rule 14.15.

(3)   If the creditor alters the value of the security with the permission of the office-holder or the court then the office-holder may only redeem at the new value.

(4)   If the office-holder redeems the security the cost of transferring it is payable as an expense out of the insolvent estate.

(5)   A creditor whose debt is secured may at any time deliver a notice to the office-holder requiring the office-holder to elect whether or not to redeem the security at the value then placed on it.

(6)   The office-holder then has three months in which to redeem the security or elect not to redeem the security.

**Derivation**—This rule derived from the Insolvency Rules 1986, SI 1986/1925, rr 2.92, 4.97, 6.117.

**[2.845]**

### 14.18 Secured creditor: test of security's value

(1)   If the office-holder is dissatisfied with the value which a secured creditor puts on a security in the creditor's proof the office-holder may require any property comprised in the security to be offered for sale.

(2)   The terms of sale will be as agreed between the office-holder and the secured creditor, or as the court may direct.

(3)   If the sale is by auction, the office-holder on behalf of the company or the insolvent estate and the creditor may bid.

(4)   This rule does not apply if the value of the security has been altered with the court's permission.

**Derivation**—This rule derived from the Insolvency Rules 1986, SI 1986/1925, rr 2.93, 4.98, 6.118.

### [2.846]

#### 14.19  Realisation or surrender of security by creditor

(1)   If a creditor who has valued a security subsequently realises the security (whether or not at the instance of the office-holder)—

(a)   the net amount realised must be treated in all respects (including in relation to any valuation in a proof) as an amended valuation made by the creditor; and

(b)   the creditor may prove for the balance of the creditor's debt.

(2)   A creditor who voluntarily surrenders a security may prove for the whole of the creditor's debt as if it were unsecured.

**Derivation**—This rule derived from the Insolvency Rules 1986, SI 1986/1925, rr 2.83, 2.94, 4.88, 4.99, 6.119.

**General note**—See *Cahillane v NALM Ltd* [2014] EWHC 1992 (Ch), [2014] BPIR 1093: if a creditor subsequently receives more than the value that he put on the security, then what he actually receives is treated as being the value of the security and any resulting excess of dividend must be repaid to the trustee for distribution amongst the remaining unsecured creditors.

### [2.847]

#### 14.20  Discounts

All trade and other discounts (except a discount for immediate or early settlement) which would have been available to the company or the debtor but for the insolvency proceedings must be deducted from the claim.

**Derivation**—This rule derived from the Insolvency Rules 1986, SI 1986/1925, rr 2.84, 4.89, 6.110.

### [2.848]

#### 14.21.  Debts in foreign currency

(1)   A proof for a debt incurred or payable in a foreign currency must state the amount of the debt in that currency.

(2)   The office-holder must convert all such debts into sterling at a single rate for each currency determined by the office-holder by reference to the exchange rates prevailing on the relevant date.

(3)   On the next occasion when the office-holder communicates with the creditors the office-holder must advise them of any rate so determined.

(4)   A creditor who considers that the rate determined by the office-holder is unreasonable may apply to the court.

(5)   If on hearing the application the court finds that the rate is unreasonable it may itself determine the rate.

(6)   This rule does not apply to the conversion of foreign currency debts in an application for a debt relief order.

**Derivation**—This rule derived from the Insolvency Rules 1986, SI 1986/1925, rr 2.86, 4.91, 6.111.

**General note**—The point at which the foreign currency is to be converted into sterling is the 'relevant date', defined in r 14.1(3).

Creditors who suffer loss because of currency fluctuations between the relevant date and the date of payment are not entitled to claim the loss as a provable debt: *In re Lehman Bros International (Europe) (in administration) (No 4)* [2017] UKSC 38, [2018] AC 465, [2017] 2 BCLC 149.

**[2.849]**

**14.22 Payments of a periodical nature**

(1)   In the case of rent and other payments of a periodical nature, the creditor may prove for any amounts due and unpaid up to the relevant date.

(2)   Where at that date any payment was accruing due, the creditor may prove for so much as would have been due at that date, if accruing from day to day.

**Derivation**—This rule derived from the Insolvency Rules 1986, SI 1986/1925, rr 2.87, 4.92, 6.112.

**'Relevant date'**—Now defined at r 14.1(3).

**[2.850]**

**14.23 Interest**

[Note: provision for the payment of interest out of a surplus remaining after payment of the debts is made by section 189(2) in respect of winding up and section 328(4) in respect of bankruptcy.]

(1)   Where a debt proved in insolvency proceedings bears interest, that interest is provable as part of the debt except in so far as it is payable in respect of any period after the relevant date.

(2)   In the circumstances set out below the creditor's claim may include interest on the debt for periods before the relevant date although not previously reserved or agreed.

(3)   If the debt is due by virtue of a written instrument and payable at a certain time, interest may be claimed for the period from that time to the relevant date.

(4)   If the debt is due otherwise, interest may only be claimed if demand for payment of the debt was made in writing by or on behalf of the creditor, and notice was delivered that interest would be payable from the date of the demand to the date of the payment, before—

    (a)    the relevant date, in respect of administration or winding up; or

    (b)    the presentation of the bankruptcy petition or the bankruptcy application.

(5)   Interest under paragraph (4) may only be claimed for the period from the date of the demand to the relevant date and, for the purposes of the Act and these Rules, must be charged at a rate not exceeding that mentioned in paragraph (6).

(6)   The rate of interest to be claimed under paragraphs (3) and (4) is the rate specified in section 17 of the Judgments Act 1838 on the relevant date.

(7)   In an administration—

    (a)    any surplus remaining after payment of the debts proved must, before being applied for any other purpose, be applied in paying interest on those debts in respect of the periods during which they have been outstanding since the relevant date;

    (b)    all interest payable under sub-paragraph (a) ranks equally whether or not the debts on which it is payable rank equally; and

    (c)    the rate of interest payable under sub-paragraph (a) is whichever is the greater of the rate specified under paragraph (6) and the rate applicable to the debt apart from the administration.

**Derivation**—This rule derived from the Insolvency Rules 1986, SI 1986/1925, rr 2.88, 4.93, 6.113.

**General note**—Interest can be paid on both secured and unsecured debts.

In *Burlington Loan Management Ltd v Lomas (Joint Administrator)* [2017] EWCA Civ 1462, [2017] BCC 759 the Court of Appeal held (affirming David Richards J's decision in *Re Lehman Brothers International (Europe) (In Administration)* [2015] EWHC 2269 (Ch), [2015] BPIR 1102 and Hilyard J's decision in *Re Lehman Brothers International (Europe) (In Administration)* [2016] EWHC 2417 (Ch) (also referred to as 'Waterfall II')) that IR 1986, r 2.88 (replaced by IR 2016, r 14.23) constituted a complete statutory code for the award of statutory interest on provable debts, statutory interest was calculated on the basis of allocating dividends first to the reduction of the principal (proved debt) and then to the payment of accrued statutory interest; it identified for each proving creditor the amount of the debt upon which interest is payable, the period or periods during which it is payable and the rate payable; where the 'rate applicable apart from the administration' was a compounding rate, accrued statutory interest did not continue to compound following the payment in full of the principal amount by way of dividends; whilst administrators were obliged to act with all reasonable speed, creditors had no entitlement to compensation for late payment of statutory interest; for any future or contingent debt at the date of administration interest was payable from the date that the company entered administration, not the date any such payment fell due; the 'rate applicable to the debt apart from the administration' could not include a foreign rate of interest applicable to a foreign judgment obtained after the date of administration nor a foreign judgment rate of interest which would have become applicable to the debt if the creditor had obtained a foreign judgment but had not done so; the 'rate applicable to the debt apart from the administration' included in the case of a provable debt that was a close-out sum under a contract, a contractual rate of interest that began to accrue only after the close-out sum became due and payable due to action taken by the creditor after the date of the commencement of the company's administration.

In *Joint Administrators of Lehman Brothers International (Europe) (In Administration) v Revenue and Customs Commissioners* [2019] UKSC 12, [2019] 1 WLR 2173, [2019] 1 BCLC 609, the Supreme Court held that statutory interest payable on proven debts in an administration amounts to 'yearly interest' under s 874 of the Income Tax Act 2007 and is therefore subject to deductions of income tax. The Supreme Court also agreed with the dicta in *Burlington Loan Management Ltd v Lomas (Joint Administrator)* that r 2.88 of the IR 1986 (replaced by IR 2016, r 14.23) constituted a complete code for the award of statutory interest on provable debts (at [7]).

## [2.851]

### 14.24 Administration: mutual dealings and set-off

(1)   This rule applies in an administration where the administrator intends to make a distribution and has delivered a notice under rule 14.29.

(2)   An account must be taken as at the date of the notice of what is due from the company and a creditor to each other in respect of their mutual dealings and the sums due from the one must be set off against the sums due from the other.

(3)   If there is a balance owed to the creditor then only that balance is provable in the administration.

(4)   If there is a balance owed to the company that must be paid to the administrator as part of the assets.

(5)   However if all or part of the balance owed to the company results from a contingent or prospective debt owed by the creditor then the balance (or that part of it which results from the contingent or prospective debt) must be paid in full (without being discounted under rule 14.44) if and when that debt becomes due and payable.

(6)   In this rule—

"obligation" means an obligation however arising, whether by virtue of an agreement, rule of law or otherwise; and

"mutual dealings" means mutual credits, mutual debts or other mutual dealings between the company and a creditor proving or claiming to prove for a debt in the administration but does not include any of the following—

(a)   a debt arising out of an obligation incurred after the company entered administration;

(b)   a debt arising out of an obligation incurred at a time when the creditor had notice that—

(i)   an application for an administration order was pending, or

(ii)   any person had delivered notice of intention to appoint an administrator;

(c)   a debt arising out of an obligation where—

(i)   the administration was immediately preceded by a winding up, and

(ii)   at the time when the obligation was incurred the creditor had notice that a decision had been sought from creditors under section 100 on the nomination of a liquidator or that a winding-up petition was pending;

(d)   a debt arising out of an obligation incurred during a winding up which immediately preceded the administration; or

(e)    a debt which has been acquired by a creditor by assignment or otherwise, under an agreement between the creditor and another party where that agreement was entered into—

    (i)    after the company entered administration,

    (ii)    at a time when the creditor had notice that an application for an administration order was pending,

    (iii)    at a time when the creditor had notice that any person had given notice of intention to appoint an administrator,

    (iv)    where the administration was immediately preceded by a winding up, at a time when the creditor had notice that a decision had been sought from creditors under section 100 on the nomination of a liquidator or that a winding-up petition was pending, or

    (v)    during a winding up which immediately preceded the administration.

(7)   A sum must be treated as being due to or from the company for the purposes of paragraph (2) whether—

    (a)    it is payable at present or in the future;

    (b)    the obligation by virtue of which it is payable is certain or contingent; or

    (c)    its amount is fixed or liquidated, or is capable of being ascertained by fixed rules or as a matter of opinion.

(8)   For the purposes of this rule—

    (a)    rule 14.14 applies to an obligation which, by reason of its being subject to a contingency or for any other reason, does not bear a certain value;

    (b)    rules 14.21 to 14.23 apply to sums due to the company which—

    (i)    are payable in a currency other than sterling,

    (ii)    are of a periodical nature, or

    (iii)    bear interest; and

    (c)    rule 14.44 applies to a sum due to or from the company which is payable in the future.

**Derivation**—This rule derived from the Insolvency Rules 1986, SI 1986/1925, r 2.85.

**General note**—Under the former administration regime under Part II of the 1986 Act there was no general power permitting an administrator to make a distribution to creditors. The absence of such a general power explains why the former regime did not include the provisions governing mandatory set-off in administration, set-off being a component part of the process of admitting proofs for distribution purposes. With the implementation of Sch B1, however, and in particular the power of the court to give permission for an administrator to make a distribution under para 65(2), r 2.85 of the IR 1986 was introduced to provide for mutual credits and set-off in administration. Although those provisions were modelled on the well-established r 4.90 applicable to liquidations, there were differences in wording which gave rise to concerns which prompted the move to harmonise the effect of set-off in liquidation and administration so as to provide greater detail and clarity regarding the meaning of the set-off rules in administration. (For observations on the original r 2.85 regime see *Isovel Contracts Ltd v ABB Building Technologies* [2002] 1 BCLC 390.)

It should be noted that, unlike in liquidation under r 14.25 where set-off is automatic, in administration set-off only applies if the administrator gives notice of the intention to make a distribution to creditors (r 14.24(1)).

For consideration of the meaning of 'future debts' for the purposes of the discounting mechanism in r 14.44 in the context of set-off, quantification of foreign debts and the treatment of interests on debts due to the company see the judgment of Norris J in *Re Kaupthing Singer & Friedlander Ltd (in administration)* [2010] 1 BCLC 222. For the treatment of interest-bearing debts which are also future debts see the clarification provided by the Court of Appeal in the same case at [2011] BCC 555 which, save for overturning the decision below in holding that future debts due to the company were to be discounted but only to the extent necessary to achieve the set-off, leaves the judgment of Norris J below undisturbed.

See the notes to s 323 and r 14.25.

[2.852]

#### 14.25 Winding up: mutual dealings and set-off

(1) This rule applies in a winding up where, before the company goes into liquidation, there have been mutual dealings between the company and a creditor of the company proving or claiming to prove for a debt in the liquidation.

(2) An account must be taken of what is due from the company and the creditor to each other in respect of their mutual dealings and the sums due from the one must be set off against the sums due from the other.

(3) If there is a balance owed to the creditor then only that balance is provable in the winding up.

(4) If there is a balance owed to the company then that must be paid to the liquidator as part of the assets.

(5) However if all or part of the balance owed to the company results from a contingent or prospective debt owed by the creditor then the balance (or that part of it which results from the contingent or prospective debt) must be paid in full (without being discounted under rule 14.44) if and when that debt becomes due and payable.

(6) In this rule—

"obligation" means an obligation however arising, whether by virtue of an agreement, rule of law or otherwise; and

"mutual dealings" means mutual credits, mutual debts or other mutual dealings between the company and a creditor proving or claiming to prove for a debt in the winding up but does not include any of the following—

    (a)    a debt arising out of an obligation incurred at a time when the creditor had notice that—

        (i)    a decision had been sought from creditors on the nomination of a liquidator under section 100, or

        (ii)    a petition for the winding up of the company was pending;

    (b)    a debt arising out of an obligation where—

        (i)    the liquidation was immediately preceded by an administration, and

        (ii)    at the time the obligation was incurred the creditor had notice that an application for an administration order was pending or a person had delivered notice of intention to appoint an administrator; and

    (c)    a debt arising out of an obligation incurred during an administration which immediately preceded the liquidation;

    (d)    a debt which has been acquired by a creditor by assignment or otherwise, under an agreement between the creditor and another party where that agreement was entered into—

        (i)    after the company went into liquidation,

        (ii)    at a time when the creditor had notice that a decision had been sought from creditors under section 100 on the nomination of a liquidator,

        (iii)    at a time when the creditor had notice that a winding-up petition was pending,

        (iv)    where the winding up was immediately preceded by an administration at a time when the creditor had notice that an application for an administration order was pending or a person had delivered notice of intention to appoint an administrator, or

        (v)    during an administration which immediately preceded the winding up.

(7) A sum must be treated as being due to or from the company for the purposes of paragraph (2) whether—

    (a)    it is payable at present or in the future;

    (b)    the obligation by virtue of which it is payable is certain or contingent; or

    (c)    its amount is fixed or liquidated, or is capable of being ascertained by fixed rules or as a matter of opinion.

(8)   For the purposes of this rule—

    (a)    rule 14.14 applies to an obligation which, by reason of its being subject to a contingency or for any other reason, does not bear a certain value;

    (b)    rules 14.21 to 14.23 apply to sums due to the company which—

        (i)    are payable in a currency other than sterling,

        (ii)   are of a periodical nature, or

        (iii)  bear interest; and

    (c)    rule 14.44 applies to a sum due to or from the company which is payable in the future.

**Derivation**—This rule derived from the Insolvency Rules 1986, SI 1986/1925, r 4.90.

**General note**—'Set-off is a claim which can be, as the name suggests, set off against another claim, ie in practice it operates as a defence to that other claim': *Hofer v Strawson* [1999] 2 BCLC 336 at 341. The scheme of insolvency set-off was discussed by Lord Briggs JSC in *Bresco Electrical Services Limited (in liquidation) v Michael J Lonsdale (Electrical) Limited* [2020] UKSC 25, paras [27]–[34]. Set-off occurs in the context of liquidation where a person or company has a claim against the company in liquidation and the latter also has a claim against the former. The process of set-off relieves the company in liquidation pro tanto of the duty of paying a dividend on a debt due to the creditor and enables the creditor pro tanto to be paid in full out of a debt which the creditor owes to the company. The creditor obtains a windfall because he or she recovers all of his or her claim, whereas, if set-off did not apply, this would not be the case. So, unlike set-off in general terms, insolvency set-off is not merely procedural, but also affects substantive rights: *Swissport (UK) Ltd v Aer Lingus Ltd* [2007] EWHC 1089 (Ch) at [43]. The rule as to set-off applies to bankruptcies, and is found in s 323. It is strange that there is no provision in the Act that deals with set-off in relation to liquidations.

For set-off to apply there must be two separate debts, and so one cannot set-off individual debits and credits pursuant to a running (current) account: *MS Fashions Ltd v BCCI (No 2)* [1993] Ch 425, affirmed on appeal *High Street Services Ltd v BCCI* [1993] BCC 360, CA.

Rule 14.25 is self-executing in the sense that it operates automatically and is not brought into force as a result of the election of either party, so attempting to prove in a liquidation is not a prerequisite to being able to claim a set-off: *National Westminster Bank Ltd v Halesowen Presswork & Associates Ltd* [1972] AC 785, HL; *Morris v Agrichemicals Ltd* [1996] BCC 204 at 208, CA; [1997] BCC 965 at 969, HL; *Re Bank of Credit and Commerce International SA (in liquidation) (No 8)* [1998] 1 BCLC 68 at 73. The rule is such that the parties involved are not able to contract out of it (*National Westminster Bank Ltd v Halesowen Presswork & Associates Ltd* at 809, 824; *British Eagle International Airlines Ltd v Cie Nationale Air France* [1975] 2 All ER 390 at 409–411, [1975] 1 WLR 758 at 780–781, HL; *Re ILG Travel Ltd* [1996] BCC 21 at 48; *Stein v Blake* [1996] AC 243 at 251, 255, HL), and the operation of the set-off rule cannot be waived: *Re Cushla Ltd* [1979] 3 All ER 415 at 423. The courts are not entitled to decide that they will not apply the rules of set-off as part of the exercise of their discretion: *Re BCCI (No 11)* [1997] Ch 213, [1996] BCC 980, [1997] 1 BCLC 80.

In the situation where a person has a claim in a winding up that partly comes within the category of a preferential debt (under ss 175, 389 and Sch 6), and partly it is a non-preferential debt, then what is owed to the company by the creditor is to be set off rateably between the preferential and non-preferential components of the claim: *Re Unit 2 (Windows) (in liquidation)* [1985] 1 WLR 1383.

The three requirements that must always be satisfied before set-off can take place are: the claims must have existed when the company entered winding up; the claims must be commensurable; and there must be mutuality.

A debt arising from a market contract cannot be set off until the completion of default proceedings (Companies Act 1989, ss 159(4), 163(1), (2)). These are proceedings brought pursuant to the relevant investment exchange or clearing house rules where default occurs.

A liquidator is entitled to assign the net balance which arises under the operation of this rule, that is, after the set-off has taken place: *Enterprise Managed Services Ltd v Tony McFadden Utilities Ltd* [2009] EWHC 3222 (Ch).

**Account**—Paragraph (2) provides that an account has to be taken, and this is, theoretically, to be taken on the date of liquidation, even though in practice the account is taken later when the liquidator is aware of the debts of the company. In taking an account, regard is had for developments occurring after the date of liquidation, such as the valuing of claims: *MS Fashions Ltd v BCCI (No 2)* [1993] Ch 425 at 432. It is not always possible in taking the account to wait for all contingencies to occur and all actual or potential liabilities which existed at the time of liquidation to be quantified, so the liquidator has to estimate the value of claims: *Stein v Blake*

[1996] AC 243 at 252. Peter Prescott QC (sitting as a deputy judge of the High Court) in *Swissport (UK) Ltd v Aer Lingus Ltd* [2007] EWHC 1089 (Ch) said that the account which is required to be taken properly involves a valuation of the cross-claim. He went on to say that 'I would reject the submission that, once any sort of cross-claim is shown to be barely arguable, it must be estimated at face value and then set off for summary judgment purposes against an undoubted claim on which summary judgment would otherwise be available': at [51].

In order to calculate the set-off account, the same principles used by administrators and liquidators to quantify the debts of a company are utilised in relation to debts that are owed to a company. Thus, those debts that are owed to the company that are contingent or payable at a future time are included for set-off purposes (see r 14.25(7)). A sum shall be regarded as being due to or from the company for the purposes of para (2) if it falls within those categories mentioned in para (7).

The Supreme Court (reversing Fraser J and the Court of Appeal below) held in *Bresco Electrical Services Limited (in liquidation) v Michael J Lonsdale (Electrical) Limited* [2020] UKSC 25 that it is open to a company in liquidation to refer a dispute over a construction contract to adjudication under s 108 of the Housing Grants, Construction and Regeneration Act 1996. Lord Briggs JSC, giving the unanimous judgment of the Supreme Court, rejected an argument (which Fraser J had accepted at first instance) that if there are cross-claims between the parties to a construction contract and one of them is in liquidation, the previous dispute is replaced by a single net balance, so that the adjudicator's jurisdiction under s 108 is not engaged. This, held Lord Briggs, would be a triumph of technicality over substance (para [48]). The further argument (which both Fraser J and the Court of Appeal had accepted) that to permit construction adjudication would be 'an exercise in futility' was also rejected. Lord Briggs pointed out that the process of proof of debt in insolvency shares many of the attractive features of construction adjudication, in terms of speed, simplicity, proportionality and economy, but that adjudication has the added advantage that a construction dispute will be more amenable to resolution in adjudication by a professional construction expert than by many liquidators (para [61]). The Supreme Court concluded that construction adjudication, on the application of the liquidator, was not incompatible with the insolvency process (para [71]). The Supreme Court recognised that an adjudicator's decision may not be summarily enforceable but held that the court was well-placed to deal with this at the summary judgment stage, by refusing it in appropriate cases or granting it but with a stay of execution (at [64]). In *John Doyle Construction Ltd (in liquidation) v Erith Contractors Limited* [2020] EWHC 2451 Fraser J, in refusing to grant summary judgment to enforce an arbitration decision, gave guidance on the principles governing a company in liquidation seeking to enforce an adjudicator's decision in its favour by summary judgment in light of *Bresco*.

**Contributories**—Where a contributory is owed money by the company in liquidation, he or she is not entitled to set-off the debt against any call that is made on the contributory by the liquidator until such time as all of the creditors of the company have been paid in full (s 149(3)). Rather, it is incumbent on the contributory to establish the debt that is claimed in the normal way, and, upon the payment of calls which are due, the contributory is then entitled to receive dividends on the debt equally with the other creditors of the company. Likewise, a contributory is not able to set-off amounts due to him or her by the company, where the liquidator requires the contributory to contribute to the assets of a company in winding up: *Re Overend, Gurney & Co; Grissell's Case* (1866) 1 Ch App 528; *Re General Works Co, Gill's Case* (1879) 12 ChD 755. In *Joint Administrators of LB Holdings Intermediate 2 Ltd v Joint Administrators of Lehman Bros International (Europe)* [2017] UKSC 38, [2018] AC 465, [2017] 2 BCLC 149 the Supreme Court held that the contributory rule can also apply in a distributing administration.

The liquidator is unable to set-off a debt due to the company from a deceased contributory, against what the contributory is due in the winding up: *Re Peruvian Railway Construction Co* [1915] 2 Ch 144, *Pearson v Primeo Fund (in official liquidation)* [2020] UKPC 3.

**Secured creditors**—Insolvency set off is now considered to apply to secured claims because 'mutual dealings' are not limited to provable debts (*Bresco* at [51]; *In re Lehman Bros International (Europe) No 4* [2017] UKSC 38, [2018] AC 465, [2017] 2 BCLC 149 at [167]–[170]).

**Claims and (Mutual) 'dealings'**—Claims must be part of mutual dealings between the company and the claimant who is a creditor of the company that is proving or claiming in the winding up.

Debts must sound, or be measurable, in money, ie they are commensurable: *Eberle's Hotels & Restaurant Co v Jonas* (1887) 18 QBD 459 at 468; *Stein v Blake* [1994] Ch 16, [1993] BCLC 1478. Dealings means anything that comes within the description of an ordinary business transaction: *Eberle's Hotels & Restaurant Co v Jonas* at 465. Older cases limited 'dealings' in precursors of r 4.90 to those involving anything that had a commercial or business flavour, so a claim for assault would not enable the set-off rule to apply (*Eberle's Hotels & Restaurant Co v Jonas* at 465). However, more recent cases have interpreted 'dealings' more broadly and have not limited claims to those arising out of contract: *Re DH Curtis (Builders) Ltd* [1978] Ch 162, [1978] 2 WLR 28; *Re Unit 2 Windows Ltd (in liquidation)* [1985] 1 WLR 1383, [1985] 3 All ER 647. The

Australian High Court has held that a fraudulent misrepresentation made in the course of negotiations leading to a contract may form part of the relevant dealing for set-off purposes: *Gye v McIntyre* (1991) 171 CLR 609, (1991) 98 ALR 393. The House of Lords has said that it does not matter how the debts claimed came into being – whether by contract, statute or tort – provided that they led to commensurable cross-claims: *State for Trade and Industry v Frid*, sub nom *Re West End* [2004] UKHL 24, [2004] 2 AC 506, [2004] 2 BCLC 1 at [8]–[9], HL. Paragraph (7) now explicitly provides that certain claims can be brought into set off. Previously the claims enumerated were permitted at common law.

Despite this more liberal approach, anyone who has been guilty of misfeasance in relation to the affairs of a company that went into liquidation is not entitled to set off-what he or she was owed by the company against an order made pursuant to misfeasance proceedings: *Manson v Smith* [1997] 2 BCLC 161, CA. The reason for this is two-fold. Firstly, because where the misfeasance occurs before winding up it does not constitute a 'dealing' with the wrongdoer; and, secondly, because the sum due from the misfeasant is not a debt until the order directing its payment is made and therefore did not exist at the date of the winding-up. The same can be said in relation to a person to whom preference payments were made before winding up and who is required to disgorge them: *Lister v Hooson* [1908] 1 KB 174 at 176–177; *Re A Debtor* [1927] 1 Ch 410. Similarly, a conversion of property cannot constitute a dealing: *Re Cosslett (Contractors) Ltd No 2* [2002] 1 AC 336, [2002] 1 BCLC 77 at [35], HL. It is not clear that sums due from a director pursuant to s 213 CA 2006 following a breach of s 197 CA 2006 cannot be set-off, but if the breach also amounts to misfeasance (for example, a breach of ss 171 or 172 CA 2006), it is not capable of being set-off (*Jackson v Casey* [2019] EWHC 1657 (Ch) at [74]–[76]).

A guarantor is not entitled to claim set-off where the right of proof of the principal debtor in relation to what was guaranteed still exists: *Re Fenton* [1931] 1 Ch 85 at 112, CA.

There can be no set-off unless mutuality exists: *Re Cushla Ltd* [1979] 3 All ER 415; *Morris v Agrichemicals Ltd* [1997] BCC 965, HL. '"Mutual" indicates the notion of reciprocity and does not mean "identical" or "the same"': *Gye v McIntyre* (1991) 171 CLR 609 at 623, (1991) 98 ALR 393 at 402 (Aust HC). Claims will only be able to be set-off where they are due between the same parties and in the same right: *Re ILG Travel Ltd* [1996] BCC 21, *National Westminster Bank Ltd v Halesowen Presswork & Assemblies Ltd* [1972] AC 785, *Secretary of State for Trade and Industry v Frid*, *Lady Moon SPV SRL v Petricca and Co Capital Ltd* [2019] EWHC 710 (Ch). So, there can be no set-off in respect of debts owing to and by a particular person in different capacities. If a debt is owed jointly by two persons to a company and the company only owes a debt to one of the persons, it cannot be said that there is mutuality, and there can be no set-off: *Re Pennington & Owen Ltd* [1925] Ch 825.

Given the principle of separate legal entity, a person is only able to set-off a claim against a company to which he or she owed money, so any money owed to the person by a connected company that is in the course of winding up, cannot be set-off against what the person owed to the first company: *BCCI v Habib Bank Ltd* [1999] 1 WLR 42, [1999] BPIR 1. Further, if a debt owed to a company is assigned by the company before liquidation to some other person, there is no mutuality so there can be no set-off in relation to the debt except to the extent of any balance which remains: *Re Asphaltic Wood Pavement Co, Lee & Chapman's Case* (1885) 30 ChD 216, CA; *Re City Life Assurance Co Ltd* [1926] Ch 191, CA.

Where there are liabilities which exist between a company and a number of government departments, mutuality will be said to exist, with the result that the Crown may set off a debt owed to the company by one government department against a debt owed by the company to another government department: *Re Cushla Ltd*; *RA Cullen Ltd v Nottingham Health Authority* (1986) 2 BCC 99, 368; *Secretary of State for Trade and Industry v Frid* [2004] UKHL 24, [2004] 2 AC 506, [2004] 2 BCLC 1. Where the Secretary of State has a claim against the company by virtue of the fact that he or she has paid to the company's employees the amounts to which they are entitled under the Employment Rights Act, the liquidator is permitted to set off any credit to which the company is entitled (and which is held by the government), against the Secretary of State's claim: *Secretary of State for Trade and Industry v Frid* (the liquidator was entitled to a VAT credit).

**The point in time of set-off**—The critical point of time is the date when the company goes into liquidation: *MS Fashions Ltd v BCCI (No 2)* [1993] BCC 70 at 73; *Secretary of State for Trade and Industry v Frid* [2004] UKHL 24, [2004] 2 AC 506, [2004] 2 BCLC 1. It is at this date that mutual dealings giving rise to obligations that are capable ultimately of being the subject of an account between the parties must occur. Obligations incurred after the winding up has commenced cannot be set off (*Ince Hall Rolling Mills v Douglas Forge Co* (1882) 8 QBD 179). However, it is not necessary for the purposes of this rule that the debt should have been due and payable before the date of the company's liquidation; rather it is sufficient that there was an obligation arising out of the terms of a contract or a statute by which a debt sounding in money would become payable when some future event occurred. According to the House of Lords in *Secretary of State for Trade and Industry v Frid*, it was not necessary for the purposes of this rule that the debt should have been due and payable before the date of the company's liquidation; rather it was sufficient that there was an obligation arising out of the terms of a contract or a statute by which a debt sounding in money would become payable when some future event occurred (at 535). This latter amount was regarded as a debt to which IR 1986, r 4.90 applied. The revamped r 14.25 makes that express. This approach to set-off reflects the approach to provable debts in general found in the decision of the Supreme Court in *Re Nortel GmbH* [2013] UKSC 52, [2014] AC 209: see notes to r 14.1.

**Exclusion of set-off**—Rule 14.25(6) provides that certain sums cannot fall under the headings of 'mutual credits', 'mutual debts' or 'mutual dealings', for purposes of set-off. Any debt acquired by a creditor by way of an agreement entered into after one of the dates provided for in para (6) cannot be taken into account for set-off.

In relation to notice mentioned in r 14.25(6), it is suggested that the kind of notice on the part of a creditor which must be established by a liquidator or administrator who is seeking to avoid set-off is actual. It is submitted that a set-off claim of a creditor cannot be repelled by a liquidator merely because the creditor was aware that the company was suffering some liquidity problems. The creditor would have to have notice of one of the following: the meeting of creditors; the presentation of a winding-up petition; the company was in administration; or the creditor was aware that administration was likely. This also applies to debts that are acquired by assignment after notice that the company was going to go into liquidation or administration, although it does not apply to debts that arose from an agreement made before notice of liquidation or administration.

Anyone with a claim which is statute-barred is not able to set off the claim against what he or she owes the company: *Pott v Clegg* (1847) 16 M & W 321, 153 ER 1212.

**'Obligation'**—In line with case law, the meaning of obligation is given a broad interpretation. See the notes accompanying s 323 and r 14.24.

For further discussion, see R Derham *Set-off* (OUP, 4th edn, 2010) and especially Chs 2–9; RM Goode *Principles of Corporate Insolvency Law* (4th edn, 2011), Ch 8.

CHAPTER 3

DISTRIBUTION TO CREDITORS IN ADMINISTRATION, WINDING UP AND BANKRUPTCY

## [2.853]

**Note**
[Note: a document required by the Act or these Rules must also contain the standard contents set out in Part 1.]

## [2.854]

**14.26 Application of Chapter to a particular class of creditors and to distributions**
(1) This Chapter applies where the office-holder makes, or proposes to make, a distribution to any class of creditors other than secured creditors.
(2) Where the distribution is to a particular class of creditors in an administration, a reference in this Chapter to creditors is a reference to that class of creditors only.

Derivation—This rule derived from the Insolvency Rules 1986, SI 1986/1925, r 2.95(5).

## [2.855]

**14.27 Declaration and distribution of dividends in a winding up**
[Note: section 324 makes provision in respect of such a declaration and distribution in a bankruptcy.]
Whenever a liquidator in a creditors' voluntary winding up or a winding up by the court has sufficient funds in hand for the purpose the liquidator must, while retaining such sums as may be necessary for the expenses of the winding up, declare and distribute dividends among the creditors in respect of the debts which they have proved.

Derivation—This rule derived from the Insolvency Rules 1986, SI 1986/1925, r 4.180.

## [2.856]

**14.28 Gazette notice of intended first dividend or distribution**
(1) Subject to paragraphs (2) and (4) where the office-holder intends to declare a first dividend or distribution the office-holder must gazette a notice containing—

(a)    a statement that the office-holder intends to declare a first dividend or distribution;

(b)    the date by which and place to which proofs must be delivered; and

(c)    in the case of a members' voluntary winding up, where the dividend or distribution is to be a sole or final distribution, a statement that the distribution may be made without regard to the claim of any person in respect of a debt not proved.

(2)   Where the intended dividend is only to preferential creditors the office-holder need only gazette a notice if the office-holder thinks fit.

(3)   The office-holder may in addition advertise such a notice in such other manner (if any) as the office-holder thinks fit.

(4)   Paragraph (1) does not apply where the office-holder has previously, by a notice which has been gazetted, invited creditors to prove their debts.

**Derivation**—This rule derived from the Insolvency Rules 1986, SI 1986/1925, rr 11.2, 2.95, 4.182A.

## [2.857]

### 14.29 Individual notices to creditors etc of intended dividend or distribution

(1)   The office-holder must deliver a notice of the intention to make a distribution to creditors or declare a dividend—

(a)    to the creditors in an administration; and

(b)    to all creditors in a winding up or a bankruptcy who have not proved (including any creditors who are owed small debts and are not deemed under rule 14.3(3) to have proved as a result of a previous notice under rule 14.29).

(2)   Where the intended dividend is only for preferential creditors, the office-holder is only required to deliver such a notice to the preferential creditors.

(3)   Where the office-holder intends to declare a dividend to unsecured creditors in an administration or winding-up the notice must also state the value of the prescribed part unless there is no prescribed part or the court has made an order under section 176A(5).

**Derivation**—This rule derived from the Insolvency Rules 1986, SI 1986/1925, rr 2.95, 11.2.

## [2.858]

### 14.30 Contents of notice of intention to declare a dividend or make a distribution

A notice under rule 14.29 must contain the following—

(a)    a statement that the office-holder intends to make a distribution to creditors or declare a dividend (as the case may be) within the period of two months from the last date for proving;

(b)    a statement whether the proposed distribution or dividend is interim or final;

(c)    the last date by which proofs may be delivered which must be—

       (i)    the same date for all creditors who prove, and

      (ii)    not less than 21 days from the date of notice;

(d)    a statement of the place to which proofs must be delivered;

(e)    the additional information required by rule 14.31 where the office-holder intends to treat a small debt as proved for the purposes of paying a dividend; and

(f)    in the case of a members' voluntary winding up, where the distribution is to be a sole or final distribution, a statement that the distribution may be made without regard to the claim of any person in respect of a debt not proved.

**Derivation**—This rule derived from the Insolvency Rules 1986, SI 1986/1925, rr 2.95(4), 11.2.

**[2.859]**

### 14.31 Further contents of notice to creditors owed small debts etc

(1)   The office-holder may treat a debt, which is a small debt according to the accounting records or the statement of affairs of the company or bankrupt, as if it were proved for the purpose of paying a dividend.

(2)   Where the office-holder intends to treat such a debt as if it were proved the notice delivered under rule 14.29 must—

(a)   state the amount of the debt which the office-holder believes to be owed to the creditor according to the accounting records or statement of affairs of the company or the bankrupt (as the case may be);

(b)   state that the office-holder will treat the debt which is stated in notice, being for £1,000 or less, as proved for the purposes of paying a dividend unless the creditor advises the office-holder that the amount of the debt is incorrect or that no debt is owed;

(c)   require the creditor to notify the office-holder by the last date for proving if the amount of the debt is incorrect or if no debt is owed; and

(d)   inform the creditor that where the creditor advises the office-holder that the amount of the debt is incorrect the creditor must also submit a proof in order to receive a dividend.

(3)   The information required by paragraph (2)(a) may take the form of a list of small debts which the office-holder intends to treat as proved which includes that owed to the particular creditor to whom the notice is being delivered.

**[2.860]**

### 14.32 Admission or rejection of proofs following last date for proving

(1)   Unless the office-holder has already dealt with them, the office-holder must within 14 days of the last date for proving set out in the notice under rule 14.29—

(a)   admit or reject (in whole or in part) proofs delivered to the office-holder; or

(b)   make such provision in relation to them as the office-holder thinks fit.

(2)   The office-holder is not obliged to deal with a proof delivered after the last date for proving, but the office-holder may do so if the office-holder thinks fit.

(3)   In the declaration of a dividend a payment must not be made more than once in respect of the same debt.

(4)   . . .

**Derivation**—This rule derived from the Insolvency Rules 1986, SI 1986/1925, rr 2.96, 11.3.

**Amendments**—SI 2019/146, as from IP completion day (as defined in the European Union (Withdrawal Agreement) Act 2020, s 39(1)–(5)).

**General note**—Applications against decisions on proofs are provided for in r 14.8. For consideration of these applications, see the notes relating to the aforementioned rule.

**[2.861]**

### 14.33 Postponement or cancellation of dividend

(1)   The office-holder may postpone or cancel the dividend in the period of two months from the last date for proving if an application is made to the court for the office-holder's decision on a proof to be reversed or varied, or for a proof to be excluded, or for a reduction of the amount claimed.

(2)   The office-holder may postpone a dividend if the office-holder considers that due to the nature of the affairs of the person to whom the proceedings relate there is real complexity in admitting or rejecting proofs of claims submitted.

(3)   Where the dividend is postponed or cancelled a new notice under rule 14.29 will be required if the dividend is paid subsequently.

**Derivation**—This rule derived from the Insolvency Rules 1986, SI 1986/1925, rr 2.96A, 11.4.

**General note**—See *Lomax Leisure Ltd v Miller* [2007] EWHC 2508 (Ch), [2008] 1 BCLC 262, [2007] BPIR 1615 where liquidators postponed and later cancelled the payment of dividends even though they had already declared the dividends and provided cheques when they became aware of a pending application by another creditor. The declaration did not impose a duty to pay a dividend in that sum and the liquidator was not personally liable to pay the dividend and so there was no claim for damages or compensation against the liquidator. The claim based on dishonouring of the cheques was dismissed as the creditors had provided no consideration for these. See also notes to r 14.45.

## [2.862]

### 14.34 Declaration of dividend

(1) The office-holder must declare the dividend in the two month period referred to in rule 14.30(a) in accordance with the notice of intention to declare a dividend unless the office-holder has had cause to postpone or cancel the dividend.

(2) The office-holder must not declare a dividend so long as there is pending an application to the court to reverse or vary a decision of the office-holder on a proof, or to exclude a proof or to reduce the amount claimed unless the court gives permission.

(3) If the court gives such permission, the office-holder must make such provision in relation to the proof as the court directs.

**Derivation**—This rule derived from the Insolvency Rules 1986, SI 1986/1925, rr 2.97, 11.5.

**General note**—In *Lomax Leisure Ltd v Miller* [2007] EWHC 2508 (Ch), [2007] BPIR 1615, [2008] 1 BCLC 262, it was held that a liquidator was not under a duty to pay a dividend that he had declared where to pay it would override the duty to retain funds to meet the expenses of the winding up.

## [2.863]

### 14.35 Notice of declaration of a dividend

(1) Where the office-holder declares a dividend the office-holder must deliver notice of that fact to all creditors who have proved for their debts (subject to paragraph (5)).

(2) The notice declaring a dividend may be delivered at the same time as the dividend is distributed.

(3) The notice must include the following in relation to the insolvency proceedings—

    (a)    the amounts raised from the sale of assets, indicating (so far as practicable) amounts raised by the sale of particular assets;

    (b)    the payments made by the office-holder in carrying out the office-holder's functions;

    (c)    the provision (if any) made for unsettled claims, and funds (if any) retained for particular purposes;

    (d)    the total amount to be distributed and the rate of dividend; and

    (e)    whether, and if so when, any further dividend is expected to be declared.

(4) In an administration, a creditors' voluntary winding-up or a winding up by the court, where the administrator or liquidator intends to make a distribution to unsecured creditors, the notice must also state the value of the prescribed part unless there is no prescribed part or the court has made an order under section 176A(5).

(5) Where the office-holder declares a dividend for preferential creditors only, the notice under paragraph (1) need only be delivered to those preferential creditors who have proved for their debts.

**Derivation**—This rule derived from the Insolvency Rules 1986, SI 1986/1925, rr 2.98, 2.99, 11.6.

## [2.864]

### 14.36 Last notice about dividend in a winding up

[Note: section 330 contains the requirement to deliver such a notice in a bankruptcy.]

(1) When the liquidator in a winding up has realised all the company's assets or so much of them as can, in the liquidator's opinion, be realised without needlessly prolonging the winding up, the liquidator must deliver a notice as provided for in this Chapter, either—

    (a)    of intention to declare a final dividend; or

    (b)    that no dividend, or further dividend, will be declared.

(2)   The notice must contain the particulars required by rule 14.30, 14.31, 14.37 or 14.38 as the case may be and must require claims against the assets to be established by a date set out in the notice.

Derivation—This rule derived from the Insolvency Rules 1986, SI 1986/1925, r 4.186.

## [2.865]

### 14.37 Contents of last notice about dividend (administration, winding up and bankruptcy)

(1)   This rule applies in an administration, winding up or bankruptcy.

(2)   If the office-holder delivers notice to creditors that the office-holder is unable to declare any dividend or (as the case may be) any further dividend, the notice must contain a statement to the effect either—

    (a)    that no funds have been realised; or

    (b)    that the funds realised have already been distributed or used or allocated for paying the expenses of the insolvency proceedings.

(3)   The information required by paragraph (2) may be included in a progress report.

Derivation—This rule derived from the Insolvency Rules 1986, SI 1986/1925, rr 2.100, 11.7.

## [2.866]

### 14.38 Sole or final dividend

[Note: see section 330 in respect of a dividend in a bankruptcy.]

(1)   Where, in an administration or winding up, it is intended that the distribution is to be a sole or final dividend, after the date specified as the last date for proving in the notice under rule 14.29, the office-holder—

    (a)    in a winding up, must pay any outstanding expenses of the winding up out of the assets;

    (b)    in an administration, must—

        (i)    pay any outstanding expenses of a winding up (including any of the items mentioned in rule 6.42 or 7.108 (as appropriate)) or provisional winding up that immediately preceded the administration,

        (ii)    pay any items payable in accordance with the provisions of paragraph 99 of Schedule B1,

        (iii)    pay any amount outstanding (including debts or liabilities and the administrator's own remuneration and expenses) which would, if the administrator were to cease to be the administrator of the company, be payable out of the property of which he had custody or control in accordance with the provisions of paragraph 99, and

        (iv)    declare and distribute that dividend without regard to the claim of any person in respect of a debt not already proved; or

    (c)    in a members' voluntary winding up may, and in every other case must, declare and distribute that dividend without regard to the claim of any person in respect of a debt not already proved.

(2)   The reference in paragraph (1)(b)(iv) and (c) to debts that have not been proved does not include small debts treated as proved by the office-holder.

(3)   The court may, on the application of any person, postpone the date specified in the notice.

Derivation—This rule derived from the Insolvency Rules 1986, SI 1986/1925, rr 2.68, 4.186.

## [2.867]

### 14.39 Administration and winding up: provisions as to dividends

[Note: see section 324(4) in respect of such provisions in bankruptcy.]

In an administration or winding up, in the calculation and distribution of a dividend the office-holder must make provision for—

    (a)    any debts which are the subject of claims which have not yet been determined; and

    (b)    disputed proofs and claims.

**Derivation**—This rule derived from the Insolvency Rules 1986, SI 1986/1925, r 4.182(1).

## [2.868]

### 14.40 Supplementary provisions as to dividends and distributions

(1)    A creditor is not entitled to disturb the payment of any dividend or making of any distribution because—

    (a)    the amount claimed in the creditor's proof is increased after payment of the dividend;

    (b)    in an administration, a creditors' voluntary winding up or a winding up by the court the creditor did not prove for a debt before the declaration of the dividend; or

    (c)    in a members' voluntary winding up, the creditor did not prove for a debt before the last date for proving or increases the claim in proof after that date.

(2)    However the creditor is entitled to be paid a dividend or receive a distribution which the creditor has failed to receive out of any money for the time being available for the payment of a further dividend or making a further distribution.

(3)    Such a dividend must be paid or distribution made before that money is applied to the payment of any further dividend or making of any further distribution.

(4)    If, after a creditor's proof has been admitted, the proof is withdrawn or excluded, or the amount of it is reduced, the creditor is liable to repay to the office-holder, for the credit of the insolvency proceedings, any amount overpaid by way of dividend.

**Derivation**—This rule derived from the Insolvency Rules 1986, SI 1986/1925, rr 2.101, 4.182(2), 11.8.

**General note**—Where all the assets of a company have been distributed, and the company has been dissolved, those creditors who are late in claiming a dividend are unable to trace the assets into the hands of those who have received them pursuant to the liquidator's distribution: *Butler v Broadhead* [1975] Ch 97.

## [2.869]

### 14.41 Secured creditors

(1)    The following applies where a creditor alters the value of a security after a dividend has been declared.

(2)    If the alteration reduces the creditor's unsecured claim ranking for dividend, the creditor must as soon as reasonably practicable repay to the office-holder, for the credit of the administration or of the insolvent estate, any amount received by the creditor as dividend in excess of that to which the creditor would be entitled, having regard to the alteration of the value of the security.

(3)    If the alteration increases the creditor's unsecured claim, the creditor is entitled to receive from the office-holder, out of any money for the time being available for the payment of a further dividend, before any such further dividend is paid, any dividend or dividends which the creditor has failed to receive, having regard to the alteration of the value of the security.

(4)    The creditor is not entitled to disturb any dividend declared (whether or not distributed) before the date of the alteration.

**Derivation**—This rule derived from the Insolvency Rules 1986, SI 1986/1925, rr 2.102, 6.109, 11.9.

**General note**—See *Cahillane v NALM Ltd* [2014] EWHC 1992 (Ch), [2014] BPIR 1093: if a creditor subsequently receives more than the value that he put on the security, then what he actually receives is treated as being the value of the security and any resulting excess of dividend must be repaid to the trustee for distribution amongst the remaining unsecured creditors.

**[2.870]**

### 14.42 Disqualification from dividend

If a creditor contravenes any provision of the Act or these Rules relating to the valuation of securities, the court may, on the application of the office-holder, order that the creditor be wholly or partly disqualified from participation in any dividend.

Derivation—This rule derived from the Insolvency Rules 1986, SI 1986/1925, rr 2.103, 11.10.

**[2.871]**

### 14.43 Assignment of right to dividend

(1)  If a person entitled to a dividend ("the entitled person") delivers notice to the office-holder that the entitled person wishes the dividend to be paid to another person, or that the entitled person has assigned the entitlement to another person, the office-holder must pay the dividend to that other person accordingly.

(2)  A notice delivered under this rule must specify the name and address of the person to whom payment is to be made.

Derivation—This rule derived from the Insolvency Rules 1986, SI 1986/1925, rr 2.104, 11.11.

**[2.872]**

### 14.44 Debt payable at future time

(1)  Where a creditor has proved for a debt of which payment is not due at the date of the declaration of a dividend, the creditor is entitled to the dividend equally with other creditors, but subject as follows.

(2)  For the purpose of dividend (and no other purpose) the amount of the creditor's admitted proof must be discounted by applying the following formula—

$$X \ / \ 1.05^n$$

where—

    (a)    "X" is the value of the admitted proof; and

    (b)    "n" is the period beginning with the relevant date and ending with the date on which the payment of the creditor's debt would otherwise be due, expressed in years (part of a year being expressed as a decimal fraction of a year).

Derivation—This rule derived from the Insolvency Rules 1986, SI 1986/1925, rr 2.89, 2.105, 4.94, 6.114, 11.13.

General note—This rule exists to facilitate the proof of liabilities such as annuities, future rent payable in respect of a lease that the liquidator has failed to disclaim, instalments to become due on contracts of hire, and a debenture repayable at a date after the beginning of winding up. With the payment of debentures, the date for repayment is accelerated, with the result that the full amount of principal together with interest to date automatically becomes due on winding up, irrespective of the date fixed for payment under the contract: *Wallace v Universal Automatic Machine Co* [1894] 2 Ch 547.

**[2.873]**

### 14.45 Administration and winding up: non-payment of dividend

[Note: see section 325(2) for equivalent provisions in respect of bankruptcy.]

(1)  No action lies against the office-holder in an administration or winding up for payment of a dividend.

(2)  However, if the office-holder refuses to pay a dividend the court may, if it thinks just, order the office-holder to pay it and also to pay, out of the office-holder's own money—

    (a)    interest on the dividend, at the rate for the time being specified in section 17 of the Judgments Act 1838, from the time when it was withheld; and

    (b)    the costs of the proceedings in which the order to pay is made.

Derivation—This rule derived from the Insolvency Rules 1986, SI 1986/1925, rr 2.70(3), 4.182(3).

**General note**—It was held in *Lomax Leisure Ltd v Miller* [2007] EWHC 2508 (Ch), [2007] BPIR 1615, [2008] 1 BCLC 262 at [34.1] that if a creditor was not paid then the remedy open to that creditor was under IR 1986, r 4.182(3) (replaced by IR 2016, r 14.45(2)). If a liquidator declared a dividend and then dissipated or paid away assets so that an application under r 4.182(3) was not possible, then a personal claim could lie against the liquidator depending on the circumstances. Save where the company had been dissolved, the claim would ordinarily only be capable of being brought as a misfeasance claim under s 212 (misfeasance procedure).

# PART 15 DECISION MAKING

## [2.874]

**Introductory commentary on Part 15: Decision making**—The decision-making process in Part 15 involves a fundamental overhaul to the way in which office-holders engage with and seek the views of creditors. Central to this overhaul are the amendments made by the Small Business, Enterprise and Employment Act 2015 by which a physical meeting is no longer the default position in seeking the approval of creditors to proposals. Physical meetings, therefore, will become less common. It should be remembered that the meeting of creditors model for decision making in insolvency proceedings is rooted in the latter part of the 1800s and that, until these latest legislative reforms, the insolvency decision making process has not kept pace with or, indeed, exploited the advantages of modern forms of electronic communication, e-communications only being first permitted by the Insolvency (Amendment) Rules 2010.

**SIP 6**—SIP 6, *Deemed consent and decision procedures in insolvency proceedings*, took effect from 1 January 2018, replacing an interim version of the SIP effective from 6 April 2017.

**Deemed consent**—With some limited exceptions (identified below) an office-holder is able to use a process of deemed consent by which the office-holder writes to creditors with a proposal and, provided the office-holder receives objections from 10% or less of creditors by value, the proposal will be deemed to be approved. In the event that 10% or more of creditors object to the proposal then the office-holder will be obliged to use an alternative decision-making process (see below). Deemed consent will not be available in three specific scenarios: first, the approval of an individual or company voluntary arrangement; secondly, the removal of an office-holder; and, thirdly, the approval of an office-holder's remuneration.

The fact that a creditor holds less than 10% of the total value of creditor claims is not fatal to that creditor (or more than one creditor holding less than 10% of such claims) where the creditor(s) objects to a proposal presented using the deemed consent procedure. The Rules allow for objection by such creditor(s) and the raising of concerns, in consequence of which the office-holder has a duty to consider whether deemed consent is the most appropriate mechanism to use. The burden also falls on the office-holder in assessing whether the 10% threshold has been reached, rather than creditors having to organise themselves to demonstrate the 10% requirement (although creditors are, of course, free to organise themselves as they wish, especially in the face of view or proposals conflicting with their wishes).

The 'deemed consent procedure' (as defined in r 1.2(2)) provisions appear in ss 246ZF (corporate insolvency) and 379ZB (personal insolvency) of the 1986 Act. Rule 15.7 makes further provision about deemed consent.

**The forms of alternative decision making and the calling of a physical meeting**—With two exceptions, the specific form an alternative decision-making process takes is at the discretion of the office-holder. Subject to those two exceptions (see below), an office-holder may choose to use a remote meeting, correspondence, a method of electronic voting, or any method by which the office-holder can engage with creditors without a physical meeting taking place. All of these matters are defined in r 15.2.

The first exception is that an office-holder may only call a physical meeting of creditors if, and only if, such a physical meeting has been requested by 10% or more by value of creditors, 10% of the total number of creditors, or ten individual creditors. That course is open to such creditors at any time that their consent or approval is sought by the office-holder. Accordingly, the expense of calling a physical meeting should only be incurred and charged to the insolvent estate where the requisite level or number of creditors has asked for this to happen. Sections 246ZE and 379ZA provide that a decision may not be made by a physical meeting of creditors unless the proscribed proportion of the creditors request in writing – see above – that the decision be made by such a meeting.

The second exception concerns the appointment of a liquidator in a creditors' voluntary liquidation. Under that procedure the only methods of seeking a decision from creditors that the company may use are a virtual meeting or deemed consent. If creditors object to the use of deemed consent then the company must immediately call a physical meeting. Creditors may still require that a physical meeting is held in any case.

**Abolition of final meetings**—The provisions of the Small Business, Enterprise and Employment Act 2015 abolished all final meetings of creditors where previously required (ie in creditors' voluntary liquidation, compulsory liquidation, and bankruptcy where someone other than the Official Receiver is trustee). Final meetings of members (shareholders) in members' voluntary liquidations are also be scrapped. It will still be necessary for the office-holder to engage with creditors by sending them a copy of the final account, and creditors will continue to be able to object to the release of the office-holder upon receipt of that document by notifying the office-holder of their objection.

**Opting out of further correspondence**—The rules now allow a creditor to opt out of receiving further correspondence where, most obviously, a creditor has no further interest in a case and requires no further information about it. Notices of intended dividends are not subject to the opt-out option and creditors also retain the ability to opt back in to receive notices.

**Continuing relevance of decisions under the Insolvency Rules 1986**—The derivation notes to the provisions in Part 15 below identify those provisions within the IR 1986 from which the 2016 provisions derive. The substance of the new provisions, and the similarity in the wording used, mean that judicial authority under the previous provisions will continue to have some relevance. This should not, however, be overstated. The 2016 Rules represent a new code. Decisions under the former provisions should, therefore, be treated with some caution unless the wording and context of the new provision is identical to the earlier equivalent provision.

## CHAPTER 1

### APPLICATION OF PART

**[2.875]**

**15.1 Application of Part**

In this Part—

    (a)    Chapters 2 to 11 apply where the Act or these Rules require a decision to be made by a qualifying decision procedure, or by a creditors' decision procedure or permit a decision to be made by the deemed consent procedure; and

    (b)    Chapter 12 applies to company meetings.

## CHAPTER 2

### DECISION PROCEDURES

**[2.876]**

**Note**

[Note: a document required by the Act or these Rules must also contain the standard contents set out in Part 1.]

**[2.877]**

**15.2 Interpretation**

(1)    In these Rules—

        "decision date" means—

        (a)    in the case of a decision to be made at a meeting, the date of the meeting;

        (b)    in the case of a decision to be made either by a decision procedure other than a meeting or by the deemed consent procedure, the date the decision is to be made or deemed to have been made;

        and a decision falling within paragraph (b) is to be treated as made at 23:59 on the decision date;

        "decision procedure" means a qualifying decision procedure or a creditors' decision procedure as prescribed by rule 15.3;

        "electronic voting" includes any electronic system which enables a person to vote without the need to attend at a particular location to do so;

"physical meeting" means a meeting as described in section 246ZE(9) or 379ZA(9);

"virtual meeting" means a meeting where persons who are not invited to be physically present together may participate in the meeting including communicating directly with all the other participants in the meeting and voting (either directly or via a proxy-holder);

(2) The decision date is to be set at the discretion of the convener, but must be not less than 14 days from the date of delivery of the notice, except where the table in rule 15.11 requires a different period or the court directs otherwise.

(3) The rules in Chapters 2 to 11 about decision procedures of creditors apply with any necessary modifications to decision making by contributories.

(4) In particular, in place of the requirement for percentages or majorities in decision making by creditors to be determined by value, where the procedure seeks a decision from contributories value must be determined on the percentage of voting rights in accordance with rule 15.39.

General note—See the Introductory note to Part 15: Decision making.

The definitions in r 15.2(1) are key to the operation of Chapter 15. Note the definitions of 'electronic voting' and 'virtual meeting' and the breadth and unrestricted nature thereof. Note the reference in r 15.2(2) to the table in r 15.11.

Rule 15.2(4) is necessary to apply the new decision-making procedures to contributories.

The definition of 'requested decision' – by which creditors or contributories may request a decision, rather than a request for a decision to be made by way of a physical meeting – appears in r 15.18.

## [2.878]

### 15.3 The prescribed decision procedures

[Note: under sections 246ZE and 379ZA a decision may not be made by a creditors' meeting (a physical meeting) unless the prescribed proportion of the creditors request in writing that the decision be made by such a meeting.]

The following decision procedures are prescribed as decision procedures under sections 246ZE and 379ZA by which a convener may seek a decision under the Act or these Rules from creditors—

    (a)    correspondence;

    (b)    electronic voting;

    (c)    virtual meeting;

    (d)    physical meeting;

    (e)    any other decision making procedure which enables all creditors who are entitled to participate in the making of the decision to participate equally.

Amendments—SI 2017/366.

## [2.879]

### 15.4 Electronic voting

Where the decision procedure uses electronic voting—

    (a)    the notice delivered to creditors must give them any necessary information as to how to access the voting system including any password required;

    (b)    except where electronic voting is being used at a meeting, the voting system must be a system capable of enabling a creditor to vote at any time between the notice being delivered and the decision date; and

    (c)    in the course of a vote the voting system must not provide any creditor with information concerning the vote cast by any other creditor.

## [2.880]

### 15.5 Virtual meetings

Where the decision procedure uses a virtual meeting the notice delivered to creditors must contain—

(a)  any necessary information as to how to access the virtual meeting including any telephone number, access code or password required; and

(b)  a statement that the meeting may be suspended or adjourned by the chair of the meeting (and must be adjourned if it is so resolved at the meeting).

**[2.881]**

### 15.6 Physical meetings

(1)  A request for a physical meeting may be made before or after the notice of the decision procedure or deemed consent procedure has been delivered, but must be made not later than five business days after the date on which the convener delivered the notice of the decision procedure or deemed consent procedure unless these Rules provide to the contrary.

(2)  It is the convener's responsibility to check whether any requests for a physical meeting are submitted before the deadline and if so whether in aggregate they meet or surpass one of the thresholds requiring a physical meeting under sections 246ZE(7) or 379ZA(7).

(3)  Where the prescribed proportion of creditors require a physical meeting the convener must summon the meeting by giving notice which complies with rule 15.8 so far as applicable and which must also contain a statement that the meeting may be suspended or adjourned by the chair of the meeting (and must be adjourned if it is so resolved at the meeting).

(4)  In addition, the notice under paragraph (3) must inform the creditors that as a result of the requirement to hold a physical meeting the original decision procedure or the deemed consent procedure is superseded.

(5)  The convener must send the notice under paragraph (3) not later than three business days after one of the thresholds requiring a physical meeting has been met or surpassed.

(6)  The convener—

(a)  may permit a creditor to attend a physical meeting remotely if the convener receives a request to do so in advance of the meeting; and

(b)  must include in the notice of the meeting a statement explaining the convener's discretion to permit remote attendance.

(7)  In this rule, attending a physical meeting "remotely" means attending and being able to participate in the meeting without being in the place where the meeting is being held.

(8)  For the purpose of determining whether the thresholds under section 246ZE(7) or 379ZA(7) are met, the convener must calculate the value of the creditor's debt by reference to rule 15.31.

**Amendments**—SI 2017/366.

**[2.882]**

### 15.7 Deemed consent (sections 246ZF and 379ZB)

[Note: the deemed consent procedure cannot be used to make a decision on remuneration of any person, or where the Act, these Rules or any other legislation requires a decision to be made by a decision procedure.]

(1)  This rule makes further provision about the deemed consent procedure to that set out in sections 246ZF and 379ZB.

(2)  A notice seeking deemed consent must, in addition to the requirements of section 246ZF or 379ZB (as applicable) comply with the requirements of rule 15.8 so far as applicable and must also contain—

(a)  a statement that in order to object to the proposed decision a creditor must have delivered a notice, stating that the creditor so objects, to the convener not later than the decision date together with a proof in respect of the creditor's claim in accordance with these Rules failing which the objection will be disregarded;

(b)    a statement that it is the convener's responsibility to aggregate any objections to see if the threshold is met for the decision to be taken as not having been made; and

(c)    a statement that if the threshold is met the deemed consent procedure will terminate without a decision being made and if a decision is sought again on the same matter it will be sought by a decision procedure.

(3)   In this rule, the threshold is met where the appropriate number of relevant creditors (as defined in sections 246ZF and 379ZB) have objected to the proposed decision.

(4)   For the purpose of aggregating objections, the convener may presume the value of relevant creditors' claims to be the value of claims by those creditors who, in the convener's view, would have been entitled to vote had the decision been sought by a decision procedure in accordance with this Part, even where those creditors had not already met the criteria for such entitlement to vote.

(5)   The provisions of rules 15.31(2) (calculation of voting rights), 15.32 (calculation of voting rights: special cases) and 15.33 (procedure for admitting creditors' claims for voting) apply to the admission or rejection of a claim for the purpose of the convener deciding whether or not an objection should count towards the total aggregated objections.

(6)   A decision of the convener on the aggregation of objections under this rule is subject to appeal under rule 15.35 as if it were a decision under Chapter 8 of this Part.

CHAPTER 3

NOTICES, VOTING AND VENUES FOR DECISIONS

**[2.883]**

**Note**
[Note: a document required by the Act or these Rules must also contain the standard contents set out in Part 1.]

**[2.884]**

**15.8 Notices to creditors of decision procedure**
(1)   This rule sets out the requirements for notices to creditors where a decision is sought by a decision procedure.

(2)   The convener must deliver a notice to every creditor who is entitled to notice of the procedure.

(3)   The notice must contain the following—

(a)    identification details for the proceedings;

(b)    details of the decision to be made or of any resolution on which a decision is sought;

(c)    a description of the decision procedure which the convener is using, and arrangements, including the venue, for the decision procedure;

(d)    a statement of the decision date;

(e)    a statement of by when the creditor must have delivered a proof in respect of the creditor's claim in accordance with these Rules failing which a vote by the creditor will be disregarded;

(f)    a statement that a creditor whose debt is treated as a small debt in accordance with rule 14.31(1) must still deliver a proof if that creditor wishes to vote;

(g)    a statement that a creditor who has opted out from receiving notices may nevertheless vote if the creditor provides a proof in accordance with paragraph (e);

(h)    in the case of a decision to remove a liquidator in a creditors' voluntary winding-up or a winding up by the court, a statement drawing the attention of creditors to section 173(2), 174(2) or 174(4) (which relate to the release of the liquidator), as appropriate;

(i)    in the case of a decision to remove a trustee in a bankruptcy, a statement drawing the attention of creditors to section 299(1) or 299(3) (which relates to the release of the trustee);

(j)    in the case of a decision in relation to a proposed CVA or IVA, a statement of the effects of the relevant provisions of the following—

    (i)    rule 15.28 about creditors' voting rights,

    (ii)    rule 15.31 about the calculation of creditors' voting rights, and

    (iii)    rule 15.34 about the requisite majority of creditors for making decisions;

(k)    except in the case of a physical meeting, a statement that creditors who meet the thresholds in sections 246ZE(7) or 379ZA(7) may, within five business days from the date of delivery of the notice, require a physical meeting to be held to consider the matter;

(l)    in the case of a meeting, a statement that any proxy must be delivered to the convener or chair before it may be used at the meeting;

(m)    in the case of a meeting, a statement that, where applicable, a complaint may be made in accordance with rule 15.38 and the period within which such a complaint may be made; and

(n)    a statement that a creditor may appeal a decision in accordance with rule 15.35, and the relevant period under rule 15.35 within which such an appeal may be made.

(4)   The notice must be authenticated and dated by the convener.

(5)   Where the decision procedure is a meeting the notice must be accompanied by a blank proxy complying with rule 16.3.

(6)   This rule does not apply if the court orders under rule 15.12 that notice of a decision procedure be given by advertisement only.

**Derivation**—This rule derived from the Insolvency Rules 1986, SI 1986/1925, rr 1.9, 1.48, 2.34, 4.50, 4.51, 4.54, 5.17, 6.79, 6.81.

**Amendments**—SI 2017/366.

**General note**—See the Introductory note to Part 15: Decision making.

## [2.885]

### 15.9 Voting in a decision procedure

(1)   In order to be counted in a decision procedure other than where votes are cast at a meeting, votes must—

(a)    be received by the convener on or before the decision date; and

(b)    in the case of a vote cast by a creditor, be accompanied by a proof in respect of the creditor's claim unless it has already been given to the convener.

(2)   In an administration, an administrative receivership, a creditors' voluntary winding up, a winding up by the court or a bankruptcy a vote must be disregarded if—

(a)    a proof in respect of the claim is not received by the convener on or before the decision date or, in the case of a meeting, 4pm on the business day before the decision date unless under rule 15.26 or 15.28(1)(b)(ii) (as applicable) the chair is content to accept the proof later; or

(b)    the convener decides, in the application of Chapter 8 of this Part, that the creditor is not entitled to cast the vote.

(3)   For the decision to be made, the convener must receive at least one valid vote on or before the decision date.

**Derivation**—This rule derived from the Insolvency Rules 1986, SI 1986/1925, rr 2.38, 3.11, 4.50, 4.51, 4.54, 6.79, 6.81.

**General note**—See the Introductory note to Part 15: Decision making.

Note the pre-requisite in r 15.9(3) for the making of a valid decision.

**[2.886]**

### 15.10 Venue for decision procedure

The convener must have regard to the convenience of those invited to participate when fixing the venue for a decision procedure (including the resumption of an adjourned meeting).

**Derivation**—This rule derived from the Insolvency Rules 1986, SI 1986/1925, rr 1.13, 2.35, 3.9, 4.60, 5.18, 6.86.

**General note**—See the Introductory note to Part 15: Decision making.


**[2.887]**

### 15.11 Notice of decision procedures or of seeking deemed consent: when and to whom delivered

Note: when an office-holder is obliged to give notice to "the creditors", this is subject to rule 1.37, which limits the obligation to giving notice to those creditors of whose address the office-holder is aware.

(1) Notices of decision procedures, and notices seeking deemed consent, must be delivered in accordance with the following table.

| Proceedings | Decisions | Persons to whom notice must be delivered | Minimum notice required |
|---|---|---|---|
| administration | decisions of creditors | the creditors who had claims against the company at the date when the company entered administration (except for those who have subsequently been paid in full) | 14 days |
| administrative receivership | decisions of creditors | the creditors | 14 days |
| creditors' voluntary winding up | decisions of creditors for appointment of liquidator (including any decision made at the same time on the liquidator's remuneration or the establishment of a liquidation committee) | the creditors | 14 days on conversion from members' voluntary liquidation, 7 days on conversion from member's voluntary liquidation where deemed consent has been objected to and in other cases, 3 business days |
| creditors' voluntary winding up or a winding up by the court | decisions of creditors to consider whether a replacement should be appointed after a liquidator's resignation | the creditors | 28 days |
| winding up by the court | decisions of creditors to consider whether to remove or replace the liquidator (other than after a liquidator's resignation) | the creditors and the official receiver | 14 days |

| | | | |
|---|---|---|---|
| creditors' voluntary winding up or a winding up by the court | other decisions of creditors | the creditors | 14 days |
| winding up by the court | decisions of contributories | every person appearing (by the company's records or otherwise) to be a contributory | 14 days |
| proposed CVA | decisions of creditors | the creditors | 7 days for a decision on proposed modifications to the proposal from the company's directors under paragraph 31(7) of Schedule A1; 7 days for consideration of proposal where physical meeting requisitioned; in other cases, 14 days |
| proposed IVA | decisions of creditors | the creditors | 14 days |
| bankruptcy | decisions of creditors to consider whether a replacement should be appointed after the resignation of a trustee | the creditors and the official receiver | 28 days |
| bankruptcy | decisions of creditors to consider removing the trustee | the creditors and the official receiver | 14 days |
| bankruptcy | decisions of creditors on appointment of new trustee following removal of previous trustee (including any decision made at the same time on the establishment of a creditors' committee) | the creditors | 7 days |
| bankruptcy | other decisions of creditors | the creditors | 14 days |
| . . . | . . . | . . . | . . . |

(2)   This rule does not apply where the court orders under rule 15.12 that notice of a decision procedure be given by advertisement only.

**Derivation**—This rule derived from the Insolvency Rules 1986, SI 1986/1925, rr 1.9, 1.48, 2.35, 3.9, 4.50, 4.54, 5.17, 6.79, 6.81.

**Amendments**—SI 2017/702; SI 2019/146, as from IP completion day (as defined in the European Union (Withdrawal Agreement) Act 2020, s 39(1)–(5)).

**CIGA 2020**—This provision is affected by temporary measures at Sch 4, para 24 of CIGA 2020.

**General note**—See the Introductory note to Part 15: Decision making.

The minimum notice required in each case in the above table should be read with r 15.2(2) which provides that the decision date (as defined in r 15.2(1)) is to be set at the discretion of the convener, but must be not less than 14 days from the date of delivery of the notice, except where the above table requires a different period or the court directs otherwise.

The final entry in the table above, 'Main proceedings in another member State', was inserted by the Insolvency Amendment (EU 2015/848) Regulations 2017 (SI 2017/702) in relation to proceedings opened on or after 26 June 2017 on which date the Recast EU Regulation (2015/848) came into force.

## [2.888]

### 15.12 Notice of decision procedure by advertisement only

(1)   The court may order that notice of a decision procedure is to be given by advertisement only and not by individual notice to the persons concerned.

(2)   In considering whether to make such an order, the court must have regard to the relative cost of advertisement as against the giving of individual notices, the amount of assets available and the extent of the interest of creditors, members and contributories or any particular class of them.

(3)   The advertisement must meet the requirements for a notice under rule 15.8(3), and must also state—

(a)   that the court ordered that notice of the decision procedure be given by advertisement only; and

(b)   the date of the court's order.

**Derivation**—This rule derived from the Insolvency Rules 1986, SI 1986/1925, rr 2.37A, 4.59, 6.85.

**General note**—See the Introductory note to Part 15: Decision making.

The making of an order for advertisement under r 15.12 disapplies r 15.11: see r 15.11(2).

## [2.889]

### 15.13 Gazetting and advertisement of meeting

(1)   In an administration, a creditors' voluntary winding up, a winding up by the court, or a bankruptcy, where a decision is being sought by a meeting the convener must gazette a notice of the procedure stating—

(a)   that a meeting of creditors or contributories is to take place;

(b)   the venue for the meeting;

(c)   the purpose of the meeting; and

(d)   the time and date by which, and place at which, those attending must deliver proxies and proofs (if not already delivered) in order to be entitled to vote.

(2)   The notice must also state—

(a)   who is the convener in respect of the decision procedure; and

(b)   if the procedure results from a request of one or more creditors, the fact that it was so summoned and the section of the Act under which it was summoned.

(3)   The notice must be gazetted before or as soon as reasonably practicable after notice of the meeting is delivered in accordance with these Rules.

(4)   Information to be gazetted under this rule may also be advertised in such other manner as the convener thinks fit.

(5)   The convener may gazette other decision procedures or the deemed consent procedure in which case the equivalent information to that required by this rule must be stated in the notice.

**Derivation**—This rule derived from the Insolvency Rules 1986, SI 1986/1925, rr 2.34, 4.50, 4.53C, 4.53D, 6.79.

**General note**—See the Introductory note to Part 15: Decision making.

## [2.890]

### 15.14 Notice to company officers, bankrupts etc in respect of meetings

(1)   In a proposal for a CVA, an administration, a creditors' voluntary winding up or a winding up by the court notice to participate in a creditors' meeting must be delivered to

every present or former officer of the company whose presence the convener thinks is required and that person is required to attend the meeting.

(2)   In a bankruptcy, notice of a meeting must be delivered to the bankrupt who is required to attend the meeting unless paragraph (3) applies.

(3)   In a bankruptcy, where the bankrupt is not required to attend the meeting, the notice must state—

  (a)   that the bankrupt is not required to attend the meeting;

  (b)   that if the bankrupt wishes to attend, the bankrupt should tell the convener as soon as reasonably practicable;

  (c)   that whether the bankrupt will be allowed to participate in the meeting is at the discretion of the chair; and

  (d)   that the decision of the chair as to what intervention, if any, the bankrupt may make is final.

(4)   Notices under this rule must be delivered in compliance with the minimum notice requirements set out in rule 15.2(2) or in compliance with an order of the court under rule 15.12.

Derivation—This rule derived from the Insolvency Rules 1986, SI 1986/1925, rr 1.16, 2.34(2), 4.58, 6.84.

General note—See the Introductory note to Part 15: Decision making.

## [2.891]

### 15.15  Non-receipt of notice of decision

Where a decision is sought by a notice in accordance with the Act or these Rules, the decision procedure or deemed consent procedure is presumed to have been duly initiated and conducted, even if not everyone to whom the notice is to be delivered has received it.

Derivation—This rule derived from the Insolvency Rules 1986, SI 1986/1925, r 12A.4.

General note—See the Introductory note to Part 15: Decision making.

The presumption in this provision, like that in the former IR 1986, r 12A.4, is a presumption only, and, as such, rebuttable.

## [2.892]

### 15.16  Decisions on remuneration and conduct

(1)   This rule applies in relation to a decision or resolution which is proposed in an administration, a creditors' voluntary winding up, a winding up by the court or a bankruptcy and which affects a person in relation to that person's remuneration or conduct as administrator, liquidator or trustee (actual, proposed or former).

(2)   The following may not vote on such a decision or resolution whether as a creditor, contributory, proxy-holder or corporate representative, except so far as permitted by rule 16.7 (proxy-holder with financial interest)—

  (a)   that person;

  (b)   the partners and employees of that person; and

  (c)   the officers and employees of the company of which that person is a director, officer or employee.

Derivation—This rule derived from the Insolvency Rules 1986, SI 1986/1925, rr 4.63, 6.88.

General note—See the Introductory note to Part 15: Decision making.

Note that the exclusions on voting in r 15.16(2) apply not only to remuneration but also the entirely separate issue of 'conduct' of the classes of office-holder prescribed by r 15.16(1).

CHAPTER 4

DECISION MAKING IN PARTICULAR PROCEEDINGS

**[2.893]**

**Note**

[Note: a document required by the Act or these Rules must also contain the standard contents set out in Part 1.]

**[2.894]**

**15.17 Decisions in winding up of authorised deposit-takers**

(1) This rule applies in a creditors' voluntary winding up or a winding up by the court of an authorised deposit-taker.

(2) The directors of a company must deliver a notice of a meeting of the company at which it is intended to propose a resolution for its winding up to the Financial Conduct Authority and to the scheme manager established under section 212(1) of the Financial Services and Markets Act 2000.

(3) These notices must be the same as those delivered to members of the company.

(4) Where any decision is sought for the purpose of considering whether a replacement should be appointed after the liquidator's resignation, removing the liquidator or appointing a new liquidator, the convener must also deliver a copy of the notice by which such a decision is sought to the Financial Conduct Authority and the scheme manager.

(5) A scheme manager who is required by this rule to be given notice of a meeting is entitled to be represented at the meeting.

   **Derivation**—This rule derived from the Insolvency Rules 1986, SI 1986/1925, r 4.72.

   **General note**—The voting rights of a scheme manager are provided for in r 15.29.

   'Authorised deposit-taker' is defined in r 1.2(2).

CHAPTER 5

REQUISITIONED DECISIONS

**[2.895]**

**Note**

[Note: a document required by the Act or these Rules must also contain the standard contents set out in Part 1.]

**[2.896]**

**15.18 Requisitions of decision**

[Note: this rule is concerned with requests by creditors or contributories for a decision, rather than requests for decisions to be made by way of a physical meeting under sections 246ZE(3) or 379ZA(3).]

(1) In this Chapter, "requisitioned decision" means a decision on nominations requested to be sought under section 136(5)(c) or a decision requested to be sought under section 168(2), 171(2)(b), 171(3A), 172(3), 298(4)(c) or 314(7) or paragraph 52(2) or 56(1) of Schedule B1.

(2) A request for a decision to be sought under paragraph 52(2) of Schedule B1 must be delivered within 8 business days of the date on which the administrator's statement of proposals is delivered.

(3) The request for a requisitioned decision must include a statement of the purpose of the proposed decision and either—

      (a)    a statement of the requesting creditor's claim or contributory's value, together with—

          (i)      a list of the creditors or contributories concurring with the request and of the amounts of their respective claims or values, and

          (ii)    confirmation of concurrence from each creditor or contributory concurring; or

    (b)    a statement of the requesting creditor's debt or contributory's value and that that alone is sufficient without the concurrence of other creditors or contributories.

(4)   A decision procedure must be instigated under section 171(2)(b) for the removal of the liquidator, other than a liquidator appointed by the court under section 108, if 25% in value of the company's creditors, excluding those who are connected with the company, request it.

(5)   Where a decision procedure under section 171(2)(b), 171(3), 171(3A) or 298(4)(c) is to be instigated, or is proposed to be instigated, the court may, on the application of any creditor, give directions as to the decision procedure to be used and any other matter which appears to the court to require regulation or control.

(6)   Where the official receiver receives a request under section 136(5)(c) and it appears that it is properly made, the official receiver must withdraw any notices previously given under section 136(5)(b) and act in accordance with Chapter 2 as if the official receiver had decided under section 136 to seek nominations.

**Derivation**—This rule derived from the Insolvency Rules 1986, SI 1986/1925, rr 2.37, 4.57, 6.83.

**General note**—See the Introductory note to Part 15: Decision making. There is some comment on this provision in *Re Birdi, Miles v Price* [2019] EWHC 291 (Ch), [2019] BPIR 498 at [101]–[104] (Adam Johnson QC).

## [2.897]

### 15.19 Expenses and timing of requisitioned decision

(1)   The convener must, not later than 14 days from receipt of a request for a requisitioned decision, provide the requesting creditor with itemised details of the sum to be deposited as security for payment of the expenses of such procedure.

(2)   The convener is not obliged to initiate the decision procedure or deemed consent procedure (where applicable) until either—

    (a)    the convener has received the required sum; or

    (b)    the period of 14 days has expired without the convener having informed the requesting creditor or contributory of the sum required to be deposited as security.

(3)   A requisitioned decision must be made—

    (a)    where requested under section 136(5)(c), within three months; or

    (b)    in any other case, within 28 days;

of the date on which the earlier of the events specified in paragraph (2) of this rule occurs.

(4)   The expenses of a requisitioned decision must be paid out of the deposit (if any) unless—

    (a)    the creditors decide that they are to be payable as an expense of the administration, winding up or bankruptcy, as the case may be; and

    (b)    in the case of a decision of contributories, the creditors are first paid in full, with interest.

(5)   The notice of a requisitioned decision of creditors must contain a statement that the creditors may make a decision as in paragraph (4)(a) of this rule.

(6)   Where the creditors do not so decide, the expenses must be paid by the requesting creditor or contributory to the extent that the deposit (if any) is not sufficient.

(7)   To the extent that the deposit (if any) is not required for payment of the expenses, it must be repaid to the requesting creditor or contributory.

**Derivation**—This rule derived from the Insolvency Rules 1986, SI 1986/1925, rr 2.37, 4.57(2), 4.61(3), (5), 6.83(2), 6.87.

**General note**—See the Introductory note to Part 15: Decision making. There is some comment on this provision in *Re Birdi, Miles v Price* [2019] EWHC 291 (Ch), [2019] BPIR 498 at

[101]–[104] (Adam Johnson QC). If the 'required sum' in r 15.19(2)(a) is not received then the otherwise mandatory requirement to initiate the procedures referred to is not triggered.

CHAPTER 6

CONSTITUTION OF MEETINGS

**[2.898]**

**15.20  Quorum at meetings**
(1)   A meeting is not competent to act unless a quorum is in attendance.
(2)   A quorum is—
    (a)   in the case of a meeting of creditors, at least one creditor entitled to vote; and
    (b)   in the case of a meeting of contributories, at least two contributories entitled to vote, or all the contributories, if their number does not exceed two.
(3)   Where the provisions of this rule as to quorum are satisfied by the attendance of the chair alone or the chair and one additional person, but the chair is aware, either by virtue of proofs and proxies received or otherwise, that one or more additional persons would, if attending, be entitled to vote, the chair must delay the start of the meeting by at least 15 minutes after the appointed time.

**Derivation**—This rule derived from the Insolvency Rules 1986, SI 1986/1925, r 12A.21.

**[2.899]**

**15.21  Chair at meetings**
(1)   The chair of a meeting must be—
    (a)   the convener;
    (b)   an appointed person; or
    (c)   in cases where the convener is the official receiver, a person appointed by the official receiver.
(2)   However, where a decision on the appointment of a liquidator under rule 6.14(2)(b), 6.14(4) or 6.14(6) is made by a meeting or a virtual meeting, the chair of the meeting must be the convener.

**Derivation**—This rule derived from the Insolvency Rules 1986, SI 1986/1925, rr 2.36, 3.10, 4.55, 4.56, 5.19, 6.82.
**Amendments**—SI 2017/366.
**Definitions**—'convener' see r 1.2; 'appointed person' see r 1.2(3).

**[2.900]**

**15.22  The chair—attendance, interventions and questions**
The chair of a meeting may—
    (a)   allow any person who has given reasonable notice of wishing to attend to participate in a virtual meeting or to be admitted to a physical meeting;
    (b)   decide what intervention, if any, may be made at—
        (i)   a meeting of creditors by any person attending who is not a creditor, or
        (ii)   a meeting of contributories by any person attending who is not a contributory; and
    (c)   decide what questions may be put to—
        (i)   any present or former officer of the company, or
        (ii)   the bankrupt or debtor.

**Derivation**—This rule derived from the Insolvency Rules 1986, SI 1986/1925, rr 4.58, 6.84.
**Complaints by excluded parties**—See the procedure in rr 15.36 and 15.46.

## CHAPTER 7

### Adjournment and Suspension of Meetings

**[2.901]**

#### 15.23 Adjournment by chair

(1)   The chair may (and must if it is so resolved) adjourn a meeting for not more than 14 days, but subject to any direction of the court and to rule 15.24.

(2)   Further adjournment under this rule must not be to a day later than 14 days after the date on which the meeting was originally held (subject to any direction by the court).

(3)   But in a case relating to a proposed CVA, the chair may, and must if the meeting so resolves, adjourn a meeting held under paragraph 29(1) of Schedule A1 to a day which is not more than 14 days after the date on which the moratorium (including any extension) ends.

Derivation—This rule derived from the Insolvency Rules 1986, SI 1986/1925, rr 1.21, 1.53, 2.35, 3.14, 4.65(3), 5.24, 6.91.

**[2.902]**

#### 15.24 Adjournment of meetings to remove a liquidator or trustee

If the chair of a meeting to remove the liquidator or trustee in a creditors' voluntary winding up, a winding up by the court or a bankruptcy is the liquidator or trustee or the liquidator's or trustee's nominee and a resolution has been proposed for the liquidator's or trustee's removal, the chair must not adjourn the meeting without the consent of at least one-half (in value) of the creditors attending and entitled to vote.

Derivation—This rule derived from the Insolvency Rules 1986, SI 1986/1925, rr 4.113, 4.114, 6.129.

**[2.903]**

#### 15.25 Adjournment in absence of chair

(1)   In an administration, administrative receivership, a creditors' voluntary winding up, a winding up by the court or a bankruptcy, if no one attends to act as chair within 30 minutes of the time fixed for a meeting to start, then the meeting is adjourned to the same time and place the following week or, if that is not a business day, to the business day immediately following.

(2)   If no one attends to act as chair within 30 minutes of the time fixed for the meeting after a second adjournment under this rule, then the meeting comes to an end.

Derivation—This rule derived from the Insolvency Rules 1986, SI 1986/1925, rr 2.35(5), 4.65(6A), 6.91(4A).

**[2.904]**

#### 15.26 Proofs in adjournment

Where a meeting in an administration, an administrative receivership, a creditors' voluntary winding-up, a winding up by the court or a bankruptcy is adjourned, proofs may be used if delivered not later than 4pm on the business day immediately before resumption of the adjourned meeting, or later than that time where the chair is content to accept the proof.

Derivation—This rule derived from the Insolvency Rules 1986, SI 1986/1925, rr 2.35, 4.65(7), 6.91(5).

**[2.905]**

#### 15.27 Suspension

The chair of a meeting may, without an adjournment, declare the meeting suspended for one or more periods not exceeding one hour in total (or, in exceptional circumstances, such longer total period during the same day at the chair's discretion).

**Derivation**—This rule derived from the Insolvency Rules 1986, SI 1986/1925, rr 1.21, 1.53, 2.35, 3.14, 4.65, 5.24, 6.90.

**General note**—For case examples on suspension of a meeting see *Re Forstater* [2015] BPIR 21 and *Rowbury v OR* [2015] EWHC 2276 (Ch).

## CHAPTER 8

### CREDITORS' VOTING RIGHTS AND MAJORITIES

**[2.906]**

**Note**

[Note: a document required by the Act or these Rules must also contain the standard contents set out in Part 1.]

**[2.907]**

### 15.28 Creditors' voting rights

(1) In an administration, an administrative receivership, a creditors' voluntary winding up, a winding up by the court and a bankruptcy, a creditor is entitled to vote in a decision procedure or to object to a decision proposed using the deemed consent procedure only if—

    (a)    the creditor has, subject to rule 15.29, delivered to the convener a proof of the debt claimed in accordance with paragraph (3), including any calculation for the purposes of rule 15.31 or 15.32, and

    (b)    the proof was received by the convener—

        (i)    not later than the decision date, or in the case of a meeting, 4pm on the business day before the meeting, or

        (ii)    in the case of a meeting, later than the time given in sub-paragraph (i) where the chair is content to accept the proof; and

    (c)    the proof has been admitted for the purposes of entitlement to vote.

(2) In the case of a meeting, a proxy-holder is not entitled to vote on behalf of a creditor unless the convener or chair has received the proxy intended to be used on behalf of that creditor.

(3) A debt is claimed in accordance with this paragraph if it is—

    (a)    claimed as due from the company or bankrupt to the person seeking to be entitled to vote; . . .

    (b)    . . ..

(4) The convener or chair may call for any document or other evidence to be produced if the convener or chair thinks it necessary for the purpose of substantiating the whole or any part of a claim.

(5) In a decision relating to a proposed CVA or IVA every creditor, secured or unsecured, who has notice of the decision procedure is entitled to vote in respect of that creditor's debt.

(6) Where a decision is sought in an administration under rule 3.52(3)(b) (pre-administration costs), rule 18.18(4) (remuneration: procedure for initial determination in an administration) or rule 18.26(2) (first exception: administrator has made statement under paragraph 52(1)(b) of Schedule B1), creditors are entitled to participate to the extent stated in those paragraphs.

**Derivation**—This rule derived from the Insolvency Rules 1986, SI 1986/1925, rr 1.17, 1.49, 2.38, 3.11, 4.67, 4.68, 5.21, 6.93, 6.93A.

**Amendments**—SI 2019/146, as from IP completion day (as defined in the European Union (Withdrawal Agreement) Act 2020, s 39(1)–(5)).

**CIGA 2020**—This provision is affected by temporary measures at Sch 4, para 25 of CIGA 2020.

**General note**—See the Introductory note to Part 15: Decision making.

**The authorities under the Insolvency Rules 1986**—The provisions in the 1986 Rules from which r 15.28 is derived (listed above) generated a considerable body of case law. Those provisions are dealt with extensively in the 5th edition of this book (2016): see the decision of the Court of Appeal in *Price v Davis* [2014] EWCA Civ 26, [2014] 1 WLR 2129 and the decision of the Northern

Ireland High Court in *Ulster Bank Ltd v Taggart* [2018] NIMaster 7. An equitable assignee of a debt is entitled to exercise voting rights: *Kapoor v National Westminster Bank plc* [2011] EWCA Civ 1083, [2011] BPIR 1680 (although on the facts of that case, there was a material irregularity arising from the circumstances and the lack of good faith in respect of the assignment).

In *Gertner v CFL Finance Ltd* [2018] EWCA Civ 1781 (a decision under the former 1986 Rules) the Court of Appeal upheld the revocation of an individual voluntary arrangement by reason of a material irregularity at the creditors' meeting. A creditor which had breached its duty of good faith should not have been allowed to vote on the proposed IVA. By entering into a settlement agreement with a related company under which it stood to gain a substantial sum, and failing to disclose the agreement, the creditor had placed itself in conflict with the interests of the other creditors.

## [2.908]

### 15.29 Scheme manager's voting rights

(1)   For the purpose of voting in a creditors' voluntary winding up or a winding up by the court of an authorised deposit-taker at which the scheme manager established under section 212(1) of the Financial Services and Markets Act 2000 is entitled to be represented under rule 15.17 (but not for any other purpose), the manager may deliver, instead of a proof, a statement containing—

    (a)    the names of the creditors of the company in relation to whom an obligation of the scheme manager has arisen or may reasonably be expected to arise;

    (b)    the amount of each such obligation; and

    (c)    the total amount of all such obligations.

(2)   The manager may from time to time deliver a further statement; and each such statement supersedes any previous statement.

**Derivation**—This rule derived from the Insolvency Rules 1986, SI 1986/1925, Sch 1, paras 2–4, 6.

### 15.30

*(Revoked)*

**Derivation**—This rule derived from the Insolvency Rules 1986, SI 1986/1925, rr 2.38, 4.67, 6.93.

**Amendments**—Revoked by SI 2019/146, as from IP completion day (as defined in the European Union (Withdrawal Agreement) Act 2020, s 39(1)–(5)).

## [2.909]

### 15.31 Calculation of voting rights

(1)   Votes are calculated according to the amount of each creditor's claim—

    (a)    in an administration, as at the date on which the company entered administration, less—

        (i)    any payments that have been made to the creditor after that date in respect of the claim, and

        (ii)    any adjustment by way of set-off which has been made in accordance with rule 14.24 or would have been made if that rule were applied on the date on which the votes are counted;

    (b)    in an administrative receivership, as at the date of the appointment of the receiver, less any payments that have been made to the creditor after that date in respect of the claim;

    (c)    in a creditors' voluntary winding up, a winding up by the court or a bankruptcy, as set out in the creditor's proof to the extent that it has been admitted;

    (d)    in a proposed CVA—

        (i)    at the date the company went into liquidation where the company is being wound up,

        (ii)    at the date the company entered into administration (less any payments made to the creditor after that date in respect of the claim) where it is in administration,

       (iii)    at the beginning of the moratorium where a moratorium has been obtained (less any payments made to the creditor after that date in respect of the claim), or

       (iv)    where (i) to (iii) do not apply, at the decision date;

  (e)    in a proposed IVA—

       (i)    where the debtor is not an undischarged bankrupt—

          (aa)    at the date of the interim order, where there is an interim order in force,

          (bb)    otherwise, at the decision date,

       (ii)    where the debtor is an undischarged bankrupt, at the date of the bankruptcy order.

(2) A creditor may vote in respect of a debt of an unliquidated or unascertained amount if the convener or chair decides to put upon it an estimated minimum value for the purpose of entitlement to vote and admits the claim for that purpose.

(3) But in relation to a proposed CVA or IVA, a debt of an unliquidated or unascertained amount is to be valued at £1 for the purposes of voting unless the convener or chair or an appointed person decides to put a higher value on it.

(4) Where a debt is wholly secured its value for voting purposes is nil.

(5) Where a debt is partly secured its value for voting purposes is the value of the unsecured part.

(6) However, the value of the debt for voting purposes is its full value without deduction of the value of the security in the following cases—

  (a)    where the administrator has made a statement under paragraph 52(1)(b) of Schedule B1 and the administrator has been requested to seek a decision under paragraph 52(2); and

  (b)    where, in a proposed CVA, there is a decision on whether to extend or further extend a moratorium or to bring a moratorium to an end before the end of the period of any extension.

(7) No vote may be cast in respect of a claim more than once on any resolution put to the meeting. . ..

(8) A vote cast in a decision procedure which is not a meeting may not be changed.

(9) Paragraph (7) does not prevent a creditor . . . from—

  (a)    voting in respect of less than the full value of an entitlement to vote; or

  (b)    casting a vote one way in respect of part of the value of an entitlement and another way in respect of some or all of the balance of that value.

**Derivation**—This rule derived from the Insolvency Rules 1986, SI 1986/1925, rr 1.17(2), (3), 1.49(3), 1.52(3), 2.38(4), 2.40(2), 3.11(4), 5.21(2), (3), 5.41(2), 6.93.

**Amendments**—SI 2019/146, as from IP completion day (as defined in the European Union (Withdrawal Agreement) Act 2020, s 39(1)–(5)).

**CIGA 2020**—This provision is affected by temporary measures at Sch 4, para 26 of CIGA 2020.

**General note**—This provision is of key practical importance. The provisions from which it is derived (listed above) have generated a considerable amount of case law. For the first time, voting rights are grouped within one provision, save for the special cases identified in r 15.32. The following guidance by reference to the case law under the Insolvency Rules 1986 should be adopted with care, in particular given minor linguistic differences between the former and present provisions.

**Entitlement to vote**—See the decision of the Court of Appeal in *Price v Davis* [2014] EWCA Civ 26, [2014] 1 WLR 2129.

**RULE 15.31(1)**

This provision is temporal in determining the point in time at which the calculation is made, as distinct from the calculation itself. The calculation of a claim for voting purposes may be different from the value at the date at which a dividend entitlement is calculated.

**RULE 15.31(2)**

This provision is almost identical to the first half of the former IR 1986, r 1.17(3): 'a creditor may vote in respect of a debt for an unliquidated amount or any debt whose value is not ascertained and for the purposes of voting (but not otherwise) his debt shall be valued at £1 unless the chairman agrees to put a higher value on it'. The following guidance applies to that provision.

' . . . a debt for an unliquidated amount or any debt whose value is not ascertained
. . . '—The origin of this provision dates back to s 16(3) of the Bankruptcy Act 1869 which
provided that a creditor was not entitled to vote in respect of any unliquidated or contingent debt
or any debt the value of which was not ascertained. In *Tager v Westpac Banking Corp* [1997]
1 BCLC 313 at 326H His Honour Judge Weeks QC, sitting as a High Court judge, identified the
following helpful guidance on the terminology from the judgment of Mellish LJ in *Ex parte Ruffle,
re Dummelow* (1873) 8 Ch App 997 at 1001:

> 'The question really is what is meant by an "unliquidated debt" . . . The fair construction of
> the clause seems to me this: "a contingent" debt refers to a case where there is a doubt that there
> will be any debt at all; "a debt the value of which is not ascertained" means a debt the amount
> of which cannot be estimated until the happening of some further event, and an "unliquidated
> debt" includes not only all cases of damages to be ascertained by a jury, but beyond that, extends
> to any debt where the creditor fairly admits that he cannot state the amount.'

' . . . unless the chairman [covener or chair] agrees to put a higher value on it . . . '—In
*Doorbar v Alltime Securities Ltd* [1995] BCC 1149, in upholding the decision of Knox J below,
confirmed in the judgment of Peter Gibson LJ (at 1157E) that the term 'agrees', in the context of
the analogous r 5.17(3), does not connote agreement between the chairman of the creditors'
meeting and a creditor. Thus:

> 'Given that the chairman is not a lawyer but an insolvency practitioner at a meeting of creditors,
> it seems to me unlikely that the draftsman contemplated the necessity of agreement with the
> creditor on each debt of this [unliquidated or unascertained] character. It is sufficient if the
> chairman expresses his willingness to put, and puts, an estimated minimum value on the debt.'

In so finding, the Court of Appeal, like Knox J, did not follow the earlier judgment of Ferris J in
*Re Cranley Mansions Ltd* [1994] 1 WLR 1610 (on r 1.17(3)) which had held that the term 'agrees'
is requiring of some bi-lateral agreement between chairman and creditor. The function of the
chairman, indeed duty, therefore, under this subrule is to place an estimated minimum value on the
creditor's debt for voting purposes which is to stand at £1 unless the chairman is able to assess the
debt at a higher value. The same approach should be adopted in relation to the present provision:
*Re Newlands (Seaford) Educational Trust, Chittenden v Pepper* [2006] EWHC 1511 (Ch), [2006]
BPIR 1230 at [23] (Morritt C).

The former r 1.17(3) required the placing of a £1 value on a claim unless the chairman can be
satisfied as to some 'higher value'. Rule 15.31(3) is cast in identical terms. A chairman should not
speculate, nor regard himself as obliged to investigate a claim; rather, he should consider the
totality of the evidence advanced by the creditor, any other relevant creditor and the debtor and
consider whether such evidence enables him to attribute a value of more than £1 to the claim: *Re
Newlands (Seaford) Educational Trust, Chittenden v Pepper* (above). In particular (at [28]), the
chairman should neither speculate nor consider himself under any obligation to investigate a
creditor's claim.

> 'If the totality of the evidence [being that put forward by the creditor or any other creditor or the
> debtor] leads him to the conclusion that he can safely attribute to the claim a minimum value
> higher than £1 then he should do so.'

For a case in which the applicant's case was initially advanced on the footing that its claim was
liquidated but subsequently amended to allege that the chairman, even if he had considered (as he
did) the applicant's claim was unliquidated, should have gone on to consider the valuation of the
unliquidated claim as being in excess of £1: see *Leighton Contracting (Qatar) WLL v Simms*
[2011] EWHC 1735 (Ch), [2011] BPIR 1395 (HHJ Simon Barker QC).

The duty of the chairman to place a minimum figure on an unliquidated or unascertained debt
does not come into operation if the creditor merely stays away from the creditors' meeting. In those
circumstances, given the potential for such a course enabling the frustration of a voluntary
arrangement, the chairman need not fix a minimum figure, notwithstanding which the absent
creditor will be bound by an approved arrangement: *Re Cancol Ltd* [1995] BCC 1133 at 1147C
(Knox J). Although a chairman is under no obligation to a creditor to put a minimum value on a
claim and to notify the creditor of that position prior to the creditors' meeting, the duty to fix a
minimum value is operative if the creditor lodges a proxy in respect of its debts but is not in
attendance in person: *Beverley Group plc v McClue* [1995] 2 BCLC 407 at 418C–418E (Knox J).

## RULE 15.31(3)

This rule is very similar to the second half of the former IR 1986, r 1.17(3) (see above).

**[2.910]**

### 15.32 Calculation of voting rights: special cases

(1)  In an administration, a creditor under a hire-purchase agreement is entitled to vote in respect of the amount of the debt due and payable by the company on the date on which the company entered administration.

(2)  In calculating the amount of any debt for the purpose of paragraph (1), no account is to be taken of any amount attributable to the exercise of any right under the relevant agreement so far as the right has become exercisable solely by virtue of—

    (a)    the making of an administration application;

    (b)    a notice of intention to appoint an administrator or any matter arising as a consequence of the notice; or

    (c)    the company entering administration.

(3)  Any voting rights which a creditor might otherwise exercise in respect of a claim in a creditors' voluntary winding up or a winding up by the court of an authorised deposit-taker are reduced by a sum equal to the amount of that claim in relation to which the scheme manager, by virtue of its having delivered a statement under rule 15.29, is entitled to exercise voting rights.

**Derivation**—This rule derived from the Insolvency Rules 1986, SI 1986/1925, r 2.42, Sch 1.

**CIGA 2020**—This provision is affected by temporary measures at Sch 4, para 27 of CIGA 2020.

**[2.911]**

### 15.33 Procedure for admitting creditors' claims for voting

(1)  The convener or chair in respect of a decision procedure must ascertain entitlement to vote and admit or reject claims accordingly.

(2)  The convener or chair may admit or reject a claim in whole or in part.

(3)  If the convener or chair is in any doubt whether a claim should be admitted or rejected, the convener or chair must mark it as objected to and allow votes to be cast in respect of it, subject to such votes being subsequently declared invalid if the objection to the claim is sustained.

**Derivation**—This rule derived from the Insolvency Rules 1986, SI 1986/1925, rr 1.17A, 1.50, 2.39, 4.70, 5.21(1)–(4), 5.22, 6.94(1), (3).

**General note**—This provision again draws heavily on the derivation provisions listed above. The case law decided under those former provisions will doubtless be of significant relevance in considering these new provisions. The three sub-paragraphs of r 15.33 mirror very closely the former IR 1986, rr 1.17A(1), (2) and (4).

RULE 15.33(2)

There is no presumption which requires the convener should err in favour of either admitting the creditor to proof for voting purposes or rejecting the creditor's claim: *Re A Company (No 004539 of 1993)* [1995] 1 BCLC 459 at 466A-466B (Blackburne J).

RULE 15.33(3)

This provision calls for the exercise of judgment on the part of a convener. A creditors' meeting is not the appropriate forum for the determination of the status or quantum of an alleged debt. Subject to the convener exercising his discretion so as to admit or reject a claim in whole or in part, this rule, in effect, gives the benefit of the doubt to the creditor, at least for voting purposes, and subject to any appeal. In practice, one course open to a convener with doubts as to the validity of a claim is to adjourn the creditors' meeting so as to allow for the production by the creditor of further evidence in support of its claim, especially where the particular creditor's claim, if admitted as asserted, would itself serve to block or carry approval of the resolution under consideration.

**[2.912]**

### 15.34 Requisite majorities

(1)  A decision is made by creditors when a majority (in value) of those voting have voted in favour of the proposed decision, except where this rule provides otherwise.

(2)  In the case of an administration, a decision is not made if those voting against it include more than half in value of the creditors to whom notice of the decision

procedure was delivered who are not, to the best of the convener's or chair's belief, persons connected with the company.

(3)  Each of the following decisions in a proposed CVA is made when three-quarters or more (in value) of those responding vote in favour of it—

(a)  a decision approving a proposal or a modification;

(b)  a decision extending or further extending a moratorium; or

(c)  a decision bringing a moratorium to an end before the end of the period of any extension.

(4)  In a proposed CVA a decision is not made if more than half of the total value of the unconnected creditors vote against it.

(5)  For the purposes of paragraph (4)—

(a)  a creditor is unconnected unless the convener or chair decides that the creditor is connected with the company;

(b)  in deciding whether a creditor is connected reliance may be placed on the information provided by the company's statement of affairs or otherwise in accordance with these Rules; and

(c)  the total value of the unconnected creditors is the total value of those unconnected creditors whose claims have been admitted for voting.

(6)  In a case relating to a proposed IVA—

(a)  a decision approving a proposal or a modification is made when three-quarters or more (in value) of those responding vote in favour of it;

(b)  a decision is not made if more than half of the total value of creditors who are not associates of the debtor vote against it.

(7)  For the purposes of paragraph (6)—

(a)  a creditor is not an associate of the debtor unless the convener or chair decides that the creditor is an associate of the debtor;

(b)  in deciding whether a creditor is an associate of the debtor, reliance may be placed on the information provided by the debtor's statement of affairs or otherwise in accordance with these Rules; and

(c)  the total value of the creditors who are not associates of the debtor is the total value of the creditors who are not associates of the debtor whose claims have been admitted for voting.

**Derivation**—This rule derived from the Insolvency Rules 1986, SI 1986/1925, rr 1.19, 1.52, 2.43, 3.15, 4.63, 5.23, 6.88.

**Amendments**—SI 2017/366.

**CIGA 2020**—This provision is affected by temporary measures at Sch 4, para 28 of CIGA 2020.

**General note**—The case law under the former provisions in the IR 1986 from which the present provision derives generated a significant degree of case law which will be of some assistance in interpreting this new provision. That case law is considered in detail in the 5th edition of this book (2016).

**Definitions**—'associate' see r 1.2(2) and s 435.

## [2.913]

### 15.35  Appeals against decisions under this Chapter

(1)  A decision of the convener or chair under this Chapter is subject to appeal to the court by a creditor, by a contributory, or by the bankrupt or debtor (as applicable).

(2)  In a proposed CVA, an appeal against a decision under this Chapter may also be made by a member of the company.

(3)  If the decision is reversed or varied, or votes are declared invalid, the court may order another decision procedure to be initiated or make such order as it thinks just but, in a CVA or IVA, the court may only make an order if it considers that the circumstances which led to the appeal give rise to unfair prejudice or material irregularity.

(4)  An appeal under this rule may not be made later than 21 days after the decision date.

(5)  However, the previous paragraph does not apply in a proposed CVA or IVA, where an appeal may not be made after the end of the period of 28 days beginning with the day—

(a)   in a proposed CVA, on which the first of the reports required by section 4(6) or paragraph 30(3) of Schedule A1 was filed with the court; or

(b)   in a proposed IVA—

(i)   where an interim order has not been obtained, on which the notice of the result of the consideration of the proposal required by section 259(1)(a) has been given, or

(ii)   otherwise, on which the report required by section 259(1)(b) is made to the court.

(6)   The person who made the decision is not personally liable for costs incurred by any person in relation to an appeal under this rule unless the court makes an order to that effect.

(7)   The court may not make an order under paragraph (6) if the person who made the decision in a winding up by the court or a bankruptcy is the official receiver or a person nominated by the official receiver.

**Derivation**—This rule derived from the Insolvency Rules 1986, SI 1986/1925, rr 1.17A, 1.50, 1.52, 2.39, 3.12, 4.70, 5.22, 5.23, 5.42, 6.94.

**General note**—The case law under the former provisions in the IR 1986 from which the present provision derives generated a significant degree of case law which will be of some assistance in interpreting this new provision. That case law is considered in the notes to r 15.31 above.

In relation to the former r 2.39, in *HMRC v Maxwell* [2010] EWCA Civ 1379, [2012] BCC 30 the Court of Appeal identified that an appeal is not merely a review of the decision below and the court must form its view based on the evidence and the arguments advanced at the appeal hearing. On the facts of that case, and the former r 2.39, the chairman was to form a view as to the nature and quantum of the debt as at the date of the creditors' meeting, not as at administration, although the chairman could take account of events between the point of administration and the meeting.

A statute-barred debt is not automatically excluded from voting: *Ulster bank Ltd v Taggart* [2018] NIMaster 7 (Northern Ireland High Court).

**Sub-rule 15.35(6) costs**—This provision provides the 'no personal liability' default position, even in the face of a successful appeal, contrary to the usual 'loser pays' default position on costs under CPR 44.2 and IR 2016, r 12.41(3), subject to contrary court order. This mirrors the position under IR 2016, r 14.9(2) which provides for the costs position on an appeal from an office-holder's decision to admit or reject a proof for dividend purposes. In the case of such a successful appeal, the office holder may only be personally liable for costs in special circumstances: *Nimat Halal Food v Patel* [2020] EWHC 734 (Ch).

There is no such express carve out against costs in the provisions in the IA 1986 under which applications are commonly made in tandem with an appeal under the present provision; the practice on costs varies where such co-joined challenges are successful, usually on the basis that it is anomalous for the convenor or chair of a meeting, at least as a default position, to be exempt from liability for costs under the present provision but absent like protection under the provisions of the Act.

In *Re Rochay Productions Ltd (in liquidation)* [2020] EWHC 1737 (Ch), [2020] BPIR 1423 ICCJ Barber dismissed an application for a personal costs order against the chairperson of a creditors' meeting but made a costs order on the indemnity basis against the creditor whose proof was successfully challenged on the application of another creditor. Judge Barber held at [5], having referenced the related provision in r 14.9(2) (above), that a costs order should only be made against a chairperson under r 15.35(6), arising out of an appeal against his or her decision to admit or reject a proof, in 'special circumstances, where the decision to admit or reject a proof was self-interested, irrational or unreasonable, or where there is otherwise good reason to do so', thereby adopting an approach equivalent to that under r 14.9(2).

On personal costs orders see *Smurthwaite v Simpson-Smith* [2006] EWCA Civ 1183, [2006] BPIR 1504 in which the Court of Appeal upheld the costs order imposed by the trial judge, HHJ Rich QC, where the conduct of the chairman of a creditors' meeting considering an IVA proposal was held not to have been dishonest but to have fallen far below that of a reasonable insolvency practitioner given the methodology by which the IVA came to be approved so as to justify that individual being fixed with personal liability for 50% of the successful applicant's costs upon the IVA being set aside. At [33] Jacob LJ identified one difficulty with the case being the insolvency practitioner having 'made common cause with the debtor' before warning of 'the inherent danger in adopting such a stance. Insolvency practitioners should be much more careful to preserve their utter independence from any party, either the debtor or any creditor'.

CHAPTER 9

EXCLUSIONS FROM MEETINGS

**[2.914]**

Note
[Note: a document required by the Act or these Rules must also contain the standard contents set out in Part 1.]

**[2.915]**

**15.36 Action where person excluded**
(1) In this rule and rules 15.37 and 15.38, an "excluded person" means a person who has taken all steps necessary to attend a virtual meeting or has been permitted by the convener to attend a physical meeting remotely under the arrangements which—
    (a)    have been put in place by the convener of the meeting; but
    (b)    do not enable that person to attend the whole or part of that meeting.
(2) Where the chair becomes aware during the course of the meeting that there is an excluded person, the chair may—
    (a)    continue the meeting;
    (b)    declare the meeting void and convene the meeting again; or
    (c)    declare the meeting valid up to the point where the person was excluded and adjourn the meeting.
(3) Where the chair continues the meeting, the meeting is valid unless—
    (a)    the chair decides in consequence of a complaint under rule 15.38 to declare the meeting void and hold the meeting again; or
    (b)    the court directs otherwise.
(4) Without prejudice to paragraph (2), where the chair becomes aware during the course of the meeting that there is an excluded person, the chair may, at the chair's discretion and without an adjournment, declare the meeting suspended for any period up to 1 hour.

Derivation—This rule derived from the Insolvency Rules 1986, SI 1986/1925, r 12A.23.

**[2.916]**

**15.37 Indication to excluded person**
(1) A creditor who claims to be an excluded person may request an indication of what occurred during the period of that person's claimed exclusion.
(2) A request under paragraph (1) must be made in accordance with paragraph (3) as soon as reasonably practicable, and in any event, not later than 4pm on the business day following the day on which the exclusion is claimed to have occurred.
(3) A request under paragraph (1) must be made to—
    (a)    the chair where it is made during the course of the business of the meeting; or
    (b)    the convener where it is made after the conclusion of the business of the meeting.
(4) Where satisfied that the person making the request is an excluded person, the person to whom the request is made under paragraph (3) must deliver the requested indication to the excluded person as soon as reasonably practicable, and in any event, not later than 4pm on the business day following the day on which the request was made under paragraph (1).

Derivation—This rule derived from the Insolvency Rules 1986, SI 1986/1925, r 12A.24.

**[2.917]**

**15.38 Complaint**
(1) A person may make a complaint who—

     (a)    is, or claims to be, an excluded person; or

     (b)    attends the meeting and claims to have been adversely affected by the actual, apparent or claimed exclusion of another person.

(2)   The complaint must be made to the appropriate person who is—

     (a)    the chair, where the complaint is made during the course of the meeting; or

     (b)    the convener, where it is made after the meeting.

(3)   The complaint must be made as soon as reasonably practicable and, in any event, no later than 4pm on the business day following—

     (a)    the day on which the person was, appeared or claimed to be excluded; or

     (b)    where an indication is sought under rule 15.37, the day on which the complainant received the indication.

(4)   The appropriate person must, as soon as reasonably practicable following receipt of the complaint,—

     (a)    consider whether there is an excluded person;

     (b)    where satisfied that there is an excluded person, consider the complaint; and

     (c)    where satisfied that there has been prejudice, take such action as the appropriate person considers fit to remedy the prejudice.

(5)   Paragraph (6) applies where the appropriate person is satisfied that the complainant is an excluded person and—

     (a)    a resolution was voted on at the meeting during the period of the person's exclusion; and

     (b)    the excluded person asserts how the excluded person intended to vote on the resolution.

(6)   Where the appropriate person is satisfied that if the excluded person had voted as that person intended it would have changed the result of the resolution, then the appropriate person must, as soon as reasonably practicable,—

     (a)    count the intended vote as having been cast in that way;

     (b)    amend the record of the result of the resolution;

     (c)    where notice of the result of the resolution has been delivered to those entitled to attend the meeting, deliver notice to them of the change and the reason for it; and

     (d)    where notice of the result of the resolution has yet to be delivered to those entitled to attend the meeting, the notice must include details of the change and the reason for it.

(7)   Where satisfied that more than one complainant is an excluded person, the appropriate person must have regard to the combined effect of the intended votes.

(8)   The appropriate person must deliver notice to the complainant of any decision as soon as reasonably practicable.

(9)   A complainant who is not satisfied by the action of the appropriate person may apply to the court for directions and any application must be made no more than two business days from the date of receiving the decision of the appropriate person.

**Derivation**—This rule derived from the Insolvency Rules 1986, SI 1986/1925, r 12A. 25.

CHAPTER 10

CONTRIBUTORIES' VOTING RIGHTS AND MAJORITIES

**[2.918]**

**15.39 Contributories' voting rights and requisite majorities**
In a decision procedure for contributories—

     (a)    voting rights are as at a general meeting of the company, subject to any provision of the articles affecting entitlement to vote, either generally or at a time when the company is in liquidation; and

     (b)    a decision is made if more than one half of the votes cast by contributories are in favour.

Derivation—This rule derived from the Insolvency Rules 1986, SI 1986/1925, rr 4.63, 4.69.

## CHAPTER 11

### RECORDS

**[2.919]**

### 15.40 Record of a decision

(1)  The convener or chair must cause a record of the decision procedure to be kept.

(2)  In the case of a meeting, the record must be in the form of a minute of the meeting.

(3)  The record must be authenticated by the convener or chair and be retained by the office-holder as part of the records of the insolvency proceedings in question.

(4)  The record must identify the proceedings, and must include—

   (a)  in the case of a decision procedure of creditors, a list of the names of the creditors who participated and their claims;

   (b)  in the case of a decision procedure of contributories, a list of the names of the contributories who participated;

   (c)  where a decision is taken on the election of members of a creditors' committee or liquidation committee, the names and addresses of those elected;

   (d)  a record of any change to the result of the resolution made under rule 15.38(6) and the reason for any such change; and

   (e)  in any case, a record of every decision made and how creditors voted.

(5)  Where a decision is sought using the deemed consent procedure, a record must be made of the procedure, authenticated by the convener, and must be retained by the office-holder as part of the records of the insolvency proceedings in question.

(6)  The record under paragraph (5) must—

   (a)  identify the proceedings;

   (b)  state whether or not the decision was taken; and

   (c)  contain a list of the creditors or contributories who objected to the decision, and in the case of creditors, their claims.

(7)  A record under this rule must also identify any decision procedure (or the deemed consent procedure) by which the decision had previously been sought.

Derivation—This rule derived from the Insolvency Rules 1986, SI 1986/1925, rr 2.44A, 3.15, 4.71, 6.95.

## CHAPTER 12

### COMPANY MEETINGS

**[2.920]**

### 15.41 Company meetings

(1)  Unless the Act or these Rules provide otherwise, a company meeting must be called and conducted, and records of the meeting must be kept—

   (a)  in accordance with the law of England and Wales, including any applicable provision in or made under the Companies Act, in the case of a company incorporated—

      (i)  in England and Wales, or

      (ii)  outside the United Kingdom other than in an EEA state;

   (b)  in accordance with the law of that state applicable to meetings of the company in the case of a company incorporated in an EEA state other than the United Kingdom.

(2)  For the purpose of this rule, reference to a company meeting called and conducted to resolve, decide or determine a particular matter includes a reference to that matter being resolved, decided or determined by written resolution of a private company passed in accordance with section 288 of the Companies Act.

(3)  In an administration—

    (a)  in summoning any company meeting the administrator must have regard to the convenience of the members when fixing the venue; and

    (b)  the chair of the meeting must be either the administrator or an appointed person.

**Derivation**—This rule derived from the Insolvency Rules 1986, SI 1986/1925, r 2.49(5A).

## [2.921]

### 15.42  Remote attendance: notification requirements

When a meeting is to be summoned and held in accordance with section 246A(3), the convener must notify all those to whom notice of the meeting is being given of—

    (a)  the ability of a person claiming to be an excluded person to request an indication in accordance with rule 15.45;

    (b)  the ability of a person within rule 15.46(1) to make a complaint in accordance with that rule; and

    (c)  in either case, the period within which a request or complaint must be made.

## [2.922]

### 15.43  Location of company meetings

(1)  This rule applies to a request to the convener of a meeting under section 246A(9) to specify a place for the meeting.

(2)  The request must be accompanied by

    (a)  a list of the members making or concurring with the request and their voting rights, and

    (b)  from each person concurring, confirmation of that person's concurrence.

(3)  The request must be delivered to the convener within seven business days of the date on which the convener delivered the notice of the meeting in question.

(4)  Where the convener considers that the request has been properly made in accordance with the Act and this rule, the convener must—

    (a)  deliver notice to all those previously given notice of the meeting—

        (i)  that it is to be held at a specified place, and

        (ii)  as to whether the date and time are to remain the same or not;

    (b)  set a venue (including specification of a place) for the meeting, the date of which must be not later than 28 days after the original date for the meeting; and

    (c)  deliver at least 14 days' notice of that venue to all those previously given notice of the meeting;

and the notices required by sub-paragraphs (a) and (c) may be delivered at the same or different times.

(5)  Where the convener has specified a place for the meeting in response to a request to which this rule applies, the chair of the meeting must attend the meeting by being present in person at that place.

**Derivation**—This rule derived from the Insolvency Rules 1986, SI 1986/1925, r 12A.22.

## [2.923]

### 15.44  Action where person excluded

(1)  In this rule and rules 15.45 and 15.46, an "excluded person" means a person who has taken all steps necessary to attend a company meeting under the arrangements which—

    (a)  have been put in place by the convener of the meeting under section 246A(6); but

    (b)  do not enable that person to attend the whole or part of that meeting.

(2) Where the chair becomes aware during the course of the meeting that there is an excluded person, the chair may—
- (a) continue the meeting;
- (b) declare the meeting void and convene the meeting again; or
- (c) declare the meeting valid up to the point where the person was excluded and adjourn the meeting.

(3) Where the chair continues the meeting, the meeting is valid unless—
- (a) the chair decides in consequence of a complaint under rule 15.46 to declare the meeting void and hold the meeting again; or
- (b) the court directs otherwise.

(4) Without prejudice to paragraph (2), where the chair becomes aware during the course of the meeting that there is an excluded person, the chair may, in the chair's discretion and without an adjournment, declare the meeting suspended for any period up to 1 hour.

**Derivation**—This rule derived from the Insolvency Rules 1986, SI 1986/1925, r 12A.23.

## [2.924]

### 15.45 Indication to excluded person

(1) A person who claims to be an excluded person may request an indication of what occurred during the period of that person's claimed exclusion.

(2) A request under paragraph (1) must be made in accordance with paragraph (3) as soon as reasonably practicable, and in any event, not later than 4pm on the business day following the day on which the exclusion is claimed to have occurred.

(3) A request under paragraph (1) must be made to—
- (a) the chair where it is made during the course of the business of the meeting; or
- (b) the convener where it is made after the conclusion of the business of the meeting.

(4) Where satisfied that the person making the request is an excluded person, the person to whom the request is made under paragraph (3) must deliver the requested indication to the excluded person as soon as reasonably practicable, and in any event, not later than 4pm on the business day following the day on which the request was made under paragraph (1).

**Derivation**—This rule derived from the Insolvency Rules 1986, SI 1986/1925, r 12A.24.

## [2.925]

### 15.46 Complaint

(1) A person may make a complaint who—
- (a) is, or claims to be, an excluded person; or
- (b) attends the meeting and claims to have been adversely affected by the actual, apparent or claimed exclusion of another person.

(2) The complaint must be made to the appropriate person who is—
- (a) the chair, where the complaint is made during the course of the meeting; or
- (b) the convener, where it is made after the meeting.

(3) The complaint must be made as soon as reasonably practicable and, in any event, no later than 4pm on the business day following—
- (a) the day on which the person was, appeared or claimed to be excluded; or
- (b) where an indication is sought under rule 15.45, the day on which the complainant received the indication.

(4) The appropriate person must, as soon as reasonably practicable following receipt of the complaint,—
- (a) consider whether there is an excluded person;
- (b) where satisfied that there is an excluded person, consider the complaint; and

(c)    where satisfied that there has been prejudice, take such action as the appropriate person considers fit to remedy the prejudice.

(5)  Paragraph (6) applies where the appropriate person is satisfied that the complainant is an excluded person and—

(a)    a resolution was voted on at the meeting during the period of the person's exclusion; and

(b)    the excluded person asserts how the excluded person intended to vote on the resolution.

(6)  Where the appropriate person is satisfied that if the excluded person had voted as that person intended it would have changed the result of the resolution, then the appropriate person must, as soon as reasonably practicable,—

(a)    count the intended vote as having been cast in that way;

(b)    amend the record of the result of the resolution;

(c)    where notice of the result of the resolution has been delivered to those entitled to attend the meeting, deliver notice to them of the change and the reason for it; and

(d)    where notice of the result of the resolution has yet to be delivered to those entitled to attend the meeting, the notice must include details of the change and the reason for it.

(7)  Where satisfied that more than one complainant is an excluded person, the appropriate person must have regard to the combined effect of the intended votes.

(8)  The appropriate person must deliver notice to the complainant of any decision as soon as reasonably practicable.

(9)  A complainant who is not satisfied by the action of the appropriate person may apply to the court for directions and any application must be made no more than two business days from the date of receiving the decision of the appropriate person.

**Derivation**—This rule derived from the Insolvency Rules 1986, SI 1986/1925, r 12A.25.

## PART 16   PROXIES AND CORPORATE REPRESENTATION

### [2.926]

**Note**

[Note: a document required by the Act or these Rules must also contain the standard contents set out in Part 1.]

### [2.927]

#### 16.1 Application and interpretation

(1)  This Part applies in any case where a proxy is given in relation to a meeting or proceedings under the Act or these Rules, or where a corporation authorises a person to represent it.

(2)  References in this Part to "the chair" are to the chair of the meeting for which a specific proxy is given or at which a continuing proxy is exercised.

    **General note**—Given their importance and common usage in the business of creditors' meetings there is relatively little authority on the subject of proxies. Concerned with Part VIII of the former IR 1986 (proxies and company representation), the judgment of Lewison LJ (Jackson and Mummery LJJ agreeing) in *Horler v Rubin* [2012] EWCA Civ, [2012] BPIR 749 continues to be of significance in analysing this important area in terms of the principles relevant to the provisions. Having referred to Carnwath J's characterisation of a proxy in *Re Cardona* [1997] BPIR 604 at 608 ('a proxy is simply a form of agency which enables the principal to express his views at the meeting without personally being present'), his Lordship went on (at [21]):

    'As rr 8.1(6) and 8.3(6) make clear it is for the proxy to decide how to vote on resolutions not dealt with in the proxy. In other words, the proxy's actual authority is to make whatever decision he thinks fit, unless his authority is actually restricted by his principal. It is important to emphasise that the authority conferred by a proxy is actual authority; not ostensible authority. In my judgment, the judge approached the question of authority from the wrong end. It was not a question of what [the principal] expressly authorized [the proxy-holder] to do: it was a question of what [the principal] expressly forbade [the proxy-holder] from doing. Whatever was not forbidden was actually authorised.'

## [2.928]

### 16.2 Specific and continuing proxies

(1) A "proxy" is a document made by a creditor, member or contributory which directs or authorises another person ("the proxy-holder") to act as the representative of the creditor, member or contributory at a meeting or meetings by speaking, voting, abstaining, or proposing resolutions.

(2) A proxy may be either—

    (a)    a specific proxy which relates to a specific meeting; or

    (b)    a continuing proxy for the insolvency proceedings.

(3) A specific proxy must—

    (a)    direct the proxy-holder how to act at the meeting by giving specific instructions;

    (b)    authorise the proxy-holder to act at the meeting without specific instructions; or

    (c)    contain both direction and authorisation.

(4) A proxy is to be treated as a specific proxy for the meeting which is identified in the proxy unless it states that it is a continuing proxy for the insolvency proceedings.

(5) A continuing proxy must authorise the proxy-holder to attend, speak, vote or abstain, or to propose resolutions without giving the proxy-holder any specific instructions how to do so.

(6) A continuing proxy may be superseded by a proxy for a specific meeting or withdrawn by a written notice to the office-holder.

(7) A creditor, member or contributory may appoint more than one person to be proxy-holder but if so—

    (a)    their appointment is as alternates; and

    (b)    only one of them may act as proxy-holder at a meeting.

(8) The proxy-holder must be an individual.

**Derivation**—This rule derived from the Insolvency Rules 1986, SI 1986/1925, r 8.1.

**RULE 16.2(2)–(6)**

A proxy may be either specific or continuing. A specific proxy relates to a specific meeting; a continuing proxy relates to all meetings in any particular matter (but does not apply as a general appointment across cases. A specific proxy main contain voting instructions, but does not need to. A continuing proxy may not contain voting instructions, but it may be superseded by a specific proxy for a particular meeting. References to specific or continuing proxies should not be confused with the longer-standing terminology of special proxy (ie a proxy with voting instructions) or a general proxy (ie a proxy with no voting instructions).

The appointment by a continuing proxy of the convener of a meeting to be the proxy-holder will apply in relation to the convener of each meeting in the particular matter.

## [2.929]

### 16.3 Blank proxy

(1) A "blank proxy" is a document which—

    (a)    complies with the requirements in this rule; and

    (b)    when completed with the details specified in paragraph (3) will be a proxy as described in rule 16.2.

(2) A blank proxy must state that the creditor, member or contributory named in the document (when completed) appoints a person who is named or identified as the proxy-holder of the creditor, member or contributory.

(3) The specified details are—

    (a)    the name and address of the creditor, member or contributory;

    (b)    either the name of the proxy-holder or the identification of the proxy-holder (eg the chair of the meeting or the official receiver);

    (c)    a statement that the proxy is either—

          (i)    for a specific meeting, which is identified in the proxy, or

          (ii)    a continuing proxy for the proceedings; and

    (d)    if the proxy is for a specific meeting, instructions as to the extent to which the proxy holder is directed to vote in a particular way, to abstain or to propose any resolution.

(4)  When it is delivered, a blank proxy must not have inserted into it the name or description of any person as proxy-holder or as a nominee for the office-holder, or instructions as to how a person appointed as proxy-holder is to act.

(5)  A blank proxy must have a note to the effect that the proxy may be completed with the name of the person or the chair of the meeting who is to be proxy-holder.

**Derivation**—This rule derived from the Insolvency Rules 1986, SI 1986/1925, r 8.2.

**Amendments**—SI 2017/366; SI 2017/1115.

**General note**—There is nothing objectionable in a faxed form of proxy: *Inland Revenue Commissions v Conbeer* [1996] BCC 189.

The concept of a 'blank' proxy, and its use, is new.

**The issue of a blank proxy with a notice of a meeting**—Rule 16.3(4) expressly prohibits on a blank proxy the name or description of any person as a proxy holder or instructions as to how a person appointed as a proxy-holder is to act. This differs from the former IR 1986, r 8.2(1) which stated that a proxy sent out with a notice of meeting must not have inserted in it the name or description of any person. Thus, r 16.3 does not prevent the issue of a proxy containing a specific resolution or the listing of specific creditors who have expressed a willingness to be appointed to a committee. What cannot be inserted, however, is the name of the proxy-holder.

Rule 16.3(2)(b) requires that a blank proxy must also state whether it is specific or continuing. Although not identified expressly, it appears that the choice of specific or continuing is that of the recipient creditor, although the provision appears to be capable of putting the choice in the hands of the convener of the meeting.

## [2.930]

### 16.4 Use of proxies

(1)  A proxy for a specific meeting must be delivered to the chair before the meeting.

(2)  A continuing proxy must be delivered to the office-holder and may be exercised at any meeting which begins after the proxy is delivered.

(3)  A proxy may be used at the resumption of the meeting after an adjournment, but if a different proxy is given for use at a resumed meeting, that proxy must be delivered to the chair before the start of the resumed meeting.

(4)  Where a specific proxy directs a proxy-holder to vote for or against a resolution for the nomination or appointment of a person as office-holder, the proxy-holder may, unless the proxy states otherwise, vote for or against (as the proxy-holder thinks fit) a resolution for the nomination or appointment of that person jointly with another or others.

(5)  A proxy-holder may propose a resolution which is one on which the proxy-holder could vote if someone else proposed it.

(6)  Where a proxy gives specific directions as to voting, this does not, unless the proxy states otherwise, prohibit the proxy-holder from exercising discretion how to vote on a resolution which is not dealt with by the proxy.

(7)  The chair may require a proxy used at a meeting to be the same as or substantially similar to the blank proxy delivered for that meeting or to a blank proxy previously delivered which has been completed as a continuing proxy.

**Derivation**—This rule derived from the Insolvency Rules 1986, SI 1986/1925, rr 8.2, 8.3.

**General note**—In keeping with the ordinary rules of agency, these provisions envisage that a proxy may be varied or withdrawn by the principal at any time prior to the meeting or resolution to which it relates and may be withdrawn or varied subsequently for the purposes of any subsequent meeting or resolution: *Re Cardona* [1997] BCC 697.

## [2.931]

### 16.5 Use of proxies by the chair

(1)  Where a proxy appoints the chair (however described in the proxy) as proxy-holder the chair may not refuse to be the proxy-holder.

(2)   Where the office-holder is appointed as proxy-holder but another person acts as chair of the meeting, that other person may use the proxies as if that person were the proxy-holder.

(3)   Where, in a meeting of creditors in an administration, creditors' voluntary winding up, winding up by the court or a bankruptcy, the chair holds a proxy which requires the proxy-holder to vote for a particular resolution and no other person proposes that resolution the chair must propose it unless the chair considers that there is good reason for not doing so.

(4)   If the chair does not propose such a resolution, the chair must as soon as reasonably practicable after the meeting deliver a notice of the reason why that was not done to the creditor, member or contributory.

**Derivation**—This rule derived from the Insolvency Rules 1986, SI 1986/1925, rr 1.15, 2.36, 4.64, 5.20, 6.89, 8.3(3).

**General note**—In *Re Shruth Ltd (in liquidation); International Brands v Goldstein* [2005] EWHC 1293 (Ch), [2005] BPIR 1455 Gloster J held that the attendance of an individual in place of a person named as proxy to which no objection is raised constitutes a waiver, or may found an estoppel preventing the company or liquidator from objecting to attendance and participation by the individual who is not the named proxy.

## [2.932]

### 16.6  Right of inspection and retention of proxies

(1)   A person attending a meeting is entitled, immediately before or in the course of the meeting, to inspect proxies and associated documents delivered to the chair or to any other person in accordance with the notice convening the meeting.

(2)   The chair must—

(a)   retain the proxies used for voting at a meeting where the chair is the office-holder, or

(b)   deliver them as soon as reasonably practicable after the meeting to the office-holder.

(3)   The office-holder must allow proxies, so long as they remain in the office-holder's hands, to be inspected at all reasonable times on any business day by—

(a)   a creditor, in the case of proxies used at a meeting of creditors;

(b)   a member of the company or a contributory, in the case of proxies used at a meeting of the company, or a meeting of contributories;

(c)   a director of the company in the case of corporate insolvency proceedings; or

(d)   the debtor or the bankrupt in the case of personal insolvency proceedings.

(4)   A creditor in paragraph (3)(a) is a person who has delivered a proof in the proceedings, but does not include a person whose claim has been wholly rejected.

(5)   However the right of inspection is subject to rule 1.58 (confidentiality of documents—grounds for refusing inspection).

**Derivation**—This rule derived from the Insolvency Rules 1986, SI 1986/1925, rr 8.4, 8.5.

## [2.933]

### 16.7  Proxy-holder with financial interest

(1)   A proxy-holder must not vote for a resolution which would—

(a)   directly or indirectly place the proxy-holder or any associate of the proxy-holder in a position to receive any remuneration, fees or expenses from the insolvent estate; or

(b)   fix or change the amount of or the basis of any remuneration, fees or expenses receivable by the proxy-holder or any associate of the proxy-holder out of the insolvent estate.

(2)   However a proxy-holder may vote for such a resolution if the proxy specifically directs the proxy-holder to vote in that way.

(3) Where an office-holder is appointed as proxy-holder and that proxy is used under rule 16.5(2) by another person acting as chair, the office-holder is deemed to be an associate of the person acting as chair.

**Derivation**—This rule derived from the Insolvency Rules 1986, SI 1986/1925, r 8.6.

**General note**—The prohibition now contained in r 16.7(1) was previously limited under the former Rules to 'remuneration'; the bar is now extended to 'remuneration, fees or expenses'. The provision also clarifies that the voting of the proxy-holder or an associate into a position to receive remuneration is additional to the prohibition on voting to fix or change the basis or amount of remuneration etc.

**[2.934]**

**Note**
[Note: section 434B(a) makes similar provision for corporate representation in company insolvency proceedings.]

**[2.935]**

**16.8 Corporate representation: bankruptcy and IVA**
(1) If a corporation is a creditor in a bankruptcy or an IVA, it may by resolution of its directors or other governing body authorise a person or persons to act as its representative or representatives in relation to any decision procedure of the bankrupt or debtor's creditors held in pursuance of the Act or of these Rules.
(2) Where the corporation authorises only one person, that person is entitled to exercise the same powers on behalf of the corporation as the corporation could exercise if it were an individual creditor.
(3) Where the corporation authorises more than one person, any one of them is entitled to exercise the same powers on behalf of the corporation as the corporation could exercise if it were an individual creditor.
(4) Where the corporation authorises more than one person and more than one of them purport to exercise a power under paragraph (3)—
    (a)    if they purport to exercise the power in the same way, the power is treated as exercised in that way; but
    (b)    if they do not purport to exercise the power in the same way, the power is treated as not exercised.

**Derivation**—This rule derived from the Insolvency Rules 1986, SI 1986/1925, r 8.7.

**[2.936]**

**16.9 Instrument conferring authorisation to represent corporation**
(1) A person authorised to represent a corporation (other than as a proxy-holder) at a meeting of creditors or contributories must produce to the chair—
    (a)    the instrument conferring the authority; or
    (b)    a copy of it certified as a true copy by—
        (i)    two directors,
        (ii)    a director and the secretary, or
        (iii)    a director in the presence of a witness who attests the director's signature.
(2) The instrument conferring the authority must have been executed in accordance with section 44(1) to (3) of the Companies Act unless the instrument is the constitution of the corporation.

**Derivation**—This rule derived from the Insolvency Rules 1986, SI 1986/1925, r 8.7.

## PART 17   CREDITORS' AND LIQUIDATION COMMITTEES

### CHAPTER 1

#### INTRODUCTORY

**[2.937]**

**17.1 Scope and interpretation**

(1)   This Part applies to the establishment and operation of—

    (a)    a creditors' committee in an administration;

    (b)    a creditors' committee in an administrative receivership;

    (c)    a liquidation committee in a creditors' voluntary winding up;

    (d)    a liquidation committee in a winding up by the court; and

    (e)    a creditors' committee in a bankruptcy.

(2)   In this Part—

    "contributory member" means a member of a liquidation committee appointed by the contributories; and

    "creditor member" means a member of a liquidation committee appointed by the creditors.

    **General note**—The relevant provisions for creditors' and liquidation committees in different insolvency processes, which were dealt with separately in the IR 1986, are now combined in one place.

### CHAPTER 2

#### FUNCTIONS OF A COMMITTEE

**[2.938]**

**17.2 Functions of a committee**

In addition to any functions conferred on a committee by any provision of the Act, the committee is to—

    (a)    assist the office-holder in discharging the office-holder's functions; and

    (b)    act in relation to the office-holder in such manner as may from time to time be agreed.

    **Derivation**—This rule derived from the Insolvency Rules 1986, SI 1986/1925, rr 2.52, 3.18.
    **General note**—See s 49 and the notes thereto.

### CHAPTER 3

#### MEMBERSHIP AND FORMALITIES OF FORMATION OF A COMMITTEE

**[2.939]**

**Note**

[Note: (1) a document required by the Act or these Rules must also contain the standard contents set out in Part 1;

(2) see sections 215, 362, 363, 365, 371 and 374 of the Financial Services and Markets Act 2000 (c 8) for the rights of persons appointed by a scheme manager, the Financial Conduct Authority and the Prudential Regulation Authority to attend committees and make representations.]

**[2.940]**

**17.3 Number of members of a committee**

[Note: section 101(1) provides that a liquidation committee in a creditors' voluntary winding up may not have more than five members.]

(1)  A committee in an administration, administrative receivership or a bankruptcy must have at least three members but not more than five members.

(2)  A liquidation committee in a creditors' voluntary winding up appointed pursuant to section 101 must have at least three members.

(3)  A liquidation committee in a winding up by the court established under section 141 must have—

    (a)    at least three and not more than five members elected by the creditors; and

    (b)    where the grounds on which the company was wound up do not include inability to pay its debts, and where the contributories so decide, up to three contributory members elected by the contributories.

**Derivation**—This rule derived from the Insolvency Rules 1986, SI 1986/1925, rr 2.50, 3.16.

**General note**—For the establishment of a creditors' committee see s 49 and the notes thereto.

While the courts are not granted express powers to pass judgment on the composition of a validly appointed committee, they may, in the course of exercising their general powers in relation to winding up, seek to affect the composition so that no creditor or class of creditors with a substantial interest is excluded from the representation which it seeks: *Re Radford & Bright Ltd* [1901] 1 Ch 272 at 277.

There is Australian authority to the effect that, as in a liquidation of an insolvent company contributories cannot expect to receive anything from the winding up then, all other matters being equal, all members of the committee should represent creditors, but if all creditors are to be paid out it is reasonable that contributories should have fair representation on the committee: *Re James; In re Cowra Processors Pty Ltd* (1995) 15 ACLC 1582.

## [2.941]

### 17.4  Eligibility for membership of creditors' or liquidation committee

(1)  This rule applies to a creditors' committee in an administration, an administrative receivership, and a bankruptcy and to a liquidation committee in a creditors' voluntary winding up and a winding up by the court.

(2)  A creditor is eligible to be a member of such a committee if—

    (a)    the person has proved for a debt;

    (b)    the debt is not fully secured; and

    (c)    neither of the following apply—

        (i)    the proof has been wholly disallowed for voting purposes, or

        (ii)    the proof has been wholly rejected for the purpose of distribution or dividend.

(3)  No person can be a member as both a creditor and a contributory.

(4)  A body corporate may be a member of a creditors' committee, but it cannot act otherwise than by a representative appointed under rule 17.17.

**Derivation**—This rule derived from the Insolvency Rules 1986, SI 1986/1925, rr 2.50, 3.16, 4.152, 6.150.

## [2.942]

### 17.5  Establishment of committees

(1)  Where the creditors, or where applicable, contributories, decide that a creditors' or liquidation committee should be established, the convener or chair of the decision procedure or convener of the deemed consent process (if not the office-holder) must—

    (a)    as soon as reasonably practicable deliver a notice of the decision to the office-holder (or to the person appointed as office-holder); and

    (b)    where a decision has also been made as to membership of the committee, inform the office-holder of the names and addresses of the persons elected to be members of the committee.

(2)  Before a person may act as a member of the committee that person must agree to do so.

(3)  A person's proxy-holder attending a meeting establishing the committee or, in the case of a corporation, its duly appointed representative, may give such agreement (unless the proxy or instrument conferring authority contains a statement to the contrary).

(4) Where a decision has been made to establish a committee but not as to its membership, the office-holder must seek a decision from the creditors (about creditor members of the committee) and, where appropriate in a winding up by the court, a decision from contributories (about contributory members of the committee).

(5) The committee is not established (and accordingly cannot act) until the office-holder has sent a notice of its membership in order to comply with paragraph (9) or (10).

(6) The notice must contain the following—

    (a)      a statement that the committee has been duly constituted;

    (b)      identification details for any company that is a member of the committee;

    (c)      the full name and address of each member that is not a company.

(7) The notice must be authenticated and dated by the office-holder.

(8) The notice must be delivered as soon as reasonably practicable after the minimum number of persons required by rule 17.3 have agreed to act as members and been elected.

(9) Where the notice relates to a liquidation committee or a creditors' committee other than in a bankruptcy the office-holder must, as soon as reasonably practicable, deliver the notice to the registrar of companies.

(10) Where the notice relates to a creditors' committee in a bankruptcy the office-holder must, as soon as reasonably practicable—

    (a)      in bankruptcy proceedings based on a petition file the notice with the court; and

    (b)      in bankruptcy proceedings based on a bankruptcy application deliver the notice to the official receiver.

**Derivation**—This rule derived from the Insolvency Rules 1986, SI 1986/1925, rr 2.51, 3.17, 4.153, 6.151.

**Amendments**—SI 2017/1115.

**General note**—Just because a notice has been delivered, this does not necessarily mean that the committee has been constituted properly and can stand (*Re W & A Glaser Ltd* [1994] BCC 199, decided under r 4.153 of the 1986 Rules, which referred to the issue of a 'certificate' rather than the delivery of a 'notice'), perhaps, for instance, because the members of the committee are not in fact creditors.

## [2.943]

### 17.6 Liquidation committee established by contributories

(1) This rule applies where, under section 141, the creditors do not decide that a liquidation committee should be established, or decide that a committee should not be established.

(2) The contributories may decide to appoint one of their number to make application to the court for an order requiring the liquidator to seek a further decision from the creditors on whether to establish a liquidation committee; and—

    (a)      the court may, if it thinks that there are special circumstances to justify it, make such an order; and

    (b)      the creditors' decision sought by the liquidator in compliance with the order is deemed to have been a decision under section 141.

(3) If the creditors decide under paragraph (2)(b) not to establish a liquidation committee, the contributories may establish a committee.

(4) The committee must then consist of at least three, and not more than five, contributories elected by the contributories; and rule 17.5 applies, substituting for the reference to rule 17.3 in rule 17.5(8) a reference to this paragraph.

**Derivation**—This rule derived from the Insolvency Rules 1986, SI 1986/1925, r 4.154.

## [2.944]

### 17.7 Notice of change of membership of a committee

(1) The office-holder must deliver or file a notice if there is a change in membership of the committee.

(2)   The notice must contain the following—

    (a)   the date of the original notice in respect of the constitution of the committee and the date of the last notice of membership given under this rule (if any);

    (b)   a statement that this notice of membership replaces the previous notice;

    (c)   identification details for any company that is a member of the committee;

    (d)   the full name and address of any member that is not a company;

    (e)   a statement whether any member has become a member since the issue of the previous notice;

    (f)   the identification details for a company or otherwise the full name of any member named in the previous notice who is no longer a member and the date the membership ended.

(3)   The notice must be authenticated and dated by the office-holder.

(4)   Where the notice relates to a liquidation committee or a creditors' committee other than in a bankruptcy the office-holder must, as soon as reasonably practicable, deliver the notice to the registrar of companies.

(5)   Where the notice relates to a creditors' committee in a bankruptcy the office-holder must, as soon as reasonably practicable—

    (a)   in bankruptcy proceedings based on a petition file the notice with the court; and

    (b)   in bankruptcy proceedings based on a bankruptcy application deliver the notice to the official receiver.

**Derivation**—This rule derived from the Insolvency Rules 1986, SI 1986/1925, rr 2.51, 3.17, 4.153, 6.151.

## [2.945]

### 17.8  Vacancies: creditor members of creditors' or liquidation committee

(1)   This rule applies if there is a vacancy among the creditor members of a creditors' or liquidation committee or where the number of creditor members of the committee is fewer than the maximum allowed.

(2)   A vacancy need not be filled if—

    (a)   the office-holder and a majority of the remaining creditor members agree; and

    (b)   the total number of creditor members does not fall below three.

(3)   The office-holder may appoint a creditor, who is qualified under rule 17.4 to be a member of the committee, to fill a vacancy or as an additional member of the committee, if—

    (a)   a majority of the remaining creditor members of the committee (provided there are at least two) agree to the appointment; and

    (b)   the creditor agrees to act.

(4)   Alternatively, the office-holder may seek a decision from creditors to appoint a creditor (with that creditor's consent) to fill the vacancy.

(5)   Where the vacancy is filled by an appointment made by a decision of creditors which is not convened or chaired by the office-holder, the convener or chair must report the appointment to the office-holder.

**Derivation**—This rule derived from the Insolvency Rules 1986, SI 1986/1925, rr 2.59, 3.25, 4.163, 6.160.

## [2.946]

### 17.9  Vacancies: contributory members of liquidation committee

(1)   This rule applies if there is a vacancy among the contributory members of a liquidation committee or where the number of contributory members of the committee is fewer than the maximum allowed under rule 17.3(3)(b) or 17.6(4) as the case may be.

(2)   A vacancy need not be filled if—

(a)  the liquidator and a majority of the remaining contributory members agree; and

(b)  in the case of a committee of contributories only, the number of members does not fall below three.

(3)  The liquidator may appoint a contributory to be a member of the committee, to fill a vacancy or as an additional member of the committee, if—

(a)  a majority of the remaining contributory members of the committee (provided there are at least two) agree to the appointment; and

(b)  the contributory agrees to act.

(4)  Alternatively, the office-holder may seek a decision from contributories to appoint a contributory (with that contributory's consent) to fill the vacancy.

(5)  Where the vacancy is filled by an appointment made by a decision of contributories which is not convened or chaired by the office-holder, the convener or chair must report the appointment to the office-holder.

**Derivation**—This rule derived from the Insolvency Rules 1986, SI 1986/1925, r 4.164.

## [2.947]

### 17.10  Resignation

A member of a committee may resign by informing the office-holder in writing.

**Derivation**—This rule derived from the Insolvency Rules 1986, SI 1986/1925, rr 2.56, 3.22, 4.160, 6.157.

## [2.948]

### 17.11  Termination of membership

A person's membership of a committee is automatically terminated if that person—

(a)  becomes bankrupt, in which case the person's trustee in bankruptcy replaces the bankrupt as a member of the committee;

(b)  is a person to whom a moratorium period under a debt relief order applies;

(c)  neither attends nor is represented at three consecutive meetings (unless it is resolved at the third of those meetings that this rule is not to apply in that person's case);

(d)  has ceased to be eligible to be a member of the committee under rule 17.4;

(e)  ceases to be a creditor or is found never to have been a creditor;

(f)  ceases to be a contributory or is found never to have been a contributory.

**Derivation**—This rule derived from the Insolvency Rules 1986, SI 1986/1925, rr 2.57, 3.23, 4.161, 6.158.

**General note**—It was confirmed in *Re Future Route Ltd; Jackson v Cohen* [2017] EWHC 3677 (Ch) that if a creditor is paid in full during the liquidation, the appointment of that member terminates. In *Future Route* the creditors had been paid in full, the committee ceased to exist, and accordingly a new committee could no longer be formed. It was held that the court had the power to fix the liquidators' remuneration in such circumstances.

## [2.949]

### 17.12  Removal

(1)  A creditor member of a committee may be removed by a decision of the creditors through a decision procedure and in the case of a liquidation committee a contributory member of the committee may be removed by a decision of contributories through a decision procedure.

(2)  At least 14 days' notice must be given of a decision procedure under this rule.

**Derivation**—This rule derived from the Insolvency Rules 1986, SI 1986/1925, rr 2.58, 3.24, 4.162, 6.159.

**General note**—The courts do not have the power to remove a member of the committee (*Re Rubber & Produce Investment Trust* [1915] 1 Ch 382), but they are able to direct the liquidator to call meetings of the creditors and contributories and they can terminate the membership, depending on whether the member is a creditor or a contributory.

**[2.950]**

**17.13 Cessation of liquidation committee in a winding up when creditors are paid in full**

(1) Where the creditors have been paid in full together with interest in accordance with section 189, the liquidator must deliver to the registrar of companies a notice to that effect.

(2) On the delivery of the notice the liquidation committee ceases to exist.

(3) The notice must—

   (a) identify the liquidator;

   (b) contain a statement by the liquidator certifying that the creditors of the company have been paid in full with interest in accordance with section 189; and

   (c) be authenticated and dated by the liquidator.

**Derivation**—This rule derived from the Insolvency Rules 1986, SI 1986/1925, r 4.171A.

CHAPTER 4

MEETINGS OF COMMITTEE

**[2.951]**

**Note**

[Note: a document required by the Act or these Rules must also contain the standard contents set out in Part 1.]

**[2.952]**

**17.14 Meetings of committee**

(1) Meetings of the committee must be held when and where determined by the office-holder.

(2) The office-holder must call a first meeting of the committee to take place within six weeks of the committee's establishment.

(3) After the calling of the first meeting, the office-holder must call a meeting—

   (a) if so requested by a member of the committee or a member's representative (the meeting then to be held within 21 days of the request being received by the office-holder); and

   (b) for a specified date, if the committee has previously resolved that a meeting be held on that date.

(4) The office-holder must give five business days' notice of the venue of a meeting to each member of the committee (or a member's representative, if designated for that purpose), except where the requirement for notice has been waived by or on behalf of a member.

(5) Waiver may be signified either at or before the meeting.

**Derivation**—This rule derived from the Insolvency Rules 1986, SI 1986/1925, rr 2.52, 3.18, 4.156, 6.153.

**General note**—At the first meeting the office holder should discuss with committee members how frequently they wish to receive reports and obtain their directions. Office holders should also discuss with committee members the type of matters that they wish to have reported to them. The first meeting should be held as early as is practical after the committee is established, and in any event within 6 weeks of the committee's establishment: r 17.14(2), and SIP 15 (version effective in respect of appointments starting on or after 1 March 2017) at para 9.

**[2.953]**

**17.15 The chair at meetings**

The chair at a meeting of a committee must be the office-holder or an appointed person.

**Derivation**—This rule derived from the Insolvency Rules 1986, SI 1986/1925, rr 2.53, 3.19, 4.157, 6.154.

**[2.954]**

**17.16 Quorum**

A meeting of a committee is duly constituted if due notice of it has been delivered to all the members, and at least two of the members are in attendance or represented.

   **Derivation**—This rule derived from the Insolvency Rules 1986, SI 1986/1925, rr 2.54, 3.20, 4.158, 6.155.

**[2.955]**

**17.17 Committee-members' representatives**

(1)   A member of the committee may, in relation to the business of the committee, be represented by another person duly authorised by the member for that purpose.

(2)   A person acting as a committee-member's representative must hold a letter of authority entitling that person to act (either generally or specifically) and authenticated by or on behalf of the committee-member.

(3)   A proxy or an instrument conferring authority (in respect of a person authorised to represent a corporation) is to be treated as a letter of authority to act generally (unless the proxy or instrument conferring authority contains a statement to the contrary).

(4)   The chair at a meeting of the committee may call on a person claiming to act as a committee-member's representative to produce a letter of authority, and may exclude that person if no letter of authority is produced at or by the time of the meeting or if it appears to the chair that the authority is deficient.

(5)   A committee member may not be represented by—

   (a)   another member of the committee;

   (b)   a person who is at the same time representing another committee-member;

   (c)   a body corporate;

   (d)   an undischarged bankrupt;

   (e)   a person whose estate has been sequestrated and who has not been discharged;

   (f)   a person to whom a moratorium period under a debt relief order applies;

   (g)   a person who is subject to a company directors disqualification order or a company directors disqualification undertaking; or

   (h)   a person who is subject to a bankruptcy restrictions order (including an interim order), a bankruptcy restrictions undertaking, a debt relief restrictions order (including an interim order) or a debt relief restrictions undertaking.

(6)   Where a representative authenticates any document on behalf of a committee-member the fact that the representative authenticates as a representative must be stated below the authentication.

   **Derivation**—This rule derived from the Insolvency Rules 1986, SI 1986/1925, rr 2.55, 3.21, 4.159, 6.156.

   **General note**—There is obvious practical utility in allowing a creditors' committee representative to be represented by another person authorised by him, subject to the requirement for a letter of authority in r 17.17(2) which must be produced under r 17.17(4).

**[2.956]**

**17.18 Voting rights and resolutions**

(1)   At a meeting of the committee, each member (whether the member is in attendance or is represented by a representative) has one vote.

(2)   A resolution is passed when a majority of the members attending or represented have voted in favour of it.

(3)   Every resolution passed must be recorded in writing and authenticated by the chair, either separately or as part of the minutes of the meeting, and the record must be kept with the records of the proceedings.

   **Derivation**—This rule derived from the Insolvency Rules 1986, SI 1986/1925, rr 2.60, 3.26, 4.165, 4.166, 6.161.

**[2.957]**

### 17.19 Resolutions by correspondence

(1) The office-holder may seek to obtain the agreement of the committee to a resolution by delivering to every member (or the member's representative designated for the purpose) details of the proposed resolution.

(2) The details must be set out in such a way that the recipient may indicate agreement or dissent and where there is more than one resolution may indicate agreement to or dissent from each one separately.

(3) A member of the committee may, within five business days from the delivery of details of the proposed resolution, require the office-holder to summon a meeting of the committee to consider the matters raised by the proposed resolution.

(4) In the absence of such a request, the resolution is passed by the committee if a majority of the members (excluding any who are not permitted to vote by reason of rule 17.25(4)) deliver notice to the office-holder that they agree with the resolution.

(5) A copy of every resolution passed under this rule, and a note that the agreement of the committee was obtained, must be kept with the records of the proceedings.

**Derivation**—This rule derived from the Insolvency Rules 1986, SI 1986/1925, rr 2.61, 3.27, 4.167, 6.162.

**[2.958]**

### 17.20 Remote attendance at meetings of committee

(1) Where the office-holder considers it appropriate, a meeting may be conducted and held in such a way that persons who are not present together at the same place may attend it.

(2) A person attends such a meeting who is able to exercise that person's right to speak and vote at the meeting.

(3) A person is able to exercise the right to speak at a meeting when that person is in a position to communicate during the meeting to all those attending the meeting any information or opinions which that person has on the business of the meeting.

(4) A person is able to exercise the right to vote at a meeting when—

    (i)    that person is able to vote, during the meeting, on resolutions or determinations put to the vote at the meeting, and

    (ii)    that person's vote can be taken into account in determining whether or not such resolutions or determinations are passed at the same time as the votes of all the other persons attending the meeting.

(5) Where such a meeting is to be held the office-holder must make whatever arrangements the office-holder considers appropriate to—

    (a)    enable those attending the meeting to exercise their rights to speak or vote; and

    (b)    verify the identity of those attending the meeting and to ensure the security of any electronic means used to enable attendance.

(6) A requirement in these Rules to specify a place for the meeting may be satisfied by specifying the arrangements the office-holder proposes to enable persons to exercise their rights to speak or vote where in the reasonable opinion of the office-holder—

    (a)    a meeting will be attended by persons who will not be present together at the same place; and

    (b)    it is unnecessary or inexpedient to specify a place for the meeting.

(7) In making the arrangements referred to in paragraph (6) and in forming the opinion referred to in paragraph (6)(b), the office-holder must have regard to the legitimate interests of the committee members or their representatives attending the meeting in the efficient despatch of the business of the meeting.

(8) Where the notice of a meeting does not specify a place for the meeting the office-holder must specify a place for the meeting if at least one member of the committee requests the office-holder to do so in accordance with rule 17.21.

**Derivation**—This rule derived from the Insolvency Rules 1986, SI 1986/1925, r 12A.26.

**[2.959]**

**17.21 Procedure for requests that a place for a meeting should be specified**

(1) This rule applies to a request to the office-holder under rule 17.20(8) to specify a place for the meeting.

(2) The request must be made within three business days of the date on which the office-holder delivered the notice of the meeting in question.

(3) Where the office-holder considers that the request has been properly made in accordance with this rule, the office-holder must—

    (a)    deliver notice to all those previously given notice of the meeting—

        (i)    that it is to be held at a specified place, and

        (ii)    as to whether the date and time are to remain the same or not;

    (b)    fix a venue for the meeting, the date of which must be not later than seven business days after the original date for the meeting; and

    (c)    give three business days' notice of the venue to all those previously given notice of the meeting.

(4) The notices required by sub-paragraphs (a) and (c) may be delivered at the same or different times.

(5) Where the office-holder has specified a place for the meeting in response to a request under rule 17.20(8), the chair of the meeting must attend the meeting by being present in person at that place.

Derivation—This rule derived from the Insolvency Rules 1986, SI 1986/1925, r 12A.27.

## CHAPTER 5

### Supply of Information by the Office-Holder to the Committee

**[2.960]**

**Note**

[Note: a document required by the Act or these Rules must also contain the standard contents set out in Part 1.]

**[2.961]**

**17.22 Notice requiring office-holder to attend the creditors' committee (administration and administrative receivership) (paragraph 57(3)(a) of Schedule B1 and section 49(2))**

[Note: in an administration paragraph 57(3) of Schedule B1 enables the creditors' committee to require the administrator to provide the committee with information: section 49(2) makes similar provision in an administrative receivership.]

(1) This rule applies where—

    (a)    a committee in an administration resolves under paragraph 57(3)(a) of Schedule B1 to require the attendance of an administrator; or

    (b)    a committee in an administrative receivership resolves under section 49(2) to require the attendance of the administrative receiver.

(2) The notice delivered to the office-holder requiring the office-holder's attendance must be—

    (a)    accompanied by a copy of the resolution; and

    (b)    authenticated by a member of the committee.

(3) A member's representative may authenticate the notice for the member.

(4) The meeting at which the office-holder's attendance is required must be fixed by the committee for a business day, and must be held at such time and place as the office-holder determines.

(5) Where the office-holder so attends, the committee may elect one of their number to be chair of the meeting in place of the office-holder or an appointed person.

Derivation—This rule derived from the Insolvency Rules 1986, SI 1986/1925, rr 2.62, 3.28.

**[2.962]**

**17.23 Office-holder's obligation to supply information to the committee (winding up and bankruptcy)**
[Note: see section 49(2) and paragraph 57(3) of Schedule B1 for the office-holder's duty in an administrative receivership and an administration to supply information to the creditors' committee.]

(1) This rule applies in relation to a creditors' voluntary winding up, a winding up by the court and a bankruptcy.

(2) The office-holder must deliver a report to every member of the liquidation committee or the creditors' committee (as appropriate) containing the information required by paragraph (3)—

    (a)     not less than once in every period of six months (unless the committee agrees otherwise); and

    (b)     when directed to do so by the committee.

(3) The required information is a report setting out—

    (a)     the position generally in relation to the progress of the proceedings; and

    (b)     any matters arising in connection with them to which the office-holder considers the committee's attention should be drawn.

(4) The office-holder must, as soon as reasonably practicable after being directed by the committee—

    (a)     deliver any report directed under paragraph (2)(b);

    (b)     comply with a request by the committee for information.

(5) However the office-holder need not comply with such a direction where it appears to the office-holder that—

    (a)     the direction is frivolous or unreasonable;

    (b)     the cost of complying would be excessive, having regard to the relative importance of the information; or

    (c)     there are insufficient assets to enable the office-holder to comply.

(6) Where the committee has come into being more than 28 days after the appointment of the office-holder, the office-holder must make a summary report to the members of the committee of what actions the office-holder has taken since the office-holder's appointment, and must answer such questions as they may put to the office-holder relating to the office-holder's conduct of the proceedings so far.

(7) A person who becomes a member of the committee at any time after its first establishment is not entitled to require a report under this rule by the office-holder of any matters previously arising, other than a summary report.

(8) Nothing in this rule disentitles the committee, or any member of it, from having access to the office-holder's record of the proceedings, or from seeking an explanation of any matter within the committee's responsibility.

**Derivation**—This rule derived from the Insolvency Rules 1986, SI 1986/1925, rr 4.155, 4.168, 6.152, 6.163.

**General note**—While the committee is granted wide powers and functions, it is not entitled to inspect, or ask the liquidator questions about, documents that are sent between the liquidator and the Department of Business Enterprise and Regulatory Reform and concerning the possibility of disqualification proceedings being brought against the directors of the company: *Re W & A Glaser Ltd* [1994] BCC 199 at 205.

**Liquidator not complying**—If a liquidator takes the view that he or she need not comply with any request for information on one or more of the grounds set out in r 17.23(5), the committee, or a member of it, could seek directions from the court under s 112, in a voluntary winding up. In relation to a compulsory winding up the committee or a member of it could seek, under s 168(5), a review of the liquidator's decision.

CHAPTER 6

MISCELLANEOUS

**[2.963]**

Note

[Note: a document required by the Act or these Rules must also contain the standard contents set out in Part 1.]

**[2.964]**

**17.24 Expenses of members etc**

(1) The office-holder must pay, as an expense of the insolvency proceedings, the reasonable travelling expenses directly incurred by members of the committee or their representatives in attending the committee's meetings or otherwise on the committee's business.

(2) The requirement for the office-holder to pay the expenses does not apply to a meeting of the committee held within six weeks of a previous meeting, unless the meeting is summoned by the office-holder.

**Derivation**—This rule derived from the Insolvency Rules 1986, SI 1986/1925, rr 2.63, 3.29, 4.169, 6.164.

**General note**—The expenses fall under r 3.51(2)(g) in an administration, r 6.42(4)(f) in a voluntary liquidation, r 7.108(4)(m) in a compulsory liquidation, and r 10.149(n) in bankruptcy.

**[2.965]**

**17.25 Dealings by committee members and others**

(1) This rule applies in a creditors' voluntary winding up, a winding up by the court and a bankruptcy to a person who is, or has been in the preceding 12 months—

 (a) a member of the committee;

 (b) a member's representative; or

 (c) an associate of a member, or of a member's representative.

(2) Such a person must not enter into a transaction as a result of which that person would—

 (a) receive as an expense of the insolvency proceedings a payment for services given or goods supplied in connection with the administration of the insolvent estate;

 (b) obtain a profit from the administration of the insolvent estate; or

 (c) acquire an asset forming part of the insolvent estate.

(3) However such a transaction may be entered into—

 (a) with the prior sanction of the committee, where it is satisfied (after full disclosure of the circumstances) that the person will be giving full value in the transaction;

 (b) with the prior permission of the court; or

 (c) if that person does so as a matter of urgency, or by way of performance of a contract in force before the start of the insolvency proceedings, and that person obtains the court's permission for the transaction, having applied for it without undue delay.

(4) Neither a member nor a representative of a member who is to participate directly or indirectly in a transaction may vote on a resolution to sanction that transaction.

(5) The court may, on the application of an interested person—

 (a) set aside a transaction on the ground that it has been entered into in contravention of this rule; and

 (b) make such other order about the transaction as it thinks just, including an order requiring a person to whom this rule applies to account for any profit obtained from the transaction and compensate the insolvent estate for any resultant loss.

(6)  The court will not make an order under the previous paragraph in respect of an associate of a member of the committee or an associate of a member's representative, if satisfied that the associate or representative entered into the relevant transaction without having any reason to suppose that in doing so the associate or representative would contravene this rule.

(7)  The costs of the application are not payable as an expense of the insolvency proceedings unless the court orders otherwise.

Derivation—This rule derived from the Insolvency Rules 1986, SI 1986/1925, rr 4.170, 6.165.

### [2.966]

### 17.26 Dealings by committee members and others: administration and administrative receivership

(1)  This rule applies in an administration and administrative receivership.

(2)  Membership of the committee does not prevent a person from dealing with the company provided that a transaction is in good faith and for value.

(3)  The court may, on the application of an interested person—

    (a)    set aside a transaction which appears to it to be contrary to this rule; and

    (b)    make such other order about the transaction as it thinks just including an order requiring a person to whom this rule applies to account for any profit obtained from the transaction and compensate the company for any resultant loss.

Derivation—This rule derived from the Insolvency Rules 1986, SI 1986/1925, rr 2.64, 3.30.

### [2.967]

### 17.27 Formal defects

[Note: section 377 makes similar provision to paragraph (1) for the validity of acts of the creditors' committee in a bankruptcy.]

(1)  The acts of a creditors' committee or a liquidation committee are valid notwithstanding any defect in the appointment, election or qualifications of a member of the committee or a committee-member's representative or in the formalities of its establishment.

(2)  This rule does not apply to the creditors' committee in a bankruptcy.

Derivation—This rule derived from the Insolvency Rules 1986, SI 1986/1925, rr 2.65, 3.30A, 4.172A.

General note–see here the notes to the analogous r 12.64.

### [2.968]

### 17.28 Special rule for winding up by the court and bankruptcy: functions vested in the Secretary of State

(1)  At any time when the functions of a committee in a winding up by the court or a bankruptcy are vested in the Secretary of State under section 141(4) or (5) or section 302(1) or (2), requirements of the Act or these Rules about notices to be delivered, or reports to be made, to the committee by the office-holder do not apply, otherwise than as enabling the committee to require a report as to any matter.

(2)  Where the committee's functions are so vested under section 141(5) or 302(2), they may be exercised by the official receiver.

Derivation—This rule derived from the Insolvency Rules 1986, SI 1986/1925, rr 4.172, 6.166.

General note—See s 141(4), (5). The former subsection applies where the official receiver is the liquidator, and the latter applies where no committee exists.

CHAPTER 7

WINDING UP BY THE COURT FOLLOWING AN ADMINISTRATION

**[2.969]**

Note

[Note: a document required by the Act or these Rules must also contain the standard contents set out in Part 1.]

**[2.970]**

**17.29 Continuation of creditors' committee**

[Note: paragraph 83(8)(f) of Schedule B1 makes similar provision to this rule for the liquidation committee to continue where the administration is followed by a creditors' voluntary winding up.]

(1) This rule applies where—

(a) a winding-up order has been made by the court on the application of the administrator under paragraph 79 of Schedule B1;

(b) the court makes an order under section 140(1) appointing the administrator as the liquidator; and

(c) a creditors' committee was in existence immediately before the winding-up order was made.

(2) The creditors' committee shall continue in existence after the date of the order as if appointed as a liquidation committee under section 141.

(3) However, subject to rule 17.8(3)(a), the committee cannot act until—

(a) the minimum number of persons required by rule 17.3 have agreed to act as members of the liquidation committee (including members of the former creditors' committee and any other who may be appointed under rule 17.8); and

(b) the liquidator has delivered a notice of continuance of the committee to the registrar of companies.

(4) The notice must be delivered as soon as reasonably practicable after the minimum number of persons required have agreed to act as members or, if applicable, been appointed.

(5) The notice must contain—

(a) a statement that the former creditors' committee is continuing in existence;

(b) identification details for any company that is a member of the committee;

(c) the full name and address of each member that is not a company.

(6) The notice must be authenticated and dated by the office-holder.

Derivation—This rule derived from the Insolvency Rules 1986, SI 1986/1925, rr 4.173, 4.174A, 4.176, 4.178.

PART 18   REPORTING AND REMUNERATION OF OFFICE-HOLDERS

**[2.971]**

Note

[Note: this Part does not apply to the official receiver acting as an office-holder.]

CHAPTER 1

INTRODUCTORY

**[2.972]**

**18.1 Scope of Part 18 and interpretation**

(1) This Part applies to administration, winding up and bankruptcy.

(2)   However this Part does not apply to the official receiver as office-holder or in respect of any period for which the official receiver is the office-holder.

(3)   In particular an office-holder other than the official receiver is not required to make any report in respect of a period during which the official receiver was office-holder.

(4)   In this Part "committee" means either or both of a creditors' committee and a liquidation committee as the context requires.

CHAPTER 2

PROGRESS REPORTS

**[2.973]**

**Note**

[Note: a document required by the Act or these Rules must also contain the standard contents set out in Part 1.]

**[2.974]**

**18.2  Reporting by the office-holder**

The office-holder in an administration, winding up or bankruptcy must prepare and deliver reports in accordance with this Chapter.

**[2.975]**

**18.3  Contents of progress reports in administration, winding up and bankruptcy**

[Note: see rule 3.53 for provisions about the contents of a final progress report in an administration.]

(1)   The office-holder's progress report in an administration, winding up and bankruptcy must contain the following—

    (a)    identification details for the proceedings;

    (b)    identification details for the bankrupt;

    (c)    identification and contact details for the office-holder;

    (d)    the date of appointment of the office-holder and any changes in the office-holder in accordance with paragraphs (3) and (4);

    (e)    details of progress during the period of the report, including a summary account of receipts and payments during the period of the report;

    (f)    the information relating to remuneration and expenses required by rule 18.4;

    (g)    the information relating to distributions required by rules 18.10 to 18.13 as applicable;

    (h)    details of what remains to be done; and

    (i)    any other information of relevance to the creditors.

(2)   The receipts and payments account in a final progress report must state the amount paid to unsecured creditors by virtue of the application of section 176A.

(3)   A change in the office-holder is only required to be shown in the next report after the change.

(4)   However if the current office-holder is seeking the repayment of pre-administration expenses from a former office-holder the change in office-holder must continue to be shown until the next report after the claim is settled.

(5)   Where the period of an administrator's appointment is extended the next progress report after the date the extension is granted must contain details of the extension.

(6)   Where an administration has converted to a voluntary winding up the first progress report by the liquidator must include a note of any information received by the liquidator from the former administrator under rule 3.60(5) (matters occurring after the date of the administrator's final progress report).

Derivation—This rule derived from the Insolvency Rules 1986, SI 1986/1925, rr 2.47, 4.49B, 4.49C, 6.78A.

**[2.976]**

**18.4 Information about remuneration**

(1) The information relating to remuneration and expenses referred to in rule 18.3(1)(f) is as follows—

<ul>
<li>(a) the basis fixed for the remuneration of the office-holder under rules 18.16 and 18.18 to 18.21 as applicable, (or, if not fixed at the date of the report, the steps taken during the period of the report to fix it);</li>
<li>(b) if the basis of remuneration has been fixed, a statement of—
<ul>
<li>(i) the remuneration charged by the office-holder during the period of the report, and</li>
<li>(ii) where the report is the first to be made after the basis has been fixed, the remuneration charged by the office-holder during the periods covered by the previous reports, together with a description of the things done by the office-holder during those periods in respect of which the remuneration was charged;</li>
</ul>
</li>
<li>(c) where the basis of the remuneration is fixed as a set amount under rule 18.16(2)(c), it may be shown as that amount without any apportionment to the period of the report;</li>
<li>(d) a statement of the expenses incurred by the office-holder during the period of the report;</li>
<li>(e) a statement setting out whether at the date of the report—
<ul>
<li>(i) in a case other than a members' voluntary winding up, the remuneration expected to be charged by the office-holder is likely to exceed the fees estimate under rule 18.16(4) or any approval given,</li>
<li>(ii) the expenses incurred or expected to be incurred are likely to exceed, or have exceeded, the details given to the creditors prior to the determination of the basis of remuneration, and</li>
<li>(iii) the reasons for that excess; and</li>
</ul>
</li>
<li>(f) a statement of the rights of creditors or, in a members' voluntary winding up, of members—
<ul>
<li>(i) to request information about remuneration or expenses under rule 18.9, and</li>
<li>(ii) to challenge the office-holder's remuneration and expenses under rule 18.34.</li>
</ul>
</li>
</ul>

(2) The information about remuneration and expenses is required irrespective of whether payment was made in respect of them during the period of the report.

Derivation—This rule derived from the Insolvency Rules 1986, SI 1986/1925, rr 2.47, 4.49B, 4.49C, 6.78A.

Amendments—SI 2017/366.

**[2.977]**

**18.5 Information about pre-administration costs**

(1) Where the administrator has made a statement of pre-administration costs under rule 3.35(10)(a)—

<ul>
<li>(a) if they are approved under rule 3.52, the first progress report after the approval must include a statement setting out the date of the approval and the amounts approved;</li>
<li>(b) while any of the costs remain unapproved each successive report must include a statement of any steps taken to get approval.</li>
</ul>

(2) However if either the administrator has decided not to seek approval, or another insolvency practitioner entitled to seek approval has told the administrator of that practitioner's decision not to seek approval then—

(a)     the next report after that must include a statement of whichever is the case; and

(b)     no statement under paragraph (1)(b) is required in subsequent reports.

**Derivation**—This rule derived from the Insolvency Rules 1986, SI 1986/1925, r 2.67A.

**General note**—This rule should be read in conjunction with r 3.1, which defines pre-administration costs. The implementation of the equivalent provisions in the IR 1986 followed the decisions in *Re Kayley Vending* [2009] BCC 578 (HHJ Cooke) and *Re Johnson Machine and Tool Co Ltd* [2010] BCC 382 (HHJ Purle QC) in which the court had exercised its discretion under para 13(1)(f) to order pre-appointment costs of the proposed administrator in pre-pack administrations to be treated as an expense of the administration.

An administrator's pre-administration costs are now specifically provided for in r 3.51(2)(i). The definition of pre-administration costs in r 3.1 appears to exclude fees and expenses incurred other than in connection with the administration; there is no reason, on that approach, why in principle the costs associated with the arrangement of a pre-pack sale of the company's business and assets to be effected in the very early course of the administration should not constitute pre-administration costs.

Sub-rule (2) introduces new content for the IR 2016 requiring disclosure of any pre-appointment costs not being sought for recovery. These need only be set out in one report.

## [2.978]

### 18.6 Progress reports in administration: timing

(1)   The administrator's progress report in an administration must cover the periods of—

(a)     six months starting on the date the company entered administration; and

(b)     each subsequent period of six months.

(2)   The periods for which progress reports are required under paragraph (1) are unaffected by any change in the administrator.

(3)   However where an administrator ceases to act the succeeding administrator must, as soon as reasonably practicable after being appointed, deliver a notice to the creditors of any matters about which the succeeding administrator thinks the creditors should be informed.

(4)   The administrator must deliver a copy of a report to the registrar of companies and the creditors within one month of the end of the period covered by the report unless the report is a final progress report under rule 3.55.

(5)   An administrator who makes default in delivering a progress report within the time limit in paragraph (4) is guilty of on offence and liable to a fine and, for continued contravention, to a daily default fine.

**Derivation**—This rule derived from the Insolvency Rules 1986, SI 1986/1925, r 2.47(3), (6).

## [2.979]

### 18.7 Progress reports in voluntary winding up: timing

(1)   This rule applies for the purposes of sections 92A and 104A and prescribes the periods for which reports must be made.

(2)   The liquidator's progress reports in a voluntary winding up must cover the periods of—

(a)     12 months starting on the date the liquidator is appointed; and

(b)     each subsequent period of 12 months.

(3)   The periods for which progress reports are required under paragraph (2) are unaffected by any change in the liquidator.

(4)   However where a liquidator ceases to act the succeeding liquidator must, as soon as reasonably practicable after being appointed, deliver a notice to the members (in a members' voluntary winding up) or to members and creditors (in a creditors' voluntary winding up) of any matters about which the succeeding liquidator thinks the members or creditors should be informed.

(5)   A progress report is not required for any period which ends after a notice is delivered under rule 5.9(1) (members' voluntary winding up) or after the date to which

a final account is made up under section 106 and is delivered by the liquidator to members and creditors (creditors' voluntary winding up).

(6) The liquidator must deliver a copy of each progress report within two months after the end of the period covered by the report to—

    (a)    the registrar of companies (who is a prescribed person for the purposes of sections 92A and 104A);

    (b)    the members; and

    (c)    in a creditors' voluntary liquidation, the creditors.

**Derivation**—This rule derived from the Insolvency Rules 1986, SI 1986/1925, r 4.49C.
**Amendments**—SI 2017/366.

## [2.980]

### 18.8 Progress reports in winding up by the court and bankruptcy: timing

(1) The liquidator or trustee's progress report in a winding up by the court or bankruptcy must cover the periods of—

    (a)    12 months starting on the date a person other than the official receiver is appointed liquidator or trustee; and

    (b)    each subsequent period of 12 months.

(2) The periods for which progress reports are required under paragraph (1) are unaffected by any change in the liquidator or trustee unless at any time the official receiver becomes liquidator or trustee in succession to another person in which case—

    (a)    the current reporting period under paragraph (1) ends; and

    (b)    if a person other than the official receiver is subsequently appointed as liquidator or trustee a new period begins under paragraph (1)(a).

(3) Where a liquidator or trustee ceases to act the succeeding liquidator or trustee must as soon as reasonably practicable after being appointed, deliver a notice to the creditors of any matters about which the succeeding liquidator or trustee thinks the creditors should be informed.

(4) A progress report is not required for any period which ends after the date to which a final account or report is made up under section 146 (winding up by the court) or section 331 (bankruptcy) and is delivered by the liquidator or the trustee to the creditors.

(5) In a winding up by the court, the liquidator must deliver a copy of the progress report to the registrar of companies, the members of the company and the creditors within two months of the end of the period covered by the report.

(6) In a bankruptcy, the trustee must deliver a copy of the progress report to the creditors within two months of the end of the period covered by the report.

**Derivation**—This rule derived from the Insolvency Rules 1986, SI 1986/1925, rr 4.49B, 6.78A(3).

## [2.981]

### 18.9 Creditors' and members' requests for further information in administration, winding up and bankruptcy

(1) The following may make a written request to the office-holder for further information about remuneration or expenses (other than pre-administration costs in an administration) set out in a progress report under rule 18.4(1)(b), (c) or (d) or a final report or account under rule 18.14—

    (a)    a secured creditor;

    (b)    an unsecured creditor with the concurrence of at least 5% in value of the unsecured creditors (including the creditor in question);

    (c)    members of the company in a members' voluntary winding up with at least 5% of the total voting rights of all the members having the right to vote at general meetings of the company;

    (d)    any unsecured creditor with the permission of the court; or

    (e)    any member of the company in a members' voluntary winding up with the permission of the court.

(2) A request, or an application to the court for permission, by such a person or persons must be made or filed with the court (as applicable) within 21 days of receipt of the report or account by the person, or by the last of them in the case of an application by more than one member or creditor.

(3) The office-holder must, within 14 days of receipt of such a request respond to the person or persons who requested the information by—

    (a)    providing all of the information requested;

    (b)    providing some of the information requested; or

    (c)    declining to provide the information requested.

(4) The office-holder may respond by providing only some of the information requested or decline to provide the information if—

    (a)    the time or cost of preparation of the information would be excessive; or

    (b)    disclosure of the information would be prejudicial to the conduct of the proceedings;

    (c)    disclosure of the information might reasonably be expected to lead to violence against any person; or

    (d)    the office-holder is subject to an obligation of confidentiality in relation to the information.

(5) An office-holder who does not provide all the information or declines to provide the information must inform the person or persons who requested the information of the reasons for so doing.

(6) A creditor, and a member of the company in a members' voluntary winding up, who need not be the same as the creditor or members who requested the information, may apply to the court within 21 days of—

    (a)    the office-holder giving reasons for not providing all of the information requested; or

    (b)    the expiry of the 14 days within which an office-holder must respond to a request.

(7) The court may make such order as it thinks just on an application under paragraph (6).

**Derivation**—This rule derived from the Insolvency Rules 1986, SI 1986/1925, rr 2.48A, 4.49E, 6.78C.

**Amendments**—SI 2017/366.

## [2.982]

**18.10 Administration, creditors' voluntary liquidation and compulsory winding up: reporting distribution of property to creditors under rule 14.13**

(1) This rule applies where in an administration, creditors' voluntary liquidation or compulsory winding up there has been a distribution of property to creditors under rule 14.13.

(2) In any account or summary of receipts and payments which is required to be included in an account or report prepared under a rule listed in paragraph (3) the office-holder must—

    (a)    state the estimated value of the property divided among the creditors of the company during the period to which the account or summary relates; and

    (b)    provide details of the basis of the valuation as a note to the account or summary of receipts and payments.

(3) Paragraph (2) applies to the following—

    (a)    rule 3.63 (administrator's intention to resign);

    (b)    rule 6.25 (liquidator's resignation and replacement);

    (c)    rule 7.61 (liquidator's resignation);

    (d)    rule 18.3 (contents of progress report); and

    (e)    rule 18.14 (contents of final account (winding up) and final report (bankruptcy)).

**Derivation**—This rule derived from the Insolvency Rules 1986, SI 1986/1925, r 4.49F.

**[2.983]**

**18.11 Voluntary winding up: reporting arrangement under section 110**

(1)   This rule applies where in a voluntary winding up there has been an arrangement under section 110 and a distribution to members has taken place under section 110(2) or (4).

(2)   In any account or summary of receipts and payments which is required to be included in an account or report prepared under a section or rule listed in paragraph (3) the liquidator must—

    (a)    state the estimated value during the period to which the account or report relates of—

        (i)    the property transferred to the transferee,

        (ii)    the property received from the transferee, and

        (iii)    the property distributed to members under section 110(2) or (4); and

    (b)    provide details of the basis of the valuation as a note to the account or summary of receipts and payments.

(3)   Paragraph (2) applies to the following—

    (a)    section 92A and rule 18.7 (members' voluntary winding up: progress report to company at year's end);

    (b)    section 94 and rule 18.14 (members' voluntary winding up: final account prior to dissolution);

    (c)    section 104A (creditors' voluntary winding up: progress report to company and creditors at year's end);

    (d)    section 106 and rules 6.28 and 18.14 (creditors' voluntary winding up: final account prior to dissolution).

**Derivation**—This rule derived from the Insolvency Rules 1986, SI 1986/1925, r 4.49F.

**General note**—Section 110 covers the situation where a liquidator in a member's voluntary liquidation is proposing to sell the company's business to another company and the members of the first company are to receive shares or other securities in the latter company as compensation.

**[2.984]**

**18.12 Members' voluntary winding up: reporting distribution to members other than under section 110**

(1)   This rule applies where in a members' voluntary winding up there has been a distribution of property to members in its existing form other than under an arrangement under section 110.

(2)   In any account or summary of receipts and payments which is required to be included in an account or report prepared under a section or rule listed in paragraph (3) the liquidator must—

    (a)    state the estimated value of the property distributed to the members of the company during the period to which the account or report relates; and

    (b)    provide details of the basis of the valuation as a note to the account or summary of receipts and payments.

(3)   Paragraph (2) applies to the following—

    (a)    section 92A (progress report);

    (b)    section 94 (final account prior to dissolution);

    (c)    rule 5.6 (liquidator's resignation).

**Derivation**—This rule derived from the Insolvency Rules 1986, SI 1986/1925, r 4.49G.

**[2.985]**

**18.13 Bankruptcy proceedings: reporting distribution of property to creditors under section 326**

(1)   This rule applies in bankruptcy where there has been a distribution of property to creditors under section 326.

(2)   In an account or report which the trustee is required to prepare under a section or rule listed in paragraph (3) the trustee must—

    (a)    state the estimated value of the property distributed among the creditors during the period to which the account or report relates; and

    (b)    provide details of the basis of the valuation in a note to the account or report.

(3)   Paragraph (2) applies to the following—

    (a)    section 331 (final report to creditors in bankruptcy);

    (b)    rule 10.77 (consideration of appointment of replacement trustee); and

    (c)    Chapters 2 and 3 of this Part.

**Derivation**—This rule derived from the Insolvency Rules 1986, SI 1986/1925, r 6.78D.

## CHAPTER 3

### FINAL ACCOUNTS IN WINDING UP AND FINAL REPORTS IN BANKRUPTCY

**[2.986]**

**Note**

[Note: a document required by the Act or these Rules must also contain the standard contents set out in Part 1.]

**[2.987]**

**18.14   Contents of final account (winding up) and final report (bankruptcy)**

(1)   The liquidator's final account under section 94, 106 or 146 or the trustee's final report under section 331 must contain an account of the liquidator's administration of the winding up or of the trustee's administration of the bankruptcy including—

    (a)    a summary of the office-holder's receipts and payments, including details of the office-holder's remuneration and expenses; and

    (b)    details of the basis fixed for the office-holder's remuneration.

(2)   The liquidator's final account under section 106 or 146(1)(a) must also include a statement as to the amount paid to unsecured creditors by virtue of section 176A.

(3)   The final account or report to creditors or members must also contain—

    (a)    details of the remuneration charged and expenses incurred by the office-holder during the period since the last progress report (if any);

    (b)    a description of the things done by the office-holder in that period in respect of which the remuneration was charged and the expenses incurred; and

    (c)    a summary of the receipts and payments during that period.

(4)   If the basis of the office-holder's remuneration had not been fixed by the date to which the last progress report was made up, the final account or report must also include details of the remuneration charged in the period of any preceding progress report in which details of remuneration were not included.

(5)   Where the basis of remuneration has been fixed as a set amount, it is sufficient for the office-holder to state that amount and to give details of the expenses charged within the period in question.

**Derivation**—This rule derived from the Insolvency Rules 1986, SI 1986/1925, rr 4.125, 4.126, 4.126A, 4.49D, 6.78B.

CHAPTER 4

REMUNERATION AND EXPENSES IN ADMINISTRATION, WINDING UP AND BANKRUPTCY

**[2.988]**

Note
[Note: a document required by the Act or these Rules must also contain the standard contents set out in Part 1.]

General note—See ss 94, 106, 146 and 331 and the comments relating to them.

**[2.989]**

**18.15  Application of Chapter**
(1)   This Chapter applies to the remuneration of—
    (a)    an administrator;
    (a)    a liquidator; and
    (b)    a trustee in bankruptcy.
(2)   This Chapter does not apply to the remuneration of a provisional liquidator or an interim receiver.

**[2.990]**

**18.16  Remuneration: principles**
(1)   An administrator, liquidator or trustee in bankruptcy is entitled to receive remuneration for services as office-holder.
(2)   The basis of remuneration must be fixed—
    (a)    as a percentage of the value of—
        (i)    the property with which the administrator has to deal, or
        (ii)    the assets which are realised, distributed or both realised and distributed by the liquidator or trustee;
    (b)    by reference to the time properly given by the office-holder and the office-holder's staff in attending to matters arising in the administration, winding up or bankruptcy; or
    (c)    as a set amount.
(3)   The basis of remuneration may be one or a combination of the bases set out in paragraph (2) and different bases or percentages may be fixed in respect of different things done by the office-holder.
(4)   Where an office-holder, other than in a members' voluntary winding up, proposes to take all or any part of the remuneration on the basis set out in paragraph (2)(b), the office-holder must, prior to the determination of which of the bases set out in paragraph (2) are to be fixed, deliver to the creditors—
    (a)    a fees estimate; and
    (b)    details of the expenses the office-holder considers will be, or are likely to be, incurred.
(5)   The fees estimate and details of expenses given under paragraph (4) may include remuneration expected to be charged and expenses expected to be incurred if the administrator becomes the liquidator where the administration moves into winding up.
(6)   An office-holder, other than in a members' voluntary winding up, must deliver to the creditors the information required under paragraph (7) before the determination of which of the bases set out in paragraph (2) is or are to be fixed, unless the information has already been delivered under paragraph (4).
(7)   The information the office-holder is required to give under this paragraph is—
    (a)    the work the office-holder proposes to undertake; and
    (b)    details of the expenses the office-holder considers will be, or are likely to be, incurred.
(8)   The matters to be determined in fixing the basis of remuneration are—

    (a)    which of the bases set out in paragraph (2) is or are to be fixed and (where appropriate) in what combination;

    (b)    the percentage or percentages (if any) to be fixed under paragraphs (2)(a) and (3);

    (c)    the amount (if any) to be set under paragraph (2)(c).

(9)   In arriving at that determination, regard must be had to the following—

    (a)    the complexity (or otherwise) of the case;

    (b)    any respects in which, in connection with the company's or bankrupt's affairs, there falls on the office-holder, any responsibility of an exceptional kind or degree;

    (c)    the effectiveness with which the office-holder appears to be carrying out, or to have carried out, the office-holder's duties; and

    (d)    the value and nature of the property with which the office-holder has to deal.

(10)  A proposed liquidator in respect of a creditors' voluntary winding up may deliver to the creditors the information required by paragraphs (4) or (6) before becoming liquidator in which case that person is not required to deliver that information again if that person is appointed as liquidator.

**Derivation**—This rule derived from the Insolvency Rules 1986, SI 1986/1925, rr 2.106, 4.127, 4.148A, 6.138.

**General note**—This provision should be read in conjunction with Part 6 of the *Practice Direction – Insolvency Proceedings* (July 2020) [2020] BPIR 1211 and Statement of Insolvency Practice SIP 9 (remuneration of insolvency office-holders). The latest version of SIP 9 is entitled 'Payments to insolvency office holders and their associates from an estate' and is effective from 1 April 2021. The SIPs can be found at Appendix 1 of this work.

In theory, liquidators have no entitlement to remuneration until the liquidation is completed, but, especially if the winding up is protracted, a liquidator will commonly draw interim fees from realised assets. Liquidators are unable to claim remuneration in relation to work which either falls outside the ambit of their duties, or was not necessary: *Reiter Bros Exploratory Drilling Pty Ltd* (1994) 12 ACLC 430 at 436. Further, no claim can be made for work done or costs incurred because liquidators have not exercised a reasonable amount of skill: *Re Silver Valley Mines* (1882) 21 ChD 381 at 392.

The remuneration of the liquidator is payable from the company's assets as part of the expenses of winding up, but if there are insufficient assets to pay the expenses of winding up, the liquidator is not permitted to take his or her remuneration and expenses before paying other expenses that are given priority in r 6.42(4) (in a voluntary winding up) and r 7.108(4) (in a compulsory winding up): *Re Salters Hall School Ltd (in liquidation)* [1998] 1 BCLC 401, [1998] BCC 503. While the court has a discretion as to the order in which the expenses of winding up are to be paid (ss 112 and 156), the power will only be exercised in exceptional circumstances, in order to permit the liquidator to take or retain his or her remuneration in priority to other expenses which would normally rank ahead of remuneration: *Re Linda Marie Ltd (in liquidation)* (1988) 4 BCC 463 at 472.

'Fees estimate'—Since 1 October 2015 liquidators have been required to provide to the creditors a fee estimate, where their work is done on a time basis and so that the creditors have some idea as to the likely cost of the liquidation, and details of the anticipated expenses prior to the setting of that basis for remuneration.

## [2.991]

### 18.17 Remuneration of joint office-holders

Where there are joint office-holders it is for them to agree between themselves how the remuneration payable should be apportioned; and any dispute arising between them may be referred—

    (a)    to the committee, to the creditors (by a decision procedure) or (in a members' voluntary winding up) the company in general meeting, for settlement by resolution; or

    (b)    to the court, for settlement by order.

**Derivation**—This rule derived from the Insolvency Rules 1986, SI 1986/1925, rr 2.106(7), 4.128(2), 6.139(2).

**Joint liquidators**—While this is not usually an issue, as in most cases where there are joint office-holders they are members of the same firm, if there is a problem, and a court decides the dispute, it is likely to decide to apportion the fees equally: *Re Langham Hotel Co* (1869) 20 LT 163.

## [2.992]

### 18.18 Remuneration: procedure for initial determination in an administration

(1) This rule applies to the determination of the officer-holder's remuneration in an administration.

(2) It is for the committee to determine the basis of remuneration.

(3) If the committee fails to determine the basis of the remuneration or there is no committee then the basis of remuneration must be fixed by a decision of the creditors by a decision procedure except in a case under paragraph (4).

(4) Where the administrator has made a statement under paragraph 52(1)(b) of Schedule B1 that there are insufficient funds for distribution to unsecured creditors other than out of the prescribed part and either there is no committee, or the committee fails to determine the basis of remuneration, the basis of the administrator's remuneration may be fixed by—

    (a)    the consent of each of the secured creditors; or

    (b)    if the administrator has made or intends to make a distribution to preferential creditors—

        (i)    the consent of each of the secured creditors, and

        (ii)    a decision of the preferential creditors in a decision procedure.

**Derivation**—This rule derived from the Insolvency Rules 1986, SI 1986/1925, rr 2.106, 2.106(5A).

**Amendments**—SI 2017/366.

## [2.993]

### 18.19 Remuneration: procedure for initial determination in a members' voluntary winding up

In a members' voluntary winding up, it is for the company in general meeting to determine the basis of remuneration.

**Derivation**—This rule derived from the Insolvency Rules 1986, SI 1986/1925, r 4.148A.

## [2.994]

### 18.20 Remuneration: procedure for initial determination in a creditors' voluntary winding up or a winding up by the court

(1) This rule applies to the determination of the office-holder's remuneration in a creditors' voluntary winding up or a winding up by the court.

(2) It is for the committee to determine the basis of remuneration.

(3) If the committee fails to determine the basis of remuneration or there is no committee then the basis of remuneration may be fixed by a decision of the creditors by a decision procedure.

(4) However where an administrator becomes liquidator in either of the following two cases the basis of remuneration fixed under rule 18.18 for the administrator is treated as having been fixed for the liquidator, and paragraphs (2) and (3) do not apply.

(5) The two cases are where—

    (a)    a company which is in administration moves into winding up under paragraph 83 of Schedule B1 and the administrator becomes the liquidator; and

    (b)    a winding-up order is made immediately upon the appointment of an administrator ceasing to have effect and the court under section 140(1) appoints as liquidator the person whose appointment as administrator has ceased to have effect.

**Derivation**—This rule derived from the Insolvency Rules 1986, SI 1986/1925, r 4.127.

**General note**—If one of two administrators of a company becomes the liquidator and he or she is joined by a new appointee, it is not necessary to obtain fresh creditor approval to fix remuneration of the liquidators, for if the administrators' remuneration was fixed under r 2.106 of the 1986 Rules (restated in r 18.16) the liquidators' remuneration is deemed to be fixed under r 4.127(5A) of the 1986 Rules (restated at sub-rules (4) and (5) of r 18.20): *Re World Design and Trade Co Ltd* ([2015] Lexis Citation 250, Chief Registrar Baister, 9 June 2015).

## [2.995]

### 18.21 Remuneration: procedure for initial determination in a bankruptcy

(1) This rule applies to the determination of the office-holder's remuneration in a bankruptcy.

(2) It is for the committee to determine the basis of remuneration.

(3) If the committee fails to determine the basis of the remuneration or there is no committee then the basis of the remuneration may be fixed by a decision of the creditors by a decision procedure.

**Derivation**—This rule derived from the Insolvency Rules 1986, SI 1986/1925, r 6.138.

## [2.996]

### 18.22 Application of scale fees where creditors fail to fix the basis of the office-holder's remuneration

(1) This rule applies where in a winding up by the court or bankruptcy, the liquidator or trustee—

    (a)    has requested the creditors to fix the basis of remuneration under rule 18.20(3) or 18.21(3) as applicable and the creditors have not done so; or

    (b)    in any event if the basis of remuneration is not fixed by the creditors within 18 months after the date of the liquidator's or trustee's appointment.

(2) The liquidator or trustee is entitled to such sum as is arrived at (subject to paragraph (3)) by—

    (a)    applying the realisation scale set out in Schedule 11 to the moneys received by the liquidator or trustee from the realisation of the assets of the company or bankrupt (including any Value Added Tax on the realisation but after deducting any sums paid to secured creditors in respect of their securities and any sums spent out of money received in carrying on the business of the company or bankrupt); and

    (b)    adding to the sum arrived at under sub-paragraph (a) such sum as is arrived at by applying the distribution scale set out in Schedule 11 to the value of assets distributed to creditors of the company or bankrupt (including payments made in respect of preferential debts) and to contributories.

(3) In a bankruptcy that part of the trustee's remuneration calculated under paragraph (2) by reference to the realisation scale must not exceed such sum as is arrived at by applying the realisation scale to such part of the bankrupt's assets as are required to pay—

    (a)    the bankruptcy debts (including any interest payable by virtue of section 328(4)) to the extent required to be paid by these Rules (ignoring those debts paid otherwise than out of the proceeds of the realisation of the bankrupt's assets or which have been secured to the satisfaction of the court);

    (b)    the expenses of the bankruptcy other than—

        (i)    fees or the remuneration of the official receiver, and

        (ii)    any sums spent out of money received in carrying on the business of the bankrupt;

    (c)    fees payable by virtue of any order made under section 415; and

    (d)    the remuneration of the official receiver.

**Derivation**—This rule derived from the Insolvency Rules 1986, SI 1986/1925, rr 4.127A, 6.138A.

**General note**—Schedule 11 sets out the percentage charge that can be made in relation to the value of assets realised and distributed.

**[2.997]**

### 18.23 Remuneration: application to the court to fix the basis

(1)   If the basis of the administrator's remuneration or the liquidator's remuneration in a voluntary winding up is not fixed under rules 18.18 to 18.20 (as applicable) then the administrator or liquidator must apply to the court for it to be fixed.

(2)   Before making such an application the liquidator or administrator must attempt to fix the basis in accordance with rules 18.18 to 18.20.

(3)   An application under this rule may not be made more than 18 months after the date of the administrator's or liquidator's appointment.

(4)   In a members' voluntary winding up—

(a)   the liquidator must deliver at least 14 days' notice of such an application to the company's contributories, or such one or more of them as the court may direct; and

(b)   the contributories may nominate one or more of their number to appear, or be represented, and to be heard on the application.

**Derivation**—This rule derived from the Insolvency Rules 1986, SI 1986/1925, rr 2.106(6), 4.127(7), 4.148A(6).

**General note**—In *Re Brilliant Independent Media Specialists Ltd, Maxwell v Brookes* [2014] BPIR 1395 Registrar Jones considered an application by former joint administrators under r 2.106 of the IR 1986 (replaced by r 18.16) for the fixing by the court of their remuneration following the refusal of the respondent creditors' committee to pay part of that remuneration. The joint administrators had been appointed for a short administration of 6 months. The creditors' committee was keen for the joint administrators to complete the administration as quickly as possible so as to allow liquidators to be appointed. The creditors' committee's position was that it had never anticipated the amount of work for which the joint administrators would subsequently claim on a time cost basis; it had approved fees from the date of the joint administrators' appointment in the sum of £180,173 together with pre-administration costs of £32,806.91, but would not agree further fees. The registrar held that, although the views of the creditors' committee were relevant to the conduct of the administration and thus the issue of the administrators' remuneration, the question of the conduct of the administration came down to and depended on the decisions of the office-holders. It did not follow that absence of creditors' committee approval for the work in issue barred the court from making an order fixing remuneration for that work. In fixing remuneration, the court was required to consider the purposes of the administration, the scope of the approved proposals and the duties and responsibilities of the administrators. The court also referred to the need under para 20.4 of the *Practice Direction: Insolvency Proceedings* (the former 2012 version [2012] BCC 265, now replaced by para 21.4 of the *Practice Direction – Insolvency Proceedings* (July 2020) [2018] BPIR 1211) for a succinct narrative of the work done and the difficulties caused by the absence of such material.

**[2.998]**

### 18.24 Remuneration: administrator, liquidator or trustee seeking increase etc

An office-holder who considers the rate or amount of remuneration fixed to be insufficient or the basis fixed to be inappropriate may—

(a)   request the creditors to increase the rate or amount or change the basis in accordance with rules 18.25 to 18.27;

(b)   apply to the court for an order increasing the rate or amount or changing the basis in accordance with rule 18.28.

**Derivation**—This rule derived from the Insolvency Rules 1986, SI 1986/1925, rr 2.17, 4.129A, 6.140A.

**[2.999]**

**18.25 Application for an increase etc in remuneration: the general rule**

(1)   This rule applies to a request by an office-holder in accordance with rule 18.24 for an increase in the rate or amount of remuneration or a change in the basis.

(2)   Subject to the exceptions set out in rules 18.26 and 18.27, where the basis of the office-holder's remuneration has been fixed by the committee an administrator, liquidator or trustee may make such a request to the creditors for approval by a decision procedure.

Derivation—This rule derived from the Insolvency Rules 1986, SI 1986/1925, rr 2.107(1), 4.129A, 6.140A.

General note—See the general note to r 18.16.

**[2.1000]**

**18.26 First exception: administrator has made a statement under paragraph 52(1)(b) of Schedule B1**

(1)   This exception applies in an administration where—
    (a)   the basis of the administrator's remuneration has been fixed by the committee; and
    (b)   the administrator has made a statement under paragraph 52(1)(b) of Schedule B1.

(2)   A request by the administrator for an increase in the rate or amount of remuneration or a change in the basis must be approved by—
    (a)   the consent of each of the secured creditors; or
    (b)   if the administrator has made or intends to make a distribution to preferential creditors—
        (i)   the consent of each of the secured creditors, and
        (ii)   a decision of the preferential creditors in a decision procedure.

Derivation—This rule derived from the Insolvency Rules 1986, SI 1986/1925, r 2.107(2).

**[2.1001]**

**18.27 Second exception: administrator who had applied for increase etc under rule 18.24 becomes liquidator**

(1)   This exception applies in a liquidation where—
    (a)   an administrator has become the liquidator;
    (b)   the remuneration had been determined by the committee in the preceding administration;
    (c)   the basis of the liquidator's remuneration is treated under rule 18.20(4) and (5) as being that which was fixed in the administration; and
    (d)   the administrator had subsequently requested an increase under rule 18.24.

(2)   A request by the liquidator for an increase in the rate or amount of remuneration or a change in the basis may only be made by application to the court.

(3)   Rule 18.28(6) to (8) apply to such an application.

Derivation—This rule derived from the Insolvency Rules 1986, SI 1986/1925, r 4.127(5A).

**[2.1002]**

**18.28 Remuneration: recourse by administrator, liquidator or trustee to the court**

(1)   This rule applies to an application by an office-holder to the court in accordance with rule 18.24 for an increase in the rate or amount of remuneration or change in the basis.

(2)   An administrator may make such an application where the basis of the administrator's remuneration has been fixed—

(a)    by the committee and the administrator has requested that the rate or amount be increased or the basis changed by decision of the creditors (by a decision procedure), but the creditors have not changed it;

(b)    by decision of the creditors (by decision procedure); or

(c)    by the approval of either the secured creditors or the preferential creditors or both in a case where the administrator has made a statement under paragraph 52(1)(b) of Schedule B1.

(3) A liquidator may make such an application where the basis of the liquidator's remuneration has been fixed—

(a)    by the committee, and the liquidator has requested that the rate or amount be increased or the basis changed by decision of the creditors (by a decision procedure), but the creditors have not changed it;

(b)    by decision of the creditors (by a decision procedure);

(c)    under rule 18.20(4) and (5) or 18.22; or

(d)    in a members' voluntary winding up, by the company in general meeting.

(4) A trustee may make such an application where the trustee's remuneration has been fixed—

(a)    by the committee and the trustee has requested that the amount be increased or the basis changed by decision of the creditors (by a decision procedure), but the creditors have not changed it;

(b)    by decision of the creditors (by a decision procedure); or

(c)    under rule 18.22.

(5) Where an application is made under paragraph (2)(c), the administrator must deliver notice to each of the creditors whose approval was sought under rule 18.18(4).

(6) The office-holder must deliver a notice of the application at least 14 days before the hearing as follows—

(a)    in an administration, a creditors' voluntary winding up, a winding up by the court or a bankruptcy—

    (i)    to the members of the committee, or

    (ii)    if there is no committee to such one or more of the creditors as the court may direct;

(b)    in a members' voluntary winding up, to the company's contributories, or such one or more of them as the court may direct.

(7) The committee, the creditors or the contributories (as the case may be) may nominate one or more of their number to appear or be represented and to be heard on the application.

(8) The court may, if it appears to be a proper case (including in a members' voluntary winding up), order the costs of the office-holder's application, including the costs of any member of the committee appearing or being represented on it, or of any creditor or contributory so appearing or being represented on it, to be paid as an expense of the estate.

**Derivation**—This rule derived from the Insolvency Rules 1986, SI 1986/1925, rr 2.108, 4.130, 6.141.

**General note**—In having recourse to the court it is incumbent on the office-holder to explain why, and in what way, the remuneration previously awarded is insufficient, and then to demonstrate to the court that an increase in remuneration was deserved: *Re Tony Rowse NMC Ltd* [1996] 2 BCLC 225, [1996] BCC 196.

## [2.1003]

### 18.29 Remuneration: review at request of administrator, liquidator or trustee

(1) Where, after the basis of the office-holder's remuneration has been fixed, there is a material and substantial change in the circumstances which were taken into account in fixing it, the office-holder may request that the basis be changed.

(2) The request must be made—

(a)    to the company, where in a members' voluntary liquidation the company fixed the basis in general meeting;

(b)    to the committee, where the committee fixed the basis;

(c)    to the creditors or a particular class of creditors where the creditors or that class of creditors fixed the basis;

(d)    by application to the court, where the court fixed the basis;

(e)    to the committee if there is one and otherwise to the creditors where, in a winding up or bankruptcy, the remuneration was determined under rule 18.22.

(3)   The preceding provisions of this Chapter which apply to the fixing of the office-holder's remuneration apply to a request for a change as appropriate.

(4)   However the exception in rule 18.27 which would require such an application to be made to the court in the circumstances there set out does not apply.

(5)   Any change in the basis of remuneration applies from the date of the request under paragraph (2) and not for any earlier period.

**Derivation**—This rule derived from the Insolvency Rules 1986, SI 1986/1925, rr 2.109A, 4.131A, 6.142A.

## [2.1004]

### 18.30 Remuneration: exceeding the fee estimate

(1)   The office-holder must not draw remuneration in excess of the total amount set out in the fees estimate without approval.

(2)   The request for approval must be made—

(a)    where the committee fixed the basis, to that committee;

(b)    where the creditors or a class of creditors fixed the basis, to the creditors or that class of creditors;

(c)    where the court fixed the basis, to the court;

and rules 18.16 to 18.23 apply as appropriate.

(3)   The request for approval must specify—

(a)    the reasons why the office-holder has exceeded, or is likely to exceed, the fees estimate;

(b)    the additional work the office-holder has undertaken or proposes to undertake;

(c)    the hourly rate or rates the office-holder proposes to charge for each part of that additional work;

(d)    the time that additional work has taken or the office-holder expects that work will take;

(e)    whether the office-holder anticipates that it will be necessary to seek further approval; and

(f)    the reasons it will be necessary to seek further approval.

**Derivation**—This rule derived from the Insolvency Rules 1986, SI 1986/1925, rr 2.109AB, 4.131AB, 6.142AB.

## [2.1005]

### 18.31 Remuneration: new administrator, liquidator or trustee

(1)   This rule applies where a new administrator, liquidator or trustee is appointed in place of another.

(2)   Any decision, determination, resolution or court order in effect under the preceding provisions of this Chapter immediately before the former office-holder ceased to hold office (including any application of scale fees under rule 18.22) continues to apply in relation to the remuneration of the new office-holder until a further decision, determination, resolution or court order is made in accordance with those provisions.

**Derivation**—This rule derived from the Insolvency Rules 1986, SI 1986/1925, rr 2.109B, 4.131B, 4.148D, 6.142B.

**[2.1006]**

**18.32 Remuneration: apportionment of set fees**

(1)  This rule applies where the basis of the office-holder's remuneration is a set amount under rule 18.16(2)(c) and the office-holder ceases (for whatever reason) to hold office before the time has elapsed or the work has been completed in respect of which the amount was set.

(2)  A request or application may be made to determine what portion of the amount should be paid to the former office-holder or the former office-holder's personal representative in respect of the time which has actually elapsed or the work which has actually been done.

(3)  The request or application may be made by—

    (a)    the former office-holder or the former office-holder's personal representative within the period of 28 days beginning with the date upon which the former office-holder ceased to hold office; or

    (b)    the office-holder for the time being in office, if the former office-holder or the former office-holder's personal representative has not applied by the end of that period.

(4)  The request or application to determine the portion must be made to the relevant person being—

    (a)    the company, where the company is in members' voluntary liquidation and it fixed the basis in general meeting;

    (b)    the committee, where the committee fixed the basis;

    (c)    the creditors or a class of creditors where the creditors or that class fixed the basis;

    (d)    the court where the court fixed the basis.

(5)  In an administration where the circumstances set out in rule 18.18(4) apply the relevant person is to be determined under that paragraph.

(6)  The person making the request or application must deliver a copy of it to the office-holder for the time being or to the former office-holder or the former office-holder's personal representative, as the case may be ("the recipient").

(7)  The recipient may, within 21 days of receipt of the copy of the request or application, deliver notice of intent to make representations to the relevant person or to appear or be represented before the court on an application to the court.

(8)  No determination may be made upon the request or application until either—

    (a)    the expiry of the 21 days, or

    (b)    if the recipient delivers a notice of intent, the recipient has been given the opportunity to make representations or to appear or be represented.

(9)  Where the former office-holder or the former office-holder's personal representative (whether or not the original person making the request or application) considers that the portion so determined is insufficient that person may apply—

    (a)    to the creditors for a decision increasing the portion, in the case of a determination by the committee;

    (b)    to the court, in the case of a decision or resolution (as the case may be) of—

        (i)    the creditors (whether under paragraph (4)(c) or under sub-paragraph (a)), or

        (ii)    the company in general meeting.

(10)  Paragraphs (6) to (8) apply to an application under paragraph (9) as appropriate.

**Derivation**—This rule derived from the Insolvency Rules 1986, SI 1986/1925, rr 2.109C, 4.131C, 4.148E, 6.142C.

**[2.1007]**

**18.33 Remuneration: variation of the application of rules 18.29, 18.30 and 18.32**

(1)  This rule applies where the basis of remuneration has been fixed in accordance with rule 18.18(4) and all of the following apply—

(a)  there is now, or is likely to be, sufficient property to enable a distribution to be made to unsecured creditors other than by virtue of section 176A(2)(a); and

(b)  the administrator or liquidator in a winding up which immediately follows an administration makes a request under rule 18.29, 18.30 or 18.32.

(2)  A request under 18.29, 18.30 or 18.32, must be made—

(a)  where there is a committee, to the committee; or

(b)  where there is no committee, to the creditors for a decision by decision procedure.

**Derivation**—This rule derived from the Insolvency Rules 1986, SI 1986/1925, rr 2.109D, 4.131D.

**General note**—This rule applies where a liquidator makes a request or application under rr 18.29, 18.30 or 18.32, the basis for remuneration having previously been approved by the secured creditors.

## [2.1008]

**18.34 Remuneration and expenses: application to court by a creditor or member on grounds that remuneration or expenses are excessive**

(1)  This rule applies to an application in an administration, a winding-up or a bankruptcy made by a person mentioned in paragraph (2) on the grounds that—

(a)  the remuneration charged by the office-holder is in all the circumstances excessive;

(b)  the basis fixed for the office-holder's remuneration under rules 18.16, 18.18, 18.19, 18.20 and 18.21 (as applicable) is inappropriate; or

(c)  the expenses incurred by the office-holder are in all the circumstances excessive.

(2)  The following may make such an application for one or more of the orders set out in rule 18.36 or 18.37 as applicable—

(a)  a secured creditor,

(b)  an unsecured creditor with either—

(i)  the concurrence of at least 10% in value of the unsecured creditors (including that creditor), or

(ii)  the permission of the court, or

(c)  in a members' voluntary winding up—

(i)  members of the company with at least 10% of the total voting rights of all the members having the right to vote at general meetings of the company, or

(ii)  a member of the company with the permission of the court.

(3)  The application by a creditor or member must be made no later than eight weeks after receipt by the applicant of the progress report under rule 18.3, or final report or account under rule 18.14 which first reports the charging of the remuneration or the incurring of the expenses in question ("the relevant report").

**Derivation**—This rule derived from the Insolvency Rules 1986, SI 1986/1925, rr 2.109, 4.131, 4.148C, 6.142.

**General note**—An application under this rule must be made in a timely manner, although the court has power to extend time in appropriate cases (*Re Birdi (in bankruptcy)* [2019] EWHC 291 (Ch), [2019] BPIR 498 at [69]–[70]).

In exercising its power of review, the court is not to be influenced by the level of remuneration set by the liquidation committee, although it might well look expectantly for any special circumstances which would justify as large an amount as had been set: *Re Carton Ltd* (1923) 39 TLR 194. In any event each case must be considered on its merits: *Re Amalgamated Syndicate Ltd* [1901] 2 Ch 181.

In *Re Calibre Solicitors Ltd (in administration), Justice Capital Ltd v Murphy* [2015] BPIR 435 Registrar Jones held that a creditor's application to challenge an administrator's remuneration and expenses under IR 1986, r 2.109 had to relate to sums already incurred, and could not challenge future sums. Equally, a separate challenge is required with respect to each progress report made by an administrator. Challenging remuneration detailed in two progress reports required two applications. It followed that the statutory period of 8 weeks within which a challenge must be made relates to each separate report and runs from the date of receipt of each report in each case. The registrar took the view that power to extend the period existed under IR 1986, r 12A.55(2), which has been replaced by r 1.3 and Sch 5. In the circumstances justice required the exercise of discretion in granting an extension of the 8-week period under that provision.

In *Re B W Estates Ltd, Randhawa v Turpin* [2015] EWHC 517 (Ch), [2016] 1 BCLC 708, creditors of a company sought to challenge the remuneration of administrators under r 2.109 of the 1986 Rules and para 74 of Sch B1. HHJ David Cooke refused the application on the grounds that the administrators had been entitled to conclude that that statutory purpose of rescuing the company as a going concern could be achieved and, save in relation to one matter, had not acted unreasonably during the administration. The motive of the company's director in effecting the appointment of the administrators was irrelevant to the administrators' statement that the statutory purpose of administration was reasonably likely to be achieved where, in the circumstances, they were entitled to take that view. The applicants were not justified in asserting that, once appointed, the administrators should have brought the administration to an end immediately, or continued it only for the purpose of complying with their statutory obligations, such as making a report on the directors. In principle, it was appropriate for them to pursue a policy of ascertaining what the assets were and obtaining control of them, and seeking to explore whether a claim asserted against the company was a genuine liability or not, with a view to taking a decision as to how to proceed when assets were available in their hands. The Judge directed that if the level of remuneration could not be agreed between the parties then a further hearing would be required to fix it.

## [2.1009]

### 18.35 Remuneration and expenses: application to court by a bankrupt on grounds that remuneration or expenses are excessive

[Note: where a bankrupt is applying for an annulment under section 282(1)(b) the bankrupt may also make an application in respect of the trustee's remuneration or expenses. See rule 10.134.]

(1)  A bankrupt may, with the permission of the court, make an application on the grounds that—

    (a)    the remuneration charged by the office-holder is in all the circumstances excessive;

    (b)    the expenses incurred by the office-holder are in all the circumstances excessive.

(2)  The bankrupt may make such an application for one or more of the orders set out in rule 18.36(4).

(3)  The application must be made no later than eight weeks after receipt by the bankrupt of the report under rule 10.87.

(4)  The court must not give the bankrupt permission to make an application unless the bankrupt shows that—

    (a)    there is (or would be but for the remuneration or expenses in question); or

    (b)    it is likely that there will be (or would be but for the remuneration or expenses in question),

a surplus of assets to which the bankrupt would be entitled.

(5)  Paragraph (4) is without prejudice to the generality of the matters which the court may take into account in determining whether to give the bankrupt permission.

**Derivation**—This rule derived from the Insolvency Rules 1986, SI 1986/1925, r 6.142.

**General note**—It was held in *Re Singh* [2018] EWHC 3277 (Ch), [2019] BPIR 216 at [21] that there are two distinct questions in an application for permission under r 18.35: first, whether the requirements of r 18.35(4) are satisfied. This is a pre-condition. It is only if they are satisfied that the second, discretionary, question is considered: whether the court should grant permission. In this respect, Nugee J declined to lay down a prescriptive test, other than to say that permission should be granted if it is appropriate to do so having regard to all the relevant circumstances (at [34]).

Note that r 18.35 is not the only means by which a trustee's costs can be challenged where there is litigation on foot. In *Ardawa v Uppal* [2019] EWHC 1663 (Ch), [2019] BPIR 1086, the bankrupt made an unsuccessful application (and then appeal) to annul his bankruptcy. The trustee argued that the legal costs were payable out of the estate and governed exclusively by rr 10.148–10.149, with the bankrupt's right of challenge determined by r 18.35, and further that the court had no jurisdiction to assess the trustee's costs of the application and appeal. That submission was roundly rejected. Roth J held that the court which heard and determined the appeal has jurisdiction to address the amount of costs which the trustee seeks to recover for his costs of that appeal, whether by summary or detailed assessment.

## [2.1010]

### 18.36 Applications under rules 18.34 and 18.35 where the court has given permission for the application

(1) This rule applies to applications made with permission under rules 18.34 and 18.35.

(2) Where the court has given permission, it must fix a venue for the application to be heard.

(3) The applicant must, at least 14 days before the hearing, deliver to the office-holder a notice stating the venue and accompanied by a copy of the application and of any evidence on which the applicant intends to rely.

(4) If the court considers the application to be well-founded, it must make one or more of the following orders—

   (a) an order reducing the amount of remuneration which the office-holder is entitled to charge;

   (b) an order reducing any fixed rate or amount;

   (c) an order changing the basis of remuneration;

   (d) an order that some or all of the remuneration or expenses in question is not to be treated as expenses of the administration, winding up or bankruptcy;

   (e) an order for the payment of the amount of the excess of remuneration or expenses or such part of the excess as the court may specify by—

       (i) the administrator or liquidator or the administrator's or liquidator's personal representative to the company, or

       (ii) the trustee or the trustee's personal representative to such person as the court may specify as property comprised in the bankrupt's estate;

   (f) any other order that it thinks just.

(5) An order under paragraph (4)(b) or (c) may only be made in respect of periods after the period covered by the relevant report.

(6) Unless the court orders otherwise the costs of the application must be paid by the applicant, and are not payable as an expense of the administration, winding up or bankruptcy.

**Derivation**—This rule derived from the Insolvency Rules 1986, SI 1986/1925, rr 2.109, 4.131, 4.148C, 6.142.

## [2.1011]

### 18.37 Applications under rule 18.34 where the court's permission is not required for the application

(1) On receipt of an application under rule 18.34 for which the court's permission is not required, the court may, if it is satisfied that no sufficient cause is shown for the application, dismiss it without giving notice to any party other than the applicant.

(2) Unless the application is dismissed, the court must fix a venue for it to be heard.

(3) The applicant must, at least 14 days before any hearing, deliver to the office-holder a notice stating the venue with a copy of the application and of any evidence on which the applicant intends to rely.

(4) If the court considers the application to be well-founded, it must make one or more of the following orders—

   (a) an order reducing the amount of remuneration which the office-holder is entitled to charge;

   (b) an order reducing any fixed rate or amount;

   (c) an order changing the basis of remuneration;

    (d)    an order that some or all of the remuneration or expenses in question be treated as not being expenses of the administration or winding up or bankruptcy;

    (e)    an order for the payment of the amount of the excess of remuneration or expenses or such part of the excess as the court may specify by—

        (i)    the administrator or liquidator or the administrator's or liquidator's personal representative to the company, or

        (ii)    the trustee or the trustee's personal representative to such person as the court may specify as property comprised in the bankrupt's estate;

    (f)    any other order that it thinks just.

(5)   An order under paragraph (4)(b) or (c) may only be made in respect of periods after the period covered by the relevant report.

(6)   Unless the court orders otherwise the costs of the application must be paid by the applicant, and are not payable as an expense of the administration or as winding up or bankruptcy.

**Derivation**—This rule derived from the Insolvency Rules 1986, SI 1986/1925, rr 2.109, 4.131, 4.148C, 6.142.

## [2.1012]

### 18.38 Remuneration of a liquidator or trustee who realises assets on behalf of a secured creditor

(1)   A liquidator or trustee who realises assets on behalf of a secured creditor is entitled to such sum by way of remuneration as is arrived at as follows, unless the liquidator or trustee has agreed otherwise with the secured creditor—

    (a)    in a winding up—

        (i)    where the assets are subject to a charge which when created was a mortgage or a fixed charge, such sum as is arrived at by applying the realisation scale in Schedule 11 to the monies received in respect of the assets realised (including any sums received in respect of Value Added Tax on them but after deducting any sums spent out of money received in carrying on the business of the company),

        (ii)    where the assets are subject to a charge which when created was a floating charge such sum as is arrived at by—

            (aa)    first applying the realisation scale in Schedule 11 to monies received by the liquidator from the realisation of the assets (including any Value Added Tax on the realisation but ignoring any sums received which are spent in carrying on the business of the company),

            (bb)    then by adding to the sum arrived at under sub-paragraph (a)(ii)(aa) such sum as is arrived at by applying the distribution scale in Schedule 11 to the value of the assets distributed to the holder of the charge and payments made in respect of preferential debts; or

    (b)    in a bankruptcy such sum as is arrived at by applying the realisation scale in Schedule 11 to the monies received in respect of the assets realised (including any Value Added Tax on them).

(2)   The sum to which the liquidator or trustee is entitled must be taken out of the proceeds of the realisation.

**Derivation**—This rule derived from the Insolvency Rules 1986, SI 1986/1925, rr 4.127B, 6.139.

## PART 19 DISCLAIMER IN WINDING UP AND BANKRUPTCY

**[2.1013]**

**Note**

[Note: a document required by the Act or these Rules must also contain the standard contents set out in Part 1.]

General comment on Part 15—This Part deals with the practice and procedure that relates to the power of only a liquidator or a trustee in bankruptcy to disclaim property. As disclaimer can be employed by either a liquidator or a trustee the rules use the neutral term 'office-holder.'

Under the previous rules there were separate parts that dealt with liquidation and bankruptcy when it came to disclaimer, but now this Part addresses both, with appropriate distinctions between disclaimer in liquidation and disclaimer in bankruptcy being made, where appropriate.

Reference should be made to ss 178–182 (liquidations) and ss 315–321 (bankruptcies) as well as the notes that relate to those sections.

Disclaimer is not permitted in relation to other formal insolvency regimes.

**[2.1014]**

### 19.1 Application of this Part

This Part applies to disclaimer by a liquidator under section 178 (winding up) and by a trustee under section 315 (bankruptcy).

Derivation—This rule derived from the Insolvency Rules 1986, SI 1986/1925, rr 4.187, 6.178.

**[2.1015]**

### 19.2 Notice of disclaimer (sections 178 and 315)

(1)   An office-holder's notice of disclaimer of property under section 178 (winding up) or section 315 (bankruptcy) must (as appropriate)—

    (a)   have the title—

        (i)    "Notice of disclaimer under section 178 of the Insolvency Act 1986" (in the case of a winding up), or

        (ii)   "Notice of disclaimer under section 315 of the Insolvency Act 1986" (in the case of a bankruptcy);

    (b)   identify the company or the bankrupt;

    (c)   identify and provide contact details for the office-holder;

    (d)   contain such particulars of the property disclaimed as will enable it to be easily identified;

    (e)   state—

        (i)    that the liquidator of the company disclaims all the company's interest in the property, or

        (ii)   that the trustee of the bankrupt's estate disclaims all the bankrupt's interest in the property.

(2)   The notice must be authenticated and dated by the office-holder.

(3)   If the property consists of registered land—

    (a)   the notice must state the registered title number; and

    (b)   the office-holder must deliver a copy of the notice to the Chief Land Registrar as soon as reasonably practicable after authenticating the notice.

(4)   The liquidator must, as soon as reasonably practicable after authenticating the notice, deliver a copy of the notice to the registrar of companies.

(5)   The trustee must, as soon as reasonably practicable after authenticating the notice, file a copy of the notice—

    (a)   with the court; or

    (b)   where the bankruptcy is based on a bankruptcy application, on the bankruptcy file.

(6)   If the property consists of land or buildings the nature of the interest must be stated in the notice.

(7) The date of disclaimer for the purposes of section 178(4)(a) (winding up) or section 315(3)(a) (bankruptcy) is the date on which the liquidator or trustee authenticated the notice.

Derivation—This rule derived from the Insolvency Rules 1986, SI 1986/1925, rr 4.187, 6.178.

General note—It is important that notice be given by the office-holder of the disclaimer of property. There is no longer any prescribed form that has to be used for an office-holder to disclaim so the rule sets out what must be included in the notice of disclaimer.

## [2.1016]

### 19.3 Notice of disclaimer to interested persons (sections 178 and 315)

(1) The office-holder must deliver a copy of the notice of disclaimer within seven business days after the date of the notice to every person who (to the office-holder's knowledge)—

    (a)    claims an interest in the disclaimed property;

    (b)    is under any liability in relation to the property, not being a liability discharged by the disclaimer; and

    (c)    if the disclaimer is of an unprofitable contract, is a party to the contract or has an interest under it.

(2) If it subsequently comes to the office-holder's knowledge that a person has an interest in the disclaimed property which would have entitled that person to receive a copy of the notice under paragraph (1) then the office-holder must deliver a copy to that person as soon as reasonably practicable.

(3) If it subsequently comes to the office-holder's knowledge that a person has an interest in the disclaimed property which would have entitled that person to receive a copy of the notice under rule 19.4 or 19.5 then the office-holder must serve a copy on that person as soon as reasonably practicable.

(4) The office-holder is not required to deliver or serve a copy of a notice under paragraph (2) or (3) if—

    (a)    the office-holder is satisfied that the person has already been made aware of the disclaimer and its date, or

    (b)    the court, on the office-holder's application, orders that delivery or service of a copy is not required in the particular case.

Derivation—This rule derived from the Insolvency Rules 1986, SI 1986/1925, rr 4.188, 6.179.

General note—Under the previous rules unprofitable contracts were referred to separately in the rule to other assets but now they are combined. Furthermore pursuant to the previous rules leasehold property and dwelling houses of bankrupts were included in this rule, but now they are considered separately in the next two rules.

## [2.1017]

### 19.4 Notice of disclaimer of leasehold property (sections 179 and 317)

Where a notice of disclaimer relates to leasehold property the office-holder must serve any copies of the notice of disclaimer which are required by either section 179 (winding up) or section 317 (bankruptcy) within seven business days after the date of the notice of disclaimer.

Derivation—This rule derived from the Insolvency Rules 1986, SI 1986/1925, rr 4.188(2), 6.179(2).

## [2.1018]

### 19.5 Notice of disclaimer in respect of a dwelling house (bankruptcy) (section 318)

(1) This rule applies in a bankruptcy where the disclaimer is of property in a dwelling house.

(2) The trustee must serve any copies of the notice of disclaimer which are required by section 318 within seven business days after the date of the notice of disclaimer.

(3) A notice, or copy notice in relation to the disclaimer by a trustee of property in a dwelling house which is to be served on a person under the age of 18 may be served on the person's parent or guardian.

Derivation—This rule derived from the Insolvency Rules 1986, SI 1986/1925, r 6.179(3), (4).

## [2.1019]

### 19.6 Additional notices of disclaimer

An office-holder who is disclaiming property may at any time deliver a copy of the notice of the disclaimer to any other person whom the office-holder thinks ought, in the public interest or otherwise, to be informed of the disclaimer.

Derivation—This rule derived from the Insolvency Rules 1986, SI 1986/1925, rr 4.189, 6.180.

## [2.1020]

### 19.7 Records

The office-holder must include in the records of the insolvency a record of—

(a) the name and address of each person to whom a copy of the notice of disclaimer has been delivered or served under rules 19.3 to 19.6, with the nature of the person's interest;

(b) the date on which the copy of the notice was delivered to or served on that person;

(c) the date on which the liquidator delivered a copy of the notice to the registrar of companies;

(d) the date on which the trustee filed a copy of the notice with the court or on the bankruptcy file; and

(e) if applicable, the date on which a copy of the notice was delivered to the Chief Land Registrar.

Derivation—This rule derived from the Insolvency Rules 1986, SI 1986/1925, rr 4.190A, 6.181A.

## [2.1021]

### 19.8 Application for permission to disclaim in bankruptcy (section 315(4))

(1) This rule applies where section 315(4) requires the trustee to obtain the court's permission to disclaim property claimed for the bankrupt's estate under section 307 or 308.

(2) The trustee may apply for permission without notice to any other party.

(3) The application must be accompanied by a report—

(a) containing such particulars of the property as will enable it to be easily identified;

(b) setting out the reasons why, the property having been claimed for the bankrupt's estate, the trustee is now applying for the court's permission to disclaim it; and

(c) stating the persons (if any) who have been informed of the trustee's intention to make the application.

(4) If the report says that any person has consented to the disclaimer, a copy of that consent must accompany the report.

(5) The court may grant the permission, and may, before doing so—

(a) order that notice of the application be delivered to all such persons who, if the property is disclaimed, will be entitled to apply for a vesting or other order under section 320; and

(b) fix a venue for the hearing of the application.

Derivation—This rule derived from the Insolvency Rules 1986, SI 1986/1925, r 6.182.

**[2.1022]**

**19.9 Application by interested party for decision on disclaimer (sections 178(5) and 316)**

(1)   This rule applies where an interested party makes an application under section 178(5) (winding up) or section 316 (bankruptcy) to the office-holder in respect of any property.

(2)   The applicant must deliver the application to the office-holder and must provide proof of delivery in accordance with rule 1.52 if requested.

(3)   If in a bankruptcy the trustee cannot disclaim the property concerned without the court's permission and the trustee applies for permission within the period of 28 days mentioned in section 316(1)(b), then the court must extend the time allowed for giving notice of disclaimer to a date not earlier than the date fixed for hearing the application.

> **Derivation**—This rule derived from the Insolvency Rules 1986, SI 1986/1925, rr 4.191A, 6.183.
>
> **General note**—The Insolvency Service provides a template for the use of an interested party: https://www.gov.uk/government/publications/rule-199-application-by-interested-party-for-decisio n-on-disclaimer-company-winding-up.
>
> **'interested party'**—Birss J held that a bankrupt is not 'a person interested in the property' for the purposes of s 316, and is accordingly unable to make a valid application, in *Frosdick v Fox* [2017] EWHC 1737 (Ch), [2018] 1 WLR 38, [2017] BPIR 1194 at [61]–[65].

**[2.1023]**

**19.10 Disclaimer presumed valid and effective**

Any disclaimer of property by the office-holder is presumed valid and effective, unless it is proved that the office-holder has been in breach of the office-holder's duties relating to the giving of notice of disclaimer or otherwise under sections 178 to 180 (winding up) or sections 315 to 319 (bankruptcy), or under this Part.

> **Derivation**—This rule derived from the Insolvency Rules 1986, SI 1986/1925, rr 4.193, 6.185.

**[2.1024]**

**19.11 Application for exercise of court's powers under section 181 (winding up) or section 320 (bankruptcy)**

(1)   This rule applies to an application under section 181 (winding up) or section 320 (bankruptcy) for a court order to vest or deliver disclaimed property.

(2)   The application must be made within three months of the applicant becoming aware of the disclaimer, or of the applicant receiving a copy of the office-holder's notice of disclaimer delivered under rule 19.3 to 19.6, whichever is the earlier.

(3)   The applicant must file with the application a witness statement stating—

    (a)    whether the application is made under—

        (i)     section 181(2)(a) (claim of interest in the property),

        (ii)    section 181(2)(b) (liability not discharged),

        (iii)   section 320(2)(a) (claim of interest in the property),

        (iv)   section 320(2)(b) (liability not discharged), or

        (v)    section 320(2)(c) (occupation of a dwelling-house);

    (b)    the date on which the applicant received a copy of the office-holder's notice of disclaimer, or otherwise became aware of the disclaimer; and

    (c)    the grounds of the application and the order sought.

(4)   The court must fix a venue for hearing the application.

(5)   The applicant must, not later than five business days before the date fixed, deliver to the office-holder notice of the venue, accompanied by copies of the application and the filed witness statement.

(6)   On hearing the application, the court may give directions as to any other persons to whom notice of the application and the grounds on which it is made should be delivered.

(7)   The court must deliver sealed copies of any order made on the application to the applicant and the office-holder.

(8)   If the property disclaimed is of a leasehold nature, or in a bankruptcy is property in a dwelling house, and section 179 (winding up), 317 or 318 (bankruptcy) applies to suspend the effect of the disclaimer, the court's order must include a direction giving effect to the disclaimer.

(9)   However, paragraph (8) does not apply if, before the order is drawn up, other applications under section 181 (winding up) or section 320 (bankruptcy) are pending in relation to the same property.

**Derivation**—This rule derived from the Insolvency Rules 1986, SI 1986/1925, rr 4.194, 6.186.

**General note**—The application must be filed within 3 months, but the period may be extended by a court: *WH Smith Ltd v Wyndham Investments Ltd* [1994] 2 BCLC 571. For a recent case where the time was extended, see *Re Cadmus Management Ltd* [2016] EWHC 330 (Ch), [2017] BPIR 317. The application for a vesting order was, however, refused.

## PART 20   DEBTORS AND THEIR FAMILIES AT RISK OF VIOLENCE: ORDERS NOT TO DISCLOSE CURRENT ADDRESS

### [2.1025]

**Note**

[Note: a document required by the Act or these Rules must also contain the standard contents set out in Part 1.]

### [2.1026]

#### 20.1  Application of this Part and interpretation

(1)   The rules in this Part apply where disclosure or continuing disclosure of the current address or whereabouts of a debtor to other persons (whether to the public generally or to specific persons) might reasonably be expected to lead to violence against the debtor or against a person who normally resides with the debtor as a member of the debtor's family.

(2)   In this Part—

"current address" means the debtor's residential address and any address at which the debtor currently carries on business; and

"family" in the expression "debtor's family" has the same meaning in relation to a debtor other than a bankrupt as is provided by section 385(1) in respect of a bankrupt.

**Derivation**—This rule derived from the Insolvency Rules 1986, SI 1986/1925, rr 5.67(2), 5A.18(1), 6.235B(2).

### [2.1027]

#### 20.2  Proposed IVA (order for non-disclosure of current address)

(1)   This rule applies where a debtor intends to make a proposal for an IVA and has received notice of consent to act from the nominee.

(2)   The debtor may make an application for an order as set out in paragraph (4) for the non-disclosure of the debtor's current address.

(3)   The application must be accompanied by a witness statement referring to this rule and containing sufficient evidence to satisfy the court that rule 20.1(1) applies.

(4)   If the court is satisfied that the circumstances set out in rule 20.1(1) apply, the court may order that if the IVA is approved—

(a)   the debtor's current address must be omitted from—

(i)   any part of the court file of the proceedings in relation to the debtor's IVA which is open to inspection,

(ii)   the debtor's identification details required to be entered on the individual insolvency register under rule 11.14,

      (iii)    any notice or advertisement under rule 8.36 of an order under section 261 to annul the bankruptcy order where an IVA is approved; and

  (b)    where there is a requirement in these Rules to identify the debtor, the debtor's identification details must not include details of the debtor's current address.

(5)   Where the court makes such an order, it may further order that the details to be entered on the individual insolvency register must include instead such other details of the debtor's addresses or whereabouts as the court thinks just, including details of any address at which the debtor has previously resided or carried on business.

Derivation—This rule derived from the Insolvency Rules 1986, SI 1986/1925, r 5.67.

## [2.1028]

### 20.3 IVA (order for non-disclosure of current address)

(1)   This rule applies where a debtor has entered into an IVA.

(2)   The following may make an application for an order as set out in paragraph (4) for the non-disclosure of the debtor's current address—

  (a)    the debtor;

  (b)    the supervisor;

  (c)    the official receiver (whether acting as a supervisor or otherwise); and

  (d)    the Secretary of State.

(3)   The application must be accompanied by a witness statement referring to this rule and containing sufficient evidence to satisfy the court that rule 20.1(1) applies.

(4)   If the court is satisfied that the circumstances set out in rule 20.1(1) apply, the court may order that—

  (a)    the debtor's current address must be omitted from—

      (i)    any part of the court file of the proceedings in relation to the debtor which is open to inspection,

      (ii)    the debtor's identification details entered or required to be entered on the individual insolvency register under rule 11.14, and

      (iii)    any notice or advertisement under rule 8.35 of an order under section 261 to annul the bankruptcy order where an IVA is approved; and

  (b)    where there is a requirement in these Rules to identify the debtor, the debtor's identification details must not include the debtor's current address.

(5)   Where the court makes such an order, it may further order that the details to be entered on the individual insolvency register must include instead such other details of the debtor's addresses or whereabouts as the court thinks just, including details of any address at which the debtor has previously resided or carried on business.

Derivation—This rule derived from the Insolvency Rules 1986, SI 1986/1925, r 5.67.

## [2.1029]

### 20.4 Debt relief application (order for non-disclosure of current address)

(1)   This rule applies where a debtor intends to make a debt relief application and has been issued with a unique identifier for the application.

(2)   The debtor may make an application for an order as set out in paragraph (4) for the non-disclosure of the debtor's current address.

(3)   The application must be accompanied by a witness statement referring to this rule and containing sufficient evidence to satisfy the court that rule 20.1(1) applies.

(4)   If the court is satisfied that the circumstances set out in rule 20.1(1) apply, the court may order that if a debt relief order is made—

  (a)    the debtor's current address must be omitted from—

      (i)    any part of the court file of the proceedings in relation to the debtor which is open to inspection, and

        (ii)    the debtor's identification details required to be entered on the individual insolvency register under rule 11.18; and

    (b)    where there is a requirement in these Rules to identify the debtor, the debtor's identification must not include the debtor's current address.

(5)   Where the court makes such an order, it may further order that the details to be entered on the individual insolvency register must include instead such other details of the debtor's addresses or whereabouts as the court thinks just, including details of any address at which the debtor has previously resided or carried on business.

Derivation—This rule derived from the Insolvency Rules 1986, SI 1986/1925, r 5A.18.

## [2.1030]

### 20.5 Bankruptcy application (order for non-disclosure of current address)

(1)   This rule applies where a debtor intends to make a bankruptcy application and has been issued with a unique identifier for the application.

(2)   The debtor may make an application for an order as set out in paragraph (4) for the non-disclosure of the debtor's current address.

(3)   The application must be accompanied by a witness statement referring to this rule and containing sufficient evidence to satisfy the court that rule 20.1(1) applies.

(4)   If the court is satisfied that the circumstances set out in rule 20.1(1) apply, the court may order that if a bankruptcy order is made—

    (a)    the debtor's current address must be omitted from—

        (i)    any part of the bankruptcy file which is open to inspection,

        (ii)    the details in respect of the debtor to be entered on the individual insolvency register under rule 11.16,

        (iii)    the details in respect of the debtor to be entered in the bankruptcy order; and

    (b)    where there is a requirement in these Rules to identify the debtor, the debtor's identification details must not include the debtor's current address.

(5)   Where the court makes an order under paragraph (4), it may further order that such other details of the debtor's addresses or whereabouts as the court thinks just, including details of any address at which the debtor has previously resided or carried on business, are to be included in—

    (a)    the details in respect of the debtor kept on or to be entered on the individual insolvency register under rule 11.16;

    (b)    the details in respect of the debtor included on the bankruptcy file; or

    (c)    the description of the debtor to be inserted in the bankruptcy order.

Derivation—This rule derived from the Insolvency Rules 1986, SI 1986/1925, r 6.50B.

## [2.1031]

### 20.6 Bankruptcy and debt relief proceedings (order for non-disclosure of current address)

(1)   For the purposes of this rule, "debtor" means a person subject to a bankruptcy order, a debt relief order, a bankruptcy restrictions order, a debt relief restrictions order, a bankruptcy restrictions undertaking or a debt relief restrictions undertaking.

(2)   The following may make an application for an order as set out in paragraph (4) for the non-disclosure of the debtor's current address—

    (a)    the debtor;

    (b)    the official receiver; or

    (c)    in respect of a bankruptcy order, a bankruptcy restrictions order or a bankruptcy restrictions undertaking, the trustee or the Secretary of State.

(3)   The application must be accompanied by a witness statement referring to this rule and containing sufficient evidence to satisfy the court that rule 20.1(1) applies.

(4)   If the court is satisfied that the circumstances set out in rule 20.1(1) apply, the court may order that—

- (a) the debtor's current address must be omitted from—
  - (i) any part of the court file or bankruptcy file of the proceedings in relation to the debtor which is open to inspection,
  - (ii) the debtor's identification details entered or required to be entered on the individual insolvency register under rule 11.16 (bankruptcy orders), rule 11.18 (debt relief orders), or the bankruptcy restrictions register or the debt relief restrictions register under 11.20 (as the case may be), and
  - (iii) the details in respect of the debtor to be entered in the bankruptcy order or debt relief order;
- (b) the full title of the proceedings must be amended by the omission of the debtor's current address; and
- (c) where there is a requirement in these Rules to identify the debtor, the debtor's identification details must not include the debtor's current address.

(5) Where the court makes an order under paragraph (4), it may further order that such other details of the debtor's addresses or whereabouts as the court thinks just, including details of any address at which the debtor has previously resided or carried on business, are to be included in—

- (a) the full title of any proceedings;
- (b) the details in respect of the debtor kept on or to be entered on the relevant register; or
- (c) the description of the debtor to be inserted in the bankruptcy order or the debt relief order.

**Derivation**—This rule derived from the Insolvency Rules 1986, SI 1986/1925, rr 5A.18, 6.235B.

## [2.1032]

### 20.7 Additional provisions in respect of orders under rule 20.6(4)

(1) This rule applies where the court is making an order under rule 20.6(4) in respect of a debtor who is subject to a bankruptcy order, a bankruptcy restrictions order or a bankruptcy restrictions undertaking.

(2) The court may make either or both of the following further orders—

- (a) that the details of the debtor required to be included in any notice to be gazetted or otherwise advertised must not include the debtor's current address; and.
- (b) that the details of the debtor required to be included in any such notice to be gazetted or otherwise advertised must instead of the debtor's current address include such other details of the debtor's addresses or whereabouts as the court thinks just, including details of any address at which the debtor has previously resided or carried on business.

(3) Where the court makes an order under rule 20.6(4) amending the full title of the proceedings by the omission of the debtor's current address from the description of the debtor, the official receiver—

- (a) must as soon as reasonably practicable deliver notice of it to the Chief Land Registrar, for corresponding amendment of the register; and
- (b) may cause notice of the order to be—
  - (i) gazetted, or
  - (ii) both gazetted and delivered in such other manner as the official receiver thinks fit.

(4) A notice of the amendment of the title of the proceedings which is published in accordance with paragraph (3)—

- (a) must omit the current address of the debtor;
- (b) must contain the amended title of the proceedings, and the date of the bankruptcy order; and
- (c) must not include the description under which the proceedings were previously published.

## PART 21  THE EU REGULATION

**[2.1033]**

**Note**

[Note: a document required by the Act or these Rules must also contain the standard contents set out in Part 1.]

**21.1, 21.1A**

*(Revoked)*

**Amendments**—Revoked by SI 2019/146, as from IP completion day (as defined in the European Union (Withdrawal Agreement) Act 2020, s 39(1)–(5)).

**21.2**

*(Revoked)*

**Derivation**—This rule derived from the Insolvency Rules 1986, SI 1986/1925, rr 1.31, 1.32, 2.130, 2.131, 5.62, 5.63.
**Amendments**—SI 2017/702; Revoked by SI 2019/146, as from IP completion day (as defined in the European Union (Withdrawal Agreement) Act 2020, s 39(1)–(5)).

**[2.1034]**

**Note**

[Note: "Local creditor" is defined in Article 2(11) of the EU Regulation.]

**21.3**

*(Revoked)*

**Derivation**—This rule derived from the Insolvency Rules 1986, SI 1986/1925, rr 1.33, 2.132, 5.64.
**Amendments**—SI 2017/1115; Revoked by SI 2019/146, as from IP completion day (as defined in the European Union (Withdrawal Agreement) Act 2020, s 39(1)–(5)).

**[2.1035]**

**21.4  Confirmation of creditors' voluntary winding up: application**
(1)  This rule applies where—
  (a)  a company has passed a resolution for voluntary winding up, and either—
      (i)  no declaration of solvency has been made in accordance with section 89, or
      (ii)  a declaration made under section 89—
          (aa)  has no effect by virtue of section 89(2), or
          (bb)  is treated as not having been made by virtue of section 96; or
  (b)  a company has moved from administration to creditors' voluntary winding up in accordance with paragraph 83 of Schedule B1.
(2)  The liquidator may apply to court for an order confirming the winding up as a creditors' voluntary winding up for the purposes of the EU Regulation.
(3)  The application must be supported by a witness statement made by the liquidator which must contain—
  (a)  identification details for the liquidator and the company;
  (b)  the date on which the resolution for voluntary winding up was passed;
  (c)  a statement that the application is accompanied by the documents required by paragraph (4);
  (d)  a statement that the documents required by paragraph (4)(c) and (d) are true copies of the originals; and
  (e)  a statement whether the proceedings will be COMI proceedings, establishment proceedings or proceedings to which the EU Regulation as it has effect in the law of the United Kingdom does not apply and the reasons for so stating.

(4)   The liquidator must file with the court—
- (a)   two copies of the application;
- (b)   evidence of having been appointed liquidator of the company;
- (c)   a copy of—
  - (i)   the resolution for voluntary winding up, or
  - (ii)   the notice of moving from administration to creditors' voluntary winding up sent by the administrator to the registrar of companies under paragraph 83(3) of Schedule B1; and
- (d)   a copy of—
  - (i)   the statement of affairs required by section 99 or under paragraph 47 of Schedule B1, or
  - (ii)   the information included in the administrator's statement of proposals under rule 3.35(1)(h).

**Derivation**—This rule derived from the Insolvency Rules 1986, SI 1986/1925, r 7.62(1)–(3).

**Amendments**—SI 2017/1115; SI 2017/702; SI 2019/146, as from IP completion day (as defined in the European Union (Withdrawal Agreement) Act 2020, s 39(1)–(5)).

## [2.1036]

### 21.5 Confirmation of creditors' voluntary winding up: court order

(1)   On an application under the preceding rule, the court may make an order confirming the creditors' voluntary winding up.

(2)   It may do so without a hearing.

(3)   If the court makes an order confirming the creditors' voluntary winding up, it must affix its seal to the application.

(4)   A member of the court staff may deal with an application under this rule.

**Derivation**—This rule derived from the Insolvency Rules 1986, SI 1986/1925, r 7.62(5)–(8).

### 21.6

*(Revoked)*

**Derivation**—This rule derived from the Insolvency Rules 1986, SI 1986/1925, r 7.63.

**Amendments**—Revoked by SI 2019/146, as from IP completion day (as defined in the European Union (Withdrawal Agreement) Act 2020, s 39(1)–(5)).

### 21.7

*(Revoked)*

**Derivation**—This rule derived from the Insolvency Rules 1986, SI 1986/1925, rr 1.34, 2.133, 4.231, 5.65, 6238, 6.239.

**Amendments**—Revoked by SI 2019/146, as from IP completion day (as defined in the European Union (Withdrawal Agreement) Act 2020, s 39(1)–(5)).

### 21.8

*(Revoked)*

**Derivation**—This rule derived from the Insolvency Rules 1986, SI 1986/1925, rr 2.133, 4.231, 6.238, 6.239, 7.64, 8.8.

**Amendments**—Revoked by SI 2019/146, as from IP completion day (as defined in the European Union (Withdrawal Agreement) Act 2020, s 39(1)–(5)).

*Note*

*(Revoked)*

**Amendments**—Revoked by SI 2019/146, as from IP completion day (as defined in the European Union (Withdrawal Agreement) Act 2020, s 39(1)–(5)).

### 21.9–21.17

*(Revoked)*

**Amendments**—Revoked by SI 2019/146, as from IP completion day (as defined in the European Union (Withdrawal Agreement) Act 2020, s 39(1)–(5)).

## PART 22 PERMISSION TO ACT AS DIRECTOR ETC OF COMPANY WITH A PROHIBITED NAME (SECTION 216)

### [2.1037]

**Note**

[Note: a document required by the Act or these Rules must also contain the standard contents set out in Part 1.]

**General comment on Part 22**—This Chapter covers the case where a person seeks leave to act as a director of a company with a prohibited name, as well as providing the exceptions when the prohibition concerning the use of a company name does not apply, and hence no leave is necessary. These rules are to be read with ss 216 and 217: *ESS Production Ltd (in administration) v Sully* [2005] EWCA Civ 554, [2005] 2 BCLC 547, [2005] BPIR 691 s 216(3). Sections 216 and 217 were introduced to deal with what is often known as the 'Phoenix syndrome' although the legislation and the case law is broader than that in effect.

There are three exceptions to liability being imposed on directors where a company operates with a prohibited name. These are found in rr 22.4, 22.6 and 22.7.

The Part used to be included in Part 4 of the previous rules which was the Part which addressed liquidation in general terms. Now that the Rules separate the three forms of liquidation (members' voluntary, creditors' voluntary and compulsory) and place them in three separate Parts of the Rules it was necessary to include the rules dealing with the use of a prohibited name in their own discrete Part. The Part applies to names of companies which have entered insolvent liquidation. Such companies could be in a creditors' voluntary or a compulsory liquidation.

See the notes accompanying ss 216 and 217.

Also, see A Keay, *McPherson and Keay's Law of Company Liquidation* (Sweet and Maxwell, 4th edn, 2018) at 1058–1067.

### [2.1038]

#### 22.1 Preliminary

(1) The rules in this Part—

    (a) relate to permission required under section 216 (restriction on re-use of name of company in insolvent liquidation) for a person to act as mentioned in section 216(3) in relation to a company with a prohibited name;

    (b) prescribe the cases excepted from that provision, that is to say, in which a person to whom the section applies may so act without that permission; and

    (c) apply to all windings up to which section 216 applies.

**Derivation**—This rule derived from the Insolvency Rules 1986, SI 1986/1925, r 4.226.

### [2.1039]

#### 22.2 Application for permission under section 216(3)

(1) At least 14 days' notice of any application for permission to act in any of the circumstances which would otherwise be prohibited by section 216(3) must be given by the applicant to the Secretary of State, who may—

    (a) appear at the hearing of the application; and

    (b) whether or not appearing at the hearing, make representations.

**Derivation**—This rule derived from the Insolvency Rules 1986, SI 1986/1925, r 4.227A.

### [2.1040]

#### 22.3 Power of court to call for liquidator's report

When considering an application for permission under section 216, the court may call on the liquidator, or any former liquidator, of the liquidating company for a report of the circumstances in which the company became insolvent and the extent (if any) of the applicant's apparent responsibility for its doing so.

**Derivation**—This rule derived from the Insolvency Rules 1986, SI 1986/1925, r 4.227A(2).

**[2.1041]**

**22.4 First excepted case**

(1) This rule applies where—

    (a)    a person ("the person") was within the period mentioned in section 216(1) a director, or shadow director, of an insolvent company that has gone into insolvent liquidation; and

    (b)    the person acts in all or any of the ways specified in section 216(3) in connection with, or for the purposes of, the carrying on (or proposed carrying on) of the whole or substantially the whole of the business of the insolvent company where that business (or substantially the whole of it) is (or is to be) acquired from the insolvent company under arrangements—

        (i)    made by its liquidator, or

        (ii)    made before the insolvent company entered into insolvent liquidation by an office-holder acting in relation to it as administrator, administrative receiver or supervisor of a CVA.

(2) The person will not be taken to have contravened section 216 if prior to that person acting in the circumstances set out in paragraph (1) a notice is, in accordance with the requirements of paragraph (3),—

    (a)    given by the person, to every creditor of the insolvent company whose name and address—

        (i)    is known by that person, or

        (ii)    is ascertainable by that person on the making of such enquiries as are reasonable in the circumstances; and

    (b)    published in the Gazette.

(3) The notice referred to in paragraph (2)—

    (a)    may be given and published before the completion of the arrangements referred to in paragraph (1)(b) but must be given and published no later than 28 days after their completion;

    (b)    must contain—

        (i)    identification details for the company,

        (ii)    the name and address of the person,

        (iii)    a statement that it is the person's intention to act (or, where the insolvent company has not entered insolvent liquidation, to act or continue to act) in all or any of the ways specified in section 216(3) in connection with, or for the purposes of, the carrying on of the whole or substantially the whole of the business of the insolvent company,

        (iv)    the prohibited name or, where the company has not entered into insolvent liquidation, the name under which the business is being, or is to be, carried on which would be a prohibited name in respect of the person in the event of the insolvent company entering insolvent liquidation,

        (v)    a statement that the person would not otherwise be permitted to undertake those activities without the leave of the court or the application of an exception created by Rules made under the Insolvency Act 1986,

        (vi)    a statement that breach of the prohibition created by section 216 is a criminal offence, and

        (vii)    a statement as set out in rule 22.5 of the effect of issuing the notice under rule 22.4(2);

    (c)    where the company is in administration, has an administrative receiver appointed or is subject to a CVA, must contain —

        (i)    the date that the company entered administration, had an administrative receiver appointed or a CVA approved (whichever is the earliest), and

        (ii)    a statement that the person was a director of the company on that date; and

(d)     where the company is in insolvent liquidation, must contain —

(i)     the date that the company entered insolvent liquidation, and

(ii)    a statement that the person was a director of the company during the 12 months ending with that date.

(4)   Notice may in particular be given under this rule—

(a)     prior to the insolvent company entering insolvent liquidation where the business (or substantially the whole of the business) is, or is to be, acquired by another company under arrangements made by an office-holder acting in relation to the insolvent company as administrator, administrative receiver or supervisor of a CVA (whether or not at the time of the giving of the notice the person is a director of that other company); or

(b)     at a time when the person is a director of another company where—

(i)     the other company has acquired, or is to acquire, the whole, or substantially the whole, of the business of the insolvent company under arrangements made by its liquidator, and

(ii)    it is proposed that after the giving of the notice a prohibited name should be adopted by the other company.

(5)   Notice may not be given under this rule by a person who has already acted in breach of section 216.

**Derivation**—This rule derived from the Insolvency Rules 1986, SI 1986/1925, r 4.228.

**General note**—This rule and rr 22.6 and 22.7 deal with three cases where the prohibition in s 216 will not apply and so a person that would be affected by s 216 will not be in breach if he or she has not secured the leave of the court to act in relation to a business that uses a prohibited name.

The rule is designed to deal with two problems, namely:

*   The danger that the business of the insolvent company has been acquired at an undervalue to the prejudice of creditors; and
*   The danger that creditors of the insolvent company might think that there has been no change in the nature of the corporate vehicle: *Penrose v Official Receiver* [1996] 1 WLR 482 at 489.

Clearly in this situation the creditors of the liquidating company must be disclosed to so that they are not misled if they agree to give credit to the company that has taken over the business: *ESS Production Ltd (in administration) v Sully* [2005] EWCA Civ 554, [2005] 2 BCLC 547, [2005] BPIR 691 at [8].

The rule as it was first drafted caused problems for anyone who was the director of a company that acquired the business of the company that was insolvent. The rule was amended as a consequence of the decision of the Court of Appeal in *Churchill v First Independent Factors and Finance Ltd* [2006] EWCA Civ 1623, [2007] 1 BCLC 293, [2007] BPIR 14. The previous version of the rule failed to make clear that the notice had to be given prospectively and before the director became involved with the successor company which had acquired the prohibited name. The rule as it is now drafted permits a director to be involved with the successor company before giving the required notice (r 22.4(4)(b)). So the rule protects a director of an insolvent company where the business of that company has been or will be acquired from a liquidator by a successor company of which the individual is already a director (the actual situation in *Churchill*), where at the date the notice is given the successor company is not known by a prohibited name (in *Churchill* the successor was, however, known by a prohibited name). Rule 22.4(3)(a) also makes it permissible for retrospective notice to be given (up to 28 days).

**RULE 22.4(1)**

This covers two situations, either the business of an insolvent company is purchased from the liquidator or, from an office-holder who is not a liquidator.

'**must state . . . the name of the person**'—a previous version of paragraph (3) used the word 'may' and there was some confusion as to whether the intention was to make it mandatory that the person to whom s 216 applies to be named. The new paragraph makes it plain that it is mandatory.

**RULE 22.4(2)**

The notice must not only be served on creditors, but also published in the Gazette.

**RULE 22.4(3)**

This paragraph sets out in detail the required contents of the notice given to creditors. The Insolvency Service provides a template for the notice: https://www.gov.uk/government/publication s/rule-224-notice-to-creditors-s216-re-use-of-a-prohibited-name.

See, Dear Practitioner Issue 87 for procedural guidance. Also, see, A Deacock 'Section 216 and phoenixism – let's hope no one notices' (2007) 23 IL & P 134.

## [2.1042]

### 22.5 Statement as to the effect of the notice under rule 22.4(2)

The statement as to the effect of the notice under rule 22.4(2) must be as set out below—
"Section 216(3) of the Insolvency Act 1986 lists the activities that a director of a company that has gone into insolvent liquidation may not undertake unless the court gives permission or there is an exception in the Insolvency Rules made under the Insolvency Act 1986. (This includes the exceptions in Part 22 of the Insolvency (England and Wales) Rules 2016.) These activities are—

(a)     acting as a director of another company that is known by a name which is either the same as a name used by the company in insolvent liquidation in the 12 months before it entered liquidation or is so similar as to suggest an association with that company;

(b)     directly or indirectly being concerned or taking part in the promotion, formation or management of any such company; or

(c)     directly or indirectly being concerned in the carrying on of a business otherwise than through a company under a name of the kind mentioned in (a) above.

This notice is given under rule 22.4 of the Insolvency (England and Wales) Rules 2016 where the business of a company which is in, or may go into, insolvent liquidation is, or is to be, carried on otherwise than by the company in liquidation with the involvement of a director of that company and under the same or a similar name to that of that company.

The purpose of giving this notice is to permit the director to act in these circumstances where the company enters (or has entered) insolvent liquidation without the director committing a criminal offence and in the case of the carrying on of the business through another company, being personally liable for that company's debts.

Notice may be given where the person giving the notice is already the director of a company which proposes to adopt a prohibited name."

**Derivation**—This rule derived from the Insolvency Rules 1986, SI 1986/1925, r 4.228.

**General note**—This rule supplements the previous rule, r 22(4). The rule is effectively a new one included in the IR 2016. It simply sets out verbatim what must be included in the notice that is sent out in accordance with r 22.4(2). The material that has to be included and that is laid out in this rule explains the effect of the notice, placing it in context by referring to s 216.

## [2.1043]

### 22.6 Second excepted case

(1)     Where a person to whom section 216 applies as having been a director or shadow director of the liquidating company applies for permission of the court under that section not later than seven business days from the date on which the company went into liquidation, the person may, during the period specified in paragraph (2) below, act in any of the ways mentioned in section 216(3), notwithstanding that the person does not have the permission of the court under that section.

(2)     The period referred to in paragraph (1) begins with the day on which the company goes into liquidation and ends either on the day falling six weeks after that date or on the day on which the court disposes of the application for permission under section 216, whichever of those days occurs first.

**Derivation**—This rule derived from the Insolvency Rules 1986, SI 1986/1925, r 4.229.

**General note**—The rule is in the same terms as IR 1986, r 4.229. The aim of the rule is to ensure that the applicant for leave is not in breach of s 216 while his or her application is pending. It is likely that where a director makes an application outside of the seven-day period mentioned in r 22.6(1) there would be a delay in the court hearing the application and granting leave, and a director would be exposed to liability during the time from the filing of the application until the making of an order, as the court would not give leave retrospectively: *ESS Production Ltd (in administration) v Sully* [2005] EWCA Civ 554 at [84].

**[2.1044]**

## 22.7 Third excepted case

The court's permission under section 216(3) is not required where the company there referred to though known by a prohibited name within the meaning of the section—

(a)    has been known by that name for the whole of the period of 12 months ending with the day before the liquidating company went into liquidation; and

(b)    has not at any time in those 12 months been dormant within the meaning of section 1169(1), (2) and (3)(a) of the Companies Act.

**Derivation**—This rule derived from the Insolvency Rules 1986, SI 1986/1925, r 4.230.

**General note**—the rule is in the same terms as the rule previously applying, IR 1986, r 4.230. The object of this rule is to take outside the scope of s 216 those companies that are not Phoenix companies, and as it is frequent for companies within the same group to share common words in their names, one could infer that Parliament intended this rule to encompass the situation where there is a group of companies: *ESS Production Ltd (in administration) v Sully* [2005] EWCA Civ 554, [2005] 2 BCLC 547, [2005] BPIR 691 at [8]. See also *Ricketts v Ad Valorem Factors Ltd* [2004] 1 BCLC 1, per Mummery LJ. So this rule could apply to save from the application of s 216 a group of companies where one in the group enters insolvent liquidation, leaving other companies with similar names: *Ricketts v Ad Valorem Factors Ltd* [2004] 1 BCLC 1 at [20].

**'Known by a prohibited name'**—This is to be interpreted consistently with s 216(6): *ESS Production Ltd (in administration) v Sully* at [62], per Arden LJ. It means that the words relate to determining whether the prohibited name company was known by a prohibited name in the 12 months prior to liquidation (*ESS Production Ltd* at [66], per Arden LJ). Provided that the prohibited name company carried on some business under the prohibited name during any part of the 12 months prior to liquidation, the respondent to a s 216 claim could rely on this rule, as Parliament did not intend that this exception should not be able to apply where a company had had a name change because a change of corporate name was not an uncommon occurrence (*ESS Production Ltd* at [68]). 'Prohibited name' includes the plural (*ESS Production Ltd* at [81]).

**Dormant**—In *First Independent Factors and Finance Ltd v Mountford* [2008] EWHC 835 (Ch), [2008] 2 BCLC 297; [2008] BPIR 515 the respondent in a s 217 action was held liable when X Ltd, the company he was managing, used a prohibited name. X Ltd had been dormant in the 12 months prior to the liquidation of Y Ltd of which the respondent had control. X Ltd operated a business that in fact had not been dormant, but had been conducted by the respondent in his personal capacity and he had then transferred the business to X Ltd after Y Ltd was liquidated. The Court held that r 22.7(b) rules out any vehicles other than companies being able to take advantage of the exception. However, the provision can apply to limited liability partnerships, although it does not apply to ordinary partnerships: *Newton v Secretary of State for Business Energy and Industrial Strategy* [2016] EWHC 3068 (Ch).

SCHEDULE 1

REVOCATIONS

Introductory rule 2

**[2.1045]**

| | |
|---|---|
| The Insolvency Rules 1986 | 1986/1925 |
| The Insolvency (Amendment) Rules 1987 | 1987/1919 |
| The Insolvency (Amendment) Rules 1989 | 1989/397 |
| The Insolvency (Amendment) Rules 1991 | 1991/495 |
| The Insolvency (Amendment) Rules 1993 | 1993/602 |
| The Insolvency (Amendment) Rules 1995 | 1995/586 |
| The Insolvency (Amendment) Rules 1999 | 1999/359 |
| The Insolvency (Amendment) (No 2) Rules 1999 | 1999/1022 |
| The Insolvency (Amendment) Rules 2001 | 2001/763 |
| The Insolvency (Amendment) Rules 2002 | 2002/1307 |
| The Insolvency (Amendment) (No 2) Rules 2002 | 2002/2712 |
| The Insolvency (Amendment) Rules 2003 | 2003/1730 |
| The Insolvency (Amendment) Rules 2004 | 2004/584 |

| | |
|---|---|
| The Insolvency (Amendment) (No 2) Rules 2004 | 2004/1070 |
| The Insolvency (Amendment) Rules 2005 | 2005/527 |
| The Insolvency (Amendment) Rules 2006 | 2006/1272 |
| The Insolvency (Amendment) Rules 2007 | 2007/1974 |
| The Insolvency (Amendment) Rules 2008 | 2008/737 |
| The Insolvency (Amendment) Rules 2009 | 2009/642 |
| The Insolvency (Amendment No 2) Rules 2009 | 2009/2472 |
| The Insolvency (Amendment) Rules 2010 | 2010/686 |
| The Insolvency (Amendment) (No 2) Rules 2010 | 2010/734 |
| The Insolvency (Amendment) Rules 2011 | 2011/785 |
| The Insolvency (Amendment) Rules 2012 | 2012/469 |
| The Insolvency (Amendment) Rules 2013 | 2013/2135 |
| The Insolvency (Commencement of Proceedings) and Insolvency Rules 1986 (Amendment) Rules 2014 | 2014/817 |
| The Insolvency (Amendment) Rules 2015 | 2015/443 |
| The Insolvency (Amendment) Rules 2016 | 2016/187 |
| The Insolvency (Amendment) (No 2) Rules 2016 | 2016/903 |

SCHEDULE 2

TRANSITIONAL AND SAVINGS PROVISIONS

Introductory rule 4

GENERAL

**[2.1046]**

**1**

In this Schedule—

"the 1986 Rules" means the Insolvency Rules 1986 as they had effect immediately before the commencement date and a reference to "1986 rule" followed by a rule number is a reference to a rule in the 1986 Rules; and

"the commencement date" means the date these Rules come into force.

REQUIREMENT FOR OFFICE-HOLDER TO PROVIDE INFORMATION TO CREDITORS ON OPTING OUT

**2**

(1)   Rule 1.39, which requires an office-holder to provide information to a creditor on the right to opt out under rule 1.38 in the first communication to the creditor, does not apply to an office-holder who has delivered the first communication before the commencement date.

(2)   However, such an office-holder may choose to deliver information on the right to opt out in which case the communication to the creditor must contain the information required by rule 1.39(2).

ELECTRONIC COMMUNICATION

**3**

(1)   Rule 1.45(4) does not apply where the relevant proceedings commenced before the commencement date.

(2)   In this paragraph "commenced" means—

(a)   the delivery of a proposal for a voluntary arrangement to the intended nominee;

    (b)    the appointment of an administrator under paragraph 14 or 22 of Schedule B1;

    (c)    the making of an administration order;

    (d)    the appointment of an administrative receiver;

    (e)    the passing or deemed passing of a resolution to wind up a company;

    (f)    the making of a winding-up order; or

    (g)    the making of a bankruptcy order.

### STATEMENTS OF AFFAIRS

**4**

(1) The provisions of these Rules relating to statements of affairs in administration, administrative receivership, company winding up and bankruptcy do not apply and the following rules in the 1986 Rules continue to apply where relevant proceedings commenced before the commencement date and a person is required to provide a statement of affairs—

    (a)    1986 rules 2.28 to 2.32 (administration);

    (b)    1986 rules 3.3 to 3.8 (administrative receivership);

    (c)    1986 rules 4.32 to 4.42 (company winding up); and

    (d)    1986 rules 6.58 to 6.72 (bankruptcy).

(2) In this paragraph "commenced" means—

    (a)    the appointment of an administrator under paragraph 14 or 22 of Schedule B1;

    (b)    the making of an administration order;

    (c)    the appointment of an administrative receiver

    (d)    the passing or deemed passing of a resolution to wind up a company;

    (e)    the making of a winding-up order; or

    (f)    the making of a bankruptcy order.

### SAVINGS IN RESPECT OF MEETINGS TAKING PLACE ON OR AFTER THE COMMENCEMENT DATE AND RESOLUTIONS BY CORRESPONDENCE

**5**

(1) This paragraph applies where on or after the commencement date—

    (a)    a creditors' or contributories' meeting is to be held as a result of a notice issued before that date in relation to a meeting for which provision is made by the 1986 Rules or the 1986 Act;

    (b)    a meeting is to be held as a result of a requisition by a creditor or contributory made before that date;

    (c)    a meeting is to be held as a result of a statement made under paragraph 52(1)(b) of Schedule B1 and a request is made before that date which obliges the administrator to summon an initial creditors' meeting;

    (d)    a meeting is required by sections 93 or 105 of the 1986 Act in the winding up of a company where the resolution to wind up was passed before 6th April 2010.

(2) Where a meeting is to be held under sub-paragraph (1)(a) to (1)(d), Part 15 of these Rules does not apply and the 1986 Rules relating to the following continue to apply—

    (a)    the requirement to hold the meeting;

    (b)    notice and advertisement of the meeting;

    (c)    governance of the meeting;

    (d)    recording and taking minutes of the meeting;

    (e)    the report or return of the meeting;

    (f)    membership and formalities of establishment of liquidation and creditors' committees where the resolution to form the committee is passed at the meeting;

(g)     the office-holder's resignation or removal at the meeting;

(h)     the office-holder's release;

(i)     fixing the office-holder's remuneration;

(j)     (*revoked*)

(k)     hand-over of assets to a supervisor of a voluntary arrangement where the proposal is approved at the meeting;

(l)     the notice of the appointment of a supervisor of a voluntary arrangement where the appointment is made at the meeting;

(m)     the advertisement of appointment of a trustee in bankruptcy where the appointment is made at the meeting;

(n)     claims that remuneration is or that other expenses are excessive; and

(o)     complaints about exclusion at the meeting.

(3)   Where, before the commencement date, the office-holder sought to obtain a resolution by correspondence under 1986 rule 2.48, 4.63A or 6.88A, the 1986 Rules relating to resolutions by correspondence continue to apply and sub-paragraph (2) applies to any meeting that those rules require the office-holder to summon.

(4)   However, any application to the court in respect of such a meeting or vote is to be made in accordance with Part 12 of these Rules.

### SAVINGS IN RESPECT OF FINAL MEETINGS TAKING PLACE ON OR AFTER THE COMMENCEMENT DATE

**6**

(1)   This paragraph applies where—

(a)     before the commencement date—

(i)     a final report to creditors has been sent under 1986 rule 4.49D (final report to creditors in liquidation),

(ii)    a final report to creditors and bankrupt has been sent under 1986 rule 6.78B (final report to creditors and bankrupt), or

(iii)   a meeting has been called under sections 94, 106, 146 or 331 of the 1986 Act (final meeting); and

(b)     a meeting under section 94, 106, 146 or 331 of the 1986 Act is held on or after the commencement date.

(2)   Where a meeting is held to which this paragraph applies, Part 15 of these Rules does not apply and the 1986 Rules relating to the following continue to apply—

(a)     the requirement to hold the meeting;

(b)     notice and advertisement of the meeting;

(c)     governance of the meeting;

(d)     recording and taking minutes of the meeting;

(e)     the form and content of the final report;

(f)     the office-holder's resignation or removal;

(g)     the office-holder's release;

(h)     fixing the office-holder's remuneration;

(i)     requests for further information from creditors;

(j)     claims that remuneration is or other expenses are excessive; and

(k)     complaints about exclusion at the meeting.

(3)   However, any application to the court in respect of such a meeting is to be made in accordance with Part 12 of these Rules.

## PROGRESS REPORTS AND STATEMENTS TO THE REGISTRAR OF COMPANIES

**7**

(1)   Where an obligation to prepare a progress report arises before the commencement date but has not yet been fulfilled the following provisions of the 1986 Rules continue to apply—

(a)   1986 rule 2.47 (reports to creditors in administration;

(b)   1986 rules 4.49B and 4.49C (progress reports—winding up); and

(c)   1986 rule 6.78A (reports to creditors in bankruptcy).

(2)   Where before the commencement date, a conversion notice under paragraph 83 of Schedule B1 was sent to the registrar of companies, 1986 rule 2.117A(1) continues to apply.

(3)   The provisions of these Rules relating to progress reporting do not apply—

(a)   in the case of a bankruptcy, where the bankruptcy order was made on a petition presented before 6th April 2010; or

(b)   in the case of a winding up, where the winding-up order was made on a petition presented before 6th April 2010.

(4)   Where a voluntary winding up commenced before 6th April 2010, 1986 rule 4.223-CVL as it had effect immediately before that date, continues to apply.

(5)   Where rules 18.6, 18.7 or 18.8 prescribe the periods for which progress reports must be made but before the commencement date an office-holder has ceased to act, or an administrator has sent a progress report to creditors in support of a request for their consent to an extension of the administration, resulting in a change in reporting period under 1986 rule 2.47(3A), 2.47(3B) 4.49B(5), 4.49C(3), or 6.78A(4), the period for which reports must be made is the period for which reports were required to be made under the 1986 Rules immediately before the commencement date.

## FOREIGN CURRENCY

**8**

(1)   Where, before the commencement date an amount stated in a foreign currency on an application, claim or proof of debt is converted into sterling by the office-holder under 1986 rule 2.86, 1986 rule 4.91, 1986 rule 5A.3 or 1986 rule 6.111, the office-holder and any successor to the office-holder must continue to use that exchange rate for subsequent conversions of that currency into sterling for the purpose of distributing any assets of the insolvent estate.

(2)   However when an office-holder, convener, appointed person or chair uses an exchange rate to convert an application, claim or proof in a foreign currency into sterling solely for voting purposes before the commencement date, it does not prevent the office-holder from using an alternative rate for subsequent conversions.

## CVA MORATORIA

**9**

Where, before the commencement date, the directors of a company submit to the nominee the documents required under paragraph 6(1) of Schedule A1, the 1986 Rules relating to moratoria continue to apply to that proposed voluntary arrangement.

## PRIORITY OF EXPENSES OF VOLUNTARY ARRANGEMENTS

**10**

1986 rule 4.21A (expenses of CVA in a liquidation) and 1986 rule 6.46A (expenses of IVA in a bankruptcy) continue to apply where a winding up or bankruptcy petition is presented or a bankruptcy application is made (as the case may be) before the commencement date.

### GENERAL POWERS OF LIQUIDATOR

**11**

1986 rule 4.184 (General powers of liquidator) continues to apply as regards a person dealing in good faith and for value with a liquidator and in respect of the power of the court or the liquidation committee to ratify anything done by the liquidator without permission before the amendments made to sections 165 and 167 of the Act by section 120(2) and (3) of the Small Business, Enterprise and Employment Act 2015 (which removed the requirements for the liquidator to obtain such permission) came into force.

### FAST-TRACK VOLUNTARY ARRANGEMENTS

**12**

Where a fast-track voluntary arrangement is in effect on the commencement date the following 1986 Rules continue to apply to it after the commencement date—

    (a)    1986 rules 5.35 to 5.50 (fast-track voluntary arrangement);

    (b)    1986 rules 5.57 to 5.59 (application by official receiver to annul a bankruptcy order under section 263D(3)); and

    (c)    1986 rules 5.60 to 5.61 (other matters arising on annulments under sections 261(2)(a), 261(2)(b) or 263D(3)).

### FIRST TRUSTEE IN BANKRUPTCY

**13**

On the commencement date the official receiver becomes trustee of the bankrupt's estate where—

    (a)    a bankruptcy order was made before the commencement date; and

    (b)    no trustee has yet been appointed.

### APPLICATIONS BEFORE THE COURT

**14**

(1) Subject to paragraph (1A), where] an application to court is filed or a petition is presented under the Act or under the 1986 Rules before the commencement date and the court remains seised of that application or petition on the commencement date, the 1986 rules continue to apply to that application or petition.

(1A) Where the 1986 Rules apply by virtue of paragraph (1) they are to apply as though—

    (a)    in rules 7.47(2)(a)(ii), (b)(iii) and (c) and 13.2(3A)(a) for "a Registrar in Bankruptcy of the High Court" there were substituted "an Insolvency and Companies Court Judge", and

    (b)    in rule 7.47(5), for the words "Registrar in Bankruptcy of the High Court" both times they appear there were substituted "Insolvency and Companies Court Judge.

(2) For the purpose of paragraph (1), the court is no longer seised of an application when—

    (a)    it makes an order having the effect of determining of the application; or

    (b)    in relation to a petition for bankruptcy or winding up when—

        (i)    the court makes a bankruptcy order or a winding up order,

        (ii)    the court dismisses the petition, or

        (iii)    the petition is withdrawn.

(3) Any application to the court to review, rescind, vary or appeal an order made under paragraph 14(2) is to be made in accordance with Part 12 of these Rules.

## FORMS

**15**

A form contained in Schedule 4 to the 1986 Rules may be used on or after the commencement date if—

    (a)    the form is used to provide a statement of affairs pursuant to paragraph 4 of this Schedule;

    (b)    the form relates to a meeting held under the 1986 Rules as described in paragraph 5(1) of this Schedule;

    (c)    the form is required for the administration of a fast-track voluntary arrangement pursuant to paragraph 12 of this Schedule;

    (d)    the form is required because before the commencement date, the office-holder sought to obtain the passing of a resolution by correspondence; or

    (e)    the form relates to any application to the court or petition presented before the commencement date.

## REGISTERS

**16**

(1)   The Secretary of State must maintain on the individual insolvency register, the bankruptcy restrictions register and the debt relief restrictions register information which is on the registers immediately before the commencement date.

(2)   The Secretary of State must also enter on the appropriate register referred to in paragraph (1) information received (but not yet entered on the register) before the commencement date.

(3)   The Court's power under Part 20 to order that information must not be entered in those registers where there is a risk of violence applies equally to information received by the Secretary of State before the commencement date but not yet entered on a register.

(4)   Any obligation in Part 11 to delete information from a register or to rectify a register applies equally to information entered on the register before these rules come into force.

## ADMINISTRATIONS COMMENCED BEFORE 15TH SEPTEMBER 2003

**17**

The 1986 Rules continue to apply to administrations where the petition for an administration order was presented before 15th September 2003.

## SET-OFF IN INSOLVENCY PROCEEDINGS COMMENCED BEFORE 1ST APRIL 2005

**18**

Where before 1st April 2005 a company has entered administration or gone into liquidation, the office-holder, when calculating any set-off must apply the 1986 Rules as they had effect immediately before 1st April 2005.

## CALCULATING THE VALUE OF FUTURE DEBTS IN INSOLVENCY PROCEEDINGS COMMENCED BEFORE 1ST APRIL 2005

**19**

Where before 1st April 2005 a company has entered administration or gone into liquidation or a bankruptcy order has been made, the office-holder, when calculating the value of a future debt for the purpose of dividend (and no other purpose) must apply the 1986 Rules as they had effect immediately before 1st April 2005.

### OBLIGATIONS ARISING UNDER FAMILY PROCEEDINGS WHERE BANK-RUPTCY ORDER IS MADE ON OR BEFORE 31 MARCH 2005

**20**

Rule 12.3 of the 1986 Rules applies, without the amendments made by rule 44 of the Insolvency (Amendment) Rules 2005 to an obligation arising under an order made in family proceedings in any case where a bankruptcy order was made on or before 31 March 2005.

### INSOLVENCY PRACTITIONER FEES AND EXPENSES ESTIMATES

**21**

(1)   Rules 18.4(1)(e), 18.16(4) to (10), and 18.30 do not apply in a case where before 1st October 2015—

    (a)    the appointment of an administrator took effect;

    (b)    a liquidator was nominated under section 100(2), or 139(3) of the Act;

    (c)    a liquidator was appointed under section 139(4) or 140 of the Act;

    (d)    a person was directed by the court or appointed to be a liquidator under section 100(3) of the Act;

    (e)    a liquidator was nominated or the administrator became the liquidator under paragraph 83(7) of Schedule B1 to the Act; or

    (f)    a trustee of a bankrupt's estate was appointed.

(2)   Paragraphs (4) and (5) of rule 18.20 do not apply where an administrator was appointed before 1st October 2015 and—

    (a)    the company is wound up under paragraph 83 of Schedule B1 on or after the commencement date and the administrator becomes the liquidator; or

    (b)    a winding-up order is made upon the appointment of an administrator ceasing to have effect on or after the commencement date and the court under section 140(1) appoints as liquidator the person whose appointment as administrator has ceased to have effect.

### TRANSITIONAL PROVISION FOR COMPANIES ENTERING ADMINISTRA-TION BEFORE 6TH APRIL 2010 AND MOVING TO VOLUNTARY LIQUIDA-TION BETWEEN 6TH APRIL 2010 AND 8TH DECEMBER 2017 INCLUSIVE OF THOSE DATES

**22**

Where—

    (a)    a company goes into administration before 6th April 2010; and

    (b)    the company goes into voluntary liquidation under paragraph 83 of Schedule B1 between 6th April 2010 and 8th December 2017 inclusive of those dates;

the 1986 Rules as amended by the Insolvency (Amendment) Rules 2010 apply to the extent necessary to give effect to section 104A of the Act notwithstanding that by virtue of paragraph 1(6)(a) or (b) of Schedule 4 to the Insolvency (Amendment) Rules 2010 those amendments to the Insolvency Rules 1986 would otherwise not apply.

**Amendments**—SI 2017/366; SI 2017/1115; SI 2018/130.

SCHEDULE 3

PUNISHMENT OF OFFENCES UNDER THESE RULES

Introductory rule 6

**[2.1047]**

| Rule creating offence | General nature of the offence | Mode of prosecution | Punishment | Daily default fine (if applicable) |
|---|---|---|---|---|
| 1.56(3) | Falsely claiming to be a person entitled to inspect a document with the intention of gaining sight of it. | 1 On indictment. 2 Summary. | 2 years, or a fine, or both. 6 months, or a fine, or both. | Not applicable. |
| 3.55(7) | Former administrator failing to file a notice of automatic end of administration and progress report. | Summary. | Level 3 on the standard scale. | One tenth of level 3 on the standard scale. |
| 3.70(2) | Failing to comply with administrator's duties on vacating office. | Summary. | Level 3 on the standard scale. | One tenth of level 3 on the standard scale. |
| 4.17(6) | Administrative receiver failing to deliver required accounts of receipts and payments. | Summary. | Level 3 on the standard scale. | One tenth of level 3 on the standard scale. |
| 6.14(13) | Directors failing to seek a decision on the nomination of a liquidator. | 1 On indictment. 2 Summary. | 1 A fine. 2 A fine. | Not applicable. |
| 18.6(5) | Administrator failing to deliver required progress reports in accordance with rule 18.6. | Summary. | Level 3 on the standard scale. | One tenth of level 3 on the standard scale. |

**Derivation**—This Schedule derived from the Insolvency Rules 1986, SI 1986/1925, Sch 5.

SCHEDULE 4

SERVICE OF DOCUMENTS

Rule 1.2(2)

**[2.1048]**

1

(1)  This Schedule sets out the requirements for service where a document is required to be served.

(2)  Service is to be carried out in accordance with Part 6 of the CPR as that Part applies to either a "claim form" or a "document other than the claim form" except where this Schedule provides otherwise or the court otherwise approves or directs.

(3)  However, where a document is required or permitted to be served at a company's registered office service may be effected at a previous registered office in accordance with section 87(2) of the Companies Act.

(4)  In the case of an overseas company service may be effected in any manner provided for by section 1139(2) of the Companies Act.

(5)  If for any reason it is impracticable to effect service as provided for in paragraphs (2) to (4) then service may be effected in such other manner as the court may approve or direct.

(6)   The third column of the table below sets out which documents are treated as "claim forms" for the purposes of applying Part 6 of the CPR and which are "documents other than the claim form" (called in this Schedule "other documents").

(7)   The fourth column of the table sets out modifications to Part 6 of the CPR which apply to the service of documents listed in the first and second columns.

(8)   Part 6 of the CPR applies to the service of documents outside the jurisdiction with such modifications as the court may approve or direct.

Service of winding-up petitions

**2**

(1)   A winding-up petition must be served at a company's registered office by handing it to a person at that address who—

(a)   at the time of service acknowledges being a director, other officer or employee of the company;

(b)   is, to the best of the knowledge and belief of the person serving the petition, a director, other officer or employee of the company; or

(c)   acknowledges being authorised to accept service of documents on the company's behalf.

(2)   However if there is no one of the kind mentioned in sub-paragraph (1) at the registered office, the petition may be served by depositing it at or about the registered office in such a way that it is likely to come to the notice of a person attending the office.

(3)   Sub-paragraph (4) applies if—

(a)   for any reason it is not practicable to serve a petition at a company's registered office;

(b)   the company has no registered office; or

(c)   the company is an unregistered company.

(4)   Where this paragraph applies the petition may be served—

(a)   by leaving it at the company's last known principal place of business in England and Wales in such a way that it is likely to come to the attention of a person attending there; or

(b)   on the secretary or a director, manager or principal officer of the company, wherever that person may be found.

**General note**—This paragraph derives from r 4.8 of the IR 1986. The rule sets out the manner in which a company may be served with a petition. A company can agree to accept service by a method other than that set out in the rule: *Re Regent United Services Stores Ltd* (1878) 8 ChD 75. In *Re Great Cwmsymtoy Silver Lead Co* (1868) 17 LT 463 the court ordered service on the subscribers to the company's memorandum, but it is arguable whether courts now will permit such service except where the company is a small private company. It has been held that where the company's registered office has been demolished, service on directors of the company at the company's place of business, although not registered on Companies House files, would suffice: In *Re Fortune Copper Mining Company* (1870) LR 10 Eq 390. This has been affirmed by para (4)(b).

A court might permit the service of a petition on a foreign company. Before doing so it would have to be convinced that the court had jurisdiction to wind up (see s 221) and there was a serious issue to be tried within the exercise of the court's jurisdiction: *Re Primera Maritime (Hellas) Ltd* ([2010] EWHC 2053 (Ch), Sir Andrew Morritt C).

It would seem, from paragraph 6(3), that there can be substituted service of the petition if an order is secured that allows it.

**3   Service of administration application (paragraph 12 of Schedule B1)**

(1)   An application to the court for an administration order must be served by delivering the documents as follows—

(a)   on the company at its registered office or if service at its registered office is not practicable at its last known principal place of business in England and Wales;

(b)   on any other person at that person's proper address.

(2)   A person's proper address is any which he has previously notified as the address for service, but if the person has not notified such an address then the documents may be served at that person's usual or last known address.

(3)   Paragraph (4) sets out the proper address for service for an authorised deposit-taker who—

(a) has appointed, or is or may be entitled to appoint, an administrative receiver of the company; or

(b) is, or may be, entitled to appoint an administrative receiver of the company under paragraph 14 of Schedule B1; and

(c) has not notified an address for service.

(4) The proper address for service is—

(a) that of an office of the authorised-deposit taker where the applicant knows the company maintains a bank account; or

(b) where the applicant doesn't know of any such office, the registered office; or

(c) if there is no such registered office the usual or last known address.

## 4 Service on joint office-holders

Service of a document on one of joint office-holders is to be treated as service on all of them.

## 5 Service of orders staying proceedings

(1) This paragraph applies where the court makes an order staying an action, execution or other legal process against—

(a) the property of a company; or

(b) the property or person of an individual debtor or bankrupt.

(2) The order may be served within the jurisdiction by serving a sealed copy at the address for service of—

(a) the claimant; or

(b) another party having the carriage of the proceedings to be stayed.

## 6 Certificate of service

(1) The service of an application or petition must be verified by a certificate of service.

(2) The certificate of service must—

(a) identify the application or petition;

(b) identify the company, where the application or petition relates to a company;

(c) identify the debtor, where the application relates to an individual;

(d) identify the applicant or petitioner;

(e) specify—

(i) the court or hearing centre in which the application was made or at which the petition was filed, and the court reference number,

(ii) the date of the application or petition,

(iii) whether the copy served was a sealed copy,

(iv) the person(s) served, and

(v) the manner of service and the date of service; and

(f) be verified by a statement of truth.

(3) Where the court has directed that service be effected in a particular manner, the certificate must be accompanied by a sealed copy of the order directing such manner of service.

*Table of requirements for service*

| Rule (or section) | Document | Whether treated as claim form or other document | Modifications to Part 6 of the CPR which apply unless the court directs otherwise |
|---|---|---|---|
| 3.8 | Administration application | Claim form | Service in accordance with paragraph 3 of this Schedule. The applicant must serve the application. |

| | | | |
|---|---|---|---|
| 3.16 (& Para 15 of Sch B1) | Notice of intention to appoint administrator by a floating charge holder | Other document | The appointer must serve the notice. |
| 3.23 (& para 26 of Sch B1) | Notice of intention to appoint administrator by company or directors | Other document | Service on the company at its registered office or if that is not practicable, at its last known principal place of business in England and Wales. |
| 7.3 | Statutory demand on a company under section 123(1) or 222(1)(a) (unregistered companies) | | Note: the requirements for service of a statutory demand are set out in sections 123(1) and 222(1)(a) respectively. |
| 7.9 and 7.29 | Winding-up petition | Claim form | Service in accordance with paragraph 2 of this Schedule. The petitioner must serve the petition. |
| 7.34 | Court order for additional deposit to be paid—provisional liquidator | Other document | |
| 7.99 | Court order to enforce payment of a call | Other document | |
| 7.102 | Court order for public examination served on examinee | Other document | |
| 10.2 | Statutory demand (bankruptcy) | Other document | Service in accordance with rule 10.2. |
| 10.14 | Bankruptcy petition (creditor's) | Claim form | Personal service. The petitioner must serve the petition. |
| 10.29 | Court order—change of carriage of petition | Other document | |
| 10.50 | Court order for additional deposit to be paid—interim receiver | Other document | |
| 10.99 | Court order for public examination served on bankrupt | Other document | |
| 10.119 | Court order for disclosure by HMRC | Other document | |
| 10.126 | Notice to recipient of after acquired property | Other document | |
| 10.166 | Court order for post redirection | Other document | |
| 11.3 | Application for debt relief restrictions order (DRRO) or bankruptcy restrictions order (BRO) | Claim form | The applicant must serve the application. |
| 11.4 | Service of evidence for DRRO or BRO | Other document | |
| 12.9 | Applications to court generally (where service required) | Claim form | The applicant must serve the application. |
| 12.19 | Court order for private examination | Other document | Personal service. The applicant must serve the order. |
| 12.28(2) | Witness statement of evidence | Other document | |

| 12.37(7) | Application for block transfer order | Claim form | The applicant must serve the application. |
|---|---|---|---|
| 12.42 | Notice requiring person to assess costs by detailed assessment | Other document | |
| 12.48 | Application for costs | Claim form | The applicant must serve the application. |
| 19.4 (& sections 179 and 317) | Notice of disclaimer (leasehold property) | Other document | |
| 19.5 (& section 318) | Notice of disclaimer (dwelling house) | Other document | |
| . . . | . . . | . . . | . . . |
| Paragraph 5(1) of this Schedule | Order staying proceedings | Other document | The applicant must serve the order. |

**Derivation**—Para 1 derived from the Insolvency Rules 1986, SI 1986/1925, rr 12A.17, 12A.20; para 2 derived from the Insolvency Rules 1986, SI 1986/1925, rr 4.8, 4.22; para 3 derived from the Insolvency Rules 1986, SI 1986/1925, r 12A.19; para 4 derived from the Insolvency Rules 1986, SI 1986/1925, rr 7.56, 12A.18; para 5 derived from the Insolvency Rules 1986, SI 1986/1925, rr 2.8, 2.9, 4.9A, 6.15A.

**Amendments**—SI 2017/366; SI 2017/1115; SI 2019/146, as from IP completion day (as defined in the European Union (Withdrawal Agreement) Act 2020, s 39(1)–(5)).

## SCHEDULE 5
## CALCULATION OF TIME PERIODS

Rule 1.3

**[2.1049]**

[Note: section 376 of the Act contains a power for the court to extend the time for doing anything required by the Act or these Rules under the Second Group of Parts (Insolvency of Individuals; bankruptcy).]

1

The rules in CPR 2.8 with the exception of paragraph (4) apply for the calculation of periods expressed in days in the Act and these Rules.

2

(1) This paragraph applies for the calculation of periods expressed in months.

(2) The beginning and the end of a period expressed in months is to be determined as follows—

    (a) if the beginning of the period is specified—

        (i) the month in which the period ends is the specified number of months after the month in which it begins, and

        (ii) the date in the month on which the period ends is—

            (aa) the day before the date corresponding to the date in the month on which it begins, or

            (bb) if there is no such date in the month in which it ends, the last day of that month;

    (b) if the end of the period is specified—

        (i) the month in which the period begins is the specified number of months before the month in which it ends, and

        (ii) the date in the month on which the period begins is—

            (aa) the day after the date corresponding to the date in the month on which it ends, or

            (bb) if there is no such date in the month in which it begins, the last day of that month.

**3**

The provisions of CPR rule 3.1(2)(a) (the court's general powers of management) apply so as to enable the court to extend or shorten the time for compliance with anything required or authorised to be done by these Rules.

**4**

Paragraph 3 is subject to any time limits expressly stated in the Act and to any specific powers in the Act or these Rules to extend or shorten the time for compliance.

> **Derivation**—This Schedule derived from the Insolvency Rules 1986, SI 1986/1925, r 12.55.
> **Amendments**—SI 2017/366.

## SCHEDULE 6

### INSOLVENCY JURISDICTION OF COUNTY COURT HEARING CENTRES
Rule 9.22

**[2.1050]**

[Note: where the entry "London Insolvency District" appears in this table, jurisdiction under Parts 1 to 7 of the Act is conferred on the High Court as a result of article 6B of the High Court and County Courts Jurisdiction Order 1991 (SI 1991/724) which was inserted by the High Court and County Courts Jurisdiction (Amendment) Order 2014 (SI 2014/821).]

| Name of county court hearing centre | Parts of the Insolvency Act under which proceedings may be commenced at a county court hearing centre or the alternative court or county court hearing centre where proceedings may be commenced | Nearest full time court or hearing centre |
| --- | --- | --- |
| Aberystwyth | Parts 1 to 11 | Cardiff |
| Aldershot & Farnham | Guildford | |
| Banbury | Parts 1 to 11 | Luton, Gloucester or Reading |
| Barnet | London Insolvency District—High Court for Parts 1 to 7 (see head note); County Court at Central London for Parts 7A to 11 | |
| Barnsley | Parts 1 to 11 | Sheffield |
| Barnstaple | Parts 1 to 11 | Exeter |
| Barrow-in-Furness | Parts 1 to 11 | Blackpool or Preston |
| Basildon | Southend-on-Sea | |
| Basingstoke | Reading | |
| Bath | Parts 1 to 11 | Bristol |
| Bedford | Parts 1 to 11 | Luton |
| Birkenhead | Parts 1 to 11 | |
| Birmingham | Parts 1 to 11 | |
| Blackburn | Parts 1 to 11 | Preston |
| Blackpool | Parts 1 to 11 | |
| Blackwood | Parts 1 to 11 | Cardiff |
| Bodmin | Truro | |
| Bolton | Parts 1 to 11 | |
| Boston | Parts 1 to 11 | Nottingham |
| Bournemouth and Poole | Parts 1 to 11 | |

| Name of county court hearing centre | Parts of the Insolvency Act under which proceedings may be commenced at a county court hearing centre or the alternative court or county court hearing centre where proceedings may be commenced | Nearest full time court or hearing centre |
|---|---|---|
| Bow | London Insolvency District— High Court for Parts 1 to 7 (see head note); County Court at Central London for Parts 7A to 11 | |
| Bradford | Parts 1 to 11 | |
| Brentford | London Insolvency District— High Court for Parts 1 to 7 (see head note); County Court at Central London for Parts 7A to 11 | |
| Brighton | Parts 1 to 11 | |
| Bristol | Parts 1 to 11 | |
| Bromley | Croydon | |
| Burnley | Parts 1 to 11 | Bolton or Preston |
| Bury | Parts 1 to 11 | Bolton |
| Bury St Edmunds | Parts 1 to 11 | Cambridge |
| Caernarfon | Parts 1 to 11 | |
| Cambridge | Parts 1 to 11 | |
| Canterbury | Parts 1 to 11 | Croydon or the High Court (London) |
| Cardiff | Parts 1 to 11 | |
| Carlisle | Parts 1 to 11 | Preston or Blackpool |
| Carmarthen | Parts 1 to 11 | Cardiff |
| County Court at Central London | London Insolvency District— High Court for Parts 1 to 7 (see head note); County Court at Central London for Parts 7A to 11 | |
| Chelmsford | Parts 1 to 11 | Southend or the High Court (London) |
| Chester | Parts 1 to 11 | |
| Chesterfield | Parts 1 to 11 | Sheffield |
| Chichester | Brighton | |
| Chippenham and Trowbridge | Bath | |
| Clerkenwell and Shoreditch | London Insolvency District— High Court for Parts 1 to 7 (see head note); County Court at Central London for Parts 7A to 11 | |
| Colchester | Parts 1 to 11 | Southend or the High Court (London) |
| Conwy and Colwyn | Caernarfon | |
| Coventry | Parts 1 to 11 | Birmingham |
| Crewe | Parts 1 to 11 | Stoke or Chester |
| Croydon | Parts 1 to 11 | |
| Darlington | Parts 1 to 11 | Middlesbrough |
| Dartford | Medway | |

| Name of county court hearing centre | Parts of the Insolvency Act under which proceedings may be commenced at a county court hearing centre or the alternative court or county court hearing centre where proceedings may be commenced | Nearest full time court or hearing centre |
|---|---|---|
| Derby | Parts 1 to 11 | |
| Doncaster | Parts 1 to 11 | Sheffield |
| Dudley | Parts 1 to 11 | Birmingham |
| Durham | Parts 1 to 11 | Newcastle |
| Eastbourne | Parts 1 to 11 | Brighton |
| Edmonton | London Insolvency District— High Court for Parts 1 to 7 (see head note); County Court at Central London for Parts 7A to 11 | |
| Exeter | Parts 1 to 11 | |
| Gateshead | Newcastle upon Tyne | |
| Gloucester and Cheltenham | Parts 1 to 11 | |
| Great Grimsby | Parts 1 to 11 | Hull |
| Guildford | Parts 1 to 11 | Croydon |
| Halifax | Parts 1 to 11 | Leeds |
| Harrogate | Parts 1 to 11 | Leeds |
| Hartlepool | Middlesbrough | |
| Hastings | Parts 1 to 11 | Brighton |
| Haverfordwest | Parts 1 to 11 | Cardiff |
| Hereford | Parts 1 to 11 | Gloucester |
| Hertford | Parts 1 to 11 | Luton |
| High Wycombe | Aylesbury | |
| Horsham | Brighton | |
| Huddersfield | Parts 1 to 11 | Leeds |
| Ipswich | Parts 1 to 11 | Norwich or Southend |
| Kendal | Parts 1 to 11 | Blackpool or Preston |
| Kettering | Northampton | |
| Kings Lynn | Norwich or Peterborough | |
| Kingston-upon-Hull | Parts 1 to 11 | |
| Kingston-upon-Thames | Parts 1 to 11 | |
| Lambeth | London Insolvency District— High Court for Parts 1 to 7 (see head note); County Court at Central London for Parts 7A to 11 | |
| Lancaster | Parts 1 to 11 | Blackpool or Preston |
| Leeds | Parts 1 to 11 | |
| Leicester | Parts 1 to 11 | |
| Lewes | Brighton | |
| Lincoln | Parts 1 to 11 | Nottingham |
| Liverpool | Parts 1 to 11 | |
| Llanelli | Swansea | |
| Llangefni | Parts 1 to 11 | |
| Luton | Parts 1 to 11 | |

| Name of county court hearing centre | Parts of the Insolvency Act under which proceedings may be commenced at a county court hearing centre or the alternative court or county court hearing centre where proceedings may be commenced | Nearest full time court or hearing centre |
|---|---|---|
| Maidstone | Parts 1 to 11 | Croydon or the High Court (London) |
| Manchester | Parts 1 to 11 | |
| Mansfield | Nottingham | |
| Mayor's and City of London | London Insolvency District— High Court for Parts 1 to 7 (see head note); County Court at Central London for Parts 7A to 11 | |
| Medway | Canterbury | Croydon or the High Court (London) |
| Merthyr Tydfil | Parts 1 to 11 | Cardiff |
| Middlesbrough | Parts 1 to 11 | |
| Milton Keynes | Parts 1 to 11 | Luton |
| Mold | Wrexham | Wrexham |
| Newcastle upon Tyne | Parts 1 to 11 | |
| Newport (Gwent) | Parts 1 to 11 | Cardiff |
| Newport (Isle of Wight) | Parts 1 to 11 | Southampton or Portsmouth |
| Northampton | Parts 1 to 11 | Luton |
| North Shields | Newcastle upon Tyne | |
| Norwich | Parts 1 to 11 | |
| Nottingham | Parts 1 to 11 | |
| Nuneaton | Coventry | |
| Oldham | Parts 1 to 11 | |
| Oxford | Parts 1 to 11 | Reading |
| Peterborough | Parts 1 to 11 | Cambridge |
| Plymouth | Parts 1 to 11 | |
| Pontypridd | Parts 1 to 11 | Cardiff |
| Portsmouth | Parts 1 to 11 | |
| Port Talbot | Parts 1 to 11 | |
| Prestatyn | Parts 1 to 11 | |
| Preston | Parts 1 to 11 | |
| Reading | Parts 1 to 11 | |
| Reigate | Guildford | |
| Rhyl | Parts 1 to 11 | Birkenhead or Chester |
| Romford | Parts 1 to 11 | |
| Salisbury | Parts 1 to 11 | Bournemouth or Southampton |
| Scarborough | Parts 1 to 11 | York, Hull or Middlesbrough |
| Scunthorpe | Parts 1 to 11 | Hull or Sheffield |
| Sheffield | Parts 1 to 11 | |
| Skipton | Bradford | |
| Slough | Parts 1 to 11 | |
| Southampton | Parts 1 to 11 | |

| Name of county court hearing centre | Parts of the Insolvency Act under which proceedings may be commenced at a county court hearing centre or the alternative court or county court hearing centre where proceedings may be commenced | Nearest full time court or hearing centre |
|---|---|---|
| Southend-on-Sea | Parts 1 to 11 | |
| South Shields | Newcastle upon Tyne | |
| Stafford | Parts 1 to 11 | Stoke |
| Staines | Guildford | |
| St Albans | Parts 1 to 11 | Luton |
| St Helens | Liverpool | |
| Stockport | Parts 1 to 11 | Manchester |
| Stoke-on-Trent | Parts 1 to 11 | |
| Sunderland | Parts 1 to 11 | Newcastle |
| Swansea | Parts 1 to 11 | Cardiff |
| Swindon | Parts 1 to 11 | Gloucester or Reading |
| Taunton | Parts 1 to 11 | Exeter or Bristol |
| Telford | Parts 1 to 11 | |
| Thanet | Canterbury | |
| Torquay & Newton Abbot | Parts 1 to 11 | Exeter |
| Truro | Parts 1 to 11 | Plymouth |
| Tunbridge Wells | Parts 1 to 11 | Croydon |
| Uxbridge | The County Court at Central London | |
| Wakefield | Parts 1 to 11 | Leeds |
| Walsall | Parts 1 to 11 | |
| Wandsworth | London Insolvency District— High Court for Parts 1 to 7 (see head note); County Court at Central London for Parts 7A to 11 | |
| Warwick | Parts 1 to 11 | Birmingham |
| Watford | Luton | |
| Welshpool & Newton | Parts 1 to 11 | Stoke or Chester |
| West Cumbria | Parts 1 to 11 | |
| Weston Super Mare | Bristol | |
| Weymouth | Bournemouth | Bournemouth |
| Wigan | Parts 1 to 11 | Bolton, Manchester or Preston |
| Willesden | London Insolvency District— High Court for Parts 1 to 7 (see head note); County Court at Central London for Parts 7A to 11 | |
| Winchester | Parts 1 to 11 | Southampton |
| Wolverhampton | Parts 1 to 11 | |
| Woolwich | Croydon | |
| Worcester | Parts 1 to 11 | Gloucester |
| Worthing | Brighton | |
| Wrexham | Parts 1 to 11 | Birkenhead, Stoke or Chester |

| Name of county court hearing centre | Parts of the Insolvency Act under which proceedings may be commenced at a county court hearing centre or the alternative court or county court hearing centre where proceedings may be commenced | Nearest full time court or hearing centre |
|---|---|---|
| Yeovil | Parts 1 to 11 | Exeter or Bristol |
| York | Parts 1 to 11 | |

**Derivation**—This Schedule derived from the Insolvency Rules 1986, SI 1986/1925, Sch 2 and the Insolvency (Commencement of Proceedings) and Insolvency Rules 1986 (Amendment) Rules 2014, SI 2014/817.

SCHEDULE 7

INFORMATION TO BE PROVIDED IN THE BANKRUPTCY APPLICATION

Rule 10.35

PART 1    DEBTOR'S PERSONAL INFORMATION

**[2.1051]**

**1**

Debtor's title.

**2**

Debtor's identification details.

**3**

Any previous name or other names by which the debtor is known or has been known during the last five years immediately before the date of the bankruptcy application.

**Derivation**—This Part of this Schedule derived from the Insolvency Rules 1986, SI 1986/1925, r 6.38, Schs 2A, 2B.

PART 2    ADDITIONAL PERSONAL INFORMATION

**[2.1052]**

**4**

Debtor's contact telephone number.

**5**

Debtor's email address (if any).

**6**

Debtor's date of birth.

**7**

Debtor's National Insurance number.

**8**

Debtor's gender.

**9**

Any previous address at which the debtor has resided during the three years immediately before the date of the bankruptcy application.

**10**

Whether the debtor is—

    (a)    single;

    (b)    married;
    (c)    divorced;
    (d)    co-habiting;
    (e)    separated;
    (f)    widowed;
    (g)    a civil partner;
    (h)    a former civil partner; or
    (i)    a surviving civil partner.

**11**

All occupants of the debtor's household and in relation to each person—
    (a)    name;
    (b)    age;
    (c)    relationship to the debtor; and
    (d)    whether or not that person is dependent on the debtor.

**12**

Any other person dependent on the debtor and in relation to each person—
    (a)    name;
    (b)    age;
    (c)    postal address; and
    (d)    reason for that person's dependency on the debtor.

### Occupation and employment details

**13**

Debtor's occupation (if any).

**14**

Debtor's employment status.

**15**

Where the debtor is employed—
    (a)    date when the debtor commenced the employment; and
    (b)    name and address of the employer.

**16**

Where the debtor is unemployed—
    (a)    date when the debtor was last employed;
    (b)    date when the debtor commenced the employment; and
    (c)    name and address of the last employer.

**17**

Where the debtor has worked for any previous employers during the 12 months immediately before the date of the bankruptcy application—
    (a)    dates of that employment; and
    (b)    name and address of those employers.

**18**

Where the debtor is, or has been, self-employed other than as a partner in a partnership, during the three years preceding the date of the bankruptcy application, in respect of each business—
    (a)    date when the business commenced trading;
    (b)    name and trading address of the business;
    (c)    name or names, other than the debtor's name, in which the debtor carried on business;
    (d)    nature of the business;

(e)      trading address or addresses of the business and any address or addresses at which the debtor has carried on business during the period in which any of the debtor's bankruptcy debts were incurred; and

(f)      the date the business ceased trading, if applicable.

**19**

Where the debtor traded in a partnership at any time in the three years immediately preceding the date of the bankruptcy application, in respect of each partnership—

(a)      date the partnership commenced;

(b)      name and trading address of the partnership;

(c)      trading address or addresses of the partnership and any address or addresses at which the partnership has carried on business during or after the time when any of the debtor's bankruptcy debts were incurred; and

(d)      date the partnership ceased, if applicable.

**20**

Where the debtor is, or has been, a director or involved in the management of a company during the 12 months immediately preceding the date of the bankruptcy application—

(a)      name and contact details for each company; and

(b)      in the case of any company mentioned in accordance with sub paragraph (a) that is subject to any insolvency proceedings, the office-holder and contact details for that office-holder.

## CREDITORS

**21**

In respect of each creditor—

(a)      name and address;

(b)      account number or reference (if known);

(c)      date the debt was incurred;

(d)      the amount the creditor claims the debtor owes the creditor; and

(e)      where the debt is secured, the property of the debtor which is claimed by the creditor to clear or reduce the creditor's debt.

**22**

Where the debtor has an interest in a property, in relation to each property, its address.

## LEGAL PROCEEDINGS

**23**

Where the debtor is, or has been in the five years immediately preceding the date of the bankruptcy application, involved in proceedings for divorce, separation or the dissolution of a civil partnership—

(a)      identity of the proceedings;

(b)      nature of the proceedings; and

(c)      date and details of any resolution of those proceedings and any agreed settlement, whether formal or informal, and any gifts or transfers of property that occurred in, or as a result, of those proceedings.

**24**

Where the debtor is involved in proceedings, other than proceedings for divorce, separation or the dissolution of a civil partnership—

(a)      identity of the proceedings;

(b)      nature of the proceedings; and

(c)      date and details of any interim settlement, whether formal or informal, and any interim orders.

ASSETS AND LIABILITIES

**25**

Total value of assets.

**26**

Total value of liabilities.

**27**

Debtor's net monthly income from all sources.

**28**

Debtor's monthly surplus income calculated by reference to paragraphs 23 to 30 of Schedule 8 (additional information to be provided in the bankruptcy application).

**Derivation**—This Part of this Schedule derived from the Insolvency Rules 1986, SI 1986/1925, r 6.38, Schs 2A, 2B.

## SCHEDULE 8

## ADDITIONAL INFORMATION TO BE PROVIDED IN THE BANKRUPTCY APPLICATION

Rule 10.35

### DISPOSAL OF ASSETS

**[2.1053]**

**1**

Where in the five years preceding the date on which the bankruptcy application is made the debtor has entered into a transaction at an undervalue within the meaning of section 339(1), given a preference within the meaning of section 340(2), has rights or excluded rights under section 342A(3) of the Act or placed an asset into a trust for the benefit of any person, including the surrender of life, endowment and pension policies, in respect of each asset—

(a)    description of the asset;

(b)    date the debtor gave away, transferred or sold the asset;

(c)    consideration given, if any;

(d)    name and address of the person to whom the debtor sold, transferred or gave away the asset;

(e)    relationship of that person to the debtor;

(f)    if relevant, name of the trustees and beneficiaries or class of beneficiaries;

(g)    estimated market value of the asset at the date of the bankruptcy application;

(h)    net proceeds (if any) (less any charges and legal fees).

**2**

Where in the five years preceding the date on which the bankruptcy application is made the debtor has disposed of or sold any property at market value or disposed of, sold at market value or realised any life, endowment and pension policies in respect of each asset—

(a)    description of the asset;

(b)    date the debtor disposed of, sold at market value or realised the asset; and

(c)    net proceeds (if any) (less any charges and legal fees).

## FINANCIAL ARRANGEMENTS WITH CREDITORS

**3**

Where the debtor has been made bankrupt in the two years immediately preceding the date of the bankruptcy application—

    (a)    date of the bankruptcy order; and

    (b)    reference allocated by the official receiver.

**4**

Where the debtor has entered into a debt relief order in the two years immediately preceding the date of the bankruptcy application—

    (a)    date of the debt relief order; and

    (b)    reference allocated by the official receiver.

**5**

Where the debtor has, or has had, an IVA in the two years immediately preceding the date of the bankruptcy application, the date of the arrangement.

**6**

Where the debtor has, or has had, an arrangement in force with creditors, other than an IVA in the two years immediately preceding the date of the bankruptcy application, the date and nature of the arrangement.

## LEGAL AND FINANCIAL ADVISERS

**7**

Where a solicitor has acted for or on behalf of the debtor in the five years immediately preceding the date of the bankruptcy application, in relation to each solicitor—

    (a)    name, address and reference of the solicitor; and

    (b)    nature and date of the transaction or transactions on which the solicitor advised or acted.

**8**

Where an accountant, book keeper or other financial adviser has acted for or on behalf of the debtor in the five years immediately preceding the date of the bankruptcy application, in relation to each accountant, book keeper and financial adviser—

    (a)    name, address and reference; and

    (b)    dates of acting for the debtor.

## BUSINESS AFFAIRS OF A SELF-EMPLOYED DEBTOR

**9**

Where the debtor traded in a partnership at any time in the three years immediately preceding the date of the bankruptcy application, in respect of each partnership—

    (a)    names and addresses of each of the partners;

    (b)    name or names, other than the partners' names, in which the partnership carried on business; and

    (c)    the nature of the partnership business.

**10**

Where the debtor is or has been self-employed (other than as a partner in a partnership) at any time in the three years immediately preceding the date of the bankruptcy application—

    (a)    Value Added Tax number, where the business was registered for Value Added Tax;

    (b)    address where the debtor's books of account and other accounting records are kept; and

(c)    where the debtor holds records on a computer, details of which records are held, what software is used (including any passwords) and where the computer is located.

**11**

Where the debtor is or has been self-employed (including a partner in a partnership) at any time in the three years immediately preceding the date of the bankruptcy application—

(a)    name and address of any person employed by the debtor immediately preceding the bankruptcy application; and

(b)    whether—

    (i)    the debtor owes any employee or former employee any money, and

    (ii)    any employee or former employee has or may claim that the debtor owes that person some money.

## FINANCIAL AFFAIRS—ASSETS

**12**

The nature and value of each asset belonging to the debtor.

**13**

Where any asset is owned jointly with another person—

(a)    name and address of that joint owner; and

(b)    relationship of that person to the debtor.

**14**

Where any asset is subject to the rights of any person (other than a joint owner), whether as a secured creditor of the debtor or otherwise, in respect of each asset—

(a)    nature of third party rights;

(b)    account number or reference of that creditor or creditors; and

(c)    amount each creditor claims is owed to them.

**15**

Where the debtor holds or has held in the last two years any bank, building society, credit union or national savings account including any joint, business or dormant accounts, in respect of each account—

(a)    name, address and sort code of the bank or supplier;

(b)    account number; and

(c)    whether or not the debtor's regular income is paid into the account.

**16**

Where the debtor owns a motor vehicle or has disposed of any vehicle during the 12 months immediately preceding the date of the bankruptcy application, in respect of each motor vehicle—

(a)    make and model;

(b)    registration number;

(c)    what the motor vehicle is or was used for by the debtor

(d)    save where the motor vehicle has been disposed of, the location of the motor vehicle; and

(e)    where the motor vehicle has been disposed of, the date of disposal and any proceeds from that disposal.

**17**

Where the debtor regularly uses a motor vehicle that the debtor does not own, in respect of each motor vehicle—

(a)    make and model;

(b)    registration number;

(c)    name and address of the owner; and

(d)    debtor's relationship to the vehicle's owner.

**18**

Where the debtor owns any property consisting of land or buildings, in respect of each property—

- (a)    type of and description of the property;
- (b)    who lives at the property and their relationship to the debtor;
- (c)    any income received by the debtor from the property; and
- (d)    nature of the insurance policy currently in force in relation to the property and the expiry date of that insurance policy.

**19**

Where the debtor rents or leases a property, in respect of each property—

- (a)    who lives at the property and their relationship to the debtor;
- (b)    monthly rent;
- (c)    name and address of the landlord and any managing agent.

**20**

Where the debtor has an interest in any other property, in respect of each property—

- (a)    nature of the interest;
- (b)    type of and description of the property;
- (c)    who lives at the property and their relationship to the debtor;
- (d)    name and address of the person who permits the debtor to use the property;
- (e)    amount paid by the debtor to the person who permits the debtor to use the property;
- (f)    any income received by the debtor from the property; and
- (g)    whether or not there is a written agreement.

**21**

Where the debtor resides at a property in which the debtor has no interest, the basis on which the debtor resides at that property.

**22**

Where the debtor has or has held within the five years immediately before the date of the bankruptcy application any occupational pension, personal pension, endowment or other life policy in relation to each policy—

- (a)    type of policy;
- (b)    name and address of the pension, endowment or life assurance company or broker;
- (c)    policy number;
- (d)    approximate date when the policy was taken out;
- (e)    estimated value of policy;
- (f)    amount (if any) being received now by the debtor and the frequency of those payments; and
- (g)    name of the beneficiary or beneficiaries of the policy.

### FINANCIAL AFFAIRS—INCOME AND EXPENDITURE

**23**

Debtor's total annual income from all sources, the sources of that income and the amount from each source.

**24**

Total annual household income from all sources, the sources of that income and the amount from each source.

**25**

Current (or last) income tax reference number.

**26**

Monthly national insurance.

**27**

Mean monthly tax.

**28**

Where the debtor has any current attachment of earnings orders in force, in respect of each attachment of earnings order—

    (a)    name of creditor;

    (b)    name of the court that made the attachment of earnings order.

**29**

Particulars of the debtor's mean monthly expenditure which the debtor claims is necessary to meet the monthly reasonable domestic needs of the debtor's family, including the objective and the amount of that expenditure.

**30**

Particulars of the debtor's monthly expenditure not otherwise provided under this Schedule.

## ENFORCEMENT OFFICERS AND ENFORCEMENT AGENTS

**31**

Where an enforcement officer or enforcement agent has visited the debtor in the last six months—

    (a)    name of the creditor by whom the relevant debt is claimed;

    (b)    date of initial visit;

    (c)    description and estimated value of property seized.

## CAUSE OF INSOLVENCY

**32**

Why the debt was incurred.

**33**

Date when the debtor first experienced difficulty in paying some or all of the debtor's debts.

**34**

Reasons for the debtor not having enough money to pay some or all of the debtor's debts.

**35**

Where the debtor has gambled any money through betting or gambling during the last two years, how much the debtor has gambled.

    **Derivation**—This Schedule derived from the Insolvency Rules 1986, SI 1986/1925, r 6.38, Schs 2A, 2B.

    **Amendments**—SI 2017/366.

## SCHEDULE 9
### INFORMATION TO BE GIVEN TO CREDITORS

Rule 10.47

**[2.1054]**

**1**

Title of the debtor.

**2**

Debtor's identification details.

**3**

Any previous name or other names by which the debtor is known or has been known during the last five years immediately before the date of the bankruptcy application.

**4**

Any previous address at which the debtor has resided at during the three years immediately before the date of the bankruptcy application.

**5**

Name and address for each creditor.

**6**

Amount each creditor claims is due.

**7**

Debtor's occupation (if any).

**8**

Debtor's employment status.

**9**

Where the debtor is, or has been, self-employed other than as a partner in a partnership, during the three years preceding the date of the bankruptcy application, in respect of each business—

- (a) name and trading address of the business;
- (b) name or names, other than the debtor's name, in which the debtor carried on business;
- (c) nature of the business;
- (d) trading address or addresses of the business and any address or addresses at which the debtor has carried on business during the period in which any of the debtor's bankruptcy debts were incurred; and
- (e) where the business has ceased trading, the date when the business ceased trading.

**10**

Total value of assets.

**11**

Total value of liabilities.

**12**

Where in the five years preceding the date of the bankruptcy application the debtor has given away, placed into a trust for the benefit of any person, given a preference within the meaning of section 340 of the Act, has rights or excluded rights under section 342A of the Act or has transferred or sold for less than its true value any assets that the debtor owned, either alone or jointly, including the surrender of life, endowment and pension policies in relation to each asset—

- (a) description of the asset;
- (b) date the debtor gave away, transferred or sold the asset;
- (c) relationship of that person to the debtor;
- (d) estimated market value or true value of the asset at the date of the bankruptcy application;
- (e) value at which the asset was given away, transferred or sold; and
- (f) net proceeds (if any) (less any charges and legal fees).

**13**

Where any asset is owned jointly with another person, the nature of the asset.

**14**

Where any asset is subject to the rights of any person (other than a joint owner), whether as a secured creditor of the debtor or otherwise, in respect of each asset, the nature of third party rights.

**15**

Where the debtor owns a motor vehicle or has disposed of any vehicle during the 12 months immediately preceding the date of the bankruptcy application, in respect of each motor vehicle—

    (a)    make, model and year of manufacture;

    (b)    what the motor vehicle is or was used for by the debtor;

    (c)    save where the motor vehicle has been disposed of, the location of the motor vehicle;

    (d)    where the motor vehicle has been disposed of, the date of disposal and any proceeds from that disposal.

**16**

Where the debtor regularly uses a motor vehicle that the debtor does not own, in relation to each motor vehicle—

    (a)    make and model; and

    (b)    debtor's relationship to the vehicle's owner.

**17**

Where the debtor owns or has an interest in any property, in respect of each property—

    (a)    address;

    (b)    type of and description of the property;

    (c)    nature of the interest

    (d)    value of that interest; and

    (e)    any income received by the debtor from the property.

**18**

Where the debtor holds or has held within the five years immediately before the date of the bankruptcy application any occupational pension, personal pension, endowment or other life policy in respect of each policy—

    (a)    type of policy;

    (b)    approximate date when the policy was taken out; and

    (c)    estimated value of policy.

**19**

Debtor's net monthly income from all sources.

**20**

Debtor's monthly surplus income after taking into account any contribution made by a member of the debtor's family to the amount necessary for the reasonable domestic needs of the debtor and the debtor's family.

**21**

Current (or last) income tax reference number.

**22**

In respect of each creditor—

    (a)    name and address;

    (b)    date the debt was incurred;

    (c)    the amount the creditor claims the debtor owes the creditor;

    (d)    where the debt is secured, the property of the debtor which is claimed by the creditor to clear of reduce the creditor's debt.

**Derivation**—This Schedule derived from the Insolvency Rules 1986, SI 1986/1925, Sch 2C.
**Amendments**—SI 2017/366.

SCHEDULE 10
DESTINATION OF APPEALS FROM DECISIONS OF DISTRICT JUDGES
IN CORPORATE INSOLVENCY MATTERS
Rule 12.59

**[2.1055]**

| Country court hearing centre | Destination of Appeal |
| --- | --- |
| Aberystwyth | Cardiff or Caernarfon District Registry |
| Banbury | Birmingham District Registry |
| Barnsley | Leeds District Registry |
| Barnstaple | Bristol District Registry |
| Barrow-in-Furness | Liverpool District Registry or Manchester District Registry |
| Bath | Bristol District Registry |
| Bedford | Birmingham District Registry |
| Birkenhead | Liverpool District Registry or Manchester District Registry |
| Birmingham | Birmingham District Registry |
| Blackburn | Liverpool District Registry or Manchester District Registry |
| Blackpool | Liverpool District Registry or Manchester District Registry |
| Blackwood | Cardiff District Registry |
| Bolton | Liverpool District Registry or Manchester District Registry |
| Boston | Birmingham District Registry |
| Bournemouth and Poole | Registrar in Bankruptcy |
| Bradford | Leeds District Registry |
| Brighton | Registrar in Bankruptcy |
| Bristol | Bristol District Registry |
| Burnley | Liverpool District Registry or Manchester District Registry |
| Bury | Liverpool District Registry or Manchester District Registry |
| Bury St Edmunds | Registrar in Bankruptcy |
| Caernarfon | Cardiff District Registry |
| Cambridge | Registrar in Bankruptcy |
| Canterbury | Registrar in Bankruptcy |
| Cardiff | Cardiff District Registry |
| Carlisle | Liverpool District Registry or Manchester District Registry |
| Caernarfon | Cardiff District Registry or Caernarfon District Registry |
| County Court at Central London | Registrar in Bankruptcy |
| Chelmsford | Registrar in Bankruptcy |
| Chester | Liverpool District Registry or Manchester District Registry |
| Chesterfield | Leeds District Registry |
| Colchester | Registrar in Bankruptcy |
| Coventry | Birmingham District Registry |

| Country court hearing centre | Destination of Appeal |
|---|---|
| Crewe | Liverpool District Registry or Manchester District Registry |
| Croydon | Registrar in Bankruptcy |
| Darlington | Newcastle District Registry |
| Derby | Birmingham District Registry |
| Doncaster | Leeds District Registry |
| Dudley | Birmingham District Registry |
| Durham | Leeds District Registry or Newcastle District Registry |
| Eastbourne | Registrar in Bankruptcy |
| Exeter | Bristol District Registry |
| Gloucester and Cheltenham | Bristol District Registry |
| Great Grimsby | Leeds District Registry |
| Guildford | Registrar in Bankruptcy |
| Halifax | Leeds District Registry |
| Harrogate | Leeds District Registry |
| Hastings | Registrar in Bankruptcy |
| Haverfordwest | Cardiff District Registry |
| Hereford | Bristol District Registry |
| Hertford | Registrar in Bankruptcy |
| Huddersfield | Leeds District Registry |
| Ipswich | Registrar in Bankruptcy |
| Kendal | Liverpool District Registry or Manchester District Registry |
| Kingston-upon-Hull | Leeds District Registry |
| Kingston-upon-Thames | Registrar in Bankruptcy |
| Lancaster | Liverpool District Registry or Manchester District Registry |
| Leeds | Leeds District Registry |
| Leicester | Birmingham District Registry |
| Lincoln | Leeds District Registry or Birmingham District Registry |
| Liverpool | Liverpool District Registry or Manchester District Registry |
| Llangefni | Cardiff District Registry or Caernarfon District Registry |
| Luton | Registrar in Bankruptcy |
| Maidstone | Registrar in Bankruptcy |
| Manchester | Manchester District Registry |
| Merthyr Tydfil | Cardiff District Registry |
| Middlesbrough | Newcastle District Registry |
| Milton Keynes | Birmingham District Registry |
| Newcastle upon Tyne | Newcastle District Registry |
| Newport (Gwent) | Cardiff District Registry |
| Newport (Isle of Wight) | Registrar in Bankruptcy |
| Northampton | Birmingham District Registry |
| Norwich | Registrar in Bankruptcy |
| Nottingham | Birmingham District Registry |
| Oldham | Liverpool District Registry or Manchester District Registry |
| Oxford | Registrar in Bankruptcy |

| Country court hearing centre | Destination of Appeal |
|---|---|
| Peterborough | Registrar in Bankruptcy |
| Plymouth | Bristol District Registry |
| Pontypridd | Cardiff District Registry |
| Portsmouth | Registrar in Bankruptcy |
| Port Talbot | Cardiff District Registry |
| Prestatyn | Cardiff District Registry or Caernarfon District Registry |
| Preston | Liverpool District Registry or Manchester District Registry |
| Reading | Registrar in Bankruptcy |
| Rhyl | Cardiff District Registry or Caernarfon District Registry |
| Romford | Registrar in Bankruptcy |
| Salisbury | Registrar in Bankruptcy |
| Scarborough | Leeds District Registry |
| Scunthorpe | Leeds District Registry |
| Sheffield | Leeds District Registry |
| Slough | Registrar in Bankruptcy |
| Southampton | Registrar in Bankruptcy |
| Southend-on-Sea | Registrar in Bankruptcy |
| Stafford | Birmingham District Registry |
| St Albans | Registrar in Bankruptcy |
| Stockport | Liverpool District Registry or Manchester District Registry |
| Stoke-on-Trent | Manchester District Registry |
| Sunderland | Newcastle District Registry |
| Swansea | Cardiff District Registry |
| Swindon | Bristol District Registry |
| Taunton | Bristol District Registry |
| Telford | Birmingham District Registry |
| Torquay & Newton Abbot | Bristol District Registry |
| Truro | Bristol District Registry |
| Tunbridge Wells | Registrar in Bankruptcy |
| Wakefield | Leeds District Registry |
| Walsall | Birmingham District Registry |
| Warwick | Birmingham District Registry |
| Welshpool & Newton | Cardiff District Registry |
| West Cumbria | Liverpool District Registry or Manchester District Registry |
| Wigan | Liverpool District Registry or Manchester District Registry |
| Winchester | Registrar in Bankruptcy |
| Wolverhampton | Birmingham District Registry |
| Worcester | Birmingham District Registry |
| Wrexham | Cardiff District Registry or Caernarfon District Registry |
| Yeovil | Bristol District Registry |
| York | Leeds District Registry |

SCHEDULE 11

DETERMINATION OF INSOLVENCY OFFICE-HOLDER'S REMUNERATION

Rule 18.22

**[2.1056]**

This table sets out the realisation and distribution scales for determining the remuneration of trustees and liquidators.

| | |
|---|---|
| The realisation scale | |
| on the first £5,000 | 20% |
| on the next £5,000 | 15% |
| on the next £90,000 | 10% |
| on all further sums realised | 5% |
| | |
| The distribution scale | |
| on the first £5,000 | 10% |
| on the next £5,000 | 7.5% |
| on the next £90,000 | 5% |
| on all further sums distributed | 2.5% |

**Derivation**—This Schedule derived from the Insolvency Rules 1986, SI 1986/1925, Sch 6.

# INSOLVENCY ACT 2000

## INSOLVENCY ACT 2000

**[3.1]**

    **General note**—The Insolvency Act 2000 received Royal Assent on 30 November 2000, but was not brought into force until 1 January 2003. In substance, the 2000 Act is an amendment Act, which addresses four broad areas identified below. Rather than include limited annotations in isolation, the approach here is to incorporate any necessary commentary on the amendments introduced by the 2000 Act into the annotations to the Insolvency Act 1986, in the earlier part of this work, which itself appears subject to those amendments. This is not the case, however, with s 14, which deals with cross-border insolvency and on which the commentary appears to that provision. Neither, it should be noted, do the provisions in ss 5–8 find any corresponding commentary elsewhere since the area of disqualification of company directors is currently not dealt with in this work.

### ARRANGEMENT OF SECTIONS

#### VOLUNTARY ARRANGEMENTS

| | | |
|---|---|---|
| 1 | Moratorium where directors propose voluntary arrangement | 3.2 |
| 2 | Company voluntary arrangements | 3.3 |
| 3 | Individual voluntary arrangements | 3.4 |
| 4 | Qualification or authorisation of nominees and supervisors | 3.5 |

#### MISCELLANEOUS

| | | |
|---|---|---|
| 9 | Administration orders | 3.8 |
| 10 | Investigation and prosecution of malpractice | 3.9 |
| 11 | Restriction on use of answers obtained under compulsion | 3.10 |
| 12 | Insolvent estates of deceased persons | 3.11 |
| 13 | Bankruptcy: interest on sums held in Insolvency Services Account | 3.12 |
| 14 | Model law on cross-border insolvency | 3.13 |

#### GENERAL

| | | |
|---|---|---|
| 16 | Commencement | 3.15 |
| 17 | Extent | 3.16 |
| 18 | Short title | 3.17 |

**[3.2]**

**1 Moratorium where directors propose voluntary arrangement**

Schedule 1 (which—

    (a)    enables directors of a company to obtain an initial moratorium

    (b)    makes provision about the approval and implementation of such a voluntary arrangement where a moratorium is obtained, and

    (c)    makes consequential amendments),

is to have effect.

**[3.3]**

### 2 Company voluntary arrangements

Schedule 2 (which—

(a)     amends the provisions about company voluntary arrangements under Part I of the Insolvency Act 1986, and

(b)     in consequence of Schedule 1 and those amendments, makes amendments of the Building Societies Act 1986),

is to have effect.

**[3.4]**

### 3 Individual voluntary arrangements

Schedule 3 (which enables the procedure for the approval of individual voluntary arrangements under Part VIII of the Insolvency Act 1986 to be started without an initial moratorium for the insolvent debtor and makes other amendments of the provisions about individual voluntary arrangements) is to have effect.

**[3.5]**

### 4 Qualification or authorisation of nominees and supervisors

(1)     Part VIII of the Insolvency Act 1986 (insolvency practitioners and their qualification) is amended as follows.

(2)     In section 388 (meaning of "act as insolvency practitioner")—

(a)     for subsection (1)(b) there is substituted—

"(b)     where a voluntary arrangement in relation to the company is proposed or approved under Part I, as nominee or supervisor",

(b)     for subsection (2)(c) there is substituted—

"(c)     where a voluntary arrangement in relation to the individual is proposed or approved under Part VIII, as nominee or supervisor", and

(c)     after subsection (2A) there is inserted—

"(2B)     In relation to a voluntary arrangement proposed under Part I or VIII, a person acts as nominee if he performs any of the functions conferred on nominees under the Part in question."

(3)     . . .

(4)     . . .

**Amendments**—Deregulation Act 2015, s 19, Sch 6, Pt 6, para 20(1), (3).

## DISQUALIFICATION OF COMPANY DIRECTORS ETC

**[3.6]**

**Sections 5–8 and Sch 4**—These provisions introduce amendments to the Company Directors Disqualification Act 1986.

## MISCELLANEOUS

**[3.7]**

**General note**—Section 9 inserted new ss 10(1)(aa) and 11(3)(ba) into Part II of the 1986 Act so as to expressly prevent a landlord's right of re-entry. The provision was in any case repealed by Sch 26 to the Enterprise Act 2002.

Section 10 amended ss 218 and 219 of the 1986 Act (prosecution of delinquent directors and members of company and obligations arising under s 218).

Section 11 inserted a new s 219(2A) (use of s 218 evidence in criminal proceedings) into the 1986 Act.

Section 12 amended s 421(1) and inserted a new s 421A (insolvent estates: joint tenancies) into the 1986 Act.

Section 13 amended s 406 (interest on money received by liquidators or trustees-in-bankruptcy and invested) and para 21 of Sch 9 of the 1986 Act (provisions as to investment of monies received by trustee-in-bankruptcy and paid into Insolvency Services Account).

Section 14 is annotated below.

**[3.8]**

**9 Administration orders**

(1)  *Part II of the Insolvency Act 1986 (administration orders) is amended as follows.*

(2)  *In section 10 (effect of application), after paragraph (a) of subsection (1) there is inserted—*

> "(aa)  *no landlord or other person to whom rent is payable may exercise any right of forfeiture by peaceable re-entry in relation to premises let to the company in respect of a failure by the company to comply with any term or condition of its tenancy of such premises, except with the leave of the court and subject to such terms as the court may impose".*

(3)  *In section 11 (effect of order), after paragraph (b) of subsection (3) there is inserted—*

> "(ba)  *no landlord or other person to whom rent is payable may exercise any right of forfeiture by peaceable re-entry in relation to premises let to the company in respect of a failure by the company to comply with any term or condition of its tenancy of such premises, except with the consent of the administrator or the leave of the court and subject (where the court gives leave) to such terms as the court may impose".*

**Amendments**—Repealed by Enterprise Act 2002, s 278(2), Sch 26, as from a date to be appointed.

**[3.9]**

**10 Investigation and prosecution of malpractice**

(1)  Section 218 of the Insolvency Act 1986 (prosecution of delinquent officers and members of company) is amended as follows.

(2)  In subsection (1), for "to the prosecuting authority" there is substituted—

> "(a)  in the case of a winding up in England and Wales, to the Secretary of State, and
>
> (b)  in the case of a winding up in Scotland, to the Lord Advocate".

(3)  Subsection (2) is omitted.

(4)  In subsection (4)—

> (a)  for the words from the beginning of paragraph (a) to "that authority" in paragraph (b) there is substituted—

"forthwith report the matter—

> (a)  in the case of a winding up in England and Wales, to the Secretary of State, and
>
> (b)  in the case of a winding up in Scotland, to the Lord Advocate,

and shall furnish to the Secretary of State or (as the case may be) the Lord Advocate",

> (b)  for "the authority" there is substituted "the Secretary of State or (as the case may be) the Lord Advocate".

(5)  For subsection (5) there is substituted—

> "(5)  Where a report is made to the Secretary of State under subsection (4) he may, for the purpose of investigating the matter reported to him and such other matters relating to the affairs of the company as appear to him to require investigation, exercise any of the powers which are exercisable by inspectors appointed under section 431 or 432 of the Companies Act to investigate a company's affairs."

(6)  In subsection (6)(b), "to the prosecuting authority" is omitted.

(7)  In section 219 of that Act (obligations arising under section 218)—

> (a)  in subsection (1), for "under section 218(5)" there is substituted "in consequence of a report made to him under section 218(4)" and for "that subsection" there is substituted "section 218(5)",

(b)   in subsection (3), for "the prosecuting authority" and "that authority" there is substituted "the Director of Public Prosecutions, the Lord Advocate",

(c)   in subsection (4), for "prosecuting authority" there is substituted "Director of Public Prosecutions, the Lord Advocate".

## [3.10]

**11  Restriction on use of answers obtained under compulsion**

In section 219 of the Insolvency Act 1986, after subsection (2) (answers given by a person pursuant to powers conferred by section 218 may be used in evidence against him) there is inserted—

"(2A)   However, in criminal proceedings in which that person is charged with an offence to which this subsection applies—

(a)   no evidence relating to the answer may be adduced, and

(b)   no question relating to it may be asked,

by or on behalf of the prosecution, unless evidence relating to it is adduced, or a question relating to it is asked, in the proceedings by or on behalf of that person.

(2B)   Subsection (2A) applies to any offence other than—

(a)   an offence under section 2 or 5 of the Perjury Act 1911 (false statements made on oath otherwise than in judicial proceedings or made otherwise than on oath), or

(b)   an offence under section 44(1) or (2) of the Criminal Law (Consolidation) (Scotland) Act 1995 (false statements made on oath or otherwise than on oath)."

## [3.11]

**12  Insolvent estates of deceased persons**

(1)   After section 421 of the Insolvency Act 1986 (power to apply provisions of Act to insolvent estates of deceased persons) there is inserted—

"**421A  Insolvent estates: joint tenancies**

(1)   This section applies where—

(a)   an insolvency administration order has been made in respect of the insolvent estate of a deceased person,

(b)   the petition for the order was presented after the commencement of this section and within the period of five years beginning with the day on which he died, and

(c)   immediately before his death he was beneficially entitled to an interest in any property as joint tenant.

(2)   For the purpose of securing that debts and other liabilities to which the estate is subject are met, the court may, on an application by the trustee appointed pursuant to the insolvency administration order, make an order under this section requiring the survivor to pay to the trustee an amount not exceeding the value lost to the estate.

(3)   In determining whether to make an order under this section, and the terms of such an order, the court must have regard to all the circumstances of the case, including the interests of the deceased's creditors and of the survivor; but, unless the circumstances are exceptional, the court must assume that the interests of the deceased's creditors outweigh all other considerations.

(4)   The order may be made on such terms and conditions as the court thinks fit.

(5)   Any sums required to be paid to the trustee in accordance with an order under this section shall be comprised in the estate.

(6)   The modifications of this Act which may be made by an order under section 421 include any modifications which are necessary or expedient in consequence of this section.

(7)    In this section, "survivor" means the person who, immediately before the death, was beneficially entitled as joint tenant with the deceased or, if the person who was so entitled dies after the making of the insolvency administration order, his personal representatives.

(8)    If there is more than one survivor—

(a)    an order under this section may be made against all or any of them, but

(b)    no survivor shall be required to pay more than so much of the value lost to the estate as is properly attributable to him.

(9)    In this section—

"insolvency administration order" has the same meaning as in any order under section 421 having effect for the time being,

"value lost to the estate" means the amount which, if paid to the trustee, would in the court's opinion restore the position to what it would have been if the deceased had been adjudged bankrupt immediately before his death."

(2)    In subsection (1) of section 421, after "apply" there is inserted "in relation".

## [3.12]

### 13 Bankruptcy: interest on sums held in Insolvency Services Account

(1)    In Schedule 9 to the Insolvency Act 1986 (individual insolvency rules), in paragraph 21, for "handled" there is substituted "invested or otherwise handled and with respect to the payment of interest on sums which, in pursuance of rules made by virtue of this paragraph, have been paid into the Insolvency Services Account".

(2)    In section 406 of that Act (interest on money received by liquidators and invested)—

(a)    for "a company" there is substituted "or paragraph 21 of Schedule 9 to this Act (investment of money received by trustee in bankruptcy) a company or a bankrupt's estate",

(b)    for the sidenote there is substituted "Interest on money received by liquidators or trustees in bankruptcy and invested".

## [3.13]

### 14 Model law on cross-border insolvency

(1)    The Secretary of State may by regulations make any provision which he considers necessary or expedient for the purpose of giving effect, with or without modifications, to the model law on cross-border insolvency.

(2)    In particular, the regulations may—

(a)    apply any provision of insolvency law in relation to foreign proceedings (whether begun before or after the regulations come into force),

(b)    modify the application of insolvency law (whether in relation to foreign proceedings or otherwise),

(c)    amend any provision of section 426 of the Insolvency Act 1986 (co-operation between courts),

and may apply or, as the case may be, modify the application of insolvency law in relation to the Crown.

(3)    The regulations may make different provision for different purposes and may make—

(a)    any supplementary, incidental or consequential provision, or

(b)    any transitory, transitional or saving provision,

which the Secretary of State considers necessary or expedient.

(4)    In this section—

"foreign proceedings" has the same meaning as in the model law on cross-border insolvency,

"insolvency law" has the same meaning as in section 426(10)(a) and (b) of the Insolvency Act 1986.

"the model law on cross-border insolvency" means the model law contained in Annex I of the report of the 30th session of UNCITRAL.

(5)   Regulations under this section are to be made by statutory instrument and may only be made if a draft has been laid before and approved by resolution of each House of Parliament.

(6)   Making regulations under this section requires the agreement—

(a)   if they extend to England and Wales, of the Lord Chancellor,

(b)   if they extend to Scotland, of the Scottish Ministers.

General note—The countries who have actually adopted the Model Law are Eritrea, Japan, Mexico and South Africa in 2000, Montenegro in 2002, Poland and Romania in 2003 and the USA in 2005. Other countries such as New Zealand and Australia have expressed a willingness to adopt the text but have not done so yet.

Section 14 came into force on 30 November 2000. The Secretary of State has now implemented the UNCITRAL Model Law and it came into force on 4 April 2006 through the Cross-Border Insolvency Regulations 2006 (SI 2006/1030). As adopted in Great Britain, there is no requirement of reciprocity before the British courts will give assistance to a foreign representative.

See Fletcher (2000) 13 *Insolvency Intelligence* 57; Omar [2000] *Insolvency Lawyer* 211; and *Dawson* [2000] 4 *Receivers and Administrators Law Quarterly* 147.

See also the introduction to the Cross-Border Insolvency Regulations 2006.

## GENERAL

**[3.14]**

General note—Section 15 (not reproduced) introduced certain amendments to the Financial Services and Markets Act 2000 with consequent repeals, whilst ss 16–18 dealt with commencement, extent and short title.

**[3.15]**

**16 Commencement**

(1)   The preceding provisions of this Act (including the Schedules) are to come into force on such day as the Secretary of State may by order made by statutory instrument appoint.

(2)   Subsection (1) does not apply to section 14 (which accordingly comes into force on the day on which this Act is passed).

(3)   An order under this section may make different provision for different purposes and may make—

(a)   any supplementary, incidental or consequential provision, and

(b)   any transitory, transitional or saving provision,

which the Secretary of State considers necessary or expedient.

**[3.16]**

**17 Extent**

This Act, except section 15(3), Part II of Schedule 2 and paragraphs 16(3) and 22 of Schedule 4, does not extend to Northern Ireland.

**[3.17]**

**18 Short title**

This Act may be cited as the Insolvency Act 2000.

. . .

# ENTERPRISE ACT 2002

## ENTERPRISE ACT 2002

**[4.1]**

**General**—On 7 November 2002 a significant piece of legislation, namely the Enterprise Act 2002 (EA), received Royal Assent. The legislation is important for this volume as one sizeable Part of the Act (Part 10) introduced provisions that deal with personal and corporate insolvency. Other Parts of the legislation addressed other areas of the law such as competition. Some of the provisions affecting insolvency law are far-reaching in impact as well as being quite revolutionary. Certainly, Part 10 of the EA represents the most significant changes to insolvency law since the enactment of the Insolvency Act 1986 (IA). Largely, the EA provisions were expressed as amending provisions in the IA and, hence, those particular provisions are not set out here; their impact can be seen in the provisions of the IA. Comments concerning them can be found after the appropriate IA provision that has been changed. What are set out after this introduction are those provisions that do not amend the IA and warrant being reproduced. We do not include any comments in relation to them, as there is nothing worthwhile to say about them.

According to the White Paper titled 'Productivity and Enterprise – Insolvency: A Second Chance' (Cm 5234, July 2001) which articulated the principles on which the insolvency provisions in the EA were based, the insolvency provisions were designed to:

'[M]odernise the framework of the law of personal and corporate insolvency. They will encourage responsible risk-taking, facilitate the rescue of viable businesses and provide certainty and fairness to creditors and other stakeholders. Our proposals will address the fear of failure and reduce the stigma of bankruptcy' (Executive Summary).

The policy background to the EA's insolvency provisions can be found in several documents that were formulated in the Insolvency Service and the Department of Trade and Industry. Following the speech of the then Secretary of State for Trade and Industry in 1999, the Honourable Stephen Byers, the Minister, and the Chancellor of the Exchequer established a Government review of corporate rescue and business reconstruction mechanisms, and in September of 1999 a consultation document was produced by a review group. The review group then produced 'A Review of Company Rescue and Business Reconstruction Mechanisms' in 2000. In the spring of 2001 the Government gave a commitment that it would reform the bankruptcy laws to ensure that people obtained a second chance where they became bankrupt as a result of no fault of their own. Following re-election in 2001, the Government published the White Paper mentioned above.

The insolvency provisions of the EA did not operate immediately on the passing of the Act. The corporate insolvency provisions became operative on 15 September 2003 and the personal insolvency provisions became operative on 1 April 2004.

Probably the main aim of the legislation, as far as corporate insolvency goes, is to provide the legal milieu for the fostering of a rescue culture. This is to be done by focusing on the administration process and making it more efficient and less costly. Allied to this is the restriction on charge holders appointing administrative receivers. Largely speaking, administrative receivers cannot be appointed in relation to debentures entered into after 15 September 2003 (ss 72A–72F of the IA, as amended by the EA, set out some exceptions where administrative receivers may be appointed). Instead, charge holders are to secure their protection by using the administration process, as they can appoint, quickly out of court, an administrator, just as they have been able to appoint receivers. Companies were also given the right to appoint administrators without a court order. It was thought that permitting the appointment of administrators without the need for court proceedings might encourage its use, as it could be invoked more quickly and less expensively.

The legislation overhauls the whole administration process in an effort to make it more efficient and attractive.

Other important features of the corporate insolvency provisions are:
- the abolition of the Crown's right to be included as a preferential creditor.
- in relation to floating charges created on or after 15 September 2003, a certain part of the net proceeds (net property) from the realisation of the property covered by charges must be set aside for the unsecured creditors. This is commented on in detail in this book, in the comments attached to s 176A of the IA.

In her Foreword to the White Paper, 'Productivity and Enterprise – Insolvency: A Second Chance', the Secretary of State for Trade and Industry, stated that the proposed changes to personal insolvency:

'[W]ill strengthen the competition and power of consumers by . . . transforming our approach to bankruptcy . . . [O]ur "Fresh Start" proposals for personal bankruptcy are based on the recognition that honest failure is an inevitable part of a dynamic market economy. Our radical liberalisation of the bankruptcy regime will mean a fresh start for many, backed by a very tough regime for those whose conduct of their financial affairs is irresponsible or reckless.'

The main aspect of the liberalisation to which the Minister referred is the reduction in the length of the period of bankruptcy. Discharge would be obtainable after one year. To complement what many would see as the Government's magnanimous approach to discharge from bankruptcy, the EA provides that 'dishonest' or blameworthy bankrupts will be subject to bankruptcy restrictions orders and bankruptcy restrictions undertakings. Clearly, the restriction scheme is modelled on the company directors' disqualification regime that applies under the Company Directors' Disqualification Act 1986. As with directors' disqualification, a person can be subject to a bankruptcy restriction order for between two and 15 years.

Other noteworthy features of the personal insolvency changes are:
- It is no longer an offence if either bankrupts fail to keep proper accounting records in the 2 years before bankruptcy or they engage in gambling in the two years before the presentation of a bankruptcy petition and it materially contributed to their bankruptcy.
- The official receiver is no longer obliged to investigate the affairs of bankrupts; he now has a discretion to do so if he chooses.
- The advent of a 'fast track' IVA procedure for undischarged bankrupts where the official receiver acts as the nominee.
- The EA abolishes some restrictions and disabilities that have traditionally attached to bankrupts.

## ARRANGEMENT OF SECTIONS

### PART 10
### INSOLVENCY
### COMPANIES ETC

| | | |
|---|---|---|
| 248 | Replacement of Part II of Insolvency Act 1986 | 4.2 |
| 249 | Special administration regimes | 4.3 |
| 254 | Application of insolvency law to foreign company | 4.4 |
| 255 | Application of law about company arrangement or administration to non-company | 4.5 |

### INDIVIDUALS

| | | |
|---|---|---|
| 256 | Duration of bankruptcy | 4.6 |
| 257 | Post-discharge restrictions | 4.7 |
| 261 | Bankrupt's home | 4.8 |
| 264 | Individual voluntary arrangement | 4.9 |
| 266 | Disqualification from office: Parliament | 4.10 |
| 267 | Disqualification from office: local government | 4.11 |
| 268 | Disqualification from office: general | 4.12 |
| 269 | Minor and consequential amendments | 4.13 |

### MONEY

| | | |
|---|---|---|
| 270 | Fees | 4.14 |

Schedules
| | | |
|---|---|---|
| | Schedule 17 Administration: Minor and Consequential Amendments | 4.15 |

## PART 6   INSOLVENCY

. . .

### Companies etc

[4.2]

**248  Replacement of Part II of Insolvency Act 1986**
(1)   The following shall be substituted for Part II of the Insolvency Act 1986 (c 45) (administration orders)—

"PART II   ADMINISTRATION

**8  Administration**
Schedule B1 to this Act (which makes provision about the administration of companies) shall have effect."
(2)   The Schedule B1 set out in Schedule 16 to this Act shall be inserted after Schedule A1 to the Insolvency Act 1986.
(3)   Schedule 17 (minor and consequential amendments relating to administration) shall have effect.
(4)   The Secretary of State may by order amend an enactment in consequence of this section.
(5)   An order under subsection (4)—
    (a)    must be made by statutory instrument, and
    (b)    shall be subject to annulment in pursuance of a resolution of either House of Parliament.

[4.3]

**249  Special administration regimes**
(1)   Section 248 shall have no effect in relation to—
    (a)    *a company holding an appointment under Chapter I of Part II of the Water Industry Act 1991 (c 56) (water and sewerage undertakers),*
    (aa)    *a qualifying licensed water supplier [water supply licensee] within the meaning of subsection (6) of section 23 of the Water Industry Act 1991 (meaning and effect of special administration order) [or a qualifying sewerage licensee within the meaning of subsection (8) of that section],*
    (b)    a protected railway company within the meaning of section 59 of the Railways Act 1993 (c 43) (railway administration order) (including that section as it has effect by virtue of section 19 of the Channel Tunnel Rail Link Act 1996 (c 61) (administration)),
    (c)    a licence company within the meaning of section 26 of the Transport Act 2000 (c 38) (air traffic services),
    (d)    a public-private partnership company within the meaning of section 210 of the Greater London Authority Act 1999 (c 29) (public-private partnership agreement), or
    (e)    a building society within the meaning of section 119 of the Building Societies Act 1986 (c 53) (interpretation).
(2)   A reference in an Act listed in subsection (1) to a provision of Part II of the Insolvency Act 1986 (or to a provision which has effect in relation to a provision of that Part of that Act) shall, in so far as it relates to a company or society listed in subsection (1), continue to have effect as if it referred to Part II as it had effect immediately before the coming into force of section 248.
(3)   But the effect of subsection (2) in respect of a particular class of company or society may be modified by order of—

(a)   the Treasury, in the case of building societies, or

(b)   the Secretary of State, in any other case.

(4)   An order under subsection (3) may make consequential amendment of an enactment.

(5)   An order under subsection (3)—

(a)   must be made by statutory instrument, and

(b)   may not be made unless a draft has been laid before and approved by resolution of each House of Parliament.

(6)   An amendment of the Insolvency Act 1986 (c 45) made by this Act is without prejudice to any power conferred by Part VII of the Companies Act 1989 (c 40) (financial markets) to modify the law of insolvency.

**Amendments**—Water Act 2003, s 101(1), Sch 8, para 55(1), (3); Flood and Water Management Act 2010, s 34, Sch 5, para 6(3), as from a date to be appointed; Water Act 2014, s 56, Sch 7, paras 128, 130, as from a date to be appointed.

. . .

## [4.4]

### 254 Application of insolvency law to foreign company

(1)   The Secretary of State may by order provide for a provision of the Insolvency Act 1986 to apply (with or without modification) in relation to a company incorporated outside Great Britain.

(2)   An order under this section—

(a)   may make provision generally or for a specified purpose only,

(b)   may make different provision for different purposes, and

(c)   may make transitional, consequential or incidental provision.

(3)   An order under this section—

(a)   must be made by statutory instrument, and

(b)   shall be subject to annulment in pursuance of a resolution of either House of Parliament.

## [4.5]

### 255 Application of law about company arrangement or administration to non-company

(1)   The Treasury may with the concurrence of the Secretary of State by order provide for a company arrangement or administration provision to apply (with or without modification) in relation to—

(a)   . . .

(b)   a society registered under section 7(1)(b), (c), (d), (e) or (f) of the Friendly Societies Act 1974 (c 46),

(c)   a friendly society within the meaning of the Friendly Societies Act 1992 (c 40), or

(d)   an unregistered friendly society.

(2)   In subsection (1) "company arrangement or administration provision" means—

(a)   a provision of Part I of the Insolvency Act 1986 (company voluntary arrangements),

(b)   a provision of Part II of that Act (administration), . . .

(c)   Part 26 of the Companies Act 2006 (compromise or arrangement with creditors), and

(d)   Part 26A of that Act (compromise or arrangement with creditors where company in financial difficulty).

(3)   An order under this section may not provide for a company arrangement or administration provision to apply in relation to a society which is—

(a)   a private registered provider of social housing, or

(b)   registered as a social landlord under Part I of the Housing Act 1996 (c 52) or under Part 2 of the Housing (Scotland) Act 2010 (asp 17).

(4)   An order under this section—
  (a)    may make provision generally or for a specified purpose only,
  (b)    may make different provision for different purposes, and
  (c)    may make transitional, consequential or incidental provision.
(5)   Provision by virtue of subsection (4)(c) may, in particular—
  (a)    apply an enactment (with or without modification);
  (b)    amend an enactment.
(6)   An order under this section—
  (a)    must be made by statutory instrument, and
  (b)    shall be subject to annulment in pursuance of a resolution of either House
         of Parliament.

**Amendments**—SI 2008/948; SI 2010/866; SI 2012/700; Co-operative and Community Benefit
Societies Act 2014, s 151(4), Sch 7; Corporate Insolvency and Governance Act 2020, s 7, Sch 9,
Pt 2, para 22.

INDIVIDUALS

**[4.6]**

**256  Duration of bankruptcy**
(1)   The following shall be substituted for section 279 of the Insolvency Act 1986
(c 45) (duration of bankruptcy)—

  **"279  Duration**
  (1)    A bankrupt is discharged from bankruptcy at the end of the period of one
  year beginning with the date on which the bankruptcy commences.
  (2)    If before the end of that period the official receiver files with the court a
  notice stating that investigation of the conduct and affairs of the bankrupt under
  section 289 is unnecessary or concluded, the bankrupt is discharged when the
  notice is filed.
  (3)    On the application of the official receiver or the trustee of a
  bankrupt's estate, the court may order that the period specified in subsection (1)
  shall cease to run until—
    (a)    the end of a specified period, or
    (b)    the fulfilment of a specified condition.
  (4)    The court may make an order under subsection (3) only if satisfied that the
  bankrupt has failed or is failing to comply with an obligation under this Part.
  (5)    In subsection (3)(b) "condition" includes a condition requiring that the court
  be satisfied of something.
  (6)    In the case of an individual who is adjudged bankrupt on a petition under
  section 264(1)(d)—
    (a)    subsections (1) to (5) shall not apply, and
    (b)    the bankrupt is discharged from bankruptcy by an order of the court
           under section 280.
  (7)    This section is without prejudice to any power of the court to annul a
  bankruptcy order."
(2)   Schedule 19 (which makes transitional provision in relation to this section)—
  (a)    shall have effect, and
  (b)    is without prejudice to the generality of section 276.

**[4.7]**

**257  Post-discharge restrictions**
(1)   The following shall be inserted after section 281 of the Insolvency Act 1986 (c 45)
(bankruptcy: effect of discharge)—

**"281A  Post-discharge restrictions**

(1)   Schedule 4A to this Act (bankruptcy restrictions order and bankruptcy restrictions undertaking) shall have effect."

(2)   The Schedule 4A set out in Schedule 20 to this Act shall be inserted after Schedule 4 to the Insolvency Act 1986.

(3)   The amendments set out in Schedule 21 (which specify the effect of a bankruptcy restrictions order or undertaking) shall have effect.

. . .

## [4.8]

### 261  Bankrupt's home

(1)   The following shall be inserted after section 283 of the Insolvency Act 1986 (definition of bankrupt's estate)—

**"283A  Bankrupt's home ceasing to form part of estate**

(1)   This section applies where property comprised in the bankrupt's estate consists of an interest in a dwelling-house which at the date of the bankruptcy was the sole or principal residence of—

    (a)   the bankrupt,

    (b)   the bankrupt's spouse, or

    (c)   a former spouse of the bankrupt.

(2)   At the end of the period of three years beginning with the date of the bankruptcy the interest mentioned in subsection (1) shall—

    (a)   cease to be comprised in the bankrupt's estate, and

    (b)   vest in the bankrupt (without conveyance, assignment or transfer).

(3)   Subsection (2) shall not apply if during the period mentioned in that subsection—

    (a)   the trustee realises the interest mentioned in subsection (1),

    (b)   the trustee applies for an order for sale in respect of the dwelling-house,

    (c)   the trustee applies for an order for possession of the dwelling-house,

    (d)   the trustee applies for an order under section 313 in Chapter IV in respect of that interest, or

    (e)   the trustee and the bankrupt agree that the bankrupt shall incur a specified liability to his estate (with or without the addition of interest from the date of the agreement) in consideration of which the interest mentioned in subsection (1) shall cease to form part of the estate.

(4)   Where an application of a kind described in subsection (3)(b) to (d) is made during the period mentioned in subsection (2) and is dismissed, unless the court orders otherwise the interest to which the application relates shall on the dismissal of the application—

    (a)   cease to be comprised in the bankrupt's estate, and

    (b)   vest in the bankrupt (without conveyance, assignment or transfer).

(5)   If the bankrupt does not inform the trustee or the official receiver of his interest in a property before the end of the period of three months beginning with the date of the bankruptcy, the period of three years mentioned in subsection (2)—

    (a)   shall not begin with the date of the bankruptcy, but

    (b)   shall begin with the date on which the trustee or official receiver becomes aware of the bankrupt's interest.

(6)   The court may substitute for the period of three years mentioned in subsection (2) a longer period—

    (a)   in prescribed circumstances, and

    (b)   in such other circumstances as the court thinks appropriate.

(7)   The rules may make provision for this section to have effect with the substitution of a shorter period for the period of three years mentioned in

subsection (2) in specified circumstances (which may be described by reference to action to be taken by a trustee in bankruptcy).

(8)    The rules may also, in particular, make provision—

    (a)    requiring or enabling the trustee of a bankrupt's estate to give notice that this section applies or does not apply;

    (b)    about the effect of a notice under paragraph (a);

    (c)    requiring the trustee of a bankrupt's estate to make an application to the Chief Land Registrar.

(9)    Rules under subsection (8)(b) may, in particular—

    (a)    disapply this section;

    (b)    enable a court to disapply this section;

    (c)    make provision in consequence of a disapplication of this section;

    (d)    enable a court to make provision in consequence of a disapplication of this section;

    (e)    make provision (which may include provision conferring jurisdiction on a court or tribunal) about compensation."

(2)    Section 313 of the Insolvency Act 1986 (c 45) (charge on bankrupt's home) shall be amended as follows—

    (a)    in subsection (2) for ", up to the value from time to time of the property secured," substitute ", up to the charged value from time to time,",

    (b)    after subsection (2) insert—

"(2A)    In subsection (2) the charged value means—

    (a)    the amount specified in the charging order as the value of the bankrupt's interest in the property at the date of the order, plus

    (b)    interest on that amount from the date of the charging order at the prescribed rate.

(2B)    In determining the value of an interest for the purposes of this section the court shall disregard any matter which it is required to disregard by the rules.", and—

    (c)    at the end insert—

"(5)    But an order under section 3(5) of that Act may not vary a charged value."

(3)    The following shall be inserted after section 313 of that Act—

### "313A  Low value home: application for sale, possession or charge

(1)    This section applies where—

    (a)    property comprised in the bankrupt's estate consists of an interest in a dwelling-house which at the date of the bankruptcy was the sole or principal residence of—

        (i)    the bankrupt,

        (ii)    the bankrupt's spouse, or

        (iii)    a former spouse of the bankrupt, and

    (b)    the trustee applies for an order for the sale of the property, for an order for possession of the property or for an order under section 313 in respect of the property.

(2)    The court shall dismiss the application if the value of the interest is below the amount prescribed for the purposes of this subsection.

(3)    In determining the value of an interest for the purposes of this section the court shall disregard any matter which it is required to disregard by the order which prescribes the amount for the purposes of subsection (2)."

(4)    The following shall be inserted after section 307(2)(a) of the Insolvency Act 1986 (c 45) (after-acquired property: exclusions)—

    "(aa) any property vesting in the bankrupt by virtue of section 283A in Chapter II,".

(5)    In section 384(2) of that Act (prescribed amounts) after "section 273;" insert— "section 313A;".

(6)    In section 418(1) of that Act (monetary limits in bankruptcy) after the entry for section 273 insert—

"section 313A (value of property below which application for sale, possession or charge to be dismissed);".

(7)   In subsection (8)—

    (a)    "pre-commencement bankrupt" means an individual who is adjudged bankrupt on a petition presented before subsection (1) above comes into force, and

    (b)    "the transitional period" is the period of three years beginning with the date on which subsection (1) above comes into force.

(8)   If a pre-commencement bankrupt's estate includes an interest in a dwelling-house which at the date of the bankruptcy was the sole or principal residence of him, his spouse or a former spouse of his, at the end of the transitional period that interest shall—

    (a)    cease to be comprised in the estate, and

    (b)    vest in the bankrupt (without conveyance, assignment or transfer).

(9)   But subsection (8) shall not apply if before or during the transitional period—

    (a)    any of the events mentioned in section 283A(3) of the Insolvency Act 1986 (c 45) (inserted by subsection (1) above) occurs in relation to the interest or the dwelling-house, or

    (b)    the trustee obtains any order of a court, or makes any agreement with the bankrupt, in respect of the interest or the dwelling-house.

(10)   Subsections 283A(4) to (9) of that Act shall have effect, with any necessary modifications, in relation to the provision made by subsections (7) to (9) above; in particular—

    (a)    a reference to the period mentioned in section 283A(2) shall be construed as a reference to the transitional period,

    (b)    in the application of section 283A(5) a reference to the date of the bankruptcy shall be construed as a reference to the date on which subsection (1) above comes into force, and

    (c)    a reference to the rules is a reference to rules made under section 412 of the Insolvency Act 1986 (for which purpose this section shall be treated as forming part of Parts VIII to XI of that Act).

. . .

## [4.9]

### 264 Individual voluntary arrangement

(1)   Schedule 22 (which makes provision about individual voluntary arrangements) shall have effect.

(2)   . . .

(3)   . . .

(4)   . . .

Amendments—Small Business, Enterprise and Employment Act 2015, s 135(3)(a).

. . .

## [4.10]

### 266 Disqualification from office: Parliament

(1)   The following shall be inserted before section 427 of the Insolvency Act 1986 (c 45) (the title to which becomes 'Disqualification from Parliament (Scotland and Northern Ireland)')—

"**426A Disqualification from Parliament (England and Wales)**

(1)   A person in respect of whom a bankruptcy restrictions order has effect shall be disqualified—

    (a)    from membership of the House of Commons,

    (b)    from sitting or voting in the House of Lords, and

    (c)    from sitting or voting in a committee of the House of Lords or a joint committee of both Houses.

(2)    If a member of the House of Commons becomes disqualified under this section, his seat shall be vacated.

(3)    If a person who is disqualified under this section is returned as a member of the House of Commons, his return shall be void.

(4)    No writ of summons shall be issued to a member of the House of Lords who is disqualified under this section.

(5)    If a court makes a bankruptcy restrictions order or interim order in respect of a member of the House of Commons or the House of Lords the court shall notify the Speaker of that House.

(6)    If the Secretary of State accepts a bankruptcy restrictions undertaking made by a member of the House of Commons or the House of Lords, the Secretary of State shall notify the Speaker of that House.

### 426B  Devolution

(1)    If a court makes a bankruptcy restrictions order or interim order in respect of a member of the Scottish Parliament, the Northern Ireland Assembly or the National Assembly for Wales, the court shall notify the presiding officer of that body.

(2)    If the Secretary of State accepts a bankruptcy restrictions undertaking made by a member of the Scottish Parliament, the Northern Ireland Assembly or the National Assembly for Wales, the Secretary of State shall notify the presiding officer of that body.

### 426C  Irrelevance of privilege

(1)    An enactment about insolvency applies in relation to a member of the House of Commons or the House of Lords irrespective of any Parliamentary privilege.

(2)    In this section "enactment" includes a provision made by or under—

    (a)    an Act of the Scottish Parliament, or

    (b)    Northern Ireland legislation."

(2)    In section 427 of the Insolvency Act 1986 the following shall cease to have effect—

    (a)    in subsection (1), the words "England and Wales or", and

    (b)    subsection (7).

(3)    The Secretary of State may by order—

    (a)    provide for section 426A or 426B of that Act (as inserted by subsection (1) above) to have effect in relation to orders made or undertakings accepted in Scotland or Northern Ireland under a system which appears to the Secretary of State to be equivalent to the system operating under Schedule 4A to that Act (as inserted by section 257 of this Act);

    (b)    make consequential amendment of section 426A or 426B of that Act (as inserted by subsection (1) above);

    (c)    make other consequential amendment of an enactment.

(4)    An order under this section may make transitional, consequential or incidental provision.

(5)    An order under this section—

    (a)    must be made by statutory instrument, and

    (b)    may not be made unless a draft has been laid before and approved by resolution of each House of Parliament.

## [4.11]

### 267  Disqualification from office: local government

(1)    The following shall be substituted for section 80(1)(b) of the Local Government Act 1972 (c 70) (disqualification for membership of local authority: bankrupt)—

       '(b)    is the subject of a bankruptcy restrictions order or interim order;'.

(2)    Section 81(1) and (2) of that Act (which amplify the provision substituted by subsection (1) above) shall cease to have effect.

[4.12]

### 268 Disqualification from office: general

(1) The Secretary of State may make an order under this section in relation to a disqualification provision.

(2) A "disqualification provision" is a provision which disqualifies (whether permanently or temporarily and whether absolutely or conditionally) a bankrupt or a class of bankrupts from—

    (a)    being elected or appointed to an office or position,

    (b)    holding an office or position, or

    (c)    becoming or remaining a member of a body or group.

(3) In subsection (2) the reference to a provision which disqualifies a person conditionally includes a reference to a provision which enables him to be dismissed.

(4) An order under subsection (1) may repeal or revoke the disqualification provision.

(5) An order under subsection (1) may amend, or modify the effect of, the disqualification provision—

    (a)    so as to reduce the class of bankrupts to whom the disqualification provision applies;

    (b)    so as to extend the disqualification provision to some or all individuals who are subject to a bankruptcy restrictions regime;

    (c)    so that the disqualification provision applies only to some or all individuals who are subject to a bankruptcy restrictions regime;

    (d)    so as to make the application of the disqualification provision wholly or partly subject to the discretion of a specified person, body or group.

(6) An order by virtue of subsection (5)(d) may provide for a discretion to be subject to—

    (a)    the approval of a specified person or body;

    (b)    appeal to a specified person or body.

(7) An order by virtue of subsection (5)(d) may provide for a discretion to be subject to appeal to a specified court or tribunal; but any such order must—

    (a)    if it relates to England and Wales, be made with the concurrence of the Lord Chief Justice of England and Wales;

    (b)    if it relates to Northern Ireland, be made with the concurrence of the Lord Chief Justice of Northern Ireland.

(8) The Secretary of State may specify himself for the purposes of subsection (5)(d) or (6)(a) or (b).

(9) In this section "bankrupt" means an individual—

    (a)    who has been adjudged bankrupt by a court in England and Wales or in Northern Ireland,

    (b)    whose estate has been sequestrated by a court in Scotland, or

    (c)    who has made an agreement with creditors of his for a composition of debts, for a scheme of arrangement of affairs, for the grant of a trust deed or for some other kind of settlement or arrangement.

(10) In this section "bankruptcy restrictions regime" means an order or undertaking—

    (a)    under Schedule 4A to the Insolvency Act 1986 (c 45) (bankruptcy restrictions orders), or

    (b)    under any system operating in Scotland or Northern Ireland which appears to the Secretary of State to be equivalent to the system operating under that Schedule.

(11) In this section—

    "body" includes Parliament and any other legislative body, and

    "provision" means—

        (a)    a provision made by an Act of Parliament passed before or in the same Session as this Act, and

        (b)    a provision made, before or in the same Session as this Act, under an Act of Parliament.

(12) An order under this section—
- (a) may make provision generally or for a specified purpose only,
- (b) may make different provision for different purposes, and
- (c) may make transitional, consequential or incidental provision.

(13) An order under this section—
- (a) must be made by statutory instrument, and
- (b) may not be made unless a draft has been laid before and approved by resolution of each House of Parliament.

(14) A reference in this section to the Secretary of State shall be treated as a reference to the National Assembly for Wales in so far as it relates to a disqualification provision which—
- (a) is made by the National Assembly for Wales, or
- (b) relates to a function of the National Assembly.

(15) Provision made by virtue of subsection (7) is subject to any order of the Lord Chancellor under section 56(1) of the Access to Justice Act 1999 (c 22) (appeals: jurisdiction).

(16) The Lord Chief Justice may nominate a judicial office holder (as defined in section 109(4) of the Constitutional Reform Act 2005) to exercise his functions under subsection (7).

(17) The Lord Chief Justice of Northern Ireland may nominate any of the following to exercise his functions under subsection (7)—
- (a) the holder of one of the offices listed in Schedule 1 to the Justice (Northern Ireland) Act 2002;
- (b) a Lord Justice of Appeal (as defined in section 88 of that Act).

**Amendments**—Constitutional Reform Act 2005, s 15(1).

## [4.13]

### 269 Minor and consequential amendments

Schedule 23 (minor and consequential amendments relating to individual insolvency) shall have effect.

MONEY

## [4.14]

### 270 Fees

(1) The following shall be inserted after section 415 of the Insolvency Act 1986 (c 45) (fees orders: individual insolvency)—

"**415A Fees orders (general)**
(1) The Secretary of State—
- (a) may by order require a body to pay a fee in connection with the grant or maintenance of recognition of the body under section 391, and
- (b) may refuse recognition, or revoke an order of recognition under section 391(1) by a further order, where a fee is not paid.

(2) The Secretary of State—
- (a) may by order require a person to pay a fee in connection with the grant or maintenance of authorisation of the person under section 393, and
- (b) may disregard an application or withdraw an authorisation where a fee is not paid.

(3) The Secretary of State may by order require the payment of fees in respect of—
- (a) the operation of the Insolvency Services Account;
- (b) payments into and out of that Account.

(4) The following provisions of section 414 apply to fees under this section as they apply to fees under that section—

(a)    subsection (3) (manner of payment),

(b)    subsection (5) (additional provision),

(c)    subsection (6) (statutory instrument),

(d)    subsection (7) (payment into Consolidated Fund), and

(e)    subsection (9) (saving for rules of court)."

(2)    An order made by virtue of subsection (1) may relate to the maintenance of recognition or authorisation granted before this section comes into force.

(3)    . . .

(4)    In section 440(2)(c) of that Act (provisions not extending to Scotland) after "415," there shall be inserted "415A(3),".

Amendments—Deregulation Act 2015, s 19, Sch 6, Pt 6, para 22(1), (13).

. . .

## SCHEDULE 17
### ADMINISTRATION: MINOR AND CONSEQUENTIAL AMENDMENTS
Section 248

## GENERAL

**[4.15]**

**1**

In any instrument made before section 248(1) to (3) of this Act comes into force—

(a)    a reference to the making of an administration order shall be treated as including a reference to the appointment of an administrator under paragraph 14 or 22 of Schedule B1 to the Insolvency Act 1986 (c 45) (inserted by section 248(2) of this Act), and

(b)    a reference to making an application for an administration order by petition shall be treated as including a reference to making an administration application under that Schedule, appointing an administrator under paragraph 14 or 22 of that Schedule or giving notice under paragraph 15 or 26 of that Schedule.

. . .

## SCHEDULE 19
### DURATION OF BANKRUPTCY: TRANSITIONAL PROVISIONS
Section 256

**[4.16]**

**1 Introduction**

This Schedule applies to an individual who immediately before commencement—

(a)    has been adjudged bankrupt, and

(b)    has not been discharged from the bankruptcy.

**2**

In this Schedule—

"commencement" means the date appointed under section 279 for the commencement of section 256, and

"pre-commencement bankrupt" means an individual to whom this Schedule applies.

**3 Neither old law nor new law to apply**

Section 279 of the Insolvency Act 1986 (c 45) (bankruptcy: discharge) shall not apply to a pre-commencement bankrupt (whether in its pre-commencement or its post-commencement form).

**4 General rule for discharge from pre-commencement bankruptcy**

(1) A pre-commencement bankrupt is, subject to sub-paragraphs (2) and (3), discharged from bankruptcy at whichever is the earlier of—

    (a)    the end of the period of one year beginning with commencement, and

    (b)    the end of the relevant period applicable to the bankrupt under section 279(1)(b) of the Insolvency Act 1986 (duration of bankruptcy) as it had effect immediately before commencement.

(2) An order made under section 279(3) of that Act before commencement—

    (a)    shall continue to have effect in respect of the pre-commencement bankrupt after commencement, and

    (b)    may be varied or revoked after commencement by an order under section 279(3) as substituted by section 256 of this Act.

(3) Section 279(3) to (5) of that Act as substituted by section 256 of this Act shall have effect after commencement in relation to the period mentioned in sub-paragraph (1)(a) or (b) above.

**5 Second-time bankruptcy**

(1) This paragraph applies to a pre-commencement bankrupt who was an undischarged bankrupt at some time during the period of 15 years ending with the day before the date on which the pre-commencement bankruptcy commenced.

(2) The pre-commencement bankrupt shall not be discharged from bankruptcy in accordance with paragraph 4 above.

(3) An order made before commencement under section 280(2)(b) or (c) of the Insolvency Act 1986 (c 45) (discharge by order of the court) shall continue to have effect after commencement (including any provision made by the court by virtue of section 280(3)).

(4) A pre-commencement bankrupt to whom this paragraph applies (and in respect of whom no order is in force under section 280(2)(b) or (c) on commencement) is discharged—

    (a)    at the end of the period of five years beginning with commencement, or

    (b)    at such earlier time as the court may order on an application under section 280 of the Insolvency Act 1986 (discharge by order) heard after commencement.

(5) Section 279(3) to (5) of the Insolvency Act 1986 as substituted by section 256 of this Act shall have effect after commencement in relation to the period mentioned in sub-paragraph (4)(a) above.

(6) A bankruptcy annulled under section 282 shall be ignored for the purpose of sub-paragraph (1).

**6 Criminal bankruptcy**

A pre-commencement bankrupt who was adjudged bankrupt on a petition under section 264(1)(d) of the Insolvency Act 1986 (criminal bankruptcy)—

    (a)    shall not be discharged from bankruptcy in accordance with paragraph 4 above, but

    (b)    may be discharged from bankruptcy by an order of the court under section 280 of that Act.

**7 Income payments order**

(1) This paragraph applies where—

    (a)    a pre-commencement bankrupt is discharged by virtue of paragraph 4(1)(a), and

    (b)    an income payments order is in force in respect of him immediately before his discharge.

(2) If the income payments order specifies a date after which it is not to have effect, it shall continue in force until that date (and then lapse).

(3) But the court may on the application of the pre-commencement bankrupt—

    (a)    vary the income payments order;

    (b)    provide for the income payments order to cease to have effect before the date referred to in sub-paragraph (2).

## 8 Bankruptcy restrictions order or undertaking

A provision of this Schedule which provides for an individual to be discharged from bankruptcy is subject to—

   (a)   any bankruptcy restrictions order (or interim order) which may be made in relation to that individual, and

   (b)   any bankruptcy restrictions undertaking entered into by that individual.

**Amendments**—SI 2003/2096.

. . .

# CORPORATE INSOLVENCY AND GOVERNANCE ACT 2020

## INTRODUCTION

**[5.1]**

On 25 June 2020 Royal Assent was given to the Corporate Insolvency and Governance Act 2020 ('CIGA 2020') and it came into force on 26 June 2020. The prime reason for its enactment at this point was to address insolvency issues surrounding the Coronavirus pandemic, but it also made good on the Government's indication some time ago that it would introduce changes to the IA 1986, having consulted the community back in 2016. A series of temporary practice directions have been issued during the pandemic in support of the *Practice Direction – Insolvency Proceedings* (July 2020) [2020] BPIR 1211. The most recent of these is the *Temporary Insolvency Practice Direction* that came into force on 30 June 2021 and at the time of writing is due to remain in force until 30 September 2021, which may be found at Appendix 3 of this work. A further practice direction titled *Practice Direction (Insolvency) Relating to the Corporate Insolvency and Governance Act 2020* [2020] BPIR 1207 may be found at Appendix 4. We summarise below the main changes which have been made to the law.

**Current position**—CIGA 2020 includes some provisions which are permanent whilst others make only temporary changes to insolvency law in light of the Coronavirus pandemic and its likely economic effects. There are three major permanent changes, namely: a new standalone Moratorium (now Part A1 of the IA 1986); a new Restructuring Plan for companies in financial difficulty (now Part 26A of the Companies Act 2006); and protection of supplies (avoiding certain *ipso facto* clauses) (now s 233B of the IA 1986). The first two reflect a desire to introduce more debtor-in-possession options for financially distressed companies, that is, the company remains under the control of its directors whilst some form of rescue or restructuring of the company occurs. Besides these major changes CIGA 2020 provides for amendments to several pieces of legislation and importantly a number of provisions in the IA 1986. Most of the permanent changes to the IA 1986 are to accommodate the three major changes identified above. The main temporary changes, imposed in response to the Coronavirus pandemic, are: restrictions on the ability to present winding-up petitions and for winding-up orders to be made for a prescribed period; suspension of liability for wrongful trading during a specified period; and the Secretary of State has power to amend insolvency law to mitigate the effect of the pandemic. A table identifying those provisions that are affected by these temporary changes, with cross-references to the relevant provision in CIGA 2020, appears immediately after this introductory note below.

**Part A1 moratorium**—The Act repealed the small companies moratorium under the former Sch A1 of the IA 1986, applying to company voluntary arrangements ('CVA'), and replaced it with the new standalone Moratorium, in Part A1 to the IA 1986. A separate introductory note may be found at the beginning of Part A1 earlier in this work.

**Part 26A restructuring plan**—A second major element of CIGA 2020 is to provide for a Restructuring Plan to 'eliminate, reduce or prevent, or mitigate the effect of, any of the financial difficulties' which have affected or will affect the ability of a company to carry on its business as a going concern. These changes are introduced by a new Part 26A to the Companies Act 2006, which is enacted by Sch 9 of CIGA 2020. A separate introductory note appears at the start of Sch 9 below.

**Ipso facto clauses**—In order to protect supplies to companies that are insolvent and enter some formal insolvency regime, and to avoid ipso facto clauses, s 233B is introduced into the IA 1986 by CIGA 2020. It prohibits clauses which allow the supplier of goods or services to terminate the contract if the company enters a formal insolvency procedure, and this includes the new Moratorium and Part 26A Restructuring Plan. Section 233B states that a provision of a contract for the supply of goods or services to the company (with some exceptions such as banking and insurance products) is of no effect when the company enters an insolvency procedure, if, under that provision the contract would terminate, or the supplier would be entitled to terminate the contract or to 'do any other thing' upon the company entering an insolvency procedure. Consequently, it prevents suppliers from terminating a supply of goods or services upon the company's insolvency but also prevents suppliers from making it a condition of continued supply that arrears are paid and from making other changes to the contract such as increasing prices. This provision complements ss 233 and 233A of the IA 1986.

**Temporary changes**—At the time of enactment, the direct applicability of the temporary provisions was due to end on 30 September 2020. This has subsequently been extended several times by the Corporate Insolvency and Governance Act 2020 (Coronavirus) (Extension of the Relevant Period) Regulations 2020 (SI 2020/1031), the Corporate Insolvency and Governance Act 2020 (Coronavirus) (Suspension of Liability for Wrongful Trading and Extension of the Relevant Period) Regulations 2020 (SI 2020/1349), the Corporate Insolvency and Governance Act 2020 (Coronavirus) (Extension of the Relevant Period) No 2) Regulations 2020 (SI 2020/1483), the Corporate Insolvency and Governance Act 2020 (Coronavirus) (Extension of the Relevant Period) Regulations 2021 (SI 2021/375) and the Corporate Insolvency and Governance Act 2020 (Coronavirus) (Extension of the Relevant Period) (No 2) Regulations 2021 (SI 2021/718).

At the time of writing, the position in relation to winding up petitions is as provided for by the Corporate Insolvency and Governance Act 2020 (Coronavirus) (Extension of the Relevant Period) (No 2) Regulations 2021 (SI 2021/718), which came into force on 22 June 2021. The relevant restrictions have been extended until 30 September 2021. A detailed note on these provisions appears immediately prior to Sch 10 in the text of CIGA 2020 below.

The suspension of liability for wrongful trading was not extended by the most recent extensions and came to an end on 30 June 2021: see reg 2 of the Corporate Insolvency and Governance Act 2020 (Coronavirus) (Extension of the Relevant Period) Regulations 2021 (SI 2021/375) and reg 2 of the Corporate

Insolvency and Governance Act 2020 (Coronavirus) (Suspension of Liability for Wrongful Trading and Extension of the Relevant Period) Regulations 2021 (SI 2021/1349).

In view of the ongoing and changeable situation, it is advisable to check the up-to-date position carefully before taking any step in reliance of the applicability or non-applicability of these measures.

It should further be noted that the effect of the changes could well be relevant even after they have come to an end, and it is likely that all involved in insolvency practice will need to remember the temporary changes that were made. An example could be where a wrongful trading action is brought in the future when there might be debate over the extent to which some of the respondent director's actions that are impugned are protected by the suspension provided for in CIGA 2020.

**Omissions and inclusions**—We have reproduced below most of CIGA 2020, with certain provisions omitted. Much of the omitted material is comprised of provisions that solely concern Northern Ireland (CIGA 2020, ss 4–6, 9, 11, 13, 16–19, 28–36, 42 and 46, as well as Schs 5–8, 11 and 13). The detail of the permanent amendments to the IA 1986 (principally in relation to the new Moratorium and the provisions concerning *ipso facto* clauses) and other legislation has also been omitted, to avoid duplication. Those new provisions appear in the IA 1986, as amended by CIGA 2020, elsewhere in this book. A separate introductory note in relation to the moratorium appears at the start of Part A1.

The remainder of CIGA 2020 has been reproduced below. There are two areas of particular note. Firstly, the text to the new Part 26A to the Companies Act 2006 is found at CIGA 2020, Sch 9. This is further supported by an amended practice direction ('*Companies: Schemes of Arrangements under Part 26 and Part 26A of the Companies Act 2006*'), which may be found at APPENDIX 5 to this book. Secondly, a large number of temporary provisions designed to deal with the Coronavirus pandemic are principally found at CIGA 2020, Schs 4 and 10. Where those temporary changes affect or have affected existing provisions in other relevant legislation, they are identified in the table that appears immediately below.

## LEGISLATION AFFECTED BY TEMPORARY MEASURES IN THE CORPORATE GOVERNANCE AND INSOLVENCY ACT 2020

[5.2]

| Legislation title | Affected provision | CIGA 2020 reference |
|---|---|---|
| Companies Act 2006 | Section 441 | Section 38(1) |
| Insolvency Act 1986 | Section A3 | Sch 4, para 5 |
| Insolvency Act 1986 | Section A3(1)(a) | Sch 4, para 6(1)(a) |
| Insolvency Act 1986 | Section A4 | Sch 4, para 5 |
| Insolvency Act 1986 | Section A4 | Sch 4, para 6(2) |
| Insolvency Act 1986 | Section A5 | Sch 4, para 5 |
| Insolvency Act 1986 | Section A6(1)(e) | Sch 4, para 6(1)(b) |
| Insolvency Act 1986 | Section A6(1)(e) | Sch 4, para 7(a) |
| Insolvency Act 1986 | Section A10(1)(d) | Sch 4, para 8(2) |

| Legislation title | Affected provision | CIGA 2020 reference |
|---|---|---|
| Insolvency Act 1986 | Section A11(1)(d) | Sch 4, para 8(2) |
| Insolvency Act 1986 | Section A13(2)(d) | Sch 4, para 8(3) |
| Insolvency Act 1986 | Section A35(1) | Sch 4, para 9 |
| Insolvency Act 1986 | Section A38(1)(a) | Sch 4, para 10 |
| Insolvency Act 1986 | Section A54(1) | Sch 4, para 13 |
| Insolvency Act 1986 | Section A54(1) | Sch 4, para 53 |
| Insolvency Act 1986 | Section 74(2)(a) | Sch 10, para 10 |
| Insolvency Act 1986 | Section 122(1)(f) | Sch 10, para 7(1)(a) |
| Insolvency Act 1986 | Section 122(1)(f) | Sch 10, para 7(5)(a) |
| Insolvency Act 1986 | Section 122(1)(f) | Sch 10, para 8(1)(b) |
| Insolvency Act 1986 | Section 123(1) | Sch 10, para 5(1)(b) |
| Insolvency Act 1986 | Section 123(1)(a) | Sch 10, para 1(1) |
| Insolvency Act 1986 | Section 123(1)(a) | Sch 10, para 2(1) |
| Insolvency Act 1986 | Section 123(1)(a) | Sch 10, para 5(2) |
| Insolvency Act 1986 | Section 123(1)(b) | Sch 10, para 2(1) |
| Insolvency Act 1986 | Section 123(1)(b) | Sch 10, para 5(2) |
| Insolvency Act 1986 | Section 123(1)(c) | Sch 10, para 2(1) |
| Insolvency Act 1986 | Section 123(1)(c) | Sch 10, para 5(2) |
| Insolvency Act 1986 | Section 123(1)(d) | Sch 10, para 2(1) |
| Insolvency Act 1986 | Section 123(1)(d) | Sch 10, para 5(2) |
| Insolvency Act 1986 | Section 123(1)(e) | Sch 10, para 2(3) |
| Insolvency Act 1986 | Section 123(1)(e) | Sch 10, para 5(3) |
| Insolvency Act 1986 | Section 123(2) | Sch 10, para 2(3) |
| Insolvency Act 1986 | Section 123(2) | Sch 10, para 5(1)(b) |
| Insolvency Act 1986 | Section 123(2) | Sch 10, para 5(3) |
| Insolvency Act 1986 | Section 124 | Sch 10, para 1(1) |
| Insolvency Act 1986 | Section 124 | Sch 10, para 1(2) |
| Insolvency Act 1986 | Section 124 | Sch 10, para 2(1) |
| Insolvency Act 1986 | Section 124 | Sch 10, para 2(3) |
| Insolvency Act 1986 | Section 124 | Sch 10, para 3(1) |
| Insolvency Act 1986 | Section 124 | Sch 10, para 3(3) |
| Insolvency Act 1986 | Section 124 | Sch 10, para 4(1) |
| Insolvency Act 1986 | Section 124 | Sch 10, para 5(1)(a) |
| Insolvency Act 1986 | Section 124 | Sch 10, para 6(1)(a) |
| Insolvency Act 1986 | Section 124 | Sch 10, para 8(1)(a) |
| Insolvency Act 1986 | Section 129(2) | Sch 10, para 9 |
| Insolvency Act 1986 | Section 147 | Sch 10, para 4(4) |
| Insolvency Act 1986 | Section 147 | Sch 10, para 7(6) |
| Insolvency Act 1986 | Section 206(1) | Sch 10, para 11 |
| Insolvency Act 1986 | Section 207(2)(a) | Sch 10, para 12 |
| Insolvency Act 1986 | Section 208(2) | Sch 10, para 13 |
| Insolvency Act 1986 | Section 214 | Section 12(1) |
| Insolvency Act 1986 | Section 214A(2) | Sch 10, para 14 |
| Insolvency Act 1986 | Section 221(5)(b) | Sch 10, para 6(2) |
| Insolvency Act 1986 | Section 221(5)(b) | Sch 10, para 6(3) |
| Insolvency Act 1986 | Section 221(5)(b) | Sch 10, para 7(1)(a) |
| Insolvency Act 1986 | Section 221(5)(b) | Sch 10, para 7(5)(a) |
| Insolvency Act 1986 | Section 221(5)(b) | Sch 10, para 8(1)(b) |

| Legislation title | Affected provision | CIGA 2020 reference |
|---|---|---|
| Insolvency Act 1986 | Section 222 | Sch 10, para 1(2) |
| Insolvency Act 1986 | Section 222 | Sch 10, para 3(1) |
| Insolvency Act 1986 | Section 222 | Sch 10, para 6(1)(b) |
| Insolvency Act 1986 | Section 222 | Sch 10, para 6(2) |
| Insolvency Act 1986 | Section 223 | Sch 10, para 3(1) |
| Insolvency Act 1986 | Section 223 | Sch 10, para 6(1)(b) |
| Insolvency Act 1986 | Section 223 | Sch 10, para 6(2) |
| Insolvency Act 1986 | Section 224 | Sch 10, para 6(1)(b) |
| Insolvency Act 1986 | Section 224(1)(a) | Sch 10, para 3(1) |
| Insolvency Act 1986 | Section 224(1)(a) | Sch 10, para 6(2) |
| Insolvency Act 1986 | Section 224(1)(b) | Sch 10, para 3(1) |
| Insolvency Act 1986 | Section 224(1)(b) | Sch 10, para 6(2) |
| Insolvency Act 1986 | Section 224(1)(c) | Sch 10, para 3(1) |
| Insolvency Act 1986 | Section 224(1)(c) | Sch 10, para 6(2) |
| Insolvency Act 1986 | Section 224(1)(d) | Sch 10, para 3(3) |
| Insolvency Act 1986 | Section 224(1)(d) | Sch 10, para 6(3) |
| Insolvency Act 1986 | Section 224(2) | Sch 10, para 3(3) |
| Insolvency Act 1986 | Section 224(2) | Sch 10, para 6(3) |
| Insolvency Act 1986 | Section 240(1)(a) | Sch 10, para 15(2) |
| Insolvency Act 1986 | Section 240(1)(b) | Sch 10, para 15(3) |
| Insolvency Act 1986 | Section 242(3)(a) | Sch 10, para 16(2) |
| Insolvency Act 1986 | Section 242(3)(b) | Sch 10, para 16(3) |
| Insolvency Act 1986 | Section 243(1) | Sch 10, para 17 |
| Insolvency Act 1986 | Section 245(3)(a) | Sch 10, para 18(2) |
| Insolvency Act 1986 | Section 245(3)(b) | Sch 10, para 18(3) |
| Insolvency Act 1986 | Section 246ZB | Section 12(1) |
| Insolvency Act 1986 | Sch ZA1, para (2)(2)(b) | Sch 4, para 7(b) |
| Insolvency Act 1986 | Sch ZA1, para 13 | Section 12(5)(a) |
| Insolvency Act 1986 | Sch ZA1, para 15 | Section 12(5)(a) |
| Insolvency Act 1986 | Sch ZA1, para 18 | Section 12(5)(b) |
| Insolvency Act 1986 | Sch ZA1, para 2(1)(b) | Sch 4, para 6(1)(c) |
| Insolvency Act 1986 | Sch ZA1, para 2(1)(b) | Sch 4, para 7(b) |
| Insolvency Act 1986 | Sch ZA1, para 2(2)(b) | Sch 4, para 6(1)(c) |
| | | |
| Insolvency (England and Wales) Rules 2016 | Rule 7.5(1) | Sch 10, para 19(3) |
| Insolvency (England and Wales) Rules 2016 | Rule 7.10 | Sch 10, para 19(2) |
| Insolvency (England and Wales) Rules 2016 | Rule 12.9 | Sch 4, para 47 |
| Insolvency (England and Wales) Rules 2016 | Rule 12.29(3) | Sch 4, para 47 |
| Insolvency (England and Wales) Rules 2016 | Rule 12.36(2) | Sch 4, para 47 |
| Insolvency (England and Wales) Rules 2016 | Rule 12.37(2) | Sch 4, para 47 |
| Insolvency (England and Wales) Rules 2016 | Rule 12.37(3) | Sch 4, para 47 |

| Legislation title | Affected provision | CIGA 2020 reference |
|---|---|---|
| Insolvency (England and Wales) Rules 2016 | Rule 12.39(3) | Sch 10, para 19(4) |
| Insolvency (England and Wales) Rules 2016 | Rule 12.39(4) | Sch 10, para 19(4) |
| Insolvency (England and Wales) Rules 2016 | Rule 12.39(5) | Sch 10, para 19(4) |
| Insolvency (England and Wales) Rules 2016 | Rule 12.48(2) | Sch 4, para 47 |
| Insolvency (England and Wales) Rules 2016 | Rule 15.11 | Sch 4, para 24 |
| Insolvency (England and Wales) Rules 2016 | Rule 15.28 | Sch 4, para 25 |
| Insolvency (England and Wales) Rules 2016 | Rule 15.31 | Sch 4, para 26 |
| Insolvency (England and Wales) Rules 2016 | Rule 15.32 | Sch 4, para 27 |
| Insolvency (England and Wales) Rules 2016 | Rule 15.34 | Sch 4, para 28 |
| Insolvency (England and Wales) Rules 2016 | [various] | Sch 10, para 19(2) |
| Insolvency (Scotland) (Company Voluntary Arrangements and Administration) Rules 2018 | Rule 5.11 | Sch 4, para 64 |
| Insolvency (Scotland) (Company Voluntary Arrangements and Administration) Rules 2018 | Rule 5.26 | Sch 4, para 65 |
| Insolvency (Scotland) (Company Voluntary Arrangements and Administration) Rules 2018 | Rule 5.28 | Sch 4, para 66 |
| Insolvency (Scotland) (Company Voluntary Arrangements and Administration) Rules 2018 | Rule 5.29 | Sch 4, para 67 |
| Insolvency (Scotland) (Company Voluntary Arrangements and Administration) Rules 2018 | Rule 5.31 | Sch 4, para 68 |
| 'Rules of Court in Scotland' [not defined] | [various] | Sch 10, para 20(2) |
| 'Rules of Court in Scotland' [not defined] | | Sch 10, para 20(4) |

# CORPORATE INSOLVENCY AND GOVERNANCE ACT 2020

## ARRANGEMENT OF SECTIONS

### *Moratorium*

| | | |
|---|---|---|
| 1 | Moratoriums in Great Britain | 5.3 |
| 2 | 2 Moratoriums in Great Britain: further amendments and transition | 5.4 |
| 3 | 3 Moratoriums in Great Britain: temporary modifications | 5.5 |
| 4–6 | (*Northern Ireland only*) | |

### *Arrangements and reconstructions for companies in financial difficulty*

| | | |
|---|---|---|
| 7 | Arrangements and reconstructions for companies in financial difficulty | 5.6 |

### *Administration: sales to connected persons*

| | | |
|---|---|---|
| 8 | Administration in Great Britain: sales to connected persons | 5.7 |
| 9 | (*Northern Ireland only*) | |

### *Winding-up petitions*

| | | |
|---|---|---|
| 10 | Winding-up petitions: Great Britain | 5.8 |
| 11 | (*Northern Ireland only*) | |

### *Wrongful trading*

| | | |
|---|---|---|
| 12 | Suspension of liability for wrongful trading: Great Britain | 5.9 |
| 13 | (*Northern Ireland only*) | |

### *Termination clauses in supply contracts*

| | | |
|---|---|---|
| 14 | Protection of supplies of goods and services: Great Britain | 5.10 |
| 15 | Temporary exclusion for small suppliers: Great Britain | 5.11 |
| 16–19 | (*Northern Ireland only*) | |

### *Power to amend corporate insolvency or governance legislation: Great Britain*

| | | |
|---|---|---|
| 20 | Regulations to amend legislation: Great Britain | 5.12 |
| 21 | Purposes | 5.13 |
| 22 | Restrictions | 5.14 |
| 23 | Time-limited effect | 5.15 |
| 24 | Expiry | 5.16 |
| 25 | Consequential provision etc | 5.17 |
| 26 | Procedure for regulations | 5.18 |
| 27 | Interpretation | 5.19 |

### *Power to amend corporate insolvency or governance legislation: Northern Ireland*

| | | |
|---|---|---|
| 28–36 | (*Northern Ireland only*) | |

### *Meetings and flings*

| | | |
|---|---|---|
| 37 | Meetings of companies and other bodies | 5.20 |
| 38 | Temporary extension of period for public company to file accounts | 5.21 |
| 39 | Temporary power to extend periods for providing information to registrar | 5.22 |
| 40 | Section 39: the listed provisions | 5.23 |

### *Powers to change periods*

| | | |
|---|---|---|
| 41 | Power to change duration of temporary provisions: Great Britain | 5.24 |
| 42 | (*Northern Ireland only*) | |

### *Implementation of insolvency measures*

| | | |
|---|---|---|
| 43 | Modified procedure for regulations of the Secretary of State | 5.25 |
| 44 | Modified procedure for regulations of the Welsh Ministers | 5.26 |
| 45 | Modified procedure for regulations of the Scottish Ministers | 5.27 |
| 46 | (*Northern Ireland only*) | |

### *General*

| | | |
|---|---|---|
| 47 | Power to make consequential provision | 5.28 |
| 48 | Extent | 5.29 |
| 49 | Commencement | 5.30 |

50          Short title                                                                  **5.31**

Schedules
          Schedule 1 Moratoriums in Great Britain: Eligible Companies              **5.32**
          Schedule 2 Moratoriums in Great Britain: Contracts Involving Financial
              Services                                                             **5.33**
          Schedule 3 (*Not reproduced*)
          Schedule 4 Moratoriums in Great Britain: Temporary Provision
          Part 1 "Relevant Period" and Powers to Turn Off Temporary Provision     **5.34**
          Part 2 Modifications to Primary Legislation                             **5.35**
          Part 3 Temporary Rules: England and Wales                               **5.36**
          Part 4 Temporary Rules: Scotland                                        **5.37**
          Part 5 Entities other than Companies
          Schedules 5–8 (*Northern Ireland only*)
          Schedule 9 Arrangements and Reconstructions for Companies in Financial
              Difficulty
          Part 1 Main Provisions                                                  **5.39**
          Part 2 Consequential Amendments                                         **5.40**
          Schedule 10 Restriction on Winding-up Petitions: Great Britain          **5.41**
          Schedule 11 (*Northern Ireland only*)
          Schedule 12 Protection of Supplies of Goods and Services: Great Britain
          Part 1 Exclusions                                                       **5.42**
          Part 2 Consequential Amendments                                         **5.43**
          Schedule 13 (*Northern Ireland only*)
          Schedule 14 Meetings of Companies and other Bodies                      **5.44**

*Moratorium*

## [5.3]

**1 Moratoriums in Great Britain**
(1)   In the Insolvency Act 1986, before Part 1 (but within the First Group of Parts) insert—
(*The text to Part A1 is not reproduced here. See introductory note to CIGA 2020 above under the heading 'Omissions and inclusions'.*)
(2)   Schedule 1 inserts into the Insolvency Act 1986 a new Schedule ZA1 (eligible companies).
(3)   Schedule 2 inserts into the Insolvency Act 1986 a new Schedule ZA2 (contracts involving financial services).

   **General note**—See note immediately prior to Part A1 above.

## [5.4]

**2 Moratoriums in Great Britain: further amendments and transition**
(1)   Schedule 3 contains consequential and other amendments to do with moratoriums under new Part A1 of the Insolvency Act 1986.
(2)   Nothing in this Act affects the operation of the Insolvency Act 1986, or any other enactment, in relation to a moratorium under Schedule A1 to that Act which comes into force before the repeal of that Schedule by Schedule 3 to this Act.
(3)   Subsection (2) is without prejudice to the operation of section 16 of the Interpretation Act 1978 (general savings).

## [5.5]

**3 Moratoriums in Great Britain: temporary modifications**
Schedule 4 makes temporary modifications to Part A1 of the Insolvency Act 1986 (moratorium) and other temporary provision in connection with that Part.

**4–6**
(*Sections 4–6 solely affect Northern Ireland and are not reproduced.*)

*Arrangements and reconstructions for companies in financial difficulty*

**[5.6]**

**7 Arrangements and reconstructions for companies in financial difficulty**
Schedule 9 contains provision about arrangements and reconstructions for companies in financial difficulty.

**General note**—See note to Sch 9 below.

*Administration: sales to connected persons*

**[5.7]**

**8 Administration in Great Britain: sales to connected persons**
(1) Paragraph 60A of Schedule B1 to the Insolvency Act 1986 (which expired in May 2020) is revived.
(2) For sub-paragraph (10) of that paragraph substitute—
"(10) This paragraph expires at the end of June 2021 unless the power conferred by it is exercised before then."

**9**
(*Section 9 solely affects Northern Ireland and is not reproduced.*)

*Winding-up petitions*

**[5.8]**

**10 Winding-up petitions: Great Britain**
Schedule 10 contains temporary provision in relation to winding-up petitions in Great Britain.

**General note**—See note to Sch 10 below.

**11**
(*Section 11 solely affects Northern Ireland and is not reproduced.*)

*Wrongful trading*

**[5.9]**

**12 Suspension of liability for wrongful trading: Great Britain**
(1) In determining for the purposes of section 214 or 246ZB of the Insolvency Act 1986 (liability of director for wrongful trading) the contribution (if any) to a company's assets that it is proper for a person to make, the court is to assume that the person is not responsible for any worsening of the financial position of the company or its creditors that occurs during the relevant period.
(2) In this section the "relevant period" is the period which—
   (a) begins with 1 March 2020, and
   (b) ends with 30 September 2020.
(3) Subsection (1) does not apply if at any time during the relevant period the company concerned is excluded from being eligible by any of the paragraphs of Schedule ZA1 to the Insolvency Act 1986 listed in subsection (4), as they apply for the purposes of this subsection (see subsection (5)).
(4) The paragraphs of Schedule ZA1 to the Insolvency Act 1986 are—
   (a) paragraph 3 (insurance companies),
   (b) paragraph 4 (banks),
   (c) paragraph 5 (electronic money institutions),
   (d) paragraph 6 (investment banks and investment firms),

    (e)      paragraph 9 (payment institutions),
    (f)      paragraph 10 (operators of payment systems etc),
    (g)     paragraph 11 (recognised investment exchanges, clearing houses etc),
    (h)     paragraph 12 (securitisation companies),
    (i)      paragraph 13 (parties to capital market arrangements),
    (j)      paragraph 15 (public-private partnership project companies), and
    (k)     paragraph 18 (certain overseas companies).

(5)   In their application for the purposes of subsection (3)—

    (a)     each of paragraphs 13 and 15 of Schedule ZA1 to the Insolvency Act 1986 has effect as if in sub-paragraph (1)—
         (i)      the words ", on the filing date" were omitted, and
         (ii)     paragraph (b) were omitted, and
    (b)     paragraph 18 of that Schedule has effect as if for "paragraph 2", in both places, there were substituted "paragraphs 2, 7 and 8".

(6)   Subsection (1) also does not apply if at any time during the relevant period the company concerned—

    (a)     has permission under Part 4A of the Financial Services and Markets Act 2000 to carry on a regulated activity, and
    (b)     is not subject to a requirement imposed under that Act to refrain from holding money for clients.

(7)   This section has effect—

    (a)     in so far as it relates to section 214 of the Insolvency Act 1986, as if it were contained in Part 4 of that Act, and
    (b)     in so far as it relates to section 246ZB of the Insolvency Act 1986, as if it were contained in Part 6 of that Act.

(8)   But this section does not have effect in relation to the following bodies (which are bodies to which provisions contained in Parts 4 and 6 of the Insolvency Act 1986 apply)—

    (a)     a society that is registered within the meaning of the Friendly Societies Act 1974 and that at any time during the relevant period carries on the regulated activity of effecting or carrying out contracts of insurance;
    (b)     a building society within the meaning of the Building Societies Act 1986;
    (c)     a society that is incorporated under the Friendly Societies Act 1992;
    (d)     a registered society within the meaning of the Co-operative and Community Benefit Societies Act 2014 that is registered under that Act as a credit union;
    (e)     a registered society within the meaning of the Co-operative and Community Benefit Societies Act 2014 that at any time during the relevant period carries on the regulated activity of effecting or carrying out contracts of insurance.

(9)   In this section "regulated activity" has the meaning given by section 22 of the Financial Services and Markets Act 2000, taken with Schedule 2 to that Act and any order under that section.

**13**

(*Section 13 solely affects Northern Ireland and is not reproduced.*)

*Termination clauses in supply contracts*

[5.10]

**14 Protection of supplies of goods and services: Great Britain**

(1)   In the Insolvency Act 1986, after section 233A insert—

(*The text to ss 233B and 233C are not reproduced here. See introductory note to CIGA 2020 above under the heading 'Omissions and inclusions'.*)

(2)   In the Insolvency Act 1986, in section 434 (Crown application), before "bind" insert "and sections 233A and 233B and Schedule 4ZZA".

(3)   Schedule 12—
- (a)   inserts a new Schedule into the Insolvency Act 1986 which provides for exclusions from the operation of section 233B of that Act, and
- (b)   contains consequential amendments.

(4)   The amendments made by this section and Schedule 12 have effect in relation to a company which becomes subject to a relevant insolvency procedure on or after the day on which this section comes into force (but in respect of contracts entered into before, as well as those entered into on or after, that day).

## [5.11]

### 15  Temporary exclusion for small suppliers: Great Britain

(1)   Section 233B of the Insolvency Act 1986 does not apply in relation to a contract for the supply of goods or services to a company where—
- (a)   the company becomes subject to a relevant insolvency procedure during the relevant period, and
- (b)   the supplier is a small entity at the time the company becomes subject to the procedure.

(2)   In subsection (1)(a) "relevant period" means the period which—
- (a)   begins with the day on which this section comes into force, and
- (b)   ends with 30 June 2021.

(3)   For the purposes of subsection (1)(b), whether the supplier is a "small entity" at the time the company becomes subject to a relevant insolvency procedure (the "relevant time") is to be determined under subsections (4) to (10).

(4)   Where the supplier is not in its first financial year at the relevant time, the supplier is a small entity at the relevant time if at least two of the following conditions were met in relation to its most recent financial year—

Condition 1: the supplier's turnover was not more than £10.2 million;
Condition 2: the supplier's balance sheet total was not more than £5.1 million;
Condition 3: the number of the supplier's employees was not more than 50.

(5)   For the purposes of Condition 1 in subsection (4), if the supplier's most recent financial year was not 12 months, the maximum figure for turnover must be proportionately adjusted.

(6)   For the purposes of Condition 2 in subsection (4), the supplier's balance sheet total means the aggregate of the amounts shown as assets in the supplier's balance sheet.

(7)   For the purposes of Condition 3 in subsection (4), the number of the supplier's employees means the average number of persons employed by the supplier in its most recent financial year, determined as follows—
- (a)   find for each month in that financial year the number of persons employed under contracts of service by the supplier in that month (whether throughout the month or not),
- (b)   add together the monthly totals, and
- (c)   divide by the number of months in the financial year.

(8)   In subsections (4) to (7) the supplier's "most recent financial year" is the financial year of the supplier which, at the relevant time, has ended most recently.

(9)   Where the supplier is in its first financial year at the relevant time, the supplier is a small entity at the relevant time if at least two of the following conditions are met—

Condition 1: the supplier's average turnover for each complete month in the supplier's first financial year is not more than £850,000;
Condition 2: the aggregate of amounts which would be shown in a balance sheet of the supplier drawn up at the relevant time is not more than £5.1 million;
Condition 3: the average number of persons employed by the supplier in the supplier's first financial year (determined as specified in subsection (7)) is not more than 50.

(10)   In this section—
"entity" means—
- (a)   a company,

      (b)    a limited liability partnership,

      (c)    any other association or body of persons, whether or not incorporated, and

      (d)    an individual carrying on a trade or business;

"relevant insolvency procedure" has the same meaning as in section 233B of the Insolvency Act 1986.

(11)   This section has effect as if it were included in Part 6 of the Insolvency Act 1986.

**Amendments—**SI 2021/375.

## 16–19

*(Sections 16–19 solely affect Northern Ireland and are not reproduced.)*

*Power to amend corporate insolvency or governance legislation: Great Britain*

## [5.12]

### 20 Regulations to amend legislation: Great Britain

(1)   The Secretary of State may by regulations amend, or modify the effect of, corporate insolvency or governance legislation so as to—

      (a)    change the conditions that must be met before a corporate insolvency or restructuring procedure applies to entities of any description (whether by adding, varying or removing any condition),

      (b)    change the way in which a corporate insolvency or restructuring procedure applies in relation to entities of any description, or

      (c)    change or disapply any duty of a person with corporate responsibility or the liability of such a person to any sanction.

(2)   Regulations under this section may—

      (a)    make different provision for different purposes;

      (b)    make provision binding the Crown.

(3)   Regulations under this section must be made in accordance with sections 21 to 26.

## [5.13]

### 21 Purposes

(1)   The Secretary of State may only make regulations under section 20(1)(a) or (b) if satisfied that the regulations are expedient for any of the following purposes—

      (a)    reducing, or assisting in the reduction of, the number of entities entering into corporate insolvency or restructuring procedures for reasons relating to the effects of coronavirus on businesses or on the economy of the United Kingdom;

      (b)    mitigating or otherwise dealing with the effect on corporate insolvency or restructuring procedures of any increase or potential increase in the number of entities entering into those procedures for the reasons referred to in paragraph (a);

      (c)    mitigating difficulties that corporate insolvency or restructuring procedures might impose on a business in view of—

          (i)    any worsening of the financial position of the business in consequence of, or for reasons relating to, coronavirus,

          (ii)    constraints on people's ability to work, or to be in proximity to each other, as a result of coronavirus, or

          (iii)   measures for public health taken in response to coronavirus.

(2)   The Secretary of State may only make regulations under section 20(1)(c) if satisfied that the regulations are expedient for the purpose of securing that the duties of persons with corporate responsibility, or the liability of those persons to any sanction, take due account of the effects of coronavirus on businesses or on the economy of the United Kingdom.

**[5.14]**

**22 Restrictions**

(1) Before making regulations under section 20 the Secretary of State must consider the effect of the regulations on persons likely to be affected by them (for example, debtors, creditors or employees).

(2) The Secretary of State may only make regulations under section 20 if satisfied—

    (a) that the need for the provision made by the regulations is urgent,

    (b) that the provision made by the regulations is proportionate to the purpose for which it is made,

    (c) that it is not practicable without legislation to bring about the result intended to be brought about by that provision, and

    (d) if the Secretary of State could make the same provision in other subordinate legislation, that doing so would risk not achieving the purpose for which the regulations are made (because of possible delay or for any other reason).

(3) Regulations under section 20—

    (a) may not create a criminal offence or civil penalty (but may modify the circumstances in which a person is guilty of an existing offence or liable for an existing civil penalty);

    (b) may not make provision so as to impose or increase a fee.

(4) Regulations under section 20 may not make provision that could be made by an Act of the Scottish Parliament unless the Secretary of State has first consulted the Scottish Ministers.

**[5.15]**

**23 Time-limited effect**

(1) Regulations under section 20 must be framed so that any provision made by them—

    (a) has effect only for a period not exceeding six months, or

    (b) applies only in relation to circumstances occurring in a period not exceeding six months.

(2) This does not prevent further regulations under section 20 from—

    (a) making the same provision for, or applying in relation to, subsequent periods (not exceeding six months at a time);

    (b) extending (by up to six months) the period for or in relation to which earlier regulations under that section apply.

(3) The Secretary of State must keep regulations under section 20 under review during the period for which they have effect or in relation to which they apply.

(4) If on such a review the Secretary of State is satisfied that that period—

    (a) is longer than expedient for the purpose for which the regulations were made, or

    (b) has ceased to be proportionate to that purpose,

the Secretary of State must by regulations under this subsection revoke or amend the regulations as appropriate.

(5) Regulations under subsection (4) may contain transitional provision or savings.

**[5.16]**

**24 Expiry**

(1) The Secretary of State may not make regulations under section 20 after 29 April 2022.

(2) Where regulations under section 20 are in force on the date specified in subsection (1), that subsection does not—

    (a) affect the continued operation of the regulations, or

    (b) prevent the making of further regulations under section 20 on one or more occasions, where those further regulations make the same provision for, or applying in relation to, subsequent periods (not exceeding six months at a time).

(3)   The Secretary of State may by regulations substitute a later date for the date for the time being specified in subsection (1).

(4)   The power in subsection (3)—

    (a)   may not be exercised so as to substitute a date which is—

        (i)   after the period of one year beginning with the date for the time being specified in subsection (1), or

        (ii)   after the period of two years beginning with the date on which this Act is passed, but

    (b)   may be exercised more than once.

Amendments—Substituted by SI 2021/441.

**[5.17]**

### 25 Consequential provision etc

(1)   The Secretary of State may by regulations make consequential, incidental or supplementary provision, or transitional provision or savings, in connection with provision made by regulations under section 20.

(2)   Regulations under this section may—

    (a)   make provision by amending or modifying the effect of any enactment (including this Act);

    (b)   make different provision for different purposes;

    (c)   make provision binding the Crown.

**[5.18]**

### 26 Procedure for regulations

(1)   Regulations under sections 20 to 25 are to be made by statutory instrument.

(2)   A statutory instrument containing—

    (a)   regulations made under section 20, other than one to which subsection (6)(a) applies, or

    (b)   regulations made under section 25 which make provision by amending an Act or an Act of the Scottish Parliament,

must be laid before Parliament as soon as reasonably practicable after being made.

(3)   Regulations contained in a statutory instrument laid before Parliament by virtue of subsection (2) cease to have effect at the end of the period of 40 days beginning with the day on which the instrument is made, unless during that period the instrument is approved by a resolution of each House of Parliament.

(4)   In calculating the period of 40 days, no account is to be taken of any time during which—

    (a)   Parliament is dissolved or prorogued, or

    (b)   both Houses of Parliament are adjourned for more than 4 days.

(5)   Where regulations cease to have effect as a result of subsection (3) that does not—

    (a)   affect anything previously done under or by virtue of the regulations, or

    (b)   prevent the making of new regulations.

(6)   A statutory instrument containing—

    (a)   regulations under section 20 which merely revoke other regulations under that section (with or without transitional provision), or

    (b)   regulations under section 23(4),

is subject to annulment in pursuance of a resolution of either House of Parliament.

(7)   Regulations under section 24(3) may not be made unless a draft of the statutory instrument containing them has been laid before, and approved by a resolution of, each House of Parliament.

(8)   A statutory instrument containing regulations under section 25 which do not make provision by amending an Act or an Act of the Scottish Parliament is subject to

annulment in pursuance of a resolution of either House of Parliament (unless the regulations were contained in a statutory instrument laid before Parliament by virtue of subsection (2)).

**[5.19]**

**27 Interpretation**
(1)   In sections 20 to 26 and this section—
"coronavirus" means severe acute respiratory syndrome coronavirus 2 (SARS-CoV-2);
"corporate insolvency or governance legislation" means—

(a)    the Insolvency Act 1986, except so far as relating to the insolvency or bankruptcy of individuals,

(b)    Part 26A of the Companies Act 2006 (arrangements and reconstructions for companies in financial difficulty),

(c)    the Company Directors Disqualification Act 1986,

(d)    this Act,

(e)    any subordinate legislation made under the enactments specified in paragraphs (a) to (d),

(f)    the Cross-Border Insolvency Regulations 2006 (SI 2006/1030), and

(g)    after IP completion day, Regulation (EU) 2015/848 on insolvency proceedings;

"corporate insolvency or restructuring procedure" means—

(a)    a moratorium under Part A1 of the Insolvency Act 1986;

(b)    a company voluntary arrangement under Part 1 of that Act (including a moratorium under section 1A of that Act in a case where such a moratorium applies after the coming into force of paragraph 30 of Schedule 3);

(c)    administration under Part 2 of that Act;

(d)    receivership to which Part 3 of that Act applies;

(e)    winding up under Part 4 or 5 of that Act;

(f)    the procedure provided for by Part 26A of the Companies Act 2006;

"enactment" includes an Act of the Scottish Parliament and an instrument made under such an Act;
"person with corporate responsibility" means—

(a)    in relation to a company, a director, manager, secretary or other officer of the body,

(b)    in relation to a partnership or limited liability partnership, a partner or member, and

(c)    in relation to any other entity, a person with responsibility for managing the entity;

"subordinate legislation" has the meaning given by section 21(1) of the Interpretation Act 1978.
(2)   References to an enactment in subsection (1) include in particular that enactment as applied by any other enactment, with or without modifications, to partnerships, limited liability partnerships or other entities.

**28–36**
(*Sections 28–36 solely affect Northern Ireland and are not reproduced.*)

*Meetings and filings*

**[5.20]**

**37 Meetings of companies and other bodies**
Schedule 14 makes provision about meetings of companies and other bodies.

**[5.21]**

**38 Temporary extension of period for public company to file accounts**

(1)   This section applies where (but for this section) the period allowed for the directors of a public company to comply with their obligation under section 441 of the Companies Act 2006 to deliver accounts and reports for a financial year to the registrar would end—

(a)   after 25 March 2020, and

(b)   before the relevant day.

(2)   The period allowed for the directors to comply with that obligation is to be taken to be (and always to have been) a period that ends with the relevant day.

(3)   The relevant day is whichever is the earlier of—

(a)   30 September 2020, and

(b)   the last day of the period of 12 months immediately following the end of the relevant accounting reference period.

(4)   Expressions used in this section and section 442 of the Companies Act 2006 (period allowed for filing accounts) have the same meaning in this section as in that section.

**[5.22]**

**39 Temporary power to extend periods for providing information to registrar**

(1)   The Secretary of State may by regulations provide that any provision listed in section 40 is to have effect as if for a reference in the provision to a period of days or months ("the existing period") there were substituted a reference to such longer period ("the substituted period") as is specified in the regulations.

(2)   The substituted period must not exceed—

(a)   42 days, in a case where the existing period is 21 days or fewer, and

(b)   12 months, in a case where the existing period is 3, 6 or 9 months.

(3)   The power conferred by this section may not be exercised in relation to a reference to a period of 12 months.

(4)   Regulations under this section may make—

(a)   different provision for different purposes;

(b)   consequential, incidental or supplementary provision (including provision modifying an enactment);

(c)   transitional provision or savings.

(5)   In subsection (4) "enactment" includes an Act of the Scottish Parliament and an instrument made under such an Act.

(6)   Regulations under this section are to be made by statutory instrument.

(7)   A statutory instrument containing regulations under this section is subject to annulment in pursuance of a resolution of either House of Parliament.

(8)   This section expires at the end of the day on 5 April 2021.

(9)   The expiry of this section does not affect the continued operation of any regulations made under this section for the purpose of determining the length of any period that begins before the expiry.

**[5.23]**

**40 Section 39: the listed provisions**

The provisions referred to in section 39(1) are—

(a)   section 9 of the Limited Partnerships Act 1907 (registration of changes to a limited partnership);

(b)   section 466 of the Companies Act 1985 (registration of alteration to a floating charge);

(c)   section 9 of the Limited Liability Partnerships Act 2000 (notice of membership changes);

(d) regulation 80C of the European Public Limited-Liability Company Regulations 2004 (SI 2004/2326) (notice of change in members of the supervisory organ);

(e) the following sections of the Companies Act 2006—

section 87 (notice of change of address of registered office);

section 114 (notice of place where register of members is kept);

section 162 (notice of place where register of directors is kept);

section 167 (notice of change in directors etc);

section 275 (notice of place where register of secretaries is kept);

section 276 (notice of change in secretaries etc);

section 442 (period allowed for filing accounts);

section 790M (register of people with significant control);

section 790N (notice of place where PSC register is kept);

section 790VA (notice of change to the PSC register);

section 853A(1) (confirmation statements);

section 859A (registration of charge);

section 859B (registration of charge contained in debentures);

section 859Q (notice of place where copies of instruments creating charges are kept);

(f) the following provisions of the Scottish Partnerships (Register of People with Significant Control) Regulations 2017 (SI 2017/694)—

regulation 7 (notice of change to the registration information);

regulation 8 (notice of ceasing to be a Scottish qualifying partnership);

the provisions of Part 5 (duties to deliver information);

regulation 35 (confirmation statements).

*Powers to change periods*

**[5.24]**

**41 Power to change duration of temporary provisions: Great Britain**

(1) The Secretary of State may by regulations made by statutory instrument amend a relevant provision so as to—

(a) curtail the period for the time being specified in that provision, or

(b) prolong that period by up to six months if the Secretary of State considers it reasonable to do so to mitigate an effect of coronavirus.

(2) In this section—

"coronavirus" means severe acute respiratory syndrome coronavirus 2 (SARS-CoV-2);

"relevant provision" means—

(a) section 12(2),

(b) section 15(2),

(c) paragraph 1 of Schedule 4, or

(d) . . . .

(3) A statutory instrument containing regulations made under subsection (1)(a) is subject to annulment in pursuance of a resolution of either House of Parliament.

(4) A statutory instrument containing regulations made under subsection (1)(b) must be laid before Parliament as soon as reasonably practicable after being made.

(5) Subsection (4) does not apply if a draft of the statutory instrument has been laid before and approved by a resolution of each House of Parliament.

(6) Regulations contained in a statutory instrument laid before Parliament by virtue of subsection (4) cease to have effect at the end of the period of 40 days beginning with the day on which the instrument is made, unless during that period the instrument is approved by a resolution of each House of Parliament.

(7) In calculating the period of 40 days, no account is to be taken of any time during which—

(a)    Parliament is dissolved or prorogued, or

(b)    both Houses of Parliament are adjourned for more than 4 days.

(8)    Where regulations relating to any relevant provision cease to have effect as a result of subsection (6), the period specified in the relevant provision ends—

(a)    at the time it would have ended under the relevant provision if the regulations had not been made, or

(b)    if later, at the end of the period of 40 days mentioned in subsection (6).

(9)    Where regulations cease to have effect as a result of subsection (6) that does not prevent the making of new regulations.

(10)    Regulations under this section may make—

(a)    different provision for the purposes of different relevant provisions;

(b)    consequential, transitional or transitory provision or savings.

Amendments—SI 2021/1091.

## 42

(*Section 42 solely affects Northern Ireland and is not reproduced.*)

*Implementation of insolvency measures*

## [5.25]

### 43 Modified procedure for regulations of the Secretary of State

(1)    During the period of six months beginning with the day on which this section comes into force, any relevant provision that may be made by the Secretary of State by regulations that are subject to the affirmative resolution procedure may be made by regulations that are subject to the made affirmative procedure.

(2)    In subsection (1) "relevant provision" means—

(a)    provision under section A50(1) or (4) of the Insolvency Act 1986 (power to modify moratorium provisions in relation to certain companies);

(b)    provision under section A51(1) of the Insolvency Act 1986 (moratorium: power to make provision in connection with pension schemes);

(c)    provision under paragraph 20 of Schedule ZA1 to the Insolvency Act 1986 to exclude private registered providers of social housing from being eligible companies for the purposes of Part A1 of that Act;

(d)    provision under section 14 or 16 of the Limited Liability Partnerships Act 2000 (insolvency etc and power to make consequential amendments) to the extent that the provision is made in connection with the application of Part A1 of the Insolvency Act 1986 to limited liability partnerships that are registered providers of social housing;

(e)    provision under section 245 of the Charities Act 2011 (insolvency etc of charitable incorporated organisations etc) to the extent that the provision applies, or is otherwise made in connection with, the new insolvency measures.

(3)    During the period of six months beginning with the day on which this section comes into force, the consultation duty in section 348(4) of the Charities Act 2011 does not apply in relation to regulations under section 245 of that Act to the extent that they contain provision which applies, or is otherwise made in connection with, the new insolvency measures.

(4)    In subsections (2) and (3) "the new insolvency measures" means the provision made by—

(a)    sections 1 to 3 and Schedules 1 to 4 (moratorium);

(b)    sections 14 and 15 and Schedule 12 (termination clauses in supply contracts).

(5)    For the purposes of this section —

(a)    "regulations that are subject to the affirmative resolution procedure" means regulations that may not be made unless a draft of the statutory instrument containing them has been laid before and approved by a resolution of each House of Parliament;

    (b)    "regulations that are subject to the made affirmative procedure" means regulations that—

        (i)    are contained in a statutory instrument that must be laid before Parliament as soon as reasonably practicable after being made, and

        (ii)    cease to have effect at the end of the period of 40 days beginning with the day on which the instrument is made, unless during that period the instrument is approved by a resolution of each House of Parliament.

(6)   In calculating the period of 40 days mentioned in subsection (5)(b)(ii), no account is to be taken of any time during which—

    (a)    Parliament is dissolved or prorogued, or

    (b)    both Houses of Parliament are adjourned for more than 4 days.

(7)   Where by virtue of this section the Secretary of State makes regulations that are subject to the made affirmative procedure and the regulations cease to have effect because they are not approved within the period mentioned in subsection (5)(b)(ii), the fact that the regulations cease to have effect does not—

    (a)    affect anything previously done under or by virtue of the regulations, or

    (b)    prevent the making of new regulations.

## [5.26]

### 44 Modified procedure for regulations of the Welsh Ministers

(1)   During the period of six months beginning with the day on which this section comes into force, any relevant provision that may be made by the Welsh Ministers by regulations that are subject to the affirmative resolution procedure may be made by regulations that are subject to the made affirmative procedure.

(2)   In subsection (1) "relevant provision" means—

    (a)    provision under section A50(2) of the Insolvency Act 1986 (power to modify moratorium provisions in relation to certain companies);

    (b)    provision under paragraph 21 of Schedule ZA1 to the Insolvency Act 1986 (exclusion of registered social landlords from eligibility under Part A1 of that Act);

    (c)    provision under section 247A of the Charities Act 2011 (regulations about moratoriums for charitable incorporated organisations that are registered social landlords).

(3)   During the period of six months beginning with the day on which this section comes into force, the consultation duty in section 247A(6) of the Charities Act 2011 does not apply in relation to regulations under section 247A of that Act.

(4)   For the purposes of this section —

    (a)    "regulations that are subject to the affirmative resolution procedure" means regulations that may not be made unless a draft of the statutory instrument containing them has been laid before and approved by a resolution of Senedd Cymru;

    (b)    "regulations that are subject to the made affirmative procedure" means regulations that—

        (i)    are contained in a statutory instrument that must be laid before Senedd Cymru as soon as reasonably practicable after being made, and

        (ii)    cease to have effect at the end of the period of 40 days beginning with the day on which the instrument is made, unless during that period the instrument is approved by a resolution of Senedd Cymru.

(5)   In calculating the period of 40 days mentioned in subsection (4)(b)(ii), no account is to be taken of any time during which Senedd Cymru is—

    (a)    dissolved, or

    (b)    in recess for more than 4 days.

(6)   Where by virtue of this section the Welsh Ministers make regulations that are subject to the made affirmative procedure and the regulations cease to have effect because they are not approved within the period mentioned in subsection (4)(b)(ii), the fact that the regulations cease to have effect does not—

(a)   affect anything previously done under or by virtue of the regulations, or

(b)   prevent the making of new regulations.

[5.27]

### 45 Modified procedure for regulations of the Scottish Ministers

(1)   During the period of six months beginning with the day on which this section comes into force, any relevant provision that may be made by the Scottish Ministers by regulations that are subject to the affirmative procedure (see section 29 of the Interpretation and Legislative Reform (Scotland) Act 2010 (asp 10)) may be made by regulations that are subject to the made affirmative procedure.

(2)   In subsection (1) "relevant provision" means—

(a)   provision under section A50(3) of the Insolvency Act 1986 (power to modify moratorium provisions in relation to certain companies);

(b)   provision under paragraph 22 of Schedule ZA1 to the Insolvency Act 1986 (exclusion of registered social landlords from eligibility under Part A1 of that Act).

(3)   For the purposes of this section "regulations that are subject to the made affirmative procedure" means regulations that—

(a)   must be laid before the Scottish Parliament as soon as reasonably practicable after being made, and

(b)   cease to have effect at the end of the period of 40 days beginning with the day on which the regulations are made, unless during that period the regulations are approved by a resolution of the Scottish Parliament.

(4)   In calculating the period of 40 days mentioned in subsection (3)(b), no account is to be taken of any time during which the Scottish Parliament is—

(a)   dissolved, or

(b)   in recess for more than 4 days.

(5)   Where by virtue of this section the Scottish Ministers make regulations that are subject to the made affirmative procedure and the regulations cease to have effect because they are not approved within the period mentioned in subsection (3)(b), the fact that the regulations cease to have effect does not—

(a)   affect anything previously done under or by virtue of the regulations, or

(b)   prevent the making of new regulations.

(6)   Section 30 of the Interpretation and Legislative Reform (Scotland) Act 2010 does not apply in relation to regulations that are subject to the made affirmative procedure by virtue of this section.

### 46

(*Section 46 solely affects Northern Ireland and is not reproduced.*)

*General*

[5.28]

### 47 Power to make consequential provision

(1)   The Secretary of State or the Treasury may by regulations make provision that is consequential on this Act.

(2)   The power in subsection (1) may, in particular, be used to amend, repeal, revoke or otherwise modify any provision of this Act or any provision made by or under primary legislation passed or made—

(a)   before this Act, or

(b)   later in the same session of Parliament as this Act.

(3)   But the power to amend or repeal any provision made by this Act may not be used after the period of 3 years beginning with the day on which it is passed.

(4)   Regulations under this section—

    (a)   may make different provision for different purposes;

    (b)   may include transitional or transitory provision or savings.

(5)   Regulations under this section are to be made by statutory instrument.

(6)   A statutory instrument containing regulations under this section that amend or repeal provision made by primary legislation (whether alone or with other provision) may not be made unless a draft of the instrument has been laid before and approved by a resolution of each House of Parliament.

(7)   Any other statutory instrument containing regulations under this section is subject to annulment in pursuance of a resolution of either House of Parliament.

(8)   In this section "primary legislation" means—

    (a)   an Act,

    (b)   an Act or Measure of Senedd Cymru,

    (c)   an Act of the Scottish Parliament, or

    (d)   Northern Ireland legislation.

## [5.29]

### 48 Extent

(1)   An amendment, repeal or revocation made by this Act has the same extent within the United Kingdom as the provision amended, repealed or revoked.

(2)   The following provisions extend to England and Wales and Scotland only—

    (a)   section 3 and Parts 1 and 2 of Schedule 4;

    (b)   section 10 and Schedule 10;

    (c)   section 12;

    (d)   section 15;

    (e)   sections 20 to 24;

    (f)   section 41.

(3)   The following provisions extend to England and Wales only—

    (a)   section 44;

    (b)   Part 3 of Schedule 4.

(4)   The following provisions extend to Scotland only—

    (a)   section 45;

    (b)   Part 4 of Schedule 4.

(5)   The following provisions extend to Northern Ireland only—

    (a)   section 6 and Schedule 8;

    (b)   section 11 and Schedule 11;

    (c)   section 13;

    (d)   section 19;

    (e)   sections 28 to 36;

    (f)   section 42.

(6)   Subject to the above, this Act extends to England and Wales, Scotland and Northern Ireland.

## [5.30]

### 49 Commencement

(1)   This Act comes into force on the day after that on which it is passed, subject to subsection (2).

(2)   Paragraph 51 of Schedule 3 comes into force on such day as the Secretary of State may by regulations appoint.

(3)   Different days may be appointed for different purposes.

(4)   The Secretary of State may by regulations make transitional or saving provision in connection with the coming into force of any provision of this Act.

(5)   The power to make regulations under subsection (4) includes power to make different provision for different purposes.

(6)   Regulations under this section are to be made by statutory instrument.

**[5.31]**

**50  Short title**

This Act may be cited as the Corporate Insolvency and Governance Act 2020.

## SCHEDULE 1
### MORATORIUMS IN GREAT BRITAIN: ELIGIBLE COMPANIES
Section 1(2)

**[5.32]**

In the Insolvency Act 1986, before Schedule A1 (which is repealed by Schedule 3 to this Act) insert—

*(The text to Sch ZA1 is not reproduced here. See introductory note to CIGA 2020 above under the heading 'Omissions and inclusions'.)*

## SCHEDULE 2
### MORATORIUMS IN GREAT BRITAIN: CONTRACTS INVOLVING FINANCIAL SERVICES
Section 1(3)

**[5.33]**

In the Insolvency Act 1986, after Schedule ZA1 (inserted by Schedule 1 to this Act) insert—

*(The text to Sch ZA2 is not reproduced here. See introductory note to CIGA 2020 above under the heading 'Omissions and inclusions'.)*

## SCHEDULE 3
### MORATORIUMS IN GREAT BRITAIN: FURTHER AMENDMENTS
Section 2

*(Sch 3 is not reproduced. See introductory note to CIGA 2020 above under the heading 'Omissions and inclusions')*

## SCHEDULE 4
### MORATORIUMS IN GREAT BRITAIN: TEMPORARY PROVISION
Section 3

### PART 1   "RELEVANT PERIOD" AND POWERS TO TURN OFF TEMPORARY PROVISION

**[5.34]**

*"Relevant period"*

1

In this Schedule "relevant period" means the period which—
    (a)    begins with the day on which this Schedule comes into force, and
    (b)    ends with 30 September 2021.

*Power to turn off particular provisions of Part 2 of this Schedule early*

**2**

(1)   The Secretary of State may by regulations made by statutory instrument provide for any provision made by Part 2 of this Schedule to cease to have effect before the end of the relevant period.

(2)   The regulations may include transitional provision or savings.

(3)   A statutory instrument containing regulations under sub-paragraph (1) is subject to annulment in pursuance of a resolution of either House of Parliament.

*Power to turn off provisions of Parts 3 and 4 of this Schedule early etc*

**3**

Rules under section 411 of the Insolvency Act 1986 may provide for any provision made by paragraphs 13 to 51 or 53 to 90 to cease to have effect before the end of the relevant period.

**4**

Rules under section 411 of the Insolvency Act 1986 may make transitional provision or savings in connection with any provision made by paragraphs 13 to 51 or 53 to 90 ceasing to have effect (whether by virtue of paragraph 3 or 12).

Amendments—SI 2021/375.

PART 2   MODIFICATIONS TO PRIMARY LEGISLATION

**[5.35]**

. . .

**5**

. . .

*Relaxation of conditions for obtaining moratorium etc*

**6**

(1)   For the purposes of obtaining a moratorium under section A3 of the Insolvency Act 1986 during the relevant period—

(a)     section A3 of that Act has effect as if subsection (1)(a) were omitted;

(b)     . . .

(c)     Schedule ZA1 to that Act has effect as if paragraph 2(1)(b) and (2)(b) were omitted.

(2)   During the relevant period, only an overseas company may obtain a moratorium under section A4 of the Insolvency Act 1986.

**7**

In relation to an application for a moratorium made under section A4 or A5 of the Insolvency Act 1986 during the relevant period—

(a)     . . .

(b)     Schedule ZA1 to that Act has effect as if paragraph 2(1)(b) and (2)(b) were omitted.

. . .

. . .

**8**

. . .

. . .

**9**

. . .

. . .

**10**

. . .

. . .

**11**

. . .

Amendments—SI 2020/1033.

PART 3   TEMPORARY RULES: ENGLAND AND WALES

**[5.36]**

*Introductory*

**12**

Paragraphs 13 to 51 cease to have effect at the end of the relevant period, subject to paragraph 3.

*Definition of "the court"*

**13**

Section A54(1) of the Insolvency Act 1986 has effect as if for the definition of "the court" there were substituted—

""the court", in relation to a company, means a court having jurisdiction to wind up the company;".

*Content of documents relating to the obtaining or extending of a moratorium: general*

**14**

A notice or statement under section A6(1), A8(2), A10(1), A11(1) or A13(2) of the Insolvency Act 1986 must state—

    (a)    the provision under which it is given or made,

    (b)    the nature of the notice or statement,

    (c)    the date of the notice or statement, and

    (d)    the identification details for the company to which it relates.

*Authentication of documents relating to obtaining or extending moratorium: general*

**15**

(1)   A notice or statement under section A6(1), A10(1), A11(1) or A13(2) of the Insolvency Act 1986 must be authenticated by or on behalf of the person giving the notice or making the statement.

(2)   A notice under section A8(2)(a) of the Insolvency Act 1986 must be authenticated by the monitor.

(3)   Rule 1.5 of the England and Wales Insolvency Rules applies for the purposes of authentication under this paragraph.

*Notice that directors wish to obtain a moratorium*

**16**

A notice under section A6(1)(a) of the Insolvency Act 1986 must state—

(a)   the company's address for service, and

(b)   the court (and where applicable, the division or district registry of that court) or hearing centre in which the documents are to be filed under section A3 or the application under section A4 or A5 is to be made.

*Proposed monitor's statement and consent to act*

**17**

(1)   A statement under section A6(1)(b) of the Insolvency Act 1986 must be headed "Proposed monitor's statement and consent to act" and must contain the following—

(a)   a certificate that the proposed monitor is qualified to act as an insolvency practitioner in relation to the company,

(b)   the proposed monitor's IP number,

(c)   the name of the relevant recognised professional body which is the source of the proposed monitor's authorisation to act in relation to the company, and

(d)   a statement that the proposed monitor consents to act as monitor in relation to the company.

(2)   In this paragraph "IP number" means the number assigned to an office-holder as an insolvency practitioner by the Secretary of State.

*Timing of statements for obtaining moratorium*

**18**

Each statement under section A6(1)(b) to (e) of the Insolvency Act 1986 must be made within the period of 5 days ending with the day on which the documents under section A6(1)(a) to (e) are filed with the court (or, if the documents are filed on different days, the last of those days).

*Notice by monitor where moratorium comes into force*

**19**

A notice under section A8(2) of the Insolvency Act 1986 must—

(a)   state that it is given by the monitor acting in that capacity, and

(b)   state the name and contact details of the monitor.

*Notice that directors wish to extend a moratorium*

**20**

A notice under section A10(1)(a) or A11(1)(a) of the Insolvency Act 1986 must state—

(a)   the company's address for service, and

(b)   the court (and where applicable, the division or district registry of that court) or hearing centre in which the notice is to be filed.

*Extension under section A10 or A11 of the Insolvency Act 1986: notices and statements*

**21**

A statement by the monitor under section A10(1)(d) or A11(1)(d) of the Insolvency Act 1986 must contain contact details of the monitor.

*Timing of statements for extension under section A10 or A11*

**22**

Each statement under section A10(1)(b) to (d) or A11(1)(b) to (e) of the Insolvency Act 1986 must be made within the period of 3 days ending with the day on which the documents under section A10(1)(a) to (d) or A11(1)(a) to (e) are filed with the court (or, if the documents are filed on different days, the last of those days).

*Obtaining creditor consent: qualifying decision procedure*

**23**

(1)   The following apply, so far as relevant, for the purposes of a decision to consent to a revised end date for a moratorium under section A12 of the Insolvency Act 1986—

    (a)    Part 15 of the England and Wales Insolvency Rules (decision making), apart from rule 15.8(3)(f) and (g);

    (b)    Part 16 of the England and Wales Insolvency Rules (proxies), apart from rule 16.7.

(2)   In its application by virtue of sub-paragraph (1), Part 15 has effect subject to the modifications set out in paragraphs 24 to 28.

**24**

Rule 15.11 of the England and Wales Insolvency Rules (notice of decision procedures etc) has effect as if, before the first entry in the table, there were inserted—

| "moratorium | decision of pre-moratorium creditors under section A12 of the Act | the pre-moratorium creditors | 5 days" |
|---|---|---|---|

**25**

Rule 15.28 of the England and Wales Insolvency Rules (creditors' voting rights) has effect as if, before paragraph (1), there were inserted—

"(A1)   A pre-moratorium creditor is entitled to vote in a decision procedure under section A12 of the Act only if—

    (a)    the creditor has delivered to the convener a proof of the debt claimed in accordance with paragraph (3) including any calculation for the purposes of rule 15.31 or 15.32, and

    (b)    the proof was received by the convener—

        (i)    not later than the decision date, or in the case of a meeting, 4pm on the business day before the meeting, or

        (ii)    in the case of a meeting, later than the time given in sub-paragraph (i) where the chair is content to accept the proof, and

    (c)    the proof has been admitted for the purposes of entitlement to vote."

**26**

Rule 15.31 of the England and Wales Insolvency Rules (calculation of voting rights) has effect as if—

    (a)    before paragraph (1) there were inserted—

"(A1)   In relation to a decision to consent to a revised end date for a moratorium under section A12 of the Act votes are calculated according to the amount of each creditor's claim at the decision date.";

    (b)    after paragraph (2) there were inserted—

"(2A)   But in relation to a decision to consent to a revised end date for a moratorium under section A12 of the Act, a debt of an unliquidated or unascertained amount is to be valued at £1 for the purposes of voting unless the convener or chair or an appointed person decides to put a higher value on it.";

    (c)    in paragraph (6), after sub-paragraph (b) there were inserted—

"(c)   where the decision relates to whether to consent to a revised end date
for a moratorium under section A12 of the Act."

**27**

Rule 15.32 of the England and Wales Insolvency Rules (calculation of voting rights:
special cases) has effect as if, before paragraph (1), there were inserted—

"(A1)   In relation to a decision to consent to a revised end date for a moratorium
under section A12 of the Act, a pre-moratorium creditor under a hire-purchase
agreement is entitled to vote in respect of the amount of the debt due and payable
by the company at the decision date.

(B1)   In calculating the amount of any debt for the purpose of paragraph (A1),
no account is to be taken of any amount attributable to the exercise of any right
under the relevant agreement so far as the right has become exercisable solely by
virtue of a moratorium for the company coming into force."

**28**

Rule 15.34 of the England and Wales Insolvency Rules (requisite majorities) has effect
as if, before paragraph (1), there were inserted—

"(A1)   Subject to paragraph (B1), a decision to consent to a revised end date for
a moratorium under section A12 of the Act is made if, of those voting—

(a)   a majority (in value) of the pre-moratorium creditors who are secured
creditors vote in favour of the proposed decision, and

(b)   a majority (in value) of the pre-moratorium creditors who are
unsecured creditors vote in favour of the proposed decision.

(B1)   But a decision to consent to a revised end date for a moratorium under
section A12 of the Act is not made if, of those voting either—

(a)   a majority of the pre-moratorium creditors who are unconnected
secured creditors vote against the proposed end date, or

(b)   a majority of the pre-moratorium creditors who are unconnected
unsecured creditors vote against the proposed end date.

(C1)   For the purposes of paragraph (B1)—

(a)   a creditor is unconnected unless the convener or chair decides that the
creditor is connected, and

(b)   the total value of the unconnected creditors is the total value of those
unconnected creditors whose claims have been admitted for voting."

*Content of application to the court for extension of moratorium*

**29**

(1)   An application by the directors of a company for the extension of a moratorium
under section A13 of the Insolvency Act 1986 must state—

(a)   that it is made under that section,

(b)   the length of the extension sought,

(c)   identification details for the company to which the application relates,

(d)   the company's address for service, and

(e)   the court (and where applicable, the division or district registry of that
court) or hearing centre in which the application is made.

(2)   The application must be authenticated by or on behalf of the directors.

(3)   Rule 1.5 of the England and Wales Insolvency Rules applies for the purposes of
authentication under sub-paragraph (2).

*Timing of statements accompanying application to court for extension of moratorium*

**30**

A statement under section A13(2) must be made within the period of 3 days ending with
the day on which the application under that section is made.

*Notices about change in end of moratorium*

**31**

(1)   A notice under section A17(1) of the Insolvency Act 1986 must be given within the period of 5 days beginning with the day on which the duty to give the notice arises.

(2)   The notice must state—

    (a)   the name of the company to which it relates, and

    (b)   the provision by virtue of which the moratorium was extended or came to an end.

**32**

(1)   A notice under section A17(2) or (3) of the Insolvency Act 1986 must be given within the period of 5 days beginning with the day on which the duty to give the notice arises.

(2)   The notice must state—

    (a)   the provision under which it is given,

    (b)   the nature of the notice,

    (c)   the date of the notice,

    (d)   that it is given by the monitor acting in that capacity,

    (e)   the name and contact details of the monitor, and

    (f)   the identification details for the company to which it relates.

(3)   A notice under section A17(2) or (3) of the Insolvency Act 1986 that is given to the registrar of companies must be authenticated by or on behalf of the monitor.

(4)   Rule 1.5 of the England and Wales Insolvency Rules applies for the purposes of authentication under sub-paragraph (3).

**33**

Where a moratorium comes to an end under section A16 of the Insolvency Act 1986 because the company has entered into a relevant insolvency procedure within the meaning of that section, the notices under section A17(1) and (2) must state—

    (a)   the date on which the company entered into the relevant insolvency procedure, and

    (b)   the name and contact details of the supervisor of the voluntary arrangement, the administrator or the liquidator.

**34**

(1)   A notice under section A17(4) of the Insolvency Act 1986 must be given within the period of 3 business days beginning with the day on which the notice under section A38(1) of that Act is filed with the court.

(2)   The notice under section A17(4) of that Act must be accompanied by the notice that the monitor has filed with the court under section A38(1) of that Act.

*Notification by directors of insolvency proceedings etc*

**35**

(1)   A notice under section A24(1) of the Insolvency Act 1986 must be given before the period of 3 days ending with the day on which the step mentioned there is taken.

(2)   A notice under section A24(2) of the Insolvency Act 1986 must be given within the period of 3 days beginning with the day on which the duty to give the notice arises.

*Notice of termination of moratorium*

**36**

*(1) A notice under section A38(1) of the Insolvency Act 1986 must be filed with the court as soon as practicable after the duty in that subsection arises.*

(2)   The notice must state—

    (a)   the provision under which it is given,

(b)    the nature of the notice,

(c)    the date of the notice,

(d)    the name and contact details of the monitor,

(e)    the identification details for the company to which it relates,

(f)    the grounds on which the moratorium is being terminated,

(g)    the monitor's reasons for concluding that those grounds are made out,

(h)    the date on which the monitor concluded that those grounds were made out, and

(i)    the court (and where applicable, the division or district registry of that court) or hearing centre in which the notice is to be filed.

(3)   The notice must be authenticated by or on behalf of the monitor.

(4)   Rule 1.5 of the England and Wales Insolvency Rules applies for the purposes of authentication under sub-paragraph (3).

*Termination of moratorium under section A38(1)(d) of the Insolvency Act 1986*

**37**

For the purposes of deciding whether to bring a moratorium to an end under section A38(1)(d) of the Insolvency Act 1986 the monitor must disregard—

(a)    any debts that the monitor has reasonable grounds for thinking are likely to be paid within 5 days of the decision, and

(b)    any debts in respect of which the creditor has agreed to defer payment until a time that is later than the decision.

*Replacement of monitor or additional monitor: statement and consent to act*

**38**

(1)   A statement under section A39(4) of the Insolvency Act 1986 must be headed "Proposed monitor's statement and consent to act" and must contain the following—

(a)    a certificate that the proposed monitor is qualified to act as an insolvency practitioner in relation to the company,

(b)    the proposed monitor's IP number,

(c)    the name of the relevant recognised professional body which is the source of the proposed monitor's authorisation to act in relation to the company, and

(d)    a statement that the proposed monitor consents to act as monitor in relation to the company.

(2)   The statement must be made within the period of 5 days ending with the day on which it is filed with the court.

(3)   In this paragraph "IP number" means the number assigned to an office-holder as an insolvency practitioner by the Secretary of State.

*Replacement of monitor or additional monitor: notification*

**39**

(1)   A notice under section A39(8) of the Insolvency Act 1986 must state—

(a)    the provision under which it is given,

(b)    the nature of the notice,

(c)    the date of the notice,

(d)    the identification details for the company to which it relates,

(e)    that it is given by the monitor acting in that capacity, and

(f)    the name and contact details of the monitor.

(2)   The notice must be authenticated by the monitor.

(3)   Rule 1.5 of the England and Wales Insolvency Rules applies for the purposes of authentication under this paragraph.

*Challenge to monitor's remuneration*

**40**

(1)   An administrator or liquidator of a company may apply to the court on the ground that remuneration charged by the monitor in relation to a prior moratorium for the company under Part A1 of the Insolvency Act 1986 was excessive.

(2)   An application under this paragraph may not be made after the end of the period of 2 years beginning with the day after the moratorium ends.

(3)   On an application under this paragraph the court may—

   (a)   dismiss the application,

   (b)   order the monitor to repay some or all of the remuneration, or

   (c)   make such other order as it thinks fit.

(4)   The costs of an application under this paragraph are, unless the court orders otherwise, to be paid as an expense of the administration or liquidation.

*Challenge to directors' actions: qualifying decision procedure*

**41**

Where the court makes an order by virtue of section A44(4)(c) of the Insolvency Act 1986 requiring a decision of a company's creditors, the following provisions of the England and Wales Insolvency Rules apply for the purposes of that decision to the extent set out in the court's order and subject to any modifications set out in the court's order—

   (a)   Part 15 (decision making);

   (b)   Part 16 (proxies).

*Priority of moratorium debts etc in subsequent winding up*

**42**

(1)   Where section 174A of the Insolvency Act 1986 applies, the moratorium debts and pre-moratorium debts mentioned in subsection (2)(b) of that section are payable in the following order of priority—

   (a)   amounts payable in respect of goods or services supplied during the moratorium under a contract where, but for section 233B(3) or (4) of that Act, the supplier would not have had to make that supply;

   (b)   wages or salary arising under a contract of employment;

   (c)   other debts or other liabilities apart from the monitor's remuneration or expenses;

   (d)   the monitor's remuneration or expenses.

(2)   In this paragraph "wages or salary" has the same meaning as in section A18 of the Insolvency Act 1986.

*Priority of moratorium debts etc in subsequent administration*

**43**

(1)   Where paragraph 64A(1) of Schedule B1 to the Insolvency Act 1986 applies, the moratorium debts and pre-moratorium debts mentioned in paragraph 64A(2) of that Schedule are payable in the following order of priority—

   (a)   amounts payable in respect of goods or services supplied during the moratorium under a contract where, but for section 233B(3) or (4) of that Act, the supplier would not have had to make that supply;

   (b)   wages or salary arising under a contract of employment;

   (c)   other debts or other liabilities apart from the monitor's remuneration or expenses;

   (d)   the monitor's remuneration or expenses.

(2)   In this paragraph "wages or salary" has the same meaning as in section A18 of the Insolvency Act 1986.

*Prescribed format of documents*

**44**

Rule 1.4 of the England and Wales Insolvency Rules (requirement for writing and form of documents) applies for the purposes of Part A1 of the Insolvency Act 1986.

**45**

(1)   The following provisions of the England and Wales Insolvency Rules apply, so far as relevant, to any requirement imposed by a provision of this Part of this Schedule—

    rule 1.8 (prescribed format of documents), and

    rule 1.9(1) (variations from prescribed contents).

(2)   In their application by virtue of sub-paragraph (1), a reference in rule 1.8 or 1.9(1) to the requirements of a rule is to be read as a reference to the requirements of the provision of this Part of this Schedule.

*Delivery of documents*

**46**

The following provisions of Chapter 9 of Part 1 of the England and Wales Insolvency Rules apply for the purposes of proceedings under Part A1 of the Insolvency Act 1986 as if rule 1.36(1) included a reference to such proceedings—

    rule 1.36(2) (delivery to registrar of companies);

    rule 1.40 (delivery of documents to authorised recipients);

    rule 1.41 (delivery of documents to joint office-holders);

    rule 1.42 (postal delivery of documents);

    rule 1.43 (delivery by document exchange);

    rule 1.44 (personal delivery of documents);

    rule 1.45 (electronic delivery of documents).

*Applications to court*

**47**

(1)   The provisions of the England and Wales Insolvency Rules specified in the Table apply, so far as relevant, for the purposes of proceedings under—

    (a)    Part A1 of the Insolvency Act 1986;

    (b)    this Part of this Schedule.

(2)   In their application by virtue of sub-paragraph (1), the provisions listed in the Table have effect with—

    (a)    the modification set out in sub-paragraph (3),

    (b)    the modifications specified in the Table, and

    (c)    any other necessary modifications.

(3)   The modification is that any reference to Part 1 of the Insolvency Act 1986 includes a reference to Part A1 of that Act and this Part of this Schedule.

(4)   This is the Table referred to in sub-paragraphs (1) and (2)—

| Insolvency Rules | Topic | Modifications |
|---|---|---|
| Rule 1.35 | Standard contents and authentication of applications | |
| Rules 12.1 and 12.2 | Court rules and practice to apply etc | |
| Rule 12.3 and Schedule 6 | Commencement of proceedings | |

| | | |
|---|---|---|
| Rules 12.7 to 12.11 and 12.13 | Making applications to court: general | Rule 12.9 has effect as if, in relation to a regulated company (within the meaning of section A49 of the Insolvency Act 1986), it also required the application to be served on the appropriate regulator (within the meaning of that section). |
| Rules 12.27 to 12.29 | Obtaining information and evidence | Rule 12.29(3) has effect as if it included a reference to the monitor in relation to a moratorium. |
| Rules 12.30, 12.31, 12.33 and 12.35 to 12.38 | Transfer of proceedings | (a) Rule 12.36(2) has effect as if the list of office-holders included the monitor in relation to a moratorium. |
| | | (b) Rule 12.37(2) and (3) have effect as if the list of provisions included section A39 of the Insolvency Act 1986. |
| Rules 12.39 and 12.40 | The court file | |
| Rules 12.41, 12.42(5), 12.47, 12.48 and 12.50 | Costs | Rule 12.48(2) has effect as if it required the applicant to serve a sealed copy of the application on the monitor and the company to which the moratorium relates. |
| Rule 12.51 | Enforcement of court orders | |
| Rules 12.58, 12.59 and 12.61 and Schedule 10 | Appeals | |
| Rules 12.63 to 12.65 | Court orders, formal defects and shorthand writers | |
| Schedule 4, paragraphs 1, 4, 5 and 6 | | These paragraphs of Schedule 4 apply only for the purposes of the rules applied by this Table. |

*Identification details for a company*

**48**

(1) Where a provision of this Part of this Schedule requires a document to contain identification details for a company that is registered under the Companies Act 2006 in England and Wales, the following information must be given—

    (a)    the company's registered name;

    (b)    its registered number;

(2) Where a provision of this Part of this Schedule requires a document to contain identification details for a company that has registered particulars under section 1046(1) of the Companies Act 2006 (registered overseas companies), the following information must be given—

    (a)    the name registered by the company under section 1047 of that Act,

    (b)    the number under which it is registered, and

    (c)    the country or territory in which it is incorporated.

(3) Where a provision of this Part of this Schedule requires a document to contain identification details for an unregistered company that does not come within sub-paragraph (2) the following information must be given—

    (a)    the company's name, and

    (b)    the postal address of any principal place of business.

*Contact details of a monitor or other office-holder*

**49**

Where a provision of this Part of this Schedule requires a document to contain contact details of a monitor or other office-holder, the following information must be given—

    (a)    a postal address for the monitor or office-holder, and

    (b)    either an email address, or a telephone number, through which the monitor may be contacted.

*"The England and Wales Insolvency Rules"*

**50**

In this Part of this Schedule "the England and Wales Insolvency Rules" means the Insolvency (England and Wales) Rules 2016.

*Interpretation: general*

**51**

Expressions used in this Part of this Schedule are to be construed as if this Part of this Schedule were contained in Part A1 of the Insolvency Act 1986.

## PART 4   TEMPORARY RULES: SCOTLAND

*Introductory*

**[5.37]**

**52**

Paragraphs 53 to 90 cease to have effect at the end of the relevant period, subject to paragraph 3.

*Definition of "the court"*

**53**

Section A54(1) of the Insolvency Act 1986 has effect as if for the definition of "the court" there were substituted—

    ""the court", in relation to a company, means a court having jurisdiction to wind up the company;".

*Content of documents relating to the obtaining or extending of a moratorium: general*

**54**

A notice or statement under section A6(1), A8(2), A10(1), A11(1) or A13(2) of the Insolvency Act 1986 must state—

    (a)    the provision under which it is given or made,

    (b)    the nature of the notice or statement,

    (c)    the date of the notice or statement, and

    (d)    the identification details for the company to which it relates.

*Authentication of documents relating to obtaining or extending moratorium: general*

**55**

(1)  A notice or statement under section A6(1), A10(1), A11(1) or A13(2) of the Insolvency Act 1986 must be authenticated by or on behalf of the person giving the notice or making the statement.

(2)   A notice under section A8(2)(a) of the Insolvency Act 1986 must be authenticated by the monitor.

(3)   Rule 1.6 of the Scottish Insolvency Rules applies for the purposes of authentication under this paragraph.

*Notice that directors wish to obtain a moratorium*

56

A notice under section A6(1)(a) of the Insolvency Act 1986 must state—

(a)     the company's address for service, and

(b)     the court in which the documents are to be lodged under section A3 or the application under section A4 or A5 is to be made.

*Proposed monitor's statement and consent to act*

57

(1)   A statement under section A6(1)(b) of the Insolvency Act 1986 must be headed "Proposed monitor's statement and consent to act" and must contain the following—

(a)     a certificate that the proposed monitor is qualified to act as an insolvency practitioner in relation to the company,

(b)     the proposed monitor's IP number,

(c)     the name of the relevant recognised professional body which is the source of the proposed monitor's authorisation to act in relation to the company, and

(d)     a statement that the proposed monitor consents to act as monitor in relation to the company.

(2)   In this paragraph "IP number" means the number assigned to an office-holder as an insolvency practitioner by the Secretary of State.

*Timing of statements for obtaining moratorium*

58

Each statement under section A6(1)(b) to (e) of the Insolvency Act 1986 must be made within the period of 5 days ending with the day on which the documents under section A6(1)(a) to (e) are lodged in the court (or, if the documents are lodged on different days, the last of those days).

*Notice by monitor where moratorium comes into force*

59

A notice under section A8(2) of the Insolvency Act 1986 must—

(a)     state that it is given by the monitor acting in that capacity, and

(b)     state the name and contact details of the monitor.

*Notice that directors wish to extend a moratorium*

60

A notice under section A10(1)(a) or A11(1)(a) of the Insolvency Act 1986 must state—

(a)     the company's address for service,

(b)     the court in which the notice is to be lodged.

*Extension under section A10 or A11 of the Insolvency Act 1986: notices and statements*

61

A statement by the monitor under section A10(1)(d) or A11(1)(d) of the Insolvency Act 1986 must contain contact details of the monitor.

*Timing of statements for extension under section A10 or A11*

**62**

Each statement under section A10(1)(b) to (d) or A11(1)(b) to (e) of the Insolvency Act 1986 must be made within the period of 3 days ending with the day on which the documents under section A10(1)(a) to (d) or A11(1)(a) to (e) are lodged in the court (or, if the documents are lodged on different days, the last of those days).

*Obtaining creditor consent: qualifying decision procedure*

**63**

(1)   The following apply, so far as relevant, for the purposes of a decision to consent to a revised end date for a moratorium under section A12 of the Insolvency Act 1986—

    (a)    Part 5 of the Scottish Insolvency Rules (decision making), apart from rule 5.8(3)(f) and (g);

    (b)    Part 6 of the Scottish Insolvency Rules (proxies), apart from rule 6.7.

(2)   In its application by virtue of sub-paragraph (1), Part 5 has effect subject to the modifications set out in paragraphs 64 to 68.

**64**

Rule 5.11 of the Scottish Insolvency Rules (notice of decision procedures etc) has effect as if, before the first entry in the table, there were inserted—

| "moratorium | decision of pre-moratorium credi-tors under sec-tion A12 of the Act | the pre-moratorium creditors | 5 days" |
|---|---|---|---|

**65**

Rule 5.26 of the Scottish Insolvency Rules (creditors' voting rights) has effect as if, before paragraph (1), there were inserted—

    "(A1)   A pre-moratorium creditor is entitled to vote in a decision procedure under section A12 of the Act only if—

    (a)    the creditor has delivered to the convener a statement of claim and documentary evidence of debt, including any calculation for the purposes of rule 5.28 or 5.29,

    (b)    the statement of claim and documentary evidence of debt were received by the convener not later than the decision date, or in the case of a meeting, at or before the meeting, and

    (c)    the statement of claim and documentary evidence of debt has been admitted for the purposes of entitlement to vote."

**66**

Rule 5.28 of the Scottish Insolvency Rules (calculation of voting rights) has effect as if—

    (a)    before paragraph (1) there were inserted—

    "(A1)   In relation to a decision to consent to a revised end date for a moratorium under section A12 of the Act votes are calculated according to the amount of each creditor's claim at the decision date.";

    (b)    after paragraph (2) there were inserted—

    "(2A)   But in relation to a decision to consent to a revised end date for a moratorium under section A12 of the Act, a debt of an unliquidated or unascertained amount is to be valued at £1 for the purposes of voting unless the convener or chair or an appointed person decides to put a higher value on it.";

    (c)    in paragraph (6), after sub-paragraph (b) there were inserted—

        "(c)    where the decision relates to whether to consent to a revised end date for a moratorium under section A12 of the Act."

**67**

Rule 5.29 of the Scottish Insolvency Rules (calculation of voting rights: hire-purchase agreements) has effect as if, before paragraph (1), there were inserted—

"(A1) In relation to a decision to consent to a revised end date for a moratorium under section A12 of the Act, a pre-moratorium creditor under a hire-purchase agreement is entitled to vote in respect of the amount of the debt due and payable by the company at the decision date.

(B1) In calculating the amount of any debt for the purpose of paragraph (A1), no account is to be taken of any amount attributable to the exercise of any right under the relevant agreement so far as the right has become exercisable solely by virtue of a moratorium for the company coming into force."

**68**

Rule 5.31 of the Scottish Insolvency Rules (requisite majorities) has effect as if, before paragraph (1), there were inserted—

"(A1) Subject to paragraph (B1), a decision to consent to a revised end date for a moratorium under section A12 of the Act is made if, of those voting—

    (a) a majority (in value) of the pre-moratorium creditors who are secured creditors vote in favour of the proposed decision, and

    (b) a majority (in value) of the pre-moratorium creditors who are unsecured creditors vote in favour of the proposed decision.

(B1) But a decision to consent to a revised end date for a moratorium under section A12 of the Act is not made if, of those voting either—

    (a) a majority of the pre-moratorium creditors who are unconnected secured creditors vote against the proposed end date, or

    (b) a majority of the pre-moratorium creditors who are unconnected unsecured creditors vote against the proposed end date.

(C1) For the purposes of paragraph (B1)—

    (a) a creditor is unconnected unless the convener or chair decides that the creditor is connected, and

    (b) the total value of the unconnected creditors is the total value of those unconnected creditors whose claims have been admitted for voting."

*Content of application to the court for extension of moratorium*

**69**

(1) An application by the directors of a company for the extension of a moratorium under section A13 of the Insolvency Act 1986 must state—

    (a) that it is made under that section,

    (b) the length of the extension sought,

    (c) identification details for the company to which the application relates,

    (d) the company's address for service, and

    (e) the court in which the application is made.

(2) The application must be authenticated by or on behalf of the directors.

(3) Rule 1.6 of the Scottish Insolvency Rules applies for the purposes of authentication under sub-paragraph (2).

*Timing of statements accompanying application to court for extension of moratorium*

**70**

A statement under section A13(2) must be made within the period of 3 days ending with the day on which the application under that section is made.

*Notices about change in end of moratorium*

**71**

(1)   A notice under section A17(1) of the Insolvency Act 1986 must be given within the period of 5 days beginning with the day on which the duty to give the notice arises.

(2)   The notice must state—

     (a)    the name of the company to which it relates, and

     (b)    the provision by virtue of which the moratorium was extended or came to an end.

**72**

(1)   A notice under section A17(2) or (3) of the Insolvency Act 1986 must be given within the period of 5 days beginning with the day on which the duty to give the notice arises.

(2)   The notice must state—

     (a)    the provision under which it is given,

     (b)    the nature of the notice,

     (c)    the date of the notice,

     (d)    that it is given by the monitor acting in that capacity,

     (e)    the name and contact details of the monitor, and

     (f)    the identification details for the company to which it relates.

(3)   A notice under section A17(2) or (3) of the Insolvency Act 1986 that is given to the registrar of companies must be authenticated by or on behalf of the monitor.

(4)   Rule 1.6 of the Scottish Insolvency Rules applies for the purposes of authentication under sub-paragraph (3).

**73**

Where a moratorium comes to an end under section A16 of the Insolvency Act 1986 because the company has entered into a relevant insolvency procedure within the meaning of that section, the notices under section A17(1) and (2) must state—

     (a)    the date on which the company entered into the relevant insolvency procedure, and

     (b)    the name and contact details of the supervisor of the voluntary arrangement, the administrator or the liquidator.

**74**

(1)   A notice under section A17(4) of the Insolvency Act 1986 must be given within the period of 3 business days beginning with the day on which the notice under section A38(1) is lodged in the court.

(2)   The notice under section A17(4) of that Act must be accompanied by the notice that the monitor has lodged in the court under section A38(1) of that Act.

*Notification by directors of insolvency proceedings etc*

**75**

(1)   A notice under section A24(1) of the Insolvency Act 1986 must be given before the period of 3 days ending with the day on which the step mentioned there is taken.

(2)   A notice under section A24(2) of the Insolvency Act 1986 must be given within the period of 3 days beginning with the day on which the duty to give the notice arises.

*Notice of termination of moratorium*

**76**

(1)   A notice under section A38(1) of the Insolvency Act 1986 must be lodged in the court as soon as practicable after the duty in that subsection arises.

(2)   The notice must state—

     (a)    the provision under which it is given,

     (b)    the nature of the notice,

(c)    the date of the notice,

(d)    the name and contact details of the monitor,

(e)    the identification details for the company to which it relates,

(f)    the grounds on which the moratorium is being terminated,

(g)    the monitor's reasons for concluding that those grounds are made out,

(h)    the date on which the monitor concluded that those grounds were made out, and

(i)    the court in which the notice is to be lodged.

(3)   The notice must be authenticated by or on behalf of the monitor.

(4)   Rule 1.6 of the Scottish Insolvency Rules applies for the purposes of authentication under sub-paragraph (3).

*Termination of moratorium under section A38(1)(d) of the Insolvency Act 1986*

**77**

For the purposes of deciding whether to bring a moratorium to an end under section A38(1)(d) of the Insolvency Act 1986 the monitor must disregard—

(a)    any debts that the monitor has reasonable grounds for thinking are likely to be paid within 5 days of the decision, and

(b)    any debts in respect of which the creditor has agreed to defer payment until a time that is later than the decision.

*Replacement of monitor or additional monitor: statement and consent to act*

**78**

(1)   A statement under section A39(4) of the Insolvency Act 1986 must be headed "Proposed monitor's statement and consent to act" and must contain the following—

(a)    a certificate that the proposed monitor is qualified to act as an insolvency practitioner in relation to the company,

(b)    the proposed monitor's IP number,

(c)    the name of the relevant recognised professional body which is the source of the proposed monitor's authorisation to act in relation to the company, and

(d)    a statement that the proposed monitor consents to act as monitor in relation to the company.

(2)   The statement must be made within the period of 5 days ending with the day on which it is lodged in the court.

(3)   In this paragraph "IP number" means the number assigned to an office-holder as an insolvency practitioner by the Secretary of State.

*Replacement of monitor or additional monitor: notification*

**79**

(1)   A notice under section A39(8) of the Insolvency Act 1986 must state—

(a)    the provision under which it is given,

(b)    the nature of the notice,

(c)    the date of the notice,

(d)    the identification details for the company to which it relates,

(e)    that it is given by the monitor acting in that capacity, and

(f)    the name and contact details of the monitor.

(2)   The notice must be authenticated by the monitor.

(3)   Rule 1.6 of the Scottish Insolvency Rules applies for the purposes of authentication under sub-paragraph (2).

*Challenge to monitor's remuneration*

**80**

(1)   An administrator or liquidator of a company may apply to the court on the ground that remuneration charged by the monitor in relation to a prior moratorium for the company under Part A1 of the Insolvency Act 1986 was excessive.

(2)   An application under this paragraph may not be made after the end of the period of 2 years beginning with the day after the moratorium ends.

(3)   On an application under this paragraph the court may—

(a)   dismiss the application,

(b)   order the monitor to repay some or all of the remuneration, or

(c)   make such other order as it thinks fit.

(4)   The expenses of an application under this paragraph are, unless the court orders otherwise, to be paid as an expense of the administration or liquidation.

*Challenge to directors' actions: qualifying decision procedure*

**81**

Where the court makes an order by virtue of section A44(4)(c) of the Insolvency Act 1986 requiring a decision of a company's creditors, the following provisions of the Scottish Insolvency Rules apply for the purposes of that decision to the extent set out in the court's order and subject to any modifications set out in the court's order—

(a)   Part 5 (decision making);

(b)   Part 6 (proxies).

*Priority of moratorium debts etc in subsequent winding up*

**82**

(1)   Where section 174A of the Insolvency Act 1986 applies, the moratorium debts and pre-moratorium debts mentioned in subsection (2)(b) of that section are payable in the following order of priority—

(a)   amounts payable in respect of goods or services supplied during the moratorium under a contract where, but for section 233B(3) or (4) of that Act, the supplier would not have had to make that supply;

(b)   wages or salary arising under a contract of employment;

(c)   other debts or other liabilities apart from the monitor's remuneration or expenses;

(d)   the monitor's remuneration or expenses.

(2)   In this paragraph "wages or salary" has the same meaning as in section A18 of the Insolvency Act 1986.

*Priority of moratorium debts etc in subsequent administration*

**83**

(1)   Where paragraph 64A(1) of Schedule B1 to the Insolvency Act 1986 applies, the moratorium debts and pre-moratorium debts mentioned in paragraph 64A(2) of that Schedule are payable in the following order of priority—

(a)   amounts payable in respect of goods or services supplied during the moratorium under a contract where, but for section 233B(3) or (4) of that Act, the supplier would not have had to make that supply;

(b)   wages or salary arising under a contract of employment;

(c)   other debts or other liabilities apart from the monitor's remuneration or expenses;

(d)   the monitor's remuneration or expenses.

(2)   In this paragraph "wages or salary" has the same meaning as in section A18 of the Insolvency Act 1986.

*Prescribed format of documents*

**84**

Rule 1.5 of the Scottish Insolvency Rules (requirement for writing and form of documents) applies for the purposes of Part A1 of the Insolvency Act 1986.

**85**

(1)   The following provisions of the Scottish Insolvency Rules apply, so far as relevant, to any requirement imposed by a provision of this Part of this Schedule—

> rule 1.9 (prescribed format of documents), and
> rule 1.10 (variations from prescribed contents).

(2)   In their application by virtue of sub-paragraph (1), a reference in rule 1.9 or 1.10 to the requirements of a rule is to be read as a reference to the requirements of the provision of this Part of this Schedule.

*Delivery of documents*

**86**

The following provisions of Chapter 9 of Part 1 of the Scottish Insolvency Rules apply for the purposes of proceedings under Part A1 of the Insolvency Act 1986 as if rule 1.32(1) included a reference to such proceedings—

> rule 1.32(2) to (3) (delivery to registrar of companies);
> rule 1.36 (delivery of documents to authorised recipients);
> rule 1.37 (delivery of documents to joint office-holders);
> rule 1.38 (postal delivery of documents);
> rule 1.39 (delivery by document exchange);
> rule 1.40 (personal delivery of documents);
> rule 1.41 (electronic delivery of documents).

*Identification details for a company*

**87**

(1)   Where a provision of this Part of this Schedule requires a document to contain identification details for a company that is registered under the Companies Act 2006 in Scotland, the following information must be given—

> (a)   the company's registered name;
> (b)   its registered number;

(2)   Where a provision of this Part of this Schedule requires a document to contain identification details for a company that has registered particulars under section 1046(1) of the Companies Act 2006 (registered overseas companies), the following information must be given—

> (a)   the name registered by the company under section 1047 of that Act,
> (b)   the number under which it is registered, and
> (c)   the country or territory in which it is incorporated.

(3)   Where a provision of this Part of this Schedule requires a document to contain identification details for an unregistered company that does not come within sub-paragraph (2) the following information must be given—

> (a)   the company's name, and
> (b)   the postal address of any principal place of business.

*Contact details of a monitor or other office-holder*

**88**

Where a provision of this Part of this Schedule requires a document to contain contact details of a monitor or other office-holder, the following information must be given—

> (a)   a postal address for the monitor or office-holder, and

(b)    either an email address, or a telephone number, through which the
monitor may be contacted.

*"The Scottish Insolvency Rules"*

**89**

In this Part of this Schedule "the Scottish Insolvency Rules" means the Insolvency
(Scotland) (Company Voluntary Arrangements and Administration) Rules 2018 (SI
2018/1082).

*Interpretation: general*

**90**

Expressions used in this Part of this Schedule are to be construed as if this Part of this
Schedule were contained in Part A1 of the Insolvency Act 1986.

## PART 5    ENTITIES OTHER THAN COMPANIES

**91**

Regulations under section 14(1) of the Limited Liability Partnership Act 2000 may
make provision applying or incorporating provision made by or under this Schedule,
with such modifications as appear appropriate, in relation to a limited liability
partnership registered in Great Britain.

**92**

An order or regulations under section 118(1)(a), (3B) or (3C) of the Co-operative
and Community Benefit Societies Act 2014 may provide for provision made by or under
this Schedule to apply (with or without modifications) in relation to registered societies
(or to registered societies of the kind mentioned there).

## SCHEDULES 5–8

*(Schedules 5–8 solely affect Northern Ireland and are not reproduced.)*

## SCHEDULE 9
## ARRANGEMENTS AND RECONSTRUCTIONS FOR COMPANIES IN
## FINANCIAL DIFFICULTY

Section 7

**[5.38]**

**Introduction**—Sch 9 of CIGA 2020 introduces a new Part 26A to the Companies Act 2006 ('CA
2006') to provide for a new form of restructuring plan ('Part 26A plan'). The procedure for the
Part 26A plan is contained in new ss 901A to 901L of the CA 2006, which in many respects is
similar to the existing Part 26 concerning schemes of arrangement. As with schemes of
arrangement, the Part 26A plan is a form of debtor-in-possession procedure that required a hearing
to determine whether class meetings should be convened, followed by a further hearing (if
appropriate) to consider whether the plan should be given sanction. A key point of distinction,
however, between a Part 26A plan and either a traditional scheme of arrangement or a CVA is the
power of the court to bind a dissenting class to a Part 26A plan. This has become known as a cross-
class cram-down.

**When Part 26A will apply**—Part 26A applies where two statutory conditions in s 901A are met.
The first condition is that the company has encountered, or is likely to encounter, financial
difficulties that are affecting, or will or may affect, its ability to carry on business as a going
concern. The second is that a compromise or arrangement is proposed between the company and
its creditors, or any class of them, or its members, or any class of them, whose purpose is to
eliminate, reduce or prevent, or mitigate the effect of financial difficulties that are affecting, or will
or may affect, its ability to carry on business as a going concern.

The practice to be followed when making an application under either Part 26 or Part 26A is set
out in a practice statement ('Companies: Schemes of Arrangements under Part 26 and Part 26A of

the Companies Act 2006') dated 26 June 2020, which may be found at Appendix 5 to this work.

Since the coming into force of CIGA 2020 on 26 June 2020, a body of first instance case law has begun to emerge. The key cases that have progressed to sanction hearings include *Re Virgin Atlantic Airways Ltd* [2020] EWHC 2191 (Ch), [2021] 1 BCLC 87 (convening) (Trower J), [2020] EWHC 2376 (Ch), [2021] 1 BCLC 105 (sanction) (Snowden J); *Re DeepOcean I UK Ltd* [2020] EWHC 3549 (Ch) (convening), [2021] EWHC 138 (Ch) (sanction) (Trower J); *Re Virgin Active Holdings Ltd* [2021] EWHC 814 (Ch) (convening), [2021] EWHC 1246 (Ch) (sanction) (Snowden J); and *Re Hurricane Energy Plc* [2021] EWHC 1418 (Ch) (convening), [2021] EWHC 1759 (Ch) (sanction) (Zacaroli J). The schemes were sanctioned in *Virgin Atlantic Airways Ltd, Re DeepOcean I UK Ltd* and *Re Virgin Active Holdings Ltd*, with cross-class cram-downs imposed in the latter two cases. The scheme in *Re Hurricane Energy Plc* was the first proposed plan under the new regime to be refused sanction.

**Convening hearing**—Section 901C provides for an application to be made for the court to order that class meetings of creditors and members be convened. Every creditor or member whose rights are affected by a proposed Part 26A plan must be permitted to participate in a meeting. This is subject to the important qualification in s 901C(4), which provides that where the court is satisfied that none of the creditors or members in a particular class has 'a genuine economic interest in the company', they need not be permitted to participate in a meeting.

Generally speaking, the well-known principles in relation to class composition in relation to a scheme of arrangement under Part 26 will apply to a Part 26A plan: *Re Virgin Atlantic Airways* [2020] EWHC 2191, [44]–[48] (Snowden J). However, Snowden J later held in *Re Virgin Active Holdings Ltd* [2021] EWHC 814 (Ch) that 'a rigid application' of the Part 26 approach may not always be appropriate to a Part 26A plan. Whereas in a Part 26 case it is necessary to take care about placing creditors into the same class when they have materially different rights, in relation to a Part 26A plan where dissentient creditors can be bound by the cram down power where not every class votes in favour, it may be necessary to take care not to place creditors into an artificially large number of classes in order to provide a basis for invoking the cram down power ([61]–[62]). In the same case, Snowden J also held (at [67]–[69]) that in identifying the substance of the relevant rights for the purposes of class composition for Part 26A plans, it was appropriate to have regard to 'the counterfactual comparator', as in Part 26 cases. Although Part 26A contained no express requirement to identify a counterfactual when determining class composition, this was present in s 901G in relation to one of the conditions to be satisfied before the court could exercise its cram-down power; in Snowden J's view, the concept of 'relevant alternative' in s 901G was clearly equivalent to the 'counterfactual comparator'.

A statement complying with s 901D explaining the effect of the Part 26A plan must be circulated or made available to creditors and members. Directors and trustees are placed under a duty by s 901E in relation to the requirements of s 901D. In *Re Virgin Active Holdings Ltd* [2021] EWHC 1246 (Ch), Snowden J observed that the court is entitled to expect companies proposing Part 26A plans to cooperate in the timely provision of information, which in an appropriate case may include information over and above that which can sensibly be contained in a concise explanatory statement, and gave other useful guidance at [130]–[132].

**Sanction hearing**—Sections 901F and 901G provide for the court to sanction a Part 26A plan. Taken in isolation, s 901F essentially reflects the position under Part 26 in relation to conventional schemes of arrangement. If 75% by value of the class meetings summoned under s 901C agree to the Part 26A plan, then the court may sanction it at a second hearing.

The first Part 26A plan to be approved was in *Re Virgin Atlantic Airways Ltd* [2020] EWHC 2376 (Ch), [2021] 1 BCLC 105. In that case, however, the cross-class cram-down power was not engaged, because each of the class meetings voted in favour of the plan. Snowden J held that the established approach in respect of a Part 26 scheme of arrangement applied when determining whether or not to sanction a Part 26A plan where the power to cram down under s 901G was not engaged ([46]).

**The test for cross-class cram-down**—Where one or more classes dissent, s 901G provides that the court may nonetheless sanction it under s 901F, if 'Condition A' in s 901G(3) and 'Condition B' in s 901G(5) are met. This is the 'cross-class cram down' power. At the time of writing, two Part 26A plans requiring a cross-class cram down have received sanction under s 901G and one has been refused.

In *Re Virgin Active Holdings Ltd* [2021] EWHC 1246 (Ch) Snowden J summarised the test for cross-class cram-down at [104] as follows:

'... where a company applies for the sanction of a restructuring plan in reliance on section 901G, three questions must be considered by the Court:

(i)    Condition A: If the restructuring plan is sanctioned, would any members of the dissenting class be any worse off than they would be in the event of the relevant alternative? This is often described as the "no worse off" test.

(ii)  Condition B: Has the restructuring plan been approved by 75% of those voting in any class that would receive a payment, or have a genuine economic interest in the company, in the event of the relevant alternative?

(iii)  General Discretion: In all the circumstances, should the Court exercise its discretion to sanction the restructuring plan?'

When identifying the 'relevant alternative', it was necessary to identify the 'relevant alternative' at the date of the sanction hearing, and the court did not need to consider whether the companies or their directors might have acted differently or to entertain a submission that the companies had failed to explore other options or narrowed their options for survival: *Re Virgin Active Holdings Ltd* [2021] EWHC 1246 (Ch), [114]–[115].

**Exercise of discretion**—As to discretion, Trower J held in *Deepocean* ([46]–[47]) that the court should not have the same reluctance to depart from the decision of a meeting as in a conventional scheme of arrangement under Part 26. This is because, by its very nature, the cross-class cram-down power in s 901G contemplates that the court can override the wishes of a class meeting. Snowden J expressed agreement with this proposition in his decision in *Re Virgin Active Holdings Ltd* [2021] EWHC 1246 (Ch) at [214].

There is, however, no presumption that because Conditions A and B in s 901G are met that the court should sanction the scheme and it would need to consider all relevant factors and circumstances: *Re Virgin Active Holdings Ltd* [2021] EWHC 1246 (Ch), [224] (Snowden J).

In *Re Virgin Active Holdings Ltd* [2021] EWHC 1246 (Ch), the plan companies had divided their landlords into five classes, some of which were to be retained under the Part 26A plans and others not. The evidence showed that if the Part 26A plans were not sanctioned, administration was almost certain to happen ([116]) and that the return to the unsecured creditors (including landlords) would be only the prescribed part ([53]). Only the secured creditors and the top class of landlords voted in favour of the Part 26A plan by the requisite 75% majority. The dissentient landlords submitted that it was unfair that the benefits of the restructuring (the 'restructuring surplus') should be enjoyed by the existing shareholders to the exclusion of prior ranking unsecured creditors, such as the lower-ranking landlords ([226]–[236]). Applying a long line of authority concerning schemes of arrangement from *Re Tea Corporation Ltd* [1904] 1 Ch 12 to *Re Bluebrook Ltd* [2010] BCC 209, Snowden J held that where the only alternative to a scheme is a formal insolvency, the business and assets in essence belong to those creditors who would receive a distribution in the formal insolvency. As such, it was for those 'in the money' creditors to decide how to divide up any value or benefits that might be generated from the business and assets in the future ([238]–[242]). This was put beyond doubt by the fact that s 901C(4) provided for classes with 'no genuine economic interest' to be excluded from participation in meetings ([247]–[249]). Since the dissentient landlords were 'out of the money', their objections to the secured creditors' differential treatment of the landlords carried no weight ([266]).

Sanction was refused to a Part 26A plan requiring a cross-class cram-down in *Re Hurricane Energy Plc* [2021] EWHC 1759 (Ch). The plan was opposed by a significant number of the existing shareholders, whose equity fell to be reduced from 100% to 5% in favour of the bondholders. There was no prospect of an immediate formal insolvency procedure and instead the company proposed to continue trading for at least a further year. The application was nonetheless brought urgently, because the dissentient shareholders had served a requisition notice requiring the company to convene a general meeting for the purpose of removing and replacing directors. It was common ground that unless the Part 26A plan was approved urgently and in advance of the shareholders' having their shares diluted, the entire board would be replaced and the plan withdrawn ([59]).

Zacaroli J considered that 'Condition A' in s 901G(3) (the 'no worse off' test) was not satisfied because there was a realistic prospect based on a range of possibilities that the company would be able to discharge its obligations. It was better for the shareholders to retain 100% of the equity in a company that was continuing to trade, with a realistic prospect of being able to repay in due course, than immediately giving up 95% of the equity with a prospect of a less than meaningful return as to the remaining 5% ([124]–[128]). Further, Zacaroli J held that the impending removal of the board was not a good reason for urgency ([129]–[132]). Finally, Zacaroli J held that sanction would have been refused in the exercise of the court's discretion, even if the 'no worse off' test had been satisfied [133]–[134].

PART 1    MAIN PROVISIONS

**[5.39]**

1

In the Companies Act 2006, after Part 26 insert—

"PART 26A   ARRANGEMENTS AND RECONSTRUCTIONS: COMPANIES IN
FINANCIAL DIFFICULTY

*Application of this Part*

**901A   Application of this Part**

(1)   The provisions of this Part apply where conditions A and B are met in relation to a company.

(2)   Condition A is that the company has encountered, or is likely to encounter, financial difficulties that are affecting, or will or may affect, its ability to carry on business as a going concern.

(3)   Condition B is that—

    (a)    a compromise or arrangement is proposed between the company and—

        (i)    its creditors, or any class of them, or

        (ii)    its members, or any class of them, and

    (b)    the purpose of the compromise or arrangement is to eliminate, reduce or prevent, or mitigate the effect of, any of the financial difficulties mentioned in subsection (2).

(4)   In this Part—

"arrangement" includes a reorganisation of the company's share capital by the consolidation of shares of different classes or by the division of shares into shares of different classes, or by both of those methods;

"company"—

    (a)    in section 901J (powers of court to facilitate reconstruction or amalgamation) means a company within the meaning of this Act, and

    (b)    elsewhere in this Part means any company liable to be wound up under the Insolvency Act 1986 or the Insolvency (Northern Ireland) Order 1989 (SI 1989/2405 (NI 19)).

(5)   The provisions of this Part have effect subject to Part 27 (mergers and divisions of public companies) where that Part applies (see sections 902 and 903).

**901B   Power to exclude companies providing financial services, etc**

(1)   The Secretary of State may by regulations provide that this Part does not apply—

    (a)    where the company in respect of which a compromise or arrangement is proposed is an authorised person, or an authorised person of a specified description;

    (b)    where—

        (i)    a compromise or arrangement is proposed between a company, or a company of a specified description, and any creditors of the company, and

        (ii)    those creditors consist of or include creditors of a specified description.

(2)   In this section—

"authorised person" has the same meaning as in the Financial Services and Markets Act 2000 (see section 31 of that Act);

"specified" means specified in the regulations.

(3)   Regulations under this section are subject to affirmative resolution procedure.

*Meeting of creditors or members*

**901C   Court order for holding of meeting**

(1)   The court may, on an application under this subsection, order a meeting of the creditors or class of creditors, or of the members of the company or class of

members (as the case may be), to be summoned in such manner as the court directs.

(2)    An application under subsection (1) may be made by—

  (a)    the company,

  (b)    any creditor or member of the company,

  (c)    if the company is being wound up, the liquidator, or

  (d)    if the company is in administration, the administrator.

(3)    Every creditor or member of the company whose rights are affected by the compromise or arrangement must be permitted to participate in a meeting ordered to be summoned under subsection (1).

(4)    But subsection (3) does not apply in relation to a class of creditors or members of the company if, on an application under this subsection, the court is satisfied that none of the members of that class has a genuine economic interest in the company.

(5)    An application under subsection (4) is to be made by the person who made the application under subsection (1) in respect of the compromise or arrangement.

(6)    Section 323 (representation of corporations at meetings) applies to a meeting of creditors under this section as to a meeting of the company (references to a member of the company being read as references to a creditor).

(7)    This section is subject to section 901H (moratorium debts, etc).

**901D  Statement to be circulated or made available**

(1)    Where a meeting is summoned under section 901C—

  (a)    every notice summoning the meeting that is sent to a creditor or member must be accompanied by a statement complying with this section, and

  (b)    every notice summoning the meeting that is given by advertisement must either—

    (i)    include such a statement, or

    (ii)    state where and how creditors or members entitled to attend the meeting may obtain copies of such a statement.

(2)    The statement must—

  (a)    explain the effect of the compromise or arrangement, and

  (b)    in particular, state—

    (i)    any material interests of the directors of the company (whether as directors or as members or as creditors of the company or otherwise), and

    (ii)    the effect on those interests of the compromise or arrangement, in so far as it is different from the effect on the like interests of other persons.

(3)    Where the compromise or arrangement affects the rights of debenture holders of the company, the statement must give the like explanation as respects the trustees of any deed for securing the issue of the debentures as it is required to give as respects the company's directors.

(4)    Where a notice given by advertisement states that copies of an explanatory statement can be obtained by creditors or members entitled to attend the meeting, every such creditor or member is entitled, on making application in the manner indicated by the notice, to be provided by the company with a copy of the statement free of charge.

(5)    If a company makes default in complying with any requirement of this section, an offence is committed by—

  (a)    the company, and

  (b)    every officer of the company who is in default.

This is subject to subsection (7).

(6)    For this purpose the following are treated as officers of the company—

  (a)    a liquidator or administrator of the company, and

    (b)    a trustee of a deed for securing the issue of debentures of the company.

(7)    A person is not guilty of an offence under this section if the person shows that the default was due to the refusal of a director or trustee for debenture holders to supply the necessary particulars of the director's or (as the case may be) the trustee's interests.

(8)    A person guilty of an offence under this section is liable—

    (a)    on conviction on indictment, to a fine;

    (b)    on summary conviction in England and Wales, to a fine;

    (c)    on summary conviction in Scotland or Northern Ireland, to a fine not exceeding the statutory maximum.

**901E  Duty of directors and trustees to provide information**

(1)    It is the duty of—

    (a)    any director of the company, and

    (b)    any trustee for its debenture holders,

to give notice to the company of such matters relating to that director or trustee as may be necessary for the purposes of section 901D (explanatory statement to be circulated or made available).

(2)    Any person who makes default in complying with this section commits an offence.

(3)    A person guilty of an offence under this section is liable on summary conviction to a fine not exceeding level 3 on the standard scale.

*Court sanction for compromise or arrangement*

**901F  Court sanction for compromise or arrangement**

(1)    If a number representing 75% in value of the creditors or class of creditors or members or class of members (as the case may be), present and voting either in person or by proxy at the meeting summoned under section 901C, agree a compromise or arrangement, the court may, on an application under this section, sanction the compromise or arrangement.

(2)    Subsection (1) is subject to—

    (a)    section 901G (sanction for compromise or arrangement where one or more classes dissent), and

    (b)    section 901H (moratorium debts, etc).

(3)    An application under this section may be made by—

    (a)    the company,

    (b)    any creditor or member of the company,

    (c)    if the company is being wound up, the liquidator, or

    (d)    if the company is in administration, the administrator.

(4)    Where the court makes an order under this section in relation to a company that is in administration or is being wound up, the court may by the order—

    (a)    provide for the appointment of the administrator or liquidator to cease to have effect;

    (b)    stay or sist all proceedings in the administration or the winding up;

    (c)    impose any requirements with respect to the conduct of the administration or the winding up which the court thinks appropriate for facilitating the compromise or arrangement.

(5)    A compromise or arrangement sanctioned by the court is binding—

    (a)    on all creditors or the class of creditors or on the members or class of members (as the case may be), and

    (b)    on the company or, in the case of a company in the course of being wound up, the liquidator and contributories of the company.

(6)    The court's order has no effect until a copy of it has been—

    (a)    in the case of an overseas company that is not required to register particulars under section 1046, published in the Gazette, or

(b)    in any other case, delivered to the registrar.

**901G  Sanction for compromise or arrangement where one or more classes dissent**

(1)    This section applies if the compromise or arrangement is not agreed by a number representing at least 75% in value of a class of creditors or (as the case may be) of members of the company ("the dissenting class"), present and voting either in person or by proxy at the meeting summoned under section 901C.

(2)    If conditions A and B are met, the fact that the dissenting class has not agreed the compromise or arrangement does not prevent the court from sanctioning it under section 901F.

(3)    Condition A is that the court is satisfied that, if the compromise or arrangement were to be sanctioned under section 901F, none of the members of the dissenting class would be any worse off than they would be in the event of the relevant alternative (see subsection (4)).

(4)    For the purposes of this section "the relevant alternative" is whatever the court considers would be most likely to occur in relation to the company if the compromise or arrangement were not sanctioned under section 901F.

(5)    Condition B is that the compromise or arrangement has been agreed by a number representing 75% in value of a class of creditors or (as the case may be) of members, present and voting either in person or by proxy at the meeting summoned under section 901C, who would receive a payment, or have a genuine economic interest in the company, in the event of the relevant alternative.

(6)    The Secretary of State may by regulations amend this section for the purpose of—

(a)    adding to the conditions that must be met for the purposes of this section;

(b)    removing or varying any of those conditions.

(7)    Regulations under subsection (6) are subject to affirmative resolution procedure.

*Special cases*

**901H  Moratorium debts, etc**

(1)    This section applies where—

(a)    an application under section 901C(1) in respect of a compromise or arrangement is made before the end of the period of 12 weeks beginning with the day after the end of any moratorium for the company under Part A1 of the Insolvency Act 1986 or Part 1A of the Insolvency (Northern Ireland) Order 1989 (SI 1989/2405 (NI 19)), and

(b)    the creditors with whom the compromise or arrangement is proposed include any relevant creditors (see subsection (2)).

(2)    In this section "relevant creditor" means—

(a)    a creditor in respect of a moratorium debt, or

(b)    a creditor in respect of a priority pre-moratorium debt.

(3)    The relevant creditors may not participate in the meeting summoned under section 901C.

(4)    For the purposes of section 901D (statement to be circulated or made available)—

(a)    the requirement in section 901D(1)(a) is to be read as including a requirement to send each relevant creditor a statement complying with section 901D;

(b)    any reference to creditors entitled to attend the meeting summoned under section 901C includes a reference to relevant creditors.

(5)    The court may not sanction the compromise or arrangement under section 901F if it includes provision in respect of any relevant creditor who has not agreed to it.

(6)    In this section—

"moratorium debt"—

    (a)    in the case of a moratorium under Part A1 of the Insolvency Act 1986, has the same meaning as in section 174A of that Act;

    (b)    in the case of a moratorium under Part 1A of the Insolvency (Northern Ireland) Order 1989, has the same meaning as in Article 148A of that Order;

"priority pre-moratorium debt"—

    (a)    in the case of a moratorium under Part A1 of the Insolvency Act 1986, has the same meaning as in section 174A of that Act;

    (b)    in the case of a moratorium under Part 1A of the Insolvency (Northern Ireland) Order 1989, has the same meaning as in Article 148A of that Order.

### 901I Pension schemes

(1) In a case where the company in respect of which a compromise or arrangement is proposed is or has been an employer in respect of an occupational pension scheme that is not a money purchase scheme, any notice or other document required to be sent to a creditor of the company must also be sent to the Pensions Regulator.

(2) In a case where the company in respect of which a compromise or arrangement is proposed is an employer in respect of an eligible scheme, any notice or other document required to be sent to a creditor of the company must also be sent to the Board of the Pension Protection Fund ("the Board").

(3) The Secretary of State may by regulations provide that, in a case where—

    (a)    the company in respect of which a compromise or arrangement is proposed is an employer in respect of an eligible scheme, and

    (b)    the trustees or managers of the scheme are a creditor of the company,

the Board may exercise any rights, or any rights of a specified description, that are exercisable under this Part by the trustees or managers as a creditor of the company.

(4) Regulations under this section may provide that the Board may exercise any such rights—

    (a)    to the exclusion of the trustees or managers of the scheme, or

    (b)    in addition to the exercise of those rights by the trustees or managers of the scheme.

(5) Regulations under this section—

    (a)    may specify conditions that must be met before the Board may exercise any such rights;

    (b)    may provide for any such rights to be exercisable by the Board for a specified period;

    (c)    may make provision in connection with any such rights ceasing to be so exercisable at the end of such a period.

(6) Regulations under this section are subject to affirmative resolution procedure (but see subsection (7)).

(7) During the period of six months beginning with the day on which this section comes into force, regulations under this section are subject to approval after being made (and subsection (6) does not apply).

(8) For the purposes of subsection (7), section 1291 has effect as if any reference in that section to a period of 28 days were to a period of 40 days.

(9) In this section—

"eligible scheme" means any pension scheme that is an eligible scheme for the purposes of section 126 of the Pensions Act 2004 or Article 110 of the Pensions (Northern Ireland) Order 2005 (SI 2005/255 (NI 1));

"employer"—

    (a)    in subsection (1), means an employer within the meaning of section 318(1) of the Pensions Act 2004 or Article 2(2) of the Pensions (Northern Ireland) Order 2005;

(b)    in subsections (2) and (3)—

      (i)    in the case of a pension scheme that is an eligible scheme for the purposes of section 126 of the Pensions Act 2004, has the same meaning as it has for the purposes of Part 2 of that Act (see section 318(1) and (4) of that Act);

      (ii)    in the case of a pension scheme that is an eligible scheme for the purposes of Article 110 of the Pensions (Northern Ireland) Order 2005, has the same meaning as it has for the purposes of Part 3 of that Order (see Article 2(2) and (5) of that Order);

"money purchase scheme" means a pension scheme that is a money purchase scheme for the purposes of the Pension Schemes Act 1993 (see section 181(1) of that Act) or the Pension Schemes (Northern Ireland) Act 1993 (see section 176(1) of that Act);

"occupational pension scheme" and "pension scheme" have the meaning given by section 1 of the Pension Schemes Act 1993;

"specified" means specified in regulations under this section.

### *Reconstructions and amalgamations*

**901J Powers of court to facilitate reconstruction or amalgamation**

(1)    This section applies where application is made to the court under section 901F to sanction a compromise or arrangement and it is shown that—

    (a)    the compromise or arrangement is proposed in connection with a scheme for the reconstruction of any company or companies, or the amalgamation of any two or more companies, and

    (b)    under the scheme the whole or any part of the undertaking or the property of any company concerned in the scheme (a "transferor company") is to be transferred to another company ("the transferee company").

(2)    The court may, either by the order sanctioning the compromise or arrangement or by a subsequent order, make provision for all or any of the following matters—

    (a)    the transfer to the transferee company of the whole or any part of the undertaking and of the property or liabilities of any transferor company;

    (b)    the allotting or appropriation by the transferee company of any shares, debentures, policies or other like interests in that company which under the compromise or arrangement are to be allotted or appropriated by that company to or for any person;

    (c)    the continuation by or against the transferee company of any legal proceedings pending by or against any transferor company;

    (d)    the dissolution, without winding up, of any transferor company;

    (e)    the provision to be made for any persons who, within such time and in such manner as the court directs, dissent from the compromise or arrangement;

    (f)    such incidental, consequential and supplemental matters as are necessary to secure that the reconstruction or amalgamation is fully and effectively carried out.

(3)    If an order under this section provides for the transfer of property or liabilities—

    (a)    the property is by virtue of the order transferred to, and vests in, the transferee company, and

    (b)    the liabilities are, by virtue of the order, transferred to and become liabilities of that company.

(4)   The property (if the order so directs) vests freed from any charge that is by virtue of the compromise or arrangement to cease to have effect.

(5)   In this section—

"property" includes property, rights and powers of every description; and "liabilities" includes duties.

(6)   Every company in relation to which an order is made under this section must cause a copy of the order to be delivered to the registrar within seven days after its making.

(7)   If default is made in complying with subsection (6) an offence is committed by—

(a)   the company, and

(b)   every officer of the company who is in default.

(8)   A person guilty of an offence under subsection (7) is liable on summary conviction to a fine not exceeding level 3 on the standard scale and, for continued contravention, a daily default fine not exceeding one-tenth of level 3 on the standard scale.

*Obligations of company with respect to articles etc*

**901K   Obligations of company with respect to articles etc**

(1)   This section applies—

(a)   to any order under section 901F (order sanctioning compromise or arrangement), and

(b)   to any order under section 901J (order facilitating reconstruction or amalgamation) that alters the company's constitution.

(2)   If—

(a)   the order amends—

(i)    the company's articles, or

(ii)   any resolution or agreement to which Chapter 3 of Part 3 applies (resolution or agreement affecting a company's constitution), and

(b)   a copy of the order is required to be delivered to the registrar by the company under section 901F(6)(b) or section 901J(6),

the copy of the order delivered to the registrar must be accompanied by a copy of the company's articles, or the resolution or agreement in question, as amended.

(3)   Every copy of the company's articles issued by the company after the order is made must be accompanied by a copy of the order, unless the effect of the order has been incorporated into the articles by amendment.

(4)   In this section—

(a)   references to the effect of the order include the effect of the compromise or arrangement to which the order relates, and

(b)   in the case of a company not having articles, references to its articles are to be read as references to the instrument constituting the company or defining its constitution.

(5)   If a company makes default in complying with this section an offence is committed by—

(a)   the company, and

(b)   every officer of the company who is in default.

(6)   A person guilty of an offence under this section is liable on summary conviction to a fine not exceeding level 3 on the standard scale.

*Power to amend Act*

**901L  Power to amend Act**

(1)   The Secretary of State may by regulations make any amendment of this Act which the Secretary of State considers necessary or expedient for the purposes of, in consequence of, or for giving full effect to this Part.

(2)   Regulations under this section are subject to affirmative resolution procedure."

## PART 2   CONSEQUENTIAL AMENDMENTS

*Finance Act 1986*

**[5.40]**

**2**

The Finance Act 1986 is amended as follows.

**3**

In section 80D (repurchases and stock lending: replacement stock on insolvency), in subsection (9)(f), after "Part 26" insert "or 26A".

**4**

In section 89AB (stamp duty reserve tax: exception for repurchases and stock lending in case of insolvency), in subsection (9)(f), after "Part 26" insert "or 26A".

*Insolvency Act 1986*

**5**

The Insolvency Act 1986 is amended as follows.

**6**

(1)   In Part 4 (winding up of companies registered under the Companies Acts), Chapter 8 (provisions of general application in winding up) is amended as follows.

(2)   In section 176ZB (application of proceeds of office-holder claims), in subsection (4)(b), after "Part 26" insert "or 26A".

(3)   In section 176A (share of assets for unsecured creditors), in subsection (4)(b), after "Part 26" insert "or 26A".

**7**

(1)   Schedule B1 (administration) is amended as follows.

(2)   In paragraph 49 (administrator's proposals), in sub-paragraph (3)(b), after "Part 26" insert "or 26A".

(3)   In paragraph 73 (protection for priority creditor), in sub-paragraph (2)(c), after "Part 26" insert "or 26A".

(4)   In paragraph 74 (challenge to administrator's conduct of company), in sub-paragraph (6)(b), after "Part 26" insert "or 26A".

*Insolvency (Northern Ireland) Order 1989 (SI 1989/2405 (NI 19))*

**8**

The Insolvency (Northern Ireland) Order 1989 is amended as follows.

**9**

In Article 150A (share of assets for unsecured creditors), in paragraph (4)(b), after "Part 26" insert "or 26A".

**10**

(1) Schedule B1 (administration) is amended as follows.

(2) In paragraph 50 (administrator's proposals), in sub-paragraph (3)(b), after "Part 26" insert "or 26A".

(3) In paragraph 74 (protection for secured or preferential creditor), in sub-paragraph (2)(c), after "Part 26" insert "or 26A".

(4) In paragraph 75 (challenge to administrator's conduct of company), in sub-paragraph (6)(b), after "Part 26" insert "or 26A".

*Water Industry Act 1991*

**11**

In section 23 of the Water Industry Act 1991 (meaning and effect of special administration order), in subsection (2D)(b), after "Part 26" insert "or 26A".

*Taxation of Chargeable Gains Act 1992*

**12**

The Taxation of Chargeable Gains Act 1992 is amended as follows.

**13**

In section 263CA (stock lending: insolvency etc of borrower), in subsection (9)(f), after "Part 26" insert "or 26A".

**14**

In Schedule 5AA (meaning of "scheme of reconstruction" for purposes of section 136), in paragraph 5(a)(i), after "Part 26" insert "or 26A".

*Value Added Tax Act 1994*

**15**

In section 26AA of the Value Added Tax Act 1994 (disapplication of disallowance under section 26A in insolvency), in subsection (8), after paragraph (k) insert—

"(ka) a compromise or arrangement sanctioned by the court and delivered to the registrar or (as the case may be) published in the Gazette in accordance with section 901F of the Companies Act 2006 is in place in relation to that person,".

*Housing Act 1996*

**16**

(1) In Part 2 of Schedule 1 to the Housing Act 1996 (registered social landlords: constitution, change of rules, amalgamation and dissolution), paragraph 13 (arrangement, reconstruction, etc of company) is amended as follows.

(2) After sub-paragraph (3) insert—

"(3A) If a court makes an order under section 901F of the Companies Act 2006 (sanction of compromise or arrangement with creditors or members) in relation to the company, the company must notify the Welsh Ministers of the order.

(3B) If a court makes an order under section 901J of the Companies Act 2006 (powers of court to facilitate reconstruction or amalgamation) in relation to the company, the company must notify the Welsh Ministers of the order."

(3) In sub-paragraph (8), after "sub-paragraph (3)" insert ", (3B)".

*Financial Services and Markets Act 2000*

**17**

The Financial Services and Markets Act 2000 is amended as follows.

**18**

In section 105 (insurance business transfer schemes), in subsection (5), for "Part 26 of that Act" substitute "Part 26 or 26A of that Act, as the case may be".

**19**

In Schedule 17A (further provision in relation to exercise of Part 18 functions by Bank of England), in paragraph 24 (insolvency)—

    (a)    in sub-paragraph (1), before paragraph (a) insert—

        "(za) sections 355A and 355B (powers to participate in proceedings under Part 26A of the Companies Act 2006);";

    (b)    in sub-paragraph (2), after "recognised investment exchange" insert "(other than the reference to "an authorised person" in section 355B(2)(a))".

**20**

(1)    Part 24 (insolvency) is amended as follows.

(2)    After section 355 insert—

    *"Arrangements and reconstructions: companies in financial difficulty*

**355A  Powers of FCA and PRA to participate in proceedings**

(1)    This section applies where Part 26A of the Companies Act 2006 ("the 2006 Act") (arrangements and reconstructions: companies in financial difficulty) applies in relation to a company which—

    (a)    is, or has been, an authorised person or recognised investment exchange;

    (b)    is, or has been, any of the following—

        (i)    an electronic money institution;

        (ii)    an authorised payment institution;

        (iii)    a small payment institution;

        (iv)    a registered account information service provider;

    (c)    is, or has been, an appointed representative; or

    (d)    is carrying on, or has carried on, a regulated activity in contravention of the general prohibition.

(2)    A relevant applicant must give notice to the appropriate regulator of—

    (a)    any application which the relevant applicant intends to make under section 901C(1) of the 2006 Act, and

    (b)    any application which the relevant applicant believes a creditor or member of the company has made, or intends to make, under section 901C(1) of that Act in relation to the company.

(3)    A relevant applicant may not make an application under section 901C(1) of the 2006 Act in relation to a company that is a PRA-regulated person without the consent of the PRA.

(4)    In this section "relevant applicant", in relation to a company, means—

    (a)    the company;

    (b)    if the company is being wound up, the liquidator;

    (c)    if the company is in administration, the administrator.

(5)    The appropriate regulator is entitled to be heard at any hearing of an application made under section 901C or 901F of the 2006 Act in relation to the company.

(6)    Any notice or other document required to be sent to a creditor of the company must also be sent to the appropriate regulator.

(7)    A person appointed for the purpose by the appropriate regulator is entitled—

    (a)    to attend any meeting of creditors of the company summoned under section 901C of the 2006 Act;

    (b)    to make representations as to any matter for decision at such a meeting.

(8)   In this section—
"the appropriate regulator" means—

    (a)   where the company is a PRA-regulated person, each of the FCA and the PRA, except that the reference in subsection (7) to a person appointed by the appropriate regulator is to be read as a reference to a person appointed by either the FCA or the PRA;

    (b)   in any other case, the FCA;

"authorised payment institution", "small payment institution" and "registered account information service provider" have the same meaning as in the Payment Services Regulations 2017 (SI 2017/752) (see regulation 2 of those Regulations);

"electronic money institution" has the same meaning as in the Electronic Money Regulations 2011 (SI 2011/99) (see regulation 2 of those Regulations).

### 355B   Enforcement of requirements imposed by section 355A

(1)   For the purpose of enforcing a requirement imposed on a company by section 355A(2) or (3), the appropriate regulator may exercise any of the following powers (so far as it would not otherwise be exercisable)—

    (a)   the power to publish a statement under section 205 (public censure);

    (b)   the power to impose a financial penalty under section 206.

(2)   Accordingly, sections 205 and 206, and so much of this Act as relates to either of those sections, have effect in relation to a requirement imposed by section 355A(2) or (3) as if—

    (a)   any reference to an authorised person included (so far as would not otherwise be the case) a reference to a company falling within any of paragraphs (a) to (d) of section 355A(1),

    (b)   any reference to a relevant requirement included (so far as would not otherwise be the case) a reference to a requirement imposed by section 355A(2) or (3), and

    (c)   "the appropriate regulator" had the same meaning as in section 355A.

(3)   In this section "the appropriate regulator" has the same meaning as in section 355A."

(3)   In section 362 (powers of FCA and PRA to participate in administration proceedings)—

    (a)   in subsection (6)—

        (i)   after "arrangement" insert "in relation to which Part 26 of the Companies Act 2006 applies", and

        (ii)   for "the Companies Act 2006" substitute "that Act";

    (b)   after that subsection insert—

"(6A)   If, during the course of the administration of a company, a compromise or arrangement in relation to which Part 26A of the Companies Act 2006 applies is proposed between the company and its creditors, or any class of them, the appropriate regulator may apply to the court under section 901C or 901F of that Act."

(4)   In section 365 (powers of FCA and PRA to participate in voluntary winding up proceedings)—

    (a)   in subsection (7)—

        (i)   after "arrangement" insert "in relation to which Part 26 of the Companies Act 2006 applies", and

        (ii)   for "the Companies Act 2006" substitute "that Act";

    (b)   after that subsection insert—

"(7A)   If, during the course of the winding up of the company, a compromise or arrangement in relation to which Part 26A of the Companies Act 2006 applies is proposed between the company and its creditors, or any class of them, the appropriate regulator may apply to the court under section 901C or 901F of that Act."

(5) In section 371 (powers of FCA and PRA to participate in proceedings for winding up by court)—

    (a)    in subsection (5)—

        (i)    after "arrangement" insert "in relation to which Part 26 of the Companies Act 2006 applies", and

        (ii)    for "the Companies Act 2006" substitute "that Act";

    (b)    after that subsection insert—

"(5A)    If, during the course of the winding up of a company, a compromise or arrangement in relation to which Part 26A of the Companies Act 2006 applies is proposed between the company and its creditors, or any class of them, the appropriate regulator may apply to the court under section 901C or 901F of that Act."

### Limited Liability Partnerships Act 2000

**21**

In section 17 of the Limited Liability Partnerships Act 2000, in subsection (5)(b) (procedure for regulations applying provisions of Companies Act 2006)—

    (a)    in the entry for Part 26 of the Companies Act 2006, after "reconstructions" insert ": general";

    (b)    after that entry insert—

"Part 26A (arrangements and reconstructions: companies in financial difficulty);".

### Enterprise Act 2002

**22**

In section 255 of the Enterprise Act 2002 (application of law about company arrangement or administration to non-company), in subsection (2), omit the "and" before paragraph (c) and after that paragraph insert ", and

    (d)    Part 26A of that Act (compromise or arrangement with creditors where company in financial difficulty)."

### Income Tax (Earnings and Pensions) Act 2003

**23**

The Income Tax (Earnings and Pensions) Act 2003 is amended as follows.

**24**

(1)    Schedule 3 (SAYE option schemes) is amended as follows.

(2)    In Part 6 (requirements etc relating to share options), in paragraph 37 (exercise of options: company events)—

    (a)    in sub-paragraph (1), after "(4)" insert ", (4ZA)";

    (b)    after sub-paragraph (4) insert—

"(4ZA)    The relevant date for the purposes of this sub-paragraph is the date when the court sanctions under section 901F of the Companies Act 2006 (court sanction for compromise or arrangement) a compromise or arrangement applicable to or affecting—

    (a)    all the ordinary share capital of the company or all the shares of the same class as the shares to which the option relates, or

    (b)    all the shares, or all the shares of that same class, which are held by a class of shareholders identified otherwise than by reference to their employment or directorships or their participation in a Schedule 3 SAYE option scheme.";

    (c)    in sub-paragraph (6C)(b), after "sub-paragraph (4)" insert "or (4ZA)";

    (d)    in sub-paragraph (6E)(a), after "(4)" insert ", (4ZA)";

    (e)    in sub-paragraph (6F)(a)(i) and (b)(i), after "(4)" insert ", (4ZA)".

(3)  In Part 7 (exchange of share options), in paragraph 38 (exchange of options on company reorganisation), in sub-paragraph (2)(b), after "section 899" insert "or 901F".

**25**

(1)  Schedule 4 (CSOP schemes) is amended as follows.

(2)  In Part 5 (requirements etc relating to share options), in paragraph 25A (exercise of options: company events)—

    (a)    in sub-paragraph (1), after "(6)" insert ", (6ZA)";

    (b)    after sub-paragraph (6) insert—

"(6ZA)  The relevant date for the purposes of this sub-paragraph is the date when the court sanctions under section 901F of the Companies Act 2006 (court sanction for compromise or arrangement) a compromise or arrangement applicable to or affecting—

    (a)    all the ordinary share capital of the company or all the shares of the same class as the shares to which the option relates, or

    (b)    all the shares, or all the shares of that same class, which are held by a class of shareholders identified otherwise than by reference to their employment or directorships or their participation in a Schedule 4 CSOP scheme.";

    (c)    in sub-paragraph (7C)(b), after "sub-paragraph (6)" insert "or (6ZA)";

    (d)    in sub-paragraph (7E)(a), after "(6)" insert ", (6ZA)";

    (e)    in sub-paragraph (7F)(a)(i) and (b)(i), after "(6)" insert ", (6ZA)".

(3)  In Part 6 (exchange of share options), in paragraph 26 (exchange of options on company reorganisation), in sub-paragraph (2)(b), after "section 899" insert "or 901F".

**26**

In Schedule 5 (enterprise management incentives), in paragraph 39 (company reorganisations), in sub-paragraph (2)(b), after "section 899" insert "or 901F".

*Energy Act 2004*

**27**

In Part 2 of Schedule 20 to the Energy Act 2004 (conduct of energy administration: modifications of Schedule B1 to the Insolvency Act 1986), in paragraph 16(2), after "section 899" insert "or 901F".

*Income Tax (Trading and Other Income) Act 2005*

**28**

In Part 2 of the Income Tax (Trading and Other Income) Act 2005 (trading income), in section 259 (meaning of "statutory insolvency arrangement"), in paragraph (b), after "Part 26" insert "or 26A".

*Insolvency (Northern Ireland) Order 2005 (SI 2005/1455 (NI 10))*

**29**

In Article 10 of the Insolvency (Northern Ireland) Order 2005 (application of law about company arrangement or administration to non-company), in paragraph (3), omit the "and" before sub-paragraph (c) and after that sub-paragraph insert ", and

    (d)    Part 26A of that Act (compromise or arrangement with creditors where company in financial difficulty)."

*Companies Act 2006*

**30**

The Companies Act 2006 is amended as follows.

**31**

In section 32(1) (constitutional documents to be provided to members), after paragraph (d) insert—

"(da) a copy of any court order under section 901F (order sanctioning compromise or arrangement for company in financial difficulty) or section 901J (order facilitating reconstruction or amalgamation);".

**32**

In section 93 (recent allotment of shares for non-cash consideration), in subsection (7)(b)(i), after "Part 26" insert "or 26A".

**33**

(1)   Part 17 (a company's share capital) is amended as follows.

(2)   In section 549 (exercise by directors of powers to allot shares etc), after subsection (3) insert—

"(3A)   Subsection (1) does not apply to anything done for the purposes of a compromise or arrangement sanctioned in accordance with Part 26A (arrangements and reconstructions: companies in financial difficulty)."

(3)   In Chapter 3 (allotment of equity securities: existing shareholders' right of pre-emption)—

(a)   in section 561 (existing shareholders' right of pre-emption), in subsection (5)(a), for "566" substitute "566A";

(b)   after section 566 insert—

**"566A   Exception to pre-emption right: companies in financial difficulty**

Section 561(1) (existing shareholders' right of pre-emption) does not apply to an allotment of equity securities that is carried out as part of a compromise or arrangement sanctioned in accordance with Part 26A (arrangements and reconstructions: companies in financial difficulty)."

(4)   In section 594 (exception to valuation requirement: arrangement with another company), in subsection (6)(a)(i), after "Part 26" insert "or 26A".

(5)   In section 616(1) (interpretation of Chapter 7), in paragraph (a) of the definition of "arrangement", after "Part 26" insert "or 26A".

(6)   In section 617 (alteration of share capital of limited company), in subsection (5)(e)(i), after "Part 26" insert "or 26A".

(7)   In section 632 (variation of class rights: saving for court's powers under other provisions)—

(a)   in the entry for Part 26, after "reconstructions" insert ": general";

(b)   after that entry (but before the "or") insert—

"Part 26A (arrangements and reconstructions: companies in financial difficulty),".

(8)   In section 641 (circumstances in which a company may reduce its share capital)—

(a)   in subsection (2C), in the definition of "scheme", after "Part 26" insert "or 26A";

(b)   in subsection (7), for the words from "the phrase" to "Part 26"" substitute "the phrases "sanctioned by the court under Part 26" and "sanctioned by the court under Part 26A"".

(9)   In section 649 (registration of order and statement of capital), in subsection (3)—

(a)   in paragraph (a), after "reconstructions" insert ": general";

(b)   after that paragraph insert—

"(aa) in the case of a reduction of share capital that forms part of a compromise or arrangement sanctioned by the court under Part 26A (arrangements and reconstructions: companies in financial difficulty)—

(i)     in the case of any company other than one to which sub-paragraph (ii) applies, on delivery of the order and statement of capital to the registrar;

(ii)     in the case of an overseas company that is not required to register particulars under section 1046, on publication of the order and statement of capital in the Gazette;

(iii)     in either case, if the court so orders, on the registration of the order and statement of capital;";

(c)     in paragraph (b), for "any other case" substitute "any case not falling within paragraph (a) or (aa)".

**34**

In section 681 (unconditional exceptions to prohibition against financial assistance), in subsection (2)(e), after "Part 26" insert "or 26A".

**35**

(1)     Part 26 (arrangements and reconstructions) is amended as follows.

(2)     The heading becomes "ARRANGEMENTS AND RECONSTRUCTIONS: GENERAL".

(3)     In section 896, at the end insert—

"(4)     This section is subject to section 899A (moratorium debts, etc)."

(4)     In section 899 (court sanction for compromise or arrangement)—

(a)     after subsection (1) insert—

"(1A)     Subsection (1) is subject to section 899A (moratorium debts, etc).";

(b)     omit subsection (5).

(5)     After section 899 insert—

*"Special cases*

**899A Moratorium debts, etc**

(1)     This section applies where—

(a)     an application under section 896 in respect of a compromise or arrangement is made before the end of the period of 12 weeks beginning with the day after the end of any moratorium for the company under Part A1 of the Insolvency Act 1986 or Part 1A of the Insolvency (Northern Ireland) Order 1989 (SI 1989/2405 (NI 19)), and

(b)     the creditors with whom the compromise or arrangement is proposed include any relevant creditors (see subsection (2)).

(2)     In this section "relevant creditor" means—

(a)     a creditor in respect of a moratorium debt, or

(b)     a creditor in respect of a priority pre-moratorium debt.

(3)     The relevant creditors may not participate in the meeting summoned under section 896.

(4)     For the purposes of section 897 (statement to be circulated or made available)—

(a)     the requirement in section 897(1)(a) is to be read as including a requirement to send each relevant creditor a statement complying with section 897;

(b)     any reference to creditors entitled to attend the meeting summoned under section 896 includes a reference to relevant creditors.

(5)     The court may not sanction the compromise or arrangement under section 899 if it includes provision in respect of any relevant creditor who has not agreed to it.

(6)     In this section—

"moratorium debt"—

(a)     in the case of a moratorium under Part A1 of the Insolvency Act 1986, has the same meaning as in section 174A of that Act;

      (b)    in the case of a moratorium under Part 1A of the Insolvency (Northern Ireland) Order 1989, has the same meaning as in Article 148A of that Order;

"priority pre-moratorium debt"—

      (a)    in the case of a moratorium under Part A1 of the Insolvency Act 1986, has the same meaning as in section 174A of that Act;

      (b)    in the case of a moratorium under Part 1A of the Insolvency (Northern Ireland) Order 1989, has the same meaning as in Article 148A of that Order."

**36**

(1)    Part 27 (mergers and divisions of public companies) is amended as follows.

(2)    In section 903 (relationship of Part 27 to Part 26)—

      (a)    in the heading, for "**Part 26**" substitute "**Parts 26 and 26A**";

      (b)    in subsection (1), for "Part 26 (arrangements and reconstructions)" substitute "Part 26 (arrangements and reconstructions: general) or Part 26A (arrangements and reconstructions: companies in financial difficulty)";

      (c)    in subsections (2) and (3), for "Part 26" substitute "Parts 26 and 26A".

(3)    In section 907 (approval of members of merging companies), in subsection (2), after "917" insert ", 917A".

(4)    In section 908 (directors' explanatory report (merger))—

      (a)    in subsection (2), for paragraph (a) (but not the "and" following it) substitute—

        "(a)   the required statement explaining the effect of the compromise or arrangement,";

      (b)    after that subsection insert—

"(2A)   In subsection (2) "the required statement explaining the effect of the compromise or arrangement" means—

      (a)    in a case where a meeting is summoned under section 896 in relation to the compromise or arrangement, the statement required by section 897;

      (b)    in a case where a meeting is summoned under section 901C in relation to the compromise or arrangement, the statement required by section 901D."

(5)    In section 912 (approval of articles of new transferee company (merger))—

      (a)    the wording of the section becomes subsection (1) of that section;

      (b)    at the end of that subsection insert—

"This is subject to subsection (2).";

      (c)    after that subsection insert—

"(2)   In the case of a compromise or arrangement to be sanctioned under Part 26A, it is not necessary for the articles of the transferee company (or a draft of them) to be approved by ordinary resolution of the company in respect of which the compromise or arrangement is proposed."

(6)    In section 915 (circumstances in which certain particulars and reports not required (merger))—

      (a)    in subsection (3), for "Section 897" substitute "In a case where a meeting has been summoned under section 896 in relation to the compromise or arrangement, section 897";

      (b)    after that subsection insert—

"(3A)   In a case where a meeting has been summoned under section 901C in relation to the compromise or arrangement, section 901D (explanatory statement to be circulated or made available) does not apply."

(7)    In section 915A (other circumstances in which reports and inspection not required (merger)), in subsection (5), after "section 900(2)" insert "or, as the case may be, section 901J(2)".

*(8) Before section 918 (but after the heading "Other exceptions") insert—*

**"917A Other circumstances in which meeting of members of transferor company not required (merger)**
In the case of a compromise or arrangement to be sanctioned under Part 26A, it is not necessary for the scheme to be approved by the members of the company in respect of which the compromise or arrangement is proposed."

(9) In section 918A (agreement to dispense with reports etc (merger))—
  (a) in subsection (2), for "the application to the court under section 896" substitute "the relevant application";
  (b) after that subsection insert—
  "(3) In subsection (2) "the relevant application" means—
      (a) in the case of a compromise or arrangement to be sanctioned under Part 26, the application to the court under section 896;
      (b) in the case of a compromise or arrangement to be sanctioned under Part 26A, the application to the court under section 901C(1)."

(10) In section 922 (approval of members of companies involved in the division)—
  (a) in subsection (1), for "compromise or arrangement" substitute "scheme";
  (b) in subsection (2), after "931" insert ", 931A".

(11) In section 923 (directors' explanatory report (division))—
  (a) in subsection (2), for paragraph (a) (but not the "and" following it) substitute—
      "(a) the required statement explaining the effect of the compromise or arrangement,";
  (b) after that subsection insert—
  "(2A) In subsection (2) "the required statement explaining the effect of the compromise or arrangement" means—
      (a) in a case where a meeting is summoned under section 896 in relation to the compromise or arrangement, the statement required by section 897;
      (b) in a case where a meeting is summoned under section 901C in relation to the compromise or arrangement, the statement required by section 901D."

(12) In section 925 (supplementary accounting statement (division)), in subsection (1)(b), after "931" insert ", 931A".

(13) In section 928 (approval of articles of new transferee company (division))—
  (a) the wording of the section becomes subsection (1) of that section;
  (b) after that subsection insert—
  "(2) Subsection (1) does not apply in the case of a compromise or arrangement to be sanctioned under Part 26A."

*(14) Before section 932 (but after the heading "Other exceptions") insert—*

**"931A Other circumstances in which meeting of members of transferor company not required (division)**
In the case of a compromise or arrangement to be sanctioned under Part 26A, it is not necessary for the scheme to be approved by the members of the transferor company."

(15) In section 933 (agreement to dispense with reports etc (division))—
  (a) in subsection (3), for "the application to the court under section 896" substitute "the relevant application";
  (b) after that subsection insert—
  "(4) In subsection (3) "the relevant application" means—
      (a) in the case of a compromise or arrangement to be sanctioned under Part 26, the application to the court under section 896;

      (b)    in the case of a compromise or arrangement to be sanctioned under Part 26A, the application to the court under section 901C(1)."

(16)   In section 939 (court to fix date for transfer of undertaking etc of transferor company), in subsection (1)(b), after "section 900" insert "or, as the case may be, section 901J".

(17)   In section 940 (liability of transferee companies for each other's defaults)—

      (a)    in subsection (2), after "If" insert ", in the case of a compromise or arrangement to be sanctioned under Part 26,";

      (b)    after that subsection insert—

"(2A)   If, in the case of a compromise or arrangement to be sanctioned under Part 26A, a number representing 75% in value of the creditors or any class of creditors of the transferor company, present and voting either in person or by proxy at a meeting summoned for the purposes of agreeing to the scheme, so agree, subsection (1) does not apply in relation to the liabilities owed to the creditors or that class of creditors."

## 37

(1)   In Part 31 (dissolution and restoration to the register), Chapter 1 (striking off) is amended as follows.

(2)   In section 1005 (circumstances in which application for voluntary striking off may not be made: other proceedings not concluded), in subsection (1)(a), after "Part 26" insert "or 26A".

(3)   In section 1009 (circumstances in which application for voluntary striking off to be withdrawn), in subsection (1)(b), after "Part 26" insert "or 26A".

## 38

In section 1078 (documents subject to disclosure requirements), in subsection (3), for "section 899 or 900" substitute "section 899, 900, 901F or 901J".

## 39

(1)   Schedule 8 (index of defined expressions) is amended as follows.

(2)   In the entry for "arrangement", after the entry for Part 26 insert—

"—in Part 26A      | section 901A(4)"

(3)   In the entry for "company", after the entry for Part 26 insert—

"—in Part 26A      | section 901A(4)"

*Housing and Regeneration Act 2008*

## 40

In Part 2 of the Housing and Regeneration Act 2008 (regulation of social housing), in section 160 (company: arrangements and reconstructions), at the end insert—

"(7)   The registered provider must notify the regulator of any order under section 901F of the Companies Act 2006 (court sanction for compromise or arrangement).

(8)   An order under section 901F of the Companies Act 2006 does not take effect until the registered provider has confirmed to the registrar of companies that the regulator has been notified.

(9)   The registered provider must notify the regulator of any order under section 901J of the Companies Act 2006 (powers of court to facilitate reconstruction or amalgamation).

(10)   The requirement in section 901J(6) of the Companies Act 2006 (sending copy of order to registrar) is satisfied only if the copy is accompanied by confirmation that the regulator has been notified."

*Corporation Tax Act 2009*

**41**

In section 1319 of the Corporation Tax Act 2009 (other definitions), in paragraph (b) of the definition of "statutory insolvency arrangement", after "Part 26" insert "or 26A".

*Corporation Tax Act 2010*

**42**

The Corporation Tax Act 2010 is amended as follows.

**43**

(1)  Part 7ZA (restrictions on obtaining certain deductions) is amended as follows.

(2)  In section 269ZH (meaning of "insolvency procedures"), in subsection (5)(a), after "Part 26" insert "or 26A".

(3)  In section 269ZY (meaning of "relevant reversal credit"), in subsection (8)(b), after "Part 26" insert "or 26A".

**44**

In Part 14 (change in company ownership), in section 724A (disregard of change in parent company), in subsection (7)(a), after "Part 26" insert "or 26A".

*Third Parties (Rights against Insurers) Act 2010*

**45**

In section 6 of the Third Parties (Rights against Insurers) Act 2010 (corporate bodies etc), in subsection (1), after "section 899" insert "or 901F".

*Housing (Scotland) Act 2010 (asp 17)*

**46**

Part 8 of the Housing (Scotland) Act 2010 (registered social landlords: organisational change etc) is amended as follows.

**47**

(1)  Section 100A (restructuring by company: proposed restructuring) is amended as follows.

(2)  In subsection (1)—

    (a)  for "This section applies" substitute "Subsections (2) and (3) apply";

    (b)  omit the "and" after paragraph (b);

    (c)  for paragraph (c) substitute—

      "(c)  the restructuring will result in a tenant under a Scottish secure tenancy ceasing to be a tenant of the company in respect of which the order is made, and

      (d)  the company is not being wound up and is not in administration."

(3)  In subsection (3), for "this section" substitute "this subsection".

(4)  After subsection (3) insert—

    "(4)  Subsections (5) and (6) apply where—

      (a)  a court order is made in respect of the company under section 901C(1) of the Companies Act 2006,

      (b)  the meeting summoned by the court order is to agree a restructuring of a type mentioned in section 901J(1) of that Act,

      (c)  the restructuring will result in a tenant under a Scottish secure tenancy ceasing to be a tenant of the company in respect of which the order is made, and

      (d)  the company is not being wound up and is not in administration.

    (5)  The company must comply with sections 115 to 120 (as applied by subsection (6)) in relation to the proposed restructuring.

(6)   Sections 115 to 120 apply in relation to a proposed restructuring to which this subsection applies as they apply in relation to a proposed disposal to which section 107(4) applies, subject to the modification that section 115A(2) has effect as if, for paragraph (b), there were substituted—

> "(b)   before the meeting summoned by the court order under section 901C of the Companies Act 2006 takes place,"".

**48**

(1)   Section 101 (restructuring of company) is amended as follows.

(2)   After subsection (1) insert—

> "(1A)   This section also applies where—
>> (a)   a court order is made in respect of a company under section 901F or 901J of the Companies Act 2006, and
>> (b)   the restructuring to which the order relates is of a type mentioned in section 901J(1) of that Act."

(3)   In subsection (2)—
> (a)   after "subsection (1)" insert "or (1A)";
> (b)   in paragraph (b), after "section 900(6)" insert "or (as the case may be) section 901J(6)".

(4)   In subsection (3)(a), after "section 100A(3)" insert "or (6) (as the case may be)".

(5)   In subsection (5), after "section 900" insert "or 901J".

*Financial Services (Banking Reform) Act 2013*

**49**

(1)   Part 6 of the Financial Services (Banking Reform) Act 2013 (special administration for operators of certain infrastructure systems) is amended as follows.

(2)   In section 111 (financial market infrastructure administration)—
> (a)   omit the "and" after paragraph (a), and
> (b)   after paragraph (b) insert ", and
>> (c)   confers power on the Bank of England to participate in proceedings under Part 26A of the Companies Act 2006 (arrangements and reconstructions: companies in financial difficulty)."

(3)   After section 124 insert—

*"Powers to participate in Part 26A proceedings*

**124A  Powers of Bank to participate in Part 26A proceedings**

(1)   This section applies where Part 26A of the Companies Act 2006 ("the 2006 Act") (arrangements and reconstructions: companies in financial difficulty) applies in relation to an infrastructure company.

(2)   A relevant applicant must give notice to the Bank of England of—
> (a)   any application which the relevant applicant intends to make under section 901C(1) of the 2006 Act, and
> (b)   any application which the relevant applicant believes a creditor or member of the company has made, or intends to make, under section 901C(1) of that Act in relation to the company.

(3)   A relevant applicant may not make an application under section 901C(1) of the 2006 Act in relation to the company without the consent of the Bank of England.

(4)   In this section "relevant applicant", in relation to a company, means—
> (a)   the company;
> (b)   if the company is being wound up, the liquidator;
> (c)   if the company is in administration, the administrator.

(5)   The Bank of England is entitled to be heard at any hearing of an application made under section 901C or 901F of the 2006 Act in relation to the company.

(6) Any notice or other document required to be sent to a creditor of the company must also be sent to the Bank of England.

(7) A person appointed for the purpose by the Bank of England is entitled—

    (a) to attend any meeting of creditors of the company summoned under section 901C of the 2006 Act;

    (b) to make representations as to any matter for decision at such a meeting.

(8) Sections 197, 198 and 202A of the Banking Act 2009, and sections 201 and 202 of that Act, so far as relating to those sections, apply in relation to a failure by an infrastructure company to comply with subsection (2) or (3) above as they apply in relation to a compliance failure within the meaning of Part 5 of that Act."

*Co-operative and Community Benefit Societies Act 2014*

**50**

In section 118 of the Co-operative and Community Benefit Societies Act 2014 (power to apply provisions about company arrangements and administration in relation to registered societies), in subsection (2), after paragraph (c) insert—

    "(d) Part 26A of that Act (compromise or arrangement with creditors where company in financial difficulty)."

*Mutuals' Deferred Shares Act 2015*

**51**

In section 2 of the Mutuals' Deferred Shares Act 2015 (restriction on voting rights), in subsection (2)(b), after "section 896" insert "or 901C".

SCHEDULE 10

RESTRICTION ON WINDING-UP PETITIONS: GREAT BRITAIN

Section 10

*Restriction on winding-up petitions*

**[5.41]**

**1**

(1) During the relevant period a creditor may not present a petition for the winding up of a company under section 124 of the 1986 Act on the ground specified—

    (a) in the case of a registered company, in section 122(1)(f) of that Act, or

    (b) in the case of an unregistered company, in section 221(5)(b) of that Act,

unless conditions A to D are met (subject to sub-paragraphs (9) to (11)).

(2) Condition A is that the creditor is owed a debt by the company—

    (a) whose amount is liquidated,

    (b) which has fallen due for payment, and

    (c) which is not an excluded debt.

(3) Condition B is that the creditor has delivered written notice to the company in accordance with sub-paragraphs (4) to (6).

(4) Notice under sub-paragraph (3) must contain the following—

    (a) identification details for the company,

    (b) the name and address of the creditor,

    (c) the amount of the debt and the way in which it arises,

    (d) the date of the notice,

    (e) a statement that the creditor is seeking the company's proposals for the payment of the debt, and

    (f) a statement that if no proposal to the creditor's satisfaction is made within the period of 21 days beginning with the date on which the notice is delivered, the creditor intends to present a petition to the court for the winding-up of the company.

(5)   Notice under sub-paragraph (3) must be delivered—
  (a)   to the company's registered office, or
  (b)   in accordance with sub-paragraph (6) if—
      (i)    for any reason it is not practicable to deliver the notice to the company's registered office,
      (ii)   the company has no registered office, or
      (iii)  the company is an unregistered company.

(6)   Where this sub-paragraph applies the notice may be delivered to—
  (a)   the company's last known principal place of business, or
  (b)   the secretary, or a director, manager or (in relation to an unregistered company) principal officer of the company.

(7)   Condition C is that at end of the period of 21 days beginning with the day on which condition B was met the company has not made a proposal for the payment of the debt that is to the creditor's satisfaction.

(8)   Condition D is that—
  (a)   where the petition is presented by one creditor, the sum of the debts (or the debt, if there is only one) owed by the company to that creditor in respect of which conditions A to C are met is £10,000 or more;
  (b)   where the petition is presented by more than one creditor, the sum of the debts owed by the company to the creditors in respect of which conditions A to C are met is £10,000 or more.

(9)   A creditor may at any time apply to the court for an order that, in respect of a specified debt—
  (a)   conditions B and C shall not apply, or
  (b)   condition C shall apply as if the reference to the period of 21 days were to such shorter period as the court may direct.

(10)   Where an order is made under sub-paragraph (9)(a), the references in sub-paragraph (8) to conditions A to C are to be read as references to condition A.

(11)   If the court makes an order under sub-paragraph (9)(b) it may—
  (a)   give such directions as to delivery of the written notice referred to in condition B as it thinks fit, or
  (b)   direct that sub-paragraphs (4) to (6) shall apply in respect of the delivery of that notice subject to such modifications it thinks fit.

### Modification of Insolvency Rules and Rules of Court

**2**

(1)   This paragraph applies in relation to a petition which is presented in England and Wales by a creditor under section 124 of the 1986 Act during the relevant period.

(2)   Rule 7.5(1) of the Insolvency Rules has effect as if it also required the petition to contain a statement—
  (a)   that the requirements in paragraph 1 of this Schedule are met, and
  (b)   that no proposals for the payment of the debt have been made, or a summary of the reasons why the proposals are not to the creditor's satisfaction (as the case may be).

**3**

(1)   This paragraph applies in relation to a petition which is presented in Scotland by a creditor under section 124 of the 1986 Act during the relevant period.

(2)   Rules of Court in Scotland have effect as if they required the petition to contain an averment—
  (a)   that the requirements in paragraph 1 of this Schedule are met, and
  (b)   that no proposals for the payment of the debt have been made, or a summary of the reasons why the proposals are not to the creditor's satisfaction (as the case may be).

*Interpretation*

**4**

(1)  In this Schedule "relevant period" means the period which—
- (a)  begins with 1 October 2021, and
- (b)  ends with 31 March 2022.

(2)  For the purposes of this Schedule, references to a petition presented by a creditor—
- (a)  do not include a petition presented by one or more creditors together with one or more other persons, but
- (b)  subject to that, do include a petition presented by more than one creditor, in which case the conditions specified in paragraph 1(2) to (7) must be met in relation to each creditor presenting the petition.

(3)  For the purposes of this Schedule—

"the 1986 Act" means the Insolvency Act 1986;

"coronavirus" means severe acute respiratory syndrome coronavirus 2 (SARS-Cov-2);

"excluded debt" means a debt in respect of rent, or any sum or other payment that a tenant is liable to pay, under—
- (a)  in England and Wales, a relevant business tenancy; or
- (b)  in Scotland, a lease as defined in section 7(1) of the Law Reform (Miscellaneous Provisions) (Scotland) Act 1985,

and which is unpaid by reason of a financial effect of coronavirus;

Insolvency Rules" means the Insolvency (England and Wales) Rules 2016 (SI 2016/1024);

"registered company" means a company registered under the Companies Act 2006 in England and Wales or Scotland;

"relevant business tenancy" means—
- (a)  a tenancy to which Part 2 of the Landlord and Tenant Act 1954 applies, or
- (b)  a tenancy to which that Part of that Act would apply if any relevant occupier were the tenant;

"relevant occupier" in relation to a tenancy, means a person, other than the tenant, who lawfully occupies premises which are, or form part of, the property comprised in the tenancy; and

"unregistered company" has the meaning given in Part 5 of the 1986 Act.

*General*

**5**

(1)  The provisions of this Schedule, so far as relating to registered companies, have effect as if they were included in Part 4 of the 1986 Act.

(2)  Sub-paragraph (1) does not apply in relation to paragraphs 2 and 3 (modification of insolvency rules).

**Amendments**—Substituted by SI 2021/1091.

**General note**—Part 2 of the original form of Sch 10 of the Corporate Insolvency and Governance Act 2020 ('CIGA 2020') is headed 'Restriction on Winding-Up Petitions and Orders' and contains restrictions on such petitions and orders in defined Covid-related circumstances relating to a petition presented during the 'relevant period', as defined in para 21(1) of the same Sch 10. The relevant period started on 24 April 2020 and, as most recently amended by the Corporate Insolvency and Governance Act 2020 (Coronavirus) (Extension of the Relevant Period) (No 2) Regulations (SI 2021/718), effective from 22 June 2021, expired on 30 September 2021, although it continues to be relevant to petitions presented on or before that date. The 'relevant period', as so defined, will not be extended further. On 10 September 2021 Parliament approved new provisions which come into effect on 29 September 2021 by way of The Corporate Insolvency and Governance Act 2020 (Coronavirus) (Amendment of Schedule 10) Regulations 2021. With effect from 28 September 2021 those Regulations were replaced with the substantively identical The Corporate Insolvency and Governance Act 2020 (Coronavirus) (Amendment of Schedule 10) (No 2) Regulations 2021 (SI 2021/1091) (which serve only to correct a technical error as to the commencement date of the revoked regulations). Those new provisions ('the New Regulations') stipulate (by sub-para 4(1)) the 'relevant time' as being 1 October 2021 to 31 March 2022.

In this commentary to CIGA Sch 10, the form of Sch 10 effective in respect of petitions presented up to 30 September 2021 is termed 'the outgoing Sch 10', and the new form of Sch 10, applicable to petitions presented between 1 October 2021 and (as matters presently stand) 31 March 2022 is termed 'the New Sch 10'. Although the two forms of Sch 10 are very different, what is termed 'the coronavirus test' is common to both, and it seems very likely that the construction of that test under the outgoing Sch 10 will inform the court's approach to the test under the New Sch 10.

**Sch 10 of CIGA 2020 and the end of the CIGA IPD's application to petitions presented after 30 September 2021**—The law and procedure relevant to the outgoing Sch 10 provisions is set out in: (a) the IA 1986 and the IR 2016; (b) CIGA 2020; and (c) the Insolvency Practice Direction relating to CIGA ('CIGA IPD'), published at [2020] BPIR 1207. The CIGA IPD supplements the 2020 Act. Para 2.1 of the CIGA IPD provides that 'Paragraphs 3 to 8 of this practice direction apply to winding-up petitions presented during the relevant period'. The term 'relevant period' is also defined in para 1.1(7) by reference to para 21(1) of Sch 10 of CIGA. The relevance of the CIGA IPD to winding-up petitions falls away in respect of any winding-up petition presented after 30 September 2021.

Prior to the coronavirus pandemic, and no doubt subsequent to it at some point, in accordance with the IR 2016, a winding-up petition would be presented to the court, listed for hearing (invariably in a winding-up list) and served on the debtor company. Notwithstanding the new provisions, it remains uncontroversial that a winding-up petition should not be used as a debt collection tool, and that a petition will be dismissed (as an abuse of the court's process, usually with costs on the indemnity basis) if the petition debt is genuinely disputed on substantial grounds. It is fair to say that the outgoing Sch 10 provisions served to provide an additional basis upon which a debtor, including the unscrupulous debtor, might seek to avoid the consequences of a winding-up petition and order. The new regime presents similar footholds.

**The outgoing Sch 10 (until 30 September 2021) and the new Sch 10 (with effect from 1 October 2021)**—According to Para 7 of the Explanatory Memorandum to the New Regulations, produced by the Department for Business, Energy and Industrial Strategy, the removal of restrictions on businesses by Government justifies the current restrictions embodied in the form of the outgoing Sch 10 being replaced with what are termed 'new tapering measures' that will help business get back to normal without facing a so-called cliff edge following withdrawal of the outgoing Sch 10. The idea, the Department suggests, is to protect companies from aggressive creditor enforcement as the economy opens up, whilst allowing business to get back to a more normal way of working. According to the Department for BEIS, albeit in somewhat abstract terms at what might be considered some remove from the coal face, 'This will enable companies that are viable but cash poor due to recent trading restrictions to make use of the range of tools available to them and where appropriate to work out a rescue, and non-viable companies that cannot be saved to exit the marketplace with their productive assets recycled to the economy'.

Para 2 of the New Regulations amends the outgoing Sch 10 by substituting an entirely new version of it. The New Sch 10 provides a reduced level of protection by way of new targeted temporary measures available to corporate debtors as the economy emerges from the effects of the pandemic. The Department for BEIS recognises that these reduced measures remain a significant intervention into the normal workings of insolvency law, in particular creditor rights, and will therefore keep the temporary measures under constant review. Nevertheless, it seems very unlikely that new regime will be withdrawn or watered down further prior to 31 March 2022.

**The relevant provisions in the outgoing Sch 10 of CIGA 2020 and the CIGA IPD**—The key provisions of the outgoing Sch 10 lie in sub-paras 2(3), 2(4), 5(3) and 21(3) (which defines terms including 'coronavirus'). The court's approach to the coronavirus test is likely to be relevant to the same test under the New Sch 10.

The condition in para 5(3) of Sch 10 embodies the coronavirus test and provides that the court may only wind up the company, 'if the court is satisfied that the ground would apply even if coronavirus had not had a financial effect on the company'. The key provisions in the CIGA IPD lie in paras 3, 4, 6, 7 and 8.

The term 'the coronavirus test', as appears in both sub-paras 8.1(a) and (b) of the CIGA IPD, is relevant for the purposes of a petition based on the alternative inability to pay grounds in s 123(1)(e) or (2) of the IA 1986 in requiring that the condition in para 5(3) of the outgoing Sch 10 (above) is met.

**The three-stage process envisaged by the combined provisions of the outgoing Sch 10 and the CIGA IPD**—The procedural position is best understood as follows, including reference to the first instance judgments of Her Honour Judge Kelly, sitting as a High Court judge, in *A v B* [2021] EWHC 2289 (Ch) (11 August 2021) ('*A v B*') and, consistent with it, the decision of Insolvency and Companies Court Judge Mullen in *Re Investin Quay House Ltd* [2021] EWHC 2371 (Ch) (20 August 2021) ('*Investin*').

Initially, the burden rests on a petitioner to meet the requirement of the pre-condition in sub-para 2(4) of the outgoing Sch 10. Rule 7.5(1) of the IR 2016 (contents of petition) is amended by sub-para 19(3) of the outgoing Sch 10 to require the statement as to the petitioner's belief of those relevant matters identified in para 2 of the outgoing Sch 10. Sub-para 3.1 of the CIGA IPD provides that the court will not accept a petition for filing unless such a statement is included in the petition. Checking for the statement is an administrative step by the court, usually undertaken without further inquiry if the requirement for the statement is found to be met.

Sub-para 4.1 of the CIGA IPD then provides that, if the petition is not rejected for filing pursuant to para 3 of the CIGA IPD, 'the petition shall be listed for a non-attendance pre-trial review with a time estimate of 15 minutes'. Sub-para 4.2 of the CIGA IPD provides the purpose of the non-attendance pre-trial review is specifically the fixing of a preliminary hearing 'in order for the court to determine whether it is likely that it will be able to make an order under section 122(1)(f) or 221(5)(b) of the . . . 1986 Act having regard to the coronavirus test' (underlined emphasis).

The third stage of the winding-up process is the hearing of the petition (usually in a winding-up list), but only if the petition survives stages one and two above. It is perfectly possible that, if disputed, the petition will go off at this third stage hearing subject to directions for evidence and listing. What might be termed non-coronavirus matters giving rise to such a procedural outcome, however, are not appropriate to being dealt with at this preliminary hearing stage which is concerned only with the coronavirus test.

**The nature of the preliminary hearing under the outgoing Sch 10**—The preliminary hearing amounts to no more than a procedural filter designed to ensure that, having regard to the coronavirus test, there is a likelihood that the court will be able to make a winding-up order. It is no coincidence that the preliminary hearing concept was introduced by the pandemic-driven CIGA 2020 and the CIGA IPD. Accordingly, at the preliminary hearing the court is not concerned with any issue other than the coronavirus test. It follows that there are only two possible outcomes at the preliminary hearing, as envisaged by the sub-paras 8.1(1) and 8.1(2) of the CIGA IPD, being dismissal at that stage or listing in the winding-up list. Apparently, there is no third way: see the ICC judge's observation to this effect in *Investin* at [18]. Stepping back, there are at least four reasons for the scope of the preliminary hearing being so restricted.

First, if the court was intended to be concerned with anything other than the coronavirus test at the preliminary hearing, then the words 'having regard to the coronavirus test' in sub-paras 8.1(1) and (2) of the CIGA IPD would be otiose and meaningless. That is an inherently implausible position. Further, the language used does not suggest consideration of any other matter. It mentions only the coronavirus test. So, nothing else is relevant, including the issue of insolvency because, if the petition is listed in the winding-up list and is found not to be the subject of a genuine dispute on substantial grounds then, at least in a non-payment of a due debt case, the non-payment of the petition debt is itself evidence of insolvency (a proposition for which *Cornhill Insurance plc v Improvement Services Ltd* [1986] 1 WLR 114 is authority). Insolvency, however, is not a matter for the preliminary hearing, although the court may well have it in mind.

Secondly, if sub-para 8.1 of the CIGA IPD went further than consideration of the coronavirus test then, in effect, the door would be open to a debtor company to dispute a petition at that stage on any grounds, coronavirus-related or not. That, it is submitted, cannot have been the intention of Parliament when it enacted the legislation or those responsible for the CIGA IPD supplementing it. Such an outcome would produce the result that solvent companies and companies wholly unaffected by the pandemic could seek the protection of the new and temporary legislation. Self-evidently, and as its long heading spells out – 'An Act to make provision about companies and other entities in financial difficulty' – the legislation was enacted to address the economic difficulties experienced by companies as a consequence of the pandemic.

Thirdly, the procedure under para 6 of the CIGA IPD does not give a petitioning creditor a right of reply to the respondent company's evidence. That is consistent with the respondent company only responding to the petitioning creditor's preceding evidence on the coronavirus test issue. It would be very odd if the petitioner had no right of response if the respondent company was free to address an unlimited range of matters in opposition to the petition which extended beyond the issue of the coronavirus test.

Fourthly, a respondent company remains at liberty to seek to apply to restrain presentation or advertisement or to dispute the petition in the winding-up list. The preliminary hearing cannot have been intended to provide another forum for non-coronavirus related disputes to be raised. A respondent company requires no such further opportunity. The idea of the preliminary hearing and a hearing in the winding-up list having the same purpose is the antithesis of the overriding objective.

**What is the question before the court at the preliminary hearing under the outgoing Sch 10?**—It follows that the question before the court at the preliminary hearing is whether or not the court is satisfied that it is likely that it will be able to make an order under s 122(1)(f) of the IA 1986 on the ground specified in s 123(1)(e) or (2) (that is, make such an order at a substantive hearing of the petition in the winding-up list) having regard to the coronavirus test. That test requires the court to be satisfied that the condition in sub-para 5(3) of the outgoing Sch 10 is met. That provision provides that the court may only wind up the company 'if the court is satisfied that the ground [ie s 123(1)(e) or (2)] would apply even if coronavirus had not had a financial effect on the company'. The constituent parts of the above test raise a number of issues.

First, the question of whether it is 'likely' that the court 'will be able to make an order' winding-up the company at the substantive hearing should be read as asking whether the court 'may well' be able to make such an order. The term 'may well' applies a threshold test that is more than fanciful but without meaning more likely than not. That was the meaning attributed to the term by Deputy ICC Judge Passfield in *In the matter of PGH Investments Limited* [2021] EWHC 533 (Ch) at [33] – correctly, it is submitted – by reference to the interpretation of the same term by Chadwick LJ in *Three Rivers DC v Bank of England (No 4)* [2002] EWCA Civ 1182, [2003] 1 WLR 210. (A decision of an ICC or deputy ICC judge is not binding on a High Court judge or a s 9 judge sitting as a High Court judge but will be of persuasive effect). So interpreted, the test is relatively modest, in terms of the likelihood of the court making an order, and, without getting into a sterile argument as to what might be the marginal differences in likelihood involve, it is submitted, amounts to something equivalent, or very close to, the threshold test on the setting aside of a statutory demand or the granting of summary judgment, if that. That is a test with which the courts are well acquainted in weeding out shadowy, implausible, unsubstantiated or imprecise arguments.

Secondly, in considering such likelihood, the court has regard to the coronavirus test, and nothing else raised by either party.

Thirdly, the burden of proving the condition in sub-para 5(3) of the outgoing Sch 10 has been held in the context of a substantive hearing to restrain advertisement of a winding-up petition to rest with the petitioner, assuming the respondent company can make out a prima facie case as regards the requirement in sub-para 5(1)(c) of the Outgoing Sch 10 that coronavirus had a financial effect on the company before presentation of the petition so as to shift the burden onto the petitioner: *Re A Company (Application to Restrain Advertisement of a Winding-Up Petition)* [2020] EWHC 1551 (Ch), [2020] 2 BCLC 307, [2020] BPIR 1100 at [46] (ICC Judge Barber). The definition of the coronavirus test in para 1 of the CIGA IPD refers to para 5(3) of the outgoing Sch 10, but the provision makes no reference to sub-para 5(1)(c). That approach was followed (with the agreement of petitioner and debtor) by HHJ Kelly in *A v B* at [24]. In *Investin* at [16], ICC Judge Mullen drew attention to the fact that the burden rested on the debtor for the first part of the test, but, if discharged, shifted onto the petitioner for the second part. In so shifting the burden, ICC Judge Barber identified in *Re A Company* at [16] that the debtor need show no more than a prima facie case (although, on the facts of *Investin*, even that prima facie test was not met by the debtor: see [23]). ICC Judge Mullen in *Investin* at [17] also drew attention to the fact that the requirement in sub-para 21(3) of the outgoing Sch 10 (the judgment erroneously refers to CIGA 2020) for establishing 'financial effect' upon the debtor is wide enough to extend to an indirect effect. The scope and limits of such indirect financial effect may need working out further under the New Sch 10.

Fourthly, as regards the burden of proof on the petitioner, and as identified above, at the preliminary hearing stage, the court is not reaching a definitive finding; it is considering only whether it is likely that the court will – 'may well' – be able to make a winding-up order having regard to the coronavirus test alone. Any conclusion reached by the court as to the meeting of the coronavirus test at the preliminary hearing need not bind the court at the substantive hearing, although it is likely to be persuasive, at least as a starting point, and subject to further evidence, for the purpose of sub-para 5(3) of the outgoing Sch 10. If the intention was that the finding at the preliminary hearing stage as to the meeting of the coronavirus test was final and definitive in the event of the petition being listed in the winding-up list, then sub-para 5(3) of the outgoing Sch 10 (which would apply at that stage) would be meaningless. Rather, in applying a relatively summary filter, the court is being asked to form a preliminary view as regards the meeting of the coronavirus test, but without that view necessarily being definitive.

**The substance of the New Sch 10 as regards presentation of a winding-up petition**—Neither the New Regulations nor the New Sch 10 impose any restriction on the service of statutory demands, although this would not prevent service of a statutory demand prompting an application to restrain presentation of a petition.

Para 1 of the New Regulations provides that a winding-up petition may not be presented by a creditor on the grounds that an registered or unregistered company (as defined in Para 4) is unable to pay its debts unless certain conditions ('conditions A to D'). Those four conditions appear in sub-paras 1(2), (3), (7) and (8) and are:

(a) The first condition is that the petition debt must be liquidated, have fallen due for payment and not be an 'excluded debt', as defined in sub-para 4(3) as 'a debt in respect of rent, or any sum or other payment that a tenant is liable to pay' under (in England) a relevant business tenancy (as defined) 'and which is unpaid by reason of a financial effect of coronavirus' (relevant given the extension of the moratorium against the forfeiture of business tenancies until 31 March 2022). Thus, a commercial landlord cannot present a petition against a tenant for outstanding rent or other sum for which the tenant is liable unless the petitioning landlord can demonstrate that the non-payment is not by reason of the effect of Covid-19, subject to the petition debt being at least £10,000 (see condition D below). There are obvious good grounds for the 'financial effect of coronavirus' test for these purposes being developed consistent with the development of the coronavirus test under the outgoing Sch 10. However approached, the evidential bar confronting a landlord in proving the negative required by the test will be a difficult one to surmount in most cases by reason of the debtor tenant being best placed in terms of first-hand information for the purpose of evidencing what financial effect coronavirus has had on it.

(b)    The second condition requires that the creditor has made a formal request to the debtor company seeking proposals for the repayment of the debt. There are prescribed contents for the request, including notice of intention to present a petition in the absence of any proposal within 21-days of delivery. This new requirement for a request for proposals amounts to a mandatory requirement on the creditor for the opening of negotiations for repayment. The creditor might actually have no interest in such a request, but the requirement is mandatory, subject to the court ordering otherwise. It seems unavoidable that any reasonable response from the debtor, taken against the particular facts of the case, will inform the court's exercise of discretion on the petition coming before it for substantive hearing. This condition, like condition C, may be varied by the court on the application of a creditor, either by the complete removal of the condition or the shortening of the 21-day period in condition C. The court will not remove or vary conditions B and/or C as a matter of course; some compelling factor or cause justifying variance with the default position will almost certainly be required, such as, for example, in the case of condition B, irrefutable evidence that the debtor has ceased operations, has no assets and/or is in no position to make any remotely reasonable proposal.

(c)    The third condition requires that 'at the end of the 21 days beginning with the day on which condition B was met the company has not made a proposal for the payment of the debt that is to the creditor's satisfaction'. One obvious question that might arise here is by what standard 'the creditor's satisfaction' is judged. An entirely subjective approach, viewed from the creditor's position alone, is implausible because it would allow any debtor's own view, however objectively unreasonable, to dictate whether or not the condition had been met. Far more likely is the fact-specific approach taken to unreasonable offers to secure or compound a bankruptcy debt for the purposes of s 271(3) of the Insolvency Act 1986. The most comprehensive analysis of that approach appears in the judgment of Chief Registrar Baister in *HMRC v Garwood* [2012] BPIR 575.

(d)    The fourth condition is that the petition debt, or sum of debts where the petition is to be presented by more than one creditor and conditions A to C are met in respect of each, is £10,000 or more.

These New Regulations provide a great deal of scope for litigation as the strictures imposed by the pandemic reduce (as presently appears to be the position). It will be interesting to see how the mandatory opening of negotiations by the creditor pursuant to Condition B works on the ground given the apathy of many creditors at the petition stage. Further, if the coronavirus test continues to be construed as extending to indirect financial effect (see *Investin* at [17]), as the wording of the provision so construed appears broad enough to admit, the knock-on financial effects of coronavirus consequences first experienced by a debtor in previous financial periods are capable, prima face, of meeting the test, subject to substantiation in evidence such that the court can be satisfied as to the domino effect of those earlier consequences. *A v B* and *Investin* each demonstrates the importance of evidence supporting and corroborating the debtor's position and the potentially terminal consequences of failing to do so.

SCHEDULE 11

*(Schedule 11 solely affects Northern Ireland and is not reproduced.)*

SCHEDULE 12
PROTECTION OF SUPPLIES OF GOODS AND SERVICES: GREAT BRITAIN
Section 14

PART 1    EXCLUSIONS

**[5.42]**

**1**

In the Insolvency Act 1986, after Schedule 4 insert—
*(The text to Schedule 4ZZA is not reproduced here. See the introductory note to CIGA 2020 above under the heading 'Omissions and inclusions'.)*

PART 2    CONSEQUENTIAL AMENDMENTS

*Amendments to Acts*

**[5.43]**

**2**

In Schedule 15 to the Building Societies Act 1986 (application of companies winding up legislation to building societies), after paragraph 32 insert—

*"Protection of supplies*

**32A**

Section 233B of the Act (protection of supplies of goods and services) does not apply."

**3**

In Schedule 15A to the Building Societies Act 1986 (application of other companies insolvency legislation to building societies), after paragraph 27F insert—

*"Protection of supplies*

**27FA**

Section 233B of the Act (protection of supplies of goods and services) is omitted."

**4**

In Schedule 10 to the Friendly Societies Act 1992 (application of companies winding up legislation to friendly societies), after paragraph 35 insert—

*"Protection of supplies*

**35A**

Section 233B of the Act (protection of supplies of goods and services) does not apply."

*Amendments to subordinate legislation*

**5**

In the Insolvent Partnerships Order 1994 (SI 1994/2421), in article 4(3)(a), for "section 233 and section 233A" substitute "sections 233, 233A and 233B and Schedule 4ZZA".

**6**

In Schedule 4 to the Limited Liability Partnerships Regulations 2001 (SI 2001/1090) (disapplications for Scotland), after the entry relating to section 233A insert—

"Section 233B to the extent that that section applies in the case of the appointment of an administrative receiver."

**7**

In Schedule 2 to the Limited Liability Partnerships (Scotland) Regulations 2001 (SSI 2001/128), after the entry relating to section 233A insert—

"Section 233B to the extent that that section applies in the case of the appointment of an administrative receiver."

**8**

In Schedule 3 to the Co-operative and Community Benefit Societies and Credit Unions (Arrangements, Reconstructions and Administration) Order 2014 (SI 2014/229), after paragraph 3 insert—

> **"3A**
>
> Section 233B (protection of supplies of goods and services) does not apply in relation to a registered society that is registered as a credit union."

SCHEDULE 13

*(Schedule 13 solely affects Northern Ireland and is not reproduced.)*

SCHEDULE 14

MEETINGS OF COMPANIES AND OTHER BODIES

Section 37

*Meaning of "qualifying body"*

**[5.44]**

**1**

In this Schedule "qualifying body" means—

(a) a registered society within the meaning of the Co-operative and Community Benefit Societies Act (Northern Ireland) 1969 (c 24 (NI)),

(b) a credit union within the meaning of the Credit Unions (Northern Ireland) Order 1985 (SI 1985/1205 (NI 12)),

(c) a building society within the meaning of the Building Societies Act 1986,

(d) a society that is registered within the meaning of the Friendly Societies Act 1974 or incorporated under the Friendly Societies Act 1992,

(e) a registered branch within the meaning of the Friendly Societies Act 1992,

(f) a Scottish charitable incorporated organisation within the meaning of Chapter 7 of Part 1 of the Charities and Trustee Investment (Scotland) Act 2005 (asp 10),

(g) a company within the meaning of section 1(1) of the Companies Act 2006,

(h) a charitable incorporated organisation within the meaning of Part 11 of the Charities Act 2011, and

(i) a registered society within the meaning of the Co-operative and Community Benefit Societies Act 2014.

*Meaning of "relevant period"*

**2**

(1)   In this Schedule the "relevant period" means the period which—

    (a)    begins with 26 March 2020, and

    (b)    ends with 30 March 2021.

(2)   The appropriate national authority may by regulations substitute for the date for the time being specified in sub-paragraph (1)(b)—

    (a)    an earlier date, or

    (b)    a later date that is not more than three months after the date for the time being so specified and is not later than 5 April 2021.

(3)   Regulations under sub-paragraph (2) may make consequential or transitional provision or savings.

(4)   In sub-paragraph (2) "the appropriate national authority" means—

    (a)    in relation to a qualifying body within paragraph 1(c), (d), (e), (g), (h), or (i), the Secretary of State,

    (b)    in relation to a qualifying body within paragraph 1(f), the Scottish Ministers, and

    (c)    in relation to a qualifying body within paragraph 1(a) or (b), the Department for the Economy in Northern Ireland.

*Meetings of qualifying bodies held during the relevant period*

**3**

(1)   This paragraph applies to a meeting within sub-paragraph (2) that is held during the relevant period.

(2)   A meeting is within this sub-paragraph if it is—

    (a)    a general meeting of a qualifying body,

    (b)    a meeting of any class of members of a qualifying body, or

    (c)    a meeting of delegates appointed by members of a qualifying body.

(3)   The meeting need not be held at any particular place.

(4)   The meeting may be held, and any votes may be permitted to be cast, by electronic means or any other means.

(5)   The meeting may be held without any number of those participating in the meeting being together at the same place.

(6)   A member of the qualifying body does not have a right—

    (a)    to attend the meeting in person,

    (b)    to participate in the meeting other than by voting, or

    (c)    to vote by particular means.

(7)   The provisions of any enactment relating to meetings within sub-paragraph (2) have effect subject to this paragraph.

(8)   The provisions of the constitution or rules of the qualifying body have effect subject to this paragraph.

*Meetings of qualifying bodies held during the relevant period: power to make further provision*

**4**

(1)   The appropriate national authority may by regulations make provision for the purposes of, or in connection with, paragraph 3.

(2)   The appropriate national authority may by regulations make provision about the means by which, the form in which, and the period within which, any notice or other document relating to a meeting to which paragraph 3 applies or is expected to apply may be given or made available.

(3)   Regulations under this paragraph may—

      (a)    disapply or modify provisions of an enactment relating to meetings within paragraph 3(2);

      (b)    disapply or modify provisions of the constitution or rules of a qualifying body;

      (c)    make different provision for different purposes;

      (d)    make consequential, incidental or supplementary provision (including provision disapplying or modifying a provision of an enactment);

      (e)    make transitional provision or savings.

(4)   In this paragraph "the appropriate national authority" means—

      (a)    in relation to qualifying bodies within paragraph 1(g) or (h), the Secretary of State,

      (b)    in relation to qualifying bodies within paragraph 1(c), (d), (e) or (i), the Treasury,

      (c)    in relation to qualifying bodies within paragraph 1(f), the Scottish Ministers, and

      (d)    in relation to qualifying bodies within paragraph 1(a) or (b), the Department for the Economy in Northern Ireland.

*Extension of period for qualifying body to hold annual general meeting*

**5**

(1)   This paragraph applies where by reason of any provision a qualifying body is or was under a duty to hold a general meeting as its annual general meeting during a period ("the due period") that ends during the relevant period.

(2)   The provision is to be read as if it imposes (and had always imposed) a duty on the qualifying body to hold a general meeting as its annual general meeting during the period that begins with the due period and ends with the relevant period (but this is subject to regulations under paragraph 6).

(3)   If by reason of regulations made under paragraph 2 the relevant period is a period that ends after 30 September 2020 this paragraph has effect as if the relevant period were a period that ends with 30 September 2020.

(4)   In this paragraph a reference to "any provision" is a reference to any provision of an enactment or of the constitution or rules of the qualifying body.

(5)   In the application of this paragraph in relation to a public company, the references to a duty to hold a general meeting as its annual general meeting are to be read as including a reference to a duty to hold an accounts meeting.

*Power to extend period for qualifying body to hold annual general meeting*

**6**

(1)   The appropriate national authority may by regulations provide for any provision that would (but for the regulations) have the effect mentioned in sub-paragraph (2) to be read as if instead it had (and always had had) the effect mentioned in sub-paragraph (3).

(2)   The effect is that of imposing on a qualifying body a duty to hold a general meeting as its annual general meeting during a period ("the overlapping period") that overlaps to any extent with the relevant period.

(3)   The effect is that of imposing on the qualifying body a duty to hold a general meeting as its annual general meeting during a period that—

      (a)    begins with the overlapping period, and

      (b)    ends with such period immediately following the end of the overlapping period as is specified in the regulations.

(4)   A period specified in regulations for the purposes of sub-paragraph (3)(b) must not exceed 8 months.

(5)   Regulations under this paragraph may—

      (a)    make different provision for different purposes;

    (b)    make consequential, incidental or supplementary provision (including provision disapplying or modifying a provision of an enactment);

    (c)    make transitional provision or savings.

(6)   In sub-paragraph (1) the reference to "any provision" is a reference to any provision of an enactment or of the constitution or rules of a qualifying body.

(7)   In this paragraph "the appropriate national authority" has the same meaning as in paragraph 4.

(8)   In the application of this paragraph in relation to a public company, the references to a duty to hold a general meeting as its annual general meeting are to be read as including a reference to a duty to hold an accounts meeting.

*Regulations made by the Secretary of State or the Treasury*

**7**

(1)   Regulations made by the Secretary of State or the Treasury under this Schedule are to be made by statutory instrument.

(2)   A statutory instrument containing regulations made by the Secretary of State under paragraph 2(2)(a) of this Schedule is subject to annulment in pursuance of a resolution of either House of Parliament.

(3)   A statutory instrument containing regulations made by the Secretary of State under paragraph 2(2)(b) of this Schedule or containing regulations made by the Secretary of State or the Treasury under paragraph 4 or 6 of this Schedule must be laid before Parliament as soon as reasonably practicable after being made.

(4)   Sub-paragraph (3) does not apply if a draft of the statutory instrument has been laid before and approved by a resolution of each House of Parliament.

(5)   Regulations contained in a statutory instrument laid before Parliament by virtue of sub-paragraph (3) cease to have effect at the end of the period of 40 days beginning with the day on which the instrument is made, unless during that period the instrument is approved by a resolution of each House of Parliament.

(6)   In calculating the period of 40 days, no account is to be taken of any time during which—

    (a)    Parliament is dissolved or prorogued, or

    (b)    both Houses of Parliament are adjourned for more than 4 days.

(7)   Where regulations cease to have effect as a result of sub-paragraph (5) that does not—

    (a)    affect anything previously done under or by virtue of the regulations, or

    (b)    prevent the making of new regulations.

*Regulations made by the Scottish Ministers*

**8**

(1)   Regulations made by the Scottish Ministers under paragraph 2(2)(a) of this Schedule are subject to the negative procedure (see section 28 of the Interpretation and Legislative Reform (Scotland) Act 2010 (asp 10)).

(2)   Regulations made by the Scottish Ministers under paragraph 2(2)(b), 4 or 6 of this Schedule must be laid before the Scottish Parliament as soon as reasonably practicable after being made.

(3)   Sub-paragraph (2) does not apply if the regulations have been subject to the affirmative procedure (see section 29 of the Interpretation and Legislative Reform (Scotland) Act 2010).

(4)   Regulations laid before the Scottish Parliament by virtue of sub-paragraph (2) cease to have effect at the end of the period of 40 days beginning with the day on which they are made, unless during that period the regulations are approved by a resolution of the Scottish Parliament.

(5)   In calculating the period of 40 days, no account is to be taken of any time during which the Scottish Parliament is—

    (a)    dissolved, or

(b)    in recess for more than 4 days.

(6)   Where regulations cease to have effect as a result of sub-paragraph (4) that does not—

    (a)    affect anything previously done under or by virtue of the regulations, or

    (b)    prevent the making of new regulations.

(7)   Section 30 of the Interpretation and Legislative Reform (Scotland) Act 2010 does not apply in relation to regulations to which sub-paragraph (2) applies.

*Regulations made by the Department for the Economy in Northern Ireland*

**9**

(1)   Regulations made by the Department for the Economy in Northern Ireland under paragraph 2(2)(a) of this Schedule are subject to negative resolution within the meaning of section 41(6) of the Interpretation Act (Northern Ireland) 1954 (c 33 (NI)).

(2)   Regulations made by the Department for the Economy in Northern Ireland under paragraph 2(2)(b), 4 or 6 of this Schedule must be laid before the Assembly as soon as reasonably practicable after being made.

(3)   Sub-paragraph (2) does not apply if a draft of the regulations has been laid before, and approved by a resolution of, the Assembly.

(4)   Section 41(3) of the Interpretation Act (Northern Ireland) 1954 applies for the purposes of sub-paragraph (3) in relation to the laying of a draft as it applies in relation to the laying of a statutory document under an enactment.

(5)   Regulations laid before the Assembly by virtue of sub-paragraph (2) cease to have effect at the end of the period of 40 days beginning with the day on which the regulations are made, unless during that period the regulations are approved by a resolution of the Assembly.

(6)   In calculating the period of 40 days, no account is to be taken of any time during which the Assembly is—

    (a)    dissolved,

    (b)    in recess for more than 4 days, or

    (c)    adjourned for more than 6 days.

(7)   Where regulations cease to have effect as a result of sub-paragraph (5) that does not—

    (a)    affect anything previously done under or by virtue of the regulations, or

    (b)    prevent the making of new regulations.

(8)   A power of the Department for the Economy in Northern Ireland to make regulations under this Schedule is exercisable by statutory rule for the purposes of the Statutory Rules (Northern Ireland) Order 1979 (SI 1979/1573 (NI 12)).

(9)   In this paragraph "the Assembly" means the Northern Ireland Assembly.

*Other interpretation*

**10**

In this Schedule—

    "accounts meeting" means a general meeting of a public company at which the company's annual accounts and reports (within the meaning given by section 471 of the Companies Act 2006) are laid;

    "constitution", in relation to a company, is to be construed in accordance with section 17 of the Companies Act 2006;

    "enactment" includes an Act of the Scottish Parliament and an instrument made under such an Act;

    "public company" has the meaning given by section 4(2) of the Companies Act 2006.

**Amendments**—SI 2020/1349, SSI 2020/421.

# REGULATION (EU) 2015/848 ON INSOLVENCY PROCEEDINGS

## INTRODUCTION

[6.1]

In the early 1990s the idea of a European Community Bankruptcy Convention was discussed among the EC Member States and eventually signed by all the states in 1996 with the exception of the UK. The UK withheld its signature as retaliation for the treatment suffered during the 'beef war' when the importation of British beef was banned by certain Member States, although it also appears that there were concerns about the special position of Gibraltar in the context of the Convention. The absence of a UK signature caused the Convention to lapse but the concept of cross-border cooperation among EU Member States was later revived. It was decided to proceed by way of a Regulation on insolvency proceedings. Proceeding by way a Regulation has the advantage that the Regulation applies automatically in all the EU Member States without the need for implementing legislation. This is with the exception of Denmark which exercised an 'opt-out'.

The original Regulation was binding and directly applicable from 31 May 2002. A recast Insolvency Regulation – Regulation (EU) 2015/848 – came into force on 26 June 2017. The changes to the original Insolvency Regulation – Regulation 1346/2000 – are largely modest and procedural.

The recast regulation has the same general philosophy and structure as the original. It is essentially a private international law measure rather than a measure of substantive harmonisation. The Regulation allocates jurisdiction to open insolvency proceedings and determines the applicable law in respect of such proceedings. It also establishes however, basic minimum European standards in respect of the treatment of foreign creditors and notification of proceedings and also, to a certain extent, on the powers and duties of insolvency practitioners – Arts 48 and 49. Art 49 is the same as Art 35 in the original whereas Art 48 is a new provision.

The preamble to the Regulation locates it in the context of creating a European area of freedom, security and justice – Recitals 2–5. It refers to the cross-border activities of business entities as European markets become more integrated and also to the need to prevent asset transfers or forum manipulation to the detriment of the general body of creditors. Jurisdiction to open main insolvency proceedings is given to the state where a debtor has its centre of main interests (COMI), with jurisdiction to open secondary proceedings given to the state where the debtor has an 'establishment'.

The Regulation reflects a philosophy of Euro universalism – Recital 23 of the preamble and *Schmid v Hertel* Case C-328/12 [2014] 1 WLR 633. Main insolvency proceedings are stated to have universal scope and aim at encompassing all the debtor's assets. The idea is that insolvency proceedings with pan-European effects are more likely to produce better returns for creditors etc than a collection of separate national proceedings. So, for example, if main insolvency proceedings are opened in Ireland in respect of a company which has assets in both Ireland and Poland, the proceedings apply not only to the assets in Ireland but also to those in Poland. There is the possibility of opening secondary insolvency proceedings in Poland but these proceedings are territorial and will apply only to the assets in Poland – Art 3(2).

The rhetoric of universalism does not quite match the reality however. Not only is there the possibility of opening secondary insolvency proceedings but the effect of Arts 8–18 is that other laws may apply to certain assets and transactions rather than the law of the main proceedings. These provisions mirror, while not exactly duplicating, Arts 5–15 of the original Regulation.

The possibility of opening secondary proceedings with territorial effects represents another significant inroad on the principle of universalism. The motivation behind such proceedings is likely in many cases to be the protection of 'local' preferential creditors. It is worth pointing out that all creditors, and not just local preferential creditors, are entitled to claim in the secondary proceedings but there may be little, if anything, left in the pot after the claims of preferential creditors have been satisfied. Recital 22 of the preamble acknowledges that the preferential rights enjoyed by creditors are in some cases completely different. It also makes the aspirational point that, at the next review of the Regulation, it will be necessary to identify further measures to improve the preferential rights of employees at European level. It is difficult to know what to make of this assertion. Preferential rights of employees are a controversial topic. In some countries preferential claims may trump security rights but in many, if not most, countries they only outrank the general body of creditors. In any event, the satisfaction of employee claims through preferential status is very uneven. It depends on there being sufficient assets within the debtor's coffers to meet the claims. Protecting employee claims through a social insurance fund offers more uniform and potentially complete protection. Establishing such a fund however, requires a substantial bureaucratic commitment and there are also 'moral hazard' and financing issues, ie whether the fund should be financed through ex ante or ex post contributions from employers.

What is noteworthy about the recast Regulation is the emphasis placed on rescue and sustaining business activity. The preamble in Recital 10 talks about promoting the rescue of economically viable but distressed businesses and giving entrepreneurs a second chance.

This focus on restructuring, however, needs to be understood in its proper context. In the original Regulation the focus was almost exclusively on liquidation. This was considered to be the typical insolvency procedure. For instance, secondary proceedings commenced after main insolvency proceedings had been opened, could only be liquidation proceedings and secondary proceedings initiated before main insolvency proceedings had been opened had to be converted into liquidation proceedings at the request of the liquidator in the main proceedings. Moreover, the person who took control of a debtor's affairs after main insolvency proceedings had been opened, was referred to throughout the Regulation as a liquidator even though that person might be charged with the task of preparing a restructuring plan. The recast Regulation opts for more neutral terminology and uses the expression insolvency practitioner (IP) throughout rather than liquidator – Art 2(5). There is also no requirement that secondary proceedings should be liquidation proceedings.

The similarities between the original and 'recast' versions of the Insolvency Regulation should ensure however that the Virgos-Schmit Report, which was written when the original Regulation was in its earlier incarnation of a Convention, remains helpful as an aid to interpretation. There are a few small changes between the Convention and the Regulation, but not sufficient to render the Report useless though it should be remembered that the Report is merely an aid to interpretation and the views expressed therein are not conclusive. The report can be found at http://aei.pitt.edu/952/.

Extensive use was made of the report in *Syska v Vivendi Universal SA* [2008] 2 Lloyd's Rep 636 (HC); [2009] EWCA Civ 677, [2010] 1 BCLC 467 where it was prayed in aid of the conclusion that the expression 'lawsuits pending' in Art 4(2)(f) Regulation 1346/2000 included references to arbitration (an interpretation confirmed by Art 18 of the recast Regulation). The court also made use of a textbook partly written by one of the co-authors of the Virgos-Schmit Report, Miguel Virgos – see M Virgos and F Garcimartín, *The European Insolvency Regulation: Law and Practice* (Kluwer, 2004).

Moreover, in *Re Olympic Airlines Ltd* [2015] UKSC 27 at paras 9, 10 the report was given almost canonical force by the Supreme Court with Lord Sumption saying that the report provides 'much the most useful source of guidance'. The Supreme Court confirmed the Court of Appeal where the decision of the lower court was overturned on the basis that it failed to pay regard to para 71 of the report on the definition of an 'establishment' and the need for external, market-facing activities.

On the other hand, in *Re BRAC Rent-a-Car International Inc* [2003] 1 WLR 1421, Lloyd J failed to glean from it any decisive guidance as to whether an administration order might be made in respect of a foreign-registered company whose centre of main interests was in the European Community. The Regulation itself answered that matter affirmatively without any outside aids. Also, in *Schmid v Hertel* Case C-328/12 [2014] 1 WLR 633 the report was ignored by the CJEU even though it appeared to cover directly the point at issue in the case.

See also on the authoritative status of the report *Shierson v Vlieland-Boddy* [2005] 1 WLR 3966 at paras 47, 65–68, 73 and 76 per Chadwick and Longmore LJJ and Sir Martin Nourse and *Re Stanford International Bank Ltd* [2011] Ch 33 at paras 36 and 53 per Sir Andrew Morritt. The report was also given decisive effect by Mann J in *Trillium (Nelson) Properties Ltd v Office Metro Ltd* [2012] BCC 829 at paras 14–16.

When interpreting the Regulation, the European Court and national courts will adopt, so far as possible, autonomous, 'European' meanings for terms that may have different meanings in national laws. Moreover, the approach to construction will be purposive or teleological with the principal aim of giving effect to the purpose underlying the various provisions of the Regulation. These matters have been addressed recently by the European Court in Case C-250/17 *Tarrago da Silveira v Massa Insolvente da Espírito Santo* [2018] 1 WLR 4148, [2018] ILPr 29. The court said at para 20 that according to its settled case law, the wording used in one language version of a provision of EU law 'cannot serve as the sole basis for the interpretation of that provision or be given priority over the other language versions. Provisions of EU law must be interpreted and applied uniformly in the light of the versions existing in all EU languages'.

The recast Insolvency Regulation sits alongside the recast Jurisdiction and Judgments Regulation (Brussels I Regulation) – Regulation (EU) 1215/2012 – referred to as the Judgments Regulation. The latter Regulation applies in civil and commercial matters but according to Art 1(2)(b) it does not apply to 'bankruptcy, proceedings relating to the winding-up of insolvent companies or other legal persons, judicial arrangements, compositions and analogous proceedings'. This exception mirrors a similar provision in the earlier Brussels Convention, which also covered jurisdiction and the enforcement of judgments in civil and commercial matters.

As Chancellor Morritt remarked in *Byers v Yacht Bull Corp* [2010] EWHC 133 (Ch) the scope of the exception in Art 1(2)(b) of the Judgments Regulation has been the subject matter of a number of decided cases both in the European courts and in England. There are also an increasing number of cases concerned with the relationship between the Judgments Regulation and the Insolvency Regulation and whether actions fall within one Regulation rather than the other.

The overall objective of the Judgments Regulation is to secure the simplification of formalities that govern the reciprocal recognition and enforcement of judgments and to strengthen the legal protection of persons. The 21st Recital in the preamble makes clear the need, in the interests of the harmonious administration of justice, to ensure that irreconcilable judgments will not be given in two EU states.

Under Art 4 of the recast Judgments Regulation persons domiciled in a Member State must be sued in the courts of that Member State though there are rules of special jurisdiction allowing proceedings to be brought in other Member States in certain circumstances. Article 31 provides that if proceedings involving the same cause of action between the same parties are brought in the courts of different Member States then any court other than the court first seised must stay its proceedings until the jurisdiction of the court first seised is established and, when it is, decline its jurisdiction in favour of that court. But under Art 31(2) of the 'recast' Regulation, if the parties have given a particular court exclusive jurisdiction, that court may go on to hear the case even if it was not first 'seised'.

The Insolvency Regulation, and indeed the Jurisdiction and Judgments Regulation and other EU private international law instruments, largely cease to apply to the UK given Britain's withdrawal from the European Union – 'Brexit' – on 31 January 2020.

For the sake of completeness, one might note that on 8 April 2020 the UK applied to accede to the Lugano Convention as an independent contracting party. That application is however subject to the agreement of the contracting parties to the Lugano Convention, including the EU, and that agreement has not yet been forthcoming.

The Convention formed the basis of the UK's private international law relationship with Norway, Iceland and Switzerland and is based on the original version of the Brussels I Regulation on Jurisdiction and Enforcement of Judgments. It might therefore be used to facilitate the pan-European recognition of UK schemes of arrangement and restructuring plans. The Lugano Convention applies between those countries and the EU, and it applied to the UK by virtue of the UK being treated as an EU Member State for the purposes of international agreements entered into by the EU. This arrangement ended at the end of the Brexit implementation period.

The Insolvency (Amendment) (EU Exit) Regulations SI 2019/146 (Insolvency Brexit Regulations) were made under the European Union (Withdrawal) Act 2018 and tackle the insolvency law consequences of the UK leaving the EU. These Insolvency 'Brexit' Regulations however, largely disapply the effect of the EU Insolvency Regulation subject to an exception for cases where main insolvency proceedings have already been opened in another EU Member State at 'Brexit' implementation period completion day which was 31 December 2020 at 11 pm.

Moreover, and in addition to the existing jurisdictional heads in the insolvency legislation, there is now a new expressly designated jurisdiction to open insolvency proceedings for the purposes of rescue, adjustment of debt, reorganisation or liquidation and the debtor's centre of main interests ('COMI') is in the UK, or the COMI is in an EU Member State and there is an establishment in the UK. The continued express reference to 'COMI' and 'establishment' as connecting factors to the UK is presumably intended to facilitate recognition of UK insolvency proceedings in the remaining EU Member States.

The Insolvency (Amendment) (EU Exit) Regulations 2020, SI 2020/647, were made on 26 June 2020 and came into force on the implementation period completion day for the UK's exit from the European Union. The Regulations provide that the EU Insolvency Regulation continues to apply with respect to main proceedings opened before the day that they come into effect. In *Re Mederco (Cardiff) Ltd* [2021] EWHC 386 (Ch) Judge Davis-White addressed the position if an English administration order had been made with retrospective effect after the Brexit implementation period completion date. He said at [67]: 'Were main proceedings to have been opened in another member state prior to the making of (say) an English retrospective administration order, but after the retrospective date to which such order was to "date back", it is difficult to see how there would be anything other than chaos were the effect to be that the English order retrospectively changed the nature of the prior opening in the other EU state. In my judgment, it is necessary to distinguish the opening of proceedings from the effect of their opening.' He recognised however that this was a provisional opinion and not based on full adversarial argument.

Currently, the UK has two main statutory vehicles for international/cross-border cooperation in insolvency matters:

(1)     the EU Regulation on Insolvency Proceedings (supplemented by sector-specific instruments);
(2)     the UNCITRAL Model Law implemented in the UK by the Cross-Border Insolvency Regulations (CBIR); and
(3)     s 426 of the Insolvency Act 1986.

Additionally, there is the common law to the extent that it has not been superseded in relation to particular matters.

Unless there is some replacement treaty, or other bilateral arrangements, the logic of Brexit suggests that the UK will then, prima facie, have to rely upon the CBIR/Model Law regime, possibly supplemented by the common law, to govern its relations with other EU countries in respect of insolvency matters. It should be noted that the Brexit implementation period concluded with the coming into force of a Trade and Co-operation Agreement between the UK and EU on 1 January 2021[1]. This agreement however, is essentially bereft of provisions on judicial cooperation in civil matters.

The Insolvency Regulation is a much more comprehensive legal instrument than the CBIR/Model Law. Therefore, it could be argued that the UK legal landscape is impoverished by withdrawal from the mutual recognition and cooperation mandate under the Regulation. A possible option for the UK, post-Brexit, would have been to maintain its provisions in force insofar as they apply to the UK[2]. This would mean, however, the UK automatically recognising insolvency proceedings opened in other Member States, and judgments handed down in the course of insolvency proceedings, whereas other EU states would not necessarily recognise similar proceedings and judgments emanating from the UK.

The problems are compounded by the fact that the great majority of other EU countries have not adopted the Model Law[3]. Therefore, to get recognition of UK insolvency proceedings and insolvency-related judgments in other Member States, one has to fall back on the national private international law rules of the relevant State. The process of seeking recognition may be complicated and arduous.

[1]  See https://ec.europa.eu/info/relations-united-kingdom/eu-uk-trade-and-cooperation-agreeme nt_en and https://assets.publishing.service.gov.uk/government/uploads/system/uploads/attach ment_data/file/948093/TCA_SUMMARY_PDF.pdf.

[2]  But see the Insolvency (Amendment) (EU Exit) Regulations 2019, SI 2019/146 (Insolvency Brexit Regulations), which largely disapply the effect of the European Insolvency Regulation subject to an exception for cases where main insolvency proceedings have already been opened in another EU Member State at the end of the Brexit implementation period completion day.

[3]  Currently, only Greece, Poland, Romania and Slovenia of the remaining members of the EU are on the list maintained by UNCITRAL of countries that have adopted the Model Law – see http://www.uncitral.org/uncitral/en/uncitral_texts/insolvency/1997Model_status.html.

# REGULATION (EU) 2015/848 OF THE EUROPEAN PARLIAMENT AND OF THE COUNCIL

of 20 May 2015

on insolvency proceedings
(recast)

THE EUROPEAN PARLIAMENT AND THE COUNCIL OF THE EUROPEAN UNION,

Having regard to the Treaty on the Functioning of the European Union, and in particular Article 81 thereof, Having regard to the proposal from the European Commission,

After transmission of the draft legislative act to the national parliaments,

Having regard to the opinion of the European Economic and Social Committee[1],

Acting in accordance with the ordinary legislative procedure[2],

Whereas:

(1) On 12 December 2012, the Commission adopted a report on the application of Council Regulation (EC) No 1346/2000[3]. The report concluded that the Regulation is functioning well in general but that it would be desirable to improve the application of certain of its provisions in order to enhance the effective administration of cross-border insolvency proceedings. Since that Regulation has been amended several times and further amendments are to be made, it should be recast in the interest of clarity.

(2) The Union has set the objective of establishing an area of freedom, security and justice.

(3) The proper functioning of the internal market requires that cross-border insolvency proceedings should operate efficiently and effectively. This Regulation needs to be adopted in order to achieve that objective, which falls within the scope of judicial cooperation in civil matters within the meaning of Article 81 of the Treaty.

(4) The activities of undertakings have more and more cross-border effects and are therefore increasingly being regulated by Union law. The insolvency of such undertakings also affects the proper functioning of the internal market, and there is a need for a Union act requiring coordination of the measures to be taken regarding an insolvent debtor's assets.

(5) It is necessary for the proper functioning of the internal market to avoid incentives for parties to transfer assets or judicial proceedings from one Member State to another, seeking to obtain a more favourable legal position to the detriment of the general body of creditors (forum shopping).

(6) This Regulation should include provisions governing jurisdiction for opening insolvency proceedings and actions which are directly derived from insolvency proceedings and are closely linked with them. This Regulation should also contain provisions regarding the recognition and enforcement of judgments issued in such proceedings, and provisions regarding the law applicable to insolvency proceedings. In addition, this Regulation should lay down rules on the coordination of insolvency proceedings which relate to the same debtor or to several members of the same group of companies.

(7) Bankruptcy, proceedings relating to the winding-up of insolvent companies or other legal persons, judicial arrangements, compositions and analogous proceedings and actions related to such proceedings are excluded from the scope of Regulation (EU) No 1215/2012 of the European Parliament and of the Council[4]. Those proceedings should be covered by this Regulation. The interpretation of this Regulation should as much as possible avoid regulatory loopholes between the two instruments. However, the mere fact that a national procedure is not listed in Annex A to this Regulation should not imply that it is covered by Regulation (EU) No 1215/2012.

(8) In order to achieve the aim of improving the efficiency and effectiveness of insolvency proceedings having cross-border effects, it is necessary, and appropriate, that the provisions on jurisdiction, recognition and applicable law in this area should be contained in a Union measure which is binding and directly applicable in Member States.

(9) This Regulation should apply to insolvency proceedings which meet the conditions set out in it, irrespective of whether the debtor is a natural person or a legal person, a trader or an individual. Those insolvency proceedings are listed exhaustively in Annex A. In respect of the national procedures contained in Annex A, this Regulation should apply without any further examination by the courts of another Member State as to whether the conditions set out in this Regulation are met. National insolvency procedures not listed in Annex A should not be covered by this Regulation.

(10) The scope of this Regulation should extend to proceedings which promote the rescue of economically viable but distressed businesses and which give a second chance to entrepreneurs. It should, in particular, extend to proceedings which provide for restructuring of a debtor at a stage where there is only a likelihood of insolvency, and to proceedings which leave the debtor fully or partially in control of its assets and affairs. It should also extend to proceedings providing for a debt discharge or a debt adjustment in relation to consumers and self-employed persons, for example by reducing the amount to be paid by the debtor or by extending the payment period granted to the debtor. Since such proceedings do not necessarily entail the appointment of an insolvency practitioner, they should be covered by this Regulation if they take place under the control or supervision of a court. In this context, the term 'control' should include situations where the court only intervenes on appeal by a creditor or other interested parties.

(11) This Regulation should also apply to procedures which grant a temporary stay on enforcement actions brought by individual creditors where such actions could adversely affect negotiations and hamper the prospects of a restructuring of the debtor's business. Such procedures should not be detrimental to the general body of creditors and, if no agreement on a restructuring plan can be reached, should be preliminary to other procedures covered by this Regulation.

(12) This Regulation should apply to proceedings the opening of which is subject to publicity in order to allow creditors to become aware of the proceedings and to lodge their claims, thereby ensuring the collective nature of the proceedings, and in order to give creditors the opportunity to challenge the jurisdiction of the court which has opened the proceedings.

(13) Accordingly, insolvency proceedings which are confidential should be excluded from the scope of this Regulation. While such proceedings may play an important role in some Member States, their confidential nature makes it impossible for a creditor or a court located in another Member State to know that such proceedings have been opened,

thereby making it difficult to provide for the recognition of their effects throughout the Union.

(14) The collective proceedings which are covered by this Regulation should include all or a significant part of the creditors to whom a debtor owes all or a substantial proportion of the debtor's outstanding debts provided that the claims of those creditors who are not involved in such proceedings remain unaffected. Proceedings which involve only the financial creditors of a debtor should also be covered. Proceedings which do not include all the creditors of a debtor should be proceedings aimed at rescuing the debtor. Proceedings that lead to a definitive cessation of the debtor's activities or the liquidation of the debtor's assets should include all the debtor's creditors. Moreover, the fact that some insolvency proceedings for natural persons exclude specific categories of claims, such as maintenance claims, from the possibility of a debt-discharge should not mean that such proceedings are not collective.

(15) This Regulation should also apply to proceedings that, under the law of some Member States, are opened and conducted for a certain period of time on an interim or provisional basis before a court issues an order confirming the continuation of the proceedings on a non-interim basis. Although labelled as 'interim', such proceedings should meet all other requirements of this Regulation.

(16) This Regulation should apply to proceedings which are based on laws relating to insolvency. However, proceedings that are based on general company law not designed exclusively for insolvency situations should not be considered to be based on laws relating to insolvency. Similarly, the purpose of adjustment of debt should not include specific proceedings in which debts of a natural person of very low income and very low asset value are written off, provided that this type of proceedings never makes provision for payment to creditors.

(17) This Regulation's scope should extend to proceedings which are triggered by situations in which the debtor faces non-financial difficulties, provided that such difficulties give rise to a real and serious threat to the debtor's actual or future ability to pay its debts as they fall due. The time frame relevant for the determination of such threat may extend to a period of several months or even longer in order to account for cases in which the debtor is faced with non-financial difficulties threatening the status of its business as a going concern and, in the medium term, its liquidity. This may be the case, for example, where the debtor has lost a contract which is of key importance to it.

(18) This Regulation should be without prejudice to the rules on the recovery of State aid from insolvent companies as interpreted by the case law of the Court of Justice of the European Union.

(19) Insolvency proceedings concerning insurance undertakings, credit institutions, investment firms and other firms, institutions or undertakings covered by Directive 2001/24/EC of the European Parliament and of the Council[5] and collective investment undertakings should be excluded from the scope of this Regulation, as they are all subject to special arrangements and the national supervisory authorities have wide-ranging powers of intervention.

(20) Insolvency proceedings do not necessarily involve the intervention of a judicial authority. Therefore, the term 'court' in this Regulation should, in certain provisions, be given a broad meaning and include a person or body empowered by national law to open insolvency proceedings. In order for this Regulation to apply, proceedings (comprising acts and formalities set down in law) should not only have to comply with the provisions of this Regulation, but they should also be officially recognised and legally effective in the Member State in which the insolvency proceedings are opened.

(21) Insolvency practitioners are defined in this Regulation and listed in Annex B. Insolvency practitioners who are appointed without the involvement of a judicial body should, under national law, be appropriately regulated and authorised to act in insolvency proceedings. The national regulatory framework should provide for proper arrangements to deal with potential conflicts of interest.

(22) This Regulation acknowledges the fact that as a result of widely differing substantive laws it is not practical to introduce insolvency proceedings with universal scope throughout the Union. The application without exception of the law of the State of the opening of proceedings would, against this background, frequently lead to difficulties. This applies, for example, to the widely differing national laws on security interests to be found in the Member States. Furthermore, the preferential rights enjoyed by some creditors in insolvency proceedings are, in some cases, completely different. At the next review of this Regulation, it will be necessary to identify further measures in order to improve the preferential rights of employees at European level. This Regulation

should take account of such differing national laws in two different ways. On the one hand, provision should be made for special rules on the applicable law in the case of particularly significant rights and legal relationships (eg rights in rem and contracts of employment). On the other hand, national proceedings covering only assets situated in the State of the opening of proceedings should also be allowed alongside main insolvency proceedings with universal scope.

(23) This Regulation enables the main insolvency proceedings to be opened in the Member State where the debtor has the centre of its main interests. Those proceedings have universal scope and are aimed at encompassing all the debtor's assets. To protect the diversity of interests, this Regulation permits secondary insolvency proceedings to be opened to run in parallel with the main insolvency proceedings. Secondary insolvency proceedings may be opened in the Member State where the debtor has an establishment. The effects of secondary insolvency proceedings are limited to the assets located in that State. Mandatory rules of coordination with the main insolvency proceedings satisfy the need for unity in the Union.

(24) Where main insolvency proceedings concerning a legal person or company have been opened in a Member State other than that of its registered office, it should be possible to open secondary insolvency proceedings in the Member State of the registered office, provided that the debtor is carrying out an economic activity with human means and assets in that State, in accordance with the case law of the Court of Justice of the European Union.

(25) This Regulation applies only to proceedings in respect of a debtor whose centre of main interests is located in the Union.

(26) The rules of jurisdiction set out in this Regulation establish only international jurisdiction, that is to say, they designate the Member State the courts of which may open insolvency proceedings. Territorial jurisdiction within that Member State should be established by the national law of the Member State concerned.

(27) Before opening insolvency proceedings, the competent court should examine of its own motion whether the centre of the debtor's main interests or the debtor's establishment is actually located within its jurisdiction.

(28) When determining whether the centre of the debtor's main interests is ascertainable by third parties, special consideration should be given to the creditors and to their perception as to where a debtor conducts the administration of its interests. This may require, in the event of a shift of centre of main interests, informing creditors of the new location from which the debtor is carrying out its activities in due course, for example by drawing attention to the change of address in commercial correspondence, or by making the new location public through other appropriate means.

(29) This Regulation should contain a number of safeguards aimed at preventing fraudulent or abusive forum shopping.

(30) Accordingly, the presumptions that the registered office, the principal place of business and the habitual residence are the centre of main interests should be rebuttable, and the relevant court of a Member State should carefully assess whether the centre of the debtor's main interests is genuinely located in that Member State. In the case of a company, it should be possible to rebut this presumption where the company's central administration is located in a Member State other than that of its registered office, and where a comprehensive assessment of all the relevant factors establishes, in a manner that is ascertainable by third parties, that the company's actual centre of management and supervision and of the management of its interests is located in that other Member State. In the case of an individual not exercising an independent business or professional activity, it should be possible to rebut this presumption, for example where the major part of the debtor's assets is located outside the Member State of the debtor's habitual residence, or where it can be established that the principal reason for moving was to file for insolvency proceedings in the new jurisdiction and where such filing would materially impair the interests of creditors whose dealings with the debtor took place prior to the relocation.

(31) With the same objective of preventing fraudulent or abusive forum shopping, the presumption that the centre of main interests is at the place of the registered office, at the individual's principal place of business or at the individual's habitual residence should not apply where, respectively, in the case of a company, legal person or individual exercising an independent business or professional activity, the debtor has relocated its registered office or principal place of business to another Member State within the 3-month period prior to the request for opening insolvency proceedings, or, in the case of an individual not exercising an independent business or professional activity, the

debtor has relocated his habitual residence to another Member State within the 6-month period prior to the request for opening insolvency proceedings.

(32) In all cases, where the circumstances of the matter give rise to doubts about the court's jurisdiction, the court should require the debtor to submit additional evidence to support its assertions and, where the law applicable to the insolvency proceedings so allows, give the debtor's creditors the opportunity to present their views on the question of jurisdiction.

(33) In the event that the court seised of the request to open insolvency proceedings finds that the centre of main interests is not located on its territory, it should not open main insolvency proceedings.

(34) In addition, any creditor of the debtor should have an effective remedy against the decision to open insolvency proceedings. The consequences of any challenge to the decision to open insolvency proceedings should be governed by national law.

(35) The courts of the Member State within the territory of which insolvency proceedings have been opened should also have jurisdiction for actions which derive directly from the insolvency proceedings and are closely linked with them. Such actions should include avoidance actions against defendants in other Member States and actions concerning obligations that arise in the course of the insolvency proceedings, such as advance payment for costs of the proceedings. In contrast, actions for the performance of the obligations under a contract concluded by the debtor prior to the opening of proceedings do not derive directly from the proceedings. Where such an action is related to another action based on general civil and commercial law, the insolvency practitioner should be able to bring both actions in the courts of the defendant's domicile if he considers it more efficient to bring the action in that forum. This could, for example, be the case where the insolvency practitioner wishes to combine an action for director's liability on the basis of insolvency law with an action based on company law or general tort law.

(36) The court having jurisdiction to open the main insolvency proceedings should be able to order provisional and protective measures as from the time of the request to open proceedings. Preservation measures both prior to and after the commencement of the insolvency proceedings are important to guarantee the effectiveness of the insolvency proceedings. In that connection, this Regulation should provide for various possibilities. On the one hand, the court competent for the main insolvency proceedings should also be able to order provisional and protective measures covering assets situated in the territory of other Member States. On the other hand, an insolvency practitioner temporarily appointed prior to the opening of the main insolvency proceedings should be able, in the Member States in which an establishment belonging to the debtor is to be found, to apply for the preservation measures which are possible under the law of those Member States.

(37) Prior to the opening of the main insolvency proceedings, the right to request the opening of insolvency proceedings in the Member State where the debtor has an establishment should be limited to local creditors and public authorities, or to cases in which main insolvency proceedings cannot be opened under the law of the Member State where the debtor has the centre of its main interests. The reason for this restriction is that cases in which territorial insolvency proceedings are requested before the main insolvency proceedings are intended to be limited to what is absolutely necessary.

(38) Following the opening of the main insolvency proceedings, this Regulation does not restrict the right to request the opening of insolvency proceedings in a Member State where the debtor has an establishment. The insolvency practitioner in the main insolvency proceedings or any other person empowered under the national law of that Member State may request the opening of secondary insolvency proceedings.

(39) This Regulation should provide for rules to determine the location of the debtor's assets, which should apply when determining which assets belong to the main or secondary insolvency proceedings, or to situations involving third parties' rights *in rem*. In particular, this Regulation should provide that European patents with unitary effect, a Community trade mark or any other similar rights, such as Community plant variety rights or Community designs, should only be included in the main insolvency proceedings.

(40) Secondary insolvency proceedings can serve different purposes, besides the protection of local interests. Cases may arise in which the insolvency estate of the debtor is too complex to administer as a unit, or the differences in the legal systems concerned are so great that difficulties may arise from the extension of effects deriving from the law of the State of the opening of proceedings to the other Member States where the assets

are located. For that reason, the insolvency practitioner in the main insolvency proceedings may request the opening of secondary insolvency proceedings where the efficient administration of the insolvency estate so requires.

(41) Secondary insolvency proceedings may also hamper the efficient administration of the insolvency estate. Therefore, this Regulation sets out two specific situations in which the court seised of a request to open secondary insolvency proceedings should be able, at the request of the insolvency practitioner in the main insolvency proceedings, to postpone or refuse the opening of such proceedings.

(42) First, this Regulation confers on the insolvency practitioner in main insolvency proceedings the possibility of giving an undertaking to local creditors that they will be treated as if secondary insolvency proceedings had been opened. That undertaking has to meet a number of conditions set out in this Regulation, in particular that it be approved by a qualified majority of local creditors. Where such an undertaking has been given, the court seised of a request to open secondary insolvency proceedings should be able to refuse that request if it is satisfied that the undertaking adequately protects the general interests of local creditors. When assessing those interests, the court should take into account the fact that the undertaking has been approved by a qualified majority of local creditors.

(43) For the purposes of giving an undertaking to local creditors, the assets and rights located in the Member State where the debtor has an establishment should form a sub-category of the insolvency estate, and, when distributing them or the proceeds resulting from their realisation, the insolvency practitioner in the main insolvency proceedings should respect the priority rights that creditors would have had if secondary insolvency proceedings had been opened in that Member State.

(44) National law should be applicable, as appropriate, in relation to the approval of an undertaking. In particular, where under national law the voting rules for adopting a restructuring plan require the prior approval of creditors' claims, those claims should be deemed to be approved for the purpose of voting on the undertaking. Where there are different procedures for the adoption of restructuring plans under national law, Member States should designate the specific procedure which should be relevant in this context.

(45) Second, this Regulation should provide for the possibility that the court temporarily stays the opening of secondary insolvency proceedings, when a temporary stay of individual enforcement proceedings has been granted in the main insolvency proceedings, in order to preserve the efficiency of the stay granted in the main insolvency proceedings. The court should be able to grant the temporary stay if it is satisfied that suitable measures are in place to protect the general interest of local creditors. In such a case, all creditors that could be affected by the outcome of the negotiations on a restructuring plan should be informed of the negotiations and be allowed to participate in them.

(46) In order to ensure effective protection of local interests, the insolvency practitioner in the main insolvency proceedings should not be able to realise or re-locate, in an abusive manner, assets situated in the Member State where an establishment is located, in particular, with the purpose of frustrating the possibility that such interests can be effectively satisfied if secondary insolvency proceedings are opened subsequently.

(47) This Regulation should not prevent the courts of a Member State in which secondary insolvency proceedings have been opened from sanctioning a debtor's directors for violation of their duties, provided that those courts have jurisdiction to address such disputes under their national law.

(48) Main insolvency proceedings and secondary insolvency proceedings can contribute to the efficient administration of the debtor's insolvency estate or to the effective realisation of the total assets if there is proper cooperation between the actors involved in all the concurrent proceedings. Proper cooperation implies the various insolvency practitioners and the courts involved cooperating closely, in particular by exchanging a sufficient amount of information. In order to ensure the dominant role of the main insolvency proceedings, the insolvency practitioner in such proceedings should be given several possibilities for intervening in secondary insolvency proceedings which are pending at the same time. In particular, the insolvency practitioner should be able to propose a restructuring plan or composition or apply for a suspension of the realisation of the assets in the secondary insolvency proceedings. When cooperating, insolvency practitioners and courts should take into account best practices for cooperation in cross-border insolvency cases, as set out in principles and guidelines on communication and cooperation adopted by European and international organisations active in the area of insolvency law, and in particular the relevant guidelines prepared by the United

Nations Commission on International Trade Law (Uncitral).

(49) In light of such cooperation, insolvency practitioners and courts should be able to enter into agreements and protocols for the purpose of facilitating cross-border cooperation of multiple insolvency proceedings in different Member States concerning the same debtor or members of the same group of companies, where this is compatible with the rules applicable to each of the proceedings. Such agreements and protocols may vary in form, in that they may be written or oral, and in scope, in that they may range from generic to specific, and may be entered into by different parties. Simple generic agreements may emphasise the need for close cooperation between the parties, without addressing specific issues, while more detailed, specific agreements may establish a framework of principles to govern multiple insolvency proceedings and may be approved by the courts involved, where the national law so requires. They may reflect an agreement between the parties to take, or to refrain from taking, certain steps or actions.

(50) Similarly, the courts of different Member States may cooperate by coordinating the appointment of insolvency practitioners. In that context, they may appoint a single insolvency practitioner for several insolvency proceedings concerning the same debtor or for different members of a group of companies, provided that this is compatible with the rules applicable to each of the proceedings, in particular with any requirements concerning the qualification and licensing of the insolvency practitioner.

(51) This Regulation should ensure the efficient administration of insolvency proceedings relating to different companies forming part of a group of companies.

(52) Where insolvency proceedings have been opened for several companies of the same group, there should be proper cooperation between the actors involved in those proceedings. The various insolvency practitioners and the courts involved should therefore be under a similar obligation to cooperate and communicate with each other as those involved in main and secondary insolvency proceedings relating to the same debtor. Cooperation between the insolvency practitioners should not run counter to the interests of the creditors in each of the proceedings, and such cooperation should be aimed at finding a solution that would leverage synergies across the group.

(53) The introduction of rules on the insolvency proceedings of groups of companies should not limit the possibility for a court to open insolvency proceedings for several companies belonging to the same group in a single jurisdiction if the court finds that the centre of main interests of those companies is located in a single Member State. In such cases, the court should also be able to appoint, if appropriate, the same insolvency practitioner in all proceedings concerned, provided that this is not incompatible with the rules applicable to them.

(54) With a view to further improving the coordination of the insolvency proceedings of members of a group of companies, and to allow for a coordinated restructuring of the group, this Regulation should introduce procedural rules on the coordination of the insolvency proceedings of members of a group of companies. Such coordination should strive to ensure the efficiency of the coordination, whilst at the same time respecting each group member's separate legal personality.

(55) An insolvency practitioner appointed in insolvency proceedings opened in relation to a member of a group of companies should be able to request the opening of group coordination proceedings. However, where the law applicable to the insolvency so requires, that insolvency practitioner should obtain the necessary authorisation before making such a request. The request should specify the essential elements of the coordination, in particular an outline of the coordination plan, a proposal as to whom should be appointed as coordinator and an outline of the estimated costs of the coordination.

(56) In order to ensure the voluntary nature of group coordination proceedings, the insolvency practitioners involved should be able to object to their participation in the proceedings within a specified time period. In order to allow the insolvency practitioners involved to take an informed decision on participation in the group coordination proceedings, they should be informed at an early stage of the essential elements of the coordination. However, any insolvency practitioner who initially objects to inclusion in the group coordination proceedings should be able to subsequently request to participate in them. In such a case, the coordinator should take a decision on the admissibility of the request. All insolvency practitioners, including the requesting insolvency practitioner, should be informed of the coordinator's decision and should have the opportunity of challenging that decision before the court which has opened the group coordination proceedings.

(57) Group coordination proceedings should always strive to facilitate the effective administration of the insolvency proceedings of the group members, and to have a

generally positive impact for the creditors. This Regulation should therefore ensure that the court with which a request for group coordination proceedings has been filed makes an assessment of those criteria prior to opening group coordination proceedings.

(58) The advantages of group coordination proceedings should not be outweighed by the costs of those proceedings. Therefore, it is necessary to ensure that the costs of the coordination, and the share of those costs that each group member will bear, are adequate, proportionate and reasonable, and are determined in accordance with the national law of the Member State in which group coordination proceedings have been opened. The insolvency practitioners involved should also have the possibility of controlling those costs from an early stage of the proceedings. Where the national law so requires, controlling costs from an early stage of proceedings could involve the insolvency practitioner seeking the approval of a court or creditors' committee.

(59) Where the coordinator considers that the fulfilment of his or her tasks requires a significant increase in costs compared to the initially estimated costs and, in any case, where the costs exceed 10% of the estimated costs, the coordinator should be authorised by the court which has opened the group coordination proceedings to exceed such costs. Before taking its decision, the court which has opened the group coordination proceedings should give the possibility to the participating insolvency practitioners to be heard before it in order to allow them to communicate their observations on the appropriateness of the coordinator's request.

(60) For members of a group of companies which are not participating in group coordination proceedings, this Regulation should also provide for an alternative mechanism to achieve a coordinated restructuring of the group. An insolvency practitioner appointed in proceedings relating to a member of a group of companies should have standing to request a stay of any measure related to the realisation of the assets in the proceedings opened with respect to other members of the group which are not subject to group coordination proceedings. It should only be possible to request such a stay if a restructuring plan is presented for the members of the group concerned, if the plan is to the benefit of the creditors in the proceedings in respect of which the stay is requested, and if the stay is necessary to ensure that the plan can be properly implemented.

(61) This Regulation should not prevent Member States from establishing national rules which would supplement the rules on cooperation, communication and coordination with regard to the insolvency of members of groups of companies set out in this Regulation, provided that the scope of application of those national rules is limited to the national jurisdiction and that their application would not impair the efficiency of the rules laid down by this Regulation.

(62) The rules on cooperation, communication and coordination in the framework of the insolvency of members of a group of companies provided for in this Regulation should only apply to the extent that proceedings relating to different members of the same group of companies have been opened in more than one Member State.

(63) Any creditor which has its habitual residence, domicile or registered office in the Union should have the right to lodge its claims in each of the insolvency proceedings pending in the Union relating to the debtor's assets. This should also apply to tax authorities and social insurance institutions. This Regulation should not prevent the insolvency practitioner from lodging claims on behalf of certain groups of creditors, for example employees, where the national law so provides. However, in order to ensure the equal treatment of creditors, the distribution of proceeds should be coordinated. Every creditor should be able to keep what it has received in the course of insolvency proceedings, but should be entitled only to participate in the distribution of total assets in other proceedings if creditors with the same standing have obtained the same proportion of their claims.

(64) It is essential that creditors which have their habitual residence, domicile or registered office in the Union be informed about the opening of insolvency proceedings relating to their debtor's assets. In order to ensure a swift transmission of information to creditors, Regulation (EC) No 1393/2007 of the European Parliament and of the Council[6] should not apply where this Regulation refers to the obligation to inform creditors. The use of standard forms available in all official languages of the institutions of the Union should facilitate the task of creditors when lodging claims in proceedings opened in another Member State. The consequences of the incomplete filing of the standard forms should be a matter for national law.

(65) This Regulation should provide for the immediate recognition of judgments concerning the opening, conduct and closure of insolvency proceedings which fall within its scope, and of judgments handed down in direct connection with such insolvency proceedings. Automatic recognition should therefore mean that the effects attributed to

the proceedings by the law of the Member State in which the proceedings were opened extend to all other Member States. The recognition of judgments delivered by the courts of the Member States should be based on the principle of mutual trust. To that end, grounds for non-recognition should be reduced to the minimum necessary. This is also the basis on which any dispute should be resolved where the courts of two Member States both claim competence to open the main insolvency proceedings. The decision of the first court to open proceedings should be recognised in the other Member States without those Member States having the power to scrutinise that court's decision.

(66) This Regulation should set out, for the matters covered by it, uniform rules on conflict of laws which replace, within their scope of application, national rules of private international law. Unless otherwise stated, the law of the Member State of the opening of proceedings should be applicable (*lex concursus*). This rule on conflict of laws should be valid both for the main insolvency proceedings and for local proceedings. The *lex concursus* determines all the effects of the insolvency proceedings, both procedural and substantive, on the persons and legal relations concerned. It governs all the conditions for the opening, conduct and closure of the insolvency proceedings.

(67) Automatic recognition of insolvency proceedings to which the law of the State of the opening of proceedings normally applies may interfere with the rules under which transactions are carried out in other Member States. To protect legitimate expectations and the certainty of transactions in Member States other than that in which proceedings are opened, provision should be made for a number of exceptions to the general rule.

(68) There is a particular need for a special reference diverging from the law of the opening State in the case of rights *in rem*, since such rights are of considerable importance for the granting of credit. The basis, validity and extent of rights *in rem* should therefore normally be determined according to the *lex situs* and not be affected by the opening of insolvency proceedings. The proprietor of a right *in rem* should therefore be able to continue to assert its right to segregation or separate settlement of the collateral security. Where assets are subject to rights *in rem* under the *lex situs* in one Member State but the main insolvency proceedings are being carried out in another Member State, the insolvency practitioner in the main insolvency proceedings should be able to request the opening of secondary insolvency proceedings in the jurisdiction where the rights *in rem* arise if the debtor has an establishment there. If secondary insolvency proceedings are not opened, any surplus on the sale of an asset covered by rights *in rem* should be paid to the insolvency practitioner in the main insolvency proceedings.

(69) This Regulation lays down several provisions for a court to order a stay of opening proceedings or a stay of enforcement proceedings. Any such stay should not affect the rights *in rem* of creditors or third parties.

(70) If a set-off of claims is not permitted under the law of the State of the opening of proceedings, a creditor should nevertheless be entitled to the set-off if it is possible under the law applicable to the claim of the insolvent debtor. In this way, set-off would acquire a kind of guarantee function based on legal provisions on which the creditor concerned can rely at the time when the claim arises.

(71) There is also a need for special protection in the case of payment systems and financial markets, for example in relation to the position-closing agreements and netting agreements to be found in such systems, as well as the sale of securities and the guarantees provided for such transactions as governed in particular by Directive 98/26/EC of the European Parliament and of the Council[7]. For such transactions, the only law which is relevant should be that applicable to the system or market concerned. That law is intended to prevent the possibility of mechanisms for the payment and settlement of transactions, and provided for in payment and set-off systems or on the regulated financial markets of the Member States, being altered in the case of insolvency of a business partner. Directive 98/26/EC contains special provisions which should take precedence over the general rules laid down in this Regulation.

(72) In order to protect employees and jobs, the effects of insolvency proceedings on the continuation or termination of employment and on the rights and obligations of all parties to such employment should be determined by the law applicable to the relevant employment agreement, in accordance with the general rules on conflict of laws. Moreover, in cases where the termination of employment contracts requires approval by a court or administrative authority, the Member State in which an establishment of the debtor is located should retain jurisdiction to grant such approval even if no insolvency proceedings have been opened in that Member State. Any other questions relating to the law of insolvency, such as whether the employees' claims are protected by preferential rights and the status such preferential rights may have, should be determined by the law of the Member State in which the insolvency proceedings (main or secondary) have been

opened, except in cases where an undertaking to avoid secondary insolvency proceedings has been given in accordance with this Regulation.

(73) The law applicable to the effects of insolvency proceedings on any pending lawsuit or pending arbitral proceedings concerning an asset or right which forms part of the debtor's insolvency estate should be the law of the Member State where the lawsuit is pending or where the arbitration has its seat. However, this rule should not affect national rules on recognition and enforcement of arbitral awards.

(74) In order to take account of the specific procedural rules of court systems in certain Member States flexibility should be provided with regard to certain rules of this Regulation. Accordingly, references in this Regulation to notice being given by a judicial body of a Member State should include, where a Member State's procedural rules so require, an order by that judicial body directing that notice be given.

(75) For business considerations, the main content of the decision opening the proceedings should be published, at the request of the insolvency practitioner, in a Member State other than that of the court which delivered that decision. If there is an establishment in the Member State concerned, such publication should be mandatory. In neither case, however, should publication be a prior condition for recognition of the foreign proceedings.

(76) In order to improve the provision of information to relevant creditors and courts and to prevent the opening of parallel insolvency proceedings, Member States should be required to publish relevant information in cross-border insolvency cases in a publicly accessible electronic register. In order to facilitate access to that information for creditors and courts domiciled or located in other Member States, this Regulation should provide for the interconnection of such insolvency registers via the European e-Justice Portal. Member States should be free to publish relevant information in several registers and it should be possible to interconnect more than one register per Member State.

(77) This Regulation should determine the minimum amount of information to be published in the insolvency registers. Member States should not be precluded from including additional information. Where the debtor is an individual, the insolvency registers should only have to indicate a registration number if the debtor is exercising an independent business or professional activity. That registration number should be understood to be the unique registration number of the debtor's independent business or professional activity published in the trade register, if any.

(78) Information on certain aspects of insolvency proceedings is essential for creditors, such as time limits for lodging claims or for challenging decisions. This Regulation should, however, not require Member States to calculate those time-limits on a case-by-case basis. Member States should be able to fulfil their obligations by adding hyperlinks to the European e-Justice Portal, where self-explanatory information on the criteria for calculating those time-limits is to be provided.

(79) In order to grant sufficient protection to information relating to individuals not exercising an independent business or professional activity, Member States should be able to make access to that information subject to supplementary search criteria such as the debtor's personal identification number, address, date of birth or the district of the competent court, or to make access conditional upon a request to a competent authority or upon the verification of a legitimate interest.

(80) Member States should also be able not to include in their insolvency registers information on individuals not exercising an independent business or professional activity. In such cases, Member States should ensure that the relevant information is given to the creditors by individual notice, and that claims of creditors who have not received the information are not affected by the proceedings.

(81) It may be the case that some of the persons concerned are not aware that insolvency proceedings have been opened, and act in good faith in a way that conflicts with the new circumstances. In order to protect such persons who, unaware that foreign proceedings have been opened, make a payment to the debtor instead of to the foreign insolvency practitioner, provision should be made for such a payment to have a debt-discharging effect.

(82) In order to ensure uniform conditions for the implementation of this Regulation, implementing powers should be conferred on the Commission. Those powers should be exercised in accordance with Regulation (EU) No 182/2011 of the European Parliament and of the Council[8].

(83) This Regulation respects the fundamental rights and observes the principles recognised in the Charter of Fundamental Rights of the European Union. In particular, this Regulation seeks to promote the application of Articles 8, 17 and 47 concerning,

respectively, the protection of personal data, the right to property and the right to an effective remedy and to a fair trial.

(84) Directive 95/46/EC of the European Parliament and of the Council[9] and Regulation (EC) No 45/2001 of the European Parliament and of the Council[10] apply to the processing of personal data within the framework of this Regulation.

(85) This Regulation is without prejudice to Regulation (EEC, Euratom) No 1182/71 of the Council[11].

(86) Since the objective of this Regulation cannot be sufficiently achieved by the Member States but can rather, by reason of the creation of a legal framework for the proper administration of cross-border insolvency proceedings, be better achieved at Union level, the Union may adopt measures in accordance with the principle of subsidiarity as set out in Article 5 of the Treaty on European Union. In accordance with the principle of proportionality, as set out in that Article, this Regulation does not go beyond what is necessary in order to achieve that objective.

(87) In accordance with Article 3 and Article 4a(1) of Protocol No 21 on the position of the United Kingdom and Ireland in respect of the area of freedom, security and justice, annexed to the Treaty on European Union and the Treaty on the Functioning of the European Union, the United Kingdom and Ireland have notified their wish to take part in the adoption and application of this Regulation.

(88) In accordance with Articles 1 and 2 of Protocol No 22 on the position of Denmark annexed to the Treaty on European Union and the Treaty on the Functioning of the European Union, Denmark is not taking part in the adoption of this Regulation and is not bound by it or subject to its application.

(89) The European Data Protection Supervisor was consulted and delivered an opinion on 27 March 2013[12],

[1]  OJ C 271, 19.9.2013, p 55.

[2]  Position of the European Parliament of 5 February 2014 (not yet published in the Official Journal) and position of the Council at first reading of 12 March 2015 (not yet published in the Official Journal). Position of the European Parliament of 20 May 2015 (not yet published in the Official Journal).

[3]  Council Regulation (EC) No 1346/2000 of 29 May 2000 on insolvency proceedings (OJ L 160, 30.6.2000, p 1).

[4]  Regulation (EU) No 1215/2012 of the European Parliament and of the Council of 12 December 2012 on jurisdiction and the recognition and enforcement of judgments in civil and commercial matters (OJ L 351, 20.12.2012, p 1).

[5]  Directive 2001/24/EC of the European Parliament and of the Council of 4 April 2001 on the reorganisation and winding-up of credit institutions (OJ L 125, 5.5.2001, p 15).

[6]  Regulation (EC) No 1393/2007 of the European Parliament and of the Council of 13 November 2007 on the service in the Member States of judicial and extrajudicial documents in civil and commercial matters (service of documents), and repealing Council Regulation (EC) No 1348/2000 (OJ L 324, 10.12.2007, p 79).

[7]  Directive 98/26/EC of the European Parliament and of the Council of 19 May 1998 on settlement finality in payment and securities settlement systems (OJ L 166, 11.6.1998, p 45).

[8]  Regulation (EU) No 182/2011 of the European Parliament and of the Council of 16 February 2011 laying down the rules and general principles concerning mechanisms for control by the Member States of the Commission's exercise of implementing powers (OJ L 55, 28.2.2011, p 13).

[9]  Directive 95/46/EC of the European Parliament and of the Council of 24 October 1995 on the protection of individuals with regard to the processing of personal data and on the free movement of such data (OJ L 281, 23.11.1995, p 31).

[10]  Regulation (EC) No 45/2001 of the European Parliament and of the Council of 18 December 2000 on the protection of individuals with regard to the processing of personal data by the Community institutions and bodies and on the free movement of such data (OJ L 8, 12.1.2001, p 1).

[11]  Regulation (EEC, Euratom) No 1182/71 of the Council of 3 June 1971 determining the rules applicable to periods, dates and time limits (OJ L 124, 8.6.1971, p 1).

[12]  OJ C 358, 7.12.2013, p 15.

HAVE ADOPTED THIS REGULATION:

**[6.2]**

**General note**—The preamble, as with other European Regulations, can be used to aid interpretation of the substantive provisions. However, it should be noted that some parts of the preamble are of more significance than simply an aid to interpretation. Recital 25 for example, states that the Regulation only has intra-community effect, so where the debtor's centre of main interests (COMI) is outside the EU, the Regulation can have no effect. The preamble will be referred to where it is appropriate, in relation to the discussion of the Regulation's Articles. However, particularly important paragraphs are noted below.

**RECITALS 2–5**

These set out the general philosophy of the Regulation. Recital 5 suggests a desire to stamp out so-called forum shopping. There is an argument however that the Regulation and its predecessor, far from preventing forum shopping, may in fact have encouraged it. A decision opening insolvency proceedings in one EU Member State must then be recognised throughout the EU, subject to the possibility of opening secondary proceedings in another State where the debtor has an establishment. The Regulation creates an incentive for parties to forum shop and literally or figuratively, to race to the courtroom in the State that is perceived to be most favourable to them.

Moreover, a distinction has been increasingly drawn in the case law and commentaries between 'good' and 'bad' forum shopping – see the opinion of Advocate General Colomer in *Staubitz-Schreiber* Case C-1/04 [2006] ECR I-701 at [71] and [72]. This seems a useful taxonomy. Maximising asset values for the benefit of creditors and other stakeholders through taking advantage of more favourable laws or procedural conditions in a particular jurisdiction is an example of 'good' forum shopping, whereas debtors making assets more difficult to trace or shielding themselves from potential liabilities represents 'bad' forum shopping.

**RECITAL 7**

This recital suggests that 'regulatory loopholes' between the Insolvency Regulation and the Brussels I Regulation should be avoided. This is a noble sentiment but while the European jurisprudence has stressed the need for a harmonious interpretation of the two instruments, it is not entirely clear what is meant by 'regulatory loopholes'. The case law is certainly not conclusive. In *Nickel & Goeldner Spedition GmbH v 'Kintra' UAB* Case C-157/13 ECLI:EU:C:2014:2145 at [21] – the CJEU said that the two Regulations 'must be interpreted in such a way as to avoid any overlap between the rules of law that those texts lay down and any legal vacuum'. In *F-Tex SIA v Lietuvos-Anglijos UAB* Case C-213/10 [2013] Bus LR 232 however, the court was asked directly whether the court hearing the insolvency proceedings had the exclusive jurisdiction to adjudicate upon insolvency related actions but it declined the opportunity to answer, stating that this was not necessary for a decision in the case at hand.

Whatever the position regarding possible overlaps, Recital 7 does concede the possibility of gaps stating that the mere fact that a national procedure is not listed in annex A does not imply that the procedure is covered by the Brussels I Regulation. The UK scheme of arrangement may be an example of such a procedure but there has not yet been an appellate court decision that reviews all the relevant authorities. Instead there have been several first instance decisions, some uncontested, where the matter has been addressed at varying length. Schemes do not appear to fit neatly under either Regulation. In *Re DAP Holdings NV* [2006] BCC 48 at [14 it was suggested that applications to sanction schemes of arrangement fell outside the Brussels I Regulation but the contrary conclusion was reached in *Re Rodenstock GMbH* [2011] EWHC 1104. Here the judge did concede that the Brussels I Regulation seems ill-equipped to deal with proceedings for the sanctioning of schemes of arrangement since, in a sense, nobody was being sued. He said (at para 60) that 'they are not, at least in form, proceedings aimed at specific defendants at all. They may nonetheless be adversarial proceedings, in the sense that affected members and creditors of the scheme company may appear and oppose the grant of sanction and, for that purpose, serve evidence and make submissions just like any ordinary defendant.'

Snowden J has commented with a degree of understatement, that '[t]his point is of some difficulty': see *Re Van Gansewinkel Groep BV* [2015] EWHC 2151 (Ch) at [45].

**RECITAL 9**

Recital 9 provides that the insolvency proceedings to which the Regulation applies are listed exhaustively in Annex A. It goes on to say that when a procedure appears in the Annex, the Regulation applies without any further examination by national courts regardless of whether the definition is in fact satisfied. It adds that where a procedure is not listed, it is not covered by the Regulation. Recital 9 states this with admirable clarity but there is nothing expressly to the same effect in the substantive provisions of the recast Regulation nor was there in the original EIR. Nevertheless, the Court of Justice of the European Union (CJEU) held in in *Bank Handlowy SA v Christianapol* Case C-116/11 [2013] BPIR 174 at [33]–[35] that once proceedings are listed in Annex A to the Regulation, they must be regarded as coming within the scope of the Regulation. In

*Ulf Kazimierz Radziejewsk8* Case C-461/11 ECLI:EU:C:2012:704 at [24] the court also held that the Regulation applied only to the proceedings listed in the annex. This had the consequence that a Swedish debt relief procedure considered in that case was not subject to the Regulation as it was not included in the Annex.

In *Re Gategroup Guarantee Ltd* [2021] EWHC 304 (Ch) Zacaroli J noted that it was up to an EU Member State to choose to submit its domestic insolvency proceedings for inclusion within Annex A of the Insolvency Regulation. Therefore, he suggested that the question whether proceedings, which on the face of it were insolvency proceedings, were excluded from Brussels I could not be answered solely on the basis that they were, or were not, listed in Annex A. In any event, certain countries that were parties to the Lugano Convention, such as Switzerland, were not also a party to the Insolvency Regulation. Proceedings in such a country could not be included in Annex A, and therefore the bankruptcy exclusion in the Lugano Convention cannot be interpreted as limited to proceedings that were listed in Annex A ([76], [81]).

This case addressed the possible relevance of the 'bankruptcy' exception in Art 1(2(b) of the Insolvency Regulation in the context of the Lugano Convention. The case concerned whether the jurisdiction of the UK court to sanction a restructuring plan in respect of a UK plan company had been affected by the Convention. The restructuring plan was proposed under Part 26A UK Companies Act and proposed the restructuring of bonds that by reason of Art 23(1) of the Convention were subject to an exclusive jurisdiction clause in favour of the Swiss Courts.

As of 1 January 2021 the UK is no longer a party to the Lugano Convention but the claim form was issued, however, on 30 December 2020. As such, by reason of reg 92(1), (2)(d) and (3) of the Civil Jurisdiction and Judgment (Amendment) (EU Exit) Regulations 2019 (SI 2019/479), the Lugano Convention continued to apply.

The company on whose behalf the Part 26A plan was put forward argued that the Lugano Convention had no application to a claim under Part 26A because it is not a 'civil and commercial matter' as it fell within the bankruptcy exception in Art 1(2)(b): 'bankruptcy, proceedings relating to the winding-up of insolvent companies or other legal persons, judicial arrangements, compositions and analogous proceedings.' But for the bankruptcy exclusion, the proceedings would be a civil or commercial matter.

The judge took the view that the question had to be approached from first principles. He said that one should identify the particular features of insolvency proceedings which mean that they require special treatment and enquire whether the Part 26A restructuring plan procedure under the Corporate Insolvency and Governance Act 2020 contained the same features.

In his view, the principal 'peculiarity' of insolvency proceedings which meant that special rules relating to jurisdiction and recognition were required is that they were a collective process, driven by the need to solve the problem that the debtor's assets are insufficient to satisfy the claims of all of its creditors, thus raising at least the possibility of competition among the debtor's creditors and stakeholders ([91]).

Modified universalism underpinned the Insolvency Regulation whereas the approach to jurisdiction and recognition in the Lugano Convention was incompatible with principles of modified universalism. The relevant provisions provided a basis or bases for assuming jurisdiction against a person by reference either to that person's place of domicile or the nature of the claim made against that particular person. There were special rules, for example, where the claim was in contract, or tort, or related to insurance or consumer contracts, or employment ([92]–[96]).

'In my judgment, proceedings designed to enable a company in financial difficulties to reach a composition or arrangement . . . with its creditors involves the same peculiar feature as a straightforward bankruptcy or winding-up. The need for the composition or arrangement arises from the company's inability to satisfy the claims of all its creditors. There is inherently competition between the company's creditors, requiring a collective solution that is fair to all . . . In any event, rules which allocate jurisdiction by reference to the domicile of each creditor, or the legal nature of each creditor's claim, or by reference to bi-lateral contractual provisions with different creditors, are as inapposite and impractical in the context of Part 26A proceedings, which are premised on the financial difficulties of the company, as they are for traditional insolvency proceedings ([100]).

Moreover, the judge concluded that proceedings under Part 26A complied with the requirements of Art 1(1) in the Recast Insolvency Regulation. They could have been listed under Annex A were the UK still an EU Member State ([83], [113], [117]).

## RECITAL 16

This recital provides that the Regulation should only apply to proceedings which are based on laws relating to insolvency.

One of the main intentions behind the recast Regulation is that it should apply to a greater range of procedures. The original Regulation was limited to collective insolvency proceedings involving the partial or total disinvestment of the debtor and the appointment of a liquidator. The language of the recast is much broader but the Regulation should not be extended to proceedings based more generally on company law rather than insolvency such as schemes of arrangement under the UK Companies Act. Schemes of arrangement which are used a mechanism to facilitate takeovers may also serve as a form of 'debtor-in-possession' restructuring. The scheme procedure enables a company to enter into a compromise or arrangement with any class of creditors, or members. In this way, the capital structure of an ailing company may be rearranged. The restructuring may involve various elements such as an extension of debt repayments, whole or partial debt forgiveness, and converting debt into shares or share warrants.

There was a full discussion of the relevant considerations applicable to schemes of arrangements by Trower J in *Re Lecta Paper UK Ltd* [2020] EWHC 382 (Ch).

## RECITAL 22

**General note**—This is equivalent to Recital 11 in Regulation 1346/2000.

**Applicable law**—The law of the state in which proceedings are opened is regarded as the law that should be applied in those proceedings. Thus, if proceedings are opened in France, whether main or secondary, the law of France is to be applied. This principle is also stated in Art 7. There are some exceptions to this general rule, eg Art 8.

## RECITALS 23, 24 AND 25

**Main and secondary proceedings**—Under the Regulation it is possible to have more than one proceeding opened in relation to the same debtor. Thus, as stated in the general note, there is no unity of proceedings, but plurality. However, in order to minimise conflict there is a hierarchy of proceedings: there can be only one main proceeding, opened where the debtor has its centre of main interests (COMI), to which to some degree other secondary proceedings are subordinate. There is no limit as to the number of secondary proceedings that may be opened, so long as the requirements of Art 3 are met (and any requirements of the national law where the proceedings are to be opened).

It is clearly stated in Recital 25 that the Regulation applies only where the debtor has its centre of main interests (COMI) in the EU. It should be noted however that the Regulation only establishes international jurisdiction and does not affect national jurisdictional rules. It is the case that within the UK, jurisdiction in insolvency proceedings is determined solely by where the company is registered. Thus in *Bank Leumi (UK) Plc v Screw Conveyor Ltd* [2017] CSOH 129, 2017 SLT 1281, it was held that the Scottish courts did not have jurisdiction to make an administration order in respect of a company that was registered in England but which carried on most of its business in Scotland. Lord Doherty said at para 9: 'the EU Regulation only applies to establish international jurisdiction. The position was the same under the EC Regulation. The Member State the courts of which may open insolvency proceedings is designated, but territorial jurisdiction within that Member State is established by the Member State's national law.'

## RECITAL 26

**Jurisdiction**—Although Art 3 outlines the jurisdiction of the Regulation, this part of the preamble states that national law must still be referred to when a court decides whether it has jurisdiction to open insolvency proceedings.

## RECITALS 27–32

The recast Regulation sticks with the 'centre of main interests' or COMI test as the basis for opening main insolvency proceedings but adds a number of provisions by way of clarification and to combat improper forum shopping.

Forum shopping by individual debtors is often seen as problematic and the practice of German and Irish debtors moving to the UK has attracted particular attention where the evidence for the move seems scanty, incomplete or to be supported by fabricated documentation. A case in point is *Irish Bank Resolution Corp v Quinn* [2012] NI Ch 1, [2012] BPIR 322 and see also *Sparkasse Hilden Ratingen Velbert v Benk* [2012] EWHC 2432 (Ch) where a debtor attempted to shift COMI from the Republic of Ireland to Northern Ireland so to avail himself of the one-year bankruptcy discharge period in Northern Ireland compared with up to 12 years in the Republic. In that case however, the court held that the evidence of the move was insufficient. On the other hand, it must be remembered that genuine relocation involves the exercise of one of the fundamental freedoms guaranteed by the EU Treaties; namely, freedom of movement and is unobjectionable even if it is done to avail of shorter bankruptcy discharge periods in a particular country. For instance, in *Shierson v Vlieland-Boddy* [2005] BCC 949. It was remarked that a debtor must be free to relocate his home and business and that it was a necessary incident of the debtor's freedom that he might choose to do so for a self-serving purpose and at a time when insolvency threatens. The court added however, that it must be a change based on substance and not on illusion.

Recital 32 suggests that in cases of doubt, self-serving assertions about COMI by the debtor should not be taken at face value in the absence of supporting evidence. Recital 30 suggests the

COMI presumption may be rebutted if the principal reason for a debtor to move his habitual residence was to file for insolvency proceeding in a new jurisdiction and such a filing would materially impair the interests of creditors whose dealings with the debtor took place prior to the relocation.

Recital 28 states that in the COMI determination, special consideration should be given to the creditors and their perception as to where a debtor conducts the administration of his interests. It goes on to state that in cases of alleged COMI shifting, this may require informing creditors of the new location from which the debtor is carrying out his activities. This recital stresses a point that that has been made in some of the case law on the original Regulation. In *Irish Bank Resolution Corp v Quinn* [2012] NI Ch 1, [2012] BPIR 322 for instance, it was stated that a debtor may not hide his COMI. The court said that the COMI should be ascertainable by a reasonably diligent creditor.

Recital 30 in the preamble also codifies the case law of the European Court on COMI, particularly statements from the *Interedil* decision Case C-396/09 [2011] ECR I-9915 – that the COMI/ registered office presumption may be rebutted where 'a comprehensive assessment of all the relevant factors establishes, in a manner that is ascertainable by third parties, that the company's actual centre of management and supervision and of the management of its interests' is located in another state.

**RECITAL 88**

**Denmark**—This reflects Recital 33 of Regulation 1346/2000. The terms of the Danish opt-out were considered in *Re Arena Corporation Ltd* [2004] BPIR 375 and it was held that Denmark was not to be considered a 'Member State' for the purposes of the Regulation. Under the Regulation, an English court has no jurisdiction to make a worldwide winding-up order in relation to a company whose centre of main interests is in another Member State but it was held that jurisdiction was not ousted by the Regulation even though the company's centre of main interests was in Denmark. This meant that an English court could exercise its traditional winding-up jurisdiction and make a worldwide winding up order in respect of the company provided that the company had sufficient connection with England.

CHAPTER I   GENERAL PROVISIONS

**[6.3]**

**Article 1** *Scope* **Application and Jurisdiction**
1.   *This Regulation shall apply to public collective proceedings, including interim proceedings, which are based on laws relating to insolvency and in which, for the purpose of rescue, adjustment of debt, reorganisation or liquidation:*

   (a)   *a debtor is totally or partially divested of its assets and an insolvency practitioner is appointed;*

   (b)   *the assets and affairs of a debtor are subject to control or supervision by a court; or*

   (c)   *a temporary stay of individual enforcement proceedings is granted by a court or by operation of law, in order to allow for negotiations between the debtor and its creditors, provided that the proceedings in which the stay is granted provide for suitable measures to protect the general body of creditors, and, where no agreement is reached, are preliminary to one of the proceedings referred to in point (a) or (b).*

*Where the proceedings referred to in this paragraph may be commenced in situations where there is only a likelihood of insolvency, their purpose shall be to avoid the debtor's insolvency or the cessation of the debtor's business activities.*

*The proceedings referred to in this paragraph are listed in Annex A.*

1.   The grounds for jurisdiction to open insolvency proceedings set out in paragraph 1B are in addition to any grounds for jurisdiction to open such proceedings which apply in the laws of any part of the United Kingdom.

1A.   There is jurisdiction to open insolvency proceedings listed in paragraph 1B where the proceedings are opened for the purposes of rescue, adjustment of debt, reorganisation or liquidation and—

   (a)   the centre of the debtor's main interests is in the United Kingdom; or

    (b)    the centre of the debtor's main interests is in a Member State and there is an establishment in the United Kingdom.

1B.  The proceedings referred to in paragraph 1 are—

    (a)    winding up by or subject to the supervision of the court;

    (b)    creditors' voluntary winding up with confirmation by the court;

    (c)    administration, including appointments made by filing prescribed documents with the court;

    (d)    voluntary arrangements under insolvency legislation; and

    (e)    bankruptcy or sequestration.

2.  This Regulation shall not apply to proceedings referred to in paragraph 1 that concern:

    (a)    insurance undertakings;

    (b)    credit institutions;

    (c)    investment firms and other firms, institutions and undertakings to the extent that they are covered by *Directive 2001/24/EC* the Credit Institutions (Reorganisation and Winding up) Regulations 2004; or

    (d)    collective investment undertakings.

**Amendments**—SI 2019/146, as from IP completion day (as defined in the European Union (Withdrawal Agreement) Act 2020, s 39(1)–(5)).

**General note**—One of the main intentions behind the recast Regulation is that it should apply to a greater range of procedures and the language of Article 1 is much broader than Art 1 in the original Regulation which was limited to collective insolvency proceedings involving the partial or total disinvestment of the debtor and the appointment of a liquidator.

The Insolvency Regulation applies to insolvency proceedings; therefore it was held not to apply where the debtor is not insolvent: see *Re Marann Brooks CSV Ltd* [2003] BCC 239, a petition under the public interest ground of Insolvency Act 1986, s 124A.

The court referred to various provisions in the preamble which suggested that the application of the Regulation was limited to winding up proceedings based on the grounds of insolvency. (See also the comments of Briggs J in *Re Rodenstock GmbH* [2011] EWHC 1104 (Ch), [2011] Bus LR 1245 at para 39 that the only form of winding up proceedings 'not affected, in terms of jurisdiction, by either the Insolvency or Judgments Regulations is winding up on the public interest ground. This is because such proceedings are brought in the public interest and are not therefore a 'civil and commercial matter' within the meaning of Art 1(1) of the Judgments Regulation: see *Re Senator Hanseatiche Verwaltungsgesellschaft mbH* [1996] 2 BCLC 562, at 577'.) Winding up by the court is, however, listed in Annex A for the UK and there is no exclusion stated for windings up on public interest grounds.

The application of the Regulation to 'non-insolvency' winding up has also been considered in *Re Arm Asset Backed Securities SA* [2013] EWHC 3351 (Ch) in the context of petitions to wind up a company on the basis that it is just and equitable to do so. The court acknowledged that there were pointers either way in the text of the Regulation and in the case law but it was not necessary to reach a definitive conclusion since the court, in the particular circumstances, could make a winding up order on the grounds of insolvency.

The CJEU looked to the definition of insolvency proceedings in the version of Art 1(1) in the original Regulation in considering what constitutes the opening of insolvency proceedings in the *Eurofood* case – *Re Eurofood IFSC Ltd* Case C-341/04 [2006] ECR I-03813, [2006] Ch 508 on a reference from the Supreme Court of Ireland.

It should be noted that the UNCITRAL Model Law on Cross Border Insolvency and the Cross Border Insolvency Regulations (SI 2006/1030) have been held to apply and allow the recognition of foreign insolvency proceedings if the relevant law under which the foreign proceedings were opened includes insolvency-specific grounds as well as other grounds – see the general discussion in *Re Agrokor* [2017] EWHC 2791 (Ch), [2018] 2 BCLC 75, [2018] BPIR 1 at [55]–[63] and the statement at [63]: 'it is clear that the requirement that the law under which the proceeding is brought be "an insolvency law" is satisfied if insolvency is one of the grounds on which the proceeding can be commenced, even if . . . insolvency could not actually be demonstrated, and there was another basis for commencing the proceeding. The matter is obviously all the clearer if insolvency can indeed be demonstrated.'

But see also *In Re Sturgeon Central Asia Balanced Fund Ltd* [2020] EWHC 123 (Ch), [2020] 1 BCLC 600, where Chief ICC Judge Briggs (sitting as a deputy High Court judge) terminated an order recognising the winding-up of a solvent company in Bermuda under the UNCITRAL Model Law on Cross-Border Insolvency, as implemented by the Cross-Border Insolvency Regulations 2006.

The judgment clarifies that the Model Law and the Cross-Border Insolvency Regulations 2006 apply only to companies which are insolvent or in severe financial distress.

The equivalent of Art 1(2) was considered in *Byers v Yacht Bull Corp* [2010] EWHC 133 (Ch), [2010] BPIR 535. Chancellor Morritt commented that the exception does not relate to investment undertakings generally, nor to investment undertakings providing any services to third parties but only to those investment undertakings which provide services to third parties of the relevant description 'services involving the holding of funds or securities for third parties'. He said that any other conclusion would ignore the express words of the Article. The exceptions in Art 1(2) are largely, though not entirely, the same as those in the original Regulation. According to recital 19 of the preamble (recital 9 of original) the specified undertakings are not covered since they are subject to special arrangements and partially at least 'national supervisory authorities have extremely wide-ranging powers of intervention'. Article 1(2) was considered briefly in *Lady Moon SPV SRL v Petricca and Co Capital Ltd* [2019] EWHC 439 (Ch).

The judge at para 29 pointed out that unlike credit institutions and insurance undertakings, which are also outside the ambit of the recast Insolvency Regulation collective investment undertakings are not the subject of any other EU insolvency regulations relevant to jurisdiction. There are no harmonised European rules on the recognition of insolvency proceedings involving collective investment undertakings and they are left solely to national supervision and regulation.

In the recast Regulation, the 'investment firms' exception has been narrowed so that now it only applies to investment firms and other firms, institutions and undertakings to the extent that they are covered by the Credit Institutions Directive – Directive 2001/24/EC. In other words, the scope of application of the Insolvency Regulation has been expanded and this point was noted implicitly by Hildyard J in *Re Lehman Brothers International (Europe)* [2018] EWHC 1980 (Ch). Under the previous regime there was the possibility that investment firms and undertakings might be subject neither to the Insolvency Regulation nor to the Credit Institutions Insolvency Directive – see also *Re Worldspreads Ltd* [2012] EWHC 1263 (Ch) but this possibility no longer appears to be available.

The 'credit institutions' exception and the sector-specific measures applicable to credit institutions have been considered by the Supreme Court in *Goldman Sachs International v Novo Banco SA* [2016] UKSC 34, [2018] 1 WLR 3683. The court recognised that the credit institutions regime imposed a greater measure of universality than under the Insolvency Regulation and cautioned against adopting interpretations that would undermine the scheme of universal recognition of measures taken by the home Member State to deal with failing financial institutions.

Lord Sumption said at para 2: 'Any pan-European scheme for dealing with the systemic risks of bank failures must depend for its efficacy on the widest possible recognition of a home state's measures in other jurisdictions where banks in the course of reorganisation may have interests or assets or under whose laws it may have contracted.' Lord Sumption also pointed out that the Bank Resolution and Recovery Directive had amended the Credit Institutions Directive so that it applied to measures taken in accordance with the new tools that Member States were required to equip themselves. Provision was also made for co-operation among Member States in giving effect to those measures.

Lord Sumption also pointed out that the Bank Resolution and Recovery Directive had amended the Credit Institutions Directive so that it applied to measures taken in accordance with the new tools that Member States were required to equip themselves. Provision was also made for co-operation among Member States in giving effect to those measures.

## [6.4]

### Article 2  Definitions
For the purposes of this Regulation:

> (1)  'collective proceedings' means proceedings which include all or a significant part of a debtor's creditors, provided that, in the latter case, the proceedings do not affect the claims of creditors which are not involved in them;

> (1A)  'Member State' means a state which is a member of the EU other than Denmark.

> (2)  'collective investment undertakings' means undertakings for collective investment in transferable securities (UCITS) as defined in Directive 2009/65/EC of the European Parliament and of the Council[1] and alternative investment funds (AIFs) as defined in Directive 2011/61/EU of the European Parliament and of the Council[2].

> (3)  'debtor in possession' means a debtor in respect of which insolvency proceedings have been opened which do not necessarily involve the appointment of an insolvency practitioner or the complete transfer of

the rights and duties to administer the debtor's assets to an insolvency practitioner and where, therefore, the debtor remains totally or at least partially in control of its assets and affairs;

(4) 'insolvency proceedings' means the proceedings *listed in Annex A* listed in Article 1(1B) which there is jurisdiction to open under Article 1(1A) and includes interim proceedings;

(5) 'insolvency practitioner' means any person or body whose function, including on an interim basis, is to:

    (i)     verify and admit claims submitted in insolvency proceedings;

    (ii)    represent the collective interest of the creditors;

    (iii)   administer, either in full or in part, assets of which the debtor has been divested;

    (iv)   liquidate the assets referred to in point (iii); or

    (v)    supervise the administration of the debtor's affairs.

The persons and bodies referred to in the first subparagraph are listed in Annex B;

(6) 'court' means:

    *(i)*     *in points (b) and (c) of Article 1(1), Article 4(2), Articles 5 and 6, Article 21(3), point (j) of Article 24(2), Articles 36 and 39, and Articles 61 to 77, the judicial body of a Member State;*

    *(ii)*    *in all other articles*, the judicial body or any other competent body *of a Member State* empowered to open insolvency proceedings, to confirm such opening or to take decisions in the course of such proceedings;

(7) 'judgment opening insolvency proceedings' includes:

    (i)     the decision of any court to open insolvency proceedings or to confirm the opening of such proceedings; and

    (ii)    the decision of a court to appoint an insolvency practitioner;

(8) 'the time of the opening of proceedings' means the time at which the judgment opening insolvency proceedings becomes effective, regardless of whether the judgment is final or not;

*(9)*   *'the Member State in which assets are situated' means, in the case of:*

    *(i)*     *registered shares in companies other than those referred to in point (ii), the Member State within the territory of which the company having issued the shares has its registered office;*

    *(ii)*    *financial instruments, the title to which is evidenced by entries in a register or account maintained by or on behalf of an intermediary ('book entry securities'), the Member State in which the register or account in which the entries are made is maintained;*

    *(iii)*   *cash held in accounts with a credit institution, the Member State indicated in the account's IBAN, or, for cash held in accounts with a credit institution which does not have an IBAN, the Member State in which the credit institution holding the account has its central administration or, where the account is held with a branch, agency or other establishment, the Member State in which the branch, agency or other establishment is located;*

    *(iv)*   *property and rights, ownership of or entitlement to which is entered in a public register other than those referred to in point (i), the Member State under the authority of which the register is kept;*

    *(v)*    *European patents, the Member State for which the European patent is granted;*

    *(vi)*   *copyright and related rights, the Member State within the territory of which the owner of such rights has its habitual residence or registered office;*

    *(vii)*   tangible property, other than that referred to in points (i) to (iv), the Member State within the territory of which the property is situated;

> (viii) *claims against third parties, other than those relating to assets referred to in point (iii), the Member State within the territory of which the third party required to meet the claims has the centre of its main interests, as determined in accordance with Article 3(1);*
>
> (10) 'establishment' means any place of operations where a debtor carries out or has carried out in the 3-month period prior to the request to open *main* insolvency proceedings a non-transitory economic activity with human means and assets;
>
> (11) *'local creditor' means a creditor whose claims against a debtor arose from or in connection with the operation of an establishment situated in a Member State other than the Member State in which the centre of the debtor's main interests is located;*
>
> (12) *'foreign creditor' means a creditor which has its habitual residence, domicile or registered office in a Member State other than the State of the opening of proceedings, including the tax authorities and social security authorities of Member States;*
>
> (13) *'group of companies' means a parent undertaking and all its subsidiary undertakings;*
>
> (14) *'parent undertaking' means an undertaking which controls, either directly or indirectly, one or more subsidiary undertakings. An undertaking which prepares consolidated financial statements in accordance with Directive 2013/34/EU of the European Parliament and of the Council[3] shall be deemed to be a parent undertaking.*

[1]  Directive 2009/65/EC of the European Parliament and of the Council of 13 July 2009 on the coordination of laws, regulations and administrative provisions relating to undertakings for collective investment in transferable securities (UCITS) (OJ L 302, 17.11.2009, p 32).

[2]  Directive 2011/61/EU of the European Parliament and of the Council of 8 June 2011 on Alternative Investment Fund Managers and amending Directives 2003/41/EC and 2009/65/EC and Regulations (EC) No 1060/2009 and (EU) No 1095/2010 (OJ L 174, 1.7.2011, p 1).

[3]  Directive 2013/34/EU of the European Parliament and of the Council of 26 June 2013 on the annual financial statements, consolidated financial statements and related reports of certain types of undertaking, amending Directive 2006/43/EC of the European Parliament and of the Council and repealing Council Directives 78/660/EEC and 83/349/EEC (OJ L 182, 29.6.2013, p 19).

**Amendments**—SI 2019/146, as from IP completion day (as defined in the European Union (Withdrawal Agreement) Act 2020, s 39(1)–(5)).

### ARTICLE 2(3)

The extension of the Insolvency Regulation to debtor in possession proceedings is quite significant and brings it into line with the UNCITRAL Model Law on Cross-Border insolvency.

### ARTICLE 2(4)

The annexes may be over-inclusive in that they cover procedures that strictly speaking do not satisfy the Art 1(1) definition though the broader language used in Art 1(1) should help to minimize the risk of any mismatches. It should be noted that schemes of arrangement under the UK Companies Act are not listed in Annex A and see *Re Drax Holdings Ltd* [2004] BCLC 10 and *Re Rodenstock GmbH* [2011] EWHC 1104 (Ch), [2011] Bus LR 1245.

It is the case on the basis of Art 2(4) and the *Eurofood* judgment – Case C-341/04 *Re Eurofood IFSC Ltd* [2006] ECR I-03813, [2006] Ch 508 that once a proceeding is listed in the Annex it is entitled to recognition. This interpretation provides certainty and was confirmed by the CJEU in Case C-116/11 *Bank Handlowy and Adamiak* [2013] BPIR 174. The court said that, once proceedings are listed in Annex A to the Regulation, they must be regarded as coming within the scope of the Regulation. 'Inclusion in the list has the direct, binding effect attaching to the provisions of a regulation.' The court added that a debtor in respect of which insolvency proceedings have been opened must be regarded as being in a situation of insolvency for the purposes of application of the Regulation.

Annex A may be under-inclusive in that certain procedures in certain EU states may satisfy the Art 1(1) definition but are not listed in the Annex. There is also a time lag in that State may introduce a new insolvency procedure but some time elapses before it appears in the Annex. See in this connection the judgment of Zacaroli J in *Re Gategroup Guarantee Ltd* [2021] EWHC 304 (Ch) ([79]).

In Case C-461/11 *Ulf Kazimierz Radziejewski* (8 November 2012) the European Court suggested that the Insolvency Regulation applied only to the proceedings listed in the Annex. This interpretation is supported by Recital 9 of the preamble to the recast.

## ARTICLE 2(6), (7)

It is clear from these provisions that, in most situations, the notion of 'court' is to be interpreted widely. It does not just mean a judicial authority but includes a person or judicial body empowered by national law to open insolvency proceedings. The Virgos-Schmit Report on the draft EU Convention on Insolvency Proceedings (which preceded and foreshadowed the provisions of the Regulation) suggested that the expression was to be construed in a very broad sense as covering (para 66): ' . . . not only the judiciary or an authority which plays a similar role to that of a court or public authority . . . but a person or body empowered by national law to open proceedings or make decisions in the course of those proceedings'.

Thus a creditors' voluntary winding up is within the Regulation and the general meeting of members voting for the winding up comes within the definition of court. Therefore the resolution passing the motion for a winding up will be a judgment for the purposes of the Regulation. It is clear from Annex A that voluntary arrangements come within the Regulation even though they do not involve confirmation by the court. So the meaning of court encompasses the meeting of creditors and the resolution is the judgment for the purposes of the Regulation.

Given the wide definition, it seems also that the appointment of administrator out of court should be regarded as a judgment opening insolvency proceeding. It should also be remembered that under the Insolvency Act, an administrator is deemed to be an officer of the court, whether or not he is actually appointed by the court – Sch B1, para 5.

## ARTICLE 2(8)

For the purposes of the Regulation the time the judgment opening proceedings becomes effective is not to be confused with the presentation of a petition, eg for the winding up of a company. The crucial point is when the judgment becomes effective. In *Eurofood* [2006] Ch 508 at para 93 Advocate General Jacobs suggested that the filing of a winding-up petition might be taken to mark the commencement of proceedings. On the other hand, the presentation of the petition does not, of itself, involve the divestment of assets and there is no certainty that a winding up order will actually be made on foot of the petition.

In the case of a creditors' voluntary winding up that is confirmed by the court, there is the question of when the proceedings are actually opened for the purpose of the Regulation. On one view the proceedings are only deemed to be opened once the court confirmation is given. Since there would not be a proceeding within the Regulation in the absence of court confirmation, the proceedings will not be regarded as opened until there has been court confirmation of the creditors' voluntary winding up. But alternatively, one could argue from the wording of the Insolvency Rules that the court process is merely rubber stamping something that has already happened and therefore the proceedings have been opened at an earlier point in time.

The influential Virgos-Schmit Report however at para 68, while pointing out the importance of the time of opening of proceedings as many questions are settled by reference to it, states that only 'in order to allow the liquidator to exercise his powers [in another State] would it be necessary to take the date of confirmation by the court as the reference'.

## ARTICLE 2(9)

Article 2(9) contains rules on the 'localization' of assets and is much more comprehensive than the provision it replaces – Art 2(g) of Regulation 1346/2000.

The guidance given by the CJEU in relation to the former Art 2(g) in Case C649/13 *Nortel Networks SA v Rogeau* (11 June 2015) is also likely to apply in relation to Art 2(9). The CJEU held that both the court opening main proceedings and the court opening secondary proceedings has jurisdiction to rule on the location of assets on the basis of the rules set out in the regulation. The court noted that both courts will apply the same set of rules – thereby minimizing the risk of incompatible judgments – and also suggested that the Article establishes a hierarchy of rules that must be applied (para 54). The Advocate General implied that the rules in the Article were exhaustive but it is not clear whether the court endorsed the same approach.

## ARTICLE 2(10)

This provision establishes a genuine 'look back' period. By virtue of the provision, even if the debtor does not have an 'establishment' in a particular state when application is made to open secondary proceedings, these secondary proceedings may still be opened if the necessary establishment existed at the time of the opening of the main proceedings or three months beforehand. The fact that the necessary time frame is calculated by reference to the main proceedings means that a different result would be reached in *Re Olympic Airlines SA* [2015] UKSC 27.

In this case, the debtor airline had gone into main liquidation proceedings in Greece before the application to commence secondary proceedings in England and during that time the affairs of the company were being wound down. Under the 'old' Regulation whether secondary proceedings could be opened depended on whether there was an establishment in England at the time of the application to open the secondary proceedings, The Supreme Court held that the definition of 'establishment' required more economic activity than the mere process of winding up and therefore no secondary proceedings could be opened. There had to be activities which by their nature involved business dealings with third parties – external, market-facing activities (para 13).Article 2(10) requires these market-facing activities at the time the main proceedings were opened in Greece. This test is clearly satisfied since the airline was trading at the time.

## [6.5]

### Article 3 *International jurisdiction* Centre of main interests

1.   *The courts of the Member State within the territory of which the centre of the debtor's main interests is situated shall have jurisdiction to open insolvency proceedings ('main insolvency proceedings').*The centre of main interests shall be the place where the debtor conducts the administration of its interests on a regular basis and which is ascertainable by third parties.

In the case of a company or legal person, the place of the registered office shall be presumed to be the centre of its main interests in the absence of proof to the contrary. That presumption shall only apply if the registered office has not been moved *to another Member State* from the United Kingdom to a Member State or to the United Kingdom from a Member State within the 3-month period prior to the request for the opening of insolvency proceedings.

In the case of an individual exercising an independent business or professional activity, the centre of main interests shall be presumed to be that individual's principal place of business in the absence of proof to the contrary. That presumption shall only apply if the individual's principal place of business has not been moved *to another Member State* from the United Kingdom to a Member State or to the United Kingdom from a Member State within the 3-month period prior to the request for the opening of insolvency proceedings.

In the case of any other individual, the centre of main interests shall be presumed to be the place of the individual's habitual residence in the absence of proof to the contrary. This presumption shall only apply if the habitual residence has not been moved *to another Member State* from the United Kingdom to a Member State or to the United Kingdom from a Member State within the 6-month period prior to the request for the opening of insolvency proceedings.

2.   *Where the centre of the debtor's main interests is situated within the territory of a Member State, the courts of another Member State shall have jurisdiction to open insolvency proceedings against that debtor only if it possesses an establishment within the territory of that other Member State. The effects of those proceedings shall be restricted to the assets of the debtor situated in the territory of the latter Member State.*

3.   *Where insolvency proceedings have been opened in accordance with paragraph 1, any proceedings opened subsequently in accordance with paragraph 2 shall be secondary insolvency proceedings.*

4.   *The territorial insolvency proceedings referred to in paragraph 2 may only be opened prior to the opening of main insolvency proceedings in accordance with paragraph 1 where*

    *(a)*    *insolvency proceedings under paragraph 1 cannot be opened because of the conditions laid down by the law of the Member State within the territory of which the centre of the debtor's main interests is situated; or*

    *(b)*    *the opening of territorial insolvency proceedings is requested by:*

        *(i)*    *a creditor whose claim arises from or is in connection with the operation of an establishment situated within the territory of the Member State where the opening of territorial proceedings is requested; or*

        *(ii)*    *a public authority which, under the law of the Member State within the territory of which the establishment is situated, has the right to request the opening of insolvency proceedings.*

*When main insolvency proceedings are opened, the territorial insolvency proceedings shall become secondary insolvency proceedings.*

**Amendments**—SI 2019/146, as from IP completion day (as defined in the European Union (Withdrawal Agreement) Act 2020, s 39(1)–(5)).

**General note**—Like its predecessor, the recast Regulation confers jurisdiction to open main insolvency proceedings on the State where the debtor has its centre of main interests (COMI) but there has been considerable criticism of the COMI concept as the basis for opening main insolvency proceedings. This criticism is based on the proposition that COMI is inherently variable and fact sensitive and may give to conflicting judicial interpretations. If a relevant party considers that the opening of insolvency proceedings in a particular jurisdiction will favour its case but there are doubts about the COMI location, it makes sense to put aside these doubts and file in the 'favoured' jurisdiction. In marginal cases, a court may well be inclined to assert, rather than to decline jurisdiction. COMI is the centrepiece of the Regulation for it determines not only jurisdiction to open main insolvency proceedings but also applicable law in most cases. Given this importance, the decided cases provide many of examples of purported COMI shifts in anticipation of an insolvency filing – 'forum shopping'.

The COMI concept is in some respects a compromise between the rival 'real seat' and 'incorporation' theories of jurisdiction in respect of companies. Under the 'real seat' theory, the law applying to the internal affairs of a company is the law of the country where it has its so-called 'real seat', ie its effective central administration, whereas the incorporation doctrine refers to the law of the state of incorporation. Common law countries apply the incorporation theory but the majority of civil law countries apply the 'real seat' theory.

COMI appears closely akin to the concept of 'real seat' but there is a nod in the direction of the incorporation theory by a presumption that, in the case of company, COMI is the same as the place of the registered office. This presumption however may be rebutted. The recast Regulation could have introduced greater certainly by making the 'COMI equals registered office' presumption rebuttable only in extreme circumstances or else by replacing COMI with a place of incorporation or place of the registered office test. However, the COMI concept is also found in the UNCITRAL Model Law on Cross-Border Insolvency at Art 16 – and importing a new test into the Insolvency Regulation would introduce an unwelcome degree of international divergence. Moreover, even within the EU there may be so-called 'letterbox' companies with little or no connection with their place of incorporation and having insolvency proceedings in the country of incorporation seems very much at variance with the factual realities on the ground.

What is completely new in Art 3(1) of the recast Regulation is the introduction of so-called 'look back' periods though these provisions do no more than state that a presumption that would have otherwise applied to determine COMI will not apply. This unlike the position with Art 2(10) on the definition of 'establishment', which applies a genuine look back rule.

In the case of individuals exercising an independent business or professional activity, COMI is presumed to be the individual's principal place of business except where the principal place of business has moved to another state within three months prior to the request for the opening of insolvency proceedings. In the case of any other individual, COMI is presumed to be the place of the individual's habitual residence save where the habitual residence has moved within six months prior to the request for the opening of insolvency proceedings. The implication is that where the previous principal place of business or habitual residence has moved during the look back period then there is no presumption one way or the other about COMI which should be determined on the totality of the evidence.

For companies, the COMI/registered office presumption only applies if the registered office has not been moved to another state within three months prior to the request for the opening of insolvency proceedings. COMI shifting can easily occur however, without moving the registered office and it may be that the new provision will have little effect in practice. Significant importance however, was placed on the registered office/COMI presumption in the recent case of *Re Melars Group Ltd* [2021] EWHC 1523 (Ch). In this case Miles J overturned a winding-up order made by Deputy ICC Judge Baister [2020] EWHC 2090 (Ch). This was done largely on the basis that the first instance judge had effectively disregarded the registered office presumption in favour of Malta and decided between two rival locations for COMI, England and Switzerland opting for England. On appeal therefore, the English winding up order was lifted. In this case, the relevant company had been incorporated in the British Virgin Islands but its registered office had been moved from there to Malta.

In general, however, English courts, when asked to open insolvency proceedings on the basis of the debtor's centre of main interests, have taken an expansive approach on matters of jurisdiction. In a sense, the decision in *Re Daisytek-ISA Ltd* [2004] BPIR 30 while providing valuable guidance on the identification of the debtor's 'main interests', also serves as a case study of this expansive approach. Furthermore, the decision highlights the issue of whether in practice courts in a different Member State will, nevertheless, recognise the decision of courts in another Member State as to the location of a debtor's centre of main interests, especially when the other decision seems counter-intuitive.

In *Re Daisytek-ISA Ltd*, Daisytek-ISA Ltd was the holding company of a group of trading companies – including French and German-incorporated subsidiaries – and the question arose whether an English court had jurisdiction to make an administration order in respect of each of the companies on the basis that their centre of main interests was in England, notwithstanding the foreign incorporation. In a bold decision, Judge McGonigal answered this question in the affirmative. His Lordship held that the court was required to consider the scale of the interests administered at a particular place and their importance and then to consider the scale and importance of its interests administered at any other place that might be regarded as its centre of main interests. On the evidence he took the view that the majority of the group's administration was conducted from its head office in Bradford and, therefore, England was the centre of main interests for each subsidiary within the group. In determining the centre of main interests of each subsidiary, Judge McGonigal held that the most important 'third parties' referred to in Recital 13 are the potential creditors. He added that in the case of a trading company the most important groups of potential creditors are likely to be financiers and its trade suppliers and the value of the debts, rather than the numerical majority of creditors, was the relevant criterion.

The expansive approach of the English courts towards jurisdiction under the EU Regulation is also demonstrated by *Re BRAC Rent-A-Car International Inc* [2003] 1 WLR 1421where it was held that an English court had jurisdiction under the Regulation to grant an administration order in respect of a non-EU company where its centre of main interests was in England. In this case the company was incorporated in Delaware in the US but it had no employees in the US. All of its employees worked in England and with contracts of employment governed by English law apart from a small number in a branch office in Switzerland. All the company's trading activities were carried out by way of contracts with subsidiaries and franchisees that were governed by English law. Lloyd J decided that in the circumstances an English court had jurisdiction. In his view, by dint of both a literal reading and also a purposive interpretation of the Regulation, the only test for the application of the Regulation in relation to a given debtor is whether the centre of the debtor's main interests is in a relevant Member State and where a debtor that is a legal person is incorporated.

There are decisions, however, where the English courts have declined jurisdiction. For example, in *Hans Brochier Holdings Ltd v Exner* [2007] BCC 127 it was decided that the centre of main interests of an English incorporated company was in Germany. The main creditors of the company were located in Germany and these creditors regarded the company as operating out of Germany and fully expected any insolvency proceedings to take place in Germany. HBH had over 700 employees in Germany and only a few in England. Moreover, almost all the company employees were employed in Germany and under contracts of employment governed by German law. Warren J also pointed out that there were perceived benefits accruing if the main proceedings were in Germany. There was a large advantage in relation to German social security law, which would give the employees a significant advantage as compared with an English administration and only an experienced German insolvency administrator would be able adequately to address those rights and interests. The company's entire business operations were run out of its German headquarters so that all the relevant information and documents were located in Germany. The vast majority of these documents were in the German language and most of the legal and contractual relationships of the company were subject to German law.

## APPROACH OF THE EUROPEAN COURT OF JUSTICE

In the *Eurofood* case (Case C-341/04 [2006] ECR I-03813) the CJEU also considered the question of 'centre of main interests'. Eurofood was an Irish-incorporated wholly owned subsidiary of Parmalat, a major global food company incorporated in Italy, and its principal business activity was that of providing financing facilities for companies in the Parmalat group. The company enjoyed tax benefits conditional upon it being managed and operated in Ireland. Moreover, the day-to-day administration of Eurofood was conducted in Ireland in accordance with the terms of an agreement, which was governed by Irish law and which contained an Irish jurisdiction clause. Following the financial troubles experienced by the Parmalat group as a whole, a petition was presented to the Irish High Court seeking the winding up of Eurofood; on the same day an application to appoint a provisional liquidator was successfully made. Some three weeks later, however, an Italian court made an order pursuant to the Insolvency Regulation opening main insolvency proceedings in respect of Eurofood on the basis that its centre of main interests was in Italy. The Irish court on the hearing of the winding-up petition took a different view. The *Eurofood* case was appealed to the Irish Supreme Court [2005] BCC 999 which referred certain matters to the CJEU for a preliminary ruling including issues concerning the concept of 'centre of main interests'.

The court responded by saying that the concept had an autonomous meaning for the purpose of the Regulation and must be interpreted independently of national legislation. There was a presumption that the centre of main interests of a company was in the state where its registered office was located and this presumption applied even if the company had a parent company with a registered office in a different state. The presumption could only be rebutted:

' . . . if factors which are both objective and ascertainable by third parties enable it to be established that an actual situation exists which is different from that which locating it at that registered office is deemed to reflect. That could be so in particular in the case of a company not carrying out any business in the territory of the Member State in which its registered office is situated. By contrast, where a company carries on its business in the territory of the Member State where its registered office is situated, the mere fact that its economic choices are or can be controlled by a parent company in another Member State is not enough to rebut the presumption laid down by the Regulation.'

The court referred to 'letter box' countries not carrying on any business in the countries where their registered offices were located. In these circumstances, the presumption of concordance between registered office and centre of main interests was easily rebutted, but not so more generally, unless there were factors that were both 'objective and ascertainable by third parties' (see para 35).

The CJEU had the opportunity to revisit the COMI issue in the Italian *Interedil* case Case C-396/09, [2011] BPIR 1639. In a somewhat opaque passage the court referred to a situation where 'from the viewpoint of third parties, the place in which a company's central administration is located is not the same as that of its registered office'. The presumption in favour of the registered office could be rebutted if (paras 52, 53):

'factors which are both objective and ascertainable by third parties enable it to be established that an actual situation exists which is different from that which locating it at that registered office is deemed to reflect. The factors to be taken into account include, in particular, all the places in which the debtor company pursues economic activities and all those in which it holds assets, in so far as those places are ascertainable by third parties . . . those factors must be assessed in a comprehensive manner, account being taken of the individual circumstances of each particular case.'

It seemed to confirm the opinion of Advocate General Kokott that the lease of property and the existence of banking facilities in another EC State were insufficient facts by themselves to rebut the registered office COMI presumption.

The *Mediasucre* reference (Case C-191/10; OJ 2012 C39/3) from the French Cour de Cassation raised the issues of the inter-relationship between the COMI test and national laws that permit the substantive consolidation of insolvency proceedings. The CJEU was asked to consider:

(i)  whether rules of substantive consolidation remain effective only if the company to be joined to the insolvency proceedings has its COMI in the Member State where the first company has been placed into insolvency proceedings; and

(ii) if this is the case, whether it can be automatically inferred, solely from the finding that the property of the two companies has been intermixed, that the company which is to be joined to the proceedings has the same COMI as the first company.

The CJEU answered the first question in the affirmative stating that otherwise there would be a risk of conflicting claims to jurisdiction between courts of different Member States. The Regulation was specifically intended to prevent this in order to ensure uniform treatment of insolvency proceedings within the EU. The second question was answered in the negative. The court referred to the presumption that the registered office is the COMI. In order to reverse this presumption, it had to be established on the basis of an overall assessment of all the relevant factors (para 39):

'in a manner ascertainable by third parties, that the actual centre of management and supervision of the company concerned by the joinder action is situated in the Member State where the initial insolvency proceedings were opened'.

The court said that the intermixing of property did not necessarily imply a single centre of main interests. Indeed, such intermixing could be organised from two management and supervision centres in two different Member States.

## GROUPS OF COMPANIES AND THE 'HEAD OFFICE FUNCTIONS' TEST

The overall approach of the CJEU in *Eurofood* seems somewhat different from the 'integrated economic unit' approach that English courts have appeared to follow when determining the centre of main interests of parent and subsidiary companies. The English courts have tended to look at the affairs of the group of companies as a whole, whereas the CJEU has concentrated the inquiry onto each individual company. Moreover, the fact that the economic purse-strings of a subsidiary are pulled from group headquarters does not of itself alter the centre of its main interests. It may be however that the comments by the court leave enough 'wriggle room' for the English courts to continue with their existing approach. It must also be remembered that the observations of the court must be read with reference to the questions referred to it by the national court.

There is a strong argument that one should acknowledge the reality of multinational corporate groups. If one applies the COMI test to each individual company within a corporate group then insolvency proceedings in relation to different group companies may, or may not, be handled in a single jurisdiction by the same court. But with the recognition of only one COMI, a corporate group could be subject to a single main insolvency proceeding. This should have the effect of improving the coordination and administration of the global estate and the net recoveries for creditors. The ability to file insolvency proceedings in respect of all group companies in the same jurisdiction brings carries brings significant strategic advantages in that a coordinated sale or restructuring plan can be developed for the entire group. At the same time, one maintains the flexibility to deal with specific local problems where this is appropriate.

In *Eurofood* Advocate General Jacobs, though not the CJEU itself, appeared to endorse a 'head office functions' test when determining the centre of main interests in the case of a group of companies. He added, however, that the focus must be on the head office functions rather than simply on the location of the head office because a 'head office' could be just as nominal as a registered office if head office functions were not carried out there. In transnational business the registered office was often chosen for tax or regulatory reasons and had no real connection with the place where head office functions were performed (*Re Eurofood IFSC Ltd* Case C-341/04 [2006] ECR I-03813, para 111 of the opinion of the Advocate General).

This test has been used by a French court in *MPOTEC Gmbh* [2006] BCC 681. The court suggested that one should refer to the concept of head-office functions for the determination of the centre of main interests. It was suggested that the notion of head-office functions was founded on the following elements:

- the place of meetings of the board of directors;
- the law governing the main contracts;
- the location of business relations with clients;
- the place where the commercial policy of the group is defined;
- the existence of a prior authorisation from the parent company to enter into certain financial arrangements;
- the location of bank creditors; and
- the centralised management of purchasing policy, staff, accounts and computing systems.

Applying this guidance, the court decided that a German incorporated member of a French group of companies had its centre of main interests in France.

In *Re Lennox Holdings Ltd* [2009] BCC 155, Lewison J applied a 'head office functions' test in deciding that an English court had jurisdiction to enter main insolvency proceedings in respect of two companies whose registered offices were in Spain. He suggested that the particular examples given by the CJEU in *Eurofood* were at two opposite and extreme ends of the spectrum and the facts of most cases lie somewhere between these two extremes. For this reason, it was suggested that the approach of Advocate General Jacobs was a particularly helpful one.

Lewison J has since resiled from this view in *Re Stanford International Bank Ltd* [2009] BPIR 1157. He said that this approach was not consistent with the decision of the CJEU itself, which emphasised that COMI must be identified by reference to criteria that are both objective and ascertainable by third parties and that the presumption in favour of COMI coinciding with the company's registered office could only be rebutted by factors that are both objective and ascertainable by third parties.

Simply to look at the place where head office functions are actually carried out, without considering whether the location of these functions is ascertainable by third parties, is the wrong.

Lewison J took the view that an important purpose of COMI was to provide certainty and foreseeability for creditors of the company at the time they enter into a transaction. He looked at Recital 13 and the statement of the CJEU that COMI has to be identified by reference to criteria that are objective and ascertainable by third parties. Information would only count as ascertainable if it was in the public domain. It was not enough that it would have been disclosed as an honest answer to a question asked by a third party. Lewison J suggested that there would be a quite unrealistic burden if every transaction had to be preceded by a set of inquiries to establish whether the underlying reality differed from the apparent facts. In the *Stanford* case it was held that the COMI of an Antiguan-registered corporation was in Antigua. Quite simply there was insufficient evidence to rebut the presumption but it is important to note that the case does not involve a 'letter box' company. The company clearly carried out economic activity in Antigua not least by reason of the facts that its physical headquarters were in Antigua and most of its employees were located there.

The decision of Lewison J was confirmed in the *Stanford* case on appeal. Arden LJ however, commented ([2010] BPIR 679 at para 152):

'In determining the location of the COMI, the key question appears to be where the head office functions are based. The COMI must be determined on an objective basis and be ascertainable by third parties. It does not appear to be a question of where the principal place of business is conducted since this would give rise to uncertainty. There can in principle only be one place where head office functions are carried out, and that makes it easier to identify the COMI. The test is designed to achieve speed and ease of recognition. There are, however, difficulties in the test . . . '

The *Eurofood* presumption that the COMI is the situation of the registered office was held however to have been rebutted in *Re Kaupthing Capital Partners II Master LP Inx* [2010] EWHC 836 (Ch). The case concerned a Guernsey limited partnership (M) that was established as a special purpose vehicle to be used in connection with an investment fund and part of a larger group of companies (the Kaupthing group). M maintained registered offices in Guernsey but day-to-day activities were managed by its operator in London – another legal entity within the Kaupthing group, and certain administrative functions were delegated to other companies within the Kaupthing group. In deciding whether the presumption had been rebutted, Proudman J looked to Recital 13 of the Regulation and asked what was ascertainable by third parties though the investors in the funds were not regarded as the type of third parties that *Eurofood* or the Court of Appeal in *Stanford* had in mind. These investors were insiders within the partnership, equivalent to company shareholders rather than persons doing business with the partnership. The judge held however that creditors of the partnership were to be regarded as 'third parties' and, on the facts, it would have been apparent to creditors that their debtors' affairs were being conducted in London on the partnership's behalf.

More controversially, the registered office/Eurofood presumption was held to have been rebutted in *Re European Directories* [2010] EWHC 3472 (Ch), [2012] BCC 46. In this case an administration order was made in respect of an insolvent Dutch company whose head office was in London. The evidence was held to rebut the presumption that its centre of main interests was in the Netherlands though all the parties before the court were effectively in agreement that the COMI in the UK. What is interesting is that the court in essence used a multi-factor balancing test of the sort used by the US courts in *Re Bear Stearns* ((2007) 374 BR 122 and affirmed (2008) 389 BR 325) in a case under the US version of the UNCITRAL Model Law on Cross-Border Insolvency – Chapter 15 of the US Bankruptcy Code. In *Re Bear Stearns* Judge Lifland said except in circumstances where there is no contrary evidence, the location of the registered office did not have any special evidentiary value. It appears that COMI in the US is determined by where the most material contacts are to be found, especially management direction and control of assets. These contacts include the location of the debtor's headquarters, the location of those who actually manage the debtor, the location of the debtor's primary assets, the location of a majority of the debtor's creditors or of a majority of creditors who would be affected by the case and the jurisdiction whose law would apply to most disputes.

The registered office equals COMI presumption was also held to have been rebutted in *Re Northsea Base Investment Ltd* [2015] EWHC 121 (Ch) where the COMI of seven Cypriot registered companies was held to have been in England even though none of the directors were based in England, and board meetings were not held in England. In deciding that the presumption had been rebutted, the court placed particular emphasis on the position of the largest creditors – the banks. The loan facilities were governed by English law and contained English jurisdiction clauses, and the banks dealt with an English based shipping agent in relation to receipt of payments. Given the fact that the evidence pointed in different directions, it may be that on the same facts a court in a different Member State would come to a different conclusion on the location of COMI.

In determining COMI, it seems that more a head office functions/ascertainability test rather than a multi-factor balancing was applied in *Re Arm Asset Backed Securities SA* [2013] EWHC 3351 (Ch). The case concerned a company with a registered office in Luxembourg and whose sole business was to issue bonds to investors and then to invest the moneys in the purchase of life insurance policies in the US that were held through a US trust. The US trustee paid the insurance premiums, collected the sums due under the policies and remitted the net proceeds to the company thereby enabling it to service the bonds. It was held on an uncontested application that the COMI was in England rather than in Luxembourg despite the fact that only one of three directors were resident in England. David Richards J said that the decisions which governed the administration and management of the company were taken in London with the director based in London being primarily involved in the affairs of the company. That person was responsible for communication of the decisions of the company to agents and professional advisors. Those persons looked to London for directions.

See also *Thomas v Frogmore Real Estate Partners* [2017] EWHC 25 (Ch) where the COMI of three Jersey registered companies was held to be in the UK even though board meetings had been held in Jersey. The judge pointed out that under an advisory agreement that was governed by English law, an agent was to take on full responsibility for providing a very large range of services to the companies. Those actions included the types of function that a head office would be expected to discharge and day-to-day dealings with third parties were carried out from the agent's offices in London. Referring to the board meetings held in Jersey, a third party would not have known where they were taking place.

The COMI test in the context of the Cross Border Insolvency Regulations (CBIR) and the Model Law on Cross Border Insolvency Law has recently been considered in *Re Videology Ltd* [2018] EWHC 2186 (Ch), [2019] BCC 195 and Snowden J confirmed (para 28) that the same test of

COMI applied in this context as in relation to the Insolvency Regulation. But he was also somewhat critical of excessive reliance on the carrying out of 'head office functions' in determining COMI. He said at [43]–[45] that the:

'definition of COMI in the Recast EIR refers to the place in which the debtor "conducts the administration of its interests". The natural meaning of that expression suggests a broader concept of administration than just the place of strategic decision-making by the board of directors or senior management . . . Secondly, Recital (30) to the Recast EIR, which encapsulates the decision in *Interedil*, refers to the presumption being capable of being rebutted if it can be shown that the "central administration" of the debtor is in another Member State. That expression naturally requires the consideration of a wider range of factors in addition to where the board or senior management act. That is also consistent with how . . . the ECJ in *Interedil* went on, in paragraph [52], to specify that the type of factors which should be taken into account include, "in particular", all the places in which the debtor company pursues economic activities and all those in which it holds assets, in so far as those places are ascertainable by third parties . . . Finally, in paragraph [53] of *Interedil*, the ECJ went on to conclude that the presumption would not be rebutted unless a comprehensive assessment of all relevant factors established, in a manner ascertainable by third parties, that the company's "actual centre of management and supervision *and of the management of its interests*" is located in the other Member State . . . That formulation . . . is clearly intended to refer to a wider set of factors than just the location of the centre of "management and supervision" alone.'

Snowden J concluded at para 47 that, in any event, 'head office functions' must include more than the function of the board of directors or senior managers in deciding upon policy for the debtor company. Other functions are likely to be carried on at and from a conventional 'head office', such as employing staff; placing of orders for goods and services; sending of invoices, making and collection of payments, and operation of a company's bank account. Such functions were also more likely to be ascertainable by third parties than the holding of board or management meetings.

### BACK TO BASICS – *RE MELARS GROUP LTD* [2021] EWHC 1523

In this case Miles J reiterated the presumption that COMI is the place of the registered office and this presumption should not be disregarded lightly in place of possible alternative COMI locations. Moreover, at [56]–[62] he enunciated principles of general application in determining COMI:

(1) The principles of legal certainty and foreseeability require that COMI should be capable of ascertainment by reference to publicly available objective features. Creditors generally should be able to predict which insolvency law will apply from ascertainable features without having to make more detailed enquiries.

(2) In the case of corporate debtors there is the statutory presumption that COMI is in the place of the registered office. This is a fact in the public domain. Creditors can, therefore, assume, absent other factors which are ascertainable, and which point the other way, that the COMI will be in that place.

(3) A corporate debtor may move its registered office, including for self-serving reasons. There is protection within the regulation itself against changes within three months of the request to open insolvency proceedings. Equally, the registered office presumption may be rebutted by other evidence. It is likely to be easier to rebut the presumption, where the registered office may be seen as a letterbox, rather than the place of actual administrative conduct but, even in such cases, there is a presumption.

(4) The burden is on a party seeking to rebut the presumption to show that there is another place where the debtor conducts the administration of its interests on a regular basis.

(5) The focus is on the place where the interests of the debtor are being administered, not where it happens to operate commercially (though these may be relevant to determining the former).

(6) The matter has to be examined at the date of the request to open insolvency proceedings. Earlier or later events may be relevant, but only in so far as they may throw helpful light on the position as at that date.

(7) COMI connotes a degree of permanence. It would be inimical for the purposes of the concept and the rules in which it is embodied if COMI could fluctuate too easily depending on the place where things happened to be occurring from time to time.

### ARTICLES 3(2)–(4)

**Territorial proceedings**—If the debtor has its centre of main interests (COMI) in a Member State, then where the debtor has an establishment, as defined in Art 2(10), territorially limited proceedings may be opened in that State. Such proceedings are limited to any assets situated in the State in which the establishment is found. If territorial proceedings are opened after main proceedings, then they are called secondary proceedings (as discussed below). However, territorial proceedings may be opened before main proceedings in certain circumstances. These two situations are identified in Art 3(4) as (a) where it is not possible to open main proceedings, or

(b) where a creditor requests the opening of proceedings if he has his domicile, habitual residence or registered office in a State where the debtor has an establishment, or whose claim arises from the operation of that establishment. These types of proceedings are called territorial proceedings because they cannot be secondary proceedings since there is no main proceeding to be secondary to.

Where no main proceedings have been opened, creditors will not be able to open proceedings in another Member State unless one or other of the conditions in Art 3(4) is met, even where the domestic law of the Member State would have allowed it.

Article 3(4) contains certain ambiguities. For a start the reference to conditions laid down by law might mean an absolute bar on main insolvency proceedings in the COMI state or it might only mean that that the particular petitioner lacks the necessary standing to bring such proceedings in the case before the court. The *Hans Brochier* case [2007] BCC 127 raised this question and the CJEU was asked for a preliminary ruling on the issue by the Belgian Supreme Court in *Zaza Retail BV* Case C-112/10 [2012] BPIR 438. The CJEU restricted the possibility of opening territorial proceedings stating that such cases should be limited to what was 'absolutely necessary'. The fact that the particular petitioner lacked locus standi to request the opening of main insolvency proceedings in the state where the debtor had its COMI was not sufficient to confer jurisdiction to open territorial proceedings. Where other persons had standing, it followed that the opening of main proceedings was indeed possible.

The court referred to the situation where main insolvency proceedings in the COMI State were confined to traders and the debtor was not a trader. It suggested that this was an example of a case where territorial proceedings could be opened. According to the court in a passage which defies easy interpretation 'the impossibility of opening main proceedings must be objective and cannot vary according to the specific circumstances in which the opening of such proceedings is requested'. It is not clear whether this statement signifies the court's acceptance of the view that the bar on opening main insolvency proceedings must be absolute.

Article 3(4)(b)(ii) however, reverses another aspect of the decision in *Zaza Retail BV* Case C-112/10 [2012] BPIR 438 where the CJEU opted for a narrow interpretation of Regulation 1346/2000, Art 3(4). It was held that 'creditors' entitled to open insolvency proceedings did not include a public authority whose task under national law is to act in the public interest, but which does not intervene as a creditor, or in the name, or on behalf of creditors. Article 3(4)(b)(ii) now specifically addresses this issue.

### ARTICLE 3(3)

**Secondary proceedings**—Secondary proceedings may be necessary in some cases to enable an efficient administration of the debtor's estate. They are defined as secondary proceedings if they are opened after main proceedings. They are different in their effect to main proceedings because they only apply to assets situated within the State in which the secondary proceedings are opened.

The fact that secondary proceedings may be opened qualifies the universality of the main insolvency proceedings. The applicable law in respect of the secondary proceedings is the law of the state where the proceedings are opened, including local priority rules in respect of the distribution of assets – Arts 7 and 35. Under a genuinely universalist system the task of an IP in secondary proceedings would be merely the collection of assets and entrusting them to the IP in the main proceedings who would then distribute them in accordance with the law applicable to the main proceedings. Secondary proceedings protect local preferential creditors whose claims would be treated as non-preferential under the law that applies to the main proceedings.

Under the original Regulation, secondary proceedings had to be liquidation proceedings. This limitation was part of the horse-trading that led to the Regulation gaining the necessary measure of political acceptance. 'By opening a local liquidation proceeding, Member States can pull an emergency brake if they feel that unlimited recognition of foreign rehabilitation proceedings is unfair to their (or to their local creditors') interests' – see M Balz, 'The European Union Convention on Insolvency Proceedings' (1996) 70 American Bankruptcy Law Journal 485, 520.

Nevertheless, the limitation acted as an impediment to the 'rescue culture' because it made a coordinated sale or rescue of the assets of a company as a whole difficult, if not impossible, to achieve. The limitation has now been removed.

There was consideration of secondary proceedings and the relationship between various provisions of the Insolvency Regulation by the European Court in Case C-327/13 *Burgo Group SpA v Illochroma SA* [2014] I L Pr 42. This is a case where winding-up proceedings in respect of a Belgian-registered company were opened in France as part of the coordinated winding-up of a group of related companies. An Italian debtor had a proof of debts rejected in the French proceedings and then sought to have secondary proceedings opened in Belgium with a view to having the claim admitted to proof in those proceedings. On a reference from Belgium, the European Court held that the fact that the company had its registered office in Belgium did not preclude the possibility of secondary proceedings being opened in Belgium provided that the company had an establishment in Belgium. The court suggested that a contrary interpretation would deny some creditors the protection afforded by the Regulation. It would give rise to discrimination against creditors established in the Member State where the debtor had its registered office, compared with the creditors established in other Member States where the debtor may have other establishments.

The potential disruption that might be caused if creditors opened secondary proceedings in different countries is illustrated by *Re Collins & Aikman* [2006] BCC 861. The administrators were alive to this possibility and gave undertakings so as to alleviate the disruption that might be occasioned. The court held that the administrator should honour promises made to creditors that local priorities would be respected in return for not opening secondary proceedings in other jurisdictions.

The recast Regulation in Art 36 now generalises and 'Europeanises' some of the practices developed by the English courts in cases like *Re Collins* and *Aikman Europe SA*.

## [6.6]

### Article 4 Examination as to jurisdiction

1. A court seised of a request to open insolvency proceedings shall of its own motion examine whether it has jurisdiction pursuant to *Article 3* Article 1(1A) (a) or (b). *The judgment opening insolvency proceedings shall specify the grounds on which the jurisdiction of the court is based, and, in particular, whether jurisdiction is based on Article 3(1) or (2)* Where there is jurisdiction to open insolvency proceedings on either of the grounds specified in Article 1(1A)(a) or (b), the judgment opening such proceedings must state which of those grounds is applicable.

2. Notwithstanding paragraph 1, where insolvency proceedings are opened *in accordance with national law* without a decision by a court, *Member States may entrust* the insolvency practitioner appointed in such proceedings *to examine whether the Member State in which a request for the opening of proceedings is pending has jurisdiction pursuant to Article 3* must examine the grounds on which there is jurisdiction to open the proceedings under Article 1(1A). *Where this is the case, the insolvency practitioner shall specify in the decision opening the proceedings the grounds on which jurisdiction is based and, in particular, whether jurisdiction is based on Article 3(1) or (2)* Where this is the case and there is jurisdiction to open insolvency proceedings on either of the grounds specified in Article 1(1A)(a) or (b), the insolvency practitioner must specify in the decision opening the proceedings which of those grounds is applicable

**Amendments**—SI 2019/146, as from IP completion day (as defined in the European Union (Withdrawal Agreement) Act 2020, s 39(1)–(5)).

**General note**—Under Art 4 there is now a duty on a court, or other person or body competent to open insolvency proceedings, to examine ex officio whether or not it has jurisdiction in the particular case. The court should also specify whether the proceedings opened are main or secondary proceedings. It may be that in practice all the requirement amounts to is an additional 'box-ticking' exercise. An attempt however, is made to give teeth to the provision by Art 5 which investing any creditor with the right to challenge the decision to open main proceedings on grounds of lack of international jurisdiction.

## [6.7]

### Article 5 Judicial review of the decision to open *main* insolvency proceedings

1. The debtor or any creditor may challenge before a court the decision opening *main* insolvency proceedings on *grounds of international jurisdiction* the grounds of jurisdiction under Article 1(1A)(a).

2. The decision opening *main* insolvency proceedings may be challenged by parties other than those referred to in paragraph 1 or on grounds other than a lack of *international* jurisdiction under Article 1(1A)(a) *where national law so provides* the relevant law (other than this Regulation) of the part of the United Kingdom in which the matter is being determined so provides.

This provision in a sense gives teeth to the Article 4 duty by investing any creditor with the right to challenge the decision to open main proceedings on grounds of lack of international jurisdiction.

**Amendments**—SI 2019/146, as from IP completion day (as defined in the European Union (Withdrawal Agreement) Act 2020, s 39(1)–(5)).

**[6.8]**

*Article 6 Jurisdiction for actions deriving directly from insolvency proceedings and closely linked with them*

1. The courts of the Member State within the territory of which insolvency proceedings have been opened in accordance with Article 3 shall have jurisdiction for any action which derives directly from the insolvency proceedings and is closely linked with them, such as avoidance actions.

2. Where an action referred to in paragraph 1 is related to an action in civil and commercial matters against the same defendant, the insolvency practitioner may bring both actions before the courts of the Member State within the territory of which the defendant is domiciled, or, where the action is brought against several defendants, before the courts of the Member State within the territory of which any of them is domiciled, provided that those courts have jurisdiction pursuant to Regulation (EU) No 1215/2012.

The first subparagraph shall apply to the debtor in possession, provided that national law allows the debtor in possession to bring actions on behalf of the insolvency estate.

3. For the purpose of paragraph 2, actions are deemed to be related where they are so closely connected that it is expedient to hear and determine them together to avoid the risk of irreconcilable judgments resulting from separate proceedings.

**Amendments**—Repealed by SI 2019/146, as from IP completion day (as defined in the European Union (Withdrawal Agreement) Act 2020, s 39(1)–(5)).

**General note**—Article 6 of the recast Regulation extends the jurisdiction of the court that opened insolvency proceedings to insolvency related actions. Essentially there is a codification of the decision in *Seagon v Deko* Case C-339/07 [2009] ECR 1–767 and a clear statement that courts opening insolvency proceedings also have jurisdiction in respect of actions that derive directly from the insolvency proceedings and are closely linked with them. Insolvency-related actions are outside the Jurisdiction and Judgments (Brussels I) Regulation but within the Insolvency Regulation. Therefore, the defendant should be sued in the state that opens the insolvency proceedings rather than in its country of domicile[1].

There is however, no guidance in Art 6 on what constitutes an insolvency linked action other than avoidance actions being highlighted as an example of the term.

Under the existing case law however, the following have been held to fall into that category of insolvency-related actions:

(1) *Actions based on insolvency law that seek to fix liability on company officers.* In the leading case of *Gourdain v Nadler* Case 133/78 [1979] 3 CMLR 180 the European Court held that an action is related to bankruptcy if it derives directly from the bankruptcy and is closely linked to proceedings for realising the assets or judicial supervision. In this case, a French court had made an order requiring a German-based director of a French company that was the subject of French insolvency proceedings to contribute to the assets of the company. The order was made under provisions of French insolvency law that appeared to impose personal liability on directors if they failed to take sufficient care to ensure that company creditors had been paid in full. In essence, the European Court held that the proceedings were insolvency-related proceedings since the basis of the action stemmed from provisions peculiar to insolvency law or from insolvency law adjustments of general legal norms. It was right therefore that the defendant should be sued in the state that opened the insolvency proceedings and not in his state of domicile.

The European Court has recently held in Case C-295/13 *Rechtsanwalt H v HK* [2014] All ER (D) 50 (Dec) that the concept of insolvency-related actions extends to actions brought by the liquidator against a company director for 'reimbursement of payments which were made after the company became insolvent or after determination of an excess of company liabilities over assets?' The court considered the relevant provisions of German law under which the director of a debtor company must reimburse payments that he made on behalf of the company after it became insolvent or after it was established that the company's liabilities exceeded its assets. The provision clearly derogated from the common rules of civil and commercial law, specifically because of the insolvency of the debtor company. It required the actual insolvency of the debtor and it did not matter for this purpose that insolvency proceedings had not formally been opened.

This interpretation has been confirmed more recently in Case C-594/14 *Simona Kornhaas v Thomas Dithmar* (10 December 2015). It was held that the courts of the Member State where insolvency proceedings have been opened are invested with jurisdiction, on the basis of Art 3(1), to hear and determine an action brought by the liquidator in the insolvency proceedings against a director of the company for reimbursement of payments made after the company became insolvent or after it had been established that the company's liabilities exceeded its assets.

(2) *Actions for a declaration that a claim exists for the purpose of its registration in insolvency proceedings.* This was held to constitute an insolvency-related action in Case C-47/18 *Skarb v Stephan Riel* (ECLI:EU:C:2019:754, 18 September 2019). The case considered aspects of Austrian insolvency legislation. The European Court pointed out that the action was brought by the applicant in the main insolvency proceedings. Moreover, it was clear from the wording of the relevant provision that the action was intended to be brought in the context of insolvency proceedings, by creditors participating in those insolvency proceedings and in the event of a dispute concerning the accuracy or ranking of claims declared by those creditors.

(3) *Actions based on provisions particular to insolvency law or to insolvency-related adjustments of general legal provision.* *Gourdain v Nadler* seems to stand as authority for a general proposition that proceedings are insolvency related if they arose from provisions that are distinctive to insolvency law or from adjustments of general legal norms that are brought about by insolvency law. This reasoning has been applied by David Richards J in *Fondazione Enasarco v Lehman Brothers Finance SA* [2014] EWHC 34 (Ch), in relation to proceedings before the Swiss Bankruptcy Court challenging the liquidator's rejection of the proof of a debt. The proceedings were held therefore to fall within the 'bankruptcy' exception to the Lugano Convention, which was similar to the Brussels I Regulation. The judge pointed out that the proceedings could only arise under Swiss insolvency law and they formed an integral part of the liquidation proceedings, designed to achieve the primary purpose of such proceedings; namely the distribution of available assets among creditors whose claims were admitted or established. The purpose of the proceedings was not simply to establish whether a party had a good contractual or other claim but also the amount and ranking of the claim for liquidation purposes. The ranking of claims was a matter that arose exclusively under the relevant insolvency law.

(4) *Actions based on insolvency law that seek to set aside pre-insolvency transactions entered into by the debtor.* The leading authority here is *Seagon v Deko* Case C-339/07 [2009] ECR 1–767. (See also the comments of Lloyd LJ in *Oakley v Ultra Vehicle Design Ltd* [2006] BCC 57 at para 42 and Rimer J in *UBS AG v Omni Holdings Ltd* [2000] 1 WLR 916 at 922).

It seems, however, that not all avoidance type proceedings are within the Insolvency Regulation. Relevant factors include whether the proceedings are brought by the liquidator or a third party and whether all the recoveries accrue for the benefit of the debtor's estate. In *Re Baillies Ltd* [2012] BCC 554 for instance, Judge Purle QC suggested that proceedings under s 423 of the Insolvency Act 1986 seeking to set aside transactions that defraud creditors were not insolvency proceedings within the European Regulations. He pointed out that the provision was applicable irrespective of whether there was a liquidation or some other form of insolvency process and any victim could have brought the proceedings at any time.

The reasoning and conclusions of the European Court in Case C-295/13 *Rechtsanwalt H v HK* [2014] All ER (D) 50 (Dec) might be used however in support of the proposition that proceedings under s 423 of the Insolvency Act are 'insolvency-related' and within the Insolvency Regulation. Proceedings under s 423, however, are not strictly speaking based on the insolvency of the debtor although they are concerned with putting assets beyond the reach of creditors or otherwise prejudicing the claims of creditors.

There is a fuller discussion of the relevant issues by the European Court in *F-Tex SIA* [2013] Case C-213/10 Bus LR 232 though the decision does not provide very much in the way of general guidance. The reasoning of the court is also somewhat contorted holding that an action was not closely connected with insolvency proceedings while avoiding any decision on the question whether the action was directly linked with the proceedings. In this case a German registered company had, while insolvent, transferred money to a Lithuanian-based recipient. The payer later became the subject of insolvency proceedings in Germany and it seems that under German law, the transfer could be set aside by the liquidator. The liquidator, however, assigned to the company creditor all the company's claims against third parties including the claim for reversal of the transfer. The court held that the exercise by the assignee of the right acquired was not closely connected with the insolvency proceedings in that the assignee could freely decide whether to exercise the right; if he did so, he acted in his own interest and for his personal benefit; the proceeds of the action were owned by him personally and did not increase the assets of the insolvent debtor. The court said that the fact that the assignee was obliged to pay the liquidator a percentage of the proceeds did 'not alter that analysis, since it is merely a method of payment'. Moreover, under German law, the closure of the insolvency proceedings did not affect the assignee's claim.

(5)  *Actions challenging the exercise of a power or discretion by a liquidator or by members of a creditors' committee in the course of insolvency proceedings.* The case law suggests that actions involving a challenge to the exercise of a power or discretion given to a liquidator by insolvency law are outside the Brussels I Regulation. For instance, in *SCT Industri AB v Alpenblume AB Case C-111/08* [2009] ECR I-5655 the European Court held that an action concerning the power of the liquidator to dispose of company assets fell outside the Jurisdiction and Judgments (Brussels I) regime. Under the relevant national law – Swedish law – the effect of insolvency was to give the liquidator exclusive power to transfer company assets and he exercised this power on behalf of creditors. The court emphasised that the liquidator intervened only after insolvency proceedings had been opened and the power to act on behalf of the company stemmed specifically from the national law governing insolvency.

The reasoning of the High Court in *Polymer Vision v Van Dooren* [2011] EWHC 2951 (Comm) was similar. In this case proceedings were brought in the UK against a Dutch bankruptcy trustee relying on the Brussels I Regulation. The proceedings alleged fraudulent misrepresentation and breach of an agreement by the bankruptcy trustee as to how he would exercise his powers under Dutch bankruptcy law. It was held, however, that the case fell within the insolvency exception under the Brussels I Regulation since the statements made in negotiations and the resulting agreements derived directly from, and were closely connected with, the Dutch insolvency proceedings.

*Polymer* was however, distinguished by Carr J in *Tchenguiz v Grant Thornton* [2015] EWHC 1864 (Comm) at paras 152–158 where proceedings were brought in England against inter alia, the member of an Icelandic winding up committee for tortious conspiracy relying on the provisions of the Lugano Convention, which are in the same terms as the Brussels I Regulation. She said that the claims were not closely connected with the winding-up proceedings. There was a connection, but it was not considered to be a sufficiently close one. The winding-up of the Icelandic entity, a bank, was not the principal subject-matter of the claims against the defendants. The gravamen and root of the claims was an alleged tortious conspiracy between three individuals, involving deliberate and malicious wrongdoing in connection with an investigation by the Serious Fraud Office. The winding-up of the bank was the relevant context but the claims did not derive directly from it. There was no reliance on any insolvency aspect of the winding-up proceedings, nor were breaches of any duties or powers by the defendant in his capacity as a member of the winding-up committee relied upon. There was no reliance placed on the defendant's status under Icelandic insolvency law nor was there any suggestion of liability under Icelandic Insolvency law.

While the facts of the case seem distinguishable from those in *Tchenguiz v Grant Thornton*. the EU Court of Justice has recently held in Case C-649/16 *Valach v Waldviertler Sparkasse Bank AG* [2018] ILPr 9 that a damages action brought against members of a creditors' committee in insolvency proceedings for rejecting a restructuring plan was an insolvency-related action. Therefore it should be brought in the State where the insolvency proceedings were taking place. The claimants in this case were shareholders, and also business counterparties, of the legal entity that was the subject of insolvency proceedings. They claimed to have suffered losses such as loss on equity investments as a result of the rejection of the restructuring plan. The insolvency proceedings were taking place in Slovakia and it was alleged that the creditors' committee members had broken their duties under Slovak insolvency law including in particular the duty to act in the interests of all the creditors.

Not surprisingly, the European Court held that the action was an insolvency-related action and was subject to the jurisdictional rules of the Insolvency Regulation. It pointed out that the liability action was the direct and inseparable consequence of the performance by the committee of creditors, a statutory body established when insolvency proceedings are opened, of the task specifically assigned to them by the provisions of Slovak national law governing such procedures. The obligations that formed the basis of the liability action originated in rules that were specific to insolvency proceedings.

The relevant case law including that of the CJEU in the *Valach* case has recently been reviewed by Cockerill J in the English case, *ING Bank NV v Banco Santander SA* [2020] EWHC 3561 (Comm). She said that if an action was the direct consequence of liquidation proceedings and concerned the scope or exercise of powers by a liquidator to transfer assets or liabilities or the consequences thereof, then it would fall within the Insolvency Regulation.

The following types of proceedings have, however, been held not to be 'insolvency-related':

(1)  *Actions by an insolvency representative seeking to establish the debtor's ownership of property.* Even though insolvency proceedings in the classic sense are all about the collection of assets and their distribution among creditors, there is considerable support in the case law for the proposition that actions concerning the debtor's 'ownership' of assets are not within the Insolvency Regulation. The leading case from the European Court is *German Graphics* Case C-292/08, [2009] ECR I-8421 where a German company had supplied machinery to a Dutch company subject to a reservation of title clause in its favour. The Dutch company went into liquidation in Holland but the German supplier brought proceedings in Germany relying on the reservation of title and asserting that the German court has jurisdiction to hear the claim under the Brussels I Regulation. The European Court agreed holding that the claim of the German supplier founded on the reservation of title clause constituted an independent claim since it was not based on insolvency law and required neither the opening of insolvency proceedings nor the involvement of a liquidator. The link with insolvency was considered 'neither sufficiently direct nor sufficiently close' to warrant the insolvency provision coming into play.

There are also a number of English cases where claims have been brought successfully under the Brussels I Regulation asserting either that an insolvent debtor does, or does not, own particular property. In *Re Hayward* [1997] Ch 45, for instance, the case concerned a claim by a trustee in bankruptcy that real property in Spain formed part of the bankruptcy estate. Rattee J explained that the claim was essentially a claim by the trustee to recover from a third party assets said to belong to the bankrupt's estate and therefore vested in the trustee. The issue between the parties did not involve any aspect of bankruptcy law and it was irrelevant that the bankruptcy trustee could only assert the claim by virtue of the bankruptcy. In *Ashurst v Pollard* [2001] Ch 595, a bankruptcy trustee was seeking an order for the sale of foreign property that was formerly co-owned by the bankrupt and now vested in the trustee. It was held that in determining whether proceedings fall within the 'insolvency' provision the mere fact that a claimant happened to be a trustee in bankruptcy was not enough. In this case, the court relied on the fact that bankruptcy was not the principal subject matter of the proceedings.

*Byers v Yacht Bull Corp* [2010] EWHC 133 (Ch), [2010] BCC 368 involved a claim by a UK liquidator that the insolvent debtor was the beneficial owner of an asset – a yacht – through having funded its acquisition. The legal owner, however, successfully contended that separate 'ownership' proceedings would need to be brought under the Brussels I Regulation in its country of domicile and that the case did not fall within the Insolvency provision.

(2)  *Actions by a debtor's insolvency representative based on general contract or commercial law that seek the recovery of monies allegedly owing to the debtor.* In Case C-157/13 *Nickel and Goeldner Spedition GmbH v 'Kintra' UAB* [ 2015] QB 96 the CJEU held on a reference from Lithuania that a breach of contract claim brought by an insolvency representative against one of the debtor's counterparties did not fall within the category of insolvency-related actions. There was nothing peculiar to insolvency law about the action even though, in the words of the referring court, the 'action is brought by an insolvency administrator, acting in the interests of all the creditors of the undertaking and seeking to restore the undertaking's solvency and to increase the amount of the assets of the insolvent undertaking so that as many creditors' claims as possible may be satisfied'.

The European Court said that the right or obligation that formed the basis of the action had its source in the common rules of civil and commercial law rather than in any special rules of derogation applying to insolvency proceedings. The action could have been brought by the creditor itself before the opening of insolvency proceedings relating to it and, in these circumstances, the action would have been governed by the ordinary rules of jurisdiction that applied to civil and commercial matters. The fact that the claim was now brought by the insolvency representative who acted in the interest of the creditors did not alter the nature of the claim, which remained subject to the same rules of law as before.

The *Nickel & Goeldner Spedition* test was held to apply a fortiori in Case C-641/16 *Tunkers France v Expert France* [2018] ILPr 7. The European Court held that an action for damages for unfair competition did not fall within the jurisdiction of the court that opened the insolvency proceedings. In the action, the assignee of part of the business acquired in the course of insolvency proceedings was accused of misrepresenting itself as being the exclusive distributor of articles manufactured by the debtor.

The court distinguished Case C-111/08 *SCT Industri* [2009] ECR I-5655 where it was held that an action challenging a transfer of shares in a company made in the course of insolvency proceedings fell within the scope of the Insolvency Regulation. In that case, however, the insolvency representative who transferred the shares was criticised for failing to use a power he derived specifically from the provisions of national law governing collective procedures. On the other hand, this particular case concerned the conduct of the assignee alone.

What proceedings are or are not insolvency related has been considered by the Court of Justice in Case C-535/17 *NK v BNP Paribas* EU:C:2019:96; [2019] ILPr 10. In this case, a Dutch-based bailiff who later incorporated, had a business bank account in Belgium but the bank in Belgium it appeared had failed to monitor and the bailiff was allowed to withdraw money in the account for personal purposes and embezzle it. The bailiff's practice fell into financial difficulties and both the legal entity and the bailiff personally entered insolvency proceedings. The insolvency representative brought an action in Holland against the bank arguing that it had failed in its monitoring duty and caused loss to the general body of the bailiff's creditors. The proceeds of a successful action would accrue to the benefit of the estate. The question for the Court of Justice was whether the Dutch court had jurisdiction to hear the action by virtue of the fact that insolvency proceedings had been opened in Holland and the action was 'insolvency-related'.

The Court of Justice however, took the view that the action fell within the scope of the Brussels 1 Regulation rather than the Insolvency Regulation. It held that the action was based on the ordinary rules of civil and commercial law and not on derogating rules specific to insolvency proceedings. It could be brought by an ordinary creditor, did not fall under the exclusive competence of the liquidator and was independent of the opening of insolvency proceedings. Therefore, it could not be considered to be a direct and inherent result of those proceedings – paras 36, 37.

The general approach articulated in Case C-535/17 *NK v BNP Paribas* was applied recently by the European Court in Case C-198/18 *CeDe Group AB v KAN Sp z oo* (21 November 2019). The European Court held that the concept of 'insolvency proceedings and their effects' did not cover an action for the payment of goods delivered under a contract concluded before the opening of insolvency proceedings. General contractual rules, rather than insolvency specific rules, applied even where the action was brought by the liquidator of an insolvent company established in one Member State against the other contracting party established in another Member State.

## TRYING TO ESTABLISH GENERAL PRINCIPLES

There is some support for the view that the Insolvency Regulation is only engaged if insolvency is the principal subject matter of the proceedings. Viewed in isolation, however, the test of whether insolvency is the principal subject matter of the proceedings does not have much explanatory power. On one view, insolvency could only properly be said to be the proper subject matter of proceedings if the question is whether a debtor should enter insolvency proceedings. This would be to give the Insolvency Regulation a very narrow operation and deprive the reference to 'analogous proceedings' in the Brussels I Regulation of any force. The European Court judgment in *Gourdain v Nadler* suggests a somewhat broader view that the insolvency provision would operate where the proceedings concerned the bankruptcy specific powers of an insolvency administrator or involved a special remedy available only in insolvency cases. The mere fact, however, that the insolvency practitioner is party to the proceedings is insufficient.

More recently, a 'close and direct links' test has found favour with the European Court but one might ask how close and direct the link must be? For instance misfeasance proceedings under s 212 of the Insolvency Act 1986 provide a summary remedy in the course of liquidation proceedings against officers of the company who are found to have misapplied, or retained, or become accountable for, any money or other property of the company, or been guilty of any misfeasance or breach of any fiduciary or other duty in relation to the company. Persons found liable under the section may be ordered to restore money or property to the company or contribute a sum to the company's assets by way of compensation for the breach of duty. Recoveries under s 212 go to the company and this was considered an important factor by the European Court in *F-Tex SIA v Lietuvos-Anglijos UAB* Case C-213/10 [2013] Bus LR 232. On the other hand, it is clear that the section creates no new rights but merely provides a summary mode of enforcing rights that could have been enforced by the company before the liquidation.

Apparent inconsistencies in the jurisprudence of the European Court have been highlighted by Advocate General Bobek in Case C-535/17 *NK v BNP Paribas* EU:C:2019:96; [2019] ILPr 10 at paras 40–70.

He suggested at para 57 that the European Court should:

'reaffirm the test essentially embraced since *Nickel & Goeldner Spedition*: does the ascertaining of the right or obligation which forms the basis of the action have its source in the ordinary rules of civil and commercial law or in derogating rules specific to insolvency proceedings? The decisive criterion would thus be linked to the first part of the test, namely whether the legal basis for the action derives directly from insolvency rules. The second condition of the test would rather serve as a verification tool for the result reached on the basis of the first part, but not as a fully-fledged criterion on its own.'

The relevant case law has recently been reviewed by Cockerill J in the English case, *ING Bank NV v Banco Santander SA* [2020] EWHC 3561 (Comm). She said that she had to ask herself explicitly 'the two questions established by the authorities: what is the legal basis of the claim – is it directly derived from the insolvency? And how closely is the claim connected with the insolvency? Secondly, to review the indications provided by that analysis in the light of the established case law, in particular that which goes in the other direction.'

Ultimately it appears to be a question of balance between the advantages of channelling all legal actions involving the insolvent debtor into the courts of the state that opened the insolvency proceedings versus the importance attached to the defendant's due process rights in being sued in his country of domicile.

This case was held to fall on the Insolvency Regulation side of the line. There was found to be a direct and close link to either the internal management of the insolvency process or the conduct of the insolvency office holder ([176]).

It has been held by the European Court that the principle enunciated in *Seagon v Deko* Case C-339/07 [2009] ECR I-767 of 'centralising' insolvency-related actions in the insolvency forum applies where the defendant in an insolvency-related action is resident outside the EU. The Virgos-Schmit report at paras 11 and 44 suggests that the Regulation does not give jurisdiction in these cases. Paragraph 11 states that the Regulation: 'deals only with the intra-Community effects of insolvency proceedings. It applies only when the centre of the debtor's main interests lies within the [EU] . . . Even then, the [Regulation] . . . does not regulate the effect of the proceedings vis-à-vis third States. In relation to third States, the [Regulation] . . . does not impair the freedom of the . . . States to adopt the appropriate rules.'

The court however in *Schmid v Hertel* Case C-328/12 took a different view from Virgos-Schmit though it did not refer to the report in this connection. It decided that the competent court under Art 3 of the Regulation to open insolvency proceedings had jurisdiction to decide an action brought by the liquidator to set aside a transaction that involved a defendant who was domiciled in a third country. It suggested that the place of residence of any potential defendant to an action brought by the liquidator in the insolvency proceedings to set a transaction aside and recover additional assets for the benefit of the creditors was irrelevant to the competence of the court to open proceedings.

The court distinguished the issue of jurisdiction from that of recognition and enforcement and was unpersuaded by the argument that a third country defendant was in a weak position. It suggested that the debtor's COMI was normally foreseeable by the defendant, who could therefore take it into account in deciding whether or not to enter into a transaction with the debtor that was liable to be set aside in insolvency proceedings. The COMI might change between the time of entering into the transaction and the opening of insolvency proceedings but the court stated that the objective of preventing forum shopping prevailed over the concern to avoid the defendant being sued in a foreign court. The court was also unmoved by the consideration that the judgment would not be enforced against the third country defendant in his country of residence pursuant to the Insolvency Regulation. This could be done by means of bilateral agreements with third countries and in any event the judgment would automatically be recognised in other EU countries pursuant to what is now Art 32.

### ARTICLE 6(2)

This provision permits the IP to bring insolvency related actions in the defendant's country of domicile as well as in the insolvency forum. This facility allows an IP to couple an insolvency-related action with, for example, an action based on the duties of directors under company law. The provision has much merit for an IP is saved the job of potentially having to bring proceedings against the same defendant in two different countries, eg, an avoidance action in the state where the insolvency proceedings are opened and an action to recover assets based on general commercial law in the state where the defendant is domiciled. Transaction costs are minimised if the actions are combined and heard together in the same state.

There is however the question about which substantive law should apply in respect of the insolvency-related action. If the action is brought in the insolvency forum, then under Art 7 of the new Insolvency Regulation (Art 4 of the original Regulation) the applicable law is generally that of the insolvency forum. But the Regulation is silent as to which law should apply if the action is brought in the state of the defendant's domicile. It may seem strange that the applicable law should vary depending on where the action is brought by an insolvency practitioner but may be equally strange that the state of the defendant's domicile should, prima facie, be applying the law of the insolvency forum as the applicable law.

---

¹ See also the judgment of the European Court in Case C-296/17 *Wiemer & Trachte GmbH, in liquidation v Tadzher*, EU:C:2018:902, [2019] BPIR 252, which holds that the courts of a Member State that opens insolvency proceedings under Art 3(1) of Regulation 1346/2000 have

exclusive jurisdiction to hear and determine an action to set a transaction aside by virtue of the debtor's insolvency that is brought against a defendant whose registered office or habitual residence is in another Member State.

**[6.9]**

*Article 7 Applicable law*

1. *Save as otherwise provided in this Regulation, the law applicable to insolvency proceedings and their effects shall be that of the Member State within the territory of which such proceedings are opened (the 'State of the opening of proceedings').*

2. *The law of the State of the opening of proceedings shall determine the conditions for the opening of those proceedings, their conduct and their closure. In particular, it shall determine the following:*

   (a) *the debtors against which insolvency proceedings may be brought on account of their capacity;*

   (b) *the assets which form part of the insolvency estate and the treatment of assets acquired by or devolving on the debtor after the opening of the insolvency proceedings;*

   (c) *the respective powers of the debtor and the insolvency practitioner;*

   (d) *the conditions under which set-offs may be invoked;*

   (e) *the effects of insolvency proceedings on current contracts to which the debtor is party;*

   (f) *the effects of the insolvency proceedings on proceedings brought by individual creditors, with the exception of pending lawsuits;*

   (g) *the claims which are to be lodged against the debtor's insolvency estate and the treatment of claims arising after the opening of insolvency proceedings;*

   (h) *the rules governing the lodging, verification and admission of claims;*

   (i) *the rules governing the distribution of proceeds from the realisation of assets, the ranking of claims and the rights of creditors who have obtained partial satisfaction after the opening of insolvency proceedings by virtue of a right in rem or through a set-off;*

   (j) *the conditions for, and the effects of closure of, insolvency proceedings, in particular by composition;*

   (k) *creditors' rights after the closure of insolvency proceedings;*

   (l) *who is to bear the costs and expenses incurred in the insolvency proceedings;*

   (m) *the rules relating to the voidness, voidability or unenforceability of legal acts detrimental to the general body of creditors.*

**Amendments**—Repealed by SI 2019/146, as from IP completion day (as defined in the European Union (Withdrawal Agreement) Act 2020, s 39(1)–(5)).

**General note**—This provision is the equivalent of Art 4 in Regulation 1346/2000. The insolvency laws of Member States are disparate and so are their approaches to choice of law rules. The Regulation tries to address some of these problems with a number of Articles that harmonise to some degree the way in which certain choice of law issues are dealt with, thereby allowing contracting parties to be aware in advance of the likely outcome if one party becomes insolvent. The basic rule is that the law of the Member State in which proceedings are opened is the law that will govern those proceedings. This rule applies to matters of procedure as well as matters of substantive law in relation to the insolvency proceedings. Article 7 applies equally to main and secondary proceedings. Thus it is the law of the State of the main proceedings that will apply to those proceedings and correspondingly the law of the State in which secondary proceedings are opened will apply to those proceedings.

The recent reference from Nugee J to the Court of Justice in *Re McNamara* [2020] EWHC 98 (Ch) gives rise to the question of what is comprised in the debtor's insolvency estate and whether this includes pension fund assets built up in another EU Member State. The case concerns the scope of the freedom of establishment under Art 49 of the Treaty on the Functioning of the European Union (TFEU). The case involved an Irish national, a property developer, who had accumulated a large pension fund in Ireland and then experienced financial difficulties in Ireland. He moved his centre of main interests to the UK and filed for bankruptcy in the UK. The court was required to determine whether an Irish pension scheme was excluded from the bankruptcy estate as an 'approved pension arrangement' under the Welfare Reform and Pensions Act 1999 s 11 and whether such an 'approved pension arrangement' should be given an expansive interpretation by virtue of TFEU Art 49. It referred to the Court of Justice of the EU the issue of whether the exclusion of pension rights on bankruptcy was something that could affect freedom of establishment, or was otherwise within the scope of Art 49.

Article 4 of Regulation 1346/2000 was considered by the European Court in Case C-594/14 *Simona Kornhaas v Thomas Dithmar*. The court referred to the fact that the lex fori concursus determines the 'conditions for the opening' of the insolvency proceedings. The court held that:

> 'in order to ensure the effectiveness of that provision, it must be interpreted as meaning that, first, the preconditions for the opening of insolvency proceedings, second, the rules which designate the persons who are obliged to request the opening of those proceedings and, third, the consequences of an infringement of that obligation fall within its scope.'

A provision of German law imposing personal liability on the directors of an insolvent company that required them to reimburse payments they had made on behalf of an insolvent company after the fact of insolvency was established was held to fall within the Article. The case concerned a company incorporated under UK law but with its centre of main interests in Germany and in respect of which insolvency proceedings had been opened in Germany. The application of the relevant provisions of Germany law was held not to infringe the EU rules on freedom of establishment. The German law was not concerned with the formation of a company in a given Member State or its subsequent establishment in another Member State since the relevant law only applied after the company had been formed and after it had become insolvent.

The same provisions of German law had been considered by the European Court in *H v HK* (Case C-295/13) and it was also concluded that the German court opening the insolvency proceedings had jurisdiction in respect of an action that sought to impose personal liability on directors of the debtor company. In *H v HK* the debtor company was incorporated in Germany and insolvency proceedings were commenced in Germany but in *Kornhaas v Dithmar* the situation was somewhat different in that the debtor company had been incorporated in England but main insolvency proceedings were commenced in Germany.

The interpretation of Art 7(2)(d) on set-off was considered by Advocate General Bobek in *CeDe Group AB v KAN Sp z oo*[1] though the European Court did not specifically address the issue (Case C-198/18, 21 November 2019). Article 7(2)(d) seems directed at the situation where a debtor commences insolvency proceedings in country X. A creditor lodges a proof in the insolvency proceedings but the debtor's insolvency representative attempts to set off against the proof, a claim that the debtor has against the creditor.

The facts of *CeDe Group AB v KAN Sp z oo* were somewhat different however. Here, the liquidator of a Polish company (PPUB), which was the subject of insolvency proceedings in Poland, lodged before the Swedish courts an application against CeDe, a Swedish company, claiming payment for goods delivered under a pre-existing contract between PPUB and CeDe that was governed by Swedish law. CeDe claimed a set-off in respect of a larger debt owed to it by PPUB. As the Advocate General pointed out, the case gave the European Court the opportunity to interpret the specific provisions on applicable law contained in the Insolvency Regulation and their interaction with the general regime contained in the Rome I Regulation[2] on the law applicable to contractual obligations. In other words, what was the applicable law in relation to a set-off claim invoked against an insolvent company where the liquidator of the insolvent company had brought proceedings for payment in a state other than that of the insolvency forum? In this particular case, did Polish or Swedish law govern the availability of set-off[3]?

The Advocate General answered essentially in favour of Swedish law. He said the mere fact that what is now Art 7(2) made reference to the conditions for invoking set-offs and to the effects of insolvency on current contracts did not mean that any claim relating to a contract where a party to that contract was subject to insolvency proceedings (and/or where a set-off is invoked against that claimant) fell automatically within Art 7(2). That conclusion was not changed merely by the fact that it was the liquidator who brought the action. In his view, any other analysis would lead to unpredictable, or even bizarre, results. The law governing the contractual claim would differ from the one that the parties agreed on and would also change repeatedly, due to subsequent assignments and/or the assignees themselves eventually becoming subject to insolvency proceedings – see paras 37, 38.

The application of the law of the insolvency forum even in respect of matters not specifically referred to in Art 4(2) was also addressed in *Re Hellas Telecommunications (Luxembourg) II SCA* [2013] BPIR 756. In this case, a company incorporated in Luxembourg had shifted its COMI to England leading to an English liquidation and the English liquidators applied for an order under ss 234 and 236 of the Insolvency Act for the production of documents 'belonging to' the company or 'relating to' its promotion, formation, business, dealings, affairs or property. An attempt was made to resist the order on the grounds of legal professional privilege under Luxembourg law. The court, however, held that English law applied in deciding whether a document was protected from inspection by reason of legal professional privilege although Luxembourg law might be relevant to the exercise of any discretion.

In *Edgeworth Capital Luxembourg Sarl v Maud* [2015] EWHC 3464 (Comm) Knowles J however seemed inclined to accept a more restricted interpretation of what is now Art 7 though he did not find it necessary to reach a definitive conclusion on the issue for the purpose of his decision in the case. Nevertheless, he seemed sympathetic to the notion that a debt arising under a contract governed by English law was not capable of being discharged by insolvency proceedings in a foreign jurisdiction even through the application of the Insolvency Regulation. The case concerned a loan made to a company with its COMI in Spain and which entered into a formal insolvency process in Spain. The debtor's obligations under the loan agreement had been guaranteed and it was argued by the guarantor that its liability under the guarantee had been discharged by the Spanish insolvency proceedings. The court held that the relevant Spanish law did not have this effect but it was suggested that even if it did, it did not produce any extra-territorial effects by virtue of the Insolvency Regulation.

It is submitted that such a suggestion is difficult to square with the European Court decision in Case C-594/14 *Simona Kornhaas v Thomas Dithmar* which gives an expansive interpretation to what is now Art 7. Moreover, if a guarantor accepts liability under the guarantee and pays the principal debt then normally it is entitled to be indemnified by the debtor and has a right of reimbursement from the debtor's estate. This enlarges the scope of the claims against the estate. What is now Articles 7(2)(g) and (h) provide that the courts of the State where insolvency proceedings are opened shall determine the claims that may be lodged against the debtor's estate as well as the rules governing the lodging, verification and admission of claims.

On a reasonable construction of the words used in Art 7, the modification of English law governed obligations under insolvency proceedings opened in other EU States should be automatically recognized and implemented throughout the EU (including the UK pre Brexit) pursuant to the Insolvency Regulation. This conclusion was recently reached in *Bank of Baroda v Maniar* [2019] EWHC 2463 (Comm). The court took the view that the effect of the Insolvency Regulation was to trump the rule that the modification of English law governed obligations was exclusively governed by English law. It cited a leading text[4] to the effect that where main insolvency proceedings in another EU State are closed and the closure has, under the law of that EU State, the effect of discharging the debtor, that discharge must be recognised in the UK even if it is not an effective discharge under the law applicable to the contract which in this case, was English law.

In Case C-212/15 *ENEFI v DGRFP* OJ C6, 09/01/2017 on a request from a Romanian court for a preliminary ruling, the European Court has confirmed the opinion of Advocate General Bobek and held that the law of the state of the opening of insolvency proceedings governed the consequences of failure to lodge proof of a claim within the time permitted by that law. These consequences could include forfeiture of the claim or suspension of the enforcement of the claim in another Member State. It did not matter for that purpose that the claim was a fiscal claim.

The non-exhaustive list in Art 7(2) specifies examples of what issues will be governed by the law of the State of the opening of proceedings (*lex concursus*). It should be noted that there are exceptions to this general rule laid down in Arts 8–18 of the Regulation where the law of another Member State or possibly the law of a third state is applicable. For example, Art 7(2)(m) should be read in conjunction with Art 16 which disapplies Art 7(2)(m) where the person who benefited from an act detrimental to the creditors can prove that the law of another Member State is applicable, and that law does not permit any challenge to that act.

The proper interpretation of what is now Art 7(2)(f) has not been considered squarely and directly by the European Court, but Art 7(2)(f) issues have arisen indirectly in a number of cases, most notably in *German Graphics* Case C-292/08 [2009] ECR I-8421. This case concerned the sale of machines by a Germany supplier to a Dutch buyer subject to a reservation of title clause under which the German supplier retained ownership of the goods until the goods were paid for. The Dutch buyer went into liquidation without having paid for the machines. The machines were located in Holland when the insolvency proceedings were opened but a German court made an order granting relief to the supplier and the European Court suggests that this result is non-problematic in terms of European law. Given the location of the machines and also the fact that the insolvency proceedings had been opened in Holland, one might think that Dutch law should govern the effectiveness of the reservation of title clause and preclude actions in the German courts by virtue of the general Art 4 (now Art 7) principle and more specifically by Art 4(2)(f) (now Art 7(2)(f)). The European Court said, however, somewhat elliptically, that Art 4(2)(b) (now Art 7(2)(b)) 'only constitutes a rule intended to prevent conflicts of law' (para 37). The judgment makes no reference to Art 4(2)(f).

The *German Graphics* case is also difficult to square with two other decisions from the European Court. The first – predating *German Graphics* – is *European Commission v AMI Semiconductor Belgium BVBA* Case-294/02 [2005] ECR I-2175 where the court said that it was clear from what is now Art 7(2)(f) that the law of the State that opens insolvency proceedings governs the effects of those proceedings on actions brought by individual creditors. The court also held that, by virtue of what is now Arts 19 and 20, the opening of insolvency proceedings in an EU State should be recognised in all the other EU States and also produce the same effects in the other EU states as it has according to the law of the State in which the proceedings are opened – see also the opinion of Advocate General Kokott at para 84. The court also stated that national laws generally precluded the initiation of separate legal proceedings once insolvency proceedings have been opened and Art 7(2)(f) prevented this principle being circumvented by the bringing of actions in other EU States (paras 69–71). The second decision – subsequent to *German Graphics* – is in the *Probud Gdynia* case Case C-444/07 [2010] BCC 453. Here the European Court held that only the opening of secondary proceedings was capable of restricting the universal effect of the main insolvency proceedings. The court reaffirmed the general principle that the insolvency proceedings had the same effects throughout the EU as they had in the State where such proceedings were opened.

What is now Art 7(2)(f) was considered in *Gibraltar Residential Properties Ltd v Gibralcon* [2010] EWHC 2595 (Ch) where a Spanish construction company Gibralcon became the subject of insolvency proceedings in Spain and sought to restrain the employer GRPL from continuing with English legal proceedings arising out of the construction contract. The contract contained an English exclusive jurisdiction clause but it seems that the English court proceedings were commenced only after the Spanish insolvency proceedings had been opened. At first blush, it would appear that Spanish law as the law of the state that opened the insolvency proceedings should pursuant to Art 7(2)(f) determine the effects of the proceedings on actions brought by 'individual creditors' and the exception in the provision for 'lawsuits pending' would not apply. But Edwards-Stuart J founded his decision largely on Art 23 of the EC Jurisdiction and Judgments Regulation – Regulation 44/2001 – which gave binding effect to a jurisdiction clause in a standard 'civil or commercial' contract like the construction agreement was in this case. He said the fact that a defendant in commercial proceedings is the subject of insolvency proceedings in another Member State was not of itself a ground for depriving the Jurisdiction and Judgments Regulation of application.

Edwards-Stuart J added, however (para 15), that the English court would not take:

> 'any step to prejudice or interfere with the Spanish insolvency proceedings. This court will do no more than determine the rights of the parties under this contract, disputes which are subject to the exclusive jurisdiction of the courts of England and Wales, and make declarations accordingly, and, in particular, determine so far as it can which party is owed money by the other and how much.'

Nevertheless, it is submitted that the decision wrongly deprives the Insolvency Regulation of much of its force. While there are oddities of language in the Regulation it seems clearly that its objective was to put the court of a Member State that opens main insolvency proceedings in the primary position of determining the effect of those proceedings on the debtor's legal relationships. That court is in the prime position of surveying the debtor's debts and legal relationships and how they should be assessed and adjusted in the new situation of insolvency. Once insolvency proceedings kick in, that court should take centre stage. The *Gibralcon* decision compromises the unity and universality of insolvency proceedings that the Insolvency Regulation is ostensibly designed to achieve.

It is submitted that the *Gibralcon* decision is inconsistent with that of Gloster J in *Lornamead Acquisitions Ltd v Kaupthing Bank HF* [2011] EWHC 2611 (Ch) though the latter decision is a decision on the interpretation of 2001/24/EC – the Credit Institutions Directive – and its implementation in the UK through the Credit Institutions (Reorganisation and Winding up) Regulations 2004 (SI 2004/1045) rather than on the Insolvency Regulation. There are certain differences between the two European instruments with the Credit Institutions Directive committed to a purer concept of unity and universalism than the Insolvency Regulation. But subject to this caveat, the Directive contains similarly worded provisions to the Insolvency Regulation and Art 10 of the Directive is similar to Art 7(2)(f) of the Regulation. (Under the Directive it is not possible to start secondary insolvency proceedings with purely territorial effects in states where the debtor has an 'establishment'. Only single main insolvency proceedings with near universal effects are allowed. As Lord Glennie observed in *Landsbanki Islands HF v Mills* [2010] Scot CS CSOH 100, [2011] 2 BCLC 437, at para [61], the purpose of the Directive is to ensure that administration or winding up proceedings are dealt with exclusively in the home state of the credit institution, and to 'ensure that such proceedings, and the decisions taken in those proceedings, are recognised and given full effect in other states'.)

The case concerned an insolvent Icelandic bank and Iceland was subject to the legal regime established by the Directive. Gloster J held that Icelandic insolvency proceedings in respect of the bank had the same effect in the UK as they did in Iceland. In particular, the moratorium created by Icelandic law on legal proceedings against the insolvent bank had an equivalent effect in the UK to that in Iceland. She suggested that a narrow definition, which gave the Icelandic insolvency measure only limited effect in the UK, would undermine the purpose of the 2001 Directive, by allowing differential treatment of claimants dependent on whether they sought to proceed in the home Member State or another state. Moreover, a bank subject to a European insolvency measure that was denied full effect in the UK would be exposed to the risk of uncontrolled litigation. She also spoke of the risk of dissipation of an insolvent bank's necessarily limited resources in litigation expenditure.

Some of the dangers spoken of by Gloster J stem from the inherent nature of banks, their vulnerability to 'runs' and the structure of the Directive but her judgment has a more general resonance. She highlighted the fact that an orderly insolvency process could be disrupted, and the estate dissipated, by proceedings brought in different jurisdictions by persons claiming that they were not debtors of the estate. An English supervisory court would want to ensure that actions against the insolvent entity were properly coordinated and disciplined. She also introduced a 'reality check' to see how one might have approached the problem if Kaupthing had been a UK institution that was subject to a UK winding-up or administration order. In those circumstances, there would have been an automatic statutory stay under the Insolvency Act that prevented proceedings against the company without leave. In such circumstances, a creditor could not issue proceedings whether in Iceland or the UK without the requisite leave. Gloster J referred to this as a 'statutory gateway, designed to protect the interests of the insolvent estate and the general body of creditors and preventing a free-for-all of proceedings'.

This general approach has been adopted by Nugee J in *Re Arm Asset Backed Securities SA (No 2)* [2014] EWHC 1097 (Ch) at paras [11]–[13] in holding that the commencement of English insolvency proceedings had the effect of blocking the initiation of regulatory proceedings against the debtor in another EU country, ie Luxembourg without the consent of the English court. By virtue of what is now Arts 7 and 20 of the Insolvency Regulation the UK insolvency stay was held to apply in other EU states.

In defence of the *Gibralcon* decision [2010] EWHC 2595 (Ch) one might draw a distinction between individual enforcement actions by creditors and lawsuits more generally. Measures for the realisation of assets would be examples of enforcement actions whereas actions to determine the existence, validity, content or amount of a claim would exemplify the latter. One might argue that what is now Art 7(2)(f) only precludes enforcement actions and not lawsuits more generally. A recent decision of the European court on the Credit Institutions Directive – Case C-85/12 *LBI hf v Kepler Capital Markets SA* [2013] EUECJ C-85/12, [2013] All ER (D) 301 – does draw a distinction between individual enforcement actions and lawsuits but does so in a context where it gives greater effect to the principle of universalism and the primacy of insolvency proceedings.

In *LBI Hf v Stanford* [2014] EWHC 3921 (Ch) Asplin J summed up the position at paras [197]–[199] in respect of the Credit Institutions Directive: 'The effect of the inter-relationship between Art 10(2)(c) and Art 32 and the materially identical provisions found in Arts 4(2)(f) and Art 15 of the Council Regulation (EC) 1346/2000 have been considered in a number of cases . . . In the *Syskia* case the Court of Appeal made clear that the law of the Member State in which insolvency proceedings were opened determines whether new lawsuits could be brought against the insolvent estate after the opening of the insolvency proceedings. Further, the decision of Gloster J (as she was then) in the *Lornamead* case is authority for the proposition that where a credit institution is subject to an EEA insolvency measure in its home Member State prior to the issue of proceedings in England, it is the law of the home Member State that will determine whether the English court is required to stay the proceedings . . . Furthermore, the judgment of the European Court of Justice in *LBI hf (formerly Landsbanki Islands hf) v Kepler Capital Markets SA* (Case C-85/12) makes clear that the exception in Art 32 applies only to lawsuits pending at the time of the opening of the winding-up proceedings in the home Member State.'

Her decision has also been applied by Carr J in *Tchenguiz v Grant Thornton UK LLP* [2015] EWHC 1864 (Comm) and upheld by the Court of Appeal – [2017] EWCA Civ 83. Briggs LJ at [46] was critical of the reasoning in the Gibralcon case. He said that if *Gibralcon* suggests that nothing in the Insolvency Instruments may be permitted to have a jurisdictional effect upon proceedings for which jurisdiction is allocated by the Jurisdiction Instruments, then it is simply wrongly decided. Briggs LJ at [55] cautioned against creating 'a large, ill-defined and wholly unstated exception with potentially disastrous consequences for the unity and universalism which is characteristic of both the Insolvency Regulation and the Winding-up Directive, and which is more rigorous in the latter'.

1    Case C-198/18, 30 April 2019. The Advocate General at paras 60–63 of his opinion referred to scholarly discussion on the scope of what is now Art 7(2)(d) – Art 4(2)(d) of Regulation 1346/2000. He said at para 60: 'There appear to be three approaches to this issue. According to the first interpretation, the existence of the right of set off is a preliminary question, governed by the law applicable to the main claim, and Article 4(2)(d) then only applies to the procedural possibility of invoking set-off in the insolvency proceedings. Under the second interpretation, Article 4(2)(d) covers the law applicable to the right of set-off itself. The third interpretation says that the specific scope of Article 4(2)(d) depends on the lex concursus. This allows Article 4(2)(d) to remain neutral and not give preference to any national system over others.' He added at para 62: 'In view of both the divergent legal frameworks for set-off in the context of

insolvency in the different Member States, and the different rationales underlying those systems, I find the third approach outlined above more reasonable in practical terms.'

2   Regulation (EC) 593/2008 of the European Parliament and of the Council of 17 June 2008 on the law applicable to contractual obligations (Rome I) (OJ 2008 L177/6) ('the Rome I Regulation').

3   See para 3 of the Advocate General's opinion.

4   *Dicey, Morris and Collins on the Conflict of Laws* (15th edition) at para 31–114.

## [6.10]

*Article 8  Third parties' rights in rem*

1.   *The opening of insolvency proceedings shall not affect the rights in rem of creditors or third parties in respect of tangible or intangible, moveable or immoveable assets, both specific assets and collections of indefinite assets as a whole which change from time to time, belonging to the debtor which are situated within the territory of another Member State at the time of the opening of proceedings.*

2.   *The rights referred to in paragraph 1 shall, in particular, mean:*

   (a)   *the right to dispose of assets or have them disposed of and to obtain satisfaction from the proceeds of or income from those assets, in particular by virtue of a lien or a mortgage;*

   (b)   *the exclusive right to have a claim met, in particular a right guaranteed by a lien in respect of the claim or by assignment of the claim by way of a guarantee;*

   (c)   *the right to demand assets from, and/or to require restitution by, anyone having possession or use of them contrary to the wishes of the party so entitled;*

   (d)   *a right in rem to the beneficial use of assets.*

3.   *The right, recorded in a public register and enforceable against third parties, based on which a right in rem within the meaning of paragraph 1 may be obtained shall be considered to be a right in rem.*

4.   *Paragraph 1 shall not preclude actions for voidness, voidability or unenforceability as referred to in point (m) of Article 7(2).*

**Amendments**—Repealed by SI 2019/146, as from IP completion day (as defined in the European Union (Withdrawal Agreement) Act 2020, s 39(1)–(5)).

**General note**—This provision is the equivalent of Art 5 in Regulation 1346/2000.

This article affords some protection for the secured creditor. Although the general rule is that the law of the State in which the insolvency proceedings are opened governs the administration of the debtor's estate, there are exceptions. Rights in rem (this includes floating charges) are to be governed by local law, so such rights are an exception to the general rule in Art 7. However, Art 8 can be applied only where the asset is within another Member State at the time of opening of proceedings, otherwise the *lex concursus* is applicable.

In *ERSTE Bank Hungary Nyrt v Republic of Hungary* Case C-527/10 [2012] I L Pr 38 the CJEU decided that what is now Art 8 also applied in the case where the debtor's relevant asset was situated within the territory of a State that became a Member State of the European Union only after the insolvency proceedings had been opened.

There has been some consideration of Art 5 by the CJEU in *Lutz v Bärle* Case C-557/13, 16 April 2015 [2015] IL Pr 21, paras 38–40. The court said that the provision enables a creditor to assert effectively, and even after the opening of insolvency proceedings, a right in rem that was established before the opening of those proceedings. Moreover, in order to enable the creditor to assert its right in rem effectively, in principle that creditor must be able to exercise the right under the lex causae after the opening of the insolvency proceedings. The particular conditions under the lex causae ie the law of the state where the assets are located, would apply rather than the law of the state of the opening of proceedings.

The Virgos-Schmit Report noted that there was no exhaustive definition of a right in rem because to create such a definition might conflict with the definition of a right in rem in the Member State where the assets were located (Recital 100). Thus the characterisation of a right in rem should be sought according to national laws.

The CJEU has held in response to a request by a German court for a preliminary ruling in the *Senior Home* case Case C-195/15 ECLI:EU:C:2016:804 that a right in rem includes a national rule pursuant to which real property tax debts are by operation of law a public charge on real property and the property owner must accept enforcement against the property.

The court referred to the existing case law and said that the basis, validity and extent of a right in rem must normally be determined according to the law of the place where the asset concerned is situated. It also rejected the proposition that Art 8 only protected in the context of commercial or credit contracts. It said that a limitation on the scope of Art 8 on the basis of the commercial origin of the right in rem concerned would be contrary to the objective of safeguarding legitimate expectations and the certainty of transactions. There could be no discrimination based on the identity of the creditor.

It is still possible to challenge the validity of rights in rem under Art 7(2)(m), so Art 8 rights are not entirely outside the scope of the law of State of opening of proceedings.

It is not entirely clear what is meant by 'shall not affect' in Art 8(1) and whether this protects the secured indebtedness as well as the security over the assets themselves. In other words, take the situation where the law of the State of the opening of insolvency proceedings enables secured indebtedness to be written down without the consent of the secured creditor but this is not permitted under the law of the State where the assets are situated. Would giving effect to the law of the State of the opening of insolvency proceedings infringe the rights of the secured creditor under Art 8? There is a strong argument that rights in rem are meaningless unless they are construed as protecting also the amount of the secured indebtedness. If the secured debt can be involuntarily written down in restructuring proceedings then the fact that the debtor may have security rights over assets is in practice largely irrelevant.

## [6.11]

### Article 9 Set-off

*1.   The opening of insolvency proceedings shall not affect the right of creditors to demand the set-off of their claims against the claims of a debtor, where such a set-off is permitted by the law applicable to the insolvent debtor's claim.*

*2.   Paragraph 1 shall not preclude actions for voidness, voidability or unenforceability as referred to in point (m) of Article 7(2).*

**Amendments**—Repealed by SI 2019/146, as from IP completion day (as defined in the European Union (Withdrawal Agreement) Act 2020, s 39(1)–(5)).

**General note**—Article 9 is the equivalent to Art 6 in Regulation 1346/2000. Article 7(2)(d) specifies that the basic rule is the lex concursus applies to any set-offs, but there is one limited exception to this under Art 9. If set-off is not applicable to the creditor's claim under the law of the state of the opening of proceedings the creditor may be able to rely on Art 9(1). See para 108 of the Virgos-Schmit Report which explains the meaning of Art 9(1) as enabling the creditor to set-off his claim against the debtor where it is permitted under the law applicable to the insolvent debtor's claim, ie the law applicable to the claim where the insolvent debtor is the creditor.

Any rights under Art 9 are still subject to the avoidance principles set out in Art 7(2)(m).

It is clear from *Re BCCI (No 10)* [1997] Ch 213 litigation that set-off rights differ significantly as between Member States, and Art 9 is a valuable safeguard for creditors who have entered into certain transactions on the basis that set-off rights would be available.

A possible ambiguity in Art 9 arises from the fact that the expression 'set-off' may be used in different Member States to refer to different legal processes and, in particular, may not catch contractual netting arrangements. The language of Art 9 refers to a debtor's claim whereas contractual netting usually involves a master agreement that disparate claims from a large number of the debtor's individual contracts will be set off against the various claims of the creditor. The end result is a net loss or profit for one party.

There was some consideration of Art 9 by Advocate General Bobek in *CeDe Group* though not by the Court of Justice itself (Case 198/18, 21 November 2019). Essentially the Advocate General took the view that what is now Art 9 will apply regardless of whether the lex concursus does not permit compensation by means of set-off generally or in a specific case (para 70 of his opinion). In his view, the provision should apply 'not only where the lex concursus entirely excludes the possibility of applying a set-off, but also in cases where the specific conditions of access to a set-off differ, so that, according to the lex concursus, set-off would not be possible in a specific case, whereas it would have been possible under the law applicable to the main claim' (para 75). In other words, the mere fact that the lex concursus allows, under certain conditions, for the possibility of set-offs does not preclude the application of Art 9. The view is that Art 9 may be used when it is more generous as regards set off than the lex concursus. In other words, it allows set-off where the law applicable to the insolvent debtor's claim permits this but this is not permitted under the lex concursus, eg in relation to future or contingent claims or even by imposing monetary limits on set offs.

It is not clear however, whether the term 'permitted by the law applicable to the insolvent debtor's claim' is a reference to the contractual set-off rules of the lex causae or the relevant insolvency set-off rules or a combination of both. The rules for set-off in formal insolvency proceedings may also be different from those that apply under the general civil law. Does the language of Art 9 refer to the set-off rules in formal insolvency or those of the general civil law? In favour of the application of insolvency set-off rules, one might argue that the insolvent debtor has entered insolvency proceedings and its insolvency practitioner who acts on behalf of the debtor is more likely to be familiar with insolvency set-off rules than general civil law rules on set off in different States. But this is by no means a given.

Moreover, if the reference is intended to be to the insolvency set-off rules, then insolvency proceedings may not have been commenced in the place of the applicable law. The question that then arises is how one determines which insolvency procedure should be considered? In the UK, for instance, there are different insolvency set-off rules with different cut-off dates in liquidation and administration. Any claims incurred or acquired by the counterparty after the cut-off date cannot be taken into account for insolvency set-off and so it is essential to determine the relevant date for this purpose[1].

Commentators are somewhat divided on the question whether Art 9 should be taken to as a reference to the insolvency rules of the particular legal system[2]. Nevertheless, the *travaux préparatoires* tends to suggest that a reference to the insolvency set-off rules is intended, however difficult this interpretation may be to apply in a particular case. This analysis appears from the Virgos-Schmit Report, which states at para 109 that what now is now Art 9 'constitutes an exception to the general application of that law in this respect, by permitting the set-off according to the conditions established for insolvency set-off by the law applicable to the *insolvent debtor's claim*'.

It should also be noted that the wording of Art 9 also differs significantly from its immediate neighbours, Arts 8 and 10, by making no reference to the law of a Member state but the significance of this difference is not patently obvious.

[1] See *Goode on Principles of Corporate Insolvency Law* (London, Thomson Reuters, 5th ed 2018 by Kristin Van Zwieten) at pp 868–867.
[2] See R Snowden in R Bork and K van Zwieten *Commentary on the European Insolvency Regulation* (Oxford, OUP, 2016) para 9.08 et seq. See also R Bork and R Mangano, *European Cross-Border Insolvency Law* (Oxford, OUP, 2016) at pp 144–145 and M Brinkmann ed *European Insolvency Regulation* (Munich, Verlag Beck, 2019) at pp 100–103 and 133.

## [6.12]

### Article 10  Reservation of title

1.  The opening of insolvency proceedings against the purchaser of an asset shall not affect sellers' rights that are based on a reservation of title where at the time of the opening of proceedings the asset is situated within the territory of a Member State other than the State of the opening of proceedings.

2.  The opening of insolvency proceedings against the seller of an asset, after delivery of the asset, shall not constitute grounds for rescinding or terminating the sale and shall not prevent the purchaser from acquiring title where at the time of the opening of proceedings the asset sold is situated within the territory of a Member State other than the State of the opening of proceedings.

3.  Paragraphs 1 and 2 shall not preclude actions for voidness, voidability or unenforceability as referred to in point (m) of Article 7(2).

**Amendments**—Repealed by SI 2019/146, as from IP completion day (as defined in the European Union (Withdrawal Agreement) Act 2020, s 39(1)–(5)).

**General note**—This is the equivalent of Art 7 under Regulation 1346/2000. Article 10 preserves seller's rights under reservation of title clauses where the assets in question are situated in a Member State other than that of the insolvency forum. While Art 9 of the Directive on late payment in commercial transactions – Directive 2011/7/EU appears to mandate the recognition of 'simple' reservation of title clauses throughout the Community, the law on the more complex variations of reservation of title differs widely between Member States. England, for instance, does not recognise claims by the original supplier to resale proceeds where goods supplied subject to reservation of title have been resold in the ordinary course of business, and also a supplier's title is deemed to have been lost where the goods have been used in a process of manufacture. If England is the insolvency forum then suppliers will continue to enjoy the possibly more extensive reservation of title rights under foreign law if the assets are located in another Member State. The fact that the assets are subsequently moved to the insolvency forum does not prejudice the supplier's rights if the assets were not located there at the time of the opening of the proceedings. It should be noted that Art 10 does not positively require that the law of the situs of the asset should govern the effectiveness and extent of the supplier's rights. It may be that some other law, such as the law of the contract of sale, has a role to play. Certain reservation of title clauses may be held to constitute registrable charges under the law of the situs but not under the law of the contract. The question arises whether the law of the contract will prevail to the exclusion of requirements to register according to the law of the situs.

Article 10 was briefly considered by the CJEU in *German Graphics v van der Schee* [2010] ILPr 1 on a preliminary reference but it submitted that the decision is somewhat unsatisfactory. The case concerned the sale of machines by a Germany supplier to a Dutch buyer subject to a reservation of title clauses. The Dutch buyer went into liquidation without having paid for the machines. At the time of the opening of the insolvency proceedings the machines were located in Holland but nevertheless a German court made an order granting relief to the supplier and this order was held to be enforceable by a Dutch court in Holland. The CJEU suggests that this result was perfectly compatible with European law. The court noted that what is now Art 10 was inapplicable because the assets were situated in the State where the insolvency proceeding were opened and not some other State. Given the location of the assets one might think that Dutch law should govern the effectiveness of the reservation of title clause by virtue of what is now Art 7(2)(b) which provides that the law of the State of opening of the insolvency proceedings determines 'the assets which form part of the estate'. The CJEU said however, somewhat elliptically, that this provision 'only constitutes a rule intended to prevent conflicts of law'. The authority of the German court to make a ruling on the validity of the reservation of title was therefore acknowledged under Regulation No 1346/2000 on the recognition and enforcement of judgments in civil and commercial matters.

## [6.13]

### Article 11  Contracts relating to immoveable property

1.   *The effects of insolvency proceedings on a contract conferring the right to acquire or make use of immoveable property shall be governed solely by the law of the Member State within the territory of which the immoveable property is situated.*

2.   *The court which opened main insolvency proceedings shall have jurisdiction to approve the termination or modification of the contracts referred to in this Article where:*

   (a)   *the law of the Member State applicable to those contracts requires that such a contract may only be terminated or modified with the approval of the court opening insolvency proceedings; and*

   (b)   *no insolvency proceedings have been opened in that Member State.*

**Amendments**—Repealed by SI 2019/146, as from IP completion day (as defined in the European Union (Withdrawal Agreement) Act 2020, s 39(1)–(5)).

**General note**—This provision replaces Art 8 of Regulation 1346/2000. According to Art 7(2)(e) what might be termed the default rule again applies to current contracts to which the debtor is a party, ie that of the law of the State of the opening of proceedings. Where the contract confers rights to acquire or make use of immoveable property which is not situated in the State where proceedings have been opened, the lex situs applies.

Article 11 was interpreted by McDonald J in the Irish High Court in *Apperley Investments Ltd v Monsoon Accessorize Ltd* [2020] IEHC 523.The decision sheds light on the extent to which a UK company voluntary arrangement (CVA) impacting property rights may be enforced, or not enforced, on landlords outside the UK. It was held that the landlords were entitled to full rent on their premises and were not bound by the CVA.

While the court opening main insolvency proceedings was entitled to exercise jurisdiction, there was no mandate within Art 11 of the Regulation that conferred any power on that court to apply its own law. Therefore, the effects of insolvency proceedings on a contract falling within Art 11(1) remain governed 'solely by the law of the Member State within the territory of which the immoveable property is situated' ([58]).

There is, however, a new rule in Art 11(2) giving the courts of the State where the insolvency proceedings have been opened the power to modify the type of contracts to which Art 11 refers in certain circumstances.

It was held by the European Court, however, in *UB v VA, Tiger SCI* Case C 493/18, 4 December 2019 that the Insolvency Regulation does not confer on the courts of the State where immovable property is located international jurisdiction to hear an action for the restitution of those assets to the bankruptcy estate. The court took the view that concentrating all the actions directly related to the insolvency proceedings before the courts of the Member State where the proceedings were opened was consistent with the objective of improving the efficiency and speed of insolvency proceedings having cross-border effects.

Article 3(1) of the Insolvency Regulation was interpreted as meaning that an action brought by a trustee in bankruptcy, appointed where the insolvency proceedings were opened, seeking a declaration that the sale of immovable property in another Member State and the mortgage over it were ineffective as against the general body of creditors, fell within the exclusive jurisdiction of the Member State where the proceedings were opened. What is now Art 32 of the recast Regulation did not invest the courts in Member States where property was located with international jurisdiction even if the bringing of the action was authorised by the courts of the Member State where the proceedings were opened.

## [6.14]

### Article 12 Payment systems and financial markets

1. *Without prejudice to Article 8, the effects of insolvency proceedings on the rights and obligations of the parties to a payment or settlement system or to a financial market shall be governed solely by the law of the Member State applicable to that system or market.*

2. *Paragraph 1 shall not preclude any action for voidness, voidability or unenforceability which may be taken to set aside payments or transactions under the law applicable to the relevant payment system or financial market.*

**Amendments**—Repealed by SI 2019/146, as from IP completion day (as defined in the European Union (Withdrawal Agreement) Act 2020, s 39(1)–(5)).

**General note**—Under this article any rights or obligations of the parties to a payment or settlement system, or a financial market will not be governed by the lex concursus, but instead by the law of the Member State applicable to that system or market. This ensures certainty for any parties involved with such systems as to the law that will govern those systems in the event of insolvency.

Unlike some of the other choice of law provisions in this part of the Regulation the avoidance rules of the law of the state of the opening of proceedings (Art 7(2)(m)) are not applicable. Avoidance measures are not precluded by this article but the relevant law is the particular law applicable to the system or market.

Recital 71 also refers to a need for 'special protection in the case of payment systems and financial markets', eg in relation to 'position-closing agreements and netting agreements to be found in such systems'. It refers to the fact that the Settlement Finality Directive – Directive 98/26/EC – contains special provisions which should take precedence over the general rules of the Insolvency Regulation.

## [6.15]

### Article 13 Contracts of employment

1. *The effects of insolvency proceedings on employment contracts and relationships shall be governed solely by the law of the Member State applicable to the contract of employment.*

2. *The courts of the Member State in which secondary insolvency proceedings may be opened shall retain jurisdiction to approve the termination or modification of the contracts referred to in this Article even if no insolvency proceedings have been opened in that Member State.*

*The first subparagraph shall also apply to an authority competent under national law to approve the termination or modification of the contracts referred to in this Article.*

**Amendments**—Repealed by SI 2019/146, as from IP completion day (as defined in the European Union (Withdrawal Agreement) Act 2020, s 39(1)–(5)).

**General note**—Article 10 of Regulation 1346/20000 provided that the effects of insolvency proceedings on employment contracts and relationships should be governed by the law applicable to the contract of employment. This law would determine, for example, whether insolvency proceedings operated to terminate or to continue the contract but other important employment law related matters were left to the law of the insolvency forum, including the preferential status of employee claims.

In the recast Regulation, Art 13 retains the basic proposition that the effect of insolvency proceedings on contracts of employment is governed by the law that applies to the contract. But courts or competent authorities of Member states where insolvency proceedings may be opened may also approve the termination or modification of the contracts. It seems that behind the new contractual termination regime is the European Commission view that 'different labour law standards may hinder an insolvency administrator to take the same actions with regard to employees located in several Member States and that this situation may complicate the restructuring of a company' – see *Report from the Commission on the application of Council Regulation (EC) No 1346/2000* COM (2012) 743 at para 12.

**[6.16]**

*Article 14 Effects on rights subject to registration*

*The effects of insolvency proceedings on the rights of a debtor in immoveable property, a ship or an aircraft subject to registration in a public register shall be determined by the law of the Member State under the authority of which the register is kept.*

**Amendments**—Repealed by SI 2019/146, as from IP completion day (as defined in the European Union (Withdrawal Agreement) Act 2020, s 39(1)–(5)).

**General note**—This is equivalent to Art 11 in Regulation 1346/2000. Frequently Member States will have some kind of system for the public registration of immoveable property and certain moveable property, such as aircraft and ships, in the state where they are routinely kept. In order to prevent conflicts between the Member State in which proceedings are opened and the Member State in which the public register is kept, Art 14 identifies the law where the register is kept as the one that governs the property and not the *lex concursus*. However, as the Virgos-Schmit Report states the omission of the word 'solely' in this article means that the *lex concursus* does have some relevance: para 130 states 'a sort of cumulative application of both laws is necessary'. This means that there should be some communication between the liquidator and the keeper of the register so that an official note should be made in the register showing that insolvency proceedings are ongoing.

**[6.17]**

*Article 15 European patents with unitary effect and Community trade marks*

*For the purposes of this Regulation, a European patent with unitary effect, a Community trade mark or any other similar right established by Union law may be included only in the proceedings referred to in Article 3(1).*

**Amendments**—Repealed by SI 2019/146, as from IP completion day (as defined in the European Union (Withdrawal Agreement) Act 2020, s 39(1)–(5)).

**[6.18]**

*Article 16 Detrimental acts*

*Point (m) of Article 7(2) shall not apply where the person who benefited from an act detrimental to all the creditors provides proof that:*

    *(a)    the act is subject to the law of a Member State other than that of the State of the opening of proceedings; and*

    *(b)    the law of that Member State does not allow any means of challenging that act in the relevant case.*

**Amendments**—Repealed by SI 2019/146, as from IP completion day (as defined in the European Union (Withdrawal Agreement) Act 2020, s 39(1)–(5)).

**General note**—This is equivalent to Art 13 in Regulation 1346/2000. In the non-exhaustive list of subjects that are governed by the law of the state of the opening of proceedings, Art 7(2)(m) identifies that avoidance provisions of the state where proceedings are commenced should apply. Article 16 provides protection for any person who benefits from a detrimental act of the debtor, eg a transaction which appears to be at an undervalue. If the person can prove that the act is subject to a law other than that of the opening of proceedings and would not be open to challenge by the law of that State, then the act cannot be challenged in the place where proceedings have been opened. A creditor cannot rely on this provision unless the act or transaction was carried out before insolvency proceedings are opened. Once insolvency proceedings have begun the lex concursus applies and the assets of the debtor are subject to that law.

Some clarification on the meaning of what is now Art 16 has been provided by the CJEU in Case C-557/13 *Lutz v Bärle* (16 April 2015, [2015] IL Pr 21) and Case C-310/14 *Nike European Operations Netherlands B V v Sportland Oy* (15 October 2015). In *Lutz v Bärle* it was held that the Art 16 defence is an exception that must be construed strictly, it applies in a broad range of situations and applies whenever either substantive or procedural rules (such as time limits or limitation periods) would prevent the bringing of the action. The court said that if what is now the Art 16 defence did not cover what were considered by the forum State to be procedural matters, that interpretation would lead to arbitrary discrimination according to the legal-theory models adopted in EU Member States and prevent a uniform application of Art 16. While the provision did not, in principle, apply to acts which take place after the opening of insolvency proceedings, the right being challenged in this particular case – a right to attach assets – had been established before the opening of the insolvency proceedings and therefore could benefit from special protection given by Art 16. The transaction was governed by Austrian law which did not allow the transaction to be challenged and this was fatal to the liquidator's challenge under the law of the forum State ie Germany.

In Case C-310/14 *Nike European Operations Netherlands BV v Sportland Oy* the laws in question were Finnish law and Dutch law. Insolvency proceedings had been opened in respect of a company in Finland and it was alleged that certain payments made by the company prior to the opening of the proceedings could be impugned under Finnish law. The counterparty was a Dutch registered entity and it asserted that the relevant transactions were governed by Dutch law which did not allow any means of challenging the transactions in the relevant case. The European court held that what is now Art 16 'must be interpreted as meaning that its application is subject to the condition that, after taking account of all the circumstances of the case, the act at issue cannot be challenged on the basis of the law governing the act ("lex causae")' (see para 22).

The court added that it is for the defendant in an action relating to the voidness, voidability or unenforceability of an act to provide proof, on the basis of the lex causae, that the act cannot be challenged. The defendant had to establish both the facts from which the conclusion can be drawn that the act is unchallengeable and the absence of any evidence that would militate against that conclusion. The applicant was not required to claim or prove that the conditions for the application of a provision of the lex causae which, in principle, would enable the act at issue to be challenged are satisfied. On the other hand, while Art 13 (now Art 16) expressly governed the burden of proof, it did not set out the ways in which evidence is to be elicited, what evidence is to be admissible before the appropriate national court, or the principles governing that court's assessment of the probative value of the evidence adduced before it. These were matters for each Member State but in accordance with the principles of equivalence and effectiveness these rules should be no less favourable than those governing similar domestic situations or make it excessively difficult or impossible in practice to exercise the rights conferred by EU. Therefore, the national procedural rules should not be so onerous as to make reliance on Art 13 impossible or excessively difficult or alternatively, not sufficiently rigorous with the effect of shifting the burden of proof laid down in Art 13 – now Art 16 – (paras 25–29).

The interaction between Arts 7 and 16 was further considered by the European Court in Case C-54/16 *Vinyls Italia SpA, in liquidation v Mediterranea di Navigazione SpA* EU:C:2017:433; [2018] 1 WLR 543. The court was asked whether a person, in order to avail of what is now the Art 16 defence, must raise a procedural objection within the periods laid down by the procedural rules of the lex fori or can simply raise the defence during the course of the avoidance proceedings. The court said that the procedural rules of the lex fori must be observed. Nevertheless, the court insisted that the defendant did not have to show that under the governing law of the contract, there was no means of challenging the payment, either in general or in the abstract. Instead, it was up the defendant to prove on the specific facts of the case that the necessary conditions for a challenge to be successful would not be satisfied even though in theory the governing law of the contract provided a means of challenge.

The court was also asked whether the Art 16 defence applies when contracting parties have their head offices in a single Member State, whose law can therefore be expected to become the lex fori in the event of insolvency of one of those parties, and the parties through a contractual choice of law clause have designated another law as the law applicable. The court said that pursuant to the Rome choice-of-law regime, the parties can designate another applicable law. The defence, however, could not be relied upon for abusive or fraudulent ends such as where the parties chose the governing law of the contract to get around the rules on insolvency with a view to gaining an undue advantage. Nevertheless, the choice of a contractual governing law other than the law of the Member States where the counterparties were established did not bring into existence a presumption that the parties had abusive or fraudulent ends.

The interaction between Arts 7 and 16, or rather the equivalent Arts 4 and 13 provisions in the original Regulation, were further considered by the CJEU in *Z.M. v E.A. Frerichs* Case C-73/20 ECLI:EU:C:2021:315 (22 April 2021). The issue arose in the context of insolvency proceedings opened in Germany that involved a German company (O). O had made a payment to a Dutch company (F) that O's liquidator sought to challenge under German avoidance law. The payment had been made to satisfy contractual obligations owed by a German company (T) which belonged to the same group as O. It was accepted that Dutch law governed the contract between F and T and though the payment could be challenged under German avoidance law, it could not under Dutch law.

The CJEU concluded that since the law applicable to a contract under Rome I Regulation[1] also governs the payment by a third party in performance of the debtor's payment obligation, that law also applies where, in insolvency proceedings, the payment is challenged as an act detrimental to the body of creditors under the Insolvency Regulation. The court said that the Insolvency Regulation must be interpreted in light of the objective of protecting the expectations of the party to the contract who received the payment. The court (at [25]–[26]) said that the provisions in the Insolvency Regulation constitute a 'lex specialis' in relation to the Rome I Regulation.

It should be remembered that in this particular case, the insolvent debtor was asked by another company from the same group to make payment under a contract concluded by the other group company. One might entertain the suspicion that the goal of the payment was to put the funds of the insolvent company beyond the reach of its creditors by releasing a company in the same group from one of its debts. From the reported facts however, there does not seem to be any evidence to support this suspicion.

Article 30 of the Credit Institutions Directive is in similar terms to Art 16 and was considered by the EFTA Court in Case E-28/13 *LBI v Merrill Lynch* [2015] All ER (D) 78 (Mar) where certain transactions entered into by an insolvent Icelandic insolvent credit institution were challenged. The Icelandic bank had issued debt securities and shortly before it entered insolvency proceedings, it redeemed these securities. The liquidator sought rescission of the redemption transactions arguing that they were invalid under Icelandic law being repayments by an insolvent actor of debts before the date of maturity.

On the other hand, the defendant contended that the situation must be qualified as a purchase by the plaintiff of its own securities and not as the repayment of a debt. In any event, it argued that, under Art 30, the measures in question could only be rescinded if this were permissible under English law and, in its view, rescission would not be possible under English law. The defendant suggested that the purpose of this provision was to ensure protection against retroactive actions by the debtor to invalidate a legal act where the creditor had legitimate expectations that the act would be binding on the debtor. It also suggested that the expression 'in the relevant case' meant that the detrimental act should not be capable of being challenged in fact, taking account of all the individual circumstances of the case at hand. It was not sufficient to determine whether the act could be challenged in the abstract.

Essentially, the court accepted the defendant's arguments holding that the counterparty to the transaction could avail of both procedural and substantive defences. It was enough if the counterparty established that there was no possibility, or no longer any possibility, of challenging the transaction in question. Moreover, there had to be a concrete assessment of the specific transaction and even if, in principle, it could be challenged under the law governing the transaction, it was sufficient if the beneficiary proved that the requirements for such a challenge were not fulfilled in the case at hand. Nevertheless, the question whether the counterparty had shown that the law governing the transaction did not allow any means of challenging it had to be assessed according to the rules of the forum state for determining the substance of foreign law.

[1]  Regulation (EC) No 593/2008 of the European Parliament and of the Council of 17 June 2008 on the law applicable to contractual obligations (Rome I) (OJ 2008 L 177.

## [6.19]

### Article 17  Protection of third-party purchasers

*Where, by an act concluded after the opening of insolvency proceedings, a debtor disposes, for consideration, of:*

(a)  *an immoveable asset;*

(b)  *a ship or an aircraft subject to registration in a public register; or*

(c)  *securities the existence of which requires registration in a register laid down by law;*

*the validity of that act shall be governed by the law of the State within the territory of which the immoveable asset is situated or under the authority of which the register is kept.*

**Amendments**—Repealed by SI 2019/146, as from IP completion day (as defined in the European Union (Withdrawal Agreement) Act 2020, s 39(1)–(5)).

**General note**—This is the equivalent of Art 14 in Regulation 1346/2000. Once a debtor enters into an insolvency proceeding this usually results in the debtor being prevented from dealing with any of his assets or property, thereby ensuring that the debtor cannot dissipate his assets to the detriment of the general body of creditors. If the debtor does try to dispose of his assets after the opening of proceedings any such actions can be declared void or the court may if it considers it appropriate declare the action valid, or valid subject to certain conditions. See for example s 127 of the Insolvency Act 1986 which limits the ability of a company to dispose of its assets when winding-up proceedings have been commenced. In some cases the debtor may transfer assets to an innocent third party who was unaware of the insolvency proceedings, perhaps entering into a transaction with the debtor before the proceedings had been made public. In order to protect the innocent third party where they have given some consideration for the asset or property and the application of the lex concursus to that transaction may be to the detriment of the third party purchaser, Art 17 may come into effect. Article 17, by applying the law of the lex situs in the case of immoveable property and in the case of a registrable asset the law of the State under whose authority the register is kept, ensures the fair treatment of third party purchasers. The article does not seem to require that the lex situs or the State where the register is kept be within the EU, ie a Member State. Thus if the asset is in a third state it would appear that Art 14 still applies.

## [6.20]

### Article 18 Effects of insolvency proceedings on pending lawsuits or arbitral proceedings

*The effects of insolvency proceedings on a pending lawsuit or pending arbitral proceedings concerning an asset or a right which forms part of a debtor's insolvency estate shall be governed solely by the law of the Member State in which that lawsuit is pending or in which the arbitral tribunal has its seat.*

**Amendments**—Repealed by SI 2019/146, as from IP completion day (as defined in the European Union (Withdrawal Agreement) Act 2020, s 39(1)–(5)).

**General note**—Article 7(2)(f) states that any proceedings brought by individual creditors, such as distress, will be governed by the law of the State of the opening of proceedings, except lawsuits pending which are governed by Art 18. In the latter case Art 18 imposes a rule whereby the law of the state in which the lawsuit is pending is solely applicable to the case. It would then be a decision of the courts of the State in which proceedings are pending to decide whether they should be suspended or not.

This provision is the equivalent of Art 15 of Regulation 1346/2000 with the notable express extension to arbitration proceedings. This change in fact confirms and 'Europeanises' the interpretation of Article 15 reached by the English courts in *Syska v Vivendi Universal SA* [2008] 2 Lloyd's Rep 636 (HC), [2009] 2 All ER (Comm) 891 (CA) where it was held that the 'lawsuits pending' exception encompassed arbitration proceedings. The court said that there was no good reason why 'lawsuit' should not include a reference to arbitration. If the draftsman intended only to exclude lawsuits pending in court, unequivocally clear phraseology could easily have been used. Moreover, if it was intended to exempt pending actions from the operation of the law of the opening state it did not make sense to leave arbitrations out of the exception. Longmore LJ in the Court of Appeal remarked that if 'litigation or arbitration has begun before insolvency occurs the natural expectation of businesses would be that it should be that law that should determine whether the proceedings should continue or come to a shuddering halt'. Longmore LJ also said until the 'validity of that particular claim is ascertained, it has no status in or relevance to the insolvency proceedings at all . . . Of course if no claim has been initiated before insolvency proceedings are opened, it is entirely appropriate that the *lex concursus* should determine how any subsequent litigation or arbitration should proceed'.

A decision of the European court on the equivalent provisions in the Credit Institutions Directive (Directive 2001/24/EC, Articles 10 and 32) – *LBI hf v Kepler Capital Markets SA* Case C-85/12 [2013] EUECJ C-85/12, [2013] All ER (D) 301 – holds that the 'lawsuits pending' exception to the primacy of the insolvency proceedings should be given a narrow interpretation. The exception was held to cover only 'proceedings on the substance' and that individual enforcement actions such as the attachment orders in that case remained subject to the law of the insolvency forum which had retrospective effects.

The detailed language of Art 18 (Art 15 of Regulation 1346/2000) was more recently explored by the European Court in Case C-250/17 *Tarrago da Silveira v Massa Insolvente da Espírito Santo* [2018] 1 WLR 4148, [2018] ILPr 29. The court 'noted that the various language versions of that provision are not unambiguous'. Nevertheless, the context and the objectives of the article required an interpretation to the effect that its scope of application could not be limited to ongoing proceedings concerning a specific asset or right of which the debtor has been divested.

The predecessor of Art 18 has been considered by the English courts on a number of occasions. If a lawsuit is pending in a particular State within the meaning of Art 18, then it seems that it is for that State to determine whether the law suit may be enlarged, modified or amended in any particular way notwithstanding that insolvency proceedings have been opened in another State pursuant to Art 3. This issues was addressed by in *Fortress Value Recovery Fund v Blue Skye Special Opportunities Fund* [2013] EWHC 14 (Comm) where the court held it was for English procedural law to determine the effect of insolvency proceedings in another Member State on any proceedings pending in England in relation to liability. English procedural law permitted amendments to claims to be made notwithstanding the insolvency of the defendant and the fact that this might not be permitted under the laws of the insolvency forum was wholly irrelevant.

The same issue arose in *Isis Investments Ltd v Oscatello Investments Ltd* [2013] EWCA Civ 1493 and the same result was reached. The factual background in the latter case is somewhat different however in that it involved the relevant provisions of the Credit Institutions directive and its application in the UK through the Credit Institutions (Reorganisation and Winding up) Regulations 2004 (SI 2004/1045) rather than the Insolvency Regulation. Nevertheless the two sets of provisions are similar and in support of its conclusion the Court of Appeal relied on para 142 of the Virgos-Schmit report. The report made it clear that it was for the procedural law of the forum to decide 'whether or not the proceedings are to be suspended' and 'how they are to be continued' and 'whether any appropriate procedural modifications are needed in order to reflect the . . . intervention of the liquidator'.

## CHAPTER II   RECOGNITION OF INSOLVENCY PROCEEDINGS

### [6.21]

#### Article 19  Principle

1.  *Any judgment opening insolvency proceedings handed down by a court of a Member State which has jurisdiction pursuant to Article 3 shall be recognised in all other Member States from the moment that it becomes effective in the State of the opening of proceedings.*

*The rule laid down in the first subparagraph shall also apply where, on account of a debtor's capacity, insolvency proceedings cannot be brought against that debtor in other Member States.*

2.  *Recognition of the proceedings referred to in Article 3(1) shall not preclude the opening of the proceedings referred to in Article 3(2) by a court in another Member State. The latter proceedings shall be secondary insolvency proceedings within the meaning of Chapter III.*

**Amendments**—Repealed by SI 2019/146, as from IP completion day (as defined in the European Union (Withdrawal Agreement) Act 2020, s 39(1)–(5)).

**General note**—This Article is the equivalent to Art 16 in Regulation 1346/2000. The Article states that an insolvency proceeding opened in a Member State will be recognised in any other Member State. Recognition occurs automatically from the time the judgment opening proceedings is effective in the Member State where proceedings have been opened. Thus, as stated in the general note to Art 2, judgment is given a wide meaning and includes for example the resolution for a creditors' voluntary winding up. In *Aria Inc v Credit Agricole* [2014] EWHC 872 (Comm) at [28]. Leggatt J summarised the effect of the provision as being that any insolvency order made anywhere in the EU is effective in other Member States. See also the comments of Eady J in *Windhorst v Levy* [2021] EWHC 1168 (QB) (26 April 2021) at [58].

Recognition occurs regardless of whether it is possible to open proceedings against the debtor in any other Member State. However, it is also expressly stated that recognition of main proceedings does not prevent the opening of secondary proceedings under Art 3(2).

The *Eurofood* case ([2006] ECR I–701) emphasises that once main proceedings are claimed to have been opened by the court of a Member State, this must be recognised in other Member States without the latter being able to review the jurisdiction of the court of the opening State.

The recognition of foreign insolvency proceedings was at issue before the CJEU in *MG Probud Gdynia sp z o o* C-444/07, [2010] BCC 453. In this case a Polish construction company with its COMI in Poland carried out certain works in Germany. The company became the subject of insolvency proceedings in Poland but, after the commencement of such proceedings, the German customs authorities attempted to attach its assets in Germany contrary to Polish insolvency law. It should be noted that secondary insolvency proceedings had not been opened in Germany. The CJEU effectively ruled that this action by the German authorities was impermissible under the terms of the EC Insolvency Regulation. It said that the judgment opening insolvency proceedings in Poland was to be recognised in all other Member States including Germany from the time it became effective, and producing the same effects as under Polish law. Because of the universal effect to be accorded to main insolvency proceedings, the proceedings opened in Poland encompassed all of the company's assets, including those situated in Germany.

The decisive consideration under the Insolvency Regulation is in which State insolvency proceedings have first been opened rather than where the application to open the proceedings has first been lodged. The French Cour de Cassation in *Re X (Application to open Insolvency Proceedings)* [2014] ILPr 35 made it clear that any conflict must be resolved in favour of the order opening the proceedings and not on the basis of the respective dates when the courts were seised of the application to open the insolvency proceedings. The case highlights the distinction between the Insolvency Regulation and the Jurisdiction and Judgments Regulation. Under the latter regulation, the relevant test is which court was first seised of the matter, rather than which court first opens the proceedings.

But what if main insolvency proceedings have been opened in an EU state even though main insolvency proceedings have already been opened in a different state. Clearly the second set of proceedings should not have been opened but are the courts in the state where the first proceedings have been opened entitled to disregard the second set? One might argue that the second proceedings are a nullity because they disregard the mutual recognition mandate that is at the heart of the EC Regulation. A different view was, however, taken in *Re Eurodis PLC* [2011] EWHC 1025 (Ch), [2012] BCC 57 where it was held that while a winding up order in respect of a company made in the Belgian court probably ought not to have been made, since the main insolvency proceedings were in the UK, it had to stand as a valid order of the Belgian court unless set aside in Belgium.

## [6.22]

### Article 20  Effects of recognition

*1.   The judgment opening insolvency proceedings as referred to in Article 3(1) shall, with no further formalities, produce the same effects in any other Member State as under the law of the State of the opening of proceedings, unless this Regulation provides otherwise and as long as no proceedings referred to in Article 3(2) are opened in that other Member State.*

*2.   The effects of the proceedings referred to in Article 3(2) may not be challenged in other Member States. Any restriction of creditors' rights, in particular a stay or discharge, shall produce effects vis-à-is assets situated within the territory of another Member State only in the case of those creditors who have given their consent.*

**Amendments**—Repealed by SI 2019/146, as from IP completion day (as defined in the European Union (Withdrawal Agreement) Act 2020, s 39(1)–(5)).

**General note**—This Article is the equivalent of Art 17 in Regulation 1346/2000. Where main proceedings have been opened, their effect is the same in any other Member State as it would be in the State in which the proceedings were opened. However, this is not the result, first, where secondary proceedings (or territorial proceedings) are opened in a Member State – in such a case where the secondary proceedings are opened they will be governed by the law of that State – or, second, where the Regulation indicates otherwise, eg the law of the State of the opening of proceedings will not apply under Arts 8–18.

## [6.23]

### Article 21  Powers of the insolvency practitioner

*1.   The insolvency practitioner appointed by a court which has jurisdiction pursuant to Article 3(1) may exercise all the powers conferred on it, by the law of the State of the opening of proceedings, in another Member State, as long as no other insolvency proceedings have been opened there and no preservation measure to the contrary has been taken there further to a request for the opening of insolvency proceedings in that State. Subject to Articles 8 and 10, the insolvency practitioner may, in particular, remove the debtor's assets from the territory of the Member State in which they are situated.*

*2.   The insolvency practitioner appointed by a court which has jurisdiction pursuant to Article 3(2) may in any other Member State claim through the courts or out of court that moveable property was removed from the territory of the State of the opening of proceedings to the territory of that other Member State after the opening of the insolvency proceedings. The insolvency practitioner may also bring any action to set aside which is in the interests of the creditors.*

*3.   In exercising its powers, the insolvency practitioner shall comply with the law of the Member State within the territory of which it intends to take action, in particular with regard to procedures for the realisation of assets. Those powers may not include coercive measures, unless ordered by a court of that Member State, or the right to rule on legal proceedings or disputes.*

**Amendments**—Repealed by SI 2019/146, as from IP completion day (as defined in the European Union (Withdrawal Agreement) Act 2020, s 39(1)–(5)).

General note—This provision is the equivalent of Art 18 in Regulation 1346/2000. Clearly, if an insolvency is to be efficiently administered it is not only the proceedings themselves that must be recognised. Article 21 was considered by the Dutch Supreme Court in *Handelsveem BV v Hill* [2011] BPIR 1024. In this case a UK court had made an order under s 366 of the Insolvency Act requiring a third party in Holland to provide a list of goods held on behalf of the bankrupt and a question arose about the enforceability of this order in the Netherlands. The Dutch court held that, in accordance with what is now Art 21(1), a bankruptcy trustee was able to exercise in another Member State all the powers conferred on him by the law of the Member State in which the insolvency procedure was opened. While what is now Art 21(3) limited the exercise of those powers to those that did not comprise the use of coercive measures, this prohibition did not apply in this particular case since the trustees were acting on the basis of a judgment that was recognised and enforceable in other Member States under what is now Art 32.

## ARTICLE 21(1)

Scope of provision—The liquidator of main proceedings is given all the powers of the State that appointed him, and these powers can be exercised in any other Member State. He may remove assets from one Member State, but must have regard to the rules laid down in Arts 8–18. Obviously, the liquidator of secondary proceedings should not have as wide powers as the liquidator in main proceedings, or conflict would be likely to ensue. As secondary proceedings are ancillary to main proceedings and are concerned only with assets in that jurisdiction, so a 'secondary' liquidator is only concerned with assets within the jurisdiction that appointed him. But he may request that assets that were originally in the jurisdiction and were subsequently removed be repatriated.

## ARTICLE 21(3)

Scope of provision—A liquidator must comply with the local law of any territory in which he seeks to act. This point was made by Leggatt J in *Aria Inc v Credit Agricole* [2014] EWHC 872 (Comm) at para 60 who suggested that the law of the situs applied with respect to procedural matters.

In the UK, the exercise of an IP's powers in other EU states was recently an issue in *Wallace v Wallace* [2019] EWHC 2503 (Ch), [2019] BCC 1224. In that case it was held that the liquidator of an insolvent company was entitled to an order under the UK Insolvency Act 1986, s 263(3) requiring the company's former bookkeeper who was resident in the Republic of Ireland, to deliver up the books and records of the company in his possession or control. Reference was made to the European Insolvency Regulation and the authority of a liquidator to exercise the powers conferred on him by UK domestic law in other Member States. Moreover, the former bookkeeper was sufficiently connected with the UK jurisdiction for it to be just and proper to make an order despite the foreign element. He had been an important part of the company's operations and if he had possession of the company's books and records, he could not complain that an order requiring him to make those books and records available on a winding up involved any excess of jurisdiction by the English court. That court had an entirely legitimate interest in requiring the bookkeeper, even if abroad, to make such documents and information available to the liquidator.

The same result was reached on the basis of somewhat different reasoning in *Re Akkurate Ltd (in Liquidation)* [2020] EWHC 1433 (Ch). Vos C held that, according to the CJEU Jurisprudence, the Regulation extended the territoriality of purely domestic insolvency provisions. Proceedings under s 236(3) of the UK Insolvency Act derived directly from, and were closely connected to, insolvency proceedings, and the aim of the Regulation was to confer jurisdiction on the courts of the Member State in which the insolvent entity had its centre of main interests. Therefore, the Regulation conferred extraterritorial jurisdiction on the English court to make orders against EU-resident parties under s 236.

## [6.24]

*Article 22 Proof of the insolvency practitioner's appointment*

*The insolvency practitioner's appointment shall be evidenced by a certified copy of the original decision appointing it or by any other certificate issued by the court which has jurisdiction.*

*A translation into the official language or one of the official languages of the Member State within the territory of which it intends to act may be required. No legalisation or other similar formality shall be required.*

Amendments—Repealed by SI 2019/146, as from IP completion day (as defined in the European Union (Withdrawal Agreement) Act 2020, s 39(1)–(5)).

General note—This provision is the equivalent of Art 19 in Regulation 1346/2000. It requires only that the liquidator's appointment is evidenced by a copy of the decision appointing him. Thus, with the minimum of fuss a liquidator will be recognised in any other Member State. The only other formality that may have to be followed is that the decision appointing him may have to be translated into one of the official languages of the Member State in which the liquidator intends to act.

**[6.25]**

### Article 23 Return and imputation

1.   *A creditor which, after the opening of the proceedings referred to in Article 3(1), obtains by any means, in particular through enforcement, total or partial satisfaction of its claim on the assets belonging to a debtor situated within the territory of another Member State, shall return what it has obtained to the insolvency practitioner, subject to Articles 8 and 10.*

2.   *In order to ensure the equal treatment of creditors, a creditor which has, in the course of insolvency proceedings, obtained a dividend on its claim shall share in distributions made in other proceedings only where creditors of the same ranking or category have, in those other proceedings, obtained an equivalent dividend.*

**Amendments**—Repealed by SI 2019/146, as from IP completion day (as defined in the European Union (Withdrawal Agreement) Act 2020, s 39(1)–(5)).

**General note**—This provision is the equivalent of Art 20 in Regulation 1346/2000. Under Art 23(1), if a creditor has acted after the opening of main proceedings to enforce his claim against assets situated in another Member State, he can be forced to turn over anything he has received to the liquidator in the main proceedings, subject to Arts 8 and 10.

The principle that Art 23(2) embodies in theory may be ineffective in practice because local creditors may be satisfied in full from secondary insolvency proceedings opened at their instigation. In these circumstances they will have no need to have recourse to the main proceedings.

**[6.26]**

### Article 24 Establishment of insolvency registers

1.   *Member States shall establish and maintain in their territory one or several registers in which information concerning insolvency proceedings is published ('insolvency registers'). That information shall be published as soon as possible after the opening of such proceedings.*

2.   *The information referred to in paragraph 1 shall be made publicly available, subject to the conditions laid down in Article 27, and shall include the following ('mandatory information'):*

   *(a)   the date of the opening of insolvency proceedings;*

   *(b)   the court opening insolvency proceedings and the case reference number, if any;*

   *(c)   the type of insolvency proceedings referred to in Annex A that were opened and, where applicable, any relevant subtype of such proceedings opened in accordance with national law;*

   *(d)   whether jurisdiction for opening proceedings is based on Article 3(1), 3(2) or 3(4);*

   *(e)   if the debtor is a company or a legal person, the debtor's name, registration number, registered office or, if different, postal address;*

   *(f)   if the debtor is an individual whether or not exercising an independent business or professional activity, the debtor's name, registration number, if any, and postal address or, where the address is protected, the debtor's place and date of birth;*

   *(g)   the name, postal address or e-mail address of the insolvency practitioner, if any, appointed in the proceedings;*

   *(h)   the time limit for lodging claims, if any, or a reference to the criteria for calculating that time limit;*

   *(i)   the date of closing main insolvency proceedings, if any;*

   *(j)   the court before which and, where applicable, the time limit within which a challenge of the decision opening insolvency proceedings is to be lodged in accordance with Article 5, or a reference to the criteria for calculating that time limit.*

3. *Paragraph 2 shall not preclude Member States from including documents or additional information in their national insolvency registers, such as directors' disqualifications related to insolvency.*

4. *Member States shall not be obliged to include in the insolvency registers the information referred to in paragraph 1 of this Article in relation to individuals not exercising an independent business or professional activity, or to make such information publicly available through the system of interconnection of those registers, provided that known foreign creditors are informed, pursuant to Article 54, of the elements referred to under point (j) of paragraph 2 of this Article.*

*Where a Member State makes use of the possibility referred to in the first subparagraph, the insolvency proceedings shall not affect the claims of foreign creditors who have not received the information referred to in the first subparagraph.*

5. *The publication of information in the registers under this Regulation shall not have any legal effects other than those set out in national law and in Article 55(6).*

**Amendments**—Repealed by SI 2019/146, as from IP completion day (as defined in the European Union (Withdrawal Agreement) Act 2020, s 39(1)–(5)).

## [6.27]

### Article 25  Interconnection of insolvency registers

1.  The Commission shall establish a decentralised system for the interconnection of insolvency registers by means of implementing acts. That system shall be composed of the insolvency registers and the European e-Justice Portal, which shall serve as a central public electronic access point to information in the system. The system shall provide a search service in all the official languages of the institutions of the Union in order to make available the mandatory information and any other documents or information included in the insolvency registers which the Member States choose to make available through the European e-Justice Portal.

2.  By means of implementing acts in accordance with the procedure referred to in Article 87, the Commission shall adopt the following by 26 June 2019:

(a)  the technical specification defining the methods of communication and information exchange by electronic means on the basis of the established interface specification for the system of interconnection of insolvency registers;

(b)  the technical measures ensuring the minimum information technology security standards for communication and distribution of information within the system of interconnection of insolvency registers;

(c)  minimum criteria for the search service provided by the European e-Justice Portal based on the information set out in Article 24;

(d)  minimum criteria for the presentation of the results of such searches based on the information set out in Article 24;

(e)  the means and the technical conditions of availability of services provided by the system of interconnection; and

(f)  a glossary containing a basic explanation of the national insolvency proceedings listed in Annex A.

## [6.28]

### Article 26  Costs of establishing and interconnecting insolvency registers

1.  *The establishment, maintenance and future development of the system of interconnection of insolvency registers shall be financed from the general budget of the Union.*

2.  *Each Member State shall bear the costs of establishing and adjusting its national insolvency registers to make them interoperable with the European e-Justice Portal, as well as the costs of administering, operating and maintaining those registers. This shall be without prejudice to the possibility to apply for grants to support such activities under the Union's financial programmes.*

Amendments—Repealed by SI 2019/146, as from IP completion day (as defined in the European Union (Withdrawal Agreement) Act 2020, s 39(1)–(5)).

**[6.29]**

*Article 27  Conditions of access to information via the system of interconnection*

1.  *Member States shall ensure that the mandatory information referred to in points (a) to (j) of Article 24(2) is available free of charge via the system of interconnection of insolvency registers.*

2.  *This Regulation shall not preclude Member States from charging a reasonable fee for access to the documents or additional information referred to in Article 24(3) via the system of interconnection of insolvency registers.*

3.  *Member States may make access to mandatory information concerning individuals who are not exercising an independent business or professional activity, and concerning individuals exercising an independent business or professional activity when the insolvency proceedings are not related to that activity, subject to supplementary search criteria relating to the debtor in addition to the minimum criteria referred to in point (c) of Article 25(2).*

4.  *Member States may require that access to the information referred to in paragraph 3 be made conditional upon a request to the competent authority. Member States may make access conditional upon the verification of the existence of a legitimate interest for accessing such information. The requesting person shall be able to submit the request for information electronically by means of a standard form via the European e-Justice Portal. Where a legitimate interest is required, it shall be permissible for the requesting person to justify his request by electronic copies of relevant documents. The requesting person shall be provided with an answer by the competent authority within 3 working days.*

*The requesting person shall not be obliged to provide translations of the documents justifying his request, or to bear any costs of translation which the competent authority may incur.*

Amendments—Repealed by SI 2019/146, as from IP completion day (as defined in the European Union (Withdrawal Agreement) Act 2020, s 39(1)–(5)).

**ARTICLES 24–27**

General note—The Regulation proposes the establishment of an ambitious new regime to enhance the publicity of insolvency proceedings. Member States are required to publish certain information concerning insolvency proceedings in a 'free' and publicly accessible electronic register though access to the register may be made dependent upon establishing a 'legitimate interest' to the competent authority. What constitutes a 'legitimate interest' is obviously prone to different interpretations in different states and it is not clear whether an autonomous Europe-wide interpretation is envisaged. The information to be published includes information concerning the court opening the insolvency proceedings, the date of opening and of closing proceedings, the type of proceedings, the debtor and IP appointed, and the deadline for lodging claims. This kind of information will assist creditors and others in their information-gathering exercises, but there is no requirement to publish details of claims that have been lodged or accepted. States however, are not precluded from requiring additional information to be included on the registers, and may also charge searchers a reasonable fee for accessing these optional extras. Because of privacy concerns, states are not required to make available on the national register information concerning individuals not exercising an independent business or professional activity but may do so.

The European Commission is charged with the responsibility of establishing a decentralised system for the interconnection of national insolvency registers and the European e-Justice Portal is intended to serve as the central public electronic access point to information from the system. The ambition of the project means that a longer period has been given to get the system up and running. In general, the changes made by the recast Regulation come into effect 2 years from the date that they are published in the Official Journal. Member States however, have 36 months to establish insolvency registers and 48 months to provide confirmation that the registers will form part of an interconnected EU Portal – Arts 24, 25, 87 and 92.

**[6.30]**

*Article 28 Publication in another Member State*

1. *The insolvency practitioner or the debtor in possession shall request that notice of the judgment opening insolvency proceedings and, where appropriate, the decision appointing the insolvency practitioner be published in any other Member State where an establishment of the debtor is located in accordance with the publication procedures provided for in that Member State. Such publication shall specify, where appropriate, the insolvency practitioner appointed and whether the jurisdiction rule applied is that pursuant to Article 3(1) or (2).*

2. *The insolvency practitioner or the debtor in possession may request that the information referred to in paragraph 1 be published in any other Member State where the insolvency practitioner or the debtor in possession deems it necessary in accordance with the publication procedures provided for in that Member State.*

Amendments—Repealed by SI 2019/146, as from IP completion day (as defined in the European Union (Withdrawal Agreement) Act 2020, s 39(1)–(5)).

General note—This provision is somewhat similar to Art 21 in Regulation 1346/2000.

**[6.31]**

*Article 29 Registration in public registers of another Member State*

1. *Where the law of a Member State in which an establishment of the debtor is located and this establishment has been entered into a public register of that Member State, or the law of a Member State in which immovable property belonging to the debtor is located, requires information on the opening of insolvency proceedings referred to in Article 28 to be published in the land register, company register or any other public register, the insolvency practitioner or the debtor in possession shall take all the necessary measures to ensure such a registration.*

2. *The insolvency practitioner or the debtor in possession may request such registration in any other Member State, provided that the law of the Member State where the register is kept allows such registration.*

Amendments—Repealed by SI 2019/146, as from IP completion day (as defined in the European Union (Withdrawal Agreement) Act 2020, s 39(1)–(5)).

**[6.32]**

*Article 30 Costs*

*The costs of the publication and registration provided for in Articles 28 and 29 shall be regarded as costs and expenses incurred in the proceedings.*

Amendments—Repealed by SI 2019/146, as from IP completion day (as defined in the European Union (Withdrawal Agreement) Act 2020, s 39(1)–(5)).

**[6.33]**

*Article 31 Honouring of an obligation to a debtor*

1. *Where an obligation has been honoured in a Member State for the benefit of a debtor who is subject to insolvency proceedings opened in another Member State, when it should have been honoured for the benefit of the insolvency practitioner in those proceedings, the person honouring the obligation shall be deemed to have discharged it if he was unaware of the opening of the proceedings.*

2. *Where such an obligation is honoured before the publication provided for in Article 28 has been effected, the person honouring the obligation shall be presumed, in the absence of proof to the contrary, to have been unaware of the opening of insolvency proceedings. Where the obligation is honoured after such publication has been effected, the person honouring the obligation shall be presumed, in the absence of proof to the contrary, to have been aware of the opening of proceedings.*

Amendments—Repealed by SI 2019/146, as from IP completion day (as defined in the European Union (Withdrawal Agreement) Act 2020, s 39(1)–(5)).

**General note**—This provision is the equivalent of Art 24 in Regulation 1346/2000. The European court has held in *Van Buggenhout v Banque Internationale à Luxembourg* Case C-251/12 [2013] WLR (D) that the provision essentially covers situations where a person makes a payment to a company that is the subject of insolvency proceedings and the payment is not made to the company liquidator. The article only applied when the company was the recipient of the payment. It did not give protection to a party such as a bank, who acting on a prior mandate, transferred the company's assets notwithstanding the commencement of insolvency proceedings and in ignorance of the fact that these proceedings had been commenced.

## [6.34]

### Article 32 Recognition and enforceability of other judgments

1. *Judgments handed down by a court whose judgment concerning the opening of proceedings is recognised in accordance with Article 19 and which concern the course and closure of insolvency proceedings, and compositions approved by that court, shall also be recognised with no further formalities. Such judgments shall be enforced in accordance with Articles 39 to 44 and 47 to 57 of Regulation (EU) No 1215/2012.*

*The first subparagraph shall also apply to judgments deriving directly from the insolvency proceedings and which are closely linked with them, even if they were handed down by another court.*

*The first subparagraph shall also apply to judgments relating to preservation measures taken after the request for the opening of insolvency proceedings or in connection with it.*

2. *The recognition and enforcement of judgments other than those referred to in paragraph 1 of this Article shall be governed by Regulation (EU) No 1215/2012 provided that that Regulation is applicable.*

**Amendments**—Repealed by SI 2019/146, as from IP completion day (as defined in the European Union (Withdrawal Agreement) Act 2020, s 39(1)–(5)).

**General note**—This provision is the equivalent of Arts 25(1) and (2) in Regulation 1346/2000. Any judgments which are concerned with the administration of insolvency proceedings that are made by a court with jurisdiction under Art 19 will be recognised. This rule of automatic recognition also applies to judgments, even those not handed down by the court with jurisdiction under Art 19, if they are judgments concerned with insolvency proceedings.

In *Handelsveem BV v Hill* [2011] BPIR 1024 it was held by the Dutch Supreme Court that an English order made under s 366 of the Insolvency Act, which required a third party in the Netherlands to provide a list of goods held on behalf of the bankrupt, derived directly from the insolvency proceedings and was closely linked with them and therefore was entitled to recognition under what is now Art 32. The *Bank Handlowy* case Case C-116/11 (2011/C 152/24) [2013] BPIR 174 raised issues about recognising the closure of insolvency proceedings that have been opened in another EU state. The CJEU, on a reference from the Polish courts, concluded that in the absence of the harmonisation of substantive insolvency law, the concept of closure of insolvency proceedings could not be given an autonomous Community interpretation and must be interpreted according to national law. The court said that it was for the national law of the Member State in which insolvency proceedings have been opened to determine at which moment the closure of those proceedings occurs.

What is now Art 32 was considered in Case C-649/13 *Nortel Networks SA v Rogeau* (11 June 2015) where the CJEU held that both the court opening main proceedings and the court opening secondary proceedings has jurisdiction to rule on the location of assets on the basis of the rules set out in Art 2. The court said at para 45:

'as the Advocate General has observed in point 60 of his Opinion, Art 25(1) of Regulation No 1346/2000 will enable the risk of concurrent judgments to be avoided, by requiring any court before which a related action, such as those before the referring court, has been brought to recognise an earlier judgment delivered by another court with jurisdiction under Article 3(1) or, as the case may be, Article 3(2) of that regulation.'

## [6.35]

### Article 33 Public policy

*Any Member State may refuse to recognise insolvency proceedings opened in another Member State or to enforce a judgment handed down in the context of such proceedings where the effects of such recognition or enforcement would be manifestly contrary to that State's public policy, in particular its fundamental principles or the constitutional rights and liberties of the individual.*

**Amendments**—Repealed by SI 2019/146, as from IP completion day (as defined in the European Union (Withdrawal Agreement) Act 2020, s 39(1)–(5)).

**General note**—This provision is the equivalent of Art 26 in Regulation 1346/2000. It will come as no surprise that a rule allowing for refusal of recognition on the basis of public policy was included in the Regulation. It should be the case that this provision will be little used, for otherwise the whole basis of the Regulation, to foster co-operation, will be undermined. Moreover, the Article states that a judgment opening proceedings may only be refused where it is 'manifestly' contrary to public policy, underlining the rare occurrence of such a refusal.

See *Re Eurofood Ltd* [2004] BCC 383, where the Irish court relied on public to refuse to recognise an Italian judgment opening main insolvency proceedings against an Irish registered company. The CJEU in the *Eurofood* [2006] ECR I–701 case stated that this exception may be used where the decision to open the proceedings was taken in flagrant breach of the fundamental right to be heard, that a person concerned with such proceedings enjoys.

In the *Daisytek* proceedings [2006] BCC 841 it was argued that the French courts should use what is now Art 33 and refuse to recognise the English insolvency proceedings on the ground that the latter had ignored the right of the employees to be represented in court and that this ran counter to French public policy. The Cour de Cassation however, looked to the ECJ ruling in *Eurofood* for guidance and suggested that Art 26 should be given a limited interpretation. The fact that the employees representatives were not heard by the English court before the decision to open insolvency proceedings did not, in itself, constitute a flagrant breach of the fundamental right to be heard, which a person concerned by such proceedings enjoyed.

What is now Art 33 was however successfully invoked in the *Hans Brochier* litigation where a German court refused to recognise English insolvency proceedings on the basis, inter alia, that an administrator appointed out of court lacked the necessary attributes of independence to satisfy the EU Regulation (804 IN 1326 1331/06, Local Court of Nuremberg, 15 August 2006).

Article 33 was also successfully invoked by McDonald J in the Irish High Court in *Apperley Investments Ltd v Monsoon Accessorize Ltd* [2020] IEHC 523. It was held that a UK company voluntary arrangement CVA impacting property rights could not be enforced on landlords outside the UK. The landlords were held entitled to full rent on their premises and were not bound by the CVA.

The procedure adopted in relation to the CVA was considered to be manifestly contrary to Irish public policy and therefore deficient under Art 33. The rights of a party to be heard before its property rights were impaired was a fundamental principle of Irish constitutional law. The mere existence of a right to challenge the CVA could not cure the defect in fair procedures in the decision of the creditors to adopt the CVA.

There was a fundamental failure to provide an appropriate opportunity to the Irish landlords to make representations in the meeting of creditors which was to take a decision that would have such significant effects on their property rights. The judge suggested that the web portal which had been used to bring drafting clarifications to the attention of all creditors could also have been used to allow representations to be made by the Irish landlords.

On public policy also note the comments of the Privy Council in *Stichting Shell Pensioenfonds v Krys* [2014] UKPC 41, [2015] 2 WLR 289 at para [42] that the 'jurisdiction of the Dutch court under its own law to authorise the attachment of an Irish debt owed to a BVI company in liquidation in the BVI may fairly be described . . . as exorbitant'. The implication is that an order of the Dutch court to this effect would not be recognised in England.

## CHAPTER III   SECONDARY INSOLVENCY PROCEEDINGS

**[6.36]**

**Introduction to Chapter III**—Secondary proceedings may be opened in states where the debtor has an establishment and the effects of the proceedings are limited to assets of the debtor within that state. The fact that secondary proceedings may be opened qualifies the universality of the main insolvency proceedings. The applicable law in respect of the secondary proceedings is the law of the state where the proceedings are opened, including local priority rules in respect of the distribution of assets. Under a genuinely universalist system the task of an IP in secondary proceedings would be merely the collection of assets and entrusting them to the IP in the main proceedings who would then distribute them in accordance with the law applicable to the main proceedings. Secondary proceedings protect local preferential creditors whose claims would be treated as non-preferential under the law that applies to the main proceedings.

Under the original Regulation, secondary proceedings had to be liquidation proceedings. This limitation was part of the horse-trading that led to the Regulation gaining the necessary measure of political acceptance.

One of the main thrusts of the recast Regulation is however, to reduce the circumstances in which secondary proceedings may be opened. It does this by generalising and 'Europeanising' some of the practices developed by the English courts in cases like *Re Collins and Aikman Europe SA* [2006] EWHC 1343 and *Re Nortel Networks SA* [2009] EWHC 206. In *Re Collins and Aikman* the court developed the notion of 'synthetic' secondary proceedings, holding that the UK Insolvency Act was sufficiently flexible so that UK IPs could observe promises made to creditors in other EU states that local priorities would be respected in return for not opening secondary proceedings in these states. Local creditors effectively got the benefits of secondary proceedings without the trouble of having to open them. These secondary proceedings were 'synthetic' or 'virtual' rather than actual.

In *Re Nortel Networks SA* a mechanism was created so that the IP in the main proceeding had a 'voice' on any decision to open secondary proceedings. IPs of certain UK based companies in the Nortel group were granted an order requesting other EU courts to give notice of applications to open secondary insolvency proceedings in respect of Nortel companies and allowing them to make submissions on such applications. The IPs wished to avoid secondary proceedings on the basis that this was likely to hinder a global restructuring and reduce the overall realisations for the benefit of creditors.

Under the recast Regulation, the court seised of a request to open secondary proceedings may turn down the request if the IP in the main proceedings gives an undertaking that adequately protects the general interests of local creditors – Arts 36 and 38(2). The European Commission pointed out that such a practice was not possible under the law of many States but the new provision, while welcome in principle, comes with a lot of complexity in its detailed design – see Proposal for a new Regulation at para 3.1.3. For instance, the undertaking has to be approved by the known local creditors. Rules on qualified majority and voting that apply in the State where the secondary proceedings could have been opened apply for the approval of the undertaking.

The court seised with a request to open secondary proceedings is also required to hear the IP in the main proceedings before making its decision – Art 38. Moreover, the new provision stipulates that where a temporary stay of individual enforcement proceedings has been granted to allow for negotiations between the debtor and creditors, the court may stay the opening of secondary proceedings for up to three months as long as suitable measures are in place to protect the interests of local creditors – Art 38(3).

## [6.37]

### Article 34  Opening of proceedings

*Where main insolvency proceedings have been opened by a court of a Member State and recognised in another Member State, a court of that other Member State which has jurisdiction pursuant to Article 3(2) may open secondary insolvency proceedings in accordance with the provisions set out in this Chapter. Where the main insolvency proceedings required that the debtor be insolvent, the debtor's insolvency shall not be re-examined in the Member State in which secondary insolvency proceedings may be opened. The effects of secondary insolvency proceedings shall be restricted to the assets of the debtor situated within the territory of the Member State in which those proceedings have been opened.*

**Amendments**—Repealed by SI 2019/146, as from IP completion day (as defined in the European Union (Withdrawal Agreement) Act 2020, s 39(1)–(5)).

## [6.38]

### Article 35  Applicable law

*Save as otherwise provided for in this Regulation, the law applicable to secondary insolvency proceedings shall be that of the Member State within the territory of which the secondary insolvency proceedings are opened.*

**Amendments**—Repealed by SI 2019/146, as from IP completion day (as defined in the European Union (Withdrawal Agreement) Act 2020, s 39(1)–(5)).

**General note**—In *Re Alitalia* [2011] EWHC 15 (Ch), [2011] 1 WLR 2049 Newey J noted that the Regulation provided for assets within the scope of secondary proceedings to be disposed of in accordance with that Member State's law. It was held that the duty of co-operation under the Regulation between liquidators in main and secondary proceedings could not extend to requiring liquidators to apply assets in a different manner especially since the duty of co-operation was expressly subject to the rules applicable to each of the proceedings.

[6.39]

*Article 36 Right to give an undertaking in order to avoid secondary insolvency proceedings*

1.  In order to avoid the opening of secondary insolvency proceedings, the insolvency practitioner in the main insolvency proceedings may give a unilateral undertaking (the 'undertaking') in respect of the assets located in the Member State in which secondary insolvency proceedings could be opened, that when distributing those assets or the proceeds received as a result of their realisation, it will comply with the distribution and priority rights under national law that creditors would have if secondary insolvency proceedings were opened in that Member State. The undertaking shall specify the factual assumptions on which it is based, in particular in respect of the value of the assets located in the Member State concerned and the options available to realise such assets.

2.  Where an undertaking has been given in accordance with this Article, the law applicable to the distribution of proceeds from the realisation of assets referred to in paragraph 1, to the ranking of creditors' claims, and to the rights of creditors in relation to the assets referred to in paragraph 1 shall be the law of the Member State in which secondary insolvency proceedings could have been opened. The relevant point in time for determining the assets referred to in paragraph 1 shall be the moment at which the undertaking is given.

3.  The undertaking shall be made in the official language or one of the official languages of the Member State where secondary insolvency proceedings could have been opened, or, where there are several official languages in that Member State, the official language or one of the official languages of the place in which secondary insolvency proceedings could have been opened.

4.  The undertaking shall be made in writing. It shall be subject to any other requirements relating to form and approval requirements as to distributions, if any, of the State of the opening of the main insolvency proceedings.

5.  The undertaking shall be approved by the known local creditors. The rules on qualified majority and voting that apply to the adoption of restructuring plans under the law of the Member State where secondary insolvency proceedings could have been opened shall also apply to the approval of the undertaking. Creditors shall be able to participate in the vote by distance means of communication, where national law so permits. The insolvency practitioner shall inform the known local creditors of the undertaking, of the rules and procedures for its approval, and of the approval or rejection of the undertaking.

6.  An undertaking given and approved in accordance with this Article shall be binding on the estate. If secondary insolvency proceedings are opened in accordance with Articles 37 and 38, the insolvency practitioner in the main insolvency proceedings shall transfer any assets which it removed from the territory of that Member State after the undertaking was given or, where those assets have already been realised, their proceeds, to the insolvency practitioner in the secondary insolvency proceedings.

7.  Where the insolvency practitioner has given an undertaking, it shall inform local creditors about the intended distributions prior to distributing the assets and proceeds referred to in paragraph 1. If that information does not comply with the terms of the undertaking or the applicable law, any local creditor may challenge such distribution before the courts of the Member State in which main insolvency proceedings have been opened in order to obtain a distribution in accordance with the terms of the undertaking and the applicable law. In such cases, no distribution shall take place until the court has taken a decision on the challenge.

8.  Local creditors may apply to the courts of the Member State in which main insolvency proceedings have been opened, in order to require the insolvency practitioner in the main insolvency proceedings to take any suitable measures necessary to ensure compliance with the terms of the undertaking available under the law of the State of the opening of main insolvency proceedings.

9.  *Local creditors may also apply to the courts of the Member State in which secondary insolvency proceedings could have been opened in order to require the court to take provisional or protective measures to ensure compliance by the insolvency practitioner with the terms of the undertaking.*

10.  The insolvency practitioner shall be liable for any damage caused to local creditors as a result of its non-compliance with the obligations and requirements set out in this Article.

11.  *For the purpose of this Article, an authority which is established in the Member State where secondary insolvency proceedings could have been opened and which is obliged under Directive 2008/94/EC of the European Parliament and of the Council[1] to guarantee the payment of employees' outstanding claims resulting from contracts of employment or employment relationships shall be considered to be a local creditor, where the national law so provides.*

[1]  Directive 2008/94/EC of the European Parliament and of the Council of 22 October 2008 on the protection of employees in the event of the insolvency of their employer (OJ L 283, 28.10.2008, p 36).

**Amendments**—Repealed by SI 2019/146, as from IP completion day (as defined in the European Union (Withdrawal Agreement) Act 2020, s 39(1)–(5)).

## [6.40]

### Article 37  Right to request the opening of secondary insolvency proceedings

1.  *The opening of secondary insolvency proceedings may be requested by:*
    (a)  *the insolvency practitioner in the main insolvency proceedings;*
    (b)  *any other person or authority empowered to request the opening of insolvency proceedings under the law of the Member State within the territory of which the opening of secondary insolvency proceedings is requested.*

2.  *Where an undertaking has become binding in accordance with Article 36, the request for opening secondary insolvency proceedings shall be lodged within 30 days of having received notice of the approval of the undertaking.*

**Amendments**—Repealed by SI 2019/146, as from IP completion day (as defined in the European Union (Withdrawal Agreement) Act 2020, s 39(1)–(5)).

## [6.41]

### Article 38  Decision to open secondary insolvency proceedings

1.  *A court seised of a request to open secondary insolvency proceedings shall immediately give notice to the insolvency practitioner or the debtor in possession in the main insolvency proceedings and give it an opportunity to be heard on the request.*

2.  *Where the insolvency practitioner in the main insolvency proceedings has given an undertaking in accordance with Article 36, the court referred to in paragraph 1 of this Article shall, at the request of the insolvency practitioner, not open secondary insolvency proceedings if it is satisfied that the undertaking adequately protects the general interests of local creditors.*

3.  *Where a temporary stay of individual enforcement proceedings has been granted in order to allow for negotiations between the debtor and its creditors, the court, at the request of the insolvency practitioner or the debtor in possession, may stay the opening of secondary insolvency proceedings for a period not exceeding 3 months, provided that suitable measures are in place to protect the interests of local creditors.*

*The court referred to in paragraph 1 may order protective measures to protect the interests of local creditors by requiring the insolvency practitioner or the debtor in possession not to remove or dispose of any assets which are located in the Member State where its establishment is located unless this is done in the ordinary course of business. The court may also order other measures to protect the interest of local creditors during a stay, unless this is incompatible with the national rules on civil procedure.*

*The stay of the opening of secondary insolvency proceedings shall be lifted by the court of its own motion or at the request of any creditor if, during the stay, an agreement in the negotiations referred to in the first subparagraph has been concluded.*

*The stay may be lifted by the court of its own motion or at the request of any creditor if the continuation of the stay is detrimental to the creditor's rights, in particular if the negotiations have been disrupted or it has become evident that they are unlikely to be concluded, or if the insolvency practitioner or the debtor in possession has infringed the prohibition on disposal of its assets or on removal of them from the territory of the Member State where the establishment is located.*

*4.   At the request of the insolvency practitioner in the main insolvency proceedings, the court referred to in paragraph 1 may open a type of insolvency proceedings as listed in Annex A other than the type initially requested, provided that the conditions for opening that type of proceedings under national law are fulfilled and that that type of proceedings is the most appropriate as regards the interests of the local creditors and coherence between the main and secondary insolvency proceedings. The second sentence of Article 34 shall apply.*

**Amendments**—Repealed by SI 2019/146, as from IP completion day (as defined in the European Union (Withdrawal Agreement) Act 2020, s 39(1)–(5)).

## [6.42]

*Article 39 Judicial review of the decision to open secondary insolvency proceedings*
*The insolvency practitioner in the main insolvency proceedings may challenge the decision to open secondary insolvency proceedings before the courts of the Member State in which secondary insolvency proceedings have been opened on the ground that the court did not comply with the conditions and requirements of Article 38.*

**Amendments**—Repealed by SI 2019/146, as from IP completion day (as defined in the European Union (Withdrawal Agreement) Act 2020, s 39(1)–(5)).

## [6.43]

*Article 40 Advance payment of costs and expenses*
*Where the law of the Member State in which the opening of secondary insolvency proceedings is requested requires that the debtor's assets be sufficient to cover in whole or in part the costs and expenses of the proceedings, the court may, when it receives such a request, require the applicant to make an advance payment of costs or to provide appropriate security.*

**Amendments**—Repealed by SI 2019/146, as from IP completion day (as defined in the European Union (Withdrawal Agreement) Act 2020, s 39(1)–(5)).

## [6.44]

*Article 41 Cooperation and communication between insolvency practitioners*
*1.   The insolvency practitioner in the main insolvency proceedings and the insolvency practitioner or practitioners in secondary insolvency proceedings concerning the same debtor shall cooperate with each other to the extent such cooperation is not incompatible with the rules applicable to the respective proceedings. Such cooperation may take any form, including the conclusion of agreements or protocols.*
*2.   In implementing the cooperation set out in paragraph 1, the insolvency practitioners shall:*

   *(a)   as soon as possible communicate to each other any information which may be relevant to the other proceedings, in particular any progress made in lodging and verifying claims and all measures aimed at rescuing or restructuring the debtor, or at terminating the proceedings, provided appropriate arrangements are made to protect confidential information;*
   *(b)   explore the possibility of restructuring the debtor and, where such a possibility exists, coordinate the elaboration and implementation of a restructuring plan;*

(c)  coordinate the administration of the realisation or use of the debtor's assets and affairs; the insolvency practitioner in the secondary insolvency proceedings shall give the insolvency practitioner in the main insolvency proceedings an early opportunity to submit proposals on the realisation or use of the assets in the secondary insolvency proceedings.

3.  *Paragraphs 1 and 2 shall apply mutatis mutandis to situations where, in the main or in the secondary insolvency proceedings or in any territorial insolvency proceedings concerning the same debtor and open at the same time, the debtor remains in possession of its assets.*

**Amendments**—Repealed by SI 2019/146, as from IP completion day (as defined in the European Union (Withdrawal Agreement) Act 2020, s 39(1)–(5)).

**[6.45]**

### Article 42  Cooperation and communication between courts

1.  *In order to facilitate the coordination of main, territorial and secondary insolvency proceedings concerning the same debtor, a court before which a request to open insolvency proceedings is pending, or which has opened such proceedings, shall cooperate with any other court before which a request to open insolvency proceedings is pending, or which has opened such proceedings, to the extent that such cooperation is not incompatible with the rules applicable to each of the proceedings. For that purpose, the courts may, where appropriate, appoint an independent person or body acting on its instructions, provided that it is not incompatible with the rules applicable to them.*

2.  *In implementing the cooperation set out in paragraph 1, the courts, or any appointed person or body acting on their behalf, as referred to in paragraph 1, may communicate directly with, or request information or assistance directly from, each other provided that such communication respects the procedural rights of the parties to the proceedings and the confidentiality of information.*

3.  *The cooperation referred to in paragraph 1 may be implemented by any means that the court considers appropriate. It may, in particular, concern:*

(a)  coordination in the appointment of the insolvency practitioners;

(b)  communication of information by any means considered appropriate by the court;

(c)  coordination of the administration and supervision of the debtor's assets and affairs;

(d)  coordination of the conduct of hearings;

(e)  coordination in the approval of protocols, where necessary.

**Amendments**—Repealed by SI 2019/146, as from IP completion day (as defined in the European Union (Withdrawal Agreement) Act 2020, s 39(1)–(5)).

**General note**—By virtue of this provision, the courts involved in the main and secondary proceedings now have an express duty to cooperate with one another. Under the original Regulation, there was no express duty of co-operation between courts but there were suggestions that such a duty should be implied in certain circumstances, see *Bank Handlowy SA v Christianapol* Case C-116/11 [2013] BPIR 174 at [62], referring to the principle of sincere cooperation laid down in Art 4(3) of the Treaty on European Union.

**[6.46]**

### Article 43  Cooperation and communication between insolvency practitioners and courts

1.  *In order to facilitate the coordination of main, territorial and secondary insolvency proceedings opened in respect of the same debtor:*

(a)  an insolvency practitioner in main insolvency proceedings shall cooperate and communicate with any court before which a request to open secondary insolvency proceedings is pending or which has opened such proceedings;

(b)  an insolvency practitioner in territorial or secondary insolvency proceedings shall cooperate and communicate with the court before which *a request to open main insolvency proceedings is pending or which has opened such proceedings; and*

(c)    *an insolvency practitioner in territorial or secondary insolvency proceedings shall cooperate and communicate with the court before which a request to open other territorial or secondary insolvency proceedings is pending or which has opened such proceedings;*

(d)    *to the extent that such cooperation and communication are not incompatible with the rules applicable to each of the proceedings and do not entail any conflict of interest.*

2.   *The cooperation referred to in paragraph 1 may be implemented by any appropriate means, such as those set out in Article 42(3).*

**Amendments**—Repealed by SI 2019/146, as from IP completion day (as defined in the European Union (Withdrawal Agreement) Act 2020, s 39(1)–(5)).

### ARTICLES 41–43

**General note**—IPs and courts are obliged to cooperate and the cooperation may take different forms depending on the circumstances of the case. IPs should exchange relevant information and cooperation by way of protocols is explicitly mentioned. This reference acknowledges the practical importance of these instruments as well as further promoting their use. Courts can cooperate by the exchange of information; by coordinating the administration and supervision of the assets and affairs of the companies as well as coordinating the conduct of hearings and the approval of protocols. Co-operation however, must be appropriate to facilitate the effective administration of the proceedings; not be incompatible with the rules applicable to the respective courts nor entail any conflict of interest.

## [6.47]

### Article 44  Costs of cooperation and communication

*The requirements laid down in Articles 42 and 43 shall not result in courts charging costs to each other for cooperation and communication.*

**Amendments**—Repealed by SI 2019/146, as from IP completion day (as defined in the European Union (Withdrawal Agreement) Act 2020, s 39(1)–(5)).

## [6.48]

### Article 45  Exercise of creditors' rights

1.   *Any creditor may lodge its claim in the main insolvency proceedings and in any secondary insolvency proceedings.*

2.   *The insolvency practitioners in the main and any secondary insolvency proceedings shall lodge in other proceedings claims which have already been lodged in the proceedings for which they were appointed, provided that the interests of creditors in the latter proceedings are served by doing so, subject to the right of creditors to oppose such lodgement or to withdraw the lodgement of their claims where the law applicable so provides.*

3.   *The insolvency practitioner in the main or secondary insolvency proceedings shall be entitled to participate in other proceedings on the same basis as a creditor, in particular by attending creditors' meetings.*

**Amendments**—Repealed by SI 2019/146, as from IP completion day (as defined in the European Union (Withdrawal Agreement) Act 2020, s 39(1)–(5)).

**General note**—This Article is the equivalent of Art 32 in Regulation 1346/2000. It enables any creditor to lodge their claim in any insolvency proceedings pending in the EU. But note Recital 63 of the preamble, which states that creditors who have their 'habitual residence, domicile or registered office in the Community' should have the right to lodge a claim, which appears to be inconsistent with this Article. However, Recital 63 does not state that only those creditors are able to lodge a claim. Therefore it can be assumed that any creditor may prove in an insolvency proceeding under the Regulation.

Liquidators are entitled to participate in other insolvency proceedings as if they were a creditor.

**[6.49]**

*Article 46   Stay of the process of realisation of assets*

1. The court which opened the secondary insolvency proceedings shall stay the process of realisation of assets in whole or in part on receipt of a request from the insolvency practitioner in the main insolvency proceedings. In such a case, it may require the insolvency practitioner in the main insolvency proceedings to take any suitable measure to guarantee the interests of the creditors in the secondary insolvency proceedings and of individual classes of creditors. Such a request from the insolvency practitioner may be rejected only if it is manifestly of no interest to the creditors in the main insolvency proceedings. Such a stay of the process of realisation of assets may be ordered for up to 3 months. It may be continued or renewed for similar periods.

2. The court referred to in paragraph 1 shall terminate the stay of the process of realisation of assets:

(a)   at the request of the insolvency practitioner in the main insolvency proceedings;

(b)   of its own motion, at the request of a creditor or at the request of the insolvency practitioner in the secondary insolvency proceedings if that measure no longer appears justified, in particular, by the interests of creditors in the main insolvency proceedings or in the secondary insolvency proceedings.

**Amendments**—Repealed by SI 2019/146, as from IP completion day (as defined in the European Union (Withdrawal Agreement) Act 2020, s 39(1)–(5)).

**General note**—This provision is broadly equivalent to Art 33 of Regulation 1346/2000 though that provision referred to the stay of liquidation rather than the stay of the process of realisation of assets which is referred to in Art 46. The court referred to in para 1 shall terminate the stay of the process of realisation of assets:

(i)    at the request of the insolvency practitioner in the main insolvency proceedings;

(ii)   of its own motion, at the request of a creditor or at the request of the insolvency practitioner in the secondary insolvency proceedings if that measure no longer appears justified, in particular, by the interests of creditors in the main insolvency proceedings or in the secondary insolvency proceedings.

**[6.50]**

*Article 47   Power of the insolvency practitioner to propose restructuring plans*

1. Where the law of the Member State where secondary insolvency proceedings have been opened allows for such proceedings to be closed without liquidation by a restructuring plan, a composition or a comparable measure, the insolvency practitioner in the main insolvency proceedings shall be empowered to propose such a measure in accordance with the procedure of that Member State.

2. Any restriction of creditors' rights arising from a measure referred to in paragraph 1 which is proposed in secondary insolvency proceedings, such as a stay of payment or discharge of debt, shall have no effect in respect of assets of a debtor that are not covered by those proceedings, without the consent of all the creditors having an interest.

**Amendments**—Repealed by SI 2019/146, as from IP completion day (as defined in the European Union (Withdrawal Agreement) Act 2020, s 39(1)–(5)).

**[6.51]**

*Article 48   Impact of closure of insolvency proceedings*

1. Without prejudice to Article 49, the closure of insolvency proceedings shall not prevent the continuation of other insolvency proceedings concerning the same debtor which are still open at that point in time.

2. Where insolvency proceedings concerning a legal person or a company in the Member State of that person's or company's registered office would entail the dissolution of the legal person or of the company, that legal person or company shall not

*cease to exist until any other insolvency proceedings concerning the same debtor have been closed, or the insolvency practitioner or practitioners in such proceedings have given consent to the dissolution.*

**Amendments**—Repealed by SI 2019/146, as from IP completion day (as defined in the European Union (Withdrawal Agreement) Act 2020, s 39(1)–(5)).

## [6.52]

*Article 49  Assets remaining in the secondary insolvency proceedings*
*If, by the liquidation of assets in the secondary insolvency proceedings, it is possible to meet all claims allowed under those proceedings, the insolvency practitioner appointed in those proceedings shall immediately transfer any assets remaining to the insolvency practitioner in the main insolvency proceedings.*

**Amendments**—Repealed by SI 2019/146, as from IP completion day (as defined in the European Union (Withdrawal Agreement) Act 2020, s 39(1)–(5)).

**General note**—This provision is equivalent to Art 35 in Regulation 1346/2000. Assets situated within the territory where secondary proceedings are opened are to be administered there. However, in the rare event that there are sufficient assets to fulfil all creditors' claim in those proceedings, any surplus must be turned over to the main liquidator for distribution to any other creditors.

## [6.53]

*Article 50  Subsequent opening of the main insolvency proceedings*
*Where the proceedings referred to in Article 3(1) are opened following the opening of the proceedings referred to in Article 3(2) in another Member State, Articles 41, 45, 46, 47 and 49 shall apply to those opened first, in so far as the progress of those proceedings so permits.*

**Amendments**—Repealed by SI 2019/146, as from IP completion day (as defined in the European Union (Withdrawal Agreement) Act 2020, s 39(1)–(5)).

## [6.54]

*Article 51  Conversion of secondary insolvency proceedings*
*1.  At the request of the insolvency practitioner in the main insolvency proceedings, the court of the Member State in which secondary insolvency proceedings have been opened may order the conversion of the secondary insolvency proceedings into another type of insolvency proceedings listed in Annex A, provided that the conditions for opening that type of proceedings under national law are fulfilled and that that type of proceedings is the most appropriate as regards the interests of the local creditors and coherence between the main and secondary insolvency proceedings.*
*2.  When considering the request referred to in paragraph 1, the court may seek information from the insolvency practitioners involved in both proceedings.*

**Amendments**—Repealed by SI 2019/146, as from IP completion day (as defined in the European Union (Withdrawal Agreement) Act 2020, s 39(1)–(5)).

## [6.55]

*Article 52  Preservation measures*
*Where the court of a Member State which has jurisdiction pursuant to Article 3(1) appoints a temporary administrator in order to ensure the preservation of a debtor's assets, that temporary administrator shall be empowered to request any measures to secure and preserve any of the debtor's assets situated in another Member State, provided for under the law of that Member State, for the period between the request for the opening of insolvency proceedings and the judgment opening the proceedings.*

**Amendments**—Repealed by SI 2019/146, as from IP completion day (as defined in the European Union (Withdrawal Agreement) Act 2020, s 39(1)–(5)).

General note—This provision is the equivalent of Art 38 in Regulation 1346/2000. A temporary administrator may request measures be taken in any Member State to preserve the assets of the debtor. This is obviously important because there may be a gap between the request for proceedings to be opened and the actual opening of proceedings.

## CHAPTER IV  PROVISION OF INFORMATION FOR CREDITORS AND LODGEMENT OF THEIR CLAIMS

[6.56]

General note Chapter IV—Foreign creditors are often disadvantaged by the opening of insolvency proceedings. These proceedings may be taking place in a faraway country according to an unfamiliar procedure and language. Foreign creditors may not be aware of the time limits for lodging claims nor of the proofs that have to be submitted. A translation of the claim into one of the official languages of the relevant state may also have been required as well as the services of a foreign lawyer or other professional. These costs may make it uneconomical to submit a claim. The European Commission has said: 'Due to high costs, creditors may choose to forgo a debt, especially when it involves a small amount of money. This problem mainly affects small and medium-sized businesses as well as private individuals' – see *Report from the Commission on the application of Council Regulation (EC) No 1346/2000* COM (2012) 743 at 16–17.

The recast Regulation tries to facilitate the lodging of claims by foreign creditors – Arts 53–55. First, it is provided that representation by a lawyer or another legal professional is not mandatory for the lodging of claims – Art 53. Secondly, it provides for the introduction of two standard notice and claim forms for all proceedings irrespective of where proceedings are commenced. One is the notice to be sent to creditors and the other is for the lodging of claims. These standard forms are made available in all EU official languages, so saving on translation costs. Thirdly, each State has to indicate whether it accepts an official EU language other than its own for the lodging of claims. Fourthly, irrespective of shorter periods under national law, foreign creditors are given at least 30 days following publication of the notice of opening of proceedings in the insolvency register to lodge their claims. Finally, foreign creditors have to be informed if their claim is contested and afforded the opportunity of providing supplementary evidence to verify their claim.

[6.57]

### Article 53  Right to lodge claims

*Any foreign creditor may lodge claims in insolvency proceedings by any means of communication, which are accepted by the law of the State of the opening of proceedings. Representation by a lawyer or another legal professional shall not be mandatory for the sole purpose of lodging of claims.*

*But for the restrictive definition of "foreign creditor" see Article 2(12) of the Regulation and also recital 63 to the preamble.*

Amendments—Repealed by SI 2019/146, as from IP completion day (as defined in the European Union (Withdrawal Agreement) Act 2020, s 39(1)–(5)).

[6.58]

### Article 54  Duty to inform creditors

*1.  As soon as insolvency proceedings are opened in a Member State, the court of that State having jurisdiction or the insolvency practitioner appointed by that court shall immediately inform the known foreign creditors.*

*2.  The information referred to in paragraph 1, provided by an individual notice, shall in particular include time limits, the penalties laid down with regard to those time limits, the body or authority empowered to accept the lodgement of claims and any other measures laid down. Such notice shall also indicate whether creditors whose claims are preferential or secured in rem need to lodge their claims. The notice shall also include a copy of the standard form for lodging of claims referred to in Article 55 or information on where that form is available.*

*3.  The information referred to in paragraphs 1 and 2 of this Article shall be provided using the standard notice form to be established in accordance with Article 88. The form shall be published in the European e-Justice Portal and shall bear the heading 'Notice of insolvency proceedings' in all the official languages of the institutions of the Union. It shall be transmitted in the official language of the State of the opening of proceedings or, if there are several official languages in that Member State, in the official language or one of the official languages of the place where insolvency proceedings have been opened, or in another language which that State has indicated it can accept, in accordance with Article 55(5), if it can be assumed that that language is easier to understand for the foreign creditors.*

4. *In insolvency proceedings relating to an individual not exercising a business or professional activity, the use of the standard form referred to in this Article shall not be obligatory if creditors are not required to lodge their claims in order to have their claims taken into account in the proceedings.*

**Amendments**—Repealed by SI 2019/146, as from IP completion day (as defined in the European Union (Withdrawal Agreement) Act 2020, s 39(1)–(5)).

**General note**—Once proceedings are opened in a State, all known foreign creditors should be informed of that fact. Thus, once again it is emphasised that the communication of information is of vital importance to ensure an efficient and fair administration of the debtor's affairs.

In *X v Service Navigation de Plaisance Boat Service* [2014] ILPr 24 the French Cour de Cassation held that it was appropriate to grant relief to a Netherlands-based unsecured creditor of a company subject to French insolvency proceedings who had registered its claim outside the four-month time limit applicable under French insolvency law. The creditor had not been given a formal notice inviting it to lodge a claim and setting out the relevant time limit. The French court pointed out that Art 40 (the version of Article 54 in Regulation 1346/2000 did not set out any penalties for failure to supply the required notice and it was for national law to determine the consequences of any failure. The relevant sanction under French law for failure to provide the notice was extension of the time for lodging a claim. Reference was made to the general provisions of what is now Art 7(2)(h) of the Regulation stating that the law of the state that opens the insolvency proceedings shall determine the rules governing the lodging, verification and admission of claims.

## [6.59]

### Article 55 *Procedure for lodging claims*

1. *Any foreign creditor may lodge its claim using the standard claims form to be established in accordance with Article 88. The form shall bear the heading 'Lodgement of claims' in all the official languages of the institutions of the Union.*
2. *The standard claims form referred to in paragraph 1 shall include the following information:*
   - (a) *the name, postal address, e-mail address, if any, personal identification number, if any, and bank details of the foreign creditor referred to in paragraph 1;*
   - (b) *the amount of the claim, specifying the principal and, where applicable, interest and the date on which it arose and the date on which it became due, if different;*
   - (c) *if interest is claimed, the interest rate, whether the interest is of a legal or contractual nature, the period of time for which the interest is claimed and the capitalised amount of interest;*
   - (d) *if costs incurred in asserting the claim prior to the opening of proceedings are claimed, the amount and the details of those costs;*
   - (e) *the nature of the claim;*
   - (f) *whether any preferential creditor status is claimed and the basis of such a claim;*
   - (g) *whether security in rem or a reservation of title is alleged in respect of the claim and if so, what assets are covered by the security interest being invoked, the date on which the security was granted and, where the security has been registered, the registration number; and*
   - (h) *whether any set-off is claimed and, if so, the amounts of the mutual claims existing on the date when insolvency proceedings were opened, the date on which they arose and the amount net of set-off claimed.*

*The standard claims form shall be accompanied by copies of any supporting documents.*
3. *The standard claims form shall indicate that the provision of information concerning the bank details and the personal identification number of the creditor referred to in point (a) of paragraph 2 is not compulsory.*

4. *When a creditor lodges its claim by means other than the standard form referred to in paragraph 1, the claim shall contain the information referred to in paragraph 2.*

5. *Claims may be lodged in any official language of the institutions of the Union. The court, the insolvency practitioner or the debtor in possession may require the creditor to provide a translation in the official language of the State of the opening of proceedings or, if there are several official languages in that Member State, in the official language or one of the official languages of the place where insolvency proceedings have been opened, or in another language which that Member State has indicated it can accept. Each Member State shall indicate whether it accepts any official language of the institutions of the Union other than its own for the purpose of the lodging of claims.*

6. *Claims shall be lodged within the period stipulated by the law of the State of the opening of proceedings. In the case of a foreign creditor, that period shall not be less than 30 days following the publication of the opening of insolvency proceedings in the insolvency register of the State of the opening of proceedings. Where a Member State relies on Article 24(4), that period shall not be less than 30 days following a creditor having been informed pursuant to Article 54.*

7. *Where the court, the insolvency practitioner or the debtor in possession has doubts in relation to a claim lodged in accordance with this Article, it shall give the creditor the opportunity to provide additional evidence on the existence and the amount of the claim.*

**Amendments**—Repealed by SI 2019/146, as from IP completion day (as defined in the European Union (Withdrawal Agreement) Act 2020, s 39(1)–(5)).

## CHAPTER V   INSOLVENCY PROCEEDINGS OF MEMBERS OF A GROUP OF COMPANIES

### SECTION 1

#### COOPERATION AND COMMUNICATION

[6.60]

*Article 56  Cooperation and communication between insolvency practitioners*
1. *Where insolvency proceedings relate to two or more members of a group of companies, an insolvency practitioner appointed in proceedings concerning a member of the group shall cooperate with any insolvency practitioner appointed in proceedings concerning another member of the same group to the extent that such cooperation is appropriate to facilitate the effective administration of those proceedings, is not incompatible with the rules applicable to such proceedings and does not entail any conflict of interest. That cooperation may take any form, including the conclusion of agreements or protocols.*

2. *In implementing the cooperation set out in paragraph 1, insolvency practitioners shall:*

    *(a)  as soon as possible communicate to each other any information which may be relevant to the other proceedings, provided appropriate arrangements are made to protect confidential information;*

    *(b)  consider whether possibilities exist for coordinating the administration and supervision of the affairs of the group members which are subject to insolvency proceedings, and if so, coordinate such administration and supervision;*

    *(c)  consider whether possibilities exist for restructuring group members which are subject to insolvency proceedings and, if so, coordinate with regard to the proposal and negotiation of a coordinated restructuring plan.*

*For the purposes of points (b) and (c), all or some of the insolvency practitioners referred to in paragraph 1 may agree to grant additional powers to an insolvency practitioner appointed in one of the proceedings where such an agreement is permitted by the rules applicable to each of the proceedings. They may also agree on the allocation of certain tasks amongst them, where such allocation of tasks is permitted by the rules applicable to each of the proceedings.*

**Amendments**—Repealed by SI 2019/146, as from IP completion day (as defined in the European Union (Withdrawal Agreement) Act 2020, s 39(1)–(5)).

## [6.61]

### *Article 57 Cooperation and communication between courts*

*1. Where insolvency proceedings relate to two or more members of a group of companies, a court which has opened such proceedings shall cooperate with any other court before which a request to open proceedings concerning another member of the same group is pending or which has opened such proceedings to the extent that such cooperation is appropriate to facilitate the effective administration of the proceedings, is not incompatible with the rules applicable to them and does not entail any conflict of interest. For that purpose, the courts may, where appropriate, appoint an independent person or body to act on its instructions, provided that this is not incompatible with the rules applicable to them.*

*2. In implementing the cooperation set out in paragraph 1, courts, or any appointed person or body acting on their behalf, as referred to in paragraph 1, may communicate directly with each other, or request information or assistance directly from each other, provided that such communication respects the procedural rights of the parties to the proceedings and the confidentiality of information.*

*3. The cooperation referred to in paragraph 1 may be implemented by any means that the court considers appropriate. It may, in particular, concern:*

    *(a)    coordination in the appointment of insolvency practitioners;*

    *(b)    communication of information by any means considered appropriate by the court;*

    *(c)    coordination of the administration and supervision of the assets and affairs of the members of the group;*

    *(d)    coordination of the conduct of hearings;*

    *(e)    coordination in the approval of protocols where necessary.*

**Amendments**—Repealed by SI 2019/146, as from IP completion day (as defined in the European Union (Withdrawal Agreement) Act 2020, s 39(1)–(5)).

## [6.62]

### *Article 58 Cooperation and communication between insolvency practitioners and courts*

*An insolvency practitioner appointed in insolvency proceedings concerning a member of a group of companies:*

    *(a)    shall cooperate and communicate with any court before which a request for the opening of proceedings in respect of another member of the same group of companies is pending or which has opened such proceedings; and*

    *(b)    may request information from that court concerning the proceedings regarding the other member of the group or request assistance concerning the proceedings in which he has been appointed;*

*to the extent that such cooperation and communication are appropriate to facilitate the effective administration of the proceedings, do not entail any conflict of interest and are not incompatible with the rules applicable to them.*

**Amendments**—Repealed by SI 2019/146, as from IP completion day (as defined in the European Union (Withdrawal Agreement) Act 2020, s 39(1)–(5)).

**[6.63]**

*Article 59 Costs of cooperation and communication in proceedings concerning members of a group of companies*
The costs of the cooperation and communication provided for in Articles 56 to 60 incurred by an insolvency practitioner or a court shall be regarded as costs and expenses incurred in the respective proceedings.

Amendments—Repealed by SI 2019/146, as from IP completion day (as defined in the European Union (Withdrawal Agreement) Act 2020, s 39(1)–(5)).

**[6.64]**

*Article 60 Powers of the insolvency practitioner in proceedings concerning members of a group of companies*
1.    An insolvency practitioner appointed in insolvency proceedings opened in respect of a member of a group of companies may, to the extent appropriate to facilitate the effective administration of the proceedings:
   (a)    be heard in any of the proceedings opened in respect of any other member of the same group;
   (b)    request a stay of any measure related to the realisation of the assets in the proceedings opened with respect to any other member of the same group, provided that:
      (i)    a restructuring plan for all or some members of the group for which insolvency proceedings have been opened has been proposed under point (c) of Article 56(2) and presents a reasonable chance of success;
      (ii)    such a stay is necessary in order to ensure the proper implementation of the restructuring plan;
      (iii)    the restructuring plan would be to the benefit of the creditors in the proceedings for which the stay is requested; and
      (iv)    neither the insolvency proceedings in which the insolvency practitioner referred to in paragraph 1 of this Article has been appointed nor the proceedings in respect of which the stay is requested are subject to coordination under Section 2 of this Chapter;
   (c)    apply for the opening of group coordination proceedings in accordance with Article 61.
2.    The court having opened proceedings referred to in point (b) of paragraph 1 shall stay any measure related to the realisation of the assets in the proceedings in whole or in part if it is satisfied that the conditions referred to in point (b) of paragraph 1 are fulfilled.
Before ordering the stay, the court shall hear the insolvency practitioner appointed in the proceedings for which the stay is requested. Such a stay may be ordered for any period, not exceeding 3 months, which the court considers appropriate and which is compatible with the rules applicable to the proceedings.
The court ordering the stay may require the insolvency practitioner referred to in paragraph 1 to take any suitable measure available under national law to guarantee the interests of the creditors in the proceedings.
The court may extend the duration of the stay by such further period or periods as it considers appropriate and which are compatible with the rules applicable to the proceedings, provided that the conditions referred to in points (b)(ii) to (iv) of paragraph 1 continue to be fulfilled and that the total duration of the stay (the initial period together with any such extensions) does not exceed 6 months.

Amendments—Repealed by SI 2019/146, as from IP completion day (as defined in the European Union (Withdrawal Agreement) Act 2020, s 39(1)–(5)).

**ARTICLES 56–60**
In the original Insolvency Regulation the focus was much very on the particular individual company of a group of companies and not on its possible status as a member of a group of

companies. In one sense, this focus was understandable for the Regulation is more a conflict-of-laws instrument than a substantive law instrument. Provisions, for example, for the pooling of assets of related companies would impinge on the fundamental principle of substantive company law, reaffirmed by the UK Supreme Court – *Prest v Petrodel Resources Ltd* [2012] 2 AC 415; *VTB Capital plc v Nutritek International Corp* [2013] 2 AC 337 – that a company is a legal entity, separate and distinct from its controlling shareholders. Nevertheless, the Regulation might have contained procedurally oriented provisions enabling the same IP to be appointed to different companies within the same corporate group and for proceedings involving related group companies to be administered from the same state.

The jurisprudence from the European court has also been generally unsympathetic to the notion of procedural consolidation of insolvency proceedings. In the *Eurofood* case – Case C-341/04 [2006] ECR 1–03813 at [1] it was held that where a company carries on its business in the territory of the Member State where its registered office is situated, the mere fact that its economic choices are or can be controlled by a parent company in another Member State is not enough to rebut the presumption laid down by the Regulation.

In other words, the presumption applied that the COMI was the place of the registered office of the subsidiary. Moreover, in *Mediasucre* Case C-191/10 [2012] All ER (EC) 239 the court rejected the proposition that a single COMI could automatically be inferred from the intermixing of the property of two companies. The court said that this could be organised from two management and supervision centres in two different Member States.

The recast Regulation does not preclude the possibility of procedural consolidation in appropriate cases; in other words following the practice in relation to highly integrated groups of companies of determining that the centre of main interests of all members of the group is located in one and the same place and, consequently, to open proceedings only in a single jurisdiction.

The main focus of the recast Regulation however, in relation to groups is to extend the principles of cooperation that apply in the context of main and secondary proceedings to insolvency proceedings that involve different companies within the same group. This means that IPs and courts are obliged to cooperate with the cooperation taking different forms depending on the circumstances of the case. IPs should exchange relevant information and cooperation by way of protocols is explicitly mentioned – Art 56(1). Courts may cooperate by exchanging information; through coordinating the administration and supervision of the assets and affairs of the group companies as well as coordinating conduct of hearings and approval of protocols – Art 57.

The IP has standing in relation to insolvency proceedings affecting another member of the same group with rights to be heard and to request a stay provided that a restructuring plan for some or all of the insolvent group members has been proposed and presents a reasonable chance of success – Art 60(1). It is also provided that IPs should consider whether possibilities exist for restructuring group members which are subject to insolvency proceedings and, if so, coordinate with regard to the proposal and negotiation of a coordinated restructuring plan – Art 56(2)(c).

Nevertheless, working relationships between IPs will have to be good to ensure that the potentially valuable procedural tools provided by the recast Regulation do not become instruments for conflict and increased transaction costs.

SECTION 2

COORDINATION

SUBSECTION 1

PROCEDURE

**[6.65]**

**General note Chapter V, Section 2, Arts 61–77**—These provisions involve the possibility of opening group co-ordination proceedings that would sit alongside the separate insolvency proceedings opened in respect of individual companies within the group. The co-ordination proceedings would allow for the appointment of a co-ordinator who would partially act as a sort of 'super-mediator' between the different IPs: Art 72(2)(b). The coordinator also has the task of proposing a 'group coordination plan that identifies, describes and recommends a comprehensive set of measures appropriate to an integrated approach' to resolving the insolvency of group members. The plan may contain proposals for the settlement of intra-group disputes or, more ambitiously, to re-establish the economic performance and financial soundness of the group or any part of it – Art 72(1)(b)(i).

The amicable settlement of intra-group disputes and disputes between IPs is undoubtedly beneficial and so too is restoring the financial soundness of a group of companies but it is questionable whether the new provisions will contribute in particular to the achievement of the latter end. They may in fact lead to further costs and delay.

First, group co-ordination proceedings may be commenced in any state that is administering an insolvency in respect of a group member but where there are different co-ordination proceedings instituted in different states, other courts are required to decline jurisdiction in favour of the courts of the state that is first seised of the matter – Arts 61(1) and 62. This rule is however subject to Article 66 which allows for an agreement between at least two-thirds of IPs conferring exclusive jurisdiction on a particular court. Such exclusive jurisdiction agreements must be recognised and enforced.

Secondly, the IPs of individual companies within the group are not obliged to join the group proceedings. They may simply opt out at the commencement stage – Arts 64 and 65. Thirdly, the group co-ordination plan is not binding on individual IPs, even on those who had opted in, though the latter have a duty to consider the plan recommendations and to explain deviations from the plan to the coordinator – Article 70. Fourthly, to ensure proper implementation of the plan, there is a stay for up to six months on separate insolvency proceedings affecting a group member – Art 72(2)(e) – and it has been suggested this this stay may act as a real deterrent for supporting any group restructuring proposal. 'Individual group companies could choose not to opt in, simply to avoid the stay applying, as the stay is expressed not to apply to those companies who have not agreed to support the group coordination proceedings.' (See Clifford Chance briefing note, *Final Text for the Amended EU Regulation on Insolvency Proceedings* (December 2014).) Finally, the costs regime in respect of group coordination proceedings may give rise to difficulties. These costs are to be met by participating companies but are only to be paid for at the end of the proceedings – Art 77. This leads to the possibility that individual companies or IPs may dispute or delay payment when they have effectively opted out of the coordination proceedings after having opted in at the commencement stage.

Group coordination proceedings are noble in intention. Nobody is obliged to participate and a would-be participant can even effectively opt out at a later stage. Moreover, before opening such proceedings a court needs to be satisfied that the proceedings are appropriate and that none of the creditors of the participating companies are financially disadvantaged. The voluntary nature of the regime however, may mean that they are unlikely to be much used in practice but they may have a use in the 'big ticket' cases where there is a high degree of coordination among IPs at the outset.

[6.66]

### Article 61  Request to open group coordination proceedings

1.   Group coordination proceedings may be requested before any court having jurisdiction over the insolvency proceedings of a member of the group, by an insolvency practitioner appointed in insolvency proceedings opened in relation to a member of the group.

2.   The request referred to in paragraph 1 shall be made in accordance with the conditions provided for by the law applicable to the proceedings in which the insolvency practitioner has been appointed.

3.   The request referred to in paragraph 1 shall be accompanied by:

(a)   a proposal as to the person to be nominated as the group coordinator ('the coordinator'), details of his or her eligibility pursuant to Article 71, details of his or her qualifications and his or her written agreement to act as coordinator;

(b)   an outline of the proposed group coordination, and in particular the reasons why the conditions set out in Article 63(1) are fulfilled;

(c)   a list of the insolvency practitioners appointed in relation to the members of the group and, where relevant, the courts and competent authorities involved in the insolvency proceedings of the members of the group;

(d)   an outline of the estimated costs of the proposed group coordination and the estimation of the share of those costs to be paid by each member of the group.

**Amendments**—Repealed by SI 2019/146, as from IP completion day (as defined in the European Union (Withdrawal Agreement) Act 2020, s 39(1)–(5)).

[6.67]

### Article 62  Priority rule

Without prejudice to Article 66, where the opening of group coordination proceedings is requested before courts of different Member States, any court other than the court first seised shall decline jurisdiction in favour of that court.

**Amendments**—Repealed by SI 2019/146, as from IP completion day (as defined in the European Union (Withdrawal Agreement) Act 2020, s 39(1)–(5)).

**[6.68]**

### Article 63 *Notice by the court seised*

1. The court seised of a request to open group coordination proceedings shall give notice as soon as possible of the request for the opening of group coordination proceedings and of the proposed coordinator to the insolvency practitioners appointed in relation to the members of the group as indicated in the request referred to in point (c) of Article 61(3), if it is satisfied that:

    (a)    the opening of such proceedings is appropriate to facilitate the effective administration of the insolvency proceedings relating to the different group members;

    (b)    no creditor of any group member expected to participate in the proceedings is likely to be financially disadvantaged by the inclusion of that member in such proceedings; and

    (c)    the proposed coordinator fulfils the requirements laid down in Article 71.

2. The notice referred to in paragraph 1 of this Article shall list the elements referred to in points (a) to (d) of Article 61(3).

3. The notice referred to in paragraph 1 shall be sent by registered letter, attested by an acknowledgment of receipt.

4. The court seised shall give the insolvency practitioners involved the opportunity to be heard.

**Amendments**—Repealed by SI 2019/146, as from IP completion day (as defined in the European Union (Withdrawal Agreement) Act 2020, s 39(1)–(5)).

**[6.69]**

### Article 64 *Objections by insolvency practitioners*

1. An insolvency practitioner appointed in respect of any group member may object to:

    (a)    the inclusion within group coordination proceedings of the insolvency proceedings in respect of which it has been appointed; or

    (b)    the person proposed as a coordinator.

2. Objections pursuant to paragraph 1 of this Article shall be lodged with the court referred to in Article 63 within 30 days of receipt of notice of the request for the opening of group coordination proceedings by the insolvency practitioner referred to in paragraph 1 of this Article.

The objection may be made by means of the standard form established in accordance with Article 88.

3. Prior to taking the decision to participate or not to participate in the coordination in accordance with point (a) of paragraph 1, an insolvency practitioner shall obtain any approval which may be required under the law of the State of the opening of proceedings for which it has been appointed.

**Amendments**—Repealed by SI 2019/146, as from IP completion day (as defined in the European Union (Withdrawal Agreement) Act 2020, s 39(1)–(5)).

**[6.70]**

### Article 65 *Consequences of objection to the inclusion in group coordination*

1. Where an insolvency practitioner has objected to the inclusion of the proceedings in respect of which it has been appointed in group coordination proceedings, those proceedings shall not be included in the group coordination proceedings.

2. The powers of the court referred to in Article 68 or of the coordinator arising from those proceedings shall have no effect as regards that member, and shall entail no costs for that member.

Amendments—Repealed by SI 2019/146, as from IP completion day (as defined in the European Union (Withdrawal Agreement) Act 2020, s 39(1)–(5)).

**[6.71]**

*Article 66  Choice of court for group coordination proceedings*
1.   Where at least two-thirds of all insolvency practitioners appointed in insolvency proceedings of the members of the group have agreed that a court of another Member State having jurisdiction is the most appropriate court for the opening of group coordination proceedings, that court shall have exclusive jurisdiction.
2.   The choice of court shall be made by joint agreement in writing or evidenced in writing. It may be made until such time as group coordination proceedings have been opened in accordance with Article 68.
3.   Any court other than the court seised under paragraph 1 shall decline jurisdiction in favour of that court.
4.   The request for the opening of group coordination proceedings shall be submitted to the court agreed in accordance with Article 61.

Amendments—Repealed by SI 2019/146, as from IP completion day (as defined in the European Union (Withdrawal Agreement) Act 2020, s 39(1)–(5)).

**[6.72]**

*Article 67  Consequences of objections to the proposed coordinator*
Where objections to the person proposed as coordinator have been received from an insolvency practitioner which does not also object to the inclusion in the group coordination proceedings of the member in respect of which it has been appointed, the court may refrain from appointing that person and invite the objecting insolvency practitioner to submit a new request in accordance with Article 61(3).

Amendments—Repealed by SI 2019/146, as from IP completion day (as defined in the European Union (Withdrawal Agreement) Act 2020, s 39(1)–(5)).

**[6.73]**

*Article 68  Decision to open group coordination proceedings*
1.   After the period referred to in Article 64(2) has elapsed, the court may open group coordination proceedings where it is satisfied that the conditions of Article 63(1) are met. In such a case, the court shall:
    (a)    appoint a coordinator;
    (b)    decide on the outline of the coordination; and
    (c)    decide on the estimation of costs and the share to be paid by the group members.
2.   The decision opening group coordination proceedings shall be brought to the notice of the participating insolvency practitioners and of the coordinator.

Amendments—Repealed by SI 2019/146, as from IP completion day (as defined in the European Union (Withdrawal Agreement) Act 2020, s 39(1)–(5)).

**[6.74]**

*Article 69  Subsequent opt-in by insolvency practitioners*
1.   In accordance with its national law, any insolvency practitioner may request, after the court decision referred to in Article 68, the inclusion of the proceedings in respect of which it has been appointed, where:
    (a)    there has been an objection to the inclusion of the insolvency proceedings within the group coordination proceedings; or
    (b)    insolvency proceedings with respect to a member of the group have been opened after the court has opened group coordination proceedings.
2.   Without prejudice to paragraph 4, the coordinator may accede to such a request, after consulting the insolvency practitioners involved, where:

(a)     he or she is satisfied that, taking into account the stage that the group coordination proceedings has reached at the time of the request, the criteria set out in points (a) and (b) of Article 63(1) are met; or

(b)     all insolvency practitioners involved agree, subject to the conditions in their national law.

3.     The coordinator shall inform the court and the participating insolvency practitioners of his or her decision pursuant to paragraph 2 and of the reasons on which it is based.

4.     Any participating insolvency practitioner or any insolvency practitioner whose request for inclusion in the group coordination proceedings has been rejected may challenge the decision referred to in paragraph 2 in accordance with the procedure set out under the law of the Member State in which the group coordination proceedings have been opened.

Amendments—Repealed by SI 2019/146, as from IP completion day (as defined in the European Union (Withdrawal Agreement) Act 2020, s 39(1)–(5)).

**[6.75]**

*Article 70  Recommendations and group coordination plan*

1.     When conducting their insolvency proceedings, insolvency practitioners shall consider the recommendations of the coordinator and the content of the group coordination plan referred to in Article 72(1).

2.     An insolvency practitioner shall not be obliged to follow in whole or in part the coordinator's recommendations or the group coordination plan.

3.     If it does not follow the coordinator's recommendations or the group coordination plan, it shall give reasons for not doing so to the persons or bodies that it is to report to under its national law, and to the coordinator.

Amendments—Repealed by SI 2019/146, as from IP completion day (as defined in the European Union (Withdrawal Agreement) Act 2020, s 39(1)–(5)).

SUBSECTION 2

GENERAL PROVISIONS

**[6.76]**

*Article 71  The coordinator*

1.     The coordinator shall be a person eligible under the law of a Member State to act as an insolvency practitioner.

2.     The coordinator shall not be one of the insolvency practitioners appointed to act in respect of any of the group members, and shall have no conflict of interest in respect of the group members, their creditors and the insolvency practitioners appointed in respect of any of the group members.

Amendments—Repealed by SI 2019/146, as from IP completion day (as defined in the European Union (Withdrawal Agreement) Act 2020, s 39(1)–(5)).

**[6.77]**

*Article 72  Tasks and rights of the coordinator*

1.     The coordinator shall:

(a)     identify and outline recommendations for the coordinated conduct of the insolvency proceedings;

(b)     propose a group coordination plan that identifies, describes and recommends a comprehensive set of measures appropriate to an integrated approach to the resolution of the group members' insolvencies. In particular, the plan may contain proposals for:

(i)     the measures to be taken in order to re-establish the economic performance and the financial soundness of the group or any part of it;

(ii) the settlement of intra-group disputes as regards intra-group transactions and avoidance actions;

(iii) agreements between the insolvency practitioners of the insolvent group members.

2. The coordinator may also:

(a) be heard and participate, in particular by attending creditors' meetings, in any of the proceedings opened in respect of any member of the group;

(b) mediate any dispute arising between two or more insolvency practitioners of group members;

(c) present and explain his or her group coordination plan to the persons or bodies that he or she is to report to under his or her national law;

(d) request information from any insolvency practitioner in respect of any member of the group where that information is or might be of use when identifying and outlining strategies and measures in order to coordinate the proceedings; and

(e) request a stay for a period of up to 6 months of the proceedings opened in respect of any member of the group, provided that such a stay is necessary in order to ensure the proper implementation of the plan and would be to the benefit of the creditors in the proceedings for which the stay is requested; or request the lifting of any existing stay. Such a request shall be made to the court that opened the proceedings for which a stay is requested.

3. The plan referred to in point (b) of paragraph 1 shall not include recommendations as to any consolidation of proceedings or insolvency estates.

4. The coordinator's tasks and rights as defined under this Article shall not extend to any member of the group not participating in group coordination proceedings.

5. The coordinator shall perform his or her duties impartially and with due care.

6. Where the coordinator considers that the fulfilment of his or her tasks requires a significant increase in the costs compared to the cost estimate referred to in point (d) of Article 61(3), and in any case, where the costs exceed 10 % of the estimated costs, the coordinator shall:

(a) inform without delay the participating insolvency practitioners; and

(b) seek the prior approval of the court opening group coordination proceedings.

**Amendments**—Repealed by SI 2019/146, as from IP completion day (as defined in the European Union (Withdrawal Agreement) Act 2020, s 39(1)–(5)).

## [6.78]

### Article 73 Languages

1. The coordinator shall communicate with the insolvency practitioner of a participating group member in the language agreed with the insolvency practitioner or, in the absence of an agreement, in the official language or one of the official languages of the institutions of the Union, and of the court which opened the proceedings in respect of that group member.

2. The coordinator shall communicate with a court in the official language applicable to that court.

**Amendments**—Repealed by SI 2019/146, as from IP completion day (as defined in the European Union (Withdrawal Agreement) Act 2020, s 39(1)–(5)).

## [6.79]

### Article 74 Cooperation between insolvency practitioners and the coordinator

1. Insolvency practitioners appointed in relation to members of a group and the coordinator shall cooperate with each other to the extent that such cooperation is not incompatible with the rules applicable to the respective proceedings.

2. In particular, insolvency practitioners shall communicate any information that is relevant for the coordinator to perform his or her tasks.

Amendments—Repealed by SI 2019/146, as from IP completion day (as defined in the European Union (Withdrawal Agreement) Act 2020, s 39(1)–(5)).

**[6.80]**

*Article 75  Revocation of the appointment of the coordinator*
*The court shall revoke the appointment of the coordinator of its own motion or at the request of the insolvency practitioner of a participating group member where:*
> *(a)      the coordinator acts to the detriment of the creditors of a participating group member; or*
> *(b)      the coordinator fails to comply with his or her obligations under this Chapter.*

Amendments—Repealed by SI 2019/146, as from IP completion day (as defined in the European Union (Withdrawal Agreement) Act 2020, s 39(1)–(5)).

**[6.81]**

*Article 76  Debtor in possession*
*The provisions applicable, under this Chapter, to the insolvency practitioner shall also apply, where appropriate, to the debtor in possession.*

Amendments—Repealed by SI 2019/146, as from IP completion day (as defined in the European Union (Withdrawal Agreement) Act 2020, s 39(1)–(5)).

**[6.82]**

*Article 77  Costs and distribution*
*1.    The remuneration for the coordinator shall be adequate, proportionate to the tasks fulfilled and reflect reasonable expenses.*
*2.    On having completed his or her tasks, the coordinator shall establish the final statement of costs and the share to be paid by each member, and submit this statement to each participating insolvency practitioner and to the court opening coordination proceedings.*
*3.    In the absence of objections by the insolvency practitioners within 30 days of receipt of the statement referred to in paragraph 2, the costs and the share to be paid by each member shall be deemed to be agreed. The statement shall be submitted to the court opening coordination proceedings for confirmation.*
*4.    In the event of an objection, the court that opened the group coordination proceedings shall, upon the application of the coordinator or any participating insolvency practitioner, decide on the costs and the share to be paid by each member in accordance with the criteria set out in paragraph 1 of this Article, and taking into account the estimation of costs referred to in Article 68(1) and, where applicable, Article 72(6).*
*5.    Any participating insolvency practitioner may challenge the decision referred to in paragraph 4 in accordance with the procedure set out under the law of the Member State where group coordination proceedings have been opened.*

Amendments—Repealed by SI 2019/146, as from IP completion day (as defined in the European Union (Withdrawal Agreement) Act 2020, s 39(1)–(5)).

CHAPTER VI    DATA PROTECTION

**[6.83]**

*Article 78  Data protection*
*1.    National rules implementing Directive 95/46/EC shall apply to the processing of personal data carried out in the Member States pursuant to this Regulation, provided that processing operations referred to in Article 3(2) of Directive 95/46/EC are not concerned.*

2.   *Regulation (EC) No 45/2001 shall apply to the processing of personal data carried out by the Commission pursuant to this Regulation.*

**Amendments**—Repealed by SI 2019/146, as from IP completion day (as defined in the European Union (Withdrawal Agreement) Act 2020, s 39(1)–(5)).

## [6.84]

### Article 79   Responsibilities of Member States regarding the processing of personal data in national insolvency registers

1.   *Each Member State shall communicate to the Commission the name of the natural or legal person, public authority, agency or any other body designated by national law to exercise the functions of controller in accordance with point (d) of Article 2 of Directive 95/46/EC, with a view to its publication on the European e-Justice Portal.*

2.   *Member States shall ensure that the technical measures for ensuring the security of personal data processed in their national insolvency registers referred to in Article 24 are implemented.*

3.   *Member States shall be responsible for verifying that the controller, designated by national law in accordance with point (d) of Article 2 of Directive 95/46/EC, ensures compliance with the principles of data quality, in particular the accuracy and the updating of data stored in national insolvency registers.*

4.   *Member States shall be responsible, in accordance with Directive 95/46/EC, for the collection and storage of data in national databases and for decisions taken to make such data available in the interconnected register that can be consulted via the European e-Justice Portal.*

5.   *As part of the information that should be provided to data subjects to enable them to exercise their rights, and in particular the right to the erasure of data, Member States shall inform data subjects of the accessibility period set for personal data stored in insolvency registers.*

**Amendments**—Repealed by SI 2019/146, as from IP completion day (as defined in the European Union (Withdrawal Agreement) Act 2020, s 39(1)–(5)).

## [6.85]

### Article 80   Responsibilities of the Commission in connection with the processing of personal data

1.   *The Commission shall exercise the responsibilities of controller pursuant to Article 2(d) of Regulation (EC) No 45/2001 in accordance with its respective responsibilities defined in this Article.*

2.   *The Commission shall define the necessary policies and apply the necessary technical solutions to fulfil its responsibilities within the scope of the function of controller.*

3.   *The Commission shall implement the technical measures required to ensure the security of personal data while in transit, in particular the confidentiality and integrity of any transmission to and from the European e-Justice Portal.*

4.   *The obligations of the Commission shall not affect the responsibilities of the Member States and other bodies for the content and operation of the interconnected national databases run by them.*

**Amendments**—Repealed by SI 2019/146, as from IP completion day (as defined in the European Union (Withdrawal Agreement) Act 2020, s 39(1)–(5)).

## [6.86]

### Article 81   Information obligations

*Without prejudice to the information to be given to data subjects in accordance with Articles 11 and 12 of Regulation (EC) No 45/2001, the Commission shall inform data subjects, by means of publication through the European e-Justice Portal, about its role in the processing of data and the purposes for which those data will be processed.*

Amendments—Repealed by SI 2019/146, as from IP completion day (as defined in the European Union (Withdrawal Agreement) Act 2020, s 39(1)–(5)).

## [6.87]

### *Article 82  Storage of personal data*

*As regards information from interconnected national databases, no personal data relating to data subjects shall be stored in the European e-Justice Portal. All such data shall be stored in the national databases operated by the Member States or other bodies.*

Amendments—Repealed by SI 2019/146, as from IP completion day (as defined in the European Union (Withdrawal Agreement) Act 2020, s 39(1)–(5)).

## [6.88]

### *Article 83  Access to personal data via the European e-Justice Portal*

*Personal data stored in the national insolvency registers referred to in Article 24 shall be accessible via the European e-Justice Portal for as long as they remain accessible under national law.*

Amendments—Repealed by SI 2019/146, as from IP completion day (as defined in the European Union (Withdrawal Agreement) Act 2020, s 39(1)–(5)).

## CHAPTER VII   TRANSITIONAL AND FINAL PROVISIONS

## [6.89]

### Article 84  Applicability in time

1.  The provisions of this Regulation shall apply only to insolvency proceedings opened after 26 June 2017. *Acts committed by a debtor before that date shall continue to be governed by the law which was applicable to them at the time they were committed.*

2.  *Notwithstanding Article 91 of this Regulation, Regulation (EC) No 1346/2000 shall continue to apply to insolvency proceedings which fall within the scope of that Regulation and which have been opened before 26 June 2017.*

Amendments—Repealed by SI 2019/146, as from IP completion day (as defined in the European Union (Withdrawal Agreement) Act 2020, s 39(1)–(5)).

## [6.90]

### *Article 85  Relationship to Conventions*

1.  *This Regulation replaces, in respect of the matters referred to therein, and as regards relations between Member States, the Conventions concluded between two or more Member States, in particular:*

    *(a)*    *the Convention between Belgium and France on Jurisdiction and the Validity and Enforcement of Judgments, Arbitration Awards and Authentic Instruments, signed at Paris on 8 July 1899;*

    *(b)*    *the Convention between Belgium and Austria on Bankruptcy, Winding-up, Arrangements, Compositions and Suspension of Payments (with Additional Protocol of 13 June 1973), signed at Brussels on 16 July 1969;*

    *(c)*    *the Convention between Belgium and the Netherlands on Territorial Jurisdiction, Bankruptcy and the Validity and Enforcement of Judgments, Arbitration Awards and Authentic Instruments, signed at Brussels on 28 March 1925;*

    *(d)*    *the Treaty between Germany and Austria on Bankruptcy, Winding-up, Arrangements and Compositions, signed at Vienna on 25 May 1979;*

    *(e)*    *the Convention between France and Austria on Jurisdiction, Recognition and Enforcement of Judgments on Bankruptcy, signed at Vienna on 27 February 1979;*

*(f)*   the Convention between France and Italy on the Enforcement of Judgments in Civil and Commercial Matters, signed at Rome on 3 June 1930;

*(g)*   the Convention between Italy and Austria on Bankruptcy, Winding-up, Arrangements and Compositions, signed at Rome on 12 July 1977;

*(h)*   the Convention between the Kingdom of the Netherlands and the Federal Republic of Germany on the Mutual Recognition and Enforcement of Judgments and other Enforceable Instruments in Civil and Commercial Matters, signed at The Hague on 30 August 1962;

*(i)*   the Convention between the United Kingdom and the Kingdom of Belgium providing for the Reciprocal Enforcement of Judgments in Civil and Commercial Matters, with Protocol, signed at Brussels on 2 May 1934;

*(j)*   the Convention between Denmark, Finland, Norway, Sweden and Iceland on Bankruptcy, signed at Copenhagen on 7 November 1933;

*(k)*   the European Convention on Certain International Aspects of Bankruptcy, signed at Istanbul on 5 June 1990;

*(l)*   the Convention between the Federative People's Republic of Yugoslavia and the Kingdom of Greece on the Mutual Recognition and Enforcement of Judgments, signed at Athens on 18 June 1959;

*(m)*  the Agreement between the Federative People's Republic of Yugoslavia and the Republic of Austria on the Mutual Recognition and Enforcement of Arbitral Awards and Arbitral Settlements in Commercial Matters, signed at Belgrade on 18 March 1960;

*(n)*   the Convention between the Federative People's Republic of Yugoslavia and the Italian Republic on Mutual Judicial Cooperation in Civil and Administrative Matters, signed at Rome on 3 December 1960;

*(o)*   the Agreement between the Socialist Federative Republic of Yugoslavia and the Kingdom of Belgium on Judicial Cooperation in Civil and Commercial Matters, signed at Belgrade on 24 September 1971;

*(p)*   the Convention between the Governments of Yugoslavia and France on the Recognition and Enforcement of Judgments in Civil and Commercial Matters, signed at Paris on 18 May 1971;

*(q)*   the Agreement between the Czechoslovak Socialist Republic and the Hellenic Republic on Legal Aid in Civil and Criminal Matters, signed at Athens on 22 October 1980, still in force between the Czech Republic and Greece;

*(r)*   the Agreement between the Czechoslovak Socialist Republic and the Republic of Cyprus on Legal Aid in Civil and Criminal Matters, signed at Nicosia on 23 April 1982, still in force between the Czech Republic and Cyprus;

*(s)*   the Treaty between the Government of the Czechoslovak Socialist Republic and the Government of the Republic of France on Legal Aid and the Recognition and Enforcement of Judgments in Civil, Family and Commercial Matters, signed at Paris on 10 May 1984, still in force between the Czech Republic and France;

*(t)*   the Treaty between the Czechoslovak Socialist Republic and the Italian Republic on Legal Aid in Civil and Criminal Matters, signed at Prague on 6 December 1985, still in force between the Czech Republic and Italy;

*(u)*   the Agreement between the Republic of Latvia, the Republic of Estonia and the Republic of Lithuania on Legal Assistance and Legal Relationships, signed at Tallinn on 11 November 1992;

*(v)*   the Agreement between Estonia and Poland on Granting Legal Aid and Legal Relations on Civil, Labour and Criminal Matters, signed at Tallinn on 27 November 1998;

*(w)*  the Agreement between the Republic of Lithuania and the Republic of Poland on Legal Assistance and Legal Relations in Civil, Family, Labour and Criminal Matters, signed at Warsaw on 26 January 1993;

(x)    the Convention between the Socialist Republic of Romania and the Hellenic Republic on legal assistance in civil and criminal matters and its Protocol, signed at Bucharest on 19 October 1972;

(y)    the Convention between the Socialist Republic of Romania and the French Republic on legal assistance in civil and commercial matters, signed at Paris on 5 November 1974;

(z)    the Agreement between the People's Republic of Bulgaria and the Hellenic Republic on Legal Assistance in Civil and Criminal Matters, signed at Athens on 10 April 1976;

(aa)   the Agreement between the People's Republic of Bulgaria and the Republic of Cyprus on Legal Assistance in Civil and Criminal Matters, signed at Nicosia on 29 April 1983;

(ab)   the Agreement between the Government of the People's Republic of Bulgaria and the Government of the French Republic on Mutual Legal Assistance in Civil Matters, signed at Sofia on 18 January 1989;

(ac)   the Treaty between Romania and the Czech Republic on judicial assistance in civil matters, signed at Bucharest on 11 July 1994;

(ad)   the Treaty between Romania and the Republic of Poland on legal assistance and legal relations in civil cases, signed at Bucharest on 15 May 1999.

2.   The Conventions referred to in paragraph 1 shall continue to have effect with regard to proceedings opened before the entry into force of Regulation (EC) No 1346/2000.

3.   This Regulation shall not apply:

(a)    in any Member State, to the extent that it is irreconcilable with the obligations arising in relation to bankruptcy from a convention concluded by that Member State the United Kingdom with one or more third countries before the entry into force of Regulation (EC) No 1346/2000;

(b)    in the United Kingdom of Great Britain and Northern Ireland, to the extent that is irreconcilable with the obligations arising in relation to bankruptcy and the winding-up of insolvent companies from any arrangements with the Commonwealth existing at the time Regulation (EC) No 1346/2000 entered into force.

**Amendments**—SI 2019/146, as from IP completion day (as defined in the European Union (Withdrawal Agreement) Act 2020, s 39(1)–(5)).

## [6.91]

*Article 86  Information on national and Union insolvency law*

1.   The Member States shall provide, within the framework of the European Judicial Network in civil and commercial matters established by Council Decision 2001/470/EC[1], and with a view to making the information available to the public, a short description of their national legislation and procedures relating to insolvency, in particular relating to the matters listed in Article 7(2).

2.   The Member States shall update the information referred to in paragraph 1 regularly.

3.   The Commission shall make information concerning this Regulation available to the public.

[1]   Council Decision 2001/470/EC of 28 May 2001 establishing a European Judicial Network in civil and commercial matters (OJ L 174, 27.6.2001, p 25).

**Amendments**—Repealed by SI 2019/146, as from IP completion day (as defined in the European Union (Withdrawal Agreement) Act 2020, s 39(1)–(5)).

**[6.92]**

*Article 87  Establishment of the interconnection of registers*

The Commission shall adopt implementing acts establishing the interconnection of insolvency registers as referred to in Article 25. Those implementing acts shall be adopted in accordance with the examination procedure referred to in Article 89(3).

Amendments—Repealed by SI 2019/146, as from IP completion day (as defined in the European Union (Withdrawal Agreement) Act 2020, s 39(1)–(5)).

**[6.93]**

*Article 88  Establishment and subsequent amendment of standard forms*

The Commission shall adopt implementing acts establishing and, where necessary, amending the forms referred to in Article 27(4), Articles 54 and 55 and Article 64(2). Those implementing acts shall be adopted in accordance with the advisory procedure referred to in Article 89(2).

Amendments—Repealed by SI 2019/146, as from IP completion day (as defined in the European Union (Withdrawal Agreement) Act 2020, s 39(1)–(5)).

**[6.94]**

*Article 89  Committee procedure*

1. The Commission shall be assisted by a committee. That committee shall be a committee within the meaning of Regulation (EU) No 182/2011.

2. Where reference is made to this paragraph, Article 4 of Regulation (EU) No 182/2011 shall apply.

3. Where reference is made to this paragraph, Article 5 of Regulation (EU) No 182/2011 shall apply.

Amendments—Repealed by SI 2019/146, as from IP completion day (as defined in the European Union (Withdrawal Agreement) Act 2020, s 39(1)–(5)).

**[6.95]**

*Article 90  Review clause*

1. No later than 27 June 2027, and every 5 years thereafter, the Commission shall present to the European Parliament, the Council and the European Economic and Social Committee a report on the application of this Regulation. The report shall be accompanied where necessary by a proposal for adaptation of this Regulation.

2. No later than 27 June 2022, the Commission shall present to the European Parliament, the Council and the European Economic and Social Committee a report on the application of the group coordination proceedings. The report shall be accompanied where necessary by a proposal for adaptation of this Regulation.

3. No later than 1 January 2016, the Commission shall submit to the European Parliament, the Council and the European Economic and Social Committee a study on the cross-border issues in the area of directors' liability and disqualifications.

4. No later than 27 June 2020, the Commission shall submit to the European Parliament, the Council and the European Economic and Social Committee a study on the issue of abusive forum shopping.

Amendments—Repealed by SI 2019/146, as from IP completion day (as defined in the European Union (Withdrawal Agreement) Act 2020, s 39(1)–(5)).

**[6.96]**

**Article 91  Repeal**

Regulation (EC) No 1346/2000 is repealed.

*References to the repealed Regulation shall be construed as references to this Regulation and shall be read in accordance with the correlation table set out in Annex D to this Regulation.*

Amendments—SI 2019/146, as from IP completion day (as defined in the European Union (Withdrawal Agreement) Act 2020, s 39(1)–(5)).

**[6.97]**

**Article 92  Entry into force**

This Regulation shall enter into force on the twentieth day following that of its publication in the *Official Journal of the European Union*.

It shall apply from 26 June 2017, with the exception of:

    (a)    Article 86, which shall apply from 26 June 2016;

    (b)    Article 24(1), which shall apply from 26 June 2018; and

    (c)    Article 25, which shall apply from 26 June 2019.

*This Regulation shall be binding in its entirety and directly applicable in the Member States in accordance with the Treaties.*

Done at Strasbourg, 20 May 2015.

Amendments—SI 2019/146, as from IP completion day (as defined in the European Union (Withdrawal Agreement) Act 2020, s 39(1)–(5)).

ANNEX A

INSOLVENCY PROCEEDINGS REFERRED TO IN POINT (4) OF ARTICLE 2

**[6.98]**

*Belgique/België*

— *Het faillissement/La faillite,*

— *De gerechtelijke reorganisatie door een collectief akkoord/La réorganisation judiciaire par accord collectif,*

— *De gerechtelijke reorganisatie door een minnelijk akkoord/La réorganisation judiciaire par accord amiable,*

— *De gerechtelijke reorganisatie door overdracht onder gerechtelijk gezag/La réorganisation judiciaire par transfert sous autorité de justice,*

— *De collectieve schuldenregeling/Le règlement collectif de dettes,*

— *De vrijwillige vereffening/La liquidation volontaire,*

— *De gerechtelijke vereffening/La liquidation judiciaire,*

— *De voorlopige ontneming van beheer, bepaald in artikel 8 van de faillissementswet/ Le dessaisissement provisoire, visé à l'article 8 de la loi sur les faillites,*

*България*

— *Производство по несъстоятелност,*

*Česká Republika*

— *Konkurs,*

— *Reorganizace,*

— *Oddlužení,*

*Deutschland*

— *Das Konkursverfahren,*

— *Das gerichtliche Vergleichsverfahren,*

— *Das Gesamtvollstreckungsverfahren,*

— *Das Insolvenzverfahren,*

*Eesti*

— *Pankrotimenetlus,*

— *Võlgade ümberkujundamise menetlus,*

*Éire/Ireland*

— *Compulsory winding-up by the court,*

— *Bankruptcy,*

— *The administration in bankruptcy of the estate of persons dying insolvent,*

— *Winding-up in bankruptcy of partnerships,*

— *Creditors' voluntary winding-up (with confirmation of a court),*
— *Arrangements under the control of the court which involve the vesting of all or part of the property of the debtor in the Official Assignee for realisation and distribution,*
— *Examinership,*
— *Debt Relief Notice,*
— *Debt Settlement Arrangement,*
— *Personal Insolvency Arrangement,*

Ελλαδα
— Η πτώχευση,
— Η ειδική εκκαθάριση εν λειτουργία,
— Σχέδιο αναδιοργάνωσης,
— Απλοποιημένη διαδικασία επί πτωχεύσεων μικρού αντικειμένου,
— Διαδικασία Εξυγίανσης,

*España*
— *Concurso,*
— *Procedimiento de homologación de acuerdos de refinanciación,*
— *Procedimiento de acuerdos extrajudiciales de pago,*
— *Procedimiento de negociación pública para la consecución de acuerdos de refinanciación colectivos, acuerdos de refinanciación homologados y propuestas anticipadas de convenio,*

*France*
— *Sauvegarde,*
— *Sauvegarde accélérée,*
— *Sauvegarde financière accélérée,*
— *Redressement judiciaire,*
— *Liquidation judiciaire,*

*Hrvatska*
— *Stečajni postupak,*

*Italia*
— *Fallimento,*
— *Concordato preventivo,*
— *Liquidazione coatta amministrativa,*
— *Amministrazione straordinaria,*
— *Accordi di ristrutturazione,*
— *Procedure di composizione della crisi da sovraindebitamento del consumatore (accordo o piano),*
— *Liquidazione dei beni,*

Κυπροσ
— Υποχρεωτική εκκαθάριση από το Δικαστήριο,
— Εκούσια εκκαθάριση από μέλη,
— Εκούσια εκκαθάριση από πιστωτές,
— Εκκαθάριση με την εποπτεία του Δικαστηρίου,
— Διάταγμα Παραλαβής και πτώχευσης κατόπιν Δικαστικού Διατάγματος,
— Διαχείριση της περιουσίας προσώπων που απεβίωσαν αφερέγγυα,

*Latvija*
— *Tiesiskās aizsardzības process,*
— *Juridiskās personas maksātnespējas process,*
— *Fiziskās personas maksātnespējas process,*

*Lietuva*
— *Įmonės restruktūrizavimo byla,*
— *Įmonės bankroto byla,*
— *Įmonės bankroto procesas ne teismo tvarka,*
— *Fizinio asmens bankroto procesas,*

**Luxembourg**
— *Faillite,*
— *Gestion contrôlée,*
— *Concordat préventif de faillite (par abandon d'actif),*
— *Régime spécial de liquidation du notariat,*
— *Procédure de règlement collectif des dettes dans le cadre du surendettement,*

**Magyarország**
— *Csődeljárás,*
— *Felszámolási eljárás,*

**Malta**
— *Xoljiment,*
— *Amministrazzjoni,*
— *Stralċ volontarju mill-membri jew mill-kredituri,*
— *Stralċ mill-Qorti,*
— *Falliment f'każ ta' kummerċjant,*
— *Proċedura biex kumpanija tirkupra,*

**Nederland**
— *Het faillissement,*
— *De surséance van betaling,*
— *De schuldsaneringsregeling natuurlijke personen,*

**Österreich**
— *Das Konkursverfahren (Insolvenzverfahren),*
— *Das Sanierungsverfahren ohne Eigenverwaltung (Insolvenzverfahren),*
— *Das Sanierungsverfahren mit Eigenverwaltung (Insolvenzverfahren),*
— *Das Schuldenregulierungsverfahren,*
— *Das Abschöpfungsverfahren,*
— *Das Ausgleichsverfahren,*

**Polska**
— *Postępowanie naprawcze,*
— *Upadłość obejmująca likwidację,*
— *Upadłość z możliwością zawarcia układu,*

**Portugal**
— *Processo de insolvência,*
— *Processo especial de revitalização,*

**România**
— *Procedura insolvenÈâ€°ei,*
— *Reorganizarea judiciară,*
— *Procedura falimentului,*
— *Concordatul preventiv,*

**Slovenija**
— *Postopek preventivnega prestrukturiranja,*
— *Postopek prisilne poravnave,*
— *Postopek poenostavljene prisilne poravnave,*
— *Stečajni postopek: stečajni postopek nad pravno osebo, postopek osebnega stečaja and postopek stečaja zapuščine,*

**Slovensko**
— *Konkurzné konanie,*
— *Reštrukturalizačné konanie,*
— *Oddlženie,*

**Suomi/Finland**
— *Konkurssi/konkurs,*
— *Yrityssaneeraus/företagssanering,*
— *Yksityishenkilön velkajärjestely/skuldsanering för privatpersoner,*

*Sverige*
— *Konkurs,*
— *Företagsrekonstruktion,*
— *Skuldsanering,*

**United Kingdom**
— *Winding-up by or subject to the supervision of the court,*
— *Creditors' voluntary winding-up (with confirmation by the court),*
— *Administration, including appointments made by filing prescribed documents with the court,*
— *Voluntary arrangements under insolvency legislation,*
— *Bankruptcy or sequestration.*

Amendments—Repealed by SI 2019/146, as from IP completion day (as defined in the European Union (Withdrawal Agreement) Act 2020, s 39(1)–(5)).

ANNEX B
INSOLVENCY PRACTITIONERS REFERRED TO IN POINT (5) OF ARTICLE 2

**[6.99]**

*Belgique/België*
— *De curator/Le curateur,*
— *De gedelegeerd rechter/Le juge-délégué,*
— *De gerechtsmandataris/Le mandataire de justice,*
— *De schuldbemiddelaar/Le médiateur de dettes,*
— *De vereffenaar/Le liquidateur,*
— *De voorlopige bewindvoerder/L'administrateur provisoire,*

**България**
— *Назначен предварително временен синдик,*
— *Временен синдик,*
— *(Постоянен) синдик,*
— *Служебен синдик,*

*Česká Republika*
— *Insolvenční správce,*
— *Předběžný insolvenční správce,*
— *Oddělený insolvenční správce,*
— *Zvláštní insolvenční správce,*
— *Zástupce insolvenčního správce,*

**Deutschland**
— *Konkursverwalter,*
— *Vergleichsverwalter,*
— *Sachwalter (nach der Vergleichsordnung),*
— *Verwalter,*
— *Insolvenzverwalter,*
— *Sachwalter (nach der Insolvenzordnung),*
— *Treuhänder,*
— *Vorläufiger Insolvenzverwalter,*
— *Vorläufiger Sachwalter,*

*Eesti*
— *Pankrotihaldur,*
— *Ajutine pankrotihaldur,*
— *Usaldusisik,*

*Éire/Ireland*
— *Liquidator,*
— *Official Assignee,*

— *Trustee in bankruptcy,*
— *Provisional Liquidator,*
— *Examiner,*
— *Personal Insolvency Practitioner,*
— *Insolvency Service,*

Ελλάδα
— Ο σύνδικος,
— Ο εισηγητής,
— Η επιτροπή των πιστωτών,
— Ο ειδικός εκκαθαριστής,

*España*
— *Administrador concursal,*
— *Mediador concursal,*

*France*
— *Mandataire judiciaire,*
— *Liquidateur,*
— *Administrateur judiciaire,*
— *Commissaire à l'exécution du plan,*

*Hrvatska*
— *Stečajni upravitelj,*
— *Privremeni stečajni upravitelj,*
— *Stečajni povjerenik,*
— *Povjerenik,*

*Italia*
— *Curatore,*
— *Commissario giudiziale,*
— *Commissario straordinario,*
— *Commissario liquidatore,*
— *Liquidatore giudiziale,*
— *Professionista nominato dal Tribunale,*
— *Organismo di composizione della crisi nella procedura di composizione della crisi da sovraindebitamento del consumatore,*
— *Liquidatore,*

Κυπροσ
— Εκκαθαριστής και Προσωρινός Εκκαθαριστής,
— Επίσημος Παραλήπτης,
— Διαχειριστής της Πτώχευσης,

*Latvija*
— *Maksātnespējas procesa administrators,*

*Lietuva*
— *Bankroto administratorius,*
— *Restruktūrizavimo administratorius,*

*Luxembourg*
— *Le curateur,*
— *Le commissaire,*
— *Le liquidateur,*
— *Le conseil de gérance de la section d'assainissement du notariat,*
— *Le liquidateur dans le cadre du surendettement,*

*Magyarország*
— *Vagyonfelügyelő,*
— *Felszámoló,*

*Malta*

— *Amministratur Proviżorju,*
— *Riċevitur Uffiċjali,*
— *Stralċjarju,*
— *Manager Speċjali,*
— *Kuraturi f'każ ta' proċeduri ta' falliment,*
— *Kontrolur Speċjali,*

**Nederland**

— *De curator in het faillissement,*
— *De bewindvoerder in de surséance van betaling,*
— *De bewindvoerder in de schuldsaneringsregeling natuurlijke personen,*

**Österreich**

— *Masseverwalter,*
— *Sanierungsverwalter,*
— *Ausgleichsverwalter,*
— *Besonderer Verwalter,*
— *Einstweiliger Verwalter,*
— *Sachwalter,*
— *Treuhänder,*
— *Insolvenzgericht,*
— *Konkursgericht,*

**Polska**

— *Syndyk,*
— *Nadzorca sądowy,*
— *Zarządca,*

**Portugal**

— *Administrador da insolvência,*
— *Administrador judicial provisório,*

**România**

— *Practician în insolvenÈâ€°ă,*
— *Administrator concordatar,*
— *Administrator judiciar,*
— *Lichidator judiciar,*

**Slovenija**

— *Upravitelj,*

**Slovensko**

— *Predbežný správca,*
— *Správca,*

**Suomi/Finland**

— *Pesänhoitaja/boförvaltare,*
— *Selvittäjä/utredare,*

**Sverige**

— *Förvaltare,*
— *Rekonstruktör,*

**United Kingdom**

— Liquidator,
— Supervisor of a voluntary arrangement,
— Administrator,
— Official Receiver,
— Trustee,
— Provisional Liquidator,
— Interim Receiver,

— Judicial factor.

**Amendments**—SI 2019/146, as from IP completion day (as defined in the European Union (Withdrawal Agreement) Act 2020, s 39(1)–(5)).

## ANNEX C
### REPEALED REGULATION WITH LIST OF THE SUCCESSIVE AMENDMENTS THERETO

**[6.100]**

Council Regulation (EC) No 1346/2000 (OJ L 160, 30.6.2000, p. 1)
Council Regulation (EC) No 603/2005 (OJ L 100, 20.4.2005, p. 1)
Council Regulation (EC) No 694/2006 (OJ L 121, 6.5.2006, p. 1)
Council Regulation (EC) No 1791/2006 (OJ L 363, 20.12.2006, p. 1)
Council Regulation (EC) No 681/2007 (OJ L 159, 20.6.2007, p. 1)
Council Regulation (EC) No 788/2008 (OJ L 213, 8.8.2008, p. 1)
Implementing Regulation of the Council (EU) No 210/2010 (OJ L 65, 13.3.2010, p. 1)
Council Implementing Regulation (EU) No 583/2011 (OJ L 160, 18.6.2011, p. 52)
Council Regulation (EU) No 517/2013 (OJ L 158, 10.6.2013, p. 1)
Council Implementing Regulation (EU) No 663/2014 (OJ L 179, 19.6.2014, p. 4)
Act concerning the conditions of accession of the Czech Republic, the Republic of Estonia, the Republic of Cyprus, the Republic of Latvia, the Republic of Lithuania, the Republic of Hungary, the Republic of Malta, the Republic of Poland, the Republic of Slovenia and the Slovak Republic and the adjustments to the Treaties on which the European Union is founded (OJ L 236, 23.9.2003, p. 33)

## ANNEX D
### CORRELATION TABLE

**[6.101]**

| *Regulation (EC) No 1346/2000* | *This Regulation* |
| --- | --- |
| Article 1 | Article 1 |
| Article 2, introductory words | Article 2, introductory words |
| Article 2, point (a) | Article 2, point (4) |
| Article 2, point (b) | Article 2, point (5) |
| Article 2, point (c) | — |
| Article 2, point (d) | Article 2, point (6) |
| Article 2, point (e) | Article 2, point (7) |
| Article 2, point (f) | Article 2, point (8) |
| Article 2, point (g), introductory words | Article 2, point (9), introductory words |
| Article 2, point (g), first indent | Article 2, point (9)(vii) |
| Article 2, point (g), second indent | Article 2, point (9)(iv) |
| Article 2, point (g), third indent | Article 2, point (9)(viii) |
| Article 2, point (h) | Article 2, point 10 |
| Article 2, points (1) to (3) and (11) to (13) | |
| Article 2, point (9)(i) to (iii), (v), (vi) | |
| Article 3 | Article 3 |
| Article 4 | |
| Article 5 | |
| Article 6 | |
| Article 4 | Article 7 |

| Regulation (EC) No 1346/2000 | This Regulation |
|---|---|
| Article 5 | Article 8 |
| Article 6 | Article 9 |
| Article 7 | Article 10 |
| Article 8 | Article 11(1) |
| | Article 11(2) |
| Article 9 | Article 12 |
| Article 10 | Article 13(1) |
| | Article 13(2) |
| Article 11 | Article 14 |
| Article 12 | Article 15 |
| Article 13, first indent | Article 16, point (a) |
| Article 13, second indent | Article 16, point (b) |
| Article 14, first indent | Article 17, point (a) |
| Article 14, second indent | Article 17, point (b) |
| Article 14, third indent | Article 17, point (c) |
| Article 15 | Article 18 |
| Article 16 | Article 19 |
| Article 17 | Article 20 |
| Article 18 | Article 21 |
| Article 19 | Article 22 |
| Article 20 | Article 23 |
| — | Article 24 |
| — | Article 25 |
| — | Article 26 |
| — | Article 27 |
| Article 21(1) | Article 28(2) |
| Article 21(2) | Article 28(1) |
| Article 22 | Article 29 |
| Article 23 | Article 30 |
| Article 24 | Article 31 |
| Article 25 | Article 32 |
| Article 26 | Article 33 |
| Article 27 | Article 34 |
| Article 28 | Article 35 |
| — | Article 36 |
| Article 29 | Article 37(1) |
| — | Article 37(2) |
| — | Article 38 |
| — | Article 39 |
| Article 30 | Article 40 |
| Article 31 | Article 41 |
| — | Article 42 |
| — | Article 43 |
| — | Article 44 |
| Article 32 | Article 45 |
| Article 33 | Article 46 |
| Article 34(1) | Article 47(1) |
| Article 34(2) | Article 47(2) |

| Regulation (EC) No 1346/2000 | This Regulation |
|---|---|
| Article 34(3) | — |
| Article 35 | Article 48 |
| — | Article 49 |
| Article 36 | Article 50 |
| Article 37 | Article 51 |
| Article 38 | Article 52 |
| Article 39 | Article 53 |
| Article 40 | Article 54 |
| Article 41 | Article 55 |
| Article 42 | — |
| — | Article 56 |
| — | Article 57 |
| — | Article 58 |
| — | Article 59 |
| — | Article 60 |
| — | Article 61 |
| — | Article 62 |
| — | Article 63 |
| — | Article 64 |
| — | Article 65 |
| — | Article 66 |
| — | Article 67 |
| — | Article 68 |
| — | Article 69 |
| — | Article 70 |
| — | Article 71 |
| — | Article 72 |
| — | Article 73 |
| — | Article 74 |
| — | Article 75 |
| — | Article 76 |
| — | Article 77 |
| — | Article 78 |
| — | Article 79 |
| — | Article 80 |
| — | Article 81 |
| — | Article 82 |
| — | Article 83 |
| Article 43 | Article 84(1) |
| — | Article 84(2) |
| Article 44 | Article 85 |
| — | Article 86 |
| Article 45 | — |
| — | Article 87 |
| — | Article 88 |

# CROSS-BORDER INSOLVENCY REGULATIONS 2006 UNCITRAL MODEL LAW

## INTRODUCTION

**[7.1]**

The UNCITRAL Model Law was adopted by the United Nations Commission on International Trade Law (UNCITRAL) on 30 May 1997 and was designed as a method by which insolvencies with an international element could be more fairly and efficiently administered. The Preamble to the Model Law sets the tone for the document as a whole and states certain policy objectives. These range from the general (greater legal certainty for trade and investment) to the particular including:

(1)     fair and efficient administration of cross-border insolvencies with protection for the interests of the creditors, the debtor and other interested parties;

(2)     maximising the value of the debtor's assets; and

(3)     facilitating the rescue of financially troubled businesses with the consequence of protecting investment and preserving employment.

The Insolvency Act 2000 enabled the Secretary of State to adopt the Model Law, but this power languished unused for six years, until 4 April 2006, when the Model Law was finally introduced into British law. In the interim, the EU Regulation on Insolvency Proceedings – Regulation 1346/2000 – now recast as Regulation 2015/848 – was brought into effect and a growing body of case-law has developed based on its application. It seems logical that time was taken to allow the application of the EU Regulation to bed into UK insolvency law. Nevertheless it has long been considered appropriate to adopt some such agreement along the lines of the Model Law because the EU Regulation is limited by its geographical scope. The EU Regulation clearly can apply only within the EU and more specifically where the centre of main interests (COMI) of the debtor is within the EU. Paragraph 14 of the preamble to Regulation 1346/2000 (and para 25 of the preamble to Regulation 2015/848) states that the Regulation only has intra-community effect, so where the debtor's COMI is outside the EU, the EU Regulation can have no effect. In other cases the opening of proceedings will be decided according to the national law of the Member State. As certain countries such as the USA are neither designated for the purposes of s 426 of the Insolvency Act 1986 nor are they within the ambit of the EU Regulation, the Model Law must become increasingly significant.

Legislation based on the UNCITRAL Model Law has been adopted in a number of countries including most recently Brazil (2021), Singapore (2017), Chile (2013), Philippines (2010), Greece (2010), Canada (2009), Australia (2008), New Zealand (2006), British Virgin Islands (2005), Poland (2003), Romania (2003), Japan (2000), South Africa (2000), as well as in the USA (2005) and the UK. The number of countries adopting legislation based on the Model Law is increasing – see the UNCITRAL website www.uncitral.org for an up-to-date list of ratifications – but it is still far from the worldwide application that must be the ultimate goal if the Model Law is to be considered a success. Successful working of the Model Law in some countries may persuade other countries however, to follow suit and also adopt it. UNCITRAL itself has recently published a digest to case law on legislative enactments of the Model Law – see https://uncitral.un.org/sites/uncitral.un.org/files/media-documents/uncitral/en /20-06293_uncitral_mlcbi_digest_e.pdf.

It has also produced a 'Judicial Perspectives' of the Model Law authored primarily by Paul Heath QC, a former Judge of the High Court of New Zealand – see https://uncitral.un.org/en/texts/insolvency/explanatorytexts/cross-border _insolvency/judicial_perspective.

In the UK, the Model Law came into effect through statutory instrument SI 2006/1030, the Cross-Border Insolvency Regulations 2006 (CBIR). In reg 2 of the regulations it is stated that the Guide to Enactment that was published by UNCITRAL can be used to assist in the interpretation of the Model Law as may any other document prepared by UNCITRAL relating to the preparation of the Model Law.

It is noteworthy that UNCITRAL in 2013 produced a revised guide to enactment of the Model Law – see www.uncitral.org. This differs slightly from the original guide to enactment of the Model Law that was in force when the UK implemented the Model Law. It remains to be seen whether these differences will have any effect on the outcome of decided cases in the UK. In *Re Sturgeon Central Asia Balanced Fund Ltd (In Liquidation)* [2019] EWHC 1215 (Ch), [2019] 2 BCLC 412, [2019] BPIR 1035, however, Falk J drew attention to some differences between the original and revised versions of the guide. She noted at para 15 that the version of the Guide referred to in CBIR reg 2(2)(c) was the original Guide dating from May 1997 and also that 'the later version must be approached with some circumspection' at para 47.

In *Re Sturgeon Central Asia Balanced Fund Ltd (In Liquidation) (No 2)* [2020] EWHC 123 (Ch), [2020] 1 BCLC 600, winding-up proceedings in Bermuda, based on the just and equitable grounds and instituted in respect of a solvent company, were not recognised by an English court as a foreign main proceeding under the CBIR. After an inter partes hearing, Chief Insolvency and Companies Court Judge Briggs (sitting as a deputy High Court judge) terminated the recognition made by Falk J. The initial application for recognition before Falk J had been attended by one party only.

Judge Briggs held that the Model Law itself and other documents mentioned in reg 2(2) of the CBIR could be referred to for the purpose of interpreting Sch 1. Those were the relevant guides to interpretation at the time the CBIR came into force. In the judge's view, the court could also consider updated guidance provided by UNCITRAL after the Regulations came into effect. Reg 2 was permissive in its language and did not prevent the court from considering other materials in order to ascertain purpose or object.

In the view of Judge Briggs, it would be contrary to the stated purpose and object of the Model Law to interpret 'foreign proceeding' to include solvent debtors and actions that were subject to a law relating to insolvency but had the purpose of producing a return to members not creditors. The foreign procedure had to relate to the resolution of insolvency or financial distress. In the vast majority of recognition applications, this fact would be obvious. In this particular case, the recognition order should not have been made and would be terminated.

The overall philosophy of the Model Law and the CBIR was discussed in passing by Hildyard J in *Bakhshiyeva v Sberbank of Russia* [2018] EWHC 59 (Ch), [2018] 2 BCLC 396 – a case also known as *Re OJSC International Bank of Azerbaijan*. He suggested (para 79) that the objective of the Model Law was to assist in the development of 'universalism' and that the ultimate objective of 'universalism' is to provide a single forum applying a single regime to all aspects of a debtor's affairs on a worldwide basis. But he also pointed out that it does not address substantive domestic insolvency provisions nor did it seek to achieve a substantive uniformity or reconciliation between different jurisdictions and their substantive laws: 'Its application, and the notion of "universalism" which it is intended to advance, is thus subject to modification according to the jurisdiction in which it has been adopted. These modifications follow the substantive law in that jurisdiction, and may be significant (para 83)'. The Court of Appeal articulated the same sentiments stating that the Model Law 'does not attempt a substantive unification of insolvency law'. Its scope was 'limited to some procedural aspects of cross-border insolvency cases' – see [2018] EWCA Civ 2802, [2019] 1 BCLC 1 at paras 35–42.

Reference was also made to the explanatory memorandum produced by the UK Insolvency Service on the implementation of the Model law in the UK and the statement in the memorandum that the Model law was designed to respect the differences amongst national procedural laws - para 88 and para 7.1 of the explanatory memorandum.

An international model law is 'soft law' and even provides that States which choose to implement it may do so in different ways which means that the desired level of uniformity and harmonisation may not be achieved. On the other hand, experience with international conventions demonstrates that the process of signature and ratification may be very slow and cumbersome. Even states which sign a convention may never get around to ratification.

The Model Law does not go nearly as far as the Insolvency Regulation and this failure to cover the same field is understandable. Zacaroli J in *Re Gategroup Guarantee Ltd* [2021] EWHC 304 (Ch) at [95] suggested however, that the Model Law was underpinned by the same general principle of modified universalism as was the European Insolvency Regulation and references in this connection the comments of Henderson LJ in *Bakhshiyeva v Sberbank of Russia* [2018] EWCA Civ 2802, [2019] 1 BCLC 1 at [31].

## IMPLEMENTATION IN THE UK

**[7.2]**
The aim of the Cross-Border Insolvency Regulations as stated in Sch 1, Article 1, of the regulations is to give assistance in Great Britain where it is sought by a foreign court or foreign representative in connection with a foreign insolvency proceeding. Additionally assistance may be sought by British representatives in a foreign State in relation to a British insolvency proceeding. The Model Law

lays down some rules with regard to the interplay between different insolvency proceedings in respect of the same debtor, that is to ensure co-operation and coordination and that creditors are given rights to participate in, and be informed of, insolvency proceedings. The provisions of the Regulations track those of the Model Law fairly closely. As the Insolvency Service explain (para 7): '[w]hen drafting the articles, we have tried to stay as close to the drafting in the Model Law as possible to try and ensure consistency, certainty and harmonization with other States enacting the Model Law and to provide a guide for other States who are considered enacting the law. Our policy has been to try and enact as drafted, which may result in the use of some terms, which may not be standard in British insolvency law.'

By way of contrast, Lewison J in *Re Stanford International Bank Ltd* [2009] BPIR 1157[1] suggested that Chapter 15 of the US Bankruptcy Code implementing the Model Law in the United States and replacing s 304 of the Bankruptcy Code contained some significant divergences from the terms of the Model Law. It may be however, that Lewison J overplayed the extent of these divergences for in the US it seems that the legislative intent was to stay loyal at least to the spirit of the Model Law. A Congressional report suggests that Chapter 15 'largely tracks the language of the Model Law with appropriate United States references', talking about 'alteration to tie into United States procedural terminology' and the expression of concepts 'more clearly in United States vernacular'[2]. The US legislative history, like the British, also stresses the international origins of the Model Law and the need to promote consistent interpretation with that in other countries. The Congressional Report refers to the crucial goal of uniformity of interpretation and suggests that to the extent that US courts rely on foreign decisions, their own decisions will more likely be regarded as persuasive elsewhere[3].

[1]  But see however the US House of Representatives report on Chapter 15 – H Rep No 109–31 (2005) at p 106 stating that Chapter 15 'largely tracks the language of the Model Law with appropriate United States references'.
[2]  See HR Rep No 31, 109th Congress 1st Session at paras 106, 107 and 109.
[3]  Ibid at para 109.

## Comparisons between the Model Law and the European Insolvency Regulation

[7.3]

The Model Law does not go so far as the EU Insolvency Regulation. This reluctance to cover the same field is understandable. The Insolvency Regulation is an emanation from the European Union whose Member States have agreed to pool their sovereignty and agreed to work towards an ever-closer Union[1]. UNCITRAL is a United Nations organ with the link between Member States being profoundly more diffuse than with EU Member States. The EU Regulation contains mandatory uniform rules on jurisdiction and conflict of laws, and to that extent represents an encroachment on the sovereignty of individual Member States. The Model Law is much looser and more exhortatory in tone. It does not purport to say which law should govern insolvency proceedings that are opened in a particular jurisdiction. Moreover, states are free to open insolvency proceedings on the basis of the presence of assets within the state whereas the Insolvency Regulation requires an 'establishment'. Recognition of insolvency proceedings opened in another EU Member State is automatic whereas under the Model Law it is dependent upon an application to the court. By virtue of the Insolvency Regulation, insolvency proceedings have the same effect in other EU States as they have in the law of the insolvency forum whereas under the Model Law the consequences of recognition depend partly on the law of the recognising state. There are many other differences, particularly of detail, between the two instruments[2]. The Model Law has, however, the same concept of 'centre of main interests' or COMI as the EU Regulation and the COMI case-law under the EU instrument was used in the Model Law context by Lewison J in *Re Stanford International Bank Ltd* [2009] BPIR 1157 at para 65. There was further consideration of the COMI concept in the context of the CBIR/Model Law in *Re Videology Ltd* [2018] EWHC 2186 (Ch), [2019] BCC 195, [2018] BPIR 1795.

[1] See Article 1 of the Treaty on European Union as resulting from the amendments introduced by the Treaty of Lisbon, signed on 13 December 2007 in Lisbon and which entered into force on 1 December 2009 which refers to the Treaty marking 'a new stage in the process of creating an ever closer union among the peoples of Europe'.

[2] For an account of some of these differences see the judgment of Sean Lane J in the Bankruptcy Court of the Southern District of New York in *In re Oi Brasil Holdings* (Bankr SDNY 4 December 2017) at pp 56–60 and stating at p 57 that despite various similarities, the EU Regulation and UNCITRAL Model Law regime are far from identical.

## RECIPROCITY AND COMPATIBILITY WITH OTHER CROSS-BORDER INSOLVENCY LEGISLATION

[7.4]

The Model Law as enacted in Great Britain does not require reciprocity before a foreign representative asks for assistance, so it is not a requirement that requests can be made only from states where the Model Law has also been adopted. In the Guide to Enactment this point is forcefully made – that to rely on reciprocity would limit the Model Law's effectiveness. South Africa however, in implementing the Model Law, introduced a reciprocity condition. Under the South African Law, a government minister is required to designate countries to which it will accord recognition provided that the recognition accorded by the law of such state to South African proceedings 'justifies the application of this Act to foreign proceedings in such State.' In the UK, more of an emphasis was placed on facilitating a global approach to the administration of cross-border insolvencies. Implementation of the Model Law was seen as providing encouragement to other countries that may be contemplating introduction of the legislation.

In implementing the Model Law it was decided to avoid making any changes to s 426, which allows UK courts to respond to requests for assistance in insolvency matters from foreign courts in designated countries or territories. The UK Court in responding to the request can apply UK or the relevant foreign insolvency law. In practice only a relatively small number of countries have been designated for the purposes of s 426 and these appear to have been chosen because of their analogous common law background[1]. Section 426 continues to operate and it would be open to a foreign insolvency representative in a designated country to ask his local court to make a 'section 426' request for assistance rather himself utilising the provisions of the Model Law and the Cross-Border Insolvency Regulations (CBIR) in respect of recognition of the foreign insolvency proceedings etc. As a result of the CBIR, the UK has essentially three statutory regimes for international/cross-border co-operation in insolvency matters – the EU Regulation on Insolvency Proceedings, the UNCITRAL Model Law and s 426 of the Insolvency Act 1986 plus the common law to the extent that it has not been superseded in relation to particular matters (see also *Re Madoff Investment Securities LLC* [2009] EWHC 442, [2009] 2 BCLC 78).

In the US, however, it has been held that Chapter 15 of the Bankruptcy Code implementing the Model Law is the sole gateway for a US court to provide assistance to a foreign court and there is no residual common law or other statutory discretion. This was the holding in *Bear Stearns High-Grade Structured Credit Strategies Master Fund Ltd* (2007) 374 BR 122 and affirmed (2008) 389 BR 325[2]. The case concerned a structured investment vehicle incorporated in the Cayman Islands that was being liquidated in the Caymans. It was held, however, that the Cayman liquidation was not entitled to recognition in the US as either 'foreign main proceedings' or 'foreign non-main proceedings'. On the facts it was held that the statutory presumption that the Caymans as the place of incorporation was the centre of main interests (COMI) was rebutted by contrary evidence. It was also held that the Cayman liquidation did not qualify as a 'foreign non-main proceeding', owing to a failure to show that the investment vehicle had any place of operations in Cayman where it carried out 'non-transitory economic activity'. More controversially, it was observed that Chapter 15 heralded a shift from a subjective comity-based process under earlier bankruptcy law to a more rigid recognition standard. The *Bear Stearns* case effectively holds that Chapter 15 is narrower than its predecessor: s 304. It may be that the *Bear Stearns* decision was motivated by concerns about the nature of the Cayman proceedings but arguably such concerns could have been dealt with by limiting the effect of recognition.

Critics have questioned how the decision is consistent with the goals of the Model Law, which is generally conceived of as being designed to provide a minimum level of assistance to foreign courts and proceedings and not to preclude more extensive modes of assistance under existing national laws[3]. They argue that it would not do any violence to the language of the statute to hold that Chapter 15 is not exclusive since it does not expressly purport to be. This argument however, while conforming to the Model Law objectives, is clearly out of line with Chapter 15's legislative history and its arrangement of provisions. In the UK, on the other hand, when the Model Law was enacted in the form of the CBIR, the possibility of repealing s 426 of the Insolvency Act was considered and rejected.

[1]   The Republic of Ireland is a designated country for s 426 purposes and requests for assistance from Irish courts can potentially be dealt with under s 426, under the Cross-Border Insolvency Regulations and under the EU Insolvency Regulation since Ireland is an EU Member State: see the discussion in *Re Integrated Medical Solutions Ltd* [2012] BCC 215 at para 7. Quinn J in Ireland in *Re Arctic Aviation Assets* [2021] IEHC 268 suggested that the dearth of recent authorities on recognition of Irish restructuring and insolvency proceedings pursuant to s 426 was largely due to the fact that the European Insolvency Regulation has been in force and has governed insolvency proceedings regarding companies having their centre of main interests in either England or Ireland.

[2]   See G Moss, 'Bitter pill delivered by Judge Sweet' (2008) *Insolvency Intelligence* 118–21.

[3]   See for example G Moss 'Beyond the Sphinx – Is Chapter 15 the Sole Gateway?' (2007) 20 Insolvency Intelligence 56.

## SCHEDULES

**[7.5]**

Schedule 1 covers the Model Law itself. Schedule 2 contains the procedural requirements for applying for relief under the Model Law in England and Wales and contained in Sch 3 the same information for Scotland. One power of the court that is worthy of specific mention is that in Sch 2, Pt 8 there is a power similar to that under s 212 and that of Sch B1, para 75 to the Insolvency Act 1986 relating to the misfeasance of the foreign representative. The court may compel the foreign representative to repay money or restore property that has been misappropriated. This ability to ensure the professional conduct of the foreign representative is not something that is contained in the Model Law itself and it is interesting that there is no comparable provision in the EU Regulation. The Cross-Border Insolvency Regulations are Britain's own interpretation of the Model Law and it is evidently important that there is some redress for creditors or the debtor where the foreign representative has not acted professionally. The EU Regulation under Art 31 for instance does require that the liquidators in main and secondary proceedings to co-operate with each other, but there is no penalty outlined in the Regulation if this does not occur and there is no penalty in the Regulation for any misfeasance of the foreign representative.

# CROSS-BORDER INSOLVENCY REGULATIONS 2006

## SI 2006/1030

### ARRANGEMENT OF REGULATIONS

| | | |
|---|---|---|
| 1 | Citation, commencement and interpretation | 7.6 |
| 2 | UNCITRAL Model Law to have force of law | 7.7 |
| 3 | Modification of British insolvency law | 7.8 |
| 4 | Procedural matters in England and Wales | 7.9 |
| 5 | Procedural matters in Scotland | 7.10 |
| 6 | Notices delivered to the registrar of companies | 7.11 |
| 7 | Co-operation between courts exercising jurisdiction in relation to cross-border insolvency | 7.12 |
| 8 | Disapplication of section 388 of the Insolvency Act 1986 | 7.13 |

Schedules
| | | |
|---|---|---|
| | Schedule 1 UNCITRAL Model Law on Cross-Border Insolvency | 7.14 |
| | Schedule 2 Procedural Matters in England and Wales | |
| | Part 1 Introductory Provisions | 7.46 |
| | Part 2 Applications to Court for Recognition of Foreign Proceedings | 7.47 |
| | Part 3 Applications for Relief Under the Model Law | 7.48 |
| | Part 4 Replacement of Foreign Representative | 7.49 |
| | Part 5 Reviews of Court Orders | 7.50 |
| | Part 6 Court Procedure and Practice with Regard to Principal Applications and Orders | 7.51 |
| | Part 7 Applications to the Chief Land Registrar | 7.52 |
| | Part 8 Misfeasance | 7.53 |
| | Part 9 General Provision as to Court Procedure and Practice | 7.54 |
| | Part 10 Costs and Detailed Assessment | 7.55 |
| | Part 11 Appeals in Proceedings Under these Regulations | 7.56 |
| | Part 12 General | 7.57 |
| | Schedule 4 Notices Delivered to the Registrar of Companies | 7.58 |

[7.6]

**1 Citation, commencement and interpretation**
(1) These Regulations may be cited as the Cross-Border Insolvency Regulations 2006 and shall come into force on the day after the day on which they are made.

(2)   In these Regulations "the UNCITRAL Model Law" means the Model Law on cross-border insolvency as adopted by the United Nations Commission on International Trade Law on 30th May 1997.

(3)   In these Regulations "overseas company" has the meaning given by section 1044 of the Companies Act 2006 and "establishment", in relation to such a company, has the same meaning as in the Overseas Companies Regulations 2009.

[7.7]

**2  UNCITRAL Model Law to have force of law**

(1)   The UNCITRAL Model Law shall have the force of law in Great Britain in the form set out in Schedule 1 to these Regulations (which contains the UNCITRAL Model Law with certain modifications to adapt it for application in Great Britain).

(2)   Without prejudice to any practice of the courts as to the matters which may be considered apart from this paragraph, the following documents may be considered in ascertaining the meaning or effect of any provision of the UNCITRAL Model Law as set out in Schedule 1 to these Regulations—

    (a)    the UNCITRAL Model Law;

    (b)    any documents of the United Nations Commission on International Trade Law and its working group relating to the preparation of the UNCITRAL Model Law; and

    (c)    the Guide to Enactment of the UNCITRAL Model Law (UNCITRAL document A/CN 9/442) prepared at the request of the United Nations Commission on International Trade Law made in May 1997.

[7.8]

**3  Modification of British insolvency law**

(1)   British insolvency law (as defined in article 2 of the UNCITRAL Model Law as set out in Schedule 1 to these Regulations) and Part 3 of the Insolvency Act 1986 shall apply with such modifications as the context requires for the purpose of giving effect to the provisions of these Regulations.

(2)   In the case of any conflict between any provision of British insolvency law or of Part 3 of the Insolvency Act 1986 and the provisions of these Regulations, the latter shall prevail.

[7.9]

**4  Procedural matters in England and Wales**

Schedule 2 to these Regulations (which makes provision about procedural matters in England and Wales in connection with the application of the UNCITRAL Model Law as set out in Schedule 1 to these Regulations) shall have effect.

[7.10]

**5  Procedural matters in Scotland**

Schedule 3 to these Regulations (which makes provision about procedural matters in Scotland in connection with the application of the UNCITRAL Model Law as set out in Schedule 1 to these Regulations) shall have effect.

[7.11]

**6  Notices delivered to the registrar of companies**

Schedule 4 to these Regulations (which makes provision about notices delivered to the registrar of companies under these Regulations) shall have effect.

**[7.12]**

**7 Co-operation between courts exercising jurisdiction in relation to cross-border insolvency**

(1)   An order made by a court in either part of Great Britain in the exercise of jurisdiction in relation to the subject matter of these Regulations shall be enforced in the other part of Great Britain as if it were made by a court exercising the corresponding jurisdiction in that other part.

(2)   However, nothing in paragraph (1) requires a court in either part of Great Britain to enforce, in relation to property situated in that part, any order made by a court in the other part of Great Britain.

(3)   The courts having jurisdiction in relation to the subject matter of these Regulations in either part of Great Britain shall assist the courts having the corresponding jurisdiction in the other part of Great Britain.

**[7.13]**

**8  Disapplication of section 388 of the Insolvency Act 1986**

Nothing in section 388 of the Insolvency Act 1986 applies to anything done by a foreign representative—

(a)     under or by virtue of these Regulations;

(b)     in relation to relief granted or cooperation or coordination provided under these Regulations.

SCHEDULE 1

UNCITRAL MODEL LAW ON CROSS-BORDER INSOLVENCY

Regulation 2(1)

CHAPTER I   GENERAL PROVISIONS

ARTICLE 1

Scope of Application

**[7.14]**

**1**

This Law applies where—

(a)     assistance is sought in Great Britain by a foreign court or a foreign representative in connection with a foreign proceeding; or

(b)     assistance is sought in a foreign State in connection with a proceeding under British insolvency law; or

(c)     a foreign proceeding and a proceeding under British insolvency law in respect of the same debtor are taking place concurrently; or

(d)     creditors or other interested persons in a foreign State have an interest in requesting the commencement of, or participating in, a proceeding under British insolvency law.

**2**

This Law does not apply to a proceeding concerning—

(a)     a company holding an appointment under Chapter 1 of Part 2 of the Water Industry Act 1991 (water and sewage undertakers) or a qualifying water supply licensee within the meaning of section 23(6) of that Act (meaning and effect of special administration order);

(b)     Scottish Water established under section 20 of the Water Industry (Scotland) Act 2002 (Scottish Water);

(c)     a protected railway company within the meaning of section 59 of the Railways Act 1993 (railway administration order) (including that section as it has effect by virtue of section 19 of the Channel Tunnel Rail Link Act 1996 (administration));

(d) a licence company within the meaning of section 26 of the Transport Act 2000 (air traffic services);

(e) a public private partnership company within the meaning of section 210 of the Greater London Authority Act 1999 (public-private partnership agreement);

(f) a protected energy company within the meaning of section 154(5) of the Energy Act 2004 (energy administration orders);

(g) a building society within the meaning of section 119 of the Building Societies Act 1986 (interpretation);

(h) a UK credit institution or an EEA credit institution or any branch of either such institution as those expressions are defined by regulation 2 of the Credit Institutions (Reorganisation and Winding Up) Regulations 2004 (interpretation);

(i) a third country credit institution within the meaning of regulation 36 of the Credit Institutions (Reorganisation and Winding Up) Regulations 2004 (interpretation of this Part);

(j) a person who has permission under or by virtue of Parts 4 or 19 of the Financial Services and Markets Act 2000 to effect or carry out contracts of insurance;

(k) an EEA insurer within the meaning of regulation 2 of the Insurers (Reorganisation and Winding Up) Regulations 2004 (interpretation);

(l) a person (other than one included in paragraph 2(j)) pursuing the activity of reinsurance who has received authorisation for that activity from a competent authority within an EEA State; or

(m) any of the Concessionaires within the meaning of section 1 of the Channel Tunnel Act 1987.

**Amendments**—SI 2017/506.

**3**

In paragraph 2 of this article—

(a) in sub-paragraph (j) the reference to "contracts of insurance" must be construed in accordance with—
　(i) section 22 of the Financial Services and Markets Act 2000 (classes of regulated activity and categories of investment);
　(ii) any relevant order under that section; and
　(iii) Schedule 2 to that Act (regulated activities);

(b) in sub-paragraph (1) "EEA State" means a State. . . which is a contracting party to the agreement on the European Economic Area signed at Oporto on 2 May 1992.

**Amendments**—SI 2019/146, as from IP completion day (as defined in the European Union (Withdrawal Agreement) Act 2020, s 39(1)–(5)).

**4**

The court shall not grant any relief, or modify any relief already granted, or provide any co-operation or coordination, under or by virtue of any of the provisions of this Law if and to the extent that such relief or modified relief or cooperation or coordination would—

(a) be prohibited under or by virtue of—
　(i) Part 7 of the Companies Act 1989;
　(ii) Part 3 of the Financial Markets and Insolvency (Settlement Finality) Regulations 1999; or
　(iii) Part 3 of the Financial Collateral Arrangements (No 2) Regulations 2003;
in the case of a proceeding under British insolvency law; or

    (b)    interfere with or be inconsistent with any rights of a collateral taker under Part 4 of the Financial Collateral Arrangements (No 2) Regulations 2003 which could be exercised in the case of such a proceeding.

**5**

Where a foreign proceeding regarding a debtor who is an insured in accordance with the provisions of the Third Parties (Rights against Insurers) Act 2010 is recognised under this Law, any stay and suspension referred to in article 20(1) and any relief granted by the court under article 19 or 21 shall not apply to or affect—

    (a)    any transfer of rights of the debtor under that Act; or

    (b)    any claim, action, cause or proceeding by a third party against an insurer under or in respect of rights of the debtor transferred under that Act.

**Amendments**—Third Parties (Rights against Insurers) Act 2010, s 20(1), Sch 2, para 4.

**6**

Any suspension under this Law of the right to transfer, encumber or otherwise dispose of any of the debtor's assets—

    (a)    is subject to section 26 of the Land Registration Act 2002 where owner's powers are exercised in relation to a registered estate or registered charge;

    (b)    is subject to section 52 of the Land Registration Act 2002, where the powers referred to in that section are exercised by the proprietor of a registered charge; and

    (c)    in any other case, shall not bind a purchaser of a legal estate in good faith for money or money's worth unless the purchaser has express notice of the suspension.

**7**

In paragraph 6—

    (a)    "owner's powers" means the powers described in section 23 of the Land Registration Act 2002 and "registered charge" and "registered estate" have the same meaning as in section 132(1) of that Act; and

    (b)    "legal estate" and "purchaser" have the same meaning as in section 17 of the Land Charges Act 1972.

**General Note**—By virtue of this provision, a fairly long list of specialist types of institutions – including banks and insurance companies are excluded from the Cross-Border Insolvency Regulations 2006. Preceding the coming into force of the Regulations, there was a certain amount of lobbying that banks and insurance companies should be included rather than excluded, since these organisations conduct business worldwide and have as much, if not greater need, for international co-operation in facilitating reorganisation and liquidation. The Insolvency Service however referred to the extensive European legislation on these types of entities and the necessity for careful drafting. It decided not to include them in the Model Law but to 'consider their inclusion by means of a further instrument under s 14 of the Insolvency Act 2000 as soon as it is practicable and possible' (see 'Implementation of UNCITRAL Model Law on Cross-Border Insolvency in Great Britain Summary of Responses and Government Reply' March 2006 at para 36).

The references in the provision are quite specific. If a foreign company, including a foreign bank, does not fall within these specific provisions then it is entitled to the benefits of the CBIR and Model Law regime including recognition as a foreign insolvency proceeding. This was the situation in *Re OJSC International Bank of Azerbaijan* [2017] EWHC 2075 (Ch) where Barling J recognised Azerbaijani proceedings to restructure the debt of the largest bank in Azerbaijan as foreign main proceedings under the CBIR and imposed a moratorium on proceedings against the company akin to the moratorium in administration proceedings under the UK Insolvency Act. The bank was involved in both retail and corporate banking and was largely state owned. The primary purpose of the proceedings in Azerbaijan was to restructure the bank's indebtedness while it continued to trade. It was not a liquidation-style process but a rescue procedure, during which it was necessary that the bank should be in a position to continue trading while it was undergoing restructuring and adjustment of its liabilities. The judge had no doubt that requirements under the CBIR had been met. There was a collective judicial process underway in Azerbaijan that relates to insolvency, and for the purposes of those proceedings the assets and affairs of the bank were subject to control of, or supervision by, the courts in Azerbaijan. This process was undergone for the purposes of reorganisation.

The same general principles were applied in *Re PJSC Bank Finance and Credit (In Liquidation)* [2021] EWHC 1100 (Ch). The court in this case recognised the liquidation of a Ukrainian bank as a foreign main proceeding under the UK version of the Model Law. The bank had entered liquidation in Ukraine in 2015 and the second applicant was a Ukrainian governmental body responsible for withdrawing insolvent banks from the market and winding down their operations via liquidation. The first applicant had been appointed as DGF's authorised officer in respect of the bank's liquidation. Under Art 15(1) of the GB Model Law, a 'foreign representative' could apply to the court for recognition of the 'foreign proceedings' in which the foreign representative had been appointed.

The court held that since full control over the bank's affairs lay with the applicants, it would have served no purpose to serve the application on the bank itself. Moreover, the bank was not a 'third country credit institution' within the Credit Institutions (Reorganisation and Winding Up) Regulations 2004 reg 36. Therefore the court held that it was not excluded from the scope of the Cross Border Insolvency Regulations by Sch 1, Art 1(2)(i) ([3]).

## ARTICLE 2

### DEFINITIONS

[7.15]

For the purposes of this Law—
    (a)    "British insolvency law" means—
        (i)    in relation to England and Wales, provision extending to England and Wales and made by or under the EU Insolvency Regulation, the Insolvency Act 1986 (with the exception of Part 3 of that Act) or by or under that Regulation or Act as extended or applied by or under any other enactment (excluding these Regulations); and
        (ii)    in relation to Scotland, provision extending to Scotland and made by or under the EU Insolvency Regulation, the Insolvency Act 1986 (with the exception of Part 3 of that Act), the Bankruptcy (Scotland) Act 1985 or by or under that Regulation or those Acts as extended or applied by or under any other enactment (excluding these Regulations);
    (b)    "British insolvency officeholder" means—
        (i)    the official receiver within the meaning of section 399 of the Insolvency Act 1986 when acting as liquidator, provisional liquidator, trustee, interim receiver or nominee or supervisor of a voluntary arrangement;
        (ii)    a person acting as an insolvency practitioner within the meaning of section 388 of that Act but shall not include a person acting as an administrative receiver; and
        (iii)    the Accountant in Bankruptcy within the meaning of section 1 of the Bankruptcy (Scotland) Act 1985 when acting as interim or permanent trustee;
    (c)    "the court" except as otherwise provided in articles 14(4) and 23(6)(b), means in relation to any matter the court which in accordance with the provisions of article 4 of this Law has jurisdiction in relation to that matter;
    (d)    "the EU Insolvency Regulation" means Regulation (EU) 2015/848 of the European Parliament and of the Council of 20 May 2015 as that Regulation forms part of domestic law on and after exit day;
    (e)    "establishment" means any place of operations where the debtor carries out a non-transitory economic activity with human means and assets or services;
    (f)    "foreign court" means a judicial or other authority competent to control or supervise a foreign proceeding;
    (g)    "foreign main proceeding" means a foreign proceeding taking place in the State where the debtor has the centre of its main interests;

(h) "foreign non-main proceeding" means a foreign proceeding, other than a foreign main proceeding, taking place in a State where the debtor has an establishment within the meaning of sub-paragraph (e) of this article;

(i) "foreign proceeding" means a collective judicial or administrative proceeding in a foreign State, including an interim proceeding, pursuant to a law relating to insolvency in which proceeding the assets and affairs of the debtor are subject to control or supervision by a foreign court, for the purpose of reorganisation or liquidation;

(j) "foreign representative" means a person or body, including one appointed on an interim basis, authorised in a foreign proceeding to administer the reorganisation or the liquidation of the debtor's assets or affairs or to act as a representative of the foreign proceeding;

(k) "hire-purchase agreement" includes a conditional sale agreement, a chattel leasing agreement and a retention of title agreement;

(l) "section 426 request" means a request for assistance in accordance with section 426 of the Insolvency Act 1986 made to a court in any part of the United Kingdom;

(m) "secured creditor" in relation to a debtor, means a creditor of the debtor who holds in respect of his debt a security over property of the debtor;

(n) "security" means—

 (i) in relation to England and Wales, any mortgage, charge, lien or other security; and

 (ii) in relation to Scotland, any security (whether heritable or moveable), any floating charge and any right of lien or preference and any right of retention (other than a right of compensation or set off);

(o) in the application of Articles 20 and 23 to Scotland, "an individual" means any debtor within the meaning of the Bankruptcy (Scotland) Act 1985;

(p) in the application of this Law to Scotland, references howsoever expressed to—

 (i) "filing" an application or claim are to be construed as references to lodging an application or submitting a claim respectively;

 (ii) "relief" and "standing" are to be construed as references to "remedy" and "title and interest" respectively; and

 (iii) a "stay" are to be construed as references to restraint, except in relation to continuation of actions or proceedings when they shall be construed as a reference to sist; and

(q) references to the law of Great Britain include a reference to the law of either part of Great Britain (including its rules of private international law).

**Amendments**—SI 2017/702; SI 2019/146, as from IP completion day (as defined in the European Union (Withdrawal Agreement) Act 2020, s 39(1)–(5)).

**General note – 'foreign proceeding'**—The Model Law applies to collective insolvency proceedings whose purpose is the reorganisation or liquidation of the debtor and where the assets and affairs of the debtor are subject to court control or supervision. The 'Court' may not strictly speaking be a court, with the model law referring to a 'judicial or other authority competent to control or supervise' proceedings. The definition of collective insolvency proceedings is sufficiently wide so as to embrace both 'debtor-in-possession' corporate reorganisation regimes along the lines of Chapter 11 of the US Bankruptcy Code 1978 and the internationally more widespread manger displacing insolvency regimes like company administration in the UK.

*Re Bud-Bank Leasing SP* [2010] BCC 255, (2009) WL 1894618 highlights the fact that the Cross-Border Insolvency Regulations are wider than the EC Insolvency Regulation in certain respects. In this case, it was held that certain Polish proceedings were entitled to recognition under the Cross-Border Insolvency Regulations 2006 but it was also noted that these proceedings did not come within the concept of 'insolvency proceedings' under the European Insolvency Regulation. The Polish proceedings took place under a specially enacted law applicable to shipyards that received state subvention and which was later held to be illegal under the rules of the EC Treaty on state aid. The need to repay the aid made the shipyard companies insolvent.

In determining whether the Cross-Border Insolvency Regulations applied, Registrar Baister looked to the UNCITRAL guide for the enactment of the Model Law, which, in paras 23 and 24, stated: 'To fall within the scope of the Model Law, a foreign insolvency proceeding needs to possess certain attributes. These include the following: basis in insolvency-related law of the originating State: involvement of creditors collectively; control or supervision of the assets and affairs of the debtor by a court or another official body; and reorganization or liquidation of the debtor as the purpose of the proceeding . . . Within those parameters, a variety of collective proceedings would be eligible for recognition, be they compulsory or voluntary, corporate or individual, winding up-or reorganization. It also includes those in which the debtor retains some measure of control over its assets, albeit under court supervision (eg suspension of payments, "debtor in possession")'.

In this particular case the Polish legislation was looked at and it was held that the proceedings were plainly collective in that they took account of the interests of all creditors and the interests of employees. The proceedings were judicial since there was provision for the court to decide certain issues. They were also administrative in that they were initiated by executive decision pursuant to a statutory power. They were proceedings 'pursuant to a law relating to insolvency' in that they had the characteristics of insolvency proceedings and specifically incorporated provisions of the Polish law on Bankruptcy and Rehabilitation. Moreover, the company was divested of its assets in favour of an administrator. The assets and affairs of the company were subject to the control of a foreign court, albeit via the administrator.

In *Rubin v Eurofinance SA* [2010] EWCA Civ 895, [2011] Ch 133, US bankruptcy proceedings were recognised as foreign main proceedings under the Cross-Border Insolvency Regulations despite the fact that the US proceedings related to a debtor which, according to English law, had no legal personality either as an individual or as a body corporate. It was held that having regard to the definition of foreign proceedings under the Regulations it would be perverse to accord the word 'debtor' a different meaning than that given to it by the foreign court in the foreign proceedings.

The Court of Appeal decision in *Rubin* has since been overturned by the Supreme Court – [2012] UKSC 46 – but the Supreme Court decision does not challenge the recognition of the US bankruptcy proceedings as foreign insolvency proceedings under the Cross-Border Insolvency Regulations.

In *Re Stanford International Bank Ltd* [2010] EWCA Civ 137, [2011] Ch 33, it was held however that a US receivership did not possess the characteristics necessary to satisfy the definition of a foreign proceeding in the Model Law and Regulations. The rationale of the US law under which the receiver was appointed was to enable the US court to grant equitable relief for the benefit of investors. The law was not a law relating to insolvency which was required for the purpose of the Model Law. While the latter did not require a statutory law it did have to relate to insolvency and to constitute collective proceedings for the purpose of reorganisation or liquidation. The US law, on the other hand, was designed for the protection of investors and in this case to safeguard the assets of a bank which was the subject of allegations of fraud. It was further held that since the US receivership was not a relevant foreign proceeding the US receiver could not be a foreign representative within the Model Law statutory scheme.

It has been held in Australia that the fact that a foreign proceeding had been recognised previously as a main proceeding by courts in other jurisdictions was an important consideration in determining whether the proceedings should be recognised in Australia under its Model Law legislation: *Backman v Landsbanki Islands hf* [2011] FCA 1430.

Many aspects of the requirement for recognition of foreign insolvency proceedings have been considered in *Re Agrokor* [2017] EWHC 2791 (Ch), [2018] 2 BCLC 75, [2018] BPIR 1. In this case, there was an application for recognition of what were referred to as 'extraordinary administration proceedings' in Croatia as a 'foreign proceeding' within Art 2(i), Sch 1 to the CBIR but the application was opposed by a Russian bank that was a major creditor of the company. The extraordinary administration proceedings were being conducted under a new Croatian law that was passed to deal with companies, or groups of companies, that were of systemic importance to the Croatian economy. The new law was not yet scheduled under the European Insolvency Regulation (EIR) Regulation 2015/848, which meant that proceedings pursuant to the law were not entitled to automatic regulation under the EIR and hence the application for recognition under the CBIR.

In Croatia the relevant proceedings involved a group of companies, but in the UK recognition was only sought in respect of a particular individual company that was a member of the corporate group. It was held that there was nothing in the Model Law or in the CBIR to preclude such recognition (para 54). The court suggested that it was sensible to allow for the recognition of the position of individual debtors caught up in a group insolvency procedure. Such groups were very common and not to do so 'would leave a significant hole in the range of possible options for international recognition' (para 53).

The court decided that the Croatian proceedings were 'collective proceedings' within the Model Law/CBIR because they related to all the assets and liabilities of the debtor. Reference was made in this connection to the decision of Lewison J (affirmed on appeal) in the *Stanford International Bank* case [2009] EWHC 1441 (Ch) at para 39 where the following comments of Judge Markell in the US Bankruptcy Court case *Re Betcorp Ltd* (2009) 400 BR 266 at p 281were approved: 'A collective proceeding is one that considers the rights and obligations of all creditors. This is in contrast to a receivership remedy instigated at the request and for the benefit of a single secured creditor.' It was also held that the purpose of the proceeding must be to allow the debtor to overcome its difficulties and resume its commercial purpose but this test was clearly satisfied in this particular case (para 100).

The court in *Re Agrokor* further decided that the Croatian proceedings were subject to control or supervision by a court as required by the Model Law/CBIR. This is not a very exacting requirement for the court held that 'that the control or supervision required can not only be potential rather than actual, but can also be indirect rather than direct' (para 79).

Reference was made to the US District Court case of *Re Ashapura Minechem Ltd* (2012) 480 BR 129 at 138. In that case the District Court said: 'Supervision or control of the company's affairs is not a demanding standard. The foreign court need not control the day to day operations of the debtor. It is sufficient, for instance, that the body monitor compliance with the repayment plan negotiated between the debtor and creditors.'

The court in *Agrokor* added (para 92) that since overall the proceedings were subject to the control and supervision of the court, it was irrelevant that the government also had powers in relation to such proceedings.

Many aspects of the Model Law recognition process and the *Agrokor* decision were also addressed in *Leite v Amicorp (UK) Ltd* [2020] EWHC 3560 (Ch). The court suggested that it would create a gap in the possible options for international recognition if English courts would not recognise proceedings affecting a distinct company within a form of 'group proceedings'. The court noted the willingness of UK courts, in extreme and unusual circumstances, to permit a liquidator to pool the assets of two or more insolvent entities. Therefore, the likely pooling of assets of related companies in respect of whom the recognition application had been made, to meet creditor claims did not preclude the proceedings from being 'collective proceedings' for the Cross Border recognition regime.

The UK Model Law recognition regime has been held not to apply however, to liquidation proceedings in respect of solvent companies. In *Re Sturgeon Central Asia Balanced Fund Ltd (In Liquidation)* [2019] EWHC 1215 (Ch), [2019] 2 BCLC 412, [2019] BPIR 1035, winding-up proceedings in Bermuda based on the just and equitable grounds and instituted in respect of a solvent company were recognised initially as a foreign main proceeding under the CBIR. Falk J also held initially that despite the fact that the application for recognition had been attended by one party only, the judgment could be cited in other courts on the basis that it established a new principle or extended the current law (at [66]). This decision however, was reviewed and overturned with the recognition terminated

Falk J acknowledged that while the Model Law was aimed at entities that were insolvent or otherwise in financial distress, confining recognition to entities that were demonstrated to have those characteristics would conflict with the plain meaning of the words used and run counter to the aim of allowing recognition on an efficient basis, because of the factual enquiry that would be required.

The focus in the law was on whether the relevant proceeding was commenced 'pursuant to a law relating to insolvency', rather than using the concept of insolvency proceeding or even defining insolvency. An objective was to achieve recognition speedily, on a summary basis, without a detailed fact-finding exercise. The intention was that a recognising court should be able to recognise a foreign proceeding where it did not know the precise extent of the entity's financial problems, and did not know whether it was in fact insolvent. The fact that an entity was solvent and the purpose of liquidation was to distribute surplus assets to shareholders and not to realise assets for creditors, even though it would have that effect, did not mean that a process that would otherwise fall within the definition of foreign proceeding fell outside it (paras 50–57).

But after a full inter partes hearing, Chief ICC Judge Briggs (sitting as a deputy High Court judge) terminated the recognition made by Falk J – see [2020] EWHC 123 (Ch), [2020] 1 BCLC 600. It was emphasised that the initial application for recognition before Falk J had been attended by one party only.

Judge Briggs held that it would be contrary to the stated purpose and object of the Model Law to interpret 'foreign proceeding' to include solvent debtors and actions that were subject to a law relating to insolvency but had the purpose of producing a return to members not creditors. The foreign procedure had to relate to the resolution of insolvency or financial distress. In the vast majority of recognition applications, this fact would be obvious. In this particular case, the recognition order should not have been made and would be terminated.

On the possible application of the Model Law to solvent liquidations see also the US Chapter 15 case *Re Betcorp Ltd* (2009) 400 BR 266 but note the difference in wording between the implementation of the Model Law in the US and UK. Under s 101(23) of the US Bankruptcy Code foreign proceeding covers proceedings in a foreign country 'under a law relating to insolvency or adjustment of debt' whereas in the UK the Cross-Border Insolvency Regulations do not specifically define foreign proceedings to include proceedings for the adjustment of debts.

'foreign main proceeding'—Foreign main proceedings are defined as proceedings taking place in the State where the debtor has the centre of its main interests. The concept of 'centre of main interests' is the same as that to be found in Art 3(1) of the EU Insolvency Regulation. Snowden J said in *Re Videology Ltd* [2018] EWHC 2186 (Ch), [2019] BCC 195 at [28] 'for so long as the UK remains a party to the Recast EIR, I can see no obvious basis upon which I should adopt any different approach in relation to the concept of COMI under the CBIR/Model Law and the Recast EIR'.

While straightforward as a concept, COMI may defy easy application in practice. This is particularly the case where a debtor has its business operations spread over several states and where head office functions are performed in a state that is not the state of incorporation that may in turn be different from the state where the bulk of economic activities are carried out. Also potentially controversial is the situation where a company's real seat or 'centre of main interests' may have shifted during the course of its corporate history especially if the change occurred in the period just prior to the commencement of formal insolvency proceedings.

'Foreign non-main proceedings'—Foreign non-main proceedings means foreign proceedings, other than foreign main proceedings, taking place in a state where the debtor has an 'establishment'. 'Establishment' is defined as 'any place of operations where the debtor carries out a non-transitory economic with human means and assets or services.' This is the same definition of 'establishment' as that found in the EU Insolvency Regulation with the addition of 'services'. Whether this is a 'useful extension' to the original version or merely tautologous remains to be seen. An 'establishment' clearly requires something more than the mere presence of assets within a jurisdiction but that 'something more' is not altogether clear.

## ARTICLE 3

### INTERNATIONAL OBLIGATIONS OF GREAT BRITAIN UNDER THE EU INSOLVENCY REGULATION

**[7.16]**

*To the extent that this Law conflicts with an obligation of the United Kingdom under the EU Insolvency Regulation, the requirements of the EU Insolvency Regulation prevail.*

Amendments—SI 2017/1119; Revoked by SI 2019/146, as from IP completion day (as defined in the European Union (Withdrawal Agreement) Act 2020, s 39(1)–(5)).

## ARTICLE 4

### COMPETENT COURT

**[7.17]**

1

The functions referred to in this Law relating to recognition of foreign proceedings and cooperation with foreign courts shall be performed by the High Court and assigned to the Chancery Division, as regards England and Wales and the Court of Session as regards Scotland.

2

Subject to paragraph 1 of this article, the court in either part of Great Britain shall have jurisdiction in relation to the functions referred to in that paragraph if—

    (a)    the debtor has—

        (i)    a place of business; or

        (ii)    in the case of an individual, a place of residence; or

        (iii)    assets,

    situated in that part of Great Britain; or

    (b)    the court in that part of Great Britain considers for any other reason that it is the appropriate forum to consider the question or provide the assistance requested.

**3**

In considering whether it is the appropriate forum to hear an application for recognition of a foreign proceeding in relation to a debtor, the court shall take into account the location of any court in which a proceeding under British insolvency law is taking place in relation to the debtor and the likely location of any future proceedings under British insolvency law in relation to the debtor.

ARTICLE 5

AUTHORISATION OF BRITISH INSOLVENCY OFFICEHOLDERS TO ACT IN A
FOREIGN STATE

**[7.18]**

A British insolvency officeholder is authorised to act in a foreign State on behalf of a proceeding under British insolvency law, as permitted by the applicable foreign law.

ARTICLE 6

PUBLIC POLICY EXCEPTION

**[7.19]**

Nothing in this Law prevents the court from refusing to take an action governed by this Law if the action would be manifestly contrary to the public policy of Great Britain or any part of it.

**General note—** This provision introduces a public policy caveat. Reciprocity is not a condition of giving assistance but the Insolvency Service has suggested that as far as 'non-friendly' states are concerned, the power of the courts under Art 6 should be sufficient to prevent the giving of assistance in a particular case that would be contrary to British public policy. This provision is similar to Art 33 of the EU Insolvency Regulation 2015/848 and the use of the word 'manifestly' implies that the public policy exception should be interpreted restrictively with national courts only invoking it where a case involves mattes that are considered to be of fundamental importance. As an alternative to waving the big stick of public policy however, Art 17(4) allows a court to modify or terminate the recognition of foreign proceedings if it is shown that the grounds for granting it were fully or partially lacking or have ceased to exist.

In *Nordic Trustee ASA v OGX Petroleo* [2016] EWHC 25 (Ch), [2016] Bus LR 121 at para [60] Snowden J remarked that notwithstanding the clear intention that the public policy exception in Art 6 should be interpreted restrictively, it was strongly arguable that the court had a residual discretion to refuse recognition if satisfied that the applicant was abusing the process of recognition for an illegitimate purpose.

The public policy exception was considered more fully in *Cherkasov v Olegovich, the Official Receiver of Dalnyaya Step LLC* [2017] EWHC 756 (Ch), [2017] All ER (D) 11 (May) (security for costs application – Rose J); [2017] EWHC 3153 (Ch) – set aside application – Chancellor Vos – where it was held that the Russian insolvency representative was in clear breach of his duty of full and frank disclosure when applying to the English court for a recognition order in respect of the foreign insolvency proceedings.

In this case, third parties affected by a recognition order that had been granted on an ex parte basis sought to have the order set aside. It was held that a foreign insolvency practitioner in seeking to resist the set-aside application had to provide security for costs under r 25.12 of the Civil Procedure Rules. The set-aside application was brought on the grounds that the making of the earlier recognition order was manifestly contrary to public policy and that the foreign insolvency representative had failed to disclose relevant facts. Essentially it was argued that the foreign insolvency proceedings conducted in Russia were part of an asset-stripping exercise by instrumentalities of the Russian state to sideline political opponents. In the security for costs application Rose J said (para 82): 'It is true that Article 6 is to be read restrictively and will only be relevant in a very small number of cases. But this case falls clearly within that small class.'

The public policy exception was also addressed in *Re Agrokor* [2017] EWHC 2791 (Ch). The judge noted that the exception was a common feature of international conventions and said (para 109): 'The inclusion of the word "manifestly" must mean something more than mere contrariness or incompatibility. So it should be harder to demonstrate that something is manifestly contrary to public policy than that it is simply contrary to it. What is not clear is how much harder. One view is that "manifestly" means "more serious", rather like "gross" in the phrase "gross negligence". Another view is that "manifestly" does not add any further depth to the requirement.

It is still the standard of being "contrary to public policy" after all. But it does add the need for clarity. Where there is any doubt or any confusion as to whether it is contrary to or incompatible with public policy, there cannot be anything "manifestly" contrary to public policy'.

The judge added (para 110) that the exception for manifest contrariness to public policy should be narrowly construed. More substantively, it was held that the fact that the scheme of distribution followed in Croatian proceedings may be different from that applying under English law did not constitute a manifest violation of English public policy. Nor was there any such violation stemming from the mere fact that the Croatian proceedings would not necessarily follow a practice of pari passu distribution. It was noted that the principle of pari passu could be overridden in appropriate cases even under English law.

## ARTICLE 7

### ADDITIONAL ASSISTANCE UNDER OTHER LAWS

[7.20]

Nothing in this Law limits the power of a court or a British insolvency officeholder to provide additional assistance to a foreign representative under other laws of Great Britain.

General note—It should be noted that the Model Law is intended to provide only threshold levels of assistance. Article 7 supplements this by enabling a UK court or insolvency representative to provide additional assistance to a foreign representative. This provision acts as a 'saver for s 426 of the Insolvency Act. Section 426 is quite far reaching. It was held by the Court of Appeal in *HSBC v Tambrook Jersey Ltd* [2013] EWCA Civ 576, [2013] BPIR 484 that there need not be any 'substantive' insolvency proceedings in motion in the relevant foreign jurisdiction or the intention to institute such proceedings before the UK court could accept the request for assistance. In this case, a Jersey court had issued a letter of request asking an English court to put a Jersey registered company into administration in England. There was no such procedure in Jersey and it was considered that an English administration would produce the best outcome for creditors and other stakeholders. At first instance it was held that since insolvency proceedings in Jersey were neither in progress nor contemplated, there was nothing to assist, and the English court lacked jurisdiction to grant the request. The Court of Appeal took a different view holding that the Jersey court, by hearing the application and issuing the letter of request, was exercising its insolvency jurisdiction. In its view, that was sufficient to fulfil the requirements of s 426 and nothing more by way of formal insolvency proceedings was needed. Davis LJ observed (at para 37): 'I would be prepared to accept that s 426 would not in itself empower the courts to issue or act upon a request in respect of a matter unrelated to insolvency . . . But, that said, I do not think that the courts should be astute to equate "having" jurisdiction with "exercising" jurisdiction in the sense of connoting a requirement for the existence of some formal insolvency proceedings in the requesting state'.

## ARTICLE 8

### INTERPRETATION

[7.21]

In the interpretation of this Law, regard is to be had to its international origin and to the need to promote uniformity in its application and the observance of good faith.

## CHAPTER II  ACCESS OF FOREIGN REPRESENTATIVES AND CREDITORS TO COURTS IN GREAT BRITAIN

### ARTICLE 9

### RIGHT OF DIRECT ACCESS

[7.22]

A foreign representative is entitled to apply directly to a court in Great Britain.

General note—An essential foundation of the Model Law is the provision of access to the domestic courts by a foreign insolvency representative. In particular there is no necessity of obtaining a licence or other form of prior authorisation from a domestic regulator. An application by itself is largely a futile exercise unless it is a prelude to application for interim relief or for the recognition of foreign insolvency proceedings. To avoid unfavourable financial consequences in the shape of an adverse costs order, the foreign representative is well advised to ascertain the probability of success in a recognition application before invoking the assistance of a domestic court.

## ARTICLE 10

### LIMITED JURISDICTION

**[7.23]**

The sole fact that an application pursuant to this Law is made to a court in Great Britain by a foreign representative does not subject the foreign representative or the foreign assets and affairs of the debtor to the jurisdiction of the courts of Great Britain or any part of it for any purpose other than the application.

**General note**—This provision makes it clear that an application to the court by a foreign representative constitutes a 'limited submission' to jurisdiction. The mere fact of the application does not invest the domestic courts with any further jurisdiction over the foreign representative or all the foreign assets and affairs of the debtor. It may be, however, that in weighing up the discretionary consequences of recognition of the foreign proceedings the domestic courts will require a more universal submission to jurisdiction on the part of the foreign representative.

It is the case that the application for recognition and the making of a recognition order does not turn the foreign insolvency representative into an officer of the English court. This was held in *Glasgow (Bankruptcy Trustee) v ELS Law Ltd* [2017] EWHC 3004 (Ch), [2018] 1 WLR 1564, [2018] 1 BCLC 339, [2018] BPIR 431, where the judge suggested that in the Regulations there was nothing to suggest that an English court was permitted to exercise its punitive and disciplinary powers against a foreign professional. The fact that the foreign representative was not an officer of the English court meant that he was not subject to the rule in *Ex parte James*, which requires such officers, while acting in the course of insolvency proceedings, to observe certain standards of behaviour such as acting 'honourably'. The court said that even if something equivalent to the rule in *Ex parte James* was in force in the relevant foreign jurisdiction, such foreign rules and standards could not be applied by the UK courts. The judge said (at [86]): 'Absent authorisation by the foreign court, this court cannot exercise the supervisory jurisdiction of that court over its own officers.'

## ARTICLE 11

### APPLICATION BY A FOREIGN REPRESENTATIVE TO COMMENCE A PROCEEDING UNDER BRITISH INSOLVENCY LAW

**[7.24]**

A foreign representative appointed in a foreign main proceeding or foreign non-main proceeding is entitled to apply to commence a proceeding under British insolvency law if the conditions for commencing such a proceeding are otherwise met.

**General note**—Under this provision the foreign representative is empowered to apply for the commencement of domestic insolvency proceedings but the provision goes only to standing and the requisite grounds for commencement of such proceedings under domestic law would still have to be met.

## ARTICLE 12

### PARTICIPATION OF A FOREIGN REPRESENTATIVE IN A PROCEEDING UNDER BRITISH INSOLVENCY LAW

**[7.25]**

Upon recognition of a foreign proceeding, the foreign representative is entitled to participate in a proceeding regarding the debtor under British insolvency law.

## ARTICLE 13

### ACCESS OF FOREIGN CREDITORS TO A PROCEEDING UNDER BRITISH INSOLVENCY LAW

[7.26]

**1**

Subject to paragraph 2 of this article, foreign creditors have the same rights regarding the commencement of, and participation in, a proceeding under British insolvency law as creditors in Great Britain.

**2**

Paragraph 1 of this article does not affect the ranking of claims in a proceeding under British insolvency law, except that the claim of a foreign creditor shall not be given a lower priority than that of general unsecured claims solely because the holder of such a claim is a foreign creditor.

**3**

A claim may not be challenged solely on the grounds that it is a claim by a foreign tax or social security authority but such a claim may be challenged—

    (a)    on the ground that it is in whole or in part a penalty, or

    (b)    on any other ground that a claim might be rejected in a proceeding under British insolvency law.

**General note**—By virtue of this provision, foreign creditors become the beneficiaries of a non-discrimination principle. They are given the same right to institute and participate in insolvency proceedings as domestic creditors. In fact, existing UK insolvency law on its face does not discriminate against foreign creditors but it was felt desirable to state this point expressly so as to provide clarity and transparency for foreign creditors and office holders.

**ARTICLE 13(2)**

Foreign creditors, and in particular foreign preferential creditors, may find that their claims do not have the same status as if they would had the matter been litigated in the foreign forum though this is a general provision to the effect that foreign creditors should not be ranked lower than the class of general non-preference domestic claims.

**ARTICLE 13(3)**

Many States including the UK have traditionally excluded foreign revenue claims from recognition in insolvency proceedings: *Government of India v Taylor* [1955] AC 491. UNCITRAL has recognised national sensitivities for its Guide for Enactment contemplates that Enacting States may wish to maintain the exclusion of foreign revenue claims. Article 13 does not avail of this potential for exclusion though under Art 13(3) foreign tax and social security claims can still be challenged on the grounds, for example, that they constitute a penalty.

## ARTICLE 14

### NOTIFICATION TO FOREIGN CREDITORS OF A PROCEEDING UNDER BRITISH INSOLVENCY LAW

[7.27]

**1**

Whenever under British insolvency law notification is to be given to creditors in Great Britain, such notification shall also be given to the known creditors that do not have addresses in Great Britain. The court may order that appropriate steps be taken with a view to notifying any creditor whose address is not yet known.

**2**

Such notification shall be made to the foreign creditors individually, unless—

    (a)    the court considers that under the circumstances some other form of notification would be more appropriate; or

    (b)    the notification to creditors in Great Britain is to be by advertisement only, in which case the notification to the known foreign creditors may be by advertisement in such foreign newspapers as the British insolvency officeholder considers most appropriate for ensuring that the content of the notification comes to the notice of the known foreign creditors.

**3**

When notification of a right to file a claim is to be given to foreign creditors, the notification shall—

    (a)    indicate a reasonable time period for filing claims and specify the place for their filing;

    (b)    indicate whether secured creditors need to file their secured claims; and

    (c)    contain any other information required to be included in such a notification to creditors pursuant to the law of Great Britain and the orders of the court.

**4**

In this article "the court" means the court which has jurisdiction in relation to the particular proceeding under British insolvency law under which notification is to be given to creditors.

**General note**—Foreign creditors must be notified and notified individually of UK insolvency proceedings unless the court considers that some other form of notification would be more appropriate or where the notification to British creditors is by advertisement by something equivalent. When notice of a right to lodge a claim is given to foreign creditors, the notification must indicate a reasonable time period for filing claims and specify a place for filing.

## CHAPTER III    RECOGNITION OF A FOREIGN PROCEEDING AND RELIEF

### ARTICLE 15

#### APPLICATION FOR RECOGNITION OF A FOREIGN PROCEEDING

**[7.28]**

**1**

A foreign representative may apply to the court for recognition of the foreign proceeding in which the foreign representative has been appointed.

**2**

An application for recognition shall be accompanied by—

    (a)    a certified copy of the decision commencing the foreign proceeding and appointing the foreign representative; or

    (b)    a certificate from the foreign court affirming the existence of the foreign proceeding and of the appointment of the foreign representative; or

    (c)    in the absence of evidence referred to in sub-paragraphs (a) and (b), any other evidence acceptable to the court of the existence of the foreign proceeding and of the appointment of the foreign representative.

**3**

An application for recognition shall also be accompanied by a statement identifying all foreign proceedings, proceedings under British insolvency law and section 426 requests in respect of the debtor that are known to the foreign representative.

**4**

The foreign representative shall provide the court with a translation into English of documents supplied in support of the application for recognition.

**General note**—In *Re 19 Entertainment Ltd* [2016] EWHC 1545 (Ch) the directors of a company in US Chapter 11 bankruptcy reorganisation proceedings were recognised as 'foreign representatives'.

The applicant for recognition though must have been duly appointed in the foreign proceedings and the application must be accompanied by a certificate from the foreign court or a certified copy of its decision1. These documents must be translated into English. The foreign representative is subject to certain disclosure requirements including an obligation to identify all foreign proceedings in respect of the debtor that are within his knowledge or later become known to him. Under Art 18 the foreign representative is subject to a continuing duty to inform the court promptly of any substantial change in the status of the recognised foreign proceedings or the status of his own appointment.

See on disclosure obligations, *Nordic Trustee ASA v OGX Petroleo* [2016] EWHC 25 (Ch), [2016] Bus LR 121, (2016) GBC 1 and *Cherkasov and Others v Olegovich, the Official Receiver of Dalnyaya Step LLC* [2017] EWHC 756 (Ch), [2017] All ER (D) 11 (May). In the latter case, Rose J stated at para [13]: 'Schedule 2 to the CBIR deals with the form and content of the various documents that must be provided to the court by a foreign representative seeking a recognition order. These include the swearing of an affidavit to be attached to the application. That affidavit must contain or have exhibited to it various items aimed at establishing to the satisfaction of the court that the requirements for recognition are met. Paragraph 4(1)(d) of Schedule 2 provides that the affidavit must contain "any other matters which in the opinion of the applicant will assist the court in deciding whether to make a recognition order"'.

## ARTICLE 16

### PRESUMPTIONS CONCERNING RECOGNITION

**[7.29]**

**1**

If the decision or certificate referred to in paragraph 2 of article 15 indicates that the foreign proceeding is a proceeding within the meaning of sub-paragraph (i) of article 2 and that the foreign representative is a person or body within the meaning of sub-paragraph (j) of article 2, the court is entitled to so presume.

**2**

The court is entitled to presume that documents submitted in support of the application for recognition are authentic, whether or not they have been legalised.

**2A**

Where the EU Insolvency Regulation applies the centre of the debtor's main interests is to be determined in accordance with that Regulation.

**Amendments**—Inserted by SI 2019/146, as from IP completion day (as defined in the European Union (Withdrawal Agreement) Act 2020, s 39(1)–(5)).

**3**

Subject to paragraph 2A, in the absence of proof to the contrary, the debtor's registered office, or habitual residence in the case of an individual, is presumed to be the centre of the debtor's main interests.

**Amendments**—Substituted by SI 2019/146, as from IP completion day (as defined in the European Union (Withdrawal Agreement) Act 2020, s 39(1)–(5)).

**General note**—One of the major advantages brought about by the UNCITRAL Model Law is to simplify procedures for the recognition of foreign proceedings with complicated legalisation requirements involving notarial or consular procedures being abolished. Under this Article a UK court is entitled to presume that documents submitted in support of the application for recognition are authentic, whether or not they have been legalised.

**ARTICLE 16(3)**

The concept of 'centre of main interests' is the same as that to be found in Art 3(1) of the EU Insolvency Regulation and case law under the European instrument has been held to be relevant to the interpretation of the CBIR. As noted, however, by Lewison J in Re *Stanford International Bank Ltd* [2009] BPIR 1157 at para 65 when enacting the equivalent of Art 16(3) in the US, the US Congress changed the wording so that the presumption may be rebutted by 'evidence' rather than 'proof' to the contrary. Consequently, in the US it has been held that the burden of proof lies on the party who is asserting that particular proceedings are 'main proceedings' and the burden of proof is never on the party who is opposing that contention[1]. Furthermore, in Re *Bear Stearns High-Grade Structured Credit Strategies Master Fund Ltd* (2007) 374 BR 122 and affirmed (2008) 389 BR 325[2], Judge Liflind said except in circumstances where there is no contrary evidence, the location of the registered office did not have any special evidentiary value. From the *Bear Stearns* case it appears that the COMI is determined by where the most material contacts are to be found, especially management direction and control of assets. These contacts 'include the location of the debtor's headquarters, the location of those who actually manage the debtor, the location of the debtor's primary assets, the location of a majority of the debtor's creditors or of a majority of creditors who would be affected by the case and the jurisdiction whose law would apply to most disputes'[3].

Lewison J in *Re Stanford International Bank Ltd* [2009] BPIR 1157 noted, however, that the approach of the ECJ under the EC Regulation was different and he suggested that the English courts should follow the ECJ approach. The American jurisprudence was of lesser significance given the difference in legislative wording in the US. Lewison J said[4]:

'In my judgment it is a reasonable inference that the intention of the framers of the Model Law was that COMI in the Model Law would bear the same meaning as in the EC Regulation, since it "corresponds" to the formulation in the EC Regulation; and one of the purposes of the Model Law is to provide EU member states with a "complementary regime" to the EC Regulation.'

The judge noted that the Model Law did not contain anything equivalent to recital 13 of the EC Regulation, which provides that the COMI should correspond to where the debtor conducts the administration of his interests on a regular basis and is therefore ascertainable by third parties. He said, however, that the Model Law framers envisaged that the interpretation of COMI in the EC Regulation, necessarily including the effect of recital 13, would be equally applicable to COMI in the Model Law.

The approach adopted by Lewison J was upheld by the Court of Appeal where Chancellor Morritt commented[5]:

'Further as both Uncitral and the EC Regulation apply in England and Wales it is essential that each should be interpreted in a manner consistent with the other. It would be absurd if the COMI of a company with its registered office in, say, Spain which is being wound up both there and in the US should differ according to whether the court in England was applying Uncitral on an application by the US liquidators for recognition as a foreign main proceeding or the EC Regulation in deciding whether the court in England may entertain a petition to wind up the Spanish company here. It follows that if there is any difference in the test promulgated by the ECJ in *Eurofood* and that applied by the courts in the US then it is right that the court in England should apply the *Eurofood* test.'

Apart however, from the rare instance of outright fraud[6] it is difficult to say that that the different viewpoints articulated in *Eurofood* and *Bear Stearns* will necessarily lead to different results in concrete cases. Take the basic facts of *Bear Stearns* with an 'offshore' hedge fund type entity incorporated as a Caymans Islands company. In *Bear Stearns* there were no employees or managers in the Caymans; the investment manager was located in New York, the back-office operations including books and records were also operated from the US and prior to the commencement of the Cayman proceeding all of the company's liquid assets were located in the US. According to Liflind J, it seems that the only business done in the Caymans was limited to those steps necessary to maintain the status of the company as a registered Caymans company. In these circumstances, Liflind J is surely justified in concluding that the offshore entities closely approximate to the 'letterbox' companies referred to in *Eurofood* and therefore, the COMI presumption, even if given substantive weight, would be rebutted. *Re Kaupthing*[7] is a somewhat analogous UK case where the *Eurofood* presumption was applied but held to have been rebutted in respect of a letter box company.

---

1.   See Judge Klein in *Re Tri-Continental Exchange Ltd* (2006) 349 BR 627 at 635.

2.   See also *Re Basis Yield Alpha Fund* (2008) 381 BR 37; *Re Ernst & Young* (2008) 383 BR 773. Judge Klein made the equation between principal place of business and COMI in one of the first US Chapter cases 15 – *Re Tri-Continental Exchange* (2006) 349 BR 627 at 634 asserting that an entity's "principal place of business" in United States jurisprudence was that entity's COMI. In *Hertz Corp v Friend* (2010) 559 US 1 the US Supreme Court concluded that 'principal place of 'business' was best read as 'referring to the place where a corporation's officers direct, control, and coordinate the corporation's activities. It is the  . . .   the corporation's "nerve center." And in practice it should normally be the place where the corporation maintains its headquarters—provided that the headquarters is the actual center of direction, control, and coordination, i.e., the "nerve center," and not simply an office where the corporation holds its board meetings  . . .  ' (at pp 14–15). The court suggested that a 'nerve center' approach was simpler to apply, compared with other possible approaches, and that administrative simplicity was a major virtue. *Hertz Corp v Friend* and the administrative nerve centre test was cited by Lifland J with apparent approval in a US Chapter 15 recognition case: *Re Fairfield Sentry Ltd* (2010) 440 BR 60 though he also cited his earlier decision in *Re Bear Stearns* (2007) 374 BR 122 that the court could not rely solely on the presumption of concordance between COMI and registered office but must consider all the relevant evidence.

3.   See Lewison J in *Re Stanford International Bank Ltd* [2009] BPIR 1157 at para 66.

[4] See Lewison J in *Re Stanford International Bank Ltd* [2009] BPIR 1157 at para 45.

[5] [2010] BPIR 679 at para 54. See also Snowden J in *Re Videology Ltd* [2018] EWHC 2186 (Ch), [2019] BCC 195 at para [28] 'for so long as the UK remains a party to the Recast EIR, I can see no obvious basis upon which I should adopt any different approach in relation to the concept of COMI under the CBIR/Model Law and the Recast EIR'.

[6] On which see *Re Ernst & Young Inc* (2008) 383 BR 773.

[7] [2010] EWHC 836 (Ch).

## ARTICLE 17

### DECISION TO RECOGNISE A FOREIGN PROCEEDING

[7.30]

**1**

Subject to article 6, a foreign proceeding shall be recognised if—

(a)   it is a foreign proceeding within the meaning of sub-paragraph (i) of article 2;

(b)   the foreign representative applying for recognition is a person or body within the meaning of sub-paragraph (j) of article 2;

(c)   the application meets the requirements of paragraphs 2 and 3 of article 15; and

(d)   the application has been submitted to the court referred to in article 4.

**2**

The foreign proceeding shall be recognized—

(a)   as a foreign main proceeding if it is taking place in the State where the debtor has the centre of its main interests; or

(b)   as a foreign non-main proceeding if the debtor has an establishment within the meaning of sub-paragraph (e) of article 2 in the foreign State.

**3**

An application for recognition of a foreign proceeding shall be decided upon at the earliest possible time.

**4**

The provisions of articles 15 to 16, this article and article 18 do not prevent modification or termination of recognition if it is shown that the grounds for granting it were fully or partially lacking or have fully or partially ceased to exist and in such a case, the court may, on the application of the foreign representative or a person affected by recognition, or of its own motion, modify or terminate recognition, either altogether or for a limited time, on such terms and conditions as the court thinks fit.

General note—The recognition requirements set out in this provision should be relatively easy to establish and Art 17(3) stipulates that the decision whether or not to recognise should be made as quickly as possible. Article 17 was recently considered by Sir Alastair Norris in *Re NMC Healthcare Ltd (In Administration)* [2021] EWHC 1806 (Ch). He said (at [14]):

> 'The purpose of this categorisation is to ensure that a basic menu of relief is immediately and automatically available at minimum expense to representatives appointed by the Court which is in a position to co-ordinate a multi-national insolvency. Article 17(2) of CBIR will in general, therefore not involve undertaking a technical or complex enquiry or the production and consideration of extensive evidence: the exceptional cases will be those in which there is more than one candidate for that role.'

Art 17 (as well as Art 2) is however silent on whether the debtor must have its COMI or an establishment within the state at the time of the opening of the relevant foreign proceedings or whether the relevant time is the time of the application for recognition. The issue does not appear to have arisen squarely for decision on any of the UK cases on COMI but it has provided extensive discussion in the US under Chapter 15 of the Bankruptcy Code. The preponderant view is now that the relevant time is the time of application for Chapter 15 recognition rather than the time of commencement of the relevant foreign proceedings. In *Morning Mist v Krys (In re Fairfield Sentry Ltd)*, 714 F 3d 127 (2d Cir 2013) the Second Circuit Court of Appeals held that the recognition issue was to be determined on the basis of the debtor's activities at or around the time of filing of the Chapter 15 petition. Where, however, there was an allegation that COMI had been manipulated in bad faith, the court said that it could review the period between the commencement of the foreign proceedings and the application for recognition.

The Second Circuit decision makes it easier for foreign proceedings to achieve recognition in the US if there is any significant interval between the commencement of the foreign proceedings and the recognition application because the appointment of a foreign liquidator is likely to result in a shift in the debtor's activities to the state that opens the proceedings. It is submitted that the decision is unsatisfactory, however, and can create international disharmony rather than the harmony and co-operation that the Model Law is intended to promote. It opens up the possibility of conflicting decisions in different countries on recognition of foreign insolvency proceedings depending on the timing of a recognition application in that particular country. Determining COMI or an establishment, as the case may, with reference to the time of commencement of the foreign insolvency proceeding would create a universally fixed time and lead to greater certainty in the decision-making process. The court in *Morning Mist*, however, based its decisions firmly on the wording of Chapter 15 of the US Bankruptcy Code rather than on more general internationalist considerations. It suggested that if the US Congress had intended bankruptcy courts to view the COMI determination through a look-back period or on a specific past date, it could easily have said so. It said that international sources were of limited use in resolving whether US courts should determine COMI on the date of the Chapter 15 petition or in some other way. There is, however, other US authority: *Re Millennium Global Emerging Credit* (2011) 458 BR 63 (Bankr SDNY 2011) – that suggests that the court, in deciding on recognition, should consider COMI as of the date of the commencement of the relevant foreign proceedings and it is submitted that this authority should be given greater weight in the UK.

It is noteworthy that UNCITRAL in 2013 produced a revised guide to enactment of the Model Law, which takes a standpoint different from that in *Morning Mist*. The revised guide states that the date of commencement of the relevant foreign proceedings provides a test that can be applied with certainty to all insolvency proceedings – see revised guide at para 159 and see generally the discussion at paras 157–160.

The revised guide was referred to in *Re Videology Ltd* [2018] EWHC 2186 (Ch), [2019] BCC 195 where Snowden J said at [49]: 'Under the Model Law, a request for recognition may be made at any time after the commencement of the foreign proceedings. Accordingly, the court considering an application for recognition must determine whether the foreign proceedings for which recognition is sought are in the place that was the debtor's COMI when the proceedings commenced' referring to para 141 of the 2013 Guide to Enactment and Interpretation of the Model Law.

In Singapore, Aedit Abdullah J took a somewhat different view in *Re Zetta Jet Pte Ltd and Others (Asia Aviation Holdings Pte Ltd, intervener)* [2019] SGHC 53 ('*Re Zetta Jet (2)*') stating at para 27 of his judgment 'I am of the view that the determination of the debtor's COMI is to be made as at the date of the application to this court for recognition, and that in assessing where the COMI lies, the court's focus would be on where the primary commercial decisions are made for the debtor. This would generally be the place of registration unless otherwise shown in a particular case. The enquiry would be dependent on the circumstances of each case and no general rule can be laid down. In many cases, it may be that the factors relevant in the assessment essentially balance each other out; in such cases, the presumption under Art 16(3) of the Singapore Model Law in favour of the place of the debtor's registered office would have to come into play.'

Moreover, it appears that on a US Chapter 11 foreign main proceeding recognition application in respect of a Bermudan oil driller, Toisa, ICC Judge Burton (29 March 2019, unreported) took the view that the COMI of a debtor should be assessed at the time of the recognition application and not at the time of the foreign insolvency petition.

But in *Re Sturgeon Central Asia Balanced Fund Ltd (In Liquidation)* [2019] EWHC 1215 (Ch), [2019] 2 BCLC 412, Falk J noted that the version of the guide referred to in CBIR reg 2(2)(c) was the original 1997 Guide and that 'the later version must be approached with some circumspection'.

Both the original and revised guides were used as interpretative aids by Chief ICC Judge Briggs (sitting as a deputy High Court judge) in *Re Sturgeon Central Asia Balanced Fund Ltd (No 2)* [2020] EWHC 123 (Ch), [2020] 1 BCLC 600.

## ARTICLE 18

### Subsequent Information

**[7.31]**

From the time of filing the application for recognition of the foreign proceeding, the foreign representative shall inform the court promptly of—

(a) any substantial change in the status of the recognised foreign proceeding or the status of the foreign representative's appointment; and

(b) any other foreign proceeding, proceeding under British insolvency law or section 426 request regarding the same debtor that becomes known to the foreign representative.

**General note**—The extent of continuing disclosure obligations was considered in *Nordic Trustee ASA v OGX Petroleo* [2016] EWHC 25 (Ch), [2016] Bus LR 121, (2016) GBC 1.

## ARTICLE 19

### Relief that may be Granted upon Application for Recognition of a Foreign Proceeding

[7.32]

**1**

From the time of filing an application for recognition until the application is decided upon, the court may, at the request of the foreign representative, where relief is urgently needed to protect the assets of the debtor or the interests of the creditors, grant relief of a provisional nature, including—

(a) staying execution against the debtor's assets;

(b) entrusting the administration or realisation of all or part of the debtor's assets located in Great Britain to the foreign representative or another person designated by the court, in order to protect and preserve the value of assets that, by their nature or because of other circumstances, are perishable, susceptible to devaluation or otherwise in jeopardy; and

(c) any relief mentioned in paragraph 1 (c), (d) or (g) of article 21.

**2**

Unless extended under paragraph 1(f) of article 21, the relief granted under this article terminates when the application for recognition is decided upon.

**3**

The court may refuse to grant relief under this article if such relief would interfere with the administration of a foreign main proceeding.

**General note**—While under Art 17(3) the decision whether or not to recognise should be made at the earliest possible time there may be certain cases nevertheless where the debtor's assets are perishable, susceptible to devaluation or otherwise in jeopardy. In these circumstances, urgent interim relief may be needed to protect the assets of the debtor or the interests of the creditors and the court is empowered to act on application by a foreign representative. Provisional relief of this kind may take various forms including staying execution against the debtor's assets or entrusting the administration of these assets to the foreign representative.

## ARTICLE 20

### Effects of Recognition of a Foreign Main Proceeding

[7.33]

**1**

Upon recognition of a foreign proceeding that is a foreign main proceeding, subject to paragraph 2 of this article—

(a) commencement or continuation of individual actions or individual proceedings concerning the debtor's assets, rights, obligations or liabilities is stayed;

(b) execution against the debtor's assets is stayed; and

(c) the right to transfer, encumber or otherwise dispose of any assets of the debtor is suspended.

**2**

The stay and suspension referred to in paragraph 1 of this article shall be—

    (a)    the same in scope and effect as if the debtor, in the case of an individual, had been adjudged bankrupt under the Insolvency Act 1986 or had his estate sequestrated under the Bankruptcy (Scotland) Act 1985, or, in the case of a debtor other than an individual, had been made the subject of a winding-up order under the Insolvency Act 1986; and

    (b)    subject to the same powers of the court and the same prohibitions, limitations, exceptions and conditions as would apply under the law of Great Britain in such a case,

and the provisions of paragraph 1 of this article shall be interpreted accordingly.

**3**

Without prejudice to paragraph 2 of this article, the stay and suspension referred to in paragraph 1 of this article, in particular, does not affect any right—

    (a)    to take any steps to enforce security over the debtor's property;

    (b)    to take any steps to repossess goods in the debtor's possession under a hire-purchase agreement;

    (c)    exercisable under or by virtue of or in connection with the provisions referred to in article 1(4); or

    (d)    of a creditor to set off its claim against a claim of the debtor,

being a right which would have been exercisable if the debtor, in the case of an individual, had been adjudged bankrupt under the Insolvency Act 1986 or had his estate sequestrated under the Bankruptcy (Scotland) Act 1985, or, in the case of a debtor other than an individual, had been made the subject of a winding-up order under the Insolvency Act 1986.

**4**

Paragraph 1(a) of this article does not affect the right to—

    (a)    commence individual actions or proceedings to the extent necessary to preserve a claim against the debtor; or

    (b)    commence or continue any criminal proceedings or any action or proceedings by a person or body having regulatory, supervisory or investigative functions of a public nature, being an action or proceedings brought in the exercise of those functions.

**5**

Paragraph 1 of this article does not affect the right to request or otherwise initiate the commencement of a proceeding under British insolvency law or the right to file claims in such a proceeding.

**6**

In addition to and without prejudice to any powers of the court under or by virtue of paragraph 2 of this article, the court may, on the application of the foreign representative or a person affected by the stay and suspension referred to in paragraph 1 of this article, or of its own motion, modify or terminate such stay and suspension or any part of it, either altogether or for a limited time, on such terms and conditions as the court thinks fit.

    **General note**—Designation of the foreign proceedings as main entails certain mandatory consequences in terms of recognition. First, upon recognition there is an automatic stay on individual proceedings against the debtor's assets though the apparent breadth of this prohibition is qualified in various respects. Legal proceedings may still be instituted to prevent an action form becoming statute-barred (Art 20(4)). Secondly, there is a stay on execution against the debtor's assets and thirdly, the right to transfer, encumber or otherwise dispose of any assets of the debtor is suspended.

    The consequences of recognition of a foreign bankruptcy order were considered in *Re Derev* [2021] EWHC 392 (Ch). The court refused to continue a worldwide freezing order against a Russian bankrupt after his bankruptcy manager had obtained an order recognising the Russian bankruptcy as a foreign main proceeding under the Cross Border Insolvency Regulations. The court said that the effect of the recognition order had been to import into the conduct of the bankruptcy the infrastructure of the insolvency legislation contained in the IA 1986, which offered other forms of protection. Therefore, there was no utility in continuing the freezing order.

The infrastructure of the insolvency regime operated to deprive the debtor of control of his worldwide assets and conferred wide-ranging powers on his trustee, all of which was subject to the general control of the court, whose powers included a power of arrest under the Insolvency Act 1986 s 364. The scheme of the Model Law was intended to put the foreign trustee or bankruptcy manager in the same position, as far as practicable, as an officeholder appointed under domestic law. Consistent with that, the effect of recognition of a foreign main proceeding was to bring into play the wide infrastructure of the insolvency legislation. Absent some exceptional reason, a freezing order would not be required or justified.

### ARTICLE 20(1)

This provision was considered in *Akers v Samba Financial Group* [2014] EWCA Civ 1516 where Cayman proceedings were recognised as foreign main proceedings and it was alleged that assets held on trust for the debtor had been transferred away to the defendant following the commencement of the foreign main proceedings. The liquidators brought proceedings in England taking advantage of the CBIR and the Model Law, rather than in the Caymans because, inter alia, the defendant had no presence in the Caymans, having its main operations in Saudi Arabia. The liquidators believed that the defendant would refuse to submit to the jurisdiction of the Cayman courts and that any judgment obtained there would be difficult to enforce. They sought an order that the transfer of assets to the defendant was void. The Court of Appeal, however, overturning the first instance judgment – [2014] EWHC 540 (Ch), refused to stay the English proceedings on the basis that there Saudi Arabia was a more appropriate forum for the resolution of the dispute about the beneficial ownership of the assets. England was considered, in reality, to be the only available forum for the claim (apart perhaps from the Cayman Islands), and the claim was thought to have a realistic prospect of success.

The first instance judgment was restored by the Supreme Court – [2017] UKSC 6. The Supreme Court judgment turned on the scope of s 127 of the Insolvency Act 1986, which voids dispositions of a company's property after the commencement of a winding-up process in respect of the company. The court held that the natural meaning of 'disposition' in the context of s 127 was a transfer by a disponor to a disponee of the relevant property but in this case only the legal title to the shares had been transferred and the relevant property was the beneficial interest.

But for a somewhat critical analysis of the decision, see Chancery Bar Association Lecture 2017 'Akers v Samba: Equity's Darling Reigns Supreme', by Sir Michael now Lord Briggs JSC available at http://www.chba.org.uk/for-members/library/annual-lectures/equitys-darling-reigns-supreme.

### ARTICLE 20(2)

This provision is drafted in a broad-brush manner and does not set out all the effects of domestic British law that the provision is intended to capture.

The winding-up stay is imposed by s 130(2) of the 1986 Act. In *Gardner v Lemma Europe Insurance Co Ltd* [2016] EWCA Civ 484, at para [2] Patten LJ said that the imposition of an automatic stay was designed to avoid the unnecessary expenditure of assets that were otherwise available for distribution among creditors and to support the replacement of a creditor's right to establish a claim by judgment in an action with a right to lodge a proof of debt. He added: 'This process is inherently less expensive and carries with it a right of access to the Companies Court in the event that the proof is rejected  . . .  Consistently with this, leave to commence proceedings will only be granted by the court when it is right and fair to do so in all the circumstances and is unlikely to be granted where the issue in the action could be dealt with as conveniently in the liquidation as in other proceedings'.

The precise nature of the stay and whether it covers the exercise of contractual termination clauses as well as the institution or continuation of judicial proceedings was considered in *Re Pan Ocean Co Ltd* [2014] EWHC 2124 (Ch). It was held that the service of a contractual notice to terminate does not involve an 'action or proceeding [being] proceeded with or commenced against the company or its property' within the meaning of s 130(2) of the Insolvency Act 1986.

It is specifically stated in Art 20(3) however, that the stay does not affect rights to enforce security, rights to repossess goods under hire-purchase and retention of title agreements, rights of set-off and rights pertaining to financial market transactions to the extent that all these rights would be exercisable in a domestic British context. It should also be noted that where the foreign proceedings are of a rescue or reorganisation rather than liquidation nature, the foreign representative at the time of applying for recognition of the foreign proceedings may apply for the effects of the stay to be modified and for more appropriate relief to be granted.

### ARTICLE 20(4)

This provision was applied in *Lehman Brothers Finance AG v Klaus Tschira Stiftung GmbH* [2014] EWHC 2782 (Ch), [2014] All ER (D) 42 and see also *SK Shipping Co Ltd v STX Pan*

*Ocean Co Ltd*, Chancery Division (Companies Court), 29 July 2014 and *Bank of Tokyo-Mitsuibishi UFJ Ltd v Sanko Mineral* [2014] EWHC 3927 (Admlty), [2014] All ER (D) 14 (Dec).

**ARTICLE 20(6)**

This discretion was exercised in *Re Pan Oceanic Maritime Inc*[1] [2010] EWHC 1734 where an 'administration stay' along the lines of para 43 of Sch B1 to the Insolvency Act 1986 was granted rather than a liquidation stay following recognition of foreign insolvency proceedings.

In *Nordic Trustee ASA v OGX Petroleo* [2016] EWHC 25 (Ch), [2016] Bus LR 121 Snowden J suggested that the applicant for recognition should put before the court any material that was relevant to the exercise of the discretion lift or modify the stay. There was a requirement of full and frank disclosure in respect of the consequences of recognition and the effect on third parties and any issues that might arise in relation to the modification or termination of the stay. Snowden J held that where a collective foreign proceeding was recognised as a foreign main proceeding under the Model Law on Cross-Border Insolvency, the automatic stay of claims against the debtor was not intended to prevent persons whose claims were not subject to the collective proceedings from pursuing their claims.

The discretion to lift the stay was considered in *Re Armada Shipping* [2011] EWHC 216 (Ch). In this case the Swiss bankruptcy of a ship charterer was recognised as foreign main insolvency proceedings but nevertheless it was considered appropriate for a dispute over entitlement to sub-hire to be arbitrated in London and therefore the stay under Art 20 of the Model Law was lifted. Briggs J pointed out that all the underlying issues were issues of English shipping law involving competing proprietary or contractual claims in relation to a single asset; namely a party's obligations to make payments under the sub-charter.

Briggs J noted that Art 20(2) incorporated the domestic regime for the imposition and management of a stay prescribed by s 130(2) of the Insolvency Act 1986, which allowed actions or proceedings against the company or its property to be proceeded with or commenced with the permission of the court and subject to such terms as the court may impose. This incorporation carried with it the jurisprudence under s 130(2) which allowed the court 'a free hand to do what is right and fair according to the circumstances of each case'. In this particular case, notwithstanding the Swiss liquidation, the balance of fairness, convenience and justice was considered as lying strongly in favour of an English arbitration.

This test was applied in *Re Kombinat Aluminjuma Podgorica* [2015] EWHC 750 (Ch) though leading to a different result in the particular circumstances. Registrar Jones said at para 50: 'Insofar as claims are not in dispute, it is obvious as an overview that the stay should not be lifted. Insofar as claims are in dispute, the question is whether they can be dealt with conveniently in the insolvency. If they can, then prima facie the stay should not be lifted. If they cannot, they will need to be dealt with somehow if there is purpose and need in doing so. In the absence of alternative options, the answer is likely to be that they should be dealt with in the arbitration'

The discretion to lift a foreign bankruptcy stay to permit either the opening or continuation of arbitration proceedings has been considered by the English courts on a number of occasions. In *United Drug (UK) Holdings Ltd v Bilcare Singapore Pte Ltd* [2013] EWHC 4335 (Ch) one member of a group of companies was the subject of an insolvency process in Singapore whereas other members of the group remained solvent. The Singapore proceedings were recognised under the CBIR but the applicant wished to have the stay lifted thereby allowing arbitration proceedings to be brought against the insolvent Singapore party and a solvent member of the same group. The court held that the balance came down squarely in favour of lifting the stay in that the applicant's reasons for wishing to proceed with the arbitration were entirely legitimate reasons and there was a lack of evidence enabling the court to measure the burden on the office holders in allowing the arbitration to go ahead.

On the other hand, in *Re Lemma Europe Insurance Co Ltd* [2016] EWCA Civ 484, [2016] All ER (D) 175 (May) the court refused to lift the stay so as to allow a claim to be adjudicated upon in arbitration rather than by the liquidator. The court said that in liquidation proceedings, the collective interest of the creditors was in ensuring that debts were handled with the least possible costs. It would be wary of imposing on liquidators the heavy costs of litigation outside the liquidation proceedings if there were cheaper and easier methods of dealing with claims within the liquidation proceedings.

In *Bannai v Erez* [2013] EWHC 3689 (Comm) a contract was governed by English law and it provided for the resolution of disputes by means of English arbitration. One of the contacting parties became subject to insolvency proceedings in Israel and the other party sought and was granted an anti-suit injunction restraining the commencement or pursuance of legal proceedings in the Israeli courts or elsewhere in respect of any matters falling within the scope of the arbitration agreement.

Although the Israeli bankruptcy court had taken a different view, Burton J decided that the dispute should be adjudicated upon in arbitration. These arbitration proceedings could be concluded relatively quickly and would then inform the outcome of the Israeli bankruptcy proceedings. He referred to s 349A of the Insolvency Act, which applies where a bankrupt in the

UK was party to a contract containing an arbitration agreement, before the commencement of his bankruptcy. The section provides that 'if the trustee in bankruptcy adopts the contract, the arbitration agreement is enforceable by or against the trustee in relation to matters arising from or connected with the contract'. The court was unmoved by the argument that the Israeli trustee in bankruptcy was likely to incur additional expense by having to utilize the procedures in England.

To the same effect is *American Energy Group Ltd v Hycarbex Asia* [2014] EWHC 1091 (Ch) where, despite the court's recognition of a winding-up order made by the High Court of Singapore, the resulting automatic stay of ICC arbitration proceedings was lifted. The court took into account the facts that the arbitration claim was ready for hearing imminently, and the liquidators' application for recognition had been made extremely late.

There was a fairly full discussion of the principles applicable in deciding whether or not to lift or modify the stay in *Ronelp Marine Ltd v STX Offshore and Shipbuilding Co* [2016] EWHC 2228 (Ch). In this case, the applicants were granted permission to continue a Commercial Court action against a Korean company that was the subject of restructuring proceedings in Korea. This was done on the basis that the action concerned difficult issues of English law, the English proceedings were at an advanced stage, and allowing the proceedings to continue would not impede the restructuring plan nor unduly advance the applicants' interests over those of the creditors as a whole. Norris J did say, however, that a creditor who sought permission to continue existing proceedings had to make out the case for relief and, in the case of an unsecured money claim, had to demonstrate a circumstance or combination of circumstances that were of sufficient weight to overcome a strong imperative to have all the claims dealt with in the same manner by the foreign insolvency court. At para 31, Norris J referred to previous authority that only in 'exceptional' cases should the court give a creditor, whose claim was simply a monetary one, a right by the taking of proceedings to override and pre-empt the statutory machinery, but he added that the term 'exceptional' was a protean one.

In this case nevertheless, the relevant issues under English law were particularly uncertain and better decided by an English trial rather than by summary review in the Korean insolvency court. Resolving the matter through the Korean insolvency process was likely to take several years whereas continuing the Commercial Court proceedings would not jeopardise the restructuring plan and could provide a judgment which would assist the Korean court. While the claim might be treated differently from other claims, this was justified by the nature of the claim and the stage reached in the Commercial Court proceedings.

---

[1]   See also *Re Transfield ER Cape Ltd* [2010] EWHC 2851 (Ch).

## ARTICLE 21

### Relief that may be Granted upon Recognition of a Foreign Proceeding

**[7.34]**

1

Upon recognition of a foreign proceeding, whether main or non-main, where necessary to protect the assets of the debtor or the interests of the creditors, the court may, at the request of the foreign representative, grant any appropriate relief, including—

- (a)   staying the commencement or continuation of individual actions or individual proceedings concerning the debtor's assets, rights, obligations or liabilities, to the extent they have not been stayed under paragraph 1(a) of article 20;

- (b)   staying execution against the debtor's assets to the extent it has not been stayed under paragraph 1(b) of article 20;

- (c)   suspending the right to transfer, encumber or otherwise dispose of any assets of the debtor to the extent this right has not been suspended under paragraph 1(c) of article 20;

- (d)   providing for the examination of witnesses, the taking of evidence or the delivery of information concerning the debtor's assets, affairs, rights, obligations or liabilities;

- (e)   entrusting the administration or realisation of all or part of the debtor's assets located in Great Britain to the foreign representative or another person designated by the court;

- (f)   extending relief granted under paragraph 1 of article 19; and

(g) granting any additional relief that may be available to a British insolvency officeholder under the law of Great Britain, including any relief provided under paragraph 43 of Schedule B1 to the Insolvency Act 1986.

**2**

Upon recognition of a foreign proceeding, whether main or non-main, the court may, at the request of the foreign representative, entrust the distribution of all or part of the debtor's assets located in Great Britain to the foreign representative or another person designated by the court, provided that the court is satisfied that the interests of creditors in Great Britain are adequately protected.

**3**

In granting relief under this article to a representative of a foreign non-main proceeding, the court must be satisfied that the relief relates to assets that, under the law of Great Britain, should be administered in the foreign non-main proceeding or concerns information required in that proceeding.

**4**

No stay under paragraph 1(a) of this article shall affect the right to commence or continue any criminal proceedings or any action or proceedings by a person or body having regulatory, supervisory or investigative functions of a public nature, being an action or proceedings brought in the exercise of those functions.

**General note**—Certain consequences follow automatically from the recognition of foreign main proceedings. According to this provision, there are no such automatic consequences from the recognition of foreign non-main proceedings though similar relief is available on a discretionary basis. Moreover, whether the foreign proceedings are 'main' or 'non-main', the provision also allows additional relief to be made available on a discretionary basis.

For a discussion of the factors that might apply to the grant of discretionary relief consequent on the recognition of foreign non-main proceedings see *Re Videology Ltd* [2018] EWHC 2186 (Ch), [2019] BCC 195 at [84]–[87].

The differences between the Art 20 stay and the discretionary Art 21 stay were also explored in *Re Pan Ocean Co Ltd* [2014] EWHC 2124 (Ch). Article 21(1)(a) refers to 'staying the commencement or continuation of individual actions or individual proceedings concerning the debtor's assets, rights, obligations or liabilities, to the extent they have not been stayed under paragraph 1(a) of article 20'. In *Re Pan Ocean Co Ltd* Morgan J referred to the ordinary and well understood meaning of the phrase 'commencement or continuation of individual actions or individual proceedings' and held that it did not include service of a contractual termination notice.

In *Picard v Fim Advisers LLP: Re Madoff Investment Securities LLC* [2010] EWHC 1299, Kitchin J suggested that Art 21 had both a jurisdictional and a discretionary component. For instance where information was sought on the basis that it concerned the debtor's assets, affairs, rights, obligations or liabilities, the court had to be satisfied that this was in fact the case. If it was so satisfied, then it had a discretion to order the delivery of that information but in exercising the discretion, it must have regard to all relevant circumstances and ensure that the interests of the person against whom the order is sought are adequately protected.

In determining what was appropriate, Kitchin J also suggested that it was proper for a UK court to have regard to the relevant principles of UK insolvency law as formulated under ss 236 and 366 of the Insolvency Act 1986. These principles he enunciated as follows (paras 25–29):

> 'First, the power is conferred to enable the office holder to discover the true facts concerning the affairs of the company so that he may be able as quickly, effectively and with as little expense as possible to complete his duties. Second, even an honest person who finds himself to have been involved in a major fraud which has had a catastrophic effect for thousands of investors must be expected to cooperate with the office holder. Third, nevertheless, the court must avoid making any order which is unnecessary or unreasonable or which is oppressive to the respondent. Fourth, one of the factors which weighs against making an order or limiting its scope in some way is the disruption, stress and expense likely to be caused to the respondent. Fifth, in assessing what order to make the court will attach considerable weight to the views of the office holder.'

Further guidance on Art 21 was given by Norris J in *Larsen v Navios International* [2011] EWHC 878 (Ch). He suggested that there was every reason to give Art 21 a broad scope since it dealt with a discretionary power that was only exercisable after all relevant interests have been taken into account. In this case, a Danish company that had entered into insolvency proceedings in Denmark was party to a number of forward freight agreements that were subject to English law and the exclusive jurisdiction of the English courts. The bankruptcy proceedings resulted in early termination of the agreements and a liability on the part of the respondent to pay a large sum to the company, which the latter sought to recover in English proceedings. The respondent raised a form of non-mutual set-off as a defence. Both Danish and English insolvency law only recognised a more limited form of set-off but the respondent argued that neither insolvency law applied since the set-offs were being deployed by way of defence in English proceedings and there was no English insolvency.

The court recognised the Danish insolvency proceedings as foreign main proceedings and as part of the recognition granted additional relief under Art 21(1)(g) precluding the respondent from relying on the wider set-off. The court said that it was appropriate to exercise the discretion in this way for the protection of the assets of the company and in the interests of the general body of creditors.

A similar approach was adopted by Newey J in *Re Chesterfield United Inc* [2012] EWHC 244 (Ch) where the court considered the relationship between Arts 21(1)(d) and 21(1)(g). Article 21(1)(d) stipulates that the grant of recognition may provide for the delivery of information concerning the debtor's assets, affairs, rights, obligations or liabilities and Art 21(1)(g) allows for any additional relief that is available under local law. According to Newey J, Art 21(1)(d) was intended to set common minimum standards for documents that foreign representatives were entitled to seek. If the local law provided for additional relief, a foreign representative was entitled to seek that under Art 21(1)(g). Therefore Newey J concluded that the precise scope of Art 21(1)(d) was unimportant for present purposes.

### ARTICLE 21(2)

It is a particularly strong form of relief to entrust the distribution of domestic assets to a foreign representative though even this possibility is catered for in this provision. The provision also opens up the possibility that a foreign representative might be able to distribute realisations of British assets on a basis different to that applying under British insolvency law though creditors should be 'adequately protected'.

Article 21(2) of the Model Law was applied by David Richards J in *Re SwissAir* [2009] BPIR 1505. This company incorporated in Switzerland carried on business as Switzerland's principal international airline but it had also established a branch office in England where it had acquired assets and incurred liabilities. It went into liquidation in both Switzerland and England and the court held that it has power to order the remittal of assets collected by the English liquidator to Switzerland. David Richards J said that there was nothing in the *HIH* case that contradicted the long-established principle that the court could order remittal of assets to a foreign liquidation where the local law provided for pari passu distribution. Under Swiss law certain liabilities were given preferential status in a liquidation but more than enough assets had been realized in Switzerland to pay such liabilities in full. Other claims would be satisfied on a pari passu basis and the assets remitted from England would be distributed on this basis. The interests of creditors in England were adequately protected and the remittal order was fully consistent with the English liquidation.

For a discussion of the court's power to order the handover of assets to a foreign insolvency representative at common law and under s 426 of the Insolvency Act 1986 see *Re HIH Casualty and General Insurance Ltd* [2008] 1 WLR 852 and see also the discussion of 'adequate protection' in the Court of Appeal and at first instance: [2006] 2 All ER 671 at paras 147–154 and [2007] 1 All ER 177 at para 54. Section 361 of the US Bankruptcy Code also uses the concept of 'adequate protection' and while the concept itself is not defined, examples of 'adequate protection' are provided. It appears that the US Congress left the concept deliberately vague so as to facilitate 'case-by-case interpretation and development. It is expected that the courts will apply the concept in light of [the] facts of each case and general equitable principles': see HR Rep No 595, 95th Congress, Ist Session 339 (1977). Interestingly however, Chapter 15 of the US Bankruptcy Code which implements the UNCITRAL Model Law on Cross-Border Insolvency in the US requires that the interests of creditors should be 'sufficiently protected' when authorising the transfer of assets to a foreign insolvency representative. According to a US congressional report the change was made to avoid "confusion with a very specialised legal term in United States bankruptcy" – see HR Rep No 31, 109th Congress Ist Session at para 115.

It is unlikely in most situations that the court would order the turnover of assets to a foreign representative in non-main proceedings though even that possibility is not foreclosed. An example might be where foreign main proceedings are impossible because of jurisdictional constraints, or otherwise, in the state where the debtor's centre of main interests is located.

While Art 21 has been given a broad interpretation in certain contexts, it was held by Morgan J in *Re Pan Ocean Co Ltd* [2014] EWHC 2124 (Ch) that it does not permit the application of foreign law. Only domestic law may be applied. Morgan J rejected the argument for a broad interpretation of the expression 'appropriate relief' in Art 21 that would permit the application of foreign insolvency law. The downside to a broad judicial discretion about which law to apply, tempered only by considerations of 'justice', is increased uncertainty and this militates against effective transaction planning and the accurate pricing of risk.

The court recognised that the words 'any appropriate relief' were capable of being accorded a wide literal meaning but the very width of their literal meaning and Art 21(1)(g) in particular led to the conclusion that such a wide interpretation was inappropriate. In coming to this conclusion, the court considered the preliminary materials leading to the elaboration of the Model Law. It appeared from these documents that it was not intended that 'any appropriate relief' should allow a recognising court to grant relief that it could not grant in relation to a domestic insolvency. The court declined to follow the US decision in *Re Condor Insurance Co Ltd* (2010) 601 F 3d 319 permitting the application of foreign insolvency law by a recognising court in certain circumstances. It suggested that the legislative context and legislative history were different in the US and the US court may have misinterpreted the background negotiations that led to the Model Law.

The court in *Re Pan Ocean Co Ltd* also derived support for its conclusions on Art 21 from the decision of the Supreme Court in *Rubin v Eurofinance SA* [2012] UKSC 46, [2013] 1 AC 236 and the statement of Lord Collins at para 28 that the Model Law provided 'the type of relief that would be available in the case of a domestic insolvency'. Rubin supported the view that Art 21 should be given a wide interpretation in relation to matters of procedure but that the relief available under Art 21 was of a procedural nature. In this particular case, the relief sought went well beyond matters of procedure and affected the substance of the rights and obligations of parties under a contract. The case concerned a contract of carriage which a Brazilian company had entered into with a Korean shipper. The contract was governed by English law and contained a clause allowing the Brazilian party to terminate the contract in certain events including if the shipper entered insolvency proceedings. The shipper entered insolvency proceedings in Korea and the Brazilian party wished to activate the termination provision. The shipper's insolvency administrator, on the other hand, sought to keep the contract alive because it was quite profitable for the shipper. It appeared that under Korean insolvency law, unlike UK insolvency law, termination clauses of this type could be overridden. Morgan J concluded that even if he had the power to do so, it would not be appropriate in this particular case to give effect to the provisions of Korean insolvency law. He said (at para 112):

'In some cases, it can be argued that anyone who does business with a foreign company which might thereafter enter a process of insolvency, governed by the insolvency law of its country of registration, should expect that the insolvency will be governed by that law . . . However, in the present case, the parties had deliberately chosen English law as the law of the contract. Whereas the parties might have expected that a Korean court would apply Korean insolvency law to the insolvency of the Company, they might have been very surprised to find that an English court would apply Korean insolvency law to the substantive rights of the parties under a contract which they had agreed should be governed by English law.'

The *Pan Ocean* decision was reaffirmed in *Bakhshiyeva v Sberbank of Russia* [2018] EWCA Civ 2802, [2019] 1 BCLC 1. The Court of Appeal suggested that if the power to grant a stay under Art 21 had been intended to override the substantive rights of creditors under the proper law governing their debts, this should have been made explicit. There was no warrant for treating the Art 21 powers as other than procedural in nature with the main object of providing a temporary 'breathing space'.

The court concluded that the enactment of the CBIR did not allow the undermining of the long established rule that the modification of English law governed obligations was a matter for English law rather than foreign law. If foreign insolvency or restructuring law purported to modify the English law governed rights and obligations of creditors without their consent or participation in the proceedings, then the English courts would not grant a permanent stay under the CBIR that would have the effect of giving effect to the to the foreign proceedings and restraining enforcement of the rights still enjoyed under English law.

The court also said that there was an important distinction between a liquidation and schemes of reconstruction. In a liquidation, substantive rights of creditors were generally unaffected, and the primary focus was on achieving a fair distribution of the company's assets between all the creditors, normally on a pari passu basis. In other than exceptional cases, the liquidation would end with the dissolution of the company. In a reconstruction, on the other hand, the object was usually the continuation of the company and the terms would typically involve significant changes to the creditors' substantive rights. In a reconstruction case, the Art 21 powers should not be used so as to circumvent the English law rights of the English creditors.

The Court of Appeal also said that there was a compelling case for concluding that relief under the Model Law should not continue beyond the date of termination of the relevant foreign proceeding. This limitation would be consistent with the procedural and supportive role of the Model Law.

The recent comments of the Privy Council in *UBS AG New York v Fairfield Sentry Ltd* [2019] UKPC 20 provides however, some encouragement for those arguing for a future change of judicial direction. The court said at para 14:

'In any event, it is by no means clear that incorporation of the UNCITRAL Model Law would disincline, let alone forbid, a court from applying a foreign insolvency law. It appears to the Board that the United States Courts have interpreted the relevant statutory provisions as permitting the application of foreign insolvency law in both their now-superseded section 304 of the US Bankruptcy Code ( *In re Metzeler* 78 BR 674 , 677 (Bkrtcy SDNY 1987) and chapter 15 of the US Bankruptcy Code, which is based on the UNCITRAL Model Law, *In re Atlas Shipping* A/S 404 BR 726 , (April 27 2009, SDNY), *In re Condor Insurance Ltd* 601 F 3d 319 (March 17 2010, 5th Cir), and *In re Hellas Telecommunications* II 535 BR 543 , 566-567 (Bkrtcy SDNY 2015)).'

## ARTICLE 22

### Protection of Creditors and other Interested Persons

[7.35]

1

In granting or denying relief under article 19 or 21, or in modifying or terminating relief under paragraph 3 of this article or paragraph 6 of article 20, the court must be satisfied that the interests of the creditors (including any secured creditors or parties to hire-purchase agreements) and other interested persons, including if appropriate the debtor, are adequately protected.

2

The court may subject relief granted under article 19 or 21 to conditions it considers appropriate, including the provision by the foreign representative of security or caution for the proper performance of his functions.

3

The court may, at the request of the foreign representative or a person affected by relief granted under article 19 or 21, or of its own motion, modify or terminate such relief.

**General note**—Insofar as the consequences of recognition are discretionary, the content of the insolvency law in the foreign state may be one of the factors that help to shape the exercise of the court's discretion. This discretion is left largely unfettered though this provision tries to fill in some of the blanks by stating that the interests of the creditors and other interests of persons are adequately protected. Furthermore, the court may subject the relief to appropriate conditions, or modify or terminate it in suitable cases.

## ARTICLE 23

### Actions to Avoid Acts Detrimental to Creditors

[7.36]

1

Subject to paragraphs 6 and 9 of this article, upon recognition of a foreign proceeding, the foreign representative has standing to make an application to the court for an order under or in connection with sections 238, 239, 242, 243, 244, 245, 339, 340, 342A, 343, and 423 of the Insolvency Act 1986 and sections 34, 35, 36, 36A and 61 of the Bankruptcy (Scotland) Act 1985.

2

Where the foreign representative makes such an application ("an article 23 application"), the sections referred to in paragraph 1 of this article and sections 240, 241, 341, 342, 342B to 342F, 424 and 425 of the Insolvency Act 1986 and sections 36B and 36C of the Bankruptcy (Scotland) Act 1985 shall apply—

    (a)    whether or not the debtor, in the case of an individual, has been adjudged bankrupt or had his estate sequestrated, or, in the case of a debtor other than an individual, is being wound up or is in administration, under British insolvency law; and

    (b)    with the modifications set out in paragraph 3 of this article.

**3**

The modifications referred to in paragraph 2 of this article are as follows—

    (a)    for the purposes of sections 241(2A)(a) and 342(2A)(a) of the Insolvency Act 1986, a person has notice of the relevant proceedings if he has notice of the opening of the relevant foreign proceeding;

    (b)    for the purposes of sections 240(1) and 245(3) of that Act, the onset of insolvency shall be the date of the opening of the relevant foreign proceeding;

    (c)    the periods referred to in sections 244(2), 341(1)(a) to (c) and 343(2) of that Act shall be periods ending with the date of the opening of the relevant foreign proceeding;

    (d)    for the purposes of sections 242(3)(a), (3)(b) and 243(1) of that Act, the date on which the winding up of the company commences or it enters administration shall be the date of the opening of the relevant foreign proceeding; and

    (e)    for the purposes of sections 34(3)(a), (3)(b), 35(1)(c), 36(1)(a) and (1)(b) and 61(2) of the Bankruptcy (Scotland) Act 1985, the date of sequestration or granting of the trust deed shall be the date of the opening of the relevant foreign proceeding.

**4**

For the purposes of paragraph 3 of this article, the date of the opening of the foreign proceeding shall be determined in accordance with the law of the State in which the foreign proceeding is taking place, including any rule of law by virtue of which the foreign proceeding is deemed to have opened at an earlier time.

**5**

When the foreign proceeding is a foreign non-main proceeding, the court must be satisfied that the article 23 application relates to assets that, under the law of Great Britain, should be administered in the foreign non-main proceeding.

**6**

At any time when a proceeding under British insolvency law is taking place regarding the debtor—

    (a)    the foreign representative shall not make an article 23 application except with the permission of—

        (i)    in the case of a proceeding under British insolvency law taking place in England and Wales, the High Court; or

        (ii)    in the case of a proceeding under British insolvency law taking place in Scotland, the Court of Session; and

    (b)    references to "the court" in paragraphs 1, 5 and 7 of this article are references to the court in which that proceeding is taking place.

**7**

On making an order on an article 23 application, the court may give such directions regarding the distribution of any proceeds of the claim by the foreign representative, as it thinks fit to ensure that the interests of creditors in Great Britain are adequately protected.

**8**

Nothing in this article affects the right of a British insolvency officeholder to make an application under or in connection with any of the provisions referred to in paragraph 1 of this article.

**9**

Nothing in paragraph 1 of this article shall apply in respect of any preference given, floating charge created, alienation, assignment or relevant contributions (within the meaning of section 342A(5) of the Insolvency Act 1986) made or other transaction entered into before the date on which this Law comes into force.

**General note**—This provision enables a foreign representative, on conditions similar to domestic insolvency office holders, to initiate proceedings for the avoidance of actions that are detrimental to creditors. The right kicks in once the foreign proceedings have been recognised but it is purely a procedural mechanism. There is no intention to alter domestic law in substantive respects though Art 23(7) that on making an order in a successful application under Art 23, the court can give directions on the distribution of any proceeds of the claim. Therefore, a foreign representative who wished to challenge ostensibly dubious transactions entered into by the debtor just before the commencement of the insolvency process would have to bring his action four square within the scope of provisions such as ss 238 and 239 Insolvency Act 1986. Section 239, for instance, allows the court to set aside acts done by the debtor in the period prior to the commencement of formal insolvency processes which have the effect of giving one creditor an advantage over other creditors in the event of the debtor's insolvent liquidation. Before however, an action can be set aside under s 239 it must be demonstrated that the debtor was influenced by a desire to prefer the creditor or a guarantor for such a creditor. A foreign liquidator, no more than a domestic liquidator, cannot escape having to satisfy the court that this condition exists.

There may also be conflicts of laws difficulties such as the claim that the relevant transaction is governed by the laws of a foreign jurisdiction, which does not allow the transaction to be impeached. These issues have been noted by the Insolvency Service[1].

Choice of law issues have arisen in the context of the US version of Art 23 – s 1523 of the US Bankruptcy Code. Section 1523 provides that a foreign representative only has the standing to invoke the US avoidance provisions where full, plenary bankruptcy proceedings have been commenced under Chapter 7 or 11 of the US Bankruptcy Code. Full bankruptcy proceedings under Chapter 7 or 11 are likely to be significantly more expensive than Chapter 15 proceedings. Moreover there are certain foreign debtors, including foreign-incorporated insurance companies, specifically precluded from using Chapters 7 and 11. This is largely the reason why in *Re Condor Insurance Ltd* (2010) 601 F 3d 319 where a foreign representative sought to use foreign fraudulent transfer law to invalidate a large transfer by the company to a US affiliate. The company was in liquidation in Nevis, its 'home' jurisdiction and Nevis law was in material respects similar to US law. The US Fifth Circuit Court of Appeals permitted the use of Nevis law to avoid the transfer in the Chapter 15 context. While conscious of conflict of law difficulties, it took the view that foreign law was not excluded. It referred to comity and the fact that debtors might otherwise be tempted to hide assets in the US out of the reach of the foreign jurisdiction. The court spoke of the cost and inconvenience of full US bankruptcy proceedings, which in any event were statutorily prohibited in this case. It also observed that if the US Congress wished to bar all avoidance actions whatever their source it could have said this explicitly but did not do so ((2010) 601 F 3d 319 at 325–327).

The court referred to the 'helpful marriage of avoidance and distribution whether the proceeding is ancillary applying foreign law or a full proceeding applying domestic law – a marriage that avoids the more difficult  . . .  rules of conflict law presented by avoidance and distribution decisions governed by different sources of law' ((2010) 601 F 3d 319 at 327).

The Condor court suggested that its interpretation of Chapter 15 was consistent with the proper interpretation of the statutory predecessor – s 304 of the Bankruptcy Code. It cited the holding of a bankruptcy court in *Re Metzeler* (1987) 78 BR 674 that only avoidance actions relying upon foreign law were permitted under s 304 whereas actions that relied on US law could only be brought under Chapter 7 or 11.

The decision in *Re Pan Ocean Co Ltd* (2014) GBC 40 [2014] EWHC 2124 (Ch), [2014] Bus LR 1041 suggests, however, that the Condor decision would not be followed in the UK. The same conclusion follows from the decision of the Cayman Court of Appeal in *Picard v Primeo Fund* (16 April 2014) and overturning the first instance decision of Andrew Jones J on 14 January 2013. The court refused to interpret the provisions of an ambiguous local statute so as to permit the application of foreign transactional avoidance law. Chadwick P said that a contrary opinion would represent so radical a departure from the common law, that, had the legislature intended that result, it could have been expected to say so in clear terms.

Therefore, one might conclude by saying that foreign law cannot be used as the basis for avoidance proceedings. Nevertheless foreign law may be used as a defence if the transaction sought to be impeached was connected strongly with a foreign jurisdiction.

---

[1] See UK Insolvency Service 'Implementation of UNCITRAL Model Law on Cross-Border Insolvency in Great Britain Summary of Responses and Government Reply' (2006) at para 135.

## ARTICLE 24

INTERVENTION BY A FOREIGN REPRESENTATIVE IN PROCEEDINGS IN GREAT BRITAIN

[7.37]

Upon recognition of a foreign proceeding, the foreign representative may, provided the requirements of the law of Great Britain are met, intervene in any proceedings in which the debtor is a party.

General note—Normally, legal proceedings involving the debtor are subject to the stay that comes into play once the foreign proceedings are recognised. The kind of proceedings envisaged by Art 24 are largely those within the exceptions to the automatic stay contemplated by Art 20. The term 'intervene' is not defined in the Cross-Border Insolvency Regulations despite some desire on the part of consultees for a measure of further legislative clarification. The Insolvency Service took the view that it would be difficult to define it in such a way as to avoid narrowing the intended rights of the foreign representative. It has been suggested that in the event of dispute the court should be able to work out on a case-by-case basis whether a particular intervention was permitted – see generally 'Implementation of UNCITRAL Model Law on Cross-Border Insolvency in Great Britain Summary of Responses and Government Reply' March 2006 at paras 144–147.

## CHAPTER IV  COOPERATION WITH FOREIGN COURTS AND FOREIGN REPRESENTATIVES

## ARTICLE 25

COOPERATION AND DIRECT COMMUNICATION BETWEEN A COURT OF GREAT BRITAIN AND FOREIGN COURTS OR FOREIGN REPRESENTATIVES

[7.38]

1

In matters referred to in paragraph 1 of article 1, the court may cooperate to the maximum extent possible with foreign courts or foreign representatives, either directly or through a British insolvency officeholder.

2

The court is entitled to communicate directly with, or to request information or assistance directly from, foreign courts or foreign representatives.

General note—A central plank of the UNCITRAL Model Law is the encouragement of co-operation between courts and insolvency representatives in different jurisdictions. In many cases, such co-operation and positive interaction can take place without specific legislative sanction. UNCITRAL however were of the view that 'irrespective of the discretion courts may traditionally enjoy in a state, the existence of a specific legislative framework is useful for promoting international co-operation in cross-border cases.

The Model Law lays down a mandatory duty on courts in the Enacting State to co-operate 'to the maximum extent possible' with foreign courts and foreign representatives. Despite the imperative language there is clearly a let-out provision in that the court may conclude that no co-operation is possible in the particular case. Nevertheless, the Model Law gives a clear signal that co-operation with foreign counterparts is what is expected of a court.

In Art 25(1) there is a notable departure from the language of the Model Law in that the word 'may' is substituted for 'shall'. It was considered that the use of the word 'may' rather than 'shall' gave the courts ultimate flexibility in accordance with the appropriate circumstances while encouraging co-operation. The Insolvency Service suggested that it was 'preferable to give the court some discretion as to whether to co-operate and believe that the court will only refuse co-operation in response to an actual request where it has good reasons for doing so'.

### ARTICLE 25(2)

Under this provision, the court is entitled to communicate directly with foreign courts or representatives with no need to go through time-consuming and cumbersome consular procedures. This ability to communicate directly is critical in cases of urgency.

The UNCITRAL Guide to Enactment of the Model Law suggests that judicial co-operation should be coupled with suitable procedural safeguards for the parties involved. Communications between courts taking place openly and save in extreme circumstances with advance notice to the parties and in the presence of the parties.

## ARTICLE 26

### COOPERATION AND DIRECT COMMUNICATION BETWEEN THE BRITISH INSOLVENCY OFFICEHOLDER AND FOREIGN COURTS OR FOREIGN REPRESENTATIVES

**[7.39]**

1

In matters referred to in paragraph 1 of article 1, a British insolvency officeholder shall to the extent consistent with his other duties under the law of Great Britain, in the exercise of his functions and subject to the supervision of the court, cooperate to the maximum extent possible with foreign courts or foreign representatives.

2

The British insolvency officeholder is entitled, in the exercise of his functions and subject to the supervision of the court, to communicate directly with foreign courts or foreign representatives.

**General note**—Article 26 follows the approach of Art 25 and imposes a similar duty of co-operation on insolvency representatives and subject to the same implied limitation. Article 26(1) also avoids difficulties for British insolvency office holders by clarifying that the co-operation obligation is limited by the office holders' duties under domestic law.

## ARTICLE 27

### FORMS OF COOPERATION

**[7.40]**

Cooperation referred to in articles 25 and 26 may be implemented by any appropriate means, including—

(a) appointment of a person to act at the direction of the court;

(b) communication of information by any means considered appropriate by the court;

(c) coordination of the administration and supervision of the debtor's assets and affairs;

(d) approval or implementation by courts of agreements concerning the coordination of proceedings;

(e) coordination of concurrent proceedings regarding the same debtor.

**General note**—This article provides an illustrative list of the forms that co-operation with foreign courts or foreign representatives may take. What constitutes 'cooperation' was briefly considered in *Rubin v Eurofinance* SA [2010] EWCA Civ 895 though the Court of Appeal found it unnecessary to express a concluded view. Ward LJ referred to the fact that the forms of cooperation provided by Art 27 do not include enforcement but, on the other hand, 'cooperation "to the maximum extent possible" should surely include enforcement, especially since enforcement is available under the common law'. In *Rubin* the common law and the UNCITRAL Model Law were used together in support of the conclusion that a monetary default judgment given in US bankruptcy proceedings could be enforced in England, even though it could not have been enforced if it had been given in the ordinary courts of law of the US. The Court of Appeal accepted as a general principle of private international law that bankruptcy, whether personal or corporate should be unitary and universal. In its view, therefore, there should be unitary bankruptcy proceedings in the court of the bankrupt's domicile which should receive worldwide recognition and also apply to all the bankrupt's assets. Recognition entailed a requirement on the part of a domestic court to give assistance by doing whatever it could do in a domestic insolvency.

The Supreme Court has now taken a different view – [2012] UKSC 46. The court pointed out that neither the Model Law nor the CBIR said anything about the enforcement of foreign judgments against third parties even though recognition and enforcement were fundamental in international cases. Lord Collins observed at para 143: 'It would be surprising if the Model Law was intended to deal with judgments in insolvency matters by implication. Articles 21, 25 and 27 are concerned with procedural matters. No doubt they should be given a purposive interpretation and should be widely construed in the light of the objects of the Model Law, but there is nothing to suggest that they apply to the recognition and enforcement of foreign judgments against third parties.'

The Supreme Court held that the Court of Appeal decision in *Rubin* should not be followed because, in its view, it was not an incremental development of existing principles, but a radical departure from substantially settled law. It said that a change in the settled law governing the recognition and enforcement of judgments had all the hallmarks of legislation, and was a matter for legislative decision rather than judicial innovation. The laws relating to the enforcement of foreign judgments and to international insolvency were not areas of law that in recent times had been left to development by judge-made law. It commented that the introduction of new rules for enforcement of judgments typically depended on a degree of reciprocity and that he European Insolvency Regulation as well as the Model Law had been the product of lengthy negotiation and consultation. According to Lord Collins (at para 130):

> 'the introduction of judge-made law extending the recognition and enforcement of foreign judgments would be only to the detriment of United Kingdom businesses without any corresponding benefit . . . a person in England who might have connections with a foreign territory which were only arguably "sufficient" would have to actively defend foreign proceedings which could result in an in personam judgment against him, only because the proceedings are incidental to bankruptcy proceedings in the courts of that territory . . . [I]t might suggest that foreigners who have bona fide dealings with the United States might have to face the dilemma of the expense of defending enormous claims in the United States or not defending them and being at risk of having a default judgment enforced abroad.'

## CHAPTER V   CONCURRENT PROCEEDINGS

### ARTICLE 28

#### COMMENCEMENT OF A PROCEEDING UNDER BRITISH INSOLVENCY LAW AFTER RECOGNITION OF A FOREIGN MAIN PROCEEDING

**[7.41]**

After recognition of a foreign main proceeding, the effects of a proceeding under British insolvency law in relation to the same debtor shall, insofar as the assets of that debtor are concerned, be restricted to assets that are located in Great Britain and, to the extent necessary to implement cooperation and coordination under articles 25, 26 and 27, to other assets of the debtor that, under the law of Great Britain, should be administered in that proceeding.

**General note**—Local proceedings opened up after foreign main proceedings have been recognised are limited to assets in Britain but there is no restriction on the jurisdictional base for opening such proceedings. Effectively, the position under existing law is preserved and this allows a foreign company to be wound up in the UK where there is 'sufficient nexus' with the UK. The concept of nexus covers more than just the presence of assets and also includes the presence of creditors and permits consideration of whether a UK liquidation would be of benefit to UK creditors.

### ARTICLE 29

#### COORDINATION OF A PROCEEDING UNDER BRITISH INSOLVENCY LAW AND A FOREIGN PROCEEDING

**[7.42]**

Where a foreign proceeding and a proceeding under British insolvency law are taking place concurrently regarding the same debtor, the court may seek cooperation and coordination under articles 25, 26 and 27, and the following shall apply—

    (a)    when the proceeding in Great Britain is taking place at the time the application for recognition of the foreign proceeding is filed—

        (i)    any relief granted under article 19 or 21 must be consistent with the proceeding in Great Britain; and

       (ii)    if the foreign proceeding is recognised in Great Britain as a foreign main proceeding, article 20 does not apply;

  (b)    when the proceeding in Great Britain commences after the filing of the application for recognition of the foreign proceeding—

       (i)    any relief in effect under article 19 or 21 shall be reviewed by the court and shall be modified or terminated if inconsistent with the proceeding in Great Britain;

       (ii)    if the foreign proceeding is a foreign main proceeding, the stay and suspension referred to in paragraph 1 of article 20 shall be modified or terminated pursuant to paragraph 6 of article 20, if inconsistent with the proceeding in Great Britain; and

       (iii)    any proceedings brought by the foreign representative by virtue of paragraph 1 of article 23 before the proceeding in Great Britain commenced shall be reviewed by the court and the court may give such directions as it thinks fit regarding the continuance of those proceedings; and

In granting, extending or modifying relief granted to a representative of a foreign non-main proceeding, the court must be satisfied that the relief relates to assets that, under the law of Great Britain, should be administered in the foreign non-main proceeding or concerns information required in that proceeding.

**General note**—This provision deals with the situation where there are both local and foreign insolvency proceedings. It is implicit in the provision though nowhere expressly stated that the existence of local proceedings does not preclude or terminate the recognition of foreign proceedings. The local proceedings have primacy however. Where an application is made for recognition of foreign proceedings after the local proceedings have already commenced, any relief granted in respect of the foreign proceedings must be consistent with the local proceedings. In addition, where the foreign proceedings are main proceedings, the normal consequences attached to recognition of the same (eg the automatic stay on proceedings or executions against the debtor) do not obtain. Everything is within the discretion of the court and must be consistent with the local proceedings. Where the local proceedings come second in point of time, any relief granted in respect of the foreign proceedings whether it was discretionary or automatic, must be reviewed to make sure that it is consistent with the local proceedings.

## ARTICLE 30

### Coordination of more than one Foreign Proceeding

[7.43]

In matters referred to in paragraph 1 of article 1, in respect of more than one foreign proceeding regarding the same debtor, the court may seek cooperation and coordination under articles 25, 26 and 27, and the following shall apply—

  (a)    any relief granted under article 19 or 21 to a representative of a foreign non-main proceeding after recognition of a foreign main proceeding must be consistent with the foreign main proceeding;

  (b)    if a foreign main proceeding is recognised after the filing of an application for recognition of a foreign non-main proceeding, any relief in effect under article 19 or 21 shall be reviewed by the court and shall be modified or terminated if inconsistent with the foreign main proceeding; and

  (c)    if, after recognition of a foreign non-main proceeding, another foreign non-main proceeding is recognised, the court shall grant, modify or terminate relief for the purpose of facilitating coordination of the proceedings.

**General note**—This provision deals with co-ordination of the position where there are two or more foreign insolvency proceedings and could be described as essentially a command to the court to follow the dictates of common sense. For example, relief granted in respect of foreign non-main proceedings must be consistent with foreign main proceedings and where the former comes first, relief granted in respect of the same must be reviewed to ensure consistency with the foreign main proceedings.

## ARTICLE 31

### PRESUMPTION OF INSOLVENCY BASED ON RECOGNITION OF A FOREIGN MAIN PROCEEDING

**[7.44]**

In the absence of evidence to the contrary, recognition of a foreign main proceeding is, for the purpose of commencing a proceeding under British insolvency law, proof that the debtor is unable to pay its debts or, in relation to Scotland, is apparently insolvent within the meaning given to those expressions under British insolvency law.

## ARTICLE 32

### RULE OF PAYMENT IN CONCURRENT PROCEEDINGS

**[7.45]**

Without prejudice to secured claims or rights in rem, a creditor who has received part payment in respect of its claim in a proceeding pursuant to a law relating to insolvency in a foreign State may not receive a payment for the same claim in a proceeding under British insolvency law regarding the same debtor, so long as the payment to the other creditors of the same class is proportionately less than the payment the creditor has already received.

**General note**—This provision reflects a principle known as 'hotchpot' that is generally found in international insolvency law. A creditor is permitted to claim and submit a proof in more than one insolvency proceeding but what it has received in one proceeding must be brought into the reckoning in determining what it should receive in the second proceeding. To give a concrete example if the creditor has received 2x in the first set of insolvency proceedings and is classed as an unsecured creditor in the second insolvency proceedings where there insufficient assets to pay unsecured creditors any more than 1x then the creditor will receive nothing in the second proceedings. If there are sufficient assets to pay creditors in the second proceedings 3x then the creditor will only receive 1x in these proceedings ie 3x minus the 2x that the creditor has already received from the first proceedings. Article 32 is stated however to be without prejudice to secured claims or rights *in rem*. In other words, a creditor who has relied on the value of his security in proceedings, A but is left with an unsecured and unpaid deficiency claim, can submit a proof for the full amount of this claim in proceedings B, and does not have to account in any way for the amount that he or she has received in respect of the security. The exception to hotchpot recognised for security rights reflects the view that the secured creditor has proprietary rights to the extent of its security and that insolvency proceedings should respect property rights so far as possible.

## SCHEDULE 2
### PROCEDURAL MATTERS IN ENGLAND AND WALES

Regulation 4

## PART 1   INTRODUCTORY PROVISIONS

**[7.46]**

**1 Interpretation**

(1)   In this Schedule—

"the 1986 Act" means the Insolvency Act 1986;

"article 21 relief application" means an application to the court by a foreign representative under article 21(1) or (2) of the Model Law for relief;

"business day" means any day other than a Saturday, a Sunday, Christmas Day, Good Friday or a day which is a bank holiday in England and Wales under or by virtue of the Banking and Financial Dealings Act 1971;

"CPR" means the Civil Procedure Rules 1998 and "CPR" followed by a Part or rule by number means the Part or rule with that number in those Rules;

"enforcement officer" means an individual who is authorised to act as an enforcement officer under the Courts Act 2003;

"file in court" and "file with the court" means deliver to the court for filing;
"the Gazette" means the London Gazette;
"interim relief application" means an application to the court by a foreign representative under article 19 of the Model Law for interim relief;
. . .

. . .

"the Model Law" means the UNCITRAL Model Law as set out in Schedule 1 to these Regulations;
"modification or termination order" means an order by the court pursuant to its powers under the Model Law modifying or terminating recognition of a foreign proceeding, the stay and suspension referred to in article 20(1) or any part of it or any relief granted under article 19 or 21 of the Model Law;
"originating application" means an application to the court which is not an application in pending proceedings before the court;
"ordinary application" means any application to the court other than an originating application;
"practice direction" means a direction as to the practice and procedure of any court within the scope of the CPR;
"recognition application" means an application to the court by a foreign representative in accordance with article 15 of the Model Law for an order recognising the foreign proceeding in which he has been appointed;
"recognition order" means an order by the court recognising a proceeding the subject of a recognition application as a foreign main proceeding or foreign non-main proceeding, as appropriate;
"relevant company" means a company that is—

    (a)    registered under the Companies Act 2006,

    (b)    subject to a requirement imposed by regulations under section 1043 of that Act 2006 (unregistered UK companies) to deliver any documents to the registrar of companies, or

    (c)    subject to a requirement imposed by regulations under section 1046 of that Act (overseas companies) to deliver any documents to the registrar of companies;

"review application" means an application to the court for a modification or termination order;
"the Rules" means the Insolvency (England and Wales) Rules 2016 and "Rule" followed by a number means the rule with that number in those Rules;
. . .

. . ..

(2)   Expressions defined in the Model Law have the same meaning when used in this Schedule.

(3)   In proceedings under these Regulations, "Registrar" means—

    (a)    an Insolvency and Companies Court Judge; and

    (b)    where the proceedings are in a district registry, the district judge.

(4)   References to the "venue" for any proceedings or attendance before the court, are to the time, date and place for the proceedings or attendance.

(5)   References in this Schedule to ex parte hearings shall be construed as references to hearings without notice being served on any other party, and references to applications made ex parte as references to applications made without notice being served on any other party; and other references which include the expression "ex parte" shall be similarly construed.

(6)   References in this Schedule to a debtor who is of interest to the Financial Conduct Authority are references to a debtor who—

    (a)    is, or has been, an authorised person within the meaning of the Financial Services and Markets Act 2000;

    (b)    is, or has been, an appointed representative within the meaning of section 39 of the Financial Services and Markets Act 2000; or

(c)   is carrying on, or has carried on, a regulated activity in contravention of the general prohibition.

(6A)  References in this Schedule to a debtor who is of interest to the Prudential Regulation Authority are references to a debtor who—

(a)   is, or has been, a PRA-authorised person within the meaning of the Financial Services and Markets Act 2000; or

(b)   is carrying on, or has carried on, a PRA-regulated activity within the meaning of the Financial Services and Markets Act 2000 in contravention of the general prohibition.

(7)  In sub-paragraphs (6) and (6A) "the general prohibition" has the meaning given by section 19 of the Financial Services and Markets Act 2000 and the reference to a "regulated activity" must be construed in accordance with—

(a)   section 22 of that Act (classes of regulated activity and categories of investment);

(b)   any relevant order under that section; and

(c)   Schedule 2 to that Act (regulated activities).

(8)  References in this Schedule to a numbered form are to the form that bears that number in Schedule 5.

**Amendments**—SI 2009/1941; SI 2013/472; SI 2017/369; SI 2017/702; SI 2017/1115; SI 2017/1119; SI 2018/130, 26 February 2018; SI 2019/146, as from IP completion day (as defined in the European Union (Withdrawal Agreement) Act 2020, s 39(1)–(5)).

## PART 2   APPLICATIONS TO COURT FOR RECOGNITION OF FOREIGN PROCEEDINGS

**[7.47]**

**2  Affidavit in support of recognition application**

A recognition application shall be in Form ML1 and shall be supported by an affidavit sworn by the foreign representative complying with paragraph 4.

**3  Form and content of application**

The application shall state the following matters—

(a)   the name of the applicant and his address for service within England and Wales;

(b)   the name of the debtor in respect of which the foreign proceeding is taking place;

(c)   the name or names in which the debtor carries on business in the country where the foreign proceeding is taking place and in this country, if other than the name given under sub-paragraph (b);

(d)   the principal or last known place of business of the debtor in Great Britain (if any) and, in the case of an individual, his usual or last known place of residence in Great Britain (if any);

(e)   any registered number allocated to the debtor under the Companies Act 2006;

(f)   brief particulars of the foreign proceeding in respect of which recognition is applied for, including the country in which it is taking place and the nature of the proceeding;

(g)   that the foreign proceeding is a proceeding within the meaning of article 2(i) of the Model Law;

(h)   that the applicant is a foreign representative within the meaning of article 2(j) of the Model Law;

(i)   the address of the debtor's centre of main interests and, if different, the address of its registered office or habitual residence, as appropriate; and

(j)   if the debtor does not have its centre of main interests in the country where the foreign proceeding is taking place, whether the debtor has an establishment within the meaning of article 2(e) of the Model Law in that country, and if so, its address.

*Amendments*—SI 2009/1941.

**4 Contents of affidavit in support**

(1)  There shall be attached to the application an affidavit in support which shall contain or have exhibited to it—

    (a)    the evidence and statement required under article 15(2) and (3) respectively of the Model Law;

    (b)    any other evidence which in the opinion of the applicant will assist the court in deciding whether the proceeding the subject of the application is a foreign proceeding within the meaning of article 2(i) of the Model Law and whether the applicant is a foreign representative within the meaning of article 2(j) of the Model Law;

    (c)    evidence that the debtor has its centre of main interests or an establishment, as the case may be, within the country where the foreign proceeding is taking place; and

    (d)    any other matters which in the opinion of the applicant will assist the court in deciding whether to make a recognition order.

(2)  . . .

(3)  The affidavit shall also have exhibited to it the translations required under article 15(4) of the Model Law and a translation in English of any other document exhibited to the affidavit which is in a language other than English.

(4)  All translations referred to in sub-paragraph (3) must be certified by the translator as a correct translation.

*Amendments*—SI 2019/146, as from IP completion day (as defined in the European Union (Withdrawal Agreement) Act 2020, s 39(1)–(5)).

**5 The hearing and powers of court**

(1)  On hearing a recognition application the court may in addition to its powers under the Model Law to make a recognition order—

    (a)    dismiss the application;

    (b)    adjourn the hearing conditionally or unconditionally;

    (c)    make any other order which the court thinks appropriate.

(2)  If the court makes a recognition order, it shall be in Form ML2.

**6 Notification of subsequent information**

(1)  The foreign representative shall set out any subsequent information required to be given to the court under article 18 of the Model Law in a statement which he shall attach to Form ML3 and file with the court.

(2)  The statement shall include—

    (a)    details of the information required to be given under article 18 of the Model Law; . . .

    (b)    . . ..

(3)  The foreign representative shall send a copy of the Form ML3 and attached statement filed with the court to the following—

    (a)    the debtor; and

    (b)    those persons referred to in paragraph 26(3).

*Amendments*—SI 2017/1119; SI 2019/146, as from IP completion day (as defined in the European Union (Withdrawal Agreement) Act 2020, s 39(1)–(5)).

PART 3   APPLICATIONS FOR RELIEF UNDER THE MODEL LAW

**[7.48]**

**7 Application for interim relief—affidavit in support**

(1)  An interim relief application must be supported by an affidavit sworn by the foreign representative stating—

    (a)    the grounds on which it is proposed that the interim relief applied for should be granted;

    (b)    details of any proceeding under British insolvency law taking place in relation to the debtor;

    (c)    whether, to the foreign representative's knowledge, an administrative receiver or receiver or manager of the debtor's property is acting in relation to the debtor;

    (d)    an estimate of the value of the assets of the debtor in England and Wales in respect of which relief is applied for;

    (e)    whether, to the best of the knowledge and belief of the foreign representative, the interests of the debtor's creditors (including any secured creditors or parties to hire-purchase agreements) and any other interested parties, including if appropriate the debtor, will be adequately protected;

    (f)    whether, to the best of the foreign representative's knowledge and belief, the grant of any of the relief applied for would interfere with the administration of a foreign main proceeding; and

    (g)    all other matters that in the opinion of the foreign representative will assist the court in deciding whether or not it is appropriate to grant the relief applied for.

**8 Service of interim relief application not required**
Unless the court otherwise directs, it shall not be necessary to serve the interim relief application on, or give notice of it to, any person.

**9 The hearing and powers of court**
On hearing an interim relief application the court may in addition to its powers under the Model Law to make an order granting interim relief under article 19 of the Model Law—

    (a)    dismiss the application;

    (b)    adjourn the hearing conditionally or unconditionally;

    (c)    make any other order which the court thinks appropriate.

**10 Application for relief under article 21 of the Model Law—affidavit in support**
An article 21 relief application must be supported by an affidavit sworn by the foreign representative stating—

    (a)    the grounds on which it is proposed that the relief applied for should be granted;

    (b)    an estimate of the value of the assets of the debtor in England and Wales in respect of which relief is applied for;

    (c)    in the case of an application by a foreign representative who is or believes that he is a representative of a foreign non-main proceeding, the reasons why the applicant believes that the relief relates to assets that, under the law of Great Britain, should be administered in the foreign non-main proceeding or concerns information required in that proceeding;

    (d)    whether, to the best of the knowledge and belief of the foreign representative, the interests of the debtor's creditors (including any secured creditors or parties to hire-purchase agreements) and any other interested parties, including if appropriate the debtor, will be adequately protected; and

    (e)    all other matters that in the opinion of the foreign representative will assist the court in deciding whether or not it is appropriate to grant the relief applied for.

**11 The hearing and powers of court**
On hearing an article 21 relief application the court may in addition to its powers under the Model Law to make an order granting relief under article 21 of the Model Law—

    (a)    dismiss the application;

    (b)    adjourn the hearing conditionally or unconditionally;

    (c)    make any other order which the court thinks appropriate.

PART 4   REPLACEMENT OF FOREIGN REPRESENTATIVE

[7.49]

**12   Application for confirmation of status of replacement foreign representative**
(1)   This paragraph applies where following the making of a recognition order the foreign representative dies or for any other reason ceases to be the foreign representative in the foreign proceeding in relation to the debtor.
(2)   In this paragraph "the former foreign representative" shall mean the foreign representative referred to in sub-paragraph (1).
(3)   If a person has succeeded the former foreign representative or is otherwise holding office as foreign representative in the foreign proceeding in relation to the debtor, that person may apply to the court for an order confirming his status as replacement foreign representative for the purpose of proceedings under these Regulations.

**13   Contents of application and affidavit in support**
(1)   An application under paragraph 12(3) shall in addition to the matters required to be stated by paragraph 19(2) state the following matters—
    (a)   the name of the replacement foreign representative and his address for service within England and Wales;
    (b)   details of the circumstances in which the former foreign representative ceased to be foreign representative in the foreign proceeding in relation to the debtor (including the date on which he ceased to be the foreign representative);
    (c)   details of his own appointment as replacement foreign representative in the foreign proceeding (including the date of that appointment).
(2)   The application shall be accompanied by an affidavit in support sworn by the applicant which shall contain or have attached to it—
    (a)   a certificate from the foreign court affirming—
        (i)   the cessation of the appointment of the former foreign representative as foreign representative; and
        (ii)   the appointment of the applicant as the foreign representative in the foreign proceeding; or
    (b)   in the absence of such a certificate, any other evidence acceptable to the court of the matters referred to in paragraph (a); and
    (c)   a translation in English of any document exhibited to the affidavit which is in a language other than English.
(3)   All translations referred to in paragraph (c) must be certified by the translator as a correct translation.

**14   The hearing and powers of court**
(1)   On hearing an application under paragraph 12(3) the court may—
    (a)   make an order confirming the status of the replacement foreign representative as foreign representative for the purpose of proceedings under these Regulations;
    (b)   dismiss the application;
    (c)   adjourn the hearing conditionally or unconditionally;
    (d)   make an interim order;
    (e)   make any other order which the court thinks appropriate, including in particular an order making such provision as the court thinks fit with respect to matters arising in connection with the replacement of the foreign representative.
(2)   If the court dismisses the application, it may also if it thinks fit make an order terminating recognition of the foreign proceeding and—
    (a)   such an order may include such provision as the court thinks fit with respect to matters arising in connection with the termination; and
    (b)   paragraph 15 shall not apply to such an order.

PART 5   REVIEWS OF COURT ORDERS

**[7.50]**

**15 Reviews of court orders—where court makes order of its own motion**

(1)   The court shall not of its own motion make a modification or termination order unless the foreign representative and the debtor have either—

(a)   had an opportunity of being heard on the question; or

(b)   consented in writing to such an order.

(2)   Where the foreign representative or the debtor desires to be heard on the question of such an order, the court shall give all relevant parties notice of a venue at which the question will be considered and may give directions as to the issues on which it requires evidence.

(3)   For the purposes of sub-paragraph (2), all relevant parties means the foreign representative, the debtor and any other person who appears to the court to have an interest justifying his being given notice of the hearing.

(4)   If the court makes a modification or termination order, the order may include such provision as the court thinks fit with respect to matters arising in connection with the modification or termination.

**16 Review application—affidavit in support**

A review application must be supported by an affidavit sworn by the applicant stating—

(a)   the grounds on which it is proposed that the relief applied for should be granted;

(b)   whether, to the best of the knowledge and belief of the applicant, the interests of the debtor's creditors (including any secured creditors or parties to hire-purchase agreements) and any other interested parties, including if appropriate the debtor, will be adequately protected; and

(c)   all other matters that in the opinion of the applicant will assist the court in deciding whether or not it is appropriate to grant the relief applied for.

**17 Hearing of review application and powers of the court**

On hearing a review application, the court may in addition to its powers under the Model Law to make a modification or termination order—

(a)   dismiss the application;

(b)   adjourn the hearing conditionally or unconditionally;

(c)   make an interim order;

(d)   make any other order which the court thinks appropriate, including an order making such provision as the court thinks fit with respect to matters arising in connection with the modification or termination.

PART 6   COURT PROCEDURE AND PRACTICE WITH REGARD TO PRINCI-
PAL APPLICATIONS AND ORDERS

**[7.51]**

**18 Preliminary and interpretation**

(1)   This Part applies to—

(a)   any of the following applications made to the court under these Regulations—

(i)   a recognition application;

(ii)   an article 21 relief application;

(iii)   an application under paragraph 12(3) for an order confirming the status of a replacement foreign representative;

(iv)   a review application; and

(b)   any of the following orders made by the court under these Regulations—

(i)   a recognition order;

(ii)   an order granting interim relief under article 19 of the Model Law;

     (iii)    an order granting relief under article 21 of the Model Law;

     (iv)    an order confirming the status of a replacement foreign representative; and

     (v)    a modification or termination order.

### 19 Form and contents of application

(1)   Subject to sub-paragraph (4) every application to which this Part applies shall be an ordinary application and shall be in Form ML5.

     (2)    Each application shall be in writing and shall state—

     (a)    the names of the parties;

     (b)    the nature of the relief or order applied for or the directions sought from the court;

     (c)    the names and addresses of the persons (if any) on whom it is intended to serve the application;

     (d)    the names and addresses of all those persons on whom these Regulations require the application to be served (so far as known to the applicant); and

     (e)    the applicant's address for service.

(3)   The application must be signed by the applicant if he is acting in person, or, when he is not so acting, by or on behalf of his solicitor.

(4)   This paragraph does not apply to a recognition application.

### 20 Filing of application

(1)   The application (and all supporting documents) shall be filed with the court, with a sufficient number of copies for service and use as provided by paragraph 21(2).

(2)   Each of the copies filed shall have applied to it the seal of the court and be issued to the applicant; and on each copy there shall be endorsed the date and time of filing.

(3)   The court shall fix a venue for the hearing of the application and this also shall be endorsed on each copy of the application issued under sub-paragraph (2).

### 21 Service of the application

(1)   In sub-paragraph (2), references to the application are to a sealed copy of the application issued by the court together with any affidavit in support of it and any documents exhibited to the affidavit.

(2)   Unless the court otherwise directs, the application shall be served on the following persons, unless they are the applicant—

     (a)    on the foreign representative;

     (b)    on the debtor;

     (c)    if a British insolvency officeholder is acting in relation to the debtor, on him;

     (d)    if any person has been appointed an administrative receiver of the debtor or, to the knowledge of the foreign representative, as a receiver or manager of the property of the debtor in England and Wales, on him;

     (e)    *if a member State liquidator has been appointed in main proceedings in relation to the debtor, on him;*

     (f)    if to the knowledge of the foreign representative a foreign representative has been appointed in any other foreign proceeding regarding the debtor, on him;

     (g)    if there is pending in England and Wales a petition for the winding up or bankruptcy of the debtor, on the petitioner;

     (h)    on any person who to the knowledge of the foreign representative is or may be entitled to appoint an administrator of the debtor under paragraph 14 of Schedule B1 to the 1986 Act (appointment of administrator by holder of qualifying floating charge); . . .

     (i)    if the debtor is a debtor who is of interest to the Financial Conduct Authority, on that Authority; and

     (j)    if the debtor is a debtor who is of interest to the Prudential Regulation Authority, on that Authority.

Amendments—SI 2013/472; SI 2019/146, as from IP completion day (as defined in the European Union (Withdrawal Agreement) Act 2020, s 39(1)–(5)).

**22 Manner in which service to be effected**

(1)   Service of the application in accordance with paragraph 21(2) shall be effected by the applicant, or his solicitor, or by a person instructed by him or his solicitor, not less than 5 business days before the date fixed for the hearing.

(2)   Service shall be effected by delivering the documents to a person's proper address or in such other manner as the court may direct.

(3)   A person's proper address is any which he has previously notified as his address for service within England and Wales; but if he has not notified any such address or if for any reason service at such address is not practicable, service may be effected as follows—

> (a)   (subject to sub-paragraph (4)) in the case of a company incorporated in England and Wales, by delivery to its registered office;
>
> (b)   in the case of any other person, by delivery to his usual or last known address or principal place of business in Great Britain.

(4)   If delivery to a company's registered office is not practicable, service may be effected by delivery to its last known principal place of business in Great Britain.

(5)   Delivery of documents to any place or address may be made by leaving them there or sending them by first class post in accordance with the provisions of paragraphs 70 and 75(1).

**23 Proof of service**

(1)   Service of the application shall be verified by an affidavit of service in Form ML6, specifying the date on which, and the manner in which, service was effected.

(2)   The affidavit of service, with a sealed copy of the application exhibited to it, shall be filed with the court as soon as reasonably practicable after service, and in any event not less than 1 business day before the hearing of the application.

**24 In case of urgency**

Where the case is one of urgency, the court may (without prejudice to its general power to extend or abridge time limits)—

> (a)   hear the application immediately, either with or without notice to, or the attendance of, other parties; or
>
> (b)   authorise a shorter period of service than that provided for by paragraph 22(1),

and any such application may be heard on terms providing for the filing or service of documents, or the carrying out of other formalities, as the court thinks fit.

**25 The hearing**

(1)   At the hearing of the application, the applicant and any of the following persons (not being the applicant) may appear or be represented—

> (a)   the foreign representative;
>
> (b)   the debtor and, in the case of any debtor other than an individual, any one or more directors or other officers of the debtor, including—
>
>> [(i)   where applicable, any person specified in particulars registered under section 1046 of the Companies Act 2006 (overseas companies) as authorised to represent the debtor;]
>>
>> (ii)   in the case of a debtor which is a partnership, any person who is an officer of the partnership within the meaning of article 2 of the Insolvent Partnerships Order 1994;
>
> (c)   if a British insolvency officeholder is acting in relation to the debtor, that person;
>
> (d)   if any person has been appointed an administrative receiver of the debtor or as a receiver or manager of the property of the debtor in England and Wales, that person;
>
> (e)   *if a member State liquidator has been appointed in main proceedings in relation to the debtor, that person;*
>
> (f)   if a foreign representative has been appointed in any other foreign proceeding regarding the debtor, that person;

(g)    any person who has presented a petition for the winding up or bankruptcy of the debtor in England and Wales;

(h)    any person who is or may be entitled to appoint an administrator of the debtor under paragraph 14 of Schedule B1 to the 1986 Act (appointment of administrator by holder of qualifying floating charge);

[(i)    if the debtor is a debtor who is of interest to the Financial Conduct Authority, that Authority;

(ia)    if the debtor is a debtor who is of interest to the Prudential Regulation Authority, that Authority; and]

(j)    with the permission of the court, any other person who appears to have an interest justifying his appearance.

**Amendments**—SI 2009/1941; SI 2013/472; SI 2019/146, as from IP completion day (as defined in the European Union (Withdrawal Agreement) Act 2020, s 39(1)–(5)).

## 26 Notification and advertisement of order

(1)   If the court makes any of the orders referred to in paragraph 18(1)(b), it shall as soon as reasonably practicable send two sealed copies of the order to the foreign representative.

(2)   The foreign representative shall send a sealed copy of the order as soon as reasonably practicable to the debtor.

(3)   The foreign representative shall, as soon as reasonably practicable after the date of the order give notice of the making of the order—

(a)    if a British insolvency officeholder is acting in relation to the debtor, to him;

(b)    if any person has been appointed an administrative receiver of the debtor or, to the knowledge of the foreign representative, as a receiver or manager of the property of the debtor, to him;

(c)    *if a member State liquidator has been appointed in main proceedings in relation to the debtor, to him;*

(d)    if to his knowledge a foreign representative has been appointed in any other foreign proceeding regarding the debtor, that person;

(e)    if there is pending in England and Wales a petition for the winding up or bankruptcy of the debtor, to the petitioner;

(f)    to any person who to his knowledge is or may be entitled to appoint an administrator of the debtor under paragraph 14 of Schedule B1 to the 1986 Act (appointment of administrator by holder of qualifying floating charge);

(g)    if the debtor is a debtor who is of interest to the Financial Conduct Authority, to that Authority;

(ga)    if the debtor is a debtor who is of interest to the Prudential Regulation Authority, to that Authority;

(h)    to such other persons as the court may direct.

(4)   In the case of an order recognising a foreign proceeding in relation to the debtor as a foreign main proceeding, or an order under article 19 or 21 of the Model Law staying execution, distress or other legal process against the debtor's assets, the foreign representative shall also, as soon as reasonably practicable after the date of the order give notice of the making of the order—

(a)    to any enforcement officer or other officer who to his knowledge is charged with an execution or other legal process against the debtor or its property; and

(b)    to any person who to his knowledge is distraining against the debtor or its property.

(5)   In the application of sub-paragraphs (3) and (4) the references to property shall be taken as references to property situated within England and Wales.

(6)   Where the debtor is a relevant company, the foreign representative shall send notice of the making of the order to the registrar of companies before the end of the period of 5 business days beginning with the date of the order. The notice to the registrar of companies shall be in Form ML7.

(7)   The foreign representative shall advertise the making of the following orders once in the Gazette and once in such newspaper as he thinks most appropriate for ensuring that the making of the order comes to the notice of the debtor's creditors—

(a)   a recognition order;

(b)   an order confirming the status of a replacement foreign representative; and

(c)   a modification or termination order which modifies or terminates recognition of a foreign proceeding,

and the advertisement shall be in Form ML8.

**Amendments**—SI 2013/472; SI 2019/146, as from IP completion day (as defined in the European Union (Withdrawal Agreement) Act 2020, s 39(1)–(5)).

**27   Adjournment of hearing; directions**

(1)   This paragraph applies in any case where the court exercises its power to adjourn the hearing of the application.

(2)   The court may at any time give such directions as it thinks fit as to—

(a)   service or notice of the application on or to any person, whether in connection with the venue of a resumed hearing or for any other purpose;

(b)   the procedure on the application;

(c)   the manner in which any evidence is to be adduced at a resumed hearing and in particular as to—

(i)   the taking of evidence wholly or in part by affidavit or orally;

(ii)   the cross-examination on the hearing in court or in chambers, of any deponents to affidavits;

(d)   the matters to be dealt with in evidence.

PART 7   APPLICATIONS TO THE CHIEF LAND REGISTRAR

**[7.52]**

**28  Applications to Chief Land Registrar following court orders**

(1)   Where the court makes any order in proceedings under these Regulations which is capable of giving rise to an application or applications under the Land Registration Act 2002, the foreign representative shall, as soon as reasonably practicable after the making of the order or at the appropriate time, make the appropriate application or applications to the Chief Land Registrar.

(2)   In sub-paragraph (1) an appropriate application is—

(a)   in any case where—

(i)   a recognition order in respect of a foreign main proceeding or an order suspending the right to transfer, encumber or otherwise dispose of any assets of the debtor is made, and

(ii)   the debtor is the registered proprietor of a registered estate or registered charge and holds it for his sole benefit,

an application under section 43 of the Land Registration Act 2002 for a restriction of the kind referred to in sub-paragraph (3) to be entered in the relevant registered title; and

(b)   in any other case, an application under the Land Registration Act 2002 for such an entry in the register as shall be necessary to reflect the effect of the court order under these Regulations.

(3)   The restriction referred to in sub-paragraph (2)(a) is a restriction to the effect that no disposition of the registered estate or registered charge (as appropriate) by the registered proprietor of that estate or charge is to be completed by registration within the meaning of section 27 of the Land Registration Act 2002 except under a further order of the court.

## PART 8   MISFEASANCE

**[7.53]**

### 29 Misfeasance by foreign representative

(1)   The court may examine the conduct of a person who—

(a)   is or purports to be the foreign representative in relation to a debtor; or

(b)   has been or has purported to be the foreign representative in relation to a debtor.

(2)   An examination under this paragraph may be held only on the application of—

(a)   a British insolvency officeholder acting in relation to the debtor;

(b)   a creditor of the debtor; or

(c)   with the permission of the court, any other person who appears to have an interest justifying an application.

(3)   An application under sub-paragraph (2) must allege that the foreign representative—

(a)   has misapplied or retained money or other property of the debtor;

(b)   has become accountable for money or other property of the debtor;

(c)   has breached a fiduciary or other duty in relation to the debtor; or

(d)   has been guilty of misfeasance.

(4)   On an examination under this paragraph into a person's conduct the court may order him—

(a)   to repay, restore or account for money or property;

(b)   to pay interest;

(c)   to contribute a sum to the debtor's property by way of compensation for breach of duty or misfeasance.

(4)   In sub-paragraph (3) "foreign representative" includes a person who purports or has purported to be a foreign representative in relation to a debtor.

## PART 9   GENERAL PROVISION AS TO COURT PROCEDURE AND PRACTICE

**[7.54]**

### 30 Principal court rules and practice to apply with modifications

(1)   The CPR and the practice and procedure of the High Court (including any practice direction) shall apply to proceedings under these Regulations in the High Court with such modifications as may be necessary for the purpose of giving effect to the provisions of these Regulations and in the case of any conflict between any provision of the CPR and the provisions of these Regulations, the latter shall prevail.

(2)   All proceedings under these Regulations shall be allocated to the multi-track for which CPR Part 29 (the multi-track) makes provision, and accordingly those provisions of the CPR which provide for allocation questionnaires and track allocation shall not apply.

### 31 Applications other than the principal applications—preliminary

Paragraphs 32 to 37 of this Part apply to any application made to the court under these Regulations, except any of the applications referred to in paragraph 18(1)(a).

### 32 Form and contents of application

(1)   Every application shall be in the form appropriate to the application concerned. Forms ML4 and ML5 shall be used for an originating application and an ordinary application respectively under these Regulations.

(2)   Each application shall be in writing and shall state—

(a)   the names of the parties;

(b)   the nature of the relief or order applied for or the directions sought from the court;

(c)   the names and addresses of the persons (if any) on whom it is intended to serve the application or that no person is intended to be served;

    (d)     where these Regulations require that notice of the application is to be given to specified persons, the names and addresses of all those persons (so far as known to the applicant); and

    (e)     the applicant's address for service.

(3)   An originating application shall set out the grounds on which the applicant claims to be entitled to the relief or order sought.

(4)   The application must be signed by the applicant if he is acting in person or, when he is not so acting, by or on behalf of his solicitor.

### 33 Filing and service of application

(1)   The application shall be filed in court, accompanied by one copy and a number of additional copies equal to the number of persons who are to be served with the application.

(2)   Subject as follows in this paragraph and in paragraph 34, or unless the court otherwise orders, upon the presentation of the documents mentioned in sub-paragraph (1), the court shall fix a venue for the application to be heard.

(3)   Unless the court otherwise directs, the applicant shall serve a sealed copy of the application, endorsed with the venue of the hearing, on the respondent named in the application (or on each respondent if more than one).

(4)   The court may give any of the following directions—

    (a)     that the application be served upon persons other than those specified by the relevant provision of these Regulations;

    (b)     that the giving of notice to any person may be dispensed with;

    (c)     that notice be given in some way other than that specified in sub-paragraph (3).

(5)   Subject to sub-paragraph (6), the application must be served at least 10 business days before the date fixed for the hearing.

(6)   Where the case is one of urgency, the court may (without prejudice to its general power to extend or abridge time limits)—

    (a)     hear the application immediately, either with or without notice to, or the attendance of, other parties; or

    (b)     authorise a shorter period of service than that provided for by sub-paragraph (5);

and any such application may be heard on terms providing for the filing or service of documents, or the carrying out of other formalities, as the court thinks fit.

### 34 Other hearings ex parte

(1)   Where the relevant provisions of these Regulations do not require service of the application on, or notice of it to be given to, any person, the court may hear the application ex parte.

(2)   Where the application is properly made ex parte, the court may hear it forthwith, without fixing a venue as required by paragraph 33(2).

(3)   Alternatively, the court may fix a venue for the application to be heard, in which case paragraph 33 applies (so far as relevant).

### 35 Use of affidavit evidence

(1)   In any proceedings evidence may be given by affidavit unless the court otherwise directs; but the court may, on the application of any party, order the attendance for cross-examination of the person making the affidavit.

(2)   Where, after such an order has been made, the person in question does not attend, his affidavit shall not be used in evidence without the permission of the court.

### 36 Filing and service of affidavits

(1)   Unless the court otherwise allows—

    (a)     if the applicant intends to rely at the first hearing on affidavit evidence, he shall file the affidavit or affidavits (if more than one) in court and serve a copy or copies on the respondent, not less than 10 business days before the date fixed for the hearing; and

    (b)     where a respondent to an application intends to oppose it and to rely for that purpose on affidavit evidence, he shall file the affidavit or affidavits (if more than one) in court and serve a copy or copies on the applicant, not less than 5 business days before the date fixed for the hearing.

(2)   Any affidavit may be sworn by the applicant or by the respondent or by some other person possessing direct knowledge of the subject matter of the application.

### 37  Adjournment of hearings; directions

The court may adjourn the hearing of an application on such terms (if any) as it thinks fit and in the case of such an adjournment paragraph 27(2) shall apply.

### 38  Transfer of proceedings within the High Court

(1)   The High Court may, having regard to the criteria in CPR rule 30.3(2), order proceedings in the Royal Courts of Justice or a district registry, or any part of such proceedings (such as an application made in the proceedings), to be transferred—

(a)    from the Royal Courts of Justice to a district registry; or

(b)    from a district registry to the Royal Courts of Justice or to another district registry.

(2)   The High Court may order proceedings before a district registry for the detailed assessment of costs to be transferred to another district registry if it is satisfied that the proceedings could be more conveniently or fairly taken in that other district registry.

(3)   An application for an order under sub-paragraph (1) or (2) must, if the claim is proceeding in a district registry, be made to that registry.

(4)   A transfer of proceedings under this paragraph may be ordered—

(a)    by the court of its own motion; or

(b)    on the application of a person appearing to the court to have an interest in the proceedings.

(5)   Where the court orders proceedings to be transferred, the court from which they are to be transferred must give notice of the transfer to all the parties.

(6)   An order made before the transfer of the proceedings shall not be affected by the order to transfer.

### 39  Transfer of proceedings—actions to avoid acts detrimental to creditors

(1)   If—

(a)    in accordance with article 23(6) of the Model Law, the court grants a foreign representative permission to make an application in accordance with paragraph 1 of that article; and

(b)    the relevant proceedings under British insolvency law taking place regarding the debtor are taking place in the county court,

the court may also order those proceedings to be transferred to the High Court.

(2)   Where the court makes an order transferring proceedings under sub-paragraph (1)—

(a)    it shall send sealed copies of the order to the county court from which the proceedings are to be transferred, and to the official receivers attached to that court and the High Court respectively; and

(b)    the county court shall send the file of the proceedings to the High Court.

(3)   Following compliance with this paragraph, if the official receiver attached to the court to which the proceedings are transferred is not already, by virtue of directions given by the Secretary of State under section 399(6)(a) of the 1986 Act, the official receiver in relation to those proceedings, he becomes, in relation to those proceedings, the official receiver in place of the official receiver attached to the other court concerned.

### 40  Shorthand writers

(1)   The judge may in writing nominate one or more persons to be official shorthand writers to the court.

(2)   The court may, at any time in the course of proceedings under these Regulations, appoint a shorthand writer to take down the evidence of a person examined in pursuance of a court order under article 19 or 21 of the Model Law.

(3)   The remuneration of a shorthand writer appointed in proceedings under these Regulations shall be paid by the party at whose instance the appointment was made or otherwise as the court may direct.

(4) Any question arising as to the rates of remuneration payable under this paragraph shall be determined by the court in its discretion.

**41 Enforcement procedures**

In any proceedings under these Regulations, orders of the court may be enforced in the same manner as a judgment to the same effect.

**42 Title of proceedings**

(1) Every proceeding under these Regulations shall, with any necessary additions, be intituled "IN THE MATTER OF . . . (naming the debtor to which the proceedings relate) AND IN THE MATTER OF THE CROSS-BORDER INSOLVENCY REGULATIONS 2006".

(2) Sub-paragraph (1) shall not apply in respect of any form prescribed under these Regulations.

**43 Court records**

The court shall keep records of all proceedings under these Regulations, and shall cause to be entered in the records the taking of any step in the proceedings, and such decisions of the court in relation thereto, as the court thinks fit.

**44 Inspection of records**

(1) Subject as follows, the court's records of proceedings under these Regulations shall be open to inspection by any person.

(2) If in the case of a person applying to inspect the records the Registrar is not satisfied as to the propriety of the purpose for which inspection is required, he may refuse to allow it. That person may then apply forthwith and ex parte to the judge, who may refuse the inspection or allow it on such terms as he thinks fit.

(3) The decision of the judge under sub-paragraph (2) is final.

**45 File of court proceedings**

(1) In respect of all proceedings under these Regulations, the court shall open and maintain a file for each case; and (subject to directions of the Registrar) all documents relating to such proceedings shall be placed on the relevant file.

(2) No proceedings under these Regulations shall be filed in the Central Office of the High Court.

**46 Right to inspect the file**

(1) In the case of any proceedings under these Regulations, the following have the right, at all reasonable times, to inspect the court's file of the proceedings—

    (a)    the Secretary of State;

    (b)    the person who is the foreign representative in relation to the proceedings;

    (c)    if a foreign representative has been appointed in any other foreign proceeding regarding the debtor to which the proceedings under these Regulations relate, that person;

    (d)    if a British insolvency officeholder is acting in relation to the debtor to which the proceedings under these Regulations relate, that person;

    (e)    any person stating himself in writing to be a creditor of the debtor to which the proceedings under these Regulations relate;

    (f)    . . .

    (g)    the debtor to which the proceedings under these Regulations relate, or, if that debtor is a company, corporation or partnership, every person who is, or at any time has been—

        (i)    a director or officer of the debtor;

        (ii)    a member of the debtor; or

        [(iii)    where applicable, any person specified in particulars registered under section 1046 of the Companies Act 2006 (overseas companies) as authorised to represent the debtor].

(2) The right of inspection conferred as above on any person may be exercised on his behalf by a person properly authorised by him.

(3) Any person may, by leave of the court, inspect the file.

(4)   The right of inspection conferred by this paragraph is not exercisable in the case of documents, or parts of documents, as to which the court directs (either generally or specially) that they are not to be made open to inspection without the court's permission.

An application for a direction of the court under this sub-paragraph may be made by the foreign representative or by any party appearing to the court to have an interest.

(5)   If, for the purpose of powers conferred by the 1986 Act or the Rules, the Secretary of State or the official receiver wishes to inspect the file of any proceedings under these Regulations, and requests the transmission of the file, the court shall comply with such request (unless the file is for the time being in use for the court's purposes).

(6)   Paragraph 44(2) and (3) apply in respect of the court's file of any proceedings under these Regulations as they apply in respect of court records.

(7)   Where these Regulations confer a right for any person to inspect documents on the court's file of proceedings, the right includes that of taking copies of those documents on payment of the fee chargeable under any order made under section 92 of the Courts Act 2003.

**Amendments**—SI 2009/1941; SI 2019/146, as from IP completion day (as defined in the European Union (Withdrawal Agreement) Act 2020, s 39(1)–(5)).

### 47  Copies of court orders

(1)   In any proceedings under these Regulations, any person who under paragraph 46 has a right to inspect documents on the court file also has the right to require the foreign representative in relation to those proceedings to furnish him with a copy of any court order in the proceedings.

(2)   Sub-paragraph (1) does not apply if a copy of the court order has been served on that person or notice of the making of the order has been given to that person under other provisions of these Regulations.

### 48  Filing of Gazette notices and advertisements

(1)   In any court in which proceedings under these Regulations are pending, an officer of the court shall file a copy of every issue of the Gazette which contains an advertisement relating to those proceedings.

(2)   Where there appears in a newspaper an advertisement relating to proceedings under these Regulations pending in any court, the person inserting the advertisement shall file a copy of it in that court.

The copy of the advertisement shall be accompanied by, or have endorsed on it, such particulars as are necessary to identify the proceedings and the date of the advertisement's appearance.

(3)   An officer of any court in which proceedings under these Regulations are pending shall from time to time file a memorandum giving the dates of, and other particulars relating to, any notice published in the Gazette, and any newspaper advertisements, which relate to proceedings so pending.

The officer's memorandum is prima facie evidence that any notice or advertisement mentioned in it was duly inserted in the issue of the newspaper or the Gazette which is specified in the memorandum.

### 49  Persons incapable of managing their affairs—introductory

(1)   Paragraphs 50 to 52 apply where in proceedings under these Regulations it appears to the court that a person affected by the proceedings is one who is incapable of managing and administering his property and affairs either—

   (a)   by reason of mental disorder within the meaning of the Mental Health Act 1983; or

   (b)   due to physical affliction or disability.

(2)   The person concerned is referred to as "the incapacitated person".

### 50  Appointment of another person to act

(1)   The court may appoint such person as it thinks fit to appear for, represent or act for the incapacitated person.

(2) The appointment may be made either generally or for the purpose of any particular application or proceeding, or for the exercise of particular rights or powers which the incapacitated person might have exercised but for his incapacity.

(3) The court may make the appointment either of its own motion or on application by—

(a) a person who has been appointed by a court in the United Kingdom or elsewhere to manage the affairs of, or to represent, the incapacitated person; or

(b) any relative or friend of the incapacitated person who appears to the court to be a proper person to make the application; or

(c) in any case where the incapacitated person is the debtor, the foreign representative.

(4) Application under sub-paragraph (3) may be made ex parte; but the court may require such notice of the application as it thinks necessary to be given to the person alleged to be incapacitated, or any other person, and may adjourn the hearing of the application to enable the notice to be given.

### 51 Affidavit in support of application

An application under paragraph 50(3) shall be supported by an affidavit of a registered medical practitioner as to the mental or physical condition of the incapacitated person.

### 52 Service of notices following appointment

Any notice served on, or sent to, a person appointed under paragraph 50 has the same effect as if it had been served on, or given to, the incapacitated person.

### 53 Rights of audience

Rights of audience in proceedings under these Regulations are the same as obtain in proceedings under British insolvency law.

### 54 Right of attendance

(1) Subject as follows, in proceedings under these Regulations, any person stating himself in writing, in records kept by the court for that purpose, to be a creditor of the debtor to which the proceedings relate, is entitled at his own cost, to attend in court or in chambers at any stage of the proceedings.

(2) Attendance may be by the person himself, or his solicitor.

(3) A person so entitled may request the court in writing to give him notice of any step in the proceedings; and, subject to his paying the costs involved and keeping the court informed as to his address, the court shall comply with the request.

(4) If the court is satisfied that the exercise by a person of his rights under this paragraph has given rise to costs for the estate of the debtor which would not otherwise have been incurred and ought not, in the circumstances, to fall on that estate, it may direct that the costs be paid by the person concerned, to an amount specified.

The rights of that person under this paragraph shall be in abeyance so long as those costs are not paid.

(5) The court may appoint one or more persons to represent the creditors of the debtor to have the rights conferred by this paragraph, instead of the rights being exercised by any or all of them individually.

If two or more persons are appointed under this paragraph to represent the same interest, they must (if at all) instruct the same solicitor.

### 55 Right of attendance for member State liquidator

For the purposes of paragraph 54(1), a member State liquidator appointed in relation to a debtor subject to proceedings under these Regulations shall be deemed to be a creditor.

### 56 British insolvency officeholder's solicitor

Where in any proceedings the attendance of the British insolvency officeholder's solicitor is required, whether in court or in chambers, the British insolvency officeholder himself need not attend, unless directed by the court.

### 57 Formal defects

No proceedings under these Regulations shall be invalidated by any formal defect or by any irregularity, unless the court before which objection is made considers that substantial injustice has been caused by the defect or irregularity, and that the injustice cannot be remedied by any order of the court.

### 58 Restriction on concurrent proceedings and remedies

Where in proceedings under these Regulations the court makes an order staying any action, execution or other legal process against the property of a debtor, service of the order may be effected by sending a sealed copy of the order to whatever is the address for service of the claimant or other party having the carriage of the proceedings to be stayed.

### 59 Affidavits

(1)   Where in proceedings under these Regulations, an affidavit is made by any British insolvency officeholder acting in relation to the debtor, he shall state the capacity in which he makes it, the position which he holds and the address at which he works.

(2)   Any officer of the court duly authorised in that behalf, may take affidavits and declarations.

(3)   Subject to sub-paragraph (4), where these Regulations provide for the use of an affidavit, a witness statement verified by a statement of truth may be used as an alternative.

(4)   Sub-paragraph (3) does not apply to paragraphs 4 (affidavit in support of recognition application), 7 (affidavit in support of interim relief application), 10 (affidavit in support of article 21 relief application), 13 (affidavit in support of application regarding status of replacement foreign representative) and 16 (affidavit in support of review application).

### 60 Security in court

(1)   Where security has to be given to the court (otherwise than in relation to costs), it may be given by guarantee, bond or the payment of money into court.

(2)   A person proposing to give a bond as security shall give notice to the party in whose favour the security is required, and to the court, naming those who are to be sureties to the bond.

(3)   The court shall forthwith give notice to the parties concerned of a venue for the execution of the bond and the making of any objection to the sureties.

(4)   The sureties shall make an affidavit of their sufficiency (unless dispensed with by the party in whose favour the security is required) and shall, if required by the court, attend the court to be cross-examined.

### 61 Further information and disclosure

(1)   Any party to proceedings under these Regulations may apply to the court for an order—

  (a)     that any other party—
      (i)      clarify any matter which is in dispute in the proceedings; or
      (ii)     give additional information in relation to any such matter,

in accordance with CPR Part 18 (further information); or

  (b)     to obtain disclosure from any other party in accordance with CPR Part 31 (disclosure and inspection of documents).

(2)   An application under this paragraph may be made without notice being served on any other party.

### 62 Office copies of documents

(1)   Any person who has under these Regulations the right to inspect the court file of proceedings may require the court to provide him with an office copy of any document from the file.

(2)   A person's right under this paragraph may be exercised on his behalf by his solicitor.

(3)   An office copy provided by the court under this paragraph shall be in such form as the Registrar thinks appropriate, and shall bear the court's seal.

### 63 "The court"

(1)   Anything to be done in proceedings under these Regulations by, to or before the court may be done by, to or before a judge of the High Court or a Registrar.

(2)   Where these Regulations require or permit the court to perform an act of a formal or administrative character, that act may be performed by a court officer.

## PART 10   COSTS AND DETAILED ASSESSMENT

**[7.55]**

**64  Requirement to assess costs by the detailed procedure**
In any proceedings before the court, the court may order costs to be decided by detailed assessment.

**65  Costs of officers charged with execution of writs or other process**
(1)   Where by virtue of article 20 of the Model Law or a court order under article 19 or 21 of the Model Law an enforcement officer, or other officer, charged with execution of the writ or other process—

(a)   is required to deliver up goods or money; or

(b)   has deducted costs from the proceeds of an execution or money paid to him,

the foreign representative may require in writing that the amount of the enforcement officer's or other officer's bill of costs be decided by detailed assessment.
(2)   Where such a requirement is made, if the enforcement officer or other officer does not commence detailed assessment proceedings within 3 months of the requirement under sub-paragraph (1), or within such further time as the court, on application, may permit, any claim by the enforcement officer or other officer in respect of his costs is forfeited by such failure to commence proceedings.
(3)   Where, in the case of a deduction of costs by the enforcement officer or other officer, any amount deducted is disallowed at the conclusion of the detailed assessment proceedings, the enforcement officer or other officer shall forthwith pay a sum equal to that disallowed to the foreign representative for the benefit of the debtor.

**66  Final costs certificate**
(1)   A final costs certificate of the costs officer is final and conclusive as to all matters which have not been objected to in the manner provided for under the rules of the court.
(2)   Where it is proved to the satisfaction of a costs officer that a final costs certificate has been lost or destroyed, he may issue a duplicate.

## PART 11   APPEALS IN PROCEEDINGS UNDER THESE REGULATIONS

**[7.56]**

**67  Appeals from court orders**
(1)   An appeal from a decision of a Registrar of the High Court in proceedings under these Regulations lies to a single judge of the High Court; and an appeal from a decision of that judge on such an appeal lies, with the permission of the Court of Appeal, to the Court of Appeal.
(2)   An appeal from a decision of a judge of the High Court in proceedings under these Regulations which is not a decision on an appeal made to him under sub-paragraph (1) lies, with the permission of that judge or the Court of Appeal, to the Court of Appeal.

**68  Procedure on appeals**
(1)   Subject as follows, CPR Part 52 (appeals to the Court of Appeal) and its practice direction apply to appeals in proceedings under these Regulations.
(2)   The provisions of Part 4 of the practice direction on Insolvency Proceedings supporting CPR Part 49 relating to first appeals (as defined in that Part) apply in relation to any appeal to a single judge of the High Court under paragraph 67, with any necessary modifications.
(3)   In proceedings under these Regulations, the procedure under CPR Part 52 is by ordinary application and not by appeal notice.

PART 12   GENERAL

[7.57]

**69 Notices**

(1)   All notices required or authorised by or under these Regulations to be given must be in writing, unless it is otherwise provided, or the court allows the notice to be given in some other way.

(2)   Where in proceedings under these Regulations a notice is required to be sent or given by any person, the sending or giving of it may be proved by means of a certificate by that person that he posted the notice, or instructed another person (naming him) to do so.

(3)   A certificate under this paragraph may be endorsed on a copy or specimen of the notice to which it relates.

**70 "Give notice" etc**

(1)   A reference in these Regulations to giving notice, or to delivering, sending or serving any document, means that the notice or document may be sent by post.

(2)   Subject to paragraph 75, any form of post may be used.

(3)   Personal service of a document is permissible in all cases.

(4)   Notice of the venue fixed for an application may be given by service of the sealed copy of the application under paragraph 33(3).

**71 Notice, etc to solicitors**

Where in proceedings under these Regulations a notice or other document is required or authorised to be given to a person, it may, if he has indicated that his solicitor is authorised to accept service on his behalf, be given instead to the solicitor.

**72 Notice to joint British insolvency officeholders**

Where two or more persons are acting jointly as the British insolvency officeholder in proceedings under British insolvency law, delivery of a document to one of them is to be treated as delivery to them all.

**73 Forms for use in proceedings under these Regulations**

(1)   The forms contained in Schedule 5 to these Regulations shall be used in, and in connection with, proceedings under these Regulations.

(2)   The forms shall be used with such variations, if any, as the circumstances may require.

**74 Time limits**

(1)   The provisions of CPR Rule 2.8 (time) apply, as regards computation of time, to anything required or authorised to be done by these Regulations.

(2)   The provisions of CPR rule 3.1(2)(a) (the court's general powers of management) apply so as to enable the court to extend or shorten the time for compliance with anything required or authorised to be done by these Regulations.

**75 Service by post**

(1)   For a document to be properly served by post, it must be contained in an envelope addressed to the person on whom service is to be effected, and pre-paid for first class post.

(2)   A document to be served by post may be sent to the last known address of the person to be served.

(3)   Where first class post is used, the document is treated as served on the second business day after the date of posting, unless the contrary is shown.

(4)   The date of posting is presumed, unless the contrary is shown, to be the date shown in the post-mark on the envelope in which the document is contained.

**76 General provisions as to service and notice**

Subject to paragraphs 22, 75 and 77, CPR Part 6 (service of documents) applies as regards any matter relating to the service of documents and the giving of notice in proceedings under these Regulations.

**77 Service outside the jurisdiction**

(1)   Sections III and IV of CPR Part 6 (service out of the jurisdiction and service of process of foreign court) do not apply in proceedings under these Regulations.

(2)   Where for the purposes of proceedings under these Regulations any process or order of the court, or other document, is required to be served on a person who is not in England and Wales, the court may order service to be effected within such time, on such person, at such place and in such manner as it thinks fit, and may also require such proof of service as it thinks fit.

(3)   An application under this paragraph shall be supported by an affidavit stating—

(a)   the grounds on which the application is made; and

(b)   in what place or country the person to be served is, or probably may be found.

**78 False claim of status as creditor**

(1)   Rule 12.18 (false claim of status as creditor, etc) shall apply with any necessary modifications in any case where a person falsely claims the status of a creditor of a debtor, with the intention of obtaining a sight of documents whether on the court's file or in the hands of the foreign representative or other person, which he has not under these Regulations any right to inspect.

(2)   Rule 21.21 and Schedule 5 of the Rules shall apply to an offence under Rule 12.18 as applied by sub-paragraph (1) as they apply to an offence under Rule 12.18.

**79 The Gazette**

(1)   A copy of the Gazette containing any notice required by these Regulations to be gazetted is evidence of any fact stated in the notice.

(2)   In the case of an order of the court notice of which is required by these Regulations to be gazetted, a copy of the Gazette containing the notice may in any proceedings be produced as conclusive evidence that the order was made on the date specified in the notice.

.   .   .

SCHEDULE 4

NOTICES DELIVERED TO THE REGISTRAR OF COMPANIES

Regulation 6

**[7.58]**

**1 Interpretation**

(1)   In this Schedule—

.   .   .

"electronic communication" means the same as in the Electronic Communications Act 2000;

"Model Law notice" means a notice delivered to the registrar of companies under paragraph 26(6) of Schedule 2 or paragraph 7(4) of Schedule 3.

(2)   Expressions defined in the Model Law or Schedule 2 or 3, as appropriate, have the same meaning when used in this Schedule.

(3)   References in this Schedule to delivering a notice include sending, forwarding, producing or giving it.

**Amendments**—SI 2009/1941.

**2 Functions of the registrar of companies**

(1)   Where a Model Law notice is delivered to the registrar of companies in respect of a relevant company, the registrar shall enter a note in the register relating to that company.

(2)   The note referred to in sub-paragraph (1) shall contain the following particulars, in each case as stated in the notice delivered to the registrar—

(a)   brief details of the court order made;

(b)   the date of the court order; and

(c)    the name and address for service of the person who is the foreign representative in relation to the company.

**3**

*(Revoked)*

Amendments—SI 2009/1941.

**4 Delivery to registrar of notices**

(1)    Electronic communications may be used for the delivery of any Model Law notice, provided that such delivery is in such form and manner as is directed by the registrar.

(2)    Where the Model Law notice is required to be signed, it shall instead be authenticated in such manner as is directed by the registrar.

(3)    If a Model Law notice is delivered to the registrar which does not comply with the requirements of these Regulations, he may serve on the person by whom the notice was delivered (or, if there are two or more such persons, on any of them) a notice (a non-compliance notice) indicating the respect in which the Model Law notice does not comply.

(4)    Where the registrar serves a non-compliance notice, then, unless a replacement Model Law notice—

(a)    is delivered to him within 14 days after the service of the non-compliance notice, and

(b)    complies with the requirements of these Regulations or is not rejected by him for failure to comply with those requirements,

the original Model Law notice shall be deemed not to have been delivered to him.

**5 Enforcement of foreign representative's duty to give notice to registrar**

(1)    If a foreign representative, having made default in complying with paragraph 26(6) of Schedule 2 or paragraph 7(4) of Schedule 3 fails to make good the default within 14 days after the service of a notice on the foreign representative requiring him to do so, the court may, on an application made to it by any creditor, member, director or other officer of the debtor or by the registrar of companies, make an order directing the foreign representative to make good the default within such time as may be specified in the order.

(2)    The court's order may provide that all costs of and incidental to the application shall be borne by the foreign representative.

**6 Rectification of the register under court order**

(1)    The registrar shall remove from the register any note, or part of a note—

(a)    that relates to or is derived from a court order that the court has declared to be invalid or ineffective, or

(b)    that the court declares to be factually inaccurate or derived from something that is factually inaccurate or forged,

and that the court directs should be removed from the register.

(2)    The court order must specify what is to be removed from the register and indicate where on the register it is and the registrar shall carry out his duty under sub-paragraph (1) within a reasonable time of receipt by him of the relevant court order.

Amendments—SI 2009/1941.

. . .

# STATEMENTS OF INSOLVENCY PRACTICE

## SIP 1 AN INTRODUCTION TO STATEMENTS OF INSOLVENCY PRACTICE

[A1.1]

**Effective Date: 1 October 2015**

### PURPOSE AND PRINCIPLES

1.   The purpose of Statements of Insolvency Practice (SIPs) is to promote and maintain high standards by setting out required practice and harmonising the approach of insolvency practitioners to particular aspects of insolvency practice. They apply in parallel to the prevailing statutory framework.

2.   SIPs should be read in conjunction with the wider fundamental principles embodied in the Insolvency Code of Ethics and should be applied in accordance with the spirit of that Code. A literal interpretation of a SIP may not be appropriate where it would be contrary to the fundamental principles of the Code.

3.   fundamental principles are:

- **Integrity**
  An insolvency practitioner should be straightforward and honest in all professional and business relationships.
- **Objectivity**
  An insolvency practitioner should not allow bias, conflict of interest or undue influence of others to override professional or business judgements.
- **Professional competence and due care**
  An insolvency practitioner has a continuing duty to maintain professional knowledge and skill at the level required to ensure that a client or employer receives competent professional service based on current developments in practice, legislation and techniques. An insolvency practitioner should act diligently and in accordance with applicable technical and professional standards when providing professional services.
- **Confidentiality**
  An insolvency practitioner should respect the confidentiality of information acquired as a result of professional and business relationships and should not disclose any such information to third parties without proper and specific authority unless there is a legal or professional right or duty to disclose. Confidential information acquired as a result of professional and business relationships should not be used for the personal advantage of the insolvency practitioner or third parties.
- **Professional behaviour**
  An insolvency practitioner should comply with relevant laws and regulations and should avoid any action that discredits the profession. Insolvency practitioners should conduct themselves with courtesy and consideration towards all with whom they come into contact when performing their work.

4.   An insolvency practitioner who becomes aware of any insolvency practitioner who they consider is not complying or who has not complied with the relevant laws and regulations and whose actions discredit the profession, should report that insolvency practitioner to the complaints gateway operated by the Insolvency Service or to that insolvency practitioner's recognised professional body.

5. In addition, insolvency practitioners should ensure that their acts, dealings and decision making processes are transparent, understandable and readily identifiable, where to do so does not conflict with any legal or professional obligation. An insolvency practitioner should inform creditors at the earliest opportunity that they are bound by the Insolvency Code of Ethics when carrying out all professional work relating to an insolvency appointment. The insolvency practitioner should, if requested, provide details of any threats identified to compliance with the fundamental principles and the safeguards applied. If it is not appropriate to provide such details, the insolvency practitioner should provide an explanation why.

## REGULATORY STATUS

6. SIPs set principles and key compliance standards with which insolvency practitioners are **required** to comply. Failure to observe the principles and/or maintain the standards set out in a SIP is a matter that may be considered by a practitioner's regulatory authority for the purposes of disciplinary or regulatory action in accordance with that authority's membership and disciplinary rules.

7. Insolvency practitioners should evidence their compliance with SIPs and should, therefore, document their strategies and decision making processes appropriately.

8. SIPs set out required practice, but they are not statements of the law or the obligations imposed by insolvency legislation itself. Where an insolvency practitioner is in doubt about any obligation imposed upon them by a SIP, they should obtain appropriate guidance.

9. SIPs are issued to insolvency practitioners under procedures agreed between the insolvency regulatory authorities, acting through the Joint Insolvency Committee. They apply to practitioners authorised by each of the bodies listed below:

Recognised Professional Bodies:

- The Association of Chartered Certified Accountants
- The Insolvency Practitioners Association
- The Institute of Chartered Accountants in England and Wales
- The Institute of Chartered Accountants in Ireland
- The Institute of Chartered Accountants of Scotland
- The Law Society
- The Law Society of Northern Ireland
- The Law Society of Scotland

Competent Authorities:

- The Insolvency Service for the Secretary of State
- The Insolvency Service, Department of Enterprise, Trade & Investment

10. No liability attaches to any body or person that prepares, issues or distributes SIPs. The obligation to comply with SIPs rests solely upon the insolvency practitioner, as does any liability arising from any failure to do so.

## SIP 2 INVESTIGATIONS BY OFFICE HOLDERS IN ADMINISTRATIONS AND INSOLVENT LIQUIDATIONS AND THE SUBMISSION OF CONDUCT REPORTS BY OFFICE HOLDERS

[A1.2]

Effective Date: 6 April 2016

### INTRODUCTION

1. In any corporate insolvency there may be concerns regarding the way in which the business was conducted, how trading was controlled, whether proper decisions were made at the time, and whether assets have been sold at an under-value or otherwise dissipated. The way in which directors have acted may also be criticised by third parties.

2. Both an administrator and a liquidator of an insolvent entity have a duty to investigate what assets there are (including potential claims against third parties including the directors) and what recoveries can be made. Each of the above matters gives rise to the need for an office holder to carry out appropriate investigations, in order to satisfy the specific duties of the office holder and to allay, if possible, the legitimate concerns of creditors and other interested parties. This statement deals specifically with the investigations of an office holder in administration or insolvent liquidation.

3. Additionally, an administrator, liquidator, administrative receiver or receiver in Scotland may have a duty to report to the Secretary of State or, in Northern Ireland the Department of Enterprise, Trade and Investment (DETI) on the conduct of those that formerly controlled the company. This statement also deals with these obligations.

### PRINCIPLES

4. This statement has been produced in recognition of the principles that:

(a)   An office holder should carry out investigations that are proportionate to the circumstances of each case.

(b)   An office holder should report clearly on the steps taken in relation to investigations, and the outcomes.

(c)   Conduct reports and any subsequent new information should be submitted in a timely manner, noting the expectation that extensions to the statutorily prescribed period will only be considered in exceptional circumstances.

### KEY COMPLIANCE STANDARDS

#### Seeking information

5. The information available to an office holder upon appointment will vary from case to case depending on the extent of the office holder's prior involvement with the company, the publicity surrounding the insolvency, the quality and completeness of the company's books and records, and whether there has been a meeting of creditors. The office holder should locate the company's books and records (in whatever form), and ensure that they are secured, and listed as appropriate.

6. In every case, the office holder should invite creditors to provide information on any concerns regarding the way in which the company's business has been conducted, and on potential recoveries for the estate, both:

(a)   at any meeting of creditors at which the office holder's appointment is made or confirmed, or, in other cases, at any later meeting convened by the office holder; and

(b)   in the first communication sent to creditors by the office holder.

7. A similar invitation should also be extended to the members of any creditors' committee, upon or soon after the formation of the committee, and to any predecessor in office.

8.   An office holder should always have in mind the need to ascertain, and if necessary investigate, what assets can be realised. Enquiries should encompass whether prior transactions by the company, or the conduct of any person involved with the company, could give rise to an action for recovery under the relevant legislation.

### Initial assessment

9.   Notwithstanding any shortage of funds, an office holder should consider the information acquired in the course of appraising and realising the business and assets of a company, together with any information provided by creditors or gained from other sources, and decide whether any further information is required or appropriate. The office holder should make enquiries of the directors and senior employees, by sending questionnaires and/or interviewing them, as appropriate.

10.   In every case, an office holder should make an initial assessment as to whether there could be any matters that might lead to recoveries for the estate and what further investigations may be appropriate.

11.   An office holder should determine the extent of the investigations in the circumstances of each case, taking account of the public interest, potential recoveries, the funds likely to be available, either from within the estate and/or from other sources, to fund an investigation, and the costs involved.

### Further steps to be taken

12.   An office holder may conclude that there are matters (for example, the conduct of management, prior transactions susceptible to challenge, or the consequences of possible criminal offences) that require early investigation, either as a matter of public policy or because there are real prospects of recoveries for the estate. It is for the office holder to decide whether investigation and subsequent legal action should proceed as quickly as possible, without consultation with, or sanction by, creditors or a creditors' committee (but subject to any statutory requirement to obtain sanction).

13.   In other cases, the office holder may decide that further investigation and legal action should be carried out only after consultation or with sanction, in particular where the office holder concludes that the outcome is uncertain and the costs that would be incurred would materially affect the funds available for distribution. In such cases, the office holder may consult with major creditors (if that is appropriate) or convene a meeting of the creditors' committee or the creditors to discuss any proposals for investigation and/or action. Alternatively, consultation and approval can be carried out/sought by written resolution.

14.   Any proposals should include sufficient information (subject to considerations of privilege and confidentiality) to enable an informed decision to be made by those consulted, and are likely to include the costs that could be incurred and the possible range of returns to creditors.

15.   There may be circumstances where there are clearly insufficient funds to carry out a detailed investigation or to take action for recovery of assets, and an office holder should consider whether it is appropriate to seek funding from creditors or others.

### Reporting to creditors

16.   Creditors should be given information regarding investigations, any action being taken, and whether funding is being provided by third parties; disclosure would be subject to considerations of privilege and confidentiality and whether investigations and litigation might be compromised.

17.   The times at which information is provided to creditors will vary from case to case, but as a minimum an office holder should:

(a)   include within the first progress report a statement dealing with the office holder's initial assessment, whether any further investigations or action were considered, and the outcome; and

(b)  include within subsequent reports a statement dealing with investigations and actions concluded during the period, and those that are continuing.

## Record keeping

**18.**  An office holder should document, at the time, initial assessments, investigations and conclusions, including any conclusion that further investigation or action is not required or feasible, and also any decision to restrict the content of reports to creditors.

## Conduct reporting requirements

**19.**  The office holder should base any conduct report on information coming to light in the ordinary course of their enquiries and is not required to carry out investigations specifically for the purpose of fulfilling their statutory reporting obligations. The submission of conduct reports is one of the statutory duties that automatically fall upon the office holder and, as such, must be complied with notwithstanding any shortage of funds.

**20.**  If the office holder has not already interviewed the subject of the conduct report, the office holder may consider seeking a meeting with the subject, with a view to confirming the office holder's understanding of the facts.

**21.**  An office holder should be mindful that the content of conduct reports are prepared for the purpose of the Secretary of State and DETI discharging their statutory functions and should not be disclosed to third parties.

**22.**  Notwithstanding the confidential nature of conduct reports, office holders should be mindful that there may be circumstances in which the content of a conduct report is made available to the subject, or potentially others. Should the subject of a conduct report request disclosure, an office holder should contact the Secretary of State or DETI (as appropriate) as soon as a request is received in order to consider whether any factors apply that may result in an exemption from disclosure being applicable. Office holders should be aware that the subject may make a disclosure request directly to the Secretary of State or DETI (as appropriate), which will usually result, (after appropriate redactions) in a copy being provided to them. Additionally, conduct reports may be disclosed by Secretary of State or DETI to other Regulatory Authorities, where disclosure is considered to be in the public interest. An office holder should also bear in mind that, if disqualification proceedings are brought, the conduct report will usually be made available to the subject during the disclosure process.

**23.**  When reporting on conduct or providing new information, the office holder should highlight whether recovery proceedings have or may be commenced against the subject of the report, as this may have an impact upon any decision taken by the Secretary of State or DETI (as appropriate) to seek a compensation order or undertaking.

## Other reporting requirements

**24.**  An office holder should report possible offences disclosed during the course of their investigations to the relevant authorities.

# SIP 3.1 INDIVIDUAL VOLUNTARY ARRANGEMENTS

[A1.3]

Effective date: 1 July 2014

## INTRODUCTION

1. An Individual Voluntary Arrangement (IVA) is a statutory contract between a debtor and his or her creditors under which an insolvency practitioner will have powers and duties. An insolvency practitioner will be central to the preparation and agreement of the proposal, and the implementation of the arrangement, whether acting as adviser, nominee or supervisor. The particular nature of an insolvency practitioner's position renders transparency and fairness in all dealings of primary importance. The debtor and creditors should be confident that an insolvency practitioner will act professionally and with objectivity in each role associated with the arrangement. Failure to do so may prejudice the interests of both the debtor and creditors, and is likely to bring the practitioner and the profession into disrepute.

## PRINCIPLES

2. An insolvency practitioner should differentiate clearly between the stages and roles that are associated with an IVA (these being, the provision of initial advice, assisting in the preparation of the proposal, acting as the nominee, and acting as the supervisor) and ensure that they are explained to the debtor and the creditors.

3. An insolvency practitioner should ensure that the information and explanations provided to a debtor about all the options available are such that the debtor can make an informed judgement as to whether an IVA is an appropriate solution.

4. An insolvency practitioner should explain to the debtor, the debtor's responsibilities and the consequences of an IVA.

5. Where an IVA is to be proposed, an insolvency practitioner should be satisfied that it is achievable and that a fair balance is struck between the interests of the debtor and the creditors.

6. An insolvency practitioner's reports should provide sufficient information to enable creditors to make informed decisions in relation to the proposal and the IVA, and report accurately in a manner that aims to be clear and useful.

## KEY COMPLIANCE STANDARDS

7. Certain key compliance standards are of general application, but others will depend on whether the insolvency practitioner is acting as adviser, nominee, or supervisor.

## STANDARDS OF GENERAL APPLICATION

### Advice to the debtor

8. The insolvency practitioner should have procedures in place to ensure that the information and explanations provided to the debtor at each stage of the process (that is, assessing the options available, and then preparing and implementing an IVA), are designed to set out clearly:

(a)     the advantages and disadvantages of each available option;
(b)     the key stages and the roles of the adviser, the nominee and the supervisor, any potential delays or complications, and the likely duration of the IVA;
(c)     what is required of the debtor;
(d)     the consequences of proposing and entering into an IVA, including the rights of challenge to the IVA and the potential consequences of those challenges; and

(e)  what may happen if the IVA is not approved or not successfully completed.

## Meeting the debtor

9.  meeting should always be offered to the debtor. At each stage of the process, an assessment should be made as to whether a face-to-face meeting with the debtor is required, depending on the debtor's attitude and the circumstances and complexity of the case.

## Assessment

10.  The insolvency practitioner needs to be satisfied, at each stage of the process, that there are procedures in place to ensure that an assessment is made of:

(a)  the solutions available and their viability;
(b)  whether the debtor is being sufficiently cooperative;
(c)  the debtor's understanding of the process, and commitment to it;
(d)  the likely attitude of any key creditors and the general body of creditors, in particular as to the fairness and balance of the proposals;
(e)  whether an IVA would have a reasonable prospect of being approved and implemented; and
(f)  whether an interim order is needed or available.

## Documentation

11.  The insolvency practitioner should be able to demonstrate that proper steps have been taken at all stages of the IVA, by maintaining records of:

(a)  discussions with the debtor, including the information and explanations provided, the options outlined, and the advantages and disadvantages of each;
(b)  comments made by the debtor, and the debtor's preferred option;
(c)  any discussions with creditors or their representatives;

If the insolvency practitioner considers it appropriate in the circumstances, summaries of these discussions should be sent to the debtor.

## Documentation

## STANDARDS OF SPECIFIC APPLICATION

## Initial advice

12.  An insolvency practitioner may be asked to give advice on a debtor's financial difficulties, and the way in which those difficulties might be resolved. The insolvency practitioner should have procedures in place to ensure, taking account of the personal circumstances of the debtor, that:

(a)  The role of adviser is explained to the debtor, at this stage advising the debtor (in the debtor's interests) but in the context of needing to find a workable solution to the debtor's financial difficulties.
(b)  Sufficient information is obtained to make a preliminary assessment of the solutions available and their viability.
(c)  The obligations of the debtor to cooperate and provide full disclosure are explained. The insolvency practitioner should be able to form a view of whether the debtor has a sufficient understanding of the situation and the consequences, and whether there will be full cooperation in seeking a solution.
(d)  When considering possible solutions, account is taken of the impact of each solution on the debtor and the debtor's assets, in particular the family home, and on any third parties that may be affected.

(e)    The debtor is provided with an explanation of all the options available, the advantages and disadvantages of each, and the likely costs of each so that the solution best suited to the debtor's circumstances can be identified. This explanation should be confirmed to the debtor in writing.

### Preparing for an IVA

**13.**    When preparing for an IVA, the insolvency practitioner should have procedures in place to ensure, taking account of the personal circumstances of the debtor and the nature of the debtor's finances, that:

(a)    The debtor has had, or receives, the appropriate advice in relation to an IVA. This should be confirmed in writing if the insolvency practitioner or their firm has not done so before.

(b)    The obligations of the debtor to cooperate and provide full and accurate disclosure, are explained and the consequences of not doing so if the insolvency practitioner has not done so before. The insolvency practitioner should be able to form a view of whether the debtor has a sufficient understanding of the process of an IVA, its likely duration and the consequences, and whether there will be full cooperation and commitment from the debtor.

(c)    Sufficient information is obtained to make an assessment of an IVA as a solution, and to enable a nominee to prepare a report, including;

    (i)    the measures taken by the debtor to avoid recurrence of their financial difficulties, if any;

    (ii)    the likely expectations of any key creditors;

    (iii)    the effect of the IVA on third parties where their view may have an effect on the viability of the IVA; and

(d)    proportionate investigations into, and verification of, income and expenditure and assets and liabilities.

### The proposal

**14.**    Where the insolvency practitioner has been asked to assist the debtor to prepare a proposal, the insolvency practitioner should have procedures in place to ensure that the proposal contains the following:

(a)    sufficient information for creditors to understand the debtor's financial and trading history (where appropriate), including:

    (i)    the background and financial history of the debtor;

    (ii)    why the debtor has become insolvent;

    (iii)    any other attempts that have been made to solve the debtor's financial difficulties, if there are any such difficulties;

(b)    a comparison of the estimated outcomes of the IVA and the outcome if the IVA is not approved, including disclosure of the estimated costs of the IVA and the bases for those estimates;

(c)    the identity of the source of any referral of the debtor, the relationship or connection of the referrer to the debtor and, where any payment has been made or is proposed to the referrer, the amount and reason for that payment;

(d)    details of the amounts and source of any payments made, or proposed to be made, to the nominee and the supervisor or their firms in connection, or otherwise, with the proposed IVA, directly or indirectly and the reason(s) for the payment(s); and

(e)    where relevant, sufficient information to support any profit and cash projections, subject to any commercial sensitivity.

### The nominee

**15.**    It is the responsibility of the nominee to report in relation to the proposed IVA. When acting as nominee, the insolvency practitioner should have procedures in place to ensure that:

(a)     The debtor has had, or receives, the appropriate advice in relation to an IVA. This should be confirmed in writing if the insolvency practitioner or his firm has not done so before.

(b)     The nominee is able to report whether or not:

    (i)     the debtor's financial position is materially different from that contained in the proposal, explaining the extent to which the information has been verified.

    (ii)    the IVA is manifestly unfair.

    (iii)   the IVA has a reasonable prospect of being approved and implemented.

(c)     The debtor's consent is sought on any modifications to the proposal put forward by creditors, and the debtor understands the impact of the modifications on the implementation of the IVA and its viability.

(d)     Where a modification is adopted, the insolvency practitioner must ensure that consent is obtained from the debtor and, if appropriate, the creditors.

(e)     In the absence of consent, the IVA cannot proceed. The debtor's consent must be recorded.

### The supervisor

**16.**   When acting as supervisor, the insolvency practitioner should have procedures in place to ensure that:

(a)     Where a proposal is modified, creditors have been made aware of the final form of the accepted IVA.

(b)     The IVA is supervised in accordance with its terms.

(c)     The progress of the IVA is monitored.

(d)     Any departures from the terms of the IVA are identified at an early stage and appropriate action is then taken promptly by the supervisor.

(e)     Any discretion(s) conferred on the supervisor are exercised where necessary, on a timely basis and that exercise s reported at the next available opportunity.

(f)     Any variation to the terms of the IVA has been appropriately approved before it is implemented.

(g)     Enquiries by the debtor and creditors are dealt with promptly.

(h)     Full disclosure is made of the costs of the IVA and of any other sources of income of the insolvency practitioner or the practice, in relation to the case, in reports.

(i)     If the costs of the IVA have increased beyond previously reported estimates, this increase should be reported at the next available opportunity; and

(j)     The IVA is closed promptly on completion or termination.

## SIP 3.2 COMPANY VOLUNTARY ARRANGEMENTS

[A1.4]

**Effective date: 1 April 2021**

### INTRODUCTION

1. A Company Voluntary Arrangement (CVA) is a statutory contract between a company and its creditors under which an insolvency practitioner will have powers and duties. An insolvency practitioner will be central to the preparation and agreement of the proposal, and the implementation of the arrangement, whether acting as adviser, nominee or supervisor. The particular nature of an insolvency practitioner's position renders transparency and fairness in all dealings of primary importance.

2. An insolvency practitioner may be asked to assist a company's directors when a CVA may be a solution to the company's financial difficulties; or an insolvency practitioner may propose a CVA as administrator or liquidator. Where the principles and key compliance standards in this statement of insolvency practice are relevant only to a CVA proposed by a company's directors these are identified as such.

### PRINCIPLES

3. An insolvency practitioner should differentiate clearly between the stages and roles that are associated with a CVA (these being, the provision of initial advice, assisting in the preparation of the proposal, acting as the nominee, and acting as the supervisor) and ensure that they are explained to the company's directors (where they are making the proposal), shareholders and creditors.

4. An insolvency practitioner should act professionally and with objectivity in each role associated with the arrangement. Failure to do so may prejudice the interests of both the company and creditors, and is likely to bring the practitioner and the profession into disrepute.

5. (*Directors' proposal*) An insolvency practitioner should ensure that information and explanations about all the options available are provided to the directors, so that they can make an informed judgement as to whether a CVA is an appropriate solution for the company.

6. An insolvency practitioner should explain to the directors, the directors' responsibilities and role before and during the CVA, and the consequences of a CVA.

7. Where a CVA is to be proposed, an insolvency practitioner should be satisfied that it is achievable and that a fair balance is struck between the interests of the company and the creditors.

8. An insolvency practitioner's reports should provide sufficient information to enable the company's shareholders and creditors to make informed decisions in relation to the proposal and the CVA, and report accurately in a manner that aims to be clear and useful.

### KEY COMPLIANCE STANDARDS

9. Certain key compliance standards are of general application, but others will depend on whether the insolvency practitioner is acting as adviser, nominee, supervisor, administrator or liquidator.

## STANDARDS OF GENERAL APPLICATION

### Advice (directors' proposal)

10.  The insolvency practitioner should have procedures in place to ensure that the information and explanations provided to the company and/or the directors at each stage of the process, as appropriate (that is, assessing the options available, and then preparing and implementing a CVA), are designed to set out clearly:

(a)     the advantages and disadvantages of each available option;

(b)     the key stages and the roles of the adviser, the nominee and the supervisor;

(c)     whether and why the company will require additional specialist assistance which will not be provided by any supervisor appointed, including the likely cost of that additional assistance, if known;

(d)     any potential delays or complications; and the likely duration of the CVA;

(e)     what is required of the company and its directors;

(f)     the consequences of proposing and entering into a CVA, including the rights of challenge to the CVA and the potential consequences of those challenges; and

(g)     what may happen if the CVA is not approved or not successfully completed.

### Meeting the directors (directors' proposal)

11.   In view of the complex nature of CVAs the initial meeting with the directors should always be in person (whether at a physical meeting or using conferencing technology).

### Assessment

12.   The insolvency practitioner needs to be satisfied, at each stage of the process, that there are procedures in place to ensure that an assessment is made of:

(a)     the solutions available and their viability;

(b)     (*Directors' proposal*) whether the directors are being sufficiently cooperative;

(c)     where the directors' compliance is required for the implementation of the CVA, the directors' understanding of the process, and commitment to it;

(d)     the likely attitude of any key creditors and the general body of creditors, in particular as to the fairness and balance of the proposals;

(e)     whether a CVA would have a reasonable prospect of being approved and implemented; and

(f)     whether a moratorium is required or available.

### Documentation

13.   The insolvency practitioner should be able to demonstrate that proper steps have been taken at all stages of the CVA, by maintaining records of:

(a)     (*Directors' proposal*) discussions with the directors, including the information and explanations provided, the options outlined, and the advantages and disadvantages of each, and an explanation of the roles of the nominee and supervisor. All advice provided to the directors should be confirmed in writing;

(b)     (*Directors' proposal*) comments made by the directors, and their preferred option;

(c)     any discussions with creditors (or their representatives) and the company's shareholders; and

(d)     a detailed note of the strategy, outlining the advantages and disadvantages of each option, including the impact of trading within a CVA for a prolonged period and the continued viability of the business during that period.

## STANDARDS OF SPECIFIC APPLICATION

### Preparing for a CVA

14.  When preparing for a CVA, the insolvency practitioner should have procedures in place to ensure, taking account of the company's circumstances and the nature of the company's finances, that:

(a)   (*Directors' proposal*) The directors have had, or receive, the appropriate advice in relation to a CVA; this should be confirmed in writing if the insolvency practitioner or their firm has not done so before;

(b)   Sufficient information is obtained to make an assessment of a CVA as a solution, and to enable a nominee to prepare a report, including;

   (i)    the measures taken by the directors or others to avoid recurrence of the company's financial difficulties, if any;
   (ii)   the likely expectations of any key creditors;
   (iii)  the effect of the CVA on third parties where their view may have an effect on the viability of the CVA; and
   (iv)  proportionate investigations into, and verification of, income and expenditure and assets and liabilities;

(c)   Creditors are given adequate time to consider what is being planned as regards the CVA. Where creditors may need assistance in understanding the consequences of a CVA, the insolvency practitioner should consider signposting sources of help.

### The proposal

15.  Whether the insolvency practitioner has been asked to assist the directors to prepare a proposal or a proposal is being prepared by an administrator or liquidator, the insolvency practitioner should have procedures in place to ensure that the proposal is considered objectively, and contains the following:

(a)   sufficient information for creditors to understand the company's financial and trading history;

(b)   the roles of the directors and key employees and their future involvement in the company, including the background and financial history of the directors where relevant;

(c)   any additional specialist assistance which may be required by the company which will not be provided by any supervisor appointed, and the reason why such assistance may be necessary;

(d)   if the company has become, or is about to become, insolvent, why;

(e)   any other attempts that have been made to solve the company's financial difficulties, and the alternative options considered, both prior to and within formal insolvency by the company;

(f)   a comparison of the estimated outcomes of the CVA and the outcome if the CVA is not approved;

(g)   where relevant, sufficient information to support any profit and cash projections, subject to any commercial sensitivity;

(h)   an explanation of the role and powers of the supervisor;

(i)    details of any discussions that have taken place with key creditors;

(j)    where it is proposed that certain creditors are to be treated differently, an explanation as to which creditors are affected, how and why, in a manner which aims to be clear and useful;

(k)   an explanation of how debts are to be valued for voting purposes, in particular where the creditors include long term or contingent liabilities;

(l)    disclosure of the estimated costs of the CVA including the proposed remuneration of the nominee and the supervisor and the bases for those estimates;

(m)   the cost of any additional specialist assistance which will not be provided by any supervisor appointed

(n)   the identity of the source of any referral of the company, the relationship or connection of the referrer to the company and, where any payment has been made or is proposed to the referrer, the amount and reason for that payment;

(o) details of the amounts and source of other payments made, or proposed to be made, to the nominee and the supervisor or their firms in connection, or otherwise, with the proposed CVA, directly or indirectly and the reason(s) for the payment(s);

(p) an explanation of how debts which it is proposed are compromised will be treated should the CVA fail;

(q) the circumstances in which the CVA may fail, and

(r) what will happen to the company and any remaining assets subject to the CVA should the CVA fail.

### The nominee

**16.** Where the nominee is not the administrator or liquidator, it is the responsibility of the nominee to report in relation to the proposed CVA. When acting as nominee, the insolvency practitioner should have procedures in place to ensure that:

(a) The nominee is able to report objectively whether or not, in the nominee's judgement:
  - (i) the company's financial position is materially different from that contained in the proposal, explaining the extent to which the information has been verified;
  - (ii) the CVA is manifestly unfair;
  - (iii) the CVA has a reasonable prospect of being approved and implemented.

(b) The proposer's consent is sought on any modifications to the proposal put forward by creditors, and the proposer understands the impact of the modifications on the implementation of the CVA and its viability.

(c) Where a modification is adopted, the insolvency practitioner must ensure that consent is obtained from the proposer of the CVA and, if appropriate, the creditors. In the absence of consent, the CVA cannot proceed in a modified form. The proposer's consent or otherwise must be recorded.

**17.** Where the nominee is the administrator or liquidator, and the directors' compliance is required, their consent shall be sought.

### The supervisor

**18.** When acting as supervisor, the insolvency practitioner should have procedures in place to ensure that:

(a) where a proposal is modified, creditors have been made aware of the final form of the accepted CVA;

(b) the CVA is supervised in accordance with its terms;

(c) the progress of the CVA is monitored;

(d) any departures from the terms of the CVA are identified at an early stage and appropriate action is taken promptly by the supervisor;

(e) any discretions conferred on the supervisor are exercised where necessary, on a timely basis and that exercise is reported at the next available opportunity;

(f) any variation to the terms of the CVA has been appropriately approved before it is implemented;

(g) enquiries by creditors and shareholders are dealt with promptly;

(h) full disclosure is made of the costs of the CVA and of any other sources of income of the insolvency practitioner, associates of the insolvency practitioner or their firm, in relation to the case, in reports; and

(i) if the costs of the CVA have increased beyond previously reported estimates, this increase should be reported at the next available opportunity and an explanation of the increase provided.

**19.** The CVA should be closed promptly on completion or termination. When the CVA concludes or fails, the supervisor should ensure that the company is dealt with appropriately in accordance with the CVA proposal. What is to happen should be reported to creditors.

## SIP 6 DEEMED CONSENT AND DECISION PROCEDURES IN INSOLVENCY PROCEEDINGS

[A1.5]

**Effective Date: 1 January 2018**

### INTRODUCTION

1. Insolvency practitioners play a key role in ensuring that persons entitled to participate in the making of decisions are able to make informed decisions and that their participation is properly facilitated. Stakeholder involvement in the making of decisions is essential to the maintenance of trust and confidence in insolvency proceedings.

2. This Statement of Insolvency Practice applies to the use of deemed consent and qualifying decision procedures conducted under the Insolvency Act 1986 (as amended) and applies in England and Wales only.

### PRINCIPLES

3. An insolvency practitioner should facilitate participation in deemed consent and decision procedures by those stakeholders with an entitlement to participate.

4. An insolvency practitioner should take reasonable steps to ensure that those entitled to participate in deemed consent and decision procedures are treated fairly and able to participate on an informed basis.

5. Requests for additional information should be viewed upon their individual merits and treated by an insolvency practitioner in a fair and reasonable way. The provision of additional information should be proportionate to the circumstances of the case.

6. The formal record of a deemed consent or decision procedure should be an accurate and contemporaneous record, sufficient to explain the business conducted and the basis upon which any discretion was exercised.

### KEY COMPLIANCE STANDARDS

#### Provisions of General Application

7. Information supplied in connection with a deemed consent or decision procedure should be presented in a manner which is transparent, consistent and useful to prospective participants, whilst being proportionate to the circumstances of the case.

8. An insolvency practitioner should have procedures in place to ensure that any deemed consent or decision procedure used is subject to sufficient and proportionate safeguards against participation by persons who are not properly entitled to participate.

9. determining the authenticity of a prospective participant's authority to participate in a decision procedure, the insolvency practitioner should exercise their reasonable professional judgement to facilitate the participation of those who appear to be properly entitled.

#### Provisions of Specific Application – CVL

10. Where an insolvency practitioner is assisting in the obtaining of deemed consent or the convening of a decision procedure, the insolvency practitioner should take reasonable steps to ensure that:

(a) the convener is made fully aware of their duties and responsibilities;
(b) that the instructions to the insolvency practitioner to assist are adequately recorded;

(c)     the convener and /or chair is informed that it may be appropriate for them to obtain independent assistance in determining the authenticity of a prospective participant's authority or entitlement to participate and the amount for which they are permitted to do so, in the event these are called into question.

11.    An insolvency practitioner should disclose the extent of their (and that of their firm and/or associates) prior involvement with the company or its directors or shareholders, any threats identified to compliance with the fundamental principles of the Insolvency Code of Ethics, and the safeguards applied to mitigate those threats. This disclosure should be made with the notices convening the deemed consent or decision procedure.

12.    An insolvency practitioner should seek to ensure that the information available in advance of a deemed consent or decision procedure for the purposes of appointing a liquidator facilitates the making of an informed decision by those that are entitled to participate. Key information likely to be of interest to prospective participants (in addition to that required by statute), will commonly be:

(a)     the date of the instructions to the insolvency practitioner to assist in the deemed consent or decision procedure and by whom those instructions were given;
(b)     disclosure of any amounts paid by or on behalf of the company in respect of those instructions and to whom they were paid;
(c)     a summary of the company's relevant trading activity and financial history, which would typically include (but may not be limited to):
     (i)      an explanation of the causes of the company's failure;
     (ii)     the name(s) and company number(s) of parent, subsidiary and associated companies;
     (iii)    extracts from the company's recent accounts (whether or not filed);
     (iv)    an explanation of any material transactions conducted in the preceding 12 months, other than in the ordinary course of business.
(d)     By way of explanation of a statement of the company's affairs:
     (i)      a deficiency account reconciling the position shown by the most recent balance sheet to the deficiency in the statement of affairs;
     (ii)     the names and professional qualifications of any valuers whose valuations have been relied upon for the purpose of the statement of affairs and a summary of the basis of valuation adopted.

Any information should ordinarily be available, on request, not later than the business day prior to the decision date and may be made available via a website.

13.    An insolvency practitioner should not accept instructions to assist in a procedure for the purpose of winding up a company unless that practitioner reasonably believes that a liquidator will be appointed.

# SIP 7 PRESENTATION OF FINANCIAL INFORMATION IN INSOLVENCY PROCEEDINGS

[A1.6]

**Effective Date: 1 April 2021**

## INTRODUCTION

1. An office holder is required to report regularly to creditors and other interested parties[1].

2. The particular nature of an insolvency office holder's position renders transparency and fairness of primary importance in all their dealings.

3. The term associate is defined in insolvency legislation. For the purposes of this statement of insolvency practice, office holders should, in addition to the definition in the insolvency legislation, consider the substance or likely perception of any association between the insolvency practitioner, their firm, or an individual within the insolvency practitioner's firm and the recipient of a payment. Where a reasonable and informed third party might consider there would be an association, payments should be treated as if they are being made to an associate, notwithstanding the nature of the association may not meet the definition in the legislation.

---

[1]  "other interested parties" means those parties with rights pursuant to the prevailing insolvency legislation to information about the office holders receipts and payments. This may include a creditors' committee, the members (shareholders) of a company, or in personal insolvency, the debtor.

## PRINCIPLES

4. Reports should be relevant to the interests of the creditors and other interested parties[1], be clear and informative, be consistent across periods and be sufficient to enable creditors and other interested parties[1] to understand the nature and amounts of the receipts and payments. The office holder should consider what the creditors and other interested parties[1] might reasonably regard as appropriate or significant in the circumstances of each insolvency appointment, whilst being proportionate to the insolvency appointment.

5. Payments made by an office holder should be fair and reasonable and proportionate to the insolvency appointment, and if significant in the context of the insolvency appointment, the office holder should report and explain why the expenditure was incurred.

6. An office holder should report in a way that will assist creditors and other interested parties[1] properly to exercise their rights under the insolvency legislation.

---

[1]  "other interested parties" means those parties with rights pursuant to the prevailing insolvency legislation to information about the office holders receipts and payments. This may include a creditors' committee, the members (shareholders) of a company, or in personal insolvency, the debtor.

## KEY COMPLIANCE STANDARDS

### Form and general presentation of accounts

7. In addition to any statutory requirement to provide an account in a specified form, receipts and payments accounts should provide figures both for the period under review and on a cumulative basis.

8.   Information provided in accordance with this statement may be in a separate document issued with the receipts and payments account or given by way of note. Unless there is statutory provision to the contrary, this does not require the repetition of information previously provided.

9.   Receipts and payments accounts should show categories of items under headings appropriatefor the insolvency appointment, where practicable following headings used in prior statements of affairs or estimated outcome statements. An analysis should be provided to enable comparison with the "estimated to realise" figures in any previously issued document.

10.   Certain statutory documents require a "statement of expenses incurred" in the period and should adopt, as far as possible, the principles of this statement but need only provide information for the period under review.

### Statement of funds held

11.   Accounts should be reconciled to the balances at bank, the case records and to any amounts due to the office holder.

12.   Disclosure should be made of where the balance of the funds is held, distinguishing between funds held on non-interest bearing accounts and interest bearing accounts in the office holder's or the insolvent estate's name, amounts held in the Insolvency Services Account and in Treasury Bills, and other forms of investments.

13.   An office holder may present multiple receipts and payments accounts in more than one currency where bank accounts are maintained in those currencies (with details of the transfers between each currency), but should explain:

(a)   Why funds have been held in currencies other than sterling;
(b)   The impact of currency holdings on the estate;
(c)   An indication of the sterling value as at the date of the account.

### Value added tax (VAT)

14.   The treatment of VAT adopted within an account should be consistent and the implications of that treatment made clear.

### Payments to insolvency office holders and their associates

15.   The following should be disclosed, either separately in the receipts and payments account or by way of note:

(a)   Office holder's remuneration, showing the amounts paid on each basis;
(b)   Amounts paid to the office holder in respect of the supervision of trading;
(c)   All other amounts required to be approved in the same manner as remuneration;
(d)   Amounts paid to the office holder from the estate in respect of pre-appointment costs;
(e)   Any amounts paid to the office holder or their associates or firm other than out of the estate, giving the amounts paid, the name of payor, their relationship to the insolvent estate and the nature of the payment;
(f)   Amounts paid to sub-contractors for work that would otherwise have to be carried out by the office holder or their staff.

16.   These disclosures should always be made whenever reporting on remuneration and/or expenses, whether incurred, accrued or paid.

### Requests for additional information

17.   Requests for additional information, including on expenses, should be viewed upon their individual merits and treated by an office holder in a fair and reasonable way. The provision of additional information should be proportionate to the circumstances of the appointment.

**18.** Creditors and other interested parties[1] may have the statutory right to seek further information about payments made by the office holder. Creditors and other interested parties[1] may also have the right to apply to the court if they consider these costs to be excessive in all the circumstances.

**19.** Adequate steps should be taken to bring the rights of creditors and other interested parties[1] to their attention. Information on how to access a suitable explanatory note setting out the rights of creditors should be given, when appropriate, in reports that present financial information.

**20.** When an office holder's appointment is followed by the appointment of another insolvency practitioner, whether or not in the same proceedings, the prior office holder should provide the successor with information in accordance with the principles and standards contained in this statement. This is in addition to any statutory obligations imposed on an office holder to provide information.

[1] "other interested parties" means those parties with rights pursuant to the prevailing insolvency legislation to information about the office holders receipts and payments. This may include a creditors' committee, the members (shareholders) of a company, or in personal insolvency, the debtor.

## OTHER PRESENTATIONAL MATTERS

### Receipts

**21.** Realisations by or on behalf of the office holder should be shown gross, with the costs of realisation shown separately as payments.

**22.** Realisations by or on behalf of the office holder of assets subject to charges should be shown as above with the amounts accounted for to the chargeholder shown separately as payments.

**23.** When assets subject to charges are sold by or on the instructions of the charge-holder (or other person with a legal right to do so), the net amount received should be shown in the account (even if "nil") with the gross realisation(s), costs of realisation and the amount retained by the chargeholder shown separately by way of note.

### Payments

**24.** Payments should be stated by category, distinguishing payments made under duress, in settlement of reservation of title claims, to secured creditors, and to preferential creditors and unsecured creditors as dividends. The dates and amounts of dividends (pence in the £) should also be stated.

### Trading under office holder's control

**25.** A separate trading receipts and payments account should be provided to the creditors and other interested parties[1] to enable an appropriate understanding of what was done, why it was done and how much it cost, and the balance should be shown as a single item in the main receipts and payments account. The office holder should also provide, by way of note or in the accompanying report, details of:

(a) The assets in existence upon appointment (e.g. stock and work in progress) that have been used in trading.
(b) Any uncollected debts and unpaid liabilities in respect of trading.
(c) Trading assets (e.g. stock and work in progress) still to be realised.

[1] "other interested parties" means those parties with rights pursuant to the prevailing insolvency legislation to information about the office holders receipts and payments. This may include a

creditors' committee, the members (shareholders) of a company, or in personal insolvency, the debtor.

## Alternative approaches to asset realisation

**26.** From time to time the office holder may adopt an alternative method of asset realisation. Whatever alternative method is adopted, the requirements of this statement still apply; creditors and other interested parties[1] should be provided with sufficient information to enable an appropriate understanding of what was done, why it was done and how much it cost. For example, funds received from a hive-down company as consideration for the sale of the business or its assets should be shown in the account classified according to the categories of assets transferred and apportioned as provided for in the hive-down agreement. The proceeds of sale of the shares in the hive-down company should be shown separately. Funds received in respect of the hive-down company should not be shown simply as the proceeds of sale of the hive-down company.

**27.** A trading account for a hive-down company should be prepared adopting the same principles as set out above, as should trading accounts for other alternative approaches.

## Third party funds

**28.** Where any monies are held which do not form part of the estate and are due to be paid to third parties, the amount should be disclosed, together with any agreed fee charged to the person entitled to the monies.

## SIP 9 PAYMENTS TO INSOLVENCY OFFICE HOLDERS AND THEIR ASSOCIATES FROM AN ESTATE

[A1.7]

**Effective Date: 1 April 2021**

### INTRODUCTION

1.   The particular nature of an insolvency office holder's position renders transparency and fairness of primary importance in all their dealings. Creditors and other interested parties[1] with a financial interest in the level of payments from an estate should be confident that the rules relating to the approval and disclosure of payments to insolvency office holders and their associates have been properly complied with.

2.   The term associate is defined in the insolvency legislation. For the purposes of this statement of insolvency practice, office holders should, in addition to the definition in the insolvency legislation, consider the substance or likely perception of any association between the insolvency practitioner, their firm, or an individual within the insolvency practitioner's firm and the recipient of a payment. Where a reasonable and informed third party might consider there would be an association, payments should be treated as if they are being made to an associate, notwithstanding the nature of the association may not meet the definition in the legislation.

3.   This statement applies to all forms of insolvency proceedings under the Insolvency Act 1986, except for the following:

(a)   Moratoriums under Part A1
(b)   Members' voluntary liquidation unless those paying the fees require such disclosures

4.   Nothing within this statement obligates an office holder to provide a fees estimate where one is not required by statute.

---

[1]   "other interested parties" means those parties with rights pursuant to the prevailing insolvency legislation to information about the office holder's receipts and payments. This may include a creditors' committee, the members (shareholders) of a company, or in personal insolvency, the debtor.

### PRINCIPLES

5.   All payments from an estate should be fair and reasonable and proportionate to the insolvency appointment.

6.   Payments to an office holder from an estate should be fair and reasonable reflections of the work necessarily and properly undertaken in an insolvency appointment.

7.   Payments to the associates of an office holder from an estate should be fair and reasonable reflections of the work necessarily and properly undertaken in an insolvency appointment.

8.   All payments should be directly attributable to the estate from which they are being made or sought.

9.   Payments that could reasonably be perceived as presenting a threat to the office holder's objectivity or independence by virtue of a professional or personal relationship, including to an associate, should not be made from the estate unless disclosed and approved in the same manner as an office holder's remuneration or category 2 expenses.

10.   Payments should not be approved by any party with whom the office holder has a professional or personal relationship which gives rise to a conflict of interest.

11.   Those responsible for approving payments from an estate to an office holder or their associates should be provided with sufficient information to enable them to make an informed judgement about the reasonableness of the office holder's requests.

**12.** Disclosures by an office holder should be of assistance to creditors and other interested parties1 in understanding what was done, why it was done, and how much it cost.

**13.** Information provided by an office holder should be presented in a manner which is transparent, consistent throughout the life of the appointment and useful to creditors and other interested parties[1], whilst being proportionate to the circumstances of the appointment.

[1]   "other interested parties" means those parties with rights pursuant to the prevailing insolvency legislation to information about the office holder's receipts and payments. This may include a creditors' committee, the members (shareholders) of a company, or in personal insolvency, the debtor.

## KEY COMPLIANCE STANDARDS

### Provisions of general application

**14.** An office holder should disclose:

(a)   all payments, arising from an insolvency appointment to the office holder or their associates;
(b)   the form and nature of any professional or personal relationships between the office holder and their associates.

**15.** An office holder should inform creditors and other interested parties[1] of their rights under insolvency legislation. Creditors should be advised how they may access suitable information setting out their rights within the first communication with them and in each subsequent report. An insolvency practitioner is not precluded from providing information, including a fees estimate, within pre-appointment communications (such as when assisting directors in commencing an insolvency process).

**16.** Where an office holder sub-contracts work that could otherwise be carried out by the office holder or their staff, this should be drawn to the attention of creditors and other interested parties[1] with an explanation of why it is being done, what is being done, and how much it will cost.

**17.** The key issues of concern to creditors and other interested parties[1] will commonly be:

(a)   the work the office holder anticipates will be done and why that work is necessary;
(b)   the anticipated payment for that work;
(c)   whether it is anticipated that the work will provide a financial benefit to creditors, and if so what anticipated benefit (or if the work provides no direct financial benefit, but is required by statute);
(d)   the work actually done and why that work was necessary;
(e)   the actual payment for the work, as against any estimate provided;
(f)   whether the work has provided a financial benefit to creditors, and if so what benefit (or if the work provided no direct financial benefit, but was required by statute).

**18.** When providing information about payments from an estate the office holder should do so in a way which clearly explains the key issues. Narrative explanations should be provided to support any numerical information supplied. Such an approach allows creditors and other interested parties[1] to better recognise the nature of an office holder's role and the work they intend to undertake, or have undertaken, in accordance with the key issues.

**19.** The following are not permissible as either remuneration or an expense:

(a)   an expense or any other charge calculated as a percentage of remuneration;
(b)   an administration fee or charge additional to an office holder's remuneration;
(c)   the recovery of any overheads other than those absorbed in the charge out rates.

[1]    "other interested parties" means those parties with rights pursuant to the prevailing insolvency legislation to information about the office holder's receipts and payments. This may include a creditors' committee, the members (shareholders) of a company, or in personal insolvency, the debtor.

## Provisions of specific application

### Basis of remuneration

20.    The office holder should provide an indication of the likely return to creditors when seeking approval for the basis of their remuneration.

21.    When approval for a set fee or a percentage basis is sought, the office holder should explain why the basis requested is expected to produce a fair and reasonable reflection of the work that the office holder anticipates will be undertaken. Where a set amount or a percentage basis is being used, an explanation should be provided of the direct costs included. The office holder should not seek to separately recover sums already included in a set amount or percentage basis fee and should be transparent in presenting any information.

22.    Where remuneration is sought on more than one basis, it should be clearly stated to which part of the office holder's activities each basis relates.

23.    When providing a fees estimate the office holder should supply that information in sufficient time for creditors (including when acting through a committee) to be able to make an informed judgement about the reasonableness of the office holder's requests. Fees estimates should be based on all of the information available to the office holder at the time that the estimate is provided.

24.    When providing a fees estimate of time to be spent, creditors and other interested parties[1] may find a blended rate[2] (or rates) and total hours anticipated to be spent on each part of the anticipated work more easily understandable and comparable than detail covering each grade or person working on the appointment. The estimate should also clearly describe what activities are anticipated to be conducted in respect of the estimated fee. When subsequently reporting to creditors, the actual hours and average rate (or rates) of the costs charged for each part should be provided for comparison purposes.

25.    The information provided in the fees estimate may not be presented on the basis of alternative scenarios and/or provide a range of estimated charges. However for other payments that an office holder anticipates will, or are likely to be, made, it is acceptable to provide a range, or repeat a range quoted by a third party, for example legal costs in litigation in any expense estimates.

26.    To provide creditors and other interested parties[1] with sufficient information to make an informed judgement, office holders should divide the narrative explanations and any fees estimate provided, into areas such as:

(a)    administration (including statutory reporting)
(b)    realisation of assets
(c)    creditors (claims and distribution)
(d)    investigations
(e)    trading (where applicable)
(f)    appointment specific matters (where applicable).

27.    These are examples of common activities and not an exhaustive list. Alternative or further sub- divisions may be appropriate, depending on the nature and complexity of the appointment and the bases of remuneration sought and/or approved. It is unlikely that the same divisions will be appropriate in all appointments and an office holder should consider what divisions are likely to be appropriate and proportionate in the circumstances of each appointment.

28.    This statement does not mandate any particular fee basis. An insolvency practitioner's business model may influence the fee basis they choose. However, whatever the business model, the insolvency practitioner's commercial approach cannot override the

principle that any work done for which payment is sought must be necessarily and properly undertaken in the context of an insolvency appointment.

1    "other interested parties" means those parties with rights pursuant to the prevailing insolvency legislation to information about the office holder's receipts and payments. This may include a creditors' committee, the members (shareholders) of a company, or in personal insolvency, the debtor.

2    "A blended rate" is calculated as the prospective average cost per hour for the appointment (or category of work in the appointment), based upon the estimated time to be expended by each grade of staff at their specific charge out rate.

## Expenses

29.    Expenses are any payments from the estate which are neither an office holder's remuneration nor a distribution to a creditor or a member. Expenses also includes disbursements. Disbursements are payments which are first met by the office holder, and then reimbursed to the office holder from the estate.

30.    Expenses are divided into those that do not need approval before they are charged to the estate (category 1) and those that do (category 2).

- Category 1 expenses: These are payments to persons providing the service to which the expense relates who are not an associate of the office holder. Category 1 expenses can be paid without prior approval.
- Category 2 expenses: These are payments to associates or which have an element of shared costs. Before being paid, category 2 expenses require approval in the same manner as an office holder's remuneration. Category 2 expenses require approval whether paid directly from the estate or as a disbursement.

31.    When seeking approval of category 2 expenses, an office holder should explain for each expense the basis on which the expense is being charged to the estate.

32.    Any shared or allocated payments incurred by the office holder or their firm are to be treated as category 2 expenses and approval sought before payment. This is irrespective of whether the payment is being made to an associate, because the office holder will be deciding how the expenses are being shared or allocated between insolvency appointments. Requiring approval of these payments enables those who are approving the expenses to confirm that the approach being taken by the office holder is reasonable.

33.    If an office holder has obtained approval for the basis of category 2 expenses, that basis may continue to be used in a sequential appointment where further approval of the basis of remuneration is not required, or where the office holder is replaced.

## Reports to creditors and other interested parties

34.    Any disclosure by an office holder of payments should be of assistance to those who have a financial interest in the level of payments from an estate in understanding what was done, why it was done, and how much it costs.

35.    Reports to creditors and other interested parties[1] should include a narrative update in respect of the office holder's activity during the period being reported upon, using consistent divisions for each part of the work reported upon, as far as possible.

36.    When reporting payments during a period, the office holder should use a consistent format throughout the appointment and provide figures for both the period being reported upon and on a cumulative basis.

37.    An office holder should endeavour to use consistent divisions throughout the appointment. The use of additional categories or further division may become necessary where a task was not foreseen at the commencement of the appointment.

38.    Requests for additional information about payments should be viewed upon their individual merits and treated by an office holder in a fair and reasonable way. The provision of additional information should be proportionate to the circumstances of the appointment.

## Pre-appointment costs

**39.** Where recovery of pre-appointment costs is expressly permitted by statute and approval is sought from creditors for payment from the estate of these costs, disclosure should follow the principles and standards contained in this statement.

[1] "other interested parties" means those parties with rights pursuant to the prevailing insolvency legislation to information about the office holder's receipts and payments. This may include a creditors' committee, the members (shareholders) of a company, or in personal insolvency, the debtor.

## Provision of information

**40.** In order to facilitate information requests under statute or to support the reporting of the office holder's remuneration, time recording systems used by office holders should record time in units of not greater than six minutes for each grade of staff used.

**41.** Where realisations are sufficient for creditors to be paid in full with interest, the creditors will not have the principal financial interest in the level of payments from the estate. Once this has been established by the office holder, they should provide the beneficiaries of the anticipated surplus, on request, with information in accordance with the principles and standards contained in this statement.

**42.** When an office holder's appointment is followed by the appointment of another office holder, whether or not in the same proceedings, the prior office holder should provide the successor with information in accordance with the principles and standards contained in this statement. This is in addition to any statutory obligations imposed on an office holder to provide information.

# SIP 11 THE HANDLING OF FUNDS IN FORMAL INSOLVENCY APPOINTMENTS

[A1.8]

**Effective Date: 1 January 2018**

## INTRODUCTION

1. This statement of insolvency practice concerns the handling of funds by insolvency practitioners in connection with their appointment as an office holder. Creditors and other interested parties[1] should be confident that funds are held appropriately and securely and that their interests are adequately protected.

2. Insolvency Practitioners will typically handle the following types of funds:

(a) Estate money
Estate money is all money deriving from the realisation of an asset, income or trading receipt of the insolvent estate received by the office holder in their capacity as such. It is held for the prevailing statutory purposes of the insolvency case. Office holders are at all times responsible for estate money and for any deductions made from the funds so held.

(b) Client Money
Client money is money belonging to a third party that is permitted to be held in accordance with the client money rules and regulations as may from time to time be in force by virtue of the insolvency practitioner's authorisation by a Recognised Professional Body. It may include (but is not limited to) third party money provided other than in consideration for the acquisition of an asset of the estate; funds held by the insolvency practitioner prior to or following their appointment as an office holder; or monies coming into the hands of an insolvency practitioner which are the property of individuals or entities for which they are acting other than in the capacity as office holder.

(c) Money belonging to the office holder or an entity in which they are working.

---

[1] "other interested parties" means those parties with rights pursuant to the prevailing insolvency legislation to information about the office holders' receipts and payments. This may include the creditors' committee, the members (shareholders) of a company, or in personal insolvency, the debtor.

## PRINCIPLES

3. An insolvency practitioner should clearly differentiate and segregate estate money, client money and the money belonging to the office holder or an entity in which they are working.

4. Estate money and client money must only be handled for their proper purposes, held securely and be subject to appropriate financial controls. Estate money must be held in accordance with the principles and standards of this SIP.

## KEY COMPLIANCE STANDARDS

### Records

5. Office holders should ensure that records are maintained to identify estate money (including any interest earned thereon) for each case for which they are the office holder and document transactions involving such funds.

## Account criteria

6.   Subject to the rules relating to the payment of funds into the Insolvency Services Account, estate money should be held in account(s) which meet the following criteria:

(a)   all funds standing to the credit of an estate is held as estate money and must be readily identifiable to that estate;

(b)   the account provider must not be entitled to combine estate money with any other funds or exercise any right to set off or counterclaim against any individual estate in respect of any money owed to it by any other individual estate, or for any other reason;

(c)   interest payable on estate money must be credited to the estate by which it was earned;

(d)   the account provider must describe estate accounts in its records to make it clear that the funds held do not belong to the office holder or an entity in which they are working.

7.   Where an office holder receives estate money in a manner such that it cannot be paid directly into an estate account, such money may be cleared through an account maintained in the name of the office holder or an entity in which they are working. Such accounts should be operated in accordance with the client money rules and regulations as may from time to time be in force by virtue of that office holder's authorisation. Funds paid into such accounts should be paid out to the estate to which they relate as soon as is reasonably practicable.

## Safeguards

8.   Office holders are responsible for safeguarding estate funds from misapplication or misappropriation. Access to estate money should only be afforded to persons in respect of whose actions adequate safeguard arrangements are in place. Those arrangements should include appropriate financial controls and may include insurance.

9.   Office holders should ensure that estate money is at all times held subject to appropriate financial controls. These controls may include (but are not limited to):

(a)   ensuring transactional processing is conducted in a timely manner;

(b)   seeking to ensure that solicitors and agents holding estate money account for those funds in a timely manner;

(c)   allowing only appropriate persons within the entity to conduct transactions;

(d)   adequate supervision of personnel with access to funds;

(e)   limiting the size of transactions that can be processed by different grades of staff;

(f)   implementing secure and robust authorisation procedures within the entity;

(g)   regular reconciliation of estate and client accounts;

(h)   periodic risk assessment of transactional processes within the entity;

(i)   requiring joint signatories or joint authentication.

10.   Financial controls and safeguards applied should be proportionate to the number of estates being administered, the quantum of funds held (individually and cumulatively), the number of transactions processed and the structure and ownership of the entity.

11.   Financial controls and safeguards, including levels of insurance cover, should be fully documented and reviewed by the office holder for their adequacy, as and when appropriate (and at a minimum annually).

# SIP 13 DISPOSAL OF ASSETS TO CONNECTED PARTIES IN AN INSOLVENCY PROCESS

[A1.9]

**Effective date: 30 April 2021**

## INTRODUCTION

1. The disposal of assets in an insolvency process to connected parties may give rise to concerns that assets or groups of assets may have been disposed of at less than market value and/or on more favourable terms than would have been available to a third party.

2. It is recognised that connected party transactions may be in the best interests of creditors but require adequate disclosure to creditors and other interested parties[1] as soon as reasonably practicable. Transparency in all dealings is of primary importance.

3. It is equally important that the insolvency practitioner acts and is seen to be acting in the interests of the creditors as a whole and is able to demonstrate this.

4. This statement of insolvency practice applies to both personal and corporate insolvency appointments, with the exception of members' voluntary liquidations. In administrations where the disposal is substantial and to a connected person[2] there are additional statutory obligations placed on the purchaser and the administrator.

5. In this Statement of Insolvency Practice, a connected party means a person with any connection to the directors, shareholders or secured creditors of the company or their associates and includes any connected person[2].

[1] "other interested parties" means those parties with rights pursuant to the prevailing insolvency legislation to information about insolvency proceedings. This may include a creditors' committee, the members (shareholders) of a company, or in personal insolvency, the debtor.

[2] Connected person has the meaning given to it in paragraph 60(A)(3) of Schedule B1 to the Insolvency Act 1986

## PRINCIPLES

6. An insolvency practitioner should be clear about the nature and extent of the role of advisor in the pre-appointment period. The roles are to be explained to the debtor, the company directors and the creditors. For the purposes of this Statement of Insolvency Practice only, the role of "insolvency practitioner" is to be read as relating to the advisory engagement that an insolvency practitioner or their firm and or/any associates may have in the period prior to commencement of the insolvency process. The role of "office holder" is to be read as the formal appointment as an office holder. An insolvency practitioner should recognise that a different insolvency practitioner may be the eventual office holder. When instructed to advise a debtor, a company or companies in a group, the insolvency practitioner should make it clear that the role is not to advise any parties connected with the purchaser, who should be encouraged to take independent advice. This is particularly important when there is a possibility that a connected party may acquire an interest in the business or assets.

7. The office holder should provide creditors and other interested parties with sufficient information such that a reasonable and informed third party would conclude that the transaction was appropriate and that the office holder has acted with due regard for the creditors' interests. As this is a connected party transaction the level of detail needs to be greater than in the reporting of a third party transaction.

## KEY COMPLIANCE STANDARDS

8. An insolvency practitioner should exercise professional judgement in advising the client whether a formal valuation of any or all of the assets is necessary. Where a valuation is relied on, other than one undertaken by an appropriate independent valuer

and/or advisor with adequate professional indemnity, this should be disclosed. The rationale for doing so and an explanation of why the officer holder was satisfied with the valuation should also be disclosed.

9.   In relation to an administration, the insolvency practitioner should ensure that any connected person[2] considering purchasing the business or assets of the company involving a substantial disposal is made aware that if the disposal takes place within 8 weeks of the day on which the company enters administration unless the connected person[2] purchaser obtains a qualifying report from an evaluator, the substantial disposal cannot be effected without creditor approval.

10.   An office holder should keep a detailed record of the reasoning behind both the decision to make a sale to a connected party and all alternatives considered. When considering the manner of disposal of the business or assets the office holder should be able to demonstrate that their duties under the legislation have been met.

## DISCLOSURE

11.   The office holder should demonstrate that they have acted with due regard to creditors' interests by providing creditors with a proportionate and sufficiently detailed justification of why a sale to a connected party was undertaken, including the alternatives considered. Such disclosure should be made in the next report to creditors after the transaction has been concluded.

12.   Additionally, where a qualifying report has been provided to an administrator by a connected person[2], the administrator is required to send the qualifying report to creditors with the proposals.

13.   Where legislation permits an office holder not to disclose information in certain limited circumstances, this Statement of Insolvency Practice will not restrict the effect of those statutory provisions.

# SIP 14 A RECEIVER'S RESPONSIBILITY TO PREFERENTIAL CREDITORS

[A1.10]

Issued June 1999

## 1 INTRODUCTION

**1.1** This statement of insolvency practice is one of a series issued by the Council of the Society with a view to harmonising the approach of members to questions of insolvency practice. It should be read in conjunction with the Explanatory Foreword to the Statements of Insolvency Practice and Insolvency Technical Reminders issued in June 1996. The statement has been prepared for the sole use of members in dealing with receiverships where any assets of the company are subject to a floating charge. Members are reminded that SPI Statements of Insolvency Practice are for the purpose of guidance only and may not be relied on as definitive statements. No liability attaches to the Council or anyone involved in the preparation or publication of Statements of Insolvency Practice. This statement applies to England and Wales only.

**1.2** This statement has been prepared to summarise what is considered to be the best practice to be adopted by receivers of the assets of companies where any of those assets are subject to a floating charge so that the office holder has legal obligations to creditors whose debts are preferential. Its purpose is to:

- ensure that members are familiar with the statutory provisions;
- set out best practice with regard to the application of the statutory provisions;
- set out best practice with regard to the provision of information to creditors whose debts are preferential and to responses to enquiries by such creditors.

Whilst this statement does not specifically address the treatment of preferential claims in liquidations, members acting as liquidators (or in any other relevant capacity) should have due regard to the principles which it contains.

**1.3** The statement has been produced in recognition of the likelihood that creditors whose debts are preferential may be concerned about the categorisation of assets as between fixed and floating charges and the manner in which costs incurred during a receivership are charged against the different categories of assets.

**1.4** The statement is divided into the following sections:

- the statutory provisions
- the categorisation of assets and allocation of proceeds as between fixed and floating charges
- the apportionment of costs incurred in the course of the receivership
- the determination of claims for preferential debts
- the payment of preferential debts
- disclosure of information and responses to queries raised by creditors whose debts are preferential
- other matters

## 2 THE STATUTORY PROVISIONS

**2.1** The rights of creditors whose debts are preferential in a receivership derive from s 40 of the Insolvency Act 1986 ('the Act').

Where a receiver is appointed on behalf of the holders of any debentures of a company secured by a charge which, as created, was a floating charge and the company is not at the time in the course of being wound up, its preferential debts shall be paid out of the assets coming into the hands of the receiver in priority to any claims for principal or interest in respect of the debentures. Where the receiver is appointed under both fixed and floating charges, this requirement does not extend to assets coming into the receiver's hands pursuant to the fixed charge(s).

Preferential debts are defined in s 386 of the Act and are set out in Sch 6 to the Act (as amended from time to time), which is to be read in conjunction with Sch 4 to the Pensions Schemes Act 1993. The date at which they are to be ascertained is the date of the appointment of the receiver (s 387(4) of the Act).

2.2   Members should note that the statutory provisions give a right to creditors whose debts are preferential to be paid those debts in priority to the claims of floating charge holders, and the corollary of this right is the obligation of the receiver to pay them. Failure by a receiver to pay preferential debts out of available assets is a breach of statutory duty. However it is recognised that circumstances may arise when it is administratively convenient or cost-effective to cooperate with a company's liquidator and arrange for him to pay the receivership preferential debts, and guidance on such arrangements is given in para 6.2 below. It should be noted that such arrangements do not exonerate the receiver from his obligations.

2.3   There are no statutory provisions requiring creditors with preferential debts in a receivership to prove those debts in any formal manner and no statutory obligation is imposed on a receiver to advertise for claims.


### 3 CATEGORISATION OF ASSETS AND ALLOCATION OF PROCEEDS

3.1   In order to ascertain what assets are subject to the statutory rights of creditors whose debts are preferential, it is necessary to distinguish, on a proper interpretation of the charging document(s), which assets are subject to a fixed charge and which are subject to a floating charge. In this statement this process is referred to as 'categorisation'.

3.2   The overriding principle, as laid down by the courts, is that it is not of itself sufficient for the charging document to state that an asset is subject to a fixed charge for it to be subject to such a charge. There have been cases where the courts have struck down charges that purported to be fixed and held that they were floating.

3.3   It is the duty of a receiver to effect the right categorisation and legal advice should be taken in cases of doubt. In some instances where there is doubt as to the correct categorisation it may be possible to consult preferential creditors and reach agreement with them and the chargeholder. However, if this is not possible and the receiver, in conjunction with his legal advisers, cannot determine the correct categorisation, it may be necessary to apply to the court for directions.

3.4   Members are reminded that:

•   it is the type of charge at the time of its creation which determines whether the assets are available to meet preferential debts. Crystallisation of a floating charge into a fixed charge prior to or upon the appointment of a receiver does not affect the rights of creditors with preferential debts to be paid out of assets subject to a crystallised floating charge;

•   the conversion, during receivership, of assets (for example, stock) subject at the date of appointment of the receiver to a floating charge into assets (for example, book debts) subject to a fixed charge, will not remove them from the pool of assets which is available to pay preferential debts.

3.5   Section 40 of the Act requires that the preferential debts 'shall be paid out of the [floating charge] assets coming to the hands of the receiver in priority to' the debenture holder. The effect is that a receiver is under a liability in tort to the preferential creditors if, having had available assets in hand, he fails to apply them in payment of the preferential debts. Where any action which he proposes to take could result in a diminution in the amount available to meet preferential debts the receiver should give the most serious consideration to the risks of such action.

3.6   When assets are sold as part of a going concern (or otherwise in parcels comprising both fixed and floating charge assets) the apportionment of the total consideration suggested by the purchaser (for example for his own financial reasons) may not properly reflect the financial interests of the different classes of creditors in the individual assets or categories of assets. In these circumstances the receiver should ensure that he will be able properly to discharge his obligations to account to holders of fixed charges on the one hand and creditors interested in assets subject to floating charges on the other.

## 4 APPORTIONMENT OF COSTS

**4.1**   The amount available to meet preferential debts is the funds realised from the disposal of assets subject to a floating charge net of the costs of realisation. It is dependent, therefore, not only on the correct categorisation of the assets but also on the appropriate allocation of costs incurred in effecting realisations.

**4.2**   These costs will normally fall into one of three categories:

* liabilities incurred by the company (the receiver being its agent until winding up supervenes) and costs incurred by the receiver and recoverable by him out of the company's assets under his statutory indemnity (other than those referred to below);
* the costs of the receiver in discharging his statutory duties;
* the remuneration and disbursements of the receiver.

**4.3**   Liabilities incurred by the company and the receiver's reasonable costs are sometimes readily identifiable as applicable to either the fixed charge or floating charge assets, but in other cases may not be so easily allocated between the two categories of assets.

Where costs are clearly identifiable as having been incurred in the realisation or collecting in of one or other of the two categories they should be recorded as such in the receiver's records so that they can be deducted from realisation proceeds in ascertaining the amount available for each class of creditors.

**4.4**   It is in the nature of receiverships, and particularly receiverships where trading is continued, that there will be continuation of employment of the company's directors and staff, ongoing occupation of its premises, purchase of supplies for manufacturing and other purposes and much of the other expenditure normally associated with a company's operations. In these circumstances it may be difficult to arrive at an appropriate allocation of costs. Many of the activities in a trading receivership will enhance the realisations of assets in both of the categories identified above. They may of necessity be incurred before full categorisation has been completed.

These factors do not affect the duty of a receiver to allocate costs appropriately but that allocation will involve the exercise of professional judgement undertaken with a full appreciation that it must be made with independence of mind and with integrity.

**4.5**   The key principles for a receiver in his consideration of the allocation of costs (including any trading losses) are:

* the statutory rights of preferential creditors as set out in the Insolvency Act 1986 and the decisions of the courts in cases under that Act and predecessor legislation;
* the provisions of the charging document(s);
* the maintenance of a proper balance as between the classes of creditors with whose interests he is required to deal in the light of their legal rights.

In order to enable a receiver to allocate costs on an appropriate basis, contemporaneous records of the dominant reasons for incurring costs should be maintained. These will also assist him in providing explanations as to how he arrived at what he considers to be an appropriate allocation and provide evidence should that allocation be challenged by any of the parties involved.

**4.6**   In allocating costs a receiver should have regard to:

* the objectives for which costs were incurred, it being recognised that certain types of costs may, properly, be allocated to the fixed charge assets in one case and to the floating charge assets in another.[1] In another case such costs may enhance realisations in both categories.
* the benefits actually obtained for those financially interested in one or other category of asset in terms of protection of those assets or their value and any augmentation of that value.
* whether the benefits to those interested in assets subject to a fixed charge has been enhanced by action which proves to be detrimental to those interested in floating charge assets (for example where trading losses are incurred to protect or enhance the value of property or book debts subject to a fixed charge).
* whether the realisation of the undertaking and assets by means of a going concern sale has resulted in a reduction in the quantum of debts which are preferential due to the transfer of employment contracts.

4.7   A receiver will incur costs in complying with his statutory duties. The extent of those duties depends upon the nature of his appointment and they are more onerous in the case of administrative receivers.

An administrative receivership arises only when there is a floating charge and the charges under which the receiver is appointed are over the whole or substantially the whole of the company's assets. There are no decided cases as to how the additional costs incurred by an administrative receiver (as opposed to a receiver not so designated) should be allocated.

In apportioning the costs of fulfilling their statutory duties and in the absence of any guidance from the courts, members should have regard to the general principle referred to in para 4.5 above of maintaining a proper balance.

4.8   The allocation of a receiver's remuneration and disbursements should be undertaken adopting the same principles as those applicable to costs and he should ensure that he maintains contemporaneous records which will enable him to make an appropriate division of his remuneration and disbursements between the different categories of assets.

¹   For example the payment of rent on a leasehold property may be to preserve the value of the lease or to enable manufacturing to continue and work in progress to be completed.

## 5 DETERMINATION OF PREFERENTIAL DEBTS

5.1   As stated in paras 2.2 and 2.3 of this statement it is a receiver's obligation to pay preferential debts out of assets available for that purpose and no proof of debt or advertisement for creditors is required.

5.2   Following initial notification to potential preferential creditors of his appointment and before beginning the process of determining preferential debts, a receiver should assess whether there are likely to be sufficient floating charge realisations to pay a distribution. Where no payment will be made, it is not necessary to agree preferential claims. However, in such circumstances the receiver should write to creditors whose claims are preferential explaining why he is unable to make a payment to them.

5.3   Where there will be a distribution to preferential creditors, the receiver should assist those creditors, where possible, by providing adequate information to enable them to calculate their claims. In the case of all preferential creditors other than employees, the receiver is entitled to assume they have full knowledge of their legal entitlements under the Insolvency Act and should invite them to submit their claims. The receiver should then check those claims, and accept or reject them as appropriate.

5.4   In determining the preferential claims of employees, the receiver is not entitled to regard an individual employee as having full knowledge of his rights and entitlements. Accordingly, the receiver should obtain information from either the company's records or from the employee before calculating the claim (other than one which is payable to the Secretary of State by way of subrogation). The employee should be provided with details of the calculation of his claim and any further explanation that he may reasonably require.

5.5   Members are reminded that Sch 6 (para 11) of the Act provides that anyone who has advanced money for the purpose of paying wages, salaries or accrued holiday remuneration of any employee is a preferential creditor to the extent that the preferential claim of the employee is reduced by such advance.

5.6   When an employee's preferential debt has been paid out of the National Insurance Fund under the provisions of the Employment Rights Act 1996, the Secretary of State is entitled, by virtue of s 189 of that Act to the benefit of the employee's preferential debt, in priority to any residual claim of the employee himself. Members are reminded that a receiver is not obliged to accept the preferential claim of the Secretary of State without satisfying himself that it is correct. If a member is not able to accept the Secretary of State's claim he should contact the Redundancy Payments Service to explain why and attempt to reach agreement on the amount to be admitted.

## 6 PAYMENT OF PREFERENTIAL DEBTS

**6.1** As soon as practicable after funds become available and the amount of the preferential debts has been ascertained, members should take steps to pay them. Under the statutory provisions preferential debts do not attract interest and payments to creditors should not be unnecessarily delayed. A receiver who does not comply timeously with his obligations under s 40 and against whom judgment is obtained may find himself ordered to pay interest by the court. While members cannot be expected to bear any financial risk by paying some preferential debts before all such debts are agreed, there are often circumstances when it is possible to make payment either in full or on account before all claims have been agreed and this course of action should be adopted whenever it is practicable to do so.

**6.2** Situations may arise where, notwithstanding a receiver's statutory duty to pay preferential debts, it may (exceptionally) be administratively convenient or cost- effective for a receiver to make arrangements for the liquidator to make payment of the preferential debts arising in the receivership. Such arrangements are made at the receiver's risk, and should not be on any basis which could result in payment of an amount less than that which would have been available to meet those debts if the receiver had himself paid them, or which would cause delay in paying them.

**6.3** The receiver should provide preferential creditors with details of any such arrangements and the reason for making them.

## 7 DISCLOSURE TO CREDITORS WITH PREFERENTIAL DEBTS

**7.1** When the funds realised from assets subject to a floating charge are inadequate to pay the preferential debts in full, the receiver should (unless he has already written to them as suggested in para 5.2) send those creditors a statement setting out:

- the assets which have, in accordance with the charging document, been categorised as subject to the floating charge;
- the costs charged against the proceeds of the realisation of those assets.

**7.2** Any further information which a creditor with a preferential debt reasonably requires should be provided promptly.

## 8 OTHER MATTERS

**8.1** Difficulties may arise in determining the rights of creditors to have debts paid preferentially in priority to a prior floating charge holder when the receiver has been appointed under a second or subsequent charge. The law in this area is complex and members should seek legal advice (and if necessary apply to the court for directions) when appointed under such a charge.

**8.2** Situations will arise where payments sent out are not encashed and the payee cannot readily be located. The insolvency legislation does not make provision for this eventuality and there have been no reported cases where the courts have decided the matter. Where a receiver decides to account to the next person entitled to such monies he should bear in mind his overriding obligation to pay preferential debts. He should make such arrangements as he considers appropriate to enable him to recover the funds from the party to whom he has paid them so that he will be able to discharge his obligation to any preferential creditor who subsequently asserts his claim to payment.

## SIP 15 REPORTING AND PROVIDING INFORMATION ON THEIR FUNCTIONS TO COMMITTEES AND COMMISSIONERS

**[A1.11]**

**Effective date:** This SIP applies to insolvency appointments starting on or after **1 March 2017**

### INTRODUCTION

1. The interests of creditors are of significant importance to office holders in fulfilling their duties. Legislation provides for creditors to assist office holders in the performance of their duties through representatives elected by creditors.

2. Legislation refers to such representatives using different terms: creditors' committee (administration, administrative receivership, receivership and bankruptcy), liquidation committee (company winding up), and commissioners (sequestration in Scotland). For the purposes of this statement the term "committee" is used to refer to the appropriate body in respect of each relevant insolvency procedures.

3. This SIP also applies where a committee is proposed or formed (as appropriate) in an individual, partnership or company voluntary arrangement or trust deed (in Scotland).

4. For the purposes only of this SIP the term "office holder" includes an insolvency practitioner providing advice or assistance to directors in connection with the appointment of a liquidator in a creditors voluntary liquidation.

### PRINCIPLES

5. Office holders should ensure that those considering nomination to committees and those who are elected to committees are provided with sufficient information for them to consider nomination and be able to carry out their duties and functions.

6. Information provided by an office holder should be presented in a manner which is transparent and useful to the committee, whilst being proportionate to the case. Requests for additional information should be treated by an office holder in a fair and reasonable way.

7. Office holders should exercise professional judgement according to the circumstances of the case whilst having regard to the views of the committee. Office holders should ensure that such views do not fetter their decision making.

### KEY COMPLIANCE STANDARDS

8. Creditors should be able to make an informed decision on whether they wish to be nominated to serve on a committee. Office holders should advise creditors (or in relation to a creditors voluntary liquidation, ensure that creditors are advised) in writing how they may access suitable information on the rights, duties and the functions of the committee prior to inviting nomination of committee members.

9. At the committee's first meeting, office holders should discuss with committee members how frequently they wish to receive reports and obtain their directions. These directions are likely to depend on the circumstances of the case. Office holders should also discuss with committee members the type of matters which they wish to have reported to them so that matters of particular concern to them are identified. The first meeting of the committee should be held as early as practical after the committee is established.

10. Office holders should on each occasion they report, identify what matters (in addition to those already identified) should be included in the report, exercising professional judgement as to which aspects of the proceedings may be of concern to the committee.

11. Office holders should ensure that any arrangements which are made for reporting to a committee are properly documented and adhered to.

**12.** The frequency of reporting and directions obtained at the outset of the case may not be appropriate throughout the course of the proceedings. The office holder should therefore consider throughout the lifetime of the case whether circumstances have altered which may change the committee's requirements for reporting frequency or their directions. Where circumstances have altered, the office holder should when next reporting to the committee set out the change of circumstances and obtain new agreement on reporting frequency and any new directions necessary.

**13.** Where an office holder considers their professional judgement should override the views of a committee, the office holder should clearly document why it is inappropriate to follow the views of the committee and provide an explanation to the committee. The office holder should also consider whether it is appropriate, in matters of contention to seek the views of creditors more widely or to seek the direction of the court or the Accountant in Bankruptcy (in Scotland).

## SIP 16 PRE-PACKAGED SALES IN ADMINISTRATIONS

**[A1.12]**

**Effective date: 30 April 2021**

### INTRODUCTION

1.   The term 'pre-packaged sale' refers to an arrangement under which the sale of all or part of a company's business or assets is negotiated with a purchaser prior to the appointment of an administrator and the administrator effects the transaction or transactions immediately on or shortly after appointment.

2.   The particular nature of an insolvency practitioner's position in these circumstances renders transparency in all dealings of primary importance. Administration is a collective insolvency proceeding - creditors and other interested parties should be confident that the insolvency practitioner has acted professionally and with objectivity; failure to demonstrate this clearly may bring the insolvency practitioner and the profession into disrepute.

3.   An insolvency practitioner should recognise the high-level interest the public and the business community have in pre-packaged sales in administration. The insolvency practitioner should assume, and plan for, greater interest in and possible scrutiny of such sales where the directors and/or shareholders of the purchasing entity are the same as those of, or are connected to, the insolvent entity.

4.   It is equally important that the insolvency practitioner acts and is seen to be acting in the interests of the company's creditors as a whole and is able to demonstrate this.

5.   This Statement of Insolvency Practice applies to all pre-packaged sales in administrations, irrespective of the who the purchaser may be. Where the sale involves a substantial disposal to a connected person[1], there are additional statutory obligations placed on the purchaser and the administrator, and additional information will need to be disclosed.

6.   In this Statement of Insolvency Practice, the expression connected is used to mean a person with any connection to the directors, shareholders or secured creditors of the company or their associates and includes any connected person[1].

---

[1]   Connected person has the meaning given to it in paragraph 60(A)(3) of Schedule B1 to the Insolvency Act 1986

### PRINCIPLES

7.   An insolvency practitioner should differentiate clearly the roles that are associated with an administration that involves a pre-packaged sale, that is, the provision of advice to the company before any formal appointment and the functions and responsibilities of the administrator following appointment. The roles are to be explained to the directors and the creditors. For the purposes of this Statement of Insolvency Practice only, the role of "insolvency practitioner" is to be read as relating to the advisory engagement that an insolvency practitioner or their firm and or/any associates may have with a company in the period prior to the company entering administration. The role of "administrator" is to be read as the formal appointment as administrator after the company has entered administration. An insolvency practitioner should recognise that a different insolvency practitioner may be the eventual administrator.

8.   The administrator should provide creditors with sufficient information ("the SIP 16 statement") such that a reasonable and informed third party would conclude that the pre-packaged sale was appropriate and that the administrator has acted with due regard for the creditors' interests. Where the purchaser is connected to the insolvent entity the level of detail will need to be greater.

## KEY COMPLIANCE STANDARDS

### Preparatory work

9.   An insolvency practitioner should be clear about the nature and extent of the role of advisor in the pre-appointment period. When instructed to advise the company or companies in a group, the insolvency practitioner should make it clear that the role is not to advise the directors or any parties connected with the purchaser, who should be encouraged to take independent advice. This is particularly important if there is a possibility that the directors may acquire an interest in the business or assets in a pre-packaged sale.

10.   An insolvency practitioner should bear in mind the duties and obligations which are owed to creditors in the pre-appointment period. The insolvency practitioner should recognise the potential liability which may attach to any person who is party to a decision that causes a company to incur credit and who knows that there is no good reason to believe it will be repaid. Such liability is not restricted to the directors.

11.   The insolvency practitioner should ensure that any connected person[1] considering a pre - packaged purchase involving a substantial disposal is made aware that unless the connected person1 purchaser obtains a qualifying report from an evaluator, the substantial disposal cannot be effected without creditor approval.

12.   Where the purchaser is connected to the insolvent entity, the insolvency practitioner should make the purchaser aware of the potential for enhanced stakeholder confidence in preparing a viability statement[2] for the purchasing entity.

13.   An insolvency practitioner should keep a detailed record of the reasoning behind both the decision to undertake a pre-packaged sale and all alternatives considered.

14.   The insolvency practitioner should advise the company that any valuations obtained should be carried out by appropriate independent valuers and/or advisors, carrying adequate professional indemnity insurance for the valuation performed.

15.   If the administrator relies on a valuation or advice other than by an appropriate independent valuer and/or advisor with adequate professional indemnity insurance this should be disclosed and with the reason for doing so and the reasons that the administrator was satisfied with the valuation, explained.

---

[2]   A viability review can be drawn up by a person connected to the insolvent entity wishing to make a pre- packaged purchase, stating how the purchasing entity will survive for at least 12 months from the date of the proposed purchase. The prospective purchaser should consider providing a short narrative detailing what the purchasing entity will do differently in order that the business will not fail ("the viability statement).

### Marketing

16.   Marketing a business is an important element in ensuring that the best available consideration is obtained for it in the interests of the company's creditors as a whole, and will be a key factor in providing reassurance to creditors. The insolvency practitioner should advise the company that any marketing should conform to the marketing essentials as set out in the appendix to this Statement of Insolvency Practice.

17.   Where there has been deviation from any of the marketing essentials, the administrator is to explain how a different strategy has delivered the best available outcome.

### After appointment

18.   When considering the manner of disposal of the business or assets the administrator should be able to demonstrate that the duties of an administrator under the legislation have been met.

### Disclosure

19.   An administrator should provide creditors with a detailed narrative explanation and justification (the SIP 16 statement) of why a pre-packaged sale was undertaken and all alternatives considered, to demonstrate that the administrator has acted with due regard for their interests. The information disclosure requirements in the appendix should be included in the SIP 16 statement unless there are exceptional circumstances, in which case the administrator should explain why the information has not been provided. In any sale where the purchaser is connected to the insolvent entity, it is very unlikely that commercial confidentiality alone would outweigh the need for creditors to be provided with this information.

20.   The explanation of the pre-packaged sale in the SIP 16 statement should be provided with the first notification to creditors and in any event within seven calendar days of the transaction(s). If the administrator has been unable to meet this requirement, the administrator will provide a reasonable explanation for the delay. The SIP 16 statement should be included in the administrator's statement of proposals filed at Companies House.

21.   The administrator should recognise that, if creditors have had to wait until, or near, the statutory deadline for the proposals to be issued there may be some confusion on the part of creditors when they do receive them, the sale having been completed some time before. Accordingly, when a pre-packaged sale has been undertaken, the administrator should seek any requisite approval of the proposals as soon as practicable after appointment and, ideally, the proposals should be sent with the notification of the sale. If the administrator has been unable to meet this requirement the proposals should include an explanation for the delay.

22.   The Insolvency Act 1986 and the Insolvency (Northern Ireland) Order 1989 permit an administrator not to disclose information in certain limited circumstances. This Statement of Insolvency Practice will not restrict the effect of those statutory provisions.

## Appendix


### MARKETING ESSENTIALS

Marketing a business is an important element in ensuring that the best available consideration is obtained for it in the interests of creditors, and will be a key factor in providing reassurance to creditors. Any marketing should conform to the following:

* **Broadcast** – the business should be marketed as widely as possible proportionate to the nature and size of the business – the purpose of the marketing is to make the business's availability known to the widest group of potential purchasers in the time available, using whatever media or other sources are likely to achieve this outcome.
* **Justify the marketing strategy** – the statement to creditors should not simply be a list of what marketing has been undertaken. It should explain the reasons underpinning the marketing and media strategy used.
* **Independence** – where the business has been marketed by the company prior to the insolvency practitioner being instructed, this should not be used as a justification in itself to avoid further marketing. The administrator should be satisfied as to the adequacy and independence of the marketing undertaken.
* **Publicise rather than simply publish** – marketing should have been undertaken for an appropriate length of time to satisfy the administrator that the best available outcome for creditors as a whole in all the circumstances has been achieved. Creditors should be informed of the reason for the length of time settled upon.
* **Connectivity** – include online communication alongside other media by default. The internet offers one of the widest populations of any medium. If the business is not marketed via the internet, this should be justified.
* **Comply or explain** – particularly with sales to those connected to the insolvent entity, where the level of interest is at its highest, the administrator needs to

explain how the marketing strategy has achieved the best available outcome for creditors as a whole in all the circumstances.

## Information disclosure requirements in the SIP 16 statement

The administrator should include a statement explaining the statutory purpose pursued, confirming that the transaction(s) enable(s) the statutory purpose to be achieved and that the outcome achieved was the best available outcome for creditors as a whole in all the circumstances.

The following information should be included in the administrator's explanation of a pre-packaged sale, as far as the administrator is aware after making appropriate enquiries:

### Initial introductions

The source (to be named) of the initial introduction to the insolvency practitioner and the date of the administrator's initial introduction.

### Pre-appointment matters

The extent of the administrator's (and that of their firm, and/or any associates) involvement prior to appointment.

The alternative options considered, both prior to and within formal insolvency by the insolvency practitioner and the company, and on appointment the administrator with an explanation of the possible outcomes.

Whether efforts were made to consult with major or representative creditors and the upshot of any consultations. If no consultation took place, the administrator should explain the reasons.

Why it was not appropriate to trade the business and offer it for sale as a going concern during the administration.

Details of requests made to potential funders to fund working capital requirements. If no such requests were made, explain why.

Details of registered charges with dates of creation.

If the business or business assets have been acquired from an insolvency process within the previous 24 months, or longer if the administrator deems that relevant to creditors' understanding, the administrator should disclose both the details of that transaction and whether the administrator, administrator's firm or associates were involved.

### Marketing of the business and assets

The marketing activities conducted by the company and/or the administrator and the effect of those activities. Reference should be made to the marketing essentials above. Any divergence from these essentials is to be drawn to creditor's attention, with the reasons for such divergence, together with an explanation as to why the administrator relied upon the marketing conducted.

### Valuation of the business and assets

The names and professional qualifications of any valuers and /or advisors and confirmation that they have confirmed their independence and that they carry adequate professional indemnity insurance. In the unlikely event that valuers and /or advisors who do not meet these criteria have been employed, the reasons for doing so should be explained.

The valuations obtained for the business or its underlying assets. Where goodwill has been valued, an explanation and basis for the value given.

A summary of the basis of valuation adopted by the administrator or the valuers and/or advisors.

The rationale for the basis of the valuations obtained and an explanation of the value achieved of the assets compared to those valuations.

If no valuation has been obtained, the reason for not having done so and how the administrator was satisfied as to the value of the assets.

### The transaction(s)

The date of the transaction(s).

Purchaser and related parties

- The identity of the purchaser.
- Any connection between the purchaser and the directors, shareholders or secured creditors of the company or their associates.
- The names of any directors, or former directors (or their associates), of the company who are involved in the management, financing, or ownership of the purchasing entity, or of any other entity into which any of the assets are transferred.
- In transactions impacting on more than one related company (e.g. a group transaction) the administrator should ensure that the disclosure is sufficient to enable a transparent explanation (for instance, allocation of consideration paid).
- Whether any directors had given guarantees for amounts due from the company to a prior financier and whether that financier is financing the new business.
- Where a viability statement has been provided, it should be attached to the SIP 16 statement.

Assets

- Details of the assets involved and the nature of the transaction(s).

Sale consideration

- The consideration for the transaction(s), terms of payment and any condition of the contract that could materially affect the consideration.
- The consideration disclosed under broad asset valuation categories and split between fixed and floating charge realisations (where applicable) and the method by which this allocation of consideration was applied.
- Any options, buy-back agreements, deferred consideration or other conditions attached to the transaction(s).
- Details of any security taken by the administrator in respect of any deferred consideration. Where no such security has been taken, the administrator's reasons for this and the basis for the decision that none was required.
- If the sale is part of a wider transaction, a description of the other aspects of the transaction.

### Connected person transactions only

Where a sale involving a substantial disposal has been undertaken to a connected person1 the additional details below should be included in the SIP 16 statement.

## Qualifying report

A copy of the qualifying report provided by the connected person1 to the administrator is to be included within the SIP 16 statement unless the proposal is being sent to creditors at the same time as the SIP 16 statement.

## SIP 17 AN ADMINISTRATIVE RECEIVER'S RESPONSIBILITY FOR THE COMPANY'S RECORDS – ENGLAND AND WALES

[A1.13]

Issued August 1997; Re-issued 2 May 2011

### INTRODUCTION

This document was issued as SIP 1 (Version 2 England and Wales) in August 1997. It was re-numbered as SIP 17 (without updating of the text) with effect from 2 May 2011.

1.   This statement of insolvency practice is one of a series issued by the Council of the Society with a view to harmonising the approach of members to questions of insolvency practice. It should be read in conjunction with the Explanatory Foreword to the Statements of Insolvency Practice and Insolvency Technical Reminders issued in June 1996. The statement has been prepared for the sole use of members in dealing with administrative receiverships in England and Wales. Members are reminded that SPI Statements of Insolvency Practice are for the purpose of guidance only and may not be relied upon as definitive statements. No liability attaches to the Council or anyone involved in the preparation or publication of Statements of Insolvency Practice. This statement applies to England and Wales only.

2.   This statement has been prepared to summarise what is considered to be the best practice in circumstances where administrative receivers are approached by liquidators or directors seeking access to or custody of a company's books and records. The best practice is considered below both with regard to company records maintained prior to the appointment of an administrative receiver and with regard to those records prepared after the administrative receiver's appointment.

### COMPANY RECORDS MAINTAINED PRIOR TO APPOINTMENT OF AN ADMINISTRATIVE RECEIVER

3.   The records which a company maintains prior to the appointment of an administrative receiver may be classified under two main headings.

4.   The first comprises the non-accounting records which the directors are required to maintain by the Companies Act 1985 (as amended) (the statutory records). These consist of various registers (eg of members) and minute books (eg of directors' meetings).

5.   The second category of records maintained by a company prior to the appointment of an administrative receiver includes accounting records required by statute and all other non-statutory records of the company (statutory accounting and other non-statutory records). Taking each in turn:

### STATUTORY RECORDS

6.   The company's statutory records should be kept at its registered office (see paragraph 11 below) having regard to the provisions of the Companies Act 1985, sections 288, 353, 383 and 407 (registers of directors, members, minute books and charges).

7.   Directors' powers to cause entries to be made in these statutory records do not cease on the appointment of an administrative receiver. Indeed, the directors' statutory duties to maintain them are unaffected by his appointment.

8.   An administrative receiver would have the power to inspect the statutory records as part of his right to take possession of, collect and get in the property of the company (cf paragraph 1 of Schedule 1 to the Insolvency Act 1986). He is not, however, placed under an obligation to maintain those records after his appointment and should not normally do so.

9.   The abolition by section 130 of the Companies Act 1989 of the requirement for a company formed under the Companies Acts to have a common seal means that in many cases the company in receivership will have no common seal. Provided that an appro-

priately worded attestation clause is used, deeds can be executed without the use of the common seal. Given that the common seal may still be used for the execution of deeds by the company, however, it is considered best practice for the administrative receiver to take possession of it.

10.   On appointment, an administrative receiver has two possible options:

(i)   To leave the statutory records in the custody of the directors so that they are in a position to continue to carry out their statutory duties to maintain them.

(ii)   To take possession of the statutory records for safe keeping. In such circumstances, the administrative receiver should remind the directors of their statutory responsibilities to maintain the records and allow them free access for this purpose. It would also be advisable for the administrative receiver to prepare a detailed receipt for all the records taken into his possession. This should be signed by a director or other responsible official of the company in receivership.

11.   The administrative receiver may change the company's registered office to that of his own firm, in which case, the statutory records should also be transferred to the new registered office and the procedure outlined in paragraph 10 (ii) above followed.

12.   Any statutory records (and if applicable any seals) taken into an administrative receiver's possession (see paragraphs 8 and 9) should be returned to the directors (or liquidator) on the receiver's ceasing to act.

## STATUTORY ACCOUNTING AND NON-STATUTORY RECORDS

13.   All such records as are necessary for the purposes of the receivership and for the discharge of the administrative receiver's statutory duties should be taken into the administrative receiver's possession and/or control and any which he will definitely not require may be left with the directors. If the administrative receiver encounters difficulty in obtaining possession of the records, the provisions of sections 234–236 of the Insolvency Act 1986 may be of assistance. These are the provisions allowing an administrative receiver to apply to the court for an order for property in the control of any party to be handed to him, placing officers and others under a statutory obligation to co-operate with the administrative receiver and allowing him to apply to the court for an order summoning officers of the company in receivership and others before it for questioning.

14.   An administrative receiver is under no statutory duty to bring these records up to date to the date of his appointment although for practical purposes (such as to give prospective purchasers some indication of the financial state of the business) it may be necessary for him to do so.

15.   If an administrative receiver does not take possession of all the records it would be advisable for him to make a list of all those not taken into his custody with a note of their whereabouts.

16.   making sales of certain assets (eg book debts or plant and machinery) it may be necessary for the administrative receiver to hand over to the purchaser company records (eg debtors' ledgers or plant registers) relating to those assets. In such circumstances, the administrative receiver should ensure that the relevant asset sale agreement specifies the need for these records to be made available to the company on request. Although this will invariably be a matter of negotiation between the administrative receiver and his purchaser, it would be preferable for him to retain the originals of such records. He may make copies available to the purchaser or allow the purchaser to retain them for a short time for the purpose of making copies. Once again, appropriate provision should be made in the asset sale agreement as to the particular circumstances and as to whom is to bear the costs.

17.   If an administrative receiver transfers the business of the company to a third party as a going concern, section 49 and paragraph 6 of Schedule 11 to the Value Added Tax Act 1994 place the obligation of preserving any records relating to the business upon the transferee. This applies unless the Commissioners of Customs & Excise, at the request of the transferor, otherwise direct.

18.   This is a wide-ranging obligation. It applies regardless of whether the VAT registration is itself transferred or whether the transfer is treated as a supply of neither goods nor services.

19. The categories of records covered by Schedule 11 paragraph 6 are wideranging. They include orders and delivery notes, purchase and sales records, annual accounts, VAT accounts and credit and debit notes.

## ENTITLEMENT OF LIQUIDATOR TO RECORDS

20. The case of *Engel v South Metropolitan Brewing & Bottling Company* ([1892] 1 Ch 442) is authority to the effect that a liquidator becomes entitled to possession of all books and records relating to the "management and business" of the company which are not necessary to support the title of the chargeholder as against a court-appointed receiver. The court held that a court-appointed receiver can be compelled to deliver such documents to the liquidator against the liquidator's undertaking to produce them to the receiver on request. While there is no equivalent authority with respect to an administrative receiver, general practice supports the proposition that delivery up of records in return for an undertaking and subsequent production on request should occur (Lightman & Moss, *Law of Receivers of Companies*, 2nd Edition, paragraph 11–17).

21. An administrative receiver has no statutory authority to destroy preappointment records and in due course these must be returned to the company's directors or, if the company is in liquidation, to its liquidator.

## POST APPOINTMENT RECORDS

### Statutory accounting records

### (i)

### Relating to the period prior to the appointment of a liquidator

22. The administrative receiver should establish appropriate accounting records as from the date of his appointment. The case of *Smiths Limited v Middleton* ([1979] 3 All ER 842) shows that he has a duty to render full and proper records to the company in order that the company (and its directors) may comply with the duties imposed by sections 221, 226, 227 and 241 Companies Act 1985 (preparation and approval of accounts).

23. An administrative receiver is also under obligation to make returns of his receipts and payments pursuant to Rule 3.32 of the Insolvency Rules 1986. The statutory requirements and the best practice to be followed in the preparation of insolvency office holders' receipts and payments accounts are summarised in the statement of insolvency practice entitled 'Preparation of Insolvency Office Holders' Receipts and Payments Accounts', to which members are referred for further information.

24. When a liquidator is appointed, the *Engel* case would seem to apply so that the liquidator becomes entitled to possession of records (see paragraph 20 above).

25. Administrative receivers have no statutory authority to destroy such records and on ceasing to act must hand these over to the company's directors or, if it is in liquidation, to the liquidator.

### (ii)

### Relating to the period after the appointment of a liquidator

26. As from the commencement of liquidation, the administrative receiver loses his status as agent of the company (section 44(1)(a) Insolvency Act 1986). The administrative receiver's obligation to make returns of receipts and payments and to maintain accounting records (paragraph 23 above) remains in force.

**27.** Section 41 Insolvency Act 1986 allows any member, creditor, the Registrar of Companies or the liquidator to enforce these duties.

## OTHER RECORDS

**28.** The remaining records, books and papers relating to a receivership may be subdivided between "company records", "receiver's personal records" and "charge-holder's records".

### (i)

### Company records

Company records will include as a minimum all those records which exist as a result of carrying on the company's business and dealing with the assets. These records fall in the same category as the non-statutory records mentioned in paragraphs 13 to 21 above. They should be treated in the same way, being returned to the company's directors or if it is in liquidation, to its liquidator when the receiver ceases to act. In the case of *Gomba Holdings UK Limited v Minories Finance Limited* ((1989) 5BCC 27) consideration was given to precisely which records fall within the definition of "company records". It was held that an administrative receiver acts in several capacities during the course of a receivership. In addition to being agent of the company, he owes fiduciary obligations to his appointor and to the company. It is only documents generated or received pursuant to his duty to manage the company's business or dispose of its assets which belong to the company.

### (ii)

### Chargeholder's records

As explained above, in the *Gomba* case quoted in paragraph 28(i) above it was held that documents containing advice and information to the appointor and "notes, calculations and memoranda" prepared to enable the administrative receiver to discharge his professional duty to his appointor or to the company belong either to the appointor (if he wishes to claim them) or to the administrative receiver. They do not belong to the company.

### (iii)

### Administrative receiver's personal records

An administrative receiver's personal records are those prepared by him for the purpose of better enabling him to discharge his professional duties. They will include, for instance, his statutory record which he is required to maintain by Regulation 17 of the Insolvency Practitioners' Regulations 1990 ("the Regulations"). The record must take the form set out in Schedule 3 to the Regulations.

## BEST PRACTICE

**29.** It is considered best practice that all records mentioned above, with the exception of a receiver's personal records (paragraph 28 (iii) above) and the appointor's records (paragraph 28 (ii) above) should be made available on request to the company acting by its directors or if it is in liquidation, its liquidator unless the administrative receiver is of the opinion that disclosure at that time would be contrary to the interests of the appointor, for instance because of current negotiations for the sale of assets (*Gomba Holdings UK Limited v Homan*, [1986] 3 All ER 94). Subject to the interests of the appointor, it appears from this case that directors are entitled to such information as they need to enable them to exercise their residual powers and to perform their residual statutory duties considered above.

30.  Disclosure of the administrative receiver's personal records is a matter for his discretion, although in any legal action brought against him it could be that if such records have not been disclosed they may be held to be discoverable.

31.  Where there is no liquidator and the directors cannot be traced (or the administrative receiver has reason to suppose that they are not reliable) he will need to consider whether he feels it necessary to present a petition for the company to be wound up using his powers under Schedule 1 to the Insolvency Act 1986. Whether or not a liquidator is appointed, the administrative receiver has no statutory power to destroy a company's records even after the expiry of the statutory period for which the company would need to retain them (usually six years). Thus, if he does so without the authority of the company or the liquidator, he does so at his peril. Note also that the record an administrative receiver is required to keep by the Regulations must be preserved for a period of ten years from the later of the date upon which the administrative receiver ceases to hold office or any security or caution maintained in respect of the company ceases to have effect (Regulation 20).

Appendix 2

# INSOLVENCY PRACTICE DIRECTION 2018 (AMENDED JULY 2020)

### PRACTICE DIRECTION: INSOLVENCY PROCEEDINGS

**[A2.1]**

Practice Direction made by order of the Chancellor of the High Court, Sir Geoffrey Vos, with the approval of the Lord Chancellor, the Right Honourable Robert Buckland QC MP, Secretary of State of Justice, on 3 July 2020.

### PART ONE: GENERAL PROVISIONS

### 1.

### Definitions

**1.1** In this Practice Direction, which shall be referred to as the "IPD", the following definitions will apply:

(1) The "Act" means the Insolvency Act 1986 and includes the Act as applied to limited liability partnerships by the Limited Liability Partnerships Regulations 2001 or as applied to any other person or body by virtue of the Act or any other legislation;

(2) The "Insolvency Rules" means the rules for the time being in force and made under s 411 and s 412 of the Act in relation to Insolvency Proceedings (currently The Insolvency (England and Wales) Rules 2016, as amended), and, save where otherwise provided, any reference to a 'rule' is to a rule in the Insolvency Rules;

(3) "CPR" means the Civil Procedure Rules and "CPRPD" means a Civil Procedure Rules Practice Direction;

(4) "EU Regulation on Insolvency Proceedings" means either the Council Regulation (EC) No 1346/2000 of 29 May 2000 on Insolvency Proceedings or the Regulation (EU) 2015/848 of the European Parliament and of the Council of 20 May 2015 on Insolvency Proceedings (known as the "Recast" EU Insolvency Regulation), as applicable

(5) "Service Regulation" means Council Regulation (EC) No. 1393/2007 or such successor regulation as may come into force replacing Council Regulation (EC) No. 1393/2007 concerning the service in the Member States of judicial and extrajudicial documents in civil and commercial matters;

(6) "Insolvency proceedings" means:

   (a) any proceedings under Parts 1 to 11 of the Act, the Insolvency Rules, the Administration of Insolvent Estates of Deceased Persons Order 1986 (S.I. 1986 No.1999), the Insolvent Partnerships Order 1994 (S.I. 1994 No. 2421) or the Limited Liability Partnerships Regulations 2001;

   (b) any proceedings under the EU Regulation on Insolvency Proceedings or the Cross-Border Insolvency Regulations 2006 (SI 2006/1030); and

   (c) in an insolvency context an application made pursuant to s.423 of the Act.

(7) References to a 'company' include a limited liability partnership and references to a 'contributory' include a member of a limited liability partnership;

(8) The following judicial definitions apply:

   (a) "District Judge" means a person appointed a District Judge under s.6(1) of the County Courts Act 1984;

(b) "District Judge Sitting in a District Registry" means a District Judge sitting in an assigned District Registry having insolvency jurisdiction as a District Judge of the High Court under s.100 of the Senior Courts Act 1981;

(c) "Circuit Judge" means a judge sitting pursuant to s.5(1)(a) of the County Courts Act 1984;

(d) "ICC Judge" means a person appointed to the office of Insolvency and Companies Court Judge (previously, Registrar in Bankruptcy) under s.89(1) of the Senior Courts Act 1981;

(e) "High Court Judge" means a High Court Judge listed in s.4(1) of the Senior Courts Act 1981.

(9) The definitions in paragraph 1.1(8) include Deputies unless otherwise specified and Deputies are defined as meaning, for each definition above respectively, a deputy District judge appointed under s.8 of the County Courts Act 1984, a deputy District Judge of the High Court appointed under s.102 of the Senior Courts Act 1981, a deputy Circuit Judge appointed under s.24 of the Courts Act 1971, a deputy ICC Judge appointed under s.91 of the Senior Courts Act 1981, and a judicial office holder acting as a judge of the High Court under s.9(1) of the Senior Courts Act 1981 or a deputy judge of the High Court appointed under s.9(4) of the Senior Courts Act 1981;

(10) "Court" means the High Court or any County Court hearing centre having insolvency jurisdiction;

(11) "Royal Courts of Justice" means the Business and Property Courts of England and Wales at the Rolls Building, 7 Rolls Buildings, Fetter Lane, London EC4A 1NL.

(12) In part six of this IPD "assessor" means a person appointed as an assessor under s.70 of the Senior Courts Act 1981 or s.63 of the County Courts Act 1984 as an assessor.


## 2.

### Coming into force

**2.1** This IPD shall come into force on 3 July 2020 and shall replace all previous Practice Directions, Practice Statements and Practice Notes relating to insolvency proceedings save for the Cooperate Insolvency and Governance Act Practice Direction dated 3rd July 2020, the Temporary Insolvency Practice Direction dated 6th April 2020, and the Practice Statement for schemes of arrangement concerning Part 26A of the Companies Act 2006 dated 30th June 2020. This IPD does not affect the PD for Directors' Disqualification Proceedings.

**2.2** If at the date of commencement of this IPD, a petition or application within or for the commencement of insolvency proceedings has already been listed for a hearing at a County Court hearing centre and such County Court hearing centre would otherwise have had jurisdiction to hear and determine that petition or application as at 24th April 2018, paragraph 3 of this IPD shall not apply and a judge at that hearing centre may proceed to determine that petition or application, unless the court considers or the parties agree that it would be appropriate to transfer the petition or application in line with paragraph 3.6 in any event, in which case paragraphs 3.8-3.10 may be considered.


## 3.

### Distribution of business

**3.1** In the High Court, all petitions and applications, save where paragraph 3.2 below provides otherwise, should be listed for an initial hearing before an ICC Judge in the Royal Courts of Justice, or a District Judge Sitting in a District Registry.

**3.2** The following applications relating to insolvent companies or insolvent individuals must be listed before a High Court Judge:

(1) applications for committal for contempt; and
(2) applications for a search order (CPR 25.1(1)(h)) and a freezing order (CPR 25.1(1)(f)).

**3.3** The following applications relating to insolvent companies or insolvent individuals may be listed before a High Court Judge or ICC Judge but, subject to paragraph 3.4 below, not before a District Judge Sitting in a District Registry or a District Judge:

(1) applications for an administration order;

(2) applications for an injunction pursuant to the Court's inherent jurisdiction (e.g. to restrain the presentation or advertisement of a winding up petition);

(3) interim applications and applications for directions or case management after any proceedings have been referred or adjourned to the High Court Judge;

(4) applications for the appointment of a provisional liquidator;

(5) applications for an injunction (other than those referred to in paragraph 3.2(2) above) pursuant to s.37 of the Senior Courts Act 1981, including an ancillary order under CPR 25.1(1)(g);

(6) applications for orders concerning moratoria contained in Chapters 1–6 of the Corporate Insolvency and Governance Act 2020; and

(7) applications for orders concerning the protection of supplies of goods and services.

**3.4** The following applications relating to insolvent companies or insolvent individuals may be listed before a District Judge Sitting in a District Registry only with the consent of the Supervising Judge for the circuit in which the District Judge is sitting, or with the consent of the Supervising Judge's nominee:

(1) applications pursuant to the Court's inherent jurisdiction (e.g. to restrain the presentation or advertisement of a winding up petition);

(2) interim applications and applications for directions or case management after any proceedings have been referred or adjourned to a High Court Judge.

**3.5** When deciding whether to hear and determine proceedings or to refer or adjourn them to a different level of judge, regard must be had to the following factors:

(1) whether the proceedings raise new or controversial points of law or have wide public interest implications;

(2) which venue can provide the earliest date for the hearing;

(3) the likely length of the hearing; and/or

(4) whether the petition or application includes or is likely to include matters that must be heard by a High Court Judge under paragraph 3.2 above.

**3.6** Where an application or petition for the commencement of insolvency proceedings, or any application or petition within existing insolvency proceedings, is issued in a County Court hearing centre having insolvency jurisdiction, unless the application or petition is Local Business, the application or petition but more usually the entirety of those insolvency proceedings shall be transferred:

(a) to a County Court hearing centre having insolvency jurisdiction located at a Business and Property Court in the same circuit; or

(b) to the Central London County Court if the application or petition was issued in a County Court hearing centre located in the South-Eastern circuit; or

(c) to one of the specialist centres specified in a list published from time to time by the Chancellor of the High Court or their nominee, and located in the same circuit as the hearing centre in which the application or petition was issued,

and be listed before a judge specialising in Business and Property Courts work as defined in paragraph 4.4 of the Business and Property Courts Practice Direction (the "specialist judge"). (The current list of specified specialist centres may be found at https://www.ju diciary.uk/insolvency-proceedings-practice-direction-specified-specialist-hearing-centre s/).

**3.7** For the purpose of paragraph 3.6 Local Business means (i) applications to set aside statutory demands; (ii) unopposed creditors' winding up petitions; (iii) unopposed bankruptcy petitions; (iv) applications for income payment orders; (v) applications for and the conduct of public and private examinations; (vi) warrants for arrest in connection with the conduct of public or private examinations; (vii) claims for possession by an office-holder against a bankrupt (whether or not the bankrupt has been discharged); (viii) claims falling under the Trusts of Land and Appointment of Trustees Act 1996 (notwithstanding the application of section 335A of the Act); (ix) claims for the granting or enforcement of charging orders pursuant to section 313 of the Act; (x) unopposed applications by the Official Receiver to suspend discharge from bankruptcy, and if the application transpires to be opposed, any application by the Official Receiver for an interim suspension pending the matter being heard following its transfer pursuant to paragraph 3.6 above; and (xi) applications for debt relief orders under Part 7A of the Act Such Local Business may be heard and determined by any judge in the County Court hearing centre in which those insolvency proceedings were issued, unless such a judge considers that it would be appropriate to transfer them in accordance with paragraph 3.6 in any event.

**3.8** Where insolvency proceedings are transferred under paragraph 3.6 or 3.7, they shall be listed for review on paper before a specialist judge in the receiving court as soon as possible. The specialist judge shall determine of their own initiative where the application (or any part of it) can most fairly be determined having regard to (i) the nature and complexity of the issues; (ii) the amounts involved in the insolvency proceedings or insolvency application; (iii) the location and needs of the parties; (iv) the available judicial resources; and (v) all the other circumstances of the case. The specialist judge shall take into account any views of the transferring judge and those of the parties to the application expressed in writing (without the need for evidence).

**3.9** The options available to the specialist judge include (but are not limited to):

(a)  Retaining the entirety of the insolvency proceedings in the receiving court;
(b)  Retaining the entirety of the insolvency proceedings in the receiving court but fixing the venue of any hearing before a specialist judge at some other hearing centre or by some means other than a physical hearing;
(c)  Returning the insolvency proceedings to the sending court to be dealt with as if it were Local Business;
(d)  Retaining the insolvency proceedings in the receiving court but transferring some part back for hearing or for management and hearing in the sending court as if it were Local Business.

**3.10** The case management decision about transfer shall be recorded in an order made of the specialist judge's own initiative.

4.

## Court documents

**4.1** All insolvency proceedings should be commenced and applications in insolvency proceedings should be made using the information prescribed by the Act, Insolvency Rules, the Business and Property Courts Practice Direction and/or other legislation under which the same is or are brought or made. Some forms relating to insolvency proceedings may be found at:

https://www.gov.uk/government/collections/bankruptcy-and-insolvency-forms

5.

## Service of Court documents in insolvency proceedings

**5.1** Schedule 4 to the Insolvency Rules prescribes the requirements for service where a Court document is required to be served pursuant to the Act or the Insolvency Rules. Pursuant to Schedule 4, CPR Part 6 applies except where Schedule 4 provides otherwise, or the court otherwise approves or directs.

**5.2** Subject to the Court approving or directing otherwise, CPR Part 6 applies to the service of Court documents both within and out of the jurisdiction.

**5.3** Attention is drawn to paragraph 6 of Schedule 4 to the Insolvency Rules which provides that where the Court has directed that service be effected in a particular manner, the certificate of service must be accompanied by a sealed copy of the order directing such manner of service.

**5.4** The provisions of CPR Part 6 are modified by Schedule 4 to the Insolvency Rules in respect of certain documents. Reference should be made to the "Table of requirements for service" in Schedule 4. Notable modifications relate to the service of: (a) a winding up petition; and (b) an application for an administration order.

**5.5** A statutory demand is not a Court document.

## 6.

### Drawing up of orders

**6.1** The parties are responsible for drawing up all orders, unless the Court directs otherwise. Attention is drawn to CPRPD 40B 1.2 and the Chancery Guide. All applications should be accompanied by draft orders.

## 7.

### Urgent applications

**7.1** In the Royal Courts of Justice the ICC Judges and the High Court Judges (and in other Courts exercising insolvency jurisdiction the High Court Judges, District Judges Sitting in a District Registry and District Judges) will hear urgent applications and time-critical applications as soon as reasonably practicable. This may involve delaying the hearing of another matter. Accordingly, parties asking for an application to be dealt with urgently must be able to justify the urgency with reasons.

## PART TWO: COMPANY INSOLVENCY

## 8.

### Administrations

**8.1** Attention is drawn to paragraph 2.1 of the Electronic Practice Direction 51O -The Electronic Working Pilot Scheme, or to any subsequent Electronic Practice Direction made after the date of this IPD, where a notice of appointment is made using the electronic filing system. For the avoidance of doubt, and notwithstanding the restriction in sub-paragraph (c) to notices of appointment made by qualifying floating charge holders, paragraph 2.1 of the Electronic Practice Direction 51O shall not apply to any filing of a notice of appointment of an administrator outside Court opening hours, and the provisions of Insolvency Rules 3.20 to 3.22 shall in those circumstances continue to apply.

**8.2** Paragraph 5.4 of the Electronic Practice Direction 51O provides that 'the date and time of payment' will be the filing date and time and 'it will also be the date and time of issue for all claim forms and other originating processes submitted using Electronic Working'.

**8.3** In the absence of special circumstances, an application for the extension of an administration should be made not less than one month before the end of the administration. The evidence in support of any later application must explain why the application is being made late. The Court will consider whether any part of the costs should be disallowed where an application is made less than one month before the end of the administration.

## 9.

### Winding up petitions

**9.1** Where a winding up petition is presented following service of a statutory demand, the statutory demand must contain the information set out in rule 7.3 of the Insolvency Rules and should, as far as possible, follow the form which appears at https://www.gov.uk/government/publications/demand-immediate-payment-of-a-debt-from-a-limited-company-form-sd1.

**9.2** Before presenting a winding up petition, the creditor must conduct a search to ensure that no petition is pending. Save in exceptional circumstances a second winding up petition should not be presented whilst a prior petition is pending. A petitioner who presents a petition while another petition is pending does so at risk as to costs.

**9.3** Payment of the fee and deposit

**9.3.1** Unless the petition is one in respect of which rule 7.7(2)(b) of the Insolvency Rules applies, a winding up petition will not be treated as having been presented until the Court fee and official receiver's deposit have been paid.

**9.3.2** A petition filed electronically without payment of the deposit will be marked "private" and will not be available for inspection until the deposit has been paid. The date of presentation of the petition will accord with the date on which the deposit has been paid. If the official receiver's deposit is not paid within 7 calendar days after filing the petition, the petition will not be accepted, in accordance with paragraph 5.3 of the Electronic Practice Direction 510 -The Electronic Working Pilot Scheme. If a petition is not accepted, a new petition will have to be filed if the petitioner wishes to wind up a company.

**9.3.3** The deposit will be taken by the Court and forwarded to the official receiver. In the Royal Courts of Justice the petition fee and deposit should be paid by cheque, or by debit or credit card over the phone. The Court will record the receipt and will impress two entries on the original petition, one in respect of the Court fee and the other in respect of the deposit. In a District Registry or a County Court hearing centre, the petition fee and deposit should be paid to the staff of the duly authorised officer of the Court, who will record its receipt.

**9.3.4** If payment is made by cheque, it should be made payable to 'HM Courts and Tribunals Service' or 'HMCTS'. For the purposes of paragraph 9.3 of this IPD, the deposit will be treated as paid when the cheque is received by the Court.

**9.4** Save where by reason of the nature of the company or its place of incorporation the information cannot be stated (in which case as much similar information as is available should be given), every creditor's winding up petition must (in the case of a company) contain the information set out in rule 7.5. Similar information (so far as is appropriate) should be given where the petition is presented against a partnership.

**9.5** Where the petitioning creditor relies on failure to pay a debt, details of the debt relied on should be given in the petition (whether or not they have been given in any statutory demand served in respect of the debt), including the amount of the debt, its nature and the date or dates on or between which it was incurred.

**9.6** The statement of truth verifying the petition in accordance with rule 7.6 should be made no more than ten business days before the date of issue of the petition.

**9.7** Where the company to be wound up has been struck off the register, the petition should state that fact and include as part of the relief sought an order that it be restored to the register. Save where the petition has been presented by a Minister of the Crown or a government department, evidence of service on the Government Legal Department or the Solicitor for the Affairs of the Duchy of Lancaster or the Solicitor to the Duchy of Cornwall (as appropriate) should be filed exhibiting the bona vacantia waiver letter.

9.8

### Notice of the petition

**9.8.1** The provisions contained in Chapter 4 of Part 1 and in particular rule 7.10 must be followed (unless waived by the Court). These provisions are designed to preserve the sanctity of the class remedy in any given winding up by the Court. Failure to comply with rule 7.10 may lead to summary dismissal of the petition on the return date. If the Court, in its discretion, grants an adjournment, this will usually be on terms that notice of the petition is gazetted or otherwise given in accordance with the Insolvency Rules in due time for the adjourned hearing. No further adjournment to comply with rule 7.10 will normally be given.

**9.8.2** Copies of every notice gazetted in connection with a winding up petition, or where this is not practicable a description of the form and content of the notice, must be lodged with the Court as soon as possible after publication and in any event not later than five business days before the hearing of the petition. This direction applies even if the notice is defective in any way (e.g. is published on a date not in accordance with the Insolvency Rules, or omits or misprints some important words) or if the petitioner decides not to pursue the petition (e.g. on receiving payment).

**9.8.3** Attention is drawn to the requirement to give notice of the dismissal of a petition under rule 7.23(1). The Court will usually, on request, dispense with the requirement where (a) presentation of the petition has not previously been gazetted or (b) the company has become the subject of some supervening insolvency process, or (c) the company consents.

### 9.9

### Errors in petitions

**9.9.1** Applications for permission to amend errors in petitions which are discovered after a winding up order has been made should be made to the member of Court staff in charge of the winding up list in the Royal Courts of Justice or to a District Judge Sitting in a District Registry or District Judge.

**9.9.2** Where the error is an error in the name of the company, the member of Court staff in charge of the winding up list in the Royal Courts of Justice or a District Judge Sitting in a District Registry or District Judge may make any necessary amendments to ensure that the winding up order is drawn up with the correct name of the company inserted. If there is any doubt, e.g. where there might be another company in existence which could be confused with the company to be wound up, the member of Court staff in charge of the winding up list will refer the application to an ICC Judge at the Royal Courts of Justice. A District Judge Sitting in a District Registry or District Judge may refer the matter to a High Court Judge.

**9.9.3** Where it is discovered that the company has been struck off the Register of Companies prior to the winding up order being made, the petition must be restored to the list as soon as possible to enable an order for the restoration of the name to be made as well as the order to wind up and, save where the petition has been presented by a Minister of the Crown or a government department, evidence of service on the Government Legal Department or the Solicitor for the Affairs of the Duchy of Lancaster or the Solicitor to the Duchy of Cornwall (as appropriate) should be filed exhibiting the bona vacantia waiver letter.

### 9.10

### Rescission of a winding up order

**9.10.1** A request to rescind a winding up order must be made by application.

**9.10.2** The application must be made within five business days after the date on which the order was made, failing which it should include an application to extend time pursuant to Schedule 5 to the Insolvency Rules. Notice of any such application must be given to the petitioning creditor, any supporting or opposing creditor, any incumbent insolvency practitioner and the official receiver.

**9.10.3** An application to rescind will only be entertained if made by a (a) creditor, or (b) contributory, or (c) by the company jointly with a creditor or with a contributory. The application must be supported by a witness statement which should include details of assets and liabilities and (where appropriate) reasons for any failure to apply within five business days.

**9.10.4** In the case of an unsuccessful application, the costs of the petitioning creditor, any supporting or opposing creditor, any incumbent insolvency practitioner and the official receiver will normally be ordered to be paid by the creditor or the contributory making or joining in the application. The reason for this is that if the costs of an unsuccessful application are made payable by the company, those costs will inevitably fall on the general body of creditors.

### 9.11

### Validation orders

**9.11.1**   A company against which a winding up petition has been presented may apply to the Court after the presentation of a petition for relief from the effects of s.127(1) of the Act, by seeking an order that a certain disposition or dispositions of its property, including payments out of its bank account (whether such account is in credit or overdrawn), shall not be void in the event of a winding up order being made at the hearing of the petition (a validation order).

**9.11.2**   Save in exceptional circumstances, notice of the making of the application should be given to: (a) the petitioning creditor; (b) any person entitled to receive a copy of the petition pursuant to rule 7.9; (c) any creditor who has given notice to the petitioner of their intention to appear on the hearing of the petition pursuant to rule 7.14; and (d) any creditor who has been substituted as petitioner pursuant to rule 7.17. Failure to do so is likely to lead to an adjournment of the application or dismissal.

**9.11.3**   The application should be supported by a witness statement which should be made by a director or officer of the company who is intimately acquainted with the company's affairs and financial circumstances. If appropriate, supporting evidence in the form of a witness statement from the company's accountant should also be produced.

**9.11.4**   The extent and content of the evidence will vary according to the circumstances and the nature of the relief sought, but in the majority of cases it should include, as a minimum, the following information:

(1)   when and to whom notice has been given in accordance with paragraph 9.11.2 above;
(2)   the company's registered office;
(3)   the company's capital;
(4)   brief details of the circumstances leading to presentation of the petition;
(5)   how the company became aware of presentation of the petition;
(6)   whether the petition debt is admitted or disputed and, if the latter, brief details of the basis on which the debt is disputed;
(7)   full details of the company's financial position including details of its assets (and including details of any security and the amount(s) secured) and liabilities, which should be supported, as far as possible, by documentary evidence, e.g. the latest filed accounts, any draft audited accounts, management accounts or estimated statement of affairs;
(8)   a cash flow forecast and profit and loss projection for the period for which the order is sought;
(9)   details of the dispositions or payments in respect of which an order is sought;
(10)   the reasons relied on in support of the need for such dispositions or payments to be made prior to the hearing of the petition;
(11)   any other information relevant to the exercise of the Court's discretion;
(12)   details of any consents obtained from the persons mentioned in paragraph 9.11.2 above (supported by documentary evidence where appropriate);
(13)   details of any relevant bank account, including its number and the address and sort code of the bank at which such account is held, and the amount of the credit or debit balance on such account at the time of making the application.

**9.11.5**   Where an application is made urgently to enable payments to be made which are essential to continued trading (e.g. wages) and it is not possible to assemble all the evidence listed above, the Court may consider granting limited relief for a short period, but there should be sufficient evidence to satisfy the Court that the interests of creditors are unlikely to be prejudiced by the grant of limited relief.

**9.11.6**   Where the application involves a disposition of property, the Court will need details of the property (including its title number if the property is land) and to be satisfied that any proposed disposal will be at a proper value. Accordingly, an independent valuation should be obtained and exhibited to the evidence.

**9.11.7** The Court will need to be satisfied by credible evidence either that the company is solvent and able to pay its debts as they fall due or that a particular transaction or series of transactions in respect of which the order is sought will be beneficial to or will not prejudice the interests of all the unsecured creditors as a class.

**9.11.8** A draft of the order sought should be attached to the application.

**9.11.9** Similar considerations to those set out above are likely to apply to applications seeking ratification of a transaction or payment after the making of a winding up order.

## 10.

### Applications

**10.1** In accordance with rule 12.2(2), in the Royal Courts of Justice an officer acting on behalf of the operations manager or chief clerk has been authorised to deal with applications:

(1) to extend or abridge time prescribed by the Insolvency Rules in connection with winding up;

(2) for permission to withdraw a winding up petition (rule 7.13);

(3) made by the official receiver for a public examination (s.133(1)(c) of the Act), where no penal notice is endorsed and no unless order is made;

(4) made by the official receiver to transfer proceedings from the High Court to a specified hearing centre within the meaning of rule 12.30;

(5) to list a hearing for directions with a time estimate of 30 minutes or less in circumstances where both parties are represented without reference to an ICC Judge;

(6) for a first extension of time to serve a bankruptcy petition.

**10.2** Outside of the Royal Courts of Justice, applications listed in paragraph 10.1 must be made to a District Judge Sitting in a District Registry or in the County Court to a District Judge.

**10.3** Where an application is made by an official receiver in respect of the matters listed in paragraph 10.1(4) above, the official receiver must comply with rule 12.32 and give any incumbent office-holder 14 days' written notice of the application.

## PART THREE: PERSONAL INSOLVENCY

## 11.

### Statutory demands

**11.1** Rule 10.1 prescribes the contents of a statutory demand. An example of a statutory demand may be found at:

https://www.gov.uk/government/collections/bankruptcy-and-insolvency-forms

**11.2** Rule 10.2 applies to service of a statutory demand whether within or out of the jurisdiction. If personal service is not practicable in the particular circumstances, a creditor must do all that is reasonable to bring the statutory demand to the debtor's attention. This could include taking those steps set out at paragraph 12.7 below which justify the Court making an order for service of a bankruptcy petition other than by personal service. It may also include any other form of physical or electronic communication which will bring the statutory demand to the notice of the debtor.

**11.3** A creditor wishing to serve a statutory demand out of the jurisdiction in a foreign country with an applicable civil procedure convention (including the Hague Convention) may and, if the assistance of a British Consul is desired, must adopt the procedure prescribed by CPR rule 6.42 and CPR rule 6.43. In the case of any doubt whether the country is a 'convention country', enquiries should be made of the Foreign

Process Section of the Queen's Bench Division, Room E16, Royal Courts of Justice, Strand, London WC2A 2LL.

### 11.4

### Setting aside a statutory demand

**11.4.1** The application and witness statement in support of setting aside a statutory demand, exhibiting a copy of the statutory demand, must be filed in Court within 18 days of service of the statutory demand on the debtor. The time limits are different if the statutory demand has been served out of the jurisdiction: see rule 10.1(10).

**11.4.2** A debtor who wishes to apply to set aside a statutory demand after the expiration of 18 days, or if service is out of the jurisdiction, after the expiration of the time limit specified by rule 10.1(10)(a) from the date of service of the statutory demand, must apply for an extension of time within which to apply to set aside the statutory demand. The witness statement in support of the application to set aside statutory demand should also contain evidence in support of the application for an extension of time and should state that to the best of the debtor's knowledge and belief the creditor(s) named in the statutory demand has/have not presented a bankruptcy petition.

**11.4.3** Unless the Court to which the application to set aside is made operates Electronic Filing and Electronic Practice Direction 510 applies, the following applies:

(1) Three copies of each document must be lodged with the application, to enable the Court to serve notice of the hearing date on the applicant, the creditor and the person named under rule 10.1(3).

(2) Where copies of the documents are not lodged with the application, any order of the Court fixing a venue is conditional upon copies of the documents being lodged on the next business day after the Court's order, otherwise the application will be deemed to have been dismissed.

**11.4.4** Where the debt claimed in the statutory demand is based on a judgment, order, liability order, costs certificate, tax assessment or decision of a tribunal, the Court will not at this stage inquire into the validity of the debt nor, as a general rule, will it adjourn the application to await the result of an application to set aside the judgment, order, decision, costs certificate or any appeal.

**11.4.5** The Court will determine an application to set aside a statutory demand in accordance with rule 10.5.

**11.4.6** Attention is drawn to the power of the Court to decline to file a petition if there has been a failure to comply with the requirement of rule 10.2.

### 12.

### Bankruptcy petitions

**12.1** All petitions presented will be listed under the name of the debtor unless the Court directs otherwise.

### 12.2

### Content of petitions

**12.2.1** The attention of Court users is drawn to the following points:

(1) A creditor's petition does not require dating, signing or witnessing, but must be verified in accordance with rule 10.10.

(2) In the heading, it is only necessary to recite the debtor's name e.g. Re John William Smith or Re J W Smith (Male). Any alias or trading name will appear in the body of the petition.

**12.2.2**   Where the petition is based solely on a statutory demand, only the debt claimed in the demand may be included in the petition.

**12.2.3**   The attention of Court users is also drawn to rules 10.8 and 10.9, where the 'aggregate sum' is made up of a number of debts.

**12.2.4**   The date of service of the statutory demand should be recited as follows:

(1)   Where the demand has been served personally, the date of service as set out in the certificate of service.

(2)   Where the demand has been served other than personally, the date as set out in the certificate of service filed in compliance with rule 10.3.

### 12.3

### Searches

**12.3.1**   The petitioning creditor shall, before presenting a petition, conduct an Official Search with the Chief Land Registrar in the register of pending actions for pending petitions presented against the debtor and shall include the following certificate at the end of the petition:

"I/we certify that within 7 days ending today, I/we have conducted a search for pending petitions presented against the debtor and that to the best of my/our knowledge, information, and belief [no prior petitions have been presented which are still pending] [a prior petition (No [ .]) has been presented and is/may be pending in the [ . . . . . . . . . Court] and I/we am/are issuing this petition at risk as to costs].

Signed . . . ..Dated . . . .".

### 12.4

### The deposit

**12.4.1**   A bankruptcy petition will not be treated as having been presented until the Court fee and official receiver's deposit have been paid. A petition filed electronically without payment of the deposit will be marked "private" and will not be available for inspection until the deposit has been paid. The date of presentation of the petition will accord with the date on which the deposit has been paid. If the official receiver's deposit is not paid within 7 calendar days after filing the petition, the petition will not be accepted, in accordance with paragraph 5.3 of the Electronic Practice Direction 51O -The Electronic Working Pilot Scheme.

**12.4.2**   The deposit will be taken by the Court and forwarded to the official receiver. In the Royal Courts of Justice the petition fee and deposit should be paid by cheque, or by debit or credit card over the phone. In a District Registry or a County Court hearing centre, the petition fee and deposit should be handed to the staff of the duly authorised officer of the Court who will record its receipt. For the purposes of paragraph 12.4.1 above, the deposit will be treated as paid when received by the Court.

**12.4.3**   If payment is made by cheque, it should be made payable to 'HM Courts and Tribunals Service' or 'HMCTS'. For the purposes of paragraph 12.4 of this IPD, the deposit will be treated as paid when the cheque is received by the Court

### 12.5

### Certificates of continuing debt and of notice of adjournment

**12.5.1**   At the final hearing of a petition, the Court will need to be satisfied that the debt on which the petition is founded has not been paid or secured or compounded. The Court will normally accept as sufficient evidence a certificate signed by the person representing the petitioning creditor in the following form:

> "I certify that I have/my firm has made enquiries of the petitioning creditor(s) within the last business day prior to the hearing/adjourned hearing and to the best of my knowledge and belief the debt on which the petition is founded is still due and owing and has not been paid or secured or compounded for save as to . . .
>
> Signed . . . . . . . . . . Dated . . . . . . . . . . . .

**12.5.2**   For convenience, in the Royal Courts of Justice this certificate is incorporated in the attendance sheet for the parties to complete when they come to Court and is to be filed at the hearing. A fresh certificate will be required on each adjourned hearing.

**12.5.3**   On any adjourned hearing of a petition, in order to satisfy the Court that the petitioner has complied with rule 10.23, the petitioner will be required to file evidence of when (the date), how (the manner), and where (the address), notice of the adjournment order and notification of the venue for the adjourned hearing was sent to:

(1)   the debtor, and
(2)   any creditor who has given notice under rule 10.19 but was not present at the hearing when the order for adjournment was made or was present at the hearing but the date of the adjourned hearing was not fixed at that hearing.

**12.5.4**   For convenience, in the Royal Courts of Justice this certificate is incorporated in the attendance sheet for the parties to complete when they come to Court and is to be filed at the hearing. A fresh certificate will be required on each adjourned hearing. It is as follows:

> "I certify that the petitioner has complied with rule 10.23 of the Insolvency Rules 2016 by sending notice of adjournment to the debtor [supporting/opposing creditor(s)] on [date] at [address]".

## 12.6

### Extension of hearing date of petition

**12.6.1**   Late applications for extension of hearing dates under rule 10.22, and failure to attend on the listed hearing of a petition, will be dealt with as follows:

(1)   If an application is submitted less than two clear working days before the hearing date (for example, later than Monday for Thursday, or Wednesday for Monday), the costs of the application will not be allowed under rule 10.22.
(2)   If the petition has not been served and no extension has been granted by the time fixed for the hearing of the petition, and if no one attends for the hearing, the petition may be dismissed or re-listed for hearing about 21 days later. The Court will notify the petitioning creditor's solicitors (or the petitioning creditor in person), and any known supporting or opposing creditors or their solicitors, of the new date and time. A witness statement should then be filed on behalf of the petitioning creditor explaining fully the reasons for the failure to apply for an extension or to appear at the hearing, and (if appropriate) giving reasons why the petition should not be dismissed.
(3)   On the re-listed hearing the Court may dismiss the petition if not satisfied it should be adjourned or a further extension granted.

**12.6.2**   All applications for an extension should include a statement of the date fixed for the hearing of the petition.

**12.6.3**   The petitioning creditor should contact the Court (by solicitors or in person) on or before the hearing date to ascertain whether the application has reached the file and been dealt with. It should not be assumed that an extension will be granted.

**12.7**

### Service of bankruptcy petitions other than by personal service

**12.7.1** Where personal service of the bankruptcy petition is not practicable, service by other means may be permitted. In most cases, evidence that the steps set out in the following paragraphs have been taken will suffice to justify an order for service of a bankruptcy petition other than by personal service:

(1) One personal call at the residence and place of business of the debtor. Where it is known that the debtor has more than one residential or business addresses, personal calls should be made at all the addresses.

(2) Should the creditor fail to effect personal service, a letter should be written to the debtor referring to the call(s), the purpose of the same, and the failure to meet the debtor, adding that a further call will be made for the same purpose on the [day] of [month] 20[. . . . . . . . . . ] at [ ] hours at [place]. Such letter may be sent by first class prepaid post or left at or delivered to the debtor's address in such a way as it is reasonably likely to come to the debtor's attention. At least two business days' notice should be given of the appointment and copies of the letter sent to or left at all known addresses of the debtor. The appointment letter should also state that:

    (a) in the event of the time and place not being convenient, the debtor should propose some other time and place reasonably convenient for the purpose;

    (b) in the case of a statutory demand as suggested in paragraph 11.2 above, reference is being made to this paragraph for the purpose of service of a statutory demand, the appointment letter should state that if the debtor fails to keep the appointment the creditor proposes to serve the demand by advertisement/ post/ insertion through a letter box as the case may be, and that, in the event of a bankruptcy petition being presented, the Court will be asked to treat such service as service of the demand on the debtor;

    (c) (in the case of a petition) if the debtor fails to keep the appointment, an application will be made to the Court for an order that service be effected either by advertisement or in such other manner as the Court may think fit.

(3) When attending any appointment made by letter, inquiry should be made as to whether the debtor is still resident at the address or still frequents the address, and/or other enquiries should be made to ascertain receipt of all letters left for them. If the debtor is away, inquiry should also be made as to when they are returning and whether the letters are being forwarded to an address within the jurisdiction (England and Wales) or elsewhere.

(4) If the debtor is represented by a solicitor, an attempt should be made to arrange an appointment for personal service through such solicitor. The Insolvency Rules permit a solicitor to accept service of a statutory demand on behalf of their client but not the service of a bankruptcy petition.

**12.8**

### Validation orders

**12.8.1** A person against whom a bankruptcy petition has been presented may apply to the Court after presentation of the petition for relief from the effects of s.284(1) – (3) of the Act by seeking an order that a certain disposition or dispositions of that person's property, including payments out of their bank account (whether such account is in credit or overdrawn), shall not be void in the event of a bankruptcy order being made at the hearing of the petition (a validation order).

**12.8.2** Save in exceptional circumstances, notice of the making of the application should be given to (a) the petitioning creditor(s) or other petitioner, (b) any creditor who has given notice to the petitioner of their intention to appear on the hearing of the petition pursuant to rule 10.19, (c) any creditor who has been substituted as petitioner pursuant to rule 10.27 and (d) any creditor who has carriage of the petition pursuant to rule 10.29.

**12.8.3** The application should be supported by a witness statement which, save in exceptional circumstances, should be made by the debtor. If appropriate, supporting evidence in the form of a witness statement from the debtor's accountant should also be produced.

**12.8.4** The extent and contents of the evidence will vary according to the circumstances and the nature of the relief sought, but in a case where the debtor is trading or carrying on business it should include, as a minimum, the following information:

(1) when and to whom notice has been given in accordance with paragraph 12.8.2 above;
(2) brief details of the circumstances leading to presentation of the petition;
(3) how the debtor became aware of the presentation of the petition;
(4) whether the petition debt is admitted or disputed and, if the latter, brief details of the basis on which the debt is disputed;
(5) full details of the debtor's financial position including details of their assets (including details of any security and the amount(s) secured) and liabilities, which should be supported, as far as possible, by documentary evidence, e.g. accounts, draft accounts, management accounts or estimated statement of affairs;
(6) a cash flow forecast and profit and loss projection for the period for which the order is sought;
(7) details of the dispositions or payments in respect of which an order is sought;
(8) the reasons relied on in support of the need for such dispositions or payments to be made;
(9) any other information relevant to the exercise of the Court's discretion;
(10) details of any consents obtained from the persons mentioned in paragraph 12.8.2 above (supported by documentary evidence where appropriate);
(11) details of any relevant bank account, including its number and the address and sort code of the bank at which such account is held and the amount of the credit or debit balance on such account at the time of making the application.

**12.8.5** Where an application is made urgently to enable payments to be made which are essential to continued trading (e.g. wages) and it is not possible to assemble all the evidence listed above, the Court may consider granting limited relief for a short period, but there must be sufficient evidence to satisfy the Court that the interests of creditors are unlikely to be prejudiced.

**12.8.6** Where the debtor is not trading or carrying on business and the application relates only to a proposed sale, mortgage or re-mortgage of the debtor's home, evidence of the following will generally suffice:

(1) when and to whom notice has been given in accordance with 12.8.2 above;
(2) whether the petition debt is admitted or disputed and, if the latter, brief details of the basis on which the debt is disputed;
(3) details of the property to be sold, mortgaged or re-mortgaged (including its title number);
(4) the value of the property and the proposed sale price, or details of the mortgage or re-mortgage;
(5) details of any existing mortgages or charges on the property and redemption figures;
(6) the costs of sale (e.g. solicitors' or agents' costs);
(7) how and by whom any net proceeds of sale (or sums coming into the debtor's hands as a result of any mortgage or re-mortgage) are to be held pending the final hearing of the petition;
(8) any other information relevant to the exercise of the Court's discretion;
(9) details of any consents obtained from the persons mentioned in 12.8.2 above (supported by documentary evidence where appropriate).

**12.8.7** Whether or not the debtor is trading or carrying on business, where the application involves a disposition of property the Court will need to be satisfied that any proposed disposal will be at a proper value. An independent valuation should be obtained for this purpose and exhibited to the evidence.

**12.8.8** The Court will need to be satisfied by credible evidence that the debtor is solvent and able to pay their debts as they fall due or that a particular transaction or series of transactions in respect of which the order is sought will be beneficial to or will not prejudice the interests of all the unsecured creditors as a class.

**12.8.9** A draft of the order should accompany the application.

**12.8.10** Similar considerations to those set out above are likely to apply to applications seeking ratification of a transaction or payment after the making of a bankruptcy order.

## 13.

### Applications

**13.1** In accordance with rule 12.2(2), in the Royal Courts of Justice an officer acting on behalf of the Operations Manager or chief clerk has been authorised to deal with applications:

(1)    by petitioning creditors to extend the time for hearing petitions (rule 10.22);
(2)    by the official receiver:
   (a)    to transfer proceedings from the High Court to a specified hearing centre within the meaning of rule 12.30.
   (b)    to amend the title of the proceedings (rule 10.165).

**13.2** Outside of the Royal Courts of Justice, applications listed in paragraph 13.1 must be made to a District Judge Sitting in a District Registry or in the County Court to a District Judge.

**13.3** Where an application is to be made under 13.1(2)(a) above, the official receiver must comply with rule 12.32, and give any incumbent office-holder 14 days' written notice of the application.

## 14.

### Orders without attendance

**14.1** In suitable cases the Court will normally be prepared to make orders under Part VIII of the Act (Individual Voluntary Arrangements), without the attendance of the parties, provided there is no bankruptcy order in existence and (so far as is known) no pending petition. The orders are:

(1)    A 14 day interim order adjourning the application for 14 days for consideration of the nominee's report, where the papers are in order, and the nominee's signed consent to act includes a waiver of notice of the application or the consent by the nominee to the making of an interim order without attendance.
(2)    A standard order on consideration of the nominee's report, extending the interim order to a date seven weeks after the proposed decision date, directing the implementation of the decision procedure and adjourning to a date about three weeks after the decision date. Such an order may be made without attendance if the nominee's report has been delivered to the Court and complies with s.256(1) of the Act, and proposes a decision date not less than 14 days from that on which the nominee's report is filed in Court under rule 8.15, nor more than 28 days from that on which that report is considered by the Court under rule 8.18.
(3)    A 'concertina' order, combining orders as under (1) and (2) above. Such an order may be made without attendance if the initial application for an interim order is accompanied by a report of the nominee and the conditions set out in (1) and (2) above are satisfied.
(4)    A final order on consideration of the report of the creditors' consideration of the proposal. Such an order may be made without attendance if the report has been filed and complies with rule 8.24. The order will record the effect of the report and may discharge the interim order.

**14.2** Provided that the conditions under sub-paragraphs 14.1(2) and 14.1 (4) above are satisfied and that the appropriate report has been lodged with the Court in due time the parties need not attend or be represented on the adjourned hearing for consideration of the nominee's report or of the report of the creditors' giving consideration of the proposal (as the case may be), unless they are notified by the Court that attendance is required. Sealed copies of the order made (in all four cases in paragraph 14.1 above) will be posted by the Court to the applicant or their solicitor and to the nominee.

**14.3**    In suitable cases the Court may make consent orders without attendance by the parties. The written consent of the parties endorsed on the consent order will be required. Examples of such orders are as follows:

(1)    On applications to set aside a statutory demand, orders:
- (a)    dismissing the application, with or without an order for costs as may be agreed (permission will be given to present a petition on or after the seventh day after the date of the order, unless a different date is agreed);
- (b)    setting aside the demand, with or without an order for costs as may be agreed.

(2)    On petitions where there are no supporting or opposing creditors (see rule 10.19), and there is a statement signed by or on behalf of the petitioning creditor confirming that no notices have been received from supporting or opposing creditors, orders:
- (a)    dismissing the petition, with or without an order for costs as may be agreed; or
- (b)    if the petition has not been served, giving permission to withdraw the petition (with no order for costs).

(3)    On other applications or orders:
- (a)    for sale of property, possession of property, disposal of proceeds of sale;
- (b)    giving interim directions;
- (c)    dismissing the application, with or without an order for costs as may be agreed;
- (d)    giving permission to withdraw the application, with or without an order for costs as may be agreed.

**14.4**    If, as may often be the case with orders under sub-paragraphs 3(a) or (b) above, an adjournment is required, whether generally with liberty to restore or to a fixed date, the order by consent may include an order for the adjournment. If adjournment to a date is requested, a time estimate should be given and the Court will fix the first available date and time on or after the date requested.

**14.5**    The above lists should not be regarded as exhaustive, nor should it be assumed that an order will be made without attendance as requested.

**14.6**    Applications for consent orders without attendance should be lodged at least two clear working days (and preferably longer) before any hearing date.

**14.7**    Whenever a document is lodged or a letter sent, the correct case number should be quoted. A note should also be given of the date and time of the next hearing (if any).

## 15.

### Bankruptcy restrictions undertakings

**15.1**    Where a bankrupt has given a bankruptcy restrictions undertaking, the Secretary of State or official receiver must file a copy in Court and send a copy to the bankrupt as soon as reasonably practicable (rule 11.11). In addition the Secretary of State must notify the Court immediately that the bankrupt has given such an undertaking in order that any hearing date can be vacated.

## 16.

### Persons at risk of violence

**16.1**    Where an application is made pursuant to rules 8.6, 20.2, 20.3, 20.4, 20.5, 20.6 or otherwise to limit disclosure of information as to a person's current address by reason of the possibility of violence, the relevant application should be accompanied by a witness statement which includes the following:

(1)    The grounds upon which it is contended that disclosure of the current address as defined by rule 20.1 might reasonably be expected to lead to violence against the debtor or a person who normally resides with them as a member of their family or where appropriate any other person.

(2)   Where the application is made in respect of the address of the debtor, the debtor's proposals with regard to information which may safely be given to potential creditors in order that they can recognise that the debtor is a person who may be indebted to them, in particular the address at which the debtor previously resided or carried on business and the nature of such business.

(3)   The terms of the order sought by the applicant by reference to the Court's particular powers as set out in the rule under which the application is made and, unless impracticable, a draft of the order sought.

(4)   Where the application is made by the debtor in respect of whom a nominee or supervisor has been appointed or against whom a bankruptcy order has been made, evidence of the consent of the nominee/supervisor, or, in the case of bankruptcy, the official receiver or any other person appointed as trustee in bankruptcy. Where such consent is not available the statement must indicate whether such consent has been refused.

**16.2**   Any person listed in 16.1(4) shall be made a respondent to the application.

**16.3**   The application shall be referred to a District Judge Sitting in a District Registry, ICC Judge, or High Court Judge where it will be considered without a hearing in the first instance but without prejudice to the right of the Court to list it for hearing if:

(1)   the Court is not persuaded by the written evidence, and consequently may refuse the application;
(2)   the consent of any respondent is not attached; or
(3)   the Court is of the view that there is another reason why listing is appropriate.

## PART FOUR: APPEALS

## 17.

### Appeals

**17.1**   CPR Part 52 and its attendant practice directions apply to insolvency appeals unless dis-applied or inconsistent with the Act or the Insolvency Rules. This IPD provides greater detail on the routes of appeal as applied to insolvency proceedings under the Act, the Insolvency Rules and CPR Part 52.

### 17.2

### Appeals in Personal Insolvency Matters

**17.2(1)**   Paragraph 17.2 applies to all applications for permission to appeal and appeals from decisions made in personal insolvency matters, save those that arise from s.263N of the Act relating to bankruptcy applications to an adjudicator.

**17.2(2)**   An application for permission to appeal relating to a decision made in a personal insolvency matter by a District Judge lies to a High Court Judge.

**17.2(3)**   An application for permission to appeal relating to a decision made in a personal insolvency matter by a District Judge Sitting in a District Registry, a Circuit Judge, or an ICC Judge lies to a High Court Judge, but not to a Deputy.

**17.2(4)**   An appeal from a decision in a personal insolvency matter made by a District Judge lies to a High Court Judge.

**17.2(5)**   An appeal from a decision in a personal insolvency matter made by a District Judge Sitting in a District Registry, a Recorder, a Circuit Judge, or an ICC Judge lies to a High Court Judge, but not to a Deputy. Supervising Judges for the Business and Property Courts may, in circumstances they consider to be appropriate, allow for an appeal from a decision in a personal insolvency matter made by a District Judge Sitting in a District Registry to be handled by a Circuit Judge acting as a judge of the High Court under s.9(1) of the Senior Courts Act 1981.

## 17.3

### Appeals from Decisions of Adjudicators

**17.3(1)** An application under s.263N(5) of the Act appealing the decision of an adjudicator to refuse to make a bankruptcy order is made to the Court, in accordance with the provisions in rule 10.48.

**17.3(2)** No prior application for permission to appeal is required.

**17.3(3)** An application under s.263N(5) of the Act will be treated as the first hearing of the matter.

**17.3(4)** It is the responsibility of the applicant to obtain from the adjudicator a copy (digital or otherwise) of the original application reviewed by the adjudicator (including the adjudicator's notice of refusal to make a bankruptcy order and notice confirming that refusal) and a record of (a) the verification checks undertaken under rule 10.38 by the adjudicator and (b) any additional information provided under rule 10.39(3) and available to the adjudicator at the date when the adjudicator refused to make a bankruptcy order.

**17.3(5)** Prior to making a final decision the Court may:

(a) direct that notice of the application be given to any interested person;
(b) give permission to any interested person and the petitioner to file evidence;
(c) make any case management order to assist in determining whether to dismiss the application or make a bankruptcy order.

## 17.4

### Appeals in Corporate Insolvency Matters

**17.4(1)** Routes of appeal for appeals from decisions in corporate insolvency matters under Parts 1 to 7 of the Act (and the corresponding Insolvency Rules) are specified in rule 12.59.

**17.4(2)** An application for permission to appeal relating to a decision made in a corporate insolvency matter by a District Judge lies to a High Court Judge or an ICC Judge but not to a Deputy ICC Judge. Whether it lies to a High Court Judge or an ICC Judge depends on the location from which the decision being appealed originates, in conformity with Schedule 10 of the Insolvency Rules.

**17.4(3)** An application for permission to appeal relating to a decision made in a corporate insolvency matter by a District Judge Sitting in a District Registry or a Circuit Judge lies to a High Court Judge, but not to a Deputy.

**17.4(4)** An application for permission to appeal relating to a decision made at first instance in a corporate insolvency matter by an ICC Judge lies to a High Court Judge, but not to a Deputy.

**17.4(5)** An application for permission to appeal relating to a decision made by an ICC Judge on appeal from a District Judge in a corporate insolvency matter lies to the Civil Division of the Court of Appeal.

**17.4(6)** An appeal from a decision in a corporate insolvency matter made by a District Judge lies to a High Court Judge or to an ICC Judge, depending on the location from which the decision being appealed originates, in accordance with Schedule 10 of the Insolvency Rules.

**17.4(7)** An appeal from a decision in a corporate insolvency matter made by a District Judge Sitting in a District Registry lies to a High Court Judge but not to a Deputy. Supervising Judges for the Business and Property Courts may, in circumstances they consider to be appropriate, allow for an appeal from a decision in a corporate insolvency matter made by a District Judge Sitting in a District Registry to be handled by a Circuit Judge acting as a judge of the High Court under s.9(1) of the Senior Courts Act 1981.

**17.4(8)** An appeal from a decision in a corporate insolvency matter made by a Recorder or a Circuit Judge lies to a High Court Judge, but not to a Deputy.

**17.4(9)**  An appeal from a decision in a corporate insolvency matter made at first instance by an ICC Judge lies to a High Court Judge, but not to a Deputy.

**17.4(10)**  An appeal from a decision in a corporate insolvency matter made by an ICC Judge on appeal from a District Judge in a corporate insolvency matter lies to the Civil Division of the Court of Appeal.

## 18

### Permission to Appeal

**18.1**  A first appeal is subject to the permission requirements of CPR Part 52, rule 3.

**18.2**  An appeal from a decision of a High Court Judge, or from a decision of an ICC Judge which was itself made on appeal, requires the permission of the Court of Appeal.

## 19

### Filing Appeals

**19.1**  An application for permission to appeal or an appeal from a decision of an ICC Judge which lies to a High Court Judge must be filed at the Royal Courts of Justice.

**19.2**  An application for permission to appeal or an appeal from a decision of a District Judge Sitting in a District Registry must be filed in that District Registry.

**19.3**  An application for permission to appeal or an appeal from a decision of a District Judge must be filed in its corresponding appeal centre, as identified in the table in Schedule 10 of the Insolvency Rules.

### PART FIVE: FINANCIAL MARKETS AND INSOLVENCY (SETTLEMENT FINALITY) REGULATIONS 1999 – REQUIRED INFORMATION

**20.**  In any case in which the Court is asked to make an order to which regulation 22(1) of the Financial Markets and Insolvency (Settlement Finality) Regulations 1999 (SI 1999/2979) applies, the party applying for the order must include in the petition or application a statement to that effect, identifying the system operator of the relevant designated system, the relevant designating authority, and the email or other addresses to which the Court will be required to send notice pursuant to regulation 22(1) if an order is made.

**20.1**  At the date of this IPD, the Regulations apply where, in respect of "a participant in a designated system" (as those terms are defined in the Regulations), an order is made for administration, winding-up, bankruptcy, sequestration, bank insolvency, bank administration, building society insolvency, building society special administration or investment bank special administration. Applicants must, before making the application, check for any amendments to the Regulations.

### PART SIX: APPLICATIONS RELATING TO THE REMUNERATION OF OFFICE-HOLDERS

**21.**  This IPD sets out the governing principles and court practice. Reference should also be made to the Act and the Insolvency Rules.

**21.1**  The objective in any remuneration application is to ensure that the amount and/or basis of any remuneration fixed by the Court is fair, reasonable and commensurate with the nature and extent of the work properly undertaken or to be undertaken by the office-holder in any given case and is fixed and approved by a process which is consistent and predictable.

**21.2**  The guiding principles which follow are intended to assist in achieving the objective:

(1) "Justification". It is for the office-holder who seeks to be remunerated at a particular level and / or in a particular manner to justify their claim. They are responsible for preparing and providing full particulars of the basis for, and the nature of, their claim for remuneration.

(2) "The benefit of the doubt". The corollary of the "justification" principle is that if after having regard to the evidence and guiding principles there remains any doubt as to the appropriateness, fairness or reasonableness of the remuneration sought or to be fixed (whether arising from a lack of particularity as to the basis for and the nature of the office-holder's claim to remuneration or otherwise), such element of doubt should be resolved by the Court against the office-holder.

(3) "Professional integrity". The Court should (where this is the case) give weight to the fact that the office-holder is a member of a regulated profession and as such is subject to rules and guidance as to professional conduct and the fact that (where this is the case) the office-holder is an officer of the Court.

(4) "The value of the service rendered". The remuneration of an office-holder should reflect the value of the service rendered by the office-holder, not simply reimburse the office-holder in respect of time expended and cost incurred.

(5) "Fair and reasonable". The amount and basis of the office-holder's remuneration should represent fair and reasonable remuneration for the work properly under-taken or to be undertaken.

(6) "Proportionality of information". In considering the nature and extent of the information which should be provided by an office-holder in respect of a remuneration application to the Court, the office-holder and any other parties to the application shall have regard to what is proportionate by reference to the amount of remuneration to be fixed, the nature, complexity and extent of the work to be completed (where the application relates to future remuneration) or that has been completed by the office-holder and the value and nature of the assets and liabilities with which the office-holder will have to deal or has had to deal.

(7) "Proportionality of remuneration". The amount and basis of remuneration to be fixed by the Court should be proportionate to the nature, complexity and extent of the work to be completed (where the application relates to future remuneration) or that has been completed by the office-holder and the value and nature of the assets and/or potential assets and the liabilities and/or potential liabilities with which the office-holder will have to deal or has had to deal, the nature and degree of the responsibility to which the office-holder has been subject in any given case, the nature and extent of the risk (if any) assumed by the office-holder and the efficiency (in respect of both time and cost) with which the office-holder has completed the work undertaken.

(8) "Professional guidance". In respect of an application for the fixing and approval of the amount and/or basis of the remuneration, the office-holder may have regard to the relevant and current statements of practice promulgated by any relevant regulatory and professional bodies in relation to the fixing of the remuneration of an office-holder. In considering a remuneration application, the Court may also have regard to such statements of practice and the extent of compliance with such statements of practice by the office-holder.

(9) "Timing of application". The Court will take into account whether any application should have been made earlier and if so the reasons for any delay.

**21.3** Hearing of a remuneration application. The general rule applies for the listing of hearings as set out in paragraph 3 of this IPD. The judge hearing the application may summarily determine the application or adjourn with directions including (but not confined to) directions as to (i) whether an assessor or costs judge should prepare a report to the Court in respect of the remuneration (ii) or whether the application should be heard by a judge and an assessor or a costs judge.

**21.4** On any remuneration application, the office-holder should provide the information and evidence referred to in paragraphs 21.4.1 to 21.4.12 below.

**21.4.1** A narrative description and explanation of:

(a) the background to, the relevant circumstances of, and the reasons for their appointment;

(b) the work undertaken or to be undertaken in respect of the appointment; the description should be divided, insofar as possible, into individual tasks or categories of task (general descriptions of work, tasks, or categories of task should (insofar as possible) be avoided);

(c)    the reasons why it is or was considered reasonable and/or necessary and/or beneficial for such work to be done, giving details of why particular tasks or categories of task were undertaken and why such tasks or categories of task are to be undertaken or have been undertaken by particular individuals and in a particular manner;

(d)    the amount of time to be spent or that has been spent in respect of work to be completed or that has been completed and why it is considered to be fair, reasonable and proportionate;

(e)    what is likely to be and has been achieved, the benefits that are likely to and have accrued as a consequence of the work that is to be or has been completed, the manner in which the work required in respect of the appointment is progressing and what, in the opinion of the office-holder, remains to be achieved.

**21.4.2**   Details sufficient for the Court to determine the application by reference to the criteria which are required to be taken into account by reference to the Insolvency Rules and any other applicable enactments or rules relevant to the fixing of the remuneration.

**21.4.3**   A statement of the total number of hours of work undertaken or to be undertaken in respect of which the remuneration is sought, together with a breakdown of such hours by individual member of staff and individual tasks or categories of tasks to be performed or that have been performed. Where appropriate, a proportionate level of detail should also be given of:

(a)    the tasks or categories of tasks to be undertaken as a proportion of the total amount of work to be undertaken in respect of which the remuneration is sought and the tasks or categories of tasks that have been undertaken as a proportion of the total amount of work that has been undertaken in respect of which the remuneration is sought; and

(b)    the tasks or categories of task to be completed by individual members of staff or grade of personnel including the office-holder as a proportion of the total amount of work to be completed by all members of staff including the office-holder in respect of which the remuneration is sought and the tasks or categories of task that have been completed by individual members of staff or grade of personnel as a proportion of the total amount of work that has been completed by all members of staff including the office-holder in respect of which the remuneration is sought.

**21.4.4**   A statement of the total amount to be or likely to be charged for the work to be undertaken or that has been undertaken in respect of which the remuneration is sought which should include:

(a)    a breakdown of such amounts by individual member of staff and individual task or categories of task performed or to be performed;

(b)    details of the time expended or to be expended and the remuneration charged or to be charged in respect of each individual task or category of task as a proportion (respectively) of the total time expended or to be expended and the total remuneration charged or to be charged.

In respect of an application pursuant to which some or all of the amount of the office-holder's remuneration is to be fixed on a basis other than time properly spent, the office-holder shall provide (for the purposes of comparison) the same details as are required by this paragraph 19.4.4, but on the basis of what would have been charged had they been seeking remuneration on the basis of the time properly spent by the office-holder and their staff.

**21.4.5**   Details of each individual to be engaged or who has been engaged in work in respect of the appointment and in respect of which the remuneration is sought, including details of their relevant experience, training, qualifications and the level of their seniority.

**21.4.6**   An explanation of:

(a)    the steps, if any, to be taken or that have been taken by the office-holder to avoid duplication of effort and cost in respect of the work to be completed or that has been completed in respect of which the remuneration is sought;

(b)    the steps to be taken or that have been taken to ensure that the work to be completed or that has been completed is to be or was undertaken by individuals of appropriate experience and seniority relative to the nature of the work to be or that has been undertaken.

**21.4.7** Details of the individual rates charged by the office-holder and members of their staff in respect of the work to be completed or that has been completed and in respect of which the remuneration is sought. Such details should include:

(a) a general explanation of the policy adopted in relation to the fixing or calculation of such rates and the recording of time spent;

(b) where, exceptionally, the office-holder seeks remuneration in respect of time spent by secretaries, cashiers or other administrative staff whose work would otherwise be regarded as an overhead cost forming a component part of the rates charged by the office-holder and members of their staff, a detailed explanation as to why such costs should be allowed or should be provided.

**21.4.8** Where the remuneration application is in respect of a period of time during which the charge-out rates of the office-holder and/or members of their staff engaged in work in respect of the appointment have increased, an explanation of the nature, extent and reason for such increase and the date when such increase took effect.

**21.4.9** Details of any basis or amount of remuneration previously fixed or approved in relation to the appointment (whether by the Court or otherwise) including in particular the bases or amounts that were previously sought to be fixed or approved and the bases or amounts that were in fact fixed or approved and the method by which such amounts were fixed or approved.

**21.4.10** Where the application is for approval to draw remuneration in excess of the total amount set out in the fees estimate, their evidence must exhibit a copy of the fees estimate and address the matters listed in rule 18.30(3).

**21.4.11** In order that the Court may be able to consider the views of any persons who the office-holder considers have an interest in the assets that are under their control and of any other persons who are required by the Insolvency Rules to be notified of the hearing of the application, the office-holder must provide details of:

(a) the names and contact details for all such persons;

(b) what (if any) consultation has taken place between the office-holder and those persons and if no such consultation has taken place, an explanation as to the reason why;

(c) the number and value of the interests of the persons consulted including details of the proportion (by number and by value) of the interests of such persons by reference to the entirety of those persons having an interest in the assets under the control of the office-holder.

**21.4.12** Such other relevant information as the office-holder considers, in the circumstances, ought to be provided to the Court.

**21.5** This paragraph applies to applications where some or all of the remuneration of the office-holder is to be fixed and/or approved on a basis other than time properly spent. On such applications in addition to the matters referred to in paragraph 21.4, the office-holder shall:

(a) Provide a full description of the reasons for remuneration being sought by reference to the basis contended for.

(b) Where the remuneration is sought to be fixed by reference to a percentage of the value of the property with which the office-holder has to deal or of the assets which are realised or distributed, provide a full explanation of the basis upon which any percentage rates to be applied to the values of such property or the assets realised and/or distributed have been chosen.

(c) Provide a statement that to the best of the office-holder's belief the percentage rates or other bases by reference to which some or all of the remuneration is to be fixed are similar to the percentage rates or other bases that are applied or have been applied in respect of other appointments of a similar nature.

(d) Provide a comparison of the amount to be charged by reference to the basis contended for and the amount that would otherwise have been charged by reference to the other available bases of remuneration, including by reference to rule 18.22 and Schedule 11 to the Insolvency Rules (scale of fees).

**21.6** The witness evidence may exclude matters set out in paragraph 21.4 above but an explanation as to why a decision to exclude such material should be included in the witness evidence.

**21.7**   The evidence placed before the Court by the office-holder in respect of any remuneration application should also include the following documents:

(a)   a copy of the most recent receipts and payments account;

(b)   copies of any reports by the office-holder to the persons having an interest in the assets under their control relevant to the period for which the remuneration sought to be fixed and approved relates;

(c)   any fees estimate, details of anticipated expenses or other relevant information given or required to be given to the creditors in relation to remuneration by the office-holder pursuant to the Insolvency Rules;

(d)   any other schedules or such other documents providing the information referred to in paragraphs 21.4 above, where these are likely to be of assistance to the Court in considering the application;

(e)   evidence of any consultation or copies of any relevant communications with those persons having an interest in the assets under the control of office-holder in relation to the remuneration of the office-holder.

**21.8**   On any remuneration application the Court may make an order allowing payments of remuneration to be made on account subject to final approval whether by the Court or otherwise.

**21.9**   Unless otherwise ordered by the Court (or as may otherwise be provided for in any enactment or rules of procedure), the costs of and occasioned by an application for the fixing and/or approval of the remuneration of an office-holder, including those of any assessor, shall be paid out of the assets under the control of the office-holder.

## PART SEVEN: UNFAIR PREJUDICE PETITIONS, WINDING UP AND VALIDATION ORDERS

### 22

### Unfair Prejudice Petitions

**22.1**   Attention is drawn to the undesirability of asking as a matter of course for a winding up order as an alternative to an order under s.994 of the 2006 Act. The petition should not ask for a winding up order unless that is the remedy which the petitioner prefers, or it is thought that it may be the only remedy to which the petitioner is entitled.

**22.2**   Whenever a winding up order is asked for in a contributory's petition, the petition must state whether the petitioner consents or objects to a validation order under s.127 of the Insolvency Act 1986 in the standard form. If the petitioner objects, the written evidence in support must contain a short statement of the petitioner's reasons.

**22.3**   If the petitioner objects to a validation order in the standard form but consents to such an order in a modified form, the petition must set out the form of order to which the petitioner consents, and the written evidence in support must contain a short statement of the petitioner's reasons for seeking the modification.

**22.4**   If the petition contains a statement that the petitioner consents to a validation order, whether in the standard or a modified form, but the petitioner changes their mind before the first hearing of the petition, the petitioner must notify the respondents and may apply on notice to the court for an order directing that no validation order or a modified order only (as the case may be) shall be made by the Court, but validating dispositions made without notice of the order made by the Court.

**22.5**   If the petition contains a statement that the petitioner consents to validation order, whether in the standard or a modified form, the Court shall without further enquiry make such an order at the first hearing unless an order to the contrary has been made by the Court in the meantime.

**22.6**   If the petition contains a statement that the petitioner objects to a validation order in the standard form, the company may apply (in the case of urgency, without notice) to the Court for an order.

# Appendix 3

# TEMPORARY INSOLVENCY PRACTICE DIRECTION

## SUPPORTING THE INSOLVENCY PRACTICE DIRECTION

### Introduction

**[A3.1]**
This Temporary Insolvency Practice Direction is intended to provide workable solutions for court users as the current COVID-19 pandemic continues together with guidance as to the type of hearings which the Insolvency and Companies Court list will endeavour to provide during the period for which this temporary practice direction is in force.

### 1. Definitions

| | |
|---|---|
| "Acceptance" | has the meaning ascribed by paragraph 5.3(1) of PD510 |
| "Act" | means the Insolvency Act 1986 |
| "Business Day" | means any day other than a Saturday, a Sunday, Christmas Day, Good Friday or a day which is a bank holiday in any part of England & Wales |
| "CE-File" | refers to the Court's Electronic Working portal and "CE-Filing" means the filing with the court of any document using Electronic Working |
| "Electronic Working" | has the meaning ascribed to it by paragraph 1.1 of PD510 which, in accordance with paragraph 1.1 (2) of PD510 is a permitted means of electronic delivery of documents to the Court for the purposes of rule 1.46 of the Rules |
| "Hybrid Hearing" | means a hearing at which some of the parties, witnesses and legal representatives appear in person before the Court and others participate remotely by audio or video technology |
| "In-person Hearing" | means a hearing at which the parties, witnesses and legal representatives appear in person before the Court |
| "Temporary IPD" | means this Temporary Insolvency Practice Direction |
| "Temporary Listing Procedure for Winding-Up and Bank-ruptcy Petitions" | means the procedure set out at paragraph 4 of this Temporary IPD |
| "Filing Submission Email" | means the email referred to at paragraph 5.3(1) of PD510, generated by automatic notification following submission of a document using Electronic Working, which email acknowledges that the document has been submitted |
| "IPD" | means the Insolvency Practice Direction made by order of the Chancellor on 4 July 2018 |
| "PD510" | means Practice Direction 510 – The Electronic Working Pilot Scheme which supplements CPR rules 5.5 and 7.12 |

"**Remote Hearing**"  means a hearing at which the parties, witnesses and legal representatives appear remotely by audio or video technology

"**Rule and Rules**"  means the Insolvency (England and Wales) Rules 2016

"**Schedule B1**"  means Schedule B1 to the Insolvency Act 1986

## 2. Application and coming into force

This Temporary IPD supplements IPD and replaces the temporary insolvency practice direction which came into force on 1 October 2020. It will apply to all insolvency proceedings throughout the Business and Property Courts, subject to any variations as directed by (in London) the Chief Insolvency and Companies Court Judge or (outside London) the relevant Supervising judge. It will come into force on 30 June 2021 and remain in force until 30 September 2021 unless amended or revoked by a further insolvency practice direction in the meantime.

## 3. Filing a notice of intention to appoint an administrator and a notice of appointment of an administrator

**3.1**  Subject to paragraphs 3.3 to 3.6 below, for the purposes of Rule 1.46(2), and notwithstanding anything to the contrary in PD510, in the case of a CE-filing of any of the Notices identified in paragraph 3.2 below, the Notice shall be treated as delivered to the court at the date and time recorded in the Filing Submission Email.

**3.2**  The Notices to which paragraph 3.1 above applies are: (1) a Notice of Intention to Appoint an Administrator filed by a company or its directors under Paragraph 27 of Schedule B1; (2) a Notice of Appointment of an Administrator filed by a qualifying floating charge holder under paragraph 18 of Schedule B1; and (3) a Notice of Appointment of an Administrator by a company or its directors under Paragraph 29 of Schedule B1.

**3.3**  Paragraph 3.1 above shall not apply to a Notice of Intention to Appoint an Administrator filed by CE-File pursuant to paragraph 27 of Schedule B1 outside the time period 10:00 hours to 16:00 hours on any day that the courts are open for business. Any such Notice filed by CE-file outside that time period shall, for the purposes of Insolvency Rule 1.46(2), be treated as delivered to the Court at 10:00 hours on the day that the courts are next open for business. Accordingly, the date on which the time period of ten days in paragraph 28(2) shall begin is the date on which the courts are next open for business.

**3.4**  Paragraph 3.1 above shall not apply to a Notice of Appointment filed by CE- File pursuant to paragraph 29 of Schedule B1 outside the time period 10:00 hours to 16:00 hours on any day that the courts are open for business. Any such Notice filed by CE-file outside that time period shall, for the purposes of Rule 1.46(2), be treated as delivered to the court at 10:00 hours on the day that the courts are next open for business.

**3.5**  Notwithstanding paragraph 3.1 above, all Notices identified in paragraph 3.2 above shall continue to be reviewed by the Court, as and when practicable, in accordance with paragraph 5.3 of PD510. The validity and time at which the appointment of an administrator is effective shall not be affected by reason only of any delay in Acceptance of the Notice.

**3.6**  Electronic Working may not be used to file a Notice of Appointment of an administrator under paragraph 14 of Schedule B1 by the holder of a qualifying floating charge outside Normal Court Opening Hours. Such a Notice may only be filed outside Normal Court Opening Hours by the procedure set out in Rules 3.20 to 3.22.

## 4. Winding-up and bankruptcy petitions

**4.1**  As from the date this paragraph is brought into effect the Court will list the hearing of any winding-up and bankruptcy petition in the manner described in this paragraph 4.

**4.2**   The hearing shall be a Remote Hearing and shall be conducted using such video conferencing technology or telephone conferencing facility as the relevant Court decides.

**4.3**   The parties must provide the Court with an email address or telephone number for the purposes of being invited to join the Remote Hearing as soon as possible and in any event no later than 2 clear Business Days before the hearing date. Failure to do so may result in the Court making an order (including a winding-up order, a bankruptcy order or dismissal of the petition as the case may be) in the absence of the party who did not provide such details.

**4.4**   Any other person who intends to appear at the Remote Hearing of a winding- up or bankruptcy petition must deliver a notice of intention to appear on the petition in accordance with Rule 7.14 or Rule 10.19 as the case may be, providing with it an email address or telephone number for the purposes of being invited to join the Remote Hearing.

## 5. Other insolvency hearings

**5.1**   Hearings may be conducted by one of three methods: an In-person Hearing, a Remote Hearing or a Hybrid Hearing.

**5.2**   The parties shall liaise with each other with a view to providing the Court with an agreed proposal for the method of hearing, as far in advance of the hearing date as reasonably practicable.

**5.3**   Where the parties are unable to reach agreement, they shall each provide the Court with their proposals for the method of hearing as far in advance of the hearing date as reasonably practicable.

**5.4**   It shall be for the Court (with the benefit, as applicable, of the agreement or proposals of the parties) to determine the method of the hearing.

**5.5**   In the case of any Remote Hearing or Hybrid Hearing, the parties must provide to the Court as far in advance of the hearing as reasonably practicable, an email address or telephone number of each person intending to join the hearing remotely, for the purposes of being invited to join the Remote Hearing or Hybrid Hearing as the case may be. Failure to do so may result in the Court making an order in the absence of the party who did not provide such details.

**5.6**   It will also be open to the Court to fix a short remote case management conference in advance of the fixed hearing to allow for directions to be made in relation to the conduct of the hearing, the technology to be used, and/or any other relevant matters.

## 6. Statutory Declarations

**6.1**   Where Schedule B1 requires a person to provide a statutory declaration, a statutory declaration that is made otherwise than in-person before a person authorised to administer the oath may constitute a formal defect or irregularity. Pursuant to Rule 12.64 it is open to the Court, on objection made, to declare that such a formal defect or irregularity shall not invalidate the relevant insolvency proceedings to which the statutory declaration relates, unless the Court considers that substantial injustice has been caused by the defect or irregularity which cannot be remedied by any order of the Court.

**6.2**   Where a statutory declaration is made in the manner described in sub- paragraphs 6.2.1 to 6.2.3 below then the defect or irregularity (if any) arising solely from the failure to make the statutory declaration in person before a person authorised to administer the oath shall not by itself be regarded as causing substantial injustice.

**6.2.1**   The person making the statutory declaration does so by way of video conference with the person authorised to administer the oath;

**6.2.2**   The person authorised to administer the oath attests that the statutory declaration was made in the manner referred to in 6.2.1 above; and

**6.2.3**   The statutory declaration states that it was made in the manner referred to in paragraph 6.2.1 above.

Appendix 4

# INSOLVENCY PRACTICE DIRECTION RELATING TO THE CORPORATE INSOLVENCY AND GOVERNANCE ACT 2020

## INSOLVENCY PRACTICE DIRECTION RELATING TO THE CORPORATE INSOLVENCY AND GOVERNANCE ACT 2020

### 1. Definitions:

**[A4.1]**

**1.1**  In this practice direction the following definitions will apply:

(1)  '1986 Act' means the Insolvency Act 1986;

(2)  '2020 Act' means the Corporate Insolvency and Governance Act 2020;

(3)  'the coronavirus test' means whether:

    (a)  In the case of a petition to wind up a registered company on a ground specified in section 123(1)(a) to (d) of the 1986 Act that the condition in paragraph 5(2) of Schedule 10 to the 2020 Act is met;

    (b)  In the case of a petition to wind up a registered company on a ground specified in section 123(1)(e) or (2) of the 1986 Act that the condition in paragraph 5(3) of Schedule 10 to the 2020 Act is met;

    (c)  In the case of a petition to wind up an unregistered company on a ground specified in section 222, 223, or 224(1)(a) to (c) of the 1986 Act that the condition in paragraph 6(2) of Schedule 10 to the 2020 Act is met; or

    (d)  In the case of a petition to wind up an unregistered company on a ground specified in section 224(1)(d) or (2) of the 1986 Act that the condition in paragraph 6(3) of Schedule 10 to the 2020 Act is met;

(4)  'IPD' means the Practice Direction - Insolvency Proceedings (July 2018);

(5)  'PO 510' means Practice Direction 510 – The Electronic Working Pilot Scheme which supplements CPR rules 5.5 and 7.12;

(6)  'preliminary hearing' means the preliminary hearing of the petition listed pursuant to paragraph 8.1 (2) below;

(7)  'relevant period' has the meaning in paragraph 21 (1) of Schedule 10 to the 2020 Act;

(8)  'Rule and Rules' means the Insolvency (England and Wales) Rules 2016.

### 2. Application and coming into force

**2.1**  Paragraphs 3 to 8 of this practice direction apply to winding-up petitions presented during the relevant period:

(1)  against a registered company under section 122(1)(f) of the 1986 Act on any of the grounds specified in section 123 of the 1986 Act; or

(2)  against an unregistered company under section 124 and 221 (5)(b) of the 1986 Act on any of the grounds specified in sections 222, 223 or 224 of the 1986 Act.

**2.2**  Paragraph 9 of this practice direction applies to obtaining a moratorium under section A3 of the 1986 Act (inserted by [section 1] of the 2020 Act).

**2.3**   This practice direction shall come into force on the day that the 2020 Act comes into force.

### 3. Contents of the winding-up petition

**3.1**   A petition will not be accepted for filing unless it contains the statement required by Rule 7.5(1) as amended by paragraph 19(3) of Schedule 10 to the 2020 Act.

**3.2**   In addition, the petition shall contain a summary of the grounds relied upon by the petitioning creditor for the purposes of the coronavirus test.

### 4. Initial listing of the petition

**4.1**   Upon presentation of a winding-up petition, provided it is not rejected for filing under paragraph 2 above, the petition shall be listed for a non-attendance pretrial review with a time estimate of 15 minutes for the first available date after 28 days from the date of its presentation.

**4.2**   The purpose of the non-attendance pre-trial review is to enable the court to give directions for a preliminary hearing in order for the court to determine whether it is likely that it will be able to make an order under section 122(1 )(f) or 221 (5)(b) of the 1986 Act having regard to the coronavirus test.

### 5. Petition to remain private

**5.1**   I Until the court has concluded that it is likely that it will be able to make an order under section 122(1 )(f) or 221 (5)(b) of the 1986 Act having regard to the coronavirus test, or further order of the court in the meantime, the petition shall (in accordance with paragraph 19(2) and (4) of Schedule 10 to the 2020 Act) remain private, save for being served on the company and delivered to such other persons as are specified in Rule 7.9. Accordingly, unless the court otherwise orders:

(1)     the petition (whether filed electronically or otherwise) shall be marked private and will not be available for inspection; and
(2)     neither the petition nor the fact of its presentation shall be revealed in response to a search by a member of the public of any court file or other record.

### 6. Filing of evidence

**6.1**   If the petitioner wishes to rely upon any evidence at the preliminary hearing, other than that contained in the petition, it must file and serve on the company a witness statement containing such evidence at the same time as the petition.

**6.2**   If the company wishes to rely upon any evidence at the preliminary hearing it must file and serve on the petitioner a witness statement containing such evidence within 14 days of service of the petition upon it.

**6.3**   At least two days before the non-attendance pre-trial review the parties shall file and serve a listing certificate stating (i) the identity of their legal representatives (if any); (ii) their availability for the preliminary hearing; and (iii) a time estimate for the preliminary hearing.

### 7. The non-attendance pre-trial review

**7.1**   At the non-attendance pre-trial review the court may:

(1)     In the event that the company does not oppose the petition and the court is satisfied that it is likely to make a winding up order under section 122(1 )(f) or 221 (5)(b) of the 1986 Act having regard to the coronavirus test it shall list the petition for a hearing in the winding-up list; or

(2)     List the preliminary hearing and give such other directions in relation to the preliminary hearing as it thinks appropriate.

## 8. The preliminary hearing

**8.1**   At the preliminary hearing:

(1)     if the court is not satisfied that it is likely that it will be able to make an order under section 122(1 )(f) or 221 (5)(b) of the 1986 Act having regard to the coronavirus test, it shall dismiss the petition; or

(2)     if the court is satisfied on the evidence before it that it is likely that it will be able to make an order under section 122(1 )(f) or 221 (5)(b) of the 1986 Act having regard to the coronavirus test it shall list the petition for a hearing in the winding-up list.

**8.2**   Upon a direction under paragraph 7.1 (1) above and 8.1 (2) above, the provisions of the Rules relating to giving notice of the petition and the further conduct of the petition shall come into effect. Taking account of any direction provided in accordance with paragraph 12 below, the court will list a final hearing of the petition within such time period as allows for notice of the petition to be given pursuant to Rule 7.10.

**8.3**   If, at any time after the court has determined that it is likely that it will be able to make an order on the Petition under section 122(1 )(f) or 221 (5)(b) of the 1986 Act having regard to the coronavirus test, it appears that the same or different court has also made such a determination in respect of another petition concerning the same company, the court shall direct that both petitions shall be listed for further hearing at the same time. In such a circumstance the court shall:

(1)     where required transfer the petition to the court dealing with the petition presented first in time; and

(2)     direct that the petition presented first in time should be heard first.

## 9. Petitions presented in the County Court

**9.1**   A winding-up petition to which this practice direction applies shall be deemed to be other than Local Business for the purpose of paragraphs 3.6 and 3.7 of the IPD, whether or not the petition is opposed. Accordingly, if the petition is issued in a County Court hearing centre having insolvency jurisdiction it shall be transferred to one or other of the hearing centres referred to in paragraph 3.6 of the IPD.

## 10. Obtaining a moratorium under section A3 of the 1986 Act

**10.1**   Where directors of a company file relevant documents with the court by means of electronic delivery (within the meaning of PO 510) for the purposes of obtaining a moratorium pursuant to section A3 of the 1986 Act, for the avoidance of doubt the documents shall be treated as being filed with the court at the date and time recorded in the email referred to at paragraph 5.3(1) of P05 10, generated by automatic notification acknowledging that the documents have been submitted.

# PRACTICE STATEMENT (COMPANIES: SCHEMES OF ARRANGEMENT UNDER PART 26 AND PART 26A OF THE COMPANIES ACT 2006)

## PRACTICE STATEMENT (COMPANIES: SCHEMES OF ARRANGEMENT UNDER PART 26 AND PART 26A OF THE COMPANIES ACT 2006)

[A5.1]

1   This practice statement replaces the *Practice Statement (Companies: Schemes of Arrangement)* [2002] 1 WLR 1345. It is directed to the practice to be followed on applications pursuant to Part 26 or Part 26A of the Companies Act 2006 (the "2006 Act") seeking the sanction of the court to a scheme of arrangement between a company and its creditors and/or members (a "Part 26 scheme" and a "Part 26A scheme" respectively). The purpose is to enable issues concerning the jurisdiction of the court to sanction the scheme, the composition of classes of creditors and/or members and the convening of meetings to be identified and if appropriate resolved early in the proceedings. To achieve these objects the following practice should be observed.

2   It is the responsibility of the applicant, in relation to both a Part 26 scheme and a Part 26A scheme, to determine whether more than one meeting of creditors and/or members is required by a scheme and if so to ensure that those meetings are properly constituted.

3   In relation to Part 26 schemes, applications under section 896 of the 2006 Act (to convene a meeting or meetings of creditors or members) may be listed before either an Insolvency and Companies Court Judge or a High Court Judge, but applications in respect of a scheme which gives rise to any of the issues identified in paragraph 6 below should be listed before a High Court Judge. Applications under section 899 of the 2006 Act (to sanction a Part 26 scheme) will be listed before a High Court Judge.

4   All applications under section 901C of the 2006 Act (to convene a meeting or meetings of creditors and/or members) and all applications under section 901F of the 2006 Act (to sanction a Part 26A scheme) will be listed before a High Court Judge.

5   Where a High Court Judge hears an application under section 896 or section 901C of the 2006 Act the same judge should, if possible, hear the application to sanction the scheme.

6   It is the responsibility of the applicant, by evidence in support of the application or otherwise, to draw to the attention of the court at the hearing for an order that meetings of creditors and/or members be held ("the convening hearing"):

a.   any issues which may arise as to the constitution of meetings of members or creditors or which otherwise affect the conduct of those meetings;

b.   any issues as to the existence of the court's jurisdiction to sanction the scheme;

c.   (in relation to a Part 26A scheme) any issues relevant to the conditions to be satisfied pursuant to section 901A of the 2006 Act and, if an application under section 901C(4) of the 2006 Act is to be made, any issues relevant to that application; and (in relation to a Part 26A scheme) any issues relevant to the conditions to be satisfied pursuant to section 901A of the 2006 Act and, if an application under section 901C(4) of the 2006 Act is to be made, any issues relevant to that application; and

d.      any other issue not going to the merits or fairness of the scheme, but which might lead the court to refuse to sanction the scheme.

7   Where an application is made to convene a meeting or meetings in respect of a scheme which gives rise to any of the issues identified in paragraph 6 above, unless there are good reasons for not doing so, the applicant should, prior to the convening hearing, take all steps reasonably open to it to notify any person affected by the scheme of the following matters:

a.      that the scheme is being promoted,

b.      the purpose which the scheme is designed to achieve and its effect,

c.      the meetings of creditors and/or members which the applicant considers will be required and their composition,

d.      the other matters that are to be addressed at the convening hearing, including the issues identified in paragraph 6 above,

e.      the date and place fixed for the convening hearing,

f.      that such persons are entitled to attend the convening and sanction hearings, and

g.      how such persons may make further enquiries about the scheme.

It is the responsibility of the applicant to ensure that such notification is given in a concise form and is communicated to all persons affected by the scheme in the manner which is most appropriate to the circumstances of the case.

8   Save for the circumstance in which there are good reasons for not giving the notification identified in paragraph 7 above, it should be given to persons affected by the scheme in sufficient time to enable them to consider what is proposed, to take appropriate advice and, if so advised, to attend the convening hearing. What is adequate notice will depend on all the circumstances. The evidence at the convening hearing should explain the steps which have been taken to give the notification and what, if any, response the applicant has had to the notification.

9   Where an issue identified in paragraph 6 above has been drawn to the attention of the court it will consider whether to determine that issue forthwith, or whether to give directions for the resolution of that issue.

10   While members and/or creditors will still be able to appear and raise objections based on an issue identified in paragraph 6 above at the sanction hearing, the court will expect them to show good reason why they did not raise the issue at an earlier stage.

11   In considering whether or not to make an order convening meetings of members and/or creditors (a "meetings order") the court will consider whether more than one meeting of members and/or creditors is required, and if so what is the appropriate composition of those meetings.

12   A meetings order may include an order giving anyone affected a limited time in which to apply to vary or discharge that order with the meetings of members and/or creditors to take place in default of any such application within the time prescribed.

13   The evidence for the convening hearing should describe how it is proposed that members and/or creditors are to be given notice of any meetings convened to consider the scheme. Where interests in the applicant's debt are held indirectly, for example through intermediaries, if it is proposed that the votes to be cast at the meetings should by some method reflect the views of persons holding such indirect interests, the evidence should set out the applicant's proposals in that respect and any facts justifying those proposals.

14   Explanatory statements should be in a form and style appropriate to the circumstances of the case, including the nature of the member and/or creditor constituency, and should be as concise as the circumstances admit. In addition to complying with the provisions of section 897 or section 901D (as the case may be) of the 2006 Act, the commercial impact of the scheme must be explained and members and/or creditors must be provided with such information as is reasonably necessary to enable them to make an informed decision as to whether or not the scheme is in their interests, and on how to vote on the scheme. Where a document is incorporated into the explanatory statement by reference, readers should be directed to the material part(s) of the document.

**15**   The court will consider the adequacy of the explanatory statement at the convening hearing. The court may refuse to make a meetings order if it considers that the explanatory statement is not in an appropriate form. However, the court will not approve the explanatory statement at the convening hearing, and it will remain open to any person affected by the scheme to raise issues as to its adequacy at the sanction hearing.

**Sir Geoffrey Vos**
**Chancellor of the High Court**
**26 June 2020**

# Index

## A

**Absconder**
bankrupt 1.486
contributory 1.210
**Accounts**
administrative receivership
receipts and payment sent to registrar
2.224
creditors' voluntary winding up
liquidator, delivery to 2.267
delivery to official receiver 2.363
liquidator's duty 1.222
receiver and manager appointed out of
court, duty 1.82
special manager, duty 2.255, 2.302
**Adjudicator**
application for bankruptcy order, to 1.371
conditions 1.373
false representations to 1.378
form of order 1.376
false representations to 1.378
further information, requests for 1.375
jurisdiction 1.372
refusal to make bankruptcy order 1.377
**Adjustment of prior transaction** 1.302
**Administration**
administrator *See* Administrator
application 2.127
directors, by 2.128
filing 2.131
hearing 2.136
holder of floating charge, by 2.135
liquidator 2.138
notice of other insolvency proceedings
2.134
notice to enforcement agents 2.133
service 2.132
supervisor of CVA, by 2.129
witness statement supporting 2.130
business of company, management during
1.680, 1.735
charged property
disposal 2.180
'company' for 1.728

**Administration** – *cont.*
creditors' claims
debts, insolvent company to rank equally
2.839
estimate of value of debt 2.841
mutual dealings and set off 2.851
provable debts 2.829
proving debt
admission for dividend 2.834
withdrawal/variation of proof 2.837
unsold assets, division 2.840
creditors' committee *See* Creditors'
committee
creditors' voluntary winding up, becoming
1.700
definitions 1.618, 2.124
dissolution of company 1.701
duration and extension 1.693, 1.694
effect 1.656
end of 1.692
administrator's application 1.696
application for order
administrator, by 2.190
creditor, by 2.191
automatic 1.693, 2.188
court order, notice of 2.192
creditor's application 1.698
discharge of order on 1.702
notice 2.189
notice to registrar/court 1.703
objective achieved 1.697
expenses 2.182
priority, order of 2.183
extension of 2.187
failure to make payment under CCA 1984
order 1.592
revocation of order, effect 1.592
fraudulent trading 1.311
general note 1.70
interim moratorium 1.661
interpretation 1.728
non-UK company, position as to 1.729
objectives 1.620, 1.697
order
applicant(s)/application 1.629, 1.651

**Administration** – *cont.*
order – *cont.*
compulsory winding up petition
dismissal 1.657
conditions for 1.628
contents 2.137
court powers 1.630, 1.654
discharge 1.702
effect 3.8
floating charge holder applicant 1.652
interim 1.630
liquidator applicant 1.655
meaning 1.627
notice 1.629, 2.139
withdrawal of application 1.629
penalties 1.716
pre-administration costs 2.124, 2.184
progress reports, timing 2.978
property, distribution
report on 2.982
relevant date for preferential debts 1.522
remuneration
procedure for initial determination
2.992
rights of action, assignment 1.314
Scotland, in 1.730–1.734
statement of affairs 1.664, 1.665
content 2.158
definitions 2.156
expenses 2.162
extension, time limit, submission 2.161
filing of 2.160
limited disclosure of 2.175, 2.177
notice requiring 2.157
publication 2.178
statement of concurrence 2.159
unpaid pre-administration costs 2.124
wrongful trading 1.312
**Administrative receiver**
administration, and
making of order, effect of 1.658
restriction on, during office of 1.641
agent, deemed 1.88
appointment
acceptance 2.207
notice and advertisement of 2.212
appointment notification 1.83, 1.90
appointment prohibition
exceptions 1.118–1.125, 1.736
charged property, order for disposal of
1.87
contracts, liability on 1.88
co-operation duty 1.299
creditors' committee See Creditors'
committee
death of 2.226
defect in appointment 1.293
definition 1.73, 1.326
directions application by 1.79

**Administrative receiver** – *cont.*
disposal of charged property 2.223
indemnity 1.88
information duties 1.90
invitation to form creditors' committee
2.222
joint/more than one 1.292
appointment 2.207
powers, general 1.86, 1.734
person dealing in good faith, position of
1.86
property, powers to get in 1.298
publicity as to appointment 1.83
qualification 1.291
ceasing to be qualified 1.89, 2.227
receipts and payments 2.224
receiver other than administrative receiver
appointment by court 2.230
powers to deal with prescribed part
2.232
report to creditors 2.231
removal from office 1.89, 1.658
report 1.92
registrar of companies 2.220
secured creditors, to 2.220
unsecured creditors, copy of 2.221
resignation 1.89, 2.225
security 2.211
statement of affairs
contents 2.214
copy with report 1.92
delivery of copy 2.214
expenses 2.218
extension, time to submit 2.217
limited disclosure 2.219
notice requiring 2.213
obligation to require 1.91
release from duty to submit 2.217
retention 2.216
statement of concurrence 2.215
verification 2.216
summary remedy against 1.270
vacation of office 1.89, 2.227
notice to registrar 2.228
validity of acts 1.293
**Administrator** *See also* **Administration**
additional, appointment of 2.203
agent, as 1.686
appointment 1.619
announcement of 1.663
ceasing to have effect 1.693
company or directors, by 1.619, 1.638,
1.646, 2.149–2.152
court, by 1.619, 1.628, 1.630, 1.652,
1.708
duration 1.693
floating charge holder, by 1.619, 1.631,
1.639, 2.141–2.144
invalid, indemnity for 1.638, 1.651

**Administrator** *See also* **Administration** – *cont.*
  appointment – *cont.*
    notice obligations  1.629, 1.635, 1.637,
      1.646, 1.662
    notice of  2.141, 2.142, 2.149–2.151
      filing at court  2.143, 2.152
      publication of  2.154
    restrictions on  1.623, 1.625, 1.626,
      1.632, 1.633, 1.640, 1.645
    statutory declaration  1.635
    time effective  1.630
  calling of meeting, by  1.678
  challenge to act of  1.691
  charged property, disposal of  1.687
    floating charge  1.687
    other charge  1.687
  consent to act  2.125
  creditors' decision  1.669, 1.672
  death of  1.707, 1.716, 2.201
  discharge from liability  1.715
  disclosure, order for  2.176
  distribution to creditors  1.682
  duties  1.684
  ending administration
    application to court for  1.696
    notice of, duties  1.703
  functions  1.673
    directions of court  1.679, 1.685
    objective of  1.620
    regulation on application to court  1.691
    speed and efficiency  1.621, 1.691
  improper motive, creditor's application for
    1.698
  joint/concurrent, provisions for  1.717
  liquidator, as, following winding up  2.276
  liquidator, becoming  1.193
  management powers  1.685
    consent to exercise of power by officer
      etc  1.680
  meaning  1.618
  misfeasance, examination and remedies
    1.692
  officer of court  1.622
  powers  1.674, 1.734
  preferential creditors, position of  1.690
  property of company, duties and powers
    1.685, 1.735
  proposals  1.666, 2.164
    advertisement  2.166
    approval  1.670, 2.167
      extension of time  2.169
    consideration by creditors  1.667, 1.668
    court powers on rejection  1.671
    creditors' decision  2.170, 2.172
    extension of time, notices  2.166
    revision of  1.670, 2.171
    statement of pre-administration costs
      2.165
  public examination  1.186
  qualification  1.623

**Administrator** *See also* **Administration** – *cont.*
  qualification – *cont.*
    ceasing to be qualified  1.706, 2.200
  removal or vacation from office  1.618,
    1.698, 1.705, 2.199
    court order  1.705
    discharge  1.715
  remuneration *See also* Remuneration
    1.716, 2.990
    exceeding fee estimate  2.1004
    joint  2.991
    new administrator  2.1005
    request for increase  2.998, 2.999,
      2.1002
      exceptions  2.1000, 2.1001
    review  2.1003
  replacement  1.703
    applicants for  1.708
    application to replace  2.202
    appointment, notification and
      publication  2.203
    company appointment, after  1.708
    court appointment, after  1.708
    court power  1.712
    creditors', application by  1.708
    directors' appointment, after  1.708
    floating charge holder appointment, after
      1.709
  resignation  1.704
    grounds for  2.196
    intention of  2.197
    notice of  2.198
  secured creditors  1.620
    consent to extension  1.695
    enforcement restriction  1.660
  statement of affairs to  1.664
  third party dealing in good faith  1.674
  unsecured, share of assets for  1.233
    disapplication  1.233
  vacation of office
    duties  2.204
**Affidavit**  1.256
**After-acquired property**
  bankrupt's duties  1.452, 2.663
  notice to trustee of  1.452
  recourse to disponee  2.664
**Agent**
  administrator  1.686
  receiver (Scotland)  1.101
**Air traffic services**
  administration, licence company  4.3
**Amendment of enactments**  1.609
**Annulment of bankruptcy order**
  application  2.672
  bankruptcy restrictions order/undertaking,
    effect on  1.751
  claim of excessive remuneration  2.674
  court power  1.395
    debts all paid or secured  1.395
    final account  2.681

**Annulment of bankruptcy order** – *cont.*
court power – *cont.*
gazette, notice in 2.680
grounds 1.395
matters to be proved 2.678
notices to creditors 2.676, 2.679
stay of proceedings 2.675
hearing 2.677
IVA approved for undischarged bankrupt
1.363
debtor's application 1.363, 2.484,
2.485
official receiver's application 1.363
order
advertisement 2.488
contents 2.486
notice 2.487
trustee's final account 2.489
restriction on institution of proceedings
after 1.478
trustee's report 2.673
**Appeals**
bankruptcy 1.502, 2.815
corporate insolvency 2.814
CPR, applicable 2.813
official receiver, decision against 2.817
procedure 2.816
**Apprenticeship**
bankruptcy, effect on 1.474
**Arbitration agreement**
bankruptcy, position of trustee 1.476
**Arrangement or compromise**
trustee in bankruptcy 1.753
**Arrest**
bankruptcy, powers in 1.490, 1.492
failure to attend public examination
1.187, 1.490
inquiry into company dealings, for 1.300
**Associate**
bankrupt, of, for preference 1.460
meaning 1.604
**Attachment**
bankruptcy, issued prior to 1.472
earnings order, of 1.428
winding up, and 1.240
avoidance 1.181
**Authorised deposit-taker**
winding up
decisions 2.894
**Avoidance**
attachment, sequestration etc 1.181
disposition of property
bankrupt, by 1.398
compulsory winding up, in 1.180

**B**

**Bailment**
credit, as
hire purchase/conditional sale, to
bankrupt 1.488
**Bank, recognised**
administration exclusion 1.626
modifications order relating to, power to
make 1.580
**Bankrupt**
arrest power 1.490
book debt assignment avoidance 1.470
contributory 1.136
correspondence, re-direction power as to
1.497
death 1.578
definition 1.514
delivery of accounts, duty 2.593
expenses 2.594
director, etc, leave to act as
application 2.667
costs 2.670
court order 2.669
official receiver's report 2.668
disclosure, state of affairs
bankruptcy order made 2.592–2.595
creditor's petition 2.584–2.591
disqualification 4.10
general 4.11
Parliament 1.587, 4.10
receiver, as 1.75
Scotland 1.95
domestic and work assets
trustee claiming and replacing 1.424
duties to trustee
breach contempt of court 1.452
information etc 1.452
notice of after-acquired property 1.452
dwelling-house
ceasing to be in estate
notification 2.713
substituted period 2.716
unregistered land 2.715
vesting application to Land Registry
2.714
charge on 2.717
'estate' of 1.396
execution or attachment enforcement
against 1.472
exempt property, replacement
money in lieu of sale 2.640
purchase 2.639
family 1.519

**Bankrupt** – *cont.*
  income payments
    agreement
      acceptance  2.652
      approval  2.651
      variation  2.653
    order  2.644
      action following  2.645
      application  2.643
      payer of income, to, administration
          2.647
      review  2.648
      variation  2.646
  income payments agreement  1.428
    duration  1.428
    third party, money from  1.428
    transitional  4.16
    variation  1.428
  income payments order  1.427
    duration  1.427
    second bankruptcy, effect  1.454
    variation  1.427
  IVA applicant  1.354
  'liability'  1.515
  property of
    disposition, restrictions on  1.398
  public examination of  2.632–2.638
    adjournment  2.637
    examination  2.638
    incapacity  2.635
    notice  2.633
    order for  2.632
    procedure  2.636
  spouse
    associate, as  1.604
    creditor  1.448
    inquiry into dealings etc, of  1.492
    matrimonial home rights  1.456
  stay, under IVA interim order  1.356, 1.362
**Bankruptcy**
  after-acquired property
    bankrupt's duties  2.663
    recourse to disponee  2.664
  amendment to title  2.711
  annulment *See* Annulment of bankruptcy
      order
  appeal  1.502
  bankrupt's estate  1.396
    definition  1.396
    dwelling-house  1.397, 1.431, 4.8
    exceptions/exclusions from  1.396,
        1.418
    second bankruptcy, provisions for
        1.454, 2.692–2.696
    tenancy  1.396
  commencement  1.390
  consolidation  1.414
  contempt of court  1.405, 1.452, 1.489
  court control  1.489

**Bankruptcy** – *cont.*
  creditor
    definition  1.516
  creditors' claims
    provable debts  2.829
  creditors' committee *See* Creditors'
      committee
  creditors' petition
    amendment  2.542
    appearances, list  2.546
    carriage of, change  2.555
    Chief Land Registrar, notice to  2.539
    contents  2.533
    copies  2.540
    court in which presented  2.537
    filing  2.538
    hearing  2.547
      adjournment  2.549
      decision  2.550
      postponement  2.548
    identification
      debt  2.535
      debtor  2.534
    non-appearance, creditor  2.552
    opposition, debtor  2.544
    persons intending to appear, notice
        2.545
    presentation  2.538
    security for costs  2.543
    service  2.540
      death of debtor, before  2.541
    substitution, petitioner  2.553, 2.554
    vacating registration on withdrawal
        2.551
    verification  2.536
  criminal bankruptcy
    annulment  2.704
    costs  2.709
    discharge
      bankrupt's application  2.705
      order, court by  2.707, 2.708
    interim receivership  2.701
    official receiver
      functions  2.700
      report  2.706
    petition  2.699
    proof of debts  2.702
    rules not applying to  2.703
  criminal order  1.379, 1.381
    distribution, restriction on  1.446
    Official Petitioner  1.557
    petition based on  1.389
    prior transaction avoidance  1.461
    transitional  4.16
  debt  1.382
    'bankruptcy level'  1.382
    concealment offence  1.482
    definition  1.515
    false, failure to inform of  1.484

**Bankruptcy** – *cont.*
debt – *cont.*
  inability to pay  1.382, 1.383
  interest  1.441, 1.447
  person indebted to bankrupt, court
    enforcement powers  1.493
  priority  1.447
  spouse, owed to  1.448
  valuation  1.441
debtor
  non-disclosure of current address,
    order for  2.1030, 2.1031
  offences, liability for  1.478
debtor's application
  bankruptcy file  2.575
  bankruptcy order
    action following  2.573
    contents  2.569
    refusal to make  2.570
      appeals  2.572
      review of  2.571
    settlement  2.569
  Chief Land Registrar, registration  2.565
  contents  2.563, 2.1050
  court in which made  2.576
  determination  2.567, 2.568
  procedure  2.564
  verification  2.566
definitions  1.512
discharge from
  application  1.392
  'automatic'  1.391
  certificate  2.685, 2.686
  conditional  1.392
  costs  2.688
  court order  1.392, 4.16
  debts surviving discharge  2.687
  effect and exceptions  1.392, 1.393
  order  1.392
  refusal  1.392
  restrictions after  4.16
  second-time bankruptcy  4.16
  suspension
    application  1.391, 2.683
    lifting  2.684
disclosure, bankrupt's state of affairs
  bankruptcy order made  2.592–2.595
  creditor's petition  2.584–2.591
    accounts
      delivery of  2.590
      expenses  2.589
disposition of property  1.398
  avoidance  1.398
  third party protection  1.398
  trustee, powers of  1.433
duration  4.6
  transitional  4.16
expenses  2.690
  priority rules  2.691

**Bankruptcy** – *cont.*
HMRC, order to
  production of documents  2.654–2.657
inquiry, court powers  1.492, 1.493
interim receiver appointed
  application for appointment  2.578
  deposit  2.579
  order of appointment  2.580
  remuneration  2.582
  security  2.581
  termination  2.583
IVA, and
  debtor's default as to IVA  1.388
  expenses of IVA  1.388
jurisdiction  1.500
monetary limits, alteration  1.575
mortgaged property
  mortgagee of land, claim by  2.660
  sale
    court, order by  2.661
    proceeds  2.662
official receiver
  bankrupt's duties to  1.405
  directions application  1.489
  powers and duties  1.401, 1.403
  public examination request  1.404
  receiver and manager of estate  1.401
  release  2.617
  relief from reporting duties  2.619
  reports  1.403, 2.596
order *See* Bankruptcy order
proceedings, court powers to stay etc
  1.399
progress reports, timing  2.980
property, distribution
  report on  2.985
re-direction of bankrupt's documents,
  application for  2.712
remuneration
  procedure for initial determination
    2.995
second  1.453
solicitor, employing  1.433
special manager
  accounting duties  2.629
  appointment  2.626, 2.630
  security  2.627
    failure to give/keep up  2.628
statutory demand  1.383, 1.385, 2.526
  service  2.527
    proof of  2.528
  setting aside
    application  2.529
    hearing  2.530
time-limit extension  1.503
transaction at undervalue  1.459
trustee in bankruptcy *See also* Trustee in
  bankruptcy
  appointment  2.598, 2.599

**Bankruptcy** – *cont.*
trustee in bankruptcy *See also* Trustee in
bankruptcy – *cont.*
appointment – *cont.*
authentication 2.604
court, by 2.602
creditors' decision 2.601
notice 2.605
replacement trustee 2.608
Secretary of State, by 2.603
ceasing to be qualified 1.412
control of 2.616
creditors' committee, invitation to form
2.607
death of 2.615
enforcement of duties 2.624
hand-over of bankrupt's estate to 2.606
release of 2.614
removal
court, by 2.611
creditors, by 2.609
procedure 2.610
notice 2.613
Secretary of State, by 2.612
resignation 2.608
notice 2.613
security 2.600
solicitation, improper 2.623
transaction of, court setting aside 2.622
vacation of office 2.618
duties following 2.621
notice 2.620
vacancy, filled by OR 1.411
void dispositions 1.398
'Bankruptcy level' 1.382, 1.575
**Bankruptcy offences** 1.476
absconding 1.486
concealment/non-delivery/destruction of
books and papers 1.483
timescale 1.483
concealment/non-delivery/loss of property
1.482
timescale 1.482
contempt of court 1.452, 1.489
fraudulent disposal 1.485
timescale 1.485
innocent intention defence 1.480
institution of proceedings 1.478
non-disclosure 1.481
outside jurisdiction 1.478
penalties 1.478, 1.593, 1.759
**Bankruptcy order**
adjudicator, applications to 1.371
conditions 1.373
determinations 1.374
information requests 1.375
jurisdiction 1.372
annulment *See also* Annulment of
bankruptcy order

**Bankruptcy order** – *cont.*
annulment *See also* Annulment of
bankruptcy order – *cont.*
application 2.672
claim of excessive remuneration 2.674
final account 2.681
gazette, notice in 2.680
hearing 2.677
matters to be proved 2.678
notices to creditors 2.676, 2.679
stay of proceedings 2.675
trustee's report 2.673
appeal 1.502
Chief Land Registrar, registration 2.574
contents 2.569
creditors' petition
Chief Land Registrar, registration 2.560
contents 2.558
delivery 2.559
notice 2.559
definition 1.514
duration 1.391
form of 1.376
refusal of order 1.377
refusal to make 2.571
registration 2.736, 2.737
rescission, review etc, court powers 1.502
restrictions on making 1.386, 1.388
settlement 2.569
**Bankruptcy petition** *See also* Bankruptcy,
creditors' petition; debtor's application 1.378
amendment 1.386
consolidation 1.414
creditor's 1.382–1.386
debt(s) 1.382
expedited 1.385
grounds 1.382
proceedings on, restriction 1.386
definition 1.514
dismissal 1.381, 1.386
presentation 1.379
withdrawal 1.381
**Bankruptcy restriction order/undertak-
ing** 1.75, 1.394, 4.16
acceptance 2.730
annulment 2.732
annulment of bankruptcy, effect on 1.751
application for order 1.750, 2.720
opposition to 2.722
service 2.721
court, made by 2.723
devolution issues 4.10
disqualification provisions 1.587, 4.10
duration of order 1.750
grounds for order 1.750
interim order 1.750, 2.725–2.728
notification 2.731
obtaining credit during order 1.488

**Bankruptcy restriction order/undertaking –** *cont.*
  offer of undertaking by bankrupt 1.750
  register of 1.751
  registration 2.740, 2.741
**Body corporate**
  offences by 1.595
**Book debt**
  assignment by bankrupt 1.470
**Books/papers, bankrupt's**
  concealment/falsification/destruction offences 1.483
  lien on, unenforceability 1.475
  seizure powers 1.490
  trustee in bankruptcy taking control of 1.429
    obligation on bankrupt to deliver up 1.430
**Books/papers, company**
  evidence, as 1.248
  inspection 1.207
  lien on, unenforceability 1.310
  seizure powers 1.475
  winding up, offences relating to
    destruction, concealment, etc 1.263, 1.266
    false entries 1.263, 1.266
    non-delivery/non-production etc 1.265
**Bribe**
  liquidator, of or by 1.216, 2.250, 2.394
  trustee in bankruptcy, of or by 2.623
**Building operations**
  urban regeneration, administrative receivership 1.121
**Building society**
  administration regime 4.3
**Business**
  company not commencing, winding up ground 1.174
  insolvency practitioner's power to carry on administrator/administrative receiver 1.735

## C

**Calls** 1.203
  contributories on
    enforcement 2.412, 2.413
    leave to make, application to court 2.410
    liquidation committee, sanction of 2.409
    liquidator, by 2.408
    order 2.411
  liquidator making 1.212
  Scotland 1.213
**Capital**
  public company share capital, winding up ground 1.174

**Capital –** *cont.*
  return, authorisation
    liquidator, application to court 2.444
    procedure 2.445
**Capital market**
  arrangement
    administrative receiver appointed pursuant to 1.118, 1.736
    investment 1.736
**Capital market arrangement**
  administrative receiver appointed pursuant to
    'agreement' 1.736
**Channel Islands** 1.586
**Charge**
  administration, charged property disposal 2.180
  administrative receiver, disposal of charged property 2.223
  bankrupt, by, offence 1.485
  bankrupt's home, order imposing on 1.431, 2.717
**Coal and steel production levies**
  preferential debt 1.521, 1.756
**Collateral security**
  charge, administrative receiver, appointment under 1.123
**Commencement**
  IA 1986 1.613
**Company**
  definition for administration purposes 1.728
  financial difficulty, in
    arrangement or compromise, proposals for 5.39
**Company meeting** *See also* **Decision procedures**
  excluded person 2.923, 2.924
    complaints 2.925
  location 2.922
  remote attendance 2.921
  when required 2.920
**Company voluntary arrangement**
  accounts
    production to Secretary of State 2.118
  expenses 2.119
  fees 2.119
  full implementation of 2.120
  hand-over of property to supervisor 2.115
  meetings
    attendance 2.105
    chair 2.109
    conduct 2.101
    majorities, requisite
      members 2.111
    members, voting rights 2.110
    notice 2.105
      non-receipt 2.107
    proposal for alternative supervisor 2.108

**Company voluntary arrangement** – *cont.*
meetings – *cont.*
    requisition by creditors  2.106
moratorium  2.84–2.98
    advertisement  2.89
    continuation  2.90
    disposal of charged property during
        2.94
    documents
        filed at court to obtain  2.88
    end
        advertisement  2.93
    extension
        court order  2.92
        notice
            decision  2.91
    nominee
        applications to court, notice of  2.98
        replacement
            by court  2.96
            notice  2.97
        statement  2.87
        withdrawal of consent to act  2.95
    statement of affairs  2.85
nominee
    authorisation/qualification  1.525
    remuneration  2.119
    time-recording information  2.122
notices  2.112
preferential debts
    relevant date for  1.522
proposal  2.73–2.75
    amendment  2.74
    consideration  2.100
        creditors, by  2.102, 2.104
        members, by  2.101
    contents  2.75
    decisions, timing of  2.103
    disclosure to assist nominee  2.81
    general principles  2.74
    nominee
        disclosure to  2.81
        not liquidator/administrator  2.77
        replacement  2.83
        report  2.82
    official receiver, information for  2.78
    statement of affairs  2.79
        information, omission of  2.80
records, production to Secretary of State
    2.118
report  2.113
revocation  2.116
supervisor
    accounts  2.117
    authorisation/qualification  1.525
    hand-over of property to  2.115
    liquidator, becoming  1.193
    reports  2.117
    time-recording information  2.122

**Company voluntary arrangement** – *cont.*
suspension  2.116
termination  2.120
**Compulsory winding up** *See also* **Winding up**
    **by court**  2.313
accounts, delivery  2.363
administration following
    information duties  2.368
avoidance
    attachment, sequestration, etc  1.181
    disposition of property, etc  1.180
commencement  1.182, 1.183
contributory/ies
    absconding, arrest power  1.210
    adjustment of rights  1.206
    calls on
        enforcement  2.412, 2.413
        leave to make, application to court
            2.410
        liquidation committee, sanction of
            2.409
        liquidator, by  2.408
        order  2.411
    information to  2.365–2.369
    list of  1.201
        settlement  2.399–2.406
    orders for debts of  1.202
court powers
    cumulative  1.211
    delegation  1.212
creditors
    information to  2.365–2.369
creditors' claims
    unsold assets, division  2.840
exclusion of creditors  1.205
expenses  1.208
financial institution
    non-preferential debts  1.230, 1.523
grounds  1.177
inspection of books  1.207
liquidation committee, invitation to form
    2.374
liquidator  2.373–2.394
    account
        dissolution, prior to  2.390
    appointment
        court, by  2.375
        creditors/contributories, by  2.372
        notice  2.378
        Secretary of State, by  2.376
    ceasing to be qualified  2.387
    death of  2.386
    duties/powers  2.395–2.398
    hand over of property to  2.379
    nominations  2.371, 2.373
    release, Secretary of State, by  2.388
    removal
        court, by  2.384
        creditors, by  2.382

**Compulsory winding up** *See also* **Winding up by court** – *cont.*
  liquidator – *cont.*
    removal – *cont.*
      creditors, by – *cont.*
        procedure 2.383
        Secretary of State, by 2.385
      reporting duties
        relief/variation 2.391
      resignation 2.380
      security, costs of 2.377
      solicitation, improper 2.394
      transaction of, court setting aside 2.393
      vacation of office
        duties 2.392
        notice of intent 2.381
  litigation expenses
    property subject to floating charge 2.436–2.442
      approval 2.439–2.442
      priority 2.438
  meetings of creditors/contributories
    final meeting 1.224
    nomination of liquidator 1.192
  official receiver
    further disclosure request 2.364
    release of 2.389
    reporting duties
      relief/variation 2.391
  order 1.182
    administration prevents 1.659
    administrator's appointment 1.625, 1.654
    company in administration 2.347
    content 2.334
    effect of 1.183
    notice/copies to official receiver 2.335, 2.336
  petition 1.176
    administration order
      application treated as 1.630
      dismissal on 1.657
    certificate of compliance 2.326
    contents 2.319
    contributories, by 2.339–2.347
      applicable rules 2.340
      contents 2.341
      hearing 2.346
      presentation 2.342, 2.344
      verification 2.343
    copies
      persons entitled to 2.325
      service of 2.323
    court powers 1.178
    dismissal 2.337
    former administrator/supervisor as liquidator 2.345
    hearing
      adjournment 2.333

**Compulsory winding up** *See also* **Winding up by court** – *cont.*
  petition – *cont.*
    hearing – *cont.*
      list of appearances 2.329
      notice of appearance 2.328
      witness statement in opposition 2.330
    notice 2.324
    presentation and filing 2.321, 2.322
      injunction to restrain 2.338
    suspension 1.180, 1.657
    verification 2.320
    withdrawal 2.327
  petitioner 1.176
    contributory 1.176
    substitution of 2.331, 2.332
  preferential charge, distrained goods 1.229
  priority of costs/expenses 2.433, 2.435
  proceedings against company 1.183
    stay of 1.179
  property of company
    distribution 1.219
    securing and custody of 1.197
    vesting in liquidator 1.198
  property, distribution
    report on 2.982
  provisional liquidator
    appointment 2.349
      deposit 2.350
      notice 2.352
      order 2.351
      security 2.353
      termination 2.355
    remuneration 2.354
  public examination of officers, etc 1.186
    adjournment 2.430
    contributory, request by 2.424, 2.425
    creditor, request by 2.423, 2.425
    examinee lacking capacity 2.428
    expenses 2.431
    notice 2.427
    order 2.426
    procedure 2.429
    promoters 2.422
  special manager 2.414–2.420
    accounting duties 2.419
    appointment and remuneration 2.416
    security 2.417
      failure to give/keep up 2.418
    termination of appointment 2.420
  special resolution 1.174
  statement of affairs 1.184, 2.356–2.364
    contents 2.358
    expenses 2.362
    limited disclosure of 2.360
    notice requiring 2.357
    release, Secretary of State, by 2.361
    statement of concurrence 2.359

**Compulsory winding up** *See also* **Winding up by court** – *cont.*
statutory demand 2.316
stay of 1.200
notice 2.369
transfer of shares, effect on 1.180
voluntary winding up, interaction with 1.176, 1.182
expenses, priority of 2.434, 2.435
wrong court 1.170
**Concealment**
company books, relating to, offence 1.263, 1.266
**Confiscation order** 1.422
**Connected person**
meaning 1.324
**Consolidated Fund** 1.562
**Contempt of court**
bankruptcy, relating to 1.405, 1.489
**Contract**
administrative receiver's liability 1.88
bankrupt 1.471
arbitration agreement in 1.476
discharge application by party 1.471
joint contractor, position as 1.471
disclaimer of unprofitable
liquidator, by 1.235
trustee in bankruptcy, by 1.434, 1.435
receiver's liability 1.81
rescission by court in winding up 1.243
**Contribution to company assets**
fraudulent trading, liability after 1.271
wrongful trading, liability after 1.272
**Contributory/ies** *See also* **Creditors**
absconding 1.210
bankruptcy 1.136
calls on
enforcement 2.412, 2.413
leave to make, application to court 2.410
liquidation committee, sanction of 2.409
liquidator, by 2.408
order 2.411
company formed under Act of Parliament, etc, of 1.137
compulsory winding up
petitioner 1.176
death 1.135
debt due 1.202
adjustment 1.206
evidence, order as 1.204
order to pay 1.202
decisions by 1.315
deemed consent procedure 1.316
definition 1.133, 1.326
liability
nature of 1.134
past director/shareholder 1.130, 1.131

**Contributory/ies** *See also* **Creditors** – *cont.*
list of, compulsory winding up 1.201, 1.217
contents 2.402
costs 2.406
settlement
court's duty, delegation to liquidator 2.400
liquidator, duty 2.401
procedure 2.403
variation 2.404, 2.405
meetings
chair 2.899, 2.900
quorum 2.898
remote attendance 1.318
public examination of officer request 1.186
reference of question to court 1.164
unlimited company formerly limited member 1.132
wishes, of, meeting to ascertain 1.251
**Coronavirus pandemic**
corporate insolvency
temporary modifications relating to, 5.13, 5.24, 5.35
**Corporate insolvency**
CIGA 2020, reform by
company meetings and filings, 5.20–5.23, 5.44
legislation, power to amend, 5.12–5.19
moratorium, 5.4, 5.5, 5.34–5.37
supply contracts, 1.296, 1.297, 1.744–1.747, 5.10, 5.11, 5.42
winding up, 5.8, 5.41
wrongful trading, 5.9
**Correspondence**
re-direction power in bankruptcy 1.497
**Costs** *See also* **Expenses; Fees; Remuneration**
applications 2.801
bankruptcy
payment out of estate, priority 2.691
CPR, applicable 2.794
detailed assessment
requirement 2.795, 2.796
execution of writs or other process, enforcement officer, etc 2.797
expenses of petitioners 2.802
final costs certificate 2.803
office-holder, awards against 2.800
paid otherwise than out of insolvent estate 2.799
petitions by insolvent companies 2.798
**County court**
bankruptcy jurisdiction 1.500
compulsory winding up
jurisdiction 1.169
**Court**
co-operation, promotion of 1.586

**Court procedure and practice**
applications
directions 2.756
filing 2.752
hearing
adjournment 2.758
notice, without 2.757
persons lacking capacity to manage
affairs 2.771, 2.772, 2.773, 2.774
private examinations 2.764–2.769
service/delivery 2.754
unsecured creditors 2.761, 2.762
urgent cases 2.755
venue 2.753
block transfer orders 2.787, 2.788, 2.789
commencement of proceedings 2.747,
2.748
costs 2.794–2.803
court file 2.791
documents, office copies 2.792
court functions, performance 2.745
CPR
application of 2.744
disclosure 2.776
enforcement procedures
court orders 2.805
enforcing compliance 2.806
warrants
debtor/bankrupt, arrest 2.808
general provisions 2.807
inquiry into dealings, insolvent
company/bankrupt 2.809
officer of company, failure to attend
public examination 2.808
search of premises not belonging to
bankrupt 2.810
formal defects 2.820
further information 2.776
London Insolvency District, proceedings
allocated to 2.749
shorthand writers 2.821
transfer of proceedings between courts
applications 2.782
commenced in wrong court 2.781
consequential transfer, other proceedings
2.784
general power 2.780
procedure 2.783
witness statements 2.777
reports, office-holder by 2.778
**Credit**
bankruptcy offences
obtaining fraudulently 1.487
property obtained on, fraudulent dealing
1.487
**Creditors** *See also* **Contributory/ies**
administration order
applicant 1.629
challenge to administrator 1.691
improper motive application 1.698

**Creditors** *See also* **Contributory/ies** – *cont.*
claims, by
debts, insolvent company to rank equally
2.839
discounts 2.847
estimate of value of debt 2.841
foreign currency, debt in 2.848
interest provable 2.850
payments of periodical nature 2.849
provable debts 2.829
proving debt
exclusion by court 2.838
submission of claim 2.830
withdrawal/variation of proof 2.837
secured creditors 2.842–2.846
unsold assets, division 2.840
claims, by proving debt
admission/rejection for dividend 2.834
appeal of decision 2.835
costs of proving 2.832
inspection of proofs 2.833
requirements 2.831
committee *See* Creditors' committee
decisions by 1.315, 1.507
deemed consent procedure 1.316, 1.508
distribution to
admission/rejection of proofs 2.860
dividends 2.855, 2.868
declaration 2.862
notices 2.863
last notice, delivery of 2.864, 2.865
notices 2.856–2.859
postponement/cancellation 2.861
sole/final 2.866
report on 2.982
enforcement of execution/attachment
against bankrupt 1.472
false representation to 1.268
IVA, meaning for 1.359
list
right to 2.70
'opted-out creditor', meaning 1.323, 1.517
public examination of officer request
1.186
receipt of notices, opting out 1.320, 1.511
request for information 2.981
unsecured, share of assets for 1.233
disapplication 1.233
voluntary winding up
administration, moving to 2.193
**Creditors' committee**
attendance of receiver 1.93
dealings by members 2.966
defect in act of 1.504
establishment 2.942
establishment and functions 1.93
expenses 2.964
formal defects 2.967
functions 2.938

**Creditors' committee** – *cont.*
invitation to form
administration 2.168
administrative receivership 2.222
bankruptcy 2.607
meetings 2.952
chair 2.953
members' representatives 2.955
remote attendance 2.958
resolutions 2.956, 2.957
venue 2.959
voting rights 2.956
membership
change to, notice 2.944
eligibility 2.941
numbers 2.940
termination 2.948
office-holder
notice to attend 2.961
supply of information, obligation 2.962
removal of member 2.949
resignation from 2.947
scope 2.937
Secretary of State, functions vested in 2.968
trustee in bankruptcy, and
notice from 1.433
sanctioning acts 1.445
vacancies
contributory members 2.946
creditor members 2.945
**Creditors' meeting** *See also* Creditors' committee; Decision procedures
adjournment 2.901–2.904
advertisement 2.889
chair 2.899, 2.900
company officers, notice to 2.890
exclusion 2.915–2.917
quorum 2.898
suspension 2.905
voting rights 2.907, 2.918
admission, procedure 2.911
appeals against 2.913
authorised deposit-taker, scheme manager of 2.908
calculation 2.909, 2.910
requisite majorities 2.912
wishes of creditors, to ascertain 1.251
**Creditors' voluntary winding up** 2.258
administration becoming 1.700
commencement 1.141
confirmation
application 2.1035
court order 2.1036
costs/expenses
priority rule 2.305, 2.306
property subject to floating charge 2.307–2.312

**Creditors' voluntary winding up** – *cont.*
creditors' claims
unsold assets, division 2.840
directors' powers 1.155
directors' reports 2.277
liquidation committee 1.154
invitation to form 2.279
liquidator
account
dissolution, prior to 2.289
appointment 1.153, 2.274, 2.281
advertisement and registration 2.284
court, by 2.283
ceasing to be qualified 2.291
creditors/contributories, information 2.275
death of 2.290
delivery of accounts to 2.267
expenses 2.268
nomination, decisions 2.278
permission to exercise powers 2.297
release, Secretary of State, by 2.294
removal
court by 2.288
creditors by 2.287
resignation 2.286
security 2.285
transaction of, court setting aside 2.295
vacancy, filling 2.282
vacation of office 2.292
duties 2.293
meeting of creditors
final meeting 1.158
members' voluntary winding up converted to 1.150
members' voluntary winding up, conversion from 2.257
creditors/contributories, information 2.273
liquidator, nomination/appointment 2.271, 2.272
progress reports, timing 2.979
property, distribution
report on 2.982
remuneration
procedure for initial determination 2.994
reporting arrangements 2.983
special manager
accounting duties 2.302
appointment 2.299
termination 2.303
security 2.300
failure to give/keep up 2.301
statement of affairs
content 2.263
directors 2.262
disclosure, limited 2.265
expenses 2.266
liquidator 2.261

**Creditors' voluntary winding up** – *cont.*
statement of affairs – *cont.*
statement of concurrence 2.264
**Cross-border Insolvency Regulations 2006
(UNCITRAL)** 7.1
British insolvency law, modification 7.8
British officeholders
assistance to foreign representatives
7.20
comparison with EU Regulation 7.3
concurrent proceedings 7.41–7.45
courts, co-operation with foreign 7.12,
7.38
definitions 7.15
foreign creditor's
notification of proceedings 7.27
implementation 7.2
international obligations 7.16
jurisdiction 7.17
limited 7.23
procedure
England and Wales 7.9
appeals 7.56
Chief Land Registrar, applications
7.52
costs 7.55
court orders 7.50
court practice 7.51, 7.54
foreign representative, replacement
7.49
misfeasance 7.53
notices 7.57, 7.58
recognition, for 7.47
relief under model law 7.48
Scotland 7.10
proceedings
foreign representative 7.24, 7.25
public policy exception 7.19
recognition of the foreign proceeding
7.28–7.37
reciprocity 7.4
scope 7.14
**Crown proceedings** 1.597


# D

**Death**
administrative receiver, of 2.226
administrator, of 1.707, 1.716
contributory, of 1.135
liquidator, of 2.245, 2.290, 2.386
official receiver 1.555
**Debt relief order**
amendment 1.339
application for 1.329, 2.496
delivery 2.497
determinations 1.331
errors/omissions, in 2.514

**Debt relief order** – *cont.*
application for – *cont.*
official receiver's consideration, of
1.330
refusal 2.507
verification checks on debtor 2.499
approved intermediary, role 2.498
concealment/falsification of documents
1.343
contents 2.504
court powers 1.340
creditors
objections 2.510
prescribed information for 2.506
debtor
non-disclosure of current address,
order for 2.1029, 2.1031
debtor's duty to assist official receiver
1.337
'debtor's family' 2.493
debtor's monthly surplus income 2.500
disqualification of directors, application for
leave 2.522
court's order 2.524
official receiver's report 2.523
excluded debts 2.494
false representations/omissions 1.342
fraudulent disposal of/dealings with
property 1.344, 1.345
inquiries 1.341
intermediaries 1.348
making of 1.332
moratorium period
death of debtor, during 2.515
extension of 2.520
objections/investigations 1.338
offences 1.346, 1.347
official receiver
complaints against 2.517
court for 2.518
duties 2.505
notices to 2.514
response to objections 2.511
other debt management arrangements, and
1.333
property of debtor, value 2.501
excluded property 2.502
qualifying debts
discharge, from 1.336
moratorium, from 1.334
period for 1.335
register 1.350
registration 2.738, 2.739
revocation 1.339
creditor's request 2.512
procedure 2.513
**Debt relief restrictions order** 1.349, 1.749
application for order 2.720
opposition to 2.722
service 2.721

**Debt relief restrictions order** – *cont.*
court, made by 2.723
interim order 2.725–2.728
registration 2.740, 2.741
**Debt relief restrictions undertaking** 1.349,
1.749
acceptance 2.730
annulment 2.732
notification 2.731
registration 2.740, 2.741
**Debts, company**
person indebted to company, enforcement
powers of court 1.301
personal liability for company debts 1.276
**Decision procedures** *See also* **Creditors'
committee; Creditors' meetings;
Liquidation committee**
decision
non-receipt of notice 2.891
remuneration and conduct 2.892
requisitions 2.896, 2.897
deemed consent 2.882
definition 2.877
meetings, creditors/contributories
adjournment 2.901–2.904
advertisement 2.889
chair 2.899, 2.900
company officers, notice to 2.890
exclusion 2.915–2.917
quorum 2.898
suspension 2.905
voting rights 2.907–2.913, 2.918
notices
advertisement 2.888
creditors, to 2.884
delivery 2.887
physical meetings 2.881
prescribed 2.878
records 2.919
venue 2.886
virtual meetings 2.880
voting 2.885
**Declaration of solvency** 1.143
liability of director 1.143
**Definitions** 1.326
**Destruction of book, etc, offences**
bankrupt 1.483
company officer 1.263
**Devolution issues**
bankruptcy restrictions 1.588, 4.10
**Director(s)**
administration of company
applicant for order for 1.629, 2.128
appointment of administrator out-of-
court 1.639
consent of administrator to management
power exercise 1.680
notice of intention to appoint 1.643,
2.149

**Director(s)** – *cont.*
administration of company – *cont.*
removal/appointment,
administrator's powers 1.677
restrictions on appointment power
1.640
statutory declaration 1.644
'associate', and 1.604
bankrupt, leave to act as
application 2.667
costs 2.670
court order 2.669
official receiver's report 2.668
company voluntary arrangement proposal
statement of affairs 2.79
definition 1.326
prohibited names provision 1.275
debt liability for contravention 1.276
prohibited names, company with
leave to act 2.1037–2.1044
shadow
connected person 1.324
definition 1.326
statement of affairs
creditors' voluntary winding up 2.262,
2.263
unlimited liability 1.202
winding up offences 1.263–1.268
fraudulent trading 1.271, 1.274
prosecution of delinquent director
1.277, 3.9
summary remedy against 1.270
wrongful trading 1.272, 1.274
**Disclaimer** 2.1012
court order for 2.1024
interested person, application by 2.1022
liquidator, by 1.238, 1.239
application by interested person 1.236
leasehold 1.236
notices 1.235
'onerous property' 1.235
rent charge, land subject to 1.237
notice of 2.1015
additional notices 2.1019
dwelling-house 2.1018
interested persons to 2.1016
leasehold property of 2.1017
records 2.1020
trustee in bankruptcy, by 1.434–1.440
application by interested person 1.435
leasehold 1.436, 1.439
leave application 1.435
notices 1.435
'onerous property' 1.433, 1.434
power 1.434
rent charge, land subject to 1.438
vesting of disclaimed property, order for
1.439
trustee, application by 2.1021
validity presumption 2.1023

Disclosure
  bankrupt, state of affairs
    bankruptcy order made  2.592–2.595
    creditor's petition  2.584–2.591
  CPR  2.776
  CVA
    to assist nominee  2.81
  limited disclosure order (statement of
      affairs)
    administrative receiver  2.219
    administrator  2.175, 2.177
    compulsory winding up  2.360
    liquidator  2.265
  non-disclosure, offence
    bankrupt  1.481
    company books, relating to  1.263,
      1.266
    officer, etc, failure to give information to
      office-holder  1.299
  restrictions on
    debtor at risk of violence  2.1027,
      2.1028, 2.1031
Disposition
  fraudulent, by bankrupt  1.485
Disqualification
  insolvency practitioner  1.528
Dissolution of company  1.256
  administration, after  1.701, 2.194
  compulsory winding up, after  1.261
  early, application for  1.258
    directions deferring, etc  1.259
    notice of  1.258
    Scotland  1.260
  voluntary winding up, after  1.257
  winding up, after
    Secretary of State, directions  2.446
Distress
  administration, effect on  1.660
  avoidance  1.181
  bankruptcy
    discharge, effect on  1.473
    limit on, and outstanding debt  1.473
    preferential debts  1.473
  IVA interim order application, and  1.355
  preferential charge  1.229
Distribution
  stay of  1.453
  winding up
    voluntary  1.159
Dividends
  administration  2.867
  bankruptcy  1.443
    court order  1.444
    final  1.449
    notices  1.443, 1.449
    unclaimed  1.561
    unsatisfied creditors' claims, provision
      for  1.444
  declaration  2.862
    notices  2.863

Dividends – *cont.*
  distribution  2.855
    notices  2.856–2.859
  last notice, delivery of  2.864, 2.865
  postponement/cancellation  2.861
  secured creditors  2.869
  sole/final  2.866
  winding up  2.867
Documents
  alteration, etc
    bankruptcy offence  1.483
    winding up, prior to, offence  1.263
  authentication  2.13
  confidentiality  2.71
  copies, right to  2.67
    charges  2.68
  court, judicial notice  1.252
  delivery
    claims, details  2.66
    creditors to, opting out  2.50, 2.51, 2.52
    document exchange  2.56
    electronic  2.58, 2.59, 2.60, 2.61
    joint office-holders  2.54
    personal  2.57
    persons other than registrar to  2.40–
      2.46
    post, by  2.55
    proof of service  2.65
    registrar to  2.30–2.38
    website, use of  2.62–2.64
  form and content  2.12
  inspection
    offences  2.69
  lien, unenforceability  1.310
  list of creditors  2.70
  prescribed format  2.16
    variations  2.17
  production
    investigation of company, during  1.277
    order against HMRC  2.654–2.657
    order against Inland Revenue  1.495
    preventing, offence by company officer
      1.265
  stamp duty exemption  1.247, 1.505
  'trading record'  1.483
Dwelling-house of bankrupt  1.397
  ceasing to be in estate  1.397, 4.8
    notification  2.713
    period for/extension  1.397
    substituted period  2.716
    unregistered land  2.715
    vesting application to Land Registry
      2.714
  charge on  2.717
  charge on, trustee's application  1.431
  definition  1.519
  disclaimer of  1.437
  disclaimer, notice of  2.1018
  estate of bankrupt, in  1.396

**Dwelling-house of bankrupt** – *cont.*
  final meeting restrictions 1.451
  low value 1.432, 4.8
  occupation rights of bankrupt 1.457
    occupation order 1.457
    payment obligation 1.458
  order for possession/sale 1.397, 1.432, 4.8
    trust of land 1.455
  spouse/former spouse
    matrimonial home rights 1.456


E

**Employee**
  associate of employer, as 1.604
  co-operation duty 1.299
  EU Regulation, protection under 6.15
  payment to provide for, liquidator's power
    1.244
  pension contribution 1.756
  remuneration as preferential debt 1.521,
    1.756
  statement of affairs
    administration 1.664
    administrative receivership 1.91
    compulsory winding up, in 1.184
    receivership, Scotland 1.110
  wages 1.88
**Employment contract**
  administrative receiver adopting, liability
    on 1.88
  receiver adopting, liability 1.81
    Scotland 1.101
**Enforcement**
  UK, within 1.586
**EU Regulation on insolvency proceedings
2015**
  applicable law 7.1, 6.9
  arbitral proceedings
    effect of insolvency proceedings on 6.20
  centre of main interests 6.5
  commencement provisions 6.97
  committee procedures 6.94
  Community trade marks 6.17
  company insolvency rules, and 1.566
  courts, co-operation with foreign 7.12,
    7.38
  creditors
    right to lodge claim 6.57
      procedure 6.59
  creditors' rights
    access to British courts, foreign 7.22,
      7.26
  cross-border regulations 7.1
  deceased debtor provision 1.578
  definitions 6.4
  detrimental acts, creditors to 6.18
  employees, protection of 6.15
  European patents 6.17

**EU Regulation on insolvency proceedings
2015** – *cont.*
  financial markets, effect of proceedings on
    6.14
  foreign proceedings 7.47
  immoveable property 6.13
    rights subject to registration 6.16
  individual insolvency rules, and 1.567
  insolvency practitioner
    duty to inform creditors 6.58
  judgment, recognition of 6.21
    costs 6.32
    effect of 6.22
    honouring obligations 6.33
    insolvency practitioner
      appointment 6.24
      powers of 6.23
    insolvency registers
      access to 6.29
      costs 6.28
      establishment 6.26
      interconnection 6.27
    other judgments, provision for
      recognition/enforceability 6.34
    principle 6.21
    publication of 6.30
    refusal of recognition of proceedings/
      judgment enforcement 6.35
    registration of 6.31
    return and imputation 6.25
  jurisdiction 6.5
    examination 6.6
  main insolvency proceedings
    jurisdiction 6.5, 6.8
    opening of 6.5
      judicial review 6.7
    subsequent opening 6.53
  members of a group of companies
    cooperation
      insolvency practitioners/courts 6.60–
        6.62
        costs 6.63
    coordination proceedings
      choice of court 6.71
      court notice 6.68
      decision to open 6.73
      group coordination plan 6.75
      inclusion of insolvency practitioner
        6.74
      objections to 6.69, 6.70, 6.72
      priority rule 6.67
      request 6.66
    coordinator 6.76
      communication, languages 6.78
      cooperation with insolvency
        practitioner 6.79
      remuneration 6.82
      revocation of appointment 6.80
      rights of 6.77
      statement of costs 6.82

**EU Regulation on insolvency proceedings 2015** – *cont.*
members of a group of companies – *cont.*
powers of insolvency practitioner 6.64
moveable property
rights subject to registration 6.16
personal data, processing
access via European e-Justice Portal 6.88
Commission, responsibilities 6.85
information obligations 6.86
national insolvency registers, in 6.84
national rules 6.83
storage 6.87
procedure 7.9, 7.10, 7.54
proceedings under 2.15
reservation of title 6.12
scope 6.3
secondary proceedings 6.36
applicable law 6.38
assets remaining in 6.52
closure of proceedings 6.51
conversion of 6.54
cooperation
insolvency practitioner/courts 6.44, 6.45, 6.46
costs 6.47
costs and expenses 6.43
creditors' rights 6.48
opening of 6.37
decision for 6.41
judicial review 6.42
right to request 6.40
preservation of debtor's assets 6.55
proposal of restructuring plans 6.50
realization of assets, staying of 6.49
undertaking to avoid 6.39
set-off of creditors' claims 6.11
settlement systems, effect of proceedings on 6.14
standard forms for 6.93
third parties' rights in rem 6.10
third party purchasers, protection of 6.19
**European Community Regulation** *See* **EU Regulation on insolvency proceedings 2015**
**Evidence**
witness statements 2.777
reports, office-holder by 2.778
**Examination**
administrator, of 1.692
official receiver applicant 1.186, 1.404
private
application 1.300
applications, content 2.765
costs 2.769
order for 2.766
procedure 2.767
record of 2.768

**Examination** – *cont.*
public, of bankrupt 1.404, 1.490, 2.632, 2.633, 2.634, 2.635, 2.636, 2.637, 2.638
application for order for 1.404
failure to attend 1.404, 1.490
public, of company officer 1.186
adjournment 2.430
contributory, request by 2.424, 2.425
creditor, request by 2.423, 2.425
examinee lacking capacity 2.428
expenses 2.431
failure to attend 1.187
notice 2.427
order 2.426
procedure 2.429
promoters 2.422
Scotland 1.254
witness(es)
commission for evidence 1.253
**Execution**
bankruptcy, issued prior to 1.472
effect of insolvency 2.811
winding up, and 1.240
avoidance 1.181
officers' duties 1.241
**Expenses** *See also* **Costs; Fees; Remuneration**
bankruptcy 2.690
individual voluntary arrangement 2.481
priority (winding up), general rule 2.305, 2.306, 2.433, 2.435
property subject to floating charge 2.307–2.312, 2.436–2.442
approval 2.439, 2.440, 2.441, 2.442
priority 2.438
winding up commencing as voluntary 2.434, 2.435
**Extent (Jurisdiction)**
IA 1986 1.612
**Extortionate credit transaction** 1.308, 1.469
meaning 1.308, 1.469

**F**

**False representation**
bankruptcy offence 1.484
IVA, relating to 1.365
winding up, during, to creditors 1.268
**False statement**
bankruptcy offences 1.484
**Fees** *See also* **Costs; Expenses; Remuneration**
expense, as, priority rules
bankruptcy 2.691
winding up 2.305, 2.306, 2.433, 2.435
individual voluntary arrangement 2.481
power to make order 1.571, 4.14
company insolvency 1.569
individual insolvency 1.570

**Financial Conduct Authority**
members' voluntary winding up
meeting of authorised deposit-takers,
notice 2.237
**Financial institution**
winding up of
non-preferential debts 1.230, 1.523
**Financial market**
administrative receiver, appointment 1.123
**Floating charge**
administration
disposal power of administrator 1.687
avoidance 1.309
onset of insolvency 1.309
relevant time 1.309
qualifying 1.631, 1.652
**Floating charge holder**
administration order applicant 1.652
intervention 1.653, 2.135
administrator
appointment by 2.141, 2.142, 2.144
out of court hours 2.145, 2.146,
2.147
appointment of administrator 1.630,
1.639
compulsory winding up petition
suspension 1.657
consent to 1.638
invalid, indemnity for 1.638
power 1.631
replacement application 1.709
restrictions 1.632, 1.633
substitution application, competing
charge holder 1.713
appointment of receiver 2.230
expenses of winding up, payment 1.231
office-holder claims, proceeds of 1.232
share of assets for unsecured creditors
1.233
disapplication 1.233
voluntary winding up, written notice of
1.138
**Floating charge holder (Scotland)**
jeopardy, in 1.174
qualifying floating charge 1.631
**Foreign company** 4.4
winding up, overseas company 1.285
**Formation**
information on, office-holder's powers
court enforcement 1.301
**Fraud**
bankruptcy, relating to 1.485
IVA, relating to 1.365
winding up, prior to 1.263
creditors, transaction in fraud of 1.264
**Fraudulent trading** 1.271, 1.274, 1.311
**Friendly society** 4.5

**G**

**Gift**
bankrupt, by 1.485
transaction at undervalue 1.582
**Goods**
bankrupt obtaining on credit, scope 1.488
supply, protection of 1.296,1.297,1.744–
1.747,5.10, 5.11, 5.42
**Gratuitous alienation** 1.306
**Guarantee, company limited by**
member's liability to contribute on winding
up 1.129
**Guarantor**
preference or transaction at undervalue,
reviving obligations of 1.305

**H**

**High Court**
bankruptcy jurisdiction 1.500
compulsory winding up
case stated from county court for 1.171
jurisdiction 1.169
**Hire purchase/conditional sale/chattel
lease** 1.488
administration
disposal of goods by administrator
1.689
repossession restriction in 1.660
**HM Revenue and Customs**
production order against 2.654–2.657

**I**

**Indemnity**
administrator 1.81, 1.88, 1.638
**Individual voluntary arrangement**
bankruptcy petition, interaction with
1.353
binding effect 1.362
ceasing to have effect
premature end 1.367
creditors' decision
challenge to 1.364
debtor
non-disclosure of current address,
order for 2.1028
debtor, proposal
approval 1.360
contents 2.450
creditors, consideration by 1.359,
2.472, 2.474
nominee
disclosure to assist 2.454
notice of consent 2.451
replacement 2.465
report 2.463, 2.466
principles 2.449

**Individual voluntary arrangement** – *cont.*
 debtor, proposal – *cont.*
  supervisor
   accounts and reports  2.479, 2.480
   alternative to nominee  2.473
 default by debtor, effect of  1.388
 definitions  2.447
 delinquent debtor, action on  1.366
 false representation/fraud by debtor  1.365
 fees/expenses  2.481
 implementation  1.368, 2.482
 information, provision of  2.491
 interim order  1.353
  action following  2.461
  application  1.354, 2.456
  ceasing to have effect  1.362
  conditions for  1.356
  contents  2.460
  court for  2.457
  duration  1.356, 1.364
  effect of application  1.355
  effect of order  1.353
  extension of  2.462, 2.464
  hearing  2.459
  stay of  2.458
 no interim order
  court  2.469
  nominee
   replacement  2.470
   report  2.468
 nominee  1.354
  authorisation/qualification  1.525
  becoming supervisor  1.368
 preferential debts  1.360
  relevant date for  1.522
 proposal by debtor  1.354, 1.357, 1.358
  approval  1.360
  effect of approval  1.362
  modifications  1.360
 registration  2.734, 2.735
 report of decision  1.361
 report on proposal  1.357, 1.358
 revocation or suspension  1.364, 2.478
  revised  1.364
 Secretary of State, report to  2.477
 secured creditors  1.360
 statement of affairs  1.357, 2.452
  omission of information from  2.453
 supervisor  1.368
  authorisation/qualification  1.525
  bankruptcy petitioner  1.379
  court appointment  1.368
  directions application by  1.368
  dissatisfaction with act etc of  1.368
  hand-over of property to  2.476
  replacement/increase in number  1.368
 termination  2.482
  premature end  1.367
 undischarged bankrupt  1.354, 1.359

**Individual voluntary arrangement** – *cont.*
 undischarged bankrupt – *cont.*
  annulment of bankruptcy order  1.363,
   2.484, 2.485, 2.486, 2.487, 2.488,
   2.489
  conduct of bankruptcy, order as to
   1.356
  trustee challenging decision  1.364
  unfair prejudice  1.364
**Inland Revenue**
 production order against  1.495
**Inquiry**
 bankrupt's dealings etc  1.492
  court enforcement powers  1.493
 company dealings  1.300
  court enforcement powers  1.301
**Insolvency administration order**
 definition  1.519
 joint tenancy, court powers  1.579, 3.11
**Insolvency districts**  1.501
**Insolvency practitioner**  1.525
 'act as', meaning  1.525, 3.5
 administrator  1.623
 appointment
  EU Regulation  6.24
 authorisation to act  1.529, 1.530
 death of, block transfer of cases  2.787,
  2.788, 2.789
 direct sanctions order
  application  1.547
  conditions  1.548
  directions instead of  1.549
  meaning  1.546
  power to make  1.547
 office-holder, as  1.291
 powers
  EU Regulation  6.23
 qualification
  acting without, offence  1.526
 regulations, power  1.576
 trustee in bankruptcy to be  1.407
**Insolvency proceedings**
 bankruptcy, 'inability to pay debt'  1.382,
  1.383
 compulsory winding up ground  1.174
  deemed  1.175
  'unable to pay debts', definition  1.175
  unregistered company  1.282, 1.283,
   1.284
 European Union *See* EU Regulation on
  insolvency proceedings 2015
 gazette notices  2.18–2.23
 non-gazette notices  2.25, 2.26, 2.27, 2.28
 'onset of', for prior transaction avoidance
  1.304, 1.309
**Insolvency register**
 individual insolvency
  bankruptcy  2.736, 2.737
  death, entry relating to  2.743
  debt relief orders  2.738, 2.739

**Insolvency register** – *cont.*
  individual insolvency – *cont.*
    IVA 2.734, 2.735
    rectification 2.742
    inspection 2.733
    maintenance 2.733
**Insolvency Regulations, cross-border** 7.1
  British insolvency law, modification 7.8
  British officeholders
    assistance to foreign representatives
      7.20
  comparison with EU Regulation 7.3
  concurrent proceedings 7.41–7.45
  courts, co-operation with foreign 7.12,
    7.38
  definitions 7.15
  foreign creditor's
    notification of proceedings 7.27
  implementation 7.2
  international obligations 7.16
  jurisdiction 7.17
    limited 7.23
  procedure
    England and Wales 7.9
      appeals 7.56
      Chief Land Registrar, applications
        7.52
      costs 7.55
      court orders 7.50
      court practice 7.51, 7.54
      foreign representative, replacement
        7.49
      misfeasance 7.53
      notices 7.57, 7.58
      recognition, for 7.47
      relief under model law 7.48
    Scotland 7.10
  proceedings
    foreign representative 7.24, 7.25
  public policy exception 7.19
  recognition of the foreign proceeding
    7.28–7.37
  reciprocity 7.4
  scope 7.14
**Insolvency Rules**
  defined terms 2.10
  identification of persons/proceedings 2.14
  scope 2.8
  time periods, caclulation 2.11, 2.1048
**Insolvency Rules Committee** 1.568
**Insolvency services**
  meaning 1.591
**Insolvency Services Account** 1.558
  annual statement 1.563
  Consolidated Fund, payment into/out of
    1.562
  Investment Account 1.558
**Insolvent partnership** 1.220, 1.414
  associates 1.604
  regulations power 1.577

**Inspection**
  company books and papers 1.207
**Insurance company**
  administration exclusion 1.626
**Interest**
  debts, winding up 1.246
    official rate 1.246
  money received by liquidator/trustee in
    bankruptcy 1.560
**Interim moratorium**
  administration application, after 1.661
**Interim order**
  administration 1.630
  bankruptcy restrictions order 1.750
**Interim receiver** 1.400, 1.494
  appointment of 1.400
  debtor's property, taking possession of
    1.400
  duration 1.400
  inquiry powers of court 1.494
  insolvency practitioner as
    qualification 1.525
  limited powers 1.400
**Investigation of bankrupt** 1.403
**Investigation of company** 1.278, 3.9
  official receiver, by 1.185
  report by liquidator, following
    answers, use as evidence 1.278
**Isle of Man** 1.586

**J**

**Joint tenancy**
  insolvent deceased 1.579, 3.11
**Judgment, recognition**
  EU Regulation 6.21
    effect of 6.22
    insolvency practitioner
      appointment 6.24
      powers of 6.23
    other judgments, provision for
      recognition/enforceability 6.34
    principle 6.21
    publication of judgment 6.30
    registration 6.31
    return and imputation 6.25
**Judicial notice** 1.252
**Jurisdiction**
  bankruptcy 1.500
  compulsory winding up 1.169–1.171
    Scotland 1.172
**Just and equitable winding up** 1.174

**L**

**Land**
  bankrupt's
    mortgagee's claim 2.660

**Land** – *cont.*
   bankrupt's – *cont.*
      sale 2.661
         proceeds 2.662
   immoveable property
   EU Regulations 6.13
**Leasehold**
   administrative
      receiver/administrator's powers as to
         1.735
   disclaimer
      liquidator, by 1.236
      trustee in bankruptcy, by 1.436, 1.439,
         1.440
   landlord's rights
      administration, effect on 1.660, 3.8
      IVA interim order application, effect on
         1.355
**Licence company**
   administration 4.3
**Lien on books or papers**
   unenforceability, extent of
      administration or liquidation 1.310
      bankruptcy 1.475
**Liquidation**
   meaning of 'to go into liquidation' 1.321
   rights of action, assignment 1.314
**Liquidation committee**
   cessation, creditors paid on full 2.950
   compulsory winding up 1.194
      Scotland, in 1.195
   creditors' voluntary winding up 1.154
      Scotland, in 1.154
   dealings by members 2.965
   establishment 2.942
      contributories, by 2.943
   expenses 2.964
   formal defects 2.967
   functions 2.938
   invitation to form
      compulsory winding up 2.374
      creditors' voluntary winding up 2.279
   meetings 2.952
      chair 2.953
      members' representatives 2.955
      remote attendance 2.958
      resolutions 2.956, 2.957
      venue 2.959
      voting rights 2.956
   members
      eligibility 2.941
   membership
      change to, notice 2.944
      numbers 2.940
      termination 2.948
   office-holder
      notice to attend 2.961
      supply of information, obligation 2.962
   removal of member 2.949

**Liquidation committee** – *cont.*
   resignation from 2.947
   scope 2.937
   vacancies
      contributory members 2.946
      creditor members 2.945
**Liquidator** 1.214
   accounts duty 1.222
   administration application 1.655, 2.138
   aggrieved person's application to court
      1.220
   appointment, compulsory winding up
      1.188
      administrator as 1.193
      court, by 1.193
      nomination at meeting 1.192
      notice of 1.190
      Scotland 1.191
      Secretary of State, by 1.190
   appointment, voluntary winding up 1.145
      court, by 1.160
      none made 1.166
      notice of 1.161
   bankruptcy petitioner, as 1.379
   bribe/inducement affecting appointment
      1.216
   business of company, carrying on 1.742
   calls 1.212
   compulsory winding up 2.370
      account
         dissolution, prior to 2.390
      appointment
         court, by 2.375
         creditors/contributories, by 2.372
         notice 2.378
         Secretary of State, by 2.376
      ceasing to be qualified 2.387
      death of 2.386
      duties/powers 2.395–2.398
      hand over of property to 2.379
      nominations 2.371, 2.373
      release, Secretary of State, by 2.388
      removal
         court, by 2.384
         creditors, by 2.382
            procedure 2.383
         Secretary of State, by 2.385
      reporting duties
         relief/variation 2.391
      resignation 2.380
      security, costs of 2.377
      solicitation, improper 2.394
      transaction of, court setting aside 2.393
      vacation of office
         duties 2.392
         notice of intent 2.381
   contributories, list of
      duty to settle 1.201
   co-operation duty 1.299

**Liquidator** – *cont.*
creditors' voluntary winding up
account
dissolution, prior to 2.289
accounts, delivery to 2.267
expenses 2.268
administrator, as 2.276
appointment 1.153, 2.274, 2.281
court, by 2.283
ceasing to be qualified 2.291
creditors/contributories, information
2.275
death of 2.290
meetings, final 1.158
nomination, decisions 2.278
permission to exercise powers 2.297
release, Secretary of State, by 2.294
removal
court by 2.288
creditors by 2.287
resignation 2.286
security 2.285
statement of affairs 2.261, 2.263
disclosure, limited 2.265
transaction of, court setting aside 2.294
vacancy, filling 1.156, 2.282
vacation of office 2.292
duties 2.293
defect in appointment 1.293
delegation of court powers to 1.212
directions of court 1.220
employee, payment for 1.244
expenses 1.167
final account 1.199, 2.987
functions, compulsory winding up 1.196
information duties
official receiver, to 1.196
pending liquidations, to registrar 1.249
joint/more than one 1.292
members' voluntary winding up
appointment 1.145, 2.236
court, by 2.238
ceasing to be qualified 2.246
court appointment 1.160
death of 2.245
effect of appointment 1.145
final account 2.243
prior to dissolution 2.244
progress reports 1.147
release, Secretary of State, by 2.248
removal by company meeting 2.242
removal by court 1.160, 1.223, 2.241
resignation 2.240
security, cost of 2.239
solicitation, improper 2.250
statement of affairs 2.257
transaction of, court setting aside 2.249
vacancy, filling 1.146

**Liquidator** – *cont.*
members' voluntary winding up – *cont.*
vacation of office
duties 2.247
money received, interest on 1.560
notification on business stationery 1.245
officer of company's non-delivery etc to
1.265
powers 1.740
legal proceedings on behalf of company
1.218
voluntary winding up 1.740
progress reports, timing 2.979, 2.980
property of company 1.217, 1.235
collection and retention duties 1.298
powers to get in 1.298
provisional 1.183, 1.184, 1.525
administration restriction after
appointment 1.634
appointment 1.188
co-operation duty 1.299
more than one 1.292
property, powers to get in 1.298
qualification 1.291
release 1.226
validity of acts where defective
appointment 1.293
provisional (compulsory winding up)
appointment 2.349
deposit 2.350
notice 2.352
order 2.351
security 2.353
termination 2.355
remuneration 2.354
public examination 1.186
purchase of member's share 1.163
qualification 1.291
reference of question to court 1.164
release
compulsory winding up 1.226
voluntary winding up 1.225
removal/vacation of office
compulsory winding up 1.224
voluntary winding up 1.160, 1.223
remuneration *See also* Remuneration
2.990
exceeding fee estimate 2.1004
joint 2.991
new liquidator 2.1005
realisation of assets on behalf of secured
creditor 2.1012
request for increase 2.998, 2.999,
2.1002
review 2.1003
report on delinquent officer or member
1.277, 3.9
return of capital, authorisation
application to court 2.444
procedure 2.445

**Liquidator** – *cont.*
returns
enforcement 1.221
solicitation, improper 1.216
statement to registrar 1.249
summary remedy against 1.270
title 1.215
unsecured, share of assets for 1.233
disapplication 1.233
validity of acts 1.293
vesting of company property in 1.198
**Local government**
disqualification from 4.11
**London Insolvency District**
proceedings allocated to 2.749


**M**

**Management of company**
prohibited name contravention 1.276
**Market charge**
administrative receiver appointed under
1.123
**Material irregularity** 1.364
**Member, company**
meaning 1.325
offence during winding up, prosecution of
1.277, 3.9
past member as contributory 1.129
reduced below two, winding up 1.176
**Members' voluntary winding up**
commencement 1.141
conversion to creditors' winding up 1.150
creditors' distinguished 1.144
creditors' voluntary winding up, conversion
to 2.257
directors' powers 1.145
final account 1.148
insolvency, effect 1.149
liquidator
appointment 2.236
court, by 2.238
ceasing to be qualified 2.246
death of 2.245
final account 2.243
prior to dissolution 2.244
release, Secretary of State, by 2.248
removal by company meeting 2.242
removal by court 2.241
resignation 2.240
security, cost of 2.239
solicitation, improper 2.250
statement of affairs 2.257
transaction of, court setting aside 2.249
vacation of office
duties 2.247
meeting of authorised deposit-takers
notice to FCA 2.237
progress reports 1.147

**Members' voluntary winding up** – *cont.*
progress reports – *cont.*
timing 2.979
remuneration
procedure for initial determination
2.993
reporting arrangements 2.983
members, distribution to 2.984
resolution for 1.138
special manager 2.251–2.256
accounting duties 2.255
appointment 2.252
termination 2.256
security 2.253
failure to give/keep up 2.254
statutory declaration of solvency 2.234
**Monetary limits**
bankruptcy, in 1.575
company winding up, power to alter 1.573
unregistered company insolvency 1.574
**Moratorium**
administration, during
enforcement, etc, proceedings, on 1.660
insolvency proceedings, on 1.659
interim 1.661
debts, priority 1.227
beginning
meaning 1.9
notification 1.10
directors
actions of, challenging 1.46
early termination 1.18
effects of
creditors on 1.22–1.25
payment of pre-moratorium debts 1.30
property, disposal of 1.31–1.34
transactions, restrictions on 1.27–1.29
eligible companies 1.4, 1.615
end 1.11
notification of change in 1.19
extension of 1.12–1.17
financial contracts, meaning 1.616
floating charge documents, void provisions 1.54
instrument involving financial services,
meaning 1.616
monetary limits
increase/reduction, regulations for 1.572
monitor
actions of, challenging 1.44
directions, applications by 1.39
duty 1.37
information, provision of, to 1.38
notification of insolvency proceedings 1.26
remuneration, challenging 1.45
replacement of 1.41
status of 1.36
termination of moratorium by 1.40

**Moratorium** – *cont.*
  monitor – *cont.*
    two or more 1.42
    validity, presumption of 1.43
  "moratorium debt", meaning 1.55
  obtaining
    company subject to winding up petition 1.6
    documents, submission, court 1.5
    oversees company, for 1.7
    relevant documents, for 1.8
  offences 1.48–1.50
  payment holidays, overview 1.20
  Pension Protection Fund
    challenge brought by 1.47
  pension schemes 1.53
  "pre-moratorium debt", meaning 1.55
  regulated companies, application 1.51
  regulations, power to make 1.57
  special rules 1.51–1.53
  temporary modifications 5.5, 5.34–5.37
  transitional provision 5.4
**Moratorium (CVA)**
  advertisement of 2.89
  beginning of, notification 2.89
  continuation 2.90
  directors, role of
    proposal to nominee 3.2
  disposal of charged property during 2.94
  documents
    filed at court to obtain 2.88
  end of, advertisement 2.93
  extension
    notice
      court order 2.92
      decision 2.91
  nominee
    applications to court, notice of 2.98
    replacement
      by court 2.96
      notice 2.97
    statement 2.87
    withdrawal of consent to act 2.95
  statement of affairs 2.85
    information, omission of 2.86
**Mutual debts**
  bankruptcy 1.442

**N**

**Name, company**
  prohibited, leave to act as director 2.1037–2.1044
  restriction on re-use after insolvent liquidation 1.275
    liability for contravention/acting on instructions 1.276
**National Debt Commissioners** 1.558, 1.559, 1.560, 1.562

**Northern Ireland**
  application of IA 1986 to 1.611
  bankruptcy in, offence in England 1.488
  co-operation of courts 1.586
  disqualification from Assembly 1.588, 1.590
  privilege, and insolvency enactments 1.589, 4.10
**Notice**
  winding up, of, on stationery etc 1.245

**O**

**Offences**
  body corporate, by 1.595
  penalties 1.478, 1.593, 1.759
  relevant offence, meaning 1.581
  summary proceedings 1.594
**Office-holder**
  co-operation duty of officers etc 1.299
  expenses, fees etc *See* Remuneration
  prior transaction, setting aside 1.302
  qualification 1.291
**Officer of company**
  co-operation duty 1.299
  investigation by liquidator 1.277
  offence/fraud relating to winding up
    creditors, defrauding etc 1.264, 1.268
    during course of 1.265
    fraudulent trading 1.271
    misfeasance/breach of duty 1.268
    penalties 1.759
    prior to 1.263
    prosecution of delinquent officer 1.277, 3.9
  private examination 1.300
  restoration of money/property, order for 1.270
  statement of affairs
    administration 1.664
    administrative receivership 1.91
    compulsory winding up, in 1.184
    material omission offence 1.267
    receivership, Scotland 1.110
    summary remedy against 1.270
**Official Petitioner** 1.557
**Official receiver**
  appointment 1.554, 2.822
  attachment to courts 1.554
  bankruptcy
    release 2.617
    reports 2.596
  compulsory winding up
    accounts, delivery 2.363
    notice of order 2.335
    release 2.389
    reporting duties
      relief/variation 2.391

Official receiver – *cont.*
  compulsory winding up – *cont.*
    reports to creditors/contributories
      2.366, 2.367
  death, of 1.555
  debt relief applications, consideration, of
    1.330
  deputy 1.556
  directions, application 2.824
  expenses 2.825
  fees as expense, priority rules
    bankruptcy 2.691
  functions 1.555
  investigation of company failure 1.185
    report 1.185
  liquidator, and
    duties to 1.196
    hand over of property to 2.379
  liquidator, as 1.189
    release 1.226
    substitute, appointment of 1.189
  meetings, calling 1.189
  nominee/supervisor of voluntary
    arrangement 1.527
  not to be appointed liquidator or trustee
    2.826
  person entitled to act on behalf 2.823
  public examination application 1.186,
    1.404
  receiver and manager, as 1.77
  staff 1.556
  statement of affairs, request for 1.184
  trustee in bankruptcy
    delivery up of property to 1.430
    enforcement of duties to 2.624
    information duties 1.416
Order
  final, Scotland 1.213, 1.738
  interim
    administration 1.630
    bankruptcy restrictions order 1.750
Overseas company
  foreign company 4.4
  winding up 1.285

**P**

Parliament
  disqualification from 1.587, 4.10
  privilege, and insolvency enactments
    1.589, 4.10
Partnership
  insolvent, wrongful trading 1.273
Pawn/pledge
  bankrupt's goods held on 1.429
  offence by officer 1.263
Pension (bankruptcy)
  excessive contribution recovery 1.463,
    1.464, 1.465, 1.466, 1.467, 1.468

Pension (bankruptcy) – *cont.*
  excessive contribution recovery – *cont.*
    information from responsible person
      1.465
    order restoring position 1.463
    pension-sharing case, provisions for
      1.466, 1.467, 1.468
  interests 1.427
Pension, occupational
  contribution as preferential debt 1.521,
    1.756
'Person' 1.737
Personal representative
  contributory, of 1.135
Preference
  bankruptcy 1.460
    meaning 1.460
    order restoring position 1.460
    'relevant time' 1.461
    trustee's application 1.460
  winding up 1.303
    possible orders 1.305
    'relevant time' 1.304
Preferential debts 1.520, 1.756
  administration 1.620, 1.690
    consent of creditor to extension 1.695
  bankruptcy 1.447, 1.521, 1.756
  categories 1.756
  compulsory winding up 1.228, 1.522
  Financial Services Compensation Scheme,
    relating to 1.756
  HMRC debts 1.756
  IVA 1.360
  ranking 1.228, 1.447
  receivership, payment in 1.84
    Scotland 1.103
  relevant dates 1.522
  voluntary winding up 1.159, 1.228
Priority of debts
  bankruptcy 1.447
    spouse as creditor 1.448
  litigation expenses 2.438
  winding up 2.432
    general rule 2.433
    voluntary winding up, interaction with
      2.434
Proceedings, legal
  administration, effect on 1.660
  bankrupt, against, court powers 1.399
  power to bring
    administrator/administrative receiver
      1.735
    liquidator 1.742
    trustee in bankruptcy 1.753
Proceeds of crime
  property released from detention 1.419
  property subject to confiscation or-
    der 1.420, 1.421
  property subject to restraint order 1.418
Prohibited company name 1.275

**Prohibited company name** – *cont.*
liability for contravention 1.276
**Project finance**
administrative receiver for 1.122, 1.736
**Promoter**
co-operation duty 1.299
private examination of 1.300
prohibited names provision 1.275
public examination 1.186
public examination of 2.422
statement of affairs, duty
administrator, to 1.664
summary remedy against 1.270
**Proof of debts**
admission for dividend 2.834
appeal of decision 2.835
costs 2.836
bankruptcy, in 1.441
mutual debts and set-off 1.442
second bankruptcy 1.454
valuation by trustee 1.441
costs of proving 2.832
exclusion by court 2.838
inspection of proofs 2.833
rejection for dividend 2.834
requirements 2.831
submitting a claim 2.830
withdrawal/variation of proof 2.837
**Property**
leasehold
disclaimer, notice of 2.1017
**Property of bankrupt**
dispositions, restrictions on 1.398
distribution in specie 1.445
exempt 1.396
inquiry into 1.492
non-delivery up/concealment/loss offence
1.482
seizure 1.491
situated in another part of UK 1.586
**Property of company**
administrator's duties/powers 1.685,
1.735
enforced delivery up 1.298
meaning 1.605
office-holder powers
inquiry of person having 1.300, 1.301
to get in 1.298
sale, power of 1.735, 1.743, 1.754
winding up, and 1.298
fraud, destruction, concealment etc,
offences 1.263, 1.264
**Proxies**
application of rules 2.927
authorisation to represent corporation
2.936
blank proxies 2.929
continuing proxies 2.928
financial interest, proxy-holder with 2.933

**Proxies** – *cont.*
inspection, right of 2.932
retention 2.932
specific proxies 2.928
use of 2.930
chair, by 2.931
**Public company**
compulsory winding up ground (share
capital) 1.172
**Public interest**
winding up ground 1.177
administration, order during 1.699
**Public policy**
refusal of recognition of
proceedings/judgment enforcement
EU Regulation 6.35
**Public-private partnership project**
administration regime 4.3
administrative receiver for 1.119
**Purchase of own shares**
liability of directors/shareholders on
winding up 1.130

### R

**Railway company**
administration regime 4.3
administrative receiver, appointment for
1.125
**Receiver (Scotland)** 1.94–1.115
administrative receiver, prohibition on
appointment 1.117–1.126
exceptions 1.118–1.125
agent, deemed 1.101
appointment 1.95
cessation of 1.106
circumstances 1.96
holder of charge, by 1.95, 1.97
notification of 1.108
company's website, on 1.108
stationery etc 1.108
ceasing to be qualified, vacation of office
1.106
charged property, authority for disposal of
1.105
contracts, liability as to 1.101
creditors' committee 1.112
definitions 1.114
directions of court 1.107
disqualification 1.95
firm 1.95
fixed security holders, position of 1.104
forms 1.115
indemnity 1.106
information duties 1.109
joint 1.95, 1.100
powers 1.99, 1.735
person dealing in good faith, position of
1.99

Receiver (Scotland) – *cont.*
  powers – *cont.*
    precedence and suspension of 1.100
  priority of debts 1.103
    order of distribution of moneys 1.104
    preferential debts 1.103
  removal from office 1.106
  remuneration 1.102, 1.106
  report 1.111
  resignation 1.106
  returns, enforcement 1.113
  statement of affairs 1.110
    release from duty to submit 1.110
Receiver and manager 1.85
  accounts duties 1.82
  appointment out of court 1.77–1.82
    information on website 1.83
    invalid, liability 1.78
    stationery etc to state 1.83
    time of 1.77
  bankruptcy
    official receiver 1.401
  contracts, liability on 1.81
  cross-border powers 1.116
  definition 1.326
  directions application by/concerning 1.79
  disqualification
    bankrupt 1.75
    body corporate 1.74
  indemnity 1.78, 1.81
  joint 1.77
  joint appointment 2.207
  official receiver appointed as 1.77
  payment of debts out of floating charge
    assets 1.84
  public examination 1.186
  publicity as to appointment 1.83
  remuneration, court fixing 1.80
  returns, enforcement 1.85
  statement of affairs 1.91, 1.110
  unsecured, share of assets provision 1.233
    disapplication 1.233
  vacation of office 1.81
Receivership *See* Administrative receiver;
  Receiver and manager
Recognised professional body
  compliance orders 1.551
  declaration 1.531
  directions 1.535, 1.536
  fees orders 1.571
  financial penalties 1.537, 1.538
    appeals 1.539
    recovery of 1.540
  information, provision of 1.550
  recognition
    application for 1.532
    revocation of 1.543, 1.544, 1.545
  regulatory functions 1.533
    meaning 1.534

Recognised professional body – *cont.*
  reprimand 1.541, 1.542
Records
  definition 1.605
Register (insolvency)
  bankruptcy restrictions 1.751
Register of members
  false entry in register offence 1.266
  rectification 1.201, 1.212
Registered social landlord
  administrative receiver, appointment for
    1.124
Registrar of companies
  administrative receiver
    notice of vacation from office 2.228
    receipts and payments, to 2.224
    report to 2.220
  compulsory winding up
    notice of order 2.336
    notice to 2.378
  documents, delivered to 2.30–2.38
Relative
  associate, as 1.604
Remuneration *See also* Costs; Expenses; Fees
  administrator 1.716
  apportionment, set fees 2.1006
  court, fixing 2.997
  creditors'/members' request for information
    2.981
  exceeding fee estimate 2.1004
  excessive expenses
    bankrupt, application by 2.1009,
      2.1010
    creditor/member, application by 2.1008,
      2.1010, 2.1011
  general principles 2.990
  initial determination of
    administration 2.992
    bankruptcy 2.995
    creditors' voluntary winding up 2.994
    members' voluntary winding up 2.993
    winding up by court 2.994
  joint office-holders 2.991
  progress report 2.976
  realisation of assets on behalf of secured
    creditor 2.1012
  request for increase 2.998, 2.999, 2.1002
    exceptions 2.1000, 2.1001
  review 2.1003
  scale fees 2.996
Rent charge, land subject to
  disclaimer 1.237, 1.438
Repeals 1.608
Reports 2.974
  distribution of property about 2.982
  final account/report 2.987
  pre-administration costs, information
    2.977
  progress report
    administration, timing 2.978

**Reports** – *cont.*
  progress report – *cont.*
    bankruptcy, timing 2.980
    voluntary winding up, timing 2.979
    winding up, timing 2.980
  progress reports 2.975
  remuneration, information 2.976
**Reservation of title** 6.12
**Restraint order**
  property subject to 1.418
**Returns**
  liquidator's
    enforcement 1.222

**S**

**Sale, order for**
  bankruptcy, in 1.432, 4.8
  trust of land 1.455
**Sale, power of**
  administrator/administrative receiver
    1.735
  trustee in bankruptcy 1.754
**Scotland**
  administration 1.730–1.734
  application of legislation to
    IA 1986 1.610
  compulsory winding up
    appeals from orders 1.214, 1.737
    calls 1.213
    jurisdiction 1.174
    liquidation committee 1.195
    liquidator 1.191, 1.221
    officer's attendance at meeting 1.209
    remittance to Lord Ordinary 1.173
  co-operation of courts 1.586
  costs of leave against company being
    wound up 1.255
  diligence, effect 1.242
  examination of persons 1.254
  gratuitous alienation 1.306
  Parliament
    disqualification from 1.588, 1.590
    privilege, and insolvency enactments
      1.589, 4.10
  sequestration in, bankruptcy offence in
    England 1.488
  unclaimed dividends 1.250
  unfair preference 1.307
  unregistered company, winding up 1.281
  voluntary winding up
    liquidation committee 1.154
**Secretary of State**
  administration time-limits, amendment
    power 1.727
  annual report to Parliament 1.506
  creditors' committee functions, exercise of
    1.413

**Secretary of State** – *cont.*
  Insolvency Services Account, payment into
    1.558
    Investment Account 1.558
  institution of proceedings for bankruptcy
    offence 1.478
  IVA
    report on and prosecution of debtor
      1.366
  liquidator, powers as to
    appointment of 1.190
    removal of 1.224
  trustee in bankruptcy
    appointment of 1.408
    removal of 1.409
**Secured creditor**
  bankruptcy, in 1.516
    petitioner 1.384
    proof of debts 1.441
    rights after discharge of order 1.393
  IVA, and 1.360
  meaning 1.322, 1.516
**Security**
  meaning 1.322
**Seizure of/search for property**
  bankruptcy, powers in 1.491
    inquiry into bankrupt's dealings, during
      1.492
    third party premises 1.491
  inquiry into company dealings, for 1.300
**Sequestration**
  avoidance 1.181
**Service**
  administration application 2.132
**Set-off**
  bankruptcy 1.442
**Setting aside**
  liquidator's transaction 2.249, 2.295,
    2.393
  prior transaction 1.302
  statutory demand, bankruptcy
    application 2.529
    hearing 2.530
**Shares**
  bankrupt's estate, in 1.429
**Society/non-company body** 4.5
**Special manager** 1.496
  bankruptcy
    accounting duties 2.629
    appointment 2.626
      termination 2.630
    security 2.627
      failure to give/keep up 2.628
  compulsory winding up 2.414–2.420
    accounting duties 2.419
    appointment and remuneration 2.416
    security 2.417
      failure to give/keep up 2.418
    termination of appointment 2.420

**Special manager** – *cont.*
  creditors' voluntary winding up
    accounting duties  2.302
    appointment  2.299
      termination  2.303
    security  2.300
      failure to give/keep up  2.301
  defect in act of  1.504
  members' voluntary winding up  2.251–
      2.256
    accounting duties  2.255
    appointment  2.252
      termination  2.256
    security  2.253
      failure to give/keep up  2.254
**Stamp duty**
  exemption
    bankruptcy  1.505
    winding up  1.247
**Statement of affairs**
  administration
    content  2.158
    expenses  2.162
    extension, time limit, submission  2.161
    filing of  2.160
    limited disclosure of  2.175, 2.177
    notice requiring  2.157
    publication  2.178
    statement of concurrence  2.159
  administration, in  1.664, 1.665
  administrative receiver, submitted to
    contents  2.214
    delivery of copy  2.214
    expenses  2.218
    extension, time to submit  2.217
    limited disclosure  2.219
    notice requiring  2.213
    release from duty to submit  2.217
    retention  2.216
    statement of concurrence  2.215
    verification  2.216
  admissibility in evidence  1.596
  bankruptcy petition, with, creditor's  1.402
    release or extension of time  1.402
  compulsory winding up  1.184, 2.356–
      2.364
    contents  2.358
    expenses  2.362
    limited disclosure of  2.360
    notice requiring  2.357
    release, Secretary of State, by  2.361
    statement of concurrence  2.359
  creditors' voluntary winding up, in  1.149
  CVA, in  2.79
    information, omission of  2.80
    moratorium case  2.85
      information, omission of  2.86
  directors  2.262
    content  2.263

**Statement of affairs** – *cont.*
  individual voluntary arrangement  2.452
    omission of information from  2.453
  IVA, in  1.357
  liquidator  2.257, 2.261
    content  2.263
  material omission offence  1.267
  receivership, in  1.91, 1.110
**Statement of solvency**
  liability of director  1.130
**Stationery**
  notification on, winding up  1.245
**Statutory declaration**
  administrator's appointment, relating to
      1.635, 1.644
**Stay of distribution**  1.453
**Stay of proceedings**
  annulment of bankruptcy  2.675
  bankruptcy, by IVA interim order  1.356,
      1.362
  bankruptcy, during  1.399
  compulsory winding up, during  1.179
  compulsory winding up, of  1.200
  IVA application, court power  1.355
**Subordinate legislation** *See also* **Insolvency
      Rules**  1.565
  company insolvency rules, power to make
      1.566, 1.757
  individual insolvency rules  1.567, 1.757
  insolvency practitioner regulations  1.576
  Insolvency Rules Committee, consultation
      with  1.568
  meaning  1.605
  provisions that can be included
    company insolvency  1.757
    individual insolvency  1.757
**Supervisor**
  CVA
    accounts  2.117
    application for administration  2.129
    hand-over of property to  2.115
    proposal for alternative  2.108
    reports  2.117
    time-recording information  2.122
**Surety**
  preference/transaction at undervalue,
      reviving obligations of  1.305
**System charge**
  administrative receiver, appointment under
      1.123


**T**

**Tenancy**
  vesting in trustee in bankruptcy  1.424,
      1.425
**Third party**
  acting in good faith (administration)  1.674

**Third party** – *cont.*
bankruptcy
protection in 1.398
search of premises 1.491
rights, EU Regulations 6.10
**Time-limit**
extension/amendment
administration, in 1.724
bankruptcy, in 1.503
**'Trading record'**
bankrupt's falsification offence, meaning for
1.483
**Transaction at undervalue** 1.302, 1.582
bankruptcy 1.459
'relevant time' 1.461
trustee's application 1.459
court powers to make orders 1.582
meaning 1.459, 1.582
possible orders 1.305
'relevant time' 1.304
victim 1.582
winding up 1.302
possible orders 1.305
**Transaction in fraud of creditors** 1.264, 1.582
order, restorative or protective
court power 1.582
**Transfer of proceedings**
bankruptcy 1.500
**Transfer of shares**
winding up, effect on
compulsory winding up 1.180
voluntary winding up 1.142
**Transitional/savings** 1.607, 1.759
company insolvency 1.759
**Transport**
licence company, administrative
receivership 1.125
**Trust of land**
bankruptcy, order for sale in 1.455
**Trustee in bankruptcy** *See also* **Bankrupt;**
**Bankruptcy**
'act as insolvency practitioner' 1.525
appointment 1.407, 2.598
acceptance 1.407
authentication 2.604
certification 2.599
court, by 2.602
creditors' decision 2.601
notice 1.408, 2.605
replacement trustee 2.608
Secretary of State, by 2.603
book debt assignment avoidance 1.470
bribe affecting appointment 2.623
business of bankrupt, power to carry on
1.753
ceasing to be qualified 2.616
contract, unprofitable 1.434
contributory, of 1.136
creditors' committee, invitation to form
2.607

**Trustee in bankruptcy** *See also* **Bankrupt;**
**Bankruptcy** – *cont.*
death of 2.615
defect in act of 1.504
delivery up of books and property to
1.429
obligation 1.430
directions application 1.414, 1.489
disposition of property 1.433
dissatisfaction with act etc of 1.414
distribution of bankrupt's estate 1.416,
1.441–1.451
criminal bankruptcy 1.446
final 1.449
in specie, with permission 1.445
stay where second bankruptcy 1.453
enforcement of duties 2.624
execution or attachment enforcement,
benefit of 1.472
extortionate credit transaction, application
for order 1.469
final report of 1.450, 2.987
first trustee in bankruptcy 1.406
functions 1.416
hand-over of bankrupt's estate to 2.606
information duty 1.416
joint 1.407
liability 1.410, 1.415
misfeasance 1.415
money received, interest on 1.560
negligence 1.415
official name of/reference to 1.416
official receiver as 1.407
creditors' committee functions, provision
for 1.413
provisions applying 1.416
release 1.410
powers 1.433, 1.752
with permission 1.433
progress reports, timing 2.980
qualification 1.407
ceasing to be qualified 1.409
receivership prior to appointment 1.401
release 1.410, 2.614
removal 1.409
annulment of order, on 1.410
court, by 2.611
creditors, by 2.609
procedure 2.610
notice 2.613
resignation 1.409
Secretary of State, by 2.612
Secretary of State, removal by 1.409
remuneration *See also* **Remuneration**
2.990
exceeding fee estimate 2.1004
joint 2.991
new trustee 2.1005
realisation of assets on behalf of secured
creditor 2.1012

Trustee in bankruptcy *See also* Bankrupt;
      Bankruptcy – *cont.*
  remuneration *See also* Remuneration –
      *cont.*
    request for increase   2.998, 2.999,
        2.1002
    review   2.1003
  replacement/filling vacancy   1.411
  reports
    relief from reporting duties   2.619
  resignation   2.608
    notice   2.613
  second bankruptcy, provisions for   2.694,
      2.695, 2.696
  security   2.600
  seizure/disposal of property   1.415
  solicitation, improper   2.623
  transaction of, court setting aside   2.622
  trust of land, order for sale   1.455
  vacation of office   2.618
    duties following   2.621
    notice   2.620
  vesting of bankrupt's estate in   1.417,
      1.424, 1.425
    confiscation order property   1.422
    receivership/administration
        order property   1.420
    restraint order, property subject to
        1.418
    tenancies   1.425


U

Unfair preference   1.307
Unfair prejudice
  individual voluntary arrangement   1.364
Unlimited company
  contributory's set-off   1.202
  formerly limited, restriction on past
      member's liability to contribute
      1.131
Unregistered company
  meaning   1.280
  winding up   1.279
    circumstances   1.281
    contributories   1.286
    cumulative provisions   1.289
    insolvency   1.574
    jurisdiction   1.281
    overseas company wound up as   1.285
    provisions applying   1.281
    stay or sist of proceedings   1.287
Urban regeneration project
  administrative receiver   1.121, 1.736
Utility
  project, administrative receiver   1.120,
      1.736
  supplier
    supplies to bankrupt   1.498, 1.499

Utility – *cont.*
  supplier – *cont.*
    supplies to insolvent company   1.294,
        1.295


V

Voluntary winding up *See also* Creditors'
      voluntary winding up; Members'
      voluntary winding up
  administrator's appointment restriction
      1.625
  circumstances for   1.138
  commencement   1.140
  compulsory winding up, interaction with
      1.176, 1.182
  court, reference of question to   1.164
  debts, payment of   1.217
  declaration of solvency   1.143
  dissolution of company   1.257
  distribution of property   1.159
  effect of   1.141
  expenses   1.167
  extraordinary resolution
    advertisement after passing   1.139
    notice prior to   1.138
  notice of resolution to floating charge
      holder   1.138
  property of company   1.217
  resolutions   1.138, 1.154
  scheme of reorganisation, company subject
      to   1.162
    dissenting member, procedure for   1.163
  shares as consideration for sale of company
      property   1.162
  special resolution   1.138
  transfer of shares avoidance   1.142
  winding up by court, saving for rights
      1.168


W

Wales
  disqualification from Assembly   1.588,
      4.10
Warrant
  execution
    criminal law provision applied   1.586
Water company   1.125, 1.294
  administration regime   4.3
Winding up (general) *See also* Compulsory
      winding up; Voluntary winding up;
      Winding up by court
  creditors' claims
    estimate of value of debt   2.841
    mutual dealings and set off   2.852
    provable debts   2.829
  examination of witnesses
    commission for evidence   1.253

Winding up (general) *See also* Compulsory
winding up; Voluntary winding up;
Winding up by court – *cont.*
examination of witnesses – *cont.*
public, of officers 1.186, 1.187
financial institution
non-preferential debts 1.230, 1.523
former unlimited company re-registered as
limited 1.131
'go into liquidation', meaning 1.321
interest on debts 1.246
malpractice
before 1.265
during, after 1.265
meetings
wishes of creditors/contributories, as to
1.251
monetary limits 1.573
pending, information to registrar 1.249
petition
temporary restrictions/prohibitions 5.8,
5.41
prohibited names 1.275
publicity 1.245
Winding up by court *See also* Compulsory
winding up
accounts, delivery 2.363
contributory/ies
calls on 2.407
enforcement 2.412, 2.413
leave to make, application to court
2.410
liquidation committee, sanction of
2.409
liquidator, by 2.408
order 2.411
information to 2.365–2.369
list of, settlement 2.399–2.406
creditors
information to 2.365–2.369
creditors' claims
debts, insolvent company to rank equally
2.839
unsold assets, division 2.840
liquidation committee, invitation to form
2.374
liquidator 2.373–2.394
account
dissolution, prior to 2.390
appointment
court, by 2.375
notice 2.378
Secretary of State, by 2.376
ceasing to be qualified 2.387
death of 2.386
duties/powers 2.395–2.398
hand over of property to 2.379
liquidator
appointment
creditors/contributories, by 2.372

Winding up by court *See also* Compulsory
winding up – *cont.*
liquidator – *cont.*
liquidator – *cont.*
nominations 2.371, 2.373
release, Secretary of State, by 2.388
removal
court, by 2.384
creditors, by 2.382
procedure 2.383
Secretary of State, by 2.385
reporting duties
relief/variation 2.391
resignation 2.380
security, costs of 2.377
solicitation, improper 2.394
transaction of, court setting aside 2.393
vacation of office
duties 2.392
notice of intent 2.381
litigation expenses
property subject to floating charge
2.436–2.442
approval 2.439, 2.440, 2.441, 2.442
priority 2.438
official receiver
further disclosure request 2.364
release of 2.389
reporting duties
relief/variation 2.391
order
company in administration 2.347
content 2.334
notice/copies to official receiver 2.335,
2.336
petition
certificate of compliance 2.326
contents 2.319
contributories, by 2.339–2.347
applicable rules 2.340
contents 2.341
hearing 2.346
presentation 2.342, 2.344
verification 2.343
copies
service of 2.323
dismissal 2.337
former administrator/supervisor as
liquidator 2.345
hearing
adjournment 2.333
list of appearances 2.329
notice of appearance 2.328
witness statement in opposition
2.330
notice 2.324
persons entitled to 2.325
presentation and filing 2.321, 2.322
injunction to restrain 2.338

**Winding up by court** *See also* **Compulsory winding up** – *cont.*
  petition – *cont.*
    verification 2.320
    withdrawal 2.327
  petitioner
    substitution of 2.331, 2.332
  priority of costs/expenses 2.433, 2.435
  progress reports, timing 2.980
  provisional liquidator
    appointment 2.349
      deposit 2.350
      notice 2.352
      order 2.351
      security 2.353
      termination 2.355
    remuneration 2.354
  public examination of officers, etc
    adjournment 2.430
    contributory, request by 2.424, 2.425
    creditor, request by 2.423, 2.425
    examinee lacking capacity 2.428
    expenses 2.431
    notice 2.427
    order 2.426
    procedure 2.429
    promoters 2.422
  remuneration
    procedure for initial determination 2.994

**Winding up by court** *See also* **Compulsory winding up** – *cont.*
  special manager 2.414
    accounting duties 2.419
    appointment and remuneration 2.416
    security 2.417
      failure to give/keep up 2.418
    termination of appointment 2.420
  statement of affairs 2.356–2.364
    contents 2.358
    expenses 2.362
    limited disclosure of 2.360
    notice requiring 2.357
    release, Secretary of State, by 2.361
    statement of concurrence 2.359
  statutory demand 2.316
  stay, notice of 2.369
  voluntary winding up, interaction with
    expenses, priority of 2.434, 2.435
**Witness**
  fraudulent or wrongful trading, to 1.274
**Wrongful trading**
  administration in 1.312
  directors' liability 1.272
  insolvent partnership 1.273
  suspension, CIGA 2020, by 5.9